HALSBURY'S
LAWS OF ENGLAND

ANNUAL ABRIDGMENT

1995

HALSBURY'S
Laws of England

FOURTH EDITION

ANNUAL ABRIDGMENT 1995

BUTTERWORTHS

LONDON 1996

UNITED KINGDOM	Butterworths a Division of Reed Elsevier (UK) Ltd Halsbury House, 35 Chancery Lane, **London** WC2A 1EL and 4 Hill Street, **Edinburgh** EH2 3JZ
AUSTRALIA	Butterworths, **Sydney**, **Melbourne**, **Brisbane**, **Adelaide**, **Perth**, **Canberra** and **Hobart**
CANADA	Butterworths Canada Ltd, **Toronto** and **Vancouver**
HONG KONG	Butterworths Asia, **Hong Kong**
IRELAND	Butterworth (Ireland) Ltd, **Dublin**
MALAYSIA	Malayan Law Journal Sdn Bhd, **Kuala Lumpur**
NEW ZEALAND	Butterworths of New Zealand Ltd, **Wellington** and **Auckland**
SINGAPORE	Butterworths Asia, **Singapore**
SOUTH AFRICA	Butterworths Publishers (Pty) Ltd, **Durban**
USA	Michie Butterworth, **Charlottesville**, Virginia

© Reed Elsevier (UK) Ltd 1996

ISBN   0 406 99615 6

Printed in Great Britain by
Clays Ltd, St Ives plc

PUBLISHERS' NOTE

This is the twenty second *Annual Abridgment* and covers the year 1995. The *Abridgment* constitutes year by year a comprehensive survey of English case law, statute law and subordinate legislation. European Community law and decisions of Commonwealth courts are given attention commensurate with their importance. Further noteworthy items are derived from government papers, reports of committees, legal periodicals and the daily press. The alphabetical arrangement and the comprehensive tables and index make the work an ideal aid to research.

Each *Annual Abridgment* is complete without recourse to any other publication.

When referring to this volume reference should be made to both the year and the relevant paragraph number: eg "1995 Abr para 3068".

This volume covers the law made in 1995 and is compiled from sources available in London on 31 December 1995.

BUTTERWORTHS

TABLE OF CONTENTS

The text of this *Abridgment* is arranged under the following titles. A list of titles currently used in *Halsbury's Laws* appears on page *13*.

Table of Contents

Table of Contents

ARRANGEMENT OF TITLES
HALSBURY'S LAWS, FOURTH EDITION &
REISSUE

The following is the title scheme of *Halsbury's Laws* as it stood in 1995. Where the titles used in the *Annual Abridgment* differ from those in the main work, the new titles appear in brackets.

Arrangement of Titles

REFERENCES AND ABBREVIATIONS

Abr...Halsbury's Abridgment
AC (preceded by date)...................Law Reports (Appeal Cases)
ACTR..Australian Capital Territory Reports
ADRLJ..Arbitration and Dispute Resolution Law Journal
ALJ...Australian Law Journal
All ER..All England Law Reports
All ER (EC) ....All England Law Reports European Cases
ALJR..Australian Law Journal Reports
ALR..Australian Law Reports
AVMA ....AVMA Medical & Legal Journal
BCLC..Butterworths Company Law Cases
BLR ....Building Law Reports
BLRev...Business Law Review
BMLR...Butterworths Medico-Legal Reports
BTR..British Tax Review
CCC ....Canadian Criminal Cases
Ch (preceded by date)....................Law Reports (Chancery Division)
CJQ..Civil Justice Quarterly
CLJ...Cambridge Law Journal
CLP..Computer Law and Practice
CLSR..Computer Law and Security Report
CLY ....Current Law Yearbook
CMLR ....Common Market Law Reports
Comp Lawyer...............................Company Lawyer
Conv ....Conveyancer and Property Lawyer
CR..Clinical Risk
Cr App Rep ....Criminal Appeal Reports
Cr App Rep (S) ....Criminal Appeal Reports (Sentencing)
Crim LR ....Criminal Law Review
CTLR ....Computer and Telecommunications Law Review
Decisions and Reports ....Decisions and Reports of European Commission on
                                                        Human Rights
DLR..Dominion Law Reports (Canada)
ECR..European Court Reports
EG..Estates Gazette
EGCS ....Estates Gazette Case Summaries
EGLR ....Estates Gazette Law Reports
EHRR ....European Human Rights Reports
EIPR...European Intellectual Property Review
ELJ ....Ecclesiastical Law Journal
Fam (preceded by date).................Law Reports (Family Division)
Fam Law.......................................Family Law (journal)
FCR..Family Court Reporter
FLR...Family Law Reports
FSR...Fleet Street Reports
HC..House of Commons Paper
HLR...Housing Law Reports
ICCR...International Company and Commercial Law Review
ICJ Reports ....International Court of Justice Reports
ICLQ ....International and Comparative Law Quarterly
ICR...Industrial Cases Reports
ILJ ....Industrial Law Journal
Imm AR...Immigration Appeal Reports
INLP ....Immigration and Nationality Law and Practice
IR ....Irish Reports
IRLR ....Industrial Relations Law Reports
JBL ....Journal of Business Law
JIBFL..Journal of International Banking and Financial Law
JP ....Justice of the Peace Reports
JP Jo ....Justice of the Peace Journal
JPL ....Journal of Planning and Environmental Law
JSWFL...Journal of Social Welfare and Family Law
LA ....Legal Action

LGR...Local Government Reports
LG Rev...Local Government Review
Lloyd's Rep..................................Lloyd's Law Reports
LMCLQ.......................................Lloyd's Maritime and Commercial Law Quarterly
LQR...Law Quarterly Review
LS..Legal Studies
LS Gaz...Law Society Gazette
LS Gaz Rep..................................Law Society Gazette Reports
Med LR..Medical Law Reports
MLJ..Malayan Law Journal
MLR...Modern Law Review
MLRep..Manx Law Reports
NI...Northern Ireland Law Reports
NLJ..New Law Journal
NLJR..New Law Journal Reports
NTR..Northern Territory Reports
NZLR..New Zealand Law Reports
OJ C...Official Journal of the European
                                                      Communities—communications and information series
OJ L...Official Journal of the European Communities—
                                                      legislation series
P & CR..Property and Compensation Reports
PIQR...Personal Injuries and Quantum Reports
PLR...(Estates Gazette) Planning Law Reports
QB (preceded by date)...................Law Reports (Queen's Bench Division)
RA..Rating Appeals
RPC..Reports of Patent Etc Cases
RRC..Ryde's Rating Cases
RTR..Road Traffic Reports
RVR..Rating and Valuation Reporter
SA..South African Law Reports
SC..Session Cases
SJ...Solicitors' Journal
SLT...Scots Law Times
STC..Simon's Tax Cases
STC (SCD)...................................Simon's Tax Cases (Special Commissioners' Decisions)
STI...Simon's Tax Intelligence
TC..Tax Cases
TR..Taxation Reports
VATTR..Value Added Tax Tribunal Reports
VR..Victorian Reports
WLR...Weekly Law Reports

WORDS AND PHRASES

The following words and phrases have been judicially interpreted and can be found at the relevant paragraph noted below.

TABLE OF STATUTES

TABLE OF STATUTORY INSTRUMENTS

Table of Statutory Instruments

Table of Statutory Instruments

Table of Statutory Instruments

Table of Statutory Instruments

Table of Statutory Instruments

Table of Statutory Instruments

TABLE OF CASES

Decisions of the European Court of Human Rights, European Commission of Human Rights, and European Court of Justice are listed numerically after the main table.

A

Decisions of the European Court of Human Rights and European Commission of Human Rights are listed below numerically. These decisions are also included in the preceeding alphabetical table.

Table of Cases

COMMAND PAPERS

QUANTUM OF DAMAGES TABLE

This table refers to examples of awards of damages in personal injury or fatal accident cases that have been summarised in the MONTHLY REVIEWS. Cases are arranged in the following order, with cases involving more than one injury being classified according to the major injury suffered.

Death
Brain damage and paralysis
Multiple injuries
Psychological damage and
emotional stress

Internal injuries
Burns
Scarring
Head
Neck and shoulder

Back, chest and abdomen
Arm and hand
Leg and foot
Minor injuries

For the purposes of this table the age of the plaintiff is at the date of the accident unless otherwise stated. In fatal accident cases, sex and age are those of the deceased unless otherwise stated.

INJURY	PSLA	SEX/AGE	CITATION & REVIEW PARA NUMBER
Brain Damage	£750,000 (Total damages)	Male/26	*L v V* (settled out of court), para 1003
	£128,000 (Including interest)	Male/4	*Wadsworth v West Lancashire Health Authority* (QBD), para 1003
	£122,000	Male/infant	*Barnett v North Bedfordshire Health Authority* (settled out of court), para 1003
	£105,500 (Including interest)	Male/22	*Thorpe v Hooper* (QBD), para 1003
Tetraplegia	£95,000	Male/17	*Stevenson v Sweeney* (Outer House), para 1004
Paralysis	£64,464 (Including interest)	Male/39	*Smith v Salford Health Authority* (QBD), para 1005
Multiple injuries	£25,000	Malc/8	*George v Tipper* (Bristol County Ct), para 1006
	£22,730 (Including interest)	Female/39	*Wilson v Clarke* (Colchester County Ct), para 1006
	£12,500	Female/17	*Tribe v Cheffey* (settled out of court), para 1006
	£8,000	Male/56	*Brown v Woodall* (Court of Appeal), para 1006

Quantum of Damages Table

INJURY	PSLA	SEX/AGE	CITATION & REVIEW PARA NUMBER
	£6,960	Female/60	*Reid v Edinburgh Acoustics* (Outer House), 1006
	£5,000	Male/42	*West v Campagnie* (Reading County Ct), para 1006
	£3,888	Female/30	*Jones v Khangura* (Birmingham County Ct), para 1006
	£3,500	Female/37	*Szulc v Howard* (Birmingham County Ct), para 1006
Psychological damage	£20,000	Female/27	*Sarjeant v Crawford*, (QBD), para 1007
	£18,000	Female/28	*Re C* (settled out of court), para 1007
	£15,000	Female/6–14	(CICB), para 1007
	£10,000	Female/35	(CICB), para 1007
	£10,000	Female/11–15	(CICB), para 1007
	£2,800	Male/87	*Horton v CAMAS Associated Asphalt* (settled out of court), para 1007
	£2,500	Male/37	*Brandman v Prior* (Dartford County Ct), para 1007
	£2,000	Female/29	*Howell v Bolton Hospitals NHS Trust* (Bolton County Ct), para 1007
Post-traumatic stress disorder	£40,000	Female/40	(CICB), para 1008
	£36,750	Male/27	(CICB), para 1008
	£25,488 (including interest)	Male/34	*Harding v British Railways Board* (Manchester County Ct), para 1008
	£15,000	Male/19	(CICB), para 1008
	£8,500	Male/50	(CICB), para 1008
	£5,000	Female/27	(CICB), para 1008
Internal injuries	£22,500 (approx)	Female/49	*S v D* (settled out of court), para 1009

INJURY	PSLA	SEX/AGE	CITATION & REVIEW PARA NUMBER
	£20,000	Female/33	*Levy v T* (settled out of court), para 1009
	£13,000	Male/33	*Cooper v Pontefract Hospital NHS Trust* (settled out of court), para 1009
	£4,000	Female/30	*Moore v Martin* (settled out of court), para 1009
	£2,750	Male/14	*Ahmed v Aquamead* (settled out of court), para 1009
	£2,500	Male/20	*Walker v Heron* (Liverpool County Ct), para 1009
Burns	(1) £16,528.69 (2) £10,057.97 (3) £12,779.47 (4) £2,979.90 (5) £11,278.37 (6) £3,000	Male/(1) 41 (2) 23 (3) 36 (4) 43 (5) 54 (6) 29	*Boyle v J C Services* (Liverpool County Ct), para 1010
	£16,000	Male/52	*Farragher v Quarmby Holdings* (Halifax County Ct), para 1010
Scarring	£8,000 (including interest)	Male/5	*Mason v Weeks* (Bristol County Ct), para 1011
	£5,500	Female/21	*Lewis v Jukes* (Stourbridge County Ct), para 1011
	£2,250	Male/15	*Crisp v Hare* (Cardiff County Ct), para 1011
	£1,500	Male/18	*Bradley v Range Security* (Liverpool County Ct), para 1011
Skin	£15,000	Male/45 (at trial)	*Netherwood v Iloman Engineering* (Isle of Man), para 1012
	£10,000	Female/39	*Maddox v Rocky Horror (London)* (QBD), para 1012
Scalp	£5,073.50	Male/29	*West v NS Hair Treatment Clinic* (Birmingham County Ct), para 1013

INJURY	PSLA	SEX/AGE	CITATION & REVIEW PARA NUMBER
Head	£55,000	Female/17	(CICB), para 1014
	£50,000	Female/35	(CICB), para 1014
	£27,500 (total damages)	Female/22	(CICB), para 1014
	£7,800 (including interest)	Female/9	*Mayor v Boardman* (Stoke-on-Trent County Ct), para 1014
	£7,500	Male/31	(CICB), para 1014
	£6,500	Male/16	*Fotheringham v Murfitt* (Oldham County Ct), para 1014
	£3,500	Male/23	(CICB), para 1014
	£3,120	Female/23	*Taylor v RS Thompson* (Mayor's and City of London County Ct), para 1014
	£2,400 (amount of payment in)	Male/11	*Curtis v Securicor* (Southampton County Ct), para 1014
	£1,000	Male/15 months	*Compton v Watson* (settled out of court), para 1014
	£900	Female/35	*Ohene v Rymer* (Lambeth County Ct), para 1014
Head and face	£22,500	Male/23	*Cory-Wright v Chapman* (Central London County Ct), 1015
Head and eye	£12,000	Male/33	(CICB), para 1016
Head and ear	£8,000	Female/2	*Lane v Evans* (Birmingham County Ct), para 1017
Head and back	£40,000	Male/57	(CICB), para 1018
Head and foot	£6,000 (total damages)	Female/56	Re H (settled out of court), para 1019
Face	£3,300 (approx)	Female/49	*McDonald v Lothian Health Board* (Outer House), para 1020
Eye	£7,500	Male/43	*McCarthy v Knowsley MBC* (Liverpool County Ct), para 1021

INJURY	PSLA	SEX/AGE	CITATION & REVIEW PARA NUMBER
	£5,000	Male/32	Names of parties witheld (settled out of court), para 1021
	£3,486.92	Male/7	*Nicoll v Lyall* (settled out of court), para 1021
	£1,000	Male/5	*Barry v Evans* (Cheltenham County Ct), para 1021
Ear	(1) £8,500; (2) £6,500; (3) £5,000	Male/(1) 23–52; (2) 27–52; (3) 16–33	(1) *Hurlow v Ford Motor Company*; (2) *Wade v Ford Motor Company*; (3) *Powell v Ford Motor Company* (Swansea County Ct), para 1022
Jaw	£7,500	Male/55	(CICB), para 1023
	£7,000	Female/7	*Fraser v Southampton City C* (Southampton County Ct), para 1023
Teeth	£13,000 (total damages)	Male/1–22	*Wills v Critchley* (settled out of court), para 1024
	£2,679.42	Female/21	*Geard v Sukevics* (settled out of court), para 1024
Teeth and face	£5,000	Male/32	*Edwards v Blackmore* (Torquay County Ct), para 1025
Neck	£9,000	Female/53	*Poulton v Manchester City C* (Manchester County Ct), para 1026
	£8,500	Male/33	*Doherty v Brown* (Reading County Ct), para 1026
	£8,000	Female/43	*Fisher v Bandwidth Vehicles Rentals* (Reading County Ct), para 1026
	£7,800	Male/48	*Winfindale v Roberts* (Truro County Ct), para 1026
	£6,500	Female/45	*Bond v West Midlands Travel* (Birmingham County Ct), para 1026

INJURY	PSLA	SEX/AGE	CITATION & REVIEW PARA NUMBER
	£4,500	Male/15	*Brown v Ledson* (Southport County Ct), para 1026
	£4,500	Female/50	*Flaherty v Acron Travel* (settled out of court), para 1026
	£4,000	Female/37	*Brinkworth v Payne & Co* (Reading County Ct), para 1026
	£3,500	Female/29	*Pollard v Blackman* (Reading County Ct), para 1026
	£2,700	Female/37	*Paul v Payne* (Epsom County Ct), para 1026
	£2,500	Female/15	*Pearce v Abraham Shaw & Co* (Halifax County Ct), para 1026
	£1,500	Male/39	*Hemsley v Hesketh* (Blackpool County Ct), para 1026
	£1,500	Female/44	*Sharp v MTL Trust Holdings* (Liverpool County Ct), para 1026
	£1,500	Male/20	*Hindle v Briggs* (Reading County Ct), para 1026
	£1,500	Female/16	*Scaife v Griffiths* (Southampton County Ct), para 1026
	£1,250	Male/26	*Bass v Medley* (Reading County Ct), para 1026
	£1,250	Male/44	(CICB), para 1026
	£1,100	Male/32	*Flaherty v Catley* (Birkenhead County Ct), para 1026
	£900	Male/33	*Jones v Mercury Communications* (Birkenhead County Ct), para 1026
	£750	Male/15	*Paxton v Newman* (Exeter County Ct), para 1026

INJURY	PSLA	SEX/AGE	CITATION & REVIEW PARA NUMBER
	£650	Male/24	*Ballard v Digital Equipment Corpn* (Wandsworth County Ct), para 1026
	£600	Female/26	*Farmer v Rylance* (Reading County Ct), para 1026
	£500	Male/22	*Nettleton v Wright* (Birkenhead County Ct), para 1026
	£500	Female/38	*Yates v Dowdeswell* (Birkenhead County Ct), para 1026
Neck and shoulder	£2,200	Female/47	*Johnson v Fairclough* (settled out of court), para 1027
Neck and back	£7,500	Female/52	*Sachs v Harvey* (Romford County Ct), para 1028
	£1,515 (including interest)	Male/73	*Stimson v Williams* (Birkenhead County Ct), para 1028
	£1,000	Female/27	*Wilson v Fenlon* (Birkenhead County Ct), 1028
Neck and hip	£4,717.50 (including interest)	Female/46	*Re Shakespeare* (Blackburn County Ct), para 1029
Shoulder	£12,500	Male/40	*Mills v Morris Motorcycles (a Firm)* (Cardiff County Ct), para 1030
	£3,250	Male/24	*Blanche v Brown* (Exeter County Ct), para 1030
Back	£22,500	Female/23	*McIlgrew v Devon CC* (Court of Appeal), para 1031
	£20,000	Male/47	*Scott v BVS International* (Mayor's and City of London County Ct), para 1031
	£15,000	Female/36	*Thomas v Bath District Health Authority* (Court of Appeal), para 1031

INJURY	PSLA	SEX/AGE	CITATION & REVIEW PARA NUMBER
	£12,000	Male/24	*Leech v Ward* (Burton-upon-Trent County Ct), para 1031
	£6,800	Female/29 (at trial)	*Downer v Murray* (Bristol County Ct), para 1031
	£6,500	Male/51	*Wheeler v Ford Motor Company* (Cardiff County Ct), para 1031
	£5,333	Female/42	*Duffy v Lanarkshire Health Board* (Outer House), para 1031
	£5,000	Female/49	*Parkinson v Longfield Care Homes* (Preston County Ct), para 1031
	£4,750	Female/20	*Shields v Vera* (Reading County Ct), para 1031
Back and scarring	£3,250	Female/28	*Hartfield v Green* (Mayor's and City of London County Ct), para 1032
Back and hip	£16,000	Female/17	*Kirk v Laine Theatre Arts* (Nottingham County Ct), para 1033
Back and knee	£1,500	Female/23 (at trial)	*Martin v Willis* (Sheffield County Ct), para 1034
Chest	£25,000	Male/52	*McKenzie v Cape Building Products* (Second Division), para 1035
	£15,650 (amount of payment in)	Female/45	*D'Arcy v Stockport Health Authority* (QBD), para 1035
Chest and lungs	£30,000	Male/63	*Stanners v Graham Builders Merchants* (Outer House), para 1036
	£8,000	Male/55 (at trial)	*McCance v Newalls Insulation* (Outer House), para 1036
Trunk	£1,325 (including interest)	Male/34 (at trial)	*McCallion v Dodd* (Bristol County Ct), para 1037

INJURY	PSLA	SEX/AGE	CITATION & REVIEW PARA NUMBER
Abdomen	£30,250 (including interest)	Male/17	*McDonnell v Woodhouse and Jones (a firm)* (QBD), para 1038
Arm	£20,000	Male/29	(CICB), para 1039
	£4,000	Male/25	*Beecham v Right* (Doncaster County Ct), para 1039
	£3,971 (including interest)	Female/6	*Morgan v Southampton City C* (Southampton County Ct), para 1039
	£850	Male/2	*Smith v Blue Band Motors* (settled out of court), para 1039
Arm and shoulder	£8,000	Male/45	*Cole v Weir Pumps* (Outer House), para 1040
Arm and hand	£6,500	Male/29	*McCutcheon v Lothian Regional Council* (Outer House), para 1041
Arm and leg	£22,500	Male/48	*Cavanagh v BP Chemicals* (Outer House), para 1042
Arm and foot	(1) £6,500 (2) £5,000	(1) Male/45 (2) Female/51	*Tweedy v Newboult* (Outer House), para 1043
Elbow	£95,000	Male/38	*Girvan v Inverness Farmers Dairy* (Court of Session), para 1044
	£8,000	Male/44	*Hunter v Clyde Shaw* (Outer House), para 1044
	£3,500	Female/33	*Clarke v Liverpool City C* (Liverpool County Ct), para 1044
Wrist	£11,995	Female/15	(CICB), para 1045
	£5,500	Female/22	*Kitching v Tesco Stores* (Leeds County Ct), para 1045
	£4,000	Male/24	*Burrow v Pontefract Hospital NHS Trust* (settled out of court), para 1045

INJURY	PSLA	SEX/AGE	CITATION & REVIEW PARA NUMBER
	£3,500	Male/13	*Hill v Dudley MBC* (Stourbridge County Ct) para 1045
	£3,000	Male/53	*Fowler v South Yorkshire Transport* (Sheffield County Ct), para 1045
	£2,250	Male/18	*Abbott v Roebuck t/a The Hollywood Bowl* (Bromley County Ct), para 1045
Wrist and fingers	£20,000	Female/21	*(CICB),* para 1046
Hand	£10,500	Male/33	*Hall v Hi-Tech Integrity Castings* (QBD), para 1047
	£7,500	Male/44	*Wheeler v Central Independent Television* (Nottingham County Ct), para 1047
	£6,000	Male/22	*Parker v Scott* (Workington County Ct), para 1047
	£5,000	Female/8	*Mallett v Committee for the Time Being of the Hanney War Memorial Hall* (Oxford County Ct), para 1047
	£3,500	Male/37	*Farnan v Liverpool City C* (Liverpool County Ct), para 1047
	£1,800	Female/17	*Brogan v Leicestershire Health Authority* (settled out of court), para 1047
	£1,000	Female/39	*Khalifa v Hardy* (Halifax County Ct), para 1047
	£950	Female/41	*Pullen v Birds Eye Walls* (Hull County Ct), para 1047
Finger	£1,000	Female/38	*Lea v William Baird* (Manchester County Ct), para 1048

INJURY	PSLA	SEX/AGE	CITATION & REVIEW PARA NUMBER
Sphincter	£30,000	Female/25	*H v F* (settled out of court), para 1049
Vagina	£9,000	Female/32	*Link v Pontefract Hospitals NHS Trust* (settled out of court), para 1050
Leg	£35,000	Male/49	*Davey v MJF Precision Welding* (Portsmouth County Ct), para 1051
	£17,000	Male/35	*Walledge v Brown* (Outer House), para 1051
	£15,000	Female/26	(CICB), para 1051
	£15,000	Male/19	*Hicks v Munley* (Birkenhead County Ct), para 1051
	£6,500	Male/7	*Tildsley v Adams* (settled out of court), para 1051
	£5,228	Female/9	*Seabridge v Scarborough BC* (Huddersfield County Ct), para 1051
	£3,250	Female/21	*Bent v Bolton MBC* (Bristol County Ct), para 1051
	£2,000	Female/42	*Turner v Dale* (Chesterfield County Ct), para 1051
	£1,250	Female/4	*Narewal v Birmingham Cable* (settled out of court), para 1051
Knee	£24,200	Male/50	*Rosen v Wheatgrove* (Central London County Ct), para 1052
	£17,500	Female/32	*Steward v Gates Hydraulics* (Peterborough County Ct), para 1052
	£8,000	Female/19	*Fisher v Strachan* (settled out of court), para 1052

INJURY	PSLA	SEX/AGE	CITATION & REVIEW PARA NUMBER
	£4,000	Male/31	*Back v Sharpe* (Dartford County Ct), para 1052
	£1,500	Male/4	*McCarthy v British Gas* (Exeter County Ct), para 1052
Ankle	£65,000 (total damages)	Male/39	*Kelk v Starbake Anglia* (settled out of court), para 1053
Foot	£10,000	Male/21	*Wright v Macclesfield Health Authority* (Altrincham County Ct), para 1054
	£5,250	Male/25	*Almond v Britt-Waight* (Halifax County Ct), para 1054
	£1,500	Female/13	*Jones v Winteringham* (settled out of court), para 1054
Ankle and foot	£6,500	Female/45	*Tweedy v Newboult* (Outer House), para 1043
Minor injuries	£1,000	Male/19	*Jinks v Ramzan* (Newport (Gwent) County Ct), para 1055
	£900	Female/—	*Kotecha v Harrow LBC* (Willesden County Ct), para 1055
	£700	Male/2	*Hewson v Lewis* (settled out of court), para 1055

TABLE OF ARTICLES

ADMINISTRATIVE LAW

AGENCY

AGRICULTURE

ANIMALS

ARBITRATION

COMMONS

COMPANIES

COMPULSORY ACQUISITION OF LAND

COMPUTERS AND INFORMATION TECHNOLOGY

CONFIDENCE AND DATA PROTECTION

CONFLICT OF LAWS

CONSTITUTIONAL LAW

CONSUMER CREDIT

CONSUMER PROTECTION

CONTEMPT OF COURT

CONTRACT

CONVEYANCING

COPYRIGHT

CORONERS

COUNTY COURTS

COURTS

CRIMINAL LAW

CUSTOMS AND EXCISE

DAMAGES AND COMPENSATION

DEEDS AND OTHER INSTRUMENTS

DISCOVERY, INSPECTION AND INTERROGATORIES

DIVORCE

EASEMENTS

ECCLESIASTICAL LAW

EDUCATION

EMPLOYMENT

ENVIRONMENT

EQUITY

EUROPEAN COMMUNITIES

Table of Articles

EVIDENCE [CIVIL]

EXECUTION

EXECUTORS AND ADMINISTRATORS

EXTRADITION AND FUGITIVE OFFENDERS

FAMILY ARRANGEMENTS, UNDUE INFLUENCE AND VOIDABLE CONVEYANCES

FINANCIAL SERVICES

FISHERIES

FOOD, DAIRIES AND SLAUGHTERHOUSES

Table of Articles

HUSBAND AND WIFE

INCOME TAXATION

INHERITANCE TAXATION

INJUNCTIONS

MEDICINE, PHARMACY, DRUGS AND MEDICINAL PRODUCTS

MENTAL HEALTH

MISREPRESENTATION

MONEY

MORTGAGE

NATIONAL HEALTH SERVICE

NEGLIGENCE

NUISANCE

PRESS, PRINTING AND PUBLISHING

PRISONS

RAILWAYS, INLAND WATERWAYS AND PIPE-LINES

RATING AND THE COUNCIL TAX

REAL PROPERTY

SETTLEMENTS
New Legislation on Settlements, John Line: Tax Journal, Issue 324, p 16

SEX DISCRIMINATION
All Dressed Up and Nowhere to Go, Ann Spowart Taylor (on employers' right to control the appearance of their staff): 139 SJ 546

EC Law and the Dismissal of Pregnant Servicewomen, Anthony Arnull: (1995) 24 ILJ 215

Equality of Treatment: A Variable Concept? Philippa Watson: (1995) 24 ILJ 33

Judicial Education on Equality, Livingston Armytage (on educating the judiciary about sex and race equality): 58 MLR 160

A Recent Problem? Barbara Hewson (on sexual harassment at the Bar): 145 NLJ 626

Rights and Remedies: Part-Time Workers and the Equal Opportunities Commission, Anne Morris: (1994) 1 JSWFL 1

Ruling Out Affirmative Action, Sionaidh Douglas-Scott (on the approach to affirmative action by the European Court of Justice in comparison with the United States Supreme Court): 145 NLJ 1586

Sexual Harassment: Moving Away from Discrimination, Janet Dine and Bob Watt: 58 MLR 343

Sexual Harassment—Opening Up Pandora's Box? Peter Townsend and Arthur Baker: 159 JP Jo 39

Sexual Orientation Discrimination and Europe, Frances Russell: 145 NLJ 338

Skirting Around Sexual Harassment, Irene Mackay and Jill Earnshaw: 145 NLJ 338

Soliciting Equality—The Way Forward, Clare McGlynn (on discrimination against women solicitors): 145 NLJ 1065

SHIPPING AND NAVIGATION
General Average Ancient and Modern, John Macdonald: [1995] LMCLQ 480

Insolvency at Sea, Sir Jonathan Mance (on the Third Party (Rights against Insurers) Act 1930): [1995] LMCLQ 34

The Master—Is He Still in Command? Frode Grotmol: 145 NLJ 1534, 1581

Multi-Party Maritime Arbitrations, Philip Yang: [1995] ADRLJ 30

Procedural Reform in Maritime Arbitration, Bruce Harris: [1995] ADRLJ 18

'Safer Ships, Cleaner Seas': The Report of the Donaldson Inquiry Into the Prevention of Pollution from Merchant Shipping, Mark Wallace: [1995] LMCLQ 404

Ships are Different: The Case for Limitation of Liability, David Steel: [1995] LMCLQ 77

The 1993 Convention on Maritime Liens and Mortgages, Francesco Berlingieri: [1995] LMCLQ 57

SOCIAL SECURITY AND SOCIAL SERVICES
Avoiding the Benefits Trap, Petra Lucioli (on the effect of personal injury settlements on welfare benefits): LS Gaz, 18 January 1995, p 18

Continuing Offences—Section 111, Social Security Administration Act 1992, T M Daber: 159 JP Jo 299

Elderly People and Residential Care, Gordon Ashton: 139 SJ 978, 1010, 1036, 1074

Incapacity Benefit, Martin Barnes: LA, May 1995, p 16

Income Support and Mortgage Interest: the New Rules, Adam Griffith: LA, October 1995, p 17

Income Support Mortgage Interest Changes, Kate Tonge: 145 NLJ 1418

Jobseekers Act 1995: Consolidation With a Sting of Contractual Compliance, Helen Carr: (1995) 24 ILJ 395

National Insurance Concessions, David Harris (on concessionary relief from National Insurance contributions): Tax Journal, Issue 306, p 16

Recoupment Planning, David Milton (on deduction of state benefits from personal injury awards): 145 NLJ 784

SOLICITORS
A Brave New World, John Peysner and Paul Balen (on conditional fees): LS Gaz, 31 Aug 1995, p 20

The Case for a National Legal Service, Bob Hoyle: 145 NLJ 189

Conditional Fees: Investing in the Future, Paul Balen: 139 SJ 678

Contingency Fees, Clive Boxer: 139 SJ 704

Equal and Decent Treatment, Henry Hodge (on the Law Society's anti-discrimination measures): 145 NLJ 303

Exploding the Myths of Conditional Fees, Barjinder Sahota: 145 NLJ 592

Forgery and Property: Effects and Remedies, Josephine Hayes (on *Penn v Bristol & West Building Society* (1995) Times, 19 June (para 2783)): 139 SJ 716

Insurance Cover for Redundancy and Sickness, Michael Wilson: 139 SJ 722

A Lack of Authority, Daniel Worsley (on *Penn v Bristol & West Building Society* (1995) Times, 19 June (para 2783)): LS Gaz, 21 June 1995, p 23

STAMP DUTIES

STOCK EXCHANGE

TELECOMMUNICATIONS AND BROADCASTING

TORT

Table of Articles

HALSBURY'S

Annual Abridgment 1995

ADMINISTRATIVE LAW

Halsbury's Laws of England (4th edn) Vol 1(1) (reissue), paras 1–300

1 Articles

Appealing Dilemmas, Francis Fitzpatrick (on judicial review of tax cases): Tax Journal, Issue 323, p 12

The Case For a National Legal Service, Bob Hoyle: 145 NLJ 189

Costs Against Justices, Alan Murdie: 159 JP Jo 599

Judicial Magicians, Michael Fordham (on procedural ingenuity found in public law): LS Gaz, 8 March 1995, p 24

Judicial Review, Ian Saunders (on judicial review of tax cases): Tax Journal, Issue 291, p 14, Issue 294, p 11

The Lord Chancellor's Role Within the Government, Lord Mackay of Clashfern: 145 NLJ 1650

Reasons for Decisions, Derek Morgan (on *R v Cambridge District Health Authority, ex p B* [1995] 2 All ER 129 (para 12)): 145 NLJ 428

Time Limits in Administrative Law, Gary Blaker: 139 SJ 1208, 1231

Transfer of Cases Between Public and Private Law Procedures: the English Law Commission's Proposals, Carl Emery: [1995] CJQ 163

2 Declaration—action—interim relief—interlocutory injunction

See *Newport Association Football Club Ltd v Football Association of Wales Ltd*, para 1707.

3 Habeas corpus—refusal to release applicant on bail

See *Re Marshall*, para 752.

4 Judicial review—appeal—error of law

See *Conoco Ltd v Customs and Excise Comrs*, para 3047.

5 Judicial review—application—adjournment of substantive hearing—adjournment pending determination of criminal proceedings

See *R v Birmingham City Coroner, ex p Najada*, para 691.

6 Judicial review—application—housing benefit—notice of proceedings—service of notice on Secretary of State

See *R v Liverpool City Council, ex p Muldoon; R v Rent Officer Service, ex p Kelly*, para 2729.

7 Judicial review—decision of Attorney General—decision not to institute contempt proceedings

See *R v A-G, ex p Taylor*, para 2394.

8 Judicial review—decision of coroner—decision not to allow persons to examine witnesses at inquest

See *R v HM Coroner for the Southern District of Greater London, ex p Driscoll*, para 689.

9   Judicial review—decision of Court of Aldermen—refusal to confirm election of alderman—failure to give reasons

See *R v Corporation of London, ex p Matson*, para 1988.

10   Judicial review—decision of government department—change of policy—legitimate expectation

The Ministry of Agriculture, Fisheries and Food changed its fishing licensing policy on the strength of which the applicant company had already purchased a beam trawler. The applicant sought judicial review of the ministry's decision, contending that it had had in law a legitimate expectation that any change in licensing policy would not be such as to frustrate the completion of the process of licence aggregation for the trawler, and that the new licensing policy should have included provisions in favour of fishermen who had irrevocably entered commitments to acquire beam trawl licences and who had demonstrated a real and genuine intent to do so. *Held*, (1) legitimacy was a function of expectations induced by government and of policy considerations which militated against their fulfilment. The balance in the first instance was for the policy-maker to strike; but if the outcome was challenged by judicial review, the court's criterion was not the bare rationality of the policy-maker's conclusion and its task was not only to recognise the constitutional importance of ministerial freedom to formulate and to reformulate policy, but also to protect the interests of those individuals whose expectations of different treatment had a legitimacy which in fairness outweighed the policy choice which threatened to frustrate it. It was not unfair, in the light of the government's legitimate policy imperatives and objectives, to exclude from the policy's transitional provisions enterprises in the position of the applicant, notwithstanding that the latter had embarked on the acquisition of transferable licence entitlements in anticipation and with the genuine intention of being able to aggregate them on to a vessel for the purpose of beam trawling. Fairness did not require the perceived need for a swift limitation of beam trawling to be sacrificed in favour of a class whose expectations, however reasonable and however genuine, might well have eventually subverted the policy. The means adopted by the ministry bore a fair proportion to the end in view. Accordingly, the application would be dismissed. Further, while the framer of a policy for the exercise of a governmental discretion should be prepared to consider making exceptions where merited, the inclusion of thought-out exceptions in the policy itself might well be exhaustive of the obligation and while any further candidates for exemption had to be considered, it would always be a legitimate consideration that to make one such exception could set up an unanswerable case of partiality or arbitrariness. A decision-maker had to balance the case for making no such exception against the case for generalising it. The ministry had acted within the band of rational policy choices.

  R v Ministry of Agriculture Fisheries and Food, ex p Hamble (Offshore) Fisheries Ltd [1995] 2 All ER 714 (Queen's Bench Division: Sedley J).

11   Judicial review—decision of government department—decision to withdraw right to compensation

See *R v Ministry of Agriculture, Fisheries and Food, ex p St Clere's Hall Farm*, para 55.

12   Judicial review—decision of health authority—decision not to finance specific treatment

A district health authority decided not to provide funding for the further medical treatment of a 10-year-old girl who was suffering from a life-threatening illness on the ground that it would not be in her best interests and that the substantial cost of the treatment in relation to the small prospect of its success would not be an effective use of the authority's limited resources. On an application for judicial review of the decision, *held*, the courts were not arbiters of the merits of cases of this kind. The authority's decision-maker had not disregarded the wishes of the girl's family. The fact that he had described the proposed treatment, which did not have a well tried track record of success, as 'experimental', was neither unfair nor inaccurate in view of the estimates of success and the opinion of the doctor who was prepared to undertake the treatment. The authority did not have unlimited resources and had to make difficult and agonising decisions over the use of its resources. It had not exceeded its powers or acted unreasonably. Its decision was lawful and, accordingly, the court could not intervene by way of judicial review. The application would be dismissed.

  R v Cambridge Health Authority, ex p B [1995] 2 All ER 129 (Court of Appeal: Sir Thomas Bingham MR, Sir Stephen Brown P and Simon Brown LJ).

13 Judicial review—decision of health authority—decision to limit availability of treatment

See *R v Sheffield Health Authority, ex p Seale*, para 2132.

14 Judicial review—decision of Home Secretary—change of prison rules

See *R v Secretary of State for the Home Department, ex p Briggs*, para 2405.

15 Judicial review—decision of Home Secretary—mandatory life sentence—decision to increase minimum period to be served by prisoner

See *R v Secretary of State for the Home Department, ex p Pierson*, para 2408.

16 Judicial review—decision of local authority—decision not to temporarily close roads to reduce traffic pollution

See *R v Greenwich London Borough Council, ex p Williams*, para 1518.

17 Judicial review—decision of local authority—provision of council housing—duty to make inquiries

See *R v Northavon District Council, ex p Palmer*, para 1529.

18 Judicial review—decision of local authority—rescission of decision to provide accommodation to homeless applicant—whether decision subject to judicial review principles

See *R v Ealing London Borough Council, ex p Parkinson*, para 1541.

19 Judicial review—decision of magistrates' court—alternative of appeal by way of case stated

It has been held that, when challenging a decision of the magistrates' court, it is preferable to appeal by way of case stated rather than apply for judicial review. This is because judicial review ought to be used as a last resort where every other avenue of challenge has been exhausted and because on an appeal by way of case stated the High Court will be presented with all the findings of fact made by the magistrates. It will be a matter of grave concern to the High Court if the circumstances of the case suggest that an applicant for judicial review may not have acted in good faith.

If, on an application for judicial review of a magistrates' court decision, there is material on which the magistrates could have reached that decision it is almost impossible for an applicant to claim *Wednesbury* unreasonableness. In particular, if proceedings for non-payment of community charge discloses a wilful refusal to pay, it is not necessary for the court to investigate the alternative of culpable neglect.

R v Oldbury Justices, ex p Smith (1994) 159 JP 316 (Queen's Bench Division: Turner J).

20 Judicial review—decision of magistrates' court—refusal to adjourn proceedings

See *R v Lincoln Justices, ex p Count*, para 2008.

21 Judicial review—decision of Secretary of State—objection to appointment of chief executive of life assurance company

See *Buchanan v Secretary of State for Trade and Industry*, para 1718.

22 Judicial review—decision of Secretary of State—refusal to confirm order prohibiting resumption of quarrying

See *R v Secretary of State for Wales, ex p Mid-Glamorgan County Council*, para 2862.

23 Judicial review—decision of university—exclusion of student

See *Joobeen v University of Stirling*, para 1195.

24   Judicial review—decision of value added tax and duties tribunal—refusal to refer question to European Court of Justice—justiciability

On an appeal by a taxpayer against an assessment to value added tax, a value added tax and duties tribunal decided that the application of Community law was clear so that a ruling from the European Court of Justice was not required. The taxpayer sought judicial review of the decision. *Held*, the Tribunals and Inquiries Act 1992, s 11 made provision for an appeal to the High Court where any party to proceedings was dissatisfied in point of law with a decision, direction or order of the tribunal. While the tribunal's refusal to refer a question was an interlocutory order, it did not follow that it was not a decision to which s 11 applied. Whether one called it a decision, direction or order, the tribunal's refusal to refer a question was plainly encompassed by the words of s 11. The present case could not be distinguished from the type of case for which the appeal procedure had been provided. As there was an alternative remedy available to the applicant that it should have adopted, its application for judicial review would be refused.

R v London Value Added Tax and Duties Tribunal, ex p Conoco Ltd [1995] STC 468 (Queen's Bench Division: Popplewell J).

25   Judicial review—disciplinary tribunal—court proceedings brought simultaneously— stay of tribunal's inquiries sought—public interest element

The large scale misappropriation of assets belonging to pension funds was discovered. The applicants, auditors of both the pension funds and of companies that were trustees and managers of the relevant assets of those funds, were expected to be defendants in various civil actions. They were also subject to inquiries relating to disciplinary proceedings by a professional tribunal. Their application for a stay of those proceedings pending the trials of the civil actions was refused by the tribunal. On their application for judicial review of that decision, it was submitted that having to defend parallel proceedings brought a serious risk of injustice, that there was no urgency in continuing the inquiry and that the continuation of the inquiry might prejudice any criminal trials. *Held*, the court was required to conduct a balancing exercise of weighing the public interest in the prompt and efficient operation of the disciplinary scheme of the tribunal against the risk of serious prejudice to the fairness of the trial of other proceedings, which might result in an injustice. There was strong public interest in the continuance of the inquiry not being delayed and there was no reason to think that the inquiry and any disciplinary measures would not be conducted fairly. Disciplinary proceedings were necessary both to ensure that regulatory questions arousing public concern were addressed within a reasonable time scale and that they were addressed by a body with power to deal with them by way of fine and disqualification. They would not be efficacious if they had to await the resolution of civil proceedings, which might happen long after the event. The case raised questions of real public concern as to the protection afforded by professional auditors. If criminal trials were to take place, the parties and the trial judge would be alive to any potential risk of prejudice. Accordingly, the application would be dismissed.

R v Chance, ex p Smith (1995) Times, 28 January (Queen's Bench Division: Henry LJ and Kay J). *R v Panel on Take-overs and Mergers, ex p Al Fayed* [1992] BCLC 938, CA (1992 Abr para 441) applied.

26   Judicial review—exemption from income tax assessment—susceptibility to judicial review

See *R v IRC, ex p Caglar*, para 1607.

27   Judicial review—government consultation paper—justiciability

Six local authorities sought leave to apply for judicial review of the consultation process by virtue of which the Secretary of State exercised his powers, under the Civil Aviation Act 1982, s 78, to regulate noise levels made by aircraft at certain airports. *Held*, the consultation document contained such patent inconsistencies and contradictions that they could be easily recognised and commented upon by those persons consulted. Such matters lay within the purview of the political process, not the law. Accordingly, the application would be dismissed.

R v Secretary of State for Transport, ex p Richmond upon Thames London Borough Council (1995) Times, 11 May (Queen's Bench Division: Sedley J).

28   Judicial review—leave to apply—time limit for applications

Council Directives (EC) 91/680, 92/12 and 94/4 permitted some duty and tax-free purchases on journeys between member states for a transitional period until 30 June 1999, notwithstanding the establishment of the internal market as from 1993. These Directives were subsequently implemented by the Value Added Tax (Tax Free Shops) Order 1992, SI 1992/3131, the Excise Duties (Personal Relief) Order 1992, SI 1992/3135 and the Value Added Tax (Tax Free Shops) Order 1994, SI 1994/686.

Channel Tunnel operators had been granted leave ex parte to apply for judicial review of the government orders which exempted sea and air carriers from the abolition of duty-free sales within the European Union. The various ferry companies and air operators opposed the application. *Held*, RSC Ord 53, r 4(1) provided that an application for judicial review should be made promptly and in any case within three months from the date on which the grounds for the application first arose. Although leave had already been granted ex parte that did not prevent it from being set aside under RSC Ord 32, r 6. The dates on which the grounds for the application first arose were the dates on which the orders were made, which was over three months before the application was made. Accordingly, the ex parte leave granted should be set aside.

R v Customs and Excise Comrs, ex p Eurotunnel plc (1995) Independent, 23 February (Queen's Bench Division: Balcombe LJ and Tucker J).

29 Judicial review and statutory appeals—Special Educational Needs Tribunal—decision

See *R v Special Educational Needs Tribunal, ex p South Glamorgan County Council*, para 1187.

30 Misconduct in public office—application of offence to local authority employees

See *R v Bowden*, para 909.

31 Natural justice—destruction of dog ordered without informing owner—breach of natural justice

See *R v Ealing Justices, ex p Fanneran*, para 102.

32 Natural justice—fair hearing—principles of fairness

It has been held that, when considering whether the decision of an administrative body is fair, the rules of natural justice depend on their context. The court should take into account factors such as the structure of the relevant decision-making body and the nature of its task. It should also be careful to avoid treating the decision-making process of such bodies as though they are judicial tribunals.

R v Avon County Council, ex p Crabtree [1996] 1 FLR 502 (Court of Appeal: Neill and Millett LJJ and Sir Ian Glidewell).

33 Parliamentary Commissioner—departments and authorities subject to investigation

The Parliamentary Commissioner Order 1995, SI 1995/1615 (in force on 31 July 1995), adds a number of arts councils and research councils to the list of departments and authorities which are subject to investigation by the Parliamentary Commissioner for Administration. In addition, two research councils which have ceased to exist are removed from the list.

ADMIRALTY

Halsbury's Laws of England (4th edn) Vol 1(1) (reissue), paras 301–564

34 Action in rem—arrest of ship—arrest of more than one ship prohibited

Scotland
The Administration of Justice Act 1956, s 47(1) provides that a ship may not be arrested to enforce a claim unless the ship is the ship with which the action is concerned or all the shares in the ship are owned by the defendant to the action.

It has been held that reference to 'a ship' in the 1956 Act, s 47 is proof that the 1956 Act is intended to incorporate the provisions of the Brussels Convention 1952 which prohibit the arrest of more than one ship owned by the defendant of an action.

Interatlantic (Namibia) (Pty) Ltd v Okeanski Ribolov Ltd (The Alfala) [1995] 2 Lloyd's Rep 286 (Outer House). *The Banco* [1971] 1 All ER 524, CA applied.

Similar provision to the 1956 Act, s 47 is made for England in the Supreme Court Act 1981, s 21(8).

35   Admiralty Court—revised procedure

Clarke J has issued the following *Practice Direction* ([1996] 1 All ER 188).

1. General
(1) Reference to the 'registry' in the following is a reference to the Admiralty and Commercial Registry.
(2) These directions should, where applicable, govern the practice to be followed in admiralty matters in the registry.
(3) These directions come into force on 11 January 1996 and supersede all previous admiralty registrar's *Practice Notes* or *Practice Directions*.

2. Application of masters' Practice Directions
In cases not covered by these directions, the masters' *Practice Directions* should, where applicable, be followed with such modifications as the circumstances require, for example, the substitution of 'Admiralty and Commercial Registry' for 'Central Office', and 'action department' and 'admiralty registrar' for 'master' and 'practice master'.

3. Forms of writs and acknowledgments of service
See RSC Ord 6, r 1, Ord 75, r 3, and Appendices A, B.
If it is desired to commence proceedings both in rem and in personam, separate writs must be issued: *Practice Direction (Admiralty: Writ)* [1979] 1 WLR 426 (1979 Abr para 2102). Where the defendants are described in the writ as 'the owners of the ship X', any acknowledgment of service, in addition to stating the description appearing in the writ, must also state the full names of the persons acknowledging service and the nature of their ownership.
In the event of there being insufficient space on the acknowledgment of service form itself, such additional information must appear on a separate document to accompany and be lodged with the acknowledgment of service form.

4. Admiralty Court Practice

Preface
1. Practice in the Commercial Court has, for some time, been governed not only by RSC Ord 72, but also by the *Guide to Commercial Court Practice* (see *The Supreme Court Practice 1995* (Vol 1, paras 72/A1–72/A30, 3rd supplement)).
2. Many of the actions heard in the Admiralty Court raise similar issues to those heard in the Commercial Court. Many of those who regularly practise in the Admiralty Court also practise in the Commercial Court. Since 1987, there has been an Admiralty and Commercial Registry. In those circumstances, it is desirable that there should be as much harmonisation as possible between the practice of the two courts, provided that care is taken to ensure that the two courts remain independent so that each may best serve the interests of those who wish to use it.
3. Those aims could best be served by improving the practice of the Admiralty Court in the following areas: the hearing of interlocutory applications by the admiralty judge, the listing of actions, and the harmonisation of the general practice of the two courts where appropriate.

A. Interlocutory Applications
4. With effect from 8 June 1993, most summonses and other interlocutory applications, including motions, which are to be heard by the admiralty judge and which are short enough to be heard on 'summons day', will ordinarily be listed for hearing on Fridays. The admiralty registrar will continue to hear interlocutory applications as before.

B. Trials
5.1 With effect from 8 June 1993, trials will thus be heard on Mondays to Thursdays and, save in exceptional circumstances, will not be heard on Fridays.
5.2 Except where the admiralty judge otherwise directs, all actions will be heard by the admiralty judge. However, the Admiralty and Commercial Registry will maintain a list of all matters to be heard in the Admiralty and Commercial Courts in order to ensure that the judicial resources of both courts are used to best effect. All such listing is to be under the direction of the Admiralty and Commercial Court listing officer.
5.3 That will enable the admiralty judge to hear actions in the Commercial Court, and it will also enable judges of the Commercial Court to hear actions in the Admiralty Court where the facts of the particular case make that course appropriate.
5.4 It is stressed that the purpose of the change is to make both courts operate as efficiently as possible. Care will be taken to ensure that an admiralty action which involves questions of

navigation, or other particular matters of an essentially admiralty nature, will be heard by the admiralty judge or, where necessary, by a judge nominated by the admiralty judge who has experience of such questions or matters.

C. Practice

6.1 With effect from 8 June 1993, the *Guide to the Commercial Court Practice* will govern the practice in the Admiralty Court so far as applications to and hearings before the admiralty judge are concerned, save where the provisions of that guide apply only to commercial actions, and save that applications in the Admiralty Court will continue to be heard by the admiralty judge or the admiralty registrar in accordance with the Rules of the Supreme Court.

6.2 Thus, the following sections of the *Guide to Commercial Court Practice* will apply to proceedings in the Admiralty Court before the admiralty judge:

II Ex parte applications
IV Service out of the jurisdiction
V Mareva and Anton Piller injunctions
VI Summonses inter partes
VII Arbitration matters
VIII Security for costs
IX Pleadings
X Amendment of pleadings
XI Discovery and interrogatories
XII The Summons for directions (except for paras 12.1, 12.2)
XIII Preliminary issues
XIV Exchange of evidence: factual witnesses
XV Exchange of evidence: expert witnesses
XVI Documents
XVII Preparation for long trials (save that the reference in para 17.2 to a single judge should be a reference to the admiralty judge, unless he otherwise directs)
XVIII Pre-trial check-list
XIX The trial

6.3 The reason that some parts of the *Guide to Commercial Court Practice* have been omitted is that they do not seem to be appropriate to an admiralty action, having regard to the express terms of Ord 75 and to the fact that Ord 72 does not apply to an admiralty action. However, suggestions from the Admiralty Court Committee, or indeed from any other user of the Admiralty Court, as to how the practice of the court could be improved in that or any other respect, are welcome.

6.4 The above direction replaces direction 4 of *Practice Direction (Admiralty: Directions)* [1973] 1 WLR 1146.

Conclusion

7.1 The above *Practice Direction* was issued with the consent of Lord Taylor of Gosforth CJ, and with the approval of Saville J as judge in charge of the Commercial Court.

7.2 The changes in the practice set out above will come into effect from 8 June 1993, subject to any adjustments which may be necessary as a result of arrangements or orders already made at that date of the *Practice Direction*.

5. Discharge of cargo under arrest from ships not under arrest and of cargo not under arrest from ships under arrest

See RSC Ord 75, r 12.

(1) Where a ship is not under arrest but cargo on board her is, and those interested in the ship wish to discharge the cargo which is under arrest, they may, without intervening in the action, request the marshal to take the appropriate steps. If the marshal considers the request reasonable and if the applicant gives an undertaking in writing satisfactory to the marshal to pay on demand the fees of the marshal and all expenses to be incurred by him, or on his behalf, in taking the desired steps, the marshal must apply to the court under Ord 75, r 12 for the appropriate order.

(2) Where those interested are unable or unwilling to arrange for such an undertaking to be given, they may intervene in the action in which the cargo is under arrest, and apply by summons for an order for discharge of the cargo and for directions as to the fees and expenses of the marshal in and about the discharge and storage of the cargo pursuant to such order.

(3) Where a ship is under arrest but cargo on board her is not, and those interested in cargo wish to secure its discharge, one or other of the procedures outlined above may be followed.

6. Use of postal facilities in the registry
See RSC Ord 1, r 10.

(1) Queen's Bench Masters' Practice Direction, dir 3 (use of postal facilities in Queen's Bench Division) will be followed in the registry, subject to the following and any other necessary modifications.

(2) Applications together with the requisite documents must be posted to the Admiralty and Commercial Registry, Room E200, Royal Courts of Justice, Strand, London WC2A 2LL.

(3) The classes of business for which the use of postal facilities is permitted in the Queen's Bench Division is extended to cover the filing and lodgment of the following classes of documents: (i) praecipes for caveats, (ii) bail bonds and affidavits under Ord 75, r 16, (iii) preliminary acts, (iv) counter-notices to summons for directions, (v) notices and counter-notices under Ord 38, (vi) agreements between solicitors under Ord 75, r 35, (vii) claims in references, and (viii) lists of undisputed items, and documents in support of claims, in references.

(4) Documents sent by post for filing or lodgment must be accompanied by two copies of a list of the documents sent and an envelope properly addressed to the sender.

(5) On receipt of the documents in the registry, the proper officer will, if the circumstances are such that had the documents been presented personally, they would have been filed or lodged, cause them to be filed or lodged and will, by post, notify the sender that that has been done. If the documents would not have been accepted if presented personally, the proper officer will not file or lodge them, but will retain them in the registry for collection by the sender, and will, by post, so inform the sender.

(6) When the documents received through the post are filed or lodged by the proper officer, they will be sealed and entered as filed or lodged on the date on which they are received in the registry.

(7) It will not be possible for the registry to enter into any correspondence or telephonic communication concerning the refusal to accept for filing or lodgment any documents sent by post.

(8) Queen's Bench Masters' Practice Direction, dir 3, para 20 (applications by post for special appointments before masters) does not apply to applications for the appointment of a date for a reference.

7. Exhibits to affidavits: return to party lodging
When an affidavit is filed in the registry in admiralty proceedings, any exhibits to it will be returned to the party lodging them when no longer required by the court. In the case of motions and summonses, those exhibits will normally be returned at the end of the hearing.

8. Compromise or settlement by person under disability etc
(1) On a summons or originating application for approval of the settlement or compromise of a claim, or for the acceptance of money paid into court, in an action in which any party is a person under a disability, the amounts of any proposed payments must be left blank.

(2) No affidavit will usually be required on the hearing of the summons or originating summons.

(3) At least two days before the date fixed for the hearing, the parties must lodge in the registry the originals or copies of all documents to which they intend to refer at the hearing.

9. References: form of schedule to registrar's decision
See RSC Ord 75, rr 41, 42.

Where a list of agreed items has been filed under Ord 75, r 41(6), or any items have been agreed at the hearing, the registrar must not in the schedule to his decision list the agreed items separately, but must set out the total of the amounts agreed in respect of them, unless any party otherwise requests at the hearing.

10. Applications relating to foreign currency funds in court, including proceeds of sale of a ship or the property sold by the marshal
(1) When proceeds of a sale are paid into court by the marshal, or payment is made by a party to an action, and such payment is in a foreign currency, the funds must not be placed to an interest-bearing account or otherwise dealt with without the direction of the court.

(2) An application to place foreign currency to an interest-bearing account, unless made at the same time as an application for sale or other prior application, may be made by summons. Notice of the placement of foreign currency to an interest-bearing account must be given to all parties interested in the fund by the party at whose instance the foreign currency is invested.

(3) Any interested party who objects to the mode of investment of foreign currency paid into court may apply by summons to the admiralty registrar for directions.

(4) Several types of deposit are usually available, and applications to place the funds to any interest-bearing account or otherwise, must specify the type of deposit required. Advice as to those matters cannot be given by the registry staff.

11. Taxation of costs

Supreme Court Taxing Office
At the request of the admiralty registrar, all costs in admiralty matters are to be taxed in the Supreme Court Taxing Office. The procedure for the commencement of taxations is as set out in the *Supreme Court Practice 1995*, paras 62/30/1–62/30/8.

A summons to review a taxation will follow the Queen's Bench Division procedure, in accordance with *Practice Direction (Taxation: Review)* [1984] 1 WLR 856 (1984 Abr para 2022).

With the agreement of the admiralty registrar, *Practice Direction (Admiralty: Taxation Review)* [1973] 1 WLR 1424 is cancelled. *Practice Direction (Admiralty: Taxation of Costs)* [1986] 1 WLR 1310 (1986 Abr para 1973) relates to the procedure to be followed on review of taxation under RSC Ord 62, r 35.

AGENCY

Halsbury's Laws of England (4th edn) Vol 1(2) (reissue), paras 1–300

36 Articles

The Agent of a Non-Resident, David Wainman: Tax Journal, Issue 305, p 8
Agents and Compensation, Julian Roberts (on the Commercial Agents (Council Directive) Regulations 1993/3053): 145 NLJ 453
Attorneys as Trustees, Richard Oerton (on sale of a co-owned property where one co-owner is represented by someone with an enduring power of attorney): LS Gaz, 22 March 1995, p 18
Unfair Contracts, Richard Lawson (on unfair contracts in relation to agency and incorporation): 145 NLJ 697

37 Agent—company director—scope of authority

See *New Zealand Guardian Trust Co Ltd v Brooks*, para 2837.

38 Agent—goods or services supplied through agent—deemed supplies—value added tax liability

See *Wirral Metropolitan Borough Council v Customs and Excise Comrs*, para 3040.

39 Agent—proceeds of sale held in account for principal—winding up—existence of trust

See *Re Fleet Disposal Services Ltd; Spratt v AT & T Automotive Services Ltd*, para 532.

40 Agent—self-employed agent—contract of engagement—restraint of trade—severance of unlawful terms

The plaintiff, a sales agent, was paid commission for business introduced to the defendant company. His contract of engagement entitled him to renewal commission provided that he could satisfy one of two conditions. He would qualify if he either did not compete with the defendant for one year after termination of his contract or if he was aged 65 at the termination date. After leaving the defendant's employment the plaintiff made a claim for renewal commission. This was refused because he was working in competition with the defendant and was not yet aged 65 years. The plaintiff commenced proceedings to claim renewal commission. *Held*, it was possible to strike out both conditions since they were inseparable parts of a clause of the contract intended to restrain trade. This could be done without altering the character of the contract since the true consideration for receiving renewal commission was not acceptance of the requirement not to compete, but the plaintiff's work procuring business before his resignation. The defendant was simply attempting to impose new conditions on the plaintiff's right to receive renewal commission that would take effect on termination of employment.

Since the conditions were unlawful they could be severed leaving the plaintiff's right to commission enforceable under the contract. Accordingly, his claim would succeed.

Marshall v NM Financial Management Ltd [1995] 4 All ER 785 (Chancery Division: Jonathan Sumption QC).

41 Estate agent—duty of care—contractual duty

The plaintiffs claimed damages against the solicitors and estate agents who had acted for them in connection with their purchase of certain property.The claims alleged breaches of duty both in contract and tort. The solicitors were held liable in both contract and tort. The estate agents, who were held not liable in contract but liable in tort, appealed against the decision, contending that the nature and extent of their responsibilites had been limited by the express and implied terms of their contract with the plaintiffs so that no further or different responsibilites, by means of a duty of care in tort, could be imposed upon them. *Held*, the duty of care in tort was, in appropriate circumstances, imposed by the general law; the contractual obligations resulted from the common intention of the parties. There was no reason in principle why a *Hedley Byrne* type of duty could not arise in an overall set of circumstances where, by reference to certain limited aspects of those circumstances, the same parties entered into a contractual relationship involving more limited obligations than those imposed by the duty of care in tort. The duty of care in such circumstances and the duties imposed by the contract would be concurrent but not co-extensive. The difference in scope between the duty of care in tort and the duties imposed by the contract would reflect the more limited factual basis which gave rise to the contract and the absence of any term in the contract which precluded or restricted the wider duty of care in tort. The plaintiffs had alleged that the estate agents had failed to investigate adequately the planning status of the property or to advise the plaintiffs to obtain appropriate written confirmation of the authorised or established use of the property. They had not pleaded that the estate agents were in breach of the duty of care in tort because of the giving of incorrect advice as to the planning position concerning the property. The plaintiffs had not pleaded that the estate agents had given them negligent advice nor a general failure to advise as to the planning position concerning the property. There were no grounds for founding a liability in tort capable of amounting to advice upon which the plaintiffs had acted to their detriment. The estate agents were not liable in tort on a basis which was within the terms of the pleaded case. Accordingly, their appeal would be allowed.

Holt v Payne Skillington (a Firm) (1995) Times, 22 December (Court of Appeal: Hirst and Peter Gibson LJJ and Forbes J). *Hedley Byrne & Co Ltd v Heller & Partners Ltd* [1963] 2 All ER 575, HL, considered.

42 Estate agent—duty of care—purchaser relying on property particulars—negligent mis-statement

An estate agent incorrectly described a property's garden, which was half an acre, as being almost one acre. The particulars contained a standard disclaimer that statements in the particulars were not to be relied on as representations of fact. When a purchaser viewed the property he was given a copy of the particulars. Following exchange of contracts, the purchaser issued a writ claiming damages due to the estate agent's negligence. At first instance, the judge found that the estate agent owed the purchaser a duty of care in respect of the negligent mis-statement but that the purchaser had not established that he had suffered any loss. On the purchaser's appeal, *held*, (1) although the estate agent knew, or ought to have known, that the purchaser was likely to rely on his representation, he also knew that the purchaser had the particulars, which included the disclaimer. The element of proximity was therefore negatived as a reasonable person, appreciating that the statement he was proposing to rely on was a statement contained in the particulars, would understand that because of the disclaimer there was no assumption of responsibility by the estate agent. (2) It would not be unfair under the Unfair Contract Terms Act 1977 for the estate agent to rely on the disclaimer. The transaction involved a sophisticated member of the public who had ample opportunity to regulate his conduct having regard to the disclaimer and who would have been assumed by all concerned to have had the benefit of legal advice before exchanging contracts. Further, the use of disclaimers by estate agents was commonplace. Accordingly, the appeal would be dismissed.

McCullagh v Lane Fox & Partners Ltd (1995) Times, 22 December (Court of Appeal: Nourse and Hobhouse LJJ and Sir Christopher Slade). Decision of Colman J [1994] 1 EGLR 48 (1994 Abr para 59) affirmed.

See also *Holt v Payne Skillington (a firm)*, para 41.

43   Estate agent—duty to client—loss suffered by client—fraud

The plaintiff, the leasehold owner of a flat, instructed the defendant estate agents to sell his flat. It was sold to the purchaser for £210,000 and was then transferred to a subpurchaser for £395,000. £210,000 was paid to the plaintiff and £185,000 was paid to the purchaser. The subsale was a bogus transaction to defraud the lender who had loaned £296,000 on the security of the flat. The plaintiff claimed damages from the defendants on the ground that they had failed to exercise the ordinary standard of care because they had either lost or ignored a fax sent to them by the landlords' solicitors seeking clarification as to the identity of the proposed purchaser. *Held*, following the receipt of the fax, negotiations for the sale of the flat had ceased temporarily. Accordingly, the defendants were justified in not pursuing the matter of who would be the purchaser if negotiations recommenced. The failure to act on the fax was not, therefore, a breach of duty. Even if the plaintiff had known of the pretended subsale, there was no evidence that he could have renegotiated the sale price to obtain a higher price at the fraudsters' expense. Although the plaintiff would have been able to retain any money paid to him as a bona fide vendor if he had in good faith negotiated a higher price, public policy prevented the court from awarding him damages for failing to obtain a share in the proceeds of a fraud. His claim would fail.

Berkowitz v M W (St John's Wood) Ltd [1995] 1 EGLR 29 (Court of Appeal: Butler-Sloss and Hoffmann LJJ and Sir Francis Purchas).

44   Fraud by agent—failure to disclose fraud—liability of principal—validity of reinsurance contract

See *PCW Syndicates v PCW Reinsurers*, para 1740.

45   Relations between principal and third persons—notice to agent—knowledge imputed to principal

See *Halifax Mortgage Services Ltd v Stepsky*, para 2110.

AGRICULTURE

Halsbury's Laws of England (4th edn) Vol 1(2) (reissue), paras 301–1133

46   Articles

Agricultural Occupancy Conditions, H W Wilkinson: 145 NLJ 608
The Agricultural Revolution, Stephen McNulty and Della Evans (on the Agricultural Tenancies Act 1995): Estates Gazette, 29 July 1995, p 82
Business Tenancies for Farms, Roger Gibbard: Estates Gazette, January 7 1995, p 106
Cowed but Unbowed, Michael Harwood (on farm animals and public paths): 139 SJ 610
Drafting Farm Business Leases, Christopher Jessel: Estates Gazette, 11 November 1995, p 126
A Farmyard Revolution, William Barr (on the Agricultural Tenancies Act 1995): 139 SJ 650
Implications of the Agricultural Tenancies Bill, Christopher Jessel: Estates Gazette, January 28 1995, p 150
Of Sheep Dips, Pesticides and Damages for Personal Injuries, Alan Care (on claims for damages for sheep dip poisoning): 139 SJ 1250
Pastures New, Roger Yates (on the Agricultural Tenancies Act 1995): 145 NLJ 1372
Raging Bull, Michael Harwood (on farm animals and public paths): 139 SJ 628
Tenant Farming: For the Good of the Nation, Susan Bright (on the Agricultural Tenancies Act 1995): [1995] Conv 445
Termination of Leases, Graham Fife (on *Pennell v Payne* (1994) Times, 13 December (1994 Abr para 65)): Estates Gazette, 14 October 1995, p 134
Views of the Countryside, Roger Yates (on the Agricultural Tenancies Bill 1995): LS Gaz, 5 April 1995 p 16

47   Agricultural business—grants

The Farm and Conservation Grant (Variation) Scheme 1995, SI 1995/890 (in force on 15 May 1995), varies the 1989 Scheme, SI 1989/128, in compliance with Council Regulation (EC) 2328/91, to provide that where expenditure is incurred on or after 15 May 1995 in providing protective fencing, grants will be payable towards the costs. The grants apply only to protective fencing on land which is the subject of management obligations in Wales under the Habitat (Water Fringe) (Wales) Regulations 1994, SI 1994/3100, or the Habitat (Coastal Belt) (Wales) Regulations 1994, SI 1994/3101, with a view to the protection or improvement of a wildlife habitat.

48 Agricultural employment—wages

The Agricultural Wages Committee (Areas) (England) Order 1995, SI 1995/3186 (in force on 1 January 1996), establishes a new agricultural wages committee for the counties of northern England.

49 Agricultural holding—garden centre—use of garden centre amounting to use as agricultural holding

Scotland
A local authority granted a lease of land in favour of a company. The lease provided that the land was only to be used for the operation of the company's seed and nursery business, including the wholesale and retail sale of the products of the business and the carrying on generally of the usual business of a retail garden centre. The authority later claimed that the predominant use of the land, rather than being agricultural, was for the business activity of selling, wholesale and retail, garden plants, garden tools, seeds, compost, chemicals and trees and that items were brought in for resale. It sought a declaration that the use of the land was not use as an agricultural holding within the meaning of the Agricultural Holdings (Scotland) Acts 1949 and 1991. *Held*, the authority had to establish that as a matter of substance the land comprised in the tenancy taken as a whole was not an agricultural holding. The reference in the lease to the usual business of a retail garden centre did not exclude the possibility that the agricultural and non-agricultural uses of the land upon which the business was carried on might amount to the land being an agricultural holding. Much depended on the relationship between the use of the land for the propagation of products and its use as a shop for the sale of plants and other goods which had been bought in. On the facts in the present case, the judge found in favour of the authority.
Aberdeen District Council v Ben Reid & Co Ltd (1995) Times, 6 October (Outer House).

50 Agricultural holding—non-payment of rent—whether agricultural holdings excluded from provisions relating to service of notices

See *Lindsey Trading Properties Inc v Dallhold Estates (UK) Pty Ltd*, para 1838.

51 Agricultural holding—partner's share in tenancy—valuation for purposes of inheritance taxation

See *Walton v IRC*, para 1698.

52 Agricultural holding—succession to tenancy—calculation of annual income of land

The Agricultural Holdings (Units of Production) Order 1995, SI 1995/2125 (in force on 12 September 1995), supersedes the 1994 Order, SI 1994/2183, and prescribes units of production for the assessment of the productive capacity of agricultural land and sets out the amount to be regarded as the net annual income from each such unit for the year 12 September 1995 to 11 September 1996. The units of production are used together with the net annual income of land to determine whether or not the land in question is a commercial unit for the purposes of the succession provisions contained in the Agricultural Holdings Act 1986.

53 Agricultural holdings—succession to tenancy—principal source of livelihood

The Agricultural Holdings Act 1986, s 36(3)(a) provides that a person may apply for a new tenancy of an agricultural holding on the death of the previous tenant if he is a close relative of the deceased, and if in the seven years ending with the date of death, his principal source of livelihood throughout a continuous period of not less than five years derived from his agricultural work on the holding.

An area of farm land was let to the appellant's father, and the appellant worked full-time on the farm as a partner with his father until his father's death. He was granted an order that he was entitled to a tenancy of the holding in succession to his father. On the landlords' appeal, it was decided that the appellant did not satisfy the eligibility condition of the 1986 Act, s 36(3)(a), because he had not shown that the farm had made sufficient profits which could have constituted the principal source of his living. On the appellant's appeal, *held*, s 36(3) had to be construed in a purposive manner, and 'livelihood' could be defined as the sum spent or consumed for the purpose of living. In the instant case, the appellant's only income came from his work on the holding, in the form of drawings on the business account of the partnership. He was entitled to make those drawings because he was engaged full-time in agricultural work on the holding. It was irrelevant that for some of the relevant years the holding had made a loss and that the drawings to fund his living expenses had therefore come from bank loans rather than from the profits of the holding. Accordingly, the appeal would be allowed.

Welby v Casswell [1995] 2 EGLR1 (Court of Appeal: Stuart-Smith, Waite and Millett LJJ). Decision of Popplewell J [1994] 35 EG 126 (1994 Abr para 67) reversed.

54 Agricultural marketing—fruit plant material

The Marketing of Fruit Plant Material Regulations 1995, SI 1995/2653 (in force on 1 December 1995), implement Council Directive (EC) 92/34, and Commission Directives (EC) 93/48, 64, 79, on the marketing of fruit plant propagating material and fruit plant within the European Community. The regulations (1) set quality standards to be met by certain genera and species of plant material when marketed and prescribe conditions to be satisfied by suppliers of plant material, subject to an exemption for small producers all of whose production and sales of plant material are intended for final use by persons on the local market who are not professionally involved in plant production; (2) provide that suppliers may not market plant material unless it is substantially free on visual inspection from harmful organisms and diseases and unless it satisfies minimum quality requirements; (3) require producers to take certain measures if organisms as described in (2) above are found; (4) prescribe additional quality requirements in respect of the marketing of plant material of the genus citrus by producers; (5) provide that plant material must be marketed with reference to the variety to which it belongs or, in the case of rootstocks which do not belong to a variety, to the appropriate species or interspecific hybrid, and that it must be accompanied by a supplier's document or, when marketed to non-professional final consumers, by appropriate product information; (6) require suppliers who are neither producers nor engaged only in the marketing of small quantities of plant material to non-professional final consumers to keep records on the buying, selling or delivery of plant material; (7) require suppliers (including producers), other than those engaged only in the marketing of plant material to non-professional final consumers, also to keep records on any mixing of plant material of different origins; (8) require producers to keep records on occurrences of harmful organisms and diseases; (9) require producers who market plant material to be accredited by the minister, such accreditation being conditional on the maintenance of production practices in accordance with requirements established by these regulations and on the keeping of prescribed records; and (10) provide that an inspector may enter the premises of a supplier to ensure compliance with these regulations and may by notice prohibit the marketing or movement of unsatisfactory plant material.

55 Agricultural marketing—milk and milk products—quota system—partnership requirements

The applicants, a number of milk producing farmers who had each been allocated a milk quota by the Ministry of Agriculture, Fisheries and Food, entered into partnerships with each other in order to enable them to recommence milk production against the quota. The ministry subsequently decided to withdraw the quotas and entitlement to compensation. The applicants sought judicial review of the decision. *Held*, the applicants had not pooled their assets, their land or their quotas. Although there did not have to be a complete merger of their assets, there had to be a pooling of assets and for the assets of each applicant to contribute to the milk production of the partnership. The applicants had failed to fulfil the test of sufficient involvement laid down in *Case C-86/90: O'Brien v Ireland* and, accordingly, their application would be dismissed.

R v Ministry of Agriculture, Fisheries and Food, ex p St Clere's Hall Farm [1995] 3 CMLR 125 (Queen's Bench Division: Tucker J).

56 Agricultural marketing—ornamental plant material

The Marketing of Ornamental Plant Material Regulations 1995, SI 1995/2651 (in force on 1 December 1995), implement Council Directive (EC) 91/682, and Commission Directives (EC) 93/49, 63, 78, on the marketing of ornamental plant propagating material and ornamental plant within the European Community. The regulations (1) set quality standards to be met by certain genera and species of plant material when marketed and prescribe conditions to be satisfied by suppliers of plant material, subject to an exemption for small producers all of whose production and sales of plant material are intended for final use by persons on the local market who are not professionally involved in plant production; (2) provide that suppliers may not market plant material unless it is substantially free on visual inspection from harmful organisms and diseases and unless it satisfies minimum quality requirements; (3) require producers to take certain measures if organisms as described in (2) above are found; (4) prescribe additional quality requirements in respect of the marketing of flower bulbs by producers; (5) provide that plant material must be marketed with reference to either the group of plants or the variety to which it belongs, and that it must be accompanied by a supplier's document or, when marketed to non-professional final consumers, by appropriate product information; (6) require suppliers who are neither producers nor engaged only in the marketing of small quantities of plant material to non-professional final consumers to keep records on the buying, selling or delivery of plant material; (7) require suppliers (including producers), other than those engaged only in the marketing of plant material to non-professional final consumers, also to keep records on any mixing of plant material of different origins; (8) require producers to keep records on occurrences of harmful organisms and diseases; (9) require producers who market plant material to be accredited by the minister, such accreditation being conditional on the maintenance of production practices in accordance with requirements established by these regulations and on the keeping of prescribed records; and (10) provide that an inspector may enter the premises of a supplier to ensure compliance with these regulations and may by notice prohibit the marketing or movement of unsatisfactory plant material.

57 Agricultural marketing—vegetable plant material

The Marketing of Vegetable Plant Material Regulations 1995, SI 1995/2652 (in force on 1 December 1995), implement Council Directive (EC) 92/33, and Commission Directives (EC) 93/61, 62, on the marketing of vegetable propagating and planting material other than seed in the European Community. The regulations (1) set quality standards to be met by certain genera and species of plant material when marketed and prescribe conditions to be satisfied by suppliers of plant material, subject to an exemption for small producers all of whose production and sales of plant material are intended for final use by persons on the local market who are not professionally involved in plant production; (2) provide that suppliers may not market plant material unless it is substantially free on visual inspection from harmful organisms and diseases and unless it satisfies minimum quality requirements; (3) require producers to take certain measures if organisms as described in (2) above are found; (4) prescribe additional quality requirements in respect of the marketing of bulbs of shallots and garlic by producers; (5) provide that, when marketed, plant material must be accompanied by a supplier's document or, when marketed to non-professional final consumers, by appropriate product information; (6) require suppliers who are neither producers nor engaged only in the marketing of small quantities of plant material to non-professional final consumers to keep records on the buying, selling or delivery of plant material; (7) require suppliers (including producers), other than those engaged only in the marketing of plant material to non-professional final consumers, also to keep records on any mixing of plant material of different origins; (8) require producers to keep records on occurrences of harmful organisms and diseases; (9) require producers who market plant material to be accredited by the minister, such accreditation being conditional on the maintenance of production practices in accordance with requirements established by these regulations and on the keeping of prescribed records; and (10) provide that an inspector may enter the premises of a supplier to ensure compliance with these regulations and may by notice prohibit the marketing or movement of unsatisfactory plant material.

58 Agricultural marketing—wine

The Common Agricultural Policy (Wine) Regulations 1995, SI 1995/615 (in force on 1 April 1995), which replace the 1994 Regulations, SI 1994/674, provide for the enforcement of specified EC regulations. The regulations designate competent authorities, agencies and a liaison authority for the purposes of enforcement, define 'medium dry' for the purposes of labelling and description and specify conditions for the use of geographical ascriptions for the designation of table wine. In addition, they exempt certain products from provisions relating to information required on labels, permit the planting for certain purposes of vine varieties whose planting would otherwise be prohibited and provide for powers of inspection and enforcement. The regulations also authorise controls on the movement of wine sector products, relieve authorised officers of personal liability for acts done by them in execution of these regulations, confer on courts before which proceedings are brought powers in relation to the analysis and examination of samples, specify the regions in the United Kingdom for producing quality wines psr, specify the list of vine varieties, minimum natural alcoholic strength, maximum yield per hectare and analytical test in the production of quality wine psr and permit the production of such wine in areas of immediate proximity to the specified regions. Offences, penalties and defences are prescribed.

59   Agricultural marketing—wine—labelling

The applicant, a Spanish producer of sparkling wine, challenged Council Regulation (EC) 3309/85, art 6(4), which reserved the use of the term 'crémant' to quality sparkling wines produced in France and Luxembourg. The term had not previously been regulated in Community law and the applicant had used the term 'Gran Cremant' as a registered trade mark in relation to such wines produced in Spain since 1924. The applicant sought the annulment of the regulation, contending that the provision, which required it to stop using the term, restricted its sales. *Held*, although the regulation was of a legislative nature, it was nevertheless of individual and direct concern to the applicant. It could sue under the EC Treaty, art 173(2). The term 'crémant' referred to a manufacturing process, not to origin. Its reservation to two member states was discriminatory in relation to other member states, contrary to arts 6, 40(3) unless it could be objectively justified. France and Luxembourg had first legislated in respect of the term in 1975 whereas the applicant had registered the term in Spain more than 50 years earlier. There was no justification for reserving the use of the term to France and Luxembourg on the ground of traditional use. Accordingly, the regulation would be annulled.

   Case C-309/89: Codorniu SA v EU Council [1995] 2 CMLR 561 (ECJ: Full Court).

Under Community regulations on the labelling of sparkling wine, terms relating to a production method could only be used to refer to the name of a geographical unit where the wine in question was entitled to use the particular geographical indication. Producers who had used the term 'méthode champenoise' were permitted to use the term until September 1994. A German association of wine growers, which had been refused permission by German authorities to use the term on their wines, nevertheless continued to use the term after that date. It fell to be determined whether the regulations under which the association was prohibited from using the term were invalid. *Held*, the prohibition infringed neither the right to own property, because, before the adoption of the regulations, all wine growers were entitled to use the term, nor the right to freedom of trade, because the regulations in question were intended to further the general economic interest such as the protection of consumers and registered designations of the geographical origins of wines. Producers were not disproportionately affected as a transitional period was provided and alternative expressions could be used. The prohibition applied to all Community producers of sparkling wine, with the exception of those entitled to use the term 'Champagne'. Accordingly, the regulations in question were valid.

   Case C-306/93: SMW Winzersekt GmbH v Land Rheinland-Pfalz [1995] 2 CMLR 718 (ECJ: Full Court).

60   Agricultural Tenancies Act 1995

The Agricultural Tenancies Act 1995 makes new provision regulating agricultural tenancies in England and Wales. The Act received the royal assent on 9 May 1995 and came into force on 1 September 1995.

Part I (ss 1–8) General Provisions
Section 1 introduces and defines the concept of farm business tenancies, setting out the conditions that a tenancy must meet in order to come within the ambit of the Act. A tenancy cannot be a farm business tenancy if it begins before 1 September 1995 or if it is a tenancy beginning on or after that date under the statutory succession provisions of the Agricultural Holdings Act 1986: s 2. Section 3 sets out the circumstances in which the exchange of notices provided for in s 1 applies to a new tenancy arising from a surrender and re-grant of an existing farm business tenancy. Section 4 disapplies the 1986 Act in relation to certain new tenancies granted on or after 1 September 1995. Sections 5–7 make provision for the giving of notice when either party wishes to end a farm business tenancy of a fixed term of more than two years or a tenancy from year to year. Section 8 enables a tenant in possession to remove any fixture affixed by him or building erected by him on the holding irrespective of whether the fixing or erecting was done during a previous tenancy agreement between the parties.

Part II (ss 9–14) Rent Review Under Farm Business Tenancy
Section 9 provides an option for the parties to agree on a fixed rent, with no reviews during the tenancy, or to agree to adjust the rent by or to a specified amount or by applying an objective formula. Where the parties do not make such an agreement, ss 10–13, which make provision

for rent payable to be referred to arbitration, apply. The entitlement to require a rent review is not affected by the grant of a new tenancy of a severed part of the revision: s 11. Section 14 deals with interpretation.

Part III (ss 15–27) Compensation on Termination of Farm Business Tenancy
Section 15 defines a tenant's improvement as any physical improvement made on the holding or any intangible advantage obtained for the holding by the tenant. Section 16 provides that a tenant is only entitled to compensation for a tenant's improvement on the termination of a tenancy so long as the improvement is not removed from the holding. Sections 17, 18 require a tenant to obtain his landlord's written consent to any improvements or planning permission in order to be eligible for compensation. A landlord's refusal or failure to give such consent is referable to arbitration: s 19. Sections 20, 21 set out the amount of compensation payable for a tenant's improvement or planning permission and s 22 provides for claims for compensation at the end of farm business tenancies to be referred to arbitration if they are not previously settled by written agreement between the landlord and the tenant. Sections 23–25 set out a tenant's entitlement to compensation for improvements where he remains in the holding during two or more tenancies (s 23), where the landlord has resumed possession of part of the holding (s 24) or where the reversionary estate in the holding is severed (s 25). Section 26 provides that a tenant is entitled to compensation under Pt III notwithstanding any agreement to the contrary and s 27 defines 'planning permission' for these purposes as having the meaning given by the Town and Country Planning Act 1990, s 336(1).

Part IV (ss 28–41) Miscellaneous and Supplemental
Sections 28–30 set out the procedure to be followed for the resolution of disputes arising under the Act or under the terms of a farm business tenancy and s 31 amends the Law of Property Act 1925, s 99 and the Agricultural Holdings Act 1986, Sch 14 so as to empower mortgage lenders to influence and control the making of leases relating to mortgaged agricultural land in the same way as in connection with any other land. A landlord under a farm business tenancy is empowered to give consents and make agreements as if he were absolutely entitled to the estate or land in question by s 32 whilst s 33 authorises certain specified statutory trustees to raise or apply capital money, or to raise money by mortgage, for the purpose of paying expenses, compensation or costs arising from the operation of the Act. Provision for the value of a tenant's improvement to be disregarded in estimating the best rent or reservation in the nature of rent for land comprised in a farm business tenancy is made by s 34. Section 35 amends the Solicitors Act 1974, s 22 so as to permit Full Members of the Central Association of Agricultural Valuers, Associates or Fellows of the Incorporated Society of Valuers and Auctioneers, and Associates or Fellows of the Royal Institution of Chartered Surveyors, to draw or prepare certain instruments relating to farm business tenancies. Section 36 makes provision as to the service of notices under the Act. Section 37 provides for the application of the Act to Crown land and ss 38, 39 make provision for the interpretation of the Act. Section 40 and the Schedule amend a number of enactments in consequence of the Act and s 41 makes provision for short title, commencement and extent.

61 Apples—apple orchards—grubbing up

The Apple Orchard Grubbing Up (Amendment) Regulations 1995, SI 1995/40 (in force on 13 January 1995), amend the 1991 Regulations, SI 1991/3, to take account of Commission Regulation (EC) 3149/94 which permits applications for the payment of premium for the grubbing up of apple orchards to be made during the month of January 1995.

62 Arable crops—compensatory payments

The Arable Area Payments Regulations 1995, SI 1995/1738 (in force on 31 July 1995), replace the 1994 Regulations, SI 1994/947. They implement and supplement provisions of Council Regulation (EC) 1765/92 which establishes a support system for producers of certain arable crops under which compensatory payments may be made. The regulations (1) make provision for the calculation of payments; (2) define the production regions in Great Britain; (3) require producers claiming compensatory payments to set aside part of their arable land; (4) require member states to take appropriate measures relating to set-aside land to ensure the protection of the environment; (5) provide for the transfer of set-aside requirements between producers; (6) prescribe plot sizes; (7) require records to be kept; (8) specify reductions in payments and interest payable on recoverable payments; (9) confer power on authorised persons and create offences and penalties.

The Arable Area Payments (Amendment) Regulations 1995, SI 1995/2780 (in force on 15 November 1995), amend the principal regulations supra. Provision is made for a system whereby a farmer may apply to the Minister of Agriculture, Fisheries and Food for approval to the exchange of ineligible and eligible land for the purpose of receipt of compensatory payment, new deadlines are set in respect of delivery notifications for producers of non-food raw materials, and penalties are imposed for late notification.

63 Common agricultural policy—agricultural methods—environmental protection— nitrate sensitive areas—limited use of nitrogen fertiliser

The Nitrate Sensitive Areas (Amendment) Regulations 1995, SI 1995/1708 (in force in part on 27 July 1995 and in part on 1 June 1996), amend the 1994 Regulations, SI 1994/1729, by expanding the criteria of eligibility of land for aid in certain cases and by amending both the undertakings to be given by farmers and the restrictions on the acceptance of applications for aid. Upgrading into the premium arable scheme is prohibited in specified circumstances. In addition, the regulations permit the withholding or recovery of payment where aid is duplicated and set out rates of payment in respect of the new nitrate sensitive areas. SI 1990/1187 and 1993/3198 are revoked.

The Nitrate Sensitive Areas (Amendment) (No 2) Regulations 1995, SI 1995/2095 (in force on 30 August 1995), further amend the 1994 Regulations supra. They make some minor and drafting amendments and enable rights to be enjoyed by virtue of Council Regulation (EC) 1460/95 establishing a support system for producers of certain arable crops. In addition, a further option to the premium arable scheme, namely the set-aside option, is established and provision is made as to the conditions for eligibility, the undertakings to be given by applicants for aid, the grounds on which an application may be refused, payment rates and the possibilities of upgrading to the premium arable scheme.

64 Common agricultural policy—agricultural methods—environmental protection—salt marshes

The Habitat (Salt Marsh) (Amendment) Regulations 1995, SI 1995/2871 (as amended by SI 1995/2891) (in force on 30 November 1995), amend SI 1994/1293 in consequence of Council Regulation (EC) 1460/95, which amends Council Regulation (EC) 1765/92, establishing a support system for producers of certain arable crops where some of their land has already been set aside pursuant to a set-aside scheme. The regulations (1) add a new payment rate for aid for set-aside land managed in accordance with the management obligations in the 1994 Regulations. The new payment rate applies to land which the beneficiary has declared in his application form that he intends to count as being set-aside land for the purposes of Council Regulation (EC) 1765/92; (2) amend the requirements concerning the information to be included in such an application and supplied at the time of claiming payment of aid; and (3) allow the minister to recover the difference between the new payment rate and the payment rate for land that was arable land at the start of the management period, if the beneficiary counts land as being set-aside for the purposes of Council Regulation (EC) 1765/92, where that land is not already set-aside land.

65 Common agricultural policy—agricultural processing and marketing—grants

The Agricultural Processing and Marketing Grant Regulations 1995, SI 1995/362 (in force on 10 March 1995), supplement Council Regulation (EC) 866/90 which contains measures for improving the processing and marketing conditions of agricultural products. The European Commission has the power to grant aid from the Guidance Section of the European Agricultural Guidance and Guarantee Fund towards investments or projects which fulfil its objectives and member states must make financial contributions towards such investments and projects if they are located on their territory. The regulations empower ministers to make grants towards expenditure in respect of investments or projects approved for the payments of aid from the Guidance Fund of amounts sufficient to enable them to qualify for that aid. Procedures for approval of expenditure for the purposes of such aid or grants and their payment are laid down. There is a duty to retain and produce expenditure records and authorised officers can enter land to require their production. It is an offence to make false statements in order to obtain aid or grants and the regulations specify the circumstances in which approval of expenditure may be revoked or aid or grants recovered. SI 1994/3137 is revoked.

66   Common agricultural policy—basic principles—non-discrimination between producers and consumers

See *Codorniu SA v EU Council*, para 59.

67   Common agricultural policy—pure-bred animals—registration

An Irish cattle breeder applied for judicial review of the defendant society's refusal to register his herd in Ireland. The British government recognised the society as one which maintained registration records in respect of that particular breed of cattle under Council Directive (EC) 77/504. *Held*, it was clear from the structure of Community law and from the directive itself that the Directive's purpose was to facilitate a range of organisations which were recognised by national governments and which operated in accordance with the same principles. Thus, the organisation could only operate within its national boundaries, where the national government could exercise its essential monitoring role. Accordingly, the society was not obliged to register the Irish cattle and the application would be dismissed.

R v Hereford Herd Book Society, ex p O'Neill (1995) Times, 19 July (Queen's Bench Division: Carnwath J).

68   Common fisheries policy

See EUROPEAN COMMUNITIES.

69   Control of pests—restrictions upon importation—potatoes originating in the Netherlands

The Potatoes Originating in the Netherlands Order 1995, SI 1995/3018 (in force on 23 November 1995), imposes certain requirements in respect of potatoes grown and harvested in the Netherlands in 1995, in order to provide safeguards against the introduction into and the spread within Great Britain of a plant pest, Pseudomonas solanacearum (smith) smith. The order (1) requires a person intending to import into Great Britain potatoes originating in the Netherlands to give to an inspector two days' prior notification in writing of that intention and to provide specified information, (2) provides that a person who gives notification of his intention to import potatoes under the order is deemed to satisfy the requirements of the Seed Potatoes Originating in the Netherlands (Notification) (Scotland) Order 1995, SI 1995/2874 in respect of those potatoes, and (3) provides that an inspector who has reasonable grounds for suspecting that a person has or will have in his possession potatoes originating in the Netherlands may exercise the powers conferred by the Plant Health (Great Britain) Order 1993, SI 1993/1320, in respect of such potatoes.

70   Eggs—marketing standards

The Eggs (Marketing Standards) Regulations 1995, SI 1995/1544 (in force on 10 July 1995), supersede the 1985 Regulations, SI 1985/1271, to provide for the implementation of European Community regulations relating to marketing standards for shell eggs and to the production and marketing of eggs for hatching and farmyard poultry chicks. The principal amendments include the introduction of more detailed labelling requirements and the implementation of public health conditions in relation to the sale of shell eggs and the use of eggs in catering kitchens. In addition, the regulations designate enforcement authorities, give authorised officers specified powers and require specified persons to keep records and supply information. The form of official mark which may be used under Community provisions is prescribed and the regulations create an offence and prescribe a penalty for failing to comply with requirements.

71   Export refunds—administrative penalties

The Export Refunds (Administrative Penalties) (Rate of Interest) Regulations 1995, SI 1995/2861 (in force on 1 December 1995), specify the rate of interest applicable for the calculation of any interest payable pursuant to Commission Regulation (EC) 3665/87, art 11 as 1 per cent above the three month sterling London interbank offered rate.

72   Feeding stuffs—regulations

The Feeding Stuffs Regulations 1995, SI 1995/1412 (in force on 30 June 1995), consolidate with amendments the 1991 Regulations, SI 1991/2840, as amended, and implement Community law. The principle changes to the previous law are as follows: (1) the list of animals prescribed for the purposes of the definition of feeding stuffs is extended to include piglets and foals; (2) conditions which must be satisfied if feeding stuffs intended for particular nutritional purposes are to be marketed are included; (3) changes are made to the labelling requirements specified for feeding stuffs intended for particular nutritional purposes; (4) an official method for calculating the energy value of feedings stuffs intended for particular nutritional purposes is added.

73 Fertilisers—regulations

The Fertilisers (Amendment) Regulations 1995, SI 1995/16 (in force on 30 January 1995), implement Commission Directive (EC) 93/69. Amendments relate to prescribed descriptions of material, meanings of names, particulars and information to be contained in the statutory statement and limits of variation. Provision is added to prohibit the sale, in specified circumstances, of ammonium nitrate.

74 Hill livestock—compensatory allowance

The Hill Livestock (Compensatory Allowances) (Amendment) Regulations 1995, SI 1995/100 (in force on 9 February 1995), amend the 1994 Regulations, SI 1994/2740, so as to (1) amend a number of definitions contained in Council regulations; (2) amend certain provisions to reflect the new rates of compensatory allowances payable for cattle and sheep; (3) delete reference in the provision relating to the withholding or recovery of compensatory allowance to the obstruction of a person accompanying an authorised person; (4) make further consequential amendments.

The Hill Livestock (Compensatory Allowances) (Amendment) (No 2) Regulations 1995, SI 1995/1481 (in force on 13 July 1995), further amend the 1994 Regulations, SI 1994/2740. A number of definitions are revised and amended and the rates of payment of compensatory allowances for cattle and sheep are further revised. In addition, the retention periods for cattle and sheep are amended, conditions for making claims for compensatory allowances are replaced and regulations relating to overgrazing are amended.

The Hill Livestock (Compensatory Allowances) (Amendment) (No 3) Regulations 1995, SI 1995/2778 (in force on 15 November 1995), further amend the 1994 Regulations, SI 1994/2740, as follows: (1) the calculation for determining the number of ewes in respect of which compensatory allowances may be paid is altered; (2) a claim for such an allowance must be made between certain dates; (3) only one claim for a compensatory allowance for sheep may be made in respect of a given year. A number of consequential amendments are also made.

75 Home-Grown Cereals Authority—levy scheme—rate of levy

The Home-Grown Cereals Authority (Rate of Levy) Order 1995, SI 1995/1439 (in force on 1 July 1995), specifies for the year beginning 1 July 1995 the rates of dealer levy, grower levy and processor levies which appear to ministers to be sufficient to meet the amount apportioned to certain cereals to finance the non-trading functions of the Home-Grown Cereals Authority under the Cereals Marketing Act 1965. The order also specifies the rate of levy in respect of the amount apportioned to certain oilseeds for the same purpose.

76 Livestock—artificial insemination—cattle

The Artificial Insemination of Cattle (Animal Health) (England and Wales) (Amendment) Regulations 1995, SI 1995/2549 (in force on 23 October 1995), further amend the 1985 Regulations, SI 1985/1861, so as to clarify the requirements for trade in deep-frozen semen. The regulations also implement Council Directive (EC) 93/60 which extends the animal health requirements applicable to trade within the European Economic Area and imports from third countries of deep-frozen bovine semen to cover fresh bovine semen. Contravention of the regulations constitutes an offence under the Animal Health and Welfare Act 1984, s 10(6).

77 Livestock—beef special premium

The Beef Special Premium (Amendment) Regulations 1995, SI 1995/14 (in force on 30 January 1995), further amend the 1993 Regulations, SI 1993/1734, so as to implement Commission Regulation (EC) 3086/92. The regulations expressly qualify the right to issue a national administrative document (which is necessary for the grant of a premium) by prohibiting its issue in relation to any animal in respect of which the identification provisions of the Bovine Animals (Records, Identification and Movement) Order 1995, SI 1995/12, are contravened.

78 Livestock—bovine embryos

The Bovine Embryo (Collection, Production and Transfer) Regulations 1995, SI 1995/2478 (in force on 13 October 1995), replace the 1993 Regulations, SI 1993/2921, and give effect to Council Directive (EC) 89/556. The regulations (1) provide for the approval of collection, production and transfer teams; (2) provide for the allocation of registration numbers for teams; (3) specify conditions to be complied with in relation to collection, production, storage, transport and transfer of bovine embryos; (4) require the use of anaesthetics in relation to the collection and transfer of the embryos; (5) require records to be kept in relation to the embryos.

The Bovine Embryo (Collection, Production and Transfer) (Fees) Regulations 1995, SI 1995/2479 (in force on 13 October 1995), supersede the 1993 Regulations, SI 1993/2920. They set the fees payable for services under the 1995 Regulations supra.

79 Livestock—extensification—moorland areas

The Moorland (Livestock Extensification) Regulations 1995, SI 1995/904 (in force on 18 April 1995), comply with Council Regulation (EC) 2078/92 and allow payments of aid to be made to farmers who reduce their ewe flocks. The regulations apply to England only. The rate of payment is set and is payable to farmers with participating production units which are within specified areas. Applicants for aid are required to give certain undertakings and their applications must include particular information and evidence. In addition, provision is made for changes in occupation of the land subject to the undertakings. Successful applicants must allow specified persons to enter land for the purpose of monitoring compliance with undertakings. Further, where a person fails to comply with his undertakings, they may be treated as terminated and withhold or recover all or part of any aid due or paid. An offence in relation to making false statements is created.

The Moorland (Livestock Extensification) (Wales) Regulations 1995, SI 1995/1159 (in force on 18 April 1995), make similar provision in relation to payments of aid to farmers as the 1995 Regulations, SI 1995/904, supra but they apply to Wales only.

80 Pesticides—maximum residue levels in crops, food and feeding stuffs

The Pesticides (Maximum Residue Levels in Crops, Food and Feeding Stuffs) (Amendment) Regulations 1995, SI 1995/1483 (in force on 30 June 1995), amend the 1994 Regulations, SI 1994/1985, and specify maximum levels of pesticide residues in accordance with Council Directives (EC) 94/29 and 94/30. The regulations confer a defence of due diligence on those charged with offences relating to residues under Community law. In addition, maximum levels of residues contained in the 1994 Regulations are removed, including those levels not required by Community law.

81 Plant breeders' rights—fees

The Plant Breeders' Rights (Fees) (Amendment) Regulations 1995, SI 1995/606 (in force on 1 April 1995), further amend SI 1990/618, so as to add leeks to the list of plant varieties for which fees are payable in respect of tests or examination in connection with an application for a grant of plant breeders' rights.

The Plant Breeders' Rights (Fees) (Amendment) (No 2) Regulations 1995, SI 1995/2947 (in force on 8 December 1995), amend the 1990 Regulations, SI 1990/618, by introducing provision for the payment of reduced renewal fees for plant breeders' rights for plant varieties in respect of which there is a subsisting Community plant variety right granted in accordance with Council Regulation (EC) 2100/94 on Community plant variety rights.

82 Plant breeders' rights—plant variety rights office—extension of functions

The Plant Variety Rights Office (Extension of Functions) Regulations 1995, SI 1995/2655 (in force on 1 November 1995), enable the United Kingdom plant variety rights office to carry out functions entrusted to it by the Community plant variety office, created by Council Regulation (EC) 2100/94. The functions include the exercise of specific administrative functions of the

Community office and the technical examination of varieties relating to compliance with qualifying criteria for protection under the Community scheme.

83   Plant breeders' rights—schemes

The Plant Breeders' Rights (Herbaceous Perennials) Scheme 1995, SI 1995/526 (in force on 24 March 1995), replaces SI 1969/1023 as amended. The scheme prescribes the varieties of herbaceous perennials in respect of which grants of plant breeders' rights may be made, and the periods for which rights are exercisable. The scheme also allows legal proceedings to be taken in respect of infringements of the rights in a registered name of a variety of ornamental plant if the infringement is committed in relation to specified varieties of herbaceous perennials. In addition, a compulsory licence granted by the Controller of Plant Variety Rights for a herbaceous perennial does not have effect for a specified number of years from the date of grant of rights in a particular variety.

The Plant Breeders' Rights (Miscellaneous Ornamental Plants) Scheme 1995, SI 1995/527 (in force on 24 March 1995), replaces SI 1990/1594, as amended. It prescribes the varieties of miscellaneous ornamental plants for which grants of plant breeders' rights may be made, and the periods for which rights are exercisable. The scheme also allows legal proceedings to be taken in respect of infringements of the rights in a registered name of specified varieties of ornamental plants. In addition, a compulsory licence granted by the Controller of Plant Variety Rights for an ornamental plant does not have effect for three years from the grant of rights in respect of that variety.

The Plant Breeders' Rights (Trees, Shrubs and Woody Climbers) (Variation) Scheme 1995, SI 1995/528 (in force on 24 March 1995), amends SI 1993/2776, so as to vary the periods for which rights are exercisable in respect of certain plant varieties. In addition, where a compulsory licence is granted by the Controller of Plant Variety Rights in respect of a plant variety, the period for which the licence does not have effect after the date of the grant of rights in that variety is reduced to two years.

The Plant Breeders Rights (Sweet Peas) Scheme 1995, SI 1995/529 (in force on 24 March 1995), prescribes the varieties of sweet peas in respect of which grants of plant breeders' rights may be made, and the periods for which rights are exercisable. The scheme also allows legal proceedings to be taken in respect of infringements of the rights in the registered name of a variety of sweet peas when the infringement is committed in connection with any other variety of sweet peas. Additionally, a compulsory licence granted by the Controller of Plant Variety Rights for a variety of sweet peas does not have effect until three years after the date of the grant of rights in that variety.

The Plant Breeders' Rights (Vegetables) (including Field Beans and Field Peas) (Variation) Scheme 1995, SI 1995/530 (in force on 24 March 1995), further amends SI 1980/319, so as to add leeks and certain varieties of cabbage and greens to the species of plant varieties for which grants of plant breeders' rights may be made. Additionally, legal action may be taken in respect of infringements of the rights in the registered name of a variety of leek or certain varieties of cabbage and greens, during the prescribed period for which the rights may be exercised.

84   Plant health—general provisions

The Plant Health (Great Britain) (Amendment) Order 1995, SI 1995/1358 (in force on 27 May 1995), amends the 1993 Order, SI 1993/1320, so as to implement Community law relating to protected zones and to certain diseases and to make provisions consequential to the accession of Austria, Finland and Sweden to the plant health single market. The definition of 'plant' is amended and an inspector may now require items, whether or not suspected of contamination, to be removed after importation to premises specified by him to facilitate inspection.

The Plant Health (Great Britain) (Amendment) (No 2) Order 1995, SI 1995/2929 (in force on 6 December 1995), amends the 1993 Order supra. The order amends the protected zones recognised in respect of various specified plant pests.

85   Plant protection products

The Plant Protection Products Regulations 1995, SI 1995/887 (in force on 17 April 1995), implement Council Directive (EC) 91/414 which establishes an authorisation system whereby plant protection products may not be placed on the market unless they have been authorised. The purpose of the system is to ensure that wherever the products are placed on the market they are effective without causing harm to human or animal health and without adversely affecting plants and ground water or the environment in general. The regulations establish an authorisation system in Great Britain and prohibit the placing on the market and use of plant protection products unless they have been approved by the relevant ministers and are placed on the market and used in accordance with any conditions or requirements specified in their approval. Provisions relate to the application for approvals, approvals for research and development, the extension, revocation and modification of approvals and the notification of information on potentially dangerous effects. Further, the regulations provide for packaging, labelling, seizure and disposal of products. Offences and penalties for contravention of the regulations are created and a general defence of due diligence is provided.

The Plant Protection Products (Fees) Regulations 1995, SI 1995/888 (in force on 17 April 1995), prescribe fees to be paid in connection with services provided and approvals granted under the 1995 Regulations, SI 1995/887. The principle services and approvals are specified and provision is made for the payment of a smaller fee at the discretion of the relevant ministers. In addition, the regulations prescribe the time at which fees are payable.

86 Poultry, farmed game bird and rabbit meat—hygiene and inspection

See para 1428.

87 Products of animal origin—imports and exports

The Products of Animal Origin (Import and Export) (Amendment) Regulations 1995, SI 1995/2911 (in force on 1 December 1995), amend the 1992 Regulations, SI 1992/3298, so as to replace the term 'divisional veterinary officer' with the term 'divisional veterinary manager' to reflect changes in the organisation of the veterinary field service.

88 Rural development grants

The Rural Development Grants (Agriculture) (No 2) Regulations 1995, SI 1995/2202 (in force on 14 September 1995), provide that financial assistance may be granted towards operations which promote rural development. The Minister of Agriculture, Fisheries and Food has the power to approve operations for such assistance, with or without attaching conditions to the approval, and to make payments. The regulations set out the circumstances in which an approval may be revoked and when financial assistance which has been paid out may be recovered. Authorised officers are given powers of entry and inspection in relation to land on which an approved operation is situated or documents relating to an approved operation are held. Beneficiaries of assistance are obliged to keep records relating to the approved operation for a specified period and to supply such information to the minister when required. It is an offence to supply false or misleading information for the purposes of obtaining financial assistance, to obstruct an authorised officer in the exercise of his powers, to fail to keep relevant records for the required period or to fail to assist an authorised officer. SI 1995/2096 is revoked.

89 Seeds—cereal seeds

The Cereal Seeds (Amendment) Regulations 1995, SI 1995/1482 (in force on 30 June 1995), implement Community Directive (EC) 95/6 on the marketing of cereal seed. The regulations also amend the 1993 Regulations, SI 1993/2005, to permit the marketing of seeds of hybrids of rye as certified seed. Conditions are established which are to be met both by the crops from which the seeds of hybrids of rye are obtained and by the seeds themselves.

90 Seeds—national lists of varieties—fees

The Seeds (National Lists of Varieties) (Fees) (Amendment) Regulations 1995, SI 1995/607 (in force on 1 April 1995), amend SI 1994/676, so as to provide for fees to be charged for testing for distinctness, uniformity and stability in respect of any of the hereditary sources of a variety which is the subject of an application for entry in a national list that the minister may require to be tested, including where an applicant is exempted from payment of such fees for the variety itself by reason of payment of fees for tests carried out on his behalf for the purposes of a grant of plant breeders' rights. The regulations also provide for fees to be charged for trials for value for cultivation and use, in respect of seeds used for such trials sown on or after 1 April 1995. Revised fees are prescribed for trials for value for cultivation and use, and the regulations also provide that fees are to be charged for such trials in respect of varieties of flax.

91 Sheep—annual premium

The Sheep Annual Premium (Amendment) Regulations 1995, SI 1995/2779 (in force on 15 November 1995), further amend the 1992 Regulations, SI 1992/2677, to make provision in relation to the date on which a producer making an application for sheep annual premium in respect of a particular marketing year must deliver his application.

92 Suckler cows—premiums

The Suckler Cow Premium (Amendment) Regulations 1995, SI 1995/15 (in force on 30 January 1995), amend the 1993 Regulations, SI 1993/1441, so as to take account of the revocation and replacement of certain orders by the Bovine Animals (Records, Identification and Movement) Order 1995, SI 1995/12.

The Suckler Cow Premium (Amendment) (No 2) Regulations 1995, SI 1995/1446 (in force on 1 July 1995), further amend the 1993 Regulations supra, by amending and inserting new definitions and by revising the closing date for premium applications. The regulations provide for certain multiple applications to be treated as a single application made by one producer and a revised regulation regarding overgrazing is inserted. In addition, provision is made permitting penalties to be applied where a producer uses unsuitable supplementary feeding methods and authorised persons are given the power to inspect land to determine whether such unsuitable methods have been used.

93 Sugar beet—research and education

The Sugar Beet (Research and Education) Order 1995, SI 1995/612 (in force on 1 April 1995), provides for the carrying into effect for the year 1995–96 of the programme of research and education in matters affecting the growing of home-grown beet. Further, it makes provision for the assessment of contributions towards the expenditure on the programme and for their collection.

94 Surplus food—regulations

The Surplus Food Regulations 1995, SI 1995/184 (in force on 20 February 1995), supplement the provisions of Council Regulation (EC) 3730/87 and Commission Regulation (EC) 3149/92, which lay down rules for the supply of food from intervention stocks to designated organisations for distribution to the most deprived persons in the Community. The regulations confer on authorised officers the power to enter land or vehicles and to inspect premises and any surplus food found on them. In addition, the officers may require the production of, and seize, records or documents and may also seize surplus food. Offences are created in relation to furnishing false information, selling surplus food and distributing such food to persons who are not prescribed as eligible recipients. Further, time limits are specified within which prosecutions must be brought and provision is made for a defence of due diligence.

ALLOTMENTS AND SMALLHOLDINGS

Halsbury's Laws of England (4th edn) Vol 2 (reissue), paras 1–200

95 Allotments—management—sale—displacement of allotment holders

A local authority proposed to sell land owned by it on which allotments had been provided for over 50 years. It sought the consent to the sale of the Secretary of State as required by the Allotments Act 1925, s 8. The allotment holders were to be relocated to another site which had such deficiencies that, in the opinion of the inspector appointed to consider the council's application for consent, the authority was not making adequate provision for the displaced allotment holders, as required by s 8. The Secretary of State disagreed with the inspector's decision on the ground that, despite the deficiencies, gardening could reasonably be undertaken on the new site. He decided to grant his consent to the sale of the land subject to the authority undertaking certain works of improvement to the new site. The applicants sought judicial review of his decision, contending that 'adequate provision' in s 8 meant that allotments of at least equal or commensurate in fitness to the existing ones had to be provided. *Held*, 'adequate provision' meant the provision of an allotment site on which allotment gardening could reasonably be undertaken by the allotment holders who would be displaced. The 1925 Act did not state that a replacement site had to be at least as advantageous to the allotment holders as that which they had to leave. If such a requirement were made, 'adequate provision' would rarely be found and the operation of s 8 would be distorted. The Secretary of State's decision was not wrong and, accordingly, the application would be dismissed.

R v Secretary of State for the Environment, ex p Gosforth Allotments and Gardens Association (1995) 70 P & CR 480 (Queen's Bench Division: Laws J).

ANIMALS

Halsbury's Laws of England (4th edn) Vol 2 (reissue), paras 201–600

96 Articles

Animal Nuisance Complaints: the Dos and Don'ts, Barry F Peachey: 139 SJ 784
Animal Transportation, Simon Brooman and Deborah Legge: 145 NLJ 1131
Blood Sports and Public Law, Alistair Lindsay: 145 NLJ 412
Cowed but Unbowed, Michael Harwood (on farm animals and public paths): 139 SJ 610
Raging Bull, Michael Harwood (on farm animals and public paths): 139 SJ 628
It Shouldn't Happen to a Vet, Charles Foster (on veterinary negligence): 139 SJ 186

97 Animal health—divisional veterinary manager

The Animal Health Orders (Divisional Veterinary Manager Amendment) Order 1995, SI 1995/2922 (in force on 1 December 1995) amends a number of orders so as to replace the term 'divisional veterinary officer' or 'divisional veterinary inspector' with the term 'divisional veterinary manager' to reflect changes in the organisation of the veterinary field service. The following are amended: SI 1963/286, 1966/507, 1974/2211, 2212, 1977/944, 1980/79, 1983/344, 1950, 1984/1943, 1987/790, 1989/878, 1991/1155, 2184, 2246, 1994/3141, 3249, 1995/11, 12, 1755.

98 Bovine animals—records, identification and movement

The Bovine Animals (Records, Identification and Movement) Order 1995, SI 1995/12 (in force on 1 April 1995), implements Council Directive (EC) 92/102 on the identification and registration of animals to the extent that it applies to bovine animals, and revokes certain other provisions to the same extent. In particular, the order requires owners and persons in charge of bovine animals on a holding to give information about the holding to the appropriate divisional veterinary officer, to keep records of their births, deaths and movement, and to keep a record of their numbers for a specified period. In addition, market operators must keep records of calves passing through the market for a specified period. Owners and persons in charge of bovine animals must also ensure that the animals are identified by ear tags containing specified particulars. The ear tags, which must be of a style approved by the Minister of Agriculture, Fisheries and Food and must not adversely affect the well-being of the animal, may be removed only on the authority of a veterinary inspector, and must not be altered or defaced. Lost or illegible ear tags must be replaced, and in certain circumstances animals may be identified by a temporary mark. Animals without an identification mark may not be moved. The order also creates offences and specifies penalties, and provides that the order is to be enforced by the local authority.

99 Deer hunting—ban by local authority—ethical and moral objections

See *R v Somerset County Council, ex p Fewings*, para 1955.

100 Diseases of animals—cattle—enzootic bovine leukosis

The Enzootic Bovine Leukosis (Amendment) Order 1995, SI 1995/13 (in force on 27 January 1995), implements Council Directives (EC) 64/432 and 77/391 which require the operation of a monitoring and testing programme in order to achieve officially enzootic bovine leukosis-free status under the directives. The 1980 Order, SI 1980/79, is amended so as to provide that (1) if any laboratory examination of a sample from a bovine animal identifies evidence of the existence of enzootic bovine leukosis, the divisional veterinary officer is to be notified; (2) those purchasing milk for resale in any form have the responsibility for quarterly sampling of the milk from the herd from which they purchase milk and for dispatching the samples to a specified animal health laboratory so that they may be tested; (3) such samples are to be labelled according to particular requirements; and (4) the laboratory must give notice of samples which test positive or inconclusive, and keep records of certain details relating to the testing on a quarterly and six monthly basis.

101   Diseases of animals—horses—equine viral arteritis

The Equine Viral Arteritis Order 1995, SI 1995/1755 (in force on 1 August 1995), extends the definition of 'disease' in the Animal Health Act 1981, s 88(1) to include equine viral arteritis. The order makes provision relating to (1) notification procedures and precautions to be taken where the presence of the disease or virus is known or suspected in a stallion or mare which has been served within the previous 14 days, (2) restrictions and requirements imposed on stallions and on their semen where presence of the disease or virus is suspected, (3) veterinary inquiries to ascertain the existence of the disease or virus. The order also provides for the publication of details of any stallion suspected of being diseased or carrying the virus, where a veterinary examination is postponed.

102   Dogs—dangerous dogs—allowing dog to be in public place without muzzle or lead—destruction of dog ordered without informing owner

The defendant pleaded guilty to being in charge of a pit bull terrier in a public place without it being muzzled, contrary to the Dangerous Dogs Act 1991. When he appeared before the justices the defendant was ordered to pay a fine and the dog was ordered to be destroyed. The applicant, who was the owner of the dog, obtained an injunction restraining the police from destroying the dog and applied for judicial review of the justices' decision. She submitted that as she was not notified of the hearing the justices' order should be quashed. *Held*, in all probability the presence of the applicant at the hearing would not have made any difference but the fact remained that she should have been told of the hearing. It was the duty of the justices to act in accordance with natural justice and that had not happened in the present case. Accordingly, the application for judicial review would be allowed. The destruction order would be quashed and the case sent back to the justices.

R v Ealing Justices, ex p Fanneran (1995) Times, 9 December (Queen's Bench Division: Staughton LJ and Rougier J).

103   Dogs—dangerous dogs—person in charge of dog

Scotland

The Dangerous Dogs Act 1991, s 3(1) provides that if a dog is dangerously out of control in a public place, the owner, or the person for the time being in charge of the dog, is guilty of an offence. If the dog injures any person whilst out of control, an aggravated offence is committed. Section 3(2) provides that in proceedings under s 3(1) against a person who is the owner of a dog but was not at the material time in charge of it, it is a defence that the dog was at the material time in the charge of a person whom he reasonably believed to be a fit and proper person to be in charge of it.

The appellant was the registered owner of a rottweiler dog, which he left in the custody, care and control of his girlfriend when they stopped living together. Whist visiting his girlfriend, the appellant noticed his dog outside in a playing field and went to retrieve it. Before he could do so, the dog attacked a young girl, biting her on the leg. When the appellant was charged with an offence under the 1991 Act, s 3(1), he relied on the defence provided by s 3(2), arguing that he had reasonably believed that the dog was in the custody of a fit and proper person, namely his girlfriend, at the material time. The defence was rejected and the appellant was convicted. On appeal, *held*, the fact that a dog was out of control in a public place did not mean that no one was in charge of it. The responsibility for keeping a dog under control lay with the person whom the owner believed was a fit and proper person to be in charge of it, and the failure to keep a dog under control did not remove that responsibility from the person. In the instant case, the appellant's girlfriend was in charge of the dog and therefore had responsibility for it at the time that it attacked the girl. Moreover, the appellant had not resumed responsibility merely because he went out to retrieve the dog. Accordingly, the appeal would be allowed.

Swinlay v Crowe 1995 SLT 34 (High Court of Justiciary).

104   Export of animals—live animals exported for slaughter—contract of employment— port authorities' discretion to exclude trade

See *R v Coventry Airport, ex p Phoenix Aviation; R v Dover Harbour Board, ex p Peter Gilder and Sons; R v Associated British Ports, ex p Plymouth City Council*, para 2313.

105   Export of animals—signing of export certificate—failure to inspect whole consignment—whether false trade description

See *Roberts v Leonard*, para 2906.

106   Export of animals—veterinary and zootechnical checks

The Animals and Animal Products (Import and Export) Regulations 1995, SI 1995/2428 (in force on 9 October 1995), replace the 1993 Regulations, SI 1993/3247, taking into account changes in EC legislation. Categories of animals permitted to be imported through authorised border inspection posts are now specified. In addition, changes have been made in accordance with the European Economic Area Agreement concerning the conditions of accession of a number of countries.

107   Import of animals—post-import controls

The Animals (Post-Import Control) Order 1995, SI 1995/2439 (in force on 9 October 1995), replaces the 1993 Order, SI 1993/14. It establishes controls with regard to cattle from areas not free from warble fly, pigs from areas not free from Aujesky's disease, cattle from Canada, cattle imported under specific EC legislation and sheep and goats from areas not free from contagious agalactia. The order empowers an inspector to serve a notice in specified circumstances requiring a person to comply with any duty imposed by the order and is enforceable by the local authority. A contravention of the order is an offence under the Animal Health Act 1981.

108   Import of animals—veterinary and zootechnical checks

See para 106.

109   Pigs—records, identification and movement

The Pigs (Records, Identification and Movement) Order 1995, SI 1995/11 (in force on 30 January 1995), implements some of the requirements of Council Directive (EC) 92/102 on the identification and registration of animals, in so far as they relate to pigs. The order replaces part of SI 1963/286, the whole of SI 1975/203 as amended, and also replaces SR & O 1925/1349 as amended and SI 1960/105 in so far as they relate to pigs. The order provides that (1) each owner or keeper of pigs must supply information about the holding to the local divisional veterinary officer, and notify him of any changes in that information, (2) a record of pig movements must be kept in the form set out in Sch 1 and retained for three years, such record including details of the identification marks of the pigs concerned, (3) pigs for export must be marked by a permanent tattoo or ear tag identifying the holding on which the mark was applied, a distinctive number allotted to the pig, and the country code, (4) pigs moved between holdings in Great Britain must be marked either as if for export or with a mark sufficient to identify them during the journey, (5) the movement of pigs other than slaughter pigs between markets and collecting centres is prohibited, (6) pigs may only be moved from a farm for certain purposes, or returned to it if they are accompanied by a declaration made by the owner, (7) it is prohibited to move any pigs off premises within 20 days of the movement of any pigs onto those premises, except in certain exempted cases, (8) pigs may be moved from premises where waste food is kept only if they are accompanied by a declaration made by the owner or keeper, and may be moved only to other premises in the same occupation or to a slaughterhouse for slaughter, (9) the movement of pigs from a collecting centre is permitted if they are accompanied by a declaration, and the movement of pigs from any other place is subject to licensing, (10) sales of pigs and collecting centres are subject to licensing, and (11) the forms of declaration and licence include requirements for cleansing and disinfection with an approved disinfectant of road vehicles used for moving pigs, and impose restrictions upon the circumstances in which pigs can be moved in a road vehicle with other categories of pigs or with other things, and on the transfer of pigs from one vehicle to another. The order also creates offences and specifies penalties, and provides that the requirements imposed by the order are to be enforced by local authorities.

110 Spring traps

The Spring Traps Approval Order 1995, SI 1995/2427 (in force on 10 October 1995), replaces the 1975 Order, SI 1975/1647, as amended. The order adds four types of traps to those already approved by the Minister of Agriculture, Fisheries and Food in accordance with the Pests Act 1954, and the circumstances in which they may be used, in order to ensure that no trap can operate as a leghold trap, the use of which is prohibited in the Community by virtue of Council Regulation (EC) 3254/91.

111 Transportation of animals—welfare—journey plans

The Welfare of Animals during Transport (Amendment) Order 1995, SI 1995/131 (in force on 23 January 1995), amends the 1994 Order, SI 1994/3249. The meaning of 'transport undertaking' is to include persons who consign animals for transport, and for journeys outside Great Britain the consignor must provide a journey plan and certificate. The person in charge of the animals must comply with the provisions of the journey plan and a breach of any obligation by that person will be considered to be a breach by the undertaking itself for certain purposes.

112 Transportation of animals—welfare—meaning of 'journey'

Under the Welfare of Animals during Transport Order 1992, SI 1992/3304, art 4(1) it is the duty of any person in charge of an animal which is being transported on a vehicle to ensure that at suitable intervals during the journey it is provided with water, food and rest. The intervals are not to exceed 15 hours: art 4(2).

Two young calves were transported from farms to auctions and then on to premises where they were collected by hauliers. The hauliers transported the calves to ports and finally to destinations in France. At no time during the 34 hours from leaving the farms to arriving at their French destinations were the calves fed, watered or rested. The hauliers were convicted under the Animal Health Act 1981, s 73(a) which provided that it was an offence to contravene the 1992 Order, art 4. On appeal, the hauliers submitted that there was no jurisdiction to try the offences which had been completed outside the United Kingdom and that the relevant journey had been from the point where they collected the calves to the point where the lorries left the country. *Held*, since the 1992 Order gave no assistance in defining 'journey' the court considered the definition in Council Directive (EC) 91/628, art 2. That defined a journey as transport from the place of departure to the place of destination. The place of departure was defined as the place at which the animal had first been loaded onto a means of transport or any place where the animal had been accommodated for at least 10 hours, watered, fed and cared for. The effect of the Directive was that 'journey' meant the whole transport from the farm to the auction and then to the final destination. The 1992 Order was to be construed to accord with the Directive and, accordingly, the appeal against conviction would be dismissed.

Ken Lane Transport Ltd v North Yorkshire County Council [1995] 1 WLR 1416 (Queen's Bench Division: Staughton LJ and Mitchell J).

Welfare of Animals during Transport Order 1992, SI 1992/3304, now Welfare of Animals during Transport Order 1994, SI 1994/3249.

113 Veterinary drugs

See MEDICINE, PHARMACY, DRUGS AND MEDICINAL PRODUCTS.

114 Veterinary surgeons—Commonwealth and foreign candidates

The Veterinary Surgeons (Examination of Commonwealth and Foreign Candidates) (Amendment) Regulations Order of Council 1995, SI 1995/2396 (made on 6 September as 1995), amend the 1967 Regulations, SI 1967/599, by further increasing the fees payable by persons holding certain Commonwealth or foreign qualifications in veterinary surgery for sitting the whole or part of the statutory examination of the Royal College of Veterinary Surgeons. In addition, the period of notice required for withdrawing from examinations in order to obtain a one half refund of the fee is increased. SI 1976/1168, 1980/999 and 1984/1072 are revoked.

115 Veterinary surgeons—practice by students

The Veterinary Surgeons (Practice by Students) (Amendment) Regulations Order of Council 1995, SI 1995/2397 (made on 6 September 1995), amend the 1981 Regulations, SI 1981/988, to exempt those students who hold recognised overseas qualifications from the effects of the Veterinary Surgeons Act 1966, s 19(1). SI 1967/1960 is revoked.

116   Veterinary surgeons—unlawful conduct—whether conduct amounting to disgraceful conduct

The appellant, a veterinary surgeon, employed two veterinary surgeons at his clinic. Both employees held recognised European qualifications in veterinary surgery which enabled them to apply to be registered as members of the Royal College of Veterinary Surgeons pursuant to the Veterinary Surgeons Act 1966. Although they had applied for registration by the time the appellant employed them, they had not actually been registered. Charges were brought against the appellant for causing or permitting his employees to provide veterinary care while they were not registered and the disciplinary committee of the college found that the appellant's conduct had been disgraceful in a professional respect. His registration was suspended for four months. On appeal, *held*, although it was of obvious importance from the point of view of both the profession and of the public that only registered veterinary surgeons should be employed, both individuals had genuinely sought to register and the appellant was aware of that. Both had the requisite qualifications and the delay in registration was to some extent due to the administrative arrangements adopted. On all the evidence, it could not reasonably be said that the appellant's conduct was disgraceful in a professional respect, albeit he was in breach of the statute employing the two surgeons. This was a special case in which it was right to allow the appeal.

Plenderleith v Royal College of Veterinary Surgeons [1996] 1 WLR 224 (Privy Council: Lords Browne-Wilkinson, Slynn of Hadley and Hoffmann).

117   Veterinary surgeons and veterinary practitioners—registration

The Veterinary Surgeons and Veterinary Practitioners (Registration) (Amendment) Regulations Order of Council 1995, SI 1995/207 (in force on 31 March 1995) approves regulations which further amend the 1967 Regulations, SI 1967/395, by increasing the fees payable in respect of the registration and annual retention of names on the registers of the Royal College of Veterinary Surgeons by approximately 3 per cent. The 1994 Order, SI 1994/305, is amended.

118   Wild birds—migratory birds—conservation

See *Association pour la Protection des Animaux Sauvages v Prefet de Maine-et-Loire*, para 3123.

119   Wildlife—protection—wild birds

The Wildlife and Countryside Act 1981 (Amendment) Regulations 1995, SI 1995/2825 (in force on 30 November 1995), amend the 1981 Act to implement Council Directive (EC) 79/409 on the conservation of wild birds. The defence available to an authorised person to the killing or injuring of a wild bird on the ground that the action is necessary to prevent serious damage extends to cover damage to inland waters. However, the regulations limit the defences by providing that an authorised person must show that the killing is necessary and, if the killing is foreseeable, a licence must be applied for as soon as reasonably practicable.

ARBITRATION

Halsbury's Laws of England (4th edn) Vol 2 (reissue), paras 601–900

120   Articles

The Adversarial Myth, Francis Miller (on the adversarial nature of arbitration), Francis Miller: 145 NLJ 734

Chapter Nine of the Latham Report: Dispute Resolution: [1995] ADRLJ 164

Client Self-Help: Practical Suggestions for Cost Saving and Effective Dispute Resolution, Graeme Bradley: [1995] ADRLJ 170

Don't Disregard Time Limits, Timothy Stone (on enforcement of time limits in appeals against arbitrators' awards): 139 SJ 976

Multi-party Maritime Arbitrations, Philip Yang: [1995] ADRLJ 30

The Politics of Arbitration Reform, Arthur Marriott: (1995) 14 CJQ 125

Procedural Reform in Maritime Arbitration, Bruce Harris: [1995] ADRLJ 18

Revised Arbitration Bill, Nicholas Cheffings and Charles Goodwyn: Estates Gazette, 30 September 1995, p 140

Simply Negotiation with Knobs on, Andrew Floyer Acland (on alternative dispute resolution):
  LA, November 1995, p 8
The Structured Avoidance of Disputes, John Uff and Joanna Higgins: [1995] ADRLJ 179
Who Wants Mediation? John Bloor: Estates Gazette, 5 August 1995, p 62

121 Arbitration agreement—clause—claim for payment—claim that payment contingent on determination by arbitrator

Scotland
The appellant and the respondent companies were parties to a contract which provided that any dispute or difference of any kind arising between them was to be referred to arbitration. The appellant made a claim for sums payable under the contract which was unsuccessful at first instance. On appeal by the appellant, the respondent submitted that the sums were contingent because they were subject to a condition in the contract which had to be fulfilled before they became payable, namely, that the arbitrator had to determine the disputed issue in favour of the appellant. *Held*, the arbitration clause did not contain any condition which was required to be fulfilled before the sum became payable. The parties were not bound to go to arbitration and if, after the action had been commenced, neither party had chosen to found upon the provisions of the arbitration clause, then no arbitration would take place. The effect of such a clause was that instead of the court, it was the arbitrator who was to inquire into and decide the merits of the claim. It had never been suggested that the fact that the court had to determine the merits of the claim itself made a claim for payment of a debt contingent. The appeal would be allowed accordingly.
  Rippin Group Ltd v ITP Interpipe SA 1995 SLT 831 (Inner House).

122 Arbitration agreement—sub-contract-clause permitting dispute to be referred to arbitration under main contract—interpretation

Scotland
An arbitration clause in a sub-contract stipulated (1) that if a dispute arose in connection with the sub-contract it was to be referred to arbitration, but (2) if a dispute also arose in connection with the main contract and the contractor considered that such dispute touched or concerned the sub-contract works, then the contractor might require any dispute which arose under the sub-contract to be referred to the arbitrator to whom the dispute under the main contract was referred.
  A contractor commenced proceedings against the sub-contractor for payment of a large sum arising out of the sub-contract. The sub-contractor issued a defence and counterclaim seeking damages in respect of an alleged breach of contract. It also sought an order to require the contractor to refer the dispute to arbitration in accordance with clause (1) of the arbitration clause. The contractor claimed that the dispute fell within clause (2) on the ground that a dispute had arisen in connection with the main contract in which it was seeking a declaration that an agreement for completion and settlement of contracts had been completed and the main dispute 'touched or concerned the sub-contract works' because the sub-contractor was not entitled to receive payment under the sub-contract until the action in respect of the main contract had been resolved. *Held*, the arbitration clause had to be looked at in its entirety when considering whether there was any justification for the contractor's opinion that the main action 'touched or concerned the sub-contract works'. The point of contact between the two disputes would have to be a matter which had a material bearing on the decision in both disputes. Having regard to the pleadings in both disputes, it was clear that the dispute under the main contract did not touch or concern the sub-contract works, albeit that it might affect the sub-contractor's right to immediate payment. There was no material connection between the disputes. Accordingly, a declaration would be made requiring the contractor to refer the matter to arbitration in accordance with clause (1) of the arbitration clause.
  Taymech Ltd v Trafalgar House Construction (Regions) Ltd 1995 SLT 1003 (Outer House).

123 Arbitrator—allegation of misconduct—return of interim payment made by one party

An arbitrator ordered the payment of an interim account in respect of fees in a rent review case. One party paid but the other refused. The arbitrator repaid the sum that was paid and the plaintiff claimed under the Arbitration Act 1950, s 23(1) that the arbitrator should be removed on the ground that he had misconducted himself. *Held*, there was no misconduct. The request for an interim payment was a proposal to both of the parties, not merely to one of them nor to whichever of them agreed to it. It was an open negotiation between the arbitrator and the parties. The mere fact that he had learned that one party was willing to pay his interim account but the other was not could not amount to improper conduct. Nor did it provide a foundation for a justifiable concern that he might be biased in favour of one party. Accordingly, the application would be dismissed and the case remitted to the arbitrator.

Turner v Stevenage Borough Council (1995) Times, 7 December (Chancery Division: Mr Anthony Grabiner QC).

124 Award—appeal against award—appeal to Court of Appeal—uncertificated issues

See *Vitol SA v Norelf Ltd*, para 660.

125 Evidence—experts' reports—production

See *London & Leeds Estates Ltd v Paribas Ltd (No 2)*, para 1844.

126 Foreign award—enforcement—stay of execution—removal of stay

The plaintiffs obtained an arbitration award in their favour in Russia under the New York Convention on the Recognition and Enforcement of Foreign Arbitral Awards. After unsuccessfully trying to enforce the award in Russia, the plaintiffs applied to the English court and were granted leave to enforce it in the same manner as a judgment or order to the same effect and to enter judgment against the defendants. The plaintiffs duly entered judgment, but a stay of execution of four months was subsequently granted by consent. On the defendants' application for a renewal of the stay while they continued to challenge the award in Russia, *held*, having elected to convert the award into an English judgment, the plaintiffs ought in principle to be subject to the same procedural rules as applied to the enforcement of such judgments, and the wording of the Arbitration Act 1975 did not suggest otherwise. The 1975 Act, s 3 provided for enforcement either by action or in the same manner as an arbitrator's award was enforceable under the Arbitration Act 1950, s 26. There was nothing in either of those provisions to suggest that, once judgment had been entered in the terms of the award, it was to be treated for enforcement purposes in a different manner from any other judgment or order. Therefore the court had, in principle, jurisdiction to entertain an application for a stay. However, the court would rarely, if ever, order a stay in respect of a convention award when, under the convention, the time for enforcement had arrived. On the facts, there was no reason for the stay to remain and the defendants' application would be dismissed.

Far Eastern Shipping Co v AKP Sovcomflot [1995] 1 Lloyd's Rep 520 (Queen's Bench Division: Potter J).

127 Reference to arbitration—delay in prosecuting claim—power to dismiss claim within limitation period

The Arbitration Act 1950, s 13A provides that, unless a contrary intention is expressed in an arbitration agreement, the arbitrator has the power to make an award dismissing any claim in a dispute referred to him if it appears that there has been an inordinate and inexcusable delay on the part of the claimant in pursuing the claim and that the delay will give rise to a substantial risk that it is not possible to have a fair resolution of the issues in the claim or that the delay has caused or is likely to cause serious prejudice to the respondent.

In 1989 the appellant company brought an arbitration claim against the respondent company over the pricing and costs of a labour only subcontract entered into between the parties. The respondent company served its defence in November 1989, a preliminary hearing was held in July 1991 and directions for the main hearing were given in October 1991. Following a delay of nine months the respondent company applied to strike out the claim but the arbitrator held that he had no power to do so. Following the decision in *L'Office Cherifien des Phosphates v Yamashita-Shinnihon Steamship Co*, that under the 1950 Act, s 13A arbitrators could take into account delay occurring prior to the commencement of s 13A, the respondent company was given leave to apply to the arbitrator to reconsider its application to strike out the claim. In making a final award in March 1994 the arbitrator struck out the appellant company's claim on the grounds that, under the 1950 Act, s 13A there had been an inordinate and inexcusable delay on its part and that the delay had given rise to a substantial risk that it would not be possible to have a fair resolution of the claim, even though the statutory limitation period had not expired. On appeal, *held*, there was nothing in the enactment of the 1950 Act, s 13A (which was inserted by the Courts and Legal Services Act 1990, s 102) to suggest that Parliament intended to give arbitrators a power to strike out which went further than the jurisdiction in litigation, extending to claims that were not time-barred. The wording of s 13A indicated that the powers to dismiss claims in arbitration and in litigation were to be exercised in the same way. Section 13A merely gave an arbitrator a discretion to dismiss claims for want of prosecution and a claim could only be dismissed within its limitation period in exceptional circumstances. Since the circumstances of the present case were not exceptional, the appeal would be allowed and the award set aside.

James Lazenby Co v McNicholas Construction Co Ltd [1995] 3 All ER 820 (Queen's Bench Division: Rix J). *L'Office Cherifien des Phosphates v Yamashita-Shinnihon Steamship Co* [1994] 1 All ER 20 (1993 Abr para 144) followed.

AUCTION

Halsbury's Laws of England (4th edn) Vol 2 (reissue), paras 901–1000

128 Auctioneer—sale of forgery—auctioneer's liability to purchaser

The defendant, a firm of auctioneers, inspected a painting using an ultra-violet lamp and a magnifying glass and by reference to a catalogue entry and an article. In the defendant's auction catalogue, the painting was described as being by S and as signed by him. The artist's initials were on the painting. The plaintiff bought the painting at an auction conducted by the defendant but she later alleged that it was a forgery within the defendant's terms and conditions of sale and claimed a refund. It was apparent that the original painting had been extensively overpainted. By the use of X-rays and infra-red reflectography S's initials had been found under the visible surface and, on the balance of probabilities, the original painting was by S. However, on the evidence, the initials visible on the painting were by another artist. The defendant claimed it owed no duty of care to the plaintiff since the painting was sold 'as is' and was correctly described. *Held*, under the defendant's conditions a buyer had five years to exercise the right to return a forged painting, unless the catalogue description was in accordance with the accepted opinion of scholars at that time or if only unreasonably expensive, impractical or damaging scientific process would establish the forgery. Further, there had to be a substantial catalogue misdescription before a lot could be said to be a forgery. Because of the overpainting, the painting could not be described as being by S and was a forgery within the defendant's conditions. The defendant had taken the risk of forgery which it could reasonably have detected. Any competent art dealer or auctioneer would have been able to tell that the painting had been substantially overpainted and, when looked at carefully, the initials had been put on by the overpainter. The defendant was not entitled to rely on any exception to liability and, accordingly, judgment would be for the plaintiff.

De Balkany v Christie Manson & Woods Ltd (1995) Independent, 19 January (Queen's Bench Division: Morison J).

AVIATION

Halsbury's Laws of England (4th edn) Vol 2 (reissue), paras 1001–1800

129 Articles

State Aid and Air Transport, Trevor Soames and Alan Ryan: [1995] 5 ECLR 290
Turbulence in the Skies of Europe, Jeffrey Goh: 145 NLJ 1665

130 Aircraft—notional weights—calculation

The Air Navigation (General) (Amendment) Regulations 1995, SI 1995/1093 (in force on 9 May 1995), amend the 1993 Regulations, SI 1993/1622, so as to (1) introduce new notional passenger and crew weights for aeroplanes and helicopters of all sizes, (2) introduce an option to use 'all adult' notional weights for aircraft with 30 or more passenger seats, (3) distinguish between the notional weights of holiday and non-holiday charter flights, (4) include hand baggage within the new definition of notional weights, (5) introduce new notional hold baggage weights which are only available for aircraft with 20 or more passenger seats, and (6) alter the co-ordinates defining Europe.

131 Air navigation—Canada—service charges

The Civil Aviation (Canadian Navigation Services) (Amendment) Regulations 1995, SI 1995/2144 (in force on 1 September 1995), further amend the 1994 Regulations, SI 1994/2325, by (1) increasing the charge for the use of air navigation services provided by or on behalf of the Government of Canada within the Gander Flight Information Region to $142.10 Canadian, and (2) increasing the charge for the use of air navigation services provided by or on behalf of the Government of Canada by the Edmonton Control Centre to $209.00 Canadian. The regulations also amend the provisions relating to the detention and sale of aircraft for unpaid charges.

The Civil Aviation (Canadian Navigation Services) (Second Amendment) Regulations 1995, SI 1995/2713 (in force on 1 November 1995), further amend the 1994 Regulations, SI 1994/2325, so as to (1) introduce a definition of 'specified airspace', (2) decrease the charge for the use of air navigation services provided by or on behalf of the Government of Canada within the Gander Flight Information Region to $142.10 Canadian, thus partially superseding SI 1995/2144, (3) introduce a new charge for the use of air navigation services provided by or on behalf of the government of Canada through certain airspace, and (3) withdraw an existing charge made for the air navigation services provided by the Edmonton Area Control Centre.

132 Air navigation—general

The Air Navigation (No 2) Order 1995, SI 1995/1970 (in force on 29 August 1995), replaces SI 1995/1038, which replaced the 1989 Order, SI 1989/2004 as amended. The order makes provision as to the registration and marking of aircraft, air operators' certificates, airworthiness and equipment of aircraft, aircraft crew and licensing, operation of aircraft, fatigue of crew, documents and records, movement of aircraft, air traffic services, aerodromes, aeronautical lights and dangerous lights, as well as general provisions. Certain provisions of this order, either by themselves or in conjunction with the definition of 'prescribed' in Council Regulation (EC) 392/91, art 118, confer on the Secretary of State power to make regulations.

133 Air navigation—Hong Kong

The Air Navigation (Hong Kong) Order 1995, SI 1995/2700 (in force in part on 1 December 1995 and in part on 1 June 1996), replaces the Air Navigation (Overseas Territories) Order 1977, SI 1977/820, as amended, and makes provision, in respect of Hong Kong, in relation to the registration and marking of aircraft, air operators' certificates, airworthiness and equipment of aircraft, aircraft crew and licensing, operation of aircraft, fatigue of crew, documents and records, control of air traffic, aerodromes, aeronautical lights and dangerous lights, and provision of general application.

134 Air navigation—Isle of Man

The Air Navigation (Isle of Man) (Revocation) Order 1995, SI 1995/1296 (in force on 22 June 1995), revokes the 1979 Order, SI 1979/929, which extended to the Isle of Man, subject to exceptions, adaptations and modifications, the Air Navigation Order 1976, SI 1976/1783. The 1979 Order has been superseded by legislation made by virtue of the Airports and Civil Aviation Order 1987 (an Act of Tynwald).

135 Air navigation—navigation services—charges

The Civil Aviation (Navigation Services Charges) Regulations 1995, SI 1995/497 (in force on 1 April 1995), replace the 1991 Regulations, SI 1991/470, and revoke the amending Regulations, SI 1992/475, 1993/499, 1176, 1994/503. They specify (1) charges payable to the Civil Aviation Authority (CAA) for navigation services provided in connection with the use of Heathrow-London, Gatwick-London, Stansted-London, Aberdeen (Dyce), Edinburgh and Glasgow aerodromes, (2) the charges payable to the CAA by the operator of a helicopter which flies from any place in the United Kingdom to a vessel or offshore installation within specified areas of the Northern North Sea and the Southern North Sea, (3) the charges payable to the CAA in respect of services provided in the Shanwick Oceanic Control Area, and (4) charges payable for services provided outside hours where the intention to land or take off is not carried out. Provision is also made for the detention and sale of aircraft, equipment, stores etc for unpaid charges.

136 Air navigation—overseas territories—amendment

The Air Navigation (Overseas Territories) (Amendment) Order 1995, SI 1995/2701 (in force on 1 December 1995), further amends the 1989 Order, SI 1989/2395, so as to reflect changes made to the law applicable to the United Kingdom. The changes relate to (1) the scope of the requirement to make available and keep up to date an operations manual, (2) the requirement to establish and comply with aerodrome operating minima, (3) air traffic controllers' responsibilities relating to fatigue, (4) the licensing of aerodromes, (5) the submission by air traffic engineers of reports of reportable occurrences, (6) crew training and tests of proficiency in using instrument approach-to-land systems, (7) the grant of permission, subject to conditions, not to carry a flight manual, (8) weight and performance requirements for specified aeroplanes, and (9) the carriage of dangerous goods by air. Amendments are made to the Rules of the Air, which are set out in Sch 13 to the 1989 Order, in relation to low flying, visual flight rules, and markings for taxi-holding positions.

137 Air navigation—route charges

The Civil Aviation (Route Charges for Navigation Services) (Amendment) Regulations 1995, SI 1995/1004 (in force on 1 May 1995), further amend the 1994 Regulations, SI 1994/3071, by (1) restricting the exemption from the 1994 Regulations for flights made exclusively for the purpose of the instruction or testing of flight crew to such flights made within the specified airspace of the United Kingdom, (2) substituting Sch 2 to the 1994 Regulations in order to reduce the unit rate in ECUs in the case of Austria and the United Kingdom, and increase the unit rate in ECUs in the case of Turkey, and (3) introducing new transatlantic charges for navigation services.

The Civil Aviation (Route Charges for Navigation Services) (Second Amendment) Regulations 1995, SI 1995/1438 (in force on 1 July 1995), further amend the 1994 Regulations supra so as to introduce new transatlantic charges for navigation services, thus partially superseding SI 1995/1004 supra.

The Civil Aviation (Route Charges for Navigation Services) (Third Amendment) Regulations 1995, SI 1995/2329 (in force on 1 October 1995), further amend the 1994 Regulations supra by (1) introducing new transatlantic charges, thus superseding SI 1995/1438, and (2) substituting Sch 2 to the 1994 Regulations in order to increase the unit rate in ECUs in the case of Norway, thus partially superseding SI 1995/1004.

The Civil Aviation (Route Charges for Navigation Services) Regulations 1995, SI 1995/3160 (in force on 1 January 1996), revoke and replace, with amendments, the 1994 Regulations supra as amended, and determine certain rates of charges payable to the Eurocontrol Organisation in respect of navigation services provided for aircraft in certain specified airspace, taking into account the new apportionment of Eurocontrol costs between member States resulting from the accession of the Czech Republic to the Eurocontrol Convention on 1 January 1996. The unit rates in ECUs and the amount of the charges in ECUs (for transatlantic flights) are calculated by reference to the costs of provision of en-route navigation services in the participating countries in the Eurocontrol charges system, the amount of traffic using each country's airspace and the relationship of each country's currency to the ECU over a period agreed by Ministers of the participating countries. In calculating the revised charges, the average of the exchange rates between the ECU and the currencies of the participating countries obtaining in the month of July 1995 have been used. The unit rate for the United Kingdom has decreased by 1.1 per cent. If the amount of the charge is not paid by the operator of the aircraft within 24 days of the date payment is demanded by Eurocontrol interest at the rate of 8.69 per cent shall be paid from that day until the date when payment is made, and provision is made for the detention and sale of aircraft where default is made in the payment of charges incurred. Changes of substance from the 1994 Regulations include the withdrawal of the exemption for flights made between points within the specified airspace of Austria and the specified airspace of France, and Bahrain, Larnaca, Venice, Helsinki, Cologne—Bonn, Moscow, Warsaw, Luxembourg, Basle, Berlin, Hanover, Salzburg and Stuttgart have been added to, and Amman and Timisoara have been deleted from, certain zones in Sch 3 to the regulations.

138   Air passenger duty—extended schemes

The Air Passenger Duty (Extended Schemes) Regulations 1995, SI 1995/1216 (in force on 1 June 1995), amend the Finance Act 1994, s 39 so as to enable extended schemes to be permitted under which all exemptions from duty may be calculated if the registered operator so desires.

See also para 2489.

139   Airport charges—detention of aircraft for unpaid charges

The Aerodromes (Designation) (Detention and Sale of Aircraft) Order 1995, SI 1995/2475 (in force on 19 October 1995) designates Barra-Traigh Mhor and Biggin Hill aerodromes as aerodromes to which the Civil Aviation Act 1982, s 88 applies. Section 88 allows the owner or manager of a designated aerodrome to detain and sell aircraft where default is made in the payment of airport charges.

140   Byelaws—designated airports

The Airport Byelaws (Designation) Order 1995, SI 1995/2474 (in force on 19 October 1995), designates Barra-Traigh Mhor airport for the purposes of the Airports Act 1986, s 63. Section 63 provides authority for the airport operator of a designated airport to make byelaws for regulating the use and operation of the airport and the conduct of all persons while within the airport.

141   Carriage by air—exclusion of airline's common law liability—landing of aircraft in war zone—distress suffered by passenger

Scotland
The plaintiff was aboard an aircraft which landed in a country at the time of its invasion by a neighbouring country. She was captured by the invading forces and imprisoned for a month, which caused her to suffer great distress necessitating medical counselling. She brought a common law action for damages against the airline claiming that it was negligent in landing in a country where the threat of imminent invasion existed. The airline claimed that the plaintiff could only bring an action under the provisions of the Carriage by Air Act 1961 which incorporated the provisions of the Warsaw Convention as amended at the Hague, 1955 and, as the Convention excluded common law rights, the plaintiff had no cause of action. At first instance, the judge found for the airline. On appeal, *held*, the 1955 Convention had been intended to achieve a uniformity in the law relating to international carriage by air and it was therefore necessary to conclude that the list of liabilities was meant to be exhaustive. The plaintiff could only pursue her case if she could bring it within the terms of the Convention, which she had failed to do and, accordingly, the appeal would be dismissed.

Abnett v British Airways plc (1995) Times, 22 June (Inner House).

142   Carriage by air—injury to passenger—cause of action—international convention—time limit

The Warsaw Convention as amended by the Hague Protocol 1955 ('the Convention'), art 17 (set out in the Carriage by Air Act 1961, Sch 1) provides that the carrier is responsible for damage sustained in the event of the death or wounding of a passenger or any bodily injury suffered by a passenger if the accident which caused the damage so sustained took place on board the aircraft or in the course of any of the operations of embarking or disembarking. Article 29 provides that the right to damages is extinguished if an action is not brought within two years, reckoned from the date of arrival at the destination, or from the date on which the aircraft ought to have arrived, or from the date on which the carriage stopped.

The appellants were passengers on an aeroplane on an international flight which stopped off for refuelling. Whilst they were waiting in the airport terminal, the airport was attacked by forces from a neighbouring country, and the appellants were held hostage for nearly three weeks. More than two years after the event, the appellants commenced proceedings against the respondent for common law negligence, seeking damages in respect of their physical and psychological injuries. The respondent successfully argued that the appellants' sole and exclusive cause of action was under the Convention, art 17, and that their claim was barred by art 29, as proceedings had not been commenced within two years. The court rejected the appellants' argument that they had a cause of action for common law negligence as well as under the Convention. On appeal, *held*, the Convention governed international carriage by air, and once such carriage was in progress, the occurrence of any event gave rise to the carrier's 'no fault' liability. It was not possible to claim damages both under the Convention and also under any alternative provisions. The Convention set out an exhaustive code for the liability of international carriers by air and was intended to provide a uniform set of rules to eliminate conflict of laws issues and jurisdictional questions as to limitation periods. It also included provisions intended to achieve uniform documentation. In the instant case, art 17 provided the only remedy available to the appellants, but as their action was brought outside the time limit provided by art 29, the proceedings had to be struck out. Accordingly, the appeal would be dismissed.

Sidhu v British Airways plc [1995] PIQR P427 (Court of Appeal: Leggatt, Swinton Thomas and Otton LJJ). *Abnett v British Airways plc* (1995) Times, 22 June (para 141) considered.

143 Carriage by air—live animals exported for slaughter—discretion to exclude trade

See *R v Coventry Airport, ex p Phoenix Aviation; R v Dover Harbour Board, ex p Peter Gilder and Sons; R v Associated British Ports, ex p Plymouth City Council*, para 2313.

144 Carriage by air—loss of goods in transit—carrier's liability—limitation of liability

The Warsaw-Hague Convention, art 22, as set out in the Carriage by Air Act 1961, Sch 1, provides that in the carriage of registered baggage and cargo, the liability of a carrier is limited to 250 francs per kilogram unless the consignor has made, at the time the package was handed over to the carrier, a special declaration of interest in delivery at destination. In that case the carrier will be liable to pay a sum not exceeding the declared sum. Article 25 provides that the limits of liability specified in art 22 do not apply if it is proved that the damage resulted from an act or omission of the carrier done with intent to cause harm or recklessly and with knowledge that damage would probably result.

The plaintiff company was the owner of a consignment of diamonds lost in transit while in the custody of the defendant airline. A special declaration of interest under art 22 had been made by the plaintiff for a sum which was a fraction of the diamonds' actual value but it brought an action to recover a sum in excess of the declared sum, under art 25. The defendant claimed that the special declaration of interest in art 22 was not one of the limits of liability specified in art 25 which, as a result, did not apply to remove the limit of liability in the special declaration. At a hearing of that preliminary issue, the judge found in favour of the plaintiff. On appeal, *held*, construing art 22 as a consistent whole, it was clear that it was to be regarded as imposing a limit of liability of the type disapplied by art 25, provided the strict criteria of that article were proved. Therefore, where a consignor had made a special declaration of interest under art 22, he could nevertheless recover damages in excess of the sum specified in the declaration where the actual value of the consignment was greater than that sum. Accordingly, the appeal would be dismissed.

Antwerp United Diamonds BVBA v Air Europe (a firm) [1995] 3 All ER 424 (Court of Appeal: Butler-Sloss, Hirst and Otton LJJ). Decision of Phillips J [1993] 4 All ER 469 (1993 Abr para 163) affirmed.

145 Civil aviation—air travel organisers' licence—provision of flight accommodation and licensing

The Civil Aviation (Air Travel Organisers' Licensing) Regulations 1995, SI 1995/1054 (in force on 10 May 1995), replace the 1972 Regulations, SI 1972/223, and the amending Regulations, SI 1974/1802, 1975/1049, 1979/5, 1981/314. The regulations make provision (1) as to the regulation of provision of accommodation in aircraft, (2) licensing, and (3) offences and penalties. The major changes from the 1972 Regulations are (a) the categories of person who may make available flight accommodation, and hold themselves out as being entitled to do so, have been extended, (b) all persons holding themselves out as being so entitled are required to disclose the capacity in which they are so entitled and, if acting as an agent of an air travel organiser's licence (ATOL), to identify their principal, (c) new provisions are introduced relating to the acceptance of payment and provision of receipts and making it an offence to contravene those requirements, (d) reg 9(1)(b), which provided that on the transfer of a business of an ATOL holder, the licence would in specified circumstances be treated as if it had been granted to the transferee, has been omitted, and (e) the fine for failure to surrender a licence and the fines for failing to comply with the terms of a licence and for furnishing false information have been increased.

146 Civil aviation—Civil Aviation Authority—borrowing

The Civil Aviation Authority (Borrowing Powers) Order 1995, SI 1995/1289 (in force on 11 May 1995), specifies £550 million for the purposes of the Civil Aviation Act 1982, s 10(6) thus increasing the maximum amount of the principal of the Civil Aviation Authority's outstanding borrowing by £50 million.

147   Civil aviation—Civil Aviation Authority—duty of care—issue of certificate of airworthiness

See *Philcox v Civil Aviation Authority*, para 2167.

148   Civil aviation—Isle of Man

The Civil Aviation (Isle of Man) (Revocation) Order 1995, SI 1995/1297 (in force on 22 June 1995), revokes SI 1952/1032, 1961/575, 1967/805, 1967/808, 1969/594, 597, 1970/951, 1971/1745, 1972/451, 1973/1762, 1980/188, 1984/132, which have been superseded by legislation made by virtue of the Airports and Civil Aviation Act 1987 (an Act of Tynwald). The revoked orders extended to the Isle of Man, subject to exceptions and modifications, various Acts of Parliament relating to civil aviation which have now been replaced.

149   Civil aviation—joint financing

The Civil Aviation (Joint Financing) (Amendment) Regulations 1995, SI 1995/3161 (in force on 1 January 1996), amend the 1994 Regulations, SI 1994/3055, so as to (1) increase the charge payable by operators of aircraft to the Civil Aviation Authority in respect of crossings between Europe and North America; and (2) increase to 17.436 per cent the sum which is to be deducted by the CAA from the charges received and remitted to the Civil Aviation Organisation in respect of air navigation services provided by it.

150   International bodies—Eurocontrol—European Community competition law

See *SAT Flugesellschaft mbH v European Organisation for the Safety of Air Navigation (Eurocontrol)*, para 3162.

BAILMENT

Halsbury's Laws of England (4th edn) Vol 2 (reissue), paras 1801–1892

151   Bailee—duty of care—damage to plaintiff's vehicle while in police possession—liability of police

See *Sutcliffe v Chief Constable of West Yorkshire*, para 2163.

152   Hire—nature of contract

Scotland

The plaintiff suppiled a photocopier to the defendant health board. Under the terms of the contract, the copier was supplied free, and the defendant undertook to purchase a minimum amount of photocopy paper from the plaintiff. The plaintiff also had a monopoly in the supply of parts and requisites. The issue arose whether the contract was a contract for hire of the copier or a contract for the supply of paper. At first instance, the contract was held to be one of hire. On appeal, *held*, the contract had to be regarded in accordance with its true commercial purpose. The contract was essentially one for hire of equipment which the plaintiff agreed to supply and service. It had all the essential elements of a contract for the location of corporeal moveables and, the fact that charges related to volumes of paper provided, with a monthly premium, was not inconsistent with such an interpretation.

Eurocopy (Scotland) plc v Lothian Health Board 1995 SLT 1356 (Inner House).

BANKING

Halsbury's Laws of England (4th edn) Vol 3(1) (reissue), paras 1–350

153   Articles

Banks and Subpoenas, Colin Passmore: 145 NLJ 89

Banks, Security and the New Legislation from Europe, Paul Stafford (on the implications for banks of the Unfair Terms in Consumer Contracts Regulations 1994, SI 1994/3159): 139 SJ 478

Electronic Cash—Welcome to the Future, Ian Hutton: 145 NLJ 1810
Independent Advice After *O'Brien*, H W Wilkinson (on *Barclays Bank plc v O'Brien* [1993] 4 All ER 417, HL (1993 Abr para 1826)): 145 NLJ 792
Money Laundering and Banking Secrecy, Gerard McCormack: 16 Comp Lawyer 10
Taking Financial Services to the Cleaners, Michael Levi (on suspicious transaction reports): 145 NLJ 26
Taking Security After *O'Brien*, Richard Hooley (on *Barclays Bank plc v O'Brien* [1993] 4 All ER 417 (1993 Abr para 1826)): [1995] LMCLQ 346

154 Account—tracing of funds—fiduciary duty to account—unjust enrichment by bank

Scotland
A company paid cheques drawn in its own and the plaintiff's favour into an overdrawn bank account with the defendant bank. The cheques were written by customers of the company for sums owed by them to the plaintiff under a credit card scheme. The company went into receivership and the plaintiff claimed the sums paid in by the cheques from the bank, on the ground that the company had been acting as an agent of the plaintiff and there was therefore a fiduciary duty to account. The bank had unsuccessfully claimed that there was no case to answer and appealed. *Held*, if this was to be regarded as merely a tracing case then the plaintiff could not bring an action because once sums had been paid into an account in order to reduce its debit balance, they ceased to exist and were therefore untraceable. In this case, however, the plaintiff had a relevant case of unjust enrichment against the bank. It was possible that if the plaintiff could show that a fiduciary relationship existed between itself and the company, and that the bank had known that sums paid into the account by the company were specifically intended to be paid to the plaintiff, then the plaintiff might be able to recover its funds. Accordingly, the appeal would be dismissed.
Style Financial Services Ltd v Bank of Scotland (1995) Times, 23 May (Inner House).

155 Bank—bank as creditor—duty of disclosure of unusual terms to guarantor

See *Levett v Barclays Bank plc*, para 1484.

156 Bank—duty owed to customer—advice on prudence of transaction

The plaintiffs owned two houses and had mortgage and overdraft facilities with a bank. They decided to buy, renovate and sell another house as a business venture. They approached their bank manager about the project and he viewed two houses with them, one of which they did not proceed with because of the manager's reservations. The project involved borrowing some £40,000 more than the value of the house on a short-term bridging loan and the plaintiffs produced figures showing that a profit would be made if property values increased by 25 per cent. However, because of renovation costs and falling house prices, the plaintiffs suffered a loss of £77,000. On their claim that the bank had been negligent, *held*, if a customer of a bank requested advice on the prudence of a particular transaction and the bank gave it, then a duty of care arose on the bank's part. In the present case, the plaintiffs specifically sought the advice of the manager on the prudence of the transaction and he advised that it was financially viable and encouraged the plaintiffs to proceed with it. Therefore, the bank owed the plaintiffs a duty of care. Detailed calculations would have clearly demonstrated that the project was not feasible and the manager ought to have known that the plaintiffs were having difficulties meeting their existing financial obligations. Their income was insufficient to meet their outgoings and the prospects of any increase in income was speculative. The bank was in breach of its duty of care having failed to heed the plaintiffs' lack of business experience, failed to check their assumptions about renovation costs and time scale, failed to advise that the property market could falter and having miscalculated the viability of the venture. Accordingly, an order would be made in the plaintiffs' favour.
Verity v Lloyds Bank plc (1995) Independent, 19 September (Queen's Bench Division: Robert Taylor J).

157 Banking co-ordination—application to Liechtenstein

The Banking Co-ordination (Second Council Directive) (Amendment) Regulations 1995, SI 1995/1217 (in force on 1 June 1995), amend the 1992 Regulations, SI 1992/3218, so as to give effect to the adaptations made to Council Directive (EC) 89/646 (co-ordination of laws relating to taking up and pursuit of the business of credit institutions) in its application to Liechtenstein by the Agreement on the European Economic Area signed at Oporto on 2 May 1992 (as amended).

158   Confidentiality—information relating to customers—obligation to give discovery of documents—effect on implied duty of confidentiality

The customers of a bank were granted orders restraining the bank from breaching its duty of confidentiality by revealing information and documents which it held about them. The bank later commenced proceedings against its accountants for the tort of deceit in respect of audit clearance given in relation to certain deposits made by the bank's customers. In the course of those proceedings, the accountants were ordered to disclose documents in their possession, power and control to the bank's solicitors, counsel and expert witnesses. The accountants therefore sought to vary the injunction granted to the customers so that they could comply with the order, but the customers opposed the application. *Held*, where the rules of discovery required disclosure of documents, an individual in possession of documents containing confidential information did not breach his duty of confidentiality if he disclosed those documents in pursuance of such an obligation. Here, the accountants had no direct contractual relationship with the customers, whereas the bank did have such a relationship which thereby gave rise to the duty to inform its customers of any disclosure of confidential information relating to them. The customers had not established that they had a right to restrain the accountants from disclosing the information which they held about them, and which they were obliged to disclose in the course of discovery and also intended to rely on in their defence. The accountants were therefore entitled to a variation of the customers' injunction and, accordingly, the application would be allowed.

Adham v Bank of Credit and Commerce International SA (No 2); El Jawhary v Bank of Credit and Commerce International SA (No 2) [1995] 2 BCLC 581 (Chancery Division: Evans-Lombe J).

159   Credit institutions—protection of depositors

The Credit Institutions (Protection of Depositors) Regulations 1995, SI 1995/1442 (in force on 1 July 1995), make provision for authorised European Economic Area (EEA) credit institutions to participate in the deposit protection scheme set up by the Banking Act 1987, or the investor protection scheme set up by the Building Societies Act 1986. They also regulate participation in deposit protection schemes in other EEA States by authorised institutions and building societies and enable non-EEA institutions to leave the deposit protection scheme. EEA institutions accepting deposits in the United Kingdom may participate in a scheme if the Deposit Protection Board is satisfied that the institution's home state scheme affords less protection than the corresponding United Kingdom scheme. A contribution must be paid to the Deposit Protection Board by an EEA institution or participation must be notified to the Investor Protection Board. Provision regarding withdrawal or exclusion from participation is made. Any withdrawal or exclusion from a United Kingdom scheme must be notified by an EEA institution to its United Kingdom depositors. A home state scheme must be consulted by the relevant Board on an EEA institution's participation in a United Kingdom scheme and the Board may enter into agreements with that scheme. It is provided that the Boards must maintain a list of participating EEA institutions, and that depositors in EEA states must be notified when United Kingdom institutions and building societies withdraw or are excluded from host state schemes. Agreements may be entered into between the Boards and host state schemes and any insolvency of a United Kingdom institution or building society must be declared to any relevant host state scheme. Provision is made for non-EEA institutions to be exempted from the need to participate in the 1987 Act scheme, in certain circumstances. Deposit Protection Board decisions are subject to appeal. Certain amendments and modifications are made to the 1986 and 1987 Acts.

160   Insurance—banking policy—cover for theft—theft by company

See *Deutsche Genossenschaftsbank v Burnhope*, para 1723.

161   Investment services—securities—implementation of EC provisions

See para 1383.

162   Letter of credit—discrepant documents—documents produced by photocopiers

It has been held that, unless otherwise stipulated in the letter of credit, a bank must accept as original documents produced or appearing to have been produced by reprographic, automated or computerised techniques, provided that such documents are marked as originals. Where no such authentication appears on a document created by a photocopier, the issuing bank is entitled to refuse payment even if the document in question is an original document.

Glencore International AG v Bank of China [1996] 1 Lloyd's Rep 135 (Court of Appeal: Sir Thomas Bingham MR, Saville LJ and Sir John Balcombe).

163 Letter of credit—fraud by third party—obligation of issuing bank

Fraudulent letters of credit, purporting to have been issued by the defendant bank, were issued in favour of the first plaintiff who retained the first letter of credit and assigned two others to the second plaintiff. The fraudsters also managed to procure the sending of 'tested telexes', by or on the defendant's behalf, to both plaintiffs. These confirmed that the letters of credit were authentic and that the defendant accepted all responsibilities and liabilities under them. The first plaintiff claimed that by virtue of the telex in relation to the first letter of credit, the defendant was estopped from denying the authenticity of the same. It sought a declaration entitling it to present a conforming document under the letter of credit. The second plaintiff claimed damages against the defendant under the other two letters of credit. *Held*, the telexes had to be treated as being authorised by the defendant unless the first plaintiff was either on notice or put on inquiry as to their authenticity. The extent of the duty to inquire and the question of what might put a party on notice depended on the circumstances of every case. The more usual the circumstances and the clearer the representation appeared to be, the less the duty to inquire and the less likely that the circumstances would be such as to put anyone on inquiry. The first plaintiff could only be deemed to have constructive knowledge of matters to which it had wilfully turned a blind eye. There was no evidence that it was put on notice that the underlying transactions or the telexes coming from the defendant were fraudulent. In addition, the first plaintiff was under no duty to investigate the transactions for the defendant's benefit despite having owed a duty to the second plaintiff to make inquiries as to the validity of the assigned letters of credit. The first plaintiff was therefore entitled to treat the telexes as authentic. Accordingly, a declaration in the terms sought would be made in its favour. The defendant was also in breach of a duty of care owed to the second plaintiff. It was immaterial that the fraudulent telexes had been sent at the latter's request. The second plaintiff would not have advanced funds by reference to the letters of credit but for the sending of the telexes, and the defendant had been negligent in sending them. Therefore, as against the second plaintiff, the defendant was also estopped from denying the validity of the letters of credit. The second plaintiff would be entitled to damages against the defendant. A further consequence of the estoppels was that the second plaintiff would not be entitled to bring a claim against the first plaintiff, either for breach or warranty or misrepresentation. On that basis, there would be no finding of contributory fault by the first plaintiff in respect of the damages claim.

Standard Bank London Ltd v Bank of Tokyo Ltd; Sudwestdeutsche Landesbank Girozentrale v Bank of Tokyo Ltd [1995] 2 Lloyd's Rep 169 (Queen's Bench Division: Waller J).

164 Letter of credit—interpretation—implied terms

It has been held that the courts will rarely imply terms into a letter of credit or first demand guarantee as a matter of business efficacy. In particular, the commercial structure of letters of credit, first demand bonds and associated cross-undertakings require that the relevant obligations owed by banks are clear and certain. That need for certainty applies with equal force when the question is whether liability under a bond or cross undertaking has commenced.

Cauxell Ltd v Lloyds Bank Ltd (1995) Times, 26 December (Queen's Bench Division: Cresswell J).

BANKRUPTCY AND INSOLVENCY

Halsbury's Laws of England (4th edn) Vol 3(2) (reissue), paras 1–878

165 Articles

Bankruptcy and Bailiffs, John Kruse: LA, June 1995, p 16
Impounding and Insolvency, John Kruse: LA, September 1995, p 24
Insolvency at Sea, Sir Jonathan Mance (on the Third Party (Rights against Insurers) Act 1930): [1995] LMCLQ 34

Legislate in Haste, Repent at Leisure, Fiona Williams (on the Insolvency Act 1986, ss 19, 44):
145 NLJ 1425
Priority of the Floating Charge in Corporate Insolvency: *Griffiths v Yorkshire Bank plc* ([1994] 1
WLR 1427 (1994 Abr para 487)), Adrian Walters: 16 Comp Lawyer 291
Proprietary Claims and Their Priority in Insolvency, A J Oakley: (1995) 54 CLJ 377
Winding Up Recalcitrant Debtors, Fidelis Oditah: [1995] LMCLQ 107

166　Bankruptcy—assignment of right of action by trustee in bankruptcy—legally-aided assignee—validity of assignment

See *Norglen Ltd (in liquidation) v Reeds Rains Prudential Ltd; Mayhew-Lewis v Westminster Scaffolding Group plc; Levy v ABN Amro Bank NV,* para 497.

167　Bankruptcy—creditor's petition—inability to pay debts

The Insolvency Act 1986, s 268(1)(b) provides that, for the purposes of s 267(2)(c) (grounds of
a creditor's petition), a debtor appears unable to pay a debt if the debt is payable immediately
and execution or another process in respect of the debt on a judgment or order of court in
favour of the petitioning creditor to whom the debt is owed has been returned unsatisfied in
whole or in part.

The debtor gave guarantees to the creditors in respect of the debts of a company. The
company went into receivership so that the debtor became potentially liable under the
guarantees. Realising he could not pay the sum that might be sought from him, the debtor put
forward a voluntary arrangement which was rejected. The creditors demanded payment and
when the demand was not met they obtained summary judgment against the debtor. The
creditors then issued a writ of execution which was delivered to the sheriff, who was unable to
gain access on visiting the debtor's house. The creditors' solicitors countermanded the execution
and the sheriff returned the writ endorsed as 'unsatisfied in whole'. The creditors then issued a
bankruptcy petition for an amount representing 'the amount by which the execution was
returned unsatisfied'. The debtor's application to strike out the application succeeded and the
creditors appealed. The issue was whether the execution had been 'returned unsatisfied in whole
or in part' within the meaning of s 268(1)(b). *Held*, s 268(1)(b) contemplated execution and
endorsement of the manner in which the execution was carried out. If the sheriff was unable to
gain access to the premises in which the execution was to be carried out, then there was no
execution and an endorsement could not be made. Accordingly, the creditors were not entitled
to present the petition and the appeal would be dismissed.

Re a Debtor (No 340 of 1992) (1995) 139 Sol Jo LB 82 (Court of Appeal: Stuart-Smith, Waite
and Millett LJJ).

168　Bankruptcy—duties of a bankrupt—injunction restraining bankrupt from leaving jurisdiction—power of court to grant injunction

The Insolvency Act 1986, s 333(1) provides inter alia that a bankrupt must give to his trustee
such information as to his affairs as the trustee may reasonably require.

The respondent had been declared bankrupt but had continued to live in luxury. His trustee
in bankruptcy suspected that he was concealing his assets and applied for an injunction restraining
him from leaving the country pending the hearing of an application by the trustee for his
committal for contempt of court. The injunction was granted on the ground that it would aid
the trustee in securing the bankrupt's compliance with his duty under the 1986 Act, s 333 to
give the trustee information as to his affairs, and that the trustee's right to information might be
lost if the bankrupt left the jurisdiction. *Held*, the duties imposed by s 333 were designed to assist
the trustee in the performance of his statutory functions. Under the 1986 Act, s 366 a trustee
could obtain a warrant for the arrest of a bankrupt who failed to comply with a summons to
appear before the court. It would be extraordinary if a trustee could not obtain the less severe
remedy of an injunction preventing the bankrupt from leaving the jurisdiction. Accordingly, the
appeal would be dismissed.

Morris v Murjani (1995) Times, 27 December (Court of Appeal: Hirst and Gibson LJJ and
Buxton J).

169　Bankruptcy—joint tenants—severance of joint tenancy—property vesting in trustee

A husband and wife owned two properties as beneficial joint tenants. The husband committed
an act of bankruptcy by failing to comply with a bankruptcy notice as a consequence of which a
bankruptcy petition was presented against him. The wife died two months later leaving her

estate to her two children in her will. Three months later, a receiving order was made against the husband and six months later he was adjudicated bankrupt. It fell to be determined whether the vesting of his property in the trustee, which severed the joint tenancies, occurred at the time of the act of bankruptcy by retrospective effect of the adjudication, in which case the wife's share as a tenant in common devolved as part of her estate, or whether it occurred at the time of the adjudication, in which case her share had passed on her death to the husband as survivor with the result that on adjudication the whole interest in the properties vested in the trustee. *Held*, where a joint tenant of property was adjudged bankrupt under the Bankruptcy Act 1914, the title of the trustee in bankruptcy to that property related back to the first available act of bankruptcy, with the result that the joint tenancy was severed as from that date and not the subsequent date of adjudication. Since the relation back of the trustee's title to the act of bankruptcy was an automatic statutory consequence he could not then lay claim to the property and at the same time deny that it had vested in him at the anterior date. It followed that while the trustee could elect to rely on the doctrine of relation back to found a claim to property formerly belonging to the debtor and to claim that a joint tenancy had been severed where it was the debtor who had died in the interim, the personal representatives of a deceased joint tenant could also rely on the doctrine to deprive the trustee of his claim to an interest which had accrued to the debtor by survivorship. The joint tenancy had been severed on the husband's act of bankruptcy and, accordingly, a one-half share in the properties formed part of the wife's estate.

Re Dennis (a Bankrupt) [1995] 3 All ER 171 (Court of Appeal: Sir Thomas Bingham MR, Kennedy and Millett LJJ). *Smith v Stokes* (1801) 1 East 363, dictum of Lord Esher MR in *Re Pollitt, ex p Minor* [1893] 1 QB 455 at 457, CA, and *Montefiore v Guedalla* [1901] 1 Ch 435 applied. Decision of Nicholls V-C [1992] 3 All ER 436 (1992 Abr para 154) reversed.

170 Bankruptcy—official receiver—contracting out of functions

See para 503.

171 Bankruptcy—order—appeal against order—application for leave to appeal out of time

A debtor had given sureties for the payment of a company's rent. When the rent was not paid, the creditor served a statutory demand on the debtor. A judgment in default was entered against the debtor in the Queen's Bench Division. Shortly afterwards a bankruptcy petition based on the judgment debt was presented in the Chancery Division. A Queen's Bench master then refused the debtor's application to set aside the judgment. Notice of appeal against this order was issued but on the day before it was listed to be heard the debtor was adjudicated bankrupt. Thus nobody appeared before the Queen's Bench judge on the following day and the appeal was dismissed. The debtor instructed different solicitors and applied for leave to appeal against the bankruptcy order out of time. His application was refused and he appealed. *Held*, on an application for leave to appeal out of time against a bankruptcy order, the registrar should consider, without hearing the appeal itself, whether he was satisfied that the appeal was unarguable or doomed to failure, the onus being on the respondent to the application. Moreover, where a bankruptcy petition was based on a judgment debt which was the subject of a bona fide appeal being prosecuted with due diligence, the registrar should adjourn the bankruptcy petition pending determination of the appeal. Accordingly, leave to appeal out of time against the bankruptcy order would be granted.

Re a Debtor (No 799 of 1994), ex p Cobbs Property Services Ltd [1995] 3 All ER 723 (Chancery Division: Harman J). *Re Yeatman, ex p Yeatman* (1880) 16 Ch D 283, CA, *Nestle v National Westminster Bank plc* (1990) Times, 23 March, CA, applied.

172 Bankruptcy—order—circumstances in which order may be made

It has been held that having regard to the Insolvent Partnerships Order 1986, SI 1986/2142, art 15(3), a creditor can rely on an unsatisfied statutory demand as the basis for petitioning for a bankruptcy order against one partner in a partnership, without the need also to petition for the winding up of the partnership or for a judgment against the partnership.

Schooler v Customs and Excise Comrs [1995] 2 BCLC 610 (Court of Appeal: Nourse, Roch and Hobhouse LJJ).

The 1986 Order has been replaced by the Insolvent Partnerships Order 1994, SI 1994/2421.

173　Bankruptcy—order—rescission of order—discretion to rescind

The appellants applied to rescind a bankruptcy order made against them. At the time of their application, the appellants had no ground for rescission but shortly afterwards they persuaded the petitioning creditor to support their application. The petitioning creditor did so because it believed that there was a serious risk that the existence of a bankruptcy order against one of the appellants would prejudice the recovery of a substantial asset for the estate. The judge dismissed the application on the grounds that there was no new matter which had not been raised and was not available at the previous hearing, and that the court should not be party to a deception created by the rescission of the order that the appellant was not bankrupt and had not been made bankrupt. On appeal, *held*, the appellants based their applications on the fact that circumstances had changed and did not simply rely on the petitioning creditor's change of mind. They relied on the fact that a large body of creditors supported the rescission of the order and none of the known creditors opposed it. The fact that the underlying circumstances which led the creditors to support the rescission had been known at the time the order was made did not prevent the creditors' change of attitude from being both new and relevant. As it had occurred since the making of the orders, it was a factor which could not be taken into account on an appeal and an application to rescind was the only means of giving effect to the creditors' wishes. Further, there was no evidence from which the judge could properly conclude that the appellants intended to embark on a course of deception if the order was rescinded. Accordingly, the appeal would be allowed.

Fitch v Official Receiver (1995) Times, 21 November (Court of Appeal: Neill and Millett LJJ and Sir Iain Glidewell).

174　Bankruptcy—petition—petition served on foreign debtor visiting England—debtor having no assets in England

The debtor was a Swedish national, living in Belgium, who entered into an agreement with the creditor, an English company. The plaintiff incurred a debt under the agreement and was shortly afterwards made bankrupt in Sweden. Whilst visiting England the plaintiff was served with a bankruptcy petition by the creditor. The registrar made a bankruptcy order, inferring that the debtor had assets within England and incorrectly assuming that the debt had been incurred after, not before, the debtor had been declared bankrupt in Sweden. The debtor appealed on the ground that the fact that he had no assets in England and was already bankrupt in Sweden made such an order an unnecessary waste of costs. *Held*, the ease with which funds could be transferred across international boundaries and the international business connections of the debtor meant that an order ought to be made, despite the fact that there were no assets in England. Such an order could assist the creditor in reaching foreign assets and, in any event, the debtor had not sufficiently discharged the burden of proof relating to whether he had assets in the jurisdiction. Accordingly, the debtor's appeal would be dismissed.

Re Thulin [1995] 1 WLR 165 (Chancery Division: Jules Sher QC).

175　Bankruptcy—priority of bankruptcy expenses

See para 506.

176　Bankruptcy—proof of debts—mutual credit and set-off—assignment of right of action by trustee in bankruptcy

The Insolvency Act 1986, s 323 provides that where there have been mutual dealings between a bankrupt and a creditor before the bankruptcy, an account must be taken of what is due from each party to the other in respect of the mutual dealings and the sums due from one party must be set off against the sums due from the other. Only the balance (if any) of the account taken is provable as a bankruptcy debt or to be paid to the trustee as part of the bankrupt's estate.

The plaintiff sued the defendant for damages for breach of contract and the defendant counterclaimed. The plaintiff was adjudicated bankrupt and his right of action against the defendant vested in his trustee in bankruptcy, who assigned it back to the plaintiff in return for a share in the net proceeds. The defendant successfully applied to have the proceedings dismissed on the ground that a claim subject to a set-off under the 1986 Act, s 323 could not be validly assigned. That decision was reversed on the plaintiff's appeal. On the defendant's appeal, *held*, bankruptcy set-off, unlike legal set-off, affected the substantive rights of the parties by enabling the bankrupt's creditor to use his indebtedness to the bankrupt as a form of security. Bankruptcy set-off also had a much wider scope than legal set-off in that it applied to any claim arising out of mutual credits or other mutual dealings, including liabilities which at the time of the bankruptcy might have been subject to contingency. Section 323 operated at the time of bankruptcy without any step having to be taken by either of the parties. The account had to be taken whenever it was necessary for any purpose to ascertain the effect of s 323. In the present case, this meant that the original chose in action ceased to exist and was replaced by a claim to the net balance. If the set-off was mandatory, self-executing and resulted, as of the bankruptcy date, in only a net balance being owing, the cross claims could not, as choses in action, each continue to exist. On the question of whether the net balance could be assigned, bankruptcy set-off did not require the trustee or anyone else to execute it. It was true that the trustee would not ordinarily be a party to the action between assignee and creditor, but there was no reason why a defendant should not, with leave, join the trustee as a defendant to his counterclaim. Accordingly, a trustee could assign the right to the net balance like any other chose in action. The appeal would be dismissed.

Stein v Blake [1996] 2 All ER 961 (House of Lords: Lords Keith of Kinkel, Ackner, Lloyd of Berwick, Nicholls of Birkenhead and Hoffmann). Decision of Court of Appeal [1993] 4 All ER 225 (1993 Abr para 182) affirmed.

177   Bankruptcy—property vesting in trustee in bankruptcy—criminal injuries compensation award as property

The Insolvency Act 1986, s 436 provides that 'property' vesting in a trustee in bankruptcy includes every description of property, wherever situated, and also obligations and every description of interest, whether present or future or vested or contingent, arising out of, or incidental to, property.

A bankrupt had suffered a serious assault and consequently applied to the Criminal Injuries Compensation Board which awarded her compensation. Her trustee in bankruptcy claimed that the compensation constituted property under the 1986 Act, but the bankrupt claimed it came outside the definition. *Held*, the word 'property' could not have been intended to refer to something that had no present existence but might come into existence on an uncertain event in the future. Accordingly, the bankrupt's hope that she would receive an award was not, at that moment, part of her property and did not vest in the trustee.

Re a Bankrupt (No 145 of 1995) (1995) Times, 8 December (Chancery Division: Knox J).

178   Bankruptcy—statutory demand—dismissal of application to set aside statutory demand—issue estoppel in bankruptcy proceedings

The petitioner supplied goods to a business of which the debtor and W were directors and shareholders. That company ceased to trade and the petitioner sought payment from the debtor of the outstanding balance. A statutory demand was served and the debtor applied under the Insolvency Rules 1986, SI 1986/1925, r 6.4 to set aside the demand. The debtor claimed that he was not in any sort of partnership with W, that W did not have the authority to place the order for the goods with the petitioner and that the order was either placed on behalf of the company or made by W personally. His application to set aside the statutory demand was dismissed. The debtor sought a review of the order dismissing his application to set aside the statutory demand. The application for review was dismissed. The petitioner then appealed against an order whereby the bankruptcy petition was stood over for the purpose of a later hearing, arguing that there were no grounds upon which the bankruptcy order should have been refused. *Held*, although an issue estoppel was created by the dismissal of a debtor's application to set aside a statutory demand where the district judge had found no substantial grounds on which the debt could be disputed, a bankruptcy court on the full hearing of the bankruptcy petition could go behind the issue estoppel and was not bound by it.

Eberhardt & Co v Mair [1995] 3 All ER 963 (Chancery Division: Evans-Lombe J).

179   Bankruptcy—transaction at an undervalue—declaration of trust

See *Midland Bank plc v Wyatt*, para 1369.

180   Bankruptcy—voluntary arrangement—material irregularity

The applicants, a number of creditors of a debtor, were dissatisfied with the voluntary arrangements approved by the majority of the creditors at a creditors' meeting. In an application brought under the Insolvency Act 1986, s 262, they challenged the decision of the meeting. They claimed that the failure of the debtor to disclose his assets and liabilities accurately in his statement of affairs constituted 'a material irregularity at or in relation to such a meeting' within s 262(1)(b). *Held*, a 'material irregularity at or in relation to . . . a meeting' was not confined to any irregularity affecting the manner in which a meeting was convened or conducted, but included any irregularity in the preparation or presentation of a debtor's proposal and statement of affairs. In cases where a creditor believed that the debtor was concealing assets or misleading him as to his financial position, it would generally be more appropriate to present a bankruptcy petition to enable a trustee in bankruptcy to investigate the debtor's affairs. However, where the irregularity merely arose from the unintentional failure of a debtor to provide adequate information, there was no reason why a creditor should not pursue an application under s 262(1)(b) requesting the court to make a direction for the summoning of a further meeting of the debtor's creditors to consider alternative proposals. In the present case, it was clear that the statement of affairs was materially inaccurate as to the debtor's assets and liabilities. Accordingly, an order would be made under s 262(4) revoking the approval of the voluntary arrangements.

Re a Debtor (No 87 of 1993) (No 2) [1996] 1 BCLC 63 (Chancery Division: Rimer J).

181 Bankruptcy—voluntary arrangement—rights of execution creditor

The Insolvency Act 1986, s 258(4) provides that a creditors' meeting may not approve any proposal or modification which affects the right of a secured creditor of the debtor to enforce his security, except with the concurrence of the creditor concerned.

The plaintiff obtained a consent judgment against the defendants and also, by way of execution, a writ of fieri facias. The sheriff took walking possession of chattels which formed part of the business of the defendants who later entered into an individual voluntary arrangement with their creditors. Application was made to the court to determine whether or not the plaintiff was a secured creditor so that the meeting of creditors which had approved the individual voluntary arrangement could not, because of the 1986 Act, s 258(4), affect or modify his rights with respect to the chattels in constructive possession of the sheriff without his consent. *Held*, where goods were seized under a writ of fieri facias the execution creditor was, as regards those goods, in the position of a secured creditor before the goods were sold. The meeting of creditors could not, because of the 1986 Act, s 258(4), modify the plaintiff's rights with respect to the chattels and the attempt to retain the chattels within the company constituted a material irregularity in the holding of the creditors' meeting. Accordingly, the court would order that the execution could proceed notwithstanding the individual voluntary arrangement.

Peck v Craighead [1995] 1 BCLC 337 (Chancery Division: M E Mann QC)

182 Bankruptcy—voluntary arrangement—secured creditor—execution creditor as secured creditor—prejudice to security

The debtors were partners in a hotel business, and had both secured and unsecured creditors. One of their creditors, who had been employed as the general manager of the hotel, commenced proceedings against them for repayment of a sum that he had invested in the hotel and for payment of arrears of salary. After judgment was entered in his favour, he issued a writ of fieri facias and a sheriff took walking possession of most of the chattels in the hotel. Thereafter, the debtors entered into voluntary arrangements with their creditors, and part of the arrangement was that the supervisor was to sell the hotel as a going concern. Relying on the Insolvency Act 1986, s 258(4), the creditor sought to challenge the voluntary arrangements on the basis that they unfairly prejudiced his rights as a secured creditor. On the question of whether or not he was a secured creditor, *held*, the fact that an execution creditor had not yet enforced his security was irrelevant, as it was sufficient that the debtor's property in the goods was bound. Moreover, the supervisor of a voluntary arrangement did not acquire property in a debtor's goods, nor did he have a priority claim to it. Where a debtor had been declared bankrupt, an execution creditor did not lose his security by virtue of the doctrine of relation back, and a sheriff was entitled to execute a writ of fieri facias even if the debtor had entered into a voluntary arrangement. An execution creditor was therefore a secured creditor and, in the instant case, his security had been prejudiced by the approval of the voluntary arrangements.

Re a Debtor (No 10 of 1992) (1995) Times, 1 February (Chancery Division: Martin Mann QC).

183 Bankruptcy—voluntary arrangement—voting rights—unliquidated amount

The Insolvency Rules 1986, SI 1986/1925, r 5.17(3) provides that a creditor may not vote in respect of a debt for an unliquidated amount or any debt whose value is not ascertained, except where the chairman agrees to put upon the debt an estimated minimum value for the purpose of entitlement to vote.

The plaintiff creditor was the landlord of property of which the defendant was the tenant's guarantor. The plaintiff served a statutory demand on the defendant for arrears and subsequently presented a bankruptcy petition. A voluntary arrangement was proposed and approved by the majority of creditors. The arrangement included all future liabilities arising under the guarantee on the property despite the plaintiff's objections to the inclusion. On an application by the plaintiff for a declaration that the arrangement did not include future rent under the lease, the court declared that a future debt of an unliquidated amount could not be included in a voluntary arrangement where there was no agreement between the debtor and the creditor. This decision was reversed on appeal. On further appeal, *held*, the context of the words in r 5.17(3) was that there was a general prohibition against creditors voting on an unliquidated sum but there was an exception if the chairman agreed. The chairman did not have to agree with the creditor or anyone in particular. It was sufficient if he expressed his willingness to put and did put an estimated minimum value on the debt. Accordingly, the plaintiff was bound by the arrangement and the appeal would be dismissed.

Doorbar v Alltime Securities Ltd (1995) Times, 7 December (Court of Appeal: Hirst and Peter Gibson LJJ and Forbes J).

184 Bankruptcy—voluntary arrangement—whether terminated by subsequent bankruptcy order

A wife had obtained orders for financial relief against her former husband in divorce proceedings. The husband was declared bankrupt and then sought to enter into a voluntary arrangement with his creditors. Under the voluntary arrangement all but two creditors were notified of a meeting by the nominee of the arrangement and in the event only a small number attended at the meeting, the wife being amongst those absent. At the meeting an arrangement was approved which was to continue until all the creditors were paid. Shortly thereafter the bankruptcy order was annulled but a new creditor obtained a bankruptcy order in respect of debts incurred after the approval of the voluntary arrangement. The supervisor applied for directions under the Insolvency Act 1986, s 263(4) as to whether the second bankruptcy order brought the voluntary arrangement to an end and, if it did not, how much of the former wife's claim ranked for dividend in the voluntary arrangement. *Held*, when the voluntary arrangement was made the supervisor became trustee of the bankrupt's assets, which he held on trust for all creditors who had notice of the meeting and were entitled to vote. Thus the bankrupt had no beneficial interest in those assets and they did not form part of his estate when the subsequent order was made. Accordingly, that order did not bring the voluntary arrangement to an end. Although the wife had been given notice of the meeting in respect of non-matrimonial debts only, under the 1986 Act, s 260(2)(b), such a creditor was allowed to participate in an arrangement in respect of all the debts owed to them. Accordingly, the wife was entitled to arrears which had accrued at the date of the first order but not to debts accruing thereafter.

Re Bradley-Hole (a Bankrupt) [1995] 4 All ER 865 (Chancery Division: Rimer J).

185 Insolvency—administration order—employees of company in administration—adoption of contracts of employment

See *Powdrill v Watson; Talbot v Cadge; Talbot v Grundy*, para 466.

186 Insolvency—administration order—uncollected community charge

See *Preston Borough Council v Riley*, para 2428.

187 Insolvency—appeals—individual insolvency—procedure

Sir Richard Scott V-C has issued the following *Practice Direction (Insolvency Appeals: Individuals)* ([1995] 1 All ER 129), which comes into effect on 1 October 1995, upon which *Practice Direction (Insolvency and Revenue Appeals in the North)* [1991] 1 All ER 608 (1991 Abr para 144) is revoked in so far as it relates to insolvency, and *Practice Direction (Insolvency Appeals: Hearings outside London)* [1992] 1 WLR 791 (1992 Abr para 1958) is revoked in its entirety.

1. An appeal from a decision made in a county court by a circuit judge, or in the High Court by a registrar in bankruptcy, lies to a single judge of the High Court: Insolvency Act 1986, s 375(2) and Insolvency Rules 1986, SI 1986/1925, r 7.48(2).

2. Such appeals must be set down and heard as follows:

(I) an appeal from a decision of a registrar in bankruptcy must, or from any decision made in any county court may, be set down and heard in London by a High Court judge of the Chancery Division, or by a deputy judge designated to sit as a judge of the Chancery Division under the Supreme Court Act 1981, s 9.

(ii) an appeal from a decision made in a county court exercising jurisdiction over an area within the Northern and North Eastern Circuits, may be set down in Leeds, Liverpool, Manchester or Newcastle upon Tyne, by the Vice-Chancellor of the County Palatine or by a circuit judge designated under the 1981 Act, s 9 to sit as a judge of the Chancery Division at the above venues and at Preston.

(iii) an appeal from a decision made in a county court exercising its jurisdiction over an area within the Birmingham, Bristol or Cardiff Chancery District Registries, may be set down in the registry appropriate to the area in which the decision was made, for hearing in Birmingham, Bristol or Cardiff by the Chancery supervising judge or by a circuit judge designated under the 1981 Act, s 9 to sit as a judge of the Chancery Division in Birmingham, Bristol or Cardiff.

3. The procedure and practice of the Supreme Court relating to appeals to the Court of Appeal apply to appeals in insolvency proceedings: 1986 Rules, r 7.49(1). Thus, RSC Ord 59 applies to insolvency appeals.

4. In relation to any appeal under the 1986 Act, s 375(2) to a single judge of the Chancery Division, any reference to the Court of Appeal in the Rules of the Supreme Court is replaced by a reference to that judge, and any reference to the Registrar of Civil Appeals is replaced by a reference to a bankruptcy registrar who deals with insolvency proceedings, referred to below as the Registrar of Bankruptcy Appeals: 1986 Rules, r 7.49(2).

5. The single judge sits in open court to hear the appeal, and hears applications for injunctions pending the substantive hearing of the appeal, and for expedition or vacation of the hearing date of an appeal.

6. The Registrar of Bankruptcy Appeals sits in chambers in London, and hears applications for an extension of time for serving a notice of appeal, an extension of time for setting down a notice of appeal, an extension of time for serving a respondent's notice, leave to amend a notice of appeal or a respondent's notice, security for costs of an appeal, and leave to adduce further evidence on an appeal.

7(i). A form of notice of appeal appropriate to insolvency appeals to a single judge is set out in *Atkins Court Forms* (Vol 7), or can be adapted from the form set out in RSC Ord 59, or be obtained in London from the fees room, Thomas More Building, Royal Courts of Justice, or from the addresses set out in paragraph 8(iv) below.

(ii) Applications to the Registrar of Bankruptcy Appeals can be made on Bankruptcy Application Form 7.2, which can be obtained from the fees room, Thomas More Building, Royal Courts of Justice or from the addresses in paragraph 8(iv) below, and must be lodged at the address at paragraph 8(iv)(a) below.

8. The following practice applies to all appeals to the single judge of the High Court, whether set down in London, or set down at one of the other venues referred to in paragraph 2 above.

(i) a notice of appeal must be served not later than 28 days, such time to run: (a) in the case of an appeal from an order made in a county court, from the date the order was made: RSC Ord 59, rr 4 and 19(3), (b) in the case of an appeal from an order made by a registrar in bankruptcy, from the date on which the order was sealed: RSC Ord 59, r 4(1).

(ii) notice of appeal must be served on all parties to the proceedings below who are directly affected by the appeal. That includes the district judge of the appropriate county court (see RSC Ord 59, r 19(2)) and, where a bankruptcy order has been made, the Official Receiver.

Service of the notice of appeal can be effected by the following methods: (a) leaving the document at the proper address of the person to be served, (b) by post, (c) through a document exchange, (d) if both appellant and respondent are represented, by solicitors by fax, together with a hard copy posted to the party concerned on the same day as the fax is sent, (e) by substituted service with the leave of the court.

(iii) after service, the appellant must set down the notice of appeal within the time limits set out in RSC Ord 59, r 5, by lodging the documents listed below:

(a) two copies of the notice of appeal, one of which must be endorsed with a certificate of the date and method of service, and stamped with the appropriate fee,

(b) a copy of the order under appeal,

(c) the estimate of time for the hearing.

(iv) the above documents may be lodged personally or by post at the address of the appropriate venue listed below:

(a) if the appeal is to be set down and heard in London, the documents must be lodged at Room 206, Thomas More Building, Royal Courts of Justice, Strand, London WC2A 2LL;

(b) if the appeal is to be set down in Manchester, the documents must be lodged at the Chancery Section, Courts of Justice, Crown Square, Manchester M3 3FL;

(c)(i) if the appeal is to be set down in Birmingham, the documents must be lodged as the district registry of the Chancery Division of the High Court, 33 Bull Street, Birmingham B4 6DS, (ii) if the appeal is to be set down in Bristol, the documents must be lodged at the Chancery

Division of the High Court, 3rd Floor, Greyfriars, Lewins Mead, Bristol, BS1 2NR, (iii) if the appeal is to be set down in Cardiff, the documents must be lodged at the District Registry of the Chancery Division of the High Court, 1st Floor, 2 Park Street, Cardiff CF1 1NR.

(v) if the documents are correct and in order, the court at which the documents are lodged will fix a hearing date and, under paragraph 8(iv)(b), (c) above, will also fix the place of hearing. That court will send letters to all the parties to the appeal, informing them of the date and place of hearing, and indicating the time estimate given by the appellant. The parties will be invited to notify the court of any alternative or revised time estimate. In the absence of any such notification, the estimate of the appellant will be taken as agreed. The court will also send a document setting out the court's requirements concerning the form and content of the bundle of documents for the use of the judge. Such bundle must be lodged by the appellant at the address of the appropriate venue as set out in paragraph 8(iv) above, not later than seven days before the date fixed for the hearing. Failure to do so may result in the appeal being dismissed by the judge.

(vi) skeleton arguments, accompanied by a written chronology of events relevant to the appeal must be lodged at the address of the appropriate venue as set out in paragraph 8(iv) above, at least two clear days before the date fixed for the hearing. Failure to lodge may result in an adverse order by the judge on the hearing of the appeal.

(vii) a notice of appeal and a respondent's notice may be amended (a) with the leave of the Registrar of Bankruptcy Appeals or the single judge, at any time, (b) without leave, by supplementary notice served (i) in the case of a notice of appeal, not later than five days after setting down the notice of appeal, (ii) in the case of a respondent's notice, not later than five days after setting down the respondent's notice.

After service, two copies of the amended notice must be lodged at the address of the appropriate venue as set out in paragraph 8(iv) above, one copy endorsed with the date on which service was effected, and stamped with the appropriate fee.

(viii) where an appellant does not wish to continue with the appeal, or where the appeal has been settled, the appeal may be dismissed by consent or on paper without a hearing. An order to that effect signed by each party or letters of consent from each party, must be lodged not later than 24 hours before the date fixed for the hearing of the appeal, at the address of the appropriate venue as set out in paragraph 8(iv) above.

9. An appeal from a decision made by a single judge lies with the leave of that judge or of the Court of Appeal, to the Court of Appeal: see 1986 Rules, r 7.48(2). Applications for such leave to appeal must be made to the single judge at the conclusion of his judgment on the appeal. If a party fails to apply, that party may apply ex parte by notice of application. Such notice, together with draft intended grounds of appeal, must be lodged at the address of the appropriate venue as set out in paragraph 8(iv) above, within 28 days of the sealing of the order made on the appeal. The application will first be considered ex parte by the judge who heard the appeal, who may refuse leave, or give such directions as he thinks fit for the disposal of the application. Applications made after the 28-day period has expired must be made directly to the Court of Appeal.

188 Insolvency—assignment of right of action—legally-aided assignee—validity of assignment

See *Norglen Ltd (in liquidation) v Reeds Rains Prudential Ltd; Mayhew-Lewis v Westminster Scaffolding Group plc; Levy v ABN Amro Bank NV*, para 497

189 Insolvency—interim order—leave of court—peaceable re-entry under forfeiture clause

See *Re Debtors Nos 13A10 and 14A10*, para 1816.

190 Insolvency—liquidator—agreement for assignment of fruits of action—champertous agreement

See *Ward v Aitken*, para 667.

191 Insolvency—practitioner—removal—loss of qualification—supervisor of voluntary arrangement—power to appoint substitute

The Insolvency Act 1986, s 263(5) provides that the court may, whenever it is expedient to appoint a person to carry out the functions of the supervisor and inexpedient, difficult or impracticable for an appointment to be made without the assistance of the court, make an order appointing a person who is qualified to act as an insolvency practitioner in relation to a debtor, either in substitution for the existing supervisor or to fill a vacancy. The Insolvency Rules 1986, SI 1986/1925, r 5.5A provides that an application to the court under the 1986 Act, Pt VIII (individual voluntary arrangements) is to be made to a court in which the debtor would be entitled to present his own petition in bankruptcy.

The Secretary of State withdrew authorisation for an insolvency practitioner to continue to act as such, upon which he automatically vacated office as the liquidator of four companies and also ceased to be qualified to act as the supervisor of 20 individual voluntary arrangements. On the Secretary of State's application for an order for another person to be appointed in the insolvency practitioner's place, the court decided that it was empowered to make the appointment in relation to the companies, as the Secretary of State was a fit and proper person to make the application. As regards the appointment of a substitute supervisor for the voluntary arrangements, *held*, where an application for an order relating to a voluntary arrangement had originally been made to a county court, the 1986 Rules, r 5.5A required the same court to consider an application under the 1986 Act, s 263. As none of the voluntary arrangements in the instant case had originated in the High Court, the High Court had no jurisdiction to make the order sought by the Secretary of State. Accordingly, the application would be dismissed.

Re Bridgend Goldsmiths Ltd [1995] 2 BCLC 208 (Chancery Division: Blackburne J).

192 Insolvency—transactions at an undervalue—discovery—communications between debtor and legal advisers

See *Barclays Bank plc v Eustice*, para 1069.

193 Insolvency—voluntary arrangement—challenge—nature of proceedings

See *Re a Debtor (No 87 of 1993)*, para 1338.

BARRISTERS

Halsbury's Laws of England (4th edn) Vol 3(1) (reissue), paras 351–536

194 Articles

The Case For a National Legal Service, Bob Hoyle: 145 NLJ 189
An Imbalance of Power, Emily Driver (on sexual harassment at the Bar): 145 NLJ 1027
The Liability of Lawyers as Suppliers of Services, Mario Monti: 139 SJ 1473
A Recent Problem? Barbara Hewson (on sexual harassment at the Bar): 145 NLJ 626
The Role of the Legal Services Ombudsman, Michael Barnes: 145 NLJ 930

195 Costs—barrister's personal liability for costs—overrun of earlier trial

See *Re a Barrister (Wasted Costs Order No 4 of 1993)*, para 2332.

196 Costs—barrister's personal liability for costs—raising of inadmissible issue

See *Sampson v John Boddy Timber Ltd*, para 2335.

197 Professional conduct—advice to client—advice to defendant not to give evidence at trial

Trinidad and Tobago
In the defendant's trial for murder, the prosecution was based on the evidence of three eye-witnesses who claimed to have seen the defendant stabbing the deceased with a knife. Their evidence was only consistent with the defendant having made an unprovoked attack. The defendant did not give evidence. This was of the greatest importance since, if the defendant was going to have any prospect of avoiding conviction, it depended on his giving evidence which conflicted with that of the eye-witnesses. The defendant had wanted to give evidence that he and the deceased had been involved in a struggle when the deceased was wounded with the knife he (the deceased) had drawn. However, during the trial his counsel had gone over to the dock and told him that he would not be sending him to the witness box. Counsel submitted that he felt duty bound to advise the defendant to remain silent after the defendant had told him something which took him by surprise. On appeal against conviction, *held*, whatever counsel

had been told, it was his duty to investigate the matter fully and explain the alternative courses open to the defendant. Counsel should, if necessary, have sought an adjournment for that purpose. He did not fulfil the duties he owed to his client by giving whispered advice during the trial. The defendant had been deprived of the chance to make an informed decision on whether or not to give evidence or at least make a statement from the dock. It was not explained to him how important his evidence would be to the outcome of the trial and that without it there was, in practice, no defence. There had been a miscarriage of justice and, accordingly, the appeal would be allowed.

Sankar v State of Trinidad and Tobago [1995] 1 All ER 236 (Privy Council: Lords Browne-Wilkinson, Bridge of Harwich, Slynn of Hadley, Woolf and Nicholls of Birkenhead).

198 Professional conduct—mistake in criminal trial—basis of appeal

See *R v Satpal Ram*, para 746.

199 Rights—remuneration—recovery of fees from solicitor

New Zealand
The plaintiff barrister was instructed by solicitors to act for a client in civil proceedings, but his instructions were withdrawn before trial. The defendant solicitor took over the matter in place of the original solicitors, and instructed another barrister to act. Following trial, a sum was paid to the solicitor's trust account, but it was insufficient to pay solicitor's costs and disbursements, which included counsel's fees. The plaintiff issued proceedings, claiming that he had a lien over the funds in priority to or ranking equally with the solicitor. *Held*, as regards competing liens where successive solicitors were employed by the same client, the general rule under English law was that a second solicitor was entitled to be paid first, regardless of whether or not there were sufficient funds for the first solicitor. Such an approach was unsatisfactory where successive solicitors had each contributed to the ultimate success of a case, as the earlier solicitor was entitled to his unpaid costs and counsel's fees. The rule in New Zealand was that where there were competing claims for costs by different solicitors against a fund recovered by the joint or successive services of each of them, the solicitors were to share in the fund equally, although that rule could be displaced if equity demanded it. However, the rule in both England and New Zealand was that a barrister had no right to sue his instructing solicitors for his fees, as their relationship was one of honour and not of debt. If the rule was otherwise, it might undermine the rule that barristers were immune from suit for litigation and matters connected with litigation. As a barrister could not sue a solicitor for fees, he was not entitled to a lien on property as against his instructing solicitors or clients, and therefore in the instant case, the plaintiff had no claim or lien against the defendant.

Atkinson v Pengelly [1995] 3 NZLR 104 (High Court).

200 Trial—change of barrister—criminal appeal

See *R v Bowler*, para 852.

BETTING, GAMING AND LOTTERIES

Halsbury's Laws of England (4th edn) Vol 4(1) (reissue), paras 1–300

201 Articles

Drinking and Dicing, David Teagle: 139 SJ 929
The Law of Supply and Demand in Licensing and Gaming, J N Spencer: 159 JP Jo 422
Running a Lottery Syndicate, H W Wilkinson: 145 NLJ 217

202 Amusements with prizes—amusement machines—licence duty

The Amusement Machine Licence Duty Regulations 1995, SI 1995/2631 (in force on 1 November 1995), replace the 1988 Regulations, SI 1988/1602, in consequence of the extension of gaming licence duty to amusement machines.

203 Amusements with prizes—amusement machines—refusal of permit—discretion of granting authority

The applicant sought judicial review challenging the dismissal by the Crown Court of an appeal under the Gaming Act 1968, Sch 9, para 11 against a refusal by the local authority to grant him a permit under s 34 to operate an amusement centre with prizes. *Held*, the 1968 Act, Pt II (gaming on licensed premises) expressly referred to the need to take demand into account in considering the granting of licences. However, the absence of any express reference to demand in Sch 9 did not indicate an intention on the part of Parliament to exclude demand from the decision-making process under the 1968 Act, Pt III (gaming by means of machines). On the contrary, Parliament had given local authorities an unfettered discretion under Pt III, in contrast to the tight statutory framework created by Pt II. Where there was opposition to the proposed introduction of an amusement centre, the authority could consider the extent to which a demand existed before granting a permit. It could not be said that no reasonable court could have held on the evidence in the present case that there was not sufficient demand to outweigh the opposition to the proposed centre. That was a question of fact for the court to determine and the court had reached its decision in a balanced way. The court did not have to indicate the threshold of demand that had to be established. There was no error in the approach of the authority or the Crown Court and accordingly, the application would be dismissed.

R v Crown Court at Chichester, ex p Forte (1995) Times, 9 March (Queen's Bench Division: Brooke J).

204 Amusements with prizes—amusement machines—small prize machines—non-monetary prizes—accumulation of small prizes to exchange for larger prize

The operators of an amusement arcade displayed a notice stating that the small prizes offered by their gaming machines had a points value and that points could be combined to redeem larger prizes. It was argued that this right of exchange gave rise to an offence under the Gaming Act 1968 since it was a benefit which was not expressly permitted under the 1968 Act, s 34(3). *Held*, under the 1968 Act, s 34(3), a person who won an item from a gaming machine received only one benefit or advantage, that is a non-monetary prize as defined in s 34(8), so that any right to exchange the prize was incidental and not prohibited by the Act. There was no prohibition on playing a game more than once and thus winning more than one prize and further, small money prizes were permitted and money by its nature could be accumulated. Consequently, it was reasonable to infer that there was no policy against accumulation and no reason why a number of small prizes could not be exchanged for a larger prize.

R v Burt and Adams Ltd (1995) Times, 22 November (Court of Appeal: Kennedy LJ, Wright and Wickham JJ).

205 Amusements with prizes—application for permit for prize bingo—existing permits for amusements with prize machines in locality

Scotland

A company applied for an amusements with prizes permit under the Lotteries and Amusements Act 1976, s 16 in order to operate prize bingo. The licensing committee refused the permit after giving consideration to the notion that a licensee holding a permit for prize bingo could also operate amusements with prize machines and that a licensee under the Gaming Act 1968, s 34 holding a permit for amusements with prize machines could also operate prize bingo. Since there were already two section 34 permits in the area it was considered that the grant of a s 16 permit would amount to overprovision. On appeal it was argued that there was a distinction between the two types of permit and that the committee had erred in deciding that there was a possibility of overprovision. *Held*, in view of the discretion conferred by the 1976 Act, Sch 3, para 7(2) a licensing committee could properly refuse to grant a permit on the grounds that to do so would result in overprovision of a particular type of facility. It was legitimate for the committee to look at the general type of activity that could be carried out on the premises in question, to look at the activity being carried out nearby under permits granted under the 1968 Act and to conclude that each activity involved low cost gaming, providing a form of amusement with prizes of low value. Further, the committee was entitled to consider possible developments in activities at premises with particular permits. Accordingly, the appeal would be refused.

Matchurban Ltd v Kyle and Carrick District Council (No 2) 1995 SLT 1211 (Second Division).

206 Amusements with prizes—monetary limits

The Amusements with Prizes (Variation of Monetary Limits) Order 1995, SI 1995/928 (in force on 1 May 1995), increases from £25 to £30 the maximum amount permitted to be taken by way of the sale of chances in any one determination of winners in amusements provided at certain fairs and other commercial entertainments. SI 1992/425 is consequently revoked.

207 Betting—duty—administration

The Betting and Gaming Duties (Payment) Regulations 1995, SI 1995/1555 (in force on 1 August 1995), amend the General Betting Duty Regulations 1987, SI 1987/1963, the Bingo Duty Regulations 1988, SI 1988/333, and the Gaming Licence Duty Regulations 1991, SI 1991/1798, so that public notices issued by the Commissioners of Customs and Excise now specify the address to which returns and payments must be sent; and the notices relating to general betting duty and bingo duty now specify the relevant forms of return.

208 Betting—licensed betting offices—changes to rules for licensed betting offices

The Betting, Gaming and Lotteries Act 1963 (Schedule 4) (Amendment) Order 1995, SI 1995/579 (in force on 6 April 1995), amends the Betting, Gaming and Lotteries Act 1963, Sch 4, so as to (1) remove the restriction regarding the size and positioning of television screens used on licensed premises; and (2) extend the range of refreshments which may be sold on licensed premises.

209 Betting—licensed betting offices—control

The Licensed Betting Offices (Amendment) Regulations 1995, SI 1995/578 (in force on 6 April 1995), amend the 1986 Regulations, SI 1986/103, by removing the prohibition on advertisements outside a licensed betting office which consist of, or include, moving displays or moving images and by extending the range of matters in respect of which text can be included in such an advertisement. They also remove the restriction whereby statutory notices setting out the terms on which persons are invited to bet were prevented from being exhibited so as to be read from outside the premises.

210 Dog racecourses—greyhound racing—deregulation

The Deregulation (Greyhound Racing) Order 1995, SI 1995/3231 (in force on 7 January 1996), removes certain burdens from the greyhound betting industry and from the operators of dog tracks. The order (1) allows the operator of a dog racecourse to make available permanent structures to bookmakers on the track, provided that the permanent structures are only used in connection with betting on events elsewhere than on the track and at times when racing is taking place on that track, (2) allows the taking of bets on a dog race by means of a totalisator in advance of the day of the race, (3) makes provision for inter-track totalisator betting, (4) permits the operator of a dog racecourse to have an interest in bookmaking on that track in respect of events elsewhere than on that track, and (5) makes minor and consequential amendments.

211 Dog racecourses—totalisators

The Dog Racecourse Totalisator Regulations 1995, SI 1995/3232 (in force on 7 January 1996), replace the 1967 Regulations, SI 1967/10, as amended, so as to prescribe the conditions which totalisators on dog racecourses must comply with and prescribe certain particulars which must be set out in notices posted on dog racecourses in connection with the operation of a totalisator. The regulations (1) prescribe the conditions for totalisators on dog racecourses, (2) prohibit the receipt of bets by such a totalisator otherwise than through a terminal forming part of the totalisator and require a totalisator to have a central recording system (for bets made through its terminals) and a public display system, (3) require a terminal to have certain recording capabilities and provide that it must not be capable of recording a transaction in certain circumstances, (4) require the totalisator to have a system to prevent its terminal accepting bets in certain eventualities or conditions, (5) require the totalisator to be designed and maintained to prevent unauthorised access to it and to protect the security of the data it records, (6) lay down requirements for the central recording system so that it must immediately and automatically record bets taken by means of the totalisator's terminals and must maintain a central record sufficient to allow the calculation of winnings, (7) require the public display system to be linked to the central recording system so as to display the number of betting units staked on each relevant pool, with different requirements depending on the immediacy of the link, (8) provide for certain adaptations to the regulations where a totalisator is being used for betting under a licensed inter-track betting scheme, and (9) set out the prescribed particulars which must be set out in notices posted on dog racecourses in connection with the operation of a totalisator.

212 Finance Act 1995

See para 2489.

213 Gaming—bingo—fees

The Gaming (Bingo) Act (Fees) (Amendment) Order 1995, SI 1995/322 (in force on 1 April 1995), amends the 1986 Order, SI 1986/833, so as to increase the fee payable to the Gaming Board for Great Britain for the issue of a certificate issued by the board to an organiser of games of multiple bingo under the Gaming (Bingo) Act 1985 to £148,000. In addition, the order increases the fee payable to the Gaming Board for Great Britain for the continuing in force of such a certificate for a period of three years to £143,000. The 1992 Order, SI 1992/430, is revoked.

214 Gaming—bingo—monetary limit

The Gaming (Bingo) Act (Variation of Monetary Limit) Order 1995, SI 1995/122 (in force on 1 February 1995), replaces SI 1992/3076, so as to increase the maximum amount to be paid as a prize in respect of a game of multiple bingo, from £75,000 to £250,000.

215 Gaming—charges

The Gaming (Small Charges) (Amendment) Order 1995, SI 1995/1669 (in force on 1 August 1995), amends the 1992 Order by increasing the maximum daily charge which may be made in clubs and miners' welfare institutes in respect of a person taking part in gaming when the only games played are bridge and whist, from £6 to £15.

216 Gaming—clubs—charges

The Gaming Club (Hours and Charges) (Amendment) Regulations 1995, SI 1995/927 (in force on 1 May 1995), further amend SI 1984/248, so as to increase the maximum charges which may be made for admission to gaming on bingo club premises from £6.60 to £6.80. SI 1994/958 is consequently revoked.

217 Gaming—fees

The Gaming Act (Variation of Fees) Order 1995, SI 1995/321 (in force on 13 February 1995), increases the fees to be charged under the Gaming Act 1968 for the matters specified in the order. SI 1992/93 is revoked.

218 Gaming—licence duty—administration

See para 207.

219 Gaming—licence duty—monetary amounts

The Betting and Gaming Duties Act 1981 (Monetary Amounts) Order 1995, SI 1995/2374 (in force on 1 October 1995), (1) increases to £8 the maximum amount in money or money's worth that a gaming machine may pay out for a single game before it ceases to qualify as a small-prize machine; (2) increases to 25p the maximum permitted amount to play a gaming machine once, under the exemption from gaming machine licence duty for gaming by machine at a pleasure fair; (3) increases, under that exemption, to £4 in cash, and to £8 in money and non-monetary prizes, the maximum permitted prize levels for a single play; (4) raises the monetary limits that must be observed for small scale commercial amusements to qualify for exemption from bingo duty by increasing to £1 the maximum amount permitted to be paid by a single player for a card, increasing to £100 the maximum amount permitted to be paid by all players for a single game, and increasing to £1 the maximum amount to be distributed as a money prize. SI 1984/431, 1992/2954, 1993/752, 1994/2967 are revoked.

220 Gaming—licence duty—specified games

The Gaming Licence Duty (Games) Order 1995, SI 1995/442 (in force on 1 April 1995), adds super pan 9 and casino stud poker to the games for which a gaming licence is required under the Betting and Gaming Duties Act 1981, s 13(3).

221 Gaming—monetary limits

The Gaming Act (Variation of Monetary Limits) Order 1995, SI 1995/926 (in force on 1 May 1995), replaces SI 1993/967, 1994/956, 957, so as to increase (1) the maximum permitted aggregate amount of winnings in respect of games of bingo played in one week simultaneously on different club premises from £10,000 to £25,000, and (2) the maximum amount by which weekly winnings on any particular bingo club premises may exceed the aggregate amount of the stakes hazarded from £2,500 to £5,500. In relation to the conditions on which gaming for prizes is permitted at licensed club premises, the maximum value of prizes is increased to £30.

The Gaming Act (Variation of Monetary Limits) (No 2) Order 1995, SI 1995/2288 (in force on 1 October 1995), increases (1) the maximum permitted charge for playing a game once on licensed or registered premises by means of a machine to which the Gaming Act 1968, Pt III applies; and (2) the maximum permitted charge and the maximum permitted amount which may be offered as a prize for playing a machine once at certain fairs, licensed club premises and commercial entertainments. SI 1985/575, 1989/2190, 1992/2647 are revoked.

222 Lotteries—Gaming Board fees

The Lotteries (Gaming Board Fees) Order 1995, SI 1995/323 (in force on 1 April 1995), increases the fees payable to the Gaming Board under the Lotteries and Amusements Act 1976 for the registration of societies' and local authorities' lottery schemes. The 1993 Order, SI 1993/3224, is revoked.

223 Lotteries—lottery syndicate—distribution of prize money—duty of members

Canada

The plaintiff and the defendants were all members of a lottery syndicate. Every Thursday, the treasurer collected four dollars from each member, to be spent equally on tickets for the draws held on the following Saturday and Wednesday. Each member was entitled to an equal share in the winnings. One Thursday, the plaintiff paid his share to the treasurer. The treasurer subsequently contacted a number of members and explained that there was a shortfall in the sums collected for the Saturday draw. Between them, it was agreed that the money collected should all go towards buying tickets for the Saturday draw. The plaintiff and one other member were not consulted. The following Monday, the treasurer asked the plaintiff to contribute a further two dollars towards the Wednesday draw. He refused on the ground that he had already paid for that ticket. The treasurer put in an additional two dollars on behalf of the other member who had not been contacted. One of the tickets for the Wednesday draw won a prize of $1.15 million. The defendants refused to give the plaintiff a share in the winnings because he had not paid the additional two dollars when he was asked for it. The plaintiff sought a declaration of co-ownership in the winning ticket. *Held*, the plaintiff had been entitled to refuse to pay additional money for the Wednesday draw. The money collected on the previous Thursday was collected for both draws and the treasurer should not have placed it all on the Saturday draw. The treasurer acted as trustee of the syndicate's funds. His duty was to apply the funds according to the terms under which each member paid. He had acted in breach of trust in using all of the plaintiff's contribution to pay for tickets for the Saturday draw. The other members of the syndicate had also acted in breach of trust in voting to exclude the plaintiff from sharing in the winnings. The plaintiff was entitled to an equal share of the winnings. Accordingly, a declaration would be made in the terms sought by the plaintiff.

Taylor v Smith (1995) 128 DLR (4th) 548 (General Division).

224 National lottery—lottery duty—instant chances

The Lottery Duty (Instant Chances) Regulations 1995, SI 1995/2815 (in force on 1 December 1995), apply to lotteries that form part of the National Lottery. The regulations (1) determine when an instant lottery chance is to be deemed to have been taken for the purposes of payment of lottery duty, (2) define the phrase 'instant chance', (3) stipulate that each instant chance must bear a unique reference number in an identifiable sequence, and (4) make provision entitling the registered promoter to claim duty credit where duty has been paid on an instant chance which is not then taken.

225 National Lottery—National Lottery Charities Board—increase in membership

The National Lottery Charities Board (Increase in Membership) Order 1995, SI 1995/1645 (in force on 26 July 1995), increases the number of members to be appointed to the National

Lottery Charities Board by the Secretary of State under the National Lottery etc Act 1993, Sch 5, para 1, from a chairman and sixteen other members to a chairman and twenty-one other members.

226 National Lottery—National Lottery Distribution Fund—distributing bodies

The National Lottery etc Act 1993 (Amendment of Section 23) Order 1995, SI 1995/2088 (in force on 1 September 1995), amends the National Lottery etc Act 1993, s 23(1) (distributing bodies for sums allocated for expenditure on or connected with the arts) by substituting the Arts Council of Northern Ireland for the Arts Council of Northern Ireland 1994.

BRITISH NATIONALITY, IMMIGRATION AND RACE RELATIONS

Halsbury's Laws of England (4th edn) Vol 4(2) (reissue), paras 1–300

227 Articles

Access to Legal Assistance for Asylum-seekers, Prakash Shah: [1995] 9 INLP 55
Appeals from the Immigration Appeal Tribunal to the Court of Appeal: a Short Guide for the
    Practitioner, Jim Gillespie: [1995] 9 INLP 92
Border Controls Revisited, Ramnik Shah: 145 NLJ 283
A Burden On the Taxpayer? Some Developments In the Role of 'Public Funds' in Immigration
    Law, Richard McKee: [1995] 1 INLP 29
Conducive to the Public Good? Richard McKee: [1995] 9 INLP 95
Detention of Asylum-seekers: A Continuing Cause for Concern: [1995] 9 INLP 59
The Immigration Appellate Authority, Judge David Pearl: 145 NLJ 761
The Immigration (European Economic Area) Order 1994, Sofia Gondal: [1995] 1 INLP 21
Immigration for Investors, Jaqueline Thompson: 139 SJ 714
The New Immigration Rules and Business Migrants, Bernard Andonian: [1995] 1 INLP 14
Racial Harassment at Work, Daniel Barnett: 145 NLJ 1614
Recent Trends in Asylum Appeals, Richard McKee: [1995] 9 INLP 52
Refugees and Safe Third Countries, Prakash Shah: [1995] 1 INLP 3
Ruling Out Affirmative Action, Sionaidh Douglas-Scott (on the approach to affirmative action
    by the European Court of Justice in comparison with the United States Supreme Court): 145
    NLJ 1586
'Social Group' for the Purposes of Asylum Claims, Michael Haran: [1995] 9 INLP 64
The Starting Point, Geoffrey Bindman (on EC measures against racism): 145 NLJ 62
Testing Time for Asylum-seekers, Richard McKee (on immigration officers' powers of
    administrative detention): 145 NLJ 321

228 British nationality—citizenship—designated service

The British Citizenship (Designated Service) (Amendment) Order 1995, SI 1995/552 (in force on 1 April 1995), further amends the 1982 Order, SI 1982/1004, so as to include in the types of service designated by the Secretary of State under the British Nationality Act 1981, s 2(3), service under the Council for the Central Laboratory of the Research Councils, service under the European Conference of Ministers of Transport, service under the International Energy Agency, and service under the Organisation for Economic Co-operation and Development.

229 British nationality—citizenship—registration—conferment of citizenship

A husband applied for registration as a British citizen before the Immigration Act 1971, ss 2(1) and 2(2)(a) were repealed by the British Nationality Act 1981, but the application was not registered until after the 1981 Act came into force. His wife was granted leave to enter the United Kingdom on the basis that she was the dependant of a British citizen, but the Secretary of State later concluded that she was an illegal entrant, and gave directions for her removal. On the wife's application for judicial review of the decision, the issue was whether or not the husband was a British citizen, *held,* having regard to the provisions of the 1981 Act and other immigration legislation, it was clear that registration, and not merely application, was a prerequisite to the grant of British citizenship. In the instant case, the wife had not acquired citizenship through her husband, because his application was not registered before the repeal of the relevant provisions of the 1971 Act. Accordingly, the application would be dismissed.

R v Secretary of State for the Home Department, ex p Amina Bibi [1995] Imm AR 185 (Queen's Bench Division: Popplewell J).

230   Immigration—aliens—registration with police

The Immigration (Registration with Police) (Amendment) Regulations 1995, SI 1995/2928 (in force on 1 January 1996), further amend the 1972 Regulations, SI 1972/1758, by increasing from £30 to £34 the fee payable by aliens who are required to register with the police.

231   Immigration—asylum—appeal—absence of applicant from appeal hearing

After arriving in the United Kingdom with a false passport, the applicant claimed asylum which was refused by the Secretary of State. He appealed against the decision, but at the date of the hearing claimed to be ill and did not attend. The adjudicator decided that he was not so ill that he could not attend, and dismissed the appeal. The dismissal was based partly on findings of fact adverse to the applicant which depended on credibility. Leave to appeal was refused, and the applicant applied for judicial review of that decision and also of the Secretary of State's decision to issue directions for his removal back to Nigeria. He argued that, in considering whether the hearing should have been adjourned, the adjudicator should have considered not whether it was actually possible for him to attend but whether if he had attended he could have done justice to his case, and that the adjudicator had erred in the findings of fact which were based on credibility. He further claimed that the Secretary of State had disregarded policy guidance in coming to his decision and had failed to give reasons for his refusal to exercise his discretion outside the rules governing asylum. *Held*, the adjudicator had not erred in concluding that the medical evidence did not justify adjourning the case. Nor had he erred in making findings of fact in the absence of the applicant when they were dependent on an assessment of credibility. Further, the Secretary of State had not erred in coming to his decision, and was not obliged to provide reasons for not exercising an extra-statutory discretion. Accordingly, the application would be dismissed.

R v Secretary of State for the Home Department, ex p Owalabi [1995] Imm AR 400 (Queen's Bench Division: Harrison J).

232   Immigration—asylum—appeal—role of Secretary of State

The Asylum and Immigration Appeals Act 1993, s 8(4) provides that where directions are given for a person's removal from the United Kingdom, the person may appeal to a special adjudicator against the direction on the ground that his removal would be contrary to the United Kingdom's obligations under the Convention relating to the Status of Refugees.

The applicant applied for political asylum on the ground that his life was in danger from terrorists who had threatened his aunt and killed his cousin and grandfather. His claim was refused, as was his application for leave to appeal, and directions were given for his removal. The applicant's solicitors then informed the Home Office that the applicant's father had also been killed by terrorists, and sent documents supporting the claim. Despite that information, the Secretary of State decided that the authorities in the applicant's country of origin would be able to protect the applicant and his family, and gave further directions for the applicant's removal. The applicant's solicitors argued that the recent information and supporting documentation constituted a fresh asylum application, but the Secretary of State decided that the documentation did not alter the fundamental basis of the applicant's claim, but merely amplified it. He therefore decided that the applicant had no right of appeal. On the applicant's application for judicial review of the decision, *held*, removal directions were given by an immigration officer, and under the Asylum Appeals (Procedure) Rules 1993, SI 1993/1661, notice of appeal had to be served on the immigration officer, who then passed it on to the special adjudicator. Only when an appeal was so constituted did the Secretary of State become involved. Moreover, it was only once an appeal was made under the 1993 Act, s 8(4) that the issue of whether or not an asylum seeker had made a fresh claim could arise, and that had to be determined by the court or tribunal to which the appeal was made, and not by the Secretary of State. As neither the 1993 Act nor the 1993 Rules provided any immediate role for the Secretary of State when a notice of appeal was lodged, the Secretary of State had erred in deciding that his decision in the instant case was final. However, on the facts, the application would be dismissed.

R v Secretary of State for the Home Department, ex p Singh (1995) Independent, 17 October (Queen's Bench Division: Carnwath J).

233 Immigration—asylum—application—detention pending outcome of application

The Asylum and Immigration Appeals Act 1993, s 6 provides that during the period beginning when a person makes a claim for asylum and ending when the Secretary of State gives him notice of the decision of the claim, he may not be removed from or required to leave the United Kingdom.

The applicants, who were illegal immigrants, applied for political asylum and were detained by immigration officers pending the determination of their applications. In successfully applying for writs of habeas corpus to secure their release, the applicants relied on the 1993 Act, s 6 in arguing that immigration officials had no power to detain them because they were not persons in respect of whom directions for their removal could be given. On appeal by the Secretary of State, *held*, although the effect of the 1993 Act, s 6 was that directions could not be given for the removal of an applicant for political asylum pending the outcome of the application, it did not mean that no directions at all could be given in respect of such a person. The Secretary of State still had the power to give directions for arrangements to be made for the removal of an asylum applicant and, pending such directions, he could be detained under powers conferred by the Immigration Act 1971, Sch 2, para 16(2). The effect of an asylum application was merely to prolong the period during which an applicant could be detained pending his removal. In the instant case, the applicants were illegal immigrants to whom the 1971 Act, Sch 2 applied because they had not been given leave to enter or remain. Although immigration officers had no power to give directions for the applicants' immediate removal, they did have power to give directions for their detention. Accordingly, the appeal would be allowed.

R v Secretary of State for the Home Department, ex p Khan [1995] 2 All ER 540 (Court of Appeal: Leggatt and Otton LJJ and Sir Ralph Gibson). Decision of Dyson J (1995) Times, 25 January, Independent, 20 January, reversed.

234 Immigration—asylum—application—fraudulent application

On his application for asylum, the applicant gave an account of his imprisonment and ill-treatment in Zaire. After hearing his evidence, a special adjudicator found the applicant to be totally devoid of any credibility and was not satisfied that he would be arrested on his return to Zaire. The applicant appealed to the Immigration Appeal Tribunal, which held that a person who put forward a fraudulent and baseless claim for asylum would not be afforded the protection of the Geneva Convention relating to the Status of Refugees 1951. On further appeal, the applicant argued that by making his application, he had proved to the requisite standard that he would be at risk of persecution if he was returned to Zaire as a failed asylum seeker. *Held*, it was erroneous as a matter of law to hold that there could never be a case in which, by the very act of claiming asylum, an applicant put himself at risk of persecution. However, to rely on the making of the application rather than its contents would be exceptional. In a fraudulent application based on false facts the applicant's credibility would be called into question and even if he could establish that he did not set up the application for asylum to create a danger of persecution, he would be likely to find it extremely difficult to demonstrate to the required standard a genuine subjective fear coming within the definition of the 1951 Convention. The greater the degree of the falsehood and bogus claims, the infinitely more difficult it would be to prove to the requisite standard the requirements of the 1951 Convention. In the present case, the tribunal's finding had been in error but, since its decision on the facts was unassailable, the appeal would be dismissed.

M v Secretary of State for the Home Department [1996] 1 All ER 870 (Court of Appeal; Butler-Sloss, Millett and Ward LJJ).

235 Immigration—asylum—certification that application without foundation—safe third country—material on which certificate based

The applicants, Somali nationals, stayed for a few days in Spain before travelling to the United Kingdom where they claimed asylum on the ground that they feared persecution in Somalia. The Home Secretary refused their claims, certifying that they were without foundation and that Spain was a safe country to which the applicants could be returned. Special adjudicators dismissed their appeals against his decision. On further appeal, it fell to be determined whether the Home Secretary was obliged to make available to the adjudicators all the material on which he had based his decision that Spain was a safe third country and whether the special adjudicators had sufficient evidence on which to decide the appeals. *Held*, Steyn LJ dissenting, in deciding whether a country was a safe third country, the Home Secretary was entitled to rely on information from a variety of sources, including the Foreign and Commonwealth Office, but he was under no duty to provide either the applicants or the special adjudicators with all the information on which he had relied. The certificates issued by him provided some evidence that Spain was a safe third country and there was no evidence before the special adjudicators that it was not a safe country. Unless the procedure followed could itself be challenged, the conclusion reached by the special adjudicators could not be faulted. The procedure had been laid down by Parliament to ensure the speedy determination of appeals and there was no justification for the court to imply a duty of disclosure on the Home Secretary. The appeals would be dismissed.

Steyn LJ believed that fundamental rights of asylum seekers were rendered ineffective by the procedure laid down which he considered to be so unfair as to be unlawful.

Secretary of State for the Home Department v Abdi; Secretary of State for the Home Department v Gawe [1994] Imm AR 402 (Court of Appeal: Neill, Steyn and Peter Gibson LJJ). Decision of Sedley J (1994) Times, 10 March (1994 Abr para 215) reversed.

This decision has been affirmed: [1996] 1 All ER 641, HL.

236   Immigration—asylum—certification that application without foundation—safe third country—matters to be taken into consideration

The applicant, a Romanian citizen, left her country because of her political activities, and travelled through several countries before arriving in the United Kingdom. Although the last two countries through which she travelled, namely Germany and Holland, were parties to the United Nations Convention relating to the Status of Refugees, 1951, the others were not. Her application for asylum was refused by the Secretary of State on the basis that Holland was a safe third country. Following the Secretary of State's certification that the claim was without foundation, he issued directions for the applicant's removal. Her appeal to a special adjudicator against the certificate was dismissed, as was her application for judicial review of that decision. On further appeal, *held,* in deciding whether or not a third country was safe, both the Secretary of State and the special adjudicator were obliged to consider whether the third country would properly entertain a claimant's substantive application for asylum in accordance with the 1951 Convention, and, if it was not prepared to do so, whether the third country would give proper consideration to whether or not it was safe to return the claimant to yet another country. In stating that Holland was a safe third country, it was implicit that both the Secretary of State and the special adjudicator had considered those matters. However, they were not obliged to consider whether the other countries to which Holland might send the applicant were safe countries. Accordingly, the appeal would be dismissed.

Martinas v Special Adjudicator [1995] Imm AR 190 (Court of Appeal: Nourse, Glidewell and Simon Brown LJJ).

237   Immigration—asylum—deportation decision—validity of decision pending outcome of asylum application

On the same day that the applicant applied for asylum, he was served with notice of the Secretary of State's intention to deport him and immediately detained. On his application for judicial review, the applicant argued that having regard to the Asylum and Immigration Appeals Act 1993, s 6, the decision to make a deportation order against him whilst his claim for asylum had not yet been determined and his consequential detention were unlawful. *Held,* there was a distinction between a decision to make a deportation order and the actual making of an order. A notice of intention to deport could be served at the same time that an asylum application was being considered, because it did not require a person to leave the United Kingdom. Accordingly, the appeal would be dismissed.

R v Governor of Wolds Prison, ex p Samateh [1995] 17 LS Gaz Rep 48 (Court of Appeal: Staughton, Beldam and Peter Gibson LJJ).

238   Immigration—asylum—refusal of application—prior refusal by safe third country— procedural impropriety in third country

Where an asylum applicant has come to the United Kingdom from another country which is a party to the United Nations Convention relating to the Status of Refugees or its Protocol and which has considered and rejected an application for asylum from him, his application in the United Kingdom may be refused without substantive consideration of his claim to refugee status: Statement of Changes in Immigration Rules 1994, para 347.

The applicants, three Romanian citizens, applied for judicial review of the decisions of the Secretary of State and two special adjudicators, to refuse their claims to be treated as refugees. The applicants had arrived from France, where they had been refused asylum. The Secretary of State made his decision pursuant to the 1994 Rules, para 347. The applicants contended that the special adjudicators had wrongly refused to hear their complaints of the way their cases had been heard in France. *Held*, the adjudicators had erred in law by directing their minds particularly to whether France was a safe third country. In a para 347 case, the key question was whether the application for asylum made in the third country had been determined rationally, according to the principles of natural justice. The phrase in para 347 'has considered and rejected' should be read to mean 'has properly considered and rejected'. However, there was no obligation to investigate the details of the hearing before the relevant foreign tribunal, since there was a presumption that a Convention country would deal properly with asylum applications. Only where they were provided with evidence of procedural impropriety were the Secretary of State or the adjudicators obliged to consider whether there had been procedural defects which constituted a breach by the third country of the principles of substantial justice. Accordingly, judicial review would be granted in the cases of the two applicants in respect of whom the special adjudicator had declined to consider the propriety of the French proceedings. The application of the third applicant, in respect of whom there was no evidence of procedural impropriety or that the French decision had been perverse, would be refused.

R v Secretary of State for the Home Department, ex p Stefan [1995] Imm AR 410 (Queen's Bench Division: Collins J).

239 Immigration—asylum—well-founded fear of persecution—matters to be taken into consideration

The appellants, who were Sri Lankan Tamils, unsuccessfully applied for asylum, and their appeals to the Immigration Appeal Tribunal and the Secretary of State were refused. Although large numbers of young male Tamils were being arrested in Sri Lanka, it was decided that in all the prevailing circumstances, such round-ups did not constitute persecution within the meaning of the 1951 Convention relating to the Status of Refugees. In particular, there was evidence that there had been an improvement in the treatment of Tamils since the appellants had made their asylum applications and since their appeals had been refused. On further appeal, the appellants argued that the court had misdirected itself in law in regarding such round-ups as justifiable arrests rather than arbitrary and unlawful acts which amounted to persecution. *Held*, the issues of whether or not a person or a group of persons had a well-founded fear of persecution and whether or not their freedom would be threatened, formed a single composite question which had to be considered in the round, taking account of all the relevant circumstances. Here, Tamils had been arrested at a time of political unrest, but their loss of liberty was relatively short, and although the arrests were based on ethnic origin, they were intended to maintain public order rather than to oppress Tamils. Moreover, even if the arrests were unlawful, that in itself was not enough to bring the matter within the ambit of the 1951 Convention. In addition, the prospective nature of asylum appeals overrode the retrospective approach that was required for all other immigration appeals. Ordinary immigration appeals were entirely specific to the individual applicant, whereas asylum appeals necessarily concerned the situation prevailing in a particular foreign country. Special adjudicators and the Secretary of State therefore had to be informed about that situation, and it would be wrong to ignore further information after the date on which the Secretary of State had refused to grant asylum. As such, in the instant cases, improvements in the situation in Sri Lanka since the appellants' asylum applications had been refused were material to the assessment of the present level of risk of persecution. Accordingly, the appeals would be dismissed.

R v Immigration Appeal Tribunal, ex p Sandralingham; R v Immigration Appeal Tribunal, ex p Rajendrakumar (1995) Times, 30 October (Court of Appeal: Nourse, Staughton and Simon Brown LJJ).

240 Immigration—deportation—notice of decision to deport—circumstances in which notice need not be given

The Immigration Appeals (Notices) Regulations 1972, SI 1972/1683, reg 3(1) provides that where any decision or action which is appealable is taken, written notice thereof must as soon as practicable be given to the person in respect of whom the decision or action is taken. Regulation 3(4) provides that it is not necessary for notice to be given if the officer or authority required to give it has no knowledge of the whereabouts or place of abode of the person to whom it is to be given.

The appellant was given leave to enter the United Kingdom as a visitor for one month. He remained in the country after the expiry of his leave, and waited until he had been ordinarily resident for five years before applying for indefinite leave to remain. However, a deportation decision had already been made against the appellant, although the immigration authorities had been unsuccessful in their inquiries as to his whereabouts in order to serve him with notice of the decision. On the appellant's appeal, he argued that he had not been given proper notice. *Held,* the immigration authorities had attempted the serve the appellant at the various addresses which he had given on his arrival. Having regard to the 1972 Regulations, reg 3(4), as they had been unable to trace the appellant's whereabouts or place of abode, they were no longer obliged to give him notice of the deportation decision. Although the Immigration Act 1971 required that written notice of a decision or action had to be given to the person affected, it was legitimate and proper for the 1972 Regulations to make an exception to that obligation if, in practice, it was impossible to serve notice. Regulation 3(4) was therefore valid. Moreover, in the instant case, the deportation decision had been made within five years of the appellant being resident in the United Kingdom. Accordingly, the appeal would be dismissed.

Singh v Secretary of State for the Home Department (1976) [1995] Imm AR 299 (Court of Appeal: Lord Denning MR, Scarman and Bridge LJJ).

1972 Regulations replaced by Immigration Appeals (Notices) Regulations 1984, SI 1984/2040.

241 Immigration—deportation—recommendation for deportation—threat to national security—sufficient evidence

The Immigration Act 1971, s 3(5)(b) provides that a person who is not a British citizen is liable to deportation if the Secretary of State deems his deportation to be conducive to the public good.

The applicant, an Iranian citizen, was granted refugee status in Kuwait and then came to the United Kingdom to study. He was later arrested and given notice by way of letter that his continued presence in the United Kingdom would not be conducive to the public good for reasons of national security, because of the likelihood of his involvement in terrorist activities. On the applicant's application for judicial review of the decision, *held,* the fact that the letter did not use the exact wording of the 1971 Act, s 3(5)(b) was irrelevant, as the Secretary of State had applied the correct test in reaching his decision. The reason given in the letter for the applicant's deportation was, by itself, insufficient to justify a deportation order. However, the court had read further affidavit evidence from an immigration officer which stated that the Secretary of State had seen material which led him to believe that the applicant was concerned in the planning of terrorist activity within the United Kingdom, and that to give further information would be damaging to national security. Accordingly, the application would be refused.

R v Secretary of State for the Home Department, ex p Jahromi (1995) Times, 6 July (Court of Appeal: Nourse, Roch and Hutchison LJJ).

242 Immigration—deportation—refugee—drug offences

The United Nations Convention relating to the Status of Refugees 1951, art 33(1) provides that no contracting state can expel or return a refugee to the frontiers of territories where his life or freedom would be threatened on account of his race, religion, nationality, membership of a particular social group or political opinion. Article 33(2) provides that the benefit of art 33(1) may not be claimed by a refugee whom there are reasonable grounds for regarding as a danger to the security of the country in which he is, or who, having been convicted by a final judgment of a particularly serious crime, constitutes a danger to the community of that country.

The appellant was granted asylum and given limited leave to enter and remain in the United Kingdom. Having been convicted of four drug offences, the appellant was sentenced to a term of imprisonment and recommended for deportation. Following the appellant's release from prison, the Secretary of State gave notice of intention to deport him and, relying on the 1951 Convention, art 33(2), refused to grant the appellant further leave to remain as a refugee. The appellant unsuccessfully appealed against the decision. On further appeal, *held,* even where a refugee had lost the benefit of the 1951 Convention, there was still a duty to carry out a balancing exercise before making a deportation order. In the instant case, the Immigration Appeal Tribunal ('the tribunal') had acknowledged that the appellant was a refugee, but had correctly regarded the issue as being whether or not the decision to make a deportation order was justified. The tribunal had taken account of the seriousness of the appellant's convictions and concluded that he had behaved in such a way that the public interest favoured his deportation. Moreover, none of the factors relating to the appellant's background weighed against deportation. In considering the appellant's refugee status, the tribunal had taken account of the risk of persecution and inhumane treatment that the appellant might suffer if he was returned to his country of origin, but decided that the risk was outweighed by the risk to the public if he was allowed to remain, especially since there was no evidence that he would be persecuted because of his political opinions. In addition, the fact that the appellant had been recognised as a refugee carried little weight, as the grounds for such recognition were unclear. The tribunal had not erred in law in its decision and, accordingly, the appeal would be dismissed.

Raziastaraie v Secretary of State for the Home Department [1995] Imm AR 459 (Court of Appeal: Sir Thomas Bingham MR, Peter Gibson and Saville LJJ).

243   Immigration—deportation—residence period

The applicant overstayed following the expiry of his limited leave to remain in the United Kingdom. The Home Office sent a letter to him at the address that he had given on his arrival, warning that he was liable to deportation if he did not leave voluntarily, but the letter was returned, giving a new address for the applicant. A deportation notice was then sent to the applicant, by ordinary post to his original address and by recorded delivery to the new address. When no reply was received, a deportation order was issued, but it was not served because the applicant could not be found. The applicant later applied for indefinite leave to remain, but his application was refused and he was personally served with the deportation order. The Secretary of State refused to review the decision to make the order. By that time, as the applicant had been in the United Kingdom for 14 years, he sought leave to remain under the 14-year concessionary rule. His application was refused, and on his application for judicial review of the decisions, *held*, the Secretary of State had applied the 14-year rule, and there were countervailing factors against granting the applicant indefinite leave to remain, in particular the fact that a deportation order had been made and served on him before the 14-year period had elapsed. Where a deportation order had been validly served, the person who was the subject of the order could not have a legitimate expectation that he would be allowed to remain if he managed to stay in the country for at least 14 years. Here, the deportation order had been validly served, as the Home Office had sent it to the applicant's last known address and it was not returned. Alternatively, if there was no known address for the applicant, the Secretary of State was not obliged to serve notice. Accordingly, the application would be dismissed.

Musah v Secretary of State for the Home Department [1995] Imm AR 236 (Court of Appeal: Glidewell, Mann and Millett LJJ). *R v Secretary of State for the Home Department, ex p Ofori* [1994] Imm AR 581 (1994 Abr para 228) and *Hussain v Immigration Appeal Tribunal* [1995] Imm AR 413 followed.

244   Immigration—deportation—threat to national security—terrorist activities

The Secretary of State made a deportation order against the applicant on the ground that it was conducive to the public good, pursuant to the Immigration Act 1971, s 3(5)(b), for reasons of national security and other reasons of a political nature. In giving reasons for the order, the Secretary of State stated that the applicant was actively involved in supporting terrorist activities being carried out in India. The applicant applied for judicial review of the decision, arguing that the Secretary of State could only deport a person for activities which affected the public good in the United Kingdom, and not for activities which took place outside the country, even if initiated from the United Kingdom. *Held*, the power conferred by the 1971 Act, s 3(5)(b) could be exercised in a whole range of circumstances, subject to *Wednesbury* principles. It was therefore impossible to delimit the circumstances in which the Secretary of State was entitled to decide that a deportation order was conducive to the public good, and his decision in the instant case was not unreasonable, especially since various consequences could flow from the existence of terrorist conspiracies in the United Kingdom, whether or not their outcome was intended to occur abroad. Accordingly, the application would be dismissed.

R v Secretary of State for the Home Department, ex p Singh [1995] Imm AR 447 (Queen's Bench Division: Laws J).

245   Immigration—displaced persons—temporary refuge—Community obligation

See para 3098.

246   Immigration—entry—illegal entry—application for housing—responsibility for determining immigration status

See *R v Westminster City Council, ex p Castelli; R v Westminster City Council, ex p Tristran-Garcia*, para 1528.

247   Immigration—entry—illegal entry—entry gained by deception—deception by silence

The applicant, a Saudi Arabian citizen, her husband and their children, were granted leave to enter the United Kingdom as visitors. The husband's subsequent claim for political asylum was refused and he was declared an illegal entrant. Directions were given for his removal to the United States of America where he had lived with the applicant and the children for a year before coming to the United Kingdom. The applicant then sought political asylum in her own right, claiming that her husband was her dependant. The Secretary of State certified that her claim was without foundation, because the United States was a safe third country. He concluded that, as the applicant had known that her husband intended to claim asylum for the whole family, she had secured entry by deception so that she too was an illegal entrant. On the applicant's appeal, a special adjudicator upheld the Secretary of State's decisions. The applicant's application for judicial review of the decisions was dismissed at first instance. On her renewed application for judicial review, *held*, on the facts and findings of the special adjudicator, it had been shown that the applicant was an illegal entrant. By the silent tendering of her passport, there had been material deception. The Secretary of State was entitled to certify, pursuant to the Asylum and Immigration Appeals Act 1993, Sch 2, para 5(3)(a), that the applicant's claim was without foundation even though she claimed to be a refugee. He was also entitled, under Sch 2, para 5(3)(b), to conclude that the application was vexatious. Accordingly, the application would be dismissed.

Al-Zahrany v Secretary of State for the Home Department [1995] Imm AR 510 (Court of Appeal: Stuart-Smith, Waite and Millett LJJ). Decision of Dyson J [1995] Imm AR 283 affirmed.

248 Immigration—entry—illegal entry—restrictions on employment

The Immigration Act 1971, Sch 2, para 21(2) provides that so long as a person is at large in the United Kingdom by virtue of paragraph 21 (temporary admission or release of persons liable to detention), he is subject to such restrictions as to his residence, employment or occupation as may from time to time be notified to him in writing by an immigration officer.

The applicants illegally entered the United Kingdom, and were therefore persons in respect of whom directions could be given for their removal. They were detained pending their removal, but successfully applied for writs of habeas corpus. On the Secretary of State's appeal, the writs were set aside and the applicants were detained again. In granting bail to the applicants, restrictions were imposed on their employment, pursuant to the 1971 Act, Sch 2, para 21(2). On their application for judicial review, *held*, once a writ of habeas corpus was granted, a successful appeal against it did not thereafter make a person liable to be detained. It followed that in the instant case, restrictions could not be imposed on the applicants as to their employment and, accordingly, the appeal would be allowed.

R v Secretary of State for the Home Department, ex p Virk; R v Secretary of State for the Home Department, ex p Taggar; R v Secretary of State for the Home Department, ex p Singh (1995) Times, 13 October (Queen's Bench Division: Popplewell J).

249 Immigration—entry—illegal entry—work permit—validity

The overseas labour section of the Department of Employment issued the applicants with work permits to work as chefs in a restaurant, and the applicants were given leave to enter the United Kingdom on that basis. Although the work permits were authentic, they were issued by an employee of the overseas labour section who had acted in breach of internal procedures. In particular, he had ignored the requirements that at least two officers had to be involved in a case, and that the processing and approval of work permit applications had to be carried out by different persons. It was also the case that the applicants did not meet the skills and experience criteria required for chefs, and that it was unusual to grant more than one work permit for the same establishment. When the irregularity was discovered, the applicants were given notice that they were illegal entrants, and that they were liable to be detained pending their removal. Their application for judicial review of the decision was refused. On appeal, *held*, in order to sustain an allegation that a person was an illegal entrant within the meaning of the Immigration Act 1971, s 33(1), it had to be shown that he had entered in breach of a provision of the Act. A person could be an illegal entrant if he obtained leave to enter fraudulently, as fraud vitiated consent to entry and was an offence under the 1971 Act, s 26(1)(c). Although it had been decided that a person was an illegal entrant if his work permit was invalidated by fraud, in the instant case the work permits were genuine, in that they had been issued by the Department of Employment, they bore the department's official stamp, and did not contain false information. Moreover, neither the restaurant owner nor the applicants had made any misrepresentation, nor had they acted with impropriety. The work permits therefore could not be described as invalid, but merely as inappropriate, as they should not have been issued because the criteria and internal rules for granting work permits were not satisfied. The applicants were not illegal entrants and, accordingly, the appeal would be allowed.

R v Secretary of State for the Home Department, ex p Ku [1995] 2 All ER 891 (Court of Appeal: Sir Thomas Bingham MR, Hobhouse and Morritt LJJ). Decision of Laws J [1994] Imm AR 183 (1994 Abr para 239) reversed. *R v Immigration Officer, ex p Chan* [1992] 1 WLR 541, CA (1992 Abr para 194) distinguished.

250 Immigration—entry—leave to enter—variation of leave—leave to remain as spouse

Scotland

The applicant, a Pakistani citizen, was granted limited leave to enter the United Kingdom to marry a British citizen. He did not apply for an extension of his leave to remain until several months after the expiry of his original leave, upon which his wife informed immigration officials that they had already divorced. Having been served with notice of intention to make a deportation order against him, the applicant married another British citizen and applied to the Secretary of State to exercise his discretion to grant him leave to remain as a spouse. The Secretary of State refused the application, and decided that deportation proceedings should go ahead. That decision was confirmed following a review of the case. The applicant applied for judicial review of the decisions on the ground that they were unreasonable, having regard to *Wednesbury* principles. *Held*, as regards the applicant's reference to the European Convention on Human Rights 1950, art 8, contracting states had a wide discretion as to how to give effect to the obligation to have respect for family life, and that could include taking account of immigration matters. As it was clear that the Secretary of State's immigration policy did not ignore that obligation, the applicant could not rely on art 8. There was a public interest in the regular administration of immigration control and the regular application of immigration rules. Fairness in immigration control was a delicate matter, and the Secretary of State was therefore entitled to regard it as important to observe immigration rules and give significant weight to them in exercising his discretion. Moreover, if the applicant was allowed to make his application for leave from the United Kingdom, even though under the rules he was obliged to do so from Pakistan, that might encourage others to seek a similar advantage. The Secretary of State was also entitled to take into account that the applicant had overstayed without seeking an extension of his leave at the proper time, and that he had not made full disclosure of his marital situation. Although it might be unreasonable for the Secretary of State to require the applicant to return to Pakistan to make an application for leave to enter, it was impossible to say that no useful purpose would be served in requiring him to do so. Accordingly, the application would be dismissed.

R v Secretary of State for the Home Department, ex p Irfan Ahmed [1995] Imm AR 210 (Outer House).

251 Immigration—entry—leave to enter—variation of leave—right of appeal—transit passenger

The appellant, a Malaysian citizen, came to the United Kingdom as a member of a touring party. The tour was scheduled to take two days and the immigration officer therefore treated the appellant as a transit passenger, granting her leave to enter for 48 hours. Her passport stamp did not indicate that the appellant was granted leave only as a transit passenger and she applied for variation of her leave to enter as a visitor. The application was refused and the Secretary of State asserted that the appellant had no right of appeal under the Immigration Act 1971, s 14(2A). Her appeal was dismissed by an adjudicator and, on further appeal to the Immigration Appeal Tribunal, *held*, it was essential that the leave granted indicated the category in which it was granted. If the passport stamp reflecting leave granted to a transit passenger did not indicate that it was in that special category of 'passenger in transit', it had to be taken to be leave granted as a visitor. It followed that as the leave given was that of a visitor, there was a right of appeal. Accordingly, the appeal would be allowed.

Low v Secretary of State for the Home Department [1995] Imm AR 435 (Immigration Appeal Tribunal).

252 Immigration—entry—leave to enter—variation of leave—right of appeal—visitor

The Immigration Act 1971, s 14(2A)(c) provides that a person is not entitled to appeal against any refusal to vary his leave if the refusal is on the ground that the variation would result in the duration of the person's leave exceeding what is permitted by the immigration rules.

The applicant was granted 6 months' leave to enter the United Kingdom as a visitor. Before that period expired, his leave was varied such that he was granted leave to remain as a working holidaymaker for two years. At the end of that period, he applied for a further three months' leave to remain as a visitor. The Secretary of State refused the application on the ground that the 6-month maximum period of stay as a visitor would be exceeded if the applicant was granted further leave to remain. The applicant was also informed that having regard to the 1993 Act, s 14(2A), he had no right of appeal. On appeal against the latter decision, *held*, the Secretary of State could have granted the applicant a lesser period of leave than that sought, equal to the unexpired portion of his leave to remain as a visitor. In deciding that any extension of leave would result in the applicant exceeding the maximum stay permitted as a visitor, the Secretary of State had erred in his approach and therefore had not established a valid ground of refusal. The applicant therefore had a right of appeal against the refusal of variation of leave and, accordingly, the appeal would be allowed.

Wong v Secretary of State for the Home Department [1995] Imm AR 451 (Immigration Appeal Tribunal).

253   Immigration—entry—leave to enter—variation of leave—right of appeal—work permit holder

The Immigration Act 1971, s 14(2A)(a) provides that a person is not entitled to appeal against any refusal to vary his leave if the refusal is on the ground that a relevant document has not been issued. The Statement of Changes in Immigration Rules 1990 (HC 251), para 122 provides that where a work permit was issued for a period other than four years, an application for an extension of stay in the employment for which the permit was issued must be referred to the Department of Employment. Only if the department is prepared to approve the continued appointment may an appropriate extension of stay be granted.

The appellant entered the United Kingdom with a work permit, and his application to the Department of Employment for an extension of his period of permitted employment was initially refused, but later granted for six months. Having regard to the department's initial refusal, the Secretary of State refused to grant the applicant further leave to remain. The appellant was also informed that having regard to the 1971 Act, s 14(2A)(a), he had no right of appeal against the refusal of leave to remain. That decision was upheld by an adjudicator. On appeal, *held*, where a continuation of an approved employment was sought, the Department of Employment did not issue a work permit but instead gave written approval for continued employment. As the Immigration Rules, para 122 did not require a document to be issued, the 1971 Act, s 14(2A)(a) did not apply in the instant case, and the Secretary of State was therefore wrong in deciding that the appellant had no right of appeal against the refusal of a variation of his leave to remain. Moreover, even if a document was required under para 122, a written approval of continued employment given by the Department of Employment did not constitute a 'relevant document' for the purposes of s 14(2A)(a). Accordingly, the appeal would be allowed.

Pang v Secretary of State for the Home Department [1995] Imm AR 470 (Immigration Appeal Tribunal).

254   Immigration—entry—refusal of leave to enter—appeal—adjudicator—matters to be stated in decision

The applicant's fiancé was refused leave to enter the United Kingdom. In dismissing his appeal, an adjudicator decided that there was insufficient evidence that the parties and their respective dependants would be able to support themselves without recourse to public funds. The Immigration Appeal Tribunal refused the applicant's application for leave to appeal against the decision. On her application for judicial review, *held*, in considering an appeal under the Immigration Act 1971, s 19, if an adjudicator was not satisfied that an appellant and his dependants would be able to support themselves without recourse to public funds, he had to state clearly the identity of the parties and their dependants, what assets they had, the source of those assets and when they would be available, and what amounts he considered to be necessary for their adequate maintenance during the relevant period. He also had to indicate in his decision whether there was a dispute between the Secretary of State and the appellant and, if so, why he was not satisfied that the appellant's contentions were correct. Such an approach would isolate questions of fact from questions of law, thereby making it easier to identify matters of law and simplifying the task of the Immigration Appeal Tribunal or the court. Accordingly, on the facts of the case, the application would be granted.

R v Immigration Appeal Tribunal, ex p Shahim Begum (1995) Times, 15 February (Queen's Bench Division: Schiemann J).

255 Immigration—entry—refusal of leave to enter—appeal—delay—change of circumstances

The applicant, a citizen of Bangladesh, was refused entry clearance to join his father in the United Kingdom, the entry clearance officer having been dissatisfied as to the relationship as claimed. The initial appeal against this decision was withdrawn by the applicant. Later, when he was of full age, a second application was made under the rules governing dependent relatives. This was refused in 1984 and, as a result of the consequent appeal being overlooked, the matter was not reconsidered until 1992. By that time, DNA evidence confirmed the relationship as claimed. An application had also been made, and refused, for the Secretary of State to consider the admission of the applicant outside the immigration rules. At first instance, discretionary relief of judicial review was refused on the ground that in the circumstances, given the long delay in time, it would be perverse for entry clearance to be granted. This was despite it being common knowledge that the adjudicator in the second appeal had erred in law in considering the applicant's circumstances at the date of the appeal and not at the date of decision of the application. The applicant appealed. *Held*, there had been no procedural impropriety during the hearing of the first appeal since, in the absence of any statutory provision to the contrary, an appeal might be withdrawn at any time. An adjudicator could only give directions to give effect to his determination, and not to frustrate it. Thus, he could not direct an entry clearance officer not to issue entry clearance. The issuing of directions was entirely at the adjudicator's discretion, but would be inappropriate where it had become apparent to him that there had been a significant change in circumstances and an applicant could no longer satisfy the relevant rule. There was no evidence that the applicant's circumstances in 1984 allowed him to qualify under the rules. Therefore, the granting of judicial review would serve no purpose. Accordingly, the appeal would be dismissed.

Rahman v Immigration Appeal Tribunal [1995] Imm AR 372 (Court of Appeal: Stuart-Smith, Hobhouse and Pill LJJ).

256 Immigration—entry—refusal of leave to enter—child applicant in foster care—jurisdiction to consider residence order—intervention by court

See *Re M (a Minor) (Immigration: Residence Order)*, para 432.

257 Immigration—entry—refusal of leave to enter—exclusion conducive to public good—judicial review

The applicant, the founder of a religious organisation based in Korea, was required by the Home Secretary to have entry clearance to visit the United Kingdom. On two previous occasions, the applicant was refused entry, but on appeal an adjudicator had directed that clearance be issued. The applicant applied to visit the United Kingdom to meet members of the organisation and make a speech. The Home Secretary refused entry clearance on the ground that the proposed visit would not be conducive to the public good. The applicant applied for judicial review of the decision on the grounds that the Home Secretary was under a continuing obligation to comply with the adjudicator's earlier direction and that the applicant had not been given the opportunity to deal with the factors taken into account by the Home Secretary. *Held*, there was no right of appeal to an adjudicator where entry clearance was refused on the ground that the Home Secretary concluded that a person's exclusion was conducive to the public good. Although the adjudicator's earlier decisions were relevant facts to which the Home Secretary had to have regard, there was no obligation in law to grant entry clearance. However, there was a want of fairness on the part of the Home Secretary in failing to afford the applicant the opportunity to deal with why, in the present case, unlike on the previous occasions, it was not in the public good for him to enter the United Kingdom. There had been a departure by the Home Secretary from the ground rule that there was an obligation to listen fairly to both sides. A declaration would be made accordingly.

R v Secretary of State for the Home Department, ex p Moon (1995) Independent, 2 November, Times, 8 December (Queen's Bench Division: Sedley J).

258 Immigration—entry—refusal of leave to enter—recourse to public funds

The Statement of Changes in Immigration Rules 1990 (HC251), para 50(e) provides that a passenger seeking admission to the United Kingdom as the spouse of a person who is present and settled in the United Kingdom must hold a current entry clearance granted for the purpose. An entry clearance will be refused unless the entry clearance officer is satisfied that the parties will be able to support themselves and their dependants without recourse to public funds.

The applicant applied for entry clearance to join his wife in the United Kingdom. His wife was on income support, as she was unable to work because of difficulties in finding adequate child care. The application was refused by an entry clearance officer because he was not satisfied that the applicant and his wife would be able to maintain themselves adequately without recourse to public funds. An adjudicator upheld the decision, and the Immigration Appeal Tribunal refused to grant the applicant leave to appeal against it. On the applicant's application for judicial review of that decision, *held*, the Immigration Act 1971, ss 1(4) and 3(2) gave the Secretary of State general power to make immigration rules which were very broad, and which could therefore include a requirement that those seeking entry clearance should not have recourse to public funds. As the 1990 Rules, para 50(e) did not go so far as to lay down rules for eligibility for social security, the Secretary of State had properly exercised his powers of immigration control in enacting the provision. As regards the reasonableness of the rule, the applicant's argument that para 50(e) discriminated against non-EEC citizens could not be accepted, as the 1971 Act, s 3(2) allowed the Secretary of State to make a distinction between EEC and non-EEC citizens. Moreover, the Race Relations Act 1976 did not expressly state that the 1976 Act applied to immigration rules. Paragraph 50(e) was therefore neither ultra vires nor unreasonable. Moreover, para 50(e) embraced indirect as well as direct reliance on public funds. Accordingly, the application would be dismissed.

R v Secretary of State for the Home Department, ex p Islam Bibi [1995] Imm AR 157 (Queen's Bench Division: Hidden J).

The Statement of Changes in Immigration Rules 1990 (HC251) has been replaced by the Statement of Changes in Immigration Rules 1994 (HC395).

259 Immigration—entry—refusal of leave to enter—returning resident—exercise of discretion

The Statement of Changes in Immigration Rules 1990 (HC 251), para 58 provides that a passenger returning to the United Kingdom from overseas is to be admitted for settlement on satisfying the immigration officer that he had indefinite leave to enter or remain in the United Kingdom when he last left, that he has not been away for longer than two years, and that he now seeks admission for the purpose of settlement. A passenger who has been away from the United Kingdom too long to benefit from para 58 may nevertheless be admitted if, for example, he has lived here for most of his life: para 59.

The respondent came to the United Kingdom from India and remained for 13 years. He then returned to India for family reasons but made a series of visits to the United Kingdom each within a two-year period in order to preserve his returning resident status. On each visit he was given indefinite leave to enter as a returning resident with leave to remain indefinitely. However, on a further visit he was granted only limited leave to enter for six months as a visitor. He returned to India shortly after and some months later he applied for entry clearance as a returning resident. The entry clearance officer refused that application. The Immigration Appeal Tribunal held that although the respondent did not have indefinite leave to enter in accordance with the 1990 Rules, para 58, that did not preclude the possibility of his enjoying the benefit of the discretion in para 59. On appeal, it was argued on behalf of the officer that the discretion could only be exercised if an applicant satisfied the requirements of para 58, except for his having been away for more than two years. *Held*, although the immigration rules were not statutes and were not to be interpreted as strictly as statutes were interpreted, the words contained in the rules had to be given their natural and ordinary meaning. Further, the rules were to be read in their statutory context and where there were several paragraphs dealing with the same matter, clearly they had to be read as a whole. Applying those rules to paras 58 and 59, the officer's interpretation had been correct and, accordingly, the appeal would be allowed.

Bombay Entry Clearance Officer v De Noronha [1995] Imm AR 341 (Court of Appeal: Glidewell, Hirst and Hoffmann LJJ).

260 Immigration—entry—refusal of leave to enter—right of appeal—student—intended student

The applicant was refused leave to enter the United Kingdom as an intended student, but was granted temporary admission pending further consideration of her application. When interviewed by an immigration officer, the applicant was advised to enrol on a course of study. Having enrolled on a three-year course and also a three-month course, the applicant was re-interviewed and later given notice that her application for leave to remain as a student was refused, on the basis that the immigration officer was not satisfied that she genuinely intended to study, and to leave the United Kingdom thereafter. The applicant was told that she had a right of appeal, but only from abroad and only in relation to the three-year course. On her application for judicial review, *held*, it was more difficult for an intended student who had not yet registered on a course to convince an immigration officer that he genuinely intended to follow a course of study, as compared with somebody who had already done so. However, the same relevant immigration rules applied in both situations, and in the instant case, the same application for entry as a student had been considered both before and after the applicant had enrolled on a course. The applicant therefore had a right of appeal from abroad because she had obtained places on two courses and, in consequence, was not entitled to seek judicial review of the refusal of leave to enter unless there were exceptional circumstances. Her allegation that it was unfair of the immigration officer to advise her to enrol on a course in order to gain leave to enter only for her application then to be refused, was a factor which an adjudicator could have taken into account if the applicant had exercised her right of appeal. Moreover, she could have provided the adjudicator with evidence that she had been accepted on a course of study. In any event, the allegation of unfairness was not an exceptional circumstance. Accordingly, the appeal would be dismissed.

Morikawa v Secretary of State for the Home Department [1995] Imm AR 258 (Court of Appeal: Glidewell, Hobhouse and Morritt LJJ).

261 Immigration—entry—refusal of leave to enter—spouse—polygamous marriage—validity

Under the Family Law Act 1986, s 46(2), an overseas divorce obtained otherwise than by means of judicial proceedings is recognised if neither party to the marriage was habitually resident in the United Kingdom throughout the year preceding the divorce. Under the Matrimonial Causes Act 1973, s 11(d), a polygamous marriage entered into outside England and Wales is invalid if either party was domiciled in England and Wales at the time of the marriage.

The applicant, a citizen of Pakistan, was refused entry clearance to the United Kingdom as the wife of a British citizen on the grounds that the marriage was not valid in English law. The applicant had been married twice before. As was permitted by Islamic law, her second husband already had one wife when he had married the applicant. He later purported to divorce the applicant, by talaq, an Islamic procedure which entitles a husband unilaterally to repudiate his marriage without recourse to court proceedings. The talaq was pronounced in the United Kingdom while he was resident there, although at that time he was domiciled in Pakistan. An Immigration Tribunal refused the applicant leave to appeal on the ground that she could not be maintained without recourse to public funds. She sought a judicial review of that decision. *Held*, the talaq pronounced in the United Kingdom was 'an overseas divorce . . . obtained otherwise than by means of proceedings' within the 1986 Act, s 46(2). It was not recognised under English law because the second husband had been habitually resident in the United Kingdom throughout the year preceding its pronouncement. Their marriage was valid notwithstanding the 1973 Act, s 11, because it had taken place outside England and Wales and neither party was habitually resident there at the time. The applicant's third husband, her sponsor, was domiciled in England and Wales when they married. Consequently, she did not have the capacity to marry him as she remained married to her second husband under English law. Where, as in the present case, an appeal would inevitably fail on one ground, a tribunal was fully entitled to refuse to consider the merits of another ground raised in the application for leave to appeal. Accordingly, the application would be dismissed.

R v Immigration Appeal Tribunal, ex p Jan [1995] Imm AR 440 (Queen's Bench Division: Tucker J). *R v Immigration Appeal Tribunal, ex p Majid Khan* [1995] Imm AR 19, followed.

262 Immigration—frontier and passport controls between United Kingdom and other member states—legality

The applicant sought judicial review of the Secretary of State's decision to maintain frontier controls and passport checks on persons moving between the United Kingdom and other member states of the European Union, contending that, by virtue of the EC Treaty, art 7(a), the internal market was to comprise an area without internal frontiers in which the free movement of goods, persons, services and capital was ensured and that the controls and checks in question were unlawful. He also sought to have certain relevant issues referred to the European Court of Justice. *Held*, art 7(a) did not have direct effect. It was for the European Court to decide the question of direct effect only where the national court was not confident what that court would decide. This was not such a case and, accordingly, no questions would be referred to that court and the application would be dismissed.

Flynn v Secretary of State for the Home Department [1995] Imm AR 594 (Court of Appeal: Leggatt and Rose LJJ and Sir Ralph Gibson). Decision of McCullough J [1995] 3 CMLR 397 affirmed.

263 Immigration—rules

The Statement of Changes in Immigration Rules 1994 (HC 395), is further amended (see HC 797 (1995)) so that a national or citizen of Gambia now requires a visa to enter the United Kingdom. The requirement that an applicant who seeks an extension of stay as a student must have been admitted to the United Kingdom with a valid student entry clearance does not apply to any application for an extension of stay for the purpose of studying made by a national of Gambia whose current leave to enter or remain was granted before 27 October 1995.

The 1994 Statement is further amended (see Cm 3073) so that a national or citizen of Tanzania now requires a visa to enter the United Kingdom. The requirement that an applicant who seeks an extension of stay as a student must have been admitted to the United Kingdom with a valid student entry clearance does not apply to any application for an extension of stay for the purpose of studying made by a national of Tanzania whose current leave to enter or remain was granted before 5 January 1996.

The 1994 Statement is further amended (see HC 274) so that a national or citizen of Kenya now requires a visa to enter the United Kingdom. The requirement that an applicant who seeks an extension of stay as a student must have been admitted to the United Kingdom with a valid student entry clearance does not apply to any application for an extension of stay for the purpose of studying made by a national of Kenya whose current leave to enter or remain was granted before 8 March 1996.

264 Immigration—transit visa

The Immigration (Transit Visa) (Amendment) Order 1995, SI 1995/2621 (in force on 24 October 1995), amends the 1993 Order, SI 1993/1678, by removing Lebanon from the list of countries the nationals or citizens of which require a visa to pass through the United Kingdom, and by adding China, Ghana and Nigeria to the list.

265 Immigration—travel documents—visa requirements—nationals of third countries— external borders of member states

See para 3138.

266 Race relations—discrimination—appeal under self-regulating organisation's rules— jurisdiction of tribunal to hear complaint

The Race Relations Act 1976, s 54(1) provides that a complaint by any person that another person has committed an act of discrimination against the complainant which is unlawful by virtue of the 1976 Act, Pt II, may be presented to an industrial tribunal. Section 54(2) provides that s 54(1) does not apply to a complaint against a qualifying body of an act in respect of which an appeal, or proceedings in the nature of an appeal, may be brought under any enactment.

The plaintiff, who was of Arab origin, applied to join the defendant organisation ('FIMBRA'), the members of which were authorised to carry on investment business under the Finance Act 1986, s 8(1). Her application was refused, as was her appeal under FIMBRA rules. She appealed to an industrial tribunal under the 1976 Act, s 54(1) but the tribunal held that it had no jurisdiction because the plaintiff's appeal under the FIMBRA rules was an appeal 'brought under any enactment' as set out in the 1976 Act, s 54(2) and she was therefore precluded from bringing a complaint under s 54(1). On the plaintiff's appeal, *held*, neither the power to make FIMBRA rules and to enforce them, nor the power to hold an appeal under them, came from the 1986 Act or legislation subordinate to it. Instead, they came from FIMBRA's articles of association. Therefore, an appeal brought under the rules was not 'brought under any enactment' under s 54(2) and, accordingly, the appeal would be allowed and the plaintiff would be entitled to present her complaint to the tribunal.

Zaidi v Financial Intermediaries Managers and Brokers Regulatory Association [1995] ICR 876 (Employment Appeal Tribunal: Smith J presiding).

267 Race relations—discrimination—control over development of land—gipsy caravan site

See *R v Runnymede Borough Council, ex p Smith*, para 2851.

268 Race relations—discrimination—employment—complaint—originating application

An employee submitted an originating application to an industrial tribunal alleging unlawful deduction from wages, unfair dismissal, and race discrimination against his employer. When the case came to be heard, the employee sought to present an additional claim of indirect race discrimination under the Race Relations Act 1976, s 1(1)(b). The employer objected, on the ground that the employee's additional claim would amount to a new claim which had not been made within the three-month time limit. Regarding it as an application to bring a claim out of time, an industrial tribunal concluded that the employee should have made his complaint of indirect race discrimination at an early stage of the proceedings, and that it would not be just and equitable to allow him to do so at such a late stage. On the employee's appeal against the dismissal of his application, *held*, an originating application which made a claim of race discrimination under the 1976 Act incorporated any claim for race discrimination, whether direct or indirect, or discrimination by victimisation. It was irrelevant that there were different ways in which discrimination could occur, under different sections of the Act. The employee's application was therefore not time-barred, as it was nothing more than an application to amend. The test which the industrial tribunal should have applied was whether or not the employer would suffer hardship or prejudice if the application was granted, so as to justify refusing the employee's application. The case was to be remitted to the industrial tribunal for consideration of that issue and, accordingly, the appeal would be allowed.

Quarcoopome v Sock Shop Holdings Ltd [1995] IRLR 353 (Employment Appeal Tribunal: Buckley J presiding).

269   Race relations—discrimination—employment—complaint—time limits—continuing act

The appellant, a Ghanaian fire safety case worker, brought a complaint of racial discrimination against his employer. The complaint gave the date when the action complained of took place as 'continuing' and the grounds for the complaint were specified as the failure to promote the appellant in respect of jobs for which he had been shortlisted, failure to shortlist him for other jobs, failure to regrade him and failure to allow him to act up to a higher grade when the opportunity arose. An industrial tribunal decided that the acts alleged were not acts of continuing discrimination within the meaning of the Race Relations Act 1976, s 68(7) and dismissed the complaint as being out of time. On appeal, *held*, the tribunal erred in law in failing to treat the acts complained of with respect to regrading and failure to give the opportunity to act up as continuing acts. An act did not extend over a period simply because the doing of the act had continuing consequences. However, an act did extend over a period of time if it took the form of some policy, rule or practice, in accordance with which decisions were taken from time to time. A succession of specific instances could indicate the existence of a practice, which in turn could constitute an act extending over a period which was a continuing act. The acts in the present case were continuing acts which were not barred by s 68. Accordingly, the appeal would be allowed and the case would be remitted.

Owusu v London Fire and Civil Defence Authority [1995] IRLR 574 (Employment Appeal Tribunal: Mummery J presiding).

270   Race relations—discrimination—employment—detriment—harassment by work colleagues—liability of employer

See *Tower Boot Co Ltd v Jones*, para 1220.

271   Race relations—discrimination—employment—detriment—service in foreign country excluded from calculation of pension entitlement

The appellants, who were East African Asians, were employed by the respondent bank in Kenya and Tanzania. They were classed as local contract staff, and were members of the pension fund for such employees. When the appellants were required to leave their respective countries, they were given a financial package by the respondent to compensate them for their loss of pension. They were also offered alternative employment in the United Kingdom, and were allowed to join the occupational pension scheme on condition that they would not be given credit for their years of service in Kenya and Tanzania. The appellants successfully claimed that the condition was discriminatory on grounds of race, but the respondent's appeal was allowed on the basis that there had been neither direct nor indirect discrimination. On further appeal, *held*, the reason why the respondent had refused to credit the appellants with their years of service in East Africa for pension purposes was that they had already been compensated for the loss of pension rights related to that service. As no race-based criterion had been applied to the appellants, there had been no direct discrimination. As regards indirect discrimination, although a condition had been applied to the appellants which they were unable to comply with, they had not suffered detriment because they had been fully aware that the compensation package was intended to represent the loss of pension rights attributable to their years of service in East Africa, and that they would not be credited for those years during their service in the United Kingdom. They therefore had no good reason for feeling dissatisfied or aggrieved, nor had they suffered injustice. Even if they had suffered detriment, the condition as to service and pension entitlement was justifiable because the appellants would otherwise have been doubly compensated following the change in their employment. Accordingly, the appeal would be dismissed.

Barclays Bank v Kapur (No 2) [1995] IRLR 87 (Court of Appeal: Balcombe and Rose LJJ, and Sir Ralph Gibson). *James v Eastleigh Borough Council* [1990] 2 All ER 607, HL (1990 Abr para 2180) followed.

272 Race relations—discrimination—employment—intention to discriminate

The Race Relations Act 1976, s 57(3) provides that as respects an unlawful act of discrimination falling within the 1976 Act, s 1(1)(b) ('indirect' discrimination), no award of damages is to be made if the respondent proves that the requirement or condition in question was not applied with the intention of treating the claimant unfavourably on racial grounds.

An employer introduced a requirement that no employee could not take any holiday during certain months. When one of its employees took a day off during that period in order to attend a Muslim festival, he was given a final warning. An industrial tribunal found that the employer had discriminated against the employee in imposing the requirement, and awarded the employee damages for upset and distress. On appeal, the employer argued that it had not intentionally treated the employee less favourably on racial grounds, having regard to the 1976 Act, s 57(3). *Held*, intention related to the state of mind of the person who, at the time that he did the relevant act, wanted to bring about the state of affairs which constituted the unfavourable treatment on racial grounds and knew that an unlawful consequence would follow from his act. Section 57(3) was not concerned with a person's motives. In the instant case, the fact that the employer imposed a no-holiday requirement in order to promote business efficiency was irrelevant, as it knew what the consequences of the requirement might be. The industrial tribunal had been entitled to conclude that the employer had intended to treat the employee unfavourably on racial grounds and, accordingly, the appeal would be dismissed.

Hussain v J H Walker Ltd [1995] IRLR 11 (Employment Appeal Tribunal: Mummery J presiding).

273 Race relations—discrimination—employment—summary dismissal—application of discrimination provisions to former employee

The Race Relations Act 1976, s 4(1)(c) provides that in relation to employment at an establishment in Great Britain, it is unlawful for a person to discriminate against another by refusing to offer him employment. Section 4(2)(c) provides that it is unlawful for a person to discriminate against an employee by subjecting him to any other detriment.

The applicant was summarily dismissed for misconduct, and her internal appeal was rejected. She complained to an industrial tribunal that white employees would not have had their appeals against dismissal rejected. On the question of whether or not the industrial tribunal had jurisdiction to consider her complaint, it was decided that the applicant was entitled to bring a claim under the 1976 Act, s 4(1)(c). On the employer's appeal, *held*, the definition of 'employee' in the 1976 Act differed from that in the Employment Protection (Consolidation) Act 1978, indicating that Parliament had not intended that a former employee should be included as an 'employee' for the purposes of the 1976 Act, s 4(2)(c). As there was no express provision in her contract of employment that the contract was to continue pending an appeal, her employment had ended on the day that she was summarily dismissed and she was therefore no longer an employee at the time of the internal appeal. Moreover, s 4(1)(c) was not intended to include former employees who sought reinstatement. The applicant therefore had no remedy for the discrimination that had occurred after her summary dismissal and, accordingly, the appeal would be dismissed.

Post Office v Adekeye (No 2) [1995] IRLR 297 (Employment Appeal Tribunal: Smith J presiding).

274 Race relations—employment and social affairs—rights of the individual—European Union resolution

See para 3177.

BUILDING CONTRACTS, ARCHITECTS, ENGINEERS AND SURVEYORS

Halsbury's Laws of England (4th edn) Vol 4(2) (reissue), paras 301–700

275   Articles

CDM—What Does it Mean to You? George Markland (on the Construction (Design and Management) Regulations 1994, SI 1994/3140): Estates Gazette, 22 July 1995, p 107

Diving in at the Deep End, Steven Gee QC (on *Ruxley Electronics and Construction Ltd v Forsyth* (1995) Times, 3 July, HL (para 277)): LS Gaz, 31 Aug 1995, p 23

The Expert's Role in Delay Claims by Building Contractors, Anthony Speaight: 145 NLJ 1052

Is Near Enough Good Enough? Isaac E Jacob (on *Ruxley Electronics and Construction Ltd v Forsyth* (1995) Times, 3 July, HL (para 277)): 139 SJ 676

A Smaller Splash, Andrew Bruce (on *Ruxley Electronics and Construction Ltd v Forsyth* (1995) Times, 3 July, HL (para 277)): 145 NLJ 1086

276   Building contract—bond—performance bond—bond as guarantee

The main contractor for a construction project entered into a sub-contract for part of the work. The sub-contractor provided a bond for a specified sum jointly with a surety. Administrative receivers were appointed over the subcontractor, which was unable to complete the sub-contract. The main contractor began proceedings against the surety under the bond. On the question of whether the bond was a guarantee so that the surety was able to rely on defences which would have been available to the sub-contractor, *held*, bonds in similar form had existed for many years and had been treated by the parties to them and by the courts as guarantees. The bond in the present case contained indications that it was intended to be a guarantee and the surety was described as such in the bond. There was also relevant authority for that conclusion. In the absence of specific provisions, it followed that questions of money due for work already done and claims of set-off against the main contractor which could have been relied on by the sub-contractor in defence to an action for damages for breach of contract could properly be relied on by the surety.

Trafalgar House Construction (Regions) Ltd v General Surety & Guarantee Co Ltd [1995] 3 All ER 737 (House of Lords: Lords Keith of Kinkel, Ackner, Jauncey of Tullichettle, Lloyd of Berwick and Steyn). *Calvert v London Dock Co* (1838) 2 Keen 638 and *Trade Indemnity Co Ltd v Workington Harbour and Dock Board* [1937] AC 1, HL considered.

277   Building contract—breach—failure to achieve precise contractual objective—assessment of damages

A householder employed builders to construct a swimming pool. The contract provided for the pool having a maximum depth of 7ft 6ins but, as built, its maximum depth was only 6ft. The trial judge found that the shortfall in depth had not decreased the value of the pool and that it would be unreasonable to reconstruct it, and only awarded the householder damages for loss of amenity. On appeal, the householder succeeded in obtaining substantially higher damages for the cost of reconstructing the pool. On appeal by the builder, *held*, damages were designed to compensate for an established loss and not to provide a gratuitous benefit to the aggrieved party. It followed that the reasonableness of an award was to be linked directly to the loss sustained. If it was unreasonable in a particular case to award the cost of reinstatement, it had to be because the loss sustained did not extend to the need to reinstate. What constituted the aggrieved party's loss was a question of fact and degree. Where the party in breach had entirely failed to achieve the contractual objective, it was likely that the loss was the necessary cost of attaining that objective. In taking reasonableness into account in determining the extent of loss, it was reasonableness in relation to the particular contract and not at large. However, where the contractual objective had been substantially achieved, the situation might be very different. Personal preference could be a factor in reasonableness and hence in determining what loss had been suffered, but it could not in itself be determinative of what the loss was. In the present circumstances, the trial judge had been entitled to find that it was unreasonable to reconstruct the pool. Accordingly, the appeal would be allowed.

Ruxley Electronics and Construction Ltd v Forsyth [1995] 3 All ER 268 (House of Lords: Lords Keith of Kinkel, Bridge of Harwich, Jauncey of Tullichettle, Mustill and Lloyd of Berwick). Decision of Court of Appeal [1994] 3 All ER 801 (1994 Abr para 262) reversed.

278   Building contract—tender accepted subject to contract—failure to complete contract—reimbursement of preparation costs

The plaintiffs offered to purchase a licence for residential development of land from the defendant owners of the land. The offer was accepted subject to contract, to the district valuer's certificate of market value, to the plaintiffs' development scheme achieving the desired design quality and to the obtaining of detailed planning permission. The conclusion of the contract was delayed by the defendants' request for further designs by new architects, the need for detailed costings, the defendants' difficulty in obtaining vacant possession of the whole of the land and the fall in the value of residential property during the period. The contract was never completed, but the plaintiffs claimed reimbursement from the defendants of various professional fees incurred in respect of the proposed development. *Held*, where negotiations intended to result in a contract were entered into on express terms that each party was free to withdraw from the negotiations at any time, each party had to be taken to know that pending the conclusion of a binding contract any cost incurred by him in preparation for the intended contract would be incurred at his own risk. By deliberate use of the words 'subject to contract' with the intention that they should have their usual effect, the parties accepted that in the event of no contract being entered into, the loss should lie where it fell. Further, the costs for which the plaintiffs sought reimbursement were incurred by them not by way of accelerated performance of the anticipated contract at the request of the defendants, but for the purpose of putting themselves in a position to obtain and then perform the contract. The reason the contract did not materialise was that the parties could not agree on the price, and not that either party decided to abandon the project. Accordingly, the claim would be dismissed.

Regalian Properties plc v London Docklands Development Corpn [1995] 1 WLR 212 (Chancery Division: Rattee J).

279   Building works—dispute—settlement—procedure

See *Chartered Society of Physiotherapy v Simmonds Church Smiles*, para 2412.

BUILDING SOCIETIES

Halsbury's Laws of England (4th edn) Vol 4(2) (reissue), paras 701–988

280   Accounts—information to be disclosed

The Building Societies (Accounts and Related Provisions) (Amendment) Regulations 1995, SI 1995/3065 (in force on 1 January 1996), further amend SI 1992/359 so as to provide for a new, shorter form of prescribed statement for the purposes of the Building Societies Act 1986, s 76(4). In particular, (1) the requirement that the summary directors' report must contain three separate sections under specified headings has been removed, (2) the report must now include a summary review of any significant events which have occurred since the end of the financial year with which the summary financial statement deals, (3) the part of the summary which deals with the results for the year has been expanded to include additional items derived from the income and expenditure account, (4) the information which must be included in the part of the summary statement which deals with the financial position at the end of the year has been expanded to include amounts in respect of subordinated liabilities and permanent interest bearing shares, and (5) the number of items required to be included in the summary of key financial ratios has been reduced, although a requirement has been introduced that an explanation must be provided as to the significance of those ratios.

281   Assets and liabilities—aggregation

The Building Societies (Aggregation) (Amendment) Rules 1995, SI 1995/1187 (in force on 1 June 1995), further amend SI 1993/2833, by removing the requirement that if the aggregate amount of class 1 assets attributed to a society exceeds 15 per cent of the society's total commercial assets, the excess is to be attributed to class 2.

282   Building Societies Commission—expenses—general charge and fees

The Building Societies (General Charge and Fees) Regulations 1995, SI 1995/711 (in force on 1 April 1995), which replace the 1994 Regulations, SI 1994/656, provide for a general charge to be paid by authorised building societies towards the expenses of the Building Societies Commission for the accounting year 1995–1996. Each building society must pay a sum determined by reference to its total assets, subject to a reduction. The regulations also require building societies to pay fees in respect of (1) particular functions of the Building Societies Commission relating to mergers of building societies and transfers of business to commercial companies, and (2) particular functions of the Central Office of the Registry of Friendly Societies. In addition, fees must be paid by persons wishing to inspect or receive copies of documents in the custody of the Central Office of the Registry of Friendly Societies.

283 Building Societies (Joint Account Holders) Act 1995

The Building Societies (Joint Account Holders) Act 1995 amends the Building Societies Act 1986 to secure the rights of second-named account holders in building society joint accounts. It enables second-named (or former second-named) joint account holders to participate in distributions following the death of the first-named account holder. The Act received the royal assent on 1 May 1995 and came into force on that date, applying in any case where the vesting date within the meaning of the Building Societies Act 1986, s 100 falls after that date.

Section 1 inserts a new s 102A into the 1986 Act and consequentially amends Sch 2, para 7. It applies where the terms of the transfer of the business of a building society make provision for part of the funds of the society or its successor to be distributed among, or for other rights in relation to shares in the successor to be conferred on, members of the society in consideration of the transfer. It introduces a description of the person who is to benefit from the new provisions. Section 2 deals with citation and application.

284 Deregulation

The Deregulation (Building Societies) Order 1995, SI 1995/3233 (in force in part on 11 January 1996 and in part on 11 June 1996), amends the Building Societies Act 1986 by (1) amending s 6 to allow a building society to acquire and hold premises overseas for the purposes of the business of a subsidiary or other associated body, (2) further amending s 7 by raising the maximum percentage limit on a society's non-retail funds and deposits to 50 per cent of the society's share and deposit liabilities, and by excluding from the calculation of that limit liabilities in respect of capital resources that may be aggregated with reserves for capital adequacy purposes, (3) repealing s 22, which imposed obligations upon a society to meet the liabilities of associated bodies in certain circumstances, (4) repealing the requirement in s 78(2) that the auditors' report be read to the annual general meeting of a society, and (5) amending Sch 4, para 1 by removing the requirement to notify the mortgagor of the sale of mortgaged land, where the person selling the land has reasonable cause to believe that a notice sent to the mortgagor's last known address will not be received by him.

285 Directors—limits on transactions

The Building Societies (Limits on Transactions with Directors) Order 1995, SI 1995/1872 (in force on 1 September 1995), amends the Building Societies Act 1986, s 64, so as to increase to £100,000 the total amount of non-cash assets that a society may acquire from its directors or persons connected with them. The order also amends the 1986 Act, s 65, in particular so as to (1) increase to £100,000 the total amount of the preferential loan or loans that a society may make to its directors for the purchase or improvement of a dwelling house, and (2) increase to £20,000 the amount of a director's expenses incurred in the performance of his duties that a society may meet.

286 Investment—power to invest in qualifying bodies—designated bodies

The Building Societies (Designation of Qualifying Bodies) Order 1995, SI 1995/1188 (in force on 1 June 1995), designates a 'financing body' as a description of body corporate which is suitable for investment and support, but not support only, by building societies, under the Building Societies Act 1986, s 18. A financing body is a company, or an industrial and provident society, or a body corporate formed in any member state or certain other specified countries, and the purposes for which it may be formed include acquiring, holding or disposing of (i) debts due from corporate and unincorporate bodies, and (ii) shares and equivalent rights acquired in connection with loans either at the time the loan is advanced (up to a maximum value of 5 per cent of the loan), or following a default or compromise. A building society may also invest and support a financing body so that it can take deposits. In addition, the order (1) amends the 1993 Orders, SI 1993/985 and SI 1993/2706, so as to (a) remove the restrictions on designated bodies carrying on a deposit-taking business in the United Kingdom, (b) add a restriction on designated bodies which trade in derivatives, and (c) substitute a new definition of 'market maker', and (2) amends SI 1993/985 so as to add companies and industrial and provident societies to the types of body in which a building society may invest and support.

The Building Societies (Designation of Qualifying Bodies) (No 2) Order 1995, SI 1995/3063 (in force on 1 July 1996), designates a 'personal lines insurance body' as a body corporate suitable for investment, or investment and support, under the Building Societies Act 1986, s 18. A 'personal lines insurance body' is a company or an industrial and provident society, or a body corporate formed in any member state, or in certain other countries. Subject to certain exceptions, the insurance business of a personal lines insurance body is restricted to the insurance of individuals.

287 Lending—syndicated lending

The Building Societies (Syndicated Lending) Order 1995, SI 1995/3066 (in force on 1 January 1996), supplements the Buildings Societies Act 1986, s 14A, which allows building societies to participate in syndicated lending. In particular, the 1995 Order (1) makes provision as regards what constitutes appropriate security where a building society participates in a syndicated loan, (2) in relation to the requirements of the 1986 Act, Pt III regarding the structure of a building society's commercial assets, makes provision for the classification of a building society's participation in syndicated lending, and (3) provides that the 1986 Act, Pt III applies with modifications to a building society's participation in syndicated lending.

288 Liquid assets—regulations

The Building Societies (Liquid Asset) (Amendment) Regulations 1995, SI 1995/550 (in force on 1 April 1995), further amend SI 1991/2580, so as to add certain other permitted security instruments to the list of liquid assets contained in the Schedule. The regulations also extend the definition of 'mortgage backed securities' to include securities guaranteed by the Federal National Mortgage Association of the United States of America or the Federal Home Loan Mortgage Corporation of the United States of America.

The Building Societies (Liquid Asset) (Amendment) (No 2) Regulations 1995, SI 1995/3064 (in force on 1 January 1996), further amend the 1991 Regulations, SI 1991/2580 so as to substitute a revised description of the liquid assets which a building society may hold for the purposes of meeting its liabilities as they arise. As a result, building societies may now hold as liquid assets rights arising from the lending by them of gilt-edged stock to any counterparty. The regulations also add a new description of liquid assets, namely rights arising from the lending, under the rules of any depository or clearing agent, of certain securities which are recorded in the records of the depository or clearing agent in the building society's name, or the name of any person who holds such securities on a building society's behalf.

289 Mergers—bonus distributions

The Building Societies (Mergers) (Amendment) Regulations 1995, SI 1995/1874 (in force on 1 September 1995), amend the 1987 Regulations, SI 1987/2005, so as to provide that the prescribed limit on any distribution among members of a society is now five per cent of the value of the society's total assets, as stated in the merger approved and sent under the Building Societies Act 1986, Sch 16, Pt I, unless the merger is a partial transfer of engagements, where the limit is now five per cent of the value of the liabilities transferred.

290 Non-retail borrowing—limit on disregard

The Building Societies (Non-Retail Funds and Deposits) (Limit on Election) Order 1995, SI 1995/1873 (in force on 1 September 1995), amends the Building Societies Act 1986, s 7, so that the limit on the amount of a society's liabilities to any person which may be disregarded pursuant to an election by the society not to count certain funds or deposits towards the limit on non-retail funds or deposits, is now £100,000.

291 Provision of services

The Building Societies (Provision of Services) Order 1995, SI 1995/1189 (in force on 1 June 1995), varies the Building Societies Act 1984, Sch 8, Pt III, so as to remove some of the restrictions relating to the provision of certain banking services to persons other than individuals. The services concerned are arranging to take deposits, providing guarantees, and arranging the provision of guarantees.

292   Transfer of business—transfer to specially formed company—restrictions

The Building Societies Act 1986, s 100(8) provides that where, in connection with any transfer of business, rights are to be conferred on members of a building society to acquire shares in priority to other subscribers, the right must be restricted to those members who held shares in the society throughout the period of two years which expired on the qualifying day specified in the transfer.

Two building societies proposed that the undertaking and engagements of the second society would be transferred to the first society and that thereafter the merged business would be transferred, under the Building Societies Act 1986, Pt X, to a public limited company specially formed for that purpose. It was proposed that (a) a fixed allocation of free shares would be made to (i) all shareholding members who held shares to the value of £100 or more on the date when the proposed merger was first announced to the public, who continued to hold shares until the completion of the transfer of the business to the successor company and who were eligible to vote on the shareholders' resolution to approve the transfer, (ii) borrowing members subject to similar conditions, and (iii) persons who were employees or pensioners of the two societies on that date; and (b) an additional variable allocation of free shares would be made to shareholding members who had held shares in the first society for a period of two years expiring on a qualifying day. On the question of whether the distribution of free shares to members other than two-year shareholders was restricted by the 1986 Act, s 100(8), *held*, the words 'in priority to other subscribers' were intended to describe and qualify the 'rights to acquire shares' which were the subject of the restriction imposed by s 100(8). The 'rights to acquire shares' were rights conferred on members by the transfer agreement in connection with and in consideration of the transfer. The 'other subscribers' referred to in s 100(8) were persons who, in connection with the transfer, subscribed for shares in the successor company, but who did so on terms which were less favourable than those conferred on members or on some class of members under the transfer agreement. Those persons could be (1) some other class of members, (2) employees or pensioners, (3) existing members of the successor company where the successor was an existing company or (4) members of the public in circumstances where, in connection with the transfer, the successor company made a public offer of its shares. However, where there was no one who, in connection with the transfer, subscribed or was entitled to subscribe to shares in the successor company other than those persons upon whom rights were conferred by the transfer agreement and who enjoyed the same rights inter se, then there could be no 'other subscribers' for the purpose of s 100(8) and no infringement of the restriction. On the basis that no offer of shares in the successor company was to be made to the public in connection with the proposed conversion and that the terms of the transfer were those put before the court, there were no persons who were or could become 'other subscribers' in respect of the fixed share allocation and accordingly there would be no infringement of the restriction in s 100(8) if the proposed conversion took place.

Building Societies Commission v Halifax Building Society [1995] 3 All ER 193 (Chancery Division: Chadwick J). *Cheltenham and Gloucester Building Society v Building Societies Commission* [1994] 4 All ER 65 (1994 Abr para 274) considered.

CAPITAL GAINS TAXATION

Halsbury's Laws of England (4th edn) Vol 5(1) (reissue), paras 1–400

293   Articles

Different Views of Fairness, David Wainman (on the implications of *Marren v Ingles* [1979] STC 637 (1979 Abr para 272)): Tax Journal, Issue 299, p 14

Leaving the Group, Brenda Coleman and David Martin (on the provisions of the Taxation for Chargeable Gains Act 1992, s 179 and the Finance Bill 1995): Tax Journal, Issue 293, p 9

Making Provision for the Mentally Disabled, Francis Fitzpatrick: Tax Journal, Issue 317, p 8

Refused Clearances—What Next? Bradley Phillips (on refusal of capital gains tax clearances): Tax Journal, Issue 321, p 10

Yes, But Will They Fly? Michael Murphy (on the taxation of venture capital trusts): Tax Journal, Issue 296, p 8

294 Disposal of assets—close company—transfer of assets—transfer at undervalue

The Inland Revenue has issued a new concession by virtue of which it will not seek to apply the Taxation of Chargeable Gains Act 1992, s 125, which reduces the allowable acquisition cost of shares held by a shareholder in a close company at the date of a transfer of assets at undervalue otherwise than at arm's length, to a transfer which has already been taxed as income or a distribution, or where the transferee is an employee of the company and has already been taxed under Schedule E on the difference between the market value of the asset and the amount actually paid for it. See further *STI*, 18 May 1995.

295 Disposal of assets—composite transaction

The taxpayer company borrowed from a bank the dollar equivalent of the sterling sum required by it to make a purchase of shares. It simultaneously entered into a forward contract to purchase on the date the loan matured sufficient dollars to repay the loan. The sterling price payable under the forward contract was less than the sterling equivalent the taxpayer had borrowed so that overall it made a small commercial profit which it had included in its accounts. It subsequently borrowed a sum interest-free from its parent company which it applied with the bank's consent in reduction of the dollar loan although the forward contract remained in place. The forward contract was subsequently modified orally so that the taxpayer's right to receive the dollars was replaced by the right to have both dollar loans extinguished. The pound depreciated substantially against the dollar so that the sterling equivalent of the dollars purchased under the forward contract increased substantially. It fell to be determined whether, for tax purposes, the dollar loan and the forward contract were to be treated as separate transactions whereby the loss on the dollar loan was not an allowable loss but the gain realised on the disposal of the taxpayer's rights under the forward contract was chargeable. *Held*, where it was shown that an agreement was apparently complete and complied with the requirements of law as to the formation of a contract but which contained no express stipulation that it was or was not to be legally binding, the inference of an intention not to enter into a binding agreement was not one that would be lightly drawn. The true and only reasonable conclusion to be drawn was that the agreement between the taxpayer and the bank was a single composite agreement under which the taxpayer could not deal with the forward contract without the consent of the bank and under which the bank was to be at liberty to use the dollars purchased in discharge of the dollar loan to the extent that it had not been repaid with the consent of the bank. It followed that the taxpayer had made no profit on the forward purchase of the dollars and made no sterling loss on the repayment of the dollar loan, except the small commercial profit which had already been brought into account.

Whittles (Inspector of Taxes) v Uniholdings Ltd (No 3) [1995] STC 185 (Chancery Division: Sir John Vinelott).

296 Disposal of assets—reorganisation of share capital—incidental costs

The Inland Revenue has issued a new concession by virtue of which the incidental costs of acquisition or disposal, which would be allowable under the Taxation of Chargeable Gains Act 1992, s 38(1)(a) or 38(1)(c), incurred on or as a result of a share exchange or company reconstruction or amalgamation within s 135 or 136, may be treated as consideration given for the shares or debentures; and (2) payments in respect of contingent liabilities, as defined in s 49(1)(c), similarly incurred are restricted to the amount that would have been allowable under s 49(1)(c) if ss 135, 136 had not applied. See further *STI*, 18 May 1995.

297 Disposal of assets—transaction otherwise than by way of bargain made at arm's length—market value

The taxpayer was one of the two directors and sole shareholders of a small private company against which another company had obtained judgment. The latter assigned the benefit of the debt to the taxpayer and his co-director who held the benefit of the debt in equal shares. The debt was paid by instalments. The taxpayer made a profit, in commercial terms, of about £60,000. He appealed against an assessment to capital gains tax, contending that he had acquired the debt in connection with his waiver of emoluments as a director so that his acquisition should be deemed, under the Capital Gains Tax Act 1979, s 29A(1)(b), to be for a consideration equal to the market value of the asset at the date of acquisition. *Held*, there was no evidence establishing any relevant connection between the assignment and a diminution of the taxpayer's emoluments which, having regard to the accounts of the debtor company, had been reduced prior to the date of the assignment of the judgment debt. To establish a relevant connection, the taxpayer would have to show that at the time of the assignment he had given up some right to emoluments then payable. As the debt had been payable by a company of which the taxpayer and his co-director were the only directors and shareholders, the payments in satisfaction of the debt had not been transactions at arm's length so that the consideration for the disposal by virtue of s 29A(1)(a) was deemed to be for a consideration equal to the market value of the debt. The valuation proposed by the taxpayer's accountant, arrived at by applying to the debt the ratio between the assets and liabilities of the debtor company, would be rejected. The actual sums paid to the taxpayer were the best evidence of market value. The appeal would be dismissed.

Whitehouse v Ellam (Inspector of Taxes) [1995] STC 503 (Chancery Division: Vinelott J).

1979 Act, s 29A(1)(b) now Taxation of Chargeable Gains Act 1992, s 17(1)(b).

298   Disposal of assets—unquoted shares—expenditure wholly and exclusively incurred in ascertaining market value

The costs reasonably incurred in making any valuation required for the purposes of the computation of the gain accruing to a person on the disposal of an asset, including in particular expenses reasonably incurred in ascertaining market value where required, are allowable as a deduction from the consideration in the computation: Capital Gains Tax Act 1979, s 32(2)(b).

The taxpayers, the administrators of the deceased's estate, sold shares held by the deceased at his death in an unquoted company. It fell to be determined whether the expenses incurred by the taxpayers in appealing against an assessment to capital gains tax, which involved a question of the value of the shares, were an allowable deduction under s 32(2)(b). A Special Commissioner decided that the appeal process was part of the determination of market value and, accordingly, that expenditure incurred up to and including the hearing of an appeal was in principle incurred in ascertaining market value for the purposes of s 32(2) and an allowable deduction in computing the chargeable gain. On appeal by the Revenue, *held*, while the costs of the initial valuation of the shares was allowable expenditure under s 32(2)(b), the natural interpretation of that provision did not extend to or include the costs incurred by the taxpayers in carrying out negotiations with the Revenue as to the valuation of the shares or in pursuing their appeal against the assessment. Accordingly, the appeal would be allowed.

Couch (Inspector of Taxes) v Administrators of Caton's Estate) [1996] STC 201 (Chancery Division: Rimer J). Decision of Special Commissioner [1995] STC (SCD) 34 reversed.

1979 Act, s 32(2)(b) now Taxation of Chargeable Gains Act 1992, s 38(2)(b).

299   Disposal of assets—unquoted shares—valuation

At the date of her death in 1987, the deceased held shares in a company which was not quoted on a recognised stock exchange. The holding represented 3 per cent of the company's issued capital. In 1988, all the issued share capital was sold. The executor was assessed to capital gains tax on the disposal of the shares by reference to an acquisition cost deemed by the Capital Gains Tax Act 1979, s 49 to be the market value of the shares at the date of the deceased's death. In calculating the market value of the shares at that date, the tax inspector took account of certain unpublished information, including an estimate of the profitability of the company for 1987, confirmation that its increased level of profitability was maintainable and information about a possible sale of the company. The executor appealed against the determination. At the end of the hearing, both parties sought costs pursuant to the Special Commissioners (Jurisdiction and Procedure) Regulations 1994, SI 1994/1811, r 21. *Held*, under the 1979 Act, s 152(3), any information, including unpublished confidential information, and even information which might prejudice the interests of the company, was assumed to be available in the hypothetical sale if it would reasonably be required by a prudent prospective purchaser of the asset in question. It was necessary to consider, in each case, what information a prudent prospective purchaser of the asset would reasonably require. In the present case, in view of the amount of the outlay required to purchase the deceased's holding, the fact that the last published accounts were more than one year out of date at the time of the proposed sale, and the fact that the approximate results of the year's trading for the year ending 30 August 1987 were available on 28 September 1987, a prudent prospective purchaser of the shareholding in question would reasonably have required up-to-date information about profits and also information as to whether that level of profits was maintainable. However, the size of the holding and of the outlay required to purchase the holding were not sufficiently large to lead to a conclusion that a prospective purchaser could reasonably have required information about a possible sale of the company.

The power to award costs pursuant to the 1994 Rules, r 21 was limited to an order in respect of costs of the hearing and only where the party against whom the order was made had acted wholly unreasonably in connection with the hearing. No award of costs should be made against the executor because he had not acted wholly unreasonably in seeking two adjournments. Accordingly, the appeal would be dismissed with no order as to costs.

Clark's Executor v Green (Inspector of Taxes) [1995] STC (SCD) 99 (Special Commissioner's decision).

1979 Act, ss 49, 150, 152 now Taxation of Chargeable Gains Act 1992, ss 62, 272, 273.

300   Exemptions and reliefs—annual exempt amount

The Capital Gains Tax (Annual Exempt Amount) Order 1995, SI 1995/3033 (made on 28 November 1995), provides that for the year 1996–97 an individual is exempt from capital gains tax on taxable gains not exceeding £6,300. This applies unless Parliament otherwise determines.

301   Exemptions and reliefs—private residence–non-adjoining land

The taxpayer owned property which comprised two non-contiguous parts on one of which her residence was located. On the other part, situated between 25 and 30 feet away, she had maintained a small garden with a washing line, had erected a shed and had allowed her family and friends to use it for relaxation. Her use of that part of her property had declined in the years leading up to its sale. She appealed against an assessment to capital gains tax on the sale, contending that the land had been occupied and enjoyed with her principal private residence so that the gains accruing on its disposal qualified for relief under the Capital Gains Tax Act 1979, s 101(1)(b), as land enjoyed with the taxpayer's residence. *Held*, the availability of relief under s 101(1)(b) was not subject to a statutory requirement that the land sold should adjoin or be contiguous with the taxpayer's residence. The distance between the land sold and the taxpayer's residence was not sufficient to disqualify the taxpayer from claiming the relief. Furthermore, her use and enjoyment of the land with her residence had continued, although at a gradually decreasing rate, up until the time of the sale. Accordingly, the appeal would be allowed.

Wakeling v Pearce (Inspector of Taxes) [1995] STC (SCD) 96 (Special Commissioner's decision).

1979 Act, s 101 now Taxation of Chargeable Gains Act 1992, s 222.

302   Exemptions and reliefs—retirement relief—chargeable business assets

'Chargeable business asset' means 'an asset (including goodwill but not including shares or securities or other assets held as investments)' which is, or is an interest in, an asset used for the purposes of a profession: Finance Act 1985, Sch 20, para 12(2).

The taxpayer retired on grounds of ill-health from a firm of accountants of which he was a partner. The partnership capital included shares in a service company whose main activity was the provision of accounting and secretarial services primarily to the partnership but also to others at a profit. The taxpayer appealed against the refusal of his claim to retirement relief on the disposal of the shares, contending that the shares were assets of the partnership whose disposal amounted to the disposal of the whole or part of a business qualifying for relief under s 69(2)(a). He contended that the shares were 'chargeable business assets' as defined by Sch 20, para 12(2), in respect of which relief was available on the gains accruing on their disposal within Sch 20, para 6 and that only shares held as investments were excluded from the category of chargeable business assets. *Held*, the words in parentheses in Sch 20, para 12(2) should be read disjunctively. Accordingly, an asset which was a share was excluded as a chargeable business asset, as was an asset which was a security and as were other assets which were held as investments. All shares, therefore, were excluded from being chargeable business assets within Sch 20, para 12(2). Moreover, the shares were a business investment which were not used for the purposes of the taxpayer's profession. The appeal, therefore, would be dismissed.

Durrant v IRC [1995] STC (SCD) 145 (Special Commissioner's decision).

1985 Act, s 69, Sch 20, paras 6, 12(2) now Taxation of Chargeable Gains Act 1992, s 163, Sch 6, paras 6, 12(2).

303   Exemptions and reliefs—retirement relief—disposal of business

The Finance Act 1985, s 69 provides that relief from capital gains tax is to be given in any case where a material disposal of business assets is made by an individual who at the time of the disposal has reached the age of 60. A disposal of business assets is defined as a disposal of the whole or part of a business.

The plaintiff was a dairy farmer who decided to give up dairy farming and therefore sold his entire dairy herd. One year later, he sold his milk quota, and claimed capital gains tax relief under the 1985 Act, s 69. The Inland Revenue claimed that the relief did not apply and the plaintiff appealed successfully. On further appeal *held*, the disposal of the quota had been disposal of an asset used in the business of the dairy farm but was not, by itself, the disposal of either the whole or part of that business. The relevant business activity had been the production and sale of milk and that activity had ceased when the herd had been sold and the subsequent sale of another asset did not constitute disposal of part of the business. Accordingly, the plaintiff was not entitled to tax relief under the 1985 Act, s 69 and the Inland Revenue's appeal would be allowed.

Wase (Inspector of Taxes) v Bourke [1996] STC 18 (Chancery Division: Mr Anthony Grabiner QC).

304 Exemptions and reliefs—rollover relief—replacement of business assets—consideration for sale of old assets applied in acquisition of new assets

Roll-over relief applies if the consideration which a person carrying on a trade obtains for the disposal of, or of an interest in, assets ('the old assets') . . . is applied by him in acquiring other assets, or an interest in, other assets ('the new assets') if the acquisition took place in the period beginning 12 months before and ending three years after the disposal of the old assets: Capital Gains Tax Act 1979, s 115(1), 3.

The taxpayer purchased certain land and buildings which he brought into use for the purposes of the business carried on by him. Within 12 months of the acquisition, he sold part of the same land and buildings and sought, under s 115(1), to 'roll over' the gain made on that disposal into the acquisition cost of the remainder of the land and buildings retained by him. *Held*, the sale was a part disposal, not a disposal of part, of the business premises, and, therefore, the sale of the premises could not constitute 'old assets' as distinct from other assets. Further, it could not be said that any quantifiable part of the consideration for the disposal of the premises was 'applied' in the acquisition of the retained part, whatever meaning was given to the word 'applied'. Accordingly, the taxpayer was not entitled to the relief sought.

Watton (Inspector of Taxes) v Tippett [1996] STC 101 (Chancery Division: Sir John Vinelott). Decision of Special Commissioner [1995] STC (SCD) 17 reversed.

1979 Act, s 115(1) now Taxation of Chargeable Gains Act 1992, s 152(1).

305 Exemptions and reliefs—rollover relief—replacement of business assets—expenditure on improvements to existing assets

The Inland Revenue has issued a revised version of Concession D22 extending rollover relief where the proceeds of a disposal of qualifying trading assets are applied in improving existing qualifying assets rather than in acquiring new qualifying assets. By virtue of the revised concession, the Taxation of Chargeable Gains Act 1992, Sch 4, by virtue of which, in certain circumstances, only half of any deferred gains are taxed, now applies to gains rolled over where the other assets are used only for the purposes of the trade or where, on completion of the work on which the expenditure was incurred, the assets are immediately taken into use and used only for the purposes of the trade. See further *STI*, 18 May 1995.

306 Finance Act 1995

See para 2489.

307 Settled property—creation of overseas trusts—assessment of gain

The Finance Act 1981, s 80(2) provides that capital gains of non-resident settlements are to be computed as the amount on which the trustees would have been chargeable to capital gains tax if they had been resident or ordinarily resident in the United Kingdom. The Finance Act 1988, Sch 10, para 1(2) provides that, in the case of settled property where the settlor has an interest, where chargeable gains accrue to trustees they are not chargeable to tax in respect of those gains which are instead treated as having accrued to the settlor.

The taxpayer was the settlor and beneficiary of a settlement, the trustees of which were not resident in the United Kingdom. He claimed that, under the 1981 Act, s 80(2), the trust gains for a particular year were the amount on which the trustees would have been chargeable to tax if they had been resident in the United Kingdom. The amount on which the trustees were chargeable was therefore to be ascertained by applying the 1988 Act, Sch 10, para 1(2) if the settlor was also a beneficiary. Accordingly, the trustees were not liable to tax on the relevant gains and the trust gains to be assessed in this instance were nil. The taxpayer's argument was rejected by special commissioners and their decision was upheld at first instance. On further appeal, *held*, the purpose of the 1988 Act, s 80(2) was to compute the amount of the charge imposed on the beneficiaries of a non-resident settlement under the 1988 Act, s 80(3) and the following subsections. The taxpayer's argument, if successful, would lead to an absurd result as it would apply a provision relating to one type of settlement to a quite different type of settlement. The 1988 Act, Sch 10, para 1(2) had to be ignored when making the computation under the 1981 Act, s 80(2) and accordingly, the appeal would be dismissed.

De Rothschild v Lawrenson (Inspector of Taxes) [1995] STC 623 (Court of Appeal: Nourse, Farquharson and Henry LJJ). Decision of Vinelott J [1994] STC 8 (1993 Abr para 283) affirmed.

1981 Act, s 80 now Taxation of Chargeable Gains Act 1992, s 87. 1988 Act, Sch 10 repealed: 1992 Act, Sch 12.

CARRIERS

Halsbury's Laws of England (4th edn) Vol 5(1) (reissue), paras 401–604

308   Carriage by air
See AVIATION.

309   Carriage by land—claim for freight charges—set-off of cross-claims
See *United Carriers Ltd v Heritage Food Group (UK) Ltd*, para 2641.

310   Carriage by rail
See RAILWAYS, INLAND WATERWAYS AND PIPE-LINES.

311   Carriage by sea
See SHIPPING AND NAVIGATION.

312   Common transport policy
See EUROPEAN COMMUNITIES.

313   International carriage of goods—perishable foodstuffs
The International Carriage of Perishable Foodstuffs (Amendment) Regulations 1995, SI 1995/1716 (in force on 3 August 1995), further amend SI 1985/1071, so as to (1) alter the fees charged for the examination of goods vehicles, railway wagons and containers carrying perishable foodstuffs on international journeys, and (2) change the basis for charging for examination at a place other than the Refrigerated Vehicle Test Centre.

CHARITIES

Halsbury's Laws of England (4th edn) Vol 5(2) (reissue), paras 1–600

314   Articles
Can the VAT Burden Be Relieved? Ian Dawes (on the VAT burden on charities): Tax Journal, Issue 319, p10
Charities and Sales Promotion, Richard Lawson: 159 JP Jo 265
Fundraising for Maintained Schools: The Charity Law Implications, Debra Morris: [1995] Conv 453
A Step In the Dark? Julie Nazerali and Karen Plumbley-Jones (on the draft Acquired Rights Directive): 139 SJ 144
VAT: A New Source of Income, Glenn Havenhand (on the reclamation of VAT by charities): Tax Journal, Issue 301, p 16

315 Accounts and audit—small charities—financial limits for accounting requirements

The Charities Act 1993 (Substitution of Sums) Order 1995, SI 1995/2696 (in force in part on 1 December 1995 and in part on 1 March 1996), amends (1) the Charities Act 1993, s 5 so as to increase the level of gross income in a registered charity's financial year above which it must state on certain documents that it is so registered from £5,000 to £10,000; (2) the 1993 Act, s 42 so as to increase the level of gross income in any financial year of a charity above which the charity is required to prepare a statement of accounts complying with the prescribed requirements from £25,000 to £100,000; and (3) the 1993 Act, s 43 so as to increase the level of gross income or total expenditure in any of the current or two preceding financial years of a charity above which the charity is required to have its accounts audited by a person who satisfies specified criteria from £100,000 to £250,000.

316 Accounts and reports—regulations

The Charities (Accounts and Reports) Regulations 1995, SI 1995/2724 (in force on 1 March 1996), make provision for the form and content of the accounts of charities, the financial years of charities, the auditing or examination of charity accounts and the annual reports of charity trustees. The form and content of accounts prepared by charity trustees under the Charities Act 1993, s 42, accounts of common investment funds and common deposit funds, and accounts of registered housing associations and charities conducting higher and further education institutions is prescribed. The financial year of a charity is defined and provision is made for the duties of auditors and the reports which they are required to make. Provision is also made for the reports of independent examiners and the circumstances in which dispensation from the requirement to have accounts audited or examined may be given by the Charity Commissioners are prescribed.

317 Charitable purpose—faith healing

Before her death, the testatrix was involved with the conduct of a small religious and healing movement at her home. The activities of the group fell into two categories, namely, healing sessions and religious services. By her will, the testatrix left her residuary estate on trust to two faith healers, directing that they were to use the estate to further the spiritual work carried on by the group. The executors of the will issued an originating summons against the trustees, arguing that the greater proportion of the religious services were open only to a small private group of working members and, since those private religious meetings were not charitable, the object of the gift was not exclusively charitable and therefore failed, regardless of whether the remainder of the group's activities were charitable. The trustees claimed that faith healing had now become recognised as a charitable purpose without any religious element included and that, where there was also a religious element, provided the healing was open to the public, it was charitable. *Held*, spiritual work in the form of faith healing was charitable, either on the basis that faith healing had become a recognised public benefit, or that in any event the religious element in the present case rendered that work a charitable purpose within which a sufficient element of public benefit for the charity to be recognised by the law was assumed, there being no contrary evidence. The spiritual healing work the group did for members of the community was the reason it was there and, although the testatrix would have regarded the private religious services as an integral part of the general work, the private element was clearly ancillary or subsidiary to the public faith healing part of the group's work and did not disqualify it from being charitable. Accordingly, the gift was a valid charitable gift.

Funnel v Stewart (1995) Times, 9 December (Chancery Division: Miss Hazel Williamson, QC).

318 Charitable purpose—relief of poverty—gift to poor and needy relatives and their issue—validity of gift

See *Re Segelman (deceased)*, para 3084.

319 Charitable purpose—religious purpose—contemplative order of nuns

An enclosed community of Anglican nuns applied for registration as a charity. The objects of the order disclosed that it was a contemplative order devoted to perpetual intercession. It was accordingly necessary for proof of public benefit to be established. The order undertook a substantial amount of counselling and support for various persons and also gave educational support to various groups. The Charity Commissioners found that the work of the order involved a real and substantial charitable element which was for the public benefit and which could not be dismissed as de minimis (the retreat facilities which it provided were not regarded as charitable). Further, the numbers of associates of various descriptions who lived outside the order but who were regarded as an integral part of it and the publicity which the order gave to its charitable work indicated that its charitable activities were performed outside the order itself. Nevertheless, the commissioners stated that they had to be satisfied that the extension of the enhanced charitable activity into a dominant purpose was supported by the order's constitution. In construing the constitution, the commissioners stated that the object of the order as there set out should not necessarily be regarded as defining the whole purpose of the order in the strict legal sense. The criterion to be applied was whether the charitable activities were the outward manifestation of the life of intercessory prayer (and, accordingly, properly regarded as the actual purpose of the order) or whether they were incidental to the contemplative life. Looking at the activities, the commissioners were satisfied that, at their lowest, the purposes of the order could be said to provide an arguable case for a construction favourable to charitable status. They recommended that the constitution be modified to put the matter beyond doubt; an appropriate amendment was duly adopted and the order was registered.

Re Society of the Precious Blood (1989) Decisions of the Charity Commissioners, Vol 3, p 11.

320   Charities Act 1993—commencement

The Charities Act 1993 (Commencement and Transitional Provisions) Order 1995, SI 1995/2695, brings into force, on 1 March 1996, Pt VI (ss 41–49), concerning charity accounts, reports and returns, and Sch 6, para 21(3). Part VI comes into force, for the purpose only of making any order or regulations under any of its provisions, on 15 October 1995. Transitional provision is also made. For a summary of the Act, see 1993 Abr para 296. For details of commencement, see the commencement table in the title STATUTES.

321   Charities (Amendment) Act 1995

The Charities (Amendment) Act 1995 makes provision for the treatment of two or more charities as a single charity for all or any of the purposes of the Charities Act 1993. The Act received the royal assent on 8 November 1995 and came into force on that date.

Section 1 amends the 1993 Act, s 96 to enable the Charity Commissioners to direct that for all or any of the purposes of the 1993 Act two or more charities having the same charity trustees are to be treated as a single charity. Section 2 deals with short title and extent.

322   Land held by charity—registration

See para 1791.

323   Non-charitable purpose—gift for benefit of individuals—subsidiary purposes

The Charity Commissioners considered a proposal for the establishment of a trust for the purposes of preserving and maintaining structures and buildings connected with the Settle and Carlisle railway line which was operated by British Rail. The commissioners, distinguishing *Trades House of Glasgow v IRC* (1969) 45 TC 178 (which, as a Scottish decision, was not binding upon them), stated that the charitable nature of the proposed purposes was not excluded by the fact that the structures etc which the charity proposed to maintain would remain largely in the ownership of British Rail. They accepted that the preservation of the structures would be meaningless unless the line was operational and that it would be beyond the resources of the proposed trust to run its own trains over the line; further, British Rail needed to retain ownership of the line and its structures if it was to fulfil its statutory functions. Any private benefit which British Rail derived from the trust should be regarded as incidental and subsidiary (applying *IRC v City of Glasgow Police Athletic Association* [1953] AC 380), provided that the trustees did not apply part of the trust funds in relieving British Rail of its legal responsibilities to maintain the line in service.

Re Settle and Carlisle Railway Trust (1990) Decisions of the Charity Commissioners, Vol 3, p 1.

324   Recreational charities—interests of social welfare

The Charity Commissioners have stated that in their view the ambit of the classes specified in the Recreational Charities Act 1958, s 1(2)(b)(i), is sufficiently ambiguous as to what constitutes a sufficiently wide class of beneficiaries to satisfy the public benefit test (see s 1(1)) to justify reference (on *Pepper v Hart* [1993] 1 All ER 42 principles (see 1992 Abr para 2498) to the parliamentary material leading to the passing of the Act. A minister's statement in 1958 indicated that the parliamentary intention was to relax the common law rule prohibiting a class within a class, so that smaller classes would suffice to satisfy the test of public benefit in the 1958 Act, s 1(1). The commissioners stated that there was no reason why such classes could not be defined by reference to race, nationality, ethnic or national origins, or religion, provided that such further classes could be properly identified and that they were in consequence in a position of social and economic need (cf s 1(2)(b)(i)). The commissioners concluded that community associations and other recreational organisations which met the requirements of the Act and were established primarily for identifiable racial minority groups could properly be regarded as being charitable where there was evidence of special need of the recreational facilities provided because of the social and economic circumstances of the group. The commissioners approved model objects for such associations and organisations.

Re Community Associations and Other Recreational Charities Established by Reference to Race, Nationality, Ethnic or National Origins or Religion (1995) Decisions of the Charity Commissioners, Vol 4, p 17.

325 Registration—exemption

The Exempt Charities Order 1995, SI 1995/2998 (in force on 30 November 1995), declares the University of Derby to be an exempt charity within the meaning of the Charities Act 1993 (exemption from registration as a charity).

326 Trustees—investments—division of funds

The Charities (Trustee Investments Act 1961) Order 1995, SI 1995/1092 (in force on 25 April 1995), directs that any division of a trust fund consisting of property held by or in trust for a charity under the Trustee Investments Act 1961, s 2(1) is to be made so that the value of the wider range part of the fund, instead of being equal to the value of the narrower range part, is three times that value.

CHILDREN AND YOUNG PERSONS

Halsbury's Laws of England (4th edn) Vol 5(2) (reissue), paras 601–1392

327 Articles

Acting for Children, Jane Leigh (on acting for children in private law proceedings): 139 SJ 40

Acting for Parents in Care Proceedings, David Fish: [1995] Fam Law 391

After the Care Order—Into Forbidden Territory, Glenn Brasse: [1995] Fam Law 31, 75

Alcohol Experts in Family Cases, Jonathan Goodliffe: 145 NLJ 633

Allocating Family Law Cases, Paul Tain: 139 SJ 192

All Secure, Hugh Howard (on the practice and procedure of secure accommodation orders): 139 SJ 1202

Appointing and Funding of Guardians in Private Law Cases, Philip Kidd and Paul Storey: [1995] Fam Law 682

Care and Supervision—Families' Experiences, Bridget Lindley: [1995] Fam Law 424

Child Abuse—Punishment or Partnership, Judge Paul Collins: [1995] Fam Law 140

Child Protection, Privacy and Covert Video Surveillance, Terry Thomas: 17 JSWFL 311

Child Protection Research, Peter Smith: [1995] Fam Law 432

Child Support Revisited, Wendy Mantle (on the Child Support Act 1995): 139 SJ 788

The Child's Best Interests v Procedures, Tony Wells: [1995] Fam Law 193

The Children Act 1989 and Early Childhood Services, Claire Cameron and Peter Moss: 17 JSWFL 417

Children and Young Persons Before the Adult Magistrates' Court—Where Are They Tried?, Elizabeth Franey: 159 JP Jo 21

Children in Care—Placement Abroad, Glenn Brasse: [1995] Fam Law 486

Children Seeking Leave to Apply Under the Children Act 1989, David Burrows: 139 SJ 396

Children's Certificates for the Bar Areas of Licensed Premises—Conditions for the Availability of Meals, J N Spencer: 159 JP Jo 242

Children's Certificates—Problem or Panacea? A M Wesson: 159 JP Jo 314

Children's Certificates Under the Deregulation and Contracting Out Act 1994, J N Spencer (on licences allowing admittance of children under the age of 14 into public bars): 159 JP Jo 171

Children's Rights: In the Name of the Child, Jeremy Roche: 17 JSWFL 261

Contact: A Compendium, Victor Smith (on the meaning of 'contact' in the Children Act 1989): 159 JP Jo 159, 188

Contact Can be Crucial, Hugh Howard (on contact promoting adopting): 139 SJ 900

Contradictions in Children's Policy: Partnering Families or Policing Them? Roger Smith: 17 JSWFL 301

The Criminal Justice and Public Order Act 1994—The Effect on Young Offenders, Leonard Jason-Lloyd: 159 JP Jo 71, 89

A Dilemma—Contact or Adoption, Robert Stevens: 159 JP Jo 501

Discovery and Disclosure in Children Cases, David Burrows: 139 SJ 60

Domestic Violence and Children, David Fish: [1995] Fam Law 82

Emotional Abuse and Expert Evidence, Carole Kaplan and Anne Thompson: [1995] Fam Law 628

Ethnicity and Child Care Placements, Hugh Howard: 139 SJ 921

Ex Parte Orders—Cherchez Le Juge, David Price (on the jurisdiction of judges to hear ex parte family applications in the county court): [1995] Fam Law 34

Grandparents Seeking Contact, Robert Stevens: 159 JP Jo 753

The Guardian Ad Litem and the Local Authority, Victor Smith: [1995] Fam Law 188

Guardians and Experts, Betty Foster and Michael Preston Shoot: [1995] Fam Law 250

In Defence of Doli Incapax, Terence Moore: 159 JP Jo 347

Is Adoption Working? Hugh Howard: 139 SJ 873

Judicial Attitudes to Contact and Shared Residence Since the Children Act 1989, Ines Weyland: 17 JSWFL 445

A Judicial Step Too Far, Adrian Jack (on the abolition of doli incapax): 145 NLJ 315

A Lifeline for the Agency, Maggie Rae (on the Government's damage limitation measures to save the Child Support Act 1991): 145 NLJ 140

The 'Mareva', the Magistrates and the Child Support Act, Susan Spencer: 159 JP Jo 821

New Rules for Juvenile Offenders, Tony Wilkinson: 139 SJ 110

Newham and *Bedfordshire*: Negligence in Residential Care, Jonathan Butler and Graham Wood (on *M v Newham Borough Council* (1995) Times, 30 June (para 2833)): 145 NLJ 1826

Obscene Material on the Internet, Stephen Dooley: 139 SJ 868

Parental Orders Under the Human Fertilisation and Embryology Act 1990, Malcolm Dodds: 159 JP Jo 448

Play-Groups and Child-Minders: The Effect of the Children Act 1989; Registration and Rights of Appeal to the Family Courts, J N Spencer: 159 JP Jo 144, 157

Presumption of Contact—What Presumption? Caroline Willbourne and Joanna Geddes: [1995] Fam Law 87

Problems in the Criminal Law of Adoption, Ralph Sandland: 17 JSWFL 149

Publicity and Children Cases, David Ormerod: [1995] Fam Law 686

Publicity in Children Cases—A Personal View, Mr Justice Wall: [1995] Fam Law 136

The Putative Father Under Rules of Court, Jacqueline Priest: [1995] Fam Law 23, 78

Residence Order or Package Order? Andrew Grand: [1995] Fam Law 201

Secure Accommodation, Carole Smith (on the Children Act 1989, s 25(3): [1995] Fam Law 369

Taking an Independent View, Barbara Mitchels and Alister Prince (on instructing an independent social work consultant): SJ Supp, 30 June 1995, p 44

Use of Experts in Children's Cases, Victor Smith: 159 JP Jo 635, 648

328 Activity Centres (Young Persons' Safety) Act 1995

The Activity Centres (Young Persons' Safety) Act 1995 makes provision for the regulation of centres and providers of facilities where children and young persons under the age of 18 engage in adventure activities, including provision for the imposition of requirements relating to safety. The Act received the royal assent on 28 June 1995 and came into force on 28 August 1995.

Section 1 gives the Secretary of State power to designate a licensing authority to exercise prescribed functions relating to the licensing of persons providing facilities for adventure activities. Regulations under s 1 may make provision for the circumstances in which licences are required and impose safety requirements. Section 2 states that regulations may provide for it to be an offence to do anything for which a licence is required otherwise than in accordance with the licence or, for the purposes of obtaining or holding a licence, to make a false statement to the licensing authority or to recklessly make a statement which is false; and sets out penalties for such offences, providing for defences to offences and the application of specified provisions of the Health and Safety at Work etc Act 1974. Sections 3–6 deal with supplementary provisions, expenses, commencement, short title and extent.

329 Adoption—Adopted Children Register—information on register—disclosure

The Adoption Act 1976, s 50(5) provides that the Adopted Children Register and other registers and books kept by the Registrar General in accordance with s 50(4) are not open to public inspection or search, and the Registrar General must not furnish any person with any information contained in, or with any copy or extract from, any such registers or books except in accordance with s 51 or under an order of certain courts, one of which is the High Court.

A woman wanted to trace her half-brother who had been put up for adoption when he was a child, and with whom all contact had been lost. She was referred to an adoption counselling organisation and, as it was impossible to trace the agency which had been responsible for the adoption, the organisation made a successful ex parte application under s 50(5) for an order that the Registrar General should furnish it with information about the half-brother. On the Registrar General's application for the order to be set aside, *held*, it was inappropriate for orders under s 50(5) to be made on an ex parte basis as there was seldom a pressing urgency for such information. The court's discretion to grant an order for disclosure of information about an adopted child did not have to be exercised sparingly, as there was no express provision to that effect in the Act. It was also the case that there was a trend towards greater transparency in matters relating to adoption. Moreover, the only means by which a blood relative who was not an adoptee could find out information about an adopted relative who had not registered himself under the Adoption Contact Register, was to make an application under s 50. As such, the burden of proof on an applicant under s 50 was no greater than the ordinary burden of establishing a case of sufficient weight and justification which persuaded a judge that it was reasonable to grant an order for disclosure of information. Here, the woman was suffering from a degenerative lung disease which might be genetic. It was therefore important for her to trace her half-brother so that he could be screened for the disease, as early detection could lead to treatment at an early stage. Accordingly, the application would be dismissed.

Re H (Adoption: Disclosure of Information) [1995] 1 FCR 546 (Family Division: Thorpe J).

330 Adoption—adoption order—application for order—foster parents

The Adoption Rules 1984, SI 1984/265, r 4, provides that in proceedings to free a child for adoption, the local authority must prepare a report in the form set out in Sch 2. Schedule 2 lists certain particulars which, so far as practicable, are to be included in the report and under para 2(i) the authority is required to state the wishes and feelings of each natural parent in relation to the adoption.

The parents of two children had a short relationship which ended before the birth of the second child and indeed the father was unaware of the existence of a second child. Shortly after its birth the mother handed over the second child to the local authority for adoption. The child was placed with foster parents who applied to adopt her and the question arose whether it was practicable to ascertain the father's wishes and feelings under the 1984 Rules. *Held*, in considering whether a course of action was desirable it was permissible to look at the end result. In this case the father had contact with the elder child and was thus likely to hear of the existence of the younger child sooner or later. From the child's point of view it would be better if the matter were dealt with now rather than when the father eventually discovered the facts. Accordingly, the court would direct that the father's wishes and feelings be included in the report under the 1984 Rules, Sch 4.

Re P (Adoption) (Natural Father's Rights) [1995] 2 FCR 58 (Family Division: Ewbank J).

331 Adoption—adoption order—application for order—unmarried couple—order in favour of one partner—joint residence order

A child in respect of whom a care order was in force was placed with unmarried foster parents. They wished to adopt the child. Accordingly, one partner applied to adopt the child and both partners applied for a joint residence order. *Held*, the child needed a permanent base and permanent family and his welfare demanded that he be adopted. Although the Adoption Act 1976, s 14 prohibited the granting of an adoption order in favour an unmarried couple, the court could grant an adoption order to one partner and make a joint residence order in favour of both partners under the Children Act 1989, s 11(4). Where it was intended that the child should live with both partners, it was not realistic to grant a residence order solely in favour of the partner who was not granted an adoption order. To do so would indicate that the child was to live only with that partner. Joint residence orders should be made only in unusual circumstances, but the present case was sufficiently unusual to warrant such a course. The granting of a joint residence order did not amount to an attempt to circumvent the provisions of the 1976 Act, because, although a residence order in favour of a partner would give him parental responsibility, he would not acquire the full rights of an adoptive parent. The applications would be granted.

Re AB (Adoption: Joint Residence) [1996] 2 FLR 27 (Family Division: Cazalet J).

332 Adoption—adoption order—application for order—unmarried natural father without parental responsibility

It has been held that it is not a mandatory requirement of law that an unmarried natural father, who does not have parental responsibility for his child under the Children Act 1989, be joined as a respondent to adoption proceedings. Under the Adoption Rules 1984, SI 1984/265, r 15, the respondents to adoption proceedings are each parent or guardian of a child. However, the correct meaning of 'parent' for the purposes of the rules is that under the Adoption Act 1976, s 72(1), which defines 'parent' as any parent who has parental responsibility for the child under the 1989 Act.

Re C (Minor) (Adoption: Parties) [1995] 2 FLR 483 (Court of Appeal: Leggatt LJ and Thorpe J).

333 Adoption—adoption order—application for order—welfare of child—natural parents—rights

A child born in The Gambia was brought to England to live with the applicants as part of an informal fostering arrangement. Her parents later sought to take her back to The Gambia and the applicants made an application to adopt her. *Held*, the correct test to be applied was whether in all the circumstances of the case an adoption order was appropriate. If so, the court had to decide whether the consent of the parents should be dispensed with. An adoption order could only be made if both criteria were satisfied. As adoption had the effect of extinguishing parental responsibility, it was right that the court should take into account concepts other than the child's welfare, such as the right of a child to be brought up by his parents in the cultural heritage of their native country. An adoption order was not appropriate in the present case and, accordingly, the application would be dismissed.

Re B (Adoption: Child's Welfare) [1995] 1 FLR 895 (Family Division: Wall J).

334 Adoption—adoption order—conditions referred to at hearing not included in order—parents' application for leave to apply for contact

The parties, who both suffered from psychiatric illness, married and had a child. The child was removed from their care and placed with prospective adopters. At the first stage of the split adoption hearing, an application to dispense with the parent's agreement was granted. However, the social worker dealing with the case said that photographs of the child and news of her schooling would be forwarded to the parents. At the hearing's second stage, the adoption order was made without conditions. Both the local authority and the adopters' solicitor refused the parents' request for photigraphs and news of the child. The parents sought leave under the Children Act 1989, s 10(9) to apply for contact with the child. At first instance, a district judge ordered a further hearing of the application before a Family Division judge at which the adopters could make representations. On the adopters' appeal against that decision, *held*, although the unfairness to the parents was real and not merely apparent, it did not follow that they were necessarily to be granted leave. The parents' remedy derived from the flawed proceedings in the county court, not from provisions of the 1989 Act. It was open to them to apply in the county court for the amendment of the adoption order to reflect the arrangements made at the first stage of the hearing. Alternatively, they could appeal against the order on the grounds that it was manifestly flawed, unfair and deficient. However, the nature of the proposed application for contact was fundamentally inconsistent with the judicial framework for the care and upbringing of the child. There was the measurable possibility of disruption that might prove harmful if the now well-constituted family were subjected to the challenge of court proceedings. Accordingly, the appeal would be allowed.

Re E (Adopted Child) (Contact: Leave) [1995] 2 FCR 655 (Family Division: Thorpe J).

335 Adoption—adoption order—contact with natural family—guidelines

Following allegations of sexual abuse within the family, the applicant's half-brothers and half-sister were taken into care. The applicant had no contact with the children after they were adopted. The adoption agency resisted an application by the applicant for contact with the children but there was an informal agreement that the adoptive parents would provide the applicant with annual progress reports. The agency later told the applicant that it would not be in the children's best interests to send reports. The applicant sought leave to apply for contact but her application was refused at first instance. On appeal, *held*, the judge had made errors in refusing to grant leave. The failure of the adoptive parents to provide a progress report was clearly a change of circumstances which justified reopening the question of contact. Further, there was no evidence before the judge that the proposed application might disrupt the children's lives to such an extent that they might be harmed by it, nor was there any material entitling the judge to infer such a risk. While it was important for adopters to have an unfettered right to bring up their adopted children without constraints and that the adoptive family be shielded from risks to its security and stability, it was also of the highest importance that adoption proceedings be conducted in a spirit of co-operation between the adopters and the natural family whenever possible. The adopters should not resile from informal agreements without giving reasons and without the court being in a position to inquire into the matter. Accordingly, the appeal would be allowed.

The court set out guidelines as to the procedure to be followed in applications for leave to apply for direct or indirect contact after adoption, which should ensure that adoptive parents were not unnecessarily disturbed by applications, and that the judge hearing the application had as much relevant information as possible. It would normally be appropriate for the court to direct that the adoption agency be given notice of the application for leave, but not for it to be a party to the application. In some cases it might be necessary to transfer applications to the High Court and to bring in the Official Solicitor but there was no reason for that to be the general rule.

Re T (Minors) (Adopted Children: Contact) [1995] 3 WLR 793 (Court of Appeal: Balcombe, Peter Gibson and Hutchison LJJ).

336 Adoption—adoption order—foreign order—English adoption proceedings—notice of proceedings—service on natural mother

A Paraguayan court made a 'simple' adoption order under Paraguayan law in respect of the youngest child of a single Paraguayan mother in favour of the applicants who were domiciled in England. Under the order, a link was maintained between the child and his natural mother. Paraguayan law did not allow a full adoption order to be made in the circumstances. English law did not recognise the simple adoption order as it did not come within the ambit of the 1965 Hague Convention on Jurisdiction, Applicable Law and Recognition of Decrees relating to Adoption or the Adoption (Designation of Overseas Adoption) Order 1973, SI 1973/19. The applicants claimed that, if the court found the agreement to adopt insufficient, the circumstances of the case justified not serving notice of the English proceedings on the natural mother. *Held*, as the Paraguayan order was not recognised by English law, the natural mother remained the child's mother in English law. The mother had only agreed to an adoption order in Paraguay and there was no evidence that she had agreed to an English adoption order being made. Under the Adoption Rules 1984, SI 1984/265, the child's natural mother was a respondent to an adoption application and had to be properly served. This was not a case in which it would be appropriate to dispense with the requirement for service and, accordingly, the mother's agreement to the making of an English adoption order would be sought.

Re G (Foreign Adoption: Consent) [1995] 2 FLR 534 (Family Division: Johnson J).

337 Adoption—adoption order—notice of proceedings—natural father

An adoption order was made in favour of a stepfather after it was decided to dispense with service of notice of the proceedings on the child's natural father. The mother and stepfather had indicated their belief that the natural father was probably overseas, but had also given notice of his last known domestic address and had made every effort to contact him through the agency of foreign embassies. The natural father heard of the adoption order some time later and sought leave to appeal out of time. The parties disputed the frequency with which the father had made contact and thus the cause of the delay in his hearing of the adoption order. *Held*, the Court of Appeal was clearly unsuited to deal with the important issue of fact but, if it refused the application and steps were taken to set the order aside in the county court, that would only result in another appeal. It would invoke its jurisdiction, under the Supreme Court Act 1981, s 15(3), assuming the authority and jurisdiction of the court or tribunal from which the appeal was brought. The appeal was brought from the county court which would have had the power to direct a preliminary issue to be tried in respect of the question of service. Under s 15(3), the court could so direct and when a determination was made the matter could be returned for consideration of the application for leave to appeal out of time.

Re T (A Minor) (Adoption Order: Leave to Appeal) [1995] 3 FCR 299 (Court of Appeal: Balcombe, Butler-Sloss and Leggatt LJJ).

338 Adoption—adoption order—order for contact with natural parent

A young child was placed with prospective adoptive parents, during which time she continued to have contact with her natural mother. With the latter's consent, an adoption order was made. Both the child's guardian ad litem and social worker recommended, and the adoptive parents agreed, that although the child should continue to have some contact with the natural mother, it should not form part of the adoption order but should be left to the adoptive parents to determine. As agreement could not be reached as to how often contact should take place, the judge decided that it should be once a year, and he made an order to that effect in addition to the adoption order. On the adoptive parents' appeal, *held*, the judge had made the contact order to give the mother some degree of security, so that if anything should go wrong, she would have some means of redress without having to apply for leave of the court. However, it was well-established that the rights of adoptive parents should not be interfered with, that constraints should not be placed upon them, and that they should not be fettered in trying to integrate an adopted child into their family. It was inconsistent with the unconditional nature of the mother's consent to the adoption that she should be given the security of a contact order. The security that she desired had to be based on trust in the adoptive parents. These particular adoptive parents had been chosen because they recognised that it was in the child's interests to see her natural mother, although they wished to have ultimate control over contact arrangements. It was therefore an unnecessary additional burden that the adoptive parents should have to return to court in order to have the contact order suspended, varied or discharged. If they wished to stop contact, they would have to give a reason to the natural mother for doing so, upon which the mother could obtain leave to challenge their decision if that seemed appropriate. Moreover, the requirement of obtaining leave was a valuable safeguard for both the adoptive parents and the child. The contact order was unnecessary, and there were good reasons why it should not have been made. Accordingly, the appeal would be allowed.

Re T (A Minor) (Contact after Adoption) [1995] 2 FCR 537 (Court of Appeal: Butler-Sloss and Millett LJJ and Sir Ralph Gibson).

339 Adoption—adoption order—setting aside

The appellant's father was a Kuwaiti Muslim and his mother was an English Roman Catholic. He was, however, adopted by an orthodox Jewish family who believed him to be Jewish and, therefore, brought him up in the Jewish faith. The appellant attempted to settle in Israel, but was asked to leave the country on suspicion that he was an Arab spy. When he later discovered the identity of his natural parents, he attempted to settle in Kuwait where his natural father resided but was refused permission to do so. His application for an order to set aside the adoption order was refused. On appeal against that decision, *held*, although adoption orders could be set aside for procedural irregularity, the court did not have an inherent power to set aside adoption orders for mistake or misapprehension nor was there a statutory provision which allowed the court to do so. Such a power would undermine the whole basis on which adoption orders were made, namely that they were final and for life as regards the adopters, the natural parents and the child. Moreover, it would gravely damage the lifelong commitment made by adopters if the validity of an adoption order could be challenged subsequently by the child or the natural parents. There had been no procedural irregularity when the adoption order was made and, accordingly, the appeal would be dismissed.

Re B (Adoption: Setting Aside) [1995] 3 WLR 40 (Court of Appeal: Sir Thomas Bingham MR, Brown and Swinton Thomas LJJ). Decision of Sir Stephen Brown P [1995] 1 FLR 1 (1994 Abr para 310) affirmed.

340 Adoption—adoption papers—confidential report—disclosure of information to parent

The Adoption Rules 1984, SI 1984/265, r 53(2) provides that an individual referred to in a confidential report supplied to the court may inspect, for the purposes of the hearing, the part of the report which refers to him, subject to certain directions given by the court.

A guardian ad litem interviewed children for a report in adoption proceedings, promising them confidentiality. The mother applied to see specific sections of the guardian's report but her application was refused. Her subsequent appeal was dismissed on the basis that the value of providing the information had to be balanced against the risk to the child. On further appeal, *held*, in such cases the judge must start from a strong presumption in favour of disclosing to a party any material relating to him. The opportunity to know of and to be able to respond to adverse material was at the heart of a fair hearing, especially when that hearing concerned issues of adoption, the determination of which could be long lasting and far-reaching. However, as r 53(2) made clear, there must be some limit to the duty of disclosure. Where it was suggested that disclosure might harm the child the court should take the matter very seriously but it should look very closely at the degree of likelihood of harm occurring and the gravity of that harm. To require harm to be certain would be to pitch the test too high. A powerful combination of likelihood and seriousness of harm would be required before the requirements of a fair trial would be overridden. Accordingly, the appeal would be allowed.

Re D (Minors) (Adoption Reports: Confidentiality) [1995] 4 All ER 385 (House of Lords: Lords Goff of Chieveley, Browne-Wilkinson, Mustill, Lloyd of Berwick and Nicholls of Birkenhead). Decision of Court of Appeal [1995] 1 WLR 356 (1994 Abr para 314) reversed.

341 Adoption—adoption papers—records held by local authority—disclosure in criminal proceedings

Under the Adoption Rules 1984, SI 1984/265, r 53(3), any person who obtains any information, in the course of, or relating to, adoption proceedings must treat that information as confidential and may only disclose it if the disclosure is necessary for the proper exercise of his duties.

In a criminal trial, a defendant charged with rape sought disclosure of adoption papers relating to the child of the alleged victim. The trial judge refused the application. Subsequently, the local authority applied by originating summons to the Family Division for guidance and a ruling as to its obligations under the Adoption Rules 1984, r 53 in respect of the adoption papers. *Held*, in the case of *Re D*, which concerned wardship, it was held that the leave of the court was required to disclose in criminal proceedings documents which were in the custody and control of the court, but that the disclosure of documents which had never been in the custody or control of the court was to be decided by the trial judge in the criminal proceedings. In the present case, although the documents were in the custody of the local authority rather than the adoption court they nevertheless fell within the ambit of r 53. The defendant was entitled to seek disclosure of the documents but was not entitled as of right to obtain disclosure since the documents prima facia attracted public interest immunity. The question of disclosure was entirely a matter for the trial judge in the criminal proceedings. Accordingly, the Family Division would not intervene and a ruling binding the criminal court would not be made.

Re H (Criminal Proceedings: Disclosure of Adoption Records) [1995] 1 FLR 964 (Family Division: Sir Stephen Brown P). *Re D* [1994] 1 FLR 346, CA followed.

342 Adoption—arrangements for adoption—restrictions

The Adoption Act 1976, s 11(1) provides that a person other than an adoption agency cannot make arrangements for the adoption of a child or place the child for adoption, unless the proposed adopter is a relative of the child or he is acting in pursuance of an order of the High Court.

Shortly after the birth of a child whose mother suffered from a mental disorder and was unable to take care of him, a local authority was granted an interim care order. At a renewal hearing the grandmother of the child indicated that the mother was willing to have the child fostered so that he could be adopted by a society approved as an adoption agency under the Adoption Act 1976, s 11. A residence order was made in favour of the grandmother and the judge recorded an agreement that the local authority would continue to accommodate the child until he was placed with adopters. This was intended to give the grandmother parental responsibility so that she could oversee adoption arrangements. At a further hearing a different district judge held that, where a mother was under a disability and thus unable to give informed consent to arrangements for placing her child, the only possible route to adoption was by means of a care order and that arrangements between the grandmother and the society would be in breach of the 1976 Act, s 11(1). That part of the order recording the agreement that the authority would continue to accommodate the child was discharged and a direction was made that the matter be listed before a judge of the High Court. The authority applied for leave to withdraw its care order under the Children Act 1989, s 31. The issues raised were whether agreements between a third party and an adoption agency with a view to placing the child for adoption contravened the 1976 Act, s 11(1) and whether the only proper method of placing the child for adoption was by means of a care order. *Held*, the 1976 Act, s 11(1) was aimed at the private placing of a child by one individual with another and could not render unlawful arrangements between a mother or person acting on her behalf and an approved adoption agency. Thus, an order of the court was not required to render arrangements between the grandmother and an approved adoption agency lawful. Accordingly, the authority would be given leave to withdraw its application for a care order.

Re W (A Minor) (Adoption: Mother Under Disability) [1995] 2 WLR 458 (Family Division: Wall J).

343 Adoption—freeing order—order for contact with father—application for variation by local authority—jurisdiction of court

Care orders in respect of three children granted a local authority orders freeing the children for adoption and dispensing with the parents' agreement. Monthly contact between the parents and the children was to continue after adoption orders were made. The children were placed with prospective adopters. The contact arrangements were subsequently varied to contact three times a year on the basis that further contact might inhibit relationships between the children and the prospective adopters. On the father's appeal, *held*, the authority was prohibited by the Children Act 1989, s 9 from making an application for the variation of an order. Although it could seek to correct an ambiguity or ask for an amendment under the slip rule, neither of those could extend to the variation of a contact order. If the children were to become part of another family, the parents' contribution had to be subsidiary to that of prospective adopters. Under its inherent jurisdiction, the court had a duty to see what the proper period of contact was prior to the adoption hearing. Accordingly, contact would be reduced to three times a year pending further determination by the High Court.

Re C (Minors) (Variation of Contact: Jurisdiction) [1995] 3 WLR 30 (Court of Appeal: Balcombe and Butler-Sloss LJJ).

344 Adoption—placement of child—illegal placement

A child was placed for adoption in unintentional contravention of the Children Act 1976, s 11. In a county court adoption application it was held that the adoption should proceed in that court. The guardian ad litem appealed. *Held*, although s 11 was silent as to the consequences of its contravention, it was certain that its purpose was the protection of children and the promotion of their welfare. Parliament could not have intended that an illegal placement should be an absolute bar to adoption. Thus, a court hearing such an adoption application was not prohibited from making an order notwithstanding the absence of a statutory dispensing power. The breach of s 11 had to be taken into account and the court had to exercise its discretion in the same way as it would for an application for authorisation of a breach under s 57. Further, it was clear that Parliament had considered that only the High Court should be able to ratify a placement which would otherwise be prohibited. The proper procedure was for the county court to exercise its power under the Children (Allocation of Proceedings) Order 1991, SI 1991/1677, art 12 and to transfer the proceedings to the High Court. Accordingly, the appeal would be allowed.

Re G (A Minor) (Adoption: Illegal Placement) [1995] 3 FCR 26 (Court of Appeal: Balcombe, Hirst and Simon Brown LJJ).

345 Adoption—proceedings—natural father—rights

See *Keegan v Ireland*, para 1582.

346 Capacity of child—consent to medical treatment—right of child to refuse essential treatment

A child aged 15 had suffered all her life from a life-threatening genetic condition so that she needed monthly blood transfusions and daily injections of iron. Her father had done this for her until she reached the age of nine when she started to inject herself. She did so irregularly with the result that her physical growth was retarded. At the age of ten, the girl began to attend meetings of Jehovah's Witnesses with her mother. Her father continued to consent to the blood transfusions. However, after the child and her mother left the family home she failed to attend the hospital for her routine transfusion, stating that it was against her faith to do so. The local authority applied to the court requesting that it exercise its inherent jurisdiction to authorise treatment. *Held*, the High Court had the power to authorise medical treatment where a child refused consent, its function being to act as the 'reasonable parent'. The court would be very reluctant to allow a child to martyr itself but would start from the position that the child's wish would be given effect unless the balance was strongly against this. In the present case, despite the girl's age, she did not seem to be '*Gillick* competent' in that she did not have a clear understanding of the manner of the suffering, distress and death which she would experience if her treatment were not resumed. Moreover, as she had endured treatment for over 15 years it seemed foolish to stop when in two years' time, having reached adulthood, she could well change her mind or alternative forms of therapy could become available. Accordingly, the application would be granted. The girl's express wish would be overridden and authority would be given to her doctor, if necessary, to force treatment upon her.

Re S (A Minor) (Refusal of Medical Treatment) [1994] 1 FCR 604 (Family Division: Johnson J). *Re R (A Minor)* [1991] 4 All ER 177, CA (1991 Abr para 316), *Re W (A Minor: Medical Treatment: Court's Jurisdiction)* [1992] 2 FCR 785, and *Re T (An Adult: Medical Treatment)* [1992] 4 All ER 649, CA (1992 Abr para 1719), considered.

347 Care order—application for discharge—application by child

A child wished to apply for the discharge of a care order made in respect of himself and the question arose whether it was necessary for him to obtain the leave of the court before making such an application. *Held*, there was a distinction between the public law provisions of the Children Act 1989, s 39(1)(b) and the private law provisions of s 10. Section 39(1)(b) provided for the discharge of a care order on the direct application of the child, whereas s 10 required a preliminary application for leave by a child who was an intended applicant in private law proceedings. Accordingly, it was not necessary that the child obtain leave before applying for the discharge of the order.

Re A (Care Order: Discharge Application by Child) [1995] 2 FCR 686 (Family Division: Thorpe J).

348 Care order—application for discharge—earlier findings of fact—review

Three children had been committed to the care of a local authority when the trial judge, relying heavily on the evidence of social workers, found that one child had been sexually abused by a friend of the mother and that the mother was aware of the abuse but was unable or unwilling to acknowledge it. The mother's friend was convicted with others of offences of sexual abuse. In care proceedings involving the children of those others the judge was not prepared to hold that the children were at significant risk and made orders for their return home. He found that the social workers had been insufficiently cautious and over-ready to believe the children's allegations. On this basis the mother wished to have the original trial judge's order set aside and she applied for an extension of time to appeal against the order. *Held*, under the Children Act 1989, s 39, a court could discharge a care order on the application of, inter alia, a parent. The issue had to be determined in accordance with s 1, which made the child's welfare paramount; in particular, under s 1(3)(e), the court was bound to have regard to any harm which the child had suffered or was at risk of suffering. In family proceedings the court had the power to review findings reached at earlier stages. However, because of the disruption which would be caused by the re-opening of past proceedings and the prejudice to the child's welfare created by any delay in reaching a final determination, the power to review earlier findings of fact would only be exercised in very limited circumstances. Accordingly, the application would be dismissed.

Re S (Minors) [1995] 2 FLR 639 (Court of Appeal: Waite and Schiemann LJJ).

349 Care order—application for order—disclosure of documents—documents held by Crown Prosecution Service in connection with unrelated charges

A child was found dead, having been left overnight by his parents at the home of a known drug abuser. Death was found to be due to natural causes but swabs taken from the child's body revealed the presence of morphine and amphetamine. The child's siblings were then made the subject of emergency protection orders and taken into foster care pending the hearing of applications for care orders. The local authority sought disclosure of certain documents from the Crown Prosecution Service ('CPS') which it was holding in connection with unrelated charges brought against the drug abuser. This was refused and an application was made for an order for disclosure. *Held*, generally in cases where a party to care proceedings sought disclosure of the social work records of a local authority, the public interest in maintaining the confidentiality of such records was balanced against the public interest in ensuring that justice was done to that party. However, the circumstances in this case were distinctive in that the authority's legitimate objective in seeking disclosure was to enable it to make a more informed decision about children who were the subject of care proceedings. In such a case, the issue of disclosure could be dealt with over two stages: disclosure by the CPS to the authority; and subsequent disclosure of those documents to other parties to the care proceedings. At either stage, disclosure could be resisted if it was thought that it could be prejudicial. Accordingly, disclosure of some but not all documents would be ordered and their circulation would be strictly limited. The court compared the exercise of its discretion to order disclosure with the power of the guardian ad litem to examine local authority records under the Children Act 1989, s 42.

Nottinghamshire County Council v H [1995] 2 FCR 365 (Family Division: Johnson J).

350   Care order—child living with grandparents—local authority withdrawing application for care order—grandparents seeking care order—factors to be considered

A local authority applied for care orders in respect of two children who lived with their mother. A series of interim orders were made and the children then lived with their maternal grandparents. Shortly afterwards, both children were diagnosed as suffering from a muscle-wasting disease which would confine them to wheelchairs within a few years. They also had developmental and behavioural problems and were emotionally disturbed. The authority wanted to withdraw its care order applications and sought supervision and residence orders in favour of the grandparents. The grandparents did not want the power or responsibility conferred by a residence order and considered that a care order would provide the support they needed. *Held*, there were circumstances in which a care order could have financial advantages for the grandparents and therefore have indirect advantages for the children. The fact that such a financial benefit would materially contribute to the childrens' welfare was a factor which could properly be regarded as relevant. It was difficult to conceive of circumstances in which it would not be wrong in principle to oblige an individual who had not applied for, and did not desire, a residence order to accept such an order and such responsibility. If the power to impose a residence order was not exercised, there would be no practicable means of preventing the parents having parental responsibility save by the making of a public law order. Although the court should be slow to make a care order where an authority did not want it, the court should not shrink from exercising the power to do so provided the threshold criteria were satisfied and the welfare of the children demanded it. In the present case, the welfare of the children demanded that a care order be made and, accordingly, an order would be made.

Re K (Care Order or Residence Order) [1995] 1 FLR 675 (Family Division: Stuart-White J).

351   Care order—child temporarily resident in England and Wales—jurisdiction of court

A mother and child from Jamaica had been living in England for several years and were facing deportation. The local authority applied for a care order in respect of the child. The question arose whether in view of the child's residential status, the court had jurisdiction to make public law orders under the Children Act 1989, Pt IV, if the threshold criteria of s 31 were met. *Held*, in deciding the jurisdictional basis for an application under Pt IV, it was necessary to consider Parliament's intention when interpreting the Act. The Act did not give any guidance on the issue, s 31(8) being of illustrative rather than defining assistance. Since the object of the Act was to provide the best solution to children's difficulties that concerned adults, courts and local authorities could provide, the least restrictive interpretation should be applied. There were strong policy reasons why the range of children in relation to whom local authorities could make applications should be equally broad as the range of children covered by private law orders under s 8. Thus, for the court to have jurisdiction to entertain a care application under Pt IV, the child concerned should either be habitually resident in England and Wales or present in England and Wales at the time when the application was made. Accordingly, the court would have jurisdiction to entertain the local authority's application.

Re R (Care Orders: Jurisdiction) [1995] 1 FLR 711 (Family Division: Singer J).

352   Care order—contact with grandparent—application for leave to seek contact—circumstances to be taken into account

Under the Children Act 1989, s 34(3), on an application made by any person who has obtained the leave of the court to make an application for contact with a child in the care of a local authority, the court may make such order as it considers appropriate with respect to the contact which is to be allowed between the child and that person.

It has been held that where a court is faced with a grandparent's application for leave to apply for a contact order, it would be anomalous were the court not to take into account for the purposes of exercising its discretion under s 34(3), the criteria specifically laid out for consideration in s 10(9). As well as having regard to all the circumstances of the case, the court should also have regard at least to (1) the nature of the contact sought, (2) the connection between the applicant and the child and, although grandparents have not been placed in a special category, contact between a child and his family is assumed to be beneficial, (3) the crucially significant factor of disruption because the need for stability and security after a child has been taken into care is usually vital, and (4) the wishes of the parents and the local authority which, although not determinative, are material.

Re M (Care: Contact: Grandmother's Application for Leave) [1995] 3 FCR 550 (Court of Appeal: Butler-Sloss, Simon Brown and Ward LJJ).

353   Care order—effect and duration

See Re L (Minors) (Sexual abuse: Standard of proof), para 355.

354   Care order—threshold conditions—likelihood of significant harm to child—determination of risk of harm

The Children Act 1989, s 31(2)(a) provides that the court may only make a care order if it is satisfied that the child concerned is suffering, or is likely to suffer, significant harm.

A mother had four daughters, two by her first husband and two by a subsequent partner. The eldest daughter alleged that she had been sexually abused by the partner, who was charged with rape. The local authority applied for care orders in respect of the younger daughters. The partner was acquitted of rape, but the authority proceeded with the applications, asking the judge to find, on the civil standard of proof, that the partner had sexually abused the eldest daughter or that there was a substantial risk that he had done so. The applications were dismissed on the ground that the judge could not be sure to the requisite high standard of proof that the eldest daughter's allegations were true, a decision affirmed on appeal. On the authority's further appeal, held, Lords Browne-Wilkinson and Lloyd of Berwick dissenting, in s 31(2)(a), 'likely' meant a real possibility, one which could not sensibly be ignored having regard to the nature and gravity of the feared harm in the particular case. In cases involving the care of children, the standard of proof was the ordinary civil standard of the balance of probabilities. The local authority based its case on the second limb of s 31(2)(a), relying on the allegation that over many years the eldest daughter had been subject to repeated abuse. The younger girls were not at risk unless the eldest had been abused by the partner in the past. If she had not been abused, there was no reason to think her sisters might be abused. To decide that they were at risk because there was a possibility that the eldest daughter had been abused would be to base the decision not on fact but on the suspicion that she might have been abused. This would lower the threshold prescribed by Parliament. Accordingly, the appeal would be dismissed.

Re H (Minors) (Child Abuse: Threshold Conditions) [1996] 1 All ER 1 (House of Lords: Lord Goff of Chieveley, Browne-Wilkinson, Mustill, Lloyd of Berwick and Nicholls of Birkenhead). Decision of Court of Appeal [1995] 1 FLR 643 affirmed.

355   Care proceedings—allegations of sexual abuse—standard of proof

The Court of Appeal has held that, in relation to allegations of sexual abuse in family cases, the standard of proof is the balance of probabilities on which there has to be cogent evidence commensurate with the seriousness of the allegations. Once a judge has correctly applied this test, there is no reason to repeat the test on every occasion that he makes reference as to whether or not he is satisfied. The Children Act 1989 removes from the court any continuing control over children after a care order is made, unless or until a further application is made to the court. The powers of the court and the exercise of discretion under s 1 are then restored for the duration of any such application. Once a care order has been made the court has no further part to play in the future welfare of the child unless a care contact order has been made under s 34. The responsibility passes to the local authority in deciding whether to place the child for adoption and with whom the child is placed.

Re L (Minors) (Sexual abuse: Standard of proof) (1995) Times, 3 July (Court of Appeal: Butler-Sloss, Henry and Pill LJJ).

356   Care proceedings—confidential statements—disclosure in criminal proceedings

It has been held that statements made by parents to social workers carrying out a risk assessment in the course of care proceedings are covered by the Children Act 1989, s 98(2). The statements therefore cannot be used in criminal proceedings, nor can they be used for any other purpose without leave of the court.

Re T (Disclosure) [1995] Fam Law 603 (Plymouth County Court: Judge Wigmore). Oxfordshire CC v P [1995] 2 All ER 225 (para 361) followed.

357 Care proceedings—discovery of documents—report disclosed in child care proceedings—criminal proceedings—court's discretion to disclose

A child was admitted to hospital after drinking a quantity of methadone in the home of her parents who were both drug addicts. Emergency protection orders were made in relation to the child and her brother and they were placed in foster homes. In support of her case in care proceedings, the mother commissioned a medical report relating to the child's consumption of the methadone. The report was filed with the court and made available to the other parties to the proceedings. Police, who were investigating whether any criminal offences had been committed, obtained an order for disclosure of the report to them. On appeal by the mother against the decision to make the order, she contended that the report was protected by legal professional privilege, which the court could not override, and that disclosure would infringe her privilege against self-incrimination. *Held*, legal professional privilege could not cover a report prepared pursuant to an order requiring it to be filed with the court and made available to all parties. Even if the report were privileged, the court was entitled to override the privilege on the grounds of the paramountcy of the child's welfare and the court's special role in care proceedings under the Children Act 1989. The privilege against self-incrimination prevented a person from being compelled or required to incriminate himself; it did not prevent him answering a question or producing a document if he wished to do so. The mother had voluntarily commissioned the report. She had then duly filed it, without being compelled to do so, and without claiming the privilege as she was entitled to do. The court had a discretion to disclose the report and had balanced the importance of confidentiality in care proceedings against the public interest in the administration of justice. Its decision to exercise its discretion to make an order in favour of the police was reasonable. Accordingly, the appeal would be dismissed.

Re L (Police Investigation: Privilege) [1995] 1 FLR 999 (Court of Appeal: Sir Thomas Bingham MR, Swinton and Morritt LJJ).

This decision has been affirmed: (1996) Times, 22 March, HL.

358 Care proceedings—discovery of documents—discovery against person not party to proceedings

During care proceedings, a father issued a subpoena duces tecum against the police to produce to the court copies of certain videos that he considered relevant to the proceedings. He had been suspected of sexually abusing his children and the videos were of police interviews with some of his children taken during the criminal investigation. These children were not themselves involved in the care proceedings. *Held*, since the police were not a party to the care proceedings, the issue of a subpoena duces tecum was the appropriate procedural course to take. The interviews could have an important bearing on the issues in question in the care proceedings. Accordingly, it would be appropriate to make an order allowing the father and the local authorities a limited number of copies.

Re M and K (Child Abuse: Video Evidence) [1996] 1 FCR 261 (Family Division: Sir Stephen Brown P).

359 Care proceedings—finding of sexual abuse by father—admissibility of finding in other care proceedings involving same father

See *Re S, S and A (Care Proceedings: Issue Estoppel)*, para 1330.

360 Care proceedings—legal representation—conflicting interests of siblings

Seven siblings were the subject of care proceedings and were to be represented by a single advocate. No objection to the care plan proposed by the local authority was made in respect of the younger children, but the second eldest child rejected the plan. At the hearing of the care proceedings, the guardian ad litem and the advocate sought the judge's leave for that child to be represented separately by a different solicitor. The judge refused on the ground that the matter had been raised so late in the proceedings that to arrange separate representation would abort the hearing. Instead, he urged the advocate to do his best to represent all the children. On the guardian ad litem's appeal, *held*, in truth, it was impossible for a single advocate to advance the position advocated by an authority in care proceedings and at the same time represent the interests of a child opposed to the care plan. Accordingly, the appeal would be allowed.

Re P (Minors) (Representation) [1996] 1 FCR 457 (Court of Appeal: Russell and Thorpe LJJ and Sir Ralph Gibson).

361   Care proceedings—non-accidental injuries to child—confession made by mother to guardian ad litem—confidentiality

Care proceedings were commenced when a 12-week-old baby suffered non-accidental injuries. A guardian ad litem was appointed and the baby's mother confessed to the guardian that she had caused the injuries. The guardian informed the social services department which informed the police who obtained a witness statement from the guardian. The Crown wanted to rely on the statement to prove criminal charges against the mother. The mother wished to be fully frank in the care proceedings but she was reluctant to file any statement in case it was used against her in the pending criminal proceedings. She had lost confidence in the guardian and made an application to have her replaced. *Held*, information received by a guardian ad litem before writing his report was as confidential as the report itself. Under the Children Act 1989, the court had to give paramount consideration to a child's welfare and there was a duty of full and frank disclosure of all matters whether or not they were favourable to a party. Proceedings under the wardship jurisdiction were confidential, the confidentiality covering reports, statements, proofs of evidence, documents filed and evidence given, and the same treatment should be accorded to proceedings under the 1989 Act. The police had been wrong to seek to make use of the admission made to the guardian and the guardian had been wrong to make a witness statement without first seeking the court's leave for its disclosure. Accordingly, to encourage frankness, the mother's application would be granted and the guardian would be replaced.

Oxfordshire County Council v P [1995] 2 All ER 225 (Family Division: Ward J).

362   Care proceedings—non-accidental injuries to child—confidential information provided by mother—disclosure in criminal proceedings

A local authority brought care proceedings under the Children Act 1989 in respect of five children following the death of a baby who was the twin sister of the youngest child. The care proceedings had been initiated after the hospital to which the baby had been admitted advised the authority's social services department of its suspicions that the baby's injuries were non-accidental. The older children were voluntarily accommodated with foster parents and the coroner and police began investigations into the cause of the baby's death. The children's mother did not make any statement about the baby to social workers or to the guardian ad litem because, while she recognised the importance of doing so, she was nervous of the consequences not only for herself but also for the baby's father. She therefore sought a direction that any statement she might make would be confidential to the care proceedings. *Held*, the clear effect of the Administration of Justice Act 1960, s 12 and the Family Proceedings Rules 1991, SI 1991/1247, r 4.23(1) was that evidence in proceedings concerning the upbringing or maintenance of a minor was confidential to the court. Any judge hearing an application for the disclosure of material in proceedings under the 1989 Act had to weigh a number of potentially conflicting factors, including (1) the interests of the child and his need to be protected not only from harm from either of the parents but also from an unjustified separation from his parents, (2) the need to encourage candour from all those involved in the proceedings, above all the parents who had the most relevant information to impart, (3) the public interest in both the proper functioning of inter-agency child protection procedures, and (4) the public interest in the proper conduct and defence of criminal proceedings. In an appropriate case, the court had power to direct that putative statements should remain confidential, albeit that such a direction would not bind future judges in the exercise of their discretion on any subsequent application for disclosure of evidence. Any incriminating statements that either parent might make were adequately protected from disclosure by the prohibition in the 1989 Act, s 98(2) and the general law against anything they said being used in criminal proceedings against them. Accordingly, the mother's application would be refused.

Cleveland County Council v F [1995] 2 All ER 236 (Family Division, Leeds: Hale J). *Oxfordshire CC v P* [1995] 2 All ER 225 (para 361) considered.

363   Care proceedings—non-accidental injuries to child—death—care proceedings in respect of second child—findings of court

Parents admitted responsibility for non-accidental injuries suffered by their daughter. She later died and it was possible that her death involved a traumatic assault. When the parents had a second child, the local authority made applications for a care order, an order terminating contact between the child and his parents and an order freeing him for adoption. A lengthy contested hearing was likely although avoidable if the parents consented or withdrew opposition to the making of the orders. The authority was concerned that such an outcome might enable the parents to claim, in future proceedings relating to as yet unborn children, that no determination of responsibility for the death of their first child was ever made in the care proceedings relating to their son. It prepared a document of proposed findings of fact which were intended to ensure that issues relating to the daughter's death could not be reopened in future litigation. The parents produced their own document amending the authority's one and the parties were unable to resolve the differences in them. *Held*, the formal admissions offered by the parents were more than sufficient to meet the threshold criteria in the Children Act 1989, s 31. They could not safely be entrusted with the care of any child. The court recognised the authority's concern to avoid a further presentation of complex medical issues at some uncertain future date, but it had to concentrate on the purposes and scope of the present proceedings, namely to settle the boy's future. The court had no definable statutory duty in relation to children as yet unborn. The authority's concerns had to be set against the benefit of concluding the contested proceedings by compromise. It was contrary to the public interest to risk the loss of the benefit of concluding proceedings by compromise through an over-complication of the means of reaching the compromise. The care and contact orders were made by consent and the parents did not oppose the order to free the child for adoption. Orders would be made accordingly.

Re D (A Minor) (Basis of Uncontested Care Order) [1995] 2 FCR 681 (Family Division: Thorpe J).

364 Care proceedings—non-accidental injuries to child—oral statements made to social worker—disclosure to police

The Family Proceedings Rules 1991, SI 1991/1247, r 4.23 provides that, notwithstanding any rule of court to the contrary, no document, other than a record of an order, held by the court will be disclosed, other than to a party, the legal representative of a party, the guardian ad litem, the Legal Aid Board, or a welfare officer, without leave of the judge or district judge.

Care proceedings were brought in relation to a child who had sustained unexplained injuries. The parents of the child made oral statements to a social worker regarding the injuries. The local authority sought to disclose those statements to the police but, at first instance, the judge held that the information was covered by the 1991 Rules, r 4.23 and should not be disclosed. On the authority's appeal, *held*, Auld LJ dissenting, although a written statement by a parent made for the purpose of care proceedings whether handed to a social worker, a guardian ad litem or the court direct, would be covered by r 4.23, oral admissions made to a social worker recorded in writing and placed in the social work file did not at that stage come within the ambit of r 4.23. There was a rather fine distinction between information in oral form provided to the social worker not being within the rule whereas substantially the same information reduced to writing by the social worker and filed with the court was within the rule. However, the wording of r 4.23 appeared to be plain: leave to disclose was only required in respect of documents held by the court. There was neither need nor justification for extending the scope of the clear words so as to require leave for the disclosure of information imparted to a social worker and recorded in case notes or a report which for one reason or another had never reached the court. Accordingly, the appeal would be allowed.

Re G (Minor) (Social Worker: Disclosure) [1996] 1 FLR 276 (Court of Appeal: Butler-Sloss and Auld LJJ and Sir Roger Parker).

365 Care proceedings—procedure—time estimates, discovery and presentation of evidence

The child of a paranoid schizophrenic mother and an alcoholic father was placed with foster parents immediately after his birth. In the course of care proceedings instituted by the local authority, it became clear that the mother was both incapable of looking after the child and that there was a high risk that she would be a danger to him. An assessment of the father concluded that he would be unable to care for the child full time on his own. The local authority decided that the child should be placed for adoption, that contact with the mother should be terminated, but that contact with the father should continue. A care order was made, and the court ordered that the child should be placed for adoption. In giving judgment, certain matters of practice were considered by the court. *Held*, the history of delay in the case emphasised the fact that all those who wished to participate in caring for a child had to show consistency in their commitment, and make their position clear as soon as possible. The case also demonstrated the need for accuracy in giving time estimates. Moreover, all parties in family proceedings, especially local authorities, had to be unbiased in presenting their evidence. A social worker's evidence had to be demonstrably fair, balanced and objective. In particular, where value judgments were made, a social worker had to include all the material, both negative and positive, on which his judgment was based and had to be able to demonstrate that he had reached a fair conclusion which was objectively based on all the disclosed material. Further difficulties in the case could have been avoided if the father's solicitors had considered what pre-trial discovery was necessary for the proper conduct of the proceedings. Although that did not mean that there could be discovery of all local authority files or social workers' notes, applications for discovery had to precede a trial and form part of the preparatory process. Applications for discovery during trial were to be discouraged.

Re JC (Care Proceedings: Procedure) [1995] 2 FLR 77 (Family Division: Wall J).

366 Care proceedings—report of guardian ad litem—disclosure

A local authority successfully applied for care orders to be made in respect of two children. At the conclusion of the case, an application was made under the Family Proceedings Courts (Children Act 1989) Rules 1991, SI 1991/1395, r 23, for the guardian ad litem's report in those proceedings to be disclosed to a family centre where the children were to receive therapeutic treatment. The justices granted leave to disclose the report. The authority appealed against part of that order on the basis that it was not necessary for leave to be granted. It submitted that the family centre was part of the authority and, since the authority was a party to the proceedings, all its officers were permitted to have sight of the documents held by the court without leave. Nobody resisted the proposal that the report should be made available to the family centre but the guardian ad litem was concerned to preserve the confidentiality of his report and to limit its distribution. *Held*, the overriding principle involved was the extent of the confidentiality of the guardian ad litem's report. The principle of confidentiality had to be strictly preserved. The dissemination of a report made to the court for the court's own information during proceedings was a matter of importance because the confidentiality was that of the court. The justices had been right to require that leave should be sought. The court should be told for whom the distribution of the report was particularly required. To make the report available to the family centre would suggest that any one of a number of different people might be afforded the opportunity to look at it. That seemed to be a matter which should concern the court at the time and some investigation should properly be made into who should be shown the report. Accordingly, the appeal would be dismissed.

Re C (Minors) (Guardian ad Litem: Disclosure of Report) [1995] 2 FCR 837 (Family Division: Sir Stephen Brown P).

367 Care proceedings—video recordings of police interviews in criminal investigation—subpoena duces tecum

See *Re M (Minors) (Care proceedings: Police videos)*, para 358.

368 Child abduction and custody—parties to conventions

The Child Abduction and Custody (Parties to Conventions) (Amendment) (No 4) Order 1995, SI 1995/1616 (in force on 1 July 1995), further amends the 1993 Order, SI 1993/3144, by adding Zimbabwe to the list of contracting states to the 1980 Hague Convention on the Civil Aspects of International Child Abduction. SI 1995/1031 is revoked.

The Child Abduction and Custody (Parties to Conventions) (Amendment) (No 3) Order 1995, SI 1995/1295 (in force on 1 March 1995), adds Italy to, and removes Malta from, the list of the contracting states to the European Convention on Recognition and Enforcement of Decisions concerning Custody of Children and on the Restoration of Custody of Children. SI 1995/264 is revoked.

369 Child abduction and custody—wrongful removal—abduction by father—order for disclosure of father's whereabouts

See *Re B (Abduction: Disclosure)*, para 1068.

370 Child abduction and custody—wrongful removal—abuse of process—delay in prosecution

An American mother and her English husband lived with their children in the United States until they separated. An order, made in American divorce proceedings, gave the mother temporary residence of the children and prohibited either party from removing them from the jurisdiction. The mother and children later flew to England. More than one year later, the father issued proceedings in England under the Hague Convention on the Civil Aspects of International

Child Abduction and the Child Abduction and Custody Act 1985. Apart from a directions hearing, no further steps were taken in the proceedings by the father for some eight months. He then applied for further directions and the mother applied to strike out his applications. *Held*, at the time of the mother's striking out application the children had been in England for two-and-a-half years. They were settled in their new environment. There was a significant delay between the children coming to England and the father commencing proceedings under the Convention. The proceedings had not been conducted with the expedition that was appropriate. Notwithstanding that more than 12 months had elapsed since the American order prohibiting the children's removal to England, the English court retained jurisdiction to entertain the application under the Hague Convention. However, the proceedings had not been properly prosecuted and now amounted to an abuse of process. Accordingly, the application to strike out the proceedings would be allowed.

Re G (Abduction: Striking Out Application) [1995] 2 FLR 410 (Family Division: Connell J).

371 Child abduction and custody—wrongful removal—acquiescence—views of child

The 1980 Hague Convention on the Civil Aspects of International Child Abduction, art 13 provides that the return of a child wrongfully removed from a contracting country may be refused if the child objects to being returned and has attained an age and degree of maturity at which it is appropriate to take account of his views.

An American national, the father of two children born in the United States of America, sought the return of the children who, he claimed, had been wrongfully retained by their mother in England. The mother claimed that the father had acquiesced in the unlawful retention and that one of the children, who did not wish to return to the United States, was old enough for her views to be taken into account. *Held*, the father could not be said to have acquiesced in the unlawful retention of the children merely because he accepted blame for the breakdown of his marriage to the mother and had waited six months before commencing proceedings under the Convention for their return. Regard should be had to the practical consequences of making an order for their return and the protection from harm afforded to them by the laws of the United States. The court was not satisfied that the child was sufficiently mature to have her views taken into account, but even if she was the court would still have exercised its discretion to order a return. Accordingly, the court would order the return of the children to the United States.

Re K (Abduction: Child's Objections) [1995] 1 FLR 977 (Family Division: Wall J).

372 Child abduction and custody—wrongful removal—child outside the jurisdiction— jurisdiction of court

The child of a United States national, his mother, and an Iraqi national, his father, lived in California with his mother after his parents separated. A Californian court ordered that the child was not to be removed from California without the consent of both parents, who had joint custody of the child, or the leave of the court. The father removed the child to Iraq but agreed to meet the mother in London to discuss the child's future. It fell to be determined whether the English court had jurisdiction, on the mother's application under the Child Abduction and Custody Act 1985, to make an order for the restoration of the child to his mother, at least temporarily, even though the child had not yet arrived in the United Kingdom. *Held*, the 1985 Act, by giving effect to the 1980 Hague Convention on the Civil Aspects of International Child Abduction, imposed a duty on the English court to co-operate with all other contracting states and to act expeditiously in making orders to secure the return of children taken wrongfully. Nothing either in the Act or the Convention expressly or impliedly limited the court's jurisdiction. Accordingly, by virtue of the wide terms of the 1985 Act, s 5, the court could give interim directions in respect of a child who was not yet in the United Kingdom. The court would make an order for the initial restoration of the child to his mother's care in England on the ground that there were substantial grounds for expecting that he would arrive in the United Kingdom with his father.

Re N (Child Abduction: Jurisdiction) [1995] 2 WLR 233 (Family Division: Wilson J).

373 Child abduction and custody—wrongful removal—custody—joint custody

Scotland

The 1980 Hague Convention on the Civil Aspects of International Child Abduction, art 3 provides that the removal or retention of a child is to be considered wrongful where it is in breach of rights of custody attributed to a person, either jointly or alone, under the law of the state in which the child was habitually resident immediately before the removal or retention, and at the time of the removal, those rights were actually exercised, either jointly or alone.

Rights of custody may arise in particular by operation of law, or by reason of a judicial or administrative decision. Article 5 provides that rights of custody include rights relating to the person of the child and, in particular, the right to determine the child's place of residence.

The parties married in Australia where the only child of the family was born. After the parties separated, the child lived with the mother but regularly stayed with the father at weekends and during the week. The mother decided that she wished to return to Scotland with the child, but the father refused to give his consent to the proposal. The mother left Australia with the child without giving the father prior notice, as she knew that he would have commenced proceedings to prevent her from doing so. Under Australian law, the parties had joint custody of the child, and on the father's application for an order for sole custody, the mother argued that she had been the only party exercising rights of custody within the meaning of art 3 of the Convention. *Held*, although the care and control that the father exercised over the child could be described as access, it was not the result of any court order to that effect and, therefore, he still had joint custody rights with the mother under Australian law. Moreover, in expressly exercising his right as guardian to refuse to allow the child to change his place of residence, the father had been exercising his joint right of custody at the time that the child was removed. The removal of the child from Australia was unlawful and, accordingly, the application would be granted.

McKiver v McKiver 1995 SLT 790 (Outer House).

374 Child abduction and custody—wrongful removal—discretion of court not to order return

The parents of three children lived in Australia. The father was diagnosed as suffering from a depressive illness and prescribed effective medication but before diagnosis he caused extraordinary stresses to the mother and children. The parents later separated and the children stayed with the mother. The father agreed to the mother taking the children to England for an extended holiday. Before their departure the mother began to suspect one of the daughters had been sexually interfered with and this was confirmed by a medical examination. Another child was referred to the local psychiatric resource with behavioural problems. The mother then took the children to England and refused to allow telephone contact with the father. The case was later referred to social services and the daughter attributed to her father the responsibility for sexual interference. When the father issued an originating summons for the return of the children to Australia, the mother conceded wrongful abduction but relied upon the defence in the 1980 Hague Convention on the Civil Aspects of International Child Abduction, art 13(b), that there was a grave risk that their returning would expose them to physical or psychological harm. *Held*, an art 13(b) defence must be weighed in the light of the immediate past and by a comparison of the risks involved in returning the children and those involved in refusing to return them. The mother had put the children at risk of grave psychological harm by removing them from their homeland by deception and obstructing contact with the father. The court must weigh the psychological harm of return against the psychological consequences of refusing return and in so doing must consider the primary purpose of the convention to ensure the swift return of abducted children. The children themselves were not opposed to returning to Australia although they did not want to be separated from their mother. She had made it clear that she would not return there under any circumstances even if it meant parting from the children. The court could not allow abducting parents to defeat the purpose of the Convention in this way and would not take the mother's ultimatum into account. Thus, the discretion under art 13(b) would not be exercised and the return of the children would be ordered.

N v N (Abduction: Article 13 Defence) [1995] 1 FCR 595 (Family Division: Thorpe J).

375 Child abduction and custody—wrongful removal—habitual residence—claims of other jurisdiction—emphasis placed on habitual residence

The parties lived in Texas and had one child. When they divorced, the Texas court made an order awarding them joint custody, with primary residence to the mother and contact to the father. With the father's consent, although in contravention of the order, the mother took the child to England. He returned to live with his father for several months but then returned to England again. It was intended that, after the child's first school term there, the mother would return him to his father. She failed to do so and, while she obtained an interim residence order in England, the Texas court awarded the father sole care and control and directed that the mother return the child to the father. When she did not, the father applied to the English court for the child's return under the Child Abduction and Custody Act 1985 and the court's inherent jurisdiction. At first instance, the judge found that the child was habitually resident in England and that the claims of the Texas jurisdiction could not prevail. On appeal, *held*, the father's initial consent to the child's removal to England constituted consent to the loss of the child's habitual residence in America and a claim of wrongful retention under the 1980 Hague Convention on the Civil Aspects of International Child Abduction was precluded. However, the judge erred in treating the claims of the Texan jurisdiction, which he would otherwise have regarded as predominant in the child's interests and those of international comity, as being displaced by the need to follow the spirit of the Convention in the emphasis placed on habitual residence. Taking into account the similarity in the Texan and English systems of law and procedure and the fact the child was a Texan child of Texan parents who had entrusted the matter of the child's upbringing to the Texas court, the court concluded that the claims of the Texas jurisdiction to decide his future were overwhelming. Accordingly, the appeal would be allowed.

Re K (Abduction: Consent: Forum Conveniens) [1995] 2 FLR 211 (Court of Appeal: Neill, Hoffmann and Waite LJJ).

376 Child abduction and custody—wrongful removal—habitual residence—declaration pending final determination by court in another jurisdiction

A father was granted a declaration that the removal of the child of the family by the mother from the jurisdiction of England and Wales was wrongful, within the meaning of the 1980 Hague Convention on the Civil Aspects of International Child Abduction, art 3. On the mother's appeal, *held*, the jurisdiction for an English court to comply with a request for a declaration as to the wrongful removal of a child was given by the Child Abduction and Custody Act 1985, s 8. Although such a declaration presupposed that a child was habitually resident in England at the time of the removal, it did not necessarily amount to a final determination of the issue. Even if a request for a declaration was made before a final decision as to a child's place of habitual residence was made in another state which was a signatory to the Hague Convention, it was still preferable for an English court to make a declaration based on the assumption that the place of habitual residence was England. It was therefore inevitable that an English court would have to consider on a provisional basis matters which were to be decided by the other state, and it could not debar itself from the power to grant a declaration where a request was properly made. Accordingly, the appeal would be dismissed.

Re P (Abduction: Declaration) [1995] 1 FLR 831 (Court of Appeal: Butler-Sloss and Millett LJJ and Sir Ralph Gibson).

377 Child abduction and custody—wrongful removal—notice of removal

A Spanish separation order awarded custody of the children of the marriage to their English mother and contact to their Spanish father. In breach of the order, the mother took the children to England without the father's consent. She commenced divorce proceedings in England and sought a residence order in respect of the children. The father protested to the court by letter but made no application under the 1980 Hague Convention on the Civil Aspects of International Child Abduction for their return. It fell to be determined whether, in the absence of convention proceedings, the court should nevertheless regard itself as having received 'notice of wrongful removal or retention of a child' within the meaning of art 16 which would prevent the court from deciding on the merits of rights of custody, and whether it had a duty to secure that the father was informed of his rights under the Convention. *Held*, nothing in art 16 restricted the word 'notice' to notice from any particular source or in any particular form. Accordingly, a court which became aware in any manner that there had been a wrongful removal or retention of a child within the meaning of art 3 was to be regarded as having received notice of that wrongful removal or retention for the purposes of art 16. Although there was no rule regulating procedure in the absence of convention proceedings, the court nevertheless had a statutory duty to comply with art 16 and should refrain from deciding the merits of rights of custody unless or until it found that no application under the Convention had been lodged within a reasonable time of its receiving notice of the wrongful removal or retention. The court had a duty to secure that the parent in the state from which the child had been removed was informed of his rights under the Convention unless it was clear that there had been acquiescence in the wrongful removal or retention in the sense of positive acceptance of the situation. The court in the present proceedings had not received an application under the Convention within a reasonable time following receipt of the notice so that it was no longer barred by art 16 from granting a residence order in respect of the children. However, as there was no evidence of any positive acceptance of the situation by the father, it would be appropriate to inform him of his rights under the Convention.

R v R (Residence Order: Child Abduction) [1995] 4 All ER 115 (Family Division: Stuart-White J).

378 Child abduction and custody—wrongful removal—removal between different United Kingdom jurisdictions

Divorced parents had a daughter who lived with her grandmother. The parents later remarried, had a son and separated again. Divorce proceedings were issued and matters relating to the residence of the son were dealt with, but no decree nisi was ever granted. A year later, the grandmother objected to the mother's plan to take her daughter on a holiday to Israel. The mother applied for a specific issue order. Meanwhile in proceedings in Scotland, the grandmother was granted an interim custody order. Following an attempt by the mother to remove the daughter from the jurisdiction, the grandmother obtained an order in the English courts for the return of the daughter to Scotland. The mother applied for a residence order in England. She also applied for the Scottish proceedings to be stayed on the ground that there was a pending residence application in England. At the same time the grandmother applied to have the English proceedings stayed on the ground that there were advanced proceedings in Scotland. The English proceedings were transferred to the High Court. *Held*, in principle, the English court had jurisdiction by reason of the divorce proceedings. Normally this would deprive the Scottish court of jurisdiction. However, on the specific facts of this case it was more appropriate for the proceedings to be dealt with in Scotland. The divorce proceedings were issued primarily to deal with the son's residence and had no continuing life or utility. The mother's residence application was issued to obstruct the Scottish proceedings. The latter proceedings were ready for trial having been issued first. In addition, the daughter was within the jurisdiction of the Scottish court and had been for most of her life. Accordingly, the court would direct that no order be made on the mother's residence application until further order.

Re S (Jurisdiction to Stay Application) [1995] 1 FLR 1093 (Family Division: Thorpe J).

379 Child abduction and custody—wrongful removal—return of child—child's own views

The 1980 Hague Convention on the Civil Aspects of International Child Abduction, art 13 provides that the return of a child wrongfully removed from a contracting state may be refused if the child objects to being returned and has attained an age and degree of maturity at which it is appropriate to take account of the child's own views.

A child lived in Ireland with his mother and her boyfriend but was removed by his natural father and taken back to England after the child made allegations that he was being maltreated. The mother made an application, under the Convention, for the child to be returned to Ireland, on the ground that he had been wrongfully removed. The judge granted an order for the return of the child to Ireland but the matter was returned to the court for reconsideration of further evidence. At that hearing, the child successfully applied to be joined as a party and appealed against the original order. The mother cross-appealed against the child being joined as a party. *Held*, although a child would only be made a party to a Convention application in exceptional cases, the issue in this case was between the child and his mother and not between the parents. Therefore, the only way to consider the validity of the child's objection was by his own legal representation, and the mother's appeal from the order joining the child as a party would be refused. Article 13 applied because the child had expressed valid and genuine objections and was mature enough for his concerns to be taken into account. There was also a substantial amount of evidence to suggest the child's well-being could be threatened if he were to return to Ireland. Accordingly, the order for the child's return would be discharged and he would, instead, be made a ward of court.

Re M (Child Abduction: Child's Objection to Return) [1995] 1 FCR 170 (Court of Appeal: Butler-Sloss, Staughton and Hoffmann LJJ).

380 Child abduction and custody—wrongful removal—return of child—risk of harm

A mother wrongfully removed her child from the United States in breach of the father's custody rights under the 1980 Hague Convention on the Civil Aspects of International Child Abduction, art 3. She claimed that there was a grave risk that the child's return would expose him to physical or psychological harm or otherwise place him in an intolerable situation, which meant that, under art 13(b), the court would not be required to order the return of the child. At first instance, the court declared that the child ought to be returned to the United States. On appeal by the mother, *held*, the threshold of proof required by art 13(b) was very high and cases where it was met were exceptional. However, the signatories to the convention had clearly envisaged that there could be circumstances in which the return of a child would expose him to a grave risk of harm or an intolerable situation and it appeared that the present case was a rare example of those criteria being met. Accordingly, the appeal would be allowed and the child would be permitted to remain in the United Kingdom.

Re F (A Minor) (Child abduction: Risk If Returned) (1995) Times, 15 February (Court of Appeal: Butler-Sloss and Millett LJJ and Sir Christopher Slade).

381 Child abduction and custody—wrongful removal—right to determine child's place of residence—removal to place outside jurisdiction of habitual residence

An English mother and a Greek father married and had a child. They lived in Greece but separated shortly after the child was born. On the mother's application, a Greek court made a provisional order committing the physical custody of the child to the mother. Her subsequent application for a substantive order to that effect did not progress because of a lawyers' strike. When the father later threatened to remove the child the mother brought the child back to England and the father issued an originating summons under the 1980 Hague Convention on the Civil Aspects of International Child Abduction for the return of the child to Greece. *Held,* the removal of a child was to be considered wrongful where it was in breach of custody rights attributed to a person either jointly or alone under the law of the state in which the child was habitually resident immediately before the removal. Under the Greek Civil Code, 'parental care' included 'the care of the person of the child' and that was defined as including the determination of the child's place of residence. The provisional order temporarily committed the care of the person of the child exclusively to the mother. There were no other relevant statutory provisions or authorities as to whether that extended to the selection of a place of residence outside the jurisdiction of the Greek court and there were no previous decisions of the superior court. The father had to demonstrate that the removal was wrong according to Greek law. He had failed to do so and, accordingly, the summons would fail.

Re M (A Minor) (Abduction) [1995] 3 FCR 99 (Family Division: Thorpe J).

382 Child abduction and custody—wrongful removal—rights of custody

Scotland

The 1980 Convention on the Civil Aspects of International Child Abduction, art 3 provides that the removal or retention of a child is to be considered wrongful where it is in breach of rights of custody attributed to a person, either jointly or alone, under the law in the state in which the child was habitually resident immediately before his removal or retention, and at the time of removal or retention, those rights were actually exercised, either jointly or alone, or would have been exercised but for the removal or retention.

A husband and wife lived in Spain, where the child of the family was born. When the parties separated, they entered into a separation agreement which was binding under Spanish law and which provided that their right of joint custody under Spanish law was to be preserved. When the wife went with the child to live in Scotland without the husband's knowledge or agreement, the husband sought an order for the child's return to Spain, relying on the Child Abduction and Custody Act 1985. The wife opposed the application, arguing that the husband did not have rights of custody within the meaning of the Convention, art 3. *Held,* as Spanish law allowed legal rights and powers in relation to a child to be shared between parents, it was necessary to have regard to the situation as a whole in order to determine whether the rights enjoyed by a parent amounted to rights of custody for the purposes of art 3. Here, although the separation agreement gave the wife care and control of the child and allowed her to change her domicile, the husband had custody rights in important respects which went beyond access, including the right to supervise the child's upbringing. Moreover, as the agreement provided that the child could only be taken out of Spain on holiday subject to certain limitations, it was implicit that the child's residence could not be changed without the husband's consent. Although the enjoyment of a right of access was not enough by itself to amount to rights of custody, having regard to the terms of the agreement, the husband had custody rights. It followed that the child's removal was a breach of his rights and amounted to wrongful removal. Accordingly, the application would be granted.

Bordera v Bordera 1995 SLT 1176 (Outer House).

383 Child abduction and custody—wrongful removal—undertaking given to court of another jurisdiction—application of Hague Convention

Two children were born in Italy of an English mother and an Italian father. Following the breakdown of the relationship between the parents, the mother applied to the Italian court for a custody order in respect of each child. Having received advice that her custody application stood little chance of success she brought the children to England where she sought a residence order.

The father started proceedings in Italy and an order was made directing that the children were to live with the father in the interim, although custody was vested in the local authority in Italy. The father then filed his answer in the English proceedings and made an application for a peremptory return order. Such an order was made at first instance but only after an adjournment resulting from concerns regarding the practical arrangements that would be made if the children were returned to Italy. Those concerns were allayed by the giving of certain undertakings by the father. The mother appealed, introducing new evidence to show that the arrangements in Italy were inadequate. *Held*, the principles to be applied in Hague Convention and non-Convention cases were prima facie the same. The father had given the judge at first instance undertakings regarding the points which had caused the mother anxiety. Although the mother had introduced new evidence, the father had given further undertakings in Italy confirming his willingness to fulfil those given to the judge at first instance. Judges in one country could assume that the courts in another country would take the same serious view of a failure to honour undertakings given to a court of any jurisdiction. Accordingly, the appeal would be dismissed.

Re M (Abduction: Non-Convention Country) [1995] 1 FLR 89 (Court of Appeal: Sir Thomas Bingham MR, Ralph Gibson and Waite LJJ).

384   Child abuse—standard of proof—weight of expert witnesses' opinions

A mother and her husband had four children who were taken into care by the local authority. The mother later had a baby by a different man. The authority suspected that the four children had been sexually abused by their mother and various of her partners, including her husband, based on statements made by the children and their foster parents, as well as the children's behaviour. Applications were made by the authority for contact between the four children and their parents to be terminated, for three of the children to be adopted and for the baby's future to be decided. Much evidence of gross sexual practices was presented from the mother, foster parents and children, and eleven experts expressed the opinion that the children had been sexually abused. *Held*, the accuracy of a child's statements in this case was a matter for the court and not for the experts and their opinion would therefore carry little weight or was inadmissible. When assessing the likelihood of future harm, allegations of past conduct by the parents must be left out of account unless the court was satisfied as to those allegations on the balance of probabilities. The court was satisfied, on the balance of probabilities, that the four older children had been sexually abused by their mother and various partners and there was also a likelihood that the fifth child would suffer significant harm if it remained with the mother and her partner. Accordingly, the authority's application with regard to the four older children would be granted. A care order in respect of the baby would be granted. An application to free her for adoption would be adjourned.

Re B (Child Sexual Abuse: Standard of Proof) [1995] 1 FLR 904n (Family Division: Johnson J).

385   Child care—local authority—duty to child in care—right of action against authority

See *X (Minors) v Bedfordshire County Council; M (a Minor) v Newham London Borough Council; E (A Minor) v Dorset County Council; Christmas v Hampshire County Council; Keating v Bromley London Borough Council*, para 2833.

386   Child care—placement of children—short-term placements

The Children (Short-term Placements) (Miscellaneous Amendments) Regulations 1995, SI 1995/2015 (in force on 25 August 1995), amend the Foster Placement (Children) Regulations 1991, SI 1991/910, the Arrangements for Placement of Children (General) Regulations 1991, SI 1991/890, the Placement of Children with Parents etc Regulations 1991, SI 1991/893, and the Review of Children's Cases Regulations 1991, SI 1991/895. The total length of time for which a series of short-term placements may last and still be regarded as one placement for certain purposes is extended, the requirements for visits to a child to supervise a series of short-term placements are modified and special provision is made for a review of cases where there is a series of short-term placements.

387   Child Support Act 1995

The Child Support Act 1995 makes provision in respect of child support maintenance and other maintenance, and provides for a child maintenance bonus. The Act received the royal assent on 19 July 1995. Certain provisions came into force on 4 September, 1 October and 18 December 1995 and on 22 January 1996: SI 1995/2302, 3262. The remaining provisions come into force on a day or days to be appointed. For details of commencement, see the commencement table in the title STATUTES.

Sections 1–9 insert ss 28A–28H into the Child Support Act 1991 ('the 1991 Act'). Where a maintenance assessment is in force, the person with care of the child or the absent parent in respect of whom the assessment was made, may apply in writing within a specified time limit to the Secretary of State for a 'departure direction'. Such a direction requires a child support officer to make a fresh maintenance assessment, and must specify the basis on which the amount of maintenance is to be fixed. The Secretary of State is obliged to give an application preliminary consideration, and he may reject it at this stage. Provision is also made for a maintenance assessment which is the subject of an application for a departure direction to be reviewed, and for the application to lapse following a review. The Secretary of State may impose on the absent parent a condition that he must continue making regular maintenance payments whilst his departure direction application is being considered. The Secretary of State can determine the application himself or refer it to a child support appeal tribunal. General principles are set out, to which the Secretary of State must have regard in determining a departure direction application, and provision is made in respect of the circumstances in which a departure direction may be given. A direction has effect for a specified period, until the occurrence of a specified event or until it is cancelled in circumstances prescribed by regulations made by the Secretary of State. The child support officer to whom the case is referred must comply with the departure direction as soon as reasonably practicable. The absent parent in respect of whom the maintenance assessment is made, or the person with care of the child, may appeal against the Secretary of State's decision to a child support appeal tribunal. Transitional provisions are made in respect of these new provisions.

Schedule 1 contains supplemental provision in respect of departure direction applications, and Sch 2 provides for the cases in which a departure direction may be given, and for controls on the provisions which may be included in a direction.

Where a person is in receipt of child maintenance and also income support or a job seeker's allowance, s 10 allows the Secretary of State to make regulations for the payment in certain circumstances of a child maintenance bonus.

Section 11 provides that if a child support officer does not have enough information to make an assessment, or conduct or complete a review, he may make an interim maintenance assessment. Where an application is made to the Secretary of State for a review of the amount of the maintenance assessment on the ground that there has been a change of circumstance, s 12 provides that the Secretary of State must refer the application to a child support officer. The officer must take account of a change of circumstance only if he knows about it or has been notified of it. In addition, s 13 provides that an officer may continue a review even if the maintenance assessment ceases to be in force during the course of the review. If he is satisfied that the maintenance assessment was not validly made, s 14 allows him to cancel it. He may also cancel an assessment in other prescribed circumstances. Section 15 gives a child support officer power to instigate reviews himself in certain circumstances.

Section 16 introduces a new provision whereby an appeal under the 1991 Act lapses if, before the appeal is heard, a review decision is made which is the same as the decision which would have been reached on a successful appeal. Section 17 allows the Lord Chancellor to provide for officers other than Child Support Commissioners to determine matters other than appeals, applications for leave to appeal, or references.

Section 18 defers the application of the 1991 Act in cases where a maintenance agreement is made before 5 April 1993, or where a maintenance order is in force and the parent concerned is not receiving a relevant benefit. In addition, s 19 provides that the Secretary of State does not have to proceed with an application for a maintenance assessment made on the basis of a benefit claim, if the benefit claim has been withdrawn or disallowed.

By s 20, a declaration of parentage may be applied for after a maintenance assessment has been made, and the courts may have regard to such declarations when making 'topping-up' maintenance orders. Section 21 enables the Secretary of State to recover DNA testing fees from an alleged parent who does not dispute the results of the test, or who is subsequently declared to be the parent of the child concerned. He may also, under s 22, impose a financial penalty for late payment of child support maintenance, as an alternative to interest.

Section 23 allows the Secretary of State to reimburse overpayments of child support maintenance, and to recover such overpayments from the recipient. Compensatory payments may be made under s 24 to the person caring for the child and receiving family credit or disability working allowance, if his child support maintenance is reduced because of changes to child support legislation. Section 25 introduces a new provision into the Social Security Administration Act 1992 such that where maintenance is being collected by the Secretary of State, income support and other benefits may be paid at a level which has not been reduced to take account of child maintenance payments and the maintenance payments retained by the Secretary of State.

Under s 26, the power to make regulations or orders under the Act is exercisable by statutory instrument. Section 27 contains interpretation provisions, s 28 contains financial provisions, and s 29 relates to Northern Ireland. Schedule 3 makes numerous minor and consequential amendments. Section 30 relates to the short title, commencement and extent of the Act.

388   Child support—child support commissioners—procedure

The Child Support Commissioners (Procedure) (Amendment) Regulations 1995, SI 1995/2907 (in force on 4 December 1995), amend the 1992 Regulations, SI 1992/2640, by providing for nominated officers to perform certain functions of a commissioner and for the consideration by a commissioner of decisions made by a nominated officer.

389   Child support—compensation for recipients of family credit and disability working allowance

The Child Support (Compensation for Recipients of Family Credit and Disability Working Allowance) Regulations 1995, SI 1995/3263 (in force on 23 January 1996), provide (1) that the relevant time, for the purposes of the Child Support Act 1995, s 24 (compensation payments for a reduction in child support maintenance attributable to changes in child support legislation), is the day immediately prior to the effective date of the revised assessment; (2) for the calculation of the compensation payment; (3) for the calculation, in particular cases, of the reduction in child support maintenance; (4) that payment of compensation is not to be made if the amount of the payment is less than a specified amount; and (5) for the payment of compensation in instalments or as a lump sum.

390   Child support—deduction from earnings order—defective order

The Child Support Act 1991, s 2 provides that where the Secretary of State or any child support officer is considering the exercise of any discretionary power conferred by the Act, he must have regard to the welfare of any child likely to be affected by his decision. The Child Support (Collection and Enforcement) Regulations 1992, SI 1992/1989, reg 22(3)(a) provides that one of the grounds on which an appeal against a deduction from earnings order may be made is that the order is defective.

Following a husband and wife's separation, the Child Support Agency assessed the husband's liability to maintain the two children of the family. When a deduction from earnings order was made against the husband, he appealed to the magistrates' court, arguing that the agency had failed to take account of the welfare principle under the 1991 Act, s 2 in making the order which should, therefore, be quashed. The justices decided that they had jurisdiction to consider whether to quash the order, but concluded that the agency had taken account of the welfare principle and so dismissed the husband's appeal. On the husband's further appeal, *held*, although s 2 required the Secretary of State, through the agency, to have regard to the welfare principle, he was not obliged to attach significant weight to it, as welfare was not a paramount or even significant consideration and had no influence on the quantification of an absent parent's liability to maintain a child. Here, the husband had been properly assessed in the manner provided for by the 1992 Regulations and the Act and, therefore, could not argue in magistrates' court proceedings that the deduction from earnings order was defective within the meaning of the 1992 Regulations, reg 22. He could, however, have applied for judicial review of the agency's decision on the ground that insufficient weight had been attached to the children's welfare. Accordingly, the appeal would be dismissed.

R v Secretary of State for Social Security, ex p Biggin [1995] 1 FLR 851 (Queen's Bench Division: Thorpe J).

391   Child support—maintenance assessment—appeal against assessment—contemporaneous application for injunction to prevent dissipation of funds

See *Department of Social Security v Butler*, para 1714.

392   Child support—maintenance order—application for judicial review—remedy provided by statute

An application for financial provision for twins was made by their mother and determined in the father's absence. He initially admitted paternity but later denied he was the father, calling for

DNA tests to establish paternity. Although he knew that the application had been made, he spent some time overseas and was unable to attend at the hearing because his solicitors were unable to inform him of its date. The justices were of the opinion that the father was intent upon avoiding proceedings and he was ordered to pay a periodic sum. He applied for judicial review of that decision. *Held*, judicial review would not be granted where there was a statutory appeal procedure under the Children Act 1989, s 94, and the remedy thereby provided was adequate as a means of resolving the complaint. The substantial delay which would result from having the application heard was also an influencing factor. Accordingly, the application would be dismissed.

R v High Peak Magistrates' Court, ex p B [1995] 3 FCR 237 (Queen's Bench Division: Cazalet J).

393 Child support—maintenance scheme—proposed changes

The Secretary of State for Social Security has presented a white paper to Parliament, *Improving Child Support* (Cm 2745), setting out the government's proposals for changes to the child support maintenance scheme. The changes include changes to the maintenance formula (which took effect from April 1995), the introduction of an element of discretion so as to allow departure from the formula assessment in certain cases (this will be dependent upon legislation) and a number of changes in the administration of the scheme. Under the changes to the formula, no one will be required (subject to exemption and subject to a minimum payment) to pay more than 30 per cent of net income, or more than 33 per cent if arrears are also being paid off. A broadly-based allowance in exempt income will be introduced in recognition of any property or capital settlement effected before April 1993, and another such allowance will be introduced to contribute towards travel to work costs where these are high. In an effort to assist absent parents who have responsibility for a step family, reasonable housing costs will be allowed in full in all cases. The 'additional element' provided by the formula will be restricted, but the right to apply to the courts for a further order in such cases will be retained. Where the revised formula results in lower receipts by recipients of family credit or disability working allowance, a non-benefit compensation payment will be available. Under proposed legislation a parent who is in receipt of income support or jobseeker's allowance and who has care of a child for each week for which maintenance is paid will receive a credit which will be payable as a lump sum when she takes up work of 16 hours or more. To enable the Child Support Agency to tackle its backlog of work, it will postpone handling cases where parents with care have been receiving income support since April 1993, and also where the parent with care has failed to reply adequately to the agency's inquiries made before July 1994. In cases of significant delay by the agency in making a maintenance assessment and in requesting payment, consideration will be given to not enforcing more than six months' arrears of maintenance provided that the absent parent gives suitable undertakings. Reviews of assessments for changes of circumstances will be implemented more quickly and periodic reviews will be carried out at two-yearly intervals, instead of each year. There will be a moratorium on the charging of the agency's fees until April 1997; on the same date penalty charges for late payment will replace interest charges. Changes are also to be introduced relating to interim maintenance assessments, and to the date of liability where the maintenance inquiry form is returned promptly. The exercise of the discretion envisaged in proposed legislation for departing from the assessment formula may be applied for by either parent and the other parent will be entitled to make representations on the issue. A plea for a departure from the formula by the absent parent will have to be supported by evidence of special circumstances and also of the hardship which would result if the formula were to be applied.

394 Child support—regulations—miscellaneous amendments

The Child Support (Miscellaneous Amendments) Regulations 1995, SI 1995/123 (in force on 16 February 1995), (1) amend the Child Support (Information, Evidence and Disclosure) Regulations 1992, SI 1992/1812, by imposing an obligation on employers to provide information for certain purposes about an alleged absent parent who denies parentage; (2) amend the Child Support (Maintenance Arrangements and Jurisdiction) Regulations 1992, SI 1992/2645, by providing that where an interim maintenance assessment has been made and at that time there was a court order in force in respect of children covered by that interim maintenance assessment, the effective date of any subsequent maintenance assessment is the effective date of that interim maintenance assessment; and (3) further amend the Child Support (Maintenance Assessment Procedure) Regulations 1992, SI 1992/1813, so as to (a) make provision for the effective date of an interim maintenance assessment reviewed under the Child

Support Act 1991, s 16 or 19(1) and to clarify the provision for the setting of the effective date of an interim maintenance assessment where a court order is in force in respect of the relevant child, (b) set out the information to be included in the notification which must be given where a Category A interim maintenance assessment is made, or a fresh such assessment issued after a review, (c) provide for the setting of the effective date of a maintenance assessment where a court order is in force in respect of the relevant children at the time the assessment is made, or was in force at the time the assessment was made which preceded the making of the maintenance assessment, and (d) make additional provision for the effective date of an assessment, reviewed because the original effective date was incorrect.

The Child Support and Income Support (Amendment) Regulations 1995, SI 1995/1045 (in force in part on 13 April 1995 and in part on 18 April 1995), (1) amend the Child Support Appeal Tribunals (Procedure) Regulations 1992, SI 1992/2641, by providing for a pending appeal to continue when a party to it dies; (2) further amend the Child Support (Arrears, Interest and Adjustment of Maintenance Assessments) Regulations 1992, SI 1992/1816, so as to remove the liability for interest in respect of any day after 17 April 1995 and to provide for overpaid maintenance to be set off against arrears of maintenance and against current maintenance payable; (3) further amend the Child Support (Collection and Enforcement) Regulations 1992, SI 1992/1989, by (a) providing for a protected earnings rate in deduction from earnings orders in respect of interim maintenance assessments and in cases where arrears are due under a previous assessment but there is no current assessment in existence, (b) defining the grounds upon which magistrates may discharge a deduction from earnings order as defective and making further provision for discharge of a deduction from earnings order by the Secretary of State; (4) further amend the Child Support Fees Regulations 1992, SI 1992/3094, by providing that no assessment fee or collection fee is payable where it would otherwise have become payable on or after 18 April 1995 and before 6 April 1997; (5) further amend the Child Support (Information, Evidence and Disclosure) Regulations 1992 supra, by requiring Crown servants to provide information in certain circumstances and providing for information given by one party to a maintenance assessment to be disclosed to the other in certain circumstances; (6) further amend the Child Support (Maintenance Arrangements and Jurisdiction) Regulations 1992 supra, by providing for maintenance orders under specified enactments to be relevant for the purposes of the Child Support Act 1991, ss 8 (role of the courts with respect to maintenance for children), 10 (relationship between maintenance assessments and certain court orders and related matters); (7) further amend the Child Support (Maintenance Assessment Procedure) Regulations 1992 supra, by providing for (a) two further categories of interim maintenance assessment, (b) periodical reviews to take place every 104 weeks, and (c) the effective date of a maintenance assessment in certain circumstances to be eight weeks after a maintenance inquiry form has been sent to an absent parent; (8) further amend the Child Support (Maintenance Assessments and Special Cases) Regulations 1992, SI 1992/1815, by (a) requiring a child support officer, in certain circumstances, to make allowances for travel to work costs and for certain property transfers in the calculation of child support maintenance, (b) providing that an absent parent must be left with not less than 70 per cent of his net income after deduction of the amount payable under a maintenance assessment and (c) removing the requirement to apportion housing costs; (9) further amend the Child Support (Miscellaneous Amendments and Transitional Provisions) Regulations 1994, SI 1994/227, by providing that the transitional provisions do not apply to Category D interim maintenance assessments and that the special provision for the amount of a maintenance assessment made following a review on a change of circumstances under the 1991 Act, s 17 where the transitional provisions apply also applies to a review of a decision of a child support officer under s 18 or a review at the instigation of a child support officer under s 19; and (10) further amend the Income Support (General) Regulations 1987, SI 1987/1967, by providing that if a person loses income support in respect of mortgage interest on receiving child support maintenance and that maintenance in specified cases is later reduced or terminated, the claimant's previous entitlement to income support on account of mortgage interest will be restored provided that the period since he was last entitled to benefit does not exceed 26 weeks.

The Child Support (Miscellaneous Amendments) (No 2) Regulations 1995, SI 1995/3261 (in force in part on 18 December 1995 and in part on 22 January 1996), (1) further amend the Child Support (Arrears, Interest and Adjustment of Maintenance Assessments) Regulations 1992 supra, by providing for the circumstances in which a parent with care must reimburse the Secretary of State for overpayments of maintenance which he has repaid to the absent parent; (2) further amend the Child Support (Collection and Enforcement) Regulations 1992 supra, by requiring that a deduction from earnings order specify the liable person's national insurance number, where known; (3) further amend the Child Support (Information, Evidence and

Disclosure) Regulations 1992 supra, so that they apply to the provision of information on reviews, set the time within which specified information must be supplied, extend the circumstances in which information can be given, and make provision for disclosure of information by the Secretary of State to a child support officer and by a child support officer to the Secretary of State; (4) further amend the Child Support (Maintenance Arrangements and Jurisdiction) Regulations 1992 supra, so as to allow an application for a maintenance assessment to be made, although a court order is in existence, where the court has decided that it has no power to vary or enforce the order; (5) further amend the Child Support (Maintenance Assessment Procedure) Regulations 1992 supra, (a) in respect of interim maintenance assessments, (b) by providing for notification of the lapsing of an appeal, (c) by providing for a periodical review to be made instead of a review in specified circumstances, (d) by requiring a child support officer to take account of matters brought to his attention by the parties, (e) by providing for effective dates of new maintenance assessments in particular cases, and (f) by providing for the circumstances in which a reduced benefit direction should not be given or will be suspended; (6) further amend the Child Support (Maintenance Assessments and Special Cases) Regulations 1992 supra, by (a) making further provision for the definition of 'relevant week', for the purposes of reviews, and the definition of 'day-to-day care', (b) stating that where housing costs consist of fees paid for residential care, the amount of those fees must be net of any housing benefit, (c) providing for adjustment of existing maintenance assessments where a new application is made in multiple application cases, and (d) providing for the value of a compensating transfer made out of assets belonging to the parent with care alone; (7) amend the Child Support and Income Support (Amendment) Regulations 1995 supra, in respect of contribution to maintenance by deduction from benefit; and (8) further amend the Child Support (Miscellaneous Amendments and Transitional Provisions) Regulations 1994 supra, in relation to interim maintenance assessments made after 22 January 1996.

The Child Support (Miscellaneous Amendments) (No 3) Regulations 1995, SI 1995/3265 (in force on 22 January 1996), make a number of amendments to the Child Support (Miscellaneous Amendments) (No 2) Regulations 1995 supra to correct certain erroneous references in specified regulations.

395 Children (Scotland) Act 1995

The Children (Scotland) Act 1995 reforms the law of Scotland relating to children but certain provisions extend to England and Wales. The Act received the royal assent on 19 July 1995 and comes into force on a day to be appointed. For details of commencement, see the commencement table in the title STATUTES.

The provisions which extend to England and Wales are: s 18 (duty of persons with parental responsibilities to notify change of address to local authority looking after child), s 26(2) (power of Scottish local authority to place child with a person in England and Wales), s 33 (effect of orders made in different parts of the United Kingdom), s 44 (prohibition of publication of proceedings at children's hearing), s 70(4) (power of children's hearing imposing supervision requirement to require child to reside at specified place in England or Wales), s 74 (further provision as respects children subject to supervision requirements), s 82 (recovery of certain fugitive children), s 83 (harbouring of fugitive children), s 93 (interpretation), s 104 (financial provision), and s 105 (extent, short title, commencement and certain minor and consequential amendments in Sch 4 and certain repeals in Sch 5).

396 Contact order—application for order—abuse of child's mother by applicant—report of court welfare officer

Six years before a child's birth, his maternal grandfather had been convicted of offences against his mother, including indecent assault. Following the breakdown of his parents' marriage, the child and his mother went to live with the maternal grandparents for approximately six months. The grandmother made allegations that the mother was not properly caring for the child and the grandparents later sought an order granting them access to the child. The mother then alleged that the grandfather had indecently assaulted her while she was living with them and later when the grandparents had visited her. The grandfather denied these allegations and the offences of which he had previously been convicted. The court welfare officer presented a report concluding that the grandfather's behavioural history constituted a risk to the child. The judge disagreed with the conclusions expressed by the court welfare officer although he was not asked to give evidence. He made no finding as to whether the grandfather had behaved inappropriately towards the mother and made an order granting access to the grandparents. *Held*, it was not open to the judge to view the grandfather's previous conviction in a qualified light nor should he have rejected the evidence of the court welfare officer without hearing evidence from him. Where such reports expressed clear recommendations and warnings, the judge could proceed to form directly opposite conclusions only after hearing further oral evidence. Accordingly, the appeal would be allowed and a retrial ordered with the court welfare officer present.

Re CB (Access: Attendance of Court Welfare Officer) [1995] 1 FLR 622 (Court of Appeal: Purchas LJ and Douglas Brown J).

397 Contact order—application for order—application by father—local authority joined as party to proceedings

The appellant was convicted of indecently assaulting the 13-year-old daughter of a woman with whom he lived and was sentenced to 18 months' imprisonment. He had three children from a previous relationship and their mother sought orders preventing the appellant's contact with them. He made a cross-application for contact and the local authority was directed to conduct an investigation into his situation under the Children Act 1989, s 37. The authority concluded that the appellant presented a serious risk to the children and that there should be no long-term unsupervised contact with them. At a directions hearing before the justices' clerk, the authority was made a party to the proceedings. It then opposed the appellant's contact application in the magistrates' court although the mother had now relented in her attitude towards contact. The magistrates made a number of findings of fact which were adverse to the appellant and dismissed his application. On his appeal, *held*, the private law remedies under s 8 were not open to the authority and the magistrates' clerk had been in error in allowing the authority to become a party. However, there was nothing to indicate that the justices would have reached an alternative conclusion had the authority not been a party. There was evidence on which the magistrates could properly base all their findings and there was no indication that matters which should not have been taken into account were taken into account. The court was unable to say that the exercise of the magistrates' discretion was plainly wrong and, accordingly, the appeal would be dismissed.

F v Cambridgeshire County Council [1995] 2 FCR 804 (Family Division: Stuart-White J). *Nottingham County Council v P* [1993] 3 All ER 815, CA (1993 Abr para 417) considered.

398 Contact order—application for order—application by father—power to prevent further applications—appropriate use of power

A father had previously applied for a contact order in respect of his children under the Children Act 1989, s 8. The mother was hostile to any contact and the court directed at that stage that the children should have the assistance of a psychiatrist and an order was made under the 1989 Act, s 91(14) prohibiting the father from making any further applications for contact without leave of the court. The father later applied for leave which the judge refused to grant on the basis that, because of the mother's hostility to contact, it would not be in the children's best interests to force contact upon them at that time. The father appealed against the refusal, submitting that the judge had failed to take account of the very limited purposes for which the original order under s 91(14) had been made. *Held*, an order under s 91(14) was a draconian sanction appropriate when there was a real fear that children might become distressed or have their security disturbed through the vexatious, ill-judged or obsessive pursuit of applications by a party. In the present case, the father was neither vexatious nor oppressive in his genuine attempts to further the welfare of his children by maintaining contact with them. The original restraint order had been granted to enable psychiatric assessment to take place and it would be inappropriate to refuse leave for future applications once it became apparent that the original purpose had failed. The judge had failed to have regard to the established principles that every child had a right to be brought up in the knowledge of his non-custodial parent and, save in exceptional circumstances, a custodial parent should not be allowed to deprive the child of that right through his or her obduracy or by adopting an attitude which resulted in the child becoming averse to contact with the non-custodial parent. Accordingly, the appeal would be allowed.

Re F (Minors) (Contact: Restraint Order) [1995] 1 FLR 956 (Court of Appeal: Nourse and Waite LJJ).

399 Contact order—application for order—interim order—circumstances of grant of interim order

A father applied for and was granted interim contact with his son pending a final hearing of his application for contact. On the mother's appeal, *held*, there were two categories of case involving contact: that where the principle of contact was accepted by both parties and the issue was one of quantum or the nature of the contact, and that where the principle of contact itself was in issue. In both cases the guiding principle was the welfare test under the Children Act 1989, s 1. Where the principle of contact was in issue, there was a danger that unless made as part of a coherent plan and unless care was taken, an interim order could be seen as prejudging the issue. There were two broad categories of circumstances in which interim contact orders were likely to be made: where the order was and was perceived to be part of the overall adjudication process, and where the court had sufficient information to be satisfied that the order was in the child's best interests, even though it was possible that it might come to a different conclusion at the final hearing, particularly where contact had continued happily for many years and had been stopped without apparent good reason. It was difficult to envisage circumstances in which an order could otherwise be made without hearing oral evidence or expert advice.

Re D (A Minor) (Contact: Interim Order) [1995] 1 FCR 501 (Family Division: Wall J).

400 Contact order—application for order—local authority ordered to intervene and obtain psychiatric reports

The Children Act 1989, s 7(1)(b) provides that a court considering any question with respect to a child under the Act may ask a local authority to arrange for (i) an officer of the authority, or (ii) such other person (other than a probation officer) as the authority considers appropriate, to report to the court on such matters relating to the welfare of that child as are required to be dealt with in the report.

The question arose whether a court had power under s 7(1)(b) to order a local authority to intervene in contact proceedings, instruct a child psychiatrist and commission a report for use by the court. *Held*, even in circumstances where it was appropriate for the report of a child psychiatrist to be available to the court, there was no power under s 7(1)(b) to impose such unwelcome obligations upon a local authority and insist that it bear the expense. Any other interpretation of s 7(1)(b) would be contrary to the philosophy of the 1989 Act which limited an authority's powers to intervene in private law proceedings.

The court also stated that the intervention of a child psychiatrist could be achieved in two ways, the most appropriate of which was to invite the parties to instruct a psychiatrist jointly. Alternatively, in exceptional circumstances the court might invoke RSC Ord 40, which applied to family proceedings by virtue of the Family Proceedings Rules 1991, SI 1991/1247, r 1.3(i) and the County Court Act 1984. On the application of any party, the court was empowered to appoint an independent expert to inquire and report on any question of fact or opinion before the court.

Re K (Contact: Psychiatric Report) [1995] 2 FLR 432 (Court of Appeal: Russell, Henry and Ward LJJ).

401 Contact order—conditions of contact—nature of conditions that may be imposed

A mother refused to co-operate with a direct contact order made in favour of her child's father. The father obtained an indirect contact order under the Children Act 1989, s 8 to which a number of conditions were attached. These required the mother to (1) send the father photographs of the child every three months, (2) send him progress reports when the child began nursery school or playgroup, (3) inform him of any significant illness and also send medical reports, (4) accept delivery of cards and presents for the child, and (5) read and show the child any such communications and give him the presents. On the mother's appeal against the order, *held*, where parents were separated and a child was in the day-to-day care of one of them, it was almost always in the child's best interests to have contact with the other parent. The 1989 Act, s 11(7) conferred a wide and comprehensive power on the court to make orders which would effectively ensure that contact took place. Where indirect contact was ordered, it was reasonable that the custodial parent should be obliged to report on the child's progress to the non-custodial parent, since he would not be able to correspond with the child in a meaningful way if he was unaware of the child's activities. Moreover, a judge could not limit a non-custodial parent's communications to a certain number of letters or cards. In the instant case, the court had power to compel the mother to read to the child the communications sent by the father, as she could not simply withhold her consent in order to defeat the order. The fact that she was unwilling to read them out was irrelevant, because the court had considered that contact was appropriate and she was therefore subject to an enforceable duty to promote it. In addition, as long as the father's communications did not contain any offensive material, the mother could not censor them. She was obliged to comply with the conditions that had been ordered and, accordingly, the appeal would be dismissed.

Re O *(Contact: Imposition of Conditions)* [1995] 2 FLR 124 (Court of Appeal: Sir Thomas Bingham MR, Simon Brown and Swinton LJJ). Re M *(A Minor) (Contact: Conditions)* [1994] 1 FLR 274 (1993 Abr para 378) doubted.

402   Contact order—evidence—failure to hear oral evidence

A father applied for a contact order in respect of his child. The application met with a series of delays, due in part to the father's failure to keep in touch with the court welfare officer. At a directions appointment, the father's application for a contact order was dismissed and he was debarred from making any further application for contact without leave of the court. *Held*, the justices' decision to dismiss the father's application was fatally flawed. The justices had failed to hear all the evidence before reaching their decision, having chosen to rely on written statements of the parties rather than to hear any oral evidence. The father's case was not so hopeless as to entitle the justices to dismiss it out of hand. Accordingly, although there had been a lengthy delay in the proceedings which was not to be welcomed, the appeal would be allowed. The case would be ordered to be reheard before a fresh bench.

Re M *(Contact)* [1995] 1 FLR 1029 (Family Division: Hollis J).

403   Contact order—leave to apply for order—application by grandmother—nature of application

The parties divorced and their three-year-old child lived with the mother. The father moved in with the grandmother and, although the father ceased to have contact with the child, the grandmother sought leave to apply for a contact order. At the hearing, the judge proceeded with the matter on the basis that leave was granted. The court welfare officer reported that there was considerable hostility between the families and that contact would not benefit the child while the hostility continued. The judge, therefore, refused contact on the basis that the application was premature, but he said contact might be possible in a couple of years when the child was older. The grandmother appealed, arguing that once she had been granted leave to apply she should have been placed in the same position as a parent on a hearing for contact and that the judge had to identify any cogent reason for refusing contact. *Held*, under the Children Act 1989, two groups of people could apply for contact: those who had a right to apply for an order and those who had to apply for leave to make such an application. The grandmother was required to apply for leave and in deciding whether to grant leave, the court had to have regard to a number of matters including the nature of the application, the applicant's connection with the child and any risk that the child's life might be disrupted to such an extent that he would be harmed by contact. Although there was a presumption that a parent should have contact unless there were cogent reasons why he should not, that was not the approach towards any other member of the family. There could be no such presumption that a grandmother who obtained leave was entitled to contact unless it could be shown by cogent reasons that she should not have it. Every judge looked at the facts of the case and had to do what was best for the child. In exercising his discretion, the judge thought it was not for the good of the child to have contact with his grandmother at that time. Accordingly, the appeal would be dismissed.

Re A *(Section 8 Order: Grandparent Application)* [1995] 2 FLR 153 (Court of Appeal: Butler-Sloss and Otton LJJ).

404   Criminal offence—decision to caution child—caution in breach of guidelines—discretion to review decision

See R v Commissioner of Police of the Metropolis, ex p P, para 755.

405   Family proceedings—application for order—power to prevent further applications

The Children Act 1989, s 91(14) provides that, on disposing of any application for an order under the 1989 Act, the court may (whether or not it makes any other order in response to the application) order that no application for an order under the Act of any specified kind may be made with respect to the child concerned by any person named in the order without the leave of the court.

The father of two children had a number of convictions for sexual offences involving young persons. Care orders were made in respect of the children and the local authority was granted an order terminating the father's contact with them. In subsequent proceedings, the father unsuccessfully opposed the authority's application to discharge the care orders and the mother's application for a residence order. On the question of whether the court should also make an order under the 1989 Act, s 91(14), *held*, where the circumstances of a case were extreme and a child's needs were great, it was important that the risk of unnecessary disturbance caused to the child by repeated or revived litigation was avoided by preventing further litigation unless the court was satisfied that there was some merit in it. The correct use of s 91(14) and the parameters of its application were a matter of judicial discretion and, in the circumstances of the instant case, an order would be made preventing the father from making any application for any order under the 1989 Act of any kind in relation to any of the children, without the leave of the court.

Re G and M (Child Orders: Restricting Applications) [1995] 2 FLR 416 (Family Division: Singer J). *Re Y (Child Orders: Restricting Applications)* [1994] 2 FLR 699 (1994 Abr para 384) followed.

406 Family proceedings—case management—preparation for and conduct of hearings

The following *Practice Direction* ([1995] 1 All ER 586) has been issued by the President of the Family Division, and applies to all family proceedings in the High Court and in all care centres, family hearing centres and divorce county courts.

1. The importance of reducing the cost and delay of civil litigation makes it necessary for the court to assert greater control over the preparation for and conduct of hearings than has hitherto been customary. Failure by practitioners to conduct cases economically will be visited by appropriate orders for costs, including wasted costs orders.

2. The court will accordingly exercise its discretion to limit discovery, the length of opening and closing oral submissions, the time allowed for the examination and cross-examination of witnesses, the issues on which it wishes to be addressed, and reading aloud from documents and authorities.

3. Unless otherwise ordered, every witness statement or affidavit will stand as the evidence-in-chief of the witness concerned. The substance of the evidence which a party intends to adduce at the hearing must be sufficiently detailed, but without prolixity. It must be confined to material matters of fact, not (except in the case of evidence of professional witnesses) of opinion, and if hearsay evidence is to be adduced, the source of the information must be declared or good reason given for not doing so.

4. It is a duty owed to the court both by the parties and by their legal representatives to give full and frank disclosure in ancillary relief applications and also in all matters in respect of children. The parties and their advisers must also use their best endeavours to confine the issues and the evidence called to what is reasonably considered to be essential for the proper presentation of their case, to reduce or eliminate issues for expert evidence and, in advance of the hearing, to agree which are the issues or the main issues.

5. Unless the nature of the hearing makes it unnecessary and in the absence of specific directions, bundles should be agreed and prepared for use by the court, the parties and the witnesses, and must be in A4 format where possible, suitably secured. The bundles for use by the court must be lodged with the court (the Clerk of the Rules in matters in the Royal Courts of Justice, London) at least two clear days before the hearing. Each bundle should be paginated, indexed, wholly legible, and arranged chronologically. Where documents are copied unnecessarily or bundled incompetently, the cost will be disallowed.

6. In cases estimated to last for five days or more and in which no pre-trial review has been ordered, an application should be made for a pre-trial review. It should when practicable be listed at least three weeks before the hearing, and be conducted by the judge or district judge before whom the case is to be heard and should be attended by the advocates who are to represent the parties at the hearing. Wherever possible, all statements of evidence and all reports should be filed before the date of the review and in good time for them to have been considered by all parties.

7. Whenever practicable and in matters estimated to last five days or more, each party should, not less than two clear days before the hearing, lodge with the court, or with the Clerk of the Rules in matters in the Royal Courts of Justice, London, and deliver to other parties, a chronology and skeleton argument, concisely summarising that party's submissions in relation to each of the issues, and citing the main authorities relied upon. It is important that the skeleton arguments should be brief.

8. In advance of the hearing, upon request and otherwise in the course of their opening, parties should be prepared to furnish the court, if there is no core bundle, with a list of documents essential for a proper understanding of the case.

9. The opening speech should be succinct. At its conclusion, the other parties may be invited briefly to amplify their skeleton arguments. In a heavy case, the court may, in conjunction with final speeches, require written submissions including the findings of fact for which each party contends.

407 Family proceedings—children interviewed in relation to criminal proceedings against father—conduct of interview

Two boys lived with their father, his partner and her three children. Charges were brought against the father alleging that he had raped his partner's daughters and interim care orders were made in respect of the two boys. The father's solicitor sought to interview the boys for the purpose of preparing the father's defence in criminal proceedings. The local authority was not opposed to an interview but wanted it to be carried out by someone trained to conduct such interviews. The solicitor accepted that a guardian ad litem or a social worker should be present, but he applied to the court for permission to enable him to interview the boys. *Held*, the court had the power to determine the matter under its inherent jurisdiction. It had to weigh any potential harm to the children against the interests of justice. Although this was a matter in which there was some parental responsibility, it did not follow that it was a matter of the children's upbringing in which the welfare of the children was paramount. Their welfare was not, therefore, the sole and overriding consideration. Although the interview was an ordeal, that had to be weighed against the advantage to the children's welfare of a fair trial being accorded to their father. Accordingly, the interests of justice required that the father's solicitor should be able to ask the questions he wished to ask. The interview would take place in the presence of a social worker and would only take place if the Crown Prosecution Service indicated its intention to continue the prosecution. The application would be allowed accordingly.

Re M (Care: Leave to Interview Child) [1995] 1 FLR 825 (Family Division: Hale J).

408 Family proceedings—costs—discretion to award costs

Two children were taken into the care of a local authority and the authority applied for permission to refuse contact between the children and their father. At the hearing, the magistrates refused to grant the authority's application and instead ordered that the children should have direct contact with their father twice a year and that monthly letters and presents should be permitted at the authority's discretion. The magistrates further ordered the authority to pay the father's costs. On the authority's appeal against the order for costs, *held*, the Family Proceedings Courts (Children Act 1989) Rules 1991, SI 1991/1395, r 22 did not give any guidance or set out any criteria which should be followed when such an application for costs was made. The normal rule in civil litigation was that costs followed the event. However, it would be unusual for a court to make an order for costs in a case involving children where the conduct of a party had not been reprehensible or the party's stance had not been beyond the band of what was reasonable. It would be a matter for the discretion of the court in the light of those criteria as to what order for costs should be made, and where a local authority carrying out its statutory duties had to exercise its balanced judgment, the authority should not feel that it was liable to be condemned in costs if, despite acting within the band of reasonableness, it might form a different view to that of a court. The magistrates were wrong in the way they exercised their discretion as to costs and, accordingly, the appeal would be allowed.

Re M (Local Authority's Costs) [1995] 1 FCR 649 (Family Division: Cazalet J).

409 Family proceedings—costs—reserved costs order

It has been held that reserved costs which ought to have been, but are not, requested at the end of original proceedings in the Family Division may be awarded by the court in a supplementary order.

S v S (Family Proceedings: Reserved Costs Orders) [1995] 2 FCR 402 (Family Division: Michael Horowitz QC).

410 Family proceedings—estoppel per res judicata—applicability of doctrine

A father applied to a magistrates' court for custody of his two children. The mother made a counter-application for custody. She alleged that the father had been violent towards her and that he had sexually abused both children. The father denied the latter allegation, arguing that the mother was an unfit parent and that she had talked about sexual abuse in front of the children. The justices made a finding that, although the daughter had sexual knowledge which was inappropriate for her age, there was no evidence that it was the result of sexual abuse by the father. They made a residence order in the mother's favour and ordered contact to the father. Following the breakdown of the contact arrangements, the father applied for a residence order. When the mother sought to raise the sexual abuse allegation in those proceedings, the father argued that she was estopped from doing so because of the justices' findings in the previous proceedings. On that issue, *held*, the doctrine of estoppel per res judicata was founded on considerations of public policy. In particular, it was based on the need for certainty, and also the fact that it was wrong for a matter to be litigated twice and for a litigant to have to defend twice the same complaint made against him. However, the doctrine of estoppel per res judicata did not apply in child care cases, as there was a countervailing public interest and public policy relating to the protection of children. In particular, it was the court's duty to have regard to the welfare of a child as the paramount consideration, and, in the instant case, it was therefore necessary to inquire whether there had been sexual abuse and whether the children could have contact with the father without suffering harm or further harm. The rules relating to estoppel were part of the law of evidence rather than the substantive law, but those rules sometimes had to be set aside in the interests of justice, as that interest was greater than the rules of evidence. On that basis, the court was not bound by the justices' finding that the father had not sexually abused the children and, therefore, the mother was not estopped from repeating the allegation.

K v P (Children Act Proceedings: Estoppel) [1995] 1 FCR 457 (Family Division: Ward J). *DSV Silo-und Verwaltungsgesellschaft mbH v Owners of the Semnar; the Semnar (No 2)* [1985] 2 All ER 104 (1985 Abr para 384) considered.

411 Family proceedings—evidence—documents used in family proceedings—disclosure in other proceedings

A mother and father who were illegal immigrants appealed against a decision made in immigration proceedings which would have resulted in them being forced to return to their country of origin with their two children. Care proceedings had already been commenced under the Children Act 1989 in respect of the children, and a care plan had been agreed upon between the parents and the local authority. The parents applied for leave to disclose the documents used in the 1989 Act proceedings to the special adjudicator in the immigration appeal. On the question of whether all or only certain of those documents could be disclosed, *held*, evidence in proceedings under the 1989 Act was confidential, and it was not desirable for it to be used in any other proceedings. However, there was no absolute rule against disclosure and, in exercising its discretion, the court had to balance the interests of the child against other relevant interests. In the instant case, one of the relevant interests was that the special adjudicator should have all the relevant information before him so that he could reach a fair and just conclusion in the immigration appeal. Although the children's best interests were not an issue for consideration in the immigration proceedings, the court had to look at the material which was to be disclosed and decide whether their welfare was likely to be prejudiced by disclosure. As the documents did not contain any confidential information about the children's lives, characters or experiences but related mainly to the father's fears about what would happen to him if he were forced to return to his country of origin, there was only a minimal risk that the children would be harmed by disclosure. The value of disclosure in terms of doing justice in the immigration proceedings outweighed the possibility of causing harm to the children and, therefore, all the documents could be disclosed to the special adjudicator. Accordingly, the application would be granted.

Re F (A Minor) (Disclosure: Immigration) [1994] 2 FLR 958 (Family Division: Coningsby J). *Brown v Matthews* [1990] 2 All ER 155, CA (1990 Abr para 1048) applied.

412 Family proceedings—evidence—video recordings and expert evidence

In a case of alleged sexual abuse, the following guidance was given in respect of video recordings and expert evidence. Where video recordings of interviews are made of a child by the police or a hospital, copies of such of those recordings which are likely to be used in court proceedings must be made available. A solicitor making a request for a copy of a video recording must justify his request, and it is reasonable to require him to give an undertaking not to copy or release the video recording, or any transcript of it, from his custody, other than to counsel or the medical experts involved in the case. Breach of undertakings given to hospitals or the police in respect of video recordings, or misuse of them, will be dealt with severely by the court. If a hospital or the police fails unreasonably to provide a copy of the video recording, the court can order them to do so and to pay the costs of the application in that respect, if costs have been wasted. As regards expert witnesses, once all the expert evidence in a case is available, the lawyers should be able to agree which issues remain to be determined, and to make a further time estimate. Expert medical witnesses have to recognise the importance of their role in sex abuse cases and that it is therefore important that their opinions should be made available to the parties in sufficient time. There is potential benefit in medical experts preparing a joint report as regards areas on which they are agreed, and setting out the matters on which they disagree. A copy of the report must be made available to all parties and, in addition, a meeting of experts should be held to discuss the remaining issues, and to agree a timetable for further preparation of the case.

Re R (Child Abuse: Video and Expert Evidence) [1995] 2 FCR 573 (Family Division: Johnson J).

413 Family proceedings—fees

The Family Proceedings Fees (Amendment) Order 1995, SI 1995/2628 (in force on 30 October 1995), amends the 1991 Order, SI 1991/2114, by modifying the rules on exemption from payment of court fees, increasing certain fees, introducing a single fee of £1 for copies of documents, and replacing, with a flat fee of £30, the scale of fees payable on the issue of a warrant of execution.

414 Family proceedings—guardian ad litem—appointment—circumstances in which appointment may be made

The Children Act 1989, s 37(1) provides that where in any family proceedings in which a question arises with respect to the welfare of any child, it appears to the court that it may be appropriate for a care or supervision order to be made, the court may direct the appropriate authority to undertake an investigation of the child's circumstances. Section 41(6)(b) defines 'specified proceedings' as any proceedings in which the court has given a direction under s 37(1) and has made or is considering making an interim care order.

A 13-year-old girl began a relationship with an older boy and ran away from home to live with him. She reurned home briefly and also went into short-term voluntary care before returning to live with the boy's parents. Following her parents' application for a residence order, a district judge made an order under the 1989 Act, s 37 directing the local authority to undertake an investigation of the girl's circumstances. He also appointed a guardian ad litem for the girl under s 41(6)(b). The authority failed to complete the assessment required for the investigation within the time limit, but indicated to the court that it would not be seeking a care or supervision order. In view of the authority's decision, the guardian ad litem sought guidance on certain issues relating to her appointment. *Held*, the appointment of a guardian ad litem was not automatic in cases where a s 37 order had been made, as the court had to consider the specified purpose of the investigation and whether or not the child's interests could be safeguarded without such an appointment. Cases which were purely concerned with private law matters, such as residence or contact, were not appropriate for s 37 orders or for the appointment of a guardian ad litem, as they did not usually involve the possibility that a care or supervision order might be made. Moreover, where an order was made under s 37, the proceedings were 'specified proceedings' within the meaning of s 41(6)(b) but ceased to be so if a local authority indicated that it would not be applying for a care or supervision order. In consequence, the appointment of a guardian ad litem ended, and it was by judicial act rather than by administrative act that the appointment was to be terminated. On the facts of the case, the guardian ad litem had been properly appointed, but once the authority indicated that it would not be seeking a care or supervision order, the proceedings ceased to be 'specified proceedings'. However, as the authority had not completed its assessment, the guardian ad litem's involvement was still necessary to protect the girl's interests, and the appointment was to continue as a fresh appointment under the Family Proceedings Rules 1991, SI 1991/1247, r 9.5 until the authority's assessment was fully completed and a final decision could be made by the court.

Re CE (A Minor) (Appointment of Guardian ad Litem) [1995] 1 FCR 387 (Family Division: Wall J).

415 Family proceedings—Official Solicitor—appointment as guardian ad litem

1. The Official Solicitor has issued the following *Practice Note* ([1995] 2 FLR 479), which supersedes *Practice Note* [1993] 2 FLR 641 (1993 Abr para 399).

Appointment as guardian ad litem of child subject to proceedings

2. In specified (public law) proceedings under the Children Act 1989, the Official Solicitor may only be appointed in the High Court, in accordance with a direction of the Lord Chancellor, reported at [1991] 2 FLR 471 (1991 Abr para 1910), where the court considers that the circumstances are that:

(1) the child does not have a guardian ad litem in the proceedings, and

(2) there are exceptional circumstances which make it desirable in the interests of the welfare of the child concerned that the Official Solicitor, rather than a panel guardian, should be appointed, having regard to:

(a) any foreign element in the case which is likely to require inquiries or other action, to be pursued outside England and Wales;

(b) the burden of having to represent several children;

(c) other High Court proceedings in which the Official Solicitor is representing the child;

(d) any other circumstances which the court considers relevant.

The Official Solicitor, in accordance with the direction, may also give advice and other assistance as he considers appropriate to any guardian ad litem in specified proceedings in the High Court.

3. In non-specified (private law) proceedings under the 1989 Act, and in proceedings under the inherent jurisdiction of the High Court, the Official Solicitor may either act in the High Court or in a county court (but not in a family proceedings court), under the Family Proceedings Rules 1991, SI 1991/1247, r 9.5. In most cases, a child's interests will be sufficiently safeguarded by a court welfare officer's report. It is only where this is not so that the question of the appointment of the Official Solicitor may arise, and even then the Official Solicitor's involvement should be exceptional rather than automatic.

4. He will accept appointment in those exceptional cases in which it has been established that a child's interests may not be adequately protected by a court welfare officer's report, and that it is desirable that the child should be separately represented. Such exceptional cases will include those where:

(1) there is a substantial foreign element;

(2) there appear to be exceptional or difficult points of law;

(3) there are unusual or complicating features, such as where one parent has killed the other, or is a transsexual;

(4) there is conflicting or controversial medical evidence;

(5) a child is ignorant of the truth as to its parentage (cf *Re R (A Minor) (Contact)* [1993] 2 FLR 762), or is refusing contact with a parent in circumstances which point to the need for psychiatric assessment; and

(6) is acting for the child in other proceedings.

5. He will almost invariably accept appointment in a case which falls into the classes of case upon which judicial guidance has been given about his appointment, that is to say:

(1) where a child has sought separate representation by solicitor but the court does not consider he is competent (*Re T (A Minor) (Wardship: Representation)* [1993] 4 All ER 518, CA (1993 Abr para 420); *Re S (A Minor) (Independent Representation)* [1993] 3 All ER 36, CA (1993 Abr para 389));

(2) if a child is separately represented but the court needs the assistance of the Official Solicitor as amicus curiae (*Re H (A Minor) (Guardian ad Litem: Requirement)* [1993] 2 FLR 552, CA (1993 Abr para 390));

(3) if difficult issues of medical confidentiality arise (*Note: Re HIV Tests* [1994] 2 FLR 116);

(4) 'special category cases', such as sterilisation and abortion, where application should be made under the inherent jurisdiction of the High Court (*Re HG (Specific Issue Order: Sterilisation)* [1993] 1 FLR 587).

Appointment as next friend and for child not subject of proceedings

6. Subject to the 1991 Rules, r 9.2A, the Official Solicitor may also act as next friend of a child seeking leave to make an application under the 1989 Act or in other family proceedings. If the court refuses leave under r 9.2A, or revokes it under r 9.2A(8), it may appoint the Official Solicitor to represent the child by virtue of r 9.2A(10). He may also accept appointment under r 9.2(1) in respect of a child who is the mother of the child subject of the proceedings.

Appointment as guardian ad litem of an adult party under mental disability

7. In the absence of any other suitable and willing person, the Official Solicitor is available to be appointed, in the High Court or in a county court pursuant to the 1991 Rules, r 9.2(4), as the guardian ad litem or next friend of an adult party who is under a disability. That is to say, an adult who is suffering from a mental disorder, within the meaning of the Mental Health Act 1983, s 1, which renders that person incapable of managing his or her property and affairs. Medical evidence to this effect must be obtained before the Official Solicitor will accept appointment. Where there are practical difficulties in obtaining such medical evidence, the Official Solicitor should be consulted.

Terms of appointment

8. Orders made appointing the Official Solicitor should be expressed as being made subject to his consent. Save in the most urgent of cases (eg where immediate medical treatment is an issue), it is unlikely that the Official Solicitor will be able to complete his inquiries in less than three months. To ensure that he has sufficient time to undertake the inquiries which he considers

necessary, a substantive hearing date less than three months ahead should not be fixed without consulting him. It is often helpful to discuss the question of appointment with the Official Solicitor or one of his staff, by telephoning 0171 911 7127. The number also operates as the guardian ad litem panel managers' helpline.

9. The Court of Appeal (Civil Division) has indicated that the Official Solicitor should always be consulted in cases where it is sought to restrain publicity about a child (*Re H (Minors) (Injunction: Public Interest)* [1994] 1 FLR 519).

10. Where the circumstances of the case justify the involvement of the Official Solicitor, a completed copy of the questionnaire which forms part of the *Practice Note*, a copy of the order appointing him (subject to his consent), and the court file should be sent to:

The Official Solicitor
81 Chancery Lane
London WC2A 1DD
DX 0012 Chancery Lane
Fax: 0171 911 7105

It is most important, if delay is to be avoided, that the court file is sent to the Official Solicitor immediately in every case.

416 Family proceedings—welfare report—court welfare officer

A mother applied for a prohibited steps order against the father of their child in order to prevent him from having contact with the child. At the first hearing in the proceedings, a consent order was made which included a provision that a local authority social worker was to prepare and file a welfare report. The father did not accept the findings of the report, but stated that he would accept the report of an independent psychologist whether or not it was favourable to him. At a directions hearing, a judge ordered a court welfare officer to prepare a welfare report. The mother appealed against the direction, arguing that a welfare report had already been prepared by a social worker, that it was of no value to the child for a further similar report to be prepared, and that it would involve unnecessary duplication and lead to unjustified delay. *Held*, court welfare officers were accustomed to the court process, to interviewing children and relevant adults, to attending court, to making written and oral recommendations, and to being questioned in court. In contrast, social workers had more limited knowledge of the court process, and their role was usually confined to fact-finding reports which did not involve making recommendations. In the instant case, the judge felt that, because of the serious nature of the mother's application, the child's interests required the introduction of the special expertise of a court welfare officer. Although the social worker's report was of use, she had not seen the child and the father together, nor had she made an assessment of the father's character. The judge had taken account of the delay that would arise as a result of his direction, but concluded that the disadvantage of delay was outweighed by the need to ensure that the court was fully informed of all the circumstances of the case. Accordingly, the appeal would be dismissed.

Re W (Welfare Reports) [1995] 2 FLR 142 (Court of Appeal: Nourse and Waite LJJ).

417 Family proceedings—wishes of child—balancing wishes and best interests of child

When the parties separated it was agreed that their two daughters would live with the mother in the matrimonial home and have contact with the father. He moved into his parents' home and later applied for a residence order in respect of the younger child. The application was based largely on that child's expressed wishes, which were stated to the father, the court welfare officer and the judge. In the officer's view, the child could live with either parent, although she did not know what life would really be like with her father because he was living with his parents and there was, therefore, a degree of artificiality about the circumstances. For that reason, the judge felt he should not give as much weight as he otherwise might to the younger child's views and found that she should continue to live with her mother. On the father's appeal, *held*, the judge approached the views of the child in a proper manner. He clearly had her wishes well in mind and correctly directed himself to have regard to her ascertainable wishes and feelings. At the same time, he concluded that the matters raised in evidence affected the weight to apply to them and that could not be said to be wrong. The judge was entitled to take account of the instinctive view of the officer based as it was on her experience. Accordingly, the appeal would be dismissed.

The court stated that the practice of requesting a child as young as 12 years to swear an affidavit in family proceedings was inappropriate and it was not fair on children that they should be dragged into the arena to be asked specifically to choose between two parents both of whom they loved.

Re M (a Minor) (Child: Wishes and Feelings) [1995] 2 FCR 90 (Court of Appeal: Butler-Sloss LJ and Ewbank J).

418 Financial provision—maintenance order—matters to be taken into consideration—Child Support Agency assessment

It has been held that where justices are determining the sum of child maintenance to be paid by an absent parent, it is useful to bear in mind what sum the Child Support Agency would have arrived at, as although the agency's assessment is not binding, it is strongly persuasive.

E v C (1995) Times, 4 December (Family Division: Douglas Brown J).

419 Financial provision—unmarried parents—transfer of property to child

A mother applied for financial provision for her child, A, under the Children Act 1989, Sch 1 against the father of the child, a wealthy man resident abroad. The mother had two other children, one older and one younger, and she claimed that the father was the father of all three children. The family had been supported by the father from the time that the mother was pregnant with the eldest child. After the birth of A, the father purchased a property as a home for the mother and children and paid large sums for their support. He visited the home from time to time but the parties never cohabited. Blood tests showed that he was not the father of the other children, although he admitted that he was the father of A. The mother began divorce proceedings against the father, but the court made a declaration that the parties had never been married and made an order for costs against the mother in view of her misconduct in bringing the proceedings. The father then terminated his financial support. The mother's application for financial provision included a claim for a transfer of the property either to herself for the benefit of the child or to the child absolutely. *Held*, the claim for the transfer of the property to A absolutely would be rejected on the ground that there were no special circumstances which required the father to do more than maintain his daughter until she was independent. The proper order was one requiring a settlement to be made for the benefit of A on terms that the property should be conveyed to trustees to hold the property for A for a period terminating six months after A attained the age of 18 or completed full-time education. The mother's misconduct in bringing the divorce proceedings meant that she would be treated by the court as someone who had fabricated a case to pervert justice. Such misconduct precluded any claim by the mother for herself, but did not affect the financial provision in relation to A, which would include an allowance for the mother on account of the discharge of her obligations in looking after A. The amount of financial provision for A would not be reduced because it might be spent in part for the benefit of the other two children.

A v A (Financial Provision for Child) [1995] 1 FCR 309 (Family Division: Ward J).

420 Parental responsibility agreement—application to terminate agreement—child's welfare

A mother discovered that the father of her illegitimate child had physically abused the child. She applied for an order under the Children Act 1989, s 4(3) to terminate their parental responsibility agreement and for an order preventing the father from making any further Children Act applications with respect to the child without leave of the court. *Held*, as a general principle the courts should encourage unmarried fathers to seek parental responsibility. At all times, however, the welfare of the child was the paramount consideration. Allowing the parental responsibility agreement to continue might put the child at risk and would send a message to others that the father had not, by his actions, forfeited responsibility for the child. It could be unsettling for the child's carers to face any further applications by the father. Consequently it was appropriate to direct that leave of the court would be required before the father made any further applications to the court in respect of the child. Accordingly, the orders sought by the mother would be made.

Re P (Terminating Parental Responsibility) [1995] 1 FLR 1048 (Family Division: Singer J).

421 Parental responsibility order—application by unmarried father—principles to be applied

The parties lived together and had one child, who was registered in the father's surname. On the parties' separation, the father continued to make regular payments towards the child's maintenance. When the father was convicted of possessing obscene literature, the mother severed contact but, because the child became deeply distressed, contact was resumed. The father applied for a parental responsibility order and defined contact. No order was made as to contact because the parties were able to agree the matter. On hearing the parental responsibility application, although the judge found that the father had paid maintenance, had regular contact with the child and was committed to her, the application was refused. On appeal, *held*, in an appropriate case, the aim was to equate the position of an unmarried father with that of a father of a legitimate child. The court, in considering whether to make an order, had to take into account a number of factors, including the degree of commitment and attachment shown by the father and the reasons for applying for the order. Where the father showed attachment and commitment and it was established that the reasons for the application were not demonstrably improper or wrong, it would be for the child's welfare that an order be made. It would not give a father a right to interfere in matters within the day-to-day management of the child's life and misuse by the father of the rights conferred by the parental responsibility order could be controlled by a prohibited steps or a specific issue order or, as a last resort, by the discharge of the parental responsibility order. Misunderstandings as to the nature of an order arose from a failure to appreciate that, in essence, the granting of the order was the granting of status. It was wrong to place undue and false emphasis on the rights, duties and powers comprised in parental responsibility and not to concentrate on the fact that what was being conferred on the father was the status of parenthood for which nature had already ordained that he bear responsibility. Accordingly, the appeal would be allowed.

Re S (A Minor) (Parental Responsibility) [1995] 3 FCR 225 (Court of Appeal: Butler-Sloss, Simon Brown and Ward LJJ).

A father applied for orders for contact and parental responsibility in respect of his two young daughters. Although he had reached an agreement with their mother in relation to contact, the magistrates refused his application for parental responsibility, stating that they did so because the level of mistrust and antagonism between the parents had given rise to concern that if an order was made it would lead to disputes as to the children's upbringing. On appeal, *held*, the magistrates had misunderstood the nature and purpose of a parental responsibility order. It would not affect the day-to-day care of the children when they were in the mother's care. Instead, it provided status for the father. In deciding whether to make such an order, the court should take into account the degree of commitment the father had shown towards the children, the degree of attachment that existed between the father and the children and the father's reasons for applying for the order. In this case, there was ample evidence of his commitment to the children and their affection for him and, accordingly, the appeal would be allowed.

Re S (A Minor) (Parental Responsibility) [1995] 3 FCR 564 (Family Division: Sir Stephen Brown P).

422 Paternity—presumption of legitimacy—recognition of child's natural father

See *Kroon v The Netherlands*, para 1586.

423 Paternity—proof of paternity—blood tests—application for order for blood tests— consent of child

The applicant mother sought a direction under the Family Law Reform Act 1969, s 20(1) that blood tests be taken to ascertain whether or not the respondent was the father of her 16-year-old child who was the subject of an application under the Child Support Act 1991, s 27. The respondent objected but the child had signed a form of consent to the test. *Held*, the 1991 Act did not specifically provide a power to direct blood tests but proceedings brought under s 27 were civil proceedings and thus the court had a power to direct such tests under the 1969 Act, s 20. In exercising that discretion, the principle to be applied was that the court should direct a blood test unless it was against the child's interests to do so. The child wished the blood test to be taken and was of an age to give consent. In the absence of any evidence that it was against his interests to do so, the court would direct that the tests be undertaken.

Re E (Child Support: Blood Tests) [1995] 1 FCR 245 (Family Division: Stuart-White J). *S v S, W v Official Solicitor* [1972] AC 24, HL, followed.

424 Proceedings involving children—allocation of proceedings

The Children (Allocation of Proceedings) (Amendment) Order 1995, SI 1995/1649 (in force on 2 October 1995), further amends the 1991 Order, SI 1991/1677, by nominating the county court at Pontypridd as an additional Family Hearing Centre and by listing it as a Care Centre in place of the county court at Merthyr Tydfil.

425 Proceedings involving children—civil proceedings—reporting restrictions—proceedings against health authority

See *R v Cambridge District Health Authority, ex p B (No 2)*, para 2392.

426 Proceedings involving children—criminal proceedings—reporting restrictions—young offender

See *R v Inner London Crown Court, ex p Barnes*, para 2397.

427 Prohibited steps order—court's power to make order—order in form of injunction

A local authority began care proceedings on the basis that a mother of four children had been unable to provide a sufficient standard of parenting to protect any of the children from significant harm. The authority originally planned to attempt rehabilitation of all four children with the mother but, by the time of the hearing, that plan had been abandoned in respect of the middle two children. At the hearing, it was held that if the eldest and youngest children were returned to the mother's care they would be exposed to serious risk of harm and supervision orders were made in respect of those two children. Further, to ensure that those children were not returned to the mother an order was made injuncting the mother from removing them from their foster home. The mother appealed against the injunction and the authority cross-appealed against the refusal to make a care order. Further evidence was admitted by the Court of Appeal from the authority which had learned that the mother had in the meantime given birth to another child, that the father of that child was considered a risk to children and that his role in the mother's household was uncertain. Consequently, the authority's plans in respect of the children had changed and it proposed that the youngest child be placed for adoption and that the eldest be placed in long-term foster care. *Held*, although the judge's order was in the form of an injunction, it was in essence a prohibited steps order under the Children Act 1989, s 8(1), which defined such an order as one which provided that no step which could be taken by a parent in meeting his parental responsibility for a child, and which was of a kind specified in the order, should be taken by any person without the consent of the court. Section 100(2)(b) further provided that the High Court's inherent jurisdiction should not be exercised with respect to children so as to require a child to be accommodated by or on behalf of a local authority. Thus the judge could not properly make the order that he had made. Even if the order was in substance an injunction, he was purporting to exercise a jurisdiction to protect children that the county court did not possess. However, it was clear that care orders in respect of the eldest and youngest child were necessary and they would be granted in respect of those two children. Accordingly, the appeal and the cross-appeal would be allowed.

Re S and D (Child Case: Powers of Court) [1995] 1 FCR 626 (Court of Appeal: Balcombe, Staughton and Rose LJJ). *D v D (Child Case: Powers Of Court)* [1994] 3 FCR 28, followed.

428 Prohibited steps order—leave to remove child from jurisdiction—matters to be taken into consideration

The parents of a child separated, upon which the mother looked after the child and the father was granted a contact order. When the father later applied for staying contact, the mother stated that she intended to emigrate to New Zealand with the child. The father was concerned that the child should remain in contact with him and his family and, therefore, applied for a prohibited steps order to prevent the mother from removing the child from the jurisdiction permanently. On the mother's application for leave to do so, *held*, a child's welfare was the first and paramount consideration in deciding whether to grant leave to remove him from the jurisdiction permanently, but leave was not to be withheld unless the interests of the child and those of the custodial parent were clearly incompatible. Although in the instant case that general principle created a presumption in favour of the mother's application, it was also necessary to consider the importance of the relationship between the father and the child, as it was through that relationship that the child had contact with members of his father's family. The father was more realistic and reasonable than the mother, whose individuality and idealism were her weaknesses, and who did not really believe that it was important for the child to maintain a relationship with his father. Those weaknesses could be compensated and safeguarded by the development of the child's relationship with his father. If the child was allowed to emigrate, he would not be able to communicate easily and spontaneously with his father by letter and telephone and it was likely that he would see his father only once a year. In all the circumstances, it would be wrong to grant the mother leave to remove the child from the jurisdiction permanently and, accordingly, her application would be dismissed.

MH v GP (Child: Emigration) [1995] 2 FLR 106 (Family Division: Thorpe J).

429   Prohibited steps order—power to make order against non-party—use of power to protect children

Under the Children Act 1989, s 8, a prohibited steps order means an order that no step which could be taken by a parent in meeting his parental responsibility for a child, and which is of a kind specified in the order, is to be taken by any person without the consent of the court. No court is to exercise its powers to make a prohibited steps order with a view to achieving a result which could be achieved by making a residence or contact order: s 9(5).

A mother lived with her six children and a cohabitee who was not their father. He sexually abused one child and clearly posed a risk to all of the children. On the local authority's application, a prohibited steps order was made against the mother to prevent contact between the children and the cohabitee. The judge refused to make such an order against the cohabitee on the ground that he had no jurisdiction to do so since the cohabitee was not a party to the proceedings. The children's guardian ad litem appealed against the refusal, but the cohabitee claimed that it would be wrong in principle to make an order against him when he was not a party. *Held*, a contact order included an order that there be no contact. The judge had no power to make a prohibited steps order against the mother since that would achieve the same result as a contact order requiring her not to allow contact with the cohabitee and could be enforced in the same way. However, a prohibited steps order which required the cohabitee not to have or to seek contact with the children would not contravene s 9(5). If a 'no contact' order had been made against the mother, the order would be directed at her as the subject of the order and the obligation would be on her to prevent any contact. There could not be a 'no contact' order directing the cohabitee not to have or to seek contact. Accordingly, the appeal would be allowed. The cohabitee would be given liberty to apply on notice to vary or discharge the prohibited steps order under s 11(7)(d), which provided that a s 8 order could make such incidental, supplemental or consequential provision as the court thought fit, and that would be sufficient to meet the justice of the case.

Re H (Minors: Prohibited Steps Order) [1995] 1 WLR 667 (Court of Appeal: Butler-Sloss LJ and Sir Ralph Gibson).

430   Residence order—allegations of sexual abuse—allegations not proved

A family consisted of a mother and father, their two children and seven stepchildren. The parents later divorced and the two children of both parents went to live with the father. They were well cared for. Several years later, one of the father's stepdaughters alleged that he had sexually abused and raped her throughout the marriage. Proceedings were then commenced by the local authority in respect of the two children who remained within his care. The mother took the children to live with her. At first instance the judge found that there was some evidence of the father having acted in an inappropriate way towards his stepdaughter. However, he also concluded that the stepdaughter's most serious allegations, and particularly the allegation of rape, had not been made out to the standard of proof on a balance of probabilities. It was possible but not probable that her allegations were true. Having considered those matters and the possibility of harm to the children if they were returned to the father, against the very strong desire of the children to be returned to their father and the emotional harm they had suffered in being removed to their mother, the judge concluded that the children should be returned to their father. The mother appealed. *Held*, this was a finely balanced case where the judge had been required to balance the possibility of sexual abuse in the future against the actuality of emotional abuse in the present and the future. The judge had not erred in principle in reaching his decision, nor had he failed to take into account any relevant factors. Accordingly, the appeal would be dismissed.

Re N (Residence: Hopeless Appeals) [1995] 2 FLR 230 (Court of Appeal: Butler-Sloss, Simon Brown and Ward LJJ).

431   Residence order—application by child—relevant factors

A child who lived with her father under a residence order, applied for leave of the court to apply under the Children Act 1989, s 8 for an order allowing her to live with her mother. *Held*, the principles set out in the 1989 Act, s 10(9), which normally apply to applications for leave to apply for s 8 orders, do not apply to applications by children and, although the best interests of the child are of importance, in cases such as the one in issue, they are not paramount. The child possessed sufficient understanding to make the application but the court had also to have regard to the likelihood of success of the application before granting leave to apply. It would be impossible to say that the application which the applicant sought to make would be one which could not succeed and, accordingly, leave to apply would be granted.

Re C (Residence: Child's Application for Leave) [1995] 1 FLR 927 (Family Division: Stuart-White J).

432 Residence order—application by foster mother—child ordered to leave jurisdiction by immigration service—intervention by court

M arrived in the United Kingdom, with his daughter F, seeking asylum. He was given temporary admission but was then detained and F was found apparently abandoned and extremely distressed. The local authority placed F with a foster mother where she made good progress. She told the foster mother that M had physically assaulted her. M also told F that her mother was dead but later said that she was alive. F did have some contact with her father, but she said that she never wished to see him again. When the immigration service informed the authority that it intended to remove M and F, the foster mother applied for a residence order and for leave to commence those proceedings. Leave was granted and a prohibited steps order was made preventing the child being removed from the foster mother or the jurisdiction until further order or under Home Office direction. Both M and F were refused leave to enter under the Immigration Act 1971, s 3(1). *Held*, (1) under the Family Law Act 1986 an English court did not have jurisdiction to make an order in a non-matrimonial case unless the child was habitually resident or present in the country. The Children Act 1989 contained no express provisions about jurisdiction and the matter was therefore governed by the 1986 Act, under which the court had primary jurisdiction. (2) Before intervening, the court had to be satisfied that the application was not a device to avoid immigration rules and that the circumstances were exceptional or most exceptional. Although the welfare of the child was paramount under the 1989 Act, there had to be a balancing exercise with the requirements of public policy and that required some extraordinary circumstances which took the case outside the normal considerations of welfare. On the facts, both elements of the test were satisfied and it was one of the rare cases in which the court should intervene on behalf of the child. Accordingly, a residence order was made in favour of the foster mother and, because F had no relatives in the country and needed protection until adulthood, the order would extend to F's eighteenth birthday.

Re M (A Minor) (Immigration: Residence Order) [1995] 2 FCR 793 (Family Division: Bracewell J).

433 Residence order—contested applications—appropriateness of testing child for HIV

After a child's mother died from an illness which was AIDS-related, the child was made a ward of court. There were to be contested residence applications and the Official Solicitor applied for an order for the taking of a sample of the child's blood in order to discover whether she was HIV positive. This application was supported by medical evidence which pointed to the usefulness of knowledge of a child's medical status at a time when the child was about to begin going to school and would be likely to encounter many childhood illnesses. Such knowledge would be fundamentally important to the treatment of such illnesses. The local authority opposed the application, pointing to the stigma associated with HIV infection and stating that such knowledge could only be beneficial if the test was negative. *Held*, when the residence applications were heard the court would be influenced by the considerations in the Children Act 1989, s 1(3)(b) which required the court to have regard to the child's physical, emotional and educational needs. There was no doubt, given the doctor's evidence, that it would be best for the child if the test were carried out. The test should be carried out immediately so that when the residence applications were being heard, the judge could take into account the results of the blood test.

Re W (A Minor) (HIV Test) [1995] 2 FCR 184 (Family Division: Kirkwood J).

434 Residence order—leave to remove child from jurisdiction—factors to be taken into account

The mother and father of a child were respectively Swedish and English, and the matrimonial home was in England. Following the parties' separation, the mother went to Sweden with the child, but eventually returned to England and was reconciled with the father. Following further separations, the father was granted an ex parte joint residence order, and the mother was granted leave to take the child to Sweden for 28 days. In determining the residence order application, the judge found that the child had dual nationality, that the mother had few ties in England and could not contemplate living in England indefinitely, and that she was the child's primary carer and would be better than the father at caring for him. The judge therefore made a residence order in the mother's favour and also gave her leave to remove the child from the jurisdiction. On the father's appeal, *held*, in addition to the judge's findings, the court welfare officer had stated that the status quo should not be altered and that although both parents were important to the child, the most important relationship for him was that with his mother. Moreover, the effect on the mother of having to remain in England was relevant to the care of the child and the child's happiness. The judge had considered all the matters listed in the Children Act 1989, s 1(3), and could not be faulted in his approach to the matter of residence. As regards removing the child from the jurisdiction, the judge had not been obliged to apply 1989 Act criteria as the father had claimed, as the Act did not alter the underlying factors which needed to be considered in deciding whether or not to allow a parent to remove a child from the jurisdiction. Moreover, the judge had borne in mind all the matters referred to in s 1(3) in considering the issue, and had also considered the difficulties and stresses that would be placed on the child, and also on the father in having to travel to Sweden to have contact with the child. The judge had been required to carry out a balancing exercise, and had done so with care. Accordingly, the appeal would be dismissed.

H v H (Residence Order: Leave to Remove from Jurisdiction) [1995] 2 FCR 469 (Court of Appeal: Staughton LJ and Wall J).

435   Secure accommodation—secure accommodation order—jurisdiction of youth court to make order where different youth court remanded young person

The Children Act 1989, s 92(2) provides that proceedings under that Act should be treated as family proceedings. Under the Criminal Justice Act 1991, s 60(3), in the case of a child or young person who has been remanded or committed to local authority accommodation by a youth court, any application for a secure accommodation order, notwithstanding the 1989 Act, s 92(2), is to be made to that court.

A 16-year-old boy who lived in Liverpool allegedly committed serious offences in Manchester. The youth court there remanded the boy to the care of the local authority in Liverpool. The authority later applied to the youth court in Liverpool to place the boy in secure accommodation, pursuant to the 1991 Act, s 60(3). That court declined jurisdiction on the ground that the application had to be made to the court which had remanded the boy to the authority's care. On the authority's appeal against that decision, *held*, s 60(3) provided that an authority in making such an application for secure accommodation should apply to the appropriate youth court rather than to the family proceedings court. The jurisdiction was not confined to the court which had remanded the boy. It was clearly appropriate that the authority should apply to its own court in relation to children remanded in its care. Accordingly, the appeal would be allowed and the matter remitted to the youth court for determination.

Liverpool City Council v B [1995] 1 WLR 505 (Family Division: Ewbank J).

436   Secure accommodation—secure accommodation order—relevant criteria—welfare of child

Under the Children Act 1989, s 25, a child who has to be looked after by a local authority may not be placed, and, if placed, may not be kept, in accommodation provided for the purpose of restricting liberty unless it appears that any accommodation other than that provided for the purpose of restricting liberty is inappropriate because (a) the child is likely to abscond from such other accommodation, or (b) the child is likely to injure himself or other people if he is kept in any such other accommodation.

A 14-year-old boy was charged with serious offences including arson with intent to endanger life. A youth court remanded him into the care of the local authority, but the boy absconded from his accommodation on 31 occasions and committed further offences. On the authority's application for a secure accommodation order, the magistrates found that the authority had satisfied the relevant criteria in s 25. They granted an order for 21 days in secure accommodation, the minimum time needed for further assessment and psychiatric treatment. The boy appealed against the order, submitting that the magistrates had erred because they were not only under a duty to satisfy themselves of the criteria in s 25 but were also specifically required to consider his welfare under s 1. *Held*, it was clear that the hearing went beyond the mere question of whether the s 25 criteria could be established and went into matters relating to the boy's welfare. Although the justices did not make any specific finding or reference to s 1 it was clear that it was not something out of the magistrates' minds. The magistrates had not erred in their approach and, accordingly, the appeal would be dismissed.

AE v Staffordshire County Council (1995) 159 JP 367 (Family Division: Kirkwood J).

437   Secure accommodation—voluntary homes and registered children's homes

The Children (Secure Accommodation) Amendment Regulations 1995, SI 1995/1398 (in force on 23 June 1995), further amend the 1991 Regulations, SI 1991/1505, by extending (for purposes connected with the extension of provision of secure accommodation by the Criminal Justice and Public Order Act 1994, s 19) the provisions which govern secure accommodation in community homes to secure accommodation in voluntary homes and registered children's homes, and by removing the prohibition of the use of accommodation for the purpose of restricting the liberty of children in voluntary homes and registered children's homes.

438   Surname—change by one parent—objection by other parent—consideration of child's wishes

A mother of three children separated from her first husband and later divorced. She was granted custody of the children and the usual order was made to prohibit her from changing the childrens' surnames without their father's consent or the leave of the court. The mother subsequently remarried and applied for leave to change their surnames to that of her second husband. The children, who were aged between 12 and 16 years, clearly wanted their surnames to be changed. They had come to be known by their stepfather's name and, for some time, had refused to have any contact with their natural father. At first instance, the application was dismissed. The mother appealed. *Held*, orders that ran contrary to the wishes of normal adolescent children were virtually unknown in family law, particularly in the realm of applications for residence or contact. However, the granting of leave to change a child's surname would only serve to injure the link between the child and his father. Accordingly, irrespective of the childrens' wishes, the granting of leave would not be in their best interests. The appeal would be dismissed.

Re B (Minors) (Change of Surname) (1995) Times, 1 December (Court of Appeal: Stuart-Smith LJ and Wilson J).

439   Wardship—jurisdiction—identification of child—injunction to restrain identification—discharge or variation of injunction

The mother of a handicapped child obtained an injunction restraining the media from revealing the identity of the child or any establishment where she was residing or being educated or treated. Following comments made by the mother in a television broadcast, she too was restrained from discussing the child's education. The child started at an institute which offered a unique method of treating problems of the kind confronting her and a television production company wanted to make a documentary about the institute's work which would involve identifying and filming the child. The mother wished to permit the film to publicise the institute's valuable work and thereby to enhance the child's welfare and esteem. The mother applied to have the injunctions discharged or varied to enable the production and broadcast of the programme. At first instance, the judge refused on the ground that it would not be in the child's best interests. On appeal, *held*, in being asked to decide whether the child could take part in the programme, the court was determining a question with respect to her upbringing and the Children Act 1989, s 1 therefore applied to make the child's welfare the paramount consideration. On that approach, the judge had been correct in his conclusion that, notwithstanding the fundamental importance of the freedom of publication of information, the welfare of the child would be harmed and not advanced by her participation in the making and publication of the programme and that she should continue to enjoy the protection against publicity which the injunctions gave her. Accordingly, the appeal would be dismissed.

Re Z (a Minor) (Freedom of Publication) [1995] 4 All ER 961 (Court of Appeal: Sir Thomas Bingham MR, Auld and Ward LJJ).

440   Wardship—proceedings—habitual residence of child disputed by parents— jurisdiction

The parties were married in Pakistan and then lived in England where they had a child. When she was eight years old, her father took her to Pakistan and enrolled her in a boarding school there. However, wardship proceedings were commenced and the father was ordered to return the child to England. The mother was awarded interim care and control of the child. The father claimed that the mother had agreed to the child's habitual residence being changed to Pakistan. The mother contended that the child had been sent to Pakistan for educational purposes only and the official solicitor argued that, even if there had been an agreement to send the child to live abroad, if the parents were both habitually resident in England and the agreement failed, the child's habitual residence would not be abroad. *Held*, one parent could not unilaterally change a child's habitual residence without the agreement of the other unless circumstances arose which, quite independently, would point to a change in the child's habitual residence. It was open to the parents to agree to change their child's habitual residence without changing their own but an agreement to send their child abroad to a boarding school would not be sufficient to change the child's habitual residence. Even if there had been such an agreement as would change the habitual residence, it would require the continued agreement of both parents to make that situation continue. Accordingly, the child was habitually resident in England and the court had jurisdiction to determine her future.

Re A (Wardship: Jurisdiction) [1995] 1 FLR 767 (Family Division: Hale J).

CHOSES IN ACTION

Halsbury's Laws of England (4th edn) Vol 6 (reissue), paras 1–200

441   Assignment—judgment debt

See *Whitehouse v Ellam (Inspector of Taxes)*, para 297.

CLUBS

Halsbury's Laws of England (4th edn) Vol 6 (reissue), paras 201–500

442   Bingo duty—administration

See para 207.

443   Bingo duty—monetary amounts

See para 219.

444   Gaming clubs—charges

See BETTING, GAMING AND LOTTERIES.

445   Licensing (Sunday Hours) Act 1995

See para 1760.

COMMONS

Halsbury's Laws of England (4th edn) Vol 6 (reissue), paras 501–800

446   Articles

Getting Greens Registered, Alec Samuels (on registration of town or village greens): 139 SJ 948
How the Local Authority Can Protect a Common, Alec Samuels: 159 JP Jo 825
Protecting Our Commons, Alec Samuels (on *Lewis v Mid-Glamorgan County Council* [1995] 1
   All ER 760, HL): 139 SJ 764.

447   Common land—recreation grounds—parish council byelaws—revocation

The Recreation Grounds (Revocation of Parish Council Byelaws) Order 1995, SI 1995/376 (in force on 31 March 1995), revokes certain specified byelaws which were made by the relevant parish councils in the exercise of powers conferred by the Local Government Act 1894, as they are substantially superseded by byelaws made under other enactments.

448 Common land—registration—removal from register—land compulsorily acquired

A water authority compulsorily acquired common land under powers conferred by a private Act of Parliament for a purpose which was abandoned before commencement. Invoking the procedure laid down in the Compulsory Purchase Act 1965, Sch 4 they convened a meeting of commoners and agreed a level of compensation of commoner's rights which was later paid. They then dated a vesting deed whereby they took the land free from commonable and all other rights. The land was later conveyed to the borough council who wanted to use it for other purposes, having a bona fide belief that it was no longer common land. In the meantime there had been no change in the use of the land, which continued to be used by the general public and grazed by commoners. The borough council applied to the county council for removal of the land from the commons register. The county council issued a summons to determine whether the land had ceased to be common land and should be excluded from the register and whether the commoners should be able to challenge the vesting deed by which the land had been taken free from commonable and other rights. On appeal by the commoners against a determination in favour of the borough council, *held*, the land had not been deprived of its status as a common. Payment to the commoners had extinguished their individual rights but the rights of access enjoyed by the general public had not been extinguished by the private Act. Thus, the land was properly registered under the Commons Registration Act 1965. The provisions of the Commons Act 1876, s 36 applied, prohibiting enclosure without the sanction of Parliament. Accordingly, the appeal would be allowed.

Lewis v Mid Glamorgan County Council [1995] 1 All ER 760 (House of Lords: Lords Jauncey of Tullichettle, Templeman, Griffiths, Ackner and Browne-Wilkinson). Decision of Court of Appeal (1993) Times, 8 November (1993 Abr para 523) reversed in part.

449 Common land—registration—town or village green—registration of land used by employees for sport and recreation

Employees of an airbase had for some years used land between the airbase and their homes for recreation and sports. A resident applied to the local authority to amend its register of town and village greens by registering the land in question under the Commons Registration Act 1965, s 13 as a village green, defined under s 22 as 'land on which the inhabitants of any locality have indulged in sports or pastimes as of right for a period of not less than twenty years'. The application was granted and the plaintiff applied to the High Court under the 1965 Act, s 14(b) for an order that the register be rectified by deleting the amendment. *Held*, in order to found a claim as user as of right it had to be shown that the user was of such character and degree of frequency to indicate an assertion of a right to perform the activity on the land in question rather than a mere toleration of the activity by the landowner. Where an employer allowed employees' children to play on its land the only reasonable inference was that such user was by tacit permission or tolerance. Residents of streets adjacent to open land could not have a right created for them in perpetuity because they did not constitute a defined body of persons recognised in law as an entity and because the land in question was not defined. Further, the requirement that the activity should have been indulged in for not less than twenty years should be interpreted as meaning twenty years immediately before the application and not any twenty-year period in the past. Accordingly, the application would be granted.

Ministry of Defence v Wiltshire County Council [1995] 4 All ER 931 (Chancery Division: Harman J).

450 Common land—registration—town or village green—user as of right—amendment of register

The Commons Registration Act 1965, s 1(2)(a) provides that after 30 July 1970, no land capable of being registered under the Act is to be deemed to be common land or a town or village green unless it is so registered. Section 22 defines a town or village green as land which has been allotted by or under any Act for the exercise or recreation of the inhabitants of any locality, or on which the inhabitants of any locality have a customary right to indulge in lawful sports and pastimes, or on which the inhabitants of any locality have indulged in such sports or pastimes as of right for not less than 20 years. Section 13(b) provides that regulations made under the Act may provide for the amendment of the common register after 30 July 1970 where any land becomes common land, or a town or village green.

The Secretary of State bought an uncultivated area of land, on which he planned to build a hospital. The applicants later applied for the land to be registered under the 1965 Act as a village green, but the Secretary of State objected to the application. When the local planning authority rejected the application, the applicants applied for judicial review of the decision. *Held*, a town or village green had to be adjunct to a town or village, and a 'locality' was a distinct and identifiable community or district, rather than merely a place or geographical area. Moreover, the main purpose of registration was to record and settle existing rights and interests, rather than add to or alter them. The important words in the 1965 Act, s 22 were 'as of right', as they indicated that mere use of the land in question was not enough. The more substantial and formal the use of the land, the stronger the inference that that was done in assertion of a right. Here, although the land had been used for recreational purposes, there was no evidence that such user was as of right, nor that such a right had arisen since 1970 for the purposes of s 13(b). Moreover, the use of the land had not been by reference to any particular locality, as the evidence pointed merely to a collection of people living in the area surrounding the land who had used it, albeit over a long period of time. As the applicants had not shown that the land was a village green, the local planning authority had not erred in refusing to register it as such. Accordingly, the application would be dismissed.

R v Suffolk County Council, ex p Steed (1995) 70 P & CR 487 (Queen's Bench Division: Carnwath J).

COMMONWEALTH AND DEPENDENCIES

Halsbury's Laws of England (4th edn) Vol 6 (reissue), paras 801–1108

451 Bahamas—capital punishment—murder—mandatory sentence

Bahamas

Under the law of The Bahamas a person who commits murder is liable to suffer death in the manner authorised by the law.

The appellants were convicted of murder and sentenced to death by hanging. Their appeals against conviction were dismissed. They complained that to sentence them to death would infringe their constitutional rights to life and not to be subjected to inhuman or degrading punishment. *Held*, although the law in question used the word 'liable', it was plain that the death sentence was the mandatory sentence for murder in The Bahamas. The common law method of executing the death sentence by hanging remained in force and was incorporated into the law of The Bahamas by statute. The constitutional rights of the appellants would not be infringed by the imposition of the death sentence.

Jones v A-G of the Commonwealth of the Bahamas [1995] 4 All ER 1 (Privy Council: Lords Keith of Kinkel, Lane, Jauncey of Tullichettle and Browne-Wilkinson and Sir John May).

452 Bahamas—capital punishment—stay of execution—constitutional motion regarding sentence—circumstances in which stay granted

Bahamas

The appellant in a death penalty case had applied for a stay of execution pending a hearing of a motion that the carrying out of the sentence would be unconstitutional. The Supreme Court of the Bahamas had refused to grant the stay and the Court of Appeal had dismissed his appeal. On further appeal, *held*, a refusal of a stay in a death penalty case would only be granted where it was plain and obvious that the constitutional motion would fail. If an arguable point was raised, even if it was considered that the motion was likely to fail, the case should not be decided under the pressures of time attending applications for a stay of execution. Even if the court decided not to grant a full stay until determination of the constitutional motion, it should grant a short stay of a few days to enable its decision to be tested on appeal. Accordingly, the appeal would be allowed.

Reckley v Minister of Public Safety and Immigration [1995] 4 All ER 8 (Privy Council: Lords Goff of Chieveley, Browne-Wilkinson and Hoffmann).

453 Bahamas—commission of inquiry—appointment and powers

The Bahamas

The Commissions of Inquiry Act 1911, s 2 provides that whenever it appears to the Governor General in Council that it is for the public benefit to do so, he may issue a commission, appointing persons not less than three in number to inquire into and report upon any matter stated in such commission as the subject of inquiry. Section 10(1)(b) provides that any commissioner has the power of a justice of the Supreme Court to call for the production of documents or things, including the power to retain and examine the same. Letters of Patent

1909, art XIII provides that the Governor may constitute and appoint all such judges, commissioners, justices of the peace, and other necessary officers in the islands as may be lawfully constituted and appointed.

The Governor General appointed a commission made up of the respondents, to inquire into certain specified matters relating to three companies. When the appellant was summoned to give evidence before the commission, he challenged the validity of the appointment of the commission and its power to summon him. His application was unsuccessful at first instance and on appeal. On further appeal, *held*, whether the commission was appointed by the Governor General in the exercise of his prerogative powers or his powers under the 1911 Act, s 11, the appointment was valid and the members of the commission had the necessary powers, and were subject to the duties, provided by the 1911 Act. Moreover, the Governor General had acted properly in appointing the commission on the advice of the government, as the Bahamian Constitution required him to do so. The 1911 Act, s 10(1)(b) empowered the commission to issue a subpoena duces tecum, but it could not order a search of persons or property. Even if it were empowered to order a search, such an order would be permitted by the Constitution as an act done in the interests of defence, public safety and public order. It was settled that the Governor General was obliged to specify the matters which were the subject of an inquiry and could not leave it to an appointed commission to determine. In the instant case, as the Governor General had expressly confined the scope of the inquiry to matters arising out of or in connection with the affairs of the three companies, he had not delegated any of his discretion. Although only a court had jurisdiction to try criminal offences, a commission could nevertheless make a report on such matters to the Governor General. Accordingly, the appeal would be dismissed.

Bethel v Douglas [1995] 3 All ER 801 (Privy Council: Lords Keith of Kinkel, Lane, Jauncey of Tullichettle, Browne-Wilkinson, and Sir John May)

454   Barbados—capital punishment—delay in execution—inhuman or degrading treatment or punishment

Barbados
The applicants sought redress for alleged infringements of their constitutional rights, claiming that the delay in carrying out death sentences imposed on them constituted inhuman or degrading punishment. *Held*, although a significant effort had been made to deduct from the period of the delay periods when the applicants had been prevaricating, the delay still amounted to over five years. However, a minute examination of such delays and apportionment of blame should be discouraged. The correct approach was that indicated in *Pratt v A-G for Jamaica*, which was to look at the total period of time which had elapsed and then to ask whether the delay was due entirely to the fault of the accused such as an escape from custody or a frivolous or time wasting resort to legal procedures which amounted to an abuse of process; where that was the case, the accused could not take advantage of the delay. In the present case, no period fell to be deducted from the total period which had elapsed since the death sentence was passed on the appellants. Accordingly, the appeals would be allowed and sentences of life imprisonment substituted.

Bradshaw v A-G for Barbados; Roberts v A-G for Barbados [1995] 1 WLR 936 (Privy Council: Lords Goff of Chievely, Lane, Slynn of Hadley, Steyn and Sir Ralph Gibson). *Pratt v A-G for Jamaica* [1993] 4 All ER 769, PC followed.

455   Brunei—criminal evidence—confession—oppression in conduct of police interview

Brunei
The appellants were arrested on suspicion of firearms offences and, in accordance with the customary 'special procedure', were manacled with their hands behind their backs and had hoods placed over their heads whilst being interrogated. A few days after their interrogations, they made and signed written confessions. In the period between the interrogations and the signing of the confessions, they were questioned by police officers and deprived of visits from relatives. The appellants were convicted of firearms offences, and on appeal, they argued that there had been oppression in the conduct of the police interviews. *Held*, the very nature of the special procedure and the relatively short gap between the time when the procedure was applied and the statements were signed, suggested that the statements were or might have been obtained by oppression. Under the Criminal Procedure Code of Brunei, s 117(2), the prosecution had the burden of proving that a statement was made voluntarily. In the instant case, the prosecution had failed to prove beyond reasonable doubt that the statements were not obtained by oppression, and they should have been ruled inadmissible. Accordingly, the appeal would be allowed.

Burut v Public Prosecutor [1995] 3 WLR 16 (Privy Council: Lords Goff of Chieveley, Jauncey of Tullichettle, Mustill, Nicholls of Birkenhead and Steyn).

456 Commonwealth Development Corporation Act 1995

The Commonwealth Development Corporation Act 1995 increases the statutory limit on borrowing by the Commonwealth Development Corporation, gives the Secretary of State power to waive interest payments on advances to the corporation and makes provision relating to the remuneration, pensions and compensation of corporation members. The Act received royal assent on 28 June 1995 and came into force on that date.

Section 1 increases the statutory limit on the outstanding amount of sums borrowed or guaranteed by the corporation to £1,100m, with provision for an increase by order to a larger sum not exceeding £1,500m. The separate statutory limit on advances to the corporation is removed. Provision is made in s 2 for the Secretary of State, with the approval of the Treasury, to make interest-free advances to the corporation and enables him, with Treasury consent, to waive interest on advances made to the corporation by him. Section 3 enables the Secretary of State to determine remuneration, allowances and pensions of corporation members, removes the requirement for Treasury consent in relation to such matters and provides for compensation payments to be made in special circumstances to a person who ceases to be a member of the corporation. Sections 4 and 5 relate to repeals, short title and extent.

457 Dependent territories—Civil Service—pensions

The Overseas Service (Pensions Supplement) Regulations 1995, SI 1995/238 (in force on 1 March 1995), consolidate the 1977 Regulations, SI 1977/320 (as amended), and provide for the payment of supplements on pensions paid to certain officers who have served governments, authorities or institutions of overseas territories. The 1995 Regulations are in a different form to that of the 1977 Regulations, but the substance of the earlier regulations remains largely unchanged.

458 Dependent territories—intelligence services

See para 588.

459 St Vincent and the Grenadines—criminal procedure—notice of appeal—defective notice—validation

St Vincent and the Grenadines
The appellant was convicted of murder and sentenced to death. His notice of application for leave to appeal against conviction and sentence failed to comply with rules of court which required that the notice be signed by the appellant within a specified time limit. At the hearing of a co-defendant's appeal, the appellant's request to have the period for lodging his notice of application extended was refused on the ground that, as the rules did not permit extension of time, the court had no jurisdiction to hear the appeal. On his appeal against that refusal, *held*, where it was in the interests of justice that non-compliance with the rules should be waived, the court had power to proceed with a criminal appeal even though the appellant had accidentally failed to comply with the rules. Although a statutory provision specifying a time limit for the lodging of an appeal could not thereby be overridden, non-compliance with requirements deriving solely from the rules could be waived. By virtue of such waiver, the notice of appeal would be validated as from the date it had been lodged. As it was in the interests of justice that the appellant's appeal should be heard, his failure to observe the rules would be waived so that his notice of appeal would be validated. Accordingly, the appeal would be allowed and the case remitted for determination.

Pollard v The Queen [1995] 1 WLR 1591 (Privy Council: Lords Jauncey of Tullichettle, Browne-Wilkinson, Mustill, Slynn of Hadley and Hardie Boys J).

460 South Africa Act 1995

The South Africa Act 1995 makes amendments to various enactments in connection with the re-admission of South Africa as a member of the Commonwealth. The Act received the royal assent on 23 March 1995 and came into force on that date.

461 South Georgia and Sandwich Islands—Commissioner

The South Georgia and South Sandwich Islands (Amendment) Order 1995, SI 1995/1621 (in force on 17 July 1995), amends the 1985 Order, SI 1985/449, so as to make fresh provision for the office of Commissioner for South Georgia and the South Sandwich Islands. The Commissioner is to be appointed by Her Majesty, and holds office at Her Majesty's pleasure. In the event that the office becomes vacant or the holder is unable to fulfil his duties, a Secretary of State is to designate a person to assume office.

462 Trinidad and Tobago—capital punishment—delay in execution—cruel and unusual punishment

Trinidad and Tobago

The appellant was convicted of murder and sentenced to death. He appealed to the Privy Council on the grounds that (1) his execution after a delay of four years and ten months in hearing his appeal was a cruel and unusual punishment contrary to the constitution and (2) giving him less than 17 hours' notice of his impending execution was a breach of his constitutional rights not to be deprived of life except by due process of law and not to be deprived of such procedural provisions as were necessary for the purpose of giving effect to his rights and freedoms. *Held*, where a person was sentenced to death in a common law jurisdiction, execution had to be carried out as swiftly as practicable after sentence, allowing a reasonable time for appeal and consideration of reprieve. In assessing what was a reasonable time for appeal, great importance had to be attached to ensuring that delay would not occur and any delay which did occur would be curtailed. The aim should be for the local court of appeal to hear and decide an appeal within 12 months of conviction and for any appeal to the Privy Council to be disposed of within a further 12 months. As those target periods had been substantially exceeded because of the failure to make available the judge's notes of the evidence at the trial for four years, the execution of the appellant would constitute cruel and unusual punishment. Justice and humanity required that a man under sentence of death should be given reasonable notice of the time of his execution to enable him to arrange his affairs. There was a settled practice that a condemned man should have at least four clear days, including a weekend, between the reading of the death warrant and his execution. Accordingly, giving the appellant less than 17 hours' notice of his execution constituted a breach of his constitutional rights. The appeal would be allowed.

Guerra v Baptiste [1995] 4 All ER 583 (Privy Council: Lords Keith of Kinkel, Goff of Chieveley, Slynn of Hadley, Nolan and Nicholls of Birkenhead).

COMPANIES

Halsbury's Laws of England (4th edn) Vol 7(1) (reissue), paras 1–1069, Vol 7(2) (reissue), paras 1070–2441

463 Articles

Attorney-General v Reid: The Company Law Implications, A J Boyle (on *Attorney-General for Hong Kong v Reid* [1994] 1 All ER 1, PC (1993 Abr para 2576)): 16 Comp Lawyer 131
Auditors - and the legal profession, Graham Potter: 145 NLJ 884
Branch Registration of an Overseas Company, Bernard Andonian: 139 SJ 47
Commencement of Trading, David Martin (on the rules governing commencement of a trade): Tax Journal, Issue 303, p 4
The Companies Act 1989—A Curate's Egg? N J M Grier (on sections of the 1989 Act relating to registration of charges which have never been brought into force): 16 Comp Lawyer 3
The Companies Maze, Rob Hann (on the Local Authorities (Companies) Order 1995, SI 1995/849): LS Gaz, 7 June, p 19
Compliance Programmes, Julian Armstrong (on *Director General of Fair Trading v Pioneer Concrete (UK) Ltd* [1995] 1 All ER 135, HL (1994 Abr para 1219)): [1995] ECLR 147
Conduct of Business Rules; What We Have and What We Can Expect, Tarjei Thorkildsen: 16 Comp Lawyer 305
Controlling Directors' Remuneration, Frances Le Grys: 139 SJ 96
Conveyancers and the Director as Purchaser, Nicholas Le Poidevin: 139 SJ 21
Corporate Criminal Liability, Bernard Robertson (on *Meridian Global Funds Management Asia Ltd v Securities Commission* (para 515)): 159 JP Jo 751
Corporate Governance and Corporate Opportunities, Gerard Bean: 15 Comp Lawyer 266
Corporate Redomicile, David Lewis: 16 Comp Lawyer 295
Debunking the Myth of the Kite Mark, Penelope Silver (on the BS5750 kite mark): 145 NLJ 19
The Director's Duties, Catherine Drew: LS Gaz, 1 March 1995, p 16
Directors' Duties and 'Self-Dealing', Andrew Griffiths: 139 SJ 1184, 1210

Directors' Handshakes: The Perspective After Greenbury, Michael Ryley: 139 SJ 987

Directors' Remuneration: Constraining the Power of the Board, Andrew Griffiths: [1995] LMCLQ 372

Disclosure of Tentative Information by Listed Companies—Pt 1, Ahal Besorai: 16 Comp Lawyer 236, 270

Fair Shares, David Cohen (on measures taken to make employee share schemes more attractive to companies): LS Gaz, 8 March 1995, p 16

Fettering Directors' Discretion, Thomas Courtney: 16 Comp Lawyer 227

Goodwill and Intangible Assets: New Proposals for Accounting Reform, Andy Simmonds: [1995] EIPR 34

Joint Venture Analysis: The Latest Chapter, Alec Burnside and Judy Mackenzie Stuart (on treatment of joint ventures under EC competition rules): [1995] ECLR 138

Legal Aspects of Management Buy-Outs, Maurice Dwyer: (1995) 4 ICCLR 129

Neither a Borrower Nor a Lender Be, Gary Morris and David Williams (on the tax dangers of making loans to directors, employees and participators): Tax Journal, Issue 316, p 11

Non-Executive Directors: Are They Truly Independent? John Cadman: 139 SJ 346

Priority of the Floating Charge in Corporate Insolvency: *Griffiths v Yorkshire Bank plc* ([1994] 1 WLR 1427 (1994 Abr para 487)), Adrian Walters: 16 Comp Lawyer 291

The Pros and Cons of Incorporation, Hywel Williams (on the taxation implications of incorporation): Tax Journal, Issue 325, p 18

Protecting the Public, Leslie Wise (on disqualified directors remaining in their posts): LS Gaz, 19 July 1995, p 24

A Quiet Revolution in Corporate Liability for Crime, Celia Wells: 145 NLJ 1326

Rethinking Corporate Crime and Individual Responsibility, Mark Stallworthy: Criminal Lawyer, Issue 55, p 5

Revised Proposals for CVAs, Andrew Campbell (on proposals from the Insolvency Service for a company voluntary arrangement): 139 SJ 656

Shares in Nominee Names, Michael Heneker: 139 SJ 531

Time for a Wellcome Change, Richard Pincher (on European notions of what constitutes a business): Tax Journal, Issue 302, p 16, Issue 303, p 11, Issue 304, p 12

Valuation of Shares in Buyout Orders, G Shapira: 16 Comp Lawyer 11

Winding Up Recalcitrant Debtors, Fidelis Oditah: [1995] LMCLQ 107

Withdrawal from the Joint Enterprise and Accessoryship Liability, Alan Reed: Criminal Lawyer, Issue 60, p 1

464   Accounts—audit—consequential amendments

The Companies Act 1989 Part II (Consequential Amendments) Regulations 1995, SI 1995/1163 (in force on 23 May 1995), make consequential amendments to the Companies Act 1985, s 717 (limited partnerships; limit on number of members), the Income and Corporation Taxes Act 1988, s 184 (independent accountants) and the Companies Act 1989 (Eligibility for Appointment as Company Auditor) (Consequential Amendments) Regulations 1991, SI 1991/1997.

The Companies Act 1989 Part II (Consequential Amendment) (No 2) Regulations 1995, SI 1995/2723 (in force on 13 November 1995), repeals the Building Societies Act 1986, Sch 11, para 5(2)(d) (body corporate not qualified for appointment as auditor of a building society) so as to enable bodies corporate to be eligible for appointment as auditors of building societies to the same extent that they are so eligible in relation to companies.

465   Accounts—audit—exemption

The Companies Act 1985 (Audit Exemption) (Amendment) Regulations 1995, SI 1995/589 (in force on 30 March 1995), amend the Companies Act 1985, s 249D so as to redefine the persons who are entitled to act as reporting accountants for the purposes of the 1985 Act, s 249C (reports required for the purposes of exemption from audit).

466   Administration order—employees of company in administration—adoption of contracts of employment

The Insolvency Act 1986, s 19(5) provides that any sums payable in respect of debts or liabilities incurred while a person was an administrator of a company under contracts of employment adopted by him in the carrying out of his functions are charged on the property of the company in his custody or under his control in priority to his own remuneration or expenses. The administrator is not to be taken to have adopted a contract of employment by reason of anything done or omitted to be done within 14 days after his appointment. Section 44 makes corresponding provision for administrative receivers.

The administrators and administrative receivers (the administrators) of companies wrote to the companies' employees advising them that they would continue to pay their salaries while a buyer for the businesses was sought. The letters stated that the administrators did not adopt or assume personal liability in respect of the employees' contracts of employment. When it became clear that a buyer would not be found, the administrators terminated the employees' contracts. The court held that the letters were ineffective and that by continuing the employment the administrators had adopted the contracts of employment. Accordingly, liabilities incurred to such employees while they had been administrators, including payments in lieu of notice and holiday pay on dismissal, were payable in priority to other debts. On appeal, the question was whether the 1986 Act, ss 19 and 44 gave the employees the right to be paid in full, and in priority to all other creditors, not only for services actually rendered during the administration or receivership but also other payments not referable to such services to which the employees were entitled under their contracts of employment. *Held*, the concept of adoption of the contract covered at least accepting liability for payment for services rendered to the administrator under the contracts he had continued. Therefore the concept of adoption was inconsistent with an ability to pick and choose between different liabilities under the contract. The contract as a whole was either adopted or not. If the employment was continued for more than 14 days after the appointment of the administrator or receiver, it was inevitable that the whole contract had been adopted. Section 19 only applied to liabilities incurred during the administration, which included liability for wages accruing during the contractual period of notice or the damages payable for failure to give such notice. The employees were therefore entitled to payment in lieu of notice, including pension contributions in respect of the notice period. However, holiday pay referable to complete months of service expiring before the administrator's appointment did not fall within s 19. The liability of a receiver was likewise restricted to liabilities incurred under the contract when he was receiver.

Powdrill v Watson; Talbot v Cadge; Talbot v Grundy [1995] 2 All ER 65 (House of Lords: Lords Keith of Kinkel, Browne-Wilkinson, Mustill, Woolf and Lloyd of Berwick). Decisions of Court of Appeal [1994] 2 All ER 513 and Lightman J [1994] 4 All ER 300 (sub nom *Re Ferranti International plc; Re Leyland Daf Ltd*) affirmed.

The effect of this decision has been abrogated for contracts adopted after 15 March 1994 by the Insolvency Act 1994.

467 Administration order—solicitor holding funds recovered on behalf of company—company unable to discharge solicitor's fees—solicitor's lien over funds

An administration order was made against a company and administrators were appointed. Bills submitted to the company by a firm of solicitors were not paid and the firm indicated to the administrators its intention to apply money held on client account, which had been recovered on behalf of the company, to discharge the bills in part. The firm transferred the money to office account and the administrators brought proceedings to recover the money pursuant to the Insolvency Act 1986, s 234(2), which gave the court power to order a person holding company property to surrender it to the company's administrators. The judge found that the firm had a general lien over the money but, in asserting it against the administrators, the firm had taken a step to enforce its security over the company's property and, under the 1986 Act, s 11(3)(c), needed the administrators' consent or the court's leave to do so. The firm paid the money back into client account and sought leave to apply it in the payment of the bill. *Held*, on the assumption that the lien over the money was destroyed by the payment to office account and that when it was paid back into client account it became the company's property for the purpose of s 234(2), the firm acquired a fresh general lien in respect of unpaid fees. Although the firm's transfer of the money to office account without the court's leave was technically in breach of s 11(3)(c), no damage resulted from the breach and s 11 could not deprive the firm of the security provided by the lien over the reconstituted client account. Accordingly, the application would be allowed.

Euro Commercial Leasing Ltd v Cartwright & Lewis [1995] 2 BCLC 618 (Chancery Division: Evans-Lombe J).

468 Administrator—powers—company pension scheme—appointment and removal of trustees

See *Denny v Yeldon*, para 2255.

469 Auditors—remuneration—non-audit work

The Companies Act 1985 (Disclosure of Remuneration for Non-Audit Work) (Amendment) Regulations 1995, SI 1995/1520 (in force on 10 July 1995), amend the 1991 Regulations, SI 1991/2128, under which remuneration of a company's auditors and their associates for non-audit work done for the company must be disclosed in notes to the company's annual accounts. The 1995 Regulations amend the definition of associate of a company's auditors to exclude any body corporate in respect of which any partner in, or director of, the company's auditors was at any time in the relevant financial year entitled to exercise, or control the exercise of, 20 per cent or more of the voting rights at any general meeting solely in his capacity as an insolvency practitioner, a receiver, a receiver or manager, or a judicial factor on the estate of any person.

470 Capital duty—reduced rate—transfer of part of business

See *Commerz-Credit-Bank AG-Europartner v Finanzamt Saarbrücken*, para 3165.

471 Capital investment—state aid—recovery

See *Spain v EC Commission*, para 3116.

472 Companies Act 1989—commencement

The Companies Act 1989 (Commencement No 15 and Transitional and Savings Provisions) Order 1995, SI 1995/1352, brings into force on 3 July 1995 ss 145, 212 (both in part), Sch 19, para 20 (which inserts the Companies Act 1985, s 744A: index of defined expressions) and certain repeals in Sch 24. Transitional and savings provisions are also made.

The Companies Act 1989 (Commencement No 16) Order 1995, SI 1995/1591, brings ss 171, 176, 181 into force on 4 July 1995. For a summary of the Act, see 1989 Abr para 231. For details of commencement, see the commencement table in the title STATUTES.

473 Deregulation and Contracting Out Act 1994—commencement

The Deregulation and Contracting Out Act 1994 (Commencement No 3) Order 1995, SI 1995/1433, brings into force on 1 July 1995 ss 13(1), 39 (in part), Schs 5, 11, para 6, relating to the striking off of non-trading private companies registered in Great Britain. For regulations made under these provisions, see paras 513, 514. For a summary of the Act, see 1994 Abr para 2760. For details of commencement, see the commencement table in the title STATUTES.

474 Director—disqualification—application for disqualification order—appeal by official receiver—role of appellate court

The official receiver brought proceedings against the defendant company director for disqualification under the Company Directors Disqualification Act 1986, s 6. The application was dismissed and the official receiver appealed. *Held*, the appeal was, because of the Insolvency Rules 1986, r 7.49, a true appeal. In exercising its appellate jurisdiction, the appellate court would normally defer to the decision of the trial judge as regards findings of primary fact with respect to the charges alleged against the director as justifying disqualification. As regards the inferences to be drawn from such facts or the evaluation of such facts, for example in determining whether a reasonable director should have concluded that the company should not have traded beyond a particular point, the appellate court was in as good a position as the trial judge to draw such inferences or make such evaluations. Likewise, the appellate court might, in certain circumstances, be in an equally good position to determine whether the conduct of the director showed unfitness to take part in the management of a company's affairs. In such cases the appellate court should not shrink from making a decision even though it was disagreeing with the trial judge's findings. On the facts, the trial judge had erred in his finding that the evidence did not indicate that the defendant was unfit to be concerned in the management of a company. Accordingly, the appeal would be allowed and the defendant would be disqualified.

Re Hitco 2000 Ltd [1995] 2 BCLC 63 (Chancery Division: Jules Sher QC).

475 Director—disqualification—application for disqualification order—delay in proceedings—public interest

Proceedings under the Company Directors Disqualification Act 1986, for a disqualification order against a director were struck out because of the Official Receiver's inexcusable and inordinate delay in prosecuting the action. On the Official Receiver's appeal, one of the issues was the correct approach to be applied in applications to strike out disqualification proceedings for want of prosecution. *Held*, the fact that disqualification proceedings were brought in the public interest to protect the public was a factor to be balanced against the prejudice caused to a respondent by the inordinate and inexcusable delay in prosecuting the action. As the primary purpose of disqualification proceedings was to protect the public, and not to punish the director, the court could strike out proceedings if there had been serious prejudice, and it was unlikely that there would be a case that was so exceptional that disqualification proceedings would be allowed to continue if there was no possibility of a fair trial. Even if a fair trial was possible, there was a statutory two-year limit for commencing proceedings to which the court was obliged to have regard in deciding whether or not to strike out proceedings for want of prosecution. It was also necessary to take account of prejudice caused by delay before the commencement of proceedings, as well as prejudice caused by any delay thereafter. However, prejudice caused by the fact that proceedings were pending was irrelevant if it was not caused by delay. Moreover, as a director's unfitness was to be judged by his past conduct, the public interest in obtaining a disqualification order did not necessarily diminish with time. The court would rarely be justified in striking out proceedings solely because of the inherent prejudice arising from disqualification proceedings. In the instant case, the inherent prejudice of the proceedings together with the additional prejudice caused by the effect of delay on witnesses' recollection of events, amounted to a serious delay which outweighed the public interest in pursuing disqualification proceedings against the respondent. Accordingly, the appeal would be dismissed.

Re Manlon Trading Ltd [1995] 1 BCLC 578 (Court of Appeal: Staughton, Beldam and Peter Gibson LJJ). Decision of Evans-Lombe J [1995] 1 All ER 988 (1994 Abr para 494) affirmed.

476 Director—disqualification—application for disqualification order—dismissal of action—prejudice to fair trial—loss of documents

The Secretary of State commenced proceedings under the Company Directors Disqualification Act 1986, s 6 for disqualification orders against the two directors of a company which had gone into voluntary liquidation. When one of the directors sought to inspect certain documents which had been in the possession of the liquidator appointed to wind up the company, the Treasury Solicitor informed the director that the documents could no longer be found. The director unsuccessfully applied for the proceedings to be struck out. On appeal, *held*, the court had to determine whether or not the director's inability to inspect and study the lost documents seriously prejudiced the possibility of a fair trial to such an extent that the disqualification proceedings ought to be struck out. It was necessary to take account of the fact that, prior to the loss of the documents, the Secretary of State had intended to rely on them in support of his application and the director had not asked to inspect them. It was also necessary to take account of the fact that the allegations against the director were both numerous and serious. Although the lost documents were of some relevance to the allegations against the director, having regard to all the circumstances, his inability to inspect them did not prejudice him so as to justify striking out the disqualification proceedings. Accordingly, the appeal would be dismissed.

Re Dexmaster Ltd [1995] 2 BCLC 430 (Chancery Division: Robert Walker J).

477 Director—disqualification—application for disqualification order—proceedings commenced in county court by official receiver

The County Courts Act 1984, s 42(1) provides that where a county court is satisfied that any proceedings before it are required to be in the High Court, it must order the transfer of the proceedings to the High Court, or, if the court is satisfied that the person bringing the proceedings knew or ought to have known of that requirement, order that they be struck out.

The official receiver commenced proceedings in a county court seeking a disqualification order against the directors of a company. The official receiver and the Secretary of State later made a joint application to the High Court to have the county court proceedings transferred to the High Court, substituting the Secretary of State for the official receiver. In the alternative, the Secretary of State sought leave to issue disqualification proceedings against the directors in the High Court even though more than two years had elapsed since the dissolution of the company. Having regard to the 1984 Act, s 42(1), the directors sought an order for the county court proceedings to be struck out on the ground that those proceedings had been issued more than two years after the dissolution of the company and therefore the county court had no jurisdiction to consider the application. *Held*, having regard to the Company Directors' Disqualification Act 1986, proceedings for the disqualification of a director had to be brought in the High Court by the Secretary of State, and could not be brought in a county court by the official receiver. As such, the county court proceedings in the instant case had been improperly constituted. Moreover, the court could not amend the parties to the action by substituting the Secretary of State for the official receiver, or adding the Secretary of State as a plaintiff, as the mistake related to the office holder and not merely his name. Having regard to the 1984 Act, s 42(1), a county court judge would have struck out the disqualification proceedings rather than transferred them to the High Court, as it would have been unjust to the directors to allow the proceedings to be transferred. In addition, having regard to the Secretary of State's delay in issuing High Court proceedings, he would not be granted leave to make a disqualification application out of time. Accordingly, the Secretary of State's application would be dismissed, and the directors' application would be allowed.

Re NP Engineering and Security Products Ltd [1995] 2 BCLC 585 (Chancery Division: Harman J).

478 Director—disqualification—de facto director—conduct of director

The Company Directors Disqualification Act 1986, s 6(1) provides that the court must make a disqualification order against a person where it is satisfied that he is or has been a director of a company which has at any time become insolvent and that his conduct as a director of that company makes him unfit to be concerned in the management of a company.

H and R set up a scrap metal company as a joint enterprise. At the time of the setting up of the company, R was a recently discharged bankrupt so his wife acted as his nominee as both shareholder and director, but took no active part in the company's affairs. During the life of the company R remained in sole charge of buying and selling, whilst H was responsible for finance and administration. The company traded at a loss and eventually became insolvent, largely due to a number of invoice deceptions perpetrated by R against H. The official receiver applied for disqualification orders to be made against both men, in R's case on the basis that he had been a de facto or shadow director. R claimed that he was not a director, even though he controlled the company's entire trading operation, which he said was because of his professional expertise in the metal trade. *Held*, the word 'director' in the 1986 Act, s 6(1) included a de facto director, who for the purpose of an application for disqualification meant someone who had in fact acted as a director, though not appointed as such. The fact that the company existed because R had invited H to join him in a business, that R was in sole charge of the company's trading with no limit to the commitments he could enter into on the company's behalf and that R received, or was authorised by the board to receive, equal remuneration and benefits, entitled the court to conclude that R was a de facto director of the company and could therefore be made subject to a disqualification order under the 1986 Act, s 6(1).

R's unlawful conduct and H's gullibility in accepting R's explanations for the bogus invoices plus his failure adequately to check the accounts meant that both were unfit to be concerned in the management of a company. Accordingly, the official receiver's application would be granted; R would be disqualified for ten years and H would be disqualified for four years.

Re Moorgate Metals Ltd [1995] 1 BCLC 503 (Chancery Division: Warner J).

479 Director—disqualification—order—administrative provisions

The Companies (Disqualification Orders) (Amendment) Regulations 1995, SI 1995/1509 (in force on 1 July 1995), amend the 1986 Regulations, SI 1986/2067, so as to prescribe new Forms DO1–DO4 for the provision of prescribed information to the Secretary of State regarding disqualification orders.

480 Director—disqualification—order—application to stay order

The defendant was disqualified from being a director by an order made under the Company Directors Disqualification Act 1986, s 6. He applied for a stay of the order, pending appeal, even though the statute did not contain an express provision to that effect. *Held*, the High Court and the Court of Appeal did have jurisdiction to stay or suspend a disqualification order but, in deciding whether to exercise that discretion, the court must consider whether, and to what extent, the protection of the public might reasonably be foregone pending the appeal. Normally, protection of the public and the interests of the director would best be served by an application for leave to act under the 1986 Act, s 17, but there would be exceptional cases where this remedy would be inadequate. However, this was not such an exceptional case. The defendant had not applied for leave to act under s 17 or presented evidence which a court considering whether to grant leave would require, and for that reason alone the application would be refused.

Secretary of State for Trade and Industry v Bannister [1996] 1 All ER 993 (Court of Appeal: Glidewell and Morritt LJJ and Sir John May).

481   Director—disqualification—order—contents of order

It has been held that in the Company Directors Disqualification Act 1986, the word 'or' between
s 1(1)(a) to (d) is conjunctive, with the consequence that a disqualification is one that disqualifies
a person holding any of the offices, or carrying on any of the activities, identified in those
subsections and an order which does not disqualify a person from doing all of those things is not
a disqualification order within the 1986 Act, s 1(1).

Re Gower Enterprises Ltd (No 2) [1995] 2 BCLC 201 (Chancery Division: Robert Reid QC).

482   Director—disqualification—proceedings—proceedings after winding up—expenses of winding up—liquidator's remuneration

The Company Directors Disqualification Act 1986, s 6(2)(a) provides that a company becomes
insolvent if it goes into liquidation at a time when its assets are insufficient for the payment of its
debts and other liabilities and the expenses of the winding up.

It has been held that the phrase 'expenses of winding up' within the 1986 Act, s 6(2)(a) is to
be interpreted in the same way as in the Insolvency Act 1986. Thus, the part of a liquidator's
remuneration which is part of the 'expenses of winding up' is that which is properly payable in
accordance with the Insolvency Rules 1986 and, where applicable, the Insolvency Regulations
1986, subject to any challenge by a creditor under the 1986 Rules, r 4.131 on the ground that
the sum so arrived at is excessive. If a liquidator's remuneration is charged in accordance with
the scheme laid down by the 1986 Rules and Regulations, then it will constitute part of the
'expenses of the winding up' for the purposes of s 6(2)(a). It is immaterial that the figure arrived
at is greater, the same, or lower than the figure that would have been arrived at by applying the
scales laid down for the official receiver in the 1986 Regulations.

Re Gower Enterprises Ltd [1995] 2 BCLC 107 (Chancery Division: Blackburne J).

483   Director—disqualification—proceedings—proceedings after winding up—preference to creditor

It has been held that before a director of an insolvent company can be disqualified for giving
preference to a creditor it must at least be shown that he was aware that there was a desire to
prefer the creditor and that it had influenced the company. Although it appeared from the
Company Directors Disqualification Act 1986 that such a director could be disqualified for
authorising a transaction which gave preference to a creditor and which could be set aside under
the Insolvency Act 1986, ss 238–240 even if he was unaware that there was a desire to give that
preference, such a consequence could not have been intended by Parliament.

Re Living Images Ltd (1995) Times, 7 August (Chancery Division: Laddie J).

484   Director—disqualification—fraudulent trading—meaning of 'creditors'

The Companies Act 1985, s 458 provides that if any business is carried on with intent to defraud
creditors of the company or creditors of any other person or for any fraudulent purpose, any
person who was knowingly a party to the carrying on of the business in that manner is liable to
imprisonment or a fine or both.

After being convicted of the offence of fraudulent trading the director of a defunct merchant
bank appealed, arguing that in s 458 the word 'creditors' denoted those customers who were
entitled to immediate repayment and did not extend to potential or contingent creditors having
an existing right to repayment at some future date. Much of the money borrowed by the bank
could not be called in immediately and thus, it was claimed, the lenders of that money did not
fall within the meaning of 'creditors' in s 458. Further, it was claimed that there was want of
jurisdiction because the offences were committed in New York and at that time the provisions
of the Criminal Justice Act 1993, Pt I were not in force. *Held*, the offence under s 458 was a
continuing one since fraudulent trading could prejudice future as well as present creditors. In s
458 the word 'creditors' denoted those to whom money was owed and whether or not that
money could presently be sued for was immaterial. Also, the English courts did have jurisdiction
to try an offence of dishonestly obtaining property under the Theft Act 1968, s 15 where, as a
result of dishonesty, funds were transferred from one overseas bank account to another which
was overseas but still operated from England. Accordingly, the appeal would be dismissed.

R v Smith (Wallace Duncan) (1995) Times, 13 November (Court of Appeal: Rose LJ, Jowitt
and Moore-Bick JJ).

485　Director—disqualification—leave to act as director—circumstances in which leave may be granted

Scotland

The Secretary of State applied for a disqualification order under the Company Directors' Disqualification Act 1986, s 6 against the director of a company which became insolvent because of its failure to pay income tax, national insurance and value added tax. Although the director accepted that he should be prevented from serving as a director or being concerned in the management of a company, he sought leave to continue acting as the director of two associated companies. *Held*, the purpose of the 1986 Act was to protect members of the public from those whose behaviour as directors showed them to be a danger to the public. On the facts of the case, the director knew or should have been aware that the company had continued to trade whilst it was insolvent, and a substantial sum of money had been involved. However, as his conduct was not so serious, the period of disqualification was to be limited to three years. The court had a discretion whether to grant leave to allow him to continue as the director of the associated companies and as to the terms and conditions on which to grant leave. The associated companies had traded successfully for some time with no hint of impropriety, and there had been no repetition of the problems that had occurred with the insolvent company. Moreover, there was evidence that the associated companies relied upon the director's goodwill for their success and would suffer if he were removed as a director. As it was unlikely that there would be a real danger to the public if he were allowed to continue as a director, leave was to be granted to allow him to do so, subject to certain conditions. Accordingly, the application would be granted.

Secretary of State for Trade and Industry v Palfreman [1995] 2 BCLC 301 (Outer House).

486　Director—disqualification—procedure

Sir Richard Scott V–C has issued the following *Practice Direction* ([1996] 1 WLR 170).

The number of applications for disqualification orders of unfit company directors under the Company Directors Disqualification Act 1986 has steadily grown, and has undergone a surge in the last 12 months. Disqualification orders should come into force at the earliest moment, both in the public interest and so that respondent directors may have the uncertainty as to their position resolved as soon as possible. Therefore delay in the processing of disqualification applications is a matter of legitimate concern.

The overall effect of the new direction is to give the court greater control over the conduct of those proceedings so as to enable them to be dealt with as expeditiously as possible.

It addresses in particular the problem of cases which are not set down for trial where they ought to be, and cases where the parties have taken no steps to obtain a hearing date for a case that has been set down. The new direction makes adjustment also to the developing procedure initiated by Ferris J in *Re Carecraft Construction Co Ltd* [1994] 1 WLR 172 for enabling applications where there is no dispute about the material facts, and no dispute about the appropriate period of disqualification, to be dealt with in a summary fashion. That procedure will enable the court to dispose of these applications more speedily than has hitherto been possible.

As to the need for there to be a court hearing at all in cases where the Secretary of State, or the Official Receiver, and the respondent director are in agreement as to the essential facts and as to the length of the appropriate disqualification period, court time should be reserved for cases where there is a dispute between the parties which has to be resolved. Under the 1986 Act, there is no alternative but for all applications for disqualification, no matter what state of agreement there may be between the parties, to be processed through the court machinery. That is unnecessary and avoidable. It is therefore recommended that the Secretary of State give consideration to the possibility of introducing amending legislation under which an agreement between a director and the Secretary of State or the Official Receiver as to the disqualification period to be applied to the director be given the same effect as a court order imposing the disqualification period. If the director is willing to bar himself from acting as a director for a period that the Secretary of State regards as being sufficient to protect the public interest, time and money need not be expended by insistence on bringing the case before the court.

1. This *Practice Direction* is to be read in conjunction with the Insolvent Companies (Disqualification of Unfit Directors) Proceedings Rules 1987, SI 1987/2023 and the Chancery Guide (*The Supreme Court Practice 1995* (Vol 2, paras 874–899)). The definitions in the 1987 Rules apply in this *Practice Direction*.

2 When the summons, which has to be an originating summons, is issued, the applicant will be given a date for the first hearing of the summons. The rules provide that the date is to be not less than eight weeks from the date of issue of the summons. The rules further provide that evidence in support of a summons must be filed when the application is issued, and that evidence

in answer and in reply must be filed within 28 days of service of the summons and 14 days from receipt of the evidence in answer, respectively. That timetable can only be extended by consent, or with the leave of the court. All evidence must be filed before the first hearing of the summons.

First hearing of the summons

3. All interlocutory directions must be sought at the first hearing of the summons so that the application can be determined at the earliest possible date. The parties must take all such steps as they respectively can to avoid successive directions hearings.

4. If at the first hearing the registrar adjourns the case for further consideration under the 1987 Rules, r 7(4), he will, so far as possible, give all the directions for trial including, where r 7(4) applies, a direction as to whether the matter is to be heard by a judge or a registrar. That direction may at any time be varied by the court, either on application or of its own motion. If the court varies the direction in the absence of the parties, notice will be given to the parties.

Setting down for trial

5.(a) At the appropriate stage, the registrar will direct the applicant to set the case down for trial within such period, usually five days, as he may order. The parties cannot extend that period by agreement. The applicant must give notice to the respondent/s when he has set the case down.

(b) If the case is to be heard by a judge, the case will be entered in the judges' Companies List.

(c) If the case is not set down within the period specified by the registrar, it may be listed before the court to show cause why it should not be struck out.

Fixing a date for trial

6.(a) Within 15 working days of setting down, or such other period as the court may allow, the parties must together attend:

(i) if the case is to be heard by a registrar, at Room 405, Thomas More Building, Royal Courts of Justice, or (ii) if the case is to be heard by a judge, before the Chancery Clerk of the Lists, in either case to fix a date for trial. For that purpose, they must produce to the Chief Clerk or the Chancery Clerk of the Lists, a written estimate of the length of the trial signed by the advocates for all the parties.

(b) The parties cannot by agreement extend the period for attendance to fix a trial date. In the event of non-compliance with para 6(a), the court will fix a date for trial and give notice of the date to the parties.

Estimates of length

7.(a) If a party does not provide an estimate of the length of trial to the court when required to do so, the court may act on the estimate of the other party.

(b) As stated in the Chancery Guide, section 5.2, the parties must inform the court immediately of any material change in an estimate.

Pre-trial review (PTR)

8. In all cases where the hearing is estimated to take 10 days or more, and in any other case where the court so directs, a PTR will be held by a registrar, or, if the case is to be heard by a judge, by a judge in chambers. If the PTR is to be heard by a registrar, the date for the hearing of the PTR will be fixed at a hearing of the summons. If the PTR is to be heard by a judge, the applicant must issue a separate summons for a PTR, and it is the responsibility of the applicant to ensure that a hearing date for a PTR is obtained so that the PTR is held between eight and four weeks before the trial date. If, where the PTR is to be heard by a judge, the applicant fails to issue a summons for a PTR or to obtain a hearing date for the summons, the case may be listed by the Chancery Clerk of the Lists (on notice to the parties) for a PTR.

9. The provisions of the Chancery Guide, section 3.10(3)–(7) apply to PTRs in disqualification cases, whether the PTR is to be heard by a judge or a registrar.

The trial

10. Skeleton arguments must be prepared by all the parties in all but the simplest cases, whether the case is to be heard by a registrar or a judge. They must comply with the guidelines in the Chancery Guide, Appendix 3.

11. The advocate for the applicant must also in all but the simplest cases, provide (a) a chronology, (b) a dramatis personae, (c) in respect of each respondent, a list of the references to the relevant evidence for each matter relied upon as constituting unfitness.

12. The above-mentioned documents must be delivered to the court not less than two clear days before the day fixed for the hearing. If the case is to be heard by a judge but the name of the judge is not known, or the judge is a deputy judge, those documents must be delivered to the Chancery Clerk of the Lists. If the name of the judge, other than a deputy judge, is known,

those documents must be delivered to the judge's clerk. If the case is to be heard by a registrar, the documents must be delivered to Room 405, Thomas More Building, Royal Courts of Justice. Copies must be provided to the other party so far as possible when they are delivered to the court.

13. The Chancery Guide, section 5.3 applies to bundles of documents for use at the trial.

Summary procedure

14. If the parties decide to make an application under the procedure adopted in *Carecraft*, they must inform the court immediately and obtain a date for the hearing of the application.

15. Whenever a *Carecraft* application is made, the applicant must (a) except in simple cases where the circumstances do not merit it or when the court otherwise directs, submit a written statement containing in respect of each respondent any material facts which, for the purposes of the application, are either agreed or not opposed by either party, and (b) specify in the written statement, or, if none, a separate document, the period of disqualification which the parties are to invite the court to order, or the bracket (that is 2–5 years, 6–10 years, 11–15 years) into which they submit the case falls.

16. Paragraph 12 above applies to the documents mentioned in paragraph 15, unless the court otherwise directs.

Hearings outside London

17. Where application for a disqualification order is made by summons issued in the Chancery District Registries in Birmingham, Bristol, Cardiff, Leeds, Liverpool, Manchester or Newcastle, this *Practice Direction* applies with the following modifications:

(a) Upon the issue of the summons, the court must endorse it with the date and time for the first hearing before a district judge. The powers exercisable by a registrar under this *Practice Direction* are exercisable by a district judge.

(b) If the district judge either at the first hearing or at any adjourned hearing before him, directs that the summons is to be heard by a High Court judge or by an authoriseD circuit judge, he must direct that the case be entered forthwith in the list for hearing by that judge, and the court must allocate (i) a date for the hearing of the trial by that judge, and (ii) unless a district judge directs otherwise, a date for the hearing of a PTR by the trial judge.

18. The documents mentioned in paragraphs 10, 11 and 15 must be delivered to the appropriate court not less than two clear days before the day fixed for the hearing. Copies must be provided to the other party so far as possible when they are delivered to the court.

487 Director—disqualification—proceedings—affidavit evidence—attendance of deponent

RSC Ord 38, r 2(3) provides that in any matter begun by originating summons, originating motion or petition, and on any application made by summons or motion, evidence may be given by affidavit unless in the case of any such cause, matter or application any provision of the Rules of the Supreme Court otherwise provides or the court otherwise directs, but the court may on the application of any party, order the attendance for cross-examination of the person making any such affidavit, and where after such an order has been made, the person in question does not attend, his affidavit cannot be used as evidence without the leave of the court.

The Secretary of State commenced proceedings against the appellant under the Company Directors Disqualification Act 1986, s 7 and the Insolvent Companies (Disqualification of Unfit Directors) Proceedings Rules 1987, SI 1987/2023, seeking a disqualification order against him. In the course of the proceedings, the Registrar of the Companies Court made an order under RSC Ord 38, r 2(3) that all deponents of affidavit evidence were to attend the hearing of the application for cross-examination, in default of which their affidavits could not be read or used in evidence without leave of the court. On appeal, the appellant argued that the registrar had no jurisdiction to make such an order because the rule did not apply to proceedings under the 1986 Act. Alternatively, he argued that the registrar had wrongly exercised his discretion. *Held*, the relevant provisions of the Rules of the Supreme Court applied to disqualification proceedings unless the 1987 Rules expressly provided otherwise. As there was no inconsistency between the 1987 Rules and RSC Order 38, r 2(3), the registrar had correctly decided that he had jurisdiction to make an order requiring the attendance of deponents for cross-examination. As disqualification proceedings were of a penal nature, the court would not compel a respondent to give evidence, but if he chose to file affidavit evidence, there was no reason why he should not be cross-examined on it. Moreover, if an order for cross-examination was made under RSC Ord 38, r 2(3) and a deponent failed to attend, a defendant could not rely on the Civil Evidence Act 1968, s 2(1) in order to adduce the affidavit as a statement unless leave of the court had been granted. Here, if the appellant's foreign resident deponents were unable to attend for cross-examination, the court could then consider whether or not in all the circumstances to allow their affidavits to be used as evidence without cross-examination. Having regard to the facts, the registrar had considered that it was desirable that all deponents should attend for cross-examination in so far as possible, and had not wrongly exercised his discretion. Accordingly, the appeal would be dismissed.

Re Dominion International Group plc [1995] 1 WLR 649 (Chancery Division: Rattee J).

488   Director—duty to disclose interest in contract—requirement to disclose interest at meeting of directors—sole director

The Companies Act 1985, s 317 provides that it is the duty of a director of a company who is interested in a contract or proposed contract with the company to declare his interest at a meeting of the directors of the company.

Whilst sole director of the plaintiff company the defendant had authorised payment to himself of sums due to him on the termination of his employment by the plaintiff. The plaintiff brought a claim for the moneys, and the issue in the defendant's application for leave to defend was whether the defendant had complied with s 317. *Held*, the object of s 317 was to ensure that the interest of any director or shadow director in any contract was an item of business at a meeting of the directors. A sole director would know of his own interest but might not know of the interest of any shadow director and s 317 ensured that he should know. Furthermore, it was most important in the case of sole directors for there to be a reminder of the director's duty and a record that the reminder was given. It followed that the legislature could not have intended the word 'meeting' in s 317 to exclude sole directors. In order to comply with s 317 the director could hold a meeting alone or with another person, such as the company secretary. If made alone, the declaration must still be recorded in the minutes. The minutes did not record any declaration but that was not conclusive and, accordingly, leave to defend would be granted.

Neptune (Vehicle Washing Equipment) Ltd v Fitzgerald [1995] 3 All ER 811 (Chancery Division: Lightman J).

489   Director—first director of company—resignation of proposed director before registration of company

A co-founder of a company was a signatory to its memorandum and articles of association as one of the first directors of the company. However, prior to the company's formation he had sent a letter, addressed to the person who was to be the chairman of the company, in which he tendered his resignation as a director. He had then purported to withdraw his resignation by sending a further letter, addressed to a person who was never an officer or a putative officer of the company. After its formation, the company filed a form with the registrar recording the resignation of the director. A conflict later arose between various factions within the company. In the ensuing proceedings, the court ordered an extraordinary general meeting to be held. Under the articles of association, the members entitled to vote at the meeting included persons who had been admitted to the company. The articles also provided that no person was to be admitted as a member of the company unless his admission was approved by the council of the company. The issues subsequently arose whether the director's resignation had been effective and whether the extraordinary general meeting had been validly constituted. *Held*, the director's letter of resignation constituted a continuing offer which was accepted by the company. Therefore, he was no longer a director of the company. The meeting was not validly constituted. Admission to membership of the company required a decision of the company's council as to whether a person should be admitted as a member. The procedure adopted by the company amounted to little more than the automatic admission on an administrative basis of any person who applied for membership. This was not sufficient to comply with the company's articles of association. Judgment would be given accordingly.

POW Services Ltd v Clare [1995] 2 BCLC 435 (Chancery Division: Jacob J).

490   Director—liability—negligence

See *New Zealand Guardian Trust Co Ltd v Brooks*, para 2837.

491   Dissolution of company—declaration that dissolution void—application for declaration by potential creditor—landlord as creditor

The Companies Act 1985, s 651(1), (2) provides that where a company has been dissolved, the court may, on an application made for the purpose by the liquidator of the company or by any other person appearing to the court to be interested, make an order on such terms as the court thinks fit, declaring the resolution void. Thereupon, such proceedings may be taken as might have been taken if the company had not been dissolved.

The plaintiff landlord granted leases of two premises to a company ('the tenant'), which covenanted to pay the rent for the whole of the term. The tenant then assigned the leases to a third party ('the first assignee'), which assigned the leases to another company ('the second assignee'). When the second assignee went into liquidation, its liquidators disclaimed the leases, and the landlord looked to the tenant for payment of rent. By that time, however, the tenant had been voluntarily wound up. The landlord sought a declaration under the Companies Act 1985, s 651 that the dissolution was void, arguing that once the tenant was revived, the tenant would have a right of indemnity against the first assignee in respect of the rent. The application was dismissed. On appeal, *held*, the purposes of the 1985 Act, s 651 were to enable a liquidator to distribute an overlooked asset and to allow a creditor to make a claim which he had not previously made. A company was entitled to seek voluntary winding up, nothwithstanding that it would thereby be unable to fulfil future or contingent obligations. Contingent creditors could make claims up to the value of their claims as at the date of the winding up, but a company could not be required to set aside a fund against the possibility that the contingency might happen. Although the liquidator was entitled to complete a winding up and file his final accounts and report thereafter, the finality of a dissolution was subject to the express provisions of s 651. The judge was therefore wrong to conclude that he could not as a matter of principle make an order under s 651. The interest of an applicant did not have to be firmly established or highly likely to succeed, as it sufficed that his interest was not merely shadowy. Here, an order under s 651 might enable the tenant to meet a liability which would otherwise remain unpaid, and that was sufficient ground for the court to exercise its discretion to grant a declaration that the dissolution was void. Accordingly, the appeal would be allowed.

Stanhope Pension Trust Ltd v Registrar of Companies (1993) 69 P & CR 238 (Court of Appeal: Sir Thomas Bingham MR, Hoffmann and Henry LJJ).

492 EC provisions

See EUROPEAN COMMUNITIES.

493 Foreign companies—execution of documents

The Foreign Companies (Execution of Documents) (Amendment) Regulations 1995, SI 1995/1729 (in force on 1 August 1995), amend the 1994 Regulations, SI 1994/950, so as to take account of the Requirements of Writing (Scotland) Act 1995, Sch 2, para 5, Sch 4, para 51, which amend the Companies Act 1985, s 36B, in relation to the rules for the signing and execution of documents by companies incorporated outside Great Britain.

494 Forms

The Companies (Forms) (Amendment) Regulations 1995, SI 1995/736 (in force on 1 April 1995), prescribe the following amended forms for the purposes of the Companies Act 1985: Forms 6, 10, 12, 30(5)(a), 30(5)(b), 30(5)(c), 43(3), 43(3)(e), 49(1), 49(8)(a), 51, 53, 54, 117, 190, 266(1), 266(3), 287, 288a, 288b, 288c, 318, 325, 353, 363a and 391. The corresponding old forms are revoked as from 1 April 1996. Forms 363b and 363s are revoked as from 1 April 1995.

495 Forms—Welsh language forms

The Companies (Welsh Language Forms and Documents) (Amendment) Regulations 1995, SI 1995/734 (in force on 1 April 1995), amend the 1994 Regulations, SI 1994/117, so as to prescribe the following new forms which are in Welsh as well as English: (1) Form 10CYM (statement of first directors, secretary and intended situation of registered office of a company); (2) Form 12CYM (statutory declaration of compliance with requirements on application for registration of a company). The regulations also prescribe the following amended additional forms in Welsh as well as English: (1) Form 287CYM (notice of change in situation of a company's registered office address); (2) Forms 288aCYM, 288bCYM, and 288cCYM (notice of particulars of appointment and resignation of directors and secretaries and of change in particulars contained in the register); (3) Form 363CYM (annual return form).

The Companies (Welsh Language Forms and Documents) (No 3) Regulations 1995, SI 1995/1508 (in force on 1 July 1995), prescribe new Welsh Forms 12CYM, 30(5)(a)CYM, 30(5)(b)CYM, and 30(5)(c)CYM for the purposes of the Companies Act 1985, ss 12 (registration of memorandum and articles) and 30 (exemption from requirement of 'limited' as part of company name).

496 Insider dealing—information in respect of offences—international co-operation

An agreement between the United Kindom and the Netherlands was signed in London on 20 July 1994 regarding mutual assistance in relation to offences concerning securities, futures and options (Cm 2932). The agreement is specifically concerned with insider dealing, market manipulation and other irregularities in relation to securities, futures and options; the regulation of investment business; the disclosure of interests in securities; the duty to make full and fair disclosure when offering or issuing securities; and certain other matters designated by the parties: art 8. It does not affect the operation, however, of the European Convention on Mutual Legal Assistance in Criminal Matters (Cm 1928) (art 6), nor inhibit other channels of assistance: art 7. The parties undertake to give each other the fullest possible measure of assistance in matters within the scope of the agreement: art 1. Requests for assistance must specify what information is required, the purpose for which it is sought, the circumstances giving rise to the request, the link between the request and the regulatory function of the requesting authority, and whether a representative of the requesting authority wishes to be present, if feasible, during the investigation: art 10. Factors to be considered when a request is received include whether the request involves the assertion of a jurisdiction not recognised by the requested authority, whether executing the request would intefere with an existing investigation, and whether it would be contrary to public interest to give the assistance sought: art 12. Where the request involves substantial costs, the parties will reach a cost-sharing arrangement before proceeding with the request: art 14. Restrictions are imposed on the uses to which information supplied under a request may be put (art 15), but the parties may agree to putting such information to other uses: art 16. Subject to waiver by the requesting authority, any request for information will be kept confidential unless disclosure is necessary to give effect to it and information, subject to waiver, supplied under a request will similarly be kept confidential: art 17). However, both the request and the information obtained may be disclosed, unless the request otherwise states, to the appropriate national enforcement and regulatory bodies: art 19. In accordance with the terms of art 22, the agreement entered into force on 1 July 1995.

497 Insolvency—assignment of right of action—legally-aided assignee—validity of assignment

In the first of three similar cases, the liquidator of an insolvent company assigned a cause of action to the company's former directors on terms that if the action succeeded, the proceeds would be applied first towards the company's debts with the balance divided equally between the assignees and the company. In the second case, a company's administrative receiver assigned a cause of action to one of the company's directors, who was also one of the company's creditors, on terms that he was to be the sole beneficiary of any proceeds of the action. In each case, the assignees were granted legal aid to apply to be substituted as plaintiffs in the respective actions, but their applications were refused. They appealed against that decision. In the third case, the court substituted the legally-aided former directors of an insolvent company as the plaintiffs in an action assigned to them by the company. The defendant in those proceedings appealed against the assignment, claiming that it was void. *Held*, it was not contrary to public policy for a trustee to assign a cause of action to a bankrupt, or for a liquidator to assign a cause of action to a former officer of an insolvent company, as the relevant provisions of the insolvency legislation absolved trustees in bankruptcy and liquidators from accusations of maintenance and champerty. Here, in the first case, the liquidator had acted sensibly in assigning the cause of action to the company's former directors, even though it enabled him to sue with the benefit of legal aid which would not otherwise have been available to him. Moreover, it was irrelevant that obtaining legal aid was the object of the assignment as well as its effect. As regards the second case, a creditor of an insolvent company had a substantial and genuine commercial interest in proceedings to recover company assets, and the assignment was not invalid merely because the motivating factor for it was the fact that the assignee, rather than the assignor, was entitled to legal aid. As neither assignment was a sham, the assignees should have been substituted as plaintiffs in the respective actions. Accordingly, in relation to the first two cases, the appeal would be allowed, and in relation to the third case, the appeal would be dismissed.

Norglen Ltd (in liquidation) v Reeds Rains Prudential Ltd; Mayhew-Lewis v Westminster Scaffolding Group plc; Levy v ABN Amro Bank NV [1996] 1 All ER 945 (Court of Appeal: Sir Thomas Bingham MR, Hobhouse and Aldous LJJ).

498   Insolvency—inquiry into company's dealings—disclosure of information—order for production of documents—circumstances in which order may be made

Scotland

Liquidators appointed to deal with the winding up of a company were unable to obtain all the information which they required about the company's assets and dealings. They therefore sought orders under the Insolvency Act 1986, ss 236 and 237 against the company's accountants and certain individuals, for the production of documents and for oral examination. The accountants and individuals opposed the applications on the grounds that such orders would be oppressive and unreasonable. *Held*, in exercising its power under the 1986 Act, s 236 to make an order for the production of documents, the court had to balance an applicant's reasonable need to see the requested documents in order to properly carry out his functions, against the fact that production of documents should not impose an unnecessary and unreasonable burden on the person against whom the order was made. However, it was irrelevant that production might be inconvenient, involve a lot of work, or might make a person liable to future claims. Here, the company had suffered the loss of a substantial portfolio of assets as a result of unauthorised transactions by a particular agent at a time when the company's accountants were acting as the company's auditors and financial advisers, and therefore had detailed knowledge of its affairs. In considering whether there were any countervailing considerations against making the order, it was a fact that the liquidators' further investigations might lead them to decide that the accountants, or those with whom the accountants had dealt, bore some responsibility for the company's losses. It was also the case that the accountants and the individual respondents had co-operated fully with the liquidators in producing documents and supplying information, and were prepared to co-operate further on specific matters. Despite those considerations, this was an exceptional case which warranted an order for production of documents, although the order would be made against the auditors only. No order for oral examination would be made, as the order for production of documents was less oppressive.

McIsaac and Wilson, Petitioners 1995 SLT 498 (Outer House). *Re British and Commonwealth Holdings plc (joint administrators) v Spicer and Oppenheim (a firm)* [1992] 4 All ER 876, HL (1992 Abr para 409) applied.

499   Insolvency—inquiry into company's dealings—ex parte application—examination by American attorney

The Insolvency Act 1986, s 236 provides that, in the case of a company in respect of which a winding-up order has been made, an office-holder (being a liquidator or the official receiver) may apply to the court to summon to appear before it any officer of the company or any person with information or documentation relating to the company and may order the production of any document or other records relating to the company.

The administrators of a company made an ex parte application to examine certain members of a firm of solicitors associated with transactions in which large sums of money had been improperly abstracted from the company prior to the administration. The registrar made an order for production of the documents sought and another for oral examination of members of the firm which he ordered could be carried out by an American attorney. The solicitors appealed on the grounds that (1) there had not been an adequate explanation by the administrators as to why the documents sought fell within the 1986 Act, s 236, (2) it was unreasonable to seek to examine the members of the firm without giving them the details of the grounds on which the administrators sought to examine them, and (3) the registrar had no jurisdiction to order that the examination be conducted by a United States attorney. *Held*, the administrators were entitled to ask for the documents under s 236 but they ought not to have made the application ex parte as no good reason had been shown why an exception could be made to the general rule that a person was entitled to be heard before an order of the court was made against him. An oral examination was more expeditious than issuing a questionnaire provided that the solicitors were supplied by the administrators with a note of the topics which the administrators wished to pursue. Under the Insolvency Rules, r 9.4(1), it was only the applicant office-holder who was entitled to put questions to a witness subsequent to an order for examination and, therefore, the court had no jurisdiction to order that the examinations be conducted by an American attorney. The appeal would be allowed in part and dismissed in part and an order would be made accordingly.

Re Maxwell Communications Corpn plc (No 3) [1995] 1 BCLC 521 (Chancery Division: Vinelott J).

500 Insolvency—inquiry into company's dealings—order for examination of company officers—ex parte order

A company was funded by a finance group by means of a loan secured on a lease of the company's premises, which were then leased back to the company. Upon being informed that the profits of the company were insufficient to cover the rent payable under the sub-lease, officers of the group held weekly management meetings with the managing director of the company. All receipts of the company were paid into an account in the name of the group and periodic transfers were made from this account to the account of the company. The company went into liquidation and the liquidator sent a questionnaire to the officers of the group designed to establish their involvement in the affairs of the company. They answered this questionnaire, but refused to answer a supplementary questionnaire which sought to discover whether they were shadow directors of the company, whether the company had been trading while insolvent and whether their conduct was such that they might be disqualified from acting as directors. The liquidator obtained an ex parte order under the Insolvency Act 1986, s 236 requiring the officers to attend before the registrar. On appeal by the officers, *held*, the reasons given for making the application ex parte were insufficient. The examination of the officers was primarily directed to showing that they were shadow directors. However, there was no prima facie case made out to show that they were shadow directors. The central point was that they were acting in defence of their own interests as creditors in making terms for the continuation of credit in the light of the threatened default. The directors were free to take the offer of terms or leave it. Accordingly, the supplementary questionnaire was oppressive, and the appeal would be allowed.

Re PFTZM Ltd (in liquidation); Jourdain v Paul [1995] 2 BCLC 354 (Chancery Division: Judge Paul Baker QC).

501 Insolvency—liquidation of international bank—approval of court—contribution and pooling agreement—objections by certain interested parties

The liquidators of an international bank and its subsidiary companies ('the companies') sought the court's approval of two agreements. A contribution agreement involved the companies agreeing to settle claims made against them by the majority shareholders in return for those shareholders contributing a sum, worked out by a specific formula, to the liquidation, which could then be paid out to creditors who gave releases of claims they might have against the majority shareholders and others. A pooling agreement involved the companies pooling their assets which could then be distributed to creditors pari passu. The distribution of the pooling fund was to take place in Luxembourg but the liquidators were to be entitled to retain some of the fund to compensate those people who would be prejudiced if they had to claim in Luxembourg. There were objections to the agreements from (1) a creditor who claimed the dividend he could expect to receive under the agreements would be less than that which he might receive if the litigation were continued; (2) ex-employees who claimed proprietary remedies over some of the companies' assets and who asserted that provision ought to be made in the agreements for the retention of sufficient funds by the liquidators to meet such claims and (3) some ex-directors of the companies who had brought anti-racketeering actions against the majority shareholders in the United States, and who feared that, unless they stopped those proceedings, the shareholders would exercise a provision in the contribution agreement enabling them to remove the ex-directors' names from a list of 'related persons' entitled to benefit from mutual releases from claims and cross-claims under that agreement. *Held*, (1) the only alternative to the resolution by compromise proposed by the liquidators was intractable, lengthy and speculative litigation, and the only chance for depositors getting a reasonably prompt return, albeit perhaps less than they would have received in damages, was for the agreements to go ahead. This had been confirmed by the approval of the agreements by the majority of creditors and therefore the court would need a very strong reason to decline to grant its approval. (2) If the ex-employees wished to pursue their claims for proprietary remedies, they ought to have made a formal application for such relief. There was insufficient evidence before the court to establish whether there was any substance to such claims for proprietary remedies and, this was therefore an insufficient ground for withholding approval of the agreements. (3) The ability given to the majority shareholders by the contribution agreement to coerce some of the ex-directors to abandon proceedings against them was an insufficient ground for refusing approval of the agreements as, if such approval was withheld, there was nothing stopping the majority shareholders immediately offering to enter into an identical agreement with the ex-directors' names removed. Accordingly, the agreements would be approved.

Re Bank of Credit and Commerce International SA (No 10) [1995] 1 BCLC 362 (Chancery Division: Sir Richard Scott V-C).

502 Insolvency—liquidator—agreement for assignment of fruits of action—champertous agreement

See *Ward v Aitken*, para 667.

503 Insolvency—official receiver—contracting out of functions

The Contracting Out (Functions of the Official Receiver) Order 1995, SI 1995/1386 (in force on 30 May 1995), enable an official receiver to authorise another person, or that person's employees, to exercise the official receiver's functions under the insolvency legislation (subject to certain exceptions). The order provides that the official receiver's right of audience before the court is only exercisable by persons who have a right of audience under the Courts and Legal Services Act 1990.

504 Insolvency—practitioner—removal—loss of qualification—supervisor of voluntary arrangement—power to appoint substitute

See *Re Bridgend Goldsmiths Ltd*, para 191.

505 Insolvency—reuse of company name—application for leave—relevance of directors' inexperience and undercapitalisation

The Insolvency Act 1986, s 216 provides that a person who was a director of a company that went into insolvent liquidation must not within a period of five years be a director of any other company that is known by a prohibited name except with leave of the court.

The appellants had been directors of a company that had been wound up by the court on the ground that it was unable to pay its debts. They applied to continue trading through a new company bearing a very similar name to the company that had gone into insolvent liquidation and appealed against the dismissal of their application. *Held*, the issue was whether it was appropriate, when considering an application for leave under s 216, to take into account the risk that the company might fail as a result of its directors' lack of experience or its undercapitalisation. The answer to that question was that the court should only have regard to the purpose of s 216 and it was wrong to treat an applicant under that section as if he had been disqualified for any of the reasons under the Company Directors Disqualification Act 1986. It was particularly wrong, in the absence of other evidence, to treat him as if he was unfit to be a director. Accordingly, leave would be granted.

Penrose v Secretary of State for Trade and Industry [1996] 2 All ER 96 (Chancery Division: Chadwick J).

506 Insolvency—rules—priority of winding up expenses

The Insolvency (Amendment) Rules 1995, SI 1995/586 (in force on 1 April 1995), amend the 1986 Rules, SI 1986/1925, so as to alter the order of priority in which the expenses of a winding up by the court and a bankruptcy are payable. The fee payable under a fees order made under the Insolvency Act 1986, ss 414 and 415 for the performance by the official receiver of his general duties as official receiver, and the repayable deposit lodged as security for that fee, are moved in the order of priority from immediately before to immediately after the payment of the other fees payable under any such fees order and the remuneration of the official receiver under general regulations.

507 Insolvency—voluntary arrangement—priority of claims—contractual nexus between company and its members

The Insolvency Act 1986, s 74(2)(f) provides that, where a company has been wound up, a sum due to any member of the company (in his character of a member) by way of dividends, profits or otherwise is not deemed to be a debt of the company, payable to that member in a case of competition between himself and any other creditor not a member of the company, but any such sum may be taken into account for the purpose of the final adjustment of the rights of the contributories among themselves.

The defendant purchased the whole issued share capital of a company (A) which it later discovered was almost worthless as a result of the way in which A had formerly been managed. The defendant and A both went into administration. The defendant brought an action against A for damages for negligent misrepresentation by which it was claimed the defendant had been induced to purchase A's shares, and also against the bank which had advised the defendant on the acquisition, for breach of duty. The bank issued a third party notice against A claiming an indemnity, contribution or damages. A scheme of arrangement was made between A and its creditors and the scheme's administrators applied by originating summons for a determination by the court of the questions whether, in the event of either the defendant being awarded damages or the bank being awarded an indemnity, contribution or damages, against A, such sums would be debts owed to the defendant in its 'character of a member' of A within the meaning of the 1986 Act, s 74(2)(f) and, if so, whether either claim gave rise to a scheme liability. *Held*, even if membership of a company was a necessary condition of a debt arising, the debt would not be caught if the condition of membership could be seen as irrelevant. In borderline cases, the court must look at the substance of the matter in deciding whether the claim could be identified as characteristically a member's claim, in the sense of arising directly from the contractual nexus between the company and its members. In the present case, the claim made by an open-market purchaser of shares in a company, as opposed to an original subscriber or allottee, and based on alleged negligent misrepresentation by the company as to its assets, though necessarily conditional upon membership of the company, was not sufficiently closely related to the corporate nexus to be characteristically a member's claim. Accordingly, the defendant was not claiming in its 'character as a member' within the meaning of s 74(2)(f).

If the claims of the defendant and the bank were within s 74(2)(f), they constituted a separate class of subordinated creditors for whom, if they were to be bound, a separate class meeting ought to have been called. Accordingly, the defendant and the bank were not bound by the scheme and their claims did not give rise to a scheme liability as they were not liabilities of the sort intended to be dealt with by the scheme.

Soden v British and Commonwealth Holdings plc [1995] 1 BCLC 686 (Chancery Division: Robert Walker J).

508 Investigation of companies—evidence acquired by inspectors—admissibility in criminal proceedings

See *R v Saunders; R v Parnes; R v Ronson; R v Lyons*, para 804.

509 Members—meeting—convening of meeting—application to court—voting procedure

The Companies Act 1985, s 371(1) provides that if for any reason it is impracticable to call a meeting of a company in any manner in which meetings of that company may be called, or to conduct the meeting in a manner prescribed by the articles or the Act, the court may either of its own motion or on the application of any director of the company or any member of the company who would be entitled to vote at the meeting, order a meeting to be called, held and conducted in any manner in which the court thinks fit.

A company's articles of association provided that all votes at annual general meetings and extraordinary meetings had to be given in person and that voting by proxy was not permitted. An extraordinary general meeting was called to vote on a resolution to abolish the article, but it was disrupted by members who were opposed to the resolution to such an extent that no orderly business could be conducted. The applicants applied for an order under the 1985 Act, s 371(1) in respect of the conduct of future meetings to consider the resolution. In particular, they sought directions that attendance should be limited to committee members only and that all other company members should be allowed to register postal votes. *Held*, 'impracticable' within the meaning of the 1985 Act, s 371(1) referred to whether a desired meeting could be conducted as a matter of practicality. In the instant case, the applicants were entitled to be concerned about the tactics that an extreme faction of the company's members might employ at future meetings. It was impracticable for the company to call any further meetings in the manner provided for by the articles of association or the 1985 Act, and the court therefore had jurisdiction to consider the application and give directions as to how future meetings should be convened and conducted for the purpose of considering the resolution. Although the directions sought by the applicants were unusual and contrary to the voting method provided by the company's constitution, the circumstances were so extreme that the directions in the terms sought would be ordered. Accordingly, the application would be granted.

Re the British Union for the Abolition of Vivisection [1995] 2 BCLC 1 (Chancery Division: Rimer J). *Re El Sombrero Ltd* [1958] Ch 900 considered.

510 Members—meeting—validity of meeting—appointment of members in accordance with company's articles of association

See *POW Services Ltd v Clare*, para 489.

511   Members—meeting—voting—corporation representative

New Zealand

A corporation which is a member of a company may, by resolution of its directors, authorise a person to act as its representative at any meeting of the company, and the person so authorised is entitled to exercise the same powers on behalf of the corporation which he represents as if it were an individual shareholder of the company: Companies Act 1985, s 375.

A company, a shareholder of another company, the defendant, appointed a proxy to attend and act on its behalf at an extraordinary general meeting of the defendant. The shareholder company attempted to fax a notice of appointment of the proxy to the plaintiff, another shareholder of the defendant, but the transmission failed. The proxy was treated throughout the meeting as the shareholder company's agent, but his vote was disallowed by the defendant's board of directors. The plaintiff subsequently sought to challenge that decision. *Held*, the proxy had attended the meeting, not only as a purported proxy, but also as a representative of the shareholder company in accordance with a law of New Zealand in similar terms to the 1985 Act, s 375, under which the right to vote depended on whether a valid resolution conferring authority to do so had been passed. It did not depend upon the production of evidence at the meeting that this had been done. The decision to reject the proxy's vote was therefore contrary both to the law and the defendant's articles. Accordingly, a declaration would be made on the basis that the vote of the proxy was valid.

Maori Development Corpn Ltd v Power Beat International Ltd [1995] 2 NZLR 568 (High Court)

512   Names—regulation of names—words requiring approval

The Company and Business Names (Amendment) Regulations 1995, SI 1995/3022 (in force on 1 January 1996), further amend the 1981 Regulations, SI 1991/1685, so as to insert the expression 'Chamber of Commerce, Training and Enterprise' into the list of words and expressions requiring the Secretary of State's approval for their use in company and business names. The 1995 Regulations also delete the words 'breed', 'breeder', and 'breeding', and 'nursing home' from the list.

513   Non-trading company—striking off—fees

The Companies (Fees) (Amendment) Regulations 1995, SI 1995/1423 (in force on 1 July 1995), amend the 1991 Regulations, SI 1991/1206, in consequence of the new procedure for the directors of a non-trading private company to apply to the registrar of companies for the company's name to be struck off the register introduced by the Deregulation and Contracting Out Act 1994, s 13(1), Sch 5. The regulations prescribe a new fee of £10 for the making of such an application.

514   Non-trading company—striking off—forms

The Companies (Forms) (No 2) Regulations 1995, SI 1995/1479 (in force on 1 July 1995), prescribe new Forms 652a (application for striking off) and 652c (withdrawal of application for striking off) for use under the new procedure for the directors of a non-trading private company to apply to the registrar of companies for the company's name to be struck off the register introduced by the Deregulation and Contracting Out Act 1994, s 13(1), Sch 5.

The Companies (Welsh Language Forms and Documents) (No 2) Regulations 1995, SI 1995/1480 (in force on 1 July 1995), prescribe Forms 652aCYM and 652cCYM in Welsh, corresponding to the forms prescribed by SI 1995/1479 supra.

515   Powers and liabilities—directing mind of company—attribution of knowledge

New Zealand

Under New Zealand law, every person who becomes a substantial security holder in a public company must give notice of that fact as soon as he knows or ought to know that he is a substantial security holder in the company.

An investment manager employed by the appellant company funded the purchase of a controlling holding in a public company by improperly using his authority to deal in shares. The appellant accepted that it had a relevant interest in the holding, but did not give the requisite notice. The appellant was held to be in breach of its duty to give notice on the ground that the manager's knowledge had to be attributed to the appellant because he was directing the mind and will of the company. On appeal, *held*, a company's primary rules of attribution, typically found in its articles of association, together with the general principles of agency, were usually sufficient to enable its rights and obligations to be determined. However, when a rule of law expressly or by implication excluded attribution on the basis of the general principles of agency or vicarious liability, the court had to create a special rule of attribution for the particular substantive rule. This was always a matter of interpretation. Although the phrase 'directing the mind and will' would often be the best description of the person designated by the relevant attribution rule, it might be better to acknowledge that not every such rule had to be forced into the same formula. The policy of the notice provision was to compel the immediate disclosure of the identity of persons who became substantial security holders. In the case of the appellant company, it knew that it had become a substantial security holder when that was known to the person who had authority to do the deal. The investment manager's knowledge was attributable to the appellant, and the fact that he did the deal for a corrupt purpose and did not give notice because he did not want his employers to find out did not affect the attribution of knowledge and the consequent duty to notify. Accordingly, the appeal would be dismissed.

Meridian Global Funds Management Asia Ltd v Securities Commission [1995] 3 All ER 918 (Privy Council: Lords Keith of Kinkel, Jauncey of Tullichettle, Mustill, Lloyd of Berwick and Hoffmann).

516 Receivership

See RECEIVERS.

517 Registration—contracting out of registration functions

The Contracting Out (Functions in relation to the Registration of Companies) Order 1995, SI 1995/1013 (in force, with certain exceptions, on 5 April 1995), enables the registrar of companies for England and Wales and the Secretary of State to authorise another person, or that person's employees, to exercise some of their functions in relation to companies.

518 Registration—restoration to register—joinder of third party in proceedings

The appellant stood surety for a company's obligations as lessee of shop premises from which it traded. The company had taken an assignment of the premises from the original tenant whose obligations were guaranteed by the respondent as surety. The company was later dissolved, leaving arrears of rent. The landlord claimed payment of the rent arrears from the respondent as surety for the original tenant's liability. The respondent joined the appellant as third party in the proceedings. He also applied under the Companies Act 1985, s 653 for the restoration of the company to the register in order to take advantage of the guarantee of the company's liabilities by the appellant. The appellant applied to be joined in the restoration proceedings so that he could oppose the respondent's application. The application for joinder was dismissed. On appeal, *held*, the court had jurisdiction under RSC Ord 15, r 6(2) to order the joinder of a third party whose rights would be affected to an application for restoration of a company to the register. However, where the third party merely wished to argue that the applicant had no claim against the company or that the proceedings which the revived company proposed to bring against him had no prospects of success, he should not be entitled to intervene in the application. By contrast, joinder would be allowed where the order for restoration would directly affect the rights of the third party irrespective of whether the applicant had any claim against the company or the company had any claim against the third party. On the facts, the applicant had an arguable case that it would not be just for the company to be restored. Firstly, restoration would have the effect of depriving him of his main defence against the landlord's claim; and secondly, the respondent had no locus standi as a creditor to make his application for restoration. The appeal would therefore be allowed.

Re Jayham Ltd [1995] 2 BCLC 455 (Chancery Division: Maddocks J).

519 Securities—public offers—prospectuses

See para 1387.

520 Securities—uncertificated securities—transfer—transfer without written instrument

The Uncertificated Securities Regulations 1995, SI 1995/3272 (in force on 19 December 1995), provide for the transfer without a written instrument of title to a unit of a security, and evidencing of title otherwise than by certificate, in accordance with a computer-based system and procedures. The system is to be centred around a person known as the operator. The regulations provide for the approval of the operator by the Treasury and give the Treasury certain powers in relation to the operator if he, or the system, fail to meet specified criteria. The conditions on which issuers may allow securities issued by them to participate in the system are set out, and provision is made for a class of shares governed by articles of association which are in all respects consistent with the regulations to become participating securities. Provision is also made for the directors of a company to pass a resolution so that other classes of shares can become participating shares notwithstanding any contrary provisions in the articles, and for the members of the company to prevent or reverse a directors' resolution. Conditions are also specified for securities other than shares to become participating securities.

The keeping of registers by participating issuers recording persons holding in uncertificated form units of a security issued by them is provided for, as is the title that such entries confer and the registration of the transfer of title to an uncertificated unit following instructions from the operator to do so. A transferee acquires a property right in uncertificated units transferred by means of the system before his name appears on the register of securities and an equitable interest in a number of units calculated in accordance with the regulations. The sending of certain instructions by means of the system is prevented and persons on whose behalf instructions are sent are prevented from denying particular matters in relation to the instructions. In certain circumstances, the operator is liable if as a result of the sending of certain instructions a person suffers loss.

521 Security for costs—company as plaintiff—discretion of court

The plaintiff company claimed a substantial sum from the defendants pursuant to a joint venture agreement. The defendants' application for an order for security for costs against the plaintiff was refused on the ground that it would stifle the plaintiff's claim. On appeal by the defendants, *held*, in exercising its discretion under the Companies Act 1985, s 726(1) to order a plaintiff company in an action to make a payment of security for the defendant's costs where it appeared that the plaintiff might be unable to pay such costs if the defendant was successful in his defence, the court would have regard to all the circumstances of the case and would not be prevented from ordering security simply on the ground that it would deter the plaintiff from pursuing its claim. The court had to balance the injustice to the plaintiff if prevented from pursuing a proper claim by an order for security against the injustice to the defendant if no security was ordered and at the trial the plaintiff's claim failed and the defendant found himself unable to recover from the plaintiff the costs which had been incurred by him in his defence of the claim. In considering all the circumstances, the court would have regard to the plaintiff's prospects of success but would not go into the merits in detail unless it could clearly be demonstrated that there was a high degree of probability of success or failure. Account also had to be taken of the conduct of the litigation, including any open offer or payment into court, any changes of stance by the parties and the lateness of the application, if appropriate. The court would not refuse to order security on the ground that it would unfairly stifle a valid claim unless it was satisfied that, in all the circumstances including whether the plaintiff could fund the litigation from outside sources, it was probable that the claim would be stifled. In this regard, it was for the plaintiff to satisfy the court that it would be prevented by an order for security from continuing the litigation. In considering the amount of security that might be ordered the court would have regard to the fact that it was not required to order the full amount claimed by way of security and it was not even bound to make an order of a substantial amount. The present appeal would be allowed.

Keary Developments Ltd v Tarmac Construction Ltd [1995] 3 All ER 534 (Court of Appeal: Butler-Sloss and Peter Gibson LJ). *Sir Lindsay Parkinson & Co Ltd v Triplan Ltd* [1973] 2 All ER 273, *Porzelack KG v Porzelack (UK) Ltd* [1987] 1 All ER 1074 (1987 Abr para 2006) and *Okotcha v Voest Intertrading GmbH* [1993] BCLC 474 applied.

522 Security for costs—order against company—company business and claim sold to individual—joinder of individual conditional on payment of costs into court

A company was ordered to pay security for the defendant's costs otherwise its action would be stayed. The company then sold its business, including the claim, to a director of the company. When the director applied to be joined as a plaintiff, the judge imposed a condition in granting the application that the plaintiff made a payment into court of the same amount previously ordered. The plaintiff appealed against the condition and was granted legal aid. The defendant cross-appealed, submitting that the assignment of the business to the plaintiff was a sham, or colourable device, or an abuse of the court's process, designed to circumvent the court's order for security and the rule that corporations were ineligible for legal aid. *Held*, (1) under CCR, Ord 15 any person could be added or substituted as a party and terms could be imposed as a condition of ordering an addition. The judge had therefore been entitled to impose appropriate conditions. However, the defendant was in no worse a position than if the company had sold its business to the plaintiff before bringing proceedings; he was a personal plaintiff who was liable to the extent of his available assets to meet any costs order made against him. There was therefore no justification for the order. (2) The court rejected the suggestion that the sale agreement was a sham. The sale might not turn out to be valid, but there was no indication that the company was to retain any interest in any recovery made by the plaintiff against the defendant. It was a device in that it was a transaction effected to circumvent a procedural disadvantage to which the company, but not the plaintiff, might be subject. (3) The legal aid board would have to consider whether the sale was effected to enable the plaintiff to prosecute the claim with the benefit of legal aid instead of through the company without that benefit, and if so whether it was unreasonable that he should have legal aid. That was a judgment the board was well fitted to make. If the grant was not unreasonable the board might not refuse it. In that event, it would not be open to the court to set aside the joinder of the plaintiff on the ground that it would open the door to an abuse of legal aid. Accordingly, the judge's order would be set aside and the cross-appeal would be dismissed.

Eurocross Sales Ltd v Cornhill Insurance plc [1995] 4 All ER 950 (Court of Appeal: Sir Thomas Bingham MR, Auld and Ward LJJ).

523 Shares—acquisition of own shares by company—covenant to maintain asset rates

See *Barclays Bank plc v British and Commonwealth Holdings plc,* para 525.

524 Shares—acquisition of own shares by company—payment in settlement of action

The defendant employee was accused of fraud by the plaintiff company on the basis of false invoices rendered by a company owned by his wife. The plaintiff claimed a declaration that the shares in the wife's company and loans to it should be assigned to the plaintiff as they had been purchased with money paid in respect of the false invoices. A Tomlin order was made staying the proceedings and under this the plaintiff was required to purchase all of the defendant's rights in the shares of the wife's company together with such rights as the defendant had in the shares of the plaintiff company, including share options. The plaintiff applied to the court for an order requiring the defendant to transfer to it all rights in shares in the plaintiff company that he had acquired by exercising an option together with his entitlement to exercise that option in relation to further shares in return for a specified sum. The issue to be determined was whether that part of the Tomlin order referring to shares in the plaintiff company was unenforceable as being in contravention of the Companies Act 1985, s 143(1), which prevented a company from purchasing its own shares. The plaintiff claimed that s 143(1) did not prohibit payments made to settle an action when the defendant had acknowledged that his shares should belong to the plaintiff company. *Held*, the provisions of the Tomlin order referring to shares and options to acquire shares were a purchase transaction falling within the 1985 Act, s 143(1). The claim in relation to the share entitlement failed. Even if the plaintiff had been entitled to recover the share and option entitlement and the sum they paid in consideration was regarded simply as money paid to settle a strong case and avoid litigation, the case would not be outside the ambit of s 143 as the claim made in relation to the shares was something that arose outside the proceedings. Similarly, the claim in relation to the option entitlement failed, being inextricably bound up with the void part of the transaction.

Vision Express (UK) Ltd v Wilson [1995] 2 BCLC 419 (Chancery Division: Knox J).

525 Shares—redeemable shares—failure to redeem—breach of covenant

The Companies Act 1985, s 151 provides that it is not lawful for a company to give financial assistance for the purpose of acquisition of its own shares. Section 178 provides that a company is not liable in damages in respect of any failure on its part to redeem or purchase any of its shares.

A company (C) purchased redeemable preference shares from the defendant, on condition that the shares were to be redeemed in four equal tranches, at the rate of one tranche per year for four years. The scheme also involved an option agreement under which, in any year that the defendant failed to redeem a tranche of shares, company C had the right to sell that tranche to a company formed for the purpose and financed by the plaintiff banks. The defendant also covenanted to conduct its affairs so as to maintain certain asset rates and any breach of that covenant would entitle the plaintiffs to bring an action for damages. The defendant was placed into administration and, as a result, failed to redeem the last two tranches. The plaintiffs claimed damages for breach of covenant but the defendant maintained that the action could not succeed as it would be in breach of the 1985 Act, ss 151 and 178. At first instance, the plaintiffs were awarded damages. On appeal by the defendant, *held*, although, under s 178, a company was not liable for failure to redeem its shares it could, as in this case, be liable for breach of a covenant to so redeem, which would not constitute a breach of that section. There had also been no breach of s 151 because the covenants' purpose was to reassure company C and did not involve giving any financial assistance for the acquisition of the shares. Accordingly, the appeal would be dismissed.

British and Commonwealth Holdings plc v Barclays Bank plc [1996] 1 All ER 381 (Court of Appeal: Kennedy and Aldous LJJ and Sir Roger Parker).

526 Shares—share option scheme—approval by Inland Revenue—effect of amendment of scheme on approval

The Inland Revenue approved a share option scheme of a company, with the effect that the charge to income tax under Schedule E did not apply to gains realised on an exercise of the option. Instead there was a charge to capital gains tax if and when the shares acquired by the option holder were disposed of. The company proposed to merge with another company and amended the scheme so as to eliminate a rule of the scheme that the options ceased to be exercisable six months after a merger. A decision of a special commissioner that the amended scheme should continue to be an approved scheme under the Income and Corporation Taxes Act 1988, Sch 9 was reversed on appeal. On further appeal by the company, *held*, in deciding whether the Revenue ought to have been satisfied that the amendments fulfilled the requirements of Sch 9, it had to be determined whether the option holders thereby obtained a right to acquire shares within Sch 9, paras 25, 29. The relevant right was a right obtained under the scheme to acquire scheme shares. Under the unamended scheme, such a right was obtained by each option holder on the grant of his option. The question of whether the option holder, by virtue of the amendments, obtained a new right to acquire scheme shares was one of degree. The amendments did not make it inevitable that all option holders would be affected by them. The impossibility of attributing any uniform practical consequence to the amendments demonstrated that their effect had to be considered irrespective of such consequences. So considered, each option holder did not obtain a new right to acquire scheme shares. Accordingly, the appeal would be allowed.

IRC v Reed International plc; Reed International plc v IRC [1995] STC 889 (Court of Appeal: Nourse, Beldam and Evans LJJ). Decision of Blackburne J [1994] STC 396 (1994 Abr para 529) reversed.

527 Shares—title to shares—foreign shares—forum for deciding title

See *Macmillan Inc v Bishopsgate Investment Trust plc (No 3)*, para 576.

528 Summary financial statements

The Companies (Summary Financial Statements) Regulations 1995, SI 1995/2092 (in force 1 September 1995), replace the 1992 Regulations, SI 1992/3075. Changes of substance are as follows: (1) the manner in which a listed public company is to ascertain whether an entitled person wishes to receive a summary financial statement in place of the full accounts and reports for the financial year is amended; (2) the provision under which a failure by an entitled person to respond to a relevant consultation impliedly countermanded any previous notification of a wish to receive full accounts and reports is revoked; (3) companies are now only required to pay for the postage on cards sent to entitled persons if those persons have addresses in the European Economic Area; (4) a summary financial statement sent to an entitled person is no longer required to be accompanied by a reply-paid card on which the entitled person can request the full accounts and reports, but the statement must contain a clear statement of the right of entitled persons to obtain a free copy of a company's full accounts and reports and of how that copy can be obtained; and (4) amendments are made consequential on revisions to the law on the content of the full statutory accounts of insurance companies and groups. Transitional provision is also made.

529 Unfair prejudice to members—conflicting interests of members—duty of directors

Where a company's affairs are being conducted in a manner which is unfairly prejudicial to the interests of some or all of its members, an action may be brought by such members for an order under the Companies Act 1985, s 459.

It has been held that where a company's affairs are conducted in a manner which affects different groups of shareholders in different ways, the directors have a duty both to act in good faith for the benefit of the company and to strike the right balance between conflicting sections of interest. The term 'unfairly prejudicial' in s 459 is wide and general. Consequently, the circumstances in which an order can be made under that provision are not exhaustive. The correct action to be taken by the directors depends on the circumstances of the case.

Re BSB Holdings Ltd; London Merchant Securities plc v Chargeurs SA (1995) Times, 2 August, Independent, 7 September (Chancery Division: Arden J).

530 Unfair prejudice to members—remedy—capacity of petitioner for relief

The plaintiff, an experienced businessman, set up a company with the intention of enabling the defendants to run their own business. The plaintiff was the company chairman, but the business was run by the defendants and they held a majority shareholding. The company's working capital was provided by a second company, which was effectively controlled by the plaintiff. The business was run on a basis of trust and no documents regulating the management of the company were ever drafted. Following the breakdown of relations between the plaintiff and the defendants, the plaintiff was removed as chairman and as a director. He thereupon petitioned for an order under the Companies Act 1985, s 459 that the defendants be required to purchase his shares, or that the company be wound up on the grounds that it was just and equitable to do so. On the question of the capacity in which a petitioner complained under s 459, held, in considering the question, the court had to take a broad approach as to what might properly be regarded as a petitioner's interest as a member of the company. That interest, in the case of a small private company in which a member had ventured capital, might include a legitimate expectation that he would continue to participate in the management of the company and be a director. The separateness of the plaintiff and the second company did not exclude him from seeking relief under s 459 on the ground that the loans by the second company were procured by the plaintiff and formed an essential part of the arrangements entered into for the venture to be carried on by the company. This was also the way the parties themselves looked at the matter. The plaintiff therefore had a legitimate expectation of being able to participate in the management of the company, at least as long as the second company remained a significant loan creditor, until a change in management and control became necessary for some other reason.

R & H Electric Ltd v Haden Bill Electrical Ltd; Re Haden Bill Electrical Ltd [1995] 2 BCLC 280 (Chancery Division: Robert Walker J).

531 Unfair prejudice to members—understanding on which shareholders associated— whether directors acting outside articles of association

The Companies Act 1985, s 459 provides that a member of a company can apply to the court by petition for an order on the ground that the company's affairs are being or have been conducted in a manner which is unfairly prejudicial to the interests of some part of the members.

A company's share capital was divided into A shares, carrying voting rights but no right to dividends or capital and B and C shares which carried no votes but were entitled in different ways to dividends and capital. It was a family-run concern with shares held by, or on trust for, various descendants of the founder. The petitioner held approximately 8 per cent of the C shares and sought a winding-up order on just and equitable grounds or an order under the 1985 Act, s 459 that the holders of the A shares purchase her shares. She alleged that the directors had kept the company in business in order to earn excessive remuneration whilst the company was operating at a loss and that they had failed to keep proper and complete accounting records. Held, in deciding whether actions were unfairly prejudicial for the purposes of s 459 it must be considered that fairness was being judged in a commercial context. The starting point would be to determine whether the conduct in question was in accordance with the articles of association. In some instances, even though the action was in compliance with the articles of association, those articles may not have reflected the understandings on which the shareholders were associated and thus the action might still be unfair. In the present case, there was no reason to suppose that the relationship between the company and its members was other than that set out in the articles of association. There was no basis for finding that the directors had abused their fiduciary powers or acted outside the articles and thus the petition would be dismissed.

Re Saul D Harrison & Sons plc [1995] 1 BCLC 14 (Court of Appeal: Neill, Hoffmann and Waite LJJ).

532 Winding up—agent holding proceeds of sale in account for principal—existence of trust

The plaintiff company acted as a selling agent for major car leasing companies. The arrangement between the company and the defendant provided that the company would pay the proceeds of any sale into a designated bank account and remit the proceeds less commission and costs within five days of receipt, all repayments to be by separate cheques. The company went into creditors' voluntary liquidation at a time when there was a credit balance in the agency account. The question arose in a summons for directions taken out by the liquidator as to whether the defendant had a proprietary claim to this sum, the other creditors agreeing that they had no such claim. *Held*, the credit balance in the agency account was held on trust for the defendant. Whether or not a trust of the proceeds in the account had been created depended on the intention of the parties and the proper construction of the agency agreement between the parties. On the facts, given that the company was to act as the defendant's agent for sale, that the credit period allowed to the company before it had to hand over the proceeds of sale was relatively short, and payment for each transaction had to be made by separate cheques, a trust relationship had been created between the parties. Accordingly, the defendant had a proprietary claim to the credit balance in the agency account.

Re Fleet Disposal Services Ltd; Spratt v AT & T Automotive Services Ltd [1995] 1 BCLC 345 (Chancery Division: Lightman J).

533 Winding up—compulsory winding up order—company in creditors' voluntary liquidation

A company incorporated in England was a member of a large group with associated companies in the United States, Switzerland and the Netherlands. It appeared to be managed from Switzerland. Two Swiss companies within the group on which the company was dependent for its main income terminated an arrangement with the company. It went into creditors' voluntary liquidation and a liquidator was appointed. The petitioning creditor believed that assets had been extracted from the company prior to the liquidation and that creditors on whom the goodwill of the company depended had been paid to the disadvantage of certain other creditors such as itself. There was strong documentary evidence of improper manoeuvring prior to the liquidation. The petitioning creditor sought the compulsory winding up of the company. The day before a creditors' meeting at which the petitioning creditor sought the removal of the liquidator, an associated company put in proof of a large debt. At the meeting, a new liquidator was appointed by the votes of the companies in the group. At the hearing of the petition, *held*, in exercising its discretion whether to order the compulsory winding up of a company already in creditors' voluntary liquidation, the court had to take account of both the quantity and the quality of the claims of the petitioning creditor on the one hand and the opposing creditors on the other hand. Where a substantial independent creditor believed that it had been prejudiced by sharp practice, fairness and commercial morality might require that it be given the opportunity to insist on the company's affairs being scrutinised by the process which followed a compulsory order. It was entitled to an investigation both independent and clearly seen to be independent even where the voluntary liquidation was already well advanced and a compulsory order might cause further expense and delay. In exercising its discretion, the court also had to take into account the fact that, where there were inter-group trading activities, particularly where the company seemed to have engaged in no other trading activity, there was much room for manipulation of profit and loss. The last-minute claim of the associated company meant that the inter-group trading activities demanded impartial investigation on behalf of the general body of creditors. The fact that the associated creditors had gone to such lengths to install the new liquidator was itself enough to disqualify him. In those circumstances, a compulsory order would be made.

Re Gordon & Breach Science Publishers Ltd [1995] 2 BCLC 189 (Chancery Division: Robert Walker J).

534 Winding up—expenses of winding up—liquidator's remuneration

See *Re Gower Enterprises Ltd*, para 482.

535 Winding up—liquidator—control of liquidator by creditors—liquidator's discretion to sell assets

The Insolvency Act 1986, s 167(3) provides that the exercise by the liquidator in a winding up of a company by the court of the powers exercisable with or without the sanction of the court is subject to the court's control, and any creditor or contributory may apply to the court with respect to any exercise or proposed exercise of any of those powers. Section 168(5) provides that if any person is aggrieved by an act or decision of the liquidator, that person may apply to the court, and the court may confirm, reverse or modify the act or decision complained of and make such order in the case as it thinks just.

It has been held that the 1986 Act, s 167(3) confers on a creditor a right to apply to the court with respect to any exercise as well as any proposed exercise of the liquidator's powers. Section 168(5) is ancillary to s 167(3) and gives to, amongst others, a creditor or contributory the right to apply to set aside a decision or act of a liquidator. The words 'persons aggrieved' in s 168(5) are no more than shorthand for the longer description 'any creditor, debtor or other person aggrieved'. However, the court will only interfere with the exercise of a liquidator's discretion to sell the assets of an insolvent company in very exceptional circumstances.

Re Edennote Ltd; Tottenham Hotspur plc v Ryman [1995] 2 BCLC 248 (Chancery Division: Sir John Vinelott).

536 Winding up—order—rescission—persons entitled to appear at hearing

Winding-up petitions were presented by the Inland Revenue against a number of companies for non-payment of income tax. The Revenue agreed to an adjournment of the petitions so that the possibility of company voluntary arrangements could be explored. However, it opposed a further extension of the adjournment and, in the absence of opposing creditors at the hearing, winding up orders were made by the registrar. The major secured creditor of the companies was in favour of the companies being put in a position to proceed with company voluntary arrangements. On the companies' appeals against the orders and, alternatively, their applications to have the orders rescinded, *held*, the registrar had jurisdiction to refuse the further adjournment and to make the winding-up orders. As the registrar had not misdirected himself on the evidence in making the orders, the appeals would be dismissed. In hearing an application for rescission of a winding-up petition under the Insolvency Rules 1986, SI 1986/1925, r 7.47(1), the court had a discretion under r 4.16(5) to give leave for creditors opposing the winding up to be heard even though they had not appeared at the earlier proceedings. In deciding whether or not to rescind the orders, the court had to be satisfied that there was a real prospect that the proposals being put forward in the voluntary arrangement would command the necessary creditor approval. On the evidence, the court was so satisfied and the orders would be rescinded.

Re Dollar Land (Feltham) Ltd [1995] 2 BCLC 370 (Chancery Division: Blackburne J).

537 Winding up—petition—application to restrain advertisement of petition—court's discretion to restrain

The Insolvency Rules 1986, SI 1986/1925, r 4.11(1) provides that, unless the court otherwise directs, an insolvency petition must be advertised.

The Secretary of State had presented insolvency petitions against two companies under the Insolvency Act 1986, s 124A on the grounds that it was expedient in the public interest that they be wound up. The companies sought to restrain advertisement of the petitions until there had been a full hearing on the merits. It was decided at first instance that a party which had presented a petition could not be prevented from proceeding with that petition, including its advertisement, unless there was prima facie evidence that the petition was more or less bound to fail. On appeal, *held*, the judge had erred in equating the test to be adopted on an application to restrain the advertisement of a petition already on the file with that adopted on an application to restrain the presentation of one which had not reached the file. This was demonstrated by the discretion exercisable under the 1986 Rules, r 4.11(1) which did not come into a decision on abuse of process. That provision required advertisement unless the court otherwise directed and it was for the company to show sufficient reason to depart from the normal practice. The court would not restrain the advertisement unless the companies could show that it might cause serious damage to their reputation and financial stability. Accordingly, the appeal would be allowed.

Re Companies (Nos 007923 and 007924 of 1994) [1995] 1 WLR 953 (Court of Appeal: Nourse and Waite LJJ). *Coulon Sanderson & Ward Ltd v Ward* (1985) Financial Times, 18 October, CA (1985 Abr para 351) distinguished. *Re a Company (No 007946 of 1993)* (1993) Times, 18 November (1993 Abr para 504) applied.

The Secretary of State presented a petition for a company to be wound up. The petition alleged that (1) the company's claims to be a market research company were bogus, (2) a scheme operated by the company to establish a database whereby members of the public were offered bonuses or prizes on joining or procuring membership of others was in fact a lottery, (3) the scheme was bound to fail, and (4) the company was using misleading promotional material. The company applied under the Insolvency Rules 1986, SI 1986/1925, r 4.11 for an order that advertisement of the petition be dispensed with or restrained until after the petition was heard, claiming that public knowledge of the petition created a real danger that membership applications might decline or cease and that members might exercise their contractual right for the return of their fees. *Held*, the purposes of the advertisement were (1) to enable creditors and interested parties to attend and put before the court material relevant to the decision whether or not to make a winding up order, and (2) to tell the public that a petition had been presented so that they might be warned that any dealing with the company should take place with caution. Commercial honesty required that existing or prospective members be informed of the truth, namely that the future of the company was in doubt, fulfilling the second purpose of the advertisement. Further, it was common ground that members of the scheme were entitled to repayment of fees if it was held to be a lottery and, since the company would be insolvent, such members might rank as creditors. There was no force in the company's complaint and, accordingly, the application would be dismissed.

Applied Database Ltd v Secretary of State for Trade and Industry [1995] 1 BCLC 272 February (Chancery Division: Lightman J).

538   Winding up—petition—bringing of derivative action on behalf of company

The plaintiff was a 50 per cent shareholder in a vehicle hire company. The remaining shares were held by the defendant who was the sole director of the company. The defendant was also a shareholder in a coach hire business and his wife was a director of that company. The plaintiff's daughter had been married to the defendant. The plaintiff commenced proceedings on behalf of the vehicle hire business alleging that the defendant and his wife had been instrumental in diverting business from the vehicle hire company to the coach hire company and that the defendant had paid money belonging to the vehicle hire company into his own bank account. The defendant had presented a petition to wind up the vehicle hire company on the grounds that it was unable to pay its debts or that it was just and equitable that the company should be wound up. He sought either to strike out the current action on the grounds that it was not a permissible derivative action or to stay the action until the hearing of the winding-up petition. His application had been dismissed. On appeal, *held*, a shareholder could bring a derivative action on behalf of the company if the action was brought bona fide in the interests of the company and there were no other remedies available. A derivative action was not available for any ulterior purpose. The opportunity to put the company into liquidation provided an alternative remedy to the derivative action. It was clear that the present action was being pursued for personal reasons rather than in the interests of the company. Accordingly, the appeal would be allowed and the action struck out.

Barrett v Duckett [1995] 1 BCLC 243 (Court of Appeal: Russell, Beldam and Gibson LJJ). Decision of Sir Mervyn Davies [1995] 1 BCLC 73 reversed.

539   Winding up—petition—disputed debt—substantial grounds for dispute

A company owned a block of flats which it managed on behalf of the long lessees of the flats. The company entered into a building contract with the petitioner for the carrying out of repairs to the building. The contract was later suspended and then terminated, the petitioner being given the right to issue an interim certificate for the value of the work and money due. The petitioner served first a statutory demand for payment followed by a petition for the winding up of the company on the grounds that it was unable to pay its debts. At the hearing it was belatedly admitted by the petitioner that there was a genuine dispute as to what money was due according to the certificate. *Held*, as the company disputed the amount of the debt in good faith and had substantial grounds for doing so, the correct course was to strike out the petition.

Re a Company (No 00212 of 1995) (1995) Times, 7 April (Chancery Division: Rattee J). *Re a Company* [1984] 3 All ER 78 (1984 Abr para 342) followed.

540   Winding up—petition—petition by Secretary of State—evaluation

The Secretary of State presented petitions under the Insolvency Act 1986, s 124A for the winding up of six companies on the ground that it was expedient in the public interest to do so. On the hearing of the petitions, *held*, on the question of whether it would be just and equitable for the companies to be wound up by the court under s 124A, the principles applicable had been set out in *Re Walter L Jacob & Co Ltd* (1989) 5 BCC 244. Where the court was faced with a petition presented by a creditor or contributory, it had to consider primarily the conflicting interests and wishes of the opposing parties to the petition and carry out a balancing exercise. In principle, the exercise to be carried out where the petitioner was the Secretary of State was the same. Whoever might be the petitioner, the court had to weigh the factors pointing to the conclusion that it would be just and equitable to wind up the company against those which pointed to the opposite conclusion. Where the reasons put forward were founded on considerations of public interest, the court itself had to evaluate those reasons to the extent necessary for it to form a view on whether they afforded sufficient reason for making a winding-up order in a particular case. With public interest petitioners, the evaluation would be carried out with the assistance of evidence and submissions from the Secretary of State and other parties, but the cogency of the submissions made on behalf of the Secretary of State fell to be considered and tested in the same way as any other submissions. On the facts of the present case, the petitions would be dismissed.

Re a Company (No 007816 of 1994), (No 007818 of 1994), (No 007819 of 1994), (No 007820 of 1994), (No 007821 of 1994), (No 007822 of 1994) [1995] 2 BCLC 539 (Chancery Division: Jonathan Parker J).

541 Winding up—petition—striking out—presentation of petition after company voluntary arrangement—adequacy of notice of creditors' meeting

The applicant company issued proceedings against the respondent. The action was dismissed and an order for costs was made against the applicant in an amount to be fixed. A notice of discontinuance of the proceedings was sent to the respondent on the day before company voluntary arrangements were approved at a meeting of the applicant's creditors. The respondent was aware from various sources of the creditors' meeting but denied having received any formal notice of the meeting. The applicant maintained that the notice had been sent in accordance with the rules. The applicant had assigned an estimated value, for voting purposes, to the respondent's claim in the event that he attended the creditors' meeting. The figure was given to the chairman at the meeting. The respondent did not, however, either attend or vote at the meeting. The legal costs for which the applicant was liable were subsequently taxed and a certificate as to costs was issued. Soon afterwards, the respondent presented a petition for the winding up of the applicant on the ground of non-payment of the costs. The applicant applied for the petition to be struck out on the ground that the respondent was bound by the voluntary arrangements. *Held,* where notice of a creditors' meeting to consider a company voluntary arrangement was sent to a creditor in accordance with the rules and the creditor had, albeit from a third party, received notice of the meeting, no injustice would be caused by regarding him as having had notice in accordance with the rules even though he had not received it. A creditor with an unliquidated or unqualified claim was entitled to vote, pursuant to the Insolvency Rules 1986, r 1.173, at a creditors' meeting held to consider voluntary arrangements only if he attended the meeting in person or by proxy and the chairman of the meeting agreed to put an estimated value on the debt for the purposes of voting at the meeting. The respondent had notice of the meeting and would have been entitled to vote had he attended. Therefore the voluntary arrangements were binding upon him and the winding-up petition would be struck out.

Beverley Group plc v McClue [1995] 2 BCLC 407 (Chancery Division: Knox J).

542 Winding up—proof of debts—quantification of claim—moneys held on trust

Under an agreement between a package tour operator and a number of travel agents, moneys paid to an agent by customers in payment for holidays were to be held on express trust for the tour operator on confirmation of the contract between the customer and the operator. The agreement also provided that should either a travel agent or the tour operator be wound up, any moneys held by a travel agent would belong absolutely to the liquidator of the tour operator. The travel agents were entitled to a commission upon the tour operator's confirmation of a holiday. Customer's moneys received by the travel agents were not paid into a separate account but were paid into their general account. The tour operator went into liquidation and the liquidator brought proceedings against travel agents holding customers' moneys for holidays booked with the operator. The liquidator claimed that the moneys were held on trust for the tour operator, that certain commission payments due to the travel agents could not be deducted from those moneys and that the travel agents were not entitled to set off against the moneys any sums due to them from the operator. *Held,* on a true construction of the agreement a trust was created under which the tour operator had a charge in equity over the moneys to secure payment of the agent's outstanding indebtedness to it. The agreement pointed clearly towards a monthly accounting in which all debits and credits were brought into account. Accordingly, the travel agents were entitled to bring into account by way of deduction from the moneys in their possession all sums for the time being owing to them by the tour operator, whether in respect of commission or otherwise.

Re ILG Travel Ltd (in administration) [1995] 2 BCLC 128 (Chancery Division: Jonathan Parker J).

543 Wrongful trading—action for contribution to company's assets—limitation period

A company went into voluntary liquidation. Four and a half years later, the joint liquidators commenced proceedings against the company's directors for wrongful trading under the Insolvency Act 1986, s 214. The directors subsequently applied to have the action dismissed for want of prosecution. The issue arose whether there was any limitation period applicable to the liquidators' claim and, if so, whether that period had expired. It also fell to be determined whether there had been inordinate and inexcusable delay in prosecuting the claim and whether the delay had caused serious prejudice to the directors. *Held*, the relevant limitation period was governed by the Limitation Act 1980, s 9(1). This provided that an action to recover any sum recoverable by virtue of any enactment could not be brought after the expiration of six years from the date on which the cause of action accrued. The cause of action created by s 214 accrued when the company went into liquidation. Therefore, the liquidators were not time-barred from bringing the action. However, as they had launched their claim more than four years into the applicable limitation period, it was incumbent upon them to prosecute their claim with a minimum of further delay. On the facts, they had failed to do so since there were two periods of delay which were both inordinate and inexcusable. Moreover, the directors had suffered prejudice because of the failing memories of the witnesses as a result of the liquidators' culpable delay in prosecuting the claim. Accordingly, the liquidators' claim would be struck out.

Re Farmizer (Products) Ltd [1995] 2 BCLC 462 (Chancery Division: Blackburne J).

COMPULSORY ACQUISITION OF LAND

Halsbury's Laws of England (4th edn) Vol 8(1) (reissue), paras 1–400

544 Articles

Betterment: Better for Whom? Simon Purcell: 139 SJ 659
Compulsory Purchase: Recent Development, Norman E Osborn: 139 SJ 115

545 Certificate of appropriate alternative development—factors to be taken into account

A borough council owned an area of land which bordered on a major road for which a county council was the highway authority. The county council devised a scheme for the improvement of the road, and required the area of land in order to carry out the scheme. Having issued a compulsory purchase order in respect of the land, the county council applied to the borough council, as the local planning authority for the land, for a certificate of appropriate alternative development. The borough council issued a certificate which stated that it would have granted planning permission for development of office, residential or hotel development if the county council had not proposed compulsorily to acquire the land. The county council appealed against the certificate, and the Secretary of State decided to cancel it and grant planning permission, but only for a car park. The borough council applied under the Land Compensation Act 1961, s 21 to quash his decision on a number of grounds. *Held*, even if the Secretary of State had accepted that the land was suitable for housing use, he would have been obliged to balance the suitability of such use against planning objections. Where an application for a certificate was made and the land in question was owned by a public authority for public purposes, it was relevant to consider the protection of potential public purposes in assessing compensation under the 1961 Act, as the need for public open space in an area could amount to a valid planning objection to a hypothetical development. The Secretary of State was therefore entitled to conclude that the need for land for housing, office or hotel use was overridden by the planning objections to the development. In deciding whether or not planning permission would have been granted by the borough council, the Secretary of State had been required to have regard to the development plan and other material considerations, and not to what landowners would have done with the land. Although he had taken account of opportunity cost as a material consideration, it was not a consideration of great weight that would have determined the issue one way or the other. The Secretary of State had not acted perversely. He had taken account of only the relevant factors, and had also followed the correct statutory procedures and had dealt with the points raised. Accordingly, the application would be dismissed.

Maidstone Borough Council v Secretary of State for the Environment (1994) 69 P & CR 1 (Queen's Bench Division: Tucker J).

546   Compensation—assessment—injurious affection to retained land—prior determination in respect of compulsorily acquired land

The claimants owned land, part of which had been compulsorily acquired. Following an appeal to the Secretary of State for the Environment, a certificate of appropriate alternative development was issued in respect of the acquired land. This stated that had that land not been acquired, planning permission would have been granted for residential development there. At the time of the acquisition, there was a firm prospect that a road would be built which would have rendered development likely on the land. A dispute arose as to the value of the compensation to be paid for the severance of the land and injurious affection to the retained land. *Held,* there was no ground for saying that the scope of the certificate was limited to the acquired land and as such was of evidential value only in relation to the retained land. The case fell squarely within the doctrine of issue estoppel, which applied to decisions to issue certificates made by the Secretary of State under the Land Compensation Act 1961, s 18. The acquiring authority was a party to those proceedings and had appeared to present its case. Subject to its right of appeal, it was duly bound by the issue of the certificate. The tribunal in those proceedings was required to determine whether planning permission would have been granted for the acquired land on the assumption that the proposed road scheme had gone ahead. In the current proceedings, the same issue required determination in relation to the retained land. The authority was therefore estopped from reopening the question. Accordingly, the authority would be bound by the certificate in determining the amount of compensation to be paid in respect of the retained land.

Porter v Secretary of State for Transport (1995) 70 P & CR 82 (Lands Tribunal: Judge Marder).

547   Compensation—assessment—land taken for highway—whether benefit to adjoining land set off against compensation

The Highways Act 1980, s 261(1)(a) provides that in assessing the compensation payable in respect of the compulsory acquisition of land by a highway authority, the Lands Tribunal must have regard to the extent to which the remaining contiguous lands belonging to the same person may be benefited by the purpose for which the land is authorised to be acquired.

Land was taken by compulsory purchase from a city council, for which it was to receive £3m, to enable a county council to construct a link road. It was agreed that the betterment of the city council's retained land on the construction of the road would amount to £4m and it fell to be determined whether the Lands Tribunal should have regard to the betterment value in assessing compensation. At the time the land was acquired various planning permissions were in existence for residential development of land which included the betterment land, but the permissions could only be partially implemented until the road was completed. The city council claimed that set-off for betterment to retained land arising from road provision on the acquired land under the 1980 Act, s 261(1)(a) should only be made where any benefit was directly attributable to the road provision and did not apply where planning permissions were granted in expectation of road provision. *Held,* the setting-off of benefit to retained land against compensation for land taken was entirely a statutory matter and depended upon the words of the applicable statute. As the development of the retained land was limited until such time as the road was completed, its value would be enhanced by the road to be constructed on the acquired land and as the enhanced value exceeded the compensation payable for the acquired land, compensation had to be assessed at nil.

Leicester City Council v Leicestershire County Council (1995) 70 P & CR 435 (Lands Tribunal: T Hoyes FRICS).

548   Compensation—assessment—relocation of business—loss caused by contemplation of effects of compulsory purchase order

The defendant owned a business on land which was made subject to a form of compulsory purchase order known as a resumption order, made by the government of Hong Kong. The Lands Tribunal awarded compensation based on the value of the business on the date of resumption, the so-called 'extinguishment basis', but on appeal it was held that the correct basis of assessment was the cost of relocation and continued operation of the interrupted business. The tribunal also determined that the defendant was able to claim damages for losses incurred due to the threat of the order but prior to it actually being made, but that decision was also reversed on appeal. On further appeal by the government in relation to the method of assessment, and cross-appeal by the defendant in relation to the time from which compensation may be claimed, *held,* the tribunal had taken account of the number of years of discontinuity between the original business ceasing to operate and the commencement of operations by the newly located business and concluded that the two were separate businesses. There was no evidence entitling the appeal court to reach a different conclusion. In such circumstances, the most appropriate method of assessment was the extinguishment basis as opposed to the relocation basis. To qualify for compensation a loss suffered as a result of compulsory purchase had to be causally connected, not too remote, and not a loss which a reasonable person would have avoided. However, a claim would not fail for lack of causal connection by reason only that the loss arose before the compulsory purchase order was made, provided it arose in contemplation of such an order and the threat which it presented. Accordingly, the appeal and cross appeal would be allowed and the defendant would be awarded damages, assessed on the extinguishment basis, caused by contemplation of the compulsory purchase order being made.

Director of Buildings and Lands v Shun Fung Ironworks Ltd [1995] 1 All ER 846 (Privy Council: Lords Keith of Kinkel, Mustill, Slynn of Hadley, Lloyd of Berwick and Nicholls of Birkenhead).

549 Compensation—claim—validity

The plaintiffs claimed compensation of 'an amount in excess of £50 to be agreed' for depreciation in the value of their property resulting from the opening of, and extensions to, an airport. It fell to be determined whether the claims were valid for the purposes of the Land Compensation Act 1973, s 3(1)(f), which requires a notice of claim to contain particulars of the amount of compensation claimed. *Held*, a notice of claim had to include the amount of compensation sought. A purely arbitrary figure was not a basis for subsequent negotiation. Although a similar requirement of particularisation of a claim in response to a notice to treat was not strictly relevant in construing the 1973 Act, it indicated the background of procedure in respect of claiming compensation from publicly authorised authorities for publicly authorised works in the context of which the 1973 Act, Pt I (ss 1–19) came to be enacted. The plaintiffs' claims were invalid and, accordingly, the tribunal had no jurisdiction to entertain them.

Fennessy v London City Airport Ltd [1995] 2 EGLR 167 (Lands Tribunal: Judge Rich QC). *Methodist Church Trustees v North Tyneside Metropolitan Borough Council* (1979) 38 P & CR 665 (1979 Abr para 421) considered.

550 Compensation—depreciation caused by use of public works—construction of bypass—noise and dirt

A dual carriageway bypass was built near to the claimant's property. As a result of the bypass, the through road in which his property was situated became a cul-de-sac, and an 'A' road to the rear of his property became a 'B' road. On the claimant's application under the Land Compensation Act 1973, for compensation for depreciation in the value of his property as a result of the noise and dirt caused by the bypass, the compensating authority disputed the claim, arguing that the bypass had made the property more desirable and quieter. *Held*, although the 1973 Act, s 1 required a claimant to prove that there had been a depreciation in the value of his land by physical factors caused by the use of public works, there was no particular way in which that had to be proved, as that was a matter of fact and opinion rather than of law. Similarly, the requirement under the 1973 Act, s 6 that compensation was to be reduced by the increase in value attributable to the public works be given effect as seemed most appropriate, and did not necessarily require a separate deduction. Here, the claimant had translated a change in the nature of the traffic noise into an increase in noise, whereas expert evidence showed that there had been no such increase. Expert evidence also showed that there was no correlation between traffic noise and volume on the one hand, and property values on the other, as prospective purchasers did not generally take account of such matters. The suggestion by the claimant's expert that it was necessary to compare the instant case with settlements and judicial decisions made in respect of land situated in other parts of the country could not be accepted as such comparables were irrelevant. Moreover, compensation had been assessed as nil for properties adjoining the claimant's property, and it was a fact that there had been a dramatic reduction in traffic on the former 'A' road and in the claimant's road as a result of the bypass. Additionally, the Lands Tribunal's own inspection of the claimant's property confirmed that the property had benefited from the bypass to a greater extent than any depreciation caused by the noise and dirt from it and, accordingly, the application would be dismissed.

Hallows v Welsh Office [1995] RVR 74 (Lands Tribunal: Judge Michael O'Donoghue and PH Clarke, FRICS).

551 Compulsory purchase order—acquisition of land for car park—offer of long lease rejected by acquiring authority—uncertainty on expiry of lease

Scotland

A compulsory purchase order was made in respect of the appellants' plot of land, together with other plots, on which a local authority wished to build a car park. The appellants' objections were the subject of a public local inquiry. Before the inquiry took place, the appellants told the authority that they would consider granting a long lease of the land, but the authority did not find the proposal acceptable. At the inquiry, the inspector noted that, in view of the long-term uncertainties such an arrangement could create, a lease would not be in the interests of the purpose of the order and he recommended that the order be confirmed. On appeal, *held*, the appellants had not raised the issue of a long lease in their objections before the inspector. The inspector had noted that the authority's policy was not to invest heavily in publicly-owned facilities on ground that they did not own, that the other plot owners were willing to sell and that the appellants had offered no particular term of years. He had also recognised that practical difficulties could arise once the plot was only a featureless portion of the car park. Although no submissions had been made regarding the practical difficulties of mixed tenure, the inspector had been entitled to take account of the fact that a long lease would create insecurity as to what would happen when it expired. In view of the facts, he could not reasonably be criticised for making his findings and the Secretary of State could not reasonably be criticised for accepting them. The appellants had not been prejudiced by the way in which the matter had been dealt with and, accordingly, the appeal would be dismissed.

Stirling Plant (Hire and Sales) Ltd v Central Regional Council (1995) Times, 9 February (Court of Session).

552 Entry onto land—entry before completion—rate of interest after entry

The Acquisition of Land (Rate of Interest after Entry) Regulations 1995, SI 1995/2262 (in force on 31 December 1995), replace the 1994 Regulations, SI 1994/468, so that the rate of interest payable where entry is made, is fixed at 0.5 per cent below the standard rate applying from time to time (calculated by reference to the base rate quoted by the seven largest banks authorised under the Banking Act 1987).

553 Lands Tribunal—jurisdiction—compensation—installation of sewer

The Public Health Act 1936, s 15(1)(a) provides that a water authority may construct a public sewer, either inside or outside their area. Section 278 provides that a local authority must make full compensation to any person who has sustained damage by reason of the exercise by the authority of any of their powers under the Act.

The respondent water authority constructed a sewer on private land belonging to the claimant, having given notice pursuant to the 1936 Act, s 15. Although it was agreed that compensation was payable, the claimant contended that the construction of the sewer constituted a compulsory acquisition of land or an acquisition of an interest or right in the land, which therefore gave the Lands Tribunal jurisdiction to determine whether or not he was entitled to interest on the agreed compensation. The respondent argued that a landowner's entitlement to compensation under the 1936 Act, s 278 was in respect of damage only, and not to interest for a delay in the payment of compensation. It also argued that disputed compensation claims could only be determined by arbitration. On the preliminary issue of the Lands Tribunal's jurisdiction, *held*, the effect of the Land Compensation Act 1961, s 1 was to transfer jurisdiction over the assessment of compensation for the construction of a sewer on private land, in the exercise of powers under the 1936 Act, from arbitration to the Lands Tribunal, provided that the construction constituted a compulsory acquisition of land. There was a distinction between the exercise by an authority of its power to lay a sewer, and the subsequent interest or rights acquired when the sewer vested in the authority. Here, the respondent was obliged to compensate the claimant for damage caused by the exercise of its power under the 1936 Act, s 15. The space occupied by the sewer vested in the respondent by virtue of the 1936 Act, s 20, and there was therefore a compulsory acquisition of land for the purposes of the 1961 Act, namely of the stratum of subsoil in which the sewer was laid. Moreover, the laying of the sewer on the claimant's land gave the respondent a right or interest in the land for the purposes of the 1961 Act. In consequence of the compulsory acquisition, the Lands Tribunal had power to award interest on the agreed compensation, and also had jurisdiction to consider a reference which related solely to the determination of the amount of such interest.

Taylor v North West Water Ltd [1995] RVR 83 (Lands Tribunal: Judge Michael O'Donoghue and PH Clarke, FRICS). *Thurrock, Grays and Tilbury Joint Sewerage Board v Thames Land Co Ltd* (1925) 90 JP 1 followed.

554 Notice to treat—withdrawal—withdrawal after entry into possession

The Land Compensation Act 1961, s 31(1) provides that where a person served with a notice to treat has delivered to an acquiring authority a notice in writing of the amount claimed by him containing the necessary particulars of the nature of his interest and the details of the amount claimed in time so as to enable the authority to make a proper offer of compensation the authority may, within six weeks after the delivery of the notice of claim, withdraw any notice to treat served on the claimant or on any other person interested in the land authorised to be acquired. Under s 52, an acquiring authority that has taken possession of land may make an advance payment on account of compensation. Where the amount of any advance payment made on the basis of the acquiring authority's estimate of the compensation exceeds the compensation as finally determined or agreed, the excess must be repaid; if after any payment has been made to any person, it is discovered that he was not entitled to it, the amount of the payment is recoverable by the authority: s 52(5).

On an application for judicial review of a decision by an acquiring authority to withdraw a notice to treat in respect of land owned by the applicant, it fell to be determined (1) whether the acquiring authority was entitled to withdraw the notice to treat even after it had entered into possession of the land, and (2) if so, the rights of the parties following the withdrawal where the authority had made an advance payment of compensation under the 1961 Act, s 52. *Held*, (1) the right to withdraw under s 31(1), unlike that under s 31(2), was not limited in a case where possession had been taken. Mere withdrawal of the notice to treat did not result in possession being recovered by the owner, but it removed his entitlement to compensation in respect of acquisition. (2) Compensation in s 52 was directed to ordinary compensation for the acquisition of the land. The purpose of s 52(5) was to contrast the position at the time of the advance payment with the position when compensation was finally determined or agreed. If at that time it was found that there was either an excess or no entitlement, then the right to payment arose. As an owner had a right to specific compensation under s 31, he could not retain a sum which was paid on an assumption which had been falsified by events and which did not represent his true loss. Accordingly, the application would be dismissed.

R v Northumbrian Water Ltd, ex p Able UK Ltd (1995) Times, 18 December (Queen's Bench Division: Carnwath J).

555 Purchase notice—validity—notice served in respect of only part of land for which planning permission refused

See *Cook v Winchester City Council*, para 2897.

CONFIDENCE AND DATA PROTECTION

Halsbury's Laws of England (4th edn) Vol 8(1) (reissue), paras 401–600

556 Articles

Controls and Constraints on Processing Personal Data, David Bainbridge and Graham Pearce: 145 NLJ 1579

Current Legal Issues in UK Data Protection, Rosemary Jay: [1995] 5 CTLR 152

Data Protection, David Bainbridge and Graham Pearce (on the new Data Protection Directive): 145 NLJ 1505

The Data Protection Directive, Susan Singleton: 11 CLP 140

An Ethical Issue of the Information Age—Computers and Privacy, Amanda Hoey: 11 CLP 126

Manual Processing, Access, Exemptions and the Registrar, David Bainbridge and Graham Pearce: 145 NLJ 1656

The Proposed Data Protection Directive and the Data Protection Act 1984, Vivianne Jabbour and Heather Rowe: [1995] 2 CTLR 38

Now We Are Eleven: The Data Protection Act 1984, Kevin Browne: 139 SJ 848

Telephone Technology and Data Protection, Valerie Collins: 11 CLP 74

Will the Data Protection Directive Prevent a Global Information Infrastructure? Jan Berkvens: 11 CLP 38

557 Access to data—protection of the individual—right of privacy

See para 3190.

558 Confidence—banking—information relating to customers

See *Adham v Bank of Credit and Commerce International SA (No 2)*, para 158.

559 Data protection—registration held by local authority—local government reorganisation

See para 1973.

CONFLICT OF LAWS

Halsbury's Laws of England (4th edn) Vol 8(1) (reissue), paras 601–1094

560 Articles

Choice of Law in Tort and Delict, Adrian Briggs (on the Private International Law (Miscellaneous Provisions) Act 1995): [1995] LMCLQ 519

Double Actionability: A Flexible Approach, Paul Friedman (on *Red Sea Insurance Co Ltd v Bouygues SA* [1994] 3 All ER 749 (1994 Abr para 574)): 145 NLJ 55

Forum Non Conveniens and the Brussels Convention, Alan Reed and T P Kennedy: 145 NLJ 1697, 1788

Jurisdiction and Beyond, Paul Friedman (on *Grupo Torras SA v Sheikh Fahad Mohammed al Sabah* [1996] 1 Lloyd's Rep 7, CA (para 567)): 145 NLJ 1158

The Negative Declaration in Transnational Litigation, Andrew S Bell: (1995) 111 LQR 674

561 Foreign divorce—divorce obtained otherwise than by means of judicial proceedings—recognition

See *R v Immigration Appeal Tribunal, ex p Asfar Jan*, para 261.

562 Foreign judgment—enforcement—reciprocal enforcement—Canada

The Reciprocal Enforcement of Foreign Judgments (Canada) (Amendment) Order 1995, SI 1995/2708 (in force on 1 December 1995), amends the text of the 1984 Ottawa Convention on the Reciprocal Recognition and Enforcement of Judgments in Civil and Commercial Matters, as set out in the Schedule to the 1987 Order, SI 1987/468, to reflect an agreement between the governments of the United Kingdom and Canada in which the United Kingdom is to assume an obligation of a kind provided for in the 1988 Lugano Convention on Jurisdiction and the Enforcement of Judgments in Civil and Commercial Matters, art 59. The United Kingdom undertakes not to recognise or enforce any judgment given in a third state that is a party to the 1988 Convention against a person domiciled or habitually resident in Canada.

563 Foreign judgment—recognition and enforcement—allegation of fraud

St Vincent and the Grenadines

In proceedings brought by the respondents in France to recover sums owed to them by the appellants under a guarantee, the latter alleged that the guarantee had been obtained by fraud. The French courts rejected the allegation and gave judgment for the respondents. When the respondents sought to enforce the judgment in St Vincent and the Grenadines, the appellants made further allegations of fraud and obtained an order for the production of the original guarantee. The Court of Appeal, in allowing the respondents' appeal against the order, decided that it would be an abuse of process to allow the appellants to continue to defend the proceedings. On appeal by the appellants, *held*, every court of justice had an inherent power to prevent misuse of its process whether by a plaintiff or a defendant. Nothing precluded a party from obtaining summary judgment or an order striking out pleadings on the ground of abuse of process where a fraud was alleged. Where allegations of fraud had been made and determined abroad, summary judgment or striking out in subsequent proceedings were appropriate remedies, in the absence of plausible evidence disclosing at least a prima facie case of fraud. The appellants' defence of fraud was an abuse of process and should be struck out. The appeal would be dismissed.

Owens Bank Ltd v Etoile Commerciale SA [1995] 1 WLR 44 (Privy Council: Lords Templeman, Jauncey of Tullichettle, Mustill, Lloyd of Berwick and Nolan). *House of Spring Gardens Ltd v Waite* [1990] 2 All ER 990, CA (1990 Abr para 1045), and dictum of Lord Diplock in *Hunter v Chief Constable of West Midlands Police* [1981] 3 All ER 727 at 729, HL (1981 Abr para 1088), applied.

564　Foreign marriage—polygamous marriage—recognition

See *R v Immigration Appeal Tribunal, ex p Asfar Jan*, para 261.

565　Interlocutory order—discovery order in English proceedings made by Scottish court—consideration of similar remedy in English court

Scotland

The plaintiff brought an action in England against the defendant for infringement of its patent. The infringement could only be inferred, rather than definitely ascertained by examination of the end product and consequently, the plaintiff applied in the Scottish court for early discovery of documents and other property which the plaintiff claimed was necessary for him to find out the precise nature of the alleged infringement. At first instance, an order of discovery was made by the Scottish court under the power granted by the Civil Jurisdiction and Judgments Act 1982, and the defendant appealed. *Held*, as a general rule, the Scottish court was entitled to make an order for discovery in proceedings brought in England if it considered that the same or similar remedy would have been granted in the English courts and that it would not be vexatious or oppressive for the order to be granted. In this case the judge had been entitled to conclude that the English court would have granted early discovery as that was a necessary step to ensure that the issues involved in the case were significantly narrowed. Accordingly, the appeal would be dismissed and the order for discovery would be made.

Union Carbide Corpn v BP Chemicals Ltd 1995 SLT 972 (Inner House).

566　Jurisdiction—breach of confidence claim—breach falling outside scope of jurisdiction clauses

The Convention on Jurisdiction and the Enforcement of Foreign Judgments in Civil and Commercial Matters 1968, art 17 (contained in the Civil Jurisdiction and Judgments Act 1982, Sch 1), provides that if parties to an agreement, one or more of whom is domiciled in a contracting state, have agreed that a court or courts of a contracting state is or are to have jurisdiction to settle any disputes which have arisen in connection with a particular legal relationship, that court or courts has or have exclusive jurisdiction. Such an agreement conferring jurisdiction must be either in writing or evidenced in writing.

The plaintiffs owned confidential information relating to the manufacture of a particular type of metal pipe. The defendants had been given access to the information during negotiations to acquire rights of manufacture of the pipes, as a result of signing two agreements both of which contained express confidentiality clauses and clauses giving jurisdiction to the English courts. In the event, the licence to manufacture was not granted to the defendants although an exclusive licence to sell was granted. It was later alleged by the plaintiffs that the defendants were manufacturing equipment to make the pipes as well as manufacturing the pipes themselves, with the collaboration of past and present employees of the plaintiffs, and brought an action for breach of contract. The defendants acknowledged that the Convention, art 17 together with the jurisdiction clauses in the agreements gave the right of jurisdiction to the English courts, but argued that the jurisdiction did not extend to non-contractual claims for misuse of confidential information. They also claimed that the contractual undertakings made only applied to information actually disclosed as a result of the undertakings and not to any information disclosed or misused at a later time, and that the Convention did not give the court any jurisdiction to hear claims relating to information not covered by the scope of the undertakings as there was no evidence that the plaintiffs were suffering direct damage within the jurisdiction. At first instance, the court declared that the plaintiffs were entitled to bring an action in the English courts. On appeal by the defendants, *held*, it would defeat the purpose of the Convention if the plaintiffs were able to give a narrow construction to the undertakings so that the plaintiffs could only bring an action in the English courts concerning information covered by those undertakings. The jurisdiction clauses not only covered breach of contract claims but also claims for misuse of confidential information closely connected with them and the English courts therefore had the necessary jurisdiction. Article 5(3) limited the application to matters relating to tort, delict or quasi-delict. The European court was considering whether restitutionary claims fell within that ambit and, as breach of contract claims were indistinguishable in principle, the court could not express a concluded view on that matter at the present time. Assuming the plaintiffs' claim did come within the ambit of the Convention, they still had to show they had suffered direct harm in England for the Convention to apply. There was no evidence that that had been the case and accordingly, the appeal would be allowed although the plaintiffs would be given an opportunity to apply for interlocutory relief only.

Kitechnology B V v Unicor GmbH Plastmaschinen [1995] FSR 765 (Court of Appeal: Sir Donald Nicholls V-C, Evans and Waite LJJ).

567 Jurisdiction—exclusive jurisdiction—object of proceedings

The 1968 Convention on Jurisdiction and the Enforcement of Judgments in Civil and Commercial Matters (implemented in the United Kingdom by the Civil Jurisdiction and Judgments Act 1982), art 16(2), as amended, provides that in proceedings which have as their object the validity of the constitution, the nullity or the dissolution of companies or other legal persons or associations of natural or legal persons, or the decisions of their organs, the courts of the contracting state in which the company, legal person or association has its seat will have exclusive jurisdiction regardless of domicile. Where proceedings involving the same cause of action and between the same parties are brought in the courts of different contracting states, any court other than the court first seised must of its own motion stay its proceedings until such time as the jurisdiction of the court first seised is established: art 21.

The plaintiffs, a Spanish company and its English subsidiary, claimed damages for fraudulent conspiracy and breach of duty and moneys alleged to be due under constructive trust. Legal proceedings involving the defendants, who were the directors, officers and advisers of the company, were brought in England and Spain. The defendants argued that (1) the proceedings were principally concerned with the decisions of the Spanish company and that consequently the Spanish courts, being the courts of the contracting state in which the company had its seat, had exclusive jurisdiction pursuant to art 16(2); and (2) the action in England should be stayed under art 21 because the proceedings involved the same cause of action and parties as proceedings pending before the Spanish courts. At first instance, the judge refused to set aside or stay the English action. On appeal, *held*, (1) the subject matter of the action was not the decisions of the Spanish company but the frauds which the defendants were alleged to have practised on the company and its subsidiary. Therefore, art 16(2) did not debar the English court from assuming jurisdiction. (2) Under Spanish law, a civil action was not definitively pending for the purposes of the 1968 Convention until it had been filed, admitted and served. Until then it merely had a provisional character. The Spanish proceedings were not served on the relevant parties until after the proceedings had been served in England and therefore the English proceedings came first. Accordingly, the appeal would be dismissed.

Grupo Torras SA v Sheikh Fahad Mohammed Al Sabah [1996] 1 Lloyd's Rep 7 (Court of Appeal: Stuart-Smith, Hobhouse and Millett LJJ).

568 Jurisdiction—foreign proceedings—injunction to restrain proceedings—application

A bank made an application by summons in an action after judgment for an injunction restraining a company from raising in proceedings in Cyprus certain matters which the bank claimed could and should have been raised in the action. The first issue was whether the bank could seek that form of relief in that manner, the second whether the court had the jurisdiction to grant such relief, and finally, whether in the circumstances of the case, it should grant the relief. *Held*, RSC Ord 29, r 1 expressly provided for the grant of injunctive relief after the trial, whether or not the injunction was claimed in the party's writ. Given that if the bank had issued an originating summons the court would have had jurisdiction to grant the relief and that the court would have power to grant a Mareva injunction on the issuing of a summons in the action, it would seem strange if the bank were put out of court by virtue of issuing a summons in the action rather than an originating summons. Also, it was not surprising that *Halsbury's Laws*, Vol 24 (reissue), para 958, contained a statement, relying on two old authorities, that it was not necessary to start a new action to claim an injunction after judgment where one party violated the spirit of the decree. The court could see no reason why, pursuant to Ord 29, r 1, it did not retain a power to grant an injunction in such circumstances. Although there was no specific authority on the point, the court could see no reason why an English court could not injunct foreign proceedings where they breached the principle that all aspects of a matter should be litigated at the same time. However, before granting an injunction against proceedings in a foreign jurisdiction the court had to exercise caution. In this case, having balanced the competing public and private interests, it was not right to grant an injunction.

Zeeland Navigation Co Ltd v Banque Worms (1995) Times, 26 December (Queen's Bench Division: Waller J).

569 Jurisdiction—foreign proceedings—injunction to restrain proceedings—oppression and injustice to plaintiffs created by foreign jurisdiction

Scotland

A helicopter took off from an oil platform off the coast of Scotland and crashed into the sea, killing a pilot and ten passengers. The plaintiffs were families of the victims who brought proceedings against the helicopter company in Scotland, as well as proceedings against a number of companies, including the owner of the oil platform, in Texas. The plaintiffs in the Texan proceedings applied for injunctions preventing the defendants from continuing, or taking any step, in the Texan proceedings or commencing fresh proceedings there or anywhere outside the United Kingdom, in respect of any claim arising out of the crash. The defendants claimed that Texas was the more appropriate forum because two of the plaintiffs were domiciled there and the others had sufficient contact with Texas to make them subject to that jurisdiction. They also contended that it would be unjust to deny them Texan jurisdiction as it presented advantages over the Scottish legal system, including contingency fees, jury trial and a higher award of damages. *Held*, any connection between the action and Texas was fragile in the extreme. The plaintiffs had established that the action had the most real and substantial connection with Scotland which was therefore the most appropriate forum. In addition, if the defendants were allowed to pursue the Texan proceedings, it would subject the plaintiffs to oppression and injustice as they would be unable to join the helicopter company as a third party or compel discovery without being held to have accepted the jurisdiction of the Texan court. The advantages of the Texan jurisdiction claimed by the defendants were bound up with the question of natural forum, but as Scotland was the natural forum, they could have no reasonable expectation of those advantages. Any benefit which the defendants would derive from the contingency fee system in the United States was not a legitimate juridical advantage when the natural forum was not in the United States. In fact, there were no legitimate juridical advantages in litigating in Texas of which it would be unjust to deprive the defendants and which would outweigh the plaintiffs' case of oppression and injustice. It was clear that the injunction to prevent the Texan proceedings to continue ought to be upheld but the law regarding comity of nations required that the Texan court be given the opportunity to stay the proceedings and for that reason alone, the injunctions would not be granted.

Shell UK Exploration and Production Ltd v Innes 1995 SLT 807 (Outer House).

570 Jurisdiction—foreign proceedings—injunction to restrain proceedings—restraint by person within the jurisdiction

It has been held that where a plaintiff abandons a claim against a defendant in another jurisdiction in order to pursue the action in England and then decides to proceed with the overseas action, the English court will not grant a stay of the English action and indeed it will grant an injunction restraining the plaintiff from suing the defendant in the foreign jurisdiction if it will cause substantial injustice to the defendant to be be sued on two fronts.

Advanced Portfolio Technologies Inc v Ainsworth (1995) Times, 15 November (Chancery Division: Harman J). *Societe Nationale Industrielle Aerospatiale v Lee Kui Jak* [1987] 3 All ER 510, PC, distinguished.

571 Jurisdiction—foreign proceedings—stay of proceedings—counterclaim—interlocutory application

The applicants, defendants and third parties in English proceedings arising out of reinsurance contracts, applied by interlocutory applications and originating summonses to restrain the plaintiffs from bringing and pursuing claims against the applicants in counterclaims as defendants in related proceedings in the United States, on the grounds that the applicants' legitimate rights under the Brussels and Lugano Conventions on Jurisdiction and the Enforcement of Judgments in Civil and Commercial Matters (set out in the Civil Jurisdiction and Judgments Acts 1982, Schs 1 and 3C) would be invaded by the American proceedings and that the prosecution of such proceedings was unconscionable, oppressive or contrary to the interests of justice. Two foreign plaintiffs in the English proceedings applied for a declaration that, since they were neither domiciled nor resident nor carrying on business in England, the court had no jurisdiction to over them in respect of the relief sought by the applicants. *Held*, (1) the court had jurisdiction to grant the injunction sought within the existing actions for the following reasons (i) RSC Ord 29, r 1 contemplated that applications for interlocutory injunctions could only be made in actions in respect of which a separate trial inter partes was contemplated and neither the applicants as third parties in the proceedings nor the foreign plaintiffs were engaged in a lis inter se wherein the relief was claimed as a matter of substance. However, Ord 29, r 1 was so wide and unqualified that, in principle, a third party could seek interlocutory relief by injunction against a foreign plaintiff on the basis that, by suing in England, the foreign plaintiff had submitted not only to the risk and incidence of a counterclaim but also to any claim against him by a third party provided leave of the court was obtained or sought under Ord 16, rr 8 and 9 for the direct determination of a claim or issue between the plaintiff and the third party. (ii) Furthermore, the court could, under its wide inherent jurisdiction to prevent injustice to a party before the court, permit a third party to apply in an appropriate case for an antisuit injunction in an action already before the court to which the foreign plaintiff was already a party, thus obviating the need to issue new proceedings by way of originating summons, in order to do what was just and equitable to prevent improper vexation or oppression and/or to do justice between the parties in relation to the trial between them. It would not always be necessary for the third party to apply to the court in the action for a question or issue to be tried directly between the third party and the plaintiff in order to found the third party's rights to apply in the action. The oppression relied on by the applicants arose from the fact that proceedings were already before the English court in the light of, or in relation to which, the pursuance of the foreign suit was said to be vexatious or oppressive, and in those circumstances it was sensible and appropriate that the application should be made in the English proceedings. (iii) The form in which an injunction was sought ought not to be determinative of whether the application could be made within the action or had to be made by the commencement of new proceedings. Although the application for an antisuit injunction was final and not interlocutory in form, it nevertheless fell within RSC Ord 29, r 1 because it did not necessarily involve or operate as a final resolution of the parties' rights, since the court would be unlikely to grant relief of a truly final nature as there would be express or implied liberty to apply in the event of a change of circumstances which resulted in that issue being withdrawn from the English court, or if for any other reason the oppression originally complained of were relieved. (2) With regard to the foreign plaintiffs, the Brussels and Lugano Conventions, art 6 applied to proceedings for an antisuit injunction simpliciter, even though that form of relief was peculiar to the United Kingdom, and since many of the defendants to the originating summonses were domiciled in England, each of the foreign plaintiffs fell within art 6(1), because they were each a person domiciled in a contracting state who was sued as one of a number of defendants in the courts for the place where a number of those other defendants were domiciled. Furthermore, there was nothing in art 6 to suggest that it was limited to cases in which there was an assertion of joint liability on the part of the defendants sued or that it was inapplicable to a situation where a number of defendants, whether jointly or severally, were, on the same facts, similarly liable to the remedy sought by the plaintiff to the suit. However, the court had no jurisdiction to grant the antisuit injunction on the grounds that by proceeding with their counterclaims in the American action the foreign plaintiffs had invaded or threatened their right to be sued in accordance with the conventions, since the applicants' right to be sued in accordance with the conventions had not been invaded by the American proceedings. (3) Although it was a prerequisite to the granting of an order that England should be the natural forum for the dispute, that was not enough in itself when the effect of the order would be to prohibit or restrict proceedings in a foreign court. The applicant also had to demonstrate unconscionable vexation and oppression and in that context a balance had to be struck between the legitimate interests of the parties. In the circumstances the ends of justice did not require, and it would not be appropriate, to grant the applicants the relief they sought. Accordingly, the application for an antisuit injunction would be dismissed.

Société Commerciale de Réassurance v Eras International Ltd (No 2) [1995] 2 All ER 278 (Queen's Bench Division: Potter J).

572 Jurisdiction—forum with which action has the most real and substantial connection—availability of legal aid

The plaintiff claimed damages for negligence against his former employer, the defendant company, after contracting throat cancer while working in an allegedly unsafe mine in Namibia. The action was stayed at first instance on the ground that it should be tried in Namibia. The plaintiff appealed. He argued that England and Wales was the most suitable jurisdiction because of the availability of legal aid, and that because he was totally without means and because legal aid was unavailable in Namibia, he would be unable to pursue his claim in that jurisdiction. *Held*, it was accepted both that the jurisdiction of Namibia was prima facie the one to which the claim had the most real and substantial connection, and that the plaintiff would get a fair trial there. There were strong humanitarian grounds for refusing a stay on the sole ground of availability of legal aid. However, there was a consensus among major common law jurisdictions that actions should be tried in the forum with which they had the most real and substantial connection. It would be unhelpful for a court considering issues of forum non conveniens, to have to make comparisons between the various forms of public assistance for litigation that were available in different countries. This was entirely consistent with the Legal Aid Act 1988, s 31(b), under which the right to legal aid does not affect the rights or liabilities of any party or the principles on which the discretion of any court is based. The availability of a plaintiff's private resources in one jurisdiction as opposed to another remained a relevant factor. The non-availability of legal aid in Namibia was irrelevant to the decision to grant a stay of the English proceedings. Accordingly, the appeal would be dismissed.

Connelly v RTZ Corpn plc [1996] 1 All ER 500 (Court of Appeal: Neill, Waite and Swinton-Thomas LJJ).

573 Jurisdiction—libel action—place where harmful event occurred

The Convention on Jurisdiction and the Enforcement of Judgments in Civil and Commercial Matters 1968, art 5(3) provides that a person domiciled in a contracting state may, in another contracting state, be sued in matters relating to tort, delict or quasi-delict in the courts for the place where the harmful event occurred.

The defendant, a French company, was the publisher of a French newspaper which printed an article about an operation carried out by French drug squad officers at a bureau de change in Paris. The plaintiff, a United Kingdom national involved in the business of bureaux de change, alleged that the article was defamatory because it suggested that his business was involved in a drug-trafficking network for which he had laundered money. When the plaintiff issued libel proceedings in England, the defendant argued that the English courts had no jurisdiction to consider the matter because no 'harmful event' had occurred in England within the meaning of the 1968 Convention, art 5(3). The House of Lords stayed the proceedings and referred several questions to the European Court of Justice as to the interpretation of art 5(3). *Held*, having regard to art 5(3), there had to be a close connection between the dispute and courts other than those of the state of the defendant's domicile in order to confer jurisdiction on those other courts in the interests of the sound administration of justice and the efficacious conduct of proceedings. In the case of a libellous newspaper article distributed in several contracting states, the place of the event giving rise to the damage was the place where the newspaper publisher was established, as that was the place from where the harmful event was issued and put into circulation. The court of that place therefore had jurisdiction to hear the action for damages. Article 5(3) allowed a plaintiff to commence proceedings in the place where the damage occurred, and the injury caused by a defamatory publication occurred in the places where the publication was distributed and where the victim was known. In those circumstances, the courts of each contracting state had jurisdiction to rule on the injury caused in that state to the victim's reputation, as they were best placed to assess the libel and to determine the extent of the damage. Moreover, as the object of the Convention was not to unify procedural rules and substantive law, the criteria for assessing whether or not a particular event was harmful and the evidence required to prove a claim were matters for the national laws of the court seised of the action.

Case C-68/93: Shevill v Presse Alliance SA [1995] 2 AC 18, [1995] 2 All ER (EC) 289 (ECJ: Full Court).

574 Jurisdiction—pending divorce proceedings in England—custody proceedings in Scotland—appropriate forum

See *Re S (Jurisdiction to Stay Application)*, para 378.

575 Jurisdiction—purchase agreement—commission to broker

The Lugano Convention on Jurisdiction and the Enforcement of Judgments in Civil and Commercial Matters 1988, art 5, provides that a person domiciled in a contracting state may be sued in another contracting state in matters relating to a contract, in the courts for the place of performance of the obligation in question.

It has been held that, where a buyer has contracted with a seller to pay commission to the broker of a purchase agreement, under the 1988 Convention, art 5, the broker has a right to sue the buyer for that commission as 'matters relating to a contract' in the jurisdiction in which the agreement to pay commission was made, rather than the jurisdiction in which the seller is domiciled.

Atlas Shipping Agency (UK) Ltd v Suisse Atlantique Société d' Armament Maritime SA [1995] 2 Lloyd's Rep 188 (Queen's Bench Division: Rix J).

576 Jurisdiction—shares—title to shares—priority between competing interests

The plaintiff, a Delaware company controlled by an individual through an English publicly-quoted company, owned a controlling interest in B Inc, a company incorporated in New York. Contrary to the plaintiff's interests, the individual agreed to pledge shares in B Inc to the defendants as security for loans made by them to his private interests. The shares were transferred to the defendants in New York. The plaintiff's claim for the return of the shares was dismissed.

On a preliminary issue in the plaintiff's appeal as to the applicable law for determining title to the shares, *held*, an issue as to who had title to shares in a company had to be decided by the law of the place where the shares were situated, the lex situs. Ordinarily, unless the shares were negotiable instruments by English law, this was the law of the place where the company was incorporated. Situs and incorporation had the advantage of pointing to one system of law which was unlikely to be transient and could not be manipulated by a purchaser of shares in order to gain priority. If a lender chose to take as security shares in companies incorporated in a number of different jurisdictions, he might have to make different inquiries so as to satisfy himself as to his title.

Macmillan Inc v Bishopsgate Investment Trust plc (No 3) [1996] 1 All ER 585 (Court of Appeal: Staughton, Auld and Aldous LJJ). For earlier proceedings, see [1995] 3 All ER 747 infra.

The plaintiff, a Delaware corporation, owned the controlling interest of B Inc, a company incorporated in New York. The plaintiff was itself a wholly-owned indirect subsidiary of an English publicly quoted company, MCC, which was part of a group of companies controlled by RM. The plaintiff resolved to allow RM to transfer the B Inc shares to the first defendant, an investment trust controlled by RM, and authorised him to sign the share transfers, without realising RM wished to do so for his own fraudulent purposes. In order to facilitate dealings in the shares, a large proportion of them were deposited in the New York central depository system (the DTC). Three tranches of these shares were subsequently used as security for loans made by the second, third and fifth defendants. The first tranche was deposited with the second defendant in London and the security was perfected by deposit in the DTC system after RM's death, the second tranche was transferred to the third defendant by a book entry made in New York through the DTC system after RM's death and the third tranche was transferred to the fifth defendant in two parcels, one parcel by a book entry made in New York through the DTC system and the other delivered in London with an executed share transfer. Following RM's death his group of companies collapsed and the plaintiff issued a writ against the second, third and fifth defendants claiming recovery of the shares or their proceeds of sale on the grounds that they had been pledged to the defendants in breach of trust, that the plaintiff's interest in the shares was superior to that of the defendants and that they were held on constructive trust by the defendants, who in turn claimed to be entitled to the shares as bona fide purchasers for value without notice of the plaintiff's interest. The question arose whether the priority of interests was to be determined according to New York or English law. *Held*, under Delaware law as under English law, the act of an agent acting within the scope of his actual or apparent authority did not cease to bind his principal merely because the agent was acting fraudulently and in furtherance of his own interests. Therefore, RM's signature on the share transfers was duly authorised notwithstanding his fraudulent purpose. The subsequent dealings with the shares had taken place without the plaintiff's knowledge or approval and therefore in breach of trust. The plaintiff's claim was properly characterised as a proprietary restitutionary claim based on the unjust enrichment of the defendants occasioned by depriving the plaintiff of its property, since there was no relationship of any kind between the plaintiff and any of the defendants in respect of the B Inc shares and no equity between the parties. The plaintiff therefore had to rely on its continuing equitable interest in the property under an express or resulting trust and not on an equity between the parties giving rise to a constructive trust. Since the second, third and fifth defendants relied for the creation of their security interests on book entries made in New York, and had derived title from the deposit of the certificates by way of security in England and that security was later perfected by book entries in New York the effect of those transactions on the plaintiff's prior interest was to be determined by the law of New York as the lex loci actus.

As the defendants had no notice at the time they took delivery of the shares by way of security that the shares belonged to the plaintiff they were at that stage bona fide purchasers for value without notice of the plaintiff's prior interest and they were entitled to obtain the legal interest after having actual notice of the plaintiff's prior interest because they had executed share transfers and therefore could do so without recourse to the plaintiff. Accordingly, the actions against all three defendants would be dismissed.

Macmillan Inc v Bishopsgate Investment Trust plc (No 3) [1995] 3 All ER 747 (Chancery Division: Millett J).

577 Private International Law (Miscellaneous Provisions) Act 1995

The Private International Law (Miscellaneous Provisions) Act 1995 makes provision regarding (1) interest on judgment debts and abitral awards expressed in a currency other than sterling, (2) marriages entered into by unmarried persons under a law which permits polygamy, and (3) the choice of law rules in respect of tort and delict actions. The Act received the royal assent on 8

November 1995, and certain provisions came into force on that date and on 8 January 1996. The remaining provisions come into force on a day or days to be appointed. For details of commencement, see the commencement table in the title STATUTES.

Part I (ss 1–4) relates to interest on judgment debts and arbitral awards. Section 1 provides that where a High Court judgment is given for a sum expressed in a currency other than sterling and is a debt which carries interest, the court may order that the interest rate is to be such as the court thinks fit, in rather than the specified statutory rate. Similar provision is made by s 2 in respect of county court judgment debts. Where an award is made following arbitration proceedings, s 3 provides that it is to carry interest as from the date of the award, and that the rate is to be either the statutory rate or, where the sum is expressed in a currency other than sterling, such rate as the arbitrator or umpire thinks fit. As a result of these provisions, consequential amendments are made by s 4 to certain enactments which refer to the interest rate payable on judgment debts.

Part II (ss 5–8) relates to the validity of marriages under a law which permits polygamy. Section 5 declares that a marriage entered into outside England and Wales between parties who were not previously married and one of whom is domiciled in England and Wales, is not to be regarded as void in England and Wales on the ground that the marriage was entered into under a law which permits polygamy. By s 6, s 5 is deemed to apply to all marriages entered into before the commencement of s 5, subject to certain exceptions and savings, including where, before the commencement of s 5, either party to a potentially polygamous marriage has remarried or obtained an annulment. Section 7 relates to Scotland, and s 8 contains supplemental provisions.

Part III (ss 9–15) relates to the choice of law in tort actions. Section 9 sets out the purpose of Pt III, stating that it applies in choosing the law to be used in determining issues relating to tort ('the applicable law'), but providing that it is for the court of the forum seised of the action to determine whether or not an issue of tort arises. In addition, s 10 abolishes the common law rule which requires a tort to be actionable under both the law of the forum and the law of another country, and also the rule which allows for the law of a single country to be applied in order to determine the issues arising from a tort claim. Section 11 establishes a new general rule that the applicable law is the law of the country in which the events constituting the tort occur. Where the events occur in more than one country, the tort is to be taken as having occurred in the country where the individual was injured (if it is a personal injury claim), where property was damaged (if it is an action for damage to property), or, in any other case, in the country in which the most significant element of the tort occurred. However, s 12 allows the general rule to be displaced if, having regard to the most significant factors connecting a claim to a country, it is more appropriate for the applicable law governing the claim to be the law of the other country. By s 13, Pt III does not apply to defamation claims. Section 14 contains transitional provisions and savings, and s 15 deals with the application of the Act to the Crown.

Part IV (ss 16–19) contains provisions relating to the commencement of the Act, its short title and the extent of its application.

578 Reciprocal enforcement—maintenance order—registration

Scotland

The parties were married in India and lived together in Scotland for a short while before the wife returned to India. Subsequent to the husband obtaining a divorce in Scotland, the wife obtained a maintenance order against him in an Indian court and registered it in Scotland under the Maintenance Orders (Reciprocal Enforcement) Act 1972. The husband challenged the validity of the registration, arguing that the maintenance order was invalid because it had been granted after the divorce and that it was therefore against public policy to enforce it. *Held*, under Indian law, the parties were regarded as married despite the divorce granted in Scotland, and the maintenance order had therefore been made on the basis that the wife was still a married woman. Having regard to the 1972 Act, India was a reciprocating country and the order made by the Indian court was a maintenance order within the meaning of s 21(1). As the wife had taken all the procedural steps necessary to register the order, it could be enforced as if it had been made in the Scottish courts. The provisions of the 1972 Act, s 6 were mandatory and unqualified in that they did not allow the court to refuse to register a maintenance order if the proper procedure had been followed. It was not contrary to public policy to enforce the order and, accordingly, the application would be dismissed.

Sethi v Sethi 1995 SLT 104 (Outer House). *Pilcher v Pilcher* [1955] 3 WLR 231, DC followed.

579 Reciprocal enforcement—maintenance order—United States

The Reciprocal Enforcement of Maintenance Orders (United States of America) Order 1995, SI 1995/2709 (in force on 1 December 1995), applies, with modifications, the provisions of the

Maintenance Orders (Reciprocal Enforcement) Act 1972, Pt I to the States specified in Schedule 1 to the Order.

The Magistrates' Courts (Reciprocal Enforcement of Maintenance Orders) (United States of America) Rules 1995, SI 1995/2802 (in force on 1 December 1995), make provision, in relation to magistrates' courts, for the various matters which are to be prescribed under the Maintenance Orders (Reciprocal Enforcement) Act 1972, Pt I (Reciprocal Enforcement of Maintenance Orders made in the United Kingdom or Reciprocating Country) as set out in the Reciprocal Enforcement of Maintenance Orders (United States of America) Order 1995. SI 1995/2709. They apply with variations for this purpose the provisions of the Magistrates' Courts (Reciprocal Enforcement of Maintenance Orders) (Hague Convention Countries) Rules 1980, SI 1980/108.

580 Stay of proceedings—forum non conveniens—different jurisdictions within United Kingdom

The plaintiff, domiciled in Scotland, brought a libel action in both England and Scotland, against the defendant Scottish newspaper which was also distributed, but to a lesser extent, in England. The defendant sought a stay of the action on the ground of forum non conveniens on the basis that Scotland was the proper jurisdiction in which the case ought to be heard. The plaintiff claimed that the English court had jurisdiction under the Civil Jurisdiction and Judgments Act 1982. *Held*, where the jurisdiction of the court was derived exclusively from the 1982 Act, s 16, Sch 4, it was free to apply the doctrine of forum non conveniens. The application of that doctrine was appropriate in this case and, accordingly, the application would be granted.

Cumming v Scottish Daily Record and Sunday Mail Ltd (1995) Times, 8 June (Queen's Bench Division: Drake J). *Foxen v Scotsman Publications Ltd* (1994) Times, 17 February (1994 Abr para 571) reversed.

581 Stay of proceedings—forum non conveniens—divorce proceedings—discretionary stay

See *R v R (Divorce: Stay of Proceedings)*, para 1110.

582 Transnational divorce—recognition

The Family Law Act 1986, s 46(1) provides that the validity of an overseas divorce obtained by means of proceedings will be recognised if (a) the divorce is effective under the law of the country in which it was obtained, and (b) at the relevant date either party to the marriage (i) was habitually resident in the country in which the divorce was obtained, or (ii) was domiciled in that country, or (iii) was a national of that country. Section 46(3) provides that 'the relevant date' means in the case of an overseas divorce obtained by means of proceedings, the date of the commencement of the proceedings.

A rabbi who served as an ecclesiastical judge received a letter from a husband applying to marry for the second time. The husband supplied details of his previous marriage and its termination by get in Israel. The get was effective as a divorce decree under Israeli law. The rabbi applied for recognition of the decree under the 1986 Act. It was accepted that a divorce by means of a get was a divorce obtained 'by means of proceedings' within s 46(1) and that in the present case the criteria laid down in s 46(1)(a) and (b) were satisfied. It fell to be determined whether the get, which had been written in London under Jewish ecclesiastical law and delivered to the wife at the district rabbinical court in Israel, was an overseas divorce within the meaning of s 46. *Held*, the reference to 'the date of the commencement of the proceedings' in s 46(3) must refer to one set of proceedings instituted in the country in which the divorce was obtained for the purposes of recognition. The proceedings should be geographically connected not only to the place where the divorce was obtained but to the place where they were instituted. Had proceedings in more than one country been envisaged, it would have been logical for the date to be when the divorce was obtained. Proceedings had to begin and end in the same place. A transnational divorce could not be recognised and, accordingly, the application would be dismissed.

Berkovits v Grinberg, A-G intervening [1995] 2 All ER 681 (Family Division: Wall J).

CONSTITUTIONAL LAW

Halsbury's Laws of England (4th edn) Vol 8, paras 801–1647

583 Articles

MPs Discover the Unwelcome Face of Parliamentary Privilege, Penelope Gorman (on libel actions brought by MPs): 139 SJ 772
A Valid Act? Trevor Tayleur (on the Parliament Act 1949): 145 NLJ 1328

584 Civil Service—civil servant—freedom of expression—membership of political party

See *Vogt v Germany*, para 1568.

585 Crown Agents Act 1995

The Crown Agents Act 1995 provides for the vesting of the property, rights and liabilities of the Crown Agents in a company nominated by the Secretary of State and for the subsequent dissolution of the Crown Agents. The Act received the royal assent on 19 July 1995 and came into force on that day.

Section 1 and Sch 1 provide for the vesting of the property, rights and liabilities of the Crown Agents, under the law of the United Kingdom or that of any other country or territory, in a successor company on a day to be appointed (see the commencement table in the title STATUTES). Section 2 provides for the Crown Agents, at the direction of the Secretary of State, to repay its commencing capital debt and for the repayments to go to the National Loans Fund. The Secretary of State is also empowered to direct that the Crown Agents be deemed to assume a debt to him: s 2. As a consequence of the vesting by virtue of s 1, the successor company must issue securities of the company to the Secretary of State at his direction, such direction only to be given while the company is wholly owned by the Crown: s 3.

Under s 4, the Secretary of State may, while the successor company is wholly owned by the Crown, acquire securities of the successor company or rights to subscribe for any such securities. Section 5 provides that the statutory accounts prepared by the successor company must be drawn up as if the vesting under s 1 took place at the end of the Crown Agents' last full accounting year before the vesting, and that the value or amounts included in the accounts of the successor company must be taken to be those included in the Crown Agents' accounts for that accounting year. Under s 6, the successor company may use the name 'Crown Agents' notwithstanding the provisions of the Companies Act 1985.

Section 7 provides for the successor company to be treated for all purposes of corporation tax as if it were the same person as the Crown Agents. Section 8 provides for the Crown Agents to continue in existence for a period after the appointed day, with a minimum of two rather than six members, in order to discharge its functions under ss 9 (functions with respect to the vesting of foreign property in the successor company) and 10 (making of final reports and accounts). Section 11 makes consequential provision in respect of the Crown Agents Holding and Realisation Board and s 12 deals with the power to make orders under the Act. Section 13 and Sch 2 contain consequential amendments and repeals, s 14 deals with interpretation and s 15 deals with citation and extent.

586 European Communities (Finance) Act 1995

The European Communities (Finance) Act 1995 makes provision for the ratification of the treaty signed at Edinburgh in 1992, the effect of which is to increase the financial contribution made by the United Kingdom to the European Union. The Act received the royal assent on 16 January 1995 and came into force on that date.

Section 1 amends the definitions of 'the Treaties' and 'the Community Treaties' in the European Communities Act 1972, s 1(2) to include the Council's decision of 31 October 1994 on the Communities' system of own resources. Section 2 deals with short title and repeals the European Communities (Finance) Act 1988.

587 Identity cards—consultation paper

The Home Secretary has issued a consultation paper, *Identity Cards* (Cm 2879), in which the benefits of the introduction of identity cards are considered, as well as the specific issues of privacy and security of issue. Experience in other countries is reviewed. The main areas of interest in the consultation paper, however, are whether identity cards, if introduced, should be voluntary or compulsory, and the form that such cards might take, with regard to advances in technology which might be applied to such cards. The introduction of voluntary cards would depend on the extent to which the benefits of cards might commend themselves to the public, and the new style driving licence which will incorporate a photograph of the driver might provide the basis for such a voluntary card (non-drivers being allowed to apply for such, in special form) although additional information would need to be included in addition to that required for driving licence purposes. Perhaps the most contentious area on which views are sought is the possible introduction of identity cards on a compulsory basis; these might be simply identity cards and nothing more, or they might be multi-purpose cards. Compulsory cards would, of necessity, lead to issues of enforcement. The government is not, however, committed to change; the option of doing nothing and allowing persons to rely on existing documents as at present (eg birth certificates, driving licences, passports) remains a possibility.

588 Intelligence services—Dependent Territories

The Intelligence Services Act 1994 (Dependent Territories) Order 1995, SI 1995/752 (in force on 5 April 1995), extends the Intelligence Services Act 1994, ss 5(1) (warrants) and 11(1) (interpretation) to the colonies specified in the Schedule to the order.

589 Judicial pensions

See COURTS.

590 Ministers—contracting out of functions—registration of companies

See para 517.

591 Ministers—designation order

The European Communities (Designation) Order 1995, SI 1995/262 (in force on 2 March 1995), amends the 1991 (No 3) Order, SI 1991/2289, and designates certain ministers who, and departments which, may exercise powers to make regulations conferred by the European Communities Act 1972, s 2(2) in relation to matters concerning (1) measures relating to the protection of the ozone layer and to substances that deplete the ozone layer, and (2) measures relating to the avoidance of discrimination in relation to the transfer of control of important manufacturing undertakings to non-residents. The order also designates any Northern Ireland department for the purpose of exercising the aforementioned powers to make regulations under s 2(2) in relation to measures under (1) supra.

The European Communities (Designation) (No 2) Order 1995, SI 1995/751 (in force on 17 April 1995), amends the 1987 (No 2) Order, SI 1987/926, and designates certain ministers who, and departments which, may exercise powers to make regulations conferred by the European Communities Act 1972, s 2(2) in relation to matters concerning (1) measures relating to equipment and protective systems intended for use in potentially explosive atmospheres, (2) measures relating to Community plant variety rights, (3) measures relating to promotion of rural development, (4) measures relating to competition in the markets for satellite communications and telecommunications services other than public voice telephony, mobile and telex services, and satellite communications and telecommunications terminal equipment, and (5) measures relating to counterfeit and pirated goods. The order also designates any Northern Ireland department for the purpose of exercising the aforementioned powers to make regulations under s 2(2) in relation to measures under (1) and (2) supra.

The European Communities (Designation) (No 3) Order 1995, SI 1995/2983 (in force on 15 December 1995), designates ministers who, and departments which, may exercise powers to make regulations conferred by the European Communities Act 1972, s 2(2), in respect of (1) measures relating to craft intended for recreational purposes, (2) measures relating to articles made of, or comprising or resembling, precious metals, and (3) measures relating to patents and trade marks. The regulations also revoke SI 1992/2870.

The European Communities (Designation) (No 4) Order 1995, SI 1995/3207 (in force on 12 January 1996), designates ministers who, and departments which, may exercise powers to make regulations conferred by the European Communities Act 1972, s 2(2), in respect of measures relating to dentistry, medicine, nursing, midwifery, pharmacy, and their specialities. The regulations also revoke SI 1987/448 and SI 1994/2791.

592　Ministers—salaries

The Ministerial and other Salaries Order 1995, SI 1995/2984 (in force on 1 January 1996), replaces the 1994 Order, SI 1994/3206, so as to increase salaries payable under the Ministerial and other Salaries Act 1975 to ministers, salaried members of the Opposition, the Speaker of the House of Commons and other paid office holders.

593　Ministers—transfer of functions

The Transfer of Functions (Treasury and Minister for the Civil Service) Order 1995, SI 1995/269 (in force on 1 April 1995), transfers to the Minster for the Civil Service some of the functions of the Treasury as follows: (1) specified functions relating to the civil service; (2) functions under the Forestry Act 1967 relating to the number and remuneration of staff appointed by the Forestry Commissioners; (3) functions under or by virtue of the provisions of specified Acts; and (4) functions in relation to allowances for MEPs and in relation to the remuneration, other terms and conditions, pensions or compensation for loss of office of various persons appointed by statute whose staff are civil servants.

The Transfer of Functions (Science) Order 1995, SI 1995/2985 (in force on 1 January 1996), transfers the functions of the Minister for the Civil Service and of the Chancellor of the Duchy of Lancaster under the Science and Technology Act 1965, ss 2, 3, Schs 1, 3 to the Secretary of State for Trade and Industry. There are also transferred to him functions under the Royal Charters of the Biotechnology and Biological Sciences Research Council, the Economic and Social Research Council, the Engineering and Physical Sciences Research Council, the Medical Research Council, the Natural Environment Research Council, the Particle Physics and Astronomy Research Council, and the Council for the Central Laboratory of the Research Councils. Further, all property, rights and liabilities to which the Minister for the Civil Service or the Chancellor of the Duchy of Lancaster are entitled or subject in connection with the functions are transferred and certain other functions will cease to be exercisable by them.

594　Northern Ireland

See NORTHERN IRELAND.

595　Public procurement—supply contracts

See para 2929.

596　Public record office—fees

The Public Record Office (Fees) Regulations 1995, SI 1995/991 (in force on 1 May 1995), prescribe new fees to be charged for the authentication of copies of records and for other services provided by the Public Record Office. The 1994 Regulations, SI 1994/1497, are revoked.

597　Public service pensions

See PENSIONS AND SUPERANNUATION.

598　United Nations—sanctions—European Community legislation—enforcement under domestic legislation

The appellants were convicted of breaches of the Customs and Excise Management Act 1979, by evading sanctions imposed by the Serbia and Montenegro (United Nations Sanctions) Order 1992, SI 1992/1302, and Council Regulations (EC) 1432/1992 and 990/1993. Questions arose as to whether the regulations were within the ambit of the Community's common commercial policy, whether the order was valid, and whether there was effective statutory machinery for enforcing the sanctions by imposing penalties. *Held,* having regard to the EC Treaty, art 113, the regulations formed part of the Community's common commercial policy, and were adopted to ensure the uniform implementation of the United Nations resolution throughout the Community. The order was neither incompatible with the regulations and nor did it seek to disapply them, as art 234 provided that the Community could not prevent the United Kingdom from performing its obligations under the United Nations Charter. However, the European

Communities Act 1972, s 2(1) provided that liabilities and restrictions arising under Community treaties, including regulations, took effect in the United Kingdom without further enactment. The enforcement of the regulations, therefore, did not require further domestic legislation, because the enforcement provisions of the 1979 Act could be applied. Moreover, the regulations themselves could form the basis for a criminal conviction under the 1979 Act. The fact that it had been wrong to refer to the order in prosecuting the appellants was not a ground on which to set aside the convictions, because the appellants had been provided with the essential elements of the nature of the charges against them. Accordingly, the appeal would be dismissed.

R v Searle; R v KCS Products Ltd; R v Borjanovic; R v BYE Ltd (1995) 16 Cr App Rep (S) 944 (Court of Appeal: Lord Taylor of Gosforth CJ, McKinnon and Judge JJ).

CONSUMER CREDIT

Halsbury's Laws of England (4th edn) Vol 22, paras 1–400

599 Articles

The Consumer Credit Counselling Service, Magda D'Ingeo: 145 NLJ 190

Time Orders, Neil Hickman, Derek McConnell and Michael Ramsden: 145 NLJ 691

Time Orders: The New Law, Jonathan Seitler (on *Southern and District Finance plc v Barnes; J and J Securities Ltd v Ewart; Equity Home Loans Ltd v Lewis* (1995) Times, 19 April, CA (para 604)): 139 SJ 560

600 Articles

Time Orders: The New Law, Jonathan Seitler (on *Southern and District Finance plc v Barnes; J and J Securities Ltd v Ewart; Equity Home Loans Ltd v Lewis* (1995) Times, 19 April, CA (para 604)): 139 SJ 560

601 Advertising—false or misleading statements—security statement and annual percentage rate given insufficient prominence

The Consumer Credit Act 1974, s 43(1) provides that the Act's provisions dealing with advertising apply to any advertisement published for the purposes of a business carried on by the advertiser indicating that he is willing to provide credit. Section 151 makes similar provision in relation to anybody who publishes an advertisement for the purposes of a business of credit brokerage whether it advertises the services of that person or the services of people to whom he effects introductions.

The defendants were mortgage brokers who were prosecuted for failing to comply with the 1974 Act and regulations made under it, in relation to advertisements that appeared in a local paper which allegedly gave insufficient prominence to both a security statement that failure to make repayments could lead to loss of a mortgagor's house, and the annual percentage rate (APR). On appeal, the defendants claimed that their advertisements did not fall within the remit of s 43(1) or s 151 and that, in any event, as they did not identify the source of the loan, they were not covered by the 1974 Act. *Held*, on the face of them, the advertisements were offering credit as well as credit brokerage services and the defendants fell within the definition of 'advertiser' set out in the 1974 Act. The fact that the source of the loan was not identified did not prevent the Act from applying but, on the contrary, made the advertisements doubly misleading because they implied that the advertiser was willing to give credit. The advertisements were covered by regulations made under the Act, but were not merely simple credit advertisements as they contained information that a person was willing to provide credit and were thus intermediate credit advertisements which were required to contain a prominent security statement and APR. Accordingly, the appeal would be dismissed.

R v Munford (1994) 159 JP 395 (Court of Appeal: Hobhouse LJ, Garland and Curtis JJ).

602 Conditional sale agreement—title to motor vehicle—liability of finance purchaser

The Hire Purchase Act 1964, s 27 applies where a motor vehicle has been bailed under a hire purchase agreement, or has been agreed to be sold under a conditional sale agreement and, before the property in the vehicle has become vested in the debtor, he disposes of the vehicle to another person. Section 27(3) provides that where the person to whom the disposition is made is a trade or finance purchaser, if the person who is the first private purchaser of the motor vehicle after that disposition is a purchaser of the vehicle in good faith without notice of the relevant agreement, the disposition has effect as if the title of the creditor to the vehicle had been vested in the debtor immediately before he disposed of it to the original purchaser. Section 27(6) provides that in a case where the debtor disposes of the motor vehicle to a trade or finance purchaser, nothing exonerates that trade or finance purchaser, or any other trade or finance purchaser who becomes a purchaser of the vehicle and is not a person claiming under the first private purchaser, from any liability to which he would be subject apart from s 27.

A car dealer sold a car to the defendant bank, which agreed to sell it to the plaintiff under a conditional sale agreement. When the plaintiff attempted to sell the car, he discovered that it was already subject to a prior finance agreement with another finance company. The plaintiff unsuccessfully commenced proceedings to rescind the conditional sale agreement. On the plaintiff's appeal, *held*, the term in the conditional sale agreement which provided that the defendant was the owner of the car at the date of the conditional sale, was a condition and not merely an express warranty or innominate term, as it was fundamental to the whole agreement that the defendant had property in the car and would retain it until the plaintiff had paid for it in full. Moreover, the object of the 1964 Act, s 27 was to protect private purchasers and those claiming under them, but not the original purchaser or hirer or any intervening trade or finance company, from civil or criminal liability. In the instant case, as the debtor was the initial hire purchaser of the car, s 27 did not exonerate him from criminal or civil liability. It followed that as the debtor then sold the car to a finance purchaser, namely the defendant, the defendant was also not exonerated from liability. The plaintiff was therefore entitled to rescind the agreement and, accordingly, the appeal would be allowed.

Barber v NWS Bank plc [1996] 1 All ER 906 (Court of Appeal: Kennedy and Peter Gibson LJJ and Sir Roger Parker).

603 Credit agreements—cancellable agreement—representations made to debtor

The Consumer Credit Act 1974, s 67 provides that a regulated agreement may be cancelled by the debtor if the antecedent negotiations included oral representations made when in the presence of the debtor by an individual acting as, or on behalf of, the negotiator. Section 189 defines 'representation' as including any condition or warranty, and any other statement or undertaking, whether oral or in writing.

A credit agreement was signed on the borrower's premises without the lending company giving the borrower notice of his right to cancel the agreement. The borrower appealed against the decision that the agreement was not a cancellable agreement within s 67 and that he was liable to pay moneys in respect of the agreement. The issue was whether oral representations had been made to the borrower. *Held*, the definition in s 189 appeared at first sight to mean that any statement was a 'representation'. However, that could not have been Parliament's intention. To constitute a representation, the statement must be one of fact or opinion or an undertaking as to the future which was capable of inducing the proposed borrower to enter the agreement. It need not be shown that it did in fact induce him to enter into the agreement, that the particular borrower would have been likely to be so induced, nor that it was intended to induce the agreement. It was sufficient that there was a statement which by its nature was capable of inducing an agreement. Such representations had been made to the borrower and accordingly the appeal would be allowed.

Moorgate Property Services Ltd v Kabir [1995] 5 CL 73 (Court of Appeal: Staughton, Beldam and Peter Gibson LJJ).

604 Credit agreements—default and termination—court's powers—time orders— moneys in respect of which time order granted

The Consumer Credit Act 1974, s 129 provides that, if it appears to the court just to do so, it may make a time order providing for the payment by the debtor of any sum owed under a regulated agreement or a security by such instalments, payable at such times as the court considers reasonable. Section 136 provides that the court may in any order made under the Act include such provision as it considers just for amending any agreement or security in consequence of a term of the order.

Three appeals were brought, one against the dismissal of an application for a time order, one against an order for possession and one against an order granting a time order. The issues before the court were, firstly, the meaning of the words 'any sum owed' in s 129 and, secondly, the scope of the power given by s 136 to include in a time order 'such provision as it considers just for amending any agreement or security in consequence of a term of the order'. *Held*, when a time order was made relating to the non-payment of money, the 'sum owed' meant every sum which was due and owing under the agreement but where possession proceedings had been brought by the creditor, that would comprise the total indebtedness. Secondly, under s 136 the court could include in a time order an amendment of the agreement which it considered just to both parties, including the amendment of the rate of interest payable.

Southern and District Finance plc v Barnes; Equity Home Loans Ltd v Lewis (1995) 27 HLR 691 (Court of Appeal: Leggatt, Roch and Aldous LJJ).

605 Credit agreements—exempt agreements

The Consumer Credit (Exempt Agreements) (Amendment) Order 1995, SI 1995/1250 (in force on 6 June 1995), further amends the 1989 Order, SI 1989/869, by adding the names of six mortgage companies to the list of specified bodies certain of whose agreements are exempt from the provisions of the Consumer Credit Act 1974.

The Consumer Credit (Exempt Agreements) (Amendment) (No 2) Order 1995, SI 1995/2914 (in force on 11 December 1995), further amends the 1989 Order supra so as to add the name of one insurance company to the list in Sch 1, Pt I to the order, and add the names of five bodies corporate to the list in Sch 1, Pt III to the order. Where the name of a body is included in either of those lists the Consumer Credit Act 1974 does not regulate certain of the agreements under which it advances money.

606 Investment services—securities—implementation of EC provisions

See para 1383.

CONSUMER PROTECTION

607 Articles

The Consumer Credit Counselling Service, Magda D'Ingeo: 145 NLJ 190

Consumer Protection: 'Clocking', Disclaimers and the Statutory Defences, Geoff Holgate: 159 JP Jo 701

Consumer Protection: Trading Standards Officer, Enforcement and the Police and Criminal Evidence Act 1984, Geoff Holgate: 159 JP Jo 284

Contract Concerns, Charles Maggs (on the Unfair Terms in Consumer Contracts Regulations 1994, SI 1994/3159 (1994 Abr para 606)): LS Gaz, 1 June 1995, p 23

Effective Diligence (Reliance on Certificates of Compliance), Victor Smith: 159 JP Jo 572, 587

Judicial Approaches to Due Diligence, Deborah Parry (on due diligence as a defence to consumer protection offences): [1995] Crim LR 695

The Law of Tips and Service Charges, Roger Peters: 139 SJ 847

Of Sheep Dips, Pesticides and Damages for Personal Injuries, Alan Care (on claims for damages for sheep dip poisoning): 139 SJ 1250

The Seller is not Liable For . . . Edward Burroughs (on the Unfair Terms in Consumer Contracts Regulations 1994, SI 1994/3159 (1994 Abr para 606)): 145 NLJ 1367

Trading Standards—Searches By Power or Consent, Victor Smith: 159 JP Jo 76

Unfair Terms in Consumer Contract Regulations 1994, Kiron Reid (on the Unfair Terms in Consumer Contracts Regulations 1994, SI 1994/3159 (1994 Abr para 606)): 16 Comp Lawyer 280

608 Consumer credit

See CONSUMER CREDIT.

609 Consumer information—Consumer Committee

See para 3118.

610 Consumer information—footwear—indication of materials used in main components

The Footwear (Indication of Composition) Labelling Regulations 1995, SI 1995/2489 (in force on 23 March 1996), implement Council Directive (EC) 94/11 on the labelling of materials used in the main components of footwear for consumer sale. The regulations require 'responsible persons' to ensure that labelling on footwear placed on the market provides information as to the material that constitutes at least 80 per cent of the surface area of the upper, at least 80 per cent of the surface area of the lining and sock, and at least 80 per cent of the volume of the outer sole. The information must be provided by way of pictogram or written indication and the retailer must ensure that consumers are informed of the meaning of any pictogram shown. Provision is made for criminal penalties for breach of the regulations and for enforcement, including service of compliance notices.

611 Consumer information—medicinal products—explanatory brochure available after purchase

See *Ter Voort*, para 3122.

612 Consumer safety—active implantable medical devices

The Active Implantable Medical Devices (Amendment and Transitional Provisions) Regulations 1995, SI 1995/1671 (in force on 8 August 1995), amend the 1992 Regulations, SI 1992/3146, so as to implement, in part, Council Directive (EC) 93/42, which amends Council Directive (EC) 90/385 (as implemented by the 1992 Regulations), and also to implement, in part, Council Directive (EC) 93/68. The regulations (1) amend certain definitions and introduce new definitions; (2) substitute 'CE Marking' for all references to ÈC Mark', and make other consequential amendments; (3) specify the language which must be used on the packaging of medical devices; (4) amend the conformity assessment procedures to be carried out in order that the CE marking may be affixed to devices; (5) provide that the Secretary of State may authorise a clinical investigation to take place before the 60 day period (referred to in the 1992 Regulations, reg 7(1)) has elapsed; (6) set out the obligations of persons other than manufacturers; (7) provide that the Secretary of State may refuse to designate, or may withdraw designation from, notified bodies when certain fees are not paid; (8) provide that the Secretary of State may inspect certain premises for the purposes of carrying out her functions in relation to notified bodies; (9) amend the provisions on prohibition on supply and the notification of decisions; (10) provide for a two-stage procedure to be used in cases in which the Secretary of State has reasonable grounds for believing that the CE marking has been wrongly affixed to a device which he does not consider to be unsafe; (11) illustrate the CE marking and prescribe requirements as to its dimensions etc; (12) amend the provisions concerning the evaluation of clinical data; and (13) set out the conformity assessment procedures to be followed by manufacturers.

613 Consumer safety—cosmetic products

The Cosmetic Products (Safety) (Amendment) Regulations 1995, SI 1995/1478 (in force in part on 30 June 1995, in part on 1 July 1995 and in part on 30 June 1996), further amend the 1989 Regulations, SI 1989/2233, so as to implement Commission Directive (EC) 94/32. The regulations impose further prohibitions on the use of certain substances in cosmetic products and expand the warning label requirements for the use of other specified substances. They also permit, subject to restrictions and certain labelling requirements, the use of strontium hydroxide in depilatory products and strontium peroxide in rinse-off hair care preparations for professional use and delete the latter from the list of substances provisionally allowed to be used in cosmetic products. The regulations extend the provisionally allowed use of certain substances and preservatives for specified periods, and permit and extend the use in cosmetic products of certain UV filters, subject to restrictions.

614 Consumer safety—failure to comply with general safety requirement—cooker hood unsafe when used with cooker—defence of due diligence

Under the Consumer Protection Act 1987, s 10(4), in any proceedings against a person for an offence under s 10 in respect of any goods, it is a defence to show that, at the time he supplied the goods or offered or agreed to supply them or exposed or possessed them for supply, he neither knew nor had reasonable grounds for believing that the goods failed to comply with the general safety requirement. In proceedings against any person for an offence to which s 39 applied, it is a defence for that person to show that he took all reasonable steps and exercised all due diligence to avoid committing the offence: s 39.

A consumer bought a cooker hood to be used with his gas cooker. When it was used with the cooker the fan in the hood could not be turned off and the switches became too hot to touch. The consumer complained and the company from which he bought the hood replaced it. He had the same problem with that hood and informed his local trading standards officer. Both the company and the importers of the hood were prosecuted and convicted under the 1987 Act. On appeal, (1) the company sought to establish a defence under s 10(4) and (2) the importers relied on a defence of due diligence under s 39. *Held*, (1) goods failed to comply with the general safety requirement in s 10 if they were not reasonably safe having regard to all the circumstances. That included not only the use of the goods in isolation but also the use that must have been contemplated. In the present case, that use was in conjunction with a gas cooker and, although the hood was not inherently safe, it became dangerous in circumstances which should have been contemplated. A defence could not be established under s 10(4) because there was material information available to the effect that a potential problem existed and there was overwhelming evidence that the company directors would have been aware of the problems encountered when a hood was used with a gas cooker. (2) If the importers had made any inquiries at all they would have known that there was a potential problem and would have taken some steps at least to do something about it. They did not satisfy the requirements of a defence under s 39. Accordingly, the appeals would be dismissed.

Whirlpool (UK) Ltd v Gloucestershire County Council (1993) 159 JP 123 (Queen's Bench Division: Russell LJ and Blofeld J).

615 Consumer safety—fireworks

The Fireworks (Safety) (Revocation) Regulations 1995, SI 1995/415 (in force on 16 March 1995), revoke the 1986 Regulations, SI 1986/1323, which prohibit any person from supplying, offering to supply or agreeing to supply fireworks to any person apparently under the age of 16. The Explosives Act 1876, s 31 which prohibits the sale of explosives, including fireworks, to a person apparently under 16 years remains in force.

616 Consumer safety—gas appliances

The Gas Appliances (Safety) Regulations 1995, SI 1995/1629 (in force partly on 18 July 1995; fully on 1 January 1996), replace the 1992 Regulations, SI 1992/711. The Regulations implement Council Directive (EC) 90/396 on the approximation of the laws of the member states relating to appliances burning gaseous fuels. Those provisions of the 1992 Regulations which required gas appliances to conform with certain essential criteria and to be safe when normally used are re-enacted. New provision is made (1) requiring manufacturers choosing the production monitoring procedures of EC verification and EC unit verification to ensure that and make a declaration that the appliance conforms with the Directive; (2) requiring the appliance category to appear on the appliance or data plate together with the CE Marking; (3) prohibiting markings likely to deceive third parties as to the meaning and form of CE Marking; (4) during the transitional period of any Directives which apply, requiring the accompanying documentation to state which Directives have been applied; (5) facilitating the issue of a compliance notice in the case of gas appliances to which the CE Marking has been unduly affixed; and (6) redefining the CE Marking. The Regulations do not apply to second-hand gas appliances but for these purposes they retain in force the Gas Cooking Appliances (Safety) Regulations 1989, SI 1989/149 and the Heating Appliances (Fireguard) (Safety) Regulations 1991, SI 1991/2693, reg 1(3).

617 Consumer safety—medical devices

The Medical Devices (Consultation Requirements) (Fees) Regulations 1995, SI 1995/449 (in force on 20 March 1995), prescribe the fees payable in accordance with Council Directive (EC) 93/42. The regulations prescribe the amount and the circumstances in which fees are payable and provision is made as to the recovery of unpaid fees.

618 Consumer safety—teats and dummies

The N-nitrosamines and N-nitrosatable Substances in Elastomer or Rubber Teats and Dummies (Safety) Regulations 1995, SI 1995/1012 (in force on 28 April 1995), implement Council Directive (EC) 93/111. The regulations apply to teats and dummies intended to be (or which are) brought into contact with foodstuffs, and concern the release of N-nitrosamines and N-nitrosatable substances from elastomer or rubber teats and dummies. They prohibit the supply of a teat or dummy not complying with the requirements of these regulations. Basic rules and criteria applicable to determining the release of N-nitrosamine and N-nitrosatable substances are also provided.

619 Consumer safety—toys

The Toys (Safety) Regulations 1995, SI 1995/204 (in force on 24 February 1995), consolidate with amendments the 1989 Regulations, SI 1989/1275 and implement the requirements of Council Directive (EC) 88/378, as amended, on the approximation of the laws of the member States concerning the safety of toys. They require toys to satisfy the essential safety requirements in Annex II of the 1988 Directive and provide for the appointment of bodies to carry out examinations and tests and to issue EC type-examination certificates. Provision is made for the CE marking of toys and for other information which must be put on toys and their packaging or accompany them. Provision is also made for the retention of information by the manufacturer, his authorised representative established in the United Kingdom or any other person established in the United Kingdom who was the first supplier of the toy in the Community, and for keeping this information available for inspection by an enforcement authority. In addition to these provisions and to minor consequential amendments, the Regulations separate the obligations placed on a person who supplies a toy from those placed on the manufacturer or his authorised representative established in the Community who supplies a toy by making an express provision for the requirement not to supply any toy which would jeopardise the safety or health of users or third parties under certain defined conditions.

620 Consumer safety—toys—reasonable steps and due diligence to avoid committing offence—British Standard

The Consumer Protection Act 1987, s 39 provides that where any person is accused of an offence under the Act it is a defence to show that he took all reasonable steps and exercised all due diligence to avoid committing the offence.

The defendant was the manufacturer of a toy which was in breach of the safety provisions of the Toys (Safety) Regulations 1989, SI 1989/1275. The manufacturer's defence to a prosecution brought by a trading standards officer was that it had ensured the toy met the British Standard which constituted a reasonable step and due diligence under the 1987 Act, s 39. The magistrates' court acquitted the manufacturer and the trading standards officer appealed. *Held*, the s 39 defence would only be made out where reasonable steps and due diligence were employed in relation to the regulations and not to another standard. The manufacturer ought to have made inquiries as to whether it was complying with the regulations which were part of the law of the land and could not assume that meeting the British Standard constituted compliance with the regulations. Accordingly, the appeal would be allowed and the case remitted.

Balding v Lew Ways Ltd (1995) 159 JP 541 (Queen's Bench Division: Pill LJ and Keene J).

621 Monopolies and mergers

See TRADE, INDUSTRY AND INDUSTRIAL RELATIONS.

622 Package holidays and tours—bonding arrangements and insurance

The Package Travel, Package Holidays and Package Tours (Amendment) Regulations 1995, SI 1995/1648 (in force on 24 June 1995), amend the 1992 Regulations, SI 1992/3228 so as to (1) permit an organiser, retailer and approved body to enter into a bonding arrangement with a person authorised in the Channel Islands or the Isle of Man to carry on the business of entering into bonds; (2) permit an approved body to have insurance cover with an insurer authorised in the Channel Islands or the Isle of Man; and (3) update the reference to a member State to include any member of the European Economic Area.

623 Package holidays and tours—consumer's contract with tour operator—tour operator's trade association offering protection against insolvency—extent of protection for consumer

See *Bowerman v Association of British Travel Agents Ltd*, para 652.

624 Price indication—misleading indication—burden of proof

It has been held that references to consumers in the Consumer Protection Act 1987, s 20 (offence of giving misleading price indication) were intended to limit the offence to those cases where the misleading indication was intended to affect the actions of a person who might wish to be supplied with goods for his own private use or consumption. However, subject to this qualification, there is nothing in the 1987 Act, ss 20 or 21 (meaning of 'misleading') requiring the prosecution to prove that a particular misleading indication of price has been given to a particular person who might wish to be supplied with the goods for his own private use or consumption.

MFI Furniture Centres Ltd v Hibbert (1995) 160 JP 178 (Queen's Bench Division: Balcombe LJ and Collins J).

625 Price marking—indication of unit price

The Price Marking (Amendment) Order 1995, SI 1995/1441 (in force on 7 June 1995), further amends the 1991 Order, SI 1991/1382. The order substitutes the date 7 June 1997 for 7th June 1995 as the date from which the indication of the unit price of certain goods pre-packed in pre-established quantities is required.

626 Restrictive trade practices

See TRADE, INDUSTRY AND INDUSTRIAL RELATIONS.

627 Trade descriptions

See TRADE DESCRIPTIONS.

CONTEMPT OF COURT

Halsbury's Laws of England (4th edn) Vol 9, paras 1–200

628 Articles

The Accused, the Jury and the Media, Damian Paul Carney: 145 NLJ 12

Press and Prejudice, Alistair Bonnington (on contrasting approaches to prejudicial pre-trial publicity): 145 NLJ 1623

Trial by Media, David Bentley (on sensational press and television coverage of trials): 139 SJ 243

629 Breach of court order—committal order—defect in order—procedure

An order was made against a father forbidding him from removing his child from the child's guardian. He breached the order twice and was sentenced to two suspended sentences totalling three months' imprisonment. He breached the order again and a further suspended sentence of six months' imprisonment was imposed to run concurrently with the previous suspended sentences. When the father appeared in court after a further breach, the draft of the previous order was placed before the judge. However, it stated that the period of six months' imprisonment was to run consecutively with the earlier sentences, making the father liable for a total of nine months' imprisonment. The father admitted the latest breaches and the judge purported to activate a nine-month order. The father appealed on grounds that (1) the order did not specify the contempts or breaches of the order for which he was committed, and (2) the judge would have activated the outstanding suspended sentence of six months rather than impose a longer sentence had he been aware of the correct form of the previous order. *Held*, (1) although the most recent breaches were not particularised in the order as they should have been, they were not themselves directly punished; they merely triggered the previous sentences. Therefore, the appellant suffered or was intended to suffer the imposition of sentences of which he knew he was in peril when he committed the breaches he had admitted. In the circumstances, the court was unable to conclude that the appellant had suffered any injustice and the sentences should stand. (2) When the judge realised that the sentences should have run concurrently, he indicated that he would have imposed a six-month sentence. Accordingly, the nine-month sentence would be quashed and a sentence of six months' imprisonment substituted.

C v Hackney London Borough Council [1995] 2 FCR 306 (Court of Appeal: Leggatt, Aldous and Hutchison LJJ).

630 Breach of court order—committal order—immediate committal to prison— direction that contemnor be brought back to court for further consideration of sentence—validity of order

A husband was found guilty in the county court of contempt of court for breach of undertakings not to use violence against his wife. He was committed to prison immediately with a direction that he be brought back before the court at a later date for a custodial sentence to be further considered. On his appeal, *held*, the committal order was bad on its face and internally inconsistent since it purported to commit the contemnor until a later date and also required his production on that date. There was no identifiable period of committal and therefore the order offended against the Contempt of Court Act 1981, s 14(1). The court had no power to direct further consideration of sentence on the later date and, in deleting the part of the order which drew the attention of the contemnor to his right to apply to purge the contempt, wrongly deprived him of that right. Apart from contempt in the face of the court, there was no power to detain an alleged contemnor prior to a finding of contempt. Neither was there power to detain after a finding of contempt but before sentence. Accordingly, the order would be quashed, the court would direct the contemnor's immediate release and would substitute a sentence of six months' imprisonment suspended until the expiry of the undertakings the contemnor had given.

Delaney v Delaney [1996] 1 All ER 367 (Court of Appeal: Sir Thomas Bingham MR and Sir John Balcombe). *Vaughan v Vaughan* [1973] 3 All ER 449, CA and *Lamb v Lamb* [1984] 5 FLR 278, CA followed.

631   Breach of court order—committal proceedings—adjournment

A wife applied for the committal of her former husband for contempt of an undertaking relating to non-molestation and assault. On the husband's application, the proceedings were adjourned until the conclusion of his criminal trial for the assault. The wife appealed against the decision to adjourn. *Held*, no evidence had been adduced by the husband to suggest that there would have been a real risk of serious prejudice that would have led to an injustice. Consequently, there was no justification for an adjournment. The committal proceedings should proceed and be dealt with swiftly and conclusively. Accordingly, the appeal would be allowed.

Keeber v Keeber [1995] 2 FLR 748 (Court of Appeal: Butler-Sloss and Otton LJJ). *Szczepanski v Szczepanski* [1985] FLR 468, CA, and *H v C (Contempt and Criminal Proceedings)* [1993] 1 FLR 787, CA, applied.

632   Breach of court order—injunctive order—appropriate sentence

A husband was in breach of an injunctive order in favour of his wife. The order prevented him from disposing of any part of his severance payment on leaving the army until an inter partes hearing. At the contempt hearing he admitted his breach of the court's order, which breach was considered so flagrant as to be punished with a sentence of nine months' imprisonment. On appeal, the issue was whether that punishment was appropriate. *Held*, the breach was a substantial one, with systematic disregard shown for the court's order. Furthermore, the wife had no prospect of recovering any amount from the appellant. The judge had made no error in principle, had not failed to exercise his discretion judicially and had given sufficient weight to all factors. The sentence was not excessive and, accordingly, the appeal would be dismissed.

Hudson v Hudson [1995] 2 FLR 72 (Court of Appeal: Roch and Ward LJJ).

633   Committal for contempt—hearing—disclosure of evidence in advance of hearing

In a contempt of court case, it has been held that the court does not have the power to compel an alleged contemnor to swear an affidavit setting out his case in advance of the hearing. In such a case, however, it does have the power to direct a respondent to a committal summons to swear affidavits or produce statements of witnesses of facts upon which he might want to rely, and to file and serve such evidence in convenient time before the hearing in order to permit proper presentation of evidence in reply. In those circumstances, the applicant in the proceedings cannot make use of the respondent's evidence until it is deployed by the respondent either by reading it or by relying upon it. Likewise, a respondent cannot be cross-examined until he deploys the evidence in support of his own case. Legal advisers to respondents in committal proceedings ought to ensure that if they file evidence in answer to the summons, but do not wish to put it in before closure of the applicant's case, that fact is made clear. The wise course for a respondent is to make a full and frank admission of his contempt or, if he denies contempt, to set out his case clearly and in detail.

Re B (a Minor) (Contempt: Evidence) [1996] 1 FCR 158 (Family Division: Wall J).

634   Interference with administration of justice—reports of judicial proceedings— decision not to institute contempt proceedings—whether decision reviewable

See *R v A-G, ex p Taylor*, para 2394.

635   Interference with the administration of justice—reports of judicial proceedings—strict liability rule—publication of report of alleged crime—identification of accused

See *HM Advocate v Caledonian Newspapers Ltd*, para 2396.

636   Obstructing police officer—contamination of identification parade—wilful obstruction

See *Connolly v Dale,* para 920.

637   Proceedings—hearing—opportunity for legal representation

The appellant was alleged to have offered a sum of money to a potential witness to persuade him not to give evidence against the appellant's brother. The judge regarded the matter as one of urgency because of its possible effect on the trial and decided to deal with it immediately, even though the appellant was unrepresented. He allowed the trial to continue because no prejudice had been caused, and postponed his finding on the appellant's alleged contempt until the conclusion of the trial. Although the appellant was represented by counsel when he was subsequently brought before the court, the judge refused to hear counsel. On appeal against the finding of contempt, *held*, a person who was accused of contempt and faced the possibility of imprisonment had to be allowed legal representation where that was practicable. Here, although the appellant was initially unrepresented, that was not the case at the subsequent hearing and the finding of contempt should not have been made before giving his counsel the opportunity to make representations on his behalf. Accordingly, the appeal would be allowed.

R v Bromell (1995) Times, 9 February (Court of Appeal: Hobhouse LJ, Pill and Steel JJ).

638   Proceedings—legal aid—remuneration of legal representatives

See para 1867.

639   Punishment—jurisdiction of Queen's Bench Divisional Court—contempt of industrial tribunal

RSC Ord 52, r 1(2)(a)(iii) gives power to the Queen's Bench Divisional Court to punish contempt of court committed in connection with proceedings in an inferior court.

On the question of whether an industrial tribunal was an inferior court within the meaning of Ord 52, r 1, *held*, an industrial tribunal was an inferior court within Ord 52, r 1 on the grounds that (1) the tribunal had many of the characteristics to which the authorities referred as being those of a court of law in that it was established by Parliament, and had a legally qualified chairman appointed by the Lord Chancellor and other members representing employers and employees drawn from panels compiled by the Secretary of State. It sat in public to decide cases affecting the rights of parties and it had power to compel the attendance of witnesses, administer oaths, control the parties' pleadings and order discovery. The parties before it could have legal representation, it could award costs and it had to give reasons for its decisions. It consequently appeared to exercise a judicial function. (2) On all three tests propounded in *A-G v British Broadcasting Corpn* [1981] AC 303, HL (1980 Abr para 465) the tribunal was a court. (3) The tribunal was a court within the meaning of the Contempt of Court 1981, s 19, which defined 'court' as including any tribunal or body exercising the judicial function of the state.

Peach Grey & Co (a firm) v Sommers [1995] 2 All ER 513 (Queen's Bench Division: Rose LJ and Tuckey J).

CONTRACT

Halsbury's Laws of England (4th edn) Vol 9, paras 201–750

640   Articles

Change of Position, Paul Key (on the availability of a defence of change of position to an action for restitution): 58 MLR 505

Consolidation or Confusion? Meryll Dean (on the EC Directive on Unfair Contract Terms (93/13/EC)): 145 NLJ 28

Developments in the Common Law Doctrine of Non Est Factum, A L R Joseph: [1994] MLJ cxxix

Excising Estoppel by Representation as a Defence to Restitution, Paul Key: (1995) CLJ 388

How Fair Art Thou? Anthony Mosawi (on the EC Directive on Unfair Contract Terms (93/13/EC)): LS Gaz, 25 January 1995, p 20

Illiterate and Ill-Read—No Defence in Contract: 159 JP Jo 647

Of Contracts and Clauses, Ronald Paterson (on the effectiveness of entire agreement clauses): LS Gaz, 22 February 1995, p 26

The Performance Interest in Contract Damages, Daniel Friedmann: (1995) 111 LQR 628

Striking the Balance in the Law of Restitution, Graham Virgo: [1995] LMCLQ 362

Title Claims and Illegal Transactions, Nelson Enonchong: (1995) 111 LQR 135

Tort or Contract? Clive Boxer (on *Henderson v Merrett Syndicate* [1994] 3 WLR 761 (1994 Abr para 1687)): 139 SJ 136

Unconscionability as a Vitiating Factor, Nicholas Bamforth (on contractual arrangements set aside as unconscionable bargains): [1995] LMCLQ 538

Unfair Contracts, Richard Lawson (on unfair contracts in relation to agency and incorporation): 145 NLJ 697

Unfair Contract Terms Regulations, Laurie Elks (on the Unfair Terms in Consumer Contracts Regulations 1994, SI 1994/3159 (1994 Abr para 606)): LA October 1995, p 15

Unfair Terms in Consumer Contract Regulations 1994, Kiron Reid (on the Unfair Terms in Consumer Contracts Regulations 1994, SI 1994/3159 (1994 Abr para 606)): 16 Comp Lawyer 280

'Unjust Enrichment', Steve Hedley: (1995) 54 CLJ 578

Unjust Enrichment Claims; A Comparative Overview, Brice Dickson: (1995) 54 CLJ 100

Unfair Terms in Land Contracts: Copy Out or Cop Out? Susan Bright and Christopher Bright: (1995) 111 LQR 655

641 Applicable law

See CONFLICT OF LAWS.

642 Breach of contract—contractual duty—negligent advice—liability in tort

See *Holt v Payne Skillington (a Firm)*, para 41.

643 Breach of contract—damages

See DAMAGES.

644 Building contracts

See BUILDING CONTRACTS, ARCHITECTS, ENGINEERS AND SURVEYORS.

645 Contractual term—implied term—contract of service—implied term that services to be carried out with reasonable skill and care

Hong Kong

The plaintiff's daughter bought a package tour of China offered by the first defendant. The tour was for an all-in price including 'transportation as specified in itinerary', and the tour brochure, which contained the terms of the contract, was headed 'everything more comprehensively and thoughtfully worked out' and referred throughout to the tour group as 'we'. At the border with China the tour was joined by a tour guide who was an employee of the second defendant. Part of the tour consisted of a lake crossing. Prior to the crossing, the tour guide informed the party that they would have to make the crossing by speedboat owned by the third defendant. Three crossings were necessary to take the whole group across, but after the first two crossings the driver of the boat refused to make the third trip. Another employee of the third defendant agreed to make the third crossing in the course of which the boat was involved in a collision, as a result of which the plaintiff's daughter drowned. The plaintiff brought proceedings against the defendants claiming damages for breach of contract and for negligence. The judge awarded damages against all three defendants. On the plaintiff's appeal against the setting aside of the judgment on the ground that the first defendant was not in breach of its contractual duty to the deceased, *held*, whether a contract was one where the defendant agreed merely as agent to arrange for services to be provided by others, in which case there was an implied term that he would use reasonable care and skill in selecting those other persons, or one where the defendant agreed to supply the services, in which case, subject to any exemption clause, there was an implied term that he would as supplier carry out the services with reasonable care and skill, was a matter of construction of the particular contract. Having regard to the terms of the contract between the plaintiff's daughter and the first defendant, the first defendant undertook to provide and not merely to arrange all the services included in the tour programme, even if some activities were to be carried out by others. It was an implied term of the contract that the services provided by the first defendant would be carried out with reasonable skill and care and the obligation under the contract that the services would be provided with reasonable skill and care continued to exist even if some of the services were to be rendered by others, and even if tortious liability existed on the part of those others. Since the crossing of the lake had not been carried out with reasonable skill and care in that no steps had been taken to see that the driver of the speedboat was of reasonable competence and experience, the first defendant was liable for breach of contract. The appeal would therefore be allowed.

Wan v Kwan Kin Travel Services Ltd [1995] 4 All ER 745 (Privy Council: Lords Goff of Chieveley, Jauncey of Tullichettle, Slynn of Hadley, Nolan and Hoffmann).

646   Contractual term—implied term—fitness for purpose

See *Saphena Computing Ltd v Allied Collection Agencies Ltd*, para 679.

647   Contractual term—implied term—mortgage contract—exercise of option within reasonable time

Under the terms of a loan agreement with the defendant bank the borrowers mortgaged a vessel as security. The contract provided that, if the borrowers had not secured employment for the vessel by a specified date, the bankers could require them to sell the vessel by serving an appropriate notice within a specified date. The borrowers did not in fact secure employment for the vessel by the specified date but the bankers did not serve their notice for some three months. The borrowers argued that the notice was invalid as it had not been served within a reasonable time of the specified date. *Held*, it was a matter both of general principle and business necessity that an option must be exercised within a reasonable time if no time limit was specified. Thus, the words 'given within a reasonable time' could be implied into the contract in relation to the serving of the notice by the bank. However, the contract also envisaged that the bank would take time to balance the possibility of future employment with the advantages of sale and thus the notice was served within a reasonable time. Accordingly, the notice was valid and the borrowers were in default of the loan agreement in failing to sell the vessel.

Zeeland Navigation Co Ltd v Banque Worms, The Foresight Driller II [1995] 1 Lloyd's Rep 251 (Queen's Bench Division: Rix J).

648   Contractual term—interpretation—ouster of jurisdiction of court

An international agreement provided for compensation for damage from oil pollution. The compensation was paid out of a fund administered by the defendant company. The agreement provided for claims to be brought within a specified time limit and for the defendant to be the 'sole judge' of any claim. The plaintiff company made a claim under the agreement. The defendant asserted that the claim had been brought out of time and that it had exclusive jurisdiction to determine whether or not a time limit had expired. The court held that any determination by the defendant as to whether a claim had been made in time could be reviewed by an English court, that the court's power of review was unrestricted, and that findings of fact as well as conclusions of law could be challenged. On the defendant's appeal, *held*, it remained the general rule of common law that an agreement wholly to oust the jurisdiction of the courts was against public policy and void. In the absence of some statutory provision, such as the Arbitration Act 1979, s 3, the rule remained in force. However, in applying the rule, questions of fact were treated differently from questions of law. The defendant accepted that decisions on questions of law could be reviewed by the court and that the court could intervene if it failed to act fairly in making any determination or if the determination could be shown to be perverse. Therefore no question as to the ouster of the court's jurisdiction arose and the problem was the definition of the court's role. The agreement was unusual as one of the functions of the defendant was to administer the fund. In most cases, the claimant would be a member of the defendant company and the company and the board of directors were there to hold a balance between members. In the context of the agreement, the words 'sole judge' were sufficient to show that the determination was to be final and binding for all purposes on matters of fact, subject to any question of unfairness, bad faith or perversity. This accorded with the nature of the scheme and took account of the importance of having the simplest possible machinery to adjudicate claims. Accordingly, the appeal would be allowed.

West of England Shipowners Mutual Insurance Association (Luxembourg) v Cristal Ltd, The Glacier Bay (1995) Times, 26 October, Independent, 1 November (Court of Appeal: Neill, Waite and Pill LJJ). Decision of Waller J [1995] 1 Lloyd's Rep 560 reversed.

649   Contractual term—levy of additional subscription by association of Lloyd's names—defaulting members—penalty—relief from forfeiture

The defendants were members of an association comprised of Lloyd's names from particular syndicates who had formed the association in order to bring actions against their managing agent and members' agents. The association voted to levy additional subscriptions under powers contained in the association agreement, but the defendants did not pay, were declared defaulting members and were therefore not entitled to a share in any damages awarded to the association. They applied to the court for a declaration as to whether the power to declare the defendants defaulting members was a contractual penalty and therefore unenforceable, whether they were entitled to relief from forfeiture and whether there was an implied term obliging the association to conduct a detailed investigation of the defendants' means before declaring them defaulting members. *Held*, it was an essential part of the arrangement between the association's members that if a member ceased to contribute his share of the cost of bringing the actions he ran the risk of being excluded from his share of the benefit of the arrangement, and therefore the exclusion did not constitute a penalty. To allow a member who had not undertaken his share of the risk by paying his subscriptions on time to come in after the litigation had been successfully concluded, so that there was no longer any risk, and still share in the fruits of the litigation on payment of his overdue subscription would undermine, rather than attain, the object of the forfeiture provision against which relief was sought as well as one of the fundamental objectives of the constitution of the association and, accordingly, relief against forfeiture was not appropriate. There was no evidence that there was an implied term in the association agreement requiring an investigation of defaulting members' means and, accordingly, no such investigation needed to be conducted.

Nutting v Baldwin [1995] 1 WLR 201 (Chancery Division: Rattee J).

650   Formation of contract—agreement—common undisclosed intention

On the trial of a preliminary issue relating to insurance contracts, it has been held that consensus requires that each party to a contract should know or be capable of knowing what he has agreed on at the time of making the contract. Accordingly, evidence that both parties had the same undisclosed intention as to the effect of the contract is inadmissible in evidence for the purpose of interpreting a written contract.

New Hampshire Insurance Co v MGN Ltd (1995) Times, 25 July (Court of Appeal: Staughton, Millett and Ward LJJ).

651   Formation of contract—condition precedent—unilateral contract

The plaintiff was a tenant of a public house and had a five-year lease with a brewery. The lease contained an option to renew for a further five years once certain conditions had been met, including one requiring that a further business agreement and business plan were to be agreed. A preliminary issue arose as to whether the brewery, having refused to agree or to offer to enter into a new business agreement or plan, was entitled to refuse to grant the tenant a new lease on the ground that a condition precedent in the lease had not been satisfied. The preliminary issue was decided in favour of the brewery and the tenant appealed. *Held*, an option to renew a lease, like any other option, was a unilateral contract under which the grantor undertook to do something if, but only if, certain conditions were satisfied. It was in general impossible to imply terms which imposed legal obligations into a unilateral contract. Accordingly it was impossible to imply any terms which imported a legal obligation on the brewery to do or to refrain from doing anything until its obligation to grant a further term had arisen. There was no basis for invoking the doctrine that a man could not take advantage of his own wrong. It further fell to be determined whether, on the true construction of the lease and in the events which had happened, it was necessary for the condition to have been satisfied. Effect could be given to the parties' obvious intentions by construing the lease as if it read that the lessee would, if so required, agree a further agreement and plan. That would impose no obligation on the brewery. Whether the brewery required a tenant to agree a new agreement or plan would be a question of fact in each case. In the present case the brewery did not require the tenant to agree a new agreement or plan and therefore the condition precedent did not need to be satisfied. Accordingly, the appeal would be allowed.

Little v Courage Ltd (1995) Times, 4 January (Court of Appeal: Sir Stephen Brown P, Kennedy and Millett LJJ). Decision of Ferris J (1994) Times, 19 January (1994 Abr para 645) reversed.

652   Formation of contract—intention to create legal relations—public notice— impression gained by reader of notice

The plaintiffs booked a skiing holiday with a tour operator who was a member of the defendant, a trade association of travel agents and tour operators that sought to protect the public against the insolvency of its members. A notice displayed in the tour operator's office described the defendant's scheme of protection under which, in the event of a member's insolvency, the defendant would reimburse a customer and seek to arrange for him to continue with a booked arrangement as far as possible. The tour operator became insolvent and the holiday was arranged with another operator who received the refund from the defendant. The refund did not include holiday insurance premiums paid by the plaintiffs. They sought a refund of the sum attributable to the insurance. *Held*, Hirst LJ dissenting, as with many cases involving the construction of a document, the case depended on impression. The notice would be understood by the ordinary member of the public as importing an intention to create legal relations with customers of members of the defendant. It contained an offer of a promise which the customer was entitled to accept by choosing to do business with a member of the defendant. The protection scheme was a scheme in relation to the defendant's members but it was a scheme of protection of the customers of those members. The defendant was offering to protect the reader of the notice, the prospective customer. It was an inevitable inference that the defendant was going to do something for the customer if the member should fail financially. The defendant would step in and deal directly with the customer. It was a financial undertaking with a financial content. It satisfied the criteria of a unilateral contract and contained promises which were sufficiently clear to be capable of legal enforcement. There was a direct contractual relationship between a customer of a failed member of the defendant and the defendant itself. Accordingly, the plaintiffs' action would succeed.

Hirst LJ considered the notice to be descriptive rather than contractual in character, there being no words of promise or any firm commitment.

Bowerman v Association of British Travel Agents Ltd [1995] NLJR 1815 (Court of Appeal: Hirst, Waite and Hobhouse LJJ). *Carlill v Carbolic Smoke Ball Co* [1893] 1 QB 256, CA, considered.

653   Formation of contract—requirement of certainty—contract of insurance permitting annual variations

It has been held that, where a company contracts to supply its employees with a medical insurance scheme, the fact that the scheme permitted an annual variation of its incidental terms did not render the contract void on the grounds of uncertainty.

Baynham v Philips Electronics Ltd (1995) Times, 19 July (Queen's Bench Division: Latham J).

654   Frustration—advance payment made before discharge—recovery of payment

Subject to the court's discretion, in cases where a contract has been frustrated, the Law Reform (Frustrated Contracts) Act 1943, s 1 allows a party to recover advance payments made to a party under the contract before the time when the parties are discharged.

The plaintiffs, pop concert promoters, agreed to promote a concert to be held by the defendant pop group at a stadium in Madrid. However, the stadium was found to be unsafe and the authorities banned its use. The permit issued to the plaintiffs to hold the concert was revoked. A suitable alternative venue could not be found and the concert was cancelled. The plaintiffs sought to recover an advance payment made to the defendants. By way of a counterclaim, the defendants sought damages for breach of contract by the plaintiffs in failing to secure the permit. *Held*, it was an implied term of the contract that the plaintiffs would use all reasonable endeavours to obtain a permit for the concert. However, they were not required to ensure that a permit would remain in force after its issue. The contract was frustrated, not because the permit had been revoked, but because the stadium had been found to be unsafe and its use banned. The 1943 Act, s 1 entitled the plaintiffs to recover the advance payments made to the defendants. The court's discretion to allow the defendants to set off their losses was broad. It could be invoked to mitigate any possible harshness of allowing all loss to lie where it had fallen. However, in all the circumstances of the case, having particular regard to the plaintiffs' loss, justice would be done by making no deduction in favour of the defendants. Accordingly, the plaintiffs' claim would succeed and the counterclaim would be dismissed.

Gamerco SA v ICM/Fair Warning (Agency) Ltd [1995] 1 WLR 1226 (Queen's Bench Division: Garland J).

655 Loan contract—attempt to reclaim money—claim for money had and received

See *Spargos Mining NL v Atlantic Capital Corpn*, para 2376.

656 Misrepresentation

See MISREPRESENTATION.

657 Mistake

See MISTAKE.

658 Parties—party contracting with himself

See *Ingram v IRC*, para 1695.

659 Payment due under contract—unlawful harassment of debtor

Under the Administration of Justice Act 1970, s 40(1) a person commits an offence if, with the object of coercing another person to pay money claimed from that other as a debt due under a contract, he harasses that other person with demands for payment which . . . are calculated to subject him or members of his family or household to alarm, distress or humiliation.

An electricity supplier was convicted of an offence under the 1970 Act, s 40(1). On appeal by way of case stated, *held*, an agreement for the supply of electricity between a tariff customer and a public electricity supplier was not a contract. There was a clear distinction in the Electricity Act 1989 between supplies governed by the terms of special agreements within the meaning of s 22 and supplies to tariff customers which were governed by the Act. In the absence of any findings to support a special agreement between the electricity supplier and the customer the relationship between the parties could only be that of a tariff customer and public electricity supplier which was not founded on contract. Since there was no contract and the debt claimed was not claimed under a contract there could be no offence under the 1970 Act, s 40(1).

The court went on to consider the proper construction of the words 'calculated to subject' in s 40(1). Following the decision of the House of Lords in *McDowell v Standard Oil Company (New Jersey)* [1927] AC 632, 'calculated' in this context meant 'likely' rather than 'intended'.

Norweb plc v Dixon [1995] 3 All ER 952 (Queen's Bench Division: McCowan LJ and Dyson J).

660 Repudiation—anticipatory repudiation—acceptance

The Arbitration Act 1979, s 1(7) provides that no appeal lies to the Court of Appeal from a decision of the High Court on an appeal against an arbitration unless the High Court or the Court of Appeal gives leave, and it is certified by the High Court that the question of law to which its decision relates either is one of general public importance or is one which for some other special reason should be considered by the Court of Appeal.

The appellants entered into a contract to buy a cargo of propane from the respondents for delivery on a specified date. Loading of the cargo was not completed until after the delivery date and the appellants wrote to the respondents repudiating the contract on the ground that delivery was overdue. The respondents later informed the appellants that loading had been completed. After five months in which there had been no communication between the parties, the respondents resold the cargo at a price lower than the contract price, and claimed the difference from the appellants. An arbitrator made an award in favour of the respondents, holding that there had been an anticipatory breach of contract on the part of the appellants and that the respondents' failure to take further steps to perform the contract was both an acceptance of the anticipatory breach and a sufficient communication of it to the appellants. On appeal, it was held that as a matter of law, mere failure to perform contractual obligations could constitute acceptance of an anticipatory repudiation by the other party. On further appeal, *held*, (1) the ability of an innocent party to choose between acceptance of a repudiation and affirmation of the contract made it necessary for the choice to be clear and unequivocal. Silence and inaction, which could be equally consistent with the affirmation of the contract, was equivocal and could not therefore constitute acceptance of a repudiation. (2) The respondent to an appeal against an arbitrator's award was not entitled, contrary to the 1979 Act, s 1(7), to raise in the Court of Appeal uncertified issues of law, let alone issues of mixed fact and law, in order to show that, even if the appellant succeeded on the certified point of law, the appeal should none the less be dismissed on other grounds. If the respondent wished to raise such a point he himself had to apply to the High Court for a certificate and was only entitled to pursue the point in the Court of Appeal if he was successful in that application and obtained leave either in the High Court or the Court of Appeal. The appeal would be allowed.

Vitol SA v Norelf Ltd, The Santa Clara [1995] 3 All ER 971 (Court of Appeal: Nourse, Kennedy and Hirst LJJ). Decision of Phillips J [1994] 1 WLR 1390 (1993 Abr para 608) reversed.

661   Repudiation—demand for payment—refusal to make payment—price greater than that originally agreed

Hong Kong

The respondents required a 25 per cent deposit for a car, which the appellant duly paid. The respondents later made a demand for payment of the balance of the purchase price, the amount of which was based on the price in their price list and was somewhat higher than the price as originally stated. They gave notice that unless the purchase price was paid they would treat the contract as at an end and forfeit the deposit. When no further payment was made the deposit was forfeited. The appellant challenged the respondents' right to receive the sum they had demanded. *Held*, the respondents were not entitled to insist on the payment of an increased price for the car. They would only be allowed to do so to reflect an increase in the costs to which they were subjected by the conditions in the contract. On the question of whether the respondents were entitled to repudiate the contract, the fact that they were acting bona fides in asking for the higher purchase price was important. Further, there was nothing to prevent the appellant from paying the amount he thought was due. Until he at least tendered that sum the respondents were not required to deliver the goods. In fact the appellant had never called for delivery and there had been no repudiatory behaviour on the part of the respondents until after the appellant had made it clear that he was not going to make the further payment. Accordingly, the appeal would be dismissed.

Vaswani v Italian Motors (Sales and Services) Ltd [1996] 1 WLR 270 (Privy Council: Lords Jauncey of Tullichettle, Woolf, Lloyd of Berwick, Steyn and Hoffmann).

662   Rescission—partial rescission—rescission in equity

See *Vadasz v Pioneer Concrete (SA) Pty Ltd*, para 1311.

663   Restitution—unjust enrichment—failure of consideration

The plaintiff local authority entered into an interest rate swap agreement with the defendant bank. Although the latter was aware that the Audit Commission had expressed concern over whether certain interest rate swaps were within the powers of local authorities, it did not consider that there was any serious risk that the agreement with the plaintiff might be invalid. Following the first payment by the defendant under the agreement, the plaintiff paid the defendant the sum due. The payment reassured the defendant that the plaintiff would continue to honour the agreement. As a result of a provisional ruling by the House of Lords that interest rate swaps entered into by local authorities were ultra vires and void, the defendant made no further payments under the agreement. The plaintiff sought to recover the net sums it had paid to the defendant. The defendant contended that it had entered into the agreement in good faith and had relied on the validity of that agreement in committing itself to parallel hedging transactions to protect its position. *Held*, the plaintiff, as net payer under the agreement, was prima facie entitled to recover the net payments made to the defendant as money had and received on the basis that it was its money in equity or on the basis that there was no consideration for the payments, since both law and equity treated the defendant as being unjustly enriched by the receipt of the plaintiff's money. The fact that the defendant had made a loss on the transaction as a whole or had entered into a transaction which proved to be void was immaterial. Moreover, even if the plaintiff was not entitled to recover the net payments in equity but only at common law, the position would in substance be the same because the plaintiff would be entitled to recover the net sums paid as money had and received to the use of the plaintiff on the basis that there was no consideration for the payment and that it was the plaintiff's money which was being paid to the defendant. If a net payee under an interest rate swap agreement could show that it had altered its position in good faith after the receipt of money from the net payer, it might in principle be entitled to rely on the defence of change of position, but it could not rely on the supposed validity of the transaction either in support of a plea of estoppel or in support of a defence of change of position because the transaction was and always had been void. It followed that if the change of position defence asserted by the net payee involved reliance on the validity of an interest rate swap transaction which was in fact void, the result would not be that events before the receipt could be taken into account but that neither events before nor after it could be relied on. Accordingly, the defendant's reliance on the validity of the original swap agreement in committing itself to a protective hedging strategy and in maintaining hedging transactions day by day thereafter did not afford the defendant, as net payee, any defence of change of position since it involved relying not on the receipt of money but on the validity of a void transaction. The defendant therefore had been unjustly enriched by the receipt of what was the plaintiff's money and, as a result, the plaintiff was entitled to the return of the net payments which it had made to the defendant.

South Tyneside Metropolitan Borough Council v Svenska International plc [1995] 1 All ER 545 (Queen's Bench Division: Clarke J). *Westdeutsche Landesbank Girozentrale v Islington London Borough Council* [1994] 4 All ER 890, CA, and dictum of Hobhouse J in *Kleinwort Benson Ltd v South Tyneside Metropolitan Borough Council* [1994] 4 All ER 972 at 984 (1994 Abr para 568) applied. *Lipkin Gorman (a firm) v Karpnale Ltd* [1992] 4 All ER 512, HL (1991 Abr para 165) considered.

664   Sale of goods

See SALE OF GOODS.

665   Specific performance

See SPECIFIC PERFORMANCE.

666   Success fee clause—construction—circumstances in which liability to pay fee arises

The defendants, who were the chief executive and non-executive chairman of a football league, entered into an agreement with the plaintiff bank whereby the plaintiff negotiated on the football league's behalf in relation to the sale of the right to televise its football matches. The plaintiff managed to negotiate a higher bid for the television rights from a satellite television company and claimed that it was therefore entitled to a success fee. In proceedings in respect of the claim, *held*, where banking and investment banking advisers sought to include success fee clauses in agreements with clients, they were to explain to their clients what they had in mind and identify in clear terms in the agreement what was required to trigger the liability to pay a success fee. In this case, although the agreement stated that one of the circumstances in which the plaintiff was entitled to a success fee was if it made a substantial contribution to the negotiation of a higher bid from the television companies, on the facts of the case the plaintiff had not made such a substantial contribution. Accordingly, the application would be refused.

Swiss Bank Corpn v Parry (1995) Times, 9 February (Queen's Bench Division: Cresswell J).

667   Void and illegal contracts—champertous agreement—liquidator's powers

The liquidator of a compulsorily wound-up company agreed to share with a third party the prospective fruits of claims mounted against former directors for alleged wrongful trading. He claimed relief under the Insolvency Act 1986, s 214 against the directors who sought a stay of the proceedings on the grounds that the liquidator's agreement with the third party was champertous. *Held*, there were three routes by which a person could dispose to another the prospect of benefiting from litigation against a third party: (1) a transfer of property with inherent rights, such as an absolute assignment of a debt, which could not be champertous as the recipient obtained a legitimate interest in the subject matter of the liquidation; (2) an assignment of a mere cause of action, divorced from any property, which was generally against public policy; (3) an assignment of the fruits of a yet to be decided action, which was unobjectionable as the assignee had no right to interfere in the proceedings but such an assignment had to be supported by a consideration and could only operate in equity. The present case involved an agreement for the assignment of the fruits. The statutory power to sell property conferred on liquidators by the 1986 Act, Sch 4, para 6 could validly be exercised without any breach of the rules governing maintenance or champerty. Because the prospective fruits of the claims under the 1986 Act, s 214 did not fall within the definition of property in s 436, they were not exempted from the law of champerty, despite the fact that the agreement had been approved by a registrar. Accordingly, the applications by the directors for a stay of proceedings would be granted and the registrar's approval of the agreement would be withdrawn.

Ward v Aitken [1995] 2 BCLC 493 (Chancery Division: Robert Walker J). *Grovewood Holdings plc v James Capel & Co* [1995] 2 WLR 70 (1994 Abr para 635) followed.

668 Void and illegal contracts—champertous agreement—solicitor's retainer— contingency fees—enforceability of agreement

In 1988, the plaintiffs retained the defendants as their solicitors under an agreement which provided for 'a 20 per cent reduction from solicitor/client costs for any lost cases'. By the time the plaintiffs terminated the retainer, they owed the defendants considerable sums in fees and disbursements. A dispute arose as to what was due to the defendants, the plaintiffs having been advised that the retainer appeared to provide for payment of contingency fees and was not only professionally improper but contrary to public policy and unenforceable with regard to fees still unpaid, and in addition that the plaintiffs were arguably entitled to recover any fees already paid. On a preliminary issue as to the enforceability of the retainer, *held*, a contingency fee for conducting litigation which was champertous and unenforceable as being contrary to public policy was not confined to a direct or indirect share of the spoils and included a differential fee dependent on the outcome of the litigation. It followed that the solicitor's retainer at issue was clearly champertous and unenforceable, and, in the circumstances, there was no question of severance of the words 'for any lost cases' in the retainer, since that would constitute an attempt at unilateral rectification by removing, to the defendants' pecuniary disadvantage, the words creating a differential fee. The plaintiffs were not therefore bound to make any further payments under the retainer. However, they were not entitled to recover fees which they had already paid to the defendants, since the parties had to remain in the position in which they found themselves. Where services had been rendered and paid for under an unenforceable contract in circumstances where it could not be suggested that the payee had, apart from entering the agreement, acted unconscionably towards the payer or been unjustly enriched at his expense, it would be unrealistic to hold that the consideration, albeit one contrary to public policy, had wholly failed and that the payer was entitled to recover the price of those services while retaining the benefit of them.

Aratra Potato Co Ltd v Taylor Joynson Garrett (a firm) [1995] 4 All ER 695 (Queen's Bench Division: Garland J). *Re Hutley's Goods* (1869) LR 1 P & D 596 and *Cole v Booker* (1913) 29 TLR 295 considered.

CONVEYANCING

Halsbury's Laws of England (4th edn) Vol 39, paras 301–800, Vol 42, paras 1–400

669 Articles

A Charter for Conveyancing, Richard Blair: LS Gaz, 15 December 1995, p 24

Conveyancers and the Director as Purchaser, Nicholas Le Poidevin: 139 SJ 21

Conveyancers' Duties, Tim Burt (on the implications of *Mortgage Express Ltd v Bowerman & Partners (a Firm)* [1995] QB 375, CA (para 2785): LS Gaz, 31 Aug 1995, p 17

Conveyancing Fees, Tony Holland: 145 NLJ 1825

Equitable Accounting, Elizabeth Cooke: [1995] Conv 391

Forgery and Property: Effects and Remedies, Josephine Hayes (on *Penn v Bristol & West Building Society* (1995) Times, 19 June (para 2783)): 139 SJ 716

French Leaseback Fears, Henry Dyson (on buying French holiday property free of VAT): 139 SJ 426

Informal Transactions in Land, Estoppel and Registration, Graham Battersby: 58 MLR 637

A Lack of Authority, Daniel Worsley (on *Penn v Bristol & West Building Society* (1995) Times, 19 June (para 2783)): LS Gaz, 21 June 1995, p 23

Land Reform, J P Garner (on ways to make conveyancing simpler and cheaper): 145 NLJ 1026

Market Adaptation, Paul Marsh: LS Gaz, 15 December 1995, p 21

Mind-boggling Act, Edward Burroughs (on the Law of Property (Miscellaneous Provisions) Act 1994): 145 NLJ 1130

New Standard Conditions of Sale, Richard Castle (on changes introduced by the Law of Property (Miscellaneous Provisions) Act 1994, Pt I): 139 SJ 602

Problems Arising on the Death of a Property Owner: Law of Property (Miscellaneous Provisions) Act 1994, Part II, Linda Clements: [1995] Conv 477

Sale by Mortgagees, Simon Miller and Jonathan Klein: 139 SJ 607

Severance Revisited, Louise Tee (on conversion of a joint tenancy to a tenancy in common): [1995] Conv 105

What Are Fixtures?—Life After the *Botham* Decision, Martin Codd (on *TSB Bank plc v Botham* [1995] EGCS 3): Estates Gazette, 10 June 1995, p112

670　Co-ownership—joint tenants—severance of joint tenancy

See *Re Dennis (a bankrupt)*, para 169.

671　Contract for sale—conditional contract—waiver of condition

Scotland

One of the conditions of a contract for the sale of land was that the contract was to remain conditional until the purchaser confirmed to the vendor that planning permission for certain purposes had been granted by the local authority. The purchaser undertook to pursue the planning permission application, and to keep the vendor informed of progress made. The contract also provided that if the purchaser failed to satisfy the condition within five years, the contract would terminate automatically. Shortly before the end of the five-year period, the purchaser indicated in a letter that the condition had been 'purified', but was unable to confirm that planning permission had been granted. On the vendor's application for a declaration that the contract was terminated, *held*, as the letter did not expressly confirm that planning permission had been granted, the condition had not been satisfied. As to whether or not the condition had been waived by the purchaser, a party could waive a suspensive condition only if the condition existed for his sole benefit. Here, the fact that the contract, and not merely an offer or acceptance, was subject to the suspensive condition, and that the vendor was entitled to appeal to the Secretary of State in relation to the planning permission application, indicated that both the vendor and the purchaser had an interest in the condition. Moreover, the provision that the contract would fail if the condition was not satisfied was another indication that the vendor had an interest in the condition. In light of those considerations, the vendor had a substantial interest in the condition, such that the purchaser could not unilaterally waive it. The parties had not contemplated that the contract would be concluded other than on the basis of obtaining planning permission and, accordingly, the application would be granted.

　　Manheath Ltd v HJ Banks & Co Ltd (1995) Times, 2 June (Outer House).

672　Contract for sale—rectification following completion—common intention of parties

Scotland

A purchaser offered to buy four areas of land from a vendor. However, the draft contract drawn up by the purchaser's solicitors referred to five areas of land, and the vendor's solicitors confirmed that five areas of land were to form the subject of the conveyance. The vendor's solicitors later wrote to the purchaser accepting the initial offer to purchase four areas of land, but the contract of sale that was executed related to five areas of land. Following completion, the vendor claimed that the transaction should be set aside because there had been a material common error. The claim succeeded, and on the purchaser's appeal, *held*, the onus was on the vendor to establish that the conveyance did not give effect to the parties' true intention. Although the conveyance did not conform to the initial offer which was accepted by the vendor, the fact that an extra piece of land had been conveyed was not enough, by itself, to establish common error. However, the inference to be drawn from the initial offer was that four areas of land were to be conveyed, and the explanation for the conveyance of an additional area of land was that a mistake had been made in the draft contract of sale when there was no binding contract between the parties. Accordingly, the appeal would be dismissed.

　　Aberdeen Rubber Ltd v Knowles & Sons (Fruiterers) Ltd 1995 SLT 870 (House of Lords: Lords Mackay of Clashfern LC, Keith of Kinkel, Jauncey of Tullichettle, Mustill, and Lloyd of Berwick).

673　Contract for sale—signature of both parties—validity of typed signature

The plaintiff company entered into an oral agreement with a woman to purchase land owned by her. A director of the company sent a typed letter for the woman to sign which also bore the typed name of the director and the address of the plaintiff. The woman signed the letter but died before the transaction was complete. The plaintiff sought specific performance of the contract but the woman's personal representatives applied to have the claim struck out on the ground that the plaintiff had not signed the letter and therefore, the requirement of the Law of Property (Miscellaneous Provisions) Act 1989, s 2, that agreements regarding land must be signed by each party, had not been met. The plaintiff contended that past authority on the Law of Property Act 1925, s 40 had established that a party's name pre-printed or typed on a document was capable of being sufficient signature for the purposes of that Act and that principle ought therefore to apply to the 1989 Act. At first instance, the judge found in favour of the personal representatives. On appeal by the plaintiff, *held*, it was an artificial use of language to treat a printed or typed name as a signature under the 1989 Act. The authorities regarding the 1925 Act, s 40 did not apply as it was wrong to clutter the 1989 Act with the ancient baggage of earlier decisions where they converted the meaning of 'signed' into something that the ordinary man would not recognise. Accordingly the appeal would be dismissed.

Firstpost Homes Ltd v Johnson [1995] 4 All ER 355 (Court of Appeal: Balcombe, Peter Gibson and Hutchison LJJ).

674 Restrictive covenants

See EQUITY.

COPYRIGHT

Halsbury's Laws of England (4th edn) Vol 9, paras 801–1000

675 Articles

Abridgements and Abstracts: Copyright Implications, David Vaver: [1995] EIPR 225

Copyright, Civil or Criminal? Brian McConnell (on the criminal provisions of the Copyright, Designs and Patents Act 1988): 145 NLJ 666

Copyright Harmonisation in the European Union and in North America, Ysolde Gendreau: [1995] EIPR 488

Copyright Theft—Summary Proceedings Under s 107, Copyright, Designs and Patents Act 1988, P W H Lydiate: 159 JP Jo 431

Copyright in Computer Programs: Back to Basics? Andrew Charlesworth: 145 NLJ 569

Design Copyright Licences of Right: How Will They Work in Practice? Caroline Bodley: [1995] EIPR 180

European Intellectual Property Rights: A Tabular Guide, Claire Burke: [1995] EIPR 466

Harmonising Intellectual Property Laws in the European Union: Past, Present and Future, Thomas Vinje: [1995] EIPR 361

International Differences in Copyright Protection for Software, Barry Sookman: [1995] 5 CTLR 142

International Intellectual Property Conventions: A Tabular Guide, Claire Burke: [1995] EIPR 477

New States of Mind, Eugene Gott and Mark Singley (on the new intellectual property antitrust guidelines proposed by the United States): LS Gaz, 5 April 1995, p 20

Planning and Copyright: Copyright and Planning, Alec Samuels: 159 JP Jo 212

Problems Over Copyright, Peter Jennings (on copyright issues in house design): Estates Gazette, 7 October 1995, p 124

The Proposed EU Directive for the Legal Protection of Databases: A Cornerstone of the Information Society? Laurence Kaye: [1995] EIPR 583

Protection of Software Fonts in UK Law, Justin Watts and Fred Blakemore: [1995] EIPR 133

Publish and Be Damned? Simon Gallant and Mary Russell (on copyright and the use of new media formats): LS Gaz, 15 February 1995, p 20

Reconceptualising Copyright in the Digital Era, Andrew Christie: [1995] EIPR 522

A Reversal of Fortune, William Sloan Coats and David Harrison Kramer (on software copyright): 10 CLP 159

Satellite Wars: Encryption, Piracy and the Law, Matthew Harris, Nick Gardner and Bill Moodie: [1995] 1 CTLR 123

676 Application to other countries

The Copyright (Application to Other Countries) (Amendment) Order 1995, SI 1995/2987 (in force in part on 15 December 1995 and in part on 1 January 1996), amends the 1993 Order, SI 1993/942, so as to take account of the accession of (1) Estonia, Georgia, Guyana, Latvia, Lithuania, Moldova, the Russian Federation, Saint Kitts and Nevis, Tanzania, and the Ukraine to the Berne Copyright Convention; (2) Belarus and Saudi Arabia to the Universal Copyright Convention; and (3) Bulgaria, Hungary, Iceland, Jamaica, and Moldova to the Rome

Convention for the Protection of Performers, Producers of Phonograms and Broadcasting Organisations.

677 Duration of copyright and rights in performances—harmonisation of term—implementation of EC provisions

The Duration of Copyright and Rights in Performances Regulations 1995, SI 1995/3297 (in force on 1 January 1996), implement the provisions of Council Directive (EC) 93/98 which harmonise the term of protection of copyright and related rights. The regulations amend the copyright, Designs and Patents Act 1988 so as to increase the existing period of copyright in literary, dramatic, musical and artistic works in the United Kingdom from the life of the author plus 50 years to the life of the author plus 70 years. The calculation of the duration of copyright in films is modified so as to be similar in length to that of other works, but based on the life of certain persons connected with the film rather than the life of the author. The starting point for the calculation of the present 50-year period is also amended and provision is made for reciprocal duration of copyright and performer's rights in the case of works and performances connected with countries that are not members of the European Economic Area. Detailed transitional provision is also made. In relation to the duration of copyright, for works in which copyright subsists on 31 December 1995, the duration of copyright is extended from 1 January 1996. For works in which copyright has expired in the United Kingdom before 1 January 1996, but which are protected on that date under the copyright legislation of any other state in the EEA, copyright revives on 1 January 1996 and expires on a date 70 years after the author's death. In relation to duration of rights in performances, provision is made for extending and reviving rights in performances where this occurs as a result of the application of the amended starting point for calculating the term of protection of existing performances.

678 Infringement—authorisation—place of authorisation—jurisdiction

The Copyright, Designs and Patents Act 1988, s 16(2) provides that copyright in a work is infringed by a person who without the licence of the copyright owner does, or authorises another to do, any of the acts restricted by the copyright.

The plaintiff claimed that the first and second defendants, which were respectively English and Danish companies, had infringed its copyright in certain sound recordings. The second defendant, which claimed to be entitled to the same copyright as the plaintiff, had granted a licence to the first defendant to manufacture and sell copies of the sound recordings in the United Kingdom. The plaintiff alleged that the second defendant had authorised the first defendant's acts, within the meaning of the 1988 Act, s 16(2), and issued a writ against both defendants. The second defendant applied to have service of the writ set aside, arguing that the plaintiff's case did not disclose a serious question to be tried. In particular, it contended that s 16(2) applied only to acts done within the jurisdiction of the United Kingdom, or, in the alternative, that it had not authorised the first defendant's acts. The application was dismissed. On appeal, *held*, as s 16(2) contained no territorial limitation as to the place from where the restricted act had to be authorised, the court had jurisdiction once such an act was done within the United Kingdom. It was therefore irrelevant that the act which preceded the consequence took place abroad, nor did there have to be a causal link between the preliminary act and its consequence. As such, the fact that the second defendant had granted a licence from Denmark to the first defendant was not a bar to the court's jurisdiction, as the first defendant's acts had taken place in the United Kingdom. Moreover, having regard to the relevant clauses of the licence, the second defendant had authorised the first defendant's acts. Accordingly, the appeal would be dismissed.

ABKCO Music and Records Inc v Music Collection International Ltd [1995] RPC 657 (Court of Appeal: Neill and Hoffmann LJJ).

679 Infringement—computer software—ownership of copyright

A supplier contracted to supply an agency with computer software. When batch software was installed, the supplier had to sort out a number of defects, but when on-line software was installed, it caused further problems with the batch software. Before the problems were resolved, the contractual arrangements were terminated by consent. On the supplier's action for breach of contract, it had to be decided whether the software supply was covered by one or two contracts. It also brought an action for copyright infringement. The agency argued that it owned the software copyright in equity, it had a right to copy the source code to repair and improve the software and the infringement had been innocent. It counterclaimed for breach of an implied term as to fitness for purpose and for failure to provide support. The parties also disputed whether the supplier's standard terms had been incorporated into any contract. *Held*, (1) there were two contracts; although an outline proposal for on-line software had been made before the parties entered the contract for batch software, it was not included in that contract. (2) The standard conditions were referred to in the first contract and were therefore incorporated. They were not incorporated into the second contract in respect of which they were not mentioned. (3) Although the software was commissioned and designed for the agency's needs specifically, the supplier intended to sell it to others and copyright was not mentioned before the first contract was made. The agency's claim failed. (4) If the contracts had provided for the agency to receive the source code, it would have been impliedly licensed to use it for repair or improvement. In fact, only the provision of the object code had been agreed because that was sufficient to fulfil the functions required. (5) The software was not entirely fit for its purpose and it could not have been the intention for defects to remain. The agency should therefore have limited use of the source code for the purpose of repairing such defects, but any further improvements would infringe the supplier's copyright. (6) The agency knew the standard terms and, on the facts, the defence of innocence failed. (7) The batch software was fit for its purpose when delivered, but was rendered unfit to some extent later. However, when the parties' relationship ended, the agency agreed to accept the software in that condition and the supplier was not then able to render the software fit. (8) An obligation to support did not arise until the software was complete and that stage was never reached.

On the agency's appeal in relation to the software's fitness for purpose, *held*, the supplier had been released from its continuing obligation to complete the contractual task of rectifying any defects. The recorder had been correct and, accordingly, the appeal would be dismissed.

Saphena Computing Ltd v Allied Collection Agencies Ltd [1995] FSR 616 (Queen's Bench Division: Mr Recorder Havery QC), (Court of Appeal: O'Connor, Dillon and Staughton LJJ). *British Leyland Motor Corpn Ltd v Armstrong Patents Co Ltd* [1986] 1 All ER 850, HL (1986 Abr para 440) considered.

680 Infringement—copyright of third party—protection

The plaintiff company, as assignee of the copyright of an author, brought an action against the defendants for infringement of copyright in an adaptation or arrangement of a song which the author had made in 1992. The arrangement was an adaptation of, and dramatically different from, the original song. The defendants contended that, by reason of the absence of any licence from the copyright owner of the original song, the arrangement at the date of its composition in 1992 was an infringing work and that the exploitation of it by the sale of copies of it in the United Kingdom continued to constitute a technical infringement of the rights in the original song so that the plaintiff was precluded from enforcing any rights of copyright against the defendants or alternatively any rights of copyright in respect of the period before a licence was obtained. *Held*, although it was well-established that the court might refuse to enforce copyright on public policy grounds, the mere existence of an infringement of the copyright of a third party, let alone an innocent as opposed to a deliberate infringement, was not sufficient to bring that jurisdiction into play. Accordingly, a plaintiff would be entitled to prevent others pirating his work, even if it infringed the copyright in another work, subject to his obligation to account to the original author for his due share of any recovery. The plaintiff was entitled to enforce its rights of copyright in the arrangement. The court would grant the plaintiff an injunction restraining further infringement. Further, the innocent and technical nature of the infringement and the long inertia of the licensee defeated any attempt by the defendants to invoke the doctrine of clean hands in answer to the plaintiff's claim for an injunction.

ZYX Music GmbH v King [1995] 3 All ER 1 (Chancery Division: Lightman J).

681 Infringement—prohibition on import of goods

The Copyright (EC Measures Relating to Pirated Goods and Abolition of Restrictions on the Import of Goods) Regulations 1995, SI 1995/1445 (in force on 1 July 1995), amend the Copyright, Designs and Patents Act 1988, s 111, which entitles a copyright owner to give notice to the Commissioners of Custom and Excise of infringing material, requesting that it may be treated as prohibited. The regulations limit such requests to goods which arrive in the United Kingdom from outside the European Economic Area or goods from within that area which have not been entered for free circulation. However, this restriction does not apply to goods entered, or expected to be entered, for free circulation, export, re-export or for a suspensive procedure in respect of which an application may be made under Council Regulation (EC) 3295/94, art 3(1) laying down measures to prohibit the release for free circulation, export, re-export or entry for a suspensive procedure of counterfeit or pirated goods.

682   Infringement—remedies—election of remedy—ability of plaintiff to postpone election

In an action for infringement of copyright the plaintiff sought either an inquiry as to damages caused by or an account of profits earned upon the defendant's pleaded infringement, a declaration that the plaintiff was entitled at its election to an assessment of damages or an account of profits and a direction that (1) the defendants furnish within two months a schedule detailing the receipts, costs and sales associated with the infringement; and (2) the plaintiff elect between its remedies within seven days of receipt of that schedule. The issue was thus whether a plaintiff could be forced to elect before he had the information, by means of discovery or otherwise, to make an informed decision. *Held*, in the absence of English authority on the point, it was open to the court to develop a procedure which allowed a plaintiff seeking alternative remedies in such a case to postpone election of the remedy until such time as he had the wherewithal to make an informed choice.

Island Records Ltd v Tring International plc [1995] 3 All ER 444 (Chancery Division: Lightman J). *Minnesota Mining & Manufacturing Co v C Jeffries* [1993] FSR 189, considered.

683   Infringement—substantial reproduction—modified architect's designs

The plaintiffs were associated companies which designed and constructed houses. Their design director (RD) produced some drawings for a standard range of house designs which were passed on to a firm of technical draughtsmen (CH) who, under RD's guidance and supervision, produced drawings of the elevations and floorplans for the new range. Twenty five designs were produced for the new range, each of which was subject to ongoing refinement and modification of a minor nature. One of the plaintiffs' directors left and joined the defendant company which wanted to develop a range of national house designs. He instructed CH to draw design ideas based on the drawings of the plaintiffs' range with amendments. The plaintiffs brought an action for breach of copyright and claimed additional damages under Copyright, Designs and Patents Act 1988, s 97(2) because the infringements had been carried out flagrantly. The defendant claimed that the original drawings by RD must have been based on pre-existing drawings and were therefore not original, that the plaintiffs had to identify the exact drawings which had been infringed because the originals had been modified from time to time and that the plaintiffs were not the owners of the copyright in the drawings. *Held*, in a case where the plaintiff produced many versions of a copyright work, each differing slightly from the others, it would frequently be almost impossible to identify precisely which one was copied by the defendant. However, copying of a substantial part of the design depicted on one drawing would therefore infringe the copyright in that drawing or, if it was not the first in the series, the copyright in the first of the series, unless the design had been profoundly changed over a period of time. Even though RD might have utilised a feature or features from preceding designs, provided an architect had put significant effort and skill into producing a new design with a new combination of features, that new design would be the subject of copyright. RD and CH were joint authors of the work as it was wrong to think that only the person who carried out the mechanical act of fixation was an author. There might well be skill and expertise in drawing clearly and well but that did not mean that it was only that skill and expertise which was relevant. Each had contributed a significant part of the skill and labour protected by the copyright and they were therefore joint authors. On the facts, it was clear there had been an infringement of the copyright in a number of the plaintiffs' designs and judgement would be given accoringly.

It was not necessary for an infringer to be aware that his acts amounted to infringement for an additional award of damages for flagrancy of infringement to be made and, although the court must have regard to such flagrancy and the benefit accruing to the defendant by reason of the infringement, there was no requirement that both or either of those features be present. In the present case, the breach of copyright had been flagrant and additional damages would therefore be awarded.

Even if the court had not found that the plaintiffs owned the copyright in the designs, it would have held that there was an implied term in the contract with CH that the plaintiffs had exclusivity and that the defendant had procured CH to breach that implied exclusivity.

Cala Homes (South) Ltd v Alfred McAlpine Homes East Ltd [1995] FSR 818 (Chancery Division: Laddie J).

684   Offences—confiscation orders

See para 2602.

685 Originality—requirement of skill and labour—photocopy of original design

The defendant produced original designs for use on handmade decorative tiles. After selecting one of the drawings, he photocopied it, enlarging it by ten per cent in the process. The photocopied designs were copied by the plaintiffs on to tins and photograph albums and the defendant successfully brought an action for infringement of copyright. The plaintiff appealed on the ground that copyright did not subsist in the enlarged photocopies. *Held*, the photocopying of his drawings by the defendant did not result in a depiction substantially different from the drawings themselves. In photocopying them he devoted no such skill and labour as conferred originality of an artistic character and the process was wholly mechanical with nothing to suggest that enlargement was for any purpose of that kind. Accordingly, the defendant could not establish copyright in the photocopies and the appeal would be allowed.

The Reject Shop plc v Manners [1995] FSR 870 (Queen's Bench Division: Leggatt LJ and Kay J).

686 Rights in performances—reciprocal protection

The Performances (Reciprocal Protection) (Convention Countries) Order 1995, SI 1995/2990 (in force in part on 15 December 1995 and in part on 1 January 1996), replaces the 1994 Order, SI 1994/264, so as to add Bulgaria, Hungary, Iceland, Jamaica and Moldova to the list of countries enjoying reciprocal protection of rights in performances under the Copyright, Designs and Patents Act 1988, Pt II. The order also makes consequential provision on the entry into force for the United Kingdom of the Agreement Establishing the World Trade Organisation and the reciprocal obligations arising therefrom under the Agreement on Trade-Related Aspects of Intellectual Property Rights, which are to take effect on 1 January 1996.

CORONERS

Halsbury's Laws of England (4th edn) Vol 9, paras 1001–1200

687 Articles

Coroners' Inquests, Anthony Barton: 1 CR 225, 2 CR 25

688 Inquest—duty to summon jury—death occurring abroad

The Coroners Act 1988, s 8(3)(d) provides that if it appears to a coroner, either before he proceeds to hold an inquest or in the course of an inquest begun without a jury, that there is reason to suspect that the death occurred in circumstances the continuance or possible recurrence of which is prejudicial to the health or safety of the public or any section of the public, he must proceed to summon a jury.

It has been held that the 1988 Act, s 8(3)(d) applies to deaths which occur abroad as well as those which occur in England and Wales.

Re Neal (Coroner: Jury) (1995) Times, 9 December (Queen's Bench Division: Staughton LJ and Rougier J).

689 Inquest—examination of witnesses—persons entitled to examine witnesses

The sisters of the deceased sought judicial review of a coroner's decision not to allow them to examine witnesses at an inquest concerning their brother's death. *Held*, by virtue of the Coroner's Rules 1984, SI 1984/552, r 20, a coroner was empowered to decide who was entitled to examine any witness at an inquest. Under r 20(2)(h), a person who, in the coroner's opinion, was a properly interested person, was so entitled. There was a public interest in not excluding anyone who appeared to have a proper interest. Blood relations who had been in contact with the deceased before his death would appear to have such an interest and a coroner would not be expected to take a restrictive approach in respect of close relatives. 'Interested' should not be given a narrow technical meaning; it was not confined to a proprietary right or a financial interest in the deceased's estate but could cover a variety of concerns. 'Properly' imported a notion that the interest must be reasonable and substantial, not trivial or contrived. The coroner would have to be satisfied that the person seeking to examine witnesses was genuinely directed to the scope of the inquest as defined in r 36. The sisters of the deceased should be considered 'properly interested persons'. Accordingly, their application would succeed.

R v HM Coroner for the Southern District of Greater London, ex p Driscoll (1993) 159 JP 45 (Queen's Bench Division: Kennedy LJ and Pill J).

690   Inquest—inquest without a body—exercise of discretion

The Coroners Act 1988, s 15(1) provides that where a coroner has reason to believe that a death has occurred in or near his district in such circumstances that an inquest ought to be held and that, owing to the destruction of the body by fire or otherwise, or to the fact that the body is lying in a place from which it cannot be recovered, an inquest cannot be held, he may report to the Secretary of State. Section 15(2) provides that where such a report is made, the Secretary of State may, if he considers it desirable to do so, direct a coroner to hold an inquest into the death.

The husband of the deceased confessed to the police that he had strangled the deceased and burnt her body in an incinerator. In criminal proceedings, however, his confession was ruled inadmissible, and he was acquitted of murder. Having regard to the 1988 Act, s 15, a coroner reported the matter to the Secretary of State, who decided that an inquest should not be held as it would mean subjecting the husband to a second judicial process which might find that he had in fact murdered the deceased. On the deceased's sister's application for judicial review of the Secretary of State's decision, *held*, a coroner could make a reference to the Secretary of State under the 1988 Act, s 15(1) even if he was not entirely certain that a death had occurred, but merely believed so. As such, in the instant case, the Secretary of State's decision to proceed on the basis that s 15(1) was satisfied, was not irrational or incorrect. Moreover, an inquest was likely to be directed towards a verdict which suggested that the husband had killed the deceased, even though a verdict of unlawful killing would not necessarily be inconsistent with his acquittal. The Secretary of State's discretion under s 15 was very wide, and it was not for the court to substitute its discretion merely because it might have come to a different conclusion had the discretion been vested in the court. Accordingly, the application would be dismissed.

R v Secretary of State for the Home Department, ex p Weatherhead (1995) Times, 19 December (Queen's Bench Division: May J).

691   Inquest—judicial review—coroner's conduct—matters to be taken into consideration—coroner's inquest

A coroner's inquest was held following the death of a doctor's patient. The coroner noticed that there were discrepancies between the doctor's notes and his oral evidence, and questioned the doctor about this when he gave evidence at the inquest. However, the doctor was not warned that he was not bound to answer self-incriminatory questions. At the end of the inquest, the coroner recorded that the patient had died of natural causes brought on by a lack of care. He also referred the matter to the General Medical Council and to the police, as a result of which the doctor was charged with manslaughter and attempting to pervert the course of justice. The doctor successfully applied for leave to apply for judicial review of the inquest and the coroner's conduct of it, but the coroner was granted an adjournment of the substantive hearing of the application pending determination of the criminal proceedings. On the doctor's appeal, *held*, an applicant for judicial review was entitled to have his application heard as soon as reasonably practicable, and a respondent seeking an adjournment of the application had to justify it. Here, the judge had been entitled to take into account whether or not the court would have granted the doctor relief if he had proved that his legal rights in relation to the inquest had been infringed. The doctor's impending criminal trial was also a relevant consideration, and the judge had been entitled to conclude that the judicial review proceedings were likely to be academic whatever the outcome of the criminal proceedings. Moreover, as the Crown Court and the High Court were concerned with different questions of law and fact, it was difficult to see how a declaratory ruling in judicial review proceedings could be used in evidence in the criminal proceedings, or what prejudice would be caused to the doctor if his answers to the coroner's questions were put in evidence in the criminal proceedings. Accordingly, the appeal would be dismissed.

R v Birmingham City Coroner, ex p Najada (1995) Times, 5 December (Neill and Auld LJJ and Sir Iain Glidewell).

692   Inquest—verdict—ingredients for verdict of neglect

The deceased, an inmate at a young offenders institute, hanged himself by a sheet in circumstances where it was likely he was seeking attention. A prison officer had previously seen him standing on a toilet with a sheet around his shoulders. The officer had not taken the matter seriously and had told the deceased to stop messing about. At the inquest, the coroner gave the jury a choice of verdicts to consider but said that they could not return a verdict indicating neglect. The deceased's mother applied to quash the coroner's ruling. *Held*, the Court of Appeal in *R v North Humberside and Scunthorpe, ex p Jamieson* [1994] 3 All ER 972 (1994 Abr para 672) set out the law governing verdicts of neglect. In the present case, the officer had not guarded against the possibility that the deceased's earlier gesture might have resulted in suicide, but that did not amount to an ingredient of neglect. It was possible for a jury to return an adjectival verdict of accident aggravated by lack of care but it was difficult to think of a case where such a verdict would be appropriate. Accordingly, the application would be dismissed.

R v HM Coroner for South Yorkshire (East Division), ex p Tremble (1995) 159 JP 761 (Queen's Bench Division: Owen J).

COUNTY COURTS

Halsbury's Laws of England (4th edn) Vol 10, paras 1–700

693 Articles

Beware the Forgotten Order, Peter Smith (on CCR Ord 9, r 10): 145 NLJ 346
Conduct of Repossession Hearings, Jonathan Armstrong: 139 SJ 449, 476, 505, 527
The Publisher in the Electronic Age: Caught in the Area of Conflict of Copyright and Competition Law, Harald Heker: [1995] EIPR 75
Removing Squatters, Andrew Blower (on the procedure for removing squatters): 139 SJ 1070

694 Automatic directions—timetable—request for hearing date—failure to comply with timetable

The County Court Rules 1981, Ord 17, r 11(3)(d) provides that when pleadings are deemed to be closed, unless a day has already been fixed, the plaintiff must within six months request the proper officer to fix a day for the hearing. By Ord 17, r 11(9), if no such request is made within 15 months of the day on which pleadings are deemed to be closed, the action must be automatically struck out.

The plaintiff commenced proceedings against the defendant for negligence and breach of statutory duty. Fifteen months after the close of pleadings, the plaintiff applied for an extension of the period for requesting a hearing date. A district judge rejected the defendant's submission that the action had to be automatically struck out under Ord 17, r 11(9). He instead decided that the request for an extension of the 15-month time limit was an implied request for a hearing date to be fixed, even though the plaintiff had not filed a note giving an estimate of the length of the trial and the number of witnesses, as required by Ord 17, r 11(8). The decision was upheld on appeal. On the defendant's further appeal, *held*, a request for a hearing date was not invalid merely because the requirements of Ord 17, r 11(8) were not satisfied, as there was no particular form in which the request had to be made. However, it was advisable for a plaintiff applying for an extension of the 15-month period to put in his notice of application, in the alternative, a request for a hearing date to be fixed. Accordingly, the appeal would be dismissed.

Ferreira v American Embassy Employees' Association (1995) Times, 30 June (Court of Appeal: Nourse, Roch and Hutchison LJJ).

In her claim for damages for personal injuries, the plaintiff failed to comply with the automatic directions provided by CCR Ord 17, r 11(3), by which she should have given discovery, filed a statement of special damage with her particulars of claim, disclosed experts' reports and witness statements within the prescribed time and requested a hearing date within six months of the date on which the timetable began to operate. Nevertheless, within the 15-month period of the date on which pleadings were deemed to have closed, she requested a hearing date. The defendants sought to have the request struck out on the ground that the plaintiff had failed to comply with Ord 17, r 11 and that it was an abuse of process. *Held*, in a case governed by Ord 17, r 11, the mere failure to comply with the rules did not amount to an abuse of process because a 15-month limit, applicable in nearly every case, had been applied to the possible period of delay. Further, it could not have been intended that, where there had been compliance with Ord 17, r 11(3)(d) within that time limit, the court had repeatedly to investigate the reasons for an earlier failure to comply with the time limits for complying with automatic directions. Although the plaintiff had not even substantially complied with the rules, her conduct did not amount to an abuse of process. Accordingly, the defendants' application would be dismissed.

Ashworth v McKay Foods Ltd (1995) Times, 16 November (Court of Appeal: Sir Thomas Bingham MR, Henry and Thorpe LJJ).

695 Central London County Court Business List—transfer of proceedings—value of claim

See para 2386.

696 Committal order—penal notice—indorsement—procedure

The applicant, who was a local authority tenant, sought an order requiring the local authority to carry out certain works to his accommodation. At the court hearing, the local authority's representative consented to the order being made but left the court before consenting to a penal notice being attached to the order, which would have named a particular local authority officer as the individual liable for committal in the event that the order was not obeyed. The court clerk refused to indorse a penal notice on the order without leave of the judge, and the judge refused to indorse a penal notice without the local authority's express consent. On the applicant's application for judicial review of the decision, *held*, the indorsement of a penal notice on an order which the court had made was a mandatory act, for which there was no discretion. An individual did not have to be named in a penal notice in order to create contingent liability for committal for contempt, as it was service of the order on him that was necessary to bring the order's existence to his attention and to place him under an obligation not to frustrate it. Where an individual was to be named, the party in whose favour the order had been granted had to obtain a direction to that effect from a county court judge or a district judge, with or without the respondent's consent. Accordingly, the application would be granted.

R v Wandsworth County Court, ex p Munn (1994) 26 HLR 697 (Queen's Bench Division: Sedley J).

697 Costs—late application to adjourn—lack of preparation by solicitors

See *Trobridges v Walker*, para 705.

698 County Court—dress

See para 717.

699 County Court Rules

The County Court (Amendment) Rules 1995, SI 1995/969 (in force on 30 April 1995), further amend the 1981 Rules, SI 1981/1687, by altering the procedure, under CCR Ord 25, r 7, to be followed where a warrant of execution is issued in one court and sent to another court for execution.

The County Court (Amendment No 2) Rules 1995, SI 1995/1582 (in force on 24 August 1995, further amend the 1981 Rules, SI 1981/1687, by inserting Ord 24, Pt II, which sets out a procedure for obtaining an interim possession order in summary proceedings for possession, and by conferring on district judges jurisdiction to make possession orders in summary proceedings under Ord 24, Pt I.

The County Court (Amendment No 3) Rules 1995, SI 1995/2838 (in force in part on 1 December 1995 and in part on 8 January 1996), further amend the 1981 Rules, SI 1981/1687, by (1) increasing the small claims limit from £1,000 to £3,000, except in relation to personal injury actions, (2) amending the small claims procedure, (3) providing for the taxation of costs where a conditional fee agreement has been made, and (4) revising the costs provisions and increasing witness allowances and fixed costs.

The County Court (Amendment No 4) Rules 1995, SI 1995/3277 (in force on 8 January 1996), further amend the 1981 Rules, SI 1981/1687, by (1) inserting a rule to enable a litigant in proceedings which are referred automatically to arbitration to recover a sum in respect of legal advice for making or defending a claim for an injunction, an order for specific performance or similar relief; (2) increasing from £112.50 to £200 the sum allowed in respect of the fees of an expert in small claims; and (3) stating, for the purpose of clarification, that an application to set aside an award made in the absence of a party must be made to the court and not to the arbitrator who gave the award.

700 County Court Rules—forms

The County Court (Forms) (Amendment) Rules 1995, SI 1995/970 (in force on 30 April 1995), further amend the 1982 Rules, SI 1982/586, by substituting a new Form N42(c) (warrant of execution), and changing references in Forms N30(CCBC) (judgment for plaintiff (in default)) and N30(1)(CCBC) (judgment for plaintiff (acceptance of offer)) to 'National Girobank' to 'Girobank plc'.

The County Court (Forms) (Amendment No 2) Rules 1995, SI 1995/1583 (in force on 24 August 1995), further amend the 1982 Rules, SI 1982/586, by inserting forms for use in proceedings for an interim possession order.

The County Court (Forms) (Amendment No 3) Rules 1995, SI 1995/2839 (in force on 8 January 1996), further amend the 1982 Rules, SI 1982/586, by substituting a new form of summons and of defence, namely, Forms N1, N1(D), NI (SPC), N2, N3, N4, N9B, N9B(SPC), N10(HP/CCA), N96 and N98, and a new Form N92 (application for administration order), (all as a consequence of the increase in the small claims limit), and by revising a note concerning the notices of hearing in arbitrations.

The County Court (Forms) (Amendment No 4) Rules 1995, SI 1995/3278 (in force on 8 January 1996), further amend the 1982 Rules, SI 1982/586, in order to make amendments to the new form of summons and a form of defence (Form N9) introduced by SI 1995/2839.

701 Default action—agreement to extend time—striking out of action

Each plaintiff had commenced an action for personal injuries in the county court by default summons and had agreed with the defendant to extend time generally for service of the defence extending, in one case, to the service of the particulars of claim. Twelve months had elapsed from the date of service of the summons without delivery of admission, defence or counterclaim or the entry of judgment. It fell to be determined whether the actions should be struck out under CCR 1981, Ord 9, r 10. *Held*, under Ord 9, r 10, no enlargement of the period of 12 months from service of a default summons could be granted under Ord 13, r 4. That must mean that the court's ordinary power of retrospective extension under Ord 13, r 4(2) was excluded but the court's power of prospective extension under Ord 13, r 4(1) was not necessarily excluded because Ord 9, r 10 was not directed to the period before 12 months had expired. When a plaintiff agreed to extend a defendant's time for serving a defence, whether indefinitely or indefinitely subject to notice, or for a definite period, he was in effect agreeing not to enter judgment in default of defence during whatever period was agreed. Although an agreement between the parties could not always override or circumvent a procedural rule, Ord 9, r 10 did not form part of a coherent code giving the court control of the progress of litigation. An agreement that time for defence should be generally extended had the effect of ousting Ord 9, r 10. Accordingly, the present actions could not be struck out under that rule.

Heer v Tutton; Pickles v Holdsworth; Lovell v Porter [1995] 4 All ER 547 (Court of Appeal: Sir Thomas Bingham MR, Peter Gibson and Saville LJJ).

Where 12 months have expired from the date of service of a default summons and no admission, defence or counterclaim has been delivered and judgment has not been entered against the defendant, the action must be struck out: CCR 1981, Ord 9, r 10.

The plaintiff commenced an action for personal injuries by default summons against the defendant employers. Brief particulars of his claim were included. No defence was delivered by the defendants and the plaintiff did not deliver detailed particulars of his claim until 18 months later. The defendants sought to have the action struck out, contending that as their defence was not served until 18 months after the issue of the summons and no default judgment had been entered, the action should automatically have been struck out after 12 months. *Held*, Ord 9, r 10 stated clearly that, if at the end of 12 months from the date of service of a default summons, neither party had taken any further steps in the action, and if there had been no order or agreement extending time for delivery of defence and if no judgment had been entered against the defendant, the action had then to be struck out. The rule was mandatory; it applied automatically even if further steps were taken after the end of the 12-month period. Accordingly, the action would be struck out.

Webster v Ellison Circlips Group Ltd [1995] 4 All ER 556 (Court of Appeal: Glidewell, Simon Brown and Peter Gibson LJJ).

The plaintiff brought proceedings against the defendant following a road traffic accident. The plaintiff's solicitor and the defendant's insurers agreed in a telephone conversation that, if the insurer sent the plaintiff an interim payment, the plaintiff's solicitor would take no further court action and there would be no need to file a defence. An interim payment was made and during the following 13 months, negotiations continued in relation to medical evidence with a view to finalising the medical position. The insurer then informed the plaintiff's solicitor that the plaintiff's action had been struck out under CCR, Ord 9, r 10 and that no further offers would be made to the plaintiff. The plaintiff's solicitors applied for the action to proceed notwithstanding the expiration of the time limit under Ord 9, r 10. *Held*, Ord 9, r 10 operated in every case to automatically strike out a claim which had not been pursued by the plaintiff within the 12-month period. However, where a defendant sought, and the plaintiff agreed to, an extension of time for filing a defence the operation of Ord 9, r 10 could be usurped. It was clearly contrary to any view of justice that, by virtue of the defendant's own prevarication which the plaintiff had consented to in good faith, the defendant could escape liability. Accordingly, the application would be allowed.

McKie v Shad Ford Trucks (24 November 1995, unreported) (Birkenhead County Court: District Judge Travers) (Kindly submitted for publication by Michael W Halsall, Solicitors). *Heer v Tutton*; *Pickles v Holdsworth*; *Lovell v Porter* (1995) Times, 5 June, CA (para 701) considered.

702 Districts—delimitation of districts

The Civil Courts (Amendment) Order 1995, SI 1995/1897 (in force in part on 29 September 1995 and in part on 27 October 1995), amends the 1983 Order, SI 1983/713, so as to close the county courts at Wisbech and Market Drayton.

The Civil Courts (Amendment) (No 2) Order 1995, SI 1995/3173 (in force in part on 29 December 1995 and in part on 2 January 1996), further amends the 1983 Order, SI 1983/713, by closing the Bargoed, Barry, Cardigan, Llandrindod Wells and Otley County Courts and transferring the County Court at Brentwood to Basildon.

703 Divorce county courts

See DIVORCE.

704 Fees

The County Court Fees (Amendment) Order 1995, SI 1995/2627 (in force on 30 October 1995), further amends the 1982 Order, SI 1982/1706, by (1) removing exemption from payment of court fees from those in receipt of income support who are also in receipt of civil legal aid, (2) setting a flat fee of £65 on non-money claims, regardless of whether such a claim is linked to a money claim; (3) replacing, with fee bands, the 10p per £ plaint fee scale; (4) replacing, with lower fees for users of the County Court Bulk Centre, the 15p per £ fee scale on issue of warrants of execution with fee bands; (5) replacing, with a flat fee of £80, with no additional fee for a money claim, the scale of fees payable on issue of warrants of delivery and possession; (6) abolishing the additional fee payable for a warrant of delivery or possession where the recovery of a sum of money is also sought; (7) replacing, with a flat fee of £50, the fee of 10p per £ payable on issue of an attachment of earnings application; (8) increasing, from 5p to 10p, the fee payable on dividends; (9) increasing, to £1 per page, the fee for copies of documents; (10) increasing, from £20 to £25, the fee on issue of a debtor's petition in bankruptcy; (11) increasing the fee on issue of a creditor's petition in bankruptcy; (12) increasing, from £50 to £55, the fee on issue of any other petition under the Companies Act 1985 or Insolvency Act 1986; (13) increasing, from £15 to £20, the fee on the hearing of an application under the 1985 Act or the 1986 Act before a district judge; and (14) abolishing the fee payable on the hearing of a public examination.

705 Hearing—fixed date—application to adjourn

One month before the date fixed for the hearing of an action, the defendant's solicitors advised the plaintiff's solicitors that their client would be abroad visiting relatives during the month of the hearing and furthermore would be unlikely to be available the month after that. The plaintiff's solicitors agreed to an adjournment and the matter was listed for hearing at a later date. In the month before the new hearing date the defendant's solicitors notified the plaintiff's solicitors that the defendant would again be abroad on the date of the hearing, this time on holiday. The plaintiff's solicitors indicated by letter that they would not consent to a further adjournment and inquired whether or not the defendant's solicitors had been aware of their client's holiday arrangements when the matter was being relisted. The defendant's solicitors produced the holiday booking form which showed that the defendant's holiday was in fact booked after the matter had been relisted. It was claimed that the booking had been made by members of the defendant's family without his knowledge. The plaintiff's solicitors again indicated their refusal to agree to an adjournment and, since no application to adjourn had apparently been made and since no documents were forthcoming from the defendant's solicitors, despite repeated requests, the plaintiff's solicitors proceeded to lodge the trial bundles with the court. Four days before the hearing date the defendant's solicitors informed the plaintiff's solicitors of their application to adjourn. At the hearing of the application the plaintiff's solicitors maintained that it should have been made earlier. *Held*, the only merit of the defendant's solicitors' application was that judgment would almost inevitably have been entered against the defendant had the matter proceeded on the date fixed, since he was not in the country. As soon as the defendant's solicitors had become aware that the plaintiff's solicitors did not consent to an application to adjourn they should have made an application to take the matter out of the list; there was nothing in the correspondence between the parties which could excuse the defendant's solicitors' failure to do so. It was a duty of solicitors to ensure that court hearings were attended. In the present case, the application would have to be granted because of the risk of injustice to the defendant, but it would be granted only because the defendant was already abroad. However, the defendant's solicitors would be ordered to pay the plaintiff's solicitors' costs of the application and the costs of trial thrown away.

Trobridges v Walker (6 September 1995, unreported) (Plymouth County Court: Judge J E Previte QC). *Joyce v King* (1987) Times, 13 July, CA (1987 Abr para 2078) and *Fowkes v Duthie* [1991] 1 All ER 337n (1990 Abr para 1872) considered. (Kindly submitted for publication by H Davies, of Trobridges, Solicitors, Plymouth).

706 Judgment—judgment in absence of party to proceedings—application by party to set aside judgment—interference with judge's exercise of discretion

A building society sought an order for possession of the appellant's business premises, charged as security for a mortgage loan, when he fell into repayment arrears. The appellant failed to attend the four-day hearing and the building society was granted an order in his absence. The appellant applied under CCR, Ord 37, r 2 to set aside the order, asserting that he missed the first two days of the hearing because court officials misled him as to the date of the hearing. He had arrived at court on the third day, but made no application to the judge and left. At first instance, the judge concluded that on the third day the appellant had deliberately chosen not to apply for a re-hearing and refused to set aside judgment. On appeal, *held*, a party's prima facie right to have the action heard in his presence had to be circumscribed by pragmatic considerations. The following matters were to be considered: (1) where a party with notice of proceedings disregarded the opportunity of participating in the trial, he would normally be bound by the decision; (2) where judgment had been given, the absent party's explanation for his absence was most important; unless it was not deliberate, but due to accident or mistake, the court would be unlikely to allow a rehearing; (3) where setting aside judgment would entail a complete retrial on matters of fact which the court had already investigated, the application would not be granted unless there were very strong reasons for doing so; (4) the court would not consider setting aside judgment regularly obtained unless the applicant enjoyed real prospects of success; (5) whether the successful party would be prejudiced by the judgment being set aside, especially if he could not be protected against the financial consequences; (6) there was a public interest in there being an end to litigation and in not having the court's time occupied by plurality of litigation. In the circumstances of the present case, there was no ground for disturbing the judge's exercise of discretion and, accordingly, the appeal would be dismissed.

National Counties Building Society v Antonelli (1995) Independent, 30 November (Court of Appeal: Stuart-Smith, Otton and Pill LJJ).

707 Jurisdiction—transfer of proceedings to High Court—adoption hearing—ratification of placement otherwise prohibited

See *Re G (a Minor) (Adoption: Illegal Placement)*, para 344.

708 Jurisdiction—transfer of proceedings to High Court—application for disqualification order in respect of company director

See *Re NP Engineering and Security Products Ltd,* para 477.

709 Person under disability—claim on behalf of person under disability—payment—approval of court

The plaintiff, an adult under disability, obtained judgment against a council for damages for personal injury. The council sought to have the judgment set aside and the plaintiff's claim struck out on the ground that, in an earlier action brought by the plaintiff's mother, a council tenant, against the council, the damages awarded to the mother included compensation for the plaintiff's loss. *Held,* the plaintiff's dependence on her mother did not create such a nexus between them that they could be regarded as the same party. Accordingly, the plea of res judicata did not apply. By virtue of CCR Ord 10, rr 10, 11, where money was claimed by a person under disability, no settlement, compromise or payment should be valid without the approval of the court. The principle that an unlitigated monetary claim was barred if it could have been advanced and established in earlier proceedings could not be extended to persons who were not party to the earlier proceedings. The doctrine of res judicata had no application in the present proceedings. The practice whereby, in proceedings brought by a council tenant alone, settlement was reached on behalf of the tenant's family, should cease because it ignored the effect of Ord 10, rr 10, 11 and might disadvantage those under disability in the family. The council's application would be dismissed.

Chin v Hackney London Borough Council (1995) Independent, 16 November (Court of Appeal: Butler-Sloss, Simon Brown and Saville LJJ).

710 Remedies—prescribed relief

The County Court Remedies (Amendment) Regulations 1995, SI 1995/206 (in force on 1 February 1995), amend the 1991 Regulations, SI 1991/1222, by providing that where proceedings are to be or are included in the Central London County Court Business List and the application is made to a circuit judge nominated by the senior presiding judge, an interlocutory injunction restraining a party from removing assets from the jurisdiction of the High Court or dealing with assets may be granted.

711 Service of process—summons—extension of time limit for service—discretion

CCR Ord 7, r 10A(1) provides that in an action for personal injuries, the summons may be served in accordance with the provisions of r 7 by the plaintiff's solicitor sending it by first-class post to the defendant at the address stated in the summons. Ord 13, r 4 provides that the period within which a person is required or authorised to do any act in any proceedings may be extended by the court on the application of any party.

The plaintiff was injured in a road traffic accident, and sought to claim damages for personal injuries from the defendant. As the defendant was uninsured, the Motor Insurers' Bureau ('the bureau') dealt with the claim. Relying on Ord 7, r 10A(1), the plaintiff issued a summons and served it at the defendant's last-known address, as his address was otherwise unknown. When no response was received, the plaintiff obtained judgment in default. Having been informed of the judgment, the bureau applied for service of the summons on the defendant and the default judgment to be set aside. The plaintiff applied for leave to extend the time limit for service of the summons, and was granted a 12-month extension. On the bureau's appeal, *held,* before an extension of time for service would be granted under Ord 13, r 4, an applicant had to explain why he had failed to comply with the relevant time limit and show good reason why he should be granted relief. Here, there had been difficulty in finding any address at which the defendant could be personally served. Although the plaintiff had attempted to surmount the problem by serving the summons at the defendant's last-known address, it was subsequently decided that that could not be done as it was a defendant's actual address at the date of issue of the summons that had to be stated on the summons. The plaintiff therefore had a good explanation for why he had not complied with the relevant time limit. In addition, the plaintiff had at all times kept the bureau informed of his intention to issue proceedings and of his actions in that respect, and there was no prejudice to the bureau in granting the relief sought. It was in the interests of justice to grant an extension of time for service of the summons and, accordingly, the appeal would be dismissed.

Blanksby v Turner [1995] PIQR P272 (Court of Appeal: Hobhouse and Merritt LJJ). *Willowgreen Limited v Smithers* [1994] 1 WLR 832, CA (1993 Abr para 646) followed.

712 Service of process—summons—service by post—address

Proceedings in respect of a road traffic accident were issued three years after the occurrence of the accident and were served at the defendant's last known address although it was clear that the defendant had not resided at that address for some time. Judgment in default was entered against the defendant who successfully applied to have the judgment set aside on the grounds that there had not been proper service. The plaintiff appealed. *Held*, the appeal turned on the court's residual discretion to extend the validity of proceedings following defective service, so as to allow for good service to be effected thereafter. The County Court Rules had never allowed service of an originating process to be effected by posting it to a person's last-known address. *Willowgreen Ltd v Smithers* had further shown that the address to be stated in a request for summons was the defendant's current address. Moreover, if the time for service was extended, this would lead to the conclusion that a defendant would be deprived of a Limitation Act defence which he would have had if proceedings had been begun afresh. Accordingly, the appeal would be dismissed.

Mather v Adesuyi and the Motor Insurers' Bureau [1995] PIQR P454 (Court of Appeal: Simon Brown and Millett LJJ). *Willowgreen Ltd v Smithers* [1994] 2 All ER 533, CA (1993 Abr para 646) followed, *Blanksby v Turner* [1995] PIQR P 272, CA distinguished.

713 Small claims—automatic referral to arbitration—interlocutory orders—appeals

It has been held that CCR Ord 13 (applications and orders in the course of proceedings) applies to interlocutory orders made in arbitration hearings and that therefore a judge has jurisdiction under Ord 13 to hear appeals against such orders.

Pickard v Centrewest London Buses (17 October 1995, unreported) (Uxbridge County Court: Judge Marcus Edwards). Kindly submitted for publication by Tracey McLevy, Barrister.

714 Small claims—automatic referral to arbitration—tenant's claim for landlord's breach of repairing obligation

In proceedings in which two tenants claimed damages against their landlords for breach of repairing obligations, a question arose as to whether such claims falling within the county court financial limit were automatically subject to the small claims arbitration procedure. *Held*, in resolving claims referred for arbitration under CCR 1981, Ord 19, district judges had jurisdiction to grant specific performance or other injunctive relief. The small claims arbitration procedure was the norm for the disposal of small and relatively simple claims. Claims made by tenants to enforce their landlord's implied repairing obligations under the Landlord and Tenant Act 1985, s 11 could not form any general exception. Section 17, which empowered the court to order specific performance of a landlord's repairing obligations, envisaged that the court dealing with that claim would have jurisdiction to grant specific performance. In cases where, in spite of the smallness of the claim, justice could not be done to an unrepresented claimant under the arbitration procedure, trial might be ordered.

Joyce v Liverpool City Council; Wynne v Liverpool City Council [1995] 3 All ER 110 (Court of Appeal: Sir Thomas Bingham MR, Hirst and Aldous LJJ).

715 Trial—allegation of fraud—right to trial with a jury

Under the County Courts Act 1984, s 66(3)(a), the proceedings will be tried with a jury where the court is satisfied that there is in issue a charge of fraud against any party to the proceedings making an application to the court for trial by jury.

The plaintiff sought reimbursement from the defendant company in respect of travellers cheques issued by it which the plaintiff claimed had been lost or stolen. In the pleadings the defendant made an allegation of fraud against the plaintiff. On the basis of that allegation, the plaintiff applied for the proceedings to be tried with a jury pursuant to the 1984 Act, s 66(3)(a). The defendant, relying on *Barclays Bank Ltd v Cole* [1966] 3 All ER 948, CA, argued that it was not a case that could be tried with a jury. The judge ordered that the proceedings be tried with a jury. On the defendant's appeal, *held*, in *Barclays Bank Ltd v Cole* the court decided that 'a charge of fraud' amounted to an actionable deceit and the court was bound by that decision. There was no actionable deceit in the present case as the defendant had not acted to its detriment. Accordingly, a charge of fraud was not in issue in the plaintiff's case and the appeal would be allowed.

Grant v Travellers Cheque Associates Ltd (1995) Times, 19 April (Court of Appeal: McCowan and Ward LJJ and Sir Roger Parker).

COURTS

Halsbury's Laws of England (4th edn) Vol 10, paras 701–1000

716 Articles

Access to Justice and Alternatives to Courts: European Procedural Justice Compared, Erhard
   Blankenburg: [1995] 14 CJQ 176
Allocating Family Law Cases, Paul Tain: 139 SJ 192
Appeals by Case Stated From the Magistrates' Court, Alan Murdie: 139 SJ 984
Applications for Pre-Legal Aid Certificates Costs—A Lawful Order? James N R Parry: 159 JP
   Jo 104
Are There Any Clothes for the Emperor to Wear? Michael Zander (on the Woolf Inquiry into
   the civil justice system): 145 NLJ 154
The Courts and Foreign Currency Obligations, Steven Stern: [1995] LMCLQ 494
Essays on the Woolf Report, Michael Zander: 145 NLJ 1866
Findings and Reasons—Easing the Burden, Peter Dawson and Robert Stevens: 159 JP Jo 483
Judicial Education on Equality, Livingston Armytage (on educating the judiciary about sex and
   race equality): 58 MLR 160
The Jurisdiction of Summary Courts to Try Children and Young Offenders, FG Davies: 159 JP
   Jo 787, 803
Technology and the Courts, Peter Fallon: 145 NLJ 10
Televising the Courts: An Appraisal of the Scots Experiment, Roderick Munday: 159 JP Jo 37,
   57.
Waffle Free Zones? Gordon Exall (on the intended effect of Lord Taylor's and Sir Richard
   Scott's Practice Direction on Civil Litigation: Case Management): 139 SJ 109
Will Woolf Work? Steven Gee (on Lord Woolf's Inquiry): 139 SJ 674
Woolf's Justice, Ramnik Shah (on Lord Woolf's Inquiry): 145 NLJ 147

717 Advocates—court dress

Lord Taylor of Gosforth CJ has issued the following *Practice Direction* ([1995] 1 WLR 648).
   1. Following *Practice Direction* ([1994] 1 WLR 1056) (1994 Abr para 690), views were sought
from organisations and individuals closely concerned with the working of the court on the dress
appropriate for advocates, in light of the extension to rights of audience under the Courts and
Legal Services Act 1990. There was no consensus among those who responded, but a majority
want the wearing of wigs to be discontinued in the future if not immediately.
   2. Solicitors who appear as advocates in courts in which they have traditionally enjoyed rights
of audience, namely courts in Scotland, county courts, crown courts and, previously, quarter
sessions have not worn wigs.
   3. Against that background, the practice of wearing wigs is not to be extended, and the
requirements of *Practice Direction* ([1994] 1 WLR 1056) are reaffirmed.
   4. Queen's Counsel must wear a short wig and a silk or stuff gown over a court coat, junior
counsel must wear a short wig and stuff gown with bands, and solicitors must wear a black stuff
gown with bands but no wigs.
   5. This *Practice Direction* applies throughout the Supreme Court, including the Crown Court
and in county courts.

718 County courts

See COUNTY COURTS.

719 Court of Appeal—appeal from Court of Appeal—refusal of certificate—second
application

See *R v Tang*, para 749.

720 Court of Appeal—practice directions

See PRACTICE AND PROCEDURE.

721 Employment Appeal Tribunal

See EMPLOYMENT.

722 European Court of Human Rights

See HUMAN RIGHTS.

723 European Court of Justice

See EUROPEAN COMMUNITIES.

724 High Court—judges—acting judge—retirement age

The Supreme Court Act 1981, s 9(1) lists the persons who may act as a judge of a specified court, or act as a judge of a division of a particular court, on the request of the Lord Chancellor. Section 9(1A) (as inserted by the Judicial Pensions and Retirement Act 1993, Sch 6, para 5(1)) provides that such a person must not act as a judge after the day on which he attains the age of 75. The 1993 Act, s 27(1) provides that a person may act as if he had not ceased to hold office for the purpose of continuing to deal with, giving judgment in, or dealing with any ancillary matter relating to any case begun before him before he ceased to hold that office. Section 27(4) provides that if and to the extent that the prohibition on holding office after the age of 75 would not be regarded as a prohibition on the holding of an office, it is to be treated as if it were a prohibition, and references in s 27 to office, or to vacating or otherwise ceasing to hold office, are to be construed accordingly.

An acting judge who was in the course of hearing a High Court action, was already over the maximum retiring age for judges when the 1993 Act came into force, but he delivered judgment thereafter. The applicant, who was the unsuccessful plaintiff in the proceedings, applied for judicial review of the Lord Chancellor's decision to permit or instruct the acting judge to continue sitting as a High Court judge after the 1993 Act came into force. In particular, he argued that the 1993 Act prohibited the acting judge from completing the case, because the post of acting judge was not an 'office' for the purposes of the 1993 Act, s 27(1). *Held*, although the post of acting judge was not expressly described in the 1993 Act as a relevant office, the 1993 Act, s 27(4) stated that the prohibition on being an acting judge was to be treated as a prohibition on holding an office. As such, s 27(1) applied to an acting judge, and the acting judge in the instant case was therefore authorised to finish conducting the action. Accordingly, the application would be dismissed.

R v Lord Chancellor, ex p Stockler (1995) Times, 4 December (Queen's Bench Division: Staughton LJ and Rougier J).

725 House of Lords—practice directions

See PRACTICE AND PROCEDURE.

726 Judicial Pensions and Retirement Act 1993—commencement

The Judicial Pensions and Retirement Act 1993 (Commencement) Order 1995, SI 1995/631, brings the Act into force on 31 March 1995. For a summary of the Act, see 1993 Abr para 1926. For details of commencement, see the commencement table in the title STATUTES.

727 Judicial pensions—additional benefits for disregarded earnings

The Judicial Pensions (Additional Benefits for Disregarded Earnings) Regulations 1995, SI 1995/640 (in force on 31 March 1995), provide for the timing, manner and clawback of payments of benefit under the Judicial Pensions and Retirement Act 1993, s 19, which enables judicial officers to derive pensions benefits from their earnings above the level of the pensions cap.

728 Judicial pensions—additional voluntary contributions

The Judicial Pensions (Additional Voluntary Contributions) Regulations 1995, SI 1995/639 (in force on 31 March 1995), provide for the payment of voluntary contributions by members of the pension scheme constituted by the Judicial Pensions and Retirement Act 1993, Pt I and members of existing judicial pension schemes towards the cost of additional benefits under their respective schemes.

729 Judicial pensions—appeals

The Judicial Pensions (Appeals) Regulations 1995, SI 1995/635 (in force on 31 March 1995), provide for the manner in which, and the time within which, appeals under the Judicial Pensions and Retirement Act 1993, s 20, and other specified enactments, against decisions of the administrators of certain judicial and other pension schemes are to be brought.

730 Judicial pensions—contributions—surviving spouses' and children's pensions

The Judicial Pensions (Contributions) Regulations 1995, SI 1995/638 (in force on 31 March 1995), prescribe the contributions to be made by qualifying office holders towards surviving spouses' and children's pensions payable under the Judicial Pensions and Retirement Act 1993.

The Judicial Pensions (Contributions) (Amendment) Regulations 1995, SI 1995/2961 (in force on 11 December 1995), amend SI 1995/638 supra so as to apply the provisions relating to refunds to office-holders to whom the pension scheme constituted under the Judicial Pensions and Retirement Act 1993, Pt I, applies by virtue of s 1(1)(d) of the 1993 Act, as well as those to whom it applies by virtue of s 1(1)(b).

731 Judicial pensions—guaranteed minimum pension

The Judicial Pensions (Guaranteed Minimum Pension etc) Order 1995, SI 1995/2647 (in force on 1 November 1995), modifies the scheme constituted by the Judicial Pensions and Retirement Act 1993, Pt I to enable it to meet the contracting-out requirements of the Pension Schemes Act 1993. The order confers on an office holder and his surviving spouse the right to receive a pension of not less than the guaranteed minimum pension calculated in accordance with the Pension Schemes Act 1993, and provides for the payment of contributions in respect of a surviving spouse's pension that may become payable by virtue of the order where the office holder marries after retirement. The order also amends the Judicial Pensions (Requisite Benefits) Order 1988, SI 1988/1420, in relation to the payment of contributions in respect of widow's pensions that may become payable by virtue of the 1988 Order where the office holder marries after retirement. The 1995 Order provides that the period of relevant service to be taken into account for the purpose of calculating the contribution to the widow's pension must not extend beyond the day appointed under the Pensions Act 1995 after which contracted out service will cease to earn rights to a guaranteed minimum pension or widow's guaranteed minimum pension.

732 Judicial pensions—miscellaneous provisions

The Judicial Pensions (Miscellaneous) Regulations 1995, SI 1995/632 (in force on 31 March 1995), set out the circumstances in which, and the conditions subject to which, a person holding a qualifying judicial office may elect for the Judicial Pensions Act 1993, Pt I (new arrangements for judicial pensions) to apply to him. The regulations also prescribe the formula for determining the annual rate of a judicial pension under the new arrangements where the appropriate annual rate is to be actuarially reduced in certain specified cases, and make provision for cases in which a member of the judicial pension scheme constituted under the new arrangements is appointed to qualifying judicial office but fails to work for a period of 12 consecutive months before ceasing to participate in the scheme. Provision is also made for the calculation of the pensionable pay of a person who is a member of the scheme but who works, or has worked, on a part-time basis only.

733 Judicial pensions—preservation of benefits

The Judicial Pensions (Preservation of Benefits) Order 1995, SI 1995/634 (in force on 31 March 1995), makes provision for reduced pensions, lump sums, surviving spouses' and children's pensions to be preserved and become payable in the case of members of the pension scheme constituted under the Judicial Pensions and Retirement Act 1993, Pt I who cease to hold qualifying office before reaching normal pension age.

734 Judicial pensions—qualifying judicial offices—City of London

The Judicial Pensions (Qualifying Judicial Offices etc) (City of London) Order 1995, SI 1995/633 (in force on 31 March 1995), amends the Judicial Pensions and Retirement Act 1993, Sch 1, Pt I so as to add the offices of Recorder of London and Common Serjeant to the list of judicial offices which may be qualifying judicial offices for the purposes of the new arrangements for judicial pensions contained in the 1993 Act, Pt I.

735 Judicial pensions—transfer between schemes

The Judicial Pensions (Transfer Between Judicial Pension Schemes) Regulations 1995, SI 1995/636 (in force on 31 March 1995), provide for the valuation of benefits transferred between existing judicial pension schemes and the pension scheme constituted by the Judicial Pensions and Retirement Act 1993, Pt I, including benefits arising out of voluntary contributions.

736 Judicial pensions—transfer of accrued benefits

The Judicial Pensions (Transfer of Accrued Benefits) Regulations 1995, SI 1995/637 (in force on 31 March 1995), deal with the transfer of accrued benefits between non-judicial pension schemes and the schemes constituted by the Judicial Pensions and Retirement Act 1993, Pt I and s 19 under Sch 2. The regulations prescribe the requirements to be satisfied by the non-judicial schemes, the limits on payments into and the type of benefits to be provided under the 1993 Act schemes, for the calculation of cash equivalents on a transfer out of those schemes, and the calculation of an annual pension and derivative benefits to reflect the transfer payments into those schemes.

737 Judicial retirement—retirement age of General Commissioners

The Retirement Age of General Commissioners Order 1995, SI 1995/3192 (in force on 1 January 1996), amends the Judicial Pensions and Retirement Act 1993, Sch 5 so as to add the office of General Commissioner to the list of judicial offices in respect of which there is a maximum retirement age of 70 years.

738 Magistrates' courts

See MAGISTRATES.

739 Practice and procedure directions

See CRIMINAL EVIDENCE AND PROCEDURE; PRACTICE AND PROCEDURE.

740 Transfer of proceedings—Chancery Division to Queen's Bench Division—action brought by Lloyd's names

See *Deeny v Littlejohn & Co (a firm); Deeny v Walker*, para 1735.

CRIMINAL EVIDENCE AND PROCEDURE

Halsbury's Laws of England (4th edn) Vol 11(1) (reissue), paras 1–800, Vol 11(2) (reissue), paras 801–1592

741 Articles

Accountability and the Crown Prosecution Service, Sybil Sharpe: 159 JP Jo 731

Amendments to the Codes, Michael Cousens (on changes to the PACE code): LS Gaz, 5 April, p 18

Arrest Without Warrant, Sze Ping-Fat: 159 JP Jo 837

Assessment and Rehabilitation in Brain Injury, Colin Hedley (on importance of assessment by an expert body): 145 NLJ 186

Beat the Defence, Neil Addison (on the right to silence in police interviews): Police Review, 14 April 1995, p 20

Beating the Bandits, Gloria B Hughes (on custody officers having a greater say on bail conditions): Police Review, 13 January 1995, p 16

BEST and the Legal Profession, Bethan Hubbard (on the national database of scientific expertise): SJ Supp, 30 June 1995, p 36

Challenging DNA Evidence, Alec Samuels: 159 JP Jo 156

Codes of Confusion, Julian Gibbons (on changes to the PACE code): Criminal Lawyer, Issue 53, p 5

Committal for Non-Payment of Local Taxes, Paul Russell: 159 JP Jo 228

Consumer Protection: Trading Standards Officer, Enforcement and the Police and Criminal Evidence Act 1984, Geoff Holgate: 159 JP Jo 284

'Corroboration' After the 1994 Act, Peter Mirfield (on the Criminal Justice and Public Order Act 1994, s 32(1)): [1995] Crim LR 448

Corroboration: Goodbye to All That? Diane Birch: [1995] Crim LR 524

Court Experts, Frederick Lawton: 139 SJ 793

CPS Charging Standards: A Cynic's View, F G Davies: 159 JP Jo 203

Cracking the Codes, Michael Cousens (on the revisions to the codes of practice under the Criminal Justice and Public Order Act 1994): LS Gaz, 1 February 1995, p 18

The Criminal Appeal Act 1995: Appeals Against Conviction, J C Smith: [1995] Crim LR 920

The Criminal Appeal Act 1995: the Criminal Cases Review Commission: How Will it Work? Kate Malleson: [1995] Crim LR 929

Criminal Appeals and the Criminal Cases Review Commission, J C Smith: 145 NLJ 533, 572

The Criminal Justice Act, Bernard George (on the Criminal Justice and Public Order Act 1994): LS Gaz, 16 December 1994, p 19, 5 January 1995, p 24

The Criminal Justice and Public Order Act 1994, Elizabeth Franey: Criminal Lawyer, Issue 55, p 3

Criminal Justice and Public Order Act 1994—Evidence and Procedure, F G Davies: 159 JP Jo 311, 327

The Criminal Justice and Public Order Act 1994: The Evidence Provisions, Ian Dennis: [1995] Crim LR 1

Criminal Justice and Public Order Act 1994—The Bail Act Provisions, F G Davies: 159 JP Jo 259, 279

Criminal Justice and Public Order Act 1994—The Transfer Provisions, F G Davies: 159 JP Jo 239

Directions for Silence (on the right to silence): 145 NLJ 1621

Doli Incapax Resurrected, Tony Wilkinson (on *C v DPP* [1995] 2 All ER 1, HL (para 761)): 139 SJ 338

Don't Let Them Have Them, Nigel Ley (on refusing rights of audience to civil servants): 145 NLJ 1124

Doubts and Burdens: DNA Evidence, Probability and the Courts, Mike Redmayne: [1995] Crim LR 464

Drafting the Indictment: Common Assault and Common-Sense, David Cowley: 145 NLJ 1820

Drugs in Sport—Chains of Custody, Edward Grayson: 145 NLJ 44

Duress of Circumstances and Joint Enterprise, Alan Reed: 139 SJ 1052

The Erosion of *Boardman v DPP*, Colin Tapper (on admission of similar fact evidence): 145 NLJ 1223

European Co-operation in Telephone Tapping, Susan Nash: 145 NLJ 954

Excess Alcohol, Incorrect Procedures and Inadmissible Evidence, Michael Hirst: (1995) 54 CLJ 600

The Fearful Witness, Nicholas Reville: 145 NLJ 1774

Finding the Best Expert Witness, David Jessel: SJ Supp, 30 June 1995, p 12

Forensic Evidence and Terrorist Trials in the United Kingdom, Clive Walker and Russell Stockdale: (1995) 54 CLJ 69

Forensic Science Help, Jeffrey Bayes: SJ Supp, 30 June 1995, p 24

The Form of Indictments: Comments of the Law Commission's Consultation Paper, Michael Bowes: [1995] Crim LR 114

From Committal Proceedings to Transfer for Trial, Robert Girvan: 159 JP Jo 379

The Fruits of the Crime, Robert Rhodes (on asset forfeiture schemes): 145 NLJ 822

Handling Convictions Admissible Under s 27(3) of the Theft Act 1968, Roderick Munday: 159 JP Jo 223, 261

Halting Criminal Prosecutions: The Abuse of Process Doctrine Revisited, Andrew L T Choo: [1995] Crim LR 864

Hospital Orders Without Conviction, Alec Samuels: [1995] Crim LR 220

Identification by Witnesses, David Kemp (on new rules for identity parades): Police Review, 5 May 1995, p 20

Inferences from Silence—A Guide for the Perplexed, Neil Corre: 159 JP Jo 468

Inferences from the Accused's Silence—Sections 34–39 Criminal Justice and Public Order Act 1994, Malcolm Dodds: 159 JP Jo 567

Instrumental Protection, Human Right or Functional Necessity? Reassessing the Privilege against Self-Incrimination, Ian Dennis: (1995) 54 CLJ 342

The Imposition and Effectiveness of Conditions in Bail Decisions, John Raine and Michael Willson: 159 JP Jo 364

Improving Legal Custodial Advice, Lee Bridges and Jacqueline Hodgson: [1995] Crim LR 101

In Defence of Doli Incapax, Terence Moore: 159 JP Jo 347

In on the Act, Keith Potter (on the Proceeds of Crime Act 1995): Police Review, 1 December 1995, p 22

Killing With Cars After Adomako: Time for Some Alternatives? Ian Brownlee and Mary Seneviratne (on *R v Adomako* [1994] 3 All ER 79, HL (1994 Abr para 889)): [1995] Crim LR 389

Liability for Inadvertence: A Lordly Legacy? L H Leigh (on *R v Adomako* [1994] 3 All ER 79, HL (1994 Abr para 889)): 58 MLR 457

Losing Sight of the Defendant: The Government's Proposals on Pre-Trial Disclosure, Roger Leng: [1995] Crim LR 704

Miscarriages of Justice: A Systems Approach, Richard Nobles and David Schiff: 58 MLR 299

Mischief or Malice? Roger Donaldson (on moves to review the law on the age of criminal responsibility): Police Review, 24 March 1995, p 16

Money Laundering and Banking Secrecy, Gerard McCormack: 16 Comp Lawyer 10

The Need for Quality Control, Eric Shepherd (on the need to avoid 'forensic twaddle' in testimony): 145 NLJ 636, 729

New Bail Powers for Custody Officers, Clifford Williams: 145 NLJ 685

The New Codes of Practice and the Questioning of Vulnerable Suspects, Neil Corre: 159 JP Jo 531

New Improved PACE, Roger Ede (on changes to the PACE code): 139 SJ 298

A New Look at Eye Witness Testimony, Maxwell McLean: Criminal Lawyer, Issue 53, p 1

New Rules for Juvenile Offenders, Tony Wilkinson: 139 SJ 110

Non-Police Station Interviews? Paul Tain: 139 SJ 299

Not Completely Appealing, Anne Owers (on the Criminal Appeal Bill 1995): 145 NLJ 353

Not Very Appealing, Stephen Gilchrist (on the Criminal Appeal Bill 1995): 139 SJ 368

Obscure, Illiberal and Inconsistent, L H Leigh (on the Criminal Procedure and Investigations Bill 1995): 145 NLJ 1791

PACE and Searches by Trading Standards Officers, Richard Lawson (on changes to the PACE code following *Dudley Metropolitan Borough Council v Debenhams plc* (1995) JP 18 (1994 Abr para 615)): 139 SJ 661

Police Surveillance, John Marston: 145 NLJ 1862

Private Prosecutions by the Victims of Violent Crime, Edward Saunders: 145 NLJ 1423

Prying Eyes, Jack English (on reading of police notebooks by defence solicitors): Police Review, 20 October 1995, p 19

Psychology and Legal Practice: Fairness and Accuracy in Identification Parades, Ian McKenzie: [1995] Crim LR 200

Psychology and the Law: Love or Hate? Yvette Tinsley: 145 NLJ 1038

Questioning and Identification: Changes Under PACE '95, David Wolchover and Anthony Heaton-Armstrong: [1995] Crim LR 356

Reassessing the Role of the 'Appropriate Adult', Brian Littlechild (on the role of the 'appropriate adult' in police interviews): [1995] Crim LR 540

Reformulating the Intoxication Rules: The Law Commission's Report, Ewan Paton: [1995] Crim LR 382

Representing People with Hearing Difficulties, Anita Gesser: LA, June 1995, p 14

Restraint Orders and Drug Trafficking, Simon Whitehead: 145 NLJ 446

The Right to Comment on Silence, David Rhodes: Police Review, 7 April 1995, p 19

The Right to Silence, Alan Murdie (on the effect of the Criminal Justice and Public Order Act 1994): 139 SJ 148

A Sample of Lawmaking, Roderick Munday (on the effect of the Criminal Justice and Public Order Act 1994, s 31): 145 NLJ 855, 895

Search Powers, David Rhodes and Brian Roberts (on new search powers for police): Police Review, 12 May 1995, p 17

Section 78 of PACE and Improperly Obtained Evidence, Roderick Munday: 159 JP Jo 663

Self-Incrimination, Corporate Misconduct, and the Convention on Human Rights, Susan Nash: [1995] Crim LR 854

Silence in Court—Some Thoughts on Sections 34–37 Criminal Justice and Public Order Act 1994, William Miles: 159 JP Jo 415

Similar Fact and Corroboration Warnings—A Strange Concoction? Ian M Hardcastle: 159 JP Jo 583

Solicitors Beware? Neill Blundell (on new rules on the appointment of private investigators): 139 SJ 762

Streamlining Bail, Mick Hayden (on new powers for custody officers to impose conditional bail): Police Review, 17 March 1995, p 16

Taking Samples, David Rhodes (on new powers to take body samples from suspects): Police Review, 28 April 1995, p 15

Taking the Burden of Proof Seriously, Paul Roberts: [1995] Crim LR 783

To See the Wood for the Trees, Chris Hine (on the use of a forensic accountant as an expert witness): SJ Supp, 30 June, p 26

Unused Prosecution Material in Summary Proceedings—Disclosure to Defence, Stephen Savage: 159 JP Jo 363

Victims, Mediation and Criminal Justice, Martin Wright: [1995] Crim LR 187

Videotape Evidence and the Advent of the Expert Ad Hoc, Roderick Munday: 159 JP Jo 547

What is the Criminal Justice System For? Brian P Block: 159 JP Jo 484

742   Appeal—application of proviso—failure to direct jury as to provocation

The appellant admitted killing the deceased. At trial, the defence proceeded solely on the basis that the appellant had been in a state of diminished responsibility at the relevant time. In summing up, the judge failed to refer to the possibility that the appellant had killed the deceased because of provocation. The appellant was convicted of murder, and on appeal he argued that the judge had erred in law in failing to direct the jury on the defence of provocation. *Held*, as there was evidence that the appellant could have been provoked to lose his self-control, there had been a misdirection because of the trial judge's failure to put the issue of provocation to the jury, even though that defence had not been raised at trial. However, the Criminal Appeal Act 1968, s 2(1) empowered the Court of Appeal to apply the proviso in those circumstances, and on the facts of the case, a reasonable jury which had been properly directed as to provocation would inevitably have concluded that a reasonable man with the relevant characteristics of the appellant would not have been provoked to act as he had done. Accordingly, the appeal would be dismissed.

R v Cox [1995] 2 Cr App Rep 513 (Court of Appeal: Stuart-Smith, Waite and Millett LJJ).

743   Appeal—evidence on appeal—disputing of fact—financial means of defendant

The Criminal Appeal Act 1968, s 11(3) provides that the Court of Appeal may, if it considers an appellant ought to have been sentenced differently, quash a sentence and substitute a more appropriate sentence which could have been imposed by the court below. Section 23(1)(c), (3) provides that the Court of Appeal, if they think it necessary or expedient in the interests of justice, may receive the evidence, if tendered, of any witness who is competent but not compellable.

The defendant was involved in a fake robbery of gemstones which allowed him to claim insurance money and was convicted of conspiracy to defraud, conspiracy to steal and conspiracy to commit false accounting. He was sentenced to five years' imprisonment and fined £559,000. He appealed on the ground that he was unable to afford the amount of the fine. It was proposed that the court order the defendant to swear an affidavit disclosing his financial circumstances but the defendant argued that the court did not have the jurisdiction to do so. He also claimed that the sentencing judge had been wrong in imposing a fine because the Powers of Criminal Courts Act 1973, s 35(4A) provided that where the court considered it appropriate to impose a fine and a compensation order, but the offender had insufficient means to pay both, the court had to give preference to compensation. *Held*, where a defendant relied in mitigation on extraneous factors not connected with the facts or circumstances of the offence itself, which would fall outside the scope of a *Newton* hearing, the Crown Court clearly had power to hear evidence from the defendant to verify his contention. Therefore, the Court of Appeal had power to receive evidence to that effect under the 1968 Act, ss 11(3) and 23(1)(c), (3). Where a defendant declined to give a proper and satisfactory explanation as to where stolen assets had gone the court was entitled to draw the inference that the defendant had the means to pay the financial penalty imposed. That principle would apply in the present case if the defendant declined an invitation to give evidence to support that part of his mitigation. Where a defendant introduced extraneous matters in mitigation which the court considered to be of doubtful validity, it was for the defendant to make the mitigation good and the prosecution was not obliged to disprove it. In relation to such extraneous matters, a civil burden of proof rested on the defendant although, in general, the sentencing judge would readily accept the accuracy of defending counsel's statements in this context. Accordingly, the court would invite the defendant to give oral evidence relating to his financial means and to produce any relevant documents.

The sentencing court ought to have given preference to compensation and so the fine would be substituted by a compensation order. Accordingly, to that extent, the appeal would be allowed.

R v Guppy (1994) 16 Cr App Rep (S) 25 (Court of Appeal: Hirst LJ, Tudor Evans and Laws JJ). *R v Newton* (1982) 77 Cr App Rep 13 (1983 Abr para 2994) applied.

744   Appeal—evidence on appeal—evidence declared inadmissible at trial

The appellant's wife was found dead in circumstances which, in view of a suicide note produced by the appellant, suggested that she had taken her own life. However, the subsequent investigation resulted in the appellant's conviction of her murder. At his trial, statements of three of the wife's friends as to what she had said to them about suicide notes were not admitted on the ground that they were inadmissible hearsay. On his appeal against conviction, the appellant requested the court to receive fresh evidence from a woman who claimed to have spoken to the wife on the day of her death and from a forensic pathologist and a handwriting expert. *Held*, the evidence of the forensic pathologist and the handwriting expert would not be received. The court, in exercising its discretion under the Criminal Appeal Act 1968, s 23(1) not only had power to receive admissible evidence which would afford a ground for allowing the appeal but also had a wider discretion, if it thought it necessary or expedient in the interests of justice, to order any witness to attend for examination and to be examined by the court whether or not he had testified at the trial. Accordingly, evidence which had been ruled inadmissible at trial might be received on the appeal if the appeal court concluded that it was relevant and admissible. The statements attributed to the wife by her three friends threw light on the wife's state of mind, one of the main issues in the case. Hearsay evidence to prove the declarant's state of mind was an exception to the rule against hearsay. The court did not consider that the fresh evidence of the woman would have been likely to have affected the jury's verdict. Although the three friends' statements were relevant and admissible under the hearsay rule, it was not necessary or expedient in the interests of justice to require the friends to give evidence. The appeal would be dismissed.

R v Gilfoyle (1995) Times, 31 October (Court of Appeal: Beldam LJ, Scott Baker and Hidden JJ).

745   Appeal—House of Lords—procedure

See *Practice Direction*, para 2362.

746   Appeal—mistake by defence counsel—counsel acting reasonably

At a murder trial, the defendant's counsel advised his client to base his defence on provocation, although self defence was an arguable alternative. A case of provocation was presented to the court and the defendant was convicted of murder. He appealed against his conviction. *Held*, there was an increasing tendency for appeals against conviction to be based on an assertion of fault on the part of the counsel for the defence. It was not in the public interest that a reasonable though mistaken decision of counsel could be the cause of a miscarriage of justice, nor was it appropriate for the legal process to be prolonged on the ground that the defendant's case might have succeeded if it had been advanced on a different basis. The defendant had failed to establish that he had been deprived of a viable ground of defence by the advice of his counsel and, accordingly, his appeal would be dismissed.

R v Satpal Ram (1995) Times, 7 December (Court of Appeal: Beldam LJ, Scott Baker and Stuart-White JJ).

747   Appeal—power to substitute conviction of alternative offence—power to substitute verdict of guilty of substantive offence when originally charged with conspiracy

See *R v Watts*, para 880.

748   Appeal—reference—hearing for directions—estimate of court time

On a preliminary hearing for directions concerning discovery of documents in an appeal against conviction on a reference by the Home Secretary under the Criminal Appeals Act 1968, s 17(1)(a), it has been held that counsel must respond to requests from the Criminal Appeals Office for estimates of the length of court time it is thought the hearing for directions will occupy. Although counsel is not expected to be precise, responses must be given to such reasonable requests and the court will take a failure to do so very seriously.

R v Stock (1995) Times, 14 June (Court of Appeal: Lord Taylor of Gosforth CJ, Forbes and Mitchell JJ).

749 Appeal—refusal of certificate that point of law of general public importance involved—second application

It has been held that where the Court of Appeal has refused without reasons a written application for a certificate under the Criminal Appeal Act 1968, s 32 that a point of law of general public importance is involved, counsel cannot make a second, oral application under the 1968 Act, s 33 to a different constitution of the same court, as only one such application may be made.

R v Tang [1995] Crim LR 813 (Court of Appeal: Lord Taylor of Gosforth CJ, Tucker and Forbes JJ).

750 Arrest—lawfulness of arrest—reasonable grounds for suspecting arrestable offence about to be committed

The Police and Criminal Evidence Act 1984, s 24(7) provides that a constable may arrest without warrant anyone whom he has reasonable grounds for suspecting to be about to commit an arrestable offence.

Police officers saw the appellants sitting in a car near a bank, but the appellants drove off when the officers approached them. When the police received information that one of the appellants owned two shotguns and had previously been involved in burglaries, they concluded that the appellants were about to commit an armed robbery and therefore arrested them on suspicion of the offence. The appellants were detained at a police station and their homes were searched, but they were eventually released without charge. It was in fact the case that no robbery took place on the day in question. On the appellants' claim for damages for assault, false imprisonment and damage to property, the judge decided that the police had had reasonable grounds for suspecting that the appellants were about to commit an arrestable offence. He therefore dismissed the case. On appeal, *held*, the test of whether there was reasonable suspicion that an arrestable offence had been or was about to be committed was an objective one, based on whether a reasonable man who knew the law and who was told of the facts of the particular case would believe that there was reasonable cause for suspicion. Although the test was not to be placed too high, it had to have a reliable factual basis. An appellate court would not interfere with a trial judge's conclusion as to reasonable suspicion unless he had misdirected himself in law or was plainly wrong, as it was for the trial judge to make the necessary findings of fact. Here, there was ample material on which the judge could have decided that the police had established that there were reasonable grounds for suspecting that the appellants had committed an arrestable offence. Accordingly, the appeal would be dismissed.

Bull v Chief Constable of Sussex (1995) 159 LGR 893 (Court of Appeal: Neill LJ and Cazalet J). *Castorina v Chief Constable of Surrey* [1988] NLJR 180, CA (1988 Abr para 504) applied.

751 Arrest and detention—Codes of Practice

See para 779.

752 Bail—breach of bail condition—bail withdrawn by recorder—effect of withdrawal—failure to bring defendant before court within time limit

The Bail Act 1976, s 7(4) provides that a person who is arrested by virtue of a breach of a bail condition must be brought as soon as practicable and in any event within 24 hours after his arrest before a justice of the peace for the petty sessions area in which he was arrested.

A recorder remanded an offender on bail on condition that he resided in a bail hostel and did not go within a certain distance of a particular locality. The following day, the applicant breached one of the conditions and was arrested. He was brought back before the court and the recorder withdrew his bail. The offender applied for a writ of habeas corpus against the prison governor and the police commissioner on the grounds that the 1976 Act, s 7(4) had not been complied with. The police commissioner sought to rely on the provision in the Supreme Court Act 1981, s 47(2) which gave the court power to vary or rescind an order within 28 days of making it. *Held*, the recorder was not a justice of the peace within the 1976 Act, s 7(4) and she had no power to withdraw bail. As a result, the offender had not been brought before a justice of the peace within the period stipulated in s 7(4). The 1981 Act, s 47(2) did not apply. That provision was intended to provide for mistakes made at the time an order was made and was not ordinarily apt to enable the court to review an order on the basis of fresh facts brought before it which had arisen subsequently. Accordingly, the application would be allowed.

Re Marshall (1994) 159 JP 688 (Queen's Bench Division: Auld and Laws JJ).

753 Bail—reconsideration of decision to grant bail—procedure

See para 2017.

754 Bail—surrender to custody—point at which surrender to custody occurs—liability of surety

The appellant, a surety for an international businessman charged with theft and false accounting, appealed against a decision refusing his application for judicial review of a decision requiring him to forfeit part of his recognisance following the businessman's abscondence. The businessman had earlier appeared and been arraigned at a preparatory hearing under the Criminal Justice Act 1987, ss 7–9. The room in which the hearing was held had no dock, so the businessman simply stood up, was formally arraigned, and pleaded not guilty to the charges put to him. The issue was whether his appearance constituted a surrender to the custody of the court so as to terminate the appellant's bail obligations. *Held*, Sir Thomas Bingham MR dissenting, a surrender to custody occurred when a defendant on bail and under a duty so to surrender attended at court and overtly subjected himself to the court's directions. This had been done, at the latest, when the businessman was arraigned at the beginning of the trial and the appellant's obligation as surety thereby ended. Accordingly, the appeal would be allowed.

R v Central Criminal Court, ex p Guney [1995] 2 All ER 577 (Court of Appeal: Sir Thomas Bingham MR, Peter Gibson LJ and Sir Michael Mann). Decision of Queen's Bench Divisional Court [1994] 1 WLR 438 reversed.

755 Caution—decision to caution child—decision in breach of guidelines—court's discretion to review decision

A 12-year-old boy was cautioned at a police station for theft although he did not admit to committing an offence. On an application for judicial review of the decision to caution, he submitted that the court could properly intervene if a caution was administered in clear breach of the guidelines in Home Office Circular 18/1994 which contained *The Cautioning of Offenders*, as amended, and the revised *National Standards for Cautioning*. *Held*, it was possible to seek judicial review of a decision to caution where none of the preconditions contained in the circular were met and in particular where no clear and reliable admission of the offence had been made. It was not necessary for the decision to caution to be mala fides or a flagrant and deliberate breach of the guidelines; a clear but unintentional breach was sufficient. On the evidence, there had been the clearest failure to comply with the condition that an offender had to admit the offence and a caution would not be appropriate without such clear and reliable admission. Further, the process was flawed by the police failure to deal with the condition for child under 14, namely the necessity to establish whether the child knew what he was doing was seriously wrong. Accordingly, the application would be allowed and the caution would be quashed and expunged from the police records.

R v Commissioner of Police of the Metropolis, ex p P (1995) Times, 24 May (Queen's Bench Division: Simon Brown LJ and Curtis J). *R v Chief Constable of Kent, ex p L* [1993] 1 All ER 756 and *C (a Minor) v DPP* (1995) Times, 17 March (para 761), HL considered.

756 Committal proceedings

See MAGISTRATES.

757 Costs—costs out of central funds—claim submitted outside time limit

The Costs in Criminal Cases (General) Regulations 1986, SI 1986/1335, reg 6 provides that no claim for costs is to be entertained unless it is submitted within three months of the date on which the costs order was made. Under reg 12(1), the time limit under reg 6 may, for good reason, be extended. Where an applicant without good reason has failed (or, if an extension were not granted, would fail) to comply with a time limit, the appropriate authority may, in exceptional circumstances, extend the time limit: reg 12(2).

It has been held that, where an application to extend time is made after the expiry of the three-month time limit, it is a misconstruction to construe reg 12(1) so as to prevent consideration of whether or not there was a good reason for the failure to apply within the time limit. Further, to construe reg 12(2) as meaning that the exceptional circumstances had to relate to the reasons for the failure to apply within three months is also a misconstruction.

R v Clerk to North Kent Magistrates, ex p McGoldrick & Co (a firm) (1996) 160 JP 30 (Queen's Bench Division: Schiemann J).

758 Costs—proceedings to detain and forfeit proceeds of drug trafficking— discontinuance of forfeiture proceedings—payment of defendant's costs

The Commissioners of Customs and Excise brought proceedings against the defendant under the Criminal Justice (International Co-operation) Act 1990, after seizing a large sum of money from him. They made several successful applications for detention of the money under the 1990 Act, s 25. However, a later application for forfeiture brought under s 26 was discontinued and the property was returned to the defendant. The justices made a costs order under the Courts Act 1971, s 52 against the commissioners in respect of both the detention and the forfeiture proceedings. The commissioners appealed against the order. *Held*, the 1971 Act, s 52 did not extend to cover both the costs of the discontinued complaint and the costs of any connected complaint. The s 25 proceedings had been heard and determined and, accordingly, fell to be assessed under the Magistrates' Courts Act 1980, s 64. It was implicit in s 52 that the court could only award costs in respect of the proceedings in question. Accordingly, the appeal would be allowed and the case remitted to the justices for them to reconsider the award in respect of the s 26 proceedings.

R v Dover Magistrates' Court, ex p Customs and Excise Comrs (1995) Times, 12 December (Queen's Bench Division: Staughton LJ and Rougier J).

1990 Act, ss 25, 26 now Drug Trafficking Act 1994, ss 42, 43.

759 Costs—wasted costs—claim by party called as witness

The Prosecution of Offences Act 1985, s 19A(1) provides that in any criminal proceedings the Court of Appeal, the Crown Court or a magistrates' court may disallow, or (as the case may be) order the legal or other representative concerned to meet, the whole of any wasted costs or such part of them as may be determined in accordance with regulations.

A firm of solicitors represented the defendant on charges of indecently assaulting a girl. The girl was being accommodated on a voluntary basis by a local authority and the solicitors required the authority to attend court and to be represented on an application for the authority to produce its social services file relating to the girl. Following the defendant's acquittal, the authority claimed payment of wasted costs. The Crown Court made an order against the solicitors on the ground that the application to produce the file was without foundation, that it had been made without proper consideration of the grounds for making it and that it was speculative, unspecific and appeared to be directed to discrediting the girl. On appeal, the solicitors contended that the authority was not a party to the proceedings and should not be awarded costs. *Held*, the words 'in any criminal proceedings' in the 1990 Act, s 19A(1) were wide enough to cover proceedings initiated by summons for the attendance of a witness before the Crown Court to produce a document or documents and a party who was served with a witness summons and who served a notice of application asking the court to declare that the summons should be of no effect was thus a party to criminal proceedings. Accordingly, the appeal would be dismissed.

Re a Solicitor (Wasted Costs Order) [1996] 1 FLR 40 (Court of Appeal: Beldam LJ, Judge J and Judge Allen).

760 Criminal Appeal Act 1995

The Criminal Appeal Act 1995 amends the provisions relating to appeals and references to the Court of Appeal in criminal cases, establishes a Criminal Cases Review Commission and confers functions on, and makes other provision in relation to the commission, and amends the Magistrates' Courts Act 1980, s 142 (power of magistrates' courts to rectify mistakes etc) and the Criminal Justice Act 1988, s 133 (compensation for miscarriages of justice etc). The Act received the royal assent on 19 July 1995. Certain provisions came into force on 1 January 1996 (SI 1995/3061) and the remaining provisions come into force on a day or days to be appointed. For details of commencement, see the commencement table in the title STATUTES.

Part I (ss 1–7) The Court of Appeal
Section 1 extends the requirement to obtain leave to appeal to all appeals to the Court of Appeal except where the judge of the court of trial certifies that the case is fit for appeal. By virtue of s 2, the Court of Appeal must allow an appeal against conviction where the conviction is unsafe and, in any other case, must dismiss the appeal. Section 3 abolishes the Secretary of State's power

to refer cases to the Court of Appeal. That court may receive fresh evidence if it considers it is capable of belief (s 4) and may direct the Criminal Cases Review Commission (see infra) to investigate and report on any matter relevant to the determination of a case being considered by the court. The Registrar of Criminal Appeals may exercise certain powers of the Court of Appeal: s 6. Provision is made by s 7 for appeals in cases of death.

Part II (ss 8–25) The Criminal Cases Review Commission
A body corporate, to be known as the Criminal Cases Review Commission, whose members are to be appointed by Her Majesty on the recommendation of the Prime Minister, is to be established: s 8. Schedule 1 makes further provision concerning the appointment and remuneration of the commission's members, employees, the procedure for meetings, and the making of annual reports to the Secretary of State and the keeping of accounts. Any conviction or sentence in a case which has been tried on indictment, or a verdict or finding arrived at on the trial on indictment of a person under a mental disability, may be referred by the commission to the Court of Appeal; any such reference is to be treated for all purposes as an appeal by the person concerned: s 9. Sections 10, 12 apply to Northern Ireland. The commission may refer to the Crown Court any case which has been tried summarily and, where appropriate, that court may grant bail to a person whose case has been referred: s 11. A reference of a conviction, finding or sentence may not be made under ss 9, 11 unless the commission has complied with the conditions set out in s 13 and, where it refers a case, it must give the Court of Appeal its reasons for doing so or, where it declines to refer a case, it must give the applicant its reasons for doing so: s 14.

Investigations by the commission following a direction by the Court of Appeal are to be conducted in accordance with s 15. The commission may consider, and give the Secretary of State its conclusions on, any matter referred to it by him which has arisen on consideration of the exercise of the royal prerogative of mercy in relation to a conviction; and it must notify the Secretary of State of any reasons which, in its view, merit his considering whether to recommend the exercise of the royal prerogative of mercy in respect of any one case: s 16.

The commission has power to obtain certain documents and other material which may be relevant in the exercise of its functions (s 17) and, by virtue of s 18, it may receive certain documents and other material in the possession or control of the Secretary of State as a result of his existing functions of making references to the Court of Appeal and recommending the exercise of the royal prerogative of mercy. Where it believes that inquiries should be made for assisting it in the exercise of any of its functions in relation to a case, the commission may require the appointment of investigating officers to carry out those inquiries: s 19. An investigation is to be carried out under the direction and supervision of the commission which may direct that an investigating officer cease to act as such; and the investigating officer must report his findings to the commission and to the person who appointed him: s 20. The powers set out in ss 17–20 do not preclude the commission from obtaining statements, opinions and reports and taking other steps to assist it in the exercise of its functions: s 21. Section 22 defines 'public body' for certain purposes.

It is an offence under s 23 for a current or former member or employee of the commission, or a current or former investigating officer, to disclose information which is subject to an obligation of secrecy except in the circumstances specified in s 24. A person who is required under s 17 to produce a document may require the commission not to disclose it without his consent: s 25.

Part III (ss 26–28) Other Provisions
Magistrates are empowered by s 26 to reopen a case regardless of the defendant's plea at the trial, and where it appears to be in the interests of justice, they may vary, rescind or replace a sentence imposed by a magistrates' court. Section 27 applies to Northern Ireland. In assessing compensation for a miscarriage of justice, the assessor must have regard to the matters set out in s 28.

Part IV (ss 29–34) Supplementary
Section 29, Schs 2, 3 deal with minor and consequential amendments and repeals, and ss 30–34 with interpretation, financial provision, commencement, extent and short title.

761 Criminal capacity—child aged between ten and fourteen—presumption as to criminal capacity

The defendant, aged 12, was convicted of interfering with a motor cycle with the intention to commit theft, the magistrates having inferred, from the fact that he had run away from police officers who had seen him tampering with the motor cycle and that the motor cycle was seriously damaged, that he knew that what he had done was seriously wrong. On his appeal against conviction, the question arose whether the doctrine of doli incapax, under which a child between the ages of 10 and 14 was deemed incapable of criminal intent unless the contrary was shown, had outlived its usefulness and should no longer be regarded as part of the common law. *Held*, the presumption that a child between those ages was deemed incapable of criminal intent unless the contrary was shown was still universally recognised as an effective doctrine of the criminal law. The prosecution had to prove beyond reasonable doubt that the child defendant did the act charged and that when doing it he knew it was a wrong act as distinct from mere naughtiness or childish mischief. The criminal standard of proof applied. The evidence relied upon to prove the defendant's guilty knowledge could not be the mere proof of the doing of the act charged, however horrifying or obviously wrong that act might be. There was no evidence in the present case outside the commission of the offence upon which the presumption could be found to have been rebutted. Accordingly, the appeal would be allowed.

C v DPP [1995] 2 All ER 43 (House of Lords: Lords Jauncey of Tullichettle, Bridge of Harwich, Ackner, Lowry and Browne-Wilkinson). Decision of Queen's Bench Divisional Court [1994] 3 All ER 190 reversed.

762 Criminal Justice and Public Order Act 1994—commencement

The Criminal Justice and Public Order Act 1994 (Commencement No 5 and Transitional Provisions) Order 1995, SI 1995/127, brings into force on 3 February 1995, ss 17, 18, 23, 24, 31–33, 40–43, 46–51, 64(1)–(3) (in part), 66(10)–(13), 67(3)–(5), (8), (9), 72–74, 84(1)–(4), 85, 86(1), 88, 91, 92, 136–137, 138(1)–(5), 139–141, 152(1), 154, 155, 157(1)–(6), (9), 160–164, 168 (in part), 169, 170, Sch 8, certain minor amendments in Sch 9, consequential amendments in Sch 10 and repeals in Sch 11. Transitional provision is also made.

The Criminal Justice and Public Order Act 1994 (Commencement No 6) Order 1995, SI 1995/721, brings into force, on 10 April 1995, ss 25–30, 34–39, 54–60, 62, 64(4)–(6), 66(1)–(5), (7)–(9), 67(1), (2), (6), (7), 156, Sch 9, para 37(3), Sch 10, paras 1, 2, 5, 6, 10, 15, 19–23, 32–34, 41–44, 48, 51, 54–58, 62, 67, 71, and certain repeals in Sch 11.

The Criminal Justice and Public Order Act 1994 (Commencement No 7) Order 1995, SI 1995/1378, brings into force on 30 May 1995 s 19 by virtue of which kinds of secure accommodation for certain young persons are extended.

The Criminal Justice and Public Order Act 1994 (Commencement No 8 and Transitional Provision) Order 1995, SI 1995/1957, brings into force (1) on 24 August 1995, ss 75, 76, Sch 10, para 3 (squatters: interim possession orders: powers of entry), (2) on 4 September 1995, s 45, Sch 5, Sch 10, para 65 (extension of procedures for guilty pleas), and (3) on 1 November 1995, s 89 (video recordings: restriction of exemptions) (except in relation to a video work of which a video recording has been supplied or offered for supply prior to that date).

For a summary of the Act, see 1994 Abr para 732. For details of commencement, see the commencement table in the title STATUTES.

763 Criminal Justice (Scotland) Act 1995

The Criminal Justice (Scotland) Act 1995 provides for the reform of the Scottish criminal justice system but certain provisions extend to England and Wales. The Act received the royal assent on 19 July 1995 and comes into force on a day to be appointed. For details of commencement, see the commencement table in the title STATUTES.

The provisions which extend to England and Wales are: s 108 (enforcement in England and Wales of Scottish orders relating to the proceeds of crime and property used in crime, such as restraint orders and forfeiture orders), s 110 and Sch 4 (sequestration, bankruptcy, winding up or receivership of persons holding realisable or forfeitable property).

764 Criminal law

See CRIMINAL LAW.

765 Criminal Procedure (Consequential Provisions) (Scotland) Act 1995

The Criminal Procedure (Consequential Provisions) (Scotland) Act 1995 makes provision for repeals, consequential amendments, transitional matters and savings in connection with the consolidation of enactments in the Criminal Procedure (Scotland) Act 1995 (para 766), the Proceeds of Crime (Scotland) Act 1995 (para 841), and the Criminal Law (Consolidation)

(Scotland) Act 1995 (para 891). Some provisions extend to England and Wales. The Act received the royal assent on 8 November 1995 and came into force on 1 April 1996.

The provisions which extend to England and Wales are: s 7 (short title, interpretation, commencement and extent), Sch 3, para 5 (transitory modification of the Criminal Procedure (Scotland) Act 1995 concerning children), and any amendment contained in Sch 4 (minor and consequential amendments) of any enactment which extends to England and Wales.

766 Criminal Procedure (Scotland) Act 1995

The Criminal Procedure (Scotland) Act 1995 consolidates certain enactments relating to criminal procedure in Scotland. Some provisions extend to England and Wales. The Act received the royal assent on 8 November 1995 and came into force on 1 April 1996.

The provisions which extend to England and Wales are: ss 44 (detention of children in residential accommodation), 47 (restriction on report of proceedings involving children), 209(3) and (7) (supervised release orders), 234(4)–(11) (probation orders: persons residing in England and Wales), 244 (community service orders: general provisions relating to persons living in England and Wales or Northern Ireland), 252 (enforcement of compensation orders: application of provisions relating to fines, but s 252 only extends to England and Wales for the purposes of the construction of the Magistrates' Courts Act 1980, s 91), s 303(4) (Secretary of State's power by order to make such provision as may be necessary for the enforcement in England and Wales or Northern Ireland of any fixed penalty which is transferred as a fine to a court in England and Wales or Northern Ireland), s 309 (short title, commencement and extent).

767 Crown Court—arraignment—judicial review by High Court—jurisdiction

The three applicants were committed in custody to the Crown Court on charges of kidnapping and causing grievous bodily harm. Before their arraignment, they each served an alibi notice. When they were arraigned, one of them refused to enter a plea on the grounds that the evidence against him was not in such a state as to enable him to plead properly. Nevertheless, the judge directed that a plea of not guilty be entered on his behalf. The other two applicants also reluctantly entered pleas of not guilty. Certain fingerprint evidence relating to one of the applicants was served on the day of arraignment. At the arraignment, after considering the length of the prospective trial and witness requirements the judge ordered that all scientific and additional evidence be served as soon as possible but no trial date was fixed. Additional fingerprint evidence was subsequently served and the following day the trial date was fixed. The maximum prescribed period of custody between the applicants' committal for trial and their arraignment then expired. The judge ruled that, as the arraignment had not been a sham, the custody time limits would be inoperative. The applicants sought judicial review of the arraignment, contending that it was a nullity since it should not have taken place until all outstanding evidence had been served on them and had been premature because at that stage no trial date could be fixed. *Held*, the arraignment of a defendant and the conduct of a plea and directions hearing generally were clearly matters 'relating to trial on indictment' within the Supreme Court Act 1981, s 29(3) since the purpose of the arraignment of a defendant who was to be the subject of a trial on indictment was to determine the plea that he wished to enter in relation to that trial. Assuming that the arraignment of the applicants had been conducted properly and not for the purpose of defeating custody time limits, s 29(3) had effect to deny the court jurisdiction to intervene by way of judicial review. The arraignment had been carried out in accordance with the relevant prescribed procedures and consonant with the practice rules relating to plea and directions hearings in the Crown Court, the purpose of which, in common with the custody time limits, was to procure an expeditious and efficient trial. It had in no sense been a sham having regard to the fact that the Crown's evidence depended mainly on the credibility of the complainant and the only further material evidence given since the arraignment was fingerprint evidence, the service of which was unlikely to have had any bearing on the pleas to be tendered by the applicants, particularly since before the arraignment occurred each of them had served an alibi notice, thereby giving an indication of the nature of their defences. The arraignment was therefore valid. Further, even if the court had jurisdiction by way of judicial review, the application would be refused, since the delay in issuing the notice of motion for judicial review had taken the proceedings beyond the prescribed custody time limits in order to enable the applicants, in the context of bail, to contend that there had been such a change of circumstance as would make admission to bail appropriate, thereby enabling them to derive an unfair advantage from the lapse of time. Accordingly, the applications would be dismissed.

R v Crown Court at Leeds, ex p Hussain [1995] 3 All ER 527 (Queen's Bench Division: Leggatt LJ and Kay J). *R v Crown Court at Manchester, ex p DPP* [1993] 2 All ER 663, HL (1993 Abr para

772) and *DPP v Crown Court at Manchester and Huckfield* [1993] 4 All ER 928, HL (1993 Abr para 671) applied.

768 Crown Court—distribution of court business

Lord Taylor of Gosforth CJ has issued the following *Practice Direction* ([1995] 2 All ER 900), which amends *Practice Direction* [1987] 3 All ER 1064.

Classification
1. For the purposes of trial in the Crown Court, offences are to be classified as follows:

Class 1: (1) any offences for which a person may be sentenced to death; (2) misprision of treason and treason felony; (3) murder; (4) genocide; (5) an offence under the Official Secrets Act 1911, s 1; (6) incitement, attempt or conspiracy to commit any of the above offences.

Class 2: (1) manslaughter; (2) infanticide; (3) child destruction; (4) abortion (Offences against the Person Act 1861, s 58); (5) rape; (6) sexual intercourse with a girl under 13; (7) incest with a girl under 13; (8) sedition; (9) an offence under the Geneva Conventions Act 1957, s 1; (10) mutiny; (11) piracy; (12) incitement, attempt or conspiracy to commit any of the above offences.

Class 3: all offences triable only on indictment other than those in classes 1, 2 and 4.

Class 4: (1) wounding or causing grievous bodily harm with intent (Offences against the Person Act 1861, s 18); (2) robbery or assault with intent to rob (Theft Act 1968, s 8); (3) incitement or attempt to commit any of the above offences; (4) conspiracy at common law, or conspiracy to commit any offences other than those included in classes 1 and 2; (5) all offences which are triable either way.

Committals for trial
A magistrates' court, on committing a person for trial under the Magistrates' Courts Act 1980, s 6, must, if the offence or any of the offences is included in classes 1 to 3, specify the most convenient location of the Crown Court where a High Court judge regularly sits, and if the offence is in class 4, must specify the most convenient location of the Crown Court.

In selecting the most convenient location of the Crown Court, the justices must have regard to the considerations referred to in the Magistrates' Courts Act 1980, s 7, and to the locations of the Crown Court designated by a presiding judge as the location to which cases must normally be committed, from their petty sessions area.

Where on one occasion, a person is committed in respect of a number of offences, all the committals must be to the same location of the Crown Court, and that location must be the one where a High Court judge regularly sits, if such a location is appropriate for any of the offences.

Committals for sentence or to be dealt with
Where a probation order, order for conditional discharge or a community service order has been made, or suspended sentence passed, and the offender is committed to be dealt with for the original offence or in respect of the suspended sentence, he must be committed as follows:

If the order was made or the sentence was passed by the Crown Court, he must be committed to the location of the Crown Court where the order was made or sentence was passed, unless it is inconvenient or impracticable to do so.

If he is not so committed and the order was made by a High Court judge, he must be committed to the most convenient location of the Crown Court where a High Court judge regularly sits.

In all other cases, where a person is committed for sentence or to be dealt with, he must be committed to the most convenient location of the Crown Court.

In selecting the most convenient location of the Crown Court, the justices must have regard to the location or locations of the Crown Court designated by a presiding judge as the locations to which cases must normally be committed from their petty sessions area.

Appeals and proceedings under the Crown's Court's original civil jurisdiction
The hearing of an appeal or of proceedings under the civil jurisdiction of the Crown Court must take place at the location of the Crown Court designated by a presiding judge as the appropriate location for such proceedings originating in the areas concerned.

Application for removal of a driving disqualification
Application must be made to the location of the Crown Court where the order of disqualification was made.

Transfer of proceedings between locations of the Crown Court
Without prejudice to the provisions of the Supreme Court Act 1981, s 76, directions may be given for the transfer between one location of the Crown Court and another of (i) appeals, (ii) proceedings on committal for sentence or to be dealt with, (iii) proceedings under the original

civil jurisdiction of the Crown Court where this appears desirable for expediting the hearing, or for the convenience of the parties.

Such directions may be given in a particular case by an officer of the Crown Court or, generally, in relation to a class or classes of case, by the presiding judge or judge acting on his behalf. If dissatisfied with such directions given by an officer of the Crown Court, any party to the proceedings may apply to a judge of the Crown Court, who may hear the application in chambers.

Allocation of business

1. General

Class 1 cases must be tried by a High Court judge. A case of murder, or incitement, attempt or conspiracy to commit murder may be released by or on the authority of the presiding judge, for trial by a circuit judge approved by the Lord Chief Justice.

Class 2 cases must be tried by a High Court judge, unless a particular case is released for trial by a circuit judge. A case of rape or a case in any class of serious sexual offence against a child may be released for trial, only by a circuit judge or recorder approved by the senior presiding judge with the concurrence of the Lord Chief Justice.

Class 3 cases may be tried by a High Court judge or, in accordance with general or particular directions given by a presiding judge, by a circuit judge or recorder.

Class 4 cases may be tried by a High Court judge, a circuit judge, a recorder or an assistant recorder. A class 4 case must not be listed for trial by a High Court judge except with his or the presiding judge's consent.

Appeals from decisions of magistrates and committals to the Crown Court for sentence must be heard by (i) a resident or designated judge, (ii) a circuit judge, nominated by the resident or designated judge, who regularly sits at the Crown Court centre, (iii) an experienced recorder specifically approved by the presiding judges for the purpose, or (iv) where no circuit judge or recorder satisfying these requirements is available and it is not practicable to obtain the approval of the presiding judges, by a circuit judge or recorder selected by the resident or designated judge to hear a specific case or cases.

With the exception of courts operating the plea and directions scheme, the following arrangements for pre-trial proceedings must apply:

Applications or matters arising before trial (including those relating to bail) must be listed where possible before the judge by whom the case is expected to be tried. Where a case is to be tried by a High Court judge who is not available, the application or matter must be listed before any other High Court judge then sitting at the Crown Court centre at which the matter has arisen, before a presiding judge, before the resident or designated judge for the centre, or, with the consent of the presiding judge, before a circuit judge nominated for the purpose.

In other cases, if the circuit judge, recorder or assistant recorder who is expected to try the cases is not available, the matter must be referred to the resident or designated judge, or, if he is not available, to any judge or recorder then sitting at the centre.

Matters to be dealt with after a trial must, where possible, be listed before the judge who originally dealt with the matter, or, if not, before a judge of the same or higher status.

2. Allocation of proceedings to a court comprising lay justices

In addition to the classes of case specified in the Supreme Court Act 1981, s 74, any other proceedings apart from cases listed for pleas of not guilty which, in accordance with these directions are listed for hearing by a circuit judge or recorder, are suitable for allocation to a court comprising justices of the peace.

3. Transfer of cases between circuits

An application that a case be transferred from one circuit to another must not be granted unless the judge is satisfied that (i) the approval of the presiding judges and circuit administrator for each circuit has been obtained, or (ii) the case may be transferred under general arrangements approved by the presiding judges and circuit administrators.

When a resident or designated judge is absent from his centre, the presiding judges may authorise another judge who sites regularly at the same centre to exercise his responsibility.

4. Presiding judges' directions

For the just, speedy and economical disposal of the business of a circuit, presiding judges must, with the approval of the senior presiding judge, issue directions as to the need where appropriate to reserve a case for trial by a High Court judge, and as to the allocation of work between circuit judges, recorders and assistant recorders, and where necessary the devolved responsibility of resident or designated judges for such allocation. In such directions. specific provision must be made for cases in the following categories:

(a) cases where death or serious risk to life, or the infliction of grave injury are involved, including motoring cases of this category arising from reckless driving and/or excess alcohol;

(b) cases where loaded firearms are alleged to have been used;

(c) cases of arson or criminal damage with intent to endanger life;

(d) cases of defrauding government departments or local authorities or other public bodies of amounts in excess of £25,000;

(e) offences under the Forgery and Counterfeiting Act 1981, where the amount of money or the value of goods exceeds £10,000;

(f) offences involving violence to a police officer which result in the officer being unfit for duty for more than 28 days;

(g) any offence involving loss to any person or body of a sum in excess of £100,000;

(h) cases where there is a risk of substantial political or racial feeling being excited by the offence or the trial;

(i) cases which have given rise to widespread public concern;

(j) cases of robbery or assault with intent to rob where gross violence was used, or serious injury caused, or where the accused was armed with a dangerous weapon for the purpose of the robbery, or where the theft was intended to be from a bank, a building society or a post office;

(k) cases involving the manufacture or distribution of substantial quantities of drugs;

(l) cases the trial of which is likely to last more than ten days;

(m) cases involving the trial of more than five defendants;

(n) cases in which the accused holds a senior public office, or is a member of a profession or other person carrying a special duty or responsibility to the public, including a police officer when acting as such;

(o) cases where a difficult issue of law is likely to be involved, or a prosecution for the offence is rare or novel.

With the approval of the senior presiding judge, general directions may be given by the presiding judges of the South Eastern Circuit concerning the distribution and allocation of business of all classes at the Central Criminal Court.

769 Crown Court—plea and directions hearings

Lord Taylor of Gosforth CJ has issued the following *Practice Direction* ([1995] 1 WLR 1318), which establishes plea and directions hearings (PDHs) in the Crown Court, and applies to all cases other than serious fraud, in Crown Court centres which have notified the magistrates' courts that PDHs have been introduced.

At the PDH, pleas will be taken and, in contested cases, prosecution and defence are expected to assist the judge in identifying the key issues, and to provide any additional information required for the proper listing of the case. The detailed operation of the rules is a matter for the judiciary of each Crown Court centre, taking the views of other agencies and the legal profession into account.

1. In every case, other than serious fraud cases in relation to which a notice of transfer to the Crown Court is given under the Criminal Justice Act 1987, s 4 and child abuse cases transferred under the Criminal Justice Act 1991, s 53, the magistrates' court must commit the defendant to appear in the Crown Court on a specific date fixed in liaison with the Crown Court listing officer, for an initial plea and directions hearing (PDH). The PDH provisions apply equally to child abuse cases, for which special arrangements will need to be made for the Crown Court to fix a PDH date on receipt of the case papers.

2. The purpose of the PDH is to ensure that all necessary steps are taken in preparation for trial, and to provide sufficient information for a trial date to be arranged. It is expected that the advocate briefed in the case will appear in the PDH wherever practicable.

3. At least 14 days' notice of the PDH must be given, unless the parties agree to shorter notice. The PDH must be within six weeks of committal in cases where the defendant is on bail, and four weeks where the defendant is in custody.

Preparation for the PDH

4. Where the defendant intends to plead guilty to all or part of the indictment, the defence must notify the probation service, the prosecution and the court as soon as that is known.

5. The defence must supply the court and the prosecution with a full list of the prosecution witnesses they require to attend at the trial. That must be provided at least 14 days prior to the PDH, or within three working days of the notice of hearing, where the PDH is fixed less than 17 days ahead.

6. For all class 1 offences and for lengthy and complex cases, a summary must be prepared by the prosecution for use by the judge at the PDH. All class 2 cases must be scrutinised by the prosecution to determine whether the provision of a summary is appropriate in any particular

case. The summary will assist the judge by indicating the nature of the case, and focusing on the issues of fact and/or law likely to be involved. The summary should also assist the judge in estimating the trial length.

Form of hearing

7. The PDH hearing will normally be held, and orders made, in open court, and all defendants must be present, except with the leave of the court. It must be conducted:

(a) in all cases other than those in class 1 or class 2 and serious sexual offences of any class against a child, by the trial judge or such judge as the presiding judge or resident judge appoints;

(b) in cases in class 1 or class 2 and serious sexual offences of any class against a child, by a High Court judge, or by a circuit judge or recorder to whom the cases have been specifically released in accordance with *Practice Direction* [1995] 1 WLR 1083, or by a directions judge authorised by the presiding judges to conduct such hearings. However, (i) pleas of guilty when entered before a directions judge in such cases must be adjourned for sentencing by a High Court judge, circuit judge or recorder to whom the case has been specifically released, and (ii) a directions judge may only deal with those matters necessary to see that such cases are prepared conveniently for trial, including identifying any issues suitable for a preliminary hearing before the trial judge, and making such necessary directions as may facilitate the conduct of such a preliminary hearing.

Conduct of hearing

8. At the PDH, arraignment will normally take place.

9. If the defendant pleads guilty, the judge must proceed to sentencing wherever possible.

10. Following a not guilty plea, and where part or alternative pleas are not accepted, the prosecution and defence will be expected to inform the court of:

(a) the issues in the case;

(b) issues, if any, as to the mental or medical condition of any defendant or witness;

(c) the number of witnesses whose evidence will be placed before the court, either orally or in writing;

(d) the defence witnesses in (c) above whose statements have been served and whose evidence the prosecution will agree and accept in writing;

(e) any additional witnesses who might be called by the prosecution, and the evidence that they are expected to give;

(f) facts which are to be admitted and which can be reduced into writing, in accordance with the Criminal Justice Act 1967, s 10(2)(b), within such time as may be directed at the hearing, and of the witnesses whose attendance will not be required at trial;

(g) exhibits and schedules which will be admitted;

(h) the order and pagination of the papers which are to be used by the prosecution at trial;

(I) any alibi, which must already have been disclosed in accordance with the Criminal Justice Act 1967;

(j) any point of law which is anticipated will arise at trial, any questions as to the admissibility of evidence which appear on the face of the papers, and any authority on which the party intends to rely;

(k) any applications which are to be made for evidence to be given through live television links by child witnesses, as defined by the Criminal Justice Act 1988, s 32, in cases involving violent or sexual offences, particulars of which must already have been lodged with the court in writing on the form in the Crown Court Rules 1982, SI 1982/1109, Sch 5, within 28 days after the date of committal of the defendant, or the referral date of a bill of indictment in relation to the case;

(l) any applications to submit pre-recorded interviews with a child witness as evidence in chief;

(m) any applications for screens for use by witnesses seeking a visual break between themselves and any relevant parties; whether any video, tape recorder, or other technical equipment will be required during a trial; where tape recorded interviews have taken place, of any dispute or agreement as to the accuracy of any transcript or summary;

(n) any other significant matter which may affect the proper and convenient trial of the case, and whether any additional work needs to be done by the parties;

(o) the estimated length of the trial, to be agreed more precisely having taken account of any views expressed by the judge and the other parties;

(p) witness availability and the approximate length of witness evidence, so that attendance can be staggered during lengthy trials, having agreed likely dates and times of attendance, having taken into consideration real hardship and inconvenience to a witness where applicable;

(q) availability of advocate;

(r) whether there is a need for any further directions.

11. Subject to the provisions of the Criminal Justice Act 1967, ss 9 and 10, admissions under para 10(f) above may be used at trial.

12. The judge may make such order or orders as lie within his or her powers as appear necessary to secure the proper and efficient trial of the case. Each party must, at least 14 days before the date of trial, confirm to the court in writing that all such orders have been fully complied with.

13. A questionnaire annexed to the *Practice Direction* provides a recommended structure for use by the judiciary in conducting a PDH. A single copy of the questionnaire, completed as far as possible with the agreement of both advocates, must be handed in to the court prior to the commencement of the PDH.

14. The defence must apply to the court for the case to be listed for mention if they are to obtain instructions from the defendant. If the defendant fails to attend court, the judge will wish to consider whether a warrant of arrest ought to be issued.

15. The rules come into force immediately, and replace Practice Rules of 25 October 1994 (unreported), which are revoked.

770 Custody—time limits—additional offence—new custody time limit created

The applicant appeared before a magistrates' court charged with rape, the custody time limit in relation to the charge having expired an additional charge of false imprisonment and included that charge in a draft indictment served on the applicant's solicitors. At a hearing before the magistrate, he refused to extend the custody time limit relating to the rape and the next day it was pointed out that a charge of false imprisonment had not yet been preferred. The applicant was therefore charged with false imprisonment and a new custody time limit was created from that day. The applicant sought judicial review on the grounds that the magistrate had been wrong to treat the charge of false imprisonment as a new offence and that, even if this was not the case, the circumstances in which the charge was preferred was an abuse of process. *Held*, the charge of false imprisonment was clearly a new offence, attracting a new time limit. It was only an abuse of process to prefer a new charge, thereby creating a new custody time limit, if the new charge had been preferred merely to avoid an existing custody time limit but it was desirable that a prosecutor ought to review the case before him to determine at the earliest possible moment whether the evidence disclosed offences other than the one for which the accused had been charged and ought to try to comply with the original custody time limit if at all possible. Accordingly, the application would be dismissed.

R v Wolverhampton Justices and Crown Court at Stafford, ex p Uppal (1994) 159 JP 86 (Queen's Bench Division: Beldam LJ and Buxton J).

771 Custody—time limits—bail on expiry of time limit

The Prosecution of Offences (Custody Time Limits) Regulations 1987, SI 1987/299, reg 6(6) provides that the Crown Court, on being notified that an accused who is in custody pending trial there has the benefit of a custody time limit and that limit is about to expire, must grant him bail in accordance with the Bail Act 1976, as from the expiry of the time limit, subject to a duty to appear before the Crown Court for trial.

The defendant was committed in custody for trial. No arraignment took place at the request of the defence and they gave an undertaking not to object to an extension of the 112-day custody time limit. Due to an oversight, however, the prosecution made no application to extend the time limit. Two weeks after the limit expired the case was listed at the request of the defence and the defendant was arraigned and remanded in custody. He sought judicial review of his remand, submitting that following the expiry of the time limit he was entitled to be granted bail until trial and that his remand in custody was beyond the powers of the Crown Court. *Held*, under the Prosecution of Offences Act 1985, s 22, the Secretary of State could make regulations with respect to a preliminary stage of proceedings up to, but not beyond, the date of arraignment, specifying the maximum period during which the accused may be in custody pending arraignment. If the Crown Court had been notified that the applicant had the benefit of the custody time limit which was about to expire, it would have been bound to grant bail as from the expiry of the time limit. If reg 6(6) was to be construed as meaning that bail was granted to the date of trial, as the defendant submitted, it would be beyond the Secretary of State's powers under the 1985 Act, s 22. However, it was possible to give reg 6(6) a meaning which would not make it ultra vires the 1985 Act because it did not state expressly that bail must continue until trial. It merely made the bail granted subject to a duty to appear before the court for trial. Accordingly, the application would be dismissed.

R v Crown Court at Croydon, ex p Lewis (1994) 158 JP 886 (Queen's Bench Division: Balcombe LJ and Schiemann J).

The Prosecution of Offences (Custody Time Limits) (Amendment) Regulations 1995, SI 1995/555 (in force on 10 April 1995), further amend the 1987 Regulations, SI 1987/299, by providing that references to a person's first appearance in proceedings in a magistrates' court for an offence include a reference to his appearance on the hearing of an application under the Magistrates' Courts Act 1980, s 43B following the grant of police bail or on reconsideration of a bail decision under the Bail Act 1976, s 5B; and (2) by making the grant of bail on expiry of a Crown Court custody time limit subject to the Criminal Justice and Public Oder Act 1994, s 25, by virtue of which bail is excluded in certain cases of homicide and rape.

772   Disclosure of prosecution case to defence—government proposals

The Home Secretary has published a consultation document, *Disclosure* (Cm 2864), setting out proposals for reforming the current arrangements for prosecution and defence disclosure in criminal proceedings. The proposals are intended to apply to trials on indictment and also to summary proceedings. The scheme avoids an open-ended obligation to disclose all material which might conceivably be relevant to the defence, and gives the defence an opportunity to narrow the issues in dispute. The proposed procedure would be for the investigator to preserve material obtained during a criminal investigation; material in specified categories would be made available to the prosecutor, together with a schedule of the other material preserved. The prosecutor would serve on the defence the material upon which the prosecution would rely, and also material in the specified categories or any other material which might undermine the prosecution case ('primary prosecution disclosure'); there would be no duty to disclose the schedule or any other unused material. The defence would be required to provide particulars of its case to enable the issues in dispute to be identified before the trial ('defence disclosure'). The prosecutor would then disclose any unused material which might assist the particular line of argument disclosed by the defence ('secondary prosecution disclosure'). A failure to disclose the defence case at this stage or attempts to overcome the limitations of prosecution disclosure by running different lines of argument in succession might be the subject of comment at the trial, and the court might draw any appropriate inferences. Any dispute as to the adequacy of disclosure would be settled by a court before the trial. If the prosecution wished to withhold material on the ground that it was sensitive (eg the material related to matters of national security or the material, if publicly known, might facilitate the commission of an offence), it would have to seek an appropriate ruling from the court.

773   Enforcement procedures—Codes of Practice

See para 779.

774   Evidence—child—competence

The appellant was charged with indecent assault on a nine-year-old girl. The police videotaped an interview with the child, at the end of which the interviewer discussed with her the difference between telling a lie and telling the truth. Before trial the prosecution applied for leave under the Criminal Justice Act 1988, s 32A for the video recording of the interview to be played to the jury as the child's evidence-in-chief. The judge watched the video recording before the trial, concluded that the child was competent to give evidence and duly granted leave. At trial the video recording was shown to the jury. On conclusion of the child's evidence, the judge realised that he had not investigated her competence as a witness in the presence of the jury by asking her whether she understood the difference between truth and lies and the importance of telling the truth. The child was therefore recalled and, in the presence of the jury, the judge satisfied himself as to her competence to give the evidence that she had already given. The appellant was convicted. On appeal, *held*, although a judge was under no duty to conduct a preliminary investigation of a child's competence to give evidence, he retained the power to do so where he considered that there was a question as to the child's knowledge of the difference between truth and falsehood and the importance of telling the truth. In those cases where a judge considered it necessary to investigate a child's competence to give evidence in addition to or without the benefit of an earlier view of a videotaped interview under s 32A of the 1988 Act, he had to do so in open court in the presence of the accused because it was a part of the trial, but need not do so in the presence of the jury. The jury's function was to assess the child's evidence, including its weight, from the evidence he or she gave on the facts of the case after the child had been found competent to give it, and the exercise of determining competence was not a necessary aid to that function. On the facts, the judge was justifiably satisfied from his pre-trial view of the video recording as to the child's competence to give evidence and that leave could properly be granted under s 32A. Accordingly, he was under no duty to investigate the matter again with her at all or in the presence of the jury and as a result there was no material irregularity. The appeal would therefore be dismissed.

R v Hampshire [1995] 2 All ER 1019 (Court of Appeal: Swinton Thomas LJ, Auld and Ward JJ).

In a trial concerning various offences against children, one child witness gave evidence which was later retracted. The defendants at the trial subsequently appealed, claiming that many of the witnesses at the trial were children who should not be regarded as competent and whose evidence should be discounted. *Held*, in deciding whether a child witness was competent the question to ask was whether he could understand the questions being asked and respond to them intelligibly and coherently though it was relevant to inquire as to his ability to distinguish between truth and fiction, fact and fantasy as part of that test. Where a child gave evidence before a jury which he then retracted, the jury should be allowed to consider all that he said to them and should be given strong warnings about the dangers of relying on such evidence. In the circumstances one of the appeals would be allowed.

R v D (1995) Times, 15 November (Court of Appeal: Swinton Thomas LJ, Waterhouse and Harrison JJ).

775　Evidence—child—evidence through live television link

The Criminal Justice Act 1988, s 32 provides that certain witnesses under the age of 14, may give evidence through a live television link if the offence is one which involves an assault on, or threat of injury to, a person.

It has been held that the term 'threat of injury' within the 1988 Act, s 32 applies to the offence and not the offender. An offence involves a 'threat of injury' if the circumstances are such that injury to a person is a real possibility, for example, where the offence is one of arson being reckless as to whether life is endangered. It does not necessarily need to involve any actual threat of injury to a person by the offender. It is the circumstances of the offender's activity viewed objectively which has to present the threat.

R v Lee [1996] 1 Cr App Rep 135 (Court of Appeal: Russell LJ, Rougier and Rhys Davies JJ).

776　Evidence—child—video recording of police interview—provision of video to jury on retirement

A stepfather appealed against his conviction of indecent assault and rape of his 12-year-old stepdaughter on the grounds that video recordings of police interviews with the child were shown in the jury room after the jury retired at the jury's request and with the judge's sanction. He claimed that the judge should not have allowed the jury to see the video and that the judge should have specified those parts which were evidence in contrast to those which were not in addition to pointing out that videos could only be used for the purposes of testing the evidence of children at trial and discovering any inconsistencies. *Held*, the judge did have the power to allow the jury to see the video provided that the jury were correctly warned as to what was evidence and what was not. In this instance the judge had emphasised that the video itself was not evidence and that its purpose was to enable the jury to compare the evidence given at trial with that which had been given earlier. When allowing juries to see videos after retirement it was advisable to repeat the direction that they were not evidence but this was not an essential requirement.

R v Atkinson [1995] Crim LR 490 (Court of Appeal: Lord Taylor of Gosforth CJ, Curtis and Gage JJ).

777　Evidence—child—video recording of police interview—second showing of video

An appeal was made against conviction after a video interview of a child witness was played for a second time during the trial. It was argued that the second playing of the video was a material irregularity. *Held*, an application for a second showing of a video of witness evidence would only be granted if made specifically by the jury. Otherwise, a replay was inappropriate and should be discouraged as a departure from the normal course of evidence. Such departures should only take place in exceptional circumstances. In the present case the replay had been requested by prosecuting counsel and there was no evidence of special circumstances. Accordingly, the appeal would be allowed and a retrial ordered.

R v M (Criminal Evidence: Replaying Video) (1995) Times, 29 November (Court of Appeal: Lord Taylor of Gosforth CJ, Kay and Brian Smedley JJ).

778   Evidence—child—video recording of police interview—transcript of recording provided to jury

The Criminal Justice Act 1988, s 32(A) permits the admission of video recordings of the testimony of child witnesses in criminal proceedings.

The defendant was convicted of indecent assault on a child. During his trial, the girl's evidence-in-chief took the form of a video of her interview with the police, and she was cross-examined via a video link. The trial judge permitted the jury to be given a typed transcript of the video recording, which it retained throughout the trial and its retirement. The defendant appealed against the conviction. *Held*, there was a serious risk that by allowing the jury to have a transcript of only the girl's evidence-in-chief the jury might have attached a disproportionate amount of weight to that evidence. That amounted to a material irregularity. Accordingly, the appeal would be allowed and the conviction would be quashed.

R v C (RE) (1995) 159 JP 521 (Court of Appeal: Russell and Pill LJJ, and Turner J).

779   Evidence—Codes of Practice

The Police and Criminal Evidence Act 1984 (Codes of Practice) (No 3) Order 1995, SI 1995/450 (in force on 10 April 1995), revokes the 1988 Order, SI 1988/1200, and the 1990 Order, SI 1990/2580, and brings into operation the following revised codes of practice under the Police and Criminal Evidence Act 1984, ss 60(1)(a) and 66: (1) the Code of Practice for the Exercise by Police Officers of Statutory Powers of Stop and Search; (2) the Code of Practice for the Searching of Premises by Police Officers and the Seizure of Property found by Police Officers on Persons or Premises; (3) the Code of Practice for the Detention, Treatment and Questioning of Persons by Police Officers; (4) the Code of Practice for the Identification of Persons by Police Officers; and (5) the Code of Practice on Tape Recording. The revised codes supersede the corresponding existing codes.

780   Evidence—confession—confession obtained in breach of Code of Practice

The appellants asked a police informant if he could cash a cheque which they had intercepted in the post. The informant told the police and introduced the appellants to two undercover officers. They had several meetings which were secretly taped, during which the appellants confessed to the offence, and they were convicted of conspiracy to handle a stolen cheque. On appeal, they submitted that (1) the officers intended to use the taped conversations as evidence in a future trial and it had been wrong of them to question the appellants in a way that circumvented the Police and Criminal Evidence Act 1984, Codes of Practice, and (2) what was said between undercover officers and defendants could never be admissible. *Held*, (1) the purpose of the codes was to ensure that where there was a reasonable possibility that a confession was unreliable, it would not go before the jury. In the present case, it was highly unlikely that the admissions were unreliable. It was not the case that the officers were used to circumvent the requirements of the codes; they had gone to discover the appellants' future plans and references to the cheque were part of establishing the appellants' credentials as criminals. In deciding whether to admit evidence under s 78 the judge had to consider all the circumstances and his discretion would only be impugned if it was *Wednesbury* unreasonable. On the facts, the discretion had been properly exercised. (2) The court rejected the line of argument that if a defendant confessed to a police officer it was not admissible, but if he did so to a member of the public it would be, purely because that person was not an officer. The appeals would be dismissed accordingly.

R v Lin [1995] Crim LR 817 (Court of Appeal: McCowan LJ, Schiemann and Mitchell JJ).

781   Evidence—confession—confession of mentally handicapped person—absence of independent person

The Police and Criminal Evidence Act 1984, s 77(1) provides that without prejudice to the general duty of the court at a trial on indictment to direct the jury on any matter on which it appears to the court appropriate to do so, where at such trial the case against the accused depends wholly or substantially on a confession by him, and the court is satisfied that he is mentally handicapped and that the confession was not made in the presence of an independent person, the court must warn the jury of the special need for caution before convicting the accused in reliance on the confession, and must explain that the need arises because of the above-mentioned circumstances.

The appellant, a mentally handicapped woman, was convicted of murder and arson on the basis of confessions that she had made to the police and to friends, although no independent person was present on those occasions. She later retracted the confessions that she had made to the police, but subsequently made further confessions to them in the presence of her social worker and solicitor. On appeal, the prosecution argued that the 1984 Act, s 77 did not apply to the appellant's confessions to her friends, and that the confessions made to the police when an independent person was not present had not formed a substantial part of the prosecution case. *Held*, the purpose of an independent person was to assist a mentally handicapped person in recalling what he had said, to give evidence as to the mental and emotional state of the handicapped person at the time of his confession, and to give him sensible advice if he was or became unfit to speak. An independent person within the meaning of the 1984 Act, s 77 had to be independent of the person to whom the confession was made. The appellant's friends could not have been independent persons, and s 77(1) therefore applied to the confessions made to them. Moreover, it was clear that the prosecution case had depended on the confessions made to the police and to the appellant's friends when no independent person was present, as the police had informed the appellant of virtually all the details about the fire at the time that she had first confessed. The judge's failure to warn the jury in accordance with s 77(1) had therefore been a material irregularity and, accordingly, the appeal would be allowed.

R v Bailey [1995] 2 Cr App R 262 (Court of Appeal: Roch LJ, Garland and Gage JJ).

782   Evidence—corroboration—capacity of witness—independent evidence

The appellant was convicted of the rape of a severely mentally ill woman. Her evidence was confused, seemingly unreliable and self-contradictory at times. In summing up, the judge identified two possible lies told by the appellant in interview as evidence capable of corroborating the woman's account of events. On appeal, the appellant argued that the woman's evidence was so flawed that there was no evidence to corroborate, and no case to answer. Furthermore, the possible lies could neither corroborate in law or in fact. *Held*, the strength or weakness of the woman's evidence depended on the view to be taken of her reliability as a witness. Her evidence could therefore be left to the jury even without corroboration. Her potential credibility did not have to be assessed by the judge in isolation from the other evidence. Her capacity as a witness could only be assessed in the light of all the evidence. The judge should identify the issues in the case and then relate the potentially corroborative evidence to them, with the appropriate warnings. There was other independent evidence or medical evidence to support the woman's evidence. The lies provided potential corroboration as to what had happened. The judge had approached the case in the correct manner and accordingly the appeal would be dismissed.

R v Morris [1995] Crim LR 495 (Court of Appeal: Hirst LJ, Auld and Holland JJ).

783   Evidence—corroboration—similar fact evidence—possibility of collusion

The appellant was convicted of sexual offences of a similar nature against his adopted daughter and his step-daughter. At his trial, the appellant denied the charges and argued that the girls had concocted the story. The trial judge directed the jury that if they were sure the girls had not collaborated to concoct a false story, the similar fact evidence of one girl provided corroboration for the evidence of the other. On appeal, the question arose as to how a trial judge should deal with such cases. *Held*, where there was an application to exclude evidence on the ground that it did not qualify as similar fact evidence and the submission raised a question of collusion, the judge had to approach the question of admissibility on the basis that the similar facts alleged were true and apply the test in *DPP v P* accordingly. Generally, collusion was not relevant at that stage. If a submission raised a question of collusion in such a way as to cause the judge difficulty in applying the test, he might be compelled to hold a voire dire. If evidence of similar facts was admitted and circumstances were adduced in the course of the trial which indicated that no reasonable jury could accept the evidence as free from collusion, the judge had to direct the jury that it could not be relied on as corroboration or for any other purpose adverse to the defence. Where that was not the case but the question of collusion had been raised, the judge had clearly to draw the importance of collusion to the attention of the jury and leave it to them to decide whether, notwithstanding such evidence of collusion as might have been put before them, they were satisfied that the evidence could be relied upon as free from collusion and tell them that if they were not so satisfied they could not properly rely on it as corroboration or for any other purpose adverse to the defence. In all such cases, the statutory discretion provided by the Police and Criminal Evidence Act 1984, s 78 and the common law discretion preserved by the 1984 Act, s 82(3) had to be kept in mind. The appeal would be dismissed.

R v H (Evidence: Corroboration) (1995) 159 JP 649 (House of Lords: Lords Mackay of Clashfern LC, Griffiths, Mustill, Lloyd of Berwick and Nicholls of Birkenhead). Decision of Court of Appeal [1994] 2 All ER 881 (1994 Abr para 753) affirmed. *DPP v P* [1991] 3 WLR 161, HL (1991 Abr para 627), *R v Ananthanarayanan* [1994] 2 All ER 847, CA (1993 Abr para 704) and *R v Ryder* [1994] 2 All ER 859, CA (1993 Abr para 749) considered.

784 Evidence—corroboration—warning to jury—guidelines

By virtue of the Criminal Justice and Public Order Act 1994, s 32(1), at a trial on indictment it is no longer obligatory for the court to give the jury a warning about convicting the accused on the uncorroborated evidence of a person merely because that person is an alleged accomplice of the accused, or, where the offence charged is a sexual offence, the person in respect of whom it is alleged to have been committed.

In separate cases, the appellants appealed against their convictions for indecent assault on a young girl. In giving guidelines as to convicting defendants on the basis of the uncorroborated evidence of unreliable witnesses, *held*, the use of the word 'merely' in the 1994 Act, s 32(1) indicated that a corroboration warning did not have to be given in every case where a witness complained of a sexual offence or where the witness was an alleged accomplice of the accused. It was a matter for a trial judge's discretion whether or not he ought to give a warning to the jury and the terms in which the warning was to be given, and that depended on the content and manner of the witness's evidence, the circumstances of the case, and the issues raised. Where it had been shown that a witness was unreliable, a judge might consider that he had to warn the jury to exercise caution before relying on the witness's uncorroborated evidence. Where it was shown that a witness had lied, made previous false complaints, or bore a grudge against the defendant, a stronger warning was appropriate. In particular, the judge might warn the jury to look for supporting material before acting on the impugned witness's evidence. However, there was no formula to which a judge was obliged to conform in giving a warning. Moreover, the court would be slow to interfere with the exercise of a trial judge's discretion, as he was better placed to assess the manner of the witness's evidence and its content. On the facts of each case, the appeals would be dismissed.

R v Makanjuola; R v Easton [1995] 3 All ER 730 (Court of Appeal: Lord Taylor of Gosforth CJ, Tucker and Forbes JJ).

785 Evidence—cross-examination—accused's previous convictions

When the appellant was charged with an offence under the Theft Act 1968 his defence was that the evidence against him had been fabricated by the police officers involved. The officers were prosecution witnesses at his trial. When the prosecutor cross-examined the appellant, he sought to call evidence of the appellant's previous convictions. The appellant objected on the ground that he had no previous convictions of a dishonest nature, but the justices exercised their discretion in favour of allowing the cross-examination because the nature of the defence was such as to involve imputations on the character of the prosecution witnesses thereby rendering evidence of the appellant's previous convictions admissible for the purposes of credibility. The appellant was convicted and, on appeal by way of case stated, *held*, where an appellant rendered himself liable to cross-examination on previous convictions under the Criminal Evidence Act 1898, s 1(f)(ii), and there were no previous convictions of a dishonest nature, the justices did not have to exercise their discretion in the appellant's favour by refusing to allow the cross-examination if, in all the circumstances of the case, they considered that it was only fair that they should know the appellant's character. The fact that the appellant had no previous convictions for dishonesty was no more than a factor for the justices to consider and it did not constitute any bar to their permitting the cross-examination. Accordingly, the appeal would be dismissed.

Fearon v DPP (1995) 159 JP 649 (Queen's Bench Division: Leggatt LJ and Buxton J).

786 Evidence—cross-examination—police officer—evidence of officer given in other trials

The appellants were convicted of robbery and conspiracy to rob, on the basis of confessions which they had allegedly made to investigating police officers. At trial, they had submitted that the confessions were false and that they had been signed only because of physical duress used by the officers. On appeal, the appellants argued that their convictions were unsafe because the same officers had been involved in several other cases subsequent to their case in which the confession evidence had been discredited because it had been fabricated. *Held*, where it was alleged that confession evidence in other cases had been fabricated by investigating police officers, the officers could be cross-examined on that issue. The usual criteria for admissibility applied in the instant case, even though cross-examination had not been possible at the time of the trial because the other cases in which the officers' evidence had been discredited had not then occurred. There was evidence of a pattern of dishonest behaviour in the conduct of interviews, and it was therefore legitimate to draw an inference that the officers had a habit of concocting false confessions where there was no other evidence against a suspect. In light of the other cases, it was not possible to have any confidence in the appellants' alleged confessions and, accordingly, the appeal would be allowed.

R v Williams [1995] 1 Cr App Rep 74 (Court of Appeal: Leggatt LJ, Morland and Bell JJ).

787 Evidence—defendant—decision not to give evidence

Lord Taylor of Gosforth CJ has issued the following *Practice Direction* ([1995] 1 WLR 657).

1. The Criminal Justice and Public Order Act 1994, s 35(2) requires that at the end of the prosecution evidence, the court must be satisfied that the accused is aware that the stage has been reached at which evidence may be given for the defence and that he may give evidence. If he chooses not to do so, or if he is sworn in and then refuses without good cause to answer any question, it is permissible for the jury to draw such inferences as appear proper from his failure to give evidence or his refusal without good cause to answer any question.

2. The 1994 Act, s 35(1) provides that s 35(2) does not apply if at the conclusion of the prosecution evidence, the accused's legal representative informs the court that the accused will give evidence. That ought to be done in the jury's presence. If the representative indicates that the accused will give evidence, the case must proceed in the usual way.

3. If the court is not informed of this, or if the court is informed that the accused does not intend to give evidence, the judge must ask the representative in the presence of the jury:

'Have you advised your client that the stage has now been reached at which he may give evidence and, if he chooses not to do so or having been sworn without good cause refuses to answer any question, the jury may draw such inferences as appear proper from his failure to do so?'

4. If the representative replies to the judge that the accused has been so advised, the case may proceed. If counsel replies that the accused has not been so advised, the judge must direct the representative to advise his client of the consequences set out in paragraph three and adjourn briefly for that purpose before proceeding any further.

5. If the accused is not represented, the judge must at the conclusion of the prosecution evidence and in the presence of the jury say to the accused:

'You have now heard the evidence against you. Now is the time for you to make your defence. You may give evidence on oath and be cross-examined like any other witness. If you do not give evidence or, having been sworn, without good cause refuse to answer any question, the jury may draw such inferences as appear proper. That means they may hold it against you. You may also call any witness or witnesses whom you have arranged to attend court. Afterwards you may also, if you wish, address the jury by arguing your case from the dock. But you cannot at that stage give evidence. Do you now intend to give evidence?'

788 Evidence—defendant—defendant declining to give evidence on counsel's advice—counsel's conduct

See *Sankar v State of Trinidad and Tobago*, para 197.

789 Evidence—disclosure—evasion of prohibition on export of goods—disclosure of government documents

See *R v Blackledge*, para 956.

790 Evidence—disclosure—medical report prepared in child care proceedings

See *Re L (Police Investigation: Privilege)*, para 357.

791 Evidence—disclosure—public interest immunity

See *Re H (Criminal Proceedings: Disclosure of Adoption Records)*, para 341.

792 Evidence—documentary evidence—business documents

The Criminal Justice Act 1988, s 24(1) provides that a statement in a document is admissible as evidence of any fact of which direct oral evidence would be admissible if the document was created or received by a person in the course of a trade, business, profession or other occupation, or as the holder of a paid or unpaid office, and the information contained in the document was supplied by a person (whether or not he was the maker of the statement) who had or may be reasonably supposed to have had personal knowledge of the matters dealt with. Section 24(4)(iii) provides that a statement prepared for the purposes of pending or contemplated proceedings or of a criminal investigation, is admissible by virtue of s 24(1) if the person who made the statement cannot reasonably be expected (having regard to the time which had elapsed since he made the statement and to all the circumstances) to have any recollection of the matters dealt with in the statement.

A supermarket customer attempted to pay for goods using a stolen credit card, but made off in a car before he could be apprehended. One of the supermarket's employees recognised the driver of the car as the customer, and noted his appearance and the registration number of his car. The details were relayed to another employee, who made a written note of the details. The prosecution sought to establish that the car which the employee had seen being driven away was the same as that which belonged to the appellant, and was given leave to introduce the employee's note as a business record under the 1988 Act, s 24. On appeal against his conviction for handling stolen goods and obtaining property by deception, the appellant argued that because the employee had attended the trial and had given oral evidence, she was not a person to whom s 24(4)(iii) applied, and that the judge had therefore erred in allowing the document to be admitted. *Held*, since the definition of 'statement' in the 1988 Act, Sch 2, para 5 included 'any representation of fact, whether made in words or otherwise', the prosecution was entitled to treat certain parts of a document as independent statements. In giving oral evidence, the employee had been able to recollect the circumstances in which she had made the document and some of the details contained in it. Those parts of the document which she could not remember, in particular the registration number of the appellant's car, were independent statements which, for the purposes of s 24(4)(iii), she could not reasonably be expected to recall. The judge had therefore not erred in granting leave to admit the document and, accordingly, the appeal would be dismissed.

R v Carrington (1993) 99 Cr App Rep 376 (Court of Appeal: Waite LJ, Hidden and Harrison JJ).

Contracts were placed with overseas companies when the appellant, an employee of the Ministry of Defence, was in a position to influence the placing of contracts. Those companies made payments to intermediate companies which were put in numbered bank accounts. The prosecution claimed that they were corrupt payments made as an inducement or reward for the appellant and he was charged with corruption. At the trial, the judge admitted documents purporting to emanate from the overseas companies which evidenced payments into the accounts, although the only evidence relating to the documents came from an investigating officer who received them after requests were made to the countries in question. The appellant was convicted and, on appeal, he submitted that the conditions required by s 24 had not been satisfied and that the document should not have been admitted. *Held*, the purpose of s 24 was to enable a document to speak for itself and that would be defeated if oral evidence was to be required in every case from a person who was either the creator or keeper of the document, or the supplier of the information contained in the document. In the present case, the appropriate authorities abroad had produced the documents and the court was entitled to infer that they had acted within the law when obtaining them from the companies. Direct oral evidence from officers in those authorities or the relevant companies was not essential. The judge had been entitled to infer that the companies had to keep proper accounts and that copies of documents relating to the payments would have been kept. The fact that the payments were corrupt did not prevent the documents from being created in the course of a company's business. Information in the documents that payments had been made to the intermediate companies was information within the personal knowledge of the document's creator. Accordingly, the appeal would be dismissed.

R v Foxley [1995] 2 Cr App Rep 523 (Court of Appeal: Roch LJ, Curtis and Stuart White JJ).

793 Evidence—documentary evidence—computer printout

The Police and Criminal Evidence Act 1984, s 69 provides that in any proceedings a statement in a document produced by a computer is not admissible as evidence of any fact stated therein unless it is shown that there are no reasonable grounds for believing that the statement is inaccurate because of improper use of the computer and that at all material times the computer was operating properly.

The defendant was convicted of possession of opium. The principal forensic scientist initially thought it was cannabis but there was some doubt and it was put into a solution and fed into a machine which subjected it to a scientific process and then produced a printout. He identified codeine and sought the opinion of a specialist in the field who identified further substances including morphine. The principal forensic scientist then gave evidence at the trial that the substance was opium. On an application for leave to appeal against conviction, it was contended that the evidence that the substance was opium was hearsay and that it should be excluded under s 69. *Held*, in almost every case in which an expert gave evidence he would rely on facts ultimately provided by a machine. The scientist's evidence was based on his own interpretation of the printout from the machine and the expert's opinion of that printout. It was not hearsay, it was an expert opinion given on evidence properly considered by him. The submission that the evidence was contrary to s 69 ignored the wording of that section, which was designed to ensure that the computer was operating properly and that the documents it produced could be relied upon. The documents in question were not even produced at the trial. Accordingly, the application would be dismissed.

R v Golizadeh [1995] Crim LR 232 (Court of Appeal: Rose LJ, Morland and Steel JJ).

794   Evidence—documentary evidence—untraceable witness

Under the Criminal Justice Act 1988, s 23(2)(c) a statement made by a person in a document is admissible in criminal proceedings as evidence of any fact of which direct oral evidence by him would be admissible if all reasonable steps have been taken to find the person who made the statement, but he cannot be found.

The appellant was charged with murder after he fatally stabbed the victim. The appellant claimed that, in the course of a struggle, he had accidentally wounded the victim. A witness made a statement to the police describing how the appellant had thrust towards the victim with a knife in his hand. She said that the appellant had then held the victim down and robbed him. At the trial, the witness failed to appear and police efforts to trace her were unsuccessful. The prosecutor applied to have her statement read pursuant to the Criminal Justice Act 1925, s 13, but, as the conditions of that section could not be satisfied, he made a further application under the 1988 Act, s 23(2)(c). The judge allowed the application. The statement was read and the appellant was convicted of murder. On appeal, *held*, once the judge had found, as a fact, that the 1925 Act, s 13 did not factually apply, it was right that he consider whether the provisions of the 1988 Act, s 23 applied. On the facts, he found that the conditions of admissibility in s 23 had been met and he rightly allowed the statement to be read. Accordingly, the appeal would be dismissed.

R v James (1995) 160 JP 9 (Court of Appeal: Swinton Thomas LJ, Latham and Morison JJ).

795   Evidence—drug offences—possession—intent to supply—evidence indicating drug dealing

The defendant had been convicted of possessing a controlled drug with intent to supply and sentenced to five years' imprisonment. A confiscation order of £912.50, found in his possession on his arrest, was made. On his appeal against conviction, the question arose whether evidence of the £912.50 had rightly been admitted. *Held*, the finding of money, whether in the defendant's home or in his possession when in conjunction with a substantial quantity of drugs was capable of being relevant to the issue of whether there had been an intent to supply drugs. The judge had to direct the jury as to how it should approach the question of whether the finding of the money was probative of the necessary intent. He had to indicate that any explanation for the money put forward by the defendant as an innocent explanation would have to be rejected by the jury before it could regard the finding of the money in the defendant's possession as relevant to the offence. The jury should also be directed that if, in its opinion, there was any possibility of the money being in the defendant's possession for any reasons other than drugs dealing, the evidence would not be probative. However, if it concluded that the finding of the money indicated not past drug dealing but on-going drug dealing, such finding of the money together with the drugs might be taken into account by the jury in considering whether the necessary intent had been proved. Although the absence of such a direction in the present case amounted to a misdirection or non-direction, the court believed that the jury would, nevertheless, have reached the same conclusion whatever direction the judge had given. There had been no miscarriage of justice and, accordingly, the appeal would be dismissed.

R v Grant [1995] Crim LR 715 (Court of Appeal: Lord Taylor of Gosforth CJ, Owen J and Sir Lawrence Verney, Recorder of London).

It has been held that, where a defendant is charged with possession of cannabis with intent to supply, evidence which may show that he is a dealer in drugs is admissible if the evidence is relevant to an issue in the case. Such evidence will usually be relevant to the question of whether the defendant had the particular drug in his possession with intent to supply it to another or whether it was for his own personal use. Different items found in the defendant's possession may require different considerations. Thus, the possession of large quantities of money, as opposed to the possession of other items such as scales, may not always be relevant. Evidence which is relevant is admissible subject to the judge's discretion to exclude it.

R v Brown [1995] Crim LR 716 (Court of Appeal: Swinton-Thomas LJ, Auld and Ward JJ). *R v Batt* [1994] Crim LR 592, CA (1994 Abr para 870), *R v Morris* (1995) 159 JP 1, CA (1994 Abr para 773), and *R v Wright* [1993] Crim LR 607, CA (1993 Abr para 780), considered.

796 Evidence—drug offences—possession—intent to supply—evidence of expensive goods owned

The appellant was convicted of possessing a Class A drug with intent to supply. At his trial considerable emphasis had been laid on his possession of large sums of money and luxury items typically owned by drug dealers. On appeal, *held*, it was clear that the intention to supply must relate to the particular drugs found in the appellant's possession and that to be admissible, evidence must be relevant and thus probative of that intention. It was the duty of the trial judge to ensure that irrelevant evidence was not heard, especially if it was prejudicial to the defence and if such evidence should be heard, it was the judge's duty to direct the jury on how to treat it or to disregard it. The fact that the appellant had large sums of money was admissible as evidence but required careful treatment. His ownership of the luxury items was not admissible since ownership of such items was not restricted to drug dealers and it had not been shown that they were used for drug dealing. Accordingly, the appeal would be allowed and, because the appellant had already served a considerable prison sentence, instead of ordering a retrial his conviction would be quashed.

R v Gordon [1995] 2 Cr App Rep 61 (Court of Appeal: Henry LJ, Rougier and Douglas Brown JJ). *R v Batt* (1994) 158 JP 883, CA (1994 Abr para 870), considered.

797 Evidence—drug offences—prohibition on import of drug—fraudulent evasion

The defendant appealed against his conviction of being knowingly concerned in the fraudulent evasion of the prohibition on the importation of a controlled drug, contending that evidence that cocaine had been found concealed in shoes worn by him when he arrived in the United Kingdom should have been excluded. *Held*, under the Customs and Excise Management Act 1979, s 78(2), any person entering the United Kingdom was required to answer any questions concerning his baggage or contained in it or carried with him. In demanding the production of the defendant's shoes, the customs officer who had found the cocaine was acting in pursuance of s 78(2). That provision must be understood to refer to carriage by sea, air, or train. This conclusion was not to be taken as extending the general permission conferred on customs authorities to conduct extensive searches of suspects' clothing under s 78. Section 164, which provided prerequisites for the exercise of the power to search and contained safeguards for the individual, made provision for such searches. The evidence in question had been rightly admitted and, accordingly, the appeal would be dismissed.

R v Lucien [1995] Crim LR 807 (Court of Appeal: Swinton LJ, Waterhouse and Wright JJ).

798 Evidence—evidence of bad character—defendant's propensity towards violence

The defendant was convicted of murdering his infant son. At his trial, there was no direct evidence as to who had inflicted the fatal injuries on the baby. However, one witness gave evidence that the defendant often became angry when the baby cried. Medical evidence also indicated that the baby had suffered injuries on earlier occasions which could not have been sustained accidentally. The defendant did not give or call any evidence, but relied upon evidence of his good character in the form of exculpatory statements made to the police and others. At his appeal, he contended that the trial judge should have excluded the evidence of the earlier injuries and of his bad temper, because the prosecution had not attempted to establish that he was responsible for the baby's earlier injuries. It was further claimed that the evidence should have been excluded because it was relevant only to his disposition and propensity to commit crimes of violence. The second ground for appeal was that the jury had been misdirected as to the effect of his good character. *Held*, the evidence in dispute was evidence of motive. It was admissible. The prosecution was entitled to produce it to show how the defendant had reacted to the baby on other occasions, so that it could invite the jury to infer that on the critical occasion the defendant was so angry that he resorted to gross violence. In consideration of the second ground for appeal, it was clear that the trial judge had misdirected the jury with regard to the effect of the defendant's good character. As the defendant did not give evidence but relied on the answers he had given to the police, the trial judge ought to have directed the jury to have regard to his good character when considering the credibility of what he had said. She should also have given a direction that good character was relevant to his alleged propensity to commit crimes of violence. Her failure to give such directions amounted to a material irregularity that rendered the conviction unsafe. Accordingly, the appeal would be allowed and the conviction quashed.

R v Fulcher [1995] 2 Cr App Rep 251 (Court of Appeal: Kennedy LJ, Kay and Keene JJ).

799 Evidence—exclusion—breach of code of practice—conduct of interview

The appellant's car was searched by police officers, and he admitted that a bag in it contained heroin. The appellant answered several questions as to the source of the heroin and the identity of the others involved, and was then arrested and cautioned. Two hours later at the police station, one of the police officers made a note of his earlier conversation with the appellant. Having taken legal advice, the appellant refused to answer questions when interviewed, and refused to sign the notes which the officer had made. A voire dire was held as to the admissibility of the conversation, and the judge concluded that there had not been a breach of the relevant code of practice. In cross-examination at trial, however, the police officer accepted that there had been a breach of the code of practice regarding the conduct of interviews, as the appellant had been deprived of his right to a solicitor and of his right to notify somebody of his arrest. The judge nevertheless decided that a fair trial was still possible. The appellant was convicted of conspiracy to supply heroin, and on appeal, *held*, it was for the judge, and not the police officer giving evidence, to decide whether or not there had been a breach of the code of practice relating to the conduct of interviews. The judge was not bound by the police officer's admission, and having reconsidered the matter in light of it, he had decided that his original decision was still correct. He was entitled to come to that conclusion having regard to the evidence as a whole, in particular to the nature of the questions that the appellant had been asked. Moreover, in summing up, the judge had explained to the jury the potential significance of any breaches, and had reminded the jury of the points made by the defence. Accordingly, the appeal would be dismissed.

R v Hassan [1995] Crim LR 404 (Court of Appeal: Kennedy LJ, Hidden and Bell JJ).

800 Evidence—exclusion—defence of entrapment

The Police and Criminal Evidence Act 1984, s 78 provides that the court may refuse to admit prosecution evidence if it appears that, having regard to all the circumstances, including those in which the evidence was obtained, it would have such an adverse effect on the fairness of proceedings that the court ought not to admit it.

An 11-year-old child acting under the instructions of officers in the Trading Standards Department purchased an 18 category film from a store. The child was not asked his age by the saleswoman. The company which owned the store was prosecuted by the local authority for an offence under the Video Recordings Act 1984, s 11(1). The company submitted that it had been entrapped and that, as a result of using the child's services, it had been induced to make the sale when no sale would otherwise have been made. At first instance, the justices found that the Trading Standards Department had acted ultra vires in instructing the child to purchase the video and the evidence was excluded under the 1984 Act, s 78. On appeal, *held*, no defence of entrapment was available under English law and it was not appropriate in the circumstances of the case to exclude evidence under s 78. The child did not act as an agent provocateur and did not commit an offence in purchasing the video. Nor did he incite, aid or abet the commission of an offence by the company. He simply played a part in a situation which rendered the company culpable. If there had been any element of persuasion of the saleswoman by the child, different considerations might have prevailed. The justices had been fundamentally in error and, accordingly, the appeal would be allowed.

Ealing London Borough v Woolworths plc [1995] Crim LR 58 (Queen's Bench Division: Russell LJ and Blofeld J). *DPP v Marshall* [1988] 3 All ER 683, DC (1988 Abr para 536) considered.

801 Evidence—exclusion—discretion to exclude relevant prosecution evidence—exclusion at request of co-defendant

Jamaica

Three robbers armed with guns carried out a robbery. During the robbery three men were shot and killed. The appellant and another man were charged with the murders and both pleaded not guilty. The appellant's counsel requested that the judge direct that a part of the co-defendant's police statement in which he implicated the appellant by name be excluded before it was admitted in evidence. The judge ruled that the statement should be admitted in its entirety. After the prosecution had closed its case and the appellant had testified the trial judge upheld a submission that the co-defendant had no case to answer and discharged him. The appellant was then convicted of all three murders. On appeal from the dismissal by the Court of Appeal of

Jamaica of his application for leave to appeal against conviction, *held*, a judge in a criminal trial had a discretionary power to refuse to admit relevant evidence on which the prosecution proposed to rely if he considered that its prejudicial effect outweighed its probative value. He had no discretionary power on that basis to exclude evidence at the request of a defendant in a joint trial which tended to support the defence of a co-defendant. Nor could he edit a statement made by a co-defendant on which he proposed to rely. In the present case, the part of the co-defendant's statement implicating the appellant was prima facie relevant and admissible evidence against the co-defendant. The Judge had warned the jury in his summing up that the statement was not evidence against the appellant. Accordingly, the appeal would be dismissed.

Lobban v R [1995] 2 All ER 602 (Privy Council: Lords Goff of Chieveley, Mustill, Slynn of Hadley, Nicholls of Birkenhead and Steyn).

802 Evidence—exclusion—evidence irregularly obtained—exclusion on grounds of fairness

The Police and Criminal Evidence Act 1984, s 78 provides that in any proceedings the court may refuse to allow evidence on which the prosecution proposes to rely to be given if it appears to the court that, having regard to all the circumstances, including the circumstances in which the evidence was obtained, the admission of the evidence would have such an adverse effect on the fairness of the proceedings that the court ought not to admit it.

The defendant's telephone number had been found on a person at an airport who had cocaine concealed in her clothing but was later acquitted of being knowingly concerned in the unlawful importation of drugs. The carrier had agreed to telephone the defendant, pretending she had not been arrested, and their conversation was recorded. The defendant was arrested and tried separately on the same charge of being knowingly concerned in the unlawful importation of the drug. On appeal against conviction, it was contended that the evidence should be excluded on the grounds of unfairness to the defendant. *Held*, the fact that the evidence was obtained by subterfuge did not necessarily lead to its exclusion. The distinction based on fairness or unfairness in s 78 had to be made taking account of all the circumstances of the case and the type of crime involved. The evidence was properly admitted in this case and the appeal would be dismissed.

R v Cadette [1995] Crim LR 229 (Court of Appeal: Evans LJ, Tucker and Longmore JJ).

803 Evidence—exclusion—evidence of accomplices—extradition proceedings

The Police and Criminal Evidence Act 1984, s 78 provides that in any proceedings the court may refuse to allow evidence on which the prosecution proposes to rely if it appears that having regard to all the circumstances, including the circumstances in which the evidence was obtained, the admission of the evidence would have such an adverse effect on the fairness of the proceedings that the court ought not to admit it. Section 82 provides that 'proceedings' means criminal proceedings.

A suspect awaiting a decision as to his extradition to the United States to stand trial on sixteen charges applied for a writ of habeas corpus following his committal to custody. The evidence against him consisted mainly of testimonies from eight former members of his gang. Each of those eight accomplices had pleaded guilty in the United States pursuant to a plea agreement with the prosecuting authorities. The applicant argued that it was self-evident that the plea agreement must have included a term that the accomplices would receive substantially reduced sentences in return for giving evidence against him since gang members who did not enter into such agreements had received much longer sentences. The magistrate ruled that the 1984 Act, s 78 did apply to extradition committal proceedings but that he would not exercise the discretion to exclude the evidence. *Held*, there were several clear distinctions between the position of examining justices in domestic proceedings and that of the metropolitan stipendiary magistrate in extradition proceedings (1) there was no opportunity to challenge evidence; (2) there was no abuse of process jurisdiction; (3) the Judges Rules and the Police and Criminal Evidence Act 1984 (s 66) Codes of Practice which repealed them did not apply; and (4) *R v King's Lynn Justices, ex p Holland* (1992) 156 JP 825, where it was held that the 1984 Act, s 78 applied to domestic committal proceedings, did not apply. Accordingly, extradition proceedings were not 'criminal proceedings' within the meaning of s 82 and s 78 had no application in extradition proceedings.

R v Governor of Belmarsh Prison, ex p Francis [1995] 3 All ER 634 (Queen's Bench Division: McCowan LJ and McKinnon J). *R v Governor of Pentonville Prison, ex p Lee* [1993] 3 All ER 504 applied.

804　Evidence—exclusion—evidence of DTI inspectors

The Police and Criminal Evidence Act 1984, s 78(1) provides that in any proceedings the court may refuse to allow evidence on which the prosecution proposes to rely to be given if it appears to the court that, having regard to all the circumstances in which the evidence was obtained, the admission of the evidence would have such an adverse effect on the fairness of the proceedings that the court ought not to admit it. The Companies Act 1985, s 434 provides that inspectors appointed by the Secretary of State to investigate the affairs of a company may examine on oath the officers of the company and an answer given by a person to a question put to him may be used in evidence against him.

The appellants were convicted of offences arising from a share support scheme during the takeover of one company by another. They appealed on the grounds that (1) interviews conducted by Department of Trade and Industry inspectors under the 1985 Act, in which the appellants were deprived of protection against self-incrimination, should have been excluded at their trial under the 1984 Act, s 78, and (2) having regard to the evidence between the appointment of the inspectors and the appellants' arrests, the 1985 Act procedure had been misused and the inspectors' inquiry should have given way to a police investigation. *Held*, Parliament had, by the 1985 Act, overridden the principle of self-incrimination and it was the court's duty to apply domestic law, which was unambiguous. The admission in evidence of answers which Parliament had said might be admitted could not be regarded as unfair per se under the 1984 Act, s 78 simply because of inherent features in the statutory regime under which they were obtained. However, in considering whether the application of the statutory regime created any unfairness, a judge could have in mind that under that regime there was an obligation to answer the inspectors' questions on pain of sanctions. Parliament had provided for inspectors in the field of company fraud to operate under the regime of the 1985 Act and for answers elicited to be admissible in criminal proceedings. It was not improper for the prosecuting authorities to permit that regime to take its course up to the point when they considered a police investigation should sensibly be started. On the evidence, there was no abuse of process or improper collusion which rendered the inspectors' interviews inadmissible. Accordingly, the appeals would be dismissed.

R v Saunders; R v Parnes; R v Ronson; R v Lyons [1995] 45 LS Gaz R 31 (Court of Appeal: Lord Taylor of Gosforth CJ, Macpherson of Cluny and Potter JJ).

805　Evidence—exclusion—trial within a trial in summary proceedings

The appellant was tried in the magistrates court on summonses alleging that he had committed offences under the Copyright Act 1956. He claimed that the evidence of an interview conducted by a copyright federation investigator should be excluded under the Police and Criminal Evidence Act 1984, s 78 because there had been breaches of the relevant codes of practice under the 1984 Act and also because he had not been cautioned or given access to legal assistance. The appellant submitted that he should be allowed to give evidence on the issue of admissibility without having to give evidence, and without being exposed to cross-examination, on the facts of the case generally (a 'voire dire'). The justices were of the opinion that they had no power to hold a voire dire where an accused in a summary trial raised the issue of the admissibility of evidence under the 1984 Act, s 78. On appeal, *held*, the guiding principle when an application to exclude evidence under s 78 was made in a summary trial was that the justices had to either consider the matter when it arose or leave it for consideration until the end of the hearing, taking the course of action which was most likely to secure a trial which was fair and just to both sides. Although justices were obliged to allow evidence to be given on a voire dire if an application to exclude evidence was made under s 76, the same rule did not apply in the case of an application to exclude evidence under s 78. In most magistrates' court proceedings, it was better that the whole of the prosecution case should be put, including the disputed evidence, before a voire dire was held because the issue of the exclusion of evidence under s 78 had to be considered having regard to all the circumstances of the case. If there were specific matters which a defendant sought to challenge, such as the manner in which an interview was conducted, he could be heard on a voire dire. In the instant case, although it would have been fair to have considered the voire dire at the end of the hearing, there had been a strong case against the appellant even without the disputed evidence. Accordingly, the appeal would be dismissed.

Halawa v Federation against Copyright Theft [1995] 1 Cr App Rep 21 (Queen's Bench Division: Ralph Gibson LJ and Smith J). *Vel v Chief Constable of North Wales* (1987) 151 JP 510, DC (1987 Abr para 1666) followed.

806 Evidence—guilty plea by co-defendant

In a joint trial for handling stolen goods one defendant pleaded guilty and both were convicted. The other defendant appealed, contending that his co-defendant's guilty plea should not have been admitted for the purposes of showing that the goods in question were stolen. *Held*, in the circumstances it was acceptable to adduce evidence of a co-accused's conviction in order to establish that the goods in question were stolen. The Police and Criminal Evidence Act 1984, s 74(2) provided that, where a person other than the accused was convicted of an offence, it should be assumed that he had committed that offence unless the contrary was proved. It was, in any case, open to the defence counsel to apply for a voir dire in order to establish that the guilty plea was misconceived. However, the appeal would be allowed on the grounds that the judge had failed to give an appropriate direction in respect of the defendant's previous good character and the effect of this on his credibility.

R v Pigram [1995] Crim LR 808 (Court of Appeal: Otton LJ, Ognall and Forbes JJ). *R v Berrada* (1989) 91 Cr App Rep 131n, CA (1989 Abr para 586) followed.

807 Evidence—hearsay—declarant's state of mind

See *R v Gilfoyle*, para 744.

808 Evidence—hearsay—exceptions—first-hand hearsay—admission of written statements

The Criminal Justice Act 1988, s 23(1), (2)(b) provides that a statement made by a person in a document is admissible in criminal proceedings as evidence of any fact of which direct oral evidence by him would be admissible if he is outside the United Kingdom and it is not reasonably practicable to secure his attendance.

The prosecution in a drugs trial applied to admit under the 1988 Act, s 23(2)(b) the statement of a key witness resident in Venezuela. As evidence that it was not reasonably practicable for that witness to attend, the prosecution also had a statement from a drugs officer in Venezuela which verified that the witness would not be able to attend. The judge ruled that it was not reasonably practicable for the officer to attend the proceedings in England, and his statement could therefore be accepted under s 23(2)(b). He also ruled that the officer's statement disclosed that it was not practicable for the witness to attend and, therefore, the witness's statement was also admissible under s 23(2)(b). The defendant appealed on the grounds that the judge ought not to have found that it was not reasonably practicable for the officer to attend and that, in any event, the officer could not give evidence on the witness's inability to attend as that would constitute second-hand hearsay. *Held*, when deciding whether to admit written statements under s 23(2)(b), the court had to consider a number of factors: (1) the importance of a witness's evidence and how prejudicial it was to the defendant if the witness did not attend. In this case, the court was concerned with the evidence of the witness and the officer's evidence was solely what he had been told by that witness. (2) The expense and inconvenience. This was not a major consideration, but, in the present circumstances, it would be a considerable expense for the officer to travel from Venezuela to give evidence which could not be seriously challenged in cross-examination. (3) The reasons given for the witness's inability to attend. These were findings of fact which ought not to be lightly interfered with on appeal and which, in this case were satisfactory.

This was not a case of second-hand hearsay because both witnesses were proving different things and there was no reason why the inability of the witness to attend could not be proved by a statement received under s 23(2)(b). Accordingly, the appeal would be dismissed.

R v Castillo (1995) Times, 2 November (Court of Appeal: Stuart Smith LJ, Ian Kennedy J and Judge Saville).

809 Evidence—hearsay—exceptions—first-hand hearsay—transcript of earlier criminal proceedings

At the first trial of the appellants for murder, evidence was given by a witness that the second appellant, while sharing a cell with the witness, had made a number of admissions to her. At the retrial, a transcript of that evidence was admitted, the witness having absconded from an open prison. On appeal against conviction, the first appellant contended that he should not have been tried jointly with the second appellant. The latter contended that, although the transcript had been admissible in evidence, it should have been excluded. *Held*, the transcript was admissible as first-hand hearsay under the Criminal Law Act 1988, s 23. In s 24, by virtue of which a statement prepared for the purposes of contemplated criminal proceedings may be admissible in the proceedings in specified circumstances, 'statement prepared for the purposes of contemplated criminal proceedings' included a statement made in the course of criminal proceedings. The transcript was also admissible as a 'business etc document' under s 24. The court had a discretion, under ss 25, 26, as to whether to admit a statement admissible under ss 23, 24. Although the bad character of the witness who had given the evidence in question was not an overriding factor, she had boasted of an ability to deceive and the jury should have had an opportunity to assess her demeanour and manner of giving evidence. In view of the potential unfairness to the second appellant in the jury having had no such opportunity, the transcript should have been excluded in the interests of justice. Her appeal would be allowed and her conviction quashed.

The trial judge had warned the jury repeatedly that the second appellant's out-of-court statements were not evidence against the first appellant. In permitting the joint trial to proceed, the judge had not exercised his discretion wrongly. The first appellant's appeal would be dismissed.

R v Lockley; R v Corah [1995] 2 Cr App Rep 554 (Court of Appeal: Pill LJ, Ognall and Buckley JJ).

810 Evidence—hearsay—Law Commission consultation

In 1993, the Law Commision recommended the abolition of the hearsay rule in civil proceedings (see 1993 Abr para 1243). It has now published a related consultation paper, *Evidence in Criminal Proceedings: Hearsay and Related Topics* (Law Commission consultation paper 138). It suggests that hearsay in criminal proceedings should continue to be governed by different rules from those applicable to civil proceedings and that the abolition of the rule in the latter should not necessarily mean that it should also be abolished in relation to criminal proceedings. The commission viewed several options and has ruled out the possibility of making no change to the present law, the possibility of the free admissibility of hearsay evidence and the possibility of introducing a rule requiring the court to seek the best available evidence. The options on which views are sought are an exclusionary rule with an inclusionary discretion; the current law plus an inclusionary discretion; categories of automatic admissibility; and categories of automatic admissibility plus a limited inclusionary discretion. The commission provisionally favours the last option. It proposes a definition of the hearsay rule: an assertion other than one made by a person while giving oral evidence in the proceedings is inadmissible as evidence of any fact or opinion that the person intended to assert. It further provisionally proposes that where evidence of a particular element in an offence includes hearsay, that element should not be regarded as proved unless the hearsay evidence is supported by direct evidence and that judicial discretion to exclude hearsay evidence should be restricted to existing common law and statutory discretions.

811 Evidence—identification—credibility of identification witness—court's duty to give warning

Jamaica
It has been held that, in cases where the credibility of an identification witness is the principal or sole line of defence, there might be exceptional cases where the trial judge need not give a warning to the jury in accordance with *Turnbull*, or where a warning could be given in briefer terms than in a case where the accuracy of identification is challenged. However, even in those exceptional cases, it will always be wise for the trial judge to tell the jury in an appropriate manner to consider whether it is satisfied that the witness was not mistaken in his identification.

Shand v R [1996] 1 All ER 511 (Privy Council: Lords Keith of Kinkel, Browne-Wilkinson, Slynn of Hadley, Hoffmann and Hardie Boys J). *R v Turnbull* [1976] 3 All ER 549, CA (1976 Abr para 601) considered.

812 Evidence—identification—group identification—appropriate place for identification

The appellant was charged with offences under the Trade Descriptions Act 1968. Trading standards officers arranged for a group identification to take place when the appellant went to the magistrates' court in connection with his bail. Before his trial began, the appellant submitted that the identification evidence should be excluded pursuant to the Police and Criminal Evidence Act 1984, s 78 because of its adverse effect on the fairness of the proceedings. Following a voir dire, the judge found that although there had been some breaches of the 1984 Act, Codes of Practice, Code D, by which the officers were bound, the evidence should nevertheless be admitted. On appeal against conviction, the appellant claimed that the judge's ruling was wrong. *Held*, there was evidence that at any one time between 20 and 30 people were in the foyer of the magistrates' court, young men mostly of an age equivalent to that of the appellant, and the venue was not considered inappropriate if a group identification was to be attempted. There was no evidence before the judge that the circumstances involved any unfairness and he was entitled to take the view that the identification could properly be admitted. Accordingly, the appeal would be dismissed.

R v Tiplady (1995) 159 JP 548 (Court of Appeal: Lord Taylor of Gosforth CJ, Popplewell and Steel JJ).

813 Evidence—identification—indentification from video recording and photographs— appropriate direction to jury

The appellant and 23 other people were charged with violent disorder following an incident at a demonstration. Although the appellant admitted that he had been present and had taken part in the demonstration, he argued that it had not been proved that he was one of those who had actively taken part in the violence that had occurred. The prosecution evidence consisted of a photograph of the appellant taken by the police when he was arrested the day after the demonstration, and of a video recording and still photographs taken at the time of the demonstration. It was alleged that the person shown in the still photographs was the appellant, and that the police photograph showed the same person who was in the still photographs. On his appeal against conviction, the appellant argued that the judge had not given a sufficient direction to the jury on the identification evidence and, in particular, that he had failed to give a full *Turnbull* warning. *Held*, where the identification of a defendant was by photographs or a video recording rather than by witness identification, one of the matters which a jury had to decide was whether the person shown committing the offence in the photographs or video recording was the same person whom they saw in court. In that respect, they had to decide whether or not the defendant's appearance had changed since the recording was made. A full *Turnbull* direction was only necessary and appropriate in the case of a witness identification. In the case of a photographic identification, the direction had to conform with *Dodson*. There was also a general requirement that a jury had to be warned of the risk of mistaken identification and of the need for care when making an identification. Here, the judge had given a proper direction in respect of not only the police photograph but also the still photographs and the video recording. He had also told the jury that they were to ignore the photographs if they were not satisfied that the person shown in them was the appellant. Accordingly, the appeal would be dismissed.

R v Blenkinsop [1995] 1 Cr App Rep 7 (Court of Appeal: Evans LJ, Curtis and Morrison JJ). *R v Turnbull* [1976] 3 All ER 549, CA (1986 Abr para 601) and *R v Dodson* [1984] 1 WLR 971, CA (1984 Abr para 668) considered.

814 Evidence—identification—identification from video recording and photographs— special knowledge of police officer

After a football match where the supporters were filmed and photographed as they arrived at the stadium, the appellants went near two public houses. A fracas ensued which was recorded by video cameras fixed to the buildings. The recording of the incident showed a confused scene with many supporters and other members of the public. A police officer studied this black and white film closely and compared it with the colour film and photographs taken at the match. At the trial the constable was allowed to give evidence as the video recording was played to the jury to indicate where acts of violence were taking place and to identify those committing the violent acts as persons, including the appellants, who were clearly shown on the colour film and still photographs. The appellants claimed that the identification was mistaken and appealed against conviction on the ground that the jury should have seen the video without assistance from the constable as to the identity of those involved since he did not know the appellants and could not be regarded as an expert witness. *Held*, the police officer had special knowledge that the court did not possess and which he had acquired by lengthy and studious application to material which was itself admissible evidence. It would be impractical to afford the jury the time and facilities to conduct the same research. Thus, it was legitimate to allow the officer to assist the jury by pointing to what he asserted was happening in the crowded scenes on the film. He was open to cross-examination and the jury were free to accept or reject his assertions. Accordingly, the appeals would be dismissed.

R v Clare; R v Peach (1995) 159 JP 412 (Court of Appeal: Lord Taylor of Gosforth CJ, Owen J and Judge Sir Lawrence Verney, Recorder of London).

815 Evidence—identification—identification parade—impracticability of holding parade

The appellant and his co-accused were charged with a robbery which the victim's friend witnessed. All of those involved were 15 years of age. Both the appellant and the co-accused asked for an identification parade but the identification officer decided that it was impracticable because the difference in their appearances meant that two juvenile parades would have to be held. Since it was a school holiday it would not be possible to approach a school for that purpose and because of the seriousness of the charge, the ages of those involved and the fact that one of the witnesses was due to go on holiday shortly, the officer decided it was not appropriate to delay the identification procedure. A group identification was held instead and the appellant was convicted. On appeal by way of case stated, it fell to be determined whether the youth court had been right to find that the officer was entitled to regard the holding of a parade as impracticable and that witnesses' evidence on a group identification was admissible. *Held*, there was no breach of the Police and Criminal Evidence Act 1984 Codes of Practice unless the officer's decision could be impugned as unreasonable. The court was sceptical of the police policy that it was impracticable to hold such parades during school holidays. In the present case, however, the officer had taken account of additional considerations which made it impossible to categorise her decision as perverse and it could not be criticised as one not open to her on the facts. The justices had been correct to hold that there had been no breach of the code and to admit the witnesses' evidence. Accordingly, the appeal would be dismissed.

Tomkinson v DPP [1995] Crim LR 60 (Queen's Bench Division: Simon Brown LJ and Morland J).

816 Evidence—identification—refusal of witness to testify—statement before jury that refusal based on threats

Two defendants were convicted of arson. They had been identified to the police by a witness who at the trial said that he would not give evidence because of threats. The judge admitted that statement as evidence under the Criminal Justice Act 1988, s 23, refusing to exercise a discretion to exclude under s 25. An appeal was made on the basis that the jury should have been discharged after hearing the witness's statement and that the statement should have been excluded under the 1988 Act, s 26, the judge having erroneously considered s 25. *Held*, where it was known that a witness was not prepared to give evidence, his reasons should be investigated in the jury's absence and his failure to appear explained to them in uncompromising terms. The judge should have considered excluding the statement under the 1988 Act, s 26 and not s 25. Whereas s 25 provided that a statement should be admitted unless the court was of the opinion that in the interests of justice it should not, s 26 provided that leave to admit a statement should not be given unless the court was of the opinion that it ought to be admitted in the interests of justice. The evidence given by the witness was, being identification evidence, of an intrinsically delicate nature and, had the judge considered the matter under s 26, it was possible that he would have decided to exclude it. Accordingly, the appeal would be allowed.

R v Jennings [1995] Crim LR 810 (Court of Appeal: Swinton Thomas LJ, Waterhouse and Wright JJ).

817 Evidence—identification—similar facts—cumulative identification

The defendant was convicted of two counts of indecent assault and one count of grievous bodily harm as a result of attacks on three women at separate times. The attacks were similar to those made on several other women in the same area, and identification of the defendant had been made by more than one of the victims. The defendant appealed on the ground that the judge had misdirected the jury regarding the approach to identification evidence in that an identification about which a jury was not sure could not support another identification about which it was not sure, even if the facts of the two offences were similar. *Held*, the jury had to be satisfied that the evidence showed that the offences had been committed by one man, before they could consider the identification evidence from more than one of the victims, in a cumulative manner. That had been made quite clear by the judge in this case and, accordingly, the defendant's appeal would be dismissed.

R v Barnes [1995] 2 Cr App Rep 491 (Court of Appeal: Lord Taylor of Gosforth CJ, and Ebsworth JJ).

818 Evidence—identification—warning to jury—circumstances in which warning is required

The defendant was convicted of causing grievous bodily harm in a nightclub. A witness had testified that she had seen him commit the crime and that he was very large. Other witnesses at the scene who did not see the offence described two men, one of whom was much larger than the other. At trial it was argued by the prosecution that the case depended on the witness's identification. The defendant claimed that he had been at the nightclub but that he was not involved in the disturbance. The judge directed the jury to look at the witness's observation but did not give a full *Turnbull* direction. On appeal it was argued that the judge should have given a full *Turnbull* direction. *Held*, a *Turnbull* direction was only required where there was a possibility of mistaken identification. That would generally arise when the issue was whether the accused had been present and a witness had claimed to identify him on the basis of a previous sighting. It was not always necessary to give the direction where the accused had been present and the issue was as to what he had been doing. In *R v Thornton* the court was not seeking to make the *Turnbull* direction necessary in such circumstances. In this instance, the defendant was of distinctive size, the witnesses had identified a tall man and there was no one at the scene of a remotely similar height. Accordingly, the appeal would be dismissed.

R v Slater (1995) 1 Cr App Rep 584 (Court of Appeal: Rose LJ, Holland and Kay JJ). *R v Thornton* (1994) 158 JP 1155, CA (1994 Abr para 791), *R v Turnbull* [1976] 3 All ER 549, CA (1976 Abr para 601) applied.

819 Evidence—identification—warning to jury—matters to be included in warning

Jamaica

The appellants were convicted of murdering a man by attacking him with a machete. The prosecution case was based on the visual identification of the appellants by four witnesses, one of whom gave evidence that the deceased had named his attackers shortly before dying. At trial, the defence claimed that the witnesses had been mistaken in their identifications, and the appellants did not give sworn evidence but made statements from the dock in which they put forward alibis. Additionally, the fourth appellant raised the defences of self-defence and provocation. On appeal, a number of issues were raised. *Held*, (1) in relation to identification evidence, it was not always incumbent on a judge to tell the jury that a mistaken witness could be a convincing witness, as *Turnbull* did not require the use of a set form of words. A judge had a broad discretion as to how to express himself when directing a jury on identification, and merely had to comply with the spirit and sense of the guidance provided by *Turnbull*. In the instant case, the judge had emphasised that an honest witness could still be mistaken, and that was appropriate to convey the fact that it was not enough that a witness was credible as he also had to be reliable. (2) An unsworn statement was evidentially inferior to that of a sworn statement, and a judge was entitled to bring that to the jury's attention. As the appellants had made unsworn statements in putting forward their alibis, the judge had not been obliged to direct the jury as to the impact that their rejection of the alibis had on the identification evidence, but only had to direct the jury to give the alibis such weight as they saw fit. (3) Dying declarations were admissible as evidence if at the time that the deceased made the declaration he was under a settled expectation that he would die. That exception to the hearsay rule was not to be abolished. In the instant case, as the deceased's last words were made almost contemporaneously with the attack on him, they constituted highly probative evidence. (4) Where counsel was engaged on behalf of more than one defendant, he had to consider whether or not there was a conflict of interest between them which might inhibit his proper and effective defence of one of them. On the facts of the instant case, there was no conflict of interest, and the fourth appellant had not required separate representation. Accordingly, the appeal would be dismissed.

Mills v R [1995] 3 All ER 865 (Privy Council: Lords Keith of Kinkel, Griffiths, Browne-Wilkinson, Lloyd of Berwick and Steyn). *R v Turnbull* [1976] 3 All ER 549, CA (1976 Abr para 601), *Ratten v R* [1971] 3 All ER 801, PC, and *Director of Public Prosecutions v Walker* [1974] 1 WLR 1090, PC (1974 Abr para 673) applied.

820 Evidence—psychiatric evidence of behaviour—defendant's refusal to speak at trial

See *R v Holman*, para 836.

821 Evidence—similar fact evidence—evidence to rebut defence—defence of lack of knowledge—evidence of drug possession admitted in trial concerning drug importation

The appellant had been convicted of being knowingly concerned in the fraudulent evasion of the prohibition on importation of a Class B prohibited drug. Quantities of the drug had been found concealed in a vehicle he was driving into the country. At his trial he denied any knowledge of the drugs. Evidence was presented of a search carried out at his home in England which had revealed small quantities of another Class B drug with related equipment. The purpose of the evidence was to show that the appellant indeed had knowledge of drugs and was not telling the truth when he claimed to have no knowledge. On appeal against conviction on the grounds that the evidence relating to the search of his home should not have been admitted, *held*, where a person portrayed himself as an innocent victim in this type of case, evidence showing that he had connections with the same type of substances in his home country was relevant and admissible, since the jury should be allowed to consider such a coincidence. However, this rule was qualified by the court's power to exclude such evidence on the grounds of unfair prejudice. Accordingly, the appeal would be dismissed.

R v Peters [1995] 2 Cr App Rep 77 (Court of Appeal: Evans LJ, Morland and Gage JJ). *R v Willis* (29 January 1979, unreported) applied.

822   Evidence—similar fact evidence—previous offence committed in Scotland— admissibility

The defendant was convicted of the murder of three young girls in England. Part of the prosecution evidence that went before the jury was the fact that the defendant had been convicted a few years earlier for assault and indecent assault of a young girl in Scotland, with similar features to the crimes in issue. The defendant appealed against his conviction on the ground that the Scottish conviction was inadmissible. *Held*, where the facts of a crime are similar to those of another, the court is entitled to take the first crime into account when considering the second, regardless of the prejudicial effect this might have. In this case, the similarities between the Scottish case and the present case were so striking that the decision to allow the facts of the Scottish case to be put before the jury was totally justified. The jury must consider whether both offences were committed by the same man, whoever that might be, and then decide whether the defendant was that man. The judge's directions in this case had been to that effect and could not therefore be criticised. Accordingly, the defendant's appeal would be dismissed.

R v Black (1995) Times, 1 March (Court of Appeal: Lord Taylor of Gosforth CJ, Ognall and Steel JJ).

823   Evidence—statement made by co-accused—evidence adduced by cross- examination of prosecution witness as to facts in statement

The three defendants, A, B and C, admitted burgling a shop. They also admitted causing a fire which resulted in the death of an occupant in the flat above the shop. B and C claimed that A had started the fire while A said that B and C had started the fire. A claimed that he had been told by B that B and C always set light to premises they had burgled and that B had confirmed that he and C had done so a week before when they burgled an office. At the defendants' trial, two prosecution witnesses gave evidence that they had seen B and C at the scene of the office burglary and the judge gave leave for A's counsel to cross-examine the witnesses to establish the truth about what B had told A. The defendants' were all convicted of manslaughter on the basis of a joint enterprise. On their appeal against conviction, B and C submitted that the judge had been wrong to admit the evidence of the prosecution witnesses. *Held*, whether A's claims that B and C had committed the previous burglary and arson were true or not were irrelevant to the issues of guilt in the present case. But if what was, according to A, said by B could be shown to have been true, then it was more likely that B had said it than if his claims were exaggerated or false. That appeared to satisfy the test of relevance because the evidence tended to show that the version of the facts put forward by one co-accused was more probable than that put forward by the other. The truth of what was alleged to have been said was clearly established by the evidence which was admitted. To have excluded it would seriously have handicapped A in his defence. The judge's ruling had been correct and, accordingly, the appeal would be dismissed.

R v Thompson; R v Sinclair; R v Maver [1995] 2 Cr App R 589 (Court of Appeal: Evans LJ, Kay and Collins JJ).

824   Evidence—use of DNA profiles from blood sample taken during previous investigation—failure to destroy sample and profiles after investigation—breach of statutory duty

The appellant was charged with the rape of two girls in 1991. During the investigation he was asked to provide a blood sample for DNA profiles which, he was told, would be destroyed pursuant to the Police and Criminal Evidence Act 1984, s 64 if he was acquitted. He was further informed that if he refused without good cause to give a sample a jury could draw inferences from his refusal. He provided a sample and his details were entered onto a DNA database. A match showed with a sample taken from a rape victim three years earlier, but, at that point, the appellant was acquitted of raping the two girls and the sample, profiles and information on the database should have been destroyed. Instead, the database operator notified the police of the apparent match. The appellant was arrested and was informed that the DNA profiles had been retained. At first instance, the appellant submitted that the judge should use his discretion to exclude the DNA evidence under s 78 on the basis that it would have such an adverse effect on the fairness of the proceedings that the court ought not to admit it. The judge rejected the submission and the appellant was convicted. On appeal, *held*, not only was there a breach of s 64, but the appellant had in effect been misled in consenting to give the sample by statements and promises which were not honoured. To allow the sample to be used in evidence at a trial four years after the alleged offences when it had been retained in breach of statutory duty and in breach of the undertakings to the appellant had to have an adverse effect on the fairness of the trial. The sample should not have been admitted and without it the evidence was insufficient to render the verdict safe and satisfactory. The admission of the DNA profiles must have played a predominant part in the jury's deliberations. Accordingly, the appeal would be allowed and the conviction quashed.

R v Nathaniel (1995) 159 JP 419 (Court of Appeal: Lord Taylor of Gosforth CJ, Owen J and Sir Lawrence Verney, Recorder of London).

825 Evidence—witness—credibility—failure to call police officer under suspension

Proceedings were brought for the alleged threatening and assaulting of police officers. At the time of the trial one of the officers involved was under suspension for unrelated reasons. The case was dismissed for abuse of process because the prosecution refused to call the suspended officer. An application was then made for an order of certiorari to quash that decision. *Held*, the credibility of a witness should be determined in relation to the content of his evidence alone unless there was reason to believe that his evidence might be untrue because, for example, he had been convicted of perverting the course of justice. Where the evidence a witness was to give was merely peripheral or corroborative of other evidence there could be no objection to the prosecution's failure to call him if they felt that it was possible to proceed without him. The situation was different where the witness was central to the incident which lead to the charge. In the present case the proper course would have been to call the officer as a witness and to establish at the outset that he was suspended. Instead of dismissing the case the justices should have used their own power to call the officer as a witness. Accordingly, the application would be granted.

R v Haringey Justices, ex p DPP [1996] 1 All ER 828 (Queen's Bench Division: Stuart-Smith LJ and Butterfield J).

826 Evidence—witness—summons for production of documents—witness's instructions to solicitor—legal professional privilege

The appellant made a statement to his solicitor in which he admitted a murder. He later retracted the statement, claiming that although he had been present at the scene, his stepfather had committed the murder. The appellant was acquitted of the murder at trial and the stepfather was subsequently charged with the murder. At the stepfather's committal proceedings, the appellant was asked about his original instructions to his solicitors. He declined to waive legal professional privilege and the magistrate issued summonses under the Magistrates' Courts Act 1980, s 97 directing the applicant and his solicitor to produce the relevant proofs of evidence. The summonses were upheld on appeal. On further appeal, *held*, the use of previous inconsistent statements was governed by the Criminal Procedure Act 1865, ss 4 and 5. The 1865 Act contemplated cross-examining counsel having the inconsistent statement in his hand so that the procedure which might culminate in the document becoming admissible could begin. The 1980 Act, s 97, however, contemplated the production by a witness of documents which were immediately admissible per se. Section 97 could not be used to obtain discovery, which was primarily what was sought in the present case, and the summonses ought not to have been granted under s 97. The second issue, which arose only if the conditions for issue of a witness summons under s 97 were satisfied, was whether the magistrate was obliged to weigh competing public interests in accordance with the decision in *R v Ataou*. The principle that ran through all the cases was that a man had to be able to consult his lawyer in confidence, since otherwise he might hold back half the truth. Legal professional privilege was a fundamental condition on which the administration of justice as a whole rested. Once it was established, no exception could be allowed to its absolute nature. *R v Ataou* had been wrongly decided and the appeal would, accordingly, be allowed.

R v Derby Magistrates' Court, ex p B [1995] 4 All ER 526 (House of Lords: Lords Keith of Kinkel, Mustill, Taylor of Gosforth CJ, Lloyd of Berwick and Nicholls of Birkenhead). Decision of Queen's Bench Divisional Court (1994) Times, 31 October (1994 Abr para 810) reversed. *R v Ataou* [1988] QB 798, CA (1987 Abr para 634) and *R v Barton* [1972] 2 All ER 1192 overruled.

827 Evidence—witness—written statement of deceased witness

Under the Criminal Justice Act 1988, s 23 a statement made by a person in a document is admissible in criminal proceedings as evidence of any fact of which direct oral evidence by him would be admissible where that person is dead if the statement was made to a police officer or some other person charged with the duty of investigating offences or charging offenders.

The prosecution alleged that the appellant, the owner of a company, failed to keep sufficient records or books showing how much value added tax was due with the intention of evading payment. The lack of documentation made it impossible to establish the precise sum owed. The appellant's accountant made a statement to Customs and Excise officers in which he said that he could establish a certain level of tax liability and that he had noticed a large discrepancy between purchase totals and sales invoices. Before the appellant was brought to trial the accountant died. At the trial, the judge admitted the accountant's statement as evidence under s 23 and the appellant was convicted. On appeal, *held*, the judge gave careful consideration to the question of admissibility and directed himself in accordance with *R v Cole* that it was appropriate to have regard to the likelihood of the appellant himself being able to refute the statement's contents. He had asked himself the appropriate questions and correctly applied the criteria set out, in particular, in s 26. Where a trial judge was required to exercise a discretion, the fact that the Court of Appeal might have exercised its discretion differently was not a good ground for allowing an appeal and did not mean that there was a material irregularity. The judge had made no error in exercising his discretion and, accordingly, the appeal would be dismissed.

R v Grafton [1995] Crim LR 61 (Court of Appeal: McCowan LJ, Scott-Baker and Blofeld JJ). *R v Cole* [1990] 2 All ER 108, CA (1990 Abr para 575) considered.

828 Indictment—charges stayed at committal proceedings—power to include stayed charges in indictment

The appellant was charged with 16 offences, including rape and bestiality, involving his wives and children. At the committal proceedings, seven charges were stayed on the ground of abuse of process because to investigate and determine charges 30 to 40 years after the alleged commission of the offences might make it improbable for the defendant to have a fair trial. The magistrate nevertheless went on to admit statements which formed the basis of the excluded charges and they were included in the committal papers. At the appellant's trial, the judge permitted the prosecution to include the stayed charges in the indictment. The appellant was convicted of 12 offences and was sentenced to a total of 12 years' imprisonment. On appeal against conviction, he submitted that it had not been open to the prosecution to resurrect charges which had been stayed. *Held*, under the Administration of Justice (Miscellaneous Provisions) Act 1933, s 2(2) the judge had the power to include in counts any offences disclosed on the depositions, whether or not the justices had committed on them. There was nothing in the 1933 Act to say that could not be done even where counts had been stayed on the ground of abuse of process as opposed to insufficiency of evidence. In addition, even where the statements had not been included in the committal bundle it would still have been open to the prosecution to have sought a voluntary bill of indictment from a High Court judge. Accordingly, the appeal would be dismissed.

R v C (1994) 159 JP 205 (Court of Appeal: McCowan LJ, Schiemann and Dyson JJ).

829 Indictment—joinder of offences—dangerous driving and aggravated vehicle-taking—abuse of process

The appellant was charged with aggravated vehicle-taking based on dangerous driving. At his trial, counts of dangerous driving were added to the indictment and the defendant pleaded guilty. He later appealed against the convictions of dangerous driving. He argued that it was repetitive to add a charge of dangerous driving to an indictment for aggravated vehicle-taking. *Held*, there was an important distinction between the offences of dangerous driving and aggravated vehicle-taking. A charge of dangerous driving could only be brought against the driver of a vehicle. Presence in the vehicle did not, of itself, make a defendant an aider and abettor of dangerous driving. By contrast a defendant who was in a vehicle and had been a party to its taking without consent could be guilty of aggravated vehicle-taking even if he was not the driver. Moreover, proof of dangerous driving was not sufficient to prove aggravated vehicle-taking. The legal characteristics of the offences and the evidence necessary to convict were quite different. Therefore, the judge had exercised his discretion correctly in allowing the indictment to contain two counts. There was no abuse of process and no basis for the argument that the counts were based on substantially the same evidence. Accordingly, the appeal would be dismissed.

R v Harding [1995] Crim LR 733 (Court of Appeal: Leggatt LJ, Latham and Harrison JJ). Dictum of Lord Morris of Borth-y-Gest in *Connelly v DPP* [1964] 2 WLR 1145 at 1157, HL considered.

830 Interception of communications—communication by means of public telecommunication system—police station switchboard

The Interception of Communications Act 1985, s 1(1), (2) provides that a person who intentionally intercepts a communication in the course of its transmission by post or by means of a public telecommunication system is guilty of an offence unless the communication is intercepted in accordance with a warrant issued by the Secretary of State or the person has reasonable grounds for believing that the person to whom, or the person by whom the communication is sent has consented to the interception.

The appellants had been convicted of conspiracy to supply controlled drugs. They had pleaded guilty after the judge ruled that transcripts of calls made by a co-defendant from a police station's pay phone were admissible against them. The calls had been routed through the police station's internal switchboard. The judge ruled that the interception was only unlawful under s 1(1) if the interception took place on the public telecommunication system. *Held*, it was clear from its wording that s 1(1) was confined to tapping or interception of lines forming part of a public system and did not extend to the tapping of lines forming part of a private system. Interception took place when, and at the place where, the electrical impulse or signal which was passing along the line was intercepted in fact. If there was an interception of a private system, the communication was not at that time passing through the public system. 'Communication' did not refer to the whole of a transmission, it referred to the electrical impulse or signal which was affected by the interception. The fact that later or earlier signals have formed or will form part of the communication does not mean that interception takes place at some other place or time.

R v Ahmed [1995] Crim LR 246 (Court of Appeal: Evans LJ, Curtis and Morison JJ).

831 Interception of communications—interception by non-resident of United Kingdom—admissibility of intercepted telephone calls

The United States government applied to the Secretary of State for the extradition of the applicant to face charges of conspiracy to cause explosions and attempting to procure arms and munitions from the United States for use by an Irish terrorist organisation. The applicant was arrested and subsequently committed to prison by the stipendiary magistrate pending the Secretary of State's decision regarding his return to the United States. Thereafter the applicant sought a writ of habeas corpus challenging his committal on the ground that the evidence against him, which was contained in three telephone calls made to him in Ireland by two co-conspirators in Florida which had been intercepted in the United States by its own government agents, was inadmissible in all proceedings in the United Kingdom. In particular, he contended (1) that the United States government agents, by intercepting telephone calls in Florida which at some stage in the course of transmission were routed to Ireland through one of the designated United Kingdom telecommunication systems, had prima facie committed an offence contrary to the Interception of Communications Act 1985, s 1, and (2) that the use of that evidence in extradition proceedings was therefore prohibited under s 9 of the Act. *Held*, on its true construction, the 1985 Act, s 1 did not create an offence triable in the United Kingdom in respect of an act committed outside the United Kingdom by a non-resident. Moreover, where an interception had been made outside the United Kingdom, there was no evidence that an offence under s 1 had been committed by a 'public telecommunications operator' or 'any person engaged in the running of a public telecommunication system' within the United Kingdom and, as a result, the conditions required by s 9 of the Act for the exclusion of evidence could not be satisfied. On the facts, there was no evidence that any person engaged in the running or operation of a public telecommunication system in the United Kingdom had been involved in the interception of the three telephone conversations. It followed that evidence of those conversations was not excluded by the provisions of the 1985 Act, s 9 and was therefore admissible in the extradition proceedings. Accordingly, the application would dismissed.

R v Governor of Belmarsh Prison, ex p Martin [1995] 2 All ER 548 (Queen's Bench Division: McCowan LJ and Gage J).

832   Investigation of offences—report to Crown Prosecution Service—discovery—public interest immunity

See *O'Sullivan v Commissioner of Police of the Metropolis*, para 1072.

833   Legal aid

See LEGAL AID.

834   Magistrates' courts

See MAGISTRATES.

835   Mutual assistance in criminal matters—agreement with Thailand

A treaty has been signed between the United Kingdom and the Kingdom of Thailand on mutual assistance in criminal matters (Cm 2792). The treaty relates to assistance in connection with investigations, prosecutions and other proceedings relating to criminal matters. Specific examples of such assistance include taking testimony and statements of persons, providing documents, records and evidence, serving documents, executing requests for searches and seizures, transferring persons in custody to give testimony, locating persons and assisting in restraint and forfeiture proceedings. Assistance will not be provided under the treaty to private parties. The treaty is expressly stated not to apply to the execution of arrest warrants or to military offences (as defined): art 1. A request for assistance may be refused on the ground that it prejudices sovereignty or the essential interests of the requested party, or that it relates to a political offence. The execution of a request may be postponed if it would interfere with an on-going criminal investigation: art 2. The contents of the request are specified in art 4. The costs of executing requests fall, with some exceptions, on the requesting party: art 6. Information and evidence obtained under the treaty may only be used, in the absence of prior consent by the requested party, for the purposes stated in the request. The request for assistance may be kept confidential at the request of the requesting party who may also impose conditions of confidentiality on the information or evidence supplied: art 7. A person summoned to give testimony, make a statement, or produce documents, etc in the territory of the requested party may be compelled to do so as in criminal investigations and prosecutions in that territory. A person specified in the request may be permitted to witness the taking of testimony, etc and may question the person whose testimony is being taken: art 8. Forms are appended to the treaty for authenticating business records and records of government offices or agencies and for certifying the continuity of custody of any article seized under the treaty, its identity and the integrity of its condition. A person in custody may be transported to the territory of the requesting party to give evidence only with that person's consent and that of the requested party (art 12); once a person has been so transported that person will entitled to safe conduct in the territory of the requesting party: art 17. Requests for the restraint of the proceeds or instruments of crime may be made in accordance with art 14 and for the confiscation of such in accordance with art 15. The treaty is subject to ratification and will enter into force on the exchange of the instruments of ratification: art 21.

836   Plea—refusal to plead—defendant mute of malice—judge entering not guilty plea—jury not empanelled to decide fitness to plead—psychiatric evidence of defendant's behaviour not admitted

The Criminal Law Act 1967, s 6(1)(c) provides that where a person is arraigned on an indictment, if he stands mute of malice or will not answer directly to the indictment, the court may order a plea of not guilty to be entered on his behalf, and he is then to be treated as having pleaded not guilty.

The appellant was charged with blackmail and other offences. When she was arraigned she did not answer orally to the indictment but shook her head when the counts were put to her. The judge directed that a plea of not guilty be entered; he did not empanel a jury to try an issue whether she was mute of malice or by visitation of God. The appellant did not speak for several months before her trial and, at her trial, she gave evidence by making written replies to oral questions. The judge heard psychiatric evidence in the jury's absence that she was suffering from hysteria but that she was not unfit to plead and had asserted to her psychiatrist that she was not guilty. The judge did not admit the psychiatric evidence before the jury. The appellant was convicted and, on appeal, she submitted that (1) the judge had been wrong to rule against the jury deciding on the issue of fitness to plead, and (2) because the jury might have drawn unflattering inferences from what might be seen as her attempt to manipulate the proceedings, psychiatric evidence should have been admitted to explain her behaviour. *Held*, (1) the judge had been correct to rule as he did. Where an accused was dumb but still able to communicate in and understand the trial proceedings, the judge was not debarred from entering a plea of not guilty by virtue of s 6(1)(c). The appellant was fit to be tried, wanted to plead guilty and communicated her case effectively if unconventionally. (2) The judge had dealt properly with the matter and told the jury to ignore why the appellant gave evidence in an unconventional way. The appellant's defence was not based on her mental state but on a complete denial of the offences. Accordingly, the appeal would be dismissed.

R v Holman [1995] Crim LR 80 (Court of Appeal: Kennedy LJ, Mitchell and Bell JJ).

837 Power of entry—entry to private premises without a warrant—prevention of breach of the peace

The plaintiff, who was divorced from her husband, was ordered by the county court to deliver up certain furniture and effects to the husband. Three days before the expiry of the time limit for complying with the order, the husband went to the plaintiff's house with two police officers, whose attendance had been arranged by the husband's solicitors. The husband went into the house and proceeded to load furniture into a van. The plaintiff then arrived on the scene and demanded that the furniture be returned to the house, but one of the police officers insisted that the van was not to be unloaded, that the husband be allowed to drive away and that any disputes would have to be sorted out later between the parties' solicitors. The plaintiff subsequently brought proceedings in the High Court against the police claiming damages for trespass and breach of duty but her action was dismissed. On appeal, *held*, at common law the police had power to enter private premises without a warrant to prevent a breach of the peace occurring there if they reasonably believed a breach was likely to occur on the premises, which power was expressly preserved by the Police and Criminal Evidence Act 1984, s 17(6). In particular, the police power of entry to prevent a breach of the peace was not restricted to entering premises where public meetings were held. However, before exercising the power of entry onto private premises, the police had to have a genuine belief that there was a real and imminent risk of a breach of the peace occurring and were required to act with great care and discretion, particularly when exercising the power of entry against the wishes of the owner or occupier of the premises. On the facts, the police officers had a lawful excuse for entering the plaintiff's property. The appeal would therefore be dismissed.

McLeod v Metropolitan Police Comr [1994] 4 All ER 553 (Court of Appeal: Neill, Hoffmann and Waite LJJ).

838 Pre-trial hearings—government consultation

The Home Office has issued a consultation document, *Improving the Effectiveness of Pre-Trial Hearings in the Crown Court* (Cm 2924), in which it suggests that judges should have the power to make binding rulings at any point after a case has been transferred to the Crown Court. Such rulings could be made at a plea and directions hearing or subsequently and might have effect, by way of example, in relation to the number and nature of the counts on which the prosecution will proceed, the identity and number of witnesses to be called, and the pleas to be entered by the defence. Such rulings would not be subject to appeal to a higher court, but a judge would have jurisdiction to vary or discharge such rulings. Subject to a pilot scheme and an assessment of the costs, it is further proposed that preparatory hearings, similar to those held under the Criminal Justice Act 1987 in cases of serious or complex fraud, should be introduced for other complex and potentially lengthy cases in the Crown Court.

839 Prisoners (Return to Custody) Act 1995

See para 2404.

840 Proceeds of Crime Act 1995

The Proceeds of Crime Act 1995 makes further provision in relation to the recovery of the proceeds of criminal conduct and for facilitating the enforcement of overseas forfeiture and restraint orders. The Act received royal assent on 28 June 1995 and certain provisions came into force on that date. The remaining provisions came into force on 28 June 1995. For details of commencement, see the commencement table in the title STATUTES.

Under s 1 it is the duty of the court to make a confiscation order if the prosecutor or the court considers that it would be appropriate. The court may, for the purpose of determining whether a defendant has benefited from relevant criminal conduct and for assessing the value of the defendant's benefit from such conduct, make the rebuttable assumption that property transferred to the defendant in the six years prior to the institution of proceedings was derived from crime: s 2. The prosecutor must tender a statement to the court as to any relevant matters to determine such conduct and any benefit from that conduct: s 3. Under s 4 a defendant may be ordered to give the court information to assist it in carrying out its functions. Section 5 provides for the review of cases where proceeds of crime were not assessed in the original proceedings. Under s 6 there may be a revision of an assessment of the proceeds of crime and s 7 provides for revision of the assessment of the amount to be recovered. Where a defendant serves a term of imprisonment in default of paying any amount due under a confiscation order, the order continues to have effect for the purposes of other methods of enforcement: s 8. Interest may be payable on sums unpaid under confiscation orders: s 9. Section 10 provides for the variation of an order on a receiver's application. Section 11 enables the court, on an application made by a police constable, to order that a person must make material available for the purposes of an investigation into whether any person has benefited from criminal conduct. A search warrant may be issued for the same purpose: s 12. Provision is made for the disclosure of information held be government departments: s 13. Section 14 provides for the enforcement of overseas forfeiture and restraint orders in the United Kingdom. Consequential and transitional amendments and repeals are made under s 15 and Sch 1. Section 16 relates to short title, interpretation, commencement and extent.

841   Proceeds of Crime (Scotland) Act 1995

The Proceeds of Crime (Scotland) Act 1995 consolidates as regards Scotland certain enactments relating to the confiscation of the proceeds of, and forfeiture of property used in, crime. Certain provisions extend to England and Wales. The Act received the royal assent on 8 November 1995 and came into force on 1 April 1996.

The provisions which extend to England and Wales are: ss 42 (enforcement of Scottish orders in England and Wales), 44 and Sch 2 (sequestration, bankruptcy, winding up or receivership of persons or companies holding realisable or forfeitable property), and s 50 (short title, commencement and extent).

842   Prosecution of offences—delay—failure to emphasise delay in summing up

The appellant had been convicted of a number of offences of indecent assault on young male relatives which had occurred up to 23 years before his trial. His appeal was based on the grounds that the trial judge had failed in his summing up to make any reference to the difficulty for the defence caused by the lapse of time between the alleged offences and their being reported. *Held*, the issue as to whether a judge should, in his summing up, make such a reference depended on the length of the delay, the cogency of the evidence and the circumstances of the case. In this instance, it had been many years before the accusations were made and the evidence was not corroborated. Accordingly, the judge should have given a direction and the appeal would be allowed.

R v E (Sexual Abuse: Delay) (1995) Times, 6 July (Court of Appeal: Lord Taylor of Gosforth CJ, Rougier and Ebsworth JJ).

843   Prosecution of offences—delay—stay of proceedings—direction by judge

The defendant was convicted of rape and indecent assault in relation to incidents that occurred between 17 and 23 years before his trial. He unsuccessfully sought a stay of the indictment on the ground that owing to the age of the complaints there was an abuse of process. On appeal by the defendant, *held*, a stay could only be employed in exceptional circumstances but a judge must give appropriate directions where there had been considerable delay which might prejudice the defendant. In this case, the judge had failed to refer to any of the difficulties faced by the defence as a result of the delay and this was a material misdirection or non-direction.

R v Birchall (1995) Times, 23 March (Court of Appeal: Hutchison LJ, Curtis J and Sir Lawrence Verney QC, Recorder of London).

844   Prosecution of offences—mode of trial procedure—co-defendants

See *R v Ipswich Justices, ex p Callaghan*, para 2019.

845   Restrictions on reporting—criminal proceedings

See PRESS AND PRINTING.

846 Search and seizure—search warrant—material relevant to overseas investigation—circumstances in which warrant may be granted

A Customs and Excise officer made an ex parte application for a warrant to search and seize documents from the premises of a firm of accountants. The application was made on the direction of the Secretary of State under the Criminal Justice (International Co-operation) Act 1990, s 7, following a request by American authorities who were investigating money-laundering offences. Although the judge had no experience of such applications, he quickly read through the application and issued the required search warrants. On the accountants' application for judicial review of the decision, *held*, a search warrant was an intrusion into the liberty of the person, and therefore great caution was required before granting an ex parte application for such a warrant. Here, the judge had relied solely on what the customs and excise officer had told him, rather than satisfying himself that the relevant statutory requirements had been met, and he could not have analysed and sorted out all of the evidence in the short time which he took to consider the application. Moreover, given that the hearing was so short and that the judge was referred to virtually no statutory provisions or other information, the judge should have given a short statement of his reasons for granting the warrant, so that it could be apparent that he had taken the appropriate matters into account. Accordingly, the application would be granted.

R v Crown Court at Southwark and HM Customs and Excise, ex p Sorsky Defries [1996] Crim LR 195 (Queen's Bench Division: McCowan LJ and Waller J).

847 Search and seizure—seizure of controlled drug—police acting on information received—effect of delay

Scotland

The Misuse of Drugs Act 1971, s 23(2) provides that, if a constable has reasonable grounds to suspect that any person is in possession of a controlled drug in contravention of the 1971 Act or any regulation made thereunder, the constable may search that person, and detain him for the purpose of searching him.

The police received information that the accused was involved in the possession and supply of controlled drugs. Some attempt was made to trace him but he could not be found. Approximately two months later, two officers recognised the accused in the street. They detained him in order to search him. He was found to be in possession of a quantity of cannabis resin and was subsequently convicted of possession of a controlled drug under the 1971 Act, s 5(2). The accused appealed against his conviction. *Held*, at the time of the detention of the accused, the police officers did not have reasonable grounds for suspecting him to be in unlawful possession of a controlled drug. The information upon which they had proceeded was too old. No other evidence formed a sound basis for their having reasonable grounds to believe that he was in possession of a controlled drug. Accordingly, they were not entitled to carry out the search in terms of s 23(2). The appeal would be allowed and the conviction quashed.

Ireland v Russell 1995 SLT 1348 (High Court of Justiciary).

848 Search and seizure—seizure of motor vehicle—damage to vehicle while in police possession—liability of police

See *Sutcliffe v Chief Constable of West Yorkshire*, para 2163.

849 Stay of proceedings—prejudice to fair trial—driving offence—destruction of vehicle before charge

The defendant was convicted of causing death by careless driving while under the influence of drink or drugs. At the defendant's appeal against his conviction, the issue arose as to whether the proceedings should have been stayed. Due to an oversight by the police, the defendant's car had been scrapped before he had been charged with an offence and, therefore, before the defence had the opportunity to inspect the vehicle. *Held*, the jurisdictional basis of the court's power to stay proceedings was the duty to uphold the law by protecting its own purposes and functions. The jurisdiction would usually be exercised in cases where the court had either concluded that the defendant could not receive a fair trial or that it would be unfair for him to be tried. Notwithstanding these underlying principles, the law remained in a stage of development and each case had to be considered on its own facts. In the present case, the question of whether the conviction was unsafe or unsatisfactory had to be considered both at the stage when the application to stay the proceedings was made, and in hindsight. The court also had to consider whether it was fair to bring the defendant to trial when the car had been destroyed. On the facts of the case, the absence of the car did not affect the fairness of the trial. Accordingly, the appeal would be dismissed.

R v Beckford [1995] RTR 251 (Court of Appeal: Neill LJ, Alliott and Rix JJ). Dictum of Sir Roger Ormrod in *R v Crown Court at Derby, ex p Brooks* (1984) 80 Cr App Rep 164 at 168, DC (1984 Abr para 714) approved. *R v Horseferry Road Magistrates' Court, ex p Bennett* [1993] 3 ALL ER 138, HL (1993 Abr para 38) considered.

850 Trial—acquittal following close of prosecution case

The appellant was charged with assault occasioning actual bodily harm following an incident in a pub. At trial, having heard the evidence of the prosecution witnesses, in particular the evidence of an independent witness which was favourable to the appellant, the judge directed the jury that they could hear evidence on behalf of the defence if they so wished or they could retire to consider their verdict on the basis of the prosecution evidence that they had heard. The jury decided to hear the defence evidence, and returned a guilty verdict. On appeal, the appellant argued that the verdict was unsafe and unsatisfactory. *Held*, the judge's direction might have given the jury the impression that the independent witness's evidence was so honest and accurate that the appellant should be acquitted. However, although a judge was entitled to remind a jury of their right to stop a case and acquit a defendant at the close of the prosecution case, he could only intimate that right and could not invite the jury to do so. If a judge thought that the case against a defendant was too unsafe or unsatisfactory to put to a jury, he was obliged to stop the case himself rather than cast that burden onto the jury. Here, the case was fit to go to the jury even though the judge had thought that an acquittal was inevitable. Although his intervention had been unwise, the jury had decided the case upon the evidence and their verdict was not unsafe or unsatisfactory. Accordingly, the appeal would be dismissed.

R v Kemp [1995] 1 Cr App Rep 151 (Court of Appeal: McCowan LJ, Morland and Buckley JJ).

851 Trial—calling of witnesses—discretion of prosecution—guidelines

It has been held that the prosecution must generally have at court all witnesses whose statements have been served as witnesses on whom the prosecution intend to rely, if the defence want those witnesses to attend. In deciding which statements to serve, the prosecution has an unfettered discretion, but must normally disclose material statements not served. The prosecution enjoys a discretion whether to call, or tender, any witness it requires to attend, but the discretion is not unfettered and must be exercised in the interests of justice, so as to promote a fair trial. In practice, the prosecution ought normally to call or offer to call all the witnesses who can give direct evidence of the primary facts of the case, unless for good reason the prosecutor regards the witness's evidence as incredible or unbelievable, but he cannot regard a witness as incredible merely because his account is not favourable to the prosecution's case. However, a prosecutor is not obliged to proffer a witness merely in order to give the defence material with which to attack the credit of other witnesses on whom the Crown relies. Moreover, because the judgment to be made is primarily that of the prosecutor, in general the court will only interfere with it if he has erred in principle.

R v Russell-Jones [1995] 3 All ER 239 (Court of Appeal: Kennedy LJ, Owen and Laws JJ).

852 Trial—change of solicitor—appeal proceedings

On appeal against her conviction of murder, the appellant criticised her trial counsel and solicitors for wrongly conceding that the victim had been murdered, for failing to adduce certain expert evidence that might have supported a defence of accidental death and for failing to call a number of character witnesses. *Held*, the court rejected entirely the criticisms. In particular, leading trial counsel had not been allowed adequate time to deal with the very serious allegations against him and, as the transcripts were made available to the court but not to him, he had been obliged to rely on his recollection. That was unfair both to him and the court. The court would re-emphasise that there ought to be professional rules of conduct to ensure that fresh solicitors and counsel instructed in criminal appeals communicated promptly with those who had appeared at the trial.

R v Bowler (1995) Times, 9 May (Court of Appeal: Swinton Thomas LJ, Latham and Morison JJ).

853 Trial—conduct of trial judge—hostility to defendant

See *R v Wood*, para 2395.

854 Trial—conviction—civil action against solicitors for negligent conduct of trial— whether abuse of process

See *Smith v Linskills (a Firm)*, para 2355.

855 Trial—fairness of trial—defendant with physical disability—fitness to plead or face trial—application for stay of proceedings

New Zealand

At a criminal trial, the accused applied for a stay of the proceedings on the basis that he suffered from a medical condition which made it impossible for him to face trial or, to obtain a fair trial. Several years previously, he had suffered two accidents which left him in considerable pain. The pain was relieved by means of an injection of morphine direct to his spine every six hours. However, the drugs had a number of undesirable side effects including sleepiness, inability to concentrate and, at times, respiratory depression. The level of pain would be reduced after each injection, but it would then increase. There was no evidence that the accused suffered from any psychiatric disability or illness. *Held*, in cases where the accused was not fit to stand trial, justice required the court to exercise its inherent jurisdiction and order a stay of proceedings. The accused had a constitutional right to a fair trial. It would not be fair if he suffered from a disability that effectively prevented him either from defending himself or, from comprehending what was taking place. Despite taking morphine, the accused was able to understand various matters relating to the court hearing and, to distinguish the various functions of the judge, prosecuting counsel and defence counsel. He understood that it was for the jury to determine his guilt or innocence. He also understood the court procedure and appeared to have the cognition and perception of an ordinary person not on medication. He was not suffering from a disability that would prevent him from entering a plea and facing trial. Accordingly, the application would be dismissed.

R v Duval [1995] 3 NZLR 202 (High Court).

856 Trial—jury

See JURIES.

857 Trial—mode of trial—cases capable of being dealt with in a magistrates' court— government consultation

See para 2012.

858 Trial—offence triable either way joined with summary offence—acquittal of offence triable either way

The Criminal Justice Act 1988, s 41(1) provides that where a magistrates' court commits a person to the Crown Court for trial on indictment for an offence triable either way, it may also commit him for trial for any summary offence with which he is charged which (a) could involve disqualification from driving, and (b) arises out of circumstances which appear to the court to be the same or connected with the offence triable either way. Under s 41(5), if the defendant is convicted on the indictment, the Crown Court must consider whether the conditions specified in s 41(1) were satisfied. Section 41(11) provides that where the Court of Appeal allows an appeal against conviction of an offence triable either way, it must also set aside the conviction of a summary offence of which the defendant had also been convicted in the Crown Court under s 41(1).

The defendant was committed to the Crown Court for trial on charges of possession of an offensive weapon (count 1), driving while disqualified (count 2) and, by virtue of the 1988 Act, s 41, on a charge of having no insurance. He was acquitted of the offence under count 1 and convicted on count 2 and of having no insurance. On his appeal against conviction, it fell to be determined whether a summary offence, such as count 2, could properly be added to an indictment containing an offence which was triable either way, such as count 1, and (2) whether the court had power to deal with the charge of having no insurance once the defendant had been acquitted of the offence which was triable either way. *Held*, the defendant had been driving his car with the offensive weapon in it at a time when he was disqualified. The offences were committed at the same time. Consequently, count 2 had been properly added to count 1 because the two offences were founded on 'the same facts and evidence' within the meaning of the 1988 Act, s 40(1)(a), which permits a count charging a person with a summary offence (ie count 2), to be included in an indictment if the charge is founded on the same facts or evidence as a count charging an indictable offence (ie count 1). The defendant, having been convicted under count

2, had been 'convicted on the indictment' within the meaning of s 41(5). Count 2 had been properly joined with count 1. As such, it was to be treated as an indictable offence just as much as count 1 was. Thus, by virtue of the conviction under count 2, s 41(5) empowered the Crown Court to sentence the defendant on the charge of having no insurance. Therefore the judge had acted within his jurisdiction and, accordingly, the appeal would be dismissed.

The court acknowledged that s 41(11) might create an anomaly by preventing the Court of Appeal from dealing with a connected summary offence in cases where a defendant had been acquitted of an indictable offence by the trial court.

R v Bird [1995] Crim LR 745 (Court of Appeal: Lord Taylor of Gosforth CJ, McKinnon and Judge JJ).

859 Trial—retrial—order for retrial—necessity for due expedition

The defendant's conviction for burglary was quashed and a retrial was ordered. It was also ordered that he was to be arraigned within two months, and that a fresh indictment was to be lodged within 14 days. Although the prosecution lodged a fresh indictment within 14 days and informed the Crown Court of the order that had been made in respect of re-arraignment, it did not arraign the defendant until after the two-month time limit. On the defendant's application for an order that a verdict of acquittal should be entered, *held*, the Criminal Appeal Act 1968, s 8(1) empowered the court to grant leave to arraign if it was satisfied that the prosecution had acted with all due expedition. In the instant case, the onus of fixing a trial date had been on the prosecution, and it had acted with all due expedition in lodging the fresh indictment within 14 days and informing the Crown Court at that time that the defendant was to be arraigned within two months. Accordingly, the application would be refused.

R v Murphy (1995) Times, 28 February (Court of Appeal: Swinton LJ, Waterhouse and Wright JJ).

860 Trial—summing up—direction to jury—accomplice direction

The appellant allegedly started a violent disorder between him and his associates and another group which resulted in someone being killed. The appellant alone was charged with murder and, with others, violent disorder. He maintained that his associates, who pleaded guilty to affray, had agreed to give evidence wrongly blaming him for the killing. At the trial, three of his associates gave evidence against the appellant and he was convicted. On appeal against conviction, he submitted that the judge wrongly declined to give a full 'accomplice' direction in respect of the three co-accused who had given evidence. The Crown argued that the judge had a discretion as to the giving of a full direction and that the court should not overturn the exercise of that discretion. *Held*, the definition of 'accomplice' referred to a participant in the offence charged and in the present case no one else had been charged with murder. However the witnesses had been charged with violent disorder, and had pleaded guilty to affray, arising out of the incident. The court did not agree with the Crown that the exercise of the judge's discretion should not be overturned because (1) the direction should have been given in relation to the charge of violent disorder, (2) the motive for the witnesses allegedly fabricating the story against the appellant was linked with the murder charge because it served to protect one of their own number, and (3) the witnesses were not themselves on trial with the appellant. Accordingly, the appeal would be allowed, the conviction would be quashed and a retrial ordered.

R v Asghar [1994] Crim LR 941 (Court of Appeal: Roch LJ, Potter and Smith JJ).

861 Trial—summing up—direction to jury—'battered woman's syndrome'

See *R v Oakes*, para 911.

862 Trial—summing up—direction to jury—defence of provocation—characteristics of accused

See *R v Dryden*, para 913.

863 Trial—summing up—direction to jury—good character of defendant

The appellants were convicted of offences relating to fraudulent evasion of value added tax. At their trial, they relied on the fact that they had no previous convictions, but they gave testimony or made pre-trial statements containing admissions. On their appeals against conviction, the question arose as to whether directions as to good character in accordance with *R v Vye* [1993] 3 All ER 241, CA (1993 Abr para 790) had to be given in all cases in which a defendant has adduced evidence of good character. *Held*, cases occurred where a defendant, who had no previous convictions, was shown beyond doubt to have been guilty of serious criminal behaviour similar to the offence charged, and a judge should not be compelled to give *Vye* directions in cases where a defendant's claim to good character was spurious. A trial judge had a limited residual discretion to decline to give any character directions in the case of a defendant without previous convictions if he considered it an insult to common sense. Prima facie the directions had to be given, and the judge would often be able to place a fair and balanced picture before the jury by giving *Vye* directions and then adding qualifying words concerning other proved or possible criminal conduct of the defendant which emerged during the trial. But if it made no sense to give such directions, the judge could in his discretion dispense with them.

R v Aziz; R v Tosun; R v Yorganci [1995] 3 All ER 149 (House of Lords: Lords Goff of Chieveley, Jauncey of Tullichettle, Browne-Wilkinson, Mustill and Steyn).

See also *R v Fulcher*, para 798.

864   Trial—summing up—direction to jury—inference to be drawn from accused's silence

The Criminal Justice and Public Order Act 1994, s 35(3) provides that the court or jury, in determining whether the accused is guilty of the offence charged, may draw such inferences as appear proper from the failure of the accused to give evidence or his refusal, without good cause, to answer any question.

The Court of Appeal has given the following guidelines on the direction to be given by a trial judge to a jury under the 1994 Act, s 35, where a defendant has not given evidence. (1) The judge has to tell the jury that the burden of proof remains on the prosecution throughout and has to tell them what the required standard is. (2) It is necessary for the judge to make it clear that the defendant is entitled to remain silent. (3) An inference from a failure to give evidence cannot on its own prove guilt. (4) Therefore, the jury has to be satisfied that the prosecution has established a case to answer before drawing any inferences from silence. (5) If, despite any evidence relied on to explain his silence or in the absence of such evidence, the jury conclude that the silence can only sensibly be attributed to the defendant's having no answer or none that will stand up to cross-examination, they may draw an adverse inference.

R v Cowan; R v Gayle; R v Ricciardi [1995] 4 All ER 939 (Court of Appeal: Lord Taylor of Gosforth CJ, Turner and Latham JJ).

865   Trial—summing up—direction to jury—intoxication—murder

The appellant and a friend fell asleep in the same room whilst they were both drunk. When the appellant was awoken by his friend making a homosexual advance towards him, he stabbed him to death. At trial, he raised the defence of automatism, claiming that he had been having a night terror. In summing up, the judge directed the jury as to the intent necessary for murder, but did not specifically refer to the effect of intoxication on the appellant's intention. He instead gave a separate direction on intoxication, stating that it was not a defence in itself and that a drunken intent was still an intent. The appellant was convicted of murder. On appeal, he argued that the judge had been obliged to give a proper direction on intoxication, as it might have prevented the formation of the necessary intent. *Held*, it was for the trial judge to decide if the evidence of intoxication was such that there should be a direction on it, regardless of whether or not the issue was raised by a defendant. In the instant case, having decided to give a direction on intoxication, the judge had not made it clear that its effect could be relevant to the question of whether or not the appellant had the necessary intent for murder. Moreover, his separate direction on the issue may wrongly have given the jury the impression that intoxication was not relevant to intent. Accordingly, the appeal would be allowed.

R v McKinley [1994] Crim LR 944 (Court of Appeal: Glidewell LJ, Alliott and Colman JJ).

866   Trial—summing up—direction to jury—intoxication—rape

Scotland

The appellant was charged with rape. At trial, the judge directed the jury that they had to decide whether it was proved that force or the threat of force had been used, and whether the will of the complainant had been overcome. In particular, the judge referred to the fact that the complainant had been drunk at the time of the incident, and told the jury that they had to decide whether the complainant's intoxication was such that she was inclined to indulge in sexual intercourse which she regretted soon after, and whether she was incapable of exercising the degree of resistance which she would have been able to do but for her intoxication. The appellant was convicted of the offence. On appeal, he argued that the judge had misdirected the jury. *Held*, the judge had correctly defined rape, and had emphasised the two elements of absence of consent and overcoming the complainant's will. A reasonable jury would have concluded from the judge's reference to the complainant's inability to resist because of her intoxication, that it would have been easier for the appellant to overcome the complainant's unwillingness to have sexual intercourse because of her intoxication. As regards the judge's direction that the complainant might have consented to intercourse more readily because of her intoxication but that she might have regretted it soon after, a reasonable jury would have concluded that rape would not be established if the complainant had agreed to intercourse in those circumstances. The judge's direction had been adequate and, accordingly, the appeal would be dismissed.

W v HM Advocate 1995 SLT 685 (High Court of Justiciary). *Sweeney v X* 1982 SCCR 509 considered.

867 Trial—summing up—direction to jury—lies—circumstances in which direction necessary and matters to be included in direction

The appellants were convicted of murder and pleaded guilty to robbery. On appeal, they argued that the trial judge had failed properly to direct the jury as to the lies that they had told in giving evidence. *Held*, a *Lucas* direction was required (1) when a defendant raised an alibi, (2) where it was desirable or necessary for a judge to suggest to the jury that they should look for corroboration of a piece of evidence from other evidence in the case, in particular from the lies told by the defendant, (3) where the prosecution sought to show that something said in or out of court in relation to a separate and distinct issue was a lie and therefore relied upon it as evidence of the defendant's guilt in relation to the offence in question, and (4) where there was a danger that the jury might regard a defendant's lies as proof that he was guilty of the offence. If a judge had properly considered whether a *Lucas* direction was necessary and how it was to be formulated, the Court of Appeal would be slow to interfere with his exercise of discretion. The direction had to be tailored to the circumstances of the case, but it was sufficient for a judge to point out that the lie had to be admitted or proved beyond all reasonable doubt, and that the mere fact that a defendant had lied was not in itself evidence of his guilt. Only if the jury was satisfied that the defendant had not lied for innocent reasons could a lie support the prosecution case. Having regard to the facts of the instant case and the direction given, the appeal would be dismissed.

R v Burge; R v Pegg (1995) Times, 28 April (Court of Appeal: Kennedy and Curtis LJJ and Buxton J). *R v Lucas* [1981] 2 All ER 1008 (1981 Abr para 732) applied.

868 Trial—summing up—direction to jury—majority verdict direction

The defendant had been convicted of murder. At his trial, the jury was not at first agreed in its verdict. After the trial judge had given a majority verdict direction, the jury retired for a second time and 40 minutes later returned with a majority verdict. The defendant applied for leave to appeal against conviction. *Held*, there was no evidence to suggest that the failure to ask the jury after its first retirement if it had reached a unanimous verdict caused any juror to feel under pressure to reach a verdict in accordance with the majority decision. Consequently the conviction was safe and leave to appeal would be refused.

R v Dudson [1995] Crim LR 502 (Court of Appeal: Lord Taylor of Gosforth CJ, Scott Baker and Longmore JJ).

869 Trial—summing up—direction to jury—presence of jury during submissions of no case to answer—judge's comments on sincerity of defence case

Jamaica

The appellant had been charged with murder in Jamaica. During the trial the judge insisted that a submission by the defence that there was no case to answer be heard in the presence of the jury. This was the prevailing practice in Jamaica at that time. Further, at the end of his summing up the judge described the defence as insincere and commented on discrepancies between the appellant's evidence and the way in which his counsel put his case in cross-examination. He asked the jury to consult amongst themselves to see if they wished to retire to consider their verdict. It was only after the foreman indicated that they did wish to retire that they did so. The appellant was convicted and he appealed to the Court of Appeal of Jamaica which dismissed his appeal but expressed doubts about the desirability of the practice of hearing and determining a submission of no case to answer in the presence of the jury. He appealed to the Privy Council, contending that the judge had committed a material irregularity in refusing to ask the jury to withdraw during submissions of no case to answer, that the judge was wrong in describing the defence as insincere and that in asking the jury whether they wished to retire, he was implying that there was really nothing for them to discuss. *Held*, a trial judge should ask the jury to withdraw during submissions of no case to answer since it was a matter for him alone whether there was sufficient evidence to place the case before the jury and they could not assist him in making that decision. Further, the judge's comments that the defence case was insincere would probably have been seen by the jury as a criticism of the appellant rather than his counsel. He should have asked for the comments of counsel in the absence of the jury before his summing up and his comments were unfair to the appellant. As to the judge asking the jury if they wished to retire, it was a cardinal rule of criminal procedure that a trial judge should avoid any hint of pressure on a jury to reach a verdict. In this case, the possibility that some of the jurors understood the judge to be conveying to them that there was nothing to discuss could not be excluded. In asking the jury whether they wished to retire and in criticising the sincerity of the defence, the judge had deprived the appellant of a fair trial. Accordingly, the appeal would be allowed.

Crosdale v R [1995] 2 All ER 500 (Privy Council: Lords Goff of Chievely, Mustill, Slynn of Hadley, Nicholls of Birkenhead and Steyn).

870   Trial—summing up—direction to jury—rape—lack of consent

A 14-year-old girl accused the appellants of raping her. The girl was said to have been asleep during the alleged offence and remembered nothing. The appellants were convicted of the offence and, on appeal, submitted that the judge should have given the jury an express direction in accordance with *R v Howard* that the prosecution had to prove that the girl physically resisted or, if she did not, that her understanding and knowledge were such that she was not in a position to decide whether to consent or resist. *Held*, under the Sexual Offences (Amendment) Act 1976, the essential element in the definition of rape was the absence of consent. Any attempt to introduce a different criterion was mistaken and contrary to the law. The jury should be directed that consent, or absence of consent, was to be given its ordinary meaning and that there was a difference between consent and submission. It did not follow that, because every consent involved a submission, a mere submission involved consent. In the present case, the judge had given a proper, adequate and full direction on the law of rape and on the presence or absence of consent, and full directions on the element of mens rea. Accordingly, the appeals would be dismissed.

R v Larter [1995] Crim LR 75 (Court of Appeal: Hobhouse LJ, Tudor Evans and Ebsworth JJ). *R v Howard* [1965] 3 All ER 684, CA, considered.

871   Trial—summing up—direction to jury—separation of jury—appropriate direction—guidelines

The Criminal Justice and Public Order Act 1994, s 43 provides that if, on the trial of any person for an offence on indictment, the court thinks fit, it may at any time (whether before or after the jury have been directed to consider their verdict) permit the jury to separate.

The appellant was charged with trading with intent to defraud, and false accounting. At the conclusion of the judge's summing up, the jurors were allowed to separate to consider their verdicts, and were sent home having been told not to discuss the case with anybody. The following day, one of the jurors brought textbooks on accounting in to court and asked the judge if he could take them into the jury room. The judge refused his request, and directed all of the jurors that textbooks could not be used and that they were to concentrate on the evidence heard and documents received during the course of the trial. The appellant was convicted of the offences. On appeal, he argued that the judge had misdirected the jury. *Held*, generally, a jury was not to be given additional evidence or material to assist them once they had retired to consider their verdict. In a case where the jury was allowed to separate during consideration of their verdict, a judge's direction ought to state that (1) it was for the jury to decide the case on the evidence and arguments that they had seen and heard in court, and not that which they had seen or heard outside the court, (2) once all the evidence had been adduced, it was wrong for a juror to seek or receive further evidence or information about the case, (3) the jury must not talk to anyone about the case or allow anyone to talk to them about it, except amongst themselves and only in the jury room, and (4) when they left the court, they should try not to think about the case again until they returned to court and retired to the jury room to continue their deliberations. There were no precise form of words which had to be used in giving such a direction, but it was desirable for it to be given in full on the first dispersal of the jury, with a brief reminder at each subsequent dispersal. In the instant case, the failure to give such a full direction was an immaterial irregularity and, accordingly, the appeal would be dismissed.

R v Oliver (1995) Times, 6 December (Court of Appeal: Roch LJ, Douglas Brown and Blofeld JJ).

CRIMINAL LAW

Halsbury's Laws of England (4th edn) Vol 11(1) (reissue), paras 1–800, Vol 11(2) (reissue), paras 801–1592

872 Articles

Affray: Who's Afraid and of What? Stuart Whitehouse: 139 SJ 503

Assault on a Police Officer: s 51(1) of the Police Act 1964, Alan Murdie: 139 SJ 548

Border Law: Sections 136–141 Criminal Justice and Public Order Act 1994, Neil Addison: Criminal Lawyer, Issue 55, p 1

Breach of the Peace and Reasonableness, Philip Plowden and Kevin Kerrigan: Criminal Lawyer, Issue 1, p 5

Causes of Crime, Brian Block: 159 JP Jo 841

Changes Relating to Certain Sexual Offences Brought About by CJPOA 1994, Anne Davies and Margaret Rodgers: Criminal Lawyer, Issue 57, p 6

Child Sex Tourism, Jessica Holroyd: 145 NLJ 1199

Clean Water and Muddy Causation: Is Causation a Question of Law or Fact, or Just a Way of Allocating Blame? Nicola Padfield (on causation in pollution offences): [1995] Crim LR 683

Computer Pornography, Colin Manchester: [1995] Crim LR 546

Conspiracy to Defraud: Some Comments on the Law Commission's Report, J C Smith: [1995] Crim LR 209

Context-Dependent Crime, Joseph Jaconelli (on 'speech crimes'): [1995] Crim LR 771

Contra Bonos Mores: Fraud Affecting Consent In Rape, Alan Reed: 145 NLJ 174

Corporate Body, Gary Slapper (on corporate responsibility and criminal liability): LS Gaz, 15 February 1995, p 18

The Criminal Justice and Public Order Act 1994: Gypsies—The Criminalisation of a Way of Life? Sue Campbell: [1995] Crim LR 28

The Criminal Justice and Public Order Act 1994: The Public Order Elements, A T H Smith: [1995] Crim LR 19

A Critique of the Correspondence Principle in Criminal Law, Jeremy Horder: [1995] Crim LR 759

Drugs in Sport—Chains of Custody, Edward Grayson: 145 NLJ 44

The Failure to Degenderise the Law of Rape: The Criminal Justice and Public Order Act and the Transsexual Victim, Andrew Sharpe: Criminal Lawyer, Issue 53, p 7

Fair Trials and Effective Policing, Sarah Cornelius (on British war crimes trials): 145 NLJ 1232

Firearms Licensing - Time for Reform, Peter Burton: 145 NLJ 882

Fraud and Insurance Claims, R W Hodgin: 145 NLJ 136

Homicide and Accomplices, Laurence Toczek: 145 NLJ 956

Homicide of Children, D J Power: 159 JP Jo 209

How Far Can You Lawfully Go in Defence of Your Property? Alec Samuels: 159 JP Jo 875

In(de)terminable Intentions, Nicola Lacey: 58 MLR 692

Intention in the Criminal Law—a Rejoinder, Jeremy Horder (in response to 'A Clear Concept of Intention—Elusive or Illusory' by Nicola Lacey, 56 MLR 621): 58 MLR 678

Interim Possession Orders, Louella Crisfield (on the new offence created by the Criminal Justice and Public Order Act 1994, s 76): LA, September 1995, p 21

Investigating Serious Fraud, Susan Nash (on the Davie Report): 145 NLJ 530

Judicial Approaches to Due Diligence, Deborah Parry (on due diligence as a defence to consumer protection offences): [1995] Crim LR 695

The Law Commission and Criminal Law Reform, Henry Brooke: [1995] Crim LR 911

The Law Commission, Conspiracy to Defraud and the Dishonesty Project: [1995] Crim LR 461

Legless Provocation? Timothy Batchelar (on the establishment of provocation as a defence to murder): Criminal Lawyer, Issue 54, p 4

Local Difficulty, Alan Beckley (on powers relating to trespass under the Criminal Justice and Public Order Act 1994): Police Review, 23 December 1994, p 18

Making them Pay, Andrew Mitchell (on the Proceeds of Crime Act 1995): Police Review, 27 October 1995, p 14

The Meaning of 'Culpable Homicide', J N Spencer: 159 JP Jo 447

Mental Injury in Assault Cases, Karla Parsons: 139 SJ 770

Money Laundering and the Legal Profession, Monty Raphael: 145 NLJ 1377

Money Laundering—the Complete Guide, Leonard Jason-Lloyd: 145 NLJ 149, 183, 219

More Justice for Battered Women, Donald Nicolson and Rohit Sanghvi (on *R v Humphries* (1995) Independent, 11 July, CA (para 911): 145 NLJ 1122

The New Regime for the Correction of Miscarriages of Justice, Dandy Malet: 159 JP Jo 716

Obscene Material on the Internet, Stephen Dooley: 139 SJ 868

Proceeds of Crime Act 1995, Kennedy Talbot: 145 NLJ 1857

Provocation, Abnormal Traits and Necessity, Alan Reed: Criminal Lawyer, Issue 61, p 1

Provocation and the Reasonable Person, L H Leigh: 145 NLJ 1308

Public Order Review, Jo Cooper: LA, September 1995, p 17

Public Policy Under Duress, Gary Slapper (on *R v Pommell* (1995) Times, 22 May, CA (para 893)): 145 NLJ 1063

A Quiet Revolution in Corporate Liability for Crime, Celia Wells: 145 NLJ 1326

Rape, Fraud and Consent: The Correct Approach, Alan Reed: 139 SJ 44

Rethinking Corporate Crime and Individual Responsibility, Mark Stallworthy: Criminal Lawyer, Issue 55, p 5

Retrospective Crime, Ralph Beddard (on the right not to be tried for a crime created retrospectively): 145 NLJ 663

Rights of Victims in the Criminal Justice System: Rhetoric or Reality? Helen Fenwick: [1995] Crim LR 843

Seasons of Mists and Mellow Fruitfulness, Mary Welstead (on the law of trespass): 145 NLJ 1499

Self-Incrimination, Corporate Misconduct, and the Convention on Human Rights, Susan Nash, Mark Furse: [1995] Crim LR 854

Sex and Consent, David Michael (on rape as a two-tier offence): Police Review, 16 June 1995, p 24

Strict Liability Offences: The Need for Careful Legal Advice to Both Corporations and Individuals, Alan Reed: Criminal Lawyer, Issue 52, p 3

Theft from Vehicles: Drugs, Network and 'Crime Surfers', P Broadbent: 159 JP Jo 451, 472

Thinking the Unthinkable, Rowan Bosworth-Davies (on financial crime): 145 NLJ 811

Treasons Past and Present, Anthony Verduyn: 145 NLJ 1884

Trespassers on Byways in the Countryside: Section 61 of the Criminal Justice and Public Order Act 1994, George Laurence: [1995] JPL 905

Trespassers Will be Prosecuted, Alan Murdie (on aggravated trespass in the Criminal Justice and Public Order Act 1994): 145 NLJ 389

Victory For Common Sense? Jonathan Cooper (on the decision of the ECHR that UK drug trafficking law is in breach of art 7(1)): LS Gaz, 15 February 1995, p 11

Wages of Sin . . . Deepak Singh (on the Proceeds of Crime Act 1995): LS Gaz, 22 November 1995, p 14

When Sport Becomes a Crime, Lancelot Robson: Criminal Lawyer, Issue 57, p 3

873   Assault—inclusion of assault count in indictment charging theft—'assault' construed as including battery

The Criminal Justice Act 1988, s 39 provides that common assault and battery are summary offences punishable by a fine not exceeding level five on the standard scale or imprisonment for a term not exceeding six months, or both. Section 40 provides that a count charging a person with common assault may be included in an indictment if the charge is founded on the same facts or evidence as a count charging an indictable offence.

The defendant was charged with shoplifting together with two other counts of criminal damage to property and common assault, all of which arose from the same incident. The assault complained of was a reference to the defendant spitting in the face of a police officer. On the recommendation of the judge, the prosecution amended the third count to read 'battery' instead of 'common assault', and the defendant was convicted. The defendant appealed on the ground that the third count could not, as a result of the prosecution's amendment, be heard at the same time as the other two counts because the 1988 Act, s 40 only applied to assault and not battery. *Held*, it was likely that the failure to include battery in s 40 was due to a drafting error and therefore, the word 'assault' in that section must be construed as including battery as well as assault. Accordingly, the appeal would be dismissed.

R v Lynsey [1995] 3 All ER 654 (Court of Appeal: Henry LJ, Garland and Sedley JJ).

874   Attempted murder—principal using firearm—secondary party charged with principal—proof required to prosecute secondary party

The appellant and his passenger were followed by a police car. The appellant, knowing that his passenger had a rifle with him, stopped and reversed his vehicle towards the police car and the passenger then fired shots at the officers in the car. Both men were convicted of attempted murder. On his appeal against conviction, the appellant argued that since the intention of the principal in attempted murder had to be to kill, a secondary party was only guilty if he knew that the principal did intend to kill; it was not sufficient to know that he might kill. *Held*, the court rejected the appellant's argument. The jury had clearly found that the appellant, knowing that the passenger had a rifle, had assisted him. If the jury had concluded that the appellant also knew that the passenger might shoot to kill, and if he had actually killed one of the police officers, the appellant would have been guilty of murder. There was no logical reason why the same knowledge should not make him guilty of attempted murder once the jury were sure that the passenger himself was guilty of that offence. Accordingly, the appeal would be dismissed.

R v O'Brien [1995] 2 Cr App Rep 649 (Court of Appeal: Glidewell LJ, Popplewell and Johnson JJ).

875   Bomb hoax—bomb in any place or location—meaning of 'any place or location'

By virtue of the Criminal Law Act 1977, s 51(2), any person who communicates any information which he knows to be false to another person with the intention of inducing in him or any other person a false belief that a bomb or other thing liable to explode or ignite is present in any place or location whatever is guilty of an offence.

On appeal against his conviction of an offence under s 51(2), the appellant contended that, although he had made a hoax emergency telephone call stating that there was a bomb, as he had not identified the location where it was, he could not be guilty of the offence. *Held*, s 51(2) was concerned with the intention of the hoaxer; that which was induced in the mind of the person receiving the information was what was relevant. 'In any place or location' in s 51(2) meant 'somewhere'. Section 51(2) did not require a specific place or location. A statement that there was a bomb necessarily implied that there was a bomb somewhere which was sufficient to comply with s 51(2); such a statement might well induce panic, disruption and wastage of emergency resources. The appeal would be dismissed.

R v Webb [1995] 27 LS Gaz R 31 (Court of Appeal: Swinton Thomas LJ, Popplewell and Harrison JJ).

876   Collective trespass or nuisance on land—powers of police—retention and disposal of vehicles

See para 2308.

877   Complicity in crime—collateral acts—joint enterprise

The appellants were convicted of manslaughter after an incident where the victim died from a fatal kick. The trial judge directed the jury that the appellants could have been engaged in a joint enterprise even if there had been no pre-arranged plan. The jury had to be convinced that the defendants attacked the victim simultaneously with a common intention or purpose that the victim should suffer harm, the fatal blow also being part of the common intention. On appeal, *held*, in cases where there was no pre-arranged plan it was not sufficient for the jury to be satisfied that the appellants had shared a common purpose to harm the victim. They must also have made it clear to each other by their actions that harming the victim was their common intention. The judge had misdirected the jury and, consequently, the appeal would be allowed.

R v Petters [1995] Crim LR 501 (Court of Appeal: Staughton LJ, Waterhouse and Morrison JJ).

878   Consent—Law Commission consultation

The Law Commission has issued a consultation paper, *Consent in the Criminal Law* (consultation paper 139) based in part on the consultation following publication of its earlier paper, *Consent and Offences Against the Person* (1994 Abr para 862). The Law Commission suggests that its main proposals relating to consent should apply to all criminal offences, and not only to offences against the person and sexual offences. The intentional or reckless causing of seriously disabling injury (as defined) to another should be an offence even if the injured person gives consent (as defined), but the term 'reckless' in this context would be strictly defined; further, in such cases the ordinary principles of secondary liability should apply to determine whether the injured person is a party to the offence. The intentional or reckless causing of an injury falling short of a seriously disabling injury should not be an offence if the injured person gives consent. The commission considers the issues of mistaken belief in consent in relation to offences against the person and sexual offences and the burden of proof in relation to consent and mistaken belief. It proposes provisionally that, in relation to any offence to which consent is or may be a defence, a valid consent may not be given by a person lacking capacity (as defined; separate proposals are made in relation to minors and to the mentally disabled and the ability to 'understand' appropriate information is defined). Consideration is given to statutory age limits in relation to a mistaken belief in consent (including the defence under the Sexual Offences Act 1956, s 6(3)). The commission proposes provisionally that a person should not be treated as having given a valid consent if he or she has been deceived as to the nature of the act or as to the identity of the other person or persons involved in it. It asks whether a fraudulent misrepresentation that a person is HIV free or free from other sexually transmitted diseases should be treated as an exception to the principle that fraud nullifies consent only when it goes to the nature of the act or the identity of the other person involved. The commission further proposes provisionally that a person should be guilty of an offence (punishable with up to five years' imprisonment) if he or she does an act which, if done without the consent of another, would be an offence so punishable and if such consent has been procured by deception. It asks whether there are circumstances in which a person who wishes to rely on the consent of another to the causing or risking of injury should be under an express duty to communicate certain information; and also more generally it asks how the law should treat non-disclosure of material facts. The commission suggests that a self-induced mistake which is known to the defendant should vitiate consent, as should threats of non-consensual force which induced a consent. Views are sought as to how the law should view consent induced by other forms of threats and, in the alternative, whether it should be an offence to procure consent by threats. The commission makes provisional proposals as to exceptions to criminal liability for injuries caused by 'proper medical treatment or care' administered with consent, and injuries caused in the course of 'properly approved medical research' and with consent. Views are sought as to whether the age limit of 18 years should be retained for tattooing and whether there should be an age limit for valid consent to piercing below the neck, branding, scarification and dangerous exhibitions. The commission proposes provisionally changing the mens rea in the Tattooing of Minors Act 1969, s 1; that the circumcision of Jewish and Muslim males for religious reasons with their parents' consent should continue to be lawful; and that no person under 18 years should be able to give valid consent to injuries intentionally caused for sexual, religious or spiritual purposes. Views are sought on lawful correction, the formulation of an exception permitting consent to injuries suffered in the course of playing (or practising) recognised sports in accordance with their rules, and definitions of 'fighting' and 'horseplay' in relation to criminal liability and an exception to such.

879 Conspiracy—conspiracy to defraud—economic loss—actual loss or risk of loss

New Zealand

The defendant was a director and deputy chairman of a company and a director of some of its subsidiaries. The group's major investment projects were handled by an investment team of which the defendant and the chairman were members. The chairman requested the defendant to establish a structure involving three overseas companies and banks in order to conceal certain payments. The structure was used in a number of transactions. The defendant was convicted of conspiring with others to defraud any one or more of the company, its subsidiaries and others by agreeing to use dishonestly a system of disguising the source and utilisation of money from legitimate inquiry. On his appeal against conviction, *held*, where a person was charged with conspiracy to defraud based on economic loss, the prosecution had to prove that the victim had a right or interest which was capable of being prejudiced by actual loss or by being put at risk. A defendant who dishonestly concealed from another person information which he was under a duty to disclose to that person, or which that person was entitled to require him to disclose, could be guilty of fraud and, since a company was entitled to recover secret profits made by its directors at its expense, a dishonest agreement by directors to impede a company in exercising its right of recovery would constitute a conspiracy to defraud. As the defendant had participated in the use of the overseas structure dishonestly to conceal information which he had been under a duty as a director to disclose to the company, he had properly been convicted and, accordingly, the appeal would be dismissed.

Adams v R [1995] 1 WLR 52 (Privy Council: Lords Templeman, Jauncey of Tullichettle, Mustill, Lloyd of Berwick and Nolan). Dictum of Viscount Dilhorne in *R v Scott* [1974] 3 All ER 1032 at 1039, HL, and *Wai Yu-tsang v R* [1991] 4 All ER 664, PC (1991 Abr para 679) applied. *R v Governor of Pentonville Prison, ex p Tarling* (1978) 70 Cr App Rep 77, HL (1977 Abr para 1271), considered.

880   Conspiracy—indictment—appeal against conviction—power to substitute verdict of guilty of substantive offence

The appellant's appeal against his conviction of conspiracy to blackmail had been allowed and his conviction had been quashed on the ground that it was inconsistent with the acquittal of two co-accused. The remaining issue was whether the court could substitute a verdict of guilty of the substantive offence of blackmail. It was claimed that such a verdict could be substituted because the allegation in the indictment, charging the appellant with conspiring with two other men to make a demand with menaces impliedly amounted to the substantive offence. *Held*, the court could not substitute a verdict of guilty of the substantive offence of blackmail because on the indictment charging the appellant with conspiracy the jury could not have found him guilty of blackmail. To have done so would have conflicted with *Practice Direction (Crime: Conspiracy)* [1977] 1 WLR 537 in which it was said that in any case where an indictment contained substantive counts and a related conspiracy count, the judge should require the prosecution to justify the joinder, or, failing justification, to elect whether to proceed on the substantive or on the conspiracy counts. The situation in the present case had arisen through the prosecution's decision to charge conspiracy rather than the substantive offence which could have been charged at the outset.

R v Watts (1995) Times, 13 April (Court of Appeal: Glidewell LJ, Popplewell and Johnson JJ).

881   Criminal damage—intent to endanger life or recklessness as to whether life endangered—causal connection between damage and danger

A person who destroys or damages any property (a) intending to destroy or damage any property or being reckless as to whether any property would be destroyed or damaged; and (b) intending by the destruction or damage to endanger the life of another or being reckless as to whether the life of another would be thereby endangered is guilty of an offence, if an object was deliberately· or recklessly thrown causing damage which endangered the life of another: Criminal Damage Act 1971, s 1(2).

In the first case, the appellants pushed a heavy coping-stone from the parapet of a railway bridge onto a passenger train passing below. The stone landed on the rear bulkhead of a carriage and a corner of the stone penetrated the roof. The passengers were showered with material from the roof but received no physical injury. The appellants were convicted of damaging property with intent to endanger life. In the second case, the appellant drove a stolen car from which a passenger threw bricks at a pursuing police car. One of the bricks smashed the rear window of the police car, showering the officers in the car with broken glass. The appellant then rammed his car into the police car several times. He too was convicted of damaging property with intent to endanger life. On appeal against conviction, *held*, on a charge of damaging property with intent to endanger life or recklessness as to whether life would be endangered under s 1(2)(b), the prosecution had to prove that the danger to life resulted from the destruction of or damage to property and it was not sufficient for the prosecution to prove that the danger to life resulted from the defendant's act which caused the destruction or damage. The words 'destruction or damage' in s 1(2)(b) referred to the destruction or damage which the defendant intended to cause or to the risk of which he was reckless, not to the destruction or damage which in fact occurred. What had to be considered was not whether and how life was in fact endangered but whether and how it was intended by the defendant to be endangered or if there was an obvious risk of it being endangered. Where a defendant dropped a stone from a bridge, the effect of s 1(2) was that if he intended that the stone itself would crash through the roof of a train or motor vehicle thereby directly injuring passengers or was reckless whether it did, s 1(2) would not apply, but if he intended that the stone would smash the roof so that material from it would or might descend upon passengers or was reckless whether it did, thereby endangering life, he was guilty of an offence under s 1(2). On the facts of the first case, the trial judge had misdirected the jury, which by its verdict must be taken to have found that the appellants intended that the stone itself would crash through the roof of the carriage and endanger life. The conviction under s 1(2) could not be sustained on that basis. However, as the jury's finding implied that the appellants must also have been reckless as to the danger to passengers from material falling from the roof, a conviction under the alternative count of damaging property, being reckless as to whether life was endangered, would be substituted. Where a defendant threw a brick at the windscreen of a moving vehicle and caused some damage to the vehicle, the question whether he committed an offence under s 1(2) did not depend on whether the brick hit the windscreen but on whether he intended to hit it and intended or was reckless as to whether any resulting damage would endanger life. On the facts of the second case, the damage caused was itself capable of endangering life by causing the driver to lose control of the vehicle and it had been open to the jury to infer an intention to endanger life by damaging the vehicle. That appeal would be dismissed.

R v Webster; R v Warwick [1995] 2 All ER 168 (Court of Appeal: Lord Taylor of Gosforth CJ, Ognall and Gage JJ). *R v Steer* [1987] 2 All ER 833, HL (1987 Abr para 515), applied.

882 Criminal damage—intent to endanger life or recklessness as to whether life endangered—recklessness—test of recklessness

The appellant was convicted of damaging property being reckless as to whether life was endangered. He had received a householder's consent before proceeding to remove cables and associated equipment and had left a live cable exposed for a short period of time. He argued that he had not been reckless in that he had not thought that there was any risk of endangering life at any stage and that after the cable had been removed he had taken the precaution of burying it. Thus, it was claimed, he fell outside the definition of *Caldwell* recklessness because he had not failed to recognise the risk nor had he acted recognising the existence of a risk. Instead he had thought about the risk and decided there was no risk. *Held*, there was a clear distinction between avoiding a risk and taking steps to remedy a risk which had already been created. If a defendant was to argue that certain steps taken by him prevented him from falling within the definition of recklessness then those steps must have been directed towards preventing the risk at all rather than remedying it once it had arisen. In the present case the appellant accepted that he had created a risk by exposing the cable and although he then took reasonable precautions to remedy the danger, he was remedying a risk he had already created. Accordingly, the appeal would be dismissed.

R v Merrick [1995] Crim LR 802 (Court of Appeal: Farquharson LJ, Hidden and Longmore JJ). *R v Caldwell* [1981] 1 All ER 961, HL (1981 Abr para 2482) applied.

883 Criminal Injuries Compensation Act 1995

The Criminal Injuries Compensation Act 1995 provides for the establishment of a scheme for compensation for victims of violent crime, and new rules for determining compensation payable under the scheme are introduced. The Act received the royal assent on 8 November 1995 and came into force on that date.

Section 1 obliges the Secretary of State to introduce a criminal injuries compensation scheme and provides definitions. The assessment of amounts payable under the scheme is to be determined under a tariff prepared by the Secretary of State and additional amounts may be available for special expenses and fatal injuries: s 2. Provision is made by s 3 for the matters to be dealt with by the scheme and for the appointment of a scheme manager and claims officers. Section 4 provides for the review of decisions taken on compensation claims and there is also provision for appeals from decisions taken as a result of such reviews (s 5). Section 6 deals with reports, accounts and financial records and s 7 makes awards inalienable. The Income and Corporation Taxes Act 1988 is amended so as to make awards granted in the form of annuities exempt from income tax: s 8. Section 9 allows the Secretary of State to pay for the scheme, including its administration and s 10 gives the Parliamentary Commissioner for Administration jurisdiction over the scheme. The Secretary of State must lay a draft of the tariff and any altered provisions before Parliament: s 11. Section 12 and the Schedule set out repeals and transitional provisions and s 13 deals with short title, and extent.

884 Criminal injuries—compensation—applicant's entitlement to oral hearing

The Criminal Injuries Compensation Scheme 1990, para 24(c), provides that an applicant is entitled to an oral hearing only if no award or a reduced award was made by the Criminal Injuries Compensation Board and there is a dispute as to the material facts or conclusions upon which the initial or reconsidered decision was based or it appears that the decision may have been wrong in law or principle.

The applicant applied to the board for compensation after an assault and robbery. His application was turned down on the ground of his own criminality, and he subsequently applied for an order of certiorari to quash the board's refusal, claiming that 'conclusion' in para 24(c) meant any conclusion drawn from the facts, including the conclusion as to the extent to which the award ought to be affected by a previous conviction. *Held*, the language of para 24(c) was not confined to raw facts but included conclusions, inferences and value judgments drawn from those facts. In this case, the dispute over the applicant's character was a dispute as to conclusions and, accordingly, the certiorari order would be granted and the board's decision quashed.

R v Criminal Injuries Compensation Board, ex p Dickson (1995) Times, 20 December (Queen's Bench Division: Carnwath J).

885   Criminal injuries—compensation—conduct of deceased—refusal of award

The widow of a murder victim applied for compensation under the Criminal Injuries Compensation Scheme. The application was refused on the ground that the deceased had been of bad character. The applicant appealed against the decision. She contended that the board had failed to take her own good character into account and that it had failed to consider ordering reduced compensation. *Held*, it was sufficient for the board to state that no award was appropriate because of the character of the deceased. It was not necessary to show that the character of both persons had been considered. In addition, it was only if the board had come to the conclusion that an award should be given that it would have been required to consider whether it should be a full award or a reduced sum. The reasons given by the board were adequate and, accordingly, the appeal would be dismissed.

R v Criminal Injuries Compensation Board, ex p Cook [1996] 2 All ER 144 (Court of Appeal: Beldam, Hobhouse and Aldous LJJ).

886   Criminal injuries—compensation—extension of scheme

The 1990 version of the Criminal Injuries Compensation Scheme has been extended to cover injuries or death caused by or to officers of the United Kingdom in the exercise of their functions in the Channel Tunnel or the control zones, within the meaning of the Channel Tunnel (International Arrangements) Order 1993, SI 1993/1813. The extension came into effect on 2 August 1993 (the date on which the order came into force). Information concerning the extension is given in the 30th report of the Criminal Injuries Compensation Board (Cm 2849). The report also states that the 1990 Scheme enabled certain categories of decisions to be delegated to staff. During 1993–94 some 14,219 cases were so delegated (19 per cent of the board's case load); this was a contributory factor to the resolution of 70 per cent of the board's case load during 1993–94 within 12 months of receipt.

887   Criminal injuries—compensation—interim award—applicant subsequently convicted of crimes—power to refuse further award

Under the Criminal Injuries Compensation Scheme 1990, para 6(c) the Criminal Injuries Compensation Board may withhold or reduce compensation if it considers that, having regard to the conduct of the applicant before, during or after the events giving rise to the claim or to his character as shown by his criminal convictions or unlawful conduct, it is inappropriate that a full award, or any award at all, be granted.

When the applicant was 11 years old he was rendered blind in one eye as a result of a violent crime. He applied for compensation under the Criminal Injuries Compensation Scheme and an interim award was made. The Board then adjourned the matter for three years because no final medical prognosis was available. Although the applicant had no criminal convictions at that time, when the matter came before the Board again some five years later, he had become involved in criminal activities and had been convicted of a number of offences. The Board, applying the 1990 Scheme, para 6(c), determined that any further award would be inappropriate. The applicant sought judicial review of the Board's decision. *Held*, an applicant's criminal convictions did not have to be related to the injury in respect of which compensation was claimed to be relevant to the Board's consideration. Those involved in criminal activity should not receive money from the public purse for an injury which they had sustained. The Board was entitled to have regard to convictions as at the date the award fell to be considered, rather than at the time of the injury. The Board's decision that the applicant was not an appropriate person to receive an award at the public expense was a matter entirely within their discretion and was not *Wednesbury* unreasonable. Accordingly, the application would be dismissed.

R v Criminal Injuries Compensation Board, ex p Thomas [1995] PIQR P99 (Queen's Bench Division: Popplewell J).

888   Criminal injuries—compensation—rape victim—effect of delay in reporting offence

The Criminal Injuries Compensation Scheme, para 6(a) provides that the burden is on a claimant to satisfy the Board, on a balance of probabilities, that he took all reasonable steps in a reasonable time to inform the police of the circumstances of the injury to which their claim relates.

The applicant had been raped at knife point and sexually assaulted. Being extremely distraught she did not report the incident to the police until six weeks later. At a committal the justices dismissed the case against the suspect she had picked out at an identification parade. Her claim for compensation was dismissed by the Criminal Injuries Compensation Board under para 6(a) on the basis of the delay in reporting the incident and the consequence that the assailant was not brought to justice. She applied for an order of certiorari to quash the Board's refusal. *Held,* the purpose of para 6(a) was to maximise the chance of prosecuting the offender and to minimise the opportunity for fraudulent claims. Thus, the effect of a delay was a relevant but not a determinative consideration. The Board should make an appraisal of the reasons for the delay, such as the victim's emotional state, and its significance in relation to the delay. In this case that had not been done and, accordingly, the order of certiorari would be granted.

R v Criminal Injuries Compensation Board, ex p S (1995) 159 JP 637 (Queen's Bench Division: Sedley J).

889   Criminal injuries—compensation—statutory provisions—decision to implement alternative scheme

The Criminal Justice Act 1988, s 171(1) provides that the Act is to come into force on such day as the Secretary of State may by order made by statutory instrument appoint, and different days may be appointed for different provisions.

The 1988 Act, ss 108–117 provided for compensation to be paid to those who had suffered personal injuries as a result of criminal behaviour, and gave effect to a similar non-statutory scheme which had been in existence for many years. The Secretary of State introduced a new non-statutory scheme to replace the statutory scheme such that compensation would no longer be assessed on the same basis as common law damages, but on a tariff basis. It was conceded that the amount payable under the tariff scheme would be considerably less than that payable under the statutory scheme. The applicants successfully challenged the Secretary of State's decision not to implement the statutory scheme, arguing that s 171(1) obliged him to introduce it at some point, even though he had a discretion as to when to do so. On the Secretary of State's appeal, *held*, the Secretary of State did not have an absolute and unfettered discretion whether or not to bring into force the provisions of the 1988 Act relating to the compensation scheme, as in enacting s 171(1), Parliament had intended that the power to implement the provisions should be exercised at an appropriate time unless there was a change of circumstances which made it inappropriate to do so. As the Secretary of State was therefore under a duty to review from time to time the question of when to bring the provisions into force, his decision that he would not do so was unlawful. Moreover, the Secretary of State could not procure events to take place and rely on them as a ground for not bringing the provisions into force. The tariff scheme was inconsistent with the statutory scheme, an abuse of prerogative power and unlawful, and in introducing it, the Secretary of State had debarred himself from exercising his powers under s 171(1) in the manner intended by Parliament. Accordingly, the appeal would be dismissed.

R v Secretary of State for the Home Department, ex p Fire Brigades Union [1995] 2 AC 513[1995] 2 All ER 244 (House of Lords: Lords Keith of Kinkel, Browne-Wilkinson, Mustill, Lloyd of Berwick, and Nicholls of Birkenhead). Decision of Court of Appeal [1995] 1 All ER 888 (1994 Abr para 859) affirmed.

890   Criminal Justice Act 1993—commencement

The Criminal Justice Act 1993 (Commencement No 8) Order 1995, SI 1995/43, brings into force, on 3 February 1995, ss 27, 28, relating to confiscation orders and postponed determinations.

The Criminal Justice Act 1993 (Commencement No 9) Order 1995, SI 1995/1958, brings into force on 14 August 1995, Sch 5, para 1, which amends the Criminal Appeal Act 1968, s 50 by replacing the definition of 'sentence'. For a summary of the Act, see 1993 Abr para 807. For details of commencement, see the commencement table in the title STATUTES.

891   Criminal Law (Consolidation) (Scotland) Act 1995

The Criminal Law (Consolidation) (Scotland) Act 1995 consolidates certain enactments creating offences and relating to the criminal law in Scotland, but certain provisions also extend to England and Wales. The Act received the royal assent on 8 November 1995 and came into force on 1 April 1996.

The provisions which extend to England and Wales are: ss 27–29 (investigation of serious or complex fraud), 35(10)–(12) (disclosure of information held by government departments), 53 (short title, commencement and extent).

892   Defences—diminished responsibility—availability of defence on appeal following conviction for murder

The appellant was one of three people involved in killing her husband. Although there was medical evidence that she was suffering from paranoid schizophrenia at the relevant time and that her responsibility for the killing was therefore materially diminished, the appellant expressly instructed both her solicitors and counsel that she did not wish to put forward a plea of guilty to manslaughter on the ground of diminished responsibility. She pleaded not guilty to murder, but was convicted of the offence on the basis of confessions that she had made to the police. She applied for leave to appeal, and for leave to introduce fresh evidence so that she could raise the defence of diminished responsibility. *Held*, there was medical evidence that the appellant was sufficiently capable of making a plea at the time that she was called upon to do so. She was fully advised as to the plea that she should make, in particular as to the availability of a plea of guilty of manslaughter on the ground of diminished responsibility. Even though she was not a normal person, she was capable in law of making a decision as to how her case should be put before the court and did so having had the benefit of proper advice. It was therefore not permissible for her to change her mind and have the matter reconsidered on the basis of a plea of diminished responsibility. Accordingly, the appeal would be dismissed.

R v Straw [1995] 1 All ER 187 (Court of Appeal: O'Connor LJ, Michael Davies and Schiemann JJ).

893 Defences—duress of circumstance—circumstances in which defence may apply

Police officers entered the appellant's home early in the morning to execute a search warrant and found him in bed with a loaded gun beside him. His explanation was that someone had visited him during the night with the gun, intending to go and shoot those responsible for killing one of his friends. The appellant had managed to persuade the person to leave the gun with him so that he could hand it over to the police the following day. The appellant was charged with possessing a prohibited weapon and ammunition without a firearm certificate. Initially, he intended to plead not guilty, relying on the defence of necessity, but the trial judge decided that the defence was not established because the appellant had failed to go immediately to the police with the gun. The appellant therefore entered a guilty plea. On appeal, *held,* where a person committed an offence in order to prevent someone else from committing a more serious offence, he could not be granted an absolute discharge, nor could the prosecuting authorities decide not to prosecute. It was for that reason that the limited defence of duress of circumstance had been developed in relation to road traffic offences, but there was no general defence of necessity. A person who raised the defence of duress of circumstance in relation to a firearms offence had to show that he had desisted from committing a crime as soon as he reasonably could. Here, the jury would have had to consider the fact that there had been a delay between the time that the appellant came into possession of the gun and the time that the police arrived at his house. An unexplained delay might mean that the defence was not available and that it was therefore unnecessary to leave it to the jury to decide whether or not the defence was proved. Here, however, the fact that the appellant had put a loaded gun in his bed did not deprive him of the defence, but was a matter which the jury could have taken into account. The judge should not have decided the issue himself but should have left it to the jury and, accordingly, the appeal would be allowed.

R v Pommell [1995] 2 Cr App Rep 607 (Court of Appeal: Kennedy LJ, Mantell and Hooper JJ).

894 Defences—marital coercion—direction to be given by judge

Under the Criminal Justice Act 1925, s 47 on a charge against a wife for any offence other than treason or murder it will be a good defence to prove that the offence was committed in the presence of, and under the coercion of, her husband.

A wife signed two passport application forms using the name of a dead child, whose birth certificate had been obtained by the husband. At her trial, she admitted signing the passports, but asserted that she had done so under coercion from her husband. She was convicted of offences of making a false statement to procure a passport and was sentenced to a conditional discharge for two years. On appeal, the wife submitted that the judge had failed to give the proper direction as to the defence of marital coercion. *Held*, the appropriate direction was used in *R v Richman* [1982] Crim LR 507, where the judge directed that coercion did not necessarily mean physical force or the threat of physical force. The coercion could be physical or moral but the wife had to prove that her will was overborne by the wishes of her husband. The judge had failed to make the distinction between coercion and duress and that amounted to a material misdirection. Accordingly, the appeal would be allowed.

R v Shortland (1996) 160 JP 5 (Court of Appeal: Kennedy LJ, Steel and Hooper JJ).

895 Drug offences—possession—intent to supply—misdirection to jury to convict of both crimes

Scotland
The defendant was accused of supplying the drug ecstasy contrary to the Misuse of Drugs Act 1971, s 4(3)(b) and possessing ecstasy with intent to supply to others, contrary to the 1971 Act, s 5(3). Both charges had been based on the evidence of a quantity of the drug at the defendant's accommodation. The judge directed the jury that, if they were satisfied that the defendant had purchased a quantity of the drug in order to split it into smaller shares for distribution to others, the proper verdict would be guilty of both charges because it would mean that the defendant was more actively involved in the chain of distribution than just being in possession with intent to supply to other people. The defendant was convicted and appealed. *Held*, the judge had given a misdirection because possession of the drug with a view to sell for profit was a typical example of an offence under the 1971 Act, s 5(3), but the defendant would have had to be involved in a number of transactions over a period of time before or after he was discovered in possession, to be guilty of an offence under s 4(3)(b). The directions had been confusing and could have led to a miscarriage of justice. Accordingly, the appeal would be allowed and the conviction under s 4(3)(b) would be quashed.
Dickson v HM Advocate 1995 SLT 703 (High Court of Justiciary).

896 Drug offences—powers of search and seizure—police acting on information received

See *Ireland v Russell*, para 847.

897 Drug offences—production of cannabis—meaning of 'production'

It has been held that the stripping of cannabis plants after they have been cut and harvested falls within the definition of 'production' of cannabis by 'manufacture, cultivation or any other method' in the Misuse of Drugs Act 1971, s 37(1), as it is done to produce that part of the plant which is a controlled drug by use of the 'other method' of discarding the parts of the plant which are not useable for the drug, and putting together those which are.
R v Harris; R v Cox [1996] Crim LR 36 (Court of Appeal: Leggatt LJ, Collins J and Judge Capstick).

898 Evidence and procedure

See CRIMINAL EVIDENCE AND PROCEDURE.

899 False trade descriptions

See TRADE DESCRIPTIONS.

900 Football spectators—licence to admit spectators—seating requirements

Football Spectators (Seating) Order 1995, SI 1995/1706 (in force on 31 July 1995), directs the Football Licensing Authority, when granting any licence to admit spectators to a number of specified football grounds, to include a condition imposing the requirement that: (1) only seated accommodation is to be provided for spectators at a designated football match; and (2) spectators will only be admitted to watch a designated football match from seated accommodation.

901 Forgery and counterfeiting—custody of counterfeit notes—defence of lawful excuse—direction to jury

Under the Forgery and Counterfeiting Act 1981, s 16(2) it is an offence for a person to have in his custody or under his control, without lawful authority or excuse, any thing which is, and which he knows or believes to be, a counterfeit of a currency note or of a protected coin. When the appellant attempted to buy foreign currency with some bank notes, he was told that they were forgeries. He was later stopped by Customs and Excise officers and when asked what he was going to do with the notes, he said that he did not know. He was charged with an offence under the 1981 Act, s 16(2). The appellant's possession of the counterfeit notes was never disputed but, at his trial, it fell to be determined whether he raised any issue which could justify the conclusion that he had a lawful excuse for his custody of the notes. The appellant claimed that indecision was a state of mind which could amount to a lawful excuse. The judge decided that there was no material on which a jury properly directed could conclude that the appellant might have a lawful excuse and, as a result, the appellant pleaded guilty to the offence. Following the appellant's conviction, he appealed on the basis that the guilty plea was entered as a consequence of an indication by the judge of his proposed direction, which was wrong in law. *Held*, the court agreed with the view of the judge. A lawful excuse could only be based in such circumstances on a settled intention to hand in the counterfeit things to an appropriate authority. Accordingly, the direction that was proposed by the judge was one which could not be challenged as being wrong in law and the appeal would be dismissed.

R v Sunman [1995] Crim LR 569 (Court of Appeal: Hobhouse LJ, Latham and Sedley JJ).

902 Harassment of debtors

See *Norweb plc v Dixon*, para 659.

903 Illegal immigration

See BRITISH NATIONALITY, IMMIGRATION AND RACE RELATIONS.

904 Industrial relations legislation—application—picketing

The Trade Union and Labour Relations (Consolidation) Act 1992, s 241(1)(c) provides that a person commits an offence who, with a view to compelling another person to do or abstain from doing any act which that person has a legal right to do or abstain from doing, wrongfully and without legal authority hides any tools, clothes or other property owned or used by that person, or deprives him of or hinders him in the use thereof. Section s 241(3) allows a constable to arrest without warrant anyone he reasonably suspects of committing an offence under the section.

The defendant occupied a crane during an anti-roads protest and refused to move, thereby preventing workmen from continuing with construction work. He was charged with committing an offence under the 1992 Act, s 241 and also with wilfully obstructing a police officer in the execution of his duty, contrary to the Police Act 1964, s 51(3). Justices decided that the 1992 Act, s 241 applied only to trade disputes or industrial action and not to anti-road protesters. They therefore dismissed the first charge, but convicted the defendant on the second charge. On the Director of Public Prosecution's appeal, *held*, having regard to the long history of the 1992 Act, s 241, Parliament had re-drafted the provision so as to widen the scope of its application beyond the employment context in which it had first been enacted. As it was therefore not confined to the context of trade disputes, the defendant could have been tried on such a charge. Accordingly, the appeal would be allowed.

DPP v Todd (1995) Independent, 5 May (Queen's Bench Division: Simon Brown LJ and Curtis J).

905 Intoxication and criminal liability—Law Commission proposals

The Law Commission has published a report, *Legislating the Criminal Code: Intoxication and Criminal Liability* (HC 153; Law Com No 229). It proposes that the present law on intoxication should be codified, with few changes; a draft Bill is appended to the report. A person should be treated as 'intoxicated' if his awareness, understanding or control is impaired by an intoxicant (ie alcohol, a drug, or any other substance which, once taken into the body, has the capacity to impair awareness, understanding or control). The circumstances in which a person's intoxication should be regarded as involuntary, including the taking of intoxicants for medicinal purposes or in circumstances that would amount to a defence to a criminal charge, are described and provision is made as to the burden of proof. The effect of taking, in addition to a known intoxicant, another substance which, unknown to the taker, is also an intoxicant is considered. In criminal proceedings where the prosecution alleges any intention, purpose, knowledge, belief, fraud or dishonesty, evidence of intoxication should be taken into account in determining whether the allegation has been made out; where any other mental element is alleged, the defendant who was voluntarily intoxicated should be treated as having been aware of anything of which he would, but for his intoxication, have been aware. Where voluntary intoxication results in automatism, liability should not be avoided solely on the ground of automatism; where automatism is caused partly by intoxication and partly by a disease of the mind, the matter should fall, as at present, within the law of insanity. An intoxicated mistake should not be available as a defence to a criminal charge in the case of voluntary intoxication if the belief would not have been held but for the intoxication and, further, the offence does not require proof of intention, purpose, knowledge, belief, fraud or dishonesty.

See also paras 865, 866.

906 Manslaughter—involuntary manslaughter—death caused by injuries consequent on vigorous sexual activity—activity consented to by deceased

The defendant, with the deceased's consent, penetrated the deceased's vagina and rectum with his hand. The deceased suffered cuts caused by the defendant's signet ring, but she did not realise the potentially serious nature of the injuries. When she later died of septicaemia as a result of the cuts the Crown alleged that the defendant was guilty of manslaughter. Although the prosecution accepted that the activity, if consensual, would not amount to an assault or any other crime, it argued that as the deceased could not have consented to the injuries themselves, their occurrence made the defendant's actions unlawful. *Held*, the sexual activity to which both the deceased and the defendant had agreed did not involve deliberate infliction of injury or harm and, but for the fact that the defendant was wearing a signet ring, no injury at all would have been caused or could have been contemplated. The question of consent to injury did not arise because neither party anticipated or considered it. The deceased sustained her unfortunate injuries as an accidental consequence of the sexual activity which was taking place with her consent. It would be contrary to principle to treat as criminal activity something which would not otherwise amount to assault merely because in the course of the activity an injury occurred. Accordingly, the count of manslaughter could not be sustained on the basis of the agreed facts.

R v Slingsby [1995] Crim LR 570 (Crown Court at Nottingham).

907 Manslaughter—joint enterprise—act outside the common purpose

The 15-year-old appellant was the passenger in a stolen car driven by his 14-year-old co-defendant. After travelling at high speed and attracting the attention of police officers, the car was slowed to a walking pace and the appellant and his co-defendant jumped out, leaving the car in gear. The car continued moving and struck a child's pram, killing the child. The co-defendant pleaded guilty to manslaughter and to taking the vehicle without authority. The appellant was tried on the same charges and the judge rejected a submission that the case should be withdrawn from the jury on the grounds that there was no evidence that the appellant had encouraged his co-defendant to act as he did and that there was insufficient evidence to enable the jury to conclude that what had happened was merely an unforeseen consequence of a joint enterprise. On appeal against conviction of manslaughter, *held*, the phrase 'reckless driving' could be applied to both that part of the co-defendant's driving during which he was at the wheel and to the abandonment of the vehicle at the end, leaving it to career on its own. However, the two elements to this chain of events were quite different in character. It was understandable that the jury might infer that the appellant had entered into a joint enterprise in which he contemplated the former kind of driving. However, the evidence did not support a contention that he contemplated the abandonment of the vehicle, leaving it in gear so that it caused the child's death. Further, there was no evidence that the appellant encouraged his co-defendant in any way. Accordingly, the case should have been withdrawn from the jury, the appeal would be allowed and the conviction for manslaughter quashed.

R v Mahmood [1995] RTR 48 (Court of Appeal: Lord Taylor of Gosforth CJ, Schiemann and Wright JJ).

908 Manslaughter—joint enterprise—variation in participants' intent—whether offence beyond contemplation of enterprise

The appellants and a co-accused took part in a robbery. The second appellant kept watch outside the shop while the first appellant, who was armed with a knife, and the co-accused, armed with a metal bar, entered the shop. The co-accused beat the shop owner, who later died as a result of his injuries; a small amount of cash was taken. The co-accused pleaded guilty to murder and robbery. The appellants pleaded guilty to robbery but submitted that the attack went beyond anything they had contemplated and did not form part of any joint enterprise. They were acquitted of murder but found guilty of manslaughter. On appeal against conviction, *held*, it was possible that a defendant, whilst being a participant in a joint enterprise, might lack a specific intent possessed by another participant. In such cases, where proof of participation was considered to prove only the mens rea appropriate to a lesser offence, only the lesser crime would be proved against the defendant. Whether an act was committed in the course of carrying out a joint enterprise was a question of fact and, if the act was not so committed, the joint enterprise ceased to provide a basis for finding the defendant guilty. It did not follow, however, that a variation in intent at the time of committing the act would preclude the act from having been done in the course of carrying out a joint enterprise. In the present case, the verdicts of manslaughter were properly open to the jury and were correctly left to them. Accordingly, the appeals would be dismissed.

R v Stewart [1995] 3 All ER 159 (Court of Appeal: Hobhouse LJ, Turner and Wright JJ).

909 Misconduct in public office—application of offence to local authority employees

It has been held that anyone who is appointed to discharge a public duty, and receives compensation in whatever shape whether from the Crown or otherwise, is capable of being charged with the offence of misconduct in a public office. The offence is not limited to officers or agents of the Crown and therefore can equally apply to local authority employees.

R v Bowden [1995] 4 All ER 505 (Court of Appeal: Hirst LJ, Hidden and Mitchell JJ).

910 Murder—death within a year and a day

The Law Commission has published its proposals for reform of the law relating to the irrebuttable presumption that a person cannot be convicted of murder where death does not occur within a year and a day of the injury that caused it, *Legislating the Criminal Code: The Year and a Day Rule in Homicide* (HC 183, Law Com No 230). The report recommends the abolition of the present rule, without retrospective effect, in relation to the offences of murder, manslaughter, infanticide, aiding and abetting suicide and any other offence to which it may apply, and to suicide for the purposes of coroners' verdicts. The position regarding the application of the rule to causing death by dangerous driving, to causing death by careless driving when under the influence of drink or drugs and to aggravated vehicle-taking causing death is not entirely clear, but the commission's view is that the rule probably applies also to those offences and, assuming that it does, that it should be abolished in relation to them. However, the commission recommends that the Attorney General's consent should be required for the prosecution of an offence involving causing the death of another where the death occurred more than three years previously, or where the act or omission causing the death has been the basis for proceedings against the accused and in respect of which a custodial sentence of two or more years has been imposed on him. The Attorney General's consent would similarly be required if the charge related to aiding, abetting, counselling or procuring a person's suicide in such circumstances. A draft Homicide Bill is appended to the report to give effect to the recommendations.

911 Murder—defence—provocation—abnormal characteristics—battered woman syndrome

The appellant came from an unhappy family background and sought attention by frequent attempts to cut her wrists. She left home at the age of 16 to work as a prostitute. She was picked up by the victim and lived with him while continuing to work as a prostitute. The victim subjected the appellant to physical abuse. The appellant subsequently lost interest in the victim and they were separated for a period. After drinking together, the appellant and the victim went to the victim's house. Fearing trouble, the appellant took two knives from the drawer. She cut her wrists with one of the knives. The victim undressed and sat near her. The appellant feared that he might force her to have sex with him. The victim taunted her that she had not made a very good job of her wrist-slashing. She lost her self-control and stabbed him. She was charged with murder and in her defence relied on the whole history of her relationship with the victim as a cumulative catalogue of provocative conduct against her, culminating in the jibe about the inefficiency of her wrist-cutting which was the trigger that snapped her self-control. Evidence was given as to the appellant being of abnormal mentality with immature, explosive and attention-seeking traits. The trial judge, directing the jury as to provocation, told them that they had to decide the effect of the jeer on a young woman in that situation who did not have a distorted and explosive personality. The appellant was convicted of murder. On appeal, *held*, there was force in the submission that the appellant's tendency to attention-seeking by wrist-slashing was closely comparable to dyslexia and anorexia and like those could be regarded as a psychological illness or disorder which was in no way repugnant or wholly inconsistent with the concept of the reasonable person. It was also a permanent condition which was abnormal. It was open to the jury to conclude that the provocative taunt relied on as the trigger inevitably hit directly at this abnormality. The appellant also argued that immaturity was an eligible characteristic of the reasonable man, and immaturity was clearly not repugnant to that concept. Therefore the judge should have left those two relevant characteristics to the jury as eligible for attribution to the reasonable woman. The judge had also failed to analyse to the jury the various strands of provocation at the successive stages starting from the first meeting with the victim and culminating in the killing. The appeal would therefore be allowed.

R v Humphries (1995) Independent, 11 July (Court of Appeal: Hirst LJ, Cazalet and Kay JJ).

It has been held that, even if suffering from battered woman syndrome, a defendant can not succeed in a defence of provocation to a charge of murder in a case of domestic violence, unless the jury is satisfied that she had suffered, or might have suffered, a sudden and temporary loss of self-control at the time of the killing. However, the severity of such a syndrome and the extent to which it was suffered by the defendant is relevant to the defence, and the medical evidence should be left to the jury for consideration. It might be relevant in two ways. Firstly, it might be important to the question of what triggered the actus reus and might lead to a jury more readily finding that a minor incident had triggered a sudden loss of control. Secondly, the trial judge should leave battered woman syndrome or personality disorder to the jury as eligible for attribution to the reasonable person.

R v Thornton (1995) Times, 14 December (Court of Appeal: Lord Taylor of Gosforth CJ, Hidden and Ebsworth JJ).

New Zealand

The appellant was physically and emotionally abused by the deceased. He threatened to kill her and her children and the appellant's daughter alleged that she had been sexually abused by him. Although the appellant obtained non-molestation and non-violence orders against the deceased and fled to a women's refuge several times, she remained with him. One night, when the appellant feared a serious beating, she gave the deceased a fatal overdose and buried him in the garden. When the body was discovered, she was charged with murder. At her trial, the appellant claimed alternatively lack of intent, self-defence or provocation based on her medical evidence of 'battered woman's syndrome' by reason of which she felt helpless against the deceased's violence, had a heightened sensitivity to threats and an impaired ability to reason rationally. The appellant was convicted and, on appeal, she claimed that the judge had failed adequately to direct the jury about the syndrome and had downplayed the history of abuse by concentrating on her evidence relating to the night of the death. *Held*, there had not been any misdirection as to battered woman's syndrome since (1) more than a brief reference to the syndrome would have required a detailed analysis of evidence adverse to the appellant, (2) extensive submissions by counsel had put the syndrome at the forefront of the case when the judge summed up, (3) the judge made it clear that all the evidence was relevant to intent, self-defence and provocation, (4) although the direction had not been comprehensive, it was not so inadequate as to be unjust, (5) in any event, there had been evidence of a deliberate, calculated crime, and (6) the appellant's evidence had not harmed her case or downplayed the history of abuse since it had gathered together all of the past and showed its dreadful climax. Accordingly, the appeal would be dismissed.

R v Oakes [1995] 2 NZLR 673 (Court of Appeal).

912 Murder—defence—provocation—question for determination by jury

When the appellant's wife was found dead he told the police that he had thrown her onto a bed. Her injuries were consistent with impact to a wooden bed end but there were too many injuries to have resulted from a single fall. The appellant's principal defence was one of accident, in that the injuries occurred when he restrained his wife from leaving home because he believed she would commit suicide. The issue of manslaughter was also raised on the basis that excessive force had been used by the appellant. His counsel did not invite the jury to consider provocation because it was inconsistent with the defence but the judge gave a direction upon it. The appellant was convicted of murder and, on appeal, he submitted that the judge gave the jury no assistance on the evidence relevant to the issue of provocation. *Held*, it was well established that the judge had to leave the jury to decide if there was evidence which suggested that the accused had been provoked, even if the defence did not raise the issue and would prefer not to do so because it was inconsistent with the primary defence. Where the judge had to do so, he should indicate, unless it was obvious, what evidence might support the conclusion that the accused lost his self-control. This was particularly important where counsel had not raised the issue. In the present case, the judge had not given any such assistance to the jury and that amounted to a non-direction. However, on the evidence there had not been a miscarriage of justice. Accordingly, the appeal would be dismissed.

R v Stewart [1995] 4 All ER 999 (Court of Appeal: Stuart-Smith LJ, Kay and Dyson JJ). *R v Rossiter* (1992) 95 Cr App Rep 326, CA (1992 Abr para 798) and *R v Cambridge* [1994] 2 All ER 760, CA considered.

The appellant was convicted of murder. Shortly before the killing, the appellant learned that his son, a drug user, had been threatened by a drug dealer. Armed with a shotgun and a cut throat razor, the appellant went to the dealer's home. After a confrontation between the men, the appellant used the razor to inflict serious injuries on the dealer. The dealer fled pursued by the appellant who fired the shotgun twice. Although the shots did not hit him directly, the dealer was killed by particles blasted from a wire mesh fence by the force of the gunshots. There was evidence that the appellant then asked a friend to fabricate an alibi for him. At trial, the appellant sought to rely on the defence of provocation on the basis of the threat to his son. The trial judge directed the jury that there was no evidence capable of giving rise to a defence of provocation other than 'self-induced' provocation arising after the appellant had entered the dealer's home. At his appeal against conviction the appellant claimed that the trial judge had misdirected the jury. *Held*, the Homicide Act 1957, s 3 moved the test of provocation from the province of the trial judge to that of the jury. Although there would be considerable difficulty in establishing a defence of provocation based on the threats to the son, it was a matter which ought to have been left to the jury. The trial judge had also misdirected the jury with regard to the appellant's attempt to procure a false alibi. She had failed to give it a clear direction specifying how, as a matter of law, it should regard the appellant's conduct after the killing and the lies he had told. Accordingly, the appeal would be allowed and a retrial ordered.

R v Baillie [1995] 2 Cr App Rep 31 (Court of Appeal: Henry LJ, Rougier and Douglas Brown JJ).

913   Murder—defence—provocation—reasonable man test

The Homicide Act 1957, s 3 provides that where on a charge of murder there is evidence on which the jury can find that the person charged was either provoked (whether by things done or by things said or by both together) to lose his self-control, the question whether the provocation was enough to make a reasonable man do as he did must be left to the jury; in determining that question, the jury must take into account everything, both done and said, according to the effect which, in their opinion, it would have on the reasonable man.

The deceased had an argument with the defendant over the defendant's addiction to glue-sniffing. A fight broke out, which was halted by a third party. The deceased wished to continue the argument and following another struggle, the deceased was fatally wounded by the defendant. The defendant pleaded not guilty to a charge of murder and relied on the defence of provocation at trial. On appeal against conviction, the question was whether when directing a jury on provocation under the 1957 Act, s 3 and in accordance with the model direction in *R v Camplin* [1978] AC 705, HL (1977 Abr para 700), the judge had to exclude from the jury's consideration characteristics and past behaviour of the defendant, at which the taunts were directed, which in the judge's view were inconsistent with the concept of the reasonable man. *Held*, the defendant's addiction to glue-sniffing should have been taken into account as affecting the gravity of the provocation. It was a characteristic of particular relevance since the words of the deceased which were said to constitute provocation were directed towards the defendant's addiction and his inability to break himself of it. Accordingly, the appeal would be allowed.

R v Morhall [1995] 3 All ER 659 (House of Lords: Lords Goff of Chieveley, Browne-Wilkinson, Slynn of Hadley, Nicholls of Birkenhead and Steyn). Decision of Court of Appeal [1993] 4 All ER 888 (1993 Abr para 829) reversed.

The appellant built a property on his land without obtaining the necessary planning permission. When the local authority obtained a demolition order in respect of the property, the appellant made a number of violent threats against the authority and, in particular, against the principal planning officer. The officer and the authority's solicitor visited the appellant on the day of the demolition and, just before the demolition began, the appellant shot and killed the officer and attempted to shoot the solicitor. The appellant was convicted of murder and attempted murder. At his trial, he had raised a defence of provocation and, on appeal, he submitted that the judge had failed to put forward obsession and eccentricity as characteristics for the jury's consideration of the issue whether a reasonable man in the appellant's position would have lost his self-control. *Held*, when determining whether a reasonable man might, in circumstances similar to the appellant, have been provoked to lose his self-control and act as the appellant did, the jury were entitled to consider those permanent characteristics or traits which served to distinguish the accused from the ordinary person in the community and were specifically relevant to the events relied on as constituting the provocation. The appellant's obsessiveness and his eccentric character were characteristics which ought to have been left to the jury for their consideration. However, while the judge's summing up was flawed, there was overwhelming evidence that the appellant was not in a state where he had lost his self-control. He had announced his violent intentions a considerable time before the event and had prepared himself. The jury would have rejected the suggestion that the appellant's deliberate action was something which someone with the self-control of a reasonable man would have done and, accordingly, the appeal would be dismissed.

R v Dryden [1995] 4 All ER 987 (Court of Appeal: Lord Taylor of Gosforth CJ, MacPherson and Steel JJ).

914 Murder—defence—self defence—failure properly to direct jury

Jamaica

The respondent was a special constable who was charged with murder following an altercation in the street in which one of two brothers was killed. He claimed that there had been a struggle in which the brothers had tried to take his gun and that he had fired a shot accidentally. His alternative defence was provocation. The issue of self defence was not raised by counsel and in summing up the judge specifically withdrew the issue of self defence from the jury. The respondent was acquitted of murder and convicted of manslaughter. Following the Court of Appeal's quashing of his conviction on the grounds that the jury should have been directed on the issue of self defence, the Director of Public Prosecutions appealed. *Held*, where there was a struggle in such circumstances, with two men trying to get hold of a gun held by another, then it was possible that the killing was murder, or that it was provoked and was manslaughter, or that it was an accident or that it happened deliberately but in self defence. Self defence in such circumstances could well include preventing an attacker from trying to get a gun which might have beenused to harm the accused. Even if the evidence in support of self defence was not strong, the issue should have been explained and left to the jury. Since the judge had failed to give such a direction the conviction for manslaughter could not stand and the appeal would be dismissed.

DPP (Jamaica) v Bailey (1995) 1 Cr App Rep 257 (Privy Council: Lords Templeman, Ackner, Mustill, Slynn of Hadley and Woolf). *DPP v Walker* [1974] 1 WLR 1090, considered.

915 Murder—excessive use of force—soldier acting in the course of duty—alternative conviction of manslaughter

The appellant, a soldier serving in Northern Ireland, was on patrol with the purpose of catching joyriders. He fired four shots at a passing stolen car, the fourth of which fatally injured a passenger in the car. It was a finding of fact that the appellant had intended to cause death or serious bodily harm, and that he had not acted in self-defence or in the defence of his colleagues because he had fired the fourth shot when the car had ceased to pose a threat to his patrol group. Moreover, there was no suggestion that he believed that the driver of the car was a terrorist or that he would have carried out terrorist offences if allowed to escape. The appellant was convicted of murder, on the basis that he had used unreasonable and excessive force. His appeal against conviction was dismissed and, on further appeal, the issue was whether in such circumstances a soldier or police officer was guilty of manslaughter and not murder. *Held*, there was little distinction between force used in self-defence and force used to prevent a crime or to arrest offenders. On the facts of the case, the defence of self-defence was not available to the appellant because he had used excessive force. Although soldiers in Northern Ireland were in a special position and it had been recommended in a 1980 report by the Criminal Law Revision Committee (Cmnd 7844) that a person should be convicted of manslaughter rather than murder when it was reasonable for him to use force in self-defence or to prevent a crime if at the time of the act he honestly believed that the force he used was reasonable in the circumstances, that recommendation and similar recommendations made by the House of Lords Select Committee on Murder and Life Imprisonment and the Law Commission had not yet been enacted. The court could develop law in accordance with recommendations before legislation was introduced, but it was not appropriate to do so in the instant case as the reduction of murder to manslaughter was essentially a matter to be decided by Parliament. Accordingly, the appeal would be dismissed.

R v Clegg [1995] 1 All ER 334 (House of Lords: Lords Keith of Kinkel, Browne-Wilkinson, Slynn of Hadley, Lloyd of Berwick and Nicholls of Birkenhead). *Palmer v The Queen* [1971] 1 All ER 1077, PC followed.

916 Murder—intent—direction to jury

The defendant was convicted of the murder of a child killed in an arson attack on his home. On appeal, *held*, the trial judge had incorrectly directed the jury as to the necessary intent for murder and at times equated foresight with intent. The jury should have been asked to consider how probable was the consequence that resulted from the defendant's voluntary act and whether he foresaw the consequences of his act. It had then to decide whether in all the circumstances, including those questions of foresight, an intention to kill or cause serious bodily harm had been made out. The trial judge had failed to emphasise to the jury that foresight was merely an evidential guide and did not necessarily imply the existence of intention. The conviction was unsafe. Accordingly, the appeal would be allowed and a verdict of manslaughter would be substituted.

R v Scalley [1995] Crim LR 504 (Court of Appeal: Russell LJ, May and Mitchell JJ). *R v Nedrick* [1986] 3 All ER 1, CA (1986 Abr para 547) applied.

917   Murder—intent—joint enterprise—secondary party lacking intent

The appellants, together with another man had called at the home of a person who was shot and killed by one of the group. It was alleged that there had been a joint enterprise but the appellants claimed that they were present purely for the purposes of purchasing cannabis. They appealed against their convictions of murder for which they had been sentenced to life imprisonment. *Held*, the judge had followed the formulation laid down in *R v Hyde* that if one party realises (without consenting to the use of such conduct) that another party may kill or cause serious injury but nevertheless continues to participate with that party in the venture, that will amount to a sufficient mental element for him to be guilty of murder if the other party kills with the requisite intent during the course of the venture. It had been strongly argued that it was anomalous to require proof against a secondary party of a lesser mens rea than that required of the principal who committed the actus reus. However, the court felt bound to follow *R v Hyde*, having regard to the approval it had received in numerous Court of Appeal decisions and the fact that it was in accordance with *R v Maxwell*. If the result presented an unacceptable anomaly it was for the House of Lords or the legislature to rectify it. Accordingly, the appeal would be dismissed and leave to appeal to the House of Lords refused.

R v Powell; R v Daniel (1995) Times, 2 June (Court of Appeal: Lord Taylor of Gosforth CJ, Tucker and Forbes JJ). *R v Hyde* [1990] 3 All ER 892, CA (1990 Abr para 654), *R v Maxwell* [1978] 1 WLR 1350, HL (1978 Abr para 578), followed.

918   Murder—unlawful injury to mother carrying child in utero—murder of child born alive

A man stabbed his pregnant girlfriend in the abdomen. She gave birth to a live infant that survived for 4 months before it died. The man pleaded guilty to wounding the girlfriend with intent to cause her grievous bodily harm and was charged with the murder of the infant. He was acquitted on that charge on the trial judge's ruling that, in law, there was no case to go to the jury. The Attorney General referred the following point of law to the court: (1) subject to proof of the requisite intent in either case, whether the crimes of murder or manslaughter could be committed where unlawful injury was deliberately inflicted (a) to a child in utero or (b) to a mother carrying a child in utero, where the child is subsequently born alive, enjoys an existence independent of the mother, thereafter dies and the injuries inflicted while in utero either caused or made a substantial contribution to the death; (2) whether the fact that the death of the child was caused solely as a consequence of injury to the mother rather than as a consequence of direct injury to the foetus could negative any liability for murder or manslaughter in such circumstances. *Held*, (1) murder or manslaughter could be committed where unlawful injury was deliberately inflicted either to a child in utero or to a mother carrying a child in utero in such circumstances. The requisite intent to be proved in the case of murder was an intention to kill or cause really serious bodily injury to the mother, the foetus before birth being viewed as an integral part of the mother. Such intention had to be appropriately modified in the case of manslaughter. (2) The fact that the death of the child was solely caused in consequence of injury to the mother rather than as a consequence of injury to the foetus did not negative any liability for murder and manslaughter provided the jury were satisfied that causation had been proved.

A-G's Reference (No 3 of 1994) [1996] 2 All ER 10 (Court of Appeal: Lord Taylor of Gosforth CJ, Kay and Steel JJ).

919   Northern Ireland—prevention of terrorism

See para 2179.

920   Obstructing a police officer—wilful obstruction—contamination of identification parade in attempt to procure alibi

After being charged with murder the applicant claimed he had an alibi. His solicitor hired a private investigator who planned to substantiate the alibi by means of showing a photograph of the applicant to a specific group of people. The police claimed that they wished to carry out an identification parade and that showing the photograph would obstruct the course of their investigation contrary to the Police Act 1964. The police asked the potential alibi witnesses not to look at the photograph. On an application against the police for committal for contempt of court, *held*, the police had no power to prevent the solicitors from approaching potential witnesses. In discharging his duties, the solicitor was not 'wilfully' obstructing a police officer under the Police Act 1964, s 51(3), even though his actions might result in the contamination of the identification parade. Accordingly, the threat to prosecute under the 1964 Act was a contempt of court.

Connolly v Dale [1995] 3 WLR 786 (Queen's Bench Division: Balcombe LJ and Buxton J).

921 Obtaining property by deception—obtaining cheques—deception where manager and employee signed cheque

The defendant made dishonest applications to a finance company for loans for equipment to be used by companies owned or controlled by him by submitting false invoices. As a result, he was convicted of obtaining property by deception, the property being cheques issued by the finance company. He appealed on the ground that the judge had misdirected the jury by telling them that it was sufficient that any employee who had been concerned with writing the cheque had been deceived. *Held*, there were two reasons why the direction had been wrong. Firstly, it was not a question of whether any employee had been deceived but whether any employee whose state of mind stood as that of the company was aware of the falsity of the transaction. If that had been the case, it was irrelevant how many other employees were not so aware. Second, the cheque was not obtained from the employees who typed it out, but from the people who signed it. Therefore, (1) where only a manager signed the offence could not be made out, (2) where a manager signed with another employee, it had to be shown that the other was deceived and (3) where two employees, who were not managers, signed, it had to be proved that one or both had been deceived and that, where one was, the other did not know of the fraud because, if they did, the company had not been deceived. The judge had not made that distinction clear to the jury and, accordingly, the appeal would be allowed and the conviction quashed.

R v Rozeik [1996] 1 WLR 159 (Court of Appeal: Leggatt LJ, Collins and Capstick JJ).

922 Obtaining property by deception—transaction effected by electronic means—property belonging to another—whether intention permanently to deprive

The Theft Act 1968, s 15(2) provides that a person is to be treated as obtaining property if he obtains ownership, possession or control of it, and 'obtain' includes obtaining for another or enabling another to obtain or to retain.

The appellants made some 40 mortgage applications which contained false particulars to building societies. In each case, a solicitor acted for both the appellants and the lender and the mortgage advances were made by electronic transfer from the lender to the solicitor. The appellants were charged with obtaining, or attempting to obtain, property by deception under the 1968 Act. They admitted making false representations but claimed that the loans would be repaid because the housing market was buoyant at that time. The appellants were convicted. On appeal, they claimed that (1) the transfer of money to the solicitor did not amount to obtaining property within s 15(2); (2) such a transfer was simply an internal transfer of the lender's assets; (3) there was no property 'belonging to another'; and (4) there could be no intent permanently to deprive a person of an intangible item such as an electronic transfer. *Held*, (1) the definition of property in s 4(1) included a transfer by electronic means. (2) When the transfer took place a contract existed which provided that the appellants would execute a mortgage in consideration of the loan and the asset was transferred to the solicitor's client account. (3) Following the transfer, although the solicitor held the funds for a limited purpose, there was an obtaining of property 'belonging to another'. (4) Where an electronic transfer occurred the court was of the opinion that it was of funds which the appellants never intended to be returned and therefore the 'intent to deprive permanently' was made out. Accordingly, the appeal would be dismissed.

R v Preddy; R v Slade [1995] Crim LR 564 (Court of Appeal: Farquharson LJ, Ebsworth and Steel JJ).

923 Outraging public decency—act taking place in private house—requirement as to commission of offence in place where public might witness act

The appellant allegedly committed an act outraging public decency in his own home. Following his conviction, he appealed on the ground that such an offence could not be committed in or at a place to which the public had no access. *Held*, it was established in *R v Mayling* [1963] 1 All ER 687, CA, that it was a necessary condition in committing an offence that at least two people must have been able to witness what happened. In the court's view, there was a further requirement that the offence was committed in a place where there existed a real possibility that members of the general public might witness what happened. In the present case, that requirement was plainly not met and, accordingly, the appeal would be allowed and the conviction quashed.

R v Walker [1995] Crim LR 826 (Court of Appeal: Lord Taylor of Gosforth CJ, Laws and Keene JJ).

924 Perverting the course of justice—actus reus—act or course of conduct

The appellant's brother was stopped whilst driving the appellant's car because it was not displaying a vehicle excise licence. A summons was issued in the appellant's name when documents relating to the car were not produced to the police. The appellant did not attend court, but was sentenced in his absence for various offences under the Road Traffic Act 1988. A fine was imposed and an order for costs made, and as the appellant failed to make any payments, a warrant for his arrest was issued. When a police officer attempted to execute the warrant, the appellant gave a different date of birth to that stated in the warrant, explaining that the date of birth on the warrant was that of his brother. The appellant was charged with perverting the course of justice, in that he had allowed informations alleging contraventions of the 1988 Act to be proved in his name even though they were actually committed by his brother. On appeal, *held,* the offence of perverting the course of justice was committed when a person acted or embarked on a course of conduct which was intended to pervert the course of public justice. In the instant case, the appellant had not appeared at court when the case was originally considered, nor had he made any representations. As he had not carried out any act or course of conduct, he did not have the necessary actus reus to commit the offence, and acquiescence was not enough to form the basis of the offence. Accordingly, the appeal would be allowed.

R v Headley (1996) 160 JP 25 (Court of Appeal: Lord Taylor of Gosforth CJ, Popplewell and Steel JJ).

925 Perverting the course of justice—failure to administer breath test

An off-duty police officer who had been drinking in a pub, was involved in a road accident. An ambulance and several police officers, two of whom included the appellants, went to the scene of the accident. Although the ambulance drivers and those attending the officer in hospital were of the opinion that his breath smelt of alcohol, the appellants did not breathalyse the officer at any stage. A member of the ambulance crew reported them for misconduct, and the appellants were charged with perverting the course of justice by failing to administer a breath test at the scene of the accident, and with misconduct in a public office by failing to administer a breath test at the scene or thereafter. On appeal against their conviction for the first offence, *held,* although the Road Traffic Act 1988, s 6 empowered police officers to administer breath tests, it did not impose a duty on them to do so in every case. It was for the jury to decided on the particular facts of a case whether a police officer had been under such a duty. Moreover, in deciding whether or not a breath test should have been administered at the scene of an accident, the test could be given at a later stage if there was a risk of causing harm or injury to a person. Here, the judge had failed to refer to that possibility in his summing up, whereas it had been an important aspect of the appellants' defence. On the facts, the appellants had been under a duty to administer a breath test because they had suspected that the officer had consumed alcohol, and in those circumstances, they were guilty of the lesser offence of misconduct in a public office rather than perverting the course of justice. Accordingly, the appeal would be allowed.

R v Ward [1995] Crim LR 398 (Court of Appeal: Staughton LJ, Owen and Holland JJ). *R v Coxhead* [1986] RTR 502, CA (1985 Abr para 1950) followed.

926 Prevention of terrorism—exclusion order—challenge

The applicant, the president of a political party with inferred links to a terrorist organisation, wished to address the House of Commons. The Home Secretary made an exclusion order to prevent the applicant entering the United Kingdom. The applicant sought judicial review of that decision but it was dismissed except on the issue of proportionality, namely whether he should have been permitted to visit for a few hours. That issue was referred to the European Court of Justice. The exclusion order was revoked shortly afterwards and the Home Secretary applied for a withdrawal of the reference and for the application for judicial review to be dismissed. The applicant then sought to add a claim for exemplary damages. *Held,* (1) awards of exemplary damages were considered in respect of action by government servants only when it was oppressive, arbitrary or unconstitutional. In the present case, such damages would be considered on the basis that while the Home Secretary was taken to have been justified in making the exclusion order, he did not attach sufficient weight to the right to free speech. Since it was contrary to national security requirements to reveal the ground on which the Home Secretary based his decision, it would be a formidable task for the applicant to persuade the court that the decision was so clearly disproportionate that it could not properly have been made. To succeed in his damages claim the applicant would be required to go even further and cause the court to view the decision as so clearly wrong as to merit the punitive form of damages. The court concluded that this was not a case where exemplary damages could be awarded. (2) Since the Home Secretary was not obliged to give reasons which it would be contrary to the public interest to disclose, those who sought to have the exclusion order reimposed could not provide a legitimate basis for the continuation of the judicial review proceedings. Accordingly, the application for judicial review had no remaining content and, accordingly, would be dismissed.

R v Secretary of State for the Home Department, ex p Adams [1995] All ER (EC) 177 (Queen's Bench Division: Leggatt LJ and Kay J). For earlier proceedings see (1994) Independent, 27 July (1994 Abr para 905).

927 Prevention of terrorism—temporary provisions

The Prevention of Terrorism (Temporary Provisions) Act 1989 (Enforcement of External Orders) Order 1995, SI 1995/760 (in force on 24 March 1995), enables certain types of order made in a designated country or territory to be enforced in the United Kingdom. The relevant orders are those made under the 1989 Act, s 11(3)(a) or (b) or orders that prohibit dealing with property subject to an external forfeiture order or regarding which such an order could be made as a result of proceedings instituted in the designated country or territory.

The Prevention of Terrorism (Temporary Provisions) Act 1989 (Continuance) Order 1995, SI 1995/816 (in force on 22 March 1995), continues in force the 1989 Act, Pts I–IV and s 27(6)(c) for 12 months from 22 March 1995, with exceptions for certain provisions that have effect in Northern Ireland.

928 Public order—public assembly—imposition of conditions—failure to comply with conditions

The Public Order Act 1986, s 14(1) provides that if the senior police officer, having regard to the time or place at which and the circumstances in which any public assembly is being held or is intended to be held, reasonably believes that it may result in serious public disorder, serious damage to property or serious disruption to the life of the community, he may give directions imposing on the persons organising or taking part in the assembly conditions as to the place at which the assembly may be held, its maximum duration, or the maximum number of persons who may constitute it.

The appellant distributed information to travellers about free festivals, using news sheets and an incoming-only telephone and answer machine. He was served with a notice under the 1986 Act, s 14 requiring him to comply with certain conditions concerning a particular festival which the police believed was due to take place. The appellant was convicted of failing to comply with the notice, even though the police were unable to adduce evidence that any actual public assembly was attributable to him. On appeal, *held*, the police did not know the exact date of the alleged event, nor even whether the event was due to be held in a public place. The requirements of the 1986 Act, s 14 had not been satisfied and, accordingly, the appeal would be allowed.

DPP v Baillie [1995] Crim LR 426 (Queen's Bench Division: McCowan LJ and Buxton J)

929 Public order—raves—powers of police—disposal of sound equipment

See para 2307.

930 Rape—award of damages to victim—award in relation to other personal injury awards

See *Griffiths v Willliams*, para 979.

931 Road traffic offences

See ROAD TRAFFIC.

932 Sentencing

See SENTENCING.

933 Theft—property belonging to another—money collected for charity

The Theft Act 1968, s 5(3) provides that where a person receives property from or on account of another, and is under an obligation to the other to retain and deal with that property or its proceeds in a particular way, the property or proceeds will be regarded, as against him, as belonging to the other.

A television company acted as a charity trust to raise money for various charities. The appellant organised a number of events and, on the recommendation of the company, he paid the money raised into a separate bank account. The company authorised the appellant to transfer the money from that account to his own bank account so that he could write a cheque for the amount owed to the charity trust. That cheque, together with others later drawn on his account, were not met. At the same time, he was withdrawing money from the account. The appellant was convicted of theft. On his appeal, *held*, by virtue of the 1968 Act, s 5(3), the appellant was under an obligation to retain, if not the actual notes and coins, at least their proceeds, that is to say the money credited in the separate bank account. When he took the money credited to that account and moved it over to his own account, it was still the proceeds of the notes and coins donated which he proceeded to use for his own purposes, thereby appropriating. Accordingly, the appeal would be dismissed.

R v Wain (1995) 2 Cr App Rep 660 (Court of Appeal: McCowan LJ, Ognall and Gage JJ).

934   Unlawful eviction—harassment of occupier—harassment by landlord's agent—statutory liability of agent

The Housing Act 1988, s 27 provides that it is unlawful for a landlord or any person acting on his behalf to cause a tenant to give up occupation of premises by acts of harassment. A landlord in breach of s 27 is liable for damages, assessed in accordance with the provisions of s 28.

The defendant landlord appointed a managing agent of a property of which the plaintiffs were tenants. The agent committed acts of harassment which caused the plaintiffs' occupation of the property to become intolerable with the result that they moved out and brought an action against the agent under the 1988 Act, ss 27, 28. At first instance, the judge dismissed the claim against the agent and the plaintiffs appealed. *Held*, the language of the 1988 Act, ss 27, 28 clearly provided that only the landlord himself, and not his agent, was liable under those sections. An agent was liable for his own personal torts. Accordingly, any claim against the agent in this case was conclusively barred and the appeal would be dismissed.

Sampson v Wilson [1995] 3 WLR 455 (Court of Appeal: Sir Thomas Bingham MR, Hirst and Aldous LJJ).

CUSTOMS AND EXCISE

Halsbury's Laws of England (4th edn) Vol 12, paras 501–1100

935   Articles

Bootlegging—Excise Goods and the Single Market, Christopher Burke: 159 JP Jo 383
New Customs, Gavin McFarlane: LS Gaz, 20 September 1995, p 20

936   Air passenger duty

See AVIATION.

937   Counterfeit and pirated goods

The Counterfeit and Pirated Goods (Customs) Regulations 1995, SI 1995/1430 (in force on 1 July 1995), make provision consequent on Community provisions for the prohibition of the release for free circulation, export, re-export or entry for a suspensive procedure of counterfeit or pirated goods. A form of application, to be completed by the holder or authorised user, or a representative, of a trade mark or other intellectual property right, and certain other aspects of the procedure to be followed by the applicant, are set out.

The Counterfeit and Pirated Goods (Consequential Provisions) Regulations 1995, SI 1995/1447 (in force on 1 July 1995), replace the Counterfeit Goods (Consequential Provisions) Regulations 1987, SI 1987/1521, and make provision consequential upon Council Regulation (EC) 3295/94, which lays down measures to prohibit the release for free circulation, export, re-export or entry for a suspensive procedure of counterfeit and pirated goods. The regulations (1) provide that such goods are rendered liable to suspension, detention and forfeiture, (2) provide that the Customs and Excise Management Act 1979, ss 139, 144–146, 152–155, Sch 3, are applied in respect of such goods, and (3) make additional provision about the burden of proof similar to s 154(2)(f) of the 1979 Act.

938 Customs duty—equivalent charge—prohibition within Community

See *Edouard Dubois et Fils SA v Garonor Exploitation SA*, para 3127.

939 Customs officers—control of persons entering or leaving the United Kingdom—anything carried with person

See *R v Lucien*, para 797.

940 Customs reviews and appeals—binding tariff Information

The Customs Reviews and Appeals (Binding Tariff Information) Regulations 1995, SI 1995/2351 (in force on 1 October 1995), provide that the Finance Act 1994, s 14, which provides for reviews and appeals to the VAT and Duties Tribunals in respect of certain decisions of the Commissioners of Customs and Excise, applies also to decisions as to (1) the determination of the tariff classification of any goods (if the determination founds a decision as to a charge, rate or amount of duty), (2) whether or not binding tariff information is to be supplied, (3) whether or not any binding tariff information is to be annulled, withdrawn or revoked, so far as any such decision is made for the purposes of the Community provisions relating to binding tariff information.

941 Customs traders—accounts and records

The Customs Traders (Accounts and Records) Regulations 1995, SI 1995/1203 (in force on 1 June 1995), require customs traders to keep and preserve records containing information about their businesses and about their dealings in customs goods as defined in the Finance Act 1994, s 20(3)(a). The regulations (1) specify the requirements for keeping and preserving commercial records; (2) require particular customs traders to keep and preserve a copy of every supplementary or simplified declaration made by them or on their behalf, or, instead, to keep and preserve a record of all the information set out in such declarations; (3) permit the Commissioners of Customs and Excise to specify, in a public notice, additional and alternative records to be kept and preserved; (4) require certain records to be kept and preserved so that it is readily apparent that they relate to a particular customs declaration; (5) specify the form that the required records may take; (6) require a customs trader who is required by or under the regulations to keep a record, to do so at the time when any information that is to be recorded is first known to him or as soon as possible thereafter; and (7) require customs traders to preserve their records for four years or such lesser period as the commissioners may require.

942 Excise duty—beer

See para 942.

943 Excise duty—drawback

The Excise Goods (Drawback) Regulations 1995, SI 1995/1046 (in force on 1 June 1995), replace the 1992 Regulations, SI 1992/3151, and amend the Excise Warehousing (Etc) Regulations 1988, SI 1988/809. Claims for drawback of excise duty are now permitted where excise goods are exported, warehoused for export, destroyed because they are not of satisfactory quality, and in certain circumstances, accidentally destroyed. The provision for drawback of excise duties to goods exported to non-member states and to goods warehoused for export is extended. Where an ineligible claimant makes a claim for drawback or an eligible claimant submits a claim for drawback for ineligible goods, he is liable to a civil penalty.

944 Excise duty—exemption for goods for personal consumption—whether goods purchased by agent included

Tobacco products were imported from Luxembourg without payment of excise duty by an agent who then delivered them to individuals whose orders had been taken by a British company. Applications for judicial review were brought challenging the detention of the goods. The applicants had argued that if a purchaser bringing back cigarettes for personal consumption from Luxembourg would only pay Luxembourg duty by virtue of Council Directive (EC) 92/12, art 8, then the same must be true if the purchaser employed an agent. The Commissioners of Customs and Excise argued that the scheme fell within the 1992 Directive, art 10, as it included products purchased by non-authorised persons and subject to excise duty in the country of destination. It was also argued that the scheme was covered by the Excise Goods (Holding, Movement, Warehousing and REDS) Regulations 1992, SI 1992/3135, and the Excise Duties (Personal Reliefs) Order 1992, SI 1992/3155, made in conformity with the directive. On appeal against the refusal of the applications, *held*, the court was unable to determine the appeal without making a reference to the European Court of Justice for answers to the following questions: (1) whether art 8 of the directive had the effect of precluding the charging of duty on goods provided by an agent from one country for individuals in another country; (2) whether it had the effect of precluding the exercise of duty on such goods when the provision by an agent resulted from a commercially devised scheme. However if the court had been able to determine the appeal, it would have been dismissed for the following reasons: the internal market was in a transitional period and not yet fully developed; some economies would suffer large losses of revenue if such schemes were allowed; an historical and purposive approach to the directive showed it as a measure seeking progress towards the internal market but envisaging the enactment of several substantive provisions regarding liability to duty; the words used in the directive made it clear that it was directed towards travellers physically taking goods with them and art 9(2) envisaged interrogation of travellers which could not operate if the goods were transported through an agent; and further, art 10 showed that in cases of distance selling or mail order operations tax would be paid in the country of destination.

R v Customs and Excise Comrs, ex p EMU Tabac Sàrl (Imperial Tobacco Co intervening) (1995) Times, 10 August, Independent, 17 August (Court of Appeal: Butler-Sloss, Aldous and Schiemann LJJ).

945 Excise duty—payment—other fuel substitutes

The Other Fuel Substitutes (Payment of Excise Duty etc) Regulations 1995, SI 1995/2717 (in force on 1 December 1995), require a producer of liquids in respect of which excise duty is charged by the Hydrocarbon Oil Duties Act 1979, s 6A, (1) before he sends out from any premises a consignment of liquid in respect of which a delivery note would be required to be issued, or as soon as practical after he makes a chargeable use of a liquid at any premises with the consequence that a duty of excise is charged by virtue of s 6A, to make entry of those premises in accordance with the Customs and Excise Management Act 1979, s 108; (2) in respect of each consignment of liquid sent out from his premises, to issue to the consignee a serially numbered delivery note containing specified particulars; (3) in relation to his premises, to pay to the commissioners the duty due, not later than the fifteenth day of the month next following the preceding month in which he has sent out or used chargeable liquids at his premises, and to furnish them with a return containing specified information; and (4) to make and keep a fuel substitutes record containing specified particulars.

946 Excise duty—rates—other fuel substitutes

The Other Fuel Substitutes (Rates of Excise Duty etc) Order 1995, SI 1995/2716 (in force on 1 December 1995), prescribes the rates of the excise duty charged on liquids comprised in the Hydrocarbon Oil Duties Act 1979, s 6A which are for use as substitutes for mineral oil motor fuel, or as additives or extenders in motor fuel or substitute motor fuel as follows: (1) the rate of excise duty charged on the setting aside or on the use of a liquid as fuel for an engine is at the same rate as that applying to light oil unless the rate is determined in accordance with head (2) or (3) infra; (2) the rate of excise duty on any chargeable liquid which is set aside must be determined by an entry in a record that the liquid is suitable only as fuel for a diesel or an aircraft's non-piston engine, or a leaded or unleaded petrol engine, or, if the liquid is not entered in the record under any of those headings, it is liable to the rate applicable to light oil, unless it is entered in that record as specially produced as fuel for a piston-engined aircraft in which case it is liable at the specified rate of duty, (3) the rate of excise duty for additives or extenders to fuel, except such additives and extenders which are not entered as suitable only for an engine fuelled by diesel oil or petrol, or not entered as multi-fuel additives or extenders, is at the rate of duty applicable to unleaded petrol, and (4) chargeable liquids which attract the specified heavy oil rate of duty must be treated thereafter as heavy hydrocarbon oil, and any chargeable liquid which attracts the light oil rate, regardless of whether that rate attracts a rebate, must be treated thereafter as light oil.

947 Excise duty—relief—fuel and lubricants imported in commercial vehicles

The Travellers' Reliefs (Fuel and Lubricants) Order 1995, SI 1995/1777 (in force on 1 August 1995), provides that the relief from excise duty given by SI 1989, SI 1989/1898, to travellers from other European Union member states in respect of lubricants and fuel in commercial vehicles, applies only in respect of fuel on which excise duty has been paid at a rate appropriate to the use to which the fuel is being or is intended to be put.

948 Excise duty—travellers' allowances

The Travellers' Allowances Amendment Order 1995, SI 1995/3044 (in force on 1 January 1996), amends the 1994 Order, SI 1994/955 by increasing the allowance for goods, other than wines, spirits, tobacco, perfume and toilet water, obtained by a person who has travelled in a third country and contained in his personal baggage (the 'other goods' allowance), from £136 to £145.

949 Excise duty—vehicle excise duty—design weight certificate

See para 951.

950 Excise duty—vehicle excise duty—designation of small islands

The Vehicle Excise Duty (Designation of Small Islands) Order 1995, SI 1995/1397 (in force on 1 July 1995), designates specified islands as small islands for the purposes of the Vehicle Excise and Registration Act 1994, Sch 1, para 18, which defines the expression 'island goods vehicle' for the purposes of Pt VIII, which sets out the annual rate of vehicle excise duty applicable to goods vehicles.

951 Excise duty—vehicle excise licence—design weight certificate

The Vehicle Excise (Design Weight Certificate) Regulations 1995, SI 1995/1455 (in force on 1 July 1995), (1) provide for applications for design weight certificates and for the issue of certificates following an examination, (2) provide for a design weight certificate to be conclusive evidence of the design weight of a vehicle at the time of the examination, (3) enable the Secretary of State to refuse to issue a vehicle excise licence if he is not satisfied that the licence applied for is the appropriate licence for the vehicle in question, (4) specify the circumstances in which he can require a design weight certificate to be produced before he decides to refuse to issue a vehicle excise licence if he is not satisfied that the licence applied for is the appropriate licence for the vehicle in question, and (5) provide for an adaptation reducing the design weight of a vehicle to be treated as permanent if and only if it is an adaptation with respect to which a design weight certificate has been issued.

952 Export of goods—control—contravention

On their appeals against convictions of contravening the Export of Goods (Control) Order 1987, SI 1987/2070 and the Export of Goods (Control) Order 1989, SI 1989/2376, the appellants contended that, as the Import, Export and Customs Powers (Defence) Act 1939, s 1(1), under which the orders were made, had lapsed, the orders were invalid. *Held*, the orders in question were validly made under powers contained in an unrepealed statute. As the 1939–45 war had not been declared to have ended by an Order in Council under the 1939 Act, s 9(3), the 1987 and 1989 Orders were not ultra vires or invalid. Accordingly, the appeals would be dismissed.

R v Blackledge; R v Grecian; R v Mason; R v Phillips (1995) 139 Sol Jo LB 139 (Court of Appeal: Lord Taylor of Gosforth CJ, Tucker and Forbes JJ).

953 Export of goods—control—dual-use and related goods

The Dual-Use and Related Goods (Export Control) Regulations 1995, SI 1995/271 (in force for the purposes of issuing general licences on 14 February 1995 and for all other purposes on 1 March 1995), implement provisions of Council Regulation (EC) 3381/94, by virtue of which a Community regime for the control of exports of dual-use goods and related matters is established. The regulations replace the export controls on such goods that were previously contained in the Export of Goods (Control) Order 1994, SI 1994/1191, as amended, in particular by (1) requiring a Community licence for the export from the Community of any specified dual-use goods and providing that such a licence is valid throughout the Community; (2) requiring a licence for the export to another member state of any specified dual-use goods; (3) prohibiting the export of certain goods without a licence; (4) applying the Customs and Excise Management Act 1979, ss 138, 145–148, 150–155 to specified dual-use goods prohibited from export from the United Kingdom to another member state and providing for the forfeiture of such goods; (5) requiring a licence for the export of goods which are to be exported for purposes connected with chemical, biological and nuclear weapons and missiles capable of delivering such weapons; (6) prohibiting, in certain circumstances, the export of goods even though a Community licence has been granted in respect of them in another member state, where the Secretary of State considers that the export would be contrary to the essential foreign policy or security interests or the fulfilment of the international obligations or commitment of the United Kingdom, and for the detention, in certain circumstances, by the proper officer of Customs and Excise, for a period of ten working days, of goods for which a Community licence has been granted; (7) setting out control measures, in relation to any licence issued by the Secretary of State and any Community licence capable of use in the United Kingdom, and for exports to other member states, regarding the making of misleading licence applications, failure to comply with licence conditions, registration, and record-keeping; (8) extending the requirements to register with the Department of Trade and Industry before, or soon after, exporting under an Open General Export Licence and to keep certain records for a specified period for inspection purposes where goods are exported under any licence under the regulations and also where any specified goods are exported to another member state; (9) providing for the inspection of records relating to licence applications; and (10) requiring that specified goods, when exported to another member state, be accompanied by commercial documentation which indicates clearly that the goods are subject to control if exported from the Community.

The Dual-Use and Related Goods (Export Control) (Suspension) Regulations 1995, SI 1995/441 (in force on 28 February 1995), suspend the coming into force of the principal regulations, SI 1995/271 supra, for all other purposes until Council Regulation (EC) 3381/94 has been published in the Official Journal of the European Communities.

The Dual-Use and Related Goods (Export Control) (Suspension No 2) Regulations 1995, SI 1995/1151 (in force on 25 April 1995), amend SI 1995/441 supra by providing for the principal regulations to come into force for all other purposes on 1 July 1995.

The Dual-Use and Related Goods (Export Control) (Amendment) Regulations 1995, SI 1995/1424 (in force on 30 June 1995), further amend the principal regulations supra by (1) revoking the definition of 'transit or transhipment'; (2) removing the export of goods which pass only through the territory of the Community and goods exported to another member state without being dispatched from the United Kingdom from the control of the principal regulations and restoring such exports to the control of the Export of Goods (Control) Order 1994, SI 1994/1191; (3) prohibiting specified goods and certain dual-use goods to which the end use control applies, from being exported to other member states without a licence if their ultimate destination is elsewhere; (4) prohibiting the export of goods which have received a licence from another member state if the Secretary of State considers that their export to a destination outside the Community would be contrary to the essential foreign policy or security interests of the United Kingdom or the fulfilment of its international obligations or commitments, subject to the goods being put at the disposal of the exporter; (5) making it an offence to fail to comply with the requirement to notify for purposes of end use control; and (6) prohibiting the export of microlight aircraft and hang-gliders and associated technology to any destination outside the Community.

The Dual-Use and Related Goods (Export Control) (Amendment No 2) Regulations 1995, SI 1995/3298 (in force on 23 January 1996), further amend the principal regulations supra by enabling a customs officer to detain goods so that the authorities may have an opportunity to inform the exporter that the goods are or may be intended for use in connection with weapons of mass destruction.

954 Export of goods—control—dual-use goods—common foreign and security policy

See para 3129.

955 Export of goods—control—enforcement of international trade sanctions

See *R v Searle*, para 598.

956 Export of goods—control—exports to Iraq—prosecutions for conspiracy to evade prohibition on exports—disclosure of documents

The appellants were charged with a conspiracy relating to the export of prohibited goods to Iraq, whereby it was alleged that licences were obtained for the shipment of goods to Jordan when their true destination was Iraq. At preliminary hearings, the appellants pleaded not guilty, arguing that the authorities were aware of Jordan being used as a conduit for exports to Iraq. They requested disclosure of policy and guideline documents governing the grant of export licences during the relevant period. The Crown denied the request on the ground that there were no Department of Trade and Industry documents that showed that the authorities were turning a blind eye to such exports. When the trial judge rejected the defence submissions, the appellants changed their pleas to guilty. Following acquittals in a similar case, documents were disclosed by the Ministry of Defence, the Foreign Office and the Security Services which supported the appellants' arguments. The appellants appealed against their convictions on the ground that if the documents had been disclosed at their trial they would not have pleaded guilty and that the non-disclosure prevented them from making properly informed decisions about their defence. *Held*, the documents ought to have been made available before the trial as they would have enabled the appellants to present an arguable case along the lines they had already indicated before seeing the documents. The documents might have left a jury in doubt as to whether the appellants' conduct was condoned by one or more limbs of the executive. The failure to disclose them amounted to a material irregularity. Documents in the possession of one or other government department involved in the inter-departmental consideration of licences were to be regarded as in the possession of the Crown as an indivisible entity. Accordingly, the appeals would be allowed.

R v Blackledge (1995) Times, Independent, 8 November (Court of Appeal: Lord Taylor of Gosforth CJ, Macpherson and Maurice Kay JJ). For earlier related proceedings, see (1995) Times, 29 May (para 952).

957 Export of goods—control—general orders

The Export of Goods (Control) (Amendment) Order 1995, SI 1995/3060 (in force on 29 November 1995), further amends the 1994 Order, SI 1994/1191, so that goods in transit, other than military goods and certain animals and animal products, may be exported to Serbia and Montenegro without a licence under conditions applying to most other destinations.

The Export of Goods (Control) (Amendment No 2) Order 1995, SI 1995/3249 (in force in part on 15 December 1995 and in part on 23 January 1996), further amends the 1994 Order supra, so that (1) meat recovered by mechanical means from the vertebral column of a bovine animal is added to the list of animal products whose export to destinations outside the Community is prohibited, except where the goods are not intended for human consumption; (2) the definition of 'bovine offal' now accords with the definition of 'specified bovine offal' in the Specified Bovine Offal Order 1995, SI 1995/1928, para 1402; (3) the prohibition on the export of certain live animals from Northern ireland to member states other than Ireland is removed; and (4) references to the United Nations protected Areas in Croatia are removed from the exclusions from the provisions on goods in transit.

958 Export of goods—export to non-member states—permissible member state restrictions

See *Criminal proceedings against Leifer*, para 3111.

959 Finance Act 1995

See para 2489.

960 Import of goods—goods from other member states—prohibition on unlicensed imports

See *EC Commission v Germany*, para 3132.

961 Import of goods—goods from other state party to EEA Agreement—application of European Community law

See *Ravintoloitsijain Liiton Kustannus Oy Restamark v Helsingin Piiritullikamari*, para 3112.

962 Import of goods—restrictions—potatoes originating in the Netherlands

See para 69.

963　Police and Criminal Evidence Act 1984—application to customs and excise

The Police and Criminal Evidence Act 1984 (Application to Customs and Excise) (Amendment) Order 1995, SI 1995/3217 (in force on 1 January 1996), applies the 1984 Act, s 24(6) to Customs and Excise. Officers of Customs and Excise are given a power of arrest in respect of arrestable offences, the investigation of which is a matter assigned to the Commissioner of Customs and Excise and for which such officers do not otherwise have a power of arrest.

964　Revenue traders—accounts and records

The Revenue Traders (Accounts and Records) (Amendment) Regulations 1995, SI 1995/2893 (in force on 1 December 1995), amend the 1992 Regulations, SI 1992/3150, so as to require that any claim for recovery of overpaid excise duty under the Customs and Excsie Management Act 1979, s 137A must be made in writing to the Commissioners of Customs and Excise and state, by reference to such documentary evidence as is in the possession of the claimant, the amount of the claim and the method by which it was calculated.

965　Statistics of trade

The Statistics of Trade (Customs and Excise) (Amendment) Regulations 1995, SI 1995/2946 (in force on 1 January 1996), further amend the 1992 Regulations, SI 1992/2790, so as to increase the assimilation thresholds set for trade in goods dispatched, or for goods received, from £150,000 to £160,000. SI 1994/2914 is revoked.

966　Value added tax

See VALUE ADDED TAX.

DAMAGES AND COMPENSATION

Halsbury's Laws of England (4th edn) Vol 12, paras 1101–1300
Contributors
Our thanks to the following, who have contributed items to this title this month:
Abenson & Co, Solicitors, Liverpool
Adlams, Solicitors, St Neots
Kate Akerman, Pupil Barrister
Robert Alford, Barrister
Allan Henderson Beecham & Peacock, Solicitors, Newcastle upon Tyne
Peter Atherton, Barrister
Bell Pope, Solicitors, Southampton
Ruth Blair, Barrister
Blakemores, Birmingham, Solicitors
Richard Booth, Barrister
Nicola Braganza, Barrister
Damian Brown, Barrister
Lawrence Caun, Barrister
Clarke Willmott & Clarke, Solicitors, Bridgwater
Edmund Cofie, Barrister
Alasdair Davidson, Barrister
Hugh Davies, Barrister
Davies and Partners, Solicitors, Bristol
David S Dixon, Barrister
Douglas-Mann & Co, Solicitors
Mererid Edwards, Barrister
Stephen Ellis-Jones, Barrister
David Evans, Barrister
Katharine Ferguson, Pupil Barrister
Gaunts, Solicitors, Halifax
Antonis Georges, Barrister
Caspar Glyn, Barrister

Christopher Goddard, Barrister
Iain Goldrein, Barrister
Allan Gore, Barrister
Tim Grover, Barrister
Michael W Halsall, Solicitors, Merseyside
William E Hanbury, Barrister
Jonathan Hand, Barrister
Hartley and Worstenholme, Solicitors, Castleford
John Hartshorne, Pupil Barrister
Hatton Scates and Horton, Solicitors, Manchester
Arthur J Healey, Solicitor
Henriques Griffiths, Solicitors, Bristol
Higgs and Sons, Solicitors, Stourbridge
Ian Groom, Barrister
Kevin Higgins, Barrister
Jon Holbrook, Barrister
Damian Horan, Bevan Ashford, Solicitors, Exeter
Christopher Hough, Barrister
James Hurd, Pupil Barrister
Abdul S Iqbal, Barrister
Jackaman Smith and Mulley, Solicitors, Ipswich
John Richard Jones, Barrister
LL Jacobs, Redfern & Co, Solicitiors, Birmingham
Linda Knowles, Barrister
Sarah Larcombe, Solicitor
Andrew Lewis, Barrister
John Livesey, Barrister
Nicholas Lumley, Barrister
Colin McEachran QC, Advocate
Tracey McLevy, Pupil Barrister
Colin Mendoza, Barrister
Simon Michael, Barrister
Richard Miller, Barrister
Stephen Murray, Barrister
Patterson, Glenton and Stracey, Solicitors, Newcastle upon Tyne
Jo-Anne Patterson, Barrister
Pattinson and Brewer, Solicitors, London
Pengilly and Ridge, Solicitors, Weymouth
Pictons, Solicitors, Stevenage
Pip Punwar, Barrister
Russell Pyne, Barrister
Rhodes Thain Collinson, Solicitors, Halifax
Susan Roach, Barrister
Karl Rowley, Pupil Barrister
Bradley Say, Barrister
Barrie Searle, Barrister
Martin Seaward, Barrister
Shoosmiths and Harrison, Solicitors, Reading
Bruce R Silvester, Barrister
Christopher J Smith, Holyoak & Co, Solicitors, Leicester
Martin Smith and Co, Solicitors, Borehamwood
Nicholas Starks, Barrister
Stephensons, Solicitors, St Helens
Christopher Taylor, Barrister
Robin Thompson and Partners, Solicitors, Cardiff
Trainor Alston, Solicitors, Coatbridge
Robert Weir, Barrister
Jeremy Western, Barrister
Mark Whitcombe, Barrister
Timothy White, Barrister
Paul Wilson, Barrister
Woollcombe Beer Watts, Solicitors, Newton Abbot

Woolwich Lander and Savage, Solicitors, Bootle
Stuart R Yeung, Barrister

967   Articles

Avoiding the Benefits Trap, Petra Lucioli (on the effect of personal injury settlements on welfare benefits): LS Gaz, 18 January 1995, p 18

Claiming for PTSD (Post Traumatic Stress Disorder), Richard Hoare: 139 SJ 736

Dancing to a New Tune, Tim Bancroft (on payments to the Compensation Recovery Unit): 139 SJ 341

Deafness is Not so Easy, Nigel Cooksley (on bringing a claim for industrial deafness): 139 SJ 1066

Expert Testimony and Cerebral Palsy, Paul Pimm: SJ Supp, 30 June 1995, p 46

Fatal Accident Multipliers, Tim Sture: LS Gaz, 15 March 1995, p 24

Food Poisoning and the PI Lawyer, Damian Horan: 139 SJ 1181

How Much is Enough? Geraldine McCool and Mark Bennett (on the Law Commission's study of personal injury compensation): 139 SJ 284

Multipliers Cannot be Fun, Stephen Irwin: 145 NLJ 628

A Nervous Breakdown, Martin Murphy (on the House of Lords ruling in *Page v Smith* [1995] 2 WLR 644, HL (para 2173)): LS Gaz, 1 June 1995, p 16

Nervous Shock, Charles Lewis (on *Page v Smith* [1995] 2 WLR 644, HL (para 2173)): 139 SJ 960

A Pain in the WRULD, Katharine Nicholas and Elisabeth Roth (on handling RSI claims): 139 SJ 64

Personal Injury Astrologers, Robert Owen (on use of actuarial evidence in assessing quantum): 139 SJ 1068

A Plea for a Lost Chance: Hotson Reconsidered, Charles Foster (on *Hotson v East Berkshire Area Health Authority* [1987] 2 All ER 909 (1987 Abr para 731)): 145 NLJ 228, 248

PTSD (Post Traumatic Stress Disorder): The Medical View, Dr Michael Beary: 139 SJ 734

Quantifying Damages in Computer Disputes, Graham Smith: 11 CLP 45

Recoupment Planning, David Milton (on deduction of state benefits from personal injury awards): 145 NLJ 784

Rehabilitation Experts: What They Do and Where to Find Them, Richard Hoare: SJ Supp, 30 June

Setting Off Interlocutory Costs Against Damages, Diana Bretherick: 139 SJ 91

The £694 Question, Roger Cohen (on the proper remedy for infringement of property rights): Estates Gazette, 4 February 1995, p 158

Trusting the Times Tables, Sir Michael Ogden QC (on the use of actuarial tables for calculating personal injury compensation): LS Gaz, 22 March 1995, p 20

Where Benefits Exceed Damages: The Insurers' Catch 22, Gary Burrell: Quantum, Issue 5/95, p 1

968   Assessment of damages—alternative remedies—difference between alternative and cumulative remedies

Hong Kong

The deceased agreed to assign a number of properties to the plaintiff, but no assignment was executed and he eventually let the properties without the plaintiff's knowledge. The plaintiff brought proceedings against the defendant, the deceased's personal representative, claiming an order that the defendant assign the properties to the plaintiff, a declaration that the plaintiff was the equitable owner of the properties, an account of all secret profits in respect of the letting of the properties and payment of all such profits, and damages for breach of trust. The plaintiff obtained summary judgment against the defendant, who produced an account showing certain profits. The plaintiff obtained a charging order over adjoining land belonging to the deceased and the defendant paid the plaintiff a sum of money in respect of the account of profits to discharge the charging order. In the assessment of damages, the plaintiff claimed under two heads: (1) damages for loss of use and occupation, and (2) damages in respect of the loss caused by the diminution in value of the property due to the wrongful use and occupation. Damages were assessed under both heads, with the deduction of the sum received by the plaintiff. On appeal, it was held that, having received payment on account of the profits made from letting the properties, the plaintiff could not thereafter claim compensation for having been kept out of possession of the properties. On further appeal, *held*, an account of the profits made from the lettings was an alternative remedy to damages for the loss of use of the properties. At the time of summary judgment, the plaintiff should have been required, so far as the two remedies were inconsistent, to choose which it would take. However, the plaintiff was not required to elect and instead the order gave it both remedies. Thereafter the plaintiff proceeded to enforce both remedies. In the circumstances, the receipt of the payment from the defendant was not an election by the plaintiff for an account of profits and against damages. Acceptance of the payment signified nothing given that the order had, wrongly, provided for the plaintiff to have both remedies and that the plaintiff was actively pursuing both. On the facts, there was no inconsistency between the awards of damages under heads (1) and (2).

Personal Representatives of Tang Man Sit v Capacious Investments Ltd [1996] 1 All ER 193 (Privy Council: Lords Keith of Kinkel, Lloyd of Berwick, Nicholls of Birkenhead and Steyn, and Hardie Boys J).

969 Assessment of damages—breach of contract—failure to achieve precise contractual objective

See *Ruxley Electronics and Construction Ltd v Forsyth*, para 277.

970 Assessment of damages—fatal accident—bereavement damages—parent causing child's death

The Fatal Accidents Act 1976, s 1A(1), (3) provides that an action in respect of a wrongful act causing death may include a claim for a statutory sum of damages for bereavement. Section 1A(4) provides that where there is a claim for damages for bereavement for the benefit of both the parents of the deceased, the sum awarded must be divided equally between them (subject to any deduction falling to be made in respect of costs not recovered from the defendant).

The negligence of the defendant caused a road accident in which one of her daughters was killed. The plaintiff, the deceased child's father, claimed damages for bereavement under the 1976 Act, s 1A. He argued that he should receive the full statutory sum as (1) he sued solely on his own behalf, and for his own benefit, and consequently s 1A(4) did not apply, and (2) the mother was the tortfeasor and it was contrary to public policy that she should be allowed to benefit. *Held*, the plaintiff was only entitled to half of the statutory sum. In bringing an action under the 1976 Act, the plaintiff was under a duty to act on behalf of any other eligible dependants who wished to benefit. The duty arose from the fact that, under the 1976 Act, s 2(3), only one action could be brought in respect of a death. The plaintiff's claim had to be construed as being for the benefit of both himself and the defendant. Consequently, s 1A(4) prevented the recovery of more than half of the sum from her.

Navaei v Navaei (6 January 1995, unreported) (Eastbourne County Court: Deputy District Judge Radcliffe) (Messrs Steven Rimmer & Co, Eastbourne, for the plaintiff; Russell Pyne, Messrs Phillips, Hove, for the defendant) (Kindly submitted for publication by Russell Pyne, Barrister).

971 Assessment of damages—fatal accident—loss of dependency—claim by child

The plaintiffs were sisters aged five and one respectively. After a road traffic accident in which they suffered personal injuries and their parents were killed, they went to live with their uncle's family. At first instance, the trial judge awarded the first plaintiff damages in the amount of £5,000 for the handicap she would experience on the labour market. In calculating both plaintiffs' net dependency on their parents, the judge rejected the conventional approach whereby 75 per cent of the family's income was attributed to the plaintiffs and the remaining 25 per cent was attributed to the parents' living expenses. The judge found that only 50 per cent should be attributed to the plaintiffs. Two reasons were given for the departure from the usual approach. Firstly, a large part of the mortgage payments from the parents' net income was to be regarded as investment in the accumulation of a property portfolio, rather than as ordinary family expenditure. The plaintiffs' interests in such investments were already provided for under another head of damages. Secondly, the parents might have had more children with whom the family income would have had to be shared. The post trial multipliers were then calculated at a discount of almost 40 per cent in respect of the first plaintiff and 35 per cent in respect of the second plaintiff. The figures were decided on the basis of the small chance that the family's income might have decreased throughout the dependencies, the very small chance that the plaintiffs might have died during their dependencies and, the discount for the advancement of the capital sum. The plaintiffs appealed against the award. *Held*, when assessing damages for handicap on the labour market, it may be equally appropriate to apply the multiplier/multiplicand approach as the assessment of a lump sum approach. Both methods were equally speculative, particularly where it was impossible to say what the plaintiff would and could have done but for the accident. Nevertheless the judge's award was too low and a figure of £12,500 would be substituted. His reasoning could not be faulted in respect the decision to take 50 per cent as the appropriate percentage for the net dependency. However, the multiplier was too low. It ought to have been calculated in the conventional way whereby a 4.5 per cent rate of discount was taken and a further allowance of about 10 per cent was made for the contingencies mentioned by the judge. The award would be reassessed on the basis of the higher multiplier and, accordingly, the appeal would be allowed in part.

Dhaliwal v Personal Representatives of Hunt (deceased) [1995] PIQR P56 (Court of Appeal: Balcombe, Henry and Auld LJJ).

972 Assessment of damages—fatal accident—loss of dependency—loss of undeclared earnings and benefits

The plaintiff claimed damages under the Fatal Accidents Act 1976 in respect of her loss of dependency arising from the death of her husband in a motor accident. For approximately six months before his death the deceased worked part-time, earning about £90 a week. Those earnings were not declared to the social security authorities, and he continued to claim full supplementary benefit and housing benefit. At first instance, the judge made a finding that the deceased had a nil prospect of employment. He awarded damages in the sum of £6,575, but refused to include an award for loss of dependency in respect of the undeclared earnings and state benefits. The plaintiff appealed against the award. *Held*, the judge had erred in his finding that the deceased had no prospect of employment. An award of £12,480 was appropriate in respect of the lost chance of full-time earnings. The judge rightly refused to make any award under the head of loss of dependency in respect of the benefits and undeclared earnings. As regards the state benefits, the plaintiff was in no sense dependent on the deceased. Both she and her husband were dependent on the state in that regard. The claim in relation the undeclared earnings would also fail. There was no force in the argument that, in calculating the figure of £12,480 a percentage abatement had been applied by the court to the figure that would have been obtained by assuming the deceased to be in full-time work and that, accordingly, the plaintiff was entitled to have the shortfall made good by treating the lost undeclared earnings as a head of lost dependency. Furthermore, the argument offended against public policy in two ways. It required the court to assume that the deceased would never have mended his ways or, been caught in the act of committing his fraud on the social security authorities. Second, the court would not treat the proceeds of illegally concealed earnings as providing a valid head of recovery by way of damages for loss or injury. Accordingly, the appeal would be allowed and the award increased to a sum of £12,480 only.

Hunter v Butler (1995) Times, 28 December (Court of Appeal: Hirst, Waite and Hobhouse LJJ). *Hassall v Secretary of State for Social Security* [1995] 3 All ER 909, CA, considered.

973 Assessment of damages—loss of enjoyment of holiday

The plaintiffs booked a tour of China and Hong Kong at a cost of £1,860 per person through the defendant tour operator. The brochure offered four nights' first class accommodation in Hong Kong at one of two specified hotels. In fact, neither of the specified hotels was used and the accommodation in Hong Kong was merely of a 'superior' standard. Furthermore, the plaintiffs were obliged to take taxis from their accommodation to the main tourist area. The plaintiffs claimed damages against the tour operators. *Held*, the plaintiffs would be awarded the taxi fares incurred in travelling from their hotel to the main tourist area and the difference in cost between the superior standard hotel and the first class hotel. The plaintiffs would also be awarded £25 each in respect of distress and loss of enjoyment to reflect the standard of their accommodation and the inconvenience caused by their having to travel by taxi to the main tourist area over the four-day period.

Clarke v Edwards & Hargreaves Ltd (19 July 1995, unreported) (Birmingham County Court: District Judge Dowley) (Nicholas Starks for the defendant). Kindly submitted for publication by Nicholas Starks, Barrister, who comments that the case is of interest as there are few reported cases dealing with claims of this kind and that the sum awarded for loss of enjoyment is low in proportion to the total cost of the holiday in question.

The two plaintiff families, five adults and three children in total, booked a fortnight's holiday to Tenerife at a cost of £2,058.25. They had requested and booked three-star hotel rooms at half board which were to be allocated on arrival, but they were actually given self-catering apartments situated on several floors, thus separating the parents and their children. The rooms were stark and uninviting, infested with cockroaches and wild dogs roamed freely over the grounds. The restaurant facility was not cleared adequately, staff allowed cats to eat food left on the tables and food served was of a very poor standard. The area around the apartments was scruffy, the outside walls were covered with graffiti, and broken glass around the swimming pool caused cuts to one of the infant plaintiffs' feet. The plaintiffs made numerous complaints to the local representatives, to the head office on the island and to their agents in England, but the defendants failed to remedy the situation, or to deal with the plaintiffs in a humane way. The plaintiffs were offered alternative apartments within the complex and three accepted, but two of these subsequent rooms were also infested with cockroaches. The plaintiffs demanded to return home, but were told that they would have to meet the cost of the journey themselves. They were awarded total damages of £8,040 (plus interest) which included £500 per family for diminution in value of holiday, £320 per family in respect of expenses incurred in eating elsewhere during the holiday and £800 per plaintiff in respect of general damages for distress and disappointment. Interest on the special damages was awarded from the date the holiday began.

Clarke v Airtours plc (17 February 1995, unreported) (Staines County Court: Judge Hucker) (Kindly submitted for publication by Tracey McLevy, Pupil Barrister).

974 Assessment of damages—loss of profit—partnership—apportionment of profits

The plaintiff suffered serious injuries when she was involved in an accident on the railway. Prior to the accident, the plaintiff and her husband had run a teashop and bed and breakfast business. They had intended to expand the business, but because of the plaintiff's injuries, they had to scale down their expansion and did not implement them until considerably later than planned. For tax purposes, the plaintiff and her husband were assessed on the profits of the business as to 60 per cent on the husband and 40 per cent on the plaintiff. In assessing damages, the judge decided that it was inappropriate to apportion loss of profits to the business as between the plaintiff and her husband, and damages for future loss of earnings were awarded using a multiplier of 12. On the defendant's appeal, *held*, the plaintiff's husband had no claim in law against the defendants because they did not owe him a duty of care, and therefore the plaintiff could not recover the full amount of the loss of takings of the business. The business was carried on in partnership, and having regard to the Partnership Act 1890, s 24, there was a presumption that it was an equal partnership. As that presumption was not rebutted by the taxation arrangement between the plaintiff and her husband, the plaintiff was entitled to 50 per cent of the profits, and could therefore recover only 50 per cent of the loss of takings attributable to the accident. As regards damages for loss of future earnings, the plaintiff was 56 years old at the time of trial and although the judge had been correct to assess damages on the basis that the plaintiff would have carried on until the age of 70 rather than 75, he had erred in using a 12-year multiplier in respect of a potential 14-year loss. Such a multiplier was too high, and was instead to be reduced to nine. Accordingly, the appeal would be allowed.

Kent v British Railways Board [1995] PIQR Q42 (Court of Appeal: McCowan and Peter Gibson LJJ, and Sir John May).

975 Assessment of damages—personal injury—investment options

It has been held that in determining the amount of damages to be awarded in personal injury cases, the court must have regard to the fact that a higher rate of return can be obtained if damages are invested in equities rather than in index-linked gilts, although the latter offers greater precision in achieving the necessary object of damages.

Thomas v Brighton Health Authority (1995) Times, 19 November (Queen's Bench Division: Collins J).

976 Assessment of damages—premises in disrepair—award for diminution in value of tenancy

See *Symons v Warren*, para 1799.

977 Assessment of damages—professional negligence—solicitor—causation of loss—action taken by third party

The plaintiff instructed the defendant solicitors regarding sale of his house to D, a potential purchaser. Due to the defendants' negligence in not sending relevant documents in time, the sale fell through and the plaintiff brought an action for damages against the defendants. The judge held that the plaintiff had to show that, on the balance of probabilities, if the defendants had delivered the documents on time, D would have bought the plaintiff's house rather than any other one. If so, the plaintiff could recover his full loss but, if not, he would not receive anything. In the event, the judge was satisfied that D would have bought the plaintiff's house and therefore awarded full damages. On appeal by the defendants, *held*, the judge had taken the wrong approach to the question of causation where the loss depended upon the action of an independent third party in circumstances which did not, in fact, arise. He ought to have evaluated the loss of the chance of the sale going ahead as a result of the defendants' negligence. In the present case, there was evidence to suggest that D might have preferred the house he actually bought even if the documents had been sent promptly and, accordingly, the chance would be assessed at 50 per cent and the judge's award would be reduced by that amount.

Stovold v Barlows (1995) Times, 30 October (Court of Appeal: Stuart-Smith, Otton and Pill LJJ).

978 Assessment of damages—professional negligence—solicitor—damages for anxiety, distress and worry

Scotland

A wife instructed solicitors to act for her in divorce and ancillary relief proceedings. As part of the financial provision arrangements, it was agreed that the husband would transfer the former matrimonial home to the wife having redeemed the outstanding mortgage and paid off a business loan secured on the property. However, the wife's solicitors failed to inform her about the loan, and failed to ensure that it had been discharged or to obtain written confirmation from the husband's solicitors that the husband accepted responsibility for the loan. The wife did not know about the loan until many years after the conclusion of the matrimonial proceedings, by which time the husband was unable to repay it. When the wife became aware that she was at risk of losing her home if the husband defaulted on the loan, she became depressed, and was prescribed medication. She commenced proceedings against her solicitors for negligence, seeking damages for the amount of the outstanding loan, and for anxiety, worry and distress. *Held*, on the facts, the wife's solicitors were guilty of negligence because they had failed to perform their contractual duty of care. Although there was evidence that the wife had been suffering from anxiety and distress prior to the matrimonial proceedings because of other personal problems, the major cause of her depression was the uncertainty as to whether or not she might lose her home because of the unpaid loan. That uncertainty had carried on for a substantial period of time, and in all the circumstances, she was entitled to damages of £3,000 for anxiety, distress and worry. Accordingly, the application would be allowed.

Curran v Docherty 1995 SLT 716 (Outer House).

979 Assessment of damages—rape—amount of award in relation to awards made in other personal injury cases

Damages of £50,000 were awarded in respect of a rape. The rapist appealed against the sum, arguing that the damages should bear a proper relationship to the awards made in other types of personal injury case. *Held*, the circumstances and consequences of rape placed it in a different category from personal injury cases in general. It was clear that attitudes to rape had developed so as to take account of this. The penalties passed by criminal courts had increased and rape within marriage had become a criminal offence. It was impossible to say that an award of £50,000 was out of all proportion and inappropriate. Accordingly, the appeal would be dismissed.

Griffiths v Williams (1995) Times, 24 November (Court of Appeal: Rose, Millett and Thorpe LJJ). *W v Meah* [1986] 1 All ER 935, not followed.

980 Assessment of damages—wrongfully dishonoured cheque—injury to credit and business reputation—damages

The issue arose whether a bank's customer who was not a trader was entitled to recover substantial rather than nominal damages for loss of business reputation when his cheque was wrongly dishonoured by the bank. *Held*, the credit rating of an individual was as important for his personal transactions, including mortgages, hire purchase and banking facilities, as it was for a person engaged in trade. In either case there was a presumption of some injury when his cheque was dishonoured by his bank. In such circumstances, an individual could obtain substantial rather than nominal damages in contract for loss of business reputation. There was no binding authority for the proposition that substantial damages were only available if special facts were proved which were known by the bank when the contract was made.

Kpohraor v Woolwich Building Society (1995) Times, 8 December (Court of Appeal: Evans and Waite LJJ, and Sir John May).

981 Breach of contract—claim for damages for distress—contract to repair motor car

The owner of a prestigious motor car took it to the manufacturer's repair shop in order for repairs to be made. The manufacturer breached the contract to repair and the owner was awarded damages at first instance. However, the owner appealed against the award claiming that it should have included an amount for disappointment, loss of enjoyment or distress. He argued that he had acquired his car for his pleasure and to drive on social occasions so that he could enjoy the experience of ownership that such a prestigious car could bring. *Held*, the general rule was that damages for distress, inconvenience or loss of enjoyment were not recoverable for breach of an ordinary commercial contract but only where the contract was one for the provision of pleasure, freedom from harassment or relaxation. The plaintiff's attempt to bring his contract for the repair of his car within that exceptional class of case failed. Although it had been the plaintiff's object to enjoy to the full the ownership of his car, it did not follow that every time it was submitted for service or repair those who undertook the work but failed to carry it out with proper care and skill would be answerable in damages for any distress, frustration, anxiety or lack of pleasure caused to the plaintiff. No liability for damages for distress arose and, accordingly, the appeal would be dismissed.

Alexander v Rolls Royce Motor Cars Ltd [1996] RTR 95 (Court of Appeal: Staughton, Beldam and Peter Gibson LJJ).

982 Breach of contract—claim for loss of bargain—lost work

The plaintiff, a printing company, obtained summary judgment with damages to be assessed against the defendant newspaper for repudiation of a contract to print its weekly newspaper. After the repudiation the plaintiff had taken steps to mitigate its loss by replacing the work, but was unable to fill up its order books completely. The plaintiff argued that the likely price of the lost work should first be assessed and then the direct expenses of carrying out the work, such as the cost of the paper and ink should be deducted. However, the judge also deducted a percentage of the plaintiff's labour costs and general overheads from the plaintiff's gross profit, to arrive at an award based on the plaintiff's perceived net profit. The plaintiff appealed. *Held*, damages for loss of profit from repudiation of a contract should represent the loss of the value of the benefit of which the innocent party was deprived through the breach. He should be compensated for the loss of his bargain. That was a question of fact in each case. It was clear, however, that where a business had spare capacity due to the effects of a recession, the quantum of damages could be equated to the loss of gross profits. It was right to take into account the fact that the effect of the breach was to reduce the business's available expenditure to pay its existing and future overheads by a sum equivalent to the gross profit, and not just of the notional net profit. Accordingly, the appeal would be allowed and there would be substituted a sum equivalent to the notional gross profit under the contract.

Western Web Offset Printers Ltd v Independent Media Ltd (1995) Times, 10 October (Court of Appeal: Nourse and Ward LJJ and Sedley J).

983 Breach of contract—claim for wasted expenditure—failure to promote exhibition

The defendant organised a trade show relating to the vehicle repair business, and the plaintiff company, which sold vehicle-straightening equipment, was an exhibitor at the show. Although the plaintiff incurred considerable expenses in appearing at the show, it gained no new business, as the show was not a success because the defendant failed to promote it properly. On the plaintiff's claim for damages, the defendant conceded that it was in breach of its contract with the plaintiff. A judge held that where such a contract was breached, a plaintiff could elect to claim either expectation damages for the profit he would have earned but for the defendant's breach, or reliance damages for the money expended in reliance on the defendant's promise to perform the contract. He concluded that in the instant case, the plaintiff's expectation of profit was well-founded and that it would have recouped all of its expenditure. He therefore awarded damages for wasted expenditure. On the defendant's appeal against quantum, *held*, the judge was satisfied that the plaintiff expected to transact sufficient business as a result of attending and exhibiting at the show in order to recover its expenditure, and that such an expectation was reasonable and justified in light of the defendant's assurances that the show would be adequately advertised and promoted. He had not merely presumed that the plaintiff's appearance at the show would have been profitable, but had required that to be proved. The judge had directed himself properly and, accordingly, the appeal would be dismissed.

Dataliner Ltd v Vehicle Builders and Repairers Association (1995) Independent, 30 August (Court of Appeal: Hirst, Henry and Swinton Thomas LJJ).

984 Breach of contract—repudiatory breach—applicability of term limiting damages for time-related costs

A limitation clause in an agreement for the sub-contracting of construction work provided for a maximum payment of damages in respect of time-related costs. Under another clause in the agreement the contractors gave to the sub-contractors notice of determination of their employment on the grounds that they had not proceeded diligently. The contractors claimed damages for breach of contract from the subcontractors, the amount of which was greater than that specified in the limitation clause. *Held*, once the contract had been determined by repudiatory breach the issue of time ceased to be of importance and thus the limitation clause did not apply. Damages flowed from the repudiation to compensate for non-performance. Further, a limitation of liability clause must be clear and unambiguous and would be construed strictly.

Bovis Construction (Scotland) Ltd v Whatlings Construction Ltd 1995 SLT 1339 (House of Lords: Lords Jauncey of Tullichettle, Browne-Wilkinson, Mustill, Lloyd of Berwick and Hoffmann).

985 Breach of contract—sub-standard service—level of damages

The plaintiffs, who carried on a mail order business, contracted with the defendant road transport operators for the delivery and collection of goods sold to customers. Terms were agreed for an enhanced level of service from the defendants. The plaintiffs accepted that the defendants had performed a basic level of service but argued that they had not provided the enhanced level. The plaintiffs claimed damages on the basis of a report commissioned by them and pleaded in their statement of claim, which adopted a complex approach to deriving the total value of the claim. The judge held that the plaintiffs were only entitled to recover nominal damages. On appeal, *held*, an innocent party who contracted for an enhanced service and received a substandard service was in principle entitled to claim more than nominal damages. However, an innocent party in such a position had to quantify, or at least provide evidence from which the court could draw an inference as to, the difference between the value of what was contracted for and the value of what was provided. The plaintiffs had not attempted to do this. They had made a sophisticated attempt to calculate the fraction of the contract consideration properly attributable to the breaches of which they complained. But this was no more than an attempt to make good a partial failure of consideration under the guise of a claim for damages. Accordingly, the appeal would be dismissed.

White Arrow Express Ltd v Lamey's Distribution Ltd [1995] NLJR 1504 (Court of Appeal: Sir Thomas Bingham MR, Rose and Morritt LJJ).

986 Compensatory damages—police—false imprisonment

The plaintiff was arrested early one morning whilst half-dressed, taken to a police station, and detained for four and a half hours before being released without charge. On her claim for damages for false imprisonment, the jury awarded her £50 exemplary damages, but made no award of compensatory damages. On her appeal, *held*, it was rare for compensatory damages not to be awarded when an award of exemplary damages was made. In this case, the appellant, who was only 15 years old at the time, had suffered fright, distress and harm, and her rights had been infringed. The jury's decision not to award her compensatory damages was perverse and irrational. The court would not order a retrial but would make its own award of compensatory damages, namely £350. Accordingly, the appeal would be allowed.

Cumber v Chief Constable of Hampshire Constabulary [1995] 08 LS Gaz R39 (Court of Appeal: Nourse and Waite LJJ, and Sir Tasker Watkins).

987 Criminal compensation order

See SENTENCING.

988 Criminal Injuries Compensation Act 1995

See para 883.

989 Infringement of copyright—flagrant infringement—additional damages

See *Cala Homes (South) Ltd v Alfred McAlpine Homes East Ltd*, para 683.

990 Interest on damages—deduction of tax

It has been held that where no regard is paid to taxation when determining the amount of damages to be awarded, the court must not automatically disregard taxation when determining interest on the damages under the Supreme Court Act 1981, s 35A. The court ought to approach each case on its own merits, placing a sensible pragmatic restraint on attempts at ascertaining a plaintiff's tax position but at the same time refraining from awarding interest for loss of use of money where it is not likely that the plaintiff has suffered the loss of use in question.

Deeny v Gooda Walker (No 4) [1995] STC 696 (Queen's Bench Division: Phillips J).

991 Liability—nervous shock—foreseeability of injury

See *Page v Smith*, para 2173.

992 Measure of damages—conversion—unlawful detention of gas cooker

The plaintiff occupied the defendant's property, and, on leaving the property, the defendant withheld the plaintiff's gas cooker. In proceedings for conversion under the Torts (Interference with Goods) Act 1977, the plaintiff obtained judgment in default. During the twelve months in which the plaintiff was without her gas cooker, she was unable to afford to purchase a new one, and had to borrow a microwave oven and a deep fat fryer. She was also unable to feed her son properly whilst he was recovering from illness, and had to spend more money than she would otherwise have done buying convenience foods. On the issue of damages, *held*, the plaintiff was entitled to damages in respect of the value of the gas cooker at the time of conversion, namely £600. She was also entitled to damages for loss of use of the gas cooker for the 12 months that she was without it, at the rate of £25 a week (£1,300 in total). Interest of £54.50 was also awarded.

Jackson v Wylie (20 November 1995, unreported) (Burnley County Court: District Judge Geddes) (Peter Anderson for the plaintiff) (Kindly submitted for publication by Pollard, Bower & Co, Solicitors).

993 Measure of damages—defamation—guidance given to jury

See *John v MGN*, para 1878.

994 Measure of damages—delay in proceedings—financial prejudice to defendant— value of money in hand during delay

See *Gahan v Szerelmey (UK) Ltd*, para 2360.

995 Measure of damages—installation of faulty heating system—landlord's liability

The plaintiff local authority brought proceedings against a tenant for alleged rent arrears. The tenant was unable to attend the proceedings and a possession order was made against him in his absence. On his application to have the possession order set aside, he counterclaimed for damages against the local authority in respect of a faulty central heating system that the local authority had installed. Although one of the two radiators in the living room and the fan heater in the bathroom worked, the other radiator in the living room and the ones in the bedroom and hallway did not work. The problem existed for four years, during which time, when it was cold, the defendant, who was in his late fifties and was frail, would light his oven for extra heat, sit in his living room wearing an overcoat and go to bed fully clothed. He also regularly visited neighbours on the pretext of making a social visit, when in reality, he wanted to escape the cold. The judge found that, although the cold periods were mostly confined to six months in each year, the experience of living alone whilst cold had been particularly discomforting. The defendant was awarded general damages of £3,800, comprising £850 per year and £600 because the cold caused the defendant's foot to feel dead.

London Borough of Newham v Hewitt (28 March, unreported) (Bow County Court: Recorder White) (Kindly submitted for publication by Jon Holbrook, Barrister). Mr Holbrook notes that this case is of particular interest because it concerns disrepair, where the sole defect was a faulty heating system.

996 Measure of damages—loss in value of negligently overvalued security—loss attributable to collapse of property market

See *Banque Bruxelles Lambert SA v Eagle Star Insurance Co Ltd*, para 3062.

**997   Measure of damages—mesne profits—reversioner ejecting lessee of property—
property rented out by reversioner—entitlement to and calculation of mesne
profits**

The Bahamas

The plaintiff was the lessee of 30 apartments within a hotel complex. The defendants, the hotel
operators and reversioners under the lease, ejected the plaintiff and used the apartments as part
of the hotel for almost 16 years until the plaintiff obtained an order for possession. He made an
application for mesne profits in respect of the defendants' trespass and, at first instance, the
registrar calculated damages by allowing a percentage of simple interest on the plaintiff's original
investment. The plaintiff appealed and the court held that the defendants were liable to pay the
plaintiff a reasonable rent for the wrongful use of the apartments. The sum was calculated to be
a percentage of the defendants' actual gross revenue from the hotel, in proportion to the total
number of rooms, for the period of the trespass and the plaintiff's award was substantially
increased. On the defendants' appeal, *held*, although the plaintiff might not have suffered any
actual loss by being wrongfully deprived of his property, and the defendants might not have
derived any actual benefit from their use of the property, the plaintiff was still entitled to recover
a reasonable rent for the wrongful use of his property by the defendants. A reasonable rent was
payable for the use of each apartment for 365 days of each year of the trespass period, even
though the actual levels of occupancy might have been lower. Since any figure based on that
calculation would be in excess of the award made by the previous court, the defendants had
failed to show that the award should be reduced and, accordingly, the appeal would be dismissed.

  Inverugie Investments Ltd v Hackett [1995] 3 All ER 841 (Privy Council: Lords Keith of Kinkel,
Griffiths, Browne-Wilkinson, Lloyd of Berwick and Steyn). *Swordheath Properties Ltd v Tabet*
[1979] 1 All ER 240, CA and *Stoke-on-Trent City Council v W & J Wass Ltd* [1988] 3 All ER
394, CA applied.

**998   Measure of damages—negligent mis-statement—loss of chance—evaluation of
chance**

The plaintiff bank financed a property transaction entered into by a client of the defendant
accountancy firm. As a result of rapidly deteriorating market conditions the bank made inquiries
to the accountancy firm as to their client's net worth. The accountancy firm enormously
overstated their client's assets and admitted shortly thereafter that their value was considerably
smaller and that they had been in breach of their duty of care to the bank. The bank then sold
the property which was the subject of the client's transaction for a relatively low price. Damages
were awarded against the accountancy firm and they appealed against the amount of the
damages. *Held*, on the balance of probabilities the bank would have sold the property involved
at an earlier date and it would have had a real or substantial chance of recouping more money
from the transaction than it actually did. The evaluation of the chance was to be taken into
account in estimating the amount of damages to be awarded. In the present case the degree of
chance was such that the amount of damages should be reduced and the appeal allowed.

  First Interstate Bank of California v Cohen Arnold & Co (1995) Times, 11 December (Court of
Appeal: Nourse and Ward LJJ, and Smedley J).

999   Non-pecuniary loss—Law Commission consultation paper

The Law Commission has issued a consultation paper, *Damages for Personal Injury: non-pecuniary
loss* (consultation paper No 140), as part of its larger review of the law of damages. The paper is
concerned with compensation for the non-pecuniary consequences of injury, but also considers
the issue of assessment of damages in defamation cases. The commission provisionally suggests
that the courts should continue to award damages for non-pecuniary loss and that such damages
should be assessed in accordance with current principles rather than the 'functional approach' (ie
the use to which damages might be put so as to provide solace to the plaintiff). Views are sought
on the scale of damages for non-pecuniary loss which should be awarded to plaintiffs who have
been rendered permanently unconscious and also to plaintiffs who, although conscious, are so
severely brain-damaged as to have little appreciation of their condition. The commission
provisionally suggests that no threshold for non-pecuniary loss should be introduced, but seeks
views from those who hold a contrary view as to the level of any such threshold. Similarly,
views are sought as to the adequacy of present awards for non-pecuniary loss (and particularly
views which are based otherwise than on intuition) and whether such awards (especially in
respect of very serious injuries) have kept pace with inflation over the past 25 to 30 years. The
report considers the possible introduction of a legislative tariff for non-pecuniary awards and
seeks views (on the assumption that such a tariff might be introduced) as to its form. As an
alternative to a legislative tariff, the possibility of establishing a compensation advisory board is

discussed and views sought on a model set out in the report. The commission suggests, provisionally, that trial by jury should not be used to provide sample awards for non-pecuniary loss and views are sought on the greater use of 'medical scoring' for comparing such awards, and on the possible use of computers and other means to assist the judiciary in assessing awards. The commission provisionally suggests that compensatory damages in personal injury cases should always be left to the judge. In relation to awards in defamation cases, it considers the proposed split between the determination of liability and damages between judge and jury as unworkable, and views are sought on this issue. It further recommends (provisionally) that, in defamation cases and in other cases where the jury assesses damages for non-pecuniary loss, the judge should inform the jury of the range of such awards in personal injury cases. Views are sought on whether there should be a ceiling on such awards in defamation cases (and, if so, the appropriate level). The commission suggests that interest should continue to be paid on damages for non-pecuniary loss in personal injury cases. Views are sought, however, as to whether such interest should be paid only on past (as opposed to future) non-pecuniary loss, whether it should be payable from the date of the accident rather than the date of the service of the writ, and whether the current rate (2 per cent) is satisfactory. The commission provisionally suggests that an injured person's right to recover damages for non-pecuniary injuries should continue to survive in the case of supervening death for the benefit of his estate and seeks views as to whether the survival should be conditional or unconditional. Finally, the commission seeks views on whether the overlap between damages for loss of earnings and damages for loss of amenity raised in *Fletcher v Autocar Transporters Ltd* [1968] 2 QB 322 gives rise to difficulties and, if so, how such difficulties might be solved.

1000   Personal injury—deduction for benefits received—incapacity pension—deduction from award for loss of retirement pension

It has been held that where a plaintiff has been awarded damages for negligence against his employer, payments made from an incapacity insurance scheme, not administered by his employer, are not deducted from the part of the award representing the loss of retirement pension as the scheme is treated as a form of insurance, the premiums of which are paid for by the injured party in the form of contributions. This is in accordance with the principle that a tortfeasor ought not to be allowed to enjoy the fruits of the plaintiff's foresight and prudence in insuring himself against an incapacitating accident.

Longden v British Coal Corpn [1995] ICR 957 (Court of Appeal: McCowan, Roch and Ward LJJ).

1001   Personal injury—entitlement to damages—trespasser engaged in criminal activities

The plaintiff attempted to break into the allotment shed of the defendant, aged 76. The defendant fired his shotgun through a hole in the shed door, hitting and injuring the plaintiff. The plaintiff pleaded guilty to various criminal offences and the defendant was prosecuted on charges of wounding, but was acquitted. The plaintiff brought an action for damages for personal injuries on the basis of trespass to the person, breach of the duty owed under the Occupier's Liability Act 1984, s 1, and negligence. The defendant raised the defences of ex turpi causa non oritur actio, accident, self-defence and contributory negligence. The judge found that the defendant used greater violence than was justified in lawful self-defence and was negligent even by the standard of care to be expected from the reasonable man placed in the defendant's situation. The plaintiff was awarded damages, although the judge found the plaintiff two-thirds responsible for his injuries. On the defendant's appeal, *held*, the judge's finding was entirely justified. With regard to the defence of ex turpi causa non oritur actio, the issue was whether the plaintiff in a personal injury claim for damages for negligence was debarred from making any recovery where he was a trespasser and engaged in criminal activities when the injury was suffered. Any broad test of causation was satisfied in such a case, as the plaintiff would not have sustained the injury caused by the defendant unless he had been where he was and acting as he was at the relevant time. These were factors which were taken into account when assessing contributory negligence. The question of whether there was a complete defence would only have relevance to the defendant's proportion of the liability. Applying the defence in the present circumstances would mean that a trespasser who was also a criminal was effectively an outlaw, who was debarred by the law from recovering compensation for any injury which he might sustain. The trespasser/criminal was clearly not an outlaw. Accordingly, the appeal would be dismissed.

Revill v Newberry [1996] 1 All ER 291 (Court of Appeal: Neill, Evans and Millett LJJ).

1002   Personal injury—provisional damages—procedure

See 2369.

Personal injury—quantum of damages

Examples of awards of damages in personal injury or fatal accident cases are arranged in the following order. Cases involving more than one injury are classified according to the major injury suffered.

Death	Internal injuries	Back, chest and
Brain damage and paralysis	Burns	abdomen
Multiple injuries	Scarring	Arm and hand
Psychological damage and	Head	Leg and foot
emotional stress	Neck and shoulder	Minor injuries

1003   *Brain damage*

Total damages: £750,000
Sex: Male
Age at accident: 26
Date of settlement: November 1995
Judge/court: settled out of court

The plaintiff was involved in a serious road traffic accident and sustained serious **head injuries** involving **brain damage** leading to **right spastic hemiparesis, fracture of the right femur** and **soft tissue injuries** to the **calf**. He was left with his **right leg and arm** being **spastic** and **hyper-reflexic** and was initially **doubly incontinent**. At first he exhibited **labile** and **uncontrolled behaviour**. He **requires nursing** for the rest of his life and is **unfit for any gainful employment**. He underwent treatment in hospital and was discharged into the care of his mother and brother after being taught basic living skills by using a series of prompts and after his behaviour was modified by treatment. His mother and brother had to learn the regime under which the plaintiff had lived so that he could be cared for at home and the home had to be modified to accommodate him. The plaintiff was left with **residual right hemiparesis** but is able to walk indoors with a rollator and knee brace. He has some functional use in the right upper limb with **continuing deformity of the right hand** and has **continuing deformity in the right leg**. He requires a **check list** and **verbal prompting** for **independent washing and dressing**. Though he enjoys conversation, this is limited because of **poor memory and lack of recall**. There was significant **front-temporal lobe dysfunction** and he is dependant on **high levels of anti-depressant** therapy.

L v V (settled out of court) (Kindly submitted for publication by Arthur J Healey, Hartley & Worstenholme, Solicitors, Castleford).

PSLA: £128,000 (including interest)
Total damages: £1,250,000 (agreed settlement after ten per cent liability discount)
Sex: Male
Age at injury/trial: 4/11
Date of injury/trial: 15 February 1988/27 June 1995
Judge/court: Harrison J/Queen's Bench Division, Manchester

Plaintiff sustained **irreversible brain damage** due to **hypoxia** whilst undergoing a circumcision operation. He was left with a **severe mental handicap** which gave rise to difficult behaviour, over-activity, problems with locomotion and manipulation and **severe epilepsy**, which was poorly controlled. His disabilities rendered him **wholly dependant** and in need of constant supervision. Prior to the trial of the action, liability was settled in the plaintiff's favour, but it was agreed that damages would be subject to a ten per cent discount to reflect possible difficulties over liability and causation. Prior to the commencement of the quantum trial, the above amount was agreed as an appropriate figure for settlement and included (1) special damages of £87,127 (plus £21,449 interest and less £18,229 benefits) comprising £23,141 travelling and transport; £44,167 gratuitous care (after allowing £11,075 invalid care allowance); £8,631 additional household expenditure; £8,669 accommodation (£4,219 excess costs to date and £4,450 costs thrown away); £2,519 aids and appliances and (2) future losses of £1,251,412 (less benefits of £4,126 per annum with a multiplier of 19.6) comprising £955,051 nursing costs (£38,899 age 11–13, £197,090 age 13–19 and £719,062 age 19 onwards); £12,439 future transport; £76,532 accommodation; £37,532 additional household costs; £17,643 future appliances (at £1,604 using a multiplier of 4); £3,571 medical expenses; £13,348 therapies; £10,340 holidays; £109,276 loss of earnings and £15,680 Court of Protection costs. Nursing costs were assessed on the basis that the plaintiff would live and be cared for at home until age 13 and would then move to a centre for the mentally handicapped (which would provide all necessary therapies), he would initially return home for about nine weeks per year but after the age of 19 would be fully residential at the centre.

Wadsworth v West Lancashire Health Authority (27 June 1995, unreported) (Michael Shorrock QC, Christopher Melton, Messrs Hatton Scates and Horton, Manchester, for the plaintiff; Brian Leveson QC, North West Health Legal Services, for the defendant) (Kindly submitted for publication by Howard Hatton, Solicitor, of Messrs Hatton Scates and Horton).

PSLA: £122,000
Total damages: £1,100,000
Sex: Male
Age at injury/settlement: Birth/14
Date of injury/settlement: 30 August 1979/18 July 1994
Earnings multiplier: 14
Judge/court: Drake J/Queen's Bench Division, London (settled out of court)

Plaintiff developed **severe cerebral palsy** at birth when there was a delay in performing a caesarean section and he was **deprived of oxygen**. He was left with **developmental delay**, speech delay and **epilepsy**. He would be totally dependent upon others for the rest of his life and required **constant care** and assistance with eating and communication. Maximum life expectancy was thought to be 50. The above award comprised £58,000 past financial losses (with £24,000 interest thereon), aproximately £325,000 future care costs, £60,000 physiotherapy, approximately £101,000 speech and occupational therapy, £60,000 travel expenses, approximately £60,000 additional aids, £60,000 additional housing costs, £40,000 additional household expenditure, £20,000 holidays, £140,000 loss of earnings, £30,000 Court of Protection costs.

Barnett v North Bedfordshire Health Authority (unreported) (Edward Bailey, Messrs Pictons, Stevenage, for the plaintiff) (Kindly submitted for publication by Mark C Wardrop, Solicitor and Susan Dugard, Legal Executive, of Messrs Pictons).

PSLA: £105,500 (including interest)
Total damages: £850,000 (including interest)
Sex: Male
Age at accident/trial: 22/26
Date of accident/trial: September 1991/13 March 1995
Earnings multiplier: 7.5
Judge/court: May J/Queen's Bench Division, London

Plaintiff, a trainee accountant, suffered **major brain injuries** in a road traffic accident. He was in a **coma** for two weeks before entering the **persistent vegetative state** in which he remained at time of trial. He underwent several **major surgical procedures** and was discharged from hospital 11 months after the accident. He was then **cared for in his parents' home**, which had been adapted for his special needs with grant aid. Plaintiff remains **entirely dependent** on the care of others and is, as far as doctors can ascertain, unaware of his condition. His parents were primary carers and although they had limited subsidised and outside voluntary help, their psychological and physical health suffered. It was agreed at trial that plaintiff would probably live for another ten years, a life expectancy largely attributable to his excellent care, near absence of infections, good nutrition and recent advances in medical care. The above award included: (1)

special damages of £106,672, with £15,322 interest thereon comprising £26,000 (past loss of earnings), £16,000 (parents' attendance at hospital), £44,500 (family care), £7,000 (non grant-aided accommodation costs), £7,137 (transport), £100 (nutrition), £5,188 (clothes and miscellaneous expenses) and £747 (physiotherapy); (2) future losses of £585,000 comprising £210,000 (loss of earnings, including the lost years), £225,000 (care), £15,000 (holidays), £50,000 (accommodation), £25,000 (transport), £10,000 (nutrition), £15,000 (clothes and miscellaneous expenses), £35,000 (private treatment) and (3) Court of Protection fees and sundries of £37,506.

Thorpe v Hooper (13 March 1995, unreported) (John Cherry QC and Martin Seaward, Messrs Booth and Blackwell, London, for the plaintiff; Christopher Purchas QC and Jonathan Waite, Messrs A E Wyeth and Co, Dartford, for the defendant) (Kindly submitted for publication by Martin Seaward, Barrister).

1004   *Tetraplegia*

PSLA: £95,000
Total damages: £644,378
Sex: Male
Age at accident/trial: 17/19
Date of accident/trial: 26 January 1992/15 June 1994
Earnings multiplier: 14
Future care multiplier: 20
Court: Outer House

Scotland
The plaintiff was a passenger in a car which was involved in a road accident. He suffered **complete paralysis of his trunk and lower limbs, lost the use of his hands**, and **could not control his bladder and bowel functions**. Although he could still move his shoulder and certain muscles in his elbow, he suffered **persistent pain in his right arm and shoulder**, and experienced **involuntary movements in his arms, trunk and legs**. After two years of extensive treatment, he could **walk with the aid of elbow crutches and a support for his left foot**, but at an **abnormally slow speed** and with **great difficulty**. His ability to wash and dress himself was severely limited because of the **spasticity and weakness of his hands**, especially his left hand. He had **gross spasticity in his limbs**, for which medication was required, and the **nerve system control of the blood supply to his feet** was affected to such an extent that he had **abnormally cold feet**. The plaintiff had to **exercise for at least an hour every day** to maintain the efficiency of the muscles which were not paralysed, and had to **wear special splints at night to prevent his hands from clawing**. The **prognosis** was that there would be **further deterioration**, and that eventually he would be **confined to a wheelchair**. In respect of damages for solatium, the plaintiff was awarded a greater sum than a 'conventional' paraplegic would be, because his ability to move with crutches was limited and he could not control or use a manual wheelchair. The plaintiff was awarded damages in respect of the services provided by his mother and other members of his family up to the date of trial. The multiplier for damages for future care was assessed by reference to actuarial tables as 20. As the plaintiff was likely to remain at home for only a further 5 and a half years, damages were awarded in respect of future care costs for that period, and also for the remaining 14 and a half years. There was only a very slight chance that the plaintiff would be able to find part-time employment, and a multiplier of 14 was therefore applied in assessing damages for future loss of earnings. Damages for other specific matters were agreed upon.

Stevenson v Sweeney 1995 SLT 29 (Outer House).

1005   *Paralysis*

PSLA: £64,464 (including £4,464 interest)
Total damages: £536,420 (including £43,584 interest)
Sex: Male
Age at injury/trial: 39/46
Date of injury/trial: November 1988/4 August 1995
Benefit multiplier: 10 (reduced from 15 to allow for possibility of changes to the benefit system)
Earnings multiplier: 8
Judge/Court: Potter J/Queen's Bench Division, Manchester

Plaintiff, a window cleaner, underwent an **occipito-cervical operation** using a Ransford loop in November 1988. After the operation, due to the defendant's alleged negligence, the plaintiff was in a state of **tetrapelgia**. His condition improved although his **limb movement remains much impaired** and he is **unable to work**. Prior to accident plaintiff led an active life, playing football, weight training, cycling and fishing. Defendant argued that the major proportion of the plaintiff's disabilities arose from his **pre-existing but previously undiagnosed ankylosing spondylitis.** Potter J found plaintiff's disability attributable 60 per cent to tetraparesis, 30 per cent to ankylosing spondylitis and 10 per cent to depression. Judge also had regard to **Ogden tables**, not to fix the multiplier but as an aid to deciding appropriate traditional multiplier. The multiplier for life was 15. The above award consisted of: pain, suffering and loss of amenity, £60,000 (plus £4,464 interest); loss of earnings, past, £67,978, future, £103,776 (earnings multiplier of 8 to take account of retirement age of 60, rather than 65, and allowing for uncertainty and possible periods of unemployment); capital costs on house, past £3,605, future, £30,000; increased running costs on house, past, £1,500, future, £6,000; medical care, past, £295, future, £20,000; transport costs, past, £1,089, future, £13,471; aids and equipment, future, £25,809; care, past, £49,000, future, £150,000; miscellaneous, past £470; less benefits, past £17,228, future (using a multiplier of 10 rather than 15 to allow for possible cuts in benefit entitlement) £16,220; interest £32,411 (including credit for interim payments).

Smith v Salford Health Authority (4 August 1995, unreported) (Caroline Swift QC, Andrew Long, Hatton, Scates & Horton, Manchester, for the plaintiff; George Davies & Co, Manchester for the defendant) (Kindly submitted for publication by Howard Hatton, Solicitor, Hatton, Scates & Horton, Solicitors).

1006 *Multiple injuries*

PSLA: £25,000
Total damages: £25,000
Sex: Male
Age at accident: 8
Date of trial: 7 February 1995
Judge/court: District Judge Bolton/Bristol County Court

Plaintiff was injured as he was crossing a zebra pedestrian crossing. He sustained an **angulated displaced fracture** of the distal third of the **right tibia and fibula**, a wound to the back of his right thigh, **multiple grazes** to his ankle and foot, cuts to his right arm and a **closed head injury**. The leg fracture united in an almost anatomical position, although there was a **10 degree reduction in flexion** in the right knee and some discomfort in the right shin. He was left with a **stable scar of 13 cms** on the back of his thigh, together with scars on the right shin and right forearm, which were not major cosmetic flaws. The plaintiff developed **behavioural problems** as a result of the head injury, which gave rise to **irritability** and regular **temper outbursts**. Carbamazepine was prescribed and he is likely to **require medication for several years**. There was some possibility that his educational performance had been affected, particularly his **memory and concentration**, although his performance had been below standard prior to the accident.

George v Tipper (7 February 1995, unreported) (Alasdair Brough, Messrs Davies and Partners, Bristol, for the plaintiff; Messrs John A Neil, Bristol, for the defendant) (Kindly submitted for publication by Ewan Lockhart of Messrs Davies and Partners, Solicitors).

PSLA: £22,730 (including interest)
Total damages: £30,456.85 (including interest)
Sex: Female
Age at accident/trial: 39/44
Date of accident/trial: August 1990/15 December 1994
Judge/court: Judge Brandt/Colchester County Court

Plaintiff was involved in a road traffic accident and sustained a **fractured right clavicle**, **severe lacerations** to her right ear and an **unstable fracture** of the **second cervical vertebra**, with a quarter body subluxation. Her right arm was placed in a sling and the lacerations required stitches. **Traction** was applied to her neck by means of **skull tongs** applied under local anaesthetic. For **six weeks she was restrained** and could not move her upper torso and neck, she was prescribed analgesics and sleeping tablets, but throughout this period she was **terrified that one movement could lead to death or paralysis**. She was then prescribed a **stiff cervical collar** and a week later, was discharged from hospital. Five weeks after this, she was given a **soft collar**, which she continued to wear for four weeks, until she returned to work. She experienced some pain due to the clavicle fracture and was left with an **obvious bump at the fracture site** and slight **scarring** to her right ear and these physical deformities were a source of **embarrassment**. Fourteen weeks after the accident, she was still wearing the soft collar and had limited **restriction of movement** in her neck in all directions, **tingling** in her fingers and hands and aching between the shoulder and elbow of her left arm. However, neurological examinations revealed **no evidence of nerve compression**. She also complained of stiffness in her back and hips and soreness on the back of her head where it had rested on the pillow during traction. Four years after the accident, these symptoms were still a problem and she was suffering from an aching pain in the neck and shoulders. These **symptoms were likely to be permanent** and the prognosis was that the neck pain and stiffness would **increase over time**, thus restricting her ability to drive and work. Plaintiff demonstrated **extreme anxiety** as a result of the accident, particularly whilst in traction and later whilst driving or being driven. A psychiatrist indicated that she would gradually recover from this emotional distress over a number of years although there was likely to be some **residual distress**. In making his assessment of damages the judge took into account (1) the serious nature of the injuries; (2) the unpleasant nature of the traction; (3) the medical evidence as regards future deterioration and (4) the psychiatric effects of the accident. Since these aspects were not anticipated in the figures noted in the Judicial Studies Board Guidelines, he awarded damages of considerably more than those indicated. The above award included special damages of £7,289.85, with interest of £437 thereon.

Wilson v Clarke (15 December 1994, unreported) (David Pugh, Messrs Jackaman Smith and Mulley, Ipswich, for the plaintiff; Richard Du Cann, Messrs Mills and Reeve, Norwich, for the defendant) (Kindly submitted for publication by Messrs Jackaman Smith and Mulley, Solicitors).

PSLA: £12,500
Total damages: £15,000
Sex: Female
Age at accident/settlement: 17/20
Date of accident/settlement: 23 August 1991/10 January 1995
Judge/court: Settled out of court

Plaintiff was involved in a road traffic accident, she suffered multiple **facial lacerations** above the hairline and above the right upper eyelid; multiple **lacerations above the left knee**; a **whiplash injury** and a complete right sided **facial palsy**. She was admitted for **neurological observation** and remained in hospital for four days. She was **off work for one month**, she wore a collar for one month and the whiplash injury resolved soon after this. The facial palsy had cleared three months after the accident. One year after the accident, she required **day surgery** to remove some glass from her face and later underwent a **surgical revision** operation of the right eyebrow and the major thigh/knee scars. This was unsuccessful and it was agreed by the court that the **scarring** was a **major cosmetic problem**. The knee scars were particularly unsightly, the plaintiff was constantly questioned about them and no longer wore short skirts. The facial scars were prominent in the right eyebrow area and plaintiff altered her hairstyle to cover it. The above award included special damages of £2,500.

Tribe v Cheffey (settled out of court) (Richard Tyson, Messrs Pengilly and Ridge, Weymouth, for the plaintiff; Messrs CA Norris, Ringwood, for the defendant) (Kindly submitted for publication by Timothy Guppy of Messrs Pengilly and Ridge, Solicitors).

PSLA: £8,000
Total damages: £15,650.59
Sex: Male
Age at accident/trial/appeal: 56/59/61
Date of accident/trial/appeal: 22 November 1989/5 November 1992/12 December 1994

The plaintiff was involved in a road traffic accident, and was still recovering from his injuries when he was involved in a second road traffic accident ('the substantive accident') five months later. As a result of the substantive accident, the plaintiff suffered an **avulsion fracture and damage to the inner and cruciate ligaments of** his **left knee**, which it was diagnosed would lead to **osteoarthritis**. He experienced **pain** in his knee when **crouching and kneeling**, and his ability to carry out his hobbies and leisure activities was restricted. The plaintiff also sustained a **blow** to his **left shoulder** which **exacerbated the effects of the first accident**, and suffered **intermittent pain** in his **left hip and neck**, attributable to the substantive accident. He was awarded damages following trial, but within a month he was involved in a **third road traffic** accident, which exacerbated the injuries from the substantive accident. On appeal as to quantum, *held*, as there were a number of separate injuries, the judge should have fixed a reasonable sum of compensation for each of them and then stood back and considered the case as a whole in order to arrive at a global aggregate figure that was reasonable compensation for the totality of the injuries. Here, in that respect, the sum of £8,000 would be substituted for the original sum of £9,000. As regards damages for future loss of earnings, having regard to the events which occurred in the two years following the original judgment, damages should have been awarded for lost earnings for a period of six months, and a lump sum for loss of earnings for the five years thereafter until retirement age.

Brown v Woodall [1995] PIQR Q36 (Court of Appeal: Staughton and Gibson LJJ, and Sir John May).

PSLA: £6,960 (including interest)
Total damages: £39,909 (one third deducted for contributory negligence)
Sex: Female
Age at accident/trial: 60/65
Date of accident/trial: 31 August 1989/18 January 1995
Earnings multiplier: 3.5
Court: Outer House

Scotland
Plaintiff tripped over a piece of timber on the steps of a railway station. She fell heavily on her right shoulder and hip, her head went through a glass panel and she became unconscious. She suffered a **subluxation** of the **right acromioclavicular joint** and a **lateral flexion injury** to her **cervical spine**. She had **considerable pain** in her hip, shoulder and neck, had **difficulty walking** for some time and had physiotherapy for three years. Five years after the accident she still had pain in her neck and shoulder and periodically suffered **numbness** in her **right hand**, with the index and middle fingers going into spasm. As a result of these injuries she could not drive and was **forced to give up her job**. She claimed she was unable to do housework or other heavy activity and felt that she had been deprived of her independence but it was held that she exaggerated the effect of her injuries. Her cervical spine had been subject to **pre-existing degenerative change** in the form of cervical spondylosis, which was exacerbated by the fall. The above award included £27,591 for loss of past wages with £2,548 in interest. £2,810 was paid in respect of the husband's services (including interest).

Reid v Edinburgh Acoustics Ltd 1995 SLT 659 (Outer House).

PSLA: £5,000
Total damages: £5,000
Sex: Male
Age at accident: 42
Date of accident/trial: September 1992/18 October 1994
Judge/court: District Judge Jolly/Reading County Court

Plaintiff was involved in a road traffic accident and sustained a **blow to his occiput** and **lost consciousness** for a short period. He also suffered a **whiplash** injury, **hyperextension** of the fingers and wrist of his left hand, injuries to his chest and a supraspinatus injury to his right shoulder. He underwent **physiotherapy**, but took **no time off work** and took no analgesics. Five months later, he began suffering from **frequent headaches**, which could become **migranous**. Moving his neck caused him **persistent pain**, he had intermittent **paraesthesia** in his right arm (which sometimes woke him at night) and pain and clicking in his right shoulder. Due to the poor economic climate, he **persevered in his job**, even though it involved a considerable amount of driving and some lifting, both of which **exacerbated his symptoms**. Five months after the accident, he was found to have a **reduced range of movement** in his neck and right shoulder and there were areas of tenderness. The injuries affected his hobbies of gardening and squash for a short period. At date of hearing, he was still suffering from headaches twice a week, some migranous, neck pains when driving for long periods and occasional clicking in the shoulder. The headaches and neck pain were expected to settle in about two and a half years and the shoulder injury by three years after the accident. No residual symptoms or degenerative changes are expected after this time.

West v Campagnie Ltd (18 October 1994, unreported) (Robert Weir, Messrs Shoosmith and Harrison, Reading, for the plaintiff) (Kindly submitted for publication by Robert Weir, Barrister).

PSLA: £3,888 (including interest)
Total damages: £7,934.54
Sex: Female
Age at accident/trial: 30/31
Date of accident/trial: 18 September 1994/29 November 1995
Judge/court: Judge Gosling/Birmingham County Court

The plaintiff was involved in a road traffic accident in which the defendant's vehicle collided with her vehicle. She suffered **pain and numbness** in the **upper part of** her **left arm**, and sustained **swelling and bruising** to the **lower part of** her **left arm**. She also suffered **neck pain and stiffness**, and had to **wear** a **soft cervical collar** and take **painkillers**. Because of **substantial restriction in her neck movement in all cardinal planes**, the plaintiff had to undergo a course of **physiotherapy**. In addition, she suffered a **lumbar sprain injury** which **intermittently** manifested itself by way of **diffuse aching**, although this was not expected to cause long-term problems. As a result of the accident, the plaintiff was **absent from work for five weeks**, her ability to participate in **sporting activities** was restricted.

Jones v Khangura (29 November 1995, unreported) (Simon Davis, Messrs Blakemores, Birmingham, for the plaintiff) (Kindly submitted for publication by Messrs Blakemores).

PSLA: £3,500
Total damages: £3,500
Sex: Female
Age at injury: 37
Date of trial: 24 February 1995
Judge/court: Judge Alton/Birmingham County Court

Plaintiff, a teacher, was **assaulted during the course of an attempted car theft**. She was **punched in the face** (causing a **laceration to the upper lip** which required **stitches**), and she sustained **bruising to the coccyx**, due to a fall during the assault. Her menstrual cycle was affected and she developed **thrush** in reaction to drugs prescribed. She was diagnosed as suffering from **depressive neurosis** with **anxiety and panic disorder**, this had a profound effect on her life; she suffered from apathy, **loss of confidence**, **fatigue**, panic attacks, recurring dreams and **fear of further attack**. Prior to the attack, she had been a very active member of the scouting movement, which involved public speaking to large numbers of people and, as a result of the attack, she was no longer able to play such a significant role. She attempted to return to work on two occasions, but found it too difficult. At time of trial, she had not had treatment for the psychiatric problems, preferring to deal with the matter within her supportive family. The prognosis was that, if she took up treatment there would be a **70 per cent chance of full recovery**, a 20 per cent chance of partial recovery and a 10 per cent chance of permanent symptoms.

Szulc v Howard (24 February 1995, unreported) (Jeremy Western, Messrs Dawkins and Grey, Birmingham, for the plaintiff) (Kindly submitted for publication by Jeremy Western, Barrister).

1007 *Psychological damage and emotional stress*

PSLA: £20,000
Total damages: £325,512 (including interest)
Sex: Female
Age at accident/trial: 27/33
Date of accident/trial: 16 December 1988/28 November 1995
Earnings multiplier: 13
Judge/court: Judge Wilcox (sitting as a High Court Judge)/Queen's Bench Division, London

Plaintiff suffered a **moderate whiplash injury** while a rear seat passenger in a taxi. Since childhood the plaintiff had had a left hemiparesis which meant that her left arm was virtually without useful function. The whiplash injury gave her pain and discomfort in her neck and across her right shoulder and down the right arm to the hand. As a result of the accident the **plaintiff developed Somatoform Pain Disorder** ('SPD'). The judge found that at the time of the trial although there was **no organic basis for the plaintiff's symptoms**, the **pain was real, acute and debilitating**. She continued to complain of pain across the top of her right shoulder and down the right arm to the wrist. The pain was worse if she undertook any activity. She had pins and needles in her right hand and limited movement in her neck. She had undergone a variety of treatments including acupuncture, local anaesthetics, steroids and physiotherapy. She was referred for neurological examination and psychiatric assessment and therapy. The prognosis was gloomy; although there was a **possibility of improvement, it was not likely**. The plaintiff **was unable to work, run a home or care for children without intensive support**. The judge rejected a suggestion that the plaintiff was a malingerer. The above award included: £20,000 general damages; £143,065 for future loss of earnings (£11,005 per annum with a multiplier of 13); £25,538 for future care; £9,018 for future costs of hairdressing and holidays, £1,251 for future equipment costs; £900 for future travelling expenses; £39,000 for future costs of a resident nanny; and £76,000 for past loss of earnings and cost of care to the date of the trial.

Sarjeant v Crawford (28 November 1995, unreported) (David Foskett QC, David Evans, Messrs Field Seymour Parkes, Reading, for the plaintiff) (Kindly submitted for publication by David Evans, Barrister).

PSLA: £18,000
Total damages: £22,000
Sex: Female
Age at accident: 28
Date of accident: 25 September 1989
Date of settlement: July 1995
Judge/court: settled out of court

After being admitted to hospital, the pregnant plaintiff was given doses of the drugs prostaglandin and syntocinon. Five days later, there were **Type 1 decelerations in the foetal heartbeat** which was recorded at 100 beats per minute and which should have given cause for concern. Further epidural was administered and syntocinon was recommenced. The cervix became fully dilated with the presenting part of the foetal head below the ischial spine. It was noted that the foetal heartbeat had **Type 1 decelerations with good recovery** but the CTG indicated **Type 2 decelerations with poor recovery** and contractions were frequent. Despite this the rate of syntocinon infusion was maintained without referral to medical staff. It was later noted that Type 1 decelerations were persisting with good recovery but it was clear that these were **Type 2 decelerations**, medical staff were not informed and syntocinon was continued. Later the **foetal heartbeat suddenly dropped to 60 beats per minute**, the plaintiff was urged to push and an **episiotomy** was performed. A **forceps delivery of a stillborn child** took place. It was alleged that the health authority was negligent in failing to interpret the CTG trace properly, that despite evident cause for concern they failed to act upon the change of foetal heart tracing, caused or permitted syntocinon to be admitted despite the foetal heart decelerations, failed to inform medical staff, failed properly to monitor despite high blood pressure and exposed the plaintiff to unnecessary risk. The plaintiff sustained **nervous shock and distress** as a consequence and suffered **pain on sexual intercourse**. Expert counsel was supportive of the claim for psychological suffering. Special damages were claimed for funeral costs, travelling costs in relation to subsequent pregnancies, gratuitous care and flowers in remembrance of the unborn child. The above award comprised £18,000 general damages, £2,180 special damages, plus interest.

Re C (settled out of court) (Andrew Buchan, Messrs Holyoak & Co, Leicester, for the plaintiff) (Kindly submitted for publication by Christopher J Smith, Holyoak & Co, Solicitors).

PSLA: £15,000
Total damages: £15,000
Sex: Female
Age at injury/hearing: 6–14/18
Date of hearing: 26 July 1995
Court: Criminal Injuries Compensation Board, York

Between the ages of 6 and 8 applicant was **sexually assaulted** by a friend of the family. She came into contact with him again between the ages of 13 and 14 when he again **touched her indecently** and encouraged her in sexual activity with him. The applicant was **withdrawn, isolated and agoraphobic**. She had not had any relationships with young boys and believed that she would **never want to marry or have children**. Prior to the second contact with the abuser she had been **raped and sexually assaulted** by another friend of the family. An application to the Board had been made in respect of this attack and an award of £12,500 made. A second application in respect of the first abuser was initially refused by the single member who made the first award on the grounds that it related to injuries which had already been compensated for in the first award. The Board indicated that it was impossible to differentiate between the injuries so it re-opened the initial application and made an award of £15,000 in respect of both applications.

W v Criminal Injuries Compensation Board (26 July 1995, unreported) (Messrs Rhodes Thain Collinson, Halifax, for the applicant) (Kindly submitted for publication by Allan Western, Messrs Rhodes Thain Collinson, Solicitors).

PSLA: £10,000
Total damages: £10,000
Sex: Female
Age at injury/hearing: 35/36
Date of injury/hearing: 20 April 1993/9 May 1994
Court: Criminal Injuries Compensation Board, Glasgow

Scotland
Applicant was **raped at knifepoint**. At trial of her attacker, applicant suffered **trauma of recalling events and humiliation** when he was acquitted of rape. Encountered attacker on bus three months later and was aware of him watching her. A week later her attacker was arrested and charged with the rape and murder of another woman at the same place. He was found guilty and sentenced to life imprisonment. Applicant had always been shy and anxious and **prone to depression and anxiety attacks**. These symptoms **severely exacerbated by attack**. Applicant had **difficulty sleeping** at night and by day was **pre-occupied with constant fear** of what might have happened to her.

A v Criminal Injuries Compensation Board (9 May 1994, unreported) (Messrs Trainor Alston, Coatbridge, for the applicant) (Kindly submitted for publication by Messrs Trainor Alston, Solicitors).

PSLA: £10,000
Total damages: £10,000
Sex: Female
Age at abuse/hearing: 11–15/24
Date of abuse/hearing: 1982–1986/4 July 1995
Judge/court: Criminal Injuries Compensation Board, York

Applicant was subjected to **sexual abuse** by her **step-father** from the **age of 11 to 15** as well as one relatively minor physical assault. When she was 16 her step-father was charged with unlawful sexual intercourse and assault. The applicant and her mother withdrew their statements before the trial. An initial application was refused on the grounds that unlawful sexual intercourse was not a crime of violence, that the intercourse was consented to and enjoyed by the applicant and because the applicant was unwilling to give evidence. At the hearing it was accepted that at the age of 11 there was certainly no consent and that great pressure was placed on the applicant not to give evidence. Medical evidence was provided that the applicant **continued to suffer nightmares** about the abuse, that it was persistently in her mind and that she **had difficulty forming lasting relationships**.

Criminal Injuries Compensation Board, York (4 July 1995, unreported) (Messrs Rhodes Thain & Collinson, Halifax for the plaintiff) (Kindly submitted for publication by Alan Western, Messrs Rhodes Thain & Collinson, Solicitors).

PSLA: £4,000 (£2,500 for psychological damage, £1,500 for physical injuries)
Total damages: £4,538.46 (including interest)
Sex: Male
Age at accident/trial: 37/40
Date of accident/trial: 29 June 1993/12 July 1995
Judge/court: Deputy District Judge Millward/Dartford County Court

Plaintiff was injured when the defendant's vehicle hit his vehicle side on with sufficient force to lift it off the ground. He sustained multiple minor injures: **soft tissue injury to the neck**, **right iliac crest bruised and tender**, **bruising over the antero-lateral joint line**. There was a lack of extension of the cervical spine of 20 degrees and lateral flexion and extension produced pain in the shoulder. The judge accepted, **without expert evidence**, the plaintiff's claims to

psychological effects of the accident: **tearfulness** for three days after the accident, **nervousness** when driving and **anxiety** when traffic approach from his left or when passing the scene of the collision.

Brandman v Prior (12 July 1995, unreported) (Bradley Say, T G Baynes of Cardigan Chambers, Bexleyheath, for the plaintiff; defendant unrepresented) (Kindly submitted for publication by Bradley Say, Barrister).

PSLA: £2,800
Total damages: £3,400
Sex: Male
Age at injury/settlement: 87/88
Date of injury/settlement: 13 October 1994/13 September 1995
Court: Settled out of court

Plaintiff was walking across a zebra crossing when he **tripped over a hole** in the road and fell into an unguarded trench, both of which had been excavated by the defendant. He suffered **cuts and nasty bruises** to his forehead, left side and leg and right hand. He did not require hospital treatment. He suffered dizzy spells and headaches which lasted for several weeks, but within three months he no longer showed any signs of physical injury. However, he is now **much less outgoing than before** the incident. He no longer goes on walks on his own, has given up DIY and gardening and **no longer has any confidence** in his ability to achieve anything. His zest for life as been markedly diminished. The above award included £600 special damages for the provision of care by immediate members of the family.

Horton v CAMAS Associated Asphalt Ltd (unreported) (Messrs Clarke Willmott & Clarke, Bridgwater, for the plaintiff; Eagle Star for the defendants) (Kindly submitted for publication by Huw Ponting, Messrs Clarke Willmott & Clarke, Solicitors). Mr Ponting notes that it is interesting that of the £2,800 agreed for pain suffering and loss of amenity approximately £2,000 was attributed to the plaintiff's loss of confidence.

PSLA: £2,000
Total damages: £2,059.26
Sex: Female
Age at accident/trial: 29/31
Date of accident/trial: 11 April 1994/16 November 1995
Judge/court: Judge MacMillan/Bolton County Court

Plaintiff was employed by the defendants as a domestic assistant at a hospital. Whilst cleaning in the opthalmology department she **suffered a needle stick injury from a syringe** which had been discarded into a refuse bag. She suffered **no physical injury** but developed a **psychological reaction** in that she became **concerned at the prospect that she might have contracted hepatitis or AIDS**. She developed a mixed anxiety depressive order which persisted for about four months. She received four injections to boost her immunity to hepatitis. She remained apprehensive until seen months after the accident when she was seen by a consultant haematologist and reassured that she was not likely to have contracted any infection. The judge found a **full recovery** took place within a very short time of being so advised. At the time of the accident the plaintiff was **attempting to become pregnant** and she was advised not to conceive until four months after her hepatitis injections were complete. The above award included £59.26 special damages for travel expenses.

Howell v Bolton Hospitals NHS Trust (16 November 1995, unreported) (Timothy White, for the plaintiff, N McEwan for the defendant) (Kindly submitted for publication by Timothy White, Barrister).

1008 *Post-traumatic stress disorder*

PSLA: £40,000
Total damages: £105,000
Sex: Female
Age at injury/trial: 40/45
Date of trial: 15 May 1995
Court: Criminal Injuries Compensation Board, York

Applicant, an area supervisor for a company, was **violently raped**, with **threats to kill**. She sustained a **fracture** to the transverse process of the **lumbar vertebrae** and **bruising** to her head, neck and left loin. She required **counselling** as regards the rape, but three years after the incident she was still suffering from **post-traumatic stress** disorder, depression and recurrent physical symptoms such as **headaches and back pain**. Five years after the incident there was little improvement in her psychological condition, she had **loss of libido** and was capable of only the **lightest work**. The **prognosis was uncertain**. The above award included £65,000 past loss of earnings, future loss of earnings and other incidental special damages.

Criminal Injuries Compensation Board, York (15 May 1995, unreported) (John Behrens, Messrs T I Clough and Co, Bradford, for the applicant) (Kindly submitted for publication by Abdul S Iqbal, Barrister).

PSLA: £36,750
Total damages: £52,144
Sex: Male
Age at injury: 27
Date of injury/assesment: March 1987/6 July 1995
Court: CICB, Durham
Earnings multiplier: 12

Applicant, a security guard, was **assaulted during an armed robbery**. He was hit over the right shoulder, neck and head and kicked while on the ground. He sustained a **comminuted fracture of the left ulna** requiring **plating and bone grafting**. He has made a good recovery from his physical injuries but is suffering **post-traumatic stress** requiring out-patient psychiatric treatment including drug therapy for depression. He continues to suffer depression, anxiety, irritability and a **generalised phobic state** with poor self esteem and feelings of inadequacy. He has gained weight and become reclusive. His **marriage has broken down** and he has **not worked since the attack**. The applicant appealed against an initial award of £20,000. On appeal he was awarded £35,000 for pain, suffering and loss of amenity, including the severe psychological effect; £1,750 for the fractured ulna; future loss of earnings at £1,137 per annum with a multiplier of 12 (reduced to take account of the possibility that the plaintiff might find alternative employment) and special damages of £1,750.

CICB, Durham (6 July 1995, unreported) (Messrs Allan Henderson Beecham & Peacock, Newcastle upon Tyne, for the plaintiff) (Kindly submitted for publication by Sir Jeremy Beecham, Messrs Allan Henderson Beecham & Peacock, Solicitors).

PSLA: £25,488 (including interest at two per cent)
Total damages: £251,220.56
Sex: Male
Age at accidents/trial: 31 and 34/38
Date of accidents/trial: March 1987 and November 1990/20 May 1995
Earnings multiplier: 9
Judge/court: Judge Fish/Manchester County Court

Plaintiff, a train driver, was involved in two separate incidents at work. In the first incident, an **object was thrown by vandals** through the windscreen of the locomotive which he was driving and in the second incident, the **brakes of his locomotive failed** as he was approaching a station, causing it to collide with a stationary coach already at the platform. At time of impact the speed of the locomotive was five to ten miles per hour and the plaintiff was thrown about by the collision and sustained **whiplash** type injuries, but avoided more serious injuries by leaving his seat just before impact. As a result of the first accident, he suffered symptoms of **acute anxiety** and was moved to **restricted driving duties**. By the date of the second accident, he had almost completed an **anxiety management course** and was making good progress. Plaintiff never returned to driving or any form of work after the second incident, his level of anxiety increased and **post traumatic stress disorder** developed to such an extent that his career was ended. He suffered **sleep disturbance**, morbidity, **personality change** (which lead to difficulties with and separations from his wife). At time of trial he was still suffering from **pain**, particularly in the **lower limbs**, although this was not at a level which would be debilitating or restrict his social activities. He undertook college courses, but was unable to complete a degree course, neither could he hold down any significant employment, and was unlikely to be able to do so in the future. The judge accepted the medical evidence that the plaintiff continued to suffer **chronic pain** from relatively **minor injuries** and the award for general damages included an element for this. The above award included £81,183.12 special damages (past loss of earnings plus interest thereon), £139,347 future loss of earnings (based on a multiplicand of £15,483 and a multiplier of 9), £5,202.44 pension loss. There was no award for loss of congenial employment.

Harding v British Railways Board (20 May 1995, unreported) (Peter Atherton, Messrs Brian Thompson and Partners, Manchester, for the plaintiff; Nicholas Brazlavski, Messrs Peter Rickson and Partners, Preston, for the defendant) (Kindly submitted for publication by Peter Atherton, Barrister and Messrs Brian Thompson and Partners, Manchester).

PSLA: £15,000
Total damages: £40,000
Sex: Male
Age at injury/hearing: 19/31
Date of injury/hearing: December 1983/12 June 1995
Court: Criminal Injuries Compensation Board, Bristol

Applicant, a barman, was assaulted by a group of youths. He sustained **a fractured skull** and bruising of chest and legs. Injuries required detention in hospital for one week and three months' convalescence. Applicant returned to work four months after assault but left after three months when he became **apprehensive and scared**. The applicant was unemployed for long periods due to **serious psychological problems** he suffered whenever he worked in public houses. Eight months before the hearing he had secured a job in a brasserie and had recently been promoted. His symptoms included **severe memory impairment, headaches** associated with **vomiting, blurred vision and photophobia** and **personality change**. A neurologist's prognosis was that these conditions were unlikely to improve and could well form part of a **post traumatic syndrome**. As a result of his **aggressive mood swings** his **marriage had collapsed**. The above award comprised £15,000 for pain, suffering and loss of amenity, £10,000 *Smith v Manchester* award, and £15,000 for past loss of earnings.

Isaacs v Criminal Injuries Compensation Board (12 June 1995, unreported) (Christopher Taylor, Messrs D'Angibau Willmott, Bournemouth, for the applicant) (Kindly submitted for publication by Christopher Taylor, Barrister).

PSLA: £8,500
Total damages: £8,500
Sex: Male
Age at injury/hearing: 50/53
Date of injury/hearing: July 1992/24 July 1995
Court: CICB, Liverpool

Applicant was **abducted and held for ransom** for two and a half days by a gang. His captors persistently threatened to kill or maim him. He was tied up and **punched in the left eye, threatened with knives and snakes**, injected with horse tranquilliser and **told that parts of him would be amputated**. A handgun was discharged near him causing him to believe for a few moments that he was dead. He suffered a **sub-conjunctival haemorrhage** in the left eye causing double vision for a short period. The eye was symptom free after eight months. For 12 months up until the criminal trial of his abductors he was unable to relax. He frequently burst into tears, suffered disrupted sleep and concentration and had vivid dreams about the event. After eighteen months he was suffering from **severe post-traumatic stress disorder** and was diagnosed as being **agoraphobic** and had severely disabling symptom levels. Three years after the incident his condition had improved although he still suffered from anxiety, agoraphobia and disturbed sleep.

CICB, Liverpool (24 July 1995, unreported) (Linda Knowles; Messrs Gamlins Storrar Cowdry, Prestatyn, for the applicant) (Kindly submitted for publication by Linda Knowles, Barrister).

PSLA: £5,000
Total damages: £12,500
Sex: Female
Age at assault/hearing: 27/31
Date of assault/hearing: 30 November 1991/5 October 1995
Court: Criminal Injuries Compensation Board, London

Applicant was **stabbed in the back** with a six inch chisel by her ex-boyfriend. She was taken to hospital where she was found to have sustained a **puncture wound in the left renal area of her back**. Due to shock she was unable to move and was fed intravenously and catheterised. The wound was clipped together and dressed and she was **discharged after four days**. The wound remained painful for two months. There is a **small but not disfiguring mark** at the wound site and no underlying injury. Prior to the assault the applicant had been employed by an agency as a social worker. She was unable to work for one month as a result of the injury. She returned to work thereafter but began to **experience symptoms of depression and shock** to such an extent that she felt **unable to carry on with her job** and no longer accepted work from the agency. She regularly suffered from **loss of self esteem and acute anxiety**. The applicant was confused about who was responsible for the incident and had a misplaced sense of guilt. She periodically experienced shaky legs, poor short term memory, sudden **extreme tiredness and mood swings which would lead to aggressive behaviour**. She received counselling on a regular basis from her GP and a professional counsellor. The applicant was **largely recovered by the date of the hearing** although she still experienced the occasional bad day. In October 1994 she had felt well enough to embark on an art degree and **hoped to return to social work** at the end of the course to work in the field of art therapy. The Board awarded £7,500, or approximately one year's earnings, in respect of loss of earnings and £5,000 for pain, suffering and loss of amenity. The Board found that the post-traumatic stress disorder was moderate in severity and that the stab wound should be treated as analogous to a simple leg fracture.

Criminal Injuries Compensation Board, London (5 October 1995, unreported) (Kate Akerman, for the applicant) (Kindly submitted for publication by Kate Akerman, Barrister).

1009   *Internal injuries*
PSLA: £22,500 approximately
Total damages: £30,000
Sex: Female
Age at injury: 49
Date of injury: October 1991
Court: Settled out of court

Plaintiff underwent a **laparoscopic cholecystectomy** (excision of the gall bladder). Post operatively she experienced **severe abdominal pains**, developed a **biliary leak** and **jaundice**. She underwent a laparotomy and the bile duct was found to be divided by the clip on the stump of the cystic duct. A **stricture** then developed and several endoscopic retrograde cholangio-pancreatograms (ERCP) and three **biliary stents** were required. Thereafter, she suffered abdominal pain for several months. The stent was removed when the stricture had developed adequate calibre. Plaintiff continued to suffer epigastric abdominal pain, usually in the evenings and after meals, her **sleep was disturbed** and her weight increased. She has been left with a **vertical scar of 12 cms** to the right of the **umbilicus** and will remain on **long term surveillance**, which may include ultrasound, ERCP, liver function tests and coagulation profile. The medical expert at the trial criticised the division of the common bile duct during the laparoscopic cholecystectomy. The plaintiff's claim included £1,185 nursing care (gratuitously provided by plaintiff's family), £1,250 transport costs and loss of earnings and an allowance of £7,590 for cost of taking out annual private health insurance (using a multiplier of 11).

S v D (unreported) (Margaret DeHaas, Messrs Hatton Scates and Horton, Manchester, for the plaintiff; Messrs Hempsons, Manchester, for the defendant) (Kindly submitted for publication by Howard Hatton, Solicitor, of Messrs Hatton Scates and Horton).

PSLA: £20,000
Total damages: £22,500
Sex: Female
Age at injury: 33
Date of injury: 25 February 1991
Court: Settled out of court

Plaintiff underwent a **laparoscopic cholecystectomy** (excision of the gall bladder) and following the operation she suffered **nausea**, vomiting, **abdominal pain**, fever and rigors. She was re-admitted to hospital and underwent a **laparotomy** and clips were found on the upper and lower ends of the divided common bile duct, she then underwent a **choledochojejunos-tomy**. Following these further operations, she continued to feel unwell and five months afterwards, she was suffering from **recurrent jaundice**. She then underwent a **percutaneous transhepatic cholangiogram** and a further laparotomy. She returned home two weeks later and the abdominal stents were removed six weeks later. Plaintiff was left with a large and **painful abdominal scar** plus scars from several drain insertions. She continued to suffer from symptoms of nausea, fatty **food intolerance**, **borborygmus**, occasional constipation, and tiredness and it is likely that these **symptoms will continue**. Medical evidence suggested that a range of complications could arise in the future including (1) a ten per cent chance of bilio-enteric stricture occurring, with a ninety per cent chance within seven years, further stricture formation would increase the risk of biliary scerosis and could ultimately require liver transplantation; (2) incisional hernia in the wound; (3) duodenal ulceration, which could give rise to bleeding, perforation or stenosis and surgery could cause epigastric fullness, abdominal distension, post prandial discomfort and exacerbation of existing symptoms of nausea, vomiting etc, or, (4) development of adhesions and intestinal obstruction. Of these possible complications some could be life threatening and could require further operations, some of which might be emergency procedures. Plaintiff was granted leave to apply for further damages at an unspecified date in the event of deterioration. The above award included £2,500 special damages.

Levy v T (unreported) (Margaret DeHaas, Messrs Hatton Scates and Horton, Manchester, for the plaintiff; Messrs Hempsons, Manchester, for the defendant) (Kindly submitted for publication by Howard Hatton, Solicitor, of Messrs Hatton Scates and Horton). Mr Hatton comments that this case illustrates the serious risks involved where the common bile duct is divided as a result of laparoscopic cholecystectomy and not noticed prior to the patient's discharge from hospital. In such a case, the long term risks need to be considered and a claim for provisional damages incorporated.

PSLA: £13,000
Total damages: £15,000
Sex: Male
Age at injury: 33
Date of injury: May 1992
Court: Settled out of court

Plaintiff, a self employed builder, underwent a **vasectomy** under **local anaesthetic**. He was **not examined** before the operation and, during the operation, the surgeon was unable to locate the vas deferens to the right testicle. He explored the scrotum and in the course of the exploration, **damaged the right testicular artery**. Plaintiff was left with an **atrophic** right testicle and following surgery, his scrotum became very **swollen and painful**. He was re-admitted to hospital for one week and the swelling and pain continued for two weeks. Plaintiff alleged that if the vas deferens was impalpable clinically, then surgery should have been under general anaesthetic, thus enabling the surgeon to make a larger incision and conduct a proper examination of the spermatic chord. The above award included approximately £1,600 for remedial surgery and interest and approximately £400 loss of earnings.

Cooper v Pontefract Hospital NHS Trust (unreported) (Peter Atherton, Messrs Hartley and Worstenholme, Castleford, for the plaintiff; Charles Foster, Yorkshire Health Legal Services, for the defendant) (Kindly submitted for publication by Arthur J Healey, Solicitor, of Messrs Hartley and Worstenholme).

PSLA: £4,000
Total damages: £52,780
Sex: Female
Age at injury/settlement: 30/35
Date of injury/settlement: April 1990/May 1995

Plaintiff had **undergone a sterilisation procedure** in 1985. In March 1990 she **missed her period** and went to see her GP. The GP saw the plaintiff on a number of occasions between 9 April 1990 and 13 August 1990 **when the correct diagnosis of pregnancy was made**. By then it was **too late to carry out a termination** and the plaintiff gave birth to a daughter on 9 December 1990. Liability was conceded before the matter came to trial and the plaintiff accepted the defendant's insurers offer of settlement. The above award was based approximately on: general damages, £4,000; creche, £1,560; loss of earnings, £1,444; future cost of clothes and shoes, £700 per annum with a multilpier of 12; cost of childminder, £920 per annum with a multilpier of 10; food, £2,500 per annum with a multilpier of 12; play school costs up to the age of 5, £1,200; and a deduction of £6,364 for child benefit and interest on the special damages of £3,340.

Moore v Martin (unreported) (B McIntyre, Messrs Hartley and Worstenholme, Castleford, for the plaintiff; Huw Lloyd, Messrs Le Brasseurs, Leeds, for the defendant) (Kindly submitted for publication by A J Healey, Hartley and Worstenholme, Solicitors).

PSLA: £2,750
Total damages: £2,750
Sex: Male
Age at injury: 14
Date of settlement: 16 May 1995
Judge/court: District Judge Sheratte/Ilford County Court (settled out of court)

Plaintiff, who was suffering from **acute lymphoblastic leukaemia**, was directed to take the **wrong dosage of methotrexate** by his pharmacist, the correct dosage was eight doses a week, which was wrongly increased to eight doses a day. Plaintiff received 12 doses of the drug over 12 days and suffered initially from a **sore throat** and mouth and **nose bleeds**. He was **unable to eat** or swallow and was admitted to hospital, where pancytopenia, or **severe anaemia** was diagnosed. He had a very **low platelet and white cell count**, dry cracked lips and large **necrotic ulcers** inside both cheeks and on his tongue. He received **intravenous antibiotics**, platelet and **blood transfusions**. After seven days in hospital, he was discharged and by this stage his mouth ulcers were healing well and he could eat and drink. According to a medical expert the plaintiff's life expectancy had not been diminished, but the overdose could have been **fatal** had it not been for the prompt treatment. The above settlement was agreed following payment in.

Ahmed v Aquamead Ltd (unreported) (Edmund Cofie, Messrs Mahmood and Southcombe, Ilford, for the plaintiff) (Kindly submitted for publication by Edmund Cofie, Barrister).

PSLA: £2,500
Total damages: £2,608.33 (including £108.33 interest)
Sex: Male
Age at injury/trial: 20/23
Date of injury/trial: October–December 1992/8 September 1995
Judge/court: Judge Bernstein/Liverpool County Court

Plaintiff, a student, was **exposed to carbon-monoxide gas** due to a faulty gas fire in his bedroom while living in shared student accommodation. He suffered **intractable headaches**, feelings of collapse, **nausea** and **behaviour aberration**. He has made a **full recovery** and has **no long term effects**.

Walker v Heron (8 September 1995, unreported) (David Geey, Messrs Abenson & Co, Liverpool, for the plaintiff; defendant unrepresented) (Kindly submitted for publication by Messrs Abenson & Co, Solicitors).

1010 *Burns*

PSLA: (1) £16,528.69, (2) £10,057.97, (3) £12,779.47, (4) £2,979.90, (5) £11,278.37, (6) £3,000
Total damages: (1) £18,000, (2) £10,384, (3) £13,756, (4) £3,000, (5) £35,000, (6) £3,000
Sex: Male
Ages at accident: (1) 41, (2) 23, (3) 36, (4) 43, (5) 54, (6) 29
Date of accident/trial: 25 April 1991/12 June 1995
Judge/court: Judge Marshall-Evans/Liverpool County Court (settled on day of trial)

Six plaintiff fire-fighters sustained **physical and psychological injuries** whilst fighting a garage fire during which acetylene cylinders exploded causing a flash-over of flame.

Plaintiff 1 sustained deep partial thickness **skin loss burns** to wrists, ears, the left side of his face and the back of his neck; distortion and loss of part of the lobe of the left ear, **permanent scarring** and **heat intolerance** to both ears, causing the ears to become red and painful in hot conditions; a **jarring injury** to his neck, causing intermittent stiffness and restriction of movement and still a problem at date of trial; psychological symptoms: **mood change**, irritability, sleep impairment, reticence and nervousness at garage fires, symptoms fell short of post traumatic stress disorder, but would impair the quality of his life. The injuries required dressings for two weeks and plaintiff was **off work for eight months**. The above award included £1,471.31 special damages and was subject to a deduction of £3,357.86 in respect of Compensation Recovery Unit (CRU).

Plaintiff 2 sustained **flash burns** to ears, scalp, back of neck and left wrist. He was left with **permanent residual pain** and numbness in both ears, exacerbated in hot or cold weather; **noticeable scarring** on both ears and the back of the left wrist; moderate severity **post-traumatic stress disorder** for two months, reduced to mild severity for one year. At time of trial continuing symptoms included wariness, **anxiety** about scarring, avoidance of discussion about accident or its effects, **irritability** and problems with personal relationships, impaired sleep and increased startle response. In general he was left more vulnerable to the effects of further accidents. He required dressings for two weeks and was **off work for nine weeks**. The above award included £326.03 special damages and was subject to a deduction of £384 in respect of CRU.

Plaintiff 3 suffered burns to the face, ears, arm and leg and was **detained in hospital** for several days. Thereafter he required **dressings and ointment** and was off work for four months. He was left with (1) permanent heat and cold intolerance to both ears, preventing him from going outside for a time; (2) flaky skin on his forehead; (3) moderate severity **post traumatic stress disorder** for two to three months and **depression**, which required medication and gave rise to sleep impairment, nightmares (initially three to four times a week, reducing to monthly), emotional responses, **reduced social confidence**, irritability (putting a strain on his marriage), **personality change** from extrovert to worrier, temporary increased startle response and increased alcohol consumption. Plaintiff has been left **vulnerable** to psychological stress in the future. The above award included £976.53 special damages and was subject to a deduction of £756 in respect of CRU.

Plaintiff 4 suffered **flash burns** to the rims of both ears and to his whole face, which required antiseptic cream for two weeks and caused temporary **tenderness** when exposed to heat and sunlight and after shaving; **swollen lips**, causing difficulties in eating and drinking for ten days and minor shock. He was off work for four weeks. The above award included £20.10 special damages and was subject to a deduction of £168 in respect of CRU.

Plaintiff 5, the **officer in charge** at the incident who had responsibility for other plaintiffs, sustained flash burns to hair and eyebrows and **partial thickness facial burns**, requiring antiseptic cream for two weeks, he had **no scarring** but was **sensitive to sunlight**; moderate severity **post-traumatic stress disorder** for several months (which reduced to mild severity, but persisted at time of trial) and feelings of guilt, tension, recurring intrusive memories, **apprehensiveness** when dealing with fires, loss of enjoyment of work, sleep disturbance, increased tendency to be emotional, irritability and personality change from extrovert to **tense and insecure**. Plaintiff returned to work after a month out of a sense of duty, despite continuing psychological upset, these continuing symptoms caused him to **retire at least two years earlier** than he otherwise would have. The above award included £23,721.63 special damages.

Plaintiff 6 suffered burns to face and eyes. He was treated with **eye drops**, detained in hospital for several hours for observation and was **off work for 20 days** with eye irritation. He suffered from **headaches**, particularly in sunlight, for which he required analgesics and was **prone to eye infections** and intermittent inflammation of the eyes and eyelids, which persisted at time of trial.

Boyle v J C Services (12 June 1995, unreported) (Allan Gore, Messrs Brian Thompson & Partners, Liverpool, for the plaintiff) (Kindly submitted for publication by Allan Gore, Barrister).

PSLA: £16,000
Total damages: £31,907.51
Sex: Male
Age at injury/trial: 52/61
Date of injury/trial: 25 January 1986/15 May 1995
Judge/Court: Judge Walker/Halifax County Court

Plaintiff was injured in an explosion at work. He suffered **extensive burns** to his hands and face of a **deep partial thickness** type and secondary burns to his body from the melted nylon material of his anorak. Injuries required two-week stay in hospital. Plaintiff unable to return to work for four months. He was left with some **permanent alteration of the pigmentation** of his hands and face. There was a **permanent degree of stiffness** in his fingers which affected his ability to maintain machinery and manipulate small objects as well as reducing his enjoyment of golf. For about two years plaintiff suffered **nightmares** and remained distressed by the sight of news reports relating to fires and had a fear of calor gas cylinders. In addition his **mental acuity was affected**. The above award comprised £16,000 general damages (apportioned at £9,000 for physical injuries and £7,000 for post traumatic stress and psychological injuries) and special damages of £15,907.51.

Farragher v Quarmby Holdings (15 May 1995, unreported) (Alistair McDonald, Messrs Rhodes Thain & Collinson, Halifax, for the plaintiff) (Kindly submitted for publication by Allan Western, of Messrs Rhodes Thain & Collinson, Solicitors).

1011 *Scarring*

PSLA: £8,000 (including interest)
Total damages: £9,370.49 (including interest)
Sex: Male
Age at injury/trial: 5/10
Date of injury/trial: 29 December 1988/12 November 1993
Judge/court: Recorder Dunkels QC/Bristol County Court

Plaintiff was **attacked** and bitten on the head **by a rottweiler dog**. He sustained a **severe laceration** to his forehead and scalp, with **tissue loss** from the upper part of the right side of his forehead. He underwent an **emergency operation** under general anaesthetic to close the forehead and anterior scalp skin defect by means of a **scalp rotation flap**. A secondary defect at the back of the scalp, caused by rotation of the flap, was healed by means of a **split skin graft** taken from his right thigh. Plaintiff required a **blood transfusion** and was kept in hospital for ten days. He developed a noticeable **bald area** and, eight months after the accident, he underwent a **further operation** to excise the secondary skin graft. A wide **undermining and advancement** of the hair-bearing normal scalp skin was successfully performed and the bald area was converted into a **linear suture line**. Plaintiff remained in hospital for a week. The scars produced by the injury and treatment were originally red and uncomfortable and unsightly, but were pain free and pale by time of trial and were **camouflaged** naturally by the plaintiff's hair, although they could be seen if the hair is brushed aside. It was thought possible that the scalp scars might stretch and widen as the plaintiff matured and that surgical revision to narrow the scars might be necessary. If the scars became visible if the plaintiff lost his hair with age, it was thought that the scars would be an understandable source of embarrassment. There was also a patch of residual numbness on the right forehead and a superficial scar on the front of the plaintiff's right thigh. The above award included special damages of £1,070.49 with interest of £300 thereon.

The plaintiff's claim was based on the defendant's breach of his liability under the Animals Act 1971, s 2, and on his breach of his common law duty of care. The claim under the 1971 Act was dismissed, but the plaintiff was successful in the claim based on the breach of the defendant's common law duty of care. The defendant's appeal against the finding was dismissed.

Mason v Weeks (12 November 1993, unreported) (Anthony Hand, Messrs Bell Pope, Southampton, for the plaintiff; Robert Davies, Messrs Allen and Partners, Bristol, for the defendant) (Kindly submitted for publication by Shaun Underhill of Messrs Bell Pope, Solicitors).

PSLA: £5,500
Total damages: £5,640.94
Sex: Female
Age at accident/trial: 21/24
Date of accident/trial: 7 February 1992/15 May 1995
Judge/court: Recorder Coates/Stourbridge County Court

Plaintiff, a payroll clerk, was dancing at a night-club when she was knocked and fell onto the floor, injuring her left (non-dominant) arm on some broken glass. She sustained a deep **four inch laceration** of the **muscular tissue**, the biceps tendon was partly divided, the wound **haemorrhaged** profusely and the **brachial artery** was visible. The following day the lacerated muscle tissue was sutured under **general anaesthetic** and the skin wound left partially open. The arm was elevated in a **Bradford sling** and she was prescribed antibiotics. Three days later she underwent further **secondary suturing** of the skin wound under local anaesthetic. She remained in hospital for five days and was **off work for one month**. Plaintiff was left with **obvious cosmetic scarring** and numbness for three quarters of an inch around the scar. She was self conscious about the scar, she no longer wore short sleeves and the scar itched and inflamed in sunny weather, although it could be masked with make-up. The above award included £125.49 special damages (loss of earnings and travel) with £15.45 interest thereon.

Lewis v Jukes (15 May 1995, unreported) (Messrs Higgs and Sons, Stourbridge, for the plaintiff; Messrs William Wright and Son, Dudley, for the defendant) (Kindly submitted for publication by Ian Shovlin, Solicitor, of Messrs Higgs and Sons).

PSLA: £2,250
Total damages: £2,250
Sex: Male
Age at accident/trial: 15/23

Date of accident/trial: 4 June 1987/13 November 1995
Judge/court: District Judge Wyn Rees/Cardiff County Court

Plaintiff was **attacked by a German Shepherd dog** in the course of his employment as a milk delivery boy. His **left hand, wrist and elbow and upper left thigh sustained multiple lacerations and puncture wounds**. He was taken to hospital where he was given a tetanus toxoid injection and an intermuscular injection of antibiotics. His wounds were cleansed and dressed with steristrips, his hand and wrist bandaged and his arm placed in a sling. He attended hospital on five subsequent occasions and was absent from school for two weeks. At the date of the trial he was left with **four small scars on the left hand and wrist**, the largest measuring **1cm x 2cm**. He had three small scars over the flexor aspect of the left elbow and a 1cm scar that was barely visible on his thigh. The scars were described by the court as **'not prominent but visible'** and their appearance will not improve. They **did not cause embarrassment but did tend to itch** in hot whether. He has also acquired a **significant phobia of large dogs**, experiencing a churning sensation in his stomach on sight of one and would cross the street to avoid passing a large dog, even if it was on a leash.

Crisp v Hare (13 November 1995, unreported) (Jo-Anne Patterson, for the plaintiff) (Kindly submitted for publication by Jo-Anne Patterson, Barrister).

PSLA: £1,500
Total damages: £1,500
Sex: Male
Age at injury: 18
Date of injury/trial: 20 August 1993/11 April 1995
Judge/court: District Judge Wolfson/Liverpool County Court

Plaintiff sustained two **puncture wounds** in the left side of his abdomen when he was attacked by an alsatian guard dog. The wounds were cleaned at hospital, but **no sutures** were required. Plaintiff had **fully recovered** from his injuries after two months. He was left with **two pink scars**, one oval in shape and 12 mms wide and the other 17 mms by 6 mms, both of which will fade in time and be of **no cosmetic significance**. As a result of the attack, plaintiff was very wary of large dogs.

Bradley v Range Security Ltd (11 April 1995, unreported) (Charles Lander for the plaintiff) (Kindly submitted for publication by Messrs Woolwich Lander and Savage, Bootle).

1012 *Skin*

PSLA: £15,000 (plus interest)
Total damages: £55,446.75 (plus interest)
Sex: Male
Age at trial: 45
Date of trial: 20 May 1993
Earnings multiplier: 12
Judge/court: Deemster Corrin/High Court, Common Law Division

Isle of Man
Plaintiff worked as a machine setter operator and contracted **dermatitis** from his contact with cooling oils. The dermatitis started on the **back of his hands and the cuticles of his finger nails**. He experienced **swelling and small blisters and the skin cracked**. He was in **constant pain** and suffered from intensive itching. The condition **spread to his arms and face** and he was ill with blood poisoning as a result of the dermatitis. The plaintiff's employer failed to remove him from contact with cooling oils and, as a result, he suffered from a **depressive illness**. Because of his condition, the plaintiff and his wife abstained from all physical contact. He became **irritable and bad tempered** and lost interest in his hobbies. The plaintiff left his employment approximately seven years after the onset of his dermatitis and became a book-keeper for his wife. His dermatitis improved but it was probable that he would **continue to suffer from contact dermatitis in the foreseeable future** at a substantially lower degree of severity and frequency, and outbreaks of the condition might be accompanied by bouts of depression. The above award included £28,080 for future loss of earnings (using a mulitplier of 12), £3,000 for future handicap on the labour market and £9,366.7575 special damages.

Netherwood v Iloman Engineering Ltd (1993–95 ML Rep 75) (Richard Penn, Solicitor, for the defendant) (Kindly submitted for publication by Richard Penn, Solicitor).

PSLA: £10,000
Total damages: £187,000 (including interest)
Sex: Female
Age at injury/trial: 39/44
Date of injury/trial: November 1990/26 May 1995
Earnings multiplier: 12
Judge/court: Waller J/Queen's Bench Division, London

Plaintiff, a versatile and talented actress and singer, was employed to play two parts in the defendant's West End musical production. Ultra-violet orange greasepaint labelled 'for hair use only' was **applied around the plaintiff's eyes** causing **a chronic irritant contact dermatitis**. Since the injury she has been unable to wear makeup. This has **decimated her career** as well as making her everyday life awkward. The above award consisted of £10,000 general damages for pain, suffering and loss of amenity, £341 interest on that sum, £5,000 general damages for loss of congenial employment, £42,000 special damages for loss of income to the date of trial, £295 special damages for expenses to the date of trial, £9,364 interest on the special damages and £120,000 for loss of future earnings calculated at £10,000 with a multiplier of 12.

Maddox v Rocky Horror (London) Ltd (26 May 1995, unreported) (Messrs Douglas-Mann & Co, London, for the plaintiff) (Kindly submitted for publication by Messrs Douglas-Mann & Co, Solicitors).

1013 *Scalp*

PSLA: £5,073.50 (including interest)
Total damages: £8,948.23
Sex: Male
Age at accident/trial: 29/31
Date of accident/trial: June 1993/16 August 1995
Judge/court: Assistant Recorder Kirkham/Birmingham County Court

The plaintiff engaged the defendant to carry out **synthetic hair implantation**. The treatment consisted of implanting **2000 artificial hair fibres** over a period of three sessions, each session involving up to **20 injections of local anaesthetic** in the scalp. However, the treatment was **unsuccessful**, and resulted in the plaintiff's **scalp** becoming **red and crusted, with pustules** forming. He also developed **red lumps on** his **back and shoulders**. The defendant then sought to **remove the artificial hair without** using **anaesthetic**, and although the redness, pustules and crusting regressed, **scars began to develop on** the **plaintiff's scalp**, which **worsened** in **hot weather**. As a result, the plaintiff became **introverted, and self-conscious** about his appearance. He **would not go out without wearing a cap** and also gave up sport. In addition, his **marriage** was **adversely affected**, and he was unable to socialise.

West v N S Hair Treatment Clinic Ltd (16 August 1995, unreported) (N E H Tarbitt, Redfern & Co, Birmingham, for the plaintiff) (Kindly submitted for publication by LL Jacobs of Redfern & Co, Solicitors).

1014 *Head*

PSLA: £55,000
Total damages: £218,773
Sex: Female
Age at injury: 17/31
Date of injury/hearing: February 1981/5 July 1995
Court: Criminal Injuries Compensation Board, London

The applicant was attacked by a group of men in 1981. She was **knocked unconscious** and may have suffered a fractured skull. About three weeks after the assault she suffered her first **epileptic convulsion**. For the **next 14 years she suffered one to two seizures a week**, usually unheralded. She would fall, suffering bruising and on one occasion a fracture. She was **incontinent in about half of the seizures** and **part ictal confusion was present**. Drug **treatment had been unsuccessful**. She also suffered from headaches once or twice a week – non-throbbing bi-frontal sensations lasting 1–2 days, together with **loss of cognitive function and loss of memory**, possibly caused by the high levels of drugs in her blood. She was **moody and depressed**. She had recently been referred to the National Society for Epilepsy who, through new drug regimes and counselling, were reasonably optimistic that the seizures could be controlled better. The applicant's **husband had given up work in 1984 to look after his** wife but there was a possibility that he might be able to leave her alone to go back to work in about three years. There was no possibility of the applicant returning to employment other than in sheltered, part-time work. It was hoped that she would be able to gain some independence in social and domestic life but at the date of the hearing she was totally house bound and reliant on her husband for shopping, cooking and housework. She had **stopped going out since having a fit in the local high street, during which she was robbed**. The above award consisted of £55,000 for pain, suffering and loss of amenity, £55,000 for past care provided by husband, £39,000 for her future loss of earnings, £60,000 for future care to be provided by husband, £6,323 for temporary professional care to relieve husband and introduce counselling, and £3,450 for the cost of adaptations to the flat. The figures for past and future care and future loss of income were round figures and the board did not state the multiplier or multiplicand.

Criminal Injuries Compensation Board, London (5 July 1995, unreported) (Christopher Hough, for the applicant) (Kindly submitted for publication by Christopher Hough, Barrister). Mr Hough notes that the case is particularly interesting for the high award for care provided by the husband.

PSLA: £50,000
Total damages: £50,000
Sex: Female
Age at injury/hearing: 35/40
Date of injury/hearing: 13 May 1990/19 May 1995
Court: Criminal Injuries Compensation Board, Durham

Applicant was repeatedly **punched in the head** during an attack. She sustained **cuts and bruises** to her face, she was **unconscious** for a short period and was detained in hospital for five days. Three months after the accident, she suffered a **grand mal seizure** and was diagnosed **epileptic**; there was **no family history** of seizures. Applicant subsequently complained of headaches and grand mal seizures once or twice a month. She was prescribed high dosages of **anti-convulsant drugs** and, although frequency of seizures was reduced, they continued to occur without warning. During two seizures she injured her shoulder and burned her hand. The medication affected her sleep, she became tense and **depressed**, she required someone to monitor her and had to **attend hospital regularly**. She had **lost confidence** and independence and was **incontinent**. At time of award, she was heavily pregnant and increased dosage of the anti-convulsants was necessary to avoid seizures during pregnancy. Applicant was unable to return to her pre-accident employment as dress designer/machinist. The Board accepted that the seizures were grand mal and accepted causation of the seizures on the balance of probability (although their cause was subject to conflicting medical opinion, since the head injury was not believed to be severe enough to cause post-traumatic epilepsy and there had been no fracture or significant loss of consciousness).

Criminal Injuries Compensation Board, Durham (19 May 1995, unreported) (Messrs Patterson, Glenton and Stracey, Newcastle upon Tyne, for the applicant) (Kindly submitted for publication by William Dryden, Solicitor, of Messrs Patterson, Glenton and Stracey).

PSLA: Global award
Total damages: £27,500
Sex: Female
Age at injury/hearing: 22/29
Date of injury/hearing: 10 March 1989/18 September 1995
Court: Criminal Injuries Compensation Board, London

Applicant was on duty as a special constable for the Metropolitan Police when called to a disturbance at a dance hall involving approximately 100 youths fighting. In the course of assisting a colleague with an arrest she was **struck from behind with a baseball bat** on the right side of the head suffering an **undisplaced fracture of the right cheekbone**. She suffered **severe and regular headaches** over the six-year period from the date of the injury to the date of the hearing. On one occasion the headache persisted for 13 hours although they **generally lasted for two to four hours**. The regularity was unpredictable: she could be free from headaches for two to three weeks and then have a sequence of one a day for a week. A **vein underneath the applicant's cheek bone would throb in an unsightly manner** during the more severe headaches. There was **no apparent neurological abnormality** and the medical diagnosis was that the headaches were a form of **post traumatic stress**. It was suggested that psychotherapy might help but there was otherwise no reliable prognosis and the headaches might continue indefinitely. A *Smith v Manchester* award was claimed on the basis that the applicant's continued absenteeism from her part-time job as a radio cab dispatcher (from which she had resigned by mutual agreement) and her medical history of incapacitating headaches would make it extremely difficult for her to secure full-time employment. She was also denied the opportunity of applying for a post as a full-time regular police officer due to the headaches. The above global award included compensation for loss of earnings. Her net earnings had been £142 per week.

Criminal Injuries Compensation Board, London (18 September 1995, unreported) (Messrs Martin Smith & Co, Borehamwood, for the applicant) (Kindly submitted for publication by Martin Smith of Martin Smith & Co, Solicitors).

PSLA: £7,800 (including interest)
Total damages: £7,800 (including interest)
Sex: Female
Age at accident/trial: 9/12
Date of trial: 3 May 1995
Judge/court: Judge Taylor/Stoke-on-Trent County Court

Plaintiff sustained a **fractured skull** in a road traffic accident. At time of accident she was a passenger in the back seat of a stationary car which was hit by another vehicle, she was holding a golf club, which hit her on the head and caused a **comminuted depressed fracture** of the **frontal bone** in the middle of the forehead. She underwent an operation under **general anaesthetic** in which the **laceration** on the forehead was extended and the wound cleaned; the depressed **fragments were removed** and the one cm **tear in the dura** was closed; one large bone fragment was replaced in the skull defect and the skin was stitched. She was discharged after five days and returned to school two and a half weeks later and from that time she suffered no fainting, blackouts, or headaches. She was left with a **permanent scar** (of five and a half cms long and one to two mms wide), which ran down the centre of her forehead. Initially she wore her hair in a fringe to conceal the scar, but at time of trial she no longer did so, the scar sometimes felt **itchy and tingly**, and people had commented upon it. Plaintiff also had a period of **post traumatic amnesia** for about 24 hours. The head injury was moderately severe, and there was some slight **contusional damage** to the underlying brain tissue, although there was **no residual neurological deficit**. There was thought to be a ten per cent risk of **epilepsy** for the first five months, falling to five per cent after two years and two per cent after eight years. The risk of epilepsy would persist throughout the plaintiff's life. The above award was provisional, the judge fixed no limit on the time period during which the plaintiff could apply to court for further damages if she should develop epilepsy in the future.

Mayor v Boardman (3 May 1995, unreported) (Hugh Davies for the plaintiff; Francis Burns for the defendant) (Kindly submitted for publication by Hugh Davies, Barrister).

PSLA: £7,500
Total damages: £7,500
Sex: Male
Age at injury/hearing: 31/35
Date of injury/hearing: 28 February 1991/22 March 1995
Court: Criminal Injuries Compensation Board, Bristol

Applicant was **attacked with a claw hammer** and sustained a **fractured skull**. An operation was carried out to remove **bone fragments** from the wound and he was left with a large indentation near the top of his skull and the scar tissue tended to weep. He also suffered **headaches** and bouts of **amnesia**, dizziness and clumsiness as a result of his injuries. By date of hearing, he was still suffering from headaches and dizziness three or four times a week and it was thought that these symptoms were likely to **continue for the foreseeable future**.

Criminal Injuries Compensation Board, Bristol (22 March 1995, unreported) (John Livesey, Messrs Kelcey and Hall, Bristol, for the applicant) (Kindly submitted for publication by John Livesey, Barrister).

PSLA: £6,500
Total damages: £6,824.11
Sex: Male
Age at accident/trial: 16/21
Date of trial: 21 March 1995
Judge/court: Judge Earnshaw/Oldham County Court

Plaintiff was thrown from the back of a lorry and sustained a **depressed left temporal fracture**, with a **lineal occipital fracture** and minor cuts and abrasions. The day after the accident, he suffered a self-limiting complex **generalised epileptic seizure**, lasting about 30 seconds. He had no further epileptic seizures after this and by date of trial, he was at no greater than average risk of epilepsy. Plaintiff remained in hospital for eight days. The minor cuts and abrasions healed within a few weeks, but he was left with slight scarring on his right arm, although this was not cosmetically disfiguring. The accident occasioned a significant **inconvenience** to the plaintiff's working and social life; he was unable to ride his motorcycle for two years and had to stop playing football, as he was told he could not head a football. It was alleged that he had undergone a **personality change** as a result of the accident, but this was not supported by the medical evidence and was rejected by the judge. The above award included £324.11 special damages.

Fotheringham v Murfitt (21 March 1995, unreported) (Alistair Webster for the plaintiff; Hugh Davies for the defendant) (Kindly submitted for publication by Hugh Davies, Barrister).

PSLA: £3,500
Total damages: £4,045
Sex: Male
Age at injury/hearing: 23/26
Date of injury/hearing: 24 January 1993/22 September 1995
Court: CICB, York

Applicant travelling to a football match when he was assaulted by a group of rival supporters. He was kicked repeatedly while on the ground and suffered a **fractured nose**, a **slight chip fracture** over the left eyebrow and **bruising** to the face and body and **concussion**. He was tired and nauseous for two days after the attack and was off work for two weeks. The **injuries healed without cosmetic defect**. Continued to suffer post-traumatic headaches once or twice a fortnight for two years after the assault as well as having some obstruction of the nasal airways.

Criminal Injuries Compensation Board, York (22 September 1995, unreported) (Mark Whitcombe, Messrs Robin Thompson & Partners, Stanmore, for the applicant) (Kindly submitted for publication by Mark Whitcombe, Barrister).

PSLA: £3,120 (including interest)
Total damages: £5,340 (including interest)
Sex: Female
Age at accident: 23
Date of accident/trial: July 1991/1 December 1994
Judge/court: District Judge Samuels/Mayor's and City of London County Court

Plaintiff, a traffic warden, suffered a **head injury** when a metal clip struck her as it fell from a scaffold. She was **dazed** for a few moments, **felt nauseous** and was left with a red mark on the side of her head. She began to get **headaches** soon after the accident, which had largely **settled after two months**, but recurred occasionally for a further 16 months. Plaintiff's enjoyment of punk rock concerts was affected by the headaches and she also **lost confidence**. She was **off work for two months**, and returned to light duties after this, but did not return to full duties until eight months after the accident. Plaintiff had made a full recovery 18 months after the accident. The above award included special damages of £2,220 (including interest).

Taylor v RS Thompson Ltd (1 December 1994, unreported) (Martin Seaward, Messrs Robin Thompson and Partners, London, for the plaintiff) (Kindly submitted for publication by Martin Seaward, Barrister).

Total damages: £2,400 (amount of payment in accepted by plaintiff)
Sex: Male
Age at accident/trial: 11/15
Date of accident/trial: 21 November 1991/6 April 1995
Judge/court: District Judge Tennant/Southampton County Court

Plaintiff suffered minor **head injuries** when he was struck by a van and thrown onto the windscreen. He was **knocked unconscious** but regained some consciousness on the way to hospital and, by the time he arrived at hospital, could localise a **painful stimulus** and make incomprehensible sounds. Lateral cervical spine and chest x-rays revealed **no spinal or cardiovascular injuries** and he was given a **hard collar**. He was transferred to the neurological centre for assessment and management of his head injury and underwent a **CT scan** and a scalp laceration was sutured. The scan revealed a **small lesion** in the **deep white matter** of the left frontal lobe, plus a lesion in the right parietal white matter. Plaintiff also sustained soft issue injuries to his right hand and bruising to the inguinal region. He remained in hospital for a week and was reviewed by the neurosurgical department four months later; no specific problems were reported and he was discharged. Plaintiff was advised to accept defendant's payment in (£548.25 special damages were pleaded).

Curtis v Securicor Ltd (6 April 1995, unreported) (Messrs Bell Pope, Southampton, for the plaintiff; Messrs Hextall Erskin and Co, for the defendant) (Kindly submitted for publication by Shaun Underhill, Solicitor, of Messrs Bell Pope).

PSLA: £1,000
Total damages: £1,000
Sex: Male
Age at injury/settlement: 15 months/3 years
Date of injury/settlement: 8 October 1993/20 September 1995
Judge/court: District Judge Garside/Bradford County Court

Plaintiff, a baby, was placed with the defendant, a registered child minder. When his father collected the plaintiff he noticed that the plaintiff had **bruising and swelling** around his **right eye** and around the **right side of his forehead**; **bruising on his left forehead**; a red mark just in front of his right eye, an area of **bruising inside his left ear**; and **bruising on the palmar surface of his fingers**. The opinion of the consultant paediatrician was that the bruising was **non-accidental** and was caused by an adult rather than another child. The police investigated but no proceedings were brought against the defendant. The plaintiff has **recovered well** and has **no recollection** of the events or the suffering.

Compton v Watson (settled out of court) (Messrs Gaunts, Halifax, for the plaintiff; Messrs Berrymans, London for the defendant) (Kindly submitted for publication by Messrs Gaunts, Solicitors).

PSLA: £900 (for defendant on counterclaim)
Total damages: £2,845.41 (for defendant on counterclaim)
Sex: Female
Age at accident/trial: 35/38
Date of accident/trial: 8 December 1995/12 May 1995
Judge/court: Recorder Nicol/Lambeth County Court

Defendant, a teacher, was involved in an accident on a mini-roundabout near the school were she taught. On impact she was thrown sideways and hit her head against the driver's door sustaining a **laceration** to the scalp which required **six stitches** and healed well. For the first week after the accident she suffered pain around the laceration and **constant throbbing** in the other side of the head. She suffered **shock** and had difficulty sleeping for a week after the accident. For three months she was **nervous about driving** in general and in particular about the mini-roundabout, which she had to use to get to her school. By the date of the trial, recovery was complete. The plaintiff's claim against the defendant was dismissed. The above award, made to the defendant on the defendant's counterclaim, included £1,945.41 special damages.

Ohene v Rymer (12 May 1995, unreported) (Richard Serlin for the plaintiff; Katharine Ferguson for the defendant) (Kindly submitted for publication by Katharine Ferguson, Pupil Barrister).

1015   *Head and face*
PSLA: £22,500
Total damages: £140,421
Sex: Male
Age at accident: 23
Date of accident/trial:14 October 1989/11 November 1994
Earnings multiplier: 8
Judge/court: Judge Hallgarten QC/Central London County Court

Plaintiff was involved in a car accident and suffered a **comminuted fracture of the left mid-line of the anterior mandible, an undisplaced fracture of the left condylar neck of the mandible, severe lacerations under chin and multiple dental fractures**. The plaintiff was taken to hospital where his **mandible was plated and wired** under general anaesthetic. He needed 37 stitches under his chin and the dental fractures required lengthy **orthodontic and**

maxillo-facial remedial work. The plaintiff also suffered **distress** and **depression**. His jaw remained wired for several weeks and he was left with **permanent mis-alignment of the jaw** leaving his face looking slightly lopsided. There was a **numb patch on his chin** and from 1990 onwards he had to wear a special **orthodontic brace** which required monthly regulation. At the time of the trial he was still undergoing dental treatment. The main effect of the injuries was mental. The plaintiff returned to work at the end of 1989 but the firm went into liquidation and at the same time he began to develop **tinnitus, a fuzzy feeling in his left cheek, giddiness, disorientation and fatigue** which were psychological in origin and likely to be amenable to improvement. He found a new job but was unable to cope with it because of his injuries and he left to run his own business. As a result of his injuries the plaintiff developed a **benign cyst** in his mouth which was enucleated. Worry about whether the cyst was malignant caused a serious relapse in his general condition and he started to suffer **panic attacks**. He took antidepressants, beta-blockers and sleeping pills and was treated for **mild to moderate post-traumatic stress disorder**. His condition improved between June 1993 and the date of the trial. He was **unlikely to work again to full capacity** or expand his business significantly. He would always suffer a degree of **depression, lack of energy and lack of concentration**. He would receive treatment for a further three years or so and continue to improve for a further five years after that. The above award included £3,807 medical and other expenses to date; £24,614 loss of earnings to trial; £15,000 agreed future medical expenses; £70,000 continuing loss of earnings (at £8,750 using a multiplier of 8); £4,500 handicap on labour market.

Cory-Wright v Chapman [1995] PIQR Q10 (Central London County Court: Judge Hallgarten QC).

1016   *Head and eye*
PSLA: £12,000
Total damages: £12,000
Sex: Male
Age at injury/hearing: 33/35
Date of injury/hearing: 4 September 1993/17 May 1995
Court: Criminal Injuries Compensation Board, Glasgow

Scotland
Applicant was **struck on the side of the face** by an opponent during a football game. He suffered an **orbital fracture in two places**, received **20 stitches** to his face and **damaged his retina**. He initially suffered from **severe impairment of vision** although this had lessened to the extent that by the time of the hearing his vision had stabilised. He is left with some **blurring to his vision** and **cannot read for more than a couple of minutes** at a time without having to rest and start again. The injury did not affect his career.

Baker v Criminal Injuries Compensation Board (17 May 1995, unreported) (Messrs Clarke Willmott & Clarke, Bridgwater, for the applicant) (Kindly submitted for publication by Huw Ponting of Clarke Willmott & Clarke, Solicitors).

1017   *Head and ear*
PSLA: £8,000
Total damages: £8,000
Sex: Female
Age at accident/trial: 2/8
Date of trial: 27 February 1995
Judge/court: Judge Potter/Birmingham County Court

Plaintiff was involved in a road traffic accident and suffered a **fractured skull**, a **left sided haemotympanum**, a convulsion and her balance was affected for ten days. The only lasting injury was mild to moderate **unilateral deafness** in her left ear, due to a **dislocation of the ossicular chain**. The deafness in the ear was on average 44 dB between 500 and 800 Hz and would be **permanent** unless she underwent **ossiculoplasty**. However, despite this, she could still hear generally well. The total cost of the surgery would be £3,000, could not take place until her mid to late teens and there would be a 70 to 85 per cent chance of this returning her hearing to near normal, but a one per cent chance of deterioration and a **risk of tinnitus**.

Lane v Evans (27 February 1995, unreported) (Nicholas Starks, Messrs Peter Rickson and Partners, Birmingham, for the plaintiff; Paul Bleasdale, Messrs Rowley Dickinson, Birmingham, for the defendant) (Kindly submitted for publication by Nicholas Starks, Barrister). Mr Starks comments on the fact that there appear to be no reported cases dealing with a unilateral partial hearing loss in so young a plaintiff.

1018   *Head and back*

PSLA: £40,000
Total damages: £50,500
Sex: Male
Age at injury/trial: 57/63
Date of injury/trial: 26 April 1989/7 March 1995
Court: Criminal Injuries Compensation Board, Plymouth

Applicant, a prison officer, sustained **cerebral and spinal injuries** arising from an **assault** by an inmate. He was **punched in the head** about five times, sustaining a **concussive head injury**, which gave rise to **post-traumatic amnesia** in the order of fifteen minutes to two hours. He also **injured his lower back** in the assault. **No surgical treatment** was required, but the head injury gave rise to the following permanent changes (which were confirmed by a neurologist, an orthopaedic surgeon and a clinical psychologist): (1) **short-term memory loss** meant that he forgot people, had problems remembering and pronouncing names, dates and places, was no longer confident in social situations and had to use a **tape recorder**, a filofax and notes to **prompt** him; reading was no longer a pleasure, as he forgot what he had read previously and he was unable to pursue his hobby of lapidary, as he could not retain the necessary details in his mind; (2) he **could not sustain concentration**. If he tried to do work requiring concentration, he suffered severe pains over one side of his head which could last for days and he had **difficulties with mental arithmetic**; (3) he became **reclusive**, withdrew from his wife, suffered from loss of self-confidence and **depression** ; (4) he **could not cope with stress**, finding that his mind went blank when he was under pressure. He got **anxious** about everyday matters such as appointments with doctors, and **slept badly**. The lower back injuries prevented him from doing physical work such as heavy digging, lifting or home decoration and his back was prone to giving out which often **confined him to bed for up to a week**. He could **no longer drink alcohol** which he had enjoyed to a moderate extent prior to the assault. The above award included £10,500 special damages.

   Criminal Injuries Compensation Board, Plymouth (7 March 1995, unreported) (Damian Horan, Messrs Bevan Ashford, Exeter, for the applicant) (Kindly submitted for publication by Damian Horan, Barrister).

1019   *Head and foot*

PSLA: (Agreed settlement not broken down)
Total damages: £6,000
Sex: Female
Age at injury/settlement: 56/59
Date of injury/settlement: 30 September 1992/6 November 1995
Court: Settled out of court

Plaintiff underwent an operation for the removal of a benign cyst on her forehead. Following the local anaesthesia she **never recovered sensation** in an area extending from her right eyebrow to the back of her head and from her ear to a line across the mid-line of her scalp **corresponding with the upper branch of the supra orbital nerve**. Following this she was referred to a neurosurgeon and underwent **a second procedure to perform a nerve graft** using a cutaneous nerve from the lateral side of the right calf. She had been warned that this would result in a small area of numbness about two inches across on the dorsal of the foot. In the event the numbness extended from the lateral two toes along the dorsal surface of the foot to the heel, the adjacent plantar surface and about a hand's breadth above the lateral mallelous. There has also been little improvement in the numbness of the scalp. Sensation to pin prick, cotton wool and temperature has been lost in the area of the left forehead above the eyebrow extending about two centimetres across the midline. The anaesthesia extends down to the ears and posteriorly to the occipital surface of the scalp. The health authority denied liability but the above settlement was agreed inclusive of £411 loss of earnings.

   Re H (settled out of court) (Harrowell Shaftoe, York, for the plaintiff) (Kindly submitted for publication by Mark Tempest, Harrowell Shaftoe, Solicitors).

1020 *Face*

PSLA: Approximately £3,300
Total damages: £11,233 (including interest)
Sex: Female
Age at accident: 49
Date of accident/trial: 25 April 1989/13 December 1994
Court: Outer House

Plaintiff was injured in the course of a **biopsy** of her right maxillary sinus when instrumental pressure caused **damage to the infra-orbital nerve**. As a result, the plaintiff suffered **paraesthesia**, which **deprived her of normal feeling on the right side of her face** below the eye, on the cheek, down the side of the nose, in her lips and in the top of her gum and the roof of her mouth. She felt **self conscious** and had a **tendency to dribble**. Since the accident she had been **reluctant to go out socially** and she never went to restaurants. The plaintiff's complaints were far from trivial and, with no prospect of betterment, reflected a very real affliction which she would have to bear for the rest of her life. The award included £1, 233 interest.

McDonald v Lothian Health Board 1995 SLT 1033 (Outer House).

1021 *Eyes*

PSLA: £7,500
Total damages: £7,500
Sex: Male
Age at accident/trial: 43/45
Date of accident/trial: 30 April 1993/6 September 1995
Judge/court: Judge Mackay/Liverpool County Court

Plaintiff tripped whilst holding a screwdriver. It entered his **right eye** causing injury. Surgery repaired the injury leaving plaintiff with **moderate reduction in vision of right eye** which is **permanent but correctable by wearing spectacles**. He has a 10 per cent risk of developing a cataract and a 5 per cent risk of developing raised intraocular pressure. General damages of £7,500 were agreed.

McCarthy v Knowsley Metropolitan Borough Council (6 September 1995, unreported) (Tim Grover, Messrs Mackrell & Thomas, Liverpool, for the plaintiff) (Kindly submitted for publication by Tim Grover, Barrister).

PSLA: £5,000
Total damages: £7,654.95
Sex: Male
Age at accident/settlement: 32/33
Date of accident/settlement: 18 May 1994/23 February 1995
Court: Settled out of court

Plaintiff, a car tyre warehouse worker, was struck in the face by a car tyre which fell from a rack. He suffered a **6 mm hyphaema** in the anterior chamber of the left eye and **extensive facial bruising**. The vision in his left eye was **permanently impaired**, being measured at 6/9, but was within the normal range of vision when wearing spectacles or contact lenses. Prior to the accident, plaintiff had normal eyesight. **No sequelae** were expected. The above award included £154.95 special damages and £2,500 future expenses for contact lenses and spectacles (calculated at £250 per year using a multiplier of 10).

Names of parties witheld (unreported) (Messrs Martin Smith and Co, Borehamwood, for the plaintiff) (Kindly submitted for publication by Messrs Martin Smith and Co).

PSLA: £3,486.92
Total damages: £4,250
Sex: Male
Age at injury/settlement: 7/11
Date of settlement: 28 October 1994
Judge/court: Settled out of court

Plaintiff underwent a series of four **operations to correct a squint in his right eye**. Two months after the last operation, he had to undergo a fifth operation to **remove a swab** which had been **left in his eye intra-operatively** and two days later **a second swab extruded** from his eye. As a result of the swabs being left in his eye, he suffered **pain and discomfort** for approximately **three months** and required the fifth and unnecessary operation. Proceedings were not issued and the defendants did not admit liability. The above award included £763.08 special damages.

Nicoll v Lyall (settled out of court) (Messrs Pattinson and Brewer, London, for the plaintiff; Messrs Le Brasseur J Tickle, London, for the defendant) (Kindly submitted for publication by Linda Levison, Solicitor, of Messrs Pattinson and Brewer). Ms Levison comments that there appears to be no directly comparable case. CICB guidelines include £3,000 for a laparotomy (although no permanent scar resulted in the present case). Judicial Studies Board Guidelines give a lower limit of £1,500 for minor eye injuries.

PSLA: £1,000
Total damages: £1,000
Sex: Male
Age at injury/trial: 5/6
Date of injury/trial: 5 March 1995/2 October 1995
Judge/Court: District Judge Greenslade/Cheltenham County Court

Plaintiff was **a rear near-side passenger** in a car, **wearing a seat belt**, when the car was hit by another vehicle travelling in the opposite direction. The plaintiff was thrown forward and hit his head on the passenger seat in front of him. He was distressed and was transferred by ambulance to hospital. On examination he was found to have a horizontally orientated **laceration of the left eyelid**. The injury was treated with wound glue. There was **swelling and bruising** around the left eye together with **headaches for the best part of a week**. The plaintiff was absent from school for one week. When his eyes are open the plaintiff has some fullness of the left eyelid but no visible scarring. When his eye is closed there is **a horizontally orientated one to two centimetre scar** on the eyelid. The scar is not tender to palpate but remains lumpy and associated some fullness to the surrounding tissues. The prognosis is that the **scar will be scarcely visible** over time and that there will be no long term legacy.

Barry v Evans (2 October 1995, unreported) (Caroline Horton, Messrs Shoosmiths & Harrison, Fareham, for the plaintiff) (Kindly submitted for publication by Caroline Horton, Barrister).

1022 *Ears*

PSLA: (1) £8,850 (reduced from £9,500 for previous damage); (2) £6,500; (3) £5,000
Total damages: (1) £8,850 (reduced from £9,500 for previous damage); (2) £6,500; (3) £5,000
Sex: Male
Age at injury/trial: (1) 23–52/52; (2) 27–52/52; (3) 16–33/33
Date of injury/trial: (1) 1966 onwards; (2) 1970 onwards; (3) 1978 onwards/12 September 1995
Judge/court: Judge Francis/Swansea County Court

Three actions were brought by employees against the same defendant employer. Plaintiff 1 worked as a cutter/grinder from 1966 onwards, plaintiff 2 worked as a machine operator from 1970 and plaintiff 3 worked as a toolroom machinist from 1978. As a result of excessive noise exposure in the course of their employment they suffered damage to their hearing. Liability was not in dispute.

Plaintiff 1: hearing loss first became apparent about six to eight years before the trial. At the time of the trial, on the basis of the DSS formula, he was suffering an **average bilateral high tone hearing loss** of 43 decibels over 1, 2 and 3 khz, 42 decibels over 1, 2 and 4 khz and at 4 khz, 65 decibels on the right and 75 decibels on the left. His main complaints were having to **turn the television up too loud**, having **difficulty on the telephone or in social situations** where there was background noise and not going out as much as before as a result. He also suffered **mild, but constant tinnitus**. The judge said he had born in mind that continuous tinnitus is always unpleasant and harms the quality of life. General damages were assessed at £9,500 but a deduction of £650 was made in line with a specialist's attribution (by way of 'informed estimate') of 67 per cent of the defendant's hearing loss to his employment previous to that with the defendant.

Plaintiff 2: hearing loss first became apparent about five years before the trial. At the time of the trial, on the basis of the DSS formula, he was suffering an **average bilateral high tone hearing loss** of 25 decibels over 1, 2 and 3 khz, 28 decibels over 1, 2 and 4 khz and at 4 khz, 60 decibels on the right and 55 decibels on the left. His main complaints were having to **turn the television up too loud**, having **difficulty on the telephone or in social situations** where there was background noise. He also suffered **mild tinnitus**. Although describing the plaintiff as 'a genuine man' the judge expressed concern at the plaintiff's claims of a dramatic increase in the tinnitus in the months leading up to the trial and stated that it was not an easy case to assess. He assessed general damages at £6,500.

Plaintiff 3: hearing loss first became apparent about six years before the trial. At the time of the trial, on the basis of the DSS formula, he was suffering an **average bilateral high tone hearing loss** of **20 decibels both at 1, 2 and 3 khz and 1, 2 and 4 khz** and at **4 khz, 25 decibels on the right and 30 decibels on the left**. His main complaints were **not hearing his wife speaking to him** unless she was face to face with him and having **difficulty in social situations** where there was background noise. He also suffered **very mild tinnitus**. The judge said that although the disability was of the very mildest nature, the plaintiff's youth attracted an appreciably enhanced award. General damages were assessed at £5,000.

(1) *Hurlow v Ford Motor Company* (12 September 1995, unreported); (2) *Wade v Ford Motor Company* (12 September 1995, unreported); (3) *Powell v Ford Motor Company* (12 September 1995, unreported) (N Hillier, Messrs Robin Thompson & Partners, Cardiff, for the plaintiffs; A Webb, Messrs Hugh James, Jones & Jenkins, Cardiff, for the defendants) (Kindly submitted for publication by Martin Khan, Legal Executive, Messrs Robin Thompson and Partners, Solicitors).

1023 *Jaw*

PSLA: £7,500
Total damages: £8,735
Sex: Male
Age at injury/hearing: 55/63
Date of injury/hearing: 19 July 1987/28 February 1995
Court: Criminal Injuries Compensation Board, London

Applicant, a ticket collector, sustained a **fractured top jaw** in an **assault**. As a result he experienced problems with his **sinuses** and the **bones below each eye**. No fixing operation was required but he continued to experience problems, particularly with his **dentures**, which no longer fitted as well as they had before the assault. He was **off work for six weeks**, he was irritable, tense and **depressed**, he had nightmares and flashbacks of the assault, and was found to have sustained chronic 'moderate' **post traumatic stress disorder**. The above award included £1,235 loss of earnings/expenses.

Criminal Injuries Compensation Board, London (28 February 1995, unreported) (Damian Brown, Messrs Pattinson and Brewer, London, for the applicant) (Kindly submitted for publication by Damian Brown, Barrister).

PSLA: £7,000
Total damages: £7,000 (plus a small amount in respect of special damages)
Sex: Female
Age at accident/trial: 7/11
Date of accident/trial: 21 August 1990/15 November 1994
Judge/court: Deputy District Judge Collins/Southampton County Court

Plaintiff was **thrown from her bicycle** when the front wheel caught in a concrete rut. She sustained **fractures to right and left mandibular condylars**, with displacement of the right condylar head, a **full laceration** to the **chin** (measuring 3 cm) **and full thickness lacerations** to the **mucosa of the lower lip** (measuring 5 mms and caused by her upper teeth becoming imbedded in lower lip), fractures of the **upper central incisors** (involving the nerve) and fractures of the upper right and left **lateral incisors**. The laceration to the chin was thoroughly explored and **sutured** under **local anaesthetic** and, as the jaw fractures prevented her from forming a normal bite, a **soft diet** was recommended. The jaw injuries were reviewed regularly, the **fracture site involved a growth centre** and the likelihood of the plaintiff developing **degenerative joint disease** in her jaw was in the region of ten to twenty per cent. A year after the accident she was still experiencing **occasional pain** over the fracture site, she could feel a lump on her lower lip and a **scar** of two and a half cms was visible on her chin, but did not warrant surgical intervention. She underwent an **extensive programme of dental treatment** over a period of many months. Both **upper incisors were dead** and it was decided that a **root fill and closure** would be attempted. The **root canals were washed, dried and filled** with **hypocal** and the open ends of the roots closed with a calcific dentine material achieved from the whole of the hollow internal passageways inside the tooth and the roots were sealed up using a gutta percha and sealants. After this, the teeth were thought to be **sixty six per cent secure for ten years**, although it was not possible to predict whether they would fail. Further treatment was required to restore the appearance of the teeth using **bonded composite filling**, but this was delayed due to **chronic infections** in both upper central incisors and by plaintiff's reluctance to attend dentist. A small figure for special damages was also agreed in respect of damage to the bicycle and clothing.

Fraser v Southampton City Council (15 November 1994, unreported) (Messrs Bell Pope, Southampton, for the plaintiff; Messrs Payne Marsh, Southampton, for the defendant) (Kindly submitted for publication by Shaun Underhill, of Messrs Bell Pope, Solicitors).

1024   *Teeth*

PSLA: (Agreed settlement not broken down)
Total damages: £13,000
Sex: Male
Age at injury/settlement: 1 onwards/22
Date of injury/settlement: 1973 onwards/July 1994
Court: Settled out of court

As an infant the plaintiff was **prescribed the antibiotic Achromycin** (under the proprietary name Tetracycline) for the treatment of bronchitis. At the time it was well known amongst medical practitioners that Achromycin **caused discoloration of the teeth**, particularly when administered to infants. Twelve of the plaintiff's teeth were affected. They had **dark yellow-grey incremental bands** across the **facial and lingual surfaces of the incisors and canine teeth of both jaws**. The plaintiff underwent 11 visits to a dental hospital between November 1990 and March 1992 to have porcelain veneers fitted. It is likely he will have to repeat the treatment in about ten years time. He has suffered a great deal of **anxiety and distress** at school as **a result of name calling** by his peers. These jibes were directly related to his discoloured teeth. He described the treatment he underwent as long and painful. The above settlement was a total figure and was not apportioned.

Wills v Critchley (settled out of court) (Leslie Thomas, Messrs John Davies & Co, Leeds for the plaintiff; Messrs Hempsons, Manchester, for the defendant) (Kindly submitted for publication by Leslie Thomas, Barrister).

PSLA: £2,679.42
Total damages: £3,000
Sex: Female
Age at accident: 21
Date of accident: 4 January 1995
Court: Settled out of court

Plaintiff, a part time karate coach, was knocked from her bicycle by a car and landed face first on the road. She **chipped** the edge of the upper **left central incisor** and there were several **cracks in the buccal surface** of the enamel, but minimal loss of enamel. The lateral incisor was more severely damaged, with the loss of a piece of tooth (measuring two mms by one and a half mms), from the mesio-incisal angle of the tooth. The trauma to the teeth caused **severe pain** for several days, but x-rays revealed **no damage to the roots** of either tooth and, after initial filling, both teeth were later **crowned**. The long term prognosis for both teeth was uncertain since **nerve damage** could manifest itself, resulting in either tooth dying and would necessitate root canal therapy and the provision of post retained bonded crowns. Plaintiff also sustained **minor bruising** of the right knee and the lateral side of the left lower femur and grazing to the chin. The above award included £320.58 special damages.

Geard v Sukevics (unreported) (Messrs Clarke Willmott and Clarke, Bridgwater, for the plaintiff) (Kindly submitted for publication by Huw W R Ponting, of Messrs Clarke Wilmott and Clarke).

1025   *Teeth and face*

PSLA: £5,000
Total damages: £6,828.40
Sex: Male
Age at injury/trial: 32/36

Date of injury/trial: 26 January 1991/3 April 1995
Judge/court: District Judge Meredith/Torquay County Court

Plaintiff, a newsagent, was punched and kicked in the face during an attack. He sustained a **traumatic fracture** of the **upper left first premolar** and lost a huge amount of the **palatal wall** aspect of the tooth, a **black eye** and a cut to the inner surface of his left upper lip, which tended to catch on the left upper third canine. The longevity of the upper left second premolar was also prejudiced. One year after the accident, he lost the remaining buccal aspect of the upper left first premolar and part of the loose root was extracted. A month after this, he lost a substantial amount of the **palatal wall** of the upper left second premolar, a composite **resin filling** was placed with **pinned core retention** to replace the cusp and **bridge/crown** treatment was expected to be necessary for this tooth within five years. Three years after the accident, he underwent an operation to **remove the residual root** of the upper left first premolar by incision and afterwards the gum was closed with stitches. Plaintiff was left with a **linear scar of 5 cms** under his chin, which required six stitches and would be prominent and permanent. There was also a smaller 'C' shaped scar, of 3 cms, near the left upper lip, but this was only slightly visible by date of trial. Plaintiff was off work for three weeks because he was embarrassed by his injuries. The above award included £150 aggravated damages (for humiliation of assault in front of his wife and stepdaughter), £750 cost of future dental treatment and £928.40 special damages.

Edwards v Blackmore (3 April 1995, unreported) (Kevin Higgins, Messrs Hooper and Wollen, Torquay, for the plaintiff) (Kindly submitted for publication by Kevin Higgins, Barrister).

1026 *Neck*

PSLA: £9,000
Total damages: £9,869.86 (including interest)
Sex: Female
Age at accident/trial: 53/56
Date of trial: 31 March 1995
Judge/court: Judge Tetlow/Manchester County Court

Plaintiff suffered a **head injury** and a wrenching injury to her **cervical spine** when she fell in a pool of water at work and struck her head on a protruding tap. The wrenching injury aggravated pre-existing but hitherto asymptomatic **degenerative changes** and caused permanent symptoms which would not have occurred in the normal course of events. Plaintiff suffered from an **aching neck** after any manual labour such as heavy housework, knitting, ironing, and carrying heavy shopping. She was still able to take part in her **leisure activities**, but endured **pain for several hours** afterwards. She was left with **scarring** above and through the left eyebrow and by time of trial the scarring had faded, but the growth of hair was interrupted and would not grow back. She was aware of, but not embarrassed by the scar. Plaintiff also suffered from **headaches** approximately twice a week, which lasted for two to three hours. All **symptoms were permanent** and would not improve. The judge considered that the scar was significant and fell in the centre of the £1,500 to £5,000 bracket set out in the Judicial Studies Board Guidelines. The above award included £559.86 special damages and £310 interest.

Poulton v Manchester City Council (31 March 1995, unreported) (John Richard Jones, Messrs Whittles, Manchester, for the plaintiff; Kevin Donnelly, Susan Orrell of Manchester City Council Legal Department, for the defendant) (Kindly submitted for publication by John Richard Jones, Barrister).

PSLA: £8,500
Total damages: £8,500
Sex: Male
Age at accident/trial: 33/35
Date of accident/trial: July 1993/29 June 1995
Judge/court: Deputy District Judge Landen/Reading County Court

Plaintiff, a carpenter, was injured in a road traffic accident and suffered a **whiplash** type injury and **damage to the articulatory cartilage** on the back of the knee. He had just started a two-week holiday, which was ruined. He was left with **intermittent neck symptoms** and would suffer from some **discomfort every day**. Symptoms were exacerbated by the heavy work that was required in his job. The plaintiff found that lifting his young son for long periods caused discomfort in the neck and he suffered from **soreness and clicking** in the knee, especially when driving for long periods or doing skirting board work.

Doherty v Brown (29 June 1995, unreported) (Robert Weir for the plaintiff) (Kindly submitted for publication by Robert Weir, Barrister).

PSLA: £8,000
Total damages: £8,050
Sex: Female
Age at injury/trial: 43/44
Date of trial: 27 September 1995
Judge/court: District Judge Keogh/Reading County Court

Plaintiff was involved in a rear shunt road traffic accident and suffered a **whiplash injury** to the neck. She had three days off work, suffered from **unsettled sleep, headaches and extreme stiffness** for three weeks following the accident. Nine months after the accident she was still unable to carry shopping more than 200 yards, had difficulty turning her head to reverse and suffered **discomfort** when driving for more than 30 minutes and **when working with a 'mouse'** in her job as a secretary. She had become more short tempered when she was suffering from pain related to the accident and had only played tennis four times during the summer whereas she had previously played three to four times a week. Her ability to take part in aerobics classes had been affected as had her DIY activities which she now paid others to perform. The prognosis was that she would **remain symptomatic permanently**. The above award included £50 special damages for the loss of the use of her car for five days.

Fisher v Bandwidth Vehicles Rentals Ltd (27 September 1995, unreported) (Caspar Glyn for the plaintiff) (Kindly submitted for publication by Caspar Glyn, Barrister).

PSLA: £7,800 (including interest)
Total damages: £12,647 (including interest)
Sex: Male
Age at accident/trial: 48/51
Date of accident/trial: 16 March 1993/11 July 1995
Judge/court: District Judge White/Truro County Court

Plaintiff, a carpenter/joiner, was injured in a traffic accident. He suffered **serious whiplash** as well as **multiple minor injuries** to his forehead, nose, tooth, chest and right ankle. He was off work for seven weeks. He continued to suffer a **diminishing** rather than improving **range of movement** in his neck at the time of trial. Extension was 20 per cent of normal, rotation 40 per cent of normal, lateral flexion 20 per cent of normal. He suffered frontal headaches and had great difficulty in looking up. This prevented him from working at heights or on cranes, although this did not really affect his income. The above award, made on the basis of full liability, included £4,847 special damages (including interest) and £300 interest on the general damages. The total award was reduced by 15 per cent for contributory negligence.

Winfindale v Roberts (17 July 1995, unreported) (Robert Alford for the plaintiff) (Kindly submitted for publication by Robert Alford, Barrister).

PSLA: £6,500
Total damages: £7,237 (including interest)
Sex: Female
Age at accident/trial: 45/49
Date of accident/trial: 28 February 1992/20 October 1995
Judge/Court: Judge Bray/Birmingham County Court

Plaintiff was the driver of a car which was struck from behind while stationary. There were two separate impacts. She sustained bruising to the anterior chest wall, caused by wearing a seat belt, which had resolved within two months of the accident. More seriously, she also sustained a **whiplash injury to her neck**. She had an immediate feeling of tightness across her chest and had difficulty in breathing. Later on the same day she developed stiffness and increasing pain at the back of her neck, together with a headache. Plaintiff **wore soft and hard collars for about two months**. Her sleep was disturbed most nights. Three courses of physiotherapy have led to a **moderate alleviation of pain**. At trial plaintiff stated she had not had a day since the accident when she had been free of pain. She experienced **constant pain down the left side of the neck** with a feeling of crushing and grinding when moving the neck. Pain radiates down the left side of the body and occasionally she gets a feeling of dragging in the left leg and tingling in the left arm. She also suffers from occipital headaches. **Rotation of the neck to the left is half of normal and to the right is three quarters of normal**. She has difficulty in carrying out household chores and is no longer able to garden, a hobby which had been her pride and joy. Other pastimes have also been affected. **Plaintiff had suffered from cervical spondylosis at C5/6 and C6/7 for approximately 10 years prior to the accident** which had caused neck pain and restriction of movement. The judge accepted the plaintiff's medical evidence that the accident had accelerated her condition by a period of five years. The above award included special damages of £507.78 and interest.

    Bond v West Midlands Travel Ltd (20 October 1995, unreported) (Stephen Murray, Messrs Sydney Mitchell, Birmingham, for the plaintiff, Stuart Clarkson, Messrs Maurice Putsman & Co) (Kindly submitted for publication by Stephen Murray, Barrister).

PSLA: £4,500
Total damages: £4,682.60
Sex: Male
Age at accident/trial: 15/17
Date of trial: 23 November 1994
Judge/court: Judge Bernstein/Southport County Court

Plaintiff was a front seat passenger in a car involved in a road traffic accident. He suffered a **strained neck** and a **strain, bruising and swelling to his right shoulder**. The bruising and swelling resolved quickly and he wore a **sling**, on and off for six weeks. He underwent **physiotherapy for ten weeks** and later, for another three weeks, but he has been left with a permanent residual discomfort of a minor nature in his neck. The above award included special damages of £40 and interest of £142.60.

    Brown v Ledson (23 November 1994, unreported) (Antonis Georges, Messrs Coyne Learmonth, Crosby, for the plaintiff; Simon Gorton, Messrs Percy Hughes and Roberts, Birkenhead, for the defendant) (Kindly submitted for publication by Antonis Georges, Barrister).

PSLA: £4,500
Total damages: £4,500
Sex: Female
Age at accident/settlement: 50/51
Date of accident: 30 September 1993

Plaintiff was a **passenger in a coach** which crashed in Spain. She sustained whiplash type **soft tissue injuries** to the neck and minor aching in the lower legs. Both of these injuries were expected to settle within two years. Her **long-standing psychological anxiety state** for which she had been treated many times over the preceding 23 years was exacerbated requiring an increase in her dosage of diazepam from 2 mg per week to 6mg per day. There were no special damages.

    Flaherty v Acron Travel (settled out of court) (David Kenny, Messrs Stephensons, St Helens for the plaintiff; Norwich Union Insurance for the defendant) (Kindly submitted for publication by Sheryl Rigby, Messrs Stephensons, Solicitors).

PSLA: £4,000
Total damages: £5,241.36 (reduced to £1,747.12 due to plaintiff's contributory negligence)
Sex: Female
Age at accident/trial: 37/38
Date of accident/trial: 22 February 1994/21 November 1995
Judge/court: Judge Catlin/Reading County Court

Plaintiff was injured in a road traffic accident. She sustained **bruising to her chest** which made **breathing difficult and painful** for two days. She also received a whiplash injury to her neck which resulted in her taking **11 weeks off work**. A year after the accident she suffered **only intermittent pain** and could go a few days at a time without any symptoms. The prognosis was that she would be **largely recovered two years after the accident**. Before the accident the plaintiff had suffered from **migraine headaches**. After the accident she suffered from an **increased frequency** of these headaches for a year. The above award included £1,241.36 special damages and was reduced due to the plaintiff's two thirds contributory negligence.

    Brinkworth v Payne & Co (21 November 1995, unreported) (Rob Weir, Shoosmiths & Harrison, Reading, for the plaintiff, Cole & Cole, Reading for the defendant) (Kindly submitted for publication by Rob Weir, Barrister).

PSLA: £3,500
Total damages: £3,500
Sex: Female
Age at accident/trial: 29/31
Date of accident/trial: November 1993/10 March 1995
Judge/court: District Judge Payne/Reading County Court

Plaintiff sustained a whiplash injury in a road traffic accident. Initially her neck was stiff and she had a very **severe headache** for 72 hours. She was given a **cervical collar**, which she wore intermittently for four weeks and she underwent three painful courses of **physiotherapy** with manipulations. All the neck symptoms had resolved within three to four weeks. One week after the accident, she developed a **low backache**, which she described as a nuisance. Plaintiff also found sleeping difficult for a few weeks after the accident, she was **off work for two weeks** and for some months she could not push her younger child in his pushchair and had to be careful when gardening and doing household tasks. She found that sitting in one position for an hour or so brought on the back pain, which would last for one to two hours. These symptoms were ongoing at date of trial and the prognosis was that the symptoms would resolve themselves within a year. Plaintiff was very shaken and upset by the accident, the stress affected her **menstrual cycle** and her first two periods after the accident were very **heavy and painful**, particularly in the pelvic area. For a long time after the accident, she was nervous and panicky when driving, but by the date of trial she was suffering from such **panic attacks** only occasionally and the prognosis was that this would settle in due course.

Pollard v Blackman (10 March 1995, unreported) (Robert Weir, Messrs Shoosmiths and Harrison, Reading, for the plaintiff) (Kindly submitted for publication by Robert Weir, Barrister).

PSLA: £2,700
Total damages: £6,380.20
Sex: Female
Age at accident/trial: 37/38
Date of accident/trial: February 1994/3 February 1995
Judge/court: Deputy District Judge Stary/Epsom County Court

Plaintiff suffered a **mild whiplash injury** to her neck and an injury to her left shoulder as a result of a road traffic accident. For a week after the accident she was unable to do any housework or shopping. By the following week her symptoms had improved, but she continued to take **analgesics** regularly, her **sleep was disturbed** and she suffered from nightmares. At time of trial, she was still suffering from **occasional twinges** and **stiffness** in her neck. The above award included £3,365.80 special damages and £314.40 interest.

Paul v Payne (3 February 1995, unreported) (Nicola Braganza, Messrs Coleman and Tilley, Surbiton, for the plaintiff) (Kindly submitted for publication by Nicola Braganza, Barrister).

PSLA: £2,500
Total damages: £2,500
Sex: Female
Age at injury/settlement: 15/16
Date of injury/settlement:11 October 1994/8 August 1995
Judge/court: District Judge Slim/Halifax County Court

Plaintiff was struck by a vehicle. She suffered **pain in her neck and right shoulder** and was off school for a week. She would usually ride her horse five times a week but was unable to ride for three months and continued to have some aching in the shoulder, especially in cold weather, for about six months. This was expected to ease within the following six to twelve months. The settlement was approved by the judge.

Pearce v Abraham Shaw & Co (unreported) (Messrs Rhodes Thain & Collinson, Halifax, for the plaintiff) (Kindly submitted for publication by Allan Western, Messrs Rhodes Thain & Collinson, Solicitors).

PSLA: £1,500
Total damages: £1,500
Sex: Male
Age at accident/trial: 39/40
Date of accident/trial: 18 March 1994/7 March 1995
Judge/court: District Judge James/Blackpool County Court

Plaintiff, a plumber, sustained a **hyperextension/flexion injury** to his **cervical spine** in a road traffic accident. He had a **constant ache** in his neck, he was **off work for two weeks** and his hobbies of badminton, motorcycling and swimming were curtailed. The pain lasted for **six months** and thereafter he had no symptoms except **occasional stiffness** in cold weather.

Hemsley v Hesketh (7 March 1995, unreported) (Karl Rowley, Messrs Boote Edgar Esterkin, Manchester, for the plaintiff) (Kindly submitted for publication by Karl Rowley, Pupil Barrister).

PSLA: £1,500
Total damages: £1,802.13
Sex: Female
Age at injury/trial: 44/45
Date of injury/trial:—/19 June 1995
Judge/Court: Judge Hedley/Liverpool County Court

Plaintiff was driving along motorway when window of a bus was blown out and struck her car. She made an emergency stop suffering a **whiplash-type** injury and **sprained ankle**. The shock and distress caused a flare up of **psoriasis** and she was **unable to shop** for two weeks. The plaintiff only visited her doctor on a couple of occasions and was driving again two days after the accident. The above award included £802.13 special damages.

Sharp v MTL Trust Holdings Ltd (19 June 1995, unreported) (Antonis Georges, Canter, Levin & Berg, of Kirkby, for the plaintiff) (Kindly submitted for publication by Antonis Georges, Barrister).

PSLA: £1,500
Total damages: £1,500
Sex: Male
Age at accident/trial: 20/22
Date of trial: 18 August 1995
Judge/court: District Judge Davidson/Reading County Court

In a road traffic accident plaintiff suffered **forced flexion of his neck** followed by **forced extension**. He received no medical attention. Plaintiff was shocked and dazed for an hour after the accident and developed a **slight neck ache** which lasted for almost a week. He suffered **bouts of disturbed sleep and crying** which also lasted for a week. He had a phobia of driving for several days and repeatedly had episodes during the day and night where he suddenly **saw headlights coming straight towards him**. After one week the phobia was slight save at roundabouts. After ten weeks the plaintiff had **made a full recovery**.

Hindle v Briggs (18 August 1995, unreported) (Caspar Glyn, for the plaintiff) (Kindly submitted for publication by Caspar Glyn, Barrister).

PSLA: £1,500
Total damages: £1,611.98
Sex: Female
Age at accident/trial: 16/17
Date of accident/trial: 22 January 1995/15 December 1995
Judge/court: District Judge Tennant/Southampton County Court

Plaintiff was a front seat passenger in a vehicle involved in a **road traffic accident**. Immediately after impact the plaintiff experienced **sudden pain in her neck** which radiated into her **left shoulder**. The plaintiff suffered **contusion of her left shoulder** and **whiplash type soft tissue injury to the cervical spine**. The injuries caused **acute pain** in the neck for two weeks and in the left shoulder for three weeks. The plaintiff continued to experience **intermittent neck ache** on average once every other week which lasted up to one day. The discomfort occurred unpredictably. The left shoulder felt painful if the plaintiff attempted any heavy lifting activities but at other times she had no symptoms. At the time of the hearing the plaintiff still experienced intermittent ache in the neck and the shoulder. The award included £111.98 special damages.

Scaife v Griffiths (15 December 1995, unreported) (Shaun Underhill, Messrs Bell Pope, Southampton, for the plaintiff) (Kindly submitted for publication by Shaun Underhill, of Messrs Bell Pope, Solicitors).

PSLA: £1,250
Total damages: £1,257.67 (including £7.67 interest)
Sex: Male
Age at accident/trial: 26/27
Date of accident/trial: 25 April 1994/20 June 1995
Judge/court: District Judge Jolly/Reading County Court

Plaintiff, a teacher, suffered a **hyperextension/flexion** injury to his cervical spine and **a mild blow to his right knee** in a road traffic accident. He attended the accident and emergency department where examination revealed a **slightly palpable spasm** in the right posterior region of the neck. He was given a soft collar which he wore for two days. The pain eased gradually over the next 7 days but the plaintiff experienced a slight twinge on the right side of his neck occasionally every two to three months on waking or making sudden movements. After the accident he was **shocked and nauseous for 2 hours**. He was off work for a week and was unable to coach or play rugby.

Bass v Medley (20 June 1995, unreported) (Caroline Horton, Messrs Shoosmiths and Harrison, Reading for the plaintiff; defendant not present) (Kindly submitted for publication by Caroline Horton, Messrs Shoosmiths and Harrison, Solicitors).

PSLA: £1,250
Total damages: £1,250
Sex: Male
Age at assault/hearing: 44/47
Date of assault/hearing: 13 August 1992/2 November 1995
Court: Criminal Injuries Compensation Board, Cardiff

Applicant, a nurse, **suffered lacerations to the neck** whilst in the process of restraining a patient. The laceration was **1.5 centimetres long** and had **penetrated the platysma muscle**. He received **four stitches** and underwent a course of antibiotics. The applicant took **no time off work** and the wound **healed within seven days**. He has been left with a **prominent scar**. The Board also took into consideration the **minor anxiety** the applicant had of contracting a virus.

Criminal Injuries Compensation Board, Cardiff (2 November 1995, unreported) (Messrs Robin Thompson & Partners, Cardiff, for the applicant) (Kindly submitted for publication by Jason Smith, Messrs Robin Thompson & Partners, Solicitors).

PSLA: £1,100
Total damages: £1,223.24
Sex: Male
Age at injury/trial: 32/33
Date of injury/trial: 22 November 1994/11 May 1995
Judge/Court: District Judge Frost/Birkenhead County Court

Plaintiff suffered **whiplash to the cervical spine** and was in severe pain for **a week to ten days**. He has made a full recovery. The above award included £1,100 general damages (plus interest of £4.58), £15 for inconvenience and special damages of £103.66.

Flaherty v Catley (11 May 1995, unreported) (Michael Pickavance, Messrs Michael W Halsall, Merseyside, for the plaintiff) (Kindly submitted for publication by Messrs Michael W Halsall, Solicitors).

PSLA: £900
Total damages: £900
Sex: Male
Age at accident/trial: 33/34
Date of accident/trial: 23 June 1995/28 November 1995
Judge/court: Judge Trigger/Birkenhead County Court

Plaintiff was involved in a **road traffic accident** and sustained a **whiplash** type injury, **bruising** and **injury to his back**. He was moderately **shocked and shaken** three to four hours after the accident. The plaintiff had **mild, persistent central low back pain** for seven hours after the accident which became **severe and persistent** for three to four days. The **pain was moderate and intermittent** thereafter. The plaintiff was unable to carry out his work as a self employed courier because of his injuries. He was anxious when travelling in cars and received four sessions of **physiotherapy** to treat his intermittent central low back pain. The plaintiff's neck symptoms resolved within six to eight weeks of the accident and at the time of the trial, the symptoms were fully resolved.

Jones v Mercury Communications Ltd (28 November 1995, unreported) (Gordon Bellis, Messrs Michael W Halsall, for the plaintiff) (Kindly submitted for publication by Messrs Michael W Halsall, Solicitors).

PSLA: £750
Total damages: £750
Sex: Male
Age at accident/trial: 15
Date of accident/trial: 9 August 1993/20 April 1995
Judge/court: Deputy District Judge Lloyd-Davies/Exeter County Court

Plaintiff sustained a **minor whiplash injury** as a result of a road traffic accident. He suffered pain in his cervical spine and lower back, but had **full mobility** in his **lumbar spine** and no symptoms in his legs. Plaintiff was unable to take part in school sports for one week, and ten days after the accident he experienced **pain** in the left side of his lower back whilst jogging. He was advised to **rest for two weeks** and after this, was able to return to sporting activities with **no further problems**. Medical evidence at trial confirmed that there was little chance of sequelae.

Paxton v Newman (20 April 1995, unreported) (Messrs Bevan Ashford, Exeter, for the plaintiff) (Kindly submitted for publication by Damian Horan, Barrister, of Messrs Bevan Ashford).

PSLA: £650
Total damages: £7,600
Sex: Male
Age at accident/trial: 24/25
Date of accident/trial: 24 January 1994/20 February 1995
Judge/court: Judge Sumner/Wandsworth County Court

Plaintiff was involved in a road traffic accident and sustained a **whiplash injury** to his **cervical spine**. He suffered **slight pain** at time of accident, but by the following day there was considerable **tenderness**, pain and **limitation of movement** over much of his neck and the back of his head. Medical examination revealed tenderness along both sides of the cervical spine and over the **occiput**, there was **no bruising**, but there was some limitation of movement. These symptoms resolved gradually over the next two to three weeks and by four weeks after the accident, plaintiff had **fully recovered**. **No lasting problems** were expected, plaintiff had not taken any time off work and his **pre-accident hobbies were unaffected**. The above award included £5,200 special damages and £1,750 loss of use of car.

Ballard v Digital Equipment Corpn (20 February 1995, unreported) (Richard Booth, Messrs Laurence Kingsley, New Malden, for the plaintiff; Erica Power, Messrs Wyeth and Co, for the defendant) (Kindly submitted for publication by Richard Booth, Barrister).

PSLA: £600
Total damages: £1,157.55
Sex: Female
Age at accident/trial: 26/28
Date of accident/trial: 14 December 1993/25 May 1995
Judge/court: District Judge Jolly/Reading County Court

Plaintiff suffered a **hyperextension/flexion** injury to her **cervical spine** in a road traffic accident. The evening after the accident she had a **pain in her neck**, over her **right shoulder** where the seat belt had been and to a lesser extent in her **lower lumbar spine**. She attended the accident and emergency department where x-rays appeared normal and she was advised to rest. The pain continued for three days during which time the plaintiff found it difficult to sit or stand for long periods. The symptoms **ceased completely within seven months**. She was off work for three days and was unable to do housework, missed her weekly aerobics class and two evening classes where she was studying for a diploma. The above award included £459.48 special damages, £45 for loss of use of car and £54.07 interest.

Farmer v Rylance (23 May 1995, unreported) (Caroline Horton, Messrs Shoosmiths and Harrison, Reading for the plaintiff; defendant not present) (Kindly submitted for publication by Caroline Horton, Messrs Shoosmiths and Harrison, Solicitors).

PSLA: £500
Total damages: £500.65
Sex: Male
Age at injury/trial: 22/22
Date of injury/trial: 28 December 1994/8 June 1995
Judge/Court: Judge Bernstein/Birkenhead County Court

Plaintiff suffered **whiplash injury** in road traffic accident. Suffered **moderate pain** for **two weeks**. He has made a full recovery. he suffered 24 hours of general shock and was apprehensive about driving. The above award included £500 general damages and special damages of £36.65 including interest.

Nettleton v Wright (8 June 1995, unreported) (Gordon Bellis, for the plaintiff) (Kindly submitted for publication by Messrs Michael W Halsall, Solicitors).

PSLA: £500
Total damages: £1,083.90 (including interest)
Sex: Female
Age at accident/trial: 38/39
Date of accident/trial: 8 July 1993/24 October 1995
Judge/court: District Judge McCullagh/Birkenhead County Court

Plaintiff was involved in a road traffic accident when her vehicle was struck in the rear by another vehicle. She sustained a **flexion hypertension injury** to her **cervical spine** causing pain and stiffness which lasted for **8 days**. She took **one day off work**. The above award included special damages of £583.90 including interest.

Yates v Dowdeswell (24 October 1995, unreported) (Andrew Menary, Messrs Michael W Halsall, Maghull, for the plaintiff; defendant in person) (Kindly submitted for publication by Messrs Michael W Halsall, Solicitors).

1027   *Neck and shoulder*

PSLA: £2,200
Total damages: £2,200
Sex: Female
Age at accident/settlement: 47/48
Court: Settled out of court

Plaintiff, a front seat passenger wearing a seat belt, was involved in a road traffic accident. She suffered immediate **chest pains** and later developed **neck and shoulder pains**, for which she was prescribed a **surgical collar** and **analgesics**. Shortly after the accident, she underwent **acupuncture** treatment to alleviate the pain and this was moderately successful. At time of settlement, pain was only occasional and a full recovery was expected some 15 to 18 months after the accident.

Johnson v Fairclough (unreported) (Messrs Stephensons, St Helens, for the plaintiff) (Kindly submitted for publication by Sheryl Rigby of Stephensons, Solicitors).

1028   *Neck and back*

PSLA: £7,500
Total damages: £7,902.58 (plus interest)
Sex: Female
Age at accident: 52
Date of accident/trial: 30 March 1992/23 August 1994
Judge/court: Judge Paynter Reece/Romford County Court

Plaintiff **injured her neck and back** in a road traffic accident. Immediately afterwards, she complained of **neck pain** and over the following twenty-four hours the **pain spread to her lower back and right arm** and she experienced **tingling and loss of sensation** in the fingers of her right hand. She attended hospital the next day, but made no complaint about the back pain, thinking that it was linked to the severe neck pain. She was prescribed **analgesics**, she wore a **hard collar** for three days and thereafter wore a **soft collar** for three months and had **physiotherapy** for six weeks. She was **off work for four weeks** and was **unable to drive** for six weeks. Three months after the accident, the back pain became worse and she developed

sciatica. Some nine months later, the pain became severe after an incident when she bent down to pick up the telephone. She spent two weeks at home in bed and was again prescribed analgesics and physiotherapy. She was referred to the **orthopaedic department** and pre-existing **degeneration** at L 4/5 was observed. At time of trial, she was still **unable to continue her pre-accident hobbies** of yoga, keep fit and swimming and required help with housework. The neck and back pain were **unlikely to improve**, the symptoms will recur and a collar will be necessary from time to time. The judge held that, although the plaintiff had no pre-accident history of back complaints, the back injury probably arose coincidentally with the accident and in making the award, the judge made some allowance for this pre-existing degeneration. The above award included £402.58 special damages.

Sachs v Harvey (23 August 1994, unreported) (Pip Punwar, Messrs E Edwards Son and Noice, Ilford, for the plaintiff) (Kindly submitted for publication by Pip Punwar, Barrister).

PSLA: £1,500 (plus £15 interest)
Total damages: £4,908.10 (including interest)
Sex: Male
Age at accident/trial: 73/74
Date of accident/trial: 2 October 1994/28 September 1995
Judge/court: Judge Crowe QC/Birkenhead County Court

Plaintiff was involved in a road traffic accident and suffered a **whiplash type injury** together with **jarring to his lower back**. He took analgesics. His neck and back ached **severely for one day** and then **moderately for two weeks**. He became **physically symptom free six weeks after** the accident. He was, however, **emotionally shaken and upset**, which residual psychological symptoms lasted **ten months**. The above award included £3,408.10 special damages including loss of use and interest.

Stimson v Williams (28 September 1995, unreported) (Nigel Lawrence, Messrs Michael W Halsall, Maghull, for the plaintiff; no appearance for the defendants) (Kindly submitted for publication by Messrs Michael W Halsall, Solicitors).

PSLA: £1,000
Total damages: £1,110
Sex: Female
Age at accident/trial: 27/27
Date of accident/trial:1 March 1995/17 August 1995
Judge/court: District Judge Frost/Birkenhead County Court

Plaintiff was involved in a road traffic accident and suffered a **whiplash type injury**. She took extra Co-proxamol for a week, having already been prescribed it for a **pre-existing lower back complaint**. On the morning after the accident she developed **moderate pain and stiffness** in the centre of her back and neck, which spread to the top of both shoulders. This pain became **mild and episodic after a week**. Although some activities which formed part of her employment as a barmaid aggravated the injury, she was completely **symptom free three months after** the accident. The above award included £110 special damages.

Wilson v Fenlon (17 August 1995, unreported) (Rob Altham, Messrs Michael Halsall, Maghull, for the plaintiff; no appearance for the defendants) (Kindly submitted for publication by Messrs Michael W Halsall, Solicitors).

1029   Neck and hip
PSLA: £4,717.50 (including interest)
Total damages: £4,717.50 (including interest)
Sex: Female
Age at injury/trial: 46/48
Date of injury/trial: 12 February 1992/18 May 1995
Judge/court: District Judge Geddes/Blackburn County Court

Plaintiff, a self-employed matron of a nursing home, sustained **soft tissue wrenching injuries** to her **neck and hip** joint regions in a road traffic accident. Immediately after the accident, she developed a headache and a feeling of stiffness in her neck, particularly on the left side and down to the left shoulder. She was not given a cervical collar, had no physiotherapy and, because she was self-employed, she could not take time off work. Five months after the accident, she was still suffering from a slight pulling sensation at the back of her neck and although she had full movement in her left hip, there was **pain at extremes of movement**, particularly on abduction and maximum flexion. Ten months after the accident, her neck **ached and felt stiff** in cold weather and when turned maximally or held in a flexed position for any length of time and the left hip was also painful when abducted or rotated maximally. There was **no indication of pre-existing degenerative change** in neck or hip joints and she was able to take part in aerobics, albeit with some discomfort in the hip. It was thought that her **symptoms would persist** for the foreseeable future, but would probably decrease marginally over time, although she would never be completely free of discomfort. Plaintiff also suffered from post traumatic stress disorder for two to three years. At time of trial all of her problems were lessening.

Re Shakespeare (18 May 1995, unreported) (Barrie Searle, Messrs Ramsbottom and Co, Darwen, for the plaintiff) (Kindly submitted for publication by Barrie Searle, Barrister).

1030   *Shoulder*

PSLA: £12,500
Total damages: £103,418.48
Sex: Male
Age at accident/trial: 40/45
Date of accident/trial: 7 September 1990/12 April 1995
Earnings multiplier: 10
Judge/court: Judge Pitchford/Cardiff County Court

Plaintiff, an RAF airframe fitter, was involved in a motorcycle accident in which he sustained a **fractured right humerus** (with insertion of the rotator cuff muscles into the humeral head affected), injuries to his neck, lumbar back, left knee and damage to and loss of teeth. Plaintiff underwent several operations on his right shoulder, including **manipulative operations** and an **arthroscopy** to remove particles of **bone debris**. There was wasting of the **infraspinatus muscle** and severe **restriction of external rotation** of shoulder, with **90 per cent loss of movement** (internal rotation was normal and he had a 0 to 90 degrees range of movement in abduction of the right shoulder). Plaintiff was left with a **permanent partial incapacity** in his right shoulder, a **considerable scar** at the injury site and two small scars at the back of his shoulder as a result of the arthroscopy. The other injuries resolved over a period of three to four years. One year after the accident, he returned to work on light duties, but was unable to return to his pre-accident job because the restriction of movement in his right shoulder prevented him from carrying out heavy work overhead. His **employment terminated** four years after the accident and he was left at a disadvantage on the open labour market, however it was recognised that he had a fairly good chance of obtaining lighter work in the aviation industry, although he would be more likely to be made redundant. Liability was not in dispute. The above award included £3,500 loss of congenial employment, £2,859 pension loss, £21,617.14 past loss of earnings, £15,545.40 to compensate during job search period for an 18-month duration (multiplied by an annual salary of £10,363.60), £17,251 future partial loss of earnings (£1,725 with a multiplier of 10), £25,909 *Smith v Manchester* award (£10,363.60 using a multiplier of 2.5), £580 miscellaneous expenses and recompense for the motorcycle, £3,656.94 interest on general and special damages.

Mills v Morris Motorcycles (a Firm) (12 April 1995, unreported) (Neil Bidder, Messrs Robin Thompson and Partners, Cardiff, for the plaintiff; Andrew Keyser for the defendant) (Kindly submitted for publication by Martin S Khan, Legal Executive, of Robin Thompson and Partners, Solicitors).

PSLA: £3,250
Total damages: £5,371 (plus interest and subject to 25 per cent reduction in respect of contributory negligence)
Sex: Male
Age at accident/trial: 24/28
Date of trial: 11 April 1995
Judge/court: Judge Ward/Exeter County Court

Plaintiff, a self-employed decorator and artexer, sustained a **partial subluxation** of his right (dominant) **acromio-clavicular joint** and some superficial **grazing** to that shoulder and both knees in a road traffic accident. His right arm was placed in a **sling**, which he wore for about a month and he was **unable to work for five weeks**. Thereafter he experienced some **difficulty at work**, but after about three months, there was only some aching in the right shoulder when **working overhead**, although this would quickly cease if he held his arm by his side. There was a **prominent end to the right clavicle**, but **no restriction of movement** in his shoulder. Prognosis was that he would continue to suffer pain when working overhead, but there was little risk of him developing increased symptoms due to future onset of arthritis. Plaintiff was unable to return to his previous sporting activities of karate and weight training for some considerable period of time after the accident. The above award included agreed special damages of £2,121.

Blanche v Brown (11 April 1995, unreported) (Marisa Smith, Messrs McKenzie and Chester, Exeter, for the plaintiff; Jonathan Hand, Messrs Wolferstans, Plymouth, for the defendant) (Kindly submitted for publication by Jonathan Hand, Barrister).

1031 *Back*

PSLA: £22,500
Total damages: £199,652.18
Sex: Female
Age at accident/trial: 23/29
Date of accident/trial: 18 January 1988/12 October 1994
Earnings multiplier: 12
Judge/court: Steyn and Hirst LJJ/Court of Appeal

Plaintiff, a care assistant at an old persons residential home, **injured her back** whilst lifting a patient. The next morning her back was very stiff and painful, she returned to work, but was sent home, has been unable to work since then and is now **severely disabled**. An **epidural injection** one month after the accident and treatment from a **chiropractor**, a **physiotherapist** and an **acupuncturist** failed to reduce the pain. Two years after the accident, she underwent an **MRI scan**, which revealed a **disc derangement** and **annular tear** at L5/S1. This was confirmed by a discogram and some nine months later, she underwent a **spinal fusion operation** to implant a **carbon fibre device at L5/S1** disc space. This was held in place with three screws and a **bone graft** was taken from the right iliac crest. Plaintiff was left with a **scar of 21 cms** across her abdomen and was in hospital for ten days. Despite some improvement immediately following the operation, she soon returned to her pre-operative state. There was **no pre-accident history of back pain** or degenerative disorder and the court was in agreement that plaintiff's present condition was entirely attributable to the accident. Plaintiff **walks with a stick**, she can only sit or stand for short periods, her **sleep is disturbed**, she cannot bend down, is **unable to lift** heavy objects and requires help with housework. She has given up her hobbies of disco dancing, aerobics, hiking and gardening and her social life has been curtailed. Plaintiff's sexual life has also been severely affected and, although her husband and herself wish to have children, and there is no clinical reason for her not to do so, this will be considerably more painful than is usual and delivery would almost certainly be by **caesarean section**. Plaintiff would never be able to return to her pre-accident employment. Appeal by defendants against award of general damages dismissed on the ground that the trial judge was correct in viewing the case as serious because the spinal fusion was not successful in alleviating the pain, thus leaving plaintiff with a very significant long term disability, and that the sexual malfunction and unsightly scarring were particularly serious for a young married woman. Appeal in respect of multiplier of 22 for continuing miscellaneous items such as assistance with housework, extra cost of petrol, prescription charges, etc allowed and multiplier reduced to 18.

McIlgrew v Devon County Council (12 October 1994, unreported) (Vivienne Gay, Messrs Brian Thompson and Partners, London, for the plaintiff; William Coley, Messrs Wray Smith and Co, London, for the defendant). Also reported at [1995] PIQR Q66.

PSLA: £20,000 (including £5,000 for separate injury to dominant hand in accident caused by same defendants)
Total damages: £162,727.16 (including interest)
Sex: Male
Age at injury/trial: 47/51
Date of injury/trial: August 1991/6 June 1995
Earnings multiplier: 6
Judge/Court: Judge Calman QC/Mayor's and City of London County Court

Plaintiff, a foreman installer of heavy duty photocopiers, was injured when a team-mate unexpectedly dropped his corner of a 7 cwt scissor table, causing plaintiff to take load. Suffered **low lumbar soft tissue injury** causing **chronic and severe low backache** at L5/S1 level. **No physiological cause** for the pain could be found but the judge accepted evidence of doctors and plaintiff that it was genuine, permanently disabling and not caused by earlier fracture of L1 and L4. Plaintiff was unable to bend forward or sideways without pain and was unable to sit, drive or stand for more than a few minutes without pain. Hobbies of golf, badminton, gardening and DIY restricted. Plaintiff had not worked since accident and would not be able to do any work involving lifting or bending. Judge accepted he might never work again. Earnings multiplier of 10 reduced to 6 to reflect risks of osteoarthritis from earlier accident, possibility of retraining and future employment and risk that plaintiff might have in any event lost employment in the future. The above award comprised £20,000 for pain, suffering and loss of amenity, special damages of £52,836.16 (including loss of earnings from date of accident and interest) and £86,100 for future loss of earnings.

Scott v BVS International Ltd (6 June 1995, unreported) (Simon Michael, for the plaintiff) (Kindly submitted for publication by Simon Michael, Barrister).

PSLA: £15,000
Total damages: £73,000
Sex: Female
Age at accident/trial: 36/40
Date of accident/trial: December 1989/22 November 1994
Earnings multiplier: 10
Judge/court: Nourse and Henry LJJ, Sir John Megaw/Court of Appeal

Plaintiff suffered a very painful **lower back injury** due to the defendant's **negligence**. **Discectomy and fusion**, a major surgical process, could resolve the problems but there was a small risk that surgery might leave her in a worse position and **possibly severely incapacitate her**. She was not prepared to take that risk while her children, aged 9 and 11 years at the date of the trial, were young but was prepared to **consider surgery in five or six years' time**. The judge took account of what the operation could achieve, the chances of success and the risks attached to it and whether and when she would or might agree to it. An award of £15,000 was made for pain, suffering and loss of amenity and the judge set the multiplier for future losses at 10, bearing in mind whether there would be an operation and if it would be successful, whether the plaintiff would work again and whether degenerative changes in her back would develop to shorten her working life. On appeal, the defendant contended that (1) the judge should have found that the plaintiff ought to have the discectomy and fusion operation in five to six years' time whatever her fears then were, and (2) that on that basis the multiplier for loss of earnings would be not more than five or six. *Held*, the judgment revealed no error of principle or misapprehension of the factual evidence and the judge's conclusions could not be faulted. Accordingly, the appeal would be dismissed.

Thomas v Bath District Health Authority [1995] PIQR Q19 (Court of Appeal: Nourse and Henry LJJ and Sir John Megaw).

PSLA: £12,000
Total damages: £19,023
Sex: Male
Age at accident/trial: 24/29
Date of trial: 9 January 1995
Judge/court: Deputy District Judge Mort/Burton-upon-Trent County Court

Plaintiff, steel erector, **fell 30 feet** from a partially constructed roof. He was **in hospital for three weeks** and sustained significant **crush fractures** to the fifth, eighth and ninth thoracic vertebrae. He also suffered an injury to the **right knee joint**, from which he subsequently made a full recovery. He experienced **tenderness over the dorsal spine**, prolonged backache, developed **psoriasis** and suffered occasional discomfort at night, when driving and when bending. He was also unable to walk for more than half a mile and could not cope with difficult terrain, he was distressed that his **weight had increased significantly** and, at time of trial, he continued to suffer chronic **residual low back pain**. Medical evidence suggested that these symptoms would continue for a finite period. Plaintiff had to **retrain as a clerical officer** with the benefits agency, a job which gave him less satisfaction and income than his previous occupation. The injury also affected his ability to play football, cricket, squash and tennis. The above award included £3,510 special damages, £1,800 *Smith v Manchester* award and £1,713 interest.

Leech v Ward (9 January 1995, unreported) (Stuart R Yeung, Messrs Glandfield and Cruddas, Uttoxeter, for the plaintiff) (Kindly submitted for publication by Stuart R Yeung, Barrister).

PSLA: £6,800
Total damages: £10,154 (including interest)
Sex: Female
Age at trial: 29
Date of accident/trial: October 1990/15 April 1995
Judge/court: District Judge Bolton/Bristol County Court

Plaintiff, a cleaner, was injured in a road accident. She initially sustained **minor whiplash**, a **blow to the head**, shock and a degree of vomiting. Eight weeks later she experienced the onset of **low back pain**. At the time of the trial she continued to suffer the following: intermittent low back pain with severe bouts at a frequency of two to three times a month; dull but constant back ache; intermittent anterior hip pain and right posterior calf to heal pain. She was diagnosed as suffering from **lumbro-sacro dysfunction** and **chronic right sacro-iliac joint strain**. She would never be symptom free but the pain would diminish over three to five years. The above award included £2,765 special damages and interest.

Downer v Murray (15 April 1995, unreported) (Messrs Henriques Griffiths, Bristol for the plaintiff) (Kindly submitted for publication by Hector Stamboulieh, Solicitor, of Messrs Henriques Griffiths, Solicitors).

PSLA: £6,500
Total damages: £6,500
Sex: Male
Age at trial: 51
Date of accident/trial: 27 November 1991/25 November 1994
Judge/court: Assistant Recorder Crowley/Cardiff County Court

Plaintiff, a works supervisor, **injured his back** when he tripped and **fell down some metal stairs** at his place of work. He was able to get up immediately, but the fall was painful and he was shaken. The back **pain became increasingly worse** in the year following the accident and at time of trial, he was still suffering from pain, **discomfort and stiffness** in his back. The accident had a considerable effect on the plaintiff's **quality of life**, he **gained weight** as a result of giving up his hobbies of long-distance and marathon running and stopped watching and coaching rugby, gardening and doing home decoration. Prior to the accident, he had suffered from **occasional mechanical back pain**, which was mild in nature and kept easily under control with analgesics. However, the judge found that the fall had **exacerbated this condition** which, in his view, would through gradual deterioration, have lead to the plaintiff's present condition within five years. In his assessment of damages, the judge treated the case as being of a similar nature to *Butler v Guildford Borough Council* (24 April 1990, unreported) (*Butterworths Personal Injury Litigation Service* at IX [1602, 1594]) and *Hawthorne v Bowater Scott* (8 May 1989, unreported) (*Butterworths Personal Injury Litigation Service* at IX [1693,1565] and X [1702]).

Wheeler v Ford Motor Company Ltd (25 November 1994, unreported) (Philip Marshall, Messrs Robin Thompson and Partners, Cardiff, for the plaintiff; Jonathan Walters, Messrs Hugh James Jones and Jenkins, Cardiff, for the defendant) (Kindly submitted for publication by Martin S Khan, Solicitor, of Robin Thompson and Partners).

PSLA: £5,333
Sex: Female
Age at accident/trial: 42/49
Date of accident/trial: 21 December 1986/24 March 1994
Court: Outer House

Scotland
The plaintiff fell whilst at work, causing **tenderness** to the **muscles on the left side of the lower thoracic spine**. Having rested for a few days, the plaintiff returned to work. However, she was **forced to give up work** seven months after the accident, as she could no longer do her job properly. Thereafter, the plaintiff's condition deteriorated such that her **pain became more severe**, affecting her **back, shoulders, neck and knees** to the extent that she **could not lift items or bend**. She had to **wear a collar and use a stick**, and also took **painkillers and sleeping tablets**. In addition, she **suffered depression, lost a substantial amount of weight**, and became **totally dependent** on her family. Having regard to expert medical evidence, the judge concluded that the plaintiff's condition was brought on by her **emotional and psychological reaction to the accident**, as the pain of which she complained was totally **out of proportion to the actual injury**. In addition, having regard to the plaintiff's medical

history, he concluded that the plaintiff was **predisdposed to develop symptoms of anxiety and depression**, and that, even if the accident had not occurred, she would have suffered from anxiety and depression. The awards for pain, suffering, and loss of amenity, and for past loss of earnings that would have been made were therefore reduced by one third, and no award was made for future loss of earnings. Damages were, however, awarded in respect of services rendered to the plaintiff by her family and for the loss of her services to her family.

Duffy v Lanarkshire Health Board 1995 SLT 1312 (Outer House).

PSLA: £5,000 (no damages awarded, plaintiff failed to establish liability)
Sex: Female
Age at accident/trial: 49/55
Date of trial: 30 March 1995
Judge/court: Recorder Sander/Preston County Court

Plaintiff, a care assistant at a nursing home, sustained a **possible fractured sacrum** when she fell down some stairs at work. Afterwards she suffered **on-going pain** in her lumbar spine and left shoulder. She had a **previous history of back complaints** and had visited her doctor on a number of occasions prior to the accident, but had not had any time off work in relation to this. X-rays taken after the accident revealed pre-existing **significant degenerative changes** in her cervical and lumbar spine. It was noted that the accident accounted for her symptoms and the **increased level of discomfort** and accelerated the onset of degenerative change by a period of three years. Plaintiff would have been forced to retire three years after the date of the accident in any event, due to increasing level of symptoms as a result of the degenerative changes. Furthermore, the plaintiff **failed to establish liability** and so no damages were awarded.

Parkinson v Longfield Care Homes Ltd (30 March 1995, unreported) (Barry Searle, for the plaintiff; Ruth Trippier, for the defendant) (Kindly submitted for publication by James Hurd, Pupil Barrister).

PSLA: £4,750
Total damages: £6,592
Sex: Female
Age at injury/trial: 20/22
Date of injury/trial: February 1993/14 August 1995
Judge/court: Judge Kenny/Reading County Court

Plaintiff suffered **whiplash** injury to **neck, thoracic spine and lumbar spine** in road traffic accident. She developed pain across front of left hip and in her left wrist. She was **off work for six weeks**. After that she continued to suffer from minor residual symptoms including nightmares, flash-backs and dizzy spells for about six months, pins and needles sensation in left arm and **difficulty lifting for about a year**, and **headaches for about two years**. By the time of the trial she was only suffering pain between the shoulder blades once every two to three months.

Shields v Vera (14 August 1995, unreported) (Rob Weir, for the plaintiff) (Kindly submitted for publication by Rob Weir, Barrister).

1032 *Back and scarring*

PSLA: £3,250
Total damages: £3,427.82 (including interest)
Sex: Female
Age at injury/trial: 28/30
Date of injury/trial: 4 June 1993/15 June 1995
Judge/Court: Judge Rich/Mayor's and City of London County Court

Plaintiff was injured in a road traffic accident. She suffered **lacerations** to her left arm and **soft tissue injuries** to her neck and back. A piece of glass had to be removed from her arm, requiring **16 stitches** and leaving **five or six small pinkish scars** on her **upper arm.** Plaintiff was unable to work for two weeks. The back injury causing **significant pain** for six months after the accident and made **sleep difficult** for two weeks. Plaintiff was a keen sportswoman and a badminton player at league level. She had been on her way to France for an active holiday when the accident occurred and had had to take a more sedentary holiday later in the year instead. The above award consisted of £3,250 pain, suffering and loss of amenity (apportioned £1,250 for the scarring and £2,000 for the back pain) and special damages of £118. The judge placed special emphasis on the restriction of plaintiff's ability to enjoy her hobbies and the loss of her chosen form of holiday.

Hartfield v Green (15 June 1995, unreported) (Catherine Brown, David Levene & Co, London, for the plaintiff; Susan Roach, Messrs Hill Dickenson Davis Campbell, London, for the defendant) (Kindly submitted for publication by Susan Roach, Barrister).

1033 *Back and hip*

PSLA: £16,000
Total damages: £18,807.40
Sex: Female
Age at accident/trial: 17/23
Date of accident/trial: May 1989/10 March 1995
Judge/court: Judge Heald/Nottingham County Court

Plaintiff, a student at a theatre arts college with the ambition of becoming a professional dancer, sustained a **severe ligamentous and capsular strain** in the **lower back and around the right hip** whilst **performing a box–splits exercise** in a jazz dancing class. She felt immediate pain in her groin and was unable to continue the class. She tried to carry on dancing for two weeks after the accident but had to stop. About a month after the accident, the pain in her lower back supervened that in the groin, she received treatment from a **physiotherapist** and osteopath and was advised to **walk with a stick** and to take **substantial rest** during the summer vacation. She returned to college in the autumn, but the back and groin pain were too severe for her to dance and she had to leave college. At time of trial, plaintiff was still experiencing **significant symptoms** and had reached her final stage of recovery. Although no significant increase in disability was expected, she would **never be able to dance professionally** and her **sporting activities** would be **restricted**. Plaintiff was currently working as an airline hostess. When making the award for general damages, the judge considered that the plaintiff's loss of ability to follow her chosen career was very different from cases where damages had been awarded for inability to follow congenial employment, such as a fireman or policeman. The plaintiff had been determined to become a professional dancer from the age of eight, she had devoted considerable spare time to this end and the judge was satisfied that there was a distinct possibility of her reaching the top level of dancers, bearing in mind how few dancers reach those heights. He therefore included an award of £10,000 for loss of ability to pursue chosen career as a dancer in the general damages. The award also included £2,807.40 special damages.

Kirk v Laine Theatre Arts Ltd (10 March 1995, unreported) (Alison Hampton, Messrs Shoosmiths and Harrison, Nottingham, for the plaintiff; Patrick Limb, Messrs Geoffrey Delaney, Peterborough, for the defendant) (Kindly submitted for publication by John Hartshorne, Pupil Barrister).

1034 *Back and knee*

Total damages: £1,500
Sex: Female
Age at trial: 23
Date of trial: 10 November 1995
Judge/court: Assistant Recorder Bullock/Sheffield County Court

Plaintiff was involved in a **road traffic accident**. She sustained **soft tissue bruises and contusions to the knee** and **ligamentous strain of the lumbar spine**. She experienced pain in the right knee within two or three hours of the accident and within two weeks she developed **low back pain**. At all times the knee remained clinically stable and it took approximately 6 to 12 weeks for the plaintiff to recover. She took analgesics for the back pain and attended a course of **physiotherapy** which gave some relief. She had difficulties in domestic activities, especially washing her hair, and full recovery took approximately nine months. It was thought unlikely that there would be any permanent disability.

Martin v Willis (Ian McLauchlan for the plaintiff) (Kindly submitted for publication by Ian McLauchlan, Barrister).

1035 *Chest*

PSLA: £25,000
Total damages: £37,139.32
Sex: Male

Age at trial: 52
Date of trial: 10 December 1993
Court: Second Division

Scotland
The plaintiff was **exposed to asbestos** in the course of his employment. He developed **pleural plaques, pleural thickening,** and **sub-pleural fibrotic changes**, which were diagnosed as signs of **asbestosis** and which rendered him **breathless**. In addition, the plaintiff had a **restrictive airways condition** caused by the **late onset of asthma,** which also contributed to his breathlessness. His **overall respiratory deficit** was assessed at **15 per cent.** There was a **risk** that he would **develop lung cancer or mesothelioma**, and that his **pleural thickening and pleural plaques** would beome **worse**. Although the plaintiff could continue working, he would be **limited as to the work that he could do** because of his condition. The above award included £15,000 for loss of future earnings (reduced on appeal to £9,139.32 on account of state benefits). In addition, £1,500 was awarded each for personal services and necessary services provided to the plaintiff.
   McKenzie v Cape Building Products Ltd 1995 SLT 701 (Second Division).

Total damages: £15,650 (amount of payment in accepted by plaintiff)
Sex: Female
Age at injury: 45
Date of injury: January 1972
Court: Queen's Bench Division, Manchester

Plaintiff was admitted to hospital to undergo an operation to remove a **lump from her right breast**, but a **complete right mastectomy** was carried out instead. Histology subsequently showed fibrocystic hyperplasia, with **no evidence of malignancy**. As a result of the mastectomy, she sustained **ugly scarring** and suffered some loss of feeling in the back. Her quality of life was adversely affected, she was embarrassed by the loss of the breast, had difficulties in adapting and using a **prosthesis** and no longer went swimming or sunbathing. Plaintiff issued a writ in 1989 having received independant medical evidence in support of her case. She claimed she was only aware of the possibility of proceeding with a claim when she read about a similar case in a newspaper 16 years after the operation. The defendant denied liability on the grounds that the plaintiff's claim was out of time under the Limitation Act 1980, s 33. Prior to the trial of the limitation point, plaintiff accepted a payment into court of £15,650.
   D'Arcy v Stockport Health Authority (unreported) (Messrs Hatton Scates and Horton, Manchester, for the plaintiff; North West Health Legal Services, for the defendant) (Kindly submitted for publication by Howard Hatton, Solicitor, of Messrs Hatton Scates and Horton).

1036   *Chest and lungs*
PSLA: £30,000
Sex: Male
Age at trial: 63
Date of trial: 24 January 1995
Court: Outer House

Scotland
The plaintiff, who was employed by the defendant, was required him to **handle asbestos** products in the course of his employment. After leaving the defendant's employment, he was **unable to work for two years** because of undiagnosed ill-health. He was later treated for **angina**, a **duodenal ulcer**, and for a **stroke** brought on by his **heavy smoking**. He also suffered from **arthritis of the knee** and **breathlessness**. Having been able to work only intermittently because of his ill-health, the plaintiff was eventually certified unfit for work. Eleven years after leaving the defendant's employment, the plaintiff was diagnosed as having **lung fibrosis**, although medical evidence suggested that his other complaints would have rendered him unfit for work in any event. At the date of trial, his **life expectancy** was **five years**. On the plaintiff's claim for damages, it was held that because his lung fibrosis was not diagnosed until several years after he had been certified unfit for work, he had failed to establish any loss of earnings. In addition, much of his complaint of breathlessness was due to his smoking, rather than to his lung fibrosis. However, the above award was made on the basis that he was suffering from asbestosis.
   Stanners v Graham Builders Merchants Ltd 1995 SLT 728 (Outer House).

PSLA: £8,000
Total damages: £12,000
Sex: Male
Age at trial: 55
Date of trial: 12 May 1995
Court: Outer House

Scotland
The plaintiff suffered from **chronic obstructive airways disease** ('COAD'), **bronchitis** and **emphysema**, and also had **pleural plaques** and **bilateral pleural thickening** in his lungs. The COAD was caused by the plaintiff's **cigarette smoking**, but the pleural thickening was caused by his **exposure to asbestos dust** over a period of **17 years** in the course of his employment with the defendant. The plaintiff **had to use inhalers**, was **unable to climb stairs**, and was **breathless even when resting**. His **home** was **specially adapted and fitted with alarms**, and he **relied** on his **sister and other relatives** to do all his housework. Having been **forced to give up work** because of his ill health, the plaintiff was dependent on social security benefits. The court concluded that the plaintiff's exposure to asbestos and the resulting pleural plaques and pleural thickening were evidence of **early asbestosis**, which shortened his life expectancy even further. He was also at **risk of** developing **lung cancer and mesothelioma**. The plaintiff's disability was, however, substantially attributable to the COAD caused by his smoking, rather than to his asbestos inhalation. Moreover, the COAD subsisted before he developed asbestosis and the latter did not significantly increase his respiratory problems. Damages were awarded for solatium and for services to be rendered to the plaintiff by his family for the remainder of his life.

   McCance v Newalls Insulation Ltd 1996 SLT 80 (Outer House).

1037   *Trunk*

PSLA: £1,325 (including interest)
Total damages: £5,553.95 (including interest)
Sex: Male
Age at trial: 34
Date of accident/trial: December 1993/3 April 1995
Judge/court: District Judge Bolton/Bristol County Court

Plaintiff, a self employed construction contractor, was involved in road traffic accident in which he sustained **soft tissue damage** to his **rib cage** and **shoulder** area and a possible injury to the cervical spine, complicated by the restraining effect of his seatbelt. He suffered **severe chest pain**, breathing difficulties and **wheezing** for five days after the accident and was prescribed analgesics, **anti-inflammatories** and antibiotics. Thereafter he developed an **acute shooting pain**, which radiated down the left side of his **chest and abdomen**, this resolved over the next four weeks, but the plaintiff was **unable to work** during this period. Plaintiff's **sleep was disturbed** for six weeks, leading to tiredness during the day. All symptoms had resolved within five months of the accident. The above award included £3,844.50 special damages, with £384.45 interest thereon.

   McCallion v Dodd (3 April 1995, unreported) (Christopher Taylor, Messrs Boote Edgar Esterkin, Manchester, for the plaintiff) (Kindly submitted for publication by Christopher Taylor, Barrister).

1038   *Abdomen*

PSLA: £30,250 (including interest at 10 cent)
Total damages: £326,255 (including interest)
Sex: Male
Age at accident/trial: 17/26
Date of accident/trial: 26 June 1986/10 April 1995
Earnings multiplier: 14
Judge/court: Waterhouse J/Queen's Bench Division

Plaintiff was operating a crane in connection with tunnelling work, when it turned over and he **fell 18 ft** down a shaft and landed on the edge of a metal skip on his abdomen. The right side of his **colon was perforated** and he underwent a **laparotomy**, followed by **construction of a colostomy** on the right side. There was considerable **contamination of the peritoneal cavity** and he remained in hospital for eight days. He was re-admitted three weeks later with abdominal pain, **vomiting and diarrhoea**, which was thought to be secondary to a **viral**

infection. Two and a half months after the accident, the **colostomy was successfully closed** and plaintiff was kept in hospital for a further nine days. Plaintiff also suffered lacerations to the forehead, knee and groin as a result of the accident, which required stitches and have left the plaintiff with scars. Although plaintiff made good recovery, he was still substantially disabled and had suffered from the following sequelae: (1) the colostomy had been very painful, his **skin had become sore** and he sometimes had accidents which were unpleasant and messy; (2) he had suffered from **shock** and had developed a **fear of tunnel shafts**, but there was **no depression** or post traumatic stress disorder; (3) there were **unsightly scars** at the incision sites of the laparotomy and the colostomy, both were subject to **herniation** and the former was six and a half inches long and one inch in diameter, **two further operations** were required, but **no substantial improvement** was expected; (4) he had **digestive problems** and for eight years had **urgency and frequency of bowel action**, at time of trial he still had to avoid spicy or greasy foods; (5) he no longer enjoyed swimming and cycling and his self confidence was affected, particularly his relationships with women; (6) he suffered **pain on heavy lifting** and was advised to refrain from work of a heavy nature, he would not be able to follow his desired career of tunnel mining and would be limited to work of a light nature. Plaintiff had no academic qualifications or skills, having left school at 16 with one CSE. The above award included £100,882 pre-trial losses (with past loss assessed from age 21), and interest of £48,423 thereon (at 48 per cent); £142,800 loss of future earnings and £3,900 agreed cost of future surgery.

   McDonnell v Woodhouse and Jones (a Firm) (10 April 1995, unreported) (George Pulman QC and Ian Ashford-Thom, Messrs Sebastian Coleman and Co, for the plaintiff; Bryan McGuire, Messrs C J Sweet, Messrs Rayfields, London and Messrs Greenfields, for the defendants) (Kindly submitted for publication by Kate Akerman, Pupil Barrister).

1039   *Arm*
PSLA: £20,000
Total damages: £147,920
Sex: Male
Age at injury/hearing: 29/34
Date of injury/hearing: 24 September 1989/22 May 1995
Earnings multiplier: 10
Court: Criminal Injuries Compensation Board, London

Applicant, a carpenter, was injured when he was **attacked with a wooden club**. He sustained a closed **fracture of the right radius**, a comminuted **intra-articular fracture** of the olecranon of the left elbow and **bruising** and pain over his chest, back and arms. He underwent an operation under **general anaesthetic** to reduce and fix the fractured right radius with a **metal plate and screws** and the left elbow was immobilised in a **plaster cast**. He remained in **hospital for three weeks** and attended the fracture clinic for nearly a year. Applicant was left with a long **surgical scar** on the right forearm, he suffered pain on waking up (which radiated up to the right shoulder and increased the more he used the arm) and he had to take analgesics. He also suffered from pins and needles, weakness in the right hand, reduced **grip power** (due to the pain) and **supination** was three quarters normal. There was pain and stiffness on the posterior aspect of the left elbow, he was unable to straighten his arm, supination was two thirds normal, flexion and extension lacked 40 degrees and there was damage and irregularity to the articular cartilage. Applicant also suffered pain on the left side of the chest when doing heavy lifting, tenderness over the tenth and eleventh ribs and increasing pain in the back, with tenderness over the spinous processes (which may have been aggravated by the injury). He was **deeply depressed** and reluctant to go out alone at night. At time of trial, there was irregularity in the left elbow, which had mal-united and this would definately lead to **osteoarthritis** in the near future. He still found it difficult to lift heavy weights, an activity which would in any case accelerate the onset of osteoarthritis. Applicant would not be able to return to his pre-accident employment as a carpenter, which was the only job that he knew and he suffered from dyslexia (unrelated to the injuries). These symptoms were permanent and would get worse. The above award included £30,000 past loss of earnings (reduced by one seventh to allow for likely gaps in work), and £97,920 future loss of earnings (using a multiplier of 10).

   Criminal Injuries Compensation Board, London (22 May 1995, unreported) (Bruce R Silvester for the applicant) (Kindly submitted for publication by Bruce R Silvester, Barrister).

PSLA: £4,000
Total damages: £4,195 (including interest)
Sex: Male

Age at accident/trial: 25/29
Date of accident/trial: 26 December 1990/22 May 1995
Judge/court: District Judge Foster/Doncaster County Court

Plaintiff was thrown from his motorbike in a road accident. He suffered **grazing to his hip** and **severe bruising to left arm,** which healed in about two months. He later developed symptoms in **back of left shoulder**. Medical evidence accepted at the trial linked this to the accident and suggested that there should be full recovery within six to eight years. Examined three years after the accident he had **pain on internal rotation** but otherwise no restriction in function. At trial plaintiff still had pain when raising arm above head height or upon lifting heavy objects. He had been unable to return to motorbike riding, which had been his great passion, due to discomfort in the shoulder caused by vibrations. The above award for pain suffering and loss of amenity was apportioned £3,000 for the shoulder and £1,000 for other injuries. It included £75 special damages and £120 interest.

Beecham v Right (22 May 1995, unreported) (Ian Groom for the plaintiff; Martin Lindsay for the defendant) (Kindly submitted for publication by Ian Groom, Barrister).

PSLA: £3,971 (including interest)
Total damages: £4,000 (including interest)
Sex: Female
Age at injury/settlement: 6/10
Date of injury/settlement: 7 January 1992/27 September 1995
Judge/court: District Judge Ainsworth/Southampton County Court

Plaintiff **fell from climbing apparatus** in defendants' housing estate playground. She suffered a **supracondylar fracture of the right humerus** (non-dominant hand). The fracture was set under general anaesthetic and she remained in hospital for three days. She was away from school for three weeks. Although two years after the accident there was still a 10 degree reduction in flexion she was making a steady recovery and the prognosis was that the **improvement would continue** with growth leaving **no visible deformity**. Special damages of £24 with £5 interest were claimed and the judge approved a total settlement of £4,000 including £3,971 damages for pain, suffering and loss of amenity.

Morgan v Southampton City Council (27 September 1995, unreported) (Messrs Bell Pope, Southampton, for the plaintiff) (Kindly submitted for publication by Shaun Underhill, Messrs Bell Pope, Solicitors).

PSLA: £850
Total damages: £850
Sex: Male
Age at injury/settlement: 2/4
Date of injury/settlement: 27 May 1993/18 September 1995
Judge/Court: Deputy District Judge Gillman/Stourbridge County Court

Plaintiff was **a rear near-side passenger** in a car, **wearing a seat belt**, when the car was hit from behind by a lorry. The car in which the plaintiff was a passenger was shunted into the vehicle in front. The plaintiff attended hospital where he received treatment for **a small superficial abrasion**. He was **extremely distressed** by the incident. Symptoms comprised **waking at night** and **a degree of reluctance to sit in the car seat**. All the symptoms appeared to have **abated within 12 months** of the accident. The case was settled prior to trial and the settlement approved by the Deputy District Judge.

Smith v Blue Band Motors Ltd (settled out of court) (Messrs Higgs & Sons, Stourbridge, for the plaintiff; Messrs Berrymans, Birmingham, for the defendant) (Kindly submitted for publication by Ian Shovlin, Messrs Higgs & Sons, Solicitors).

1040 *Arm and shoulder*
PSLA: £8,000
Total Damages: £11,000
Sex: Male
Age at accident/trial: 45/48
Date of accident/trial: 18 April 1991/2 February 1994
Court: Outer House

Scotland

The plaintiff was visiting the factory premises of a potential client when he **fell whilst negotiating steps**. He **broke his right arm just below the elbow** and **sustained soft tissue injury to** his **lower arm and wrist**. Although the plaintiff was absent from work for only two weeks whilst the injury **healed satisfactorily**, he later began to suffer from severe pain emanating from his neck and causing pain in his shoulders. This was diagnosed as **brachial neuritis** for which there was no curative treatment, and expert evidence indicated that it had been **brought on by the trauma of the accident**. As a result, the plaintiff could carry out only **limited gardening work, could not drive for long periods of time**, and experienced **pain in his arm at night** which **interrupted his sleep**. The prognosis was that it was unlikely that his condition would improve. The trial judge accepted the plaintiff's testimony as to how the condition had arisen, even though there was no medical evidence to support the alleged causal connection between the accident and the plaintiff's subsequent pain. Damages were awarded for solatium, and for services rendered to him by his relatives immediately after the accident (£500). Damages for loss of earnings were restricted to £2,500, as there was no evidence that the plaintiff was likely to lose his job.

Cole v Weir Pumps Ltd 1995 SLT 12 (Outer House).

1041   Arm and hand

PSLA: £6,500
Total damages: £7,500
Sex: Male
Age at injury: 29
Date of injury/ hearing: 28 February 1992/ 28 October 1994
Court: Outer House

Scotland

Plaintiff, a janitor, was injured in the course of his employment when his arm broke a window while he was working on a ladder. He sustained **severe laceration** to his right forearm, with **division of the ulner nerve and some muscle tissue**. Treatment included some **skin grafting**. The plaintiff recovered from his injury and returned to work after three months. He was left with **scarring** on his arm and his thigh, the donor site of the skin graft and a **slight clawing of the right ring and small fingers**, the small finger tending to lie in abduction. He also suffered **reduced grip power** and a permanent weakness in his right dominant hand. For past loss of earnings he was awarded £500 and a further £500 was awarded for the services rendered by his wife while his arm was in a splint.

McCutcheon v Lothian Regional Council 1995 SLT 917 (Outer House)

1042   Arm and leg

PSLA: £22,500 (excluding interest)
Total damages: £117,000 (excluding interest)
Sex: Male
Age at accident/trial: 48/53
Date of accident/trial: 11 December 1990/2 March 1995
Earnings multiplier: 3.5
Judge/court: Lord Clyde/Outer House

Scotland

The plaintiff, a self-employed shuttering joiner was injured in a fall. He **fractured** his right **tibia and fibula** and his left **radius and ulna**. The **leg fracture failed to unite** properly and following several unsuccessful operations to correct the problem, the **plaintiff had to wear a calliper**. The **leg became distorted** but further operative treatment later carried out made a **significant improvement** to his condition. At the time of the trial, it was hoped that the **leg would heal in the next six months**. It still gave the plaintiff discomfort and he tired easily. As a result of the misalignment of the leg, the plaintiff's **ankle distorted**. He **used a stick to walk**, although he could walk about the house and for short distances outside without it. If the pain continued the plaintiff would use the stick for the foreseeable future. The problems with his ankle meant the plaintiff could not stand for a long time and he continued to have **stiffness and restriction of movement** in it. It was unlikely that he would recover full mobility of his ankle. An initial operation on the plaintiff's arm failed but some improvement could be achieved by a further operation. The **limb had misaligned** because one bone had healed and the other had not. While proper alignment might be achieved, the movement of the arm would not necessarily improve. It was believed that there would **never be a full rotation of the arm**. The plaintiff could no longer play golf and until a year before the trial, when he had started to do some gardening, he had been unable to enjoy cycling and gardening. He had periods of **depression** and had been **unable to return to work**. The above award included £51,000 past loss of earnings, £42,500 future loss of earnings (using a multiplier of 3.5 and £1,000 for services provided by the plaintiff's wife. £22,159 was deducted from the total award in respect of benefits.

Cavanagh v BP Chemicals Ltd 1995 SLT 1287 (Outer House).

1043   *Arm and foot*

PSLA: (1) £6,500; (2) £5,000
Total damages: (1) £18,500; (2) £21,500
Sex: (1) Female; (2) male
Age at accident/trial: (1) 45/49; (2) 51/55
Date of accident/trial: 17 June 1991/7 April 1995
Court: Outer House

Scotland
The two plaintiffs were involved in a road traffic accident. Plaintiff 1 sustained a **laceration of the left big toe**, an **abrasion on her left foot**, and a **fractured left ankle**. Six months after the accident, the plaintiff continued to suffer **tenderness and discomfort in her ankle**, particularly towards the end of the day. Those **symptoms** were still **persisting over three years later**, and there was evidence that the plaintiff had developed **osteo-arthritis** in her ankle. In addition, she had to take **pain killers on a regular basis** and wear a **support bandage** on her ankle.

Plaintiff 2 sustained **swelling and tenderness** to his **right elbow**, a **laceration** over the tip of his **right middle finger**, **bruising and swelling to his right middle and ring fingers, thumb and wrist**, and also **grazing to his left forearm and nose**. The plaintiff had to wear an **arm sling**, and his right elbow remained painful for several weeks after the accident. Six months thereafter, the plaintiff found that he was **unable to move his right elbow fully**, and he also experienced **aching discomfort in the elbow and in his right hand**, especially when the weather was cold and damp and when he used his elbow. He also had less sensation in the tip of his right middle finger, and his right thumb was swollen. These **symptoms persisted**, and at trial there was evidence that they would continue and that the **aching discomfort** in his elbow **would increase**.

Prior to the accident, the plaintiff and her husband had run a general provisions shop and a cafe. In the weeks immediately following the accident, their relatives helped them to run the shop, although the plaintiff and her husband still had to shut the shop earlier than they would otherwise have done, and the cafe was closed for approximately six weeks. The plaintiff and her husband also had to stop the take away food service which they had previously provided in the shop, and that business was not resumed thereafter. As a result of having to permanently reduce their work capacity and working hours, their business suffered losses. Damages for loss of profit were awarded as a lump sum, rather than on a multiplier and multiplicand basis, as the court was of the opinion that it was difficult to assess how the business would have fared had it not been for the accident.

Tweedy v Newboult 1996 SLT 2 (Outer House).

1044   *Elbow*

PSLA: £95,000
Total damages: £165,530
Sex: Male
Age at accident/trial: 38/45
Date of accident/trial: 1989/11 May 1995
Judge/court: Lord Gill and a jury/Court of Session

Scotland
Pursuer, a farmer and international clay target shooter, was injured in a **road traffic accident**. He sustained **lacerations** to his head and knee and very serious **multiple fractures** of the **right arm and elbow**. He was left with pieces of **bone protruding** from the right elbow and amputation was considered. However this was not necessary, and he underwent an operation to insert a **pin from elbow to wrist**. The pin was removed two years later, by which time the arm had stiffened considerably and there was only **50 degrees of flexion**, a disability which

would be permanent. Pursuer could not bring a cup to his lips with his right hand, tie a tie or do up shirt buttons and required the help of his wife with driving and operation of complicated farm machinery. He had **continuing pain** which was worst in wet weather, his sleep was disturbed and he had to take pain killers. As a result of the accident, he could no longer take part in **international clay target shooting competitions** in which he had **previously won cash and other prizes**; he won the European Championship in 1988 and a bronze medal in the Commonwealth Games. The award for pain, suffering and loss of amenity included a portion to compensate the pursuer for this loss of opportunity and comprised £35,000 for past loss and £60,000 for future loss. The above award also included £4,000 past losses in pursuer's share in partnership profits, £2,000 future losses in pursuer's share in partnership profits; £30,000 past loss of prizes, £20,000 future loss of prizes; £2,000 wife's services to date of trial, £3,000 wife's services in future; £1,800 services pursuer unable to render to his family to date of trial, £6,000 future services pursuer unable to render to his family; £1,680 travelling costs and £50 damage to clothing.

   Girvan v Inverness Farmers Dairy (11 May 1995, unreported) (Colin McEachran QC and Raymond Docherty, Messrs Dundas and Wilson, Edinburgh, for the pursuer; M S Jones QC and Lesley Shand, Messrs Brodies, Edinburgh, for the defendant) (Kindly submitted for publication by Colin McEachran QC, Advocate). Mr McEachran comments that this case is of particular interest because it involves a second jury trial in a situation where the first award of £120,000 for pain, suffering and loss of amenity (see 1993 Abr para 950) was overturned on appeal as being excessive.

PSLA: £8,000
Total damages: £72,264.86
Sex: Male
Age at injury/hearing: 44/48
Date of injury/trial: 1990/1994
Earnings multiplier: 3
Court: Outer House

Scotland
The plaintiff, an industrial radiographer, developed **lateral epicondylitis** in **both elbows** (bilateral tennis elbow) as a result of his working conditions. As **physiotherapy and injections failed** to ease his condition, an **operation** was performed on his **left elbow** to **release the common extensor origin from the prominence of the lateral epicondyle**. A **similar operation** performed on his **right elbow** was **less successful**. After the operations, the plaintiff **continued** to suffer from **general weakness in both arms** and **pain** when **squeezing and gripping,** thereby **affecting** his ability to carry out his **usual activities** and **hobbies**. In particular, he was unable to **lift heavy articles, write, and to carry out certain domestic and personal tasks**. He was also **unable** to **resume** his **former employment**, although medical evidence suggested that he would make a full recovery within five years. It was also suggested that he could undertake **other work** in the **meantime**. Damages were awarded for solatium. For past loss of earnings, he was awarded a total of £29,198.17, with interest, and for future loss of earnings, a multiplier of three was applied to an annual salary of £10,000. Damages were also awarded for lost pension benefits. Damages were not given for services rendered to the plaintiff by his wife, but £1,000 was awarded in respect of the plaintiff's inability to continue to care for his mother-in-law.
   Hunter v Clyde Shaw plc 1995 SLT 474 (Outer House).

PSLA: £3,500
Total damages: £3,500
Sex: Female
Age at accident/trial: 33/35
Date of accident/trial: 15 February 1994/6 November 1995
Judge/court: Judge Trigger/Liverpool County Court

Plaintiff **fell on pavement** suffering **fractures of the head of the radius (elbow) in each arm**. Blood was aspirated from both elbow joints and the arms immobilised in **slings which were worn for four weeks**. During this time the **plaintiff was unable use either of her arms and needed assistance** with dressing, eating, washing and attending to her toilet. Once the slings were removed she underwent a course of physiotherapy for eight weeks over which time she gradually **recovered the use of her arms and symptoms settled** to a manageable level. The plaintiff continued to be troubled by pain in her elbows and pins and needles in her hands for about two months after the accident. The fractures had united soundly but according to medical evidence there was a **remote possibility** that within the next 25–30 years she **might develop a moderate degree of arthritis**.

Clarke v Liverpool City Council (6 November 1995, unreported) (Tim Grover, John Hassall, Messrs Canter, Levin & Berg, Liverpool, for the plaintiff) (Kindly submitted for publication by Tim Grover, Barrister).

1045 *Wrist*

PSLA: £11,995
Total damages: £12,000
Sex: Female
Age at accident/hearing: 15/19
Date of hearing: 13 January 1995
Court: Criminal Injuries Compensation Board, York

Applicant was **pushed off a wall** in an unprovoked attack and sustained a **fractured distal radius** and an **ulna styloid fracture** to the left (non-dominant) wrist. The fractures were placed in a **plaster of Paris** back slab for six weeks. However, the ulna styloid **fracture did not unite** and now lies in a **displaced position**. At date of hearing, applicant had **reduced range of movement** in the left wrist, poor grip strength in the left hand and fine crepitus was noted on rotation of the left forearm. She experienced difficulties when **holding or lifting** anything with her left hand, when opening doors and with other day to day activities. The wrist condition was expected to be **permanent** and there was some risk of **painful post traumatic osteoarthritis** and arthroscopy of the wrist and **further surgery**. The file was not destroyed and leave was given to make a **further application** should arthritis develop in the future. The above award included a nominal sum of £5 for loss of earnings.

Criminal Injuries Compensation Board, York (13 January 1995, unreported) (David S Dixon, Messrs Atherton and Godfrey, Doncaster, for the applicant) (Kindly submitted for publication by David S Dixon, Barrister).

PSLA: £5,500
Total damages: £8,188 (including interest)
Sex: Female
Age at accident/trial: 22/26
Date of accident/trial: 26 July 1991/24 August 1995
Judge/court: Judge Bush/Leeds County Court

Plaintiff injured in the course of her employment as a grocery assistant when she put out her hands to stop a case of soft drinks from falling on her. She sustained a **severe soft tissue injury** to her **right (dominant) wrist**. She was required to wear a **plaster cast for nearly four months**, during which time she was **off work**. She was then fitted with a brace but could only carry out light duties when she returned to work. By the date of the trial she had still not been able to return to her previous duties. She suffered **continuous pain in the wrist for eight months** and thereafter continued to suffer pain radiating along her forearm whenever she tried to carry out strenuous tasks. There is some pain on extremes of movement. The pain caused difficulties in carrying out normal household tasks and writing. The plaintiff had been unable to continue swimming and her pen-friend hobby had been affected. There had been **some improvement in the symptoms** with the aid of painkillers (which the plaintiff still took at the date of the trial) but the **disability and pain would be permanent**, although there was an uncertain possibility of some improvement over the course of time. The above award included £1,000 *Smith v Manchester* award and special damages of £1,120.

Kitching v Tesco Stores Ltd (24 August 1995, unreported) (Paul Wilson, Messrs Whittles, Leeds, for the plaintiff) (Kindly submitted for publication by Paul Wilson, Barrister).

PSLA: £4,000
Total damages: £7,000
Sex: Male
Age at accident: 24
Date of accident: 7 July 1991
Court: Settled out of court

Plaintiff, a self employed hod carrier, fell and injured his **left wrist**. He attended hospital, **no x-ray** was taken and he was advised that he had sprained the wrist. After struggling for a few months, he visited his doctor, who commissioned an x-ray, which revealed a **fracture of the left scaphiod bone** with **non union**. Ten months after the accident, the plaintiff underwent a **bone grafting** procedure and the **fracture was fixed** with a Herbert screw. The above award included approximately £3,000 special damages.

Burrow v Pontefract Hospital NHS Trust (unreported) (Bruce McIntyre, Messrs Hartley and Worstenholme, Castleford, for the plaintiff; Charles Foster, Yorkshire Health Legal Services, for the defendant) (Kindly submitted for publication by Arthur J Healey, Solicitor, of Messrs Hartley and Worstenholme).

PSLA: £3,500
Total damages: £3,500
Sex: Male
Age at injury/trial: 13/14
Date of injury/trial: 3 June 1993/13 March 1995
Judge/court: District Judge Hearne/Stourbridge County Court

Plaintiff was climbing unsupervised on climbing apparatus in the defendant's leisure centre when he fell eight feet onto the floor. He suffered a **greenstick fracture** of the **lower metaphysis** with slight dorsal angulation on the left wrist and a **greenstick fracture** of the **distal radius metaphysis** on the right wrist. He was in hospital for two days and was discharged from the fracture clinic eight weeks after the accident. He missed school for three days, could not play piano or violin for eight weeks and could not participate in sporting activities for three months.

Hill v Dudley Metropolitan Borough Council (13 March 1995, unreported) (Ian Shovlin, Messrs Higgs and Sons, Stourbridge for the plaintiff; Messrs Wragge & Co, Birmingham for the defendant) (Kindly submitted for publication by Ian Shovlin, Messrs Higgs and Sons, Solicitors).

PSLA: £3,000
Total damages: £3,486.98
Sex: Male
Age at accident: 53
Date of trial: 17 February 1995
Judge/court: Judge Sutcliffe/Sheffield County Court

Plaintiff sustained a **fractured left non-dominant wrist**, a laceration above his left eye and a minor bruise when he **fell off a step ladder** at work. His wrist was in plaster for five weeks and he was off work for seven weeks. The **laceration** healed, leaving no scar. Nine months after the accident he had only **minor discomfort** in the wrist and had recovered the full range of movement, there was no risk of osteoarthritis and by date of trial he had only minor discomfort in cold weather. The above award included special damages of £486.98, comprising £466.98 agreed lost earnings and £20 miscellaneous medical expenses.

Fowler v South Yorkshire Transport Ltd (17 February 1995, unreported) (William E Hanbury, Messrs Morrish and Co, Leeds, for the plaintiff; Toby Stewart, Messrs Ashington Denton, Sheffield, for the defendant) (Kindly submitted for publication by William E Hanbury, Barrister).

PSLA: £2,250 (plus £70.77 interest)
Total damages: £4,731.73 (plus £944.12 interest)
Sex: Male
Age at accident/trial: 18/22
Date of accident/trial: 9 December 1991/10 October 1995
Judge/court: Assistant Recorder Christopher Smyth/Bromley County Court

Plaintiff **slipped on the floor** of the kitchen at the restaurant in which he was working. He put his left (non-dominant) hand out to break his fall and fell upon it, sustaining **a suspected fracture of the left trapezium bone** in the wrist joint. He was taken to hospital complaining of pain at the base of his left thumb. An X-ray showed no bone injury but in view of the possibility of a fracture of the scaphoid bone a plaster cast was applied. He was given Brufen tablets and referred to the fracture clinic. X-rays taken ten days later showed changes **suggestive of a fracture of the trapezium**, but confirmed there was no fracture of the scaphoid bone. A plaster cast was re-applied and not removed until 38 days after the fall. At the time of the removal the pain and swelling in the wrist had largely resolved and he was discharged from the clinic. As a result of his injuries the **plaintiff was off work for six weeks**, after which time he was **dismissed from his employment**. On examination 15 months after the accident he was complaining of an aching discomfort at the base of his left thumb from time to time, especially when engaged in lifting anything heavy. He was aware of this discomfort roughly once every week but if he had no lifting to do his wrist did not trouble him at all. There was no indication the plaintiff had injured his wrist permanently and the ongoing symptoms found on examination after 15 months were expected to resolve within another three to six months. **No degenerative changes** were anticipated and the judge described the injury as a minor one from which the young plaintiff had made a very good recovery. General damages of £2,250 plus £70.77 interest were awarded. Special damages of £2,481.73 were awarded, made up of: £2,973.08 for loss of earnings (at £135.14 per week for 6 weeks off work before dismissal and 16 weeks unemployment); £440 loss of benefit of tips (at £20 per week for the same period); and travel and sundry expenses of £26.80. A deduction of £958.15 was made for statutory sick pay received. Interest of £873.35 on the special damages was awarded.

Abbott v Roebuck t/a The Hollywood Bowl (10 October 1995, unreported) (Colin Mendoza, Messrs Braund & Fedrick, Sidcup, for the plaintiff; Messrs Robbins Olivey & Herrington for the defendants) (Kindly submitted for publication by Colin Mendoza, Barrister and Sarah Larcombe, Messrs Braund & Fedrick, Solicitors). Mr Mendoza notes that the consultant orthopaedic surgeon who was called to give evidence for the plaintiff described the injury as 'extremely rare'.

1046 *Wrist and fingers*

PSLA: £20,000
Total damages: £125,432
Sex: Female
Age at injury/hearing: 21/30
Date of injury/hearing: August 1986/21 July 1995
Earnings multiplier: 12
Court: Criminal Injuries Compensation Board, Plymouth

Applicant, a nurse, was injured when attempting to lift a psychiatric patient. The patient resisted, **forcing middle and ring fingers of right (dominant) hand back over wrist**. There was a 'scrunching sound' and **immediate and significant pain**. The fingers were put in to a splint and strapped. She was diagnosed as suffering from a **forcible hyper-extension injury** to the wrist and fingers together with **traumatic reflex sympathetic dystrophy**. A **thoracic sympathectomy** was carried out in April 1987. There was no real improvement after the operation and the applicant was reduced to lighter duties as a receptionist. A further reduction in her duties lead to her resignation in October 1989. She has tried several non-nursing jobs but been unable to maintain them due to her injury. She is now studying to qualify for Pre-school Playgroups Association diploma. Her references stated that she would have gone on with her nursing career and would have qualified to at least State Enrolled Nurse and possibly Staff Nurse grade. All pain relief and treatment possibilities had been exhausted and the **disability is permanent**. For the purposes of Industrial Injury Benefit she was assessed as being **15% disabled for life**. **Constant pain in her wrist and fingers** is **only partially relieved** by pain killers and a tens machine. The wrist is continually in a support and she suffers impaired pain perception and severely restricted wrist movement. The extensor tendons to the hands stand out as though in spasm and there is a lack of sweating within the skin of the fingers. The applicant can pick up small objects using an unusual technique but not with index finger pad to thumb pad and she is unable to pick up heavy objects. Her **quality of life has been severely restricted**: she cannot play properly with her daughter, tie her shoelaces, or do simple manual tasks like peeling vegetables, or opening tins and bottles and she can only drive for short distances.

Criminal Injuries Compensation Board, Plymouth (21 July 1995, unreported) (Roger Henderson, Messrs Woollcombe Beer Watts, Newton Abbot, for the applicant) (Kindly submitted for publication by Roger Henderson of Messrs Woollcombe Beer Watts, Solicitors).

1047 *Hand*

PSLA: £10,500
Total damages: £26,103
Sex: Male
Age at accident/trial: 33/35
Date of accident/trial: 29 April 1992/11 October 1995
Judge/court: Court of Appeal/Butler-Sloss and Simon-Brown LJJ

The plaintiff suffered **crush injuries** to the **tips of the middle, ring and little fingers** of his dominant right hand whilst transporting castings as part of his work as an industrial radiographer. The **ring finger was amputated through the distal segment**. He had **physiotherapy** and was **off work** for **16 weeks**. After that he returned to work and has worked ever since. He has **tenderness and numbness** in the tips of the middle and little fingers. The stump of the partially amputated finger is **tender and hypersensitive**. His **power of grip** and **writing ability** have been affected and he has lost the **dexterity** necessary for manipulating small objects and lifting heavy weights. On examination the little and middle fingers were found to be **scarred but with full movements**. His ring finger was **two and a half centimetres short**. His **reduction in grip** was found to be **20 per cent**, he has a **permanent cosmetic blemish** and **permanent changes in sensitivity**. Though he adapted to his injury the judge at first instance found that he was affected in four areas of his life: (1) at work, where his job involved intricate and manual work, sometimes requiring a full grip and often requiring a great deal of writing. He is now prone to **clumsiness** and has to call upon colleagues for **help**. He has some **tenderness and pain**; (2) at home, where he is unable to carry out a lot of domestic tasks; (3) generally in that he suffers, for instance, difficulty in handling money; (4) in his leisure time in that his sporting activities and hobbies have been somewhat curtailed. The defendants appealed against the award under two heads of damage in the first instance decision. It was held on appeal that the award of £10,500 for pain, suffering and loss of amenity and the award of £11,180 for his loss of earnings and his future handicap on the labour market, though both quite high, were not sufficiently so to warrant interference.

Hall v Hi-Tech Integrity Castings Ltd (11 October 1995, unreported) (Kindly submitted for publication by Richard Copnall, Barrister).

PSLA: £7,500
Total damages: £22,500
Sex: Male
Age at accident: 44
Date of accident/trial: March 1993/3 January 1995
Judge/court: Recorder Apsley/Nottingham County Court

Plaintiff, a television scenery and props man, suffered a **crush injury to the index, middle and ring fingers** of his right **non-dominant hand**. There were **compound fractures** to the distal phalanges of the middle and ring fingers, **damage to the nail beds** and subungual haematoma of the index finger. He was off work for six weeks. The middle and ring finger tips healed in position of **curving backwards** and there was **ridging** of the ring and middle finger nails. Plaintiff was **embarrassed** by the appearance of the finger tips and nails. He was able to return to work, although he had some difficulties: **inco-ordination** of the finger tips meant that he had great difficulty tying knots, a task frequently required in his work; his **fingers ached after heavy work and in cold weather** and the finger tips were **sore if knocked**. The accident had brought forward pre-existing but symptomless **osteoarthritis** in the finger joints, and at age 60 to 65, he will suffer some lack of dexterity in the fingers. The judge noted that the plaintiff's injury increased the risk of him being made **redundant**, he had had more than 20 years' experience in this work and, having **no formal qualifications or transferable skills**, would have to take a substantial drop in earnings if he had to obtain work outside television. The above award included £15,000 for handicap on the labour market.

Wheeler v Central Independent Television plc (3 January 1995, unreported) (Christopher Goddard, Messrs Robin Thompson and Partners, Nottingham, for the plaintiff; Anthony Snelson, Messrs Richard Steer and Co, Teddington, for the defendant) (Kindly submitted for publication by Christopher Goddard, Barrister).

PSLA: £6,000
Total damages: £14,925
Sex: Male
Age at injury/trial: 22/24
Date of injury/trial: 18 December 1992/29 July 1995
Judge/court: Judge R Brown/Workington County Court

Plaintiff was injured when a barman caused a glass to smash in his hand. He suffered a **deep laceration** between the thumb and index finger on his **right (dominant) hand** which **divided the tendons and nerves**. Surgery repaired the superficial and deep flexor tendons to the index finger. He required a **nerve graft** from the dorsal aspect of the hand to bridge the gap between the ulnar side digital nerve to the index finger and the radial side digital nerve to the middle finger. He was in a **plaster cast for approximately 6 to 8 weeks**. Eighteen months after the injury the plaintiff was **unable to fully straighten the right index and middle fingers**. The index finger suffered an **extensor deficit of 15 degrees** both at the metacarpal phalangeal and the proximal interphalangeal joints and **10 degrees** at the distal interphalangeal joints. By the trial he was able to bend his index and middle fingers to within 1 centimetre of the palm, although there was some permanent loss of sensation in the index finger, and had recovered some of the **loss of power in the hand to between 50–75 per cent** of the left hand. The plaintiff suffered no difficulty in his employment as a result of the injury. The above award included special damages of £5,415 and a *Smith v Manchester* award of £3,510 based on the equivalent of six months net loss of earnings.

Parker v Scott (29 July 1995, unreported) (Hugh Davies for the plaintiff; Nicholas Kewtrell for the defendant) (Kindly submitted for publication by Hugh Davies, Barrister).

PSLA: £5,000
Total damages: £5,000
Sex: Female
Age at injury/trial: 8/9
Date of injury/trial: 11 March 1994/25 April 1995
Judge/Court: District Judge Campbell/Oxford County Court

Plaintiff suffered a **crush injury** when her **left (non-dominant) index finger** was trapped in a door at the defendant's premises. Examination under general anaesthetic revealed **loss of pulp tissue, laceration of the nail bed** and a **fracture** of the finger. Two skin grafts were carried out, the first having failed to take. Plaintiff was initially reluctant to look at her finger but her anxieties appeared to be resolved. The injury affected her horse riding and recorder playing for three to six months. The **finger nail was curved** and **prone to infection**, the finger was **slightly shortened** and there was a **slight loss of grip and dexterity**. There was no risk of long term deformity other than to the nail.

Mallett v Committee for the Time Being of the Hanney War Memorial Hall (25 April 1995, unreported) (Mr Singer, Linnels of Oxford, for the plaintiff; Stephen Ellis-Jones, Davies Lavery of Maidstone, for the defendant) (Kindly submitted for publication by Stephen Ellis-Jones, Barrister).

PSLA: £3,500
Total damages: £14,969.62 (including interest)
Sex: Male
Age at accident/trial: 37/39
Date of trial: 27 February 1995
Judge/court: Judge Lachs/Liverpool County Court

Plaintiff suffered a **displaced fracture** of the head and neck of the **proximal phalanx of the right thumb** when he tripped on a damaged area of pavement and **fell onto his outstretched hand**. The fracture was reduced with a small screw under **general anaesthetic** and two **K wires** were placed through the head of the proximal phalanx in case of further fracturing. Plaintiff underwent **physiotherapy** and was left with a dorsal scar measuring one and three quarters of an inch and a radial scar of one inch. There was no residual discomfort and only **minimal restriction** of movement, although this did not present a problem. It was thought probable that he would develop **osteoarthritis**, which would involve some additional discomfort. The above award included £10,176 special damages and £1,273.62 interest.

Farnan v Liverpool City Council (27 February 1995, unreported) (Antonis Georges, Messrs Malcolm J Ross, Liverpool, for the plaintiff) (Kindly submitted for publication by Antonis Georges, Barrister).

PSLA: £1,800
Sex: Female
Age at accident/settlement: 17/20
Date of accident/settlement: 9 June 1992/October 1995
Judge/court: settled out of court

The plaintiff **cut her right hand** on **broken glass**, suffering a **laceration** to the **palmar surface of the hand**, a **large cut** at the **base of** her **thumb**, and a **small cut** at the **distal palmar crease** level in the line of the web beneath her little and ring fingers. On attending a hospital accident and emergency department, the plaintiff's **wounds were cleaned** and she was told that there was **no glass in** the **wound. Stitches** were **inserted** and **removed after a week. Three months later**, however, the plaintiff was referred back to the accident and emergency department, as by that time she had **reduced sensation over the whole** of the **palmar surface of** her **index finger and a radial half of** her **middle finger**. This was diagnosed as a **division of** the **deep palmar branch of** the **ulnar nerve, damage to** the **common digital nerve of the index and middle fingers,** and **damage to the radial branch of** the **digital nerve of** her **index finger**. The plaintiff had an **operation** which **successfully repaired the nerves**, and later made a **complete recovery**. Compensation was agreed in respect of the three month's pain and suffering which she had endured.

Brogan v Leicestershire Health Authority (unreported) (Margaret de Haas, Holyoak & Co, Leicester, for the plaintiff). (Kindly submitted for publication by C J Smith of Holyoak & Co, Solicitors).

PSLA: £1,000
Total damages: £1,250
Sex: Female
Age at accident/trial: 39/42
Date of trial: 12 July 1995
Judge/court: District Judge Lamb/Halifax County Court

Plaintiff, a waitress, fell at work and **severed the tendons of her thumb**. The thumb and wrist were in a plaster of paris cast for three weeks. For **five weeks she was unable to carry out housework, drive, dress or wash herself**. After nine weeks she had made a full recovery. The above award included £250 special damages.

Khalifa v Hardy (12 July 1995, unreported) (Messrs Rhodes Thain & Collinson, Halifax for the plaintiff) (Kindly submitted for publication by Alan Western, Messrs Rhodes Thain & Collinson, Solicitors).

PSLA: £950
Total damages: £950
Sex: Female
Age at accident/trial: 41/43
Date of trial: 17 March 1995
Judge/court: District Judge Evans/Hull County Court

Plaintiff, a process worker, sustained a **soft tissue injury** to the **little finger** and nail of her right (dominant) hand, when it became **caught in a conveyor belt**. Two unsuccessful attempts were made to remove the nail under **local anaesthetic**, causing the plaintiff **extreme pain** and the nail was subsequently **repaired with adhesive**. She was **off work for three weeks**, during which time she was unable to use her right hand, the injured finger was acutely painful and she **could not drive her car**. For six weeks she found it **difficult to use her right hand** to fasten buttons, laces etc and her **leisure activities were curtailed**. The prognosis was that the finger would be **sensitive to heat** and cold for 18 to 24 months and that there was permanent **incomplete re-attachment of the nail bed**.

Pullen v Birds Eye Walls Ltd (17 March 1995, unreported) (Henry Witcomb, Messrs Robin Thompson and Partners, Hull, for the plaintiff; Nicholas Lumley, Messrs Wansbrough Willey Hargrave, Leeds, for the defendant) (Kindly submitted for publication by Nicholas Lumley, Barrister).

1048 *Finger*
PSLA: £1,000
Total damages: £1,064.78 (including interest)
Sex: Female
Age at accident/trial: 38/41
Date of trial: 28 April 1995
Judge/court: Judge Fawcus/Manchester County Court

Plaintiff, a sewing machinist, was sewing when a **needle pierced** her left (non-dominant) **index finger and nail**. The needle and her nail were **removed under a ring block**, but a tiny **fragment of metal** remained in the finger as it was too small to remove. The injury was **extremely painful** and she was **off work for one week**. After three weeks there was 95 per cent recovery, although she continued to experience **sensitivity** in the finger in cold weather.

Plaintiff was left with a faint mark on the pad of her finger where the needle had protruded and the nail re-grew in a flaky manner for three months, but by the time it had grown out fully it was of normal appearance. The above award included £45.65 special damages and £19.13 interest.

Lea v William Baird plc (28 April 1995, unreported) (Antonis Georges, Messrs Whittles, Manchester, for the plaintiff) (Kindly submitted for publication by Antonis Georges, Barrister).

1049 *Sphincter*

PSLA: £30,000
Total damages: £32,500
Sex: Female
Age at accident: 25

The plaintiff gave birth to a daughter on 17 February 1987. An **episiotomy** was performed and the hospital staff called for a general medical practitioner to attend to **suture** the wound. The defendant attended as part of the general practitioner's deputising service for night cover. At episiotomy damage was caused to the **sphincter**. The plaintiff alleged that the duty obstetrician should have been called and asked to examine her and that her wound should have been sutured with long acting reabsorbable sutures by an obstetrician under general or regional anaesthetic. The wound was in fact sutured by the general practitioner. The **sphincter was not properly sutured** and the plaintiff suffered a **disruption of the internal sphincter mechanism**. She suffered **faecal incontinence** when walking, after opening her bowels and during sexual intercourse. This was caused by **weakness in the anterior aspect** and to the **right of the anal sphincter** and a **low anal tone**. On 1 February 1993 the plaintiff underwent repair surgery which involved undergoing a **left iliac fossa defunctioning colostomy** to minimise the risk of infection. The colostomy was reversed in August 1993. Although the plaintiff's condition improved she has not fully recovered in that she must wash herself whenever she defecates and there is a lack of sensation during sexual intercourse. The above award comprised £2,500 special damages.

H v F (unreported) (settled out of court) (Peter Atherton, Hartley & Worstenholme, Castleford, for the plaintiff; Julian Goose, Le Brasseur J Tickle, London, for the defendant) (Kindly submitted for publication by Arthur J Healey, Hartley & Worstenholme, Solicitors, Castleford).

1050 *Vagina*

PSLA: £9,000
Sex: Female
Age at accident: 32
Date of accident: March 1993
Judge/court: settled out of court

The plaintiff, a married woman with no children, was advised by the defendant to undergo a **small cone biopsy**. After the procedure, she was in **considerable pain** and started to **leak urine**. She was later **diagnosed** as having a **vesico-vaginal fistula**, which was corrected by **excision of the fistula tract** and **repair to the vagina and bladder**. In addition, the **greater omentum** was **mobilised and interposed between the bladder and the vagina** to prevent recurrence. As a result of the injury, the plaintiff was temporarily **unable to have sexual intercourse** or **take part in sporting activities**. There was also evidence of a **risk of future stress incontinence**, particularly if she were to have a child. The matter was settled before trial as regards general damages, special damages, and payment of the plaintiff's costs.

L v Pontefract Hospitals NHS Trust (unreported) (settled out of court) (Margaret de Haas, Hartley & Worstenholme, Castleford, for the plaintiff; Michael Taylor, W J M Lovel, for the defendant) (Kindly submitted for publication by Arthur J Healey, Hartley & Worstenholme, Solicitors).

1051 *Legs*

PSLA: £35,000
Total damages: £123,117.50 (subject to a reduction of one third in respect of contributory negligence)
Sex: Male
Age at accident/trial: 49/55

Date of accident/trial: 20 November 1989/6 February 1995
Judge/court: Judge Burford QC/Portsmouth County Court

Plaintiff, a fabricated welder, suffered **serious leg injuries** following a fall from a wall. There was a **comminuted fracture** of the lower shaft of the **left femur**, involving the left knee joint and a **bi-malleolar fracture of the right ankle**. The right ankle was **manipulated under anaesthetic** and supported with a **plaster back slab**, a pin was passed through the left upper tibia to apply traction to the left femoral fracture, and the lateral and medial side of the right ankle was internally **fixed with a plate and screws**. After two weeks plaintiff had a good range of movement in the ankle and some movement in left knee with help from a machine. One month after the accident, a **cast brace** was applied to the left leg to give him to mobility and he was discharged the following week. An x-ray three months after the accident also revealed a fracture of the left patella. One month later, the plaster cast and metal plates were removed from the right ankle, but it continued to be painful and subject to swelling and stiffness and there is **permanent loss of movement** and a risk of **osteoarthritis**. Plaintiff still had major problems with the left knee at time of trial and, due to **degenerative changes**, an **artificial replacement** will be necessary within five to ten years. Plaintiff is **substantially disabled** and walks with a stick and is in **constant pain**. He can only stand for short periods, his walking is restricted, he cannot kneel or climb stairs, do any home decorating, ride a bicycle, drive (except for short distances), or play golf or judo. He has **not worked since the accident** and there is little prospect of him securing future employment. The above award was reduced by one third in respect of contributory negligence and included £35,000 past loss of earnings, £40,000 future loss of earnings and handicap on labour market, £6,375 for an operation to replace the knee joint, £4,790 purchase of automatic car, £1,750 DIY and car maintenance and £202.50 miscellaneous costs.

Davey v MJF Precision Welding (6 February 1995, unreported) (Mark Lomas, Messrs Bell Pope, Southampton, for the plaintiff; Mr Matovu, Messrs Jarvis and Bannister, London, for the defendant) (Kindly submitted for publication by Shaun Underhill, Solicitor, of Messrs Bell Pope).

PSLA: £17,000
Total damages: £33,756.63
Sex: Male
Age at accident/trial: 35/40
Date of accident/trial: 28 August 1990/21 June 1995
Court: Outer House

Scotland
The plaintiff sustained a **compound fracture of the left tibia** in a road traffic accident. He had **extensive in-patient and out-patient hospital treatment**, and was unable to resume his full-time work as a social security benefit fraud investigator until a year and four months after the accident. There was medical evidence that the **plaintiff** would **develop osteo-arthritis** in the **lateral compartment of** his **left knee** over the next **five to ten years**, and some **wasting of the quadriceps muscles** had already occurred. Although the plaintiff could use his knee for ordinary everyday activities, he had **difficulty** carrying out certain activities **in the course of his employment**, such as visiting building sites and climbing over rough and uneven ground. Such activities were instead carried out by his colleagues, but it was the case that if the plaintiff developed osteo-arthritis to the extent that his activities were further restricted, he would not be able to continue his employment and would have to **retire early** on medical grounds. Having regard to the ordinary vicissitudes of life, damages of £4,000 were awarded for loss of future earning capacity. The parties agreed damages for loss of past earnings, the value of the plaintiff's car and other incidental losses.

Walledge v Brown 1996 SLT 95 (Outer House).

PSLA: £15,000
Total damages: £25,000
Sex: Female
Age at injury/hearing: 26/30
Date of hearing: 28 February 1995
Court: Criminal Injuries Compensation Board, Birmingham

Applicant, who was five and a half months **pregnant**, was **beaten about the legs** with an **iron bar** during a **violent assault**. She sustained an **open fracture** of the **left tibia** and cuts and bruises to both legs. The wounds were **débrided** and the **fracture manipulated** under **general anaesthetic**. She was in hospital for three weeks and her leg was in **plaster** for seven months, which caused her some **difficulties during childbirth**. The fracture healed well, but her leg was **shortened by one cm** and had a **15 degree bow**. She was left with a **limp**, which placed stress upon her abdomen and caused further pain and she could only walk short distances with the aid of a **walking stick**. The fracture site was more painful in cold weather and she generally felt cold more in that leg. Applicant also suffered from **depression** and was diagnosed as suffering from **post traumatic stress disorder**, she was afraid to leave the house and her sleep was disturbed. She was **dependant upon her husband for eleven months** after the attack, during which time he cared for their children, washed her and carried out household tasks. At time of trial she still required assistance with shopping and heavier household chores. The above award included £10,000 special damages for past care.

Criminal Injuries Compensation Board, Birmingham (28 February 1995, unreported) (Alasdair Davidson for the applicant) (Kindly submitted for publication by Alasdair Davidson, Barrister).

PSLA: £15,000
Total damages: £19,150.37 (including interest)
Sex: Male
Age at accident/trial: 19/21
Date of accident/trial:8 December 1994/24 October 1995
Judge/court: Judge Morgan/Birkenhead County Court

Plaintiff was involved in a collision with a motor vehicle while driving his motorcycle. He sustained a **fracture to the right fibula**, a **fracture dislocation to the right ankle**, **deep lacerations** to the outer aspect of the **right thigh** and abrasions to the left knee. He was admitted to hospital and had surgery to his ankle with **internal fixation of the lateral malleolar fracture**. The **thigh wound was debrided** and initially left open though later closed in a secondary procedure. The plaintiff was **in hospital for ten days**. He had a plaster cast for a further ten weeks and was on non-weight bearing crutches during that period. The metalwork in his leg was removed in 1994. By May 1995 **full function had returned to the left leg** which still had residual scarring. The right leg still ached occasionally, particularly if the plaintiff stood for long periods. There was some slight residual stiffness in the right ankle but **no later complications were expected**. The **scarring to the right thigh was permanent**. The plaintiff had returned to full time employment. The above award included £4,150.57 special damages including interest.

Hicks v Munley (24 October 1995, unreported) (Andrew Menary, Messrs Michael W Halsall, Maghull, for the plaintiff; no appearance for the defendants) (Kindly submitted for publication by Messrs Michael W Halsall, Solicitors).

PSLA: £6,500
Total damages: £6,500
Sex: Male
Age at accident/settlement: 7/9
Date of accident/settlement: 6 May 1993/19 June 1995
Judge/court: Deputy District Judge Munro/Leigh County Court (settled prior to trial)

Plaintiff was crossing quiet estate road when hit by defendant's vehicle. He suffered a **transverse fracture** of the **mid shaft of the left femur** and **grazing** to the back of the head and left buttock. He was in hospital in traction for seven weeks, then mobilised in a caliper for a further seven weeks. When examined 13 months after the accident the **fracture had healed well**, leg lengths had equalised, no limping was evident and no further complications were expected. There was a **permanent scar** on the left buttock but it was in the area normally covered by underwear and would not cause any undue embarrassment. The case was settled prior to trial and the settlement approved by Deputy District Judge Munro.

Tildsley v Adams (19 June 1995, settled prior to trial) (Messrs Stephensons, St Helens, advised by Phillip Grundy, for the plaintiff; Rowley Dickinson, Manchester) (Kindly submitted for publication by Sheryl Rigby, Messrs Stephensons, Solicitors).

PSLA: £5,228
Total damages: £5,500
Sex: Female
Age at injury/settlement: 9/12

Date of injury/settlement: 19 July 1992/21 August 1995
Judge/Court: District Judge Harrison/Huddersfield County Court

Plaintiff **fell as she walked down a grass bank** adjacent to a swimming pool. The slope of the bank was increasingly steep and ended in an **unfenced and hidden drop of five or six feet** into a car park. The plaintiff suffered **abrasions to her forehead and the bridge of her nose** which settled after two or three weeks and left no mark; an **abrasion to her right knee** which settled after two to three weeks and left a very small area of marking which is no trouble to her; a **chip to a lower tooth** which was filled by a dentist; and **a fracture of the mid shaft of the left femur**. The plaintiff was placed in **traction on a splint for six weeks** after which she was placed in a brace and mobilised. After eight weeks the fracture was chemically united, she was out of the brace and advised to begin weight-bearing. By **ten weeks she no longer needed crutches** and was able to **resume her normal activities three to four months after the accident**. There is a minimal degree of external rotation at rest and some marking on the posterior aspect of the left femur but **no future problems are anticipated**.

Seabridge v Scarborough Borough Council (21 August 1995, unreported) (Messrs Oates Hanson, Huddersfield, for the plaintiff; Messrs Hammond Suddards, Leeds, for the defendant) (Kindly submitted for publication by Messrs Oates Hanson, Solicitors).

PSLA: £3,250
Total damages: £4,110.46 (including interest)
Sex: Female
Age at accident/trial: 21/25
Date of accident/trial: 21 October 1991/17 July 1995
Judge/court: Judge MacMillan/Bury County Court

Plaintiff was injured when tread on stairs gave way. She suffered a **fractured right fibula**. She was in **plaster for seven weeks**, then wore an elasticated support and underwent physiotherapy. She had made a good recovery, although she was still aware of tenderness especially in cold weather. She is reluctant to wear anything other than flat shoes. She was expected to be **entirely symptom free in the near future**. The above included £860.46 special damages and was agreed between counsel after a contested hearing as to liability.

Bent v Bolton Metropolitan Borough Council (17 July 1995, unreported) (Timothy G White for the plaintiff; Michael Smith for the defendant) (Kindly submitted for publication by Timothy G White, Barrister).

PSLA: £2,000
Total damages: £2,133.87 (including interest)
Sex: Female
Age at accident: 42
Date of accident/trial: 6 January 1995
Judge/court: District Judge Reeson/Chesterfield County Court

Plaintiff sustained a **deep laceration** to her posterior **left thigh** as a result of sitting on a **toilet seat** with a jagged broken edge. The wound **bled profusely** and required **seven stitches** under local anaesthetic. Two weeks after the accident, the wound became **inflamed** and **antibiotics** were prescribed. Plaintiff was **off work for ten days** and had difficulties sitting down and sleeping on her back for six to eight weeks. She was left with a **scar** of 3cm by 2mm, which **itched** from time to time. She is **conscious of the scar** and no longer wears shorts or exposes that part of her leg to the sun and remains nervous of using any toilet other than her own.

Turner v Dale (6 January 1995, unreported) (Mererid Edwards, Messrs Elliot Mather Smith, Chesterfield, for the plaintiff) (Kindly submitted for publication by Mererid Edwards, Barrister).

PSLA: £1,250
Total damages: £1,250
Sex: Female
Age at accident: 4
Date of accident/settlement: 4 November 1994/27 November 1995
Judge/court: Settled out of court

Plaintiff leant over a glass top table from which a nail was protruding. The **nail pierced the front of her left leg** below the knee. First aid was administered and the wound was cleaned. Two days later, the wound was still tending to bleed. The plaintiff had a **limp for a week** and the wound took approximately **two weeks to heal** during which time it had to be redressed once. The plaintiff was left with a **scar** 5cm below the lower border of the knee which measured 6mm in diameter and was depressed by approximately 1mm. The scar was a slightly different colour to the surrounding skin and, although the cosmetic defect was relatively slight, the plaintiff did work for a number of modelling agencies which might not use her where a close-up photograph of legs was required.

Narewal v Birmingham Cable Ltd (settled out of court) (Graham Marsh, Messrs Lovsey Marsh, Birmingham for the plaintiff; Messrs Buller Jefferies, Birmingham, for the defendant) (Kindly submitted for publication by Graham Marsh, of Messrs Lovsey Marsh, Solicitors).

1052 *Knees*

PSLA: £24,200
Total damages: £48,964.72 (including interest)
Sex: Male
Age at injury/trial: 50/54
Date of injury/trial: 28 December 1990/27 June 1995
Judge/Court: Colin Smith QC/Central London County Court

Plaintiff, London taxi-cab driver, was injured when his taxi collided with the defendant's lorry. He suffered a **laceration** over his right eye; **pain** in his elbows; **whiplash** which has resulted in a **permanent 20 per cent reduction in rotation** of his neck; and, developing three years after the accident, **early accelerated degenerative process in right hip**. His most serious injury was to his knee and **constant pain in his knee** with a **patello-femoral catch**. The knee was **prone to giving way** and he **may need a joint replacement** in 15 years due to early osteoarthritis. The injuries caused constant pain in his neck and knee making it impossible to drive long distances, he suffered from stress and hypertension, his inability to work fully had caused financial hardship and he lost his home due to inability to maintain mortgage repayments. He was unable to jog or dance and the injury interfered with his sex life. The above award comprised £24,200 general damages (apportioned £7,500 for the neck, £12,000 for the knee, £3,500 for the hip and £1,200 for the elbows and laceration) and £24,000 special damages plus interest.

Rosen v Wheatgrove Ltd (27 June 1995, unreported) (Lawrence Caun, Messrs Alexander Johnson, of London, for the plaintiff; Christopher Bamford, Messrs Edwards, Son & Noice, of London, for the defendant) (Kindly submitted for publication by Lawrence Caun, Barrister).

PSLA: £17,500
Total damages: £19,250 (plus interest and subject to a reduction of one third for contributory negligence)
Sex: Female
Age at accident/trial: 32/38
Date of accident/trial: 14 April 1989/28 November 1994
Judge/court: Judge Crane/Peterborough County Court

Plaintiff **injured her right knee** on the pedestal of her desk at work. Ten months after the accident, an **arthroscopy** was performed and some **softening and fibrilation of the medial pole** of the patella was apparent and a **lateral release operation** was performed. She returned to work one month later, but suffered from increasingly **severe pain**. She was found to have marked **retro-patella tenderness and crepitus** and was provided with **analgesics**. She made little progress and two months after the first operation, she was re-admitted to hospital and underwent an **arthrotomy** of the right knee, which revealed marked **chondral degeneration** and a **blister type lesion** over the medial pole of the patella. The abnormal articular cartilege was excised and 32mm **carbon patch** was inserted into the retro-patella surface. Plaintiff was in hospital for four days and was **off work for a total of 23 weeks** between the first operation and her return to work some nine months after the second operation. She now **walks with a stick**; suffers severe pain if the leg is accidentally knocked; is in constant **pain in cold weather**; finds it **difficult to negotiate stairs** and can no longer kneel down or squat; she has limited sexual activity and can no longer enjoy gymnastics, netball, swimming or walking. She cannot lift bulky objects; cannot do the gardening, drive a car, wear high heels or get up and down quickly, but she can hold down a clerical job similar to her employment prior to the accident. The above award included £1,750 special damages and was reduced by one third due to contributory negligence.

Steward v Gates Hydraulics Ltd (28 November 1994, unreported) (Simon Tattersall, Messrs Adlams, St Neots, for the plaintiff; James Dingemans, Messrs Berrymans, London, for the defendant) (Kindly submitted for publication by Paddy Willmer, F Inst L Ex, of Adlams, Solicitors).

PSLA: £8,000
Total damages: £19,000 (including interest)
Sex: Female
Age at accident/settlement: 19/25
Date of accident/settlement: September 1989/20 September 1995
Court: Settled out of court

Plaintiff **suffered from a medical problem** in respect of the **dislocation of the patella** on average once every four months. The **defendant consultant carried out a tibial tubercle transposition of the right patella** on the plaintiff in September 1989. Despite six months' physiotherapy the **plaintiff continued to experience problems and further dislocation.** In October 1990 she fell in a restaurant and her knee dislocated and was plastered. This was the subject of a separate action against the restaurant which was compromised. The knee had taken on an unpleasant appearance which made the plaintiff feel self conscious. The plaintiff was seen on several occasions by the defendant who thought the problem was caused by insufficient physiotherapy on the part of the plaintiff. In September 1992 the **problem was diagnosed by a different consultant** as being **due to the incorrect repositioning of the plaintiff's patella** by the defendant. A second operation was carried out by the second consultant. The plaintiff claimed that the defendant's failure to reposition the patella in the correct place was negligent and lead to three years' unnecessary pain and suffering. The matter was settled out of court and the above settlement includes £7,500 for loss of earnings.

Fisher v Strachan (settled out of court) (Messrs Martin Smith & Co, Borehamwood, for the plaintiff, Messrs Hempsons, London, for the defendant) (Kindly submitted for publication by Martin Smith of Messrs Martin Smith & Co, Solicitors).

PSLA: £4,000
Total damages: £5,565.69
Sex: Male
Age at injury/trial: 31/33
Date of injury/trial: 29 August 1993/2 March 1995
Judge/Court: Recorder Digney/Dartford County Court

Plaintiff was knocked off his motor-cycle by the defendant and sustained multiple minor injuries including **grazing to left shoulder**, **mild contusion** of the **left elbow** and, most seriously, **severe bruising** and **contusion** of the **left knee** and **left upper tibia** with **probable bruising to the bone** caused by a **subperiostal haematoma**. He took five weeks off work. Most of the injuries settled quickly but the knee injury continued to cause sharp pain whilst kneeling, stiffening when held in one position for too long, discomfort in the medial side of the knee when jogging and discomfort during sexual intercourse.

Back v Sharpe (2 March 1995, unreported) (Stephen Ellis-Jones, T G Baynes, Dartford, for the plaintiff) (Kindly submitted for publication by Stephen Ellis-Jones, Barrister).

PSLA: £1,500
Total damages: £1,500
Sex: Male
Age at accident: 4
Date of accident/trial: 8 June 1993/28 April 1995
Judge/court: District Judge Moon/Exeter County Court

Plaintiff sustained injuries to both knees when he tripped over a board covering a hole in the pavement which had been placed there by the defendants. There was **no fracture**, but both knee caps sustained a direct blow, resulting in **bruised bone syndrome**, which affected the **patella articular cartilage** and underlying bone. The injury was exacerbated, and recovery delayed, by the plaintiff's **diabetes** and by two **previous fractures** (of the right tibia and right femur respectively), which had only just healed by date of accident. In normal circumstances he would have been expected to make a full recovery within a few months, but it took **16 months** for the injuries to settle. During this time he had difficulty in walking and could not ride his bicycle. It was thought unlikely that there would be any long term sequelae.

McCarthy v British Gas plc (28 April 1995, unreported) (Messrs Bevan Ashford, Exeter, for the plaintiff) (Kindly submitted for publication by Damian Horan, Barrister, of Messrs Bevan Ashford).

1053 *Ankle*

PSLA: (Agreed settlement not broken down)
Total damages: £65,000
Sex: Male
Age at injury/settlement: 39/44
Date of injury/settlement: 2 May 1991/October 1995
Court: Settled out of court

Plaintiff worked as a driver for the defendant and his duties included loading and unloading goods from vehicles at the defendant's premises. Plaintiff was unloading empty mobile bread racks in the raised concrete loading and unloading area of the defendant's premises. The area was congested with a number of racks. **A rack** at the top of the loading area was pushed by another employee so that it **fell and struck the plaintiff's right ankle**. He suffered a **3 to 4 inch laceration** to the back of the **right ankle** and a **partial division of the right Achilles tendon**. The injury has lead to **significant functional disability** and he has been assessed as **20 per cent disabled** by the DSS. Despite emergency surgery on the day of the accident, subsequent physiotherapy and a pain relieving injection into a neuroma in the scar he continues to suffer pain. The ankle remains very sensitive and is aggravated by cold and damp conditions. At the time of the settlement he was **still unable to resume his job** as a driver as he can only drive for about 12 miles before having to stop and walk around because his ankle is stiff. Sexual relations with his wife have been affected and the strain of the injury has also affected the plaintiff's family life. He has also lost confidence and suffered mood changes. His injury **severely limited his recreational interests** of dog training and freshwater and seawater fishing. He finds standing for any period of time causes pain. In addition an expert's report stated that the plaintiff suffered '**moderately severe reactive depression and an anxiety state**'. It was anticipated that the plaintiff would recover full movement of his ankle within five years of the injury. The above settlement was a total figure and not apportioned.

Kelk v Starbake Anglia (settled out of court) (Leslie Thomas, for the plaintiff; B J K Lewis for the defendant) (Kindly submitted for publication by Leslie Thomas, Barrister).

1054 *Foot*

PSLA: £10,000
Total damages: £10,000
Sex: Male
Age at accident/trial: 21/25
Date of trial: 14 March 1995
Judge/court: Judge Carter QC/Altrincham County Court

Plaintiff sustained a **soft tissue injury** to his **left leg** during the course of a game of rugby. He was negligently treated by the defendants who **failed to carry out surgery** which would have resolved his condition and enabled him to make a good recovery with no **neurovascular problems** (although he would have had a surgical scar and some muscle protrusion). As a result of the lack of treatment he suffered a **complete foot drop**. He walked with **crutches** for six weeks and then with a **drop foot splint** for six months which **severely restricted his mobility**. He made a **reasonable recovery**, although there was some **residual loss of inversion** and eversion of the ankle. He could walk normally, but was unable to jog for more then a mile and he could **no longer play rugby or squash**. Prior to the accident he had been a very proficient rugby player, playing competitively to a high standard and his inability to play caused him **considerable distress**. There was no likelihood of further deterioration.

Wright v Macclesfield Health Authority (14 March 1995, unreported) (Timothy White, Messrs Slater Heelis, Sale, for the plaintiff; James McKeon, Messrs Hill Dickinson Davis Campbell, for the defendant) (Kindly submitted for publication by Timothy White, Barrister).

PSLA: £5,250
Total damages: £5,250

Sex: Male
Age at accident: 25
Date of trial: 29 March 1995
Judge/court: Judge Bush/Halifax County Court

Plaintiff, an electronics engineer, sustained a **double fracture** of the right **os calcis** (heel bone) in a road traffic accident. The fractures extended into the sub talar joint and one was slightly displaced and comminuted. Plaintiff was in hospital for two days with the **leg elevated** and **packed in ice**, after this he used non-weight bearing **crutches** for three weeks. Once the swelling was reduced, a plaster was applied below the knee for a further three weeks and then he was mobilised with a walking stick. He was **off work for seven weeks** and returned to full duties two and a half months after the accident. Prior to the accident, he had undertaken a high level of sporting activity, but he was unable to cycle for four months and only returned to his other hobbies of running, climbing and fell walking one year after the accident, whereon he experienced significant pain and required a course of physiotherapy. He reached a stable and final state one and a half years after the accident, experiencing only **occasional pain** in his right heel lasting up to an hour after performing high levels of sporting activity. Eversion of the ankle was limited by five degrees and a small lump on the back of the heel caused discomfort when he was wearing ordinary shoes. These continuing symptoms would not affect his employment prospects, although they would intrude upon, but not prevent him from taking part in sporting activities. There was a long term risk of symptomatic **osteoarthritis** which was assessed at ten per cent.

Almond v Britt-Waight (29 March 1995, unreported) (Andrew Lewis, Messrs Walker Morris, Leeds, for the plaintiff; Richard Copnall, for the defendant) (Kindly submitted for publication by Andrew Lewis, Barrister). Mr Lewis comments that this case is of interest because there do not appear to be any comparable cases reported where a good recovery has been made after an os calcis fracture.

PSLA: £1,500 (settlement approved by court)
Total damages: £1,500 (settlement approved by court)
Sex: Female
Age at injury/settlement: 13/14
Date of injury/settlement: 22 October 1994/27 October 1995
Judge/Court: District Judge Slim/Halifax County Court

Plaintiff, **seat-belted back seat passenger** in car involved in road traffic accident. After the accident she complained of **pain in right foot and ankle**. X-rays did not show any bone injury. She was **absent from school** for two-and-a-half weeks and was **using crutches** for three-and-a-half weeks. For about a month she was unable to use the foot pedals on her piano and had considerable difficulty bathing, washing and dressing. She developed blisters on her hand due to using the crutches. At the date of the hearing she reported that she had **fully recovered**, apart from very occasional aching in the foot, which lasted only for a short time. Settlement of £1,500 general damages was approved by the court.

Jones v Winteringham (settled out of court) (Messrs Rhodes Thain & Collinson, Halifax, for the plaintiff; Messrs Irwin Mitchell, Leeds, for the defendant) (Kindly submitted for publication by Allan Western, Messrs Rhodes Thain & Collinson, Solicitors).

1055   *Minor injuries*
PSLA: £1,000
Total damages: £1,944.82
Sex: Male
Age at accident/trial: 19/21
Date of trial: 14 February 1995
Judge/court: Judge Morgan/Newport (Gwent) County Court

Plaintiff was involved in a road traffic accident and was **thrown from his motor cycle**, over the roof of the car and onto the ground. He sustained very **painful injuries** to the **left shoulder** and **right thumb**, with associated **restriction of movement** in these joints, pain in the **left ankle**, a cut to the lower inside lip and **minor abrasions** to the left side of the body. No history of **concussion** was noted and there was **no bone injury**. Plaintiff was off work for two weeks, after which time the symptoms had completely resolved. The judge noted that plaintiff had suffered a **nasty shock,** but the injuries were of a minor nature. The above award included £944.82 special damages.

Jinks v Ramzan (14 February 1995, unreported) (Richard Miller, Messrs Roger James Clements and Panting, Newport, for the plaintiff) (Kindly submitted for publication by Richard Miller, Barrister).

PSLA: £900
Total damages: £950
Sex: Female
Date of trial: 12 April 1995
Judge/court: Judge Rowntree/Willesden County Court

Plaintiff, a final year law student, was driving along a road towards a junction which had been recently resurfaced, the give way lines which should have indicated the approach to a junction had been obliterated by the resurfacing and there were no signs warning of the junction. The plaintiff did not stop at the junction and was in collision with a car proceeding along the major road. The plaintiff sued the highway authority for negligence and claimed personal injury damages for **minor bruises to her cheek, forehead and thigh, a small laceration to her lower lip, tenderness to her chest and back pain** (which interfered with her preparation for her examinations and prevented her from doing aerobics). All of the injuries had resolved after two to three weeks. Both parties sought to rely on the authority of *Bird v Pearce and Somerset County Council* [1979] RTR 369, (1979) 77 LGR 753, CA. On the basis of full liability the plaintiff would have received £900 general damages, however it was adjudged that the highway authority was 25 per cent liable for the collision and the plaintiff was 75 per cent liable and so the award was subject to a 75 per cent reduction. Plaintiff was also awarded £50 salvage value of her car.

Kotecha v London Borough of Harrow (12 April 1995, unreported) (Willesden County Court: Judge Rowntree) (Kindly submitted for publication by Ruth Blair, Barrister).

PSLA: £700
Total damages: £700
Sex: Male
Age at accident: 2/5
Date of accident/settlement: 15 April 1993/21 September 1995
Judge/court: Settled out of court

Plaintiff was involved in a **road traffic accident** and sustained **bruising to the left ribs**. He had no bony injury or underlying lung injury. He made a **full recovery** and had little or no memory of the accident.

Hewson v Lewis (settled out of court) (Katharine Ferguson, for the plaintiff) (Kindly submitted for publication by Katharine Ferguson, Barrister).

1056   Psychiatric damage—professional rescuers—police as witnesses to football ground disaster

See *Frost v Chief Constable of South Yorkshire*, para 2172.

DEEDS AND OTHER INSTRUMENTS

Halsbury's Laws of England (4th edn) Vol 12, paras 1301–1566

1057   Articles

Execution of a Mortgage Deed, C I Howells: 145 NLJ 286

1058   Deed—rectification—mistake

See *Racal Group Services Ltd v Ashmore*, para 1661.

DISCOVERY, INSPECTION AND INTERROGATORIES

Halsbury's Laws of England (4th edn) Vol 13, paras 1–200

1059 Articles

Controlling a Juggernaut, Colin Passmore (on the curbing of the scale of discovery by the courts): LS Gaz, 25 October 1995, p 20

Disclosure Dilemma, Simon Whitehead (on disclosure of assets by drug traffickers): LS Gaz, 28 June 1995, p 20

Discovery and Disclosure in Children Cases, David Burrows: 139 SJ 60

Discovery: Redaction in Action, Colin Passmore and Jonathan Goodliffe: 145 NLJ 313

PII [Public Interest Immunity] and the Police, Stephen McNamara: 139 SJ 262

1060 Anton Piller orders

See INJUNCTIONS.

1061 Discovery of documents—assessment forms used in selecting employees for redundancy—redundant employees' seeking discovery of retained employees' forms

See *British Aerospace v Green*, para 1240.

1062 Discovery of documents—disclosure of information by company—documents in possession of subsidiary company

Australia

After selling shares in a credit business the plaintiff made various claims against the defendant purchaser under the sale agreement. The plaintiff sought from the defendant discovery of various documents which were in the possession of the credit business. The defendant objected to the production of the documents on the ground that they were in the possession of one of its subsidiaries and thus not within its power and not discoverable. *Held*, the court had a general power to order discovery under RSC Ord 14 and whether or not it would exercise that power would depend on the facts of the case. In this instance the defendant company and its subsidiary did not seem to be operating as separate legal entities and the defendant effectively had possession, power and control over the documents even though they were physically in the possession of its subsidiary. Accordingly, orders for discovery would be made.

Linfa Pty Ltd v Citibank Ltd [1995] 1 VR 643 (Supreme Court of Victoria).

1063 Discovery of documents—documents relating to exercise of trustee's discretion

See *Wilson v Law Debenture Trust Corpn plc*, para 2262.

1064 Discovery of documents—medical records—disclosure to medical and legal advisers

A former nurse claimed that she had suffered illness as a consequence of her exposure to a particular substance in the course of her employment. The health authority's application under the County Courts Act 1984, s 53 for an order of discovery of her medical records to their legal advisers was dismissed. The authority appealed against that dismissal, arguing that the court could not adjudicate on which documents were relevant and thus subject to disclosure under s 53. *Held*, under the 1984 Act, s 53 the records could not be disclosed to medical advisers alone, to the exclusion of legal advisers; disclosure could only be to both. Nor could the medical advisers peruse the records to decide which should be disclosed to the legal advisers. Further, in such an action where liability, causation and damages were all at issue the medical records were almost certainly relevant. Accordingly, the appeal would be allowed.

Hipwood v Gloucester Health Authority [1995] ICR 999 (Court of Appeal: McCowan and Simon Brown LJJ).

1065 Discovery of documents—order made by Scottish courts—proceedings brought in England

See *Union Carbide Corpn v BP Chemicals Ltd*, para 565.

1066   Discovery of documents—persons not parties to the proceedings—power to order disclosure against third party

See *Re D (Restraint Order: Non-party)*, para 2594.

1067   Discovery of documents—privilege—legal professional privilege—client bringing civil proceedings against solicitor—waiver of privilege

It has been held that, where a plaintiff brings an action against his former solicitor, that solicitor is entitled to discovery and inspection of files of the plaintiff's other earlier solicitors held by his present solicitors since, by bringing the action, the plaintiff has impliedly waived legal professional privilege.

Kershaw v Whelan [1996] 1 WLR 358 (Queen's Bench Division: Ebsworth J).

1068   Discovery of documents—privilege—legal professional privilege—disclosure of client's whereabouts—client abducting his children—extent of disclosure

A father abducted his two young children and disappeared. He later wrote to his solicitor but asked him not to reveal the father's whereabouts. On an application for disclosure by the mother and the central authority, the solicitor was ordered to disclose the father's whereabouts, together with any documents in his possession relating to those whereabouts, and to keep the mother's solicitor informed of any future change of address if it came into his possession. The mother and the central authority appealed against the order on the basis that it was very narrow and was inadequate for the amount of information which might become available. They claimed that the father's solicitor should have been ordered to disclose his entire file, together with any documents which might come into his possession in the future, to use his best endeavours to ascertain the father's whereabouts, and not to tell the father of the disclosures he had made. *Held*, the effect of the judge's order was that the father's legal professional privilege was overridden to the extent that the solicitor was entitled and obliged to disclose any information or communications from his client which might assist in ascertaining his whereabouts. It was not, however, overridden in any other respect. There had to be a balance between the duty to a client and a duty to comply with a court order, and the solicitor could not properly be ordered to lie or otherwise to mislead his client. It was a matter for the solicitor's honest professional judgment to decide how those principles were to be applied to the documents and information in his possession. Accordingly, the appeal would be dismissed.

Re B (Abduction: Disclosure) [1995] 1 FLR 774 (Court of Appeal: Butler-Sloss and Hoffmann LJJ).

1069   Discovery of documents—privilege—legal professional privilege—documents relating to client defrauding creditors

Under the Insolvency Act 1986, s 423, where a debtor makes a transaction at an undervalue, the court may declare the transaction void if it is satisfied that the transaction was entered into to put assets beyond the reach of a creditor or otherwise prejudice his interests.

A bank applied under the Insolvency Act 1986, s 423 for an order declaring void various transfers of property by a debtor to his sons. The bank obtained an order requiring the debtor to disclose all documents containing or evidencing communications between himself and his legal advisers that related to the transactions. On appeal by the debtor, *held*, in the absence of a prima facie case, legal professional privilege would be available for the documents in question. The court had to be satisfied that a transaction had been entered into at an undervalue and for a prohibited purpose. The transfers in question had been made at an undervalue to members of the family at a time when action by the creditor was expected by the debtor. Since the assets remaining in the hands of the debtor barely covered the value of the debt, there was a strong prima facie case that the purpose of the transactions was to prejudice the interests of the creditor. Legal advice sought or given to effect an iniquity was not privileged. There was no public interest in maintaining the confidential nature of communications between a client and his solicitor in such cases. The judge's order for discovery would be upheld and, accordingly, the debtor's appeal would be dismissed.

Barclays Bank plc v Eustice [1995] 4 All ER 511 (Court of Appeal: Butler-Sloss, Aldous and Schiemann LJJ).

1070   Discovery of documents—privilege—legal professional privilege—non-legal advice by solicitor—waiver of privilege

The plaintiff company wished to purchase the share capital of some insurance companies, but before doing so, it consulted a team of advisers including accountants and legal advisers. After the sale had gone through, the insurance companies were exposed to huge claims due to the insufficiency of their retrocession cover and the plaintiff sued its advisers claiming that it would not have entered into the agreement without their negligent advice. The plaintiff's accountants requested that the plaintiff gave discovery of communications with its legal advisers relating to general advice on the commercial advisability of entering into the agreement which they claimed were not privileged as they did not contain purely legal advice. They also claimed that such communications were not confidential between members of the same team of advisers. Alternatively, if the documents were privileged, the plaintiff had waived such privilege in the same way that a client who sues his solicitor for negligence waives privilege in respect of documents containing legal advice passing between his solicitor and himself. *Held*, a solicitor's professional duty or function was not limited to purely legal advice but included advice on the commercial wisdom of entering into a particular transaction. In such a case, a solicitor had a discretion on whether or not it was necessary to disclose communications between himself and his client to non-legal advisers. If he decided not to exercise that discretion then those communications would remain confidential. A plaintiff was deemed to have waived privilege in relation to an action brought by him against his solicitor as enforcement would deprive the solicitor of the means of defending the claim but this principle did not apply outside the solicitor-client relationship where privilege prevented defendants gaining access to evidence that might assist in the defence. Otherwise, it would constitute a fundamental inroad into the scope of legal professional privilege. It was clear that the documents in question were privileged by reason of the legal professional relationships between the plaintiff and its legal advisers and, accordingly, the application for disclosure would be dismissed.

Nederlandse Reassurantie Groep Holding NV v Bacon & Woodrow (a firm) [1995] 1 All ER 976 (Queen's Bench Division: Colman J).

1071 Discovery of documents—privilege—legal professional privilege—privilege overridden by court

See *D v D (Production Appointment)*, para 1104.

1072 Discovery of documents—privilege—public interest immunity—police report to Crown Prosecution Service

The plaintiff was arrested and charged with assaulting a police officer. The charge was subsequently dismissed at trial and the plaintiff brought an action against the police for wrongful arrest and malicious prosecution. He sought discovery of the initial report form on which the police provided a summary of the case for the Crown Prosecution Service. The police resisted discovery on the ground that public interest immunity attached to that class of document. The plaintiff argued that where objection on the ground of public interest immunity was taken before trial, the decision to object had to be taken by a government minister or the permanent head of the relevant department. *Held*, the route for raising the public interest immunity claim suggested by the plaintiff might be appropriate in cases where the interests of the state were directly affected, as in applications for disclosure of high level government documents. However, there was no rule that precluded the claim being raised in other ways. Where there was clear authority to support the assertion that class immunity applied, it was sufficient for the claim to be raised by a responsible official within the relevant organisation. There was a clear distinction between the primary documents generated in an investigation into alleged criminal conduct, such as witness statements and exhibits, and secondary documentation comprising a report based on that primary material directed to the CPS. The fact that the document in question was the first such report to be produced did not take it outside the secondary class of document. Accordingly, the document belonged to a class of documents to which public interest immunity attached and the plaintiff's application would be dismissed.

O'Sullivan v Metropolitan Police Comr (1995) 139 Sol Jo LB 164 (Queen's Bench Division: Butterfield J). *Taylor v Chief Constable of Greater Manchester* [1995] 2 All ER 420, CA (para 2301) followed. *R v Chief Constable of West Midlands Police, ex p Wiley* [1994] 3 All ER 420, HL (1994 Abr para 2159) distinguished.

1073 Production of documents—privilege—legal professional privilege—inadvertent disclosure

The plaintiff company commenced proceedings in England against the defendant company for passing off and infringement of a registered trade mark. Similar proceedings were commenced against the defendant's associated company in America. The parties agreed that an order should be made enabling discovery in the English proceedings to be used in the American proceedings, and a similar order was made in the American proceedings. The defendant completed discovery within the specified time limit in the English proceedings, and it was agreed that the plaintiff's solicitors would photocopy the relevant disclosed documents and forward them to its American lawyers. When the plaintiff's solicitors became aware that the defendant might have been able to claim privilege in respect of certain documents which had been disclosed, namely legal bills and the advice of an American attorney, they informed the defendant of their intention to use them. The defendant claimed that they were privileged and had been disclosed by mistake, and sought an injunction for their return. *Held*, where a party sought to prevent the use of privileged documents, the general rule was that, in the absence of fraud, an injunction would not be granted after inspection had occurred unless disclosure of the documents had occurred by mistake. The mistake had to be obvious to a hypothetical reasonable solicitor rather than to whoever happened to receive the document, and the court had to take account of the extent of the privilege claimed, the nature of the disclosed documents, the complexity of the discovery, and the manner in which it had been carried out in deciding whether a reasonable solicitor would have realised that privilege had not been waived. In the instant case, the legal bills and the written advice were privileged, and in view of the short time available to the defendant to comply with the order for discovery and the fact that discovery of a large number of documents had been given without due care, there was no reason to suppose that the defendant had intended to waive privilege. The plaintiff's argument that the written advice was not a privileged document because it had been prepared by an American attorney who was not a practitioner in English law could not be accepted. In deciding whether a document was privileged, it was necessary to look at the substance and form of the disputed document, the circumstances in which it had come into existence, and its purpose. Here, the advice had been given in respect of contemplated litigation which would affect the defendant's worldwide business interests, and was to be used to decide what business and legal strategies should be adopted. Accordingly, the application would be granted.

International Business Machines Corpn v Phoenix International (Computers) Ltd [1995] 1 All ER 413 (Chancery Division: Aldous J).

1074 Production of documents—privilege—public interest immunity—class claim

The plaintiffs brought an action for negligence against the defendant bank arising out of the defendant's conduct in the management of the plaintiff's investmants. The plaintiffs applied under RSC Ord 24, r 11(1) for the production of documents which the defendant had already disclosed to the Security and Futures Authority (SFA) (its regulatory body) and the Bank of England. The defendant resisted the application principally on the grounds of public interest immunity. *Held*, public interest immunity could be claimed on the grounds that the documents were either part of a class which ought to be immune (so that they were to be treated as immune without reference to their contents) or that they ought by virtue of their contents to be treated as immune. It was vigorously reiterated in *R v Chief Constable of the West Midlands, ex p Wiley* that a heavy onus lay on a person who sought to establish a new class claim to public interest immunity. It had been claimed that class immunity was essential to the proper working of the SFA as a self-regulatory organisation under the Financial Services Act 1986, ss 7, 8, since if documents were discoverable member firms might be less candid in their disclosures, confining them to the information which was essential to comply with the rules of membership. However, where a serious breach occurred, a member firm would know that its activities were likely to become public knowledge and it was unlikely that the issue of immunity would affect its candour. Yet the need to promote candour could not justify the withholding of the whole class identified by the defendant. The communication might amount to no more than the member firm was bound to provide under the rules of membership and thus their motivation would be to comply with those rules. A class based immunity could hardly be necessary to the proper functioning of the SFA in cases where the communication was designed to mislead the SFA. The member firm might have disclosed less than it ought to have done. The system could be abused by companies putting all the material which was likely to be sensitive in civil litigation into an SFA report. Further, the purpose of the 1986 Act was the protection of investors and a class-based claim to public interest immunity might in fact result in the withholding of information from those investors. Accordingly, the claim to class-based public interest immunity would not be allowed.

Kaufmann v Credit Lyonnais Bank (1995) Times, 1 February (Chancery Division: Arden J). *R v Chief Constable of the West Midlands, ex p Wiley* [1994] 3 WLR 433, HL followed.

1075   Production of documents—privilege—public interest immunity—Police Complaints Authority

See *Taylor v Chief Constable of Greater Manchester,* para 2301.

DISTRESS

Halsbury's Laws of England (4th edn) Vol 13, paras 201–500

1076   Distress for rent—landlord's rights against assignee—rent owed by assignor

The tenant of a commercial property assigned its lease to the plaintiff company, even though the lessee owed rent to the defendant landlord at the time. Soon after the assignment, the defendant demanded that the plaintiff should pay the tenant's rent arrears. When the plaintiff refused to do so, the defendant instructed a bailiff to levy distress. The plaintiff managed to secure the release of the distrained goods, and successfully commenced proceedings for damages for excessive distress. On the defendant's appeal, *held,* the essence of the right to distrain was that it gave a landlord rights over goods in which he had no proprietary interest. One of the circumstances in which the right arose was in respect of a tenant's breach of his obligation to pay rent. However, just as a landlord had no right to sue an assignee for rent arrears incurred by the original tenant, he had no right to distrain on the goods of an assignee of the original tenant for rent arrears which accrued prior to assignment. Moreover, although a landlord was entitled to distrain against whatever goods he found on the demised premises whether they belonged to the tenant or a stranger, one of the exceptions to that rule was that a landlord could not distrain on the goods of a third party brought onto the demised premises with his consent. It followed that a landlord could not consent to an assignment and then distrain on the assignee's goods for pre-existing rent arrears. Accordingly, the appeal would be dismissed.

Wharfland Ltd v South London Co-operative Building Co Ltd [1995] 2 EGLR 21 (Queen's Bench Division: John Crowley QC).

1077   Distress for rent—reputed ownership—ownership of vehicle subject to hire agreement

The Law of Distress (Amendment) Act 1908, s 4(1) provides that in relation to a tenant whose rent is in arrears, the Act does not apply to goods in the possession of such a tenant by the consent and permission of the true owner under such circumstances that such tenant is the reputed owner of the goods.

The plaintiff hired out a van to a company which owed rent to the defendant landlords. The defendant distrained for arrears of rent, and a walking possession agreement was made between the defendant and the company in respect of the goods on the company's premises, including the hired van. The plaintiff successfully instituted proceedings against the defendant for damages in respect of the van. On the defendant's appeal, the issue was whether or not the company had been the 'reputed owner' of the van within the meaning of the 1908 Act, s 4(1). *Held,* one of the features of the law of distress was that another person's property could be distrained and sold without his knowledge. In order to establish that the goods in the company's possession were in its reputed ownership, the defendant had to establish that a reasonable person with knowledge of the general course of business and who had made all reasonable inquiries, would have inferred that the goods were owned by the company. Judicial notice had to be taken of the fact that there had been an increase in hiring and hire purchase since the 1908 Act was originally passed, especially in respect of motor vehicles. The defendant should have made inquiries of the Driver and Vehicle Licensing Centre in order to establish the ownership of the van, or could have made similar inquiries of Hire Purchase Information Ltd. Such inquiries would have shown that the van was not in the company's 'reputed ownership', and therefore could not have been the subject of distraint. Accordingly, the appeal would be dismissed.

Salford Van Hire (Contracts) Ltd v Bocholt Developments Ltd [1996] RTR 103 (Court of Appeal: Nourse and Hirst LJJ and Sir Ralph Gibson).

1078   Distress for taxes—collector—fees, costs and charges

See para 1628.

DIVORCE

Halsbury's Laws of England (4th edn) Vol 13, paras 501–1352

1079 Articles

Affidavits of Means—Past Their Sell-By Date? Maggie Rae: [1995] Fam Law 186
Agreements and Marriage Breakdown, David Burrows (on pre-divorce agreements): 139 SJ 294
Barry Orders and Interim Financial Provision, David Burrows (on *Barry v Barry* [1992] 3 All ER 405 (1992 Abr para 955)): 139 SJ 496
Divorce and Religion, Helen Conway: 145 NLJ 1618
Divorce Reform—Do We Need Fault? Peter Townsend and Arthur Baker: 159 JP Jo 206
Divorce Reform—Peering Anxiously into the Future, Gwynn Davies: [1995] Fam Law 564
The Divorce White Paper—Some Reflections, Stephen Cretney: [1995] Fam Law 302
The Effect of Divorce on Wills, Roger Kerridge: [1995] Conv 12
An End to the Quickie Divorce, Maggie Rae: 145 NLJ 657
The Future for Divorce, Siân Blore (on the white paper on divorce reform): 139 SJ 416
How Adults Cope with Divorce—Strategies for Survival, Shelley Day Sclater and Martin Richards: [1995] Fam Law 143
How Final is a Foreign Divorce Settlement? Alan Reed: [1995] Fam Law 246
Interest On Lump Sum, Georfon Lingard: [1995] Fam Law 29
Intestacy, Divorce and Wills, Gareth Miller: 145 NLJ 1693
The Limits of Mediation, Shelley Day Sclater: [1995] Fam Law 494
Mediation and Divorce Law Reform—the Lawyer's View, Peter McCarthy and Janet Walker: [1995] Fam Law 361
Mediation and the Ground for Divorce, Jean Graham Hall: 159 JP Jo 349
Pension Deal, Andrew White (on *Brooks v Brooks* (1995) Times, 3 July, HL (para 1098)): LS Gaz, 19 July 1995, p 18
Pensions After *Brooks*, Maggie Rae (on *Brooks v Brooks* [1995] 3 All ER 257, HL (para 1098)): 145 NLJ 1009
Pensions After *Brooks*: Part II, District Judge Isobel Plumstead and David Salter (on *Brooks v Brooks* [1995] 3 All ER 257, HL (para 1098)): [1995] Fam Law 490
Pensions and Divorce: Time for a Change, Maggie Rae: 145 NLJ 310
Rhetoric and Reality in Divorce Reform, Rebecca Bailey-Harris: [1995] Fam Law 618
Working Together After Re M, Andrew Grand (on threshold conditions for care orders): [1995] Fam Law 26

1080 Costs—order against non-party—expert witness

A husband, who was the petitioner in ancillary relief proceedings against his wife, applied to have his wife's accountant joined as a second respondent in an application for an order that the accountant pay the husband's costs incurred in the ancillary relief proceedings. The application also sought leave to serve on the accountant, if so joined, points of claim with a view to the development of pleadings as a preliminary to the determination of the application for costs. *Held*, an order against a non-party was always exceptional and any application to that effect ought to be treated with considerable caution. Ordinarily, the determination of an application for costs against a non-party ought to be by summary procedure. Sufficient notice and formality was achieved by arranging a hearing convenient to the non-party and by giving the non-party full particulars of how the application will be put in solicitor correspondence. Since the power invoked was a power to invoke costs against a non-party, it was unnecessary and illogical to devise a procedure that first joined the potential payer as a party before exercising the discretion invoked. Normally, witnesses in civil proceedings enjoyed immunity from any form of civil action in respect of evidence given in those proceedings and the readiness of forensic accountants to contribute their expert guidance ought not to be shaken by the risk that if their evidence was critically received they might be ordered to pay part of the litigation costs. In this case, although there were specific criticisms of the accountant, the principal causative factor was the wife's unfounded and resolute conviction that the husband had concealed assets and, accordingly, the application would be refused.
S v S (Application for Costs against Witness) [1995] 1 FCR 185 (Family Division: Thorpe J).

1081 Costs—taxation—basis of taxation and appropriate care and control allowance

An Iranian husband issued divorce proceedings in Iran, and his Irish wife commenced divorce and ancillary relief proceedings in England. The English divorce proceedings were stayed following an agreement that the wife could pursue ancillary relief proceedings in the English courts. The husband was a wealthy businessman with substantial, worldwide assets, and an order was made granting a lump sum to the wife and periodical payments for the children of the family. The husband was also ordered to pay the wife's costs on an indemnity basis in respect of the ancillary relief proceedings, and on a standard basis in respect of the discontinued proceedings. At the inter partes taxation of the wife's costs, to which the Matrimonial Causes Rules 1988, SI 1988/1328, applied in part, a district judge decided that he could not interfere with the wife's claim in respect of work done prior to 3 October 1988 (the date on which the rules came into effect), and therefore allowed an hourly charging rate of £70 for work done before that date, with a care and control allowance of 150 per cent for both interlocutory and main items. For work done after that date, he allowed an hourly rate of £75 an hour, with a care and control allowance of 150 per cent for main items, but only 75 per cent for interlocutory items. The husband disputed the district judge's decision on a number of grounds, and applied for a review of the decision. *Held*, costs in respect of work carried out before the 1988 Rules came into force had to be taxed on a party and party basis. Thereafter, taxation could be on either a standard basis or an indemnity basis. Moreover, a district judge was entitled to interfere with a claim for work carried out prior to 3 October 1988. Here, it was a finding of fact that the husband had failed to make full disclosure and that he was an unreliable witness. He had instructed at least six firms of solicitors in the course of the proceedings, and at certain stages had acted as a litigant in person. He had also made serious allegations against the wife and her solicitor. In addition, the matter was fiercely contested by the parties, and was complicated by the fact that substantial assets and two jurisdictions were involved. However, the hourly rate for work prior to 3 October 1988 was too high, and a more appropriate rate was £60. As regards the general care and control allowance, a case had to be extraordinary, and not merely exceptional, in order to justify an allowance of 150 per cent. Although this was not a ground-breaking case, it had been unusual, and exceptionally burdensome for the wife's solicitors. An allowance of 75 per cent for interlocutory items was therefore justified, but for main items, an allowance of 100 per cent was more appropriate.

F v F (Family Division: Taxation of Costs) [1995] 1 FCR 674 (Family Division: Cazalet J).

1082 Custody of children

See CHILDREN AND YOUNG PERSONS.

1083 Decree absolute—appeal—whether sufficient time to appeal from decree nisi— whether question to be determined by Court of Appeal

The Family Proceedings Rules 1991, SI 1991/1247, r 2.42(8) provides that where a party wishes to appeal against a decree absolute of divorce, the question whether he has had the time and opportunity to appeal from the decree nisi must be determined on an application for a re-hearing under that rule.

A divorcee applied to the Court of Appeal for a declaration under the Supreme Court Act 1981, s 18(1)(d) that he should not be precluded from serving and setting down a notice of appeal from a decree absolute of divorce. *Held*, previously the Court of Appeal would have dealt with the question of whether a person seeking to appeal from a decree absolute of divorce had had the time or opportunity to appeal from the decree nisi in question. However, this position had been altered by the 1991 Rules and the words 'an application for a re-hearing under this rule' made it clear that it referred to an application in the court by which the original decree of divorce was granted. This view was reinforced by r 2.42(9) which stated that any other application for a re-hearing was to be by way of an appeal to the Court of Appeal.

Clark v Clark [1995] 2 FLR 487 (Court of Appeal: Balcombe, Roche and Pill LJJ).

1084 Decree absolute—right of respondent to apply—time requirements

Following the breakdown of her marriage a wife had applied for a decree nisi of divorce which had been granted on 27 July 1994. Her husband had then applied for a decree absolute which had been granted on 20 September 1994. The wife had then applied for the decree absolute to be set aside on the grounds that the necessary period of time under the Matrimonial Causes Act 1973, s 9(2) had not elapsed before the application was made and that no notice of it had been given to her. The court refused to set aside the decree on the grounds that, being an action in rem it was voidable, not void. On appeal, *held*, allowing the appeal, the decree was a nullity and not merely voidable as the court purporting to grant it had lacked the jurisdiction to do so since it was in contravention of the time provisions laid down in the 1973 Act, s 9(2).

Manchanda v Manchanda [1995] 2 FLR 590 (Court of Appeal: Leggatt LJ and Thorpe J).

1085 Decree nisi—appeal—order of district judge

The Family Proceedings Rules 1991, SI 1991/1247, r 8.1(1) provides that any party may appeal from an order or decision made or given by the district judge in family proceedings in a county court, to a judge on notice.

It has been held that having regard to r 8.1(1), where decree nisi is pronounced by a district judge in relation to a cause of action that is in the special procedure list, an appeal against the order lies to a county court judge and not to the Court of Appeal.

Marya v Marya [1995] 2 FLR 911 (Court of Appeal: Balcombe, Peter Gibson and Hutchison LJJ).

1086 Divorce reform—government proposals

The Lord Chancellor has published the government's proposals for reform of the law of divorce, *Looking to the future: Mediation and the ground for divorce* (Cm 2799). The white paper describes the objectives of a better divorce process as supporting the institution of marriage, providing practical steps to prevent the irretrievable breakdown of marriage, ensuring that parties understand the consequences of divorce before taking any irretrievable decision, where divorce is unavoidable, minimising the bitterness and hostility between the parties and the trauma for any children, and minimising the costs to the taxpayer and the parties. The government proposes that the sole ground for divorce should be that the marriage has irretrievably broken down. This ground would be evidenced by the passing of a period of time (at least 12 months) for reflection and consideration; this would enable the couple to address what had gone wrong in the marriage, whether there was any hope of reconciliation and, if divorce was inevitable, to make proper arrangements for living apart before a divorce order was made. The period of reflection and consideration might be suspended in order to facilitate reconciliation. The couple would also be required as a precondition to divorce, subject to exceptions, to attend, by appointment, an information-giving session at which they would be introduced to the benefits of marriage guidance and counselling, and information on the emotional, psychological, financial and legal aspects of separation and divorce and its effects on parents and children. The objectives of family mediation would also be explained and the benefits of working together on arrangements for the parties' future described. The information-giving session would include 'legal information', but not 'legal advice', and might be held as a group session rather than as an individual interview. The responsibility of the initiating spouse and the non-initiating spouse for attending the information-giving session would be different, but the latter would normally be required to attend if that spouse wished to make an inter partes application to the court, eg for a residence or contact order. The requirement to attend information-giving sessions might in due course be extended to other forms of dispute, eg those concerning residence and contact with children. No charge would be made for the information-giving sessions. During the period of reflection and consideration the court would have power, of its own motion or on application, to make orders relating to any children of the marriage, financial provision and property adjustment orders; property adjustment orders would normally only take effect after the divorce. The making of arrangements for children, property and finances would be a precondition of the grant of a divorce, unless dispensed with by the court. The present bar to divorce in five-year separation cases on the ground that grave hardship would be caused by the dissolution would be retained and made available in all cases. The option of judicial separation as an alternative to divorce would remain available on the sole ground of irretrievable breakdown of the marriage, and subject also to the 12-month period for reflection and consideration; an order for judicial separation would be capable of conversion to an order of divorce on the application of either or both parties.

No change is proposed at present to the law of nullity. It is proposed to remove the existing grounds of behaviour and desertion as grounds for financial provision orders under the Domestic Proceedings and Magistrates' Courts Act 1978, s 2.

The government is of the view that a more constructive means of making arrangements for a life apart should be made available to couples, but should not be a mandatory requirement, in the form of mediation. Mediators would be expected to remind parents of the duty to take account of the welfare of their children and also their children's views, where these are ascertainable. Statutory privilege would attach to statements made in the course of mediation. The cost of dissolving a marriage would fall primarily on the couple and the eligibility criteria for the mediation services would be the same as for legal aid for legal services (ie subject to a means test, contributions payable by those who could afford it, and reasonable behaviour on the part of those receiving publicly funded assistance). The Legal Aid Board would be responsible for the funding of mediation through block-funded contracts to local mediation services, underpinned by quality standards in respect of professional practice and value for money. Public funding would be available for limited types of legal advice and assistance as part of the mediation process (eg translating a mediated agreement into an enforceable agreement, advice as to the tax and/or state benefit implications of the agreement), but not for uncontrolled access to lawyer representation throughout the mediation process. In respect of certain matters, the couple might obtain advice from the same solicitor and the government would discuss the implementation of such a proposal with the appropriate professional bodies.

The government proposes to launch a widespread public information campaign for the purpose of encouraging couples whose marriages are in difficulties to seek appropriate help in good time and for the purpose of informing the public about the new divorce process.

The divorce process would be initiated by a statement of marital breakdown in prescribed form filed by one or both the spouses in the Divorce County Court. The statement would be served on the non-initiating spouse who would be able to file in response a statement of facts relating to children, home and finance. After the period of reflection and consideration, either party, or both parties, would be able to apply for judicial separation or divorce. The present practice of district judges in relation to the examination of consent ancillary relief applications and where one on the parties is acting without legal representation or advice would be applied to mediated agreements. The new arrangements are to be the subject of a pilot project.

1087 Family proceedings—fees

See para 413.

1088 Financial provision—appeal—leave to appeal out of time—new events—husband accepting redundancy package

At an ancillary relief hearing, a wife was awarded 70 per cent of the proceeds of the sale of the matrimonial home and an endowment policy and any benefit from a relocation package which was provided by the husband's employers. The husband was later made redundant and received a lump sum and a pension. The wife applied for leave to appeal out of time against the original order on the ground that new events undermined the basis of that order. A district judge granted leave to appeal out of time to a circuit judge but, on appeal, the circuit judge found that the district judge did not have the power to grant leave in those circumstances. The circuit judge re-heard the application and held that the particular circumstances did not constitute new events. He refused leave to appeal. It fell to be determined whether that decision was correct. *Held*, under the Family Proceedings Rules 1991, SI 1991/1247, r 8.1(4), or in respect of ancillary relief hearings under CCR, Ord 13, r 4, Ord 37, r 6, a district judge had the power to grant leave to appeal out of time to a circuit judge. However, the district judge had not applied the right principles to the matter and the circuit judge had rightly decided to re-hear the application for leave to appeal. The circuit judge's refusal to grant leave to appeal would be upheld and an order would be made accordingly.

Ritchie v Ritchie (15 December 1995, unreported) (Court of Appeal: Hirst LJ and Bennett J). (Kindly submitted for publication by Richard Martin, Barrister)

1089 Financial provision—conduct—bigamy

A husband was granted a decree of nullity on the basis of his wife's bigamy. On the wife's claim for ancillary relief, the husband was ordered to pay her a lump sum. The husband appealed against the order, arguing that the wife should not have been entitled to make a claim for financial provision because it was contrary to public policy to allow her to benefit from her crime. *Held*, bigamy was a serious offence, and a female bigamist was to be treated in the same way as a male bigamist. The judge had been wrong to allow the wife to make a claim for financial provision for herself and the children of the family, as that meant that a bigamist was entitled to assert a claim which she would not otherwise have been able to make but for her deception and had she remained merely as a cohabitee. Although the Matrimonial Causes Act 1973, s 25(2)(g) obliged the court to have regard to any conduct of the parties which it would be inequitable to disregard, Parliament did not intend that the public policy principle that a person should not profit from his crime could not be applied in matrimonial situations. The judge had given little consideration to the seriousness of the offence, which struck at the heart of the institution of marriage. Where a criminal act undermined the fundamental notions of monogamous marriage, the court would be slow to allow a bigamist to make a claim for ancillary relief. The innocent party to the marriage should, however, be entitled to claim financial relief. Here, the wife could not be allowed to profit from her crime and, accordingly, the appeal would be allowed.

Whiston v Whiston [1995] 2 FCR 496 (Court of Appeal: Russell, Henry and Ward LJJ). Decision of Thorpe J [1994] 2 FCR 529 (1994 Abr para 1057) reversed.

1090   Financial provision—consent order—draft order—death of one party

See *Hunter v Babbage*, para 2472.

1091   Financial provision—distribution of income and capital—improper pressure on third parties

A husband and wife separated after twelve years of marriage. The wife had no capital of her own, but the husband was the joint managing director of a successful family business. He had a substantial income, and assets which included shares and a pension. He was also a Lloyd's name. Although the matrimonial home was of substantial value, it was subject to a mortgage and bank guarantees to cover contingent liabilities to Lloyd's and a Lloyd's loan. In ancillary relief proceedings, the judge decided that the husband could provide alternative security for his Lloyd's liabilities and that his income could be increased. He therefore ordered the sale of the matrimonial home and payment by the husband of a substantial lump sum to the wife, periodical payments for the benefit of the children of the family, and payment of the children's school fees. On the husband's appeal, *held*, the court was not obliged to limit its orders to existing capital or income, as it could take account of the potential availability of wealth from sources owned or administered by third parties. Although the court would not put improper pressure on third parties to act in a way which enhanced the financial means of the spouse ordered to maintain the other spouse, a judge was entitled to make an order which encouraged third parties to provide the maintaining spouse with the means to comply with a financial provision order. Here, the husband had substantial income and assets which were not readily available to him. Although the terms of the order were a powerful inducement to his family to help him, they did not impose improper pressure on them. Accordingly, the appeal would be dismissed.

Thomas v Thomas [1995] 2 FLR 668 (Court of Appeal: Glidewell and Waite LJJ).

1092   Financial provision—financial resources of parties—husband's failure to make full and frank disclosure

A husband and wife divorced and in ancillary relief proceedings she was awarded a lump sum of £10,000, as a final capital settlement, together with periodical payments of £4,000 per annum. The lump sum was made on the basis that the husband had assets of £90,000 and the wife had assets of £60,000. Further applications were made by the wife for upward variation of the periodical payments and she subsequently suffered medical problems which prevented her from taking up full-time employment. The wife suspected that the husband had failed to make full and frank disclosure of his financial position and she obtained evidence showing that he owned shares in a fish farm, was a member of Lloyds, made payments into a pension fund and had bank accounts abroad, none of which information had been disclosed to the court. The wife was granted leave to appeal out of time against the previous orders approximately 15 years after the parties separated. *Held*, despite the difficulty in quantifying the husband's financial circumstances, in the light of his absence from the proceedings and the deceitful manner in which he had conducted himself over a long period, the court was entitled to draw inferences against him and to give particular weight to the needs of the wife. The orders which had been obtained as a result of the clearly fraudulent conduct of the husband would be set aside. The wife's medical condition was a material factor in quantifying her entitlement. Taking into account the back calculation of revised orders and the arrears accruing, the correct lump sum order was £150,000 and the periodical payments would be increased to £14,000 per annum, to be continued until the lump sum order had been made. Further, the husband would pay the costs of the wife's application for upwards variation and the appeal. The appeal would be allowed accordingly.

C v C (Financial Provision: Non-Disclosure) [1995] 1 FCR 75 (Family Division: Thorpe J).

Substantial assets had already been transferred to a wife under a separation deed when she filed a petition for divorce and applied for financial relief. Her husband swore an affidavit in which he confirmed his total net worth was in excess of £10 million. He contended that it was not necessary for him to disclose his actual net worth since he would be able to meet any order for financial provision made by the court. He further contended that since his wife had resources worth more than £3 million it was in any event inconceivable that an order would be made in her favour. The wife sought directions claiming that her husband had failed to disclose his income and provided insufficient details of his capital and that she ought to be aware of any pension rights she might be losing. *Held*, in order to comply with the Matrimonial Causes Act 1973, s 25, the court needed a minimum of information. It was not sufficient for the husband to say that his assets were not less than a particular value and that he could therefore meet any order. Accordingly, (1) since the size of the husband's income would go directly to the standard of living he could enjoy, he should give an estimate of his total income, (2) he should give a summary of all assets worth more than £100,000 with an estimated value of each asset, although supporting evidence was not required, and (3) if the wife might lose her pension rights following the divorce she was at the very least entitled to know what she had lost.

Van G v Van G (Financial Provision: Millionaires' Defence) [1995] 2 FCR 250 (Family Division: Ewbank J).

1093 Financial provision—husband committing assault on wife—husband's share of capital settled on children—factors to be considered

The parties married and had three children. The husband became depressed and suicidal when the wife enrolled on a degree course and the parties separated. The wife remained in the matrimonial home with the youngest child. On one occasion the husband visited the wife and, without provocation, he struck her with a kitchen knife causing superficial wounds. He then attempted to commit suicide. On the parties' divorce, both applied for financial relief and a judge ordered that the husband's interest in the matrimonial home be settled on the children. On appeal by the husband, *held*, although the assault was conduct which it would be inequitable to disregard, it was only one of the factors to be taken into account under the Matrimonial Causes Act 1973, s 25. That factor should not have driven the court to conclude that the husband should be deprived of his entire capital, particularly bearing in mind his psychological disturbance. The application of capital from a spouse to children was not a permissible objective of the statutory powers. In exercising discretion as to financial provision the parties' joint entitlement to the matrimonial home had to be adjusted to reflect conduct, responsibility, needs and contribution. The wife had overall responsibility for the care of the children until they reached independence and therefore all the capital should be available to the wife until that responsibility was discharged. In the present case, a clear and final order was desirable. Accordingly the husband would be ordered to transfer all his interest in the matrimonial home to the wife and she would be ordered to pay him a lump sum, to be deferred until she had completed responsibility for the children, in particular responsibility to provide them with a home.

A v A (Financial Provision) [1995] 2 FCR 137 (Family Division: Thorpe J).

1094 Financial provision—lump sum payment—conduct—financial mis-management

On the parties' marriage, the wife agreed to invest a substantial sum of her own money in the husband's dairy farm business, which at that time was subject to many liabilities. As a result of the husband's mismanagement and misfortune over a number of years, the dairy farm incurred considerable losses and became further indebted. A separation agreement made between the parties and approved by the court, included a provision that the dairy farm was to be sold, upon which the wife was to receive a substantial sum in full and final settlement of any claims which she might make under the Matrimonial Causes Act 1973. However, the husband did not proceed with the sale, and he was eventually made bankrupt by his secured creditors, and a possession order was made in respect of the dairy farm. Despite receiving property and a sum of money as one of the secured creditors in the husband's bankruptcy, the wife did not receive all of the sum agreed upon in the separation agreement. In ancillary relief proceedings subsequent to the parties' divorce, the husband applied for a lump sum order. At that time, he was on state benefit and living with his parents, whereas the wife had substantial assets and owned a considerable property. *Held*, although the husband and wife had reached a formal agreement as to financial provision, the circumstances that had transpired were totally different from those contemplated at the time that it was made, and it was not a case in which one party sought to depart unreasonably or capriciously from a formal settlement. As such, although the separation agreement was important, it was only part of the history of the marriage, and the case had to be determined on the basis of the criteria under the 1973 Act, s 25. In considering the parties' conduct, it would be inequitable to disregard the husband's responsibility for the mismanagement of the dairy farm, which had resulted in the dissipation of his own money and that of his wife, family, friends, and commercial creditors. However, the disparity in the present position of the parties was so great that it would not be a fair application of the s 25 criteria if no financial provision was made for the husband. The wife was therefore to pay him a lump sum, but only in so far as it would enable him to purchase basic accommodation. Accordingly, the application would be granted.

Beach v Beach [1995] 2 FCR 526 (Family Division: Thorpe J). *Edgar v Edgar* [1980] 3 All ER 887 (1980 Abr para 958) distinguished.

1095   Financial provision—lump sum payment—payment out of capital sum due to husband on leaving Royal Navy—retrospective effect of provisions

Under the Naval Discipline Act 1957, s 128G(1), inserted by the Armed Forces Act 1991, s 16, every assignment of or charge on, and every agreement to assign or charge, any pay, pensions, grants or other allowances payable to any person in respect of his service will be void. No order will be made by any court the effect of which would be to restrain any person from receiving anything which he is precluded from assigning and to direct payment thereof to another person: s 128G(2).

The parties divorced in 1982. An order was made that the husband was to pay the wife a proportion of any lump sum he received on leaving the Royal Navy, which he was due to do in 1986. Although the Naval and Marine Pay and Pensions Act 1865 provided that any assignment of any pay or grant by a serviceman would be void there was no restriction in relation to court orders. However, the husband did not leave the service or receive his capital sum until 1993, by which time the 1957 Act, s 128G had been inserted. On the husband's appeal against the order, the judge held that it imposed a charge on the husband's prospective lump sum entitlement on leaving the Royal Navy which was rendered invalid by the voiding provisions of s 128G. The wife appealed against that decision. *Held*, there was no room in the statutory scheme of s 128G for the implication of a deeming provision under which an order that would be prima facie voidable already for infringement of s128G(2) was to be treated notionally as imposing a charge and therefore void also under s 128G(1). The judge was wrong to have treated the order as a charge and, even if he had been right to do so, he would have been wrong to have regarded the 1991 Act as capable of having any retrospective effect so as to invalidate supposed charges created by orders made before the commencement of the Act. Accordingly, the appeal would be allowed.

Legrove v Legrove [1995] 1 FCR 102 (Court of Appeal: Ralph Gibson and Waite LJJ).

1096   Financial provision—maintenance order—overseas maintenance order—registration and enforcement

See *Sethi v Sethi*, para 578.

1097   Financial provision—overseas divorce—application for leave to apply for financial provision—delay

Where a marriage has been dissolved by means of an overseas divorce, the Matrimonial and Family Proceedings Act 1984, s 13 states that no application for an order for financial relief can be made unless leave of the court has been obtained, and the court will not grant leave unless it considers that there is substantial ground for the making of an application for such an order. In deciding whether to grant leave, the court must have particular regard to a number of factors specified in s 16(2), including the length of time that has elapsed since the date of the divorce.

A husband and wife separated and the husband obtained a divorce decree in Belgium. Over a period of several years, the wife made unsuccessful attempts to enforce Belgian maintenance orders through her local magistrates' court. Much of the delay was caused by unhelpful legal advice. Eventually, some twelve years after the divorce, she applied under the 1984 Act, s 13 for leave to apply for ancillary relief in England and Wales. Leave was refused and she appealed. *Held*, the judge's refusal was based on a finding that there was no substantial ground for the making of an application, the issue of delay having been deemed to be so overwhelming that it was extremely unlikely that the wife would succeed in any claim. The judge was entirely right to consider the issue of the delay. However, but for the delay the wife's claim satisfied the grounds set out in the 1984 Act, s 16(2) and, there was some prospect of success if her husband had assets. Although the test under s 16 was stringent, account ought to have been taken of the circumstances of the delay. The delay was not because she had not wanted relief, her claim having always been in the hands of her legal advisors. The issue of the delay would be highly relevant in the final hearing, but it did not preclude her from attempting to claim financial relief from the husband. Accordingly, the appeal would be allowed.

Lamagni v Lamagni [1995] 2 FLR 452 (Court of Appeal: Butler-Sloss, Morritt and Hutchison LJJ).

1098   Financial provision—pension—variation of pension scheme

The Matrimonial Causes Act 1973, s 24(1)(c) provides that on granting a decree of divorce, the court may make an order varying the terms of a marriage settlement.

A husband set up an exempt approved pension fund scheme through his company. Rule 1 of the scheme provided that at his retirement the husband could elect to give up part of his pension to provide, from the date of his death, a deferred pension for life for his spouse or other dependents. Under rule 2, this benefit was payable at the discretion of the company to members of a class including the husband's spouse and children and any persons nominated by him in his lifetime. On the parties' divorce, the court varied the pension scheme to provide a pension for the wife, a decision that was affirmed on appeal. On further appeal by the husband, *held*, the authorities had correctly given a wide meaning to 'settlement' in this context. In considering the purpose of the husband when entering it, the scheme had to be looked at in the round and in the context of the circumstances then subsisting. Viewed in that light, the husband was to be taken to have entered into the scheme with the intention of providing for the retirement of himself and his wife by the tax efficient means afforded by the scheme. Such a disposition fell within the wide meaning of 'marriage settlement' in the 1973 Act, s 24(1)(c) because of the presence of rules 1 and 2. Where a scheme provided something other than benefits payable exclusively to the scheme member, the natural inference was that all the benefits, including those payable to the scheme member, formed part of the marriage settlement. Accordingly, the court had power to vary the scheme so far as it concerned a settlement made by the husband. A distinction had to be drawn between the benefits provided by the scheme and the surplus where a benefit exceeded the maximum amount of benefit permissible under an exempt approved scheme. The court could only make a variation order in respect of the settled property. Under the scheme, the surplus belonged to the company, but the settlor was the husband. Thus the surplus did not form part of the settled property. The appeal would be dismissed.

Brooks v Brooks [1995] 3 All ER 257 (House of Lords: Lords Keith of Kinkel, Ackner, Lloyd of Berwick, Nicholls of Birkenhead and Steyn). Decision of Court of Appeal [1994] 4 All ER 1065 (1994 Abr para 1069) affirmed.

1099 Financial provision—periodical payments—consent order—duration of periodical payments

The Matrimonial Causes Act 1973, s 23 (1)(a), (b) provides that on granting a decree of divorce, nullity of marriage or judicial separation, the court may make an order that either party must make to the other such periodical payments as may be specified in the order. Section 28(1A) provides that where such a periodical payments order is made, the court may direct that the receiving party shall not be entitled to apply for an extension of the term specified in the order.

A consent order disposed of financial relief proceedings between husband and wife following the breakdown of their marriage. It provided for a lump sum to be paid to the wife and periodical payments diminishing over a period of seven years. At the end of that period the wife's claim for periodical payments would be dismissed and she would not be entitled to make any application under the Matrimonial Causes Act 1973, s 23 (1)(a) or (b). However, the order did not contain a direction under s 28(1A). The one child of the marriage remained with the wife. Four years later the wife sought a variation of the consent order extending the duration of the periodical payments. *Held*, the correspondence between the solicitors acting for the parties at the time of the order clearly indicated that there should be no application by the wife to extend the seven-year period. However, the legal advice given to the wife was so manifestly bad and so manifestly the principal factor contributing to the consent order that the periodical payments order ought to be extended and enlarged. Consideration should have been given not just to the husband's capital but to his high earning capacity compared with the low earning capacity of the wife and his pension rights should have been investigated. It should have been clear to the wife's legal advisers that she would be unlikely to survive without periodical payments for life. Where a contract precluded application under s 23, the courts could grant relief in exceptional circumstances. Moreover, s 31 of the Act provided that the court's first consideration should be the welfare of any child of the family. In this instance it was likely that the child would continue to be dependant on the mother for some time. Accordingly, the application would be allowed and the periodical payments order extended.

B v B (Consent Order: Variation) [1995] 1 FLR 9 (Family Division: Thorpe J).

1100 Financial provision—periodical payments—variation—effect of cohabitation

A husband and wife separated after 24 years of marriage, and later divorced. On the wife's application for ancillary relief, the former matrimonial home was transferred to the wife outright, and the husband was ordered to make annual periodical payments of £30,000 for an unlimited period. The order was made on the basis that although the wife had a boyfriend, she was not living with him, nor was she financially dependent on him, nor did she intend to remarry. Four months after the conclusion of the proceedings, the wife began cohabiting with her boyfriend in the former matrimonial home. When the husband discovered this three years later, he applied for a variation of the periodical payments order. A senior district judge reduced the annual sum to £18,000, but the husband appealed against the order, arguing that periodical payments should have been reduced to a nominal sum. The wife also appealed against the order, arguing that the sum should not have been reduced to less than £25,000. *Held*, although the relationship between the wife and her cohabitee had continued in the three years following the original order, cohabitation could not be equated with marriage. It was a relevant factor to be taken into account in considering the wife's financial circumstances and needs, but was not decisive. What was more important was the fact that the profits of the cohabitee's business had increased substantially since they began cohabiting, suggesting that he had the capacity to make a reasonable contribution in return for the support, benefits and services provided to him by the wife. The cohabitee had made no capital contribution to the former matrimonial home, and yet it was because of the provision of a home and the wife's direct and indirect support that he had been able to build up his business. However, there was no certainty as to whether their relationship would continue, and it was also the case that the wife was entitled to some financial independence following 24 years of marriage to the husband. Having regard to other relevant facts and to the circumstances of the case as a whole, periodical payments would be reduced to an annual sum of £10,000.

A v A (Financial Provision: Variation) [1995] 2 FCR 353 (Family Division: Thorpe J).

1101 Financial provision—pre-nuptial agreement—relevance of agreement to application for financial provision

A husband and wife, who were German, entered into pre-nuptial contracts. The first contract was in German, and was intended to be governed by German and Swiss law. The second contract was in English, and was intended to be governed by American law, as the husband owned property in America. The contracts provided that the wife would be entitled only to the equivalent of a German judge's pension in the event of divorce, even though the husband was an extremely wealthy businessman. Although the parties had homes in several countries, they settled in England with their three children. Following the parties' separation, the husband commenced divorce proceedings. On the issue of (1) the amount of maintenance pending suit payable to the wife, and (2) the relevance of the pre-nuptial contracts, *held*, (1) in cases involving large sums of money, it was unnecessary to have a full-scale investigation of interim provision. However, in such cases, reasonable interim provision had to be determined on the basis of the standard of living of the ultra-rich and not that of ordinary people. Here, the husband had understated the standard of living which the wife had enjoyed before their separation, and had failed to take account of the fact that the wife and children had been undermaintained since the separation. The wife, however, had made some unjustifiable claims as to her reasonable requirements. (2) Pre-nuptial contracts were of limited significance in England, as the rights and responsibilities of husbands and wives were regulated by statute and could not be influenced by contractual terms devised to control and limit standards which were intended to be of universal application. Even if the contracts were enforceable under German law, it was possible that the wife could have argued that there had been inequality of bargaining power or undue influence, or that the contracts were inconsistent with German social policy. As such, little weight would be attached to the contracts.

F v F (Ancillary Relief: Substantial Assets) [1995] 2 FLR 45 (Family Division: Thorpe J).

1102 Financial provision—proceedings—solicitor's wrongful termination of retainer—defective application by client in person—liability of solicitor

See *Young v Purdy*, para 2786.

1103 Financial provision—production appointment—application for appointment—ex parte or on notice

It has been held that where in financial relief proceedings a party applies for a production appointment against any person, the application should be made inter partes and should ordinarily be supported by an affidavit. An ex parte application may be made if there is a legitimate anxiety that notice may lead to the destruction or invasion of the document. If the district judge does not consider that the anxiety is legitimate, he may direct that the proceedings be adjourned to be heard on notice.

B v B (Production Appointment: Procedure) [1995] 1 FLR 913 (Family Division: Thorpe J).

1104   Financial provision—production appointment—application for disclosure against accountant—limit of discovery at court's discretion

During their marriage, the parties' lifestyle was dependent on the wife's wealthy father. When the husband petitioned for divorce he applied for ancillary relief. Both parties disclosed that they had no significant assets although the wife later conceded she had not made a full and frank disclosure. The wife's father died and the husband applied for a production appointment against the father's accountant, an executor of the will. The accountant claimed that he could make no disclosure because of professional and client privilege. When the husband applied to have the production summons argued out before a judge, the accountant submitted that production should be limited to documents relevant to the wife's affairs, the order should limit production to a five-year period and documents relating to particular companies and trusts should be excluded. The husband claimed that the inquiry should extend beyond the marriage breakdown to an earlier period when financial arrangements were made in respect of the wife's family. *Held*, where there was such manifest avoidance of the duty of full and frank disclosure, the exercise of discretion as to the bounds of production should be broad. If the boundary was narrow there was a risk that information as to the nature and extent of the wife's financial circumstances might be lost. An investigative accountant instructed on the husband's behalf would be able to exclude irrelevant documents or material and would avoid incurring unnecessary costs. The husband was entitled to see the documentation that evidenced the financial arrangement preceding the marriage breakdown. Once the production order was put in place and it was made plain to the accountant and the wife that the privilege which would ordinarily shield the material had been overridden by the court's jurisdiction, the investigative accountant and the father's accountant could act co-operatively in the efficient and economical exchange of relevant information. The father's accountant's professional costs in complying with the production order would become costs in the ancillary relief application with the probability that they would ultimately fall to be discharged by the wife.

D v D (Production Appointment) [1995] 3 FCR 183 (Family Division: Thorpe J).

1105   Financial provision—property adjustment order—order for sale of matrimonial home—discretion to defer sale

The defendants were a husband and wife who had separated. The husband lived in a house owned by his wife while she remained in the matrimonial home with their young children. The plaintiff bank lent money to the husband, secured by a charge over the matrimonial home. The husband defaulted and the plaintiff obtained an order absolute that possession of the matrimonial home be delivered to the plaintiff for sale. The wife appealed on the ground that the court ought to have used its discretion to defer the sale until the children had reached 18 years of age or had left full-time education. *Held*, the rule was that the interests of a chargee took priority over those of a spouse save for exceptional circumstances. In this case, the wife was in a comparatively favourable position because she owned another house and moving would not involve the children having to change school. The property did not have a collateral purpose as the matrimonial home because the husband was no longer living there and had charged his interest as co-owner to the plaintiff and no exceptional circumstances had therefore been proved. An order for possession ought to allow sufficient period of time for the innocent spouse to move out with the minimum of distress and dislocation but this period had to be as short as possible and any period longer than a few weeks had to be avoided if it caused hardship to the chargee. Accordingly, the appeal would be dismissed and an order made requiring the wife to vacate the property during the school holidays.

Barclays Bank plc v Hendricks [1996] 1 FLR 258 (Chancery Division: Laddie J). *Re Citro (a Bankrupt)* [1990] 3 All ER 952, CA (1990 Abr para 157) and *Lloyds Bank plc v Byrne* [1993] 1 FLR 369, CA (1993 Abr para 1442) followed.

1106   Financial provision—property adjustment order—order for sale of matrimonial home—revised valuation

In ancillary relief proceedings an order was made that a matrimonial home should be sold with a lump sum payment to be made to the wife. From a valuation taken at the time it was anticipated that the balance would be sufficient to enable the husband to rehouse himself. Later, when the wife sought to enforce the sale it was discovered that the property was worth considerably less than the original valuation. The husband unsuccessfully applied for leave to appeal out of time. On appeal, *held*, the grounds upon which the district judge had made his order were invalidated by a new event, namely the discovery either that the original valuation was unsound, or alternatively that the house could not be sold at its assumed market price. Any appeal would be likely to succeed since the husband was now unable to rehouse himself with his share of the proceeds of sale. Although there had been a lengthy delay between making the order and the application for leave to appeal, this was justifiable in all the circumstances of the case taking account of the situation in which the husband found himself. He could not be criticised for his attempts to raise money to avoid the need to sell the home, or for his reluctance to sell the property in an unfavourable market. Accordingly, the appeal would be allowed and the matter remitted for hearing before a circuit judge.

Heard v Heard [1995] 1 FLR 970 (Court of Appeal: Sir Thomas Bingham MR, Kennedy and Millett LJJ).

1107 Financial provision—transfer of business—dissolution of partnership—husband and wife as partners

A husband and wife were partners in the business of a residential care home to which the wife had contributed the majority of the initial capital secured by a charge on the matrimonial home. The value of the business, however, did not outweigh the couple's liabilities. The relationship broke down and the husband moved to a room in the residential home whilst the wife remained in the matrimonial home with her three children. The wife petitioned for divorce and an order was obtained from the county court in which the judge declared that as the business was no longer viable, the wife's position ought to be protected as much as possible as she stood to lose more and therefore, the matrimonial home, subject to the charge, would become her sole property. The residential home was also transferred to the wife subject to a charge for the husband over a third of the business and its profits. The husband was awarded a weekly sum on account of his share of the profits and was ordered to vacate his room in the residential home. The husband appealed against the order on the ground that the court did not have jurisdiction to make it and that the judge had exercised his discretion improperly in determining the husband's share in the business. *Held*, the order came within the Matrimonial Causes Act 1973, ss 24, 24A and it was established law that the court had the power to order the husband to transfer his share of the partnership assets to the wife. There was enough evidence for the court to conclude that the partnership had been dissolved on the date of the final hearing before the district judge and the judge had jurisdiction to order that the wife hold the partnership assets on trust with certain capital and income provision made for the husband. The order had been imperfectly drafted, particularly in concluding that because partnership assets exceeded liabilities, there was nothing that could be transferred. The assets included the bricks and mortar of the residential home which could be assumed by the wife but it was wrong to make an order specifying that, although the wife was the sole owner of the business, the husband was still liable for a share of future losses. It was impracticable for the husband to be re-instated as a partner in the business and for him to return to live at the business address. The award of shares in the business fell within the judge's discretion under the 1973 Act, and accordingly, the husband's appeal would be allowed to the limited extent only of perfecting the order of the county court judge.

Belcher v Belcher [1995] 2 FCR 143 (Court of Appeal: Balcombe and Hobhouse LJJ).

1108 Foreign proceedings—recognition

See CONFLICT OF LAWS.

1109 Matrimonial home—exclusion order

See HUSBAND AND WIFE.

1110 Petition—stay of proceedings—discretionary stay—concurrent foreign proceedings—appropriate forum

The parties, who were Swedish citizens, were married in Sweden. When they came to live in England, they entered into a marriage contract whereby the wife was to receive a specified sum of money in the event of a divorce. The contract was in Swedish form and registered in Sweden. When the husband returned to live in Sweden, the wife remained in England and commenced divorce proceedings. The husband filed a divorce petition in Sweden, but the Swedish courts granted the wife a stay of his petition because the English proceedings had been issued first in time. On the husband's application under the Domicile and Matrimonial Proceedings Act 1973, s 9, Sch 1 for a stay of the wife's divorce petition and all proceedings flowing from it, *held*, although the parties were Swedish, had married and lived in Sweden, and the marriage contract was in Swedish form, they had been habitually resident in England for 10 years, and the wife and one of the children of the family intended to remain in England. It was therefore not clear whether England or Sweden was the more appropriate forum for the trial of the action. However, the court had to consider where the balance of fairness, including convenience, lay, and in that respect, the wife would be likely to receive less by way of financial relief under Swedish law than she would under English law. For that reason, justice demanded that the English courts should deal with the divorce petition, and that the proceedings should not be stayed. Accordingly, the application would be refused.

R v R (Divorce: Stay of Proceedings) [1994] 2 FLR 1036 (Family Division: Ewbank J). *de Dampierre v de Dampierre* [1987] 2 WLR 1006, HL (1987 Abr para 342) followed.

1111 Transnational divorce—recognition

See *Berkovits v Grinberg, A-G intervening*, para 582.

EASEMENTS AND PROFITS A PRENDRE

Halsbury's Laws of England (4th edn) Vol 14, paras 1–300

1112 Articles

Abandonment of an Easement: Is It a Question of Intention Only? Dr Christine J Davis: [1995] Conv 291

1113 Easements—right of way—obstruction—gate across path

The plaintiffs and defendants owned neighbouring properties at either end of a row of terraced cottages. Following the purchase of their property the defendants discovered that the plaintiffs had a right of way to pass and repass along a pathway across their garden. All other properties in the terrace were similarly burdened with rights of way and enjoyed the benefit of the right of way across the other owners' land. The purpose of the right of way was to enable the owners of the dwellings rear access to their properties and access to the public highway at the front of the properties. The defendants were concerned about the security of their property and about the safety of their young son who on occasions had gone out of the garden and onto the main road. They did not deny the existence of the right of way but erected a wooden gate with a lock across it. Although the defendants offered to provide the plaintiffs and other owners of properties in the terrace with a key to the gate, the plaintiffs issued proceedings claiming damages and a declaration that the defendants were not entitled to obstruct the right of way by means of the gate. The plaintiffs further sought an order restraining the defendants from erecting or placing any obstruction on the right of way and a mandatory injunction to remove the gate. The defendants relied on the decision in *Dawes v Adela Estates Ltd* (1970) 216 Estates Gazette 1405 where an automatic lock on a door in a block of flats did not amount to substantial interference. *Held*, for the plaintiffs to succeed the gate must represent a substantial obstruction to their easement. If the gate was either unlocked or, if locked, the plaintiffs were provided with a key, and so long as nothing else was done to impede the right of passage, no substantial interference had occurred. Accordingly, the defendants were entitled to erect a gate across the right of way and mandatory and restraining injunctions would be refused.

Hall v Shepherd (22 June 1993, unreported) (St Albans County Court: District Judge Hewetson-Brown). *Pettey v Parsons* [1914] 2 Ch 653, CA applied. (Messrs Bretherton & Co, for the plaintiff; Messrs Martin Smith & Co, for the defendant) (Kindly submitted for publication by Martin Smith, Solicitor, of Messrs Martin Smith & Co).

1114 Easements—right of way—prescription—illegal use

See *Robinson v Adair*, para 1517.

1115 Easements—right to water supply—prescription by lost modern grant—loss of right by execution of licence

The defendant owned a house which, under an easement granted in 1858, had received its water supply from a tank and pipes situated in the plaintiff's field. In 1948 the plaintiff and defendant's predecessors in title executed a licence to construct a new water tank and lay new pipes in the field which would supply water to the house at a minimal charge. Thirty two years later, the defendant gave notice of discontinuance of the licence in accordance with its relevant terms, but maintained that she still had the right to a continuing water supply. The plaintiff disagreed and brought an action. At first instance, the judge declared that, although the 1858 grant was perpetuitous and void, the defendant had acquired a right to procure water by prescription through the doctrine of lost modern grant. On appeal, the plaintiff introduced a new argument that from 1858 until 1948 the occupiers of the house and the field were lessees and not fee simple owners and, therefore, the defendant's predecessor could not acquire an easement against his own landlord. The defendant argued that the plaintiff ought not to be allowed to introduce this new argument in the Court of Appeal. *Held*, there could be no objection to admission of the new point as it was founded on evidence given in the court below and which was available in the Court of Appeal. Although it was correct that a tenant could not acquire an easement by presumed grant or prescription against his own landlord or another tenant, that principle did not apply where a lessee had the unilateral right by statute at any time and without anyone else's consent to enlarge his leasehold interest into the fee simple. In this case that right was created by the Law of Property Act 1925, s 153 and the Conveyancing Act 1881, s 65, as amended by the Conveyancing Act 1882, s 11. Before the 1948 licence was executed the predecessors of the defendant had acquired a prescriptive right to take water for domestic use by the doctrine of lost modern grant but that right could not have been exercised at the same time as the right created by the licence. The acceptance of the licence by the defendant's predecessor, the subsequent destruction of the old water tank and installation of its replacement meant that the previous prescriptive right was impliedly abandoned and, accordingly, the appeal would be allowed.

Bosomworth v Faber (1992) 69 P & CR 288 (Court of Appeal: Dillon, Farquharson and Simon Brown LJJ).

ECCLESIASTICAL LAW

Halsbury's Laws of England (4th edn) Vol 14, paras 301–1435

1116 Articles

Blasphemy, Cultural Divergence and Legal Relativism, Clive Unsworth: 58 MLR 658

1117 Church of England (Miscellaneous Provisions) Measure 1995

The Church of England (Miscellaneous Provisions) Measure 1995 makes provision for a number of matters affecting the Church of England. The Measure received the royal assent on 19 July 1995 and comes into force on a day or days to be appointed. For details of commencement, see the commencement table in the title STATUTES.

Section 1 makes it lawful for ministers of the Church of Ireland to officiate in England. Section 2 makes it lawful for the constitution and statutes of Christ Church, Oxford to provide for the appointment of not more than two lay canons. Under s 3, the bishop of a diocese may confer the designation of archdeacon emeritus on any person who retires immediately after holding the office of archdeacon. Section 4 amends the law relating to the resignation of deans, residentiary canons and archdeacons.

Section 5 amends the Ecclesiastical Commissioners Act 1840, s 27 in relation to the qualification of deans, archdeacons and canons and s 6 amends the Church Commissioners Measure 1947, s 6 in relation to the composition of the Assets Committee. Section 7 and the Schedule make various amendments to the Church Funds Investment Measure 1958 and s 8 amends the constitution of the Church of England Pensions Board. Section 9 amends provision concerning ecclesiastical judges and s 10 that dealing with searches of certain register books. Section 11 makes various amendments to the Pastoral Measure 1983 and s 12 amends the discharge of certain functions of bishops. Section 13 makes revised provision relating to trees in churchyards and s 14 amends a number of enactments in connection with General Synod procedure. Section 15 deals with short title, commencement and extent.

1118 Church Representation Rules

The Church Representation Rules (Amendment) Resolution 1995, SI 1995/3243 (in force in part on 1 January 1996, in part on 1 May 1996, and in part on 1 May 1997), amends the Church Representation Rules (contained in the Synodical Government Measure 1969, Sch 3) so as to make provision for independent examiners and auditors as required by the Charities Act 1993, and for modifications concerning provincial episcopal visitors appointed under the Episcopal Ministry Act of Synod 1993.

1119 Clergy—curates' conditions of employment—termination of curacy—right to claim compensation for unfair dismissal

See para 1208.

1120 Faculty—churchyard—installation of plaque

The incumbent and churchwardens of a church sought a faculty for the installation of a commemorative plaque. The plaque was dedicated to a Roman Catholic priest convicted of high treason under an Act of 1594 and subsequently executed. *Held*, there were a number of factors to be considered before granting a faculty including whether the grant was proper, whether the granting of a faculty in a churchyard would unnecessarily curtail the rights of parishioners buried there, and whether it might cause offence. Thus, a plaque could be erected to commemorate outstanding service to the Church of England, the country or mankind in general, or to record something significant in local or national history. Whilst the commemoration of a Roman Catholic priest might fulfil these latter factors, it was inappropriate that it should take place in an Anglican churchyard when the priest was not regarded as a martyr by that denomination. Moreover, the court could not sanction a memorial to a person convicted of high treason and not subsequently pardoned. Accordingly, the petition would be dismissed.

Re St Edmund's Churchyard, Gateshead [1995] 3 WLR 253 (Durham Consistory Court: Bursell QC, Ch).

1121 Faculty—confirmatory faculty—sale of church items

Following the merger of two parish churches, certain items were surplus to requirement and never used in public worship, namely some flagons, chalices and patens. The parish, which was in financial difficulty, was advised by the rural dean that the items could be sold, although he failed to advise that a faculty was necessary to authorise the sale. With the consent of the parochial church council, the items were sold by auction to third parties, and later resold. Following the diocesan registrar's inquiry as to why a faculty had not been sought, the auctioneers, the incumbent of the parish and the churchwardens petitioned for a confirmatory faculty. On a hearing for directions, *held*, having regard to the Faculty Jurisdiction Rules 1992, SI 1992/2882, r 25, the matter could be disposed of by way of written representations, provided that all parties consented and that all the purchasers had been given an opportunity to make representations, as it was not a case in which evidence had to be heard in open court. As the sale of church items without a faculty was illegal, purchasers acquired no title to them, and legal title remained with the churchwardens of the parish. Here, if a faculty had been sought prior to the sale, further inquiry would have been made in respect of the objections that had been raised to the petition, but it was impossible to say what the outcome of such an inquiry would have been. The items had been redundant for several years and, in view of the parish's financial needs and the fact that the items had been sold and resold, there was no practical justification for refusing to grant a confirmatory faculty. Accordingly, the petition would be granted.

Re St John's with Holy Trinity, Deptford [1995] 1 WLR 721 (Southwark Consistory Court: RMK Gray QC, Ch).

1122 Faculty—contents of churches—introduction of contents

A faculty was sought for the introduction of a pair of altar standards, two votive candle stands, a pair of candelabra, a set of sanctuary bells, two portable acolytes' chairs and a thurible and stand. A confirmatory faculty was also sought for two holy water stoups. *Held*, (1) the altar standards were a modern form of candlestick and as such were legal. (2) In the light of the sweeping away of the rigorist interpretation of the Book of Common Prayer, processions, with or without lighted candles, the ceremonial use of incense and the ringing of sanctuary bells during Holy Communion were prima facie doctrinally acceptable. Therefore the introduction of the acolytes' chairs, the thurible and stand and the sanctuary bells for use in these practices was permissible. (3) Items that assisted private devotions could be admitted into a church as long as they did not detract from the devotions of others nor from the services and ministrations within the church itself. The votive candle stands would therefore be permitted, although only until further order so that the court could retain control in the event that they acquired superstitious uses. (4) As the ceremonial use of holy water was provided for in services commended by the House of Bishops and as such was not contrary to the doctrine of the Church of England, holy water stoups could no longer be regarded as illegal or inappropriate ornaments. Accordingly, the faculty would be granted.

Re St John the Evangelist, Chopwell [1995] 3 WLR 606 (Durham Consistory Court: Judge Bursell QC, Ch). *Re St Thomas, Pennywell* [1995] 2 WLR 154 (para 2786) applied.

1123 Faculty—reservation of the sacrament—removal to safe and suitable reservation

In a parish church the sacrament had been reserved in an aumbry in the lady chapel for several years. When the aumbry became damp the incumbent and churchwardens petitioned to have it replaced with a sacrament house. The petition was fully supported but, at the court's request, the archdeacon entered an objection to determine whether reservation was lawful and whether the sacrament house was an unlawful ornament. *Held*, the reservation was lawful because, so long as it was required for communion, the elements of the sacrament could be reserved. Reservation was lawful and theologically permissible and it was for the bishop to judge whether the manner in which it took place was reverent and whether the incumbent's and congregation's attitude to the sacrament was theologically acceptable. When used in a safe and seemly manner, the sacrament house was not an illegal ornament but an article consistent with and subsidiary to the church's ministrations. Further, the aumbry was damp and unsafe and unsuitable to the continued reservation of the sacrament. Accordingly, the faculty would be granted.

Re St Thomas, Pennywell [1995] 2 WLR 154 (Durham Consistory Court: RDH Bursell QC, Ch).

1124 Fees—ecclesiastical judges and legal officers

The Legal Officers (Annual Fees) Order 1995, SI 1995/1959 (in force on 1 January 1996), revokes the 1994 Order, SI 1994/2010, increases the annual fees payable to diocesan registrars and makes minor amendments to the list of duties covered by the fees. The order also adds new items to the list of work not covered by the annual fee and for which a fee calculated in accordance with the Solicitors' (Non-Contentious Business) Remuneration Order 1994, SI 1994/2616, is to be paid.

The Ecclesiastical Judges and Legal Officers (Fees) Order 1995, SI 1995/1961 (in force on 1 January 1996), revokes the 1994 Order, SI 1994/2009, increases the fixed fees in relation to faculty proceedings and extends and clarifies the application of those fees. The order also increases the additional fees for appeals and the fees for taxation of costs, applies those fees to faculty proceedings, and increases the fees payable to provincial registrars and Vicars–General.

1125 Fees—parochial fees

The Parochial Fees Order 1995, SI 1995/1960 (in force on 1 January 1996), revokes the 1994 Order, SI 1994/2011, and establishes a new table of fees in respect of baptism, marriages and burials, the erection of monuments in churchyards, and searches in various church registers and copies of entries in those registers.

1126 Legal aid—rules

The Church of England (Legal Aid) Rules 1995, SI 1995/2034 (in force on 1 October 1995), consolidate, with amendments, the 1988 Rules, SI 1988/1175, the 1990 Rules, SI 1990/1438, and the 1993 Rules, SI 1993/1840. The 1995 Rules make express provision for the business of the Legal Aid Commission to be carried out by correspondence in certain circumstances and extend the power to grant interim legal aid certificates. The rules extend the requirement for an assisted person's solicitor to apply to the commission for authority to incur specified costs to cover all types of appeal and all cases where counsel is instructed. New provision is also made for the commission to appoint a committee to carry out taxations and assessments of costs in cases where the commission has not directed that the matter is to be dealt with by the full commission.

1127 Team and Group Ministries Measure 1995

The Team and Group Ministries Measure 1995 amends existing legislation concerning team ministries with the aim of ensuring that such ministries operate as effectively as possible. The Measure received the royal assent on 28 June 1995 and s 2 came into force on that day. The remainder of the Measure comes into force on a day or days to be appointed. For details of commencement, see the commencement table in the title STATUTES.

Section 1 and Sch 1 amend the Pastoral Measure 1983, s 20 (establishment of team ministries) so as to make provision for the service of deacons in a team ministry and for the assignment to any member of the team who is not a member of the team chapter of a special responsibility for pastoral care in respect of a part of the area of a benefice. Section 2 provides that in the case of team ministries established for the area of any benefice under a pastoral scheme made under the Pastoral Measure 1968, the scheme is deemed to contain provisions for the pastoral care of persons in that area by those who are to share the cure of souls therein together with all other persons authorised by the bishop to serve in that area as members of the team. Section 3 amends provisions for the alteration of team and group ministries in the 1983 Measure, s 22 and s 4 amends the provisions for compensation of clergy in the 1983 Measure, s 26 to include deacons in team ministries.

Under s 5, the powers exercisable by pastoral order in relation to team ministries are extended. Section 6 makes supplementary provision regarding pastoral schemes and orders and ss 7–9 amend a number of enactments concerned with property occupied by team ministries. Section 10 inserts a new definition of 'minister' into the Churchwardens (Appointment and Resignation) Measure 1964 to deal with the situation where a special responsibility for pastoral care in respect of the parish has been assigned to a member of the team in a team ministry but a special cure of souls in respect of the parish has not been assigned to a vicar in the team ministry. Sections 11 and 12 make provision relating to parochial church councils and the sharing of church buildings. Under s 13, deaconesses, licensed lay workers, readers and other lay persons may be licensed to serve in the area of a benefice in respect of which a team ministry is established.

Sections 14 and 15 amend provisions relating to the powers of diocesan boards of finance to deal with glebe land and the licensing of ministers, deaconesses, lay workers and readers. Section 16 amends the definition of 'minister' in the Care of Churches and Ecclesiastical Jurisdiction Measure 1991 to take account of the case where a special responsibility for pastoral care in respect of the parish has been assigned to a member of the team in a team ministry but a special cure of souls in respect of the parish has not been assigned to a vicar in the team ministry. Section 17 amends provision for sequestration of profits during the vacancy of a benefice and s 18 and Sch 2 contain transitional provisions. Section 19 deals with extent and s 20 with short title, commencement and interpretation.

EDUCATION

Halsbury's Laws of England (4th edn) Vol 15 (reissue), paras 1–300

1128 Articles

Compulsory School Attendance in Britain, Anwar Khan: 24 Journal of Law & Education 91 (USA)

Education Law—a 1995 Report, Jonathan Robinson: 145 NLJ 1864

Fundraising for Maintained Schools: The Charity Law Implications, Debra Morris: [1995] Conv 453

Learning Under the Law—Part I: The Legacy of Educational Legislation, J N Spencer: 159 JP Jo 87, 109

Negligent Teaching, Oliver Hyams (on *X v Bedfordshire County Council* (1995) Times, 30 June, HL (para 2833)): 139 SJ 746

New Structures in Education, Stephen Simblet (on the Education Act 1993 increasing the potential for litigation in education): 139 SJ 296

A New Year and a New Tribunal, Jonathan Robinson (on the Special Educational Needs Tribunal): 145 NLJ 15

Schools, Colleges and Universities, David Rudling (on VAT relating to education): Tax Journal, Issue 318, p 15

1129 Disability Discrimination Act 1995

See para 1215.

1130 Educational rights—right to educational grant—child of Community migrant worker

See *Landesamt für Ausbildungsförderung Nordrhein-Westfalen v Gaal*, para 3137.

1131 Education association—recommendation that school be closed—duty to consult

The pupils of a school through their next friends applied for judicial review of a report of an education association, its recommendation that the school be closed and the Secretary of State's decision to discontinue the education association and consequently close the school. It was argued on behalf of the Secretary of State that there was no suggestion that before an education association prepared its report it should consult. *Held*, the absence of a statutory obligation was marked. It was clear from amendments made to the Education Act 1980, s 12 by the Education Act 1993 that there was no obligation generally to consult. However, it must have been known to Parliament that there was an implicit obligation on the Secretary of State to consult before closing. The obligation did not apply in the present case where the steps taken constituted a special measure: the school was failing its pupils, it had not improved and there was an urgent requirement that all the pupils receive the best education. Accordingly, there was no obligation to consult and the appeal would be dismissed.

R v Secretary of State for Education and Employment, ex p Morris (1995) Times, 15 December (Queen's Bench Division: Popplewell J).

1132 Education association—schools conducted by education associations— contracting and proprietorial powers

The Education (Schools Conducted by Education Associations) (Amendment) Regulations 1995, SI 1995/61 (in force on 6 February 1995), amend the 1993 Regulations, SI 1993/3103, and the 1994 Regulations, SI 1994/1084, so as to remove from the powers conferred on an education association named in an order made under the Education Act 1993, s 220, Sch 4 (which concerns the exercise of powers by the education association before the transfer date), the powers in para 2 of that Schedule to enter into contracts and to acquire and dispose of property.

1133 European dimension in education—development—'Socrates' programme

See para 3176.

1134 European Year of Lifelong Learning

See para 3089.

1135 Fees and awards—foreign students

The Education (Fees and Awards) (Amendment) Regulations 1995, SI 1995/1241 (in force on 1 June 1995), amend the 1994 Regulations, SI 1994/3042, so as to include part-time courses within the scope of Part II, which relates to fees for tuition. These amendments do not apply as respects the charging of relevant fees in respect of students attending a course which begins before 1 September 1995.

1136 Finance—discretionary awards—policy not to make discretionary awards

A prospective law student applied for judicial review of his local council's refusal to give him a grant to attend a course leading to a professional qualification. He argued that if local education authorities were allowed to adopt policies whereby awards were not made to students attending such courses, they would become the preserve of the affluent. *Held*, the decision not to give grants to students at private institutions was a political decision, and as such would not be criticised by the court. Moreover, there were other publicly funded institutions at which the course was taught. Whether students who could not otherwise afford to attend postgraduate courses should be given grants was a matter for local education authorities. The application would be dismissed.

R v Southwark London Borough Council, ex p Udu (1995) Times, 30 October (Court of Appeal: Staughton, Henry and Pill LJJ).

A law student applied for judicial review of a county council's decision not to make an award under the Education Act 1962, s 2 to assist him to study on the legal practice course. In his application he stated that, working as a criminal lawyer with low remuneration, he would be unable to repay the loan required to finance the course. The council's general policy was to not make discretionary awards, but to consider each case individually to determine whether exceptional circumstances existed under its published criteria, such as an absence of other sources of funding, or the existence of a disability or of health or personal difficulties. *Held*, a local authority was entitled to have a policy whereby it made no discretionary education awards except in exceptional circumstances. Parliament had left it to local authorities to decide to whom to distribute public bounty and there was nothing irrational in generally excluding from potential recipients those who had access to other sources of funds. Accordingly, the application would be dismissed.

R v Warwickshire County Council, ex p Williams [1995] ELR 326 (Queen's Bench Division: Schiemann J).

The Education Act 1962, s 1(1) provides that it is the duty of every local education authority, subject to and in accordance with regulations made under the Act, to bestow on persons ordinarily resident in their area awards in respect of their attendance on courses to which s 1 applies. Section 1(6) provides that, without prejudice to the duty imposed by sub-s (1), an authority has the power to bestow on any person an award in respect of his attendance on a course to which s 1 applies, where he is not eligible for an award under sub-s (1) in respect of that course.

The applicant had received a mandatory award for her first degree in Biochemistry. Whilst studying for that degree she informed the respondent that she intended to read medicine as a second degree and was told that, under its discretionary awards policy, she would be considered for an award for the final three years of clinical study. Three years later, when she was offered a place to read medicine she was told that, as a result of a change in policy, her course was not included amongst those considered for awards. The respondent had concluded that any discretionary awards, which would have been made under s 1(6), would have to be paid at the full rate, including amounts for both tuition and maintenance. They resolved that no maintenance awards would be made for courses leading to NVQ levels 3, 4 and 5 (the applicant's course was one leading to NVQ level 4) and that effectively awards under s 1(6) would cease to be available. The respondent informed the applicant that it would have liked to have made an award in respect of her tuition fees but that the 1962 Act precluded partial awards. The applicant sought judicial review of the decision, contending that the authority had misdirected itself on the interpretation of s 1(6) and that it had unlawfully fettered its discretion in its adoption of its policy on awards for students and in the manner in which that policy was applied to the applicant. *Held*, under the Education (Mandatory Awards) Regulations 1992, SI 1992/1270, regs 10, 12 the respondent was under no duty to grant an award to a person who had already attended a designated course. The applicant had already received a mandatory award and was not eligible for an award under the 1962 Act, s 1(1). The authority had a discretion to make an award under s 1(6) and once it was exercised, the student was to be treated in the same way as those under sub-s (1) so that the authority had a discretion to make a full award (including a maintenance grant) or no award at all. However, a local authority could not adopt a policy precluding the exercise of its discretion with total disregard to the merits of individual cases. To have an effective exceptions procedure, they must have available to them information by reference to which special circumstances could be assessed. Accordingly, the decision would be quashed by an order of certiorari.

R v London Borough of Bexley, ex p Jones [1995] ELR 42 (Queen's Bench Division: Legatt LJ).

The Education (Mandatory Awards) Regulations 1992, SI 1992/1270 were superseded by the 1993 Regulations, SI 1993/2914, themselves replaced by SI 1994/3044, as from 1 September 1995.

1137 Further education—information

The Education (Further Education Institutions Information) (England) Regulations 1995, SI 1995/2065 (in force on 1 September 1995), which apply to educational institutions in England, replace, with modifications, the 1993 Regulations, SI 1993/1993, and the Education (Distribution by Schools of Information about Further Education Institutions) (England) Regulations 1993, SI 1993/3197. The regulations (1) require the governing bodies of institutions within the further education sector to publish specified information about the educational achievements of their students and their occupations after completing their courses, (2) prescribe how the information is to be determined, and the time and manner of publication, and (3) require the governing bodies of maintained, grant-maintained and grant-maintained special schools which provide secondary education, and the proprietors of city technology colleges and city colleges for the technology of the arts, to distribute to pupils in the second year of the fourth key stage the published information which is provided to them.

1138   Grant-maintained schools—acquisition of grant-maintained status—ballot expenditure

The Education (Ballot Expenditure) Regulations 1995, SI 1995/628 (in force on 1 April 1995), specify the limits on expenditure which a local education authority may incur for the purpose of influencing the outcome of parental ballots held under the Education Act 1993, s 28 (in relation to schools eligible for grant-maintained status). The limit is determined by a formula which, in addition to a fixed sum, takes account of the number of ballots notified in a financial year and the number of registered pupils at the school in respect of which a ballot is held. Provision is also made concerning requirements in relation to the keeping of accounts.

1139   Grant-maintained schools and grant-maintained special schools—finance

The Education (Grant-maintained and Grant-maintained Special Schools) (Finance) Regulations 1995, SI 1995/936 (in force on 1 April 1995), replace the Education (Grant-maintained Schools) (Finance) Regulations 1994, SI 1994/938, and the Education (Grant-maintained Special Schools) (Finance) Regulations 1994, SI 1994/2111. The regulations confer functions on the Funding Agency for Schools regarding the determination and redetermination of amounts of maintenance grant payable to schools, the payment of capital and special purpose grants to schools, and the imposition of requirements to be observed by governing bodies in receipt of grant. The principal changes are (1) the relevant local education authority percentages are revised; (2) provision is made in relation to the calculation of maintenance grant to be paid to schools which become grant-maintained schools pursuant to proposals published by promoters under the Education Act 1993, s 49; (3) provisions relating to cash protection for schools are modified; (4) additional provision is made in respect of expenditure on employment of teaching staff to make special provision for pupils belonging to ethnic minorities where the local education authority's scheme makes no such provision for the financial year in question; (5) provision is made in relation to deficits and deductions in respect of the budget shares of schools, which become grant-maintained, in the period during which they were county or voluntary schools, and such deficits or deductions are to be taken into account in determining the amount of the school's maintenance grant; (6) provision is made for the funding authority to make additional payments in respect of schools which provide education for wide ranges of pupils; and (7) provision is made for the funding authority to add to or deduct from amounts determined in respect of a school, other than a special school, which is situated in the area of a local authority which is not the area of the local authority which previously maintained it.

The Education (Grant-maintained and Grant-maintained Special Schools) (Finance) (Amendment) Regulations 1995, SI 1995/1554 (in force on 14 July 1995), amend SI 1995/936 supra so as to correct drafting errors.

1140   Grant-maintained schools—finance—calculation of grant

The Education (Grant-maintained Schools) (Finance) (Wales) Regulations 1995, SI 1995/587 (in force on 1 April 1995), replace the 1994 Regulations, SI 1994/610, and make provision for the calculation of the amount of maintenance grant which may be paid and the kinds of capital and special purpose grants which may be paid, by the Secretary of State to the governing bodies of such schools.

1141   Grants—education support and training

The Education (Grants for Education Support and Training) (England) Regulations 1995, SI 1995/605 (in force on 1 April 1995), replace the 1994 Regulations, SI 1994/612. The regulations make provision as to (1) expenditure in respect of which grants are payable; (2) grants in respect of payments to third parties; (3) the rate of grant; (4) conditions for payment of grant; (5) requirements to be complied with; (6) the Secretary of State's power to require local education authorities to delegate decisions about the spending of grant to persons determined in accordance with the regulations; and (7) the purposes for or in connection with which grants are payable.

The Education (Grants for Education Support and Training) (England) (Amendment) Regulations 1995, SI 1995/1705 (in force on 1 August 1995), amend the 1995 Regulations supra so as to enable grant to be paid for, or in connection with, the provision of training courses for the training of specialist teacher assistants to provide assistance and support for qualified teachers in teaching subjects including reading, writing and mathematics to primary school pupils.

1142 Grants—education support and training—Wales

The Education (Grants for Education Support and Training) (Wales) Regulations 1995, SI 1995/501 (in force on 1 April 1995), replace the 1994 Regulations, SI 1994/612, so far as they apply in relation to local education authorities in Wales. The regulations make provision as to (1) expenditure in respect of which grants are payable; (2) grants in respect of payments to third parties; (3) the rate of grant; (4) conditions for payment of grant; (5) requirements to be complied with, and (6) the purposes for, or in connection with which, grants are payable.

1143 Grants—travellers and displaced persons

The Education (Grants) (Travellers and Displaced Persons) (Amendment) Regulations 1995, SI 1995/543 (in force on 1 April 1995), amend the 1993 Regulations, SI 1993/569, reducing the rate of grant payable in England and providing that refugees and displaced persons in respect of whom grant is paid under the Local Government Act 1966, s 11 are not eligible for grant under the Education Reform Act 1988, s 210.

1144 Higher education—awards—mandatory awards

The Education (Mandatory Awards) Regulations 1995, SI 1995/3321 (in force on 1 September 1996), replace the 1994 Regulations, SI 1994/3044, and the amending SI 1995/1240. Changes of substance from the provisions of the 1994 Regulations, other than changes in the rates of grant and allowance, are as follows: (1) the list of subjects studied on a course for the degree of Bachelor of Education which attract a second full mandatory award for the course is amended; (2) an amendment is made to the provision for the reduction of grant in case of absence due to illness; (3) provision for the payment of fees charged by colleges of the Universities of Kent, Lancaster and York is made; (4) all students who live away from their parent's home are now entitled to the ordinary maintenance requirement applicable to students living away from their parent's home irrespective of whether they could conveniently attend their courses from home; (5) the right of certain students to be able to claim travel expenses has been extended; and (6) provision is made to allow payments under the European Community programme known as 'Leonardo da Vinci' to be disregarded in calculating a student's income for the purposes of ascertaining his entitlement to maintenance grant.

1145 Independent schools—assisted places scheme

The Education (Assisted Places) Regulations 1995, SI 1995/2016 (in force on 25 August 1995), which relate to the scheme for assisted places at independent schools required to be established by the Education Act 1980, s 17, consolidate, with amendments, the 1989 Regulations, SI 1989/1235 and the amending SI 1990/1546, 1991/1767, 1992/1798, 1993/1936 and 1994/2034. Part I of the regulations makes general and introductory provision. Part II deals with eligibility for assisted places. Eligibility is subject to specified conditions, being conditions relating to residence in the British Islands or the European Economic Area or refugee status, minimum age, selection at sixth form level, declarations of income by the child's parents, and academic ability. The condition relating to residence has been revised so as to remove the requirement that a child who is a national of a member state of the European Community be resident in the British Isles on the relevant date, and so as to take account of the European Economic Area Agreement. Part III makes provision for remission of fees in certain circumstances. Provision is made for the computation of income, the determination of remission questions, the calculation of remission and the scales of remission. The reduction to be made in relevant income in respect of dependent relatives has been increased from £1,140 to £1,165. Part IV contains administrative arrangements as to reimbursement claims, time limits, forms etc and miscellaneous requirements, including requirements as to the publication of information in relation to the assisted places scheme, the proportion of pupils to be selected from publicly maintained schools, the fees payable, increases in fees, returns required by the Secretary of State and the school accounts to be kept. Part V contains miscellaneous requirements, the main changes from the previous regulations relating to the auditing of school accounts, and the assessment of total income for the purposes of the regulations. The regulations also make transitional provision.

The Education (Assisted Places) (Incidental Expenses) Regulations 1995, SI 1995/2017 (in force on 25 August 1995), consolidate, with amendments, the 1989 Regulations, SI 1989/1237 and the amending SI 1990/1547, 1991/1830, 1992/1661, 1993/1937 and 1994/2035, and complement the Education (Assisted Places) Regulations 1995, SI 1995/2016 supra. The regulations relate to the incidental expenses of pupils holding assisted places at schools by virtue of the scheme established pursuant to the Education Act 1980, s 17. They provide for grants towards expenditure on uniform and other clothing (including sports clothing) and travel, for the remission of charges for meals where the parents are in receipt of income support, and for the remission of charges for certain field study courses. The grants are subject to a means test, the provisions for which have been amended so as to raise the limit of relevant income for payment of uniform grant in the first year, with corresponding increases in the maximum amounts of grant payable where relevant income is below that figure. Travel grant is payable in full where the relevant income does not exceed £9,585 and at reduced rates where the relevant income exceeds that figure. Charges for meals are remitted in full where the parents of an assisted pupil are in receipt of income support. Charges for field study courses are remitted in full where the parents of an assisted pupil are entitled to any remission of fees under SI 1995/2016. General provision is made relating to grants and remission of charges and to the reimbursement of schools for the amount of all grants made and charges remitted. The Secretary of State may specify the time, manner and form in which parents are to apply for grants or remission of charges or to furnish information, and is required to reimburse schools for the grants made and charges remitted under these regulations or the revoked regulations.

1146   Local education authority—exercise of education function—school admissions policy—exclusion of Roman Catholic children from non-denominational schools

In a local education authority's catchment area there was an unusually large number of Roman Catholic schools. Those schools and the authority had entered into an agreement under the Education Act 1980, s 6(6) whereby only a small number of non-Roman Catholic children would be admitted to such schools. Because there was consequently a large number of places for Roman Catholic children at such schools, the authority adopted a reciprocal policy whereby places at non-denominational schools would only be allocated to Roman Catholic children after other applications had been met. A Roman Catholic child had attended a Roman Catholic primary school. When he came to transfer to secondary school his parents expressed a preference for a particular non-denominational school. He was refused a place at that school but offered a place at another school. His parents sought judicial review, challenging the authority's selection policy. *Held*, such a policy would at first seem discriminatory and unsustainable. However, because of the arrangements made between the diocesan authorities and the local education authority pursuant to s 6(6), very few non-Roman Catholic children could be accommodated at Roman Catholic schools if they so wished. Accordingly, the application would be refused.

R v Lancashire County Council, ex p Foster [1995] 1 FCR 212, (1995) ELR 33 (Queen's Bench Division: Kennedy LJ and Alliott J).

1147   Local education authority—finance—schemes for financing county and voluntary schools

The Local Government Changes for England (Local Management of Schools) Regulations 1995, SI 1995/3114 (in force on 31 December 1995), make incidental and transitional provision of general application for the local management of schools in England in connection with schemes for the financing of county and voluntary schools under the Education Reform Act 1988, Pt I, Chapter III. The regulations (1) make provision in relation to the schemes of transferee authorities which will become local education authorities by virtue of changes made by an order under the Local Government Act 1992, s 17, (2) make provision in relation to the schemes of transferor and transferee authorities which are already local education authorities and whose areas are not abolished, (3) make specific provision regarding consultation with the governing bodies of grant-maintained special schools, (4) make provision concerning the suspension of schools' delegated budgets, and (5) provide that where the special schools of a local education authority are required to be covered in any financial year by a scheme made by the authority, s 33 of the 1988 Act shall have effect for certain purposes in relation to that authority, as if any reference to a county school maintained by an authority included a reference to a special school of that authority.

1148   Local education authority—provision of transport for attendance at school—duty to provide safe transport—seat belts

A mother sought judicial review of a local authority's decision that they would not provide seat belts or other methods of restraint in its minibuses, which were used by her son in travelling to and from school. *Held*, a local authority had a positive duty to provide transport which enabled a child to travel to and from school in safety and reasonable comfort. In considering whether or not that obligation had been satisfied, it was necessary to look at government recommendations, the practice of other education authorities, and the law in respect of seat belts. Here, not only had the local authority consulted the relevant ministers and considered the issue of seat belts in detail in various committees, but it had also considered the safety record of its vehicles and the financial implications of fitting seat belts. The local authority had not erred in their approach to their duty, and the decision that it was not necessary or essential to fit seat belts in school transport was neither wrong nor perverse within *Wednesbury* principles. The local authority could not be required to take a decision which was not currently considered as proper or necessary and, accordingly, the application would be dismissed.

  R v Gwent County Council, ex p Harris [1995] 2 FLR 1021 (Queen's Bench Division: Macpherson of Cluny J). *R v Hereford and Worcester County Council, ex p P* [1992] 2 FCR 732 (1992 Abr para 1017) considered.

1149 National curriculum—assessment arrangements—key stage 1

The Education (National Curriculum) (Assessment Arrangements for the Core Subjects) (Key Stage 1) (England) Order 1995, SI 1995/2071 (in force on 7 August 1995), which replaces the 1993 Order, SI 1993/1983, and the amending SI 1994/2099, specifies the assessment arrangements for the core subjects in the final year of the first key stage, as they apply to maintained and grant-maintained special schools (not established in a hospital) in England. The main changes from the 1993 Order relate to the determination of levels of attainment in English, mathematics and science.

The Education (National Curriculum) (Assessment Arrangements for English, Welsh, Mathematics and Science) (Key Stage 1) (Wales) Order 1995, SI 1995/2207 (in force on 31 August 1995), which applies to schools in Wales only, and replaces the 1993 Order, SI 1993/2190 and the amending SI 1994/646, 2226, specifies the assessment arrangements for pupils studying 'the relevant subjects' (defined as mathematics, science and, in relation to schools and classes which are Welsh speaking, Welsh, or, in relation to schools and classes which are not Welsh speaking, English) of the National Curriculum in the final year of the first key stage. The main changes from the 1993 Order relate to the determination of levels of attainment in the relevant subjects.

1150 National curriculum—assessment arrangements—key stage 2

The Education (National Curriculum) (Assessment Arrangements for the Core Subjects) (Key Stage 2) (England) Order 1995, SI 1995/2072 (in force on 7 August 1995), which replaces the 1994 Order, SI 1994/2100, specifies the assessment arrangements for the core subjects in the final year of the second key stage, as they apply to maintained and grant-maintained special schools (not established in a hospital) in England. The main changes from the 1994 Order relate to the determination of levels of attainment in English, mathematics and science.

The Education (National Curriculum) (Assessment Arrangements for English, Welsh, Mathematics and Science) (Key Stage 2) (Wales) Order 1995, SI 1995/2208 (in force on 31 August 1995), which applies only to schools in Wales, and replaces the 1994 Order, SI 1994/2227, specifies the assessment arrangements for pupils studying 'the relevant subjects' (defined as English, Welsh, mathematics and science) of the National Curriculum in the final year of the second key stage. The main changes from the 1994 Order relate to the determination of levels of attainment in the relevant subjects.

1151 National curriculum—assessment arrangements—key stage 3

The Education (National Curriculum) (Assessment Arrangements for the Core Subjects) (Key Stage 3) (England) Order 1995, SI 1995/2073 (in force on 7 August 1995), which replaces the 1994 Order, SI 1994/2101, specifies the assessment arrangements for the core subjects in the final year of the third key stage, as they apply to maintained and grant-maintained special schools (not established in a hospital) in England. The main changes from the 1994 Order relate to the determination of levels of attainment in the core subjects.

The Education (National Curriculum) (Assessment Arrangements for English, Welsh, Mathematics and Science) (Key Stage 3) (Wales) Order 1995, SI 1995/2209 (in force on 31 August 1995), which applies only to schools in Wales, and replaces the 1994 Order, SI 1994/2228, specifies the assessment arrangements for pupils studying 'the relevant subjects' (defined as English, Welsh, mathematics and science) of the National Curriculum in the final year of the third key stage. The main changes from the 1994 Order relate to the determination of levels of attainment in the relevant subjects.

1152   National Curriculum—attainment targets and programmes of study—art

The Education (National Curriculum) (Attainment Targets and Programmes of Study in Art) (England) Order 1995, SI 1995/58 (in force on 1 August 1995), replaces the 1992 Order, SI 1992/598, and applies to pupils at maintained schools and grant-maintained special schools in England only. Provision is made for the attainment targets and programmes of study specified in relation to key stages one, two and three of a pupil's compulsory schooling in the document entitled 'Art in the National Curriculum (England)' published by HMSO (ISBN 0 11 270890 0) to have effect for the purpose of specifying those elements of the National Curriculum for art.

The Education (National Curriculum) (Attainment Targets and Programmes of Study in Art) (Wales) Order 1995, SI 1995/71 (in force on 1 August 1995), replaces the 1992 Order, SI 1992/757, and makes provision for the study of art in Welsh schools. The attainment targets and programmes of study set out in the document entitled 'Art in the National Curriculum (Wales)', published by HMSO (ISBN 0 11 701818 X) are to have effect in relation to key stages one, two and three of a pupil's compulsory schooling.

1153   National Curriculum—attainment targets and programmes of study—English

The Education (National Curriculum) (Attainment Targets and Programmes of Study in English) Order 1995, SI 1995/51 (in force on various dates between 1 August 1995 and 1 August 1997), replaces the 1989 Order, SI 1989/907, and the 1990 Order, SI 1990/423, so as to provide for the attainment targets and programmes of study specified in relation to the various stages of a pupil's compulsory schooling in the document entitled English in the National Curriculum' by HMSO (ISBN 0 11 270882 X) to have effect for the purpose of specifying those elements of the National Curriculum for English.

1154   National Curriculum—attainment targets and programmes of study—geography

The Education (National Curriculum) (Attainment Targets and Programmes of Study in Geography) (England) Order 1995, SI 1995/55 (in force on 1 August 1995), replaces the 1991 Order, SI 1991/2562, and applies to pupils at maintained schools and grant-maintained special schools (other than those established in a hospital) in England only. Provision is made for the attainment targets and programmes of study specified in relation to key stages one, two and three of a pupil's compulsory schooling in the document entitled 'Geography in the National Curriculum (England)' published by HMSO (ISBN 0 11 270886 2) to have effect for the purpose of specifying those elements of the National Curriculum for geography.

The Education (National Curriculum) (Attainment Targets and Programmes of Study in Geography) (Wales) Order 1995, SI 1995/72 (in force on 1 August 1995), replaces the 1991 Order, SI 1991/751, and makes provision for the study of geography in maintained and grant-maintained schools in Wales. The attainment targets and programmes of study set out in the document 'Geography in the National Curriculum (Wales)', published by HMSO (ISBN 0 11 701816 3) are to have effect in relation to key stages one, two and three of a pupil's compulsory schooling.

1155   National Curriculum—attainment targets and programmes of study—history

The Education (National Curriculum) (Attainment Targets and Programmes of Study in History) (England) Order 1995, SI 1995/54 (in force on 1 August 1995), replaces the 1991 Order, SI 1991/681, and applies to pupils at maintained and grant-maintained schools in England only. Provision is made for the attainment targets and programmes of study specified in relation to key stages one, two and three of a pupil's compulsory schooling in the document entitled 'History in the National Curriculum (England)' published by HMSO (ISBN 0 11 270885 4) to have effect for the purpose of specifying those elements of the National Curriculum for history.

The Education (National Curriculum) (Attainment Targets and Programmes of Study in History) (Wales) Order 1995, SI 1995/73 (in force on 1 August 1995), replaces the 1991 Order, SI 1991/752, and makes provision for the study of history in Welsh schools. The attainment targets and programmes of study set out in the document entitled 'History in the National

Curriculum' published by HMSO (ISBN 0 11 701819 8) are to have effect for key stages one, two and three of a pupil's compulsory schooling.

1156   National Curriculum—attainment targets and programmes of study—mathematics

The Education (National Curriculum) (Attainment Targets and Programmes of Study in Mathematics) Order 1995, SI 1995/52 (in force on various dates between 1 August 1995 and 1 August 1997), replaces the 1991 Order, SI 1991/2896. The order provides for the attainment targets and programmes of study specified in relation to the various key stages of a pupil's compulsory schooling in the document entitled 'Mathematics in the National Curriculum' published by HMSO (ISBN 0 11 270883 8) to have effect for the purpose of specifying those elements of the National Curriculum for mathematics.

1157   National Curriculum—attainment targets and programmes of study—modern foreign languages

The Education (National Curriculum) (Attainment Targets and Programmes of Study in Modern Foreign Languages) Order 1995, SI 1995/57 (in force on various dates between 1 August 1995 and 1 August 1997), replaces the 1991 Order, SI 1991/2563, and provides for the attainment targets and programmes of study specified in relation to key stages three and four of a pupil's compulsory schooling in the document entitled 'Modern Foreign Languages in the National Curriculum' published by HMSO (ISBN 0 11 270889 7) to have effect for the purpose of specifying those elements of the National Curriculum for modern foreign languages.

1158   National Curriculum—attainment targets and programmes of study—music

The Education (National Curriculum) (Attainment Targets and Programmes of Study in Music) (England) Order 1995, SI 1995/59 (in force on 1 August 1995), replaces the 1992 Order, SI 1992/597, and applies to pupils at grant-maintained and grant maintained special schools in England only. Provision is made for the attainment targets and programmes of study specified in relation to key stages one, two and three of a pupil's compulsory schooling in the document entitled 'Music in the National Curriculum (England)' published by HMSO (ISBN 0 11 270891 9) to have effect for the purpose of specifying those elements of the National Curriculum for music.

The Education (National Curriculum) (Attainment Targets and Programmes of Study In Music) (Wales) Order 1995, SI 1995/70 (in force on 1 August 1995), replaces the 1992 Order, SI 1992/758, and makes provision for the study of music in Welsh schools. The attainment targets and programmes of study specified in the document entitled 'Music in the National Curriculum (Wales)', published by HMSO (ISBN 0 11 701817 1) are to have effect for the purpose of specifying those elements of the National Curriculum for music in relation to key stages one, two and three of a pupil's compulsory schooling.

1159   National curriculum—attainment targets and programmes of study—physical education

The Education (National Curriculum) (Attainment Targets and Programmes of Study in Physical Education) Order 1995, SI 1995/60 (in force on various dates between 1 August 1995 and 1 August 1997) replaces the 1992 Order, SI 1992/603, and provides for the attainment targets and programmes of study specified in relation to the various key stages of a pupil's compulsory schooling in the document entitled 'Physical Education in the National Curriculum' published by HMSO (ISBN 0 11 270892 7) to have effect for the purpose of specifying those elements of the National Curriculum for physical education.

1160   National Curriculum—attainment targets and programmes of study—science

The Education (National Curriculum) (Attainment Targets and Programmes of Study in Science) Order 1995, SI 1995/53 (in force on various dates between 1 August 1995 and 1 August 1997), replaces the 1991 Order, SI 1991/2897, and provides for the attainment targets and programmes of study specified in relation to the various key stages of a pupil's compulsory schooling in the document entitled 'Science in the National Curriculum' published by HMSO (ISBN 0 11 270884 6) to have effect for the purpose of specifying those elements of the National Curriculum for science.

1161 National Curriculum—attainment targets and programmes of study—technology

The Education (National Curriculum) (Attainment Targets and Programmes of Study in Technology) Order 1995, SI 1995/56 (in force on various dates between 1 August 1995 and 1 August 1997) replaces the 1990 Order, SI 1990/424, so as to provide for the attainment targets and programmes of study specified in the documents published by HMSO entitled 'Design and Technology in the National Curriculum' (ISBN 011 270888 9) and 'Information Technology in the National Curriculum' (ISBN 0 11 270887 0) to have effect for the purpose of specifying those elements of the National Curriculum for technology.

1162 National curriculum—attainment targets and programmes of study—Welsh

The Education (National Curriculum) (Attainment Targets and Programmes of Study in Welsh) Order 1995, SI 1995/69 (in force on various dates between 1 August 1995 and 1 August 2000), replaces the 1990 Order, SI 1990/1082, and provides for the attainment targets and programmes of study set out in the document entitled 'Welsh in the National Curriculum' published by HMSO (ISBN 0 11 701815 5) to have effect for the four key stages of pupils' compulsory schooling. The 1990 Order and its amending instruments are to continue to apply to the extent to which the present order is not yet in force.

1163 National curriculum—exceptions

The Education (National Curriculum) (Exceptions) (Wales) Regulations 1995, SI 1995/1574 (in force on 1 August 1995), replace the 1989 Regulations, SI 1989/1308, so as to (1) disapply the provisions of the Education (National Curriculum) (Attainment Targets and Programmes of Study in English) Order 1989, SI 1989/907, in relation to pupils in the first key stage in a class which is taught more than half of the subjects specified wholly or partly through the medium of Welsh, and (2) refer to the National Curriculum in English in general terms, rather than to any specific order under which that curriculum is from time to time established. SI 1989/907 is replaced by SI 1995/51 as from 1 August 1995. The regulations extend to grant-maintained special schools (other than those established in hospitals), as well as to the other types of maintained schools covered by the 1989 Regulations.

1164 National Curriculum—individual pupils' achievements—information

The Education (Individual Pupils' Achievements) (Information) (Amendment) Regulations 1995, SI 1995/924 (in force on 21 April 1995), amend the 1993 Regulations, SI 1993/3182. Several changes are made, including the following (1) the educational achievements of pupils in the final year of the second key stage are to be reported in the headteacher's report, both in relation to the individual pupil and in relation to all such pupils at the school; (2) in the case of pupils on the final year of the first or third key stage, the report must include the national comparative information about the educational achievements of all pupils at schools in England who were at those stages in the preceding school year; (3) in the case of pupils in the final year of the second or third key stage, only the result of whichever National Curriculum ('NC') tests or tasks indicates the pupil's highest level of attainment must be included in the report; and (4) the information on the individual educational achievements of pupils in the final year of the first key stage is to include, where applicable, the results of any key stage two NC tests administered to the pupil pursuant to the Education (National Curriculum) (Assessment Arrangements for the Core Subjects) (Key Stage 2) (England) Order 1994, SI 1994/2100.

The Education (Individual Pupils' Achievements) (Information) (Wales) (Amendment) Regulations 1995, SI 1995/522 (in force on 1 April 1995), amend the 1994 Regulations, SI 1994/959. The regulations require head teachers to report the results of key stage two assessments. The reports to parents should include the results of key stage two and three tests as provided by the external marketing agency. Where a head teacher has requested but not received before the end of the summer term a review of the results provided by the external marketing agency in respect of any National Curriculum tests taken by a pupil in the final year of the first, second or third key stage the report must now indicate that those results are provisional. Once the outcome is known the reviewed results must be reported to parents.

1165 Professional education and training—mutual recognition of qualifications

See para 3147.

1166   Pupils—registration

The Education (Pupil Registration) Regulations 1995, SI 1995/2089 (in force on 1 September 1995), which consolidate, with amendments, the Pupils' Registration Regulations 1956, SI 1956/357, and regs 11 and 12 of the Education (Schools and Further Education) Regulations 1981, SI 1981/1086, make provision in respect of admission and attendance registers (including the form, content, inspection and preservation of, and extracts and deletions from, such registers), leave of absence, dual registration, returns, and the use of computers. The main changes are that (1) where the reason for a pupil's absence cannot be established at the commencement of a session, that absence is to be recorded as unauthorised until it has been ascertained that the absence was authorised and the register accordingly amended, (2) the name of a pupil may only be deleted from the attendance register when that pupil's name has been deleted from the admission register in accordance with these regulations, (3) a pupil's name is to be deleted from the admission register in cases where the pupil has not returned to the school within ten days of the expiry of an extended leave of absence and where the proprietor is satisfied that the failure to return is not due to sickness or unavoidable cause, (4) where a pupil has been continuously absent for a period of four weeks, his name may only be deleted from the admission register when both the school and the local education authority have failed, after reasonable inquiry, to locate the pupil, and (5) where the proprietor has been notified by a parent that a pupil is receiving education otherwise than at school, and has deleted that pupil's name from the register in accordance with these regulations, a return must be made to the local education authority within the ten school days immediately following that deletion.

1167   School Curriculum and Assessment Authority—transfer of functions—Wales

The Education (School Curriculum and Assessment Authority) (Transfer of Functions) Order 1995, SI 1995/903 (in force on 21 April 1995), provides for the transfer of functions from the School Curriculum and Assessment Authority to Awdurdod Cwricwlwm Ac Asesu Cymru (the Curriculum and Assessment Authority for Wales) in relation to subjects other than Welsh, of the examination and assessment of pupils in the fourth key stage and above. All other functions of the authority had previously been transferred by SI 1994/645.

1168   Schools—attendance order—form to be used by local education authority

The Education (School Attendance Order) Regulations 1995, SI 1995/2090 (in force on 1 September 1995), which replace the School Attendance Order Regulations 1944, SR & O 1944/1470, prescribe the form of a school attendance order for the purposes of the Education Act 1993, s 192, whereby a local education authority is required to serve a school attendance order on the parent of a child who fails to satisfy the authority that the child is receiving suitable education and the authority is of the opinion that the child should attend school.

**1169   Schools—discipline—exclusion of pupil—hearing before school governors—
          appeal against exclusion**

A pupil was said to have sworn in the presence of a teacher and was excluded from school indefinitely by the headteacher. At a hearing before the governors, they misunderstood the procedure believing that the pupil had no right to be heard. The governors decided not to order the pupil's reinstatement and his exclusion was made permanent. On appeal to the school's appeals committee, the pupil was notified that the permanent exclusion was a reasonable response to his behaviour. He applied for judicial review of the decisions of the school's governing body and the committee, submitting that because the governors had misunderstood their powers to hear from him at the first hearing, the subsequent proceedings were similarly flawed and should be struck out and, further, that the imposition of the exclusion order was unreasonable. *Held*, it was necessary to consider what took place before the committee and, on the evidence, it had performed its function not only by conducting a full review of the evidence obtained by the headmaster at the stage of his inquiry, but specifically, they permitted the pupil to give evidence concerning the incident. To allow him to give an account of the matter was an act of obvious fairness as well as an express requirement of the Revised Code of Practice for Appeals under the Education Acts 1980 and 1981 and the Education (No 2) Act 1986. It was plain that, by its decision, the committee had accepted the pupil had been responsible for the behaviour complained of and that the decision permanently to exclude was a reasonable response. In the present case, it was reasonable to believe that the pupil and his father understood what transpired at the hearing. It was not apparent that the committee had misdirected itself in any way. The pupil failed to establish that a reasonable head teacher could not have arrived at the same decision. Accordingly, judicial review would be refused.

R v Governors of St Gregory's RC Aided High School, ex p Roberts [1995] ELR 290 (Queen's Bench Division: Turner J).

1170   Schools—financial delegation—mandatory exceptions

The Education (Financial Delegation to Schools) (Mandatory Exceptions) Regulations 1995, SI 1995/178 (in force on 24 February 1995), replace the 1994 Regulations, SI 1994/277. They prescribe expenditure to be left out of account (in addition to that expenditure already set out in the Education Reform Act 1988, s 38(4)(a), (b)) in determining the part of the general schools budget of any local education authority in England for any financial year beginning on or after 1 April 1995 which is available for allocation to individual schools under a scheme under the 1988 Act, s 33. The prescribed expenditure is (1) that falling to be taken into account in determining specified central government grants; (2) that falling to be taken into account in determining specific grants from the EC which support activities in schools; (3) expenditure of the kind referred to in the Local Government Act 1966, s 11, in respect of posts approved by the Secretary of State; (4) expenditure in respect of the costs of compensation, redundancy and certain other payments; (5) expenditure on services provided by education welfare officers and education social workers; (6) expenditure on services provided by education psychologists; and (7) expenditure in connection with a local education authority's duties to make assessments of, and to make, maintain and review statements for, children with special educational needs.

1171   Schools—financial statements—prescribed particulars

The Education (School Financial Statements) (Prescribed Particulars etc) Regulations 1995, SI 1995/208 (in force on 24 February 1995), replace the 1994 Regulations, SI 1994/323, in relation to local education authorities in England, for a financial year beginning on or after 1 April 1995. The regulations prescribe the form in which budget and outturn statements are to be prepared, specify the particulars and information additional to that set out in the Education Reform Act 1988, s 42 which are to be contained in budget and outturn statements respectively and prescribe the manner in which and the times by which, such statements are to be published. The 1994 Regulations continue to apply for the financial year beginning on 1 April 1994; the 1993 Regulations, SI 1993/113, continue to apply for the financial year beginning on 1 April 1993; and the 1990 Regulations, SI 1990/353, continue to apply for earlier financial years (except in so far as they impose requirements in respect of the Education Reform Act 1988, s 42(4)(f)–(i), being provisions repealed by the Education Act 1993, s 275).

The Education (School Financial Statements) (Prescribed Particulars etc) (Amendment) Regulations 1995, SI 1995/532 (in force on 31 March 1995), amend the 1994 Regulations supra. In relation to financial years beginning on or after 1 April 1995, outturn statements are required to include additional information relating to reductions and increases in a school's budget share taking place by virtue of the Education Act 1993, s 262(4), in consequence of the permanent exclusion of pupils from the school or the admission of pupils permanently excluded from other schools.

1172   Schools—information

The Education (School Information) (England) (Amendment) Regulations 1995, SI 1995/2480 (in force on 16 October 1995), further amend the 1994 Regulations, SI 1994/1421, which require the governing body of a county school, a voluntary school, a special school maintained by a local education authority which is not established in a hospital, a grant-maintained school or a grant maintained special school which is not established in a hospital to publish a prospectus for distribution to parents and others. The 1994 Regulations are amended so as to (1) require information relating to the assessment results of pupils in the final year of the second key stage to be included in the prospectus, (2) make provision in relation to the information in the prospectus concerning GCE 'A' level and GCE 'AS' level examinations where a pupil is entered for both examinations in the same subject, (3) require additional information to be given concerning the percentage of pupils in the final year of the first key stage, where the number of pupils is ten or more, who were either exempted from teacher assessment but assessed by the administration of National Curriculum tests, or who were assessed by the administration of National Curriculum tests but exempted from teacher assessment in each of mathematics and the specified attainment targets in English, (4) make similar provision to that in (3) for pupils in the final year of the third key stage, and (5) provide that where a governing body have already published the annual prospectus before the commencement of these regulations, the additional information required by these regulations need not be published in that school year.

The Education (School Information) (Wales) (Amendment) Regulations 1995, SI 1995/2070 (in force on 30 August 1995), amend the 1994 Regulations, SI 1994/2330, so as to (1) make amendments to para 15 of Sch 2 to those regulations consequential on the revocation and replacement of regulations referred to in that paragraph by the Education (School Information) (Wales) Regulations 1995, SI 1995/1904, and (2) provide that the information to be published by governing bodies will now be required to include information about key stage 2 assessments.

1173   Schools—performance—information

The Education (School Performance Information) (England) (Amendment) Regulations 1995, SI 1995/1561 (in force on 13 July 1995), amend the 1994 Regulations, SI 1994/1420, so as to (1) require the governing body of a county or voluntary school, any special school maintained by a local education authority which is not established in a hospital, and any grant-maintained school or grant-maintained special school which is not established in a hospital, to provide the Secretary of State with information relating to assessment results of pupils at or near the end of the second key stage, (2) revoke the provisions concerning the provision of information on lesson time, and (3) make minor drafting amendments.

The Education (School Performance Information) (Wales) Regulations 1995, SI 1995/1904 (in force on 19 August 1995), which apply to schools and local education authorities in Wales, replace the 1994 Regulations, SI 1994/2254, and relate to the provision to the Secretary of State, and publication, of information about the performance of schools and certain other specified information. The regulations impose duties on head teachers to provide specified information to governing bodies of maintained secondary schools and on governing bodies of maintained secondary schools (including grant-maintained and grant-maintained special schools) and non-maintained special schools and proprietors of independent schools with pupils over the age of eleven to provide the Secretary of State with specified information in relation to their school. The governing bodies of certain schools are required to provide parents and others with specified information by making it available at the school, and the governing body of every maintained secondary school with pupils in the final year in the fourth key stage and every maintained primary school with pupils in the final year of the second key stage is required to make available and distribute, a booklet to be published by the Secretary of State which contains information provided to him under the regulations. Those same published particulars are not required to be made available to any person on more than one occasion. The regulations also prescribe the information that is required to be given about examination results, background information about the school in question, information about authorised and unauthorised absence, and the determination of averages over relevant three year periods.

1174   Schools—school reorganisation and admissions
See para 1968.

1175   Sex discrimination—designated educational establishments

The Sex Discrimination (Designated Educational Establishments) (Revocation) Order 1995, SI 1995/2019 (in force on 1 September 1995), revokes the 1975 Order, SI 1975/1902, and the amending SI 1980/1860 and SI 1993/560. The 1975 Order is revoked in consequence of amendments made to the Sex Discrimination Act 1975, s 22, which makes it unlawful for any educational establishment to which that section applies to discriminate on the grounds of sex.

1176   Special educational needs—assessments and statements—Wales

The Education (Special Educational Needs) (Prescribed Forms) (Welsh Forms) Regulations 1995, SI 1995/45 (in force on 13 February 1995), modify the 1994 Regulations, SI 1994/1047, so as to prescribe Welsh versions of the notice to parents and the statement of special educational needs set out in those regulations.

1177   Special educational needs—local education authority—duty of care

See *X (Minors) v Bedfordshire County Council; M (a Minor) v Newham London Borough Council; E (a Minor) v Dorset County Council; Christmas v Hampshire County Council; Keating v Bromley London Borough Council*, para 2833.

1178 Special educational needs—schools—approval of closure by Secretary of State—matters to be disclosed in consultation process

The Education Act 1993, s 183(2), (6) provides there where a local education authority intend to discontinue a special educational needs school, they must serve notice on the Secretary of State and such persons as may be prescribed of their proposals. By s 184(2) any person may submit objections to the proposals to the body which served the notice.

The Secretary of State decided to approve the closure of a special educational needs school following a proposal from the local education authority. The main reasons given for the Secretary of State's decision were that (1) the school lacked necessary specialist facilities, (2) there was difficulty in providing the national curriculum, (3) there had been a decline in the number of children in the school, and (4) a school inspector had reported that the school's achievements were poor. A number of parents challenged the decision, arguing in particular that they had not previously been informed of the inspector's findings, thereby denying them the opportunity to reply to them. *Held*, the Secretary of State had been entitled to take a particular year, rather than any other year, as the basis on which to conclude that the number of children in the school had fallen in successive years, and it was not for the court to interfere with that decision on the ground that there had been an error of fact. Had the parents known that an inspector had visited the school and criticised it in a report which was taken into account by the Secretary of State, they would have replied to those criticisms. In particular, the parents would have argued that the national curriculum had changed since the report, that the national curriculum was of little relevance to children with special educational needs, and that a subsequent, favourable report on the school had been made by an inspector. Although in an administrative appeal concerning special educational needs, the Secretary of State was not obliged to disclose advice given to her by a school inspector because such advice formed part of the decision-making process, new material or new issues introduced in the course of the consultation process had to be disclosed so that comments could be obtained from those participating in the consultation process. In the instant case, the inspector's findings amounted to a new issue or new material, and the parents and other objectors had not been given the opportunity to make representations in that respect. The Secretary of State's failure to allow them to do so vitiated her decision and, accordingly, the application would be allowed.

R v Secretary of State for Education, ex p Skitt [1995] ELR 388 (Queen's Bench Division: Sedley J). *R v Secretary of State for Education, ex p S* [1995] ELR 71, CA applied.

1179 Special educational needs—statement—allocation of cash sums to various bands of special needs

It has been held that a local education authority was not fettering itself in the discharge of its obligation under the Education Act 1981 to make provision for children with special educational needs by virtue of its policy of allocating pupils with those needs to various bands, each of which was ascribed a cash figure for expenditure on provision for those needs. The sum was ascribed in order to enable the authority to make budgetary provision and it did not indicate any unwillingness on the part of the authority to secure special educational provision for the children in question.

R v Cumbria County Council, ex p P [1995] ELR 337 (Queen's Bench Division: Schiemann J).

Education Act 1981 repealed by the Education Act 1993, ss 303, 307, Sch 21, Pt I. For provision for children with special educational needs, see the 1993 Act, ss 156–191.

1180 Special educational needs—statement—annual review

The Education (Special Educational Needs) (Amendment) Regulations 1995, SI 1995/1673 (in force on 14 August 1995), amend the 1994 Regulations, SI 1994/1047, so as to (1) define 'qualified teacher' in relation to the transitional provisions governing annual reviews of statements of special educational needs, and (2) correct a drafting error.

1181 Special educational needs—statement—attendance at fee-paying school—obligation to pay school fees

In a statement of special educational needs, the local educational authority named a fee-paying school as appropriate for a child's education. The child's parents had strongly wished him to attend the school, which was an orthodox Jewish school, and the authority had determined that it would be suitable provided that the assistance of a special needs assistant was made available to the child. It also expressed a willingness to pay for such assistance. The child subsequently claimed the full cost of the school fees from the authority. *Held*, the naming, in a statement of special educational needs, of a particular fee-paying school as appropriate for a child's education, did not automatically impose a duty upon the authority to pay all the child's school fees. In the present case, the named school was not necessary as part of the child's special educational provision. He could equally have attended an ordinary school in the area. The fee-paying school had only been named in the statement because it was acceptable to the parents. As such, the authority could not be held responsible for the entire cost of the school's fees. Accordingly, the child's claim would be dismissed.

R v Hackney London Borough Council, ex p C (1995) Times, 7 November (Court of Appeal: Staughton, Henry and Pill LJJ).

1182   Special educational needs—statement—recommendation that child attend mainstream school—expectation of provision of mobility aids

A mother sought judicial review of a local authority's decision not to provide a lift at her child's school. The child had mobility problems and it had been advised that she should not climb stairs. However, the organisation of the school was such that it was necessary for her to attend some classes and facilities that were not on the ground floor. Her inability to do so led to a feeling of exclusion and her work began to suffer. A statement of special educational needs had recommended that the child attend a mainstream school and receive a high level of attendance support. It was argued that once the child was accepted for mainstream schooling, any aid that was necessary to enable her to participate fully in the curriculum should be regarded as special educational provision and the authority was in breach of that obligation so to provide. Further, that the authority's decision was *Wednesbury* unreasonable and that the applicant had had a legitimate expectation that the lift would be installed, which expectation should be fulfilled. *Held*, if the provision of the lift was necessary, it was necessary to improve the child's mobility and not as special educational provision. The authority had acted reasonably, given its information and resources, both of which were limited. Even if the court had not been convinced of this it would not have exercised its discretion to grant relief because the complaint was one of omission rather than commission and it would be more appropriate to send the matter back for reconsideration. Further, there was no question of legitimate expectation since the authority had made no representation that it would provide a lift for the child's use. A reassessment of the child's educational and non-educational needs would be ordered.

R v Lambeth London Borough, ex p MBM [1995] ELR 374 (Queen's Bench Division: Owen J).

1183   Special educational needs—statement—statement not maintained—arrangements made by local education authority

A child suffered from severe dyslexia. She was initially educated in schools maintained by the local education authority but her education was plainly unsatisfactory and her parents sent her to an independent fee paying school where she flourished. The local education authority later granted her a statement of special educational needs. This provided for her to attend the fee paying school and for the authority to provide part funding of the fees. When the child reached the age of 16 the authority ceased to maintain the statement of special educational needs and thus the funding. On an application by the parents to quash the decision to cease to maintain the statement, *held*, the parents had not made suitable arrangements for the child's education within the meaning of the Education Act 1981, s 7(1) merely by placing her in a fee paying school which they could not afford. Under s 7 it had to be the authority or the parents who had made the arrangements and it could not be both. The parents had made the placement at the school only in the light of the authority's failure to provide a place at a school which could meet the child's educational and other needs. The authority had made the 'arrangements' by making its belated statement and then agreeing to part fund the arrangement contained in the statement. In any case, the parents could not, to the authority's knowledge, continue to pay the fees, the education at the school could not continue without payment and thus the parents had not made suitable arrangements within s 7(1). Accordingly, the application to quash the decision would be allowed.

R v Kent County Council, ex p W [1995] 2 FCR 342 (Queen's Bench Division: Turner J). 1981 Act, s 7 now Education Act 1993, s 168.

1184   Special educational needs—supplies—payment for supplies—terms of payment

The Education (Payment for Special Educational Needs Supplies) (Amendment) Regulations 1995, SI 1995/629 (in force on 1 April 1995) further amend the 1994 Regulations, SI 1994/650, so as to (1) prescribe an amount for meeting the cost of supplies under the Education Act 1993, s 162(1), included in Part 1 of a local education authority's budget statement by reference to the planned expenditure in respect of which it is so included, rather than by reference to these regulations in accordance with which it is so included, and (2) replace references to the provisions of the Education Act 1981, which have been repealed (with savings), with references to the relevant provisions of the 1993 Act.

1185 Special educational needs—tribunal—appeal against tribunal's decision—appeal by child

On the application of a child, a Special Educational Needs Tribunal refused to amend the name of the school specified in a statement of special educational needs. The child's appeal was dismissed at first instance on grounds of merit. On further appeal, the issue arose whether the High Court had correctly determined that it had the jurisdiction to entertain the child's appeal. *Held*, the Tribunals and Enquiries Act 1992, s 11(1) permitted a 'party to proceedings' to bring an appeal from the tribunal to the High Court on a point of law. Therefore, whether the High Court had jurisdiction in the present case depended on whether, the child in question was rightfully 'a party' to the original appeal to the tribunal. Neither the Education Act 1993, nor the Special Educational Needs Tribunal Regulations 1994, SI 1994/1910, made provision for the child to bring the appeal to the tribunal himself. The provisions consistently identified the parent as the person bringing the appeal. The child was merely the beneficiary of the litigation and, was not a 'party to the proceedings' for the purposes of the 1992 Act, s 11(1). Therefore the Special Educational Needs Tribunal did not have the jurisdiction to entertain the child's appeal and, the High Court did not have the jurisdiction to entertain any further appeal by the child. Accordingly, the court had no jurisdiction to entertain the present appeal and it would be dismissed.

S (a Minor) v Special Educational Needs Tribunal [1996] 1 WLR 382 (Court of Appeal: Leggatt and Millett LJJ and Sir Ralph Gibson). Decision of Latham J (1995) Independent, 28 September affirmed

1186 Special educational needs—tribunal—constitution and procedure

The Special Educational Needs Tribunal Regulations 1995, SI 1995/3113 (in force on 8 December 1995), replace the 1994 Regulations, SI 1994/1910, making provision in relation to the establishment and procedure of the Special Educational Needs Tribunal constituted by the Education Act 1993, s 177. Provision is made as to: (1) the members of the lay panel and the establishment of tribunals to exercise the jurisdiction of the Special Educational Needs Tribunal; (2) the making of an appeal to the tribunal and the reply by the local education authority; (3) the preparation for the hearing; (4) the determination of appeals; and (5) the additional powers of, and general provisions relating to, the tribunal.

1187 Special educational needs—tribunal—decision—judicial review and statutory appeals

It has been held that the correct procedure for challenging a decision of the Special Educational Needs Tribunal is by way of an appeal to the High Court under RSC Ord 55 and not by way of judicial review under RSC Ord 53, since the judicial review process should not be allowed to supplant the normal statutory appeal procedure.

R v Special Educational Needs Tribunal, ex p South Glamorgan County Council (1995) Times, 12 December (Court of Appeal: Rose, Millett and Thorpe LJJ).

1188 Teachers—employment

The Education (Teachers) Amendment Regulations 1995, SI 1995/602 (in force on 1 April 1995), amend the 1993 Regulations, SI 1993/543. The regulations provide that (1) licences and authorisations allowing unqualified persons to teach in schools will after 31 March 1995 be granted by the Teacher Training Agency rather than the Secretary of State; (2) such licences and authorisations will be granted on the recommendation of governing bodies alone and the consent of the local education authority, with one exception, will not be required; (3) a licence or authorisation will lapse if the teacher ceases to be employed in the post particularised in the licence; (4) licences and authorisations to teach in schools in Wales continue to be granted by the Secretary of State; (5) in relation to registered teachers, after 31 March 1995 registrations will be effected by the Teacher Training Agency and not the Secretary of State; (6) spent provisions in the 1994 Regulations, SI 1994/222, and the Education (Pupil Referral Units) (Application of Enactments) Regulations 1994, SI 1994/2103 are revoked.

The Education (Teachers) (Amendment) (No 2) Regulations 1995, SI 1995/2594 (in force on 1 November 1995), further amend the 1993 Regulations supra in relation to the barring or restricting of the employment of persons in relevant employment (as defined by the 1993 Regulations) by the Secretary of State. The regulations provide that where a person is convicted of committing, or attempting to commit, an offence specified by these regulations involving a child under the age of 16, the Secretary of State is under a duty (1) where that person is in relevant employment, to direct his employers to terminate his employment and to direct that he is not to be subsequently appointed to or employed in relevant employment, and (2) where that person is not in relevant employment, to direct that he is not to be subsequently appointed to or employed in relevant employment. In certain circumstances, such a direction may be withdrawn or varied. Where a direction is varied, it may be varied so that the person concerned is only to be appointed to or employed in relevant employment subject to any specified conditions. The regulations provide that where the Secretary of State is considering making a direction, or is considering withdrawing or varying a direction, or where a direction is required to be made following a person's conviction of, or attempt to commit, a specified offence, the Secretary of State may require that the person concerned is to be medically examined, and if the person fails to do so without good reason, the Secretary of State may reach a decision on the evidence and information available. The Secretary of State is no longer under an obligation to arrange a medical examination at the request of the person concerned.

1189   Teachers—pay and conditions

The Education (School Teachers' Pay and Conditions) (No 2) Order 1995, SI 1995/1743 (in force on 1 September 1995), which revokes the 1994 Order, SI 1994/1231 and the 1995 Order, SI 1995/1015, and which applies to all school teachers (as defined in the School Teachers' Pay and Conditions Act 1991, s 5(1), (2)) in England and Wales, directs that the provisions set out in the document entitled 'School Teachers' Pay and Conditions Document 1995' shall have effect from 1 September 1995, with the exception of para 21.6 (relating to teachers receiving the Inner London Area Supplement) which shall have effect as from 1 September 1994 (the retrospective effect is authorised by the 1991 Act, s 2(4)(f)).

1190   Teachers—superannuation

See PENSIONS AND SUPERANNUATION.

1191   Teachers—training—bursaries

The Education (Bursaries for Teacher Training) (Amendment) Regulations 1995, SI 1995/603 (in force on 1 April 1995), amend the 1994 Regulations, SI 1994/2016, so as to take into account amendments made to the Education (Teachers) Regulations 1993, SI 1993/543, by the amending SI 1995/602. These regulations amend the definition of 'course of initial teacher training' so as to refer, in addition to such courses which are approved by the Secretary of State, to such courses at institutions which are accredited by the Teacher Training Agency or the Higher Education Funding Council for Wales.

1192   Teachers—training—funding

The Education (Funding For Teacher Training) Designation Order 1995, SI 1995/1704 (in force on 1 August 1995), designates the City Technology Colleges Trust Limited as an institution eligible for funding under the Education Act 1994, Pt I for the purposes of the provision of teacher training, the provision of facilities, and the carrying on of other activities in connection with the provision of teacher training.

1193   Teachers—training—Teacher Training Agency—additional functions

The Teacher Training Agency (Additional Functions) Order 1995, SI 1995/601 (in force on 1 April 1995), confers on the Teacher Training Agency additional functions in respect of the licensing or otherwise authorising of unqualified teachers to be employed as teachers in schools and in respect of the requirements imposed on persons carrying on city technology colleges or city colleges for the technology of the arts as to the training and teaching experience of persons who seek to become qualified teachers.

1194   University—commissioners—duties and powers—continuation

The Education (University Commissioners) Order 1995, SI 1995/604 (in force on 31 March 1995), continues the powers and duties of the university commissioners, which would otherwise have ceased on 1 April 1995, until 1 April 1996.

1195   University—exclusion of student—non-payment of fees

Scotland

The applicant was offered a place on a diploma course and, having paid a non-returnable deposit towards the course fees, he was registered as a student. When he failed to pay the outstanding amount of the fees within the period prescribed by the university's regulations, he was excluded from the university and his registration for the course was terminated. On his application for judicial review of the university's decision, *held*, the university's regulations provided that a student's registration would be cancelled unless outstanding fees were paid in full by the end of the calendar month after the student was registered, or unless the university's finance officer received satisfactory evidence that the fees would be paid subsequently in full. On the facts of the case, the university had been entitled to rescind its contract with the applicant for non-payment of fees. Moreover, although the relationship between a student and a university could give rise to situations which were amenable to judicial review, the instant case was concerned with merely contractual rights and obligations. The action therefore should have been a claim in contract and not an application for judicial review. Accordingly, the application would be dismissed.

Joobeen v University of Stirling 1995 SLT 120 (Outer House).

1196   Youth exchanges—'Youth for Europe' programme

See para 3175.

ELECTIONS

Halsbury's Laws of England (4th edn) Vol 15 (reissue), paras 301–883

1197   Ballot papers—form of words in Welsh

The Elections (Welsh Forms) Order 1995, SI 1995/830 (in force on 1 April 1995), prescribes a form of words in Welsh for certain words used on ballot papers to be used at parliamentary, European Parliamentary and local government elections in Wales. Corrections are also made to the Welsh translation of certain words prescribed for use in directions in notices used in polling station and in official poll cards issued to voters.

1198   Election expenses—expenses incurred for promoting a candidate—advertisements

Scotland

The Representation of the People Act 1983, s 75(1)(b), (c) provides that no expenses with a view to promoting or procuring the election of a candidate at an election may be incurred by any person other than the candidate, his election agent and persons authorised in writing by the election agent, on account of issuing advertisements, circulars or publications, or of otherwise presenting to the electors the candidate or his views or the extent or nature of his backing or disparaging another candidate.

The defendant, a trade union, undertook at its own expense an advertising campaign which attacked the national government and many of its policies. The defendant placed advertisements on billboards throughout Scotland and in wards where the plaintiffs were standing as candidates, and also intended to place advertisements in national newspapers. The advertisements effectively urged voters not to vote for the political party which the plaintiffs represented. Arguing that the defendant's actions contravened the 1983 Act, s 75(1), the plaintiffs sought an injunction preventing the defendant from incurring further expenditure in its advertising campaign, and also sought an order for the removal of advertisements that had already been posted. *Held*, advertisements in the form of a generalised attack on one or more of the policies of a political party did not contravene s 75, even if it incidentally assisted a particular candidate. Section 75 was, instead, intended to prohibit expenditure above the statutory maximum allowed for each candidate in a particular constituency, incurred on the authorisation of the candidate's election agent. Moreover, even though the election in the instant case was limited to Scotland, it was still a national election, albeit for local government, in which the national political parties were involved. Accordingly, the application would be dismissed.

Walker v UNISON 1995 SLT 1226 (Outer House). *R v Tronoh Mines Ltd* [1952] 1 All ER 697 and *DPP v Luft* [1976] 2 All ER 569 (1976 Abr para 948), HL considered.

1199 Election petition—City of London ward election—joinder of successful candidates—meaning of returning officer

The Representation of the People Act 1983, s 128(2) provides that a person whose election is questioned by an election petition, and any returning officer of whose conduct the petition complains, may be made a respondent to the petition.

The petitioners were candidates nominated for election in two City of London wards. It was prohibited for a candidate to stand for election in more than one ward at a time so they delivered notices of withdrawal in relation to one of the wards to the alderman who was the presiding officer. The alderman refused to accept the notices as they were not attested and the plaintiffs were consequently deemed to have withdrawn their candidatures from both ward elections. In the second ward, there were no more candidates than vacancies and those candidates were elected without a poll. The petitioners petitioned, as the sole respondent, the alderman as the returning officer under the 1983 Act, s 128(2), seeking a determination that their notices of withdrawal were valid and that they had been validly nominated for the second ward. The alderman applied to have their petition struck out. *Held*, 'returning officer' referred to the person in charge of the election procedure whether or not a poll is taken and the alderman in this case came within that definition and had been properly joined. Any successful candidate impugned by an election petition had the right to be heard and also had to be joined as a respondent. In this case, the time limits for such a joinder had expired and the court had no discretion to extend those time limits. Accordingly, the alderman's application to strike out would be granted.

Absalom v Gillett [1995] 1 WLR 128 (Queen's Bench Division: Laws and Forbes JJ).

1200 Local elections—right to vote and stand as candidate—European Union citizens

The Local Government Elections (Changes to the Franchise and Qualification of Members) Regulations 1995, SI 1995/1948 (in force in part on 6 August 1995 and in part on 1 January 1996), extend the franchise and change the qualification for election and holding office as members of local authorities. The regulations (1) amend the Local Government Act 1972 and the City of London (Various Powers) Act 1957 (together with certain Scottish and Northern Ireland Acts), to extend the right to stand at local government elections in England, Wales and Scotland, local elections in Northern Ireland, and Common Council elections in the City of London, to citizens of all member States of the European Community on the same terms as Commonwealth citizens; and (2) amend the Representation of the People Act 1983, the City of London (Various Powers) Act 1957 (together with certain Scottish and Northern Ireland Acts) so as to extend the right to vote in the elections referred to in (1) above to all citizens of member States of the European Community on the same terms as Commonwealth citizens. SI 1986/1081, 2209, 2214, 2215 are consequently amended.

1201 Parliamentary constituencies

See PARLIAMENT.

1202 Returning officer—parliamentary constituencies

The Returning Officers (Parliamentary Constituencies) (England) Order 1995, SI 1995/2061 (in force in part on 25 August 1995, and in part on the issue of a proclamation by Her Majesty summoning a new Parliament), designates the returning officers for parliamentary constituencies where they are not determined by the Representation of the People Act 1983. The 1983 Order, SI 1983/468, as amended, is revoked.

1203 Returning officer—parliamentary constituencies—Wales

The Returning Officers (Parliamentary Constituencies) (Wales) Order 1995, SI 1995/1142 (in force in part on 10 May 1995 and in part on the issue of a proclamation by Her Majesty summoning a new Parliament), amends the 1983 Order, SI 1983/468, so far as it relates to Wales, so as to designate the acting returning officers for the county constituencies in Wales and the returning officer for the borough constituency of Cardiff South and Penarth, where appointment of a returning officer is not determined by the Representation of the People Act 1983, s 24(1)(b).

ELECTRICITY AND ATOMIC ENERGY

See FUEL AND ENERGY.

EMPLOYMENT

Halsbury's Laws of England (4th edn) Vol 16 (reissue), paras 1–650

1204 Articles

All Dressed Up and Nowhere to Go, Ann Spowart Taylor (on employers' right to control the appearance of their staff): 139 SJ 546

An Alternative Forum to Industrial Tribunals, James Pyke (on the Joint Industry Board's Exempted Dismissal Procedures Agreement): 139 SJ 268

Compliance Programmes, Julian Armstrong (on *Director General of Fair Trading v Pioneer Concrete (UK) Ltd* [1995] 1 All ER 135, HL (1994 Abr para 1219)): [1995] ECLR 147

The Conceptualization of European Labour Law, Brian Bercusson: (1995) 24 ILJ 3

Countering Disability Discrimination, Christine Clayson and Geoff Holgate: 139 SJ 442

Disability Discrimination Act, Christine Clayson and Geoffrey Holgate: 139 SJ 1254

Disability Discrimination Bill, Edward Myers: 145 NLJ 1156

Does a Subcontractor Have Restitutionary Rights Against the Employer? Peter Watts: [1995] LMCL 398

Employees and the Unfair Contract Terms Act, Loraine Watson: (1995) 24 ILJ 323

EC Law and the Dismissal of Pregnant Servicewomen, Anthony Arnull: (1995) 24 ILJ 215

Equality of Treatment: A Variable Concept? Philippa Watson: (1995) 24 ILJ 33

Financial Futures and Options, Nigel Doran and Ashley Greenbank (on the taxation of futures and options): Tax Journal, Issue 302, p 14, Issue 303, p 16, Issue 304, p 16

The Future of Labour Law, Bob Hepple: (1995) 24 ILJ 303

Future Directions in European Union Social Policy Law, Erika Szyszczak (on the impact of the European Union on British labour law): (1995) 24 ILJ 19

The Government's Proposals to Amend UK Legislation Concerning Consultation About Collective Redundancies and Business Transfers, Karl Larrad: 159 JP Jo 621

In Restraint of Trade, Lynette Warren: 139 SJ 1005

Joint Liability for Unfair Dismissal on Transfers, Trevor Bettany: 139 SJ 43

The Law of Tips and Service Charges, Roger Peters: 139 SJ 847

Racial Harassment at Work, Daniel Barnett: 145 NLJ 1614

Rights and Wrongs, Michael Ryley (on *Milligan v Securicor Cleaning* [1995] IRLR 288 (para 1248)): LS Gaz, 13 July 1995, p 20

Ruling Out Affirmative Action, Sionaidh Douglas-Scott (on the approach to affirmative action by the European Court of Justice in comparison with the United States Supreme Court): 145 NLJ 1586

Sexual Harassment—Opening Up Pandora's Box? Peter Townsend and Arthur Baker: 159 JP Jo 39

Skirting Around Sexual Harassment, Irene Mackay and Jill Earnshaw: 145 NLJ 338

A Step In the Dark? Julie Nazerali and Karen Plumbley-Jones (on the draft Acquired Rights Directive): 139 SJ 144

Thou Shalt Not Covet the Boss's Clients or Employees, M Walsh (on restrictive covenants): 145 NLJ 1400

TUPE [Transfer of Undertakings (Protection of Employment) Regulations 1981, SI 1981/1794] and the Employee Who is Unaware of the Transfer, John McMullen: 139 SJ 366

Unfair Dismissal: Employer's Variation of Employment Contracts, Geoffrey Holgate: 139 SJ 958

When is an Employee Entitled to Receive Payment in Lieu of Notice? Geoffrey Mead (on *Abrahams v Performing Rights Society Ltd* [1995] ICR 1028 (para 1212)): 139 SJ 816

Whisper Those Sweet Nothings: The Trouble with Employee References, Mark Watson-Gandy: 159 JP Jo 315

Whistleblowers and Job Security, David Lewis: 58 MLR 208

Whistleblowing—Time for a Change? Nicholas Rose (on the need for a change in the law relating to employment fidelity and confidentiality): 145 NLJ 113

Workers of the World, Michael James (on disputes under international employment contracts): 139 SJ 768

1205 Continuity of employment—part-time employment—rights under EC law

Scotland
The EC Treaty, art 119 provides that each member state must maintain the principle that men and women should receive equal pay for equal work.

The applicant was employed part-time by a club for three years, normally working less than 16 hours a week. When she was dismissed her unfair dismissal claim failed because she did not have the five years' service necessary to bring a claim under the Employment Protection (Consolidation) Act 1978. Following the decision in *Equal Opportunities Commission v Secretary of State for Employment*, where the House of Lords held that a 16-hour qualifying condition was held to be indirectly discriminatory against women, the applicant made a further claim for unfair dismissal under the EC Treaty, art 119. The industrial tribunal held that the application should be treated as timeous and directed that the claim should be heard on its merits. The club appealed on the ground that (1) a further claim, where an application had already been made and refused, offended against the principle of legal certainty, and (2) it was doubtful whether the House of Lords' decision applied to cases claiming compensation for unfair dismissal. *Held*, (1) although the initial application was dismissed, the tribunal had jurisdiction to entertain the claim under art 119. The principle of res judicata did not apply because no reference was made to art 119 in the previous proceedings and the claim was not barred by the principle of issue estoppel because the applicant was not seeking to challenge findings of fact. The claim had been presented within a reasonable time of the House of Lords' decision and had to be regarded as timeous. (2) The tribunal agreed with the decision in *Mediguard Services Ltd v Thame* that compensation for unfair dismissal fell to be regarded as 'pay' for the purposes of art 119. Accordingly, the appeal would be dismissed and the case remitted to the industrial tribunal for a hearing on its merits.

Methilhill Bowling Club v Hunter [1995] IRLR 232 (Employment Appeal Tribunal: Lord Coulsfield presiding). *Equal Opportunities Commission v Secretary of State for Employment* [1994] 1 All ER 910, HL (1994 Abr para 2532) and *Mediguard Services Ltd v Thame* [1994] ICR 751, EAT (1994 Abr para 1201) followed.

1206   Contract of employment—breach of contract—employer seeking to avoid onerous term—unambiguous term

The plaintiff pilot's contract of employment stated that the seniority of pilots would be determined by reference to the date of their joining the defendant company. New entrants would start as first officers and work their way up the seniority scale. The defendant took over another airline and recruited many of its pilots. The new pilots were not employed as first officers, but were granted seniority according to their seniority with their former employers. The plaintiff brought a claim for damages for breach of contract. *Held*, the plaintiff's contract of employment clearly indicated that the term 'new entrant' meant every new pilot. There was no justification for the defendant's claim that pilots joining it as a result of a merger were excluded from the term 'new entrant'. The merger might have been jeopardised had the defendant insisted that the new pilots joined it as first officers. However, notwithstanding this fact, there was no authority for the proposition that the court should have substituted what it believed to be a reasonable result in place of the contract's meaning, which was unambiguous. Accordingly, the plaintiff's claim would succeed.

Adams v British Airways plc [1995] IRLR 577 (Queen's Bench Division: Laws J).

1207   Contract of employment—duty to employer—fidelity—extent of duty

The respondent, a small industrial cleaning company, secured a substantial cleaning contract, and the appellant, who was employed by the respondent as a foreman, was involved in the contract. When the contract came up for renewal, tenders were invited. The appellant told the respondent that he had tendered for the contract, and was dismissed when he refused to sign an undertaking that he would not compete with the respondent for industrial cleaning contracts whilst in their employment. In dismissing his complaint of unfair dismissal, an industrial tribunal held that the appellant had been in breach of his duty of fidelity by refusing to give the undertaking sought, and that the respondent had therefore been entitled to terminate his employment. On appeal, *held*, although an employee soliciting for his former employer's customers after leaving their employment was a factually different situation from an employee tendering for the future business of an employer's customers in competition with the employer whilst still in their employment, in both cases there was a breach of the obligation to give faithful service. In the latter situation, as in the instant case, an employer was entitled to expect that an employee would not compete with him for contracts with the existing customers. Accordingly, the appeal would be dismissed.

Adamson v B & L Cleaning Services Ltd [1995] IRLR 193 (Employment Appeal Tribunal: Pill J presiding).

1208   Contract of employment—existence of contract—clergyman—right to claim compensation for unfair dismissal

A clergyman had been taken on as an assistant curate at a church on the understanding that he would remain there until he secured an independent appointment. He was dismissed at the end of a three-year training period following differences with his vicar. He was then given a temporary appointment at another church for six months, following which he was taken off the diocesan pay-roll. In response to his claim for unfair dismissal, the church argued that the tribunal had no jurisdiction to hear the complaint. At a preliminary hearing, *held*, the applicant was entitled to pursue a claim against the Church of England seeking compensation for unfair dismissal and reinstatement. Notwithstanding the spiritual nature of his duties, an Anglican clergyman had a secular contract of employment with the Church of England and could thus bring a claim against it for unfair dismissal.

Coker v Diocese of Southwark [1995] ICR 563 (Industrial Tribunal, South London).

1209   Contract of employment—fraudulent employer—stigma compensation

The appellants were employees of a bank which operated in a corrupt and dishonest manner. The bank collapsed and, although the appellants were innocent of any wrongdoing, they claimed they were stigmatised by reason of their previous employment. They claimed compensation for the loss consequently suffered arguing that there should be implied into their contracts of employment a term that their employer would not conduct itself in a manner calculated as likely to destroy or seriously damage the relationship of confidence and trust between employer and employee. At first instance, the judge concluded that such a term could not be implied because it was not part of a contract to prepare an employee for service with future employers and the claims were struck out as failing to disclose a reasonable cause of action. The appellants submitted on appeal that their claims were justified on general principles as the pecuniary loss flowed from a breach of the implied term. *Held*, the appellants did not claim damage to goodwill as recognised by law, and the object of the contract of employment was to employ, not to promote or preserve existing reputations or to prepare for future employment. In those circumstances, the damages claimed were not legally recoverable as the appellants would be compensated for damage to reputation alone. Accordingly, the appeals would be dismissed.

Malik v Bank of Credit and Commerce International SA (in liquidation) [1995] 3 All ER 545 (Court of Appeal: Glidewell, Morritt and Aldous LJJ). Decision of Evans-Lombe J (1994) Times, 23 February affirmed.

1210   Contract of employment—illegal contract—employee's right to bring claim for sex discrimination

See *Leighton v Michael*, para 2651.

1211   Contract of employment—restrictive covenant—severance of unlawful terms

See *Marshall v NM Financial Management Ltd*, para 40.

1212   Contract of employment—termination of contract—payment in lieu of notice—contractual entitlement

The plaintiff was employed on a five-year contract, under which he was entitled to two years' notice of termination of employment, or an equivalent payment in lieu, if his employment was terminated at the end of the five-year period or at any time during the last two years of the contract. After the five years expired, the parties were unable to agree on the terms of a new contract, but it was agreed that the plaintiff was to remain in his post for a further two years, subject to the same terms as the previous contract. When the plaintiff was dismissed seven months later, he commenced proceedings for payment in lieu of notice for the remainder of the two-year period. The defendant entered a defence which included an assertion that the plaintiff was obliged to mitigate his losses. That part of the defence was struck out, and on the defendant's appeal, *held*, the provisions of the old contract relating to notice and payment in lieu applied to the two-year contract of employment. As the defendant had lawfully elected to terminate the contract before the end of the two-year notice period, it was bound to pay the plaintiff the amount due in lieu of notice for the remainder of that period. It followed that the sum due to the plaintiff was a contractual entitlement and not liquidated damages for breach of contract, and there was therefore no duty to mitigate. However, even if the sum was due as damages, there was still no duty to mitigate. Accordingly, the appeal would be dismissed.

Abrahams v Performing Rights Society Ltd [1995] IRLR 486 (Court of Appeal: Aldous and Hutchison LJJ).

1213   Contract of employment—terms of employment—annual hours of work—calculation of overtime

The appellants were employed as hourly-paid workers by a company and were paid at a higher rate for any overtime. The company agreed a payment system with the recognised unions under which each employee was to be paid a standard weekly wage, based on a notional 40-hour week, with overtime becoming payable only after a certain number of hours had been worked each year. The system was included in collective agreements and, where necessary, incorporated into contracts of employment. The appellants were made redundant part of the way through the pay year and although they had worked, pro rata, more than 40-hour weeks, they did not receive any additional payment for overtime as they had not worked the requisite annual total of hours. The appellants claimed that the company had made unauthorised deductions within the Wages Act 1986, but an industrial tribunal rejected the claim. On appeal, *held*, it could not have been the intention of the parties that an employee was expected to perform hours of work but was not entitled to be paid for them. The tribunal erred in law in refusing to imply a term which would entitle an employee, whose employment was terminated by his employer before the end of the pay year, to be paid the standard hourly rate, as stipulated in the terms and conditions of employment, for the hours actually worked by him in excess of 40 hours a week. The implication of such a term filled an obvious gap in the incidental detail of the express terms affecting those whose contracts were terminated before the end of the relevant year. Accordingly, the appeal would be allowed and the case would be remitted to the industrial tribunal to calculate the excess hours worked by each appellant.

Ali v Christian Salvesen Food Services Ltd [1995] IRLR 624 (Employment Appeal Tribunal: Mummery J presiding).

1214   Contract of employment—terms of employment—restraint of trade—notice period

The defendant was employed as a money broker by the plaintiff company under a one-year contract, which provided that the contract could be terminated by either party giving six months' written notice. The contract also provided that if the defendant gave inadequate or no notice, the plaintiff could waive the breach and compel the defendant to abide by the termination clause for a maximum of six months, if it was reasonably likely that he would be interested in or concerned in any other money-broking business. In addition, the defendant covenanted that he would not be concerned in the same or similar business as that of the plaintiff for a period of six months after the termination of his employment. When the defendant was offered employment with a rival company, he resigned with immediate effect, but the plaintiff sought to hold him to the six months' notice requirement by giving him 'garden leave' for that period. As the defendant refused to agree to it, the plaintiff applied for an interlocutory injunction restraining the defendant from directly or indirectly engaging or being concerned with any business likely to compete with its own, in particular the defendant's new employer. *Held*, it was in the plaintiff's interest to protect the customer connection which had been established at its own expense and which formed part of its goodwill. There would also be potential and unquantifiable damage to the plaintiff if it was unable to put new traders in place to deal with the defendant's customers. The defendant would not suffer damage if injunctive relief was granted, as his employment with the rival company would not be prejudiced, nor was there evidence that his skills would be adversely affected if he was temporarily prevented from working. Moreover, six months was not an unnecessarily long period, as the defendant had willingly entered into the contract subject to the six months' notice requirement. Although it was necessary to consider whether or not a six-month injunction would reduce the defendant to a condition of idleness, that was not a decisive factor. Additionally, it was not a pre-requisite to granting an injunction to enforce a garden leave provision that an employee had to be offered work of a similar type, rather than remaining idle. Here, there was a serious issue to be tried and the balance of convenience lay in granting the relief sought. Accordingly, the application would be granted.

Euro Brokers Ltd v Rabey [1995] IRLR 206 (Chancery Division: Judge Robert Reid QC). *American Cyanamid Co v Ethicon Ltd* [1975] 1 All ER 504, HL (1975 Abr para 1864) applied.

1215   Disability Discrimination Act 1995

The Disability Discrimination Act 1995 provides for the establishment of a statutory right of non-discrimination for disabled people in employment, and for access to goods, facilities and services. A National Disability Council is established to advise the government on the elimination of discrimination against disabled people. The Act received the royal assent on 8 November 1995 and certain provisions came into force on that date and on 1 January 1996: SI 1995/3330.

The remaining provisions come into force on a day or days to be appointed. For details of commencement, see the commencement table in the title STATUTES.

Part I (ss 1–3, Schs 1, 2) Disability
Section 1 defines 'disabled person'. Schedule 1, paras 1–6 set out supplementary definitions. Schedule 1, para 7 provides that people who were on the register of disabled persons on 12 January 1995 and the date when that paragraph comes into force, will continue to be deemed to have been disabled during the initial period, even after that period is over. Schedule 1, para 8 provides that a person with a progressive condition will be regarded as a disabled person under the Act from the time when the condition first has an effect (even if it is not substantial) provided that substantial effects are likely in the future. Section 2 and Sch 2 provide that the Act's definition of 'disability' and the provisions dealing with the new employment right and the right of access to goods and services apply, with modifications where appropriate, to a person who has had a disability, in the same way as they apply to someone who is currently disabled. Section 3 enables the Secretary of State to issue guidance for determining whether an impairment has a substantial adverse effect or a long-term effect. The guidance must be laid in draft before both Houses of Parliament for 40 days and cannot be issued if either House resolves not to approve it.

Part II (ss 4–18, Sch 3, Pt I, Sch 4, Pt I) Employment
Section 4 is in the same terms as the Sex Discrimination Act 1975, s 6, and the Race Relations Act 1976, s 4 and makes it unlawful for employers to discriminate against disabled persons. Section 5 provides that an employer discriminates against a disabled person when he treats him less favourably than he treats or would treat others without being able to show that the treatment in question is justified. This test may be satisfied by a failure, without justification, to comply with the duty under s 6 to make reasonable adjustments. Regulations under s 5(6) may stipulate that the additional cost of any benefit is a valid ground of justification. Section 6 imposes on an employer the duty to make the reasonable adjustments referred to in s 5. The duty of reasonable adjustment is disapplied for occupational pensions and certain similar benefits. Section 7 provides that nothing in Pt II applies to an employer with fewer than 20 employees. Within five years the Secretary of State is to review the operation of the employment provisions in relation to small firms, and there is a power for the Secretary of State to lower the threshold number below 20 but never to raise it above. Section 8 and Sch 3, Pt I, provide for the enforcement of Pt II to be by complaint to an industrial tribunal and require officers of the Advisory, Conciliation and Arbitration Service (ACAS) to provide conciliation. Where a tribunal finds that a complaint presented to it is well-founded, it may make a declaratory order, award compensation, or recommend the taking of specified action. Section 9 renders void any term in a contract of employment or other agreement requiring the contravention of Pt II or limiting its operation. Section 10 contains exceptions from Pt II for charities and persons who provide 'supported employment' under the Disabled Persons (Employment) Act 1944, s 15, as amended by the 1995 Act, s 61(1)–(5). Section 11 enables an industrial tribunal to make assumptions about an employer's reason for refusing employment to a disabled person where he has published an advertisement suggesting that he will discriminate against disabled persons. Section 12 makes it unlawful for a principal, in relation to contract work, to discriminate against a disabled person. Section 12 also applies the provisions of Pt II to any principal in relation to contract work as if he were the employer of the contract worker. Section 13 makes it unlawful for a trade union, employers' association or analogous body to discriminate against a disabled person in relation to the terms on which it admits him to membership, or by refusing to accept, or deliberately not accepting, his application for membership. Section 14 defines 'discrimination' in this context and provides for the making of regulations. Section 15 places a duty on trade organisations to make reasonable adjustments. Section 16 provides for the modification of leases which ostensibly prohibit modification where the lessee is under a duty to make reasonable adjustments to the premises. Section 17 implies into the rules of occupational pension schemes a rule of non-discrimination against disabled people. Section 18 covers the situation where an employer makes arrangements with an insurance company for insurance benefits to be received by employees.

Part III (ss 19–28, Sch 3, Pt II, Sch 4, Pt II) Discrimination in Other Areas
Section 19 provides that it is unlawful for a service provider to discriminate against a disabled person by not providing goods, facilities and services that he provides for other members of the public, or by providing them on different terms or to a different standard. Section 20 defines 'discrimination' for the purposes of Pt III, providing that a service provider discriminates against a disabled person when he treats him less favourably than he treats others, he cannot show that the treatment in question is justified, and that this test may be satisfied by a failure, without justification, to comply with the duty under s 21 to make reasonable adjustments. Section 21

places a duty on service providers to remove or alter physical and communication barriers, to amend policies, procedures and practices which prevent disabled people using a service and to provide auxiliary aids or services. Section 22 provides that it is unlawful for landlords and others disposing of or selling property to discriminate against a disabled person. Section 23 exempts 'small dwellings' from those provisions. Section 24 defines 'discrimination' for these purposes. Section 25 and Sch 3, Pt II set out the enforcement procedure and remedies available when a claim of unlawful discrimination is made. A disabled person who believes he has been discriminated against has recourse to the county court, where the remedies are damages, including damages in compensation for injuries to feelings. Section 26 renders void any contract term contravening, limiting or excluding any provision relating to the right of access to goods, facilities and services, enabling a county court to replace or modify such terms. Section 27 provides for certain leases to be modified to allow otherwise improper alterations. Schedule 4, Pt II makes provision for the enforcement of the duty through the county court. Section 28 provides that the Secretary of State may make arrangements for the provision of advice and assistance to persons for the settlement of disputes.

Part IV (ss 29–31) Education
Section 29 amends the Education Act 1993, s 161, to require all schools to set out their policies of non-discrimination against pupils with disabilities, and the Education Act 1994, s 1, placing a duty on the Teacher Training Agency to have regard to the requirements of disabled persons. Section 30 amends the Further and Higher Education Act 1992, ss 5, 8, 62, 65 and the Education Act 1944, s 41, placing a duty on the further education funding councils to require individual colleges to produce information on the facilities for education for students with disabilities, and requiring councils to produce an annual report to the Secretary of State on the progress made in the provision of further education for students with disabilities and the councils' plans for future provision, placing a duty on the higher education funding councils to have regard to the needs of disabled students, ensuring that disabled persons and the funding councils have access to information about available provision and placing a duty on local education authorities to publish disability statements. Section 31 applies to Scotland only.

Part V (ss 32–49) Public Transport
Sections 32, 33 enable the Secretary of State to make regulations defining standards of access which new taxi cabs will be required to meet, requiring taxi drivers to carry disabled passengers in a safe and appropriate manner, requiring vehicles used under a contract to provide hire car services at designated transport facilities and the drivers of such vehicles to be subject to the 'taxi provisions' of this Act. Section 34 provides that a licensing authority may, after a certain date, only license taxis which comply with the construction requirements set out in the taxi accessibility regulations. Section 35 enables the Secretary of State to make regulations enabling a licensing authority to apply for an order granting exemption from the requirements. Section 36 sets out the duties applying to drivers of regulated taxis hired by a disabled person. Any driver who fails to comply with these duties will be guilty of an offence. Provision is made for a licensing authority to exempt a taxi driver on the grounds of health. Section 37 imposes duties on taxi drivers to convey a disabled person accompanied by a guide dog or a hearing dog. Section 38 provides for an appeal within 28 days to a magistrates' court against a decision of a licensing authority to refuse an exemption certificate under s 36 or 37. Section 39 applies to Scotland only. Section 40 gives the Secretary of State powers to make regulations covering access to public service vehicles for disabled people. Section 41 provides for 'accessibility certificates' to be issued by vehicle examiners. Section 42 provides for a type of approval whereby an initial 'type vehicle' is approved, and subsequent vehicles of the same type are issued with approval certificates. Section 43 allows special operating authorisation for vehicles which do not conform to the accessibility regulations or for which a certificate has not been granted. Section 44 provides for an appeals system. Section 45 gives the Secretary of State power to require fees to be paid on applications for certificates, type approvals and appeals. Sections 46, 47 deal with access to rail services. Section 48 deals with offences which are committed by corporate bodies. Section 49 creates offences and sets penalties for forgery or misuse of certificates.

Part VI (ss 50–52, Sch 5) The National Disability Council
Section 50 provides for the establishment of the National Disability Council, setting out its duties and functions. It has the power to advise on matters relevant to the elimination of discrimination against disabled people. Schedule 5 makes further detailed provision regarding the Council. Sections 51, 52 provide for the Council to prepare proposals for, and reviews of, codes of practice.

Part VII (ss 53–58) Supplemental
Section 53 enables the Secretary of State to issue codes of practice containing practical guidance for the purposes of eliminating discrimination against disabled persons in employment. Such a code is admissible in evidence in any proceedings under the Act. Section 54 lays down the procedure for issuing a code of practice. Section 56 imposes a duty on the Secretary of State to prescribe forms for the use of parties in deciding whether to take proceedings against him under Pt II. Section 57 provides that a person who knowingly aids another to do an act which is unlawful under the Act is to be treated as committing the same kind of unlawful act. Section 58 prescribes that an act done by a person in the course of his employment is to be treated as also done by his employer and that an act done by an agent with the authority of another person is to be treated as done by that person. Section 59 provides that the Act does not make an act unlawful if it is carried out under legislation, or in order to comply with a condition or requirement imposed by a minister by virtue of an enactment.

Part VIII (ss 60–70, Schs 6-8) Miscellaneous
Section 60 authorises the Secretary of State to appoint persons to advise and assist him in connection with matters relating to the employment of disabled persons and confers on him the power to repeal certain related enactments. Section 61 amends and repeals provisions of the Disabled Persons (Employment) Act 1944. Sections 62, 63 provide for a limited extension of the restricted reporting order powers covering disability discrimination cases heard by tribunals. Section 64 deals with the application of the provisions of the Act to the Crown, exempting from the employment provisions of Pt II members of the armed forces, the police, MoD police, specially constituted national police forces, fire fighters, and prison officers. Section 65 deals with the application of the Act to Parliament and s 66 deals with the application of Pt II to government appointments which would otherwise fall outside the ambit of the employment provisions. Section 67 contains ancillary powers. Section 68 provides definitions and other interpretative provisions. Section 69 contains financial provisions. Schedule 6 makes consequential amendments. Schedule 7 sets out the provisions repealed by the Act and Sch 8 relates to Northern Ireland. Section 70 deals with short title, commencement and extent.

1216 Discrimination—language assistant from other member state—fixed term contract

See *Case C-272/92: Spotti v Freistaat Bayern*, para 3139.

1217 Employer—duty of care

See HEALTH AND SAFETY AT WORK.

1218 Employer—insolvency—applicant working under temporary contracts—payments due to applicant—application to Secretary of State for payments—whether applicant 'employee'

The Employment Protection (Consolidation) Act 1978, s 122 provides that if, on an application made to him by an employee, the Secretary of State is satisfied that the employer of that employee has become insolvent and that on the relevant date the employee was entitled to be paid the whole or part of any debt, the Secretary of State will pay the employee the amount to which, in the opinion of the Secretary of State, the employee is entitled. An employee means an individual who has entered into or works under a contract of employment: s 153.

The appellant worked for an employment agency on a series of temporary contracts. The conditions of service stated that he provided his services as a self-employed worker rather than under a contract of service. Under the conditions the appellant was under no obligation to accept an assignment but, if he did, he had to comply with conditions of fidelity, confidentiality and obedience to instructions. He was not obliged to work a specific number of hours and did not receive holiday or sickness pay. The agency could instruct him to terminate an assignment at any time and he could be summarily dismissed for improper conduct. His weekly wage was calculated at an hourly rate from time sheets and deductions were made for income tax and national insurance. On the agency's insolvency, the appellant applied for payment of monies owed to him by it pursuant to the 1978 Act, s 122. The Secretary of State withheld payment on the ground that the appellant was not an employee within the meaning of s 153 and an industrial tribunal upheld that decision. On further appeal, *held*, the parties' relationship was governed by the conditions of service. Where the relevant contract was wholly contained in such a document, the question whether the contract was one of employment was a question of law to be determined upon the true construction of the document in its factual matrix. On the totality of the conditions of service, although they were described as relating to temporary self-employed workers, they created an employment relationship between the agency and the appellant. The appellant was entitled to a payment from the Secretary of State and the appeal would be allowed accordingly.

McMeechan v Secretary of State for Employment [1995] ICR 444 (Employment Appeal Tribunal: Mummery J presiding).

1219 Employer—insolvency—guaranteed payments

The Insolvency of Employer (Excluded Classes) Regulations 1995, SI 1995/278 (in force on 9 March 1995), give effect to certain obligations arising from the European Economic Area Agreement 1992, as adjusted by the Protocol signed at Brussels on 17 March 1993. The regulations provide that those who ordinarily work in Austria, Finland, Iceland, Norway or Sweden, in accordance with the terms of their contracts of employment, come within the ambit of the Employment Protection (Consolidation) Act 1978, Pt VII, relating to the entitlement of employees to recover outstanding payments on the insolvency of their employer.

1220 Employer—vicarious liability—act done in course of employment—unauthorised way of doing authorised act

An employee, who was of mixed race, resigned from his employment after being subjected to racial harassment by his work colleagues. One employee had deliberately burned his arm with a hot screwdriver, metal bolts were thrown at him and he was subjected to racist taunts. An industrial tribunal found that the racial harassment amounted to unlawful discrimination. The employer was held to be vicariously liable for the harassment on the grounds that the acts were done 'in the course of employment' of the employees concerned, within the meaning of the Race Relations Act 1976, s 32(1). The employer appealed. *Held*, the meaning of the phrase 'in the course of employment' was well-established in law. The relevant test was whether, in all the circumstances of the case, the unauthorised wrongful act of the servant was so connected with that which he was employed to do as to be a mode of doing it. The tribunal had been wrong in its finding that the assaults could be regarded as modes of carrying out employment tasks, and that any other decision would have amounted to a finding that an employer could only be liable for the expressly authorised acts of its employees. The appeal would therefore be allowed. The case would be remitted to a differently constituted industrial tribunal to be reheard on the alternative ground that the employer had been aware of the racial abuse and subjected the employee to the detriment of exposing him to further abuse. While such an alternative case had not been presented to the tribunal for consideration, there was a factual basis for it in the employee's originating application. The interests of justice required the matter to be considered properly.

Tower Boot Co Ltd v Jones [1995] IRLR 529 (Employment Appeal Tribunal: Buckley J presiding).

1221 Employment Appeal Tribunal—time limit for appeal to tribunal—extension of time limit

See *United Arab Emirates v Abdelghafar*, para 1445.

1222 Employment rights—time off for public duties

The Time Off for Public Duties Order 1995, SI 1995/694 (in force on 1 April 1995), amends the Employment Protection (Consolidation) Act 1978, s 29(1), by including in the list of bodies whose members are covered by that section, police authorities appointed under the Police Act 1964, Sch 1B.

1223 Equal pay and treatment—working and family life for men and women—equal opportunities—European Union action programme for 1996–2000

See para 3181.

1224 Health and safety at work

See HEALTH AND SAFETY AT WORK.

1225   Industrial training boards—levy—construction industry

The Industrial Training Levy (Construction Board) Order 1995, SI 1995/25 (in force on 10 January 1995), imposes a levy on employers in the construction industry for the purpose of raising money towards meeting the expenses of the Construction Industry Training Board. The levy is limited to 0.25 per cent of payroll in respect of employees employed under contracts of service or apprenticeship, and 2 per cent of payments made by employers to persons under labour-only agreements. The levy is in respect of the thirtieth levy period commencing on 10 January 1995 and ending on 31 March 1995. Provision is made for the levy to be assessed by the Board, and for a right of appeal to an industrial tribunal against an assessment.

1226   Industrial training boards—levy—engineering construction

The Industrial Training Levy (Engineering Construction Board) Order 1995, SI 1995/26 (in force on 10 January 1995), imposes a levy on employers in the engineering construction industry for the purpose of raising money towards the expenses of the Engineering Construction Industry Training Board. The levy is to be imposed in respect of the thirty-first levy period commencing on 10 January 1995 and ending on 31 August 1995. Subject to specified exemptions, the levy is assessed by the Board and there is a right of appeal against an assessment to an industrial tribunal.

1227   Industrial tribunal—contempt of tribunal—punishment—jurisdiction of Queen's Bench Divisional Court

See *Peach Grey & Co (a firm) v Sommers*, para 639.

1228   Industrial tribunal—jurisdiction—diplomatic immunity—waiver of immunity— entry of notice of appearance

An employee submitted a complaint of unfair dismissal against his former employer, the Nigerian High Commission ('the commission'). The application was served on the Ministry of Foreign Affairs in Nigeria by the British High Commission, and the Foreign and Commonwealth Office ('the Foreign Office') also sent a copy to the commission, together with a notice of appearance form, for information purposes. The commission replied to the Foreign Office by returning the form uncompleted, undated and unsigned, and sending a note stating that the employee had been dismissed because of his incompetence and lack of qualifications. It also requested the Foreign Office to forward the form and note to the appropriate authority. The commission later made a claim to diplomatic immunity. On a preliminary issue, an industrial tribunal decided that it had jurisdiction to consider the complaint because the commission had waived its right to immunity by submitting a notice of appearance, such notice being constituted by the returned form and note. On the commission's appeal, *held*, having regard to the State Immunity Act 1978, s 2(3)(b), immunity could be waived either by express submission or by a state taking a step in the proceedings, such as serving a defence. The commission's return of the notice of appearance form and a note did not constitute a notice of appearance nor a step in the proceedings, as the form was returned blank, whereas the Industrial Tribunals (Rules of Procedure) Regulations 1985, SI 1985/16, r 3(1) required a notice of appearance to set out the respondent's name and address, state whether or not he intended to resist the application, and the grounds on which he did so. Here, the note did not state whether or not the commission intended to resist the application. Moreover, although the note gave reasons for the employee's dismissal, that was a diplomatic communication between the representatives of foreign states which therefore did not satisfy r 3(1). Equally, the fact that the commission requested the Foreign Office to send the note to the appropriate authority did not mean that the Foreign Office was entering a notice of appearance on the commission's behalf. Accordingly, the appeal would be allowed.

London Branch of the Nigerian Universities Commission v Bastians [1995] ICR 358 (Employment Appeal Tribunal: Mummery J presiding).

1985 Regulations replaced by 1993 Regulations, SI 1993/2687.

1229   Industrial tribunal—procedure—power of tribunal to order exclusion of members of public from hearing

Under the Industrial Tribunals (Constitution and Rules of Procedure) Regulations 1993, SI 1993/2687, Sch 1, r 14 in any case which involves allegations of sexual misconduct the tribunal may make a restricted reporting order.

In the course of an application involving allegations of sexual assault on the applicant, an industrial tribunal made an order under r 14. However, the applicant alleged that the order had been breached in an article in a national newspaper and the respondent claimed that he could be identified from the details in the article by anyone who frequented his place of work. The parties made a joint application for the proceedings to be heard in camera. Although r 8 provided the tribunal with a discretion to sit in private, it did not believe that it had the power to do so and instead the tribunal exercised its general discretion under r 9(1) to order that the press and public could be present until evidence considered to be of a salacious or sensitive nature was led, at which stage the tribunal would be cleared of press and public. The tribunal was adjourned while an application was made for judicial review to declare the order under r 9(1) ultra vires. *Held*, the tribunal did not have the power to make the order and it had erred in considering that its wide discretion under r 9(1) included such a power. The power of the tribunal to sit in private or public was governed by r 8. It was anxiety about the type of evidence in the present case which resulted in Parliament giving tribunals additional power under r 14 to make restricted reporting orders, to balance the needs of the press with those of the tribunals. Tribunals therefore had to look to an order under r 14 in order to exercise a power to prohibit evidence which could lead to the identification of the persons involved in a case involving allegations of sexual misconduct. The order under r 9(1) was ultra vires and, accordingly, the application would be allowed.

R v Southampton Industrial Tribunal, ex p INS News Group Ltd [1995] IRLR 247 (Queen's Bench Division: Brooke J).

1230 Insolvency of employer—pay in lieu of notice—discrimination on grounds of maternity

The EC Treaty, art 119 defines 'pay' as the ordinary basic or minimum wages or salary and any other consideration which the worker receives, directly or indirectly, in respect of his emploment from his employer.

Shortly after the applicant started maternity leave her employers went into liquidation and her employment was terminated. She claimed from the Secretary of State under the Employment Protection (Consolidation) Act 1978, s 122 a sum equivalent to 12 weeks' pay in lieu of notice which she was entitled to receive from her employer on dismissal. The Secretary of State refused payment on the ground that s 122 did not apply and the industrial tribunal upheld the refusal on the ground that the applicant was not ready or willing to work and was not rendered incapable of working by sickness under the 1978 Act, Sch 3. On appeal it was argued that the EC Treaty, art 119 gave her an independent right to payment and that that provision should prevail over the 1978 Act in the event of inconsistency. *Held*, sums payable by an employer to an employee for failing to give notice were 'pay' within the meaning of art 119, which the applicant could invoke directly. The principle of equal pay contained in art 119 was breached by the failure of the 1978 Act to extend its benefits to women absent from work for reasons of pregnancy and thus those women were treated less favourably than other employees absent from work through no fault of their own. Accordingly, the appeal would be allowed and the applicant was entitled to payment out of the national insurance fund of a sum equivalent to the pay in lieu of notice she would have received from her employer on dismissal.

Clark v Secretary of State for Employment [1995] ICR 761 (Employment Appeal Tribunal: Mummery J presiding).

1231 Jobseekers Act 1995

See para 2750.

1232 Part-time employees—equal treatment

The Employment Protection (Part-time Employees) Regulations 1995, SI 1995/31 (in force on 6 February 1995), repeal those parts of the Employment Protection (Consolidation) Act 1978 and the Trade Union and Labour Relations (Consolidation) Act 1992 which have until now excluded part-time employees from entitlement to (1) the right to written particulars of employment, (2) certain rights which do not depend on a qualifying period of employment, and (3) the right to time off for trade union duties and activities. The regulations also provide that periods of part-time employment are to count in the computation of periods of employment under the 1978 Act.

1233 Racial discrimination

See BRITISH NATIONALITY, IMMIGRATION AND RACE RELATIONS.

1234 Redundancy—acceptance of alternative position—resignation after dispute over terms—claim that redundancy amounted to unfair dismissal—power to disregard dismissal

Under the Employment Protection (Consolidation) Act 1978, s 84(1) if an employee's contract of employment is renewed, or he is re-engaged under a new contract of employment in pursuance of an offer made by his employer before the ending of his employment under the previous contract, and the renewal or re-engagement takes effect either immediately or after an interval of not more than four weeks thereafter, then the employee will not be regarded as having been dismissed by his employer by reason of the ending of his employment under the previous contract.

An employee was seconded from his department, where he was a sheet metal worker, to a different section because of a shortage of work. After being there six months, his employer told him the transfer would be permanent and that his wages would be reduced. The employee refused to accept the reduction and was made redundant. Shortly after his employment was terminated, he was offered a vacancy in the sheet metal department on the basis that there would be no break in his service and his entitlements would be the same as before. He returned to work but left within three weeks because the parties were unable to agree the terms of his employment. On the employee's claim that his redundancy amounted to unfair dismissal, the employer contended that the 1978 Act, s 84(1) applied to extinguish that dismissal. At first instance, an industrial tribunal found that, although the reason for dismissal was redundancy, s 84 applied only where claims were made for payments owing to redundancy under the 1978 Act, Pt VI, not to a claim of unfair dismissal under Pt V. On appeal, *held*, it was the substantive reason for the dismissal which determined the applicability of s 84, not the procedural aspects of such a dismissal which determined whether it had been fair or unfair. Section 84 was there to provide the employer with a defence to an employee's claim substantially based upon the redundancy situation and in the present case, since the reason for dismissal was redundancy, s 84 applied. There was a break in time between the date of the dismissal and the employee's re-employment and it was necessary to determine whether the second contract was a renewal or a re-engagement within the meaning of s 84(1). Accordingly, the appeal would be allowed and the matter remitted to the tribunal.

Ebac Ltd v Wymer [1995] ICR 466 (Employment Appeal Tribunal: Judge Byrt QC presiding).

1235 Redundancy—continuity of employment—local government service

The Redundancy Payments (Local Government) (Modification) (Amendment) Order 1995, SI 1995/1157 (in force on 1 June 1995), further amends the 1983 Order, SI 1983/1160, so as to add further employers to the list of employers whose employees are deemed to be in continuous employment for the purposes of certain redundancy payments provisions under the 1983 Order.

1236 Redundancy—duty to consult with workers' representatives—regulations

The Collective Redundancies and Transfer of Undertakings (Protection of Employment) (Amendment) Regulations 1995, SI 1995/2587 (in force on 26 October 1995), amend the Trade Union and Labour Relations (Consolidation) Act 1992 so as to (1) require that where there are to be redundancies or a transfer of an undertaking, an employer must consult either elected representatives where there is no recognised trade union, or representatives of a recognised trade union, (2) limit the duty to consult about redundancies to cases where at least 20 redundancies are proposed, (3) provide protection for elected representatives (in addition to trade union representatives) against dismissal and against being subjected to any other detriment, and also confer on them a right to time off without pay to carry out their functions. The regulations also amend the 1981 Regulations, SI 1981/1794, so as to make it clear that the right to complain about a dismissal because of a transfer of an undertaking does not apply if the employee does not meet the normal qualifying conditions.

1237 Redundancy—duty to consult with workers' representatives—trade union as workers' representative—application of EC directive

The defendant company was formed following the privatisation of the water industry. The company did not recognise the union which represented a minority of its employees, and instead formed a staff council consisting of elected employees and senior management, and established a staff consultative committee. When the company decided to make large-scale redundancies, it consulted with the staff council and the staff consultative committee as to alternatives to redundancy and as to the selection criteria to be applied where redundancies were unavoidable.

A group of employees and their union commenced proceedings seeking a declaration that Council Directive (EC) 75/129, art 2 was directly enforceable against the company in relation to the proposed redundancies, and that the company was obliged to consult with the union even though it did not recognise it. *Held*, the company performed a public service, for which it had special powers. It was necessary to consider whether the service provided by the company was under the Secretary of State's control, and in that respect it was irrelevant that the company was a commercial concern which did not carry out the traditional functions of the state, that it was not an agent of the state, and that the state did not have everyday control of its activities. The company's appointment as a water and sewerage undertaker was made by the Secretary of State, and he and the director of the water industry regulatory body controlled the company by way of the conditions attached to its instrument of appointment, in particular as to the manner in which the company carried out its functions. The company's activities were therefore under the control of the state. The company was not, however, a public administrative body within the meaning of art 1(2)(b). In identifying for the purposes of art 2 the workers' representatives with whom an employer was obliged to consult when contemplating making collective redundancies, there was no obligation on an employer to consult with a trade union just because it represented an employee. Where there was no agreement between an employer and his employees as to who was the employees' representative for the purpose of consulting over collective redundancies, the directive allowed member states to introduce laws, regulations or administrative provisions to designate the representatives. As member states had a wide discretion in that respect, art 2 was not unconditional and sufficiently precise such that it could be directly enforced against the company. In any event, the union could not be described as the employees' representative, because it was not recognised by the company. Accordingly, the application would be dismissed.

Griffin v South West Water Services Ltd [1995] IRLR 15 (Chancery Division: Blackburne J). *Case C-188/89: Foster v British Gas* [1990] 3 All ER 897, ECJ (1990 Abr para 2695) applied.

1238   Redundancy—payments—calculation—increase of limits

See para 1261.

1239   Redundancy—pension scheme—additional credit under scheme—pro rata credit for part-time employees—claim of indirect discrimination against women

The EC Treaty, art 119 provides that each member state must maintain the principle that men and women should receive equal pay for equal work.

A teacher was employed part-time by the local authority, although she also undertook supply and temporary full-time teaching work. When she was made redundant the authority credited her with additional service to increase her pension because she met certain age and service requirements. However, the authority decided that part-time teachers who were eligible for credit should have their compensation calculated proportionally to that of a full-time teacher who was similarly eligible and it therefore took no account in its calculation of her additional teaching work. The teacher brought a claim against the authority under the Sex Discrimination Act 1975 and the EC Treaty, art 119 on the basis that the policy of allowing full-time teachers to have additional service calculated by reference to their actual past service, while the service of part-time workers was calculated only by reference to their permanent contract, directly discriminated against women. An industrial tribunal upheld the complaint under art 119, finding that, since more women than men were in part-time employment, the condition affected a far greater number of women than men. On appeal by the authority, *held*, the tribunal erred in finding that the condition to be full-time for the purpose of calculating the additional credit discriminated against the part-time female employee contrary to art 119. The same test as that applied under the 1975 Act should have been applied, namely, the tribunal should have asked whether the proportion of women who could comply with the condition was considerably smaller than the proportion of men who could comply. In the present case, the tribunal concluded from the proposition that more women than men worked part-time that the employer's decision was unlawfully discriminatory. If it had asked itself the correct question, the tribunal would have reached the same conclusion as it had under the 1975 Act, that the proportion of women teachers who could comply with the condition was not considerably smaller. Accordingly, the appeal would be allowed.

Staffordshire County Council v Black [1995] IRLR 234 (Employment Appeal Tribunal: Morison J presiding).

1240 Redundancy—selection for redundancy—assessment forms completed for all employees—discovery of retained employees' forms by dismissed employees

An employer was required to reduce his workforce. Assessment forms were completed for each employee whereby marks were awarded according to certain criteria to determine employees' eligibility. Those employees who scored lowest were dismissed. They claimed that their selection had been unfair and successfully applied to an industrial tribunal for discovery of the assessment forms of the retained employees to compare their ratings with those of the dismissed employees. The Employment Appeal Tribunal overturned the order for discovery and on the employees' appeal against that decision, *held*, to succeed with their application for discovery the employees had to demonstrate that discovery was necessary for disposing fairly of the proceedings. Unless a document was relevant to some issue in dispute, its disclosure and production could not be necessary for such fair disposal. Discovery would not be ordered to allow an applicant to discover whether there was an issue he could raise. In the present case, discovery could be relevant only to the fairness of the manner in which the selection process was performed. When the industrial tribunal directed itself to the question of what discovery was necessary, it should have taken into account the fact that the application of the assessment system was not attacked in any specific respect. There was therefore no issue at that stage to which the retained assessments could be claimed to be relevant and, accordingly, the appeal would be dismissed.

British Aerospace plc v Green [1995] IRLR 433 (Court of Appeal: Stuart-Smith, Waite and Millett LJJ).

1241 Redundancy—selection for redundancy—grounds relating to trade union activities

Throughout his employment, an employee, a trade union activist, had failed to comply with work arrangements regulating the amount of time he spent on his union duties and on his work. The employer needed to make redundancies and adopted a method of selection based on six criteria, including quantity of work. The employee was assessed as being 'very poor' on this ground, despite allowance being given for a reasonable amount of involvement in trade union activity. He was selected for redundancy on the basis of the assessment. An industrial tribunal later ruled that he had been unfairly dismissed. However, his claim that he had been unfairly selected for redundancy by reason of his trade union activities was rejected by the industrial tribunal on the ground that the employer had not deliberately selected him because he was a union activist. The employee appealed. *Held*, a dismissal was automatically unfair if an employer selected an employee for redundancy by reason of his participation in union activities at an appropriate time. There was no requirement that the employer must have deliberately intended to be rid of a trade unionist. The industrial tribunal had found that the feature of the employee's work history that had made the employer select him was that he had been spending too much time on his union activities. This was the same as saying that the employer's reason for selecting him was that he had spent too much time on trade union duties. Had the tribunal approached the question correctly, it would have come to the conclusion that the employee was selected for redundancy because he had taken part in trade union activities when, in accordance with the employer's albeit reluctant consent, it was permissible for him to do so. Accordingly, the appeal would be allowed, a finding that the employee had been unfairly selected by reason of his trade union activities would be substituted, and the degree of contributory fault by the employee would be re-assessed.

Dundon v GPT Ltd [1995] IRLR 403 (Employment Appeal Tribunal: Smith J presiding).

1242 Redundancy—selection for redundancy—pool of comparators

The Employment Protection (Consolidation) Act 1978, s 59 provides that where the reason or principal reason for the dismissal of an employee was that he was redundant, but it is shown that the circumstances constituting the redundancy applied equally to one or more employees in the same undertaking who held positions similar to that held by him and who have not been dismissed by the employer, and that the reason for which he was selected for dismissal was one of those specified in s 58(1), the dismissal must be regarded as unfair.

The appellant was employed by the respondent as a technical services operator. By arrangement, he spent 50 per cent of his time carrying out his duties as a trade union shop steward, and the remainder of his time working as a packaging operator. When his job became redundant, he was interviewed by other department managers with a view to alternative employment. The department managers took account of his trade union activities, and did not offer him an alternative post. An industrial tribunal dismissed the appellant's complaint of unfair dismissal under the 1978 Act, s 59. On appeal, *held*, the industrial tribunal should have limited its consideration to the appellant's status as a skilled manual worker, the nature of his work as a packaging operator, and the terms and conditions of his employment as a technical services operator. There were no other employees employed by the respondent to whom the redundancy situation applied equally, who held positions similar to that of the appellant and who had not been dismissed, as the two other technical service operators who had not been made redundant could not be comparators because they did that job all of the time, whereas the appellant did not. Moreover, the appellant had not shown that the reason or principal reason for his selection for redundancy was his trade union activities. Accordingly, the appeal would be dismissed.

O'Dea v ISC Chemicals Ltd [1995] IRLR (Court of Appeal: Balcombe, Peter Gibson and Hutchison LJJ).

1243 Redundancy—selection for redundancy—selection criteria—application of criteria—procedural unfairness

Scotland

The appellant company and their employees' unions agreed upon the selection criteria for redundancy, and supervisors were required to assess each employee in their department in accordance with the criteria. The assessments were then reviewed by senior managers, who made the final decision as to which employees were to be made redundant out of those who had scored the lowest points in each department. When the respondents were selected for redundancy, they disputed the accuracy of their assessments and complained of unfair dismissal. It was later discovered that the supervisors had made errors in carrying out the assessments. In concluding that the dismissals were unfair, an industrial tribunal stated that the selection criteria were not applied fairly to the respondents, and that there had been a lack of proper consultation because of the failure to disclose and discuss the assessment marks. On the appellant's appeal, *held*, the appellant's senior management had made their selections on the basis of information given to them by departmental supervisors. As they had been entitled to assume that the supervisors had conducted the assessments properly, there was no reason why they should not have relied on that information. All that an employer had to prove was that the method of selection for redundancy was fair in general terms, and that it was applied reasonably by the senior officials responsible for choosing employees for dismissal. Here, it was not necessary for the supervisors who had conducted the assessments to give evidence as to why they had marked each employee as they had done. The appellant had set up a good selection system, which had been administered honestly and reasonably. Moreover, the appellant had not been obliged to disclose to the respondents their individual assessment marks and discuss them. The appellant had acted reasonably in all the circumstances and, accordingly, the appeal would be allowed.

Eaton Ltd v King [1995] IRLR 75 (Employment Appeal Tribunal: Lord Coulsfield presiding). *Buchanan v Tilcon Ltd* [1983] IRLR 417 (1983 Abr para 3463) applied.

1244 Redundancy—selection for redundancy—selection criteria—employee's trade union activities

See *Dundon v GPT Ltd*, para 1241.

1245 Sex discrimination

See SEX DISCRIMINATION.

1246 Statutory sick pay

See para 2766.

1247 Trade unions

See TRADE, INDUSTRY AND INDUSTRIAL RELATIONS.

1248 Transfer of undertakings—continuity of employment—categories of employee

The Transfer of Undertakings (Protection of Employment) Regulations 1981, SI 1981/1794, reg 8 provides that where, either before or after a relevant transfer, any employee of the transferor or transferee is dismissed, that employee shall be treated for the purposes of the Employment Protection (Consolidation) Act 1978, Pt V as unfairly dismissed if the transfer or a reason connected with it is the reason or principal reason for the dismissal.

Two employees were dismissed when a local authority's cleaning operations were contracted out to a private company. An industrial tribunal held that they had insufficient qualifying service to entitle them to make complaints of unfair dismissal. Neither employee had two years' continuous service within the 1978 Act, s 54. On an interlocutory appeal, *held*, the statutory position had been changed by the 1981 Regulations, implementing Council Directive (EEC) 77/187, and they had to be read in the light of the wording and purpose of the directive. The directive provided that there could be an exemption made in respect of certain specified categories of employee. However, the structure and language of reg 8 did not confer an exemption on a specific category such as employees with less than two years' service. It was a deeming provision treating dismissal by reason of a transfer as unfair dismissal. This was consistent with the purpose of the directive, which was to provide absolute protection against dismissal to all employees in the event of a change of employer. The reference to the 1978 Act was a reference to the fact that the dismissal was to be treated as unfair and was thus not subject to the detailed requirements of s 57. Accordingly, the appeal would be allowed and leave to appeal would be granted.

Milligan v Securicor Cleaning [1995] IRLR 288 (Employment Appeal Tribunal: Mummery J presiding).

1249 Transfer of undertakings—continuity of employment—failure to inform employee of transfer

The Transfer of Undertakings Regulations 1981, SI 1981/1794, reg 5(1) provides that a relevant transfer does not operate so as to terminate the contract of employment of any person employed by the transferor in the undertaking transferred, but any such contract which would otherwise be terminated by the transfer has effect after the transfer as if originally made between the person so employed and the transferee. Regulation 5(1) will not operate to transfer a contract of employment and the rights powers, duties and liabilities under or in connection with it if the employee informs the transferor or the transferee that he objects to being employed by the transferee: reg 5(4A).

The respondent was employed as a salesman by the appellant company. When the appellant's business was transferred to another company, a memorandum was sent to all staff informing them that their contracts of employment were to be transferred to it. The respondent claimed that he did not receive the memorandum, and it was a finding of fact that he continued to be paid by the appellant. When the respondent was later told that he would have to be employed on a self-employed basis because of the appellant's financial difficulties, he refused to accept such employment and was dismissed. His complaint of unfair dismissal was upheld. On appeal, one of the appellant's arguments was that the respondent had been employed by the other company at the time of his dismissal. *Held*, at common law, the substitution of one employer for another could only be effected by a novation of the contract of employment, and that required both the knowledge and consent of the employee. Although the need for an employee's consent had been abrogated by the decision in *Berg and Busschers v Besselsen*, there was still a need for all parties affected by a transfer to be informed of it. Having regard to the 1981 Regulations, reg 5(1), the transfer of an undertaking did not affect an employee's employment contract until he was told of the fact of the transfer and the identity of the transferee. Moreover, the right given to an employee by reg 5(4A) could not be exercised unless he was informed of the transfer. As the respondent was not aware of the transfer of the appellant's business, he continued to be employed by it and, accordingly, the appeal would be dismissed.

Photostatic Copiers (Southern) Ltd v Okuda [1995] IRLR 11 (Employment Appeal Tribunal: Peppitt J presiding). *Cases C-144, 145/87: Berg and Busschers v Besselsen* [1990] ICR 396, ECJ (1990 Abr para 2710) considered.

1250 Transfer of undertakings—employer's duty to inform and consult trade unions—lodging of complaint by union before transfer

The Transfer of Undertakings (Protection of Employment) Regulations 1981, SI 1981/1794, reg 10(2) provides that the transferor of an undertaking must, long enough before that transfer takes place, inform any representatives of his employees' trade unions of details and implications of the transfer in order that consultations may take place. Regulation 11 provides that a complaint by a union that the employer has failed to comply with reg 10 must be presented to an industrial tribunal before the end of three months from the date of the transfer.

A health authority intended to transfer a hospital to a National Health Service trust, and informed the relevant trade union representatives two months beforehand. The union representatives claimed that they had not been informed sufficiently long enough before the transfer, in breach of reg 10(2), and lodged a complaint with the industrial tribunal two weeks before the transfer took place. The health authority claimed that the tribunal had no jurisdiction because the earliest a complaint could be presented under reg 11 was the date the relevant transfer took place and that the complaint was, in any event, premature. At first instance the health authority's argument was rejected. On further appeal, *held*, reg 11 was a limitation provision prohibiting an industrial tribunal from considering complaints presented after a certain date but it did not specify a start date and consequently it was acceptable for a complaint to be presented before a particular transfer took place. Regulation 10(2) clearly stated that the duty to consult and inform union representatives had to be carried out long enough before a transfer to enable consultations to take place, and therefore, a complaint presented two weeks before the transfer could not be considered premature. Accordingly, the health authority's appeal would be dismissed.

South Durham Health Authority v Unison [1995] ICR 495 (Employment Appeal Tribunal: Mummery J presiding).

1251   Transfer of undertakings—relevant transfer—automatic transfer of contract of employment

Scotland

The respondent was the company secretary and chief accountant of a parent company and its subsidiary company, and his contract of employment was with the parent company. Receivers were appointed for the parent company and its subsidiary, and when the subsidiary company was sold to the appellant company, part of the parent company was also transferred to it. The respondent was told by the receivers that his contract remained with the parent company. When the respondent was subsequently made redundant, he made a complaint of unfair dismissal against the appellant. On a preliminary issue, an industrial tribunal decided that he had been employed in the part of the parent company which had been transferred, that it was a transfer to which the Transfer of Undertakings (Protection of Employment) Regulations 1981, SI 1981/1794, applied, and that the respondent's contract had therefore been transferred to the appellant. On the appellant's appeal, *held*, the 1981 Regulations, reg 5 was imperative in its terms, and had to be applied if the conditions for its application were satisfied. Here, there had been a transfer not only of the subsidiary company, but also of that part of the parent company to which the respondent had been assigned. The receivers were mistaken in informing the respondent that his contract of employment continued with the parent company even after the transfer of the part of it in which the respondent was employed, as they had failed to take account of the 1981 Regulations. Although an employee could elect to continue working for a transferor after a transfer, that could occur only if a new agreement to that effect was made between the parties. As the respondent had not resigned, nor had he been dismissed by the appellant, neither the respondent's uncertainty as to his employment status nor the receivers' mistake could prevent the application of the 1981 Regulations. Moreover, it could not be inferred that the respondent had chosen to enter into a new contract of employment with the parent company, even though he had continued to work for it under the direction of the receivers after the transfer. The 1981 Regulations therefore continued to apply to his employment and, accordingly, the appeal would be dismissed.

Sunley Turriff Holdings Ltd v Thomson [1995] IRLR 184 (Employment Appeal Tribunal: Lord Coulsfield presiding).

1252   Transfer of undertakings—relevant transfer—liability of transferee for sex discrimination

Under the Transfer of Undertakings (Protection of Employment) Regulations 1981, SI 1981/1794, reg 5(2)(b) anything done before the transfer is completed by or in relation to the transferor in respect of that contract or a person employed in that undertaking or part, is deemed to have been done by or in relation to the transferee.

An employer forced an employee to retire when she reached the age of 60, but later re-employed her on a part-time basis. Soon after, the employer sold some of its assets to the transferee, and the employee continued to work for the transferee until she was made redundant. On the employee's claim of sex discrimination in relation to the decision to force her to retire at 60, an industrial tribunal ruled that the transferee was liable even though the discrimination did not arise out of the contract of employment existing at the time of the transfer, but out of the employee's previous employment contract. On the transferee's appeal, *held*, reg 5(2)(b) applied not only to things done before a transfer in respect of a particular contract, but also to anything done before a transfer in respect of a person employed in the transferred undertaking. As the general aim of the 1981 Regulations was to ensure that an employment relationship continued unchanged in so far as possible following a transfer, an employer's liability could be transferred to the transferee of an undertaking even if there had been a change in the contractual relationship between the transferor and employee before the transfer. Accordingly, the appeal would be dismissed.

DJM International Ltd v Nicholas [1996] IRLR 76 (Employment Appeal Tribunal: Mummery J presiding).

1253   Transfer of undertakings—relevant transfer—liability of transferor or transferee

Scotland

The Transfer of Undertakings (Protection of Employment) Regulations 1981, SI 1981/1794, reg 5(2)(a) provides that all the transferor's rights, powers, duties and liabilities under or in connection with any contract of employment are transferred to the transferee.

It has been held that art 5(2)(a) unambiguously and expressly excludes a transferor's liability, as the word 'transfer' denotes that all of his liabilities pass to the transferee and that he is no longer subject to them. Moreover, the proviso to Council Directive (EC) 77/187, art 3(1) confirms that a transferor's liabilities do not continue following a transfer unless member states have made provision to that effect in their national laws. In addition, it is irrelevant whether or not there has been a break in the relevant employees' employment before a transfer, as the 1981 Regulations also apply to those who would have been employed immediately before the transfer if they had not been unfairly dismissed before the transfer for a reason connected with it.

Stirling District Council v Allan [1995] IRLR 301 (Inner House).

1254   Transfer of undertakings—relevant transfer—retention of identity of undertaking

Employees of a company were dismissed in the month following the dissolution of the company. An industrial tribunal awarded them redundancy payments in proceedings to which the applicants, the two directors and sole shareholders of the company, who had carried on the business after the dissolution, had failed to enter an appearance within the prescribed time and whose request for an extension of time had been refused. Their application for a review of the tribunal's decision was refused on the ground that, as they had failed to enter an appearance, they were not entitled to apply for a review. The Employment Appeal Tribunal granted them leave to appeal out of time from the industrial tribunal's refusal to grant them an extension of time. *Held*, where an industrial tribunal refused an extension of time to enter an appearance, an applicant who still wished to contest the originating application should appeal against the refusal. The prohibition in the Industrial Tribunals (Rules of Procedure) Regulations 1985, SI 1985/16, r 3(2) on a respondent taking any part in the proceedings referred to proceedings before the industrial tribunal. It did not preclude the party in default from appealing, both from a decision refusing to extend time and a subsequent decision on the merits, to the Employment Appeal Tribunal. When considering whether there had been a transfer of an undertaking by 'some other disposition' within the meaning of the Transfer of Undertakings (Protection of Employment) Regulations 1981, SI 1981/1794, reg 3(2), it should be considered whether the undertaking had retained its identity. Although the company had been dissolved, the business had retained its identity in the applicants' hands with the same assets and employees. The fact that the ownership of the undertaking had not been transferred to them was irrelevant for the purposes of the 1981 Regulations. Accordingly, the regulations applied and the employees were entitled to redundancy payments. The appeal would be dismissed.

Charlton v Charlton Thermosystems (Romsey) Ltd [1995] ICR 56 (Employment Appeal Tribunal: Mummery J presiding).

1255   Transfer of undertakings—relevant transfer—stable economic activity

See *Case C-48/94: Ledernes Hovedorganisation, acting on behalf of Ole Rygaard v Dansk Arbejdsgiverforening, acting on behalf of Strø Mølle Akustik A/S*, para 3179.

1256   Transfer of undertakings—relevant transfer—transfer of economic activity

Scotland

A local authority set up a direct services organisation which successfully tendered for a contract to clean schools buildings. Although the direct services organisation was responsible for the cleaning, it had no assets of its own and the cleaners were employed by the local authority, which provided the necessary materials and transport. When the contract expired, the direct services organisation tendered for the contract again, but it was awarded instead to the respondent company. The appellant, who was employed by the local authority as a cleaner, refused to accept the alternative employment offered to her following the loss of the contract, and was made redundant. In dismissing her complaint of unfair dismissal and unfair selection for redundancy, an industrial tribunal decided that there had not been a transfer of an undertaking from the local authority to the respondent, as no recognisable economic activity had been transferred. On appeal, *held*, in interpreting the Transfer of Undertakings (Protection of Employment) Regulations 1981, SI 1981/1794, so as to comply with Council Directive (EC) 77/187, it was necessary to consider whether the economic activity in question remained identifiable, even if not identical, after the alleged transfer, having regard to the activities in which the relevant employees had been employed. Here, the cleaning of school buildings by the local authority's employees through its direct services organisation had been ancillary to its activities in the provision of educational services. That part of its undertaking had been transferred when the respondent took over the cleaning contract and continued to use a large number of the cleaners who had previously been employed by the local authority. The identity of the undertaking previously carried on by the local authority had therefore survived the change of responsibility for its operation and, accordingly, the appeal would be allowed.

Kelman v Care Contract Services Ltd [1995] ICR 260 (Employment Appeal Tribunal: Mummery J presiding). *Case C-392/92: Schmidt v Spar- und Leihkasse der früheren Ämter Bordesholm, Kiel und Cronshagen* [1994] IRLR 302, ECJ (1994 Abr para 3038) applied.

1257   Transfer of undertakings—relevant transfer—transfer of labour-only economic activity

A local authority which owned an airport, contracted out the airport's firefighting and baggage-handling services. The contractor undertook to provide sufficient staff to provide firefighting and baggage-handling services, and the local authority undertook to supply the contractor with all the necessary firefighting and other equipment. When the local authority terminated the contract, five employees who had originally been employed by the local authority and subsequently by the contractor, were made redundant. They complained that there had been a transfer of an undertaking to which the provisions of the Transfer of Undertakings Regulations 1981, SI 1981/1794, applied, and made successful claims on that basis. On the local authority's appeal, *held*, in deciding whether or not there had been a transfer of an undertaking within the meaning of Council Directive (EC) 77/187, art 1(1), and consequently the 1981 Regulations, the court had to adopt a purposive approach to interpreting the directive. An economic entity could be comprised of just employees and activities, particularly in the service industry, and did not have to be the same both before and after the transfer. Moreover, the fact that no goodwill was transferred because the old economic entity had ended and the transferee had started up a new business, did not mean that there had not been a relevant transfer. The court had to identify the economic entity before the transfer, making inquiries as to its activities, and identifying its assets and the work done by the relevant employees. Having examined the same matters in relation to the period after the transfer, the court then had to ask whether the economic entity had retained its identity after the transfer, rather than whether the same business was still in existence. In the instant case, the contractor had performed an economic activity for the local authority which involved the provision of services, and it was an activity which was capable of being transferred even though it was a labour-only activity. Not only had the local authority carried on the same activity after the termination of the contract, but also the employees' jobs had continued to exist. The fact that the local authority had directly or indirectly controlled the employees' work when the services had been contracted out was irrelevant, as it was the contractor who had carried on the activity and had profited from it. There had been a transfer of an undertaking and, accordingly, the appeal would be dismissed.

Isles of Scilly Council v Brintel Helicopters Ltd [1995] ICR 249 (Employment Appeal Tribunal: Morison J presiding).

1258   Transfer of undertakings—relevant transfer—transfer of services—services in the nature of a commercial venture

Under the Transfer of Undertakings (Protection of Employment) Regulations 1981, SI 1981/1794, reg 2(1) (as amended by the Trade Union Reform and Employment Rights Act 1993), 'undertaking' includes any trade or business but does not include any undertaking or part of an undertaking which is not in the nature of a commercial venture.

The applicants were employed in a local authority's cleansing department. The authority contracted out its cleansing work to a company but, instead of employing the applicants, the company took on a number of new staff. The applicants complained to an industrial tribunal on the ground that they had been unfairly dismissed. An industrial tribunal held that there was a relevant transfer of the authority's undertaking in which the applicants were engaged to the company under the 1981 Regulations and, in consequence, that the applicants' contracts of employment were transferred to the company by operation of law. On the company's appeal, it fell to be determined whether the undertaking was one to which the 1981 Regulations applied. *Held*, the words 'in the nature of' in reg 2(1) showed that an enterprise was not required to be a commercial venture to qualify as an undertaking under the regulations. Apart from the fact that it was not the function of an authority to trade for profit in the sense of making a profit for distribution, in every other sense the authority had been carrying on a cleansing business before the transfer which was 'in the nature of a commercial venture' and to which the regulations therefore applied. Accordingly, the appeal would be dismissed.

UK Waste Control Ltd v Wren [1995] ICR 974 (Employment Appeal Tribunal: Morison J presiding).

1259 Transfer of undertakings—relevant transfer—transfer of subsidiary company

A parent company had a number of subsidiary companies, four of which were located in the same premises as the parent company. The parent company's chief executive, who was employed by the parent company and not by any of the subsidiary companies, was responsible for the financial management and running of all the subsidiaries. Following financial difficulties, receivers were appointed to the parent company and its subsidiaries. The chief executive was made redundant and, shortly afterwards, the four subsidiary companies which shared the same premises as the parent company were sold, although the parent company was not a party to the transaction. On the chief executive's complaint of unfair dismissal, an industrial tribunal decided that the transferred assets were owned by the parent company, that the parent and its subsidiaries formed one economic entity, and that part of the parent company had therefore been transferred on the sale of the four subsidiary companies. The industrial tribunal concluded that it was a transfer to which the Transfer of Undertakings (Protection of Employment) Regulations 1981, SI 1981/1794, applied, and that the chief executive had been dismissed to make the sale of the parent company more attractive to potential purchasers, rather than because of a redundancy situation. On the parent company's appeal against the finding of unfair dismissal, *held*, the industrial tribunal's conclusion was based on a decision made in relation to competition law which suggested that an economic approach was necessary to determine the identity of the transferor of an undertaking. However, such an approach could not be applied to the 1981 Regulations or to employment situations generally, nor was it appropriate to apply the concept of a single economic unit. Here, the parent company was not a party to the sale, nor could it be regarded as forming a single economic entity with the subsidiary companies, even though it owned the goodwill of the subsidiary companies and the premises used by them. The chief executive was therefore not employed by the transferor of the four subsidiary companies. Moreover, he was not employed by the part of the parent company that was transferred, as he was not assigned or allocated to it. Accordingly, the appeal would be allowed.

Michael Peters Ltd v Farnfield [1995] IRLR 190 (Employment Appeal Tribunal: Tucker J presiding). *Case 186/83: Botzen v Rotterdamsche Droogdok Maatschappij BV* [1986] 2 CMLR 50, ECJ (1986 Abr para 2963), applied. *Hydrotherm Geratebau GmbH v Compact Del Dott Inq Maria Androli & Sas* [1985] CMLR 224, ECJ, distinguished.

1260 Unfair dismissal—appeal against industrial tribunal decision—extension of time limit

The appellant was employed by the respondent health authority for 20 years under a contract of employment which involved work of less than eight hours a week. Following the termination of his employment, the appellant made a claim of unfair dismissal, but an industrial tribunal decided that it did not have jurisdiction to consider the complaint because the appellant had not worked for at least eight hours a week during his employment. Two years later and following the decision in *R v Secretary of State for the Employment, ex p Equal Opportunities Commission* ('the EOC case') [1994] 1 All ER 910, HL (1994 Abr para 2532) that the hours per week qualifying condition was contrary to Community law, the appellant applied for an extension of time for lodging his appeal. *Held*, although it had been decided that time did not begin to run until the United Kingdom had amended national rules on time limits in order to comply with certain Community directives on equal pay and equal treatment, that principle applied only to time limits for initiating proceedings, and not to time limits for appealing against decisions. Moreover, the existing time limits for lodging appeals in industrial tribunal matters were not incompatible with Community law, as they were no less favourable than time limits for similar claims, nor did they make it difficult or virtually impossible for a person to enforce his Community rights. As regards the appellant's reliance on the EOC case, an appellant applying for an extension of time could not simply rely on a subsequent decision of a superior court in order to argue that his case had been wrongly decided. The proper approach was to look at all the circumstances of each particular case in order to determine if it was just to extend the time. A case could not be determined by reference to a general principle, such as the necessity for finality in litigation or certainty, although they were factors to be taken into consideration. Here, the court had made a binding decision on the basis of the legal position at the time. That decision had been accepted, and the appellant had not appealed within the relevant time limit. He could have put forward the arguments that were put forward two years later in the EOC case, but did not do so. It would therefore be wrong to extend the time for appealing merely because the law had changed subsequent to the decision in the appellant's case. The law was subject to change, and the appellant's claim was subject to the hazards of time inherent in change. Accordingly, the appeal would be dismissed.

Setiya v East Yorkshire Health Authority [1995] ICR 799 (Employment Appeal Tribunal: Mummery J presiding). *Emmott v Minister for Social Welfare* [1991] IRLR 387, ECJ distinguished.

1261   Unfair dismissal—compensation—awards—increase of limits

The Employment Protection (Increase of Limits) Order 1995, SI 1995/1953 (in force on 27 September 1995), revokes SI 1992/312, 313 and 1993/1348, increases certain limits which must be reviewed annually under the Employment Protection (Consolidation) Act 1978, s 148, and raises certain other limits under the 1978 Act, ss 75, 75A and the Trade Union and Labour Relations (Consolidation) Act 1992, ss 156, 158. The limit of guarantee payment in respect of any day is increased to £14.50, and the limit of the amount for the purpose of calculating the sum payable by the Secretary of State in respect of the debt due to an employee whose employer has become insolvent, is increased to £210. The limit of the amount of a 'week's pay' for the purpose of calculating redundancy payments and the basic and additional awards of compensation on a complaint of unfair dismissal, is increased to £210. The limit of the amount of compensation which can be awarded by an industrial tribunal in unfair dismissal claims as the compensatory award or as the compensation for failure to comply fully with an order of reinstatement or re-engagement, is increased to £11,300. The minimum basic award is increased to £2,770, and the maximum amounts of the special awards payable on a complaint of unfair dismissal on trade union grounds and health and safety grounds are increased to £13,775, £27,500 and £20,600 respectively.

1262   Unfair dismissal—compensation—contributory fault—industrial action—discriminatory failure to re-engage

The appellant was one of a number of employees who were dismissed by the respondent following an industrial dispute, but some of the dismissed employees were later re-employed. An industrial tribunal upheld the appellant's complaint of unfair dismissal. On the respondent's appeal, however, it was decided that contributory fault should have been taken into account in deciding whether or not to reduce the appellant's compensation, even though it was a case of discriminatory failure to re-engage. On the appellant's appeal, *held*, where a group of employees was dismissed for participating in industrial action and some of them were re-engaged, an industrial tribunal had to decide whether the employer's failure to re-engage some of them was discriminatory and, if so, whether an employee who was not re-engaged had contributed to his dismissal such that his compensation should be reduced. In that respect, an employee's compensation was not to be reduced solely because of conduct in which the re-engaged employees had also participated, but if the employee had carried out acts of his own which, although connected with the common action, were sufficiently blameworthy and which had contributed to the decision to dismiss him, it might be just and equitable to reduce his compensatory award. Here, there had been a discriminatory failure to re-engage the appellant, and the industrial tribunal should not have considered whether there had been contributory fault, as that fault arose solely from the industrial action. Accordingly, the appeal would be allowed.

Crosville Wales Ltd v Tracey (No 2) [1996] IRLR 91 (Court of Appeal: Beldam, Waite and Otton LJJ).

1263   Unfair dismissal—compensation—deduction of invalidity benefit

The Employment Protection (Consolidation) Act 1978, s 74(1) provides that the amount of the compensatory award is such amount as the tribunal considers just and equitable in all the circumstances having regard to the loss sustained by the complainant in consequence of the dismissal in so far as that loss is attributable to action taken by the employer.

An employee successfully claimed that she had been unfairly dismissed. Although she was awarded compensation, the total amount of the invalidity benefit that she had received was deducted from the award. On the employer's appeal against the finding of unfair dismissal, the employee cross-appealed as regards the deduction from her award. *Held*, the status of invalidity benefit was unclear, as although entitlement to it was based on contributions, it could not properly be described as an insurance or pension fund which was managed on actuarial principles. Moreover, invalidity benefit fell within the Social Security Contributions and Benefits Act 1992, Pt II, in which unemployment benefit was also included, and it was settled at common law that that was a benefit which was deductible from an award of damages. However, the 1978 Act, s 74(1) could not be equated with the common law of damages, and an important feature of it was that compensation had to be just and equitable. In addition, s 74(1) allowed the court to take account of analogous situations, such as damages awards in personal injury cases. Taking such matters into consideration, it was clear that Parliament intended that employers and employees were to be treated equally, either by deducting all of the relevant benefit or by dividing the value of it between the parties. In the instant case, it was just and equitable that half of the invalidity benefit received should be deducted from the employee's compensation award. Accordingly, the appeal would be dismissed and the cross-appeal would be allowed in part.

Rubenstein v McGloughlin (1995) Times, 28 December (Employment Appeal Tribunal: Judge Hicks presiding).

1264   Unfair dismissal—compensation—reduction of basic and compensatory awards— bases of reduction

Two employees were summarily dismissed having been caught stealing property belonging to their employer. An industrial tribunal decided that they had been unfairly dismissed because the employer had failed to follow contractual procedural requirements. However, the industrial tribunal reduced the employees' compensatory awards by 100 per cent on the basis of their contributory fault, and also reduced their basic awards by 50 per cent. One of the grounds of the employer's appeal was that the basic award also should have been reduced by 100 per cent. *Held*, under the Employment Protection (Consolidation) Act 1978, s 74(1), (6), regarding compensatory awards, an industrial tribunal was obliged to calculate the losses sustained by an employee and then determine the extent to which the employee had contributed to or caused his dismissal, reducing the award as it considered just and equitable. Even if that test had been applied in the instant case, the industrial tribunal would still have decided to reduce the compensatory awards to nil, because of the employees' conduct. In calculating the amount of the basic award, although there were certain matters for which an employee had to be compensated, the 1978 Act, s 73(7B) permitted an industrial tribunal to take account of an employee's conduct so as to reduce the award, and it was unnecessary to make findings as to causation or contributory fault. Although different considerations applied to ss 73(7B) and 74(6), such considerations sometimes overlapped. In the instant case, the reductions were not wrong in principle, but reflected the discretion given to an industrial tribunal by the Act. Accordingly, the appeal would be dismissed.

Charles Robertson (Developments) Ltd v White [1995] ICR 349 (Employment Appeal Tribunal: Holland J presiding). *Rao v Civil Aviation Authority* [1994] ICR 495, CA (1994 Abr para 1253) applied.

1265   Unfair dismissal—compensation—reduction of basic award—payment made by employer

The Employment Protection (Consolidation) Act 1978, s 73(9) provides that the amount of the basic award must be reduced by the amount of any redundancy payment awarded by the tribunal in respect of the same dismissal, or any payment made by the employer to the employee on the ground that the dismissal was by reason of redundancy.

An employee was dismissed, and one of the terms of his dismissal was that he was to receive a sum from his employer which included his statutory entitlement to redundancy pay. An industrial tribunal subsequently decided that the employee had in fact been unfairly dismissed rather than dismissed for redundancy. In making orders for basic and compensatory awards of compensation, the industrial tribunal did not reduce the employee's basic award by the amount given to him by his employer in respect of his statutory redundancy entitlement. The employer successfully appealed against the failure to reduce the basic award in accordance with the 1978 Act, s 73(9). On the employee's appeal, the issue was whether the payment should have been taken into account or whether a dismissal had to be by reason of redundancy before such a reduction could be made. *Held*, the 1978 Act, s 73(9) applied only where there had been dismissal by way of redundancy, and it was irrelevant whether the redundancy payment was awarded by an industrial tribunal or made by an employer. In the instant case, the payment made by the employer should not have been taken into account, as the employee had not in fact been dismissed by reason of redundancy. Section 73(9) was therefore irrelevant and, accordingly, the appeal would be allowed.

Boorman v Allmakes Ltd [1995] IRLR 553 (Court of Appeal: Nourse, Evans and Rose LJJ).

1266   Unfair dismissal—complaint to industrial tribunal—time limit—excluded employment—age limit—normal retiring age

The Employment Protection (Consolidation) Act 1978, s 67(4) provides that an industrial tribunal must consider a complaint if, where the dismissal is with notice, the complaint is presented after the notice is given notwithstanding that it is presented before the effective date of termination.

The respondent was employed as a matron in a rest home under a contract of employment which did not specify any retirement age. Following a change in ownership of the rest home, the appellant employer introduced new contracts of employment which provided for a normal retiring age of 60 for all employees. Although the respondent refused to accept the new terms, she was given 10 weeks' notice terminating her employment on the ground that she would have reached retirement age by the end of the notice period. Whilst still under notice, the respondent made a complaint of unfair dismissal to an industrial tribunal, upon which the appellant summarily dismissed her. An industrial tribunal decided that it had jurisdiction to consider the complaint notwithstanding the summary dismissal, and concluded that the respondent had been unfairly dismissed. The employer's appeal was dismissed, and on further appeal, *held*, the conditions of the 1978 Act, s 67(4) were satisfied even before the respondent was summarily dismissed, as she had made a complaint of unfair dismissal after receiving notice of dismissal but before the expiry of the notice period. The industrial tribunal had therefore been correct in deciding that it had jurisdiction to consider her complaint, and it was not invalidated by the subsequent summary dismissal. As regards retirement, it had been the policy of the previous employer to consider the circumstances of employees on an individual basis. Moreover, the respondent's reasonable expectation had not been that she would have to retire at 60, and she had resisted the appellant's attempts to impose a retirement age of 60 on her. The fact that other employees had been persuaded to accept such a retirement age was irrelevant, as their jobs involved less responsibility. There was therefore no normal retirement age for an employee holding the same senior position that the respondent held and, accordingly, the appeal would be dismissed.

Patel v Nagesan [1995] ICR 989 (Court of Appeal: Balcombe and McCowan LJJ, and Sir Tasker Watkins).

1267   Unfair dismissal—complaint to industrial tribunal—time limit—party joined after expiry of limit—exercise of tribunal's discretion to join party

The Industrial Tribunals (Constitution and Rules of Procedure) Regulations 1993, SI 1993/2687, Sch 1, r 17 provides that a tribunal may at any time on the application of any person direct any person against whom any relief is sought to be joined as a party.

A local authority employee was dismissed when the authority contracted out part of its operations to a company. The employee presented a complaint of unfair dismissal naming the authority as respondent but the authority suggested that the claim should have been brought against the company. Although the three-month time limit on unfair dismissal claims had already expired the employee successfully asked an industrial tribunal to join the company as a second respondent. The company then sought to be dismissed from the proceedings on the ground that the employee's application was made after the time limit expired. At first instance, the tribunal held that the company had been properly joined in accordance with r 17. It found that, although the delay did not prejudice the company, the employee might suffer hardship if he was denied the chance to bring his claim against them. The company appealed, submitting that a tribunal could only exercise its discretion under r 17 in the same way that the High Court exercised its corresponding jurisdiction and therefore, where a time limit had expired, there was a discretion only where a party had been misnamed or misdescribed, not where an applicant had mistakenly decided to sue the wrong party. *Held*, the addition of a party was a matter of discretion for a tribunal, even where the time limit had expired. Under r 17 a tribunal could direct the addition or substitution of a party at any time and it was not accepted that a tribunal had to exercise its powers to amend in the same way as the High Court exercised its analogous jurisdiction. In the present case, the tribunal had exercised its discretion properly and there were no grounds for interfering with its decision. Accordingly, the appeal would be dismissed.

Drinkwater Sabey Ltd v Burnett [1995] IRLR 238 (Employment Appeal Tribunal: Judge John Hall QC presiding).

1268   Unfair dismissal—complaint to industrial tribunal—time limit—right to bring complaint

The appellant was a teacher who worked for less than 21 hours a week. She was dismissed, but did not make a complaint of unfair dismissal until nearly 18 years later, following the decision in *R v Secretary of State for the Employment, ex p Equal Opportunities Commission* ('the EOC case') [1994] 1 All ER 910, HL (1994 Abr para 2532) that the qualifying thresholds for part-time workers indirectly discriminated against women and were contrary to the EC Treaty, art 119. An industrial tribunal dismissed the appellant's complaint because it had not been made within the three-month time limit provided by the Employment Protection (Consolidation) Act 1978, s 67(2). On appeal, *held*, the EOC case did not deal with the issue of time limits for unfair dismissal or redundancy claims made by part-time workers. The appellant's claim was a private law claim for compensation for unfair dismissal, rather than a claim against the respondent as an emanation of the state for failing to implement a Community law which would have created substantive individual rights. An industrial tribunal did not have jurisdiction to entertain unfair dismissal claims presented after the expiry of the statutory three-month time limit except in limited circumstances, and the time limit applied even if the claim involved directly enforceable Community law rights. Moreover, an industrial tribunal was obliged to apply the statutory time limit unless it could be shown that it was less favourable than that provided for in similar types of actions, or unless the time limit made it impossible in practice to exercise the rights given by art 119. Neither of those situations arose in the instant case. In any event, the appellant could have made her complaint within the three-month time limit and argued, at that stage, that the qualifying conditions were ineffective. The industrial tribunal had not erred in its decision and, accordingly, the appeal would be dismissed.

Biggs v Somerset County Council [1995] ICR 811 (Employment Appeal Tribunal: Mummery J presiding).

This decision has been affirmed on appeal: (1996) Times, 29 January, CA.

1269   Unfair dismissal—complaint to industrial tribunal—time limit—whether presentation of complaint within time limit reasonably practicable

The Employment Protection (Consolidation) Act 1978, s 67(2) provides that an industrial tribunal must not consider a complaint unless it is presented before the end of the period of three months beginning with the effective date of termination or within such further period as the tribunal considers reasonable in a case where it is satisfied that it was not reasonably practicable for the complaint to be presented before the end of the period of three months.

The applicant was dismissed from his position as a sales representative in July. His employer offered him the opportunity to continue selling its products on a commission-only basis and the applicant did so for just over three months until the employer ended the arrangement. The applicant immediately presented a complaint claiming that he had been unfairly dismissed in July. Although he did not present his complaint within the three month time limit, an industrial tribunal held, pursuant to s 67(2), that, given the applicant's need to remain on reasonable terms with his employer for financial reasons, it had not been reasonably practicable to present his complaint in time, but that he had done so promptly when the arrangement was terminated. On the employer's appeal, *held*, the commission arrangement entered into made it highly inappropriate for the applicant to issue proceedings against the employer immediately. However, it was a matter of commercial convenience and interest, entered into in good faith, and that was not something which made it 'not reasonably practicable' within the meaning of s 67(2) to present the complaint in time. Accordingly, the appeal would be allowed.

Birmingham Optical Group plc v Johnson [1995] ICR 459 (Employment Appeal Tribunal: Judge Hull QC presiding).

An employee submitted a complaint of unfair dismissal, claiming that he had been unfairly selected for redundancy ('the first ground'). He later amended his originating application to add that he had been unfairly dismissed for reasons relating to his capability ('the second ground'). However, he did not submit his application until after the expiry of the three-month time limit, as it was not until after that period that he became aware of the facts of each ground of complaint. An industrial tribunal decided that it had jurisdiction to consider the second ground but not the first. On the employers' appeal, that decision was upheld. On the employers' further appeal, *held*, a disadvantage of the industrial tribunal procedure for pleadings and discovery was that the information which an employee needed in order to know the full circumstances and motives for his dismissal sometimes came to light only slowly and gradually. Where that occurred, an employee was to be given an opportunity to add to or amend his grounds of complaint, and it was not contrary to justice or fairness to allow him to raise a second ground of complaint within a reasonable period. Moreover, having regard to the Employment Protection (Consolidation) Act 1978, s 67(2), supra, the moment at which an employee first believed that he had a right to claim unfair dismissal did not fix for all time the point at which it was reasonably practicable for him to submit a complaint. The reasonable practicability of presenting a complaint within the time limit and the reasonableness of any subsequent period elapsing before a complaint was presented, were matters which had to be considered separately under each head of unfair dismissal upon which a complaint was founded. Accordingly, on the facts, the appeal would be dismissed.

Marley UK Ltd v Anderson [1996] IRLR 163 (Court of Appeal: Russell, Waite and Schiemann LJJ). Decision of Employment Appeal Tribunal [1994] IRLR 152 (1993 Abr para 1185) affirmed.

1270 Unfair dismissal—constructive dismissal—conduct entitling employee to resign—employer's failure to implement grievance procedure

An employee, who was paid on a commission basis, was concerned about changes in sales methods introduced by the employer company, which led to a substantial reduction in his take-home pay. The employer had no established procedure for dealing with his grievance, and the employee had never been given a written statement of his terms and conditions specifying the method of pursuing a grievance. Discussions between the employee and his manager about his drop in take-home pay came to nothing, as did his subsequent attempts to take his grievance up with the managing director and the chairman of the company. The managing director merely told him that the matter would be dealt with in time. The employee then resigned. An industrial tribunal subsequently upheld his claim to have been constructively dismissed, and made a finding of unfair dismissal. The employer appealed. *Held*, there was an implied term in the employee's contract of employment that the employer would reasonably and promptly provide him with an opportunity to obtain redress for any grievance he might have. The Employment Protection (Consolidation) Act 1978, s 1 required employers to provide their employees with a written statement of their employment which included a note specifying to whom and in what manner the employee might apply if he had any grievance. It was clear, therefore, that Parliament considered that good industrial relations required employers to implement a method of dealing with grievances in a proper and timeous manner. Moreover, an employee's right to obtain redress against a grievance was fundamental. In the present case, the employer's failure to provide and implement a procedure to deal with the employee's grievance, amounted to a breach of his contract of employment. That breach was sufficiently serious to justify the employee to resign and be treated as having been constructively dismissed. Accordingly, the appeal would be dismissed.

WA Goold (Pearmak) Ltd v McConnell [1995] IRLR 516 (Employment Appeal Tribunal: Morison J presiding).

1271 Unfair dismissal—effective date of termination of employment—ratification of invalid decision

At a meeting of the executive committee of the respondent students union, it was decided that the appellant was to be summarily dismissed. The appellant was informed of the decision at a meeting held two days later, and the sum to which he was entitled in consequence of his dismissal was calculated as of the date of the second meeting. On the appellant's complaint of unfair dismissal, an industrial tribunal decided that the complaint was out of time because it had not been made within three months of the effective date of the termination of his employment. On appeal, the appellant argued that as the decision reached at the executive committee's first meeting was invalid because the meeting had not been properly convened, his dismissal had not taken place until he had received a letter from the executive committee confirming his dismissal. That letter had been received within three months of the date on which he had presented his complaint. *Held*, the effective date of termination of employment for the purposes of the Employment Protection (Consolidation) Act 1978, s 67(2) was a matter of fact, which was to be decided in a practical and commonsense manner having regard to what the parties understood at the time of the dismissal. The dismissal in the instant case could not have taken effect on the date on which the appellant received the letter, as that had merely confirmed the earlier decision to dismiss him, and at the time of the second meeting, both the appellant and the executive committee understood that the appellant's employment was to be terminated. Where a dismissal occurred as a result of a void resolution, the decision was not necessarily a nullity. Even though the executive committee members who informed the appellant of his dismissal were acting as the unauthorised agents of the executive committee when doing so, their decision was later ratified by the executive committee, thereby retrospectively validating their actions. Moreover, in ratifying the decision, the executive committee had been aware of all the relevant facts, in particular that the committee meeting had not been properly convened. The appellant had therefore not presented his complaint within the prescribed time limit and, accordingly, the appeal would be dismissed.

Newman v Polytechnic of Wales Students Union [1995] IRLR 72 (Employment Appeal Tribunal: Judge Hague QC presiding).

1272   Unfair dismissal—excluded employment—age limit—normal retiring age

The appellants were employed by the respondent bank as messengers. Although their contractual retirement age was 60, there was an established practice that messengers could apply for annual extensions allowing them to continue working up to the age of 65. When the respondent issued an official circular which stated that there was to be a common retiring age of 60 for all employees, it made an exception in the case of messengers who were aged 55 and over on 7 November 1987 so that they could continue with the usual practice if certain conditions were satisfied. The appellants were informed of this exception in writing, and when they were subsequently made redundant, they claimed that they had been unfairly dismissed. Having regard to the Employment Protection (Consolidation) Act 1978, s 64(1)(b), the respondent submitted that the industrial tribunal had no jurisdiction to entertain the complaints because the appellants were over retirement age at the time of their dismissals. The industrial tribunal decided that there was no normal retiring age for the appellants because messengers were allowed to retire at different ages. The respondent's appeal against the decision was allowed, and on further appeal, *held*, where there was a contractual retirement age which applied to all or nearly all employees of a particular group, there was a rebuttable presumption that the contractual retiring age was the normal retiring age for that group of employees. An employee's reasonable expectation in respect of retirement had to be considered on an objective basis. In this case, prior to the circular and the letters sent to the appellants, all messengers could have expected to be allowed to continue working past the contractual retirement age of 60 up to the age of 65. Thereafter, however, the circular imposed a normal retiring age of 60, subject to the exception made in the case of those messengers who were over 55 but under 60 as at a particular date. An exception limited in time and made for a relatively small category of employees within a particular age range did not destroy a normal retiring age policy. The policy announced by the circular was genuine and not a sham, nor had it been abandoned, and the exception made in respect of the appellants had not destroyed that policy. Accordingly, the appeal would be dismissed.

O'Brien v Barclays Bank plc [1995] 1 All ER 438 (Court of Appeal: Glidewell, Peter Gibson and Henry LJJ).

Under the Employment Protection (Consolidation) Act 1978, s 64(1)(b) the statutory right not to be unfairly dismissed does not apply to the dismissal of an employee if, on or before the date of termination, he attained the normal retiring age for an employee holding the position which he held if the undertaking in which he was employed has a normal retirement age and, in any other case, the age of 65.

An employer sought to reduce the normal age of retirement from 65 years to 64 years of age. Although no agreement was reached in negotiations with the union, the employer gave all employees a written notice of the change and sent them each a letter purported to be individual notice of that change. Some time later, a 64-year-old employee had his employment terminated. The employee claimed he had been unfairly dismissed. An industrial tribunal held that the employer's action in reducing the age at which employees had to retire to 64 established a new normal retiring age of 64 and that, since the employee had attained that age when his employment was terminated, he was precluded from claiming that his dismissal was unfair. On the employee's appeal, *held*, an employer could not reduce the normal retiring age below the contractual age of retirement. The contractual retirement age for employees in the relevant position established a presumption as to the normal retirement age which could not be changed to the disadvantage of an employee without taking the steps necessary to obtain a change in the contractual retiring age, typically by either a consensual variation or by terminating the contracts by lawful notice and offering fresh ones. The tribunal had erred in its finding. Accordingly, the appeal would be allowed and the case would be remitted for re-hearing.

Bratko v Beloit Walmsley Ltd [1995] IRLR 629 (Employment Appeal Tribunal: Judge Hicks QC presiding).

1273 Unfair dismissal—qualifying period—compatibility with EC sex discrimination provisions

See *R v Secretary of State for Employment, ex p Seymour-Smith*, para 2654.

1274 Unfair dismissal—reason for dismissal—sufficiency of reason—final written warning—expiry of warning

Having been given an oral warning about his work, an employee was later given a final written warning by way of letter because of his sickness absence and conduct. It was stated that the letter would remain on his file for 12 months from the date of the letter, and that any further misconduct would be considered as grounds for dismissal. Exactly a year to the date of the letter, the employee committed a further act of misconduct. At a disciplinary hearing, the employer decided to dismiss him on the basis that the final written warning had still been in force at the time of the final incident of misconduct. On the employee's complaint of unfair dismissal, an industrial tribunal decided that the final written warning had expired the day before the final incident of misconduct, and that the employer could not reasonably have dismissed the employee on the basis of the single act of misconduct. On the employer's appeal against the finding of unfair dismissal, *held*, it was a question of construction whether the first day of the final written warning was included or excluded from the computation of the 12-month period for which the employee was subject to the written warning, as there was no general rule in that respect. Since the commencement date of the warning was ambiguous, it was to be construed strictly against the employer. Such ambiguity could have been avoided by clearly specifying the time, day and date on which the warning was to commence and also that on which it was to expire. As the employer had failed to do so, the warning was to be construed in favour of the employee. The industrial tribunal had therefore not erred in deciding that the employee was not subject to the final written warning at the time of the final act of misconduct and, accordingly, the appeal would be dismissed.

Bevan Ashford v Malin [1995] ICR 453 (Employment Appeal Tribunal: Mummery J presiding).

1275 Unfair dismissal—reason for dismissal—trade union activities

An employee was involved in giving presentations at induction courses run by his employer for new employees. He was also a trade union shop steward. The employer and the union had good relations and the employer allowed the union to use the induction courses as a forum for recruitment. The employee attended an induction course as part of the management team and also gave a presentation on behalf of the union. During the course of his union presentation, the employee made remarks about the employers to which they took exception. In particular, he said that in matters of health and safety, it was the union and not the company who would fight for the employees, the company being primarily concerned with profits. The employee was subsequently demoted, treating this as a constructive dismissal and claiming that he had been dismissed because of his trade union activities, contrary to the Trade Union and Labour Relations (Consolidation) Act 1992, s 152. On the employers' appeal against a decision upholding the employee's claim, *held*, the employee had been dismissed for a reason relating to his trade union activities within s 152. The union had been permitted to use the course as a forum for recruitment and consent to recruit had to include consent to underline the services that the union provided. This could reasonably involve a submission that the union could provide a service which the employer did not. A consent which prevented the recruiter from saying anything adverse about the employer was not a real consent. It could not be regarded as an abuse of privilege by the employee for him to make remarks which were critical of the employer. Accordingly, the appeal would be dismissed.

Bass Taverns Ltd v Burgess [1995] IRLR 596 (Court of Appeal: Balcombe and Pill LJJ and Sir Ralph Gibson).

1276 Unfair dismissal—re-engagement or reinstatement—terms

An employee held the position of field supervisor for a company. His salary was less than £17,000 and he was not entitled to a company car. When the company dismissed him, he issued an application claiming unfair dismissal and at an industrial tribunal he sought re-engagement.

The company said that the employee's dismissal was due to redundancy but did accept that it had been unfair. The tribunal ordered that the company re-engage the applicant in a vacant position as national technical specialist. The salary range for that post was £18,000–£21,000 and the employee would be entitled to a company car. On the company's appeal against the tribunal's decision, *held*, the tribunal fell into error in concluding that it could direct re-engagement in respect of employment which was on substantially better terms than the employment formerly held by the employee. The Employment Protection (Consolidation) Act 1978, s 69(6) provided that it was not permissible for a tribunal to order re-engagement in respect of employment significantly more favourable than that which the employee might have obtained if reinstatement had been ordered. In addition, it was, in general, undesirable for an industrial tribunal to order re-engagement in respect of a specific job, as distinct from identifying the nature of the proposed employment. Accordingly, the appeal would be allowed and the case would be remitted to the tribunal to consider the appropriate remedy.

Rank Xerox (UK) Ltd v Stryczek [1995] IRLR 568 (Employment Appeal Tribunal: Judge Butter QC presiding).

1277 Wages—deduction—discretionary payment of proportion of service charge

A restaurant waiter's contract of employment provided that in addition to being paid a set fee for each session that he worked, he was to be paid a proportion of the service charge. The service charge was pooled and apportioned between employees on a weekly basis, such proportions being determined at the discretion of the restaurant's management. The waiter's share of the service charge was reduced when part of the service charge was allocated to the restaurant's turnover and put towards another employee's wages. As his overall weekly wages were reduced as a result, the waiter complained that there had been a deduction from his wages without his written agreement or consent, contrary to the Wages Act 1986, ss 1(1)(b) and 8(3). His complaint was dismissed and, on appeal, *held*, although the allocation of the service charge was a matter for the discretion of the restaurant's management, that discretion was limited to the proportions in which the service charge was allocated amongst the employees who actually gave service. Management was not entitled to allocate part of the service charge to the restaurant's income, and as the waiter had not agreed or consented to it, there had been an unlawful deduction from his wages within the meaning of the 1986 Act. Accordingly, the appeal would be allowed.

Saavedra v Aceground Ltd (t/a Terrazza Est) [1995] IRLR 198 (Employment Appeal Tribunal: Holland J presiding).

1278 Wages—deduction—unlawful deduction or error of computation—unlawful demotion

The appellant was employed as a section leader at a college, a job which involved certain administrative duties. Following his suspension from those duties, disciplinary proceedings were commenced against him. At the time of the proceedings, control of the college was being transferred from the respondent local authority to the governing body of the college. The governing body operated the disciplinary panel procedure, and the revised code of discipline gave it discretion to transfer or demote an employee to another post at the same or lower grade. The charges against the appellant were upheld and he was demoted, with the result that the local authority, acting on the instructions of the college's governing body, paid the appellant at a reduced rate thereafter. The appellant claimed that the reduction was an unlawful deduction within the meaning of the Wages Act 1986, s 1(1), but an industrial tribunal decided that there had been an error of computation, within the meaning of the 1986 Act, s 8(3). On appeal, *held*, an 'error of computation' referred to a mistake through inadvertence or ignorance, and 'computation' referred to reckoning the amount due to an employee by the process of counting and calculation. In the instant case, the reduction of the appellant's wages had occurred because of the deliberate decision by the disciplinary panel to demote him and reduce his wages. The fact that the panel's decision was the result of a legal and factual error was irrelevant, as it was the decision that had led to the reduction in the appellant's wages, and not an error of computation. As the governing body did not have the power to demote the appellant, it did not have the right to require the local authority to reduce the appellant's wages. The reduction in the appellant's wages was therefore a 'deduction' within the meaning of the 1986 Act, s 1(1). Moreover, the appellant's claim did not have to be for damages for breach of contract but could be made under the 1986 Act, as his contract of employment still existed because he had not accepted the repudiatory breach of contract brought about by the reduction in his wages. Accordingly, the appeal would be allowed.

Morgan v West Glamorgan County Council [1995] IRLR 68 (Employment Appeal Tribunal: Mummery J).

1279   Wrongful dismissal—earlier proceedings for unfair dismissal—plea of res judicata

See *Clink v Speyside Distillery Co Ltd*, para 1332.

ENVIRONMENT

1280   Articles

Chartered Surveyors and Land Quality Statements, Philip Wilbourn: Estates Gazette, March 4 1995, p 311

The Clean-Up Clause, Richard Burnett-Hall (on the Environment Bill 1995): LS Gaz, 26 April 1995, p 18

Clean Water and Muddy Causation: Is Causation a Question of Law or Fact, or Just a Way of Allocating Blame? Nicola Padfield (on causation in pollution offences): [1995] Crim LR 683

Contaminated Ground Rules, Derek Jerram: Estates Gazette, 2 December 1995, p 100

Contaminated Land, Richard Stein and Sean Humber: 139 SJ 270

Criminal Liability for Damage, Neil Turner and Stuart Gronow (on liability of landlords for environmental pollution caused by their tenants): Estates Gazette, 25 November 1995, p 143

Environment Act 1995, Simon Payne: 139 SJ 1100, 1118

Environmental Bill—New Controls, Hugh Barrett (on contaminated land): Estates Gazette, January 28 1995, p 146

Environmental Protection; 'Causing' Pollution—The Final Word? Geoff Holgate: 159 JP Jo 127

The Greening of European Rights Law, Alastair Mowbray: 139 SJ 840

High Talk and Low Cunning: Putting Environmental Principles into Legal Practice, Stephen Tromans: [1995] JPL 779

The Impact of Environmental Assessment on Public Inquiry Decisions, Carys Jones and Christopher Wood: [1995] JPL 890

Insurance Cover for Damage to the Environment, Robert Holmes and Michael Broughton: Estates Gazette, 1 April 1995, p 123

PPG 9 'Nature Conservation'—A New Initiative? Lynda Warren and Victoria Murray: [1995] JPL 574

Remedies and Remediation: Foundational Issues in Environmental Liability, Jenny Steele: 58 MLR 615

Structure Plans—the Conduct and Conventions of Examination in Public, Richard Phelps: [1995] JPL 95

Tree Preservation and Nuisance, Leslie Rutherford and Sheila Bone: [1995] JPL 102

Tree Roots: a Foreseeable Nuisance, Barry Stanton and Gordon Wignall: 139 SJ 1146

Water Pollution and the Causing Offence, Neil Parpworth: 159 JP Jo 244

1281   Air quality standards

The Air Quality Standards (Amendment) Regulations 1995, SI 1995/3146 (in force on 31 December 1995), amend the 1989 Regulations, SI 1989/317, so as to (1) revoke temporary provisions relating to suspended particulates which have become spent, and (2) amend the implementation of the definition of 'limit value' in Council Directive (EC) 85/203, art 2 on air quality standards for nitrogen dioxide, previously implemented by the 1989 Regulations.

1282   Antarctic Act 1994—commencement

The Antarctic Act 1994 (Commencement) Order 1995, SI 1995/2748, brings into force, on 1 November 1995, ss 1, 2, 8–32, 33 (in part), 34–36. For a summary of the Act, see 1994 Abr para 1285. For details of commencement, see the commencement table in the title STATUTES.

1283   Antarctica

The Antarctic Regulations 1995, SI 1995/490 (in force on 1 November 1995: SI 1995/2741), prescribe the procedure for applying for permits under the Antarctic Act 1994, and in certain circumstances applicants must submit initial environmental evaluations or comprehensive environmental evaluations. Permits must be produced when requested, and may be revoked or suspended. The Antarctic Act Tribunal is established in order to hear appeals against revocations and suspensions, and the regulations set out provisions relating to the tribunal's constitution and procedural matters. In relation to offences committed under the Act, the regulations contain provisions as to arrest, physical evidence and the attendance of witnesses. Additionally, the regulations designate certain areas as restricted areas, Antarctic historic sites and monuments, and protected places.

1284 Antarctica—Antarctic Act Tribunal

The Tribunals and Inquiries (Antarctic Act Tribunal) Order 1995, SI 1995/2877 (in force on 1 December 1995), brings the Antarctic Act Tribunal, established by SI 1995/490, under the Council on Tribunals.

1285 Antarctica—Guernsey

The Antarctic Act 1994 (Guernsey) Order 1995, SI 1995/1033 (in force on the coming into force of specified provisions of the Antarctic Act 1994), extends those provisions to the Bailiwick of Guernsey, subject to specified modifications.

1286 Antarctica—Isle of Man

The Antarctic Act 1994 (Isle of Man) Order 1995, SI 1995/1035 (in force on the coming into force of specified provisions of the Antarctic Act 1994), extends those provisions to the Isle of Man, subject to specified modifications.

1287 Antarctica—Jersey

The Antarctic Act 1994 (Jersey) Order 1995, SI 1995/1034 (in force on the coming into force of specified provisions of the Antarctic Act 1994), extends those provisions to Jersey, subject to specified modifications.

1288 Antarctica—overseas territories

The Antarctic Act 1994 (Overseas Territories) Order 1995, SI 1995/1030 (in force in part on 15 May 1995, in part on such day or days as may be appointed by the governor of each territory to which the order applies), extends the provisions of the Antarctic Act 1994 relating to environmental protection, including enforcement provisions, to the territories of Anguilla, Bermuda, British Antarctic Territory, the Cayman Islands, the Falkland Islands, Montserrat, St Helena and Dependencies, South Georgia and the South Sandwich Islands, Turks and Caicos Islands, and the Virgin Islands, subject to certain modifications. The order also partially revokes the Antarctic Treaty Order in Council 1962, SI 1962/401.

1289 Environment Act 1995

The Environment Act 1995 provides for the establishment of a body corporate to be known as the Environment Agency and a body corporate to be known as the Scottish Environment Protection Agency; the transfer of functions, property, rights and liabilities to those bodies and for the conferring of other functions on them; various matters with respect to contaminated land and abandoned mines; matters in relation to National Parks; the control of pollution, the conservation of natural resources and the conservation or enhancement of the environment; obligations on certain persons in respect of certain products or materials; matters in relation to fisheries. The Act received the royal assent on 19 July 1995. Certain provisions came into force on that date, and on and between 28 July 1995 and 1 April 1996, and certain provisions come into force on 1 January 1999: SI 1995/1983, 2765, 2950. The remaining provisions come into force on a day or days to be appointed. For details of commencement, see the commencement table in the title STATUTES.

Part I (ss 1–56) The Environment Agency and the Scottish Environment Protection Agency

Chapter I The Environment Agency
Section 1, Sch 1 establish the Environment Agency, to which the functions, property, rights and liabilities of certain environmental statutory bodies, including the National Rivers Authority and the London Waste Regulation Authority, are transferred by ss 2, 3, Sch 2. Section 4 sets out the principal aim and objectives of the agency. Provision is made regarding the duties of the agency

in relation to pollution control (s 5), water (s 6), general environmental and recreational functions (s 7) and sites of special interest (s 8). Section 9 empowers the Secretary of State and the Minister of Agriculture, Fisheries and Food ('the ministers') to approve codes of practice to which the agency must have regard, and s 10 deals with incidental functions of the agency. Section 11 provides for the establishment and maintenance of an advisory committee in Wales connected with the carrying out of the agency's functions whilst the agency is required to establish and maintain environment protection advisory committees throughout England and Wales (s 12, Sch 3), as well as regional and local fisheries advisory committees: s 13. Section 14, Sch 4 provide for the establishment of regional flood committees with the same areas as the existing flood committees. The regional flood committees' composition must be in accordance with the provisions of s 15, and changes to the composition are dealt with by s 16. The agency may make a local defence scheme for the creation of a local defence committee (s 17), the composition of which must be in accordance with the provisions of s 18. Section 19, Sch 5 deal with the membership and proceedings of regional and local flood committees.

Chapter II The Scottish Environment Protection Agency
Sections 20–36, Sch 6 apply to Scotland.

Chapter III Miscellaneous, General and Supplemental Provisions Relating to the New Agencies
Section 37 deals with incidental general powers of the new agencies and s 38 permits any minister to delegate any of his eligible functions to the agency. The agency has a duty to consider the costs and benefits before exercising any of its powers: s 39. Section 40 provides that the ministers may give general or specific directions to the agency with respect to the carrying out of any of its functions. The agency may make charging schemes in relation to the issuing of licences and other activities (s 41) which must be submitted for approval to the Secretary of State who must have regard to specified matters when considering the scheme: s 42. Section 43 sets out an incidental power of the new agency to impose charges. Section 44 empowers the ministers to determine the financial duties of the agency and s 45 makes provision for the accounts and records to be kept by the agency. The agency's accounts must be audited by an auditor appointed by the Secretary of State and inspected by the Comptroller and Auditor General: s 46. The ministers may make grants to the agency, with the approval of the Treasury, on such terms as they think fit: s 47. Borrowing powers of the agency are set out in s 48 and the ministers' power to grant government loans, with the approval of the Treasury, is set out in s 49. Section 50 provides for government guarantees of the agency's borrowings and the duty of the ministers to place a statement relating to such borrowing before both Houses of Parliament. The ministers may direct specified information to be provided by the agency (s 51) which must prepare and publish an annual report that is to be placed before both Houses of Parliament: s 52. Section 53 contains supplemental provisions relating to local inquiries and other hearings and s 54 enables a person authorised by the agency, although not of counsel or a solicitor, to prosecute in proceedings before a magistrates' court, on behalf of the agency. Section 55 provides for the continuity of exercise of the functions transferred to the agency and s 56 contains interpretation provisions in relation to Pt I of the Act.

Part II (ss 57–60) Contaminated Land and Abandoned Mines
Section 57 inserts new definitions for 'contaminated land' and other key terms in the Environmental Protection Act 1990 and new provisions dealing with statutory nuisance in relation to contaminated land. In addition, new provisions on abandoned mines are inserted in the Water Resources Act 1991: s 58. Section 59 applies to Scotland. The defence against prosecution for pollution and the exemption from recovery of expenses under the Water Resources Act 1991, do not apply to mines abandoned after 31 December 1999, under s 60, which also permits the agency to carry out pollution investigations and claim costs.

Part III (ss 61–79) National Parks
Section 61 sets out new provisions dealing with the purposes of National Parks and new provisions are also made by s 62, in regard to the duty of specified authorities to consider the economic and social well-being of local communities within the National Park when exercising functions which might affect it. Section 63, Sch 7 provide that existing authorities which deal with National Parks may be wound up by the Secretary of State and replaced by new National Park authorities and sets out their constitution and procedure, whilst s 64 deals with National Park authorities specific to Wales. Section 65, Sch 8 provide for the general purposes and powers as well as supplemental and incidental powers, of National Park authorities. Section 66 requires every National Park authority to prepare a National Park Management Plan within three years after its operational date, which formulates policy for management of the relevant Park and carrying out of its functions. A National Park Authority is the sole local planning authority in relation to the area of the Park (s 67) and has the same functions as a local planning authority

does under specified statutes: ss 68–70, Sch 9. Section 71 empowers National Park Authorities to issue levies to local councils who appoint authority members, every financial year, and s 72 allows the Secretary of State, with Treasury approval, to make grants to National Park Authorities for such purposes, amounts, terms and conditions as he sees fit. Capital finances and borrowing powers of National Park Authorities are dealt with by s 73, and s 74 validates certain grants to local authorities for expenditure in connection with National Parks. Section 75 gives the Secretary of State power, when making an order under Pt III of the Act, to make incidental, supplemental, consequential or transitional provision whilst, under s 76, any public authorities affected by an order made under Pt III may make agreements with respect to incidental matters. Section 77 applies to the Isles of Scilly. Section 78, Sch 10 make minor and consequential amendments. Interpretation provisions relating to Pt III are contained in s 79.

Part IV (ss 80–91) Air Quality
Section 80 requires the Secretary of State to prepare and publish a national air quality strategy after consultation with the agency and other representative bodies. The agency must have regard to the strategy in discharging its pollution control functions (s 81) and every local authority must carry out a review of air quality in its area from time to time: s 82. If it appears from a local authority review that a particular area has not met air quality standards, it must be designated an air quality management area (s 83) and the duties of the local authority in relation to such management areas are set out in s 84. Reserve powers of the Secretary of State in relation to air quality are dealt with in s 85. Where a district council is comprised in an area for which there is a county council, the county council may make recommendations and proposals to the district council regarding air quality matters and the Secretary of State has the power to direct a county council to fulfil its obligations in this respect: s 86. Section 87 enables regulations to be made in respect of Pt IV matters and s 88 allows the Secretary of State to issue guidance to local authorities regarding their Pt IV duties. Section 89 applies to the Isles of Scilly. Section 90, Sch 11 set out supplementary provisions regarding air quality and s 91 contains interpretation provisions for Pt IV.

Part V (ss 92–125) Miscellaneous, General and Supplemental Provisions
Section 92, Sch 12 require the Secretary of State to prepare a national waste strategy and s 93 empowers him to make regulations for the purpose of promoting or securing an increase in the re-use, recovery or recycling of products or materials. Specific provisions which may be included in any regulations made by the Secretary of State, are set out in s 94 together with supplementary provisions, and offences and penalties for breach of any regulation, are dealt with in s 95. Section 96, Schs 13, 14 deal with review of old mineral planning permissions and periodic review of mineral planning permissions. Section 97 empowers the ministers to make regulations concerning the protection of important hedgerows in England or Wales. Section 98 provides for the ministers, with Treasury consent, to make grants for purposes conducive to conservation of the countryside or for the promotion of the enjoyment of the countryside by the public. The Minister of Agriculture, Fisheries and Food must consult certain bodies and persons before making or modifying specified subordinate legislation promoting conservation: s 99. Section 100 extends the meaning of 'drainage' in certain enactments and s 101 permits the ministers to give grants for preliminary and post-project studies relating to drainage and flood-defence works. Section 102 allows a person with knowledge of, or expertise in, marine environmental matters to be appointed to a local fisheries committee and also permits such a committee to make byelaws for marine environmental purposes. The ministers may make an order restricting fishing for marine environmental purposes and the agency may make byelaws for marine or aquatic environmental purposes: s 103. Section 104 introduces a fixed penalty system for certain offences relating to salmon or freshwater fisheries and s 105, Sch 15 contain minor and consequential amendments relating to fisheries. Sections 106, 107, Schs 16, 17 apply to Scotland. Section 108, Sch 18 provide that a person who appears suitable to a relevant authority may be given powers of entry, inspection, seizure and other related powers in order to enforce the pollution control functions of that authority and s 109 gives an authorised person power to seize an article or substance found by him which he considers to be a cause of imminent danger of serious pollution of the environment or serious harm to human health, and render it harmless. Offences relating to powers of entry, in particular, obstruction of an authorised person, are dealt with in s 110. Section 111 repeals certain provisions which restrict the admissibility in evidence of information obtained from samples in pollution proceedings. Section 112, Sch 19 amend certain offences relating to false or misleading statements or false entries. Section 113 permits the disclosure of information by specified people and bodies to other specified people or bodies for the purpose of facilitating the carrying out by the agency, a minister or a local enforcing authority of their relevant functions under the Act. The Secretary of State has the power to delegate his functions of determining an appeal or referring a matter involved in an appeal, to any person he has

appointed for this purpose: s 114, Sch 20. The Act binds the Crown subject to specified provisions (s 115) as do certain enactments set out in s 116, Sch 21. Sections 117, 118 apply the Act to the Isles of Scilly. Section 119 makes provision in relation to stamp duty on transfers made under Pt I of the Act and s 120, Schs 22–24, make minor and consequential amendments, transitional and transitory provisions, savings and repeals. Section 121 provides that the Secretary of State or the minister may amend any local statutory provision if he considers it appropriate as a result of an enactment made under the Act. Section 122 deals with the form and procedure for giving directions under the Act, and s 123 deals with service of documents. Section 124 contains general interpretation provisions and s 125 deals with short title, commencement and extent.

1290 Environment Act 1995—national park authorities—Wales

See para 1973.

1291 Environmental Protection Act 1990—commencement

The Environmental Protection Act 1990 (Commencement No 17) Order 1995, SI 1995/2152, brings into force on 11 August 1995 s 62, under which the Secretary of State may make special provision by regulations for the treatment, keeping or disposal of certain dangerous or intractable waste. For a summary of the Act, see 1990 Abr para 1032. For details of commencement, see the commencement table in the title STATUTES.

1292 Home Energy Conservation Act 1995

The Home Energy Conservation Act 1995 makes provision for the drawing up of local energy conservation reports in relation to residential accommodation and gives the Secretary of State functions in connection with energy conservation authorities. The Act received the royal assent on 28 June 1994 and came into force in England on 15 January and 1 April 1996: SI 1995/3340. The Act comes into force in Wales on a day or days to be appointed. For details of commencement, see the commencement table in the title STATUTES.

Section 1 contains definitions of 'energy conservation authority', 'energy conservation measures' and 'residential accommodation' and describes the area of an energy conservation authority. Every energy conservation authority must prepare a report setting out energy conservation measures and an assessment of the effect such measures will have in terms of cost, savings, employment, environmental impact and other matters it considers appropriate: s 2. The authority may consult appropriate persons when preparing the report which must be published and a copy sent to the Secretary of State. Section 3 sets out the functions of the Secretary of State in relation to reports, including the setting of a timetable for the preparation of energy conservation reports and the preparation of a report by the Secretary of State himself, on the progress made by energy conservation authorities. The Secretary of State may give guidance to energy conservation authorities to which such authorities must have regard: s 4. If instructed to do so by the Secretary of State, an authority may modify a report or prepare further reports: s 5. Section 6 contains supplementary provisions and s 7 deals with expenses. Section 8 relates to Northern Ireland. Section 9 deals with citation and commencement.

1293 Litter—offence of leaving litter—definition of litter

The Environmental Protection Act 1990, s 87(1), (5) provide that it is an offence to deposit in a specified place and leave any thing whatsoever in such circumstances as to cause, or contribute to, or tend to lead to, the defacement by litter of any such place.

It has been held that trade or commercial refuse bagged up awaiting collection is litter in the ordinary sense of the word for the purposes of the 1990 Act, s 87.

Westminster City Council v Riding (1995) Times, 31 July (Queen's Bench Division: Stuart-Smith LJ and Butterfield J).

1294 Nuclear testing—underground testing—challenge to testing by France

See *New Zealand v France*, para 1438.

1295 Pollution control—air pollution—emission of dark smoke—scope of offence

Under the Clean Air Act 1993, s 2(1) dark smoke must not be emitted from any industrial or trade premises and if, on any day, dark smoke is so emitted the occupier of the premises and any person who causes or permits the emission is guilty of an offence.

The owner of a farm lit a fire on his land. An environmental officer saw a plume of smoke from the fire and formed the view that the smoke constituted dark smoke. The farm came within the definition of trade premises and the owner was convicted of an offence under the 1993 Act, s 2(1). On appeal, he claimed that 'emission' in s 2(1) meant emission beyond the boundaries of the land occupied by the owner and that the 1993 Act did not prohibit dark smoke in the part of the environment occupied by him. The appeal was dismissed, and on further appeal by way of case stated, *held*, the expression 'emitted from land' in s 2(1) included a movement above the surface of the ground within the boundaries of the land occupied. There was no reason why emissions would be limited to a movement beyond those boundaries. An important purpose of the 1993 Act was to abate the pollution of the air and to give effect to that purpose and the operation of s 2 was not limited to the air above neighbours' land. Accordingly, the appeal would be dismissed.

O'Fee v Copeland Borough Council (1995) 160 JP 20 (Queen's Bench Division: Pill LJ and Keene J).

1296 Pollution control—discharge of waste—discharge into controlled waters—causing pollution—circumstances in which offence may be committed

The Water Act 1989, s 107(1)(a) provides that a person contravenes s 107 if he causes or knowingly permits any poisonous, noxious or polluting matter to enter any controlled waters, and s 107(6) provides that a person who contravenes s 107 is guilty of an offence, and liable to a penalty.

The first respondent collected and disposed of highly toxic waste and oils in an area where the second respondent was a sewerage undertaker with statutory duties to provide and maintain sewerage disposal systems. The third respondent was a local authority which, by a commercial agreement, performed certain duties delegated to it by the sewerage undertaker. When highly toxic sewage entered a stream and flowed into a river causing the destruction of marine life, the respondents were charged with causing polluting matter to enter controlled waters contrary to the 1989 Act, s 107(1)(a). On their acquittal, the Attorney-General referred several questions as to the interpretation and application of s 107(1)(a). *Held*, it was a question of fact whether a respondent 'caused' polluting matter to enter controlled waters, but 'cause' was not qualified by the word 'knowingly'. It was to be given its plain, commonsense meaning, and involved some active participation in the operation or chain of operations resulting in the pollution of controlled waters. An offence under s 107(1)(a) could be committed by more than one person, where they each carried out different and separate acts which either contributed to the polluting matter entering the waters, or without any of which the polluting matter would not have entered the water. If a sewerage company set up and owned a plant or system to carry out its statutory duties and the sewerage passing through it polluted controlled waters, the company had participated in the active operation or chain of operations resulting in the pollution of the controlled waters, and could therefore be guilty of causing pollution. Where a respondent had undertaken the day-to-day running and maintenance of a sewerage system but failed to properly maintain it, a jury was entitled to find it guilty of causing pollution to enter controlled waters. Moreover, if a person removed the pumps required to avoid pollution, he could also be guilty of causing pollution.

A-G's Reference (No 1 of 1994) [1995] 1 WLR 599 (Court of Appeal: Lord Taylor of Gosforth CJ, Alliott and Rix JJ). *Alphacell Ltd v Woodward* [1972] 2 All ER 475, HL, and *National Rivers Authority v Yorkshire Water Services Ltd* [1994] 3 WLR 1202, HL (1994 Abr para 1293) followed.

1297 Pollution control—discharge of waste—discharge into controlled waters—causing pollution—river bed as part of controlled waters

It has been held that a river bed is part of controlled waters and that a person does not cause polluting matter to enter the waters within the meaning of the Water Resources Act 1991, s 85(1) merely by stirring up mud and silt from the river bed, as those substances are already present.

National Rivers Authority v Biffa Waste Services Ltd (1995) Times, 21 November (Queen's Bench Division: Staughton LJ and Rougier J).

1298 Pollution—control—discharge of waste—discharge into controlled waters—meaning of 'controlled waters' and 'pollute'

The Water Resources Act 1991, s 85(1) provides that a person is in contravention of this Act if he causes or knowingly permits any poisonous, noxious or polluting matter to enter any controlled waters.

After higher than normal levels of ammonia were found in a water source, pollution control officers inspected a stream near a water compound. They found that the stream had jumped its normal course through a field because of siltation and was running over another field. A company had caused slurry to be put on both fields with the result that the raw subterranean water became contaminated. The company was convicted of pollution contrary to the 1991 Act, s 85(1). On appeal, it contended that (1) water was only 'controlled water' while it was flowing in the watercourse and, therefore, the stream was not controlled water when it jumped its normal course; (2) the prosecution had to show that some harm had resulted to the water amounting to 'pollution' and since ammonia levels were within permitted limits, no such harmful effect was shown; and (3) the judge should have acceded to a submission of no case to answer because it had not been proved that the company was the owner or occupier of the land or that it carried on the farming enterprise on the land. *Held*, (1) the words 'through which water flows' in the definition of watercourses in the 1991 Act, s 221 governed only sewers and passages, not streams. Watercourses did not cease to be watercourses simply because they were dry. (2) The ordinary dictionary definition of 'pollute' was to be applied and it was clear that it was intended to have a different meaning from poisonous or noxious. Whether matter polluted the water was a question of fact and degree. It was not necessary in such a case to establish actual harm; the likelihood or capability of causing harm to animal or plant life or those who used the water was sufficient. (3) The court was, however, bound to come to the conclusion that no evidence had been put forward to establish that the company was the owner or occupier of the land or carried on the farming enterprise. Accordingly, on that ground, the appeal would be allowed.

R v Dovermoss Ltd (1995) 159 JP 448 (Court of Appeal: Stuart-Smith LJ, Potts and Mitchell JJ).

1299 Pollution—control—prescribed processes and substances

The Environmental Protection (Prescribed Processes and Substances) (Amendment) Regulations 1995, SI 1995/3247 (in force on 8 January 1996), amend the 1991 Regulations, SI 1991/472, which relate to integrated pollution control and local air pollution control under the Environmental Protection Act 1990, Pt I. The regulations amend the descriptions of the following processes: gasification and associated processes, combustion processes, non-ferrous metals, petrochemical processes, manufacture and use of organic chemicals, inorganic chemical processes, pesticide production, pharmaceutical production, paper and pulp manufacturing, coating processes and printing, and the treatment and processing of animal or vegetable matter. In addition, minor amendments and transitional provisions are made.

1300 Pollution—control—traffic pollution—powers of local authority—temporary closure of roads

See *R v Greenwich London Borough Council, ex p Williams*, para 1518.

1301 Protection of environment—financial assistance

The Financial Assistance for Environmental Purposes Order 1995, SI 1995/150 (in force on 15 February 1995), varies the Environmental Protection Act 1990, s 153(1). The order enables financial assistance to be given for the purposes of (a) national or international architectural award schemes or competition schemes relating to the protection, improvement or better understanding of the environment, and (b) the National Forest Company, whose main objects are to promote and implement the National Forest strategy for the creation of the National Forest in the Midlands area of England and related matters.

The Financial Assistance for Environmental Purposes (No 2) Order 1995, SI 1995/554 (in force on 28 March 1995), amends the Environmental Protection Act 1990, s 153(1), to enable the Secretary of State, with the consent of the Treasury, to give financial assistance to or for the purposes of the Energy Saving Trust Limited, a company limited by guarantee whose main objects are to promote and provide for the efficient and rational use of energy in the United Kingdom.

The Financial Assistance for Environmental Purposes (No 3) Order 1995, SI 1995/1085 (in force on 16 May 1995), amends the Environmental Protection Act 1990, s 153(1) so as to enable financial assistance to be given to, or for the purposes of, the Convention on Biological Diversity, the objectives of which are the conservation of biological diversity and the sustainable use of its components, and the United Nations Framework Convention on Climate Change, which aims to achieve stabilisation of greenhouse gas concentrations in the atmosphere at a safe level.

The Financial Assistance for Environmental Purposes (No 4) Order 1995, SI 1995/3099 (in force on 31 December 1995), amends the Environmental Protection Act 1990, s 153(1) to enable the Secretary of State, with the consent of the Treasury, to give financial assistance to the programme administered by the National Radiological Protection Board for conducting radon measurements in premises in England.

1302 Protection of environment—genetically modified organisms—applications for consent for release into the environment

The Genetically Modified Organisms (Deliberate Release) Regulations 1995, SI 1995/304 (in force on 8 March 1995), implement Commission Directive (EC) 94/15 by amending the 1992 Regulations, SI 1992/3280. Separate provision is made for information required in relation to applications to release or market higher plants and that required in relation to applications to release or market other organisms. The regulations amend the provisions relating to applications for consent to release in order to take account of Commission Directive (EC) 94/730. In addition, amendments are made to the requirements for advertising applications for consent to release organisms, the cases and circumstances in which a marketing consent is required and the provisions relating to keeping the public register.

1303 Protection of environment—land drainage—improvement works—assessment of environmental effects

The Land Drainage Improvement Works (Assessment of Environmental Effects) (Amendment) Regulations 1995, SI 1995/2195 (in force on 21 September 1995), amend SI 1988/1217 as follows: (1) modifications are made to the procedure which must be followed by a drainage body where it considers that an environment statement should, or should not, be prepared for proposed improvement works, (2) where a drainage body is required to provide further information to the appropriate minister so that he can decide whether or not to consent to the proposed works, the drainage body must comply with the same requirements as to publicity and consultation as apply in relation to the preparation of an environmental statement, and (3) when notifying its decision as to whether proposed works should be carried out, the drainage body must confirm in writing that it has considered the proposals, the environmental statement, and any representations made in that respect, and the appropriate minister is under a similar duty.

1304 Protection of environment—transport and works—assessment of environmental effects

See para 2425.

1305 Waste—collection and disposal—recycling of waste

The Environmental Protection (Waste Recycling Payments) (Amendment) Regulations 1995, SI 1995/476 (in force on 1 April 1995), substitute the amounts for the determination of a waste disposal authority's net saving in waste disposal costs per tonne of expenditure for the purposes of the Environmental Protection Act 1990, s 52(1) or (3) as set out in the 1992 Regulations, SI 1992/462.

1306 Waste—waste management licensing

The Waste Management Licensing (Amendment etc) Regulations 1995, SI 1995/288 (in force on 1 April 1995), amend the 1994 Regulations, SI 1994/1056, and the Controlled Waste Regulations 1992, SI 1992/588. The 1992 Regulations are amended to provide that scrap metal will become controlled waste for the purposes of the Environmental Protection Act 1990. Amendments to the 1994 Regulations are made in respect of (1) mobile plant; (2) the exclusion from waste management licensing of activities under certain control regimes; (3) exemptions from waste management licensing; (4) registration in connection with exempt activities; (5) provisions relating to activities exempt from waste management licensing; (6) the waste framework directive; (7) the registration of brokers of controlled waste; (8) technical competence.

The Waste Management Licensing (Amendment No 2) Regulations 1995, SI 1995/1950 (in force on 29 July 1995), amend the 1994 Regulations, SI 1994/1056, and the 1995 Regulations,

SI 1995/288, so as to (1) extend to 31 March 1996 a transitional exemption from waste management licensing for certain activities involving the biological or physico-chemical treatment of waste where the person carrying on the activities has done so since before 1 May 1994 and where those activities were not subject to licensing under the Control of Pollution Act 1974, Pt I (waste on land); and (2) extend the transitional period during which the 1994 Regulations, reg 4, which specifies that persons are only to be treated as technically competent to manage certain waste facilities if they hold a relevant certificate of technical competence, does not apply to a person to whom the transitional exemption from licensing applies.

EQUITY

Halsbury's Laws of England (4th edn) Vol 16 (reissue), paras 651–950

1307 Articles

The End is Nigh, Steven Fogel and Emma Slessenger (on the Landlord and Tenant (Covenants) Bill 1995): Estates Gazette, 8 July 1995, p 143

The Law of the Land, David Knight (on the Landlord and Tenants (Covenants) Act 1995): LS Gaz, 26 July 1995, p 17

Leasehold Covenants, Indemnities and Group Reconstructions, Alice Belcher: [1995] Conv 199

Transfer of Property Orders and Cohabitees, Kim Everett and Mark Pawlowski: [1995] Fam Law 417

A Trustee's Lot is Not a Happy One, Robin Towns (on the position of trustees and personal representatives under the system of implied covenants for title): 145 NLJ 1410

Undue Influence, Misrepresentation and the Doctrine of Notice, John Mee (on *Barclays Bank plc v O'Brien* [1993] 4 All ER 417, HL (1993 Abr para 1826)): (1995) CLJ 536

1308 Equitable jurisdiction—fraud—constructive knowledge—duty to investigate

See *Standard Bank London Ltd v The Bank of Tokyo Ltd; Sudwestdeutsche Landesbank Girozentrale v The Bank of Tokyo Ltd*, para 163.

1309 Equitable jurisdiction—fraud—gift

See *Langton v Langton*, para 1482.

1310 Equitable licence—revocation of licence—public entry into shopping centre

The defendants were young men who were creating a nuisance in a shopping centre owned by the plaintiff. The plaintiff sent letters to each of the defendants, informing them that any licence to enter the centre they possessed had been revoked. At first instance it was held that the public had an equitable right to enter the centre provided their conduct was reasonable. On appeal by the plaintiff, *held*, there was no legal right of the public to enter the shopping centre as it had not been dedicated as a highway and there had not been a walkway agreement under the Highways Act 1980, s 35. An equitable licence was not revocable where a person occupying or using land had acted in reliance upon the representation or acquiescence of the person having a proprietary interest in the land. That was not the case here as there was no representation by the plaintiff and no member of the public had altered his position in reliance upon any such representation. It was doubtful whether the principle could apply to create rights for the public at large as the acts or omissions of individuals relying on a representation could not create rights in favour of the public. Accordingly, the appeal would be allowed and the case remitted on the basis that the plaintiff had the right to prevent the defendants from entering in the shopping centre.

    CIN Properties Ltd v Rawlins [1995] 2 EGLR 130 (Court of Appeal: Balcombe, Roch and Saville LJJ).

1311 Equitable remedies—rescission of contract—fraudulent misrepresentation

Australia

The appellant, a company director, signed a personal guarantee of his company's debts in favour of a creditor, the respondent company. The debts related to goods supplied by the respondent to the appellant's company. The guarantee related to all money owed, or which might at any time be owed, to the respondent. It later sued the appellant under the guarantee for a sum representing the total indebtedness of his company to it. At first instance, the trial judge found that the officers of the respondent company had misrepresented to the appellant that he was to guarantee only the future indebtedness of his company. He ordered that the appellant was entitled in equity to rescind the guarantee in so far as it related to any debts owed to the respondent before the guarantee was signed. The appellant appealed arguing that he was entitled to have the guarantee rescinded in its entirety. *Held*, a contract could not be rescinded ab initio unless the parties could be restored substantially to the status quo. As the appellant was unable to return the consideration he had received under the contract for the supply of the goods and had not offered the value of the goods supplied under it, unconditional relief could not be granted. Equity, however, could operate to set aside a contract entirely even though the parties could not be restored substantially to their original positions. In a case involving fraud, the defrauding party should, where possible, be prevented from enjoying the benefit of his fraud. Thus the court could order that the relief was conditional on the party seeking equity doing equity. In the present case, independent of any misrepresentation by the respondent, the appellant was willing to guarantee the future indebtedness of his company. The contract could be enforced to that extent. Accordingly, the appeal would be dismissed.

Vadasz v Pioneer Concrete (SA) Pty Ltd (1995) 130 ALR 570 (High Court). *Barclays Bank plc v O'Brien* [1993] 4 All ER 417, HL (1993 Abr para 1826), applied. *O'Sullivan v Management Agency and Music Ltd* [1985] 3 All ER 351, CA (1984 Abr para 1074), *Erlanger v New Sombrero Phosphate Co* (1878) 3 App Cas 1218, HL, and *Spence v Crawford* [1939] 3 All ER 271, HL, followed. *TSB Bank plc v Camfield* [1995] 1 All ER 951, CA (1994 Abr para 1994), not followed.

1312 Fiduciary relationship—tracing of assets—building society mortgage—discharge of previous charge—fiduciary relationship between building society and purchasers' solicitor

The defendant charged his property to a building society (H). Three years later, the plaintiff secured a charge over the property as a judgment creditor. The defendant exchanged a contract for sale of the property and the purchasers of the property obtained a mortgage advance from their building society (AN) secured by a first legal charge over the property. AN sent the balance of the purchase money by telegraphic transfer to the purchasers' solicitors, who then transmitted the funds to the first defendant's solicitors who in turn transferred the funds to H. The plaintiff brought an action for enforcement of his charging order against AN and the defendant and AN brought a counterclaim. *Held*, AN's money could be traced to the payment to H and was used to discharge H's legal charge. Therefore, AN was entitled to be subrogated to H's legal charge to the extent that AN's money had redeemed the charge, in which case there was nothing left to which the plaintiff's charging order could attach. One could only trace in equity where there was a fiduciary relationship which attracted the equitable jurisdiction. In this case, that requirement was satisfied because as soon as the purchasers' solicitors received the money it was held in trust for AN which had never intended to be an unsecured creditor but wished to retain beneficial interest in its money until that money became a first legal mortgage on the property. Accordingly, the plaintiff's action would be dismissed and AN's counterclaim would be granted.

Boscawen v Bajwa; Abbey National plc v Boscawen [1995] 4 All ER 769 (Court of Appeal: Stuart-Smith, Waite and Millett LJJ).

1313 Fiduciary relationship—tracing of assets—proceeds of share fraud—tracing—pleading rights of a third party

The plaintiff brought an action against a company based on the knowing receipt by that company of £2.325m, part of the proceeds of a massive share fraud. On a remission to the Chancery Division by the Court of Appeal for the purpose of a decision on quantum (1) it was established that the company's share-pushing operation was wholly fraudulent, worthless shares being sold to about 4,000 would-be investors; (2) it appeared that the plaintiff's action had been the only individual claim brought against the company; and (3) the plaintiff and the trustee in bankruptcy had agreed that the proceeds of the present action should be divided 70:30 between the plaintiff and the other victims. The plaintiff submitted that in the light of the 70:30 agreement and the near certainty that no further individual claim would now be made by any of the other victims, there was nothing inequitable in an order for the payment of the whole of the £2.325m to the plaintiff, his lost assets being specifically traceable. The company contended that it was open to any of the other victims similarly to trace their losses and argued that not the whole, but only a fraction of the £2.325m could belong in equity to the plaintiff, the balance belonging in equity to the other victims. *Held*, it was almost inconceivable that any of the other victims would now try to mount an individual claim. The evidence indicated that, in practice, all their interests were being looked after by the trustee in bankruptcy. Whether it was possible for the rights of a third party to be raised by way of defence to a claim to trace would depend on the nature of the claim and the surrounding circumstances. In the present case such a plea was inappropriate and, accordingly, there would be an order that the company pay to the plaintiff the whole sum of £2.325m.

El Ajou v Dollar Land Holdings plc (No 2) [1995] 2 All ER 213 (Chancery Division: Robert Walker J). For earlier related proceedings see [1994] 2 All ER 685, CA (1993 Abr para 470).

1314 Notice—constructive notice—restrictions—imputation of agent's knowledge to principal

See *Halifax Mortgage Services Ltd v Stepsky*, para 2110.

1315 Presumption of advancement—home inhabited by father and son—property conveyed into son's sole name—intestate death of father

The defendant and his father lived in a property conveyed to the defendant in his sole name. A deed was drawn up by the father's solicitors whereby the defendant held the property on trust for his father and himself in unequal shares. The deed was never sent to the father and remained unsigned at the time of his death when the plaintiff, the defendant's sister, claimed that she was entitled to a share in the property. The defendant disagreed and, at first instance, the judge stated that the plaintiff had failed to rebut the presumption of advancement which vested the property in the defendant. On appeal by the plaintiff, *held*, the presumption of advancement and resulting trust was useful in solving questions of title but was easily rebutted by relatively slight evidence. Here, the fact that the father had never informed his son that he had instructed his solicitors not to proceed with the trust and that no reason had been expressed for the father wishing to divest himself of all interest in the house, was sufficient to rebut the presumption and, accordingly, the appeal would be allowed.

McGrath v Wallis [1995] 2 FLR 114 (Court of Appeal: Nourse and Hirst LJJ and Sir Ralph Gibson).

1316 Principles of equity—clean hands doctrine—beneficial interest in house—fraudulent purpose of registration of house

See *Nelson v Nelson*, para 2988.

1317 Principles of equity—clean hands doctrine—transfer of property—illegal purpose—whether presumption of advancement rebutted by illegal purpose

A father transferred shares to his son for no consideration with the illegal purpose of deceiving creditors into believing that the father did not own any shares in the company. The illegal act was never carried out as the transfer was not shown to the creditors. The father sought to recover the property, relying on the illegality of the transaction to rebut the presumption of advancement, and claiming that he was able to do so because the illegal purpose was never carried out. *Held*, the father was entitled to recover the property. The presumption of advancement was rebutted by the illegal purpose since it was clear that the father intended to retain a beneficial interest in the property. The father could rely on evidence of the illegal purpose in order to rebut the presumption since the purpose had not been carried into effect. The fact that he had withdrawn from the illegal transaction provided an exception to the general rule that the court would not lend its aid to a person who founded their action on an illegal act.

Tribe v Tribe (1995) Times, 14 August (Court of Appeal: Nourse, Millett and Otton LJJ). *Perpetual Executors and Trustees Association of Australia Ltd v Wright* (1917) 23 CLR 185, *Palaniappa Chettiar v Arunasalam Chettiar* [1962] AC 294, PC followed.

1318 Restrictive covenant—discharge or modification—benefit to sole objector

The applicants sought the discharge or modification of a restrictive covenant which prevented the use of an annexe in the grounds of their house as an independent dwelling house for which they had obtained planning permission. They contended that the restriction conferred no practical benefit on the local council, which objected to the application on the ground that, if the application succeeded, its ability to control undesirable forms of development would be jeopardised. *Held*, the restriction impeded a reasonable user without securing to the council a practical benefit of substantial value or advantage. Accordingly, the restriction would be modified so as to allow the occupation of the annexe as an independent dwelling house, subject to a condition restricting its further development. The use of the annexe as an independent dwelling would not affect the locality any more than did its present use so that the council's policy of attempting to prevent obtrusive development in the open countryside would not be undermined. The fact that planning permission had been granted for the proposed use was a matter to be taken into account but did not bind the tribunal in the exercise of its statutory jurisdiction to discharge or modify a restrictive covenant.

Re Williamson's Application (1994) 68 P & CR 384 (Lands Tribunal: Judge Marder QC).

1319 Restrictive covenant—discharge or modification—general building scheme—benefit to objectors

The Law of Property Act 1925, s 84(1)(aa) provides that on the application of any person interested in any freehold land affected by any restriction arising under a covenant or otherwise as to the user of the building thereon, the Lands Tribunal may wholly or partially discharge or modify any such restriction on being satisfied that the continued existence thereof would impede reasonable user of the land for public or private purposes, or would unless modified so impede such user.

The applicant, a property development company, bought a semi-detached house which was situated on an estate of semi-detached houses. All the properties on the estate, including the applicant's property, were subject to a restrictive covenant which provided that the owners would not use their property for any purpose other than that of a private dwelling house or as the residence of a doctor, dentist, or surgery ('the covenant'). The applicant also owned a neighbouring area of land, and was granted conditional planning permission to demolish the semi-detached house, build new houses, and construct an access road. As construction of the road would have breached the covenant, the applicant sought to discharge or modify it, having regard to the 1925 Act, s 84(1)(aa). The application was opposed by a number of residents living on the estate ('the objectors'). *Held*, a general building scheme existed, as both the applicant and the objectors had derived title from a common vendor, and the covenant was consistent with a general development scheme and was intended to benefit the properties. Such a scheme established a system of local law which applied to the whole estate, and those with the benefit of it were entitled to enforce it even if they might be only temporarily or indirectly affected by any development on the estate. There was therefore a greater presumption that the covenant would be upheld, and a greater onus of proof on the applicant to show that the requirements of the 1925 Act, s 84 were satisfied. Here, the proposal to build an access road did not amount to reasonable user of the land for private purposes. Although the covenant impeded the proposed development, such an impediment was a practical benefit of substantial value to the objectors, as it resulted in the maintenance of the status quo. In particular, the objectors would be able to retain the street scene which would otherwise be spoilt by new houses, avoid the increase in traffic that would be generated by an access road, and would not be disturbed by demolition and construction work. Moreover, refusing to discharge the covenant was not contrary to public interest. Accordingly, the application would be dismissed.

Re Bromor Properties Ltd's Application (1995) 70 P & CR 569 (Lands Tribunal: PH Clarke FRICS).

1320 Restrictive covenant—enforceability—covenant against carrying on specified business

The first plaintiffs sold land to a local authority subject to a restrictive covenant for the benefit of land retained by them that the purchasers and their successors in title would not at any time carry on or permit to be carried on upon the land conveyed any business comprising the sale and purchase of fuel. The authority sold on the burdened land and the purchaser of that land subsequently sold a small portion of it to the owners of adjoining land between the burdened land and the plaintiffs' retained land. Part of the adjoining land was then acquired by the defendants for the construction of a supermarket. The first plaintiffs gave possession of part of their retained land to the second plaintiff for the purposes of a filling station. The defendants contracted to acquire the remainder of the adjoining land, including the small portion of the burdened land, proposing to use the small portion of land (which remained subject to the restrictive covenant) for access to the remainder of the land (which was not subject to the covenant), on which they proposed to run a filling station. The plaintiffs sought a declaration that the defendants' proposal would be a breach of the restrictive covenant. *Held*, the use of the burdened land to facilitate business on land not subject to the covenant did not amount to the carrying on of business on the burdened land. Unless and until some business was carried on on the burdened land, the covenant was not infringed. The restrictive covenant in the present case was a restriction on the use of a specific piece of land in a particular way. The burdened land was not being used for an infringing trade and it was not possible to extend the burden of the covenant on the basis that customers came to the burdened land with the intention of trading on land not subject to the covenant. Accordingly, the declaration would be refused.

Elliott v Safeway Stores plc [1995] 1 WLR 1396 (Chancery Division: Judge Paul Baker QC).

1321   Specific performance

See SPECIFIC PERFORMANCE.

1322   Subrogation—legal charge to bank—charge discharged by finance company— company's entitlement to be subrogated to bank

See *Castle Phillips Finance v Piddington*, para 2108.

ESTOPPEL

Halsbury's Laws of England (4th edn) Vol 16 (reissue), paras 951–1091

1323   Estoppel by conduct—negligence

See *Standard Bank London Ltd v The Bank of Tokyo Ltd; Sudwestdeutsche Landesbank Girozentrale v The Bank of Tokyo Ltd*, para 163.

1324   Estoppel by conduct—statutory tenancy—second succession of family member

See *Daejan Properties Ltd v Mahoney*, para 1852.

1325   Estoppel by deed—doctrine of 'feeding estoppel'—application to registered land

The defendant purported to charge a property by way of legal mortgage to a bank by means of a legal charge. At the date of the charge, the defendant was not, and was not entitled to be, registered as proprietor of the property, although he had agreed with the registered proprietor to buy his interest in the property. The registered proprietor subsequently executed a transfer of the property to the defendant, who was duly registered as proprietor. The bank then applied for the charge to be registered. The defendant objected to registration and the judge ruled that the bank was not entitled to have the existing charge registered and had to obtain a fresh charge. On appeal, the bank argued that although the defendant could not create a legal charge on the date he purported to do so, the effect of the legal charge was to create a legal mortgage by estoppel. When the defendant later obtained the legal title by representation, the estoppel was fed and the bank became entitled to register the legal charge without the need to obtain a fresh charge. *Held*, estoppel by deed did not depend upon the presence of any recital or other express representation of title and the companion doctrine of feeding the estoppel operated automatically without further assurance in such a case. If the case had concerned unregistered land, the bank would have acquired a legal mortgage by estoppel on the date of the purported charge and a legal mortgage in interest when the defendant later obtained the legal estate. There was nothing in the land registration legislation which precluded the registration of a legal charge granted by the person who was afterwards registered as proprietor, but executed before he became entitled to be so registered. Accordingly, the doctrine applied to the creation of a legal charge of registered land. The appeal would be allowed.

First National Bank plc v Thompson [1996] 1 All ER 140 (Court of Appeal: Staughton, Millett and Ward LJJ).

1326   Estoppel by statement—local housing authority—undertaking not to evict squatter

See *Southwark London Borough Council v Logan*, para 1810.

1327   Issue estoppel—bankruptcy proceedings—dismissal of application to set aside statutory demand

See *Eberhardt & Co v Mair*, para 178.

1328 Issue estoppel—determination in respect of compulsorily acquired land— subsequent proceedings to determine compensation in respect of retained land

See *Porter v Secretary of State for Transport*, para 546.

1329 Issue estoppel—Lloyd's litigation

See *Barrow v Bankside Members Agency Ltd*, para 1738.

1330 Issue estoppel—proceedings concerning children—specific finding of fact—finding of sexual abuse by parent

A local authority commenced proceedings concerning three children whom it believed to be at risk of sexual abuse by the father of one of them. The only ground for its application was that the father had sexually abused children in two other families of which he was a member. In proceedings relating to the second of those families, the judge had made a finding of fact that the father had sexually abused the children of the first family, and had stated that there was a real possibility that he had also abused a child of the second family. At a preliminary hearing, the issue arose as to whether the doctrine of issue estoppel prevented the parties in the current proceedings from challenging the judge's findings of fact in the earlier proceedings. *Held*, where the issue of the perpetration of sexual abuse was directly relevant in earlier proceedings, was fully investigated by the court and was the subject of an express finding against a party in accordance with the appropriate standard of proof, then it would not be appropriate to challenge that finding in later proceedings. To that extent, the doctrine of issue estoppel was to be imported into children cases. In the present case, the finding of fact relating to the first family was not 'necessary' to the judge's decision regarding the second family, and was not fully argued since the father was not present at the hearing. The finding was also made solely on the judge's reading of written evidence, and was expressed to be made on a balance of probabilities. It was now doubtful whether a finding on such a low standard of proof would have validity. The judge's observations in regard to the child of the second family did not amount to a finding of fact. Thus, neither of the judge's findings were sufficiently established to give rise to an estoppel situation. Accordingly, a declaration would be made that the judge's findings were not findings which had been established for the purposes of the instant proceedings, and fell to be established by evidence.

Re L (Minors) (Care Proceedings: Issue Estoppel) [1995] 1 FCR 221 (Family Division: Wilson J).
See also *K v P (Children Act Proceedings: Estoppel)*, para 410.

1331 Proprietary estoppel—reliance on promises—detriment—burden of proof

The plaintiff lived with the deceased in a homosexual relationship for all except one year during a 16-year period, until the deceased's death. The plaintiff helped the deceased to run several commercial ventures during that period, and also acted as his chauffeur and companion. In return, the deceased gave the plaintiff pocket money and paid for all his living and clothing expenses. During the latter part of their relationship, the deceased repeatedly promised the plaintiff that he would leave him his property. The deceased made a will naming a particular property as his gift to the plaintiff, but he failed to alter his will when he subsequently sold that property and bought another, and the original gift was therefore adeemed on his death. As a result, the plaintiff received only a minimal legacy, and therefore made a claim against the deceased's estate based on the principle of proprietary estoppel. On the basis of the plaintiff's trial testimony, the judge concluded that it had not been proved that the plaintiff had acted in reliance on the promises made to him. On appeal, *held*, to establish proprietary estoppel, a plaintiff had to show that there was a sufficient link between the promises relied upon and the conduct which constituted the detriment, although the promises did not have to be the sole inducement for the conduct. Once that had been shown, it was for the defendant to prove that the plaintiff had not relied on those promises. Here, the plaintiff had believed that he would inherit the deceased's property, and that belief had been encouraged by the deceased. The plaintiff had suffered detriment in that he had received minimal wages throughout his years of service to the deceased. The trial judge had erred in his conclusion, as there was evidence that promises were made to the plaintiff and that the plaintiff's conduct was such that inducement could be inferred, and the defendants had not discharged the burden of proving that the plaintiff had not relied on those promises. Accordingly, the appeal would be allowed.

Wayling v Jones (1995) 69 P & CR 170 (Court of Appeal: Balcombe, Leggatt and Hoffmann LJJ). *Re Basham (deceased)* [1987] 1 All ER 405 (1986 Abr para 965) applied.

1332   Res judicata—application to unfair dismissal and wrongful dismissal proceedings

Scotland

An industrial tribunal dismissed an unfair dismissal claim after finding that the claimant had voluntarily left her employment. She then brought a further action against the employer claiming that she had been dismissed without notice in breach of her contract. In its defence, the employer pleaded res judicata on the basis of the tribunal's earlier findings. *Held*, the subject matter of the proceeding before the tribunal was whether the employee had a well-founded claim that she had been unfairly dismissed and should be accorded the statutory remedies consequential on such a dismissal. This did not depend upon whether there had been a breach of contract. The character of that claim was different to that of the present proceedings and, therefore, the doctrine of res judicata did not apply. The employer's plea would be dismissed.

   Clink v Speyside Distillery Co Ltd 1995 SLT 1344 (Outer House).

1333   Res judicata—mother and child with disability bringing separate actions for damages—whether principle applies

A mother brought an action against a local authority for damages for illness arising from disrepair to the council house in which she and her family lived. She reached a settlement with the authority but her child, who suffered from Down's Syndrome, then brought a claim for damages by her stepfather and next friend. At first instance, the judge found that the child's dependence on her mother created a sufficient nexus between them that they should be regarded as the same party. On the child's appeal, *held*, the judge's decision stretched the bounds of the doctrine of res judicata beyond breaking point. His reasoning meant that although the child's claim would be defeated because of her disability and dependence on her mother, her older brothers, lacking that same nexus with their mother, could bring their own separate actions. Accordingly, the appeal would be allowed.

   C v Hackney London Borough Council [1996] 1 All ER 973 (Court of Appeal: Butler-Sloss, Simon Brown and Saville LJJ).

1334   Res judicata—unlitigated monetary claim—person not party to earlier proceedings

See *Chin v Hackney London Borough Council*, para 709.

EUROPEAN COMMUNITIES

In conformity with the arrangement of titles in *Halsbury's Laws*, this title appears as the final title, on pages 945–978 post.

EVIDENCE [CIVIL]

Halsbury's Laws of England (4th edn) Vol 17, paras 1–400

1335   Articles

Access to Expertise, Nikki Honey (on a new directory of expert witnesses): SJ Supp, 30 June 1995, p 14
Alcohol Experts in Family Cases, Jonathan Goodliffe: 145 NLJ 633
Are There Any Clothes for the Emperor to Wear? Michael Zander (on the Woolf Inquiry into the civil justice system): 145 NLJ 154
Audit Negligence: The Expert Accountant's Role, George Sim: SJ Supp, 30 June 1995, p 32
BEST and the Legal Profession, Bethan Hubbard (on the national database of scientific expertise): SJ Supp, 30 June 1995, p 36
Calling in Evidence, Steven Baker: LS Gaz, 1 June 1995, p 20
Challenging DNA Evidence, Alec Samuels: 159 JP Jo 156
Court Experts, Frederick Lawton: 139 SJ 793
Emotional Abuse and Expert Evidence, Carole Kaplan and Anne Thompson: [1995] Fam Law 628
Essays on the Woolf Report, Michael Zander: 145 NLJ 1866

Expert Tax Witnesses, Peter Vaines: 145 NLJ 1035
Expert Testimony and Cerebral Palsy, Paul Pimm: SJ Supp, 30 June 1995, p 46
Experts on Trial, John Ellison (on Lord Woolf's recommendations on expert witnesses): 139 SJ 744
Forensic Science Help, Jeffrey Bayes: SJ Supp, 30 June 1995, p 24
Guardians and Experts, Betty Foster and Michael Preston Shoot: [1995] Fam Law 250
The Independent? Julian Cohen (on the conflicting role and duties of expert witnesses): 145 NLJ 1048
Proving Comparables, Jim Cotter (on the effect of the Civil Evidence Bill on use of comparable evidence in valuations): Estates Gazette, 5 August 1995, p 66
Rehabilitation Experts: What They Do and Where to Find Them, Richard Hoare: SJ Supp, 30 June 1995, p 18
Use of Experts in Children's Cases, Victor Smith: 159 JP Jo 635, 648
Waffle Free Zones? Gordon Exall (on the intended effect of Lord Taylor's and Sir Richard Scott's Practice Direction on Civil Litigation: Case Management): 139 SJ 109
Will Woolf Work? Steven Gee (on Lord Woolf's Inquiry): 139 SJ 674
Woolf's Justice, Ramnik Shah (on the Woolf Inquiry into the civil justice system): 145 NLJ 147

1336   Affidavit evidence—affidavits, exhibits and documents—form

Lord Taylor of Gosforth CJ has issued the following *Practice Direction* ([1995] 1 WLR 510).
Paragraph 1 of *Practice Direction (Evidence: Documents)* [1983] 3 All ER 33 (1983 Abr para 2585) is amended as follows to add a new requirement (iv) namely:
'the identifying initials and number of each exhibit to the affidavit'.
The existing requirement (iv) is renumbered as (v), and 'EWJ3, 4 and 5' is added to the end of the example given.
In all other respects *Practice Direction (Evidence: Documents)* [1983] 3 All ER 33 is affirmed.

1337   Affidavit evidence—disclosure of evidence prior to hearing—contempt of court committal proceedings

See *Re B (a Minor) (Contempt: Evidence)*, para 633.

1338   Affidavit evidence—hearsay—nature of proceedings

RSC Ord 41, r 5(1) provides that in any final proceedings affidavit evidence may contain only such facts as the deponent is able of his own knowledge to prove. Under RSC Ord 41, r 5(2) an affidavit sworn for the purpose of being used in interlocutory proceedings may contain hearsay evidence
The applicants, who were disgruntled creditors of a debtor, applied to the court under the Insolvency Act 1986, s 262 to challenge the voluntary arrangements made by the majority of the creditors. They claimed the proceedings were interlocutory and an affidavit consisting almost entirely of hearsay evidence, was admissible under RSC Ord 41, r 5(2). *Held,* the court was required to give a final ruling on the challenge to the voluntary arrangements made by the majority of the creditors. Thus, the application under the 1986 Act, s 262 would decide the rights of the parties. The fact that the court might make consequential orders after the final judgment did not mean that these were interlocutory proceedings. The proceedings were final proceedings and hearsay evidence was not admissible on the application. Accordingly, the applicants' request to be permitted to adduce the affidavit in evidence would be refused.
Re a Debtor (No 87 of 1993) [1996] 1 BCLC 55 (Chancery Division: Rimer J).

1339   Cases involving children

See CHILDREN AND YOUNG PERSONS.

1340   Civil Evidence Act 1995

The Civil Evidence Act 1995 makes provision for the admissibility of hearsay evidence, the proof of certain documentary evidence and the admissibility and proof of official actuarial tables in civil proceedings. The Act received the royal assent on 8 November 1995 and comes into force on a day or days to be appointed. For details of commencement, see the commencement table in the title STATUTES.
Section 1 abolishes the rule against the admission of hearsay in civil proceedings. Hearsay evidence which is already admissible by virtue of other statutes is not affected by the provisions

of the Act. Section 2 requires parties, subject to rules of court and unless they agree otherwise, to give fair notice of their intention to adduce hearsay evidence. Section 3 provides for a power to call for cross-examination a person whose statement has been tendered as hearsay evidence and s 4 sets out the considerations relevant to the weighing of hearsay evidence. Section 5 makes provision in relation to the competence and credibility of the makers of statements and s 6 applies the provisions of the Act to previous statements of witnesses. Section 7 provides for specified common law rules relating to hearsay to be superseded by the provisions of the Act and for other specified common law rules to continue to have effect.

Section 8 provides for the proof of statements contained in documents and copies of documents and allows copies of copies to be received in evidence. Section 9 provides for the receipt in evidence of records of a business or a public authority (as defined) without further proof. Under s 10, the actuarial tables (together with explanatory notes) for use in personal injury and fatal accident cases issued by the Government Actuary's Department are admissible in evidence for the purpose of assessing, in personal injury actions, the sum to be awarded as general damages for future pecuniary loss. Section 11 defines 'civil proceedings', s 12 provides for the making of rules of court necessary for carrying into effect the provisions of the Act, and s 13 deals with interpretation. Section 14 contains savings, s 15 and Schs 1, 2 contain consequential amendments and repeals, and s 16 deals with short title, commencement and extent.

1341 Criminal cases

See CRIMINAL EVIDENCE AND PROCEDURE.

1342 Documentary evidence—transcript of judge's summing up

The Civil Evidence Act 1968, s 4(1) provides that a statement contained in a document is admissible as evidence of any fact stated therein of which direct oral evidence would be admissible, if the document is or forms part of a record compiled by a person acting under a duty from information supplied by a person (whether acting under a duty or not) who had, or may be reasonably supposed to have had, reasonable knowledge of the matters dealt with in that information and which, if not supplied by that person to the compiler of the record directly, was supplied to him by the compiler of the record indirectly through one or more intermediaries each acting under a duty.

The plaintiff company brought civil proceedings against a number of people who had been involved in a gold bullion robbery on its premises. Although the defendant had not been tried for any offence in connection with the robbery, the plaintiff claimed that he had had dealings with a person who had been convicted of conspiring to the robbery. In particular, it was alleged that the defendant had laundered part of the proceeds of sale of the stolen gold. On his application for an order that judges' summings up in the criminal proceedings were inadmissible evidence in the civil proceedings, *held*, transcripts of judges' summings up were not 'any other admissible evidence' within the meaning of the 1968 Act, s 11(2)(b), and were second-hand hearsay for the purposes of the 1968 Act, s 2(1). However, having regard to the 1968 Act, s 4(1), official transcripts of evidence given in the ordinary course of legal proceedings formed part of a record. As there was therefore scope for regarding transcripts of judges' summings up in the same way, such transcripts were also admissible as evidence. Accordingly, the application would be dismissed.

Brinks Ltd v Abu Saleh [1995] 4 All ER 74 (Chancery Division: Rimer J).

1343 Exchange of witness statements—witness unable to recall facts in statement—admissibility of statement

RSC Ord 38, r 2A(2) provides that at the summons for directions in an action commenced by writ, the court must direct every party to serve on the other parties written statements of the oral evidence which the party intends to adduce on any issues of fact to be decided at trial. Rule 2A(7)(a) provides that the court may direct that the statement served is to stand as the evidence-in-chief of the witness.

The plaintiff commenced proceedings against the defendant for breach of professional duty in relation to advice given on the purchase of an insurance company. As a great deal of evidence was to be involved in the case, one of the plaintiff's main witnesses was interviewed on a number of occasions by the plaintiff's solicitors, and a lengthy witness statement was produced and signed by him three years later, based on the interviews. At trial, the witness confirmed that his witness statement was true and that it contained his evidence, but on cross-examination it emerged that he could no longer remember some of the events described in his statement. On the defendant's application for an order that the witness statement was inadmissible as evidence-in-chief, *held*,

Ord 38, r 2A was introduced to save trial time, as it made examination-in-chief unnecessary, enabled the parties to know in advance what the remaining factual issues were, and also enabled them to prepare cross-examination in advance. The fact that a witness made an assertion of fact in his witness statement which he could not subsequently remember during cross-examination, did not necessarily make his statement inadmissible, although it might render it less reliable. In those circumstances, it was necessary for the court to evaluate the witness's assertion that his evidence-in-chief in the witness statement was true. Where the facts of a case were numerous and complex and the witness's memory had faded between the time that proofs of evidence were taken and the time that he signed his witness statement, the court could exercise its discretion to allow the statement to be used as long as the witness was available for cross-examination. In those circumstances, there could be no real prejudice or unfairness to the opposing party, and in the instant case, the defendant had had the main witness statement for several months before trial, enabling it to prepare detailed cross-examination. The witness statement was therefore admissible and, accordingly, the application would be dismissed.

Nederlandse Reassurantie Groep Holding NV v Bacon & Woodrow (No 2) [1995] 2 Lloyd's Rep 404 (Queen's Bench Division: Colman J).

1344 Exclusion of evidence—exclusion of admissible oral evidence—justices' failure to hear oral evidence

See *Re M (Contact)*, para 402.

1345 Expert evidence—appointment of court expert

Proceedings for professional negligence were brought against the defendant surveyors in respect of a large number of mortgage valuations. The surveyors made applications to call an expert in respect of each of the properties and the plaintiff applied for the appointment of a court valuation officer under RSC Ord 40. *Held*, in considering whether to allow the calling of such a large number of experts the question to be asked was whether it was likely to assist in the just, expeditious and economical disposal of the action. There would be advantages in having a local expert for each property but the court was concerned with doing justice, not with achieving an expensive and unnecessary perfection, and the appointment of a court expert would obviate unfairness by placing the parties in the same position. A court appointed expert was not merely a witness and, in giving him instructions under RSC Ord 40, the court could order him to conduct his inquiry by any fair means authorised by those instructions, even if that involved the incorporation in his report of material such as comparables outside his own experience which in the evidence of a witness would be inadmissible as hearsay. Accordingly, the plaintiff's application would be allowed and the surveyors' applications would be dismissed.

Abbey National Mortgages plc v Key Surveyors Nationwide Ltd [1995] 40 EG 130 (Official Referee's Business: Judge Hicks QC).

1346 Expert evidence—expert witnesses—matters in respect of which evidence may be given

The plaintiff was awarded damages against the defendant for negligence following a road traffic accident, although the amount were reduced by 25 per cent in respect of his contributory negligence. On the defendant's appeal, *held*, the admissibility of expert evidence was governed by the Civil Evidence Act 1972 and rules of court. Although the court could restrict the number of expert witnesses, it could not do so on the grounds that their evidence was irrelevant or unnecessary. Although expert witnesses could assist a judge in making primary findings of fact, they were not entitled to draw conclusions from the statements of witnesses to the accident, or to draw conclusions as to how the accident could have been avoided. They were matters for the trial judge to determine, and expert evidence which attempted to deal with such matters was both irrelevant and inadmissible. Moreover, the need for expert evidence in road traffic accidents ought be the exception rather than the rule. On the facts of the case, the appeal would be allowed.

Liddell v Middleton (1995) Times, 17 July (Court of Appeal: Stuart-Smith, Peter Gibson and Hutchison LJJ).

1347 Expert evidence—personal injury action—examination of plaintiff—request by defendant for plaintiff to be examined by magnetic resonance scan

See *Hill v West Lancashire Health Authority*, para 1350.

1348   Oaths—prescribed bodies

The Commissioners for Oaths (Prescribed Bodies) Regulations 1995, SI 1995/1676 (in force on 31 July 1995), provide that the Institute of Legal Executives is a prescribed body and therefore members of the institute are able to act as commissioners for oaths.

1349   Parol evidence—written contract—common undisclosed intention—relevance

See *New Hampshire Insurance Co v MGN Ltd*, para 650.

1350   Personal injury—evidence—medical examination of plaintiff—request by defendant for plaintiff to be examined by magnetic resonance scan

The plaintiff claimed damages for personal injuries from the defendant health authority arising from allegedly negligent medical treatment surrounding his birth. The plaintiff alleged that he suffered from spastic hemiplegia microcephaly and intellectual impairment. The defendant requested the right to carry out a magnetic resonance imaging scan on the plaintiff, but the plaintiff refused. On the defendant's application to the court, the judge ordered that the defendant be afforded the opportunity to examine the plaintiff as requested, failing which there was to be a stay of the proceedings. On the plaintiff's appeal, *held*, the first thing that had to be decided was whether or not the request for the test to be carried out was a reasonable request. If the court decided the request was reasonable, it then had to determine whether any refusal was reasonable. If the court concluded that both the request and the refusal were reasonable, it had to determine, on a balance between the reasonableness of the request and the reasonableness of the refusal, what was the right decision. In the present case, the request was a reasonable one. The refusal was also reasonable. On the question of balancing, the defendant submitted that the risks involved in the test were negligible, that the test was useful and that the reasonableness of the request outweighed the reasonableness of the refusal. The plaintiff submitted that where tests involved any risk to health, it was a risk that the plaintiff ought not to undergo. The question would be decided in favour of the plaintiff on the ground that the risk, whether it be low, very low or minimal, remained a risk to health. There was a danger to the plaintiff, and this was not a case where a patient was asked to accept a risk in the course of treatment, and could choose to accept such a risk balanced against the advantages of the treatment. It was a test which the plaintiff was being asked to undergo for the purposes of enabling the other party in the litigation to make an assessment of his injury. Balancing the risk against the prospective results, the reasonableness of the refusal outweighed the reasonableness of the request. Accordingly, the appeal would be allowed.

Hill v West Lancashire Health Authority (26 May 1995, unreported) (Queen's Bench Division, Liverpool: Gage J) (Iain Goldrein, Messrs Evill & Coleman, for the plaintiff; Nicholas Braslavsky, West Lancashire Health Authority, for the defendant). Kindly submitted for publication by Iain Goldrein, Barrister.

EXECUTION

Halsbury's Laws of England (4th edn) Vol 17, paras 401–700

1351   Articles

Bankruptcy and Bailiffs, John Kruse: LA, June 1995, p 16
Impounding and Insolvency, John Kruse: LA, September 1995, p 24
Walking Possession Redefined, John Kruse: 145 NLJ 1337

1352   Writ of fieri facias—seizure of goods—tools of trade

See *Brookes v Harris*, para 2640.

EXECUTORS AND ADMINISTRATORS

Halsbury's Laws of England (4th edn) Vol 17, paras 701–1591

1353 Articles

Administration of Estates, Philip Rossdale (on the Law of Property (Miscellaneous Provisions) Act 1994): 139 SJ 747
The Executor's Duty to Inform, James Sunnucks: 145 NLJ 1408
Firearms—Advice for Executors, Peter Sarony: 145 NLJ 1405
Probate and Administering Estates: Dealing With Delay, Philip Rossdale: 139 SJ 424
A Trustee's Lot is Not a Happy One, Robin Towns (on the position of trustees and personal representatives under the system of implied covenants for title): 145 NLJ 1410
When a Grant of Representation Should be Renounced, Philip Rossdale: 139 SJ 10

1354 Family provision—application by cohabitant—assessment of maintenance

The applicant, a 56-year-old woman, lived with and was wholly maintained by the deceased for 19 months until his death. He had deceived the applicant into believing he was a widower although his wife of 30 years was still alive and the marriage was still subsisting. The relationship between the applicant and the deceased had been foundering for several months before the death and the applicant had been looking for employment. The deceased made no provision for the applicant in his will and she therefore applied for maintenance out of his estate under the Inheritance (Provision For Family and Dependants) Act 1975, s 1(1)(e). *Held*, in all the circumstances, a reasonable testator in the deceased's position would have provided the applicant with lifetime maintenance, although he would not have provided a home. A needs figure of £7,500 per annum was adopted and the applicant was awarded capitalised maintenance of £101,500, together with costs, out of the estate.

Re P (14 December 1995, unreported) (Taunton District Registry: District Judge Turner) (Kindly submitted for publication by Messrs Clarke Willmott & Clarke, Solicitors).

1355 Family provision—application by illegitimate child—leave to apply out of time

A deceased's will provided for his substantial estate to be left to his sister subject to a power vested in trustees to appoint in favour of a wide class within two years of his death. He had an illegitimate child who came into that class. Although the mother of that child knew of his death, a claim was not made until two and a half years later, after probate had been granted and the trustees had exercised their power of appointment in favour of the deceased's widow, their son and her two children. The child appealed against the refusal to allow her to pursue her claim outside the limitation period prescribed by the Inheritance (Provision for Family and Dependants) Act 1975, s 4. *Held*, although the mother could not adequately explain the delay, and although there was no general rule whereby permission could be granted to allow a child to make an application out of time, the claim was brought by the child herself and it would be unfortunate if she suffered as a result of the mother's omission. Further, there had been no physical distribution of the estate and the child's claim had a very good prospect of success. Accordingly, the appeal would be allowed.

Re W (A Minor) [1995] 2 FCR 689 (Family Division: Wilson J). *Re Salmon (deceased)* [1980] 3 All ER 532 (1980 Abr para 2195) applied.

1356 Family provision—application by son—moral obligation to give effect to mutual wills made in favour of adult son

See *Goodchild v Goodchild*, para 3086.

1357 Intestacy—father killed by son—son's entitlement to father's estate—application of forfeiture rule

The plaintiff killed his parents while he was suffering from a mental disease. He was convicted of their manslaughter on grounds of diminished responsibility and a hospital order was made in respect of the plaintiff under the Mental Health Act 1983, s 37. The plaintiff's parents died intestate. Although the plaintiff accepted the well-established rule of public policy, known as the forfeiture rule, which precluded a person who had unlawfully killed another from acquiring a benefit in consequence of the killing, he contended that the decision in *Gray v Barr* did not require a court to apply the forfeiture rule in every case of manslaughter, but only in those where the person making the claim had been guilty of deliberate, intentional and unlawful violence or threats of violence. *Held*, in *Royse v Royse* the court held that the plaintiff, having been convicted of the manslaughter of her husband, could not have disputed that she was disqualified from taking any benefit under his will, or on his intestacy, even though the sentence passed upon her was one of detention for hospital treatment. The court in the present case was bound by that decision and it was impossible to distinguish the instant case on its facts. Even if it had been permissible to apply the test in *Gray v Barr*, the test would have been abundantly fulfilled since there were deliberate and intentional acts of violence which resulted in two deaths. Accordingly, the plaintiff's application had to fail on grounds of public policy.

Jones v Roberts [1995] 2 FLR 422 (Chancery Division: Kolbert J). *Royse v Royse* [1984] 3 All ER 339, CA (1984 Abr para 1057) applied and *Gray v Barr* [1971] 2 All ER 949, CA considered.

1358 Law Reform (Succession) Act 1995

The Law Reform (Succession) Act 1995 amends the law relating to the distribution of the estates of deceased persons and makes provision as to the effect of the dissolution or annulment of marriages on wills and appointments of guardians. The Act received the royal assent on 8 November 1995 and came into force on that day.

Section 1 makes provision for the distribution of estates on intestacy and partial intestacy. A survivorship provision as between spouses is introduced into the statutory rules governing distribution on intestacy to the effect that a spouse of a deceased person takes in accordance with those rules only if he or she survives the deceased for at least 28 days. The 'hotchpot' rule, under which certain payments made by a person dying intestate, and certain interests acquired under the will of a person who dies partially intestate, must be brought into account by the recipient against the share in the estate to which he would otherwise be entitled, is abolished. Section 2 provides that a person may apply under the Inheritance (Provision for Family and Dependants) Act 1975 for financial provision out of a deceased person's estate if, though not married to the deceased, he or she lived with the deceased as husband or wife.

Section 3 changes the effect on a will of the testator's divorce or the annulment of his marriage so that, unless a contrary intention appears in the will, any provision of the will appointing the former spouse as trustee or executor takes effect as if the former spouse had died on the date on which the marriage was dissolved or annulled and any property left by the will to the testator's former spouse will pass as if the former spouse had died on that date. Section 4 provides that, on a divorce or annulment of a marriage, any appointment by one of the former spouses of the other former spouse as guardian of a child is revoked unless a contrary intention appears from the appointment. Section 5 and the Schedule contain repeals and s 6 deals with citation and extent.

EXTRADITION AND FUGITIVE OFFENDERS

Halsbury's Laws of England (4th edn) Vol 18, paras 201–300

1359 Articles

Extradition and Human Rights, Susan Nash: 145 NLJ 429

1360 European Convention on Extradition—Croatia and Slovenia

The European Convention on Extradition Order 1990 (Amendment) (No 2) Order 1995, SI 1995/1962 (in force on 1 September 1995), further amends the 1990 Order, SI 1990/1507, by adding Croatia and Slovenia to the states parties to the European Convention on Extradition. The Order in Council embodying the extradition treaty between the United Kingdom and Serbia, so far as it applies to extradition between Croatia and Slovenia and the United Kingdom, the Channel Islands and the Isle of Man, is revoked; the entry for the Czech Republic and Slovak Federal Republic is replaced by entries for the Czech Republic and Slovakia; and the reservation made by the Czech and Slovak Federal Republic in relation to transit now applies in respect of both the Czech Republic and Slovakia.

1361   European Convention on Extradition—French and Dutch overseas territories

The European Convention on Extradition Order 1990 (Amendment) Order 1995, SI 1995/1624 (in force on a date to be notified in the London Gazette), further amends SI 1990/1507 so as to extend the application of the European Convention on Extradition as between the United Kingdom and France to certain French overseas territories, and as between the United Kingdom and the Netherlands, to certain Dutch overseas territories.

1362   European Convention on Extradition—Lithuania

The European Convention on Extradition Order 1990 (Amendment) (No 3) Order, SI 1995/2703 (in force on 1 December 1995), further amends the 1990 Order, SI 1990/1507, by adding Lithuania to the list of parties to the European Convention on Extradition.

1363   Extradition crimes—drug trafficking—Falkland Islands and Gibraltar

The Extradition (Drug Trafficking) (Falkland Islands and Gibraltar) Order 1995, SI 1995/1620 (in force in part on 11 July 1995, in part on a date to be notified in the London Gazette), extends the operation of the Extradition (Drug Trafficking) Order 1991, SI 1991/1701, to the Falkland Islands and Gibraltar, and adds Croatia, Slovenia and Slovenia to the list of foreign states which are parties to the Convention and with which extradition treaties are in force.

1364   Extradition crimes—torture

The Extradition (Torture) (Bermuda) Order 1995, SI 1995/3209 (in force on 12 January 1996), extends to Bermuda the Extradition (Torture) Order 1991, SI 1991/1702, in implementation of the United Nations Convention against Torture and other Cruel, Inhuman or Degrading Treatment or Punishment (4 February 1985).

1365   Extradition proceedings—evidence—accomplices—exclusion of evidence

See *R v Governor of Belmarsh Prison, ex p Francis*, para 803.

1366   Extradition proceedings—evidence—intercepted telephone calls—interception by non-resident of United Kingdom

See *R v Governor of Belmarsh Prison, ex p Martin*, para 831.

1367   Extradition proceedings—procedures between member states—judicial co-operation

See para 3097.

FAMILY ARRANGEMENTS, UNDUE INFLUENCE AND VOIDABLE CONVEYANCES

Halsbury's Laws of England (4th edn) Vol 18, paras 301–400

1368   Articles

Independent Advice After *O'Brien*, H W Wilkinson (on *Barclays Bank plc v O'Brien* [1993] 4 All ER 417, HL (1993 Abr para 1826)): 145 NLJ 792

Taking Security After *O'Brien*, Richard Hooley (on *Barclays Bank plc v O'Brien* [1993] 4 All ER 417 (1993 Abr para 1826)): [1995] LMCLQ 346

Undue Influence, Misrepresentation and the Doctrine of Notice, John Mee (on *Barclays Bank plc v O'Brien* [1993] 4 All ER 417, HL (1993 Abr para 1826)): (1995) CLJ 536

1369   Family arrangements—deed of arrangement—intention—avoidance of creditors—proof of intention

A matrimonial home was registered in the joint names of a husband and wife. They executed a legal charge to secure a mortgage loan from a bank. The husband then entered into a deed of arrangement giving his equity interest in the home to his wife and two daughters. The bank was not aware of the trust deed, and the wife was not aware of its effects. Later the husband negotiated further loans from the bank to finance his business interests on the security of his interest in the home. In a debt action brought by the bank, the husband sought to rely on the trust deed to resist the making absolute of a charging order nisi obtained by the bank on his interest in the home. *Held,* at the time of executing the trust deed the husband's true intention was to protect his family from commercial risk rather than to endow them with an interest in the property. To establish that the deed was a sham it was not necessary to prove that there had been a fraudulent motive; nor was it necessary to establish that both the husband and wife intended the deed to have no effect. The transaction was a sham and was void and unenforceable. In addition, the attempt to transfer the interest to the daughters was a transaction entered into without consideration and was voidable under the Insolvency Act 1986, s 423. Accordingly, the charging order in favour of the bank would be made absolute.

Midland Bank plc v Wyatt [1995] 1 FLR 697 (Chancery Division: D E M Young QC).

1370 Family provision—application under Inheritance (Provision for Family and Dependants) Act 1975

See EXECUTORS AND ADMINISTRATORS.

1371 Undue influence—gift—setting aside

See *Langton v Langton,* para 1482.

1372 Undue influence—legal charge—constructive notice

See MORTGAGE.

FINANCIAL SERVICES

1373 Articles

PIA [Personal Investment Authority] Complaints Procedure, Gary Envis: 145 NLJ 815

A POSitive Framework for Offers of Unlisted Securities, Michael Howlett (on the Public Offers of Securities Regulations 1995, SI 1995/1537): 139 SJ 1018

Taking Financial Services to the Cleaners, Michael Levi (on suspicious transaction reports): 145 NLJ 26

VAT on Financial Services, Peter Hewitt: Tax Journal, Issue 308, p 14

1374 Advertising—restrictions on advertising—exemptions

The Financial Services Act 1986 (Investment Advertisements) (Exemptions) Order 1995, SI 1995/1266 (in force on 19 June 1995), consolidates and amends the exemptions from the restrictions on advertising imposed by the Financial Services Act 1986, s 57. The order deals with the following kinds of advertisements: (1) advertisements which are issued by a body corporate other than an open-ended investment company where particular investments issued by the body corporate or its holding company are traded or dealt in on a specified market or where the advertisement consists of specified documents; (2) advertisements relating to bearer securities which are issued by a body corporate other than an open-ended investment company; (3) advertisements issued in connection with employee share schemes; (4) advertisements issued within groups of bodies corporate; (5) advertisements between participants or potential participants in a joint enterprise; (6) investment advertisements issued in connection with the sale of goods or supply of services; (7) advertisements issued by persons without a permanent place of business in the United Kingdom to persons with whom they have an existing relationship established abroad; (8) advertisements issued to certain persons sufficiently expert to understand the risks involved; (9) advertisements issued to persons regarded as having an existing and common interest in the subject matter of the advertisement; (10) advertisements issued by trustees and personal representatives; (11) advertisements issued by operators of recognised collective schemes who are not authorised under the 1986 Act; (12) advertisements relating to publications or programmes which contain advice which does not fall within the 1986 Act, Sch 1, para 15 by virtue of Sch 1, para 25 or 25A; (13) advertisements relating to the facilities offered by specified markets; (14) advertisements relating to shares in a private company established to manage the fabric or common parts of residential or business property or to supply services to such property; (15) advertisements issued for the purpose of remedying injustice stated by the Parliamentary Commissioner for Administration to have occurred.

The Financial Services Act 1986 (Investment Advertisements) (Exemptions) (No 2) Order 1995, SI 1995/1536 (in force on 19 June 1995), further consolidates and amends the exemptions from the restrictions on advertising imposed by the 1986 Act supra, s 57. The order deals with the following kinds of advertisements: (1) advertisements issued by certain bodies corporate in connection with the promotion or encouragement of industrial or commercial activity or enterprise in the United Kingdom; (2) certain advertisements issued in connection with takeovers of private companies; (3) advertisements which are issued in connection with certain sales of shares in a body corporate; (4) advertisements issued by persons holding permissions granted under the 1986 Act, Sch 1, para 23; (5) advertisements directed at informing or influencing persons of a specified kind; (5) advertisements relating to an investment falling within the 1986 Act, Sch 1, paras 1–5 which is traded or dealt in on a specified market, or which is permitted by a body which regulates such a market or the offer or issue of such advertisements on such a market; (6) advertisements issued by specified markets; (7) advertisements which are prospectuses issued in accordance with the Public Offers of Securities Regulations 1995, SI 1995/1537 (see para 1387) publications publicising such prospectuses, or documents required for admission to trading on a specified market; (8) advertisements the issue of which is required or authorised under other legislation. The order also makes provision for where a publication is sent to a person who has placed an advertisement in it and for advertisements issued to persons involved in advertising, gives indications as to whether an advertisement may be regarded as being directed at informing or influencing persons of the relevant kind, and deals with the issue by industrial and provident societies of advertisements relating to their debentures.

1375 Credit institutions—prudential supervision
See para 3145.

1376 Credit institutions—solvency ratios
See para 3144.

1377 Fiduciary duties—Law Commission proposals
The Law Commission has published a report, *Fiduciary Duties and Regulatory Rules* (Cm 3049; Law Com No 236), concerning the possibility of conflicting duties to different customers and conflicts of interests within businesses concerned with financial markets. Its recommendations (which are enshrined in a draft Bill appended to the report) differ from the provisional conclusions set out in the commission's consultation paper which was published in May 1992 (consultation paper 124; see 1992 Abr para 1177). The recommendations in the report apply to persons who are covered by the Financial Services Act 1986, s 48(2)(h), but the protection to be afforded by legislation would apply without prejudice to any express contractual provisions entered into with customers or any other defence available to the business concerned. The commission recommends that a business should not be liable by reason of any fiduciary duty owed to a customer for withholding information by reason of an established Chinese wall arrangement (as defined) which complies with regulatory requirements, nor if the business places itself in a position whereby its own interests on one side of such a Chinese wall conflict with a duty owed to a customer of a department on the other side of the Chinese wall (and, because of the Chinese wall, neither department is aware of the conflict of interests), nor where a business owes conflicting duties to customers of different departments on different sides of such a Chinese wall and (in consequence) neither department is aware of the conflict. It is proposed that the legislation should apply only where different departments of the same legal entity are separated by a Chinese wall or where a person is lawfully carrying on another business in connection with his investment business and a Chinese wall is erected between the investment business and the connected business.

1378 Financial markets and insolvency—money markets—application of insolvency law
The Financial Markets and Insolvency (Money Market) Regulations 1995, SI 1995/2049 (in force on 15 August 1995), apply (with modifications) the Companies Act 1989, Pt VII (financial markets and insolvency) to certain aspects of the settlement arrangements relating to the money markets provided by persons admitted to a list maintained by the Bank of England under the

1989 Act, s 171. The regulations also provide for the supervision by the Bank of persons it has admitted to the list.

1379 Financial Services Act 1986—commencement

The Financial Services Act 1986 (Commencement) (No 13) Order 1995, SI 1995/1538, brings into force on 19 June 1995 s 212(3) (in part), and certain repeals in Sch 17 relating to the Companies Act 1985. For a summary of the Act, see 1986 Abr para 1791. For details of commencement, see the commencement table in the title STATUTES.

1380 Investment advice—protection of investor—investor in another member state

See *Alpine Investments BV v Minister van Financiën*, para 3141.

1381 Investment business—authorisation—exemption

The Financial Services Act 1986 (Miscellaneous Exemptions) Order 1995, SI 1995/202 (in force on 22 February 1995), provides for additional specified persons to be exempt from the requirement to obtain authorisation under the Financial Services Act 1986 in respect of any investment business they carry on, namely the Church of Ireland Trustees and the Commonwealth Development Corporation (when acting in exercise of its powers under the Commonwealth Development Act 1978).

1382 Investment services—extension of scope of statutory regulation

The Financial Services Act 1986 (Investment Services) (Extension of Scope of Act) Order 1995, SI 1995/3271 (in force on 1 January 1996), amends the scope of the Financial Services Act 1986 so as to give effect to Council Directive (EC) 93/22 (investment services in the securities field). The order adds certain instruments to the list of investments in the 1986 Act, Sch 1, Pt I (certain shares in industrial and provident societies and certain bills of exchange). The order also extends the activities that are to constitute the carrying on of investment business and amends the meaning of 'investment business' in the 1986 Act, s 1 to include the provision of all investment services to which the directive applies.

1383 Investment services—securities—implementation of EC provisions

The Investment Services Regulations 1995, SI 1995/3275 (in force in part on 1 January 1996 and in part on 1 January 1997), implement Council Directive (EC) 93/22 (investment services in the securities field) and Council Directive (EC) 93/6 (capital adequacy of investment firms and credit institutions). The regulations provide for the recognition of certain investment firms authorised in other EEA states for the purposes of providing listed services in the United Kingdom. Provision is made for the implementation of certain decisions of the EC Commission or the EC Council and for the carrying on of listed activities in other member states by United Kingdom authorised investment firms. The regulations also amend the Financial Services Act 1986 and the Consumer Credit Act 1974, and introduce new requirements obliging persons who wish to acquire or increase holdings in United Kingdom authorised investment firms in excess of certain specified sizes to notify the relevant regulators before doing so.

1384 Investors Compensation Scheme—claims for compensation—assessment of compensation

The Financial Services (Compensation of Investors) Rules 1990, r 2.04(1) provides that the basic compensatable claims are claims for property held and claims arising from uncompleted transactions, and an application for compensation relating to any other claim is to be met only where the Investors Compensation Scheme considers that it is essential in order to provide fair compensation to the investor.

The applicants entered into home income plans advertised by a firm of financial advisers whereby they took out loans secured by mortgages. The money borrowed was invested in a bond from which the applicants could draw an income. The firm went into liquidation and at that date the applicants' funds were worth much less than their mortgage debts. They had also incurred professional fees for the firm's work. The applicants sought compensation under the Investors Compensation Scheme (ICS), set up under the Financial Services Act 1986. It was common ground that the measure of compensation should be the difference between the debts and the value of the bonds at the relevant date, but the ICS said that any sums the applicants received as income should be deducted and the amounts claimed for professional fees should be limited. At first instance the court found in favour of the applicants but, on appeal, *held*, Lord Steyn dissenting, the language of the 1990 Rules, r 2.04(1) provided for a broad discretion to include within the definition of a compensatable claim either the claim as a whole or those elements of it that the ICS considered essential to provide fair compensation and to exclude those that it did not. Since the ICS had a discretion to disallow sums received by the applicants as income, it could not be said that its decision to do so was one that no reasonable public authority, exercising the functions imposed by the 1986 Act and the 1990 Rules, could have reached. Therefore, there were no grounds on which the court could interfere with that decision. As to professional costs, the ICS had been entitled to take the view that a cap should be imposed and the limit imposed in the present case was reasonable in the circumstances. Accordingly, the appeal would be allowed.

R v Investors Compensation Scheme Ltd, ex p Bowden [1995] 3 All ER 605 (House of Lords: Lords Keith of Kinkel, Browne-Wilkinson, Lloyd of Berwick, Nicholls of Birkenhead and Steyn). Decision of Court of Appeal [1994] 3 WLR 1045 (1994 Abr para 1374) reversed.

1385   Investors' Compensation Scheme—claims for compensation—liability to contribute

The Financial Services Act 1986, s 54(3)(b) provides that a compensation scheme made under s 54 cannot be made so as to apply to persons who are members of a recognised self-regulatory organisation except after consultation with that organisation, and no scheme applying to such persons may be made unless the Secretary of State is satisfied that the rules establishing it make sufficient provision for securing that the amounts which members are liable to contribute reflect the amount of the claims made or likely to be made.

The plaintiff was a member of the Personal Investment Authority ('the PIA'), a self-regulatory organisation in the investment industry. The PIA was responsible for administering compensation payable by its members, to whom it passed on levies made by the Investors' Compensation Scheme. The Securities and Investments Board approved certain rules made by the PIA relating to the liability of its members to contribute to the compensation scheme. On an application for judicial review, the plaintiff challenged some of the rules, arguing that the 1986 Act, s 54 prohibited compulsory contributions to the compensation scheme, and that the SIB could not delegate to the PIA the power to determine its members' liability to contribute to the scheme. *Held*, the 1986 Act, s 54(3) required rules to be made to produce contributions from PIA members, the amount of which was sufficient to discharge claims made or likely to be made against members of the PIA or their predecessors. The purpose of s 54(3) was not to allocate liability, but to provide a means of discharging that liability. The 1986 Act therefore did not impose any limitation on the way in which liability for claims was allocated amongst PIA members and, accordingly, the application would be dismissed.

R v Securities and Investments Board, ex p Sun Life Assurance Society plc (1995) Times, 9 October (Queen's Bench Division: Sedley J).

1386   Regulated markets—European Economic Area regulated—exemption

The Financial Services Act 1986 (EEA Regulated Markets) (Exemption) Order 1995, SI 1995/3273 (in force on 1 January 1996), makes provision for an exemption from the scope of the authorisation requirement imposed by the Financial Services Act 1986, Pt I, so that a person may, without having to obtain authorisation under the 1986 Act, provide within the United Kingdom trading facilities constituting a market which operates without any requirement for a person dealing on the market to have a physical presence either in the EEA State from which the trading facilities are provided, or on any physical floor that the market may have, provided that the market appears on a list drawn up by another EEA State pursuant to the provisions of Council Directive (EC) 93/22, art 16.

1387   Securities—public offers—prospectuses

The Public Offers of Securities Regulations 1995, SI 1995/1537 (in force on 19 June 1995), give effect to Council Directive (EC) 89/298 on the co-ordination of the requirements for the drawing up, scrutiny and distribution of a prospectus when transferable securities are to be offered to the public. They also give effect, in relation to the mutual recognition of prospectuses and listing particulars, to certain provisions of Council Directive (EC) 80/390. The regulations provide for persons offering transferable securities to the public in certain circumstances to prepare and publish a prospectus according to specified requirements. These provisions replace the Companies Act 1985, Pt III for most purposes. The regulations also amend the Financial Services Act 1986, Pt IV to enable a prospectus to be prepared and approved, in certain circumstances, in accordance with listing rules. The 1986 Act, Pt V (offers of unlisted securities) (not in force) is repealed.

FIRE SERVICES

Halsbury's Laws of England (4th edn) Vol 18, paras 401–600

1388 Fire authority—duty of care—duty owed to the general public

Scotland

Under the Fire Services Act 1947, s 1(1), every fire authority must secure the services for its area of such a fire brigade and such equipment as may be necessary to meet efficiently all normal requirements. It must also make efficient arrangements for dealing with calls for the assistance of the fire brigade in the case of fire.

The fire brigade was called to the house adjoining the plaintiff's twice in one evening. After the first call, it had unknowingly left the scene when the house was still on fire. Upon its return, it could not bring the fire under control, and the plaintiff's house was destroyed. The plaintiff brought an action against the defendant fire authority for damages in negligence. *Held*, although the 1947 Act did not impose an express duty on the defendant to exercise reasonable care in its firefighting operations, its actions did not stem from an exercise of pure discretionary power. The defendant had acted in performance of an express duty imposed by s 1. Consequently, the duty of care owed by the defendant to the plaintiff extended beyond simply ensuring that it did not add to the damage that the plaintiff would have suffered had the defendant done nothing. Furthermore, public policy did not grant an immunity for negligence to a fire brigade in its firefighting operations. Accordingly, as a matter of law the plaintiff would not be prevented from bringing a claim against the defendant.

Duff v Highland and Islands Fire Board (1995) Times, 3 November (Outer House). *East Suffolk Rivers Catchment Board v Kent* [1941] AC 74, HL, doubted.

1389 Fire authority—supply contracts—procedure

See para 2929.

1390 Firefighters—appointment and promotion

The Fire Services (Appointments and Promotion) (Amendment) Regulations 1995, SI 1995/2109 (in force on 1 September 1995), further amend the 1978 Regulations, SI 1978/436, by replacing references to the Fire Service Drill Book in certain provisions relating to practical examinations for promotion by references to the Fire Service Training Manual.

FISHERIES

Halsbury's Laws of England (4th edn) Vol 18, paras 601–1000

1391 Articles

Whose Fish Are they Anyway? Marc Weller (on the United Nations Convention on the Law of the Sea 1982): 145 NLJ 536

1392 Environment Act 1995

See para 1289.

1393 Fisheries and aquaculture structures—grants

The Fisheries and Aquaculture Structures (Grants) Regulations 1995, SI 1995/1576 (in force on 22 June 1995), implement European Community regulations laying down the criteria and arrangements regarding structural financial assistance in the fisheries and aquaculture sector and the processing and marketing of its products. The regulations provide for and regulate the payment of grants by ministers towards expenditure in respect of certain types of investments or projects which have been approved and regulate the payment of financial assistance in respect of relevant operations approved by ministers. The procedure for making applications for approval is laid down and the rate of grant payable and the method of payment is specified. Applicants are required to keep certain records relating to an operation for a required period and must give assistance to authorised officers when required. Authorised officers are given powers of entry and inspection for specified purposes and provision is made for the reduction, withholding and recovery of financial assistance paid in certain circumstances. In addition, offences are created in relation to the making of false statements in order to obtain financial assistance, the obstruction of officers in the exercise of their powers and the failure to comply with an authorised officer's request.

1394 Fishing vessels—certification of deck officers and engineer officers

The Fishing Vessels (Certification of Deck Officers and Engineer Officers) (Amendment) Regulations 1995, SI 1995/1428 (in force on 1 August 1995), amend SI 1984/1115 so that in relation to fishing vessel Class I officers, fishing vessel Class II officers and fishing vessel Class III officers, it gives effect to Council Directive (EC) 92/51 relating to a second general system for the recognition of professional education and training. The 1995 Regulations provide for the recognition of equivalent foreign certificates issued by certain authorities abroad, and for the issue of certificates of equivalent competency for the holders of such certificates. This enables the holders to serve as qualified officers on United Kingdom fishing vessels in the appropriate position. Where foreign certificates are not equivalent to United Kingdom certificates, the regulations make provision for aptitude tests or adaptation periods. In addition, a saving provision provides that certificates of equivalent competency are not required until 1 August 1997 by those who have certificates issued before that date by countries where certificates were recognised before 1 August 1995.

1395 Fishing vessels—decommissioning scheme

The Fishing Vessels (Decommissioning) Scheme 1995, SI 1995/1610 (in force on 5 July 1995), provides for the making of grants by the Minister of Agriculture, Fisheries and Food or other relevant Secretary of State, for the decommissioning, by scrapping, of vessels registered in the United Kingdom. Owners of vessels applying for a grant must meet specified requirements and follow a specified procedure. An application must be in respect of one vessel only and a bid for the amount of grant for which an applicant offers to scrap the vessel must be included. Provision is made for the method by which bids are selected for approval. An applicant must notify the relevant minister of the details of the scrapping at least two weeks before it takes place and must surrender his licence and secure his vessel's removal from the register. Ministers must be provided with certain information by the applicant in the event of substantial damage or destruction of the vessel. Provision is made for the amount of the grant, the method of payment and undertakings to be given by applicants. Applicants have a duty to give assistance to authorised officers, who have prescribed powers. Provision is also made for the reduction, withholding and recovery of grant in certain circumstances.

1396 Fishing vessels—safety improvements—grants

The Fishing Vessels (Safety Improvements) (Grants) Scheme 1995, SI 1995/1609 (in force on 29 June 1995), enables grants to be made towards expenditure incurred in making improvements to certain vessels so that the owners of such vessels may obtain a certificate under the Fishing Vessels (Safety Provisions) Rules 1975, SI 1975/330. The scheme lays down the procedure for making and approving applications for approval of improvements and expenditure and the criteria to be used in selecting qualifying applications. Eligibility for a grant is dependent on proof of expenditure incurred and proper execution of the relevant improvement. The scheme specifies the rates of grant. Applicants may be required to give undertakings, must keep certain records for a period of three years after the last payment of a grant and must give assistance to authorised officers who have powers of entry and inspection. Grants may be reduced, withheld or recovered in certain circumstances. In addition, offences are created in respect of the production of false statements or documents and the wilful refusal to supply information, make returns or produce documents.

See also para 2684.

1397   Salmon and freshwater fisheries—fish health regulations

The Fish Health (Amendment) Regulations 1995, SI 1995/886 (in force on 17 April 1995), amend the 1992 Regulations, SI 1992/3300, so as to implement Commission Decisions (EC) 94/817 and 94/865.

1398   Salmon and freshwater fisheries—protection of fisheries—unclean or unseasonable salmon

Scotland

The Salmon and Freshwater Fisheries Act 1975, s 2 provides that a person who takes or has in his possession any unclean or unseasonable salmon is liable to a penalty.

The appellant had been charged with having in his possession unclean or unseasonable salmon contrary to s 2 on the last day of the season for taking salmon in the relevant fishery district. The appeal raised the question of the meaning of the word 'unseasonable' in s 2. *Held*, a salmon was 'unclean' if it had already begun to spawn or had not yet recovered from spawning. It was 'unseasonable' if it had already begun to spawn or was full of spawn and on the point of spawning in that if the belly was gently pressed towards the vent, spawn or milt was discharged. This was clear from the fact that the purpose of s 2 was to protect fish which were breeding and those which were in a state of exhaustion consequent upon breeding, irrespective of the time at which they were taken.

Brady v Procurator Fiscal, Stonehaven (1995) Times, 27 February (High Court of Justiciary).

1399   Sea fishing—Community provisions—enforcement

The Third Country Fishing (Enforcement) Order 1995, SI 1995/907 (in force on 18 April 1995) (as amended by SI 1995/2437), makes it an offence to breach certain specified articles of European Community regulations for the purposes of United Kingdom law where they occur within British fishery limits. These include regulations concerned with methods of fishing, holding and observing licences, keeping log books and making radio reports. The master of an offending vessel will be liable to a fine and forfeiture of fish and fishing gear. The maximum fine for offences related to keeping logbooks and observing licence conditions is £50,000. Powers of enforcement are conferred on British sea-fishery officers. Anyone found guilty of obstructing or assaulting an officer will be punished. SI 1994/1681 is revoked.

1400   Sea fishing—quotas—enforcement

The Sea Fishing (Enforcement of Community Quota Measures) Order 1995, SI 1995/908, replaces the 1994 Order, SI 1994/1679, to make provision for the enforcement of restrictions and obligations set out in Council Regulation (EC) 3362/94 which fixes total allowable catches and quotas for 1995. The order creates offences in respect of breaches of the regulations and imposes penalties, which may include the forfeiture of fish, nets and other fishing gear, in respect of those offences. Powers of enforcement are conferred on British sea-fishery officers in relation to fishing boats and on land and in relation to the seizure of fish and fishing gear. Anyone found guilty of obstructing or assaulting an officer may be punished.

FOOD, DAIRIES AND SLAUGHTERHOUSES

Halsbury's Laws of England (4th edn) Vol 18, paras 1001–1400

1401   Articles

Food Hygiene and the Law, Katharine Thompson: 145 NLJ 1335
Keep it Clean, Jeremy Stranks (on defences to food law offences): 139 SJ 624

1402   Bovine offal

The Specified Bovine Offal Order 1995, SI 1995/1928 (in force on 15 August 1995), controls specified bovine offal which is material that may contain the agent containing bovine spongiform encephalopathy. The order extends current provisions relating to such offal. Provision is made to control the sale and use of offal for human and animal consumption and to regulate the initial treatment of such offal. Consignments of offal, once removed from the carcass, are regulated and the order controls plants, centres, incinerators and other premises by requiring them to be approved and by regulating the way in which they deal with the offal. In addition, veterinary and laboratory premises are regulated and provisions are made as to export, sampling, transport and storage. Provisions in the Bovine Spongiform Encephalopathy Order 1991, SI 1991/2246, are revoked and amended.

The Bovine Offal (Prohibition) (England, Wales and Scotland) (Revocation) Regulations 1995, SI 1995/1955 (in force on 15 August 1995), revoke the 1989 Regulations, SI 1989/2061, as amended, which control specified bovine offal. Specified bovine offal is now controlled by the Specified Bovine Offal Order 1995, SI 1995/1928 supra. The regulations amend the Animal By-Products (Identification) Regulations 1995, SI 1995/614. In addition, SI 1995/613 is revoked.

1403 Bread and flour—composition and labelling

The Bread and Flour Regulations 1995, SI 1995/3202 (in force on 1 January 1996), replace the 1984 Regulations, SI 1984/1304. Subject to certain exemptions, the regulations (1) continue to require that wheat flour be fortified with specified essential ingredients, (2) restrict the use of specified ingredients in the preparation of flour and bread and require that an indication of the presence of a flour treatment agent be given in the case of both prepacked and non-prepacked bread, (3) prohibit the use of 'wholemeal' and 'wheat germ' in the labelling or advertising of bread save in relation to bread that complies with specified compositional requirements, (4) create offences and prescribe penalties, (5) specify the enforcement authorities, (6) create a defence in relation to exports in certain circumstances, (7) provide that for a transitional period a defence is available where there would not have been any contravention of the revoked regulations, and (8) apply various sections of the Food Safety Act 1990.

1404 Cheese and cream—composition and labelling

The Cheese and Cream Regulations 1995, SI 1995/3240 (in force on 1 January 1996), replace the Cheese Regulations 1970, SI 1970/94, and the Cream Regulations 1970, SI 1970/752. In certain circumstances, cream and cheese imported into England from a European Economic Area State are exempt from the regulations if suitably labelled to give the nature of the cream or cheese. The regulations retain the existing controls on the use of enzymes in the manufacture of cheese and the restriction on the use of certain names of cheese. Cream may now be sold without its having to bear a description chosen from a closed list of prescribed descriptions. However, if offered for sale as clotted cream, double cream, whipping cream, whipped cream, sterilised cream, cream or single cream, sterilised half cream or half cream, it must contain the minimum percentage of fat prescribed by the regulations. Cream must be clotted if sold as clotted cream and it must be whipped if sold as whipped cream. Failure to comply with the regulations is an offence punishable on summary conviction with a fine not exceeding level 5 on the standard scale. In certain circumstances a defence is provided in relation to exports.

1405 Dairies—dairy produce—hygiene

The Dairy Products (Hygiene) (Charges) Regulations 1995, SI 1995/1122 (in force on 12 May 1995), re-enact the charging provision contained in the 1990 Regulations, SI 1990/1584. Charges are £94 for a general dairy farm visit and £63 for a sampling dairy farm visit. Exemptions from charges are restricted to specified sampling dairy farm visits.

1406 Dairies—dairy produce—quotas

The Dairy Produce Quotas (Amendment) Regulations 1995, SI 1995/254 (in force on 28 February 1995), further amend the 1994 Regulations, SI 1994/672, in consequence of the reorganisation of the arrangements in relation to the marketing of milk in Northern Ireland.

1407 Food—additives—conditions of use

See para 3120.

1408 Food—animal by-products—identification

The Animal By-Products (Identification) Regulations 1995, SI 1995/614 (in force on 1 April 1995), make provision for the sterilisation and staining of animal by-products and for the control of their movement. The regulations (1) require the immediate staining or sterilisation of certain animal by-products at a slaughterhouse, game processing facility or at any animal by-products premises; (2) prohibit the freezing of any animal by-product in such slaughterhouses, facilities or premises; (3) prohibit the storage of unsterilised by-products in the same room as products intended for human consumption or, if the by-products are not properly packed and labelled, prohibit their storage in the same premises as products fit for human consumption; (4) prohibit, except in certain circumstances, the movement of unstained or unsterilised animal by-products from any slaughterhouse or relevant facility or premises; (5) create offences and prescribe penalties. SI 1982/1018 is revoked and consequential amendments are made to SI 1989/2061.

1409 Food—food additives—colouring

The Colours in Food Regulations 1995, SI 1995/3124 (in force on 1 January 1996), implement Council Directive (EC) 94/36 on the colours for use in foodstuffs and Commission Directive (EC) 95/45 which lays down specific criteria of purity concerning colours for use in foodstuffs. The provisions (1) prohibit the use of any colour in or on any food other than a permitted colour, (2) prohibit the use of any permitted colour in or on any food, otherwise than in accordance with the regulations, (3) prohibit the use of any colour except certain permitted colours for the health marking etc of certain meat and meat products, (4) prohibit the use of any colour other than a permitted colour on eggshells, (5) prohibit the sale for use in or on any food of any colour other than a permitted colour, and permit only certain permitted colours to be sold directly to consumers, (6) prohibit the sale of any food containing any added colour other than a permitted colour used in or on it in accordance with the regulations, (7) make provisions in relation to compound foods, (8) make provisions in relation to the condemnation of food, (9) create offences, prescribe a penalty and provide for the regulations to be enforced by food authorities, (10) provide a defence in relation to exports, (11) incorporate specified provisions of the Food Safety Act 1990, and (12) contain a transitional provision and exemption.

1410 Food—infant formula and follow-on formula

The Infant Formula and Follow-on Formula Regulations 1995, SI 1995/77 (in force on 1 March 1995), implement Commission Directives (EC) 91/321 and 95/52 to make provision in relation to infant and follow-on formula. The regulations (1) prohibit the sale of food labelled as infant or follow-on formulae unless it complies with requirements as to composition, labelling, appearance and packaging; (2) require exported formulae to comply with similar compositional standards unless the importing country requires products to be labelled in an appropriate language; (3) limit the advertising of infant formulae to specified types of publications and restrict the content of advertisements for infant and follow-on formulae; (4) prohibit special displays or promotions of infant formulae at retail outlets; (5) prohibit the promotion of infant formulae by providing such formulae free or at reduced prices; (6) lay down requirements as to information to be contained in materials, which deal with the feeding of infants, intended to reach pregnant women and mothers of infants and young child and also regulate when manufacturers and distributors may make gifts of informational or educational equipment or materials.

1411 Food—miscellaneous food additives

The Miscellaneous Food Additives Regulations 1995, SI 1995/3187 (in force on 1 January 1996), implement Council Directive (EC) 95/2 which makes provision in relation to food additives, other than colours and sweeteners, and their use in foodstuffs intended for human consumption. The use of any miscellaneous additives in or on any food, or the sale of such additives for use in or on food or direct to a consumer, is prohibited unless it is a specified permitted additive. In addition, the sale or use of such additives primarily as a carrier or carrier solvent is restricted. It is an offence to contravene the regulations and a penalty is prescribed. The regulations are to be enforced by food authorities.

1412 Food—miscellaneous revocations and amendments

The Food (Miscellaneous Revocations and Amendments) Regulations 1995, SI 1995/3267 (in force on 1 January 1996), revoke SI 1944/42, 1950/589, 1960/2331, 1964/760 and 1967/1866, together with any amending instruments.

1413 Food—spreadable fats—marketing standards

The Spreadable Fats (Marketing Standards) Regulations 1995, SI 1995/3116 (in force on 1 January 1996), make provision for the enforcement and execution of Council Regulation (EC) 2991/94, which lays down standards for spreadable fats, and make provision as to the vitamin content of margarine. The regulations (1) specify the authorities which enforce and execute the regulations; (2) create offences, prescribe a penalty and contain a limited exemption in respect of any spreadable fat to which the EEA Agreement applies and which is brought into Great Britain from an EEA State other than a member state; (3) provide a defence in relation to exports so as to implement Council Directive (EC) 89/397 on the official control of foodstuffs; (4) incorporate specified provisions of the Food Safety Act 1990. SI 1966/1074, 1252, 1967/1867 and 1970/1286 are revoked.

1414 Food—surplus food regulations

See para 94.

1415 Food—sweeteners

The Sweeteners in Food Regulations 1995, SI 1995/3123 (in force on 1 January 1996), implement Council Directive (EC) 94/35 on sweeteners for use in foodstuffs and Council Directive (EC) 95/31 which lays down specific criteria of purity concerning sweeteners. The regulations prohibit the sale of any sweetener intended for sale to the ultimate consumer or for use in or on any food, other than a permitted sweetener, and prohibits the use of any sweetener in or on foods for infants and young children where the foodstuffs are intended for particular nutritional uses. In addition, the sale of table-top sweeteners is prohibited unless they are permitted sweeteners and are labelled in accordance with the regulations. Offences are created and penalties are prescribed for contravention of the regulations, which are to be enforced by food authorities. Provision is made for a defence in relation to exports and the regulations incorporate specified provisions of the Food Safety Act 1990. SI 1983/1211, 1497, 1988/2084, 2112 are revoked in full and SI 1985/67, 1068, 1991/1476 are revoked in part.

1416 Food production—extraction solvents

The Extraction Solvents in Food (Amendment) Regulations 1995, SI 1995/1440 (in force on 30 June 1995), amend SI 1993/1658, so as to include cyclohexane as an extraction solvent which may be used in the preparation of flavourings from natural flavouring materials, subject to a prescribed maximum residue limit.

1417 Food safety—confectionery manufacturer's duty of care—chocolate containing knife blade

The defendant was a manufacturer of chocolate sweets, one of which contained a knife blade that cut a woman's tongue. At first instance, the court fined the defendant £25,000, but the defendant appealed on the ground that this amount was excessive. *Held*, there was a very high duty on manufacturers of confectionery and other foodstuffs to ensure that no foreign bodies as dangerous as knife blades were contained in any of their products and they ought to take all precautions necessary to prevent this occurring. The court did not want to give the impression that a company with a good record would go unpunished on a first transgression in circumstances similar to those in the present case. Therefore a substantial fine had to be imposed, but in this case the fine was excessive and, accordingly, would be reduced to £7,000.

R v F & M Dobson Ltd (1995) 16 Cr App Rep (S) 957 (Court of Appeal: Lord Taylor of Gosforth CJ, Owen J and Sir Lawrence Verney QC).

1418 Food safety—defence of due diligence—piece of bone found in food—bone as evidence of failure to use due diligence

Under the Food Safety Act 1990, s 14 any person who sells to the purchaser's prejudice any food which is not of the nature or substance or quality demanded by the purchaser is guilty of an offence. In any proceedings for an offence under the Act, it is a defence for the person charged to prove that he took all reasonable precautions and exercised all due diligence to avoid the commission of the offence by himself or by a person under his control: s 21.

A complaint was laid against a baby food manufacturer that a piece of bone had been found in a jar of food. The manufacturer, charged under the 1990 Act, s 14, sought to rely on a defence of due diligence under s 21, giving as evidence details of its production process. The magistrate found that, although the manufacturer took all reasonable precautions, the existence of the bone meant that it could not have exercised all due diligence. The manufacturer applied for the magistrate to state a case, but he refused to do so on the ground that the manufacturer's application was frivolous under the Magistrates' Courts Act 1980, s 111. The manufacturer applied for judicial review of the magistrate's decision. *Held*, the defence of due diligence under the 1990 Act, s 21 could only be relevant in circumstances where there was some offence under s 14 so for the magistrate to say that the existence of the bone was evidence that the manufacturer had not exercised due diligence was difficult to understand. Whether due diligence had been exercised depended upon the facts. The manufacturer's application had not been frivolous and, accordingly, the application would be allowed.

R v Bow Street Magistrates' Court, ex p Cow and Gate Nutrition plc (1994) 159 JP 120 (Queen's Bench Division: Balcombe LJ and Schiemann J).

1419 Food safety—general food hygiene

The Food Safety (General Food Hygiene) Regulations 1995, SI 1995/1763 (in force on 15 September 1995), implement Council Directives (EC) 93/43, on the hygiene of foodstuffs, and 80/778, on the use of water for food production purposes. 'Potable water' is defined and the quality standard for water used for food production purposes is set. Various obligations are imposed on the proprietor of a food business. He must ensure that specified operations are carried out in a hygienic way and requirements for food premises are set out. The rules of hygiene also cover transportation, requirements as to equipment, food waste, water supply, personal hygiene and training. A proprietor must identify activities which are critical to ensuring food safety and ensure that adequate safety procedures are identified, implemented, maintained and reviewed. In addition, a proprietor must be notified of medical conditions suffered by certain food handlers. Provision is also made in relation to offences, penalties, enforcement and revocations.

A revised version of Code of Practice No 9 under the Food Safety Act 1990, *Food Hygiene Inspections* (September 1995), has been issued. The code provides guidance for food authorities on the frequency and nature of inspections undertaken to assess the hygiene of premises and the public health protection aspects of food law. It includes advice on the enforcement of the Food Safety (General Food Hygiene) Regulations 1995, SI 1995/1763 supra and advice on a scheme to determine the minimum frequency of inspection based on an evaluation of the potential risk. The revised code came into force on 15 September 1995.

1420 Food safety—proceedings—condemnation—cross-examination of expert witness

Scotland

A cheese manufacturer was charged with an offence under the Food Safety Act 1990, alleging that certain batches of his cheese were unfit for human consumption because they were contaminated with a particular bacteria. Although evidence was adduced by expert witnesses for both the manufacturer and the local authority as to the existence of the bacteria, the justice refused to allow cross-examination of the local authority's expert. On the manufacturer's appeal against conviction, *held*, although it had been decided that a justice condemning food was acting in an administrative capacity rather than a judicial capacity, his decision was nevertheless likely to affect adversely a defendant's rights and interests. A justice was therefore under a duty to exercise his powers in accordance with natural justice, especially where he was statutorily obliged to reach his decision on the basis of evidence. Although a refusal to allow cross-examination was not always unfair, here, the manufacturer's livelihood had been affected by the justice's decision, as a valuable quantity of cheese had been condemned. Moreover, since the scientific evidence was in dispute, there was a need for it to be tested by careful and thorough cross-examination, and for the qualifications and experience of the expert witnesses to be investigated. In refusing to allow cross-examination, the justice had been unable to reach a fully informed decision. Accordingly, the appeal would be allowed.

Errington v Wilson 1995 SLT 1193 (Outer House). *R v Cornwall Quarter Sessions, ex p Kerley* [1956] 1 WLR 906, doubted.

1421 Food safety—temperature control

The Food Safety (Temperature Control) Regulations 1995, SI 1995/2200 (in force on 15 September 1995), apply to all stages of food production, except for primary production, but do not apply to activities of food businesses, except those relating to fishery products. The regulations contain new food temperature control requirements with respect to chilled food, including provision for the upward variation of the standard temperature in appropriate circumstances. There are also defences which relate to the tolerance periods for which food may be held outside temperature control. In addition, the regulations contain requirements relating to food which needs to be kept hot and include defences which allow for downward variation of the minimum temperature in appropriate circumstances. A new general temperature control requirement is added which prohibits the keeping of perishable foodstuffs at temperatures which would result in a risk to health. Further, provision is made in relation to the cooling of food. The regulations also deal with offences, penalties and enforcement.

1422 Fruit juices and fruit nectars—manufacturing

The Fruit Juices and Fruit Nectars (England, Wales and Scotland) (Amendment) Regulations 1995, SI 1995/236 (in force on 1 March 1995), amend the 1977 Regulations, SI 1977/927 and 1026, to implement Commission Directive (EC) 93/45 concerning the manufacture of nectars. Fruit nectar may be manufactured using apricots, other specified fruit or any admixture thereof without the addition of sugar or honey, where the naturally high sugar content of such fruit so warrants.

1423 Materials in contact with food

The Plastic Materials and Articles in Contact with Food (Amendment) Regulations 1995, SI 1995/360 (in force on 10 March 1995), amend the 1992 Regulations, SI 1992/3145, and implement EC Regulations laying down the basic rules necessary for testing migration of the constituents of plastic materials and articles intended to come into contact with foodstuffs.

1424 Meat—fresh meat—licensing of premises

The Fresh Meat (Hygiene and Inspection) Regulations 1995, SI 1995/539 (in force on 1 April 1995), replace the 1992 Regulations, 1992/2037, to give effect to Community law (1) on health problems affecting the trade in fresh meat to extend it to the production and marketing of fresh meat, (2) concerning public health and animal health problems affecting the production and placing on the market of farmed game meat, and (3) on public health and animal health problems relating to the killing and placing on the market of wild game. The regulations provide for the licensing of slaughterhouses and other establishments and for the appointment of veterinary surgeons and inspectors to supervise such premises. The relevant minister must provide health marking equipment and arrange for the mark to be applied to fresh meat which is fit for human consumption. Fresh meat may not be sold for human consumption unless it is obtained from licensed premises, meets hygiene requirements and is accompanied by a commercial document or health certificate. Certain conditions must be complied with before a dead or slaughtered animal is brought into a slaughterhouse or farmed game processing facility. Occupiers of licensed premises must keep certain records and responsibility for the execution and enforcement of regulations is transferred from local authorities to the minister.

The Fresh Meat (Hygiene and Inspection) (Amendment) Regulations 1995, SI 1995/3189 (in force on 1 January 1996), amend the 1995 Regulations, SI 1995/539, to incorporate the amendments made to Council Regulation (EC) 64/443 on conditions for the production and marketing of fresh meat. The regulations amend the number of animals which constitutes a 'livestock unit' and make provision for the extension of the deadline for the completion of work needed to bring premises up to the required standard. In addition, certain throughput limits for 'low throughput slaughterhouses' are increased and provision is made for the microbiological testing for salmonella of meat destined for Sweden and Finland. Further, provision is made regarding the removal of certain lymph nodes from specified bovines.

1425 Meat—hygiene, inspection and examinations for residues—charges

The Meat (Hygiene, Inspection and Examinations for Residues) (Charges) Regulations 1995, SI 1995/361, implement provisions concerning the level of fees to be charged for health inspections and controls on meat contained in Council Directive (EC) 85/73, as amended, on the financing of health inspections and controls on fresh meat and poultry. The regulations (1) require the minister to make a charge for the performance of his functions relating to health inspection and control exercises in respect of domestic animal or domestic bird meat and to examinations for the presence of residues; (2) provide for the calculation of charges for health inspections and control exercises carried out at slaughterhouses, cutting premises, rewrapping centres and cold stores; (3) make provision for calculating charges for examinations for the presence of residues and authorise the minister to charge for health inspections and control exercises in respect of game meat; (4) require that before he fixes charges, the minister gives notice of the amount of the proposed charge and considers representations made concerning the charge by any person whom he has notified; (5) require that the minister is provided with the necessary information to calculate charges under these regulations and with any evidence necessary to verify such information. In addition the regulations revoke or amend the following: SI 1990/2494, 1991/2843, 1992/2037, 2353, 1993/1359, 1360, 1994/1029.

The Meat (Hygiene, Inspection and Examinations for Residues) (Charges) (Amendment) Regulations 1995, SI 1995/2836 (in force on 24 November 1995), amend the 1995 Regulations supra so as to introduce new charging rates for examinations for the presence of residues.

1426 Meat—minced meat and meat preparations—hygiene

The Minced Meat and Meat Preparations (Hygiene) Regulations 1995, SI 1995/3205 (in force on 1 January 1996), implement Council Directive (EC) 94/65 which lays down the requirements for the production and placing on the market of minced meat and meat preparations. The regulations require premises producing relevant meat and meat preparations to be approved and conditions for the consignment or sale for consignment of minced meat and meat preparations are specified. In addition, certain requirements relating to transportation are to be met. Food authorities must provide required information to the relevant minister regarding the execution of their duties and enforcement authorities are responsible for the supervision of premises and the enforcement of the regulations. Further, offences are created and penalties prescribed for contravention of any provision. The regulations do not apply to certain premises producing or storing such meat or preparations or to certain mechanically recovered meat.

1427 Milk—Milk Development Council

The Milk Development Council Order 1995, SI 1995/356 (in force on 7 February 1995), establishes the Milk Development Council for the milk industry in Great Britain. The order assigns functions to the council, provides for the appointment of members and council proceedings as well as the keeping of a register of producers. It empowers the council to require registered producers to furnish returns containing prescribed information and to impose charges for expenses incurred in the exercise of their functions. Provision is made for the borrowing and investment of money and offences and penalties are prescribed.

1428 Poultry, farmed game bird and rabbit meat—hygiene and inspection

The Poultry Meat, Farmed Game Bird Meat and Rabbit Meat (Hygiene and Inspection) Regulations 1995, SI 1995/540 (in force on 1 April 1995), replace the 1994 Regulations, SI 1994/1029, and give effect to Council Directives (EC) 71/118, 91/495 and, in part, 91/494. The regulations provide for the licensing of slaughterhouses, cutting premises, cold stores and re-wrapping centres, and also make provision for applications, revocations and appeals in relation to licences. Official veterinary surgeons are designated and appointed, and inspectors are appointed, to supervise licensed premises, and surgeons' powers are specified. The use of a slaughterhouse for slaughtering a bird or rabbit not intended for sale for human consumption is prohibited. Authorisations of persons as plant inspection assistants may be made and provisions relating to such authorisations are specified. The regulations require the minister to arrange for pre-slaughter and post-mortem health inspections of birds and rabbits and to make provisions in relation to the application of the health mark. The operation of licensed premises without giving advance notice to the minister is prohibited except in certain circumstances and certain conditions must be complied with in relation to the sale of fresh meat for human consumption. In addition, documents required for the transport of fresh meat are specified, slaughter in certain circumstances may be prohibited and surgeons must keep specified records and notify the presence of specified diseases. Occupiers and producers are under specified duties and the regulations create offences and prescribe penalties. Provision is made in relation to the minister's recovery of costs, food authorities are required to supply him with particular information and enforcement authorities are specified. Further, provisions are made for the application of the Food Safety Act 1990 and the import of meat from Northern Ireland, the Channel Islands and the Isle of Man.

1429 Slaughter or killing of animals—welfare

The Welfare of Animals (Slaughter or Killing) Regulations 1995, SI 1995/731 (in force on 1 April 1995), give effect to Council Directive (EC) 93/119 on the protection of animals at the time of slaughter or killing. The regulations apply to the movement, lairaging, restraint, stunning, slaughter and killing of animals bred and kept for the production of meat, skin, fur or other products, to the killing of animals for the purpose of disease control and to the killing of surplus chicks and embryos in hatchery waste. Provisions cover the slaughter or killing of animals in slaughterhouses, knackers' yards or elsewhere and the slaughter of animals by a religious method. The regulations provide for the powers of authorised officers and, in addition, create offences and penalties in relation to any contravention of the regulations.

1430 Spirits—description and definition

The Spirit Drinks (Amendment) Regulations 1995, SI 1995/732 (in force on 3 April 1995), amend the 1990 Regulations, SI 1990/1179, to update various references to EC legislation and to make provision for the enforcement and execution of further legislation which lays down detailed implementing rules on the definition, description and presentation of spirit drinks and applies the agreements between the European Union and third countries on the mutual recognition of certain spirit drinks.

1431 Welfare foods

See SOCIAL SECURITY AND SOCIAL SERVICES.

1432 Wild game meat—hygiene and inspection

The Wild Game Meat (Hygiene and Inspection) Regulations 1995, SI 1995/2148 (in force on 20 September 1995), give effect, in part, to Council Directive (EC) 92/45 on public health and animal health problems relating to the killing of wild game and the placing on the market of wild game meat. The regulations require wild game processing facilities, which consign or sell for consignment wild game meat, to be licensed. A licence will only be issued if the facilities comply with prescribed requirements. A licence may be refused or granted subject to conditions and may be revoked. Licensed premises will be supervised by official veterinary surgeons and inspectors and the times of operation of such premises are controlled. The regulations provide that a health mark is to be applied to all wild game meat produced in licensed premises which is fit for human consumption. Records must be kept in respect of inspections and occupiers of premises must also keep specified records. In addition, the regulations specify the duties of occupiers and create offences and penalties.

FOREIGN RELATIONS LAW

Halsbury's Laws of England (4th edn) Vol 18, paras 1401–1908

1433 Asylum

See BRITISH NATIONALITY, IMMIGRATION AND RACE RELATIONS.

1434 Consular fees

The Consular Fees Order 1995, SI 1995/1617 (in force on 20 July 1995), replaces SI 1994/2793 and SI 1994/3202, so as to increase by approximately 60 per cent some consular fees. This is intended to meet the increased cost of providing the services, and is a step towards eventual full cost recovery. The order also repeals the fee for issuing an excursion document for travel to France, and makes new provision for a multiple entry clearance to be issued, valid for one year.

1435 European Communities

See EUROPEAN COMMUNITIES.

1436 Geneva Conventions (Amendment) Act 1995

The Geneva Conventions (Amendment) Act 1995 makes provision for the amendment of the Geneva Conventions Act 1957 to enable effect to be given to the protocols additional to the Geneva Conventions of 1949 (protection of victims of international and non-international armed conflicts). The Act received the royal assent on 19 July 1995 and comes into force on a day or days to be appointed. For details of commencement, see the commencement table in the title STATUTES.

Section 1 amends the 1957 Act, s 1 to provide that any grave breach of the first protocol constitutes an offence on the same basis as a grave breach of any of the Geneva Conventions.

Section 2 amends the 1957 Act, s 6 (unauthorised use of Red Cross or Red Crescent emblem). The function of giving authority for such use is conferred on the Secretary of State and the international sign of civil defence and the international distinctive signals for identifying medical units and transports are added to the list of signs and signals protected under s 6(1), (2). The maximum fine for breach of the 1957 Act, s 6(1), (2) is increased from level 3 to level 5 on the standard scale and the power of forfeiture is extended to articles other than goods: s 2.

Section 3 inserts a new s 6A into the 1957 Act to enable the Secretary of State to make regulations conferring general authority for the use of anything mentioned in s 6(1), (2) or otherwise regulating the use for the purposes of any of the scheduled conventions, or the first or second protocol of any emblem, designation, sign or signal. Section 4 amends the 1957 Act, s 7 to modify and insert definitions and to add supplementary material. For the purposes of the 1995 Act, the protocols inserted into the 1957 Act by the 1995 Act, s 6, Schedule are to be read subject to any reservations or declarations made on ratification by the United Kingdom, the text of which is certified by an order in council: s 4. An order in council may be made revoking or revising an earlier order to take account of the withdrawal or partial withdrawal of any reservation or declaration: s 4. Section 5 contains repeals and s 7 deals with short title, commencement and extent.

1437 Human rights
See HUMAN RIGHTS.

1438 International Court of Justice—judgment—request to reopen judgment—jurisdiction
The International Court of Justice gave judgment in a case involving atmospheric nuclear testing brought by New Zealand against France. The judgment stated that New Zealand could request an examination of the situation in accordance with the relevant statute. Twenty years later, following the resumption of underground nuclear tests by France, New Zealand requested an examination of the situation in accordance with the judgment. On the hearing of the request, *held*, the question consisted of two elements, the first concerning the courses of procedure envisaged by the court in the judgment when it stated that New Zealand could request an examination of the situation and the second concerning the effect on the basis of the judgment. With regard to the first element, in laying down that New Zealand could request an examination of the situation in specified circumstances, the court could not have intended to limit the application to legal procedures such as the filing of a new application, a request for interpretation or a request for revision. Neither had the court excluded a special procedure in the event that the specified circumstances arose. Such a procedure was indissociably linked with the existence of those circumstances, and if they did not arise the procedure was unavailable. With regard to the second element, the basis of the judgment was France's undertaking not to conduct any further atmospheric nuclear tests. It was only in the event of resumption of such tests that the basis of the judgment would have been affected and that hypothesis had not materialised. The court could not, therefore, take into account questions relating to underground nuclear tests. Accordingly, the basis of the judgment had not been affected, and the request would be dismissed on the ground that it did not fall within the judgment.

New Zealand v France (1995) Times, 6 October (International Court of Justice).

1439 International Court of Justice—jurisdiction—requirement for state's consent to jurisdiction
Following Indonesia's entry into East Timor, East Timor became an Indonesian province. Indonesia and Australia concluded a treaty on the exploitation of the continental shelf lying between Australia and East Timor. Portugal, the administering power of East Timor, contended that, in taking measures to apply the treaty, Australia had violated the rights of the people of East Timor to self-determination and violated Portugal's rights as an administering power. Portugal applied to the International Court of Justice to determine the matter. *Held*, before assessing Australia's behaviour, the court necessarily had to determine whether, having regard to the circumstances in which Indonesia had entered and remained in East Timor, it could or could not have acquired the power to enter into treaties on behalf of East Timor relating to the resources of the continental shelf. The court would therefore have to rule on the lawfulness of Indonesia's conduct as a prerequisite for deciding on Portugal's contention. Indonesia had not accepted the jurisdiction of the International Court of Justice and its rights and obligations would therefore constitute the subject matter of a judgment made in the absence of the state's consent. Such a judgment would run directly counter to the well established principle of international

law that the court could only exercise jurisdiction over a state with the state's consent. Accordingly, the court found that it could not rule on Portugal's claims on the merits whatever the importance of the questions raised by those claims and of the rules of international law which they brought into play.

Case concerning East Timor (Portugal v Australia) (1995) Times, 18 July (International Court of Justice). *Monetary Gold removed from Rome in 1943* [1954] ICJR 32 considered.

1440 International organisations—Asian Development Bank—extension of limit on guarantees

The Asian Development Bank (Extension of Limit on Guarantees) Order 1995, SI 1995/1502 (in force on 25 May 1995), increases to £230m the limit on the aggregate amount of sums payable under the Overseas Development and Co-operation Act 1980, s 7(1)(a) (which provides that the Secretary of State must pay out of money provided by Parliament any sum which may be required to make payments in fulfilment of any undertaking given by the United Kingdom Government in pursuance of art 3, para 3 of the Agreement for the establishment and operation of the Asian Development Bank).

1441 International organisations—Asian Development Bank—payments to capital stock

The Asian Development Bank (Further Payments to Capital Stock) Order 1995, SI 1995/1503 (in force on 25 May 1995), provides for (1) the payment to the Asian Development Bank of a subscription not exceeding the equivalent of US $435,866,318.50 to the increased authorised capital stock of the bank pursuant to arrangements made with the bank in accordance with Resolution 232 adopted by the Board of Governors of the bank on 22 May 1994; (2) payments to maintain the value of the subscription to the increased authorised capital stock and for the redemption of non-interest-bearing and non-negotiable notes issued by the Secretary of State in payment of the subscription; and (3) any sums which may be received by the government of the United Kingdom in pursuance of the arrangements to be paid into the Consolidated Fund.

1442 International organisations—legal capacity—recognition by English law

The defendant was an international organisation formed through a treaty signed by Egypt and the Gulf States, for the purpose of the manufacture of arms. The treaty expressly stated that the defendant was to have a juridical personality and was not subject to the law of any member state. Due to the signature of a peace treaty between Egypt and Israel, the other member states declared that the defendant would be liquidated, but the Egyptian government purported, by the making of domestic laws, to continue its existence as an exclusively Egyptian organisation. The plaintiff company had entered into a joint venture with the defendant, which was cancelled. As a result of arbitration proceedings arising from the cancellation, the plaintiff obtained a garnishee order against six banks holding deposits belonging to the defendant. The Egyptian organisation intervened to have the garnishee order struck out on the ground that it was the same as the defendant and therefore was the true owner of the bank accounts. On a preliminary issue as to the whether the Egyptian organisation was the same as the defendant, *held*, English law only recognised a foreign entity as having a legal personality if it had been accorded legal personality under the law of a foreign state recognised by England. The fact that several states had accorded it legal capacity under their law did not mean that there was more than one international organisation for the English courts to recognise, but merely that there was more than one factual basis upon which recognition could be accorded to the same organisation. Once such recognition had been accorded, questions of nationality and domicile became irrelevant. The proper law governing the defendant was public international law as it would be contrary to the comity of nations if the court applied the law of only one member state as governing law, particularly when the founding treaty had expressly indicated that the organisation must not be subject to any domestic law. As the Egyptian organisation's claim that it was the same organisation as the defendant was based on a non-justiciable issue of Egyptian law, it was unable to prove its claim.

Westland Helicopters Ltd v Arab Organisation for Industrialisation [1995] 2 WLR 126 (Queen's Bench Division: Colman J).

1443 Privileges and immunities—diplomatic immunity—industrial tribunal proceedings

See *London Branch of the Nigerian Universities Commission v Bastians*, para 1228.

1444   Privileges and immunities—jurisdictional immunity—commercial activities

RSC Ord 65, r 3 provides that where a writ is served on a body corporate in accordance with Ord 10, r 1(2), that rule has effect as if for the reference to the knowledge of the defendant there were substituted a reference to the knowledge of the mayor, chairman or president of the body, or the town-clerk, secretary, treasurer or other similar officer thereof. The State Immunities Act 1978, s 14(2) provides that a separate entity is immune from the jurisdiction of the United Kingdom courts if the proceedings relate to anything done by it in the exercise of sovereign authority and the circumstances are such that a state would have been so immune. By s 3, a state is not immune in respect of proceedings relating to commercial transactions, which are any activities in which a state engages otherwise than in the exercise of sovereign authority.

Following Iraq's invasion of Kuwait, the Iraqi government ordered the defendant, a state-owned company, to take over the plaintiff's aircraft. The defendant used the aircraft as part of its own fleet, and also in accordance with instructions given by the Iraqi government. When the Kuwaiti government regained power, the plaintiff issued a writ in England against the defendant and the Iraqi government in respect of the aircraft. The Commonwealth and Foreign Office sent the documents for service on the Iraqi government to the Iraqi Embassy in London, with a letter requesting the Embassy to forward them to the relevant minister in Iraq. However, that was not done. The documents for service on the defendant were served on one of the defendant's employees. Upon judgment in default being entered against the defendant and the Iraqi government, the Iraqi government applied for judgment to be set aside, and the defendant claimed that it was entitled to immunity under the 1978 Act, s 14(2). The defendant's application was dismissed, but the Iraqi government's application was allowed. On appeal, the defendant's appeal was allowed. On further appeal, *held*, the defendant had been validly served, as the employee on whom the writ had been served was an 'other similar officer', within the meaning of RSC Ord 65, r 3. As regards service on the Iraqi government, the delivery of the writ by the Commonwealth and Foreign Office to the Iraqi Embassy was, at best, a request to forward the writ to Iraq. As that had not been done, service had not been properly effected. As regards the defendant's claim of immunity from jurisdiction, although the defendant had been acting in the exercise of sovereign authority in removing the plaintiff's aircraft to Iraq and using them as directed by the Iraqi government, after the aircraft had been incorporated into its fleet, the defendant could not be said to have been acting in the exercise of sovereign authority. It therefore could not claim immunity. Accordingly, on the issue of immunity, the plaintiff's appeal would be allowed, but on the issue of the validity of service on the Iraqi government, the plaintiff's appeal would be dismissed.

Kuwait Airways Corpn v Iraqi Airways Co [1995] 3 All ER 694 (House of Lords: Lords Goff of Chieveley, Jauncey of Tullichettle, Mustill, Slynn of Hadley, Nicholls of Birkenhead). Decision of Court of Appeal (1993) Times, 27 October (1993 Abr para 1314) reversed in part.

1445   Privileges and immunities—state immunity—exception—contract of employment

The applicants complained of unfair dismissal against their employer which entered a notice of appearance claiming state immunity and named a legal representative. Notice of a preliminary hearing was sent to the representative although the tribunal had been informed that he no longer acted for the employer. In the employer's absence, an industrial tribunal decided that the State Immunity Act 1978, s 4(1), by virtue of which proceedings in relation to contracts of employment were excluded from the general immunity granted to a foreign state, gave the tribunal jurisdiction to hear the applicants' complaints. The employer appealed against a refusal to extend the time for appealing. *Held*, the 1978 Act, s 1(2) conferred a positive duty on a court or tribunal to satisfy itself that effect had been given to the immunity conferred by the Act. If the industrial tribunal which had heard the original proceedings had not given effect to that immunity, the appeal tribunal had a duty to do so by correcting the error. The employer had shown a reasonably arguable case that the industrial tribunal had failed to apply the law of state immunity correctly. Accordingly, the appeal would be allowed and the time for appealing would be extended even though the employer had not offered an acceptable excuse for failing to comply with the time limit.

United Arab Emirates v Abdelghafar [1995] ICR 65 (Employment Appeal Tribunal: Mummery J presiding).

1446   Privileges and immunities—World Trade Organisation

The World Trade Organisation (Immunities and Privileges) Order 1995, SI 1995/266 (in force on a date to be notified in the London Gazette), confers privileges and immunities on the World Trade Organisation, its officials and representatives of its members.

1447 United Nations—arms embargo—dependent territories

The United Nations Arms Embargoes (Dependent Territories) Order 1995, SI 1995/1032 (in force on 16 May 1995), applies to certain dependent territories. The order imposes restrictions pursuant to decisions of the Security Council of the United Nations (Resolution 713 of 25 September 1991, Resolution 733 of 23 January 1992, Resolution 788 of 19 November 1992 and Resolution 918 of 17 May 1994) which made provision for states to implement a general and complete embargo on all deliveries of weapons and military equipment to the former Yugoslavia.

1448 United Nations—sanctions—enforcement under domestic legislation

See *R v Searle*, para 598.

FORESTRY

Halsbury's Laws of England (4th edn) Vol 19(1) (reissue), paras 1–100

1449 Plant health—protective measures—Community requirements

The Plant Health (Forestry) (Great Britain) (Amendment) Order 1995, SI 1995/1989 (in force on 21 August 1995), amends the 1993 Order, SI 1993/1283, to reflect changes in the recognised protected zones agreed in accordance with the procedure laid down by Council Directive (EC) 77/93 on protective measures against the introduction of organisms into the Community, and their spread within the Community, which are harmful to plants or plant products. Provision is also made to improve protection against the introduction and spread of tree pests.

FRIENDLY SOCIETIES

Halsbury's Laws of England (4th edn) Vol 19(1) (reissue), paras 101–500

1450 Corporation Tax Acts—application—modification

The Friendly Societies (Modification of the Corporation Tax Acts) (Amendment) Regulations 1995, SI 1995/1916 (in force on 10 August 1995), amends the 1992 Regulations, SI 1992/1655. The 1992 Regulations are made by the Treasury and modify the application of the Corporation Tax Acts in their application to life or endowment business carried on by friendly societies and the 1995 Regulations make various amendments to the modifications.

1451 Finance Act 1995

See para 2489.

1452 Friendly Societies Commission—general charge

The Friendly Societies (General Charge and Fees) Regulations 1995, SI 1995/709 (in force on 1 April 1995), replace the 1993 Regulations, SI 1993/547, and provide for a general charge to be paid by friendly societies towards the expenses of the Friendly Societies Commission. Each society is required to pay a sum equal to 0.24 per cent of its specified income, as indicated by its contributions from members and interest on investments reported in its annual return for the year ended 31 December 1993, subject to a maximum charge of £19,500. The regulations also increase the fees payable for matters transacted under the Friendly Societies Act 1974 or the Friendly Societies Act 1992.

1453 Life or endowment business—management and capital allowances expenses—exemption from tax

See *Homeowners Friendly Society Ltd v Barrett (Inspector of Taxes)*, para 1632.

1454 Regulation of societies—transitional provision

The Friendly Societies Act 1992 (Transitional and Consequential Provisions) Regulations 1995, SI 1995/710 (in force on 1 April 1995), make transitional and consequential provision as a result of the coming into force of provisions of the Friendly Societies Act 1992. The transitional provisions continue the effect of specified provisions relating to long term insurance business and permit, for specified periods, a friendly society or registered branch to prepare its balance sheet as formerly permitted to registered societies and registered branches under the Friendly Societies Act 1974, s 30 (true and fair view of assets and liabilities) rather than under the 1992 Act, s 70 (true and fair view of the state of affairs).

1455 Subsidiary—activities

The Friendly Societies (Activities of a Subsidiary) Order 1995, SI 1995/3062 (in force on 1 January 1996), amends the Friendly Societies Act 1992, Sch 7 (activities which may be carried on by a subsidiary of, or body jointly controlled by, an incorporated friendly society) so as to add the new activities of personal deposit taking and personal lines general insurance. The order also extends the activity of providing administrative services to friendly societies or other bodies whose business consists of any activity falling within Sch 7 so that such services may be provided to a body whose business consists of one of the new activities.

1456 Transfer of business—taxation

The Friendly Societies (Taxation of Transfers of Business) Regulations 1995, SI 1995/171 (in force on 17 February 1995), provide that the provisions of the Corporation Tax Acts which apply on the transfer of the whole or part of the long term business of an insurance company to another company have effect where the transferee is a friendly society. The regulations also modify the application of the Corporation Tax Acts and the Income and Corporation Taxes Act 1988, s 440 (charge to corporation tax on chargeable gains) in their application to the business of friendly societies.

FUEL AND ENERGY

Halsbury's Laws of England (4th edn) Vol 19(1) (reissue), paras 501–800, Vol 19(2) (reissue), paras 801–1921

1457 Articles

Electricity: The Time to Act? Martyn Day and James Cameron (on the difficulties involved in litigation over health dangers from electricity supply): 139 SJ 67

1458 Atomic energy and radioactive substances—hospitals—exemption

The Radioactive Substances (Hospitals) Exemption (Amendment) Order 1995, SI 1995/2395 (in force on 3 October 1995), amends the 1990 Order, SI 1990/2512, by extending the exemptions from registraion under the Radioactive Substances Act 1993, s 7 for the keeping and use of certain radioactive materials on hospital premises. Subject to specified conditions, the order also excludes certain radioactive waste kept on hospital premises from the provisions of s 13(1).

1459 Atomic energy and radioactive substances—nuclear installations—safety— international convention

A convention on nuclear safety was signed in Vienna on 20 September 1994 (Cm 2927). The contracting parties undertake to take the necessary steps to secure the safety of existing nuclear installations and to ensure that all reasonably practicable improvements to upgrade such installations are made as a matter of urgency. Suitable legislation must be enacted and retained in force. Primary responsibility for the safety of nuclear installations must reside with the licensed operators. All organisations concerned with such installations must ensure that due priority is given to matters of safety, but contracting parties must ensure that adequate funds are available to support each installation throughout its life, that appropriately qualified staff are available, that quality assurance programmes are established and implemented, that safety assessments are carried out and that the physical state of installations is verified. Contracting parties are also required to take appropriate steps to ensure that the radiation exposure of all staff and the public is kept to the minimum reasonaby achievable and that suitable plans are prepared to deal with emergencies. The responsibilities of contracting parties in relation to the siting of installations, their design, construction and operation are also set down. The convention will enter into force 90 days after the deposit of the 22nd ratification etc, provided that at least 17 states with operative nuclear installations have so ratified. The United Kingdom has not ratified the convention.

1460 Atomic Energy Authority Act 1995

The Atomic Energy Authority Act 1995 makes provision for the transfer of property, rights and liabilities of the United Kingdom Atomic Energy Authority. The Act received the royal assent on 8 November 1995 and came into force on that date.

Section 1 imposes on the United Kingdom Atomic Energy Authority ('the authority') a duty to make schemes for the transfer of property, rights and liabilities (with the exception of nuclear site licences) in accordance with the directions of the Secretary of State, and Sch 1 contains detailed provisions as to the making of schemes, including the payment of compensation to third parties whose interests or rights are diminished in value or extinguished. Section 2 sets out the powers of the Secretary of State to give directions to the authority. Section 3 confers supplementary powers on the authority. Section 4 enables the authority and the Secretary of State to enter into agreements with third parties with respect to transfer schemes. Under s 5, the authority must provide any information and assistance required by the Secretary of State in connection with the exercise of his powers. Section 6 and Sch 2 provide for the financial structure and control of successor companies while they are publicly owned. By virtue of s 7, the authority must not dispose of any securities of any successor company without the consent of the Secretary of State and the Treasury. Section 8 and Sch 3 provide for the tax consequences of a transfer to a successor company and the tax effects of issuing securities and of extinguishing liabilities. Section 9 and Sch 4 enable employees of the authority to remain in the authority's pension schemes after a transfer to a successor company so long as the company remains publicly owned. Under s 10 the Secretary of State may, with the consent of the Treasury extinguish certain of the authority's liabilities. Section 11 reduces the minimum number of members of the authority from seven to four and removes the need for members of the authority to possess certain expertise and experience. Sections 12 to 14 contain supplementary provisions as to expenses, interpretation, short title and extent.

1461 Electricity—electricity supply—cables—link with cancer—application for issue of guidelines

It has been held that the Secretary of State is under no duty, either under domestic or European law, to issue regulations to control emissions of electromagnetic fields from high-voltage cables forming part of the national grid. Where there is a clear risk of personal injury or damage to property arising from the transmission of electricity through such power cables, the Secretary of State is under a duty to protect the public from that risk by the making of appropriate directions. However, an unproven possibility that such emissions might cause childhood leukaemia in the locality of the power cables is not sufficient to impose such a duty on him.

R v Secretary of State for Trade and Industry, ex p Dudridge (1995) Independent, 20 October, Times, 26 October (Court of Appeal: Kennedy and Peter Gibson LJJ and Sir Iain Glidewell). Leave to appeal against decision of Queen's Bench Divisional Court (1994) Independent, 4 October (1994 Abr para 1438) refused.

1462 Electricity—electricity supply—connection charge—dispute—reference to Director General

The Electricity Act 1989, s 23(1) provides that any dispute arising under ss 16–22 between a public electricity supplier and a person requiring a supply of electricity may be referred to the Director General of Electricity Supply by either party, and on such a reference, the dispute must be determined by order made either by the director or an arbitrator appointed by him.

The licensed public electricity supplier for the area in which a building company had built new houses, increased the amount charged for connecting the houses to the electricity supply system. The building company considered that the charges were unreasonable, but nevertheless paid them. Other builders, who had not paid the connection charges, referred the matter to the Director General, who decided that the charges were excessive. When the building company sought to refer the reasonableness of their connection charges to the director, he was advised that he had no power to determine a reference once a charge had been paid. On the building company's application for judicial review, *held*, a broad interpretation had to be given to the 1989 Act, s 23, as the Act did not state that a reference had to be made within a given time limit or prior to payment of a disputed charge. Moreover, if a narrow interpretation was given to s 23(1), the parties and the director would lose the opportunity of having a test case heard, and it would cause other practical and substantive difficulties for customers who wished to dispute a charge even after they had paid it. Although the Act made electricity suppliers vulnerable to being forced to make connections, customers were also vulnerable because of the monopoly position held by suppliers. In the instant case, a dispute had arisen, and the director was obliged to determine it if it was referred to him. Accordingly, the application would be granted.

R v Director General of Electricity Supply, ex p Redrow Homes (Northern) Ltd (1995) Times, 21 February (Queen's Bench Division: Schiemann J).

1463 Electricity—electricity supply—non-fossil fuel sources

The Electricity (Non-Fossil Fuel Sources) (England and Wales) (Amendment) Order 1995, SI 1995/68 (in force on 17 January 1995), amends the 1994 Order, SI 1994/3259, so as to remove the obligation on public electricity suppliers in England and Wales to make arrangements to secure the availability during certain periods (defined in the order) of generating capacity from non-fossil fuel generating stations of the descriptions specified in the order. The order also amends the definition of one of the periods and reduces certain aggregate amounts of generating capacity in respect of one of the periods.

1464 Electricity—electricity supply—relationship between supplier and customer— whether agreement to supply amounting to contract

See *Norweb plc v Dixon*, para 659.

1465 Electricity—electricity supply—requirement of consent for overhead lines—power to award costs

A proposal had been made by a licence holder under the Electricity Act 1989 for a new overhead line crossing the applicant's land. An application for compulsory wayleave was made but before the hearing could be completed the inspector fell ill. The applicant requested that the Secretary of State exercise his power to award the costs of the hearing against the licence holder and applied for judicial review of the decision that there was no provision for one party to a wayleave hearing to pay the costs of another. *Held*, the Secretary of State did not have power to make an award of costs following a wayleave hearing under the 1989 Act. There had been no assimilation of provisions on costs in wayleave hearings under the 1989 Act as there had been in relation to inquiries. Accordingly, the application would be dismissed.

R v Department of Trade and Industry, ex p Healaugh Farms (1995) Times, 27 December (Queen's Bench Division: Carnwath J).

1466 Electricity—electricity supply—rateable values

See para 2465.

1467 Electricity—electricity supply—standards of performance

The Electricity (Standards of Performance) (Amendment) Regulations 1995, SI 1995/687 (in force on 1 April 1995), revoke and replace Schs 2–4 and 6–14 of the 1993 Regulations, SI 1993/1193, so as to revise the periods in respect of the matters referred to in regs 5(2)(a), (b) (installation of a meter and provision of an electricity supply), 9(4)(b) (meter disputes), and 10(2)(a), (b) (queries about charges and payments) of the 1993 Regulations.

1468 Energy—European Energy Charter—implementation

See para 3124.

1469 Finance Act 1995

See para 2489.

1470 Fuel—hydrocarbons licensing—authorisations for prospection, exploration and production—criteria

The Hydrocarbons Licensing Directive Regulations 1995, SI 1995/1434 (in force on 30 June 1995), give effect in part to Council Directive (EC) 94/22, on the conditions for granting and using authorisations for the prospection, exploration and production of hydrocarbons. The regulations (1) restrict the criteria which the Secretary of State may take into account when considering an application for a licence made in accordance with regulations under the Petroleum (Production) Act 1934; (2) provide that the criteria determining applications are to be published, together with the notice inviting applications, in the Official Journal of the European Communities; (3) provide that an application may be refused on the grounds of national security if the applicant is effectively controlled by nationals of a state which is not a member state but otherwise the criteria may not be applied in a discriminatory manner; (4) provide that when an application is unsuccessful, the applicant is to be notified on request of the reasons for the decision; (5) limit the terms and conditions which may be imposed on the grant of a licence: (6) provide that such terms and conditions must be applied in a non-discriminatory manner; (7) provide that where the Secretary of State has invited applications for a licence he must make available to interested parties a statement of the terms and conditions upon which the licence will be granted, and any changes made in those terms and conditions prior to the grant of the licence must be made available to any person who has requested such a statement; (8) require the Secretary of State to limit the term of any licence granted to the period necessary for the proper performance of the activities authorised by the licence and restrict the circumstances in which the Secretary of State may extend a licence; and (9) limit the Secretary of State's powers to request information from a licensee and to monitor the activities of the licensee.

1471 Fuel—offshore installations—health and safety at work

See para 1509.

1472 Gas Act 1995

The Gas Act 1995 amends the Gas Act 1986, Pts I and II to make provision for requiring the owners of certain gas processing facilities to make them available to other persons and for connected purposes. The Act received the royal assent on 8 November 1995 and certain provisions came into force on that date. The remaining provisions come into force on a day or days to be appointed. For details of commencement, see the commencement table in the title STATUTES.

Section 1 amends the 1986 Act, s 4 relating to the general duties of the Secretary of State and the Director General of Gas Supply ('the Director'). Section 2 inserts a new s 4A into the 1986 Act which imposes additional duties on the Secretary of State and the Director in relation to safety and requires them, in carrying out their functions under the 1986 Act, Pt I, to consult the Health and Safety Executive in respect of safety matters. For the 1986 Act, s 5 a new provision is substituted making it an offence for a person to convey, supply or ship gas unless he is authorised to do so by licence. Exceptions to that prohibition are contained in the 1995 Act, Sch 1, inserted as Sch 2A into the 1986 Act. The 1986 Act, s 6A is substituted and empowers the Secretary of State after consultation with the Director to grant by order an exemption to the requirement for a licence: s 4. The exemption may be subject to conditions and may be revoked if a condition is breached. Section 5 substitutes the 1986 Act, s 7 to make provision for the licensing of public gas transporters. The Director may grant licences authorising a person to convey gas through pipes in his authorised area, as specified in the licence, or to convey it through pipes to any pipe-line system operated by another public gas transporter or to any such system specified in the licence. Notice of the grant or extension of a licence must be given and any representations or objections to it considered. Section 6 inserts a new s 7A into the 1986 Act which deals with the licensing of gas suppliers and gas shippers. Such a licence will not be granted to the holder of a licence under the 1986 Act, s 7. The licences may not artificially exclude premises occupied by disabled people or pensioners, or those who are likely to default in the payment of charges. A new s 7B is inserted into the 1986 Act making provision as to the procedure for applying for licences and for the inclusion of conditions: s 7. Section 8, substituting the 1986 Act, s 8, makes provision for determining standard conditions for inclusion in licences. Section 9 inserts a new s 8B into the 1986 Act which provides for the new gas code, setting out the obligations of licence holders and consumers. The code is in Sch 2, inserted as Sch 2B in the 1986 Act, and it contains many of the provisions of the 1986 Act, Sch 5. Further amendments to the 1986 Act, Pt I are made by s 10, Sch 3 and include provisions relating to the assignment and modification of licences, the powers and duties of public gas transporters, quality standards, safety regulations, the construction of pipe-lines, the determination of disputes and the functions of the Director. Provisions in the 1986 Act, ss 33A–33E relating to standards of service will cease to have effect four years after the new framework for the industry comes into place: s 10. Amendments to the 1986 Act, Pt III are made by s 11. Section 12 provides that the Secretary of State may grant applicants the right to make use of gas processing facilities other than those operated by a public gas transporter. Under s 13 the Director must give information, advice and assistance to the Secretary of State in the exercise of any functions under the 1995 Act. Section 16, Sch 4 contain minor and consequential amendments. Transitional provisions, savings and repeals are contained in s 17 and Schs 5, 6. Section 18 deals with short title, commencement and extent.

1473 Gas—arrangements for supply to electricity generating stations—authority

The Electricity Generating Stations (Gas Contracts) Order 1995, SI 1995/2450 (in force on 16 October 1995), gives a general authority for a person to enter into arrangements for obtaining a supply of natural gas as a fuel for an electricity generating station without giving notice to the Secretary of State under the Energy Act 1976, s 14(2), provided that the duration of such arrangements is expressly limited to a period not exceeding one year.

1474 Gas—meters

The Gas (Meters) (Amendment) Regulations 1995, SI 1995/1251 (in force on 6 June 1995), further amend SI 1983/684 by replacing the reference to fees calculated in accordance with another provision of the regulations, with a reference to the requisite fee. It also declares that only meter examiners in the civil service of the Crown have the duty to re-examine meters.

1475 Home Energy Conservation Act 1995

See para 1292.

1476 Offshore installations and pipeline works—management and administration

The Offshore Installation and Pipeline Works (Management and Administration) Regulations 1995, SI 1995/738 (in force in part on 20 June 1995, and in part on 20 June 1997), contain requirements for the purposes of health and safety which give effect to certain provisions of Council Directive (EC) 92/91. In particular, (1) most of the duties contained in the regulations are imposed on the duty holder, who is defined as being, in relation to a fixed installation, the 'operator', and, in relation to a mobile installation, the 'owner', (2) the duty holder must notify the Health and Safety Executive of the date of the intended entry or departure of an installation into or from relevant waters, and where there is a change of duty holder, an operation cannot take place until details of the change have been notified to the Health and Safety Executive, (3) an installation manager must be appointed, and the regulations set out further requirements in relation to him, (4) the installation manager must take reasonable measures against a person for health and safety reasons, including restraining or putting him ashore, (5) everyone on an installation must co-operate with the installation manager in so far as is necessary to ensure compliance with certain statutory provisions, and they must also co-operate with both the installation manager and the helicopter landing officer in certain circumstances; in addition, installations managers must co-operate with each other for certain health and safety reasons, (6) a record must be kept on the installation, and ashore, of the persons who are on the installation, (7) a 'permit to work' system must be introduced on an installation where it is necessary for health and safety reasons, (8) written instructions must be given as to the procedures which must be observed for health and safety reasons, (9) information must be kept regarding the weather and other matters, (10) those on an installation, or engaged in certain other offshore activities, must have access to the relevant address and telephone number of the Health and Safety Executive, and (11) exemption certificates may be granted by the Health and Safety Executive. Requirements are also set out as regards effective communication, helideck operations, health surveillance, adequate provisions, the ready availability of drinking water, and visual identification of an installation. In addition, the Employers' Liability (Compulsory Insurance) Act 1969 applies to the regulations, with certain modifications and extensions, and certain provisions of the Mineral Workings (Offshore Installations) Act 1971 are repealed or modified, as are certain other instruments.

1477 Offshore installations—prevention of fire and explosion—emergency response

The Offshore Installations (Prevention of Fire and Explosion, and Emergency Response) Regulations 1995, SI 1995/743 (in force on 20 June 1995), give effect to certain provisions of

Council Directives (EC) 92/91 and 89/391, in relation to offshore installations in territorial waters adjacent to Great Britain or in the United Kingdom sector of the continental shelf. Most of the duties are imposed on the 'duty holder' who is, in relation to a fixed installation, the 'operator', and, in relation to a mobile installation, the 'owner'. In particular the regulations (1) impose a general duty on the duty owner to take measures to protect persons on the installation from fire and explosions, and their effects, and for securing effective emergency response, (2) require the duty holder to perform, repeat, and keep a record of an assessment of measures for effective evacuation, escape, recovery and rescue, to avoid or minimise any major accident, and otherwise protect persons from a major accident involving fire or explosion, (3) require the duty holder to establish the organisation and arrangements which are to have effect in an emergency, ensuring that instructions and training are provided on the action to be taken and that written information is provided on the use of emergency plant, (4) require the duty holder to ensure the availability of equipment if an accident occurs involving a helicopter, (5) require the duty holder to prepare and up-date an emergency response plan, which must be available, tested, and its contents known, (6) identify certain kinds of measures which the duty holder can take to prevent fire and explosion, (7) require the duty holder to take appropriate measures for detecting fire and other events which may require emergency response, and for conveying information on certain incidents to places where control action can be instigated, (8) require the duty holder to make arrangements for controlling emergencies and for giving warning of an emergency, (9) require muster areas, evacuation and escape points to be created, and persons assigned to such areas, (10) require the duty holder to ensure that arrangements exist for safe evacuation of persons to a safe place, and for their recovery thereafter, (11) require the duty holder to ensure that a means of escape from the installation exists where the evacuation arrangements fail, (12) require the duty holder to discharge certain duties regarding personal protective equipment, (13) require the duty holder to ensure that plant on an installation is suitable and maintained in a sufficient state, working order and good repair, and that a suitable written scheme is prepared and operated by a competent and independent person for systematic examination of certain plant. The regulations also contain other requirements regarding life-saving appliances and the availability of information on the location of hazardous areas, and a number of statutory provisions are consequently revoked.

See also para 1510.

1478 Petroleum production—landward areas

The Petroleum (Production) (Landward Areas) Regulations 1995, SI 1995/1436 (in force on 30 June 1995), make provision for applications for licences to search for and get petroleum in Great Britain and its adjacent islands and waters known as landward areas, and make revisions to model clauses in such licences. New model clauses for methane drainage licences are set out and a new single exploration and development licence is introduced. The regulations also introduce a new procedure for applications for licences to explore and produce hydrocarbons. Details of the blocks to be licensed, the latest date for applications and the period within which the licences are to be granted are published in the Official Journal of the European Communities. There is also a new procedure enabling a licensee to apply for a licence for an area contiguous to the area or areas covered by its existing licence if the Secretary of State decides that geological or production considerations justify the grant of such a licence. Model clauses for a supplementary seismic survey licence are now contained in the regulations. SI 1991/981 and SI 1982/1000 are revoked.

1479 Petroleum production—seaward areas

The Petroleum (Production) (Seaward Areas) (Amendment) Regulations 1995, SI 1995/1435 (in force on 30 June 1995), amend the 1988 Regulations, SI 1988/1213. The regulations introduce a new procedure for applications for production licences and provide that details of the blocks to be licensed, the latest date for applications and the period within which licences may be granted are published in the Official Journal of the European Communities. They also introduce a procedure for a licensee to apply for a licence for an area contiguous to the area or areas covered by its existing licence if the Secretary of State decides that geological or production considerations justify the grant of such a licence, and make revisions to model clauses in petroleum production licences and exploration licences.

1480 Petroleum revenue tax—tariff receipts—tariff receipts allowance

A participator of a user oil field owned an interest in a pipeline entitling it to pass a specified number of barrels of oil through the pipeline each day. It acquired a right to pass more oil through the pipeline on payment of a tariff for each additional barrel of oil. Such tariff receipts were brought into the charge to petroleum revenue tax subject to a tariff receipts allowance of 250,000 metric tonnes for each chargeable period for each user field. Under the Oil Taxation Act 1983, s 9(1), the amount of the qualifying tariff receipts received by a participator to be taken into account in computing his assessable profit or allowable loss fell to be reduced by his share of the cash equivalent of the tariff receipts allowance given by a formula set out in Sch 3, para 2(1). The question arose whether the tariff receipts allowance to which the participators of the principal field were entitled was to be calculated by reference only to oil in respect of which the tariff was paid or by reference to all oil passed through the pipeline. *Held*, the evident purpose of the 1983 Act was to give to the participators in a principal field who allowed the facilities of that field to be used by a user field in exchange for a tariff an allowance of the cash equivalent of 250,000 tonnes before qualifying tariff receipts had to be brought into charge. Section 9(4), Sch 3 was to have effect for determining for the purposes of s 9 the cash equivalent of a participator's share of the tariff receipts allowance in respect of a user field for a chargeable period. It would be inconsistent with the purposes of s 9 to include in the 250,000 tonnes oil for which no tariff had been paid.

Chevron UK Ltd v IRC [1995] STC 712 (Chancery Division: Sir John Vinelott).

GAS

See FUEL AND ENERGY.

GIFT AND ESTATE TAXATION

See INHERITANCE TAXATION.

GIFTS

Halsbury's Laws of England (4th edn) Vol 20 (reissue), paras 1–100

1481　Articles

A Problem in the Construction of Gifts to Unincorporated Associations, Paul Matthews: [1995] Conv 302

1482　Gift inter vivos—undue influence

The plaintiff, who had been sentenced to life imprisonment for killing his wife, was released after 13 years in prison. Five years later, his only son, who had not contacted the plaintiff during those 18 years and whose business had recently collapsed, suggested that he and his wife, the defendants, should move into the plaintiff's house to look after him. The plaintiff transferred the house to the defendants by way of gift but, subsequently, relations between the parties having deteriorated, he sought to set aside the gift. *Held*, the equitable doctrine relating to unconscionable bargains did not apply to gifts. It was a question of fact whether there was actual undue influence. The plaintiff had to show that he was forced by the defendants' conduct by word, deed or omission, to enter into a deed of gift. In the present case, there was either actual undue influence or, alternatively, presumed undue influence by virtue of the nature of the relationship between the plaintiff and the defendants and the degree of trust the plaintiff placed in them. The gift of the house together with a non-exclusive licence to the plaintiff was improvident and made the plaintiff dependent on the defendants. In order to discharge the presumption of undue influence, the defendants might show that the plaintiff entered into the gift freely on independent advice. They had not done so and, accordingly, the plaintiff's application would be granted and the transfer set aside.

Langton v Langton [1995] 3 FCR 521 (Chancery Division: AWH Charles QC).

GUARANTEE AND INDEMNITY

Halsbury's Laws of England (4th edn) Vol 20 (reissue), paras 101–400

1483 Articles

Guarantees, Daron Gunson (on the risks of guaranteeing another person's business loan): Tax Journal, Issue 293, p 12

Undue Influence, Misrepresentation and the Doctrine of Notice, John Mee (on *Barclays Bank plc v O'Brien* [1993] 4 All ER 417, HL (1993 Abr para 1826)): (1995) CLJ 536

1484 Guarantee—disclosure of unusual terms to surety—duty of disclosure

The plaintiffs acted as sureties using their short dated government stock as security, on condition that the debtors undertook that the stock would be returned to them before its maturity date. The debtors, without the plaintiffs' knowledge, entered into an agreement with the creditor bank for a bridging loan whereby the stocks would be put in the bank's name so that on maturity the funds would go directly to paying the bridging loan. The plaintiffs brought an action against the bank for failure to disclose material differences between the loan agreement and what the plaintiffs, as sureties, were entitled to expect. *Held,* a creditor had a duty to disclose any unusual terms of a loan agreement to a surety. Terms were automatically unusual where they were different from what a guarantor was entitled to expect. There had therefore been a material non-disclosure in this case which had caused loss as the plaintiffs would have acted differently if they had been made aware of the true position. Accordingly, judgment would be given in the plaintiffs' favour.

   Levett v Barclays Bank plc [1995] 2 All ER 615 (Queen's Bench Division: Michael Burton QC).

1485 Guarantee—guarantee obtained by fraudulent misrepresentation—rescission in equity

See *Vadasz v Pioneer Concrete (SA) Pty Ltd*, para 1311.

1486 Guarantee—guarantor of tenant—action for arrears of rent—limitation period

See *Romain v Scuba TV Ltd*, para 1896.

1487 Guarantee—guarantor's rights against creditor—guarantor's rights after payment—guarantor acting as security for part of debt only—right to share rateably in any security given for whole debt

A businessman acquired a company in order to develop specific property, borrowing over £30m to do so. A bank then made available to the company £32m to provide working capital and to replace the existing loan. The bank took full security in the form of fixed and floating charges over all the assets and undertakings of the company as security for all moneys due or owing or incurred to the bank by the company. By subsequent facility letters the facility was raised to £58m on the same security as the original advance. A further security of £10m was granted specifically to permit the redemption of redeemable shares in the company. The security for this was a memorandum of deposit and charge under which the businessman was to deposit securities of greater value than the redemption advance. The company went into default under the second facility and the bank appointed receivers who sold the businessman's shares, realising over £10m. This amount was credited to suspense accounts in the bank's name. The issue before the court was whether the businessman as surety for part of a larger debt, and who had discharged the full amount for which he was surety, was entitled to share rateably with the bank as principal creditor in any security given for the whole debt (such as the original charge over the company's assets). *Held,* the principle in *Goodwin v Gray* remained good law. Any security given by the principal debtor for the whole debt had to be shared between the principal creditor, the remainder of whose debt remained outstanding, and the surety. Accordingly, the businessman was entitled to be subrogated amd to participate in the security provided to the bank by the company.

   Re Butler's Wharf Ltd [1995] 2 BCLC 43 (Chancery Division: Richard Sykes QC). *Goodwin v Gray* (1874) 22 WR 312 followed.

1488 Guarantee—inference of fraud—injunction restraining the making of demands on guarantor

The purchasers of a business brought an action for fraudulent misrepresentation against the sellers before the payment of the second and third instalments of the purchase price. The third instalment had been secured by a performance guarantee obtained from a third party. The purchasers alleged that at the time of the execution of the agreement the sellers had become aware that, although the purchase price was based on an assumption that demand from a major customer would continue, this was no longer true, and that the sellers failed to disclose this development. On an application by the purchasers for an injunction restraining the making of demands under the guarantee it was held that they had satisfied the onus of showing, for the purpose of interlocutory relief, that it was arguable at trial that fraud was the only realistic inference. On appeal by the sellers, *held*, letters of credit, performance bonds and guarantees were generally to be treated as autonomous contracts with which the court would not interfere on grounds extraneous to the contract itself. The only exception to this rule involved instances of fraud and even then it was recognised that a guarantor had a prima facie right to be the sole arbiter on whether payment under the guarantee should be refused. However, where the issue was simply between the buyer and the seller and no demand had yet been made on the guarantor, the judge had the power to grant an injunction restraining the making of demands without proof of fraud on concluding that fraud was the only reasonable inference. Accordingly, the appeal would be dismissed.

Themehelp v West [1995] 4 All ER 215 (Court of Appeal: Balcombe, Evans and Waite LJJ).

1489 Guarantee—sub-contractor's bond—bond granted jointly with surety

See *Trafalgar House Construction (Regions) Ltd v General Surety & Guarantee Co Ltd*, para 276.

1490 Guarantee—undue influence—constructive notice

See *Halifax Building Society v Brown*, para 2111.

HEALTH AND SAFETY AT WORK

Halsbury's Laws of England (4th edn) Vol 20 (reissue), paras 401–951

1491 Articles

CDM—What Does it Mean to You? George Markland (on the Construction (Design and Management) Regulations 1994, SI 1994/3140 (1994 Abr para 1463)): Estates Gazette, 22 July 1995, p 107

A Constructive Move on Site Safety, Roger Peters (on the Construction (Design and Management) Regulations 1994, SI 1994/3140): 139 SJ 451

Corporate Body, Gary Slapper (on corporate responsibility and criminal liability): LS Gaz, 15 February 1995, p 18

Employer's Liability: Reconstructing Section 3(1) of the Health and Safety at Work etc Act 1974, Geoff Holgate: 159 JP Jo 369, 385

A Flood of Claims? John Messham (on *Walker v Northumberland County Council* [1995] 1 All ER 737 (1994 Abr para 1470)): 139 SJ 732

'Foreseeability' and Workplace Safety, Geoffrey Holgate: 139 SJ 1158

Pressure of Work, Saleem Sheikh (on *Walker v Northumberland County Council* [1995] 1 All ER 737 (1994 Abr para 1470)): LS Gaz, 15 March 1995, p 18

Safety Nets, Robert Hann (on the implications of health and safety legislation for employers): LS Gaz, 8 March 1995, pp 18

Warning: Work Can Damage Your Health, David Conn (on *Walker v Northumberland County Council* (1994) Times, 24 November (1994 Abr para 1470)): 139 SJ 576

1492 Activity Centres (Young Persons' Safety) Act 1995

See para 328.

1493 Asbestos—risks—duty to assess

Industrial cleaners undertook to clean asbestos cement roofs although they did not hold themselves out as having expertise in relation to the health hazards which might be created. As a result of their application of water in a high pressure jet to the roofs, they caused extensive contamination of the surrounding area. In proceedings against them for breach of contract, claiming half the costs of remedial work thereby occasioned, *held*, any contractor who undertook work on materials containing asbestos should have been aware, at the latest by 1988 when the Control of Asbestos at Work Regulations 1987, SI 1987/2115, came into force and as a result of the extensive publicity concerning asbestos, of the serious health hazards connected with such work. A contractor who was not aware of such risks had a duty to find out about them before undertaking the work. The cleaners had failed to exercise reasonable care and skill to perform the task safely and were liable for breach of contract. Accordingly, the claim would succeed.

Barclays Bank plc v Fairclough Building Ltd (No 2) [1995] IRLR 605 (Court of Appeal: Nourse and Beldam LJJ and Sir Tasker Watkins).

1494 Borehole sites—operations—safety

The Borehole Sites and Operations Regulations 1995, SI 1995/2038 (in force on 1 October 1995), provide minimum requirements for improving the safety and health of workers in industries involving mineral extracting through drilling. It is required that owners provide operators with relevant information and operators exercise control of borehole sites and co-ordinate prescribed measures. Duties imposed on an employer by the regulatiuons are also imposed on an operator. Employers of borehole workers must co-operate with the operator and notice of the commencement of drilling operations and the abandonment of boreholes must be given to the Health and Safety Executive, including the filing of prescribed particulars. The regulations provide that no borehole operation can be commenced at a site unless a 'health and safety document' has been prepared and a duty is imposed on an operator to ensure that every workplace on a borehole site is designed and built to certain standards and provides adequate means of escape. There is also a duty to provide health surveillance and the regulations contain a special defence to any of the offences created.

1495 Deregulation and contracting out—repeals and revocations

The Health and Safety (Repeals and Revocations) Regulations 1995, SI 1995/3234 (in force in part on 1 January 1996, and in part on 1 January 1997), repeal and revoke (1) the Home Work Orders 1911, 1912, 1913, 1929, and 1938, (2) the Horizontal Milling Machines (Amendment) Regulation 1934, S R & O 1934/207, (3) the Railway Running Sheds Orders 1961, SI 1961/1250, 1251, 1768, (4) the Slaughterhouses Orders 1962, SI 1962/2345, 2346, 2347, (5) the Hours of Employment (Convention) Act 1936, and (6) the Factories Act 1961, s 133.

1496 Electrical equipment—explosive atmospheres

The Electrical Equipment for Explosive Atmospheres (Certification) (Amendment) Regulations 1995, SI 1995/1186 (in force on 26 May 1995), further amend the 1990 Regulations, SI 1990/13, to give effect to Commission Directives (EC) 94/26 and 94/44, which adapt Council Directives (EC) 79/196 and 82/130. A manufacturer of electrical equipment may apply to a certification body for a certificate of conformity attesting that the equipment conforms to the harmonised standards provided by the 1990 Regulations. Now, the 1995 Regulations enable a manufacturer of electrical equipment which applies for a certificate of conformity to have that equipment certified by reference to the harmonised standards set out in the 1990 Regulations which are in force before 26 May 1995, in which case the application is treated as if it had been made under the 1990 Regulations. Applications for certificates of conformity made before 26 May 1995 must continue to be dealt with under the 1990 Regulations. However, a certification body cannot issue such a certificate of conformity after 29 February 1996 in respect of electrical equipment to which Council Directive (EC) 79/196 applies, or after 31 December 1996 in respect of electrical equipment to which Council Directive (EC) 82/130 applies. A certificate of conformity issued before 1 March 1996 in respect of electrical equipment to which Council Directive (EC) 79/196 applies, or before 1 January 1997 in respect of electrical equipment to which Council Directive (EC) 82/130 applies, is to be regarded as in force until 1 July 2003 for the purposes of the provisions of the 1995 Regulations relating to use of the distinctive Community mark. In addition, the 1995 Regulations preserve until 1 July 2003 the position in respect of certificates of conformity issued in accordance with the transitional provisions relating to the 1990 Regulations.

**1497   Employer—breach of statutory duty—duty to persons other than employees—
duty to customers**

The Reporting of Injuries, Diseases and Dangerous Occurrences Regulations 1985, SI
1985/2023, reg 3(1)(b) provides that where any person as a result of an accident arising out of
or in connection with work, dies or suffers an injury specified in those regulations, the
responsible person must within seven days send a report to the enforcing authority.

A shopper was injured in the respondents' store and because the accident was not reported to
the appropriate authority under the 1985 Regulations, reg 3(1)(b), that authority prosecuted the
company, alleging that it was in breach of the Regulations. The prosecution was dismissed on
the grounds that the duty contained in reg 3(1)(b) was confined to accidents involving employees,
trainees and the self-employed. The authority appealed. *Held*, the Regulations were made under
the Health and Safety at Work etc Act 1974, s 15. Section 1 of that Act provided that the
purposes of the Act were to secure the health, safety and welfare of persons at work and to
protect persons other than those at work from risks arising out of or in connection with the
activities of persons at work. Accordingly, the purpose of the Regulations was to protect persons
other than persons at work and the appeal would be allowed.

Woking Borough Council v BHS plc (1994) 159 JP 427 (Queen's Bench Division: Beldam LJ
and Buxton J).

**1498   Employer—breach of statutory duty—duty to persons other than employees—
level of fine imposed on employer**

The Health and Safety at Work Act 1974, s 3(1) provides that it is the duty of every employer
to conduct his undertaking in such a way as to ensure, so far as is reasonably practicable, that
persons not in his employment who may be affected thereby are not thereby exposed to risks to
their health or safety.

A combination carrier, which had previously carried a petroleum cargo, entered a harbour
with a new cargo. Standard procedure required the ship's master to complete a document
declaring whether there were spaces on board which might contain toxic or flammable gases.
However, the harbour company did not require the return of that document, nor did it identify
whether the vessel was a combination carrier or whether it had carried an oil cargo. Part of the
petroleum cargo had remained in the cargo line and when a workman used cutting equipment
to remove the hatch covers, there was an explosion and a fire. Two men were killed and others
were injured. The company pleaded guilty to an offence under the 1974 Act, s 3(1) and was
fined £250,000. On appeal, the company claimed it had been entitled to rely upon the ship's
master whose primary responsibility was safety and, although the fine would be appropriate for
somebody in that position, the company's responsibility was at a much lower level and a much
lower fine would have been appropriate. *Held*, the duty imposed by statute upon persons in the
position of the company was that the company itself had responsibility. It was a duty which the
company was not entitled to delegate and it was a duty which it had taken only superficial and
inadequate steps to carry out. The fine was entirely appropriate and it was apparent that any
lesser fine would have failed to bring home to the company the seriousness of its breach of duty.
The fine was not wrong in principle, nor was it manifestly excessive. Accordingly, the appeal
would be dismissed.

R v Mersey Docks and Harbour Co (1995) 16 Cr App Rep (S) 806 (Court of Appeal: Hobhouse
LJ, Pill and Steel JJ).

**1499   Employer—breach of statutory duty—duty to prevent falls through fragile
material**

The Construction (Working Places) Regulations 1966, SI 1966/94, reg 36(2) provides that no
person may pass or work near material which would be liable to fracture if his weight were to
be applied to it and so situated that if it were to be so fractured he would be liable to a fall, unless
provision is made by means of such one or more of all or any of the following, that is to say
suitable guard rails, coverings, or other means as are necessary for preventing, so far as reasonably
practicable, any person so passing or working from falling through the material.

Three workers were carrying out repairs to the roof lights at the appellant's factory when, in
disobedience to instructions, one of them climbed onto the roof and fell through a roof light
and on to the concrete floor of the building. He later died of his injuries. The appellant was
convicted of failing to discharge its duty under the Health and Safety at Work Act 1974, s 3(1),
and failing to comply with the 1966 Regulations, reg 36(2). On appeal, *held*, a code of practice,
a system of work, a body of instruction, and even the provision of a supervisor were not enough
to prevent a person falling through fragile material, as such an accident might occur as a result of

inattention or inadvertence. Where guard rails or coverings could not be provided, some other form of physical device was required, such as a safety harness. As none of those things had been provided in the instance case, the appellant had failed to comply with reg 36(2). Moreover, the words 'so far as reasonably practicable' related to the capacity of the safety devices provided to prevent accidental falls, rather than to the obligation to provide them. As regards the appellant's breach of the 1974 Act, s 3, it was unnecessary to consider whether that duty was affected by the fact that the deceased worker had disobeyed instructions in climbing onto the roof. It was also irrelevant that the worker in respect of whom the appellant was found to be in breach of its duty under s 3 was not the deceased worker but an uninjured worker. Accordingly, the appeal would be dismissed.

R v Rhone-Poulenc Rorer Ltd (1995) Times, 1 December (Court of Appeal: Kennedy LJ, Wright J, and Judge Wickham).

1500 Employer—breach of statutory duty—duty to provide protective footwear

The Factories Act 1961, s 29(1) provides that there must, in so far as is reasonably practicable, be provided and maintained safe means of access to every place at which any person has at any time to work, and every such place must be made and kept safe for any person working there. The Foundries (Protective Footwear and Gaiters) Regulations 1971, SI 1971/476, reg 5(2) provides that the employer of every person to whom the regulations apply must give every such person footwear which is suitable and which, when worn by that person, prevents so far as is reasonably practicable risk of burns to his feet and ankles. Where footwear had been lost, destroyed or is so defective as to be unsuitable, the employer must give that person suitable replacement footwear: reg 6.

The plaintiff, an experienced worker, prepared a seal for a mould and began to pour molten metal into the mould. He noticed a leak in the seal but carried on pouring the metal which then erupted through the seal burning his foot. The plaintiff had previously complained that the boots he was wearing were worn and defective, but he did have two other suitable pairs. Only liability fell to be determined and, at first instance, the plaintiff's action was dismissed. On appeal, it fell to be determined whether (i) there had been a breach of the 1961 Act, s 29(1), (ii) the employers were negligent in common law, and (iii) there had been a breach of the 1971 Regulations. *Held*, (i) the danger which had arisen did not arise from any static condition of the place of work, but from the operation upon which the plaintiff was engaged, and there was therefore no breach of s 29(1). (ii) The employers had been entitled to entrust the task of sealing the mould to an experienced worker. No one was able to suggest any alternative process which could have eliminated the possibility of the metal escaping. If anyone was negligent, it was the plaintiff for failing to construct a sufficient seal. (iii) Although the plaintiff was fully aware of the importance of wearing appropriate footwear, he chose to wear the boots about which he had complained although he had alternative boots which were suitable for the operation on which he was engaged. Even if it could be demonstrated that there was technically a breach of the 1971 Regulations, the plaintiff's own fault in the particular circumstances extinguished any breach of statutory duty on the employers' part. Accordingly, the appeal would be dismissed.

Homer v Sandwell Castings Ltd [1995] PIQR P318 (Court of Appeal: Russell LJ and Hollis J).

1971 Regulations revoked: Personal Protective Equipment at Work Regulations 1992, SI 1992/2966.

1501 Employer—breach of statutory duty—duty to provide safe place of work— foreseeability of risks or dangers

Scotland

The Factories Act 1961, s 29(1) provides that there must, in so far as is reasonably practicable, be provided and maintained safe means of access to every place at which any person has at any time to work, and every such place must be made and kept safe for any person working there.

An employee was injured when a machine part unexpectedly moved. He claimed damages from his employers under the 1961 Act, s 29(1). At first instance, the judge held that the movement of the machine could not be explained and had been quite unforeseeable and on that ground he rejected the employee's claim. On appeal, the issue between the parties was simply whether reasonable foreseeability was a necessary prerequisite in determining whether or not a place of work had been made and kept safe within the meaning of s 29(1). *Held*, as considerations of reasonable practicability involved weighing the degree and extent of risk against the time, trouble and expense of preventing it, foreseeability came into the matter as it was impossible to assess the degree of risk in any other way. To that extent reasonable foreseeability could play its part, but only at the later stage of considering whether the employers had discharged the onus upon them of showing that there were no reasonably practicable precautions which could have been taken. Section 29 did not impose an intolerable burden upon employers because they had the opportunity of establishing that there were no practicable precautions which could have been taken. It followed that reasonable foreseeability had no part to play in the initial consideration of whether or not the employers had complied with their obligation to make and keep a working place safe and, accordingly, the appeal would be allowed.

Mains v Uniroyal Engelbert Tyres Ltd [1995] IRLR 544 (Inner House).

The 1961 Act, s 29(1) is repealed as from 1 January 1996 by the Workplace (Health, Safety and Welfare) Regulations 1992, SI 1992/3004.

1502   Employer—breach of statutory duty—duty to provide safe system of work—eye protection

The Protection of Eyes Regulations 1974, SI 1974/1681, Sch 1, para 27 provides that the processes for which approved eye protectors or approved shields or approved fixed shields are required include the spraying of material by means of apparatus to which air is supplied under pressure, where there is a reasonably foreseeable risk of injury to the eyes of any person engaged in the work from particles or fragments thrown off or from intense light or other radiation.

The appellant was employed in a factory as a glaze sprayer. Her duties involved applying glaze to earthenware jars using a compressed air gun, a process which required her to keep her head very near to the air gun and the jar. The effect of the process was that the compressed air created a cloud of air and glaze which sometimes got into her hair and irritated her eyes. It was not the practice of the defendant employer or other employers in the industry to supply employees with safety goggles or any other type of eye protection, but few employees had suffered eye injuries. It was also the case that the earthenware jars were not inspected for foreign particles between the time that they were produced and the time that they were sprayed. The appellant was seriously injured when a small foreign particle in one of the earthenware jars flew into her eye whilst she was spraying it. Her action for damages for personal injury resulting from the defendant's alleged breach of a number of statutory provisions, including the 1974 Regulations, was dismissed. On appeal, *held*, even a small risk was foreseeable if a reasonable man would not have disregarded it. On the facts of the case, there had been a reasonably foreseeable risk of eye injury, and the defendant had therefore been under an absolute duty under the 1974 Regulations to provide the appellant with eye protectors or a shield. Accordingly, the appeal would be allowed.

Gerrard v Staffordshire Potteries Ltd [1995] ICR 502 (Court of Appeal: Kennedy LJ and Hale J).

The 1974 Regulations have been replaced by the Personal Protective Equipment at Work Regulations 1992, SI 1992/2966.

1503   Employer—duty of care—damages for personal injury—liability of primary and secondary employer

An employer ('the first employer') agreed that one of its employees could work temporarily under the direction of another employer ('the second employer'). The second employer's supervisor told the employee to use a ladder to do some paint work, but failed to ensure that the ladder was footed. When the employee began climbing up the ladder, the foot of it slipped, and caused him to fall and injure himself. The employee was awarded damages for personal injury against the second employer. On the second employer's appeal, the issue was whether or not the first employer was also liable. *Held*, a general employer remained liable for the safety of an employee even when he was not exercising control over him, but if there was negligence on the part of a supervisor to whom the employee had been entrusted, the supervisor's employer might be vicariously liable, in addition to the liability of the general employer. Having regard to the Civil Liability (Contribution) Act 1978, ss 1 and 2, liability could be apportioned if it was just and equitable to do so. Here, the first employer could not have anticipated that the second employer's supervisor would instruct the employee to use a long ladder on a slippery floor without anyone to foot it. The accident was therefore wholly attributable to the second employer and, although the employee was entitled to recover damages against both employers, the first employer was entitled to a complete indemnity against the second employer. Accordingly, the appeal would be dismissed.

Nelhams v Sandells Maintenance Ltd (1995) Times, 15 June (Court of Appeal: Nourse, Kennedy and Auld LJJ). Dictum of *Morris v Breaveglen* [1993] ICR 766, CA (1992 Abr para 1269) applied.

1504 Employer—duty of care—duty to provide adequate supervision of employees

Scotland

During a ball game played by two employees in their employer's workshop, the ball hit the plaintiff causing him injuries. The duties of the foreman at the workshop included supervising the employees, but he was also required to go to other parts of the building and the nature of his duties there required him to be absent from the workshop for long periods of time. The plaintiff brought an action for damages on grounds that the employer was vicariously liable for the employees' fault and negligence, that the employer was directly liable, and that the employer was vicariously liable for the foreman's failure to supervise. The judge found that the employer was directly liable on the ground that it was in breach of its duty to adequately supervise its employees. The plaintiff had alleged that the breach took the form of the foreman failing in his duty of supervision by being present when the employees were playing, but not doing anything to stop them. However, the judge found that the foreman was not present when the employees were playing and that the breach took the form of the foreman's absence from the workshop for lengthy periods. On appeal, the employer argued that it had been held to be in breach of duty on a ground not alleged on record. *Held*, the employer's duties were so broadly expressed in the plaintiff's allegations that it was not possible to say that a failure to provide supervision at all times in the workshop was a new, separate and distinct ground of fault of which no notice had been given to the employer. The case of fault was in essence a failure to provide adequate supervision and the judge had therefore been entitled to find that, although the breach of that duty took a different form to that which appeared from the plaintiff's allegations, it was nevertheless within the case argued against the employer. Accordingly, the appeal would be dismissed.

Gibson v British Rail Maintenance Ltd 1995 SLT 953 (Inner House).

1505 Employer—duty of care—duty to provide safe system of work—refuse collection

The plaintiff was employed as a dustman by the defendant local authority. Householders collected refuse in plastic bags, which were thrown into collection vehicles by dustmen. This system replaced the previous method whereby refuse had been emptied into collection vehicles from metal bins. An alternative refuse collection system involved emptying refuse into collection vehicles from wheeled bins. The plaintiff was throwing a plastic refuse bag into a collection vehicle when a piece of glass protruding from the bag scratched him on the leg. He then fell over and sustained a minor shoulder injury. He successfully claimed damages for negligence against the defendant, alleging in particular that the defendant should have used wheeled bins to collect refuse. On the defendant's appeal, *held*, where it was alleged that an employer had failed to provide a safe system of work for his employees, the court was obliged to consider whether he had taken reasonable steps to do so, having regard to the dangers inherent in their duties. Where it was alleged that an employer should have adopted an alternative system of work, the court was obliged to compare the competing systems, having regard to practicability, commercial viability and safety. Here, the judge had concluded that the defendant was negligent because the plastic bag refuse collection system was not as safe as the wheeled bin system. However, he had made only a general inquiry into the commercial viability of the use of wheeled bins, and had heard virtually no evidence as to the comparative practicability of the systems, having regard to the terrain, house layout, and street and pavement design in the defendant's area. The judge had also heard no evidence as to the health or safety hazards involved in using each system. Since he had decided to place great emphasis on the wheeled bin system, the judge should have considered all the evidence necessary to assess the merits and drawbacks of the system, and to discover the extent to which the use of such bins had become an established practice in refuse collection. As he had failed to do so, his decision could not be supported and, accordingly, the appeal would be allowed.

Nilsson v Redditch Borough Council [1995] PIQR P199 (Court of Appeal: Staughton, Waite and Peter Gibson LJJ).

1506 Employer—duty of care—liability to independent contractor

The appellant, who had traded on his own account and had acquired self-employed status for tax purposes, was employed by the defendants on a particular job, and paid at a daily rate. He was subsequently asked to re-roof part of a building, and it was agreed that he would be paid a set fee and that he would use his own tools but would not provide the materials. Whilst carrying out the work, he fell from a ladder and suffered injuries which caused brain damage. A judge ruled that the defendants did not owe to the appellant the common law or statutory duty of care owed by an employer to his employees because the appellant was an independent contractor at the relevant time and had therefore been responsible for his own safety. On appeal, *held*, because of the importance of safety at work, there was a public interest in recognising the employer/employee relationship where it existed. In order to decide who was responsible for the overall safety of the men doing a job of work, it was necessary to apply the control test to determine matters such as who gave the orders as to what was to be done, and when and how it was to be done. As the control test was not decisive, it was also necessary to consider who owned the business, in particular where the financial risk lay. There was a distinction between a situation where an employer engaged men on 'the lump' to do labouring work, and a situation where a specialist sub-contractor was employed to perform a particular part of a general building contract. In the instant case, the appellant had been employed on 'the lump' rather than as a specialist sub-contractor, and the defendants had been responsible for the job at which the appellant was injured. They therefore owed him a duty of care and, accordingly, the appeal would be allowed.

Lane v Shire Roofing Co (Oxford) Ltd [1995] IRLR 493 (Court of Appeal: Nourse, Henry and Auld LJJ). *Ferguson v John Dawson & Partners (Contractors) Ltd* [1976] 3 All ER 817, CA (1976 Abr para 974) considered.

1507 Fees

The Health and Safety (Fees) Regulations 1995, SI 1995/2646 (in force on 3 November 1995), replace the 1994 Regulations, SI 1994/397. The regulations fix or determine the fees payable by an applicant to the Health and Safety Executive in respect of an application made for (1) an approval under mines and quarries legislation; (2) an approval of certain respiratory protective equipment; (3) an approval of plant or equipment under the Agriculture (Tractor Cabs) Regulations 1974, SI 1974/2034; (4) an approval of a scheme or programme under the Freight Containers (Safety Convention) Regulations 1984, SI 1984/1890; (5) a licence under the Asbestos (Licensing) Regulations 1983, SI 1983/1649; (6) an approval of dosimetry services and for type approval of radiation generators or apparatus containing radioactive substances under the Ionising Radiations Regulations 1985, SI 1985/1333; (7) an approval, authorisation or licence etc under the Explosives Act 1875 and certain instruments thereunder, for a licence under the Petroleum (Consolidation) Act 1928 and for the classification of an article, substance, combination, or unit load under the Classification and Labelling of Explosives Regulations 1983, SI 1983/1140; (8) an explosives licence under the Dangerous Substances in Harbour Areas Regulations 1987, SI 1987/37, Pt IX; (9) an examination of specified appliances or equipment on offshore installations; (10) a vocational training certificate under the Road Traffic (Training of Drivers of Vehicles carrying Dangerous Goods) Regulations 1992, SI 1992/744; (11) a notification under the Genetically Modified Organisms (Contained Use) Regulations 1992, SI 1992/3217 and (12) a notification or application under the Notification of New Substances Regulations 1993, SI 1993/3050.

The regulations also fix the fees to be paid in respect of medical examinations and surveillance by an employment medical adviser which are required under certain of the relevant statutory provisions and fix maximum fees which may be charged under the Explosives Act 1825, the Petroleum (Consolidation) Act 1928 and the Petroleum (Transfer of Licences) Act 1936.

1508 Information for employees—modifications and repeals

The Health and Safety Information for Employees (Modifications and Repeals) Regulations 1995, SI 1995/2923 (in force in part on 1 January 1996, in part on 1 January 1997, and in part on 1 January 1998), amend the 1989 Regulations, SI 1989/682, by (1) applying the 1989 Regulations to certain premises and activities outside Great Britain, (2) adding provisions to the 1989 Regulations which enable the Health and Safety Executive to approve posters or leaflets which are specific to particular classes of employment, so that employers in those classes may display or provide those specific leaflets or posters rather than general leaflets or posters, and (3) repeal a number of provisions in health and safety legislation relating to the display of notices or posters and the provision of information.

1509 Injuries, diseases and dangerous occurrences—reporting

The Reporting of Injuries, Diseases and Dangerous Occurrences Regulations 1995, SI 1995/3163 (in force on 1 April 1996), revoke and re-enact in a consolidated form the Reporting of Injuries, Diseases and Dangerous Occurrences Regulations 1985, SI 1985/2023, the Railways (Notice of Accidents) Order 1986, SI 1986/2187, and certain provisions of the Offshore Installations (Inspectors and Casualties) Regulations 1973, SI 1973/1842, and the Submarine Pipe-lines (Inspectors etc) Regulations 1977, SI 1977/835. The regulations also repeal or amend certain provisions of the Regulation of Railways Act 1871, the Railways Employment (Prevention of Accidents) Act 1900, and the Transport and Works Act 1992. The regulations retain the requirement that the responsible person must notify and send a report to the Health and Safety Executive ('the HSE'), or notify the local authority, of fatal and non-fatal accidents arising out of, or in connection with, work, specified diseases contracted by persons at work, and specified dangerous occurrences. In particular, the regulations (1) define 'accident' as including acts of violence done to persons at work, and suicides on railways and other relevant transport systems, (2) confine the injuries which must be reported in respect of persons who are not at work to deaths, injuries which cause the person to be taken from the site of the accident to a hospital, and major injuries arising out of, or in connection with, work at a hospital, (3) update the list of dangerous occurrences which must be reported so that it now consists of general provisions and requires occurrences in respect of mines, quarries, relevant transport systems and offshore workplaces to be reported, (4) update the list of reportable diseases, (5) provide that the report which must be sent to the HSE, or the local authority, may be sent either on a form approved by the HSE or by another means approved by the HSE, (6) provide that the persons responsible for reporting gas incidents include those approved under the Gas Safety (Installation and Use) Regulations 1994, SI 1994/1886, and (7) give the HSE limited power to grant exemptions from the requirements imposed by the regulations.

1510   Legislation—application outside Great Britain—offshore installations, wells and piplines

The Health and Safety at Work etc Act 1974 (Application outside Great Britain) Order 1995, SI 1995/263 (in force on 15 March 1995), replaces, with amendments, the 1989 Order, SI 1989/840, so as to apply the Health and Safety at Work etc Act 1974, ss 1–59, 80–82, outside Great Britain, and (1) to offshore installations within territorial waters adjacent to Great Britain and areas designated under the Continental Shelf Act 1964, and activities on or in connection with them, and to certain diving activities, (2) within the same waters and areas, to wells, to most activities in connection with them and to activities immediately preparatory to such activities, (3) within the same waters and areas, to pipelines, pipeline works and certain activities connected to such works, (4) to the working of a mine and work for the purpose of or in connection with the working of any mine, within such waters or extending beyond them, and (5) within such waters to various construction and other activities. The relevant sections of the 1974 Act apply to individuals, whether or not British subjects, and to bodies corporate, whether or not incorporated under the law of the United Kingdom. With one exception, this order does not limit or prejudice the effect of other enactments in territorial waters or elsewhere.

1511   Mines—escape and rescue

The Escape and Rescue from Mines Regulations 1995, SI 1995/2870 (in force on 28 December 1995), apply to all mines apart from certain provisions that do not apply to tourist mines and others that only apply to coal mines. The manager of every mine must prepare and maintain a written emergency plan, provide accommodation for rescuers, ensure emergency equipment in good condition and plans of the mine are always available, establish warning and other communication systems, authorise only certain people to enter the mine in an emergency situation, provide self-rescuers and ensure that mine workers are sufficiently trained to deal with emergency situations. It is provided that effective arrangements for rescue must be made in relation to mines and that inspections of emergency arrangements be made. Various provisions are made relating to rescue teams and the conduct of rescue operations including the number, fitness, qualifications and training of rescue team members. The Health and Safety Executive may make exemptions from the prohibitions and requirements of the regulations.

1512   Mines—health and safety

The Mines Miscellaneous Health and Safety Provisions Regulations 1995, SI 1995/2005 (in force on 26 October 1995), revoke the Coal and other Mines (Working Plans) Rules 1956, SI 1956/1782, and the Coal and other Mines (Abandonment Plans) Rules 1956, SI 1956/1783, and amend the Electricity at Work Regulations 1989, SI 1989/635, the Management of Health and Safety at Work Regulations 1993, SI 1993/1897, and the Mines (Shafts and Winding) Regulations 1993, SI 1993/302. The regulations give effect in part, in relation to mines, to Council Direction (EC) 92/104 concerning the minimum requirements for improving the safety and health protection of workers in surface and underground mineral-extracting industries. The regulations (1) implement the directive with respect to safety instructions, the drawing up of a 'health and safety document' and the co-ordination of health and safety measures, health surveillance, written instructions and work permits, smoking and the use of open flame, protection from explosion risks, protection plans where toxic gases are present in the atmosphere, fire protection plans, fire-equipment signs, provision of emergency lighting and personal lamps, operating plans for rockbursts and gas outbursts, and flammable materials, (2) require the owners of every mine to ensure that no work is carried out at the mine unless a health and safety document has been prepared which demonstrates that the risks to which persons at work at the mine are exposed have been assessed and that adequate measures have and will be taken to safeguard their health and safety, (3) provide that, where appropriate, specified plans should be included in the document, and require the owner to ensure that the measures set out in the document are taken and that any plans included in the document are followed, (4) provide that the owner shall co-ordinate the implementation of all measures relating to the health and safety of the persons at work at the mine, (5) provide that every employer of persons at work at a mine and every owner of a mine must ensure that specified additional health and safety requirements are complied with, (6) require an employer of a person engaged in work at a mine to ensure that that person is provided with such health surveillance as is appropriate, (7) require the manager of every mine to ensure so far as is reasonably practicable that only hydraulic fluids which are difficult to ignite and satisfy fire resistance and hygiene specifications approved by the Health and Safety Executive are used at the mine, and to minimise risk where this is not possible, and (8) provide that the Mines and Quarries Act 1954, s 157 (which provides a defence in legal proceedings in certain circumstances), does not apply to prosecutions or other proceedings based on an alleged contravention of the regulations.

1513　Quarries—health and safety

The Quarries Miscellaneous Health and Safety Provisions Regulations 1995, SI 1995/2036 (in force in part on 26 October 1995 and in part on 26 July 1998), give effect in part, in relation to quarries and mines above ground, to Council Directive (EC) 92/104 concerning the minimum requirements for improving the safety and health protection for workers in surface and underground mineral-extracting industries, and Council Directive (EC) 92/91 concerning the minimum requirements for improving the safety and health protection of workers in the mineral-extracting industries through drilling. The regulations (1) require the owner of every quarry to ensure that no work is carried out at the quarry unless a health and safety document has been prepared which demonstrates that the risk to which persons at work in the quarry are exposed have been assessed and that adequate measures have and will be taken to safeguard their health and safety, (2) provide that, where appropriate, specified plans should be included in the document, (3) require the owner to ensure that the measures set out in the document are taken and that any plans included in that document are followed, (4) provide that the owner must co-ordinate the implementation of all measures relating to the health and safety of the persons at work at the quarry, (5) provide that every employer of persons at work at a quarry must co-operate with the owner to the extent requisite to enable the owner to comply with the statutory provisions, (6) require the owner of every quarry of coal, within three months of the date on which the quarry was last worked, to give notice to the Health and Safety Executive of that fact, (7) require the owner of every quarry to ensure that adequate means of escape and rescue are provided and maintained and that adequate means of communication and warning are provided to enable assistance, escape and rescue operations to be launched, (8) provide that every employer of persons at work at a quarry and every owner of a quarry must ensure that the additional health and safety requirements set out in Pts I and II of the Schedule to the 1995 Regulations are, as appropriate having regard to specified matters, complied with, and (9) require an employer of a person engaged in work at a quarry to ensure that the person is provided with such health surveillance as is appropriate. The regulations extend the scope of the Workplace (Health, Safety and Welfare) Regulations 1992, SI 1992/3004, to quarries and mines above ground, and provide that the Mines and Quarries Act 1954, s 157, is not to apply to prosecutions or other proceedings based on an alleged contravention of the regulations.

HIGHWAYS, STREETS AND BRIDGES

Halsbury's Laws of England (4th edn) Vol 21 (reissue), paras 1–895

1514　Articles

Cowed but Unbowed, Michael Harwood (on farm animals and public paths): 139 SJ 610
Highways and Development, Gill Castorina: Estates Gazette, 21 January 1995, p 113

Modification, 'Definitiveness' and the Recording of Public Rights of Way, François Barker:
[1995] Conv 188
Trespassers on Byways in the Countryside: Section 61 of the Criminal Justice and Public Order
Act 1994, George Laurence: [1995] JPL 905

1515 Highway—adoption by local highway authority—adoption agreement—overriding interest

It has been held that where a local authority has entered into an agreement under the Highways
Act 1980, s 38 to maintain a highway, it is important that the authority protects its interest so as
to bind a subsequent purchaser of the land over which the highway is to run. If it does not, a
purchaser will not be bound, notwithstanding the fact that he was aware of the agreement when
he acquired the land. Accordingly, where an authority fails (1) to express that the agreement is
made under the Local Government (Miscellaneous Provisions) Act 1982, s 33, whereby the
covenant that the work will be carried out is binding on any successors in title to the covenantor,
or (2) to register an estate contract as a land charge or to lodge a relevant caution or notice, the
rights created by the agreement are not public rights within the meaning of the Land Registration
Act 1925, s 70(1)(a) and in consequence do not bind a subsequent purchaser of the land.

  Overseas Investment Services Ltd v Simcobuild Construction Ltd (1995) 70 P&CR 322 (Court of
Appeal: Staughton, Beldam and Peter Gibson LJJ). Decision of Judge Colyer QC (1993) Times,
2 November (1993 Abr para 1364) reversed.

1516 Highway—control of dogs on roads—orders—procedure

The Control of Dogs on Roads Orders (Procedure) (England and Wales) Regulations 1995, SI
1995/2767 (in force on 11 December 1995), replace the 1962 Regulations, SI 1962/2340, as
amended. The regulations no longer empower local authorities to hold public inquiries. The
procedures to be followed by local authorities when making orders under the Road Traffic Act
1988, s 27, specifying lengths of roads on which dogs must be held on a lead, are prescribed.

1517 Highway—dedication—deemed dedication

Certain common land was accessible by vehicles from the public road via a metalled road. In
proceedings arising from the defendant's acquittal of obstructing a highway, the plaintiff alleged
that the defendant had blocked free passage along the metalled road. His contention that the
metalled road was presumed to be a dedicated highway by means of the Highways Act 1980, s
31(1), because it had been used by vehicular traffic for over 20 years, was rejected on the ground
that the use of the road by the vehicles was a criminal offence under the Road Traffic Act 1988,
s 34(1)(a) and that an easement could not be acquired by conduct which, when it took place,
was prohibited by public statute. His alternative contention that the metalled road was presumed
to be a dedicated highway because it had been used by pedestrians for over 20 years was also
rejected. On appeal by way of case stated, *held*, there was no distinction between a claim for an
easement by prescription and a claim concerning a deemed dedication of a highway. The law
would not countenance the creation of rights based on long user which was prohibited by public
statute: this principle applied both to claims to easements by prescription and to claims to
deemed dedication of a highway. The court was uncertain as to why the plaintiff's alternative
contention had been rejected. The case would be remitted to the Crown Court for
reconsideration on that alternative point.

  Robinson v Adair (1995) Times, 2 March (Queen's Bench Division: McCowan LJ and Dyson
J).

1518 Highway—diversion of traffic—temporary prohibition or restriction on use of roads—closure of roads to reduce air pollution

The Road Traffic Regulation Act 1984, s 14 permits an authority to restrict or prohibit
temporarily the use of a road where it is satisfied that traffic should be restricted or prohibited by
reason of the likelihood of danger to the public.

  The applicants were campaigners for the temporary closure of a main road to reduce the
danger to the public from air pollution caused by road traffic. They applied for judicial review
of the highway authority's decision not to establish a scheme for the occasional restriction of
traffic on the road during periods of high pollution. *Held*, using ordinary principles of
construction and common sense, it was clear that s 14 was not designed to allow the temporary
closure of roads because of pollution. It might occasionally operate because of extreme
environmental circumstances, for example to temporarily close a road affected by a heath fire,

but it was usually invoked, for example, to close roads where adverse weather or spillages rendered the road unsafe for public use. There was no power under s 14 for the authority to close the road temporarily in order to reduce the dangers of traffic pollution. Any other finding would cause chaos on the roads and might not, in any event, have the desired effect. Accordingly, the application would be dismissed.

R v Greenwich London Borough Council, ex p Williams (1995) Times, 29 December (Queen's Bench Division: Macpherson of Cluny J).

1519 Highway—functions—contracting out

The Contracting Out (Highway Functions) Order 1995, SI 1995/1986 (in force on 25 July 1995), makes provision to enable the Secretary of State for Transport to authorise another person, or that person's employees, to exercise certain of his functions in relation to maintenance, improvement and other dealings with highways in respect of which he is the highway authority. The order confers functions on the Secretary of State in specified capacities (and subject, in some cases, to specified exceptions) under (1) specified provisions of the Highways Act 1980; (2) the Walkways Regulations 1973, SI 1973/686, regs 3(1), 4(1), 5(3), 6; (3) specified provisions of the New Roads and Street Works Act 1991; (4) the Street Works (Inspection Fees) Regulations 1992, SI 1992/1688, reg 3; (5) the Street Works (Reinstatement) Regulations 1992, SI 1992/1689, regs 3, 10; (6) the Street Works (Sharing of Costs of Works) Regulations 1992, SI 1992/1690; (7) the Street Works (Maintenance) Regulations 1992, SI 1992/1691, regs 3, 4; (8) the Street Works (Registers, Notices, Directives and Designations) Regulations 1992, SI 1992/2985, regs 3(2), (3), 5, 7, 8, 11(3), 12(3), 13(3); (9) the Public Health Act 1875, s 153; (10) the Public Health Act 1925, s 14; (11) the Local Government (Miscellaneous Provisions) Act 1953, s 5(1), (2); (12) the Parish Councils Act 1957, s 5(1), (2); (13) the Public Health Act 1961, ss 45, 81; (14) the Litter Act 1983, s 5(6), Sch 1; (15) the Road Traffic Regulation Act 1984, s 72(1); and (16) the Cycle Tracks Act 1984, ss 4, 5(1).

1520 Highway—obstruction—displays outside shops on pedestrianised street— whether obstructions fractional—reasonableness of use of highway

Two shop owners who had shops in a pedestrianised shopping street displayed goods outside their shops. The displays projected across no more than five per cent of the total width of the street and were only there during daylight hours. The local authority alleged that the displays amounted to wilful obstruction of the highway, contrary to the Highways Act 1980, s 137. At first instance, the justices acquitted the owners on the grounds that any obstruction that was de minimis might be disregarded and a restriction of the highway which occupied such a small fraction of the highway's width could not be an obstruction. On the authority's appeal by way of case stated, *held*, (1) the de minimis principle was reserved for cases of fractional obstructions, such as the case of a newsagent hanging out a rack of papers, and that clearly could not be applied in the present case. (2) It was necessary to consider whether the particular use of the highway was or was not reasonable. That was a question of fact depending on all the circumstances, including the nature, location and duration of the obstruction, the purpose for which it was used and whether it caused an actual rather than a potential obstruction. The court was in no doubt that it was not reasonable to use such a substantial part of the highway for such periods of time so as to enlarge the owners' shop areas or to attract customers into their premises. Accordingly, the appeal would be allowed and the case would be remitted to the justices with a direction that they convict the respondents.

Torbay Borough Council v Cross (1995) 159 JP 682 (Queen's Bench Division: McCowan LJ and Dyson J).

1521 Highway—protection of highway—nuisance—removal of object deposited on highway—meaning of deposited

The Highways Act 1980, s 149(1) provides that if anything is deposited on a highway so as to constitute a nuisance, the highway authority for the highway may, by notice, require the person who deposited it there to remove it forthwith. If he fails to comply with the notice, the authority may make a complaint to a magistrates' court for a removal and disposal order.

The plaintiff sold hot chestnuts from a cylindrical brazier mounted on a four-wheeled barrow which was positioned on a public highway. As he did not have a street trader's licence, the local authority decided that the barrow constituted a nuisance and removed it. The plaintiff successfully sought the return of the brazier on the basis that the removal had been unlawful. On the local authority's appeal, *held*, the word 'deposited' could be used in a number of contexts, and unless that context was clearly stated, it was to be given a broad interpretation. A brazier which was stationed on the highway while attendants sold chestnuts from it was to be regarded as having been 'deposited' on the highway, within the meaning of the 1980 Act, s 149. The local authority had had reasonable grounds for believing that the public were at risk of being burnt by the brazier and were therefore correct to remove it. Accordingly, the appeal would be allowed.

Scott v Westminster City Council (1995) 93 LGR 370 (Court of Appeal: Nourse and Waite LJJ and Sir Tasker Watkins).

1522   Rail crossings, public paths, and definitive maps and statements—orders

The Rail Crossing Extinguishment and Diversion Orders, the Public Path Orders and the Definitive Maps and Statements (Amendment) Regulations 1995, SI 1995/451 (in force on 29 March 1995), amend SI 1993/9, 10, 11, 12 by amending the areas in respect of which persons are to be served with notice of orders, and by making minor and drafting amendments. The regulations also substitute SI 1993/11, Sch 1, which prescribes the forms of orders.

1523   Street works—registers, notices, directions and designations

The Street Works (Registers, Notices, Directions and Designations) (Amendment) Regulations 1995, SI 1995/990 (in force on 1 July 1995), amend the 1992 Regulations, SI 1992/2985, by imposing a new requirement on street authorities with regard to the form in which they must keep street works registers under the New Roads and Street Works Act 1991, s 53 and by making the relevant undertaker, instead of the highway authority, responsible for securing the registration of certain information.

The Street Works (Registers, Notices, Directions and Designations) (Amendment No 3) Regulations 1995, SI 1995/2128 (in force on 11 September 1995), further amend the 1992 Regulations supra by (1) referring to road traffic regulation orders in Greater London made under the Road Traffic Regulation Act 1984, s 6, and making it clear that the prohibition or restriction of the parking of vehicles referred to must be for at least one hour during the specified hours, and (2) enabling street authorities in Greater London to designate a street as traffic-sensitive where it is a priority route or, in the opinion of the Traffic Director for London, is one which is likely to be affected by a priority route. SI 1995/1154 is revoked.

HIRE PURCHASE AND CONSUMER CREDIT

Halsbury's Laws of England (4th edn) Vol 22, paras 1–400

See CONSUMER CREDIT.

HOUSING

Halsbury's Laws of England (4th edn) Vol 22, paras 401–900

1524   Articles

The Effect of Death on the Right to Buy Under Pt V of the Housing Act 1985, A H R Brierley: [1995] Conv 114

HIV and Homelessness: Lobbying, Law, Policy and Practice, David Cowan: (1995) 1 JSWFL 43

Interim Possession Orders, Louella Crisfield (on the new offence created by the Criminal Justice and Public Order Act 1994, s 76): LA, September 1995, p 21

1525   Council tax benefit

See SOCIAL SECURITY AND SOCIAL SERVICES.

1526   Home Energy Conservation Act 1995

See para 1292.

1527 Home energy efficiency grants—regulations

The Home Efficiency Grants (Amendment) Regulations 1995, SI 1995/49 (in force on 1 March 1995), further amend SI 1992/483, by extending the definition of 'householder' so that grants may additionally be paid to assured agricultural occupiers, protected occupiers, almshouse licensees whose licences meet certain conditions and to cottars. The regulations also omit a requirement that a grant is to be subject to a condition for repayment where the work was not carried out or did not comply with specified standards.

1528 Homeless persons—duty of local authority to provide accommodation—illegal immigrant—immigration status

It has been held that a housing authority has the power to decide that an applicant for housing has no right to reside in the United Kingdom and, accordingly, that it owes him no duty to provide accommodation under the Housing Act 1985, Pt III. Following the decision in *R v Secretary of State for the Environment, ex p Tower Hamlets London Borough Council* [1993] 3 All ER 439, CA (1993 Abr para 1381), a person who has illegally entered the United Kingdom and has acquired no right to remain, is owed no duty by a local authority under the 1985 Act, Pt III. That principle extends to a person who has been informed by the Immigration and Nationality Department that he has no enforceable right to reside in the United Kingdom but will not be forced to leave. In such circumstances, it is for the housing authority and not the immigration department, to determine his status and rights under the 1985 Act, Pt III.

R v Westminster City Council, ex p Castelli; R v Westminster City Council, ex p Tristran-Garcia [1996] 1 FLR 534 (Queen's Bench Division: Roger Henderson QC).

This decision has been reversed on appeal: (1996) Times, 27 February, CA.

1529 Homeless persons—duty of local authority to provide accommodation—inquiries—breach of duty by authority

The applicant lived as a squatter with her husband and two sons. They applied for housing to the respondent housing authority but the application was not processed until a housing charity intervened over a year later. The authority decided that the applicant was not homeless or threatened with homelessness and the applicants sought judicial review of the authority's decision. The application was adjourned and the authority reconsidered its decision, declaring that the applicant was homeless after all. The applicant sought damages on the ground that the authority had acted in breach of its statutory duty by failing to make adequate inquiries as to whether the applicant was homeless under the Housing Act 1985, s 62. At first instance, the application was dismissed. On appeal, *held*, duties owed by a housing authority pursuant to the 1985 Act, s 62 were owed for the benefit of the public and, if breached, did not give rise to any private cause of action for damages. Further, no private law duty arose on the part of the respondents to secure accommodation for the applicant under either the 1985 Act, s 63 or s 65, until the authority had come to a decision that the conditions necessary to give rise to a duty under either section were satisfied. Accordingly, the appeal would be dismissed.

R v Northavon District Council, ex p Palmer [1996] 1 FLR 142 (Court of Appeal: Sir Thomas Bingham MR, Auld and Ward LJJ). Decision of Roger Toulson QC (1994 Abr para 1499) affirmed.

1530 Homeless persons—duty of local authority to provide accommodation—inquiries—delegation to housing association

A local housing authority transferred its housing stock to a housing association under an agreement whereby the association was to investigate cases of persons claiming to be homeless. On completing its inquiries, the association was to report to the authority with its conclusions and recommendations and the authority would then decide whether a person was homeless, in priority need or intentionally homeless, and whether there was a local connection under the Housing Act 1985, s 62. When the applicant and her husband separated, she applied to the authority for housing for herself and her son. She was told by the association that the officer dealing with her case had said the applicant could not have any accommodation until she had custody of her son and even then she was unlikely to be offered anything. The applicant's solicitor wrote to the association in support of her application, referring to the stress the situation was causing to the son. However, the association made no further inquiries and made a recommendation, which the authority accepted, that the applicant was not homeless. The applicant sought judicial review of the authority's decision. *Held*, an authority could not delegate its duty to make inquiries into cases of homelessness or threatened homelessness under s 62.

Although it could enlist the assistance of third parties it had to take an active and dominant part in the investigative process. In the present case, since the authority did not retain such control, the making and implementation of the agreement was flawed in public law. As a result, the authority's decision in respect of the applicant was tainted by that flawed implementation. Accordingly, the appeal would be allowed.

R v West Dorset District Council, ex p Gerrard (1994) 27 HLR 150 (Queen's Bench Division: Roger Henderson QC).

1531 Homeless persons—duty of local authority to provide accommodation—intentional homelessness—eviction following conviction for assault

The applicant lived with his former wife and two sons as a bare licensee. His former wife obtained an eviction order against him after he was convicted of assaulting one of their sons. On his application for housing, the local authority accepted that he was homeless and had a priority need, but rejected his application on the ground that he had made himself intentionally homeless within the meaning of the Housing Act 1985, s 60(1), because his violence had led to his eviction. On his application for judicial review of the decision, *held*, where the reasonable result of a person's deliberate act was his eviction and the act had caused the eviction, he was intentionally homeless, even if he did not appreciate that it would lead to his eviction. The local authority in the instant case had not addressed the question of whether the eviction was the reasonable result of the applicant's violence towards his son, but had instead considered the matter purely as one of consequence. The case had to be reconsidered in the light of the reasonable result test and, accordingly, the application would be granted.

R v Westminster City Council, ex p Reid (1994) 26 HLR 690 (Queen's Bench Division: Robert Carnwath QC). *Robinson v Torbay Borough Council* [1982] 1 All ER 726 (1982 Abr para 1525) applied.

1532 Homeless persons—duty of local authority to provide accommodation—intentional homelessness—evidence of reasons for local authority's decision

The applicant made a housing application to a local authority. He claimed that he and his family had to leave their home in Greece because they had experienced harassment. The authority sent the applicant a decision letter, pursuant to the 1985 Act, s 64, stating that he was intentionally homeless because he had accommodation in Greece and that it was not satisfied that the applicant had experienced any harassment. When the authority later admitted that the reason given was inaccurate and sought to supplement it by affidavit, the applicant applied for judicial review of the decision letter. The applicant was unsuccessful at first instance and, on appeal, it fell to be determined whether the judge had erred in having regard to reasons given by the authority in an affidavit when those reasons were fundamentally different from the reasons given in the decision letter. *Held*, the court could, and in appropriate cases should, admit evidence to elucidate or, exceptionally, correct or add to the reasons given but it should be very cautious about doing so. The function of such evidence should generally be elucidation not fundamental alteration. Certainly, there seemed to be no warrant for receiving and relying on as validating the decision evidence which indicated that the real reasons were wholly different from the stated reasons. If no reasons or wholly deficient reasons were given, the applicant was prima facie entitled to have the decision quashed as unlawful. In the present case, the reality was that no reasons were given and, accordingly, the appeal would be allowed.

R v Westminster City Council, ex p Ermakov (1995) Times, 29 November (Court of Appeal: Nourse, Hutchison and Thorpe LJJ). Decision of Sir Louis Blom-Cooper QC (1994) 27 HLR 168 reversed.

1533 Homeless persons—duty of local authority to provide accommodation—intentional homelessness—joint application for housing

The Housing Act 1985, s 75 provides that accommodation is to be regarded as available for a person's occupation only if it is available for occupation both by him and by any other person who might reasonably be expected to reside with him.

The applicant left her home in Nigeria in order to live in England, with the intention of pursuing her studies and bettering her way of life. Soon after, her then fiancé left Nigeria with the same intention. They did not begin living together until they were in England, following which they married and had a child. Having lived in a series of temporary residences, the applicant and her husband applied to the respondent for housing on the basis of their homelessness. Although the application was made jointly, the respondent treated them separately in considering whether or not they were intentionally homeless. It decided that although the applicant was homeless and had a priority need, she had made herself intentionally homeless because she had left accommodation in Nigeria which it was considered reasonable for her to continue occupying. It was also the case that she had not studied, and that she had come to England knowing that she had no permanent accommodation. On the applicant's application for judicial review of the decision, *held*, the respondent had not been obliged to consider the applicant and her husband as a family unit in determining the issue of intentionality, as it was necessary to concentrate on their actions and intentions as individuals. The respondent had therefore been entitled to find that the applicant's last settled accommodation was in Nigeria and that she had deliberately left it, separately from her husband. Moreover, as there was no evidence that the applicant and her husband had lived together in Nigeria, nor that they had intended to establish a family at the time that they each came to England, and as it was also the case that they did not live together until 15 months after they had both been in England, there had been no reason for the respondent to conclude that there was any expectation of joint residence. The 1985 Act, s 75 was therefore not applicable in the instant case, as it had to be applied as at the time that the applicant and her husband each left Nigeria and not at the date of their housing application or at the time that it was refused. As such, the respondent had been entitled to conclude that the applicant was intentionally homeless and, accordingly, the application would be dismissed.

R v Barking and Dagenham London Borough Council, ex p Okuneye [1995] 3 FCR 311 (Queen's Bench Division: Sir Louis Blom-Cooper QC).

1534   Homeless persons—duty of local authority to provide accommodation— intentional homelessness—priority need—dependent children

Under the Housing Act 1985, s 59(1)(b) a person with whom dependent children reside or might reasonably be expected to reside has a priority need for accommodation. The Act does not define dependent child, but the Code of Guidance under the Act to which a local authority must have regard, although by which it is not bound, includes within the definition all children under 16, and all children aged 16 to 18 who are in, or about to begin, full-time education or training and who live at home.

The applicant applied for local authority accommodation for himself and his 16-year-old son. His son had just started a two-year youth training scheme. The authority, having had regard to the Code of Guidance, decided that as the son was not a dependent child within the 1985 Act, s 59(1)(b) the applicant was not in priority need of housing. On an application for judicial review of the decision, the judge, in dismissing the appeal noted that trainees on youth training schemes received a weekly allowance and concluded that a 16 or 17-year-old on such a scheme was not within the meaning of the words 'full-time education or training'. The applicant appealed. *Held*, it might be that a 16-year-old who was not financially independent was within s 59(1)(b), but once he went into full-time employment he could not be. The judge had been correct and, accordingly, the appeal would be dismissed.

R v Kensington and Chelsea Royal London Borough, ex p Amarfio [1995] 2 FCR 787 (Court of Appeal: Nourse, Kennedy and Evans LJJ). Decision of Sir Louis Blom-Cooper QC [1994] 3 FCR 255 (1994 Abr para 1512) affirmed.

1535   Homeless person—duty of local authority to provide accommodation—intentional homelessness—priority need—unlawful eviction

The Housing Act 1985, s 59(1)(d) provides that a person who is homeless or threatened with homelessness as a result of an emergency such as flood, fire or other disaster, has a priority need for accommodation.

The applicant was a tenant of a room in a property in multiple occupation. On his return from holiday, he discovered that he had been unlawfully evicted from the room by his landlord. He applied to the respondent local authority for housing, claiming that he was unintentionally homeless and that he had a priority need. The respondent rejected his claim, arguing that his illegal eviction was not a disaster within the meaning of s 59(1)(d). The applicant successfully applied for judicial review of the decision. The respondent appealed. *Held*, as the word 'emergency' in s 59(1)(d) was qualified by the phrase 'such as flood, fire or other disaster', it followed that Parliament did not intend that every emergency which resulted in a person becoming homeless created a priority need. The type of event which gave a homeless person a priority need was one which was both an emergency and a disaster, and Parliament intended that only emergencies which resulted in physical damage to an applicant's accommodation so as to make it uninhabitable, such as deliberate or accidental fires or floods, should confer a priority need. Unlawful eviction was not such an emergency and, accordingly, the appeal would be allowed.

R v Bristol City Council, ex p Bradic [1995] 3 FCR 204 (Court of Appeal: Nourse, Roch and Hobhouse LJJ). Decision of Sir Louis Blom-Cooper QC (1995) Times, 6 February reversed.

1536   Homeless persons—duty of local authority to provide accommodation—intentional homelessness—refusal of short-term accommodation

A local authority placed the applicant in short-term accommodation until, in accordance with its duty under the Housing Act 1985, s 65(2) to secure that accommodation became available for her occupation, it could find her suitable permanent accommodation. When she refused the permanent accommodation subsequently offered to her by the authority, it evicted her from the short-term accommodation. A second authority refused her accommodation on the ground that, as she had refused the accommodation offered by the first authority, she was now intentionally homeless. She sought judicial review of the decision, contending that the accommodation to which s 60(1), which described the concept of intentional homelessness, referred had to be 'settled' and not temporary as the short-term accommodation provided by the first authority had been. Held, 'accommodation' in s 58(1), which described the concept of homelessness, and s 60(1) meant accommodation fairly described as such which it would be reasonable for the applicant to continue to occupy having regard to general housing conditions in the authority's district. There was no additional requirement that it should be settled or permanent. The mere fact that accommodation was temporary did not mean that the applicant could not reasonably be expected to continue to occupy it within the meaning of s 60(1). As it would have been reasonable for the applicant to stay in the short-term accommodation, she was intentionally homeless and, accordingly, her application would be dismissed.

The House of Lords added that a local authority's duty to an unintentionally homeless person in priority need under s 65(2) is merely to secure that accommodation becomes available for his occupation. By virtue of s 69(1), the accommodation must be 'suitable' but this does not import any requirement of permanence.

R v Brent London Borough Council, ex p Awua [1995] 3 WLR 215 (House of Lords: Lords Goff of Chieveley, Jauncey of Tullichettle, Slynn of Hadley, Taylor of Gosforth and Hoffmann). Hillingdon London Borough Council [1986] 1 All ER 467, HL (1986 Abr para 1136), applied. Dyson v Kerrier District Council [1980] 3 All ER 313, CA (1980 Abr para 1434) considered. Decision of Court of Appeal (1994) HLR 26 539 (1994 Abr para 1510) affirmed.

1537   Homeless persons—duty of local authority to provide accommodation—intentional homelessness—settled accommodation

The applicant, a British citizen, married and went to live with her husband in India. She subsequently went to live with relatives in Bangladesh. When she returned to England with her children, she lived with her parents, but her father later gave her formal written notice to quit. On her application for housing, the local authority decided that although she was homeless and had a priority need, she had made herself intentionally homeless within the meaning of the Housing Act 1985, s 60(1) by leaving her settled accommodation in Bangladesh. In successfully applying for judicial review of the local authority's decision, she relied on the defence in the 1985 Act, s 60(3), claiming that she had unexpectedly encountered difficulty in finding employment on her return to England, and that had prevented her from being able to afford suitable accommodation. She also argued that it was her dispute with her parents in England that had been the cause of her homelessness. On the local authority's appeal, held, the matters relating to the applicant's prospects of employment and housing were matters of hope rather than relevant facts, and the local authority had therefore not acted unreasonably having regard to Wednesbury principles in refusing to take them into account when reaching their decision. Moreover, the applicant's settled home was in Bangladesh, notwithstanding the fact that she left that home and thereafter lived with her parents in England. She became homeless when she left Bangladesh, and in deliberately choosing to leave that home, she had made herself intentionally homeless. Accordingly, the appeal would be allowed.

R v Ealing London Borough Council, ex p Sukhija (1994) 26 HLR 726 (Court of Appeal: Sir Stephen Brown P, Staughton and Rose LJJ). R v Basingstoke and Deane Borough Council, ex p Bassett (1983) 10 HLR 125 (1983 Abr para 1690) doubted.

1538　Homeless persons—duty of local authority to provide accommodation—intentional homelessness—subsequent event making homelessness intentional

The applicant became homeless when an order for possession was obtained against him. He applied for local authority accommodation but the local housing authority decided that he had become homeless intentionally and referred to acts he had done after becoming homeless to establish the intentionality. On his application for judicial review of the authority's decision, the applicant contended that the acts could not have caused him to become homeless and lose settled accommodation because he was already homeless. The authority submitted that it was reasonable to hold that unintentional homelessness under the Housing Act 1985, s 58 could be made intentional by a subsequent event. *Held*, present homelessness could not logically be caused by an act or omission postdating its onset. Accordingly, the authority's decision would be quashed.

R v Islington London Borough Council, ex p Hassan [1995] 2 FCR 830 (Queen's Bench Division: Roger Toulson QC).

1539　Homeless persons—duty of local authority to provide accommodation—priority need—vulnerable person

The Housing Act 1985, s 59(1)(c) provides that a person has a priority need for accommodation if he is a person who is vulnerable as a result of old age, mental illness or handicap, or physical disability, or other special reason.

The applicant, an alcoholic and a drug addict, lost her accommodation when she was admitted to a hospital detoxification unit for treatment. Shortly before she was due to be released from the unit, she applied to the respondent local authority for rehousing, arguing that she had a priority need because she was a vulnerable person within the meaning of the 1985 Act, s 59(1)(c). It was medically certified that the applicant would suffer problems if she did not acquire suitable accommodation when discharged. The application was refused, and the applicant unsuccessfully applied for judicial review of the decision. On appeal, *held*, in order to satisfy the test of vulnerability, an applicant had to show that to some material extent he was less able to secure suitable accommodation than an ordinary person, and that if he failed to obtain it, he would suffer more than most. Here, there was no evidence that the applicant would have particular difficulty in finding suitable accommodation and, accordingly, the appeal would be dismissed.

Ortiz v City of Westminster (1993) 27 HLR 364 (Court of Appeal: Simon Brown and Hobhouse LJJ). *R v Waveney District Council, ex p Bowers* [1982] 3 All ER 727 (1982 Abr para 1526), CA followed.

1540　Homeless persons—duty of local authority to provide accommodation—request for assistance to housing association—performance of duty by association

Under the Housing Act 1985, s 72 where a local authority requests a registered housing association to assist it in the discharge of its functions under s 65, the association to whom the request is made must co-operate in rendering such assistance in the discharge of the functions to which the request relates as is reasonable in the circumstances.

A local authority agreed to transfer its housing stock to a housing association. The applicant applied to the authority for accommodation and the authority found that it had a duty under s 65 to provide accommodation. The association offered her accommodation but she refused because she wanted to live elsewhere. The authority decided that its offer was reasonable and that no further offers would be made. The applicant sought judicial review of the decision on the ground that the authority's duty to provide accommodation under s 65 could not be discharged by an association. She relied on the decision in *R v West Dorset District Council, ex p Gerrard*, where the court held that the local authority's duty under the 1985 Act, s 62 to inquire into homelessness could not be delegated to a housing association. *Held*, s 72 preserved the exclusively statutory duties of decision-making to the authority. So long as the decision-making was kept exclusively within the authority, there seemed no basis for reading into s 72 any limitation on the exercise of all powers of investigation being legitimately performed by an outside agency which was statutorily acknowledged. The court was not bound to follow the decision in *Gerrard*. In that case the issue involved the performance of the authority's duty to make inquiries as to homelessness, while the present case involved a request for assistance in finding accommodation pursuant to s 65. The authority in offering the applicant accommodation had performed its duty under s 65 and in the process it had not exceeded its powers under s 72. Accordingly, the application would be dismissed.

R v Hertsmere Borough Council, ex p Woolgar (1995) 27 HLR 703 (Queen's Bench Division: Sir Louis Blom-Cooper QC). *R v West Dorset District Council, ex p Gerrard* (1994) 27 HLR 150 (para 1530) considered.

1541 Homeless persons—duty of local authority to provide accommodation—rescission of authority's decision to provide accommodation—whether rescission subject to judicial review

A local authority found the applicant to be unintentionally homeless. It decided to offer him suitable accommodation but the applicant had failed to disclose to the authority that suitable accommodation had been made available to him by a housing association. When the authority found out, it rescinded its decision to make the offer of accommodation. It fell to be determined (1) on a preliminary issue, whether the applicant could apply for judicial review of the authority's decision, and (2) in the substantive hearing, whether the applicant could apply for compensation for the authority's failure to perform its statutory duty under the Housing Act 1985 to provide him with secure accommodation. *Held*, (1) after the authority executed its duty under the 1985 Act by notifying the applicant of its decision, any second thoughts by the authority could not assume the shape of a decision under the Act because it made no provision for such a historical decision. That decision therefore, not being an administrative one under statutory functions, was not subject to judicial review principles. (2) The applicant's case stood or fell according to whether the complaint went to the exercise of a decision-making public law function or to the exercise of an executive function. That distinction was firmly established by case law; in any given case a claim of damages could not run unless the act or omission complained of demonstrably lay on the executive side of the line. In the present case, the applicant's complaint went to the composite duty, lying in the public domain. Therefore, on principle and in light of the force of authority binding upon the court, the damages claim was misconceived. Accordingly, the application would be dismissed.

R v Ealing London Borough Council, ex p Parkinson (1995) Times, 13 November (Queen's Bench Division: Laws J).

1542 Homeless persons—duty of local authority to provide accommodation—suitability of accommodation—duty to give reasons for decision

A local authority found the applicant to be unintentionally homeless and in priority need. She was offered accommodation in a seventh-floor flat but the applicant, who was arthritic and had a young child, did not consider the accommodation to be suitable since the lift did not work. She appealed under the authority's voluntary appeals procedure but the authority informed her that the flat was suitable and that its duty to provide accommodation had been discharged. The applicant sought judicial review of that decision on the grounds that (1) the offer was unreasonable, and (2) the authority had failed to give reasons for its decision. The authority claimed that the lack of lift was temporary and that there was an acute shortage of accommodation. The application was dismissed at first instance and, on appeal, *held*, (1) the authority had to strike a balance between the applicant's needs and difficulties and those of other families on the housing waiting list. It was for the authority to make the assessment and the court should be very slow to interfere with that process except in the clearest case. On the facts, it was impossible to say that the authority acted unreasonably or reached a conclusion that no reasonable authority could have reached. (2) No general obligation was imposed on administrative authorities to give reasons for their decisions, although such a duty might be implied in appropriate circumstances. In the present case, the authority's decision was in line with its general policy and involved a difficult balancing exercise. It would be wrong to impose any general legal duty to give reasons for an authority's finding in a particular case that accommodation offered was suitable. Accordingly, the appeal would be dismissed.

R v Kensington and Chelsea Royal London Borough Council, ex p Grillo (1996) 28 HLR 94 (Court of Appeal: Neill, Hirst and Roch LJJ).

1543 Homeless persons—duty of local authority to provide accommodation—suitability of accommodation—inquiries as to suitability

A local authority accepted that it had a duty under the Housing Act 1985, s 65(2) to secure housing for the applicant. She indicated her preferred districts for rehousing but when offered accommodation in one of those districts she said the accommodation was not suitable because of its condition. She appealed against the offer but the appeal was refused. The applicant then wrote to the authority explaining that she did not want to live at the offered accommodation because her stepfather, who had sexually abused her, lived nearby. The authority treated that letter, in effect, as a further appeal which it refused, forming the view that the real reason for refusing the accommodation related to its condition. The applicant's solicitor wrote to the authority setting out in detail the abuse she had suffered but the authority carried out no further inquiries. It wrote to the solicitor stating that its duty towards the applicant had been discharged and that no additional information had been provided to add to that considered at the time it's duty was discharged. The applicant sought judicial review of that decision. *Held*, the authority's decision was erroneous in law. No reasonable authority could have concluded that the solicitor's letter contained no new information. Where an authority entirely disbelieved an account given by an applicant for housing, where the circumstances in that account were critical to the issue of whether accommodation ought to be offered in a particular area, the authority was bound to put the matters that concerned it to the applicant. An applicant had to be given an opportunity to deal with an adverse decision. Accordingly, the application would be allowed and the authority's decision quashed.

R v London Borough of Hackney, ex p Decordova (1994) 27 HLR 108 (Queen's Bench Division: Laws J).

1544 Homeless persons—duty of local authority to provide accommodation—suitability of accommodation—meaning of suitable accommodation

It fell to be determined whether a local authority could discharge its duty, under the Housing Act 1985, s 65(2), to secure suitable accommodation for a person who was unintentionally homeless with priority need, by arranging for a private landlord to grant the person in question an assured shorthold tenancy, where there was a reasonable prospect of renewal of the tenancy. *Held*, 'accommodation' in s 65(2) meant some period other than temporary accommodation. 'Settled' was more appropriate than 'permanent' to describe the nature of the accommodation to be secured because it encompassed not only sustained occupancy but also short-term residence. As permanency was not an ingredient of the accommodation required to satisfy a s 65(2) duty, an assured shorthold tenancy was capable of qualifying as 'settled accommodation'; it was not necessary to determine whether an assured shorthold tenancy was accommodation which was likely to continue indefinitely as a statutory tenancy. 'Suitable accommodation' described the nature and quality of the accommodation; it did not relate to the length of the tenancy. An authority offering an assured shorthold tenancy to a homeless person had to satisfy itself that that there was a real prospect that the tenancy would survive beyond its fixed term. Accordingly, provided that there was a reasonable prospect of renewal of the tenancy, the authority's duty under s 65(2) would be discharged.

R v Wandsworth London Borough Council, ex p Crooks (1995) 27 HLR 660 (Queen's Bench Division: Sir Louis Blom-Cooper QC).

1545 Homeless persons—duty of local authority to provide accommodation—suitability of accommodation—pregnant applicant

The Housing Act 1985, s 75 provides that accommodation is to be regarded as available for a person's occupation only if it is available for occupation both by him and by any other person who might reasonably be expected to reside with him.

A homeless woman and her husband refused a local housing authority's offer of one bedroom accommodation on the ground that she was pregnant. The authority decided to treat the refusal as unreasonable but, at first instance, its decision was quashed when the judge held that the unborn child was a 'person' under s 75. On the authority's appeal, *held*, the ordinary and natural meaning of the word 'person' was a living person and there was nothing within the context of the 1985 Act, Pt III which undermined that interpretation of the word in s 75. It was therefore to be given the meaning of a person who was alive when the offer of accommodation was made and, accordingly, the appeal would be allowed.

R v Newham London Borough Council, ex p Dada [1995] 2 All ER 522 (Court of Appeal: Glidewell, Hirst and Hoffmann LJJ). Decision of Sir Louis Blom-Cooper QC (1994) Times, 29 July reversed.

1546 Homeless persons—duty of local authority to provide accommodation—suitability of accommodation—risk of domestic violence

The applicant left the accommodation which she shared with her partner because of his violence towards her. The local authority accepted that she was a homeless person with a priority need and that she was not intentionally homeless. The applicant stated that there was only one particular area in which she did not wish to live, namely the area in which her former partner still resided. The area was therefore excluded as unsuitable, and the applicant was offered permanent accommodation in a neighbouring area. She refused to accept it and appealed, stating that her former partner had friends in that area whom he often visited. In assessing the suitability of accommodation offered to victims of domestic violence, it was the local authority's policy to take account of visits made by an aggressor to his immediate family, but not to friends, who lived in the area in which the accommodation offered to his victim was situated. As the applicant's former partner had no immediate family in the area in which the accommodation was situated, the local authority did not seek further information on the matter, and rejected the applicant's appeal. On her application for judicial review, *held*, the code of practice issued under the Housing Act 1985, s 71 stated that care had to be taken in allocating accommodation to those who had suffered violence or threats of abuse in order to reduce the risk of similar problems occcuring. If an aggressor was likely to visit people who lived in the same area as the accommodation offered to his victim, there was a risk of further violence, but the degree of risk depended on the proximity of the place visited by him and the frequency of his visits to that place. There was no difference between visiting family members and visiting friends, and therefore the local authority should have considered the risk posed to the applicant by her former partner's visits to his friends in the area in which the accommodation offered to her was situated. The case had to be reconsidered so that the local authority could seek further information on the matter and, accordingly, the application would be allowed.

R v of Southwark London Borough, ex p Solomon (1994) 26 HLR 693 (Queen's Bench Division: Popplewell J).

1547 Homeless persons—duty of local authority to provide accommodation— temporary accommodation—eviction by local authority

See *Mohamed v Manek*, para 1812.

1548 House in multiple occupation—inadequate provision of fire escape—landlord required to remedy provision—tenant's application for alternative housing

A tenant lived with his wife and young child in the top floor flat of a house in multiple occupation. There was a real risk of fire in the house and no adequate means of escape. The local authority therefore proposed serving a notice on the owner of the house pursuant to the Housing Act 1985, s 352, requiring him to remedy the inadequate means of escape within a specified time limit. The tenant applied to the authority for housing under the 1985 Act, Pt III on the basis that until the necessary improvements had been made, he and his family were not protected. The authority found that he was not homeless within s 58 and the tenant sought review of that decision. At first instance, the judge quashed the authority's decision, concluding that no delay whatever was acceptable and that the authority's proposal to give the owner an opportunity to remedy the situation was not within the range of reasonable responses. On the authority's appeal, *held*, once the problem had been identified it was plainly necessary that effective action should be taken either to provide a means of escape or to ensure that the flat was vacated and, in either event, no lengthy delay could be properly contemplated. However, if the judge's decision was upheld, anyone in the applicant's position who could demonstrate a lack of adequate means of escape from fire in a house in multiple occupation could, in effect, demand to be rehoused by the authority at once. Bearing in mind the difficulties faced by authorities in discharging their duties under the Act and that there were 4,500 households in houses of multiple occupation in the authority's area, the judge had erred in regarding the authority's decision to pursue a solution in the first instance with the owner of the house as perverse and irrational. Accordingly, the appeal would be allowed.

R v Royal Borough of Kensington and Chelsea, ex p Ben-El-Mabrouk [1995] 3 FCR 812 (Court of Appeal: Sir Thomas Bingham MR, Peter Gibson and Saville LJJ).

1549 Housing benefit

See SOCIAL SECURITY AND SOCIAL SERVICES.

1550 Housing renovation grants—forms and particulars

The Housing Renovation etc Grants (Prescribed Forms and Particulars) (Amendment) Regulations 1995, SI 1995/839 (in force on 17 April 1995), amend the 1994 Regulations, SI 1994/565. The amendments are consequential to amendments made by the Housing Renovation etc Grants (Reduction of Grant) (Amendment) Regulations 1995, SI 1995/838, and the regulations also make minor and drafting amendments.

The Housing Renovation etc Grants (Prescribed Forms and Particulars) (Welsh Forms and Particulars) (Amendment) Regulations 1995, SI 1995/857 (in force on 17 April 1995), amend the 1994 Regulations, SI 1994/693. The regulations translate into Welsh the amendments make by the Housing Renovation etc Grants (Prescribed Forms and Particulars) Regulations 1994, SI 1994/565, as amended.

1551 Housing renovation grants—reduction of grant

The Housing Renovation etc Grants (Reduction of Grant) (Amendment) Regulations 1995, SI 1995/838 (in force on 17 April 1995), amend the 1994 Regulations, SI 1994/648, so as to reflect recent changes to housing benefit rules, including the replacement of sickness and invalidity benefits by incapacity benefit and the introduction of a new test of incapacity for work, under the Social Security (Incapacity for Work) Act 1994. They also make minor and drafting amendments to the 1994 Regulations (1) changing the multipliers in reg 10 (reduction in the amount of grant), (2) amending reg 16(1) to require deductions to be made in respect of relevant child care charges, (3) adding reg 16A (treatment of child care charges), and (4) amending Sch 1 by uprooting the applicable amounts and premiums, changing references to invalidity pension to incapacity benefit, and substituting provisions relating to the new test for incapacity for work. Transitional provision is made.

1552 Housing repair grants—mandatory works—amount of grant—landlords

The Local Government and Housing Act 1989, s 110(2) provides that, subject to the other provisions of s 110 and to s 116(5), the amount of a grant towards completing mandatory works is such as may be determined by the local housing authority, having regard to (a) the cost of the relevant works, (b) if the dwelling is currently let or subject to a statutory tenancy, the amount of rent payable and of any increase which might reasonably be expected in that rent to take account of the relevant works when completed, (c) if (b) does not apply, the amount of the rent which might reasonably be expected to be obtained on a letting of the dwelling on the open market under an assured tenancy, and (d) such other matters as the Secretary of State may direct.

Landlords were served with notice requiring them to execute certain works to render their premises fit for occupation. Having complied with the notice, the landlords applied to the local authority for payment of a grant towards the costs which they had incurred. It was the local authority's general policy to award mandatory grants at the rate of 20 per cent of the costs incurred, or at a level determined by use of the formula applied under the 1989 Act, s 110, whichever was the lesser. However, if the Director of Housing Services considered that there were extenuating circumstances, such as proven hardship, the Housing Committee could consider awarding a higher level of grant. When the landlords were awarded 20 per cent of the cost of the works, they sought judicial review of both the award and the local authority's policy on grants. *Held*, in deciding the amount of a grant, the local authority was limited to the matters expressly mentioned in s 110(2)(a)–(d), and did not have a general discretion. In particular, it had no discretion to impose an arbitrary limit on the amount payable, nor could it take account of its own financial resources, or absence of resources, or those of an applicant. The amount payable had to be determined by reference to the particular factors set out in s 110(2), as the provision was exhaustive. Such an interpretation was reinforced by the statutory framework as a whole, and was the fairest way to approach the matter. If it was otherwise, landlords who had been obliged to spend money on their property would be left without a proper grant to reimburse them. The local authority's policy was therefore outside its statutory powers and, accordingly, the application would be granted.

R v Sunderland City Council, ex p Redezeus Ltd (1994) 27 HLR 477 (Queen's Bench Division: Judge J).

1553 Local authority housing—discretion to rehouse tenants—matters to be taken into consideration

The applicant, a tenant of the respondent local authority, applied for a transfer to other local authority accommodation on medical grounds, and was given priority medical status. Whilst waiting to be re-accommodated, the applicant built up substantial rent arrears, as a result of which the respondent informed her that they would not actively consider her application. Guidelines additional to the respondent's housing transfer policy included a provision that an application for rehousing by a tenant with rent arrears would only be considered if he agreed to pay the current rent plus a regular contribution to reduce the arrears. In contrast, an instruction note issued by the Director of Housing stated that if a tenant had failed to enter into an agreement for paying off the arrears, or had failed to abide by it, it was highly unlikely that he would be rehoused. The respondent later commenced possession proceedings against the applicant because of her rent arrears, and refused to reconsider their decision not to deal with her transfer application. On the applicant's application for judicial review of the decision, *held*, the part of the additional guidelines which stated that a rehousing application by a tenant with rent arrears would only be considered if he agreed to pay the current rent plus a regular contribution to reduce the arrears, was unlawful because it did not allow for any exceptions and thereby fettered the exercise of the respondent's discretion. However, it did not automatically follow that because part of the guidelines were unlawful, the decision in the instant case was unlawful. The Director of Housing's instruction note allowed for exceptions, and it was on the basis of those lawful guidelines that the respondent had reached its decision. Although it was lawful to take account of rent arrears in considering a transfer application, the respondent had taken exclusive account of the applicant's rent arrears, whereas other matters should also have been considered, in particular, the fact that she had priority status for rehousing because of her medical condition. That was a relevant exceptional circumstance which had not been taken into account and, accordingly, the application would be allowed.

R v of Islington London Borough, ex p Aldabbagh (1994) 27 HLR 271 (Queen's Bench Division: Harrison J).

1554 Local authority housing—right to buy

See LANDLORD AND TENANT.

1555 Local authority housing—secure tenancy

See LANDLORD AND TENANT.

1556 Local authority housing—squatter—squatter with priority need under housing policy—undertaking not to evict squatter—possession proceedings

See *Southwark London Borough Council v Logan*, para 1810.

1557 Local housing authority—welfare services—housing revenue accounts

The Housing (Welfare Services) (Wales) Order 1995, SI 1995/2720 (made on 9 October 1995), removes, in relation to local housing authorities in Wales and in relation to specified services, the discretion of local housing authorities in Wales to account for housing welfare services in their housing revenue accounts, as conferred by the Leasehold Reform, Housing and Urban Development Act 1993, s 127.

HUMAN RIGHTS

Halsbury's Laws of England (4th edn) Vol 18, paras 1625–1722

1558 Articles

Countering Disability Discrimination, Christine Clayson and Geoff Holgate: 139 SJ 442
A Day Out in Strasbourg, Fiona Ferguson (on the human rights of taxpayers): Tax Journal, Issue 297, p 12
Extradition and Human Rights, Susan Nash: 145 NLJ 429
Free Speech and the [European Court of Human Rights], Anthony Mosawi: 145 NLJ 227
Human Rights and the Journalist, Geoffrey Bindman: 145 NLJ 720
A Human Rights Bill, Lord Lester of Herne Hill: 145 NLJ 141
Poll Tax Committals and the European Court, Rona Epstein and Ian Wise (on *Benham v United Kingdom* (para 1588)): 139 SJ 588
Protecting Human Rights in the UK, John Wadham and Philip Leach: 145 NLJ 1135
Retrospective Crime, Ralph Beddard (on the right not to be tried for a crime created retrospectively): 145 NLJ 663
Transsexuals: The Goals in Sight, Terrence Walton: 145 NLJ 1828
Victory For Common Sense? Jonathan Cooper (on the recent decision of the ECHR that UK drug trafficking law is in breach of art 7(1)): LS Gaz, 15 February 1995, p 11

1559 Capital punishment—delay in execution—cruel and unusual punishment

See *Guerra v Baptiste*, para 462.

1560   Capital punishment—delay in execution—inhuman or degrading treatment or punishment

See *Bradshaw v A-G for Barbados; Roberts v A-G for Barbados*, para 454.

1561   Capital punishment—stay of execution—circumstances in which stay granted

See *Reckley v Minister of Public Safety and Immigration*, para 452.

1562   Data protection

See CONFIDENCE AND DATA PROTECTION.

1563   European Court of Human Rights—jurisdiction—delay in referring case to court

Proceedings for unfair dismissal by a former employee of the applicant security firm lasted for more than nine years. The applicant's complaint of a violation of its right to a fair hearing within a reasonable time, guaranteed by the European Convention on Human Rights, art 6(1), was declared admissible by the European Commission of Human Rights but was not referred to the European Court of Human Rights until one day after the three-month time limit for referral of cases. *Held*, by virtue of art 47, the court could only deal with a case within the period of three months prescribed by art 32. The operative date was that upon which the case was lodged with the court, not the date of the Commission's decision to refer the case. By the terms of the French text of art 47, the court might only 'être saisir d'une affaire' within the period of three months provided for in art 32. In order to seise a court, it was not sufficient to decide to seise it. The decision had to be implemented. The same principle applied to the word 'refer'. The commission having exceeded the time allowed, even though by only one day, the request bringing the case before the court was inadmissible. Accordingly, the court could not deal with the case.

Instituto di Vigilanza v Italy (Application 13567/88) (1993) 18 EHRR 367 (European Court of Human Rights).

1564   Freedom of association—membership of political party—civil servant

See *Vogt v Germany*, para 1568.

1565   Freedom of expression—dissemination of information—medicinal products—explanatory brochure

See *Ter Voort*, para 3122.

1566   Freedom of expression—distribution of military journal—interference by military authorities

A magazine containing material critical of military life was published by the first applicant and distributed to soldiers in the Austrian army by a soldier, the second applicant. The army sent out other military journals, along with its official publications, at its own expense but refused to authorise the distribution of the magazine and ordered the second applicant to stop distributing it. The applicants complained of a violation of their right to freedom of expression, guaranteed by the European Convention on Human Rights, art 10. *Held*, the military authorities had assumed responsibility at their own expense for the regular distribution of military journals which they sent out with their own official publications. This was bound to have an influence on the level of information imparted to members of the armed forces. The magazine published and distributed by the applicants was the only one denied distribution by the military authorities so it was reasonable for the first applicant to claim that the situation should be remedied; the refusal of the Minster of Defence to do so was an interference with the first applicant's right to impart information and ideas. Rules for military discipline had to be formulated broadly to cover diverse types of conduct but had also to afford protection against arbitrariness and make it possible for the consequences of their application to be foreseen. The rules were accessible to certain servicemen who would be aware that the minister might consider himself as bound to refer to the rules. The interference with the distribution of the magazine, for the purpose of preserving order in the armed forces, was prescribed by law. Freedom of expression applied to information or ideas that offended, shocked or disturbed the state or any section of the population. The proper functioning of the army was barely imaginable without legal rules designed to prevent the undermining of military discipline by servicemen. Exceptions to freedom of expression had to be interpreted narrowly. The applicants' magazine represented no threat to discipline; it did not recommend disobedience or violence and did not question the purpose of service in the armed forces. It could not be seen as a serious threat to military discipline. The refusal to distribute the magazine was disproportionate to the legitimate aim pursued. There had been a violation of art 10.

Vereinigung Demokratischer Soldaten Österreichs v Austria (Application 15153/89) (1994) 20 EHRR 56 (European Court of Human Rights).

1567 Freedom of expression—libel proceedings—award of damages

In an action for libel, damages of £1.5m were awarded, an amount which was three times the highest libel award previously made. The writer of the libellous material claimed that under the European Convention on Human Rights, art 6, there had been a violation of his right to access to court in that his appeal had been dismissed after the court decided he had little chance of success and after he had failed to furnish a substantial sum required as security for costs. He further contended that his right to freedom of expression under art 10 had been violated. *Held,* there had been no violation of art 6. The security for costs order had a legitimate aim, which was to protect the subject of the libel from the possibility of an irrecoverable bill for legal costs and, further, the making of such an order ensured the fair administration of justice. The sum required was reasonable and the court had made a full examination of all factors in setting it. However, there had been a violation of art 10, viewed in conjunction with the national law of the time, in that the award was so much larger than any other award previously made. In contrast, the granting of an injunction preventing the writer from releasing similar material was not in breach of art 10 in that there was nothing to suggest that its purpose went beyond that of preventing the writer from repeating his remarks.

Tolstoy Miloslavsky v United Kingdom (Application 18139/91) (1995) 20 EHRR 442 (European Court of Human Rights). *Rantzen v Mirror Group Newspapers (1986) Ltd* [1993] 4 All ER 975, CA (1993 Abr para 892), approved.

1568 Freedom of expression—membership of political party—civil servant

In 1979, the applicant, a teacher at a state secondary school, was appointed to a permanent teaching post as a civil servant with tenure for life. Disciplinary proceedings instituted against her in 1982, on the ground that she had failed to comply with her duty of political loyalty because of her involvement in various political activities, led to her dismissal in 1987 although she had been suspended from her duties and paid 60 per cent of her salary in 1986. Following the repeal of a law prohibiting the employment of extremists in the civil service, she was re-employed as a teacher in 1991. She complained that her dismissal because of her political activities constituted violations of her rights to freedom of expression, guaranteed by the European Convention on Human Rights, art 10, and to freedom of association, guaranteed by art 11. *Held,* although the right to recruitment for the civil service was deliberately omitted from the Convention, a person appointed as a civil servant might nevertheless complain of being dismissed from the service if the dismissal violated a right under the Convention, which required all rights and freedoms thereunder to be enjoyed by everyone within the jurisdiction of a contracting state without discrimination on any ground. As a general rule, guarantees in the Convention extended to civil servants so that the applicant, on her appointment, had not lost the protection of art 10. While a democratic state was entitled to require civil servants to be loyal towards the constitution and, in view of Germany's experience under the Weimar Republic, the duty of political loyalty had a special importance there, the dismissal of a teacher was a very severe sanction, affecting the reputation of the person concerned, causing the loss of livelihood and the virtual impossibility of finding an equivalent post. The adjective 'necessary' in art 10(2), which permitted states to impose restrictions 'necessary in a democratic society', implied the existence of a 'pressing social need'. The political party of which the applicant was a member was not banned in Germany. She had not taken advantage of her position to indoctrinate or exert improper influence on her pupils. As she had not been removed from her post until more than four years after the institution of the disciplinary proceedings, the authorities had shown that they did not consider it a pressing need to remove the pupils from her influence. There was no evidence that the applicant had made anti-constitutional statements even outside her work at school. As she had been dismissed because of her refusal to dissociate herself from a particular political party, there had been an interference with her right to freedom of association under art 11. There had been violations of arts 10 and 11.

Vogt v Germany (Application 17851/91) (1995) 21 EHRR 205 (European Court of Human Rights).

1569 Prohibition of discrimination—normal civic obligations—fire service

The applicant appealed unsuccessfully against a requirement that he pay a fire service levy under a law which made it compulsory for men, but not women, to serve in the fire brigade or pay a financial contribution in lieu of such service. He claimed to be the victim of discrimination on the ground of sex in breach of the European Convention on Human Rights, art 14 taken in conjunction with art 4(3)(d) which excluded any work or service which formed part of normal civic obligations from the prohibition of forced or compulsory labour under art 4(2). *Held*, compulsory fire service was one of the 'normal civic obligations' envisaged by art 4(3)(d). The financial contribution payable in lieu of service was considered to be a compensatory charge, and the obligation to pay also fell within art 4(3)(d). A difference in treatment was discriminatory for the purposes of art 14 if it had no objective and reasonable justification, or if there was no reasonable relationship of proportionality between the means employed and the aim sought to be realised. Although contracting states enjoyed a certain margin of appreciation in assessing what justified a difference in treatment, very weighty reasons had to be put forward before a difference of treatment based exclusively on the ground of sex could be regarded as compatible with the Convention. Regardless of whether there could now be any justification for treating men and women differently in respect of compulsory service in the fire brigade, the obligation to perform such service, which was exclusively one of law and theory, finally determined the matter. As there were a sufficient number of volunteers for the service, no male person was in practice obliged to serve in a fire brigade. The financial contribution had lost its compensatory character and had become the only effective duty. The imposition of such a financial burden on the ground of sex could hardly be justified. Accordingly, there had been a violation of art 14 taken in conjunction with art 4(3)(d).

Schmidt v Germany (Application 13580/88) (1994) 18 EHRR 513 (European Court of Human Rights).

1570 Prohibition of retrospective laws—criminal law—drug offences

The European Convention on Human Rights, art 7(1) provides that no one can be held guilty of any criminal offence on account of any act or omission which did not constitute a criminal offence under national or international law at the time when it was committed, nor can a heavier penalty be imposed than one that was applicable at the time that the criminal offence was committed.

The applicant was convicted of drug-related offences and sentenced to 22 years' imprisonment. In addition, a confiscation order was made against him under the Drug Trafficking Offences Act 1986, in default of payment of which he was liable to serve a consecutive two-year prison sentence. The Act was applied to the applicant even though it came into force after he had committed the offences. On his complaint that there had been a violation of the right guaranteed by art 7(1), a question arose as to whether a confiscation order was a 'penalty' within the meaning of art 7(1). *Held*, the wording of art 7(1) indicated that the starting point in assessing whether a measure was a penalty was whether the measure was imposed following a conviction for a criminal offence. Other relevant factors were the nature and purpose of the measure, its characterisation under national law, the procedures involved in making and implementing it, and its severity. In the instant case, a confiscation order under the 1986 Act could only be made following a conviction for a drug trafficking offence. The Act empowered the courts to confiscate proceeds which had been converted into other forms of assets, and was intended to prevent the use of such assets in future drug trafficking operations, and also to show that crime did not pay. However, the fact that the Act assumed that all property passing through an offender's hands over a six-year period was the fruits of drug trafficking unless he could prove otherwise, that a confiscation order was directed to all the proceeds of drug dealing and was not limited to actual enrichment or profit, that a trial judge had discretion to take account of the degree of culpability of the offender in fixing the amount of the order, and that an offender faced the possibility of imprisonment if he failed to pay the sum, gave a strong indication that the Act also had a punitive element. A confiscation order was therefore a penalty, and it was clear that the applicant had been subject to a more severe penalty as a result of the confiscation order than that to which he was liable at the time that he committed the offences. Accordingly, the application would be granted.

Welch v United Kingdom (Application 17440/90) (1995) 20 EHRR 247 (European Court of Human Rights).

1986 Act now Drug Trafficking Act 1994.

1571 Prohibition of retrospective laws—criminal law—removal of marital immunity from rape

The European Convention on Human Rights, art 7(1) provides that no one will be held guilty of any criminal offence on account of any act or omission which did not constitute a criminal offence under national or international law at the time when it was committed.

The two applicants were charged with the rape and attempted rape of their wives. In each case, the court found that the marital immunity from rape no longer existed and both applicants were convicted and sentenced to terms of imprisonment. The applicants claimed that their rights under art 7 had been violated because, at the time they had committed the offences, the general common law principle that a husband could not be found guilty of rape upon his wife was still effective. *Held*, art 7 could not be read as outlawing the gradual clarification of the rules of criminal liability through judicial interpretation from case to case, provided that the resultant development was consistent with the essence of the offence and could reasonably be foreseen. At the time the offences in the present case were committed there was significant doubt as to the validity of the alleged marital immunity for rape and there were strong indications that wider interpretation by the courts of the inroads on the immunity was probable. There was no doubt under the law as it stood at that time that a husband who forcibly had sexual intercourse with his wife could, in various circumstances, be found guilty of rape. Moreover, there was an evident evolution, which was consistent with the very essence of the offence, of the criminal law through judicial interpretation towards treating such conduct generally as within the scope of the offence of rape. That evolution had reached a stage where judicial recognition of the absence of immunity had become a reasonably foreseeable development of the law. Accordingly, the court found that there had been no violation of the applicants' rights under art 7.

SW v United Kingdom (Case No 47/1994/494/576); CR v United Kingdom (Case No 48/1994/495/577) [1996] 1 FLR 434 (European Court of Human Rights).

1572 Right to fair and public hearing—civil proceedings—appeal—failure of appeal court to deal with submissions made at first instance

The applicant successfully defended proceedings brought by his landlord to evict him. The landlord's appeal against the decision was allowed. The applicant complained of a violation of his right to a fair hearing, guaranteed by the European Convention on Human Rights, art 6(1), on the ground that the appeal court had failed to deal in its judgment with a submission, made by him at first instance, that the proceedings brought by the landlord were time-barred. *Held*, under Spanish law, the applicant, having been successful at first instance, had no standing to appeal. Although art 6(1) required a court to give reasons for its judgment, that did not require a detailed answer to every argument. The extent of that duty might vary according to the nature of the decision and the question whether a court had failed to fulfil that duty could only be determined in the light of the circumstances of the case. It was for the national courts, not the European Court of Human Rights, to examine whether the applicant's limitation plea was well-founded. However, that plea was relevant and would have been decisive so that the appeal court should have dealt with it in its judgment. As it had not done so, the European Court could not ascertain whether it merely neglected to deal with it or intended to dismiss it and, if so, its reasons for doing so. Accordingly, there had been a violation of art 6(1).

Ruiz Torija v Spain (Application 18390/91) (1994) 19 EHRR 553 (European Court of Human Rights).

The applicant alleged that, in proceedings brought by a Japanese company for the removal from the industrial property register of a trade mark owned by her, the Supreme Court, which quashed a judgment in her favour, failed to refer to one of the three submissions made by her at first instance although it rejected her other two submissions. She complained of a violation of her right to a fair hearing, guaranteed by the European Convention on Human Rights, art 6(1). *Held*, although art 6(1) required a court to give reasons for its judgment, that did not require a detailed answer to every argument. The extent of that duty might vary according to the nature of the decision and the question whether a court had failed to fulfil that duty could only be determined in the light of the circumstances of the case. It was for the national courts, not the European Court of Human Rights, to determine such questions as trade mark priority. The applicant's submission on this point was relevant and required an answer. As the Supreme Court had failed to answer it, the European Court could not ascertain whether it merely neglected to deal with that submission or intended to dismiss it and, if so, its reasons for doing so. It was immaterial that the Supreme Court had previously rejected the same submission in other proceedings between the same parties in an identical context. There had been a violation of art 6(1).

Hiro Balani v Spain (Application 18064/91) (1994) 19 EHRR 566 (European Court of Human Rights).

1573 Right to fair and public hearing—civil proceedings—impartial and independent tribunal—medical practitioners' disciplinary board

Following a hearing concerning complaints by patients that the applicant doctor charged excessive fees, a disciplinary board ordered that he be suspended from practising medicine for three months. He complained that members of the appeals board which heard his appeal against the decision were biased because they were, or had been, officials of medical unions who opposed the way in which he practised medicine and bore a grudge against him because of the views he expressed, and that his right to a fair hearing by an impartial and independent tribunal established by law, guaranteed by the European Convention on Human Rights, art 6(1), had been violated. *Held*, the manner of appointment of members of the appeals board provided no cause for treating them as biased. Although they were elected by provincial councils of their unions, they acted not as representatives of the unions but in their personal capacity. The fact that, if the board was challenged, there was no tribunal to which jurisdiction could be transferred, did not suffice to establish that it lacked impartiality or independence. The personal impartiality of each of the members of the board challenged had to be presumed until there was proof to the contrary. Problems might arise where judges participated in a decision relating to challenges against one of their colleagues if identical challenges were directed against them. The applicant had not referred to specific, material facts that could have revealed personal animosity or hostility towards him. The vague objections made by him were not well-founded. There had been no breach of art 6(1).

Debled v Belgium (Application 13839/88) (1994) 19 EHRR 506 (European Court of Human Rights).

1574 Right to fair and public hearing—civil proceedings—impartial and independent tribunal—patent appeal procedure

A company submitted two separate claims to the Dutch patent office for a patent for an invention relating to cigarettes. The patent office considered that the multiple application was inappropriate and therefore refused to grant the patent. On the company's appeal, the Appeal Division of the Patent Court ('the Appeal Division') quashed the earlier decision. However, it also decided that the invention lacked the required inventive step and therefore upheld the refusal to grant the patent. On the company's complaint that it had not had a fair hearing before an independent and impartial tribunal established by law, having regard to the European Convention on Human Rights, art 6(1), *held*, patents were so technical that there might be good reason for opting for a body other than the usual judicial courts to adjudicate on them. Even if proceedings before the Appeal Division did not comply with art 6(1), there was no violation of the article if it could be shown that there was a remedy by which the company's civil rights could be determined by an independent judicial body with sufficient jurisdiction and which provided the safeguards required by art 6(1). If the company had argued in civil proceedings in the Dutch courts that the Appeal Division was not a tribunal which satisfied the requirements of art 6(1), the civil courts would have been obliged to decide whether or not the company's argument was correct. If it was, the courts would then have had full jurisdiction to review the Appeal Division's decision. The company should have submitted a claim to the Dutch civil courts first of all, and as it had not done so, it was not for the European Court of Human Rights to find in the abstract that the remedies available under Dutch law for asserting the right to a patent did not meet the requirements of art 6(1). Accordingly, there had been no violation of art 6(1).

British-American Tobacco Co Ltd v Netherlands (Case No 46/1994/493/575) (1995) Times, 11 December (European Court of Human Rights).

1575 Right to fair and public hearing—civil proceedings—length of proceedings

The applicant obtained a law degree after retiring at the age of 50 from a career in the army. His application to the Bar Council for enrolment as a pupil advocate was rejected on the ground that he had already completed a full career and, further, had not taken the oath to become an advocate. His application to have the decision set aside was finally determined eight years later, judgment having been reserved for four years. He complained of a violation of his right to a fair and public hearing within a reasonable time, guaranteed by the European Convention on Human Rights, art 6(1). *Held*, as there were arguable grounds for the applicant being able to claim a civil right to enrolment on the list of pupil advocates, the Bar Council was required to determine a dispute concerning that right so that art 6(1) was applicable. The applicant could not be criticised for failing to file a fresh criminal complaint for denial of justice because that remedy was directed essentially at the same end as the remedies of which he had already availed himself and the government had failed to show that such a remedy would have been effective. The proceedings before the Bar Council were unfair; the reason for rejecting his application did not fall within the scope of the applicable legislation. Those proceedings were not required to be, and had not been, held in public but there was no justification for them to have been held in private. The proceedings had lasted from the time when the applicant sought to set aside the Bar Council's decision until the final decision eight years later. The applicant's conduct could not be criticised. Although the case was complex and sensitive, there was no explanation for the period of four years for which judgment had been reserved. There had been a violation of art 6(1).

De Moor v Belgium (Application 16997/90) (1994) 18 EHRR 372 (European Court of Human Rights).

The applicants were shareholders in a Moroccan company, which owned agricultural land in Morocco, and majority shareholders in a French company, which owned shares in the Moroccan company. When agricultural land in Morocco belonging to foreigners was nationalised, the applicants received compensation in respect of their shares in the Moroccan company, in accordance with a Franco-Moroccan Protocol providing for the financial consequences of the nationalisation of French citizens' assets. They were refused compensation in respect of their shares in the French company. Proceedings brought by them to recover such compensation lasted for eight years. They complained of a violation of their right to a fair hearing within a reasonable time, guaranteed by the European Convention on Human Rights, art 6(1). *Held*, although the dispute originated in an expropriation measure and related to the principle and/or the extent of reparation, it directly affected the applicants' property right, which was a civil right. The outcome of the dispute, which depended on the interpretation of the protocol, was directly decisive for a right of that nature. Accordingly, art 6(1) applied. The applicants prolonged the proceedings by nine months by bringing proceedings in the wrong court and by not filing their pleadings until four months after lodging their appeal. The wording of the protocol and the procedure followed to obtain an official interpretation of it made the case complicated. However, no explanation was forthcoming for the long periods during which the proceedings stagnated, the period of 20 months after the commencement of proceedings before the appropriate government department filed pleadings, or for the five years which the court took to hold its first hearing. A lapse of time of more than eight years was not reasonable and, accordingly, there had been a violation of art 6(1).

Beaumartin v France (Application 15287/89) (1994) 19 EHRR 485 (European Court of Human Rights).

1576 Right to fair and public hearing—civil proceedings—planning enforcement notice—appeal against notice

A planning enforcement notice served on the applicant required him to demolish two buildings on his property on the ground that they had been erected without planning permission. He appealed against the notice, first, unsuccessfully, to the Secretary of State and then, also unsuccessfully, to the High Court. He contended that the proceedings did not conform with the European Convention on Human Rights, art 6(1), which required that he receive a fair hearing by an independent and impartial tribunal. *Held*, the inspector responsible for determining the applicant's planning appeal had to make his decision in a quasi-judicial, independent and impartial, and also fair, manner. However, the Secretary of State's power to issue a direction, even while proceedings were in progress, revoking an inspector's power to decide an appeal, deprived the inspector of the requisite appearance of independence, even though the Secretary of State rarely exercised such power. The review by the inspector, therefore, did not conform with art 6(1). As the applicant's appeal to the High Court was on points of law it could not cover all aspects of the inspector's decision as to the enforcement notice. The court's jurisdiction over the facts was limited and it could not substitute its own decision. Nevertheless, the inspector's decision could have been quashed by the High Court if it had been made by reference to irrelevant factors or without regard to relevant factors, or if the inspector had relied on evidence incapable of supporting a finding of fact, or based his decision on an inference from facts which was perverse or irrational. Any alleged shortcomings in the procedure before the inspector could have been subject to review by the High Court. The applicant had not challenged the inspector's findings of fact and each of his submissions before the High Court had been adequately dealt with. The scope of the review by the High Court was sufficient to comply with art 6(1). As the remedies available to the applicant satisfied the requirements of art 6(1), there had been no violation of that provision.

Bryan v United Kingdom (Case No 44/1994/491/573) (1995) Times, 8 December (European Court of Human Rights).

1577 Right to fair and public hearing—civil proceedings—proceedings relating to child—access to confidential documents

A care order was granted to a local authority in respect of a child whose unmarried mother was suffering from mental illness. The child was placed with foster parents and the mother and father were denied access to him. In further proceedings relating to the child, certain documents, including social workers' reports, were not disclosed to the mother. The mother and father subsequently married, but in making an order to free the child for adoption, the court dispensed with their consent on the basis that it had been unreasonably withheld. Following the child's adoption by his foster parents, the mother and father complained that there had been violations of their rights to respect for family life and to a fair trial, and the father claimed that he had been discriminated against at the time that he had been an unmarried father. *Held*, the right to a fair trial meant that a person had to be given the opportunity to know and make comments on the evidence against him. The mother had been deprived of such information, in particular vital social workers' reports, and that had affected her ability to present her case and to assess the prospects of a successful appeal. The failure to disclose the social workers' reports to her had therefore been a breach of her right to a fair trial. Although the decision-making process leading up to measures in respect of care, custody and access had to be fair, the fact that there had been a violation of the right to a fair trial did not necessarily mean that there had also been a violation of the right to family life, as the nature of the interests protected by each of those rights was different. On the facts of the case, there had been no violation of the right to family life. Different treatment was discriminatory if it did not pursue a legitimate aim or if it was not proportionate to the aim pursued. The father could not claim that he had been discriminated against when he was an unmarried father, as he had a legal right to apply for parental rights, but had chosen not to do so.

McMichael v United Kingdom (Application 16424/90) (1995) 20 EHRR 205 (European Court of Human Rights).

1578 Right to fair and public hearing—civil proceedings—public law—infringement of private pecuniary rights

A local authority adopted a plan to use certain land adjoining the applicant's land as building land. The applicant's appeal against the issuing of building permits to the owners of the land and her complaints that the plan was unlawful and that she would suffer substantial nuisance because of the proposed buildings were dismissed. She complained of a violation of her right to a fair hearing before a court or tribunal, guaranteed by the European Convention on Human Rights, art 6(1), on the ground that neither the administrative court nor the constitutional court which had heard her complaints could be regarded as tribunals within the meaning of art 6(1). *Held*, although the applicant had alleged that certain provisions of building legislation had not been complied with, she nevertheless sought to avoid the infringement of her pecuniary rights on the ground that the building works on the land adjoining her property would jeopardise her enjoyment of her property and would reduce its market value. She was seeking to protect a civil right within art 6(1). As the constitutional court, which could only review the lawfulness of the use of the land and the plans for its development, could not consider all the facts of the case, it did not have the competence required by art 6(1). The administrative court, however, which examined all the applicant's complaints, was a tribunal for the purposes of art 6(1).

Ortenberg v Austria (Application 18064/91) (1994) 19 EHRR 524 (European Court of Human Rights).

1579 Right to fair and public hearing—civil proceedings—trial court's failure to give reasons for decision

The Revenue exercised its right of pre-emption over land recently purchased by the applicant on the ground that the purchase price was too low. She challenged the pre-emption unsuccessfully and complained of a violation of her right to a fair hearing, guaranteed by the European Convention on Human Rights, art 6(1), that she had not been allowed to adduce evidence that the price paid was a fair one and that she had acted in good faith, so that her right to be presumed innocent, guaranteed by art 6(2) had also been violated. She complained also of a violation of her right to the peaceful enjoyment of her possessions, guaranteed by Protocol 1, art 1. *Held*, states were entitled to arrange their fiscal policies to ensure that taxes were paid; the prevention of tax evasion was a legitimate objective which was in the public interest. The pre-emption operated arbitrarily and selectively against the applicant and was scarcely foreseeable. It was unaccompanied by basic procedural safeguards: there were no adversarial proceedings complying with the principle of equality of arms, enabling submissions on the question of the underestimation of the price of the land and, therefore, on the Revenue's position. Both the trial court and the appeal court had interpreted the domestic law as allowing the state to avail itself of its right to pre-emption without having to indicate reasons of fact and law for its decision. The state could discourage tax evasion in other ways: legal proceedings to recover unpaid tax, the imposition of tax fines, where necessary, and the threat of criminal proceedings would all, if used systematically, provide an adequate weapon. It was not sufficient compensation to reimburse the price paid, increased by 10 per cent, to a purchaser for the loss of his property, and the costs and fair expenses of the contract, where the property had been acquired with no fraudulent intent. The applicant had borne an individual and excessive burden which could have been made legitimate only if she had been able to challenge effectively the measure taken against her. The balance between the protection of the right of property and the requirements of the general interest had been upset. Nevertheless, the implementation of the pre-emption measure was not tantamount to a declaration of guilt. There had been a violation of art 6(1) and Protocol 1, art 1.

Hentrich v France (Application 13616/88) (1994) 18 EHRR 440 (European Court of Human Rights).

1580   Right to fair and public hearing—criminal proceedings—length of proceedings

The first applicants were officials of opposition political parties in Turkey. On returning to that country after a long absence, they were arrested and kept in detention pending trial for two and a half years. When they were brought to trial, they were acquitted. The second applicant was extradited to Turkey on a charge of exporting drugs and spent seven years in detention pending trial before being found guilty. The applicants, relying on the European Convention on Human Rights, arts 5(3) and 6(1), complained of the length of their detention pending trial and of the criminal proceedings against them. *Held*, having regard to the wording of the declaration made under art 46 of the Convention whereby Turkey recognised the court's compulsory jurisdiction, the court could not entertain complaints about events which had occurred before the date when the declaration was deposited ('the declaration date'). However, when examining the complaints, it would take account of the state of the proceedings at the declaration date. With regard to art 5(3), the court could only consider the period which had elapsed between the declaration date and, in the first case, the date of release or, in the second case, the date of conviction. However, when determining whether the applicants' continued detention after the declaration date had been justified, the court had to take into account the period for which the applicants had already been in custody. The danger of an accused's absconding could not be gauged solely on the basis of the severity of the sentence risked. It had to be assessed with reference to a number of other factors. The expression 'state of the evidence' used by the Turkish court to confirm the applicants' detention meant the existence and persistence of serious indications of guilt. In general these might be relevant factors, but in the present cases they could not on their own justify the continuation of the detention. There had therefore been a contravention of art 5(3). With regard to art 6(1), the court could only consider the period between the declaration date and the date of, in the first case, the date of acquittal or, in the second case, the date of the upholding of the conviction, but it had to take into account the fact that, at the declaration date, the proceedings had already lasted more than two and seven years respectively. The reasonableness of the length of the proceedings was to be assessed in the light of the particular circumstances, regard being had to the criteria laid down in the court's case law, in particular the complexity of the case, the applicants' conduct and that of the competent authorities. In the present cases, the length of the criminal proceedings in issue contravened art 6(1).

Yagci v Turkey (Applications 16419/90 and 16426/90); Mansur v Turkey (Application 16026/90) (1995) 20 EHRR 505, 535 (European Court of Human Rights).

1581   Right to fair and public hearing—criminal proceedings—nature of criminal charge—information as to charge

The applicant had been convicted of obtaining property by deception. He complained that his right to be informed of the nature of the criminal charge against him, guaranteed by the

European Convention on Human Rights, art 6(3)(a), had been violated because the prosecution had failed to refer to the statutory provision under which he had been convicted. *Held*, the applicant had been fully aware of all the components of the charge against him, in particular because the facts cited by the prosecution were identical to those established in the committal proceedings. The discrepancy complained of was clearly the result of a mere clerical error, committed when the prosecution submissions were typed and subsequently reproduced on various occasions. Accordingly, there had been no violation of art 6(3)(a).

Gea Catalán v Spain (Application 19160/91) (1995) 20 EHRR 266 (European Court of Human Rights).

1582 Right to family and private life—adoption proceedings—rights of natural father

Although the applicant and his girl friend had intended to marry, their relationship broke down and their daughter, born soon after they had ceased to cohabit, was placed for adoption without the applicant's knowledge or consent. This was in accordance with Irish law, under which the natural father of a child born outside marriage had no constitutional right to take part in the adoption process. The applicant successfully applied to be the child's guardian and was awarded custody of the child. The Supreme Court subsequently decided that, if the prospective adopters could achieve a quality of welfare significantly better than that which the natural father could offer, then his wishes should be disregarded. On the rehearing of the case before the High Court, a consultant psychiatrist stated that if the placement of the child with her prospective adopters was disturbed after a period of more than a year, she would be likely to suffer trauma and to have difficulty in forming relationships of trust. The court declined to appoint the applicant as guardian and an adoption order was made. The applicant complained of a violation of his right to respect for his family life, guaranteed by the European Convention on Human Rights, art 8. *Held*, 'family' in art 8 was not confined solely to marriage-based relationships and might encompass other de facto 'family' ties where the parties lived together outside marriage. A child born as a consequence of such a relationship was ipso jure part of that family unit from the moment, and by the very fact, of his birth. A bond amounting to family life existed between the child and the parents even though the latter were no longer cohabiting by the time the child was born or their relationship had ended. Although the secret placement of the child for adoption without the applicant's knowledge was in accordance with Irish law, and had led to the bonding of the child with the proposed adopters and to the making of the adoption order, the applicant's ties with the child had been irreversibly damaged and placed him at a disadvantage in seeking custody of the child. There were no reasons relevant to the child's welfare to justify this; such interference with the applicant's rights was not necessary in a democratic society. The applicant had no right under Irish law to take part in the adoption proceedings; his only recourse to impede the adoption was to bring guardianship and custody proceedings but, by the time those proceedings had concluded, the scales concerning the child's welfare had been tilted inevitably in favour of the prospective adopters. There had been a violation of art 8 and the applicant's right to a fair hearing, guaranteed by art 6(1), had also been violated.

Keegan v Ireland (Application 16969/90) (1994) 18 EHRR 342 (European Court of Human Rights).

1583 Right to family and private life—gipsies—caravans on land in contravention of planning controls

The applicant, a gipsy, and her children lived in caravans on her land. She unsuccessfully applied for planning permission and lived there in contravention of planning controls for three years. She was subject to enforcement measures and was prosecuted in respect of her failure to cease occupation. The applicant complained that she was prevented from living with her family on her land and from following the traditional gipsy lifestyle, which violated her right to respect for her private and family life, guaranteed by the European Convention on Human Rights, art 8. *Held*, living in a caravan was an integral part of the applicant's lifestyle and case law indicated that the traditional lifestyle of a minority could attract the guarantees of art 8. The enforcement measures and prosecution to which the applicant was subject constituted an interference. That interference was in accordance with the law and the legitimate aims of the economic well-being of the country. However, the notion of 'necessity' implied that the interference corresponded to a pressing social need and that it was proportionate to the aim pursued. Therefore, the community's interests in effective planning controls had to be weighed against the applicant's rights, with regard to whether an excessive burden was placed on her. It was apparent that there was insufficient room on the official site for the number of gipsies and records indicated a not insignificant level of disorder, crime and violence connected with the site. It was unreasonable to expect the applicant to apply for a place on a site which offered distinct disadvantages compared to her present location and the possibility of moving to a private site was not reasonably open to her. Further, it would be a criminal offence for her to station a caravan on waste ground or at the side of a road. In the circumstances, the burden placed upon the applicant was excessive and disproportionate, and the interference could not be regarded as necessary. Accordingly, there had been a violation of art 8.

Buckley v United Kingdom (Application 20348/92) [1995] JPL 633 (European Commission of Human Rights).

1584   Right to family and private life—members of armed forces—discharge for homosexuality

See *R v Secretary of State for Defence, ex p Smith*, para 2551.

1585   Right to family and private life—nuisance—failure of local authority to take action against nuisance

A waste-treatment plant sited near the applicant's home had begun operating without the requisite licence from the municipal authorities and had immediately caused health problems and nuisance to many residents of the town. The applicant complained that her right not to be subjected to degrading treatment, guaranteed by the European Convention on Human Rights, art 3, and her right to respect for her family life and home, guaranteed by art 8, had been violated because of the smells, noise and polluting fumes from the plant. *Held*, while the conditions in which the applicant and her family lived for some years had been difficult, they did not constitute degrading treatment within art 3. Severe environmental pollution might affect an individual's well-being and prevent him from enjoying his home in such a way as to affect adversely his private and family life without seriously endangering his health. A fair balance had to be struck between the competing interests of the individual and the community as a whole. In that context, the state enjoyed a certain margin of appreciation. In spite of that, the state had not struck a fair balance between the economic well-being of the town of the applicant's residence and her effective enjoyment of her home and her private and family life. Accordingly, there had been a violation of art 8.

Lopez Ostra v Spain (Application 16798/90) (1994) 20 EHRR 277 (European Court of Human Rights).

1586   Right to family and private life—paternity of child—recognition of child's natural father

The applicant, a Dutch national, was married to a Moroccan national from whom she had separated about seven years before the birth of her son. The child was registered as the son of the applicant and M, another Moroccan national with whom the applicant lived. The applicant instituted divorce proceedings one month after the child's birth. The Dutch courts refused to recognise M as the child's father on the ground that, as the applicant was still married to her husband at the time of the child's birth, the child was the legitimate child of the applicant and her husband unless the latter, with whom the applicant had lost contact at the time of their separation and who had left the Netherlands almost two years before the child's birth, brought proceedings to deny paternity. The applicant complained that her right to respect for her family life, guaranteed by the European Convention on Human Rights, art 8, had been violated. *Held*, the notion of family life was not confined solely to marriage-based relationships and might encompass other de facto 'family ties' where parties were living together outside marriage. Although living together might be a requirement for such a relationship, other factors might also serve to demonstrate that a relationship had sufficient constancy to create de facto 'family ties'. Such was the present case, three more children having been born to the parties. A child born of such a relationship was ipso jure part of that 'family unit' from the moment of his birth and by the very fact of it. Accordingly, there existed between the child in question and M a bond amounting to family life, whatever the contribution of the latter to his son's care and upbringing. The competent authorities had a duty to allow complete family ties to be formed between M and the child as expeditiously as possible. Step-parent adoption and joint custody were incompatible with the notion of respect for family life which required that the biological and social reality be permitted to prevail over a legal presumption which flew in the face of both established fact and the wishes of those concerned without actually benefiting anyone. There had been a violation of art 8.

Kroon v Netherlands (Application 18535/91) (1994) 19 EHR 263 (European Court of Human Rights).

1587   Right to liberty—detention pending criminal proceedings—length of detention

See *Yagci v Turkey; Mansur v Turkey*, para 1580.

1588   Right to liberty—lawfulness of detention—enforcement of community charge—community charge proceedings as criminal proceedings

A liability order was made against the applicant in respect of his unpaid community charge, and he was subsequently summoned to court for his continued failure to pay the charge. At the hearing, at which the applicant was unrepresented, the justices decided that his failure to pay the charge was due to his culpable neglect, even though he was unemployed, was not entitled to claim income support, and had no personal assets or income. He was committed to prison for 30 days, but was released following a successful application for judicial review of the justices' decision. On his complaint of violations of the right to liberty and the right to a fair trial as guaranteed by the European Convention on Human Rights, arts 5, 6, *held*, the justices had failed to conduct an adequate inquiry into whether the applicant's failure to pay the charge was due to his culpable neglect, and his detention under a committal order had therefore been unlawful and in breach of his right to liberty under art 5(1). Since there was no domestic law under which he could make a claim for compensation for his unlawful detention, there had also been a violation of his right to compensation under art 5(5). In relation to the right to a fair trial, 'criminal offence' for the purposes of art 6(3) did not refer exclusively to criminal law offences but could include tax enforcement proceedings which had a punitive element. As legal aid for representation at the committal hearing had not been available to the applicant even though he had faced the possibility of immediate deprivation of his liberty, there had been a violation of his right under art 6(3)(c) to defend himself by means of free legal assistance. Accordingly, the applications would succeed.

Benham v United Kingdom (1995) Independent, 8 February (European Commission of Human Rights).

1589   Right to life—deprivation of life—defence from unlawful violence—use of unnecessary force

The European Convention on Human Rights, art 2(1) provides that everyone's right to life is protected by law. However, deprivation of life is not regarded as inflicted in contravention of this requirement when it results from the use of force which is no more than absolutely necessary in defence of any person from unlawful violence: art 2(2).

The United Kingdom authorities obtained information that a terrorist organisation was planning a car bomb attack on Gibraltar, the bomb probably being detonated by remote control. The terrorist suspects involved were considered likely, if confronted by security forces, to use weapons or detonate the bomb. It was decided that soldiers would arrest them. The soldiers shouted a command to stop. The suspects made movements and the soldiers, fearing that remote control devices were being set off, fired several shots at close range, killing them. No weapons or detonators were found on their bodies and the car they were travelling in did not contain an explosive device, although another car hired by them did contain such a device. The parents of the suspects complained that the killings constituted a violation of art 2. *Held*, there had been no execution plot at the highest level of command and the soldiers had neither been instructed nor decided on their own initiative to kill the suspects irrespective of any justification for the use of lethal force. The authorities were presented with a dilemma, on the one hand being required to protect the lives of the people of Gibraltar and on the other to have minimum resort to the use of lethal force. However, the court questioned why the suspects were not arrested immediately on their arrival in Gibraltar. Further, a number of the authorities' key assessments turned out to be erroneous and insufficient allowances were made for other assumptions. In the light of these matters and of the automatic recourse to lethal force when the soldiers opened fire, the court was not persuaded that the killings constituted a use of force which was no more than absolutely necessary in defence of persons from unlawful violence within art 2(2). Accordingly, there had been a violation of art 2.

McCann v United Kingdom (Application 18984/91) (1995) 21 EHRR 97 (European Court of Human Rights).

1590   Right to peaceful enjoyment of possessions—appropriation of property by state

See *Hentrich v France*, para 1579.

1591 Right to peaceful enjoyment of possessions—transfer of land to state

The rules of administration of the patrimony of the applicants, eight monasteries in Greece, were modified by statute and most of the monastic estate was transferred to the Greek state. Three of the monasteries were parties to an agreement under which their agricultural and forest property was transferred to the state. The applicants complained that they had been arbitrarily deprived of their property, contrary to the European Convention on Human Rights, Protocol 1, art 1, and of a violation of their rights to freedom of religion under art 9, and to freedom of association under art 11. *Held,* Protocol 1, art 1 guaranteed the right of property. The law under which the applicants had been deprived of their property created a presumption of state ownership. They could assert their ownership of the land only if it derived from a duly registered title deed, from statute or from the decision of a final court against the state. The applicants were primordial constituent parts of the Greek Church, established long before the Greek state, and had accumulated substantial immovable property over the centuries. Title deeds acquired long ago would have been lost or destroyed and any adverse possession to be relied on as against the state and third parties would have been completed before the legislation in question came into effect. An interference with peaceful enjoyment of possessions had to strike a fair balance between the demands of the general interests of the community and the requirements of the protection of an individual's fundamental rights. There had been a breach of Protocol 1, art 1 in respect of the five monasteries which were not party to the transfer agreement. The Greek law had been enacted to end illegal sales of certain land, encroachments on it and its uncontrolled development. The taking of property with no provision for compensation imposed a considerable burden on the five applicant monasteries which had not signed the agreement. There was no breach of Protocol 1, art 1 in respect of the other three monasteries, in respect of which there was no evidence that they had acted under duress. The legislation in question did not concern objects intended for the celebration of divine worship and, therefore, did not interfere with the right to freedom of religion under art 9. A complaint that an increase in the number of monks would be prevented and that the faithful would be deterred from making gifts to the applicants were hypothetical and did not constitute a violation of their right to freedom of association under art 11.

Holy Monasteries v Greece (Applications 13092/87, 13984/88) (1994) 20 EHRR 1 (European Court of Human Rights).

HUSBAND AND WIFE

Halsbury's Laws of England (4th edn) Vol 22, paras 901–1178

1592 Articles

Alcohol and the Family, Jonathan Goodliffe: 145 NLJ 755, 825
Alcohol Experts in Family Cases, Jonathan Goodliffe: 145 NLJ 633
A Counsel of Perfection, Eric Dumbill and John Snape (on the debt enforcement issues when a wife stands as surety for a husband's loan): LS Gaz, 15 March 1995, p 20
Domestic Violence Applications: An Empirical Study of One Court, Geoffrey Jones, Deborah Lockton, Richard Ward, Elham Kashefi: (1995) 1 JSWFL 67
Effects of Inheritance on Financial Provision, David Burrows: 139 SJ 954
Independent Advice After *O'Brien,* H W Wilkinson (on *Barclays Bank plc v O'Brien* [1993] 4 All ER 417, HL (1993 Abr para 1826)): 145 NLJ 792
Injunctions v Bail Conditions, Margaret Crissel (on the comparison between injunctions and conditional bail in domestic violence cases): [1995] Fam Law 85
Joint Property, David Burrows (on the law of co-ownership as it affects the family home): 139 SJ 1176
Keeping Alive the Tenancy in the Matrimonial Home, David Mendes da Costa: [1995] Fam Law 622
Prenuptial Contracts, Helen Conway: 145 NLJ 1290
Production Appointments and Khanna Hearings, David Burrows: [1995] Fam Law 199
Time for Lesbian and Gay Marriages? Craig Lind: 145 NLJ 1553

1593 Divorce

See DIVORCE.

1594   Marriage—place of marriage—approved premises

The Marriages (Approved Premises) Regulations 1995, SI 1995/510 (in force on 1 April 1995), relate to the approval by local authorities of premises for the purpose of conducting civil marriages. The regulations set out the application procedure and the criteria on which approval will be granted or refused. Where approval is granted, it is valid for three years. A local authority must attach standard conditions to it and may also attach additional conditions. A local authority is also obliged to keep a register of approved premises. The regulations provide for the renewal of approvals after the expiry of the three-year period, and set out the grounds on which approval may be revoked. An aggrieved applicant may seek a review of a local authority's decision to refuse an approval or to attach additional conditions to it. A local authority may charge a fee for (1) the approval of premises, (2) the renewal of approvals, and (3) the solemnisation of a marriage before a superintendent registrar in approved premises.

1595   Marriage Act 1994—commencement

The Marriage Act 1994 (Commencement No 2) Order 1995, SI 1995/424, brings into force (1) on 24 February 1995, s 1(2), (3), and the Schedule, para 5, in so far as they insert the Marriage Act 1949, ss 46A, 46B(2), 51(1A), thereby enabling the Secretary of State to make regulations relating to the approval of premises by local authorities for use as a venue for civil marriages; and (2) on 1 April 1995, s 1(1), Schedule, paras 1–4, 6–9, and ss 1(2), (3), 2(1) (so far as not already in force), which allow civil marriages to take place on approved premises, impose certain requirements in respect of such marriages and make consequential amendments. For a summary of the Act, see 1994 Abr para 1572. For details of commencement, see the commencement table in the title STATUTES.

1596   Matrimonial home—beneficial interest—inference of beneficial interest

A husband and wife purchased the matrimonial home by way of mortgage, with the balance of the purchase price coming out of the husband's savings and a gift from his parents. Both parties worked and although the wife did not make any direct payments of the mortgage, she discharged other household outgoings. The original mortgage was replaced by one in favour of the plaintiff bank granted to the husband in his sole name and charging the property to the bank to secure repayment of the business overdraft of the husband's company. A second charge was subsequently executed on the property to secure the parties' liability under a joint guarantee as security for a business loan, and the property was transferred into the parties' joint names. The bank brought proceedings claiming payment of sums due under the mortgage and possession in default. The wife argued that she was entitled to a one half interest in the property overriding any interests of the bank. The judge found that she was only entitled to a beneficial interest of 6.5 per cent, being the proportion borne by her half of the gift from the husband's parents. On the wife's appeal, *held*, absence of express agreement as to the proportion of the beneficial interest did not in every case preclude inference of presumed agreement. Positive evidence, as in the present case, that the parties neither discussed nor intended any agreement as to the proportions of their beneficial interest did not preclude the court from inferring one on general equitable principles. On the facts, there was a clear agreement that the parties share everything equally. Accordingly, their presumed intention was to share the beneficial interest in the home in equal shares, and the appeal would be allowed.

Midland Bank v Cooke [1995] 4 All ER 562 (Court of Appeal: Stuart-Smith, Waite and Schiemann LJJ).

See also *Halifax Building Society v Brown*, para 2111.

1597   Matrimonial home—beneficial interest—title registered in name of one spouse only—constructive trust

See *Drake v Whipp*, para 2983.

1598   Matrimonial home—joint tenancy—severance of tenancy—agreement to sever

See *Hunter v Babbage*, para 2472.

1599   Matrimonial home—joint tenancy—trustees for sale—breach of trust

See *Crawley Borough Council v Ure*, para 2990.

1600 Matrimonial home—legal charge—charge signed by wife—husband obtaining loan by deceit on same security—extent of wife's liability

See *Castle Phillips Finance v Piddington*, para 2108.

1601 Matrimonial home—legal charge—husband's intention to defeat wife's ancillary relief claim—lender's notice of intention

See *B v B (P intervening) (Reviewable Disposition) (No 2)*, para 2109.

1602 Matrimonial home—local authority housing—injunction against wife—wife's notice to quit—possession proceedings amounting to contempt

See *Harrow London Borough Council v Johnstone*, para 1829.

1603 Matrimonial home—order for possession obtained by chargee—priority given to chargee—lack of exceptional circumstances

See *Barclays Bank v Hendricks*, para 1105.

1604 Matrimonial injunction—contempt—sentence of imprisonment

See *Hudson v Hudson*, para 632.

1605 Matrimonial injunction—domestic violence—power of arrest

The parties lived together as husband and wife. The respondent was found to have caused the applicant actual bodily harm while they were still living together, and the applicant was granted a non-molestation injunction with a power of arrest attached. The respondent received suspended sentences totalling three months imprisonment for breach of the injunction and the applicant was granted a fresh injunction to which a power of arrest was again attached. On the respondent's appeal, *held*, (1) the judge had taken account of all the relevant factors and was entitled to have regard to the deterrent element in any sentence passed. The total sentence was not excessive or out of line with the authorities. (2) Cohabitation at the time an injunction was applied for was not a necessary precondition of the court's jurisdiction to order a power of arrest. However, in the case of people living together, the acts of violence complained of must have occurred before the cohabitation had ceased. In the present case, there was no allegation of injury having occurred since before the hearing at which the original injunction was granted. The original power of arrest had expired, and the judge was entitled to order a fresh power of arrest by reference to the injury that had occurred if he was satisfied, in accordance with the Domestic Violence and Matrimonial Proceedings Act 1976, s 2, that the respondent had caused actual bodily harm to the applicant and considered that he was likely to do so again. It was not necessary that the previous occasion of injury had occurred at any particular time as the 1976 Act was concerned with the prevention of injury in the future. Accordingly, the appeal would be dismissed.

McCann v Wright [1996] 1 All ER 204 (Court of Appeal: Nourse, Beldam and Evans LJJ).

IMMIGRATION

See BRITISH NATIONALITY, IMMIGRATION AND RACE RELATIONS.

INCOME TAXATION

Halsbury's Laws of England (4th edn) Vol 23 (reissue), paras 1–1747

1606 Articles

The Agent of a Non-Resident, David Wainman: Tax Journal, Issue 305, p 8

All Change for Gilts and Bonds, David Marks (on the proposals for reforming the taxation of gilts and bonds): Tax Journal, Issue 311, p 5

Appealing Dilemmas, Francis Fitzpatrick (on judicial review of tax cases): Tax Journal, Issue 323, p 12

Branches, Local Currency and Matching Elections, Roger Muray and David Small (on the new foreign exchange rules): Tax Journal, Issue 312, p 7, Issue 313, p 16

The Canadian General Anti-Avoidance Rule, Brian J Arnold: [1995] BTR 541

Capital Allowances and Contracts of Sale, Paul Blakeley (on capital allowances for plant and machinery included in property sales): Estates Gazette, 18 November 1995, p 182

Clang of the Prison Gates—The Sentencing of Income Tax Offenders, W Azlan Ahmad and M Hingun: [1995] BTR 581

Commencement of Trading, David Martin (on the rules governing commencement of a trade): Tax Journal, Issue 303, p 4

A Conceptual Approach to Below Market or Beneficial Corporate Loans, Professor Yitzhak Hadari: [1995] BTR 557

Current Year Basis of Assessment—Drafting Difficulties, John C Labrum: [1995] BTR 263

A Day Out in Strasbourg, Fiona Ferguson (on the human rights of taxpayers): Tax Journal, Issue 297, p 12

Development of the *Ramsay* Principle, Sarah Falk: Tax Journal, Issue 323, p 4

Employee Relocation Expenses, Michael Kaltz: Tax Journal, Issue 291, p 18

The Employer Becomes a Tax Expert, David Maclean (on self-assessment for tax): Tax Journal, Issue 310, p 8

The End of the Road, Daron Gunson (on tax planning on the cessation of a corporate business): Tax Journal, Issue 321, p 13

Equipment Leasing, James Savory (on the deductibility of payments under finance leases): Tax Journal, Issue 299, p 12

An Equitable Approach to Quasi-Equity, Sue Porter (on taxation of convertible bonds): Tax Journal, Issue 314, p 7

The Finality of General Commissioners' Determinations, Chantal Stebbings: [1995] BTR 397

Financial Assistance, Philip Moss (on whether a private company can give assistance for the purchase of its own shares): Tax Journal, Issue 295, p 8

How They Got it All Wrong in *Pepper v Hart*, Francis Bennion: [1995] BTR 325

The Implications of Illegal Trading, Mary Mullholland and Roger Cockfield: [1995] BTR 572

Income From Property, David Williams (on Schedule A rules): Tax Journal, Issue 313, p 12, Issue 314, p 25, Issue 315, p 10

Investment Management, James Benger (on the Finance Bill 1995): Tax Journal, Issue 295, p16

Investment Managers Revisited, James Benger (on amendments to the Finance Bill 1995): Tax Journal, Issue 300, p 10

The Law of Tips and Service Charges, Roger Peters: 139 SJ 847

Leaping Through the Window, Roger Muray and David Small (on the transitional provisions of the forex regime): Tax Journal, Issue 299, p 16

Matching and Mixing, Roger Muray and David Small (on the new foreign exchange rules): Tax Journal, Issue 305, p 16

A More Flexible Approach ? Ian Saunders (on the judicial approach to tax avoidance): 139 SJ 742

National Insurance Concessions, David Harris (on concessionary relief from National Insurance contributions): Tax Journal, Issue 306, p 16

Neither a Borrower Nor a Lender Be, Gary Morris and David Williams (on the tax dangers of making loans to directors, employees and participators): Tax Journal, Issue 316, p 11

New Relationships, Richard Ballard and Ben Staveley (on taxation of corporate debt): Tax Journal, Issue 335, p 4

Offshore Funds Demystified, Robert Gaut: Tax Journal, Issue 305, p 12

The Pros and Cons of Incorporation, Hywel Williams (on the taxation implications of incorporation): Tax Journal, Issue 325, p 18

Retirement Annuity Contracts, John Hayward: Tax Journal, Issue 306, p 7, Issue 310, p 10

Share Options: What Should Happen on a Take Over? David Wainman: Tax Journal, Issue 292, p 12

Sidewind of Simplification, Kevin Prosser (on changes effected by the simplification of income tax settlement provisions): Tax Journal, Issue 301, p 8

Small Self-Administered Schemes, John Hayward (on the tax-related and practical advantages of such schemes): Tax Journal, Issue 302, p 21

Something for Nothing? Daron Gunson (on expenditure that does not attract tax relief): Tax Journal, Issue 312, p 14

The Spanish Net, George Horsman (on general anti-avoidance provisions): Tax Journal, Issue 310, p 14, Issue 312, p 10

The Spring Bank Holiday Hand Grenade, Stephen Edge (on the proposals regarding the treatment of returns on debt securities): Tax Journal, Issue 311, p 8

Tax Alchemy and Deep Discount Securities, Adrian Brettell: Tax Journal, Issue 290, p 9

Tax Pitfalls on Business Start-Ups, Daron Gunson: Tax Journal, Issue 316, p 16

Taxation of P I Annuities, Gordon Pickering (on tax law changes to enable personal injury victims to receive periodic payments under a structured settlement free of tax and direct from a life office): 139 SJ 590

Taxing Commissions, J C Gordon Pickering (on taxation of insurance and pension commissions): 139 SJ 482

Taxing Family Relationships, Jonathan Peacock: LS Gaz, 6 September 1995, p 20

This Sporting Life, Jonathan Peacock (on taxation of sportsmen): Tax Journal, Issue 302, p 11

Training Costs, Patrick Moon (on the reliefs and deductions available for training costs): Tax Journal, Issue 304, p 7

Venture Capital Trusts, Brian Armitage: [1995] BTR 263

Venture Capital Trusts, Francis Sandison: Tax Journal, Issue 294, p 8, Issue 295, p 11

Who Foots the Bill? Bill Docherty and Steve Crocker (on claiming compensation against the Inland Revenue): Tax Journal, Issue 293, p 16

Why Irish Eyes Are Smiling at Securitisation, John Cullinane and Colin Rowlinson (on tax issues surrounding securitisation): Tax Journal, Issue 318, p 12

Yes, But Will They Fly? Michael Murphy (on the taxation of venture capital trusts): Tax Journal, Issue 296, p 8

1607 Appeal—appeal by case stated—availability of procedure

The applicant was the head of the London mission of the Turkish Republic of Northern Cyprus, a republic not recognised by the United Kingdom. He sought judicial review of a decision to assess the salaries of officials of the mission to income tax, contending that the Income and Corporation Taxes Act 1988, s 321 precluded the assessment of income tax on income arising from any office or employment of an official agent in the United Kingdom for any foreign state. *Held*, the correctness or otherwise of an assessment could be challenged by way of judicial review. However, even if judicial review applied in principle, exceptional circumstances would be required to justify the court in proceeding by way of judicial review where there was a normal statutory appeal procedure. There were no such exceptional circumstances in the present case. Accordingly, the application would be dismissed.

R v IRC, ex p Caglar [1995] STC 741 (Queen's Bench Division: Popplewell J).

1608 Assessment—power to determine accounting periods—subjective nature of test

The Income and Corporation Taxes Act 1970, s 247(8) provides that, where it appears to an inspector of taxes that the beginning or end of any accounting period of a company is uncertain, he may make an assessment on the company for such period, not exceeding 12 months, as appears to him appropriate and that period must be treated as an accounting period of the company.

The taxpayer company appealed against a decision that an assessment in respect of corporation tax for a specified accounting period could be revised under s 247(8). *Held*, s 247(8) imported a subjective and not an objective test. Thus, because the Revenue could not demonstrate that the inspector in the present case had been uncertain as to the terminal date of an accounting period, it could not invoke s 247(8). The appeal would be allowed.

Kelsall (Inspector of Taxes) v Stipplechoice Ltd [1995] STC 681 (Court of Appeal: Sir Thomas Bingham MR, Peter Gibson and Saville LJJ). Decision of Vinelott J [1992] STC 842 (1992 Abr para 1389) reversed.

1970 Act, s 247(8) now Income and Corporation Taxes Act 1988, s 12(8).

1609 Avoidance—transactions between associated persons—sales at an undervalue or overvalue

Inquiries by the Board of Inland Revenue into transfer pricing activities that might have taken place between some or all of the taxpayers and associated companies overseas had resulted in notices of assessment to corporation tax on the taxpayers against which their appeals had not yet been determined. Accordingly, they had open assessments going back for many years. The Revenue was out of time for the making of further assessments in respect of many of the years of account in dispute. It fell to be determined whether the combination of the open assessments and a subsequent direction made by the Revenue under the Income and Corporation Taxes Act 1970, s 485(3) was sufficient to enable the assessments to be increased. The taxpayers contended that such a direction was ineffective unless followed by a new assessment to tax within the appropriate statutory time limit. *Held*, by virtue of the Taxes Management Act 1970, s 50(7), the General or Special Commissioners were entitled to increase an assessment if the evidence showed that to be appropriate. Section 50(6) allowed them to do so only on evidence and it was clear that they were entitled to receive evidence which would lead to an increase in the assessment. Such evidence could be tendered by a tax inspector or obtained by the commissioners pursuant to a request by an inspector. The inspector, whose functions at the hearing of an appeal were not restricted to matters expressly authorised by s 50(3), was a party to an appeal in which the assessment was at large in that it might be increased, reduced or extinguished. He could ask the commissioners to exercise any of their powers and he could adduce evidence in support of his application. Any tax adjustments necessary to give effect to a direction under the 1970 Act, s 485(3) could be made by increasing an existing open assessment to corporation tax.

Glaxo Group Ltd v IRC [1996] STC 191 (Court of Appeal: Leggatt and Millett LJJ and Sir Ralph Gibson). Decision of Robert Walker J [1995] STC 1075 affirmed.

1970 Act, s 485 now Income and Corporation Taxes Act 1988, ss 770, 773.

1610 Avoidance—transfer of assets by individual resident abroad

Shortly before his retirement, the taxpayer, a professor at the University of Hong Kong, put a lump sum into a personal portfolio bond with the Isle of Man subsidiary of an insurance company. At the time he was resident in Hong Kong but after retirement he returned to the United Kingdom. After returning, the taxpayer's wife acquired two further bonds. The scheme of the single premium portfolio bond was that an individual transferred money to the insurance company by way of premium and the insurance company issued policies of life insurance. The individual then nominated investments up to the value of the money transferred, the value insured under the policies then being linked to the performance of those investments. The taxpayer and his wife were assessed under the Income and Corporation Taxes Act 1988, s 739 on the income of the investments in the portfolios attached to the bonds. A special commissioner discharged the assessments to income tax and further determined that the taxpayer's acquisition of the bond did not have as its purpose, or one of its purposes, the avoidance of income tax so that the exemption from s 739 which was contained in the 1988 Act, s 741 would in any event apply. The Crown appealed. *Held*, s 739 had been enacted for the purpose of preventing individuals avoiding tax by the transfer of assets to persons resident abroad. However, the section did not apply to a transfer of assets made by an individual at any time when he was not ordinarily resident in the United Kingdom. With regard to the exemption point, the Crown submitted that the hallmark of a bond not effected for the purpose of avoiding a liability to tax was that the investments to which the bond was linked were pooled and the choice of individual investment did not lie with the holder of the bond. That submission was not accepted. The genuine application of a taxpayer's money in the acquisition of a species of property for which Parliament had determined a special tax regime did not amount to tax avoidance merely on the ground that the taxpayer might have chosen a different application which would have subjected him to less favourable tax treatment. The taxpayer and his wife had established that they were entitled to have all the assessments made on them under s 739 discharged. Accordingly, the Crown's appeal would be dismissed.

IRC v Willoughby [1995] STC 143 (Court of Appeal: Glidewell, Hobhouse and Morritt LJJ).

1611 Basic rate limit and personal reliefs—indexation

The Income Tax (Indexation) Order 1995, SI 1995/3031 (made on 28 November 1995), prescribes the basic rate limit and the personal reliefs for 1996–97, increased in accordance with the percentage increase in the retail price index for September 1995 over that for September 1994. The basic rate limit will be £25,300. The lower rate limit will be £3,400. The personal allowance will be £3,665, or £4,810 (for those aged 65–74), or £4,990 (for those aged 75 and over); the enhanced reliefs on account of age are reduced where a claimant's total income for the year of assessment exceeds £15,200. The married couple's allowance is increased to £1,790, or £3,115 (for those aged 65–74), or £3,155 (for those aged 75 and over); the enhanced reliefs on account of age are reduced where a claimant's total income for the year of assessment exceeds £15,200. The amounts have effect unless Parliament otherwise determines.

1612 Building societies—dividends and interest

The Income Tax (Building Societies) (Dividends and Interest) (Amendment) Regulations 1995, SI 1995/1184 (in force on 3 May 1995), further amend the 1990 Regulations, SI 1990/2231, so that deemed payments of interest under the Income and Corporation Taxes Act 1988, s 730A (treatment of price differential on sale and repurchase of securities) are payments from which income tax is not required to be deducted.

1613 Capital allowances—expenditure on scientific research—grants—corresponding Northern Ireland grants

The Capital Allowances (Corresponding Northern Ireland Grants) Order 1995, SI 1995/611 (in force on 1 April 1995), specifies certain grants the amounts of which are not to be deducted from the recipient's capital expenditure when his capital allowances are calculated. The order succeeds the 1993 Order, SI 1993/2705, which applies to grants made under agreements entered into before 1 April 1995.

1614 Capital allowances—machinery and plant—car wash site

The defendant company operated a number of car wash sites. Each site consisted of a building which incorporated the machinery and control equipment, and a surrounding tarmac area on which cars queued and parked. Special commissioners decided that each site was to be treated as a single unit which qualified as 'plant' for the purposes of the Capital Allowances Act 1990, ss 22 and 24, and therefore allowed the defendant's capital allowances claim in respect of expenditure incurred on the car wash sites and structures. On appeal by an inspector of taxes, *held*, it was necessary to apply the 'premises' test to identify those parts of an entity which were plant and those parts which were premises. The test involved considering whether the entity in question was part of the premises in which a business was carried on, or whether it was part of the plant with which the business was carried on. Moreover, premises and plant were not necessarily mutually exclusive. Here, the site on which the car wash business was operated and the building in which the machinery was situated constituted premises for the purpose of the 1990 Act, as they performed functions which were typical of a commercial building. Although a purpose-designed site could function as a single unit, that did not make it a single unit of plant, but simply meant that the whole entity was used for business purposes. Neither the site as a whole nor the building could be regarded as a single unit of plant and, accordingly, the appeal would be allowed.

Attwood (Inspector of Taxes) v Anduff Car Wash Ltd [1996] STC 110 (Chancery Division: Carnwath J).

1615 Capital allowances—machinery and plant—expenditure incurred by incoming lessee

The taxpayer ran a railway line which was built between 1862 and 1874 by a company whose operations were subsequently taken over by another company which operated the line until 1948 when the line became part of British Rail. In 1971, the line was closed. During British Rail's ownership, most of the improvements previously implemented were removed so that the line, when closed, resembled the original line as laid down. The line was reopened in 1975 when a county council purchased the freehold. In 1989, the council granted the taxpayer a 99-year lease of the line which comprised a 22-mile corridor of land with railway track, stations, signal boxes and ancillary equipment. The taxpayer claimed that part of the premium paid in respect of the lease related to plant and machinery and that it was entitled to an allowance under the Finance Act 1985, s 59, Sch 17, para 6(c) on the ground that, at the time of the grant of the lease, no person had previously become entitled to an allowance in respect of any capital expenditure incurred on the provision of the fixtures. *Held*, the taxpayer had to discharge the onus of proving that no person had previously become entitled to an allowance in respect of capital expenditure incurred on the provision of the fixtures. That involved proving a negative over a period from 1975 to the last century, an almost impossible task. Given that improvements had been made to the line over that period and that some improvements must have remained after British Rail had closed the line, it was likely, on the balance of probabilities, that either of the taxpayer's predecessors had previously become entitled to an allowance in respect of capital expenditure on the railway line. The taxpayer had failed to comply with the conditions contained in Sch 17, para 6(c). Accordingly, its claim would fail.

West Somerset Railway plc v Chivers (Inspector of Taxes) [1995] STC (SCD) 1 (Special Commissioner's decision).

1985 Act, Sch 17, para 6(c) now Capital Allowances Act 1990, s 56(c).

1616 Capital allowances—machinery and plant—glasshouse at garden centre

The taxpayer garden centre incurred expenditure on the construction of a planteria in which plants could be maintained in good condition until sold. It fell to be determined whether that expenditure qualified for first-year capital allowance as capital expenditure laid out on the provision of 'plant' within the meaning of the Finance Act 1971, s 41. The taxpayer contended that the planteria performed a distinct function in the taxpayer's trade by creating a unique environment in which plants grew and maintained their quality of growth and that although it might be regarded as part of the premises in which the business was carried on, it might also be regarded as part of the apparatus with which the business was carried on. *Held,* although some plants might remain in the planteria for considerable periods and others required special treatment when there, the planteria was a structure to which plants were brought already in a saleable condition. The plants in the planteria were available for selection by customers who could pass freely between the benches on which the plants were displayed and take them to a point of purchase. Even though the planteria might be described as a purpose-built structure, and though it provided the function of nurturing and preserving plants while there, it was nothing more than part of the premises in which the business was carried on and did not constitute 'plant' for the purpose of s 41. Accordingly, it did not qualify for a first-year capital allowance.

Gray (Inspector of Taxes) v Seymours Garden Centre (Horticulture) [1995] STC 706 (Court of Appeal: Nourse, Beldam and Otton LJJ). Decision of Vinelott J [1993] STC 354 (1993 Abr para 1461) affirmed.

1971 Act, s 41 now Capital Allowances Act 1990, s 22.

1617 Capital allowances—machinery and plant—machinery and plant installed in dwelling house—furnished letting

The Inland Revenue has published a concession concerning the way that the furnished lettings wear and tear allowance operates. The Capital Allowances Act 1990, s 61(2) specifically excludes a capital allowance claim on plant and machinery let for use in a dwelling house but, in practice, a wear and tear allowance may be made by deducting 10 per cent of net rent received. The concession, which is reclassified as a concession, was previously published as Inland Revenue Statement of Practice SP A19 and makes no change to the existing treatment. See further *STI,* 5 October 1995.

1618 Capital allowances—machinery and plant—machinery and plant installed in lessor's premises

The Finance Act 1971, s 44(1) provides that where a person carrying on a trade has incurred capital expenditure on the provision of machinery or plant for the purposes of the trade, and in consequence of his incurring the expenditure, the machinery belongs, or has belonged, to him . . . allowances must be made to him. The Finance Act 1985, s 59(1), Sch 17 apply to determine entitlement to certain allowances under the 1971 Act in respect of expenditure incurred after 11 July 1984 which does not consist of the payment of sums payable under a contract entered into before that date on the provision of machinery or plant which is so installed or otherwise fixed in or to a building or any other description of land as to become, in law, part of that building or other land.

The taxpayer finance companies carried on the business of acquiring and hiring out equipment to local authorities. It fell to be determined whether the taxpayers were entitled to capital allowances under the 1971 Act, s 44(1) in respect of expenditure incurred on central heating leased to authorities for installation in council houses and on other equipment such as boilers, swimming pool equipment, cremators, alarm systems, car park lifts and boilers installed on land occupied by the authorities. *Held,* for the purposes of s 44, property belonged to a person if he was, in law or in equity, the absolute owner of it. The taxpayers had never been owners of the equipment either in law or in equity. The equipment became a fixture, and therefore the property of a local authority, before a lease was entered into and unless and until the authority was in default or decided not to renew the lease. The taxpayers had no right to possession of the equipment or to direct how it should be used. Their only property right was a contingent right to become the owner at a future date. An agreement between the fixer of the chattel and the owner of the land could not affect the determination of the question whether, in law, the chattel had become a fixture and therefore in law belonged to the owner of the soil. The equipment in question was attached to the land in such a manner that it formed part of the land and was intended so to do. Such fixtures were, in law, owned by the owner of the land. Accordingly, the taxpayers were not entitled to allowances on expenditure incurred before 11 July 1984 on plant and machinery. The 1985 Act, Sch 17 provided a comprehensive code regulating the entitlement to capital allowances in relation to expenditure on fixtures incurred after 11 July 1984. The definition of 'interest in land' in Sch 17, para 1(2)(d) referred to an easement in English law and the equivalent concept in the law of Scotland, a servitude. The taxpayers' rights did not constitute an easement in English law and the law of Scotland had no application to the present cases. The taxpayers had not demonstrated any 'interest in land' so as to qualify for capital allowances under Sch 17, paras 2, 4.

The court also stated that the relaxed rule relating to reference to parliamentary materials as an aid to construction, if properly used, could be a valuable aid to construction when Parliament had directly considered the point in issue and passed the legislation on the basis of the ministerial statement. However, it provided no assistance to a court and was capable of giving rise to much expense and delay if attempts were made to widen the category of materials that could be looked at. Judges should be astute to check such misuse of the new rule by making appropriate orders as to costs wasted.

Melluish (Inspector of Taxes) v BMI (No 3) Ltd [1995] 4 All ER 453 (House of Lords: Lords Goff of Chieveley, Browne-Wilkinson, Slynn of Hadley, Nicholls of Birkenhead and Steyn). Decision of Court of Appeal [1994] STC 802 (1994 Abr para 1585) affirmed. *Hobson v Gorringe* [1897] 1 Ch 182, CA, and *Stokes (Inspector of Taxes) v Costain Property Investments Ltd* [1984] 1 All ER 849, CA (1984 Abr para 1326), applied. *Simmons v Midford* [1969] 2 Ch 415 overruled in part. *Pepper (Inspector of Taxes) v Hart* [1993] 1 All ER 42, HL (1993 Abr para 2498), applied.

1619   Construction industry—sub-contractors—tax deduction scheme

The Income Tax (Sub-contractors in the Construction Industry) (Amendment) Regulations 1995, SI 1995/217 (in force on 6 April 1995), amend the 1993 Regulations, SI 1993/743, by increasing to £600 the specified amount which enables a contractor to account to the collector on a quarterly basis if he has reasonable grounds for believing that the average monthly total amount to be paid to the collector in the year of assessment in respect of amounts liable to be deducted from such payments and in respect of PAYE tax and national insurance contributions will not exceed the specified amount.

The Income Tax (Sub-contractors in the Construction Industry) (Amendment No 2) Regulations 1995, SI 1995/448 (in force on 6 April 1995), further amend the 1993 Regulations supra so that the collector is no longer required first to make a demand for amounts liable to be paid by the contractor to the collector before issuing notice of the specified amount to be paid by the contractor and the specified amount no longer need be certified by the collector as an amount of unpaid tax.

1620   Corporation tax—advance corporation tax—set-off against corporation tax—claim

The taxpayer company wrote to the Inland Revenue seeking postponement of payment of corporation tax under the Taxes Management Act 1970, s 55 so that excess advance corporation tax could be set off against liability arising in earlier accounting periods. Repayment of overpaid tax was made by the Inland Revenue a few days later. The taxpayer claimed repayment supplement on the sums repaid. *Held*, no repayment supplement was due as the repayment of tax was in consequence of a claim made by the taxpayer under the Income and Corporation Taxes Act 1988, s 239(3). Its letter constituted a formal claim under that provision even though it contended that its letter referred to its intention to make a future claim. The repayment of overpaid tax was made in consequence of the taxpayer's letter. Accordingly, its claim would fail.

Savacentre Ltd v IRC [1995] STC 867 (Court of Appeal: Balcombe, Henry and Auld LJJ). Decision of Morritt J [1993] STC 344 affirmed. *Proctor & Gamble Ltd v Taylerson (Inspector of Taxes)* [1990] STC 624, CA (1990 Abr para 1290) followed.

1621   Corporation tax—advance corporation tax—set off against corporation tax—pre-ordained series of tranasctions for avoidance of tax liability

A parent company was liable to pay large amounts of advance corporation tax because of dividends that it received from a subsidiary company. It was unable to recover any of the tax because the subsidiary claimed double taxation relief in respect of the dividends, which came from overseas subsidiaries. The parent company sought to remedy the situation by buying a company which paid mainstream corporation tax and which had sums which were potentially available for carry-back under the Income and Corporation Taxes Act 1988, s 239(3), as it was the intention that the subsidiary should pay the dividend to the newly-acquired company rather than to the parent company. The parent company therefore (1) bought the taxpayer company and (2) transferred its shares in the subsidiary to the taxpayer, as a result of which (3) the defendant received a dividend from the subsidiary company and then (4) paid it to the parent company. A Special Commissioner decided that although the transactions were a series of pre-ordained steps not for commercial business reasons but in order to avoid tax liability, the taxpayer's claim for repayment under the 1988 Act, s 239(3) was valid because the steps taken were not a composite set of steps. On the plaintiff's appeal, *held*, although the four steps constituted a pre-ordained series of transactions designed to avoid tax liability, the court had to have regard to the share structure that resulted from those steps. As long as the taxpayer owned all the shares in the subsidiary company, the subsidiary had to make dividend payments to the taxpayer. It was a normal commercial transaction which resulted in a tax advantage for the parent company. As the transactions could not be treated as a composite whole, the taxpayer was entitled to claim repayment under s 239(3). Accordingly, the appeal would be dismissed.

Pigott (Inspector of Taxes) v Staines Investments Co Ltd [1995] STC 114 (Chancery Division: Knox J). *W T Ramsay Ltd v IRC* [1981] 1 All ER 865, HL (1981 Abr para 360) applied.

1622 Corporation tax—allowances—charges on income—yearly interest debited but not paid

The Income and Corporation Taxes Act 1970, s 248(3)(a) provided that payments referred to in s 248 (2) as 'charges on income' included any yearly interest. Section 248(3)(b) provided that any other interest payable on an advance from a bank was included in that category. The remainder of the section provided that any interest payable 'as mentioned in paragraph (b) above' was to be treated as having been paid on its being debited to the company's account in the books of the person to whom it was due.

Moneys were debited to a company's bank account in respect of interest capitalised under a loan agreement. A parent company claimed for group relief in respect of the interest under the 1970 Act, s 248 but it was claimed that, as the interest had been debited but not paid it was not allowable as a charge on income since it was yearly interest under s 248(3)(a). *Held*, the amounts of interest were to be treated as having been paid at the time they were debited to the account of the company in the bank's books. Section 248(3) was not to be construed as confining relief to debited non-yearly interest under s 248(3)(b) but also related to debited yearly interest. The words 'as mentioned in paragraph (b) above' constituted an adverbial phrase qualifying the word 'payable' and not the word 'interest'.

Macarthur (Inspector of Taxes) v Greycoat Estates Mayfair Ltd [1996] STC 1 (Chancery Division: Sir John Vinelott).

1970 Act, s 248 now Income and Corporation Taxes Act 1988, s 338.

1623 Corporation tax—capital duty—reduced rate

See *Commerz-Credit-Bank AG-Europartner v Finanzamt Saarbrücken*, para 3165.

1624 Corporation tax—close companies—returns—duty of disclosure

It has been held that the obligation of disclosure of a close company under the Taxes Management Act 1970, s 10 (notice of liability to corporation tax) is not limited to notice that it is a close company, but extends to notice that it is, or might be, chargeable to tax under the Income and Corporation Taxes Act 1970, s 286.

Earlspring Properties Ltd v Guest (Inspector of Taxes) [1995] STC 479 (Court of Appeal: Balcombe, Evans and Waite LJJ). Decision of Vinelott J [1993] STC 473 (1993 Abr para 1499) affirmed.

1970 Act, s 286 now Income and Corporation Taxes Act 1988, ss 419, 420.

1625 Corporation tax—management expenses—investment company

A company was incorporated to acquire and maintain certain land and buildings comprising a number of houses and garages. It covenanted with the freeholders of the houses, the company's shareholders, to carry out repairs and maintenance; the freeholders covenanted with the company to pay an annual subscription. The company's profits, which were not distributable, were to be used for maintenance. The company appealed against assessments to corporation tax on interest received from subscription income which had been placed on deposit contending that it was an investment company under the Income and Corporation Taxes Act 1988, s 130 and, therefore, entitled to deduct management expenses under s 75(1). *Held*, the company had not been incorporated for the purpose of turning the land to account for profit nor for making distributions to shareholders. It did not hold the land to make money but provided maintenance services to which its investment activities were subsidiary. The principal part of its income was not derived from the making of investments but from the membership subscriptions and from the interest thereon. Such subscriptions were not derived from the holding of the freehold land but from the existence of the covenants with the freeholders of the houses. The company was not an investment company for the purposes of s 130 and, therefore, could not deduct management expenses under s 75(1). Accordingly, its appeal would be dismissed.

Tintern Close Residents Society Ltd v Winter (Inspector of Taxes) [1995] STC (SCD) 57 (Special Commissioner's decision).

1626 Corporation tax—set-off of trading losses against trading income—investment income as trading receipt

The Income and Corporation Taxes Act 1988, s 393 provides that a company may set off trading losses sustained in an accounting period against trading income in succeeding accounting periods provided the company continues to carry on the trade.

The taxpayer carried on the business of generating electricity from nuclear fuel. Funds set aside by it to meet future liabilities were invested but were not segregated from other money and the taxpayer was not obliged to maintain such funds or to use the income therefrom to meet future liabilities. An assessment to corporation tax was made, against which the taxpayer successfully appealed on the ground that income received from the investments was a trading receipt, and that accordingly trading losses carried forward could be set against it by virtue of the 1988 Act, s 393. On appeal by the Revenue, *held*, authorities showed a company's investment income could be treated as a trading receipt where the making and holding of investments at interest was an integral part of the trade, to the same extent as the supply of the product or service to customers. In this case, the taxpayer had long term liabilities which made it possible to carry on its business without the need for maintenance of an investment fund. In addition, the liabilities for which provision had been made were not to customers, but exclusively to third parties. Both of these factors were proof that the making and holding of investments was not an integral part of the business of generating and supplying electricity by nuclear reaction and, therefore, the taxpayer's trading losses could not be set against its investment income. Accordingly, the appeal would be allowed.

Nuclear Electric plc v Bradley (Inspector of Taxes) [1995] STC 1125 (Court of Appeal: Sir Thomas Bingham MR, Millett and Schiemann LJJ). Decision of Sir John Vinelott [1995] STC 285 reversed.

This decision has been affirmed: [1996] STC 405, HL.

1627 Deposit-takers—interest payments—discretionary or accumulation trusts

The Deposit-takers (Interest Payments) (Discretionary or Accumulation Trusts) Regulations 1995, SI 1995/1370 (in force on 14 June 1995), (1) provide for the form of notification given by the trustees of a discretionary or accumulation trust for the purposes of the Income and Corporation Taxes Act 1988, s 481(5B); (2) make provision in relation to the circumstances in which a deposit-taker is entitled to delay deducting tax from payments of interest to any such trust following receipt of a notification; and (3) provide for the cancellation of a notification by the Commissioners of Inland Revenue.

1628 Distress for taxes—collector—fees, costs and charges

The Distraint by Collectors (Fees, Costs and Charges) (Amendment) Regulations 1995, SI 1995/2151 (in force on 8 September 1995), amend the 1994 Regulations, SI 1994/236, by making new provision in respect of the fees chargeable on, or in connection with, the levying of distress where a visit is made to premises, and with respect to the costs and charges recoverable where distress has been levied, and goods are subsequently sold.

1629 Double taxation relief—arrangements

Double taxation relief arrangements have been made with the following countries:

Country	Relevant statutory instrument (SI 1995 No)
Azerbaijan	762
Belarus	2706
Bolivia	2707
Malta	763
Republic of Ireland	764
Spain	765

1630 Double taxation relief—manufactured overseas dividends

The Double Taxation Relief (Manufactured Overseas Dividends) (Amendment) Regulations 1995, SI 1995/1551 (in force on 1 July 1995), amend the 1993 Regulations, SI 1993/1957, by extending the conditions for enabling a manufactured overseas dividend to be paid without deduction of tax to include a person in receipt of, but not beneficially entitled to, the payment, if he is entitled to relief from double taxation in respect of the payment under the appropriate article of arrangements made between the United Kingdom and the territory concerned for such relief, and he satisfies the other specified conditions.

1631 Exchange gains and losses—transitional provisions

The Exchange Gains and Losses (Transitional Provisions) (Amendment) Regulations 1995, SI 1995/408 (in force on 23 March 1995), amend the 1994 Regulations, SI 1994/3226, so as to ensure that the application of the provisions relating to gains and losses which have accrued, as respects debts of fixed amounts, to a company before its commencement day, is confined to debts where both the amount and the term are fixed.

1632 Exemptions—corporation tax—friendly society—life or endowment business— management and capital allowances expenses

A registered friendly society carried on both taxable and tax exempt life or endowment business. The taxable part of its business was chargeable to corporation tax on the income minus expenses basis whereunder in computing the total profits for any accounting period any sums disbursed as expenses of management were deductible. It fell to be determined whether the amount to be relieved pursuant to the exemption on profits arising from life or endowment business under the Income and Corporation Taxes Act 1988, s 460(1) was the sum of the income and chargeable gains attributable to exempt life or endowment business reduced by so much of the expenses of management and capital allowances as were attributable to exempt business. The society contended that the 'profits' arising from life or endowment business which qualified for exemption from corporation tax under s 460(1) were its investment income and chargeable gains before deducting expenses of management and capital allowances so that the amount to be charged to corporation tax was its total profits reduced by the amount attributable to tax exempt life or endowment business and then further reduced by amounts disbursed as expenses of management, and by capital allowances. *Held*, on general principles, income and capital gains together were 'profits'. The 'profits' which qualified for exemption from corporation tax under s 460(1) were the income and gains referable to 'tax exempt life or endowment business' before deducting management expenses or capital allowances. As there was no provision which resulted in an expense attributable to exempt income or gains ceasing to qualify for relief and in the absence of clear words to the contrary the society was entitled to relief with respect to expenses attributable to exempt income or gains. There was no provision requiring any proportion of capital allowances to cease to qualify for relief where a friendly society carried on tax exempt business.

Homeowners Friendly Society Ltd v Barrett (Inspector of Taxes) [1995] STC (SCD) 90 (Special Commissioner's decision).

1633 Exemptions—stock lending

The Income Tax (Stock Lending) (Amendment) Regulations 1995, SI 1995/1283 (in force on 19 June 1995), further amend the 1989 Regulations, SI 1989/1299, by updating the definition of 'other United Kingdom securities' so that it refers to the Alternative Investment Market of the Stock Exchange, which opened for trading on 19 June 1995, instead of to the Third Market of the Stock Exchange, which closed on 31 December 1990.

The Income Tax (Stock Lending) (Amendment No 2) Regulations 1995, SI 1995/3219 (in force on 2 January 1996), further amend the 1989 Regulations supra by (1) inserting definitions of 'approved agent', 'approved lender'; 'approved nominee', 'approved stock borrowing and lending intermediary', in relation to stock lending arrangements, and 'first borrower' and 'last lender', in relation to a chain of such arrangements, and replacing the definition of 'gilt-edged securities'; (2) providing that the Income and Corporation Taxes Act 1988, s 129 applies to a stock lending arrangement for the transfer of gilt-edged securities even though the arrangement was not entered into to enable the borrower to fulfil a contract under which he was required to sell securities; (3) providing that s 129 applies also to loans under which securites are borrowed to meet a demand for the return of other securities; (4) providing that s 129 applies in cases where stock lending arrangements terminate on redemption of the securities transferred under the arrangements; (5) specifying the conditions to be fulfilled if transfers, disposals and acquisitions made under such arrangements are to be disregarded for tax purposes; and (6) where any of those conditions are not fulfilled, modifying the operation of the Taxation of Chargeable Gains Act 1992 in respect of such disposals and acquisitions.

1634 Exemptions—tax-exempt special savings accounts

The Tax-exempt Special Savings Account (Amendment) Regulations 1995, SI 1995/1929 (in force on 11 August 1995), amend the 1990 Regulations, SI 1990/2361. The 1995 Regulations provide that the amount deposited in a follow-up account, as defined, may not exceed £3,000 in the first year for which the account is held, unless the building society or institution with which it is held has a certificate from the society or institution with which the matured account was held showing the amount deposited at the date of maturity or, if it is the same society or institution, maintains computer or paper records evidencing that amount. The regulations also require the society or institution with which the matured account was held to provide such a certificate at the request of the account-holder.

See also para 2488.

1635 Finance Act 1995

See para 2489.

1636 Income and Corporation Taxes Act 1988—appointed day

The Income and Corporation Taxes Act 1988, section 737A, (Appointed Day) Order 1995, SI 1995/1007, appoints 1 May 1995 (ie the day on which the Finance Act 1995 was passed) as the appointed day for the purposes of the 1988 Act, s 737A in relation to agreements to sell United Kingdom equities and United Kingdom securities entered into on or after that day.

1637 Income and Corporation Taxes Act 1988—commencement

The Income and Corporation Taxes Act 1988, section 51A, (Appointed Day) Order 1995, SI 1995/2932, provides that s 51A, inserted by the Finance Act 1995, s 77, by virtue of which interest on gilt-edged securities is to be paid without deduction of income tax and interest so paid is chargeable under Schedule D, Case III, does not apply to any interest paid before 2 January 1996. For a summary of the Act, see 1988 Abr para 1196. For details of commencement, see the commencement table in the title STATUTES.

1638 Lloyd's underwriters—gilt-edged securities—periodic accounting for tax on interest

The Lloyd's Underwriters (Gilt-edged Securities) (Periodic Accounting for Tax on Interest) Regulations 1995, SI 1995/3225 (in force on 2 January 1996), make provision in relation to the periodic returns to the Commissioners of Inland Revenue by Lloyd's Underwriters, who are prescribed by the regulations as persons to whom payments of interest on gilt-edged securities may be made without the deduction of income tax. The regulations (1) provide for a managing agent of a syndicate to make returns of amounts of any payments of interest on gilt-edged securities made without the deduction of tax to premiums trust funds of that syndicate, and of amounts of tax for which he is to be accountable under these regulations in respect of those payments; (2) specify the periods for which such returns ('quarterly returns') are to be made and provide that a quarterly return must be made within 14 days from the end of the quarter; (3) make provision for the amounts which are to be shown in a quarterly return and define the 'amount of excess gilt interest received' and 'amount of excess gilt interest paid'; (4) make provision for a managing agent to be accountable for income tax at the basic rate on the amount of excess gilt interest received for each quarter, and for amounts in respect of which tax has been so accounted to be treated for the purposes of repayment of tax as income on which income tax has been borne by deduction; (5) enable a managing agent to claim that tax nominally attributable to excess gilt interest paid may be set against amounts for which he is liable to account for previous quarters and that, where a claim is not made, the tax nominally attributable to the excess gilt interest paid must be carried forward to be set against tax payable in respect of the next quarter; (6) require a managing agent to make a special return in respect of the quarter ending on 31 March specifying the estimated amount of tax to be paid for that quarter; (7) provide that the tax required to be specified in a return is due at the time by which the return is made; (8) make provision for assessments to be made if an inspector is dissatisfied with a return, and for a managing agent to make a single payment in respect of all syndicates administered by him; (9) make provision for collection proceedings in connection with claims under the regulations; (10) provide for the provisions of the Income Tax Acts to apply to an assessment made under these regulations; and (11) make provision for interest to be payable by a managing agent on unpaid amounts of tax, and for interest to be payable to a managing agent where a payment on account made by him for the quarter ending on 31 March exceeds the total amount of tax due.

1639 Manufactured dividends—Tradepoint

The Income Tax (Manufactured Dividends) (Tradepoint) Regulations 1995, SI 1995/2052 (in force on 25 August 1995), make provision in relation to payments of manufactured dividends in respect of shares of companies resident in the United Kingdom where such payments are made by persons acting in a clearing capacity for transactions on the Exchange known as Tradepoint. The regualtions prescribe the circumstances in which such payments rank as approved manufactured payments for the purposes of the Income and Corporation Taxes Act 1988, Sch 23A; limit the amount of tax to be accounted for in respect of such payments when made by clearing participants who are not United Kingdom resident companies; and provide for returns and accounting for tax by such persons.

1640 Manufactured interest

The Income Tax (Manufactured Interest) (Amendment) Regulations 1995, SI 1995/3221 (in force on 2 January 1996), amend the 1992 Regulations, SI 1992/2074, by (1) providing a definition of 'gilt-edged securities'; (2) in the definition of 'unapproved manufactured payment', omitting manufactured gilt interest; (3) omitting the provisions which provided for the gross payment of certain manufactured interest; and (4) in the definition of 'qualifying person', excluding from the scope of the Taxes Management Act 1970, s 21 (information powers in respect of transactions of brokers and market makers), companies for which approved manufactured payments of gilt interest are the only approved manufactured payments that they may make.

1641 Manufactured overseas dividends

The Income Tax (Manufactured Overseas Dividends) (Amendment) Regulations 1995, SI 1995/1324 (in force on 7 June 1995), amend the 1993 Regulations, SI 1993/2004, (1) by replacing the definition of 'chargeable period'; (2) by providing that the offsetting of tax payable by overseas dividend manufacturers against tax in respect of overseas dividends received by them is only possible where the overseas dividends received constitute income of the overseas dividend manufacturer and not income of another person; (3) by providing that double taxation relief may not be claimed by an overseas dividend manufacturer where overseas dividends or manufactured overseas dividends received by him are matched against manufactured overseas dividends paid by him or, except to the extent of any excess credit balance which results, where there is offsetting of tax; (4) in relation to the order of priority in which overseas dividends and manufactured overseas dividends received by an overseas dividend manufacturer in any chargeable period fall to be matched against manufactured overseas dividends paid by him in that period.

1642 Occupational pension schemes

See PENSIONS AND SUPERANNUATION.

1643 Overpayment of tax—repayment

The Inland Revenue has issued Statement of Practice SP 6/95, which replaces Statement of Practice SP 1/80, explaining that overpayments of tax will not automatically be repaid where a Schedule E check shows an overpayment of £10 or less, where a payment to the collector of taxes exceeds the amount due by £1 or less, or where for inheritance tax an overpayment is £25 or less. See further *STI*, 6 April 1995.

1644 Overseas life assurance—compliance

The Insurance Companies (Overseas Life Assurance Business) (Compliance) Regulations 1995, SI 1995/3237 (in force on 2 January 1996), provide for the determination of overseas life assurance business for the purposes of the Income and Corporation Taxes Act 1988, s 431D, inserted by the Finance Act 1995, Sch 8, para 2, for insurance companies to obtain certificates on the happening of specified events, for sanctions for a failure to comply with the regulations, and for the keeping and inspection of records and the provision of information. The regulations have effect in relation to accounting periods beginning on or after 1 November 1994. Authority for the retrospective effect of the regulations is conferred by the 1995 Act, Sch 8, para 58.

1645 Overseas life assurance—tax credit

The Insurance Companies (Overseas Life Assurance Business) (Tax Credit) Regulations 1995, SI 1995/3238 (in force on 2 January 1996), provide that an insurance company is entitled to a tax credit under the Income and Corporation Taxes Act 1988, s 431 where a distribution is made in respect of any asset of the company's overseas life assurance fund; and provide for the amount of such tax credit, for the determination of the territories in which relevant overseas policy holders reside and for the keeping and inspection of records and the provision of information. The regulations have effect in relation to accounting periods beginning on or after 1 November 1994. Authority for the retrospective effect of the regulations is conferred by the Finance Act 1995, Sch 8, para 58.

1646 PAYE—regulations

The Income Tax (Employments) (Amendment) Regulations 1995, SI 1995/216 (in force on 6 April 1995), further amend the 1993 Regulations, SI 1993/744, by increasing from £450 to £600 the amount which entitles an employer to account to the collector of taxes for tax liable to be deducted under PAYE from payments to employees made by the employer in any quarterly period because he has reasonable grounds for believing that the average monthly total amount to be paid to the collector in the year of assessment in respect of PAYE tax, national insurance contributions and deductions from payments to sub-contractors in the construction industry will not exceed that specified amount.

The Income Tax (Employments) (Amendment No 2) Regulations 1995, SI 1995/447 (in force on 6 April 1995), further amend the 1993 Regulations supra by (1) providing that the collector or the Board of Inland Revenue may make a direction that an amount of tax is to be recovered from the employee where it appears to them that the employer has failed to deduct that amount from emoluments paid to the employee and the other specified conditions are satisfied; (2) by abolishing the requirement that the collector first make a demand for tax liable to be paid by the employer before issuing notice of the specified amount to be paid by the employer; (3) removing the requirement that the specified amount should be certified by the collector as an amount of unpaid tax; (4) clarifying the circumstances in which a direction may be made by the Board that tax which the employer failed to deduct is to be recovered from the employee, and the consequences of making such a direction; (5) including documents and records relating to particulars required to be included in a return by an employer in the documents and records which the employer may be required to produce to an officer of the Board for inspection; and (6) making it clear that, where a direction is made that an amount of tax is to be recovered from the employee, that amount may not be claimed as a credit by the employee in calculating the amount of tax which he is liable to pay under an assessment.

The Income Tax (Employments) (Incapacity Benefit) Regulations 1995, SI 1995/853 (in force on 13 April 1995), further amend the 1993 Regulations by providing for the operation of PAYE, with effect for the year 1995–96 and subsequent years of assessment, on payments of taxable incapacity benefit made to a claimant by the Department of Social Security.

The Income Tax (Employments) (Amendment No 3) Regulations 1995, SI 1995/1223 (in force on 25 May 1995), further amend the 1993 Regulations by omitting the reference to summary proceedings in the regulation relating to the recovery of tax.

The Income Tax (Employments) (Amendment No 4) Regulations 1995, SI 1995/1284 (in force on 6 April 1996), further amend the 1993 Regulations by (1) requiring that the certificate of tax deducted be given by the employer to the employee not later than 56 days after the end of the year of assessment to which it relates; (2) requiring that an employer include in the return containing particulars of benefits and other additional emoluments provided or paid to employees, particulars in relation to business entertainment and benefits charged under certain provisions of the Income and Corporation Taxes Act 1988 which provide for the charging of cash equivalents to income tax in respect of those benefits, and that the employer report items which have been provided by a third party, but the employer has arranged or facilitated the provision; (3) providing for a current employee and if he so requires, a former employee, to be given a statement by his employer containing the particulars supplied in a return in so far as those particulars relate to him, and certain particulars relating to car allowances and motor mileage allowances paid to the employee; (4) providing that where any person has paid or provided emoluments to an employee of another and the employer is not required, in his own return, to provide particulars of those emoluments, the person who has paid or provided such emoluments must give a statement to the employee containing particulars of them.

1647   Penalty—information—failure to furnish information

A notice was issued against the taxpayer under the Taxes Management Act 1970, s 51, requiring him to disclose details of his bank and building society accounts. The General Commissioners found that he had failed to satisfy the notice and that there had been continuing default. His appeal against the decision was dismissed, but he still failed to provide the required information. As more than two years had elapsed since the notice was originally issued, the clerk to the commissioners wrote to the taxpayer informing him that his continuing failure to comply with the notice was to be considered at a further appeal hearing, and that the commissioners would also consider whether to impose a penalty. He was informed that if he could not attend the hearing, he could be represented either by a qualified accountant or another suitable person, or submit written representations. The taxpayer did not attend the hearing, and a penalty was imposed on him in his absence. On appeal, he argued that the penalty was unjust and unreasonable. *Held*, the taxpayer was a professional person, and had been warned that a penalty might be imposed on him because of his continuing failure to comply with the notice. He had been given the opportunity to provide the information required, either in writing, in person or by a representative, but had failed to do so. There was no evidence to suggest that the commissioner's findings of fact were wrong, or that their decision was invalid in law. Accordingly, the appeal would be dismissed.

Stoll v High Wycombe General Comrs [1995] STC 91 (Chancery Division: Harman J).

1648   Personal pension schemes

See PENSIONS AND SUPERANNUATION.

1649   Reinsurance business—investment return—taxation

The Insurance Companies (Taxation of Reinsurance Business) Regulations 1995, SI 1995/1730 (in force on 28 July 1995), make provision in respect of the calculation of the investment return, for the purpose of its taxation under the Income and Corporation Taxes Act 1988, s 442A, on an insurance policy or annuity contract, where the insurance company concerned has reinsured any risk under the policy or contract. The regulations exclude certain reinsurance arrangements and policies and certain reinsurance business from the operation of s 442A. Certain reinsurance business is also excluded from ss 431C (classes of life assurance business) and 439A (taxation of pure insurance business).

1650   Relief—life assurance—deductible expenses—management expenses

The taxpayer sustained a substantial Schedule D, Case I loss in carrying on its life assurance business and claimed relief under the Income and Corporation Taxes Act 1988, s 393(2). Its computation included the deduction of management expenses. It fell to be determined whether those expenses were to be excluded from deduction in an assessment to corporation tax on the taxpayer computed on the income minus expenses basis provided for by s 75 (as applied to insurance companies by s 76) which allowed the deduction of management expenses except such expenses as were deductible in computing profits apart from s 75. *Held*, s 76(1) provided that s 75 should apply for computing the profits of an insurance company as it applied in relation to an investment company. However, if expenses were forbidden to be deducted in computing the profits of an insurance company because they could be deducted in a Schedule D, Case I computation (which could never be the case for an investment company), s 75 could not be applied for computing the profits of an insurance company as that provision applied in relation to an investment company. Accordingly, the exception in s 75(1) was not to be construed as preventing the deduction in an income minus expenses computation of the expenses of a life insurance company which were deductible in a Schedule D, Case I computation.

Prudential Assurance Co Ltd v Johnson (Inspector of Taxes) [1995] STC (SCD) 70 (Special Commissioner's decision).

1651 Relief—losses—trade—letting of furnished holiday accommodation—letting on commercial basis with view to profit

The taxpayer, an experienced commercial property analyst, acquired two flats with the intention of letting them as furnished holiday accommodation. Prior to the acquisition, he prepared a five-year projection plan, based on advice from agents specialising in letting holiday accommodation and his own expectations, which predicted losses in the first two years and increasing profits in the next three years. An economic recession had a severe impact on holiday lettings. Occupancy rates in the taxpayer's flats were lower than expected, partly due to his agents' incompetence. He incurred further losses as a result of defective building works. His claim for loss relief for the first two years under the Income and Corporation Taxes Act 1988, ss 380, 381 was rejected on the grounds that the flats had not been let 'on a commercial basis' 'with a view to the realisation of profits' within s 504(2)(a), by virtue of which the taxpayer would have been entitled to treat his activities as a trade for tax purposes, and within s 384(1) (so as to qualify for relief for losses under s 380); and that relief under s 381 was precluded by s 381(4) because profits in the trade could not reasonably be expected to be realised in the period in respect of which the loss was sustained or within a reasonable time thereafter. He appealed. *Held*, the question of whether the flats had been let on a commercial basis with a view to the realisation of profits was a subjective test. The taxpayer's purpose had been the realisation of profits. The requirements of s 504(2)(a) and, accordingly, s 384(1) were satisfied. Section 381(4) presupposed that, when an individual began a trade, losses might be suffered for four years or over a longer period according to the nature of the trade and the economic circumstances. The issue was whether profits could reasonably be expected to be realised within a reasonable time having regard to the way in which the trade was carried on. It could not have been said at the outset that the taxpayer could not reasonably have expected to have realised profits within four years of the commencement of the trade or within a reasonable time thereafter. The adverse economic circumstances which had brought about the losses could not have been predicted objectively prior to the event. The taxpayer had satisfied the objective test in s 381(4) and, accordingly, his appeal would be allowed.

Walls v Livesey (Inspector of Taxes) [1995] STC (SCD) 12 (Special Commissioner's decision).

1652 Relief—manufactured payments and transfer of securities

The Manufactured Payments and Transfer of Securities (Tax Relief) Regulations 1995, SI 1995/3036 (in force on 2 January 1996), provide that payments of manufactured dividends, manufactured interest and manufactured overseas dividends made to certain pension schemes and pension funds are exempt from income tax, and that such payments made to insurance companies carrying on pension business are exempt from corporation tax where the payment is referable to the pension business of the company. Similar provision is made in relation to amounts which are deemed to be payments of interest under the Income and Corporation Taxes Act 1988, s 730A(2) (treatment of price differential on sale and repurchase of securities), in cases where the deemed payments are made to the pension schemes, pension funds and insurance companies.

1653 Relief—mortgage or loan interest—administration

The Income Tax (Interest Relief) (Amendment) Regulations 1995, SI 1995/1213 (in force on 4 May 1995), further amend the 1982 Regulations, SI 1982/1236, in relation to the administration of the mortgage interest relief at source scheme as a consequence of statutory changes relating to the recovery of certain amounts deducted by borrowers, or paid by the Board of Inland Revenue under the scheme. A lender is no longer required to send to the Board a copy of the statutory notice received from a borrower certifying that he meets the required conditions for the operation of the relief in connection with loan interest. The Board may now recover by way of assessment amounts paid in certain circumstances to a borrower under the scheme to which he is not entitled and, in such cases, it may impose penalties for any false statement made fraudulently or negligently by the borrower in connection with the payment of such amounts, or for unreasonable delay on the part of the borrower in notifying the Board that interest on a loan has ceased to qualify for relief. Certain amendments are made to reflect statutory changes by virtue of which the Board may now recover amounts deducted under the scheme that should not have been deducted.

1654 Relief—mortgage or loan interest—housing associations

The Income Tax (Interest Relief) (Housing Associations) (Amendment) Regulations 1995, SI 1995/1212 (in force on 24 May 1995), amend the 1988 Regulations, SI 1988/1347, in order to reflect statutory changes to mortgage interest relief at source provisions.

1655 Relief—mortgage or loan interest—property used for residential and business purposes

The Inland Revenue has published a concession allowing relief for interest on a loan to buy property which is used for both residential and business purposes in part under the provisions relating to mortgage interest (see Income and Corporation Taxes Act 1988, ss 353, 369) and in part as a deduction in computing business profits. The concession applies where (1) a part of a property, which is the borrower's only or main residence, is used exclusively for business purposes. In such circumstances, the loan in question may be apportioned on the basis of the proportionate part of the property so used; and (2) a property, which is the borrower's only or main residence, is used only sometimes for business purposes, on which occasions it is used for a significant amount of time and exclusively. In these circumstances, the loan in question may be apportioned on any reasonable basis that takes account of both the proportion of the property so used and the duration of such use. In both cases, following the apportionment of the loan, mortgage interest relief may be claimed for the interest on the part of the loan attributable to residential use and a deduction may be allowed for the interest on the part of the loan attributable to business use. See further *STI*, 12 May 1995.

1656 Relief—retirement annuity—premiums paid out of income—Lloyd's syndicates

The taxpayer was an external name at Lloyd's on the affairs of which he spent three to four hours a week. Under the standard agency agreement between a name and his member's agent, the latter had sole control and management of the underwriting business and the name was to interfere in no way with the exercise of such control and management. The taxpayer paid a premium under an annuity contract out of income which he had received from the syndicates to which he belonged. He claimed retirement annuity relief, under the Income and Corporation Taxes Act 1988, s 619(1), on the ground that the income he received from Lloyd's was 'immediately derived by him from the carrying on or exercise by him of his trade as an individual' within s 623(2)(c) and was therefore 'relevant earnings' for the purposes of s 619(1). *Held*, an external name did not carry on any trade at all. Through the medium of his member's agent he subscribed to risks selected on behalf of each syndicate by its managing agent. The trade out of which the taxpayer's income arose consisted of the business of underwriting, including the identification, selection, assessment, and acceptance of risks. That trade was carried on not by him as an individual but for him by the managing agents of the syndicates and also by his member's agent. The income received by the taxpayer from Lloyd's did not constitute relevant earnings for the purposes of s 619(1) and, accordingly, his appeal would be dismissed.

    Koenigsberger v Mellor (Inspector of Taxes) [1995] STC 547 (Court of Appeal: Leggatt, Simon Brown and Ward LJJ). Decision of Lindsay J [1993] STC 408 (1993 Abr para 1486) affirmed.

1657 Relief—tax-exempt special savings account—relevant European institutions

The Tax-exempt Special Savings Account (Relevant European Institutions) Regulations 1995, SI 1995/3239 (in force on 2 January 1996), require European authorised institutions within the meaning of the Banking Co-ordination (Second Council Directive) Regulations 1992, SI 1992/3218, which may accept deposits in the United Kingdom in accordance with those regulations ('relevant European institutions') and which operate tax-exempt special savings accounts, to appoint tax representatives to discharge prescribed duties of the institution or make other arrangements with the Commissioners of Inland Revenue for the discharge of those duties. Provision is also made as to the appointment, termination of appointment, powers and liabilities of tax representatives. Relevant European institutions are added to the societies and institutions which may operate accounts, the information to be provided by relevant European institutions intending to operate accounts is specified, and the circumstances in which a society or institution ceases to be entitled to operate accounts and the requirements for the inspection of records of a society or institution are revised.

1658 Relief—vocational training—public financial assistance and disentitlement to tax relief

The Vocational Training (Public Financial Assistance and Disentitlement to Tax Relief) (Amendment) Regulations 1995, SI 1995/3274 (in force on 8 January 1996), further amend the 1992 Regulations, SI 1992/734, by adding new types of public financial assistance (namely Modern Apprenticeships or Accelerated Modern Apprenticeships and Jobmatch) which preclude the giving of tax relief for payments in respect of qualifying courses of vocational training, extending existing types of public financial assistance to cover locally named schemes within the same type and removing that known as Training Credits Scheme.

1659   Repayment of tax—insurance companies—pension business

The Insurance Companies (Pension Business) (Transitional Provisions) (Amendment) Regulations 1995, SI 1995/3134 (in force on 31 December 1995), further amend the 1992 Regulations, SI 1992/2326, by prescribing 10 per cent as the appropriate percentage by which the amount of a provisional repayment of tax on pension business investment income should be reduced for an accounting period ending after 31 December 1994 and before 1 January 1996, and 7 per cent for an accounting period ending after 31 December 1995.

1660   Schedule A—non-residents—income from land

The Taxation of Income from Land (Non-residents) Regulations 1995, SI 1995/2902 (in force on 1 December 1995), provide for the collection of tax on income of a Schedule A business carried on by a non-resident. In certain circumstances, the income is to be collected from the person acting as agent for the business in question or from a person by whom rent is payable to the non-resident.

1661   Schedule D—annuities and other annual payments—agreement for payment without deduction of tax—rectification of agreement

Under a deed, the taxpayer company covenanted to pay an annual sum to a charitable trust. The annual payments were made with tax deducted on the basis that they were deemed to be income of the trust which recovered the tax from the Inland Revenue. However, the deed did not satisfy the requirements of the Income and Corporation Taxes Act 1988, s 660(3) for a qualifying covenant in favour of a charity as the payments to be made did not exceed three years. The taxpayer, therefore, was not entitled to deduct tax. It sought to rectify the deed by stating that payments would be made on the same day in each of the following three years. At first instance, the court refused to grant rectification on the ground that there was no issue between the parties and the court would not grant rectification if the only effect was to improve the fiscal position of the taxpayer, and because the taxpayer had failed to establish that the deed did not give effect to its intention. On appeal by the taxpayer, *held*, there was an issue capable of being contested between the taxpayer and the trust. That was whether the taxpayer was entitled to deduct income tax from the covenanted payments. The court could not rectify a document merely on the ground that it failed to achieve the taxpayer's fiscal objective. The taxpayer's specific intention as to how the objective was to be achieved had to be shown if the deed was to be rectified. It had failed to establish that the deed did not give effect to its intention. Accordingly, its appeal would be dismissed.

Racal Group Services Ltd v Ashmore [1995] STC 1151 (Court of Appeal: Kennedy and Peter Gibson LJJ and Sir Ian Glidewell). *Whiteside v Whiteside* [1949] 2 All ER 913, CA; *Thomas Bates and Son Ltd v Wyndham's (Lingerie) Ltd* [1981] 1 All ER 1077, CA (1980 Abr para 1742); and *Sherdley v Sherdley* [1986] 2 All ER 202, CA (1986 Abr para 799) considered. Decision of Vinelott J [1994] STC 416 affirmed.

1662   Schedule D—gilt-edged securities—gross payments of interest

The Income Tax (Gilt-edged Securities) (Gross Payments of Interest) Regulations 1995, SI 1995/2934 (in force on 23 November 1995), impose conditions and requirements in connection with arrangements for the holding of gilt-edged securities the interest on which may be paid without deduction of tax in accordance with the Income and Corporation Taxes Act 1988, s 51A. The regulations (1) set out the conditions to be satisfied in relation to the holding of gilt-edged securities; (2) specify the requirements in relation to a Central Gilts Office (CGO) member or intermediary who is not resident and does not have a business establishment, in the United Kingdom; (3) provide for the declarations that must be made by owners of gilt-edged securities before those securities can be placed in an account designated by the CGO; (4) require a CGO member to ensure that certain conditions are satisfied in relation to any gilt-edged securities before he is entitled to place those securities in an account under (3); (5) impose similar requirements to that in (4) that an intermediary must ensure that he has satisfied in relation to any gilt-edged securities before he may arrange for those securities to be placed in an account under (3); (6) specify the circumstances in which a CGO member or intermediary must remove gilt-edged securities from an account under (3); (7) provide for the furnishing of information to the Board of Inland Revenue by a CGO member or intermediary, or by an owner of gilt-edged securities; (8) make provision for the inspection by an officer of the board of documents in the possession or control of a CGO member or intermediary relating to gilt-edged securities; and (9) provide for the keeping of records, and the retention of declarations, instructions and other documents, by persons referred to in (7).

1663   Schedule D—gilt-edged securities—periodic accounting for tax on interest

The Gilt-edged Securities (Periodic Accounting for Tax on Interest) Regulations 1995, SI 1995/3224 (in force on 2 January 1996), exercise the powers conferred on the Treasury by the Income and Corporation Taxes Act 1988, s 51B, by virtue of which the Treasury may by regulations provide that persons to whom payments of interest on gilt-edged securities are made without deduction of tax ('gross payments') must make periodic returns to an officer of the Commissioners of Inland Revenue. The regulations (1) specify the persons (resident and non-resident companies) who must make periodic returns; (2) provide for a company to make returns of amounts of any gross payments it receives and of amounts of tax for which it is to be accountable in respect of those payments; (3) specify periods, any of which is to be called a 'return period, for which returns are to be made; (4) require that a return for any specified return period be made within 14 days from the end of that period; (5) provide for the payments which are to be shown in a return made by a resident company and make corresponding provision in respect of a non-resident company; (6) define an 'amount of excess gilt interest received', an 'amount of excess gilt interest paid' and an 'aggregate amount of excess gilt interest received'; (7) provide that a company is accountable for income tax at the basic rate on the amount of excess gilt interest received for each return period; (8) enable the company, in certain circumstances, to claim that income tax on the aggregate amount of excess gilt interest received is to be set against income tax which it is liable to pay under the 1988 Act, Sch 16; (9) enable a company, in certain circumstances, to claim that income tax nominally attributable to an amount of excess gilt interest paid be set against income tax on amounts for which it is liable to account for previous return periods; (10) require a company, in certain circumstances, to carry forward income tax nominally attributable to an amount of excess gilt interest paid to the next return period; (11) provide for a company which is not a building society to make a special return in respect of a special return period which includes the month of March, showing the estimated amount of income tax for which it is accountable and make corresponding provision in the case of a company which is a building society, and provide for such a company to make a further special reconciliation return; (12) provide that income tax set against other tax cannot also be taken into account under s 7(2) or 11(3); (13) provide that tax is due at the time by which the return is to be made, and provide for assessments to be made on a company if an inspector is dissatisfied with a return; (14) make provision for collection proceedings in connection with claims under the regulations; (15) provide for the provisions of the Income Tax Acts to apply to an assessment under the regulations; and (16) provide for interest to be payable on certain amounts, and for interest to be paid to a company where the payment on account exceeds the relevant amount of tax due.

The Insurance Companies (Gilt-edged Securities) (Periodic Accounting for Tax on Interest) Regulations 1995, SI 1995/3223 (in force on 2 January 1996), (1) provide that an insurance company carrying on life assurance business is not required to include in its return for any return period the amount of tax on the amount of excess gilt interest received which is referable to the company's pension business provided that the amount of tax is identified in a claim made by the specified date, (2) modify the Income and Corporation Taxes Act 1988, Sch 19AB where payments of interest on relevant gilt-edged securities are made without deduction of tax to insurance companies carrying on pension business. The regulations apply to friendly societies carrying on pension business as they apply to insurance companies carrying on pension business.

1664   Schedule D—profits—allowable deductions—revenue payment made wholly or exclusively for purposes of taxpayer's trade

The appellant company formed two subsidiary companies to run a cellular mobile network and to sell cellular mobile telephones. It also entered into an agreement with an American company whereby it was to pay 10 per cent of its pre-tax profits to the American company for a 15-year period in return for its know-how and technical support. The agreement was ended after only three years, upon the appellant making a large payment to the American company. An inspector of taxes decided that although it was a revenue payment, it was not wholly and exclusively expended for the purposes of the appellant's trade and therefore could not be treated as a deduction for the purposes of the Income and Corporation Taxes Act 1970, s 130(a). The decision was upheld by special commissioners. On the appellant's further appeal, *held*, a payment made under a contract which did not go to the heart of the structure of a company's profit-generating apparatus was not a capital payment. The special commissioners had therefore not erred in deciding that it was a revenue payment. The appellant and its subsidiary companies were regarded as one trading entity and not as three separate companies with their own distinct business. Since the payment was intended to benefit the trade of all three companies, the special commissioners were correct in deciding that the payment was not made wholly and exclusively for the benefit of the appellant's business. Accordingly, the appeal would be dismissed.

Vodafone Cellular Ltd v Shaw (Inspector of Taxes) [1995] STC 353 (Chancery Division: Jacob J). 1970 Act, s 130 now Income and Corporation Taxes Act 1988, s 74.

1665   Schedule D—profits—annual profits or gains arising or accruing from profession or vocation

The taxpayer, a poet and novelist, sold his manuscripts and working papers to a university for a sum payable in three yearly instalments. He retained copyright in all his works. He appealed against an assessment to income tax on the first instalment of the purchase price, contending that he had sold only his notebooks and memorabilia, not his completed works, and that as such material was not a professional product the payment received in respect of it was not taxable as a profit of his profession. He contended that as there was no relief where working papers and manuscripts were sold similar to that granted under the Income and Corporation Taxes Act 1988, ss 534, 535 to authors and others who received lump sum payments in return for selling the copyright in their work, Parliament could not have intended proceeds from sales of working papers and manuscripts to be taxable as income. *Held*, the taxpayer had sold part of the fruits of his profession. All property rights created in the course of any profession and turned to profit were taxable as part of the activities of the profession if created during the continuation of the profession. Accordingly, the sum in question was taxable as a profit under Schedule D, Case II. Further, when the provisions granting relief to authors who sold copyright in their work were first enacted, Parliament would have been aware of the interest in authors' working papers and manuscripts but had not, for whatever reason, granted relief to authors who sold manuscripts without copyright. The appeal would be dismissed.

Wain v Cameron (Inspector of Taxes) [1995] STC 555 (Chancery Division: Harman J).

1666   Schedule D—profits—life assurance business—apportionment of receipts of participating funds—applicable percentage

The Life Assurance (Apportionment of Receipts of Participating Funds) (Applicable Percentage) (Amendment) Order 1995, SI 1995/1211 (in force on 24 May 1995), further amends the 1990 Order, SI 1990/1541, by providing for the calculation of the specified net investment yield to be made by reference to 'linked assets' within the meaning of the Income and Corporation Taxes Act 1988, s 432ZA instead of by reference to assets linked solely to a particular category of business.

1667   Schedule D—receipts of insurance and personal pension scheme commissions

The Inland Revenue has issued Statement of Practice SP 5/95, which replaces Statement of Practice SP 3/79, concerning the taxation implications of receipts of commission on the sale of any insurance policies, life annuity contracts, capital redemption policies and personal pension schemes. The statement covers commissions on policies and contracts for a policyholders own benefit, commissions arising from policies sold to third parties and commissions in respect of an employee's own policy. The statement also explains the effects of commission on the qualifying status of life insurance policies, on tax charges that may arise with certain types of insurance and on tax relief for contributions to personal pension schemes. See further *STI*, 6 April 1995.

1668   Schedule D—trading—determination of whether activity a trade

A sports association was a company limited by guarantee whose objects were to encourage interest in the Olympic games and to organise and co-ordinate British participation in the games. One of its chief functions was to assist the preparation, and to fund the sending, of a British team to each Olympic games. Funds were raised by granting to commercial sponsors the right to exploit the association's logo, by licensing the production of articles bearing the logo, and from public donations. Its other functions included upholding the ideals of the Olympic movement and conveying such ideals to the youth of Great Britain. It was assessed to corporation tax on the basis that it was carrying on a trade of exploiting its logo and granting the status of sponsor. On appeal, *held*, in determining whether a venture was in the nature of trade the question was whether the operations involved in the venture were of the same kind, and carried on in the same way, as those which were characteristic of ordinary trading in the line of business in which the venture was made. The association carried out numerous operations and activities in pursuance of its various objects but those activities were so intertwined that it was not possible to isolate any one of them for the purposes of determining whether or not a trade was being carried on. The earning of the sponsorship income was not derived simply from the grant by the association of the right to use its logo but was connected to other activities of the association which were of a non-commercial nature. Its activities as a whole were non-commercial so that it could not be said that it was carrying on a trade. Accordingly, its appeal would be allowed.

British Olympic Association v Winter (Inspector of Taxes) [1995] STC (SCD) 85 (Special Commissioner's decision). Dicta of Lord President Clyde in *IRC v Livingstone* (1927) 11 TC 538 at 542, CS, applied.

1669 Schedule E—emoluments from office or employment—car for private use—cost of insurance paid by employee

Scotland

The taxpayer's employers provided him with a car which was available for his private use. He paid an amount towards the private use of the car and was also responsible for arranging and financing its insurance for both private and business use, although his employers contributed towards the cost of insurance in respect of each mile travelled on business. It fell to be determined whether, in calculating the cash equivalent of the benefit, the cost of insurance was deductible. *Held,* a reduction of the cash equivalent of the benefit under the Income and Corporation Taxes Act 1988, Sch 6, para 4 was permissible only if (1) the payments were payments which the employee was required to make as a condition of the car being available for his private use. Voluntary payments by him for whatever purpose could not be brought into account; and (2) the payments were made by the employee for the use of the car for his private use. Payments made by him for some other purpose, or to entitle him to some other benefit, had also to be left out of account. It was clear that the taxpayer had been required to pay for the insurance by his agreement with his employers. The payments had, however, been made in respect of, or in exchange for, the insurance of the vehicle, not for the use of it. Thus, the payments which the taxpayer had made for the insurance were made for a purpose different than for the private use of the vehicle. He was not entitled to bring the payments which he had made for the insurance into account by way of reduction of the cash equivalent of the benefit of the car for his private use.

IRC v Quigley [1995] STC 931 (Inner House).

1670 Schedule E—emoluments from office or employment—car for private use—payment by employee to obtain more expensive car

In order to obtain a more expensive car than that which he would otherwise have been entitled to as an essential car user within his employer's grading system, the taxpayer agreed to pay to his employer the difference between the respective cost of each car. The car was available for the taxpayer's private use but he was not required to contribute for such use. He was assessed to income tax, under the Income and Corporation Taxes Act 1988, s 157, on an amount equal to the cash equivalent of the benefit of the car. He appealed against the refusal of his claim to exemption from payment of tax on the sum which he had contributed to his employer, contending that he should not be taxed on a benefit which he had in fact provided for himself, that his contribution towards the cost of the car was not a benefit and that he was to be taxed on the perceived benefit and not on the car. *Held,* a reduction in the cash equivalent of the benefit of the car was provided for in the event of the employee being required as a condition of the car being available for his private use to pay any amount of money for that use. There was no provision for a reduction in the cash benefit in the event of the employee paying to the employer a sum of money in order to obtain a better car than the employer was prepared to provide. Further, no reduction could be claimed under s 157(3), which dealt not with payments by the employee but with payments made to him or on his behalf. Accordingly, the appeal would be dismissed.

Brown v Ware (Inspector of Taxes) [1995] STC (SCD) 155 (Special Commissioner's decision).

1671 Schedule E—emoluments from office or employment—car fuel—cash equivalent of benefit

The Income Tax (Cash Equivalents of Car Fuel Benefits) Order 1995, SI 1995/3035 (in force on 6 April 1996), replaces the tables, set out in the Income and Corporation Taxes Act 1988, s 158(2), which specify the flat rate cash equivalents of the benefit of any car made available for a person's private use by reason of his employment.

1672 Schedule E—emoluments from office or employment—expenses—travelling expenses

The taxpayer owned a company ('the first company') of which he was a director and the sole employee. It supplied computer and management consultant services to a second company. The first company's registered office was at the taxpayer's place of residence which was about 80 miles away from the premises at which he provided his services to the second company. The taxpayer purchased a flat near those premises; he used the flat on weekdays while he worked at the second company's offices and returned to the first company's registered office and worked there on its affairs at weekends. It fell to be determined whether his expenses in travelling between the first company's registered office and the second company's offices was deductible under the Income and Corporation Taxes Act 1988, s 198. *Held*, the question was whether the expenditure on journeys made by the taxpayer from his home to his work place at the second company's offices was incurred 'wholly, exclusively and necessarily in the performance of' the duties of his employment within the meaning of s 198(1). At all material times, he was a computer consultant employed by his own company. He purchased the flat to save himself the trouble of two daily journeys of about 80 miles between his home and the second company's offices. He could have moved and established his own company's registered office near the second company's offices. In his journeys between the latter offices and his home, he was merely going to and from his home. His travel costs so incurred were not necessarily incurred by him in the performance of his duties and, accordingly, were not deductible under s 198.

Miners v Atkinson (Inspector of Taxes) (1995) Times, 28 November (Chancery Division: Arden J). Decision of Special Commissioner [1995] STC (SCD) 64 affirmed. *Taylor v Proven* [1974] 1 All ER 1201, HL (1974 Abr para 1694), applied.

1673 Schedule E—emoluments from office or employment—office accommodation in employee's home

The taxpayer lived and worked in London. He was offered a post with a company based in Warwickshire commencing on 1 May 1991. As he wished neither to move nor commute to Warwickshire, the company agreed to pay for the conversion of the loft at his home to an office. It paid the builders for the estimated cost of the works in full before 1 April 1991. The loft was available for the taxpayer to work in by September 1991 until which time he worked in another room in the house. From 1 April 1991, the company paid rent to the taxpayer in respect of the part of the house occupied by it. The taxpayer was assessed to income tax under Schedule E on the whole cost of the conversion as the provision of a benefit in kind within the Income and Corporation Taxes Act 1988, s 154. He appealed against the assessment, contending that the benefit was not assessable as it had been provided during the tax year 1990–91 which was before the commencement of his employment with the company. *Held*, the use of the word 'provide' in s 154 rather than other terminology such as 'make available' supported the view that the term had been used in the sense of making future provision rather than physically providing. Moreover, the company had done everything before 6 April 1991 which it had to do in order to fulfil its commitment: it had agreed with the taxpayer that it would pay for the conversion; it had contracted with the builders for the work, and had made payment in full; and it had agreed with the taxpayer that it would become his tenant in respect of the loft at a specified rent. The benefit, therefore, had been provided in the year 1990–91. As the taxpayer's employment with the company had not commenced until 1 May 1991, it did not fall within the terms of s 154. The appeal would be allowed.

Jacobs v Templeton (Inspector of Taxes) [1995] STC (SCD) 150 (Special Commissioner's decision).

1674 Schedule E—emoluments from office or employment—profit-related pay—shortfall recovery

The Profit-Related Pay (Shortfall Recovery) Regulations 1995, SI 1995/917 (in force on 19 April 1995), replace the 1988 Regulations, SI 1988/640, and now provide for unpaid amounts of shortfall in deductions made under PAYE to carry interest. SI 1993/2276 is amended.

1675 Schedule E—emoluments from office or employment—voluntary payment—bonus

The taxpayer received a bonus payment from his employers in respect of the tax year 1987–88, when the top rate of tax was 60 per cent. Payment of the bonus was deferred until the beginning of the tax year 1988–89, when the top rate of tax had been reduced to 40 per cent. It fell to be determined whether the bonus was assessable to tax for 1987–88 or 1988–89. *Held*, there was no presumption that a payment was for the year in which it was paid. The employers had resolved to make the bonus payment in the tax year 1987–88 in respect of that year but had invited the taxpayer to defer his receipt of the payment until the following tax year. The bonus could not be made taxable in a year to which it did not relate simply by deferring its payment and, accordingly, should be treated as the taxpayer's income for 1987–88.

Griffin (Inspector of Taxes) v Standish [1995] STC 825 (Chancery Division: Sir John Vinelott). Dictum of Lord Oliver of Aylmerton in *Bray (Inspector of Taxes) v Best* [1989] 1 All ER 969, HL (1989 Abr para 1254) applied.

1676 Securities—dealers in securities—Tradepoint

The Income Tax (Dealers in Securities) (Tradepoint) Regulations 1995, SI 1995/2050 (in force on 25 August 1995), provide exemption, in certain circumstances, from the bond washing provisions in the Income and Corporation Taxes Act 1988, s 732 for dealers in securities on the Exchange known as Tradepoint who are clearing participants in that Exchange, and for The London Clearing House Limited through whom transactions in Tradepoint are cleared.

1677 Securities—sale and repurchase—deemed manufactured payments

See para 1636.

1678 Securities—sale and repurchase—modification of enactments

The Sale and Repurchase of Securities (Modification of Enactments) Regulations 1995, SI 1995/3220 (in force on 2 January 1996), modify the Income and Corporation Taxes Act 1988 and the Taxation of Chargeable Gains Act 1992, in relation to the tax treatment of transactions involving the sale and repurchase of securities, in circumstances where the securities are redeemed instead of repurchased, and where other securities are substituted for those originally transferred.

1679 Special classes—Lloyd's underwriters

The Lloyd's Underwriters (Tax) Regulations 1995, SI 1995/351 (in force on 9 March 1995), provide for the taxation of underwriting members of Lloyd's by supplementing provisions contained in the Finance Act 1993 relating to individual members, and the Finance Act 1994 relating to corporate members. The regulations have effect from the year of assessment 1992–93 in their application to members who are individuals, and from the underwriting year 1994 in their application to corporate members. The definitions of 'managing agent' are extended and provision is made for the assessment and collection of tax on the profits arising from a member's underwriting business, on insurance money payable to an individual member under a stop-loss insurance in respect of a loss in his underwriting business or in connection with an amount payable to a member out of the High Level Stop Loss Fund in respect of such a loss and similar provision is made in connection with insurance money payable to a corporate member. Provision is made for an extension of time for delivery of a return of a syndicate profit or loss or a return apportioning a syndicate profit or loss, and for reasonable excuse for failure to deliver such a return. Provision is also made in relation to the taxation of an individual member and his business upon cessation of the business. SIs 1974/896, 1330, and 1990/2524 are revoked.

The Lloyd's Underwriters (Tax) (1992–93 to 1996–97) Regulations 1995, SI 1995/352 (in force on 9 March 1995), which have effect for the years of assessment from 1992–93 to 1996–97, make provision in relation to the assessment and collection of tax from underwriting members of Lloyd's. They extend the definition of 'members' agent' in the Finance Act 1993, specify the dates on which tax charged by an assessment on underwriting profits or syndicate gains is payable, and extend the time limits for certain tax assessments. Provision is also made for relief if an error is made in a return by a members' agent and for profits and losses of running off syndicates to be allocated to underwriting years.

The Lloyd's Underwriters (Special Reserve Funds) Regulations 1995, SI 1995/353 (in force on 9 March 1995), make provision relating to special reserve funds of Lloyd's underwriting members other than corporate members. They provide that a member's profits or losses arising from membership of a syndicate in a run-off underwriting year are attributable to the last underwriting year but one preceding the relevant run-off year. The time limits for payments out of or into a special reserve fund and the manner of determining the value of such a fund, are specified.

Provision is made regarding personal representatives of a deceased member who carry on his underwriting business. The definitions of 'the penultimate underwriting year', 'the relevant underwriting year' and 'the relevant year of assessment' in the Finance Act 1994 are extended to cover certain situations occurring on the death of a member. Except where otherwise provided, the regulations have effect for the year of assessment 1992–93 and subsequent years of assessment.

The Lloyd's Underwriters (Special Reserve Funds) (Amendment) Regulations 1995, SI 1995/1185 (in force on 23 May 1995), amend SI 1995/353 supra, by (1) extending the meaning of 'special reserve fund' in certain provisions of the Finance Act 1993, Sch 20, Pt I, so as to include income arising after the death of an underwriting member from assets of his special reserve fund where the income is retained by the trustees and invested, and profits arising from the investment of that income; (2) extending Sch 20, para 9, concerning tax exemption for profits arising from assets of special reserve funds, so that the tax exemptions thereby conferred apply to profits arising after the death of the member from retained income; (3) extending Sch 20, para 11, concerning the tax consequences of cessation, so that the charge to tax under that provision applies to payments made to a member out of his special reserve fund to payments of retained income made after the member's death to his personal representatives.

1680 Taxation of damages—damages awarded to Lloyd's names

See *Deeny v Gooda Walker Ltd,* para 1737.

1681 Transaction in securities—tax advantage—abnormal amount by way of dividend

The taxpayer, as trustee of an approved pension scheme, was entitled to exemption from income tax. It participated in the development of a business park by lending £25m to the development company, and by subscribing for shares in the company which carried with them an option entitling the holder to require the company's parent company to buy the shares for 7.5 per cent of a net asset valuation of the company's interest in the development. In consideration of the option, the rate of interest on the loan to the company was fixed below the market rate. The taxpayer decided to realise its investment and, accordingly, to exercise the option. The figure at which the company's parent company was required to purchase the shares was valued at £3,517,000 but, after negotiations, it was agreed that the company would purchase the shares itself instead for £2,662,750. That payment gave rise to a distribution of £2,562,750 by the company which, when aggregated with the associated tax credit of £854,250, resulted in the taxpayer receiving £3,517,000 in total. It received repayment of the tax credit but was subsequently informed that an adjustment was required under the Income and Corporation Taxes Act 1988, s 703(3) on the basis that the taxpayer had obtained a tax advantage, in the circumstances mentioned in s 704, para A, by receiving an abnormal amount by way of dividend which had been taken into account for an exemption from tax. On appeal by the taxpayer, *held,* in the absence of evidence as to the reason for the change in the purchaser of the A shares, the substitution of a sale for a consideration of £2,662,750 in place of a right to sell for £3,517,000 could not be viewed as carried out for bona fide commercial reasons nor as in the ordinary course of making or managing investments. However, the consideration provided by the taxpayer for the shares had included its agreement to accept a lower rate of interest on its loan to the company. In addition, the investment was speculative and a speculative investment would normally attract a higher rate of return. The Inland Revenue had failed to discharge its burden of proving that the distribution was of an abnormal amount. In any event, an exemption from tax of the type enjoyed by the taxpayer did not result in the obtaining of a tax advantage. The appeal would be allowed.

Universities Superannuation Scheme Ltd v IRC [1995] STC (SCD) 21 (Special Commissioner's decision). *Sheppard (Trustees of the Woodlands Trust) v IRC (No 2)* [1993] STC 240 (1993 Abr para 1482) applied.

1682 Unpaid tax—interest

The Taxes (Interest Rate) (Amendment) Regulations 1995, SI 1995/2436 (in force on 6 October 1995), further amend the 1989 Regulations, SI 1989/1297, by providing for an official rate of interest of 8 per cent per annum in connection with beneficial loans generally.

1683 Venture capital trusts

The Venture Capital Trust Regulations 1995, SI 1995/1979 (in force on 16 August 1995), make provision for the approval of a company as a venture capital trust for the purposes of the

Income and Corporation Taxes Act 1988, s 842AA, and for the reliefs from income tax in respect of investments in, and distributions by, such trusts. The regulations also make provision for the delivery to the Commissioners of Inland Revenue of returns containing particulars of investments, for the records to be kept, for the provision of information to the commissioners and the inspection of records by their officer.

INDUSTRIAL AND PROVIDENT SOCIETIES

Halsbury's Laws of England (4th edn) Vol 24 (reissue), paras 1–200

1684 Credit unions

The Industrial and Provident Societies (Credit Unions) (Amendment of Fees) Regulations 1995, SI 1995/712 (in force on 1 April 1995), which revoke SI 1994/658, further amend the 1979 Regulations, SI 1979/937, so as to increase by about 13 per cent the fees to be paid for matters transacted under the Industrial and Provident Societies Acts 1965 and 1967 and the Credit Unions Act 1979. The fees have been revised and restructured so that costs are spread more equitably by requiring all societies to pay an annual fee (as is already the case for the vast majority of friendly societies). The new annual fee will first apply to annual returns for societies' financial years on or after 31 August 1995. In the meantime, the charges for transactions during the 1995–96 financial year have been revised to relate them more closely to the cost of delivering services. Charges for inspection of documents have been increased from £4.50 to £8, and associated fees have been increased by a comparable amount.

1685 Fees

The Industrial and Provident Societies (Amendment of Fees) Regulations 1995, SI 1995/713 (in force on 1 April 1995), which revoke SI 1994/660, further amend the 1965 Regulations, SI 1965/1995, and the 1967 Regulations, SI 1967/1310, so as to increase by about 13% the fees to be paid for matters transacted under the Industrial and Provident Societies Acts 1965 and 1967. The fees have been revised and restructured so that costs are spread more equitably by requiring all societies to pay an annual fee (as is already the case for the vast majority of friendly societies). The new annual fee will first apply to annual returns for societies' financial years on or after 31 August 1995. In the meantime, the charges for transactions during the 1995–96 financial year have been revised to relate them more closely to the cost of delivering services. Charges for inspection of documents have been increased from £4.50 to £8, and associated fees have been increased by a comparable amount.

INHERITANCE TAXATION

Halsbury's Laws of England (4th edn) Vol 24 (reissue), paras 401–800

1686 Articles

Crystal Ball Gazing, Gareth Jones (on long-term inheritance tax planning advice): 139 SJ 828
Making Provision for the Mentally Disabled, Francis Fitzpatrick: Tax Journal, Issue 317, p 8

1687 Agricultural property—definition for purposes of inheritance tax

It fell to be determined whether a two and a half acre site, containing a substantial six-bedroomed farmhouse and an assortment of outbuildings together with several small areas of enclosed land, used by the deceased as part of a medium-sized farm which carried on mixed farming, constituted agricultural land or pasture qualifying for agricultural property relief from inheritance tax under the Inheritance Tax Act 1984, s 116. Agricultural property is defined in s 115(2) as agricultural land or pasture and includes woodland and any building used in connection with the intensive rearing of livestock or fish if the woodland or building is occupied with agricultural land or pasture and the occupation is ancillary to that of the agricultural land or pasture; and also includes such cottages, farm buildings and farmhouses, together with the land occupied with them, as are of a character appropriate to the property. *Held,* the Interpretation Act 1978, s 5, Sch 1 required 'land' to be read as including 'buildings and other structures' unless the contrary intention appeared. The intention that 'buildings and other structures' should not be read into the word 'land' had to appear, if at all, from other parts of the definition or the Act. The third part of the definition in the 1984 Act, s 115(2) referred expressly to the buildings and structures that would be most obviously included in the words 'agricultural land' if the 1978 Act applied in full. Considering the definition as a whole, with the exception of the inclusion of 'woodland' all that followed the words 'agricultural land or pasture' in the 1984 Act, s 115(2) was concerned with buildings which were to be included. The general structure of the definition showed a contrary intention sufficient to exclude from the inclusions in the word 'land' otherwise required by the 1978 Act, s 5, Sch 1 the words 'buildings and other structures'. Accordingly, the property in question did not fall within the definition of agricultural property and did not qualify for relief from inheritance tax.

Starke v IRC [1995] STC 689 (Court of Appeal: Stuart-Smith, Morritt and Ward LJJ). Decision of Blackburne J [1994] STC 295 (1994 Abr para 1640) affirmed.

1688 Delivery of accounts

The Inheritance Tax (Delivery of Accounts) Regulations 1995, SI 1995/1461 (in force on 1 July 1995), amend the 1981 Regulations, SI 1981/880, by increasing the amount of the value of an estate in respect of which no account need be delivered from £125,000 to £145,000 in respect of deaths on or after 6 April 1995.

1689 Exempt transfers and reliefs—business property—exclusion from relief—holding investments

The deceased owned a house divided into four furnished flats which were let on assured shorthold tenancies. The letting of the flats had been carried on by her as a business. Her executor's claim to business property relief was refused on the ground that the property was not relevant business property as the deceased's business had consisted mainly of holding investments and was therefore excluded from relief by the Inheritance Tax Act 1984, s 105(3). Her executor appealed, contending that the deceased's business had been an active one which had amounted to more than, and had been essentially different to, one consisting of making or holding investments. *Held*, a distinction had to be drawn between activities of a property letting business which were carried out qua landlord of the investment property and activities that were independent of that relationship. Activities of the former class were activities of 'holding investments' however onerous the landlord's obligations might be and however much the landlord had been involved in the control or management of the property letting business. In the present case, the whole gain derived by the deceased from the property came to her as rent. It arose entirely from the investment in the property and the leases granted out of it. The business was, therefore, wholly one of making or holding investments and so the property was excluded from being 'relevant business property' by the words of s 105(3). Accordingly, the appeal would be dismissed.

Burkinyoung (Burkinyoung's executor) v IRC [1995] STC (SCD) 29 (Special Commissioner's decision). *Martin (executors of Moore deceased) v IRC* [1995] STC (SCD) 5, para 1690, applied.

1690 Exempt transfers and reliefs—business property—relevant property

The deceased had carried on a business of owning and letting industrial units on three-year leases at fixed rents. In the course of that business, she sought and chose tenants, granted and renewed leases, complied with landlord's covenants and managed the premises. The Inland Revenue refused to grant business property relief to her executors on the ground that, by virtue of the Inheritance Tax Act 1984, s 105(3), the property was not relevant business property as the deceased's activities had constituted a business consisting wholly or mainly of making or holding investments. On appeal by the executors, *held*, the words of exclusion in a relieving provision should not be given an unnaturally restricted meaning. Section 105(3) did not distinguish between an active and passive investment business and there was no implication that the words 'business . . . of . . . holding investments' in that provision were to be confined to passive investment. The deceased's activities had fallen into three categories: the making of investments, such as finding tenants and granting leases; compliance, such as exterior painting and repairs; and management, such as handling tenants' complaints. The first two categories were clearly activities of, or attributable to, the making or holding of investments; and the third category covered activities that were incidents of the business of holding investments. All of the activities were part and parcel of the business of making or holding investments, and business property relief was therefore excluded by s 105(3). Accordingly, the appeal would be dismissed.

Martin (executors of Moore deceased) v IRC [1995] STC (SCD) 5 (Special Commissioner's decision). *Fry (Inspector of Taxes) v Salisbury House Estate Ltd* (1929) 15 TC 266, CA, considered.

1691 Exempt transfers and reliefs—business property—shareholder—control of business—portion of shares held by infant

The Inheritance Tax Act 1984, s 269(1) provides that, for the purposes of the Act, a person has control of a company at any time if he then has control of powers of voting on all questions affecting the company as a whole which if exercised would yield a majority of the votes capable of being exercised on them.

The executors of an estate appealed against a notice of determination by the Inland Revenue that at the time of her death a shareholder did not have control of a business so that the property comprised in her estate did not qualify for relief under the 1984 Act, s 104. Almost a quarter of the shares were held by an infant and it was argued that, as the child was not in a position to exercise his voting rights, the deceased shareholder had control of the business at the time of her death. *Held*, the 1984 Act, s 269(1) was concerned with the ambit of powers of voting and not with the particular capabilities of the shareholders in whose names the votes were registered. Such a construction afforded to all shareholders an equal right to claim relief irrespective of their mental or physical capacities. Accordingly, it was correct to take account of the infant's shareholding when making a determination under s 269(1) and the appeal would be dismissed.

Walding's Executors v IRC [1996] STC 13 (Chancery Division: Knox J).

1692 Exempt transfers and reliefs—gift to charity—exclusively charitable purposes

See *Re Segelman (deceased)*, para 3084.

1693 Exempt transfers and reliefs—normal expenditure out of income—transfer of surplus income

By his will the testator bequeathed his shares in a family company and the residue of his estate to his trustees on trust to pay the income to his widow for her life and subject thereto to his three sons, the taxpayers. Prior to the sale by the trustees of their holding in the company in return for shares in another company and a cash consideration, the gross income of the trust fund was small but adequate for the needs of the widow. After the sale, the income of the trust increased enormously. The widow had a modest lifestyle and she told the taxpayers that while she lived she wanted them to have the surplus income of the trust beyond the limited periodic payments she needed to meet her needs. She executed a form of authority addressed to the trustees authorising them to distribute equally between the taxpayers 'all or any of the income arising in each accounting year as is surplus to my financial requirements of which you are already aware'. Payments were made to each of the taxpayers pursuant to the authority. Those payments did not amount to the entire surplus income in the relevant accounting years as a conservative approach had been adopted in the administration of the trust which had resulted in delays in determining the surplus available for distribution. The widow died unexpectedly and the Revenue took the view that the gifts by her were potentially exempt transfers which became subject to inheritance tax on her death. The taxpayers appealed contending that the gifts were exempt transfers by virtue of the Inheritance Tax Act 1984, s 21 in that they had been made as part of the normal expenditure of the widow. *Held*, in the context of s 21, the term 'normal expenditure' connoted expenditure which at the time it took place accorded with the settled pattern of expenditure adopted by the transferor. The existence of such a settled pattern might be established either by reference to a sequence of payments by the transferor out of past expenditure, or by proof of a prior commitment or resolution adopted by the transferor regarding his future expenditure. In the instant case, the evidence had established that the widow had made a considered determination for the rest of her life to give to the taxpayers all her surplus income from the trust beyond what she reasonably required for maintenance, and that her determination had been implemented by the execution of the authority requesting the trustees to act accordingly and their so acting. That the trustees had acted in accordance with her determination was none the less so because they had acted conservatively in assessing the distributable income and hence the surplus available to the taxpayers. The widow had therefore adopted a pattern of expenditure in respect of the surplus income, and the payments to the taxpayers had been made in accordance with that pattern and were accordingly part of her normal expenditure within the meaning of s 21. The Revenue's determinations would therefore be quashed.

Bennett v IRC [1995] STC 54 (Chancery Division: Lightman J).

1694 Finance Act 1995

See para 2489.

1695 Lifetime transfer—reservation of benefit—gift of part of property

Under a scheme designed to avoid inheritance tax, the taxpayer transferred certain freehold property to her solicitor who, on the same day, declared that he held the property as nominee for the taxpayer. The following day, the solicitor granted two 20-year, rent-free, leases, extending to the whole of the property, to the taxpayer. The next day, the solicitor transferred the property, subject to the leases, to the trustees, the taxpayer's two sons and her grandson. They executed two declarations of trust constituting themselves as trustees of a settlement under which the property, subject to the leases in the taxpayer's favour, was to be held for the benefit of certain beneficiaries. On the taxpayer's death, the property was assessed to inheritance tax on the basis that it was 'property subject to a reservation' within the Finance Act 1986, s 102(2) and was, therefore, to be treated as property to which the taxpayer was beneficially entitled immediately before her death. On the executors' appeal against the assessment, *held*, a contract of lease involved the creation of mutual rights and obligations which could only be given any meaning if the contract was between two independent parties. A nominee could not grant an effective lease to his principal because no person could contract with himself. The leases purportedly granted by the solicitor to the taxpayer were a nullity. The trustees, having taken the legal estate in fee simple as volunteers on the basis that it was subject to leases in favour of the taxpayer, could not claim, on behalf of their beneficiaries, to take the legal estate free from the interests purportedly granted to the taxpayer by the leases. Equity would compel them to recognise and give effect to those interests, so that in equity the taxpayer had interests equivalent to those which she thought she had acquired in law by virtue of the leases. The taxpayer had acquired those interests simultaneously with the execution of the declarations of trust, which brought into existence for the first time beneficial interests in the property in favour of persons other than the taxpayer. At no time had the trustees and beneficiaries a more extensive interest out of which the leasehold interests had been carved. The subject matter of the gift made by the taxpayer was the property shorn of those leasehold interests. It was not property subject to a reservation for the purposes of s 102 and, accordingly, the appeal would be allowed.

Ingram v IRC [1995] STC 564 (Chancery Division: Ferris J). *Grey v Ellison* (1856) 1 Giff 438, *Henderson v Astwood* [1894] AC 150, PC, and dicta of Lord Radcliffe in *St Aubyn v A-G* [1952] AC 15 at 49, HL, applied. *Kildrummy (Jersey) Ltd v IRC* [1990] STC 657, Inner House (1990 Abr para 2355), followed. *Nichols v IRC* [1975] 2 All ER 120, CA (1975 Abr para 1632), considered.

1696 Overpayment of tax—repayment

See para 1643.

1697 Rate of tax

The Inheritance Tax (Indexation) Order 1995, SI 1995/3032 (made on 28 November 1995), prescribes a single rate of inheritance tax of 40 per cent on a person's chargeable transfers in excess of the nil rate threshold of £160,000. The order applies to chargeable transfers on or after 6 April 1996 unless Parliament otherwise determines.

1698 Valuation—assets—partnership—share of agricultural tenancy

The Finance Act 1975, s 38(1) provides that the value at any time of any property for the purposes of capital transfer tax is the price which the property might reasonably be expected to fetch if sold on the open market at that time.

The deceased carried on a farming partnership with his son. The freehold of the farm was jointly owned by himself and his two sons. The agricultural tenancy by which the farm was let to the farming partnership required a partner to live in the farm house and prohibited its assignment without the consent of the freeholders. It fell to be determined how, for the purposes of the 1975 Act, s 38, the deceased's share of the partnership assets, and particularly his share in the agricultural tenancy, should be valued. *Held*, the property that was the subject of the deemed transfer was the deceased's undivided beneficial interest in the partnership's assets including the undivided beneficial interest in the tenancy. It was wrong to value the partnership assets as a whole for the purposes of s 38 and then divide by two. Section 38 required there to be a hypothetical sale of the undivided beneficial interest in the tenancy. However, it was not necessary for the operation of the statutory hypothesis of a sale in the open market that the freeholder be treated as a hypothetical person. The sale was to be assumed to take place in the real world and, accordingly, the personal characteristics of the actual freeholder were to be taken into account. Consequently, it was material that the deemed transferee in the present case would not have been able to offer the tenancy on the open market, since it was unassignable without the freeholders' consent. Likewise, as the deceased owned an interest in a tenancy that was a partnership asset, it was material that any transferee would not be able to assign the interest in the tenancy without the consent of the actual surviving partner.

Walton v IRC [1996] STC 68 (Court of Appeal: Evans, Peter Gibson and Henry LJJ).

1975 Act, s 38 now Inheritance Tax Act 1984, s 160.

INJUNCTIONS

Halsbury's Laws of England (4th edn) Vol 24 (reissue), paras 801–1100

1699 Articles

Injunctions v Bail Conditions, Margaret Crissel (on the comparison between injunctions and conditional bail in domestic violence cases): [1995] Fam Law 85

Losing Privilege by Mistake, Tony Davies (on whether a party who mistakenly discloses a privileged document can prevent its being used in evidence): 139 SJ 584

The 'Mareva', the Magistrates and the Child Support Act, Susan Spencer: 159 JP Jo 821

Mercedes and Mareva, Steven Gee (on *Mercedes-Benz AG v Leiduck* [1995] 3 All ER 929, PC (para 2375)): 139 SJ 1076

Progress on Piller, Richard Fox (on Practice Direction (Anton Piller Orders and Mareva Injunctions) [1994] 4 All ER 52 (1994 Abr para 1648)): LS Gaz, 7 June 1995, p 22

The £694 Question, Roger Cohen (on the proper remedy for infringement of property rights): Estates Gazette, 4 February 1995, p 158

1700 Anton Piller order—trademark infringement—order to supply information—self-incrimination—risk of violence to defendant

The plaintiffs claimed that the defendant was a member of a large-scale criminal organisation which had infringed the plaintiffs' trademark. They obtained an Anton Piller order against the defendant which required him to provide them with addresses used by the organisation and the names of other people involved. The defendant applied for a discharge of that part of the order on the ground that the information would incriminate him in criminal proceedings and put him and his family at risk of violent reprisals from the other members of the organisation. *Held*, the first ground for the defendant's application had no substance since, under the Supreme Court Act 1981, s 72, the fact that a person might incriminate himself in criminal proceedings did not excuse him from complying with an order made in proceedings for trademark infringement or passing off. Furthermore, the public interest and the right of the plaintiffs to obtain the information necessary to protect and preserve their interests outweighed the defendant's interests in avoiding any risk of violence to which disclosure might expose him. Accordingly, the defendant's application would be dismissed and he would be ordered to comply with the order for disclosure without delay.

Coca-Cola Co v Gilbey [1995] 4 All ER 711 (Chancery Division: Lightman J).

1701 Damages in lieu of injunction—discretion—grant of restricted injunction

In an action for patent infringement, the court found that the plaintiff's patent was valid (save for certain claims not sued upon) and infringed, but that the defendant had a defence under the Patents Act 1977, s 44. The plaintiff amended the patent by deleting the invalid claims and varied the agreements which had given rise to the s 44 defence. It then issued proceedings against the same defendant for infringement of the same patent, and sought summary judgment under RSC Ord 14. By consent, inquiries as to damages were ordered, but the question of whether injunctions should be granted was reserved. The defendant did not oppose the grant of the injunctions, but argued that they should be limited in scope and stayed pending appeal. *Held*, the court had power under the Supreme Court Act 1981, s 50 to award damages instead of an injunction, and this included the power to award a restricted injunction and to award damages as compensation for the restriction. In exercising the discretion under s 50, the court had to follow the guidelines in *Shelfer v City of London Electric Lighting Co* [1895] 1 Ch 287. In most cases the approach suggested in *Shelfer* would be sufficient to decide whether damages should be granted instead of an injunction. However, in appropriate circumstances, the court had to take account of the interests of persons who would be affected by the grant of the injunction. That might involve considering the interests of the public. It was inherent in any patent system that a patentee would acquire a monopoly, thereby restricting competition and maintaining prices. This was contrary to the public interest, but safeguards to protect the public against the abuse of those rights were contained in the 1977 Act and an injunction would normally be granted restraining infringement unless the contrary was indicated in the 1977 Act. Something more had to be established before the court would depart from this rule. In the present case, the injunctions would not be limited and would not be stayed.

Chiron Corpn v Organon Teknika Ltd (No 10); Chiron Corpn v Murex Diagnostics Ltd (No 10) [1995] FSR 325 (Chancery Division: Aldous J).

1702 Foreign proceedings—injunction to restrain

See CONFLICT OF LAWS.

1703 Injunction to restrain bankrupt from leaving jurisdiction—power of court to grant injunction—duties of bankrupt

See *Morris v Murjani*, para 168.

1704 Injunction to restrain copyright infringement—innocent and technical infringement—public policy

See *ZYX Music GmbH v King*, para 680.

1705 Injunction to restrain media from identifying child—proposed television documentary concerning child's education and treatment—mother's application to discharge or vary injunction

See *Re Z (a Minor) (Freedom of Publication)*, para 439.

1706 Injunction to restrain passing off—deception—unintended deception

See *British Diabetic Association v Diabetic Society Ltd*, para 2951.

1707 Interlocutory injunction—action for declaration—jurisdiction

The defendant Welsh football association resolved to prevent Welsh football clubs from playing in leagues organised by the English football association in an effort to promote similar Welsh leagues. Thereafter, the plaintiffs, three Welsh football clubs, resigned from the defendant association and joined the English association, as they wished to continue to take part in the English leagues. The defendant responded by objecting to their playing home matches in Wales, and the English association, honouring that objection, insisted that the plaintiffs played home matches in England. The result was that the plaintiffs' revenue from their home gates and from sponsorship decreased considerably, threatening their continued existence. Having failed to persuade the defendant to reconsider the position, they brought an action seeking (1) declarations to the effect that the defendant's decisions excluding them from playing at home were void as being in unreasonable restraint of trade, and (2) injunctions to prevent the defendant acting in unreasonable restraint of trade. In the meantime, the plaintiffs applied for an interlocutory injunction to allow them to play their home matches in Wales for the following season. The defendant contended that where a declaration was sought in respect of a non-contractual relationship the court had no jurisdiction to grant an interlocutory injunction. *Held*, (1) although a contract or other arrangement in unreasonable restraint of trade was merely void and unenforceable and as such created no wrong, the right of an injured party to bring proceedings for a declaration that the arrangement was null and void was nevertheless a cause of action, giving those words their ordinary English meaning, and that right did not depend on the party being in a contractual relationship with the defendant, so long as he was sufficiently affected by the arrangement. Given that a claim for a declaration of rights was a cause of action, and that the existence of a cause of action founded the jurisdiction to grant an injunction, there were no grounds for saying that an injunction could only be granted in such a case on the final determination of the issues. Rather, the court had the same power to grant an interlocutory injunction where the cause of action was a claim for a declaration as it had where the cause of action was for the invasion of a right, simply on the basis that the claim might be good. Moreover, while it was true that a declaration could only be granted by way of final judgment, an interim injunction in support of a claim for a declaration was not tantamount to the grant of an interim declaration, as it was not a decision on the merits of the claim. It followed that the court had power to grant an interlocutory injunction where the only cause of action was a claim for a declaration by a trader that an arrangement or contract was in unreasonable restraint of trade and that the arrangement or contract was damaging his trade. (2) On the facts, there was a serious issue to be tried. Although the plaintiffs' delay of two years in applying for an interlocutory injunction would normally lead to their application being refused, the present case was wholly exceptional. The plaintiffs' application would therefore be allowed and an injunction granted accordingly.

Newport Association Football Club Ltd v Football Association of Wales Ltd [1995] 2 All ER 87 (Chancery Division: Jacob J).

1708   Interlocutory injunction—injunction to restrain breach of restraint of trade clause—period of injunction

See *Euro Brokers Ltd v Rabey,* para 1214.

1709   Interlocutory injunction—injunction to restrain harassment—exclusion zone order

It has been held that in common law proceedings for harassment, an injunction may be granted to restrain a defendant from entering a designated area if the exclusion zone is necessary for the protection of the plaintiff. Save in respect of Anton Piller orders and Mareva injunctions, a county court has the same power to grant interlocutory injunctions as the High Court. An injunction need not restrain conduct which is in itself tortious or otherwise unlawful. Consequently, an 'exclusion zone' order can be made even though a defendant will not commit a tort or an unlawful act by his mere presence in a particular area. A plaintiff will usually be protected by an injunction restraining the tort which has been or is likely to be committed. However, where the defendant may be tempted to loiter outside the plaintiff's home, his behaviour may be highly stressful to the plaintiff. In such cases a greater measure of restraint may be necessary to protect the rights of the plaintiff, and an exclusion zone order may be appropriate.

Burris v Azadani [1995] 4 All ER 802 (Court of Appeal: Sir Thomas Bingham MR, Millett and Schiemann LJJ).

1710   Interlocutory injunction—injunction to restrain obstruction of justice—articles relating to judicial review proceedings

New Zealand

The applicants had sought judicial review of a decision of a minister fixing various fishing quotas. During the proceedings two of the respondents sought an injunction to prevent the applicants from publishing a series of articles allegedly concerning issues in the proceedings. *Held*, it was not in the interests of justice to exercise the court's discretion in favour of an injunction, since no contempt or likely contempt by the applicants had been identified in respect of the real issues in the proceedings. The matters in respect of which the respondents sought the injunction did not determine the issues relating to the substantive proceedings. Furthermore, they were live public issues which required determination by the minister from year to year. The granting of an injunction would give rise to a clear injustice as it would be impossible to interpret fairly and police. It might also inhibit the applicants' ability to make submissions to the minister in future years. Accordingly, the application for injunctive relief would be refused.

Greenpeace New Zealand Inc v Minister of Fisheries [1995] 2 NZLR 463 (High Court of New Zealand)

1711   Interlocutory injunction—injunction to restrain passing off—misrepresentation

See *Hodge Clemco Ltd v Airblast Ltd,* para 2950.

1712   Mareva injunction—assets within the jurisdiction—service out of the jurisdiction

See *Mercedes-Benz AG v Leiduck,* para 2375.

1713   Mareva injunction—plaintiff's undertaking in damages—discontinuance of action

The plaintiff obtained a Mareva injunction against the defendant with an undertaking that it would comply with any order relating to damages incurred by the defendant resulting from the making of the injunction. The plaintiff subsequently discontinued its action against the defendant because otherwise it was unlikely to recover any more damages and would incur considerable costs. The defendant applied for an order for an inquiry into damage sustained by him as a result of the injunction, and for liberty to enter judgment against the plaintiff for damages. The application was refused and the defendant appealed. *Held*, where an action was discontinued as opposed to abandoned, the court had to consider the circumstances in which it was discontinued before deciding on whether to enforce the plaintiff's undertaking in damages. In this case, the injunction had been obtained properly and the plaintiff had been justified in continuing the action and had only discontinued it when it became apparent that the action could not be usefully continued. Accordingly, the defendant's appeal would be dismissed and the plaintiff's undertaking in damages would not be enforced.

Goldman Sachs International Ltd v Lyons (1995) Times, 28 February (Court of Appeal: Stuart-Smith, Hobhouse and Pill LJJ).

1714   Mareva injunction—substantive claim in magistrates' court governed by statute—application for ancillary relief

A father appealed against the amount of a maintenance assessment made against him although he accepted that he might be liable for arrears under the assessment. The appeal was heard in a magistrates' court under the Child Support Act 1991. The Secretary of State meanwhile applied for an injunction to prevent the father from instructing his solicitors to release funds held by them so as to dissipate the total below a certain amount. It fell to be determined whether the High Court had jurisdiction to order an injunction to support the exercise of a magistrates' court's jurisdiction. *Held*, the first question to consider was whether the power to interpose existed in relation to a magistrates' court. There was no precedent whereby the court's power to interpose had been exercised in respect of actual or anticipated proceedings before justices, although this factor was not conclusive. The second question to consider was whether the court could entertain an application for ancillary or non-substantive relief where it did not have jurisdiction in respect of the substantive claim. The Secretary of State had argued that he had a cause of action in the form of his right to obtain a liability order from justices in respect of maintenance assessments made under the 1991 Act, s 1(3). However, the statutory powers under the 1991 Act were comprehensive. Ancillary jurisdiction was not granted to the High Court nor was the Secretary of State given any power to anticipate liability orders which he might obtain from justices. Under the Act, all questions pertaining to the enforcement of an assessment were to be dealt with by the Secretary of State, the magistrates or the county court. Further, policy considerations dictated against the granting of such orders in that it could not have been Parliament's intention for statutory proceedings before justices to be duplicated and shadowed by ancillary proceedings in the High Court. Accordingly, the appeal would be dismissed.

Department of Social Security v Butler [1995] 4 All ER 193 (Court of Appeal: Simon Brown, Evans and Morritt LJJ). *Channel Tunnel Group Ltd v Balfour Beatty Construction Ltd* [1993] 1 All ER 664, HL (1992 Abr para 129), and *The Vera Cruz* [1992] 1 Lloyd's Rep 353, CA (1991 Abr para 1425), considered.

1715   Matrimonial injunctions

See HUSBAND AND WIFE.

INSURANCE

Halsbury's Laws of England (4th edn) Vol 25 (reissue), paras 1–1000

1716   Articles

Another Eventful Year in Insurance, Michael Wilson (on the annual report of the Insurance Ombudsman Bureau): 139 SJ 300
Fraud and Insurance Claims, R W Hodgin: 145 NLJ 136
Happily Ever After? Michael Wilson (on insurance for long term care): 139 SJ 1259

Insolvency at Sea, Sir Jonathan Mance (on the Third Party (Rights against Insurers) Act 1930): [1995] LMCLQ 34

Insurance Cover for Damage to the Environment, Robert Holmes and Michael Broughton: Estates Gazette, 1 April 1995, p 123

Insurance Cover for Redundancy and Sickness, Michael J Wilson: 139 SJ 722

Long Term Care Insurance, Michael Wilson: 139 SJ 250

Third Party Rights Against Insurers, Andrew Quick (on *Cox v Bankside Members Agency Ltd* (1995) Times, 27 January): 145 NLJ 918

Tort, Insurance and Ideology, Jane Stapleton: 58 MLR 820

Where Benefits Exceed Damages: The Insurers' Catch 22, Gary Burrell: Quantum, Issue 5/95, p 1

1717   Insurance brokers—registration

The Insurance Brokers (Registration) Act 1977 (Amendment) Order 1995, SI 1995/2906 (in force on 1 January 1997), amends the Insurance Brokers (Registration) Act 1977, s 3 so as to delete as qualifications for registration as an insurance broker those set out in s 3(1)(d)–(h) and amend the qualifications set out in s 3(1)(c).

1718   Insurance companies—appointment of chief executive—Secretary of State's objection to appointment—disclosure of evidence relied upon

Scotland

The Insurance Companies Act 1982, s 60(4) provides that the Secretary of State is not obliged to disclose to the company or the person proposed to be appointed any particulars of the ground on which he is considering the service on a company of a notice of objection to the appointment of a chief executive of an insurance company.

The applicant was the managing director of a life assurance company when he accepted a position as chief executive with a similar company. The Secretary of State notified him that service of a notice of objection under the 1982 Act, s 60 was being considered on the ground that he was not a fit and proper person to be appointed as chief executive. The applicant made representations to the Secretary of State, but notice was duly served. He applied for judicial review to set aside the notice on the ground that he was not warned that an employee of his previous company would give evidence, or that the nature of his proposed new duties would be raised. His interpretation of s 60(4) provided that there was a duty to disclose evidence of primary fact, although the disclosure of provisional or tentative reasoning was afforded protection. *Held*, the Secretary of State had a duty to act fairly and that would often require him to inform a candidate of the gist of the case which he had to answer. Parliament's intention in s 60(4) was to protect sources of information which were valuable in reaching a conclusion as to the fitness of a candidate for appointment. 'Particular' in s 60(4) was intended to cover any material placed before the Secretary of State relevant to the ground on which he was considering the service of the notice, including evidence of primary fact. There was, therefore, no obligation to disclose any detailed information relating to the ground on which an objection was being considered. In the present case, there had in fact been extensive disclosure and the Secretary of State had indicated the source of his information although precise terms had not been disclosed. Since the precise nature of the information before the Secretary of State was not known, the court was unable to say whether he had acted in an unfair manner with regard to the extent of the disclosure. However, it appeared that he had not relied on material which had not been canvassed in some way with the applicant and it should have been obvious to the applicant that the Secretary of State would wish to satisfy himself about the nature of his new office. The Secretary of State's approach could not be criticised and, accordingly, the application would be dismissed.

Buchanan v Secretary of State for Trade and Industry (1995) Times, 1 March (Outer House).

1719   Insurance companies—fees

The Insurance (Fees) Regulations 1995, SI 1995/688 (in force on 1 April 1995), replace the 1994 Regulations, SI 1994/643, and prescribe the fees payable to the Secretary of State under the Insurance Companies Act 1982, s 94A. The fees are payable by insurance companies when depositing their accounts and other documents under the 1982 Act, s 22(1) and by the Council of Lloyds when the statement in respect of Lloyds is deposited under s 86(1).

1720 Insurance companies—insurance business—regulation

The Insurance Companies (Amendment) Regulations 1995, SI 1995/3248 (in force on 31 December 1995), amend the 1994 Regulations, SI 1994/1516, in relation to the treatment of assets and liabilities of a United Kingdom authorised insurance company for specified purposes of the Insurance Companies Act 1982 and the methods by which benefits payable to policyholders under linked long term contracts of insurance are determined. The amendments introduce new provision in relation to (1) the treatment of specified sale and repurchase transactions, (2) the valuation of securities and beneficial interests in a limited partnership, (3) the valuation of beneficial interests in a collective investment scheme, (4) the valuation of deferred acquisition costs, (5) the treatment of derivatives, (6) contracts and assets having the effect of derivative contracts, and (7) assets to be taken into account only to a specified extent. The regulations also contain transitional provisions.

1721 Insurance companies—prudential supervision

See para 3145.

1722 Insurance Companies (Reserves) Act 1995

The Insurance Companies (Reserves) Act 1995 makes new provision to require insurance companies to maintain reserves in respect of prescribed descriptions of insurance business. The Act received the royal assent on 19 July 1995 and ss 2, 4 came into force on that date. Sections 1, 3 come into force on a day to be appointed. For details of commencement, see the commencement table in the title STATUTES.

Section 1 amends the Insurance Companies Act 1982 by requiring certain insurance companies to maintain reserves in accordance with regulations made by the Secretary of State and by providing for such reserves to be treated as a liability for the purpose of calculating a company's margin of solvency. Section 2 confers power on the Secretary of State to provide in regulations for the application of the 1982 Act, s 68 in relation to the reserves. The Companies Act 1985 concerning the treatment of reserves in financial accounts is amended by s 3. Section 4 deals with citation, commencement and extent.

1723 Insurance policy—bankers policy—cover for theft—theft by company

The plaintiff bank was insured under a banker's policy for loss arising out of 'burglary, robbery, theft or false pretences committed by persons present on the premises of the bank'. A company which was a customer of the bank had a credit line secured by treasury bills and bank certificates of deposit. With the agreement of the bank, a junior employee of the company took possession of the securities in exchange for a letter undertaking that the company would deliver alternative securities. The alternative securities were never delivered, the activities of the company were suspended, and the chairman of the company was charged with fraudulent trading. The company was wound up and the credit line loan was never repaid. The bank claimed to be entitled to recover the amount of the loan under the insurance policy, but the insurers denied liability. On a preliminary issue as to whether the facts alleged by the bank disclosed a good cause of action under the policy, *held* (Lord Steyn dissenting), the relevant clause could only relate to crimes committed by persons physically on the bank's premises. The parties could not reasonably be supposed to have had in view the Law of Property Act 1925, s 61 (which provides that in all contracts 'person' includes a corporation unless the context otherwise requires) so as to have in contemplation that a company might be present on the premises of the bank and commit theft there.

Deutsche Genossenschaftsbank v Burnhope [1995] 4 All ER 717 (House of Lords: Lords Keith of Kinkel, Lloyd of Berwick, Nicholls of Birkenhead, Steyn and Hoffmann).

1724 Insurance policy—exclusion clause—damage arising from method of waste disposal—meaning of disposal

An escape of gas from a landfill site owned by the plaintiffs caused an explosion which destroyed a nearby house. In the ensuing litigation the plaintiffs were found to be liable for the explosion, and were ordered to pay damages to the homeowner. They then sought an indemnity from their insurers, the defendant. The defendant refused to pay and at the hearing at first instance the plaintiffs' claim was upheld. The defendant appealed. *Held*, the insurance policy contained an exemption clause which excluded the defendant from liability in respect of loss arising from the disposal of waste materials unless such loss arose from an accident 'in the method of disposal'. Although the plaintiffs had clearly suffered loss as a result of an accident, that accident did not arise 'in the method of disposal' of the waste. Giving the term 'disposal' its ordinary meaning of 'putting away' or 'getting rid of', it was clear that the waste had been disposed of when the plaintiffs had buried it on the landfill site. The disposal had gone according to plan, and without mishap. The unintended and unforeseen result of the disposal was the escape of gas and the explosion. It was not the disposal of the waste that caused the accident, but its subsequent decomposition. Therefore, the defendant was entitled to rely on the exemption clause in the contract. Accordingly, the appeal would be allowed.

Middleton v Wiggins (1995) Independent, 31 August (Court of Appeal: McCowan, Aldous and Hutchison LJJ).

1725 Insurance policy—exclusion clause—property insurance—goods in transit

New Zealand

Two business partners decided to move premises and engaged the services of a freight company together with its forklift truck and drivers for those purposes. The machinery was moved to the new site and then one of the business partners supervised its positioning. In the face of protest he did not secure the machinery to the forklift truck. It fell and was damaged. The partners attempted to claim under their insurance policy which contained an exclusion clause whereby property in transit was not covered and under which the insured had to exercise due care and diligence to prevent damage. *Held*, in determining whether the machinery was in transit, the word 'transit' must be given its ordinary meaning and the purpose of the insurance contract, to protect property whilst it was on the premises, must be considered. On that basis, the machinery was no longer in transit once it had arrived at the premises and the exclusion clause did not operate. However, the requirement of due care and diligence applied to the partnership as a single entity and one partner could not make a claim where the other partner had been reckless. Accordingly, no claim could be allowed under the policy and the appeal would be dismissed.

Kelly v National Insurance Co of New Zealand Ltd [1995] 1 NZLR 641(Court of Appeal).

1726 Insurance policy—illegal and ultra vires policy—policy issued by unauthorised body—availability of stop-loss cover

The Financial Services Act 1986, s 132 provides that a contract of insurance which is entered into by a person in the course of carrying on business in contravention of the Insurance Companies Act 1982, s 2 is unenforceable against the other party, and that party is entitled to recover any money or other property transferred by him under the contract, together with compensation for any loss sustained as a result of having parted with it.

The plaintiffs were Lloyds names who brought claims under the 1986 Act, s 132 for stop-loss cover against insurance companies who were not permitted to carry on insurance business under the 1982 Act. They had entered into the contracts of insurance before the commencement of s 132 and it was claimed in the insurance companies' defence that s 132 should not be applied retrospectively. *Held*, the prima facie presumption against retrospection was expressed in *Yew Bon Tew v Kenderaan Bas Mara* [1982] 3 All ER 833. There it was stated that a statute was retrospective if it took away or impaired a vested right acquired under existing laws, or created a new obligation or duty in respect of events already past. Section 132 did not create a new obligation because its provisions were already enshrined in common law and its purpose was merely to clarify the position. Furthermore, no one in the insurance market would have thought that a contract was unenforceable merely because the insurer was not authorised under the 1982 Act, s 2. Thus, s 132 was retrospective in effect and gave a remedy to claims arising before its commencement.

Bates v Barrow Ltd, Ansell v Barrow Ltd [1995] 1 Lloyd's Rep 680 (Queen's Bench Division: Gatehouse J).

1727 Insurance policy—sale—commission—taxation

See para 1667.

1728 Insurance policy or annuity contract—reinsurance arrangement—investment return—taxation

See para 1649.

1729 Insurance premium tax—regulations

The Insurance Premium Tax (Amendment) Regulations 1995, SI 1995/1587 (in force on 17 July 1995), amend the 1994 Regulations, SI 1994/1774, by requiring registrable persons to notify the Commissioners of Customs and Excise of errors made in previous notifications and of certain changes in circumstances.

1730   Insurance premium tax—reinsurance business

See para 2489.

1731   Insurance proposal form—insured completing form—answers contained in form not amounting to continuing warranty

The insured completed an insurance proposal form before an insurance policy was made in respect of his premises. In answer to one of the questions on the form, the insured confirmed that his premises were fitted with an intruder alarm system. When the insured later made a claim on his policy the underwriters unsuccessfully sought to dismiss it. On appeal, the underwriters submitted that the insured's answer on the form amounted to a continuing warranty that the premises were fitted with an intruder alarm, that the alarm was operational and that it would be habitually set by the insured when the premises were unattended. *Held*, there was no special principle of insurance law requiring answers in proposal forms to be read as importing promises as to the future. The question in the proposal form was in the present tense and did not seek on its face any information as to the practice of the insured with regard to the alarm. There was no suggestion that an affirmative answer entailed an undertaking as to the future. A continuing warranty was a draconian term and any breach produced an automatic cancellation of cover. The fact that a loss might have had no connection at all with that breach was irrelevant. If underwriters wanted such protection then it was up to them to stipulate for it in clear terms. Accordingly, the appeal would be dismissed.

Hussain v Brown (1995) Times, 15 December (Court of Appeal: Leggatt, Rose and Saville LJJ).

1732   Liability insurance—'all risks policy'—exception for loss resulting from improvements—rectification of defects

Sub-contractors claimed under an 'all risks' insurance policy after carrying out remedial works necessitated by defects in design, construction and workmanship. Their insurance policy provided that they would be indemnified in respect of 'physical loss of or damage to the property insured howsoever caused' except in relation to, inter alia, 'costs of introducing improvements, betterments or corrections in the rectification of the design, material or workmanship causing such loss or damage'. The insurance company refused to pay for the costs of rectification of the defects which had caused the damage necessitating the remedial works. *Held*, the costs of rectifying defects which had caused the physical damage were included in the obligation to indemnify.

Cementation Piling v Commercial Union Insurance Co plc (1995) BLR 98 (Court of Appeal: Russell and Waite LJJ and Sir Ralph Gibson).

1733   Liability insurance—construction of policy—deductible clause—meaning of component part

The plaintiff sub-contractors claimed under an insurance policy after carrying out remedial work in respect of 94 installations they had made. The installations were each surrounded by cementitious board which was defective. The insurance policy indemnified the insured against any loss or damage subject to a deductible clause which provided for a deductibility amount 'in respect of each and every loss in respect of any component part'. The insurers argued that the deductible applied to each installation, thus effectively extinguishing the claim. *Held*, the cementitious board was one component part and not 94 component parts and the words 'each and every loss' applied to a composite claim caused by the cementitious board meant that the deductible should be applied once as their was one composite loss.

Mitsubishi Electric UK Ltd v Royal London Insurance (UK) Ltd (1995) 74 BLR 87 (Court of Appeal: Sir Thomas Bingham MR, McCowan and Hirst LJJ).

1734   Liability insurance—policy excluding claims arising from business

Canada

The insured had a home-owners' insurance policy which included coverage for personal liability. That coverage excluded claims arising from business except for those arising out of the insured's work for someone else as a collector or claims arising out of activities during the course of the insured's trade, profession or occupation which were ordinarily incidental to non-business pursuits. The insured was a taxi-driver and he and his employer shared the fares he billed. When a passenger failed to pay his fare, there was an altercation during which the passenger was fatally stabbed by the insured. The deceased's estate brought an action in negligence seeking damages from the insured. He claimed that his insurer should defend him and obtained an order to that effect. On the insurer's appeal against the order, *held*, the entire altercation arose over a disputed taxi fare and had to be regarded as arising from the insured's business. The events were not incidental to non-business pursuits and, although the insured gathered fares incidental to his occupation, that did not make him a collector. The insured's claim therefore fell within the ambit of the exclusion and, accordingly, the appeal would be allowed.

Re Kaler and Red River Valley Mutual Insurance Co (1995) 126 DLR (4th) 700 (Manitoba Court of Appeal).

1735   Lloyd's—action brought by names—transfer from Chancery Division to Queen's Bench Division

The plaintiffs were Lloyd's names who brought actions against the defendant insurance brokers and auditors alleging breach of duty of care causing the plaintiffs substantial losses. The defendants applied for an order transferring the case from the Chancery Division to the Queen's Bench Division for hearing in the Commercial Court. *Held*, transfer from one division to another was not encouraged by the courts. High standards had to be met before such a transfer could be considered and it would have to be shown that it was inappropriate for the case to proceed in the division in which it had commenced with special circumstances requiring, rather than merely warranting, a transfer to be made. In this case, there were two compelling reasons why transfer was appropriate. Firstly, there was the innovative and proactive case management of Lloyd's cases introduced in the Commercial Court. Secondly, the bulk of Lloyd's litigation relating to the losses which were the subject of the present action had been commenced in the Commercial Court and this was now a generally accepted practice. Accordingly, the order would be granted and the action transferred to the Commercial Court.

Deeny v Littlejohn & Co (a firm); Deeny v Walker (1995) Times, 19 January (Chancery Division: Arden J).

1736   Lloyd's—action for negligence—extension of limitation period

See *Hallam-Eames v Merrett*, para 1908.

1737   Lloyd's—action for negligence by names against managing agents—damages awarded to names—taxation of damages

The plaintiffs were Lloyd's names who had recovered damages after bringing a successful negligence action against the defendants, their managing agents. On the question of income tax payable on the damages, the court had held that they were taxable under Schedule D in the plaintiffs' hands and were not to be reduced by the amount of any tax saved by the plaintiffs in connection with their Lloyd's underwriting business. The defendants appealed on the ground that the damages were not taxable. *Held*, Saville LJ dissenting, the damages were paid for the trading loss caused to the plaintiffs through the negligent conduct of the names' underwriting business by the defendants with the intention of putting the plaintiffs in the same position as if the underwriting had been competently performed. Had the defendants protected the plaintiffs' exposure to risk by adequate reinsurance, the plaintiffs would have received the proceeds of that reinsurance. There was no difference between recovering compensation through insurance and through damages. The source of the right to damages was the negligence of the defendants acting as the agents of the plaintiffs in conducting the plaintiffs' underwriting business and it was therefore clear that the compensation arose from that trade and was liable to income tax under Schedule D. Accordingly, the appeal would be dismissed.

Deeny v Gooda Walker Ltd [1996] STC 39 (Court of Appeal: Simon Brown, Peter Gibson and Saville LJJ). Decision of Potter J [1995] STC 439 affirmed. *London and Thames Haven Oil Wharves Ltd v Attwooll (Inspector of Taxes)* [1967] 2 All ER 124, CA and *Donald Fisher (Ealing) Ltd v Spencer (Inspector of Taxes)* [1989] STC 256, CA (1989 Abr para 1194) applied.

This decision has been affirmed: [1996] 1 All ER 933, HL.

1738   Lloyd's—action for negligence by names against members' agent—raising issues available in former action

The plaintiff was a Lloyd's name who, as part of an action group, had succesfullly brought an action against the defendant, who was his members' agent, together with his managing agent, for negligent underwriting relating to certain syndicates. He later brought another action against the defendant claiming damages for a different breach of duty, namely the agent's negligence in advising him to join the syndicates in issue in the first action. The defendant appealed on the ground that the rule in *Henderson v Henderson* ((1843) 3 Hare 100) required parties to an action to bring their whole case before the court so that all aspects of it could be decided upon at the same time. *Held*, the *Henderson* rule had been designed on public policy grounds to prevent litigation from dragging on longer than necessary and to avoid a defendant being oppressed by succesive suits when only one was needed. Due to the number and complexity of the cases brought against Lloyd's, claimants had formed themselves into action groups and the Commercial Court had decided to manage the cases on the basis of the generic classes into which they fell. This meant that the plaintiff's action in issue, which fell into a different category from his first action, would not, in any case, have been decided prior to the present hearing, and there was consequently no prejudice to the defendant as a result of the plaintiff failing to plead the new claim at the outset. Even if that conclusion were wrong, the special nature of the administration of Lloyd's cases constituted special circumstances which could excuse the plaintiff from any duty to bring his whole case at the outset. Accordingly, the appeal would be dismissed.

Barrow v Bankside Agency Ltd [1996] 1 All ER 981 (Court of Appeal: Sir Thomas Bingham MR, Peter Gibson and Saville LJJ). For guidance on the progress and management of the Lloyd's litigation, see para 1747.

1739 Lloyd's—association of Lloyd's names—levy of additional subscription— defaulting members

See *Nutting v Baldwin*, para 649.

1740 Lloyd's—fraud perpetrated by names' agents—failure to disclose fraud by agents—validity of reinsurance contract

The Marine Insurance Act 1906, s 19 provides that where an insurance is effected for an assured by an agent, the agent must disclose to the insurer (a) every material circumstance which is known to himself, and an agent to insure is deemed to know every circumstance which in the ordinary course of business ought to be known by, or to have been communicated to, him, and (b) every material circumstance which the assured is bound to disclose.

A group of Lloyd's names brought an action against the defendant reinsurers for breach of a reinsurance agreement. The defendants argued that the names' agents had been defrauding the names and were obliged to disclose this fact under the 1906 Act, s 19. Failure to do so had vitiated the insurance. At first instance, the court declared the reinsurance contract was valid and the defendants appealed. *Held*, the names did not know, nor ought they to have known, that the fraud was being committed and it was implausible that an agent would disclose to his principal that he was defrauding him. If the agent's dishonesty was not something which ought to have been known to the principal it could not be held against the principal under s 19 merely because the agent was an agent to insure. Knowledge of a fraud could not be imputed to a principal where the principal's rights were affected if the agent did not make a disclosure to a third party. As a result, in this case, the reinsurance contract could not be avoided on the ground of non-disclosure by the names' agents and, accordingly, the appeal would be dismissed.

PCW Syndicates v PCW Reinsurers [1996] 1 All ER 774 (Court of Appeal: Staughton, Rose and Saville LJJ).

1741 Lloyd's—liability of underwriting names' agents—deferral of adjudication of liability

RSC Ord 33, r 4(2) provides that in any action one or more questions or issues may be ordered to be tried before the others.

It has been held that the High Court has jurisdiction under Ord 33, r 4(2), to postpone the adjudication of the liability of an underwriting name's agent who has negligently taken on risks, some of which are on outstanding potential claims. The normal rule that damages are to be decided in a single definitive award does not apply where the extent of potential third party liability is uncertain or the future loss position cannot be predicted with reasonable confidence, both of which are the case with the Lloyd's litigation.

Deeny v Gooda Walker Ltd [1995] 4 All ER 289 (Queen's Bench Division: Phillips J).

1742   Lloyd's—litigation—application for stay of proceedings—exceptional circumstances

The plaintiffs were Lloyd's names who brought an action against the defendants, who were issuers of errors and omissions insurance. The defendants had provided professional indemnity insurance to the plaintiffs' managing and members' agents. An application for a stay of the proceedings was made by the defendants under the Arbitration Act 1950, s 4, on the ground that the plaintiffs and defendants had agreed in writing to refer the matters in issue to arbitration if a dispute arose. *Held*, this case was one of the exceptional cases where it was appropriate to refuse a stay of proceedings even though there was an arbitration clause relating to the matters in issue. It was not fair to expect other interested parties, who might wish to bring actions under the 1950 Act, to intervene in arbitration proceedings as their position had to be properly protected. The issues in question were better resolved by the rules of evidence that applied in the Commercial Court and the construction of the clause had not been dealt with in any previous case and was of wide interest, although that factor was of limited weight. Accordingly, the application for a stay would be refused.

Rew v Cox (1995) Times, 29 November (Queen's Bench Division: Cresswell J).

1743   Lloyd's—litigation—case management—Queen's Bench Division Commercial Court

It has been held that the overall case management of Lloyd's litigation can only be conducted in an efficient and consistent manner if all future actions relating to Lloyd's are commenced in the Queen's Bench Division Commercial Court.

Deeny v Littlejohn & Co (1995) Times, 23 February (Queen's Bench Division: Cresswell J).

1744   Lloyd's—litigation—enforcement of successful claims—rule of chronological priority

The plaintiffs were groups of names whose actions against agents and errors and omissions underwriters were scheduled to be amongst the last heard in the Lloyd's litigation. They claimed that claims ought to be settled on a principle of rateable allocation and not on a first past the post basis. At first instance, this argument was rejected and the plaintiffs appealed. *Held*, the basic rule was that claims ought to be settled according to chronological priority and any departure from that rule would have to be justified. The maxim that equality was equity did not apply to situations like the present. There was no implied agreement that any settlement would be rateably allocated because such a term was not necessary for business efficacy and it was not an obvious but unarticulated intention. There was also nothing in the Third Parties (Rights against Insurers) Act 1930 that would support the plaintiffs' argument. The agents did not hold insurance proceeds on trust for all the names as beneficiaries because the essential elements of a trust such as certainty of terms and beneficiaries and a clear intention that the property be held for the benefit of others were missing. Although the management plan devised by the Commercial Court for dealing with the Lloyd's litigation caused obvious hardship to those names not at the front of the queue, it avoided the injustice of names who have brought successful actions being declared bankrupt before they were able to enforce the judgments they had obtained. In any event, the claims of those names at the back of the queue could not be adequately protected and on balance it did not seem that the scheme of rateable allocation would create more fairness than the rule of chronological priority. Accordingly, the appeal would be dismissed.

Cox v Bankside Members Agency Ltd [1995] 2 Lloyd's Rep 437 (Court of Appeal: Sir Thomas Bingham MR, Peter Gibson and Saville LJJ). Decision of Phillips J (1995) Times, 27 January affirmed.

1745   Lloyd's—litigation—foreseeability of loss suffered by Lloyd's name

See *Brown v KMR Services Ltd*, para 2146.

1746   Lloyd's—litigation—hearings in open court

It has been held that cases in the Lloyd's litigation must be heard in open court rather than in camera. The court will, where appropriate, give directions in order to avoid making unnecessary reference to matters that might prove commercially damaging as long as the parties were not inhibited from bringing their cases. Any applications for such directions ought to be made at least six weeks in advance of the hearing date.

Hallam-Eames v Merrett Syndicates Ltd (1995) Times, 16 June (Queen's Bench Division: Cresswell J).

1747 Lloyd's—litigation—progress and management

A statement in open court has been made by the judge in charge of the Commercial List in reference to the progress and management of the Lloyd's litigation. The litigation has been divided into the following categories: (1) LMX cases, (2) long tail cases, (3) personal stop loss cases, (4) portfolio selection cases, (5) central fund litigation and (6) other cases. A number of preliminary issues common to more than one category of case have been identified and decided and the House of Lords and Court of Appeal have assisted in the expedition of a number of appeals. Lead or pilot cases have been selected from each category in order to establish questions of liability and general principles of quantum which can be used as broad guidance for other cases in the same category. Case management techniques have been developed in relation to group cases and a liaison committee has been set up to facilitate the distribution of information to parties involved in the Lloyd's litigation. The judge has also reported on the specific progress made in each category of case.

Lloyd's Litigation: Report on Progress and Management (1995) Times, 5 May (Queen's Bench Division: Cresswell J).

1748 Lloyd's—members' agents—duty of care—duty delegable to managing agents

The plaintiffs were Lloyd's syndicates who brought actions for breach of contract and negligence against their members' agents and an action for negligence against their managing agents. The actions arose out of a reinsurance contract entered into by the plaintiffs with another syndicate which that syndicate successfully avoided due to the managing agents' failure to disclose information material to the assessment of the underwritten risk. The plaintiffs claimed that the members' agents had a non-delegable duty of care at common law towards the names they represented. *Held*, a members' agent did not have a common law duty of care concurrent with his contractual duty, unless that common law duty could be shown to be non-delegable. The authorities disclosed no policy provision which dictated a finding of non-delegable duty and therefore the members' agents in this case were not liable in tort. In addition, the managing agents duty of care was owed not only to the existing names who were members of the plaintiff syndicates, but also to future names even if the managing agents had not acted for them at the time of the negligence.

Aitken v Stewart Wrightson Members Agency Ltd [1995] 3 All ER 449 (Queen's Bench Division: Potter J).

1749 Lloyd's—reinsurance—insurance contract—application of term to reinsurance

Members' agents at Lloyd's were insured against liability for professional negligence and fraud. The professional liability insurers in turn effected reinsurance. A clause in the reinsurance contract provided that all loss settlements made by the reinsured were unconditionally binding upon reinsurers provided such settlements were within the conditions of the original policies and within the terms of the reinsurance. It fell to be determined whether the clause meant that the number of losses, for the purpose of the reinsurance contract, had been conclusively determined by the decision in *Cox v Bankside Members Agency Ltd* (1995) Times, 27 January that the liability of managing and members' agents established in the earlier case of *Deeny v Gooda Walker Ltd* (1994) Times, 7 October (1994 Abr para 1690) arose out of three originating causes under the professional liability insurance contract. *Held*, the first question was whether the reinsurers were bound not merely by the result in *Cox*, but also by decisions which the court reached on the way to that result. The reinsurers were to be bound by any compromise or judgment to the extent that it held the liability insurers liable to the members' agents and determined the amount of that liability. Good sense required that the reinsurers in the present case should be bound by the decision in *Cox* as to the meaning of the liability insurance contracts. Where there was an effort to restrict the capacity of Lloyd's to spawn litigation, as there was in the clause in question, it should receive full credit from the courts. The settlement referred to in the clause included a determination that the claims of all the members' agents arose out of three originating causes and the reinsurers were bound by the determination of that issue. If the first question was answered in the affirmative, the second question was whether the meaning of every loss in the reinsurance contract was necessarily the same as the meaning given in *Cox* to the limiting provision in the liability insurance contracts in that case. There was no relevant difference between the two clauses. As the reinsurers were bound to follow the decision in *Cox*, they were tied to the conclusion that there were three events out of which all the members' agents claims arose.

AXA Reinsurance UK plc v Field [1996] 1 Lloyd's Rep 26 (Court of Appeal: Nourse, Staughton and Simon Brown LJJ). *Cox v Bankside Members Agency Ltd* affirmed on appeal: [1995] 2 Lloyd's Rep 437, CA (para 1744).

1750   Lloyd's—underwriters—income taxation

See para 1679.

1751   Lloyd's—underwriters—special reserve funds

See para 1679.

1752   Marine insurance—insurance policy—assured—duty of disclosure—material circumstances

The Marine Insurance Act 1906, s 18(1) provides that the assured must disclose to the insurer, before the contract is concluded, every material circumstance which is known to the assured; if the assured fails to make such disclosure, the insurer may avoid the contract. By s 18(2), every circumstance is material which would influence the judgment of a prudent insurer in fixing the premium or determining whether he will take the risk. Section 18(3)(a) provides that an insured need not disclose any circumstance which diminished the risk.

The plaintiff underwriters subscribed to a contractors all risks policy under which they provided the three defendant companies with construction works insurance in respect of a joint venture by them to build several large administration buildings. An insurance submission, placed with the plaintiffs by the defendants' brokers, described the proposed buildings as being constructed on piled foundations. After their construction, the buildings suffered severe subsidence damage and the plaintiffs then learned that piled foundations had not been employed. Instead, much shallower spread foundations had been constructed. It also transpired that the defendants had failed to disclose to the plaintiffs two reports which questioned whether spread foundations were appropriate for the relevant ground conditions. The plaintiffs obtained a declaration that they could avoid the policy for misrepresentation and non-disclosure. The defendants appealed. *Held*, the insurer's right of avoidance of a contract only arose when the misrepresentation or non-disclosure was 'material' and the insurer could prove that he was induced by the same to enter into a contract on terms which he would not have accepted if the material fact had been known to him. There was no reason why a 'material' misrepresentation or non-disclosure was limited to factors which were seen to increase a risk. 'Material' referred to a relationship with the subject matter rather than a prediction of its effect. The effect of the 1906 Act, s 18(3)(a) was that an insurer had no right to avoid a policy on the ground that a circumstance which did not diminish the risk was not disclosed. That did not mean that the circumstance was not 'material' within the definition in s 18(2), since if it were not material there would be no need for the Act to provide that it need not be disclosed. The pre-contract failure by the defendants to disclose to the plaintiffs that the contractors intended to use spread foundations rather than piled foundations amounted to a misrepresentation. Furthermore, given the ground conditions, the conflicting reports on the use of spread foundations ought to have been disclosed to the plaintiffs. Both the misrepresentation and the non-disclosure of the reports were 'material', since they would certainly have affected the prudent underwriter's estimate or appreciation of the risk. There was also an implied, if not express, representation when the nature of the project and the contractors' intentions were disclosed to the plaintiffs. It could either be said that the implied representation was untrue or that material facts were not disclosed. There was a breach of duty in either case. On the facts, it was clear that the plaintiff had been induced by the misrepresentations and non-disclosure to enter into the contract. Accordingly, the defendants' appeal would be dismissed.

St Paul Fire and Marine Insurance Co (UK) Ltd v McConnell Dowell Constructors Ltd [1996] 1 All ER 96 (Court of Appeal: Nourse, Evans and Rose LJJ). *Pan Atlantic Insurance Co Ltd v Pine Top Insurance Co Ltd* [1994] 2 Lloyd's Rep 427, HL (1994 Abr para 1673) considered.

1753   Motor insurance—backdated insurance policy—commencement of policy

Scotland

A driver was stopped by the police and charged with the offence of using a motor vehicle on a road without a valid insurance policy contrary to the Road Traffic Act 1988, s 143(1), (2). The offence took place at around midday on 6 January. The previous day, the driver had telephoned his insurers to arrange car insurance. He was told that he would be insured from midnight on 5 January provided that he paid a standing charge and the first premium on the following day. A backdated insurance certificate was subsequently issued on the agreed terms, but not until after the driver had been stopped and charged. At an appeal against his conviction under s 143, the driver claimed to have held a valid insurance policy at the time that the offence allegedly took place. *Held*, the question of whether there was a contravention of s 143 was to be tested at the point in time at which the breach was said to have occurred. At that moment, the driver was not covered by any insurance policy. Therefore he had no defence to the charge. Accordingly, the appeal would be dismissed.

McCulloch v Heywood 1995 SLT 1009 (High Court of Justiciary).

1754   Motor insurance—blank bogus insurance certificates—possession with intent to deceive—whether possession of blank certificates constitutes intent

When police searched the appellant's flat they found a pad of blank forms of bogus insurance certificates purported to be issued by an insurance company. The appellant was charged with possessing a document with intent to deceive contrary to the Road Traffic Act 1988, s 173. At his trial, he submitted that he had no case to answer because the prosecution had to show an intent to deceive and until a form was completed such intent could not be established. The submission was rejected and the appellant was convicted. On appeal against conviction, *held*, if the forms had been completed they would have been likely to deceive anyone to whom they were produced. But clearly the uncompleted forms might be likely to deceive anyone seeking insurance cover for a car. In that sense, the forms could constitute a document covered by the 1988 Act, s 173 and, accordingly, the appeal would be dismissed.

R v Aworinde (1995) 159 JP 618 (Court of Appeal: Hutchison LJ, Tucker and Holland JJ).

1755   Motor insurance—permitted uninsured driving—conditional permission

Scotland
The appellant agreed that a friend could drive her car to a garage to have it repaired. Before giving him permission to do so, she told him that she did not have third party insurance, but he told her that his own insurance was comprehensive and would therefore cover the situation. The appellant relied on this advice, but it transpired that the advice was wrong, and the appellant was later charged with causing or permitting another person to use a motor vehicle on public roads without there being in force a third party insurance policy, contrary to the Road Traffic Act 1988, s 143(1), (2). In convicting the appellant, the court held that the offence was one of strict liability. On the appellant's appeal, *held*, it was a fact that the appellant would not have allowed her friend to drive her car had she known that he was not insured. Moreover, the permission which the appellant had given her friend was conditional, as it depended on him being insured to drive her car. As the friend had not fulfilled that condition, the appellant had not committed an offence. Accordingly, the appeal would be allowed.

MacDonald v Howdle 1995 SLT 779 (High Court of Justiciary). *Lyons v May* [1948] 2 All ER 1062, DC distinguished; *Newbury v Davies* [1974] RTR 367, DC (1974 Abr para 1788) followed.

1756   Property insurance—policy—fire insurance—mortgagee's interest in policy—charge over insurance proceeds

New Zealand
The plaintiff bank advanced money to the mortgagors of a residential property. The loan was secured by a second mortgage on the property. Under New Zealand law, there was implied in the mortgage a covenant by the mortgagor to insure the property and keep it insured against loss or damage by fire, such insurance to be effected in the name of the mortgagee. There was an express covenant in the memorandum of mortgage to the same effect. In fact, the mortgagors effected insurance cover with the defendant insurers in the name of one of the mortgagors causing the bank to write to the insurers to give notice of its interest as second mortgagee and asking for that interest to be noted. The insurers issued a certificate of insurance on which the bank's interest as second mortgagee was noted as a party interested in the insurance. When the mortgagors' house was subsequently destroyed by fire, the first mortgagees exercised their power of sale, repaid their mortgage out of the proceeds and paid the balance to the bank, leaving a large shortfall owing under the second mortgage. Immediately after the fire the bank wrote to the insurers notifying them of its claim under the insurance policy and later submitted a formal claim for the proceeds of the policy but, notwithstanding that notification, the insurers paid the mortgagor who had effected the insurance in full and final settlement of all claims under the policy. The bank succesfully brought proceedings against the insurers, claiming that it was entitled to the policy monies. On appeal by the insurers, *held*, the purpose of a covenant for insurance was to ensure that if the value of the security was depreciated by the occurrence of a fire or other insurable risk, the proceeds of the policy would provide a fund to make up the shortfall. That purpose could be achieved only if the covenant gave the mortgagee an interest by way of charge, and no more than an interest by way of charge, in the proceeds. The purpose of

provisions in standard insurance covenants such as the requirements that the insurance be effected in the name of the mortgagee was merely to protect the mortgagee's interest by way of charge over the proceeds of the policy rather than to create that interest. A fundamental assumption of the covenant was that such an interest existed and the mortgagor's failure to comply with one or other of the protective terms could not destroy it. If the policy was effected in the name of the mortgagor, the mortgagee still had an interest by way of charge in the proceeds and that interest necessarily took effect by way of assignment, and on giving notice, which did not have to be in a particular form, the mortgagee's interest as assignee was protected. It was standard practice for mortgagees to ask for their interests to be noted for the purpose of protecting their interests in the policy proceeds. That was how the defendant insurers themselves had treated the notice from the bank. In the context of a notice to an insurance company by a mortgagee of the insured property, the notice from the bank was a plain and unambiguous notice of assignment. The bank was therefore entitled to the proceeds of the policy and the appeal would accordingly be dismissed.

Colonial Mutual General Insurance Co Ltd v ANZ Banking Group (New Zealand) Ltd [1995] 3 All ER 987 (Privy Council: Lords Goff of Chieveley, Jauncey of Tullichettle, Browne-Wilkinson, Nolan and Hoffmann).

1757 Reinsurance—liability of reinsurer—sums actually paid by reinsured

The plaintiff and defendant were parties to a reinsurance contract containing a net loss clause which stated that the reinsurer was liable for 'the sum actually paid' by the reinsured. On the meaning of the phrase 'the sum actually paid' held, the phrase applied to sums which were immediately payable but had not been actually paid. The words had to be construed in their context. For example, it was unlikely that an excess of loss reinsurance contract would make a reinsurer's duty to pay conditional upon prior disbursement by the reinsured of incoming insurance claims. Also, the phrase was contained in an ultimate net loss clause which was mainly concerned with the measurement of reinsurance recoveries and where it would be surprising to find a condition requiring prior disbursement. The only effect of the introduction of a condition of prior payment would be that it could not at times be satisfied, thereby causing the reinsurance contract to be thwarted and the reinsurer to receive a pure windfall gain. That could not have been the mutual intention of the parties.

Charter Reinsurance Co Ltd v Fagan [1996] 1 All ER 406 (Court of Appeal: Nourse, Staughton and Simon Brown LJJ).

INTOXICATING LIQUOR

Halsbury's Laws of England (4th edn) Vol 26, paras 1–500

1758 Articles

Children's Certificate—a Practitioner's Perspective, Alan Thompson: 159 JP Jo 519
Children's Certificates for the Bar Areas of Licensed Premises—Conditions for the Availability of Meals, J N Spencer: 159 JP Jo 242
Children's Certificates—Problem or Panacea? A M Wesson: 159 JP Jo 314
Children's Certificates Under the Deregulation and Contracting Out Act 1994, J N Spencer (on licences allowing admittance of children under 14 into public bars): 159 JP Jo 171

1759 Beer—regulations

The Beer (Amendment) Regulations 1995, SI 1995/3059 (in force on 1 January 1996), amend the 1993 Regulations, SI 1993/1228, so that where beer is held on any registered premises where the records relating to removal are kept by means approved for this purpose by the Commissioners of Customs and Excise, it must be deemed to have left those premises at the time of its constructive removal or, if earlier, the time it actually left them.

1760 Licensing (Sunday Hours) Act 1995

The Licensing (Sunday Hours) Act 1995 amends the provisions of the Licensing Act 1964 relating to permitted hours in licensed premises and clubs on Sundays and Good Friday. The

Act received the royal assent on 19 July 1995 and came into force on 6 August 1995: SI 1995/1930.

Section 1 amends the Licensing Act 1964, s 60 so as to provide that in licensed premises on Sundays and Good Friday the permitted hours are from 12 noon to 10.30 pm, thereby dispensing with the afternoon break. Section 1 also provides for permitted hours in off-licensed premises on those days to begin at 10 am. Section 2 makes corresponding provision in respect of the afternoon break for registered clubs. Under s 3, magistrates may make restriction orders re-imposing an afternoon break on Sundays and Good Friday in the case of on-licensed premises and clubs. Section 4 and Schs 1, 2 contain consequential amendments and repeals. Section 5 deals with commencement and s 6 with short title and extent.

1761 Permitted hours—special hours certificate—start of special hours

It has been held that a special hours certificate governs, for the day on which it operates, all the opening hours for the premises to which it relates for that day, thereby ensuring that the police have greater control over how the premises operate and over licensing policy.

Chief Constable of West Midlands Police v Marsden (1995) 159 JP 405 (Queen's Bench Division: Owen J).

1762 Spirits—description and definition

See para 1430.

JUDGMENTS AND ORDERS

Halsbury's Laws of England (4th edn) Vol 26, paras 501–600

1763 Articles

Don't Forget the Affidavit (on *Barclays Bank v Piper* (1995) Times, 31 May, CA (para 1771)): 139 SJ 1125

1764 Foreign judgments—reciprocal enforcement

See CONFLICT OF LAWS.

1765 Judgment in default—application to set aside—adjournment of bankruptcy petition pending determination

See *Re Debtor (No 799 of 1994), ex p Cobbs Property Services Ltd*, para 171.

1766 Judgment in default—overseas enforcement of judgment—discretion to proceed to full trial where default judgment unenforceable in overseas jurisdiction

After the issue of a writ and following the defendant's failure to acknowledge service or take steps to defend the claim, the plaintiff became entitled to enter final judgment against the defendant in accordance with RSC Ord 13, r 1 and Ord 19. The plaintiff wished to enforce the judgment in an overseas jurisdiction where a default judgment was effectively unenforceable, having been obtained without any judicial examination of the merits of the plaintiff's claim. Consequently, having given the defendant full notice of the application, the plaintiff applied to the court for permission to proceed to a full trial of the claim in the defendant's absence. *Held*, where the court was presented with material to suggest that a judgment obtained by an automatic method might prove to be unenforceable in a foreign jurisdiction in which the defendant was known to reside or where there were reasonable grounds for believing he may have assets, it would be appropriate for the court to exercise its jurisdiction and proceed to a full trial of the claim. It was immaterial that the plaintiff could obtain precisely the same judgment under the automatic procedures provided both by Ord 13 and Ord 19. Accordingly, the application would be granted.

Berliner Bank v Karageorgis (1995) Times, 27 November (Queen's Bench Division: Colman J).

1767 Order—variation of order—interlocutory application—liberty to apply

The plaintiff had built a miniature robot which he had used to film inside a part of one of the pyramids at Giza which had never been seen before. A television company was at that time interested in the possibility of a documentary programme on the subject. It entered into discussions with the plaintiff and he gave a filmed interview. A television company broadcast pieces of footage from his film and extracts from the interview without the plaintiff's consent. They claimed that only the Egyptian authorities could give licence to them to use the film, that this had been done and they had broadcast the film in good faith on that footing. Being particularly concerned that the company might sell the programme overseas, the plaintiff brought proceedings for infringement of copyright. The company gave to the court undertakings until after judgment or further order that it would not sell, distribute or reproduce the material in question, though it had claimed to have evidence that the plaintiff did not own the copyright in the film. At the time the undertakings were given, the television company made it clear that it wished to reserve the right to apply at a later date to be released from the undertakings. Although such a provision was included in the draft order, no express provision for liberty to apply appeared in the final order. When the company later made such an application, the plaintiff claimed that it could not do so without showing good grounds. *Held*, on interlocutory applications as much as final trials the court was concerned to balance the intentions of the applicants to make subsequent applications with the interests of finality. In the present case there was no common intention between the parties but as a general rule the court would not compel a defendant to contest an interlocutory motion if he was prepared to give undertakings whilst evidence was being sought. It would not be reasonable to expect the defendant to fight merely to reserve the liberty to apply instead of giving undertakings. Moreover, in the circumstances the defendant had not acquiesced in the deletion of the liberty to apply clauses. Accordingly, the application would be allowed without the necessity of showing special circumstances.

Gantenbrink v British Broadcasting Corporation [1995] FSR 162 (Chancery Division: Sir Donald Nicholls V-C). *Chanel Ltd v FW Woolworth* [1981] 1 All ER 745, CA (1980 Abr para 1622), *Butt v Butt* [1987] 3 All ER 657, CA (1987 Abr para 1370), applied.

1768   Order for costs

See PRACTICE AND PROCEDURE.

1769   Private International Law (Miscellaneous Provisions) Act 1995

See para 577.

1770   Summary judgment—action to enforce earlier judgment—court's discretion whether appropriate to give judgment

Judgment was given in favour of the plaintiffs granting leave to enforce an award of an arbitrator against the defendant. That judgment was outstanding for almost six years. The defendant had not honoured the judgment and despite the best efforts of the plaintiffs, only a small amount of the very considerable judgment sum had been recovered. The plaintiffs made an application for summary judgment to enforce the judgment. *Held*, the court had a discretion as to whether or not it was appropriate to give judgment in a case which brought an action on an earlier judgment of a judge of co-ordinate jurisdiction. Such an action would be an abuse of the process of the court if the ordinary processes of execution were available. In the present case, in exercising that discretion the main fact was that the judgment had been outstanding for nearly six years and it was clear not merely that the defendant had assets which he was using in instructing lawyers in countries other than England but that he was doing all he possibly could to avoid payment of the award and the English judgment. In all the circumstances, the discretion should be exercised to enforce the original judgment and it was appropriate to do so by way of summary procedure since the court had heard the full argument and it was difficult to see what further evidence there could be. Accordingly, summary judgment would be given in the plaintiffs' favour.

E D & F Man (Sugar) Ltd v Haryanto (1995) Times, 24 November (Queen's Bench Division: Longmore J).

1771   Summary judgment—application for summary judgment—contents of supporting affidavits

A bank commenced proceedings against a debtor by a specially endorsed writ alleging that he owed substantial amounts of money from a loan account and from his current account. The statement of claim pleaded that the bank had demanded repayment in writing but that this had not been made. The debtor appealed against the consequent order for summary judgment on the grounds that affidavits made in support of the bank's application were defective. *Held*, in an application for summary judgment pursuant to RSC Ord 14, the technical requirements relating to the contents of supporting affidavits had to be observed. The purpose of those requirements was to demonstrate that the case was a proper case for summary judgment for, unlike interlocutory injunctions, Ord 14 judgments finally disposed of an action in a summary manner. In the present case, the bank's solicitor could easily have procured the information required in the affidavit by persons having knowledge of the debtor's loan account. Accordingly, the appeal would be allowed and the Ord 14 judgment set aside.

Barclays Bank v Piper (1995) Independent, 24 May, (1995) Times, 31 May (Court of Appeal: Neill and Roch LJJ).

1772 Summary judgment—application for summary judgement—second application— separate basis for application

It has been held that there is no objection in principle to more than one application being made under RSC Ord 14 provided that the legal or factual basis of the claim in the second application is quite separate from that relied upon in the pleading underlying the first application.

Bristol and West Building Society v Brandon (1995) Times, 9 March (Queen's Bench Division: Colman J).

1773 Summary judgment—leave to defend—civil proceedings following criminal convictions

Following the theft of a large quantity of gold from the plaintiff's possession, many of the robbers and handlers involved were caught and convicted of criminal offences. The plaintiff commenced civil proceedings against a number of persons including some of the robbers and handlers, and applied for summary judgment under RSC Ord 14. Two of the defendants opposed the application. *Held*, the fact that the plaintiff had delayed in making the application was irrelevant. Moreover, it would be an abuse of process to allow the defendants to rely on the Civil Evidence Act 1968, s 11(2)(a) in order to claim that their criminal convictions were wrong, as no new evidence had come to light since the criminal trial. Where an application for summary judgment was made, it was for the applicant to prove that there was no fair or reasonable probability that the defendant had a real or bona fide defence. In this case, one of the defendants could not allege that there was no positive evidence that he had handled the stolen gold, as that defence was neither real nor bona fide. Similarly, it was not open to the other defendant to claim that certain shareholdings and sums held in various accounts were not derived from the proceeds of the stolen gold, as that defence had already failed in the criminal trial and to allow him to re-litigate the matter would amount to an abuse of process. The proceeds of the robbery were held on constructive trust for the plaintiff, as it was settled law that if a trustee mixed trust funds with his own money and the two could not be distinguished, the funds belonged to the trust entirely. Accordingly, the application would be granted.

Brinks Ltd v Abu-Saleh [1995] 4 All ER 65 (Chancery Division: Jacob J).

JURIES

Halsbury's Laws of England (4th edn) Vol 26, paras 601–700

1774 Articles

The Evolving Criminal Trial Jury, in Myth and Reality, Gregory Durston: Criminal Lawyer, Issue 57, p 2
The Jury—A Suitable Case for Treatment? Alistair Bonnington: 145 NLJ 847
Racism, Impartiality and Juries, Peter Herbert: 145 NLJ 1138

1775 Juror—bias—juror's husband employed as prison officer—defendants on remand at same prison

Prior to their trial, the appellants were held in prison on remand on charges of robbery. Both worked in the prison kitchen and came in close contact with the catering officer. When the officer's wife was called for jury service she asked to be excused on the basis that her husband was a prison officer. An official, on behalf of the chief clerk of the Crown Court, informed her that she could not be excused but pointed out that she could appeal against the decision. She did not do so and in due course was called as a juror at the appellants' trial. They were convicted and, on appeal, they submitted that there was a real danger, arising from the relationship between the juror and her husband, that in carrying out her duties she might consciously or unconsciously have been guilty of bias. *Held*, it was a great pity that the juror had not been excused attendance for jury service because this situation was one which ought to have been within the contemplation of the Crown Court. The community was comparatively small and the chance that such a situation might arise was not a remote one. There was a real danger of bias and, accordingly, the appeal would be allowed and the convictions quashed. A retrial would be ordered.

R v Wilson; R v Sprason (1995) Times, 24 February (Court of Appeal: Russell LJ, Turner and Hooper JJ).

1776 Juror—bias—witnesses known to juror

The appellant was charged with indecent assault and rape. At his trial, two of the witnesses, the complainant and her mother, were known to one of the jurors. The juror, however, did not indicate to the court that she knew them. When the appellant's solicitors became aware of this, they took steps themselves to follow the juror and also instructed an inquiry agent to follow her. The appellant was convicted and on his appeal, *held*, (1) this was a highly sensitive case and the witnesses known to the juror were vital. The court felt that there was a real danger of bias in the sense that the juror might have unfairly regarded the appellant's case. (2) The conduct of the defence solicitors was most ill-advised and should never be repeated. It was perfectly permissible for them to take steps to clarify the position concerning their client but not without the leave of the Court of Appeal. Accordingly, the appeal would be allowed and a retrial would be ordered.

R v K (Jury: Appearance of Bias) (1995) 16 Cr App Rep (S) 966 (Court of Appeal: Hutchison LJ, Alliott and Curtis JJ).

1777 Juror—discharge—court's discretion—need for proper investigation

It has been held that where a judge is aware that untoward events have occurred involving a member of the public, he is entitled to question that person in the absence of the jury and to have the matter investigated by the police or court officials. If he suspects that a jury or members of it have been tampered with in some way, he has a duty to carry out investigations including the questioning of the jury or individual members. Such investigations must be to establish whether the jury's independence has been compromised and not to question their deliberations. After the investigation, the judge has a discretion to discharge an individual juror or the whole jury.

R v Blackwell; R v Farley; R v Adams [1995] 2 Cr App Rep 625 (Court of Appeal: Evans and Auld LJJ and Morland J).

1778 Juror—discharge—court's discretion—physical disability—profound deafness

The Juries Act 1974, s 9B provides that a person may be brought before a judge where it appears that, on account of physical disability, there is some doubt about his ability to act effectively as a juror. The judge must then affirm the summons unless he is of the opinion that, on account of his disability, the person will not be capable of acting effectively as a juror.

A juror who was profoundly deaf asked for the services of an interpreter. On the juror being brought before the judge under the 1974 Act, s 9B, *held*, the principle of fairness to the defendant required that every juror should have a similar opportunity to listen to the evidence and to assess the reliability of witnesses. If an interpreter was used there was a risk that the juror might lose the nuances from the manner and tone in which questions were answered. When the jury retired it would be difficult for a juror with an interpreter to make an equal contribution to the deliberations and the presence of an interpreter in the jury room would contradict the long held principle that it was an incurable irregularity for an independent person to retire with a jury even though they may take no part in the discussions. Accordingly, he would not be capable of acting effectively as a juror and would be discharged.

Re Osman [1995] 1 WLR 1327 (Central Criminal Court: Sir Lawrence Verney, Recorder of London).

1779 Verdict—change of verdict—jury hearing evidence of previous convictions

The appellant had been charged under the Offences Against the Person Act 1861, s 18 with the offence of wounding with intent to do grievous harm. The jury acquitted him of that offence and convicted him of the lesser offence of unlawful wounding contrary to s 20. He appealed against his conviction. After the verdict had been accepted and while the jury remained in the box, prosecuting counsel dealt with his previous convictions, which included other offences of violence. After the jury had been discharged, a juror told the court usher that the foreman had given the wrong verdict. The judge decided to reconvene the jury and when asked to explain themselves they indicated that the wrong verdict had been returned. The judge clarified the possible verdicts and a unanimous verdict of guilty of the more serious offence was returned. On appeal, *held*, the original verdict was plain and unequivocal and no adequate explanation of the jury's state of mind had been put forward. After the first verdict the jury had heard material which they had no right to hear and consequently the second verdict was unsafe and unsatisfactory. Accordingly, the appeal would be allowed and the original verdict would be reinstated.

R v Bills [1995] 2 Cr App Rep 643 (Court of Appeal: Russell LJ, Turner and Hooper JJ).

1780 Verdict—majority verdict—pressure to reach verdict

See *R v Dudson*, para 868.

LAND CHARGES

Halsbury's Laws of England (4th edn) Vol 26, paras 701–900

1781 Articles

Feeding the Estoppel at the Land Registry, Peter Cowell (on the dating of land charges): 139 SJ 1040

Independent Advice After *O'Brien*, H W Wilkinson (on *Barclays Bank plc v O'Brien* [1993] 4 All ER 417, HL (1993 Abr para 1826)): 145 NLJ 792

Land Charges, John Manthorpe (on the rules protecting equitable charges on the land register): LS Gaz, 29 March 1995, p 22

1782 Local land charges—requisitions—electronic means

The Local Land Charges (Amendment) Rules 1995, SI 1995/260 (in force on 1 March 1995), amend the 1977 Rules, SI 1977/985, to provide for the use of electronic means in the making of requisitions for, and the issue of certificates of, official searches of the Local Land Charges Register under the Local Land Charges Act 1975, s 9.

1783 Rules

The Land Charges (Amendment) Rules 1995, SI 1995/1355 (in force on 1 July 1995), amend the provisions of the 1974 Rules, SI 1974/1286, relating to applications for an official search in the index under the Land Charges Act 1972, s 10(1)(b) or for an office copy of an entry via the registrar's computer. The 1974 Rules are also amended to take account of amendments made to the 1972 Act by the Law of Property (Miscellaneous Provisions) Act 1994, s 15.

LAND REGISTRATION

Halsbury's Laws of England (4th edn) Vol 26, paras 901–1490

1784 Articles

Cautions Against Dealings, J F Bechelet: 139 SJ 1183

Feeding the Estoppel at the Land Registry, Peter Cowell (on the dating of land charges): 139 SJ 1040

Pending Land Actions, Dr Jean Howell: [1995] Conv 309

Title Guarantees: New Rules (and Points to Ponder), John Sarginson and Sue Cullen: 139 SJ 508

1785 Assignment—completion of assignment—completion by registration—effect of failure to register

See *Brown & Root Technology Ltd v Sun Alliance and London Insurance Co Ltd*, para 1795.

1786 Compulsory registration—extension—proposals

The first report of a joint working party (the Land Registry, the Law Commission and the Lord Chancellor's Department) on the implementation of the Law Commission's third and fourth reports on land registration (Law Com Nos 153, 178) has been published under the title *Transfer of Land: Land Registration* (Cm 2950; Law Com No 235). The report recommends that the Land Registration Act 1925, s 123 (compulsory registration) should be extended to cover assents, vesting deeds, conveyances by way of gift, conveyances pursuant to a court order and first legal mortgages. For the sake of certainty, it is suggested that express reference should also be made in s 123 to re-conveyances which are made after any first conveyance has become void for non-registration. Future extensions of s 123 should thereafter be made by statutory instrument. It is also suggested that express provision should be made to the effect that although unregistered (registrable) transactions would be ineffective to transfer or grant a legal estate or to create a legal right over land they should nevertheless take effect in equity. Specially reduced fees should be charged to encourage registration and such should be specified in Fees Orders. The report recommends that a person who suffers loss as a result of an error in, or omission from, the register should be entitled to an indemnity, regardless of whether the register is rectified. Any indemnity should, however, be proportionately reduced if the loss was in part caused by a lack of proper care on the part of the claimant. A cause of action in relation to indemnity should, for the purposes of the Statute of Limitations, be deemed to have arisen when the claimant knew (or, but for his own default, might have known) of the existence of the claim. The Land Registry's rights of recourse should be extended so that it would be subrogated to the rights of any person to whom indemnity was paid and the registry would have a statutory right to enforce any cause of action which a party who obtains rectification of the register might otherwise have had. A draft Bill which would give effect to these recommendations is appended to the report. In the foreword to the report, it is stated that it is the intention of the Lord Chancellor to implement its recommendations when a suitable opportunity presents itself.

1787 District land registries—transfer of responsibilities

The Land Registration (District Registries) Order 1995, SI 1995/2962 (in force on 1 April 1996), replaces the 1991 Order, SI 1991/2634. The districts of the district registries remain unaltered except for the transfer of responsibility for the registration of titles as follows: (1) in South Gloucestershire and Bristol from the Plymouth to the Gloucester District Land Registry, (2) in Wiltshire from the Gloucester to the Weymouth District Land Registry, and (3) in West Sussex from the Weymouth to the Portsmouth District Land Registry.

1788 Legal charge—charge created under doctrine of 'feeding estoppel'

See *First National Bank plc v Thompson*, para 1325.

1789 Law of Property (Miscellaneous Provisions) Act 1994—commencement

The Law of Property (Miscellaneous Provisions) Act 1994 (Commencement No 1) Order 1995, SI 1995/145, brings into force on 15 February 1995 s 21(1) (in part) and Sch 1, para 2, which amends the Land Registration Act 1925, s 38(2), thereby enabling the Lord Chancellor to make rules for prescribing the effect of covenants implied by virtue of the 1994 Act in dispositions of registered land. For a summary of the Act, see 1994 Abr para 2348. For details of commencement, see the commencement table in the title STATUTES.

1790 Registered dispositions—implied covenants for title

The Land Registration (Implied Covenants for Title) Rules 1995, SI 1995/377 (in force on 1 July 1995), amend the Land Registration Rules 1925, SR & O 1925/1093, so as to give effect to the Law of Property (Miscellaneous Provisions) Act 1994, Pt I (implied covenants for title on dispositions of registered land). The 1994 Rules allow registered dispositions to include references to the new terms which imply covenants for title, namely 'with full title guarantee' or 'with limited title guarantee'. Such covenants take effect as if the disposition had been expressly made subject to specified entries on the register and to the overriding interests of which the person to whom the disposition was made had notice. No reference to the implied covenants may be entered on the register, except where the registered disposition incorporating such a reference is of leasehold land. The rules also provide for the cases where a person may, in a registered disposition, continue to be expressed to execute, transfer or charge as beneficial owner, settlor, trustee, mortgagee, personal representative or under an order of the court so as to imply covenants for title under the Law of Property Act 1925, s 77 and to imply covenants for title under the 1925 Act, s 76 where that section applies to the disposition by virtue of the 1994 Act, s 11(1).

1791 Rules

The Land Registration Rules 1995, SI 1995/140 (in force on 3 April 1995), amend the 1925 Rules, SR & O 1925/1093, to provide for a certificate to be given to the registrar as to the appropriate restriction to be entered on the register where a charity which already owns land applies voluntarily to register that land. The 1994 Rules also provide that where a charity which is already registered as a proprietor of land makes an application to register new trustees it must also make an application for the appropriate restriction to be entered on the register if the existing restriction is no longer appropriate. Further, the rules provide that it is no longer possible to apply for the entry on the register of a notice of deposit or a notice of intended deposit of a certificate, although the effect of any existing entry made on the register is preserved.

The Land Registration (No 2) Rules 1995, SI 1995/1354 (in force in part on 19 June 1995 and in part on 11 September 1995), amend the 1925 Rules, SR & O 1925/1093, to provide for revised forms of entry of creditors' notices and bankruptcy inhibitions. They also amend the Land Registration (Open Register) Rules 1991, SI 1992/122, to enable any person, during the currency of a relevant notice under r 13 and subject to the limitations in that notice, to obtain day list information in respect of pending applications, pending official searches with priority, and land and charge certificates deposited at the Land Registry.

The Land Registration (No 3) Rules 1995, SI 1995/3153 (in force on 1 January 1996), amend the 1925 Rules, SR & O 1925/1093, the Land Registration (Matrimonial Homes) Rules 1990, SI 1990/1360, the Land Registration (Open Register) Rules 1991, SI 1992/122, and the Land Registration (Official Searches) Rules 1993, SI 1993/3276. 'Proper office' is defined for the purposes of all the above sets of rules as the district registry within whose district the land, or any part of the land, to which an application relates is situated. Provision is made for transfers of land held under new tenancies within the meaning of the Landlord and Tenant (Covenants) Act 1995 (ie leases granted on or after 1 January 1996 otherwise than in pursuance of an agreement entered into, an option granted or a court order made before that date) in addition to transfers of land held under leases which are not new tenancies. Provision is also made to reflect the fact that covenants implied by the Land Registration Act 1925, s 24 and the Law of Property Act 1925, s 77 (repealed in relation to new tenancies) can only apply to transfers of land held under leases that are not new tenancies.

The 1925 Rules, r 76 (transfer of land subject to a rentcharge and leasehold land as beneficial owner so as to imply covenants by the transferor implied by the Law of Property Act 1925, s 77) is revoked and new provision is made to permit the appropriate covenants to be incorporated in transfers without the transfer being made as beneficial owner. New Forms 32 (transfer of leasehold land (whole or part)), 33 (transfer of leasehold land (whole) being part of the land originally comprised in the lease, where the rent has already been apportioned), 34 (transfer of land held under a new tenancy (part) in which the rent is apportioned or land exonerated), 34A (transfer of land held under an old tenancy (part) in which the rent is apportioned or land exonerated) and 34B (transfer of land subject to a rentcharge (part) in which the rent is apportioned or land exonerated) are substituted for Forms 32, 33 and 34 in the 1925 Rules.

LANDLORD AND TENANT

Halsbury's Laws of England (4th edn) Vol 27(1) (reissue), paras 1–986, Vol 27(2) (reissue), paras 987–1739

1792 Articles

Abolition of Privity: Values at Risk, Chris Osmond: 139 SJ 1213

Acceptance of Repudiatory Breach in Leases, Mark Pawlowski: [1995] Conv 366

The Agricultural Revolution, Stephen McNulty and Della Evans (on the Agricultural Tenancies Act 1995): Estates Gazette, 29 July 1995, p 82

The Anchor Tenant and the 'Keep Open' Clause, Geoffrey Dale (on valuation problems which arise from a breach of a keep open clause): 139 SJ 94

An Answer to the Tenant's Nightmare? Patricia Vassallo and David Lyons (on tenants' restructuring of their leases): 139 SJ 899

Assignment and Assignor's Rent Arrears, J E Adams: 139 SJ 794

Assignment, Consent and a Novel Proposition, Michael Haley (on *Olympia & York Canary Wharf Ltd v Oil Property Investment Ltd* [1994] 29 EG 121 (1994 Abr para 1730)): 139 SJ 68

Commercial Leases: the New Code, Richard Castle and Alister McFarquhar: 145 NLJ 1166

Commonhold—A Prospect of Promise, D N Clarke (on the proposals for a statutory form of commonhold title): 58 MLR 486

Continuation and Termination of Business Tenancies, Kaz Stepien: 139 SJ 690

Criminal Liability for Damage, Neil Turner and Stuart Gronow (on liability of landlords for environmental pollution caused by their tenants): Estates Gazette, 25 November 1995, p 143

Dilapidations Disputes, Patricia Vassallo and Jennifer Hargreaves: 139 SJ 530

Disclaimer of Leases and Non-Payment of Rent, Mark Pawlowski (on the effect of liquidators' disclaimers of leases): 145 NLJ 892

Double Trouble, Kerry Stephenson (on the problem of double-rented property): 139 SJ 454

The Effect of Death on the Right to Buy Under Pt V of the Housing Act 1985, A H R Brierley: [1995] Conv 114, 224

Effect of Lease Termination on Subtenancies, Kaz Stepien: 139 SJ 122

Effect on Tenant's Liability of Payments Made by a Guarantor (*on Milverton Group Ltd v Warner World Ltd* [1995] EG 70, CA (para 1798)): 139 SJ 1130

The End is Nigh, Steven Fogel and Emma Slessenger (on the Landlord and Tenant (Covenants) Bill 1995): Estates Gazette, 8 July 1995, p 143

Enfranchisement Under the Leasehold Reform Act 1993: A Note on the Nominee Purchaser, J C Hicks: [1995] Conv 46

Full Repairing Covenants, H W Wilkinson: 145 NLJ 718

Going it Alone, Alan Harrison (on termination of a local authority tenancy by a joint tenant): 139 SJ 561

Harassment and Eviction, Nic Madge: 145 NLJ 937, 1060

Headline Rents—The Current Problems, Richard Porter and Michael Langdon: Estates Gazette, January 14 1995, p 130.

How Long is a Lease? Kaz Stepien (on using the word 'from' to specify the commencement date of a lease term): 139 SJ 452

Is it Ever Too Late? Nic Madge (on the prevention of eviction after a possession order): 145 NLJ 1852

Landlord and Tenant (Covenants) Act 1995, Trevor Aldridge: 139 SJ 918, 950

A Landlord's Control Over Assignments of Leases, Graham White: Estates Gazette, 15 April 1995, p 98

The Landlord's Costs of a Tenant's Breach, Darryl Greer: 145 NLJ 1538

Landlords' Repair Covenants—When is the Breach? H W Wilkinson (on *British Telecommunications plc v Sun Life Assurance Society plc* [1995] 4 All ER 44 (para 1806)): 145 NLJ 1793

The Law of the Land, David Knight (on the Landlord and Tenants Covenant Act 1995): LS Gaz, 26 July 1995, p 17

Lease Renewals: Tenants Beware, Chris Osmond: 139 SJ 429

Leasehold Covenants, Indemnities and Group Reconstructions, Alice Belcher: [1995] Conv 199

Leasehold Enfranchisement: Limits to a Loophole, David Clarke (on landlords seeking to sever the freehold in order to prevent a collective enfranchisement): 139 SJ 314

Leases and Side Agreements, Robert Wakefeld (on *System Floors Ltd v Ruralpride Ltd* [1995] 07 EG 125 (para 1809)): 139 SJ 604

Litigation Costs: Charging Through the Back Door? Graham Fife (on recovering litigation costs through service charges): Estates Gazette, 18 November, p 180

A New Lease of Life, Jan Russell and Gordon Porter (on variable rent review clauses in leases): LS Gaz, 11 May 1995, p 18

No Protection for Professional Associates? Jonathan Cole (on the failure of the Landlord and Tenant Act 1954 to protect tenants working in association): 139 SJ 1020

Open All Hours, Vivien King and Martin Wright (on the effect of Sunday opening and longer hours on landlords and tenants): Estates Gazette, 1 April 1995, p 126

Original Tenant Liability, Gary Webber (on *Hindcastle Ltd v Barbara Attenborough Associates Ltd* [1994] 4 All ER 129 (1993 Abr para 1732)): 139 SJ 196

Original Tenant Liability Redefined, Kaz Stepien (on *Friends Provident Life Office v British Railways Board* (1995) Independent, 14 September (para 1796)): 139 SJ 878

Over-rented Property: Is the Problem Over? Kerry Stephenson: 139 SJ 350

Pastures New, Roger Yates (on the Agricultural Tenancies Act 1995): 145 NLJ 1372

Rent Review Clauses: Hacking Through the Thickets, David Clarke: 139 SJ 36

Scarcity and Fair Rents, A M Prichard: 145 NLJ 210

Shortening the Shorthold: Landlords Beware: Stuart Bridge: 145 NLJ 1307

Sureties—Dangerous Variations, H W Wilkinson (on landlords releasing sureties): 145 NLJ 1141

Termination of Leases, Graham Fife (on *Pennell v Payne* (1994) Times, 13 December (1994 Abr para 65)): Estates Gazette, 14 October 1995, p 134

The Three Month Shorthold Assured Tenancy, Adrian Jack: 145 NLJ 925

Unattainable Reality, Arthur Lovitt and Sarah Crone (on arguments used by landlords and tenants to defeat each others' rent review claims): Estates Gazette, 7 October 1995, p 122

Variation of Lease or New Tenancy? Alan Dowling (on drawing the line between variation of a lease and substitution of a new one): [1995] Conv 124

Variations in Leases—An Escape Route for Tenants and Guarantors? Linda Harrison: Estates Gazette, 9 December 1995, p 117

Views of the Countryside, Roger Yates (on the Agricultural Tenancies Bill 1995): LS Gaz, 5 April 1995, p 16

What Next on Leases? Kerry Stephenson (on the implications of abolishing privity of contract for new cases): 139 SJ 798

What Value a Tenant's Break Option? Tim Cameron-Jones: 139 SJ 992

1793 Agricultural tenancies

See AGRICULTURE.

1794 Assignment—consent—application to underlet—landlord's failure to consent within reasonable time

The Landlord and Tenant Act 1988, s 1(3) provides that where there is served on a person who may consent to a proposed transaction a written application by the tenant for consent to the transaction, he owes a duty to the tenant within a reasonable time to give consent, except where it is reasonable not to give consent, and to serve on the tenant written notice of his decision whether or not to give consent.

A tenant of office buildings made a written application for consent to sublet part of the property. The landlord refused to give its consent, claiming to be justified in doing so until it had received an undertaking from the tenant's solicitors as to its costs of dealing with the consent. The costs claimed were £4,500, which the tenant claimed were unreasonable. The tenant commenced proceedings claiming damages for breach of statutory duty in the landlord's failure to give consent within a reasonable time or to serve on the tenant written notice of the reasons for withholding consent. The landlord contended that, as a matter of construction, a 'reasonable time' under the 1988 Act, s 1(3) did not begin to run until the landlord was offered a satisfactory undertaking as to costs. *Held*, s 1(3) did not require a tenant when seeking consent to a proposed transaction to include in his application an undertaking for the landlord's costs. If the landlord's argument was correct and a right to require a costs undertaking could be made a condition for his proceeding to consider a tenant's application, that could only apply where the undertaking was for a reasonable sum or for reasonable costs. The demand for costs in the present case was not reasonable and the landlord was in a position to give, or ought to have given, at least conditional consent. The landlord was in breach of its statutory duty and a declaration would be made accordingly.

Dong Bang Minerva (UK) Ltd v Davina Ltd [1995] 1 EGLR 41 (Chancery Division: Hazel Williamson QC).

1795 Assignment—date on which assignment takes effect—failure to register assignment

The defendant granted a lease to the first plaintiff, a partly-owned subsidiary of the second plaintiff, and the lease was registered at the Land Registry. The lease entitled the tenant to give notice to terminate, but the right to do so ceased on the assignment of the lease. The first plaintiff subsequently became a wholly-owned subsidiary of the second plaintiff and it was decided that all lease obligations would be undertaken by the second plaintiff. The defendant granted a licence to assign and the relevant conveyancing documents were executed. Thereafter the rent was invoiced to, and paid by, the second plaintiff. However, no registration of the assignment ever took place. The first plaintiff served a notice purporting to terminate the lease. The defendant claimed that the notice was invalid on the ground that the lease had been assigned prior to the service of the notice. On its application for a declaration that the notice was valid, the first plaintiff relied on the Land Registration Act 1925, s 22(1), which provides that the transferor of a leasehold interest is deemed to remain the proprietor of the registered estate until the transfer is registered. *Held*, where it was necessary to fix a date on which an assignment took place, that date was the date on which the assignment was completed. The assignor gave up the property on that date and he had no control over the stamping of the transfer or its submission to the Land Registry. The landlord also did not have such control, and neither the assignor nor the landlord could compel the assignee to submit the transfer for registration. Accordingly, the lease had been validly assigned and it could not be terminated by a notice served by the first plaintiff.

Brown & Root Technology Ltd v Sun Alliance and London Insurance Co Ltd [1995] 3 WLR 558 (Chancery Division: Judge Paul Baker QC).

1796   Assignment—deed of variation of assignment—liability of original underlessee

A landlord brought an action against an underlessee for arrears of rent. The arrears had accrued following the insolvency of the second assignee of the lease. The underlessee denied any liability to pay the arrears, claiming that its lease had been surrendered when the first assignee had executed a deed of variation with the landlord, thereby increasing the rent payable for the premises. At first instance, the landlord's claim was dismissed. On appeal, *held*, unless a legal estate was altered by a change in the extent of the demised premises or the terms on which they were held, a lessor and assignee could alter the terms of a lease without the law implying its surrender and re-grant for the remainder of the term of the lease. Therefore, the deed of variation did not effect a surrender of the lease. The underlessee remained liable to pay rent under its personal covenants. However, the nature of its obligations could not be varied or increased by the subsequent agreement between the landlord and the assignee. There was a distinction between a lessee's contractual liability under its personal covenants, and an assignee's liability for the obligations of the covenants 'imprinted' on the legal estate. The underlessee remained liable for the original rent, but could not be held to account for the excess rent. Accordingly, the appeal would be allowed in part.

Friends Provident Life Office v British Railways Board [1996] 1 All ER 336 (Court of Appeal: Beldam and Waite LJJ and Sir Christopher Slade).

1797   Assignment—obligation to pay rent—liability of original lessee—assignee entering into voluntary arrangement with creditors

The plaintiff landlord and defendant tenants entered into a 25-year lease of business premises. The lease was subsequently assigned. The assignee ran into financial difficulties and entered into an individual voluntary arrangement with his creditors, including the plaintiff, to whom he owed arrears of rent. Under the arrangement, funds were to be distributed to the assignee's creditors in full and final settlement of their claims against him in a specified order of priority, the plaintiff ranking seventh among the other unsecured creditors. The plaintiff sought payment of the arrears from the defendants and issued proceedings for summary judgment under RSC Ord 14 for the amount owing. The plaintiff's claim was struck out on the ground that the arrangement, in absolving the assignee from liability under the lease, also absolved the defendants. The plaintiff appealed. *Held*, where the assignee of a lease entered into a voluntary arrangement with his creditors, then, unless that arrangement provided for the forfeiture, disclaimer or variation of the lease or made express provision in relation to the original tenants, the liability of those tenants to the landlord under the lease was preserved, notwithstanding that the arrangement absolved the assignee of all liability. It followed that the defendants remained liable on their covenants under the lease. The appeal would accordingly be allowed.

Mytre Investments Ltd v Reynolds [1995] 3 All ER 588 (Queen's Bench Division: Michael Burton QC). *Deanplan Ltd v Mahmoud* [1992] 3 All ER 945 (1992 Abr para 535) applied.

1798   Assignment—surety covenants—payment by surety in consideration of release from liability—appropriation of payments

A lease, granted to the defendant, was assigned twice. Both deeds of licence to assign contained personal covenants by a surety that the assignee would pay the rent and, in default, the surety would do so. The second assignee became insolvent and defaulted on the rent. The plaintiff landlord subsequently claimed against the defendant for payment of four quarters of rent. The latter maintained that part of the rent had already been paid. It sought to rely on payments made to the plaintiff by the sureties in consideration for their release from any further obligations under the lease. At first instance, the defendant was found to be liable to pay all but that first instalment, that instalment alone having been outstanding at the time of execution of the first deed of release. The defendant appealed. *Held*, payment by a surety of a lessee's rent discharged the lessee from his liability to pay. However, the defendant had to show that the payments were appropriated to those instalments of rent for which he was being sued. By granting the deeds of release, the plaintiff had accepted performance of the obligations in the lease in part. A recital, in the first deed of release, of a demand for payment of the rent outstanding at that time, was impliedly an appropriation by the plaintiff of part of the payment towards the rent arrears. Therefore, the plaintiff was not entitled to claim that first instalment from the defendant. The plaintiff could appropriate the balance of the payments to the instalments which subsequently fell due. However if he so wished, he was entitled to defer any further appropriation and recover the remaining three rent instalments from the defendant. The defendant was not entitled to appropriate, and thus to set off, those payments against the remaining instalments. Accordingly, the appeal would be dismissed.

Milverton Group Ltd v Warner World Ltd [1995] 2 EGLR 28 (Court of Appeal: Glidewell, Kennedy and Hoffmann LJJ).

1799 Assured shorthold tenancy—mandatory grounds for possession—two-month notice period—computation of time

Before the grant of an assured shorthold tenancy, a landlord's agent purported to deliver to the prospective tenant the requisite notice under the Housing Act 1988, s 20; however, the notice had not been signed by the landlord or his agent and the landlord's name was misspelled. For five months of the tenancy the light and the extractor fan in the bathroom of the tenant's flat did not work. The bathroom had no natural light or ventilation and the tenant had to bathe and shave by candle light. Unpleasant odours lingered in the flat causing the tenant inconvenience and embarrassment as a result of which he did not invite friends to visit his home. The landlord was resident in the basement flat of the building in which the tenant's flat was situated and although he was asked to repair the defect on three occasions he failed to carry out the repair. A notice requiring the tenant to give up possession was dated and served on 1 March and was stated to expire on 30 April. The tenant resisted the claim for possession and counterclaimed for damages for disrepair. *Held*, the failure to identify the landlord properly in the s 20 notice and the failure by the landlord or its agent to sign the notice invalidated it and accordingly the tenant was an assured tenant of the premises. The notice requiring the tenant to give up possession of the premises was also ineffective. Under the 1988 Act, s 21, the tenant had to be given not less than two months' notice. In relation to notices given in respect of periodic tenancies, the rule was that the first day or the last day of the notice was disregarded. Accordingly, the notice gave one day less than the two months' notice required under s 21. As to the measure of damages to be awarded, it was estimated that the tenant had only been able to make half of the proper use of the bathroom which could have been expected. Since the bathroom was one of five rooms in the flat (ie 20 per cent of the flat) it could be said that the value of the flat to the tenant had been diminished by 10 per cent. Accordingly, damages of £1,000 would be awarded to the tenant comprising £17.50 per week for the diminution in value of the tenancy (representing 10 per cent of the weekly rental) and general damages of £30 per week over the period of actionable disrepair.

Symons v Warren (22 August 1995, unreported) (Clerkenwell County Court: District Judge Armon Jones). Kindly submitted by Declan O'Mahoney, Barrister.

1800 Business tenancy—application for new tenancy—opposition—landlord's intention to demolish or reconstruct

The Landlord and Tenant Act 1954, s 30(1)(f) provides that a landlord may refuse to grant a new tenancy if on the termination of the current tenancy, he intends to demolish or reconstruct the premises comprised in the holding or a substantial part of those premises, or to carry out substantial work of construction on the holding or part thereof, and cannot reasonably do so without obtaining possession of the holding.

The plaintiffs were the tenants of an area of land which consisted of buildings and rough vegetation, and which they used as a small farm. Their application for a new tenancy was opposed by the landlords under the 1954 Act, s 30(1)(f). The landlords had entered into an agreement with a company whereby they would grant a four-year lease of the land to the company, on condition that the company demolished the buildings on the land and converted the area into a car park with a landscaped surrounding. A judge decided that the landlords had not made out a case under s 30(1)(f), because their real motive was to sell the freehold of the land. On the landlords' appeal, *held*, a landlord's motive was irrelevant, provided that there was a genuine intention to demolish or reconstruct. Moreover, a landlord was not obliged to carry out the demolition or reconstruction himself, as that could be done by an agent or a tenant on his behalf. Here, the landlords intended the demolition work to be carried out by the company to whom it proposed to grant a short-term lease, and the fact that the proposed new lease was for a short period was strong evidence of that intention. It was irrelevant that the landlords' real motive was the eventual sale of the freehold. As they had made out a case under the 1954 Act, s 30(1)(f), they were entitled to refuse to grant the tenants a new tenancy. Accordingly, the appeal would be allowed.

Turner v London Borough of Wandsworth (1994) 69 P & CR 433 (Court of Appeal: Staughton LJ and Sir Francis Purchas).

1801 Business tenancy—termination—notice to quit—whether premises occcupied for the purposes of carrying on a business

The plaintiff was the tenant of business premises in which it let out space for market stalls. Each stallholder had access to facilities supplied by the plaintiff and paid a weekly charge and service charge for his stall. In addition, the plaintiff provided a superintendent during trading hours and no stallholder had access to the market outside normal shopping hours. The defendant landlord served a notice under the Landlord and Tenant Act 1954, Pt II, stating that it wished to terminate the plaintiff's lease, but the plaintiff served a counter-notice contending that it occupied the market hall for the purpose of its business under the 1954 Act, s 23(1) and was therefore entitled to security of tenure under the 1954 Act, Pt II. The Court of Appeal held that the plaintiff was entitled to security of tenure and the defendant appealed. *Held*, the word 'occupied' in the 1954 Act implied a physical use of the property by the tenant for the purposes of his business. Property which was occupied by someone other than a tenant would not form part of a tenant's holding, although the tenant could claim occupation of the retained parts of the premises provided the holding was still used by it for the purpose of its business. In this case, once the reversion to the stalls vested in the defendant, the plaintiff ceased to collect rents and its business in the market went. Accordingly, the business property not occupied by the plaintiff ceased to be property for which it was able to obtain a new tenancy or recover compensation and the appeal would be allowed.

Graysim Holdings Ltd v P & O Property Holdings Ltd [1995] 4 All ER 831 (House of Lords: Lords MacKay of Clashfern LC, Goff of Chieveley, Jauncey of Tullichettle, Lloyd of Berwick and Nicholls of Birkenhead). Decision of Court of Appeal (1994 Abr para 1739) reversed.

1802 Business tenancy—termination—tenant's notice—effective date

A tenant of commercial property sought to exercise its right to determine its fixed term lease. The notice was expressed to expire on the day before the expiry date specified in the lease. At first instance, it was held that the notice was effective to determine the lease. The landlord appealed. *Held*, the notice could not have taken effect at any time later than the last moment of the date specified in it. There was no authority for the proposition that the last moment of that day was the same as the first moment of the following day. An incorrect date given in a tenant's notice could only be corrected in circumstances where it was either impossible to comply with the expiry date specified in the lease or it was on some other ground inconceivable that it was the date intended. Accordingly, the tenant's notice was ineffective and the appeal would be allowed.

Mannai Investment Co Ltd v Eagle Star Life Assurance Co Ltd [1996] 1 All ER 55 (Court of Appeal: Nourse, Roch and Hobhouse LJJ).

1803 Business tenancy—termination—tenant's notice—tenant giving up occupation before expiration of contractual term

A landlord and tenant entered into a five-year sublease of commercial premises at a rent payable in advance. The tenant took possession and occupied the premises until several months before the contractual term of the lease expired. It intended to terminate the tenancy on the March quarter day in accordance with the terms of the lease, but failed to serve a valid notice within the time limits prescribed under the Landlord and Tenant Act 1954, s 27(2). A valid notice was eventually served which terminated the tenancy on the following quarter day in June. The landlord claimed rent for the period between the contractual expiry of the lease and the June quarter day. The tenant refused to pay on the ground that, as it had given up occupation before the term date, the lease had expired by effluxion on its contractual expiry and that formal notice under s 27(2) was therefore unnecessary. *Held*, a tenancy which fell within the protection of the 1954 Act would continue unless it had been determined in accordance with the provisions of the Act, even if the tenant had ceased occupation before its lease had expired by effluxion of time. The tenant's notice, which purported to terminate the tenancy on the June quarter day, was effective. Thus, both the tenancy and the tenant's liability for rent continued until that date. Accordingly, the landlord's claim would succeed.

Esselte AB v Pearl Assurance plc [1995] 2 EGLR 61 (Chancery Division: Judge Colyer QC).

1804 Covenant—covenant against alteration of user—structural alteration

The Landlord and Tenant Act 1927, s 19(3) provides that, where a lease contains a covenant against the alteration of user without licence or consent, that covenant, if the alteration does not involve any structural alteration of the premises, is deemed to be subject to a proviso that no fine is payable for or in respect of such licence or consent.

Tenants held two underleases of premises from the landlords. Negotiations commenced between the parties in which the tenants sought consent to use the ground floor of the premises for any use within the Town and Country Planning (Use Classes) Order 1987, SI 1987/764, Schedule, class A2 and the landlords looked for a break clause. The landlords' agent set out their terms in a letter, which stated that consent would be given to a change of use of the ground floor on terms including (1) an increased rent; (2) payment of legal fees; and (3) payment of a service charge. Evidence was given that the tenants proposed certain alterations to an exterior wall of the premises. The tenants sought a declaration that they were entitled to use the premises for any class A2 use, relying on the Landlord and Tenant Act 1927, s 19(3) and *West v Gwynne*. *Held*, the requirements of the letter amounted to requirements for a fine within the 1927 Act, s 19(3). However, the proposed alterations to the exterior wall were part and parcel of the proposal to alter the use. Thus, the alteration of user involved a structural alteration and s 19(3) did not apply. Accordingly, the tenants' application would be dismissed.

Barclays Bank plc v Daejan Investments (Grove Hall) Ltd [1995] 18 EG 117 (Chancery Division: Judge Rich QC). *West v Gwynne* [1911] 2 Ch 1, CA, distinguished.

1805 Covenant—covenant to keep open shop premises—breach—remedies

See *Co-Operative Insurance Society Ltd v Argyll Stores (Holdings) Ltd*, para 2794.

1806 Covenant—covenant to repair—circumstances in which covenant breached

A covenant in a lease required the landlord to keep the premises in 'complete good and substantial repair and condition'. The lessees occupied part of a building and when damage occurred to another part of the building the question arose whether the landlord was in breach of his covenant to repair those parts of the building which ceased to be in repair immediately or after the expiration of a reasonable time for carrying out the repairs. The landlord appealed from a decision that it was in breach of covenant when the building fell into disrepair. *Held*, the covenant obliged the landlord to keep the building in good repair at all times and the covenant was breached as soon as a defect occurred. The only exception to this rule occurred when the damage occurred in the demised premises themselves. Then the landlord was only in breach of his obligation when he had knowledge of the existence of damage such as would alert a reasonable landlord as to the necessity of repairs and he then failed to carry out works with reasonable expedition. Accordingly, the appeal would be dismissed.

British Telecom plc v Sun Life Assurance Society plc [1995] 4 All ER 44 (Court of Appeal: Nourse, Roch and Hutchison LJJ). Decision of Aldous J [1994] 43 EG 158 (1994 Abr para 1743) affirmed.

1807 Covenant—covenant to repair—recovery of costs of remedial work

The Leasehold Property (Repairs) Act 1938, s 1(1) provides that where a lessor serves on a lessee a notice that relates to a breach of covenant or agreement to keep or put in repair all or any of the property comprised in the lease, the lessee may, within 28 days from that date, serve on the lessor a counter-notice to the effect that he claims the benefit of the 1938 Act. Section 1(3) provides that where a counter-notice is served by a lessee, no proceedings may be taken by the lessor for the enforcement of any right of re-entry or forfeiture under any proviso or stipulation in the lease, for breach of the covenant or agreement, or for damages for breach thereof, otherwise than with the leave of the court

A covenant in a lease obliged the tenant to keep the demised premises in good tenantable repair and condition, and to maintain and repair them. The covenant also allowed the landlord to enter the premises for inspection purposes, and to give written notice to the tenant of any defects or want of repair, requiring the tenant to remedy the defects within three months, failing which the landlord was entitled to do the work himself and recover the cost from the tenant. When the landlord served a notice specifying the remedial work which needed to be done, the tenant failed to carry it out. The landlord therefore sought to exercise his right to do the work himself and recover the cost from the tenant. On the tenant's refusal to allow him entry, the landlord was granted an injunction restraining the tenant from preventing him from doing so. On appeal, the tenant argued that having regard to the 1938 Act, s 1, the landlord was obliged to obtain leave of the court to enter and carry out the work. *Held*, the landlord was not making a claim for damages for breach of the tenant's covenant to repair, but for reimbursement of sums spent in carrying out the repairs himself. He had carried out the repairs for the benefit of himself and the tenant, rather than because the property was in disrepair, and his claim was one of debt. The landlord's contractual right to enter the premises and carry out repairs himself because the tenant had failed to do so was not a situation which fell within the 1938 Act, s 1, and therefore he was not obliged to obtain leave of the court. Accordingly, the appeal would be dismissed.

Jervis v Harris [1996] 1 All ER 303 (Court of Appeal: Sir Stephen Brown P, Millett and Otton LJJ). *Swallow Securities Ltd v Brand* (1981) 45 P & CR 328 (1981 Abr para 1798) overruled.

1808 Covenant—covenant to repair—scope—relevance of current commercial life

On an appeal by a tenant from part of an interim award in a rent review concerning commercial premises and a tenant's covenant to repair, it was contended that the arbitrator had erred in accepting the landlord's submission that it was relevant to determine the life-span of the building as seen at the commencement of the term, as distinct from its now remaining commercial life. The commercial life of the building was substantially less than that envisaged at the commencement of the lease as a result of structural defects. *Held*, in assessing the scope of the tenant's covenant to repair the premises, the length of its current commercial life was irrelevant, even though it was now discovered to be substantially less than was predicted on the grant of the lease. Accordingly, the appeal would be dismissed.

Ladbroke Hotels Ltd v Sandhu [1995] 2 EGLR 92 (Chancery Division: Robert Walker J). *Anstruther-Gough-Calthorpe v McOscar* [1924] 1 KB 716, CA followed.

1809 Covenant—restrictive covenant—covenant for surrender of lease—covenant binding on successor in title to reversion

The appellant company was granted leases of three commercial properties by the second defendant. In addition to the leases, the appellant was given a letter which contained further rights and obligations relating to the properties, one of which obliged the second defendant to accept the appellant's surrender of the leases if certain conditions were satisfied. The letter was expressed to be personal to the appellant. The second defendant sold the freehold reversion to the properties to the first defendant, who was unaware of the letter. A judge dismissed the appellant's claim that it was entitled to surrender the leases, stating that the letter did not bind the first defendant because the rights and obligations contained in it were personal to the appellant and the second defendant. On appeal, *held*, the commercial reality of the leases was that the second defendant and the appellant must have intended that the burdens imposed by the terms of the letter would pass on the sale of the reversionary interest in the properties. Moreover, where a covenant affected the land itself or its value and was intended to be binding on those entitled to the reversion, it fell within the Law of Property Act 1925, s 142(1), because it referred to the subject matter of the lease. Here, the letter gave the appellant the right to require the lessor for the time being to accept the surrender of the leases, and the right to underlet the properties, and also exempted the appellant from liability for certain repairs. The covenants were expressed in terms which showed that they were intended to be binding on those entitled to the reversion, even though the benefit of them was personal to the appellant. Accordingly, the appeal would be allowed.

System Floors Ltd v Ruralpride Ltd [1995] 1 EGLR 48 (Court of Appeal: Leggatt, Millett and Morritt LJJ).

1810 Creation of tenancy—squatter with priority housing need—undertaking by local housing authority not to evict until alternative accommodation found

A council tenant, who had suffered severe racial harassment, was placed on the register for a transfer on the basis that her flat was overcrowded. The defendant housing authority later adopted a policy on racial harassment which entitled the tenant to be transferred to accommodation of equal or higher standard. Some time later, the tenant moved her family into an empty council house that the authority had offered to another family. She refused to leave and the authority obtained a possession order against her. It did not, however, seek to enforce the order at that stage. Instead it informed her that, owing to her priority status under the racial harassment policy, the order would only be enforced if she unreasonably refused an offer of suitable, alternative accommodation. The authority later served a notice to quit on the tenant and an order for possession was made in its favour. The tenant appealed, claiming to be a secure tenant of the property. *Held*, the undertaking given by the authority to the tenant that it would not enforce the possession order, did not form the basis of a binding contract between the parties entitling the tenant to remain. No term had been agreed as to payment, an essential term of any contract, and no other form of consideration had been provided by the tenant. Furthermore, neither the undertaking nor the authority's policy of giving priority to victims of racial harassment gave rise to an estoppel. The tenant had taken the decision to move out of her flat on her own initiative and, consequently, she did not suffer any detriment in reliance upon the authority's undertaking. Taking into consideration the fact that three of the tenant's children were now adult, it would, on balance, be inequitable to allow her to remain in possession of the property. The tenant had no right of occupation in the property in which she was squatting and the authority was entitled to evict her. Accordingly, the appeal would be dismissed.

Southwark London Borough Council v Logan (1995) Times, 3 November (Court of Appeal: Neill and Auld LJJ).

1811 Distress for rent

See DISTRESS.

1812 Eviction—protection from eviction—local authority as landlord—temporary accomodation provided to homeless person

The Protection from Eviction Act 1977, s 3 provides that a person cannot be evicted by the owner of premises occupied as a dwelling under a tenancy or licence, otherwise than as a result of court proceedings, with the exception of a tenancy of a hostel provided by a council.

The plaintiff claimed to be homeless under the Housing Act 1985, s 65, with the result that the local housing authority arranged temporary accommodation for him at a bed and breakfast hotel. The authority carried out investigations, concluded that the plaintiff did not have a priority need and terminated the temporary accommodation. The plaintiff successfully claimed that the authority was prevented from terminating his accommodation by the 1977 Act, s 3. On appeal by the local authority, *held*, the authority was not an 'owner' under the 1977 Act, s 3 and its conduct in terminating the plaintiff's temporary accommodation was not covered by that section. The 1977 Act was not intended to apply to temporary accommodation provided by a local authority and it was contrary to the public interest to require a local housing authority to secure accommodation for somebody to whom it had no duty at the expense of others to whom it did have a duty. In addition, it was not within the ordinary use of language to describe temporary accommodation in a hotel or hostel as premises 'occupied as a dwelling under a licence'. Accordingly, the appeal would be allowed.

Mohamed v Manek and the Royal Borough of Kensington and Chelsea (1995) 27 HLR 439 (Court of Appeal: Nourse, Henry and Auld LJJ).

1813 Forfeiture—forfeiture effected by service of writ—compromise of proceedings—effect on lease

The landlord of residential premises served notice on the tenant under the Law of Property Act 1925, s 146 and later issued and served a writ on the tenant claiming possession on the grounds that the lease was forfeit. The tenant counterclaimed for relief from forfeiture. The lease was transferred to the respondent tenant and the freehold was assigned to the appellant landlord. The parties to the forfeiture action agreed to dismiss the action. The respondent sought to acquire the freehold of the property. The county court dismissed the appellant's argument that, by reason of the service of the writ, the lease had been forfeited, the respondent was not a tenant and therefore did not qualify for enfranchisement. On appeal, *held*, the dismissal of the forfeiture action meant that the forfeiture had not been established. The lease, whatever may have been its status pending that action, had to be taken to be fully restored when the action was dismissed. There was no need for a grant of relief to restore the lease from the shadowy state it had enjoyed to a full existence. The dismissal of the claim that had driven it into the shadows had that effect. Accordingly, the appeal would be dismissed.

Twinsectra Ltd v Hynes (1995) 71 P & CR 145 (Court of Appeal: Leggatt, Aldous and Hutchison LJJ).

1814 Forfeiture—relief against forfeiture—nature and terms of relief

Long leases granted to tenants for a premium at a low rent had been mortgaged by the tenants. They had covenanted to pay service charges and rent but had defaulted under their mortgages as well as under their leases. The mortgagees sought relief against forfeiture, contending that relief could be granted retrospectively and on terms that they paid arrears of rent and service charge. Although the landlords accepted that relief was available, they contended that relief could only be granted as from the date of the order granting it and on terms that they paid arrears of rent and service charges up to the date of forfeiture and thereafter mesne profits until the date of the order. *Held*, relief could be granted to a mortgagee of the property retrospectively and on terms that it paid all arrears of rent and service charges. Relief was available in the county court under the County Courts Act 1984, s 138(2), in the High Court under the Supreme Court Act 1981, s 38 and in cases relating to proceedings brought under the Law of Property Act 1925, s 146(2).

Escalus Properties Ltd v Robinson; Escalus Properties Ltd v Dennis; Escalus Properties Ltd v Cooper-Smith; Sinclair Gardens Investments (Kensington) Ltd v Walsh [1995] 4 All ER 852 (Court of Appeal: Nourse, Roch and Henry LJJ).

1815 Forfeiture—tenant's acceptance of forfeiture—subsequent liability of former tenant for non-domestic rates

A landlord issued proceedings against the defendant tenant of commercial premises which included a claim for forfeiture of the lease. The defendant did not seek relief against forfeiture but rather vacated the premises, returned the keys and confirmed to the landlord that he relinquished the tenancy. It subsequently fell to be decided whether the rating authority was entitled to look to the defendant for payment of the non-domestic rates for a period after he had vacated the premises. At first instance, the authority's claim against the defendant was dismissed. On the authority's appeal, *held*, a claim by a landlord for forfeiture of a lease could be accepted by a tenant whether or not the claim was justified. The tenant's liability for the premises would terminate on acceptance of that prior repudiation. The defendant had accepted the landlord's termination of the lease by vacating the premises. Consequently, he had ceased to be entitled to possession of the premises and any future liabilities for the premises were thereby terminated. Accordingly, the appeal would be dismissed.

Kingston upon Thames Borough Council v Marlow (1995) Times, 25 October (Queen's Bench Division: Simon Brown LJ and Scott Baker J).

1816 Forfeiture—unpaid rent—demand for rent and re-entry

Landlords granted tenants a 25-year lease of business premises. The lease contained a forfeiture clause. The landlords sought arrears of rent for two quarters unpaid. It fell to be determined whether, by claiming the rent and then re-entering the premises, the landlords had waived their right to forfeit the lease, and whether they required leave, under the Insolvency Act 1986, s 252(2), to forfeit the lease. *Held*, once an instalment of rent had not been paid in the period permitted by the lease, a landlord could both re-enter and claim or receive the rent in question. The right of re-entry arose as soon as the rent was unpaid within the specified period by virtue of that non-payment. Any demand for, or acceptance of, the instalment of rent outside the permitted period did not affect that right. The leave of the court was not required under s 252(2) for peaceable re-entry under the forfeiture clause.

Re Debtors (Nos 13A10 and 14A10 of 1994) [1995] 2 EGLR 33 (Chancery Division: Rattee J).

1817 Housing benefit—claim by tenant—payment direct to landlord—overpayment

See *Warwick District Council v Freeman*, para 2731.

1818 Landlord and Tenant (Covenants) Act 1995

The Landlord and Tenant (Covenants) Act 1995 implements the recommendations of the Law Commission report, *Landlord and Tenant Law: Privity of Contract and Estate* (Law Com No 174) and makes provision for persons bound by covenants of a tenancy to be released from such covenants on the assignment of the tenancy. The Act received the royal assent on 19 July 1995 and came into force on 1 January 1996: SI 1995/2963.

Section 1 provides that the provisions of the Act only apply to tenancies granted after 1 January 1996 and s 2 specifies covenants to which the Act does not apply. Under s 3, the benefit and burden of all covenants in a tenancy pass on an assignment of the premises demised to the tenant; similarly, the landlord's right of re-entry also passes on an assignment under s 4. Section 5 releases a tenant who assigns premises demised to him from liability under the covenants of the tenancy and ss 6, 7 make similar provision for landlords except that the release from liability is not automatic but must be applied for under s 8. The assignor and assignee may agree to apportion liability where the assignor has assigned part only of his interest in the premises (s 9) and s 10 lays down the procedure for making such an apportionment binding on the other party to the tenancy. Section 11 makes provision for the operation of ss 5 to 10 where an assignment has been made in breach of covenant or by operation of law. Section 12 applies where a third party has certain liabilities under a covenant of a tenancy. Where two or more persons are bound by the same covenant, they are so bound jointly and severally: s 13. Section 14 provides for the abolition of indemnity covenants implied by statute. Section 15 provides for the enforcement of covenants. Section 16 provides that the provisions of the Act do not preclude a tenant from entering into an authorised agreement (within the meaning of s 16) guaranteeing performance of a covenant by the assignee. Under s 17 a former tenant or his guarantor is not liable to pay rent or any service charge or any liquidated sum payable in the event of a failure to comply with a covenant, unless the landlord has served notice on him within six months of the date when the payment became due. Similarly, under s 18 a former tenant or his guarantor is not liable to pay an amount in respect of a covenant where a variation of the tenancy has been effected after the assignment. Sections 19 and 20 contain provisions entitling a former tenant or his guarantor to a grant of an overriding lease of the premises demised by the tenancy where the former tenant or his guarantor has made full payment of an amount payable under s 17. Section 21 limits the rights of forfeiture or disclaimer to part only of the demised premises where as a result of an assignment a person is tenant of that part of the premises. Section 22 imposes conditions regulating the giving of the landlord's consent to assignments. Any liability or rights arising under a covenant as a result of an assignment and by virtue of the Act do not relate to any time before the assignment: s 23. Similarly, any release of a person from a covenant by virtue of the Act does not affect any liability arising from a breach occurring before the release: s 24. Under s 25 any agreement is void if it restricts the operation of the Act. Section 26 provides for miscellaneous savings. Section 27 contains a regulation-making power for the purpose of prescribing the form of notices to be served under the Act. Section 28 deals with interpretation. Section 29 provides for the Act to bind the Crown. Sections 30–32, Schs 1 and 2 provide for consequential amendments and repeals, commencement, short title and extent.

1819 Landlord and Tenant (Covenants) Act 1995—assignment of covenants—notices

The Landlord and Tenant (Covenants) Act 1995 (Notices) Regulations 1995, SI 1995/2964 (in force on 1 January 1996), prescribe the forms of notices to be used for the purposes of the Landlord and Tenant (Covenants) Act 1995. The forms relate to (1) notification by a landlord to a former tenant or guarantor that sums for which he is liable under a covenant have become due and are unpaid and that the landlord intends to recover them; (2) further notice that such a sum is greater than that specified in the original notice and that the landlord intends to recover the sum; (3) an application by a landlord for release from the covenants in a tenancy on an assignment of his interest and for the tenant's response to the application; (4) a landlord's application for release from the covenants in a tenancy to an appropriate extent on the assignment of part of his interest and for the tenant's response to the application; (5) a former landlord's application for release from covenants on a subsequent assignment of part of or the whole of the landlord's interest; (6) a former landlord's application for release from covenants to an appropriate extent on a subsequent assignment of the landlord's interest where the former landlord assigned only part of the reversion, and for the tenant's response to the application; (7) an application by an assignor and an assignee tenant where only part of the assignor's interest has been assigned to make an apportionment of their interests binding on the other party to the tenancy and for the other party's response to the application; (8) an application by an assignor and assignee landlord where only part of the assignor's interest has been assigned to make an apportionment of their liability under certain covenants binding on the other party to the tenancy, and for the other party's response to this application.

1820 Landlord and Tenant (Covenants) Act 1995—overriding leases—prescribed statement

The Land Registration (Overriding Leases) Rules 1995, SI 1995/3154 (in force on 1 January 1996), prescribe the statement which is required, by the Landlord and Tenant (Covenants) Act 1995, s 20(2), to be inserted into an overriding lease granted under the 1995 Act, s 19.

1821 Lease—exclusive possession—employees of children's home

The plaintiff company acquired a lease of property on which it built a children's home. As a result of the Children and Young Persons Act 1969, management of the home became the responsibility of the local authority, although the Act was not intended to alter ownership of the home. The plaintiff's property also included a number of houses and flats, and the local authority allowed its employees who worked in the children's home to occupy them exclusively, paying rent to the local authority. The plaintiff did not, however, require the local authority to account for such rent. When the local authority gave notice of its intention to withdraw from management of the children's home, it also issued notices to quit to employees occupying the houses and flats, including the defendant. In unsuccessfully opposing the plaintiff's application for a possession order, the defendant argued that the local authority had acted as the plaintiff's agent and had granted him a service tenancy as part of its statutory authority to manage the home, as a result of which he was a sub-lessee protected from eviction under the Rent Act 1977 or the Housing Act 1988. On the defendant's appeal, *held*, it was clear from certain provisions of the 1969 Act, Pt II that a local authority which was responsible for managing a children's home did not thereby acquire a proprietary interest in the home. Here, the managers of the home were not authorised to do anything on the plaintiff's behalf, and their powers related to the management of the home rather than to management of the land on which the home was built. Although the local authority had acted in its own name and on its own behalf in creating an adverse interest in the plaintiff's property by granting tenancies to employees and taking rent, the 1969 Act had not given it the power to do so. The plaintiff was therefore entitled to possession of the flats and houses and, accordingly, the appeal would be dismissed.

Redbank Schools Ltd v Abdullahzadeh (1995) Times, 20 November (Court of Appeal: Nourse, Roch and Hobhouse LJJ).

As to provisions relating to children's homes, see now the Children Act 1989, Pt VI.

1822   Lease—grant of lease by nominee to principal—validity

See *Ingram v IRC*, para 1695.

1823   Lease—option to determine—validity of notice—commencement of term and breach of condition precedent

An agreement for a 25-year lease was made between tenants and their landlord. The tenants went into possession before the execution of the lease, and the lease stated that the commencement of the term was the date on which the agreement had been made rather than the later date on which it was executed. The lease also contained a clause allowing the tenants to terminate the lease at the end of the tenth year of the term if certain conditions were satisfied, namely that they gave six months' written notice, and that they performed all of their obligations and paid the due rent until the expiration of the notice. When the tenants exercised their right to terminate the lease, they calculated the commencement of the term from the date of the execution of the lease, but at that time, they were in breach of their repairing obligations. The landlord therefore claimed that the breach invalidated the notice. On the tenants' application for a declaration as to the validity of the notice, *held*, the date for giving notice was to be calculated by reference to the date stated in the lease to be the commencement of the term, and not the date of the execution of the lease. As the tenants had given notice at the wrong time, the notice was therefore ineffective. The provision which required the tenants to have complied with all their obligations at the date of the termination of the notice was a condition precedent to the effective exercise of their right to determine the lease. Even if they had served notice at the correct time, the notice would have been invalid because they were in breach of the covenant to repair at the time of the expiration of the notice period. Accordingly, the application would be dismissed.

Trane (UK) Ltd v Provident Mutual Life Assurance [1995] 1 EGLR 33 (Chancery Division: Cooke J).

1824   Lease—surrender—acceptance of surrender—evidence of intention

It was held that the lease of a dwelling house had not been surrendered by a tenant's receiver's request to the landlord to accept an informal surrender and the subsequent compliance with the landlord's request for the return of the keys. On appeal by the receiver, *held*, the taking of keys by a landlord, when coupled with other acts, could indicate the taking of possession by him. In the present case, however, there had been no other act that evidenced an intention to resume possession by the landlord. Accordingly, the lease had not been surrendered and the appeal would be dismissed.

Proudreed Ltd v Microgen Holdings plc (1995) Times, 17 July (Court of Appeal: Butler-Sloss, Aldous and Schiemann LJJ).

1825 Lease—term of lease—date on which term commences

A company granted a 19-year lease of commercial premises to the Secretary of State, and the lease specified the date from which the term of the lease was to commence and the date on which it was to end. A clause provided that if the Secretary of State wished to terminate the lease after the end of the first 10 years, he had to give the company 6 months' written notice. When he served the prescribed notice, the company claimed that it was invalid because the first 10 years of the lease had not yet expired. On the question of whether the term commenced on the specified date or the day after the specified date, *held*, there was a presumption that where it was stated that a term was to commence from a specified date, that date was not to be included in the term and that the term therefore commenced on the following day. The presumption could, however, be rebutted by indications in the lease to the contrary. In the instant case, the lease did not demise the property for a period of years from a specified date but for a term expressed to be from a specified date until another specified date. In those circumstances, the term of the lease included both of those days and all the intervening days.

Meadfield Properties Ltd v Secretary of State for the Environment [1995] 1 EGLR 39 (Chancery Division: Warner J).

1826 Leasehold enfranchisement—acquisition of freehold—reference to leasehold valuation tribunal—costs

The Leasehold Reform Act 1967, s 9(4)(c) provides that where a person gives notice of his desire to have the freehold of a house and premises, there must be borne by him the reasonable costs of or incidental to any valuation of the house and premises. Schedule 22, para 5 provides that the costs which a person may be required to bear under s 9(4) do not include costs incurred by a landlord in connection with a reference to a leasehold valuation tribunal.

When a tenant gave notice to his landlords of his intention to buy the freehold of the property which he occupied, the landlords instructed a surveyor to set the matter down for hearing at the leasehold valuation tribunal. Although the parties subsequently agreed on a price for the property, the landlords argued that the tenant should also pay their surveyor's fees. The tenant refused and a judge ruled in his favour. On the landlords' appeal, *held*, the 1967 Act, Sch 22, para 5 was primary legislation, which had to be given its ordinary meaning and effect. It expressly referred to the 1967 Act, s 9(4), and was an exclusionary provision. Paragraph 5 required an objective inquiry, and there had to be a link between the reference to the leasehold valuation tribunal and the costs incurred. However, it did not have to be shown that that was the sole reason for the costs being incurred, and it was irrelevant that the costs were incurred before the reference. On the facts of the instant case, it was clear that the tenant was not obliged to pay the landlords' surveyor's fees and, accordingly, the appeal would be allowed.

Covent Garden Group Ltd v Naiva (1994) 27 HLR 295 (Court of Appeal: Butler-Sloss and Steyn LJJ).

1827 Licence—revocable licence—notice of revocation—requirement of reasonable time for vacating premises

An umbrella charitable institute for various educational activities owned a site which was occupied by a school. Although the school had become a major part of the institute's activities, it was seen as part of the institute's wider purpose. The school had become a voluntary aided school under the Education Act 1944 and later the institute executed a deed styled as a declaration of trust whereby the arrangement between itself as owner of the site and the education authorities could be formalised. The deed contained a clause enabling the institute to vary or revoke any of its provisions. Over the years the Department of Education and the local education authority made large contributions to the running of the school and the cost of repairs and renovations. The institute served a notice revoking its declaration of trust and purportedly terminating the school's right to occupy its premises. The notice was accompanied by a letter stating that the school could continue to use the premises for a limited period on payment of rent. The school and the education authorities brought proceedings for an order that the notice was invalid. *Held*, it was unacceptable for a body conducting a public function, with the concurrence of the landowner, to be given a notice specifying an impossibly short period which in practice was not intended to be implemented. A valid notice had to give sufficient time to enable practical arrangements to be made to safeguard the public service. The primary guide as to what would have been reasonable notice was the statute under which the licensee was operating. Accordingly, the notice terminating occupation of the school was of no effect and the school was not obliged by it to vacate the site.

Governing Body of the Henrietta Barnett School v Hampstead Garden Suburb Institute (1995) 93 LGR 470 (Chancery Division: Carnwath J).

1828 Management of premises—codes of practice

The Approval of Codes of Management Practice (Residential Property) (No 2) Order 1995, SI 1995/3149 (in force on 1 January 1996), replaces the earlier order, SI 1995/2782, which contained an error, and specifies The Association of Retirement Housing Managers' Code of Practice for the Management of Leasehold Sheltered Housing as a code of practice approved by the Secretary of State for the purposes of the Leasehold Reform, Housing and Urban Development Act 1993, ss 87, 100.

1829 Notice to quit—injunction obtained by husband preventing his exclusion from property—notice to quit given by wife—local authority's possession proceedings amounting to contempt

A husband and wife were joint weekly tenants of a house owned by a local authority. The wife left the matrimonial home after difficulties arose between her and her husband and, after she had left, the husband obtained an injunction forbidding his wife from excluding him from the property, where he remained in occupation. In order to rehouse the wife and her children, the authority required her to terminate the joint tenancy, which she did by signing a declaration that she intended to deliver possession of the home to the authority. Although the authority had now learned of the husband's injunction, it applied to the county court for an order for possession. At the hearing, the husband served a defence stating that his wife was in breach of the injunction and in contempt of court by giving notice to quit. The judge held that the authority was aiding and abetting the wife's breach and was itself in contempt and that the possession proceedings were an abuse of process. On the authority's appeal, *held*, the authority would be regarded as in contempt in the sense that, with knowledge of the injunction, it sought possession although the husband was protected from eviction at the suit of his wife. It did not matter that the authority was not a party to the obtaining of the injunction. The institution of the proceedings involved an interference with the administration of justice in that those proceedings sought to achieve a result which, while the injunction remained in force, was not open to the wife, who was an essential link in the chain of the authority seeking possession. The notice to quit could not be relied upon as determining the tenancy so long as the injunction was extant and, accordingly, the appeal would be dismissed.

Harrow London Borough Council v Johnstone [1995] 3 FCR 132 (Court of Appeal: Russell and Hobhouse LJJ and Sir Roger Parker).

1830 Notice to quit—periodic tenancy—service at last-known place of abode or business—validity

The Law of Property Act 1925, s 196(3) provides that any notice required or authorised by the Act to be served, is sufficiently served if it is left at the last-known place of abode or business in the United Kingdom of the person to be served. Section 196(5) provides that the provisions of s 196 extend to notices required to be served by any instrument affecting property executed or coming into operation after the commencement of the Act, unless a contrary intention appears.

A local authority was granted an order for possession of one of its properties. On appeal, the issue was whether or not the notice to quit had been validly served within the meaning of the 1925 Act, s 196. *Held*, the 'acceptance of offer' document signed by the tenants had contained the essential terms of their tenancy agreement and was therefore an 'instrument' within the meaning of the 1925 Act, s 196(5). However, a tenancy agreement which did not make express provision for the service of a notice to quit to determine the tenancy did not require such notice to be served, and therefore s 196(5) did not apply. If landlords wished to effect valid service of a notice to quit by leaving it on the premises which were the subject of the tenancy without having to prove that it had come to the tenant's attention, they had to make express provision for such a method of service in the tenancy agreement. They also had to prove the terms of the agreement in their action for possession following service of such a notice. That had not been done in the instant case and, accordingly, the appeal would be allowed.

Wandsworth London Borough v Attwell [1995] EGCS 68 (Court of Appeal: Glidewell and Waite LJJ).

1831 Possession—recovery—non-payment of rent—agreement to pay rent arrears—effect of subsequent non-payment of rent

A council obtained a final possession order against a tenant for non-payment of rent and an order for payment of arrears. The parties subsequently agreed that the tenant could continue to live in the flat provided that she paid her rent and made regular contributions towards the arrears. Following her failure to comply with the agreement, the council applied for a warrant to enforce the possession order. The order was refused and the council appealed. *Held*, the plain intention of the agreement was to allow the tenant to remain in exclusive possession of the property at a rent. It did not have the effect of suspending the order for possession, as the council had intended, but rather created a new tenancy or licence. This gave the tenant the same protection as under the terminated tenancy, including security of tenure. The basis for the issue of a warrant for possession had ceased to exist on the granting, by operation of law, of the new tenancy. The tenant could not be evicted without a further order for possession. Accordingly, the appeal would be dismissed.

Burrows v Brent London Borough Council (1995) 27 HLR 748 (Court of Appeal: Butler-Sloss, Otton and Auld LJJ).

1832 Possession—recovery—order for possession—breach of terms of tenancy—judge's discretion to make order

A tenant rented a flat owned by a local authority. The lease stated that the tenant and any visitors should use the premises in a manner which did not cause nuisance to or damage to the personal property of other people. However, the tenant's visitors made fire bombs in the flat and as a result it was seriously damaged by a fire. A number of windows in other flats were also damaged. Although the flat was restored and the tenant was allowed back into occupation, the authority commenced possession proceedings against him on the basis of his breach of the terms of the tenancy. At first instance, the judge held that although the tenant was in breach it was not reasonable to order possession. He found that the tenant had not taken an active part in the events leading up to the fire, was not properly aware of what was happening and, in particular, had been allowed back into occupation with no further complaints about his conduct. On the authority's appeal, *held*, the fact that the tenant was allowed back into possession was not a valid reason for the judge to exercise his discretion not to order possession. In exercising his discretion, the judge had to look at the position of the landlord and tenant and at any relevant circumstances up to the date when the action for possession was heard. In the circumstances, the judge had made the proper order and, accordingly, the appeal would be dismissed.

London Borough of Wandsworth v Hargreaves (1994) 27 HLR 142 (Court of Appeal: Russell LJ and Sir John Megaw).

1833 Possession—recovery—right of re-entry—residential occupier

The plaintiff, a sub-tenant of the defendant, wished to remain in the leased property after the expiry of the tenancy agreement between the defendant and the college attended by the plaintiff. His request to do so was refused but, nevertheless, he remained in occupation. He paid the sums requested by the defendant for his continued occupation of the property. The defendant subsequently returned such sums and took steps to prevent the plaintiff from entering the property. The plaintiff's claim for damages for unlawful eviction and for breach of the implied term for peaceful enjoyment succeeded. On appeal by the defendant, *held*, the defendant had accepted the plaintiff's continued occupation purely as a matter of sufferance. In accepting compensation for a short period, he did not intend to convert the relationship between him and the plaintiff into one of landlord and tenant. There was insufficient evidence to infer any tenancy agreement. Accordingly, the appeal would be allowed.

Vaughan-Armatrading v Sarsah (1995) 27 HLR 631 (Court of Appeal: McCowan and Simon Brown LJJ).

1834 Possession—recovery—unlawful eviction—assessment of damages

The plaintiffs were joint assured tenants of a flat owned by the defendant. Six months after they moved in, the local authority had paid no housing benefit and no rent had been paid. The plaintiffs were peacefully evicted when the defendant and his family moved into the flat. When the plaintiffs returned the next day to collect their clothes and personal possessions, the defendant's wife refused to let them in. The defendant did not respond to a request for re-admission from the plaintiffs' solicitor and the plaintiffs therefore obtained an interlocutory injunction. They were finally admitted to the property fifteen days after the eviction. They had been sleeping at friends' houses and had been denied access to all their possessions. On returning to the flat, they found that the defendant had thrown out the beds and refrigerator which he had previously provided. The level of damages fell to be assessed. *Held*, each plaintiff was awarded general damages of £2,250, being £150 per night for the time they were refused re-admission, together with aggravated damages of £1,000, owing to the defendant's failure to re-admit the plaintiffs as they and their solicitor had requested and owing to his removal of the beds and refrigerator. Unpaid rent was to be set off from that total and interest was payable on the balance.

Altun v Patel (20 November 1995, unreported) (Edmonton County Court: Judge Tibber) (Kindly submitted for publication by Jon Holbrook, Barrister).

The Housing Act 1988, s 27(3) provides that a landlord is liable to pay a former residential occupier damages in respect of his loss of the right to occupy premises as his residence. Section 27(5) provides that nothing affects the right to enforce any liability which arises apart from s 27(3) in respect of a tenant's loss of the right to occupy premises as his residence but damages will not be awarded both in respect of such a liability and in respect of a liability arising by virtue of s 27(5) on account of the same loss.

It has been held that common law damages for breach of covenants, such as a covenant for quiet enjoyment, may be awarded in addition to damages for loss of occupation under ss 27, 28.

Kaur v Gill (1995) Times, 15 June (Court of Appeal: Nourse, Kennedy and Auld LJJ).

1835 Possession—recovery—unlawful eviction—reinstatement by landlord

The Housing Act 1988, s 27(1) provides that where a landlord unlawfully deprives the residential occupier of his occupation of the whole or part of the premises, he is liable to pay him damages. Liability also arises under s 27(2) where the landlord attempts to deprive the residential occupier of occupation, or interferes with his peace or comfort, knowing or believing that the conduct is likely to cause the occupier to leave, and the occupier does leave. However, by s 27(6), no liability arises if the landlord reinstates the occupier before the proceedings brought under s 27 are finally disposed of.

A landlord excluded his tenant from her flat and moved some of her possessions onto the street. The police arrived and the landlord allowed the tenant back into occupation and took no further steps against her. Several weeks later the tenant vacated the premises and commenced an action for damages under s 27 and for damages for trespass to her goods. The tenant obtained judgment in default and was awarded substantial damages. At a hearing to make a charging order against the landlord absolute, the landlord applied for the order to be set aside. The application was refused and the charging order was made absolute. The landlord appealed. *Held*, it was doubtful whether liability arose under s 27(1) because of the reinstatement. With regard to s 27(2), the tenant could not simply rely on the deprivation of occupation. Such deprivation was only relevant as conduct calculated to cause the tenant to leave. The landlord's actions did not have that effect for several weeks after the reinstatement during which period the tenant appeared to have accepted the reinstatement. Accordingly, the award of substantial damages under s 27 represented a serious injustice to the landlord. The judgment in default, the assessment of damages and the charging order absolute would be set aside in so far as they were based on s 27. However, with regard to the trespass to goods, the tenant's claim was unanswerable and judgment had been rightly entered in her favour.

Murray v Aslam (1994) 27 HLR 284 (Court of Appeal: Sir Thomas Bingham MR, Simon Brown LJ and Sir Ralph Gibson).

1836 Possession—recovery—warrant—application to suspend or set aside after execution

CCR Ord 26, r 5 provides that a warrant of execution cannot issue without the leave of the court where six years or more have elapsed since the date of the judgment or order.

After a local authority had granted a secure tenancy in 1982 the tenant failed to pay rent. An order for possession was issued by the court in September 1985 and this was suspended on the basis that she pay the current rent and arrears. However, arrears continued to grow and a warrant for possession was issued in 1986. In 1993 a district judge gave leave to issue a warrant. Following various applications to stay execution of the order, further warrants were issued in May 1994 and April 1995. Following the latter warrant the applicant was evicted. She appealed against the dismissal of her application to set aside the execution of the warrant, relying on Ord 26, r 5. *Held*, where six years had elapsed since the date of an order for possession, the leave of the court was required before a warrant of execution could be issued. The court's assessment was required since, for example, the position of the tenant could have changed radically. In the present case, the warrants of May 1994 and April 1995 were clearly defective on those grounds. Following *Hammersmith and Fulham London Borough Council v Hill*, once a warrant was executed, relief could only be obtained if an applicant could show that the possession order on which it was issued had been set aside or if the warrant was obtained by fraud, abuse of process or oppression. In the circumstances of the present case, a warrant improperly obtained without the court's leave was an abuse of process. Such a grant of leave was much more than a mere formality. Further, the failure to obtain leave under Ord 26, r 5 was a clear breach of the mandatory requirements of that rule and could not be saved by an application under Ord 37, r 5. Accordingly, the appeal would be allowed and the execution set aside.

Hackney London Borough Council v White (1995) Times, 17 May (Court of Appeal: Russell, Hirst and Rose LJJ). *Hammersmith and Fulham London Borough Council v Hill* [1994] 03 EG 124, CA (1994 Abr para 1755) followed.

1837 Protected tenancy—sub-tenancy—forfeiture of headlease—effect on sub-tenant

The Rent Act 1977, s 137(2) provides that where a statutorily protected tenancy of a dwelling-house is determined any sub-tenant to whom the dwelling-house or any part of it has been lawfully sublet is deemed to become the tenant of the landlord on the same terms as if the tenant's statutorily protected tenancy had continued.

On an appeal, it fell to be determined whether, on the forfeiture of a headlease, a protected sub-tenant became a protected or a statutory tenant of a landlord. *Held*, the 1977 Act, s 137(2) plainly meant that the sub-tenant's relationship with the landlord was to be on the same terms as with the former tenant. Therefore, if the sub-tenant's tenancy had been a statutory tenancy, he became a statutory tenant of the landlord and if the tenancy had been a protected tenancy, the sub-tenant became a protected tenant of the landlord.

Keepers and Governors of the Free Grammar School of John Lyon v James [1995] 4 All ER 740 (Court of Appeal: Leggatt, Rose and Saville LJJ).

1838 Rent—arrears—validity of notice to pay outstanding rent

The Landlord and Tenant Act 1987, s 48(1) provides that a landlord of premises must by notice furnish a tenant with an address at which notices may be served on him by the tenant. Where a landlord fails to comply with s 48(1), any rent or service charge due from the tenant will be treated for all purposes as not being due at any time before the landlord does so supply an address. Section 48 applies to premises which consist of or include a dwelling and are not held under a tenancy to which the Landlord and Tenant Act 1954, Pt II applies: 1987 Act, s 46(1).

A landlord leased an agricultural and sporting estate to a tenant. The tenant fell into arrears of rent and the landlord served a first notice requiring the payment of outstanding rent. The tenant failed to do so and was later served with a notice to quit. The tenant's solicitor inquired whether the first notice had been served under the 1987 Act, s 48. The landlord's agent confirmed that its address was a service address and that it had not only issued notices from that address but had received counter-notices for the landlord there. The landlord then delivered a letter to the tenant reaffirming the first notice and confirmed that the agent's address was the address for service of all notices for the purpose of s 48. The tenant sought a declaration that on the true construction of s 48 no rent was due when the first notice was served nor when the landlord wrote to the tenant, and that the purported notices to pay rent were invalid and of no effect. At first instance, the judge found in the tenant's favour. On appeal, the landlord contended that s 46(1) was not intended to apply to agricultural tenancies. *Held*, (1) the word 'premises' for the purposes of s 46 meant the subject matter of the letting. There was no conflict between the provisions applicable to agricultural tenancies and the additional provision made applicable by s 46. Therefore, it could not be said that Parliament had not intended s 46 to apply to agricultural tenancies. (2) Although the first notice was defective, the landlord's letter could be properly construed as being an effective notice and, at the time the tenant received the letter, the rent said to be due was in fact due. The tenant had not been misled by the earlier misstatement. The requirement with which the tenant was notified that he had to comply had been accurately stated. The notice identified the payments which it was alleged by the landlord had not been made, and did not affect the clarity of the notice as to what the tenant was required to do or what the effect would be if the tenant did not comply with it. The statutory purpose of the notice had been fully satisfied and, accordingly, the appeal would be allowed.

Lindsey Trading Properties Inc v Dallhold Estates (UK) Pty Ltd (1993) 70 P & CR 332 (Court of Appeal: Ralph Gibson, Hirst and Peter Gibson LJJ).

1839 Rent—liability of original tenant—dissolution of tenant company—circumstances in which dissolution may be declared void

See *Stanhope Pension Trust Ltd v Registrar of Companies,* para 491.

1840   Rent—registration of rent—registration areas

The Local Government Changes (Rent Act Registration Areas) Order 1995, SI 1995/3264 (in force on 1 April 1996), redefines the registration areas required for the purposes of the Rent Act 1977, Pt IV in consequence of the abolition of the counties in Avon, Cleveland, Humberside and the reorganisation of North Yorkshire, by the Local Government Act 1992.

1841   Rent—rent assessment committee—method of assessment—use of comparables

In determining a fair rent in respect of flats let on regulated tenancies, a rent assessment committee used the registered fair rents of nearby properties as comparables. On appeal against the determination, the landlord of the flats contended that the committee should have used as comparables the assured tenancy rents of flats within the same block. His appeal succeeded and the committee appealed. *Held*, the fair rent was the market rent for the flats discounted to remove the effect of scarcity. The existence of scarcity was not a sufficient reason to reject the assured tenancies as comparables. Assured tenancy rents for virtually identical flats within the same block could be used as comparables. The security of tenure attached to a regulated tenancy was substantially the same as that under an assured tenancy; it was not a personal circumstance to be disregarded. If the committee had wished to adopt some other comparable, it should have explained why and had failed in its duties if it did not do so. Accordingly, its appeal would be dismissed.

Spath Holme Ltd v Greater Manchester and Lancashire Rent Assessment Committee (1996) 28 HLR 107 (Court of Appeal: Glidewell and Morritt LJJ and Sir John May). Decision of Harrison J (1994) 27 HLR 243 (1994 Abr para 1762) affirmed.

1842   Rent—reversioner letting holiday apartments after ejecting lessee—trespass to property—measure of damages

See *Inverugie Investments Ltd v Hackett*, para 997.

1843   Rent—review—agreement for review upwards and downwards—whether agreement on arms' length commercial terms

New Zealand

A government agency was privatised and its assets vested in a government-held company. The shares in that company were sold by the government to an insurance company. The assets included a number of government buildings which were occupied by government departments. The occupancies were not the subject of formal leases, being recorded informally in correspondence, and the government agreed with the insurance company that the arrangements had to be formalised. The terms originally negotiated by the government agency and one of the departments provided for an initial rent at the start of the term in 1985 with rent reviews at intervals of four years. At the first review the annual rent had tripled. The agency wanted reviews to be upwards only but the department would not accept that. They finally agreed that, provided the rent did not fall to less than it had been at the commencement of the lease, review could be upwards or downwards and the government tendered a lease to the insurance company to that effect. The company unsuccessfully claimed that such a lease would not be on arms' length commercial terms and, on appeal, *held*, the intention of the phrase 'on arms' length commercial terms' was that the terms of a lease, taken as a whole and including the rent and term, should be such as would have been negotiated between commercial parties bargaining at arms length. In the present case, it seemed that there were no grounds for regarding the terms of the lease as anything else. The agency and the department had negotiated as if between parties at arms' length and there was no evidence that any uncommercial concession had been made. There was nothing to displace the prima facie assumption that the formalised leases should incorporate the terms actually agreed and, accordingly, the appeal would be dismissed.

Norwich Union Life Insurance Society v A-G [1995] EGCS 85 (Privy Council: Lords Goff of Chieveley, Mustill, Slynn of Hadley, Nicholls of Birkenhead and Hoffmann).

1844   Rent—review—arbitration—production of experts' reports—reports used in earlier proceedings

In the course of a rent review arbitration, the landlord's expert gave evidence as to the changes in the office market in relation to the review date and was cross-examined about evidence he had given on behalf of tenants in two earlier arbitrations. Following the cross-examination, the tenant issued two subpoenas duces tecum, one to the landlord's expert to produce his proofs of evidence in the earlier arbitrations and the other to its own expert to produce the landlord's expert's proof in the second earlier arbitration, the tenant's expert having been the arbitrator in that earlier arbitration. The landlord's expert and the landlord applied to set aside the subpoenas. Prior to the hearing, the tenant's expert complied with the subpoena addressed to him. *Held*, the landlord's expert, as a witness, had standing to object to the subpoenas addressed to him and to the tenant's expert. The landlords had no standing to object to the subpoenas. In the light of the Criminal Procedure Act 1865, ss 4 and 5 and the Civil Evidence Act 1968, s 3(1)(a) a prior inconsistent statement which was not admitted by a witness in cross-examination was admissible in evidence. If a witness were proved to have expressed himself in a materially different sense when acting for different sides, that was a factor which ought to be brought out in the interests of individual litigants involved and in the public interest. There was a legitimate basis for admitting the landlord's expert's proof in the first of the earlier arbitrations which outweighed objections on the grounds of privacy and confidentiality. The same considerations did not apply to the proof in the second earlier arbitration as there were no particulars of possible disparities and the subpoena relating to this proof was no more than a fishing expedition and was not necessary for the fair disposal of the arbitration. Even though the tenant's expert had already produced the proof relating to the second arbitration, it was not too late to set aside the subpoena addressed to him. Accordingly, the applications of the landlord's expert in relation to the proof in the second arbitration and in relation to the subpoena addressed to the tenant's expert would be allowed, and the remaining applications would be dismissed.

London & Leeds Estates Ltd v Paribas Ltd (No 2) [1995] 02 EG 134 (Queen's Bench Division: Mance J).

1845 Rent—review—expert's reliance on adjoining retail comparables—negligence

A tenant leased premises from a landlord. The lease contained a covenant preventing the tenant from using the premises other than as a restaurant. When the rent was due for review, the tenant submitted that the existing rent should not be increased while the landlord contended that the rent should be increased. An expert was appointed and made a determination as to rent. At first instance, the tenant unsuccessfully claimed that the expert's valuation was negligent because he had paid attention to comparables other than restaurants. On appeal, *held*, in an action for negligence against an expert it was not enough to show that another expert would have given a different answer. Valuation involved questions of judgment on which experts might differ without forfeiting their claim to professional competence. In the present case, although the covenant might reduce the value of the premises and meant that the landlord had to accept a lesser rent than if the premises had freedom of user, it did not follow that lettings of similar premises for other uses were irrelevant. It was up to the notional landlord whether he preferred to let the premises with or without a covenant. The expert's regard to retail comparables could be supported by a respectable body of professional people. Accordingly, the appeal would be dismissed.

Zubaida v Hargreaves [1995] 1 EGLR 127 (Court of Appeal: Steyn, Hirst and Hoffmann LJJ).

1846 Repair—faulty heating system—damages

See *London Borough of Newham v Hewitt*, para 995.

1847 Reverse premiums—shopping centre—developer's reasonable endeavours to obtain lettings

The plaintiff developer constructed a shopping centre, with the cost of the development being financed by the defendant. Under the terms of the funding agreement, the defendant agreed to provide funds up to a specified level and any costs in excess of this level were to be met by the plaintiff. Included in the definition of development costs were reverse premiums, subject to the defendant's consent. A clause of the agreement also specified that both parties were to use their reasonable endeavours to obtain a letting of each lettable part of the shopping centre. The defendant reached its agreed level of funding but several units within the shopping centre remained unlet. The defendant argued that the plaintiff's reasonable endeavours included paying tenants reverse premiums if a reasonable landlord would do the same in the circumstances, having regard to the market conditions. At first instance, the court found in favour of the defendant but this decision was reversed on appeal. On further appeal by the defendant, *held*, the clause in issue did not oblige the plaintiff to use endeavours to agree reasonable terms but, instead, obliged the plaintiff to use reasonable endeavours to agree terms. In other words, it was the endeavours that had to be reasonable, not the terms of the letting. It was impossible to envisage the clause as reading anything other than a three stage process of first, the parties using reasonable endeavours to obtain a letting, secondly, as a result of those endeavours, actual agreement between the plaintiff, the defendant and the owner of the developed land and thirdly, the grant of an underlease on those agreed terms in the agreed form of the underlease. In any event, an obligation to agree reasonable terms would prove unworkable as, if the parties disagreed as to whether or not a reverse premium was reasonable, the question would have to be referred to arbitration thereby creating delay prejudicial to the commercial necessity of reaching speedy agreement with a tenant. Accordingly, the appeal would be dismissed.

P & O Property Holdings v Norwich Union Life Insurance Society (1994) 68 P & CR 261 (House of Lords: Lords Templeman, Ackner, Goff of Chieveley, Browne-Wilkinson and Mustill).

1848 Secure tenancy—change of landlord

The Housing (Change of Landlord) (Payment of Disposal Cost by Instalments) (Amendment) Regulations 1995, SI 1995/854 (in force on 18 April 1995), further amend SI 1990/1019 so as to increase from 8.13 per cent to 8.37 per cent the rate of interest on outstanding disposal costs which are payable by instalments under the Housing Act 1988, Pt IV. The regulations also revoke SI 1994/2916, but preserve the previous interest rate for any period before 18 April 1995.

The Housing (Change of Landlord) (Payment of Disposal Cost by Instalments) (Amendment No 2) Regulations 1995, SI 1995/2823 (in force on 30 November 1995), further amend SI 1990/1019 so as to decrease from 8.37 per cent to 7.99 per cent the rate of interest on outstanding disposal costs which are payable by instalments under the Housing Act 1988, Pt IV. The regulations also revoke SI 1995/854 supra but preserve the previous interest rate for any period before 30 November 1995.

1849 Secure tenancy—right to buy—charges on dwelling houses—priority of charges

The Housing (Right to Buy) (Priority Charges) Order 1995, SI 1995/211 (in force on 20 February 1995), adds fourteen additional bodies to the list of approved lending institutions for the purposes of the Housing Act 1985, s 156.

The Housing (Right to Buy) (Priority of Charges) (No 2) Order 1995, SI 1995/2066 (in force on 21 August 1995), adds six additional bodies to the list of approved lending institutions for the purposes of the Housing Act 1985, s 156.

1850 Secure tenancy—right to buy—discounts—division of discounts between joint tenants

The plaintiff had lived in a council house with her husband, who had been the sole tenant. When they divorced the tenancy passed to the plaintiff. The defendant, who was the boyfriend of the plaintiff, moved in and, because the plaintiff could not raise a mortgage, a joint mortgage loan was obtained and the tenancy was transferred into joint names. The plaintiff wished to exercise her right to buy option under the Housing Act 1985, and her discount under the scheme was assessed at 41 per cent, taking account of the length of her tenure. The relationship between the plaintiff and the defendant broke down and they decided to sell the house. The court treated the right to buy discount as a direct financial contribution by the plaintiff and gave her a larger share of the sale proceeds to include credit for the discount. The defendant appealed on the ground that he was entitled to an equal share of the discount. *Held*, the statutory provisions dealing with right to buy discounts were only concerned with the position between the tenant and the local authority or the landlord regarding length of tenure and not the respective contributions made to the purchase price. Therefore, although the 1985 Act allowed joint tenants the right to buy jointly, it did not follow that it also applied the discount equally. The court was right to take account of the discount when considering the financial contributions made by the parties, whether as part of the purchase price or as a matter which might lead to inferences about the parties' intentions. Accordingly, the appeal would be dismissed.

Evans v Hayward [1995] 2 FLR 511 (Court of Appeal: Dillon and Staughton LJJ).

1851 Secure tenancy—tenancy acquired under mesne landlord—surrender of intermediate lease—continuance of tenancy

A local authority demised to a mesne landlord garage premises for a term of fifteen years. In breach of covenant he converted part of the premises into a residential flat, which was occupied by a tenant on a weekly rent. The tenant became a protected tenant of the mesne landlord as the flat was a dwelling house for the purposes of the Rent Act 1977. The mesne landlord surrendered the unexpired term of the lease of the main premises to the council and the council brought possession proceedings against the tenant. It was conceded that the tenant became the direct tenant of the council and the issue was whether the tenant enjoyed a secure tenancy under the Housing Act 1985 or a simple weekly tenancy which was capable of being brought to an end by a month's notice at common law. *Held*, the tenant became a secure tenant under the Housing Act 1985 upon the surrender of the mesne tenancy. The hallmarks of a secure tenancy were laid down in the 1985 Act, s 79 as being a tenancy under which a dwelling house is let as a separate dwelling at any time when the landlord and tenant conditions in ss 80, 81 are satisfied. It being accepted that the tenancy was of a dwelling house and that the landlord and tenant conditions were satisfied, the question was whether the flat was let as a separate dwelling. It had been argued that though the flat was presently let as a separate dwelling, the crucial moment was that of the surrender of the mesne landlord's lease, when it was not. However, the use of the term 'at any time' showed that s 79 was intended to have ambulatory effect, with occupiers passing in and out of secure tenant status. Accordingly, the appeal would be allowed and a declaration that the tenancy was secure would be substituted.

Basingstoke and Dean Borough Council v Paice (1995) 27 HLR 433 (Court of Appeal: Stuart-Smith, Waite and Millett LJJ).

1852 Statutory tenancy—succession by member of family—second succession—landlord estopped from denying joint statutory tenancy

M lived with her father and mother in a flat owned by landlords. Her father was originally the statutory tenant and, on his death, her mother became statutory tenant by succession. M continued to live at the property with her mother. Under the Rent Act 1977, M would have been entitled to become the statutory tenant by second succession on her mother's death, but under the amendments made to the 1977 Act by the Housing Act 1988, instead of becoming a statutory tenant, M was only entitled to an assured tenancy. M obtained a letter from the managing agents which acknowledged that she and her mother were joint tenants of the flat. M believed as a result that she was secure and refused an offer of rehousing. When her mother died, however, the landlords claimed that M was an assured rather than a statutory tenant. A county court found in favour of the landlords and, on M's appeal against that decision, *held*, (1) the letter which M sought to rely on did not constitute an agreement under the 1977 Act, Sch 1, Pt II, para 13, whereby M could be deemed to be the statutory tenant. That required an agreement in writing between the mother and M to which the landlords were parties. (2) However, the landlords were estopped from denying that M was a joint statutory tenant. Although only one person could succeed to a statutory tenancy on the death of a statutory tenant, there appeared to be no reason why, if joint tenants held a protected tenancy, they should not both become statutory tenants if they held over on expiry of the contractual term. (3) There was no reason why the landlords should not be bound by a representation that they would treat M and her mother as if they were joint tenants. (4) The estoppel allowed the transfer to the statutory tenancy to take place without the agreement required by the 1977 Act. That requirement was imposed for the protection of individual parties rather than in the public interest and the parties were entitled to waive it. Accordingly, the appeal would be allowed.

Daejan Properties Ltd v Mahoney [1995] EGCS 4 (Court of Appeal: Sir Thomas Bingham MR, Hoffmann and Saville LJJ).

LEGAL AID

Halsbury's Laws of England (4th edn) Vol 27(2) (reissue), paras 1851–2075

1853 Articles

Enhanced Rate for Care Proceedings, Ian Robertson (on *Re Children Act 1989 (Taxation of Costs)* [1994] 2 FLR 934 (1994 Abr para 1802)): [1995] Fam Law 365

Costs Against the Legal Aid Board, Alastair Logan (on the Legal Aid Act 1988, s 18): 145 NLJ 59

Costs and the Legal Aid Act 1988, David Burrows: [1995] Fam Law 315

It's Legal Aid, Jim, But Not as We Know It, Bill Montague (on the Legal Aid Green Paper): 139 SJ 494

Legal Aid and Title to Land, Judge Nicholas Brandt: 145 NLJ 597

Legal Aid Payment for Work Undertaken Prior to the Conclusion of Criminal Proceedings, F
  G Davies: 159 JP Jo 631, 715
Legal Aid: Wrong Way Forward, Eileen Pembridge: 139 SJ 1102
The Practical Points, Steve Orchard (on the Legal Aid Green Paper): LS Gaz, 21 June 1995, p
  18
Twelve Reasons for Rejecting the Legal Aid Green Paper, Michael Zander: 145 NLJ 1098

1854 Administration of legal aid scheme—new approach to structuring of scheme—consultation paper

The Lord Chancellor's Department has issued a consultation paper, *Legal Aid—Targeting Need*
(Cm 2854). The paper sets out a new approach to the structuring of the legal aid scheme. The
principles behind the changes are that funds must be targeted on needs and priorities; high
quality services must be provided under the scheme, and suppliers must have incentives to
improve the quality of services and to find new and better ways of delivering them; incentives
must also be provided to suppliers to provide the most effective and economical solutions to
problems; and the revised scheme must operate within an overall fixed budget. The most
important mechanism for achieving the principles set out is the use of block funded contracts to
provide legal services. Block contracting would involve franchising solicitors for all legal aid
services and non-solicitor agencies (eg citizens' advice bureaux) for advice and assistance in social
welfare law. The objective of block contracting would be to improve access to justice by
establishing a means of setting priorities for legal aid and targeting expenditure where there was
the greatest need. It is not intended to create a new body to act as the contracting agent; it is
hoped that an existing organisation with a suitable local network (eg the legal aid board, local
authorities or the courts) might undertake the work. The allocation of funds to local offices
would be in accordance with guidelines laid down by Parliament, with a central budget retained
for cases incurring exceptionally high costs (which are the subject of separate and specific
consideration) or unforeseeable and urgent need. The contracting process would be by tender
for the provision of specified services, and quality standards would be an inherent part of the
contractual arrangements. Contract monitoring and auditing would be undertaken by a local
office. In the cases of civil non-family cases, social welfare cases and civil family cases, the grant
of legal aid would depend on the assessment by the supplier of the strength and nature of each
case; this assessment would be continuous throughout the life of the case. The type of work
offered under the contract would vary according to the nature of the case, eg mediation would
be included within the block contract for family cases. In criminal cases, advice and assistance
and representation would all be covered by the block contract; but legal aid would only be
available if the client used a solicitor who included police station duty work. If more than one
firm of solicitors had a block contract for the provision of duty solicitor services at the same
court, coverage would be organised on a rota basis. Solicitors would have freedom within the
contract to decide on the most effective manner of running a case, taking account of all
circumstances including cost. Representation would still depend on the criteria of financial
eligibility and the interests of justice; the possibility of the interests of justice criterion being
applied by the contracted solicitor or the legal aid board is considered, as is the possibility of
developing different criteria for determining the interests of justice which would be easier to
apply and to audit. The financial criteria for criminal legal aid and the various forms of civil legal
aid are the subject of specific consideration.

1855 Advice and assistance—assistance by way of representation—scope

The Legal Advice and Assistance (Scope) (Amendment) Regulations 1995, SI 1995/1987 (in
force on 22 July 1995), amend the 1989 Regulations, SI 1989/550, in consequence of the
abolition of committal for trial by the Criminal Justice and Public Order Act 1994 and the
substitution of a new procedure of transfer for trial. The 1995 Regulations exclude an oral
hearing under the new procedure from the scope of assistance by way of representation.

1856 Advice and assistance—duty solicitor—remuneration

The Legal Advice and Assistance (Duty Solicitor) (Remuneration) (Amendment) Regulations
1995, SI 1995/951 (in force on 24 April 1995), amend the 1989 Regulations, SI 1989/341, so
as to increase the rates of remuneration payable for legal advice and assistance by a duty solicitor.
The 1995 Regulations make provision for a higher rate of remuneration for franchisees.

1857 Advice and assistance—eligibility

The Legal Advice and Assistance (Amendment) Regulations 1995, SI 1995/795 (in force on 10 April 1995), amend the 1989 Regulations, SI 1989/340, so as to increase the income limits for legal advice and assistance (other than assistance by way of representation (ABWOR)) from £70 to £72, for non-contributory ABWOR from £63 to £64, and for contributory ABWOR from £153 to £156.

1858 Advice and assistance—police stations—remuneration

The Legal Advice and Assistance at Police Stations (Remuneration) (Amendment) Regulations 1995, SI 1995/950 (in force on 24 April 1995), amend the 1989 Regulations, SI 1989/342, so as to increase the rates of remuneration payable for legal advice and assistance at police stations. The 1995 Regulations make provision for higher rates of remuneration for franchisees.

1859 Advice and assistance—remuneration

The Legal Advice and Assistance (Amendment) (No 2) Regulations 1995, SI 1995/949 (in force on 24 April 1995), amend the 1989 Regulations, SI 1989/340, so as to increase the rates of remuneration payable for legal advice and assistance. The 1995 Regulations make provision for higher rates of remuneration for franchisees.

1860 Civil proceedings—assessment of resources

The Civil Legal Aid (Assessment of Resources) (Amendment) Regulations 1995, SI 1995/797 (in force on 10 April 1994), amend the 1989 Regulations, SI 1989/338, so as to increase the income limit for non-contributory civil legal aid from £2,382 to £2,425, the upper income limit from £7,060 to £7,187, and the upper income limit for personal injury cases from £7,780 to £7,920.

1861 Civil proceedings—costs—pre-legal aid certificate costs

See *Joyce v Kammac (1988) Ltd*, para 2777.

1862 Civil proceedings—costs awarded against assisted person—enforcement—charging order

The plaintiffs and defendants were neighbours involved in proceedings concerning a disputed right of way. Judgment was entered for the plaintiffs for damages with costs, such costs not to be enforced without leave of the court. Both parties had been granted legal aid during the course of the proceedings. The plaintiffs subsequently obtained charging orders against the defendants' property in respect of the judgment and the costs. Thereafter the plaintiffs applied for the enforcement of both charging orders by the sale of the defendants' property. At the hearing of the application, the judge (who had earlier dismissed the defendants' application for an adjournment because they had not managed to obtain legal aid) ordered (i) in respect of the costs incurred by the plaintiffs before the defendants had been granted legal aid and the damages, that the plaintiffs were entitled to enforce the charge against the defendants' property, and (ii) in respect of the costs incurred after the grant of legal aid, that the charge could be enforced against any balance of proceeds of sale of the defendants' property. The defendants appealed against the charging order in respect of costs, the refusal of the adjournment and the enforcement order. *Held* (1) for the purposes of the Legal Aid Act 1988 a charging order was a form of execution, since it was a process for enforcing the judgment of the court and the rights of a judgment creditor, and as such was prohibited by s 17(3)(b) of the Act, which provided that a legally assisted person's dwelling house should not be subject to execution to enforce an order for costs against him. It followed that the judge was not entitled to impose a charging order against the defendants' property to secure payment of costs incurred by the plaintiffs after the defendants had been granted legal aid. (2) Since at the time of the defendants' application for an adjournment, the judge could not have known whether the defendants would obtain legal aid if he adjourned the hearing of the application for sale, and understandably did not discern the arguments which might be open to them, his order refusing an adjournment could not fairly be criticised. (3) Having regard to the fact that the judge was not entitled to impose a charging order over an assisted person's dwelling house to enforce payment of costs incurred after the grant of legal aid, it was clear that he had no power to authorise enforcement of a charge against the proceeds of sale of the house in relation to those costs. It followed that that part of the enforcement order relating to the plaintiffs' costs after the defendants had obtained legal aid could not stand. The appeal would be allowed in part.

Parr v Smith [1995] 2 All ER 1031 (Court of Appeal: Sir Thomas Bingham MR, Staughton and Peter Gibson LJJ).

1863 Civil proceedings—costs awarded against assisted person—enforcement—order for sale of property

In proceedings brought by the plaintiff to establish the beneficial interests of the parties in a freehold property, a declaration was made that the first and second defendants held the property upon trust for the plaintiff and the first defendant as tenants in common in equal shares. It was further ordered that a deed of transfer, by which the property had been transferred out of the joint names of the plaintiff and the first defendant and into the joint names of the first and second defendants, should be cancelled and that the defendants should pay the plaintiff's costs, such costs not to be enforced without further order of the court. All the parties were legally aided. The defendants subsequently applied for an order for the sale of the property. The plaintiff did not oppose the application but applied for an order entitling him to enforce the order for costs against the first defendant's half share in the proceeds of sale. It fell to be determined whether the Legal Aid Act 1988, s 17(3)(a), which provided that a legally assisted person's dwelling house could not be subject to execution or any corresponding process to enforce an order for costs, prevented the court from permitting the enforcement of an order for costs against the proceeds of sale of such a dwelling house. *Held*, a fund representing the proceeds of sale of a former dwelling house was not within the restriction in s 17(3)(a) and, therefore, the court had jurisdiction to make an order which led to the enforcement of an order for costs against such a fund in such amount as the court thought reasonable. When determining whether such an order ought to be made in the exercise of its discretion, the court would consider the consequences of refusing the order, and in circumstances where both parties were legally aided it could not be regarded as a fair result if any share in property recovered by the plaintiff in successful litigation would be lost to him by virtue of the statutory charge conferred on the Legal Aid Board by s 16(6)(b) while the defendant's share remained available to the defendant to assist in the purchase of a new dwelling house. In all the circumstances of the case, it would be reasonable for the defendants to pay an amount equal to the share of the first defendant in the net proceeds of sale of the property. The court would direct that the proceeds of sale of the property be paid into an account in the names of the solicitors having conduct of the sale and that the whole share of the first defendant be paid out of that account towards the liability of the defendants under the order for costs.

Chaggar v Chaggar [1995] 4 All ER 795 (Chancery Division: Chadwick J). *Parr v Smith* [1995] 2 All ER 1031, CA (para 1862) considered.

1864 Civil proceedings—costs awarded to assisted person—costs on an indemnity basis

In the course of proceedings between the plaintiff and the defendant, the defendant was ordered to pay the plaintiff's costs on an indemnity basis. On appeal, the defendant argued that having regard to the Legal Aid Act 1988 and the Civil Legal Aid (General) Regulations 1989, SI 1989/339, it should not have been ordered to do so because the plaintiff was legally-aided. *Held*, the effect of the 1989 Regulations was that (1) a legally-aided party's legal representatives could only recover payment for work done under a legal aid certificate from the Legal Aid Board, (2) a legally-aided party could only be required to pay his legal costs to the extent of his assessed contributions and any costs which were secured as a charge on the property recovered, (3) the Legal Aid Board's liability to pay his legal representatives was limited to costs taxed on a standard basis, and (4) if costs were awarded to a legally-aided party on an indemnity basis, they could not be awarded so as to reimburse the legally-aided party, his legal representatives or the Legal Aid Board. As such, a defendant could not be ordered to pay costs on an indemnity basis to a plaintiff who was legally aided throughout the proceedings. Accordingly, the appeal would be allowed.

Willis v Redbridge Health Authority (1995) Times, 22 December (Court of Appeal: Beldam, Hobhouse and Aldous LJJ).

1865 Civil proceedings—statutory charge—operation

See *Brookes v Harris*, para 2640.

1866 Civil proceedings—statutory right to legal aid—effect on discretion of court

See *Connelly v RTZ Corpn plc*, para 572.

1867 Contempt proceedings—remuneration

The Legal Aid in Contempt Proceedings (Remuneration) Regulations 1995, SI 1995/948 (in force on 24 April 1995), replace the 1991 Regulations, SI 1991/837 (as amended). The 1995 Regulations (1) provide for a fixed division of the standard fee between an advocate and any other legal representative instructed, (2) create rights of review and appeal where a legal representative is dissatisfied with the remuneration allowed, and (3) provide increased rates of remuneration.

1868 Criminal and care proceedings—applications—records of applications

The Legal Aid in Criminal and Care Proceedings (General) (Amendment) Regulations 1995, SI 1995/542 (in force on 1 May 1995), amend the 1989 Regulations, SI 1989/344, so as to (1) require magistrates' courts to provide copies of legal aid application forms free of charge; (2) require the proper officer of each court to which applications for criminal legal aid are made to keep records of the applications, showing the court's reasons for granting or refusing legal aid; (3) require the proper officer to supply the applicant with a copy of that record where legal aid has been refused on the ground that it was not in the interests of justice to grant legal aid; and (4) exempt the applicant from the duty of providing a statement of means where no means test applies because he, his parent or guardian (or their spouses) receives income support, family credit or disability working allowance.

1869 Criminal and care proceedings—costs

The Legal Aid in Criminal and Care Proceedings (Costs) (Amendment) Regulations 1995, SI 1995/952 (in force on 24 April 1995), amend the 1989 Regulations, SI 1989/343, so as to increase the rates of remuneration for legal aid work in criminal proceedings. The 1995 Regulations make provision for higher rates of remuneration for franchisees for work done by solicitors in magistrates' courts. The regulations also change the date after which certain work may be remunerated at discretionary rates instead of prescribed rates from 30 June 1995 to 30 June 1996.

1870 Criminal and care proceedings—income limit

The Legal Aid in Criminal and Care Proceedings (General) (Amendment) (No 2) Regulations 1995, SI 1995/796 (in force on 10 April 1995), amend the 1989 Regulations, SI 1989/344, so as to increase the income limit for non-contributory criminal legal aid from £46 to £47 per week.

1871 Criminal proceedings—Crown Court—two counsel order

Lord Taylor of Gosforth CJ has issued the following *Practice Direction* ([1995] 1 WLR 261) in consequence of the amendment of the Legal Aid in Criminal and Care Proceedings (General) Regulations 1989, SI 1989/334, by the Legal Aid in Criminal and Care Proceedings (General) (Amendment) (No 2) Regulations 1994, SI 1994/3136.

1. The 1989 Regulations, reg 48(14)(a), as amended, empowers a High Court judge or a circuit judge to make or subsequently amend a legal aid order to provide for the services of two counsel (a two counsel order) or a Queen's Counsel alone in specified proceedings in the Crown Court.

2. The 1989 Regulations, reg 48(14)(b), as amended, empowers a High Court judge or an anticipated trial judge to make or subsequently amend a legal aid order to provide for the services of three counsel (a three counsel order) in specified proceedings in the Crown Court, where the prosecution is being brought by the Serious Fraud Office.

3. An application made to the Crown Court for a two counsel order, Queen's Counsel alone, or any subsequent amendment must be placed before the resident or designated judge of that Crown Court or, in his absence, a judge nominated by a presiding circuit judge, who must determine the application. Where, however, the application relates to a case which is to be heard before a named High Court judge or a named circuit judge, the application must be referred to the named judge for determination.

4. Paragraph 3 above does not apply where an application for a two counsel order is made either during a pre-trial review or during a trial, as it is for the judge seised of the case to determine the application.

5. In the event of any doubt as to the proper application of the direction, reference must be made by the judge concerned to the presiding circuit judge, who must give such directions as he sees fit.

6. This Practice Direction supersedes Practice Direction (Crown Court: Two Counsel Order) [1989] 1 WLR 618.

1872   Criminal proceedings—grant of legal aid—grant after conclusion of proceedings— circumstances in which order may be made

The Legal Aid in Criminal and Care Proceedings (General) Regulations 1989, SI 1989/344, reg 44(7) provides that where in proceedings in a magistrates' court, representation or advice is given before a legal aid order is made, that representation or advice is to be deemed to be representation or advice given under the order if (1) the interests of justice required that representation or advice be provided as a matter of urgency, (2) there was no undue delay in making an application for legal aid, and (3) the representation or advice was given by the solicitor who was subsequently assigned under the legal aid order.

A firm of solicitors was instructed to represent a defendant charged with criminal damage. As the trial was to take place on the same day that the firm received its instructions, it applied for a legal aid order later that day, after the conclusion of the trial. The justices' clerk refused to consider the application because the defendant failed to submit supporting documentary evidence of his means with the application. That information was not supplied by the defendant until nearly two weeks after the conclusion of the trial, upon which the justices' clerk decided that it was too late to make a legal aid order, as an order could not be backdated or have retrospective effect. On the firm's application for judicial review of the decision, *held*, although justices' clerks could not backdate a legal aid order or grant a conditional legal aid order, an order could be made after proceedings had concluded if the conditions of the 1989 Regulations, reg 44(7) were satisfied. Regulation 44(7) protected the legal aid fund against the possibility of paying legal aid where supporting documentary evidence of a defendant's means was never produced, and also avoided the kind of situation that had occurred in the instant case. Here, the application for legal aid had been made contemporaneously with the work undertaken. Moreover, as no contribution was immediately recoverable from the defendant because of the rule in the 1989 Regulations, reg 29(1), the justices' clerk should have made a legal aid order to enable the firm to be paid under reg 44(7) for the work that it had done earlier on the day of the application. Accordingly, the application would be allowed.

R v Highbury Corner Magistrates' Court, ex p DJ Sonn & Co (a firm) [1995] 4 All ER 57 (Queen's Bench Division: Simon Brown LJ and Curtis J).

1873   Criminal proceedings—grant of legal aid—proceedings in respect of a sentence— enforcement of compensation order

Under the Legal Aid Act 1988, s 19(5), 'criminal proceedings' includes proceedings for dealing with an offender for an offence or in respect of a sentence.

Having been convicted of conspiracy to defraud, the applicant was sentenced to five years' imprisonment and fined. On appeal, a compensation order was substituted for the fine, subject to three years' imprisonment in default of payment. His application for legal aid in proceedings for the enforcement of the compensation order was refused by magistrates on the basis that they were dealing with the enforcement of a previously imposed sentence and not the sentence itself, having regard to the 1988 Act, s 19(5). On the applicant's application for judicial review of the decision, *held*, proceedings for the enforcement of a compensation order are criminal proceedings for the purposes of s 19(5) since they are 'proceedings . . . in respect of a sentence'. Legal aid should accordingly be granted in such proceedings.

R v Redbridge Magistrates' Court, ex p Guppy (1995) 159 JP 622 (Queen's Bench Division: McCowan LJ and McKinnon J).

1874   Criminal proceedings—refusal of legal aid—application for removal of driving disqualification—payment for private medical report

As part of a sentence passed on him at the Crown Court for causing death by reckless driving, the applicant was disqualified from driving for life. He was also sentenced to three years' probation with a condition of treatment for a psychiatric condition. He wished to apply to the Crown Court for removal of the disqualification in accordance with the Road Traffic Offenders Act 1988, s 42. To support his application he required a medical report and, being unable to pay for a private medical report, he applied for legal aid. The Crown Court refused his application for legal aid on the basis of a policy that legal aid representation was unnecessary and unavailable to an applicant for the removal of a disqualification. On his application for judicial review of the decision, *held*, an applicant for the removal of a disqualification under the Road Traffic Offenders Act 1988, s 42 was eligible to apply for representation under the Legal Aid Act 1988, Pt V. The Legal Aid Act 1988, s 19, when combined with s 43, defined criminal proceedings as including any proceedings in respect of an order made on a person's conviction for an offence. Accordingly, the application would be granted.

R v Liverpool Crown Court, ex p McCann [1995] RTR 23 (Queen's Bench Division: Balcombe LJ and McCullough J).

1875 Family proceedings—taxation of costs—parents receiving separate legal aid certificates

The defendants were a husband and wife whose child had been made the subject of wardship proceedings by a local authority. Both had received legal aid separately and both were represented by separate solicitors and counsel. The district judge questioned the need to have separate representation and wrote to the Legal Aid Board for an explanation. The board stated that applications for legal aid for each defendant had been made on different dates, by different firms of solicitors, in different names and when the defendants were unmarried. The board had, therefore, not connected the two applications until substantial work had been undertaken by their respective solicitors and it was then too late to take any action. The district judge accepted this explanation but recommended that the taxing officer reduce costs allowed to account for the unnecessary duplication of legal advisers. The taxing officer disallowed half the profit costs claimed by each solicitor and reduced the fees of the wife's counsel from £2,500 to £1,000 to bring them in line with the those of the husband's counsel. On appeal against the taxation, *held*, the husband's case had been substantially less difficult and complex than the wife's and her counsel had several years more seniority than the husband's counsel. The disparity in the two counsels' fees was therefore justified and the fees of the wife's counsel would be allowed at £1,750. The not very substantial reductions by the judge for care and conduct of the case due to the number of welfare attendances on the client which did not advance the case were justified as the judge had taken an objective overall view before reaching that conclusion. The judge had been correct in stating that a competent solicitor would have realised that involvement of two solicitors in a case such as the one in issue was inefficient and inappropriate. However, the board had sanctioned separate representation and it was therefore not unreasonable as the solicitors were doing what they were authorised to do. Accordingly, the profit costs ought not to have been halved and an order would be made to that effect.

Re B and H (Minors) (Costs: Legal Aid) [1995] 2 FCR 409 (Family Division: Ward J).

1876 Legal Aid Advisory Committee—dissolution

The Legal Aid Advisory Committee (Dissolution) Order 1995, SI 1995/162 (in force on 26 January 1995), dissolves the Legal Aid Advisory Committee in existence under the Legal Aid Act 1988, s 35.

LIBEL AND SLANDER

Halsbury's Laws of England (4th edn) Vol 28, paras 1–300

1877 Articles

The Defamation Bill, Patrick Milmo (on the 1995 Bill): 145 NLJ 1340
Defamation on the Internet, Duncan Calow: [1995] 11 CLSR 199
Defamation on the Internet, Stephen Dooley: [1995] 6 CTLR 191
The Internet and Bulletin Board Defamations, Nick Braithwaite: 145 NLJ 1216
Logging on to Libel Laws (on Defamation by E-mail), Brian Napier: LS Gaz, 4 October 1995, p 21
MPs Discover the Unwelcome Face of Parliamentary Privilege, Penelope Gorman (on libel actions brought by MPs): 139 SJ 772
Strewth! Madge and Harold Have No Remedy in Libel Law, Penelope Gorman (on *Charleston v News Group Newspapers Ltd* (1995) Times, Independent, 31 March (para 1885)): 139 SJ 440

1878   Defamation—damages—guidance given to jury

It has been held that public opinion is offended by damages for defamation often being greater than damages for personal injuries which leave a plaintiff insensate or helplessly crippled. Therefore, juries in defamation actions ought to be given guidance by references to appropriate awards and brackets of awards by counsel and the judge. A jury is not bound by the submission of counsel or the judge's indication and, if it makes an award outside the upper or lower brackets, weight must be given, on appeal, to the possibility that their judgment is to be preferred to that of the judge. Reference to awards given in personal injuries actions may be made, not in order to act as a precise correlation, but to indicate the reasonableness or otherwise of an award. Exemplary damages ought never to exceed the minimum sum necessary to meet the purpose of punishing the defendant, showing that tort does not pay and deterring others.

John v Mirror Group Newspapers Ltd [1996] 2 All ER 35 (Court of Appeal: Sir Thomas Bingham MR, Neill and Hirst LJJ).

1879   Defamation—defence—breach of parliamentary privilege

The plaintiff, a member of Parliament, brought a libel action against the defendants, a political journalist and the editor of the newspaper which had published an article critical of the plaintiff in relation to his behaviour in Parliament. The defendants sought to have the action stayed. *Held*, in order to defend the action, the defendants were seeking to bring evidence concerning the plaintiff's conduct in the House of Commons. The courts would not allow them to do so because that would constitute breach of parliamentary privilege. As the plaintiff was able to enjoy the benefits of that privilege, it would be unjust to deprive the defendants of their defence. Accordingly, the action would be stayed.

Allason v Haines [1995] NLJR 1576 (Queen's Bench Division: Owen J).

1880   Defamation—defence—justification—hearsay and rumour

The plaintiff holiday company and its directors brought a defamation action against the defendant, a rival company. The corporate action was settled but the directors' action was continued. The defendant claimed that the statements complained of did not defame the directors but that, even if they did, the defence of justification still applied. The directors claimed that the plaintiff's defence of justification ought to be struck out because it could not apply where there was reliance on hearsay and rumour as there was a danger that the jury would then presume that the rumours were well founded. At first instance, the directors' application was dismissed. On appeal, *held*, although hearsay and rumour could not justify an assertion of fact that a rumour was well-founded, there were circumstances in which a person could repeat a rumour before ascertaining its truth. In such circumstances, it was possible to plead in justification that there were in truth such rumours and, accordingly, the appeal would be dismissed.

Aspro Travel Ltd v Owners Abroad Group plc [1995] 4 All ER 728 (Court of Appeal: Stuart-Smith, Waite and Schiemann LJJ).

1881   Defamation—defence—matters of public interest—public figure immunity

It has been held that in libel proceedings under English law, immunity cannot be claimed on the ground that it is in the public interest to indict a person's character because he is a public figure.

Bennett v Guardian Newspapers Ltd (1995) Times, 28 December (Queen's Bench Division: Sir Michael Davies).

1882   Defamation—defence—qualified privileged—privileged occasion

A newspaper which had defamed a person published an apology in the terms requested by that person's solicitors. The apology contained an allegedly defamatory reference to the plaintiff, who sought damages in libel against the newspaper. The solicitors were joined as third party tortfeasors. Both the newspaper and the solicitors sought to rely on the defence of common law qualified privilege. As a preliminary issue, it was held that neither party was protected by the privilege against the plaintiff's claim. The newspaper and the solicitors appealed. *Held*, the position of the newspaper and that of the solicitors had to be considered separately. The two parties had very different circumstances and the origins of their respective publications differed widely. It would be impossible to do them justice if they were not entitled to separate consideration. The newspaper was not entitled to rely on the defence of qualified privilege since it was not rebutting an attack on itself and the terms of the published apology were not justified by any duty to right the wrong done to the recipient of the apology. Having regard to the origin and circumstances of the publication of the allegedly defamatory apology by the newspaper, the necessary conditions by which protection should be given had not been satisfied. By contrast, the circumstances associated with the origin and publication of the defamatory matter by the solicitors did satisfy the conditions by which the protection of qualified privilege could be obtained. They had acted as the representative of their client. Since he had been the victim of an attack, he had a right to reply in order to rebut the accusation made against him. This could be done with a considerable degree of latitude, so long as wholly irrelevant and extraneous material was not included. Although the offending words were unnecessary, they fell squarely within the bounds of qualified privilege. The protection of qualified privilege extended to the solicitors who had acted on their client's behalf to rebut the attack made on him. Accordingly, their appeal would be allowed and the third party notice struck out. The appeal by the newspaper would be dismissed.

Watts v Times Newspapers Ltd [1996] 1 All ER 152 (Court of Appeal: Hirst and Henry LJJ and Sir Ralph Gibson). *London Association for Protection of Trade v Greenlands Ltd* [1916] 2 AC 15, HL applied. *Toogood v Spyring* [1834] 1 Cm & R 181 at 193 considered.

1883 Defamation—delay in prosecuting action—absence of legal aid

It has been held that an absence of legal aid in libel proceedings which leads to a plaintiff's delay in prosecuting his action is a matter which should elicit sympathy from the court and should be considered as a ground of excuse when deciding whether or not to strike out the action.

Gilberthorpe v Hawkins (1995) Times, 3 April (Court of Appeal: McCowan LJ, Ward J and Sir Roger Parker).

1884 Defamation—meaning of defamatory words—natural and ordinary meaning

A campaigner brought legal proceedings to procure the withdrawal of a circular to general practitioners which stated that it was permissible to give contraceptive advice to under-age girls without parental consent. Her action succeeded at first instance but then failed on appeal. Later, during a live television programme a journalist, referring to the period of the campaigner's initial success, said that there had been at least two reported suicides by pregnant girls. The campaigner brought an action against the journalist and the television company alleging that the journalist's words were defamatory. As a preliminary issue, the judge found in the campaigner's favour that the words were capable of bearing a defamatory meaning. On appeal, the journalist and the company accepted that the reasonable viewer could infer there was a clear link between the campaigner's success and the suicides, but argued that the programme did not suggest she was culpable. *Held*, Millett LJ dissenting, in *Skuse v Granada Television Ltd*, the court held that (1) any material complained about should be given its natural and ordinary meaning which it would have conveyed to the ordinary reasonable viewer watching the programme, and (2) a statement should be taken to be defamatory if it would tend to lower a plaintiff in the estimation of right-thinking members of society generally, or be likely to affect a person adversely in the estimation of reasonable people generally. In the present case, within the reasonable spectrum of meanings of which the words were reasonably capable, was the meaning that the campaigner was in some sense to blame for the girls' deaths and therefore morally responsible to a culpable degree. The suicide of two or more young girls would have been a most distressing event and reasonable viewers might well have taken a most unfavourable view of anyone who was even remotely responsible for the girls' actions. The court was satisfied that a jury might properly conclude that the words used would have been likely to affect the campaigner adversely in the estimation of reasonable persons generally and, accordingly, the appeal would be dismissed.

Gillick v British Broadcasting Corpn (1995) Times, 20 October (Court of Appeal: Neill, Evans and Millett LJJ). *Skuse v Granada Television Ltd* (1993) Independent, 2 April, CA (1993 Abr para 1672) considered.

1885 Defamation—proof of publication—newspaper headlines and photograph

The plaintiffs, actors in a popular television soap opera, brought an action for defamation against a tabloid newspaper which had published an article about the makers of a pornographic video game who had used the plaintiffs' likenesses without their permission. The article was accompanied by photographs, in which the heads of the plaintiffs were superimposed on to the bodies of models in pornographic poses. The plaintiffs conceded the article was not, in itself, defamatory but claimed that readers who only read the headline or saw the photograph would draw an inference injurious to the plaintiffs' reputations. At first instance, it was held that the article was incapable of bearing a defamatory meaning. On appeal by the plaintiffs, it was held that, although the plaintiffs had been treated very badly, the law as yet provided no remedy for them. On further appeal, *held*, where no legal innuendo was alleged, the natural and ordinary meaning to be ascribed to the words of an allegedly defamatory publication was the meaning, including any inferential meaning, which the words would convey to the mind of the ordinary, reasonable and fair-minded reader. The jury in a libel action were therefore required to determine the single meaning which the publication conveyed to the notional reasonable reader and base their verdict and any award of damages on the assumption that that was the one sense in which all readers would have understood it. It would be destructive of this principle to allow the plaintiff to invite the jury to infer that different groups of readers read different parts of the entire publication, such as headlines, and for that reason understood it to mean different things, some defamatory, some not. Accordingly, the plaintiffs' appeal would be dismissed.

Charleston v News Group Newspapers Ltd [1995] 2 WLR 450 (House of Lords: Lords Goff of Chieveley, Bridge of Harwich, Jauncey of Tullichettle, Mustill and Nicholls of Birkenhead).

1886   Defamation—trial of preliminary issue—matters for jury—malice

Following the plaintiff's appointment as the chairwoman of a regional health trust, the defendant non-executive directors of the trust made a written statement which implied that the plaintiff was incompetent and had acted with impropriety in her position as chairwoman. The statement was circulated, and eventually appeared in several national newspapers. On the plaintiff's action for damages for libel, the defendants claimed that they were entitled to the protection of the Public Health Act 1875, s 265, under which proceedings cannot be taken against a person for bona fide acts done in the execution of any duty under the National Health Service and Community Care Act 1990. In deciding that the entitlement to rely on s 265 was to be determined as a preliminary issue by a judge alone, the judge rejected the plaintiff's argument that the defence related to the substance of the libel action. On her appeal, *held*, the issue of whether or not the defendants had acted bona fides was indistinguishable from the issue of whether or not they had acted with malice. The latter issue had to be determined by a jury, as only in certain limited circumstances could a judge do so. Moreover, the fact that a plaintiff had a statutory right to have questions of fact decided by a jury was a decisive factor which a judge was obliged to take into account in exercising his discretion whether or not to determine the issue of malice himself. In any event, the 1875 Act, s 265 did not provide immunity from suit but merely a special defence. Accordingly, the appeal would be allowed.

Kirby-Harris v Baxter (1995) 25 BMLR 135 (Court of Appeal: Nourse and Evans LJJ).

1887   Slander—limitation period—expiry—discretion to extend

See *Oyston v Blaker*, para 1901.

LIBRARIES AND SCIENTIFIC AND CULTURAL INSTITUTIONS

Halsbury's Laws of England (4th edn) Vol 28, paras 301–500

1888   British Museum—authorised repositories

The British Museum (Authorised Repositories) Order 1995, SI 1995/1224 (in force on 1 June 1995), further amends the British Museum Act 1963, Sch 3, Pt 1 so as to add 23 Blythe Road, London to the list of authorised repositories of the British Museum.

1889   London exhibition halls—electrical contracting services

The Electrical Contracting (London Exhibition Halls) Order 1995, SI 1995/3299 (in force in part on 1 February 1996 and in part on 1 September 1996), makes provision in relation to electrical contracting services provided to exhibitors at exhibition halls in Greater London with more than 2,500 square metres of exhibition space. The order prohibits owners of exhibition halls from imposing restrictions on who may provide electrical contracting services to exhibitors at exhibitions organised by persons unconnected with the hall owner except on objectively justified grounds. Where there is a connection between the hall owner and the exhibition organiser, the power of the organiser to require the use of a particular electrical contractor is restricted. Hall owners are prohibited from receiving any valuable benefit from contractors in return for requiring or promoting the use of their services.

1890 Research councils—Central Laboratory

The Council for the Central Laboratory of the Research Councils Order 1995, SI 1995/261 (in force on 1 April 1995), declares the Council for the Central Laboratory of the Research Councils to be established as a research council for the purposes of the Science and Technology Act 1965 and specifies the objects of the Council.

1891 Research councils—transfer of property

The Research Councils (Transfer of Property etc) Order 1995, SI 1995/630 (in force on 1 April 1995), provides for the transfer of property, rights, liabilities and obligations from the Engineering and Physical Sciences Research Council to the Council for the Central Laboratory of the Research Councils. The order also permits the continued participation in a pension scheme administered by the United Kingdom Atomic Energy Authority of certain persons employed by the Engineering and Physical Sciences Research Council whose contracts of employment are transferred to the Council for the Central Laboratory of the Research Councils.

LIEN

Halsbury's Laws of England (4th edn) Vol 28, paras 501–600

1892 Articles

The 1993 Convention on Maritime Liens and Mortgages, Francesco Berlingieri: [1995] LMCLQ 57

1893 Solicitors—lien for costs

See SOLICITORS.

LIMITATION OF ACTIONS

Halsbury's Laws of England (4th edn) Vol 28, paras 601–1000

1894 Articles

Alleviating the Effects of s 24 of the Limitation Act 1980, Tom Keevil: 145 NLJ 1691
Limitations and Chemical Poisoning, Alan Care:(on *Dobbie v Medway Health Authority* [1994] 4 All ER 450 (1994 Abr para 1830)): 139 SJ 17

1895 Limitation period—exclusion—action by beneficiary under trust

The Limitation Act 1980, s 21(1)(b) provides that no period of limitation prescribed by the Act applies to an action by a beneficiary under a trust, being an action to recover from the trustee trust property or the proceeds of trust property in the possession of the trustee, or previously received by the trustee and converted to his use.

The plaintiff, a musician, commenced proceedings against the defendant, his former manager, claiming money received by the defendant whilst acting as his manager, damages for alleged infringement of copyright in certain works, and also the delivery up of certain master recordings. On the question of whether or not any limitation period applied to the action, *held*, the defendant had been under a fiduciary duty to account annually to the plaintiff, but had breached that duty. A constructive trust thereby arose, and therefore no limitation period applied, as the case fell within the 1980 Act, s 21(1)(b). Although not all fiduciary relationships gave rise to a constructive trust, such a situation arose in the instant case.

Nelson v Rye (1995) Times, 5 December (Chancery Division: Laddie J).

1896 Limitation period—expiry—addition of claims

The Limitation Act 1980, s 35(1)(b) provides that any new claim made in the course of any action is deemed to be a separate action and to have commenced on the same date as the original action. Section 35(3) prohibits the court from allowing a new claim, other than an original set-off or a counterclaim, to be made in the course of an action after the expiry of any limitation period which would affect a new action to enforce that claim. Section 35(5)(a) provides for an exception to this general prohibition in the case of a claim involving a new cause of action if the new cause of action arises out of substantially the same facts as are already in issue on any claim previously made in the original action.

The plaintiff contracted mesothelioma and later died. His widow, in her capacity as his personal representative, was granted leave to carry on an action for damages commenced by him against his former employers, in which he alleged that the disease had been caused by their negligent failure to provide him with a safe system of work. The widow was subsequently granted leave by a district judge to amend the writ, to include a claim for damages for her own benefit under the Fatal Accidents Act 1976. By the time of the application for leave to amend any claim under that Act had become statute-barred. The decision to grant leave was upheld on appeal. On further appeal it was argued that, as a matter of law the 1980 Act, s 35(5) did not apply, and the proposed amendment was therefore prohibited. *Held*, s 35(5) introduced a limited exception to the old rule of practice that a proceeding could not be amended to introduce a cause of action which did not exist at the date of the writ. Section 35 was not to be construed restrictively so as to apply merely to remediable defects of form and procedure. There was no reason why a claim arising out of death could not be raised at the same time as a claim based on loss of expectation of life. In assessing whether the new claim fell within s 35(5), the relevant degree of substantial identity which had to be established lay between the facts of the new claim and those facts which were 'already in issue' in the original action. Precisely the same facts were relevant to the issue of liability in the two claims, save that in the new claim the employers would not accept that the plaintiff died from mesothelioma. Similarly, the facts which related to the issue of quantum of damages were very closely related. Accordingly, the appeal would be dismissed.

Booker v Associated British Ports [1995] PIQR P375 (Court of Appeal: Butler-Sloss, Waite and Aldous LJJ).

The Limitation Act 1980, s 8 provides that no action upon a specialty can be brought after the expiry of twelve years from the date on which the cause of action accrued. Section 19 provides that no action may be brought, or distress made, to recover arrears of rent, or damages in respect of arrears of rent, after the expiration of six years from the date on which the arrears became due.

The defendant was the guarantor for the plaintiffs' tenant, who breached his covenant to pay rent. The plaintiffs brought an action against the defendant but delayed in its prosecution. The defendant applied to have the action struck out on the ground of inordinate and inexcusable delay. The question before the court was whether the limitation period for the plaintiffs' claim was six years under the 1980 Act, s 19 or twelve years under s 8. If the limitation period was twelve years, the plaintiffs could bring new proceedings and it would therefore be wrong to strike out their action. *Held*, the plaintiffs' claim was for damages in respect of arrears of rent and was covered by s 19 which applied to actions against a guarantor as well as a lessee. The fact that s 19 did not expressly state that it applied to a surety was insignificant, as was the fact that the lease and the guarantee were under seal. Accordingly, the correct limitation period for the plaintiffs' action was six years and it could therefore be struck out for want of prosecution.

Romain v Scuba TV Ltd [1995] NLJR 1850 (Court of Appeal: Evans and Waite LJJ and Sir John May).

1897   Limitation period—expiry—change of parties—date of accrual of cause of action

See *Industrie Chimiche Italia Centrale v Alexander G Tsavliris & Sons Maritime Co*, para 2372.

1898   Limitation period—expiry—discretion to extend—breach of parental duty to protect child

The Limitation Act 1980, s 11(1) (special time limit in respect of actions for personal injuries) applies to any action for damages for negligence, nuisance or breach of duty (whether the duty exists by virtue of a contract, or of a provision made by or under a statute, or independently of any contract or any such provision) where the damages claimed consist of or include damages in respect of personal injuries to the plaintiff or any other person.

A daughter alleged she was physically and sexually abused by her father when she was a child and that her mother was aware of such conduct. The father later pleaded guilty to charges of incest, and was sentenced to a term of imprisonment. Eight years after reaching the age of majority, the daughter commenced proceedings against both her mother and father for damages. The claim against her mother was for breach of duty as a parent in respect of her failure to prevent or protect the daughter from abuse by her father, and the claim against the father was for personal injuries arising from the sexual and physical abuse. The judge considered that both claims were for trespass to the person, and struck them out on the basis that more than six years had elapsed since the cause of action accrued, having regard to the 1980 Act, s 2. The daughter appealed successfully in relation to the claim against her mother, and those proceedings were restored. On the mother's appeal, *held*, the court had a discretion to extend the limitation period under s 11, but did not have such power in relation to s 2. Here, the daughter's claim against the mother was not a claim relating to direct physical contact, as in the case of the claim against the father, but was a claim for an independent tort involving acts of omission, in particular a breach of the common law duty to take care of the daughter and not expose her to unnecessary risk of injury or further injury. The claim against the mother therefore fell within s 11 and, accordingly, the appeal would be dismissed.

Seymour v Williams [1995] PIQR P470 (Court of Appeal: Russell and Millett LJJ, and Sir Ralph Gibson). *Stubbings v Webb* [1993] 1 All ER 322, HL (1992 Abr para 1629) distinguished.

1899 Limitation period—expiry—discretion to extend—date at which injury arose—plaintiff's knowledge

Scotland

The Prescription and Limitation (Scotland) Act 1973, s 17(2)(b)(i) provides that no action for damages for personal injuries can be brought unless it is commenced within three years after the date on which the pursuer in the action became, or on which in the opinion of the court it would have been reasonably practicable for him in all the circumstances to become, aware that the injuries in question were sufficiently serious to justify his bringing an action of damages. Section 19A provides that where a person would be entitled, but for any provisions of s 17, to bring an action, the court may if it seems to it to be equitable to do so, allow him to bring the action notwithstanding that provision.

The plaintiff, a prison officer, was assaulted during a prison disturbance, as a result of which he sustained bruising to his shoulder and serious back pain. Although he continued to suffer from back problems, he was assured by medical experts that his condition would improve. On the advice of his union, he submitted a claim to the Criminal Injuries Compensation Board ('the CICB'), and accepted an award two and a half years after the incident. However, the plaintiff's back condition did not improve, and he eventually had to have surgery to alleviate a protruding disc. It was not until four years after the incident that the plaintiff commenced proceedings for negligence against the defendant. As a preliminary issue, the defendant argued that the plaintiff's action was time barred, but the plaintiff sought to rely on the 1973 Act, ss 17(2)(b)(i) and 19A. *Held*, having regard to the test under s 17(2)(b)(i), it was irrelevant that the plaintiff was unaware of the true extent of his back condition until after the limitation period had expired, as the test under s 17(2)(b)(i) related to the seriousness of the situation at the time that the limitation period arose. Since the plaintiff had settled his claim against the CICB within the three-year period, he must have been aware that his injuries were sufficiently serious to warrant him commencing proceedings. As such, he could not rely on s 17(2)(b)(i) to bring his claim out of time. In considering s 19A, however, the plaintiff had been the victim of unfortunate advice, in that his union had not advised him that he ought to commence proceedings for negligence as well as the CICB claim. In addition, the initial medical advice had been unduly optimistic as to the chances of the plaintiff's back condition improving, as further medical evidence showed that his condition had been serious even before the limitation period arose. It would therefore cause greater prejudice to the plaintiff to refuse to grant his application to bring the action out of time, than to allow the action to proceed. The defendant would still be entitled to put forward arguments as to causation and the merits of the claim. Accordingly, the application would be granted.

Ferla v Secretary of State for Scotland 1995 SLT 662 (Outer House).

1900 Limitation period—expiry—discretion to extend—exercise of discretion

The Limitation Act 1980, s 33 provides that the court may direct that the limitation provisions set out in the Act are waived in relation to a particular action if it appears to the court that it would be equitable to do so. The court must have regard to all the circumstances of the case and in particular to the duration of any disability of the plaintiff arising after the date of the accrual of the cause of action: s 33(3)(d).

The plaintiff injured his back while employed by the defendant. He did not consult solicitors regarding a possible claim until five years later and the defendant was not notified of the claim for a further year while counsel was consulted and legal aid obtained. Proceedings were then commenced alleging the defendant's negligence and breach of statutory duty. The defendant claimed the proceedings were statute-barred but the plaintiff successfully applied to have the limitation provisions waived in accordance with s 33. The judge held that (1) the degree of prejudice to the defendant, taking all the circumstances into account, was not of sufficient weight by itself to justify rejecting the plaintiff's application, (2) in respect of s 33(3)(d), the duration of the plaintiff's physical disability was relevant, and (3) although it would have been sensible for the plaintiff's solicitors to have given the earliest possible notification of the claim, it was understandable that they waited for favourable advice and confirmation of legal aid before commencing proceedings. On appeal, *held*, (1) while the judge's finding as to the degree of prejudice was open to proper criticism it was nevertheless one which the judge was entitled to make. (2) For the purposes of s 33(3)(d) 'disability' was limited to the context of a person under a disability by reason of being an infant or a patient under the Mental Health Act 1983. However, physical disability fell to be considered by the judge in the overall exercise of his discretion under the 1980 Act, s 33, and the fact that he erroneously took it into account under s 33(3)(d) did not detract from that. (3) The judge was entitled to take the view that the plaintiff's solicitors could defer writing a letter before action until the necessary information to support the claim was obtained. There was no requirement that a defendant had to be put on notice of a likely claim. Accordingly, the appeal would be dismissed.

Yates v Thakeham Tiles Ltd [1995] PIQR P135 (Court of Appeal: Nourse LJ and Wall J).

1901 Limitation period—expiry—discretion to extend—libel and slander

The Limitation Act 1980, s 4A provides that the limitation period for libel or slander actions is three years from the date the cause of action accrued. Section 32A provides that where a person has not brought an action within that period because all or any of the relevant facts did not become known to him until after the expiration of that period, such an action may be brought by him within one year from the earliest date on which he knew all the facts relevant to that cause of action, but not without the leave of the High Court.

The plaintiff made an ex parte application to the court under the 1980 Act, s 32A for leave to bring an action for slander outside the limitation period. The court refused to grant leave under s 32A and the plaintiff appealed. *Held*, the grant of leave under s 32A was discretionary and there were no limits on the exercise of that discretion. Furthermore, such leave could not be applied for ex parte as RSC Ord 32, r 9(3) made it mandatory for applications to be made by originating summons with notice. The court's inherent jurisdiction to permit an ex parte application only came into effect where there was a procedural gap in the rules, which was not the case here. Accordingly, the appeal would be dismissed.

Oyston v Blaker [1996] 2 All ER 106 (Court of Appeal: Butler-Sloss, Henry and Pill LJJ).

1902 Limitation period—expiry—discretion to extend—onus of proof

The Limitation Act 1980, s 33(3) sets out the criteria to be considered by a court in exercising its discretion to override a time limit in actions in respect of personal injury or death.

A mechanic claimed that his hearing had been seriously damaged by the excessive noise his employers negligently exposed him to and brought an action outside the statutory limitation period. On appeal by the employers against a judgment in favour of the plaintiff in which the judge exercised his discretion to override the limitation period, *held*, the judge had erred in conducting the same exercise in relation to the Limitation Act 1980, s 33 as would have been necessary if he were considering striking out an action for want of prosecution. The essential difference in the two procedures was that in a striking-out application the onus was on the defendant to prove the delay and that he had been prejudiced by it. In an action under s 33 that onus was on the plaintiff, and s 33(3) provided a useful checklist for the court's reference. In this case, the appeal would be allowed since the delay was the fault of the plaintiff, his evidence lacked cogency and hence the prejudice to the defendants outweighed the prejudice to the plaintiff resulting from the application of the limitation period.

Barrand v British Cellophane plc (1995) Times, 16 February (Court of Appeal: Glidewell, Hirst and Hoffmann LJJ). *Buck v English Electric Co Ltd* [1978] 1 All ER 271 (1976 Abr para 1624) disapproved.

1903 Limitation period—expiry—substitution of parties

RSC Ord 15, r 7(2) provides that where at any stage of the proceedings in any cause or matter the interest or liability of any party is assigned or transmitted to or devolves upon some other person, the court may, if it thinks it necessary to ensure that all matters may be effectually and completely determined, order that other person to be made a party to the cause or matter and the proceedings to be carried on as if he had been substituted for the first mentioned party. The Limitation Act 1980, s 35(1) provides that any new claim made in the course of any action is deemed to be a separate action and to have been commenced on the same date as the original action. Under s 35(2), a new claim means any claim involving either (a) the addition or substitution of a new cause of action, or (b) the addition or substitution of a new party.

It has been held that the first limb of the 1980 Act, s 35(2) is confined to claims which involve a new cause of action but which do not involve the addition or substitution of a new party. Claims which involve the addition or substitution of a new party as well as a new cause of action fall within the second limb. However, the second limb does not include claims which involve the addition or substitution of a new party, but which do not involve a new cause of action. It is outside the scope of the 1980 Act to alter the law relating to the kind of substitution where the party substituted succeeds to a claim or liability already represented in the action, which involves no question of limitation, as against a kind where the party substituted has not so succeeded. Accordingly, the substitution of a new party under Ord 15, r 7 does not involve the making of a new claim as defined in s 35(2).

Yorkshire Regional Health Authority v Fairclough Building Ltd [1996] 1 All ER 519 (Court of Appeal: Neill, Evans and Millett LJJ).

1904 Limitation period—time from which period runs—date at which damage suffered—extension of lease

The plaintiff retained the defendant solicitors to act for him in the purchase of the unexpired term of a leasehold interest in a property. Eight years later, he brought proceedings against the defendants alleging that they had failed to advise him that the lease had already been extended under the Leasehold Reform Act 1967 and that no further extension was available. The defendants contended that the action was statute-barred because the limitation period ran from the date when the plaintiff purchased the property. *Held*, the plaintiff suffered damage from the date of his purchase, when he acquired an interest that was worth less to him than it would have been had it not already been extended, although the loss was not quantifiable until the time when he became entitled to acquire the freehold. Accordingly, his claim was statute-barred.

Sullivan v Layton Lougher & Co [1995] 49 EG 127 (Court of Appeal: Leggatt, Aldous and Hutchison LJJ).

1905 Limitation period—time from which period runs—date at which damage suffered—negligent valuation

In reliance on a valuation provided by a firm of valuers, a bank made an offer of advance to borrowers. The borrowers became insolvent, and the security taken for the advance proved to be insufficient to recoup the amount owed. In commencing proceedings against the valuers, the bank claimed that they had been negligent in their valuation and that the advance would not have been made if a proper valuation had been carried out. The valuers claimed that the action was statute barred because the writ was issued 6 years and 10 months after the valuation was given. The bank unsuccessfully argued that because the valuers' breach of duty had not caused it any loss until a later date when the security proved to be insufficient, the cause of action had not accrued until that time. On appeal, *held*, the valuers owed a duty of care to the bank, and had they performed their duty properly the bank would not have made the advance. Even though the advance was the measure of the bank's loss, the loss did not necessarily accrue when the advance was actually made, because the value of the security exceeded the advance at that time. As there were then readily available means of recouping the advance, the bank would have been unable to establish at that stage that it had suffered any loss. The cause of action had accrued when the bank's loss had crystallised, namely when the security was sold, and the mere fact of the advance had therefore not created an actual loss sustained more than six years before the issue of the writ. Accordingly, the appeal would be allowed.

First National Commercial Bank plc v Humberts [1995] 2 All ER 673 (Court of Appeal: Neill, Waite and Saville LJJ). *Swingcastle Ltd v Gibson (a firm)* [1991] 2 All ER 353, HL (1991 Abr para 2573) applied.

1906 Limitation period—time from which period runs—date at which injury arose—unsuccessful sterilisation

The plaintiff became pregnant and gave birth to a child after an unsuccessful sterilisation operation. She brought an action for damages for the cost of bringing up the unwanted child. At first instance, it was held that the action was a claim for 'damages in respect of personal injuries', within the meaning of the Limitation Act 1980, s 11(1). Since the cause of action had accrued more than three years before the proceedings had been commenced, the plaintiff's claim was statute-barred. She appealed. *Held,* whether her claim fell within s 11(1) was a question of substance rather than a matter of pleading. The negligent treatment had caused her to sustain a personal injury at the moment of conception, that personal injury resulting in the unwanted pregnancy and birth of the child. The three-year time limit under s 11(1) ran from the time of conception. As that time was more than three years before the commencement of the proceedings, the plaintiff's claim was statute-barred and, accordingly, her appeal would be dismissed.

Walkin v South Manchester Health Authority [1995] 4 All ER 132 (Court of Appeal: Neill, Roch and Auld LJJ).

1907   Limitation period—time from which period runs—deliberate concealment of facts

The Limitation Act 1980, s 32(1)(b) provides that where any fact relevant to a plaintiff's cause of action has been deliberately concealed from him by the defendant, the period of limitation does not begin to run until the plaintiff has discovered the concealment.

The plaintiffs, who were Lloyd's names, brought an action for breach of contract or duty against the defendant underwriters outside the six-year limitation period set out in the 1980 Act. They claimed their action was still valid under the 1980 Act, s 32(1)(b) because the defendants had deliberately concealed facts relevant to their right of action after the cause of action had arisen, and that if the section did not apply it would cause unfairness as, in most negligence cases featuring concealment, the defendant would discover and conceal his error some time after the breach. The plaintiffs' case was upheld at first instance. On appeal by the defendants it was held that there was nothing in the 1980 Act, s 32(1)(b) to suggest that the draftsman meant the section to apply where the concealing acts were done after the cause of action had arisen. On further appeal, *held,* on its true construction, the 1980 Act, s 32(1)(b) operated to postpone the running of time in every case where there was deliberate concealment by the defendant of facts relevant to the plaintiffs' cause of action, regardless of whether such concealment was contemporaneous with or subsequent to the accrual of the cause of action. In the case of subsequent concealment time did not begin to run until the concealment was or ought to have been discovered. Accordingly, if after the accrual of the cause of action the defendant took steps to conceal relevant facts, the plaintiffs had the full six-year period from the date of the discovery of such concealment to bring his action. Accordingly, the appeal would be allowed and the judge's order that the plaintiffs were entitled to rely on s 32(1)(b) of the Act to overcome the statutory time bar would be restored.

Sheldon v R H M Outhwaite (Underwriting Agencies) Ltd [1995] 2 All ER 558 (House of Lords: Lords Keith of Kinkel, Browne-Wilkinson, Mustill, Lloyd of Berwick and Nicholls of Birkenhead). Decision of Court of Appeal [1994] 4 All ER 481 (1994 Abr para 1825) reversed.

1908   Limitation period—time from which period runs—knowledge of plaintiff

The Limitation Act 1980, s 14(1)(b) provides that a person's date of knowledge refers to the date on which he had knowledge that his injury was attributable in whole or in part to the act or omission alleged to constitute negligence. Section 14(3) provides that a person is not fixed with knoweldge of a fact ascertainable only with expert advice so long as he has taken all reasonable steps to obtain that advice.

The appellant received treatment at an accident and emergency department and a few months later was told that the treatment was ineffective and an operation was required immediately. He continued to suffer pain and was dismissed from his employment after a number of years when his injuries made him unfit to continue. A medical report stated that much of his condition was attributable to the lack of appropriate treatment at the accident and emergency department. He therefore commenced proceedings against the health authority some eleven years after the treatment was given and it was held that the subsequent operation and the fact that he had been told that the inital treatment was ineffective had put him on notice at such an early stage that his claim was now statute-barred. On appeal, *held,* the appellant did not fall within the Limitation Act 1980, s 14(1)(b) as he only recently acquired knowledge of the fact that his injury was attributable to the allegedly negligent act. The fact that he had been told before his operation that the first course of treatment had not worked was not enough to put him on notice since it was not the same as imbuing him with knowledge of the omission to operate. Further, it would not be reasonable to expect a plaintiff to seek a second opinion in order to fulfil s 14(3). Accordingly, the appeal would be allowed.

Smith v West Lancashire Health Authority (1995) 25 BMLR 34 (Court of Appeal: Russell and Wall LJJ).

The Limitation Act 1980, s 14A provides that, in negligence actions where facts relevant to a cause of action are not known at the date of accrual, the limitation period runs from the earliest date on which the plaintiff had knowledge both of the material facts about the damage in respect of which an action in damages is being brought, and of other specified facts relevant to the current action.

A number of Lloyd's names brought actions for negligence against the defendant underwriters in relation to certain run-off policies and reinsurance to close contracts, which had been arranged by the defendants and resulted in the plaintiffs incurring heavy losses. The actions in relation to the policies and contracts in question were begun outside the six-year limitation period and the plaintiffs applied for the limitation period to be extended under the Limitation Act 1980, s 14A as they did not have the requisite knowledge of the facts giving rise to the negligence. The defendants claimed that letters and documents supplied to the plaintiffs three years before issue of the first writ provided sufficient information for the requisite knowledge to be obtained. At first instance the plaintiffs claim was dismissed on the ground that it was statute-barred. On appeal by the plaintiffs, *held*, the act or omission of which a plaintiff had to have knowledge had to be causally relevant for the purposes of an allegation of negligence. He did not have to know that he had a cause of action or that the defendant's acts could be characterised as negligent or as falling short of some standard of professional behaviour, but he had to have knowledge of the essence of the act or omission to which the damage was attributable. In this case, the documents alone were not sufficient to establish that the plaintiffs had the requisite knowledge at the earlier time contended by the defendants and, accordingly, the appeal would be allowed.

Hallam-Eames v Merrett Syndicates Ltd [1995] 1 WLR 243 (Court of Appeal: Sir Thomas Bingham MR, Hoffmann and Saville LJJ).

The plaintiff claimed damages for psychiatric injury allegedly suffered consequent on the witnessing of a disaster almost twenty four years before the commencement of her action. *Held*, the claim was time-barred under the Limitation Act 1980, ss 11, 14 since the plaintiff had knowledge of the facts eleven or twelve years before the commencement of her action. At that time she had sufficient knowledge to justify embarking on legal proceedings. The fact that she did not have full knowledge and only later through therapy realised the full impact of the event was a relevant factor but not one which weighed heavily with the court.

Crocker v British Coal Corpn (1995) Times, 5 July (Queen's Bench Division: Mance J).

1909   Limitation period—time from which period runs—wrongful trading action
See *Re Farmizer (Products) Ltd*, para 543.

LOCAL GOVERNMENT

Halsbury's Laws of England (4th edn) Vol 28, paras 1001–1403

1910   Articles
Advising the Advisers, Gill Murphy and Leslie Rutherford (on the extent to which a prudent local authority should rely on the decision in *Tidman v Reading Borough Council* (1994) Times, 10 November (1994 Abr para 2050)): 139 SJ 112
Blood Sports and Public Law, Alistair Lindsay: 145 NLJ 412
Community Care: Duties Towards Mentally Ill People, David Fish: LA, November 1995, p 20
The Companies Maze, Rob Hann (on the Local Authorities (Companies) Order 1995, SI 1995/849): LS Gaz, 7 June, p 19
Credit Where it is Not Due, Nicholas Dobson (on *Credit Suisse v Allerdale Borough Council* (1994) Times, 17 June (1994 Abr para 1855)): LS Gaz, 3 May 1995, p 20
Fraud in Public Sector Contracting, Stephen Cirell and John Bennett: 139 SJ 238
Local Authority Prosecutions: When Does 'Time' Begin to Run? John Whisson: 159 JP Jo 718
Sex Establishments: If at First You Don't Succeed . . . Christine Clayson: 159 JP Jo 521
Sex Shops, Alec Samuels: 159 JP Jo 91

1911   Competition—financial services—England
The Local Government Act 1988 (Competition) (Financial Services) (England) Regulations 1995, SI 1995/2916 (in force on 5 December 1995), make provision under the Local

Government Act 1988, Pt I regarding the defined activity of financial services. The regulations apply s 6 of the 1988 Act to a specified proportion of that activity from specified dates so that defined authorities are required to compete for such work if they wish to carry it out themselves.

1912 Competition—information technology—England

The Local Government Act 1988 (Competition) (Information Technology) (England) Regulations 1995, SI 1995/2813 (in force on 29 November 1995), make provision under Pt I of the Local Government Act 1988 regarding the defined activity of information technology services. The 1988 Act is applied to a specified proportion of this activity from specified dates so that defined authorities are required to compete for such work if they wish to carry it out themselves.

1913 Competition—works contracts—defined activities

The Local Government Act 1988 (Competition) (Defined Activities) Order 1995, SI 1995/1915 (in force in part on 20 July 1995 and in part on 20 August 1995), amends the Local Government Act 1988, Pt I (competition), so as to (1) add financial services, information technology services and personnel services to the list of existing defined activities which may only be carried out by defined authorities if they have previously been put out to tender in accordance with the provisions of the Act, (2) remove the exemption for work consisting of the cleaning of police buildings, except in so far as such work consists of the cleaning of buildings used for the purposes of regional crime squads, and (3) make supplementary and transitional provision.

The Local Government Act 1988 (Defined Activities) (Competition) (Amendment) (England) Regulations 1995, SI 1995/2546 (in force on 26 October 1995), amend the Local Government Act 1988 (Competition) (Legal Services) (England) Regulations 1994, SI 1994/3164, the Local Government Act 1988 (Competition) (Construction and Property Services) (England) Regulations 1994, SI 1994/3166, and further amend the Local Government Act 1988 (Defined Activities) (Competition) (Supervision of Parking, Management of Vehicles and Security Work) (England) Regulations 1994, SI 1994/3165, which applied the compulsory competitive tendering requirements of Pt I of the Local Government Act 1988 respectively to legal services, to construction and property services and to the supervision of parking, management of vehicles and security work. These regulations apply, from 1 October 1997, the requirements in (1) SI 1994/3164 (legal services) and SI 1994/3166 (construction) to county councils and non-metropolitan district councils which are not subject to a structural change pursuant to local government reorganisation, and (2) SI 1994/3165 (supervision of parking, etc) to county councils which are not subject to a structural change pursuant to local government reorganisation.

The Local Government Act 1988 (Defined Activities) (Competition) (Supervision of Parking) (Amendment) (England) Regulations 1995, SI 1995/3108 (in force on 31 December 1995), amend the Local Government Act 1988 (Defined Activities) (Competition) (Supervision of Parking, Management of Vehicles and Security Work) (England) Regulations 1994, SI 1994/3165, so as to alter the date from which the compulsory competitive tendering requirements of the Local Government Act 1988 in respect of the supervision of parking apply to county councils and non-metropolitan district councils which are not subject to a structural change pursuant to local government reorganisation. The Local Government Act 1988 (Defined Activities) (Competition) (Amendment) (England) Regulations 1995, SI 1995/2546, are consequently amended.

1914 Competition—works contracts—defined activities—exemption—fire services

The Local Government Act 1988 (Defined Activities) (Exemption) (Fire Services) (England and Wales) Order 1995, SI 1995/2901 (in force on 11 December 1995), relates to the Local Government Act 1988, Pt I, which provides that work falling within certain defined activities may be carried out by local authorities and certain other authorities only if particular conditions are fulfilled. This order exempts from the requirements of Pt I the provision of certain information technology services for the purposes of a fire authority.

1915 Competition—works contracts—defined activities—exemption—housing management

The Local Government Act 1988 (Defined Activities) (Exemption) (Housing Management) (England) Order 1995, SI 1995/1182 (in force on 26 May 1995), relates to the Local

Government Act 1988, Pt I, which provides that work falling within certain defined activities may be carried out by local authorities only if particular conditions are fulfilled. The order exempts from the requirements of Pt I housing management carried out by a relevant authority (defined in art 1(2)), so long as (1) it is carried out in relation to houses in respect of which such an authority has delegated some or all of its housing management functions to a relevant organisation (also defined in art 1(2)), (2) it is carried out by staff employed by the relevant authority who are under the direction of the committee or board of directors of the relevant organisation, and (3) it is carried out before 1 April 2001 (or in the case of some relevant authorities, before 1 April 2002). In addition, for the purposes of the Local Government Act 1988 (Defined Activities) (Exemption) (England) Order 1988, SI 1988/1372, the cost to a relevant authority of carrying out housing management includes the cost of any work which is exempted from the requirements of Pt I of the 1988 Act by the 1995 Order.

1916 Competition—works contracts—defined activities—exemption—police authorities

The Local Government Act 1988 (Defined Activities) (Exemptions) (Police Authorities) Order 1995, SI 1995/3303 (in force on 26 January 1996), exempts certain activities from those subject to competitive tendering requirements under the Local Government Act 1988, Pt I. The activities exempted include certain legal work carried out by police authorities, the work of those authorities' architectural liaison officers and certain works contracts for legal and construction and property services carried out on behalf of police authorities before specified dates.

1917 Competition—works contracts—defined activities—exemption—police buildings

The Local Government Act 1988 (Defined Activities) (Cleaning of Police Buildings) (Exemption) (England and Wales) Order 1995, SI 1995/2449 (in force on 1 October 1995), relates to the Local Government Act 1988, Pt I, which provides that work falling within certain defined activities may be carried out by local authorities only if particular conditions are fulfilled. The order exempts from the requirements of Pt I the cleaning of buildings carried out by a police authority, where the authority have estimated that the cost of carrying out this activity during the preceding financial year through their direct labour or similar organisation does not exceed £125,000.

1918 Competition—works contracts—defined activities—exemption—sports and leisure management

The Local Government Act 1988 (Defined Activities) (Exemption) (Sports and Leisure Management, Catering and Maintenance of Ground) Order 1995, SI 1995/828 (in force on 17 April 1995), relates to the Local Government Act 1988, Pt I, which provides that work falling within certain defined activities may be carried out by local authorities only if particular conditions are fulfilled. This order exempts from the requirements of Part I the management of sports and leisure facilities, catering and the maintenance of ground so long as in each case it is undertaken by specified authorities and before specified dates.

1919 Competition—works contracts—defined activities—exemption—Wales

The Local Government Act 1988 (Defined Activities, Exemptions) (Wales) (Amendment) Order 1995, SI 1995/2996 (in force on 1 January 1996), amends the 1994 Order, SI 1994/339, which provides an exemption during the period of local government reorganisation in Wales for Welsh local authorities (other than community councils) and Welsh combined fire authorities from the competition requirements of the Local Government Act 1988, Pt I, so as to extend the period of exemption until 30 September 1997.

1920 Competition—works contracts—defined activities—scope

The Local Government Act 1988 (Defined Activities) (Cleaning of Police Buildings) (England and Wales) Regulations 1995, SI 1995/1973 (in force on 17 August 1995), apply the competitive tendering requirements of the Local Government Act 1988, Pt I (competition) to specified proportions of the cleaning of police buildings as from 1 October 1996. They consequently disapply the Local Government Act 1988 (Defined Activities) (Competition) (England) Regulations 1988, SI 1988/1371, and the Local Government Act 1988 (Defined Activities) (Competition) (Wales) Regulations 1988, SI 1988/1468, in relation to the specified work. The regulations also specify the minimum and maximum periods for which police authorities may resolve to undertake building cleaning work, prior to putting the work out to competitive tender.

1921 Competition—works contracts—defined activities—specified periods

The Local Government Act 1988 (Defined Activities) (Specified Periods) (England) Regulations 1995, SI 1995/2484 (in force on 19 October 1995), which disapply the 1988 Regulations, SI 1988/1373, the Local Government Act 1988 (Defined Activities) (Competition) (England) Regulations 1990, SI 1990/1564, and the Local Government Act 1988 (Defined Activities) (Specified Periods) (Inner London) Regulations 1990, SI 1990/2468, in respect of work to which these regulations apply, specify the new minimum and maximum periods for which authorities may invite offers to carry out work in respect of some of those activities which must be open to competition under the Local Government Act 1988, Pt I. The regulations make different provision in respect of work all or the majority of which is undertaken at or connected with educational establishments, and work which is not undertaken at those establishments or does not substantially involve such work.

1922 Competition—works contracts—defined activities—supervision of parking

The Local Government Act 1988 (Defined Activities) (Competition) (Supervision of Parking) (Amendment) (England) Regulations 1995, SI 1995/3108 (in force on 31 December 1995), further amend the 1994 Regulations, SI 1994/3165, so as to alter the date the date from which the compulsory competitive tendering requirements of the Local Government Act 1988 in respect of the supervision of parking apply to county councils and non-metropolitan district councils which are not subject to a structural change pursuant to local government reorganisation. In relation to county councils, the regulations substitute the date of 1 April 1997 for 1 October 1997, and, in relation to non-metropolitan district councils, the regulations substitute the date of 1 April 1997 for 1 January 1996.

1923 Competition—works contracts—direct labour organisations

The Local Government (Direct Labour Organisations) (Competition) (Amendment) (Crown Courts) Regulations 1995, SI 1995/1377 (in force on 26 June 1995), further amend the 1989 Regulations, SI 1989/1588, and provide for work undertaken for the purposes of a Crown Court to be exempt from the Local Government, Planning and Land Act 1980, Pt III which requires local authorities, before undertaking construction or maintenance work through their direct labour organisations, to have satisfied certain requirements as respects competitive tendering.

1924 Competition—works contracts—direct service organisations

The Local Government (Direct Service Organisations) (Competition) (Amendment) Regulations 1995, SI 1995/1336 (in force on 14 June 1995), amend the 1993 Regulations, SI 1993/848, so as to make provision in respect of the conduct of competitive tendering for the carrying out of certain works by local authorities and certain other authorities. The regulations (1) provide that the periods for response to notices and invitations to tender apply only in respect of tendering in pursuance of the Local Government Act 1988; (2) provide that for periods elapsing before commencement of work, the requirement for an interval between a decision and work being undertaken in respect of work consisting of certain defined activities, is removed; (3) provide that the provisions relating to preparation of bids apply in respect of conduct by elected members and in relation to police authorities; (4) make special provision for housing management work in relation to the time by which an authority must have announced the results of tendering; (5) amend the formula by reference to which allowable costs are calculated in evaluating tenders; (6) add certain indemnities to the costs which, if taken into account in evaluating tenders, are not to give rise to action in respect of anti-competitive behaviour; and (7) make minor amendments to the method of calculating the present value of savings.

1925 Competition—works contracts—legal services and construction and property services—police authorities

The Local Government Act 1988 (Competition) (Legal and Construction etc Services) (Police Authorities) Regulations 1995, SI 1995/3302 (in force on 26 January 1996), apply the competitive tendering requirements in the Local Government Act 1988, Pt I to the defined activities of legal services and construction and property services. The regulations apply the 1988 Act, s 6 to a specified proportion of each activity of a police authority from specified dates so that such authorities must compete for such work if they wish to carry it out themselves.

1926 Competition—works contracts—local government reorganisation

The Local Government Changes for England and Local Government Act 1988 (Competition) (Miscellaneous Amendment) Regulations 1995, SI 1995/1326 (in force on 12 June 1995), amend SI 1994/3167 so as to (1) enlarge the description of authorities affected by the competition requirements of the Local Government Act 1988 to include any authority subject to a structural or boundary change resulting from the implementation of a recommendation of the Local Government Commission made in pursuance of a direction given before 17 May 1995; and (2) provide for exemption, for a period calculated by reference to SI 1994/3167, from the competition requirements of the 1988 Act in respect of functional housing management work carried out by a local authority affected by the implementation of such recommendations. Consequential amendments are also made to SI 1994/3165.

1927 Competition—works contracts—part acceptance of tender

Scotland
A council exposed 60 per cent of its ground maintenance work to compulsory competitive tendering. It received two tenders, one from a private contractor and the other from its own direct services organisation. Overall, the private contractor's bid was the lowest. However, the bill of quantities in the tender documents set out 13 separate items, and the council claimed the right to accept a tender in whole or in part. The private contractor's bid for item 1 was the lowest, and its tender for that item was accepted by the council. For items 2 to 13 the council's own organisation's tender was accepted, its bid being lower. The council refused to allow the private contractor to adjust the price for item 1. The private contractor then stated that it did not consider there to be a binding contract, and the bid of the council's own organisation was immediately accepted in respect of item 1 as well. The Secretary of State decided that, by refusing to allow the private contractor to adjust its tender in respect of item 1, the council had acted in a manner having the effect or intended or likely to have the effect of restricting, distorting or preventing competition contrary to the Local Government Act 1988, s 7. He gave a direction to the effect that the council would only have the power to carry out the ground maintenance works if they were put out to tender anew. The council applied for judicial review of that decision. *Held*, the terms of the tender documents entitled the council to accept a tender in respect of some items, but not others. Consequently, there was a binding contract between the council and the private contractor in respect of item 1. It was immaterial that the private contractor had misunderstood the effect of the tender documents. The Secretary of State had therefore misdirected himself in law by basing his decision upon the premise that there was no such binding contract between the parties. Furthermore, there was no justification for the view that the council had acted in breach of s 7. Accordingly, an order would be made to set aside the direction of the Secretary of State.

Ettrick and Lauderdale District Council v Secretary of State for Scotland 1995 SLT 996 (Outer House).

1928 Competition—works contracts—personnel services—England

The Local Government Act 1988 (Competition) (Personnel Services) (England) Regulations 1995, SI 1995/2101 (in force on 7 September 1995), apply the Local Government Act 1988, s 6 to a specified proportion of personnel services so that from specified dates, the following authorities are required to compete for such work if they wish to carry it out themselves (1) a local authority which is subject to, or created by, a structural change or substantial boundary change effected by an order made under the Local Government Act 1992, s 17 ('a structural change') where that structural change takes effect from 1 April 1995, 1 April 1996, or 1 April 1997, (2) county councils or non-metropolitan district councils which are not subject to a structural change, and (3) any other defined authority except those mentioned in ss 1(1)(b), (c), (d), (f) and (g) of the 1992 Act and a police authority. SI 1995/2100 makes similar provisions for certain other defined authorities.

1929   Competition—works contracts—personnel services—fire and civil defence authorities

The Local Government Act 1988 (Competition) (Personnel Services) (Fire and Civil Defence Authorities) (England) Regulations 1995, SI 1995/2100 (in force on 7 September 1995), apply the Local Government Act 1988, s 6 to a specified proportion of personnel services so that from 1 October 1996, a fire authority constituted by a combination scheme, a metropolitan county fire and civil defence authority or the London Fire and Civil Defence authority are required to compete for such work if they wish to carry it out themselves. SI 1995/2102 makes similar provision for certain other defined authorities.

1930   Competition—works contracts—security work—exemption

The Local Government Act 1988 (Security Work) (Exemption) (England) Order 1995, SI 1995/2074 (in force on 29 August 1995), exempts from the requirements of the Local Government Act 1988, Pt I (1) security work carried out by a defined authority through an employee whose work may involve the exercise of a power to take action to deal with a breach of certain enactments in a controlled place (as defined in the order), where that power cannot be exercised by anyone other than an employee of the defined authority or a constable, and the greater part of whose work is carried out in relation to a controlled place, (2) security work by a defined authority in England so long as it is carried out in relation to a court-house, (3) security work by the Common Council of the City of London so long as it is carried out at the premises in the City of London known as the Guildhall, and those premises remain vested in the Common Council, in any capacity, and (4) security work by the Greenwich London Borough Council so long as it is carried out in relation to the Woolwich Ferry and the operation of the Ferry is carried out in accordance with the terms of the agreement of 27 March 1986 made between the Secretary of State for Transport and that council.

1931   Competition—works contracts—sports and leisure management, cleaning of buildings and repair and maintenance of vehicles—exemption

The Local Government Act 1988 (Sports and Leisure Management, Cleaning of Buildings and Repair and Maintenance of Vehicles) (Exemption) Order 1995, SI 1995/2794 (in force on 23 November 1995), relates to the Local Government Act 1988, Pt I, which provides that work falling within certain defined activities may be carried out by local authorities only if particular conditions are fulfilled. The order exempts from the requirements of Pt I (1) the management of sports and leisure facilities by the Peterborough City Council so long as it is undertaken at the Lido, Peterborough, before 1 April 1997, (2) the management of sports and leisure facilities by the Croydon London Borough Council so long as it is undertaken at the Water Palace, Croydon, before 1 September 1996, (3) the management of sports and leisure facilities by the Tower Hamlets London Borough Council so long as it is undertaken at York Hall, during the period beginning on 1 January 1996 and ending with 31 December 1996, and at the Mile End Stadium and the Langdon Park Sports and Community Centre, during the period beginning on 1 April 1996 and ending with 31 December 1996, (4) the cleaning of buildings by the Harrow London Borough Council before 1 July 1996, so long as it is undertaken at certain specified schools and other sites before 1 April 1996, (5) the repair and maintenance of vehicles by the Sutton London Borough council before 1 July 1996, so long as it is undertaken in respect of any vehicle used by the Council in connection with any of their functions, and (6) the repair and maintenance of vehicles by the joint committee of the councils of the boroughs of Bradford, Calderdale, Kirklees, Leeds and Wakefield, so long as it is undertaken in respect of any vehicle used by the committee in connection with any of their functions.

1932   Councillors—failure to pay community charge—restrictions at council meetings

See *DPP v Burton*, para 2431.

1933   Employees—compensation for loss of remuneration

The Local Government Reorganisation (Compensation for Loss of Remuneration) Regulations 1995, SI 1995/2837 (in force on 28 November 1995), provide for the payment of compensation to persons who suffer a loss or reduction of remuneration as a consequence of any provision of an order made under the Local Government Act 1992, s 17 (implementation of local government changes for England), or by or under any provision of the Local Government (Wales) Act 1994. The regulations (1) provide that the persons to whom the regulations apply are local government employees whose remuneration in relevant employment is reduced as a result of any boundary or structural change made by or under the 1992 Act or the 1994 Act, (2) provide that a person who is entitled to local government redundancy compensation or the immediate payment of benefits under the Local Government Pension Scheme is not entitled to compensation under these regulations, (3) provide for the calculation by a relevant employer of the amount of compensation payable to an eligible person, (4) make administrative provision relating to the notification by a relevant employer of decisions about the amount of compensation payable to an eligible person, and the payment of compensation by way of instalments during the relevant compensation period, and (5) specify the circumstances in which compensation ceases to be payable.

1934 Employees—compensation for redundancy and premature retirement

The Local Government (Compensation for Redundancy and Premature Retirement) (Amendment) Regulations 1995, SI 1995/817 (in force on 14 April 1995), further amend the 1982 Regulations, SI 1982/1009, so as to (1) substitute new categories of employment for further and higher education institutions in the 1982 Regulations, Sch 1, Pt II, which changes are consequent upon the Further and Higher Education Act 1992; (2) make consequential amendments to a provision dealing with the paying authority for educational establishments; (3) substitute a reference to 1992 Act, s 85 in place of a repealed Chapter of the Education Reform Act 1988. The regulations have effect from April 1993. However, no individual, who is qualified to participate in the benefits for which the 1982 Regulations provide, is to be placed in a worse position than he would have been in if the regulations had effect only from the date of their making.

1935 Employees—remuneration—assistants for political groups

The Local Government (Assistants for Political Groups) (Remuneration) Order 1995, SI 1995/2456 (in force on 19 October 1995), which replaces the 1991 Order, SI 1991/2150, increases from £13,500 to £25,044 the amount specified for the purposes of the Local Government and Housing Act 1989, s 9 as the highest amount of annual remuneration for persons holding appointments as assistants for political groups.

1936 Employees—Wales—limitation of compensation

The Local Government Reorganisation (Wales) (Limitation of Compensation) Regulations 1995, SI 1995/1039 (in force on 4 May 1995), exclude the application of the Local Government (Wales) Act 1994, s 45 (which provides for entitlement to compensation for certain employees of existing county or district councils with contracts made before 1 December 1993 which would have continued but for the abolition of their employers and which are not transferred to a new employer) in certain cases where such employees have been able to obtain a new contract by agreement.

1937 Finance—capital finance—approved investments

The Local Authorities (Capital Finance and Approved Investments) (Amendment) Regulations 1995, SI 1995/850 (in force on 1 April 1995), further amend the Local Authorities (Capital Finance) Regulations 1990, SI 1990/432, so as to (1) provide that expenditure on the acquisition or preparation of a computer program is expenditure for capital purposes if the program is acquired or prepared for use for a period of at least one year, (2) make provision in respect of the initial cost of leases of land acquired by a local authority, (3) allow an authority to reduce the initial cost of a lease where its interest in another lease for which it provided credit cover has ceased before the end of its term, (4) provide that where a lease of land falling within reg 7(3) of these regulations is varied by the grant of a new lease of the same land, the adjusted cost of the credit arrangement for the purposes of the Local Government and Housing Act 1989, s 50(4)(b), is nil, provided that the new lease would, if granted when the original lease expired, fall within reg 7(5F) of these regulations, (5) provide that the reserved part of a local authority's capital receipts is (a) 25 per cent in specified cases where a receipt is received within a specified period in respect of a disposal of share capital or loan capital in a bus company or an airport company, or (b) 50 per cent in the case of the receipt derived from a disposal by a local authority of share or loan capital which (i) was acquired before 10 March 1988, or for the purposes of providing financial assistance under s 33 of the 1989 Act, and was issued by a company not concerned with the provision of housing or housing services, (ii) is in a company formed by, or with the participation of, the authority for any of the purposes referred to in the Local Government Act 1972, s 145(1), or (iii) is in a waste disposal company formed by, or with the participation of, the authority, (6) provide that where a local authority acquires shares in a company in consideration for the disposal of an asset, the reserved part of the notional capital receipt is nil if the asset was not acquired for housing purposes and if expenditure on acquiring the asset would be expenditure for capital purposes, (7) make provision in relation to credit ceilings, minimum revenue provision, and use of amounts set aside to meet credit liabilities, to take account of the new police authorities established under the Police Act 1964, s 3, and (8) provide that in determining a local authority's credit ceiling no account is to be taken of amounts set aside as credit cover under the Local Authorities (Companies) Order 1995, SI 1995/849. The regulations also further amend the Schedule to the Local Authorities (Capital Finance) (Approved Investments) Regulations 1990, SI 1990/426, in order to take account of new police authorities.

The Local Authorities (Capital Finance and Approved Investments) (Amendment No 2) Regulations 1995, SI 1995/1982 (in force on 24 August 1995), further amend the 1990 Regulations, SI 1990/432, so as to (1) make provision as to the consequences of a default in the payment of principal or interest under certain approved investments, (2) provide that if specified conditions are met, expenditure on making an investment in substitution for a relevant approved investment, and expenditure which consists of the application for specified purposes, or the transfer, of amounts set aside as provision for credit liabilities, is not expenditure for capital purposes and does not have to be charged to a revenue account, (3) provide that where a lease of land is varied by the grant of a new lease of the same land, the adjusted cost of the credit arrangement is nil, provided that the new lease would, if granted when the original lease expired, meet certain conditions specified in the 1990 Regulations, (4) provide that, if specified conditions are met, the sums received in respect of the disposal of an investment which, at the time of disposal, is not an approved investment are not capital receipts, (5) provide that if specified conditions are met (a) the reserved part of a local authority's capital receipts is 10 per cent where a receipt is received within a specified period in respect of a disposal of land which is used as a car park, or comprises a crematorium or, in whole or in part, comprises shops, and (b) a local authority is not required to set aside part of its capital receipts as provision to meet credit liabilities notwithstanding that they still have certain outstanding debt, (6) provide that an authority may have the use of amounts set aside as provision to meet credit liabilities notwithstanding that they still have outstanding debt, (7) take account of the new police authorities established under the Police Act 1964, s 3 (as substituted by the Police and Magistrates' Courts Act 1994, s 2), (8) provide that the credit ceiling of a local authority is to be increased where the authority applies the amount set aside as provision to meet credit liabilities to meet any levy payable under the Leasehold Reform, Housing and Urban Development Act 1993, s 136, (9) modify the way an authority which is required to keep a housing revenue account calculates the housing and non-housing amounts for the purposes of minimum revenue provision, and (10) provide that an authority may meet the conditions for their longer-term investments to be approved investments notwithstanding that they still have certain outstanding debt.

1938 Finance—capital finance—controls

The Local Authorities (Capital Finance) (Amendment) Regulations 1995, SI 1995/1526 (in force on 10 July 1995), further amend the 1990 Regulations, SI 1990/432, so as to (1) make provision for a further reduction which a local authority may make in their capital receipts before setting aside the reserved part as provision for credit liabilities; (2) reduce the capital receipt derived from the disposal of a dwelling where, among other conditions, (a) the consideration for the disposal includes the assignment or surrender of the lease of a flat granted under the Housing Act 1985, Pt V (the right to buy) or under ss 32, 43 of that Act with the benefit of a discount of 44 per cent or more of the value of the lease, and (b) there is attributed, as part of the consideration for the acquisition of the dwelling by the former tenant, an amount equal to the price paid on the grant of the lease which is assigned or surrendered; and (3) make consequential amendments.

1939 Finance—capital finance—credit arrangements

The Local Authorities (Capital Finance) (Rate of Discount for 1995/96) Regulations 1995, SI 1995/535 (in force on 1 April 1995), prescribe 9.1 per cent for the financial year beginning on 1 April 1995 for the purposes of the Local Government and Housing Act 1989, Pt IV, which makes provision for the capital finance of local authorities.

1940 Finance—capital finance—local government changes

The Local Government Changes for England (Capital Finance) Regulations 1995, SI 1995/798 (in force in part on 31 March 1995 and in part on 1 April 1995), make provision of general application for the purposes of and in consequence of orders giving effect to recommendations made by the Local Government Commission for England which relate to revenue accounts and capital finance of local authorities under the Local Government and Housing Act 1989.

1941 Finance—capital finance—transactions—bodies under local authority control

The Passenger Transport Executives (Capital Finance) (Amendment) Order 1995, SI 1995/1431 (in force on 30 June 1995), further amends the 1990 Order, SI 1990/720, so that (1) sums paid by the British Railways Board or Railtrack plc to a passenger transport executive, pursuant to deeds of assumption made by the board or Railtrack plc, relating to payments in respect of capital grants provided by an executive, are not treated as capital receipts; and (2) sums paid by the British Railways Board or Railtrack plc to a passenger transport executive pursuant to deeds of assumption are not subject to the provisions of the 1990 Order, art 5.

1942 Finance—capital finance—Wales—transitional provision

The Local Government Reorganisation (Wales) (Capital Finance) Order 1995, SI 1995/1041 (in force on 4 May 1995), makes provision with respect to the application of the Local Government and Housing Act 1989, Pt IV (revenue accounts and capital finance of local authorities) to new Welsh local authorities elected on 4 May 1995, for the transitional period from 4 May 1995 to 31 March 1996. The order (1) disapplies s 44(6) of the 1989 Act to borrowing by existing authorities if s 51 of the 1994 Act, which requires the consent of the new authorities to certain contracts, is contravened, (2) modifies, for the transitional period, the scope of new authorities' borrowing powers and the requirements for them to make minimum revenue provision, (3) disapplies, for new authorities in the transitional period, the provisions of the Local Authorities (Capital Finance) (Approved Investments) Regulations 1990, SI 1990/432, relating to minimum revenue provision, and (4) amends the Local Authorities (Capital Finance) Regulations 1990, SI 1990/426, to ensure that all the new authorities are included in the list of bodies with whom approved investments can be made.

1943 Finance—collection fund—surpluses and deficits

The Local Government Changes for England (Collection Fund Surpluses and Deficits) Regulations 1995, SI 1995/2889 (in force on 30 November 1995), make consequential and transitional provisions for the application of the Local Authorities (Funds) (England) Regulations 1992, SI 1992/2428, in relation to authorities subject to a reorganisation order by the Secretary of State, other than those to which the Local Government Changes for England (Collection Fund Surpluses and Deficits) Regulations 1994, SI 1994/3115, apply. The regulations make provision in connection with the apportionment of the estimated surplus or deficit in the collection fund of a billing authority which is an abolished or relinquishing authority (as defined in these regulations) among its successors and the apportionment of a precepting authority's share of the estimated balance and final balance among its successors. The regulations provide for payments to be made in respect of an authority's share in the estimated balance and the amount of the difference between this and its share in the final balance, and for the billing authority to make transfers between its collection and general funds in respect of its share in the estimated balance and the amount of the difference between this and its share in the final balance. The regulations modify the Local Government Finance Act 1992, ss 33, 43, 44 so that the payments and transfers required by these regulations in relation to estimated and final balances fall to be treated by a billing or major precepting authority within their calculations of their budget requirement and council tax in the same way as transfers required under the Local Government Finance Act 1988, s 97(3) and (4) and payments required under SI 1992/2428. Provision is made for certain payments between a designated authority in relation to an abolished billing authority and other successor authorities and between a relinquishing authority and its acquiring authorities in respect of balances in the collection fund in connection with certain community charge items.

1944 Finance—discharge of precepts by billing authorities

The Local Authorities (Precepts) (Wales) Regulations 1995, SI 1995/2562 (in force on 31 October 1995), which apply to Wales only, make provision for the discharge by a billing authority of its liabilities to pay amounts of precepts from its council fund. The regulations (1) make provision for a billing authority to make certain payments in accordance with a schedule of instalments and otherwise, and for the circumstances in which certain liabilities of the authority are to be treated as discharged, (2) make provision for a billing authority to determine a schedule of instalments in accordance with the prescribed rules, (3) make provision as to the payment of interest where amounts payable in accordance with a schedule of instalments is not paid, and (4) provide that the Local Authority (Funds) (Wales) Regulations 1992, SI 1992/2929, cease to have effect in relation to any financial year beginning on or after 1996.

1945 Finance—discretionary expenditure—annual limits

The Local Authorities (Discretionary Expenditure Limits) (England) Order 1995, SI 1995/651 (in force on 1 April 1995), specifies a sum appropriate for county and district councils under the Local Government Act 1972, s 137(4), which provides that the annual limit on the amount of expenditure which a local authority may incur for unauthorised purposes is to be determined by multiplying the relevant population of the authority's area by the sum appropriate to the authority.

1946 Finance—funds—payment of precepts

The Local Authorities (Funds) (England) (Amendment) Regulations 1995, SI 1995/2910 (in force on 4 December 1995), which extend to England only, amend the 1992 Regulations, SI 1992/2428, so as to require the schedule of instalments relating to amounts payable by billing authorities in respect of precepts to be determined so as to require the first instalment to be paid or transferred to principal authorities within a shorter period than 5 weeks of the start of the financial year. The period is a number of days reducing from 32 to 21 between the financial years beginning in 1996 and 1999. The final instalment, for financial years beginning in and after 1996, is to be paid or transferred by no later than 14 days prior to the end of the financial year.

1947 Finance—local government changes—amendment

The Local Government Changes for England (Finance) (Amendment) Regulations 1995, SI 1995/2862 (in force on 28 November 1995), amend the 1994 Regulations, SI 1994/2825, so as to provide (1) that the valuation list supplied under reg 46(4) of the 1994 Regulations is an authority's valuation list for the purposes of the Local Government Finance Act 1992, Pt I, Ch II, (2) for references to a designated authority to be substituted by references to a successor authority, and (3) that the rights and duties of the abolished authority pass to the designated authority in respect of payments under specified provisions of the Housing Act 1985 and the Local Government and Housing Act 1989 in respect of improvement for sale schemes, defective dwellings, Housing Revenue Account subsidy, slum clearance subsidy and financial assistance towards services for owners and occupiers of houses.

1948 Finance—local government changes—transitional and consequential provision

See para 2442.

1949 Finance—payments to designated authorities

The Local Government Changes for England (Payments to Designated Authorities) (Minimum Revenue Provision) Regulations 1995, SI 1995/2895 (in force on 1 December 1995), make provision in respect of local authorities affected by a reorganisation under the Local Government Act 1992, Pt II who are designated authorities for the purposes of the Local Government Changes for England (Property Transfer and Transitional Payments) Regulations 1995, SI 1995/402, Pt III. The regulations (1) provide definitions of 'designated authority', 'successor authorities', 'abolished authority', 'the relinquishing authority in relation to a transferred area', 'the acquiring authority', 'participant authorities', and 'the reorganisation date', (2) require an abolished authority to provide estimates of borrowings and other specified amounts to the designated authority, (3) provide for the circumstances in which participant authorities are liable to make payments to designated authorities, for the discharge of that liability, and that agreements may be made between the authorities as to the calculation of components making up the payments and the making of payments, (4) make provision in respect of the default of such agreements as referred to in (3) above, (5) provide for the times at which the components are to be calculated, (6) regulate the making of the payments, (7) make provision for the payment of interest on late payments, (8) enable a participant authority, after giving notice to the designated authority, to make voluntary additional payments to discharge its liability at any time, (9) modify the Local Authorities (Capital Finance) Regulations 1990, SI 1990/432, so as to enable participant authorities to make voluntary additional payments otherwise than from a revenue account and require the designated authority to treat such payments as capital receipts of which 100 per cent must be set aside as provision to meet credit liabilities, (10) require the designated authority to supply information, on request, to participant authorities, and (11) provide for arbitration in case of dispute about any calculation or determination by the designated authority.

1950   Local authority—closure of accounts—Wales

The Local Authorities (Closure of Accounts) (Wales) Order 1995, SI 1995/1043 (in force on 4 April 1995), designates certain new councils established by the Local Government (Wales) Act 1994 who will be responsible for the closure of accounts of specified existing authorities abolished on 1 April 1996.

1951   Local authority—disposal of dwelling houses—payment of levy

The Local Authorities (Payment of Levy on Disposals) Regulations 1995, SI 1995/1981 (in force on 24 August 1995), provide that the amounts which may be applied under the Leasehold Reform, Housing and Urban Development Act 1993, s 136, whereby a local authority is required to pay a levy in respect of a disposal of dwelling-houses which is a qualifying disposal for the purposes of s 136 and may apply amounts set aside as provision to meet credit liabilities to meet any liability for such levy (other than liability for interest), must not exceed a specified percentage of the levy concerned.

1952   Local authority—expenditure powers

The Local Authorities (Expenditure Powers) Order 1995, SI 1995/3304 (in force on 26 January 1996), specifies, for the purposes of the Local Government Act 1972, s 137(4B), a description of expenditure by a parish or community council which is not to be included by them when determining whether they have exceeded the limit on expenditure set out in s 137(4). The expenditure in question is that which is defrayed by a payment made to the parish or community council by a county, county borough or district council under their powers under s 137 made in respect of expenditure which would otherwise form part of the parish or community council's gross expenditure under s 137.

1953   Local authority—goods and services

The Local Authorities (Goods and Services) (Public Bodies) (Meat Hygiene) Order 1995, SI 1995/2626 (in force on 8 November 1995) designates the Minister of Agriculture, Fisheries and Food in relation to England, and the Secretary of State in relation to Wales as public bodies for the purposes of the Local Authorities (Goods and Services) Act 1970. The order allows local authorities to provide goods and services connected with the exercise of the ministers' functions in relation to the inspection of meat or animals.

1954   Local authority—members—allowances

The Local Authorities (Members' Allowances) (Amendment) Regulations 1995, SI 1995/553 (in force on 1 April 1995), further amend the 1991 Regulations, SI 1991/351, as follows: (1) authorities are empowered, rather than required, to make schemes which provide for the payment of special responsibility allowances to elected members; (2) financial restrictions are removed on the amounts which may be payable under allowance schemes; (3) provision is made for the publication of allowance schemes within an authority's area; (4) provision is made for circumstances (in addition to attendance at certain meetings) in which an attendance allowance may be payable to elected members; (5) the maxima which may be payable to parish and community councillors and to non-elected members of local authorities by way of allowances under the Local Government Act 1972, ss 173(1), 175, is increased by 2.8 per cent; (6) the maximum payable by way of allowances under s 173(4) is increased by 3.9 per cent.

1955   Local authority—powers—ban on deer hunting—ethical and moral objections

A council had banned deer hunting on common land belonging to the council because of opposition on ethical grounds. The land had been acquired under the Local Government Act 1972, s 120(1)(b) which states that a council may acquire land for the benefit, improvement, or development of their area. Members of the hunt brought an action for judicial review of the council's decision, and the question arose as to whether the subjective opinion of the majority of councillors that deer hunting was morally repulsive was a consideration which the council was entitled to regard as relevant at law. At first instance it was held that the council was not able to use moral considerations in deciding to impose the ban. On appeal by the council, *held*, the councillors in this case had not had their attention brought to the 1972 Act, s 120(1)(b) and had been wrongly invited to give full rein to their personal views without considering the advantages and benefits to the land of banning deer hunting. They had equated their position with that of a private landowner without appreciating the overriding statutory constraint. Accordingly, the council was not entitled to make the decision it did on the grounds it relied on and its appeal would be dismissed.

R v Somerset County Council, ex p Fewings [1995] 3 All ER 20 (Court of Appeal: Sir Thomas Bingham MR, Simon Brown and Swinton Thomas LJJ). Decision of Laws J [1995] 1 All ER 513 (1994 Abr para 1859) affirmed.

1956   Local authority—powers—housing benefit—payment of interest on withheld benefit

The Local Government Act 1972, s 111(1) provides that a local authority has power to do anything which is calculated to facilitate, or is conducive or incidental to, the discharge of any of its functions. The Social Security Administration Act 1992, s 5 and regulations made thereunder make detailed provision for the payment of social security benefits, including housing benefit.

A tenant, who was receiving housing benefit, was in dispute with his landlord. The local authority lawfully withheld his benefit pending the outcome of legal proceedings. The tenant requested the council to place the money due to him into an interest bearing account as he was concerned that if the court ruled in the landlord's favour it might also award interest on the back rent due. The local authority refused and the tenant sought judicial review of the decision. On the question of whether a local authority had the power under the 1972 Act, s 111(1) and the 1992 Act, s 5 to pay interest on benefits, *held*, the provisions under the 1992 Act, s 5 relating to the payment of housing benefit were very detailed yet made no reference to the payment of interest on retained benefit. The legislature could not have intended to specify every aspect of the administration of the scheme, and consequently the local authority had an implied power to make administrative arrangements incidental to or consequential on its powers and duties relating to housing benefit. However, the special status of the authority's power to make payments and the financial consequences of placing the money in an interest bearing account meant that the payment of interest on retained benefit was not impliedly authorised by the 1992 Act. Likewise the 1972 Act, s 111(1) did not apply unless the power being claimed under it facilitated or was conducive or incidental to the function which was supposed to be performed. In the present case, the payment of interest did not assist the payment of benefit. Accordingly, the application would be dismissed.

R v Kensington and Chelsea Royal London Borough Council, ex p Brandt (1995) Times, 21 December, (1996) Independent, 11 January (Queen's Bench Division: Dyson J).

1957   Local authority—powers—power to enter guarantee and indemnity

A company made a loan to an unregistered housing association. The loan was intended for the purchase of housing which was to be leased to the local authority for use in alleviating homelessness and the authority guaranteed the repayments and indemnified the outstanding advances under the loan. When the company made a claim for payment from the authority, it fell to be determined whether the authority had acted beyond its powers in guaranteeing and indemnifying the loan. The company argued that the authority had the power to give the guarantee by virtue of the Local Government Act 1972, s 111(1) because the guarantee was conducive or incidental to the discharge of one of the authority's functions, namely its duty under the Housing Act 1985, s 65 to house the homeless. *Held*, the authority did not have the power to give the guarantee. Although the giving of the guarantee was incidental to its duty to house the homeless, the authority's powers were subject to the provisions of any subsequent enactment, including the Housing Associations Act 1985, s 60(1), which provided that an authority could make or give loans and guarantees to a housing association only if the association was registered. Both the guarantee and the indemnity were therefore ultra vires and void ab initio. Accordingly, the company's claim would be refused.

Morgan Grenfell & Co Ltd v Sutton London Borough Council (1995) 93 LGR 554 (Queen's Bench Division: Clarke J).

1958 Local authority—powers—power to incur expenditure

See *South Tyneside Metropolitan Borough Council v Svenska International plc*, para 663.

1959 Local authority—promotion of economic development—restrictions

The Local Government (Promotion of Economic Development) (Amendment) Regulations 1995, SI 1995/556 (in force on 1 April 1995), removes the restrictions imposed by the 1990 Regulations, SI 1990/763, on principal councils in the exercise of their economic development powers.

1960 Local authority—publication of staffing information—England

The Local Government (Publication of Staffing Information) (England) Regulations 1995, SI 1995/2006 (in force on 1 September 1995), require authorities in England to whom the Local Government Planning and Land Act 1980, s 2 applies (ie local authorities and certain other authorities) to publish the information about their staffing levels which is specified in the Local Government (Publication of Staffing Information) (England) Code 1995 (contained in the Annex to the Department of the Environment Circular 14/95, dated 28 July 1995), in the manner and form and on the occasions specified in the Code.

1961 Local authority—regulated companies—requirements

The Local Authorities (Companies) Order 1995, SI 1995/849 (in force in part on 1 April 1995 and in part on 1 July 1995), contains requirements applicable to companies subject to the influence or control of local authorities within the meaning of the Local Government and Housing Act 1989, Pt V, other than companies which satisfy the conditions described in the Schedule to the order.

1962 Local Government and Housing Act 1989—commencement

The Local Government and Housing Act 1989 (Commencement No 17) Order 1995, SI 1995/841, brings s 71(1) (for certain purposes), (4), (5) (in part), (6), (8) into force on 1 April 1995 in so far as those provisions, which concern minor interests held by local authorities in limited companies, are not already in force. Transitional provision is also made. For a summary of the Act, see 1989 Abr para 1464. For details of commencement, see the commencement table in the title STATUTES.

1963 Local government areas—changes

The Local Government Changes for England Regulations 1995, SI 1995/590 (in force on 9 March 1995), amend the 1994 Regulations, SI 1994/867, so as to provide that the Local Government Act 1972, s 79, which provides that a person is qualified to be elected as a member of a local authority if he has occupied premises, resided or worked in the area of that authority for 12 months preceding the nomination day, is to have effect in relation to a candidate for election to a shadow authority as if the area of that authority had been established not less than 12 months before that day.

The Local Government Changes for England (No 2) Regulations 1995, SI 1995/1055 (in force on 4 May 1995), make further provision of general application for the purposes, or in consequence of, orders under the Local Government Act 1992, s 17 with respect to local government changes in England. The 1994 Regulations, SI 1994/867, are further amended and provision is made in respect of the first meetings of 'shadow authorities' established by such orders and the functions of those authorities.

1964 Local government reorganisation—consequential amendments—Wales

The Local Government Reorganisation (Wales) (Consequential Amendments) Order 1995, SI 1995/115 (in force on 17 February 1995), amends the definition of 'local authority' in the Local Government Act 1988, s 1(2), to include the new authorities to be established in Wales in consequence of the Local Government (Wales) Act 1994.

The Local Government Reorganisation (Wales) (Consequential Amendments No 2) Order 1995, SI 1995/1510 (in force on 16 June 1995), amends the definition of 'local authority' in the Value Added Tax Act 1994, s 96(4), so as to bring all the newly elected councils and county borough councils created as a result of the Local Government (Wales) Act 1994 within that definition.

1965   Local government reorganisation—finance—Wales

The Local Government Reorganisation (Wales) (Finance) (Miscellaneous Amendments and Transitional Provisions) Order 1995, SI 1995/3150 (in force on 1 January 1996), makes transitional provisions in relation to local government finance, responsibility for which county and county borough councils, created as a result of the Local Government (Wales) Act 1994, will take over. The application of SI 1989/1058, 1992/554, 3171 is modified and SI 1992/613, 2904, 2929 are amended.

1966   Local government reorganisation—local authority functions—consequential provision

The Local Government Changes (Rent Act) Regulations 1995, SI 1995/2451 (in force on 13 October 1995), amend the Rent Act 1977 to take account of local government reorganisation in England under the Local Government Act 1992. The amendments, which relate to local authority functions, are made in respect of the meaning of registration area, schemes for appointment of rent officers, powers of local authorities under the 1977 Act, Pt V in respect of restricted contracts, powers of local authorities to prosecute for illegal premiums for furniture and powers of local authorities to give information.

1967   Local government reorganisation—local authority functions—miscellaneous provisions

The Local Government Changes for England (Miscellaneous Provision) Regulations 1995, SI 1995/1748 (in force in part on 1 August 1995 and in part on 1 April 1996), make incidental, consequential, transitory and supplementary provision of general application for the purposes or in consequence of orders made under the Local Government Act 1992, s 17. The regulations (1) make provision with respect to preparations for the implementation of a structural change by which a county council's functions are transferred to one or more existing district councils in the county, (2) provide that councillors for any electoral area wholly comprised in a part of an existing county or district which is affected by a structural or boundary change must not take part in the county or district council's decisions on precepts or council tax for the financial year beginning on the date the structural or boundary change takes place, (3) make provision to enable a district council in a county which has the same boundaries as the district, but which has no county council, to change the name of the county, (4) amend the Sheriffs Act 1887 by inserting a definition of 'county' for the purposes of the Act in relation to England, (5) amend the Reserve Forces Act 1980 to provide that, for the purposes of the provision of that Act relating to the lieutenancy in England, the meaning of 'county' is to be the same as in the 1887 Act, (6) make other minor and drafting amendments in earlier sets of regulations of general application.

1968   Local government reorganisation—school reorganisation—consequential provision

The Local Government Changes for England (School Reorganisation and Admissions) Regulations 1995, SI 1995/2368 (in force on 2 October 1995), make incidental and transitional provision of general application in the fields of school reorganisation and admissions in consequence of orders made under the Local Government Act 1992, s 17 (which make boundary and structural changes to local government areas in England). The regulations (1) provide for transferee authorities, which will exercise the functions of a local education authority in consequence of an order under the 1992 Act, s 17 during the period before the change made by the order takes effect, to make proposals or applications relating to the establishment, alteration or discontinuance of schools and certain matters in connection with school admissions; and (2) bring into effect in relation to transferee authorities the Secretary of State's direction of July 1994, made under the Education Act 1993, s 297, concerning the composition of local authority committees dealing with education matters.

1969   Local government reorganisation—transfer of property—agreements between local authorities and fire authorities

The Local Government Changes for England (Property Transfer and Transitional Payments) (Amendment) Regulations 1995, SI 1995/2796 (in force on 23 November 1995), amend the 1995 Regulations, SI 1995/402, which made provision of general application for the transfer of the property, rights and liabilities of local authorities which are subject to structural or boundary changes under the Local Government Act 1992. The regulations amend the 1995 Regulations so as to include specific provision in respect of the property of existing fire authorities, and in particular, to exclude a category of property, rights and liabilities of fire authorities from the scope of Pt II of those regulations. They disapply the 1995 Regulations in respect of property of fire authorities which is held or used partly for fire purposes and partly for other purposes. Such property will instead be dealt with in accordance with new regulations inserted by these regulations, which will enable that property to be vested in accordance with agreements made between affected local authorities and combined fire authorities. The regulations provide for residual rights and liabilities of abolished authorities to vest in accordance with the categories of description inserted by these regulations, and enable the relinquishing and the acquiring authority in relation to a transferred area to make agreements, during the six months following a reorganisation date, in respect of property, rights or liabilities which were not identified before that date. Provision is made enabling the provisions in the 1995 Regulations relating to arbitration to also apply where property, rights or liabilities are vested by an order under s 17 of the 1992 Act.

1970   Local government reorganisation—transfer of property—designated authorities

The Local Government Changes for England (Designation of Authorities) Order 1995, SI 1995/2894 (in force on 1 December 1995), makes provision relating to the restructuring of local government in respect of the transfer of property and finance. The order specifies, as respects authorities abolished by orders already made under the Local Government Act 1992, s 17, the authorities which are designated authorities for the purposes of provisions of the Local Government Changes for England (Property Transfer and Transitional Payments) Regulations 1995, SI 1995/402.

1971   Local government reorganisation—transfer of property—local government changes

The Local Government Changes For England (Property Transfer and Transitional Payments) Regulations 1995, SI 1995/402 (in force on 14 March 1995), make provision for the purposes of orders made under the Local Government Act 1992, s 17, which give effect to structural or boundary changes recommended by the Local Government Commission for England in respect of local authorities. The regulations make comprehensive provision for the vesting of the property, rights and liabilities of a local authority which is abolished by an order under s 17 and make provision for the vesting, in accordance with any agreement, of the property, rights or liabilities of an authority which is subject to a structural or boundary change but which is not abolished by such an order. Provision is also made for the vesting of property held subject to a charitable trust and the rights or liabilities in respect of it. In addition, the regulations provide for the disposal of surplus land by the authority in whom it is vested, for the distribution of sale proceeds and for the recovery by the custodian authority of its expenditure in respect of the management of the land or its disposal. Further, provision is made in relation to financial matters and disputes arising under the regulations.

1972   Local government reorganisation—Wales—special grant

The Local Government Reorganisation (Wales) (Special Grant) Order 1995, SI 1995/128 (in force on 26 January 1995), makes provision for the new principal authorities established under the Local Government (Wales) Act 1994 to be treated as relevant authorities within the meaning of the Local Government Finance Act 1988, s 88B, so that the Secretary of State may pay special grants under that section to the new principal authorities.

1973   Local government reorganisation—Wales—transitional provision

The Local Government Reorganisation (Wales) (Transitional Provisions) Order 1995, SI 1995/570 (in force on 1 April 1995), further modifies the Local Authorities (Members' Allowances) Regulations 1991, SI 1991/351, in relation to transition committees (established by the Local Government (Wales) Act 1994, s 46), so as to provide that members serving on such committees may be paid a special responsibility allowance for the full period of existence of the transition committee on which they are serving. See also SI 1995/1042, 1161.

The Local Government Reorganisation (Wales) (Transitional Provisions No 4) Order 1995, SI 1995/2563 (in force on 31 October 1995) relates to the new county and county borough councils which will take over responsibility for the discharge of functions relating to local government in Wales from the old county and district councils, and makes provision in respect of national park authorities in Wales created as a result of the Environment Act 1995. The order (1) imposes an obligation until 31 March 1997 on each new council and national park authority to provide information and assistance to any other new council or national park authority where such information and assistance is required to enable the new body requesting it to discharge its functions; (2) makes provision with respect to public access to documents held by existing authorities where there is a continuing obligation for such documents to be held by a new council, or national park authority, and to be available for inspection; (3) make provision with respect to the Local Government Act 1972, s 115 (accountability of officers) to enable directions to be given by new councils, national park authorities and combined fire authorities for the purposes of s 115 where an officer leaves the employment of an existing authority within the three month period immediately before 1 April 1996; and (4) makes provision with respect to the Data Protection Act 1984 whereby a registration held by an existing council in the register maintained under s 4 of the 1984 Act, which expires during the period beginning with 1 November 1995 and ending on 31 March 1996, is not required to be removed from the register until 1 April 1996.

1974 Local Government Residuary Body—England

The Local Government Residuary Body (England) Order 1995, SI 1995/401 (in force on 1 April 1995), establishes the Local Government Residuary Body (England) ('the body') to take over the residual property, rights or liabilities of local authorities which are abolished by virtue of orders made under the Local Government Act 1992, s 17. Provision is made in relation to the constitution and membership of the body and in respect of its accounting and annual reporting. The body has a general duty to arrange for the transfer to other persons of any property, rights or liabilities vested in it or to make proposals to the Secretary of State for effecting such transfers by order. The Secretary of State is empowered to give directions to the body in respect of the exercise of its functions and he may require the body to submit a scheme for its winding up. The body has the power to issue levies and a duty to distribute surplus money.

1975 Local Government (Wales) Act 1994—commencement

The Local Government (Wales) Act 1994 (Commencement No 3) Order 1995, SI 1995/546, brings into force, on 20 March 1995, ss 1(5), (8) (for certain purposes of interpretation), 2, 4, 17 (for certain purposes), 66(5)–(8) (in part), Sch 15, para 6, Sch 16, paras 68(6), (7) (in part), (8), (9), (13)–(16), (19), Sch 17, paras 7, 8, and certain repeals in Sch 18. Transitional provision is also made.

The Local Government (Wales) Act 1994 (Commencement No 3) (Amendment) Order 1995, SI 1995/851 (in force on 20 March 1995), amends a transitional provision in SI 1995/546, concerning the first elections to the new authorities established by the 1994 Act so as to remove the requirement that nomination papers be delivered at the offices of the existing council which nominated the returning officer.

The Local Government (Wales) Act 1994 (Commencement No 4) Order 1995, SI 1995/852, brings into force, on 3 April 1995, ss 1(3), (5), (6), (8) (for certain purposes), 5, 14, 15, 18(1)–(6), 19, 20(4) (in part), 22(1), (4) (in part), 23(2)–(6), 25–38, 42, 44, 45, 51, 53, 56–60, 66(5)–(8) (in part), Sch 2, paras 8, 9, Sch 6, paras 2–4, 11, 12, 21, 23, 24(1)(b), Sch 7, para 1, Sch 10, para 14, Sch 12, Sch 15, paras 3, 20, 23, 26, 55, Sch 16, paras 57(1)–(5), 82(1)–(4), 82(5) (in part), 84–86, 88, 96, 97, 106, Sch 17, paras 2, 3, 5, 10–14, 18–23, and certain repeals in Sch 18. Transitional provision is also made.

The Local Government (Wales) Act 1994 (Commencement No 5) Order 1995, SI 1995/2490, brings into force on 1 October 1995 ss 1(3) (in part), (5), (8) (both for certain purposes), 20(4) (in part), 22(1), (2) (both in part), 66(5), (6), (8) (each in part), Sch 2, para 13, Sch 6, para 24(10)(b), (17)(a), Sch 7, para 27(4), Sch 8, para 3(2), Sch 15, paras 10(1), 52, 58–61, Sch 16, paras 12, 26, 98, and certain repeals in Sch 18.

The Local Government (Wales) Act 1994 (Commencement No 6) Order 1995, SI 1995/3198, brings into force (1) on 1 January 1996, s 66(6) (in part), (8) (in part), Sch 16, para 54(2) and a repeal in Sch 18, and (2) on 1 April 1996, ss 1 (3) (in part), (5), (6), (8), 8–13, 16, 18(7), 20(1)–(3), 23(1), 49, 50, 62, 66(7) (in part), Sch 2, paras 1–3, 6, 7, 10–12, Schs 4, 5, Sch 16, para 54(2), Sch 17, paras 15, 17.

For a summary of the Act, see 1994 Abr para 1866. For details of commencement, see the commencement table in the title STATUTES.

1976 Misconduct in public office—application of offence to local authority employees

See *R v Bowden,* para 909.

1977 Principal areas—Wales—appointment of returning officers for elections

The Returning Officers (Principal Areas: Wales) Order 1995, SI 1995/151 (in force on 31 January 1995), designates, for the purposes of the first elections of councillors for the new principal areas in Wales established under the Local Government (Wales) Act 1994, the existing councils which are to appoint the returning officer for each such area.

1978 Registration service—Wales

The Local Government (Registration Service in Wales) Order 1995, SI 1995/3106 (in force on 22 December 1995), provides for changes to the local registration service in Wales in consequence of the reorganisation of local government from 1 April 1996, under the Local Government (Wales) Act 1994. The order (1) provides for schemes to be made by the councils of the new counties and county boroughs establishing registration districts and sub-districts, determining the location of registration offices and the number of superintendent registrars, registrars of births and deaths and other officers required for the purpose of the Registration Acts, (2) provides that registration officers holding office immediately before 1 April 1996 are transferred on that date to one of the new authorities, (3) provides for the allocation of the posts described in the registration scheme to individual officers transferred, and (4) makes transitional provision with regard to notices given and certificates issued under the Marriage Act 1949, marriages to be solemnised before registration officers, and the registration of births and deaths.

1979 Residuary Body for Wales—appointed day

The Residuary Body for Wales (Appointed Day) Order 1995, SI 1995/103 (in force on 18 January 1995), makes provision consequent upon the Local Government (Wales) Act 1994. Where the assets, rights and liabilities of district and county councils are not transferred to new unitary authorities, a body corporate known as a Residuary Body is to inherit and manage those assets, rights and liabilities, and is responsible for the transfer and disposal of any residual assets as necessary. This order appoints 1 February 1995 for the purposes of s 39 of the 1994 Act, which provides for the establishment of that body corporate, which is to be known as the Residuary Body for Wales or Corff Gweddilliol Cymru.

1980 Residuary Body for Wales—capital finance

The Residuary Body for Wales (Capital Finance) Regulations 1995, SI 1995/101 (in force on 1 February 1995), (1) prescribe the Residuary Body for Wales as a body to which the Local Government and Housing Act 1989, Pt IV, applies; (2) modify certain provisions of Pt IV of the 1989 Act as they relate to the Residuary Body; (3) provide for sums received by the Residuary Body not to be capital receipts; and (4) provide for any lease transferred to the Residuary Body from a former local authority, which would otherwise be a credit arrangement not to be a credit arrangement.

1981 Residuary Body for Wales—levies

The Residuary Body for Wales (Levies) Regulations 1995, SI 1995/2306 (in force on 1 October 1995), confer a power on the Residuary Body for Wales to issue levies to the new principal councils created by the Local Government (Wales) Act 1994 for the purpose of meeting the Residuary Body's expenditure in respect of financial years beginning in or after 1996. The regulations make provision as to when levies are to be issued, the issue of substitute levies, the payment of levies and interest on unpaid levies, the method of apportioning the amount to be raised by levies between all the new authorities, the supply of information by the new authorities to the Residuary Body and the anticipation by a new authority of a levy which may be issued to it.

1982 Residuary Body for Wales—publication of performance information

The Residuary Body for Wales (Miscellaneous Provisions) Order 1995, SI 1995/102 (in force on 1 February 1995), modifies the application of the Local Government Act 1992, ss 1–3 (which provide for the Audit Commission to give directions to certain local and other authorities requiring them to publish information as to their performance) by treating the Residuary Body for Wales as a body to which those sections do not apply. The order also provides that the Residuary Body is to be treated as a local authority for the purposes of the Income and Corporation Taxes Act 1988, s 842A (which defines local authorities). The Local Authorities (Capital Finance) Regulations 1990, SI 1990/432, are modified so that certain provisions therein are applied in relation to the Residuary Body.

1983   Revenue support grant—specified bodies

The Revenue Support Grant (Specified Bodies) (Amendment) Regulations 1995, SI 1995/3184 (in force on 1 January 1996), further amend the 1992 Regulations, SI 1992/89, in relation to any financial year beginning on or after 1 April 1996, so as to add one name to, and delete a name from, the list of specified bodies to which revenue support grant is payable.

1984   Service agency agreements—Wales—exclusions

The Local Government (Wales) (Service Agency Agreements) Regulations 1995, SI 1995/1040 (in force on 4 May 1995), make provision consequent on the Local Government (Wales) Act 1994, s 25(1), which allows the new Welsh principal councils to enter into agreements whereby one council provides services to the other for the purposes of, or in connection with, the discharge of that council's functions ('service agency agreements'). These regulations provide that work which is subject to competition requirements imposed under the Local Government, Planning and Land Act 1980, Pt III (direct labour organisations), and the Local Government Act 1988, Pt I (competition), is to be excluded from the power given in section 25(1) of the 1994 Act, subject to limited exceptions.

1985   Staff—local government changes

The Local Government Changes for England (Staff) Regulations 1995, SI 1995/520 (in force on 31 March 1995), make incidental, consequential, transitional and supplementary provisions of general application in relation to staff matters for the purposes of and in consequence of orders giving effect to recommendations by the Local Government Commission for England. Provision is made in relation to employees whose employment is transferred from an abolished authority and to the rights, powers and duties of the new employer. Staff who are not transferred and whose employment would have continued but for the abolition of the employing authority are entitled to treat themselves as having been dismissed on grounds of redundancy. Elected members of a continuing or shadow authority who on reorganisation are employed by the successor authority are not disqualified from continuing in employment with the successor authority by virtue of the Local Government Act 1972, s 116. All chief officer posts must be filled by open competition.

1986   Superannuation

See PENSIONS AND SUPERANNUATION.

LONDON GOVERNMENT

Halsbury's Laws of England (4th edn) Vol 29, paras 1–200

1987   City of London wards—election—election petition—joinder of successful candidates—meaning of returning officer

See *Absalom v Gillett*, para 1199.

1988   Court of Aldermen—election of alderman—refusal to confirm election

The applicant was elected as an alderman in the City of London but, after appearing before the Court of Aldermen, he was informed by the Lord Mayor that the court was unable to confirm his election. No reasons were given for this decision. On appeal by the applicant against the refusal of his application for judicial review of the decision, *held*, the election of an alderman took place in two stages, the first stage being an election which was statutorily recognised. The second stage, confirmation by the Court of Aldermen, remained customary. It applied irrespective of whether the fitness and qualification of an elected alderman had been called into question by the petition of an interested party. In deciding whether to confirm an election, the court had to consider not only whether there were any matters which told against the elected person, but also whether his experience, achievements and character fitted him for the position. On the evidence, given the lack of reasons, it was impossible to say whether the decision of the court was flawed for procedural unfairness. The appropriate rules had been followed, and the applicant's suitability for the position had been deliberated on for a considerable time. However, fairness and natural justice required the decision to be explained. The applicant had been elected with a substantial majority and, without reasons, he could not know the basis for the refusal to confirm his election or whether he should stand again. Accordingly, the matter would be remitted for reconsideration by the Court of Aldermen with a direction to give reasons.

R v Corpn of London, ex p Matson (1995) Independent, 27 September (Court of Appeal: Neill, Waite and Swinton-Thomas LJJ).

1989 Sex establishments—control

See *Willowcell Ltd v Westminster City Council*, para 2825.

MAGISTRATES

Halsbury's Laws of England (4th edn) Vol 29, paras 201–600

1990 Articles

Allocating Family Law Cases, Paul Tain: 139 SJ 192
Appeals by Case Stated From the Magistrates' Court, Alan Murdie: 139 SJ 984
Calculating Days in Default for Non-Payment of Fines, F G Davies: 159 JP Jo 499
Changes to the Mode of Trial Decision Process: 159 JP Jo 699
Children and Young Persons Before the Adult Magistrates' Court - Where Are They Tried? Elizabeth Franey: 159 JP Jo 21
From Committal Proceedings to Transfer for Trial, Robert Girvan: 159 JP Jo 379
Magistrates in the Dock, Ian Wise and Rona Epstein (on magistrates' power to imprison): 145 NLJ 567
Poll Tax Committals—The Marshalsea Revisited? Ian Wise and Rona Epstein: 159 JP Jo 453
Unused Prosecution Material in Summary Proceedings—Disclosure to Defence, Stephen Savage: 159 JP Jo 363

1991 Appeal—appeal by way of case stated—alteration of case stated

The applicant was found guilty of assaulting a police officer in the execution of his duty. He put a properly formulated question to the justices for them to state a case to the High Court and both the applicant and the Crown Prosecution Service (CPS) made representations on the drafted case. The justices invited further comments from the CPS but not from the applicant. He sought the adjournment of the hearing of the case stated. *Held*, the procedure for stating a case required frankness of the parties, all of whom had to attempt to define the questions for the High Court's opinion. A properly framed question should not be fundamentally altered without the party which framed the question having an opportunity to comment on the change. The application would be allowed and the case remitted for reconsideration.

Waldie v DPP (1995) 159 JP 514 (Queen's Bench Division: Pill LJ and Keene J).

1992 Appeal—appeal by way of case stated—appeal as alternative to judicial review

See *R v Oldbury Justices, ex p Smith*, para 19.

1993 Bail hostels and probation hostels

The Approved Probation and Bail Hostel Rules 1995, SI 1995/302 (in force on 6 March 1995), replace the 1976 Rules, SI 1976/626. The principal changes include (1) the conferring of greater flexibility, with the approval of the local probation committee, in respect of the constitutions of management committees of hostels run by persons other than the probation service, (2) a requirement that such management committees publish annual reports, (3) the application, with modifications, to both management committees and probation committees of general duties in respect of the manner in which hostels are to be run, the control of expenditure and staff matters, (4) a requirement that committees adopt an admissions policy in respect of each hostel managed by them and that they inform the local courts of such policy, (5) the removal of the requirement for the Secretary of State's approval to the appointment of a person as a hostel warden (now referred to as a hostel manager), and (6) the omission of the enumeration of the specific facilities, except medical facilities, to be afforded to residents.

1994 Committal proceedings—evidence—written statement—statement made by deceased witness

The Magistrates' Courts Act 1980, s 6(2) provides that a magistrates' court inquiring into an offence as examining justices may, if satisfied that all the evidence before the court consists of written statements tendered to the court under s 102, commit a defendant for trial for the offence without consideration of the contents of those statements. In committal proceedings a written statement by any person is admissible as evidence if certain conditions are satisfied: s 102.

The appellant allegedly entered the victim's house, attacked her and took some money. The victim made a written statement following the attack but she died several weeks later. The appellant was charged with assault with intent to rob and, at committal proceedings, the victim's witness statement was tendered pursuant to the 1980 Act, s 102. The justices committed the appellant for trial under s 6(2). At her trial, the appellant submitted to the judge that, at the time of the committal, the written statement was not a statement 'by any person' under s 102 because the victim had died and was no longer a person. The judge rejected the submission and the appellant was convicted. On appeal against conviction, *held*, when the victim's written statement was made and signed she was a person and the statement was therefore 'a written statement by any person' within the terms of s 102. Accordingly, the appeal would be dismissed.

R v Sinclair (1995) 160 JP 63 (Court of Appeal: Lord Taylor of Gosforth CJ, Owen J and Sir Lawrence Verney, Recorder of London).

1995 Complaint—statutory nuisance—injunction obtained simultaneously—refusal of magistrates' clerk to issue summons

See para 2189.

1996 Confiscation orders—extension of power to make orders—orders in respect of intellectual property offences

See para 2602.

1997 Custody—time limits—first appearance for an offence

See para 771.

1998 Domestic proceedings—matrimonial injunctions

See HUSBAND AND WIFE.

1999 Evidence—exclusion—trial within a trial

See *Halawa v Federation against Copyright Theft,* para 805.

2000 Family proceedings

See CHILDREN AND YOUNG PERSONS.

2001 Justices—acceptance of jurisdiction for summary trial—subsequent decision to commit to Crown Court for sentence—extent of justices' discretion

Under the Magistrates' Court Act 1980, s 38(2)(a) if the court is of the opinion that an offence or the combination of the offence and other offences associated with it was so serious that greater punishment should be inflicted for the offence than the court has power to impose, the court may commit the offender to the Crown Court for sentence.

The applicant appeared before a magistrates' court where he pleaded guilty to charges of theft. He was remanded in custody for pre-sentence reports and subsequently appeared before the same court on burglary charges in respect of which the justices declined jurisdiction. They then decided to commit the applicant to the Crown Court for sentence in respect of the theft offences. On an application for judicial review of that decision, the proper construction of s 38(2)(a) fell to be determined. *Held*, under s 38(2)(a) the court's opinion could be formed at any moment up to the time when the case was committed for sentence, and it did not have to be formed as a result of information received after the court had decided to proceed by way of summary trial. There was nothing unreasonable or illogical in permitting a court to form a view at the stage of deciding mode of trial and another view at the stage of deciding whether or not to commit for sentence. The purpose of s 38(2)(a) was to give the justices an open textured discretion not tied to a decision on mode of trial. The court should, however, continue to think carefully when deciding to accept jurisdiction because normally an accused should be able to conclude that once jurisdiction had been accepted, he would not on the same facts be committed to the Crown Court for sentence. In the present case, the justices had relied partly on information which emerged after the directions stage that the applicant had committed the offences whilst subject to a conditional discharge, a combination order and a probation order. In deciding to commit the applicant, they could not be said to have acted irrationally. Accordingly, the application would be dismissed.

R v North Sefton Magistrates' Court, ex p Marsh (1994) 159 JP 9 (Queen's Bench Division: Steyn LJ, Kay and Smith JJ). *R v Dover Magistrates' Court, ex p Pamment* (1994) 158 JP 670, DC considered. *R v Manchester Magistrates' Court, ex p Kaymanesh* (1994) 158 JP 401, DC, disapproved.

2002 Justices—breach of natural justice—refusal to allow cross-examination of expert witness—food safety legislation

See *Errington v Wilson*, para 1420.

2003 Justices—decision—consultation with clerk

The applicant was convicted of handling stolen goods and offences of deception. He sought an order of certiorari quashing his conviction arguing that the magistrates' court clerk ought not to have retired with the magistrates without being invited to do so in open court. *Held*, by joining the magistrates in the retiring room, suspicions were bound to be raised that the clerk was influencing the decision making. Even though it had been the regular practice for 20 years for the clerk so to join the magistrates, there was no justification for his presence where his assistance on a point of law was not required. The practice was contrary to practice direction and the common law and should cease immediately. Accordingly, the appeal would be allowed and the conviction quashed.

R v Birmingham Magistrates, ex p Ahmed [1995] Crim LR 503 (Queen's Bench Division: McCowan LJ and Buxton J).

2004 Justices—decision—costs—circumstances in which decision may be quashed

When a company sought an order for costs following its successful appeal against an abatement notice, the justices decided to disallow the costs of leading counsel who had represented the company at the substantive hearing. On the company's application for judicial review of the decision, *held*, lay justices were advised by their clerk as to matters of law and could not be expected to adopt the same standard of accuracy in expressing their decisions and reasoning as that of lawyers. As such, unless the decision of the justices in the instant case was so perverse that no reasonable magistrates' court could have concluded that the assessment of costs was just and reasonable, the court could not set it aside. The justices had properly reached their decision and, accordingly, the application would be dismissed.

R v Newcastle-under-Lyme Magistrates' Court, ex p Cloudside Outdoor Pursuits Ltd (1995) Times, 7 April (Queen's Bench Division: Turner J).

2005 Justices—decision—reasonableness of decision

See *R v Oldbury Justices, ex p Smith*, para 19.

2006 Justices—discretion—discretion to permit representations in chambers

The two applicants were charged, together with two co-accused, with affray. The solicitor for one of the co-accused wished to consult the magistrate as to whether a guilty plea to a lesser charge by the first applicant could be accepted without a fresh charge being laid. For this purpose, all the advocates and the magistrates' clerk went into the magistrate's room. No record was made of the ensuing discussion. The applicants sought judicial review of their convictions. *Held*, a magistrate, whether lay or stipendiary, had an inherent discretion to permit representations in chambers during the course of a trial. The discretion had to be exercised sparingly and with caution. The magistrate had to consider whether, if he allowed such representations, his role as fact finder would be compromised. Careful consideration had to be given to the procedure, with all parties knowing that the hearing in chambers was taking place and with all parties being represented, unless the case involved public interest immunity. A contemporaneous note had to be taken, usually by the clerk. Although there was no apparent reason why any technical problem concerning the first applicant's plea should not have been heard in open court, and although no contemporaneous note was made of the hearing in chambers, there was no material irregularity and no evidence of impropriety in the trial. Accordingly, the application would be dismissed.

R v Nottingham Magistrates' Court, ex p Furnell (1995) Times, 18 December (Queen's Bench Division: Schiemann LJ and Holland J).

2007   Justices—disqualification—discretion to disqualify themselves—admissibility of evidence attracting public interest immunity

The prosecution in a summary trial, indicated in a schedule of unused material that a particular document had not been disclosed on the basis of public interest immunity. The justices excluded the accused and his solicitors whilst they heard representations on the issue from the prosecution and the police, and determined that the document was evidentially immaterial. The accused's solicitor claimed that it was contrary to the interests of justice for the justices to go on to hear the case as they might have been prejudiced by what they had heard in the accused's absence. The prosecution claimed that authorities indicated that the justices had to determine both the public interest immunity issue and any triable issues that subsequently arose. The trial was adjourned and an application made to determine the issue. *Held*, the justices had a discretion to order that a trial be heard by a different bench. In the circumstances of the present case, the justices had to exercise their discretion to disqualify themselves from the case as it would be unreasonable to do otherwise.

R v South Worcestershire Magistrates, ex p Lilley [1995] 4 All ER 186 (Queen's Bench Division: Rose LJ and Potts J).

2008   Justices—order for costs against justices—judicial review proceedings

The applicant applied for judicial review of a decision by justices to commit her to prison for failing to pay her community charge. The justices had refused to adjourn the proceedings for the attendance of the applicant, having been advised by the clerk that they had no such power. At the judicial review hearing the committal order was quashed and an order for costs made against the justices. They applied for a discharge or variation of that order for costs. *Held*, an order for costs would not be made against justices merely because they had made a mistake in law. However, such an order would be appropriate where justices had acted improperly, that is perversely or with a flagrant disregard for the elementary principles of justice which every court ought to obey. The justices had acted on the advice given to them by their clerk and as such were answerable for it. The advice was incomprehensible since it was an implicit part of every magistrates' court's jurisdiction that, in the absence of express statutory power, a case should be adjourned where the interests of justice required it. That was an elementary principle of justice and its disregard was so serious that the justices ought to be held responsible for the error. Accordingly, their application for a discharge or variation of the order for costs made against them would be refused. The order for costs would stand.

R v Lincoln Justices, ex p Count [1995] RVR 195 (Queen's Bench Division: Sedley J).

2009   Justices—powers—power to commit to prison for failure to pay community charge—means inquiry

See *R v South Tyneside Justices, ex p Martin*, para 2430.

2010   Justices—powers—power to make hospital order

Under the Mental Health Act 1983, s 37(3) where a person is charged before a magistrates' court with any act or omission as an offence and the court would have power, on convicting him of that offence, to make an order under s 37(1) in his case as being a person suffering from mental illness, then, if the court is satisfied that the accused did the act charged, the court may, if it thinks fit, make such an order without convicting him.

The applicant, who had a history of schizophrenic illness, was charged with offences of aggravated robbery. When he appeared before the justices at a committal hearing, they declined to make a hospital order under the 1983 Act, s 37(3) for want of jurisdiction. The applicant sought judicial review of the justices' decision. He submitted that s 37(3) gave magistrates a very wide discretion to take the medical rather than the penal route where a defendant was obviously mentally ill, whether cases were triable summarily or on indictment. *Held*, s 37(3) by its clear terms assumed the court would have power to try the person concerned. If the court had no power to try, as in the present case because aggravated robbery was an indictable offence, it could not convict him of that offence. Any other interpretation ran contrary to the intention of the 1983 Act and, accordingly, the application would be dismissed.

R v Chippenham Magistrates' Court, ex p Thompson (1995) Times, 6 December (Queen's Bench Division: Staughton LJ and Rougier J).

2011 Justices—size and chairmanship of bench

The Justices of the Peace (Size and Chairmanship of Bench) Rules 1995, SI 1995/971 (in force on 1 May 1995), replace the 1990 Rules, SI 1990/1554. The rules provide, in particular, (1) for the reduction from seven to three of the maximum number of justices who may sit to deal with a case in a magistrates' court, other than such a court sitting as a youth court, family proceedings court or a licensing or betting licensing committee; (2) for election to the offices of chairman and deputy chairman of the justices; (3) a nomination procedure, instead of a short list procedure, for chairman and for a maximum period of office as chairman; and (4) for the establishment of a chairmanship committee the purpose of which is to maintain a list of approved court chairmen eligible to preside in court.

2012 Magistrates' courts—cases capable of being dealt with in a magistrates' court—mode of trial—government consultation

The government is anxious to ensure that cases capable of being properly dealt with in a magistrates' court should be dealt with there. The Home Office has published a consultation document, *Mode of Trial* (Cm 2908), setting out various possibilities for retaining more cases in the magistrates' courts. These include the reclassification of more offences as triable only summarily (a list of possible offences for reclassification is annexed to the document), the removal of a defendant's unfettered right to elect trial by jury in offences triable either way, and the amendment of the Magistrates' Courts Act 1980 to oblige defendants to enter a plea before the decisions as to the mode of trial are taken. Mention is also made of the need for greater visibility of discounts in magistrates' courts to encourage defendants to plead guilty; the discount following such a plea might encourage magistrates to regard certain cases as suitable for their retention.

2013 Magistrates' courts—forms

The Magistrates' Courts (Forms) (Amendment) Rules 1995, SI 1995/1909 (in force on 4 September 1995), amend the 1981 Rules, SI 1981/553, Forms 27 and 28, in consequence of the amendments made to the procedure for pleading guilty by post introduced by the Criminal Justice and Public Order Act 1994, s 45, Sch 5.

2014 Magistrates' courts—justices' chief executives and justices' clerks—appointment

The Justices' Chief Executives and Justices' Clerks (Appointment) Regulations 1995, SI 1995/686 (in force on 1 April 1995), set out the procedure for the submission to the Lord Chancellor by a magistrates' courts committee of an application for approval of one or more persons for appointment to the office of justices' chief executive or justices' clerk under the Justices of the Peace Act 1979, s 24D or 25.

2015 Magistrates' courts—justices' clerks and assistants—compensation—variation

The Justices of the Peace Act 1949 (Compensation) (Variation) Regulations 1995, SI 1995/41 (in force on 3 February 1995), vary the 1978 Regulations, SI 1978/1682, by providing that they apply only to justices' clerks and their assistants in office on or before 2 February 1995.

2016 Magistrates' courts—powers to rectify mistakes
See para 760.

2017 Magistrates' courts—rules

The Magistrates' Courts (Amendment) Rules 1995, SI 1995/585 (in force on 10 April 1995), further amend the Magistrates' Courts Rules 1981, SI 1981/552, and the Magistrates' Courts (Forms) Rules 1981, SI 1981/553, by providing for the procedure to be followed on an application under the Magistrates' Courts Act 1980, s 43B for bail following a grant of conditional police bail and on reconsideration under the Bail Act 1976, s 5B of a decision to grant bail.

The Magistrates' Courts (Amendment) (No 2) Rules 1995, SI 1995/2619 (in force on 1 November 1995), further amend the 1981 Rules, SI 1981/552, for the purpose of setting out the procedures arising out of the Criminal Justice Act 1988, Pt VI (ss 71–103), concerning confiscation of the proceeds of an offence.

2018 Maintenance orders

See DIVORCE; HUSBAND AND WIFE.

2019 Mode of trial procedure—co-defendants—election by some of defendants for trial on indictment—committal of all defendants

The applicant was jointly charged with two co-defendants with offences of burglary and attempted theft. At the mode of trial hearing, he consented to summary trial, but his co-defendants elected Crown Court trial. Acting on the advice of their clerk and without hearing further representations, the justices decided that the matter was not suitable for summary trial. The applicant applied for judicial review of the decision. *Held*, under the Magistrates' Court Act 1980, s 19, justices had to decide whether an offence was more suitable for summary trial or trial on indictment, and one of the matters to which they had to have regard were the relevant circumstances of the offence. The 1980 Act, s 20(3) gave a defendant the right to chose the mode of trial, and that right was not affected by the fact that a co-defendant chose a different mode of trial. The decision required under s 19 was separate from that which had to be made under s 20, and had to be reached before following the procedure under s 20. As such, if a case was suitable for summary trial, co-defendants could elect to be tried separately in different courts. The justices in the instant case had been wrong to base their decision on the fact that the applicant's co-defendants had elected Crown Court trial and, accordingly, the appeal would be allowed.

R v Ipswich Magistrates' Court, ex p Callaghan (1995) 159 JP 748 (Queen's Bench Division: Pill LJ and Keene J). *R v Brentwood Justices, ex p Nicholls* [1991] 3 All ER 359, HL (1991 Abr para 1626) applied.

2020 Police and Magistrates' Courts Act 1994—commencement

See para 2298.

2021 Probation rules

The Probation (Amendment) Rules 1995, SI 1995/2622 (in force on 4 December 1995), further amend the 1984 Rules, SI 1984/647, by omitting the rule which required probation officers to hold a specified certificate of qualification in social work or an approved equivalent qualification.

2022 Witness summons—summons for production of documents—witness's instructions to solicitor—legal professional privilege

See *R v Derby Magistrates' Court, ex p B*, para 826.

MARKETS AND FAIRS

Halsbury's Laws of England (4th edn) Vol 29, paras 601–716

2023 Creation of market—establishment by local authority—grant of planning permission to rival market

The Food Act 1984, s 50 provides that the council of a district may establish a market within their district as long as it does not interfere with any rights, powers or privileges enjoyed within the district by any person, without that person's consent.

A local authority applied for an injunction restraining the defendant from operating a Saturday market just three miles from their own, in exercise of their common law right to prevent a rival market from operating within a distance of six and two-thirds miles. The defendant claimed that the authority had no right to the injunction because the defendant's predecessors had been granted planning permission to hold a market, which amounted to the establishment of a market under the 1984 Act, s 50, which the defendant had the right to run. The defendant also claimed that planning permission amounted to statutory authority giving immunity from suit, that the grant of permission was lawful and therefore there could be no nuisance and that the authority was in breach of its duty to act in the public good which included acting fairly towards a private citizen. *Held*, any right granted by planning permission was in relation to planning law and was not a universal, positive right having nothing to do with planning law and overriding the rights of others. Planning permission was relevant in considering the nature of the area involved in the nuisance claim but did not constitute statutory authority. There had been no breach of public duty by the local authority and, accordingly, the injunction applied for by the local authority would be granted.

Delyn Borough Council v Solitaire (Liverpool) Ltd (1995) 93 LGR 614 (Chancery Division: Jacob J).

MEDICINE, PHARMACY, DRUGS AND MEDICINAL PRODUCTS

Halsbury's Laws of England (4th edn) Vol 30 (reissue), paras 1–1000

2024 Articles

Manslaughter and the Doctor, Margaret Puxon: 1 CR 129
Medicinal Products and the 'Gulf War Syndrome', Richard Goldberg: 145 NLJ 1443
Meningitis: Medico-Legal Aspects, Harvey Marcovitch: 2 CR 77
Reasons for Decisions, Derek Morgan (on *R v Cambridge District Health Authority, ex p B* (1995) Times, 15 March, Independent, 14 March, CA (para 12)): 145 NLJ 428
Through the Keyhole, B Mahendra (on professional misconduct relating to keyhole surgery): 145 NLJ 1475
Thrown to Woolf, B Mahendra (on the importance of giving good instructions to medical experts): 145 NLJ 1375
Treatment of the Unconscious Patient, Robert Francis: 1 CR 160
Who Decides? The Prudent Patient or the Reasonable Doctor? Anthony Barton (on consent to medical treatment): 1 CR 86
Withdrawal of Artificial Feeding, Carol Lockett: 139 SJ 1155
Withdrawal of Medical Treatment—The Emergency Case, Adrian Palmer: [1995] Fam Law 195
A Worrying Conception, Charles Foster (on failed sterilisation cases): 139 SJ 893

2025 Consent to treatment—foreign stroke patient—jurisdiction of court—locus standi of carer

The plaintiff lived with a Norwegian man who gave her power of attorney over his bank accounts. The man suffered a severe stroke and was placed in hospital care paid for by the plaintiff with money from the accounts. The man's son arranged for his father to be taken to a Norwegian nursing home but the plaintiff obtained an interim injunction preventing the transfer. The plaintiff applied for a declaration that removal to Norway was not in the father's best interests and an injunction restraining the son from removing his father from the jurisdiction. On the question of whether the court had jurisdiction to grant the injunction and whether the plaintiff had the necessary locus standi to obtain it, the court of first instance held that the court had jurisdiction to make the declaration sought and that the plaintiff had the requisite locus standi. On appeal, *held*, although every person had the right of physical autonomy, this right did not apply to minors or those suffering from mental illness. It was a more problematic issue where a patient had been rendered unconscious or inarticulate by illness and was therefore unable to give or withhold consent. In such instances, where there was an element of controversy or a momentous and irrevocable decision had to be made, the question of what was in the best interest of the patient was justiciable by the court. Although the consequences of any decision in this case were not momentous, there was a serious justiciable issue which involved the happiness and welfare of a helpless human being. The plaintiff had clearly assumed the duty of caring for the patient and was neither a stranger nor an officious busy-body and that was enough to give the court jurisdiction. This was an area where the common law ought to respond to social needs as they were manifested case by case. Accordingly, the appeal would be dismissed.

Re S (Hospital Patient: Court's Jurisdiction) [1995] 3 All ER 290 (Court of Appeal: Sir Thomas Bingham MR, Kennedy and Millett LJJ). Decision of Hale J [1995] 2 WLR 38 affirmed.

See also *Re S (Hospital Patient: Foreign Curator)*, para 2074.

2026 Consent to treatment—sterilisation operation—duty to inform of risk of failure—responsibility of health authority

A mother had given birth to two children by Caesarean section and agreed to be sterilised during the third such birth. She was not told of the risk of failure of the operation before it took place and there was no warning of the risk on the consent form she signed. It had been found that a post-operative warning given four days after the birth was not, in view of its timing and conditions, of such a nature in terms of force and emphasis as to impinge on the plaintiff's thoughts. On a preliminary issue of the health authority's liability over the birth of the mother's fourth child, judgment was given in favour of the mother. On appeal, *held*, an emphatic and clear warning was required, together with an assuredness that the warning was being taken in. No proper warning had at any stage been given to the plaintiff or her husband and accordingly the appeal would be dismissed.

Lybert v Warrington Health Authority (1995) 25 BMLR 91 (Court of Appeal: Nourse, Millett and Otton LJJ).

2027 Consent to treatment—vasectomy operation—duty to inform of risk of failure—responsibility of Department of Health

The Ministry of Health Act 1919, s 2 provides that it is the duty of the minister to take all such steps as may be desirable to secure the preparation, effective carrying out and co-ordination of measures conducive to the health of the people, including measures for the initiation and direction of research, the collection, preparation, publication, and dissemination of information and statistics relating to the prevention and cure of diseases, the avoidance of fraud in connection with alleged remedies therefor, and the treatment of physical and mental defects.

A study on the results of vasectomy operations performed over a 10-year period reported that restoration of fertility could occur at any time, even up to 10 years after the operation. The study concluded that although the possibility of the late failure of a vasectomy operation was relatively rare, it was a factor which ought to be taken into account in pre-operative counselling and in letters confirming the achievement of sterility. It was general practice to warn patients that a vasectomy operation could sometimes fail and that fertility might reoccur, but it was not general practice to draw attention to the findings of the study. Having undergone a vasectomy operation and thereafter given two negative samples, the plaintiff was informed that he could regard himself as sterile and incapable of further parenthood. However, at no stage was he advised that the operation might not render him permanently and irreversibly sterile. Six years after the operation, the plaintiff's wife became pregnant. In claiming damages against the defendant, the Department of Health, the plaintiff alleged that the defendant had been under a duty to disseminate the results of the study to the public, and that it was in breach of its duty under the 1919 Act, s 2 in failing to do so. In the alternative, the plaintiff claimed that the defendant had been negligent. *Held*, in deciding whether or not to issue a warning to the public, the defendant had to strike a balance between causing upset and fear to large numbers of persons who were not likely to be affected by the warning, and the desire to ensure that proper advice was given to those who needed it. It was also necessary to weigh the risks involved in not giving general publicity to a problem and balance them against the expense of doing so. However, as the 1919 Act was intended to benefit the general public and did not contain any enforcement provisions in relation to s 2, there was no presumption that it gave individuals a private law right of civil action against the defendant. Moreover, although the Act obliged the minister to disseminate relevant information, that was a matter of policy in respect of which he was entitled to exercise his discretion and could not form the basis of an action for breach of statutory duty. As regards the plaintiff's claim in negligence, he had failed to establish that there was a relationship of proximity between himself and the defendant. Even after the publication of the study, the defendant had been justified in leaving it to the medical profession to decide what advice to give to those undergoing vasectomies, as the study did not significantly change what was known about the risk of failure of vasectomy operations, but merely enabled practitioners to make a clearer assessment of the risks involved. Accordingly, the application would be dismissed.

Danns v Department of Health (1995) 25 BMLR 121 (Queen's Bench Division: Wright J).

2028   Consent to treatment—vasectomy operation—duty to inform of risk of failure—responsibility of health authority

A husband and wife decided that the husband should have a vasectomy, and were counselled by a professor of obstetrics and gynaecology employed by the defendant health authority. They were told that the wife would have to continue using contraception after the vasectomy operation until the husband had two negative sperm tests. Although they followed the advice, the wife became pregnant. The husband and wife commenced proceedings against the health authority, claiming that they had been given negligent advice. In particular, it was alleged that the professor had told them that following the two clear sperm counts, there was no possibility that the wife could conceive again by the husband. Although the husband and wife were advised about the failure rate of the operation, the wife claimed that they were not advised that there was a risk that the operation might fail even after two clear sperm counts. The consent form which the husband and wife signed stated that the risk of pregnancy occurring after the operation was one in one thousand. However, the husband claimed that the professor told him that such a risk could be disregarded, as further research had shown that the risk was actually one in ten thousand, and could be as high as one in twenty thousand. He further claimed that he was told that the failure rate referred to on the consent form related to the failure rate before two clear sperm counts were obtained. *Held*, in order to obtain valid consent to a vasectomy, it was necessary to inform the parties concerned that there was a risk that the operation might fail. Here, the professor who advised the husband and wife was a serious and responsible clinician, and an expert in his field. It was unbelievable that he would have omitted to mention the matters of which the husband and wife complained, and that he would have stated some of the matters which the husband alleged. The husband and wife had conditioned themselves in advance of their consultation with the professor to believe that a vasectomy operation was the only possible solution for them. There was evidence that the professor had properly explained every part of the consent form to them, and that he had made every effort to ensure that the husband and wife understood that there was a risk that the wife might conceive despite the operation. The professor had fully and adequately discharged his duty of care towards the husband and wife and, accordingly, the application would be dismissed.

Stobie v Central Birmingham Health Authority (1994) 22 BMLR 135 (Queen's Bench Division: Turner J).

2029   Controlled drugs—licence fees

The Misuse of Drugs (Licence Fees) (Amendment) Regulations 1995, SI 1995/506 (in force on 1 April 1995), amend the 1986 Regulations, SI 1986/416, so as to increase by approximately 4 per cent the fee payable in relation to a licence to produce, supply or offer to supply or possess controlled drugs.

2030   Controlled drugs—list—modification

The Misuse of Drugs Act 1971 (Modification) Order 1995, SI 1995/1966 (in force on 1 September 1995), amends SI 1986/2330 and further amends the Misuse of Drugs Act 1971, so as to delete propylhexedrine from the list of Class C drugs which are subject to control under the 1971 Act.

The Misuse of Drugs (Designation) (Variation) Order 1995, SI 1995/2047 (in force on 1 September 1995), varies the 1986 Order, SI 1986/2331, by removing dronabinol and its stereoisomers from the control of the Misuse of Drugs Act 1971, s 7(4).

The Misuse of Drugs (Amendment) Regulations 1995, SI 1995/2048 (in force on 1 September 1995), further amend the 1985 Regulations, SI 1985/2066, by transferring dronabinol and its stereoisomers from Sch 1 to Sch 2, and by removing propylhexedrine from Sch 4.

The Misuse of Drugs (Amendment) (No 2) Regulations 1995, SI 1995/3244 (in force on 15 January 1996), amend SI 1985/2066, so as to transfer the drug temazepam from Sch 4 to Sch 3, thereby making temazepam subject to the restrictions on the import and export of controlled drugs under the Misuse of Drugs Act 1971, and removing the exemption from restrictions on possession of controlled drugs in relation to possession of temazepam when in the form of a medicinal product. The regulations also have the effect of applying to temazepam certain other provisions of the 1985 Regulations regarding the supply of controlled drugs and the duty to preserve records relating to such drugs.

2031   Dangerous drugs—offences

See CRIMINAL LAW.

2032   Dental services—general services

The National Health Service (General Dental Services) Amendment Regulations 1995, SI 1995/3092 (in force on 21 December 1995), further amend the 1992 Regulations, SI 1992/661, to make provision in relation to dentists who have been suspended from providing general dental services by the NHS Tribunal or whom the tribunal has declared not fit to be engaged in any capacity in the provision of those services. The family health services authorities are able to transfer existing arrangements for the care and treatment of the patients of suspended dentists to another dentist and to transfer them back if the suspended dentist is reinstated. In addition, the regulations prevent the employment of any suspended dentist, who is the subject of a declaration by the tribunal that he is not fit to be engaged in any capacity in the provision of general dental services, as an assistant or deputy. Further, provision is made in relation to payments of suspended dentists.

2033   Fund-holding practices—functions of family health services authorities

The National Health Service (Fund-holding Practices) (Functions of Family Health Services Authorities) Regulations 1995, SI 1995/3280 (in force on 9 January 1996), amend the 1993 Regulations, SI 1993/567, to confer on family health services authorities ('FHSAs') certain functions in relation to fund-holding practices. Applications for recognition as a fund-holding practice are to be sent to the FHSA which is to forward them to the regional health authority ('RHA') together with the FHSA's observations on the practice's suitability for fund-holding status. FHSAs are to gather and make available to RHAs information relevant to possible removal from the scheme and must also gather information relevant to the RHA's determination of a fund-holding practice's allotted sum and to propose to the RHA an allotted sum in relation to each fund-holding practice.

2034   General Medical Council—registration—fees

The General Medical Council (Registration (Fees) (Amendment) Regulations) Order of Council 1995, SI 1995/2786 (made on 19 October 1995), approves regulations which amend the regulations approved by SI 1986/149, so as to provide that, from 1 May 1996, doctors whose names are included in the overseas list of the register of medical practitioners must pay annual retention fees.

2035   General medical services—suspension of general medical practitioners

The National Health Service (General Medical Services) Amendment (No 2) Regulations 1995, SI 1995/3093 (in force on 1 January 1996), further amend the 1992 Regulations, SI 1992/635, to make provision in relation to the suspension of general medical practitioners from providing general medical services by the NHS Tribunal, either pending its investigation or pending an appeal from its decision, and in relation to practitioners who are disqualified by the tribunal from providing general medical services and who are declared unfit to provide such services in any capacity. A suspended doctor is protected from removal from the medical list on the ground that he has not provided general medical services for six months. A family health services authority is required to make temporary arrangements for the provision of general medical services to a suspended doctor's patients with one or more other doctors and provides that the patients are to be temporarily transferred to the lists of such other doctors and transferred back again if the suspended doctor is reinstated. Provision is made for payments to be made to a suspended doctor. Further, doctors' terms of service are amended to prevent a doctor employing as an assistant or a deputy either a suspended doctor or a doctor who has been disqualified and who is subject to a declaration by the tribunal that he is not fit to be engaged in any capacity in the provision of general medical services. In addition, the list of drugs and other substances which may not be prescribed by general medical practitioners for supply in the course of pharmaceutical services under the National Health Service Act 1977 is amended.

2036   Medical devices—consumer safety

See para 617.

2037   Medical devices—fees

The Medical Devices Fees Regulations 1995, SI 1995/2487 (in force on 17 October 1995), prescribe the fees payable in connection with the services provided by the Department of Health in pursuance of the Secretary of State's functions under Council Directive (EC) 90/385 on the approximation of the laws of member states relating to active implantable medical devices, and Council Directive (EC) 93/42 concerning medical devices.

2038   Medical practitioner—degree of skill and care required—delay in performing Caesarean section

The plaintiff child sued by her mother as next friend for damages for personal injury, loss and damage caused by the alleged negligence of the defendant health authority. In the seventh month of pregnancy the mother had noticed a decrease in foetal movement. She was admitted to hospital for monitoring of the foetal heartbeat. The quality of the traces was poor but the early traces showed some deceleration of heartbeat and there was increasing evidence of abnormalities in later traces. After the seventh test the registrar decided to perform a Caesarean section and the plaintiff was delivered on the fourth day after the mother's admission to hospital. The plaintiff was in a poor condition at birth and suffered severe disability and illness. The plaintiff claimed that, given the evidence of abnormalities on the monitoring tests, any reasonable doctor would have performed the Caesarean section earlier and that the delay in delivery caused or materially contributed to her condition. *Held*, no reasonably competent doctor in the position of the registrar would have acted as he did. The decision to perform a Caesarean section should have been made earlier. There was a delay of between one and a half to two hours which was attributable to the registrar and for which the defendants were vicariously liable. However, most of the damage was probably caused before the three days preceding the birth and could have been caused at any time after the 32nd week of gestation although it was impossible to identify precisely what caused the damage or when it occurred. Thus, while the injuries found to have been suffered at the birth could have made some contribution to the brain damage, on the balance of probabilities they could not have made any material or significant contribution to the final state. Accordingly, the plaintiff's claim would be dismissed.

   Robertson (an infant) v Nottingham Health Authority (1995) 22 BMLR 49 (Queen's Bench Division: Otton J).

2039   Medical practitioner—degree of skill and care required—failure to advise pregnant mother of risks to foetus

Canada
The plaintiff was pregnant when she contracted chicken pox and she asked her physician whether the illness presented any risks to the foetus. The physician failed to tell the plaintiff that there was a small possibility of brain damage. When the child was born she was brain damaged. The physician was found to be negligent and the plaintiff brought an action for damages for the cost of the child's care. At first instance, the trial judge dismissed the action on the ground that the plaintiff would have chosen to carry the foetus to full term even if she had been fully informed of the risk. The judge took into account the risk of abortion and the fact that a therapeutic abortion committee would have had to give permission for an abortion. He also relied on the fact that the pregnancy was carefully planned and that the plaintiff had refused an ultrasound scan. On the plaintiff's appeal, *held*, the finding of the trial judge on causation was not supported by the evidence, and he should not have taken into account factors peculiar to the plaintiff. Accordingly, the appeal would be allowed and a new trial would be held on causation and damages.

   Arndt v Smith (1995) 126 DLR (4th) 705 (British Colombia Court of Appeal).

2040   Medical practitioner—degree of skill and care required—failure to make correct diagnosis

Scotland
A wife brought an action alleging negligence after her husband had died from what appeared to be a minor ailment. He had visited a casualty department and had been diagnosed as suffering from a viral infection and told to contact his doctor if there was any deterioration. The next day his condition was such that he asked a neighbour to telephone his doctor. The doctor made a

diagnosis over the telephone and arranged for a prescription to be prepared for collection. A few hours later an ambulance had to be called. The patient was dead on arrival at hospital. The wife alleged negligence on the grounds that the doctor had failed to recognise that the patient's symptoms merited a house call and that she had not asked questions pertinent enough to discover the nature of those symptoms. *Held*, it was not shown that the doctor's actions differed from those of a reasonably competent doctor. Although there might be a duty to ask further questions for clarification of symptoms, the existence of the duty depended on the particular circumstances of the case and on the individual doctor being satisfied that sufficient information had been disclosed for an informed opinion to be made. Moreover, the condition from which the patient was suffering was so rare that it was unlikely to be encountered in general practice.

Morrison v Forsyth (1994) 23 BMLR 11 (Outer House).

2041 Medical practitioner—degree of skill and care required—failure to recognise risks to child

Scotland

The plaintiffs called a general practitioner out to their son in the early evening. The child had been vomiting over a 30-hour period. His appearance had become sallow and he was unable to walk or stand unaided because his foot had become inverted. The practitioner prescribed an antibiotic and antiemetic but the prescription could not be administered because the child continued to vomit. Another doctor was called out in the early hours of the morning and at that time the child was taken to hospital. On the way, he had a cardiac arrest which caused irreversible brain damage resulting in his death. The plaintiffs brought an action claiming damages for negligence. They alleged that the practitioner who had made the first visit had been negligent in failing to appreciate that the child was at risk of suffering deterioration and failing to arrange for the situation to be reviewed later in the evening. *Held*, the practitioner had been negligent in failing to ensure that further attention be paid to the situation in the event of the prescribed treatment being unsuccessful. Had that happened, the child would have been referred to the hospital earlier and would have arrived there before he had the cardiac arrest which led to his death. Damages would be awarded accordingly.

Fisher v McKenzie (1994) 26 BMLR 98 (Outer House). *Hunter v Hanley* 1995 SLT 213 applied.

2042 Medical practitioner—degree of skill and care required—responsible body of medical opinion

The plaintiff brought an action for medical negligence against two consultant surgeons and at first instance it was decided that they were not negligent, having satisfied the test laid down in *Bolam v Friern Hospital Management Committee*, that they were acting in accordance with a practice accepted as proper by a responsible body of medical men. On the plaintiff's appeal, she claimed that it was implicit in that test that the body in question had to be a substantial body in a quantitative sense. *Held*, the judge had not fallen into error in failing to consider whether the body of surgeons had to be substantial. It was sufficient if he was satisfied that they were a responsible body, however small, and that they would have considered the surgeons' decision justified. Accordingly, the appeal would be dismissed.

De Freitas v O'Brien [1995] PIQR P281 (Court of Appeal: Legatt, Swinton Thomas and Otton LJJ). *Bolam v Friern Hospital Management Committee* [1957] 2 All ER 118, applied. *Hills v Potter* [1983] 3 All ER 716 (1983 Abr para 2444) considered.

2043 Medical practitioner—degree of skill and care required—whether disabilities caused by negligence of obstetrician

The plaintiff was born with brain damage following a protracted labour which resulted in his being born with the use of an extraction instrument and forceps. He claimed that his disabilities were caused by the doctor's use of the extraction instrument, his decision to apply forceps instead of carrying out a caesarian section and his use of untoward force for an untoward length of time. *Held*, the standard of care and skill required in deciding whether there was negligence was that laid down in *Bolam v Friern Hospital Management Committee*: that of the ordinary skilled man having the special skill of an obstetrician at that time. The plaintiff had proved, on the balance of probabilities, that the doctor had failed to act as a reasonable obstetrician would have acted at that time, and that his injuries resulted from the doctor applying an inappropriate amount of force to the extraction instrument and the forceps. The regional health authority were vicariously liable for that negligence.

Townsend v Worcester and District Health Authority (1994) 23 BMLR 31 (Queen's Bench Division: Harrison J). *Bolam v Friern Hospital Management Committee* [1957] 2 All ER 118, applied.

2044 Medical practitioner—disciplinary proceedings—nature of proceedings determined by health care trust

A doctor was employed by a health care trust. Any questions concerning her professional conduct or competence were to be determined by her peers, against which she had a right of appeal. Her contract provided that, in the case of personal misconduct, if the regional medical officer found reasonable grounds to believe there had been misconduct, he was obliged to interview the doctor and could then institute disciplinary proceedings. There was no right of appeal in such a case and it was for the trust to decide under which category a case fell. The trust, believing that there had been personal misconduct, called the doctor to an interview. She was given no details of the allegations and declined to attend. The trust sent her a letter setting out details of her misconduct and informing her that the matters referred to might be viewed as serious misconduct and could result in her dismissal. The doctor applied for an injunction to restrain the trust from proceeding with disciplinary proceedings against her. *Held*, it was for the trust to decide on a common sense basis the essential character of the case in question and which category it should fall into. It was an implied term that in making that decision the trust had to act in good faith and reach a decision which it could reasonably reach. Its decision could not be impugned merely because the doctor or court would have characterised the case differently although, if the court thought the trust intended to determine complaints of professional conduct and competence in proceedings for personal misconduct, it could find that the trust could not reasonably characterise the proceedings in the way it had done. On careful examination of the letter, the court was satisfied that the matters of complaint were to be investigated and determined only so far as they related to and constituted personal misconduct. Further, the contract imposed no requirement that information regarding the subject matter under investigation should be supplied to the doctor before the interview. The application would accordingly be refused.

Kramer v South Bedfordshire Community Health Care Trust [1995] ICR 1066 (Chancery Division: Lightman J).

2045 Medical practitioner—registration—overseas doctor—conditions

The Medical Act 1983, s 25 provides that a person who is or has been registered with limited registration may apply to the General Medical Council to be registered fully and if the council thinks fit so to direct, having regard to the knowledge and skill shown and the experience acquired by the applicant, he may be registered as a fully registered medical practitioner.

A doctor with medical qualifications and experience in India and Malaysia acquired limited registration under the 1983 Act, s 25 which entitled him to practice medicine for a maximum five-year period under supervision. He held a senior house post during that time. His later application for full registration was refused by the General Medical Council (GMC). The doctor successfully applied for the GMC's decision to be quashed, although the judge would not order declaratory relief. On appeal by the GMC, *held*, the 1983 Act made a distinction between the registration of doctors qualifying in the United Kingdom and elsewhere in the European Union and the registration of doctors qualifying overseas. Furthermore, there was a distinction between those with recognised overseas qualifications eligible to full registration immediately and those with acceptable overseas qualifications who were only eligible for limited registration. Only a small number of overseas institutions were subject to regular inspections by the GMC and were recognised for the purpose of full registration. The position with regard to limited registration was entirely different; there were several hundred other institutions with so many wide variations of quality that comparison was impossible. Section 25 laid down no particular or single standard and gave the GMC a wide discretion. The judge at first instance had therefore erred in reading into s 25 an unwarranted assumption that there was a single standard to be measured against an equivalent standard of United Kingdom and European Union qualifiers. Accordingly, the appeal would be allowed.

R v General Medical Council, ex p Virik (1995) 24 BMLR 8 (Court of Appeal: Hirst and Peter Gibson LJJ and Forbes J). Decision of Carnwath J (1995) 24 BMLR 8 reversed.

2046   Medical practitioner—serious professional misconduct—test to be applied to misconduct

As a result of a doctor's diagnosis of three patients and his failure to refer them to hospital, two patients died and the third was admitted to hospital in a serious condition. The professional conduct committee of the General Medical Council found the doctor guilty of serious professional misconduct. In giving reasons for the finding, the chairman stated that the care provided fell deplorably short of the standard patients were entitled to expect. The doctor appealed against the committee's determination, submitting that the wrong test had been applied to determine what amounted to serious professional misconduct. He claimed that such misconduct could not be determined simply by deciding whether the treatment measured up to an objective standard. *Held*, in *Doughty v General Dental Council* [1987] 3 All ER 843, PC (1987 Abr para 1673) it was held that misconduct was to be judged by proper professional standards in the light of the objective facts about the individual patients. That test was equally applicable to treatment by doctors. Once it was accepted that seriously negligent treatment could amount to serious professional misconduct the present appeal had to fail. The committee had come to the conclusion that the doctor's treatment of his three patients fell deplorably short of the standard patients were entitled to expect and, in the circumstances, it was scarcely surprising that the committee concluded that the doctor was guilty of serious professional misconduct. There was no basis for interfering with the committee's conclusion and, accordingly, the appeal would be dismissed.

McCandless v General Medical Council [1996] 1 WLR 167 (Privy Council: Lords Goff of Chieveley, Nicholls of Birkenhead and Hoffmann).

2047   Medical (Professional Performance) Act 1995

The Medical (Professional Performance) Act 1995 amends the Medical Act 1983 to make provision relating to the professional performance of registered medical practitioners and the voluntary removal of names from the register of medical practitioners. The Act received the royal assent on 8 November 1995 and comes into force on a day or days to be appointed. For details of commencement, see the commencement table in the title STATUTES.

Section 1 inserts s 36A into the 1983 Act and provides that where the Committee on Professional Performance finds that a doctor's standard of professional performance is seriously deficient, it may impose conditions on or suspend the doctor's registration. Subject to specified conditions, the committee is empowered to review, extend, revoke or vary any such direction for suspension or for conditional registration. The doctor concerned must be served with a notification of the direction or variation and of his right to appeal against the decision. Section 2 inserts s 31A into the 1983 Act and empowers the General Medical Council to make regulations to enable the registrar to remove, and subsequently restore, a doctor from the Medical Register at the doctor's request. It may also make provision requiring any such restoration to be subject to its approval or the approval of one of its statutory committees.

Section 3 together with the Schedule contain supplementary and consequential amendments, principally to the 1983 Act. Provision is made for the establishment of the Assessment Referral Committee and the Committee on Professional Performance, and for the carrying out of assessments of professional performance by assessment panels. Various powers are given to assessment panels to inspect records relating to the doctor's professional performance and, having obtained a warrant, to enter and search premises. It is an offence to obstruct the exercise of such powers. Sections 5, 6 deal with interpretation, commencement and extent.

2048   Medicinal products—animal feeding stuffs

The Medicines (Medicated Animal Feeding Stuffs) (Amendment) Regulations 1995, SI 1995/799 (in force on 7 April 1995), further amend the 1992 Regulations, SI 1992/1520, by (1) replacing the fees payable in respect of the entry or retention in, or restoration to, the Register of Manufacturers of Animal Feeding Stuffs, and (2) prescribing 1 July in every year as the latest date by which a certified copy of the register has to be supplied to the minister and 1 June in the year in question as the latest date by which it must be certified as being a true copy of the register.

2049   Medicinal products—animal use—applications for licences and certificates and marketing authorisations—fees

The Medicines (Products for Animal Use-Fees) Regulations 1995, SI 1995/2364 (in force on 29 September 1995), replace the 1994 Regulations, SI 1994/1554. They prescribe fees in connection with applications and inspections relating to marketing authorisations granted under the Marketing Authorisations for Veterinary Medicinal Products Regulations 1994, SI 1994/3142, and licences and certificates granted under the Medicines Act 1968 insofar as they apply to medicinal products for animal use.

2050 Medicinal products—fixing of fees

The Medicines (Fixing of Fees Relating to Medicinal Products for Human Use) Amendment Order 1995, SI 1995/871 (in force on 1 April 1995), amends the 1989 Order, SI 1989/684, so as to take account of the disestablishment of the Committee on Review of Medicines by the Medicines (Committee on the Review of Medicines) (Revocation) Order 1992, SI 1992/606, and the Committee on Dental and Surgical Materials by the Medicines (Committee on Dental and Surgical Materials) (Revocation) Order 1994, SI 1994/3120. SI 1989/684 is also extended so that, in fixing fees under the Medicines Act 1971, account is taken of the functions of the licensing authority under the Medicines for Human Use (Marketing Authorisations Etc) Regulations 1994, SI 1994/3144, and of persons appointed under Sch 2 to those regulations and of functions relating to the enforcement of those regulations.

2051 Medicinal products—general sale list—products other than veterinary drugs

The Medicines (Products Other Than Veterinary Drugs) (General Sale List) Amendment Order 1995, SI 1995/3216 (in force on 1 January 1996), further amends the 1984 Order, SI 1984/769, which specifies the class of medicinal products which can be sold or supplied otherwise than by or under the supervision of a pharmacist. The order amends the list of medicinal products, other than products the subject of a product licence of right, on general sale, inserts entries into the list of medicinal products for internal or external use and amends the list of such products for external use only.

2052 Medicinal products—homoeopathic medicinal products—advisory board on registration

The Medicines (Advisory Board on the Registration of Homoeopathic Products) Order 1995, SI 1995/309 (in force on 20 February 1995), replaces the 1994 Order, SI 1994/102. The order makes new provision for the establishment of the Advisory Board on the Registration of Homoeopathic Products, clarifying the purposes for which the board is established, namely, for giving advice with respect to the safety and quality of any homoeopathic medicinal product which meets specified conditions set out in the order and any homoeopathic medicinal product which satisfies the conditions set out in Council Directive (EC) 92/74 and to which any relevant provision of the Medicines Act 1968 applies.

2053 Medicinal products—homoeopathic medicinal products—certificates of registration

The Medicines (Homoeopathic Medicinal Products for Human Use) Amendment Regulations 1995, SI 1995/541 (in force on 1 April 1995), further amend the 1994 Regulations, SI 1994/105, as follows: (1) to exclude from the duty on licensing authorities to consult the Advisory Board on the Registration of Homoeopathic Products the case where a refusal of a certificate is required by virtue of the 1994 Regulations, reg 5(2)(c) on the ground that the product has an insufficient degree of dilution within the meaning of reg 5(3); and (2) to amend the fees in respect of applications for the grant of, and for variations of, certificates under the 1994 Regulations.

2054 Medicinal products—human use—fees

The Medicines (Products for Human Use-Fees) Regulations 1995, SI 1995/1116 (in force on 21 April 1995), replace the 1991 Regulations, SI 1991/1474, as amended. They make provision for the fees payable under the Medicines Act 1971 in respect of marketing authorisations, licences and certificates relating to medicinal products for human use. Provision is made for capital fees to be payable in connection with applications for, or variations to, authorisations, licences or certificates and associated inspections. A new fee category is introduced in relation to applications for marketing authorisations in respect of which recognition is sought of any authorisation already granted by another member state. In addition a new scheme for the classification of fees for variations to authorisations is imposed. Periodic fees of varying amounts are imposed in connection with the holding of certain authorisations and licences. Administrative provisions deal with time of payments and waiver or refund of capital and periodic fees in specified circumstances. Special arrangements are provided in respect of the time of payment of capital fees by small companies and a new concession is introduced in respect of small companies which make complex applications for marketing authorisations.

2055 Medicinal products—labelling—expiry dates

See *EC Commission v Germany*, para 3133.

2056 Medicinal products—presentation

See *Ter Voort*, para 3122.

2057 Medicinal products—sale or supply

The Medicines (Sale or Supply) (Miscellaneous Provisions) Amendment Regulations 1995, SI 1995/3215 (in force on 1 January 1996), further amend the 1980 Regulations, SI 1980/1923, which limit the pack size on retail sale or supply of certain medicinal products on a general sale list. Provision is made for ibuprofen and clotrimazole, which are medicinal products for human use on the general sale list, to be sold or supplied by retail elsewhere than at a registered pharmacy in certain containers or packages which do not contain more than specified amounts of the product.

2058 Medicines—administration of radioactive substances

The Medicines (Administration of Radioactive Substances) Amendment Regulations 1995, SI 1995/2147 (in force on 11 September 1995), amend the 1978 Regulations, SI 1978/1006, which prohibit the administration of radioactive medicinal products except by doctors or dentists holding prescribed certificates or by persons acting under their directions. The 1995 Regulations make provision for: (1) directions and notices to be given in writing; (2) the grant of further certificates to doctors or dentists holding certificates, to authorise the administration of descriptions or classes of radioactive substances for diagnosis or treatment specified in the certificates; (3) the administration of such products under further certificates; (4) the giving of written particulars regarding the suspension, revocation or variation of certificates; (5) the cessation of certain procedural requirements where certificates are varied.

2059 Medicines—advertisements and representations—relevant medicinal product

The Medicines Act 1968 (Amendment) Regulations 1995, SI 1995/2321 (in force on 29 September 1995), add the 1968 Act, s 96(7) which provides that s 96 does not apply in relation to any medicinal product governed by the provisions of the Medicines (Advertising) Regulations 1994, SI 1994/1932, for which there is required to be in existence a summary of product characteristics, as defined in the 1994 Regulations, reg 2.

2060 Medicines—licences—exemptions—clinical trials

The Medicines (Exemption from Licences) (Clinical Trials) Order 1995, SI 1995/2808 (in force on 8 December 1995), amends the 1981 Order, SI 1981/164, and grants exemption from the restrictions on dealings in medicinal products imposed by the Medicines Act 1968, s 7. The exemption applies to selling, supplying, or procuring the sale, supply, manufacture or assembly of, a medicinal product for the purposes of a clinical trial, and is subject to conditions and limitations. The supplier must notify the licensing authority of his intention to sell or supply or procure the sale, supply, manufacture or assembly of specified medicinal products for the purposes of a clinical trial and give (1) particulars relating to the trial, including summaries of pharmaceutical data and of reports made and tests performed in relation to the medicinal products to be used; (2) a certificate signed by a medical adviser employed by, or a consultant to, the supplier as to the accuracy of the summaries and stating that in his opinion it is reasonable for the proposed trial to be undertaken; and (3) a notice containing certain information relating to usage, including the name of the medicinal product, a description of each clinical use to be investigated, details of the patients (including selection criteria) on whom the trials will be conducted, and a description of the safety procedure to be adopted. The supplier must also undertake to inform the licensing authority immediately of (1) any adverse reactions or effects associated with administration of the product that are both serious and unexpected, or any other matter which might reasonably cause the product to be regarded as unsafe for the purposes of the trial; (2) any changes in the matters specified in his notice; and (3) any refusal to approve the trial by a health committee or board or the Medical Research Council. The licensing authority may, within an extendable period of 35 days after acknowledging receipt of the supplier's notice, notify the supplier that the exemption is not to apply to the proposed trial. Otherwise, the exemption takes effect on the expiry of that period and continues for a period of 3 years unless terminated by notice sent by the authority to the supplier. The order also provides the conditions and limitations to which the Medicines (Exemption from Licences and Certificates) (Clinical Trials) Order 1995, SI 1995/2809, is subject.

The Medicines (Exemption from Licences and Certificates) (Clinical Trials) Order 1995, SI 1995/2809 (in force on 8 December 1995), replaces the 1981 Order, SI 1981/164, and grants exemption from the restrictions on dealings in medicinal products imposed by the Medicines Act 1968, s 31(2). The exemption applies to selling, supplying, or procuring the sale, supply, manufacture or assembly of a medicinal product for the purposes of a clinical trial, and is subject to certain conditions and limitations contained in the Medicines (Exemption from Licences) (Clinical Trials) Order 1995 supra.

2061   Medicines—prescription only drugs

The Medicines (Products Other Than Veterinary Drugs) (Prescription Only) Amendment Order 1995, SI 1995/1384 (in force on 30 June 1995), further amends the 1983 Order, SI 1983/1212, so as to exclude from the categories of prescription only medicines certain products containing specified substances, to amend the list of substances which render a medicinal product a prescription only medicine except in certain circumstances, to amend the list of medicinal products specified by name and product licence number that are prescription only medicines and to amend the list of medicinal products specified by name and product licence number that are not prescription only medicines.

The Medicines (Products Other Than Veterinary Drugs) (Prescription Only) Amendment (No 2) Order 1995, SI 1995/3174 (in force on 29 December 1995), further amends the 1983 Order, SI 1983/1212, which specifies descriptions and classes of prescription only medicines which are included in a class of such medicines by reason of the substances contained in them, subject to their being excluded in certain specified circumstances. The order (1) makes amendments relating to interpretation, (2) extends the exclusion for products containing beclomethasone dipropionate, (3) introduces a new exclusion for products containing budesonide, and (4) adds to the list of substances which render a medicinal product a prescription only medicine.

2062   Nurses, midwives and health visitors—periodic registration

The Nurses, Midwives and Health Visitors (Periodic Registration) Amendment Rules Approval Order 1995, SI 1995/967 (in force on 1 April 1995), approves rules made by the United Kingdom Central Council for Nursing, Midwifery and Health Visiting. The rules amend the 1983 Order, SI 1983/873, making provision for renewal of registration, continuing registration and return to practice courses.

2063   Pharmacies—application for registration and fees

The Medicines (Pharmacies) (Applications for Registration and Fees) Amendment Regulations 1995, SI 1995/3029 (in force on 1 January 1996), further amend the 1973 Regulations, SI 1973/1822, so as to increase the fees for registration of premises at which a retail pharmacy business is, or is to be, carried on, the subsequent annual, or retention, fees and the penalty for failure to pay retention fees. SI 1994/2936 is revoked.

2064   Pharmacies—pharmaceutical lists—application for inclusion on list—minor relocation

The National Health Service (Pharmaceutical Services) Regulations 1992, SI 1992/662, reg 4(3)(a) provides that where an applicant intends to change within the neighbourhood the premises from which he provides pharmaceutical services, being the same services as he intends to provide from the new premises, and the Family Health Services Authority ('the FHSA') is satisfied that the change is a minor relocation and that the provision of pharmaceutical services will not be interrupted, the application must be granted by the FHSA.

The applicants sought judicial review of the respondent health authority's decision to allow three pharmacists to move their premises to new locations. In each case, the relocations would have involved the pharmacists being situated near to the applicants' pharmacies. The application was dismissed. On appeal, *held*, the scheme created by the 1992 Regulations was intended to protect the interests of those who might need to use pharmaceutical services. The words 'minor relocation' in reg 4(3) meant exactly what they said, and it was therefore a question of geography and topography whether a move from one location to another was a minor one. In deciding that issue, a FHSA was not obliged to take into consideration as a material factor the effect that such a move might have on competing pharmacies, as the regulation said nothing about commercial competition. In the instant case, the FHSA had been entitled to conclude that the proposed moves amounted to minor relocations and, accordingly, the appeal would be dismissed.

R v Yorkshire Regional Health Authority, ex p Suri; R v Yorkshire Regional Health Authority, ex p Gompels (1995) Times, 5 December (Court of Appeal: Russell and Thorpe LJJ, and Sir Ralph Gibson). Decision of Popplewell J (1994) Times, 15 August (1994 Abr para 1943) affirmed.

2065 Service committees and tribunal—procedure

The National Health Service (Service Committees and Tribunal) Amendment Regulations 1995, SI 1995/3091 (in force on 21 December 1995), further amend the 1992 Regulations, SI 1992/664, as follows: (1) provision is made for the appointment of a deputy chairman of the tribunal; (2) the rights of appeal to the Secretary of State against the tribunal's decisions and applications to him for the lifting of any disqualification directed to the tribunal are abolished; (3) provision is made for the procedure relating to applications for interim suspension and for continuation of suspension pending appeal; (4) practice directions may be given by the tribunal's chairman; (5) amendments relating to costs, evidence, witnesses and referral of matters to professional bodies are made; (6) provision in relation to the suspension of practitioners only applies to doctors and dentists.

2066 Veterinary drugs—pharmacy and merchants' list

The Medicines (Veterinary Drugs) (Pharmacy and Merchants' List) (Amendment) Order 1995, SI 1995/3193 (in force on 1 January 1996), further amends the 1992 Order, SI 1992/33, so as to (1) alter the fees payable on registration, retention of registration and restoration of registration of agricultural merchants and saddlers under the 1992 Order, and (2) make amendments which take account of product licences or marketing authorisations granted, withdrawn or expired since 3 January 1995.

MENTAL HEALTH

Halsbury's Laws of England (4th edn) Vol 30 (reissue), paras 1001–1305

2067 Articles

Community Care: Duties Towards Mentally Ill People, David Fish: LA, November 1995, p 20
Delaying Discharge Under the Mental Health Act 1983, Rabinder Singh: LA, June 1995, p 16
Force Feeding and the Mental Health Act 1983, Phil Fennell: 145 NLJ 319
Hospital Orders Without Conviction, Alec Samuels: [1995] Crim LR 220
The Law Commission Proposals on Mental Incapacity, Philip Fennell: [1995] Fam Law 420
Making Provision for the Mentally Disabled, Francis Fitzpatrick: Tax Journal, Issue 317, p 8
Medical Treatment and Mental Incapacity, Julie Stone: 139 SJ 267
The Mentally Disordered Suspect at the Police Station, Judith Laing: [1995] Crim LR 371
On Mental Incapacity, Derek Morgan (on the Law Commission's Report on Mental Incapacity):
   145 NLJ 352
Sentencing Policy and Mentally Abnormal Offenders, Ralph Henham: Criminal Lawyer, Issue
   60, p 4
Supervision Registers for Mentally Disordered People, Terry Thomas: 145 NLJ 565
Wills and the Mentally Disabled Beneficiary, Gordon Ashton: 145 NLJ 1578

2068 Carers (Recognition and Services) Act 1995

See para 2118.

2069 Hospital order—powers of justices to make order

See *R v Chippenham Magistrates' Court, ex p Thompson*, para 2010.

2070 Mental Health Act Commission—management board

The Mental Health Act Commission (Amendment) Regulations 1995, SI 1995/2630 (in force on 1 November 1995), amend the 1983 Regulations, SI 1983/894, so as to provide for the appointment of a management committee of the Mental Health Act Commission in place of the central policy committee. The committee is to be known as the Management Board and provision is made in respect of its membership and proceedings.

2071 Mental Health (Patients in the Community) Act 1995

The Mental Health (Patients in the Community) Act 1995 makes provision in respect of mentally disordered patients who are to be released from detention in hospital, and in respect of patients who are absent without leave or on leave of absence from hospital. The Act received the royal assent on 8 November 1995 and comes into force on a day or days to be appointed. For details of commencement, see the commencement table in the title STATUTES.

Section 1 inserts ss 25A–25J into the Mental Health Act 1983. It introduces new arrangements for the supervision of mentally disordered patients aged 16 years or over, who are to be released into the community after detention in hospital for treatment. An application may be made for a patient to be supervised by a nominated supervisor upon his release. The supervisor's role is to secure that he receives the after-care services to be provided to him by the responsible health authority or local authority under the 1983 Act, s 117. Subject to certain exceptions, the provisions apply to patients on leaving hospital or at the end of any period of leave of absence. A supervision application is made by the patient's responsible medical officer ('RMO'), and must be addressed to the health authority responsible for the after-care under s 117. The RMO must be satisfied that there would be a substantial risk of serious harm to the safety of the patient or other persons, or of his being seriously exploited, if he were not to receive such after-care. Certain interested parties, including the patient, must be consulted prior to and on acceptance of the application. A patient, who is subject to after-care under supervision, may be required to reside at a specified place or to attend a place for the purpose of medical treatment, occupation, education or training.

Where a patient refuses to receive any of the after-care services, or does not comply with any requirement, the responsible authority must review the services provided for him under s 117. It must also consider whether it would be appropriate to re-admit him to hospital for further treatment under the 1983 Act. The authority may, upon certain conditions being satisfied, modify the after-care services provided.

A patient, who is subject to after-care supervision, is so subject for the period beginning when he leaves hospital and ending six months after the supervision application is accepted. The period is renewable, initially for six months and thereafter from year to year. The RMO may direct at any time that a patient's after-care should cease. Alternatively a patient may apply to a Mental Health Review Tribunal to end supervision. The Act also makes provision in relation to mentally disordered persons who are subject to community care orders in Scotland and intend to take up residence in England and Wales. Schedule 1 contains supplemental provisions in respect of after-care under supervision.

Section 2 replaces the 1983 Act, s 18(4), which deals with patients who are absent without leave from hospital. It alters the period within which such a patient may be taken into custody and returned to hospital. The period is extended either to six months after the date on which the patient absconded or to the end of the existing authority for his detention or guardianship, whichever is the later date. Section 21 is also replaced and ss 21A, B are inserted. The new provisions extend by up to one week the authority for detention or guardianship of the patient after his return. The authority for detention may also be renewed. A patient who is taken into custody or returns more than 28 days after absconding must be reassessed within seven days of his return to ascertain whether his detention or guardianship is still warranted.

Section 3 amends the 1983 Act, s 17(5) and removes the six-month limit on the period for which leave of absence may be granted to detained patients. Under the supervision of his RMO, a detained patient may be released on leave of absence for a maximum of one year before his liability to be detained under the 1983 Act ends.

Sections 4 to 6 and Sch 2 make equivalent provision for Scotland. Section 7 relates to the short title, commencement and extent of the Act.

2072 Mental incapacity—decision-making procedures—Law Commission proposals

The Law Commission has published a report, *Mental Incapacity* (HC 189; Law Com No 231), on the making of decisions on behalf of persons who are unable to make decisions for themselves. The report states that the law as it stands at present is unsystematic and 'full of glaring gaps'; it does not rest on clear or modern foundations of principle, and has failed to keep up with social and demographic changes. The commission recommends that the existing law should be replaced by a single body of legislation and that it should be complemented by codes of practice. There should be a presumption against any lack of capacity and any question as to capacity should be determined on a balance of probabilities. The legislation would provide for the circumstances in which a person would be deemed to be without capacity at a particular time. Anything which was done on behalf of a person who lacked capacity should be done in the 'best interests' of that person; the factors to be taken into account in determining what are the best interests of that person are described. The legislation would provide a 'general authority to act' under which it would be lawful to do anything for the personal welfare or health care of a person who was without capacity in relation to the matter in question if it was, in all the circumstances, reasonable for it to have been done by the person who did it. Where reasonable actions for the personal welfare or health care of the person lacking capacity cost money, the person who took the action would be entitled to be reimbursed by the other person and certain payments due to the person lacking capacity might be made, under a statutory scheme, to a person acting on his behalf. Certain restrictions would, however, be placed on the power to act for another under a general authority and it would be an offence for any person to ill-treat or neglect a person in relation to whom he had powers under the proposed legislation. Express provision would be made for 'advance refusals of treatment', as defined. In the absence of indication to the contrary, an advance refusal of treatment might be overridden by the persons having care over the person who made it if the refusal would endanger that person's life, or, in the case of a pregnant woman, that of the foetus. An advance refusal which was in writing, signed and witnessed would be presumed to be valid, but would be subject to alteration or withdrawal. The concealment or destruction of an advance refusal with intent to deceive would be an offence. The authorisation of the court would be necessary before a person lacking capacity was given certain treatment or certain medical procedures were applied; in some cases a certificate from an independent medical practitioner would be necessary. The discontinuation of artificial nutrition and hydration of a patient who was unconscious, had no activity in the cerebral cortex and no prospect of recovery would be lawful in certain circumstances, provided that the decision was taken with due regard to the best interests of the patient. Enduring powers of attorney would be replaced by a statutory form of continuing powers of attorney, which would be registrable. A continuing power of attorney would enable a donee to make and implement decisions on behalf of the donor which the latter was without capacity to make. The power might include matters relating to the donor's personal welfare, health care and property and affairs. The donee of such a power would have to act in the donor's best interests and would not be able to give or refuse consent to treatment unless the donor lacked the requisite capacity, and would not be able to consent to the donor's admission to hospital for assessment or treatment for mental disorder against the donor's wishes. A number of restrictions would be applied to the matters in respect of which the donee's consent could be given under a continuing power of attorney. The donor's bankruptcy would only revoke such part of the power as related to property and financial affairs. The scope of a donee's powers under a continuing power of attorney would be subject to extension or restriction by the court. The court would be given express power to make a declaration in relation to the capacity of a person and in relation to the validity/applicability of an advance refusal of treatment. Apart from itself making any decision on behalf of a person who lacked capacity to make such decision, the court would also be empowered to appoint a manager to make a decision or decisions on behalf of a person who lacked capacity, but the powers conferred on a manager would be limited in scope and duration; any manager would be subject to the supervision of the Public Trustee. The court's powers would cover a wide range of matters, eg where a person who lacked capacity should live, restrictions on contact with such a person, obtaining statutory benefits, and the approval of health care; but the court would not be able to approve the withholding of basic care nor any treatment refused by an advance refusal of treatment. The court's powers over the property and affairs of a person who lacked capacity would include the control and management of property, the acquisition and disposal of property, carrying on a business, dissolution of a partnership, carrying out a contract, discharging a debt or obligation, making a settlement of property, making a will and exercising powers vested in the person concerned. Local authorities would be put under a duty, where they had reason to believe that a vulnerable person, as defined, in their area was suffering, or was likely to suffer, significant harm, as defined, or serious exploitation, to make necessary inquiries to enable them to decide whether the person was in fact so suffering, or likely so to suffer and, if so, whether community care services should be provided or arranged. Authorised officers of local authorities would have powers to enter and inspect premises where vulnerable persons were believed to be at risk and to interview them in private. Vulnerable persons would be assessable by local authorities to determine whether they were at risk and temporary protection orders would be available on application to the court authorising the removal of persons to protective accommodation, only for the shortest possible time. The existing office of the Supreme Court known as the Court of Protection would be abolished. A new superior court of record, to be known as the 'Court of Protection', would be established, with its own President; it would be able to sit anywhere in England and Wales. The division of proceedings between different kinds of judges, High Court judges, circuit judges and district judges, would be made by order. A draft Bill, the Mental Incapacity Bill, which would give effect to the Law Commission's proposals, is appended to the report.

2073 Patient—admission to hospital for assessment—patient's refusal to stay in hospital after assessment—second application for admission for assessment

Under the Mental Health Act 1983, s 2(4) a patient admitted to hospital in pursuance of an application for admission for assessment may be detained for a period not exceeding 28 days but may not be detained after the expiration of that period unless, before it has expired, he has become liable to be detained by virtue of a subsequent application, order or direction under the Act.

A social services department applied to have the applicant, who suffered from paranoid schizophrenia, admitted to hospital for assessment under the 1983 Act, s 2. During the 28-day period a consultant psychiatrist recommended that the applicant should remain in hospital for treatment. He was considered too dangerous to be released. The applicant refused to consent to stay and his nearest relative objected to the applicant's detention for treatment under the 1983 Act, s 3. The department therefore needed to make an application under s 29 for an order directing that the functions of the nearest relative should be exercisable by another person, and then apply under s 3 for the applicant's detention for treatment. However, the department considered that prompt action should be taken and it therefore applied for another s 2 order for the applicant's detention. *Held*, s 2(4) excluded the possibility of a second s 2 admission being applied for during the currency of the first. A s 2 order was intended to be of short duration for a limited purpose and there was nothing in the Act which justified successive applications under the section. The powers under s 2 were not intended for the purpose of further detaining a patient for the purposes of assessment beyond the 28-day period or to be used as a stop-gap procedure. Accordingly, the decision to refuse to discharge the applicant was unlawful.

R v Wilson, ex p Williamson (1995) Independent, 19 April (Queen's Bench Division: Tucker J).

2074 Patient—appointment of foreign curator—jurisdiction of English court

S was a Norwegian who lived in England with A in a house registered in A's name. He suffered a disabling stroke and was admitted to a private hospital near A's house. A was given power of attorney by S to deal with a number of his business affairs. S's son attempted to remove his father from the hospital and take him back to Norway but A secured an injunction to restrain the son from doing so. The Norwegian court appointed a guardian of S, and A subsequently applied to the court for a declaration that it would be unlawful to remove S from the jurisdiction because it would not be in his best interests to do so. At the hearing, the question arose as to the effect in English law of the appointment of the Norwegian guardian who obtained leave to become a party to the proceedings. *Held*, the jurisdiction of the English court to decide upon the legality of any proposed action by way of declaratory or other relief in relation to the care of an incapable adult person was based upon that person's presence within the jurisdiction whatever his or her nationality or domicile. The appointment of a curator or guardian in the country of the incapable person's nationality or domicile, even if that appointment was valid under the laws of that country, did not displace the jurisdiction of the English court to determine what course of action was in the best interests of the person concerned. However, in the absence of any international agreement relating to the case of mentally incapacitated adults, the courts had to consider the comity of nations in approaching the question of what would be in the best interests of such a person in the future, not only in relation to his assets but also in relation to his person, and had to start from the assumption that it would be better for a person in the position of S to be returned to his country of domicile, the burden of proof being on those who asserted to the contrary. On the facts and taking into account all the relevant circumstances, including as far as was known S's own wishes and intentions before he suffered his incapacitating stroke, it was in the best interests of S that he return to Norway. Accordingly, the plaintiff's application would be refused and a declaration would be made in favour of the validly appointed foreign curator.

Re S (Hospital Patient: Foreign Curator) (No 2) [1995] 4 All ER 30 (Family Division: Hale J).
See also *Re S (Hospital Patient: Court's Jurisdiction)*, para 2025.

2075   Patient—detention of patient—procedure for renewal

The Mental Health Act 1983, s 20(8) provides that, where a report is duly furnished, the authority for detention or guardianship of a patient must be renewed for a prescribed period.

The applicant was detained under the Mental Health Act 1983, s 3. Her detention was renewed for two further periods of six months under the 1983 Act, s 20. On both occasions the renewal report was furnished before the expiry of the current period but the hospital managers did not consider it until after that period had expired. Proceedings were begun to determine whether it was lawful to force-feed the patient and these were adjourned to enable her to challenge the lawfulness of her detention by way of judicial review and habeas corpus. *Held*, the language of s 20 was clear. It required that the report be completed and delivered to the managers. It was not necessary for the report to be considered by the managers before the renewal took place. Accordingly, the detention was lawful and the appeal would be dismissed.

R v Managers of Warlingham Park Hospital, ex p B (1994) 22 BMLR 1 (Court of Appeal: Sir Thomas Bingham MR, Staughton and Kennedy LJJ). For earlier related proceedings, see *B v Croydon Health Authority* (1994) 22 BMLR 13, CA (1994 Abr para 1955).

2076   Patient—detention of patient—unlawful detention

The applicant was admitted to and detained in hospital under the Mental Health Act 1983, s 3, pursuant to an application for treatment made by an approved social worker. The social worker stated on the application form that the applicant's nearest relative was his mother, that he had consulted her, and that she did not object to the application. Having been detained in hospital and then placed on home leave, the applicant unsuccessfully applied for a writ of habeas corpus. On appeal, *held*, the social worker knew at the time that he applied for the applicant's admission and detention that the applicant's nearest relative was in fact his father, that the father objected to the application, and also that the father had not delegated his role as nearest relative to the applicant's mother. As such, the social worker's statement on the application form was entirely false, and it followed that the applicant's detention was unlawful. Judicial review was not an appropriate remedy, as the object of the applicant's application was not to overturn an administrative decision but to show that there had never been any jurisdiction to detain him. As the social worker's application appeared to comply with the requirements of the 1983 Act, the hospital managers had been entitled to detain the applicant, but the detention was nevertheless unlawful. Habeas corpus was therefore an appropriate remedy and, accordingly, the appeal would be allowed.

Re S-C (Mental Patient: Habeas Corpus) [1996] 1 All ER 532 (Court of Appeal: Sir Thomas Bingham MR, Neill and Hirst LJJ). *R v Secretary of State for the Home Department, ex p Muboyayi* [1991] 4 All ER 72, CA (1991 Abr para 1328) followed.

2077   Patient—medical treatment—order for treatment without consent—costs—award of costs against health authority

When an order was made regarding the force-feeding of an applicant who was held under the Mental Health Act 1983, it was further ordered that the health authority should pay a proportion of the Official Solicitor's costs. The applicant's appeal against the substantive order was unsuccessful. The authority then sought a variation of the costs order, arguing that it should not pay the Official Solicitor's costs because the proceedings had not been brought by the authority and because it was not in the public interest that parties should be deterred from seeking declarations in difficult cases by costs considerations. *Held*, the issue of costs in such circumstances was a matter for the discretion of the judge, who had not erred, and the appeal against his decision would be dismissed. However, as regards the Court of Appeal costs, it was just and equitable that these be paid out of public funds. The applicant would pay the authority's costs, which would be assessed at nil since the applicant was legally aided. The balance of the Court of Appeal costs, and in effect the whole of the costs in that court, would be paid by the Legal Aid Board.

LB v Croydon District Health Authority (No 2) [1995] 3 FCR 44 (Court of Appeal: Neill, Hoffmann and Henry LJJ). *Northampton Area Health Authority v The Official Solicitor and the Governors of St Andrews Hospital* [1994] 2 FCR 206, CA (1994 Abr para 2191) followed.

2078   Patient—restricted patient—conditional discharge—date of discharge

Under the Mental Health Act 1983, s 75(2) where a restricted patient has been conditionally discharged but has not been recalled to hospital he may apply to a mental health review tribunal in the period between the expiration of 12 months and the expiration of 2 years beginning with the date on which he was conditionally discharged and in any subsequent period of 2 years.

Following his conviction for wounding with intent, the applicant was detained in hospital under the 1983 Act as a restricted patient. A mental health review tribunal directed the applicant's conditional discharge and he left hospital seven months later. Eight months after leaving the hospital, he applied under s 75(2) to be absolutely discharged. The tribunal would not accept the application because it believed it to be premature. On an application for judicial review of that decision, it fell to be determined whether the words 'conditionally discharged' in s 75(2) crystallised at the time of the original decision to conditionally discharge the applicant or only at the time of his actual release from hospital. *Held*, s 75(1) and (2) postulated a patient conditionally discharged and a patient recalled to hospital. That use of words made it plain that 'conditionally discharged' related to the period following release from hospital. A restricted patient in hospital had the right to apply for review more frequently than a patient who had been conditionally discharged and the purpose of that distinction was that a patient conditionally discharged had to prove his social integration before he sought absolute discharge. That could only be achieved if the patient was actually released and living in the community. Therefore, for the purpose of calculating time in s 75(2) 'conditionally discharged' meant the date of actual release from hospital and not any earlier date when a decision was made that a restricted patient be discharged subject to conditions being met. Accordingly, the application would be dismissed.

R v Canons Park Mental Health Review Tribunal, ex p Martins (1995) Times, 13 June (Queen's Bench Division: Ognall J).

2079　Patient—restricted patient—conditions for making restriction order

The appellant was arrested after he kicked a young woman who was walking in a street. He pleaded guilty to assault occasioning actual bodily harm and was committed to the Crown Court for sentencing under the provisions of the Mental Health Act 1983. Three psychiatric reports recommended that a hospital order under the 1983 Act, s 37 should be made in respect of the appellant. Only one psychiatrist felt that the appellant's previous history warranted a s 41 restriction order, limited in time, to protect the public from serious harm. The appellant was sentenced to a hospital order and a restriction order without limit of time. On appeal against the restriction order, *held*, it was not necessary to wait until someone was seriously injured before making a restriction order. Under s 41, the court had to judge whether an order was necessary to protect the public from serious harm having regard to the nature of the offence, the antecedents of the offender and the risk of his committing further offences if set at large. In the present case, the assault had been unprovoked and directed at a wholly unsuspecting member of the public, and it had been necessary to make the order. Further, the court had been right to impose the order without limit of time. To put a limit on the order would have been unwise unless there was some foundation in the medical evidence for saying that the patient could be cured within a particular period. Accordingly, the appeal would be dismissed.

R v Nwohia (1995) 26 BMLR 157 (Court of Appeal: Pill LJ and Buckley J). *R v Gardiner* [1967] 1 All ER 895, CA, considered.

MINES, MINERALS AND QUARRIES

Halsbury's Laws of England (4th edn) Vol 31, paras 1–1000

2080　Coal Industry Act 1994—commencement

The Coal Industry Act 1994 (Commencement No 4) Order 1995, SI 1995/159, brings into force on 31 January 1995 s 24, which abolishes the Domestic Coal Consumers' Council.

The Coal Industry Act 1994 (Commencement No 5) Order 1995, SI 1995/273, brings into force on 1 March 1995 certain repeals in Sch 11, Pt III.

The Coal Industry Act 1994 (Commencement No 6) and Membership of the British Coal Corporation (Appointed Day) Order 1995, SI 1995/1507, appoints 30 June 1995 for the purposes of s 23(1) (relating to the membership of the corporation) and brings certain related repeals into force on the same date.

For a summary of the Act, see 1994 Abr para 1968. For details of commencement, see the commencement table in the title STATUTES.

2081   Coal industry—British Coal Corporation—extinguishment of liabilities

The Coal Industry Act 1994 (British Coal Corporation) Extinguishment of Loans Order 1995, SI 1995/509 (in force on 25 March 1995), is made under the Coal Industry Act 1994, s 20, which gives the Secretary of State power to extinguish the liabilities of the British Coal Corporation to make repayments of capital and payments of interest in respect of sums lent to them out of money provided by Parliament under the Coal Industry Act 1980, s 2. The order extinguishes the liabilities of the British Coal Corporation to make repayments of capital of £1,598,400,000 and payments of interest of £34,466,803.

2082   Coal industry—British Coal Corporation—quorum

The British Coal Corporation (Change of Quorum) Regulations 1995, SI 1995/1506 (in force on 30 June 1995), amend the 1946 Regulations, SI 1946/1094, reg 4 by substituting a quorum of three for the quorum of five required under reg 4. In addition, certain references to the deputy chairman are deleted.

2083   Coal Industry—Domestic Coal Consumers' Council—abolition

The Coal Industry (Abolition of Domestic Coal Consumers' Council) Order 1995, SI 1995/255 (in force on 1 March 1995), appoints 1 March as the date for the abolition of the Domestic Coal Consumer's Council in accordance with the Coal Industry Act 1994, s 24.

2084   Coal industry—restructuring—grants

The Coal Industry (Restructuring Grants) Order 1995, SI 1995/1454 (in force on 9 June 1995), provides that grants may be made by the Secretary of State to the British Coal Corporation for the financial year ending March 1996. The order lists the matters which are eligible for a grant, and sets limits for each head of expenditure.

**2085   Coal industry—successor companies—government shareholding—target
        investment limit**

The Coal Industry (Coal Mining Successor Companies Target Investment Limit) Order 1995, SI 1995/1477 (in force on 23 June 1995), fixes target investment limits for the Government shareholding in specified successor companies which, at a time when they were wholly owned by the Crown, became entitled or subject to, in accordance with restructuring schemes, certain property, rights and liabilities. Those successor companies acquired the former coal mining interests of the British Coal Corporation and are no longer owned by the Crown. The government shareholding must normally be kept below the limit specified.

2086   Environment Act 1995

See para 1289.

2087   Health and safety

See HEALTH AND SAFETY.

2088   Miners' welfare—Coal Industry Social Welfare Organisation

The Miners' Welfare Act 1952 (Transfer of Functions of Coal Industry Social Welfare Organisation) Order 1995, SI 1995/855 (in force on 23 March 1995), prescribes the persons to whom the functions of the Coal Industry Social Welfare Organisation are to be transferred in accordance with the Miners' Welfare Act 1952, s 12(3) (under the Coal Industry Act 1994, s 22(3), all functions were transferred whether or not they arose under the 1952 Act).

2089   Mines—subsidence—compensation—appropriate forum

Scotland
The Coal Mining Subsidence Act 1991 makes provision for payment of compensation to owners of property that has been damaged by subsidence caused by coal mining. Section 40 provides that any question arising out of the Act must, in default of agreement, be determined by the Lands Tribunal.
    The plaintiff brought an action against the defendant for compensation under the 1991 Act, in respect of subsidence damage to his property. The action was raised in the Court of Session,

basing jurisdiction on the defendant's domicile. The defence admitted that the court had jurisdiction but included pleas that the action was incompetent and irrelevant and should be dismissed. There was no extrajudicial agreement that the action should be determined by the court. The issue arose whether the court had jurisdiction to determine the action. *Held*, 'in default of agreement' in the 1991 Act, s 40(1) included default of agreement on the method and forum for resolution of any disputed question between the parties. The decision on the question of forum had not been referred to the Lands Tribunal in unqualified terms and, accordingly, it was not incompetent for the plaintiff to bring the action at common law. However, the defendant's admission that the court had jurisdiction referred only to the territorial jurisdiction of the court. No agreement had been reached between the parties that the action should be determined by the Court of Session rather than the Lands Tribunal. In the absence of any such agreement, the Lands Tribunal had exclusive jurisdiction. Accordingly, the action would be dismissed.

Osborne v British Coal Property 1995 SLT 1349 (Outer House).

2090 Mines—subsidence—subsidence damage—withdrawal of support

Scotland

The Coal Mining Subsidence Act 1991, s 1(1) provides that 'subsidence damage' means any damage to land, or to any buildings, structures or works on, in or over land, caused by the withdrawal of support from land in connection with lawful coal mining operations. Section 2(1) provides that it is the duty of the British Coal Corporation to take, in respect of any subsidence damage to any property, remedial action.

Following the subsidence of the respondents' car park, the respondents discovered that a mine shaft had been sunk beneath the land on which the car park was situated about 150 years earlier for the purpose of extracting ironstone. The shaft was subsequently used for mining coal, but was later infilled and abandoned. On the respondents' claim that the appellant was obliged to take remedial action in consequence of the subsidence, the Lands Tribunal found that the collapse or movement of the infill amounted to a withdrawal of support in connection with lawful coal mining operations, within the meaning of the 1991 Act, s 1(1). On appeal, *held*, having regard to the purpose of the 1991 Act, it was not appropriate to adopt a restrictive interpretation of 'withdrawal of support' for the purposes of s 1(1). The phrase did not necessarily mean that the removal of support was an active process, as it could cover any disappearance of support, including a passive withdrawal caused by the natural movement of infill downwards into the unfilled part of a shaft. Moreover, the words 'in connection with' had to be given their ordinary meaning, and could not be equated with 'caused by' or 'resulting from'. Withdrawal of support could therefore be connected with lawful coal mining operations even if the withdrawal did not directly result from coal mining operations and even if the operations had long-since been abandoned. Here, the partial infill of the shaft was a process connected with coal mining operations, and the fact that the infill had fallen into the unfilled part of the shaft amounted to a withdrawal of support. The appellant was therefore obliged to take remedial action and, accordingly, the appeal would be dismissed.

British Coal Corpn v Netherlee Trust Trustees 1995 SLT 1038 (Inner House).

2091 Quarries—order prohibiting the resumption of quarrying—Secretary of State's refusal to confirm order—application for judicial review

See *R v Secretary of State for Wales, ex p Mid-Glamorgan County Council*, para 2862.

MISREPRESENTATION

Halsbury's Laws of England (4th edn) Vol 31, paras 1001–1137

2092 Articles

Independent Advice After *O'Brien*, H W Wilkinson (on *Barclays Bank plc v O'Brien* [1993] 4 All ER 417, HL (1993 Abr para 1826)): 145 NLJ 792

Taking Security After *O'Brien*, Richard Hooley (on *Barclays Bank plc v O'Brien* [1993] 4 All ER 417 (1993 Abr para 1826)): [1995] LMCLQ 346

2093 Contractual misrepresentation—material misrepresentation—contract of insurance—estimate of risk insured—avoidance of contract

See *St Paul Fire and Marine Insurance Co (UK) Ltd v McConnell Dowell Constructors Ltd*, para 1752.

2094 Fraudulent misrepresentation—guarantee—guarantee obtained by fraudulent misrepresentation—avoidance of guarantee

See *Vadasz v Pioneer Concrete (SA) Pty Ltd*, para 1311.

2095 Legal charge—misrepresentation—constructive notice

See MORTGAGE.

MISTAKE

2096 Legal consequences of mistake—specific performance—mistake induced by misrepresentation—enforceability of contract

The Law of Property (Miscellaneous Provisions) Act 1989, s 2 provides that a contract for the sale or other disposition of an interest in land must be in writing and incorporate all the terms which the parties have agreed in one document or, if they have exchanged contracts, in each.

The defendant's predecessor in title became a tenant of commercial premises on an underlease from the plaintiff's predecessor. The parties had made three other agreements by deed. One was a 'put option', which was a covenant by the plaintiff's predecessor to take an assignment of the underlease from the defendant's predecessor under certain conditions. The other agreements were a 'larger premises option' allowing the underlessee to opt to transfer to larger premises and a 'side land option' allowing the underlessee to acquire land alongside the existing premises. The defendant later acquired the unexpired residue of the term of the underlease by assignment. The defendant tried to obtain from the plaintiff the put option which had previously been enjoyed by its predecessor. Its aim was to obtain the option without the plaintiff realising and so it pretended to be negotiating for the side land option. It was agreed that the defendant should acquire the rights and benefits enjoyed by its predecessor and the defendant immediately purported to exercise the put option. The plaintiff sought rectification of the agreement. On appeal from a decision that the plaintiff was not entitled to rectification because it had not been shown that the defendant knew of the plaintiff's mistake, *held*, the contract did not include the put option. Where one party to a contract intended the other to be mistaken as to the terms of their agreement and made false and misleading statements to divert the other party's attention from discovering the mistake, he could not insist on performance of the contract to the letter. Rather, he might be bound by the agreement which the other party mistakenly thought was being made, even where it could not be shown that the mistake was induced by any misrepresentation. Furthermore, under the 1989 Act, s 2, an oral agreement for the sale or other disposition of land was not binding unless there was a document recording the agreement of the parties or an exchange of formal contracts, not mere correspondence. Accordingly, the appeal would be dismissed.

Commission for the New Towns v Cooper (Great Britain) Ltd [1995] 2 All ER 929 (Court of Appeal: Stuart-Smith, Farquharson and Evans LJJ).

2097 Rectification—common intention of parties—mistake as to extent of land to be conveyed

See *Aberdeen Rubber Ltd v Knowles & Sons (Fruiterers) Ltd*, para 672.

2098 Rectification—covenanted payment to charity—fiscal objective—failure to achieve objective

See *Racal Group Services Ltd v Ashmore*, para 1661.

MONEY

Halsbury's Laws of England (4th edn) Vol 32, paras 101–400

2099 Articles
Money Laundering—the Complete Guide, Leonard Jason-Lloyd: 145 NLJ 149, 183, 219

2100 Commercial transactions—contractual payment periods—compensation for late payment
See para 3125.

2101 Companies Act 1989—commencement
See para 472.

2102 Offences—unlawful harassment of debtors
See *Norweb plc v Dixon*, para 659.

2103 Premium Savings Bonds—minimum purchase and multiple units
The Premium Savings Bonds (Amendment) Regulations 1995, SI 1995/1002 (in force on 1 May 1995), amend the 1972 Regulations, SI 1972/765, so as to remove the provisions regulating the minimum amount of premium savings bonds which may be purchased at any time and the multiples of bond units in which bonds may be purchased.

MORTGAGE

Halsbury's Laws of England (4th edn) Vol 32, paras 401–1052

2104 Articles
Barclays Bank v O'Brien Revisited, David Wolfson (on the effect of misrepresentation or undue influence by the principal debtor on a surety): 145 NLJ 22
Conduct of Repossession Hearings, Jonathan: 139 SJ 449, 476, 505, 527
A Counsel of Perfection, Eric Dumbill and John Snape (on the debt enforcement issues when a wife stands as surety for a husband's loan): LS Gaz, 15 March 1995, p 20
Debt to Society, Neil Hickman, Derek McConnell and Michael Ramsden (on the courts' powers to assist borrowers in difficulty with secured loans): LS Gaz, 26 April 1995, p 17
Execution of a Mortgage Deed, C I Howells: 145 NLJ 286
Income Support and Mortgage Interest: the New Rules, Adam Griffith: LA, October 1995, p 17
Income Support Mortgage Interest Changes, Kate Tonge: 145 NLJ 1418
Independent Advice After *O'Brien*, H W Wilkinson (on *Barclays Bank plc v O'Brien* [1993] 4 All ER 417, HL (1993 Abr para 1826)): 145 NLJ 792
A Matter of Mortgages, Ian Muirhead (on the role of endowment mortgages): LS Gaz, 1 February 1995, p 15
Mortgagees and Purchasers: Separate Solicitors? C I Howells: 145 NLJ 193
Mortgagees and the Right to Possession, Simon Miller and Jonathan Klein: 139 SJ 1154
Negligence—A Field Day for Lenders and Borrowers, Marcel Haniff and Dolf Darnton (on the implications of negligent valuations for lenders and borrowers): Estates Gazette, 6 May 1995, p 113
The 1993 Convention on Maritime Liens and Mortgages, Francesco Berlingieri: [1995] LMCLQ 57
O'Brien Revisited, Judge Stephen Gerlis (on *Barclays Bank plc v O'Brien* [1993] 4 All ER 417 (1993 Abr para 1826)): [1995] Fam Law 150
A Sad Demise? Ian Hardcastle (on the effect of the Law of Property (Miscellaneous Provisions) Act 1989 on equitable mortgages by deposit of title deeds): 139 SJ 246
Sale by Mortgagees, Simon Miller and Jonathan Klein: 139 SJ 607

A Skeleton in the Cupboard, Paul Judkins and Howard Meek (on a loophole found in mortgage indemnity policies): LS Gaz, 12 April 1995, p 16

Taking Security After *O'Brien*, Richard Hooley (on *Barclays Bank plc v O'Brien* [1993] 4 All ER 417 (1993 Abr para 1826)): [1995] LMCLQ 346

Undue Influence, Misrepresentation and the Doctrine of Notice, John Mee (on *Barclays Bank plc v O'Brien* [1993] 4 All ER 417, HL (1993 Abr para 1826)): (1995) CLJ 536

2105 Discharge of mortgage—discharge by building society—subrogation of charge—priority over prior creditor

See *Boscawen v Bajwa; Abbey National plc v Boscawen*, para 1312.

2106 Discharge of mortgage—mortgage obtained by fraud—retention of surplus funds by building society

See *Halifax Building Society v Thomas*, para 2845.

2107 Equitable interest—declaration of trust—voidability

See *Midland Bank plc v Wyatt*, para 1369.

2108 Legal charge—charge discharged by finance company—subrogation of charge

A husband sought to obtain a loan from Bank A. It required a legal charge over the matrimonial home, which was in the wife's sole name, as security. On the bank's advice the wife spoke to a solicitor before she signed the charge. The husband then transferred his banking affairs to Bank B. He told his wife that the loan he arranged with Bank B was to pay for roof repairs. The wife therefore executed a charge in favour of Bank B. The bank did not advise her to seek legal advice. She was not aware that the charge secured not only the cost of roof repairs but also Bank A's indebtedness and all moneys due in the future from the husband on his new account. When Bank B called in its loan, the husband arranged to discharge the debt with a loan from a finance company. In order to do that the husband forged a transfer of the matrimonial home into joint names and the wife's undertaking to be jointly responsible for the loan, which was secured by the property. When the husband later defaulted on the loan, the company commenced proceedings against the husband and wife claiming that it was entitled to be subrogated to Bank B since it discharged the debt owed to Bank B. At first instance, the judge found that the third charge was void against the wife. He held that she was bound only to the extent that she had full understanding of her transaction with Bank B, namely the roofing repair account, and in respect of Bank B's charge which related to the outstanding debt paid to Bank A. On the wife's appeal, *held*, (1) on the basis of *Barclays Bank plc v O'Brien*, once Bank B's charge was liable to be set aside the judge had no discretion to set the charge aside in part only and had been wrong to hold that the wife was bound to the extent of her understanding of the transaction with Bank B. The company was not subrogated to Bank B in respect of that amount. (2) Bank B was entitled to Bank A's security by subrogation when it discharged the debt to Bank A, thinking that it was to obtain an effective security for its money. When the company discharged the debt to Bank B on the same basis it became entitled to the same security as Bank B had held. The company was entitled by subrogation to Bank A's charge and the appeal would be allowed to that extent.

  Castle Phillips Finance v Piddington [1995] 1 FLR 783 (Court of Appeal: McCowan and Peter Gibson LJJ and Sir John May). *Barclays Bank plc v O'Brien* [1993] 4 All ER 417, HL applied.

2109 Legal charge—matrimonial home—lender's notice of claim to ancillary relief by wife—wife's application to set aside charge

Under the Law of Property Act 1925, s 199(2) a purchaser will not be prejudicially affected by notice of any fact or thing unless in the same transaction with respect to which a question of notice to the purchaser arises it has come to the knowledge of his solicitor as such, or would have come to the knowledge of his solicitor as such if such inquiries and inspections had been made as ought reasonably to have been made by the solicitor.

  The parties' marriage failed and the husband agreed to buy the wife's interest in the matrimonial home. Only part of the payment for the interest had been made when the husband persuaded the wife to transfer the property into his sole name so that he could charge the property to raise money to help his business. In fact, he obtained a large loan from a company and put it into a new business which failed. The husband and the company used the same firm of solicitors. The wife, who had applied for ancillary relief, sought to have the loan set aside under the Matrimonial Causes Act 1973, s 37. At first instance the judge held (1) that the husband acted with the intention of defeating the wife's ancillary relief claim, that the company had notice of that intention and the transaction was therefore reviewable under the 1973 Act, s 37(4), and (2) that the company's solicitor should have asked the husband's solicitor what the matrimonial position was. The legal charge was set aside. The company unsuccessfully appealed and, on further appeal, *held*, (1) the company's solicitor did not have actual knowledge of the husband's intention to defeat the wife's claim. The critical question was whether he ought reasonably to have made inquiries which would reveal that the wife did have a claim. That involved the proposition that, where a lender knew that a borrower was involved in divorce proceedings, he was under an obligation not only to inquire of the borrower as to whether the wife had any interest or potential interest in the property sought to be charged, but to check through other sources whether or not that information was correct. To impose such a duty would require far too much of a person dealing in land in a case where the wife was not in occupation of the property. (2) The judge's finding was entirely inconsistent with the 1925 Act, s 199(2)(b). The information obtained by the husband's solicitor had not been obtained in his capacity as solicitor to the mortgagee but as solicitor to the husband. Accordingly, the appeal would be allowed.

B v B (P Intervening) (Reviewable Disposition) [1995] 2 FCR 670 (Court of Appeal: Butler-Sloss and Hoffmann LJJ and Sir Francis Purchas).

2110 Legal charge—misrepresentation—constructive notice

A wife received a substantial lump sum as part of the financial settlement following her divorce, and used it to purchase a property which was registered in her sole name. The husband raised the money to fund the lump sum by representing to the plaintiff bank that he was to be the joint owner of the property. Following a reconciliation between the husband and wife, the wife agreed to offer her house as security for a loan that the husband needed for a particular business transaction. The wife in fact signed forms which were for several loan and current account facilities, and also signed a mandate authorising either of them to sign cheques on the joint accounts. The bank did not fully explain the mandate to the wife, nor that her property was to be security for all of the accounts and loans. The wife visited a solicitor recommended by the bank and signed a mortgage document in his presence, although the husband told the solicitor that there was no need to explain the document. The bank subsequently sought to enforce its security on the wife's property. It commenced possession proceedings and also sought a money judgment for sums owing on the overdrawn joint accounts. *Held*, the wife had signed the account mandate and executed the mortgage over her property because of a misrepresentation made to her by the husband on which she had relied. A creditor's interest was subject to a wife's equity if the wife had agreed to stand surety for the husband's debts as a result of undue influence or misrepresentation in circumstances such that the creditor was put on inquiry. A creditor was put on inquiry if the transaction was not to the wife's financial advantage, if there was a substantial risk that the husband had committed a legal or equitable wrong in procuring the wife to act as his surety, and if the creditor was aware that the parties were cohabiting, that there was an emotional tie between them, or that the surety placed trust and confidence in the principal debtor. The same principles applied to cohabitees. Here, the bank was aware that the loan and current account facilities were required for the husband's sole benefit in relation to his business and personal interests, and it was the bank that had insisted that the current account should be in the parties' joint names. The bank's belief that the parties were still married and living together was sufficient to put it on notice, and there were other facts which put the bank under an obligation to make further inquiries. The bank had not taken steps to avoid being fixed with constructive notice, as it had not properly advised the wife as to the risks involved in standing as surety. Moreover, the wife had not been fully advised by an independent solicitor, as the bank had failed to pass on relevant information to the solicitor. Accordingly, the entire transaction had to be set aside.

Allied Irish Bank v Byrne [1995] 1 FCR 430 (Family Division: Ferris J). *Barclays Bank v O'Brien* [1993] 4 All ER 417, HL (1993 Abr para 1826), and *CIBC Mortgages plc v Pitt* [1993] 4 All ER 433, HL (1993 Abr para 1827) applied.

The Law of Property Act 1925, s 199(1)(ii)(b) provides that a purchaser is not prejudicially affected by notice of any other instrument or matter or any fact or thing unless, in the same transaction with respect to which a question of notice to the purchaser arises, it has come to the knowledge of his solicitor or other agent, as such, or would have come to the knowledge of his solicitor or other agent, as such, if such inquiries and inspections had been made as ought reasonably to have been made by the solicitor or other agent.

A firm of solicitors was instructed to act for both borrower and lender in a mortgage transaction in which the lender granted a loan to a husband and wife, secured on their matrimonial home. The husband intended to use the money to redeem an existing mortgage and to use the surplus to pay business debts, but the wife thought the surplus would be used for home improvements. When default occurred in the making of the payments due under the mortgage, the lender obtained a possession order in respect of the property. The wife's appeal against the order was dismissed on the ground that the knowledge of the solicitors as to the purpose of the loan could not be imputed to the lender. On further appeal, *held*, the information as to the true purpose of the loan imparted by the husband came to the knowledge of the solicitors as solicitors for the husband and wife alone because they were not instructed to act for the lender until a week later. Once that knowledge was acquired, it remained with the solicitors and could not be treated as coming to them again when they were instructed on behalf of the lender. It followed that knowledge of the relevant matters did not come to the solicitors as the solicitors for the lenders. Accordingly, it did not come to them 'as such'. Consequently, s 199(1)(ii)(b) precluded the solicitors' knowledge of the relevant matters or facts being imputed to the lender, and the appeal would be dismissed.

Halifax Mortgage Services Ltd (formerly BNP Mortgages Ltd) v Stepsky [1996] Ch 1 (Court of Appeal: Kennedy, Morritt and Ward LJJ). Decision of Edward Nugee QC [1995] 4 All ER 656 affirmed.

2111 Legal charge—undue influence—constructive notice—charge on matrimonial home

A husband was the sole registered proprietor of the matrimonial home. He executed a charge in favour of a building society ('the first chargee') as security for a loan, and later executed another charge to a company ('the second chargee') as security for another loan. In relation to the second charge, the wife signed a letter ('the occupier's letter') postponing any interest that she might have in the property to that of the second chargee. Subsequently, both chargees were granted possession orders, and warrants for possession were issued. Prior to execution of the warrants, the wife was joined as a party to both actions and successfully applied for the warrants to be suspended. She also successfully argued that, having regard to the Land Registration Act 1925, s 70(1)(g), she had an overriding interest in the property by virtue of being in actual occupation. The chargees' appeal against that decision was allowed, and on the wife's further appeal, it fell to be decided whether there was a triable issue as to (1) whether or not the wife had an overriding interest, and (2) if so, whether it was postponed to the second chargee's interest. The latter depended on whether she had signed the occupier's letter because of the husband's misrepresentation or undue influence, of which the second chargee had constructive notice. *Held*, (1) since the husband's mother had lent the husband and wife the deposit sum that they had needed to purchase their first matrimonial home, there was evidence of a common intention to share the property beneficially, and that therefore gave rise to a constructive trust. It was irrelevant that the husband and wife had sold the original matrimonial home and bought subsequent properties, as the purchase price of the latter was derived from the former. As such, there was a triable issue on whether the wife had a beneficial interest in the property. (2) Although there was no evidence of misrepresentation, the wife's evidence that she relied completely on the husband in all financial matters and trusted him implicitly, raised a presumption of undue influence, and that was therefore a triable issue. As the second chargee had done little more than inform the wife of her right to seek independent legal advice as to the occupier's letter, it was not possible to say that there was no triable issue on the question of constructive notice. Accordingly, the appeal would be allowed.

Halifax Building Society v Brown (1995) 27 HLR 511 (Court of Appeal: Balcombe and Roche LJJ). *Lloyd's Bank plc v Rosset* [1990] 1 All ER 1111, HL (1990 Abr para 1414) and *Barclays Bank plc v O'Brien* [1993] 4 All ER 417, HL (1993 Abr para 1826) applied; *Banco Exterior Internacional v Mann* [1995] 1 All ER 936, CA (1994 Abr para 1996) considered.

2112 Legal charge—undue influence—constructive notice—independent legal advice

The defendant and her husband and son executed a legal charge over their residential property in favour of the plaintiff bank, as security to guarantee the debts of a company owned by the husband and son. Before executing the charge, the defendant received legal advice and signed a certificate to that effect. The certificate also stated that she had been informed of her right to take independent legal advice as to the effect of the charge. When the plaintiff sought possession of the property, the defendant claimed that she had executed the charge under her husband's undue influence and that the transaction had been to her disadvantage. Although the bank was unable to rebut the claim, the judge decided that the plaintiff had not been put on inquiry that the matter had not been dealt in a competent manner, and that it was entitled to rely on the fact that a solicitor had given the defendant legal advice. On the defendant's appeal, *held*, the plaintiff was aware that the defendant and her husband and son had been advised by a solicitor. It was entitled to assume that each of them had been properly advised and, in particular, that the defendant had been advised of the importance of separate legal advice. Moreover, the plaintiff had obtained a certificate signed by the defendant stating that the appropriate advice had been given, and her signature had been countersigned by the solicitor. For the plaintiff to have questioned whether the certificate was correct would have amounted to questioning the solicitor's probity and honesty. It was not required to make such inquiry and therefore did not have constructive notice of the husband's undue influence. Accordingly, the appeal would be dismissed.

Bank of Baroda v Rayarel (1995) 27 HLR 387 (Court of Appeal: Glidewell, Hirst and Hoffmann LJJ). *Barclays Bank plc v O'Brien* [1993] 4 All ER 433, HL (1993 Abr para 1826) and *Midland Bank plc v Massey* [1994] 2 FLR 342, CA (1994 Abr para 1993) considered.

2113 Legal charge—undue influence—constructive notice—knowledge of borrower's solicitor

A bank secured a charge over the property of the first defendant which he owned jointly with his wife, the second defendant. The first defendant's solicitor explained the charge to the second defendant who, after a meal with the first defendant at which a considerable amount of alcohol was consumed, signed the charge and a certificate which stated that she had been advised of the risks and possible consequences of doing so. The bank claimed possession of the property following the failure of the first defendant to pay sums guaranteed by the bank. The second defendant claimed that the charge was not binding on her as she had signed it as a result of undue influence of which the bank had constructive notice. At first instance, the bank was granted possession of the property. On appeal by the second defendant, *held*, the first defendant's solicitor had not been acting as an agent for the bank and what he knew about undue influence on the second defendant could not therefore be imputed to the bank. The fact that the bank knew she had been advised by the solicitor was sufficient to discharge its duty to ensure that she was aware of all the risks involved. The bank was entitled to take possession of the property and, accordingly, the appeal would be dismissed.

Midland Bank plc v Serter [1995] 1 FLR 1034 (Court of Appeal: Glidewell, Pill and Aldous LJJ).

2114 Mortgagee—action for possession—possession order—discretion to suspend enforcement of order

A husband and wife borrowed a substantial sum from a building society, secured by way of mortgage over their home. The building society's standard terms and conditions provided that it was entitled to possession of the property if monthly mortgage repayments fell into arrears for more than a month, but its statement of current practice provided for means of helping borrowers who were in difficulty, such as by lengthening the mortgage term, temporarily deferring interest payments, and capitalising interest. The building society was granted a possession order against the husband and wife, and the wife unsuccessfully applied for suspension of the issue of a warrant for possession. On her appeal, *held*, the court had to consider what constituted a reasonable period within which to allow a borrower to pay off arrears of mortgage instalments. Taking the remaining part of the original full term of the mortgage as the starting point, the court had to consider whether a borrower would be able to pay off the arrears by instalments over that period. Such an approach involved a detailed analysis of present figures and future projections, an assessment of how much of the outstanding debt was to be attributed to interest and how much to the principal sum, and consideration of whether or not the lender's security would be put at risk by postponing payment of arrears. Moreover, as the full term of a mortgage was the most favourable period for a borrower in calculating what was a reasonable period for payment of arrears, a lender would be justified in seeking a warrant for possession if the borrower failed to maintain the revised mortgage payments as a condition of suspension of the warrant. Applying those principles to the instant case, the appeal would be allowed.

Cheltenham and Gloucester Building Society v Norgan [1996] 1 All ER 449 (Court of Appeal: Evans and Waite LJJ, and Sir John May).

2115   Mortgage indemnities—recognised bodies

The Mortgage Indemnities (Recognised Bodies) Order 1995, SI 1995/210 (in force on 20 February 1995), adds thirteen additional bodies to the list of recognised bodies for the purposes of the Housing Act 1985, ss 442, 443.

The Mortgage Indemnities (Recognised Bodies) (No 2) Order 1995, SI 1995/2053 (in force on 21 August 1995), adds four additional bodies to the list of recognised bodies for the purposes of the Housing Act 1985, ss 442, 443.

2116   Receiver—appointment under statutory powers—powers as to application of income—accountability for tax

See *Sargent v Customs and Excise Comrs*, para 3046.

NATIONAL HEALTH SERVICE

Halsbury's Laws of England (4th edn) Vol 33, paras 1–300

2117   Articles

The Clinical Negligence Scheme for Trusts—Risk Management—A New Approach, John Hickey: 1 CR 43, 132
Contracts in the National Health Service Internal Market, Pauline Allen: 58 MLR 321
Incident Reporting and Claims, Brian Capstick: 1 CR 165
The NHS: Taking the Cadbury Report Seriously, Christopher Brophy: 139 SJ 324
Who Decides? Edward Myers (on health authorities denying patients access to their medical records): 139 SJ 504

2118   Carers (Recognition and Services) Act 1995

The Carers (Recognition and Services) Act 1995 makes provision for individuals who provide, or intend to provide care on a regular or substantial basis to have the legal right to request and to have an assessment of their needs carried out by local authorities. The Act received the royal assent on 28 June 1995 and came into force on 1 April 1996.

Section 1 provides for the circumstances in which, when local authorities are making a decision as to whether a person's needs call for the provision of any community care services, a non-professional carer may request the authority to carry out an assessment of his ability to provide care. This provision relates to England and Wales and consequential amendments and modifications are made. Section 2 applies to Scotland only. Under s 3 the Secretary of State may by statutory instrument make provision for the application of s 1 as if the Isles of Scilly were a local authority within the meaning of that section. Section 4 makes the necessary financial provision. Section 5 makes provision for short title, commencement and extent.

2119   Charges—dental services—maximum charge

The National Health Service (Dental Charges) Amendment Regulations 1995, SI 1995/444 (in force on 1 April 1995), further amend the 1989 Regulations, SI 1989/394, by increasing the maximum charge for dental treatment and appliances from £275 to £300, where the contract for the treatment or the appliances is made after 1 April 1995.

2120   Charges—drugs and appliances

The National Health Service (Charges for Drugs and Appliances) Amendment Regulations 1995, SI 1995/643 (in force on 1 April 1995), further amend the 1989 Regulations, SI 1989/419, by increasing the charge for items on prescription or supplied to outpatients from £4.75 to £5.25. In addition, the charges for specified medical appliances and the sums prescribed for the grant of repayment certificates are increased. The entitlement for a refund of pre-payment certificate fees to those entitled to remission of charges is extended, in certain circumstances also to in-patients in hospital, and time limits are introduced within which an application for a refund must be made. The regulations also make transitional arrangements in respect of pre-payment certificates and appliances ordered before the coming into force of the regulations.

The National Health Service (Charges for Drugs and Appliances) Amendment (No 2) Regulations 1995, SI 1995/2737 (in force on 20 October 1995), further amend the 1989 Regulations, SI 1989/419, so as to provide that all persons who have attained the age of 60 years shall be exempt from paying charges for such drugs and appliances.

2121 Charges—ophthalmic services

The National Health Service (General Ophthalmic Services) Amendment Regulations 1995, SI 1995/558 (in force on 1 April 1995), amend the 1986 Regulations, SI 1986/975, extending the categories of eligibility for free sight tests to include people in receipt of disability working allowance whose capital resources were £8,000 or less at the time that allowance was claimed, and certain relatives of such people.

2122 Charges—optical services

The National Health Service (Optical Charges and Payments) Amendment Regulations 1995, SI 1995/34 (in force on 1 February 1995), further amend the 1989 Regulations, SI 1989/396, so as to amend the definition of 'NHS sight test fee' by increasing the amount by which entitlement to assistance towards the cost of a private sight test carried out at a place where the patient normally resides, and the value of a voucher towards such cost or towards the supply (in certain circumstances) of glasses or contact lenses, is calculated from £34.22 to £35.09.

The National Health Service (Optical Charges and Payments) Amendment (No 2) Regulations 1995, SI 1995/691 (in force on 1 April 1995), further amend the 1989 Regulations supra so as to (1) insert a definition of disability working allowance; (2) require the ophthalmic medical practitioner, optician or other responsible authority completing an optical voucher to include on it the patient's date of birth; (3) extend the categories of eligibility for payments towards the cost of optical appliances; and (4) increase the value of vouchers issued towards the cost of supplying and replacing contact lenses, glasses and optical appliances.

The National Health Service (Optical Charges and Payments) Amendment (No 3) Regulations 1995, SI 1995/2307 (in force on 1 October 1995), further amend the 1989 Regulations supra, so as to amend the definition of 'NHS sight test fee'. Where a sight test is carried out in a patient's home, the value of assistance towards the cost of a private sight test and the value of vouchers towards the cost of a private sight test or towards the supply of glasses or contact lenses is increased from £35.09 to £36.65. In all other cases, the figure is increased from £13.15 to £13.41.

2123 Charges—remission and payment—travelling expenses

The National Health Service (Travelling Expenses and Remission of Charges) Amendment Regulations 1995, SI 1995/642 (in force on 1 April 1995), further amend the 1988 Regulations, SI 1988/551, so as to (1) define 'disability working allowance' and amend the definition of 'family'; (2) provide that a person who is in receipt of disability working allowance and whose capital is not more than £8,000 is entitled to full remission of charges and full payment of travelling expenses, and that a member of that person's family is similarly entitled; (3) provide for the assessment of capital, mentioned above, to be in accordance with the 1988 Regulations in certain cases, and to provide that in such cases notice of entitlement to remission of payment claimed under the 1988 Regulations is effective until the award of disability working allowance current at the date of claim ceases to be payable; (4) make provision for the manner in which a person's requirements are to be calculated, in consequence of the introduction of incapacity benefit; and (5) make transitional provision which provides that claims for repayment of charges or expenses paid before 1 April 1995 must be calculated as if the regulations had not been made.

The National Health Service (Travelling Expenses and Remission of Charges) Amendment No 2 Regulations 1995, SI 1995/2352 (in force on 2 October 1995), amend the 1988 Regulations, SI 1988/551. The 1988 Regulations provide that, for the purposes of calculating a person's resources and requirements, the Income Support (General) Regulations 1987, SI 1987/1967, apply. The 1995 Regulations provide that, in applying the 1987 Regulations, the Social Security (Income Support and Claims and Payments) Amendment Regulations 1995, SI 1995/1613, and the Income Support (General) Amendment and Transitional Regulations 1995, SI 1995/2287, are to be disregarded.

2124   District health authorities—decision not to finance specific treatment—lawfulness of decision

See *R v Cambridge District Health Authority, ex p B*, para 12.

2125   District health authorities—determination of districts

The National Health Service (Determination of Districts) (No 2) Order 1995, SI 1995/533 (in force on 1 April 1995), further amends the 1981 Order, SI 1981/1837, so as to abolish specified districts and determine a new one for the purposes of the National Health Service Act 1977. The order makes provision for the transfer of officers from the employment of the authority which is abolished and for the transfer of rights and liabilities.

The National Health Service (District Health Authorities) (No 2) Order 1995, SI 1995/534 (in force on 1 April 1995), abolishes specified district health authorities and establishes a new district health authority in relation to the areas previously covered. The 1990 Order, SI 1990/1756, is consequentially amended.

The National Health Service (Determination of Districts) Order 1995, SI 1995/562 (in force on 1 April 1995), amends the 1981 Order, SI 1981/1837, so as to abolish certain specified districts and determine new ones for the purpose of the National Health Service Act 1977. The order also makes provision for the transfer of officers from health authorities abolished on 1 April 1995 by the National Health Service (District Health Authorities) Order 1995 infra to the relevant new authorities established by that order, and for the transfer of rights and liabilities of the abolished authorities.

The National Health Service (District Health Authorities) Order 1995, SI 1995/563 (in force on 1 April 1995), abolishes certain district health authorities as reflected in changes to the districts of the abolished authorities and the establishment of new districts by the National Health Service (Determination of Districts) Order 1995, SI 1995/562. Further amendments are also made to the 1990 Order, SI 1990/1756, to reflect these changes.

2126   Family Health Services Appeal Authority—appointment and tenure of office

The Family Health Services Appeal Authority Regulations 1995, SI 1995/622 (in force on 1 April 1995), revoke the 1992 Regulations, SI 1992/660. The regulations provide for the appointment and tenure of office of members of the Family Health Services Appeal Authority which is a special health authority established under the National Health Service Act 1977 by the Family Health Services Appeal Authority (Establishment and Constitution) Order 1995, SI 1995/621. The regulations make provision relating to (1) the appointment and tenure of office of the chairman and members of the Authority; (2) the termination of office and eligibility of members for reappointment; (3) disqualification for appointment and the cessation of such disqualification; (4) the vice-chairman of the Authority; and (5) the appointment of, and exercise of functions by, its committees and sub-committees and its meetings and proceedings, including provision for disability for participation in proceedings on account of pecuniary interest.

2127   Family Health Services Appeal Authority—establishment and constitution

The Family Health Services Appeal Authority (Establishment and Constitution) Order 1995, SI 1995/621 (in force on 1 April 1995), provides for the establishment and constitution of a special health authority, to be known as the Family Health Services Appeal Authority, to exercise on behalf of the Secretary of State certain of her appellate and other functions (to be specified in directions given by the Secretary of State), in connection with decisions and functions of family health services Authorities, which were previously exercised on her behalf by the Northern and Yorkshire Regional Health Authority. The order also makes provision for the constitution of the Family Health Services Appeal Authority, for the transfer of staff to the Authority, for the enforcement of rights by, and liabilities against, the Authority, and for the remuneration of members of the Authority who are not also its officers.

2128   Family health services authorities—functions

The National Health Service (Functions of Family Health Services Authorities) (Prescribing Incentive Schemes) Regulations 1995, SI 1995/692 (in force on 1 April 1995), confer a new statutory function on family health services authorities. The new function is to establish and operate schemes, in accordance with directions made by the Secretary of State, under which those authorities make payments to GP practices in their localities which contain their prescribing costs.

2129 Fund-holding practices

The National Health Service (Fund-holding Practices) Amendment Regulations 1995, SI 1995/693 (in force on 1 April 1995), amend the 1993 Regulations, SI 1993/567, so as to create two levels of fund-holding practice: community fund-holding practices with at least 3,000 patients; and standard fund-holding practices with at least 5,000 patients. Provision is also made relating to the recognition of fund-holding practices, the list of goods that may be purchased for patients, the payment of management allowances, the expenditure of savings, the provision of information about proposed and past expenditure, and the list sizes for different types of fund-holding practice.

2130 General medical services—allocated funds—reimbursement of general practitioners—unlawful use of funds

The National Health Service Act 1977, s 97(1) provides that it is the Secretary of State's duty to pay in respect of each financial year to each regional health authority, sums not exceeding the amount allotted by him to the authority for that year towards meeting the expenditure attributable to the performance by the authority of their functions in that year, including functions with respect to such expenditure of family health services authorities as is attributable to the reimbursement of persons providing services in the pursuance of Pt II of the Act (general medical, dental, ophthalmic and pharmaceutical services), and of a description specified in the allotment. By s 97(3), the Secretary of State may give directions to a regional health authority with respect to the application of such sums.

A regional family health services authority ('the FHSA') had a surplus of funds allocated for the provision of local general medical services, in particular for the reimbursement of claims by general practitioners for practice staff costs, rent, and premises improvement grants. It decided to use those funds to appoint eight facilitators to arrange or assist in the provision of general medical services in the region and to carry out general administrative tasks. However, the FHSA did not consult with the general practitioners to whose practices the facilitators were appointed, nor did it consult with the local medical committee ('the committee') before making the appointments. It was also the case that general administrative tasks were not connected with the provision of general medical services. When the committee became aware of the appointments, an internal inquiry was held which concluded that the FHSA had acted contrary to Department of Health guidelines, and also queried the validity of the appointments and the appointments procedure. The committee sought the return of the money expended on the facilitators and asked the Secretary of State to take action under the relevant provisions of the 1977 Act. Upon her refusal to do so, the committee sought a declaration that the funds provided to the FHSA for the reimbursement of general practitioners had been used unlawfully. *Held*, having regard to the Department of Health's guidelines and the relevant paragraphs of the administrative handbook relating to fees and allowances for general practitioners for the provision of local medical services, it was clear that the Secretary of State had issued directions as to the use of the funds, within the meaning of the 1977 Act, s 97(3). The funds had been allocated for the reimbursement of specified costs incurred by general practitioners, and could be used only for that particular purpose. As the appointment of facilitators did not fall within the matters for which the funds should have been used, the FHSA had used them unlawfully. Accordingly, the application would be granted.

R v Secretary of State for Health, ex p Manchester Local Medical Committee (1995) 25 BMLR 77 (Queen's Bench Division: Collins J).

2131 General medical services—regulations

The National Health Service (General Medical Services) Amendment Regulations 1995, SI 1995/80 (in force on 6 February 1995), further amend the 1992 Regulations, SI 1992/635, by (1) removing the need for a family health services authority (FHSA) to make a resolution to give no more notices of a practice vacancy in certain circumstances; (2) amending doctors' terms of service to enable them to treat patients at premises other than their practice premises outside their normal hours of availability, having obtained FHSA approval and informed their patients of the address of any such premises; (3) providing that such premises must be proper and sufficient and may be inspected; (4) amending doctors' terms of service so that a deputy doctor may not treat patients at any premises approved under the new provision unless the doctor for whom he is acting has obtained the necessary approval; and (5) amending doctors' terms of service to add providing or prescribing drugs against developing malaria to the list of services for which a doctor may charge a fee.

2132   Health authority—refusal to provide treatment—decision to impose limitations on availability of treatment—lawfulness of decision

The plaintiff applied for judicial review of the defendant health authority's refusal to provide her with in vitro fertilisation treatment on the ground that she was outside the upper age limit within which the authority provided treatment. She claimed that the age restriction was illegal, and was contrary to the National Health Service Act 1977, s 3, under which the Secretary of State was under a duty to provide medical services to meet all reasonable requirements. She also claimed that the decision was irrational, not being founded on any sustainable clinical approach. *Held*, the authority was not bound, simply because it had undertaken to provide a service, to provide it on demand to any individual patient for whom the service may be beneficial. It was entitled to identify the circumstances in which the service would be provided, and to take into account its finite budget and other considerations. The authority's decision was not illegal. It was not irrational for the authority, acting on advice that the success of in vitro fertilisation treatment decreased with age, to take age into account as an appropriate criterion when balancing the need for such a provision against its ability to provide it and all other services, imposed upon it under the legislation. It was not *Wednesbury* unreasonable for the authority to look at the matter of whom to treat in the context of financial resources. Accordingly, the plaintiff's application would be refused.

R v Sheffield Health Authority, ex p Seale (1994) 25 BMLR 1 (Queen's Bench Division: Auld J). *Associated Provincial Picture Houses Ltd v Wednesbury Corporation* [1947] 2 All ER 680, CA, applied.

2133   Health Authorities Act 1995

The Health Authorities Act 1995 reforms the administrative structure of the National Health Service. The Act received the royal assent on 28 June 1995 and comes into force on that date for certain purposes; the substantive provisions take effect on 1 April 1996. For details of commencement, see the commencement table in the title STATUTES.

Under s 1, regional health authorities (RHAs), district health authorities (DHAs) and family health services authorities (FHSAs) are abolished and are to be replaced by health authorities. Section 2 introduces Sch 1 which makes provision for consequential amendments. Provision is made to enable RHAs, DHAs and FSHAs to prepare for the reorganisation, in particular by exercising each other's functions: s 3. Section 4 and Sch 2 make, and confer power to make transitional provision. Section 5 and Sch 3 contain repeals and revocations. Section 6 provides for any power to make an order or regulations under the Act to be exercisable by statutory instrument, subject to certain exceptions. Financial provision is made in s 7. Sections 8, 9 and 10 relate to commencement, extent and short title.

2134   Injury benefits

The National Health Service (Injury Benefits) Regulations 1995, SI 1995/866 (in force on 13 April 1995), replace SI 1974/1547, as amended. The regulations provide for payment of injury benefit to specified persons engaged in the National Health Service who sustain injury, contract a disease, or die in the course of their employment, where that injury, disease or death is attributable to their employment. The regulations set out the scale of benefits, and define the meaning of service for the purposes of the regulations. As regards benefits following the death of an injured person, the regulations set out the grounds of entitlement for benefit, the widow's, widower's, child's, and dependant relative's allowances, and state the circumstances in which allowances are to be restricted. The regulations also provide for the review and adjustment of allowances, the loss of the right to benefit, and the offsetting of benefit where there is criminal activity, negligence or fraud. Where officers are transferred in consequence of reorganisation, provision is made for supplementary payments to be made. Damages, compensation, or other benefits received by a person may be taken into account in determining entitlement to injury benefit so as to avoid duplicate benefits, and a person may be required to submit to a medical examination. In addition, certain persons who may be detrimentally affected by some of the provisions of the regulations may elect that those provisions should not apply.

2135   National Health Service (Amendment) Act 1995

The National Health Service (Amendment) Act 1995 makes provision in respect of persons disqualified or subject to proceedings under the National Health Service Act 1977, s 46, and in respect of the constitution of the tribunal established for that purpose. The Act received the royal assent on 19 July 1995 and certain provisions came into force on that date and on 21 December 1995: SI 1995/3090. The remaining provisions come into force on a day or days to be appointed. For details of commencement, see the commencement table in the title STATUTES.

Section 1 amends the 1977 Act, s 46(2), so as to provide that where the tribunal makes a finding that the inclusion of a person's name in a list under the 1977 Act, Pt II would be prejudicial to the efficiency of the services to which the list relates, it may also declare that the person is not fit to be engaged in any capacity in the provision of those services. New provisions are inserted by s 2, so as to provide that where a health authority has made representations for a person's disqualification, it may at any time before the case is considered by the tribunal, apply for a direction that the person be removed from any relevant list in which his name is included, disqualified from inclusion in any relevant list in which his name is not included, and declared unfit to practice. Such interim suspension ceases to have effect once the tribunal has disposed of a case, although it may order the continuation of the suspension order pending an appeal, if it is considered necessary to protect patients. However, interim suspension ceases to have effect once the specified time limit for appealing against a disqualification order has expired (where no appeal is made), or once the appeal process has been exhausted. Before an interim suspension order can be made, the affected person is entitled to make representations, call witnesses, and produce other evidence, and regulations may be made in respect of the procedure for determining applications for interim suspension orders. Regulations may also be made as regards making payments to a person who has been suspended from practice.

As regards the right to appeal to the Secretary of State from a disqualification order, s 3 replaces the existing provisions. It is now provided that where the tribunal has directed that a person's name is to be removed from or not included in any list, the relevant health authority must remove the person's name from the lists, but not until the end of the period for lodging an appeal (where no appeal is made), or until the appeal process has been exhausted.

Section 4 provides that a person must remain disqualified until the tribunal gives a direction to the contrary, and s 5 provides that the power to make regulations for prescribing the procedure for holding inquiries now includes the power to make regulations as to the disqualification procedure.

As regards the constitution of the tribunal, s 6 provides that it is to consist of a chairman appointed by the Lord Chancellor, any number of deputy chairmen appointed by the Lord Chancellor, and any number of persons, medical practitioners, medical practitioners with specified qualifications, dental practitioners, ophthalmic opticians and registered pharmacists appointed by the Secretary of State. The chairman and deputy chairman must be practising barristers or solicitors with at least ten years' standing, and the Secretary of State must consult with representatives of health authorities before appointing persons to the tribunal. Medical practitioners, dental practitioners, ophthalmic opticians and registered pharmacists are appointed after consultation with representatives of each of those professions. The functions of the tribunal are exercised by three members, namely the chairman or deputy chairman, a person appointed by the Secretary of State after consultation with health authority representatives, and a person of the same profession as the person to whom the proceedings relate.

Sections 7 to 12 make equivalent provision for Scotland, and s 13 relates to Northern Ireland. Section 14 deals with the title and extent of the Act, and with consequential repeals.

2136 National Health Service trusts—originating capital debt

The National Health Service Trusts (Originating Capital Debt) Order 1995, SI 1995/407 (in force on 15 March 1995), specifies the amount of the originating capital debt of NHS Trusts established under the National Health Service and Community Care Act 1990, s 9 with an operational date of 1 April 1994. The order also provides for the splitting of the originating capital debts into loan and public dividend capital.

The National Health Service Trusts (Originating Capital Debt) (Wales) Order 1995, SI 1995/394 (in force on 3 March 1995), determines the amount of the originating capital debt, provided for in the National Health Service and Community Care Act 1990, s 9, of NHS trusts established under that Act with an operational date of 1 April 1993. It also provides for the splitting of the originating capital debts into loan and public dividend capital.

The National Health Service Trusts (Originating Capital Debt) (Wales) (No 2) Order 1995, SI 1995/2783 (in force on 10 November 1995), determines the amount of the originating capital debt, provided for in the National Health Service and Community Care Act 1990, s 9, of specified Welsh NHS trusts established under that Act with an operational date of 1 April 1994.

It also provides for the splitting of the originating capital debts into loan and public dividend capital.

2137 Pharmaceutical services—extension of services

The National Health Service (Pharmaceutical Services) Amendment Regulations 1995, SI 1995/644 (in force on 1 April 1995), further amend the 1992 Regulations, SI 1992/662, by (1) extending the scope of supplemental services so as to enable any chemist on the pharmaceutical list of a family health services authority ('FHSA') to provide advice as to the safekeeping and correct administration of drugs in any residential care home or any nursing home registered under the Registered Homes Act 1984 and in certain homes which are not required to be registered under that Act; (2) removing the requirement that a chemist who has undertaken to provide additional professional services must display such posters and publications as the FHSA may require; (3) enabling the Secretary of State to designate, in the Drug Tariff, family health service authorities as the determining authority for remuneration in respect of specified pharmaceutical services, and requiring the FHSA to consult the Local Pharmaceutical Committee prior to the making of such a determination and publishing any determination made; (4) amending chemists' terms of service relating to the days, and to the hours within which pharmaceutical services are required to be provided and the hours that the FHSA may direct them to be provided, and provides for an appeal against such a direction of an FHSA. The FHSA may direct that a pharmacist be available outside such hours in specified circumstances, provided that a fee or other remuneration to be paid to any chemist so directed has been determined; and (5) making provision relating to fair wages for staff.

2138 Provision of accommodation and care—severely handicapped child—recovery of local authority expenses—retrospective charge for services

The first defendant's son was seriously injured at birth owing to fetal anoxia caused by the negligence of the second defendant health authority. As a result, he was severely handicapped, both physically and mentally, until he died at the age of 13. For most of his life he was cared for in a home, the cost having been borne by the plaintiff local authority under its duties under the National Assistance Act 1948, s 29 and the National Health Service Act 1977, Sch 2. Two years before the boy's death the first defendant secured damages from the second defendant for the negligence that caused her son's injuries. The agreed sum included the cost of future care at the home but specifically excluded the cost of the care provided prior to the settlement of the claim. The plaintiff subsequently sought to recover the full cost of the care from the deceased son's estate. *Held*, no statutory provision expressly prevented a local authority from retrospectively recovering the cost of services previously supplied. The only implied restriction on a local authority's power to recover such expenses was that the authority must act reasonably, and the plaintiff had acted reasonably. Therefore, the plaintiff's claim would succeed subject to the question of limitation. The date when the cause of action accrued was the date when the services were supplied and, therefore, part of the plaintiff's claim was statute-barred. Accordingly, the plaintiff's claim would succeed in part.

Avon County Council v Hooper (1995) 25 BMLR 26 (Queen's Bench Division: Taylor J).

2139 Social security

See SOCIAL SECURITY AND SOCIAL SERVICES.

2140 Special health authorities—Family Health Services Appeal Authority

The Health Service Commissioner (Family Health Services Appeal Authority) Order 1995, SI 1995/753 (in force on 17 April 1995), designates the Family Health Services Appeal Authority as a special health authority which is subject to investigation by the Health Service Commissioner.

2141 Special health authorities—National Health Service Litigation Authority— establishment and constitution

The National Health Service Litigation Authority (Establishment and Constitution) Order 1995, SI 1995/2800 (in force on 20 November 1995), provides for the establishment and constitution of the National Health Service Litigation Authority, to exercise on behalf of the Secretary of State certain of his functions as he may direct in connection with the establishment and, subsequently, the administration of a scheme under the National Health Service and Community Care Act 1990, s 21, for meeting liabilities of health service bodies to third parties for loss, damage or injury arising out of the exercise by those bodies of their functions. Provision is also made for the remuneration of members of the authority who are not also its officers.

2142 Special health authorities—National Health Service Litigation Authority— membership and procedure

The National Health Service Litigation Authority Regulations 1995, SI 1995/2801 (in force on 20 November 1995), make provision concerning the membership and procedure of the National Health Service Litigation Authority. Provision is made (1) for the appointment and tenure of office of the chairman and members of the Authority; (2) for the termination of office and the eligibility of members of the Authority for re-appointment; (3) for disqualification and the cessation of such disqualification; (4) relating to the vice-chairman of the authority, the appointment of and exercise of functions by its committees and sub-committees and its meetings and proceedings; (5) for dealing with conflicts of interest; and (6) for requiring the authority to furnish reports and certain other information to the Secretary of State.

2143 Superannuation

See PENSIONS AND SUPERANNUATION.

2144 Vaccine damage—specified disease

The Vaccine Damage Payments (Specified Disease) Order 1995, SI 1995/1164 (in force on 31 May 1995), adds haemophilus influenzae type b infection to the diseases to which the Vaccine Damage Payments Act 1979 applies.

NEGLIGENCE

Halsbury's Laws of England (4th edn) Vol 34, paras 1–200

2145 Articles

Audit Negligence: The Expert Accountant's Role, George Sim: SJ Supp, 30 June 1995, p 32

Class Action, James Burnett-Hitchcock and Suzanne Burn: LS Gaz, 22 November 1995, p 16

Damages and BBL: A Better Way? John Murdoch (on *Banque Bruxelles Lambert SA v Eagle Star Insurance Co Ltd* (1995) Times, 21 February, Independent, 24 February, CA (para 3062)): Estates Gazette, 11 March 1995, p 115

Damages for Nervous Shock: A Developing Area? Philip Noble: 145 NLJ 720

Duty of Care: Peripheral Parties and Alternative Opportunities for Deterrence, Jane Stapleton: (1995) LQR 301

If Disaster Strikes—Could You be Liable? John Mawhood and Richard Raysman (on liability for technology failure): 10 CLP 164

The Expert and the Medical Negligence Action, Charles J Lewis: 2 CR 68

It Shouldn't Happen to a Vet, Charles Foster (on veterinary negligence): 139 SJ 186

The Lords' View of a Solicitor, Clive Boxer (on *White v Jones* [1995] 1 All ER 691, HL (para 2780)): 139 SJ 372

Negligence—A Field Day for Lenders and Borrowers, Marcel Haniff and Dolf Darnton (on the implications of negligent valuations for lenders and borrowers): Estates Gazette, 6 May 1995, p 113

Negligent Teaching, Oliver Hyams (on *X v Bedfordshire County Council* (1995) Times, 30 June, HL (para 2833)): 139 746

Negligent Valuations, Thomas Grant and Hugh Tomlinson: 139 SJ 237

A Nervous Breakdown, Martin Murphy (on *Page v Smith* [1995] 2 WLR 644, HL (para 2173)): LS Gaz, 1 June 1995, p 16

Nervous Shock, Charles Lewis (on *Page v Smith* [1995] 2 WLR 644, HL (para 2173)): 139 SJ 960

Newham and *Bedfordshire*: Negligence in Residential Care, Jonathan Butler and Graham Wood (on *M v Newham Borough Council* (1995) Times, 30 June (para 2833)): 145 NLJ 1826

Occupiers' Liability to Pedestrians, Brenda Barrett: 145 NLJ 283

Of Sheep Dips, Pesticides and Damages for Personal Injuries, Alan Care (on claims for damages for sheep dip poisoning): 139 SJ 1250

A Plea for a Lost Chance: Hotson Reconsidered, Charles Foster (on *Hotson v East Berkshire Area Health Authority* [1987] 2 All ER 909 (1987 Abr para 731)): 145 NLJ 228, 248

Shock, Horror!—Yet Again, Blaise Smith (on nervous shock): 139 SJ 608

Solicitors' Professional Negligence, Christian Kessel (on *White v Jones* [1995] 1 All ER 691, HL (para 2780)): 145 NLJ 499, 537

Traffic Accidents and Nervous Shock, Barbara Harvey and Andy Robinson: 145 NLJ 1100

The Value Judgment, Myfanwy Badge (on *Banque Bruxelles Lambert SA v Eagle Star Insurance Co Ltd* (1995) Times, 21 February, Independent, 24 February, CA (para 3062)): LS Gaz, 22 March 1995, p 16

2146 Causation—foreseeability—irrelevancy of scale of loss—loss suffered by Lloyd's name

The plaintiff, who was a Lloyd's name, had brought a successful action for negligence and breach of contract against the defendant, his members' agent, on the ground that the defendant had failed to give adequate warning and advice in relation to investment in high-risk syndicates. The defendant appealed on the ground that the scale of the plaintiff's loss was unprecedented and unforeseeable and therefore unrecoverable. The plaintiff cross-appealed on the ground that the judge at first instance had been wrong in setting off profits the plaintiff had made in earlier years from the syndicates against the losses which were the subject of the present litigation. *Held*, the scale of the loss was not relevant, but rather whether the loss was of a type that was foreseeable or foreseen. In this case, the loss had been foreseeable and was therefore recoverable. The plaintiff had an independent and separate cause of action for each year he had suffered a loss, which was a legal one arising from contract law to which any equitable or restitutionary principle did not apply. The court thus had to award damages equal to the loss sustained in each cause of action without set-off and, accordingly, the defendant's appeal would be dismissed and the plaintiff's cross-appeal would be allowed.

Brown v KMR Services Ltd [1995] 4 All ER 598 (Court of Appeal: Stuart-Smith, Peter Gibson and Hobhouse LJJ). Decision of Gatehouse J [1994] 4 All ER 385 (1994 Abr para 1688) affirmed in part.

2147 Cause of action—construction works—deposit of dust on homes

See *Hunter v Canary Wharf Ltd; Hunter v London Docklands Development Corpn*, para 2183.

2148 Cause of action—fatal accident—dependant—former wife

For the purposes of the Fatal Accidents Act 1976, 'dependant' includes, under s 1(3)(a), the wife or husband or former wife or husband of the deceased and, under s 1(3)(b), any person who was living with the deceased in the same household immediately before the date of death for at least two years before that date, and who was living during the whole of that period as the husband or wife of the deceased.

The plaintiff was divorced from the deceased, but resumed cohabitation with him after her second marriage failed. When the deceased was fatally injured in the course of his employment, the defendant employer admitted liability to pay damages to the deceased's child, but denied that the plaintiff was also entitled to damages. On a preliminary issue, it was decided that the plaintiff was a dependant of the deceased within the meaning of the 1976 Act, s 1(3)(b) and was therefore entitled to make a claim for damages under the Act. On the defendant's appeal, *held*, although the 1976 Act, s 1(3) provided an elaborate list of entitled dependants, it would have been simpler to have enacted a provision such that any person who could show a relationship of dependency on the deceased was entitled to make a claim under the Act. Moreover, in its current form, s 1(3) was capable of causing hardship to family members who were still not included in the list. In the instant case, the wife ought to be given the opportunity of proving that she had been dependent on the deceased, and she did not have to show that she had been living with him in the same household for a two-year period, as if she was a common law wife. Accordingly, the appeal would be dismissed.

Shepherd v Post Office (1995) Times, 15 June (Court of Appeal: Balcombe, Otton and Aldous LJJ).

2149 Cause of action—fatal accident—dependant—partner living in same household as deceased

For the purposes of the Fatal Accidents Act 1976, 'dependant' includes, under s 1(3)(b), any person who was living with the deceased in the same household immediately before the date of the death for at least two years before that date, and who was living during the whole of that period as the husband or wife of the deceased.

Following the deceased's death as a result of an accident during the course of his employment, his mother made a claim for damages under the Fatal Accidents Act 1976 against his employer. The deceased's girlfriend, by whom he had two children, claimed that she was also entitled to damages, as she had been living with the deceased for more than two years immediately prior to his death. On the preliminary issue of whether or not the deceased's girlfriend was a dependant within the meaning of the 1976 Act, s 1(3)(b), *held*, the deceased had been associated with his girlfriend for 10 years at the time of his death, although there were periods when they did not live together, including a 3-month period during which the girlfriend lived in a refuge. Although the deceased used his parents' address for official documents, gave their name and address as his next of kin, and sometimes stayed with them for weeks at a time, there was evidence from friends and neighbours that the deceased was living with his girlfriend at her flat for the majority of the time. Brief absences did not necessarily mean that a person had ceased to live continually at a particular place for the purposes of the 1976 Act, s 1(3). On the facts, the girlfriend had been living in the same household as the deceased as his wife for at least two years prior to his death.

Pounder v London Underground Ltd [1995] PIQR P217 (Queen's Bench Division: judge not named).

2150 Damages

See DAMAGES AND COMPENSATION.

2151 Duty of care—bank—duty owed to customer—advice on prudence of transaction

See *Verity v Lloyds Bank plc*, para 156.

2152 Duty of care—classification society—physical damage—whether imposition of duty fair, just and reasonable

A short time after a cargo-loaded vessel had embarked cracks in its hull were reported. It entered a harbour where repairs were carried out. A surveyor, acting on behalf of a classification society, recommended that the vessel continue on its intended voyage and that the repairs be further inspected and dealt with at the earliest opportunity following the discharge of the cargo. The day after the vessel had left the harbour the repairs cracked and the vessel sank. On appeal, it fell to be determined whether the classification society owed a duty of care to the cargo owners. *Held*, Lord Lloyd of Berwick dissenting, even if there was sufficient proximity between the cargo owners and the classification society, it was not fair, just and reasonable to impose such a duty in view of the effects it would have on international trade. Classification societies were independent entities operating for the sole purpose of promoting the safety of lives and ships at sea. If a duty of care was held to exist, the cost of insurance would pass to shipowners. This consequence would have the effect of usurping the contractual structure governing relations between shipowners and cargo owners which was based on a system of double or overlapping insurance of cargo and the limitation of shipowners' liability to cargo owners under the Hague Rules, the Hague Visby Rules and tonnage limitation provisions. Furthermore, a further layer of insurance would be required with the attendant litigation and arbitration. It followed that the classification society did not owe a duty of care to the cargo owners.

Marc Rich & Co AG v Bishop Rock Marine Co Ltd, The Nicholas H [1995] 3 All ER 307 (House of Lords: Lords Keith of Kinkel, Jauncey of Tullichettle, Browne-Wilkinson, Lloyd of Berwick and Steyn). Decision of Court of Appeal [1994] 3 All ER 686 (1994 Abr para 2054) affirmed.

2153 Duty of care—coastguard—duty to mariner

An action for damages was brought in respect of alleged negligence by a coastguard in failing to respond to a distress signal by a fishing vessel. *Held*, the Coastguard Act 1925 was administrative and not directive and did not in terms place a statutory duty on the coastguard. Adopting an incremental approach, whereby the scope of the duty of care could be widened only by analogy, there had been no successful action against the coastguard before nor any other precedent of successful action against the rescue services. The coastguard in its ordinary function of watching and listening and in its rescue co-ordination activities did not owe a duty of care to mariners or members of the public even in an emergency. The effects of possible legal action would lead to defensiveness and a diminution in the coastguard service which would be contrary to public interest. Accordingly, the action for damages would be dismissed.

Skinner v Secretary of State for Transport (1995) Times, 3 January (Queen's Bench Division: Judge Gareth Edwards QC).

2154 Duty of care—company director—vicarious liability of company

See *New Zealand Guardian Trust Co Ltd v Brooks*, para 2837.

2155 Duty of care—confectionery manufacturer—chocolate containing knife blade

See *R v F & M Dobson Ltd*, para 1417.

2156 Duty of care—Department of Health—duty to disseminate information about risk of failure of surgery—vasectomy

See *Danns v Department of Health,* para 2027.

2157 Duty of care—doctor

See MEDICINE, PHARMACY, DRUGS AND MEDICINAL PRODUCTS.

2158 Duty of care—employer—duty to independent contractor

See *Lane v Shire Roofing Co (Oxford) Ltd*, para 1506.

2159 Duty of care—estate agent

See AGENCY.

2160 Duty of care—fire authority—duty owed to general public

See *Duff v Highland and Islands Fire Board*, para 1388.

2161 Duty of care—Law Society—investigation of complaints

See *Wood v Law Society*, para 2781.

2162 Duty of care—local authority—swimming pool—failure to prohibit diving

The plaintiff visited a swimming pool run by the defendant local authority. The maximum depth of the pool was less than that of a conventional pool, and the rules and regulations governing its use stated that diving was inadvisable because of the pool's shallow nature. In addition, lifeguards were instructed that there was to be no diving in the shallow end, and that swimmers were to be told to use a shallow style dive. Depths were indicated at various points along the side of the pool. When the plaintiff dived into the pool at the deepest end, he hit his head on the bottom, causing injuries which rendered him tetraplegic. On his claim for damages, a judge decided that the defendant had been negligent in not prohibiting diving and in failing to instruct lifeguards to enforce such a prohibition. He also held that the plaintiff had been contributorily negligent because he had ignored the clearly-marked depth of the water and had failed to perform a shallow dive. On the defendant's appeal, *held*, the defendant had been under a duty to take such care as was reasonably necessary to ensure that the plaintiff would be reasonably safe in using the swimming pool. The defendant was aware that diving was inadvisable, as not only was that stated in the rules for use of the pool, but also staff were instructed that unsafe dives were to be prevented. Lifeguards could not, however, prevent a swimmer from diving in an unsafe area or making inappropriate dives if there were no signs designating the unsafe areas or telling swimmers that only shallow dives were permitted. Having regard to all the circumstances, the only safe system was to prohibit diving altogether. The judge had therefore not erred in his decision as to liability, nor could it be said that his decision as to the apportionment of liability was demonstrably wrong. Accordingly, the appeal would be dismissed.

O'Shea v Royal Borough of Kingston-upon-Thames [1995] PIQR P208 (Court of Appeal: Neill, Hoffmann and Henry LJJ).

2163 Duty of care—police—seizure of motor vehicle—damage to vehicle while in police possession—liability of police

The police believed that the plaintiff's car incorporated a number of stolen parts. They therefore seized the car and took it to the police yard where it remained for some two months. The yard was enclosed by a 10-foot wall and, although the entrance gates were left open for operational purposes, the yard was continually busy, well lit and overlooked by police inside the building.

However, someone entered the yard and set fire to the plaintiff's car causing considerable damage. The plaintiff claimed that the police had been in breach of their duty of care as bailees and, at first instance, he was awarded damages. On appeal, *held*, while the police were in possession of the car, they had a duty to take reasonable care to prevent damage to the car by third parties. The attack in the present case was not reasonably foreseeable. There had never been a previous incident of vandalism in the yard and, in the circumstances in which the car was being kept, the risk of vandalism was remote. The vandal had shown ingenuity and daring against which reasonable precautions could not avail. Accordingly, the appeal would be allowed.

Sutcliffe v Chief Constable of West Yorkshire (1995) 159 JP 770 (Court of Appeal: Nourse, Waite and Otton LJJ).

2164   Duty of care—pure economic loss—loss consequential on physical damage

Containers of dangerous substances were loaded onto a ship and when they leaked the vessel had to be thoroughly cleaned. When the containers were opened it was found that the drums inside them were in a state of disorder. The charterers of the vessel claimed in negligence against the supplier of the drums, alleging that it had failed to secure the drums within the containers so as to enable them to withstand the ordinary risks of transport by sea. The supplier applied to strike out the points of claim and dismiss the action, arguing that the contamination did not amount to physical damage and that the only loss was the financial cost of cleaning. *Held*, the supplier was liable in tort to the charterers for negligence in the stowing of the containers and the charterers were entitled to recover such loss as might have flowed from that negligence or which might have been incurred in the mitigation thereof. However, there was no basis on which the charterers could recover pure economic loss not flowing from or incurred in mitigation of the damage. Accordingly, the application would be refused.

Losinjska Plovidba v Transco Overseas Ltd, The Orjula [1995] 2 Lloyd's Rep 395 (Queen's Bench Division: Mance J).

2165   Duty of care—Royal Navy—drunkenness

A naval airman died when he choked on his own vomit after drinking a large amount of alcohol at a naval base. The deceased, who had been celebrating a birthday and a promotion, was known to be a heavy drinker. The trial judge considered that it was just and reasonable in the circumstances to impose a duty of care on the Ministry of Defence and held that it was in breach of that duty because it had failed to enforce its own disciplinary codes on the sale and consumption of alcohol. The judge awarded damages to the deceased's widow under the Fatal Accidents Act 1976 and the Law Reform (Miscellaneous Provisions) Act 1934 but reduced the damages by 25 per cent for the deceased's own contributory negligence. The Ministry of Defence appealed, denying the existence of a duty of care and contending that the deceased alone was to blame for his collapse. *Held*, the mere existence of regulatory duties did not of itself create a special relationship imposing a duty in private law. There was no reason why it should not be fair, just and reasonable for the law to leave a responsible adult to assume responsibility for his own actions in consuming alcoholic drink. To dilute self-responsibility and blame one adult for another's lack of self-control was neither just nor reasonable and would take the development of the law of negligence an increment too far. The judge's finding that the ministry was under a duty to take reasonable care to prevent the deceased from abusing alcohol to the extent that he did would be reversed. Until the deceased collapsed, he in law alone was responsible for his condition. Thereafter, when the ministry assumed responsibility for him, the measures taken fell short of the standard reasonably to be expected. Medical assistance was not summoned and the supervision provided was inadequate. However, the deceased's fault was a continuing and direct cause of his death and a greater share of the blame should rest on him. Accordingly, the deceased's contributory negligence would be increased to two-thirds, the damages awarded would be reduced and the appeal would be allowed.

Barrett v Ministry of Defence [1995] 3 All ER 87 (Court of Appeal: Neill, Beldam and Saville LJJ). Decision of Phelan J (1993) Independent, 3 June (1993 Abr para 1882) reversed.

2166   Duty of care—solicitor

See SOLICITORS.

2167   Duty of care—supervising authority—whether duty owed to person supervised— issue of certificate of airworthiness by Civil Aviation Authority

The plaintiff claimed that the Civil Aviation Authority had been negligent in failing properly to inspect his aircraft and then issuing it with a certificate of airworthiness. One month after the certificate was issued the aircraft had crashed. He appealed against a decision that the Civil Aviation Authority was not liable in damages for negligence. *Held*, the crucial question was whether it was fair, just and reasonable to impose a duty of care upon a body which Parliament had entrusted with the duty of supervising others, especially where it was claimed that that duty was owed to the person who was to be supervised. It was the task of the owner to maintain his aircraft properly and the Civil Aviation Authority supervised to ensure that the owner had carried out his responsibilities. Its function was to protect the public against the owner's failures, not to protect an owner against his own failures. Accordingly, it would not be fair, just or reasonable to hold that the Civil Aviation Authority owed a duty to inform an aircraft owner if he had not carried out his main duty of properly maintaining his aircraft. The appeal would be dismissed.

Philcox v Civil Aviation Authority (1995) Times, 8 June (Court of Appeal: Staughton, Millett and Ward LJJ). *Marc Rich & Co v Bishop Rock Marine Co* [1994] 3 All ER 686, CA (1994 Abr para 2054), *Yuen Kun Yeu v A-G of Hong Kong* [1987] 2 All ER 705, PC (1987 Abr para 1863), *Mariola Marine Corp v Lloyd's Register of Shipping* [1990] 1 Lloyd's Rep 547 (1990 Abr para 2204), *Murphy v Brentwood District Council* [1990] 2 All ER 908, HL (1990 Abr para 1688), considered.

2168 Duty of care—valuer

See VALUERS AND APPRAISERS.

2169 Duty of care—youth centre—liability for accident—nature of duty owed—contributory negligence

The plaintiff attended a youth centre with gymnastics facilities. A youth worker showed him how to perform a somersault and the plaintiff attempted the same move while unsupervised. He laid the mats too close to the wall and when he over-rotated he hit the wall sustaining serious injuries. He alleged that the defendant, the owner and occupier of the centre, allowed mats to be laid without proper supervision, allowed unsupervised access to the mats and failed to provide proper qualified supervision. At first instance, the judge found that the defendant owed a duty of care which had been breached by its failure to provide a proper system of control, but held the plaintiff to be two-thirds to blame for the accident. The defendant appealed against the finding of liability and the plaintiff cross-appealed as to the finding of contributory negligence. *Held*, (1) the immediate causes of the accident were the absence of supervision during the practice of a dangerous exercise and the position of the mats. The judge had been entitled to conclude that the defendant was negligent because it issued no form of warning or prohibitory notice and took no steps to intervene to control the use of the mats in the absence of supervision. Proper instruction would have included the necessity of placing mats in a safe position and proper supervision would have ensured that unsupervised practice would have been discontinued and discouraged. (2) It was obvious to any reasonably intelligent person that the plaintiff was taking a real and considerable risk in performing the somersault so close to the wall when he knew of the possibility of over-rotation. The court would not accept that the plaintiff's conduct did not amount to fault within the Law Reform (Contributory Negligence) Act 1945 and, in the circumstances, the apportionment of liability was reasonable. Accordingly, the appeal and cross-appeal would be dismissed.

Fowles v Bedfordshire County Council [1995] PIQR P380 (Court of Appeal: Nourse, Millett and Otton LJJ).

2170 Foreseeability—liability of tortfeasor for suicide

Malaysia

The deceased was injured in a road accident. He was unable to work and was disturbed that he had to rely on his wife and family for his needs. Nine months after the accident, he committed suicide. His widow brought proceedings against the defendants, who were responsible for the accident. No medical evidence as to the state of the deceased's mind was adduced, but the widow stated that she did not expect the deceased to commit suicide. She also stated that the deceased was healthy before the accident, and there was no evidence that he suffered from a latent physical or psychological predisposition to a particular injury or illness. She argued that the defendants were liable on the principle that a tortfeasor had to take his victim as he found him. The defendants argued that they were not liable because the deceased's death through suicide was not foreseeable having regard to the rule in *The Wagon Mound*. *Held*, the rule in *The Wagon Mound* that a defendant was liable if the damage to the plaintiff was of a such a kind as a reasonable man would have foreseen did not abrogate the rule that a tortfeasor took his victim as he found him. Provided that the need for treatment for an injury was foreseeable, the question of foreseeability of the type of consequences did not arise. In the present case, the deceased's suicide was not a normal reaction to his injuries and was not foreseeable. Neither was his suicide an abnormal reaction coming within the thin skull rule, as there was no evidence that the deceased suffered from a psychological predisposition towards depression. Accordingly, the widow's claim would be dismissed.

Sivakumaran v Yu Pan [1995] 1 MLJ 12 (High Court of Malaysia). *Overseas Tankship (UK) Ltd v Morts Dock & Engineering Co Ltd, The Wagon Mound* [1961] 1 All ER 404, PC considered.

2171   Nervous shock—entitlement to damages—proximity

Scotland
The plaintiff was working on a bridge managed by his employer, the defendant. Whilst driving behind an open truck in which a fellow worker was sitting, he witnessed the other worker being blown over the side of bridge and falling to his death. He claimed damages for nervous shock from the defendant but his claim was dismissed at first instance. On appeal, *held*, a person could only claim for nervous shock if his relationship with the injured party was of the sort found within the closest ties of friendship or family, which was not the case in this instance. Although it was different where an employee had been an active participant in the event causing injury, where he was merely a bystander or witness to a fellow employee's injury, the ordinary rule applied and it had to be assumed that he had sufficient fortitude to enable him to endure the shock experienced as a result. Accordingly, the appeal would be dismissed.

Robertson v Forth Bridge Joint Board (1995) Times, 13 April (Inner House).

2172   Nervous shock—liability—employer—damage suffered by professional rescuers— police as witnesses of football ground disaster

The plaintiffs were police constables who claimed compensation for psychiatric damage sustained as a result of involvement in a football ground disaster in which a number of people were crushed to death. *Held*, professional rescuers were people of extraordinary phlegm who were hardened to events that ordinary bystanders would find horrific. A contract between a chief constable and his officers imposed a stricter criterion for recovery of damages for psychiatric injury and it would be inconsistent if a chief constable sent his officers out to the scene of an horrific accident and yet was in breach of contract if they attended and suffered damage. On the facts, only one policeman was a rescuer involved in the aftermath of the disaster but he was not performing a task which would make it fair and reasonable to place him within the area of proximity when a spectator who had only viewed the scene could not claim. Accordingly, the claims would be dismissed.

Frost v Chief Constable of South Yorkshire (1995) Times, 3 July (Queen's Bench Division: Waller J).

2173   Nervous shock—liability—foreseeability of injury

The plaintiff, who suffered from myalgic encephalomyelitis (ME), was involved in a road accident in which his car collided with a car driven by the defendant. He was physically uninjured, but he claimed that his condition had become permanent as a result of the accident. He claimed damages for personal injury caused by the defendant's negligence. His claim was successful at first instance, but the defendant's appeal was allowed on the basis that the plaintiff's injury was not reasonably foreseeable. On the plaintiff's appeal, *held* (Lords Keith of Kinkel and Jauncey of Tullichettle dissenting), (1) in nervous shock cases it was essential to distinguish between primary and secondary victims. In the earlier decided cases, the plaintiff had been the secondary victim, in the position of a spectator. In the present case, the plaintiff was the primary victim and the earlier cases were not in point. (2) In claims by secondary victims, in order to limit the number of potential claimants, the defendant would not be liable unless psychiatric injury was foreseeable in a person of normal fortitude. This control did not apply to cases where the plaintiff was the primary victim. (3) In claims by secondary victims, it might be legitimate to use hindsight in order to be able to apply the test of reasonable foreseeability at all. There was no place for hindsight where the plaintiff was the primary victim. (4) Subject to these qualifications, the question in all cases had to be whether the defendant could reasonably foresee that his conduct would expose the plaintiff to the risk of personal injury, whether physical or psychiatric. If the answer was yes, the duty of care was established, even though physical injury did not in fact occur. There was no justification for regarding physical and psychiatric injury as different kinds of damage. (5) A defendant who was under a duty of care to the plaintiff, whether as primary or secondary victim, was not liable for damages for nervous shock unless the shock resulted in some recognised psychiatric illness. It was not relevant that the illness took a rare form or was of unusual severity. The defendant had to take his victim as he found him. Accordingly, in the present case the appeal would be allowed.

Page v Smith [1995] 2 All ER 736 (House of Lords: Lords Keith of Kinkel, Ackner, Jauncey of Tullichettle, Browne-Wilkinson and Lloyd of Berwick). Decision of Court of Appeal [1994] 4 All ER 522 (1994 Abr para 959) reversed. Bourhill v Young [1943] AC 92, HL, McLoughlin v O'Brian [1983] 1 AC 410, HL (1982 Abr para 2132) and Alcock v Chief Constable of South Yorkshire Police [1992] 1 AC 310, HL (1991 Abr para 787) distinguished.

2174 Nervous shock—psychiatric illness caused without physical injury—Law Commission consultation

The Law Commission has published a consultation paper on the liability for negligently inflicted psychiatric illness (often referred to as 'nervous shock') which is caused without any physical injury to the plaintiff, Liability for Psychiatric Illness (Law Commission consultation paper No 137). The paper contains a number of provisional views and matters for consultation. It is suggested that the law on the subject is in need of reform and that reform should be effected by Act of Parliament. The commission provisionally proposes that there should continue to be liability for such negligently inflicted psychiatric illness and that the precondition that the illness sustained by the plaintiff should have arisen as a result of physical injury (actual or apprehended) to the plaintiff should not be re-introduced. The commission also proposes that special limitations, beyond matters within reasonable foreseeability, should continue to be applied to claims where the person negligently injured or imperilled is a person other than the plaintiff who claims compensation. Views are sought on the emphasis in such claims on the plaintiff's reasonable fortitude and on the means of establishing a close tie of love and affection between a plaintiff and the primary victim of the defendant's negligence. The commission provisionally proposes that where there is a close tie of love and affection between the plaintiff and the primary victim of the defendant's negligence the preconditions of closeness in time and space and perception through unaided senses should be abandoned, but views are sought on whether mere by-standers should be able to recover damages for shock-induced psychiatric illness, and whether 'professional rescuers' should be able to claim for negligently inflicted psychiatric illness sustained in the course of the performance of their duties. The commission provisionally proposes that a plaintiff should be able to recover for psychiatric illness where the defendant has put the plaintiff in the position of being, or of thinking that he is about to be, or has been, the involuntary cause of another's death or injury, where the illness of the plaintiff stems from the shock of the consciousness of this supposed fact (cf Alcock v Chief Constable of South Yorkshire Police [1992] 1 AC 310 at 408, HL, per Lord Oliver of Aylmerton (1991 Abr para 787)). Views are sought as to whether the requirement in secondary victim cases that the psychiatric illness must have been induced by shock should be abandoned, and whether damages should be available for psychiatric illness where the primary victim is the defendant. The commission proposes that the normal principles of causation should be applicable to determine whether the communication of true news breaks the chain of causation between the defendant's negligence and the plaintiff's psychiatric illness consequent on the communication of the news. The commission also proposes that criteria analogous to those applicable where human safety or injury to a third party is involved should apply where psychiatric illness is caused by damage, or danger, to the property of a third party. Views are sought on the possible liability for the negligent communication of news to a plaintiff which causes a foreseeable psychiatric illness. The commission further proposes that an employer who negligently over-burdens an employee with work, thereby foreseeably bringing on a psychiatric illness, should be liable in negligence, subject to the standard defences.

2175 Occupier's liability—duty owed to visitor—duty to warn visitor—visitor aware of danger

A local authority was the occupier of a harbour wall to which the public had access. The wall sloped downwards towards the sea and in the winter months the lower part was covered in algae which was plainly visible. The plaintiff sustained serious injuries when he slipped on the algae-covered slope and fell off the wall. He sued the authority, claiming that it should have erected a sign warning users that the wall was slippery, particularly when wet, and that special care should be taken. At first instance, the judge concluded that (1) the authority was negligent and in breach of the common duty of care in failing to erect warning signs, (2) if a warning sign had been erected the accident would have been avoided, and (3) the level of contributory negligence was 40 per cent. On the authority's appeal against the judge's decision, held, (1) the duty under the Occupier's Liability Act 1957 was a duty owed by the occupier to the individual visitor so it could only be said that there was a duty to warn if without a warning the visitor in question would have been unaware of the nature and extent of the risk. If the danger was obvious and the visitor was able to appreciate it no warning was required. In the present case, the plaintiff admitted that he could see the wall was covered in spray and knew it might be slippery because of the algae along its outer edge and a warning sign would not have told him anything he did not know. (2) If there had been a notice the plaintiff might have behaved with greater circumspection, but a bare possibility was insufficient to establish causation. The judge had been wrong to find liability was established and, accordingly, the appeal would be allowed.

Staples v West Dorset District Council [1995] PIQR P439 (Court of Appeal: Nourse, Kennedy and Evans LJJ).

2176 Occupier's liability—duty owed to visitor—visitor's injuries caused by third party

Canada

The plaintiff was injured during a brawl in a bar owned by the defendant. In the space of a few minutes, he had been witness to three separate assaults. Two of the assaults were occasioned upon persons who had gone to the first victim's assistance. The plaintiff then intervened in an attempt to stop the violence and was injured by an unidentified assailant. He subsequently brought an action for damages against the defendant, under a provision that created a duty similar to the duty of care owed by an occupier of premises to his lawful visitor under the Occupiers' Liability Act 1957, s 2. *Held*, the defendant had failed to take reasonable steps to protect the plaintiff from a danger which it ought to have recognised once the first victim had been attacked. There was more than enough time for the defendant's security staff to intervene. It was their failure to do so that led to the plaintiff's intervention. He did not, therefore, voluntarily accept the risk of the intervention. However, while he had not voluntarily accepted the risk, he had knowingly exposed himself to the possibility of injury. That amounted to contributory negligence. The plaintiff and the defendant were equally at fault and, accordingly, liability would be divided equally between the parties.

Jeffrey v Commodore Cabaret Ltd (1995) 128 DLR (4th) 535 (Supreme Court).

2177 Proof of negligence—plea of res ipsa locitur—medical negligence claim

The plaintiff underwent surgery for the removal of his gall bladder under general anaesthetic. Although the removal of the gall bladder was successful, she suffered damage to the brachial plexus. This caused her pain and pins and needles in the left hand and clawing of two fingers. In a claim for damages against the defendant, the plaintiff alleged that the damage was caused during administration of an intravenous drip. It was claimed that the nerves in her hand were excessively strained because her arm had been hyper-abducted, that is, placed at an angle of over 90 degrees from her body and externally rotated. At first instance, the trial judge made a finding of fact that the arm had not been placed, even accidentally, in any position during surgery that could have caused the injury. The action was dismissed. The plaintiff appealed against the trial judge's finding of fact. She contended that the only possible cause of the injury was hyper-abduction of the arm, and that the maxim res ipsa locitur should apply. *Held*, it was the trial judge who had heard the witnesses in person and arrived at findings of fact on the basis of their evidence. It was well established that the Court of Appeal could only interfere with such a finding if convinced that the judge was wrong. There was no basis to contradict the findings of the judge in the present case, as there was nothing to suggest that the anaesthetist had departed from accepted practice. The maxim res ipsa locitur did not apply and, even if it had been a proper case for the application of the doctrine, it was rebutted by evidence that the anaesthetist had acted in compliance with universally accepted practice. Moreover, it was doubtful whether the doctrine could be of much assistance in a case of medical negligence. Medical science was not so precise as to anticipate the exact result of carrying out a routine medical procedure. There was always room for a wholly unexpected result to occur in the human body even where the correct procedures were followed. The appeal would be dismissed.

Delaney v Southmead Health Authority (1992) 26 BMLR 111 (Court of Appeal: Dillon, Butler-Sloss and Stuart-Smith LJJ).

NORTHERN IRELAND

Halsbury's Laws of England (4th edn) Vol 8, paras 1637–1647

2178 Emergency provisions—codes of practice

The Northern Ireland (Emergency Provisions) Act 1991 (Codes of Practice) Order 1995, SI 1995/1896 (in force on 1 September 1995), brings into operation a revised code of practice (published by HMSO) made under the Act. The revision reflects certain changes introduced by the Criminal Justice and Public Order Act 1994 by virtue of which an authorised investigator exercising his powers under the 1991 Act, Sch 5 may now specify the manner in which information is furnished to him. SI 1993/2761 is revoked.

2179 Emergency provisions—continuance

The Northern Ireland (Emergency and Prevention of Terrorism Provisions) (Continuance) Order 1995, SI 1995/1566 (in force on 16 June 1995), continues in force, with exceptions, the temporary provisions of the Northern Ireland (Emergency Provisions) Act 1991 for twelve months from 16th June 1995, and the provisions referred to in the Prevention of Terrorism (Temporary Provisions) Act 1989, s 27(11).

2180 Government—extension of provisions

The Northern Ireland Act 1974 (Interim Period Extension) Order 1995, SI 1995/1895 (in force on 14 July 1995), extends, until 16 July 1995, the period specified in the Northern Ireland Act 1974, s 1(4), as previously extended, for the operation of specified temporary provisions for the government of Northern Ireland.

2181 Northern Ireland (Remission of Sentences) Act 1995

The Northern Ireland (Remission of Sentences) Act 1995 provides for the release on licence of persons serving sentences to which the Northern Ireland (Emergency Provisions) Act 1991, s 14 applies. The Act received the royal assent on 8 November 1995 and comes into force on a day to be appointed. For details of commencement, see the commencement table in the title STATUTES.

Section 1 provides for the release on licence of persons serving sentences subject to restricted remission. Section 2 deals with commencement. Sections 3 and 4 confer power on the Secretary of State to make orders suspending or reviving the operation of s 1. Section 5 deals with short title and extent.

NUISANCE

Halsbury's Laws of England (4th edn) Vol 34, paras 301–400

2182 Articles

Does Only the Careless Polluter Pay? A Fresh Examination of the Nature of Private Nuisance, Gerry Cross: 111 LQR 445

Encroachment of Tree Roots, Mark Pawlowski: Estates Gazette, 15 April 1995, p 100

Planning Decisions and Nuisance, Gill Murphy and Leslie Rutherford: 139 SJ 388

Quiet, Please!, Simon Jackson (on the three lines of attack open to an individual faced with a noise nuisance): 139 SJ 578

Statutory Nuisance Appeals with Special Reference to Smells, Delwyn Jones: [1995] JPL 797

Tree Roots: a Foreseeable Nuisance, Barry Stanton and Gordon Wignall: 139 SJ 1146

2183 Dust nuisance—actionability in negligence

In the first action, the plaintiffs claimed damages for nuisance against the defendant developers of a tall building for interference with their television reception. In a separate action, the plaintiffs claimed damages for negligence and nuisance against the defendant developers of a road for the deposit on their properties of dust created by the construction of the road. On appeals by the plaintiffs and the defendants against judgments made on a number of preliminary issues, *held*, (1) the erection of a building in the line of sight between a television transmitter and other properties was not actionable as an interference with the use and enjoyment of land. Accordingly, interference with television reception was not capable of constituting actionable private nuisance. However, the powers and duties conferred on planning authorities were not such that, in granting planning permissions, they were conferred an immunity in nuisance on works pursuant to the permissions. Neither was interference with television reception as pleaded capable of constituting a public nuisance at the suit of the plaintiffs. (2) A substantial link between the person enjoying the use and the land on which he was enjoying it was essential to a claim in private nuisance for interference with use and enjoyment of land. Occupation of property as a home conferred on the occupant a capacity to sue in private nuisance. (3) The deposit of dust on property was capable of giving rise to an action in negligence. Whether it did depended on proof of physical damage and that depended on the evidence and the circumstances.

Hunter v Canary Wharf Ltd; Hunter v London Docklands Development Corpn [1996] 1 All ER 482 (Court of Appeal: Neill, Waite and Pill LJJ). For earlier proceedings, see (1994) Independent, 20 December (1994 Abr para 2069).

2184 Environment Act 1995

See para 1289.

2185 Interference with television reception—actionability in nuisance

See *Hunter v Canary Wharf Ltd; Hunter v London Docklands Development Corpn*, para 2183.

2186 Private nuisance—defence—planning permission—authorisation of nuisance by grant of planning permission

The defendants had obtained planning permission for two pig weaning houses. They were held liable in nuisance to the plaintiff neighbouring landowners in respect of the smell emanating from the pigs. On appeal, the defendants submitted that since they had obtained planning permission, any smell emanating from the pigs could not amount to a nuisance. *Held*, unless one was prepared to accept that any planning decision authorised any nuisance which must inevitably flow from it, the argument that the nuisance had been authorised by planning permission in the instant case had to fail. In *Gillingham Council v Medway Dock Co* [1993] QB 343 (1991 Abr para 1771) an alleged public nuisance was held to be authorised by the grant of planning permission and so was not actionable. However, the principle applied in the *Gillingham* case could not be taken to apply to every planning decision. The court should be slow to acquiesce in the extinction of private rights without compensation as a result of an administrative decision which would be difficult to challenge. The judge had been entitled to conclude in the instant case that the planning consents did not prevent the plaintiffs succeeding in their claim in nuisance. The defendants were not immune from liability for nuisance and, accordingly, the appeal would be dismissed.

Wheeler v J J Saunders Ltd [1995] 2 All ER 697 (Court of Appeal: Staughton and Peter Gibson LJJ and Sir John May).

2187 Private nuisance—remedy—abatement—availability

A wall on the defendant's land started to bulge and lean over the land of the plaintiff. In discussions that followed between the parties, the defendant's representative refused to accept that the wall was dangerous but stated that the plaintiff could carry out repairs but at their own expense. The plaintiff demolished the wall, rebuilt it, and subsequently claimed the cost of the work from the defendant. At first instance, the judge found that the wall was a nuisance and allowed the plaintiff's claim. The defendant appealed. *Held*, it was clear that the courts discouraged plaintiffs from taking the law into their own hands. However, the right to abate a nuisance did operate to allow an occupier the right to the cost of removal of a potential source of danger to its property. The plaintiff feared for the safety of persons on its property and, accordingly, it was entitled to recover the cost of demolishing the wall. However, there was no basis on which it could recover the cost of rebuilding the wall. The defendant owed no duty to the plaintiff to fence its land, and the plaintiff only had permission to rebuild the wall at its own expense. If it wished to provide for the safety of its visitors, the plaintiff could reasonably have done so on its own property. Accordingly, the appeal would be allowed in part.

Co-operative Wholesale Society Ltd v British Railways Board (1995) Times, 20 December (Court of Appeal: Beldam, Hobhouse and Aldous LJJ).

2188 Statutory nuisance—abatement notice—appeal

The Statutory Nuisance (Appeals) Regulations 1995, SI 1995/2644 (in force on 8 November 1995), make provision with respect to appeals to magistrates' courts against abatement notices served under the Environmental Protection Act 1990, ss 80, 80A. The regulations set out the grounds on which an appeal may be made and prescribe the procedure in the case of an appellant who claims that a notice should be served on some other person. Provision is made in relation to the action which the court may take to give effect to its decision on an appeal. In addition, the regulations prescribe the cases in which an abatement notice is to be suspended pending the abandonment of, or a decision by a magistrates' court on, an appeal. SI 1990/2276 and 2483 are revoked.

2189 Statutory nuisance—complaint against local council—complaint by council tenant—civil proceedings brought at same time as complaint

The Environmental Protection Act 1990, s 82 provides that any person aggrieved by a statutory nuisance may bring proceedings in the magistrates court. Amongst the definitions of 'statutory nuisance' set out in the 1990 Act, s 79 is 'any premises in such a state as to be prejudicial to health or a nuisance'.

The applicant was the tenant of a local authority house subject to an agreement whereby the authority were obliged to keep the property in repair. A surveyor employed by the applicant inspected the property and concluded that, due to structural defects and inadequate heating, insulation and ventilation, it was prejudicial to health and therefore a statutory nuisance. He also concluded that the authority were in breach of their covenant to repair. The applicant requested the defendant magistrates' court to issue and serve a summons on the authority under the 1990 Act, s 82 and commenced civil proceedings against the authority for breach of the repairing covenant, as a result of which an injunction was obtained, requiring the authority to carry out repairs. The chief clerk of the magistrates' court refused to issue the summons, claiming that as civil proceedings had already been commenced, criminal proceedings were unjustified. The applicant claimed that the relief sought in the civil and criminal courts was different as it was necessary for the authority to carry out repairs in order to deal with the design defects but the chief clerk once again refused to issue a summons. On an application for judicial review of the chief clerk's decision, *held*, although it was not clear that the statutory nuisance would still exist once the authority had carried out the repairs specified in the injunction there was material which showed that it could. An applicant was entitled to an order for abatement of a statutory nuisance which could not be required of a landlord under a contractual or other statutory duty and, therefore, on the material before the chief clerk, he had no choice but to issue the summons. He could not refuse merely because he thought it wrong that the authority could be made to face a penalty in addition to an order to carry out repairs. Accordingly, the application would be granted.

R v Highbury Corner Magistrates' Court, ex p Edwards (1993) 26 HLR 683 (Queen's Bench Division: Ralph Gibson LJ and Smith J).

2190 Statutory nuisance—complaint against local council—complaint by council tenant—prevention of remedial work by tenant

The plaintiff was the tenant of a council flat which suffered from condensation, damp and mould. The council tried to install electric convector heaters but the plaintiff refused access on the ground that he preferred gas central heating, which he considered to be cheaper. The plaintiff brought a complaint as a person aggrieved by a statutory nuisance under the Environmental Protection Act 1990, s 82. A magistrates' court held that recurrence of the nuisance was not the fault of the council but of the plaintiff because he had refused access to the council. On appeal by the plaintiff, *held*, the council was not a person responsible for the nuisance, as defined in the 1990 Act, s 79(7) as it was not the person to whose act, default or sufferance the nuisance was attributable. It was not relevant that specific provision for the council's defence was not made under the 1990 Act, s 82. If the council had been held to be responsible for the nuisance, this would have created an absurdity as it would mean that, by preventing remedial work being undertaken, one person could procure a criminal conviction against another. Accordingly, the plaintiff's appeal would be dismissed.

Carr v Hackney London Borough Council (1995) 95 LGR 606 (Queen's Bench Division: McCowan LJ and McKinnon J).

2191 Statutory nuisance—noise—construction plant and equipment

The Construction Plant and Equipment (Harmonisation of Noise Emission Standards) (Amendment) Regulations 1995, SI 1995/2357 (in force on 29 September 1995), amend the 1988 Regulations, SI 1988/361, by making certain amendments consequential on the amendment of Council Directive (EEC) 89/514 by Council Directive (EC) 95/27.

2192 Statutory nuisance—noise—person responsible for nuisance—works required in abatement notice

Under the Environmental Protection Act 1990, s 79(1)(g) noise emitted from premises so as to be prejudicial to health or a nuisance constitutes a 'statutory nuisance'. A 'person responsible' in relation to a statutory nuisance means the person to whose act, default or sufferance the nuisance is attributable: s 79(7)(a). Section 80(1) provides that where a local authority is satisfied that a statutory nuisance exists it must serve an abatement notice specifying the time within which requirements are to be complied with (a) requiring the abatement of the nuisance or prohibiting or restricting its occurrence or recurrence, and (b) requiring the execution of such works, and the taking of such other steps, as may be necessary for any of those purposes.

A housing association, which owned the freehold of a block of flats, laid sound insulation boards between all the flats except Flats A and B. The leaseholder of Flat A complained that she was suffering noise nuisance due to noise from Flat B. The local authority served a notice on the appellant pursuant to the 1990 Act, s 79(1)(g) requiring it to provide suitable and effective sound insulation between those flats. The appellant unsuccessfully challenged the notice in the magistrates' court. On appeal by way of case stated, *held*, (1) the facts of the case were sufficient to support the magistrates' conclusion that the appellant was a 'person responsible' under s 79(7)(a); the lack of sound-proofing constituted the nuisance and that nuisance could only be attributed to the appellant. (2) The court rejected the appellant's argument that, although it owned the void between the flats, the noise in question was 'emitted' from Flat B and was only 'transmitted' through the void. It was preferable to approach the wording of the Act simply and 'emit' in s 79(1)(g) meant no more than 'goes out from', not 'produced by'. (3) The noise occurred only as a result of everyday living and the notice could not be impugned on the basis that it should have been served on the leaseholder of Flat B in addition to, or instead of, the appellant. (4) The matter involved a notoriously difficult question of sound levels and nuisance and the authority should have decided on the required work and stated that in the notice. Accordingly, the matter would be remitted to the magistrates' court to consider whether the notice would be quashed or varied further in the appellant's favour.

Network Housing Association v Westminster City Council (1994) 27 HLR 189 (Queen's Bench Division: Simon Brown LJ and Buckley J).

OPEN SPACES AND HISTORIC BUILDINGS

Halsbury's Laws of England (4th edn) Vol 34, paras 401–1000

2193 Articles

Abolition of an Unenforced Duty, Andrew Beale and Roger Geary (on repeal of the Caravan Sites Act 1968): 145 NLJ 47
Cowed but Unbowed, Michael Harwood (on farm animals and public paths): 139 SJ 610
The Criminal Justice and Public Order Act 1994: Gypsies—The Criminalisation of a Way of Life? Sue Campbell: [1995] Crim LR 28
Defining the Traveller: From Legal Theory to Practical Action, Roger Geary and Clare O'Shea (on the legal definition of 'gypsy'): 17 JSWFL 167
Fixture or Fitting?—The Case of Leighton Hall, Montgomeryshire, Gareth Thomas (on the illegal removal of fixtures from a listed building): [1995] JPL 187
Gypsy Law, Gary Blaker: [1995] JPL 191
Historic Parks and Gardens: A Review of Legislation, Policy Guidance and Significant Court and Appeal Decisions, David Lambert and Vincent Shaclock: [1995] JPL 563
In Defence of Common Humanity, Stephen Cragg and Ravi Low-Beer (on *R v Wealden District Council, ex p Wales* (1995) Times, 22 September (para 2902)): 145 NLJ 1342
New Age Gypsies? Andrew Beale and Roger Geary (on the definition of 'gypsy' under the Caravan Sites Act 1968): 138 SJ 112
PPG 9 'Nature Conservation'—A New Initiative? Lynda Warren and Victoria Murray: [1995] JPL 574
A Privileged Position? Gypsies, Land and Planning Law, Hilaire Barnett: [1994] Conv 454

2194 Environment Act 1995

See para 1289.

2195   Green belt—objection to inclusion of land in green belt—local plan inquiry—burden of proof

See *Swan Hill Developments Ltd v Southend-on-Sea Borough Council*, para 2876.

2196   Listed building—enforcement notice—appeal against notice—administrative error

The decision letter informing the applicant that his appeal, under the Planning (Listed Buildings and Conservation Areas) Act 1990, s 39, against a listed building enforcement notice had been refused wrongly advised him that he could appeal against the refusal under the Town and Country Planning Act 1990, s 288. He followed that advice but was subsequently informed of the correct method of appeal and was advised to recommence proceedings. He failed to do so and the Secretary of State sought to have the applicant's originating notice of motion struck out. *Held*, the applicant had failed to establish that the court had jurisdiction or that there was a right of appeal under s 288. An appeal from a decision under the Planning (Listed Buildings and Conservation Areas) Act 1990, s 39 could only be brought under s 65 and such proceedings could only be heard with leave of the High Court. No such leave had been obtained. There being no right of appeal under the Town and Country Planning Act 1990, s 288, the court had no jurisdiction and, accordingly, the originating notice of motion would be struck out.

O'Brien v Secretary of State for the Environment and Fenland District Council (1993) 68 P & CR 314 (Queen's Bench Division: Hidden J).

2197   National parks—national park authorities—Wales

The National Park Authorities (Wales) Order 1995, SI 1995/2803 (in force on 23 November 1995), establishes a national park authority for each of the national parks in Wales. The authorities will on a specified date become the local planning and hazardous substances authorities for the parks in place of county and county borough councils. The relevant councils and the Secretary of State for Wales will appoint members to each of the authorities. The order makes provision as to the resignation of office by members, the filling of vacancies, notices of appointment, the meetings and proceedings of an authority and the sending of copies of reports to the Countryside Council for Wales and to the county and county borough councils. The authorities are able to keep a general fund for the receipt and payment of monies and to keep accounts. In addition, provision is made as to the continuity of the exercise of functions between the current councils and the authorities and the transfer of staff to, and employment by, the authorities. The order contains transitional provisions, including those relating to capital finances and competitive tendering.

The National Park Authorities (Levies) (Wales) Regulations 1995, SI 1995/3019 (in force on 21 December 1995), provide for the issue of levies to billing authorities by national park authorities in Wales, established by the National Park Authorities (Wales) Order 1995, SI 1995/2803, and apply to levies issued by such authorities for the purpose of meeting their expenses in respect of financial years beginning on or after 1 April 1996. The regulations provide for (1) the issue of levies; (2) the apportionment of levies between councils; (3) the maximum amount of levies; (4) the issuing of substituted levies; (5) the payment of levies and the interest thereon; (6) a council to anticipate a levy which may be issued to it.

2198   Scheduled monument—consent to works—damage to scheduled monument—definition of area—extent of Secretary of State's consent

A company obtained written consent from the Secretary of State for construction works above the site of a scheduled monument. The extent of the monument was defined in a map attached to a statutory notice which had previously been published. Permission was given for specific additional work and sub-contractors were later employed to excavate a manhole. No notice of that excavation work was given and the company was charged with causing works to be executed damaging a scheduled monument. The company submitted that there was no case to answer because (1) the map could not be taken as definitive of the extent of the scheduled monument and the jury should decide as a question of fact whether the company caused damage; (2) the true construction of the Secretary of State's consent extended to the excavation work; (3) the Crown was estopped from denying that the Secretary of State consented to the work. The company was convicted and, on appeal, *held*, (1) the judge correctly construed that the map was incorporated into the notice and any ambiguities in the description of the site did not affect the map. For the jury to make a decision on the description of the monument would mean they were re-doing the scheduling work of the Secretary of State and introducing uncertainty as to whether an offence had been committed. (2) The original consent was granted because of the limited ground level work and could not be read to extend to the excavation work in question. It was a matter of law whether the consent could be construed to extend to that, not a question of fact for the jury. (3) Nothing in the documents suggested that consent to the excavation work was to be taken for granted; specific approval was given for other additional works after the consent. The estoppel argument was misconceived and, although abuse of process could be invoked, this was not an appropriate case in which to do so. Accordingly, the appeal would be dismissed.

R v Bovis Construction Ltd [1994] Crim LR 938 (Court of Appeal: Farquharson LJ, Pill and Laws JJ).

PARLIAMENT

Halsbury's Laws of England (4th edn) Vol 34, paras 1001–1506

2199 Articles
Sleaze and the Law, Leslie James: 159 JP Jo 73

2200 European Parliament—pay and pensions—transfer of functions
The Transfer of Functions (European Parliamentary Pay and Pensions) Order 1995, SI 1995/2995 (in force on 27 December 1995), transfers to the Lord President of the Council the functions of the Secretary of State under the European Parliament (Pay and Pensions) Act 1979 and any order made under that Act. Those functions relate to allowances, grants and pensions payable to or in respect of representatives and former representatives to the European Parliament who have been elected for constituencies in the United Kingdom.

2201 Parliamentary constituencies—England
The Parliamentary Constituencies (England) Order 1995, SI 1995/1626 (in force on 12 July 1995), gives effect, without modification, to the Boundary Commission for England proposals for changes to parliamentary constituencies following a review by the Commission of Representation in the House of Commons.

2202 Pensions
See PENSIONS AND SUPERANNUATION.

2203 Privilege—freedom of speech, debates and proceedings in Parliament—defence to libel action
See *Allason v Haines*, para 1879.

PARTNERSHIP

Halsbury's Laws of England (4th edn) Vol 35 (reissue), paras 1–300

2204 Articles
New Partnership Rules, Mark Nichols (on the new system of income tax for partnerships): Estates Gazette, 20 May 1995, p 126

2205 Creation—joint venture—evidence of partnership
Scotland
The defendant landowner and the plaintiff property developer arranged for the defendant to lease land to the plaintiff, which would provide capital for the development of the land by the defendant. The plaintiff sub-leased the land to the defendant for an annual rent to be calculated so as to ensure that the plaintiff would receive the proportion of rents paid by commercial sub-

sub-tenants which would be equivalent to the amount of capital provided by the plaintiff. Following forfeiture proceedings for non-payment of rent under the sub-lease, the plaintiff sought to recover its investment and an accounting in respect of certain rents due, contending that the arrangement between it and the defendant constituted a partnership or, alternatively, that the defendant had been unjustifiably enriched at its expense. *Held*, none of the features of a partnership, such as the sharing of profits and losses and mutual agency, appeared to be present in the arrangement between the plaintiff and defendant. Their arrangement had been constituted as a commercial lease and a sub-lease. It was typical of many commercial arrangements in the field of property development and exploitation. The scheme could operate effectively without a partnership between the parties being inferred. Although no provision had been made for compensation to the plaintiff for the value of its investment in the event of a forfeiture of the sub-lease, that was not by itself sufficient for a partnership to be inferred. The common economic interest of the parties to the venture, in the absence of other indications of a partnership, was not sufficient to create a joint venture. There was no authority to support the plaintiff's alternative claim of unjust enrichment. Accordingly, the action would fail.

Dollar Land (Cumbernauld) Ltd v CIN Properties Ltd (1995) Times, 21 April (Outer House).

2206   Dissolution—profits made after dissolution—apportionment of profits

The plaintiff and defendant entered into a partnership for the purpose of carrying on the business of a newsagent, acquiring leasehold premises to do so. The defendant provided far more capital than the plaintiff and in return the parties agreed that the plaintiff would put in most of the labour. The partnership was determinable at will and when it did end the defendant carried on the business on his own. An action was brought to determine how the post-determination profits and the proceeds of the sale of the business should be apportioned. *Held*, the post-determination profits had to be apportioned according to the principles laid down in *Manley v Sartori*, applying the principles of the Partnership Act 1890, s 42(1). Thus they should be apportioned on a pro rata basis, subject first to the defendant receiving a proper allowance for carrying on the business. It was clear from *Barclays Bank Trust Co Ltd v Bluff* that the provisions of s 42(1) did not apply to the profit made on the sale of the business where the partners had made unequal contributions to the partnership assets. In such circumstances the profit had to be apportioned in the same proportion as the partners' original contribution to the partnership assets.

Popat v Shonchhatra [1995] 1 WLR 908 (Chancery Division: David Neuberger QC). *Manley v Sartori* [1927] 1 Ch 157, *Barclays Bank Trust Co Ltd v Bluff* [1981] 3 All ER 232 (1981 Abr para 2122), followed.

2207   Implied authority—recklessness of one partner—ability of other partner to claim under insurance contract

See *Kelly v National Insurance Co of New Zealand Ltd*, para 1725.

2208   Insolvent partnership—creditor's petition against one partner only

See *Schooler v Customs and Excise Comrs*, para 172.

PATENTS AND REGISTERED DESIGNS

Halsbury's Laws of England (4th edn) Vol 35 (reissue), paras 301–900

2209   Articles

Additional Subject-Matter and Claim Broadening, David Musker: [1995] EIPR 594

Biotechnology Patenting: The Wicked Animal Must Defend Itself, Stephen Crespi: [1995] EIPR 431

Can an English Court Restrain Infringement of a Foreign Patent? Christopher Floyd and Iain Purvis: [1995] EIPR 110

European Intellectual Property Rights: A Tabular Guide, Claire Burke: [1995] EIPR 466

International Intellectual Property Conventions: A Tabular Guide, Claire Burke: [1995] EIPR 477

Patenting Software-Related Inventions in the US and European Patent Offices, John Richards and Martyn Molyneaux: [1995] 1 CTLR 117

Publish and Be Damned? The EPO's Enlarged Board of Appeal Decision in G03/93, George Schlich: [1995] EIPR 327

Supplementary Protection Certificates for Agrochemicals: The Draft EC Regulation, Nigel Jones and Lisa Patten: [1995] EIPR 446

2210 Patents—amendment—additional matter

The Patents Act 1977, s 76(3) provides that no amendment of the specification of a patent is to be allowed under the 1977 Act, s 75 if it results in the specification disclosing additional matter.

The respondent patented a drug for use in the treatment of coughs, cold-like and 'flu symptoms. The patent claimed that the drug consisted of new types of non-steroidal anti-inflammatory drugs ('NSAIDs') mixed with an antihistamine, a decongestant, an expectorant, and a cough suppressant. It also claimed that particular mixtures were capable of producing synergistic combinations. On the applicant's petition for the revocation of the patent, the respondent admitted that the patent was invalid as it stood and sought leave to amend the patent so as to reduce the ambit of its claims. The applicant argued that (1) amendment would result in the specification disclosing additional matter, within the meaning of the 1977 Act, s 76(3), and that (2) the patent should be revoked because of a lack of an inventive step, or obviousness. *Held*, (1) the test of additional matter was whether or not a skilled man would look at the amended specification and learn anything new about an invention which he could not learn from the unamended specification. Here, a skilled man would see that only some of the mixtures originally claimed were still in the specification. As there was nothing new in that, there was no disclosure of additional matter, and therefore the amendment to the patent was to be allowed. (2) The claim in the patent was obvious, as it involved merely substituting one NSAID with an already existing NSAID in order to improve the performance of the resulting composition, having regard to properties which the composition was already known to contain. Accordingly, the application to revoke the amended patent would be granted.

Reckitt & Colman Products Ltd v Richardson-Vicks Ltd; Smith Kline Beecham v Richardson-Vicks Inc (1995) 25 BMLR 63 (Chancery Division: Jacob J).

2211 Patents—application—appeal procedure—independent and impartial tribunal

See *British-American Tobacco Company Ltd v The Netherlands*, para 1574.

2212 Patents—construction of new claims—purposive construction

The Patents Act 1977, s 125 provides that claims must be interpreted according to the Protocol on the Interpretation of Article 69 of the European Patents Convention 1973. This provides that an invention for a patent must not be interpreted in the sense that the extent of the protection conferred is to be understood as that defined by the strict, literal meaning of the wording used in the claims; the descriptions and drawings being employed only for the purposes of resolving an ambiguity found in the claims. Nor must it be interpreted in the sense that the claims serve only as a guideline and that the actual protection extends to what the patentee has contemplated, having regard to the consideration of the descriptions and drawings by a person skilled in the art. Instead it must be interpreted as defining a position between these two extremes, combining a fair protection for the patentee with a reasonable degree of certainty for third parties.

The holder of a patent appealed from a decision that his patent for a machine for paper interleaving and cutting had been infringed by the defendants. *Held*, the protocol's requirement was fulfilled by using the purposive construction enunciated in *Catnic Components v Hill and Smith Ltd*, together with the guidance given in *Improver Corporation v Remington Consumer Products Ltd*. The purposive construction consisted in asking whether persons with practical knowledge and experience of the kind of work involved would understand that strict compliance with a particular descriptive word or phrase was intended by the patentee to be an essential part of the patent so that any variant would fall outside it. Following the *Improver* case the court should ask (1) whether the variant had a material effect on the way the invention worked. If it did, the variant was outside the claim; (2) if it did not, was it obvious to a person skilled in the art that the variant had no material effect at the date of publication of the claim? If it was not then the variant was outside the claim; (3) if it was, would a person skilled in the art have understood that the patentee intended that strict compliance with the primary meaning was an essential requirement? If that was so, the variant was outside the claim. If it was not, the court must conclude that the patentee intended the word or phrase to have a figurative rather than a literal meaning, denoting a class of things including the variant. Accordingly, the appeal would be allowed.

Kastner v Rizla Ltd [1995] RPC 585 (Court of Appeal: Balcombe, Otton, and Aldous LJJ). *Catnic Components v Hill and Smith Ltd* [1981] FSR 60, HL (1981 Abr para 2149), *Improver Corporation v Remington Consumer Products Ltd* [1989] RPC 69, CA (1989 Abr para 1706), followed. *PLG Research Ltd v Ardon International Ltd* [1995] FSR 116, CA (1994 Abr para 2095) distinguished.

2213 Patents—fees

The Patents (Fees) Rules 1995, SI 1995/2164 (in force on 4 September 1995), replace the 1992 Rules, SI 1992/616. The principal changes are as follows: (1) a fee of £50 is introduced for commencing proceedings before the comptroller on filing Form 2/77, although no fee is payable if the proceedings relate to an offer to surrender a patent; (2) a uniform fee of £40 is introduced for requesting amendment or correction on Form 11/77; (3) a fee of £50 is introduced for giving notice of opposition on Form 15/77; (4) a reduced fee of £50 is payable for registering or giving notice of a transaction, instrument or event; and (5) a uniform fee of £5 is introduced for requesting an uncertified copy of material from a file or the register, and for requesting renewal information or inspection of the register.

2214 Patents—infringement—declaration of non-infringement

The plaintiffs manufactured transparent envelopes for use with overhead projector systems in the United Kingdom, France and Germany. The defendants were the proprietors of a patent granted in the United Kingdom, France and Germany, which related to an invention for such envelopes. When the defendants alleged that the plaintiffs had infringed their patent in the United Kingdom, the plaintiffs sought a declaration under the Patents Act 1977, s 71 that their activities in France, Germany and the United Kingdom were not an infringement of the defendants' patent. The defendants' applied for an order striking out those parts of the proceedings which referred to France and Germany, arguing that the court had no jurisdiction to make a declaration in respect of acts carried out in those countries, and that they had not alleged that the plaintiffs had infringed their French or German patents. *Held*, the court's power to make a declaration under the 1977 Act was confined to acts within the United Kingdom. Moreover, a party against whom no claim was made could not sue for a declaration of non-liability. Here, the defendants had written to the plaintiffs about an infringement of their patent, but the complaint related only to their United Kingdom patent. In addition, the plaintiffs' reply to that letter drew a distinction between the defendants' United Kingdom patent and those in France and Germany. Accordingly, the application would be allowed.

Plastus Kreativ AB v Minnesota Mining and Manufacturing Co [1995] RPC 438 (Chancery Division: Aldous J).

2215 Patents—infringement—direct infringement of patented processes

The Patents Act 1977, s 60(1)(c) provides that a person infringes a patent for an invention if, while the patent is in force, he does the following in the United Kingdom in relation to the invention without the consent of the proprietor of the patent, that is to say, where the invention is a process, he disposes of, offers to dispose of, uses or imports any product obtained directly by means of that process, or keeps any such product whether for disposal or otherwise.

The plaintiffs alleged that the defendants had infringed several of their European patents relating to the manufacture of optical discs. In particular, they alleged that the defendants manufactured discs in Germany using the processes of the patents, and then sold them in the United Kingdom. The defendants denied the allegation, arguing that although they manufactured optical discs using the same processes as those involved in the plaintiffs' patents, their discs were not obtained directly by means of those processes. In particular, they pointed to the fact that their discs were physically distinct from the product produced by the patented processes. On the defendants' application for an order striking out the plaintiffs' writ and statement of claim, *held*, the 1977 Act, s 60(1)(c) was introduced to give effect to obligations under the European Patent Convention and the Community Patent Convention. Having regard to the section's German origins, the phrase 'obtained directly' was to be construed as meaning 'without intermediary'. The court therefore had to ascertain whether the allegedly infringing product was produced by the patented process, in the sense that it was the immediate or direct result of that process. Here, the defendants' discs were materially different to those which resulted from the patented processes, as the defendants' discs involved using three further production steps which were important and material in arriving at the end product. The fact that there was a causal link between the production methods was important but insufficient, as the defendants' discs were not directly obtained by the patented method. Accordingly, the application would be granted.

Pioneer Electronics Capital Inc v Warner Music Manufacturing Europe GmbH [1995] RPC 487 (Patents Court: Aldous J).

2216   Patents—infringement—erroneous statement in patent specification—statement withdrawn by patentee—patentee not estopped from bringing action for infringement

See *Gerber Garment Technology Inc v Lectra Systems Ltd*, para 2217.

2217   Patents—infringement—partially invalid patent—date from which damages for infringement reckoned

The Patents Act 1977, s 63(2) provides that, where in any proceedings it is found that a patent is only partially valid, the court will not award damages, costs or expenses, except where the plaintiff proves that the specification for the patent was framed in good faith and with reasonable skill and knowledge and, in that event, the court may grant relief in respect of that part of the patent which is valid and infringed, subject to the discretion of the court as to costs or expenses and as to the date from which damages ought to be reckoned.

The plaintiff brought an action for infringement of two of its patents for automatic cutting machines for use in the garment industry. The first patent was held to be partially valid and infringed, and it was ordered that damages be reckoned from the date of first infringement. The plaintiff requested the court's permission to resile from a statement that a particular process was already known at the time the patent was registered, which was made in the specification for the second patent. If the statement had remained it would have rendered the plaintiff's claims invalid for obviousness. The defendants appealed on the grounds that (1) the plaintiffs were not entitled to resile from the statement made in the specification, and (2) where a patent is only partially valid and there were no special circumstances such as deliberate infringement, damages must not be awarded from a date prior to the judgment. *Held*, (1) although a recital in a patent specification constituted an admission which must necessarily carry great weight, it did not estop the patentee or debar him from leading evidence to contradict it. It would be contrary to all principles to hold a party to be estopped as against another party by an erroneous statement on which that other party had not relied. (2) The discretion conferred by the 1977 Act, s 63 could not arise unless the defendant had infringed a valid claim and the plaintiff had maintained an invalid claim on the register. The correct approach to s 63 was to begin by recognising that it had swept away the old rule that the presence of an invalid claim rendered the whole patent invalid. Such a patent was now treated as partially valid, and the court could grant relief in respect of the valid claims found to have been infringed. The court had an unfettered discretion to decide from what date any award of damages ought to run, and in exercising that discretion it had to take all relevant considerations into account, including the conduct of both parties and the position of the general public. If the presence of the invalid claims had induced the defendant to act as he did, then it would be unjust to order him to pay damages prior to the date on which the invalidity of the claims was established. If, however, the presence of the invalid claims had no effect upon the defendant's conduct, as in this case, then ordinarily it would not be just to deprive the plaintiff of any part of his damages. Accordingly, the defendant's appeal would be dismissed.

Gerber Garment Technology Inc v Lectra Systems Ltd [1995] FSR 492 (Court of Appeal: Leggatt, Millett and Morritt LJJ).

2218   Patents—infringement—partially invalid patent—insufficiency of description— discretion to delete invalid claims

The plaintiffs alleged that the defendants had infringed some of the claims in their patent. A judge upheld the allegation, and also decided that certain other claims in the patent, which were not the subject of the proceedings, were invalid because they were insufficient. The judge allowed the plaintiffs' application to delete both the invalid claims and also a related passage in the body of the specification, despite the defendants' argument that the plaintiffs should be required to amend their principal claim and all of those claims which were dependent on it, so that they would all be supported by the description in the patent. On the defendants' appeal, *held*, the Patents Act 1977 distinguished between the grounds on which a specification could be rejected or curtailed before a patent was granted, and the grounds on which a patent could be revoked after being granted. The court could authorise an amendment after the trial of an infringement action in which a patent was valid in respect of all the claims that were infringed and invalid only in respect of minor or consequential claims. Here, the minor claims were dependent on the principal claim, but the principal claim was not dependent on the invalid minor claims. Where an amendment was sought in circumstances such as in the instant case, there had to be a nexus between the amendment and the circumstances giving rise to the need for an amendment. Here, the deletion sought by the plaintiffs was a natural consequence of the judge's finding that certain claims in the patent were invalid, and those invalid claims were not in issue in the proceedings. Accordingly, the appeal would be dismissed.

Chiron Corpn v Organon Teknika Ltd (No 11) [1995] FSR 589 (Court of Appeal: Dillon, Leggatt and Henry LJJ). Decision of Aldous J (1994) 21 BMLR 121 affirmed.

See also *Chiron Corpn v Murex Diagnostics Ltd (No 9)*, para 2286; *Chiron Corpn v Organon Teknika Ltd (No 10), Chiron Corpn v Murex Diagnostics Ltd (No 10)*, para 1701.

2219　Patents—infringement—proceedings—amendment of claim by adding fresh ground of objection—order for costs

The respondents had applied to the United Kingdom Patent Office for the grant of a patent and, one year later, applied to the European Patent Office for a European patent to take priority over the United Kingdom patent. The petitioner applied for revocation of the United Kingdom patent and, at the hearing for directions for trial, sought leave to add a fresh ground of objection. The judge made a *See v Scott-Paine* ((1932) 50 RPC 56) order whereby the respondents were given one month in which to elect whether to withdraw their answer and consent to revocation of the United Kingdom patent, on condition that, should it elect to do so, the petitioner had to pay all costs incurred between service of the previous and newly amended particulars. The respondents withdrew their answer and consented to the revocation of the United Kingdom patent. The petitioner claimed that the *See v Scott-Paine* order was intended to force the respondents to undertake not to sue the petitioner for infringement of any divisional patent of the European patent, if granted. They therefore applied to have the order amended to that effect, or another order granted. Alternatively, they sought to discharge the order because of a material change in circumstances or to have leave to appeal against the order. *Held*, the purpose of a *See v Scott-Paine* order was to penalise a defendant in costs for failing to include a matter in the pleadings at an earlier stage and not to provide freedom from infringement proceedings to a petitioner or respondent if the patentee elected to revoke the patent. The judge had no considerations other than those expressed in the order, the intention and meaning of which was clear on the face of it. There was no duty to inform the court or the petitioner of the divisional application and, although there was a jurisdiction to discharge an order on a change of circumstances, it was inapplicable in this case because the matters relied on lay outside the action and the terms of the order. In addition, the exercise of a legal right which existed both before and after an order was made could not constitute a change of circumstances. The order, made by consent, created a contract against which leave to appeal could not be granted and, accordingly, the application would be dismissed.

Aumac Ltd's Patent [1995] FSR 501 (Patents Court: Jacob J).

2220　Patents—infringement—reference to European Court of Justice—construction of earlier decision

The plaintiffs alleged that the defendants had infringed their patents relating to three pharmaceutical products by importing the products into the United Kingdom from certain member states. The plaintiffs did not have patents for the products in those member states because patent protection was unavailable there, and it was also the case that the products were cheaper in those other member states than in the United Kingdom. In the course of proceedings in respect of the alleged infringement, the court was asked to make a reference to the European Court of Justice for a preliminary ruling on whether or not the plaintiffs' attempt to stop importation of the products was contrary to the EC Treaty, art 36, relating to free movement of goods. On the question of whether or not a reference was to be made, *held*, the rule in *Merck v Stephar* was that where a patentee sold a product in a member state in which patent protection existed and then marketed the product in another member state in which such protection did not exist, he could not use the protection granted in the first member state to prevent the product being imported from the second member state into the first member state. Although it was normal for the court to make findings of fact when making a reference for a preliminary ruling, that would not be done in the instant case, as the issues raised by the rule in *Merck v Stephar* were of general application to the pharmaceutical industry. However, the plaintiffs' contention that the rule in *Merck v Stephar* should be modified was a relevant point, in particular their argument that drug companies had an ethical obligation to supply their products in all member states and therefore did not have freedom to chose whether or not to market their products in countries where patent protection did not exist. Their argument that there was a legal obligation to supply, both under national law and under the EC Treaty, art 86, was equally valid. As regards interlocutory relief in the case, the court was under a duty to apply an existing rule of Community law unless and until changed by a higher court. Accordingly, the case would be referred to the European Court of Justice for a preliminary ruling.

Merck & Co Inc v Primecrown Ltd [1995] FSR 909 (Patents Court: Jacob J). *Merck & Co Inc v Stephar BV* [1981] ECR 2063, ECJ considered.

2221 Patents—licensing—block exemption

See para 3156.

2222 Patents—Patents Court—rules of evidence—hearsay

The Comptroller General of Patents, Designs and Trade Marks has issued the following *Practice Direction* ([1995] 12 RPC 381).

Following the decision of the High Court in *St Trudo Trade Mark* [1995] RPC 370 that the Registrar of Trade Marks is a tribunal to which the strict rules of evidence apply within the meaning of the Civil Evidence Act 1968, s 18, the Patent Office will proceed on the basis that the judicial functions of the Comptroller under the Registered Designs Act 1949, the Patents Act 1977, the Copyright, Designs and Patents Act 1988, and the Trade Marks Act 1994 are subject to the strict rules of evidence, and the following directions apply in relation to any hearsay evidence sought to be adduced.

1. Hearsay evidence of matters of fact can only be admitted in proceedings before the Comptroller under the above Acts, under the provisions of the Civil Evidence Act 1968, Pt I, and expert evidence or opinion only if it comes within the provisions of the Civil Evidence Act 1972.

2. Where evidence is given before the Comptroller by way of affidavit or statutory declaration, the deponent is required to identify any facts which are not within his personal knowledge, to identify the source of the information to which he deposes, and his grounds for believing that the information is true. Any part of an affidavit or statutory declaration which appears to the Comptroller to relate to matters not within the deponent's knowledge and which does not comply with this requirement, will not be admitted in evidence, and no account will be taken of it by the Comptroller.

3. No other document which includes hearsay (including any document exhibited to an affidavit or statutory declaration) will be admitted in evidence, unless it either falls within an established exception to the hearsay rule, or notice has been given in accordance with RSC Ord 38, Pt III at the time of filing the document. Any such document and the accompanying notice must be filed not later than 28 days prior to the hearing.

4. Where evidence is given orally before the Comptroller, no witness may give evidence of any hearsay unless it either falls within an established exception to the hearsay rule, or the requirements of RSC Ord 38, Pt III have been complied with in relation thereto.

5. Where hearsay evidence is identified in an affidavit or a statutory declaration, or notice is given under paragraph 3 or 4 above, any other party is entitled, within 21 days of service of the affidavit, statutory declaration or notice, to serve a counter-notice, requiring the maker of the statement referred to, to be called as a witness, and the provisions of RSC Ord 38, rr 26, 27 apply thereto.

6. The foregoing directions are without prejudice to the Comptroller's power under the Civil Evidence Act 1968, s 8(3)(a) to admit hearsay statements in relation to which those directions or the requirements of a counter-notice served under paragraph 5 above have not been complied with. Accordingly, notwithstanding the foregoing directions, the Comptroller may, having regard to all the circumstances, admit hearsay evidence even though such directions have not been followed, if it appears to him to be just to do so.

2223 Patents—Patents Court—summons—interlocutory application—hearings by telephone

Jacob J has issued the following *Practice Statement* ([1995] 1 WLR 1578).

1. Telephone summons

For short (20 minutes or less) matters before the Patents Court, the patent judges are willing, unless a matter of general public importance is involved, to hear summonses by telephone conference. The procedure is as follows:

(a) Unless the matter is very urgent, the parties must agree that a telephone hearing is appropriate.

(b) Where it is known that the hearing is to be by telephone in advance of issue of the summons, it must be marked 'by telephone'. Where the summons has already been issued, a letter or fax from the party issuing it must be sent to the patent judge's clerk indicating that a telephone hearing is desired. Where a notice of motion has already been issued, the court may treat the hearing as if by summons.

(c) Any bundles to be used must be agreed and sent in advance to the judge's clerk. Any last minute documents may be sent by fax. The judge's clerk must be informed by telephone of any such documents, and it would be prudent in any event to check with the clerk that the necessary papers are present and correct.

(d) The time for hearing should be agreed with the judge's clerk. It should normally be between 9.30 am and 10.15 am.

(e) The party issuing the summons is responsible for setting up the conference call. That can be done by contacting British Telecom on 0800 778877. The call must commence with the judge at precisely the time agreed with the judge's clerk.

(f) The costs of the call are to be treated as part of the costs of the summons.

(g) Loudspeaker telephones may be used unless they interfere with the hearing.

(h) To avoid any misunderstandings, the parties must agree a minute of order immediately following the hearing of the summons. That may most conveniently be done by one party faxing a signed copy of the minute to the other and that other signing a copy and faxing the complete agreed order to the judge, but other arrangements may be agreed. The judge's clerk will arrange for the order to be drawn up in the same way as an agreed order.

(i) Jacob J and Laddie J have arranged for a recording of any telephone summons to be made. It will not be transcribed. The tape will be kept by the judge's clerk for a period of six months. Arrangements for transcription, if needed, must be made by the parties.

(j) Currently, the relevant numbers are 0171 936 6771 (clerk to Jacob J) and 0171 936 6624 (fax).

(k) The procedure may be used for most short disputed interlocutory matters. The parties must use it where it would save costs, but the procedure is not a substitute for the even cheaper procedure of an agreed interlocutory order.

2. Agreed interlocutory orders

Where the parties are agreed as to the terms of an interlocutory order, it may be made without the need for a hearing. Two drafts of the agreed order and the written consent of the parties' respective solicitors or counsel must be supplied to the clerk of the judge in charge of the patents list.

Where a draft has been amended by hand, it is helpful for a disk of the unamended version to be supplied in accordance with paragraph 7.2 of the *Chancery Guide*. (The Guide can be obtained from Room E01, Royal Courts of Justice, Strand, London WC2A 2LL.) Unless the judge considers that a hearing is needed, he will make the order in the agreed terms by initialling it. It will be drawn up accordingly and sent to the parties.

3. Information sheets on hearing of summons for directions

The formal preparation of an information sheet for a summons for directions in accordance with appendix 5 of the *Chancery Guide* is not necessary in a matter before the Patents Court. None the less, it is good practice for the parties to consider the matters referred to in appendix 5 and any other matter which may shorten or affect the trial.

4. Pre-trial reviews in patent actions

Paragraph 3.9 of the *Chancery Guide* indicates that such a review must be held in a case of over ten days' estimated duration. However, in a matter before the Patents Court, unless any party considers that it would be helpful, there is no need for a pre-trial review.

5. Rights of audience on hearing of summons

Practitioners are reminded that solicitors have rights of audience on any summons in chambers before the High Court. So, although in patent proceedings most interlocutory matters come by summons directly before a patent judge, solicitors have rights of audience on such a summons.

6. Patents judges able and willing to sit out of London

If the parties so desire, for the purpose of saving time or costs, the Patents Court will sit out of London. That also applies to any other intellectual property case. If such a sitting is desired, a request must be made in the first instance to the clerk to Jacob J, whether the matter is proceeding in a district registry or in London.

7. Widening of scope of and change of name of users' committee

With the consent of the Vice-Chancellor and the judges of the Chancery Division, the Patents Court Users' Committee will, in future, consider the problems and concerns of intellectual property litigation generally. Accordingly, the membership of the committee will be widened to include another Chancery judge and a representative of the Institute of Trade Mark Agents.

Any practitioner having views concerning the improvement of intellectual property litigation is invited to make his or her views known to the committee, preferably through the relevant professional representative on the committee.

2224 Patents—proceedings—rules

See para 2374.

2225 Patents—protection of industrial property—convention countries

The Patents (Convention Countries) (Amendment) Order 1995, SI 1995/2989 (in force in part on 15 December 1995, in part on 25 December 1995, and in part on 1 January 1996), amends the 1994 Order, SI 1994/3220, and declares the following to be new convention countries for the purpose of the protection of industrial property: Albania, Antigua and Barbuda, Azerbaijan, Bahrain, Belize, Bolivia, Botswana, Brunei Darussalam, Colombia, Costa Rica, Djibouti, Dominica, Guatemala, Jamaica, Kuwait, Macau, Maldives, Mozambique, Myanmar, Namibia, Nicaragua, Peru, Saint Kitts and Nevis, Saint Lucia, Saint Vincent and the Grenadines, Sierra Leone, Singapore, Thailand, Turkmenistan, and Venezuela.

2226 Patents—restoration—renewal fee—payment—failure to pay

The Patents Act 1977, s 28(3) provides that if the comptroller is satisfied that the proprietor of a patent took reasonable care to see that any renewal fee was paid within the prescribed period, or that that fee and any prescribed additional fee were paid within the six months immediately following the end of that period, the comptroller must by order restore the patent on payment of any unpaid renewal fee and any prescribed additional fee.

A company was granted a patent in the United Kingdom and in Malaysia. The renewal fee for the United Kingdom patent was paid for a number of years, in consequence of which the Malaysian patent also remained in force. When the company was taken over, the successor company was notified by its agent that the renewal fee was due to be paid, but decided not to pay it. As a result, the patent lapsed in the United Kingdom and also in Malaysia. It was accepted that the successor intended to maintain the Malaysian patent and would have paid the renewal fee for the United Kingdom patent had it appreciated that the validity of the former depended on the maintenance of the latter by payment of the renewal fee. The successor unsuccessfully applied for the restoration of the patent. On appeal, *held*, the 1977 Act, s 28(3) was concerned with the fee due in respect of the patent for which restoration was sought, and not with payment of renewal fees generally. A patentee had to show that he intended, or had already taken steps, to pay the renewal fee for a particular patent. A deliberate decision not to pay the fee was inconsistent with that requirement and therefore precluded the application of s 28(3). Moreover, where such a decision had been taken, the court would not restore a patent on the ground that mistake had induced that decision, as the obligation was to take reasonable care to ensure that the fee was paid rather than to decide whether or not to pay it. Here, the successor was advised that the renewal fee was payable and, although it was unaware of the significance of such payment, it reached a deliberate decision not to do so. Section 28(3) was therefore not applicable, and the patent could not be restored. Accordingly, the appeal would be dismissed.

Atlas Powder Co's Patent [1995] RPC 666 (Court of Appeal: Butler-Sloss, Morritt and Hutchison LJJ).

2227 Patents—revocation—European patent

It has been held that in seeking to implement the European Patent Convention 1973, the Patents Act 1977, s 6(1) in particular, does not follow the actual language of the convention, and if the convention itself is obscure, it is not for Parliamentary draftsmen to try and clarify that obscurity.

Beloit Technologies Inc v Valmet Paper Machinery Inc [1995] RPC 705 (Chancery Division: Jacob J).

2228 Patents—revocation—obviousness of invention

See *Reckitt & Colman Products Ltd v Richardson-Vicks Ltd; Smith Kline Beecham v Richardson-Vicks Inc,* para 2210.

2229 Patents—rules

The Patents Rules 1995, SI 1995/2093 (in force on 4 September 1995), consolidate, with amendments, the 1990 Rules, SI 1990/2384 (as amended). The principal amendments are as follows: (1) the number of prescribed forms under the Patents Act 1977 has been reduced and the forms have been modified; (2) revised provision is made for declarations of priority in the case of new applications under the 1977 Act, s 15(4) and for the documents to be provided in connection with such declarations; (3) revised provision is made for applications where all parties have consented as to who should be mentioned as the inventor of the patent; (4) additional provision is made for the voluntary amendment of the description, claims or drawings in a patent application; (5) applications and requests are required to be advertised only in the Official Journal (Patents) and uniform procedures are prescribed in respect of opposition to any matter; (6) provision for applications to register transactions, instruments and events and for applications to settle licences of right is revised; (7) periods are prescribed in respect of international applications for a patent which are to be treated as applications for a patent under the 1977 Act and which applications are to proceed earlier in the national phase; and (8) the rules relating to international preliminary examinations under the Patent Co-operation Treaty have not been reproduced to reflect the fact that the United Kingdom Patent Office no longer carries out such examinations.

2230 Patents—validity—partially valid patent—insufficiency of description—court's discretion to delete invalid claims

In earlier proceedings the plaintiff's patent for producing a hepatitis C virus was declared partially invalid on the grounds of insufficiency in relation to certain claims. The plaintiffs applied to amend the patent to remove the invalid claims but the defendants contended that the amendments should not be allowed in the discretion of the court because, by maintaining the validity of the invalid claims the plaintiffs had recklessly disregarded their duty. In addition, the defendants argued that no relief by way of damages, costs or expenses in respect of the valid claims in the plaintiff's patent should be awarded on the grounds that the original specification for the patent was not framed in good faith and with reasonable skill and knowledge. *Held,* a specification ought to be framed in the form in which a person, with reasonable skill in drafting patent specifications and knowledge of the law and practice relating thereto, would produce it with the patentee's knowledge of the invention. There was no foundation for the defendants' claim that the amendment ought to be refused and the patent revoked. The plaintiff had believed there was no insufficiency and had been advised that amendments were not necessary. Their trial submissions had been reasonable and proper and they had acted in good faith. The invalid claims ought to be deleted as there had been no culpable delay and the defendants had not suffered any detriment by the inclusion of the invalid claims. For the purposes of awarding damages in respect of the valid elements of the plaintiff's patent the court considered the specification was framed in good faith and with reasonable skill and knowledge. Accordingly, the plaintiff's application to amend would be granted.

    Chiron Corpn v Organon Teknika Ltd (No 5); Chiron Corpn v Murex Diagnostics Ltd (1994) 21 BMLR 121 (Chancery Division: Aldous J).

2231 Patents—validity—process made available to the public—further discovery as to operation of process

The first plaintiff had been granted a patent for an anti-histamine. After the patent had expired the defendants began to sell the drug. Having carried out research into the way the drug worked in the human body, the plaintiffs discovered that 99.5 per cent of it was metabolised in the liver and that the acid metabolite was almost exclusively responsible for the anti-histamine activity of the drug. A patent for the acid metabolite was granted to the first plaintiff, the second plaintiff being the exclusive licensee. The plaintiffs claimed injunctions to prevent the defendants from infringing the acid metabolite patent. They claimed that the defendants were infringing the patent by supplying a means for putting the acid metabolite invention into effect. The patent was found to be bad for lack of novelty and ordered to be revoked. The plaintiffs appealed, arguing that neither the acid metabolite nor any information about it had been made available to the public in any way before the priority date of the patent and that for a product to be made available to the public, publicly available information had to identify it and, in the present case, its formula. *Held*, notwithstanding that the acid metabolite was previously unknown, the claim to patent it lacked novelty because the anti-histamine patent had disclosed how the anti-histamine was made and that it should be taken for its anti-histamine effect. The inevitable result of following those instructions was to make the acid metabolite. Further, in the Patents Act 1977, s 2(2) the reference to matter made available to the public did not purport to confine the state of the art about products to knowledge of their chemical composition. An invention was part of the state of the art if the information disclosed enabled the public to know the product under a description sufficient to work the invention. Accordingly, the appeal would be dismissed.

Merrell Dow Pharmaceuticals Inc v HN Norton & Co; Merrell Dow Pharmaceuticals Inc v Penn Pharmaceuticals [1996] RPC 76 (House of Lords: Lords Jauncey of Tullichettle, Browne-Wilkinson, Mustill, Lloyd of Berwick and Hoffmann). Decision of Court of Appeal [1995] RPC 233 affirmed.

2232 Registered designs—fees

The Registered Designs (Fees) (No 2) Rules 1995, SI 1995/2913 (in force on 4 December 1995), replace the earlier 1995 Rules, SI 1995/2165 (which replaced the 1992 Rules, SI 1992/617), so as to (1) provide for an application on Form 9A to extend the period of protection into a fourth and fifth five-year period, at fees of £310 and £450 respectively; (2) increase the additional fee payable in respect of extra time for making application to extend the period of protection from £18 to £24 for each extra month up to a maximum of 6 months; and (3) provide that the fee when applying on Form 19A for settlement of the terms of a licence of right is to be £50. The rules also align fees in respect of several matters with fees prescribed for corresponding patents matters.

2233 Registered designs—protection of industrial property—convention countries

The Designs (Convention Countries) (Amendment) Order 1995, SI 1995/2988 (in force in part on 15 December 1995, in part on 25 December 1995, and in part on 1 January 1996), amends the 1994 Order, SI 1994/3219, and declares the following to be new convention countries for the purpose of the protection of industrial property: Albania, Antigua and Barbuda, Azerbaijan, Bahrain, Belize, Bolivia, Botswana, Brunei Darussalam, Colombia, Costa Rica, Djibouti, Dominica, Guatemala, Jamaica, Kuwait, Macau, Maldives, Mozambique, Myanmar, Namibia, Nicaragua, Peru, Saint Kitts and Nevis, Saint Lucia, Saint Vincent and the Grenadines, Sierra Leone, Singapore, Thailand, Turkmenistan, and Venezuela.

2234 Registered designs—rules

The Registered Designs Rules 1995, SI 1995/2912 (in force on 4 December 1995), consolidate the 1989 Rules, SI 1989/1105. The principal changes are as follows: (1) the prescribed forms under the Registered Designs Act 1949 are reduced in number and amended; (2) the provision in respect of the address for service to be given by applicants for registration and by persons concerned in any proceedings to which the rules relate is revised; (3) the procedure to be followed by applicants when responding to objections made to an application by the registrar is amended; (4) the provision concerning time limits for completing an application is revised to refer also to applications for registration of a design excluded from an earlier application; (5) provision in respect of applications for the registration of title by any person becoming entitled, inter alia, by assignment, transmission or operation of law is amended; (6) the provision for requests to alter a person's address or address for service in the register, or on an application or other document, is revised to require also that the relevant entry be identified in the register, application or document.

PENSIONS AND SUPERANNUATION

Halsbury's Laws of England (4th edn) Vol 33, Supp paras 1078–1158

2235 Articles

Effects of the Budget, John Haywood (on the 1994 Budget's effect on pension schemes): Tax Journal, Issue 293, p 18

Equal Treatment and Pensionable Age, Phil Shiner: LA, December 1995, p 23

Income Withdrawal, John Hayward: Tax Journal, Issue 318, p 18

Long Term Care Insurance, Michael Wilson: 139 SJ 250

Loss of Tax Approval, John Hayward: Tax Journal, Issue 290, p 16

Paying for the Bill, Robin Ellison (on the effects of the Pensions Bill 1995 on pension schemes): 139 SJ 162

Pension Deal, Andrew White (on *Brooks v Brooks* (1995) Times, 3 July, HL (para 1098)): LS Gaz, 19 July 1995, p 18

Pension Options, David Chatterton: 139 SJ 470

Pensions After *Brooks*, Maggie Row (on *Brooks v Brooks* (1995) Times, 3 July, HL (para 1098)): 145 NLJ 1009

Pensions and Divorce: Time for a Change, Maggie Rae: 145 NLJ 310

Pensions and Matrimonial Breakdown, David Burrows: 145 NLJ 223

The Pensions Bill, John Hayward (on the Pensions Bill 1994): Tax Journal, Issue 298, p22

Retirement Annuity Contracts, John Hayward: Tax Journal, Issue 306, p 7, Issue 310, p 10

Second-Hand Endowment Policies, John Hayward: Tax Journal, Issue 323, p 18

Self-Invested Personal Pension Schemes, John Hayward: Tax Journal, Issue 315, p 5

Small Self-Administered Schemes, John Hayward (on the tax-related and practical advantages of such schemes): Tax Journal, Issue 302, p 21

VAT Issues for Pension Funds, Peter Hewitt: Tax Journal, Issue 314, p 22

2236 Civil service—compensation scheme—pensions increase

The Pensions Increase (Civil Service Compensation Scheme 1994) Regulations 1995, SI 1995/1680 (in force on 25 July 1995), apply the provisions of the Pensions (Increase) Act 1971 to any pensions payable under the Civil Service Compensation Scheme 1994 as if they were pensions specified in the 1971 Act, Sch 2, Pt I. The regulations also permit increases in respect of any pension beginning on or after 1 January 1995, by virtue of the power provided by the 1971 Act, s 5(4) (power to provide for increases to take effect retrospectively).

2237 Civil Service—overseas territories—pensions supplement

See para 457.

2238 Civil Service—superannuation—admission of related employments

The Superannuation (Admission to the Principal Civil Service Pension Scheme) Order 1995, SI 1995/1293 (in force on 6 June 1995), adds the following to the employments and offices listed in the Superannuation Act 1972, Sch 1, so that the Principal Civil Service Pension Scheme, the Civil Service Additional Voluntary Contribution Scheme, and the Civil Service Compensation Scheme may apply to them: (1) employment by the Legal Services Ombudsman, with effect from 1 January 1991; (2) employment by the Pensions Ombudsman, with effect from 1 April 1991; (3) employment by the Local Government Commission for England, with effect from 1 July 1992; (4) the office of chairman of the Local Government Staff Commission (England), with effect from 13 May 1993; (5) the office of the Pensions Ombudsman, with effect from 1 September 1994; and (6) the office of the Data Protection Registrar, with effect from 1 September 1994.

2239 Civil service—supplementary earnings cap scheme—pensions increase

The Pensions Increase (Civil Service Supplementary (Earnings Cap) Pension Scheme 1994) Regulations 1995, SI 1995/1683 (in force on 25 July 1995), apply the provisions of the Pensions (Increase) Act 1971 to any pensions payable under the Civil Service Supplementary (Earnings Cap) Scheme 1994 as if they were pensions specified in the 1971 Act, Sch 2, Pt I. The regulations also permit increases in respect of any pension beginning on or after 2 March 1992, by virtue of the power provided by the 1971 Act, s 5(4) (power to provide for increases to take effect retrospectively).

2240 Commutation

The Pensions Commutation (Amendment) Regulations 1995, SI 1995/2648 (in force on 1 December 1995), further amend the 1968 Regulations, SI 1968/1163, so as to substitute new tables giving the rates to be used in calculating the capital sum to be paid in commutation of a pension or a portion of a pension.

2241 Invalidity pension—age restriction—sex discrimination
See *Graham v Secretary of State for Social Security*, para 3196.

2242 Judicial pension scheme
See COURTS.

2243 Local government—pension scheme
The Local Government Pension Scheme Regulations 1995, SI 1995/1019 (in force on 2 May 1995), revoke and consolidate with amendments the Local Government Superannuation Regulations 1986, SI 1986/24 (except Pts K and L and other provisions so far as they relate to those Parts), and revoke, either in full or in part, to the extent that they amend or modify the revoked provisions of SI 1986/24, 1986/380, 1987/293, 1579, 2110, 1988/466, 1989/371, 372, 1462, 1624, 1815, 1990/503, 1709, 2480, 1991/1203, 2471, 2522, 1992/172, 3083, 1993/366, 1367, 1810, 1814, 1848, 2531, 2783, 3030, 3043, 1994/1909, 3026, 1995/901, 963, which constitute the occupational pension scheme for persons engaged in local government employment other than teachers, policemen and firemen. The regulations make provision in respect of membership (including eligibility, joining and leaving the scheme and membership periods); members' contributions (including standard contributions, effect of absences on contributions, additional payments to improve benefits, incomplete payments and return of contributions, deduction and recovery of contributions, limitations on payments and payments under old legislation); retirement benefits (including entitlement to immediate payment of benefits on retirement, entitlement to deferred benefits, adjustment to standard benefits and overriding provisions); death grants (including death of a member, death of a pensioner and general provisions relating to death benefits); surviving spouses' pensions (including death of a member, death of a deferred pensioner, death of a pensioner, general provisions relating to surviving spouses' pensions and contracting out requirements: GMP rule); children's pensions (including death of a member, death of a deferred pensioner, death of a pensioner and general provisions relating to children's pensions); general provisions concerning benefits; determinations and appeals; interchange (including transfers in and out, interfund adjustments on changes of local government employment, transfers of certain members who are eligible to join approved non-local government schemes, payments for combined benefits, transfers to and from Scottish local government employment and overseas employment); pension funds and payments by authorities (including pension funds, management and investment of funds, valuations and rates of contributions and adjustments, employer's liability to make payments, transfers, recovery and retention from funds in misconduct cases, certain statutory payments to be met out of appropriate funds and modification in respect of the National Rivers Authority funds); and miscellaneous and supplemental provisions. SI 1985/1922, 1986/24, 380, 1987/293, 1579, 2110, 1989/1815, 1993/2783, 1994/948, 963, 3026 and 1995/901 (so far as unrevoked), are consequently amended.

2244 Local government—pension scheme—augmentation of period of scheme membership
The Local Government Pension Scheme (Augmentation) Regulations 1995, SI 1995/2953 (in force on 11 December 1995), amend the Local Government (Compensation for Premature Retirement) Regulations 1982, SI 1982/1009, and the Local Government Pension Scheme Regulations 1995, SI 1995/1019 (see para 2243), so as to (1) make provision which gives certain employing authorities the discretion to augment the period of pension scheme membership of certain members whose employment has ceased on redundancy; (2) enable those authorities to convert the whole of an award under the 1982 Regulations into an additional period of pension scheme membership for a member whose employment so ceased before 11 December 1995; (3) prescribe a time limit within which payment for the purchase of additional membership must be made to the administering authority; (4) prevent the award of a credited period under the 1982 Regulations where an authority has exercised its discretion under the provisions in the 1995 Regulations to augment scheme membership; (5) bring the Commission for the New Towns and urban development corporations within the 1982 Regulations; and (6) make consequential and saving provision.

2245 Local government—pension scheme—pensionable remuneration
The Local Government Pension Scheme (Pensionable Remuneration Amendment) Regulations 1995, SI 1995/2249 (in force on 28 September 1995), further amend the Local Government

Pension Scheme Regulations 1995, SI 1995/1019 (see para 2243), so as to (1) allow local authorities to readjust the amount of pensionable remuneration of certain pensioners who retired between 1 April 1979 and 31 August 1993 and whose pensionable remuneration was, after their retirement, decreased with a consequential reduction in their pensions (such an adjustment also affects the level of widow's/widower's/children's pensions which are calculated by reference to the pensioner's pensionable remuneration); (2) extend the local authority's discretion to pensions that have been paid or are in the course of payment and provide that back-dated payments of pension bear interest; and (3) provide that a local authority must exercise its discretion to make any adjustment within six months of 28 September 1995.

2246 Local government—pension scheme—reorganisation—Wales

The Local Government Pension Scheme (Local Government Reorganisation in Wales) Regulations 1995, SI 1995/1985 (in force on 24 August 1995), make provision for various matters consequent upon local government reorganisation in Wales under the Local Government (Wales) Act 1994 which affect the local government pension scheme constituted by the Local Government Pension Scheme Regulations 1995, SI 1995/1019 (see para 2243). The regulations (1) provide that on 1 April 1996 ('the reorganisation date') the pension funds, rights and liabilities of the administering authorities (which are abolished with effect from that date) are transferred to the new local authorities in Wales which will be the administering authorities after the reorganisation date ('the successor authorities'); (2) provide that any admission agreement in force immediately before the reorganisation date will continue in force with the successor authorities; (3) provide for the apportionment of certain funds which will be affected from the reorganisation date; (4) require successor authorities to begin the process of obtaining an actuarial certificate for the period 1 April 1996 to 31 March 1999 in respect of the fund for which they will be the administering authority as soon as possible after these regulations come into force; (5) set out an employer contribution rate for new authorities elected on 4 May 1995 for the period before the reorganisation date; (6) allow a successor authority, during a specified period, to obtain actuarial valuations of the fund they administer at different times than is otherwise provided for under the 1995 Regulations; and (7) make various consequential amendments to SI 1995/1019.

2247 Local government—superannuation—equality and maternity absence

The Local Government Superannuation (Equality and Maternity Absence) Regulations 1995, SI 1995/901 (in force on 24 April 1995), amend the Local Government Superannuation Regulations 1986, SI 1986/24, so as to (1) make drafting changes to clarify the 1986 Regulations, reg C3A (introduced by the Local Government Superannuation (Maternity Absence) Regulations 1993, SI 1993/2531); (2) allow a man to elect to receive an actuarially reduced pension at 60 if that pension were less than his guaranteed minimum (payable from the age of 65) and to allow such elections to be made with retrospective effect to 17 May 1990; (3) remove the requirement that the pension of a man retiring at 60 with less than 25 years' service is subject to an actuarial reduction of up to 33 per cent (compared to the pensions of women which are not subject to actuarial reductions); (4) provide that between 17 May 1990 and 1 May 1995, both men's and women's pensions enjoy the protection afforded by the Social Security Pensions Act 1975, and (5) confer a right for a person, in certain circumstances, to opt that these regulations do not apply. The provisions in head (1) have effect as from 1 January 1993, and in head (2) and (3) from 17 May 1990.

2248 Local government—superannuation—gratuities

The Local Government Superannuation (Gratuities) Regulations 1995, SI 1995/1497 (in force on 6 July 1995), amend the Local Government Superannuation Regulations 1986, SI 1986/24, referred to above, so as to (1) separate out the power to pay gratuities so that they can be paid under the different powers contained in the 1995 Regulations in three specific circumstances: death in service, redundancy or retirement; (2) reduce the accrual rate for all the different sorts of gratuity payments from 5 per cent to 3.75 per cent; (3) make amendments consequential on the commencement of the Local Government Pension Scheme Regulations 1995, SI 1995/1019 (see para 2243); and (4) make other consequential amendments. By virtue of the Superannuation Act 1972, s 12, heads (1) and (4) above are made retrospective with effect from 6 April 1991, and head (3) above is made retrospective with effect from 2 May 1995.

2249 Local government—superannuation—limitation on earnings and reckonable service

The Local Government Superannuation (Limitation on Earnings and Reckonable Service) Regulations 1995, SI 1995/900 (in force on 24 April 1995), amend the Local Government Superannuation Regulations 1986, SI 1986/24, so as to reflect overriding legislation introduced by the Finance (No 2) Act 1987 and the Finance Act 1989, with which the local government superannuation scheme already complies. The regulations (1) insert a new provision reflecting different categories of members depending upon whether the individual joined, or is deemed to have joined, the scheme before 17 March 1987, on or after 17 March 1987 and before 1 June 1989, or on or after 1 June 1989; (2) clarify that the limit on employees' contributions under the scheme, other than additional voluntary contributions, is linked to remuneration as defined in the 1986 Regulations and not to the employees' taxable earnings; (3) limit the maximum reckonable service to 40 years for the purposes of the calculation of benefits for members who joined the scheme after 1 June 1989; (4) limit pensionable remuneration for the purpose of calculating the retiring allowance in the case of a person who joined the scheme on or after 17 March 1987 and before 1 June 1989; (5) add definitions which are required in connection with the amendments referred to in heads (1), (2), (3), and (4) above, and (6) clarify that the limit on contributions by employees in respect of additional voluntary contributions is different from that imposed in the 1986 Regulations, Pt C in respect of employee contributions under the scheme.

2250 Local government—superannuation—miscellaneous provisions

The Local Government Superannuation (Miscellaneous Provisions) Regulations 1995, SI 1995/963 (in force on 27 April 1995), amend the Local Government Superannuation Regulations 1986, SI 1986/24, and the Local Government Superannuation (Amendment) Regulations 1994, SI 1994/3026, so as to (1) require interest to be paid on late payments of the annual retirement pension, widow's and widower's pension and children's pension as well as on the lump sum retiring allowance, ill-health retirement grant and death grant (the pension payment must be twelve months overdue for interest to be payable); (2) amend certain cross-references in the 1986 Regulations; (3) extend the period for giving notice under the 1986 Regulations, regs J13 or J14 as amended, from 3 months to 6 months in the case of a person who would have been entitled to give notice before the 1994 Regulations came into force had the 1994 Regulations come into force on 1 April 1986, and (4) allow persons who have made additional voluntary contributions and who leave the scheme, whether on leaving employment or on opting out of the scheme to choose between a range of options for the disbursement of the accumulated value of their invested additional contributions. Specified provisions of the 1995 Regulations have retrospective effect.

2251 National Health Service—pensions

The National Health Service Pension Scheme Regulations 1995, SI 1995/300 (in force on 6 March 1995), consolidate with amendments the National Health Service (Superannuation) Regulations 1980, SI 1980/362. The amendments are as follows: (1) the payment of a voluntary early retirement pension, where the employing authority agrees to meet the cost, for all members except medical and dental practitioners (with no enhancement or reduction of benefits); (2) the payment of a voluntary early retirement pension, for all members, which allows retirement between the ages of 50 and 60 with actuarially reduced benefits; (3) an increase in the amount of the lump sum benefit payable where a member dies in service to twice the member's final year's pensionable pay; (4) the extension of the provisions under which female nurses, midwives, physiotherapists and health visitors are currently allowed to retire at the age of 55 to men in those jobs in relation to pensionable service from 17 May 1990 (although these provisions are withdrawn in relation to those who first become members of the scheme after the coming into force of the regulations and in relation to those previous members who have a break in pensionable service of five years' or more ending after that date); (5) the withdrawal of mental health officer status in relation to those who first become members of the scheme after the coming into force of the regulations and for those who have a break of more than five years in their pensionable service ending after that date; (6) the suspension of pension in relation to those who return to National Health Service employment within one month of their pension becoming payable; and (7) the application of the abatement of pension for those who continue in or return to National Health Service employment after their pension becomes payable only up to age 60.

2252 Occupational and personal pension schemes—miscellaneous amendments

The Occupational and Personal Pension Schemes (Miscellaneous Amendments) Regulations 1995, SI 1995/35 (in force on 7 February 1995), amend SI 1984/380, 1985/1929, 1987/1101, 1110, 1117, 1988/137, and 1991/167 so as to (1) revise the list of bodies in SI 1984/380 with whom an insurance policy or annuity contract may be taken out for the purpose of securing guaranteed minimum pensions; (2) revise the conditions in SI 1985/1929 which an insurance company must satisfy if a policy of insurance or annuity contract is to be appropriate for the purposes of the Pension Schemes Act 1993, s 19; (3) substitute the definitions in SI 1987/1101 of a 'friendly society' and 'recognised Stock Exchange' and revise the conditions subject to which insurance policies and annuity contracts may be permitted investments; (4) update references in SI 1987/1110 to the Insurance Companies Regulations 1994, SI 1994/1516; (5) revise the list in SI 1987/1117 of insurance companies which may provide for rights by way of annuities; (6) make consequential amendments in SI 1988/137 to reflect changes in the Income and Corporation Taxes Act 1988 and revise the list of bodies therein which may establish personal pension schemes; and (7) revise the means by which short service benefits may be secured in SI 1991/167. SI 1976/598 is also revoked.

The Occupational and Personal Pension Schemes (Miscellaneous Amendments) (No 2) Regulations 1995, SI 1995/3067 (in force on 1 February 1996), make further provision relating to occupational and personal pension schemes. The regulations (1) amend SI 1991/167 so as to remove references to the conditions necessary for a discharge under the Pension Schemes Act 1993, s 81 in certain provisions which relate to the securing of short service benefit (or its alternatives) by an insurance policy or annuity contract, and (2) amend SI 1987/1110 so as to place an obligation on the trustees or managers of a personal pension scheme to inform a member within 3 months if they do not receive a payment of contributions in respect of him on the due date.

2253 Occupational and personal pensions—Pensions Ombudsman—levy

The Occupational and Personal Pension Schemes (Levy) Regulations 1995, SI 1995/524 (in force on 1 April 1995), replace the 1990 Regulations, SI 1990/2277, and make provision for the levy towards meeting the cost of the Pensions Ombudsman, the register of occupational and personal pension schemes and certain grants made to advisory bodies by the Occupational Pensions Board to be paid in future on a yearly rather than a three yearly basis. The regulations (1) require the trustees or administrators of a registrable scheme with at least two active members to pay the levy in respect of each registration year, and provide that the three-year payment cycle ceases to have effect after 31 March 1997; (2) set out how the amount of the levy is to be determined; (3) make provision, subject to certain exceptions, for the levy to be payable to the registrar of occupational and personal pension schemes in advance at the beginning of each registration year; (4) make provision to avoid duplication of payments where a levy is payable under equivalent provisions having effect in Northern Ireland; and (5) make provision for the payment together, in certain cases, of the levy for the registration years commencing 1 April 1995 and 1 April 1996 and for schemes which, under the 1990 Regulations, have already paid a levy in respect of those years.

2254 Occupational and personal pension schemes—Pensions Ombudsman—procedure

The Personal and Occupational Pension Schemes (Pensions Ombudsman) (Procedure) Rules 1995, SI 1995/1053 (in force on 10 May 1995), provide for the procedure to be followed where a complaint or dispute relating to an occupational or personal pension scheme is referred to the Pensions Ombudsman under the Pension Schemes Act 1993. In particular, the rules provide for the form of a reference, the giving of notice, the submission of evidence, and the conduct of the investigation.

2255 Occupational pension schemes—appointment and removal of trustees—insolvent company

By a definitive trust deed, a pension fund was set up for the employees of a company. The deed provided for five trustees, three appointable and removable by the company and two appointable and removable by the members of the fund. The plaintiff was a company-appointed trustee. An administration order was made in respect of the company, appointing the first and second defendants as administrators to approve a voluntary arrangement and realise the company's assets. Upon the appointment of the administrators, the Social Security Pensions Act 1975, s 57C applied, requiring them by s 57C(2) to satisfy themselves at all times as to the independence of at least one of the trustees and to appoint an independent trustee in the event that they were not so satisfied. The administrators, purporting to act under the powers conferred on them by the administration order and by s 57C, entered into a deed with the company, amending the definitive deed to reduce the number of trustees to two, vesting the power of appointment and removal of trustees in the trustees, and removing all the trustees except the plaintiff. The third defendant was appointed as an independent trustee. A point was reached when there were no employees of the company and the scheme was fully paid-up within the meaning of the Occupational Pension Schemes (Independent Trustee) Regulations 1990, SI 1990/2075, reg 4, since there were no members in pensionable service. The third defendant resolved, as independent trustee, that the scheme should be wound up. The administrators subsequently purported to appoint the fourth defendant as the independent trustee, replacing the third defendant on the grounds that his independence was in question. The plaintiff sought the directions of the court on the questions (1) whether the amendment of the definitive deed, giving the trustees of the scheme power to appoint and remove trustees, was valid and (2) at what point in time the 1990 Regulations, reg 4(2) operated to disapply s 57C. *Held*, (1) the powers of an administrator included any power exercisable by the directors of the company prior to the making of the administration order. On its true construction the general power conferred by the Insolvency Act 1986, s 14(1) to do all such things as might be necessary for the management of the 'affairs' of the company at least covered matters which realistically touched or concerned the company's business or property and, having regard to the fact that the company's objects clause empowered the directors to set up an employee pension scheme, it was clear that the administration of the scheme was an integral part of the management of the company's business. It followed that the administrators had power to act for the company in amending the definitive trust deed and the amendments were accordingly valid. (2) The power and duty of an administrator to replace an independent trustee of a pension scheme under s 57C(2) ceased by operation of the 1990 Regulations, reg 4(2) when the pension scheme was paid up and the employer company had no further trust connection with its management. Having regard to the language of s 57C, and in particular the phrase 'if and as long as', which clearly contemplated a period beginning when s 57C applied and ending when it was disapplied, the disapplication could occur at any time commencing from the date on which the administrator was appointed and s 57C first became applicable.

Denny v Yeldon [1995] 3 All ER 624 (Chancery Division: Jacob J).
1975 Act, s 57C now Pension Schemes Act 1993, ss 119, 120.

2256 Occupational pension schemes—equal access to membership

The Occupational Pension Schemes (Equal Access to Membership) Amendment Regulations 1995, SI 1995/1215 (in force on 31 May 1995), amend the 1976 Regulations, SI 1976/142, and modify the equal access requirements in the Pension Schemes Act 1993, s 118 so as to implement requirements of the EC Treaty, art 119. The regulations (1) remove the provision for the fixing of different maximum age limits for membership in the case of schemes with different normal pension ages for men and women; (2) make provision for the extension of the equal access requirements; and (3) provide for the additional resources to be provided by employers, in certain cases, to relate to periods of membership after the coming into force of the regulations.

2257 Occupational pension schemes—equal treatment

The Occupational Pension Schemes (Equal Treatment) Regulations 1995, SI 1995/3183 (in force on 1 January 1996), supersede the Occupational Pension Schemes (Equal Access to Membership) Regulations 1976, SI 1976/142, and supplement the requirements for equal treatment in connection with occupational pension schemes provided for in the Pensions Act 1995, ss 62–66. The 1995 Regulations provide (1) for the Equal Pay Act 1970 to have modified effect in relation to an equal treatment rule; (2) that a court or tribunal may not make a financial award for a claim relating to breach of an equal treatment rule and that an employer has a right to appear and be heard in such proceedings before a tribunal; (3) for a court or tribunal to have power to make a declaration as to an applicant's rights to equal treatment and for employers to provide any additional resources required; (4) for the making of a financial award to a pensioner member in respect of a breach of an equal treatment rule and for employers to provide any additional resources required; (5) for corresponding provision in relation to the breach of an equality clause in a contract of employment; and (6) for permitted exceptions to an equal treatment rule.

2258 Occupational pension schemes—guaranteed minimum pensions—increase

The Guaranteed Minimum Pensions Increase Order 1995, SI 1995/515 (in force on 6 April 1996), made following a review by the Secretary of State under the Pension Schemes Act 1993, s 109(1), specifies 2.2 per cent as the percentage by which that part of any guaranteed minimum pension attributable to earnings factors for the tax year 1988–89 and subsequent years and payable by occupational pension schemes is to be increased.

2259 Occupational pension schemes—non-resident taxpayer—discrimination

See *Wielockx v Inspecteur der Directe Belastingen*, para 3143.

2260 Occupational pension schemes—revaluation

The Occupational Pensions (Revaluation) Order 1995, SI 1995/3021 (in force on 1 January 1996), specifies the revaluation percentage for each revaluation period for the purposes of the revaluation of benefits under occupational pension schemes.

2261 Occupational pension schemes—sex discrimination—applicability of Community provisions

See *Bestuur Van Het Algemeen Burgerlijk Pensioenfonds v Beune*, para 3184.

2262 Occupational pension schemes—trustee of scheme—discretionary powers

A division of a company, the first company, was sold to a second company to whose employment existing employees in the division were transferred. Under the terms of sale, the second company was admitted temporarily as a participating company into the first company's pension scheme until it set up its own scheme. When it did so, most of the employees, including the plaintiffs, who had been members of and contributed to the first company's pension scheme, became members of the second company's pension scheme. At that time the pension scheme fund of the first company was in substantial actuarial surplus. The trust deed of the first company's pension scheme provided that the trustee was to appropriate and transfer to the second company's pension scheme such part of the assets of the scheme as the trustee determined to be appropriate having taken actuarial advice in all the circumstances. Although, in the years preceding the transfer, the first company had, as a result of the fund being in surplus, not been required to make any contributions, the trustee determined to transfer to the second company's pension scheme an amount equal only to the past service reserve of the transferring employees, leaving the whole of the surplus in the scheme. The plaintiffs issued a summons seeking disclosure of all the trust documents in the trustee's possession which indicated or might indicate the reasons for its determination. *Held*, where a discretion was entrusted to a trustee by the relevant trust instrument, the trustee was not required to give reasons for the exercise of that discretion and, in the absence of evidence apart from such disclosure that the trustee had acted improperly, whether from an improper motive or by taking account of factors which the trustee should not have taken into account or not taking into account factors which the trustee should have taken into account, the court would not interfere with the exercise of the trustee's discretion since, in general, the principles applicable to private trusts as a matter of trust law applied equally to pension schemes. The trust deed conferred a clear discretion on the trustee of the pension scheme to which the well-established principles of trust law applied, so that, in the absence of any evidence of impropriety, the trustee was under no obligation to disclose documents containing evidence of its reasons for the manner in which it exercised that discretion. Accordingly, the originating summons would be dismissed.

Wilson v Law Debenture Trust Corpn plc [1995] 2 All ER 337 (Chancery Division: Rattee J).

2263 Parliamentary pensions—accrual rate for service as a member of Parliament

The Parliamentary Pensions (Amendment) Regulations 1995, SI 1995/2867 (in force on 1 December 1995), amend the Parliamentary Pensions (Consolidation and Amendment) Regulations 1993, SI 1993/3253, so as to improve the accrual rate for service as a member of Parliament before 20 July 1983 from sixtieths to fiftieths for members in service on 1 April 1995 and alter the provisions for gratuities payable in respect of members of Parliament and the holders of ministerial and other offices who die in service on or after that date. Consequential provision is also made and the regulations have retrospective effect from 1 April 1995.

2264 Parliamentary pensions—dependants of Prime Minister or Speaker

The Pensions for Dependants of the Prime Minister or Speaker (Designated Provisions) Regulations 1995, SI 1995/1443 (in force on 29 June 1995), replace SI 1992/1701 and designate, for the purposes of the Parliamentary and other Pensions Act 1972, s 27 (which relates to payment of pensions to dependants of the Prime Minister or Speaker) those provisions of the Parliamentary pension scheme contained in the Parliamentary Pensions (Consolidation and Amendment) Regulations 1993, SI 1993/3253, regs K1–K3. The designated provisions will consequently apply in relation to the widows, widowers or children of deceased Prime Ministers or Speakers.

2265 Parliamentary pensions—European Parliament—United Kingdom representatives—pensions—additional voluntary contributions scheme

The European Parliamentary (United Kingdom Representatives) Pensions (Additional Voluntary Contributions Scheme) (No 2) Order 1995, SI 1995/739 (in force on 4 April 1995), (1) provides for participants in the pension scheme for United Kingdom representatives to the European Parliament to pay additional voluntary contributions in order to secure additional benefits within limits determined by the Board of Inland Revenue; (2) provides for the Secretary of State to appoint financial institutions to accept contributions and to provide pension benefits and for the administration of the scheme by the managers of the principal scheme; (3) imposes a limit on the total amount of regular and lump sum contributions; (4) provides for the investment of contributions in accordance with any instructions given by the contributor, including any instructions to pay all or part of the contributions to secure a lump sum death benefit in the event of death while paying such contributions; (5) describes the benefits which may be provided and the time when they are available; (6) provides for the payment of lump sums on death; (7) provides for the purchase of pensions on retirement; (8) provides for the circumstances in which the realisable value of a contributor's investments may be transferred, before retirement, to another pension scheme, used to purchase an annuity, or returned to him; (9) sets out the maximum benefits payable under the order; (10) provides that the contributor may choose to use the excess to increase or to provide another permitted benefit; (11) permits the Secretary of State to require an institution to surrender the whole or part of the value of contributions invested with it and requires the managers to reinvest the amount surrendered; (12) specifies that the costs of establishing and administering the additional voluntary contributions scheme are to be paid out of money provided by Parliament; and (13) prohibits the assignment or charge of any benefits payable under the scheme. SI 1995/720, which was defective and was not published, is revoked.

2266 Pension scheme—variation on divorce

See *Brooks v Brooks*, para 1098.

2267 Pensions Act 1995

The Pensions Act 1995 makes new provision with regard to occupational pensions, state pensions and personal pensions in response to Professor Goode's Pension Law Review Committee. The Act received the royal assent on 19 July 1995 and certain provisions came into force on that date. Further provisions came into force on on 2 October and 4 December 1995 and 1 January 1996: SI 1995/2548, 3104. The remaining provisions come into force on a day or days to be appointed. For details of commencement, see the commencement table in the title STATUTES.

Part I (ss 1–125) Occupational Pensions
Section 1 and Sch 1 provide for the establishment and constitution of the Occupational Pensions Regulatory Authority ('the authority'). Section 2 requires the authority to provide an annual report on its activities to the Secretary of State. Sections 3–15 detail the authority's power to investigate non-compliance, to impose sanctions and to appoint, suspend and disqualify trustees. Sections 16–21 make provision for member-nominated trustees and directors, requiring the trustees of a trust scheme to make arrangements for selecting member-nominated trustees and directors so that they amount to at least one third of the trustees and directors. Sections 22–26 relate to independent trustees, providing for the circumstances in which it is necessary to appoint an independent trustee and the powers of an independent trustee. Sections 27–31 make general provision with regard to trustees, preventing a person from acting as trustee, actuary or auditor of the same scheme, detailing classes of persons disqualified from being trustees and providing that the assets of a scheme must not be used to reimburse a trustee for any fine or penalty he is

required to pay. Sections 32–41 set out the functions of trustees. Sections 42–46 relate to employee trustees, providing that employers must allow employees who are trustees to take reasonable time off for the purpose of performing their duties as trustees, that they must provide payment for such time off and that employees must not suffer any detriment in their employment or be unfairly dismissed by reason of the performance of their functions as trustees. Sections 47, 48 deal with the role of professional advisers, requiring the trustees to appoint an auditor and an actuary, who take instructions from and report to the trustees rather than the employer and who report breaches of statutory obligations to the authority. Section 49 requires trust moneys to be kept in separate bank accounts and s 50 requires trustees or managers of occupational pension schemes to implement arrangements for the resolution of disputes between prescribed persons.

Sections 51–55 provide for the indexation of pensions, providing that a pension under a tax approved occupational pension scheme that is not a public service scheme must be increased annually by a minimum of a specified percentage. The first such increase must take effect no later than a year after the date on which the pension was first paid. There are restrictions on increases where a member is under the age of 55 and not permanently incapacitated from employment by reason of physical or mental infirmity or retired on those grounds. Where a pension has been increased at a rate higher than the required rate, the trustees may deduct the increase from the increase required in the following tax year. Sections 56–61 establish a minimum funding requirement under which the value of a scheme's assets must not exceed its liabilities. Trustees must obtain actuarial valuations and certificates as to the adequacy of contributions in relation to the overall level of funding. They must prepare and maintain a schedule of contributions certified by the actuary as sufficient to ensure that the scheme meets the minimum funding requirement over a prescribed period. Where contributions have not been paid in accordance with that schedule, the trustees or managers must notify the authority and they must prepare a report where the scheme fails to meet the minimum funding requirement. If at valuation the assets of the scheme are less than 90 per cent of the value of liabilities the employer must ensure that they are increased to a minimum of 90 per cent within a prescribed period. Sections 62–66 make provision for an equal treatment rule in relation to women members, which rule all occupational pension schemes must be treated as containing in connection with membership of schemes and treatment of members. The rule must be treated as applying to benefits attributable to pensionable service on or after 17 May 1990. An exception to the rule is provided in circumstances where the difference is attributable to differences between men and women in state pensions under the Social Security Contributions and Benefits Act 1992, ss 43–55. Differences are also permitted where they are the result of the application of actuarial factors which differ for men and women. Trustees or managers may thus resolve to alter schemes to comply with the rule and such alterations might be retrospective in effect. Sections 67–72 relate to the modification of schemes, providing that a right to modify must not be exercised where it would affect an already accrued right or entitlement unless specific requirements are met. Trustees are able by resolution to modify a scheme in order to extend the class of beneficiaries of benefits resulting from the death of a member and to enable the scheme to conform with other provisions of the Act. The authority is also able, on the application of specific persons, to authorise the modification of or itself modify a scheme in certain circumstances if it is satisfied that certain requirements are met, and such a modification can have retrospective effect. A minister or designated government department can similarly modify a public service scheme. Sections 73–77 deal with the winding up of pension schemes, specifying the priority order of asset allocation in the winding up of a scheme to which the rules regarding minimum funding requirements apply. Accordingly, provision is made for the ways in which trustees of such schemes can discharge their liability to members. The Pension Schemes Act 1993, s 144 is re-enacted so that a deficiency when a scheme is wound up or when an employer becomes insolvent becomes a debt due to the trustees from the employers. Where an exempt approved scheme within the meaning of the Income and Corporation Taxes Act 1988, s 592(1) is being wound up the power to distribute surplus assets to the employer can only be exercised with the consent of the trustees in specific circumstances. Where such assets remain undistributed the trustees can employ those assets to provide additional benefits or distribute them to the employer.

Sections 78–80, Sch 2 deal with the establishment, powers and constitution of the Pensions Compensation Board ('the board'). The board operates independently of the authority and the purpose behind the new compensation scheme is to cover the dishonest removal of funds by insolvent employers. Sections 81–86 make specific provision with regard to compensation, detailing the situations in which the compensation provisions apply, the time limits and other requirements applying to applications for payments under the compensation provisions, the amount of compensation the board can pay and the payment of compensation in anticipation. After consultation with the board the Secretary of State can require it to distribute among occupational pension schemes any surplus funds it holds and the board can invest surplus funds.

Sections 87–90 relate to money purchase schemes, requiring the trustees or managers of such schemes to ensure the preparation and maintenance of a payment schedule, and penalising trustees who fail to comply with this requirement. Where a due payment is not made it becomes a debt of the employer and the trustees must notify the authority. The Pension Schemes Act 1993, s 124 is accordingly amended in relation to the sum payable by the Secretary of State in the event of employer insolvency in respect of unpaid contributions. Sections 91–95 relate to assignment, forfeiture and bankruptcy, providing that an accrued right or entitlement under an occupational pension scheme is inalienable except in relation to specific circumstances. Provision is made for the provisions relating to inalienability and forfeiture in relation to public service pension schemes to be modified by regulations. The Insolvency Act 1986 is amended by the insertion of new ss 342A–342C, providing for the recovery of excessive pension contributions in the event of bankruptcy. Sections 96, 97 relate to the questioning of decisions of the authority, providing that, subject to an application for review, the authority's decision is final, although a question can be referred to the High Court where the authority deems fit or where any person is aggrieved by its determination.

Sections 98–103 provide for the gathering of information in relation to the authority. The authority is empowered to require a trustee, manager, professional adviser, employer or any person holding relevant information to disclose any information essential for the carrying out of its functions. Inspectors appointed by the authority are enabled to enter certain premises to make necessary inquiries. Further, a justice of the peace can issue a warrant for the entry into premises for the purpose of procuring relevant documents. Persons named in the warrant are required to provide explanations of documents or to disclose where they might be located. Provision is made for penalties for non-compliance with these provisions. The authority can, if it considers appropriate, publish a report of such investigations. Sections 104–106 relate to the disclosure of information by the authority, providing that the authority must not disclose information without the consent of the person to whom it relates unless the disclosure is for the purposes of enabling the authority to carry out its functions or is to certain specified persons for facilitating the discharge of their functions. Similar provisions apply to information supplied by corresponding overseas authorities, except that such information may also be disclosed for the purposes of criminal proceedings. The authority can disclose information to the Secretary of State where to do so is considered to be in the interests of the members of the scheme or in the public interest. Tax information must also be disclosed to the Authority. Sections 110–114 relate to the gathering of information in relation to the board. Trustees, professional advisers and any person holding relevant information must disclose such information to the board. Provision is made for penalties in the event of a refusal or neglect to provide such information. As with the provisions relating to the authority, there are savings with respect to certain privileges. The board can also publish reports of its investigations and certain specified persons are required to disclose information to the board, and the board is required to disclose information to certain specified persons. Sections 115–125, Sch 3 contain general and supplementary provisions.

Part II (ss 126–134) State Pensions
Section 126 introduces Sch 4, which provides for parity in the pensionable ages of women and men progressively over 10 years beginning on 6 April 2010. Provision is also made for the equalisation of women and men in certain state pensions and benefits. Sections 127–134 amend the Social Security Contributions and Benefits Act 1992. A new s 45A is inserted into the 1992 Act, which provides that family credit and disability working allowance must be considered in calculating earnings factors for the enhancement of pensions. The 1992 Act, s 44 is amended so that, in relation to those reaching retirement age after 5 April 2000 and people widowed after that date whose spouses had not reached pensionable age, where additional pension is being calculated, revaluation is carried out only in relation to the earnings factor surplus for a particular year. The Social Security Administration Act 1992, s 152 is substituted, making provision for the up-rating of pensions increased under the Social Security Contributions and Benefits Act 1992, s 52.

Part III (ss 135–151) Certification of Pension Schemes and Effects on Members' State Scheme Rights and Duties
Section 135 relates to the commencement of Pt III. Section 136 amends the Pension Schemes Act 1993, Pt III, detailing new requirements for schemes contracted-out of SERPS. Sections 137–140 relate to reductions in contributions to the state scheme, reductions in state scheme benefits and payments of rebates. The Pension Schemes Act 1993, ss 41–42, 45, 48, 55, Sch 4, are amended, making new provision in relation to the contracted-out rebate and introducing age-related rebates for money purchase schemes; age-related minimum contributions are introduced in relation to appropriate pension schemes; provision is made as to the verification of ages in connection with rebates; new provisions provide that a contracted-out earner is treated

as not having paid National Insurance contributions for the purpose of calculating additional pension. Section 141 concerns premiums and the return to the state scheme, amending the 1993 Act, s 55 so as to provide for the arrangements by which it will be possible to buy back SERPS rights. Provision is made for regulations to prescribe the extent to which a member has been in SERPS where a scheme has been wound up and there are insufficient resources to restore all of the member's SERPS rights. Sections 142–146 relate to protected rights, amending the 1993 Act, s 28, allowing a member to draw a specified yearly income between the ages of 60 and 75 as an interim arrangement before drawing an annuity. The Secretary of State is entitled to information from the scheme regarding interim arrangements. The age requirements in the 1993 Act, s 29 are amended and new provision is made in relation to insurance policies giving effect to the protected rights of a scheme member on the winding up of the scheme. Sections 147–151 make miscellaneous provision, including the dissolution of the Occupational Pensions Board, and Sch 5 makes amendments consequential on that dissolution.

Part IV (ss 152–181) Miscellaneous and Supplemental
Sections 152–154 relate to transfer values, amending the 1993 Act so as to extend the right to receive a cash equivalent transfer value and making provision as to the notification to members of the amount of the cash equivalent at the guarantee date. Section 155 amends the 1993 Act, s 168, increasing the penalties that may be imposed on summary conviction for the breach of certain regulations under that Act and making new provision for penalties for the provision of false information. Sections 156–160 relate to the Pensions Ombudsman, providing for the employment of staff by the ombudsman and the delegation of functions to such staff and amending the 1993 Act, ss 146–151, extending the ombudsman's jurisdiction and providing for the award of costs or expenses by the ombudsman. The ombudsman can disclose to the authority and other specified bodies information obtained during his investigations and he is required to pay interest where benefits are paid late. The 1993 Act, ss 136–143 are repealed by s 161. Sections 162–164 relate to personal pensions, providing for an annual increase in the rate of personal pensions of an appropriate percentage and amending the 1993 Act, s 44, enabling the Secretary of State to reject a notice of a person's choice of pension scheme where it does not comply with certain provisions of the act. Section 165 replaces the 1993 Act, s 175, providing for the levy on pension schemes to cover the expenditure of the authority and the board. Section 166 relates to pensions on divorce, inserting new ss 25B–25D into the Matrimonial Causes Act 1973, strengthening the existing duty of the courts to have regard to the value of pensions in reaching a divorce settlement. In particular, the new s 25B allows the courts to direct trustees to pay maintenance to a former spouse from a pension when it is due to a scheme member. The payment may be by way of a one-off lump sum or by periodical payments, preventing the need for former spouses to maintain contact. Section 25B also contains extensive regulation-making powers. The new s 25C deals with death benefits, giving a divorced party access, if the court deems appropriate, to such share of any lump sum payments from a pension scheme as they might have had access to had the couple not divorced. Section 167 relates to Scotland. Sections 168, 169 relate to pensions for war widows and the effects of their remarriage. Sections 170–172 relate to official and public service pensions and effect is given to Sch 6, containing consequential amendments, by s 173. Sections 174, 175 provide for subordinate legislation. Sections 176–181 provide for interpretation, repeals (introducing Sch 7), extent, short title and commencement.

2268 Personal equity plans—regulations

The Personal Equity Plan (Amendment) Regulations 1995, SI 1995/1539 (in force on 6 July 1995), further amend the 1989 Regulations, SI 1989/469, by (1) extending, to preference shares and convertible preference shares of companies incorporated in member states of the European Union and to bonds and convertible bonds of companies incorporated in the United Kingdom, the range of investments which may be held under general plans; (2) setting out the conditions which corporate bonds must satisfy before they can be held under plans or by unit or investment trusts whose units and shares or securities are held under plans; and (3) excluding venture capital trusts from the investments which can be held under single company plans.

The Personal Equity Plan (Amendment No 2) Regulations 1995, SI 1995/3287 (in force on 9 January 1996), further amend the 1989 Regulations supra by (1) providing that a European institution which may carry on home-regulated investment business in accordance with the Banking Co-ordination (Second Council Directive) Regulations 1992, SI 1992/3218, or a relevant authorised person (under the Financial Services Act 1986, s 31) must appoint a tax representative to discharge the duties of a plan manager, or make other arrangements with the Commissioners of Inland Revenue for such duties to be discharged; (2) providing for the appointment of tax representatives to be terminated; and (3) setting out the powers and liabilities of such representatives.

2269 Personal pension schemes—appropriate schemes

The Personal Pension Schemes (Appropriate Schemes) Amendment Regulations 1995, SI 1995/1612 (in force on 19 July 1995), amend the 1988 Regulations, SI 1988/137, so as to provide that a scheme can only be an appropriate pension scheme if it contains a rule requiring any minimum contributions falling to be applied so as to provide benefits in respect of a member to be so applied from the date on which they are paid to the scheme and to be allocated to a member's account within three months of that date.

2270 Personal pension schemes—independent financial advisers—statement requiring self-assessment—validity

The Securities and Investments Board ('SIB') issued a statement imposing self assessment tasks on independent financial advisers in respect of transactions with clients who had opted out of occupational pension schemes, who had not joined such schemes on commencing employment or who had transferred accrued benefits in favour of a personal pension scheme. The Independent Financial Advisers Association applied for judicial review of the SIB's decision to publish the statement and a decision of the Insurance Brokers Registration Council to adopt the statement and direct their members to follow it. *Held*, the SIB was a designated agency given functions by the Secretary of State under the Financial Services Act 1986, s 114. However, it had no power to enforce the provisions of the statement against independent financial advisers except in the few cases of those who were directly regulated by the SIB. The statement was not unlawful or ultra vires because the SIB was not purporting to exercise powers it did not have and the regulatory bodies and their members would not have been so deceived. It had also been claimed that the publication of the statement had made insurance for independent financial advisers unobtainable. This was not so. Insurance had simply become more expensive. Accordingly, the application would be dismissed on an undertaking by the SIB that it would inform every recognised self-regulatory organisation, every recognised professional body and every body affected by it that nothing in the statement was to be interpreted as requiring a firm to take steps which would invalidate its insurance cover.

R v Securities and Investments Board, ex p Independent Financial Advisers Association [1995] 2 BCLC 76 (Queen's Bench Division: Staughton LJ and Mitchell J).

2271 Personal pension schemes—sale—commission—taxation

See para 1667.

2272 Public service pensions—increased rates

The Pensions Increase (Review) Order 1995, SI 1995/708 (in force on 10 April 1995), provides for percentage increases in rates of public service pensions and deferred lump sums. The increase is the percentage (or in some cases a fraction of the percentage) by which the Secretary of State has, by direction given under the provisions of the Social Security Administration Act 1992, s 151(1) increased the sums referred to in the 1992 Act, s 150(1)(c). For pensions which began before 11 April 1994, the increase is 2.2 per cent, and for pensions which began on or after 12 April 1993, the increases are calculated on a pro rata basis based on 2.2 per cent. The order provides for increases on certain deferred lump sums which became payable on or after 11 April 1994 and before 10 April 1995. The order also makes provision for the amount by reference to which any increase in the rate of official pension is to be calculated to be reduced by the amount equal to the rate of the guaranteed minimum pension entitlement deriving from the employment which gives rise to the official pension.

2273 Railways Pension Scheme

See para 2422.

2274 Retirement annuity—premiums paid out of income—relevant earnings

See *Koenigsberger v Mellor (Inspector of Taxes)*, para 1656.

2275　Retirement benefits schemes—indexation of earnings cap

The Retirement Benefits Schemes (Indexation of Earnings Cap) Order 1995, SI 1995/3034 (made on 28 November 1995), specifies £82,200 as the earnings cap for the year of assessment 1996–97.

2276　Retirement benefits schemes—information powers

The Retirement Benefits Schemes (Information Powers) Regulations 1995, SI 1995/3103 (in force on 1 January 1996), prescribe the information and documents that are to be furnished to the Commissioners of Inland Revenue in relation to retirement benefits schemes, specify the persons responsible for furnishing them, and the time within which they are to be furnished.

2277　Retirement pension

See SOCIAL SECURITY AND SOCIAL SERVICES.

2278　Royal Navy—naval medical compassionate fund

The Naval Medical Compassionate Fund (Amendment) Order 1995, SI 1995/1965 (in force on 1 December 1995), further amends the Order in Council dated 28 July 1915, SR & O 1915/769, by providing for the President and Trustees of the Fund to be appointed by the Admiralty Board of the Defence Council and for the Honorary Treasurer and the Honorary Secretary to be appointed by the President of the Fund. In addition, amendments are made to the Schedule of the Order in Council by the substitution of a new table, which changes the multipliers by which the life subscriptions are calculated.

2279　Teachers—superannuation

The Teachers' Superannuation (Amendment) Regulations 1995, SI 1995/2004 (in force on 1 September 1995, but having effect as from 1 May 1995), further amend the Teachers' Superannuation (Consolidation) Regulations 1988, SI 1988/1652, so as to (1) provide that part-time employment in all capacities described in Sch 2 to the 1988 Regulations is pensionable (if the employee so elects) on the same terms as full-time employment, (2) require employers to record the full-time equivalent salary of part-time employees, (3) alter the definition of 'part-time' by removing the requirement that remuneration must be expressed as a proportion of an annual, termly or monthly rate for full-time employment, and (4) make consequential amendments. The regulations also make a consequential amendment to the definition of 'pensionable employment' in the Teachers' Superannuation (Additional Voluntary Contributions) Regulations 1994, SI 1994/2924.

2280　War—civilians' pensions

The Personal Injuries (Civilians) Amendment Scheme 1995, SI 1995/445 (in force on 10 April 1995), further amends the 1983 Scheme, SI 1983/686, so as to increase the amounts of allowances, pensions and awards payable under the scheme to or in respect of civilians who were killed during the 1939–45 war, and increase the amounts of income to be disregarded for the purposes of certain parts of the scheme.

2281　War—service pensions

The Naval, Military and Air Forces etc (Disablement and Death) Service Pensions Amendment Order 1995, SI 1995/766 (in force on 10 April 1995), further amends the 1983 Order, SI 1983/883, by (1) raising the maximum amount of annual earnings which may be received by a disabled person while he is deemed to be unemployable for the purposes of unemployability allowances under the 1983 Order; (2) increases the amount of a widow's pension payable under the 1983 Order; and (3) varies the rates of retired pay, pensions, gratuities and allowances in respect of disablement or death due to service in the armed forces.

2282　War—shore employments

The Injuries in War (Shore Employments) Compensation (Amendment) Scheme 1995, SI 1995/979 (in force on 30 March 1995), further amends the 1914 Scheme, by increasing the maximum weekly allowance payable to ex-members of the Women's Auxiliary Forces who suffered disablement from their service overseas during the 1914–1918 war, from £98.90 to £101.10. The amendment takes effect from 10 April 1995.

2283   War—war pensions committees

The War Pensions Committees (Amendment) Regulations 1995, SI 1995/3119 (in force on 1 January 1996), amend the 1990 Regulations, SI 1990/1349, so as to provide that the areas for which the committees are established reflect the structure of local government as it will exist on 1 April 1996. The regulations also permit the two Welsh war pensions committees to be known by Welsh names, and provide such names for them.

PERSONAL PROPERTY

Halsbury's Laws of England (4th edn) Vol 35 (reissue), paras 1201–1279

2284   Articles

Rights of Finders, Carrie Dahl-Devonshire (on *Waverley Borough Council v Fletcher* (1995) Times, Independent, 14 July (para 2285)): 139 SJ 1186

2285   Possession—possession by finder—rights as against owner of land in which object found

A local authority owned parkland subject to a covenant that it was to be used for the public's recreation. Although there was no byelaw preventing the use of metal detectors there, the authority's policy was not to permit their use. The respondent found a medieval brooch in the park by means of a metal detector and by digging up the ground. It was held not to be treasure trove and both the respondent and the authority claimed the brooch was their property. At first instance, the judge held that metal detecting was a recreation which included a right to excavate and carry away objects found and that the respondent was therefore entitled to keep the brooch. On appeal, *held*, in the case of an object found in the ground, its original owner was unlikely in most cases to be there to claim it and the law looked for a substitute owner of the land in which the object was lodged. It was well established that where an article was found in or attached to land, as between the owner or lawful possessor of the land and the finder of the article, the owner or lawful possessor had the better title. In the present case, neither the respondent's metal detecting, digging or removal of the brooch was within any of the purposes for which the authority was permitted to allow the public use of the park. The authority as owner of the park was a trustee for the general public and as such had a superior right to the brooch over the respondent who, in the absence of a licence from the authority, had no entitlement to dig and remove it. There was no basis for not applying the established general rule and, accordingly, the authority's appeal would be allowed.

Waverley Borough Council v Fletcher [1995] 4 All ER 756 (Court of Appeal: Sir Thomas Bingham MR, Auld and Ward LJJ).

PETROLEUM PRODUCTION

See FUEL AND ENERGY.

PETROLEUM REVENUE TAXATION

See FUEL AND ENERGY.

PLEADING

Halsbury's Laws of England (4th edn) Vol 36, paras 1–100

2286   Defence—amendment—principles for grant of leave to amend

The defendant in an action for patent infringement applied for leave to amend its defence to plead abuse of a dominant position contrary to the Treaty of Rome, art 86. The plaintiff opposed the application on the grounds that (1) the proposed defence was the same as that which had been struck out in an earlier action against the same defendant and in respect of the infringement of the same patent; (2) having granted summary judgment (subject to the standing over of certain matters) under RSC Ord 14 prior to the application, the court was functus officio and had no jurisdiction to allow the amendment, and (3) even if the court had discretion to allow the amendment, this was not a case in which that discretion should be exercised. *Held*, the art 86 defence sought to be introduced into the present action was the same as that struck out in the earlier action. If the defence was to be litigated, then it had to be litigated in the earlier action and to seek to raise it again amounted to an abuse of the process of the court. The order made at the Ord 14 hearing reserved 'other claims in this action' for further hearing. On a strict reading of this order, the court was not functus officio and had power to allow amendment of the pleadings to include further claims. Even if the matter had not been res judicata, the court would exercise its discretion not to allow the amendment.

Chiron Corpn v Murex Diagnostics Ltd (No 9) [1995] FSR 318 (Chancery Division: Aldous J).

2287 Statement of claim—order for further and better particulars—matters in respect of which order is necessary

A number of employees commenced proceedings against their employer for damages for personal injury resulting from the employer's negligence or breach of statutory duty. In particular, the employees alleged that they had been exposed to welding fumes. An order was made for further and better particulars of their claims, requiring them to name each fume complained of, its chemical composition, the source of the fume, and the facts relied on in support of the claim that the employer impliedly knew or ought to have known that the employees' health was at risk in working in such conditions. The order was later reversed, and on the employer's appeal, *held*, many different gases and dusts were given off by the various welding processes from time to time, and the fumes had not been inhaled individually but as a cocktail of fumes, some of which were more noxious than others. In an action for breach of statutory duty or negligence, it was not necessary to prove that the alleged breach was the whole or main cause of the damage, as it was sufficient to show that it materially contributed to the damage. Here, the particulars given by the employees and the information given in the medical reports describing their conditions and the injury that they had suffered, fully informed the employer of the nature of the claim against it. It was both impossible and unnecessary to determine in detail for the purpose of the proceedings the composition and concentration of the fumes to which the employees had been exposed. Moreover, the employer should have foreseen not merely that there was a risk of injury, but also that some form of chronic respiratory deterioration could have developed. Accordingly, the appeal would be dismissed.

Gallon v Swan Hunter Shipbuilders Ltd (1995) Times, 18 May (Court of Appeal: Nourse, Millett and Otton LJJ).

2288 Striking out—failure to set action down—action reinstated by judge—inspection of reasons tendered for default

A district judge ordered that the plaintiff's action was to be struck out if he failed to set it down within four months. The plaintiff failed to do so and, as a result, the action was struck out. Meanwhile, however, the judge made an order by consent extending the time for serving the amended defence. The judge subsequently reinstated the action, moved by the fact that the purpose and effect of his order to strike out had been overtaken by the mutual error of the parties. The defendant appealed against the judge's order to reinstate the action. *Held*, the court was concerned with marrying two conflicting principles, namely that its orders were expected to be complied with and that a party should only be expelled from the legal process as a last resort. While a deliberate flouting of the court's order could never be excused, and while breaches through neglect would cease to be excusable if they were repeated, it was for the court in other cases to inspect the reasons or excuses tendered for the default. If those could truly be described as extraneous circumstances, the default would be excusable. If not, it was for the court to decide whether in all the circumstances, including both its causes and effects, the default was such that the defaulter should have another chance on whatever terms were appropriate. On the facts in the present case, the action would be reinstated on appropriate conditions as to the future conduct of the action. Accordingly, the appeal would be dismissed.

Hogg v Aggarwal (1995) Times, 1 August (Queen's Bench Division: Sedley J).

PLEDGES AND PAWNS

Halsbury's Laws of England (4th edn) Vol 36, paras 101–200

2289   Consumer credit
See CONSUMER CREDIT.

POLICE

Halsbury's Laws of England (4th edn) Vol 36, paras 201–400

2290   Articles

Beating the Bandits, Gloria Hughes (on custody officers having a greater say on bail conditions): Police Review, 13 January 1995, p 16

Cop Talk: the Changing Rhetoric of the Police Service, Tess Newton: 145 NLJ 1362

Criminal Justice and Public Order Act 1994: Police Powers to Give Directions, Alan Murdie: LA, October 1995, p 19

Double Danger, Jack English (on the burden of proof in police disciplinary proceedings): Police Review, 7 July 1995, p 26

Judging Police Protection (on *R v Chief Constable of Sussex, ex p International Trader's Ferry* [1995] 4 All ER 364 (para 2310)): 145 NLJ 1860

Legal Advice, Mick Hayden (on a suspect's right to legal advice in a police station): Police Review, 14 April 1995, p 24

The Mentally Disordered Suspect at the Police Station, Judith Laing: [1995] Crim LR 371

The Metropolitan Police Assault—Charging Offences—Are They Based on Law? John Woods: 159 JP Jo 42

New Bail Powers for Custody Officers, Clifford Williams: 145 NLJ 685

Non-Police Station Interviews? Paul Tain: 139 SJ 299

Paying For Blame, Sarah Gibbons (on the Hillsborough tragedy and ability of on duty police officers to sue for compensation): Police Review, 10 February 1995, p 18

PII [Public Interest Immunity] and the Police, Stephen McNamara: 139 SJ 262

Police Powers and Individual Rights, Robert Roscoe: 145 NLJ 1067

Preventive Medicine, Mick Hayden (on new stop and search powers of police): Police Review, 24 March 1995, p 18

Privacy and the Unauthorised Publication of Photographs, Rabinder Singh (on *Hellewell v Chief Constable of Derbyshire* (1995) Times, 13 January (para 2291)): 139 SJ 771

Prying Eyes, Jack English (on reading of police notebooks by defence solicitors): Police Review, 20 October 1995, p 19

Questioning and Identification: Changes Under PACE '95, David Wolchover and Anthony Heaton-Armstrong: [1995] Crim LR 356

Reassessing the Role of the 'Appropriate Adult', Brian Littlechild (on the role of the 'appropriate adult' in police interviews): [1995] Crim LR 540

Squatters Squeezed, Alan Beckley (on police powers for dealing with squatters under the Criminal Justice and Public Order Act 1994): Police Review, 3 February 1995, p 16

Streamlining Bail, Mick Hayden (on new powers for custody officers to impose conditional bail): Police Review, 17 March 1995, p 16

Targeting Touts, Mike Baker (on police powers against ticket touts under the Criminal Justice and Public Order Act 1994): Police Review, 10 February 1995, p 16

Thomas v Sawkins: Revisited But Not Resolved, Alex Carroll (on a policeman's right of entry): 159 JP Jo 296

2291   Breach of confidence—defence—use of suspect's photograph for the purpose of detection of crime—public interest

Traders in a shop watch scheme had requested the police to provide photographs of individuals known for shoplifting and harassment so as to allow new members of staff to recognise them and bar them from the premises. The plaintiff had been photographed while in custody at a police station in accordance with Code D of the Police and Criminal Evidence Act 1984 Codes of

Practice. A photograph of the plaintiff had been copied from the police file and handed to shop watch members. The nature of the photograph, with the plaintiff's name, a number and a date, was such that it had clearly been taken in police custody. It would thus at least convey the information that the plaintiff was known to the police. The plaintiff discovered that his photograph was in use and sought declaratory relief and an injunction restraining the disclosure of any photograph of him taken while in custody. The chief constable applied to strike out the plaintiff's claim. *Held*, there was no doubt that in some circumstances disclosure of a photograph might be actionable as a breach of confidence. Where the police took a photograph of a suspect at the police station in circumstances where, at least, the suspect's consent was not required, they were not by law free to make whatever use they wished of the picture so obtained. The police could only make reasonable use of the photograph for the purpose of the prevention and the detection of crime, the investigation of alleged offences and the apprehension of suspects or persons unlawfully at large. Where the use of the photograph lay within those bounds, the police would have a public interest defence to any action brought against them for breach of confidence. In the present case, the police had acted in good faith for the prevention or detection of crime and had done so to a limited and specific extent by distributing the plaintiff's photograph only to persons who had reasonable need to make use of it. They had acted obviously and unarguably in the public interest and, accordingly, the plaintiff's claim would be struck out.

Hellewell v Chief Constable of Derbyshire [1995] 4 All ER 473 (Queen's Bench Division: Laws J).

2292 Conditions of service—pay and emoluments

The Police Regulations 1995, SI 1995/215 (in force on 8 March 1995), consolidate with amendments the 1987 Regulations, SI 1987/851. The amendments are as follows (1) provisions relating to authorised establishment are not reproduced; (2) provisions as to deputy chief constables have been omitted consequent on the abolition of the rank under the Police and Magistrates' Courts Act 1994; (3) the rank of chief superintendent has been abolished; (4) provision has been made for days in lieu where the exigencies of duty have precluded the allowance of a day's leave on public holidays and the granting of rest days; and (5) the maximum amount of removal allowance has been increased.

The Police (Amendment) Regulations 1995, SI 1995/547 (in force on 13 April 1995), amend the principal regulations supra in relation to ranks, part-time appointments, beats, sections, sub-divisions and divisions, appointment of chief constable, fixed term appointments for certain ranks, requirements to advertise vacancies in certain ranks, probationary service in the rank of constable, retirement, variable shift arrangements, overtime, public holidays and rest days for ranks below inspector, rate of pay, deductions from pay of social security benefits and statutory sick pay, modification for part-time service, and determination of pay.

The Police (Amendment No 2) Regulations 1995, SI 1995/2020 (in force on 26 August 1995), amend the principal regulations supra so as to (1) set out adaptations as respects the ranks in the Metropolitan and City of London police forces; (2) make provision concerning the temporary salary when a member of a police force acts for a member of a higher rank, and (c) increase certain allowances. Certain of these provisions have retrospective effect.

2293 Discipline

The Police (Discipline) (Amendment) Regulations 1995, SI 1995/1475 (in force on 10 July 1995), amend the 1985 Regulations, SI 1985/518, so as to enable a chief constable to delegate the hearing of disciplinary charges to an assistant chief constable designated to act in the absence of the chief constable under the Police Act 1964, s 6.

The Police (Discipline) (Amendment No 2) Regulations 1995, SI 1995/2517 (in force on 1 November 1995), amend the 1985 Regulations supra in relation to disciplinary hearings and appeals in the metropolitan police force, so as to enable officers of the rank of commander appointed by the Metropolitan Police Commissioner to exercise the same disciplinary functions as deputy assistant commissioners.

2294 Duty of care—seizure of motor vehicle—damage to vehicle while in police possession—liability of police

See *Sutcliffe v Chief Constable of West Yorkshire*, para 2163.

2295 Investigation of offences—report to Crown Prosecution Service—discovery—public interest immunity

See *O'Sullivan v Metropolitan Police Comr*, para 1072.

2296 Ministry of Defence Police—Police Committee

The Ministry of Defence Police (Police Committee) Regulations 1995, SI 1995/939 (in force on 1 May 1995), revoke the Ministry of Defence Police (Police Committee) Regulations 1988, SI 1988/1098, which provided for the membership of the Ministry of Defence Police Committee.

2297 Police and Criminal Evidence Act 1984—Codes of Practice

See para 779.

2298 Police and Magistrates' Courts Act 1994—commencement

The Police and Magistrates' Courts Act 1994 (Commencement No 5 and Transitional Provisions) (Amendment) Order 1995, SI 1995/246, amends SI 1994/3262 in consequence of defects in certain of the specified transitional provisions.

The Police and Magistrates' Court Act 1994 (Commencement No 5 and Transitional Provisions) (Amendment No 2) Order 1995, SI 1995/899, makes amendments to SI 1994/3262 and SI 1995/246 supra, in consequence of certain defects in the transitional provisions.

The Police and Magistrates' Courts Act 1994 (Commencement No 6 and Transitional Provisions) Order 1995, SI 1995/42, brings into force on 3 February 1995, Sch 8, para 19(1), (2), which amends the Justices of the Peace Act 1979, s 59(1), by virtue of which the Lord Chancellor is empowered to pay grant to local authorities in respect of compensation for loss of office or employment or loss or diminution of emoluments by justices' clerks and their assistants. Transitional provision is also made.

The Police and Magistrates' Courts Act 1994 (Commencement No. 8 and Transitional Provisions) Order 1995, SI 1995/685, brings into force, on 1 April 1995, ss 72, 73, 75–77, 79 (for all remaining purposes), 80, 81, 83(1), (2) (in part), 84, 88(6), 91(1) (in part), (2), (3), 93 (in part), Sch 8, paras 5, 10–16, 18, 19(1), (3), 20, 21, 25–34, and certain repeals in Sch 9. Certain of those provisions come into force in relation to certain areas on 1 April or 1 October 1995 or on 1 January 1996. Transitional provision is also made.

For a summary of the Act, see 1994 Abr para 2154. For details of commencement, see the commencement table in the title STATUTES.

2299 Police areas—Wales

The Police Areas (Wales) Order 1995, SI 1995/2864 (in force in part on 11 December 1995 and in part on 1 April 1996), amends police areas in Wales to take account of the reorganisation of local government in Wales under the Local Government (Wales) Act 1994. The order (1) amends the Police Act 1964, Sch 1A, so as to describe police areas by reference to the new local government areas in Wales and ensure that the existing police authorities continue to exist; (2) makes transitional provision so that councillors from the new local government councils can participate as members of the police authorities in certain decisions in respect of the budget and policing plan for the financial year beginning 1 April 1996; (3) makes transfers of property consequential on the changes to police areas; and (4) transfers certain civilian staff from the South Wales police authority to the Gwent police authority.

2300 Police authority—supply contracts—procedure

See para 2929.

2301 Police Complaints Authority—documents—disclosure—public interest immunity—civil proceedings for damages

Following his acquittal on charges of dishonesty offences, the plaintiff commenced proceedings against the defendant chief constable for damages for malicious prosecution, misfeasance in public office and conspiracy. In view of the number of allegations made against the police, the judge ordered the trial of the action to be by judge alone. He also ruled that reports prepared by investigating officers of the Police Complaints Authority were not subject to public interest immunity and should be produced to the plaintiff. On the defendant's application for leave to appeal against the decision, *held*, by virtue of RSC Ord 24, rr 1(1) and 2(1), the defendant was obliged to give discovery of all documents in his possession, control or power which related to matters at issue in the action. The requirement that a document had to be produced if it was necessary to fairly dispose of the matter existed in order to ensure that no party had an unfair advantage or suffered unfair disadvantage in the litigation. However, the fact that a party was merely curious to see a document was not a reason to order production. Applying the test to the case, inspection was not necessary. Although it had been decided that public interest immunity did not attach to statements obtained for the purposes of an independent investigation under the Police and Criminal Evidence Act 1984, the Act did not expressly provide that an investigating officer's report was to be seen by anyone other than the police authority which commissioned it and the Police Complaints Authority. Moreover, there was a fundamental public interest in ensuring that those responsible for maintaining law and order were uncorrupt and law abiding. Investigating officers had to be able to freely report on fellow colleagues or members of the public without fear that their opinions would be revealed to those persons, and their reports were therefore covered by public interest immunity. Accordingly, the application would be granted.

Taylor v Anderton [1995] 2 All ER 420 (Court of Appeal: Sir Thomas Bingham MR, Rose and Morritt LJJ). *R v Chief Constable of West Midlands, ex p Wiley* (1994) Times, Independent, 15 July, HL (1994 Abr para 2159) considered.

2302   Police Federation—elections

The Police Federation (Amendment) Regulations 1995, SI 1995/2768 (in force on 15 November 1995), amend the 1969 Regulations, SI 1969/1787, so as to (1) provide that men and women can vote in the elections in which previously either only men or only women could vote; (2) remove the sex qualification of the persons to be elected; (3) require certain elections to be held on the same day; and (4) make consequential amendments.

2303   Police officer—female officer—sex discrimination

See *Waters v Metropolitan Police Comr*, para 2663.

2304   Police officer—wilful obstruction of officer—contamination of identification parade in attempt to procure alibi

See *Connolly v Dale*, para 920.

2305   Police officer—witness to football ground disaster—claim for compensation for psychiatric injury

See *Frost v Chief Constable of South Yorkshire*, para 2172.

2306   Powers—decision to formally caution child—decision in breach of guidelines— court's ability to review decision

See *R v Commissioner of Police of the Metropolis, ex p P*, para 755.

2307   Powers—powers in relation to raves—disposal of sound equipment

The Police (Disposal of Sound Equipment) Regulations 1995, SI 1995/722 (in force on 10 April 1995), provide for the disposal of sound equipment in the possession of the police, the forfeiture of which has been ordered by the court under the Criminal Justice and Public Order Act 1994, s 66(1), on the summary conviction of a person for an offence in relation to a rave under s 63, provided that not less than six months have expired from the date on which the order was made, and either no application by a claimant of the equipment has been made under s 66(5), or no such application has succeeded. The regulations require the police to sell such equipment unless a police officer not below the rank of superintendent is satisfied that because of the nature of the equipment it is not in the public interest to do so, in which case it may be disposed of according to his directions; and for any proceeds of sale to be paid to the police authority and to be kept in a separate fund. Provision is made for expenditure from, and auditing of, the fund.

2308 Powers—powers to remove trespassers on land—retention and disposal of vehicles

The Police (Retention and Disposal of Vehicles) Regulations 1995, SI 1995/723 (in force on 10 April 1995), provide for the retention, safe keeping, disposal and destruction, by the police or persons authorised by them, of vehicles seized by them by virtue of their powers under the Criminal Justice and Public Order Act 1994, s 62, in relation to trespassers on land, and under s 64, in relation to raves. The police officer, or other authorised person having custody of such a vehicle must serve a notice on the person from whom it has been seized, requiring him to claim it within 21 days, and indicating to him that prescribed charges are payable and that it may be retained until they are paid. Where the authority is unable to serve a notice on such person, or that person fails to remove the vehicle from police custody, the authority must take steps to identify and serve a similar notice on the owner of the vehicle, if he is a different person. The vehicle may be destroyed or disposed of if the police are unable to find the owner or if he fails to remove it. Where it is sold, the net proceeds of sale are payable to the owner if he makes a claim within a year of the sale.

2309 Powers—search and seizure—drugs offence—delay in acting on information received

See *Ireland v Russell*, para 847.

2310 Preservation of peace—limiting of police protection for export of livestock—quantitative restrictions on exports

A company which transported livestock for export brought an application for judicial review of a chief constable's decision that policing to protect the transport of livestock from protesters would only be provided on two days each week. The company claimed that his decision and subsequent refusal to change it or delay its implementation amounted to a breach of his duty to keep the peace, alternatively that his actions amounted to a breach of the EC Treaty, art 34, being a quantitative restriction on exports. *Held*, the chief constable was not in breach of his duty to keep the peace and enforce the law. His actions were not *Wednesbury* unreasonable and the courts would not normally interfere with a decision made by a chief constable in the exercise of his discretion. However, his actions amounted to a prima facie breach of art 34 and he could not rely on the effect of civil disturbances as affording a public policy defence under art 36 if there were resources available to deal with such disturbances.

R v Chief Constable of Sussex, ex p International Trader's Ferry Ltd [1995] 4 All ER 364 (Queen's Bench Division: Balcombe LJ and Popplewell J). *Harris v Sheffield United Football Club Ltd* [1987] 2 All ER 838, CA (1987 Abr para 1960), approved. *R v Coventry City Council, ex p Phoenix Aviation* [1995] 3 All ER 37 (para 2313), followed.

2311 Prisoners (Return to Custody) Act 1995

See para 2404.

PORTS AND HARBOURS

Halsbury's Laws of England (4th edn) Vol 36, paras 401–600

2312 Harbours—detention of unsafe ship—powers of harbourmaster

See *Ullapool Harbour Trustees v Secretary of State for Transport*, para 2682.

2313 Port authorities—authorities excluding export of live animals for slaughter following unlawful disruption by protesters—authorities' discretion to exclude trade

The lawful export of live animals for slaughter attracted widespread concern and resulted in highly publicised protests. Following unlawful disruptions, certain port authorities refused the trade in such exports. The authorities denied that their refusal was motivated by animal welfare considerations. Exporters applied for judicial review of the authorities' refusal to handle the shipping of livestock, and it fell to be determined whether the authorities had the discretion to refuse to trade. *Held*, in each case, the authority had no discretion to distinguish between lawful trades or to refuse trade which was lawful and no emergency existed which could justify their non-compliance with that duty to accept lawful trade. Even if the authorities were to be regarded as having a discretion to determine which legal trades to handle they could not properly exercise it here in favour of the ban on the ground that the trade would generate unlawful disruption. Public authorities had to beware of surrendering to the dictates of unlawful pressure groups. A variation or even short term suspension of trade might be justified on occasion, but it was one thing to respond to unlawful threats and quite another to submit to them. None of the authorities had given the least thought to the awesome implications for the rule of law of doing what they proposed. The police had ample powers to control unlawful protest. The only body properly able to ban the lawful trade was Parliament unless even that would be unlawful under European Community law. Accordingly, the applications for judicial review would be granted.

R v Coventry Airport, ex p Phoenix Aviation; R v Dover Harbour Board, ex p Peter Gilder & Sons; R v Associated British Ports, ex p Plymouth City Council (1995) Independent, 13 April, Times, 17 April (Queen's Bench Division: Simon Brown LJ and Popplewell J).

PRACTICE AND PROCEDURE

Halsbury's Laws of England (4th edn) Vol 37, paras 1–1000

2314   Articles

Appeals from the Immigration Appeal Tribunal to the Court of Appeal: a Short Guide for the Practitioner, Jim Gillespie: 9 INLP 92

Are There Any Clothes for the Emperor to Wear? Michael Zander (on the Woolf Inquiry into the civil justice system): 145 NLJ 154

Automatic Striking Out: Notice or Green Book? Daniel Barnett: 139 SJ 446

The Costs Question, Kevin Browne (on interlocutory costs orders): LS Gaz, 24 May 1995, p 20

The Courts and Foreign Currency Obligations, Steven Stern: [1995] LMCLQ 494

Cutting Costs, John Lambert (on wasted costs orders): LS Gaz, 21 June 1995, p 20

Defendants: Beware Rule Changes Bearing Gifts, Stephen Evans (on rule changes in personal injury cases): 139 SJ 1253

Don't Let Them Have Them, Nigel Ley (on refusing rights of audience to civil servants): 145 NLJ 1124

Essays on the Woolf Report, Michael Zander: 145 NLJ 1866

Judicial Management, Nick Armstrong: LA, September 1995, p 6

Key Dates and Headaches, Richard Barr (on the problems caused by the automatic striking out rules): 139 SJ 376

Losing Privilege by Mistake, Tony Davies (on whether a party who mistakenly discloses a privileged document can prevent its being used in evidence): 139 SJ 584

A Matter of Opinion, Tim Constable and Nick Hallchurch (on RSC Ord 40): LS Gaz, 6 September 1995, p 16

Mercedes and Mareva, Steven Gee (on *Mercedes-Benz AG v Leiduck* [1995] 3 All ER 929, PC (para 2375)): 139 SJ 1076

New Rules for Juvenile Offenders, Tony Wilkinson: 139 SJ 110

Only on Instruction, Fidelma White and Robert Bradgate (on the issuing of writs without the proper authority): LS Gaz, 20 September 1995, p 22

A Proactive Court for Ancillary Relief Cases, Maggie Rae: [1995] Fam Law 133

Procedures at Inquiries—the Duty to be Fair, Sir Richard Scott V-C: (1995) 111 LQR 596

Setting Off Interlocutory Costs Against Damages, Diana Bretherick: 139 SJ 91

Some Serious Thoughts from Essex on Civil Justice, Judge Nicholas Brandt: 145 NLJ 350

Waffle Free Zones? Gordon Exall (on the intended effect of Lord Taylor's and Sir Richard Scott's Practice Direction on Civil Litigation: Case Management): 139 SJ 109

Will Woolf Work? Steven Gee (on Lord Woolf's Inquiry): 139 SJ 674

A Woolf in Sheep's Clothing (on Lord Woolf's Inquiry), Bill Onwusah: 145 NLJ 1095

Woolf's Justice, Ramnik Shah (on Lord Woolf's inquiry into the civil justice system): 145 NLJ 147

2315   Anton Piller orders

See INJUNCTIONS.

2316 Appeal—appeal on finding of fact

See *Delaney v Southmead Health Authority*, para 2177.

2317 Appeal—leave to appeal—grant of leave—application to set aside

On an application to set aside leave to appeal granted by a single lord justice, *held*, the full Court of Appeal would not set aside leave granted by a single lord justice even if it considered that it would not itself have granted leave or that the lord justice had been over-indulgent in granting leave. The requirement of leave was intended to provide a filter to save unnecessary time and expense on appeals which had no hope of succeeding. A single lord justice, who would make his decision on paper, would refuse leave if it was clear to him that the appeal was not arguable, although he would be anxious not to stifle appeals which might succeed even though he was sceptical as to their chances of success. A grant of leave followed by an application to set aside would frustrate the object of the procedure. The grant of leave would be treated in all but the most obvious cases as conclusive. An application to set aside leave would only succeed if it satisfied a high threshold test. The application would be dismissed.

First Tokyo Index Trust Ltd v Morgan Stanley Trust Co (Ashurst Morris Crisp, third parties) (1995) Times, 6 October (Court of Appeal: Sir Thomas Bingham MR, Henry and Thorpe LJJ).

2318 Appeal—leave to appeal out of time—jurisdiction of Court of Appeal

See *Re T (a Minor) (Adoption Order: Leave to Appeal)*, para 337.

2319 Appeal—leave to appeal out of time—subsequent invalidity of basis on which original order made

See *Heard v Heard*, para 1106.

2320 Appeal—notice of appeal—notice served by defendant after service of defence—waiver of appeal

The plaintiffs were South Africans claiming damages for personal injuries sustained as a result of exposure to harmful chemicals whilst working for a South African subsidiary of the defendant company. The defendant applied for a stay of the proceedings in favour of litigation in South Africa. At first instance, the application was refused but the action was ordered to be temporarily stayed for 28 days to enable the defendant to make an application to the Court of Appeal for a general stay pending an appeal. At the end of that 28 day period, the defendant served a defence to the action and, one month later, it served notice of appeal on the plaintiffs. The plaintiffs applied for the notice of appeal to be struck out on the ground that it was too late for the appeal to proceed. *Held*, the unqualified service of a defence was a paradigm example of conduct indicating a willingness to have the merits of a matter considered by the court. It was not relevant that the issue had arisen when it was an appeal rather than an original application which was sought to be made. In this case, the defence had been served and was unqualified which was the clearest indication that the appeal would not be pursued and, accordingly, the application would be granted and the notice of appeal struck out.

Ngcobo v Thor Chemicals Holdings Ltd (1995) Times, 10 November (Court of Appeal: Neill, Evans and Millett LJJ).

2321 Barristers

See BARRISTERS.

2322 Chancery Division—case management—preparation for and conduct of hearings

Lord Taylor of Gosforth CJ has issued the following *Practice Direction* ([1995] 1 All ER 385), which applies to all lists in the Queen's Bench and Chancery Divisions, except where other directions specifically apply.

1. The paramount importance of reducing the cost and delay of civil litigation makes it necessary for judges sitting at first instance to assert greater control over the preparation for and conduct of hearings than has hitherto been customary. Failure by practitioners to conduct cases economically will result in appropriate costs orders, including wasted costs orders.

2. The court will accordingly exercise its discretion to limit (a) discovery, (b) the length of oral submissions, (c) the time allowed for the examination and cross-examination of witnesses, (d) the issues on which it wishes to be addressed, and (e) reading aloud from documents and authorities.

3. Unless the court orders otherwise, every witness statement is to stand as the evidence-in-chief of the witness concerned.

4. RSC Ord 18, r 7 will be strictly enforced. In advance of trial, the parties must use their best endeavours to agree on the issues or the main issues, and it is their duty in so far as possible to reduce or eliminate the expert issues.

5. RSC Ord 34, r 10(2)(a)–(c) will be strictly enforced. Documents to be used in court must be in A4 format where possible, contained in suitably secured bundles, and lodged with the court at least two clear days before the hearing of the application or trial. Each bundle must be paginated, indexed, wholly legible, arranged chronologically, and contained in a ring binder or a lever-arch file. Where documents have been copied unnecessarily or bundled incompetently, the cost will be disallowed.

6. A pre-trial review must be applied for, or in default may be ordered by the court, in cases estimated to last for more than 10 days. The review must, where practicable, be conducted by the trial judge between four and eight weeks before trial, and must be attended by the advocates who are to represent the parties at trial.

7. Unless the court orders otherwise, a completed pre-trial check-list in the form set out below must be lodged with the listing officer (or equivalent) on behalf of each party no later than two months before the date of trial.

8. Not less than three clear days before the hearing of any action or application, each party must lodge a skeleton argument with the court (with copies sent to the other parties), concisely summarising that party's submissions in relation to each of the issues, and citing the main authorities relied on. The authorities may also be attached. Skeleton arguments must be as brief as the nature of the issues allow, and must not exceed 20 pages of double-spaced A4 paper without leave of the court.

9. An opening speech must be succinct, and at the end of it other parties may be invited briefly to amplify their skeleton arguments. In a heavy case, the court may require written speeches as well as final speeches, including the findings of fact for which each party contends.

PRE-TRIAL CHECK-LIST

Short title of action:
Folio number:
Trial date:
Party lodging check-list:
Name of solicitor:
Names(s) of counsel for trial (if known):

Setting Down
   (1) Has the action been set down?

Pleadings
   (2)(a) Do you intend to make any amendment to your pleadings?
   (a) If so, when?

Interrogatories
   (3)(a) Are any interrogatories outstanding?
   (b) If so, when served and upon whom?

Evidence
   (4)(a) Have all orders in relation to expert, factual and hearsay evidence been complied with? If not, specify what remains outstanding.
   (b) Do you intend to serve/seek leave to serve any further report or statement? If so, when, and what report or statement?
   (c) Have all other orders in relation to oral evidence been complied with?
   (d) Do you require any further leave or orders in relation to evidence? If so, please specify, and say when you will apply.
   (5)(a) What witnesses of fact do you intend to call? [names]
   (b) What expert witnesses do you intend to call? [names]
   (c) Will any witness require an interpreter? If so, which?

Documents
   (6)(a) Have all orders in relation to discovery been complied with?
   (b) If not, what orders are outstanding?
   (c) Do you intend to apply for any further orders relating to discovery? If so, what and when?
   (7)(a) Will you not later than seven days before trial have prepared agreed paginated bundles of fully legible documents for the use of counsel and the court?

Pre-trial review
(8)(a) Has a pre-trial review been ordered?
(b) If so, when is it to take place?
(c) If not, would it be useful to have one?

Length of trial
(9) What are counsel's estimates of the likely minimum and maximum lengths of the trial? [The answer should ordinarily be supported by an estimate of length signed by the counsel to be instructed.]

Alternative dispute resolution
(See *Practice Statement (Commercial Court: Alternative Dispute Resolution)* [1994] 1 WLR 14.)
(10) Have you or counsel discussed with your client(s) the possibility of attempting to resolve this dispute (or particular issues) by alternative dispute resolution?
(11) Might some form of alternative dispute resolution procedure resolve or narrow the issues in this case?
(12) Have you or your client(s) explored the possibility of resolving this dispute (or particular issues) by alternative dispute resolution?
[Signature of solicitor, date]

Note: This check-list must be lodged not later than two months before the date of hearing with copies to other parties.

Sir Richard Scott V-C, has issued the following *Practice Direction* ([1995] 2 All ER 512).

The provisions of the *Chancery Guide* apply to litigation in the Chancery Division. In the case of inconsistency between the provisions of the *Chancery Guide* and the provisions of any previous direction (including *Practice Direction* [1995] 1 WLR 262), the provisions of the *Chancery Guide* must prevail. The provisions of the guide are subject to any subsequent *Practice Direction* that may be made.

The *Chancery Guide* can be obtained from Room E01, Royal Courts of Justice, Strand, London WC2A 2LL.

2323 Costs—acceptance of payment in—claim for costs by plaintiff

The plaintiff was a police driver who sustained a minor whiplash injury as a result of a collision with a stolen vehicle he was pursuing. The injury completely resolved within two weeks and the plaintiff took no time off work, but he did not participating in sports for three months. The Domestic Regulatons Insurer offered £750 to settle the plaintiff's claim for damages. The plaintiff's solicitors indicated that they were prepared to accept the offer so long as their costs were also met, failing which they would commence proceedings. The defendant rejected the request and proceedings limited to £3,000 were issued. The defendant applied for the proceedings to be referred to arbitration but the judge decided that the claim for damages in excess of £1,000 was borderline but not unsustainable and therefore refused the application. Two weeks after the judge's refusal, the defendant made a payment in of £800 which was accepted by the plaintiff, before he had taken any further action. The plaintiff applied for payment out of court and costs on scale one. *Held*, the plaintiff and his solicitors had clearly decided that they would accept a payment in below £1,000 before the defendant's request to have the proceedings referred to arbitration and, in the circumstances, they would only be allowed to recover the issue fee whilst being ordered to pay those of the defendant's costs incurred after the payment in, including those of the final hearing, on scale one.

Horner v White (12 January 1995, unreported) (Clerkenwell County Court: District Judge Southcombe) (Kindly submitted for publication by Pip Punwar, Barrister).

2324 Costs—award of costs—reduction of award in proportion to time spent pursuing unrealistic points

As a result of injuries sustained in a road traffic accident involving the defendant, the plaintiff mechanic was permanently disabled from heavy work. At trial the losses resulting from his inability to continue to expand his business as he had planned were discussed at length. *Held*, the plaintiff would receive damages consisting of amounts for general damages, loss of profit in his present business and the planned expansion, future disadvantage in the labour market, and miscellaneous items connected with and purchases resulting from his injuries. However, at least half of the lengthy court hearing had been concerned with special damages and with points raised by the plaintiff on which he had failed. The case was made much more difficult and lengthy by virtue of the raising of issues which were in many respects unrealistic and which should not have been raised. Accordingly the plaintiff would only be allowed to recover 60 per cent of his costs.

Smith v Huntley [1995] PIQR P475 (Queen's Bench Division: Mance J).

2325 Costs—Calderbank offer—refusal of offer—effect on costs after compromise of action

A third party in proceedings between the plaintiff and the defendant sent the plaintiff a letter which was expressed to be 'without prejudice save as to costs' and offered to settle the matter. The terms of settlement included payment by the third party to the plaintiff of £50,000 in full and final settlement of the third party proceedings and the plaintiff's costs incurred up to the date of the letter, both in relation to those proceedings and the defendant's counterclaim. The letter also stated that if the offer was not accepted, the third party reserved the right to bring the letter to the notice of the judge on the issue of costs and that it was, as far as possible, to be regarded as the equivalent of a payment into court. The offer was not accepted but the proceedings were subsequently compromised in a consent order, the terms of which included a payment by the third party to the plaintiff of £50,000 and payment by the third party and the plaintiff of the defendant's costs of its counterclaim against the third party, with liability for those and other costs to be determined by the court in default of agreement between the parties. On the plaintiff's application for orders as to liability for costs, *held,* (1) where an offer of settlement had been made, whether by way of a payment into court, another form of offer permitted by the Rules of the Supreme Court, or by way of a *Calderbank* letter, the court's determination of liability for costs of the person who made the offer turned principally on a comparison of what was offered and what was achieved, and thereafter on whether the person to whom the offer was addressed ought reasonably to have accepted the offer. Further, the court's approach to the interpretation of RSC Ord 62, r 9(1)(d) and the general question of the interpretation and effect of a letter of settlement expressed to be 'without prejudice save as to costs' was informed by its policy of encouraging every proper means whereby a party was made to realise that steps should actively be taken by him to bring the litigation to an end. Ord 62, r 9(1)(d) did not prevent the court from considering the third party's letter when assessing liability as to costs because the third party, in making the settlement offer, did so not merely as a defendant to the counterclaim but primarily as a third party to the main proceedings, with the objective of disposing of all claims being made against it, and therefore could not have protected its position on costs without writing some form of letter. On an analysis of the position ultimately reached in the consent order, the plaintiff achieved no more as a result of not accepting the third party's offer when it was first made, and probably was worse off because the offer included an offer to pay all the costs of the defendant's counterclaim against the plaintiff to date even though the third party could not have been liable in respect of them. Moreover, regardless of whether the reasonableness of the offer was judged at the time it was made or at some later time when the plaintiff's conduct in response to it could be taken into account, the offer was clearly one which the plaintiff ought reasonably to have accepted and consequently could and should be taken into account by the court in the exercise of its discretion as to costs under Ord 62, r 9(1). The third party's letter took effect as a *Calderbank* letter and, as such, it displaced and altered the plaintiff's position as to costs. Accordingly, the plaintiff's application would be dismissed.

Padmanor Investments Ltd v Soundcraft Electronics Ltd (Derrick Wade & Waters (Southern) Ltd, third parties) [1995] 4 All ER 683 (Queen's Bench Division, Official Referees' Business: Judge Humphrey Lloyd QC). *Cutts v Head* [1984] 1 All ER 597 (1983 Abr para 1463) and *Chrulew v Borm-Reid & Co (a firm)* [1992] 1 All ER 953 (1991 Abr para 1887) considered.

2326 Costs—claim against non-party—insurer of party—discretion to award costs

On the question of whether the court should use its discretion under the Supreme Court Act 1981, s 51 to make an order for costs against an insurer of a party to litigation (in the present case a P & I club of which the party was a member), it has been held that if, in an application for the award of costs under s 51, a non-party's liability for costs is to be based on some personal cause of action against him, the court should be cautious not to use a summary procedure to side step the normal process.

Tharros Shipping Co Ltd v Bias Shipping Ltd (No 3) [1995] 1 Lloyd's Rep 541 (Queen's Bench Division: Rix J).

2327 Costs—conditional fee agreements

See para 2788.

2328 Costs—criminal cases

See CRIMINAL EVIDENCE AND PROCEDURE.

2329 Costs—divorce cases

See DIVORCE.

2330 Costs—family proceedings

See CHILDREN AND YOUNG PERSONS.

2331 Costs—legal representative's liability for costs—wasted costs order—action wrongly maintained against defendant

Scotland
The plaintiff sustained injuries in an accident. She obtained legal aid and commenced proceedings for damages against three defendants. After the evidence had been heard, the plaintiff decided not to pursue her case against the first defendant. No evidence had been led against the first defendant but the plaintiff's solicitor had maintained the case against that defendant on counsel's advice. The first defendant sought its costs from the plaintiff's solicitor on the basis that it ought to have been clear before the evidence was led that no evidence against it existed. *Held*, the plaintiff's counsel had committed a serious error of judgment in advising that the action should be continued against the first defendant. However, it was not right that the solicitor who acted on counsel's advice should be found personally liable in expenses. It seemed unfair that the solicitor in such circumstances might be personally liable while counsel was not. Accordingly, the application would be refused.

Reid v Edinburgh Acoustics Ltd (No 2) 1995 SLT 982 (Outer House).

2332 Costs—legal representative's personal liability for costs—wasted costs order—adjournment requested after difficulties with time estimates

A barrister had accepted a brief for a two-day trial immediately prior to another trial in which he was due to appear and which was to take place in another city. It was particularly important that he have conduct of the second trial, which involved a mentally retarded defendant whose confidence he had gained. However, the first trial started late and progressed more slowly then anticipated. Counsel sent a pupil to ask for an adjournment in the second trial and the judge listed the case for mention so that the barrister could explain why he was not ready. Having heard his explanation the judge made a wasted costs order. On appeal, *held*, although the barrister had been over-optimistic in failing to anticipate delays in the first trial, his conduct could not be described as unreasonable. A wasted costs order was a draconian measure and, in considering whether to make the order, the judge had to remember that he was removed from the daily demands of practice and to make allowances for difficulties with time estimates. Accordingly, the appeal would be allowed.

Re a Barrister (Wasted Costs Order No 4 of 1993) (1995) Times, 21 April (Court of Appeal: Auld LJ, Mantell and Sachs JJ).

2333 Costs—legal representative's personal liability for costs—wasted costs order—exercise of trial judge's discretion

The respondents were the solicitors and counsel acting for a litigant in civil proceedings. At the end of the trial, the judge severely criticised the respondents' conduct of the case. In particular, he found that they had deliberately misled the court, had grossly underestimated the likely length of the trial, and had not been selective in adducing evidence. The judge therefore made an order requiring the respondents to show cause why a wasted costs order should not be made against them in respect of the plaintiff's costs. He later decided that he himself should not hear the application, but that it would be unreasonable for another judge to do so as that would involve rehearing the original litigation. The judge therefore decided not to pursue the wasted costs application. On the plaintiff's appeal against that decision, *held*, the wasted costs application was made unmanageable by the number of allegations that the plaintiff intended to make against the respondents, none of which he was prepared to withdraw. Moreover, it was a matter for a judge's discretion whether or not there was to be a wasted costs hearing, and, generally, it was always for the trial judge to adjudicate on the matter. However, in the instant case, the judge had made grave allegations which struck at the heart of the respondents' professional standing, and had not given them the opportunity to reply. In those exceptional circumstances, as it would be difficult for the judge to achieve an appearance of fairness in determining the matter, he was entitled to decide not to pursue the wasted costs application. Accordingly, the appeal would be dismissed.

Re Freudiana Holdings Ltd (1995) Times, 4 December (Court of Appeal: Rose, Millett and Thorpe LJJ).

2334　Costs—legal representative's personal liability for costs—wasted costs order—solicitor acting without fee

Substantial damages were awarded against a party to a libel action. That party did not make any payment, having neither the means nor the intention of doing so. Aware of this, a firm of solicitors chose to act for him without fee, issuing proceedings on his behalf claiming that the libel action had been won by fraud and perjury. The proceedings were struck out as an abuse of process. On the solicitors' appeal against an order that they should personally pay a proportion of the defendant's costs in the unsuccessful action, *held*, there were three categories of conduct which could give rise to an order for costs against a solicitor: (1) conduct within the wasted costs jurisdiction of the Supreme Court Act 1981, s 51(6), (7); (2) conduct which was otherwise a breach of duty to the court; and (3) conduct which involved acting outside the role of solicitor. The order should have been made within the wasted costs jurisdiction of the 1981 Act, s 51(6), (7). Acting without a fee and doing so in a hopeless case did not of itself justify the making of a wasted costs order. However, the solicitors should have considered whether the claim could properly be pursued, there was a lack of propriety in the conduct of the litigation and an abuse of process such that their conduct was unreasonable within the wider sense of *Ridehalgh v Horsefield*. Accordingly, the appeal would be dismissed.

Tolstoy Miloslavsky v Aldington (1995) Times, 27 December, (1996) Independent, 3 January (Court of Appeal: Rose, Roch and Ward LJJ). *Ridehalgh v Horsefield* [1994] 3 All ER 848, CA (1994 Abr para 2188) applied.

2335　Costs—legal representative's personal liability for costs—wasted costs order—use of inadmissible document

The plaintiff sought compensation from the defendant's insurer. During the course of negotiations, the insurer stated in a letter, which was not headed 'without prejudice', that it was prepared to negotiate a settlement on a compromise basis. No settlement was reached and on the morning of the trial, the plaintiff's barrister told the insurer's counsel that he proposed to rely on the letter. Despite objection from counsel on the basis that the letter was inadmissible, the barrister referred to the letter in his opening as one which partially admitted liability. On counsel's intervention, the judge ruled that the letter was inadmissible. Counsel alleged that the letter was so manifestly inadmissible that it had been negligent of the barrister to show it to the judge and successfully applied for a wasted costs order against the barrister. On his appeal, *held*, evidence as to negotiations between parties seeking to resolve a dispute was not in general admissible whether or not they were stated to be without prejudice. In the present case, the letter was a bona fide offer of settlement and was made without prejudice although not marked as such. The barrister should not have proceeded to use the letter until he was as sure as he could reasonably be of the legal position. However, it was difficult to condemn him in negligence for raising an issue which could have been of substantial benefit to his client's case. A barrister was able to take a point which was fairly arguable and was under a duty to do so if it was in his client's interest, and it was fairly arguable in the present case that the letter did not fall within the 'without prejudice' rule. Accordingly, the appeal would be allowed.

Sampson v John Boddy Timber Ltd [1995] NLJR 851 (Court of Appeal: Sir Thomas Bingham MR, Evans and Aldous JJ). *Ridehalgh v Horsefield* [1994] 3 All ER 848 (1994 Abr para 2188), CA applied.

2336　Costs—mental health proceedings

See *LB v Croydon District Health Authority (No 2)*, para 2077.

2337　Costs—security for costs—exercise of discretion—party resident abroad

It has been held that there is no settled practice preventing the exercise of the court's discretion to order security for costs where the party against whom the order is sought is a company incorporated and resident in Northern Ireland.

Dynaspan (UK) Ltd v H Katzenberger Baukonstruktionen GmbH & Co KG [1995] 1 BCLC 536 (Chancery Division: Robert Walker J). *DSQ Property Company Ltd v Lotus Cars Ltd* [1987] 1

WLR 127 (1987 Abr para 2005) followed. *Wilson Vehicles Distributions Ltd v Colt Car Company Ltd* [1984] BCLC 93 (1983 Abr para 2564) not followed.

2338   Costs—security for costs—nominal plaintiff—circumstances in which order may be made

It has been held that before a person can be required to give security for costs under RSC Ord 23, r 1(1)(b) on the basis that he is a nominal plaintiff, it has to be shown that there is an element of deliberate duplicity, in particular that the person with a real cause of action has deliberately divested himself of all right to retain any benefit from the action, in order to cheat the defendant.

Envis v Thakkar (1995) Times, 2 May (Court of Appeal: Nourse, Kennedy and Evans LJJ).

2339   Costs—security for costs—order against company

See *Eurocross Sales Ltd v Cornhill Insurance plc*, para 522, and *Keary Developments Ltd v Tarmac Construction Ltd*, para 521.

2340   Costs—security for costs—plaintiff financed by third party—power to make order

RSC Ord 23, r 1 states the circumstances in which, on the application of a defendant to an action or other proceedings in the High Court, the court may order a plaintiff to give security for the defendant's costs. Rule 3 provides that the order is without prejudice to the provisions of any other enactment that empowers the court to require security to be given for the costs of any proceedings.

The defendant obtained an order that the plaintiff provide security for costs with respect to a libel action being brought by the plaintiff against the defendant. The plaintiff had been adjudged bankrupt and his claim was being financed by his mother. She had given an undertaking to pay any court order in respect of the defendant's costs but that undertaking was later withdrawn. The plaintiff successfully appealed against the order and the defendant further appealed. *Held*, it was conceded that the plaintiff did not fall within the scope of Ord 23, r 1, which was directed at plaintiffs who were shielding themselves behind a nominal plaintiff. Rule 1 was clearly intended to be exhaustive as to the circumstances in which an order could be made, and did not apply. No other rule gave the court power to order security for costs. Accordingly, the appeal would be dismissed.

Condliffe v Hislop [1996] 1 All ER 431 (Court of Appeal: Kennedy and Peter Gibson LJJ and Sir Roger Parker).

2341   Costs—taxation—review

In proceedings concerning trust property, the trustees had been joined as defendants although they had submitted to act as directed by the court. Fearing that a question of breach of trust and fraud on a power might arise at trial, when they might be cross-examined, the trustees instructed leading and junior counsel. However, the proceedings were compromised after commencement of trial. The plaintiff was ordered to pay the trustees' costs on an indemnity basis, such costs to be taxed if not agreed, pursuant to RSC Ord 62, r 12(2), by virtue of which on a taxation on the indemnity basis 'all costs' would be allowed except in so far as they were of an 'unreasonable amount' or had been 'unreasonably incurred'. The plaintiff sought a review of the taxation of costs. *Held*, where a given item of expenditure was examined on a taxation on the indemnity basis, if it fell within the expression 'all costs' in Ord 62, r 12(2), the item had to be allowed to the receiving party, unless it was beyond any doubt either of an unreasonable amount or had been unreasonably incurrred. Although it might have been reasonable for the trustees, who had raised no issue on the pleadings and had agreed to submit to judgment, to have instructed no counsel at all or a junior on his own, the question for the court under Ord 62, r 12(2) was whether it concluded beyond any doubt that it was unreasonable for the trustees to have instructed both leading and junior counsel. The plaintiff had failed to object to indications by the trustees or their solicitors that they proposed to instruct both counsel, and had failed to reply to the defendants' solicitor's suggestion that there should be discontinuance against them. As there was a possibility that the trustees would be subject to hostile cross-examination and that the subject of fraud on a power might be raised against them, and as the claim for costs against them had not been abandoned or qualified, it was not beyond any doubt unreasonable, but was indeed reasonable, for the trustees, as professional men with reputations to preserve, to instruct both leading and junior counsel. The fact that the trial proved to be so short was no indication that the fees of either counsel were excessive. They had been required to read the files and to keep their diaries clear for three weeks or more, and it could not have been predicted that their attendance would only be required for the first ten minutes. The instruction of a junior had been seen as a potential cost-saving measure, to avoid the necessity of leading counsel's attendance throughout the whole trial. In the circumstances, the level of agreed remuneration could not be categorised as unreasonable. The solicitors' hourly rates claimed by the plaintiff were less than the rates ascertained by a recent survey of firms in the relevant territorial area and during the relevant period, which provided the closest available guide to the rates charged by an average solicitor in the average firm in that area, and were therefore not unreasonable.

Re a Company (No 004081 of 1989) [1995] 2 All ER 155 (Chancery Division: Lindsay J). *Bruty v Edmundson* [1918] 1 Ch 112 considered.

See also *Joyce v Kammac (1988) Ltd*, para 2777.

2342 Costs—town and country planning cases

See TOWN AND COUNTRY PLANNING.

2343 County courts—procedure

See COUNTY COURTS.

2344 Court of Appeal—citation of authority

Sir Thomas Bingham MR has issued the following *Practice Direction* ([1995] 3 All ER 256), which supersedes paragraph 5 of *Practice Note* [1989] 1 All ER 891 (1989 Abr para 1798), and *Practice Note* [1991] 1 All ER 1055 (1991 Abr para 1934).

When authority is cited, whether in written or oral submissions, the following practice must in general be followed.

If a case is reported in the official law reports published by the Incorporated Council of Law Reporting for England and Wales, that report must be cited. Those are the most authoritative reports. They contain a summary of argument, and they are the most readily available.

If a case is not or not yet reported in the official law reports, but is reported in the Weekly Law Reports or the All England Law Reports, that report must be cited.

If a case is not reported in any of those series, a report in any authoritative specialist series may be cited. Such reports may not be readily available. Photocopies of the leading authorities, or the relevant parts of such authorities, must be annexed to written submissions, and it is helpful if photocopies of the less frequently used series are made available in court.

It is recognised that occasions arise when one report is fuller than another, or when there are discrepancies between reports. On such occasions, the practice outlined above does not need to be followed. It is always helpful if alternative references are given.

Where a reserved written judgement has not been reported, reference must be made to the official transcript if that is available, and not to the handed down text of the judgment.

Counsel are reminded that lists of authorities, including textbooks, to which they wish to refer, must be delivered to the head usher's office not later than 5.30 pm on the working day before the day when the hearing of the application or appeal is due to commence: see *The Supreme Court Practice 1995* (Volume 1, p 926).

Counsel must also seek confirmation that an adequate number of copies are available for the use of the court and, if that is not the case, must themselves provide an appropriate number of photocopies.

2345 Court of Appeal—presentation of appeals

Sir Thomas Bingham MR has issued the following *Practice Direction* ([1995] 3 All ER 850). **Part I—General**

INTRODUCTION
1. This *Practice Direction* supersedes *Practice Statement* [1986] 1 WLR 1318 (which deals with appeal bundles), *Practice Note* [1987] 3 All ER 434 (in so far as it deals with time estimates and listing), *Practice Note* [1989] 1 All ER 891 and *Practice Note* [1990] 2 All ER 318 (both of which deal with skeleton arguments), and *Practice Note* [1990] 2 All ER 1024 (which deals with handed-down judgments in lieu of transcripts).

2. In this *Practice Direction*:
(1) 'Advocate' means either a barrister, or a solicitor holding a Higher Courts Advocacy Qualification entitling him to act as advocate for the party concerned in the Court of Appeal. References to 'counsel' in any other relevant *Practice Statement* or *Practice Direction* is, unless the context otherwise requires, to be construed as including any such advocate.

(2) The singular includes the plural.

(3) References to a skeleton argument include a letter from the respondent's advocate in lieu of a skeleton argument where such is permissible (see para 39 below).

(4) 'Fixture' and 'second fixture' have the meanings assigned to them by paras 27 and 28 respectively.

(5) Save to the extent that this *Practice Direction* makes specific provision for particular types of application, references to appeals are to be construed as including full court applications, whether listed for hearing with the appeal or separately.

3. The provisions of this *Practice Direction* are subject to any specific directions which the court may make in any individual case,. in particular, in exceptionally urgent cases which need to be heard within days or hours of the matter coming to the attention of the Court of Appeal, and cases where an expedited hearing within weeks is sought, or ordered. Subject to that, the directions set out below must be complied with in all cases.

4. This *Practice Direction* comes into force on 4 September 1995.

APPLICATIONS FOR LEAVE TO APPEAL

5. Many applications to the Court of Appeal for leave to appeal are considered in the first instance by a single Lord Justice on paper, but in some cases the court directs that the application should proceed straight to an oral hearing. In neither case should the applicant burden the court with documents which are not relevant to the application. The letter from the Civil Appeals Office acknowledging entry of the application in the records of the court sets out the court's requirements concerning application bundles.

6. In any case where the applicant is legally aided and the single Lord Justice has refused leave to appeal on paper, the applicant's solicitor must send to the relevant legal aid office a copy of the single Lord Justice's order, including any reasons he gave for refusing leave, as soon as it has been received from the Civil Appeals Office. The court will require confirmation that this has been done in any case where an application for leave to appeal is renewed before the full court on legal aid.

Applications for leave dealt with on paper

7. Applicants must provide the single Lord Justice with a clear and succinct summary of the grounds on which leave to appeal is sought, unless these are made plain in the draft notice of appeal.

8. If the single Lord Justice, on consideration of the paper application, grants leave or directs an oral hearing of the application, directions may be given on paper as to: (1) the maximum time to be allowed to each party for oral argument on the appeal or the oral hearing of the leave application, as the case may be, and (2) the lodging and service of skeleton arguments.

Applications for leave listed for oral hearing

9. Where an application for leave to appeal is listed for oral hearing, whether initially or after a decision on paper, the following directions will apply:

(1) in all cases where the application is listed inter partes, the applicant's solicitors, or the applicant if acting in person, must, on receipt of notification from the Civil Appeals Office that an inter partes hearing has been directed, forthwith supply the respondent's solicitors, or the respondent, if in person, with a copy of the application bundle, including a copy of the transcript or note of judgment, in exactly the same form as the bundles lodged for the use of the Court of Appeal. For the purposes only of providing the copy of the application bundle to the respondent's side, photocopies of transcripts of judgment and, where relevant, evidence may be used. The costs of providing that bundle must be borne by the applicant initially, but will form part of the costs of the application.

(2) where the applicant is represented, the applicant's advocate must lodge with the Civil Appeals Office three copies of a skeleton argument, not later than seven days before the date fixed for hearing and, if the application is listed inter partes, provide a copy of it to the respondent's advocate, or the respondent if in person, on or before the date on which the skeleton argument is lodged with the Civil Appeals Office.

(3) where an application for leave is listed inter partes, the respondent's advocate must lodge with the Civil Appeals Office three copies of a skeleton argument, not later than three days before the hearing date, and provide the applicant's advocate with a copy of it on or before the date on which it is lodged with the Civil Appeals Office.

(4) the applicant's advocate, or the applicant if appearing in person, will be expected to complete his oral argument within a maximum of 20 minutes. That time limit will be extended only if the court considers that more extended argument is required.

10. Where an application for leave to appeal is listed for hearing, with the appeal to follow if leave is granted, para 9(2) to (4) do not apply. Instead, the timetable for skeleton arguments will

be the same as in the case of an appeal (see below), and the amount of time allowed for oral argument will depend on the time estimate for the appeal.

RENEWED APPLICATIONS FOR LEAVE TO MOVE FOR JUDICIAL REVIEW

11. Where leave to move for judicial review has been refused after an oral hearing in the High Court and the application is being renewed before the Court of Appeal, the applicant's advocate, or the applicant if appearing in person, will be expected to complete his oral argument within a maximum of 30 minutes. That time limit will be extended only if the court considers that more extended argument is required.

12. The applicant's advocate, and where any respondent will be represented at the Court of Appeal hearing, that party's advocate, must lodge four copies of their skeleton arguments with the Civil Appeals Office 14 days before the hearing (see paras 43 to 45 below).

13. Paragraphs 11 and 12 of this *Practice Direction* apply only to renewed applications for leave to move for judicial review. Where leave to move has been granted and the substantive application for judicial review has been dealt with in the High Court, any application to the Court of Appeal for leave to appeal against that decision will be governed by paras 5 to 10 above.

APPEALS

Time estimates and limitations on oral argument

14. In all cases where there are solicitors acting for the appellant, they must cause to be lodged with the Civil Appeals Office within 28 days after an appeal has been entered in the records of the court, an estimate of the length of the appeal hearing, exclusive of judgment. That time estimate must be on the form sent to the solicitors with the letter from the Civil Appeals Office acknowledging that the appeal has been entered in the records of the court. The procedure is as follows:

(1) the form must be duly completed and signed by the appellant's advocate.

(2) within that 28-day time limit, the original of that completed form must be sent or delivered to the Civil Appeals Office and a photocopy must be sent to the respondent's advocate, either directly or through the respondent's solicitors.

(3) the respondent's advocate must consider the appellant's estimate as soon as it has been received, and notify the Civil Appeals Office by lodging the photocopy of the form with the respondent's section of it completed and signed, if his own estimate differs from that of the appellant's advocate. In the absence of such notification, the respondent's advocate will be deemed to have accepted the estimate from the appellant's side.

15. Where the court directs that an application for leave to appeal is to be listed for hearing with the appeal to follow if leave is granted, and the court has not specified what length of time is to be allowed for oral argument, the appellant's advocate must provide a certified time estimate of the length of the hearing on the assumption that leave will be granted and the court will hear argument on the appeal. The procedure is the same as in para 14, save that: (1) the time limit will be 14 days after the date of the direction that the application be listed with appeal to follow, and (2) the estimate need not be on any special form.

16. The court and its listing officers place considerable reliance on advocates' time estimates in fixing dates and managing the list. It is therefore essential that realistic time estimates should be given and that, where practicable, the advocates on each side should consult with each other about the estimate.

17. A copy of the certified estimate must be placed and kept with each advocate's papers. Each time the advocate for any party is asked to give any advice or to deal with anything in connection with the appeal, he must look at the estimate and check whether it is still correct.

18. Any revised time estimate must be lodged with the Civil Appeals Office in writing, signed by the advocate concerned; no account will be taken of revised time estimates given by any other means. If an increased time estimate is lodged with the Civil Appeals Office after a hearing date has been fixed, the appeal may well have to be adjourned to a much later date, particularly if the estimate has been revised at a late stage. It is therefore in everyone's interests that reliable estimates should be finalised before any hearing date is fixed.

19. Whatever the estimated length of a hearing, the court will whenever possible form its own estimate, based on the judgment appealed from, the notice of appeal, and the skeleton arguments, if available, of the time which it considers oral argument of the case should take. In such cases, it will then inform the parties' representatives how much time will be allowed for oral argument.

Appeal bundles

20. Part II of this *Practice Direction* sets out revised requirements concerning the form and content of appeal bundles.

21. On lodging the appeal bundles with the Civil Appeals Office, the appellant's solicitors must supply the respondent's solicitors, or the respondent if in person, with a set of the appeal bundles in exactly the same form as the bundles lodged for the use of the Court of Appeal. The costs of provision of bundles for the respondent must be borne by the appellant initially, but will form part of the costs of the appeal.

22. Appellants will not, however, be required to furnish respondents with transcripts of judgment and evidence. In relation to transcripts, save to the extent provided by para 9(1) above, the present practice will continue. The appellant's solicitors, or the appellant if in person, must notify the respondent's solicitors, or the respondent if in person, of what transcripts have been provided for the court so that they can bespeak transcripts for their own use and also make representations if they consider that further transcripts will be required. Respondents must bespeak and pay for transcripts for the use of their solicitors and advocates.

Listing

23. In order to ensure, so far as possible, that cases are heard in their proper place in the list, each appeal is given a target date, known as its 'hear-by date'. Because of the large number of pending appeals and the consequent pressure on the Court of Appeal lists, there is now a considerable time lag between the lodging and hearing of most appeals. Because some types of appeal are inherently more urgent than others, for instance, family cases, different hear-by dates are set for different species of appeals.

24. From time to time, it may be necessary to revise hear-by dates in the light of the state of the Court of Appeal lists. Having target dates which cannot be met is unworkable and raises false hopes. Where hear-by dates are revised, the new targets will normally be applied both to appeals which do not already have a hearing date when the revision takes place, as well as to appeals set down thereafter.

25. The aim is that appeals should be listed so that they are heard neither significantly earlier nor significantly later than their respective hear-by dates. In the interests of flexibility, the listing officer has a discretion to fix the hearing date within a reasonable band on either side of the hear-by date. That system will not always apply to appeals assigned to the short warned list; such cases may be put into the list considerably earlier than their hear-by dates and may not be called on for hearing until some time thereafter.

26. Appeals will only be expedited so as to be heard well in advance of their hear-by dates, or deferred significantly thereafter, if there is a judicial direction to that effect. Requests for expedition, or for cases to be stood out of the list, should be made to the Registrar of Civil Appeals, initially by letter (see further below).

Fixtures

27. A 'fixture' means a hearing date fixed in advance: it means that the hearing is fixed to begin on a specified date or on the next following sitting day at the option of the court.

Appeals other than (a) those assigned to the short warned list, (b) those given second fixtures, and (c) cases where special listing directions have been given, will be given fixtures.

If it does not prove to be possible for the court concerned to take the appeal on the specified date or on the following sitting day and the Listing Office is unable to transfer the appeal to another court, the hearing date will have to be rearranged.

Second fixtures

28. Some appeals are designated by the court as 'second fixtures'. A second fixture is a hearing date arranged in advance on the express basis that the list is fully booked for the period in question and therefore the case will be heard only if a suitable gap occurs in the list. Any second fixture for which space does not become available will be given a first fixture on the earliest convenient date.

The short warned list

29. Cases assigned to the short warning list are put 'on call' from a specified date and are called on for hearing as and when gaps occur in the Court of Appeal list. Short warned list cases are not called in chronological order of setting down or assignment to that list. Which case will be called on will depend upon the length of the gap, the subject matter of the case and the constitution of the court. Because the number of last-minute settlements in the Court of Appeal varies enormously, it is not possible to predict when any particular short warned list case will be called on for hearing.

30. The system applicable to cases assigned to the short warned list is as follows:

(1) The parties' solicitors are notified by letter from the Civil Appeals Office that the case has been assigned to the short warned list.

(2) It is the duty of the solicitors to all parties, whether appellants or respondents, on receipt of that letter from the Civil Appeals Office: (a) to inform their advocates forthwith of the fact

that the case has been assigned to the short warned list, and of the date on which the skeleton arguments are due (see para 44 below), and (b) to provide their advocates with all necessary instructions and papers to enable them to lodge their skeleton arguments timeously.

(3) When the skeleton arguments have been lodged, the Listing Office will notify counsel's clerks by telephone of the date from which the case will be 'on call', and it will remain in the short warned list liable to be called on either on half a day's notice or, if the registrar has so directed, on 48 hours' notice. The listing officers will put short warned list cases 'on call' in such numbers and from such dates as the state of the list requires.

(4) It is the duty of solicitors to inform their lay clients when a case has been assigned to the short warned list and what the consequences of that will be. It is important that this is done so that the clients are not taken by surprise if, as is quite likely, they have to be represented at the Court of Appeal hearing by a different advocate.

31. The Registrar of Civil Appeals will consider applications to remove appeals from the short warned list and give them a fixture or second fixture, provided that the application is made at the correct time and on valid grounds. Any such application must be made as soon as the solicitors have received the letter referred to in para 30(1) above. It is far too late to do so when, or after, the case has been put 'on call'. It is not a valid ground for taking a case out of the short warned list that the parties' advocates of first choice may not be available to represent them at the appeal hearing. A case assigned to the short warned list will only be taken out of that list and given a fixture or second fixture if it is, viewed objectively, one which cannot be properly presented save by a particular advocate.

32. If any party's advocate of first choice is, for whatever reason, not available to appear on the date for which a short warned list case is called on, then a substitute advocate must be instructed immediately. Time should not be spent asking that the case should not be called on for that particular date because the advocate is unavailable, nor should the transfer of instructions to a substitute advocate be delayed in the hope that something will occur which will enable the original advocate to appear.

Expedition

33. In the interests of saving costs, the registrar deals with as many requests for expedition as possible on paper without a hearing. Requests for expedition should initially be made to the registrar by letter, or if time is short by fax, setting out succinctly and in short compass the grounds on which expedition is sought, and, if it is granted, how soon the appeal needs to be heard. At the same time, a copy of that letter or fax must be sent to the other party's solicitors so that they know at the earliest possible stage that an expedited hearing is being sought, and why.

34. Subject to the qualification referred to below, the letter to the registrar requesting expedition should be accompanied by a transcript or note of the judgment being appealed, draft grounds of appeal, and a realistic advocate's time estimate of the anticipated length of the appeal. Where, however, a hearing is needed within days or weeks, the letter requesting expedition should be sent to the registrar with copy to the other side, without waiting for the transcript or note of judgment and the draft grounds of appeal, so that the court has the maximum possible notice that such a high degree of expedition is sought.

35. Because of the immense pressures on its lists, the Court of Appeal is no longer able to expedite as many cases as hitherto.

Skeleton arguments

36. Skeleton arguments are compulsory in the case of all appeals and full court applications to the Civil Division of the Court of Appeal, except in cases which are heard as a matter of great urgency and any individual case where the court otherwise directs.

37. The purpose of a skeleton argument is to identify and summarise the points, not to argue them fully on paper. A skeleton argument should therefore be as succinct as possible. In the case of an appeal against a final order which is likely to last between one to two days, skeleton arguments should not normally exceed 10 pages in the case of an appeal on law, and 15 pages in the case of an appeal on fact. Advocates should not, however, assume that longer cases justify proportionately longer skeleton arguments, and in the case of interlocutory and shorter final appeals, it should normally be possible to do justice to the relevant points in a skeleton argument of considerably less than 10 pages. In the case of points of law, the skeleton argument should state the point and cite the principal authority or authorities in support, with references to the particular page(s) where the principle concerned is enunciated. In the case of questions of fact, it should state briefly the basis on which it is contended that the Court of Appeal can interfere with the finding of fact concerned, with cross- references to the passages in the transcript or notes of evidence which bear on the point.

38. The appellant's advocate's skeleton argument must be accompanied by a written chronology of events relevant to the appeal, cross-referenced to the core bundle or appeal

bundle. This must be a separate document, in order that it may easily be consulted in conjunction with other papers.

39. In the case of respondents who wish only to contend that the judgment of the court below is correct for the reasons given, the respondent's advocate can send in a letter to that effect in lieu of a skeleton argument. Where, however, the respondent is going to rely on any authority or refer to any evidence which is not dealt with in the judgment of the court below, a respondent's skeleton argument must be lodged. The respondent's advocate must always lodge a skeleton argument in any case where there is a respondent's notice.

Timetable for skeleton arguments
40. The arrangements relating to skeleton arguments will, in future, be as follows: if the court so directs, para 41 will apply. Generally the court is likely to make such a direction in the case of heavy or complex appeals, but it may also do so if it thinks it appropriate in other cases. Where no para 41 direction has been made, the timetable will be that prescribed in paras 42 to 45 below.

41. Where the court has directed that this paragraph shall apply:

(1) within 28 days after the entry of the appeal in the list of forthcoming appeals, the appellant's advocate must serve on the respondent's advocate a skeleton argument summarising the arguments for the appellant on the appeal, and must notify the Civil Appeals Office in writing of the date on which it was so served.

(2) within 28 days of receipt of the appellant's skeleton argument, the respondent's advocate must serve on the appellant's advocate a skeleton argument summarising the arguments for the respondent on the appeal and on any respondent's notice, and must notify the Civil Appeals Office in writing of the date on which it was so served.

(3) within 21 days of receiving the respondent's skeleton argument, the appellant's advocate may serve on the respondent's advocate a further skeleton argument summarising the appellant's arguments in answer to points raised by the respondent on the appeal and any respondent's notice.

(4) within 28 days of the date on which the respondent's advocate served his skeleton argument, each of the advocates concerned must lodge four copies of their respective skeleton arguments with the Civil Appeals Office.

42. Where no para 41 direction has been made, the timetable for skeleton arguments will continue to be as follows: subject to the proviso in para 45 below, the time limit for lodging skeleton arguments will be 14 days; in cases which have fixtures or second fixtures, it will be 14 days prior to the hearing date (see para 43 below), and in short warned list cases it will be 14 days after notification to the parties' solicitors that the case has been assigned to that list (see para 44 below). The final deadline for lodging skeleton arguments is 4 p m on the fourteenth day.

43. In cases which have fixtures or second fixtures, each advocate must lodge four copies of his skeleton argument with the Civil Appeals Office not later than 14 days before the earliest date on which the hearing is due to commence. A copy of the skeleton argument must also be sent to the opposing advocate on or before the date on which the skeleton is lodged with the Civil Appeals Office.

44. In cases assigned to the short warned list, the time limit for lodging skeleton arguments will also be 14 days, but it is not calculated by reference to any hearing date or 'on call' date: instead, that 14-day time limit runs from the date on which the parties' solicitors are notified by letter from the Civil Appeals Office that the case has been assigned to the short warned list. It will be the duty of the solicitors to all parties on receipt of the letter, to inform their respective advocates forthwith of the fact that the case has been assigned to the short warned list, and of the date on which the skeleton arguments are required. Each advocate must then ensure that four copies of his skeleton argument are lodged within that 14-day period. A copy of the skeleton argument must also be sent to the opposing advocate on or before the date on which it is lodged with the Civil Appeals Office.

45. In any case where the 14-day time limit would expire on a bank holiday or other day on which the Civil Appeals Office is closed, the skeleton arguments must be lodged with the office on the working day preceding the fourteenth day.

46. Advocates must lodge their skeleton arguments directly with the Civil Appeals Office, not via their instructing solicitors.

47. To facilitate filing of skeleton arguments in the Civil Appeals Office, advocates must in future ensure: (1) that their names are typed at the end of their skeleton arguments, and (2) that the correct Court of Appeal reference number is shown on the front page. Where a skeleton argument covers two or more appeals or applications which are due to be heard together, the reference numbers for all of them must be given.

48. If any barrister does not have instructions or all necessary papers sufficiently far in advance to be able to complete and lodge the skeleton argument on time, he should contact the registrar immediately. It is not satisfactory to leave it to his clerk to chase for the papers and then hope to obtain an extension of time for lodging the skeleton argument when the deadline is fast approaching or has already expired.

49. Any advocate who is unable to comply with the relevant skeleton argument timetable should inform the registrar by letter or fax well before the date on which the skeleton argument is due to be lodged, explain why, and seek an extension of time. Any application for an extension must be made by the advocate personally, and not by his clerk or instructing solicitor. Only exceptionally will there be any good reason for failure to lodge skeleton arguments on time, and generally the court expects the 14-day time limit to be strictly adhered to.

50. Requests for extensions of time, and cases of failure to lodge skeleton arguments timeously, are now dealt with, in the first instance, by the Civil Appeals Office senior lawyer, or in his absence, the chief clerk, but where necessary the matter will be referred to the registrar or the presiding Lord Justice.

Pre-appeal directions hearings

51. When it appears to the court that it would for any reason be advantageous to do so, the court will invite the parties' advocates and any party acting in person to attend a directions hearing held in advance of the main hearing. Such directions hearings may be conducted by the full court, a single Lord Justice or the registrar.

LITIGANTS IN PERSON

Appeal and application bundles

52. In order to assist appellants and applicants who are acting in person, two leaflets have been prepared, one for appeals and one for applications, explaining as clearly as possible how they should prepare bundles of documents for the use of the Court of Appeal. The Civil Appeals Office will send a copy of the relevant leaflet to the litigant with the letter acknowledging that the case has been entered in the records of the court. In future, the obligation of an appellant or applicant acting in person will be to lodge bundles which comply with the appeal bundle leaflet or the application bundle leaflet, as the case may be.

53. With the relevant bundle leaflet, there is a check-list which is designed to provide further help by highlighting the key requirements. Litigants in person must make sure that their bundles comply with the relevant leaflet in all respects, and in particular, the requirements set out in that check-list. When they are sure that their bundles do comply, they must complete and sign the check-list and return it to the Civil Appeals Office with their bundles.

54. In some cases, however, particularly certain types of leave to appeal applications, the court may require only limited documentation rather than formal application bundles. Except in cases which are so urgent that there is not time to do so, the Civil Appeals Office will indicate to litigants in person by letter whether limited documentation or full bundles are required.

Skeleton arguments

55. In the interests of avoiding placing undue burdens on them, litigants in person are not required to lodge skeleton arguments in support of their appeals and applications, but may do so if they wish. If an appellant or applicant in person does decide to put in a skeleton argument, he must: (1) lodge four copies of it with the Civil Appeals Office within the time limit which would apply if an advocate were acting, and (2) provide the respondent's advocate with a copy of it no later than the date on which the copies are lodged with the Civil Appeals Office.

Part II—Documentation

The following are directions of the Court of Appeal concerning bundles of documents for the purposes of appeals and full court applications.

It is the duty of those acting for appellants to ensure that the bundles of documents lodged for the use of the court, comply with the relevant rules and directions. It is also their duty to lodge the bundles within the time limit prescribed by RSC Ord 59, r 9(1). Neglect of these duties may lead to the appeal or application being dismissed.

Scrutiny of the bundles submitted shows that there are still errors and omissions which occur all too frequently. For that reason, attention is drawn, in particular, to the following requirements.

TRANSCRIPTS

All transcripts lodged, whether of evidence or of the judgment, must be official copies provided by the shorthand writers or transcribers. Appellants are not permitted to lodge photocopies which they have had taken.

Where proceedings in any court have been officially recorded in shorthand, by stenographic machine or on tape, official transcripts of the judgment and, where relevant, the evidence, must be lodged with the Court of Appeal. Unless the court otherwise directs, notes of judgment or evidence will not be accepted. Normally the court will only accept notes in lieu of transcripts where the case requires such an urgent hearing that there is not time to obtain them.

Where, however, either in any division of the High Court or in a county court, the judge handed down his judgment, photocopies of the text of that handed-down judgment signed by the judge, can be lodged for the purposes of an appeal to the Court of Appeal in lieu of official transcripts of the judgment.

NOTES OF JUDGMENT

In cases where the judge's judgment was not officially recorded and was not handed down, the counsel or solicitor who appeared for the appellant in the court below must prepare a note of the judge's judgment, agree it if possible with the counsel or solicitor who appeared for the respondent, and submit it to the judge for approval. If the parties' counsel or solicitors are not able to reach agreement about the note speedily, they should submit their rival notes of judgment to the judge, stating that they are unable to agree a note. A copy of the approved note of judgment must be included in each bundle. It should be noted in the case of county court appeals, that concluding lines in the judge's notebook reading 'Judgment for the defendant with costs on Scale 2' or the like are not 'the judge's own note of his judgment'. What is required is a note of the reasons for the decision.

In the majority of cases where the judge gives an ex tempore judgment, he will not have a full written text of it. Time should therefore not be taken up by writing to the judge's clerk, or to the county court, asking for the judge's note of judgment. In all such cases, a typed version of the appellant's counsel's or solicitor's note of the judgment must be prepared, agreed if possible, and submitted to the judge for approval. Much delay has been caused in numerous cases by failure to put this in train promptly and expeditiously. To obviate such delays, in future the following procedure must be adopted in cases where the judgment was not officially recorded or handed down:

(i) the appellant's solicitor should make arrangements for the note of judgment to be prepared, agreed with the respondent's counsel or solicitor if possible, and then submitted to the judge as soon as the notice of appeal has been served. The appellant's solicitor should not wait until the appeal has entered the list of forthcoming appeals. If that system is adopted, the approved note of judgment should be ready for inclusion in the bundles within the 14-day time limit for lodging documents, and no extension should be needed.

(ii) where both sides were represented by counsel in the court below, counsel for the appellant should submit his note of judgment directly to counsel for the respondent.

(iii) where the note of judgment has not been received back from the judge by the time the bundles are ready to be lodged, copies of the unapproved note of judgment should be lodged with the bundles. The approved note of judgment should then be substituted as soon as it is to hand.

(iv) in those cases where the appellant is appealing in person, counsel or solicitors for the respondent must make available their notes of judgment without charge, whether or not the appellant has made any note of the reasoned judgment.

COUNTY COURT NOTES OF EVIDENCE

In county court cases where the evidence was not officially recorded, a typed copy of the judge's notes of evidence must be obtained from the county court concerned, and a photocopy of those notes must be included in each bundle. Directives have been sent to county courts asking them to arrange for the notes of evidence to be transcribed as soon as the notice of appeal has been served on the county court, unless the evidence was tape recorded. The notes should then be ready for dispatch to the appellant's solicitors, or the appellant if in person, as soon as they formally request them and make provision for the copying charges. A directive has also been sent to county courts to the effect that the old practice of refusing to make the notes of evidence available until an agreed note of judgment has been submitted, is to be discontinued.

CORE BUNDLES

In cases where the appellant seeks to place before the court bundles of documents comprising more than 100 pages, exclusive of the judgment appealed against, the appellant's solicitors must prepare and lodge with the court the requisite number of copies of a core bundle containing the documents central to the appeal (see further below). In such circumstances, it will not usually be necessary to lodge multiple copies of the main bundle. It will be sufficient if a single set of the full trial documents is lodged so that the court may refer to it if necessary.

Each core bundle must always include the notice of appeal, the order appealed against, any other relevant orders made in the court below, the respondent's notice, if any, and the note of judgment and notes of evidence, if relevant. If it is a case where there are transcripts of the judgment/evidence, then those should not be bound in the core bundle, but kept separate. In addition, the core bundle should contain only those documents in support of, or in opposition to, the appeal which the Lords Justices will need to pre-read, or which are likely to be referred to in the course of oral argument. Core bundles should contain as much material as is necessary to satisfy the above test and no more.

Where the court is of the opinion, having heard an appeal or application, that documents have been copied and included in bundles which could not reasonably have been thought necessary for determination of the point or points at issue, it will not hesitate to make such costs order as may be appropriate.

Core bundles, including documents in those bundles which were also in the trial bundles, must have their own continuous pagination, using the method prescribed below, though leaving the trial bundle page numbers visible along with the new core bundle numbers. Where documents which have been included in the core bundles are referred to in the transcripts by reference to their trial bundle page numbers, either the transcripts supplied for the use of the court must be annotated with the new core bundle page numbers, or that information must be given in the skeleton arguments.

PAGINATION

Bundles must be paginated. At present, many bundles are numbered merely by document. This is incorrect. Each page must be numbered individually and consecutively, starting with page 1 at the top of the bundle and working continuously through to the end. Other numbering systems, such as 1.1, 1.2, or 2A, 2B etc must not be used. Page numbers should be placed in the bottom right-hand corner of the page. Where the documents are too numerous to fit into one file or bundle, each file or bundle should be marked with a letter and the page numbering should continue consecutively on from the end of one bundle into the next.

INDEX

There must be an index at the front of the bundle listing the documents and giving the page references for each. In the case of documents such as letters, invoices, bank statements, they can be shown in the index by a general description. It is not necessary to list every letter or invoice separately, but if a letter or other such document is particularly important to the case, then it should be listed separately in the index so that attention is drawn to it. In particular, in the case of appeals and applications in judicial review proceedings, the letter or other document which constitutes the decision sought to be reviewed, must be separately itemised in the index whether or not it forms part of the exhibit to an affidavit. Where each set of bundles consists of more than one file or bundle, an index covering all of them should be placed at the beginning of bundle A. There should not be separate indexes for each physical bundle comprised in the set.

BINDING OF BUNDLES

All the documents, with the exception of transcripts, must be bound together in lever-arch files, ring-binders, plastic binders, or laced through holes in the top left-hand corner. Loose documents will not be accepted. Lever-arch files and ring-binders must not be overfilled, and care must be taken to ensure that the rings close and fit properly so that the pages can be turned over easily. Where each set of bundles consists of more than one file, the spines should be prominently labelled.

LEGIBILITY

All documents must be legible. In particular, care must be taken to ensure that the edges of pages are not cut off by the photocopying machine or rendered illegible by the binding. If it proves impossible to produce adequate copies of individual documents, or if manuscript documents are illegible, typewritten copies of the relevant pages should also be interleaved at the appropriate place in the bundle.

APPLICATIONS FOR LEAVE TO ADDUCE FURTHER EVIDENCE

Where, as is often the case, the court has directed that an application for leave to adduce further evidence is to be listed for hearing at the same time as the appeal, separate bundles must nevertheless be lodged in respect of that application so that the further evidence can readily be distinguished from the evidence which was before the court below.

TIME LIMITS

Time limits must be complied with, and will be strictly enforced except where there are good grounds for granting an extension. The appellant's solicitor, or the appellant if in person, should therefore set about preparing the bundles well in advance of the date on which they are due without waiting for the appeal to enter the list of forthcoming appeals. In that way, in most cases, the bundles should be ready to be lodged within the 14-day time limit prescribed by Ord 59, r 9. The court will be reluctant to grant any extension of time where the failure to lodge the bundles, transcripts, notes of judgment or notes of evidence within the prescribed time limit is due to failure on the part of the appellant's solicitors, or the appellant if in person, to start soon enough on the preparation of the bundles, ordering of transcripts, or obtaining of notes of judgment or evidence.

RESPONSIBILITY OF SOLICITOR ON THE RECORD

It seems likely that the work of documentation is often delegated to very junior members of the solicitor's staff, sometimes without referring them to the relevant rule and practice direction. Delegation is not, as such, objectionable, but: (a) the member of staff must be instructed fully on what is required and be capable of ensuring that these requirements are met, and (b) the solicitor in charge of the case must personally satisfy himself that the documentation is in order before it is delivered to the court. London agents too have a responsibility: they should be prepared to answer any questions which may arise as to the sufficiency of the documentation.

2346 Court of Appeal—procedure

Sir Thomas Bingham MR has issued the following *Practice Note* ([1995] 3 All ER 847).

1. As reported in successive Reviews of the Legal Year, there has been an alarming increase in the backlog of unheard appeals, and a corresponding increase in the delay before most appeals are heard. That has occurred despite increases in the judicial strength and the professional and administrative support of the court, and despite measures introduced to weed out appeals with no prospect of success.

2. It is now generally accepted that steps must be taken to improve existing procedures and, in particular, to shorten the time currently spent on oral argument of cases in court. With the help of the Court of Appeal Users' Committee, representing judges, barristers, solicitors, and citizens' advice bureaux, the judges of the Court of Appeal have considered at some length how to achieve those ends without undermining the quality or the fairness of the court's decisions.

3. The *Practice Direction* below ([1995] 3 All ER 850), which comes into force on 4 September 1995, aims to ensure that applications and appeals are handled and decided as efficiently and expeditiously as practicable in current circumstances, consistently with fairness and sound decision-making.

4. Paper applications for leave to appeal can be more expeditiously and efficiently considered if the documents submitted are limited to those truly necessary to enable a Lord Justice to decide whether the prospective appellant has an arguable ground of appeal. The same is true of applications for leave which proceed to an oral hearing. The present frequent practice to burden the court with much irrelevant documentation must cease. The Lord Justice's decision will also be facilitated by a clear summary of the argument which the prospective appellant wishes to pursue. Where a Lord Justice has granted leave or ordered a hearing of the leave application inter partes, it will often be possible for directions to be given for the lodging of sequential, and therefore responsive, skeleton arguments, and for a maximum period to be allotted to each party for oral presentation of its case in court.

5. In the absence of specific directions, the court will normally expect oral argument in support of (i) applications for leave to appeal to be confined to a maximum of 20 minutes, and (ii) renewed applications for leave to move for judicial review to a maximum of 30 minutes. It is hoped that it may prove possible, in the light of experience, to shorten those periods without detriment to the fairness of the outcome. In either of those cases, short skeleton arguments are required.

6. Consultations conducted by the court, and its own experiences, suggest that pre-hearing procedures should, in many cases, differ, depending on the expected length of the hearing.

7. For shorter appeals, the existing procedures on the whole operate satisfactorily, provided the time limit for delivery of skeleton arguments is observed, as it too frequently is not. The court hopes that it may increasingly be able to read the judgment appealed from, the notice of appeal, the skeleton arguments, and the key documents, sufficiently far in advance of the hearing to enable it to judge and inform the parties of the time to be allowed to each party for oral argument.

8. For longer appeals, it will often be desirable that skeleton arguments should be prepared and lodged at an earlier stage. The advantages are that:

(I) they can be exchanged sequentially, with the benefit that they are responsive to each other;

(ii) in some cases, it may be advantageous to invite the parties to attend a directions hearing, probably conducted by a single Lord Justice, in advance of the main hearing, with a view to simplifying and streamlining the conduct of the hearing;

(iii) consideration can be given to allotting periods of time for the presentation of oral argument, with knowledge of what is to be argued.

9. The court is reluctant, unless obliged, to lay down rules governing the length, format and layout of skeleton arguments. It is, however, concerned at the observable tendency of some counsel to settle skeleton arguments which exceed all reasonable bounds. In a one to two day appeal on a point of law against a final order, the skeleton argument ought not to exceed a maximum of 10 pages. If the appeal is on fact, a maximum of 15 pages will ordinarily suffice. In longer appeals, it may be necessary to submit a somewhat longer skeleton. The specified maxima are not to be treated as establishing a norm. A sound argument can usually be briefly summarised, and such a summary is ordinarily the more effective for being more readily assimilated.

10. A large percentage of skeleton arguments are currently lodged late, often very late. The consequence is that much administrative time in the Civil Appeals Office is devoted to pursuing overdue skeleton arguments, and also that the court is denied the opportunity of considering the argument when pre-reading the case. The reason for lateness sometimes is that solicitors fail to provide the papers and instructions to counsel in time for the latter to draft the skeleton, and sometimes that counsel fail to set aside time to undertake that task in good time before the deadline for lodging it. Timely delivery of skeletons calls for realistic co-operation between solicitors and counsel. The court would remind solicitors of their duty to give counsel all necessary papers and instructions in good time: while some cases require more time, it is suggested that counsel should be provided with all necessary papers and instructions to draft the skeleton at least two to three weeks before the deadline for lodging it. The court would also remind counsel and their clerks of their duty to ensure that enough time is set aside for the task to be completed in time.

11. In light of the court's experience and technical changes in recent years, the current *Practice Directions* governing the documentation in appeals and applications call for revision.

12. By the time cases come before the Court of Appeal, whether on applications or appeal, the issues have usually been narrowed, and much of the documentation placed before the court below, if ever relevant, is no longer so. Parties must take care to ensure that the materials placed before the Court of Appeal are those reasonably thought to be necessary for decision of the issues before it. If anything of relevance is omitted, it can be called for. There is no justification for the cost and labour involved in the preparation of bundles which are never read or referred to. Attention is drawn to the court's powers under RSC Ord 62, r 11, and to its power to invite the taxing master to consider the cost of unnecessary copying.

13. Particular attention must be paid to the preparation and provision of core bundles which are, in cases other than the shortest, an indispensable aid to effective pre-reading. A core bundle is required in any case where the appeal bundle, excluding the judgment appealed against, comprises more than 100 pages. The provision of core bundles is frequently overlooked, and there are a number of misconceptions about them. It is supposed by some that the core bundle itself must not exceed a set number of pages, and that it need only contain documents not in the trial bundles in the court below, such as the notice of appeal and the order appealed against. The court expects the rules on core bundles to be strictly observed.

14. The practice hitherto has been that appellants are not required to provide respondents with copies of appeal bundles, but merely with a copy of the index. The court has decided to change that practice to avoid the time and expense, which can be considerable, of the respondent's solicitors having to prepare bundles for themselves and their advocate from an index, and to reduce the number of occasions on which the parties' advocates find themselves working with different bundles.

15. Since the issue of *Practice Statement* [1986] 3 All ER 630, recording facilities have been introduced for hearings before Queen's Bench judges in chambers and in certain county courts, and the practice of judges handing down judgments has become more widespread. To take account of those and other changes, that *Practice Statement* has been amended, and appears in its revised form as Part II of the *Practice Direction* below.

16. The court hopes that it may be possible to identify cases which may be susceptible to settlement by mediation. Such resort to mediation cannot, in the absence of rule changes, be other than voluntary, and it is not thought likely that mediation will be fruitful in a majority of appeals. It is, however, thought that some appeals may be capable of resolution by mediation, and it is hoped to introduce a trial scheme. If any party to an appeal, appellant or respondent, considers that the appeal may be resolved by mediation, an indication to that effect may be given in confidence to the Registrar of Civil Appeals.

2347   Court of Appeal—reserved judgment—procedure on handing down judgment

Sir Thomas Bingham MR has issued the following *Practice Note* ([1995] 3 All ER 247).

When the court reserves judgment, it has become the practice in recent years for the written judgment to be handed down without, as in the past, being read aloud. In that way, much time is saved for the court, practitioners and litigants.

Unless the court otherwise orders, copies of the written judgment are made available to the parties' legal advisers on the afternoon before judgment is due to be pronounced, on condition that the contents are not communicated to the parties before the listed time for pronouncement of judgment.

Delivery to legal advisers is to enable them to consider the judgment and decide what consequential orders they should seek. The condition is imposed to prevent the outcome being publicly reported before judgment is given, since the judgment is confidential until then.

The court may order early delivery to parties' legal advisers if it appears that they may, with more time, be able to agree the orders consequential on the judgment, and so obviate the need for, and cost of, a further attendance in court.

If for any reason a party's legal advisers have special grounds for seeking a relaxation of the usual condition restricting disclosure to the party, a request for relaxation may be made informally through the clerk to the presiding Lord Justice.

A copy of the written judgment will be made available to any party who is not legally represented at the same time as to the legal advisers. It must be treated as confidential until judgment is given.

When the court hands down its written judgement, it will pronounce judgment in open court. Copies of the written judgment will then be made available to recognised law reporters and representatives of the media.

In cases of particular interest to the media, it is helpful if requests for copies can be intimated to the presiding Lord Justice's clerk in advance of judgment, so that the likely demand for copies can be accurately estimated.

If any member of the public, not being a party or a law reporter or a representative of the media, wishes to read the written judgment when it is handed down, a copy will be made available for him or her to read and note in court, on request made to the associate or the clerk to the presiding Lord Justice. The copy must not be removed from the court, and must be handed back after reading. The object is to ensure that such a person is in no worse a position than if the judgment has been read aloud in full. Copies of the judgment may be obtained from the official shorthand writers on payment of the appropriate fee.

Anyone who is supplied with a copy of the handed down judgment, or who reads it in court, will be bound by any direction which the court may give under the Children and Young Persons Act 1933, s 39, or any other form of restriction on disclosure or reporting of the information in the judgment.

2348 Court of Protection—authority for solicitors to act for patients or donors

The Master of the Court of Protection has issued the following *Practice Direction* ((1995) 145 NLJ 1403).

1. In Court of Protection matters, problems may arise for solicitors in knowing for whom they act. In *Re EG* [1914] 1 Ch 927, it was established that where a receiver has been appointed, the solicitor acting in the matter is acting for the patient and not for the receiver. The decision leaves undecided the question of who is the patient's solicitor in cases where more than one solicitor has been instructed to make an application for receivership or where a patient himself wishes to instruct another solicitor for a particular area of his affairs, eg where he remains of testamentary capacity and wishes to instruct a different solicitor to draw up a will for him. Where more than one solicitor has been instructed, perhaps each by a different member of the patient's family, this places the solicitors in a position of uncertainty as to who is acting for the patient on the principle of *Re EG*.

2. A further difficulty may arise as a result of *Yonge v Toynbee* [1901] 1 KB 215, which decided that the retainer of a solicitor came to an end when the patient lost capacity (as an extension of the general rule that, except in the case of an enduring power of attorney, the mental incapacity of the principal revokes any agency). Nevertheless, incapacitated people may need solicitors to act for them and them alone.

3. Assuming that a patient or donor is within the jurisdiction of the Court of Protection, the solicitor's authority to act for him can be expressly confirmed by the Court of Protection. Solicitors are also entitled to look upon themselves as acting for a patient or donor and not for the person who has given them instructions (if that is not the patient or donor) from the time that an application which is in order is received by the Court of Protection or the Public Trust Office. This may, for example, be an application for the appointment of a receiver, for an order determining proceedings, for the appointment of a new receiver, for confirmation of the revocation of an enduring power of attorney or for some other relief or authorisation. Where two or more solicitors have been instructed (expressly or by implication) to act for the same

patient or donor, preliminary directions should be sought from the court as to who will be deemed to be the solicitor in the matter.

4. A solicitor instructed by an applicant for receivership (or by an attorney) will be treated by the court as the patient's (or donor's) solicitor until an objection to the application, or a competing application, is received by the court. As soon as this happens, the solicitor instructed by the first applicant must elect whether to continue representing the patient or to represent the first applicant. If the solicitor elects to represent the first applicant, then it is for the court to decide whether the patient needs separate representation and if so, to instruct a different private solicitor or the Official Solicitor (if he agrees) to act for him. If the solicitor elects to remain as the patient's solicitor, then the first applicant will have to instruct another firm.

5. Solicitors will no doubt wish to make clear to the person from whom they take initial instructions relating to patients or donors that their client will be the patient or donor and that the solicitors will have a duty of confidentiality to the patient or donor, even if the instructions come from somebody else.

6. The court would like applicants and solicitors to be aware that if a reference which is received by the court in respect of an applicant is not satisfactory, no further inquiry will be made as to the applicant's suitability but the applicant will not be appointed as receiver. This may be considered unfair to the applicant but in the court's view, the best interests of the patient must come first.

2349   Court of Protection—costs—taxation of costs

The Master of the Court of Protection and the Chief Master of the Supreme Court Taxing Office have issued the following *Practice Direction* ((1995) 145 NLJ 1403).

1. Solicitors are reminded that the court's jurisdiction extends to the management and administration of a patient's financial affairs only and it cannot be concerned with aspects of a patients affairs which are not financial; and the costs of work beyond these limit will not be the subject of an order by the court or a direction by the Public Trust Office. Consequently, no such costs will be allowed by the Supreme Court Taxing Office on taxation.

2. If solicitors believe that an item in their bill is properly chargeable as work relating to financial affairs, but that contention is not accepted by the Supreme Court Taxing Office, they should bring in objections and, if that is unsuccessful, take the question to appeal. The Court of Protection itself cannot assist by reinstating any costs disallowed by the Supreme Court Taxing Office, since the function of deciding the quantum of costs belongs to them, by reason of the Court of Protection Rules 1994, SI 1994/3046, r 89 and RSC Ord 62.

3. In cases where the receiver is not a professional person, he is nonetheless expected to be able to carry out the whole range of a receiver's duties, as outlined in the Receiver's Handbook issued by the Public Trust Office. The court may, however, in suitable cases authorise a receiver (under the 1994 Rules, r 90) to employ at the patient's expense a solicitor or other professional person to do any work not usually requiring any professional assistance. This authority should always be sought in appropriate cases. However, the rule does not extend the limits of a receiver's authority beyond financial affairs. Out-of-pocket expenses are allowed to non-professional receivers.

4. If the receiver is a solicitor, costs are allowed for the whole range of receivership duties, subject to taxation, and there is no need for him to seek authority under r 90. Accountant-receivers are allowed remuneration fixed by the court and their fees are not liable to taxation. As regards visits by solicitor-receivers to patients, or attendances by solicitor-receivers at case conferences, it has become apparent that, with more patients living in the community, patients may need a visit or require the receiver's help in connection with case conferences or similar attendances, which may be necessary in order to safeguard the financial interests of the patient. In such cases, the Supreme Court Taxing Office will accept well-founded arguments that the costs should be allowed on taxation.

2350   Courts and Legal Services Act 1990—commencement

The Courts and Legal Services Act 1990 (Commencement No 10) Order 1995, SI 1995/641, brings into force, on 6 March 1995, s 82, which amends the Judicial Pensions Act 1981 by allowing regulations to be made entitling a member of a judicial pension scheme constituted under the 1981 Act to make voluntary contributions towards the cost of the provision of additional benefits under the scheme. For a summary of the Act, see 1990 Abr para 1861. For details of commencement, see the commencement table in the title STATUTES.

2351   Criminal proceedings

See CRIMINAL EVIDENCE AND PROCEDURE.

2352 Declaration—action—interim relief—interlocutory injunction

See *Newport Association Football Club Ltd v Football Association of Wales Ltd*, para 1707.

2353 Declaration—refusal to make declaration—facts not yet in existence

A company wished to commence manufacturing goods similar to those produced by another company and sought a declaration of non-liability to protect it from the possibility of copyright claims. On appeal against the striking out of its application, *held*, the facts that could found a cause of action were not yet in existence and thus the court was being asked to make a declaration on a theoretical question, which it would not do. Accordingly, the appeal would be dismissed.

Wyko Group plc v Cooper Roller Bearings Co Ltd [1996] FSR 126 (Chancery Division: Ferris J).
Russian Commercial Bank v British Bank for Foreign Trade [1921] 2 AC 438, HL, followed.

2354 Discovery of documents

See DISCOVERY.

2355 Dismissal of action—abuse of process—action against solicitors for negligence in conduct of criminal proceedings

The plaintiff was convicted of aggravated burglary and sentenced to seven years' imprisonment, a conviction upheld on appeal. After serving his sentence, the plaintiff brought civil proceedings against the solicitors who had acted for him in relation to the trial, claiming damages for negligence in the preparation and conduct of his defence. The claim was struck out as an abuse of the process of the court on the basis that it was contrary to public policy for a conviction in a criminal court to be impugned in a civil action by a person seeking to relitigate the same issue. The plaintiff appealed successfully, the judge holding that the matter was not beyond argument and that the plaintiff's allegations in relation to new evidence which had not been available at his trial might constitute an exception to the public policy rule. On the trial of a preliminary issue, namely whether, if the solicitors had been negligent and the plaintiff had been convicted as a result of that negligence, the plaintiff's claim was sustainable in law and/or should be allowed to proceed, *held*, a plaintiff's claim for damages in such circumstances was prima facie an abuse of the process of the court in that it amounted to the initiation of proceedings for the purpose of mounting a collateral attack on the final decision of a criminal court of competent jurisdiction. As such, it was contrary to public policy and unsustainable in law unless, at the very least, new and reliable evidence was available that entirely changed the aspect of the criminal case. Accordingly, where the plaintiff had had a full opportunity to contest the original trial and verdict of the jury on appeal (even assuming demonstrable incompetence in the preparation or conduct of his defence) and was unable to adduce new and reliable evidence to establish that the conviction was wrong, the interests of certainty and finality in the proper administration of justice required the court to apply the public policy rule and strike out his claim. On the facts, the plaintiff had wholly failed to provide the court with sufficiently compelling new evidence, or to demonstrate the possible existence of any such material. Accordingly, his case was not sustainable in law and should not be allowed to proceed.

Smith v Linskills (a Firm) [1995] 3 All ER 226 (Queens Bench Division, Manchester: Potter J).

This decision has been affirmed on appeal: (1996) Times, 7 February, CA.

2356 Dismissal of action—prejudice to fair trial—loss of documents—disqualification proceedings

See *Re Dexmaster Ltd*, para 476.

2357 Dismissal of action—want of prosecution—delay—absence of legal aid—libel proceedings

See *Gilberthorpe v Hawkins*, para 1883.

2358 Dismissal of action—want of prosecution—delay—delay before expiry of limitation period

See *Re Farmizer (Products) Ltd*, para 543.

2359   Dismissal of action—want of prosecution—delay—evidence of delay

The plaintiff commenced proceedings against the defendant for negligence and breach of statutory duty arising out of an accident which occurred during the course of his employment. The plaintiff was the sole witness to the accident, and the defendant had only one witness. The plaintiff did not apply to set the matter down until over four and a half years after the date by which he should have done so. The defendant successfully applied for an order striking out the proceedings for want of prosecution, on the ground that the delay was inordinate and inexcusable and such as to create a substantial risk of serious prejudice to the defendant should the trial proceed. In particular, the judge found that the prejudice lay mainly in the effect of the delay on the ability of the defendant's witness and the plaintiff to recall the events. On the plaintiff's appeal, *held*, there had to be evidence other than the mere fact of delay from which a court could infer that a lengthy delay was likely to have impaired witnesses' memories, thereby causing a likelihood of serious prejudice to a defendant. Moreover, the onus of proving prejudice or the impossibility of a fair trial lay with the person who asserted it. It was for the trial judge to assess the prejudice, the risk, and the adequacy of the evidence in light of the circumstances of each case. Here, there was evidence as to the witness upon whom the defendant intended to rely, the nature of the issue to which that witness's evidence related, and the way in which the defendant would be prejudiced in relation to the assessment of damages. Although it was a borderline case, there was sufficient material on which the judge could have concluded that serious prejudice had been caused to the defendant as a result of the plaintiff's delay. Accordingly, the appeal would be dismissed.

Slade v Adco Ltd (1995) Times, 7 December (Court of Appeal: Neill and Auld LJJ, and Sir Iain Glidewell).

2360   Dismissal of action—want of prosecution—delay—prejudice to defendant

The plaintiff was injured in an accident at his workplace but delayed his action for damages for some years. The defendant company sought to have the action struck out on the grounds that the delay had caused it financial prejudice. On the plaintiff's appeal against the striking out of the action, *held*, the defendant had to take into account the value of having in hand the money which, but for the delay, it would have had to pay in damages. Account had to be taken of the fall in the spending power of that money during the period of delay and any interest or capital depreciation it might have been able to earn on the sum. Such computations may well be difficult but the difficulties involved might deter defendants from relying on financial prejudice except in clear and obvious cases. Accordingly, the appeal would be allowed.

Gahan v Szerelmey (UK) Ltd [1996] 1 WLR 439 (Court of Appeal: Nourse and Hobhouse LJJ and Sir Christopher Slade). *Hayes v Bowman* [1989] 1 WLR 456, CA (1988 Abr para 620) followed.

The plaintiff was born with a small dimple in his lower sacral area. Seven months later he was diagnosed as having a pilonidal sinus. At three years, it was clear that he was severely and permanently disabled. Shortly before his 21st birthday, he commenced proceedings against the defendant health authority alleging negligence in the administration of an injection when he was eight months old. The writ was served ten months later after an unsuccessful search for the plaintiff's medical records. The defendant agreed to a reasonable extension of time for service of the statement of claim to give the plaintiff time to resolve the problem of the medical records. More than two years later, an unless order was made for service of the document. The plaintiff complied with the order. However, by that time his legal aid certificate had been discharged and he was acting in person. He ignored repeated requests for further and better particulars, but was eventually granted a new legal aid certificate and instructed new solicitors. The following year, the defendant made an unsuccessful application for dismissal of the action for want of prosecution. The plaintiff then served an amended statement of claim. This pleaded an alternative claim based on an alleged failure of the defendant to anticipate the likelihood of infection to the plaintiff's lower sacral area. Thereafter the plaintiff instructed yet further solicitors, to whom the defendant's solicitors wrote threatening to issue a further summons for dismissal of the action. A summons was served almost two years later. At the first hearing, the proceedings were adjourned to allow the plaintiff's solicitors time to file an affidavit in reply. Further extensions of time were agreed to allow them to obtain a medical report. These deadlines were not met and the summons was eventually restored. The plaintiff was aged 28 years when the action was dismissed for want of prosecution by a master. His appeal to the judge was dismissed. On further appeal, *held*, the delay being accepted as inordinate, the issue was whether it could be excused. Although difficulties encountered by a plaintiff in obtaining legal aid, medical records and evidence were capable of excusing inordinate delay, neither separately nor cumulatively did they do so here.

However, the defendant had failed to establish that it had suffered serious prejudice as a result of the inordinate delay. There was no basis for dismissing the action because the plaintiff's mother had been improving her evidence as the case proceeded or because the defendant would have difficulty in adducing expert evidence to deal with the state of medical knowledge when the plaintiff was born. That difficulty arose substantially from the fact that the writ was not served until just before the plaintiff's 21st birthday. Thereafter any delay in prosecuting the case was relatively insignificant. But for the delay the case would probably have come to trial before the changes to the indemnification of health authority doctors were introduced in 1990. The changes would produce a less favourable outcome for the defendant if the plaintiff succeeded. However, that was not a sufficient basis for the defendant to establish that it had suffered prejudice. Accordingly, the appeal would be allowed.

Theodorou v Islington Health Authority (1995) 26 BMLR 1 (Court of Appeal: Nourse, Beldam and Kennedy LJJ).

2361 European Communities—Community decisions

See EUROPEAN COMMUNITIES.

2362 House of Lords—appeal—leave to appeal—petition—procedure

The House of Lords has issued a *Practice Direction* ([1995] 2 Cr App Rep 162), which amends the *Practice Directions* applicable to civil appeals ('the Blue Book'), and criminal appeals ('the Red Book'). The following provisions are included in the amendments to the Blue Book:

(1) Petitions are not admissible for presentation if they fall into one of the following categories:

(a) petitions for leave to appeal to the House of Lords from a refusal by the Court of Appeal to grant leave to appeal to that court from a judgment of a lower court, or from any other preliminary decision of the Court of Appeal in respect of a case in which leave to appeal to the Court of Appeal was not granted;

(b) petitions for leave to appeal to the House of Lords against a refusal by the Court of Appeal or a Divisional Court of the Queen's Bench Division to grant an ex parte application for leave to apply for judicial review under RSC Ord 53;

(c) petitions for leave to appeal to the House of Lords barred by the Housing Act 1985, Sch 11, para 13(4), or Sch 22, para 7(4);

(d) petitions for leave to appeal to the House of Lords brought by a petitioner in respect of whom the High Court has made an order under the Supreme Court Act 1981, s 42 (restriction of vexatious legal proceedings), unless leave to present such a petition has been granted by the High Court or a judge thereof, pursuant to that section;

(e) petitions for leave to appeal from a decision of the Court of Appeal on any appeal from a county court in any probate proceedings;

(f) petitions for leave to appeal from a decision of the Court of Appeal on an appeal from a decision of the High Court on a question of law under the Representation of the People Act 1983, Pt III.

Inadmissible petitions will not be accepted for presentation to the House. Where there is doubt as to the admissibility of a petition, it may, at the direction of the principal clerk, be accepted for presentation to the House so that its admissibility may be decided by an Appeal Committee.

(2) In cases involving civil contempt of court, an appeal may be brought under the Administration of Justice Act 1960, s 13. Leave to appeal is required, and application for such leave must first be made to the court below. If that application is refused, a petition for leave to appeal may be presented to the House of Lords. Where the decision of the court below is a decision on appeal under the same section of the same Act, leave to appeal to the House of Lords will only be granted if the court below certifies that a point of law of general public importance is involved in that decision and if it appears to that court or to the House that the point is one that ought to be considered by the House. Where the court below refuses to grant the certificate required, a petition for leave to appeal will not be accepted for presentation to the House.

(3) A petition for leave to appeal in a case involving civil contempt of court must be lodged in the Judicial Office within 14 days beginning from the date of the refusal of such leave by the court below. The application to the court below must itself be made within 14 days beginning from the date of the decision of that court from which leave to appeal is sought.

(4) The names of parties to the original action who are not parties to the petition to the House must still be included in the title, and the names of all parties must be given in the same order as in the title used in the court below.

(5) In any petition concerning minors or where, in the courts below, the title used has been such as to conceal the identity of one or more parties to the action, this fact should be clearly drawn to the attention of the Judicial Office at the time the petition is lodged, so that the title adopted in the House of Lords may take due account of the need to protect the identity of the minors or parties in question. (Petitions involving minors are normally given a title in the form 'Re X', where X is the initial letter of the child's surname).

(6) In any appeal concerning minors, parties should also consider whether it would be appropriate for the House to make an order under the Children and Young Persons Act 1933, s 39, and must, in any event, inform the Judicial Office if such an order has been made by a court below. A request for such an order must be made in writing, preferably on behalf of all parties to the appeal, as soon as possible after the appeal has been presented and not later than two weeks before the commencement of the hearing.

The following provisions are included in the amendments to the Red Book:

(1) In cases involving criminal contempt of court, an appeal lies to the House of Lords at the instance of the defendant and, in respect of an application for committal or attachment, at the instance of the applicant from any decision of the Court of Appeal (Criminal Division), the Courts-Martial Appeal Court, or Divisional Court of the Queen's Bench Division.

(2) A certificate is not required in contempt of court cases where the decision of the court below was not a decision on appeal.

2363 Interest on damages—deduction of tax

See *Deeny v Gooda Walker (No 4)*, para 990.

2364 Judge—procedural decisions made by judge—discretion to make decisions

The plaintiff commenced proceedings against the defendant. The trial judge concluded that certain issues raised in the action should be tried ahead of others because, if those issues were decided against the plaintiff, its action had to fail and the costs of exploring other issues could be avoided. The plaintiff applied for leave to appeal against that decision on the grounds that the judge's formulation of the issues was unsatisfactory, that there had already been delays, that it posed a risk of duplication of evidence and of increased costs if further issues had to be tried after the first one and that witnesses would be inconvenienced. Leave was granted because the application raised issues touching on the procedural powers to be exercised by trial judges and on the proper approach of the Court of Appeal when such powers were exercised. *Held*, although the judge's decision might not save time and expense if the issues were determined in the plaintiff's favour, or if the decision was in the defendant's favour and an appeal was successful, it was the type of decision which fell fairly and squarely within the growing procedural decision-making ambit of the trial judge. The Court of Appeal would be most reluctant to interfere unless satisfied that the trial judge was wrong. In the present case, the trial judge had been right. He made an appropriate order and had not overlooked any relevant factor. There was no ground on which there could be proper interference and, accordingly, the appeal would be dismissed.

Thermawear Ltd v Linton (1995) Times, 20 October (Court of Appeal: Sir Thomas Bingham MR, Henry and Thorpe LJJ). *Practice Direction (Civil Litigation: Case Management)* [1995] 1 WLR 508 considered.

2365 Legal aid

See LEGAL AID.

2366 Mareva injunctions

See INJUNCTIONS.

2367 Queen's Bench Division—case management—preparation for and conduct of hearings

See para 2322.

2368 Queen's Bench Division—jury list—setting down

The following *Practice Direction* ([1995] 1 WLR 364) has been issued by Drake J.

1. The state of the jury list continues to be satisfactory. There are few delays, and actions can enter the warned list and come on for trial almost immediately after they have been set down

for trial. In order to maintain this satisfactory state of affairs, it is essential that parties obey directions that are given, especially directions as to setting down.

2. There are still a large number of cases in which orders to set down are ignored. If a party has been ordered to set down a case but is not ready for trial, an application must be made to the judge in charge of the jury list for an order that the trial is not to be heard before some future date.

3. It is not for the parties to agree between themselves that the time for setting down is to be extended. Once a case has been set down, all further interlocutory applications will normally have to be heard by the judge in charge of the jury list, and the court will exercise full control over the pre-trial conduct of the action.

4. In future, if an order for setting down is not obeyed, the party in default may face severe penalties including, where appropriate, an order that the action be struck out. Any party who is at present in default must hasten to remedy the position.

2369 Queen's Bench Division—provisional damages—personal injuries—procedure

Lord Taylor of Gosforth CJ has issued the following *Practice Direction* ([1995] 1 WLR 507).

Practice Direction (Provisional Damages: Procedure) [1985] 2 All ER 895 (1985 Abr para 2030) is amended by the addition of the following:

9A. In any case in which the Court of Appeal allows an appeal from the whole or part of a judgment for provisional damages, all the provisions of Part A of this Practice Direction still apply, both as to the judgment at first instance and mutatis mutandis, the judgment and directions of the Court of Appeal.

2370 Parties—substitution of parties—effect on limitation period

See *Yorkshire Regional Health Authority v Fairclough Building Ltd*, para 1903.

2371 Parties—substitution of parties—jurisdiction—substitution of pension scheme beneficiaries for scheme trustees as plaintiffs

The trustees of an occupational pension scheme, at the request of the employers and on the advice of the defendant firm of solicitors, repaid sums to the employers as surplus and loaned them a further sum. The employers went into administrative receivership and the plaintiffs were appointed independent trustees of the scheme. The plaintiffs discovered that the value of the scheme was insufficient to cover existing and future pension entitlements, and issued proceedings against the defendants alleging that the advice given to their predecessors had been negligent. The plaintiffs were subsequently advised that they might be exposed to personal risk in relation to the costs of the proceedings, and obtained an order allowing them to cease to continue the action. On an application by two of the beneficiaries of the scheme who had not reached pensionable age to be substituted as plaintiffs, *held*, the applicants had no cause of action against the defendants, being at one remove in that any cause of action was that of their trustees. As such they were not parties to the action in any sense. RSC Ord 15, r 14(2) did not justify the handing over of the conduct of an action against a third party which the trustees had started but wished to abandon. The conduct of the trustees did not amount to a failure by them in the performance of their duty to protect the trust estate. Although they were also unwilling to incur personal liability, the trustees were entitled to take the view that they should not put the fund at risk in indemnifying them against the defendants' costs. There was no justification in giving the applicants leave to sue the defendants as they had no property in the subject matter of the action. The trustees and no one else had a cause of action against the defendants and, in all probability, it would not protect the trust against the risk of being resorted to for the defendants' costs if the action failed. Accordingly, the application would be dismissed.

Bradstock Trustee Services Ltd v Nabarro Nathanson (a firm) [1995] 1 WLR 1405 (Chancery Division: Judge Paul Baker QC).

2372 Parties—substitution of parties—substitution of successor company as plaintiff—application of limitation period

RSC Ord 15, r 7 provides that if in any action the interest or liability of any party devolves upon some other person, the court may order that other person be made a party to the proceedings as if he had been substituted for the first party.

The plaintiff was a company which merged with another company after it had brought an action against the defendant for breach of a salvage agreement. Although the merger occurred after the limitation period had expired, the plaintiff claimed that the newly formed company was entitled to be substituted as the new plaintiff in the action under RSC Ord 15, r 7. *Held*, there was nothing in Ord 15, r 7 to prevent it applying in the present circumstances. Provided the action had been brought within the limitation period, it did not matter that the substitution was executed once that period had expired. Accordingly, the application would be granted.

Industrie Chimiche Italia Centrale v Alexander G Tsavliris & Sons Maritime Co (1995) Times, 8 August (Queen's Bench Division: Mance J).

2373 Pleading

See PLEADING.

2374 Rules of the Supreme Court

The Rules of the Supreme Court (Amendment) 1995, SI 1995/2206 (in force in part on 1 October 1995 and in part on 1 December 1995), (1) amends the rules concerning revenue appeals so as to (i) introduce a new rule for appeals direct to the Court of Appeal from the Special Commissioners, (ii) amend existing provision in Ord 91 to take account of changes to the rules governing proceedings before the Special and General Commissioners, and (iii) extend the time limit for certain appeals from the value added tax tribunal; (2) imposes a requirement to seek leave to appeal in certain proceedings; (3) introduces a new rule for the taxation of fees arising under a conditional fee agreement between a solicitor and his client; (4) amends Ord 115 (confiscation and forfeiture in connection with criminal proceedings) in consequence of the Drug Trafficking Act 1994; (5) makes various miscellaneous amendments, including (i) enabling the court to penalise a defaulting defendant in originating summons proceedings by debarring evidence or striking out the defence or counterclaim, (ii) enabling a defendant to apply ex parte for an injunction, (iii) increasing the costs allowable in relation to a charging order absolute, (iv) allowing a defendant to apply for summary judgment on a counterclaim in an action for specific performance, (v) omitting the requirement for an application under the Companies Act 1985, s 651 to be begun by originating motion, (vi) amending the procedure relating to applications for the revocation of a patent and the procedure for discovery in patents proceedings, (vii) clarifying the orders to which Ord 114 (references to the European Court) applies, (viii) introducing new forms of acknowledgement of service, and (ix) amending the notice of motion so as to require the place of hearing to be specified.

The Rules of the Supreme Court (Amendment No 2) 1995, SI 1995/2897 (in force on 1 December 1995), (1) increases the costs allowed to a litigant in person and the fixed costs recoverable under RSC Ord 62, App 3; and (2) assigns appeals on a point of law from the Pensions Ombudsman to the Chancery Division and imposes a requirement for leave on any appeal from that Division.

The Rules of the Supreme Court (Amendment No 3) 1995, SI 1995/3316 (in force on 15 January 1996), (1) substitutes Ord 100 so as to make provision for proceedings under the Trade Marks Act 1994, the Olympic Symbol etc (Protection) Act 1995, the service of documents and the service of orders on the registrar; (2) amends Ord 104 (proceedings relating to patents) to make provision for the service of documents; (3) provides for a praecipe for caveats against release in Admiralty proceedings to be filed when the Admiralty Registry is closed; (4) makes amended provision for limitation actions in Admiralty proceedings; and (5) extends the provisions of Ord 115 (confiscation and forfeiture in connection with criminal proceedings) to apply to the enforcement of Northern Ireland confiscation orders and amends Ord 115 in consequence of the Proceeds of Crime Act 1995.

2375 Service of process—service out of the jurisdiction—attachment of assets within the jurisdiction

Hong Kong

A writ may be served out of the jurisdiction with the leave of the court under RSC Ord 11, r 1(1)(b), where an injunction is sought ordering the defendant to do or refrain from doing anything within the jurisdiction, or under r 1(1)(m), where the claim is brought to enforce any judgment.

The plaintiff commenced civil proceedings in Monaco where the defendant was in custody. The court there attached the defendant's assets in Monaco but refused to attach his assets in Hong Kong. The plaintiff sought the leave of the Hong Kong court, under rules corresponding to Ord 11, r 1, to serve a writ on the defendant out of the jurisdiction claiming Mareva relief to freeze his assets in Hong Kong pending the conclusion of the proceedings in Monaco. *Held*, the claim would not be 'brought to enforce' a judgment within Ord 11, r 1(1)(m) because, unlike a suit founded on the cause of action created by a judgment, the Mareva injunction did not enforce anything; it merely prepared the ground for a possible execution by different means in the future. The injunction did not enforce a 'judgment'; it was intended to hold the position until a judgment came into existence. When the injunction was sought and granted, there was no judgment. The plaintiff was merely hopeful that a favourable judgment would at some future time be obtained in an action which, when the application for leave was made, might not even have commenced. The question as to whether leave might be granted under Ord 11, r 1(1)(b) was whether an extraterritorial jurisdiction grounded only on the presence of assets within the territory was one which that provision was intended to assert. A ruling in respect of an application for Mareva relief decided no rights and called into existence no process by which the rights would be decided. The Mareva injunction did not enforce the plaintiff's rights even when a judgment had ascertained that they existed; it merely ensured that, once the mechanisms of enforcement were set in motion, there was something physically available upon which they could work. Order 11 was confined to originating documents which set in motion proceedings designed to ascertain substantive rights; the court had no power to order the service of a form of process limited to a claim for Mareva relief. Accordingly, the plaintiff's application would be dismissed.

Mercedes-Benz AG v Leiduck [1995] 3 All ER 929 (Privy Council: Lords Goff of Chieveley, Mustill, Slynn of Hadley, Nicholls of Birkenhead and Hoffmann).

2376 Service of process—service out of the jurisdiction—defects in writ and statement of claim—whether order for service abuse of process

The plaintiff had deposited a sum of money with the defendant pursuant to a loan contract and brought proceedings for the return of the money. He obtained an order for service of the proceedings out of the jurisdiction. The defendant sought to have the order set aside as an abuse of process, contending that the plaintiff's writ and statement of claim put forward a claim for money had and received where no such claim existed and that the only possible claim was under a contract of deposit. *Held*, although there was no direct authority on the point it had never been open to a creditor to sue for an outstanding debt as money had and received. The only way of advancing the claim was to sue on the subsisting contract of loan. However, there was no obligation to set aside the order because of defects in the writ and statement of claim and the proper course was to require the plaintiff to apply to have those documents amended. Accordingly, the application would be dismissed.

Spargos Mining NL v Atlantic Capital Corpn (1995) Times, 11 December (Queen's Bench Division: Colman J).

2377 Service of process—service out of the jurisdiction—establishment of good arguable case for service

The plaintiff, an English company, organised an American tour of regimental bands for the defendant, a Scottish heritage society based and operating in America. After the tour, the plaintiff claimed that the defendant breached the terms of the contract in respect of expenses and fees and sought leave to serve proceedings against the defendant outside the jurisdiction. The plaintiff was granted leave to serve outside the jurisdiction but that was then set aside. On appeal by the plaintiff, the judge, applying the test in *Attock Cement Co Ltd v Romanian Bank for Foreign Trade* [1989] 1 All ER 1189 (1989 Abr para 1846), CA, found that the plaintiff had made out a good arguable case. On the defendant's appeal, *held*, although, on the facts, the appeal would be dismissed, the judge had been wrong to apply the test in *Attock*, which required the plaintiff to satisfy the court to the civil burden of proof. That test was not approved by the House of Lords in *Seaconsar Far East Ltd v Bank Markazi Jomgouri Islami Iran* [1993] 4 All ER 456, CA (1993 Abr para 2060) and the court did not accept that the requirement to show a good arguable case required the plaintiff to satisfy the court that at the end of the day it was more probable than not that it would win the action. The plaintiff had satisfied the court that it had a good arguable case, even though the court did not believe it was possible on the present evidence to predict the outcome of the case or to find that the plaintiff was more likely than not to win.

Agrafax Public Relations Ltd v United Scottish Society Inc (1995) Times, 22 May (Court of Appeal: Russell, Henry and Rose LJJ).

2378 Service of process—service within jurisdiction—service on other similar officer

See *Kuwait Airways Corpn v Iraqi Airways Co*, para 1444.

2379 Service of process—service within jurisdiction—usual or last known address—insertion through letter box—validity of service

RSC Ord 10, r 1(2)(a) provides that a writ for service on a defendant may, instead of being personally served on him, be served by sending a copy of the writ by ordinary first-class post to the defendant at his usual or last known address. Rule 1(3)(a) provides that where a writ is served in accordance with r 1(2)(a), the date of service is deemed to be the seventh day after the date on which the copy was sent to or inserted through the letter box for the address in question, unless the contrary is shown.

The plaintiff issued a writ against the defendant, and it was purportedly served on the defendant within the relevant time limit. However, the defendant had already moved from the address to which the writ was sent and therefore did not see it. The defendant challenged the validity of service, but a district judge decided that the writ had been effectively served because it had been sent by first-class post to the defendant's last known or usual address and was not returned through the post. The decision was affirmed on appeal. On the defendant's further appeal, *held*, having regard to Ord 10, r 1(3)(a), it did not make sense to treat the seventh day after the insertion of a letter through a letter box as the deemed date of service, as service was concerned not merely with delivery but also with notice. The only reason for the generous seven-day time limit was to allow for the possibility that a letter might not come to a defendant's notice immediately. A defendant could therefore rebut the presumption in Ord 10, r 1(3)(a) by showing that proceedings had not come to his notice until the seventh day or that they had not come to his notice at all. Moreover, such a construction was reinforced by Ord 10, r 1(3)(b). As postal service was an alternative to personal service, it was not irrelevant whether or not the proceedings came to a defendant's notice. Accordingly, the appeal would be allowed.

Forward v West Sussex County Council [1995] 4 All ER 207 (Court of Appeal: Sir Thomas Bingham MR, Rose and Hobhouse LJJ)

2380 Settlements—approval—settlement of claim by person under a disability—declarations for the aid of foreign courts

The wife of a man who was killed when a derrick barge sank made a provisional settlement of her claim against the operator of the barge in an action in a United States court. The settlement purported to settle all claims that she and her three infant children might have against the operator relating to the death and was subject to approval by the English High Court. There were other dependants of the deceased who were not party to the claim and at least one of the parties to the claim was known to be reluctant to agree to the settlement. The wife then sought to have the settlement set aside by the American court on the grounds that it was inadequate. The operator sought a declaration in the High Court that the court had the power and jurisdiction to approve the settlement and applied subsequently for summary judgment. On appeal from the refusal of the High Court to grant the declaration, the first issue was whether the wife could have obtained High Court approval for the settlement and the second was whether the court should issue a declaration. *Held*, the omission of some of the deceased's dependants from the claim, the reluctance of one party to the claim to settle and the outstanding challenge to its validity in a competent court meant that the High Court would have refused to grant approval under RSC Ord 80, rr 10, 11. These rules were coherent, comprehensive, and in such claims exhaustive and there was no inherent jurisdiction for a court to exercise outside the requirements of Ord 80. As to the grant of a declaration, the court restated the general rule that the jurisdiction of the court was to settle rights contested between the parties before it not to give advisory opinions. Although there was a trend for courts to occasionally grant declarations to aid a foreign court, in this instance the declaration sought was of no practical utility and would be likely to mislead a foreign court as to the true position in English law. Accordingly, the appeal would be dismissed.

McDermott International Inc v Hardy (1995) Times, 28 December (Court of Appeal: Simon Brown and Auld LJ and Macpherson of Cluny J).

2381 Stay of proceedings—foreign proceedings—counterclaim in foreign proceedings—interlocutory application

See *Société Commerciale de Réassurance v Eras International Ltd (No 2)*, para 571.

2382 Stay of proceedings—matters to be dealt with by arbitration—exceptional circumstances justifying refusal

See *Rew v Cox*, para 1742.

2383 Summary judgment

See JUDGMENTS AND ORDERS.

2384 Supreme Court—dress

See para 717.

2385 Supreme Court—fees

The Supreme Court Fees (Amendment) Order 1995, SI 1995/2629 (in force on 30 October 1995), further amends the 1980 Order, SI 1980/821, so as to (1) remove exemption from payment of court fees for those on income support who are also in receipt of civil legal aid; (2) increase various fees relating to the Supreme Court; (3) replace the fees payable on obtaining copies of documents with a single fee; (4) revoke the fee payable on the hearing of a public examination; (5) modify the fee for searches so as to charge £5.00 per file rather than £5.00 per hour; and (6) introduce a new fee for personal searches of bankruptcy and companies records.

2386 Transfer of proceedings—transfer to Central London County Court Business List— value of claim

The High Court and County Courts Jurisdiction (Amendment) Order 1995, SI 1995/205 (in force on 1 February 1995), amends the 1991 Order, SI 1991/724, to provide that where the High Court or a county court is considering whether to transfer proceedings to or from the Central London County Court Business List, it will not be presumed that the action should be tried in the High Court unless the value of the action exceeds £200,000. The 1995 Order also provides that judgments given in proceedings arising out of an agreement regulated by the Consumer Credit Act 1974 may only be enforced in a county court.

2387 Trial—trial of separate issues—adjudication of liability—deferment of adjudication

See *Deeny v Gooda Walker Ltd*, para 1741.

2388 Writ—validity—renewal—service out of time—deemed issue and service of writ

The plaintiffs applied for an extension of the validity of their writ against the defendant, which had been served outside the limitation period, but were refused because they had failed to disclose a satisfactory explanation for the delayed service. The judge, however, directed that the writ was deemed to have been issued and served when it came to the attention of a partner from the defendant firm on a date that was within the relevant limitation period. On appeal by the defendant, *held*, there was no jurisdiction to allow the judge to make the order that he did. A writ could not be deemed to have been issued months before or after it actually had been because it could be prejudicial, not only to the parties, but to third parties as well. Even if he had had the power to grant the extension requested, to do so would have been an impermissible exercise of discretion as the situation was one in which such an extension was not justified. Accordingly, the defendant's appeal would be allowed and the writ declared invalid.

    Harrison v Touche Ross (a Firm) (1995) Times, 14 February (Court of Appeal: Sir Thomas Bingham MR, Rose and Morritt LJJ).

PRESS, PRINTING AND PUBLISHING

Halsbury's Laws of England (4th edn) Vol 37, paras 1001–1100

2389 Articles

The Accused, the Jury and the Media, Damian Paul Carney: 145 NLJ 12

Human Rights and the Journalist, Geoffrey Bindman: 145 NLJ 720

Press and Prejudice, Alistair Bonnington (on contrasting approaches to prejudicial pre-trial publicity): 145 NLJ 1623

Pressing for De-Regulation, Santha Rasaiah and David Newell (on media regulation): LS Gaz, 15 March 1995, p 16

Trial by Media, David Bentley (on sensational press and television coverage of trials): 139 SJ 243

2390 Net book agreement—breach of competition rules—exemption

See *Publishers Association v Commission of the European Communities*, para 3161.

2391 Newspapers—media ownership—government proposals

See para 2814.

2392 Reports of judicial proceedings—civil proceedings—prohibition of publication of names or other matters arising in proceedings—child—proceedings against health authority

In judicial review proceedings, a father had challenged a health authority's decision not to fund the further medical treatment of his daughter, now aged 11. Orders were made, under the Children and Young Persons Act 1933, s 39, directing that the child's identity should not be revealed in reports of the proceedings. A national newspaper offered to pay for the further funding of the treatment if it was allowed to publish a detailed story about the child, including her name. The father, therefore, sought the revocation of the s 39 orders. *Held*, this was a case in which there was a legitimate public interest in the child, who was suffering from a life-threatening illness. The father wished to raise money to fund the further treatment of his daughter, who now had some knowledge of her illness. Although it was regrettable that her medical problems had to be exploited for financial gain, if the maintenance of the reporting restrictions would deprive her of treatment which might, or would, be of therapeutic and possibly life-saving benefit to her, those restrictions could not be justified. Accordingly, the father's application would be granted and the orders revoked.

R v Cambridge District Health Authority, ex p B (No 2) [1996] 1 FLR 375 (Court of Appeal: Sir Thomas Bingham MR, Sir Stephen Brown P and Sir John Balcombe). For judicial review proceedings, see [1995] 2 All ER 129 (para 12).

2393 Reports of judicial proceedings—civil proceedings—prohibition of publication of names or other matters arising in proceedings—power of court

Under the Contempt of Court Act 1981, s 11, where the court has power to allow a name or other matter to be withheld from the public in proceedings, it may give such directions prohibiting the publication of that name or matter as it considers appropriate.

The applicants challenged a council's refusal to exercise its duty to house them under the Housing Act 1985. Both applicants were HIV positive and made applications in motions for judicial review, seeking orders that the matters be listed in the cause list by reference only to their initials, that they be granted anonymity during the main hearing, and that orders be made under s 11 preventing publication of their names, addresses and photographs. The applications were listed in the usual way with full names, and the notices of motion, which were open to inspection by the press, contained information of the HIV virus. *Held*, the court's power to grant anonymity under s 11 was very limited and could not be invoked simply to protect privacy or avoid embarrassment. The application for leave to move for judicial review constituted separate proceedings from the hearing of the main application. Thus, an order granting anonymity made in relation to the main hearing could not relate back to the application for leave to move. The court had no power to make any order in relation to the applications for leave to move, since that would render ineffectual any order it might make with regard to the main hearing. In any event, substantial publicity had already occurred as a result of the hearing in open court of the applications for leave to move for judicial review. The applicants had already lost their anonymity and the exercise of the court's power was inappropriate. Consequently, the applications would be refused.

R v Westminster City Council, ex p Castelli; R v Westminster City Council, ex p Tristran-Garcia [1996] 1 FLR 534 (Queen's Bench Division: Latham J).

2394 Reports of judicial proceedings—criminal proceedings—alleged contempt of court—decision by Attorney General not to institute proceedings—whether decision reviewable

The applicants were convicted of murder at a trial which had received extensive media coverage. Their convictions were subsequently quashed on the grounds that they were unsafe and unsatisfactory and that the extensive media coverage precluded a fair retrial. A reference was made to the Attorney General to consider contempt of court proceedings with respect to the media coverage. After taking specialist advice and hearing representations from newspaper editors it was decided that no proceedings for contempt of court should be taken and that detailed reasons for that decision would not be given to the public. The applicants sought judicial review of the decision. *Held*, it was well established that the courts could not review an exercise of discretion by the Attorney General in respect of decisions taken in his public office. This resulted from the Attorney General's unique constitutional position. Further, under the Contempt of Court Act 1981, s 7, committal proceedings could only be brought by the Attorney General and if Parliament had intended to make his contempt decisions reviewable it would have done so. Accordingly, the application would be dismissed.

R v A-G, ex p Taylor (1995) Independent, 31 July (Queen's Bench Division: Stuart-Smith LJ and Butterfield J).

2395 Reports of judicial proceedings—criminal proceedings—risk of prejudice

The defendant, a man with suspected links with a proscribed organisation, was convicted of possessing explosives with intent to endanger life. He appealed against the conviction, arguing that during his trial there was highly prejudicial press coverage that could have put pressure on the jury to convict him. It was further argued that the trial judge's manner during the trial and certain aspects of the summing up had been hostile to the defendant. *Held*, although it was important to maintain the freedom of the press in its reporting on the criminal justice system, fairness demanded that juries should not be put under any pressure by the press or anyone else. The Court of Appeal ought not to act on allegations of hostile behaviour by the trial judge, unless those allegations were either agreed between counsel or supported by evidence. There was no such evidence available to the court and very little agreement between counsel. Neither the prejudicial press coverage nor the judge's demeanour could of itself render the conviction unsafe or unsatisfactory. However the two factors, when combined, did lead to that conclusion. Accordingly, the appeal would be allowed and the conviction quashed.

R v Wood (1995) Times, 11 July (Court of Appeal: Staughton LJ, Scott Baker and Butterfield JJ).

2396 Reports of judicial proceedings—criminal proceedings—strict liability rule—reports of inactive proceedings—risk of prejudice to active proceedings

Scotland
The 'strict liability rule' means the rule of law whereby conduct may be treated as a contempt of court as tending to interfere with the course of justice in particular legal proceedings regardless of intent to do so: Contempt of Court Act 1981, s 1. The rule only applies to publications that create a substantial risk that the course of justice in those proceedings will be seriously impeded or prejudiced: s 2(2).

The defendant, a newspaper publisher, published articles relating to an accused's escape from prison while awaiting trial for assault and robbery. The first article stated that he had been in custody awaiting trial for armed robbery and gave details of his release from custody two years earlier after twice standing trial on the same murder charge. Later articles made no reference to the fact that he was an untried prisoner awaiting trial but wrongly stated that he had a conviction for culpable homicide. All articles showed photographs of the accused. Two petitions and complaints were brought against the publishers alleging that the articles were in contempt of court under the 1981 Act. *Held*, prejudice was to be assessed at the time of publication of the articles without regard to what might have already happened or might happen afterwards. The degree of risk had to be substantial, and the degree of impediment or prejudice had to be serious. Any impediment or prejudice was serious if it affected the outcome of the trial in regard to such matters as the evidence of witnesses or the jury's evaluation of the evidence. However, it would only be relevant if it affected the proceedings which were active at the time of publication. The later articles referred only to the earlier charges, which were no longer active, and contained no link between the accused and the active charges. Consequently, in respect of those articles, there was no contempt. The first article would not have breached the strict liability rule had it not been for the publication of the accused's photograph. This factor, when taken together with the contents of the article, created a risk that the evidence of witnesses might be affected, particularly with regard to identification of the accused. Accordingly, a finding of contempt would be made.

HM Advocate v Caledonian Newspapers Ltd 1995 SLT 926 (High Court of Justiciary).

2397 Reports of judicial proceedings—criminal proceedings—young offender—identification

It has been held that in considering whether to impose reporting restrictions prohibiting the publication of a young offender's identity under the Children and Young Persons Act 1933, s 39(1) the court should not refuse to make an order under s 39 for the sole purpose of publicising a rule or principle. An offender should not be named merely to give the case a greater impact on the public than if it is reported anonymously. Such an approach will not give sufficient, or indeed any, weight to the offender's interests, which must be taken into account under s 39. Where, however, in naming him a judge considers it appropriate to take account both of the general deterrent and the disgrace and the deterrence directed at the offender himself, such an approach will be unchallengeable. The effect of publicity on the offender's family is not in itself to be taken into account under s 39. However, where there is cogent evidence beyond mere speculation that any difficulties caused to the family will impede their playing a full part in the offender's rehabilitation process, these concerns may be of some significance. There must be good reason for making an order under s 39, and considerable weight should be given to the offender's age and to the possible damage to him of public identification before he reaches adulthood. Where a trial judge takes such factors into account in deciding whether to impose reporting restrictions, the courts will be reluctant to interfere with the decision.

R v Crown Court at Inner London Sessions, ex p Barnes (1995) Times, 7 August (Queen's Bench Division: Balcombe LJ and Buxton J).

PRISONS

Halsbury's Laws of England (4th edn) Vol 37, paras 1101–1300

2398 Articles

Our Ageing Prisoners, David Biles: Criminal Lawyer, Issue 52, p 6
Prisoners (Return to Custody) Act 1995—A Review, Leonard Jason-Lloyd: 159 JP Jo 754
Time for the Crime, John Hirst (on the meaning of 'life'): 145 NLJ 1571

2399 Attendance centres—rules

The Attendance Centre Rules 1995, SI 1995/3281 (in force on 30 December 1995), consolidate the 1958 Rules, SI 1958/1990 (as amended) so as to reformulate the regime for attendance centres, and provide new powers to deal with offenders who arrive late or who are required to leave because of misconduct.

2400 Prison rules

The Prison (Amendment) Rules 1995, SI 1995/983 (in force on 25 April 1995), amend the 1964 Rules, SI 1964/388, in relation to contact between unconvicted prisoners and convicted prisoners, the temporary release of prisoners, and the powers of governors in respect of disciplinary offences committed by prisoners.

The Prison (Amendment) (No 2) Rules 1995, SI 1995/1598 (in force on 17 July 1995), amend the 1964 Rules, SI 1964/388. Changes are made to the rules relating to privileges for prisoners and the rules relating to prisoners' clothing.

2401 Prisoner—application for parole—refusal based on denial of guilt

An offender sought orders of certiorari and mandamus to quash a decision by the Secretary of State and the Parole Board to refuse to grant him parole and to require them to reconsider their decision. The decision had as its basis the offender's continued denial of the offence of which he was convicted, which the Board interpreted as a failure to address his offending. Held, the authorities should avoid attaching too much weight to a refusal by such a prisoner to admit his guilt. There might be many reasons behind such a refusal, including a genuinely wrongful conviction, an unwillingness to accept past untruths or a genuine belief that the necessary intent had been absent. Each case depended on its own circumstances and there were no universally applicable rules. Accordingly, the orders of certiorari and mandamus would be granted.

R v Secretary of State for the Home Department and the Governor of Frankland Prison, ex p Zulfikar; R v Secretary of State for the Home Department and the Parole Board, ex p Zulfikar (1995) Times, 26 July (Queen's Bench Division: Stuart-Smith LJ and Butterfield J).

2402 Prisoner—high escape-risk prisoner—closed visits regime—power of Secretary of State

It has been held that the Home Secretary has power to impose a closed visits regime, whereby physical contact between exceptional escape-risk prisoners and their visitors is impossible. The test to be applied is whether there is a self-evident and pressing need for closed visits. The Prison Act 1952, s 47(1) confers on the Home Secretary a power to regulate and manage prisons and control persons detained therein. This necessarily confers a power to regulate the circumstances of visits to prisoners, so as to minimise or prevent the introduction of contraband. The reasonableness of such regulations depends on all the circumstances, including the effectiveness of the scrutiny procedures, the category and escape risk of the prisoner concerned, and the need to protect his absolute right to communicate confidentially with his legal advisers. The introduction of a closed visits regime is reasonable if it is necessary in the interests of security and the prisoner's access to confidential advice is not inhibited. Likewise, the need to maintain security might outweigh the disadvantages that closed family visits may cause to a prisoner and his family.

R v Secretary of State for the Home Department, ex p O'Dhuibhir; R v Same, ex p O'Brien (1995) Times, 26 October (Queen's Bench Division: Rose LJ and Wright J).

2403 Prisoner—segregation—legality of segregation

See *Hill v The Queen*, para 2836.

2404 Prisoners (Return to Custody) Act 1995

The Prisoners (Return to Custody) Act 1995 makes new provision for the punishment and return to lawful custody of persons unlawfully at large. The Act received the royal assent on 28 June 1995 and came into force on 5 September 1995: SI 1995/2021.

Section 1 introduces and defines the circumstances in which a person is guilty of the new offence of remaining at large after temporary release. Section 2 amends the Police and Criminal Evidence Act 1984, s 17 and the Children and Young Persons Act 1969, s 32, conferring powers of entry to arrest persons unlawfully at large. Section 3 makes provision for short title, commencement and extent.

2405 Prisoner—temporary release—rules for temporary release—changes to rules

On his admission to prison, the applicant was issued with a notice setting out the then existing criteria for eligibility for home leave. He also signed an inmate compact which referred to home leave. The eligibility of the applicant to apply for home leave was adversely affected by changes to the eligibility rules subsequently introduced by the Home Secretary. The applicant commenced proceedings for judicial review of the decision to change the rules on the ground that the changes ought to have been implemented in a manner which protected his established rights. *Held*, it was common ground that the compact gave the applicant no rights enforceable under private law, and that the concept of legitimate expectation in public law normally applied to alleged defects in procedure. In the present case, there was no evidence that the Home Secretary, in making his decision to change the rules, had failed to have regard to the applicant's expectation in relation to home leave. In addition, it could not be argued that the applicant had a legitimate expectation of obtaining a substantive benefit. The most that a convicted prisoner could legitimately expect was to have his application for home leave decided by reference to the criteria current at the time of his application. No representation had been made to prisoners that the policy for home leave was invariable. The rules had been changed in accordance with the powers given to the Home Secretary by Parliament, and he was bound to reconsider his policy in the light of the criteria set out in the amended rule. Accordingly, the application for judicial review would be dismissed.

R v Secretary of State for the Home Department, ex p Briggs (1995) Independent, 26 September (Queen's Bench Division: Kennedy LJ and McCullough J).

2406 Release on licence—life sentence—discretionary life prisoner—recall to prison

The Criminal Justice Act 1991, s 39(1) provides that, if recommended to do so by the parole board in the case of a long-term or life prisoner who has been released on licence, the Secretary of State may revoke his licence and recall him to prison.

The applicant was convicted of buggery and indecent assault involving schoolboys and sentenced to life imprisonment. Having served 18 years of the sentence, he was released on licence. A year later, when it became known that the applicant was associating with vulnerable young men, the Home Secretary recommended his recall to prison, and the parole board confirmed the decision. On the applicant's subsequent application for release, the parole board's discretionary life panel, which was aware of the confirmation of the applicant's recall, decided that there was a high risk that the applicant would commit further sexual offences and that it was necessary to protect the public. The panel therefore refused to release the applicant. On the application for judicial review of the decision, *held*, the parole board panel's decision was not affected by the fact that the parole board had confirmed the applicant's recall. A parole board's recommendation for recall was not a bar to a subsequent hearing of the merits of an application by a parole board panel, as the panel conducting the hearing was bound to be aware that there must have been a recommendation either before recall or sanctioning the recall. Moreover, the 1991 Act, s 39 did not lay down any criteria for recall, and the test adopted by the parole board panel, namely whether it was necessary for the protection of the public that a prisoner be confined, was the correct test to apply. Here, there was ample material on which the panel could have concluded that the applicant's recall was justified and, accordingly, the application would be dismissed.

R v Parole Board, ex p Watson (1995) Independent, 22 November (Queen's Bench Division: Popplewell J).

This decision has been affirmed: (1996) Times, 11 March, CA.

2407   Release on licence—life sentence—discretionary life prisoner—time for referral of cases to Parole Board

The applicants, members of a terrorist organisation, were sentenced to life imprisonment for attempted murder and conspiracy to cause explosions. They were notified that their tariff period was 20 years, on the expiration of which the Parole Board would decide whether a further period should be served if there was a risk to the public. The Home Secretary refused the applicants' request to refer the cases to the board so that they would be heard immediately on the expiration of the tariff period. On their applications for judicial review of the Home Secretary's decision, *held*, the European Court of Human Rights had held that prisoners had the right to be released if there was no longer a risk to the public, and prisoners were entitled under the European Convention on Human Rights, art 5(4) to a judicial determination of the question of risk. The Home Secretary's policy under the Criminal Justice Act 1991, s 34 of not referring cases until after the expiration of the tariff period unless there was a compelling reason was unreasonable and unlawful. The implementation of the policy meant that prisoners who were judged no longer dangerous were required to serve sentences approximately six months longer than they should. The policy flouted the principles of common law and the European Convention in that the common law required a discretionary life prisoner to be released after completion of the tariff period unless he continued to be dangerous and art 5(4) required a speedy review of the lawfulness of the detention. Where it was clear that the statutory provision which created the exercise of executive discretion was passed in order to bring domestic law in line with the convention, the court had to take account of the convention when considering the lawfulness of the exercise of the discretion. Accordingly, the Home Secretary should have referred the applicants' cases to the board at such times as would have ensured that their cases were heard immediately on the expiration of the tariff period.

R v Secretary of State for the Home Department, ex p Norney (1995) Independent, 4 October, Times, 6 October (Queen's Bench Division: Dyson J).

2408   Release on licence—life sentence—mandatory life prisoner—tariff—Home Secretary's discretion—judicial review

The applicant was convicted of murdering his parents and sentenced to two mandatory life sentences. In accordance with his scheme for fixing the penal element of mandatory life sentences, the Home Secretary invited the judiciary to advise him of the period that should be served for the purposes of retribution and deterrence (the 'tariff' period). The judiciary recommended that 15 years was an appropriate period but the Home Secretary decided not to adopt their view. He concluded that 15 years would have been appropriate for a single murder but that, since this was a premeditated double murder, a longer period of 20 years was appropriate. At the applicant's request the succeeding Home Secretary later reconsidered the matter and accepted that the murders were not premeditated and were part of a single incident. However, he maintained that the 20-year period fixed by his predecessor was appropriate. The applicant applied for a judicial review of the Home Secretary's decision, contending that his decision was irrational and unfair, and that it was not open to him to fix a longer tariff period unless significant new information of an adverse character had emerged. The application was allowed and the Home Secretary appealed. *Held*, the Criminal Justice Act 1991, s 35 and the Home Secretary's stated policy for the sentencing regime relating to mandatory life prisoners conferred a wide discretion on the minister to fix the tariff period for a life prisoner's sentence. In reviewing the tariff period, the current Home Secretary was entitled to exercise his discretion and take a more serious view of the case than his predecessor had. Consequently, his decision to fix the tariff period at the same level as his predecessor, despite his concession that aggravating factors initially relied upon were absent, was neither irrational nor unfair. Accordingly, the appeal would be allowed.

R v Secretary of State for the Home Department, ex p Pierson [1996] 1 All ER 837 (Court of Appeal: Sir Thomas Bingham MR, Neill and Hirst LJJ). Decision of Turner J (1995) Times, 14 November, reversed.

2409   Young offenders—young offender institutions—rules

The Young Offender Institution (Amendment) Rules 1995, SI 1995/984 (in force on 25 April 1995), amend the 1988 Rules, SI 1988/1422, in relation to the temporary release of inmates, the powers of governors in respect of disciplinary offences committed by inmates, and disciplinary punishments of adult female inmates.

The Young Offender Institution (Amendment) (No 2) Rules 1995, SI 1995/1599 (in force on 17 July 1995), amend the 1988 Rules, SI 1988/1422. Changes are made to the rules relating to privileges for inmates and the rules relating to inmates' clothing.

PUBLIC HEALTH

Halsbury's Laws of England (4th edn) Vol 38, paras 1–700

2410   Air pollution

See ENVIRONMENT.

2411   Building regulations—approved inspectors and public bodies

The Building (Approved Inspectors etc) (Amendment) Regulations 1995, SI 1995/1387 (in force on 1 July 1995), amend the 1985 Regulations, SI 1985/1066, so as to (1) make provision relating to the withdrawal of the approval of an approved inspector; (2) amend certain time limits; (3) allow the supervision of work involving the underpinning of a building in which an approved inspector has a professional or financial interest; (4) impose a duty regarding the calculation and notification of energy ratings; (5) make provision relating to the issue of notices where there is a contravention of the building regulations; and (6) amend the requirements in the final certificate concerning buildings or extensions over a sewer and consultation with the fire authority.

2412   Building regulations—building works—disputes between owners—settlement of disputes

A dispute arose as to whether building works carried out on certain land in London had caused damage to a building on adjoining land. A surveyor appointed to determine the issue identified the works as the cause of the damage. On appeal against that decision, under the London Building Acts (Amendment) Act 1939, s 55(n)(i), a preliminary issue arose as to whether the court was entitled to receive additional evidence which had not been before the surveyor. *Held*, under s 55(n)(i), the court had jurisdiction to rescind or modify an award in such manner as it thought fit. For that purpose, it might receive evidence, of fact or opinion, relevant to an issue raised by the appeal, including evidence which had not, or could not have, been available to the surveyor when he made his award. The award was not an arbitration award but was in the nature of an expert determination. If an appeal against the award was made, the award might be completely reopened. The court had wide powers to alter an award and, accordingly, must have power to substitute its own finding or conclusion for that made by the surveyor. It had to decide itself what award to make, taking into account all facts established by admissible evidence.

Chartered Society of Physiotherapy v Simmonds Church Smiles [1995] 1 EGLR 155 (Official Referees' Court: Judge Humphrey Lloyd QC).

2413   Building regulations—building works—material change of use and unauthorised building work

The Building Regulations (Amendment) Regulations 1995, SI 1995/1356 (in force on 1 July 1995), further amend SI 1991/2768, so as to amend the definition of material change of use and the requirements relating to it, and to amend the requirements relating to the regularisation of unauthorised building works.

2414   Environment Act 1995

See para 1289.

2415   Offensive trades or businesses—establishment and carrying on—repeal of provisions

The Repeal of Offensive Trades or Businesses Provisions Order 1995, SI 1995/2054 (in force on 1 September 1995), repeals the Public Health Act 1936, ss 107, 108, which made provision as to the establishment and carrying on of offensive trades or businesses carried on within local authorities' districts.

2416   Ships and aircraft—Isle of Man

The Public Health (Ships and Aircraft) (Isle of Man) (Revocation) Order 1995, SI 1995/267 (in force on 1 March 1995), revokes the 1982 Orders, SI 1982/1671 and 1672, which extended the 1979 Regulations, SI 1979/1434 and 1435, to the Isle of Man. They have been superseded by regulations made under the Public Health Act 1990 (an Act of Tynwald).

2417   Sports grounds—safety—designated grounds

The Safety of Sports Grounds (Designation) Order 1995, SI 1995/1990 (in force on 25 August 1995) designates a particular sports ground as one requiring a safety certificate under the Safety of Sports Grounds Act 1975. SI 1985/1064 and SI 1986/1296 are varied by omitting entries for certain sports grounds which no longer provide accommodation for more than 10,000 spectators.

2418   Waste—unwanted surplus substance—ash and building rubble

Scotland
The Control of Pollution Act 1974, s 30(1) provides that waste includes any substance which constitutes a scrap material or an effluent or other unwanted surplus substance arising from the application of any process, and any substance or article which requires to be disposed of as being broken, worn out, contaminated or otherwise spoiled.

A waste disposal authority served a notice on the appellant company requiring it to remove controlled waste from a site which it occupied. The waste consisted of ash and building rubble which the appellant had bought from other companies. The appellant unsuccessfully appealed against the notice, and on further appeal argued that the ash and building rubble did not fall within the definition of waste under the 1974 Act, s 30(1), as it was not 'unwanted' because it was a valuable resource for which the appellant and its customers were willing to pay. *Held*, the ash and building rubble was 'waste' in the hands of the companies which had sold them to the appellant, as it was 'unwanted' at that stage because it was surplus substances arising from a process applied by those companies. Until a further physical process was applied so as to change the character of the ash and building rubble, it was irrelevant that a third party wished to buy it. As such, although the ash and building rubble was not 'unwanted' to the extent that the appellant intended to sell it, it constituted waste in the context of the 1974 Act. Accordingly, the appeal would be dismissed.

H L Friel & Son Ltd v Inverclyde District Council 1995 SLT 1310 (Inner House).

RACE RELATIONS

See BRITISH NATIONALITY, IMMIGRATION AND RACE RELATIONS.

RAILWAYS, INLAND WATERWAYS AND PIPE-LINES

Halsbury's Laws of England (4th edn) Vol 38, paras 701–1102

2419 Articles

Human Error? Early Railways and the Law, Ronald Pearsall: 159 JP Jo 98

2420 Pipe-lines—inquiries—procedure

The Pipe-lines (Inquiries Procedure) Rules 1995, SI 1995/1239 (in force on 1 June 1995), prescribe the new procedure to be followed at public inquiries in connection with applications in England and Wales under the Pipe-lines Act 1962, Sch 1, Pt I, paras 4(1), 6A, and Sch 2, Pt I, para 4(1). The rules (1) make provision for pre-inquiry meetings to be held at the request of either the Secretary of State or the inspector, (2) provide for the appointment by the Secretary of State of a person to sit with an inspector at an inquiry and to advise the inspector on specified matters, (3) introduce procedures for serving of statements of case and proofs of evidence, including a timetable under which the statements and proofs of evidence must be served, (4) contain provision for summaries of proofs of evidence to be used, and (5) prescribe the procedure to be followed where a decision by the Secretary of State has been quashed in proceedings before any court. The new procedure is similar to that provided by the Electricity Generating Station and Overhead Lines (Inquiry Procedure) Rules 1990, SI 1990/528, and is intended to facilitate inquiries under the Electricity Act 1990, s 62 being held jointly with those under the Pipe-lines Act 1962 in circumstances where the Secretary of State considers that the matters should be heard together. SI 1967/1769 is consequently revoked, but continues to apply to any inquiry which commenced before these rules came into force.

2421 Railways—health and safety at work—reporting of accidents

See para 1509.

2422 Railways—pensions—Railways Pension Scheme

The Railway Pensions (Substitution and Miscellaneous Provisions) Order 1995, SI 1995/430 (in force on 12 March 1995), (1) terminates, from 13 April 1995, the Secretary of State's liability to make payments under the Transport Act 1980, s 52(1) in respect of certain sections of the Railways Pension Scheme, and provides for payments to be made instead; (2) specifies the capital value of the unfunded obligations in respect of each of those sections as at 13 April 1995; (3) requires the Secretary of State to make payments in respect of the capital values of the unfunded obligations and provides for the accrual and payment of interest on the outstanding balances of those capital values; (4) provides for the liability of the Secretary of State to make payments under the scheme to be discharged in the event of the winding up of both sections; and (5) provides for the amendment of the Railway Pensions (Substitution) Order 1994, SI 1994/2388.

2423 Railways—provision of railway services—functions of franchising director— setting of minimum service levels after privatisation

The Railways Act 1993 established a scheme for the transfer of operations of rail passenger services into private ownership. The franchising director, appointed under the Act, was given the statutory duty to fix the minimum service levels for rail passenger services after privatisation. To assist him in fixing those levels, the Secretary of State for Transport issued an instruction which, stated that they were to be 'based on' the service levels provided by British Rail immediately before privatisation. In two applications for judicial review, the applicants challenged the director's decisions to fix the minimum service levels for various franchises at levels below those previously provided by British Rail. At first instance, the applications were refused on the ground that the director had not acted unlawfully in permitting a major reduction in services after privatisation. On appeal, *held*, the guidance document provided by the Secretary of State defined and circumscribed the statutory duty of the franchising director. 'Based on' was not a term of art, nor was it an exact term. It gave the director some flexibility to make changes to the minimum service levels. However, there was a limit to the changes that the director could make without ceasing to comply with Secretary of State's instructions and acting unlawfully. The document could not be read as a warrant for anything more than a marginal change. Accordingly, where there was a finding that the minimum service levels set by the director were significantly lower than those maintained before privatisation, it was apparent that the director had not correctly understood or had failed to comply with the Secretary of State's instructions. To that extent, the appeal would prima facie be allowed. However, the application for certiorari and mandamus in respect of the first case would be refused, on the ground that there had been an undue delay in making the initial application for judicial review.

R v Director of Passenger Rail Franchising, ex p Save Our Railways (1995) Times, 18 December (Court of Appeal: Sir Thomas Bingham MR, Waite and Otton JJ).

2424 Railways—provision of railway services—non-franchised passenger services—proposals to discontinue

Scotland

Notice of a proposal to discontinue all the non-franchised railway passenger services on any line or from any station must be given within the specified period before the services are to cease: Railways Act 1993, s 37(1). In determining whether all the services on a line or from any station are such services, any services which are provided otherwise than as regular scheduled services for that line are to be left out of account: s 37(2)(c).

The defendants proposed to discontinue certain railway passenger services that were the sole users of three short sections of railway line in Scotland. They did not give notice of their proposals under s 37 as they intended to replace the discontinued services with substitute services, so that, they contended, the closure procedure under s 37 did not come into effect. The substitute services would run late at night, once a day and would be of a local nature. In judicial review proceedings, it fell to be determined whether the substitute services would be 'railway passenger services' within the meaning of s 37 and so would have the effect of preventing the closure procedure from coming into operation. *Held*, the defendants proposed to provide three new services on the same three sections of line in order to avoid the necessity of initiating the closure procedure. The services were unlikely to be of benefit to the travelling public. If it was proposed to discontinue all the passenger services on any line or from any station, the public had a right to know. It could not have been intended that the statutory closure procedure could be defeated by the provision of a service which was admitted to be of no benefit to the travelling public. The word 'for' in s 37(2)(c) directed attention to the purpose for which the service was provided. Although s 82(1) gave a very wide definition of 'services', in the context of s 37(2)(c) there had to be a service 'for' the line. A service whose sole purpose was to prevent the operation of the closure procedure was not such a service. The defendants were acting in bad faith because the sole purpose of their actions was to defeat the legitimate interests of the public who wished to see the services maintained. The defendants had acted outside their powers and were in breach of the statutory procedure.

Highland Regional Council v British Railways Board (1995) Times, 6 November (Inner House).

2425 Transport and works—assessment of environmental effects

The Transport and Works (Assessment of Environmental Effects) Regulations 1995, SI 1995/1541 (in force on 1 August 1995), amend the Transport and Works Act 1992, s 14, by requiring the Secretary of State (1) to confirm that he took into consideration environmental statements relating to projects for the construction or operation of railways, tramways and other guided transport systems, inland waterways and works interfering with rights of navigation and any opinions expressed relating to them before making or refusing orders authorising such projects, and (2) to send copies of the relevant notice of determination to those who made objections and representations, where this is not already required by the 1992 Act.

RATING AND THE COUNCIL TAX

Halsbury's Laws of England (4th edn) Vol 39, paras 1–300

2426 Articles

Committal for Non-Payment of Local Taxes, Paul Russell: 159 JP Jo 228
Poll Tax Committals and the European Court, Rona Epstein and Ian Wise (on *Benham v United Kingdom* (1995) Independent, 8 February (para 1588)): 139 SJ 588

Poll Tax Committals—The Marshalsea Revisited? Ian Wise and Rona Epstein: 159 JP Jo 453
Rating Revaluation: Is the Outcome Appealing? Philip Redman: 139 SJ 194

2427 Community charge—administration and enforcement

See para 2436.

2428 Community charge—enforcement—administration order

A county court may make an order providing for the administration of the estate of a debtor
who is unable to pay the amount of a judgment obtained against him and who alleges that his
whole indebtedness amounts to a sum not exceeding the county court limit, inclusive of the
debt for which the judgment was obtained: County Courts Act 1984, s 112.

The plaintiff council, which had obtained liability orders against the defendants in respect of
unpaid community charge, objected to the inclusion of the charges in administration orders
made in favour of the defendants under s 112. The orders were amended. The defendants
appealed against the amendment, contending that the unpaid charges constituted a debt for the
purpose of s 112. *Held*, the remedy of an action in debt was available for a wide range of
liquidated monetary liabilities and served for the recovery of statutory penalties. The defendants'
liability properly fell within the term debt. The words 'debt' and 'indebtedness' in s 112 were
unqualified and, on their ordinary meaning, included the liability for the unpaid community
charges. There was nothing in Pt VI (ss 112–117) to show that a narrower meaning was
intended. If some classes of debts were to be excluded from the scheme of Pt VI, which was
intended to be comprehensive, it was difficult to see how the orders would work in practice.
Under the Community Charge (Administration and Enforcement) Regulations 1989, SI
1989/438, the liability orders were deemed to be a debt for the purposes of a creditor's petition
for a bankruptcy order or a winding up order. That did not affect the status of the liability. The
unpaid community charge was a debt for the purposes of the 1984 Act, Pt VI and part of the
defendants' indebtedness within s 112, and had to be included in the administration orders.
Accordingly, the appeal would be allowed.

Preston Borough Council v Riley [1995] RA 227 (Court of Appeal: Russell and Hobhouse LJJ
and Sir Roger Parker).

2429 Community charge—enforcement—committal to prison—lawfulness of detention

See *Benham v United Kingdom*, para 1588.

2430 Community charge—enforcement—committal to prison—power to commit

The Community Charges (Administration and Enforcement) Regulations 1989, SI 1989/438,
permit justices to issue a warrant of commitment for failure to pay the community charge or to
postpone doing so on conditions. Before making an order the court must make inquiries into
the debtor's means and into whether the failure to pay was due to wilful refusal or neglect. An
order can only be made if the failure was due to such refusal or neglect.

The applicant was committed to prison by justices for breach of conditions relating to non-
payment of the community charge. He applied for judicial review of their decision to commit
him. *Held*, the justices had erred in reaching their decision that the applicant was guilty of
culpable neglect to pay the community charge by considering the evidence before them on the
balance of probabilities. Before issuing a warrant of commitment or fixing a term of imprisonment
and postponing the issue of the warrant, justices had to be sure, following a full means inquiry,
that the debtor's failure to pay had been due to his wilful refusal or culpable neglect. Alternatively,
if the appropriate standard of proof was a civil standard then only the highest standard of
probability was commensurate with the exercise of the power. The justices had applied neither
standard. They had also failed to conduct a proper means inquiry since, even on the lowest
standard of proof applied by the justices, the data produced by their inquiries was not capable,
of itself, of supporting a finding of culpable neglect. Accordingly, the application would be
allowed and the decision quashed.

R v South Tyneside Justices, ex p Martin (1995) Independent, 20 September (Queen's Bench
Division: Sedley J).

2431 Community charge—enforcement—councillors' failure to pay charges—
restrictions at council meetings—effect of agreements to pay charges

The Community Charges (Administration and Enforcement) Regulations 1989, SI 1989/438,
reg 17(3) provides that a charging authority and a chargeable person may agree that the estimated

amount of community charge liability which is required to be paid should be paid in such manner as is provided by the agreement.

Three councillors, who had community charge arrears, attended a council meeting held to determine local taxation. Under the Local Government Finance Act 1992, s 106(2), a councillor who left his community charges unpaid for at least two months and who was present at a council meeting dealing with community charges had to, as soon as practicable after the meeting began, disclose that fact and should not vote on any question with respect to that matter. The councillors were charged with offences of failing to disclose arrears and of voting contrary to s 106(2). The charges were dismissed by a magistrate because the prosecution was not able to adduce evidence that the councillors had voted at the meeting as well as having failed to disclose their arrears. On the prosecution's appeal by way of case stated, the councillors argued that they were not in breach of s 106(2) in any event because they had made agreements in relation to the outstanding payments with the local authority under the 1989 Regulations, reg 17(3). *Held*, (1) s 106 was intended to create two offences. The two mischiefs targeted were speaking and voting. If the only mischief was voting then the failure to disclose element would have no purpose. (2) The argument in relation to the agreements made with the authority was rejected. The words 'the amount which is required to be paid' in reg 17(3) looked to the future and referred to something which was to be paid, not to something which should have been paid. Accordingly, the appeal would be allowed.

DPP v Burton (1995) Times, 8 June (Queen's Bench Division: McCowan LJ and Mitchell J).

2432   Community charge—enforcement—power to remit debt after term of imprisonment fixed or warrant of committal issued

The Community Charges (Administration and Enforcement) Regulations 1989, SI 1989/438, reg 41(3) provides that, on an application by a charging authority under s 41, if the court is of the opinion that a debtor's failure to pay the community charge was due to his wilful refusal or culpable neglect it may if it thinks fit issue a warrant of commitment against the debtor, or fix a term of imprisonment and postpone the issue of the warrant until such time and on such conditions as the court thinks just. Where an application under reg 41 is made, and after the necessary inquiries have been made no warrant is issued or term of imprisonment fixed, the court may remit all or part of the appropriate amount mentioned in the liability order to which the application related: reg 42(2).

The defendant was found guilty of culpable neglect in failing to pay his community charge. The justices committed him to a term of 28 days' imprisonment which was postponed on the condition that he paid the debt at a weekly rate. Some months later the defendant came before the justices again because of his failure to pay. The justices decided, after considering the defendant's changed circumstances, to remit part of the debt and they fixed a term of imprisonment postponed on condition that he paid the remainder of the debt. On the local authority's appeal against the justices' decision, *held*, the only power of remission open to the justices was that contained in the 1989 Regulations, reg 42(2), which expressly provided that no term of imprisonment must have been fixed or warrant issued. In the present case, a term of imprisonment had been fixed at the first hearing and the power to remit was not available. It followed that the power to remit could not be exercised after the powers in reg 41(3) had been exercised even if, after the term had been postponed, there was a change in circumstances rendering remission appropriate. Accordingly, the appeal would be allowed.

Harrogate Borough Council v Barker (1995) 159 JP 809 (Queen's Bench Division: Harrison J).

2433   Community charge—enforcement—suspended committal order—circumstances in which suspended committal order may be made

A liability order was made against the applicant in respect of her non-payment of the community charge. On the local authority's application for a committal order, justices decided that the applicant's failure to pay the charge was due to her culpable neglect. They therefore issued a warrant for her committal, suspended on the terms that she was to pay a weekly sum to the local authority in respect of the sum owed. On her application for judicial review, the applicant argued that the justices had improperly exercised their committal powers under the Community Charges (Administration and Enforcement) Regulations 1989, SI 1989/438, reg 41(3)(a), (b) because all other methods of obtaining payment had not yet been exhausted. *Held*, justices had a discretion as to what order to make depending on the facts of each case. The 1989 Regulations, reg 41(3)(a), (b) did not, however, oblige them to exhaust all possibilities of recovering the money owed before they could make a suspended committal order, as different principles governed the proper exercise of discretion where a committal order was sought under the regulations. Suspended committal orders were intended to have a coercive effect, whereas orders for immediate committal were intended to have a punitive effect. There was no difference in principle between the exercise of the power to make a suspended committal order under the 1989 Regulations and any other power to do so to recover a civil debt. Accordingly, the application would be refused.

R v Preston Justices, ex p McCosh (1995) Times, 30 January (Queen's Bench Division: Turner J).

2434 Community charge—valuation and community charge tribunals

See para 2448.

2435 Community charge benefit

See SOCIAL SECURITY AND SOCIAL SERVICES.

2436 Council tax—administration and enforcement

The Community Charges (Administration and Enforcement) (Amendment) Regulations 1995, SI 1995/21 (in force on 1 April 1995), further amend the 1989 Regulations, SI 1989/438, so as to (1) delete the reference to a constituent council of a police authority because, by virtue of the constitution of police authorities as corporate bodies under the Police and Magistrates' Courts Act 1994, no local authority will obtain information in its capacity as such a council, and because no charging authority has had this capacity in relation to a police authority; and (2) provide that, for the purpose of calculating the sum to be deducted under an attachment of earnings order, the employer is to disregard any deduction from the debtor's earnings made by reason of the repayment by the debtor of a loan made to him by the employer.

The Council Tax (Administration and Enforcement) (Amendment) Regulations 1995, SI 1995/22 (in force in part on 1 February 1995 and in part on 1 April 1995), further amend the 1992 Regulations, SI 1992/613, so as to (1) amend the provision relating to the use of information by a billing authority because, by virtue of the constitution of police authorities as corporate bodies under the Police and Magistrates' Courts Act 1994, no local authority will obtain information in its capacity as a constituent council of a police authority, and because no billing authority has had this capacity in relation to a police authority; (2) provide that, for the purpose of calculating the sum to be deducted under an attachment of earnings order, the employer is to disregard any deduction from the debtor's earnings made by reason of the repayment by the debtor of a loan made to him by the employer; (3) provide that, where the calculation of instalments would produce an instalment of less than £5, the demand notice may require the amount of the first instalment to be the sum of the amounts which would otherwise be the first and second instalments; and (4) provide that, where a billing authority revises its estimate of a person's council tax liability, it must, in adjusting the remaining instalments, take into account any amounts paid before the day on which the adjustment takes effect which were due to be paid after that day.

The Local Government Changes for England (Community Charge and Council Tax, Administration and Enforcement) Regulations 1995, SI 1995/247 (in force on 1 April 1995), make transitional and consequential modifications to the Community Charges (Administration and Enforcement) Regulations 1989, SI 1989/438, which provide for the administration and enforcement of community charges arising under the Local Government Finance Act 1988, and the Council Tax (Administration and Enforcement) Regulations 1992, SI 1992/613, which provide for the administration and enforcement of council tax under the Local Government Finance Act 1992.

2437 Council tax—assessment of dwellings—annexe considered as separate dwelling

It has been held that, when a valuation tribunal is assessing, for council tax purposes, whether an annexe or 'granny flat' is a self-contained unit used as a separate dwelling, the following are irrelevant considerations: (1) terms of planning consent and its restrictions on the form of use. Even if this were a relevant factor, it would be wholly wrong to treat it as the sole factor, as opposed to one of a number of facts to be considered; (2) the degree of community living between the annexe and the main dwelling. The purpose of annexes or granny flats is to furnish separate accommodation for an older generation affording mutual privacy and a certain degree of community. Although the actual degree of community living is significant it cannot assist in answering the question whether the annexe was constructed or adapted for use as a separate dwelling; (3) the practicability of selling the annexe on the open market. Saleability is a useful test in confirming that the premises are self-contained but a view that they cannot be sold separately cannot assist in deciding whether they are to be treated as a self-contained unit for council tax purposes. It is a point going towards valuation not the essential physical character of the premises.

Rodd v Ritchings; Gilbert v Childs; Batty v Burfoot; Batty v Merriman [1995] 2 EGLR 142 (Queen's Bench Division: Ognall J).

2438   Council tax benefit

See SOCIAL SECURITY AND SOCIAL SERVICES.

2439   Council tax—billing authorities—anticipation of precepts

The Billing Authorities (Anticipation of Precepts) (Amendment) Regulations 1995, SI 1995/235 (in force on 23 February 1995), amend the 1992 Regulations, SI 1992/3239, so as to provide that (1) amounts in respect of precepts not yet issued by local precepting authorities which are to be included by billing authorities in the calculation of their budget requirements under the Local Government Finance Act 1992, s 32, are to include any increase or decrease in the retail prices index, and (2) whether or not a local precept is anticipated in the calculations of the billing authority's budget requirements, the billing authority is to pay the amount of the precept, if it is issued before 1 March of the year in which the calculations are made, or before the calculations are completed, and is to pay the lesser of that amount and the amount which could have been anticipated, if the precept is issued on or after this date or after completion of the calculations.

2440   Council tax—billing authorities—calculation of budget requirement—amount of a precept issued by a new parish council

The Local Government Finance (Miscellaneous Provisions) (England) Order 1995, SI 1995/161 (in force on 15 February 1995), makes transitional provisions in relation to the Local Government Finance Act 1992, ss 32, 41, 54 (providing for the calculation of budget requirements by billing authorities, the issue of precepts by local precepting authorities and the power for the Secretary of State to designate authorities). The order enables there to be taken into account in the calculation of a billing authority's budget requirement for the purposes of ss 32(2) and 54(1) of the 1992 Act, instead of the amount of a precept issued by a new parish council or the chairman of the parish meeting, or an amount anticipated in respect of that precept, an amount specified in an order made under the Local Government Act 1972, s 9 (which makes provision for a new parish council to be established for a parish by an order made by the district council of the area in which the parish is situated). The order also extends the period for a new parish council to issue its precept to October in the financial year in which the parish is created.

2441   Council tax—calculation of the council tax base by billing authorities and precepting authorities—Wales

The Local Authorities (Calculation of Council Tax Base) (Wales) Regulations 1995, SI 1995/2561 (in force on 10 November 1995), which apply to Wales in the financial years beginning on or after 1 April 1996, prescribe the rules for the calculation of the council tax base, which is an amount required by the Local Government Finance Act 1992 to be used in the calculation of the council tax by billing authorities and major precepting authorities and in the calculation of the amount of a precept payable by each billing authority to a major precepting authority. The regulations (1) provide for the calculation of the amount of a billing authority's council tax base for the purposes of the calculation of its council tax, (2) provide for the calculation of a billing authority's council tax base for a part of its area for the purposes of the calculation of its council tax similarly to the way in which the council tax base is to be calculated for the whole of a billing authority's area under head (1) above, (3) provide for the calculation of the council tax base of the area or part of the area of a billing authority for the purposes of the calculation of a major precepting authority's council tax and the amount payable by a billing authority to a major precepting authority, based on the rules as applied in heads (1) and (2) above, (4) prescribe a period for the notification by a billing authority of the council tax base of its area or a part of its area to a major precepting authority, (5) provide for how the council tax base is to be determined where a billing authority fails to notify its calculation to a major precepting authority within the period prescribed in head (4) above, and (6) amend the Local

Authorities (Calculation of Council Tax Base) Regulations 1992, SI 1992/612, so as to disapply them to calculations made by the new Welsh local authorities and Welsh police authorities.

2442 Council tax—demand notices

The Local Government Changes for England (Council Tax and Non-Domestic Rating, Demand Notices) Regulations 1995, SI 1995/23 (in force on 31 January 1995), make transitional and consequential amendments to SI 1993/191, which provides for the content of council tax demand notices and rate demand notices issued by billing authorities in England. The 1995 Regulations apply the 1993 Regulations to (a) authorities which have the functions of billing authorities, or major precepting authorities, in advance of the date for reorganisation ordered by the Secretary of State so as to give effect to recommendations for change made by the Local Government Commission ('a reorganisation order'), (b) valuation lists, or alterations to the lists, supplied under the 1993 Regulations in advance of the date for reorganisation. The 1995 Regulations also (i) disapply or amend certain requirements whereby information must be provided in the first year of reorganisation, (ii) amend references to boundary changes to include changes under reorganisation orders, and (iii) require new authorities or those to which additional functions are transferred under a reorganisation order, to provide a general explanation of the services provided before and after reorganisation.

The Council Tax (Demand Notices) (Wales) (Amendment) Regulations 1995, SI 1995/160 (in force on 16 February 1995), amend the 1993 Regulations, SI 1993/255, so as to reflect the establishment of new police authorities under the Police Act 1964, s 3 (as substituted by the Police and Magistrates' Courts Act 1994, s 2). The regulations make transitional amendments to the provisions in Sch 2, Pt I to the 1993 Regulations relating to council tax demand notices served by billing authorities for the financial year 1995/96 to reflect the fact that some authorities will cease to have police functions, and that new police authorities will not be able to supply all the information required by that Part.

2443 Council tax—discount disregards and exempt dwellings

The Council Tax (Discount Disregards and Exempt Dwellings) (Amendment) Order 1995, SI 1995/619 (in force in part on 1 April 1995 and in part on 13 April 1995), amends SI 1992/548, and further amends SI 1992/558, so as to (1) amend the conditions in SI 1992/548, to which a person who is severely mentally impaired or who is a student is subject for the purposes of determining whether that person is to be disregarded when establishing whether the amount of council tax payable in respect of a dwelling is to be subject to a discount; and (2) amend Class N in SI 1992/558 in relation to a person who is the spouse of a student and who is not a British citizen, and add Classes S, T and U in relation to dwellings occupied only by persons aged under 18 years, unoccupied annexes and dwellings occupied only by the severely mentally impaired, respectively.

2444 Council tax—liability for owners—additional provisions for discount disregards

The Council Tax (Liability for Owners and Additional Provisions for Discount Disregards) (Amendment) Regulations 1995, SI 1995/620 (in force on 1 April 1995), further amend SI 1992/551 and 552, so as to (1) amend Class C (house in multiple occupation) in SI 1992/551, and provide that the Diocesan Board of Finance is liable where a dwelling is owned by a minister of the Church of England only if the minister is in receipt of a stipend; and (2) add an additional class to SI 1992/552 of students' spouses or dependants who are from overseas and who fulfil specified conditions.

2445 Council tax—limitation—maximum amounts

The Council Tax Limitation (England) (Maximum Amounts) Order 1995, SI 1995/1545 (in force on 16 June 1995), sets maximum limits for the budget requirements for the financial year beginning in 1995 for certain named councils.

2446 Council tax—setting of amount—calculations to be made by billing authority

The Local Authorities (Alteration of Requisite Calculations and Funds) Regulations 1995, SI 1995/234 (in force on 3 February 1995), amend the Local Government Finance Act 1992, ss 32, 43, which set out how a billing authority and a major precepting authority are to calculate their budget requirements for a financial year. The regulations amend s 32 by requiring billing authorities not to take into account certain sums which they estimate will be payable into their general funds in respect of certain special grants and police grants. In addition, s 43 is amended to require major precepting authorities not to take account of certain payments which they estimate will be made to them in respect of certain special grants and police grants. Consequential amendments are made to ss 33, 44.

2447   Council tax—transitional reduction scheme

The Council Tax (Transitional Reduction Scheme) (England) Regulations 1995, SI 1995/209 (in force on 28 February 1995), which have effect in relation to the financial year beginning on 1 April 1995, provide for the reduction in certain cases of the amount that a person is liable to pay to a billing authority in England by way of council tax. The regulations (1) provide that a person is eligible for a reduction for any day as regards which his liability relates to a dwelling which is on that day, and was on 31 March 1993, the sole or main residence of an individual; (2) provide that the amount of the reduction allowed will be an amount by which the reduction allowed in respect of the dwelling on 1 April 1993 under the Council Tax (Transitional Reduction Scheme) (England) Regulations 1993, SI 1993/175, exceeds a specified amount which varies according to the valuation band applicable to the dwelling in question on that date; (3) provide that, unless the Council Tax (Reductions for Disabilities) Regulations 1992, SI 1992/554, applied on 1 April 1993, the relevant valuation band is the one to which the dwelling was assigned in the billing authority's valuation list on that date, and provide that where those regulations applied, account is taken of the lower valuation band applicable for the purposes of those regulations; (4) provide that any discount provided for in the Local Government Finance Act 1992, s 11, is also to be taken into account in calculating the amount of the reduction allowed; (5) provide that where there is an entitlement to council tax benefit, the amount of the benefit is deducted from the amount an eligible person is liable to pay after calculation of relief under the regulations; (6) enable a billing authority to obtain information for the purpose of establishing whether or not the regulations apply to any person; and (7) provide for appeals in connection with the regulations to be considered by a review board of the billing authority rather than by a valuation tribunal. The 1992 Regulations are modified in relation to appeal procedure.

2448   Council tax—valuation lists—alteration of lists and appeals

The Local Government Changes for England (Community Charge and Council Tax, Valuation and Community Charge Tribunals and Alteration of Lists and Appeals) Regulations 1995, SI 1995/624 (in force on 1 April 1995), amend the Valuations and Community Charge Tribunal Regulations 1989, SI 1989/439, and the Council Tax (Alteration of Lists and Appeals) Regulations 1993, SI 1993/290, where recommendations for change are made pursuant to the Local Government Act 1992. The regulations provide: (1) for proposals and appeals affecting an authority which is abolished by a reorganisation order to be continued in relation to the successor authority for the area in which the relevant property is situated; (2) that where there is a proposal in relation to a property which, as a result of a reorganisation order, moves from the area of one authority to that of another, the relevant authority is the acquiring authority and the relevant listing officer and tribunal are those for that authority; (3) that where an appeal has been listed before the date for reorganisation, the relevant authority is the relinquishing authority and the relevant listing officer and tribunal are those for that authority; (4) that where such a proposal affects a year before reorganisation, both the acquiring and relinquishing authorities are relevant authorities, the listing officer is that for both authorities and the valuation tribunal is that for the acquiring authority.

2449   Council tax—valuation lists—dwelling—composite hereditament—maisonette over shop

The appellant occupied a maisonette above a shop, and also occupied the shop itself. He argued that the maisonette should not be included in the valuation list, as it was not self-contained. It was the case that the only access to the maisonette was through the shop, and the majority of the rooms in the maisonette were used in conjunction with the shop. A valuation tribunal decided that the test to be applied was whether or not the maisonette could be separately occupied. It concluded that it could be, and that it was therefore to be entered on the valuation list. On the appellant's appeal, *held*, a composite hereditament consisted of property which was used wholly for the purposes of living accommodation, and provided that at least one room in it was occupied or used exclusively as a dwelling, the dwelling was a composite hereditament. The value of a composite hereditament and the fact that it could not be occupied separately were irrelevant to whether or not it ought to be included in the valuation list. It was on the basis of the valuation of the room or rooms in a composite hereditament that the appropriate council tax band was arrived at, and at that stage it might be relevant to consider whether there was separate occupation or whether the room or rooms were used in conjunction with other premises. Here, although the valuation tribunal had erred in the test that it had adopted, on the facts, the property was a composite hereditament and was therefore properly included in the valuation list. Accordingly, the appeal would be allowed.

Williams v Bristol District Valuation Officer [1995] RA 189 (Queen's Bench Division: Collins J).

2450 Distress for rates

See DISTRESS.

2451 Housing benefit

See SOCIAL SECURITY.

2452 Non-domestic rating—chargeable amounts

The Non-Domestic Rating (Chargeable Amounts) (Amendment) Regulations 1995, SI 1995/961 (in force on 31 March 1995), have been made in consequence of a defect in the 1994 Regulations, SI 1994/3279, which are amended so that the rateable value shown in the central list for hereditaments for 1 April 1995 is reduced to reflect any changes to the class of hereditaments between 1 April 1994 and 1 April 1995.

The Non-Domestic Rating (Chargeable Amounts) (Amendment No 2) Regulations 1995, SI 1995/1678 (in force on 4 July 1995), further amend the 1994 Regulations, SI 1994/3279, so as to (1) extend the special provision for hereditaments which, before they became subject to rates, were exempt because of Crown exemption, to certain hereditaments of new police authorities established from 1 April 1995 by virtue of changes made by the Police and Magistrates' Courts Act 1994; (2) amend the conditions for which Pt IV of the 1994 Regulations makes provision for determining the chargeable amount, to include the case where the hereditament was in a local non-domestic rating list on 31 March 1995; (3) update statutory references; and (4) include in the calculation of the base liability in relation to splits and mergers for the year after the year in which the creation day falls, the assumption that the hereditament was occupied and that none of the mandatory or discretionary reliefs applied to it.

The Non-Domestic Rating (Chargeable Amounts) (Amendment No 3) Regulations 1995, SI 1995/3322 (in force on 20 December 1995), further amend the 1994 Regulations, SI 1994/3279, so as to limit the amount of increase in the annual change in rates bills as between the financial year beginning in 1995 and the financial year beginning in 1996.

2453 Non-domestic rating—collection and enforcement—liability of tenant after forfeiture of business tenancy

See *Kingston-upon-Thames Borough Council v Marlow*, para 1815.

2454 Non-domestic rating—collection, enforcement and discretionary relief

The Local Government Changes for England (Non-Domestic Rating, Collection and Enforcement and Discretionary Relief) Regulations 1995, SI 1995/212 (in force on 28 February 1995), modify SI 1989/1058, so as to provide that where an authority is to be abolished under a reorganisation order, its rights and liabilities which existed prior to the date for reorganisation become those of the successor authority in relation to the area in which the relevant property is situated. However, the rights and liabilities of a local authority which ceases to have functions in relation to a part of its area ('a relinquishing authority') under a reorganisation order remain its rights and liabilities. The regulations also apply the 1989 Regulations to authorities which, under the Local Government Changes for England (Finance) Regulations 1994, SI 1994/2825, have the functions of billing authorities in advance of the date for reorganisation set by a reorganisation order. In addition, the regulations modify SI 1989/1059, by providing that any decision or determination of a relinquishing authority under a reorganisation order in relation to a property which, as a result of such an order, is transferred to the area of another authority, is to have effect as if it were the decision or determination of the acquiring authority.

2455 Non-domestic rating—contributions

The Non-Domestic Rating Contributions (England) (Amendment) Regulations 1995, SI 1995/3181 (in force on 31 December 1995), further amend the 1992 Regulations, SI 1992/3082, with respect to the rules for 1996 for calculating the contributions which billing authorities are required to pay to the Secretary of State under the Local Government Finance Act 1988, Sch 8, Pt II. The regulations alter certain figures used in the calculation of contributions and provisional amounts and make provision, for the purposes of calculating provisional amounts, in relation to areas ceasing to be enterprise zones during the year.

The Non-Domestic Rating Contributions (Wales) (Amendment) Regulations 1995, SI 1995/3235 (in force on 31 December 1995), make various technical amendments to the 1992 Regulations, SI 1992/3238.

2456 Non-domestic rating—demand notices

The Council Tax and Non-Domestic Rating (Demand Notices) (England) Amendment Regulations 1995, SI 1995/121 (in force on 15 February 1995), modify and amend the 1993 Regulations, SI 1993/191, so as to take account of the establishment of new police authorities under the Police Act 1964, s 3 (as substituted by the Police and Magistrates' Courts Act 1994, s 2) and to take account of the revaluation of hereditaments for non-domestic rating in 1995. The regulations (1) make transitional provisions which modify the provisions relating to council tax demand notices served by billing authorities and to non-domestic rating demand notices for the financial year 1995–96 to reflect the fact that some authorities will cease to have police functions and that new police authorities will not be able to supply all the information required by the 1993 Regulations; (2) amend the 1993 Regulations to require a statement of the estimated amount of police grant payable under the 1964 Act, s 31 (as substituted by the 1994 Act, s 17) for the year to be included in the information statement supplied with a council tax or non-domestic rating demand notice; and (3) make amendments to the explanatory notes sent to ratepayers which take account of the revaluation in 1995 of hereditaments subject to non-domestic rating.

The Non-Domestic Rating (Demand Notices) (Wales) (Amendment) Regulations 1995, SI 1995/284 (in force on 2 March 1995), further amend the 1993 Regulations, so as to reflect the establishment of new police authorities under the Police Act 1964, s 3 (as substituted by the Police and Magistrates' Courts Act 1994, s 2), and to reflect the revaluation of hereditaments for non-domestic rating in 1995. The regulations (1) modify the provisions relating to non-domestic rating demand notices served by billing authorities for the financial year 1995–96 to reflect the fact that some authorities will cease to have police functions, and that new police authorities will not be able to supply all the information referred to in the 1993 Regulations, Sch 3, Pt I; (2) disapply the 1993 Regulations, reg 9 (other information required to be supplied) as regards new police authorities for 1995–96; and (3) make amendments to the explanatory notes for ratepayers, to reflect the revaluation in 1995 of hereditaments subject to non-domestic rating.

See also para 2442.

2457 Non-domestic rating—hereditaments—British Railways Board—rating of booking office

The Central Rating Lists Regulations 1989, SI 1989/2263, reg 2, Schedule, provide that hereditaments belonging to the British Railways Board must be registered in the central rating list unless they are excepted hereditaments. Included in the definition of excepted hereditaments are premises used wholly or mainly as office premises which are not situated on operational land.

A valuation officer determined that a railway booking office which was situated on the first floor of a shopping centre adjacent to a railway station ought to be entered on the local rating list as it came within the definition of an excepted hereditament under the 1989 Regulations, but a local valuation tribunal decided that registration ought to be effected on the central rating list. On appeal by the valuation officer, *held*, the appeal property ought to be inserted in the local list because it was office premises not situated on operational land. It was office premises because at least 50 per cent of the floor space was used for office purposes and all the remaining floor space was used by staff for purposes clearly ancillary to that use. Although part of the property was used as a lobby by travelling ticket collectors, this was a minor use and therefore not relevant. The property was not situated on operational land because it rested on shops and a highway and had a potential for less specialised use. Accordingly, the appeal would be allowed and the property placed on the local list.

Halliday (VO) v British Railways Board [1994] RA 297 (Lands Tribunal: M St J Hopper, FRICS).

2458   Non-domestic rating—hereditaments—holiday accommodation for disabled

Under the Local Government Finance Act 1988, Sch 5, para 16(1) a hereditament is exempt from non-domestic rating to the extent that it consists of property used wholly for (a) the provision of facilities for training or keeping suitably occupied persons who are disabled, and (b) the provision of welfare services for disabled persons.

The owner of four self-contained holiday cottages designed and adapted them to meet the needs of physically handicapped guests. The cottages were used primarily as holiday accommodation for families having one or more disabled member. Disabled guests had to have an able-bodied carer with them and approximately five per cent of the lettings had been to able-bodied persons who were unaccompanied by a disabled person. A valuation tribunal decided that the hereditament was to be deleted from the valuation list as exempt from non-domestic rating by virtue of the 1988 Act, Sch 5, para 16(1). On appeal by the valuation officer, *held*, (1) para 16(1)(a) did not apply in the present case. The words 'keeping suitably occupied' were required to be read with 'training' so as to impart the sense of providing 'training or occupation', and the provision of a holiday cottage could not fall into that category. (2) Although it was obvious that the cottages were being used to provide what could properly be called a 'welfare service' for disabled people or members of their family, they could not be said to be 'used wholly' for that purpose. Accordingly, the appeal would be allowed and the hereditament would be restored to the non-domestic rating list.

Chilcott (Valuation Officer) v Day [1995] RA 285 (Lands Tribunal: Judge Marder QC presiding).

2459   Non-domestic rating—hereditaments—occupier of part—liability

The Non-Domestic Rating (Collection and Enforcement) (Miscellaneous Provisions) Regulations 1990, SI 1990/145, reg 3 applies the provisions relating to deemed notices and payment of non-domestic rates in any case where there would at a particular time be more than one occupier of a hereditament which is shown in a local non-domestic rating list, or of part of such a hereditament, or more than one owner of the whole of an unoccupied hereditament so shown.

It has been held that it is not intended that the 1990 Regulations, reg 3 imposes on an occupier of part of a hereditament liability to pay rates on the whole of the hereditament.

Ford v Burnley (1995) 159 LG Rev 669 (Queen's Bench Division: Pill LJ and Keene J).

2460   Non-domestic rating—hereditaments—police authorities

The Non-Domestic Rating (Police Authorities) Order 1995, SI 1995/1679 (in force on 7 July 1995), extends the application of the Local Government Finance Act 1988, s 64(6), which displaces certain rules as to Crown exemption, to hereditaments provided and maintained by a police authority established under the Police Act 1964, s 3 (as substituted by the Police and Magistrates Courts Act 1994) for purposes connected with the administration of justice, police purposes or other Crown purposes.

2461   Non-domestic rating—hereditaments—unoccupied hereditaments—exemption from rating—buses parked overnight in depot—parking not amounting to storage

Under the Local Government Finance Act 1988, s 45(1) the owner of an unoccupied hereditament is, provided certain conditions are satisfied, subject to a non-domestic rate if the hereditament is not one which is exempt. The Non-Domestic Rating (Unoccupied Property) Regulations 1989, SI 1989/2261, reg 2(2) provides that qualifying industrial hereditaments are exempt from s 45(1). Regulation 2(5)(b) provides that a qualifying industrial hereditament means any industrial hereditament other than a retail hereditament in relation to which all buildings comprised in the hereditament are constructed or adapted for use in the course of a trade or business, and is constructed or adapted for use for storage (including the storage or handling of goods in the course of their distribution).

It has been held that, although there is force in the argument that buses are being stored if they are kept at premises prior to being commissioned into use or if they are being kept prior to despatch having been decommissioned, the word 'storage' in reg 2(5)(b) does not include the parking of buses when parking is an integral part of their normal daily operation. Therefore, buses which are parked overnight in bus depots as a normal incident of their everyday use are not being stored and, consequently, non-domestic rates are payable on such depots.

Barnet London Borough Council v London Transport Property [1995] RA 235 (Queen's Bench Division: Harrison J).

2462 Non-domestic rating—hereditaments—unoccupied hereditaments—exemption from rating—financial limits

The Non-Domestic Rating (Unoccupied Property) (Amendment) Regulations 1995, SI 1995/549 (in force on 1 April 1995), amend the 1989 Regulations, SI 1989/2261, so as to increase from £1,000 to £1,500, the limit under which the 1989 Regulations, reg 2(2)(g) exempts from non-domestic rates a hereditament shown in a non-domestic rating list compiled on or after 1 April 1995.

2463 Non-domestic rating—rateable occupation—show house

The defendant, a property company involved in developing residential housing estates, established sales offices at each development site which remained open until all the houses on the estates had been sold. The defendant also opened show houses at each development site, consisting of completed houses which were carpeted and furnished, and view homes, which were carpeted and had curtains but remained unfurnished. The view homes and show houses were shown to prospective purchasers as examples of finished properties of the same type. In addition, fences were erected around the properties to discourage people from entering them without first going into the sales office. A valuation tribunal decided that the show houses, view homes, and sales offices were to be deleted from the rating list because they were not actually occupied and therefore there was no reason to treat them differently from the residential houses on the estates. The plaintiff, a valuation officer, appealed against the decision. *Held*, there was rateable occupation of the properties, as the defendant had exclusive occupation of them. Moreover, the designation and use of the properties was of benefit to the defendant, as the ability of prospective purchasers to see how a finished house would look facilitated the sale of the properties on the estates. It was also the case that the duration of occupation was not an important factor, as the character and nature of occupation was relevant in determining the quality of occupation. Here, there was a degree of permanent occupation, as the show houses and view homes were used for as long as necessary to assist sales. Moreover, the properties were not domestic as they were not used as private residences, and they were all single rateable hereditaments. As such, they were to be entered in the rating list and, accordingly, the appeal would be allowed.

Walker (VO) v Ideal Homes Central Ltd [1995] RA 347 (Lands Tribunal: A P Musto, FRICS presiding).

2464 Non-domestic rating—rateable values—council property—whether value calculated on basis of profits or cost of construction

A city council claimed that the assessment of the rateable value of a visitor centre was excessive and on appeal the issue in question was which method of assessment was the more appropriate: a test based on a contractor's valuation of the building or one based on a percentage of the centre's receipts. *Held*, the centre did not operate at a profit and was instead run for socio-economic reasons, including the general promotion of tourism in the area. Accordingly, an assessment of its rateable value based on a percentage of receipts method would produce a minimal rateable value and was inappropriate. If a choice had to be made between the two tests, the contractor's valuation test would be chosen and the valuation would be based upon a costing of the existing building rather than a costing of a substitute.

Plymouth City Council v Hoare (Valuation Officer) [1995] RA 69 (Devon Valuation Tribunal: JB Sharp FRICS, IRRV, Chairman).

2465 Non-domestic rating—rateable values—electricity supply industry

The Electricity Supply Industry (Rateable Values) (Amendment) Order 1995, SI 1995/962 (in force on 1 April 1995), amends the 1994 Order, SI 1994/3282, so as to allow for differences between the estimates of the declared net capacities (as defined in the 1994 Order) of National Power plc, PowerGen plc and Nuclear Electric plc, and their actual declared net capacities as at 31 March 1995.

2466   Non-domestic rating—rating lists—alteration of lists—appeals

The Non-Domestic Rating (Alteration of Lists and Appeals) (Amendment) Regulations 1995, SI 1995/609 (in force on 31 March 1995), further amend the 1993 Regulations, SI 1993/291, so as to (1) make provision in relation to proposals made after 1 April 1995 to alter a non-domestic rating list compiled on 1 April 1990; (2) make provision in relation to proposals to alter a non-domestic rating list compiled on or after 1 April 1995; (3) alter the provisions concerning the action to be taken when the valuation officer considers that a proposal to alter a list is well founded; and (4) make amendments consequent upon the removal of certain hereditaments from prescribed assessment for the purposes of non-domestic rating and the certification of rateable values by valuation officers under the Non-Domestic Rating (Chargeable Amounts) Regulations 1994, SI 1994/3279.

The Local Government Changes for England (Non-Domestic Rating, Alteration of Lists and Appeals) Regulations 1995, SI 1995/623 (in force on 1 April 1995), amend the Non-Domestic Rating (Alteration of Lists and Appeals) Regulations 1993, SI 1993/291, in relation to local authorities affected by structural change under the Local Government Act 1992. The regulations provide that proposals affecting an authority which is abolished by a reorganisation order under the 1992 Act are to be continued in relation to the successor authority for the area in which the hereditament is situated. Where proposals are moved from one list to another as a result of such an order, the relevant authority is the acquiring authority. Further, where an appeal in relation to such a proposal is listed before the reorganisation date, the relevant authority is the relinquishing authority. If a proposal affects a year before the reorganisation, provision is made for both the acquiring and the relinquishing authorities to be relevant authorities.

2467   Non-domestic rating—valuation—enterprise zones

The Valuation for Rating (Former Enterprise Zones) Regulations 1995, SI 1995/213 (in force on 1 April 1995), replace the 1991 Regulations, SI 1991/278, and the amending 1992 Regulations, SI 1992/698, and make provision for the existence of enterprise zones to be disregarded in making an assessment in relation to so much of a hereditament as is situated in a former zone.

2468   Valuation and community charge tribunals—membership and procedure—England

The Valuation and Community Charge Tribunals (Amendment) (England) Regulations 1995, SI 1995/363 (in force on 10 March 1995), further amend the 1989 Regulations, SI 1989/439, which established the valuation tribunals for dealing with appeals in connection with community charges, appeals against completion notices for non-domestic rating purposes, and appeals in connection with council tax and penalties for council tax purposes. The regulations provide (1) for employees of a tribunal not to be eligible for membership of that tribunal, (2) for the number of members of a tribunal who are members of a principal council not to exceed one third, (3) for a president or chairman whose period of membership has expired to continue in office until there has been an election to fill the vacancy, or the opportunity for such an election, (4) for the president's functions to be performed by another chairman if he is unable to perform them as a result of illness or absence abroad, and (5) for the president to be one of the chairmen. In addition, these regulations amend SI 1989/439, and further amend the Council Tax (Alteration of Lists and Appeals) Regulations 1993, SI 1993/290, and the Non-Domestic Rating (Alteration of Lists and Appeals) Regulations 1993, SI 1993/291, so as to allow appeals affecting former employees or members of a tribunal to be transferred to another tribunal.

2469   Valuation tribunals—membership and procedure—Wales

The Valuation Tribunals (Wales) Regulations 1995, SI 1995/3056 (in force in part on 1 January 1996, and in part on 1 April 1996), establish new valuation tribunals in Wales. In particular, Pts II and III (1) establish tribunals for each of the four areas of jurisdiction set out in the regulations, (2) provide for the number of members for each tribunal, the number of members to be appointed by each appointed council, the appointment of members, and the duration of their membership, (3) deal with the appointment of the tribunal's president and chairmen, (4) provide for the circumstances in which a person is to be disqualified from membership, (5) provide for allowances payable to members, and (6) contain provisions relating to administration, accommodation, and equipment. Part IV contains transitional provisions relating to transferred appeals, the winding up of existing tribunals, and initial appointments of members. Parts V and

VI set out the procedure for dealing with appeals regarding the community charge and the council tax, and Pt VII amends SI 1989/439 so as to disapply those regulations in relation to the tribunals established by the 1995 Regulations.

REAL PROPERTY

Halsbury's Laws of England (4th edn) Vol 39, paras 301–800

2470 Articles

Attorneys as Trustees, Richard Oerton (on sale of a co-owned property where one co-owner is represented by someone with an enduring power of attorney): LS Gaz, 22 March 1995, p 18

Commonhold—A Prospect of Promise, D N Clarke (on the proposals for a statutory form of commonhold title): 58 MLR 486

French Leaseback Fears, Henry Dyson (on buying French holiday property free of VAT): 139 SJ 426

The Home: Excuses and Contributions, Patrick Milne (on the developing law of beneficial co-ownership under constructive and resulting trusts): 145 NLJ 423, 456

Joint Property, David Burrows (on the law of co-ownership as it affects the family home): 139 SJ 1176

Keeping Alive the Tenancy in the Matrimonial Home, David Mendes da Costa: [1995] Fam Law 622

Native Land Rights in Australia, Peter Butt: [1995] Conv 33

Pending Land Actions, Dr Jean Howell: [1995] Conv 309

Phasing: Pain or Relief? Dennis Mabey (on the phasing of business rate bills): Estates Gazette, 17 June 1995, p 137

Poll Tax Committals and the European Court, Rona Epstein and Ian Wise (on *Benham v United Kingdom* (para 1588)): 139 SJ 588

Removing Squatters, Andrew Blower: 139 SJ 1070

Severance Revisited, Louise Tee (on conversion of a joint tenancy to a tenancy in common): [1995] Conv 105

The £694 Question, Roger Cohen (on the proper remedy for infringement of property rights): Estates Gazette, 4 February 1995, p 158

2471 Conveyancing

See CONVEYANCING.

2472 Joint tenancy—agreement to sever tenancy—draft agreement

A husband and wife were joint tenants of their matrimonial home. In the course of divorce proceedings, the wife sought ancillary relief including a property adjustment order. Proposals for the division of the proceeds of sale of the home were embodied in a draft consent order but final agreement had not been reached at the time of the husband's death. It fell to be determined whether the joint tenancy had been severed before his death. The wife claimed that the tenancy had not been severed so that, on the basis of her right of survivorship as a joint tenant, she was entitled to the entire proceeds of sale of the property. *Held*, the joint tenancy had been severed at common law so that the parties held the property in equal shares. The wife's affidavit in support of her notice of application for ancillary relief constituted sufficient notice of intention to sever the joint tenancy under the Law of Property Act 1925, s 36 although, as she had expressed a wish to sever in the future, it was not a notice of severance under s 36. The correspondence between the parties and the affidavit indicated that they had agreed that the tenancy would eventually be severed. A mutual agreement at common law to sever a joint tenancy could include an agreement to deal with the property in a way which involved severance. The severance operated independently of the agreement itself. As the agreement had not been implemented and had no legal effect, the property was held by the wife and the husband's estate in equal shares and not on the terms of the proposed agreement. Accordingly, the wife's claim would fail.

Hunter v Babbage (1994) 69 P & CR 548 (Chancery Division: John McDonnell QC).

2473 Law of Property (Miscellaneous Provisions) Act 1994—commencement

The Law of Property (Miscellaneous Provisions) Act 1994 (Commencement No 2) Order 1995, SI 1995/1317, brings the remaining provisions of the Act into force on 1 July 1995. For a summary of the Act, see 1994 Abr para 2348. For details of commencement, see the commencement table in the title STATUTES.

RECEIVERS

Halsbury's Laws of England (4th edn) Vol 39, paras 801–1000

2474 Powers—collection of debts—accountability for tax

See *Sargent v Customs and Excise Comrs*, para 3046.

2475 Remuneration—assessment by taxing officer—order for taxation on standard or indemnity basis

It has been held that RSC Ord 30, r 3, as amended, and Ord 62, r 13 enable a court to order an assessment of a receiver's remuneration by a taxing officer on either a standard or an indemnity basis. A receiver cannot seek to interfere with a judge's exercise of discretion in favour of one particular basis.

   Alliance & Leicester Building Society v Edgestop Ltd (No 2) [1995] 2 BCLC 506 (Court of Appeal: Nourse, Evans and Rose LJJ).

REGISTRATION CONCERNING THE INDIVIDUAL

Halsbury's Laws of England (4th edn) Vol 39, paras 1001–1200

2476 Births and deaths—registration—Welsh language forms

The Registration of Births and Deaths (Welsh Language) (Amendment) Regulations 1995, SI 1995/818 (in force on 1 April 1995), further amend the 1987 Regulations, SI 1987/2089, by substituting Forms 1 (particulars of birth), 2 (declaration/statement for the registration/re-registration of a birth), 5 (statement for the re-registration of a birth), 6 (statement by parent for the re-registration of a birth), 7 (particulars of still-birth) and 9 (declaration as to still-birth), contained in Sch 2 thereto, so as to delete any reference to an NHS number, to insert a specific reference to the occupation of the mother and to make other minor changes in layout. These regulations revoke the provision in the 1987 Regulations that in the case of any discrepancy between an English text and a Welsh text permitted by those regulations, the English text prevails.

2477 Births, deaths and marriages—registration—fees

The Registration of Births, Deaths and Marriages (Fees) Order 1995, SI 1995/3162 (in force on 1 April 1996), replaces the 1994 Order, SI 1994/3257, and in doing so increases certain fees relating to the registration of births, deaths and marriages.

2478 Registration officers—appointment—removal of age restrictions

The Registration of Births, Deaths and Marriages (Miscellaneous Amendments) Regulations 1995, SI 1995/744 (in force on 1 April 1995), further amend the 1968 Regulations, SI 1968/2049, and the Registration of Marriages Regulations 1986, SI 1986/1442, so as to (1) provide for the relevant particulars to be entered by the registrar in the form of attestation of marriage set out in the 1986 Regulations, such requirement being consequent upon the coming into force of those provisions of the Marriage Act 1994 which enable civil ceremonies of marriage to take place on premises approved by the local authority; and (2) remove the age restrictions on appointment to a registration office in the 1968 Regulations.

REVENUE

Halsbury's Laws of England (4th edn) Vols 5(1) (reissue), 12, 19(2) (reissue), 23 (reissue), 24 (reissue), 44(1) (reissue)

2479 Articles

Appealing for Simplicity, David R Harris (on ideas for reform of the tax appeals system): Tax Journal, Issue 317, p 11

Details of the Proposals, Paul Hockey (on the 1995 Budget): Tax Journal, Issue 335, p 10, Issue 336, p 11, Issue 337, p 8

Making the Sums Simpler, Christopher Norfolk (on the 1995 Budget): LS Gaz, 6 December 1994, p 23

New Codes of Practice, Andrew Watt (on the Inland Revenue's elite investigation units): Tax Journal, Issue 303, p 14

Partisan Explanations, Robin Mathew (on tax investigations): Tax Journal, Issue 310, p 6

Reshaping Tax Appeals, Stephen Oliver: Tax Journal, Issue 303, p 8, Issue 304, p 10, Issue 305, p 14

2480 Appropriation Act 1995

The Appropriation Act 1995 applies the sum of £112,783,415,000 out of the Consolidated Fund to the service of the year ending 31 March 1996, appropriates the sum of £210,796,770,897.35 for supply of services, and repeals the following enactments: Consolidated Fund (No 3) Act 1992, Consolidated Fund Act 1993, Consolidated Fund (No 2) Act 1993, Consolidated Fund (No 3) Act 1993 and the Appropriation Act 1993. The Act received the royal assent on 19 July 1995 and came into force on that date.

2481 Budget—summary

The Chancellor of the Exchequer delivered his budget speech on 28 November 1995. The following is a brief summary of the proposals contained in it.

Income tax

The lower and higher rates of income tax remain at 20 per cent and 40 per cent respectively for 1996–97. The basic rate is reduced to 24 per cent. The lower rate band is extended by £700 to £3,900 and the higher rate threshold by £1,200 to £25,500. The personal allowance and the personal age allowances are indexed by more than the rate of inflation. The married couple's allowance and married couple's age allowances are increased in line with inflation, as are the widow's bereavement allowance and the additional personal allowance, which are kept at the same level as the married couple's allowance. From 6 April 1996, income tax personal allowances are to be extended to citizens of all states within the European Economic Area. To match the reduction in the basic rate, the rate applicable to income of discretionary and accumulation trusts is to be reduced from 35 per cent to 34 per cent for 1996–97.

The rate of deduction for sub-contractors in the construction industry is to be reduced to 24 per cent with effect from 1 July 1996. Mandatory registration cards for those sub-contractors who do not hold exemption certificates are likely to be introduced from August 1998.

A range of measures connected with the introduction of self-assessment are to be included. For 1996–97 and subsequent years, the tax charge on savings income such as bank or building society interest will be reduced to 20 per cent for basic rate taxpayers. Higher rate taxpayers will continue to pay tax at their marginal rate. Savings income will normally be treated as the top slice of income.

Certain insurance benefits will no longer be taxable. Where such benefits are provided in times of sickness, disability or unemployment to meet existing obligations, the proposals will have retrospective effect (as outlined in a Treasury Press Release dated 2 May 1995), but in all other cases the relief will take effect from 6 April 1996.

It is proposed to extend vocational training relief, to cover courses other than those counting towards a National or Scottish Vocational Qualification. The proposal will extend relief to cover any trainee who is aged 30 or over, and who is engaged in a full-time course which lasts more than four weeks but no more than a year, and which is wholly aimed at learning or practising knowledge skills for gainful employment. Qualifying payments to training providers made after 5 May 1996 will be accepted for this purpose. The tax treatment of work incentive payments and social security benefits paid under government pilot schemes is to be set, with effect from 6

April 1996, by secondary rather than primary legislation. Payments of jobfinder's grant are to be exempted from income tax. This exemption will apply to all payments of the grant made since April 1995.

Employment

It is proposed to introduce a new three year savings contract for savings-related share option (SAYE) schemes. This will be in addition to the existing five and seven year contracts. The minimum amount which may be saved each month under a SAYE scheme is also to be reduced from £10 to £5. These changes will be introduced in the spring of 1996. It is also intended that SAYE schemes should be able to be operated in conjunction with qualifying employee share ownership trusts. At present, shares allocated to an employee under an approved profit sharing scheme must be held in trust for a five-year period before they can be disposed of without giving rise to an income tax charge. It is proposed to reduce this period to three years.

A new relief is to replace the relief for options granted under approved executive share option schemes. The relief applies to options granted on or after 17 July 1995, the date on which the former relief was abolished. To qualify for the new relief, an employee must not at any one time hold options over shares which were, at the time the options were granted, valued at more than £20,000; further, the exercise price of the option must not be manifestly less than the market value of the shares at the time when the option was granted. All other conditions for the new relief are the same as those which applied for executive share option schemes. Existing approved executive share option schemes will be deemed to have incorporated the new rules unless they make an application to the contrary to the Revenue. They will cease to be approved from the date of the application.

With effect for options granted after 27 November 1995, any capital gains liability of employers in respect of the grant of options will be computed by reference to the amount received for the options rather than the market value; similarly capital gains liabilities of employees on the sale of shares will be computed by reference to the amount paid for the options rather than their market value.

The annual limit on charitable donations qualifying for relief under the payroll giving scheme is to be increased to £1,200 with effect from 6 April 1996.

The Revenue has been asked to prepare a consultative paper on possible changes to simplify the current rules covering travel and subsistence expenses incurred by employees in the performance of their duties. The paper is particularly intended to address those issues affecting site-based employees, and employees who travel directly from their home to a temporary place of work. The scale charges on the benefit of free fuel provided for private motoring in company cars are to be increased by 5 per cent for both petrol and diesel cars, with effect from 6 April 1996. With effect from 1996–97, it is proposed that any employee who uses his own car for business travel can use the mileage rates set by the Fixed Profit Car Scheme (FPCS) to calculate any taxable profit on car allowances or motor mileage allowances they may receive, even if their employer has not entered the FPCS. Any employee may also use the FPCS rates to support a tax deduction for allowable business motoring expenses regardless of whether they receive car or mileage allowances from their employer.

Changes to the rules for taxing job-related accommodation are proposed for 1995–96, and for earlier years where the tax liability has not yet been agreed. By concession, where accommodation is provided to more than one employee in the same period, the total charge on the employees will be restricted to the amount which would have arisen on a single employee. If the open market rental value of accommodation is used to calculate the benefit in kind, and an additional charge also arises, for example because the accommodation is overseas, then by concession this additional charge will not be applied. With effect from 6 April 1996, legislative changes are to be introduced to counteract 'cash alternative' schemes under which the employee is given the option of taking accommodation or extra salary.

At present, employers may supply details of minor expenses payments and benefits in kind, given to individual employees, by way of an annual voluntary settlement. This allows the employer to pay, in a lump sum, the tax due on those items covered by the settlement, and the employer does not need to include the items in the end of year return. It is proposed to provide a statutory framework for such arrangements in order to encourage more employers to use them; enabling powers, permitting the introduction of regulations governing the operation of such arrangements, are to be made.

Pensions

From 6 April 1996, the earnings cap, by reference to which the maximum relief on contributions to personal pension schemes and benefits under certain occupational schemes are calculated, is increased from £78,600 to £82,200. The Revenue is to consult with representatives of pensions bodies on the possibility of allowing defined benefit occupational pension schemes to pay variable pensions so that a person could choose, if he wished, to take a small pension in the early years of retirement and a larger pension in later years.

Compensation for mis-sold personal pensions during the period covered by the Securities and Investments Board review will be exempt from tax if the compensation is paid into specified schemes or contracts. The exemption will not apply to annuities or other annual payments made to individuals arising from compensation. An Update will be issued by the Pension Schemes Office in due course.

Corporation tax

With effect from 1 April 1996 the small companies' rate of corporation tax is to be reduced to 24 per cent, in line with the basic rate of income tax. The full rate remains unchanged at 33 per cent. The lower and upper limits used for calculating marginal relief also remain unchanged at £300,000 and £1,500,000 respectively but the fraction used in calculating marginal relief is changed from $\frac{1}{50}$ to $\frac{9}{400}$.

A new relief is to be introduced for amounts transferred into equalisation reserves set up in respect of certain types of volatile non-life insurance business, including property, consequential loss, mortgage indemnity, marine and nuclear insurance business. The relief will apply for accounting periods ending after 22 December 1996. Transfers out of such reserves will be taxable.

The tax rules governing the approval of investment trust companies are to be modified to enable them to invest without restriction in certain residential property. The companies must hold freehold or long leasehold interests in the properties, and must let them on assured tenancies. The companies will be subject to corporation tax at the small companies rate on rental income, after deduction of expenses, and will be exempt from tax on gains arising from the sale of such property.

The rules governing the tax charge on loans to participators in close companies are to be simplified with effect for accounting periods ending after 30 March 1996. The principal change is that any tax due under these provisions will become payable nine months, instead of 14 days, after the end of the accounting period. The tax will not need to be paid at all if the loan is repaid before the tax falls due; if the loan is repaid after that date, the tax becomes due for repayment nine months after the end of the accounting period in which the loan is repaid. The rules will no longer apply to loans made to companies which are not resident in the United Kingdom.

Criteria established in court decisions that are at present used to determine whether an institution is recognised as a bank are no longer to be used. Instead, institutions which meet relevant Bank of England regulatory requirements will automatically be recognised as banks for tax purposes.

Financial matters

A range of proposals seek to facilitate the smooth operation of the financial markets. Fees received by pension funds under approved stock lending arrangements entered into after 1 January 1996 are to be exempt from tax. A simpler alternative to the existing rules for deducting tax from manufactured overseas dividends is to be introduced in 1996. As a result of changes at the Stock Exchange, references in tax legislation to 'quoted' securities are to be replaced by references to 'listed' securities although this will not change the tax treatment of the securities concerned. Regulations have been laid before the House of Commons which exempt from tax manufactured payments and profits from repo transactions in the hands of exempt pension schemes. The exemption also applies to life insurance companies, in so far as the income relates to pension business. The regulations will come into effect on 2 January 1996, and once operational, will make extra-statutory concession C19 obsolete.

A number of detailed changes are to be made to the foreign income dividend (FID) scheme. In particular, the rules defining international headquarters companies are to be amended to include a company owned by a foreign quoted company indirectly through more than one intermediate holding company. The basis of calculation of the distributable foreign profit and the notional foreign source advance corporation tax will also be changed to allow greater relief for foreign tax. Further amendments will be made to clarify the tax position of non-resident companies receiving FIDs and to make it clear that only United Kingdom resident companies can pay FIDs.

Further details are announced regarding the reform in the tax treatment of debt which will take effect from 1 April 1996. It is proposed to repeal a variety of complex rules and replace them with a single set of rules covering all debts, which in general will only apply to companies. The present rules will continue to apply to individuals and trustees.

Proposals have been made which will limit the circumstances in which collecting agents, mainly banks and stockbrokers, have to deduct tax from foreign dividends and interest. Clearer rules are proposed to allow certain investors, such as United Kingdom charities and overseas residents, to receive their foreign interest and dividends without deduction of tax.

Anti-avoidance
It is proposed to introduce legislation to clarify the Revenue's existing practice of relying on 'open' tax assessments as a means of giving effect to transfer pricing adjustments. The acceptable distribution policy rules for trading controlled foreign companies are to be amended. With effect for accounting periods beginning after 27 November 1995, a trading company will be subject to the same distribution test as a non-trading company. In order to satisfy the test for a particular accounting period, it will be required to pay a dividend to United Kingdom residents which, together with relevant dividends for preceding periods, equals at least 90 per cent of the company's net chargeable profits for the relevant period.

The provisions exempting companies whose securities are authorised to be dealt in on the Stock Exchange from certain anti-avoidance provisions intended to cancel tax advantages from artificial transactions in securities are to be tightened. The exemption will be restricted to companies whose securities are listed on the Official List. However, companies whose securities are traded on the Unlisted Securities Market will remain exempt until the market closes at the end of 1996.

Charities
It is proposed to introduce legislation which will exempt charities from tax on certain investment income. This legislation will remove the need for extra-statutory concession B9 and will apply for 1996–97 and subsequent tax years, and, for companies, in respect of accounting periods ending after 31 March 1996. The concession will continue to operate until the legislation takes effect.

Capital gains tax
For 1996–97, the annual exempt amount is to be increased, in line with indexation, to £6,300 for individuals and certain trusts for the disabled and to £3,150 for trusts generally. The age at which retirement relief becomes automatically available is to be reduced to 50 with effect for disposals made after 27 November 1995.

At present, if a chargeable gain arises to a closely held non-resident company, the proportion of that gain which may be attributed to a United Kingdom resident shareholder in the company is determined by reference to the assets to which the shareholder would be entitled on a winding up of the company. It is proposed to amend the legislation, with effect for gains arising after 27 November 1995, so that the proportion of the gain chargeable on a United Kingdom resident participator will depend on the extent of that person's participation in the non-resident company.

National insurance contributions
It is proposed that with effect from 1996–97, the allowance of 50 per cent of Class 4 national insurance contributions, currently given as a deduction against Schedule D trading profit, should be withdrawn, and the rate of Class 4 contributions should be cut from 73 per cent to 6 per cent to compensate. This amendment is intended to remove a complication in the run up to self-assessment.

Inheritance tax
The inheritance tax threshold for 1996–97 is increased to £200,000 although the rate of inheritance tax remains unchanged at 40 per cent.

It is proposed to extend 100 per cent business property relief to all holdings of unquoted shares in qualifying companies, where the shares have been held for two years, regardless of the size of holding or voting entitlement. Provision is to be made to clarify the availability of the 100 per cent relief in respect of farmland subject to agricultural tenancies where the land was acquired as a result of the death of the previous tenant. Legislation, effective for transfers after 27 November 1995, is to be introduced to clarify the operation of the rules governing transfers of qualifying business assets and agricultural assets within seven years before the death of the transferor.

Value added tax
With effect from 29 November 1995, the annual registration threshold has been increased to £47,000. The deregistration limit will rise to £45,000. The Intrastat threshold will be increased to £160,000 with effect from 1 January 1996. The payments on account scheme is to be amended, with effect from 1 June 1996, and a number of deregulatory measures are to be introduced. Anti-avoidance measures are introduced with effect from 29 November 1995 to counter abuse of the value added tax grouping rules.

Landfill tax
There are to be two rates of tax which will be introduced from 1 October 1996. Inactive waste, which does not decay, pollute or contaminate will be taxed at the rate of £2 per tonne and all other waste at a standard rate of £7 per tonne.

2482 Capital gains tax
See CAPITAL GAINS TAXATION.

2483 Capital transfer tax
See INHERITANCE TAXATION.

2484 Consolidated Fund Act 1995
The Consolidated Fund Act 1995 applies the sum of £167,222,897.35 for the year ending 31 March 1994, and the sum of £1,171,475,000 for the year ending 31 March 1995. The Act received the royal assent on 23 March 1995 and came into force on that date.

2485 Consolidated Fund (No 2) Act 1995
The Consolidated Fund (No 2) Act 1995 applies the sum of £1,915,196,000 for the year ending 31 March 1996, and the sum of £95,393,128,000 for the year ending 31 March 1997. The Act received the royal assent on 19 December 1995 and came into force on that date.

2486 Customs and excise
See CUSTOMS AND EXCISE.

2487 Finance Act 1993—commencement
The Finance Act 1993, section 11, (Appointed Day) Order 1995, SI 1995/2715, appoints 1 December 1995 as the day on which s 11 comes into force. Section 11 adds the Hydrocarbon Oil Duties Act 1979, s 6A, which provides for duty to be charged on fuel substitutes, superseding the existing provisions for petrol substitutes and power methylated spirits, amends s 22(1) (offence of using duty on which fuel has not been paid) and substitutes the Excise Duties (Surcharges or Rebates) Act 1979, s 1(1)(b) (surcharges or rebates in respect of excise duties on hydrocarbon oil etc). For a summary of the Act, see 1993 Abr para 2169. For details of commencement, see the commencement table in the title STATUTES.

2488 Finance Act 1994—appointed day
The Finance Act 1994, section 105, (Appointed Day) Order 1995, SI 1995/3125, appoints 1 January 1996 for the coming into force of s 105(3), (4)(b), which amend the Taxes Management Act 1970, s 98 so as to reflect the new information powers of the Commissioners of Inland Revenue, under the Income and Corporation Taxes Act 1988, s 605, relating to retirement benefits schemes. For a summary of the Act, see 1994 Abr para 2361. For details of commencement, see the commencement table in the title STATUTES.

2489 Finance Act 1995
The Finance Act 1995 grants certain duties, alters other duties, amends the law relating to the National Debt and the Public Revenue, and makes further provision in connection with finance. The Act received the royal assent on 1 May 1995 and certain provisions came into force on that date. For details of commencement, see the commencement table in the title STATUTES.

Part I (ss 1–20) Duties of Excise
Section 1 amends the definition of wine and cider so as to exclude wines and ciders of a strength not exceeding 1.2 per cent. Sections 2, 3, Sch 1 amend the rates of duty on wines, beers and ciders, s 4 introduces a new relief for dutiable ingredients of low strength beverages, chocolates, etc, and s 5, Sch 2 provide similar relief for denatured alcohol. Sections 6, 7 increase the rates of duty on hydrocarbon oil, and s 8 amends the definition of road vehicle for the purposes of the Hydrocarbon Oil Duties Act 1979. A provision of that Act by virtue of which there was no charge on the use of gas if delivered or stocked before 3 July 1972 is repealed: 1995 Act, s 9. The rates of tobacco product duty are increased by ss 10, 11, and the rate of pool betting duty is reduced by s 12. Section 13 introduces a new table of rates of gaming machine licence duty in

relation to licences applied for after 30 November 1994. With effect from 1 November 1995, the duty will also be charged on amusement machines: s 14, Sch 3. European Community destinations in respect of which there is a reduced rate of air passenger duty are redefined in the light of the European Economic Area Agreement, and provision is made for the assessment of interest on overdue air passenger duty which is now included in the list of preferential debts in an insolvency: ss 15–17. The rate of vehicle excise duty on private cars and other vehicles in the same category is increased; and trailer supplements are also increased: s 18. Schedule 4 provides numerous changes to the exemptions and concessions in respect of vehicle excise duty. Section 19 provides for the repayment of overpaid duty. There is a right of appeal against any refusal of a claim for repayment: s 20.

Part II (ss 21–34) Value Added Tax and Insurance Premium Tax
Value added tax in respect of supplies of fuel and power for domestic or charity use continues to be charged at the rate of 8 per cent (s 21), and value added tax on certain items imported from outside the Community is to be charged at an effective rate of 2.5 per cent: s 22. By virtue of s 23, goods supplied from a member state, or imported from outside the Community, through an agent are treated as supplied to him by the supplier and then by him to the customer. The margin scheme rules are to be replaced by new more extensive rules giving the trader the option to pay value added tax on his gross profit margin in relation to works of art, antiques etc, motor vehicles, secondhand goods and goods supplied through agents in circumstances to be specified in regulations: s 24. Supplies of goods or services by one member of a group of companies to another are ignored only if both companies continue to be members of the group until the goods have been made available or the services performed: s 25.

By virtue of s 26, the grant, assignment or surrender of an interest by co-owners is treated as the grant etc by a single person. The interest payable on an overpayment of value added tax which is due from the Commissioners of Customs and Excise is set off as a credit although this is not required in certain cases involving insolvencies in specified circumstances: s 27. Section 28 provides for the export of goods by a charity to a place outside the Community to be treated as a supply in the United Kingdom in the course or furtherance of a business; and s 29 provides for the making of regulations to enable taxable persons to defer the payment of value added tax on the supply of goods subject to the warehousing regime.

Section 30 provides a new table of fuel scale charges in respect of fuel for private use. Value added tax or duty shown in a return must be paid even though an appeal is against a requirement to provide security in respect of an appeal against the tax: s 31. By virtue of s 32, the specified percentages of penalties for failure to notify liability to register for value added tax or for the unauthorised issue of invoices are reduced except in the case of supplementary assessments made before 1 January 1995. Certain errors made in the consolidation of the value added tax legislation are rectified by s 33. Section 34, Sch 5 make further provision in respect of insurance premium tax.

Part III (ss 35–145) Income Tax, Corporation Tax and Capital Gains Tax
For 1995–96, the lower, basic and higher rates of income tax remain at 20 per cent, 25 per cent and 40 per cent; the lower rate band is increased to £3,200 and the threshold for the higher rate is increased to £24,300: s 35. The personal allowance is increased to £3,525; the married couple's allowance remains at £1,720; the age related personal allowance is £4,630 for those aged 65 and over and £4,800 for those aged 75 and over: s 36. By virtue of ss 37, 38, the rate of corporation tax remains at 33 per cent, the small companies' rate remains at 25 per cent and the marginal relief fraction is one fiftieth.

Income arising under Schedule A is to be computed, for income tax purposes, on a Schedule D Case I basis, income from furnished lettings is brought within Schedule A, income from partnership lettings is computed in one sum but the deemed business is deemed to have commenced on 6 April 1995 if the letting commenced before that date and the Schedule D Case II rules for partnership changes apply: s 39, Sch 6. Regulations will provide for the collection of tax from non-resident landlords with income falling under the new Schedule A provisions (s 40), although a separate computation is required where the taxpayer also has Schedule A income: s 41. In the case of a company which is neither a trading company nor an investment company, the deduction for interest as a charge depends on whether the interest relates to a loan to acquire property which is let commercially: s 42, Sch 7. The car benefit rules apply even though an employee is offered a cash alternative instead of a car; the cash alternative is included in the calculation of emoluments even if that is higher than the cash equivalent benefits: s 43. Equipment which is designed solely for use by a chronically sick or disabled person and which is fitted to his car does not give rise to a further benefit: s 44. The provisions which ensure a continuation of fringe benefit liability where certain employment ceases are extended to replacement loans: s 45.

Section 46 relaxes some of the exclusions of certain types of trading company as qualifying companies for the purposes of reinvestment relief. If the qualifying investment was acquired from the reinvestor's spouse, the amount of gain rolled over cannot exceed the spouse's base cost; and multiple claims in respect of the same reinvestment are given effect in such order as the reinvestor may determine, but the total amount of gains rolled over cannot exceed the cost or market value of the new investment: s 47. Rollover relief is available, by virtue of s 48, if the disposal company was a group member at the time of the disposal and the acquiring member was a member of the same group at the time of acquisition; the relief is not available for intra-group acquisitions. The rules on degrouping charges are tightened up to counteract a more elaborate version of the 'envelope trick': s 49. Section 50 excludes quoted indexed securities from the definitions of a corporate bond.

Sections 51, 52, Sch 8 make numerous changes to the taxation of life assurance business; and s 53, Sch 9 make numerous technical amendments to the taxation of overseas life companies. Section 54, Sch 10, in relation to friendly societies, increase to £270 per annum the maximum premiums which may be paid into qualifying exempt policies and remove the special limit on early surrenders.

Sections 55–57 relate to insurance policies, ss 58–61, Sch 11 make provision in relation to pensions, and ss 62–69 deal with savings and investment.

Sections 70–73, Schs 14–16, relating to venture capital trusts, set out the conditions for approval of a company as a venture capital trust, the conditions for relief from income tax (which is limited to £100,000 in any tax year and is given at the lower rate of tax only), anti-avoidance provisions and provide for reinvestment relief by way of postponement of gains where a subscriber for qualifying assets has made previous capital gains.

Sections 74–76, Schs 17, 18, concerning settlements and estates, provide that income arising under a settlement is deemed to be that of the settlor unless he has completely divested himself of any interest in the settled property.

Securities are dealt with in ss 77–85, Sch 19. In certain circumstances, interest on gilts may be paid gross; regulations will set out details for periodic accounting for tax on interest on gilt-edged securities: ss 77, 78. Where securities are transferred under an agreement to sell them, the accrued income scheme provisions are disapplied (s 79) and the price difference is deemed to be an amount of interest on a deemed loan from or to the 'interim holder' depending on whether the repurchase price is greater or less than the sale price: s 80. The bond-washing provisions are also disapplied in the case of a repo where the interim holder makes a payment to the other party representing the interest arising on the security: s 81. The requirement to account for tax on manufactured dividends is removed in relation to cases to be specified in regulations: s 82. The Treasury is empowered to make regulations to deal with special cases (s 83) and to amend the rules relating to provisions affecting dealers in securities: s 84. Where cash collateral is provided the interest is treated as the income of the stock borrower and the lender is not required to deduct tax on paying the interest to the borrower: s 85.

The term 'relevant deposit' now includes deposits by the trustees of discretionary or accumulation trusts: s 86. Where interest payable by a United Kingdom resident company to a non-resident company, which was treated as a distribution if the United Kingdom company was a 75 per cent subsidiary of the non-resident company or if both were subsidiaries of a United Kingdom company but less than 90 per cent of the share capital of the United Kingdom company was owned by a United Kingdom resident company, as from 29 November 1994, the distribution element is confined to the excess of the interest over the amount which would have been payable in the absence of a special relationship between the companies: s 87. Sections 88, 89 amend the accrued income scheme rules, deep discount securities rules and deep gain securities rules as they apply to interest receivable by United Kingdom companies from overseas associated companies so that references to the 'resident company' are now references to the 'creditor company'.

Where it is not possible to set off post-cessation expenses against post-cessation receipts, certain post-cessation expenditure now qualifies for relief against total income in the year in which it is defrayed: s 90. Where an employee pays a claim for negligence, or expenses in connection with such claim, or an insurance premium on a contract covering such a liability, he may claim a deduction from his emoluments for the amount paid. If his employer pays, that payment does not give rise to a fringe benefit: s 91. If such an amount is paid after the employment ceases, it is allowable as a deduction against total income of the year in which it is paid: s 92. Payments by employers up to £5 per night for absence from home on business in the United Kingdom and £10 for absence abroad are not treated as emoluments: s 93.

A new relief provides that the balancing charge on ships may be deferred if and to the extent that the shipowner incurs expenditure on new shipping within six years after the date of the event giving rise to the balancing charge; deferment must be claimed: ss 94–98. A person entitled to a 'highway concession' is deemed to have an interest in the road concerned; a balancing event occurs when that concession comes to an end but there is no balancing allowance or charge if the concession is extended or a new concession is granted: s 99. On a disposal of a new and unused building, or a building in an enterprise zone, the disposal value is increased to what it would have been but for the arrangements: s 100. A warehouse may now qualify as an import warehouse where the goods have arrived in the United Kingdom via the Channel Tunnel: s 101. Section 102 defers the application of certain provisions relating to capital allowances.

As far as the notice of liability provisions of trustees are concerned, the relevant trustees are, in relation to income, the persons who are trustees when the income arises and any persons who subsequently become trustees, and in relation to chargeable gains, the trustees in the year of assessment in which the gains arise and subsequent trustees; the same trustees may be required to file a return. Interest, penalties and surcharges may be recovered from any of the relevant trustees: s 103. Detailed changes are made by ss 104, 105 to the content of the self-assessment returns and partnership statements and to the requirement to keep records. As from 1996–97, employers will be required to make returns of emoluments, expenses and benefits including a computation of the taxable benefits: s 106. By virtue of s 107, Sch 20, a claim for relief must be quantified at the time it is made except where it relates to a refund of tax deducted under PAYE or to the amendment of a PAYE code number; a claim to set a loss etc of the current year against income of an earlier year need not be made in a return; effect is given to the claim in the year in which the loss arises, but the tax relief is calculated by reference to the year of claim. Section 108 makes minor changes to correct defects in the original legislation concerning payments on account of income tax. The provisions concerning surcharges on unpaid income tax are extended to cover income tax or capital gains tax for 1995–96 or earlier years which is not assessed until after 5 April 1998: s 109. Section 110 replaces the existing provisions on interest on overdue tax. An assessment, which includes a self assessment, is no longer necessary where the PAYE deductions discharge the taxpayer's liability for the year: s 111. In a case where a loan has never qualified as a relevant loan for mortgage interest relief at source ('MIRAS') purposes, the borrower may be assessed to income tax to enable the Revenue to recover the tax wrongly deducted under MIRAS: s 112.

Capital gains tax losses must now be notified to the Revenue and the notice must qualify the loss; the claims procedure applies, with the usual right of appeal where the figures are not agreed; losses agreed under this new procedure are set off before other capital gains tax losses brought forward: s 113. Capital gains tax due may be charged on any one of the trustees or personal representatives, although a trustee who ceased before the migration of a trust is not liable in respect of gains on migration if at the time he ceased there was no proposal for migration: s 114. Section 115 deals with minor amendments and repeals. The normal income tax payment on account requirements are modified for 1996–97 for which year there are no corresponding figures for 1995–6: s 116, Sch 21.

Detailed provisions, set out in s 117, deal with change of accounting date and with non-business income and losses. A loss sustained in 1995–96 from a trade, profession or vocation can be set off against income of 1996–97 where the business commenced before 6 April 1994: s 118. A loss on unquoted shares sustained in 1994–95 may be set off against income in 1993–94: s 119. Relief on pre-trading expenditure is extended to individuals in relation to trades commencing on or after 6 April 1995: s 120. Any apportionment of profit is in proportion to the number of days in the period rather than months and fractions of months: s 121. The definition of transitional overlap profit is changed to avoid double relief; capital allowances and balancing charges are ignored in calculating the overlap profit except in the case of a partnership including individuals and companies: s 122. Given that some profits will fall out of assessment on the transition from proceeding year basis to current year basis, provision is made to counteract the avoidance of tax by 'managing' profits into a period part or all of the profits of which drop out of assessment: s 123, Sch 22.

Where an individual who carries on a trade or profession wholly or partly outside the United Kingdom changes his residence status, that change is treated as the occasion of a cessation and recommencement of the business; this does not apply if the business was carried on in partnership with others: s 124. The self assessment rules are to apply to partnerships controlled abroad from 1997–98 generally and from 1995–96 where the business commenced on or after 6 April 1994: s 125. Obligations are imposed on a non-resident's United Kingdom representative in relation to the computation of profits, income and gains of its United Kingdom branch or agency: s 126, Sch 23. Section 127 provides that certain persons, such as investment brokers investment managers etc, are not to be treated as United Kingdom representatives. The United Kingdom tax liability of a non-resident is limited to tax on his total income less 'excluded income', assuming no personal allowances or double tax treaty relief, plus any tax deducted at source from excluded income: s 128. For accounting periods ending after 5 April 1995, the corporation tax liability of non-resident companies is limited to tax on profits other than 'excluded income' plus income tax deducted at source from excluded income: s 129.

A number of technical amendments are made to the exchange gains and losses legislation: s 130, Sch 24. The no gain-no loss capital gains tax rules are not to apply to the disposal of a 'qualifying asset' by one qualifying company to another before the first company's commencement day but after the second company's commencement day: s 131. Section 132 makes minor amendments to currency contracts provisions. A controlled foreign company may compute its profits in the currency in which its accounts are drawn up: s 133, Sch 25. Only offshore funds which are collective investment schemes are within the definition as regards a person having a material interest: s 134.

The carry forward of excess management expenses where the change of ownership of an investment company is associated with a major change in the business etc is prohibited: s 135, Sch 26. The items which may be excluded from the calculation of profit under a profit-related pay scheme are redrafted: s 136. The law is changed to allow part-time workers to participate in a profit-related pay scheme: s 137. The profits from an approved lottery are exempt from tax if applied for charitable purposes: s 138. As from an appointed day, but not before 1 August 1998, the rate of deduction of tax from sub-contractors in the construction industry is to be reduced; and the operation of the deduction scheme is to be tightened up: s 139, Sch 27. Where a trade is transferred between connected persons, the value to be brought into the Case I or Case II computations is the arm's length price, but the parties may elect to substitute the greater of cost or actual transfer price where both figures are less than the arm's length price: s 140. The 'initial period of incapacity' in relation to incapacity benefit is redefined so as to exclude from tax short-term benefits paid at a rate other than the higher rate: s 141. Annuities for injury damages are now exempt from income tax: s 142. Under the new special reserve scheme for Lloyd's underwriters, it is provided that income from special type reserve funds is accumulated and that withdrawals are permitted only in accordance with the rules: s 143. Section 144 extends the definition of local government residuary body. The requirement to deduct tax at source from certain rents payable by mineral extraction, transport and similar businesses is removed (s 144); and the corresponding right of the lessor to recover tax deducted is also removed, although the lessor may deduct management expenses from the rental income: s 145.

Part IV (ss 146–148) Petroleum Revenue Tax
The amount of unrelievable field losses is reduced by the amount of any unrelated expenditure which was allowed in computing the profits of the field: s 146. The time limit for claims for such losses is removed: s 147. Where an interest in the field is transferred, there is a similar restriction on the amount of transferred losses: s 148.

Part V (ss 149–151) Stamp Duty
The 90 per cent group relationship required for exemption is reduced to 75 per cent: s 149. Section 150 applies to Northern Ireland. There is a new exemption for the grant of a lease or letting between companies within the 75 per cent group relationship: s 151.

Part VI (ss 152–163) Miscellaneous and General
The Treasury is empowered to make regulations applying the tax legislation to open ended investment companies: s 152. Section 153, Sch 28 make provision for facilitating the lodgment of certain tax returns and documents required in connection with them. The cultivation of short rotation coppice, which is now treated as farming and not forestry, is brought within Schedule D Case I: s 154. Inheritance tax relief for tenanted agricultural land is increased to 100 per cent where the tenancy starts on or after 1 September 1995; transfers of land and buildings used for cultivation of short rotation coppice will qualify for the relief as from 6 April 1995: s 155. Section 156 applies to Scotland. New rules provide compensation, where a taxpayer surrenders a certificate of tax deposit for cash and then has to pay interest on a 'qualifying liability', in respect of the different interest rates applying on the certificate of tax deposit surrender and the overdue tax: s 157. A technical amendment in s 158 deals with the deduction of repayments plus interest from gross revenues by the Inland Revenue and Customs and Excise: s 158. A relevant former port authority is provided with an appeal procedure for dealing with certain assessments: s 159. The Inland Revenue is to prepare a report for the Treasury on tax simplification by 31 December 1995: s 160. Sections 161–163, Sch 29 deal with interpretation, repeals and short title.

2490 Government trading funds

The Defence Evaluation and Research Agency Trading Fund Order 1995, SI 1995/650 (in force on 1 April 1995), extends the operations of the Defence Research Agency Trading Fund to further Ministry of Defence operations including those which carry out operational analysis and technical programmes functions. The Defence Research Agency and its additional operations are renamed the Defence Evaluation and Research Agency, and the Defence Research Agency Trading Fund is renamed the Defence Evaluation and Research Agency Trading Fund. In addition, provision is made for certain additional assets and liabilities to be appropriated to the Fund, and for the treatment of those assets and liabilities.

The Buying Agency Trading Fund (Extension) Order 1995, SI 1995/1665 (in force on 1 July 1995), extends the funded operations of the Buying Agency to include operations of the fuel branch of the Department of the Environment and consequently (1) amends the description of the funded operations in the 1991 Order, SI 1991/875; (2) provides for the additional assets and liabilities appropriated to the Fund; and (3) provides for £250,000, being part of the difference between the value of the additional assets and the amounts of the additional liabilities, to be treated as public dividend capital of the fund.

2491 Income and corporation tax

See INCOME TAXATION.

2492 Inheritance tax

See INHERITANCE TAXATION.

2493 Petroleum revenue tax

See FUEL AND ENERGY.

2494 Revenue proceedings—rules

See para 2374.

2495 Stamp duties

See STAMP DUTIES.

2496 Value added tax

See VALUE ADDED TAX.

ROAD TRAFFIC

Halsbury's Laws of England (4th edn) Vol 40, paras 1–993

2497 Articles

Drink Driving: Proper Procedural Steps When Providing a Specimen of Blood or Urine, Christine Clayson: Criminal Lawyer, Issue 52, p 1

Killing With Cars After Adomako: Time for Some Alternatives? Ian Brownlee and Mary Seneviratne (on *R v Adomako* [1994] 3 All ER 79, HL (1994 Abr para 889)): [1995] Crim LR 389

Nervous Shock, Charles Lewis (on *Page v Smith* [1995] 2 WLR 644, HL (para 2173)): 139 SJ 960

Proof of Prior Disqualification for the Offence of Driving Whilst Disqualified, J N Spencer: 159 JP Jo 853

The Use of Endorsement and Disqualification for Road Traffic Offenders, F G Davies: 159 JP Jo 399, 418

Who Cares About Traffic Offences?, Brian Block: 159 JP Jo 19

2498 Accident—hospital charges

The Road Traffic Accidents (Payments for Treatment) Order 1995, SI 1995/889 (in force on 17 April 1995), increases the maximum amount payable under the Road Traffic Act 1988, s 157(2) for hospital treatment of traffic casualties to £2,949 for in-patients and to £295 for out-patients. The amount payable under s 158(2) in respect of the emergency treatment fee is increased to £21.30 and in respect of a medical practitioner's travelling expenses to 41p per mile.

2499 Carriage by road

See CARRIERS.

2500 Careless driving—causing death by careless driving when under the influence of alcohol or drugs—admissibility of evidence of defendant's alcohol consumption

It has been held that in applying the appropriate test as to whether a defendant drove without due care and attention, the jury is entitled to look at all the circumstances of the case including evidence that the defendant was affected by drink or that he had taken such an amount of drink as would be likely to affect a driver.

R v Millington (1995) 160 JP 683 (Court of Appeal: Beldam LJ, McKinnon and Judge JJ). *R v McBride* [1962] 2 QB 167, CA applied.

2501 Careless driving—driving in a public place—school grounds as public place

Scotland

The Road Traffic Act 1988, ss 2, 3 provide that it is an offence to drive a mechanically propelled vehicle dangerously or carelessly on a road or other public place.

The defendant was riding a motorcycle in the grounds of a school. Although there were no signs prohibiting access to the premises, it was well known that pupils played in the grounds after school hours and that other children went there to play. The defendant collided with a boy, causing the boy injuries, and was convicted of driving carelessly in a public place. He appealed on the ground that the school grounds were not a road or public place under the 1988 Act, ss 2, 3. *Held*, the purpose of the 1988 Act, whether one was dealing with a road or other public place, was to secure the safety of the public in places where the public may be expected to be or to have access. The school grounds were a public place because they were open to the public and because the public were permitted to have access to them. Accordingly, the appeal would be dismissed.

Rodger v Normand 1995 SLT 411 (High Court of Justiciary).

2502 Common transport policy

See EUROPEAN COMMUNITIES.

2503 Cycle racing on highways

The Cycle Racing on Highways (Amendment) Regulations 1995, SI 1995/3241 (in force on 26 January 1996), further amend the 1960 Regulations, SI 1960/250, by increasing the maximum number of competitors in races not promoted by the British Cycling Federation from 60 to 80.

2504 Dangerous driving—causing death by dangerous driving—obvious defect

The Road Traffic Act 1988, s 2A(2) provides that a person is to be regarded as driving dangerously if it would be obvious to a competent and careful driver that driving the vehicle in its current state would be dangerous.

The appellant was involved in a road accident in which his car hit an oncoming car, causing it to catch fire and killing its driver. The appellant was charged with two counts of dangerous driving arising out of the car's defective brakes (count 1) and its corrosion (count 2). Although a submission of no case to answer was allowed in respect of the first count, the appellant was convicted on the second count. On appeal, *held*, there was expert evidence that the corrosion would have been apparent only if the appellant had gone underneath the car to inspect it. However, the 1986 Act, s 2A(2) required a defect to have been obvious. Although there was some evidence that the appellant was aware or ought to have been aware of the defective condition of the car, there was insufficient evidence on which to properly convict him. Accordingly, the appeal would be allowed.

R v Strong [1995] Crim LR 428 (Court of Appeal: Rose LJ, Tucker and Smith JJ).

2505 Dangerous driving—indictment—joinder of offences

See *R v Harding*, para 829.

2506 Disqualification—discretionary disqualification—disqualification until test passed—motor vehicle used to facilitate wounding offence

The Powers of Criminal Courts Act 1973, s 44 provides that, where a person is convicted of an offence punishable on indictment with imprisonment for a term of two years or more and the court is satisfied that a motor vehicle was used for the purpose of committing, or facilitating the commission of, the offence in question, the court may order the person so convicted to be disqualified from driving for such period as it thinks fit. The Road Traffic Offenders Act 1988, s 36 provides that where a person is convicted of an offence involving obligatory or discretionary disqualification, the court may order him to be disqualified until he passes the test of competence to drive prescribed by virtue of the Road Traffic Act 1988, s 89(3).

The defendant was convicted of wounding with intent to cause grievous bodily harm. The victim was a passenger in a car that pulled out rather close in front of the defendant as he was driving. The passenger made obscene gestures in the defendant's direction and the defendant lost his temper. When both cars stopped at traffic lights, the defendant got out of his car and assaulted the passenger with a gear lever lock. There was evidence that the defendant had also deliberately driven his car in such a way as to force the other car to stop. At trial, he was sentenced to nine months' imprisonment and disqualified from driving for three years. An order was also made under the 1988 Act, s 36, requiring him to pass an extended driving test. He was granted leave to appeal only in respect of the disqualification and requirement to take an extended test. *Held*, the defendant had clearly used his car to facilitate the commission of the offence of wounding with intent. Therefore the trial judge had jurisdiction under the 1973 Act, s 44 to disqualify him from driving. The disqualification period would not normally exceed the length of the prison sentence; otherwise a defendant's employment prospects upon his release from prison might be adversely affected. However, a longer disqualification period might be justified where there was bad driving or the disqualification was intended to serve as an additional punishment. In the present case, the disqualification period of three years was too long. A period of one year would be substituted. The power under the 1988 Act, s 36, to disqualify until a further test had been taken applied only in cases of manslaughter and certain named driving offences. There was no power in respect of an offence of wounding and, accordingly, the judge's order in that respect would be quashed.

R v Patel [1995] RTR 421 (Court of Appeal: Roch LJ, Curtis and Stuart-White JJ).

2507 Disqualification—driving while disqualified—disqualified person in passenger seat—vehicle's engine warm—inference to be made

Scotland

The appellant, who had previously been disqualified from driving, was found lying across the passenger seat of a van parked on a road. The ignition key was found under his seat. Police officers took the appellant to the police station and on their return to the van some 15 minutes later they discovered that the engine was warm. The van was in exactly the same position as before and there was no one at the van. At the appellant's trial, the judge inferred that the appellant had been driving the van before the officers arrived and convicted the appellant of driving while disqualified and without insurance contrary to the Road Traffic Act 1988, ss 103(1)(b) and 143(1) and (2). On appeal, the appellant claimed that the judge had erred in drawing that inference. *Held*, all the established facts were consistent with the most probable explanation that the van had been driven to the place in question at about the material time. There were no established facts inconsistent with that explanation, nor was there any evidence pointing to any other explanation. Accordingly, the judge had been entitled to make the inference and the appeal would be dismissed.

Henderson v Hamilton 1995 SLT 968 (High Court of Justiciary).

2508 Drink-driving—blood specimen—analysis of specimen—possibility of maltreatment of specimen

Scotland

The appellant was suspected of driving with excess alcohol in his blood, contrary to the Road Traffic Act 1988, s 5(1)(a). At the police station he supplied a specimen of blood which was split into two parts, one part being given to the appellant. The Crown analysis showed that the blood specimen contained excess alcohol. A confirmatory test was made and spot checks were carried out to test quality control. The appellant's independent analysis showed the level of alcohol in the blood to be equivalent to the prescribed limit. No confirmatory test was carried out and the specimen was not analysed until 11 days after its receipt by the appellant. At the trial, the court took the view that it was entitled to look behind the analyses to see exactly how they had been carried out. Having done so, it decided that the Crown analysis truly reflected the blood alcohol content of the blood and that the appellant's analysis did not raise a reasonable doubt about the accuracy of the Crown analysis. The court also found as a fact that, while the alcohol content of a specimen could be reduced by its maltreatment, it could not be increased by such maltreatment. The appellant was convicted and, on appeal, *held*, the question whether the proportion of alcohol in the appellant's blood was in excess of the prescribed limit had been a question of fact for the court to determine upon a consideration of all the evidence. It was not bound to accept the result of the appellant's analysis nor was it bound to attach any weight to that analysis. The possibility of the maltreatment of the appellant's specimen at some time during the 11-day period, taken together with the absence of a confirmatory test, provided a sound basis for the court's conclusion that it was entitled to reject the appellant's analysis. Accordingly, the appeal would be dismissed.

Jordan v Russell 1995 SLT 1301 (High Court of Justiciary).

2509 Drink-driving—blood specimen—procedure to be followed by police—exercise of jurisdiction to quash conviction entered on guilty plea

The applicants pleaded guilty to and were convicted of driving motor vehicles when the proportion of alcohol in their blood exceeded the statutory limit. They applied for orders of certiorari to quash their convictions on the basis that the police had taken specimens for analysis without following the procedure laid down in *DPP v Warren* [1992] 4 All ER 865, HL (1992 Abr para 2189). *Held*, the judge's analysis in *R v Burton upon Trent Justices, ex p Woolley* (1994) Times, 17 November, DC (1994 Abr para 2382) was adopted, which led the court to consider whether the conduct of the prosecution in the present cases could properly be described as analogous to fraud. There had been no falsifying or suppression of evidence that might have secured an acquittal. On the contrary, there was no suggestion that the crucial evidence of the analysis of the blood samples was in any way open to doubt. Each applicant no doubt pleaded guilty on the basis of the analyses and on recognition that they had consumed alcohol to such an extent that such a reading was likely. Although there was a procedural error in the obtaining of such evidence, the conduct of the prosecution in neither case was analogous to fraud. There was no injustice to the applicants and, accordingly, the applications would be dismissed.

R v Dolgellau Justices, ex p Cartledge; R v Penrith Justices, ex p Marks (1995) Times, 4 August (Queen's Bench Division: Stuart-Smith LJ, Turner and Butterfield JJ).

2510 Drink-driving—breath, blood or urine specimen—failure to provide specimen—duplicity of charge

The Road Traffic Act 1988, s 7(6) provides that a person who, without reasonable excuse, fails to provide a specimen when required to do so is guilty of an offence.

The appellant was charged with an offence under the 1988 Act, s 7(6). The charge stated that the appellant had failed without reasonable excuse to provide a specimen of 'breath/blood/urine'. Following his conviction, he appealed on the ground that the charge was bad for duplicity. *Held*, s 7(6) created only one offence. Although the penalties provided for the offence depended on whether the investigation was under s 4 or s 5, they were not dependent on the type of sample or specimen requested. Accordingly, the appeal would be dismissed.

Worsley v DPP [1995] Crim LR 572 (Queen's Bench Division: Simon Brown LJ and Buckley J). *DPP v Butterworth* [1994] 3 All ER 289, HL, considered.

2511 Drink-driving—breath or blood specimen—failure to provide specimen—hospital patient

The Road Traffic Act 1988, s 9(1)(a) provides that while a person is at hospital as a patient, he cannot be required to provide a specimen of breath for a breath test or to provide a specimen for laboratory test unless the medical practitioner in immediate charge of his case has been notified of the proposal. If the requirement is then made, it is for the provision of a specimen at the hospital.

The appellant was taken to hospital following a road accident. She refused to give a breath specimen whilst still a patient and was therefore required to provide a blood specimen. However, she was discharged from hospital before complying with that requirement. As the appellant was no longer a patient, she was arrested for her earlier failure to provide a specimen, upon which a blood specimen was taken and she was charged with driving with excess alcohol. On appeal against her conviction for the offence, *held*, having regard to the 1988 Act, s 9(1), the appellant had been lawfully required to provide a blood specimen, and that requirement had not come to an end merely because she had ceased to be a patient. It was only if a police officer gave a clear indication that the procedure under s 9(1) no longer applied that the requirement to give a specimen was abrogated. No such indication had been given in the instant case. Moreover, the 1988 Act did not expressly provide that the specimen had to be given in hospital. Accordingly, the appeal would be dismissed.

Webber v DPP (1995) Times, 20 December (Schiemann LJ and Holland J).

2512 Drink-driving—breath test—evidence—challenge to admissibility of intoximeter evidence

It has been held that if an accused seeks to challenge the admissibility of evidence from a Lion Intoximeter 3000 machine which has been programmed, with the approval of the Home Office, to reduce alcohol level readings where the presence of acetone is detected, he must do so under the Police and Criminal Evidence Act 1984, s 78, and not s 69.

Ashton v DPP (1995) Times, 14 July (Queen's Bench Division: Balcombe and Buxton LJJ).

2513 Drink-driving—breath test—evidence—intoximeter mistakenly believed to be unreliable—subsequent admissibility of reading

The defendant was convicted of driving with excess alcohol, contrary to the Road Traffic Act 1988, s 5. At the police station he provided two positive samples of breath on an intoximeter, but the police officer believed that the machine had failed to give accurate readings. He therefore made a request for a blood sample under the 1988 Act, s 7(3)(b), but the defendant refused to comply. It subsequently transpired that the intoximeter was in satisfactory working order and the breath samples were accurate. On appeal, the issue arose whether the justices had erred in admitting the breath test results in evidence. *Held,* the test to be applied as to whether the intoximeter was reliable was not absolute. It was dependent upon the reasonable belief of the police officer in charge. The police officer had reasonably believed the machine to be inaccurate. Thus the breath samples remained potentially admissible in evidence until replaced by an admissible blood sample. The defendant had failed to give a sample of blood and consequently the breath test results, being accurate, were admissible in evidence. The appeal would accordingly be dismissed.

Hague v DPP (1995) Times, 14 November (Queen's Bench Division: Simon Brown LJ and Scott Baker J). *DPP v Winstanley* [1993] RTR 222 (1993 Abr para 2185) considered.

2514 Drink-driving—breath test—evidence—production of intoximeter printout

A driver was convicted of driving with excess alcohol on his breath. In evidence a police officer had produced a printout of an intoximeter, giving evidence on the lowest reading. He had not been cross-examined on the functioning or calibration of the machine but had handed the printout to the prosecutor who then closed the case. The defence submitted that there was no case to answer because the printout had not been produced in evidence. The driver applied for judicial review of the refusal to state a case. *Held,* once an exhibit was produced it came under the court's jurisdiction and the court could examine it whenever it chose. The court only came to examine the exhibit when the defence made a submission of no case to answer. A defence lawyer could not make a submission of no case when he saw fit, failing to point out an exhibit until that point. He was under a duty to lay the ground for his submission by calling evidence or by cross-examination.

R v Pydar Justices, ex p Foster (1995) 160 JP 87 (Queen's Bench Division: Simon Brown LJ and Curtis J). *Hasler v DPP* [1989] RTR 148 (1989 Abr para 1983) distinguished.

2515 Drink-driving—option of providing blood or urine specimen—consideration of medical reason

Under the Road Traffic Act 1988, s 7(4) if the provision of a specimen other than a specimen of breath is required the question whether it is to be a specimen of blood or a specimen of urine is to be decided by the constable making the requirement, but if a medical practitioner is of the opinion that for medical reasons a specimen of blood cannot or should not be taken the specimen must be a specimen of urine.

The appellant gave a specimen of breath which was found to be positive. He was arrested and taken to a police station. No reliable breath test device was available and the appellant was told that a specimen of blood or urine was required. When asked whether there were any reasons why a blood specimen should not be taken the appellant told the officer that he took tablets but also said that he agreed to supply a blood specimen. The blood sample was taken and the appellant was convicted. On appeal, he contended that when he told the officer that he took tablets, that was a medical reason and the officer should either have required a urine specimen or informed the doctor of the reason and allowed the doctor to decide whether the specimen should have been blood or urine in accordance with the 1988 Act, s 7(4). *Held*, on the face of it, the reason proffered by the appellant was capable of being a medical reason. If the officer had doubts about it, he could have questioned the appellant as to the nature of the tablets and the condition for which he took them. If he had concluded that there was no medical reason, he could have required blood but otherwise, if he was left in a state of doubt about the matter, he should have taken the view of a doctor. Accordingly, the appeal would be allowed and the conviction quashed.

Wade v DPP (1995) 159 JP 555 (Queen's Bench Division: McCowan LJ and Dyson J).

2516 Drink-driving—option of providing blood or urine specimen—duty to explain driver's rights—effect of failure to do so on subsequent correctly obtained specimen

The respondent provided a positive roadside breath test and was arrested. As no breath test machine was available at the police station the respondent was asked to provide a specimen of blood or urine. The officer failed to ask the respondent, in accordance with the Road Traffic Act 1988, s 7(4), whether there were any medical reasons why a blood sample should not be taken. When the doctor attempted to take blood, the respondent's vein collapsed and urine samples were taken instead. Those samples indicated that the respondent was over the prescribed statutory limit contrary to the 1988 Act, s 5(1)(a) and he was convicted of an offence. On appeal, the justices ruled that the urine evidence was inadmissible because of the officer's procedural defect in failing to ask if there was a reason why a blood sample should not be taken. The prosecutor appealed against that decision. *Held*, an officer was entitled to change his mind as to the type of specimen to be required up to the time at which the blood sample was actually taken. Once blood was given, the officer's right to change his mind ended. If that was the proper interpretation of the statutory provisions, an invalid but unproductive request for a specimen of blood did not render inadmissible evidence of the analysis of a subsequently correctly taken specimen of urine. Accordingly, the appeal would be allowed and the case would be remitted to the magistrates for the hearing to continue.

DPP v Garrett (1995) 159 JP 561 (Queen's Bench Division: Kennedy LJ and Waterhouse J). *Hayes v DPP* [1994] RTR 163 (1994 Abr para 2389) considered.

2517 Driving at excessive speed—speed measuring device—approval by Secretary of State

Scotland

The Road Traffic Offenders Act 1988, s 20(4) provides that a record produced or measurement made by a prescribed device is not admissible as evidence of a fact relevant to proceedings unless the device is of a type approved by the Secretary of State and unless any conditions subject to which the approval was given are satisfied.

The appellant was found guilty of driving at excessive speed. On appeal, he argued that the prosecution's evidence was unreliable and, in particular, that the Gatso mini radar device which police officers had used to measure his speed, was not a device which was approved for that purpose by the Secretary of State. *Held*, there was no evidence that the police officers had received special training in the use of the Gatso mini radar, nor that it was used regularly and in the course of routine work. As there was insufficient evidence to prove that the Gatso mini radar was approved by the Secretary of State, the court should not have drawn an inference to that effect. Accordingly, the appeal would be allowed.

Pickard v Carmichael 1995 SLT 675 (High Court of Justiciary). *Roberts v DPP* [1994] RTR 31, DC (1993 Abr para 2187) considered.

2518 Driving instruction—fees

The Motor Cars (Driving Instruction) (Amendment) Regulations 1995, SI 1995/1218 (in force on 29 May 1995), amend the 1989 Regulations, SI 1989/2057, by increasing the fees payable for the driving ability and fitness test and for the instructional ability and fitness test from £55 to £60 and by increasing the fee for the retention of a person's name in the register and the entry of a person's name in the register from £180 to £190.

2519 Driving licence—requirements

The Motor Vehicles (Driving Licences) (Amendment) Regulations 1995, SI 1995/1200 (in force on 29 May 1995), further amend the 1987 Regulations, SI 1987/1378, by increasing, for test applications made on or after 29 May 1995, the fees for ordinary driving tests and London taxi drivers' tests and some of the fees for extended driving tests ordered by the court under the Road Traffic Offenders Act 1988, s 36. The test fees applicable for ordinary driving tests are (1) for vehicles in Categories A and P, £36 for tests taken between 8.30 and 16.30 on a weekday and £47.50 for tests taken in the evening or at the weekend, and (2) for vehicles in other categories (not LGV/PCV), £28.50 for tests taken between 8.30 and 16.30 on a weekday and £38.50 for tests taken in the evening or at the weekend. Test fees for extended tests are (1) for vehicles in Categories A and P, £72 for tests taken between 8.30 and 16.30 on a weekday and £95 for tests taken in the evening or at the weekend, and (2) for vehicles in other categories (not LGV/PCV), £57 for tests taken between 8.30 and 16.30 on a weekday and £77.50 for tests taken in the evening or at the weekend. London taxi drivers' test fees, conducted at any time by the Metropolitan Police Commissioner, are £28.50.

The Motor Vehicles (Driving Licences) (Amendment) (No 2) Regulations 1995, SI 1995/2076 (in force on 15 August 1995), further amend the 1987 Regulations supra by redefining Category N of the categories of motor vehicles for driving test purposes so that it corresponds with those classes of vehicle specified in the Motor Vehicles (Driving Licences) (Large Goods and Passenger-Carrying Vehicles) Regulations 1990, SI 1990/2612, as amended, which are not used on roads which are repairable at the public expense or are so used for only short distances.

2520 Goods Vehicles (Licensing of Operators) Act 1995

See para 2962.

2521 Hackney carriage—licence—hackney carriage as private hire vehicle

The Local Government (Miscellaneous Provisions) Act 1976, s 46(1)(a) provides that, except as authorised by the Act, no person being the proprietor of any vehicle not being a hackney carriage or London Cab in respect of which a vehicle licence is in force, can use or permit the same to be used in a controlled district as a private hire vehicle without having for such a vehicle, a current licence for private hire vehicles.

It has been held that for the purposes of the 1976 Act, s 46, the fact that a vehicle has been licensed as a hackney carriage by one local authority does not mean that it cannot also be licensed as a private hire vehicle by another local authority.

Kingston-upon-Hull City Council v Wilson (1995) Times, 25 July (Queen's Bench Division: Balcombe LJ and Buxton J).

2522 Motor Cycle Noise Act 1987—commencement

The Motor Cycle Noise Act 1987 (Commencement) Order 1995, SI 1995/2367, brings the Act into force on 1 August 1995. For a summary of the Act, see 1987 Abr para 2259.

2523 Motor cycles—silencers and exhaust systems

The Motor Cycle Silencer and Exhaust Systems Regulations 1995, SI 1995/2370 (in force on 1 August 1996), impose requirements with respect to the supply in the course of carrying on a business of motorcycle silencers and exhaust systems. The regulations generally prohibit a person from supplying, offering or agreeing to supply, or exposing or having in his possession for the purpose of supplying, a silencer or exhaust system comprising a silencer for a motorcycle, moped or motor scooter, unless the silencer is marked in a manner specified in the regulations. The regulations also impose requirements as to packaging, labelling and the provision of accompanying instructions.

2524 Motor cycles—type approval

The Motor Cycle (EC Type Approval) Regulations 1995, SI 1995/1513 (in force on 10 July 1995), provide for (1) applications to the Secretary of State for EC type approval for motor cycles or parts of motor cycles, (2) the grant of such EC type approval by him, (3) the duties, including a duty to supply an EC certificate of conformity with each vehicle and to affix an approval mark to each part that conforms with the approved type, of holders of type approval so granted, and (4) for the withdrawal or suspension of such EC type approval granted by the Secretary of State.

2525 Motoring events—authorisation—off road events

The Motor Vehicles (Off Road Events) Regulations 1995, SI 1995/1371 (in force on 15 June 1995), replace the 1992 Regulations, SI 1992/1370, prescribing bodies which can grant an authorisation for a motoring event for the purposes of the Road Traffic Act 1988, s 13A (by virtue of which ss 1–3 of the same Act (offences of causing death by dangerous driving, dangerous driving, and careless and inconsiderate driving) are disapplied for authorised motoring events), requiring an authorisation to contain a condition that specified information about the event in question is to be given to the police and requiring payment by an applicant for authorisation of a fee specified by the relevant authorising body.

2526 Motor insurance

See INSURANCE.

2527 Motor vehicles—designation of approval marks

The Motor Vehicles (Designation of Approval Marks) (Amendment) Regulations 1995, SI 1995/3342 (in force on 5 February 1996), further amend the 1979 Regulations, SI 1979/1088, so as to prescribe a new marking relating to centre mounted stop lamps. The amendment is consequential upon amendments to ECE Regulation 7.

2528 Motor vehicles—removal and disposal—meaning of obstruction

The Removal and Disposal of Vehicles Regulations 1986, SI 1986/183, reg 3 provides that a constable may remove or arrange for the removal of a vehicle which has broken down, or been permitted to remain at rest, on a road in such a position or in such condition or in such circumstances as to cause obstruction to persons using the road or as to cause danger to such persons.

The appellant had claimed damages and declaratory and injunctive relief after police officers towed away his converted coach and family home from the position it had occupied for a considerable time for causing an obstruction to persons using the road within the meaning of the 1986 Removal Regulations, reg 3. On appeal from the dismissal of his claim, *held*, the term 'obstruction' was to be construed differently in the 1986 Removal Regulations, reg 3 from the Highways Act 1980, s 137 and the Road Vehicles (Construction and Use) Regulations 1986, SI 1986/1078. An obstruction for the purposes of the latter provisions was established by proof that any part of the highway had been obstructed so as to deny the public access to that part, and such obstruction had to be wilful, without lawful excuse and constitute an unreasonable use of the highway. However, the obvious intent of the 1986 Removal Regulations was to permit the removal, in cases of actual obstruction, of vehicles which could well be an obstruction not involving unreasonable use of the highway. The absence of any qualification as to reasonableness was a strong indication that 'obstruction' in these regulations did not have the same meaning as the other provisions. It referred to an obstruction to the use of the road by persons who were using it or might be expected to use it, hindering or preventing them from getting past. Thus, it permitted the removal of vehicles actually obstructing a road user and vehicles obstructing a road user whose arrival at that place could be expected. The police gave evidence that they were concerned mainly with the length of time the vehicle had been parked, and did not justify the removal on the basis of actual obstruction. Accordingly, the appeal would be allowed.

Carey v Chief Constable of Avon and Somerset [1995] RTR 405 (Court of Appeal: Butler-Sloss, Morritt and Hutchison LJJ).

2529 Motor vehicles—special types—authorisation

The Motor Vehicles (Authorisation of Special Types) (Amendment) Order 1995, SI 1995/3052 (in force on 1 January 1996), further amends the 1979 Order, SI 1979/1198, by (1) increasing to 2.55 metres, the maximum permitted overall width of certain motor vehicles constructed or adapted for use as grass cutters or hedge trimmers and which are authorised for use on roads, and (2) amending the provision relating to agricultural motor vehicles, agricultural trailers, agricultural trailed appliances and agricultural motor vehicles towing an off-set agricultural trailer or trailed appliance, as a consequence of amendments made to the 1986 Regulations by SI 1995/3051 (see para 2543).

2530 Motor vehicles—tests

The Motor Vehicles (Tests) (Amendment) Regulations 1995, SI 1995/1457 (in force on 1 July 1995), further amend the 1981 Regulations, SI 1981/1694, by exempting from the prohibition against using a vehicle without a test certificate vehicles that are used on roads for distances not exceeding an aggregate of 6 miles a week.

The Motor Vehicles (Tests) (Amendment) (No 2) Regulations 1995, SI 1995/2438 (in force on 9 October 1995), further amend the 1981 Regulations supra, by (1) empowering the Secretary of State to give an examiner notice that a specified person has not attended a course when required to do so by the Secretary of State or has attended such a course when required to do so but failed to complete it successfully, and requiring the examiner, on receipt of the notice, in such circumstances, to arrange that the specified person no longer carries out or supervises examinations, or signs test certificates; (2) where the Secretary of State gives an examiner notice terminating his authorisation to carry out tests, extending to 35 days the period from the date of the notice when the authorisation will cease, where the notice states that the Secretary of State considers it necessary that it should have early effect; (3) setting out three new cases (namely, where the vehicle emits a substantial amount of avoidable smoke, where items such as bonnets, tailgates etc cannot readily be opened, and where an examination cannot be carried out without risk of injury or damage) where an examiner is under no obligation to carry out or continue with an examination; (4) providing for a re-examination to be carried out free of charge after a failure if the re-examination is on the same or the next day, at the same station as the original examination and limited to certain items; (5) increasing the fee payable for the test examination of a motor bicycle not having a side car attached, from £11.14 to £11.52; (6) increasing the fee payable for the test examination of a motor bicycle with a side car attached, from £18.78 to £19.42; (7) increasing the fee payable for the test examination of vehicles in Class III ('light motor vehicles' other than motor bicycles), from £21.98 to £22.74; (8) increasing the fee payable for the test examination of vehicles in Class IV ('motor cars' and 'heavy motor cars' not being vehicles within Classes III, V, VI, or VII), from £26.10 to £27.38; (9) increasing the fee payable for the test examination of vehicles in Class V ('large passenger-carrying vehicles', particular public service vehicles and 'play buses'), from £33.04 to £34.18; (10) increasing the fee payable for the test examination of vehicles in Class VII (goods vehicles with a design gross weight of more than 3,000 kgs but not more than 3,500 kgs), from £28.84 to £29.84; and (11) increasing the fee payable on an appeal, where a notice of the refusal of a test certificate has been issued, and the fee for a duplicate test certificate.

2531 Motor vehicles—type approval—alternative requirements

The Motor Vehicles (Type Approval) (Great Britain) (Amendment) Regulations 1995, SI 1995/1322 (in force on 12 June 1995), further amend the 1984 Regulations, SI 1984/981, by (1) applying to a vehicle regardless of its date of manufacture the type approval requirements relating to noise emissions; (2) revising the type approval requirements relating to exhaust emissions; (3) revising the type approval requirements relating to noise; and (4) introducing an option for low volume type approval vehicles in respect of exhaust systems containing fibrous materials.

The Motor Vehicles (Type Approval for Goods Vehicles) (Great Britain) (Amendment) Regulations 1995, SI 1995/1323 (in force on 12 June 1995), further amend the 1982 Regulations, SI 1982/1271, by (1) applying to a vehicle, regardless of its date of manufacture, the type approval requirements relating to noise emissions; (2) revising the type approval requirements relating to exhaust emissions; (3) revising the type approval requirements relating to noise; (4) revising the form of the appropriate information document for a goods vehicle which must accompany an application for both type approval and a minister's approval certificate; (5) limiting the use of the existing form of minister's approval certificate for a goods vehicle of a type covered by a previous certificate to goods vehicles with a maximum gross weight not exceeding 3,500 kg; (6) introducing a new form of minister's approval certificate for a goods vehicle of a type covered by a previous certificate for use both as an alternative in the case of goods vehicles with a maximum gross weight not exceeding 3,500 kg and in all cases of goods vehicles with a maximum gross weight exceeding 3,500 kg; (7) limiting the use of the existing form of certificate of conformity for a goods vehicle to goods vehicles with a maximum gross weight not exceeding 3,500 kg; and (8) introducing a new form of certificate of conformity for use both as an alternative in the case of goods vehicles with a maximum gross weight not exceeding 3,500 kg and in all cases of goods vehicles with a maximum gross weight exceeding 3,500 kg.

The Motor Vehicles (EC Type Approval) (Amendment) Regulations 1995, SI 1995/2328 (in force on 1 October 1995), amend the 1992 Regulations, SI 1992/3107, so as to refer to amended

Community provisions relating to the interior fittings, wiper and washer systems, and wheel guards, of motor vehicles and to the mechanical coupling devices of motor vehicles and their trailers and their attachment to those vehicles.

2532   Motor vehicles—type approval—fees

The Motor Vehicles (Type Approval and Approval Marks) (Fees) Regulations 1995, SI 1995/925 (in force on 24 April 1995), replace the 1994 Regulations, SI 1994/1265. The regulations (1) prescribe the fees payable for the examination of vehicles and vehicle parts, for the examination of complete vehicles and for the issue of documents in connection with the type approval of vehicles and vehicle parts and the authorisation of the application of approval marks to vehicle and vehicle parts for the purposes of certain Community provisions, and the national scheme for the type approval of vehicles and vehicle parts; (2) prescribe the fees payable for the examination of premises with a view to their being approved for the purposes of carrying out examinations in accordance with a type approval scheme or certain Community provisions; and for advising a manufacturer as to whether his arrangements for securing conformity of production are likely to be accepted by the Secretary of State; (3) modify the basis on which fees are charged for a prescribed notification of differences of design, construction, equipment or marking when the vehicle is in category N1 (a goods vehicle with a gross vehicle weight not exceeding 3,500 kg); (4) prescribe an annual fee of £30 regardless of whether there was more than one notification during that year; (5) introduce a number of new fees relating to tests for light goods vehicles and tests for lighting installation, statutory plates, space for fitting rear registration plates, passenger hand holds, horns and stands for motorcycles; and (6) introduce new standards for protective steering for passenger cars and light goods vehicles and mechanical coupling devices for vehicles with four or more wheels.

2533   Motor vehicles—vehicle parked on road—requirement for insurance and test certificate where vehicle immobilised

The appellant parked a motor vehicle, which was in working order, on a road. He cancelled the insurance policy in respect of the vehicle and did not drive it for several months. The MOT test certificate then expired and no new certificate was obtained. The appellant was charged with offences of using a motor vehicle on a road without either a valid test certificate or insurance policy contrary to the Road Traffic Act 1988, ss 47(1) and 143(1). When the vehicle was found it would not have been possible to move it without making repairs but the prosecution alleged that by reason of the presence of the vehicle on the road the appellant was using it for the purposes of ss 47(1) and 143(1). Although the justices found that the appellant had taken no positive action to immobilise the vehicle and that it was clear the vehicle could neither be driven nor towed unless it was literally dragged, the appellant was convicted. On appeal by way of case stated, *held*, provided that a vehicle was a 'motor vehicle' within the definition of s 185 and that the vehicle was on a road, the owner of that vehicle had the use of it on the road whether at the material time it could move on its own wheels or not. In the present case, the appellant's vehicle was on the road and it was a motor vehicle as defined within the Act, notwithstanding that one aspect of its condition was reversible immobility. The appellant was under the obligations imposed upon him by ss 47(1) and 143(1) and, accordingly, the appeal would be dismissed.

Pumbien v Vines [1996] Crim LR 124 (Queen's Bench Division: Mitchell J).

2534   Motorways—use by traffic—restrictions on use

The Motorways Traffic (England and Wales) (Amendment) Regulations 1995, SI 1995/158 (in force on 1 January 1996), further amend the 1982 Regulations, SI 1982/1163, so that passenger vehicles which are constructed or adapted to carry more than eight seated passengers in addition to the driver and which have a maximum laden weight that exceeds 7.5 tonnes are prohibited from using the outside lane of motorways where a carriageway has three or more lanes.

2535   Parking places—controlled parking zone—consultation with residents

A local authority decided to make a designation order under the Road Traffic Regulation Act 1984 introducing a controlled parking zone. The applicants, members of a local action group, applied to have the order quashed, contending that the authority had failed (1) to consider whether its policy of progressively introducing such schemes ought to be modified in the present case, (2) to consult residents and businesses about the need for a scheme, and (3) to give them an opportunity to present alternative proposals. It fell to be determined whether the order creating the scheme was lawful. *Held*, it was clear that the applicants' suggestions had sometimes been ignored by the traffic management division, or were incompletely reported, and were always accompanied by assertions intended to lead the committee considering the scheme to reject the suggestions. By contrast, the benefits of the scheme were always emphasised. Citizens and representative organisations were entitled to expect objectivity in those whose duty it was to convey to the decision-makers what they had suggested. The representatives of residents and businesses were entitled to better treatment and should have been consulted at the beginning before a decision was made. The applicants' had made allegations about the lawfulness of the authority making so much profit from the scheme which raised serious issues entitled to consideration. No such consideration had been given. To succeed, it was enough for the applicants to demonstrate that there was a significant risk that the decision to introduce the scheme might have gone the other way. They had been substantially prejudiced by the defects in the consultation process. Accordingly, the designation order would be quashed.

R v Camden London Borough Council, ex p Cran [1995] RTR 346 (Queen's Bench Division: McCullough J).

2536 Parking places—special parking areas

The Road Traffic Act 1991 (Amendment of Section 76(3)) Order 1995, SI 1995/1437 (in force on 3 July 1995), amends the Road Traffic Act 1991, s 76(3) so as to specify additional parking restrictions which do not have effect in special parking areas.

2537 Passenger and goods vehicles

See TRANSPORT.

2538 Person in charge of a motor vehicle—person having consumed excess alcohol—likelihood of driving vehicle—passenger supervising learner driver

Scotland

Under the Road Traffic Act 1988, s 5(2) it is a defence for a person charged with an offence under s 5(1)(b) (being in charge of a vehicle with excess alcohol) to prove that at the time he is alleged to have committed the offence the circumstances were such that there was no likelihood of his driving the vehicle whilst the proportion of alcohol in his breath, blood or urine remained likely to exceed the prescribed limit.

The appellant was in the passenger seat of his car while his wife, a learner driver, was driving. At the time he was over the prescribed limit. The appellant accepted that his wife's driving was imperfect and that he would straighten the steering wheel if she was heading in the wrong direction. He was convicted of an offence under the 1988 Act, s 5(1)(b) on the basis that it was likely that he would have to take control of the steering wheel at some point while the wife was driving the car. On appeal, *held,* the question was not whether there was evidence that the appellant was likely to drive but whether he had succeeded in establishing the defence that there was no likelihood of his driving the car. Since the appellant accepted that he might take control of the car as a last resort, the judge at first instance had been entitled to conclude that the defence under s 5(2) had not been made out. Accordingly, the appeal would be dismissed.

Williamson v Crowe 1995 SLT 959 (High Court of Justiciary).

2539 Public service vehicles

See TRANSPORT.

2540 Registration marks—sale

The Sale of Registration Marks Regulations 1995, SI 1995/2880 (in force on 18 December 1995), replace the 1989 Regulations, SI 1989/1938, as amended. A new scheme is established providing for registration marks to which the Vehicle Excise and Registration Act 1994, s 27 applies to be assigned to vehicles registered in the name of persons (or their nominees) who have acquired rights under the scheme to have the marks so assigned. Registration schemes made under the 1989 Regulations, and amendments, continue to apply to unexercised rights granted on or before 17 December 1995.

2541 Road Traffic (New Drivers) Act 1995

The Road Traffic (New Drivers) Act 1995 makes new provision for the retesting of inexperienced drivers who commit traffic offences. The Act received the royal assent on 28 June

1995 and comes into force on a day or days to be appointed. For details of commencement, see the commencement table in the title STATUTES.

Section 1 provides that a person's 'probationary period' for the purposes of the Act is a period of two years beginning with the date on which the person in question becomes a qualified driver by passing a recognised driving test. Section 2 provides that where six or more penalty points have been attached to a driver's licence in consequence of his having committed an offence during his probationary period, the court must send the licence and its counterpart to the Secretary of State for revocation. Section 3 requires the Secretary of State to revoke licences thus sent to him so that the person whose licence has been revoked reverts to the position of being a learner driver driving under the terms of a provisional licence, until such time as he passes another test of competence to drive or his licence is otherwise restored. Section 4 prohibits the Secretary of State from granting a new licence until the person in question has passed a further test of competence to drive. Section 5 provides for the restoration of licences without retesting in certain circumstances. Section 6 and Sch 1 make provision applying the provisions of the Act to the case of a newly qualified driver who has a provisional licence and test certificate. Section 7 provides for the early termination of a person's probationary period. Section 8 applies the Act to persons in the public service of the Crown. Section 9 is concerned with interpretation and with the mode of service of notices required under the Act. Section 10 makes provision for the short title, commencement and extent of the Act and introduces Sch 2, which makes consequential amendments.

2542 Road traffic offences—sentencing

See SENTENCING.

2543 Road vehicles—construction and use

The Road Vehicles (Construction and Use) (Amendment) Regulations 1995, SI 1995/551 (in force on 1 April 1995), further amend the 1986 Regulations, SI 19861078, by (1) requiring that motor vehicles first used on or after 1 April 1995 and trailers manufactured on or after that date comply with specified Community provisions; (2) requiring that coaches first used on or after 1 April 1996 comply with certain conditions relating to the behaviour of vehicles on a road surface having reduced adhesion; (3) providing that certain motor vehicles first used on or after 1 April 1996 must not be fitted with an integrated retarder unless either the motor vehicle is fitted with an anti-lock device which acts on the retarder and meets specified requirements, or the retarder is fitted with a cut-out device which allows the combined control to apply the service braking system alone and which can be operated by the driver from the driving seat; (4) exempting vehicles with a maximum speed not exceeding 25 km/h and vehicles fitted for an invalid driver from compliance with the braking systems requirements of specified Community provisions; (5) requiring the maintenance of certain vehicles to comply with braking efficiency requirements and exempting industrial tractors from such requirements; (6) requiring that a bus first used on or after 15 August 1928 and before 1 January 1968 meet braking efficiency requirements that are similar to the requirements for a goods vehicle in like circumstances; (7) so that a bus first used on or after 1 April 1982 will not be regarded as meeting the braking efficiency requirements unless it is capable of meeting those requirements when the vehicle is so laden that its gross weight is its maximum gross weight, as defined; (8) requiring that the tyres of certain vehicles first used on or after 1 April 1991 be marked with an EC approval mark or comply with specified Community regulations; (9) exempting from specified requirements, in certain circumstances, a tyre designed so as to be capable of being fitted to an agricultural vehicle if it is marked with a speed symbol and a load capacity index; (10) prohibiting the use of certain trailers, which are manufactured on or after 1 October 1982 and are not fitted with a device designed to stop the trailer automatically in the event of the separation of the main coupling on a road, unless a secondary coupling is attached to the drawing vehicle and trailer; and (11) prohibiting the use on a road of certain trailers manufactured on or after 1 October 1982 and fitted with a device which is designed to stop the trailer automatically in the event of the separation of the main coupling where the operation of the device depends on a secondary coupling linking the device to the drawing vehicle unless the secondary coupling is properly attached to the drawing vehicle and trailer.

The Road Vehicles (Construction and Use) (Amendment) (No 2) Regulations 1995, SI 1995/737 (in force on 31 March 1995), correct an error in SI 1995/551 supra.

The Road Vehicles (Construction and Use) (Amendment) (No 3) Regulations 1995, SI 1995/1201 (in force on 1 June 1995), further amend the 1986 Regulations supra, by removing the 4.2 metre height restriction on the bodywork of goods vehicles with a total laden weight exceeding 35,000 kg, and removing regulations relating to wheels not fitted with pneumatic tyres, the power to weight ratio of heavy vehicles and noise limits for vehicles first used before 1 October 1983.

The Road Vehicles (Construction and Use) (Amendment) (No 4) Regulations 1995, SI 1995/1458 (in force on 1 July 1995), further amend the 1986 Regulations by exempting from the requirement to be fitted with a speed limiter goods vehicles that are used on roads for distances not exceeding an aggregate of 6 miles a week.

The Road Vehicles (Construction and Use) (Amendment) (No 5) Regulations 1995, SI 1995/2210 (in force in part on 25 September 1995 and in part on 1 January 1996), further amend the 1986 Regulations, (1) by introducing compulsory compliance with specified limits on emissions from vehicles with spark ignition engines first used on or after 1 January 1997 and providing for other vehicles whenever first used to comply with those limits as an alternative to existing requirements; (2) so that no person may use, or cause or permit to be used on a road, a vehicle first used on or after 1 August 1975 and propelled by a four-stroke spark ignition engine, if it is in such a condition and running on such fuel that (a) when the engine is idling the carbon monoxide content of the exhaust emissions from the engine exceeds, in the case of a vehicle first used before 1 August 1986, 4.5 per cent, or, in the case of a vehicle first used on or after 1 August 1986, 3.5per cent of the total exhaust emissions from the engine by volume; and (b) when the engine is running without load at a rotational speed of 2,000 revolutions per minute, the hydrocarbon content of those emissions exceeds 0.12 per cent of the total exhaust emissions from the engine by volume; (3) so that certain light vehicles with spark ignition engines first used before 1 August 1992, some such vehicles first used before 1 August 1994 and some such vehicles first used before 1 August 1996 may not be used on a road if their carbon monoxide content exceeds a specified amount at idling speed, the carbon monoxide content of the exhaust emissions exceeds 0.3 per cent at fast idling speed, the hydrocarbon content of the emissions exceeds 0.02 per cent at fast idling speed, or the ratio of air to petrol vapour in the mixture entering the combustion chambers is outside specified limits; (4) by prohibiting the use on a road of certain vehicles with diesel engines if they are in such a condition and running on such fuel that specified limits concerning the emissions are exceeded.

The Road Vehicles (Construction and Use) (Amendment) (No 6) Regulations 1995, SI 1995/3051 (in force on 1 January 1996), further amend the 1986 Regulations so as to (1) increase the maximum overall width, from 2.5 metres to 2.55 metres, in the case of (a) any motor vehicle other than a locomotive (not being an agricultural motor vehicle) and a refrigerated vehicle, (b) a trailer drawn by a motor vehicle having a maximum gross weight exceeding 3,500 kg, (c) an agricultural trailer, (d) an agricultural trailed appliance, (e) an off-set combination of an agricultural motor vehicle drawing a wheeled trailer, or (f) an agricultural, horticultural or forestry implement mounted rigidly but not permanently on a wheeled agricultural motor vehicle, agricultural trailer or agricultural trailed appliance, and (2) revise the definition of 'overall width' so that, in calculating the overall width of a vehicle, any guide-wheels fitted to a bus can be disregarded provided that they do not project more than 75 mm beyond the side of the bus.

2544 Road vehicles—registration and licensing

The Road Vehicles (Registration and Licensing) (Amendment) Regulations 1995, SI 1995/1470 (in force on 1 July 1995), amend the 1971 Regulations, SI 1971/450, in consequence of amendments made to the Vehicle Excise and Registration Act 1994, s 7, which now requires the form of the declaration to be made, and the particulars to be furnished, when a vehicle licence is taken out to be specified by the Secretary of State instead of prescribed by regulations. The special provision as to the identification of certain types of exempt vehicle made by the 1971 Regulations is omitted, all exempt vehicles, except pedestrian controlled vehicles, must now exhibit a document in the form of a licence, and regulations concerning an application for a new licence where a vehicle becomes chargeable to duty at a higher rate), an applications for a trade licence), a vehicle's horse-power and unladen weight are omitted.

2545 Taxi cabs

See TRANSPORT.

2546 Traffic signs and general directions

The Traffic Signs General (Amendment) Directions 1995, SI 1995/2769 (in force on 10 November 1995), amend the 1994 Regulations, SI 1994/1519, in relation to the placing of traffic signs to indicate speed limits at junctions between roads that are subject to differing speed limits. Other minor amendments are also made.

The Traffic Signs (Amendment) Regulations and General Directions 1995, SI 1995/3107 (in force on 5 January 1996), further amend the 1994 Regulations supra by (1) substituting a wider definition of a 'tourist attraction', (2) prescribing the new tourist facility signs set out in the Schedule, (3) making provision regarding the permitted variants and illumination of such signs, and (4) providing that the new signs may not be placed on motorways.

2547 Transport

See TRANSPORT.

2548 Vehicle excise duty

See CUSTOMS AND EXCISE.

ROYAL FORCES

Halsbury's Laws of England (4th edn) Vol 41, paras 1–600

2549 Articles

EC Law and the Dismissal of Pregnant Servicewomen, Anthony Arnull: (1995) 24 ILJ 215

Sexual Orientation and Military Employment, Robert Wintemute (on *R v Ministry of Defence, ex p Smith* (1995) Independent, 8 June (para 2551)): 145 NLJ 1477

2550 Army, Air Force and Naval Discipline Acts—continuation

The Army, Air Force and Naval Discipline Acts (Continuation) Order 1995, SI 1995/1964 (in force on 26 July 1995), continues in force the Army Act 1955, the Air Force Act 1955 and the Naval Discipline Act 1957 until 31 August 1996.

2551 Discipline—discharge of homosexuals—legality of policy

The appellants were homosexual members of the armed forces who were discharged under a Ministry of Defence policy that homosexual orientation was an absolute bar to membership of the forces. They applied for judicial review of the policy on the grounds that it was irrational, breached the right to respect for private life in the European Convention on Human Rights, and breached the Equal Treatment Directive. The ministry argued that its reasons for the policy related to morale and unit effectiveness, the special conditions of communal living and the services' in loco parentis role in relation to new recruits under 18. On appeal against the dismissal of the applications, *held*, the progressive development and refinement of public and professional opinion at home and abroad was an important feature of the case. Such opinion continued to develop, but the lawfulness of the appellants' discharge fell to be judged as of the date of their discharge in 1994. The test of irrationality was that the court could not interfere with the exercise of an administrative decision on substantive grounds except where it was satisfied that the decision was unreasonable in that it was beyond the range of responses open to a reasonable decision-maker. The human rights context was important, and the more substantial the interference with human rights, the more the court would require by way of justification before it was satisfied that the decision was reasonable. It was not the constitutional role of the court to regulate the conditions of service in the armed forces, nor did the court have the expertise to do so, but it had the role and duty of ensuring that the rights of citizens were not abused by the unlawful exercise of executive power. The ministry's policy was not irrational at the time when the appellants were discharged. It was supported by Parliament and by the ministry's professional advisers and there was no evidence which invalidated that advice. The court could not answer questions on the breach of the European Convention on Human Rights as it had seen none of the evidence relating to such questions. Further, there was nothing in the Equal Treatment

Directive which suggested that it addressed itself to discrimination on the grounds of sexual orientation. Accordingly, the appeals would be dismissed.

R v Ministry of Defence, ex p Smith [1996] 1 All ER 257(Court of Appeal: Sir Thomas Bingham MR, Henry and Thorpe LJJ). Decision of Queen's Bench Divisional Court (1995) Times, 13 June affirmed.

2552 Discipline—leave to appeal to Court-Martial Appeal Court—matters to be included in application

It has been held that in applying for leave to appeal to the Court-Martial Appeal Court, an applicant must provide fresh grounds of appeal which properly and fully set out the grounds on which the application is made, and he cannot merely rely on the notice of application together with the petition which has already been submitted to the service board.

R v Hiley (1995) Times, 10 March (Court of Appeal: Lord Taylor of Gosforth CJ, Alliott and Owen JJ).

2553 Pensions

See PENSIONS AND SUPERANNUATION.

2554 Royal Navy—capital sum awarded on leaving service—payment to another person

See *Legrove v Legrove*, para 1095.

2555 Servicewomen—dismissal—pregnancy—compensation—assessment

See *Ministry of Defence v Wheeler*, para 2648.

2556 Servicewomen—pension—provision excluding payment of pension to husband on servicewoman's death

See *Howard v Ministry of Defence*, para 2664.

SALE OF GOODS

Halsbury's Laws of England (4th edn) Vol 41, paras 601–692

2557 Articles

Consolidation or Confusion? Meryll Dean (on the EC Directive on Unfair Contract Terms (93/13/EC)): 145 NLJ 28

Goodbye to Merchantable Quality, Patrick Milne (on the Sale and Supply of Goods Act 1994): 145 NLJ 683

How Fair Art Thou? Anthony Mosawi (on the EC Directive on Unfair Contract Terms (93/13/EC)): LS Gaz, 25 January 1995, p 20

On the Receiving End, Richard Lawson (on the Sale and Supply of Goods Act 1994): LS Gaz, 5 January 1995, p 20

Product Liability, Computer Software and Insurance Issues—The St Albans and Salvage Association Cases, E Susan Singleton: 10 CLP 167

Sale of Goods: Changes to the Ownership Rules, Sheila Bone and Leslie Rutherford (on the Sale of Goods (Amendment) Act 1995): 139 SJ 866

2558 Conditional sale agreement—title to motor vehicle—liability of finance purchaser

See *Barber v NWS Bank plc*, para 602.

2559 Consumer protection

See CONSUMER PROTECTION.

2560   Implied terms—quality and fitness—breach—sale by agent for undisclosed principal

The Sale of Goods Act 1979, s 14(2) provides that where a seller sells goods in the course of a business, there is an implied condition that the goods are of merchantable quality. Where the seller sells goods in the course of a business and the buyer makes known any particular purpose for which the goods are being bought, there is an implied condition that the goods are reasonably fit for that purpose: s 14(3). These provisions apply to a sale by a person who in the course of a business is acting as agent for another as they apply to a sale by a principal in the course of a business, except where that other is not selling in the course of a business and either the buyer knows that fact or reasonable steps are taken to bring it to the notice of the buyer before the contract is made: s 14(5).

The owner of a vessel instructed an agent to sell it on his behalf under a brokerage and agency agreement. The purchaser bought the vessel, but it had defects which rendered it unseaworthy and the parties agreed that it had been unfit for the purpose for which it was bought. The purchaser was under the impression that the agents were the owners of the vessel. He successfully brought a claim for damages against the seller. On appeal, the court held that the seller was within the ambit of the 1979 Act, s 14(5) and rejected his argument that s 14(5) enabled action to be taken only against an agent acting for an undisclosed principal and not against the principal himself. On further appeal, *held*, if the seller's argument were correct, the exception to s 14(5) would be superfluous. Where an agent was acting for an undisclosed principal, a purchaser could not possibly know of the business of the unknown principal. However, the exception clearly presupposed that there would be a principal of whose existence the buyer would be aware prior to the contract of sale. The seller's restricted construction would not only give no effect to the words of the exception, but also create statutory alterations to the normal common law rules that where an agent contracted on behalf of a disclosed principal, the latter alone was liable on the contract and that an undisclosed principal might be sued on any contract made on his behalf. This construction was incorrect. Section 14(5) applied to any sale by an agent on behalf of a principal, whether disclosed or undisclosed, where circumstances giving rise to the exception did not exist. Accordingly, the appeal would be dismissed.

Boyter v Thomson [1995] 3 All ER 135 (House of Lords: Lords Jauncey of Tullichettle, Lloyd of Berwick, Nolan, Nicholls of Birkenhead and Hoffmann).

1979 Act, s 14(2) now as substituted by the Sale of Goods Act 1994, s 1.

2561   Price marking

See CONSUMER PROTECTION.

2562   Sale of Goods (Amendment) Act 1995

The Sale of Goods (Amendment) Act 1995 amends the Sale of Goods Act 1979 in relation to the sale of unascertained goods forming part of an identified bulk and the sale of undivided shares in goods. The Act received the royal assent on 19 July 1995 and came into force on 19 September 1995.

Section 1 describes the circumstances in which property may pass in goods where there is a contract for the sale of a specified quantity of unascertained goods forming part of an identified bulk. The section allows a buyer of unascertained goods to become the owner in common of an identified bulk of goods, defines the legal relationship between buyer and seller in such circumstances and gives statutory effect to the doctrine of 'ascertainment by exhaustion'. Section 2 provides a definition for 'bulk' and clarifies the meaning of the terms 'goods' and 'specific goods' to include the circumstances where there is a sale of an undivided share in goods or specific goods. Section 3 makes provision for short title, commencement and extent.

SALE OF LAND

Halsbury's Laws of England (4th edn) Vol 42, paras 1–400

See CONVEYANCING.

SENTENCING

Halsbury's Laws of England (4th edn) Vol 11(2) (reissue), paras 1187–1351

2563 Articles

Advise, Assist and Befriend, Bryan Gibson (on changes to the probation service): 145 NLJ 568

Bespoke Tailoring Won't Suit Community Sentences, Andrew Ashworth, Andrew von Hirsch, Anthony Bottoms, Martin Wasik: 145 NLJ 970

Calculating Days in Default for Non-Payment of Fines, F G Davies: 159 JP Jo 499

Confiscation Instead of Custody, J A Davis: 159 JP Jo 819

Defining 'Violent Crimes' for Sentencing Purposes, Gavin Dingwall (on the courts' interpretation of the Criminal Justice Act 1991, s 1(2)(b)): 139 SJ 422

An Early Face-Lift for Pre-Sentence Reports, Nigel Stone: 159 JP Jo 140

Effectiveness and the Probation Service, Philip Whitehead: 159 JP Jo 226

Electronic Monitoring of Curfew orders: Added Value or Alien Gimmick? Nigel Stone: 159 JP Jo 615

Fines, Proportionality and the Criminal Justice and Public Order Act 1994, Gavin Dingwall: 159 JP Jo 403

Justice and Economy—The Case for Community Service Hours Guidelines, Philip Lloyd: 159 JP Jo 502

Magistrates in the Dock, Ian Wise and Rona Epstein (on magistrates' power to imprison): 145 NLJ 567

Putting the Boot Into Young Offenders, Mark Mackarel (on positivism in juvenile sentencing): 145 NLJ 701

Sentencing for Dangerous Driving, A R Ostrin: 139 SJ 922

Sentencing Policy and Mentally Abnormal Offenders, Ralph Henham: Criminal Lawyer, Issue 60, p 4

Time for the Crime, John Hirst (on the meaning of 'life'): 145 NLJ 1571

2564 Aggravated vehicle taking—appellant's plea of guilty—whether imposition of maximum sentence appropriate

The appellant drove a stolen vehicle in a built-up area for several miles. He ignored traffic lights and signs and travelled at speeds of up to 70 mph in 30 mph areas until he crashed into a wall. He was charged with, and pleaded guilty to, aggravated vehicle taking. On his conviction, the justices said that the maximum penalty of two years' detention for the offence might be said to be far too little and, in spite of the guilty plea, the appellant was sentenced to two years' detention in a young offender institution. On appeal, *held*, if the justices intended to indicate that their view of the maximum sentence was such that they intended to impose that sentence without any regard for the circumstances in the case or for any discounts to which the appellant would reasonably be expected to be entitled, that approach would be wrong in principle. The maximum sentence should be reserved for the most serious offences of that kind while any appropriate discount should be made from a level of sentence which was commensurate with the seriousness of that offence. In the present case, no one was hurt as a result of the appellant's driving and there was no evidence that any road user was put into any imminent danger. There was no accident except for the appellant's impact with the wall but the potential for a serious accident was always present when a vehicle was driven in such a way. Although the appellant might have had little option but to admit his guilt, he had nevertheless done so. Taking all the circumstances into account, the maximum sentence was excessive and, accordingly, the appeal would be allowed to the extent that a sentence of 18 months' detention would be substituted.

R v Carroll (1995) 16 Cr App Rep (S) 488 (Court of Appeal: Hobhouse LJ, Turner and Wright JJ).

2565 Arson—mitigating factors

The appellants admitted starting two fires which caused extensive damage to property, and pleaded guilty to arson. The first appellant, who asked for eight other arson offences to be taken into account, was of previous good character, and of normal intelligence and psychological profile. As it was accepted that he was unlikely to commit further arson offences, he was sentenced on the basis of the seriousness of the offence to 30 months' detention in a young offender institution. The second appellant had committed two other arson offences and had instigated the instant offences. There was evidence that he had an abnormal personality and that he would be likely to cause further fires. He was sentenced under the Criminal Justice Act 1991, s 2(2)(b) to a longer sentence than would normally be imposed because it was concluded that he represented a danger to the public. On appeal against their sentences, *held*, the fact that the first appellant did not suffer from any psychiatric illness or abnormality and that he was a young man of normal intelligence was not a mitigating factor. The argument that he had been led astray on an impulse by the second appellant could not be accepted in view of the fact that he had committed eight other arson offences. He had to accept responsibility for his part in a serious course of conduct, and the sentence that had been imposed was therefore not too long. There was evidence that the second appellant had not learnt from his convictions and that he would be likely to re-offend. The judge had therefore been correct to sentence him under the 1991 Act, s 2(2)(b) and, accordingly, the appeals would be dismissed.

R v Bestwick (1995) 16 Cr App Rep (S) 168 (Court of Appeal: Roch LJ, Potter and Smith JJ).

2566 Attempted murder—discretionary life sentence—consideration of medical evidence regarding offender—ability of court to consider other factors in imposing sentence

The appellant received a life sentence in respect of an attempted murder and indecent assault. At the trial, medical reports suggested that he was of sound mind. He thus appealed against the sentence on the grounds that the criteria for the imposition of a discretionary life sentence as enunciated in *R v Hodgson* had not been satisfied. *Held*, *R v Hodgson* established three conditions which had to be satisfied before a discretionary life sentence could be justified: the offence had to be grave enough to warrant a very long sentence; it had to appear from the offender's history that he was a person of unstable character likely to commit offences in the future; and the likely consequences of such future offences, if committed, had to be serious. The fulfilment of the second criterion was thus being questioned. The medical evidence suggested that there was nothing in the appellant's physical or psychological constitution to suggest that he was likely to re-offend. Further, it was well established that, whilst medical evidence was normally required in considering the second criterion, the judge could also make inferences from other indicators such as a series of similar previous convictions or the fact that the case in question involved a number of offences. As the medical evidence suggested he was unlikely to re-offend and as he was connected with the commission of only one offence, a shorter sentence would be substituted.

R v Roche (1995) 16 Cr App Rep (S) 849 (Court of Appeal: Lord Taylor of Gosforth CJ, McKinnon and Judge JJ). *R v Hodgson* (1967) 52 Cr App Rep 113, CA followed.

2567 Commission of offence—statutory offence reformulated prior to plea—sentencing under reformulated offence

Hong Kong

Under the Hong Kong Bill of Rights, art 12(1) if, subsequent to the commission of an offence, provision is made by law for the imposition of a lighter penalty, the offender will benefit thereby.

The appellant was charged with two offences of possession of forged and blank credit cards, which carried maximum sentences of seven and 14 years imprisonment. After the commission of the offences but before the appellant pleaded guilty, the sections relating to those offences were replaced and in each case maximum sentences of three years and 14 years were provided, the greater sentence applicable where a specific intent was involved in the offence. The appellant was convicted of both offences and was sentenced to three and a half years for each offence. He unsuccessfully appealed against the sentences and, on further appeal, he claimed that the correct approach was to identify the elements of conduct which defined the old category of offence and then search the new categories for one whose elements corresponded substantially. He argued that, in his case, the offences did not correspond to the new sections because they called for a specific intent which was not previously required and that the court had to fall back on the offences of simple possession under the new sections and pass sentence in accordance with the three year maximum. *Held*, the appellant's argument was incorrect. Unless the new legislation was a simple re-enactment, a comparison of categories would often be impossible and the effect of the appellant's argument would be to relieve him from the increased burden of the new regime and give him a benefit which he would in practice never have enjoyed. It would spare the appellant from the increase from seven to 14 years which his criminal conduct would have attracted, and substitute a maximum of three years, a term which in the revised regime was insufficient to reflect the criminality of what he did. The question to be asked was not how the new definition of the offence corresponded with the old, but how the defendant would have stood if he had been convicted and sentenced for what he did under the new law rather than the old law. Accordingly, the appeal would be dismissed.

Chan v R [1995] 3 WLR 742 (Privy Council: Lords Keith of Kinkel, Mustill, Lloyd of Berwick, Nicholls of Birkenhead and Steyn).

2568 Common assault—aim of sentence—consideration of victim's injuries

It has been held that it is a fundamental principle of sentencing that the consequences to the victim should be taken into account by the court when it is considering the gravity of the offence and the appropriate sentence. Where the prosecution elects to charge an accused with common assault contrary to the Criminal Justice Act 1988, s 39 as opposed to the more serious offence of occasioning actual bodily harm, the court is not precluded from considering the injuries sustained by the victim merely because a more serious charge could have been brought. One of the aims of the criminal law is to redress the grievance of a victim and assuage his feelings by inflicting an appropriate punishment on the offender.

R v Crown Court at Nottingham, ex p DPP (1996) 160 JP 78 (Queen's Bench Division: Stuart Smith LJ and Butterfield J).

2569 Community service order—breach of requirement—violent behaviour exhibited towards community service officer—failure to perform work

The appellant was sentenced to 120 hours of community service for bankruptcy and other offences. Subsequently, on two occasions, the appellant threatened to slap the face of a community service officer and was summoned for breach of his community service on the ground that he had failed to work to the required standard. The court found the breach proved and the appellant appealed on the ground that, although his behaviour had been unacceptable, it did not amount to a failure to comply with the requirement that he perform work. *Held*, there was implicit in the word 'perform' an obligation to behave in a reasonable manner during the required performance and, therefore, unacceptable and violent behaviour exhibited towards a community service officer could amount to a failure, without reasonable excuse, to comply with any of the requirements of the relevant order. Accordingly, the appeal would be dismissed.

Caton v Community Service Office (1995) 159 JP 444 (Queen's Bench Division: Rose LJ and Tuckey J).

2570 Community service order—comprehensive legislative code—proposals for enactment

The Home Office has published a green paper seeking views on its proposals for enacting a comprehensive legislative code embodying the various community sentences (probation orders, community service orders, combination orders, curfew orders, supervision orders and attendance centre orders), *Strengthening Punishment in the Community* (Cm 2780). The proposals include increasing the discretion of the courts to determine the content of community sentences in individual cases by reference to pre-sentence reports and supervision plans which would take into account any preliminary indications given by the commissioning court as to the seriousness of the offence and any appropriate emphasis on reparation and the prevention of re-offending. A further proposal is that consent should no longer be required for the imposition of a community sentence.

2571 Consecutive sentences—defendant causing severe injury and manslaughter— concurrent sentences inappropriate

The defendant supplied K with methadone with the result that he suffered severe brain damage and was left severely disabled in the long term. Charges were brought against the defendant in relation to K and, while the defendant was on bail some six weeks later, he provided M with methadone resulting in M's death. The defendant pleaded guilty to charges of (1) supplying a class A controlled drug to K, (2) causing a noxious substance to be taken by K, (3) supplying methadone to M, and (4) M's manslaughter from its supply. He was sentenced concurrently to four years' imprisonment for the first three offences and five years' imprisonment for manslaughter. The Attorney General made an application for the court to review the sentences on the ground that, although they were not outside the proper range of sentences, the fact that they were concurrent made them unduly lenient. He submitted that the most serious aggravating feature of the offences was that the defendant had deliberately supplied methadone to M when he knew that K had suffered severe injury as a result of his supply. *Held*, the court was satisfied that it was inappropriate to pass concurrent sentences since the effect was to add only one year for manslaughter to what would have been appropriate sentences for the offences in respect of K alone. Accordingly, the sentences in relation to K would remain. However, in relation to M, the sentence of five years for manslaughter would be substituted for a four-year sentence to run concurrently with the four years for supplying, but both would be consecutive with the sentences in respect of K, making a total of eight years' imprisonment.

R v Johnson (A-G's Reference) (No 5 of 1995) [1996] 1 Cr App (S) 85 (Court of Appeal: Lord Taylor of Gosforth CJ, Tucker and Forbes JJ).

2572 Consecutive sentences—offences committed on separate occasions

The defendant pleaded guilty to various counts, namely robbery, wounding with intent to cause grievous bodily harm, perverting the course of justice, driving whilst disqualified, and making off without payment at a petrol station. He was sentenced to three years' imprisonment for the robbery and four years' imprisonment for wounding with intent to cause grievous bodily harm, the sentences to run concurrently. He was also given shorter prison sentences for the other offences, which were also made concurrent. In referring the case for review on the basis that the sentence was unduly lenient, the Attorney General submitted that there were a number of aggravating features to the offences, in particular that the two most serious offences were premeditated, and were committed whilst the defendant was on bail. *Held*, the robbery offence was committed on a separate occasion from that of wounding with intent to cause grievous bodily harm, and the defendant had not shown any remorse. The Attorney General was correct in arguing that the series of offences was so grave that the sentences for the two most serious offences should have been made consecutive rather than concurrent.

A G's Reference (No 4 of 1994) (1994) 16 Cr App Rep (S) 81 (Court of Appeal: Lord Taylor of Gosforth CJ, Garland and Curtis JJ).

2573 Conspiracy to cause explosions—organisation no longer engaged in terrorist activity—effect on length of sentence

It has been held that sentences of 30 years' imprisonment for conspiring to cause a series of explosions as part of a campaign of terrorism were not excessive. The length of sentence was not affected by the fact that the organisation of which the appellants were members was no longer engaged in terrorist activities.

R v Taylor; R v Hayes (1995) 16 Cr App Rep (S) 873 (Court of Appeal: Lord Taylor of Gosforth CJ, McKinnon and Judge JJ).

2574 Conspiracy to commit arson with intent to cause damage to property—political purpose—deterrent sentence

The two appellants, in pursuit of what they believed to be the interests of the Irish Republican movement, had placed incendiary devices in five shops in a city. The devices were intended to go off in the early hours of the morning so as to risk the minimum harm to individuals. One shop was seriously damaged and two shops suffered minor damage. The appellants pleaded guilty to conspiracy to commit arson with intent to cause, or being reckless as to, damage to property. The first appellant was sentenced to 20 years' imprisonment and the second appellant to 15 years' imprisonment. On appeal against sentence, *held*, the appellants' actions, which were motivated by their political beliefs, constituted an attack on the community as a whole. Such actions, intended to destabilise the community or exert pressure, would be met with severe deterrent sentences. The appellants had not intended to injure or kill individuals and, although the political climate in Northern Ireland had changed, the need to deter such offences remained. The appellants' actions were intended to be an attack on property, not on human life and limb although there was always a risk to life and limb in such cases. The sentences were too high and, accordingly, the appeals would be allowed and the sentences reduced to 16 and 11 years' imprisonment respectively.

R v Cruickshank; R v O'Donnell (1994) 16 Cr App Rep (S) 728 (Court of Appeal: Lord Taylor of Gosforth CJ, Alliott and Rix JJ).

2575 Criminal Justice (Scotland) Act 1995

See para 763.

2576 Determination of sentence—disputed facts giving rise to ambiguous verdict—sentencing based on version of facts most favourable to defendant

Two parents were charged on a count of wilful neglect after their baby suffered injuries consistent with being squeezed and swung against a wall. The prosecution alleged that there had been wilful neglect during a fourteen-day period, but medical evidence indicated that the baby suffered internal bleeding only during the last three days of that period. The prosecution was unwilling to amend the indictment by adding a count alleging wilful neglect during that three-day period. The parents were convicted by a jury and the judge indicated that he was not bound to accept the version of facts most favourable to the parents as the basis for sentencing. He sentenced each to five years' imprisonment. On appeal, *held*, the verdict of guilty followed a standard direction which allowed the jury to convict as long as they were sure and satisfied as to any wilful neglect within the period specified. They were not invited to specify the basis for their verdict and there was therefore a dilemma as to the proper approach to sentencing. An amendment to the indictment could easily have been made to secure a finding of the jury on the point in issue but the prosecution had chosen not to do so. The judge should have taken the jury's verdict to relate to the shorter period and sentenced accordingly. The sentences would be reassessed on a more favourable factual basis, but bearing in mind the considerable public abhorrence for conduct of this kind. Accordingly, the appeal would be allowed to the extent that sentences of three years' imprisonment would be substituted.

R v Efionayi (1994) 16 Cr App Rep (S) 380 (Court of Appeal: Hirst LJ, Auld and Holland JJ). *R v Stosiek* (1982) 4 Cr App Rep (S) 205, CA applied.

2577 Disqualification from driving—road traffic offences

See ROAD TRAFFIC.

2578 Driving offence—causing death by careless driving under influence of alcohol or drugs—comparison with causing death by dangerous driving

The defendant pleaded guilty to causing death by driving without due care and attention, having consumed alcohol above the prescribed limit contrary to the Road Traffic Act 1991, s 3A. He was sentenced to six years' imprisonment and disqualified from driving for ten years. He appealed against sentence. *Held*, the offence was committed after the statutory increase in the maximum sentence for the offences of causing death by dangerous driving and causing death by careless driving while under the influence of excess alcohol. The significance of the statutory changes was considered in *R v Shepherd; R v Wernet* [1994] 2 All ER 242. It seemed to the court that, by increasing the maximum penalties for the offences, Parliament intended to indicate the significance that was attached to the aggravating feature of driving while unfit through drink or drugs. Both offences now held the same maximum sentence. As such, it was unlikely that the offence of causing death by dangerous driving, which could be committed without the aggravating factor of driving with excess alcohol, was necessarily a graver type of offence than causing death by careless driving while under the influence of excess alcohol. In giving sentence, the sentencer commented that it would be difficult to imagine a worse case of causing death by careless driving while under the influence of alcohol. However, there would be cases involving higher levels of alcohol, worse driving and more deaths. In addition, the defendant had pleaded guilty and experienced genuine remorse. The case was towards the top of the scale, but the sentencer's starting point of eight years was too high. Accordingly, the sentence would be reduced to four-and-a-half years' imprisonment.

R v Locke (1995) 16 Cr App Rep (S) 795 (Court of Appeal: Henry LJ and Tuckey J). *R v Shepherd (A-G's Reference (No 14 of 1993)); R v Wernet (A-G's Reference (No 24 of 1993))* [1994] 2 All ER 242 (1993 Abr para 2250), CA, applied.

2579 Driving offence—causing death by careless driving under influence of alcohol or drugs—mitigating factors

The offender lost control of his car and collided with a lamp post, killing his passenger. It was estimated that the offender was driving at 40 mph in a 30 mph speed limit and the level of alcohol in his blood was almost twice the prescribed limit. He pleaded guilty to causing death by careless driving, having consumed alcohol so as to be above the prescribed limit and was sentenced to a combination order consisting of 80 hours of community service and 12 months' probation. He was also disqualified from driving for 12 months. On a referral by the Attorney General on the ground that the sentence was unduly lenient, *held*, a custodial sentence would normally be appropriate in such cases except in exceptional cases where the alcohol level was only just over the borderline, the carelessness was momentary and there was strong mitigation. In the present case, the deceased was the former husband of the offender's sister, and the offender had a close relationship with the deceased's son, his nephew. That was a quite exceptional circumstance and the family, rather than looking for a custodial sentence to reflect the loss of life, would be harmed were the offender to be sentenced to imprisonment. Although the sentence was considered by the court to be lenient and, now that the maximum sentence had been increased, would be unduly lenient in most cases, the court had regard to the fact that the offence was committed before that increase and to the exceptional mitigation. Accordingly, the sentence would not be increased.

A-G's Reference (No 8 of 1994) (1994) 16 Cr App Rep (S) 327 (Court of Appeal: Lord Taylor of Gosforth CJ, Ognall and Gage JJ).

The offender was found guilty of causing death by driving without reasonable consideration for other road users, with twice the legal limit of alcohol in his breath, contrary to the Road Traffic Act 1988, s 3A, and was sentenced to 18 month's imprisonment. On referral by the Attorney General on the grounds of the leniency of the sentence it was claimed in mitigation that the offender had suffered extreme remorse, being admitted to hospital with a depressive illness. *Held*, personal elements of mitigation, feelings of guilt and temporary depression should not deflect the court from passing a sentence appropriate to the gravity of the case. Accordingly, the sentence would be increased to four year's imprisonment.

R v Brown (1995) Times, 2 February (Court of Appeal: Lord Taylor of Gosforth CJ, McKinnon and Judge JJ).

2580   Driving offence—causing death by careless driving under influence of alcohol or drugs—substantial excess over prescribed alcohol limit

Under the Road Traffic Act 1988, s 3A if a person causes the death of another person by driving without due care and attention and has consumed so much alcohol that the proportion of it in his breath, blood or urine at that time exceeds the prescribed limit, he is guilty of an offence.

The appellant, the driver of a vehicle, failed to negotiate a bend in a road. The vehicle went out of control and struck a tree resulting in the death of the appellant's passenger. The appellant was breathalyzed and the blood/alcohol figure showed that he was substantially over the prescribed limit. He pleaded guilty to an offence under the 1988 Act, s 3A and was sentenced to two years' imprisonment and disqualified from holding or obtaining a licence for seven years. On his application for leave to appeal against the sentence, *held*, an offence under s 3A commanded the same maximum penalty as causing death by dangerous driving. In exceptional cases, if the alcohol level at the time of the offence was just over the prescribed limit and the carelessness was momentary, a non-custodial sentence might be imposed. In the present case, however, the blood/alcohol figure was substantially over the limit and the appellant had been previously convicted of driving with excess alcohol. The sentence imposed was appropriate and, accordingly, the application would be refused.

R v Deery (1994) 159 JP 202 (Court of Appeal: Lord Taylor of Gosforth CJ, MacPherson and Steele JJ). *R v Shepherd (A-G's Reference (No 14 of 1993))*; *R v Wernet (A-G's Reference (No 24 of 1993))* [1994] 2 All ER 242, CA, applied.

2581   Driving offence—causing death by careless driving under influence of alcohol or drugs—unduly lenient sentence

The defendant, a lorry driver, was driving just over the permitted speed limit when his lorry mounted a grass verge, hit a pedestrian and knocked him into the path of a passing car. The pedestrian was killed. The defendant later pleaded guilty to causing death by careless driving while under the influence of drink or drugs, contrary to the Road Traffic Act 1988, s 3A. By way of mitigation, it was said that he had an exemplary driving record, showed genuine remorse and had been guilty of nothing more than momentary inattention, the accident having occurred as he was checking his delivery tickets. The trial judge found that there would be no useful purpose in imposing a custodial sentence and sentenced him to 240 hours' community service and disqualified him from driving for three years. On a reference by the Attorney General on the ground that the sentence was unduly lenient, *held*, the offence was committed after the maximum punishment for the offence had been increased by Parliament from five to ten years. Parliament had clearly intended that, save in exceptional circumstances, the court should impose a custodial sentence where death by careless driving was coupled with driving over the prescribed alcohol limit. Such offences were often committed by persons who were genuinely remorseful and otherwise of good character. To say that no useful purpose would be served by sending such persons to prison was to ignore the deterrent factor. There was also a need to make it known to drivers that they could expect to receive a custodial sentence if they killed someone while driving under the influence of alcohol or drugs. Accordingly, taking into account all the mitigating factors in the present case, justice would be served by substituting a sentence of two years' imprisonment.

R v Taziker [1995] RTR 413 (Court of Appeal: Lord Taylor of Gosforth CJ, Alliott and Rix JJ).

2582   Driving offence—causing death by dangerous driving—aggravating factors

After spending an evening consuming several alcoholic drinks the applicant was aware that he should not drive but did so, at one point actually pausing in a car park to avoid a police car. There was no suggestion that he drove at an excessive speed and although it was dark, visibility was good, when his car struck and killed three women, all dressed in black, who were crossing a pelican crossing. The lights of the crossing were green at the time. A breath test showed that he had more than twice the prescribed limit of alcohol in his blood. He pleaded guilty to three counts of causing death by dangerous driving having consumed alcohol above the prescribed limit contrary to the Road Traffic Act 1988, s 3A and was sentenced to three years' imprisonment concurrently on each count and disqualified for five years. He applied for leave to appeal against sentence. *Held*, the applicant had produced several testimonials to his good character but this could not be a major factor where his alcohol level was so high and three people had been killed. At the time of the offence the Road Traffic Offenders Act 1988, Sch 2, Pt I prescribed a maximum sentence of five years. One week later the Criminal Justice Act 1993, s 67(1) came into force, amending the 1988 Act, Sch 2, Pt I so as to increase the maximum sentence to ten years. Although those new higher levels of sentencing had not come into force at the time of the offence, the courts had already indicated that the sentence for this type of offence should be higher. Accordingly, the sentence was appropriate and leave to appeal would be refused.

R v McCabe [1995] RTR 197 (Court of Appeal: Lord Taylor of Gosforth CJ, Scott Baker and Longmore JJ). *R v Shepherd (A-G's Reference (No 14 of 1993)); R v Wernet (A-G's Reference (No 24 of 1993))* [1994] RTR 49 (1993 Abr para 2250) approved.

The defendant was seen by police officers whilst driving a stolen car. In attempting to avoid them, the defendant drove at excessive speed, went through red traffic lights, mounted the pavement, drove on the wrong side of the road, and knocked over an elderly woman who later died as a result of multiple injuries. The defendant eventually abandoned the car. When arrested, he gave a false name, changed his appearance, and declined to answer questions when interviewed. However, his fingerprints were found on the vehicle and he was identified by witnesses as the driver of the car at the relevant time. He pleaded guilty to causing death by dangerous driving, driving a vehicle taken without authority, and driving whilst disqualified. He also admitted being in breach of a conditional discharge order and a community service order, and was still subject to a deferred sentence imposed for other motoring offences. For the offence of causing death by dangerous driving, he was sentenced to four years' imprisonment, disqualified from driving for ten years, and given ten penalty points. For the other offences, he was given a total of six penalty points and was ordered to take an extended driving test. No penalty was imposed for breach of the conditional discharge, and the community service order was rescinded. The Attorney General sought a review of the sentence on the ground that it was unduly lenient. *Held*, although the judge had taken account of all the aggravating features, he had given the defendant a low sentence because of his youth. It was necessary to have regard to the fact that since the sentence was originally imposed, the maximum penalty for causing death by dangerous driving had been increased from five to ten years' imprisonment. Although the case did not involve a drink factor, which was often a serious aggravating feature in driving offences, the defendant's driving had been prolonged and bad, and his conduct at the time was in itself an aggravating feature. The sentence was certainly lenient and verged on the unduly lenient, and in similar cases, the court would expect a longer sentence to be imposed. However, in the instant case, taking account of the need to discount for the element of double jeopardy, it would not be justifiable to increase the sentence.

R v Sergeant [1995] RTR 309 (Court of Appeal: Lord Taylor of Gosforth CJ, Jowitt and Cresswell JJ).

The offender was involved in an accident in which his vehicle went out of control, causing a collision between two lorries in which the drivers of both lorries were killed. Prior to the accident, the offender was seen driving at an excessive speed and in an erratic manner. He was found to have a breath alcohol level of three times the legal limit. The offender pleaded guilty to two offences of causing death by dangerous driving while affected by alcohol and was sentenced to 15 months' imprisonment and disqualified from driving for life. On the Attorney General's application for a review of the sentence on the ground that it was unduly lenient, *held*, five of the aggravating features in *R v Boswell* (1984) 6 Cr App R (S) 257, CA (1984 Abr para 2365) were present, namely the high level of alcohol, excessive speed, a prolonged course of bad driving, a previous conviction for driving with excess alcohol, and the fact that there was more than one victim. The offender had pleaded guilty, had expressed remorse and was of good character in matters other than driving. However, in a bad case such as this, the amount of discount that could be allowed for generally good previous character was limited. The sentence was, in circumstances where Parliament had recently doubled the maximum sentence for the offence, undoubtedly unduly lenient. Accordingly, concurrent sentences of five years' imprisonment on each of the two counts would be substituted and the disqualification would stand.

A-G's Reference (No 22 of 1994) [1995] RTR 333 (Court of Appeal: Lord Taylor of Gosforth CJ, French and Longmore JJ).

2583 Driving offence—causing death by dangerous driving—driver under influence of alcohol—deterrent factors

The appellant, having consumed a considerable amount of alcohol so as to be above the prescribed limit, had inattentively driven an articulated goods vehicle after dark along a dual carriageway. The vehicle had run off the road onto the grass verge and hit a man who was killed instantly. The appellant pleaded guilty to causing death by dangerous driving when under the influence of drink. He was sentenced to a community service order for 240 hours and disqualified from driving for three years. On a reference by the Attorney General on the ground that the sentence was unduly lenient, *held*, the offence had been committed since the maximum sentence had been increased from five to ten years. Where an offender was not just substantially over the permitted limit but two or three times over the limit, a substantial sentence should be imposed. It was clear that Parliament intended that where death was caused by careless driving coupled with driving over the permitted limit, the court, save in exceptional circumstances, would be expected to impose a custodial sentence. The deterrent factor and the need to establish, to the knowledge of the public, particularly the driving public, that where one drove with a substantial amount of drink, and one drove in such a way as to kill somebody, meant that a sentence of imprisonment would almost always be required. The appellant had a good driving record prior to the offence. He had indicated always that he intended to plead guilty, he had not attempted to evade responsibility and had completed almost three-quarters of the community service order. In consequence of the offence, he had lost his job, his wife and his home for which reasons the court would discount his sentence by a considerable amount. The appeal would be allowed and a sentence of two years' imprisonment substituted.

A-G's Reference (No 36 of 1994) (1994) 16 Cr App Rep (S) 723 (Court of Appeal: Lord Taylor of Gosforth CJ, Alliott and Rix JJ).

2584 Driving offence—causing death by dangerous driving—unduly lenient sentence

The offender was driving towards a pedestrian crossing at approximately 27 mph on a road with a 30 mph speed limit. Other vehicles travelling in both directions had slowed down or stopped at the crossing but the offender made no attempt to do so. He struck and killed a girl as she stepped onto the crossing from a central reservation. The offender had two relevant previous convictions for failing to comply with a traffic signal and speeding. At his trial, he was convicted of causing death by dangerous driving contrary to the Road Traffic Act 1988, s 2A and was sentenced to 28 days' custody and disqualified for three years. Since the offender had spent 14 days in custody on remand he was released immediately. On a reference by the Attorney-General on the ground that the sentence was unduly lenient, *held*, applying the guidelines set out in *R v Boswell* [1984] 3 All ER 353, CA (1984 Abr para 2365), the sentence imposed was unduly lenient and an appropriate sentence was six months' imprisonment. This was more than a 'momentary reckless error of judgment'. It involved the offender in failing to look ahead, to see the crossing, to see the girl crossing the other side of the road to the central reservation and to see the traffic ahead of him stop to allow her to go further. However, taking into account the element of double jeopardy, especially where an offender had to return to custody after being released, and the offender's state of health, it was not in the public interest to increase the sentence.

A-G's Reference (No 34 of 1994) (1994) 159 JP 237 (Court of Appeal: Lord Taylor of Gosforth CJ, Jowitt and Cresswell JJ).

2585 Driving offence—dangerous driving—mitigating factors—guilty plea

The appellant, who had never held a full driving licence, was chased by police as he drove at speeds of up to 90 mph. At times he drove with the car headlights turned off, he caused another vehicle to have to avoid an accident, drove on the wrong side of the road, through red traffic lights, collided with another vehicle, and came to rest on the pavement, and his breath test proved positive. He appealed against a two-year sentence given under the Road Traffic Offenders Act 1988, Sch 2 after his plea of guilty to a charge of dangerous driving. *Held*, the appellant had never held a full driving licence, seemed to have an obsession with driving cars, had had many convictions and had received several sentences. The only possibly mitigating factor was his plea of guilty, for which he could not be credited, the incident being an extreme example of dangerous driving for which he was caught red-handed. In reality the appellant had no option but to plead guilty. Accordingly, the appeal would be dismissed.

R v Hastings (1995) 159 JP 744 (Court of Appeal: Lord Taylor of Gosforth CJ, Tucker and Forbes JJ).

2586 Driving offence—endorsement of licence—consideration of previous convictions

Scotland

The Road Traffic Offenders Act 1988, s 31(1) provides that where a person is convicted of an offence involving an obligatory or discretionary disqualification and his licence is produced, (a) any existing endorsement on his licence is prima facie evidence that the matter is endorsed, and (b) the court may, in determining what order to make in pursuance of the conviction, take those matters into consideration.

The defendant was convicted of a speeding offence. In determining sentence, the sheriff considered the defendant's record of previous speeding convictions and, on that basis, imposed a maximum of six penalty points on his licence. This led to his disqualification from driving under the totting up procedure. The defendant appealed against the sentence. He claimed that the gravity of the offence was the only relevant consideration in deciding the appropriate number of penalty points to be imposed. He argued that if the court took previous convictions into account and that in turn led to the bringing into effect of the totting up procedure, the previous convictions would, in effect, be used twice in the same case and that would be unfair. *Held*, there was no suggestion in the 1988 Act that the court could only take into account the gravity of the offence in deciding the appropriate number of penalty points to be imposed. The statutory provisions were entirely general and did not exclude consideration of previous convictions. Accordingly, the appeal would be dismissed.

Nicholson v Westwater 1995 SLT 1018 (High Court of Justiciary).

2587 Drug offence—confiscation and forfeiture orders—High Court procedure—amendment

See para 2374.

2588 Drug offence—confiscation order—confiscation of profits relating to earlier drug trafficking conviction

The Drugs Trafficking Offences Act 1986, s 2(5) provides that, for the purposes of assessing the value of the defendant's proceeds of drug trafficking in a case where a confiscation order has previously been made against him, the court shall leave out of account any of his proceeds of drug trafficking that are shown to the court to have been taken into account in determining the amount to be recovered under that order.

In proceedings that preceded the 1986 Act, a defendant was convicted and sentenced for the offence of conspiracy to import cannabis. At that time the court had no power to make a confiscation order. The defendant admitted on oath to having benefited from drug trafficking, and his sentence included a fine equivalent to a large sum of money found in his possession upon his arrest. In later proceedings, the defendant was convicted of conspiracy fraudulently to evade the prohibition on importing cannabis. A confiscation order was made under the 1986 Act, the majority of which reflected benefits the defendant had received in relation to the earlier drug trafficking conviction. The defendant appealed against the order in so far as it took into account the earlier benefits. *Held*, even where there had been previous proceedings for a drug trafficking offence and a confiscation order had been made, the 1986 Act, s 2(5) specifically permitted the court to make a confiscation order in respect of benefits not covered by that earlier confiscation order. The power to make the confiscation order was a power exercised in connection with drug trafficking, and not a power exercised in connection with the proceedings for the earlier drug trafficking offence. Therefore it was irrelevant that the 1986 Act did not confer any powers on the court in connection with proceedings instituted before the commencement of that Act.

The judge had rightfully taken the earlier benefits into account and, accordingly, the appeal would be dismissed.

R v Taylor (1995) Times, 7 December (Court of Appeal: Lord Taylor of Gosforth CJ, Kay and Smedley JJ).

2589   Drug offence—confiscation order—determination—standard of proof

See para 890.

2590   Drug offence—confiscation order—enforcement—Northern Ireland orders

The Drug Trafficking Act 1994 (Enforcement of Northern Ireland Confiscation Orders) Order 1995, SI 1995/1967 (in force on 1 September 1995), provides for the enforcement in England and Wales of orders for the confiscation of the proceeds of drug trafficking offences.

The Criminal Justice Act 1988 (Enforcement of Northern Ireland Confiscation Orders) Order 1995, SI 1995/1968 (in force on 1 September 1995), provides for the enforcement in England and Wales of orders for the confiscation of the proceeds of offences other than drug trafficking offences.

2591   Drug offence—confiscation order—offender's realisable property

The appellant was arrested after his co-accused was found carrying drugs into the country by ferry. The drugs were seized as soon as they were found and they were never thereafter in the appellant's control or possession. He was convicted of being knowingly concerned in the fraudulent evasion of the prohibition on the importation of goods and was sentenced to 5 years' imprisonment. Further, a confiscation order was made under the Drug Trafficking Offences Act 1986 for the estimated purchase price of the drugs. On appeal, it fell to be determined whether that sum was, at the time the order was made, realisable property. *Held*, once the drugs had been seized they ceased to be property held by the appellant. There was therefore no basis upon which it could be held that the appellant was in any position to realise that property as an asset. Accordingly, the appeal would be allowed and the order would be quashed.

R v Thacker (1995) 16 Cr App Rep (S) 461 (Court of Appeal: Russell LJ, Ebsworth and Curtis JJ).

It has been held that, where a court is minded to make a confiscation order under the Drug Trafficking Offences Act 1986 in relation to the equity in the matrimonial home, it should proceed with extreme caution. A number of obvious difficulties arise in making such an order. If the property is co-owned it may be necessary to ascertain the nature and extent of the offender's interest. Consideration might also need to be given to the likely costs to be incurred in selling the property. It might also prove to be impossible to sell the property at all, particularly if the offender's family remain in occupation.

R v Gregory (1995) Times, 31 October (Court of Appeal: Beldam and Scott Baker LJJ and Stuart-White J).

2592   Drug offence—drug trafficking—ecstasy

The appellant pleaded guilty to importing a substantial quantity of ecstasy tablets and cannabis resin, and was sentenced to eight years' and six years' imprisonment respectively for the offences. The appellant's father was a convicted drug smuggler, and the appellant had become involved as a result of his father's influence. The appellant had travelled abroad on a number of occasions to obtain the drugs, attempting to conceal them in a vehicle transporter owned by his father. On his appeal against sentence, *held*, although the appellant had no previous convictions and had acted out of loyalty to his father, he must have been aware of the gravity of the offences, as ecstasy tablets were a Class A drug with a potentially lethal effect. Moreover, although a number of people had been involved in the drug smuggling operation, the appellant had acted as more than just a courier, as he had played a responsible part in organising the transportation of the drugs. The trial judge had been correct in taking a sentence of 12 years as the starting point for the ecstasy offence, and had been generous in giving a discount of four years in that respect. That sentence was therefore within the range of sentences appropriate for the offence, but the sentence for importing cannabis would be reduced to four years.

R v Blackburn (1995) 16 Cr App Rep (S) 902 (Court of Appeal: Hirst, Auld and Pill LJJ).

2593   Drug offence—drug trafficking—restraint order—external confiscation order

By virtue of the Drug Trafficking Offences Act 1986 (Designated Countries and Territories) Order 1990, SI 1990/1199, art 3(2), the 1986 Act applies, in relation to a designated country, subject to the modifications specified in the 1990 Order, Sch 2. The 1986 Act, as so modified, is set out in the 1990 Order, Sch 3. The 1986 Act, s 8(1) provides that the High Court may issue a restraint order which prohibits any person from dealing with any realisable property subject to conditions and exceptions specified in the order. The power to issue restraint orders is exercisable under s 7, as so modified, where proceedings have been issued against the defendant in a designated country, the proceedings have not been concluded and either an external confiscation order has been made or it appears that there are reasonable grounds for believing that such an order may be made. Section 1, as so modified, provides that a person against whom an external confiscation order has been made in a designated country is referred to as a defendant in the 1990 Order. The United States is a designated country for the purposes of the 1990 Order.

A drug trafficker opened bank accounts in London in the joint names of his wife's parents and allegedly deposited therein the proceeds of his unlawful drug trafficking in the United States. The United States government subsequently commenced proceedings to recover the proceeds held in the London accounts. It obtained an external confiscation order in civil proceedings commenced in New York in which the bank accounts were the named defendants. No criminal proceedings were ever brought against the drug trafficker himself. Thereafter, in proceedings brought in England, the United States government obtained a restraint order under the 1986 Act, s 8(1) which prohibited the drug trafficker and the named account holders from dealing with the money in the London accounts. One of the named account holders subsequently sought to have the restraint order set aside, but her application was refused. At her appeal the issue arose as to whether a restraint order could be made when the relevant foreign order was a civil judgment in rem. *Held*, s 7 gave the court power to make a restraint order prohibiting any dealing with the alleged proceeds of drug trafficking referred to in the external confiscation order made by a foreign court in proceedings in rem where property rather than a person was named as the defendant. Section 7 was concerned to identify the stage of proceedings instituted to obtain an external confiscation order at which a restraint order might be made. It did not require a particular form of proceedings (ie proceedings in personam), and did not use the term 'the defendant' in the limited sense described in s 1(3). The New York order recognised that the persons who were or might be interested in the relevant funds had the opportunity to intervene. Thus, the persons known or believed to have an interest in the defendant funds were clearly within the contemplation of the court order when it was made. The expression 'proceedings . . . against the defendant' in s 7 was to be construed as including proceedings in rem in which the standing of persons with a financial interest in the outcome was, as in the New York proceedings, plainly recognised. Accordingly, the appeal would be dismissed.

Re S-L [1995] 4 All ER 159 (Court of Appeal: Evans, Otton and Pill LJJ). *The Deichland* [1989] 2 All ER 1066, CA (1989 Abr para 25) applied.

2594   Drug offence—drug trafficking—restraint order—non-party to trial holding realisable property—power to make restraint order against non-party

Under the Drug Trafficking Offences Act 1986, s 8 the High Court may by order prohibit any person from dealing with any realisable property, subject to such conditions and exceptions as may be specified in the order.

A restraint order pursuant to s 8 was made against the applicant who was holding property on behalf of defendants in a criminal trial. The order also required the applicant to swear an affidavit of disclosure in respect of moneys received from certain defendants and in respect of bank transactions. The applicant sought by summons an order that he be discharged from complying with the original order. *Held*, the words 'any person' in s 8 were wide in effect. If it had been Parliament's intention to limit the powers of the court only to make such orders against parties to drug offence proceedings, it would have done so. It would be absurd that, by the simple device of passing realisable property to a third party, a person who was a party to criminal proceedings could defeat one of the main purposes of the 1986 Act. It followed that, in addition to the power to make restraint orders, there was also a power to make all such ancillary orders as appeared to the court to be just and convenient, including an order to make an affidavit of disclosure. As to the use which could properly be made of the information or evidence arising from compliance with the disclosure order in the present case, the court was satisfied that the terms of the order that the disclosure was not to be used in the prosecution of an offence alleged to have been committed by the applicant required strengthening in order to protect the applicant. Accordingly, the summons would be dismissed but the order would be varied by further prohibiting the use in any prosecution of evidence obtained as a direct result of the disclosure.

Re D (Restraint Order: Non-party) (1995) Times, 26 January (Queen's Bench Division: Turner J).

2595 Drug offence—drug trafficking—restraint order—privilege against self-incrimination

It has been held that where a defendant is the subject of a restraint order under the Drug Trafficking Offences Act 1986 and the order states that no disclosure made in compliance with it will be used in evidence in the prosecution of an offence alleged to have been committed by the defendant, additional wording should be added to the order stating that no use will be made of evidence obtained as a direct result of such disclosure. The courts will not countenance any inroads into the privilege of refusing to incriminate oneself unless either it is required by statute that the privilege takes second place to a wider public interest or that there is some adequate protection afforded. The discretion under the Police and Criminal Evidence Act 1984, s 78 to refuse to admit evidence if it will have an adverse effect on the fairness of proceedings is not to be regarded as an adequate and independent safeguard; anything involving reliance on an exercise of discretion does not constitute an adequate substitute for the absolute privilege against self-incrimination.

Re C (Restraint Orders: Identification) (1995) Times, 21 April (Queen's Bench Division: Ognall J).

2596 Drug offence—importation—guidelines

In separate cases, the appellants were convicted of offences relating to the importation of cocaine (a Class A drug) and possession of cocaine with intent to supply. In accordance with guidelines for offences involving Class A drugs, their sentences were based on the street value of the drugs. As well as imprisonment, two of the appellants were recommended for deportation, and a confiscation order was made against another appellant. On appeal against sentence, *held*, although the relative significance of any seizure of a Class A drug was measured by street value rather than by weight, street value was often difficult to assess accurately and gave rise to different judicial responses where the value was disputed. Moreover, if the street price of drugs continued to fall as drugs became more readily available, that would have the effect of reducing sentencing levels. Sentencing guidelines therefore had to be revised so as to be expressed in terms of weight rather than street value. Where the weight of the drugs at 100 per cent purity was at least 500 grams, sentences of 10 years and more were appropriate. Where the weight at 100 per cent purity was at least 5 kilograms, sentences of 14 years or more were appropriate. Having regard to the new guidelines and to all the other relevant circumstances of each case, the sentences were not excessive or inappropriate. Accordingly, the appeals would be dismissed.

R v Aranguren; R v Aroyewumi; R v Bioshogun; R v Littlefield; R v Gould (1994) 99 Cr App Rep 347 (Court of Appeal: Lord Taylor of Gosforth CJ, Waterhouse and Bell JJ). *R v Aramah* (1982) 147 JP 217, CA (1982 Abr para 2666), *R v Bilinski* (1987) 86 Cr App Rep 146, CA (1987 Abr para 2431) not followed.

It has been held that when sentencing for offences involving the drug ecstasy, the criteria to be used should be based on the weight of the active ingredient of most tablets as being about 100mg. It is to be assumed that Parliament intends crimes involving drugs of the same class, here Class A, to be treated similarly. Thus the tariff for offences involving ecstasy should be kept at around the same level as other Class A drugs. Accordingly, for 5,000 tablets of ecstasy or more, a sentence of 10 years or more is appropriate and, for 50,000 tablets or more, a sentence of 14 years or more is appropriate. The quantity of tablets or the weight of the active ingredient is only one factor to be considered in deciding the appropriate sentence. Other relevant factors include the offender's role, his plea and the assistance, if any, given to the authorities. The Court of Appeal so stated when decreasing the sentences of two appellants who had been convicted of illegally importing the drug.

R v Warren; R v Beeley [1995] Crim LR 838 (Court of Appeal: Lord Taylor of Gosforth CJ, Rougier and Ebsworth JJ). *R v Aranguren* supra applied.

2597 Fine—level of fine—harbour company's failure to take adequate precautions to prevent explosion on ship

See *R v Mersey Docks and Harbour Company*, para 1498.

2598 Firearms—possession of firearm with intent to commit robbery—unduly lenient sentence

The offender was seen loitering near a building society and a bank. He had a hood pulled over his head and was carrying an object. When arrested he was found to be in possession of an imitation pistol. He pleaded guilty to having an imitation firearm with intent to commit an offence of robbery and was sentenced to a probation order for two years. He had previous convictions for dishonesty and violence and, at the time of the offence, he was on bail in respect of an offence of deception. The Attorney General made an application for the court to review the sentence on the ground that it was unduly lenient, submitting that the offence was aggravated by the offender's admitted intention to rob a bank or building society at gunpoint, the offender's disguise and the fact that the offence was premeditated and was committed while he was on bail. *Held*, the appropriate sentence for such an offence was a custodial sentence. The court had a duty to the public and it was necessary to mark such an offence in a way which the public regarded as appropriate and which would act as a deterrent to any others minded to equip themselves for robbery and perhaps to carry it through. A sentence of 30 months had been passed in a similar case, but allowance would be made in the present case for the fact that the offender had been allowed his freedom only to be called back to court some time later. Accordingly, the appeal would be allowed and a sentence of 12 months' imprisonment would be substituted.

A-G's Reference (No 10 of 1994) (1995) 16 Cr App Rep (S) 285 (Court of Appeal: Lord Taylor of Gosforth CJ, Ognall and Gage JJ).

2599 Firearms—possession of shotgun—possession while committing offence—offender unaware shotgun was loaded

The appellant believed that a man who owed him money was at a particular address. When the appellant went to the premises the occupier refused to let him in and the appellant pointed a sawn-off shotgun through the letter box. The police arrived and the appellant threatened them with the shotgun, which went off when the police tried to disarm him. The appellant pleaded guilty to possessing a firearm at the time of committing an offence and he was sentenced to five years' imprisonment. On appeal, *held*, the use of firearms, and in particular sawn-off shotguns, was becoming increasingly prevalent, and the courts should not be inhibited from passing sentences designed to deter those minded to use a firearm for whatever purpose and in whatever context. In the present case, however, the sentencer had accepted that the appellant did not know the shotgun was loaded. Accordingly, the appeal would be allowed to the extent that the sentence would be reduced to three years' imprisonment.

R v Francis (1994) 16 Cr App Rep (S) 95 (Court of Appeal: Russell LJ, Alliott and Mance JJ).

2600 Firearms—possession of shotgun—possession without certificate

Police officers searched premises where the appellant was staying and found a sawn-off shotgun together with ammunition. The appellant pleaded guilty to possessing a shotgun without a certificate and he was sentenced to three years' imprisonment. On appeal, he submitted that the sentence was too high. *Held*, in reported cases a sentence of three years, where there were no aggravating features, was too high; the sentences ranged between one and two years' imprisonment. The court had in mind the fact that there was an increase in the use of firearms by criminals and it concluded that it was time for the authorities to be reviewed. However, the court reluctantly allowed the appeal to the extent that the sentence should be reduced to two years' imprisonment although, without the authorities, the court would not have disturbed the original sentence.

R v Ecclestone (1994) 15 Cr App Rep (S) 9 (Court of Appeal: Russell LJ, Alliott J and Sir Tasker Watkins). *R v Kennedy* (1988) 10 Cr App Rep (S) 398, CA, considered.

2601 Grievous bodily harm—rugby player striking opposing player during match

During a rugby match, the appellant struck another player in the face causing him injuries. The appellant was convicted of grievous bodily harm contrary to the Offences Against the Person Act 1861, s 20 and was sentenced to six months' imprisonment. On appeal against sentence, *held*, the sentence was not wrong in principle and, on the facts, it was not manifestly excessive. However, the appellant had been prohibited from playing rugby for 14 months and, by reason of the sentence, he had lost the opportunity to return to full-time employment after a year during which he had been out of work as a result of redundancy. The appellant had in one way

or another paid a high price for the offence and, accordingly, the appeal would be allowed to
the extent that the sentence would be reduced to four months' imprisonment.

R v Goodwin (1995) 16 Cr App Rep (S) 885 (Court of Appeal: Hirst and Auld LJJ and
Mitchell J).

2602   Intellectual property offence—confiscation order

The Criminal Justice Act 1988 (Confiscation Orders) Order 1995, SI 1995/3145 (in force on 1
January 1996), amends the Criminal Justice Act 1988, Sch 4, Pt I so as to add offences under the
Copyright, Designs and Patents Act 1988, ss 107 (making or dealing with infringing articles),
198 (making, dealing with or using illicit recordings), and the Trade Marks Act 1994, s 92
(unauthorised use of trade marks in relation to goods) to the list of offences in respect of which
magistrates' courts may make confiscation orders under the 1988 Act, Pt VI. The order only
applies to offences committed on or after 1 January 1996.

2603   Manslaughter—mother's partner violent towards child—mother's failure to
protect child

After the mother of a small child allowed her boyfriend to move in with them, a number of
people saw signs of injury on the child. She died as a result of a blow, or a series of blows, to her
chest and was found to have numerous injury marks on her body. The boyfriend was convicted
of murder and the mother was found guilty of manslaughter on the ground that she knew her
boyfriend was going to punish the child but had failed to protect her. The mother was sentenced
to 10 years' imprisonment and was also convicted of offences of wilful ill-treatment and wilful
neglect for which she was sentenced to six years' and four years' imprisonment respectively. All
sentences were to run concurrently. On the mother's appeal, held, no previous cases existed to
indicate what sentence should be imposed in such a case. Although ten years' imprisonment was
a long period, that was a matter for the trial judge to decide. He had listened to the evidence
and was able to form a view of what share of responsibility the mother had to bear for the death.
There was no error in his reasoning and there was nothing to show that he exceeded the
sentence generally considered appropriate for such an offence. Accordingly, the appeal would
be dismissed.

R v White (1995) 16 Cr App Rep (S) 705 (Court of Appeal: Staughton LJ, Waterhouse and
Morison JJ).

2604   Mitigation—inability to pay fine—dispute of facts

See R v Guppy, para 743.

2605   Murder—mandatory life sentence—recommendation as to minimum period of
imprisonment

The appellant was convicted of murder. In passing a mandatory life sentence on him, the judge
recommended that he should serve a minimum of 20 years' imprisonment. On appeal, held, the
Criminal Appeal Act 1968, s 50 defined 'sentence', but did not deal with whether statements
about the minimum period were recommendations or declarations. Although an offender could
make representations following a judicial recommendation, ultimately it was a matter to be
determined by the Secretary of State. However, there was an anomalous distinction between
mandatory life sentences and discretionary life sentences. The Criminal Justice Act 1991, s 34,
which applied to the latter, empowered judges to state the 'relevant part' of a sentence which
was appropriate for punishment and deterrence, leaving aside risk to the public. As the 'relevant
part' was part of a judge's order and not merely a recommendation, there was a right of appeal
against it. In contrast, there was no right of appeal against a recommendation made under the
Murder (Abolition of Death Penalty) Act 1965, s 1(2) as to the minimum sentence in the case of
mandatory life sentences. If a judge did not make a recommendation, a written report was sent
to the Secretary of State stating the minimum period necessary for punishment and deterrence,
again leaving aside the risk to the public. It was not clear that judges' recommendations made
under the 1965 Act, s 1(2) were always made on that basis, and in the instant case, the
recommended period had taken account not only of the need for punishment and deterrence,
but also may have reflected the risk that the appellant posed to the public. However, the court
was bound by authority and by statute and, accordingly, the appeal would be dismissed.

R v Leaney [1996] 1 Cr App Rep (S) (Court of Appeal: Lord Taylor of Gosforth CJ, Mantell
and Keene JJ).

2606 Plea bargaining—indication of likely sentence—departure from indication

The defendant's counsel in a criminal trial was persuaded to approach the judge to ask for an indication of the sentence the defendant might expect if he were to change his plea to guilty. On the basis of the information so received the defendant changed his plea. He appealed against the sentence eventually passed, claiming he had been given an expectation from which the judge subsequently departed. *Held*, counsel should not have approached the judge to ask for such an indication, nor should the judge have given such an indication. However, the appeal would be allowed on other grounds, namely that the sentence should be commensurate with the offence.

R v Thompson (1995) 159 JP 568 (Court of Appeal: Hobhouse LJ, Pill and Steel JJ).

2607 Plea of guilty—discretion of sentencing judge—unsatisfactory inquiry

The appellant had been sentenced to 18 months' imprisonment following his plea of guilty to possessing a class A controlled drug with intent to supply. The judge had expressed concern as to the plea agreed between the parties that the appellant was only going to sell the drug to two or three friends and he had insisted on a *Newton* hearing and on questioning the appellant. *Held*, where a person was pleading guilty the judge was entitled to make known any concerns he might have, to insist on a *Newton* hearing and to question the defendant, especially where it seemed that the Crown had taken a mistaken view of the facts. In the present case, it seemed that in the *Newton* hearing the judge had interrupted prematurely and had given the impression that he had made up his mind on the papers without regard to the appellant's evidence. The sentence passed was appropriate on the basis of the plea tendered but, having regard to the unsatisfactory nature of the *Newton* hearing and the manner in which the judge expressed himself when sentencing, a sentence of 12 months would be substituted.

R v Myers [1996] Crim LR 62 (Court of Appeal: Roch LJ, Curtis and Denison JJ). *R v Newton* (1982) 77 Cr App Rep 13 applied.

2608 Plea of guilty—divergence between prosecution and defence as to facts—duty of defence counsel and sentencing judge

The appellant was charged with assault occasioning actual bodily harm. The prosecution alleged that he had jabbed his wife in the face with a fork, pulled her up the stairs by her arm, punched her repeatedly about the face, head and neck, and threatened to strangle her. Although those were the facts presented to the court when the appellant entered his guilty plea, when the appellant came to be sentenced at a later date, his counsel stated that the appellant disputed the prosecution's version of events. In particular, the appellant claimed that he had not jabbed his wife in the face with a fork, and that he had slapped, rather than punched, her. The appellant was sentenced to six months' imprisonment on the basis of his limited admission, although that was not made clear by the sentencing judge. On appeal against sentence, *held*, where there was a substantial dispute between the prosecution's allegations and the extent to which a defendant accepted those allegations, it was for defence counsel to state the basis on which the guilty plea was entered, and for the sentencing judge to make clear the basis on which he was imposing sentence. If a factual dispute was not resolved by a sentencing judge, the Court of Appeal had to approach the matter on the basis of the facts accepted by the appellant. Here, even on the basis of the appellant's admission that he had only slapped his wife about the head, a serious incident had occurred. The appellant had assaulted his wife in the presence of their teenage children for no good reason other than that he was angry at what she had cooked for him. Although the wife's injuries were not serious, they could have been and, in any event, she had suffered pain. A custodial sentence was warranted, but it should have been three, rather than six, months. Accordingly, the appeal would be allowed.

R v McFarlane (1994) 16 Cr App Rep (S) 315 (Court of Appeal: Glidewell LJ, Blofeld and Buxton JJ).

2609 Plea of guilty—plea agreed on unreal and untrue facts—judge's rejection of agreed facts

It has been held that a court should seek to sentence an offender on a true basis. Where a defendant has pleaded guilty and the prosecution lends itself to an agreement founded on an unreal and untrue set of facts, the following principles apply: (1) the judge is entitled in such a case to direct the trial of an issue so that he can determine the true factual basis. (2) Such a direction does not create a ground on which the defendant can be allowed to vacate his guilty plea. (3) The decision that there should be a trial of an issue means that the judge is entitled to expect the prosecuting counsel to assist him by the presentation of prosecution evidence and in testing any evidence called by the defence. The prior agreement between prosecution and defence must be considered as conditional on the approval of the judge. It would offend and obstruct justice were the prosecution to be bound unconditionally. (4) Before the trial of an issue is embarked upon it is appropriate to consider whether there is any part of the agreement to which the prosecution should be held to be bound. Counsel should also consider which of the prosecution statements or documents read bear upon the issues to be tried.

R v Beswick (1996) 160 JP 33 (Court of Appeal: Stuart-Smith LJ, Jowitt and Steel JJ).

2610　Pre-sentence report—further adjournment for assessment—satisfactory alternative to custodial sentence—appropriateness of custodial sentence

The appellant pleaded guilty to attempted burglary. The offence was committed when he was on bail for other offences. At his trial, the appellant was remanded on bail for the preparation of pre-sentence reports and the matter was then further adjourned so that the appellant could be assessed to determine whether he was suitable for a probation order which required his attendance on a specific course. A probation officer confirmed that he should attend the course if a probation order with an appropriate condition was made. However, when the matter came before the court again, the appellant was sentenced to 18 months' imprisonment. On appeal, *held*, in *R v Gillam* (1980) 2 Cr App Rep (S) 267, CA, it was held that where a judge purposely postponed sentence so that an alternative to prison could be examined and that alternative was found to be a satisfactory one in all respects, the court should adopt that alternative as a feeling of injustice would otherwise arise. That principle applied in the present case. Nothing was said by the judge to displace any expectations which might have been created in the appellant's mind as to the likely outcome of the sentencing process in the event that he was found to be suitable for the recommended course. There was a necessity for sentencers to explain clearly what the position was when they ordered adjournments for investigation or assessment of defendants and that a custodial sentence was not in any way ruled out, whatever any further report or inquiry might reveal. Accordingly, the appeal would be allowed and a probation order with the necessary condition would be substituted.

R v Chamberlain (1994) 16 Cr App Rep (S) 473 (Court of Appeal: Stuart-Smith LJ, Buckley and Wright JJ).

2611　Proceeds of Crime Act 1995

See para 840.

2612　Proceeds of crime—confiscation—orders—statements in connection with orders

The Crown Court (Amendment) Rules 1995, SI 1995/2618 (in force on 1 November 1995), amend the 1982 Rules, SI 1982/1109, in consequence of procedures introduced by the Proceeds of Crime Act 1995. In particular, the 1995 Rules make provision for statements in connection with confiscation orders and applications for revised assessments.

2613　Reduction of sentence—reduction by periods spent in custody pending sentence—periods attributable to offence for which sentence imposed

The Criminal Justice Act 1967, s 67(1), (1A) provides that the length of any sentence of imprisonment must be treated as reduced by any relevant period and that a 'relevant period' includes any period during which the offender was in police detention in connection with the offence for which the sentence was passed. The Criminal Justice Act 1991, s 51(2) provides that, in the definition of 'term of imprisonment', consecutive terms and terms which are wholly or partly concurrent are to be treated as a single term.

A prisoner applied for judicial review of the refusal by the prison governor to include as relevant periods all time spent on remand in calculating her release date. She had been sentenced to 30 months' imprisonment for burglary, theft and handling. She had spent 28 days on remand for various offences but these were not the offences for which she was sentenced. *Held*, the challenge turned on the proper construction of the 1967 Act, s 67. In *R v Governor of Blundeston Prison, ex p Gaffney* and *R v Secretary of State for the Home Department, ex p Read*, it had been held that under s 67 individual sentences would attract credit only for the periods spent in custody before sentencing which were attributable to the offence for which sentence was imposed. It had been argued that the phrase 'sentence of imprisonment' in the 1967 Act, s 67 should be interpreted to mean the same as 'term of imprisonment' in the 1991 Act, s 51(2), which was formerly the 1967 Act, s 104(2). If that were so, every element of a concurrent sentence carried with it the right to credit pre-sentence periods of custody irrespective of the offences they related to. Clearly, the 1991 Act, s 51 did not relate to the issue of time spent on remand. The 1967 Act, s 67 expressly adopted a specific approach as opposed to the global approach of the 1991 Act, s 51. Accordingly, the application would be dismissed.

R v Governor of Styal Prison, ex p Mooney [1996] 1 Cr App Rep (S) 74 (Queen's Bench Division: Simon Brown LJ and Curtis J). *R v Governor of Blundeston Prison, ex p Gaffney* [1982] 2 All ER 492 (1982 Abr para 2676), *R v Secretary of State for the Home Department, ex p Read* (1987) 9 Cr App Rep (S) 206, CA (1987 Abr para 2105) followed.

2614 Review of sentence—unduly lenient sentence—extension of power of review

The Criminal Justice Act 1988 (Reviews of Sentencing) Order 1995, SI 1995/10 (in force on 8 February 1995), extends the range of cases which the Attorney-General can refer to the Court of Appeal where he considers that a sentence imposed in the Crown Court was unduly lenient to include fraud cases which are tried in the Crown Court following a notice of transfer given under the Criminal Justice Act 1987, s 4 and cases in which one or more of the counts in respect of which sentence is passed relates to a charge which was dismissed under the 1987 Act, s 6(1) and on which further proceedings were brought by means of the preferment of a voluntary bill of indictment.

2615 Robbery—offender threatening to use knife—unduly lenient sentence—community service order

The offender together with an accomplice demanded money from a youth by threatening to use a knife. Following his conviction for robbery, the offender was sentenced to 120 hours of community service. The Attorney General applied for the court to review the sentence on the ground that it was unduly lenient. He submitted that the offence was aggravated by taking place at night, that the victim was alone and in a vulnerable position, that the offence was carried out by two men and a threat was made to use a knife. *Held*, an offence of this kind required an element of deterrence in the sentence and a substantial period of custody was the norm. Even a first time offender should expect a custodial sentence for such a robbery in a public place. The sentencer had been influenced by the offender's good character and the fact that he had played a lesser part in the offence than his accomplice. However, those factors did not justify a departure from the norm so striking as to result in a non-custodial sentence. The fact that the offender had completed a substantial part of the community service order did not prevent the court declaring that the sentence was unduly lenient, although it would be taken into account together with the element of double jeopardy. Accordingly, a sentence of 18 months' imprisonment would be substituted.

A-G's Reference (No 6 of 1994) (1994) 16 Cr App Rep (S) 343 (Court of Appeal: Lord Taylor of Gosforth CJ, Ognall and Gage JJ).

2616 Robbery—offender's accomplice threatening to use knife—unduly lenient sentence—probation order

The offender and his accomplice approached a woman who had three young children with her. The accomplice produced a knife and demanded jewellery. He held the knife to the youngest child's chest threatening to cause injury if the woman did not immediately comply. The offender acted as a lookout while the offence took place and, although he was also carrying a knife, he did not produce it. When they were later arrested, the offender admitted that they had planned the robbery and he pleaded guilty to the offence. The accomplice was sentenced to 30 months' imprisonment and the offender to a probation order for two years. The Attorney General applied for the court to review the offender's sentence on the ground that it was unduly lenient. He submitted that the offence had been aggravated by planning, the use of lethal weapons and the choice of a vulnerable victim. Further, although the offender had acted as the lookout, he had accepted his share of the proceeds of the robbery. *Held*, mitigating factors in the offender's favour included his early admissions, his guilty plea, his limited role in the offence, a relatively minor criminal record, his weak character and his remorse. However, the court had previously held that robbery involving the use of a knife should result in severe sentences and, in the present case, the sentence had been unduly lenient. It should have been one involving several years of custody. The court had regard to the sentence imposed on the accomplice for his part in the offence and the fact that the offender had to be sentenced a second time. Accordingly, a sentence of two years' imprisonment would be substituted.

A-G's Reference (No 11 of 1994) (1994) 16 Cr App Rep (S) 373 (Court of Appeal: Lord Taylor of Gosforth CJ, Ognall and Gage JJ).

2617   Sentencing practice—unduly lenient sentence—effect on offenders

It has been held that the idea that the courts should consider the plight of the offender and that
the prime consideration was the need to rehabilitate him was misconceived. Sentencing courts
do no favour to offenders by imposing unduly lenient sentences on them, for in the end, bearing
in mind the double jeopardy of a reference by the Attorney General, this usually works to the
disadvantage of an offender.

A-G's Reference (No 14 of 1994) [1994] Crim LR 955 (Court of Appeal: Lord Taylor of
Gosforth CJ, Rougier and Ebsworth JJ).

2618   Sexual offence—attempted rape—guidelines

The appellant met a woman at a conference and they arranged to attend a ball together. The
woman was to stay in a friend's flat on the night of the ball and the appellant arranged to stay
elsewhere. Both drank a great deal of alcohol at the ball and when they returned to the flat it
was agreed that the appellant would sleep on a sofa in the woman's room. She undressed and
went to sleep, but was woken when the appellant attempted to have sexual intercourse with
her. The appellant was convicted of attempted rape and was sentenced to three years'
imprisonment. On appeal against conviction and sentence, *held*, the parties did not live together,
nor had they had sexual intercourse before, and there was no suggestion or promise of intercourse
before the incident. The guidelines in *R v Billam* were applicable and the case fell between the
extremes of a violent rape or attempted rape between strangers and intercourse without consent
after a victim had previously consented or indicated that she might consent. The court was
bound to sentence in accordance with the verdict and the sentencer was correct to hold that a
non-custodial sentence could not be justified and that the guidelines indicated a notional starting
point in excess of three years. The offence was mitigated by the appellant desisting from
committing the full offence and further allowance for that and other mitigating factors could
have been made, despite the fact that he had not pleaded guilty. Accordingly, the appeal against
sentence would be allowed to the extent of substituting a period of two years' imprisonment.

R v Diggle (1994) 16 Cr App Rep (S) 163 (Court of Appeal: Evans LJ, Judge and Bracewell
JJ). R v Billam [1986] 1 All ER 985, CA (1986 Abr para 2368) considered.

2619   Sexual offence—rape—aggravating factors

The defendant obtained entry to his victim's house using a key that had been given to him by a
former occupant of the house. When he falsely claimed that he had been locked out of his own
house, the victim, who knew the defendant through a mutual friend, agreed that he could stay
the night in the house in a separate room. After the victim had gone to bed, the defendant
entered her bedroom and demanded sexual intercourse. He used force to overpower her and
then raped her. He pleaded guilty to rape and was sentenced to six and a half years' imprisonment.
An order was also made that he was to be subjected to full-term licence. The Attorney General
referred the case for review on the basis that the sentence was unduly lenient because of the
aggravating features of the case, in particular the fact that the defendant had gained access to the
victim's house and to her bedroom by deceit and in breach of trust, that he had used excessive
violence to commit the rape, that the rape was premeditated, and that he had previous
convictions for rape and attempted rape. *Held,* in cases of rape, a plea of guilty was generally
regarded as being significant because it usually meant that the victim would not have to attend
court to give evidence. In the instant case, however, the defendant had originally pleaded not
guilty and had changed his plea only at the door of the court when the victim was present and
waiting to give evidence. In those circumstances, he could not expect to receive as great a
discount as he would have done had he pleaded guilty at the outset. The aggravating features of
a rape case as identified in *Billam* were present in the instant case, and the sentence was unduly
lenient having regard to the sentencing guidelines laid down by that case. Accordingly, a
sentence of eight years' imprisonment would be substituted.

A-G's Reference (No 28 of 1993) (1995) 16 Cr App Rep (S) 103 (Court of Appeal: Lord Taylor
of Gosforth CJ, Hutchison and Buxton JJ). R v Billam [1986] 1 All ER 985, CA (1986 Abr para
2368) applied.

2620   Sexual offence—rape—marital rape

A wife told her husband that their marriage was at an end. That evening, after he had been out
drinking, she said that he could sleep in the same bed with her as long as he left her alone. He
later had sexual intercourse with her against her wishes. He did not use violence on her beyond
having intercourse against her will and was remorseful about what he had done. He immediately

admitted the offence to the police and was convicted and sentenced to three years' imprisonment. On appeal, *held*, in *R v W* (1993) 14 Cr App Rep (S) 256, CA (1992 Abr para 2295) it was held that although a different and lower scale of sentencing did not automatically attach to a rape by a husband, where the parties were cohabiting normally and the husband insisted on intercourse without violence or threats, the previous relationship would be an important factor in reducing the level of sentencing. There was a distinction between an estranged husband who returned to the house as an intruder and raped his wife and a case, such as the present one, where the husband still lived in the same house and with consent occupied the same bed as his wife. Although there had to be a custodial sentence, in the circumstances a three year sentence was too long. Accordingly, the appeal would be allowed to the extent that the sentence would be reduced to 18 months' imprisonment.

R v M (1995) 16 Cr App Rep (S) 770 (Court of Appeal: Lord Taylor of Gosforth CJ, Jowitt and Cresswell JJ).

2621 Sexual offence—sexual abuse of child—child previously sexually abused— whether previous abuse to be taken into account in reducing sentence

The offender pleaded guilty to sexual offences against his 11-year-old niece. At his trial, the judge in passing a sentence totalling three years' imprisonment said that the fact the niece had been sexually abused previously was a matter which he was entitled to take into account in reducing the sentence. On appeal, *held*, the fact that a victim had been abused on a previous occasion in no way reduced, and indeed might increase, the gravity of further offending by an adult thereafter. In the present case, it was unlikely that the offender was unaware of the previous trouble with his niece. If, by reason of being corrupted or precocious, a victim instigated offences against herself, that was an aspect which the judge was entitled to take into account. That was only a proper matter of mitigation in a negative sense, namely, that the child was not being treated in a way she was personally resisting or found repugnant at the time. It did not, however, redound to the credit of the offender that he succumbed to the provocation of an 11-year-old girl. The central point to the sentencing exercise in such cases was that young girls were to be protected from themselves as much as from anybody else. If a girl was precocious or provocative, the adult had a duty not to succumb but to dissuade the child from that kind of conduct. The judge had allowed too much by way of discount. Accordingly, the sentence would be quashed and one totalling five years' imprisonment would be substituted.

R v D (A-G's Reference (No 36 of 1995)) (1995) Times, 24 November (Court of Appeal: Lord Taylor of Gosforth CJ, Kay and Smedley JJ).

2622 Sexual offence—unlawful sexual intercourse—unduly lenient sentence— probation order

The offender, aged 40 years, was the leader of a majorette troupe. He admitted having sexual intercourse on six or eight occasions and participating in oral sex with a 12-year-old member of the troupe. He pleaded guilty to counts of unlawful sexual intercourse with, and indecent assault on, the girl and was sentenced to a probation order for two years, with a condition of psychiatric treatment. The Attorney General made an application for the court to review the sentence on the ground that it was unduly lenient, submitting that the offence was aggravated by the age difference, the position of trust and the fact that the girl's mother had expressed concern to the offender about the nature of the girl's relationship with him prior to the sexual activity. *Held*, an offence of unlawful sexual intercourse with a girl under 13 years normally resulted in a prison sentence, especially where aggravating features existed, although probation orders had been imposed in cases where an offender was of borderline subnormal intelligence or where there were psychiatric factors. In the present case, the order made by the sentencer had been for the benefit of the offender and had laid more emphasis on the need to assist him than on aspects of deterrence of the offender and others who were in positions of trust towards young girls. The element of psychiatric need was not such as to bring the offender into the rare category of those who could be regarded as having lesser criminal responsibility and, in the circumstances, a custodial sentence was required. The appropriate sentence at first instance would have been four years' imprisonment but the court had to bear in mind the fact that the offender was being re-sentenced after probation. Accordingly, a sentence of three years' imprisonment would be substituted.

A-G's Reference (No 20 of 1994) (1994) 16 Cr App Rep (S) 578 (Court of Appeal: Lord Taylor of Gosforth CJ, Scott Baker and Longmore JJ).

2623 Theft—'ringing' of motor cars—appropriate sentence

The defendant was convicted of offences involving the 'ringing' of motor cars, in which cars were stolen, handled, disguised and subsequently disposed of. He was sentenced to concurrent sentences of three years' imprisonment on each of two counts of theft and one count of obtaining property by deception, and six months and thirty months on each of two counts of handling stolen goods. On appeal, *held*, the ringing of cars ought to attract a sentence of four to five years for a ringleader who has pleaded not guilty. In the case of someone involved in the offence who is not the ringleader and who pleads not guilty, a sentence of three years is more appropriate. In this case, the judge had not taken account of the fact that the defendant was not the ringleader and had pleaded guilty and accordingly, the appeal would be allowed and the sentence reduced to 27 months' imprisonment.

R v Evans (1995) Times, 26 June (Court of Appeal: Evans LJ, Garland and Connell JJ).

2624 Variation of sentence—original unlawful sentence rescinded—power to re-sentence offender

A judge sentenced the defendant to terms of imprisonment for possession of, and intent to supply, drugs and adjourned proceedings in relation to a confiscation order under the Drug Trafficking Act 1986. Although a judge had a power to adjourn such proceedings under the Drug Trafficking Act 1994, there was no such power under the 1986 Act and the judge therefore rescinded the sentences of imprisonment with a view to re-sentencing. A week later, he reimposed the original sentences of imprisonment and made a confiscation order under the 1986 Act. The defendant appealed on the basis that the sentences of imprisonment were wrong in law because there was no jurisdiction to re-sentence after rescission. He relied on *R v Smith* (13 March 1995, CA, unreported) where the court had doubted whether, once a sentence was rescinded, it was open to the sentencing court to re-sentence. *Held*, the court was of the clear view that it was lawful and might well be preferable to rescind an unlawful sentence, while making it clear that it had been done with a view to re-sentencing after the further necessary steps had been taken, rather than leaving the unlawful sentence in being and open to an immediate application for leave to appeal. However, the eventual sentence had to be passed within the 28-day time limit prescribed in the Supreme Court Act 1981, s 47(2). Further, the course of rescinding and re-sentencing was only open to the court if it was of the opinion that rescission did not of itself prevent that course. In the present case, the appeal would accordingly be dismissed.

R v Dunham [1996] Crim LR 65 (Court of Appeal: Beldam LJ, Scott Baker and Stuart-White JJ).

2625 Violent or sexual offence—longer than normal sentence—appropriateness where public protection provided by commensurate sentence

The Criminal Justice Act 1991, s 2(2)(b) states that where an offence is of a violent or sexual nature, the custodial sentence is to be for such longer term (not exceeding the maximum) as in the opinion of the court is necessary to protect the public from serious harm from the offender.

The appellant was convicted of three offences of robbery and linked offences of having a firearm or imitation firearm with him with intent to commit an indictable offence. The judge considered that, on the basis of the facts and the appellant's previous convictions, longer sentences than would have been considered commensurate with the seriousness of the offences were called for. Sentences of 16 years' imprisonment for the counts of robbery and nine years for each firearms count were imposed, to run concurrently. On appeal, *held*, although the appellant had demonstrated his willingness to commit offences of the gravest nature involving the use of a firearm, the sentences exceeded the starting point in *R v Turner*, the starting point for the gravest type of armed robbery, and the court found that the sentences were not to be characterised in that way. The guidelines in *R v Turner* contained an inherent factor which reflected not merely the seriousness of the offences but also the necessity to protect the public from persons who were likely to be regarded as dangerous to them. It was incumbent upon the court when considering whether to apply s 2(2)(b) to guard against the danger of effectively imposing an element of the sentence twice over where the commensurate sentence for the offence itself was likely to contain an element which was designed to achieve the protection of the public. The sentences imposed were excessive and, accordingly, the appeal would be allowed to the extent that sentences of 12 years' imprisonment would be substituted.

R v Christie (1995) 16 Cr App Rep (S) 469 (Court of Appeal: Stuart-Smith LJ, Buckley and Wright JJ). *R v Turner* (1975) 61 Cr App Rep 67, CA considered.

2626 Violent or sexual offence—longer than normal sentence—armed robbery

The Criminal Justice Act 1991, s 31(1) provides that 'violent offence' means an offence which leads, or is intended or likely to lead, to a person's death or to physical injury to a person.

The appellant pleaded guilty to three counts of armed robbery. Although he had been armed with a knife whilst committing the robberies, it was accepted that he had no intention of using it. The trial judge considered that the offences were violent offences within the meaning of the 1991 Act, s 31(1) and that having regard to the 1991 Act, s 1(2)(b), the public had to be protected from serious harm. He therefore imposed a sentence of seven years' imprisonment on each count, the sentences to run concurrently. On appeal, the issue was whether armed robbery was an offence likely to lead to physical injury within the meaning of s 31(1). *Held*, as the appellant had not intended to use the knife, he had not committed an offence which could properly be described as a violent offence. The trial judge could have relied instead on the 1991 Act, s 1(2)(a) in passing sentence. Having regard to the circumstances of the offence, the sentence imposed was too long and, accordingly, the appeal would be allowed and the sentence would be reduced to six years' imprisonment, concurrent on each count.

R v Bibby (1995) 16 Cr App Rep (S) 127 (Court of Appeal: Lord Taylor of Gosforth CJ, Hutchison and Buxton JJ).

2627 Violent or sexual offence—longer than normal sentence—child abuse—offences committed within the family circle

The Criminal Justice Act 1991, s 2(2)(b) provides that, where an offence is a violent or sexual offence the custodial sentence may be for such longer term (not exceeding the maximum) as in the court's opinion is necessary to protect the public from serious harm from the offender.

Over a number of years the appellant indecently assaulted the young son of the woman he lived with. Ten years later the son reported the abuse on learning that the appellant was living with another woman and her three children. After being confronted, the appellant eventually admitted that he had been abusing the two foster children. He made full admissions at a police station. He pleaded guilty to four counts of indecent assault on a male, two of indecency with a child and two of indecent assaults on a female. He was sentenced to seven years' imprisonment the judge being of the opinion that such a term was necessary for the protection of the public within the meaning of the 1991 Act, s 2(2)(b). On appeal, *held*, an extended sentence was not necessary to protect the public from serious harm as there was no evidence of any likelihood of offending outside the family circle, there was no real likelihood of him acquiring another family circle and, furthermore, he had begun to confront his pattern of offending.

R v S (1995) 16 Cr App Rep (S) 303 (Court of Appeal: Hirst LJ, Auld and Longmore JJ).

2628 Violent or sexual offence—longer than normal sentence—circumstances where longer than normal sentence should be imposed

The Criminal Justice Act 1991, s 2(2)(b) states that where an offence is of a violent or sexual nature, the custodial sentence is to be for such longer term (not exceeding the maximum) as in the opinion of the court is necessary to protect the public from serious harm from the offender.

It has been held that the court should only use its power to impose a longer than normal sentence under the 1991 Act, s 2(2)(b) where a proper basis is laid for the exercise of the power. Sentencing judges should only make use of the section if the evidence before them is such as to justify the conclusion that it is necessary to protect the public from serious harm from the offender. It is only in those circumstances that a sentence longer than the term that is commensurate with the seriousness of the offence, or the combination of the offence with other offences associated with it, is permissible.

R v Samuels (1995) 16 Cr App Rep (S) 856 (Court of Appeal: Hobhouse LJ, Ognall and Pill JJ).

2629 Violent or sexual offence—longer than normal sentence—general considerations

The Criminal Justice Act 1991, s 2(2)(b) provides that where an offence is a violent or sexual offence, a sentence ought to be for such longer term, not exceeding the maximum, as is in the opinion of the court necessary to protect the public from serious harm from the offender.

It has been held that it is not every case of violence or sex offending which requires that the 1991 Act, s 2(2)(b) should be invoked. If the offence before the court is an isolated one and there is no reason to fear a substantial risk of further violence or sex offending, then clearly s 2(2)(b) will not apply. However, the circumstances of the offence or offences before the court, the nature and circumstances of previous offences, medical or other evidence about the offender, statements of intent by the offender himself, or a combination of any of these and other sources, may raise in the opinion of the sentencing judge a substantial risk of the offender committing violent or sexual offences in the future which may cause serious harm. If that is so, s 2(2)(b) will apply. Where it does, some allowance will usually be made, even in the worst cases, for a plea of guilty. Account must also be taken of the age of the offender. A sentence imposed under s 2(2)(b) should, while being long enough to give necessary protection to the public for an extended period, still bear a reasonable relationship to the offence for which it is being imposed.

R v Crow; R v Pennington (1995) 16 Cr App Rep (S) 409 (Court of Appeal: Lord Taylor of Gosforth CJ, Curtis and Gage JJ).

2630   Violent or sexual offence—longer than normal sentence—protection of public—inference of danger from medical evidence

Under the Criminal Justice Act 1991, s 2(2)(b) where an offence is a violent or sexual offence, the custodial sentence is to be for such longer term (not exceeding the permitted maximum) as in the opinion of the court is necessary to protect the public from serious harm from the offender.

The appellant attacked an elderly lady with a brick causing severe bruising and swelling, puncture wounds and reduced vision in one eye. The appellant pleaded guilty to wounding with intent to cause grievous bodily harm. She had previous convictions for criminal damage, arson, wounding and common assault and a psychiatric report indicated that she had a long history of psychiatric treatment. She suffered from a marked personality disorder and her condition was unlikely to change. The court sentenced the appellant to seven years' imprisonment, passed a longer than normal sentence under the 1991 Act, s 2(2)(b). On appeal, *held*, in approaching sentence under s 2(2)(b), a court could consider all information about an offender and should call for a medical report before sentencing if the danger posed to the public was due to a medical or personality problem, in order to exclude a medical disposal. Having considered all relevant matters, the sentencer had to be satisfied, to the criminal standard, that the sentence was necessary to protect the public from serious harm. In the present case, there was evidence of the appellant's irrational conduct over many years, the assault was a very serious one and the appellant was not amenable to a hospital order under the Mental Health Act 1983. The sentencer had passed a sentence which could not be impeached and, accordingly, the appeal would be dismissed.

R v Fawcett (1995) 16 Cr App Rep (S) 55 (Court of Appeal: Hobhouse LJ, Garland and Curtis JJ).

2631   Violent or sexual offence—longer than normal sentence—telephoned or mailed threats—whether threats amount to violent offence

Under the Criminal Justice Act 1991, s 2(2)(b), the custodial sentence for a violent offence is for such longer term (not exceeding that maximum) as in the opinion of the court is necessary to protect the public from serious harm from the offender. A 'violent offence' means an offence which leads, or is intended or likely to lead, to a person's death or to physical injury to a person: s 31(1).

The appellant inundated the victim with abusive telephone calls after their relationship ended. He threatened to put a bullet in her head and said that the bullet would have her name on it. She later received an envelope containing a bullet with her name engraved on it. She had previously seen the appellant fire a handgun with live ammunition. The appellant was found guilty of threatening to kill, and was sentenced to five years' imprisonment pursuant to the 1991 Act, s 2(2)(b). On his appeal, *held*, threats made over the telephone or by post could not lead to physical injury, nor was there evidence that they were intended to lead to such injury. In those circumstances it was impossible to say that the offence was a violent offence. It would be beneficial for courts if the definition of 'violent offence' was amended to include words to indicate that it meant an offence leading to a reasonable apprehension of violence in the victim. The effect the offence had on a victim had to be taken into account in substituting any sentence. In the present case, the offence had been serious and gave an apprehension of violence and the threats were no doubt intended to have that effect. Accordingly, the sentence would be reduced to three and a half years' imprisonment.

R v Richart (1995) 16 Cr App Rep (S) 977 (Court of Appeal: Lord Taylor of Gosforth CJ, Owen J and Sir Lawrence Verney QC, Recorder of London).

2632 Violent or sexual offence—longer than normal sentence—threats to kill—intention or likelihood of causing physical injury

The Criminal Justice Act 1991, s 2(2)(b) states that where an offence is of a violent or sexual nature, the custodial sentence is to be for such longer term (not exceeding the maximum) as in the opinion of the court is necessary to protect the public from serious harm from the offender. Section 31(1) defines a violent offence as one which leads, or is intended or likely to lead, to a person's death, or to physical injury to a person.

It has been held that the offence of threatening to kill is not a 'violent offence' within the meaning of s 31(1) and consequently does not justify the imposition of an extended custodial sentence pursuant to s 2(2)(b) unless it can be established that the defendant intended death or injury to result from the threat itself, or such a consequence was likely to flow from the threat itself.

R v Ragg [1995] 4 All ER 155 (Court of Appeal: Pill LJ, Buckley and Laws JJ).

2633 Young offender—concurrent sentences—detention in young offender institution and regional secure unit

The defendant was sentenced to two years and seven months' detention under the Children and Young Persons Act 1933, s 53(2) for false imprisonment and nine months' detention in a young offender institution for assault occasioning actual bodily harm, to run concurrently. He appealed on the grounds that the judge had been wrong to impose the two sentences concurrently and that the overall sentence ought to have been reduced to take account of the period of time spent on remand in local authority care, as this would not be done automatically. *Held, R v Fairhurst* [1986] 1 WLR 1374, CA (1986 Abr para 2375) had established that a court ought not to impose a sentence of youth custody concurrently with a sentence of detention under the 1933 Act, s 53(2). Even though that case has been decided prior to changes introduced by the Criminal Justice Act 1991, the 1991 Act had not removed the impracticalities which would follow from concurrent sentences in the circumstances in issue, and therefore *R v Fairhurst* still applied. Accordingly, the sentence of detention in a young offender institution would be quashed. The Criminal Justice Act 1967, s 67(1A)(c) provided that, in connection with a particular offence, time spent in 'any accommodation provided for the purpose of restricting liberty' would be automatically deducted from any sentence subsequently imposed for that offence. Although the defendant had been detained in a unit which was not a remand centre, licensed secure accommodation or a prison, the 1967 Act, s 67(1A)(c) was not necessarily limited to 'secure accommodation' but applied to any accommodation intended to restrict liberty. In this case, the unit in which the defendant was remanded fell within that category and it was therefore unnecessary for the court to reduce the offence as this would be done automatically under the 1967 Act.

R v Collins (1994) 16 Cr App Rep (S) 156 (Court of Appeal: McCowan LJ, Douglas Brown and Waller JJ).

2634 Young offender—confiscation order—detention in default of payment

The appellant pleaded guilty to unlawful wounding, possessing heroin with intent to supply, and supplying heroin, and was sentenced to a total of four years' detention in a young offender institution. In addition, a confiscation order was made under the Drug Trafficking Act 1986 for a sum which was payable within three months, in default of which the appellant was liable to three months' consecutive detention. On appeal against sentence, *held*, a confiscation order could be enforced as if it were a fine only if the order was made against a person who was under 21 but at least 18 years of age. As the appellant was only 17, the part of the confiscation order relating to detention in default of payment would be quashed. The 15-month sentence for unlawful wounding made under the Children and Young Persons Act 1933, s 53(2) would also be quashed, as such detention could be ordered only in respect of an offence for which an adult could be imprisoned for at least 14 years.

R v Basid (1996) 160 JP 1 (Court of Appeal: Beldam LJ, Scott Baker and Stuart White JJ).

2635 Young offender—offender in local authority care—compensation order against authority—reasonableness of order

The Children and Young Persons Act 1933, s 55 provides that where a young person is convicted or found guilty of any offence and the court is of the opinion that the case would best be met by the imposition of a fine or costs or the making of a compensation order, whether with or without any other punishment, it is the duty of the court to order that the fine, costs or compensation awarded be paid by the parent or guardian of the young person unless it would be unreasonable to make an order for payment, having regard to the circumstances of the case. In relation to a young person for whom a local authority has parental authority and who is in its care, references to his parent or guardian are construed as references to that authority: s 55(1B).

It has been held that where a local authority is found to have done everything that it reasonably and properly can to protect the public from a young offender, it is wholly unreasonable and unjust that the authority should bear a financial penalty as that would place it in a position worse than that of a natural parent under the 1933 Act.

D v DPP; R v DPP; R v Burnley Crown Court, ex p Lancashire County Court; R v Preston Crown Court, ex p Lancashire County Court [1995] 3 FCR 725 (Queen's Bench Division: Leggatt LJ and Buxton J).

2636 Young offender—restrictions on sentencing—custodial sentence—consecutive sentences—excessive sentence

The Criminal Justice Act 1982, s 1B(4) provides that a court must not pass on an offender aged 15, 16 or 17 a sentence of detention in a young offender institution whose effect would be that the offender would be sentenced to a total term which exceeds 12 months. 'Total term' is defined in s 1B(6) as meaning, in the case of an offender sentenced (whether or not on the same occasion) to two or more terms of detention in a young offender institution which are consecutive or wholly or partly concurrent, the aggregate of those terms. The Criminal Justice Act 1991, s 40(4) provides that the period for which a person is ordered to be returned to a young offender institution must (a) be taken to be a sentence of imprisonment, (b) either be served before and be followed by, or served concurrently with, the sentence imposed for the new offence, and (c) be disregarded in determining the appropriate length of that sentence.

The appellant was sentenced to nine months' detention in a young offender institution, and was released on licence having served half of the sentence. Within a few weeks of his release, he committed an offence of burglary. In sentencing him to 11 months' detention in a young offender institution for that offence, the court also ordered that his licence be revoked and that he serve the remainder of the first sentence consecutive to the second sentence. On appeal, it was argued that the sentence was unlawful having regard to the 1982 Act, s 1B. *Held*, if an order was made that a person was to be returned to a young offender institution, he was not being sentenced to a term of detention, but was being ordered to serve part of a sentence which had already been imposed. As such, in the instant case, the appellant had not been sentenced on the same occasion to two or more terms of detention within the meaning of the 1982 Act, s 1B(6). The 1991 Act, s 40(4) gave the court power to order an original sentence to be served consecutive to, but not concurrent with, a new sentence imposed for a new offence. In the instant case, the 11-month sentence which was ordered to be served consecutive to the remainder of the first sentence was contrary to the 1982 Act, s 1B(4), because the effect of it was that the appellant was sentenced to a total term of detention which exceeded 12 months. Although he had not been sentenced to two terms on the same occasion, he had been sentenced to two terms of detention which were consecutive and the aggregate of which was more than 12 months. Moreover, the 1991 Act, s 40(4)(c) was not sufficiently specific so as to create an exception to the 1982 Act, s 1B(4). Accordingly, the appeal would be dismissed.

R v Foran [1996] 1 Cr App Rep (S) 149 (Court of Appeal: Kennedy LJ, Mantell and Hooper JJ).

2637 Young offender—restrictions on sentencing—custodial sentence—contempt of court

The defendant, who was 17 years old, was a prosecution witness in an indecent assault trial. After giving evidence in the morning, he did not reappear after lunch and, on the following day, admitted that his evidence had not been true. He was sentenced to three months in a young offender institution for contempt of court and appealed. *Held*, the Criminal Justice Act 1982, s 1(1) provides that a person under 21 years of age cannot be committed to prison for any reason, including contempt of court. The exception to the rule under the 1982 Act, s 9 only applied to defendants over 18 years of age since amendment by the Criminal Justice Act 1991, s 63(5). Accordingly, the appeal would be allowed and the sentence would be quashed.

R v Byas (1995) 159 JP 458 (Court of Appeal: Henry LJ, Ian Kennedy and Tuckey JJ).

2638 Young offender—restrictions on sentencing—custodial sentence—judge's failure to specify statutory provision

The Children and Young Persons Act 1933, s 53(2) provides that where a young person is convicted on indictment of any offence punishable in the case of an adult with imprisonment for 14 years or more, the court may sentence the offender to be detained for a period specified by the court in such place and on such conditions as the Secretary of State may direct.

The defendant, a 16-year-old boy, attacked a policeman who was trying to arrest him after he was caught trying to steal a car. As part of the attack, anti-freeze was thrown in the policeman's face causing temporary blindness and pain. The defendant was sentenced to three years' detention for causing grievous bodily harm with intent to resist arrest together with nine months for burglary and assault occasioning actual bodily harm, to run concurrently. He appealed on the ground that the judge had failed to specify that he was imposing the longer sentence under the 1933 Act, s 53(2), thereby rendering the sentence invalid. *Held*, the judge ought to have made plain the precise provisions of the legislation he was invoking. It was established authority that it was what the judge pronounces in his sentencing remarks that amounts to the sentence rather than what was recorded on the court record in the event of a discrepancy between the two. Although the record in this case referred to the 1933 Act, s 53(2), the judge had not made reference to the Act and therefore the sentence of three years' detention was not lawful as it stood and would be deemed by the Criminal Justice Act 1982, s 1B(5) to take effect as a sentence of 12 months' detention. Accordingly, the appeal would be allowed.

R v Wilkins (1994) 16 Cr App Rep (S) 49 (Court of Appeal: Rose LJ, Mantell and Bell JJ).

The appellants, M and S, grabbed the victim's bag causing her to fall to the ground. The victim, aged 88 years, sustained a skull fracture which left her in constant pain. The appellants, aged 16 and 17 years, were convicted of robbery. Immediately after conviction, the judge indicated that he had in mind a sentence under the Children and Young Persons Act 1933, s 53(2). However, when they were sentenced to seven years' detention pursuant to s 53(2), the judge did not refer to the 1993 Act. M was also sentenced to six months' consecutive detention for other offences. On appeal, it fell to be determined whether: (1) the sentences were imposed lawfully and properly pursuant to the 1933 Act; (2) seven years was the correct sentence for robbery; and (3) a distinction should be drawn between M and S to reflect the extra matters taken into consideration. *Held*, (1) the record made it entirely clear what sentence the judge purported to pass, because it showed that the sentences were imposed pursuant to s 53(2). While it was what the judge said in court that counted, not what the record showed, what the judge said had to be looked at in the light of everything he said in the course of the sentencing exercise. (2) When sentencing a young offender, a sentence shorter than one which would be appropriate for an adult was almost always likely to be appropriate. It was not inappropriate to impose a deterrent sentence, but it was necessary to keep a balance between that aspect, the youth of the offender and the effect of a long sentence. The case did not involve grave violence, but there was serious violence with forseeably grave consequences. The sentences of seven years would therefore be quashed and sentences of five years' detention substituted. (3) The six-month sentence was unlawful because there was no power under s 53(2) to impose a sentence of detention after there had been a committal for sentence. Accordingly, the appeals would be allowed to that extent.

R v Marriott (1994) 16 Cr App Rep (S) 428 (Court of Appeal: Farquharson LJ, Ebsworth and Steel JJ).

SET-OFF AND COUNTERCLAIM

Halsbury's Laws of England (4th edn) Vol 42, paras 401–600

2639 Set-off—action brought by Lloyd's name against managing agent—set-off of profits against losses

See *Brown v KMR Services Ltd*, para 2146.

2640 Set-off—award of costs against plaintiff in favour of defendant—debt owed to plaintiff by defendant—ability of plaintiff to set-off costs

In order to purchase a dwelling the defendant and his wife borrowed from a building society on a first mortgage and from the plaintiff on a second legal charge on the property. They fell into arrears on both and the plaintiff obtained an order for possession and repayment of the borrowed sum with interest. However, the building society obtained possession of the property and sold it for a sum which was barely sufficient to cover their mortgage. The plaintiff caused a writ of fieri facias to be issued and the sheriff entered into walking possession of a substantial collection of records, tapes and compact discs. The defendant, who was the presenter of musical programmes on radio and television, issued a summons seeking an order that the sheriff withdraw, on the grounds that the collection constituted tools of his trade and was therefore exempt from seizure. A master ruled in his favour but the terms of a formal order and the question of costs were left for a later date. The matter was in fact heard by a different master on that date, who ruled that the plaintiff should pay the costs of the defendant's challenge to the execution. The plaintiff claimed he should be entitled to set off the costs against the unsatisfied judgment owing to him from the defendant. The defendant argued that there should be no set-off, as he would then lose his collection to pay for legal aid received because of the operation of the legal aid statutory charge. A set-off was allowed since the master doubted whether the collection was to be regarded as 'property recovered' within the Legal Aid Act 1988, s 16(6). On appeal, *held*, the special feature of the case was the existence of the inflexible charge in favour of the Legal Aid Board, which it had no discretion not to enforce. The only persons to suffer were the defendant if the set-off were allowed and the plaintiff if it were not. The balance tipped in favour of the defendant and accordingly the plaintiff had to pay the defendant's costs, amounting to over £10,000, even though the defendant owed the plaintiff £135,000.

Brookes v Harris [1995] 1 WLR 918 (Chancery Division: Ferris J).

2641 Set-off—carriage of goods by land—freight charges

The plaintiffs were carriers engaged by the defendant retailers to transport and deliver Christmas hampers. They brought a claim for their carriage charges for effecting those deliveries. The defendants sought to set-off cross-claims for short delivery and other breaches of contract against the plaintiff's claim. The plaintiffs argued that their claim was for freight charges, from which the rule was that there could be no deduction by way of abatement or set-off. The defendants accepted that such a rule applied to freight claimed in shipping cases under voyage charterparties, but submitted that the rule should not apply to charges for domestic carriage by land. *Held*, the rule of abatement or set-off in relation to shipping cases under voyage charterparties, as enunciated in *Aries Tanker Corpn v Total Transport Ltd* [1977] 1 All ER 398, had little intrinsic value but was a rule of antiquity on the basis of which contracts were formed. It was difficult to apply that rule to carriage of goods by land where it was unlikely that contracts had been formed on its basis. However, the rule had been applied to carriage of goods by land in *A S Jones Ltd v Burton Gold Metal Biscuits* (unreported, 11 April 1984) and the court was bound by that decision as a result of the cumulative weight of authority and the fact that it was indistinguishable from the present case. Accordingly, there could be no deduction by way of abatement or set-off from the claim for freight charges.

United Carriers Ltd v Heritage Food Group (UK) Ltd [1995] 4 All ER 95 (Queen's Bench Division: May J).

SETTLEMENTS

Halsbury's Laws of England (4th edn) Vol 42, paras 601–1100

2642 Articles

New Legislation on Settlements, John Line: Tax Journal, Issue 324, p 16

SEX DISCRIMINATION

Halsbury's Laws of England (4th edn) Vol 16, Supp paras 767–771:38

2643 Articles

An Imbalance of Power, Emily Driver (on sexual harassment at the Bar): 145 NLJ 1027
Soliciting Equality—The Way Forward, Clare McGlynn (on discrimination against women solicitors): 145 NLJ 1065

2644 Discrimination—civic obligations—fire service

See *Schmidt v Germany*, para 1569.

2645 Discrimination—employment—dismissal—compensation

The Sex Discrimination and Equal Pay (Remedies) Regulations 1993, SI 1993/2798, reg 2 abolished the upper limit for awards for compensation for sex discrimination formerly imposed by the Sex Discrimination Act 1975, s 65(2).

An employee was dismissed by her employer in circumstances which led to an industrial tribunal finding that she had been unfairly dismissed and unlawfully discriminated against on the grounds of her sex. The industrial tribunal applied the upper limit on compensation for sex discrimination to the employee's compensation award. On her appeal, *held*, although the act of discrimination complained of took place before the date on which the 1993 Regulations came into force, the industrial tribunal had erred in law in applying an upper limit on the award. The regulations were enacted by Parliament to remedy a breach of Community law by the 1975 Act, s 65(2). Parliament could not have intended legislative provisions that breached Community law to be construed in a way which perpetuated the breach. The correct construction of the regulations was that they had a retrospective effect and removed the statutory limit on compensation in respect of all compensation awards made after their commencement date. Accordingly, the appeal would be allowed.

Harvey v Institute of the Motor Industry (No 2) [1995] IRLR 416 (Employment Appeal Tribunal: Morison J presiding).

2646 Discrimination—employment—dismissal—pregnancy—absence from work due to pregnancy-related illness

Scotland
One of the conditions of the appellant's employment was that employees would be dismissed if they were on sick leave for a continuous period of more than 26 weeks, and the condition applied to both male and female employees. The appellant, who was pregnant, was dismissed after she had been off work for more than 26 weeks because of illness due to medical complications connected with her pregnancy. On her complaint of sex discrimination contrary to the Sex Discrimination Act 1975, s 1(1)(a), an industrial tribunal decided that the appellant had been treated in the same way that a male employee would be treated if he was absent through long-term illness. On her appeal against the dismissal of her complaint, *held*, having regard to the 1975 Act, it was not relevant that the precise reason for the appellant's illness was a condition which affected only women, namely pregnancy. On the basis of the 1975 Act alone, therefore, there had been no discrimination. Moreover, having regard to decisions of the European Court of Justice, the appellant could not rely on Council Directive (EC) 76/207, art 5(1) because there was no distinction between illness arising out of pregnancy or confinement and illness for any other reason. As such, pregnancy-related illnesses were subject to an employer's general rules in respect of illness. There was, however, a distinction between pregnancy on the one hand, and illness, including pregnancy-related illness, on the other hand. As the appellant's absence had been due to illness, the directive did not apply to her claim and, accordingly, the appeal would be dismissed.

Brown v Rentokil Ltd [1995] IRLR 211 (Court of Session). *Webb v Emo Air Cargo (UK) Ltd* [1992] 4 All ER 929, HL (1992 Abr para 2313) and [1994] 1 IRLR 482, ECJ, and *Handels-og Kontorfunktionaerernes Forbund i Danmark v Dansk Arbejdsgiverforening* [1992] ICR 332, ECJ considered.

2647 Discrimination—employment—dismissal—pregnancy—employment with company through employment agency—inability to return to same position following pregnancy

Scotland
An agency had a contract to provide staff to a company. The staff were paid by the agency who then invoiced the company. The applicant worked for the company under this arrangement until she stopped due to pregnancy. When she approached the company with a view to returning, she was told that she could not go back to her previous position. She claimed that she had been discriminated against on the grounds of sex. An industrial tribunal held that, although the applicant was not an employee of the agency or company, she was in an employment relationship with both of them within the Sex Discrimination Act 1975, s 82. On the company's appeal against the tribunal's decision, the applicant further contended that she was entitled to make a complaint pursuant to s 9 that she had been discriminated against as a contract worker by not being permitted to return to work after absence during maternity. *Held*, (1) s 9 was not restricted to prohibiting discrimination against a contract worker who was actually working. Its purpose was to outlaw discrimination in the selection by the principal from among workers

supplied under an agency arrangement. The company had work available to be done by individuals employed by the agency and there was a contract between them for the supply of such workers. The applicant was therefore entitled to bring a complaint under s 9. (2) The tribunal had erred in finding that the contractual arrangements entered into meant that the applicant was in an employment relationship with the company. The definition of 'employment' in s 82 had to be taken to refer to a contract between a party doing the work and the party for whom the work was done. Accordingly, the company's appeal would be dismissed and the case remitted to the industrial tribunal.

BP Chemicals Ltd v Gillick [1995] IRLR 128 (Employment Appeal Tribunal: Lord Coulsfield presiding). For earlier related proceedings, see [1993] IRLR 437 (1993 Abr para 1185).

2648   Discrimination—employment—dismissal—pregnancy—member of armed forces—compensation—assessment

It has been held that the correct method for assessing compensation in cases of sex discrimination where servicewomen are dismissed by reason of pregnancy, is to subtract the earnings the applicant received, or would have received if she had acted reasonably to mitigate her loss, after her discharge from the amount that she would have earned had she not been dismissed. A percentage, assessed by the industrial tribunal, should then be deducted to reflect the possibility that the applicant would have remained in the services had she not been dismissed. This approach is to be preferred to the alternative of deducting the percentage from the potential earnings before the actual earnings are deducted, since the latter approach would not enable the loss actually sustained to be made good in full.

Ministry of Defence v Wheeler (1995) Times, 22 December (Employment Appeal Tribunal: Kay J presiding). *Marshall v Southampton and South West Hampshire Health Authority (Teaching) No 2* [1993] ICR 893, ECJ (1993 Abr para 2754) applied.

2649   Discrimination—employment—dismissal—pregnancy—temporary unavailability for work

The Sex Discrimination Act 1975, s 5(3) provides that a comparison of the cases of persons of different sex must be such that the relevant circumstances in the one case are the same, or not materially different, in the other. Council Directive (EC) 76/207, art 2(1) provides that the principle of equal treatment means that there must be no discrimination whatsoever on grounds of sex either directly or indirectly by reference, in particular, to marital or family status.

The appellant was engaged to replace one of the defendant's employees who was to take maternity leave. Shortly afterwards, when the appellant discovered that she herself was pregnant and was due to have her child at about the same as the employee whom she was to replace, she was dismissed. An industrial tribunal decided that the dismissal did not amount to unlawful sex discrimination, and the decision was upheld on appeal. Following a reference to the European Court of Justice for a preliminary ruling as to the construction of Council Directive (EC) 76/207, art 2(1), the European Court ruled that art 2(1) precluded the dismissal of an employee who was recruited for an unlimited term to replace another employee during the latter's maternity leave but who could not do so because she herself became pregnant. In reconsidering the appeal, *held*, the European Court's ruling that it was a relevant circumstance that the appellant had been engaged for an indefinite period suggested that there might be a distinction between such a situation and a situation where a pregnant woman was absent for the whole of the fixed period for which she had been engaged. The only way in which the 1976 Act, ss 1(1)(a) and 5(3) could be interpreted in accordance with the European Court's ruling was to hold that, where a woman was engaged for an indefinite period, the fact that the reason why she would be temporarily unavailable for work at a time when she knew that her services would be particularly required was pregnancy was a relevant circumstance, as it was a circumstance which could not apply to a hypothetical man. Accordingly, the appeal would be allowed.

Webb v Emo Air Cargo (UK) Ltd (No 2) [1995] 4 All ER 577 (House of Lords: Lords Keith of Kinkel, Griffiths, Browne-Wilkinson, Mustill and Slynn of Hadley). For earlier proceedings, see [1994] 4 All ER 115, ECJ (1994 Abr para 3029) and [1993] ICR 175, HL (1992 Abr para 2313).

2650   Discrimination—employment—equal pay

The Equal Pay Act 1970, s 1(3) provides that an equality clause does not operate in relation to a variation between a woman's contract and a man's contract if the employer proves that the variation is genuinely due to a material factor which is not the difference of sex.

The appellants were dinner ladies employed by the respondent local authority. Following a job evaluation scheme, their work was rated as equivalent to that of certain male comparators employed by the respondent, and their pay was accordingly altered to the same rate as that of their comparators. When the provision of school meals was put out to competitive tendering, the respondent formed a direct services organisation which successfully tendered for one of the contracts. It was also decided that the appellants' wages would have to be reduced if the organisation was to win the remaining contracts. On the appellants' complaints under the 1970 Act, an industrial tribunal held that the respondent had failed to establish the defence under s 1(3). In particular, it found that although market forces were a factor in the decision to reduce the appellants' pay, the reduction was for a sex-based reason because, generally, catering staff were almost exclusively women. That decision was reversed on appeal. On the appellants' further appeal, *held*, the 1970 Act had to be interpreted without making a distinction between direct and indirect discrimination, as the relevant question was whether equal treatment had been accorded to men and women employed on work rated as equivalent. Here, the appellants were engaged in work equivalent to that of men, and it was impossible to say that the industrial tribunal had erred in deciding that the difference between the appellants' pay and that of their male comparators was not due to the difference of sex. Although the respondent had reduced the appellants' wages in order to be more competitive in tendering for the school dinner contracts, the appellants were paid less than their male comparators, and had to accept such pay as they could not have found other work that suited their domestic situations. That amounted to sex-based discrimination and, accordingly, the appeal would be allowed.

Ratcliffe v North Yorkshire County Council [1995] IRLR 439 (House of Lords: Lords Keith of Kinkel, Browne-Wilkinson, Slynn of Hadley, Nicholls of Birkenhead, and Steyn). Decision of Court of Appeal [1994] IRLR 235 (1994 Abr para 2515) reversed.

See also *Specialarbejdforbundet i Danmark v Dansk Industri*, para 3187.

2651 Discrimation—employment—illegal contract of employment

The Sex Discrimination Act 1975, s 6(2)(b) provides that it is unlawful for a person, in the case of a woman employed by him, to discriminate against her by dismissing her or subjecting her to any other detriment. Section 82(1) defines 'employment' as employment under a contract of service, or a contract personally to execute any work or labour.

It has been held that an employee is not precluded from bringing a claim of sex discrimination against her employer under s 6(2)(b) by reason of illegality in the fact of, or in the performance of, her contract of employment. In determining whether an employee is entitled to such protection against sex discrimination, it is necessary to consider whether she is 'employed' within the meaning of s 82(1). However, the claim of sex discrimination is not founded on the contract of employment. It is a claim based on a right not to be discriminated against conferred by the 1975 Act on persons who are employed. There is nothing in the statute, or public policy, which excludes a person employed under an illegal contract from protection.

Leighton v Michael [1995] ICR 1091 (Employment Appeal Tribunal: Mummery J presiding).

2652 Discrimination—employment—indirect discrimination—application of requirement—mobility clause

An employee was offered promotion, subject to a variation of her contract of employment which would have required her to be available to serve in any part of the United Kingdom that her employer directed. The mobility clause applied to both male and female employees above a certain grade, but the employee complained that it amounted to unlawful sex discrimination within the meaning of the Sex Discrimination Act 1975, ss 1(1)(b) and 6(1). Her complaint was dismissed, and on appeal, *held*, judicial notice had to be taken of the fact that a higher proportion of women than men would find it in practice impossible to comply with a term of employment which required them to move house. The point in time at which a term of a contract of employment was applied to an employee was that at which the term was incorporated into the contract. Having regard to the 1975 Act, s 6(1)(b), the mobility clause in the instant case amounted to unlawful indirect discrimination. However, it was likely that the discrimination was justifiable, as all that the employer had to show was that there was a need to be able to direct employees above a certain grade to work elsewhere in the United Kingdom, even if they was unable to comply with the requirement in practice. Even if the clause was not justifiable in its present form, it could be modified so that compliance would not be required from employees who were unable to comply with it in practice. Accordingly, the appeal would be allowed and the case would be remitted to the county court.

Meade-Hill v British Council [1995] ICR 847, Independent, 26 April (Court of Appeal: Stuart-Smith, Waite and Millett LJJ).

2653 Discrimination—employment—indirect discrimination—application of requirement—relevant pool of comparators

The respondent, a single parent, was employed as a train driver, and her duty roster was such that she could be at home with her child in the mornings and the evenings. A new shift system proposed by the appellant employer would have altered shift hours and would have resulted in the respondent having to work longer hours so that she could still be at home in the mornings and evenings with her child, although she would not have received additional pay for the extra work. The respondent refused to agree to the new duty roster, and resigned when the appellant and the unions failed to reach agreement about special arrangements for single parents. She successfully complained that the new duty roster indirectly discriminated against women, contrary to the Sex Discrimination Act 1975, s 1(1)(b). On the appellant's appeal, *held*, the industrial tribunal had concluded that a considerably smaller proportion of female single parents than male single parents could comply with the requirement to work the unsociable or extended hours proposed under the new shift system, whereas the comparison should have been between the proportion of women train drivers and men train drivers who could comply with the requirement. The industrial tribunal had therefore erred in selecting the pool for comparison, as it should have consisted of all train drivers to whom the new shift system was to apply, and not a subdivision of train drivers. Moreover, there was no evidence as to either the number of single parents in the workforce or the number of male and female train drivers who were unable to comply with the rostering requirement. The fact that there were more single mothers than single fathers generally did not necessarily mean that the proportion of single mothers able to comply with the rostering requirement was considerably smaller than that of single fathers, either amongst train drivers or in general. Accordingly, the appeal would be allowed.

London Underground Ltd v Edwards [1995] ICR 574 (Employment Appeal Tribunal: Mummery J presiding).

2654 Discrimination—employment—indirect discrimination—unfair dismissal—qualifying period—compatibility with EC Directive

The applicants had been employed for approximately 15 months when they were dismissed. Their unfair dismissal complaints were rejected by an industrial tribunal because the two-year qualifying period prescribed by the Unfair Dismissal (Variation of Qualifying Period) Order 1985, SI 1985/782, was not satisfied. Their application for judicial review of the 1985 Order on the grounds that it indirectly discriminated against women and was contrary to Council Directive (EC) 76/207, was dismissed. On appeal, *held*, it was necessary to consider the operation of the two-year qualifying period requirement at the time that the applicants made their complaints to the industrial tribunal, and to consider its effect in the light of Council Directive (EC) 76/207. There was evidence that during the period leading up to the applications and thereafter, there had been, and continued to be, a considerable and persistent difference between the numbers and percentages of men and women who could comply with the two-year qualifying period requirement. It was therefore indirectly discriminatory and, moreover, could not be objectively justified, because there was no evidence that it achieved its objective of increasing employment opportunities. The requirement was contrary to the directive and, accordingly, the appeal would be allowed.

R v Secretary of State for Employment, ex p Seymour-Smith [1995] IRLR 464 (Court of Appeal: Neill, Roch and Schiemann LJJ). Decision of Queen's Bench Divisional Court [1994] IRLR 448 (1994 Abr para 2518) reversed.

2655 Discrimination—employment—promotion—automatic priority where women under-represented

See *Kalanke v Freie Hansestadt Bremen*, para 3188.

2656 Discrimination—employment—sexual harassment—detriment—single act of harassment as detriment

A male employee of the appellant company was alleged to have made grossly offensive remarks of a sexual nature to the respondent, a female employee, on several occasions. The respondent was so distressed as a result of one particular remark that she complained to the appellant. The employee denied the allegation, and following a dispute between the respondent and the appellant as to how the incident ought to have been dealt with, the respondent resigned. Her complaint of constructive unfair dismissal was rejected, but her complaint of sex discrimination was upheld on the basis that a single act of sexual harassment could constitute detriment within the meaning of the Sex Discrimination Act 1975, s 6(2)(b). On the appellant's appeal, *held,* the question of whether or not an employee suffered detriment was a matter of fact for an industrial tribunal, and detriment meant nothing more than disadvantage. In the instant case, an employee had made a sexual remark to a female employee which had caused her distress, and it was an unacceptable form of bullying which was likely to create an intimidating, hostile and humiliating work environment for her. Moreover, the question of whether or not a single act of verbal sexual harassment was sufficient to found a complaint was a question of fact and degree, and there was no requirement that the act had to be expressly rejected before it could be said to have been unwanted. Accordingly, the appeal would be dismissed.

Insitu Cleaning Co Ltd v Heads [1995] IRLR 4 (Employment Appeal Tribunal: Morison J presiding).

2657 Discrimination—employment—transfer of undertakings—liability of transferee for sex discrimination

See *DJM International Ltd v Nicholas,* para 1252.

2658 Discrimination—occupational pension scheme—criterion for determining whether scheme is occupational pension scheme

See *Bestuur Van Het Algemeen Burgerlijk Pensioenfonds v Beune,* para 3184.

2659 Discrimination—social security—exemption from prescription charges

See *R v Secretary of State for Health, ex p Richardson,* para 3192.

2660 Discrimination—social security—family credit

See *Meyers v Adjudication Officer,* para 3193.

2661 Discrimination—social security—invalidity benefit

See *Graham v Secretary of State for Social Security,* para 3196, and *Van Gemert-Derks v Bestuur van de Nieuwe Industriële Bedrijfsvereniging,* para 3197.

2662 Discrimination—social security—retirement pension

See *Bramhill v Chief Adjudication Officer,* para 3200, and *Van Munster v Rijksdienst voor Pensioenen,* para 3199.

2663 Discrimination—victimisation—policewoman assaulted by colleague—employer's vicarious liability

The Sex Discrimination Act 1975, s 4(1)(d) provides that a person discriminates against another person if he treats the victimised person less favourably than others in specific circumstances because the victimised person has alleged that the discriminator or any other person has committed an act which would amount to contravention of the 1975 Act. Section 41(1) provides that anything done by a person in the course of his employment is to be treated, for the purposes of the 1975 Act, as done by his employer as well as him, whether or not it was done with the employer's knowledge or approval.

The plaintiff policewoman claimed that she had been sexually assaulted by a colleague in her room when both were off-duty, but no disciplinary or criminal proceedings were brought against him. Three years later, the plaintiff claimed that her removal from a list of specially trained police officers was victimisation by her employer in breach of the 1975 Act, s 4(1)(d), and was done as a result of her earlier allegation of sexual assault. Her claim was rejected by an industrial tribunal. On appeal, *held,* the only act which the plaintiff alleged her employer had committed was a deemed vicarious act under s 41(1). However, the vicarious act, namely the sexual assault, would not amount to a contravention of the 1975 Act unless it was done by her colleague in the course of his employment, which was not the case. In any event, the assault did not amount to unlawful discrimination because the plaintiff's colleague had not been her employer and so neither the plaintiff's colleague or her employer were guilty of discrimination. Accordingly, her appeal would be dismissed.

Waters v Metropolitan Police Comr [1995] ICR 510 (Employment Appeal Tribunal: Mummery J presiding).

2664 Equal treatment—armed forces—servicewoman's pension—application for pension to be paid to husband on servicewoman's death

The applicant's wife retired from the army in 1973 and received a pension. When she died in 1979 the applicant sought a dependant's pension. His request was rejected because there was no provision within the relevant pension scheme for the payment of a pension to the male survivor of a deceased servicewoman. Some years later, the applicant complained to an industrial tribunal that the refusal to afford equality of treatment to servicemen and servicewomen over the provision of survivors' pensions was, and always had been, discriminatory and contrary to the EC Treaty, art 119. The tribunal held that the application was time barred under the temporal restrictions imposed by *Barber v Guardian Royal Exchange Assurance Group: C-262/88* [1990] 2 All ER 660, ECJ (1990 Abr para 2706), since the applicant had not raised an equivalent claim under national law prior to 17 May 1990. On the applicant's appeal, *held*, even if he had taken steps after his wife's death which could be construed as the raising of an equivalent claim, the direct effect of art 119 could not be relied upon by the applicant to claim entitlement to an occupational pension acquired in connection with periods of service by his wife served prior to 8 April 1976. For that reason alone, the applicant was not entitled to make the claim to a widower's pension. In any event, the direct effect of art 119 could not be relied upon in order to claim entitlement to an occupational pension acquired in connection with periods of employment served prior to 1 January 1973, when the United Kingdom joined the European Community. Further, an equivalent claim in national law had to be something equivalent to legal proceedings and the assertion of a claim was not enough. The tribunal's decision had been correct and, accordingly, the appeal would be dismissed.

Howard v Ministry of Defence [1995] ICR 1074 (Employment Appeal Tribunal: Mummery J presiding). *Defrenne v Sabena (Case 43/75)* [1976] ICR 547, ECJ (1976 Abr para 1111) applied.

2665 Equal treatment—part-time workers—continuous employment

Scotland

An employee worked part-time on alternate Fridays, although occasionally she worked every Friday. She was dismissed from her job and claimed unfair dismissal but her claim for compensation was dismissed on the ground that she had not satisfied the condition of continuous employment under the Employment Protection (Consolidation) Act 1978, Sch 13, as the continuity of her employment was terminated every Friday she did not work. The tribunal held that even if the relevant provisions of Sch 13 were indirectly discriminatory because they were detrimental to part-time workers, who were mainly women, the requirement to work weekly did not unfairly prejudice the employee because she could not comply with it. On appeal by the employee, *held*, the requirements of Sch 13 were discriminatory against women in general and contrary to the EC Treaty, art 119, relating to equal pay for men and women. The fact that the employee was unable to establish that she had been discriminated against personally was irrelevant. Periods of part-time employment had to be counted when assessing continuous employment and, accordingly, the employee's case would be referred back to the tribunal for a hearing on the merits.

Colley v Corkindale [1995] ICR 965 (Employment Appeal Tribunal: Mummery J presiding). *Equal Opportunities Commission v Secretary of State for Employment* [1994] 1 All ER 910, HL (1994 Abr para 2532) applied.

SHIPPING AND NAVIGATION

Halsbury's Laws of England (4th edn) Vol 43, paras 1–1247

2666 Articles

General Average Ancient and Modern, John Macdonald: [1995] LMCLQ 480

Insolvency at Sea, Sir Jonathan Mance (on the Third Party (Rights against Insurers) Act 1930): [1995] LMCLQ 34

The Master—Is He Still in Command? Frode Grotmol: 145 NLJ 1534, 1581

Multi-party Maritime Arbitrations, Philip Yang: [1995] ADRLJ 30

The 1993 Convention on Maritime Liens and Mortgages, Francesco Berlingieri: [1995] LMCLQ 57

Procedural Reform in Maritime Arbitration, Bruce Harris: [1995] ADRLJ 18

'Safer Ships, Cleaner Seas': The Report of the Donaldson Inquiry Into the Prevention of
Pollution from Merchant Shipping, Mark Wallace: [1995] LMCLQ 404
Ships are Different: The Case for Limitation of Liability, David Steel: [1995] LMCLQ 77

2667   Admiralty jurisdiction
See ADMIRALTY.

2668   Carriage of goods by sea—goods of a dangerous nature—duty properly to stow goods
See *Losinjska Plovidba v Transco Overseas Ltd, The Orjula*, para 2164.

2669   Carriage of passengers by sea—sea transport between member states—freedom to provide services
See *EC Commission v France*, para 3151.

2670   Costs—claim for costs against P & I club—club not party to litigation—discretion to award costs
See *Tharros Shipping Co Ltd v Bias Shipping Ltd*, para 2326.

2671   Fishing vessels
See FISHERIES.

2672   Hovercraft—application of enactments
The Hovercraft (Application of Enactments) (Amendment) Order 1995, SI 1995/1299 (in force
on 17 May 1995), amends the 1972 Order, SI 1972/971, consequential on the Insurance
Companies Act 1982 and the Merchant Shipping (Salvage and Pollution) Act 1994.

2673   Insurance
See INSURANCE.

2674   Merchant shipping—deck and marine engineer officers—certification
The Merchant Shipping (Certification of Deck and Marine Engineer Officers) (Amendment)
Regulations 1995, SI 1995/1429 (in force on 1 August 1995), amend SI 1985/1306 and SI
1986/1935 so that in relation to deck officers Class I (master mariner) and marine engineering
officers Class I, the 1995 Regulations give effect to Council Directive (EC) 89/48, which relates
to a general system for the recognition of higher education diplomas awarded on completion of
professional education and training of at least three years' duration. In relation to other specified
certificates, the regulations give effect to Council Directive (EC) 92/51 on a second general
system for the recognition of professional education and training. The regulations provide for
the recognition of equivalent foreign certificates which were issued by certain authorities abroad,
and for the issue of certificates of equivalent competency for the holders of such certificates, so
as to enable the holders to serve as qualified officers on United Kingdom ships in the appropriate
position. Where such foreign certificates are not equivalent to United Kingdom certificates,
provision is made for aptitude tests or adaptation periods. In addition, a saving provision provides
that certificates of equivalent competency are not required until 1 August 1997 by certain
holders of certificates issued before that date by countries whose certificates were recognised
before 1 August 1995.

2675   Merchant shipping—deck officers and engineer officers—certification
See para 1394.

2676   Merchant shipping—designation of Marine Safety Agency—inspection and detention of ships
The Merchant Shipping (Port State Control) Regulations 1995, SI 1995/3128 (in force on 1
January 1996), implement Council Directive (EC) 95/21 concerning the enforcement, in
respect of shipping using community ports and sailing in the waters under the jurisdiction of the

member States, of international standards for ship safety, pollution prevention and shipboard living and working conditions (port state control). The regulations apply to ships which are not British ships calling at, or anchored off, United Kingdom ports and offshore installations. They designate the Marine Safety Agency as the competent authority for the United Kingdom for the purposes of the Council Directive and these regulations, and set out the powers and commitments of the Agency in relation to inspections of ships, and the procedures for such inspections. The regulations provide for the powers for detention of ships in the Merchant Shipping Act 1995 and statutory instruments under that Act to be used in the circumstances required by the Directive. Provision is made in relation to rights of appeal and compensation, for the follow up to inspections and detentions, qualifications of inspectors, duties of pilots and port authorities to make reports, publication of the detention information, and fees and offences, and for inspection of the familiarity of the crew with essential procedures and operations relating to the safety of the ship. The Merchant Shipping (Fees) Regulations 1995, SI 1995/1893, are amended so as to provide for the payment of fees in connection with any inspection under these regulations.

2677 Merchant shipping—employment of young persons

The Merchant Shipping (Employment of Young Persons) Regulations 1995, SI 1995/972 (in force on 1 May 1995), re-enact, with modifications, certain provisions of the Employment of Women, Young Persons and Children Act 1920 and the Merchant Shipping (International Labour Conventions) Act 1925, and also implement ILO Conventions 7 and 58. The regulations (1) prescribe the only circumstances in which those under school-leaving age may be employed in a ship, (2) prescribe the conditions under which persons up to the age of 18, including children, may be employed in a ship, and (3) prohibit the employment of such persons as trimmers or stokers.

2678 Merchant shipping—fees

The Merchant Shipping (Fees) Regulations 1995, SI 1995/1893 (in force on 1 August 1995), replace the 1991 Regulations, SI 1991/784 (as amended). They prescribe changes in certain rates charged by the Department of Transport and Customs and Excise. Fees for tonnage measurement have been increased by about 3 per cent, the bottom range of the scale has been removed and maximum fees have been created. Radio survey fees have been increased by about 4 per cent and fees have been set for certificates of equivalent competency. The regulations also introduce a new fee in connection with the administration of marine examinations.

2679 Merchant shipping—light dues

The Merchant Shipping (Light Dues) (Amendment) Regulations 1995, SI 1995/525 (in force on 1 April 1995), further amend SI 1990/364 so as to remove the light dues surcharge for Ro/Ro vessels whose liability for light dues is assessed by reference to a tonnage certificate issued in accordance with the International Convention on Tonnage Measurement of Ships 1969.

2680 Merchant shipping—officer nationality

The Merchant Shipping (Officer Nationality) Regulations 1995, SI 1995/1427 (in force on 1 August 1995), provide that United Kingdom ships of 500 tons or more, and fishing vessels of 24 metres or more in length, which serve a strategic function, must carry as master persons who are Commonwealth citizens or nationals of other EEA or NATO states. The maximum penalties for breaches of the regulations are set out in the Merchant Shipping Act 1970.

2681 Merchant shipping—pollution—dangerous or polluting cargo—reporting requirements

The Merchant Shipping (Reporting Requirements for Ships Carrying Dangerous or Polluting Goods) Regulations 1995, SI 1995/2498 (in force on 31 October 1995), which revoke SI 1981/1077 and SI 1994/3245, implement Council Directive (EC) 93/75, relating to vessels bound for or leaving community ports which are carrying dangerous or polluting goods. In particular, the regulations (1) require the operator of a ship departing from a port to inform the competent authority of that port about the nature, quantity and location of any dangerous goods aboard, and its destination and intended route, although ferries on short sea voyages of less than an hour are exempt from the requirement if the ferry operator can supply the information to the competent authority immediately on request, (2) require the above-mentioned information to be lodged with the competent authority of the member state of the first port of call within the Community if the ship departs from a port outside the Community, (3) designate the Coastguard Agency of the Department of Transport as the competent authority for the United Kingdom, (4) require the master to provide details of the ship, its equipment, crew and survey certificates to a pilot, or to the competent authority, on demand, (5) require the master to provide information about the cargo aboard to the competent authority of the member state concerned if the ship gets into difficulty or is involved in an accident which is likely to pose a threat to any member state's coastline or related interests, and (6) implement the requirement in SOLAS and MARPOL to report the loss or likely loss of dangerous or polluting goods to the nearest coastal state, wherever such incidents occur, although the master may discharge this obligation by indicating which competent authority in the Community holds the information.

2682 Merchant shipping—safety—detention of unsafe ship—determination of sea limit

Scotland

The Secretary of State made orders under the Merchant Shipping Act 1988, s 30A, detaining three ships within a harbour and prohibiting the ships from going to sea because they were not fit to do so. The orders defined the sea as a line joining a point in the harbour to a neigbouring town. The harbour's limit was several miles beyond this point. The harbourmaster considered that the ships could be anchored more safely in a bay which was within the harbour limits but beyond the line mentioned in the orders. The harbour's trustees sought judicial review of the Secretary of State's orders. *Held*, although a harbourmaster may have special local knowledge, a marine safety officer had the power, which a harbourmaster did not, to board vessels and assess their safety. Therefore the legislation clearly envisaged that a safety officer was best placed to determine the seaworthiness of a particular vessel. To allow the ships to be towed to the bay would be favouring the harbourmaster's opinion over that of the officer and would thus be against the intention of the legislation. In addition, the limit determined in the orders was decided by reference to safety factors whereas the harbour limits were not. Accordingly, the application would be dismissed

Ullapool Harbour Trustees v Secretary of State for Transport (1995) Times, 13 April (Outer House).

2683 Merchant shipping—safety—hours of work

The Merchant Shipping (Hours of Work) Regulations 1995, SI 1995/157 (in force on 28 February 1995), give effect, in part, to the Merchant Shipping (Minimum Standards) Convention 1976, which requires the establishment of safety standards regarding hours of work. The regulations (1) place general duties on operators, employers and masters of United Kingdom sea-going merchant ships, other than fishing vessels and pleasure craft, to ensure that masters and seamen do not work on a ship for more hours than are safe, (2) require the working hours and rest periods for (i) masters and seamen whose work includes regular watchkeeping or ship handling, and (ii) chief engineers, chief officers and second engineer officers, to be set out in a schedule of duties which must be produced and displayed on all vessels, (3) place a general duty on seamen to use their best endeavours to be adequately rested before and during a voyage, and (4) prescribe penalties for breaches of the regulations, and provide for the power to detain ships.

2684 Merchant shipping—safety—medical stores

The Merchant Shipping and Fishing Vessels (Medical Stores) Regulations 1995, SI 1995/1802 (in force on 1 August 1995), which replace SI 1986/144 and 1988/1547, implement Council Directive (EC) 92/29 relating to the minimum safety and health requirements for improved medical treatment on board vessels, in so far as the directive relates to the carriage of medicines and other medical stores.

2685 Merchant shipping—safety—ships' doctors

The Merchant Shipping (Ships' Doctors) Regulations 1995, SI 1995/1803 (in force on 1 August 1995), replace SI 1981/1065, and implement Council Directive (EC) 92/29 (minimum safety and health requirements for improved medical treatment on board vessels) as regards the requirement to have a doctor on board ship. In particular, United Kingdom ships are required to have a doctor on board if they are carrying 100 or more persons on an international voyage of more than three days, or on a voyage during which the ship is more than one and a half days' sailing time from a port with adequate medical equipment.

2686 Merchant shipping—safety—surveys and certification

The Merchant Shipping (Survey and Certification) Regulations 1995, SI 1995/1210 (in force on 1 June 1995), (1) repeal, revoke, and re-enact the requirements contained in various Acts and instruments regarding the survey and certification of passenger ships and cargo ships, (2) give effect to the requirement imposed by the Safety of Life at Sea Convention 1974 regarding surveys and the issue of certificates, and also provide similar requirements for ships which are not subject to the Convention, (3) delegate some passenger ship surveys to the classification societies, (4) remove the requirement whereby ships on international voyages must have a passenger certificate as well as a (SOLAS) Passenger Ship Safety Certificate, (5) provide for an arbitration procedure in relation to appeals against surveys, and (6) make consequential amendments to the Merchant Shipping Acts 1894 and 1979, and the Fishing Vessels (Safety Provisions) Act 1970.

2687 Merchant shipping—seamen's documents

The Merchant Shipping (Seamen's Documents) (Amendment) Regulations 1995, SI 1995/1900 (in force on 1 September 1995), amend SI 1987/408 so as to remove the requirement that a discharge book, and an application for a discharge book, must contain the seaman's national insurance number.

2688 Merchant Shipping Act 1970—commencement

The Merchant Shipping Act 1970 (Commencement No 11) Order 1995, SI 1995/965, brings into force on 1 May 1995 ss 51, 100(3) (in part), and certain repeals in Sch 5.

The Merchant Shipping Act 1970 (Commencement No 12) Order 1995, SI 1995/1426, brings into force, on 1 August 1995, the repeal by Sch 5 of the Aliens Restriction (Amendment) Act 1919, s 5, which prohibited the employment of aliens as masters, chief engineers and skippers in British vessels.

For details of commencement, see the commencement table in the title STATUTES.

2689 Merchant Shipping Act 1995

The Merchant Shipping Act 1995 consolidates the Merchant Shipping Acts 1894 to 1994. The Act received the royal assent on 19 July 1995 and comes into force on 1 January 1996, subject to certain exceptions. For details of commencement, see the commencement table in the title STATUTES. A table showing the destination of enactments consolidated appears opposite.

DESTINATION TABLE

This table shows in column (1) the enactments repealed by the Merchant Shipping Act 1995 and in column (2) the provisions of that Act corresponding thereto.

In certain cases the enactment in column (1), though having a corresponding provision in column (2) is not, or not wholly, repealed as it is still required, or partly required, for the purposes of other legislation. A "dash" in the right hand column means that the repealed provision to which it corresponds in the left hand column is spent, unnecessary or for some other reason not specifically reproduced.

† Not repealed
* Repealed in partt

1	2
Merchant Shipping Repeal Act 1854 (c 120)	**Merchant Shipping Act 1995 (c 21)**
s 7	Rep 1993 c 22, s 8(4), Sch 5, Pt II
Lloyd's Act 1871 (c xxi)	**Merchant Shipping Act 1995 (c 21)**
s 33	—
Merchant Shipping Act 1894 (c 60)	**Merchant Shipping Act 1995 (c 21)**
s 66	Rep 1981 c 45, s 30, Schedule, Pt I
s 76(1)	s 7(1), (2), (5)
s 76(2)	s 7(3), (4)
s 82	s 11
s 84(1)	s 12(1)–(3)
s 84(2), (3)	s 12(4), (5)
s 287(1)	s 101(1), (4), (6)
s 287(2)	s 101(2), (4)
s 287(3)	s 101(3)
s 287(4)	s 101(5)
s 288	s 102
s 422(1)	s 92(1)
s 422(2)	Rep 1911 c 57, s 4(2)
s 422(3)	s 92(4)
s 449(1)	s 87(1), (2)
s 449(2)	s 87(3), (4)
s 449(3)	s 87(5)
s 458(1)	s 42(1), (2)
s 458(2)(a).	s 42(3)
s 458(2)(b)	Rep 1993 c 22, s 8(3), (4), Sch 4, para 7(b), Sch 5, Pt II
s 510	s 255(1)
s 511(1)	ss 231(1), (5), 232(1), (2)
s 511(2)	s 232(3), (4)
s 512	ss 231(1), 233
s 513	ss 231(1), 234
s 515	ss 231(1), 235(1)–(3), (5)
s 516(1)	s 231(2)
s 516(2)	s 231(3), (4)
s 518(1)	s 236(1)–(3)
s 518(2)	Applies to Scotland
s 519	s 237
s 520	s 238
s 521(1)	s 239(1)
s 521(2)	s 239(2), (3)
s 522	s 240
s 523	s 241
s 524	s 242
s 525	s 243
s 527	s 244

1	2
s 530	s 252(1)–(8)
s 531(1)	s 253(1)
s 531(2)–(4)	s 253(2)–(4)
s 532	s 252(1)–(9)
s 533	s 254
s 534	s 252(10)
s 535	s 245
s 536(1)	s 246(1),(2), (4), (5)
s 536(2)	s 246(3), (5)
s 537(1)	s 247(1), (2)
s 537(2)	s 247(3)
s 551(1)	s 225(1), (2)
s 551(2), (3)	s 225(3), (4)
s 552	s 226(1)–(4)
s 553(1) . . . . , . .	s 227(1), (2)
s 553(2)	s 227(3)
s 555(1)	s 228(1)–(3)
s 555(2)	s 228(4), (6)
s 555(2A).	s 228(5)
s 555(3)	s 228(7)
s 556	s 229(1)–(3)
s 557	s 230(3)–(5)
s 566	s 248
s 567(1)	ss 249(1), (2), 306
s 567(2), (3)	s 249(3), (4)
s 567(4)	—
s 568(1)	s 250(1)–(3)
s 568(2)	s 250(4)
s 569(2)	s 251
s 570	Applies to Scotland
s 571	Sch 14, para 11
s 634(1)	ss 193(1), (2), (4), (5), 195(1)
s 634(2)	s 195(2)
s 634A.	s 196
s 635	s 194
s 636(1)	s 200(1)
s 636(2)	s 200(2), (3)
s 638	ss 197(1), 223(2)
s 639(1), (2)	s 197(5), (7)
s 639(1A).	s 917(6)
s 642	s 197(4)
s 643	s 205(1), (2), (4)
s 643A.	s 206
s 647	s 205(6)
s 648(1)	Rep 1988 c 12, ss 48, 57(5), Schs 5, 7
s 648(2), (3)	s 205(7), (8)
s 648(4)	s 205(9)
s 649(1)	s 207(1), (2)
s 649(1A).	Applies to Scotland
s 649(2)	s 207(4)
s 650(1)	s 208(1), (4)
s 650(2)	s 208(2), (3)
s 650(3)	s 208(5)
s 651	s 209
s 652	s 198
s 653(1), (2)	s 199(1), (2)

1	2	1	2
s 653(3)	s 199(3)	s 686(1)	s 281
s 653(4)	—	s 686(2)	Rep 1993 c 22, s 8(4), Sch 5, Pt II
s 653(5)	s 199(4)	s 687	s 282
s 654(1)	s 204(1)	s 687A	s 277
s 654(2)	s 223(2)	s 687B	Applies to Scotland
s 655(1), (3)	Rep 1964 c 40, ss 29(1), 63(3), Sch 6	s 688★	Applies to Scotland
s 655(2)	s 210(3), (4)	s 689(1)	s 283(1), (2)
s 656	s 210(9), (10)	s 689(2)	s 283(3)–(5), (9)
s 657★	—	s 689(3)	s 283(6)
s 658	s 211(2)(a)	s 689(4)	s 283(7), (9)
s 659	s 212	s 689(5)	s 283(8)
s 660(1)	s 213(1)	s 690	Rep 1970 c 36, s 100, Sch 5
s 660(2)	s 213(2), (3)	s 691(1), (2)	s 286(1), (2), (4)
s 660(3)	s 213(4)	s 691(3), (4)	s 286(3), (4)
s 662	s 215	s 692(1)	s 284(1)–(3)
s 662A	ss 216, 306	s 692(2)	s 284(4), (5)
s 662B	s 217	s 692(3), (4)	s 284(6), (7)
s 664	s 218	s 692(5)	s 284(8)
s 666(1)	s 219(1)	s 693	s 285
s 666(1A)	s 219(2)	s 695(1)	s 288(1)
s 666(2)	s 219(3)	s 695(2)	s 288(2)–(4)
s 667(1)	s 220(1), (2)	s 695(3)	s 188(5)
s 667(2), (3)	s 220(3), (4)	s 695(3A), (4), (5)	Apply to Scotland
s 667(4)	s 220(5)–(7)	s 696	s 291
s 667(4A)	Applies to Scotland	s 697(1)	s 290(1), (2)
s 668(1)	Sch 8, para 1(1), (2)	s 697(2)	s 290(3)
s 668(2)	Sch 8, para 4	ss 702, 703, 710	Apply to Scotland
s 668(3)	Sch 8, para 2(1)	ss 711, 712	—
s 668(4)	Sch 8, para 2(2)	s 713	s 292(1)
s 668(5)	Sch 8, para 3	s 714	s 299(1), (2)
s 668(6)	Sch 8, para 5	s 715	s 299(3)
s 669	Sch 14, para 9(2), (3)	s 717	s 292(2)
s 676(1)(a)	s 305(1)(a)	s 718	s 303
s 676(1)(b), (e), (k)	—	s 720(1)	s 300(1), (6)
s 676(1)(c)	Rep 1993 c 22, s 8(4), Sch 5, Pt II	s 720(2)–(5)	s 300(2)–(5)
s 676(1)(d), (f)	Rep 1970 c 36, s 100(3), Sch 5	s 721(a)	—
		s 721(b)	s 221(4)
s 676(1)(g)	Rep1908 c 49	s 721(c)	s 221(5)
s 676(1)(h)	s 305(1)(b)	s 722(1)	Rep 1981 c 45, s 30, Schedule, Pt I
s 676(1)(i)	Rep 1988 c 12, ss 48, 57(5), Schs 5, 7	s 722(2)(a)	Rep 1970 c 36, s 100(3), Sch 5
s 676(1)(l)	s 305(1)(c)	s 722(2)(b)	s 300(7)
s 676(2)	s 305(2)	s 723(1)	s 257(1), (2)
s 677(1)(a), (e)	Rep 1970 c 36, s 100(3), Sch 5	s 723(2)	s 257(3), (4)
		s 724(1)	s 256(2)–(4), (9)
s 677(1)(b)	s 304(1)(b)	s 724(2)	s 256(5)
s 677(1)(c), (k), (n)	—	s 724(3)	—
s 677(1)(d)	s 304(1)(b)	s 724(4)	Rep 1979 c 39, ss 43(3), 50(4), Sch 6, Pt VI, para 12, Sch 7, Pt II
s 677(1)(f)	s 304(1)(e)		
s 677(1)(g)	s 304(1)(d)		
s 677(1)(h)	s 304(1)(f)	s 724(5)	Rep 1993 c 22, s 8(3), (4), Sch 4, para 78, Sch 5, Pt II
s 677(1)(i)	Rep 1988 c 12, ss 48, 57(5), Schs 5, 7		
s 677(1)(l)	s 304(1)(g)	s 726	s 299(4)–(6)
s 677(1)(m)	Rep 1979 c 39, ss 34(2), 50(4), Sch 7, Pt II	s 727	—
		s 728	s 256(1), (9)
s 677(1)(o)	s 304(1)(h)	s 731	s 221(1), (2)
s 677(2)	s 304(1)	s 732	s 222
s 679	s 211(4), (5)	ss 735, 736	—
s 680	passim	s 738(1)	—
s 681(1)	—	s 738(2)	ss 2(4), 308(3)
s 681(2)	ss 207(1), (2), 220(7), 236(3)	s 739	Cf ss 291(1), 306(5)
		s 741	s 308(1)
s 683(1)	s 274(1)	s 742	ss 223(1), 255(1), 313(1)
s 683(2)	s 275	s 743	—
s 683(3)	—	s 745(1)(a)–(e)	—
s 683(4)	Rep 1986 c 12	s 745(1)(f)	Sch 14, para 13
s 684	s 279	s 745(2), (3)	—
s 685	s 280		

1	2
ss 746, 747. . . . .—	
Schs 17, 19 . . . .—	

1	2
Mersey Channels Act 1897 (c 21)	Merchant Shipping Act 1995 (c 21)
. . . .—	

1	2
Merchant Shipping Act 1897 (c 59)	Merchant Shipping Act 1995 (c 21)
s 1(1). . . . .—	
s 1(2).	Rep 1988 c 12, s 57(5), Sch 7
s 2. . . . .—	

1	2
Merchant Shipping (Mercantile Marine Fund) Act 1898 (c 44)	Merchant Shipping Act 1995 (c 21)
s 1(1).	ss 211(1), 212(1), (2), 213(1), 218, 303
s 1(2).	s 211(3)(a)
s 1(3).	—
s 1(4).	passim
s 1A(1)	s 214
s 1A(2)	Rep 1972 c 41, s 134, Sch 28, Pt IV
s 2(3)★.	s 211(2)(d)
s 2A(1)	s 211(2)(b)
s 2A(2)	s 211(3)(b)
s 2B	s 211(2)(c)
s 5(1).	s 205(3)
s 5(2).	ss 205(5), 306
s 9. . . . .—	
Sch 3★.	s 211(2)(d)

1	2
Merchant Shipping (Liability of Shipowners and others) Act 1900 (c 32)	Merchant Shipping Act 1995 (c 21)
s 2(1).	s 191(1), (2), (4), (7)
s 2(2), (3).	Rep 1979 c 39, ss 19, 50(4), Sch 5, para 1(2), (3), Sch 7, Pt I
s 2(4), (5).	s 191(9)
s 2(6).	s 191(8)
s 3.	s 191(3)
ss 4, 5 . . . .—	

1	2
Merchant Shipping Act 1906 (c 48)	Merchant Shipping Act 1995 (c 21)
s 72.	s 236(1)
s 75(1).	s 256(2)–(4)
s 75(2), (3). . . . .—	
s 75(4).	s 256(5)
s 76.	s 107
s 78.	s 294
s 79(1).	s 301(1), (2)
s 79(2), (3).	s 301(3), (4)
s 80(1).	s 308(2)
s 80(2). . . . .—	
s 80(3).	s 308(4)
ss 84, 86 . . . .—	

1	2
Maritime Conventions Act 1911 (c 57)	Merchant Shipping Act 1995 (c 21)
s 1(1)	s 187(1)–(2), (4), (5)
s 1(2)	ss 187(6), (7), 188(3)
s 2	s 188(1), (3)
s 3(1)	s 189(1), (3)
s 3(2)	s 189(4)
s 4(2)	s 92(3)
s 5	Rep 1925 c 49, s 226, Sch 6; 1934 c 17, s 34(1), Sch 5, Pt I
ss 6, 7	Rep 1994 c 28, ss 1(6) 10(3), Sch 2, para 2(1), (2)
s 8	s 190
s 9(1), (3) . . . .—	
s 9(2)	Rep 1927 c 42
s 9(4)	ss 187(3), 188(2), 189(2)
s 10. . . . .—	

1	2
British Mercantile Marine Uniform Act 1919 (c 62)	Merchant Shipping Act 1995 (c 21)
s 1	s 57
ss 2, 3 . . . .—	

1	2
Aliens Restriction (Amendment) Act 1919 (c 92)	Merchant Shipping Act 1995 (c 21)
s 5	Rep 1970 c 36, s 100(3), Sch 5

1	2
Merchant Shipping (Amendment) Act 1920 (c 2)	Merchant Shipping Act 1995 (c 21)
s 1	s 212(1)
s 2 . . . .—	

1	2
Merchant Shipping (Scottish Fishing Boats) Act 1920 (c 39)	Merchant Shipping Act 1995 (c 21)
. . . .	Applies to Scotland

1	2
Merchant Shipping Act 1921 (c 28)	Merchant Shipping Act 1995 (c 21)
s 2	s 99(1), (2)
s 3	s 99(3)
s 4 . . . .—	

1	2
Fees (Increase) Act 1923 (c 4)	Merchant Shipping Act 1995 (c 21)
Sch 1† . , ...	s 288(4)

1	2
Statute of Westminster 1931 (c 4)	Merchant Shipping Act 1995 (c 21)
s 5 . . . .—	

1	2	1	2
		ss 7, 8 . . . .—	
Merchant Shipping (Safety and Load Line Conventions) Act 1932 (c 9)	Merchant Shipping Act 1995 (c 21)	Arbitration Act 1950 (c 27)	Merchant Shipping Act 1995 (c 21)
		s 29★ . . . .—	
s 5(2), (3) . . . .—		Administration of Justice Act 1956 (c 46)	Merchant Shipping Act 1995 (c 21)
s 8 . . . .—			
s 24(1) . . . . s 91(1), (2)		s 47(2)(n)★ . . . . .Applies to Scotland	
s 24(2), (3) . . . . s 91(3), (4)		s 49(1) . . . . .Applies to Scotland	
s 24(4) . . . . s 91(5)–(7)		Sch 1, Pt I, para 1★. . . . . .—	
s 24(5) . . . . s 91(7)			
s 24(6) . . . . Rep 1950 c 6		Ghana Independence Act 1957 (c 6)	Merchant Shipping Act 1995 (c 21)
s 62(1), (3) . . . .—			
ss 69, 73, 74 . . . .—		Sch 1, para 4 . . . .—	
Sch 1 . . . .—		Sch 2, paras 7, 8 . . . .—	
Pensions (Navy, Army, Air Force and Mercantile Marine) Act 1939 (c 83)	Merchant Shipping Act 1995 (c 21)	Federation of Malaya Independence Act 1957 (c 60)	Merchant Shipping Act 1995 (c 21)
s 6(3) . . . .—		Sch 1, paras 9, 10 . . . .—	
Ceylon Independence Act 1947 (c 7)	Merchant Shipping Act 1995 (c 21)	Cyprus Act 1960 (c 52)	Merchant Shipping Act 1995 (c 21)
Sch 1, para 3 . . . .—		Schedule, para 10 . . . .—	
Crown Proceedings Act 1947 (c 44)	Merchant Shipping Act 1995 (c 21)	Nigeria Independence Act 1960 (c 55)	Merchant Shipping Act 1995 (c 21)
s 5 . . . . ss 185(3), 186(4), 192(1)			
ss 6, 7 . . . . s 192(1)		Sch 1, para 4 . . . .—	
s 8 . . . . s 230(1), (2)		Sch 2, paras 7, 8 . . . .—	
s 30 . . . . Cf s 190		Tanganyika Independence Act 1961 (c 1)	Merchant Shipping Act 1995 (c 21)
s 38(2)† . . . . ss 192(2), 230(7)			
Merchant Shipping Act 1948 (c 44)	Merchant Shipping Act 1995 (c 21)	Sch 1, para 4 . . . .—	
		Sch 2, paras 7, 8 . . . .—	
s 5(1) . . . . Sch 14, para 3(1)		Sierra Leone Independence Act 1961 (c 16)	Merchant Shipping Act 1995 (c 21)
s 5(2) . . . . Sch 14, para 3(2), (3)			
s 5(3)–(5) . . . . Sch 14, para 3(4)–(7)		Sch 2, para 4 . . . .—	
s 5(6) . . . .—		Sch 3, paras 8, 9 . . . .—	
Consular Conventions Act 1949 (c 29)	Merchant Shipping Act 1995 (c 21)	South Africa Act 1962 (c 23)	Merchant Shipping Act 1995 (c 21)
s 5(2) . . . . s 239(2)		Sch 3, para 6 . . . .—	
Merchant Shipping (Safety Convention) Act 1949 (c 43)	Merchant Shipping Act 1995 (c 21)	Northern Ireland Act 1962 (c 30)	Merchant Shipping Act 1995 (c 21)
s 22(1), (2) . . . . s 93(1)–(3)		s 25(1)(a) . . . .—	
s 22(3)–(5) . . . . s 93(4)–(6)		Jamaica Independence Act 1962 (c 40)	Merchant Shipping Act 1995 (c 21)
s 22(6), (7) . . . . Rep 1970 c 36, s 100(3), Sch 5			
s 22(8) . . . . s 93(7)		Sch 1, para 4 . . . .—	
s 25 . . . . s 304(1)(c)		Sch 2, paras 7, 8 . . . .—	
ss 32, 34 . . . .—			
s 35(1) . . . .—			
s 36★ . . . .—			
s 37 . . . .—			
Sch 1, para 1 . . . .—			
Merchant Shipping Act 1950 (c 9)	Merchant Shipping Act 1995 (c 21)		

1	2	1	2

1	2
Trinidad and Tobago Independence Act 1962 (c 54)	Merchant Shipping Act 1995 (c 21)
Sch 1, para 4 . . . .—	
Sch 2, paras 7, 8 . . . .—	
Uganda Independence Act 1962 (c 57)	Merchant Shipping Act 1995 (c 21)
Sch 1, para 4 . . . .—	
Sch 3, paras 7, 8 . . . .—	
Kenya Independence Act 1963 (c 54)	Merchant Shipping Act 1995 (c 21)
Sch 1, para 4 . . . .—	
Sch 2, paras 7, 8 . . . .—	
Zanzibar Act 1963 (c 55)	Merchant Shipping Act 1995 (c 21)
Sch 1, para 8 . . . .—	
Licensing Act 1964 (c 26)	Merchant Shipping Act 1995 (c 21)
s 158 . . . .—	
Harbours Act 1964 (c 40)	Merchant Shipping Act 1995 (c 21)
s 29(2). . . . . .s 210(2)	
s 29(3). . . . . .s 210(1)	
s 30(2). . . . . .s 210(5)	
s 30(3)★. . . . . .s 210(6)	
s 30(4)†. . . . . .s 210(7)	
s 35. . . . . .Sch 10	
Malawi Independence Act 1964 (c 46)	Merchant Shipping Act 1995 (c 21)
Sch 1, para 4(a) . . . .—	
Sch 2, paras 7, 8. . . . .—	
Merchant Shipping Act 1964 (c 47)	Merchant Shipping Act 1995 (c 21)
s 9★. . . . .—	
s 11. . . . .—	
s 16. . . . . .s 91(2)	
ss 19, 20 . . . .—	
Malta Independence Act 1964 (c 86)	Merchant Shipping Act 1995 (c 21)
Sch 1, para 4(a) . . . .—	
Sch 2, paras 7, 8. . . . .—	
Gambia Independence Act 1964 (c 93)	Merchant Shipping Act 1995 (c 21)
Sch 1, para 4(a) . . . .—	
Sch 2, paras 7, 8. . . . .—	

1	2
Administration of Estates (Small Payments) Act 1965 (c 32)	Merchant Shipping Act 1995 (c 21)
s 6(1)(c). . . . .—	
Merchant Shipping Act 1965 (c 47)	Merchant Shipping Act 1995 (c 21)
s 1(1) . . . . .ss 19(1), 306	
s 1(2)–(4) . . . . .s 19(2)–(4)	
s 1(5)	
s 1(6) . . . . .s 19(5)	
s 1(6A) . . . . .s 19(6)	
s 1(7) . . . . .s 306	
s 2 . . . . .Rep 1967 c 27, s 33, Sch 2	
s 3 . . . .—	
s 4 . . . . .Rep 1968 c 32, s 18(2), Sch 4	
s 5(1) . . . .—	
s 5(2) . . . . .Rep 1979 c 39, s 50(4), Sch 7, Pt I	
s 6 . . . . .Rep 1993 c 22, s 8(5), Sch 5, Pt II	
s 7(1) . . . .—	
s 7(2) . . . . .Rep 1974 c 22	
s 8 . . . .—	
Sch 1 . . . . .s 12(3)	
Sch 2 . . . . .Rep 1974 c 22	
Guyana Independence Act 1966 (c 14)	Merchant Shipping Act 1995 (c 21)
Sch 1, para 4(a) . . . .—	
Sch 2, paras 7, 8 . . . .—	
Singapore 1966 (c 29)	Merchant Shipping Act 1995 (c 21)
Schedule, paras 10, 11 . . . .—	
Barbados Independence Act 1966 (c 37)	Merchant Shipping Act 1995 (c 21)
Sch 1, para 4(a) . . . .—	
Sch 2, paras 7, 8 . . . .—	
Merchant Shipping (Load Lines) Act 1967 (c 27)	Merchant Shipping Act 1995 (c 21)
s 1 . . . . .Sch 3, para 1	
s 2 . . . . .Sch 3, para 2	
s 3 . . . . .Sch 3, para 3	
s 4 . . . . .Sch 3, para 4	
s 5 . . . . .Sch 3, para 5	
s 6 . . . . .Sch 3, para 6	
s 7 . . . . .Sch 3, para 7	
s 8 . . . . .Sch 3, para 8	
s 9 . . . . .Sch 3, para 9	
s 10(1). . . . . .Sch 3, para 10(1)	
s 10(2). . . . . .Sch 3, para 10(2), (3)	
s 10(3), (4) . . . . .Sch 3, para 10(4), (5)	
s 11(1). . . . . .Sch 3, para 11	
s 11(2). . . . . .Rep 1979 c 39, ss 28(6), 50(4), Sch 7, Pt II	
s 12. . . . . .Sch 3, para 12	
s 13. . . . . .Sch 3, para 13	

1	2
s 14	Sch 3, para 14
s 15	Sch 3, para 15
s 16	Sch 3, para 16
s 17	Sch 3, para 17
s 18	Sch 3, para 18
s 19	Sch 3, para 19
s 20	Sch 3, para 20
s 21	Sch 3, para 21
s 22	Sch 3, para 22
s 24	Sch 3, para 24
s 25	—
s 27(1)	Sch 3, para 25
s 27(3)	Sch 3, paras 26, 27(1)
s 27(5)	Sch 3, para 28
s 30(1)	Sch 3, para 30
s 30(2)	—
s 30(3)	s 306
s 30(4)	Rep 1968 c 32, s 18(2), Sch 4
s 31	Sch 3, para 29
s 32(1)	Sch 3, para 31(1)
s 32(2), (3)	Sch 3, para 32(3), (4)
s 32(4)	Sch 3, para 31(1), (2)
s 32(5)–(7)	Sch 3, para 32(5)–(7)
s 32(8)	—
ss 33, 34.	—
Schs 1, 2	—

Mauritius Independence Act 1968 (c 8)	Merchant Shipping Act 1995 (c 21)
Sch 1, para 4(a)	—
Sch 2, paras 7, 8	—

Sea Fisheries Act 1968 (c 77)	Merchant Shipping Act 1995 (c 21)
s 17†	s 255(2)

Post Office Act 1969 (c 48)	Merchant Shipping Act 1995 (c 21)
s 3(1)*	Cf s 91(7)
s 3(6)*	—

Fishing Vessels (Safety Provisions) Act 1970 (c 27)	Merchant Shipping Act 1995 (c 21)
s 1(1)	s 121(1)
s 1(2)	s 121(2), (3)
s 1(3), (4)	s 121(4), (5)
s 2(1)	s 122(1)
s 3(1)–(3)	s 123
s 3(4)	s 124(1)–(5)
s 3(5)	s 124(7)
s 4(1)–(3)	s 125
s 4(4)	—
s 5(1)	s 126(1), (2)
s 5(2)	s 126(3)
s 7	s 306
s 9	—
s 10	s 304(1)(a)
s 11	—

Merchant Shipping Act 1970 (c 36)	Merchant Shipping Act 1995 (c 21)
s 1	s 25
s 2	s 26

1	2
s 3	s 27
s 4	s 28
s 5	s 29
s 7(1)–(3)	s 30(1)–(3)
s 7(3A)–(3C)	s 30(4)–(6)
s 7(4)–(6)	s 30(7)–(9)
s 7(7)	s 30(10)
s 8(1)–(3)	s 31(1)–(3)
s 8(3A)	s 31(4)
s 8(4), (5)	s 31(5), (6)
s 9	s 32
s 10	s 33
s 11(1)–(3)	s 34(1)–(3)
s 11(4), (4A)	s 34(5)
s 12	s 35
s 13	s 36
s 14	s 37
s 15	s 38(1)–(3)
s 16	s 39
s 17	s 40
s 18	s 41
s 20	s 43
s 22	s 44
s 25	s 53
s 26	s 45(1), (2)
s 27	s 58
s 28	s 117(1)
s 30	s 59
s 32	s 106(1)
s 33	ss 58(6), 117(2)
s 39(1)–(3)	s 70(1)–(3)
s 39(4)	Applies to Scotland
s 40	s 71
s 41	s 72
s 43	s 47
s 44	s 48
s 45	s 49(1)
s 46	s 52
s 47	s 50
s 48	s 51
s 49	s 46
s 50	s 54
s 51	s 55
s 52	s 61
s 53	s 62
s 54	s 63
s 56(1)	s 268(1)
s 56(1A)	s 268(2)
s 56(2)	s 268(3)
s 56(3)	Applies to Scotland
s 56(4)	s 268(5)
s 56(5), (6)	s 268(8), (9)
s 56(6A)	s 268(10)
s 56(7)	s 268(11)
s 57	ss 64, 269
s 58	ss 65, 270
s 59	ss 66, 268(6)
s 60	ss 67, 268(7), 269(5)
s 61(1)	s 271(1)
s 61(1A), (1B)	s 271(2), (3)
s 61(2)–(4)	s 271(4)–(6)
s 62	s 73(1)–(7)
s 63	s 74
s 64	s 75
s 67	s 73(8)
s 68	s 77
s 69	s 78
s 70	s 79
s 71(1)	s 80(1)
s 71(2)	s 80(3)
s 72(1)(a), (b)	s 108(1)–(4)

1	2
s 72(1)(c)	s 108(5), (6)
s 72(2)–(5)	s 108(7)–(10)
s 74	s 81
s 75	s 287
s 75A	s 289
s 76(1)	s 258(1), (2)
s 76(2)–(4)	s 258(3)–(5)
s 77	s 103
s 78	s 104
s 79	s 105
s 80(1)	s 295(1)–(3)
s 80(2)	s 295(4)
s 81	s 296
s 82(1)	s 297(1)
s 82(1A)	s 297(2)
s 82(2)	s 297(3)
s 83	s 297(4), (5)
s 85	—
s 86(1)	s 90(1), (2)
s 86(2)	s 90(3)
s 88	—
s 91	s 19(5), (6)
s 95(1)	ss 24(3), 106(3), 110, 112, 119(1)
s 95(2)	s 114
s 95(3)	—
s 95(4)	s 113
s 95(5)	s 120
s 95(6)	Rep 1993 c 22, s 8(4), Sch 5, Pt II
s 96(1)	s 24(1), (2)
s 96(2)(a)	s 106(2)
s 96(2)(b)	s 49(2)
s 97(1)	s 84(1)
s 97(2)–(4)	s 84(2)–(4)
s 97(5)	ss 45(3), 108(11)
s 97(6)	s 84(5)
s 97(7)	—
s 98(1)	s 304(1)(a)
s 98(2)	s 305(1)(c)
s 99	s 306
ss 100, 101	—
Sch 1	—
Sch 2, Pt I, para 1	s 109
Sch 2, Pt I, para 2	Rep 1979 c 39, ss 23(7), 50(4), Sch 7, Pt II
Sch 2, Pt I, para 3	s 116
Sch 2, Pt I, para 4	s 115
Sch 2, Pt I, para 5	s 272
Sch 2, Pt II	ss 110, 112
Sch 3, para 1	Rep 1992 c 52, s 300(1), Sch 1
Sch 3, para 2	s 283(1)
Sch 3, para 3	s 288(1), (2)
Sch 3, para 4	s 313(1)
Sch 3, paras 5–7	—
Sch 3, para 8	Rep 1984 c 26, s 10(2), Sch 2
Sch 3, paras 9–11	—
Sch 3, para 12	Sch 3, para 10(2)
Sch 3, para 13	s 310
Sch 3, para 14	—
Schs 4, 5	—

1	2
Fiji Independence Act 1970 (c 50)	Merchant Shipping Act 1995 (c 21)
Sch 1, para 4(a)	—
Sch 2, para 6	—

1	2
Attachment of Earnings Act 1971 (c 32)	Merchant Shipping Act 1995 (c 21)
s 27(3)†	s 113

1	2
Merchant Shipping (Oil Pollution) Act 1971 (c 59)	Merchant Shipping Act 1995 (c 21)
s 1	s 153, Sch 4, Chapter III (s 153)
s 1A	s 154, Sch 4, Chapter III (s 154)
s 2	s 155, Sch 4, Chapter III (s 155)
s 2A	Sch 4, Chapter III (s 155A)
s 3	s 156, Sch 4, Chapter III (s 156)
s 3A	Sch 4, Chapter III (s 156A)
s 4	ss 157, 306, Sch 4, Chapter III (s 157)
s 5(1), (2)	s 158(1), (2), Sch 4, Chapter III (s 158(1), (2))
s 5(2A)	s 158(3), Sch 4, Chapter III (s 158(3)–(6))
s 5(3)–(6)	s 158(4)–(7), Sch 4, Chapter III (s 158(7)–(10))
s 5(7)	s 158(8)
s 6(1)	s 159(1), Sch 4, Chapter III (s 159(1))
s 6(2)	Applies to Scotland
s 7	s 160, Sch 4, Chapter III (s 160)
s 8	s 161, Sch 4, Chapter III (s 161)
s 8A	Rep 1979 c 39, s 50(4), Sch 7, Pt I
s 9	s 162, Sch 4, Chapter III (s 162)
s 10(1)–(8)	s 163, Sch 4, Chapter III (s 163)
s 10(9)	s 306
s 11(1)–(5)	s 164, Sch 4, Chapter III (s 164)
s 11(6)	s 309
s 12	s 165, Sch 4, Chapter III (s 165)
s 13	s 166, Sch 4, Chapter III (s 166)
s 14	s 167, Sch 4, Chapter III (s 167)
s 15(1), (1A), (1B)	Rep 1994 c 28, ss 6(1)–(3), 10(3), Sch 3, Pt I, para 5(a), Pt II, para 7(a), Sch 4
s 15(2)	s 168, Sch 4, Chapter III (s 168)
s 16	s 169, Sch 4, Chapter III (s 169)
s 17	s 310
s 18	Rep 1993 c 22, s 8(4), Sch 5, Pt II
s 19	s 152, Sch 4, Chapter III (s 152)
s 20	s 170, Sch 4, Chapter III (s 170)
s 21	—

1	2
Prevention of Oil Pollution Act 1971 (c 60)	Merchant Shipping Act 1995 (c 21)
s 2(2A), (2B)	s 131(1), (2)
s 2(3)†	s 131(5), (6)
s 2(4)†	s 131(3)
s 5	s 132
s 6(1)(a)	s 133
s 7	s 134
s 8(2)	s 151(1), (2)
s 10	s 135
s 11(1)★	s 136(1)
s 11(2)	s 136(2)
s 11(3)†	s 136(3)
s 12	s 137
s 13	s 138
s 14	s 139
s 15	s 140
s 16	s 141
s 17(1)–(4)	s 142(1)–(4)
s 17(5)	s 142(6)–(8)
s 17(6)	s 142(9)
s 18(1)(a)†, (b)†	s 256(1)
s 18(2)†	s 256(8)
s 18(3)(b)†	s 259(4)
s 18(4)	—
s 18(5)†	s 259(3)
s 18(6)†	s 259(6)
s 18(7)†	s 259(7)
s 19(1)†	s 143(1)
s 19(2)★	s 143(4)
s 19(3)†	s 143(5)
s 19(4)†	s 274(1)
s 19(4A)†	s 143(6), (7)
s 19(4B)†	s 143(6)
s 19(5)†	s 279
s 19A(1)–(7)	s 144(1)–(7)
s 19A(8)	s 145(2),(4)
s 19A(9)	Applies to Scotland
s 19A(10)	s 144(8)
s 20	s 146
s 21	s 147
s 23★	s 148
s 24(1), (2)	s 149
s 24(3)	—
s 25(2), (3)	—
s 26†	s 150
s 27(4)	s 142(5)
s 28(1)†	s 304(1)(a)
s 29(1)★	s 142(10)
s 29(2)	s 151(3)
s 29(3)†	s 151(4)
s 29(4), (5)	s 151(5), (6)
s 29(6)	—
s 30(1), (2)	—
s 30(3)†	s 259(5)
s 30(4)†	s 143(2), (3)
s 30(4A)†	s 143(3)
s 31†	s 310
s 32†	s 151(7)

1	2
Water Act (Northern Ireland) 1972 (c 5)	Merchant Shipping Act 1995 (c 21)
s 32(3)	—

1	2
Superannuation Act 1972 (c 11)	Merchant Shipping Act 1995 (c 21)
s 17(1)	s 214
s 17(2)	—

1	2
Bahamas Independence Act 1973 (c 27)	Merchant Shipping Act 1995 (c 21)
Sch 1, para 4(a)	—
Sch 2, para 5	—

1	2
Bangladesh Act 1973 (c 49)	Merchant Shipping Act 1995 (c 21)
Schedule, para 6	—

1	2
Merchant Shipping Act 1974 (c 43)	Merchant Shipping Act 1995 (c 21)
s 1	ss 172, 181, Sch 4, Chapter IV (ss 172, 181)
s 2(1)–(7)	s 173(1)–(7), Sch 4, Chapter IV (s 173(1)–(7))
s 2(8)	ss 173(8), (9), 306, Sch 4, Chapter IV (s 173(9))
s 2(9)	s 173(10), Sch 4, Chapter IV (s 173(10))
s 2(10)	s 173(1), Sch 4, Chapter IV (s 173(1))
s 3	s 174, Sch 4, Chapter IV (s 174)
s 4	s 175, Sch 4, Chapter IV (s 175)
s 4(1)–(9)	s 175(1)–(9), Sch 4, Chapter IV (s 175)
s 4(9A)	s 175(10)
s 4(10)–(12)	Sch 4, Chapter IV (s 176(1)–(3))
s 4(13)	Sch 4, Chapter IV (s 176(4)–(6))
s 4A	ss 176, 306
s 5(1)–(5)	Sch 4, Chapter IV (s 176A(1)–(5))
s 5(6)	s 306, Sch 4, Chapter IV (s 176A(6))
s 5(7)	Sch 4, Chapter IV (s 176A(7))
s 5(8)	Sch 4, Chapter IV (s 176A(8))
s 6	s 177, Sch 4, Chapter IV (s 177)
s 7	s 178, Sch 4, Chapter IV (s 178)
s 8	s 179, Sch 4, Chapter IV (s 179)
s 8A	s 180
s 16(1)	s 88(1)
s 16(2)	s 88(4)
s 17(1)	s 88(2)
s 17(2)	s 306
s 17(3)	s 88(3)
s 18(1)	—
s 18(2)	Sch 8, para 1(2)
s 18(3)	Sch 8, paras 2(2), 3
s 19(1),(3), (5), (6)	—
s 19(4)	s 59
s 21	s 305(1)(c)
s 23(1), (4)	—

1	2
s 23(2).	Sch 4, Chapter IV (s 181(2))
s 23(3).	s 306(5)
s 24.	—
Sch 1.	Sch 5
Sch 5.	Sch 2

Petroleum and Submarine Pipe-lines Act 1975 (c 74)	Merchant Shipping Act 1995 (c 21)
s 45(2)†.	s 148

Seychelles Act 1976 (c 19)	Merchant Shipping Act 1995 (c 21)
Schedule, para 6.	—

Solomon Islands Act 1978 (c 15)	Merchant Shipping Act 1995 (c 21)
Schedule, para 4.	—

Tuvalu Act 1978 (c 20)	Merchant Shipping Act 1995 (c 21)
Sch 1, para 4(a)	—
Sch 2, para 4	—

Customs and Excise Management Act 1979 (c 2)	Merchant Shipping Act 1995 (c 21)
Sch 4, para 1†	ss 125(3), 163(4), 173(10), 209, 250(4), 251, 284(1), (4), (6), (7), 298, 299(1), Sch 3, paras 9(2), 16(1), Sch 4, Chapter III (s 163(5)), Chapter IV (s 173(10))

Kiribati Act 1979 (c 27)	Merchant Shipping Act 1995 (c 21)
Schedule, para 5.	—

Merchant Shipping Act 1979 (c 39)	Merchant Shipping Act 1995 (c 21)
s 14(1), (2).	s 183(1), (2)
s 14(3).	—
s 14(4)–(7).	s 183(3)–(6)
s 15(1), (3).	—
s 15(2).	ss 183(7), 306
s 16(1), (4).	—
s 16(2), (3).	s 184(1), (2)
s 16(5).	s 184(3), (4)
s 16(6).	s 184(5)
s 17.	s 185(1), (2)
s 18(1)–(3).	s 186(1)–(3)
s 18(4).	s 186(5)
s 19(1), (4).	—
s 19(2), (3).	Rep 1993 c 22, s 8(4), Sch 5, Pt II
s 20(1)–(3).	s 128(1)–(3)
s 20(3A)	—
s 20(4).	s 128(4)
s 20(4A)	s 128(5)
s 20(4B)(a).	s 128(6)
s 20(4B)(b)	s 306
s 20(5).	s 128(7)

1	2
s 20(6).	s 128(8), (9)
s 20(7), (8)	Rep SI 1984/703 (NI 2), art 19(2), Sch 7
s 20A	s 129
s 21(1)–(3).	s 85(1)–(3)
s 21(3A)	s 85(4)
s 21(4)–(6).	s 85(5)–(7)
s 21(7), (8)	Rep SI 1984/703 (NI 2), art 19(2), Sch 7
s 22(1).	s 86(1)
s 22(2).	s 86(4)
s 22(3).	s 86(2)
s 22(4).	s 86(3)
s 23(1).	s 60(1)–(8)
s 23(2).	s 119(2), (3)
s 23(3).	s 60(9), (10)
s 23(4).	s 306(4)(a)
s 23(5), (6)	s 80(2), (4)
s 23(7).	—
s 24.	s 111
s 25(1).	s 118(1), (2)
s 25(2).	s 118(3), (4)
s 25(3)–(5).	s 118(5)–(7)
s 26.	—
s 27(1).	s 259(1), (2)
s 27(2)–(7).	s 259(7)–(12)
s 28(1), (2)	s 260(1)
s 28(3).	s 260(2)
s 28(4).	s 260(3)–(5)
s 28(5).	s 256(9)
s 28(6).	—
s 28(7)(a), (c).	—
s 28(7)(b)	ss 271(4), 272(2)
s 29(1)(a).	s 271(1)
s 29(1)(b)	s 271(2), (3)
s 29(2).	s 271(5)
s 29(3).	—
s 30(1).	s 108(5), (6)
s 30(2).	s 273
s 31.	Rep 1988 c 12, s 57(5), Sch 7
s 32(1).	—
s 32(2), (3)	Rep 1988 c 12, s 57(5), Sch 7
s 33(1).	—
s 33(2).	Sch 8, para 2(2)
s 34(1), (2)	—
s 34(3).	s 223(3)
s 35(1).	—
s 35(2).	s 185(4)
s 36(1).	—
s 36(2).	ss 205(5), 306
s 36(3).	Sch 14, para 9(5)
s 37(1).	s 38(4)
s 37(2), (3)	Sch 14, para 4
s 37(4).	Rep 1988 c 12, s 57(5), Sch 7
s 37(5).	s 258(1)
s 37(6), (7)	—
s 37(8).	s 148
s 38(1)(a).	Sch 4, Chapter III (s 157(1))
s 38(1)(b)	—
s 38(2).	s 153(3), Sch 4, Chapter III (s 158(3)–(6))
s 38(3).	Sch 4, Chapter III (ss 163(2), 164(1), 167(2))
s 38(4)(a), (f)	—
s 38(4)(b)	Sch 4, Chapter IV (s 173(7))

1	2	1	2
s 38(4)(c)	Sch 4, Chapter IV (s 176(4)–(6))	Sch 6, Pt III.	ss 25(8), 44(4), 77(6), 79(4), 90(3), 91(4), 115(2), 163(6), 219(3), 236(2), 237(2), 246(5), Sch 4, Chapter III (s 163(7))
s 38(4)(d)	Sch 4, Chapter IV (s 176A(1))		
s 38(4)(e)	Sch 4, Chapter IV (s 176A(8))		
s 38(4)(f)	Sch 4, Chapter IV (s 177(5))	Sch 6, Pt IV.	ss 43(6), 47(5), 51(2), 54(1), 174(5), 258(5), 283(7), Sch 3, para 5, Sch 4, Chapter IV (s 174(5))
s 38(4)(g)	Sch 5, Pt II		
s 38(5)	—		
s 38(6)	Cf Sch 14, para 8	Sch 6, Pt V	ss 49(1), 52(1). 121(5), 125(2), Sch 3, paras 3, 4(4), 9(3), 13(3), 24(4)
s 39(1)	—		
s 39(2)	Rep 1987 c 18, s 108(3), Sch 8		
		Sch 6, Pt VI, para 1	Rep 1988 c 12, s 57(5), Sch 7
s 39(3)	s 34(4)		
s 41(1)	s 311	Sch 6, Pt VI, paras 2, 3. . .	—
s 41(2)	s 306(4)(c)	Sch 6, Pt VI, para 4	ss 77(5), 78(5), 79(2), 80(3),108(9)
s 42(1)	s 274(1), (2)		
s 42(2), (3)	s 274(3), (4)	Sch 6, Pt VI, para 5	—
s 42(4)	—	Sch 6, Pt VI, para 6	s 19(2), (6)
s 42(5)	Applies to Scotland	Sch 6, Pt VI, para 7	—
s 43	—	Sch 6, Pt VI, para 8	ss 26(2), 27(4), 73(6)
s 45(1)	Rep 1988 c 12, s 57(5), Sch 7	Sch 6, Pt VI, para 9	s 103(1)
		Sch 6, Pt VI, para 10	s 220(4)
s 45(2)	s 117(1)	Sch 6, Pt VI, para 11	s 257(3), (4)
s 45(3)	s 119(1)	Sch 6, Pt VI, para 12	—
s 48	s 310	Sch 6, Pt VI, para 13	s 107(3)
s 49(1)–(4)	ss 223(4), 306	Sch 6, Pt VI, paras 14–16 .	—
s 49(4A), (4B)	s 86(5), (6)	Sch 6, Pt VI, para 17	s 142(8)
s 49(5)	Sch 7, Pt II, para 8(2)	Sch 6, Pt VI, para 18	s 174(6), Sch 4, Chapter IV (s 174(6))
s 50	—		
s 51(1)	s 304(1)(a)	Sch 6, Pt VI, para 19	—
s 51(2)	—	Sch 6, Pt VI, para 20	Sch 2, para 3
s 51(3)	s 305(1)(c)	Sch 6, Pt VII, paras 1–5 . .	—
s 52	—	Sch 6, Pt VII, para 6.	s 92(4)
Sch 3, Pt I	Sch 6, Pt I	Sch 6, Pt VII, paras 7, 8 . .	—
Sch 3, Pt II, paras 1–4. . .	Sch 6, Pt II, paras1–4	Sch 6, Pt VII, para 9.	passim
Sch 3, Pt II, para 5	Sch 6, Pt II, para 5	Sch 6, Pt VII, para 10. . . .	s 284(2)
Sch 3, Pt II, paras 6–11. .	Sch 6, Pt II, paras 6–11	Sch 6, Pt VII, para 11. . . .	s 284(5)
Sch 3, Pt II, para 12	Sch 6, Pt II, para 13	Sch 6, Pt VII, para 12. . . .	—
Sch 3, Pt II, para 13	Sch 6, Pt II, para 12	Sch 6, Pt VII, paras 13, 14 Apply to Scotland	
Sch 3, Pt III, paras 1–3 . .	Sch 6, Pt I	Sch 6, Pt VII, para 15. . . .	s 99(1)
Sch 3, Pt III, para 4	Sch 6, Pt II, para 5	Sch 6, Pt VII, para 16. . . .	—
Sch 4, Pt I	Sch 7, Pt I	Sch 6, Pt VII, para 17(a) . .	Sch 3, para 4(2)
Sch 4, Pt II, paras 1, 2. . .	Sch 7, Pt II, paras 1, 2	Sch 6, Pt VII, para 17(b). .	Sch 3, para 4(3)
Sch 4, Pt II, para 3(1), (2)	Sch 7, Pt II, para 3	Sch 6, Pt VII, paras 18, 19	—
Sch 4, Pt II, para 3(3) . . .	—	Sch 6, Pt VII, para 20. . . .	s 117(1)
Sch 4, Pt II, para 4(1) . . .	Sch 7, Pt II, para 4(1)	Sch 6, Pt VII, para 21. . . .	s 59
Sch 4, Pt II, para 4(2), (3)	Sch 7, Pt II, para 4(2), (3)	Sch 6, Pt VII, para 22. . . .	—
Sch 4, Pt II, para 5	Sch 7, Pt II, para 5	Sch 7.	—
Sch 4, Pt II, para 6(1) . . .	Sch 7, Pt II, para 6(1)		
Sch 4, Pt II, para 6(2) . . .	Sch 7, Pt II, para 6(2)		
Sch 4, Pt II, para 7	Sch 7, Pt II, para 7		
Sch 4, Pt II, para 8(1) . . .	Sch 7, Pt II, para 8(1)		
Sch 4, Pt II, para 8(2) . . .	Sch 7, Pt II, para 8(3)		
Sch 4, Pt II, paras 9–13. .	Sch 7, Pt II, paras 9–13		
Sch 5, para 1	s 191(4)–(6)		
Sch 5, para 2	Rep 1983 c 21, s 69(3), Sch 4		
Sch 5, para 3	ss 185(3), 186(4), 192(1)		
Sch 5, paras 4, 5.	—		
Sch 5, para 6(1)	ss 158(5), 160, Sch 4, Chapter III (ss 158(5), 160)		
Sch 5, para 6(2)	s 168, Sch 4, Chapter III (s 168)		
Sch 6, Pt I	ss 31(6), 101(4), (5), 112(5), 300(7)		
Sch 6, Pt II	ss 44(4), 50(2), 55(4), 66, 81(2), 116(2), 135(5), 246(5), 268(6), 299(6)		

1	2
Papua New Guinea, Western Samoa and Nauru (Miscellaneous Provisions) Act 1980 (c 2)	Merchant Shipping Act 1995 (c 21)
Schedule, paras 4, 5	—

1	2
New Hebrides Act 1980 (c 16)	Merchant Shipping Act 1995 (c 21)
Sch 1, para 5	—

1	2
Magistrates' Courts Act 1980 (c 43)	Merchant Shipping Act 1995 (c 21)
Sch 7, para 90†	s 268(3)

1	2
Merchant Shipping Act 1981 (c 10)	Merchant Shipping Act 1995 (c 21)

. . . .—

1	2
Belize Act 1981 (c 52)	Merchant Shipping Act 1995 (c 21)

Sch 1, para 4(a) . . . .—
Sch 2, para 4 . . . .—

1	2
Supreme Court Act 1981 (c 54)	Merchant Shipping Act 1995 (c 21)

s 153(4)★ . . . .—
Sch 5★. . . . . ss 166(1), 177(1), Sch 4, Chapter III (s 166(1)), Sch 4, Chapter IV (s 177(1))

1	2
British Nationality Act 1981 (c 61)	Merchant Shipping Act 1995 (c 21)

s 51(3)† . . . . ss 73(4), 85(2),108(3), (10)
Sch 7† . . . . s 79(3)

1	2
Judgments Enforcement (Northern Ireland) Order 1981 (SI 1981/ 226 (NI 6))	Merchant Shipping Act 1995 (c 21)

Sch 2, para 17 . . . . s 113

1	2
Crown Proceedings Order 1981 (SI 1981/ 233)	Merchant Shipping Act 1995 (c 21)

Art 30(1)† . . . . ss 192(3), 230(8)

1	2
Magistrates' Courts (Northern Ireland) Order 1981 (SI 1981/ 1675 (NI 26))	Merchant Shipping Act 1995 (c 21)

Sch 6, Pt I, para 18 . . . . . s 268(11)
Sch 6, Pt I, para 19 . . . . . s 113

1	2
Civil Aviation Act 1982 (c 16)	Merchant Shipping Act 1995 (c 21)

s 97(1). . . . .—

1	2
Civil Jurisdiction and Judgments Act 1982 (c 27)	Merchant Shipping Act 1995 (c 21)

s 32(4)★ . . . .—

1	2
Criminal Justice Act 1982 (c 48)	Merchant Shipping Act 1995 (c 21)

s 49(1). . . . . passim
s 49(2)(a), (b) . . . . s 128(3)
s 49(2)(c) . . . .
s 49(2)(d) . . . . Rep SI 1984/703 (NI 3), art 19(2), Sch 7
s 49(3)(a) . . . . s 85(7)

s 49(3)(b) . . . . Rep SI 1984/703 (NI 3), art 19(2), Sch 7
s 49(4). . . . .—
s 81(13). . . . . s 315(2)
Sch 7, para 1 . . . . Applies to Scotland
Sch 14, para 2 . . . . passim
Sch 15, para 3 . . . . passim
Sch 15, paras 4, 5. . . . . . Apply to Scotland

1	2
Merchant Shipping Act 1984 (c 5)	Merchant Shipping Act 1995 (c 21)

s 1 . . . . s 261(1)–(3)
s 2(1)–(3) . . . . s 262(1)–(3)
s 2(4) . . . . s 262(4)
s 3 . . . . s 263
s 4(1)–(5) . . . . s 264(1)–(5)
s 4(5A) . . . . s 264(6)
s 4(6) . . . . s 264(7)
s 4(7) . . . . Applies to Scotland
s 4(8) . . . . s 264(9)
s 5(1)–(4) . . . . s 265(1)–(4)
s 5(5) . . . . Applies to Scotland
s 6 . . . . s 266
s 7(1), (2) . . . . s 256(6), (7)
s 7(3) . . . . s 259(1)
s 8 . . . . Cf s 291
s 9 . . . . s 310
s 10. . . . . s 304(1)(a)
s 11. . . . . ss 261(1), 262(1)
s 12(1), (3) . . . .—
s 12(2). . . . . Sch 4, Chapter III (s 157(2))
s 14. . . . .—
Sch 1 . . . . s 261
Sch 2 . . . .

1	2
County Courts Act 1984 (c 28)	Merchant Shipping Act 1995 (c 21)

s 27(11). . . . .—

1	2
Brunei and Maldives Act 1985 (c 3)	Merchant Shipping Act 1995 (c 21)

Schedule, para 1 . . . .—

1	2
Companies Consolidation (Consequential Provisions) Act 1985 (c 9)	Merchant Shipping Act 1995 (c 21)

Sch 2† . . . . ss 140(1), 173(10), Sch 4, Chapter IV (s 173(10))

1	2
Dangerous Vessels Act 1985 (c 22)	Merchant Shipping Act 1995 (c 21)

s 4 . . . .—

1	2
Australia Act 1986 (c 2)	Merchant Shipping Act 1995 (c 21)

s 4 . . . .—

1	2
Prevention of Oil Pollution Act 1986 (c 6)	Merchant Shipping Act 1995 (c 21)

s 1(1) . . . . s 131(1), (2)

1	2		1	2

1	2
Merchant Shipping (Provisions and Water) Regulations 1989 (SI 1989/102)	Merchant Shipping Act 1995 (c 21)
Reg 1(3)(b)† . . . . ss 44(1), 258(4)	
Limitation (Northern Ireland) Order 1989 (SI 1989/1339 (NI 11))	Merchant Shipping Act 1995 (c 21)
Sch 3, para 11 . . . . Sch 6, Pt II, para 7	
Social Security Act 1989 (c 24)	Merchant Shipping Act 1995 (c 21)
s 5(5)† . . . . s 40(2)	
Aviation and Maritime Security Act 1990 (c 31)	Merchant Shipping Act 1995 (c 21)
s 51(2)★ . . . . —	
Sch 3, para 2(1) . . . . s 104	
Sch 3, para 2(2) . . . . —	
Courts and Legal Services Act 1990 (c 41)	Merchant Shipping Act 1995 (c 21)
Sch 10, para 55(1) . . . . . . s 264(5)	
Sch 10, para 55(2) . . . . . . s 264(6)	
Environmental Protection Act 1990 (c 43)	Merchant Shipping Act 1995 (c 21)
s 148(1), (3) . . . . —	
s 148(2) . . . . s 128(3)	
Sch 14, para 1★ . . . . —	
Sch 14, para 2★ . . . . Cf s 143(6), (7)	
Sch 14, para 3★ . . . . ss 144, 145(2), (4)	
Sch 14, para 4★ . . . . s 146(1)	
Sch 14, para 5★ . . . . s 149(2)	
Sch 14, para 6★ . . . . —	
Sch 14, para 7★ . . . . s 145(3)	
Ports Act 1991 (1991 c 52)	Merchant Shipping Act 1995 (c 21)
s 31(1), (2) . . . . s 201(1), (2)	
s 31(3) . . . . s 193(2)(a)	
s 31(4), (5) . . . . s 197(2), (3)	
s 31(6) . . . . s 199(3)	
s 31(7) . . . . s 201(3)	
s 32(1), (2) . . . . Sch 9, para 1	
s 32(3), (4) . . . . Sch 9, para 2	
s 32(5) . . . . Sch 9, para 3	
s 32(6), (7) . . . . Sch 9, para 4	
s 32(8) . . . . Sch 9, para 5	
s 33(1) . . . . s 203	
s 33(2) . . . . s 223(2)	
s 33(3) . . . . s 204(2)	
s 33(4) . . . . s 223(2)	
s 34(1) . . . . s 211(2)(a)	
s 34(2) . . . . —	
s 34(3) . . . . s 193(4)(b)	
s 36(2)(c) . . . . s 221(3)	
s 41(1)★, (2) . . . . —	

1	2
s 42(2) . . . . —	
Dangerous Vessels (Northern Ireland) Order 1991 (SI 1991/1219 (NI 10))	Merchant Shipping Act 1995 (c 21)
Art 6 . . . . —	
Judicial Pensions and Retirement Act 1993 (c 8)	Merchant Shipping Act 1995 (c 21)
Sch 6, para 59 . . . . s 297(2)	
Merchant Shipping (Registration, etc) Act 1993 (c 22)	Merchant Shipping Act 1995 (c 21)
s 1(1) . . . . s 8(1), (7)	
s 1(2)–(6) . . . . s 8(2)–(6)	
s 1(7) . . . . —	
s 2 . . . . s 9	
s 3(1)–(7) . . . . s 10(1)–(7)	
s 3(8) . . . . s 306	
s 3(9) . . . . s 10(8)	
s 3(10) . . . . s 302(3)	
s 4 . . . . s 14	
s 5(1) . . . . s 15(1)	
s 5(2) . . . . ss 15(2), 306	
s 5(3)–(9) . . . . s 15(3)–(9)	
s 6 . . . . s 16	
s 7(1)–(9) . . . . s 17(1)–(9)	
s 7(10)(a) . . . . s 17(10)	
s 7(10)(b) . . . . s 306	
s 7(11) . . . . s 17(11)	
s 8 . . . . —	
s 9(1) . . . . —	
s 9(2) . . . . s 23(1)	
s 9(3) . . . . s 23(2)	
s 9(4) . . . . Sch 14, para 2	
s 9(5) . . . . s 10(9)	
s 9(6) . . . . ss 306, 314(4)	
s 10 . . . . —	
Sch 1 . . . . Sch 1	
Sch 2, para 1 . . . . Cf Sch 13, para 2	
Sch 2, para 2(a) . . . . s 11	
Sch 2, para 2(b) . . . . s 313(1)	
Sch 2, para 3 . . . . s 308(2)	
Sch 2, para 4 . . . . Cf Sch 13, para 34	
Sch 2, para 5 . . . . Cf Sch 13, para 36	
Sch 2, para 6 . . . . Cf Sch 13, para 38(a)	
Sch 2, para 7 . . . . Cf Sch 13, para 38(b)	
Sch 2, para 8 . . . . Cf Sch 13, para 38(c)	
Sch 2, para 9 . . . . Cf Sch 13, para 43(c)	
Sch 2, para 10 . . . . Cf Sch 13, para 49	
Sch 2, para 11 . . . . —	
Sch 2, para 12 . . . . Cf Sch 13, para 53(3)	
Sch 2, para 13 . . . . Cf Sch 13, para 68	
Sch 2, para 14 . . . . Applies to Scotland	
Sch 2, para 15(1) . . . . —	
Sch 2, para 15(2)(a)–(c) . . s 18(1)–(3)	
Sch 2, para 15(2)(d) . . . . . s 18(5)	
Sch 2, para 15(3)(a) . . . . . s 309(3), (5)	
Sch 2, para 15(3)(b) . . . . . —	
Sch 2, para 15(4) . . . . s 21(1), (3)	
Sch 3, para 1(1), (2) . . . . . s 1(1), (2)	
Sch 3, para 1(3) . . . . s 306	
Sch 3, para 2 . . . . s 2(1)–(3)	
Sch 3, para 3(1)–(4) . . . . . s 4(1)–(4)	
Sch 3, para 3(5) . . . . s 4(5)	

1	2
Sch 3, para 4(1), (2)	s 5(1), (2)
Sch 3, para 4(3)	—
Sch 3, para 5	s 3
Sch 3, para 6	s 6
Sch 3, para 7	s 13
Sch 4, para 1(1)	s 1(3)
Sch 4, para 1(2)	s 306
Sch 4, para 2	s 313 and passim
Sch 4, para 3	—
Sch 4, para 4(1)–(4)	s 315(2)–(5)
Sch 4, para 4(5)	—
Sch 4, para 5	s 307
Sch 4, para 6(1)(a)	ss 42(1), 257(1), (2)
Sch 4, para 6(1)(b)	s 186(1)
Sch 4, para 6(2)(a)	s 92(2)
Sch 4, para 6(2)(b)	—
Sch 4, para 6(2)(c)	s 93(1)–(3)
Sch 4, para 6(3)	—
Sch 4, para 6(4)	s 85(1)
Sch 4, para 7(a)	s 42(1)
Sch 4, para 7(b)	—
Sch 4, para 8	—
Sch 4, para 9	Applies to Scotland
Sch 4, para 10	s 40(10)
Sch 4, para 11(1)	—
Sch 4, para 11(2)(a)	s 87(1)
Sch 4, para 11(2)(b)	s 87(3)
Sch 4, para 11(2)(c)	s 87(5)
Sch 4, para 12(1)	—
Sch 4, para 12(2)	ss 94(1), (3), 95
Sch 4, para 12(3)	ss 96(1)–(8), (10), 97(1), (2)
Sch 4, para 12(4)(a)	ss 96(1), 97(1)
Sch 4, para 12(4)(b)	s 96(1)
Sch 4, para 12(4)(c)	s 96(2)
Sch 4, paras 12(4)(d)	s 96(3)
Sch 4, para 12(4)(e)	s 96(5)
Sch 4, para 12(5)	Applies to Scotland
Sch 4, para 12(6)	Sch 3, para 3(4)
Sch 4, para 13(1)	s 85(4)
Sch 4, para 13(2)	—
Sch 4, para 13(3)	s 86(1)
Sch 4, para 14(a)	s 101(1)
Sch 4, para 14(b)	s 101(2)
Sch 4, para 14(c)	s 101(3)
Sch 4, para 15	s 107(3)
Sch 4, para 16(a)	s 124(3)
Sch 4, para 16(b)	s 124(5)
Sch 4, para 17	ss 151(6), 256(1), 256(8), 259(5), (6)
Sch 4, paras 18–20	—
Sch 4, para 21(a)	s 231(2)
Sch 4, para 21(b)	—
Sch 4, para 22(a)	—
Sch 4, para 22(b)–(d)	s 236(1), (3)
Sch 4, para 22(e)	Applies to Scotland
Sch 4, para 23	s 238(1), (2)
Sch 4, para 24	s 240(1)
Sch 4, para 25	s 242(1)
Sch 4, paras 26, 27	—
Sch 4, para 28	s 247(3)
Sch 4, para 29	—
Sch 4, para 30	ss 226(3), 228(1), 229(1)
Sch 4, para 31	s 248(2), (3)
Sch 4, para 32	ss 249(1), 306
Sch 4, paras 33–36	—
Sch 4, para 37	s 223(2)
Sch 4, para 38	s 197(6)
Sch 4, para 39	s 197(4)
Sch 4, para 40	s 205(2)
Sch 4, para 41	s 206
Sch 4, para 42	s 205(6)
Sch 4, para 43	s 205(9)
Sch 4, para 44(a)	s 207(1), (2)
Sch 4, para 44(b)	Applies to Scotland
Sch 4, para 45(a)	—
Sch 4, para 45(b)	s 208(2)
Sch 4, para 45(c)	s 208(5)
Sch 4, para 46	s 209
Sch 4, para 47	s 210(11)
Sch 4, para 48	—
Sch 4, para 49	s 218
Sch 4, para 50	s 219(1), (2)
Sch 4, para 51(a)	—
Sch 4, para 51(b)	s 220(6)
Sch 4, para 51(c)	Applies to Scotland
Sch 4, para 52	—
Sch 4, para 53	s 211(4), (5)
Sch 4, para 54	—
Sch 4, para 55	s 210(5)
Sch 4, para 56(a), (b)	s 256(1)
Sch 4, para 56(c)	s 256(9)
Sch 4, para 57	s 259(2)
Sch 4, para 58	ss 207(1), (2), 220(7), 236(3)
Sch 4, para 59	ss 274(1), 275
Sch 4, para 60	s 279
Sch 4, para 61	s 281
Sch 4, para 62	s 282
Sch 4, para 63	s 277
Sch 4, para 64(a)	s 283(4)
Sch 4, para 64(b)	—
Sch 4, para 65	s 285
Sch 4, para 66	s 146(1)
Sch 4, para 67(a)	s 288(3)
Sch 4, para 67(b)	s 288(5)
Sch 4, para 67(c)	Applies to Scotland
Sch 4, para 68	s 291
Sch 4, para 69	s 290
Sch 4, para 70(a)	—
Sch 4, para 70(b)	—
Sch 4, paras 71–73	Apply to Scotland
Sch 4, para 74	passim
Sch 4, paras 75–77	Apply to Scotland
Sch 4, para 78	—
Sch 4, para 79(1)	s 302(1)
Sch 4, para 79(2)	s 302(3)
Sch 5 (saving)	Sch 14, para 7(1)

Child Support Act 1991 (Consequential Amendments) Order 1993 (SI 1993/785)	Merchant Shipping Act 1995 (c 21)
Art 5†	s 34(5)

Child Support (Northern Ireland) Order 1991 (Consequential Amendments) Order (Northern Ireland) Order 1993 (SR 1993/157)	Merchant Shipping Act 1995 (c 21)
Art 5†	s 34(5)

Merchant Shipping (Salvage and Pollution) Act 1994 (c 28)	Merchant Shipping Act 1995 (c 21)
s 1(1)–(3)	s 224(1)–(3)

1	2
s 1(4)	s 224(4), (5)
s 1(5)	s 224(6)
s 1(6)	—
s 1(7)	s 224(7)
s 2(1)	s 128(1)
s 2(2)	s 128(9)
s 3(1), (2)	—
s 3(3)	s 128(4)
s 3(4)	ss 128(5), (6), 306
s 4	s 129
s 5(1)	ss 152(1), 172(1)
s 5(2)	—
s 5(3)	ss 171(2), 182(2)
s 5(4)(a)	s 171(3)
s 5(4)(b)	s 182(3)
s 6	—
s 7(1)(a)	s 179(1), Sch 4, Chapter IV (s 179(1))
s 7(1)(b)	—
s 7(2)	—
s 8(1)–(5)	s 293
s 8(6)	s 137(9)
s 9	s 304(1)(a)
s 10	—
Sch 1, Pt I	Sch 11, Pt I
Sch 1, Pt II, paras 1–4	Sch 11, Pt II, paras 1–4
Sch 1, Pt II, para 5(1), (2)	Sch 11, Pt II, para 5
Sch 1, Pt II, para 5(3)	—
Sch 1, Pt II, paras 6, 7	Sch 11, Pt II, paras 6, 7
Sch 2, para 1(1), (2)	—
Sch 2, para 1(3)	s 226(4)
Sch 2, para 1(4)	s 228(5)
Sch 2, para 1(5)	s 229(2)
Sch 2, para 2	—
Sch 2, para 3	s 230(1)
Sch 2, para 4	Applies to Scotland
Sch 2, para 5	Sch 7, Pt II, para 4
Sch 2, paras 6, 7	—
Sch 3, Pt I, para 1	Sch 4, Chapter III (s 154)
Sch 3, Pt I, para 2	Sch 4, Chapter III (s 155A)
Sch 3, Pt I, para 3	Sch 4, Chapter III (s 156A)
Sch 3, Pt I, para 4	Sch 4, Chapter III (s 162)
Sch 3, Pt I, para 5(a)	—
Sch 3, Pt I, para 5(b)	Sch 4, Chapter III (s 168)
Sch 3, Pt I, para 6	Sch 4, Chapter III (s 170(2))
Sch 3, Pt II, para 1	s 153(2)
Sch 3, Pt II, para 2	s 154
Sch 3, Pt II, para 3	s 155
Sch 3, Pt II, para 4(a)	s 156(1)
Sch 3, Pt II, para 4(b)	s 156(2)
Sch 3, Pt II, para 5	s 162
Sch 3, Pt II, para 6(a)	s 166(2)
Sch 3, Pt II, para 6(b)	s 166(3)
Sch 3, Pt II, para 7(a)	—
Sch 3, Pt II, para 7(b)	s 168
Sch 3, Pt II, para 8	s 170(1)
Sch 3, Pt III, para 1	s 154
Sch 3, Pt III, paras 2, 3	—
Sch 3, Pt III, para 4	s 162
Sch 4	—

Local Government (Scotland) Act 1994 (c 39)	Merchant Shipping Act 1995 (c 21)
Sch 13, para 7(a)	Sch 8, para 1(2)
Sch 13, para 7(b)	Sch 8, para 2(1)
Sch 13, para 7(c)	Sch 8, para 5

Merchant Shipping (Survey and Certification) Regulations 1995 (SI 1995/1210)	Merchant Shipping Act 1995 (c 21)
Reg 1(6)†	s 101(6)
Reg 1(7)†	s 102
Reg 1(8)†	Sch 3, para 23(1)
Reg 1(9)†	Sch 7, Pt II, para 6(1)

2690 Salvage—recovery of costs—claim by cargo-owner

A cargo owner chartered a ship to transport fertiliser but before the ship completed its journey the fertiliser began to decompose. The cargo owner advised the dock master in preparation for the ship's arrival, arranged for a fire-fighting team to board it and made provision for the testing of gases. Both the ship and cargo were salved. The cargo owner claimed salvage remuneration, arguing that it had rendered salvage services to the ship as a volunteer. The shipowner claimed that the cargo owner could not do so because it was not within the recognised categories of salvor, there was no good reason to allow it to claim salvage, the cargo owner had a duty to render such assistance it could to salve the ship and cargo and, further, a cargo owner who rendered a salvage service in preservation of its own property ought not to be treated as a volunteer. *Held,* (1) there was no logical reason why, if a shipowner was entitled to claim salvage against the owner of cargo carried on his ship, a cargo owner should not be entitled to claim salvage against a ship carrying his cargo. (2) There were no rigid categories of salvor; they included any volunteer who rendered services of a salvage nature. There was no reason why they should not include cargo owners who personally rendered salvage services. (3) The submission that the cargo owner was not a volunteer was rejected; the limiting criterion could not be solely that to be debarred from claiming salvage the person concerned had to owe a duty to the particular owner of the salved property. (4) The principle that a passenger or crew member could not ordinarily recover in respect of services which he could ordinarily be expected to carry out in his capacity as a passenger or crew member should apply to cargo owners. There was no reason why services which went beyond such services could not be regarded as voluntary services in respect of which the cargo owner should be entitled to a salvage award. An order would be made accordingly.

The Sava Star [1995] 2 Lloyd's Rep 134 (Queen's Bench Division: Clarke J).

2691 Ship—explosion in ship—harbour company's failure to take adequate precautions to prevent explosion—level of fine

See *R v Mersey Docks and Harbour Company,* para 1498.

2692 Ship—mortgage of ship as security—implied term as to exercise of option within reasonable time

See *Zeeland Navigation Co Ltd v Banque Worms, The Foresight Driller,* para 647.

2693 Ship—sale of ship—sellers' obligation to notify classification society of matters affecting class

A standard form contract made between the defendant sellers and the plaintiff buyers in respect of the sale of a vessel provided, in particular, that the vessel would be at the sellers' risk and expense until delivered to the buyers, and that the vessel would be taken over by the buyers in the condition that it was in at the time of inspection. The contract also provided that the vessel would be delivered with present class free of recommendations, subject to the sellers' obligation to notify the classification society of any matters coming to their knowledge prior to delivery which might lead to the vessel's class being withdrawn or otherwise affected. The buyers inspected the vessel a few days before the contract was signed, and this was recorded in the contract. Immediately prior to delivery, the vessel passed a class survey. However, disputes arose about the condition of the vessel when it was delivered to the buyers. The matter was referred to arbitration, where the arbitrators decided that the proper construction of the relevant clause was that the sellers' obligation to notify their classification society of matters affecting class arose only as from the date of the contract. On appeal, it was held that this obligation arose as from the date of the last inspection of the vessel by the classification society. On the sellers' appeal against this decision, it was held that a plain reading of the relevant clause led to the conclusion that the sellers' promise related only to knowledge acquired by them about the vessel's condition between the date of the contract and the delivery of the vessel. On further appeal by the buyers, *held,* the phrase 'coming to their knowledge' had no temporal significance in itself and covered knowledge acquired both before and after the contract and meant matters known to the sellers, neither more nor less. In practice, it was not usually necessary to look back further than the latest relevant survey. Accordingly, the buyers' appeal would be allowed.

Niobe Maritime Corpn v Tradax Ocean Transportation SA, The Niobe [1995] 1 Lloyd's Rep 579 (House of Lords: Lords Mackay of Clashfern LC, Keith of Kinkel, Jauncey of Tullichettle, Browne-Wilkinson and Lloyd of Berwick). Decision of Court of Appeal [1994] 1 Lloyd's Rep 487 (1994 Abr para 2569) reversed.

2694 Shipping and Trading Interests Act 1995

The Shipping and Trading Interests Act 1995 consolidates certain provisions of the Merchant Shipping Acts 1974 and 1988 relating to the protection of shipping and trading interests. The Act received the royal assent on 19 July 1995 and came into force on 1 January 1996. A table showing the destination of enactments consolidated appears overleaf.

DESTINATION TABLE

This table shows in column (1) the enactments repealed by the Shipping and Trading Interests Act 1995 and in column (2) the provisions of that Act corresponding thereto.

In certain cases the enactment in column (1), though having a corresponding provision in column (2) is not, or not wholly, repealed as it is still required, or partly required, for the purposes of other legislation.

A "dash" in the right hand column means that the repealed provision to which it corresponds in the left hand column is spent, unnecessary or for some other reason not specifically reproduced.

† Not repealed

1	2	1	2
Merchant Shipping Act 1974 (c 43)	Shipping and Trading Interests Act 1995 (c 22)	Merchant Shipping Act 1979 (c 39)	Shipping and Trading Interests Act 1995 (c 22)
s 14(1)...............	s 1(1)	s 40(1)(b)	s 3(4)
s 14(2)...............	s 1(2)	Sch 6, Pt IV†	s 3(4)
s 14(3)...............	s 1(3)	Sch 6, Pt VI, para 19† ...	s 3(5)
s 14(4)...............	s 1(4)		
s 14(5)...............	ss 1(5), 2(1), (2)	Merchant Shipping Act 1988 (c 12)	Shipping and Trading Interests Act 1995 (c 22)
s 14(6)...............	s1(6), (7)		
s 14(7)...............	s 1(8)		
s 14(8)–(10)...........	s 3(4)–(6)	s 38(1)...............	—
s 14(9)...............	s 3(5)	s 38(2)...............	s 1(1)
s 14(11).............	s 1(9)	s 38(3)...............	s 1(3)
s 14(11A)............	s 1(10)	s 38(4)...............	s 1(4)
s 14(12)..............	—	s 38(5)...............	s 2(1), (2)
s 15(1), (2)...........	s 4(1), (2)	s 38(6)...............	s 1(9), (10)
s 15(2A)	s 4(3)	s 38(7)(a)............	s 4(1)
s 15(3), (4)...........	s 4(4), (5)	s 38(7)(b)	s 4(3)
s 21†................	s 2(6)	s 38(7)(c)............	s 4(5)
s 23(1)†.............	s 7(1)	s 38(8)...............	s 2(3), (4)
Sch 4, para 1(1)–(3)	s 3(1)–(3)	s 39................	s 5
Sch 4, para 2(1)	s 2(3)	s 40(1)–(8)...........	s 6(1)–(8)
Sch 4, para 2(2), (3)	s 2(4)	s 40(9)...............	—
Sch 4, para 2(4)	s 2(5)	s 40(10)..............	s 7(2)
Sch 4, para 2(5)	s 2(3)	s 40(11)..............	s 7(3)
Sch 4, para 3	s 3(6)	s 40(12)..............	s 6(9)
Sch 4, para 4	s 1(9)	s 57(1)†..............	s 7(1)

2695 Shipping consortia—international liner transport services between Community ports—agreements, decisions and concerted practices between companies

See para 3150.

SOCIAL SECURITY AND SOCIAL SERVICES

Halsbury's Laws of England (4th edn) Vol 33, paras 301–1077

2696 Articles

Avoiding the Benefits Trap, Petra Lucioli (on the effect of personal injury settlements on welfare benefits): LS Gaz, 18 January 1995, p 18

Continuing Offences—Section 111 Social Security Administration Act 1992, T M Daber: 159 JP Jo 299

Elderly People and Residential Care, Gordon Ashton: 139 SJ 978, 1010, 1036, 1074

Incapacity Benefit, Martin Barnes: LA, May 1995, p 16

Income Support and Mortgage Interest: the New Rules, Adam Griffith: LA, October 1995, p 17

Income Support Mortgage Interest Changes, Kate Tonge: 145 NLJ 1418

Jobseekers Act 1995: Consolidation With a Sting of Contractual Compliance, Helen Carr: (1995) 24 ILJ 395

National Insurance Concessions, David Harris (on concessionary relief from National Insurance contributions): Tax Journal, Issue 306, p 16

Recoupment Planning, David Milton (on deduction of state benefits from personal injury awards): 145 NLJ 784

2697 Attendance allowance—entitlement—provision of accommodation—residential care home

The Social Security (Attendance Allowance) (No 2) Regulations 1975, SI 1975/598, reg 4(1)(a) provides that attendance allowance is not payable in respect of a person who has attained the age of 16 for any period during which that person is living in accommodation provided for him in pursuance of the National Assistance Act 1948, Pt III or the National Health Service Act 1977, Sch 8, para 2 (accommodation funded out of public or local funds).

The claimant lived in a residential care home owned and run by the local authority, and paid the full charge for her accommodation. When the local authority established a company to take over management of its residential care homes, the claimant elected to remain in the same home rather than move to other local authority accommodation, and she continued to pay the full charge for the accommodation. It was decided that the claimant was entitled to attendance allowance, and the Chief Adjudication Officer unsuccessfully appealed against the decision. On his further appeal, *held*, a local authority did not have the power to pay for the costs of a person's accommodation unless and until it had made arrangements for the accommodation, or once the accommodation had been provided. Here, once the company took over management of the residential home in which the claimant lived, the continued provision of her accommodation was no longer pursuant to the 1948 Act, Pt III. As the local authority had not made arrangements for the claimant's accommodation, which she had paid for at all times, it had no power to pay for her accommodation pursuant to the 1948 Act. As the 1975 Regulations therefore did not apply, the claimant was entitled to attendance allowance. Accordingly, the appeal would be dismissed.

Steane v Chief Adjudication Officer (1995) Times, 19 December (Court of Appeal: Hirst and Aldous LJJ, and Forbes J).

The Social Security (Attendance Allowance) (No 2) Regulations 1975, SI 1975/598, reg 4(1)(c) provides that attendance allowance is not payable in respect of a person who has attained the age of 16 for any period during which that person is living in accommodation provided for him in circumstances in which the cost of the accommodation may be borne wholly or partly out of public or local funds.

A social security commissioner decided that the claimant, who suffered from illness and was accommodated by the health authority in a hostel, was entitled to attendance allowance. On the Chief Adjudication Officer's appeal against the decision, he argued that it did not matter that the claimant's accommodation was not provided under any arrangement made by the local authority, as it could have been, in which case the 1975 Regulations, reg 4(1)(c) applied. *Held*, reg 4(1)(c) applied where a local authority either paid or had the power to pay some or all of the cost of accommodation provided by a third party. One of the purposes of the regulation was to prevent local authorities from refusing or ceasing to pay the cost of accommodation for which they themselves ought to be responsible in order that a person might be entitled to attendance allowance. However, a local authority did not have the power to pay for accommodation costs unless and until it had made arrangements for accommodation to be provided, or once the accommodation was actually being provided. In the instant case, as the local authority had not made arrangements to provide the claimant with accommodation even though it could have done, the claimant was not disqualified from entitlement to attendance allowance. Accordingly, the appeal would be dismissed.

Chief Adjudication Officer v Kenyon (1995) Times, 14 November (Court of Appeal: Butler-Sloss, Simon Brown and Saville LJJ). *Decision R(A) 3/83* (1983 Abr para 3100) distinguished.

2698 Attendance allowance—reference to Scottish legislation

The Social Security (Attendance and Disability Living Allowances) Amendment Regulations 1995, SI 1995/2162 (in force on 14 September 1995), further amend the Social Security (Attendance Allowance) Regulations 1991, SI 1991/2740, and the Social Security (Disability Living Allowance) Regulations 1991, SI 1991/2890. The 1991 Regulations contain references to legislation which applies only in England and Wales, but the 1995 Regulations amend the 1991 Regulations so as to insert references to the corresponding legislation which applies in Scotland.

2699 Benefits—adjudication

The Social Security (Adjudication) Regulations 1995, SI 1995/1801 (in force on 10 August 1995), replace the 1986 Regulations, SI 1986/2218, so as to re-enact their provisions to take account of the Social Security Contributions and Benefits Act 1992, the Social Security Administration Act 1992 ('the 1992 Acts'), and the Social Security (Incapacity for Work) Act 1994. In relation to the determination of claims and questions under the 1992 Acts, the regulations contain provisions (1) common to the proceedings of all medical and non-medical adjudicating authorities, (2) for each of the adjudicating authorities, namely the Secretary of State, adjudication officers, social security appeal tribunals, disability adjudication and medical adjudication, and (3) relating to prescribed industrial diseases, income support and the review of decisions.

2700 Benefits—claims and payments

The Social Security (Claims and Payments) Amendment Regulations 1995, SI 1995/3055 (in force on 1 April 1996), further amend the 1987 Regulations, SI 1987/1968, so as to reduce from £0.80 to £0.77 the fee which qualifying lenders pay for the purpose of defraying administrative expenses incurred by the Secretary of State in making payments in respect of mortgage interest direct to qualifying lenders.

The Social Security (Income Support, Claims and Payments and Adjudication) Amendment Regulations 1995, SI 1995/2927 (in force on 12 December 1995), (1) amend the 1995 Regulations, SI 1995/1801, so as to (i) limit the occasions when reductions in the capital outstanding on a loan are considered to be relevant changes of circumstances for the purpose of the review of decisions, and (ii) make similar provision as regards changes in the rate of interest which affect the amount of a claimant's income which is disregarded, (2) amend the 1987 Regulations supra to correct an error in the citation of paragraphs, and (3) amend the 1987 Regulations, SI 1987/1967, so as to (i) widen the definition of a disabled person, (ii) correct a rule on temporary absence, so that it continues to cover people who have to leave their home because of violence from non-family members, (iii) provide that a claim must be made within 12 weeks from the end of a previous claim for housing costs, (iv) provide for when eligible capital outstanding on a loan is to be determined, (v) omit the provision whereby the amount of a remortgage entered into after 2 October 1995 is to be new housing costs, (vi) provide that carers and lone parents may, in certain circumstances, be treated as entitled to income support, even though their income and/or capital exceeds certain thresholds, and (vii) make various minor and consequential amendments.

2701 Benefits—income-related benefits

The Income-related Benefits Schemes (Miscellaneous Amendments) Regulations 1995, SI 1995/516 (in force in part on 10 March 1995, in part on 10 April 1995, and in part on 11 April 1995), further amend the Income Support (General) Regulations 1987, SI 1987/1967, the Family Credit (General) Regulations 1987, SI 1987/1973, and the Disability Working Allowance Regulations 1991, SI 1991/2887, as follows: (1) the term 'voluntary organisation' is substituted in place of 'voluntary body', and the new term is defined, (2) provision is made regarding the recognised cycle of work of school and other ancillary workers, (3) provision is made regarding matters on which an adjudication officer must be satisfied in determining a claimant's notional income in considering whether it is reasonable for a person to provide his services free of charge, and (4) the provisions specifying sums to be disregarded in calculating a person's income other than earnings are amended, in particular, the circumstances in which a payment made by a person to a claimant for benefit as a contribution towards that person's accommodation costs are to be disregarded. SI 1987/1973 and 1991/2887 are amended so as to (1) exclude from the definition of relevant child care charges, certain payments made between a claimant and his partner, (2) extend that definition to include charges made by establishments exempted from registration under the Children Act 1989, (3) provide that the age of a child, for the purpose of the treatment of child care charges in calculating a claimant's income, is to be determined at the date on which the claimant's benefit period for the relevant benefit begins, and (4) amend the conditions specifying when a member of a couple is incapacitated, (5) substitute for references to the Social Security Act 1986, in respect of a claimant's maximum rate of benefit, references to the Social Security Contributions and Benefits Act 1992, and (6) provide that payments made by the Secretary of State to compensate for a reduced maintenance assessment under the Child Support Act 1991 are to be disregarded in calculating income and capital. SI 1991/2887 is further amended as regards entitlement to disability working allowance in prescribed circumstances. SI 1987/1967 is further amended as regards (1) the definitions of 'prisoner' and 'residential accommodation' in relation to the calculation of applicable amounts in special cases and the circumstances in which a person is not treated as being in residential accommodation, (2) the sums to be disregarded in calculating the income of a claimant for benefit in cases of urgency, (3) the conditions governing entitlement to the higher pensioner and disability premiums, (4) housing costs, including mortgage interest payments, on so much of a loan as exceeds £100,000, and which are not to be met from income support, (5) the accommodation charges for residents in accommodation provided under the Polish Resettlement Act 1947 which may be met from income support, and (6) a claimant's entitlement to a disability premium in respect of a period before the date of a claim.

The Income-related Benefits Schemes (Miscellaneous Amendments) (No 2) Regulations 1995, SI 1995/1339 (in force on 17 July 1995), (1) amend SI 1987/1973 and SI 1991/2887 so as to provide for entitlement to an additional allowance or credit of £10 per week where either the claimant or his partner or both of them work not less than 30 hours per week, and for the manner in which those hours are calculated, (2) amend the Housing Benefit (General) Regulations 1987, SI 1987/1971, and the Council Tax Benefit (General) Regulations 1992, SI 1992/1814, so that any additional disability working allowance or additional family credit which is awarded to the claimant, is to be disregarded from a claimant's income in calculating his entitlement to council tax benefit and housing benefit.

The Income-related Benefits Schemes Amendment (No 2) Regulations 1995, SI 1995/2792 (in force on 28 October 1995), amend SI 1992/1814, 1991/2887, 1987/1967, 1971 and 1973, so that there is uniform treatment of those benefits in relation to pensions payable to women who are, or have been, widows of members of the Royal Navy, the Army, or the Royal Air Force under the Naval, Military and Air Forces Etc (Disablement and Death) Service Pensions Order 1983, SI 1983/883. The 1995 Regulations also empower local authorities to modify their council tax benefit and housing benefit schemes so as to disregard pensions payable under the 1983 Regulations to such women, to the extent that they are not required to be disregarded under the council tax or housing benefit regulations.

The Income-related Benefits Schemes and Social Security (Claims and Payments) (Miscellaneous Amendments) Regulations 1995, SI 1995/2303 (in force in part on 2 October 1995, and in part on 3 October 1995), introduce the following amendments: (1) SI 1992/1814, 1991/2887, 1987/1967, 1971 and 1973 are amended so as to (a) insert new definitions of 'pension fund holder' and 'retirement annuity contract', and amend the definition of 'personal pension scheme', (b) extend the provision governing the calculation of notional income to personal pensions and retirement annuity contracts, (c) exclude personal pension schemes and retirement annuity contracts from the calculation of a person's notional capital, (d) amend the provision governing the treatment of a person's entitlement to capital which is jointly held, (e) amend the provisions specifying the sums to be disregarded in calculating income other than earnings, and (f) amend the provisions specifying the sums to be disregarded in calculating capital, (2) SI 1992/1814 and 1987/1971 are also amended as regards the information that must be provided to an appropriate authority on a claim for council tax or housing benefit by a claimant and by any person or organisation which manages his personal pension scheme or administers his retirement annuity contract, (3) SI 1991/2887 is further amended as regards the disabilities which put a person at a disadvantage in getting a job, (4) SI 1987/1971 is further amended as regards the circumstances in which benefit may be withheld if a rent officer is not given access to a dwelling, and, subject to a transitional saving, as regards the effect of the termination of a rent assessment committee's determination of a reasonable rent, (5) in SI 1992/1814, 1987/1971 and 1967, the additional condition relating to entitlement to a higher pensioner or disability premium is amended as regards those who are treated as incapable of work, (6) SI 1987/1968 is amended so as to specify the information which must be provided by claimants for disability working allowance, family credit and income support, and by the person or organisation which manages his personal pension scheme or administers his retirement annuity contract. In addition, transitional provision is made in respect of those who are incapable of work on 12 April 1995 as regards their entitlement to benefit whilst temporarily absent from Great Britain, and as regards disabled students who are incapable of work. Transitional provision is also made as regards the amount of benefit to which certain claimants are entitled where an adjudication officer first determined on or after 13 April 1995 that the claimant did not satisfy the incapacity for work test and an appeal against the determination was outstanding on 2 October 1995. The transitional provisions in SI 1995/626 are also amended as regards a person's entitlement to a disability premium where he was entitled to it on 12 April 1995 and is treated as incapable of work from 13 April 1995.

2702 Benefits—overpayment—liability to repay—mental incapacity of claimant

The Social Security Act 1986, s 53(1) provides that where it is determined that, whether fraudulently or otherwise, any person has misrepresented or failed to disclose any material fact, and in consequence of the misrepresentation or failure a payment has been made in respect of a benefit to which the section applies, the Secretary of State is entitled to recover the amount of any payment which he would not have made or any sum which he would have received but for the misrepresentation or failure to disclose.

The respondent was an elderly woman who was incapable of understanding her affairs. She was admitted to a nursing home, where someone completed a claim form for income support on her behalf, which she then signed. The form contained a declaration that the respondent had no savings, whereas she had substantial savings. The Social Security Appeal Tribunal ordered the respondent to repay the amount of overpaid benefit, but that decision was set aside by a social security commissioner. On the Chief Adjudication Officer's appeal, *held*, the 1986 Act, s 53(1) covered both innocent and fraudulent misrepresentation, and it was not necessary for the person making the representation to know that he had misrepresented a material fact, nor even that he was making a representation. Here, although the claim form was completed by someone at the nursing home, the claim was made by the respondent by signing the form which contained the misrepresentation. Since she had the capacity to make the claim, she had the capacity to make the misrepresentation. Accordingly, the appeal would be allowed.

Chief Adjudication Officer v Sheriff (1995) Times, 10 May (Court of Appeal: Nourse, Millett and Otton LJJ).

Social Security Act 1986, s 53(1) now Social Security Administration Act 1992, s 71(1).

2703 Benefits—overpayment—misrepresentation

The Social Security Administration Act 1992, s 71(1) provides that where it is determined that, whether fraudulently or otherwise, any person has misrepresented or failed to disclose any material fact and in consequence of the misrepresentation or failure a payment has been made, the Secretary of State is entitled to recover the amount of any payment which he would not have made but for the misrepresentation or failure to disclose.

The appellant's entitlement to income support was calculated on, amongst other things, figures that she gave as representing the interest rates for the two mortgages that she was paying. On each occasion that the appellant collected her income support, she signed a declaration to the effect that she had correctly reported facts which could affect the amount of her entitlement.

The Department of Social Security later discovered that the interest rate for one of the appellant's mortgages had in fact been reduced following her initial application for income support, and that, as a result, the appellant had been paid more income support than that to which she was entitled. The appellant had not known of the interest rate reduction. An order was made against her in respect of the overpaid benefit, and that decision was upheld on appeal. On the appellant's further appeal, *held*, the declaration which the appellant signed was a representation that there were no facts known to her at the time that she signed the declaration which could affect the amount of her entitlement and which she had not reported. As there could not be non-disclosure of facts which were not known to a person, the appellant had not made any misrepresentation. Accordingly, the appeal would be allowed.

Franklin v Chief Adjudication Officer (1995) Times, 29 December (Court of Appeal: Staughton, Evans and Swinton Thomas LJJ). *Jones v Chief Adjudication Officer* [1994] 1 WLR 62, CA (1993 Abr para 2359) followed.

2704 Benefits—recovery from compensation payments—period for furnishing certificate of total benefit

The Social Security (Recoupment) (Prolongation of Period for Furnishing of Certificate of Total Benefit) Order 1995, SI 1995/1152 (in force on 27 April 1995), provides that for the purposes of the Social Security Administration Act 1992, s 96(1)(c), the time limit designated in the 1992 Act, s 95(1) for the furnishing of a certificate of total benefit is increased from four weeks to three months.

2705 Benefits—students

The Social Security Benefits (Miscellaneous Amendments) Regulations 1995, SI 1995/1742 (in force on 11 July 1995), further amend SI 1983/1598, 1987/1967, 1971, 1973, 1991/2887 and 1992/1814, so as to (1) amend the definition of 'student' in each of those provisions so that a person who has started a course of study remains a student even if he is temporarily absent from the course, (2) increase the amount allowed for books and equipment in calculating a student's grant income, and (3) increase the amount of the deduction made in calculating a student's eligibility for housing benefit.

2706 Benefits—up-rating

The Social Security Benefits Up-rating Order 1995, SI 1995/559 (in force on various days in April 1995), revokes the 1994 Order, SI 1994/542, and provides for the up-rating of various social security benefits. In particular, the order (1) alters the benefits and increases of benefit (except age addition) under the Social Security Contributions and Benefits Act 1992, Sch 4, Pts I, III–V, (2) increases the rates and amounts of certain pensions and allowances under the 1992 Act, and the sums payable as part of a Category A or Category B pension under the Pension Schemes Act 1993, ss 15(1), 17(2), (3), (3) increases the rates of certain workmen's compensation and industrial diseases benefits in respect of employment before 5 July 1948, (4) specifies earnings limits for child dependency increases, (5) specifies the weekly rates of statutory sick pay, (6) increases the lower rate of statutory maternity pay, (7) increases the rate of graduated retirement benefit under the National Insurance Act 1965, (8) increases the rates of disability living allowance, (9) increases the weekly rates of child benefit and one parent benefit, (10) increases the weekly rates of age addition to long-term incapacity benefit, (11) increases the rates of transitional invalidity allowance in long-term incapacity benefit, (12) specifies the applicable amount for family credit and the amount of credits for an adult, child or young person which determines a family's maximum family credit and other miscellaneous amounts, (13) specifies the applicable amount for disability working allowance and the amount of allowance for an adult, child or young person which determines the appropriate maximum disability working allowance, (14) states the amount of sums relevant to the applicable amount for the purposes of income support, (15) provides for the percentage increase of sums payable by way of special transitional additions to income support, (16) states the amount of the sums relevant to the applicable amount for the purposes of housing benefit, setting out the personal allowances and premiums, and (17) states the amount of the sums relevant to the applicable amount for the purposes of council tax benefit, setting out the personal allowances and premiums.

The Social Security Benefits Up-rating Regulations 1995, SI 1995/580 (in force in part on 10 April 1995, and in part on 13 April 1995), revoke SI 1994/559, amend SI 1994/2946, and further amend SI 1977/343, 1982/1408, and 1983/1598. The 1995 Regulations (1) provide that where a question has arisen about the effect of SI 1995/559 on a benefit already in payment, the altered rates does not apply until that question has been determined by an adjudicating authority in accordance with the provisions of the Social Security Administration Act 1992, (2) apply the provisions of the Social Security Benefit (Persons Abroad) Regulations 1975, SI 1975/563, reg 5, so as to restrict the application of increases in certain benefits where the beneficiary lives abroad, (3) raise the earnings limit which applies to unemployability supplement from, £2236.00 to £2288.00 a year, (4) raise one of the earnings limits for child dependency increases payable with invalid care allowance, from £120.00 to £125.00, (5) raise the earnings limit which applies to those undertaking work in certain circumstances while receiving sickness or invalidity benefit, from £43.00 to £44.00, although this provision has effect only for the period 10 April 1995 to 12 April 1995. The regulations also raise the limit of earnings from a councillor's allowance in relation to incapacity benefit from £43.00 to £44.00.

2707 Benefits—widows' pensions—disregard

The Income-related Benefits Schemes (Widows' etc Pensions Disregards) Amendment Regulations 1995, SI 1995/3282 (in force on 20 December 1995), amend the Council Tax Benefit (General) Regulations 1992, SI 1992/1814, the Disability Working Allowance (General) Regulations 1991, SI 1991/2887, the Family Credit (General) Regulations 1987, SI 1987/1973, the Housing Benefit (General) Regulations 1987, SI 1987/1971, the Income Support (General) Regulations 1987, SI 1987/1967, and the Income-related Benefits Schemes Amendment (No 2) Regulations 1995, SI 1995/2792, so as to (1) ensure that the first £10 of pensions paid to soldiers' widows under the Pensions and Yeomanry Pay Act 1884 are disregarded for the purpose of the above-mentioned benefits, and (2) allow local authorities to modify their housing benefit and council tax benefit schemes so as to disregard the balance of those pensions for the purposes of those schemes.

2708 Community provisions

See EUROPEAN COMMUNITIES.

2709 Contributions—defaulting sub-contractor—liability of main contractor

See *Rheinhold & Mahla NV v Bestuur van de Bedrijsfsvereniging voor de Metaalnijverheid*, para 3191.

2710 Contributions—regulations

The Social Security (Contributions) Amendment Regulations 1995, SI 1995/514 (in force on 6 April 1995), further amend the 1979 Regulations, SI 1979/591, so as to reduce the special rate of Class 2 contributions payable by share fishermen from £7.75 to £7.30.

The Social Security (Contributions) Amendment (No 2) Regulations 1995, SI 1995/714 (in force on 6 April 1995), further amend the 1979 Regulations supra so as to (1) increase the lower weekly earnings limit from £57 to £58, and increase the upper weekly earnings limit from £430 to £440, for Class 1 contributions for the tax year beginning on 6 April 1995, (2) reduce the abatement of percentage rates of Class 1 contributions payable by and in respect of serving members of the forces from 0.5% to 0.4%, and (3) decrease the weekly rate of Class 2 contributions payable by volunteer development workers from 5.6% to 5% of the lower earnings limit, so that for the tax year beginning on 6 April 1995 the weekly contributions for such workers decreases from £3.19 to £2.90.

The Social Security (Contributions) Amendment (No 3) Regulations 1995, SI 1995/730 (in force on 6 April 1995), further amend the 1979 Regulations supra so as to (1) revoke the provision which prevented interest being paid when Class 4 contributions were refunded to a contributor more than a year after the end of the tax year in respect of which they had been paid, (2) increase the average monthly total amount of PAYE tax and Class 1 contributions due to the Collector of Taxes, and on the basis of which an employer can pay Class 1 contributions quarterly, from £450 to £600, (3) remove the requirement that the Collector of Taxes must make a demand for the earnings-related or the Class 1A contributions due to be paid by the employer before issuing notice to the employer of the specified amount, and (4) remove the requirement that the specified amount should be certified by the Collector of Taxes as an unpaid amount of contributions.

The Social Security (Contributions) Amendment (No 4) Regulations 1995, SI 1995/1003 (in force on 6 April 1995), further amend the 1979 Regulations supra so as to provide that where a payment of earnings is made by conferring a beneficial interest in certain assets for which trading arrangements exist, the amount of the payment is to be established by reference to the amount obtainable under those arrangements. As regards the list of assets which are not excluded from the computation of a person's earnings, the regulations add other assets, including vouchers, for which trading arrangements exist, and also define the term 'trading arrangements' by reference to the Income and Corporation Taxes Act 1988, s 203K(2)(a).

The Social Security (Contributions) Amendment (No 5) Regulations 1995, SI 1995/1570 (in force on 18 July 1995), further amend the 1979 Regulations supra so as to provide that (1) payments made by an employer up to certain limits to defray or contribute towards personal incidental expenses incurred by a person when he stays away from home overnight in relation to an office or employment, are to be excluded from the computation of his earnings for the purpose of earnings-related contributions, and (2) payments made by an employer to defray or contribute to expenses incurred by an employed person in respect of liability insurance cover and uninsured liabilities in relation to an office or employment, are to be excluded from the computation of his earnings for the purpose of earnings-related contributions.

2711   Contributions—re-rating and national insurance fund payments

The Social Security (Contributions) (Re-rating and National Insurance Fund Payments) Order 1995, SI 1995/561 (in force on 6 April 1995), amends the Social Security Contributions and Benefits Act 1992 by increasing (1) the amounts of weekly earnings specified in the secondary earnings brackets, (2) the rates of Class 2 and Class 3 contributions, and also the small earnings exception from Class 2 contributions, (3) the amount of earnings specified below which an earner may be excepted from liability for Class 2 contributions, and (4) the lower and upper limits of profits or gains between which Class 4 contributions are payable. The order also makes provision as to the maximum amount that Parliament is to pay into the National Insurance Fund for the year 1995–1996.

2712   Council tax benefit—general

See para 2726.

2713   Council tax benefit—local government areas—changes

See para 2730.

2714   Council tax benefit—permitted total—war widows

See para 2728.

2715   Council tax benefit—subsidy—rates

See para 2733.

2716   Credits—family credit

The Social Security (Credits) Amendment Regulations 1995, SI 1995/2558 (in force on 1 November 1995), further amend the 1975 Regulations, SI 1975/556, so as to insert a new provision which applies for the purpose of entitlement to a Category A or B retirement pension, widowed mother's allowance or widow's pension. It provides that a person is to be credited with earnings equal to the lower earnings limit in respect of weeks for which family credit is paid to him. Where family credit is paid to one of a married or unmarried couple, provision is made as to which of them is to be credited with earnings. The new provision applies only to those due to reach pensionable age after 5 April 1999, and has effect in relation to the 1995–96 and subsequent tax years.

2717   Disability living allowance—care component—attention required in connection with bodily functions—assistance for deaf person to carry out reasonable level of social activity

Under the Social Security Contributions and Benefits Act 1992, s 72(1)(b)(i) a person is entitled to the care component of a disability living allowance for any period throughout which he is so severely disabled physically or mentally that, by day, he requires from another person frequent attention throughout the day in connection with his bodily functions.

The claimant, a qualified nursery nurse, was born deaf and had great difficulty speaking. She claimed that she was entitled to disability living allowance on the basis that she required attention pursuant to the 1992 Act, s 72. A social security commissioner decided that it was right to include in the aggregate of attention that was reasonably required such attention as might enable the claimant to carry out a reasonable level of social activity. On appeal by the Secretary of State, he submitted that assistance or attention to enable the claimant to live a normal social life was not reasonably required and only attention which was essential could be said to be reasonable. *Held*, Hobhouse LJ dissenting, *Mallinson v Secretary of State for Social Security* [1994] 2 All ER 295, HL (1994 Abr para 2571) established that assistance given to a blind person to help him when he went out walking was attention in connection with a bodily function. The attention given to a profoundly deaf person to enable that person to carry on, so far as possible in the circumstances, an ordinary life was capable of being attention that was reasonably required. There was nothing in s 72 or statutory provisions generally which led to the conclusion that only attention which was necessary in order to maintain life was reasonably required. The commissioner's decision was correct in law and, accordingly, the appeal would be dismissed.

Secretary of State for Social Security v Fairey (1995) 26 BMLR 63 (Court of Appeal: Glidewell, Hobhouse and Swinton Thomas LJJ).

2718 Disability living allowance—reference to Scottish legislation

See para 2698.

2719 Disability working allowance—general

The Disability Working Allowance and Income Support (General) Amendment Regulations 1995, SI 1995/482 (in force in part on 11 April 1995, and in part on 13 April 1995), amend the Income Support (General) Regulations 1987, SI 1987/1967, and the Disability Working Allowance Regulations 1991, SI 1991/2887. In relation to the latter, the regulations (1) further define 'training for work', and list the days which are to be disregarded in establishing whether a person was engaged in a period of training for work, (2) provide an additional allowance in respect of a disabled child in determining the maximum disability working allowance, and (3) make transitional arrangements as a result of the abolition of invalidity pension and the introduction of incapacity benefit. In relation to the former, the regulations (1) provide that a claimant may be entitled to income support whilst absent from Great Britain if he was incapable of work for 364 days before the absence began, or 196 days in the case of a claimant who is terminally ill or who is entitled to the highest rate of the care component of disability living allowance, (2) provide that a claimant who has failed the incapacity for work test and is appealing against that decision is not required to be available for work or to register for employment, although a claimant in such circumstances who has failed the 'all-work' test is to have the personal allowance element of his applicable amount reduced by 20 per cent, (3) provide that a person is exempt from the requirement to be available for work where he is incapable of work, or where he fails the incapacity test solely on grounds of misconduct or similar matters, (4) provide that a student may be entitled to income support if his applicable amount includes a disability premium or severe disability premium, or if he has been incapable of work for 196 days, and (5) extend the qualifying period for the disability premium on grounds of incapacity for work from 28 weeks to 364 days, except for claimants who are terminally ill. The regulations also permit the disability premium to be excluded from the applicable amount in respect of any period during which a claimant fails the incapacity test on grounds of misconduct or similar matters.

2720 Disability working allowance—reduction in child support maintenance— compensation payment

See para 389.

2721 Earnings factors—family credit

The Social Security (Effect of Family Credit on Earnings Factors) Regulations 1995, SI 1995/2559 (in force on 1 November 1995), are made for the purpose of the Social Security Contributions and Benefits Act 1992, s 45A, which provides for family credit to be taken into account in calculating the additional pension in a Category A retirement pension. In cases where family credit is paid to one member of a married or unmarried couple, the regulations determine to which member of the couple the 1992 Act, s 45A applies.

2722 Earnings factors—revaluation

The Social Security Revaluation of Earnings Factors Order 1995, SI 1995/1070 (in force on 11 May 1995), increases the earnings factors which are relevant to the calculation of the additional pension in the rate of any long-term benefit or of any guaranteed minimum pension, or which are relevant to any other calculation required under the Pension Schemes Act 1993, Pt III for certain tax years, by specified percentages of their amount. The percentage for the tax year 1994–95 is 4.4 per cent, and the percentages for certain earlier tax years have been increased so that the earnings factors for those years are revalued at 1994–1995 earnings levels. The order also provides that fractional amounts are to be rounded off for earnings factors relevant to the calculation of the additional pension in the rate of any long-term benefit.

2723 Family credit—eligibility—discrimination—application of Community legislation

See *Meyers v Adjudication Officer*, para 3193.

2724 Family credit—reduction in child support maintenance—compensation payment

See para 389.

2725 Housing benefit—amount—reduction—suitable alternative living accommodation

The Housing Benefit (General) Regulations 1987, SI 1987/1971, reg 10 provides that the payments in respect of which housing benefit is payable are (1) payments of or by way of rent; (2) payments in respect of a licence or permission to occupy the dwelling; (3) payments in respect of the use and occupation of the dwelling; and (4) payments in respect of service charges, on which the right to occupation depends. Regulation 11(2)(c) provides that where the appropriate authority considers that the rent payable for a dwelling is unreasonably high by comparison with the rent payable in respect of suitable alternative accommodation, they may treat the eligible rent as reduced.

The applicant appealed to the Housing Benefits Review Board against a reduction in the housing benefit eligible to be paid to him. He paid £40 for the right to occupy his room conditional upon a payment of a further £34.84 service charge. The board dismissed his appeal because his rent was unreasonably high compared with suitable alternative accommodation. He applied for judicial review of the board's decision, submitting firstly that reg 11(2)(c) had to be construed strictly so that only the £40 element of his rent would be compared with the rents payable for alternative accommodation. Secondly, in taking account of figures for alternative accommodation, it was unclear whether services of the type included in the applicant's rent were included. Thirdly, the Board had not given adequate reasons for its decision. *Held*, there were substantial arguments for reading the word 'rent' in reg 11(2)(c) more widely than elsewhere in the regulations. In giving adequate reasons for such a decision the correct approach was (1) to establish the rent, in the wider sense of the word, payable; (2) to indicate the type of alternative accommodation regarded as suitable, expressing a view on the services which were requisite before the alternative accommodation was regarded as suitable; (3) to indicate what rent, in the wider sense of the word, would be payable for the alternative accommodation; (4) to make a finding as to whether the rent payable on the claimant's dwelling was unreasonably high in comparison with the rent payable on suitable accommodation elsewhere; (5) if so, to indicate an amount by which the claimant's eligible rent is to be reduced; and (6) to indicate how that amount was arrived at. This approach had not been adopted. Accordingly, the decision would be quashed and the matter remitted to the board.

R v East Yorkshire Borough of Beverley Housing Benefits Review Board, ex p Hare (1995) 27 HLR 637 (Queen's Bench Division: Schiemann J).

2726 Housing benefit—general

The Housing Benefit (General) Amendment Regulations 1995, SI 1995/1644 (in force on 2 January 1996), further amend the Housing Benefit (General) Regulations 1987, SI 1987/1971. The regulations (1) make, and further amend, provisions relating to maximum eligible rent where housing benefit is payable, including conferring a discretion on local authorities to pay, in certain cases, a lesser or greater sum than would otherwise be payable under the regulations, (2) require local authorities to request rent officers to determine or redetermine housing benefit claims in certain circumstances, and (3) make saving provisions in relation to housing benefit claimants whose entitlement commenced before 2 January 1996. This protection extends to the partners of such claimants, members of the household of deceased claimants in certain circumstances, and occupants of exempt accommodation.

The Housing Benefit (General) Amendment (No 2) Regulations 1995, SI 1995/2868 (in force on 2 January 1996), further amend the 1987 Regulations supra so as to (1) prevent double deduction of ineligible charges and ensure that they are in fact deducted, (2) provide for the consequences of a reduction of rent following a pre-tenancy determination by a rent officer, and for the treatment of deductions for fuel, meals and water charges when there is a rent officer's determination, (3) require local authorities to provide certain information when making references to the rent officer, (4) permit local authorities to have regard to rent officers' determinations when determining any payment on account of rent allowances, and (5) introduce a new provision which specifies when a local authority must or must not make a reference to a rent officer where the landlord is a registered housing association.

The Housing Benefit and Council Tax Benefit (Amendment) Regulations 1995, SI 1995/511 (in force on 6 March 1995), further amend the 1987 Regulations supra and the Council Tax Benefit (General) Regulations 1992, SI 1992/1814, by amending the provisions relating to the date on which change of circumstances is to take effect in respect of income received in arrears. The regulations also make transitional provisions.

The Housing Benefit and Council Tax Benefit (Miscellaneous Amendments) Regulations 1995, SI 1995/560 (in force on 10 March 1995), further amend the 1987 Regulations supra and the 1992 Regulations supra. The regulations (1) insert the definition of 'voluntary organisation', and substitute all references to voluntary bodies with references to voluntary organisations, (2) make provision in respect of school and other ancillary workers regarding recognisable cycles of work, (3) make provision regarding the entitlement of prisoners on temporary release to housing benefit, (4) expand on the definition of child care charges, (5) amend the calculation of a claimant's notional income where he is working for a charitable or voluntary organisation or is a volunteer, (6) make provision as regards the date on which housing benefit or council tax benefit ceases in relation to income support, (7) make provision as to the circumstances in which benefit may be withheld, and (8) make provision concerning abatement of attendance allowance. In relation to the 1971 Regulations alone, the 1995 Regulations make provision in respect of excessive high rents, and require the relevant local authority to refer a dwelling for re-determination by a rent officer where there has been a change in the composition of the household.

The Housing Benefit and Council Tax Benefit (Miscellaneous Amendments) (No 2) Regulations 1995, SI 1995/626 (in force in part on 1 April 1995, in part on 3 April 1995, in part on 13 April 1995, and in part on 17 April 1995), further amend the 1987 Regulations supra, the 1992 Regulations supra, and SI 1988/662, so that in respect of housing benefit and council tax benefit the regulations (1) extend the qualifying period for the disability premium on grounds of incapacity for work, from 28 weeks to 364 days, except for claimants who are terminally ill, making provision that the qualifying period may be broken by intervals of up to 56 days, (2) specify further information which the Secretary of State may supply to a local authority, and the information which the local authority must supply to the Secretary of State, and (3) make additional minor consequential, transitional and saving amendments.

The Housing Benefit, Council Tax Benefit and Income Support (Amendments) Regulations 1995, SI 1995/625 (in force on 10 March 1995), further amend the 1992 Regulations supra, the 1987 Regulations supra, and SI 1987/1967. The regulations (1) make, and further amend, provisions relating to a person's temporary absence from a dwelling which he normally occupies as his home, (2) make saving provision in relation to housing benefit and income support claimants whose temporary absence from a dwelling commenced before 10 March 1995, and (3) make transitional provision in respect of council tax benefit recipients who were absent from their dwelling before 10 March 1995.

2727 Housing benefit—grant of benefit—permitted totals

The Housing Benefit (Permitted Totals) Order 1995, SI 1995/1954, 3151 (in force on 2 January 1996), which replaces the 1994 Order, SI 1994/579, sets out the basis for calculating the permitted total of rent rebates or rent allowances for the year 1995/1996 for authorities which grant housing benefit under the Social Security Administration Act 1992, Pt VIII. The order also limits the amount by which housing benefit payments may be increased under the discretion provided by the Housing Benefit (General) Regulations 1987, SI 1987/1971, reg 61(2), (3).

2728   Housing benefit—grant of benefit—permitted totals—war widows

The Housing Benefit (Permitted Totals) and Council Tax Benefit (Permitted Total) (Pension for War Widows) Amendment Order 1995, SI 1995/2793 (in force on 27 October 1995), sets out the basis for calculating the permitted total of rent rebates, rent allowances and council tax benefit for the year 1995/1996 for authorities which modify the housing benefit and council tax benefit schemes under the Social Security Administration Act 1992, ss 138(8)(b), 139(6)(b). Those provisions were extended so that the schemes may disregard as income the whole or part of a pension payable to a woman as a widow under the Naval, Military and Air Forces etc (Disablement and Death) Service Pensions Order 1983, SI 1983/883.

2729   Housing benefit—judicial review—circumstances in which Secretary of State may be served with notice of proceedings

RSC Ord 53, r 5(3) provides that in relation to an application for judicial review, the notice of motion must be served on all persons directly affected.

The applicants applied for judicial review of the decisions of a local authority and a rent authority refusing their applications for housing benefit. The Secretary of State unsuccessfully sought to be joined as a respondent to the proceedings. On appeal, he argued that he was directly affected by every case concerning payment of housing benefit because he had a financial interest and was therefore entitled to be a party to the proceedings. *Held*, the mere fact that the Secretary of State had a financial interest in cases concerning housing benefit did not mean that he was directly affected by every application for judicial review of decisions made in that respect. The question of whether or not he was 'directly affected' within the meaning of Ord 53, r 5(3) depended on the circumstances of each case, and the rule was not to be given a broad interpretation. If that were so, excessive burdens would be placed on judicial review applicants, although if an application showed that a particular housing benefit regulation was ultra vires, it was arguable that the Secretary of State was entitled to notice of the proceedings. Accordingly, the appeal would be dismissed.

R v Liverpool City Council, ex p Muldoon; R v Rent Officer Service, ex p Kelly (1995) 94 LGR 1 (Court of Appeal: Russell, Hobhouse and Morritt LJJ).

2730   Housing benefit—local government areas—changes

The Local Government Changes for England (Housing Benefit and Council Tax Benefit) Regulations 1995, SI 1995/531 (in force on 1 April 1995), (1) make consequential, incidental, transitional and supplementary provision for housing benefit and council tax benefit for the purposes of and in consequence of orders made by the Secretary of State following recommendations for change made by the Local Government Commission for England, (2) supplement the Local Government Changes for England Regulations 1994, SI 1994/867, by providing that in relation to various provisions of the Social Security Administration Act 1992, references to an authority which has been abolished or which has relinquished part of its area are also references to the authority acquiring that area, and (3) provide that an authority acquiring an abolished or relinquished area must terminate any benefit period granted by the previous authority.

2731   Housing benefit—overpayment—review—person affected

The plaintiff council paid housing benefit due to the tenant direct to her landlord. The tenant left the rented premises two months prior to giving the landlord one month's notice to terminate her tenancy. The plaintiff claimed from the landlord sums overpaid for a period of three months when the tenant was no longer entitled to benefit. The landlord's request for an internal review of the decision was refused on the ground that such procedure was only applicable to the person who claimed benefit. The plaintiff's claim against the landlord for the recovery of the sums in question failed at first instance. It appealed. *Held*, the questions whether there had been an overpayment, whether it could be recovered, whether under the Housing Benefit (General) Regulations 1987, SI 1987/1971, reg 100, it was to be recovered and from whom it should be recovered under reg 101, were matters to be determined under Pt XI. The plaintiff had failed to follow the Pt XI procedure. It had neither informed the landlord that he was entitled to a review nor his solicitor of the right to seek a review by the Housing Benefit Review Board. Part XI applied to any 'person affected'. A person from whom an overpayment was to be recovered was a 'person affected' by a determination. An overpayment caused by official error within reg 99(3) was one where the claimant, a person acting on his behalf, or any other person to whom the payment was made, did not cause or materially contribute to the error. By failing to disclose information to the plaintiff, the tenant had contributed to the error. As the regulations did not state that an overpayment could only be recovered from the person who contributed to the error, it was sufficient if any of those people contributed. It was recoverable if any of those people should have realised that the payment in question was an overpayment. While the plaintiff might have been able to decide both that the overpayment was recoverable and that it was recoverable from the defendant, it had failed to go through the correct procedure for doing so and, therefore, had not been entitled to bring proceedings for recovery. Accordingly, its appeal would be dismissed.

Warwick District Council v Freeman (1994) 27 HLR 616 (Court of Appeal: Kennedy LJ and Hale J).

2732 Housing benefit—service charges—provision of counselling by landlord—exclusion of service charges from benefit

The Housing Benefit (General) Regulations 1987, SI 1987/1971, Sch 1, para 1(f) provides that charges in respect of general counselling or other support services (whether or not provided by social work professionals), except those related to the provision of adequate accommodation or those provided by the landlord in person or someone employed by him who spends the majority of his time providing services for which the charges are not ineligible, are not eligible to be met by housing benefit.

The claimants, who all suffered from mental disorder or mental illness, lived in private rented accommodation. Their rent included a charge in respect of time spent by their respective landlords counselling and offering them support, as well as for the accommodation itself. Housing benefit review boards decided that the claimants' applications for housing benefit in respect of such support and counselling services were ineligible, as the landlords had not spent the majority of their time providing such services, having regard to the 1987 Regulations, Sch 1, para 1(f). The claimants successfully applied for judicial review of the decisions. On the Secretary of State's appeal, *held*, if charges were made for counselling or other support services relating to the provision of adequate accommodation, it was unnecessary to consider who actually provided such services, and charges in that respect were eligible for housing benefit. If the counselling or other support services did not relate to the provision of adequate accommodation, it was necessary to consider whether they were provided by the landlord himself, in which case a charge for such services was eligible for housing benefit. Once it was shown that the landlord provided services for a claimant, it was irrelevant to consider how he spent the remainder of his time. It was only if the services were provided by a person employed by the landlord that it was necessary to consider whether the employee spent the majority of his time doing so. Accordingly, on the facts of the instant cases, the appeal would be dismissed.

R v North Cornwall District Council, ex p Bateman; R v North Cornwall District Council, ex p Singer; R v North Cornwall District Council, ex p Barrett (1995) 27 HLR 622 (Court of Appeal: Glidewell, Mann and Millett LJJ). Decision of Queen's Bench Divisional Court (1993) 26 HLR 360 (1994 Abr para 2607) affirmed.

The 1987 Regulations, Sch 1, para 1(f) is now as amended by the Housing Benefit (General) Amendment Regulations 1994, SI 1994/1003.

2733 Housing benefit—subsidy—rates

The Housing Benefit and Council Tax Benefit (Subsidy) Order 1995 SI 1995/872 (in force on 20 April 1995), makes provision for the calculation of housing benefit and council tax benefit subsidy payable under the Social Security Administration Act 1992 to authorities administering housing benefit or council tax benefit. The order (1) sets out the manner in which the total figure for an authority's housing benefit subsidy in respect of rent rebates and allowances for the year ending 31 March 1995 is calculated, and the manner of calculating the additional sum payable to an authority in respect of the costs of administering housing benefit, (2) makes provision for additions and deductions to subsidy in respect of rent rebates or allowances, (3) sets out the manner in which the total figure for the appropriate authority's subsidy in respect of council tax benefit for the year ending 31 March 1995 is calculated and the manner of calculating the additional sum payable to an appropriate authority in respect of the costs of administering council tax benefit and (4) makes provision for additions and deductions to subsidy in respect of community charge benefits and council tax benefits.

The Housing Benefit and Council Tax Benefit (Subsidy) Amendment Regulations 1995, SI 1995/874 (in force on 20 April 1995), amend the 1994 Regulations, SI 1994/781, to provide for the particulars which must be provided by a local authority to the Secretary of State on making claims for housing benefit subsidy and council tax benefit subsidy. Details must be given of (1) rent allowance expenditure which exceeds certain determinations made by rent officers, (2) rents of dwellings of authorities in Scotland and the Development Board for Rural Wales on 31 March 1995, and on a specified date in March 1994, and (3) savings in benefits resulting from investigation of benefit fraud. The 1994 Regulations will continue to apply to any claims for subsidy for any relevant year before 1 April 1994.

2734 Housing benefit—subsidy—rent officers' functions

The Rent Officers (Additional Functions) Order 1995, SI 1995/1642 (in force on 2 January 1996), revokes and replaces, with modifications, the 1990 Order, SI 1990/428, as amended. The order (1) confers functions on rent officers in connection with housing benefit and rent allowance subsidy, (2) requires rent officers to make determinations and redeterminations relating to actual or prospective tenancies and licences of dwellings, and (3) requires rent officers to determine local reference rents and indicative rent levels. The order removes the requirement for rent officers to make interim determinations. Provision is made for exceptions to the requirement to make determinations and redeterminations and for special cases.

The Rent Officers (Additional Functions) (Amendment) Order 1995, SI 1995/2365 (in force in part on 2 October 1995 and in part on 2 January 1996), (1) makes further amendments to the 1990 Order supra, and (2) amends SI 1995/1642 so as to add a requirement for rent officers to notify local authorities where a determination requested by the authority is not one to which that order applies, and to give local authorities additional information if the rent under a tenancy, or licence fee under a licence, includes a charge for meals or fuel and is determined to be exceptionally high.

The Rent Officers (Additional Functions) (Amendment No 2) Order 1995, SI 1995/3148 (in force on 2 January 1996), confers functions on rent officers in connection with housing benefit and rent allowance subsidy, requiring them to make determinations and re-determinations in respect of tenancies and licences of dwellings. In particular, the order (1) alters the criteria for local reference rent determinations stated in SI 1995/1642, providing that rooms shared with a person other than a member of a tenant's household, a non-dependant, or a person who pays rent to the tenant, are not to be taken into account when deciding if the tenant has the use of more than one room, (2) provides that where the landlord is a charity, rents under tenancies and licences of dwellings provided in pursuit of charitable purposes are not to be taken into account when making determinations, and (3) alters the criteria for indicative rent level determinations so as to amend the definition of 'room' to exclude a room which the tenant shares with the persons mentioned in the amended definition.

2735 Incapacity benefit—regulations

The Social Security (Incapacity Benefit) (Transitional) Regulations 1995, SI 1995/310 (in force on 13 April 1995), make provision for the transition to incapacity benefit from sickness benefit and invalidity benefit for the purposes of the Social Security (Incapacity for Work) Act 1994. Days before 13 April 1995 may be taken into account for the purposes of incapacity benefit, and days of incapacity for work after 13 April 1995 may form part of a period of incapacity for work beginning before 13 April 1995. Those who were deemed to be incapable of work before 13 April 1995 may continue to be so deemed thereafter. Provision is also made for late claims for sickness benefit and invalidity benefit, and for the disqualification and suspension of payment of incapacity benefit. Awards of sickness benefit are to be treated as awards of short-term incapacity benefit, and may be paid at the transitional rate on the termination of employment after a period of entitlement to disability working allowance or a period engaged in training for work, in certain circumstances. Where a person was entitled to sickness benefit in respect of an industrial injury, the contribution conditions are to be taken as satisfied for the purpose of entitlement to short-term incapacity benefit. Awards of invalidity benefit are to be treated as awards of long-term incapacity benefit, and provision is made as to the rate at which it is payable in transitional cases. In certain circumstances, awards of incapacity benefit may be paid at the transitional rate on termination of a period of entitlement to disability working allowance or on termination of a period engaged in training for work, and where a person is incapacitated because of an industrial injury. The regulations provide for the adjustment of benefit where a guaranteed minimum pension is paid. Transitional provisions are made in respect of an increase of a Category A retirement pension for incapacity, and for an increase in the rate of long-term incapacity benefit for dependants and severe disablement allowance for dependants. Miscellaneous provisions are also made in respect of the rate of payment of incapacity benefit in the week that the benefit is introduced. In respect of the new tests of incapacity for work, transitional provisions are to apply to existing cases where incapacity is in question, although certain categories of persons are exempt from the new all work test. Additionally, days of incapacity arising before 13 April 1995 may be taken into account for the purposes of the new medical tests.

The Social Security (Incapacity for Work) (General) Regulations 1995, SI 1995/311 (in force on 13 April 1995), contain provisions affecting the determination of a person's capacity for work for the purposes of the Social Security Contributions and Benefits Act 1992. Part I contains interpretation provisions. In Pt II, a definition of 'remunerative work' is given for the purposes of the 'own occupation test'. The regulations specify the information that is required to determine whether a person is capable or incapable of work, and a person is to be treated as capable of work if he fails without good cause to provide the requested information within the prescribed periods. In particular, a person is to be treated as capable of work if he fails to attend a medical examination when requested. Those suffering from certain severe medical conditions are to be treated as incapable of work, as are hospital in-patients, those with infectious or contagious diseases, those receiving certain regular treatment, and certain pregnant women. In some circumstances, a person who works is to be treated as capable of work even if it has been determined that he is incapable of work, unless he does work which is in an exempt category and within defined limits. Moreover, a person is to be disqualified from entitlement to incapacity benefit or severe disability allowance if he has become incapable of work through his own misconduct or if he fails to observe rules of behaviour. An adjudication officer's determination as to a person's capacity for work for the purposes of his entitlement to a particular benefit is conclusive for the purposes of entitlement to any other benefit. In Pt III, a definition of the 'all work test' is given, and the regulations state the method of assessment for the test, which is based on a points system. The Schedule sets out the mental and physical disabilities which may make a person incapable of work.

The Social Security (Incapacity for Work) Miscellaneous Amendments Regulations 1995, SI 1995/987 (in force in part on 3 April 1995, and in part on 13 April 1995), amend SI 1995/310, 311, and further amend SI 1976/615. SI 1995/311 is amended so as to (1) exclude claims for unemployment benefit from the evidence requirements of those regulations relating to the determination of a claimant's capacity for work, (2) make provision for treating claimants as capable of work when they claim unemployment benefit, (3) increase the earnings limit for persons who undertake certain work on the advice of a doctor, and (4) make further provision as to the questions which must be determined by an adjudication officer. SI 1995/310 is amended so as to (1) make provision for claims for incapacity benefit in cases where the period of interruption of employment and period of incapacity for work link, (2) make transitional provision for entitlement to severe entitlement after a period engaged in training for work, (3) clarify the provisions in respect of the cases which fall into the list of cases which are exempt from the new medical test, and (4) add further categories of persons who are to be treated as incapable of work under the new medical test. SI 1976/615 is amended so as to set out the medical evidence required for the purposes of determining incapacity for work.

The Social Security (Incapacity Benefit) (Consequential and Transitional Amendments and Savings) Regulations 1995, SI 1995/829 (in force on 13 April 1995), amend or further amend SI 1974/2010, 1975/494, 529, 555, 556, 563, 1976/1409, 1977/956, 1978/393, 529, 1698, 1979/591, 597, 1982/894, 1408, 1983/506, 1598, 1984/457, 1986/625, 1960, 2218, 1988/35, 664, 1990/322, and 1994/2945 so as to make consequential amendments and transitional provisions as a result of the replacement of sickness benefit and invalidity benefit by incapacity benefit, introduced by the Social Security (Incapacity for Work) Act 1994. Part I of the 1995 Regulations contains commencement and interpretation provisions. Part II provides that references in the amended provisions to sickness benefit are replaced by references to incapacity benefit and, in addition (1) SI 1975/555 is further amended so that a beneficiary is to be regarded as having a dependant for the purposes of the 1975 Regulations if he either satisfies a condition for an increase in benefit in respect of an adult dependant, or would have done so had the conditions for increases for dependants in respect of sickness or invalidity benefit continued to apply after 12 April 1995, (2) SI 1975/556 is further amended to provide for the meaning of 'a day of incapacity for work' in relation to credits, (3) SI 1978/529 is amended to prescribe how Category A retirement pensions are to be determined for widows and widowers, (4) SI 1977/956 is further amended so as to apply those regulations to invalidity benefit, (5) references to sickness and invalidity benefit are removed from SI 1978/393, Sch 1, so that the 1978 Regulations, which deal with the rate of benefit payable to those over pensionable age, apply to unemployment benefit and certain transitional payments of incapacity benefit only, (6) SI 1979/597 is further amended so that where widow's pension is paid at a reduced rate with long-term incapacity benefit, those benefits cannot be adjusted by reference to each other; the provisions for adjustment where part-week payments of more than one benefit are adjusted are also amended, (7) SI 1983/1598 is further amended by omitting references to sickness benefit and invalidity benefit, (8) SI 1994/2945 is amended so as to provide that where a woman receives increases of benefit for a dependant spouse under SI 1995/310, such benefit is to be treated in the same manner as increases of incapacity benefit made under the Social Security Contributions and Benefits Act 1992 for the purposes of claiming adult dependency increases of retirement pension, and (9) SI 1983/506, 1984/457, and 1986/625 are further amended to include references to incapacity benefit. Part III of the 1995 Regulations makes transitional provisions and savings relating to sickness and invalidity benefit in respect of the review of decisions, the recoupment of benefit and entitlement to credits.

2736 Income support—applicable amounts—housing costs—occurrence of major change of circumstances

The Income Support (General) Regulations 1987, SI 1987/1967, Sch 3, para 10(1) provides that the aggregate amount of the housing costs element of income support for mortgage interest payments is initially restricted to the amount of the eligible rent immediately before the acquisition of the property in question. Paragraph 10(2) provides that para 10(1) ceases to apply if its application becomes inappropriate by reason of any major change in the circumstances of a family affecting their ability to meet the expenditure on housing costs.

The plaintiff and her husband, who received income support and housing benefit, lived in a house as secure tenants. The couple were given a mortgage to enable them to purchase the property but a month later the husband began living apart from the plaintiff, who applied for income support in her own right. The adjudication officer restricted the amount of income support under the 1987 Regulations, para 10(1), to the amount of housing benefit payable prior to the purchase of the property. On appeal, a tribunal held that the plaintiff's separation from her husband was a major change of circumstances under para 10(2) and the restriction would therefore not apply. The adjudication officer appealed to the Commissioner, who held that the major change had to occur after the restriction applied. On further appeal by the plaintiff, who also claimed that para 10(1) did not apply where the property was purchased before the date on which a claim for income support was made, *held*, there was nothing in para 10(1) to suggest that it only applied where a claim was made before an interest in the property was acquired. The clear structure of para 10(2) was that the major change of circumstances had to take place after some event, namely the restriction imposed under para 10(1). Accordingly, the appeal would be dismissed.

Kaur v Chief Adjudication Officer [1995] 2 FLR 559 (Court of Appeal: Stuart-Smith, Morritt and Ward LJJ).

2737 Income support—assessment of capital—beneficial joint tenant—tenancy agreement

It has been held that when assessing the capital of a claimant for income support who has an interest in a beneficial joint tenancy, the value of that interest is its current market value and not the value of the entire beneficial interest divided by the number of beneficial interests held in the property. In addition, any property owned by a claimant but subject to a tenancy agreement is to be disregarded for assessment purposes.

Chief Adjudication Officer v Palfrey; Same v Dowell; Same v McDonnell; Same v Pelter; Same v McNamara [1995] 11 LS Gaz R39 (Court of Appeal: Nourse and Hobhouse LJJ and Sir Ralph Gibson).

2738 Income support—claims and payments

The Social Security (Income Support and Claims and Payments) Amendment Regulations 1995, SI 1995/1613 (in force on 2 October 1995), further amend the 1987 Regulations, SI 1987/1967, in order to alter the way in which housing costs are calculated for the purposes of income support. The regulations (1) provide for a standard rate of interest for all loans which qualify as housing costs, (2) divide housing costs into 'existing housing costs' and 'new housing costs', (3) provide that 50 per cent of existing housing costs are to be met if the claimant has been entitled to income support for a continuous period of at least eight weeks but less than 26 weeks, and in full thereafter, and that new housing costs are to be met if the claimant has been entitled to income support for a continuous period of 39 weeks, (4) make changes to the provisions of the

1987 Regulations relating to direct payment of mortgage interest payments to lenders in cases where the claimant is a borrower, and (5) provide that money used from a housing costs payment insurance policy is, in part, not to be taken into account in determining a claimant's income.

2739 Income support—cohabitation—claimants' relationship akin to husband and wife—factors to be considered

The applicant, a disabled man, lived in the same household as a woman who claimed income support for both herself and the applicant. The applicant applied to receive income support separately but was turned down by an adjudication officer. An appeal to a social security tribunal was dismissed on the ground that the applicant was living with the woman in a relationship akin to husband and wife rather than patient and carer, and was therefore not eligible for separate income support. On further appeal, *held*, the paramount factor when determining whether a couple were living in relationship akin to husband and wife was the general relationship between the couple rather than reference to specific criteria. Matters such as financial support of each other, public declarations that they are married or sexual relations between the couple were all signposts, but not necessarily conclusive, that the couple lived as husband and wife. If there had never been sexual relations between the couple, strong alternative reasons for treating them as husband and wife would have to be found and this might therefore mean that the couple would have to be questioned about their sexual relationships. In this case, the tribunal had failed to give adequate reasons for their conclusion that the applicant and the woman were living as husband and wife. Accordingly, the tribunal's decision would be quashed and the matter referred to a differently constituted tribunal.

Re J (Income Support: Cohabitation) [1995] 1 FLR 660 (Social Security Commissioner's decision).

2740 Income support—general

See para 2719.

2741 Income support—housing costs—rate of interest

The Income Support (General) Amendment and Transitional Regulations 1995, SI 1995/2287 (in force on 2 October 1995), further amend the 1987 Regulations, SI 1987/1967, so as to increase the standard rate of interest applicable to loans which qualify for income support under the 1987 Regulations, Sch 3, from 8.35 per cent to 8.39 per cent. The regulations also provide that arrears which have accrued in certain circumstances and loans which were made to the partner of a claimant who has been deserted, or in respect of certain repairs and improvements, are to continue to qualify as housing costs for awards of income support to a specified extent.

The Income Support (General) Amendment Regulations 1995, SI 1995/3320 (in force on 21 January 1996), amend the 1987 Regulations supra so as to alter the standard rate of interest applicable to a loan which qualifies for income support under the 1987 Regulations, Sch 3, to 8 per cent.

2742 Income support—mortgage interest—loss on receipt of child support maintenance—compensation payment

See para 394.

2743 Income support—residence condition—habitual residence

The first applicant, who was born in Pakistan, had acquired British nationality but then returned to Pakistan. The second applicant, who was born in Ethiopia, was naturalised as a French citizen. The third applicants, a mother and son, were German nationals. The son sought employment in the United Kingdom. All of the applicants were refused income support on the ground that they were not habitually resident in the United Kingdom. They sought judicial review of such decisions, contending that the Income-related Benefits Schemes (Miscellaneous Amendments) (No 3) Regulations 1994, SI 1994/1807, by virtue of which the Secretary of State had introduced the concept of habitual residence in the United Kingdom as a condition of eligibility for income support under the Social Security Contributions and Benefits Act 1992, were unlawful. A question also arose as to whether a person who was not a worker, but only seeking work, was by virtue of the EC Treaty, art 48, which provided for freedom of movement for workers within the Community, entitled to non-contributory welfare benefits in a Community country of which he was not a national. *Held*, under the 1992 Act, physical presence in Great Britain was a necessary, but not a sufficient, condition for eligibility for income support. A test of habitual residence was not outside the rule-making powers of the Secretary of State. Under Community law, rights of movement and rights of residence within the Community did not necessarily carry with them maintenance rights. The applications would be dismissed.

R v Secretary of State for Social Security, ex p Sarwar (1995) Times, 19 June, (1995) Independent, 12 April (Queen's Bench Division: Balcombe LJ and French J). *Cases 316/85: Centre Public d'Aide Sociale, Courcelles v Lebon* [1987] ECR 2811, ECJ (1987 Abr para 3061) and *197/86: Brown v Secretary of State for Scotland* [1988] ECR 3205, ECJ (1988 Abr para 2721) applied.

2744   Income support—students taking substantial period of time off during full-time course—eligibility for income support

The Income Support (General) Regulations 1987, SI 1987/1967, reg 61 provides that a student is a person who is attending a full-time course of study at an educational establishment, and that a person who has started on such a course is to be treated as attending the course throughout any period of term or vacation within it until the last day of the course or such earlier date as he abandons it or is dismissed from it.

The first claimant had commenced a three-year degree course and was given permission by her university to defer the final year of the course until the following academic year. The second claimant, who had also commenced a three-year degree course, fell ill during the final year of her course and was permitted to defer her final year until the following academic year. The Social Security Commissioner decided that they were entitled to income support during the year in which they were not attending their courses because they had abandoned their courses and therefore were not students within the meaning of the 1987 Regulations, reg 61. On appeal, the Chief Adjudication Officer argued that 'abandoned' meant 'to give up finally' and that the resumption of a course after a break of a year did not amount to abandoning it. *Held* (Hirst LJ dissenting), although the Chief Adjudication Officer was correct in arguing that 'abandon' could be used in a sense which was final, it was necessary to have regard to the overall context and purpose of the regulations in order to determine who was a student. The regulations were introduced to prevent students who were available for work from claiming entitlement to unemployment benefit during the vacations. Moreover, student loans were introduced by the Education (Student Loans) Act 1990 so that students could obtain loans to help support themselves throughout the calendar year. As such, although students were excluded from entitlement to social security benefits, they were eligible for educational awards and student loans. A 'student' was therefore someone who attended a course not only during term time but also during the vacations. As the claimants were not 'students' during their year out, nor had they abandoned their courses, they were entitled to claim income support. Accordingly, the appeal would be dismissed.

Chief Adjudication Officer v Clarke; Chief Adjudication Officer v Faul [1995] ELR 259 (Court of Appeal: Glidewell, Hirst and Hoffmann LJJ).

2745   Industrial injuries—disablement pension and unemployability supplement—permitted earnings

The Social Security (Industrial Injuries) (Dependency) (Permitted Earnings Limits) Order 1995, SI 1995/581 (in force on 10 April 1995), amends the Social Security Contributions and Benefits Act 1992, Sch 7, para 4(4), so as to provide that where a disablement pension with unemployability supplement is increased in respect of a dependent child and the beneficiary is one of two persons who are spouses residing together, or an unmarried couple, the increase is not payable in respect of the first child if the other person's earnings are £125 a week or more. In respect of any further child, the increase is not payable for each complete £16 where the other person's earnings exceed £125.

2746   Invalid care allowance—earnings

The Social Security (Invalid Care Allowance) Amendment Regulations 1995, SI 1995/2935 (in force on 12 December 1995), amend the 1976 Regulations, SI 1976/409, reg 8. The 1976 Regulations, reg 8(1) provides that a person is not to be treated as gainfully employed on any day in a week unless his earnings in the immediate preceding week have exceeded a specified amount, and reg 8(2)(b) provides that a person's earnings for any week throughout which he is absent from his employment with the authority of his employer are to be disregarded for the purposes of reg 8(1). The 1995 Regulations revoke the 1976 Regulations, reg 8(2)(b), but make a saving in respect of persons to whom it applied immediately before 12 December 1995.

2747   Invalidity benefit—age restriction—sex discrimination

See *Graham v Secretary of State for Social Security*, para 3196.

2748   Invalidity benefit—entitlement—member of family of migrant worker

See *Schmid v Belgium*, para 3195.

2749   Invalidity benefit—widow's pension—withdrawal—sex discrimination

See *Van Gemert-Derks v Bestuur van de Nieuwe Industriële Bedrijfsvereniging*, para 3197.

2750   Jobseekers Act 1995

The Jobseekers Act 1995 replaces unemployment benefit and income support for the unemployed, and is also intended to promote the employment of the unemployed and assist those without a settled way of life. The Act received the royal assent on 28 June 1995. Certain provisions came into force on 12 December 1995 and on 1 January, 1 April and 6 April 1996: SI 1995/3228. The remaining provisions come into force on a day or days to be appointed. For details of commencement, see the commencement table in the title STATUTES.

Part I (ss 1–25) Entitlement to the Jobseeker's Allowance
Section 1 provides for the payment of a weekly jobseeker's allowance if a claimant satisfies certain requirements specified in s 1 and either the contribution-based conditions set out in s 2 (based on a claimant's Class 1 contributions for the two years preceding the beginning of the benefit year in which he claims the allowance, and subject to a prescribed maximum earnings limit), or the income-based conditions set out in s 3 (based on a prescribed income limit, and subject to a requirement that neither the claimant nor any member of his family is entitled to income support). Sections 12 and 13 provide that a claimant's capital must also be taken into account. Depending on which conditions a claimant satisfies, s 4 sets out the amount payable to by way of a jobseeker's allowance. The contribution-based jobseeker's allowance is payable for 182 days, although a claimant may be entitled to it for a further period in certain circumstances: s 5.

Sections 6 and 7 define the circumstances in which a claimant is available for, and actively seeking, employment, and by regulations made under s 8 he may be required to attend at a place to give information and evidence in that respect. If he fails to do so without good reason, he may lose his entitlement to the allowance. Further provision is made by ss 19–21 and Sch 1 as to the circumstances in which a person is not entitled to a jobseeker's allowance, subject to certain exemptions.

One of the requirements of s 1 is that a claimant must enter into a jobseeker's agreement, and this is dealt with in detail in s 9. The agreement is made between a claimant and an employment officer if the officer believes that the claimant is available for, and actively seeking, employment, although the matter may be referred to an adjudication officer for determination. By s 10, a jobseeker's agreement may be varied by agreement between the claimant and the employment officer, or the matter may be referred to an adjudication officer. Section 11 gives a claimant a right of appeal against an adjudication officer's decision, and also allows a claimant or an employment officer to seek a review of an adjudication officer's decision by a different adjudication officer.

By s 14, a person is not entitled to a jobseeker's allowance if he stops working because of his involvement in a trade dispute, except in certain circumstances. Similarly, by s 15, the amount payable to a claimant receiving an income-based jobseeker's allowance is reduced if a member of his family is involved in a trade dispute.

In relation to a person aged 16–18 who is not entitled to a jobseeker's allowance or income support and who is registered for, but not receiving, training, s 16 provides that an income-based jobseeker's allowance may be paid if he would otherwise suffer severe hardship. In the circumstances stated in s 17, the amount payable to a young person may be reduced, and s 18 makes provision for the recovery of severe hardship payments.

Miscellaneous provisions in ss 22–25 relate to the application of the Act to those in the armed forces, the alteration of the rates of the jobseeker's allowance, aged-based increases to the amount of income-based jobseeker's allowance payable, and the recovery of sums paid by way of an income-based jobseeker's allowance from the spouse of the person to whom the allowance is paid.

Part II (ss 26–29) Back to Work Schemes
Section 26 provides that in circumstances prescribed by regulations, those who have been or are entitled to a jobseeker's allowance or income support, are entitled to a 'back to work bonus'. In

addition, s 27 allows a former claimant's employer to make deductions from the employer's contributions payments, in certain circumstances.

By s 28, regulations may be made for expediting housing benefit and council tax benefit claims made by those who cease to claim income support or a jobseeker's allowance.

Short-term pilot schemes may also be made under s 29 to ascertain whether regulations made under the Act or under certain other related enactments encourage or facilitate the obtaining of work.

Part III (ss 30–41) Miscellaneous and supplemental provisions
Section 30 provides that resettlement grants may be paid to those who are given temporary accommodation. By s 31, a claimant's entitlement to a jobseeker's allowance, or that of his wife or partner, may be terminated if he, his wife or partner would be entitled to income support on such termination. Provision is also made by s 32 as to the effect of a jobseeker's allowance in relation to a claimant against whom a bankruptcy order has been made. Section 33 specifies inspectors' powers, and s 34 specifies offences under the Act. Section 35 contains interpretation provisions, and ss 36 and 37 deal with the power to make regulations or orders under the Act and Parliamentary control of such regulations. Section 38 deals with financial arrangements in relation to payment of the jobseeker's allowance, s 39 relates to Northern Ireland and s 40 provides that transitional provisions may be made. Section 41 sets out the short title, commencement and extent of the Act, and Schs 2 and 3 deal with consequential amendments to, and the repeal of, other provisions.

2751 Jobseeker's allowance—transitional provisions

The Jobseeker's Allowance (Transitional Provisions) Regulations 1995, SI 1995/3276 (in force on 7 October 1996), provide for continuity between, on the one hand, unemployment benefit and income support for those who are required to be available for and actively seeking employment, and, on the other hand, a jobseeker's allowance. In particular, the regulations (1) include an extended definition of the term 'jobseeking period', specifying certain other periods which are to be taken into account in determining whether a jobseeking period is continuing, (2) provide that awards of income support made to those required to be available for and actively seeking employment are to be terminated and replaced by awards of jobseeker's allowance, (3) set out the conditions which a claimant must satisfy if an award of a jobseeker's allowance is to continue, (4) provide that transitional protection is to be given for a limited period to those formerly entitled to unemployment benefit or income support, (5) provide that the rules which applied to unemployment benefit and income support as regards the calculation of earnings, disqualification for benefits and students, are to apply to some claimants whose entitlement to a jobseeker's allowance arises under these regulations, and (6) enable claims for a jobseeker's allowance to be treated also as claims for unemployment benefit or income support, or both.

2752 Maternity—statutory maternity pay—compensation of employers

The Statutory Maternity Pay (Compensation of Employers) Amendment Regulations 1995, SI 1995/566 (in force on 6 April 1995), amend the 1994 Regulations, SI 1994/1882, so as to increase the additional amount that a small employer may recover in respect of payments of statutory maternity pay, from 4 per cent to 5 per cent of the payment of statutory maternity pay.

2753 National assistance—assessment of resources

The National Assistance (Assessment of Resources) (Amendment) Regulations 1995, SI 1995/858 (in force on 13 April 1995), further amend the 1992 Regulations, SI 1992/2977. In consequence of the Social Security (Incapacity for Work) Act 1994, the 1995 Regulations replace the disregard for sickness benefit, invalidity pension or severe disablement allowance with one which relates to incapacity benefit or severe disablement allowance. In order to have an amount disregarded in the calculation of earnings for the purpose of a claim for incapacity benefit of severe disablement allowance, a person must have provided medical evidence at least 28 weeks previously, and it must not have been determined already that he is not entitled to the benefit or allowance. The regulations also remove a provision whereby fuel charges which are included in the housing costs of a person temporarily in accommodation arranged by the local authority may be disregarded only if he intends to return to the accommodation for which the costs are payable.

The National Assistance (Assessment of Resources) (Amendment No 2) Regulations 1995, SI 1995/3054 (in force on 20 December 1995), further amend the 1992 Regulations supra. The

1992 Regulations concern the assessment of a person's ability to pay for accommodation arranged by local authorities under the National Assistance Act 1948, Pt III. In particular, the 1992 Regulations, Sch 4 sets out the sums to be disregarded in calculating such a person's capital, and some of those sums are specified by reference to the Income Support (General) Regulations 1987, SI 1987/1967. The 1995 Regulations amend the 1992 Regulations, Sch 4 so as to provide a disregard in respect of any interest in property which a resident will or may possess in the future, but does not possess at the time that his ability to pay for accommodation is assessed. However, the disregard does not apply where the property in question is land or premises in respect of which the resident has granted a lease, tenancy, sub-lease or sub-tenancy.

2754 National assistance—sums for personal requirements

The National Assistance (Sums for Personal Requirements) Regulations 1995, SI 1995/443 (in force on 10 April 1995), which replace the 1994 Regulations, SI 1994/826, set a weekly sum of £13.35 as the amount which local authorities are, in the absence of special circumstances, to assume that residents in accommodation arranged under the National Assistance Act 1948, Pt III, will need for their personal requirements.

2755 Occupational pensions

See PENSIONS AND SUPERANNUATION.

2756 Personal pensions

See PENSIONS AND SUPERANNUATION.

2757 Reciprocal agreements—general

The Social Security (Reciprocal Agreements) Order 1995, SI 1995/767 (in force on 13 April 1995), amends SI 1953/884, 1955/420, 874, 1956/1897, 1957/1879, 1958/597, 771, 772, 1263, 1960/211, 707, 1961/584, 1202, 1966/270, 1968/1655, 1969/384, 1971/1742, 1972/1587, 1975/415, 1979/921, 1981/605, 1983/1698, 1894, 1984/125, 354, 1817, 1985/1202, 1987/1830, 1988/590, 1989/2002, 1991/767, 1992/812,1312, 1994/1646 and 2802, which give effect to agreements made between the governments of the UK and other countries providing for reciprocity in certain social security matters. The amendment takes account of changes made to social security legislation by the Social Security (Incapacity for Work) Act 1994, which replaced sickness benefit and invalidity benefit with incapacity benefit.

The Social Security (Canada) Order 1995, SI 1995/2699 (in force on 1 December 1995), makes provision for the modification of the Social Security Administration Act 1992, the Social Security Contributions and Benefits Act 1992, and regulations made or having effect thereunder, so as to give effect to the consolidated arrangements contained in letters exchanged between the governments of the United Kingdom and Canada. The arrangements relate to child benefit, unemployment benefit, and retirement pension. The order consequently revokes the 1959 Order, SI 1959/2216, as amended, and amends the 1976 Orders, SI 1976/225 and 1976/963.

2758 Residential care home—sale of care home by local authority—mixed economy of care

A local authority decided to close one of its directly managed residential care homes for the elderly and sell three others to the private sector. It arranged for a third party to provide and manage accommodation for the elderly whilst the authority itself would maintain accommodation for the disabled. A former resident of the care home being closed sought judicial review of the authority's decision on the ground that it was in breach of the National Assistance Act 1948, s 21, which imposed a duty on local authorities to provide accommodation for certain classes of people in need of care and attention. Section 26 of the 1948 Act, as amended, provided that arrangements under s 21 may include arrangements made with a voluntary organisation or with any other person who was not a local authority, where that organisation or person managed premises which provided accommodation for reward. At first instance, it was held that the authority had a duty under the 1948 Act to provide accommodation for all classes of persons in need and could not hive off this duty in regard to one particular class. That decision was overturned on appeal. On further appeal by the resident, *held*, the draftsman of s 26 did not mean that homes in the private sector might be included in the collective of homes that the authority had to provide. Instead, the concept of 'arrangement' used to define the authority's duty included arrangements with the private sector, thereby extending the meaning of the concept by which the authority's duty was defined. Any arrangements falling within that definition would satisfy the authority's duty. Accordingly, the appeal would be dismissed.

R v Wandsworth London Borough Council, ex p Beckwith [1996] 1 All ER 129 (House of Lords: Lords Goff of Chieveley, Griffiths, Jauncey of Tullichettle, Browne-Wilkinson and Hoffmann). Decision of Court of Appeal (1995) Times, 29 June, affirmed.

2759 Retirement benefit—graduated retirement pension—up-rating

The Social Security (Graduated Retirement Benefit) Amendment Regulations 1995, SI 1995/2606 (in force on 1 November 1995), further amend the 1978 Regulations, SI 1978/393, so as to (1) provide for the annual up-rating of graduated retirement benefit, in particular for additional graduated retirement benefit derived from the contributions of a deceased spouse to be included in the sum up-rated, and (2) provide that a person who has elected to defer his retirement pension or who has withdrawn his claim is not to be treated as entitled to a retirement pension for the purpose of enabling him to receive a graduated retirement pension on its own.

2760 Retirement pension—entitlement—qualifying periods of employment—migrant worker—discrimination

See *McLachlan v Caisse Nationale d'Assurance Vieillesse des Travailleurs Salariés de la Région d'Ile-de-France*, para 3198.

2761 Retirement pension—increase in respect of dependent spouse—sex discrimination

See *Bramhill v Chief Adjudication Officer*, para 3200 and *Van Munster v Rijksdienst voor Pensioenen*, para 3199.

2762 Social fund—award—recovery—deduction from income support payable to bankrupt

Scotland
The Social Security Administration Act 1992, s 78(1) provides that a social fund award which is repayable must be recovered by the Secretary of State, and s 78(2) provides that he may do so by deduction from prescribed benefits.

The applicant, who was entitled to income support, was made bankrupt. Her estate was sequestrated, but she continued to be entitled to income support which was paid to her rather than to her trustee in bankruptcy. The Secretary of State sought to recover social fund loans which had been made to the applicant prior to her bankruptcy by making deductions from her income support. The applicant successfully applied for judicial review, arguing that the common law rule that a creditor was not entitled to retain from a bankrupt after the date of sequestration sums in compensation for, or set-off against, sums due by the bankrupt prior to the date of sequestration, also applied to social security legislation. On the Secretary of State's appeal, *held*, the common law rule on which the applicant had relied usually applied in the context of the relationship between a trustee and a creditor where the creditor sought to exercise his right of set-off, and the trustee sought to enforce a debt due to the estate on behalf of all creditors. The rule did not apply in the context of a relationship such as that between the applicant and the respondent, as the right to receive income support after the date of sequestration did not pass to the trustee with the rest of the applicant's estate. Moreover, the respondent was not trying to exercise a right of set-off with the applicant's trustees so as to obtain an unfair preference in relation to other creditors, but was exercising a right given by the 1992 Act, s 78(2). As the common law rule did not apply to social security legislation, the respondent was entitled to recover social fund loans by making deductions from the applicant's income support. Accordingly, the appeal would be allowed.

Mulvey v Secretary of State for Social Security 1995 SLT 1064 (Inner House).

2763 Social fund—cold weather payments

The Social Fund Cold Weather Payments (General) Amendment Regulations 1995, SI 1995/2620 (in force on 1 November 1995), further amend the 1988 Regulations, SI 1988/1724, so as to (1) increase the amount payable in respect of each period of cold weather, from £7 to £8.50, and (2) make changes to the areas linked to national climatological message stations by way of Post Office postcodes, as set out in the 1988 Regulations, Sch 1.

2764 Social fund—community care grant—refusal—review by social fund inspector— matters to be taken into consideration

The Social Security Administration Act 1992, s 66(4) provides that on a review, a social fund inspector has the power to (a) confirm the determination made by a social fund officer, (b) make any determination which a social fund officer could have made, and (c) refer the matter to the social fund officer for determination.

The applicant applied for a community care grant for several items, including in respect of heating. Following the refusal of her application by a social fund officer, the decision was reviewed by a social fund inspector who confirmed the refusal. The inspector reached her decision on the basis that changes in the law made between the date that the application was first refused and the date on which she reviewed the refusal were such that heating was excluded from the matters for which a grant could be awarded. On her application for judicial review of the inspector's decision, the applicant argued that the inspector should have applied the law in force at the time that the initial decision was taken. The inspector argued that she was required to apply the law in force at the time that she reviewed the initial decision. *Held*, on a proper construction of the 1992 Act, s 66(4)(b) did not refer to the particular officer who took the decision under review by an inspector, but to a notional officer. Moreover, it could be interpreted as referring to either a decision that an officer could have made 'at the time of the determination under review', or to a decision that the officer could have made 'if he had now been making his determination'. The latter interpretation was to be preferred, as it did not offend against the presumption against retrospectivity. As such, s 66(4) obliged an inspector to have full regard to any changes in the law at the time that she made her decision and not to the law as it stood at the time of the officer's determination. Here, the inspector was required to take account of the fact that heating was excluded from the matters in respect of which a grant could be awarded and, accordingly, the application would be dismissed.

R v Social Fund Inspector, ex p Ledicott (1995) Times, 24 May (Queen's Bench Division: Sedley J).

2765 Social fund—funeral expenses

The Social Fund Maternity and Funeral Expenses (General) Amendment Regulations 1995, SI 1995/1229 (in force on 5 June 1995), further amend the 1987 Regulations, SI 1987/481, so as to (1) redefine 'close relative' and 'partner', (2) limit funeral directors' fees to £500, and limit the costs that may be claimed by a person who is not a funeral director but who arranges the funeral, and (3) specify the expenses in respect of which funeral payments may be made. The amendments do not apply to deaths which occur before 5 June 1995 where the funeral takes place on or before 5 September 1995.

2766 Statutory sick pay—percentage threshold

The Statutory Sick Pay Percentage Threshold Order 1995, SI 1995/512 (in force on 6 April 1995), provides that an employer is entitled to recover payments of statutory sick pay which exceed 13 per cent of the amount of his liability for Class 1 contributions payments in any income tax month. The order sets out the payments of statutory sick pay which must be excluded in calculating the amount to which an employer is entitled, and the entitlement is recoverable by making deductions from his contributions payments for that month or for any following income tax month within six years from the end of the tax year in which he became entitled to recover that amount. The Secretary of State must repay the amount that an employer is entitled to deduct if it exceeds the amount of his contributions payments.

The Statutory Sick Pay Percentage Threshold Order 1995 (Consequential) Regulations 1995, SI 1995/513 (in force on 6 April 1995), are consequential on the coming into force of the 1995 Order supra. The regulations provide for savings in respect of regulations which provide for relief for small employers who have made payments of statutory sick pay. Additionally, a new provision is inserted into the Statutory Sick Pay (General) Regulations 1982, SI 1982/894, which provides that an employer who elects to be treated as different employers for income tax purposes is to be treated as one employer for the purposes of provisions relating to the recovery of statutory sick pay.

2767 Training for work—payments

The Training for Work (Miscellaneous Provisions) Order 1995, SI 1995/1780 (in force on 15 August 1995), replaces the 1983 Order, SI 1993/348, and provides that for the purposes of the

Social Security Contributions and Benefits Act 1992, Pt I and specified subordinate legislation, a person using facilities provided under the training for work programme and receiving training allowances in connection with the use of the facilities, is to be treated as participating in arrangements for training under the Employment Training Act 1973, s 2. Any payment made to such a person in connection with his use of those facilities, is to be treated in the same way as a payment made in respect of such training. However, a person who uses facilities provided under the training for work programme and receives remuneration instead of training allowances in connection with the use of the facilities, is to be treated as employed by that employer. Any payment made to such a person by the employer in connection with his use of those facilities, is to be treated as earnings.

2768　Unemployment benefit—entitlement—days of unemployment

The Social Security (Unemployment, Sickness and Invalidity Benefit) Amendment Regulations 1995, SI 1995/2192 (in force on 25 September 1995), further amend the 1983 Regulations, SI 1983/1598, so that (1) where a person is on standby for employment in manning or launching a lifeboat or for the performance of duty as a part-time member of a fire brigade, any earnings derived from a retainer payable in respect of the hours when he is on standby are to be disregarded for the purposes of treating a day as a day of unemployment, and (2) the reference to a part-time fireman is substituted by a reference to a part-time member of a fire brigade.

2769　Unemployment benefit—entitlement—Venture Trust trainees

The Social Security (Unemployment, Sickness and Invalidity Benefit) Amendment (No 2) Regulations 1995, SI 1995/3152 (in force on 1 January 1996), further amend the 1983 Regulations, SI 1983/1598, so as to provide that Venture Trust trainees are available for, and actively seeking, employment up to a period of five weeks in a year.

2770　Welfare foods—dried milk

The Welfare Food (Amendment) Regulations 1995, SI 1995/1143 (in force on 22 May 1995), further amend the 1988 Regulations, SI 1988/536, so as to (1) increase the price paid for dried milk by persons entitled to purchase it, to £3.55, (2) add two more brands of dried milk to the list of those which may be purchased, and (3) take account of a change of manufacturer of two specified dried milk products.

2771　Welfare services—disabled persons—matters to be taken into account in assessing needs

A local authority made plans for the provision of services for the disabled on the basis of expected government funding. Following the withdrawal of the funding, the local authority decided to give greater priority to the more seriously disabled. The applicants were consequently informed that the services provided to them under the Chronically Sick and Disabled Persons Act 1970, s 2(1) would be reduced, although the local authority did not reassess the applicants' individual needs in light of the revised policy before reaching that decision. On their application for judicial review, *held*, a local authority was entitled to take account of its resources when assessing a disabled person's needs and when deciding whether or not to make arrangements to meet those needs. However, a local authority was not acting reasonably if it relied on the fact of a lack of resources as the reason for deciding that arrangements did not need to be made to meet a disabled person's needs. Instead, it was necessary to balance the needs of a particular person against the needs of another person and available resources. Once a local authority decided that it was necessary to make arrangements, it was under an absolute duty to the person concerned to carry them out, and the obligation was not dependent on the availability of resources. In the instant cases, the local authority should have reassessed the applicants' needs taking account of all the relevant factors, including its reduced resources. As the local authority had failed to do so and had treated the loss of resources as the sole factor to be taken into account, the decision to cut the services provided to the applicants was unlawful. Accordingly, the application would be granted.

　　R v Gloucestershire County Council, ex p Mahfood; R v Same, ex p Barry; R v Same, ex p Grinham; R v Same, ex p Dartnell; R v Islington London Borough Council, ex p McMillan (1995) Times, 21 June, Independent, 20 June (Queen's Bench Division: McCowan LJ and Waller J).

2772　Widow's benefit—entitlement

The Social Security (Widow's Benefit and Retirement Pensions) Amendment Regulations 1995, SI 1995/74 (in force on 10 February 1995), further amend the 1979 Regulations, SI

1979/642, so as to provide that a voidable marriage, in respect of which a decree absolute of nullity of marriage was granted before 1 August 1971, is to be treated as if it was a valid marriage terminated by divorce at the date of annulment.

2773 Workmen's compensation—pneumoconiosis—amount of payments

The Pneumoconiosis etc (Workers' Compensation) (Payment of Claims) (Amendment) Regulations 1995, SI 1995/1514 (in force on 1 July 1995), further amend the 1988 Regulations, SI 1988/668, so as to increase by 2.2 per cent the amount of payments made under the Pneumoconiosis etc (Workers' Compensation) Act 1979, in any case in which a person first becomes entitled to a payment on or after the coming into force of these regulations.

2774 Workmen's compensation—supplementation

The Workmen's Compensation (Supplementation) (Amendment) Scheme 1995, SI 1995/746 (in force on 12 April 1995), further amends the 1982 Scheme, SI 1982/1489, by making adjustments to the lower rates of incapacity allowance in consequence of the increase in the maximum rate of that allowance.

SOLICITORS

Halsbury's Laws of England (4th edn) Vol 44(1) (reissue), paras 1–800

2775 Articles

A Brave New World, John Peysner and Paul Balen (on conditional fees): LS Gaz, 31 Aug 1995, p 20

Conditional Fees: Investing in the Future, Paul Balen: 139 SJ 678

Contingency Fees, Clive Boxer: 139 SJ 704

The Case for a National Legal Service, Bob Hoyle: 145 NLJ 189

Equal and Decent Treatment, Henry Hodge (on the Law Society's anti-discrimination measures): 145 NLJ 303

Exploding the Myths of Conditional Fees, Barjinder Sahota: 145 NLJ 592

Forgery and Property: Effects and Remedies, Josephine Hayes (on *Penn v Bristol & West Building Society* (1995) Times, 19 June (para 2783)): 139 SJ 716

Insurance Cover for Redundancy and Sickness, Michael J Wilson: 139 SJ 722

A Lack of Authority, Daniel Worsley (on *Penn v Bristol & West Building Society* (1995) Times, 19 June (para 2783)): LS Gaz, 21 June 1995, p 23

Lack of Good Will, Andrew Paton (on *White v Jones* [1995] 1 All ER 691, HL (para 2780)): LS Gaz, 1 March 1995, p 15

The Legal Services Ombudsman: Form Versus Function? Rhoda James and Mary Seneviratne: 58 MLR 187

The Liability of Lawyers as Suppliers of Services, Mario Monti: 139 SJ 1473

Mortgagees and Purchasers: Separate Solicitors? C I Howells: 145 NLJ 193

The Role of the Legal Services Ombudsman, Michael Barnes: 145 NLJ 930

Small Practices, Hugh Howard (on advance fee fraud): 139 SJ 137

Soliciting Equality—The Way Forward, Clare McGlynn (on discrimination against women solicitors): 145 NLJ 1065

Solicitors and VAT, Stanley Dencher: 139 SJ 528

Solicitors' Liability in Negligence to Third Parties—A Resurrection, Ian Hardcastle: 15 BLRev 255

Solicitors' Professional Negligence, Christian Kessel (on *White v Jones* [1995] 1 All ER 691, HL (para 2780)): 145 NLJ 499, 537

Tort or Contract? Clive Boxer (on *Henderson v Merrett Syndicate* [1994] 3 WLR 761 (1994 Abr para 1687)): 139 SJ 136

Woolf's Justice, Ramnik Shah (on Lord Woolf's Inquiry): 145 NLJ 147

2776 Breach of trust—damages for breach—measure of damages

See *Target Holdings Ltd v Redferns (a firm)*, para 2981.

2777 Costs—pre-legal aid certificate costs—contract with client for costs

In an appeal to review taxation of a successful plaintiff's costs, it has been held that a contractual retainer which purports to make a plaintiff potentially liable to his solicitors for their pre-legal aid certificate costs over and above the green form costs is illegal. It is a sham to enable the solicitor to recover costs incurred outwith the green form scheme from the defendant and, in seeking to create a potential primary liability upon the client for his solicitor's costs, is a device to enable the solicitor to recover costs from the defendant if the plaintiff is unsuccessful.

Joyce v Kammac (1988) Ltd [1996] 1 All ER 923 (Queen's Bench Division: Morland J).

2778 Discipline—intervention in solicitor's practice—dishonesty—circumstances in which intervention takes place

The Solicitors Act 1974, Sch 1, para 1(1)(a) provides that the Law Society may exercise its powers of intervention in a solicitor's practice where the Council of the Law Society has reason to suspect dishonesty on the part of a solicitor in connection with that solicitor's practice.

It has been held that the word 'dishonesty' in the 1974 Act, Sch 1, para 1(1)(a) is not limited to stealing or the occasioning of financial harm and extends to the making of false entries in a solicitor's records.

Re a Solicitor (No S2700 of 1995) (1995) Times, 11 July (Chancery Division: Blackburne J).

2779 Discipline—intervention in solicitor's practice—dishonesty—validity of intervention notice

Under the Solicitors Act 1974, Sch 1, Pt I, para 1(1)(a), the powers to intervene in a solicitor's practice are exercisable where the Law Society has reason to suspect dishonesty on the part of a solicitor in connection with that solicitor's practice.

A solicitor was found to have a shortfall in his client account and the Law Society resolved to order that moneys held by the solicitor should be vested in it. A notice of intervention was sent to the solicitor stating, pursuant to the 1974 Act, Sch 1, Pt I, para 1(1)(a), that it had reason to suspect dishonesty on the solicitor's part. The solicitor's application to have the notice withdrawn was dismissed at first instance. On appeal, he submitted that when a solicitor was given a notice of intervention based on the grounds set out in para 1(1)(a) he had a right to be given, either in the notice or contemporaneously with it, particulars of the suspected dishonesty and the reasons for suspecting it, in default of which the notice was invalid and should be withdrawn. *Held*, in *Yogarajah v Law Society* (unreported, 21 May 1982), the judge rejected a solicitor's submission that the rules of natural justice required that not only was he to be given notice of the case against him, but also a fair opportunity to meet it before the notice was given. Further, the judge held that Sch 1 provided a sensible, statutory scheme which enabled the society to act swiftly when the possibility of mischief became apparent while also enabling the solicitor against whom such action was taken to apply as swiftly to the court to obtain a suspension of such activity on the society's behalf. He saw no necessity for complicating the scheme and depriving it of its swiftness of action by the introduction of the concept of natural justice in a situation where it did not sensibly fit. For those reasons and on a careful construction of the provisions of Sch 1, the court in the present case found that there was no requirement at the time a notice was given for the solicitor to be given particulars of the suspected dishonesty or the reasons for suspecting it. Accordingly, the appeal would be dismissed.

Giles v Law Society (1995) Times, 20 October (Court of Appeal: Nourse and Ward LJJ and Sedley J).

2780 Duty of care—failure to prepare new will—duty to intended beneficiary

After a family argument, the testator instructed the defendant solicitors to draw up a will disinheriting his two daughters. Following a reconciliation, the testator asked the defendants to prepare a new will, under which the daughters were to be the main beneficiaries. The defendants negligently delayed the preparation of the new will and the testator died before it was executed. The daughters brought proceedings against the defendants for negligence on the basis that the defendants' failure to draw up the new will resulted in their not receiving their intended legacies. On the defendants' appeal against a decision that they were in breach of their duty of care to the daughters, *held* (Lords Keith and Mustill dissenting), the nature of the transaction was such that if the solicitors were negligent and their negligence did not come to light until after the death of the testator, there would be no remedy for the ensuing loss unless the intended beneficiaries could claim. In such cases, a remedy under the principle in *Hedley Byrne & Co Ltd v Heller & Partners Ltd* [1964] AC 465, HL was available on the basis that the assumption of responsibility by a solicitor towards his client should be held in law to extend to the intended beneficiary who, as the solicitor could reasonably foresee, might as a result of the solicitor's negligence, be deprived of his intended legacy in circumstances in which neither the testator nor his estate would have a remedy against the solicitor. Accordingly, the appeal would be dismissed.

White v Jones [1995] 1 All ER 691 (House of Lords: Lords Keith of Kinkel, Goff of Chieveley, Browne-Wilkinson, Mustill and Nolan). Decision of Court of Appeal [1993] 3 All ER 481 (1993 Abr para 2423) affirmed.

2781 Duty of care—Law Society—investigation of complaints

A solicitor arranged a mortgage for the plaintiff, secured on the plaintiff's home, but did not disclose that her husband, a partner in the firm, was a proprietor of the lender, nor that she was acting for both parties to the mortgage. The plaintiff failed to meet the repayments on the loan and the solicitor's firm, acting on behalf of the lenders, brought proceedings against the plaintiff and obtained possession of her home. The plaintiff wrote a letter of complaint about the solicitor's conduct to the defendant, which replied that the firm had a duty to act for their client, the lender, and owed no duty to a third party. The plaintiff pointed out that she was also a client, but the defendant merely referred her to the courts for redress. In response to further letters from the plaintiff, the defendant stated that, in the absence of misconduct, it would not get involved. A report subsequently commissioned by the defendant concluded that the solicitor's failure to reveal her husband's interest in the lenders was conduct unbefitting a solicitor. The plaintiff brought an action for damages against the defendant for negligence over its handling of her complaints. On her appeal against the dismissal of the action, *held*, to establish a cause of action the plaintiff had to prove that the loss of her home had been caused by a breach of duty by the defendant. The judge at first instance had held that the loss was caused by a failure to find alternative finance to pay off her creditors, and the court would not interfere with that finding. The function of a regulatory body such as the defendant was to investigate complaints and not to relieve the distress felt by a complainant, although it might afford some satisfaction if the complaint was proved. If the defendant had owed a duty of care to the plaintiff, which it was not necessary to decide, it was not a duty to give peace of mind or freedom from distress. The defendant had no prospect of showing that a failure by the defendant to investigate her complaints properly or timeously was capable of sounding in damages. Accordingly, the appeal would be dismissed.

Wood v Law Society (1995) Times, 2 March, Independent, 1 March (Court of Appeal: Leggatt, Aldous and Hutchison LJJ).

2782 Duty of care—negligent advice in take-over—loss of chance dependent on hypothetical action of third party

The plaintiffs wished to expand their business by 'cherry-picking' businesses and properties belonging to another group of companies. Covenants against alienation and planning consents personal to the subsidiary company in which some of the properties were vested prevented those properties from being conveyed directly to the plaintiffs. The defendant solicitors advised that to surmount those problems the plaintiffs could acquire all of the shares in the subsidiary company, hiving off to another company the unwanted properties and liabilities. A draft agreement was sent to the solicitors acting for the group of companies which contained a warranty to the effect that the group had no existing or contingent liabilities in respect of any former or current interest in any property. The draft agreement was returned with the warranty deleted and a clause in its place which provided for an adjustment of the purchase price in accordance with any liabilities found to exist after an examination of the subsidiary company's accounts. The sale proceeded on that basis. A claim was later brought by the lessor of a property which the subsidiary company had leased as first tenant before assigning the lease to a sub-lessee who had defaulted made it apparent that the subsidiary company had first tenant liabilities which led to claims being made against the plaintiffs. The plaintiffs were unable to claim damages under the adjustment of purchase price clause and thus brought an action for damages against the defendants to recover as damages substantial losses resulting from the defaults. On the trial of a preliminary issue as to liability the judge held that the defendants were in breach of duty in failing to advise of the effect of deleting the warranty; on the issue of causation, that if they had given advice as to first tenant liability the plaintiffs would have taken steps to protect themselves; and that on the balance of probabilities the group of companies would have offered some form of protection against first tenant liability if asked. The defendants appealed, arguing that the plaintiffs had not proved on the balance of probabilities that the group of companies would have accepted the risk of first tenant liability or that the plaintiffs would not have proceeded with the deal if they had refused to accept liability. *Held*, where the plaintiff's loss resulting from the defendant's negligence depended on the hypothetical action of a third party then that was an issue of quantification of damages rather than causation. Thus, once the plaintiffs had shown on the balance of probabilities that they would have taken action to avoid the risk, they did not have to go on to prove on the balance of probabilities that the third party would have taken action to avoid risk to the plaintiff. Instead the plaintiff would succeed if he showed that there was a substantial and not merely speculative chance that the third party would have so acted. The evaluation of a substantial chance was a matter of damages for the judge determining quantum in the light of further evidence. Accordingly, the appeal would be dismissed.

Allied Maples Group Ltd v Simmons & Simmons (a firm) [1995] 4 All ER 907 (Court of Appeal: Stuart-Smith, Hobhouse and Millett LJJ).

2783 Duty of care—sale of property—failure to ascertain instructions of co-owner— husband attempting to sell house without wife's knowledge.

A wife applied for declarations relating to the purported contract of sale of a house owned jointly by herself and her husband. The husband had instructed a firm of solicitors to act in the sale of the house which was subject to a mortgage. The proposed purchaser was an accomplice of his who had obtained a mortgage from a building society, itself instructed by the same firm of solicitors. The deeds for the house showed that the wife was a co-owner yet the husband's solicitors did not contact her to obtain her instructions. The husband forged the wife's signature on an alleged contract of sale and the building society advanced the purchase price to his accomplice. *Held*, the wife's beneficial interest remained unaffected by the forged transaction as did the legal estate vested in the husband and wife. Although the wife was not a client of the solicitors she was necessarily within their contemplation when they received the title deeds and her interest as co-owner was sufficiently proximate to the transaction for them to owe her a duty of care. Thus, their failing to ascertain her instructions meant that they were liable in negligence to the wife. The solicitors were also liable to the building society which had provided the mortgage to the purchaser because they had represented that they had the authority to act for the vendors in the transaction.

Penn v Bristol and West Building Society [1995] 2 FLR 938 (Chancery Division: Judge Kolbert). *White v Jones* [1995] 1 All ER 691, HL (para 2780) followed.

2784 Duty of care—sale of property—failure to inform mortgagee of material facts

A firm of solicitors was instructed by a building society in respect of an offer of advance made to a purchaser. The solicitors were instructed to advise the building society of any matters which might prejudice its advance and security, and of matters which were at variance with the mortgage offer. Although the solicitors became aware that the property was to be sold to a company owned by a third party at a price less than the advance before being sold to the purchaser, they failed to disclose this to the building society. The solicitors were similarly instructed in relation to an offer of advance made to the third party in respect of another property, but failed to notify the building society that the third party had already paid a sum of money to the vendor of that property. When the respective purchasers defaulted on their mortgage payments, the building society claimed damages against the solicitors for breach of contract and breach of trust. *Held*, having regard to the terms of their instructions, the solicitors should have disclosed to the building society the matters relating to the first transaction, as they were relevant to the society's security in respect of both transactions, and the advances would not have been made had the building society been aware of all the facts. Since the solicitors' liability was contractual and was not dependent on negligence, the contributory negligence of the valuers in relation to the first property did not provide them with a defence. Accordingly, the society was entitled to damages for breach of contract. The solicitors had held the advance on trust, to be applied in accordance with the building society's instructions. In paying the advance before notifying the building society of relevant matters and obtaining its consent, the solicitors had also acted in breach of trust and were therefore liable to repay the amount of the advance.

Bristol and West Building Society v A Kramer & Co (1995) Independent, 26 January (Chancery Division: Blackburne J).

2785　Duty of care—sale of property—solicitor acting for lender and borrower—failure to provide lender with material information

The defendant solicitors acted for both lender and borrower in a purchase of property valued at £199,000. The plaintiff lenders were to advance £180,150 to the borrower, to be secured by way of a charge. The purchase price of the property was £220,000. The defendants learned that the property was the subject of two recent sales, the most recent, simultaneous with the sale to the borrower, being for a purchase price of £150,000. The defendants communicated that information to the borrower but not to the plaintiffs. The judge found that if the plaintiffs had been informed, they would have arranged for a second valuation and the parties agreed that if this had been done, the figure would have been sufficiently different to have caused the plaintiffs to withdraw their offer to the borrower. Judgment on the issue of liability was accordingly given in favour of the plaintiffs. On the defendants' appeal, *held*, there was no principle that any information which a solicitor in these circumstances gave to one party should always be given to the other. Where a solicitor acting for a borrower and lender received information common to both, the question of whether it should be passed on and to whom depended entirely on the relevant interest of each client which the solicitor was engaged to serve. Neither was the duty owed by the defendants to the plaintiffs simply to report to them on title. If in the course of investigating title a solicitor discovered facts which a reasonably competent solicitor would realise might have a material bearing on the value of the lender's security, or on some ingredient of the lending decision, then it was his duty to point that out. The present transaction might have been explained by special circumstances, but an obvious alternative explanation was that the property had been overvalued. The defendants should have alerted themselves to that possibility and to the need to inform the plaintiffs. The appeal would accordingly be dismissed, although the judgment of the court and of the judge at first instance was closely dependent on the facts and did not extend the duties to which solicitors were subject.

Mortgage Express Ltd v Bowerman & Partners (a Firm) [1995] QB 375 (Court of Appeal: Sir Thomas Bingham MR, Millett and Schiemann LJJ). Decision of Arden J [1994] 34 EG 116 (1994 Abr para 2655) affirmed in part. For proceedings as to the measure of damages in this case, see *Banque Bruxelles Lambert SA v Eagle Star Insurance Co Ltd* [1995] 2 All ER 769, CA.

2786　Duty of care—wrongful termination of retainer—client making application in person following termination—application defective—whether termination cause or occasion of loss

A solicitor acting for a client in ancillary relief proceedings against the client's former husband was instructed that the client had no foreseeable intention of remarrying. The client was aware that an application for relief had to be lodged before any remarriage. When the solicitor wrongfully terminated the retainer, the client lodged her own application for relief. However, the application was defective and before it could be remedied she remarried, effectively barring herself from making a claim for financial provision. The client brought an action for damages against the solicitor for breach of contract in negligence for an alleged improper unilateral termination of the retainer. At first instance, the judge found in the client's favour that there was a causal relationship between the solicitor's wrongful termination and the client's subsequent actions, and he applied judicial common sense following *Galoo Ltd v Bright Grahame Murray*. On appeal, the solicitor claimed the breach of contract did not cause the loss of the client's right to seek financial relief for herself, nor was such loss foreseeable from the breach. The client contended that if the solicitor had continued to act, she would not have acted on her own negligently. *Held*, the test in *Galoo* was an unsure guide in seeking to ascertain whether a particular breach of a duty of care which resulted in loss was to be judged in law as having caused it. That depended essentially on whether the breach relied on was the effective cause of the loss or was merely an occurrence without which no loss would have been sustained. In the present case, the breach of contract afforded the client the opportunity to act negligently. She took that opportunity and suffered damage. The solicitor's negligence was the occasion of the damage, not the cause of it. The loss of the client's right to claim was due to her failure to lodge a correct application and her remarrying before its rectification. The solicitor could not reasonably have been expected to foresee those matters and, accordingly, the appeal would be allowed.

Young v Purdy (1995) Times, 7 November (Court of Appeal: Leggatt, Morritt and Schiemann LJJ). *Galoo Ltd v Bright Grahame Murray* [1995] 1 All ER 16, CA (1994 Abr para 2036) considered.

2787 Duty to client—duty to disclose information—disclosure of privileged documents—documents mistakenly disclosed by opponents

The *Guide to the Professional Conduct of Solicitors* (6th edition, 1993), para 16.05 provides that where it is obvious that privileged documents have been mistakenly disclosed to a solicitor, the solicitor should immediately refuse to read the documents, inform the other side and return the documents. Before informing the other side, the solicitor should consider whether to obtain instructions from the client, and if deciding to do so should advise the client that the court will probably grant an injunction to prevent the overt use of any information gleaned from the documents and that both the client and the solicitor might find costs awarded against them in respect of such an injunction.

A junior clerk in the chambers of the plaintiff's counsel mistakenly sent papers relating to the plaintiff's case to the offices of the defendant's solicitor. The defendant's solicitor realised the error and, in accordance with the *Guide*, obtained instructions from his client and warned the client about the possibility of an injunction being granted. The client instructed the solicitor to read the papers, and he duly did so before returning them to the plaintiff's solicitors and saying they had been sent in error. The solicitor and his client offered undertakings that neither of them would make any use of any information derived from any of the papers and that there would be delivery up of any note that had been prepared from them. However, they refused to agree that neither the solicitor nor his firm would continue to act for the client in the action. The plaintiff sought an injunction restraining them from acting. *Held*, it offended elementary notions of fairness and justice if the client, having knowingly taken advantage of mistaken delivery of counsel's papers, could nevertheless continue to have the services in the action of people who, having read them all, had a very accurate perception of the advice given to the plaintiff. To deny the plaintiff an injunction would risk undermining the safeguard in *Ridehalgh v Horsefield* [1994] 3 All ER 848, CA (1994 Abr para 2188) that parties had to be free to unburden themselves to their legal advisers without fearing that what they said might provide ammunition for their opponent. Accordingly, the injunction would be granted.

Blackburne J observed that it was surprising that para 16.05 should, after stating that the solicitor should cease to read the documents, inform the other side and return them, go on to state that, before informing the other side, the solicitor should consider whether to obtain instructions from his client.

Ablitt v Mills & Reeve (a firm) (1995) Times, 25 October (Chancery Division: Blackburne J).

2788 Fees—conditional fee agreements

The Conditional Fee Agreements Order 1995, SI 1995/1674 (in force on 5 July 1995), provides that, for the purposes of the Courts and Legal Services Act 1990, s 58, the conditional fee agreements relating to the following specified proceedings are not unenforceable by reason only of their being conditional fee agreements: (1) proceedings for personal injury, (2) proceedings by companies in administration or winding up or by their administrators or liquidators and by trustees in bankruptcy, and (3) proceedings before the European Commission of Human Rights and the European Court of Human Rights. Proceedings are not specified for these purposes where a client is legally-aided. The maximum permitted percentage by which fees may be increased in respect of the specified proceedings is 100 per cent.

The Conditional Fee Agreements Regulations 1995, SI 1995/1675 (in force on 5 July 1995), prescribe the requirements with which an agreement between a client and his legal representative must comply in order to be a conditional fee agreement for the purposes of the Courts and Legal Services Act 1990, s 58. The regulations also apply, with modifications, to agreements between a legal representative and an additional representative (as defined).

2789 Fees—contingency fees—agreement—enforceability

See *Aratra Potato Co Ltd v Taylor Joynson Garrett (a firm)*, para 668.

2790 Law Society—duty of care—investigation of complaints

See *Wood v The Law Society*, para 2781.

2791 Negligence—assessment of damages

See DAMAGES AND COMPENSATION.

2792 Partner—partner's previous firm acting for one party—partner later acting for opposing party—risk of communicating confidential information

The defendant had formerly been a partner in the intellectual property department of a firm of solicitors which acted on behalf of the plaintiffs in patent litigation. The defendant was never involved in the litigation. He left the firm to work for another and two years later one of the plaintiffs' opponents in the patent litigation wished to instruct the defendant. The plaintiffs sought to restrain him from acting on the ground that, although he had no present recollection of any communicated information, his recollection might be triggered by future events as the litigation proceeded. The defendant maintained that he was possessed of no confidential information belonging to the plaintiffs and should be available to serve his new client. *Held*, the defendant had to show that there was no reasonable prospect of any conflict between his duty to his previous client, and his personal interest in obtaining the new retainer and his duty to his new client. Accordingly he had to show not merely that he was not in possession of any relevant confidential information but that there was no real risk that he had such information. On the facts in the present case there was no real risk that he possessed such information. The plaintiffs' evidence had only suggested the possibility of such communication. Further, the overwhelming probability was that if any confidential information was ever communicated to the former partner, with the lapse of time, the progress of the proceedings and the disclosures in evidence and on discovery in the proceedings and having regard to the highly technical issues, there could be no real risk that such information would any longer be confidential, relevant and recallable. Accordingly, the grant of the injunction would be refused.

Re a Firm of Solicitors [1995] 3 All ER 482 (Chancery Division: Lightman J).

2793 Remuneration—lien for costs

See LIEN.

SPECIFIC PERFORMANCE

Halsbury's Laws of England (4th edn) Vol 44(1) (reissue), paras 801–1000

2794 Scope of remedy—'keep open' covenant in lease—lease of supermarket premises

A lease of supermarket premises constituting the anchor unit in a shopping centre contained a covenant by the tenant to keep the premises open for retail trade during the usual hours of business in the locality (the 'keep open' covenant). The store traded at a loss and the tenant owner decided to sell it. The landlord asked it to keep the store open until an assignee of the lease could be found, being anxious about the effect of closure on the rest of the centre. However, the owner closed the store and stripped it. The landlord obtained summary judgment against the owner for breach of covenant and an order for damages to be assessed. However, the judge refused an order for specific performance requiring the owner to keep the store open for the remainder of the term of the lease. On the landlord's appeal, *held* (Millett LJ dissenting), the case was one in which it was proper to grant specific performance. If the court followed the usual practice of not granting mandatory injunctions requiring persons to carry on business, the result would be that the common form of words of the covenant would rarely, if ever, be construed as meaning what they said. If the parties wanted to contract that a failure to keep open would sound only in damages, they were at liberty to do so. But where a responsible and substantial company such as the owner had undertaken to keep one of its shops open for a stipulated period, it should be held to its bargain. The owner was provided with a means of escape by the provision for assignment of the lease, and it had stripped the store at its own peril. The landlord would have considerable difficulty in proving its loss, and an award of damages would be unlikely to compensate it fully. There was no reason why the court's willingness to grant specific performance should not be affected by a sense of fair dealing. Accordingly, the appeal would be allowed.

Co-operative Insurance Society Ltd v Argyll Stores (Holdings) Ltd [1995] 09 EG 128 (Court of Appeal: Leggatt, Roch and Millett LJJ).

STAMP DUTIES AND STAMP DUTY RESERVE TAX

Halsbury's Laws of England (4th edn) Vol 44(1) (reissue), paras 1001–1200

2795 Articles

Avoiding Stamp Duties on Transfers of Shares, G R Bretten: 139 SJ 1232
Stamp Duty: The Associated Companies Exemption, G R Bretten: 139 SJ 904
Stamping New Ground, Richard Pincher (on uncertainties in the field of stamp duty): Tax Journal, Issue 314, p 10

2796 Conveyance—agreement for sale—agreement for sale of equitable interest in property

The vendor, a partnership, carried on the business of farming on land which it owned absolutely. It agreed to sell the business as a going concern for a consideration which represented the aggregated value of the property and the other assets of the business. By the deed of agreement, the sale and purchase were be completed immediately upon exchange of the agreement, at which time the vendor was to deliver to the purchaser such of the assets as were capable of being delivered, such documents as were required by the purchaser to complete the sale and purchase of the assets, including an assignment of goodwill and book debts, and all title deeds in relation to the property. The vendor was to hold the land as nominee for the purchaser and execute such assignments, transfers or conveyances of the property to such persons as the purchaser might require. In due course, it was proposed that the land would be sold to a third party either as a whole or in parcels and that stamp duty would be incurred by the sub-purchasers. The Commissioners contended that the deed was an agreement for the sale of an equitable interest in property which was chargeable under the Stamp Act 1891, s 59(1) with the same ad valorem duty as if it were an actual conveyance on sale of the equitable estate in the property or, alternatively, whether it was a 'conveyance on sale' of an equitable interest in the property within s 54 as it vested in the purchaser an equitable interest in the property which was intended to be the vendor's only document of title. The vendor contended that the deed was an agreement for the sale of the legal estate in freehold land and was not within s 59(1) and was not a conveyance within s 54(1). *Held*, an executory agreement was completed when the parties performed their obligations under it. Following completion and the delivery of the assets and the requisite documentation, there was nothing more to be done under the deed and there was nothing capable of being specifically performed; the vendor held the land for the purchaser as a bare trustee and not as a constructive trustee. The vendor was required to execute such assignments, transfers or conveyances of the property to such persons as the purchaser might require but it did not have the right, as a vendor under an uncompleted contract would have, of requiring the purchaser to take a conveyance and so relieve it of the potentially burdensome legal title. Accordingly, while it made no practical difference whether liability arose under s 54 or s 59(1), strictly the agreement operated as a transfer of the equitable estate in the freehold property, and not as an agreement for the sale of the equitable estate. The agreement was chargeable to ad valorem duty under s 54 as a transfer of an equitable interest in the land.

Peter Bone Ltd v IRC [1995] STC 921 (Chancery Division: Sir John Vinelott).

2797 Finance Act 1995

See para 2489.

2798 Stamp duty reserve tax—exemption—Tradepoint Investment Exchange

The Stamp Duty Reserve Tax (Tradepoint) Regulations 1995, SI 1995/2051 (in force on 25 August 1995), exempt from stamp duty reserve tax certain agreements to transfer equity securities made in the course of trading in those securities on Tradepoint Investment Exchange. The agreements exempted are those involving clearing participants in that exchange, and nominees of such clearing participants, and The London Clearing House Limited through whom transactions on Tradepoint are cleared, and a nominee of that clearing house.

2799 Stamp duty reserve tax—stock lending transactions

In view of the introduction by the Stock Exchange of a new Dematerialised Stock Lending Service which permits stock lenders to hold their stock in the Stock Exchange's nominee company (SEPON), the Inland Revenue has published two concessions giving relief from stamp duty reserve tax on certain stock lending transactions. The concessions are concerned with stamp duty reserve tax, which is to be reduced to 50p, on transfers of stock by lenders into SEPON and with stamp duty reserve tax, which is to be limited to 50p if stamp duty would have been limited to 50p if there had been a paper transfer, on the return of stock from the market maker to the lender at the end of the loan. The Stock Exchange will collect stamp duty reserve tax where appropriate.

A third concession concerns relief from stamp duty reserve tax where, because of changes made to standard stock lending agreements to strengthen the security given to lenders, a stamp duty reserve tax liability would have strictly arisen. See further *STI*, 5 October 1995.

STATUTES

Halsbury's Laws of England (4th edn) Vol 44(1) (reissue), paras 1201–1526

2800 Commencement of Statutes

The following table contains detailed commencement provisions of all statutes passed in 1995. Repealed provisions are omitted. Schedules are included but not those sections which simply introduce schedules. The table also contains details of all commencement orders made in 1995, which in certain cases relate to statutes passed before 1995. Revoked orders are omitted.

An asterisk (*) indicates that a section, subsection or schedule is in force only in part or only for certain purposes.

The table refers to statutes only in so far as they relate to England and Wales.

STATUTE	COMMENCEMENT	AUTHORITY
Activity Centres (Young Persons' Safety) Act 1995	28 August 1995	s 5
Agricultural Tenancies Act 1995	1 September 1995	s 41(2)
Antarctic Act 1994		
• ss 1, 2, 8–32, 34–36, Schedule*	1 November 1995	s 35; SI 1995/2748
Appropriation Act 1995	19 July 1995	
Atomic Energy Act 1995	8 November 1995	
Building Societies (Joint Account Holders) Act 1995	1 May 1995	
Carers (Recognition and Services) Act 1995	1 April 1996	s 5(2)
Charities Act 1993		
• ss 41–49*	15 October 1995	s 99(2); SI 1995/2695
• ss 41–49*, 69, Sch 6 (para 21(3))	1 March 1996	s 99(2); SI 1995/2695
Charities (Amendment) Act 1995	8 November 1995	

STATUTE	COMMENCEMENT	AUTHORITY
Child Support Act 1995		
• ss 1–8, 9★, 10, 11, 22, 26(4)(a), 27, 28, Schs 1, 2, 3 (paras 1★, 5–7, 9, 13, 17, 20)	no date	s 30(4)
• s 30(1)–(4), (6)	19 July 1995	s 30(3)
• ss 18–21, 23★, 26(1)–(3), (4)(b), (5), (6), 27, 28, Sch 3 (paras 2, 3(2), 4, 8, 10, 14–16, 19)	4 September 1995	s 30(4); SI 1995/2302
• ss 12(1), (5)★, (7)★, 23★, 24, 25, 26(4)(c), Sch 3 (paras 1★, 3(1), 11, 12)	1 October 1995	s 30(4); SI 1995/2302
• ss 16, 17, Sch 3 (para 18)	18 December 1995	s 30(4); SI 1995/3262
• ss 9★, 11, 12(2)–(4), (5)★, (6), (7)★, 13–15	22 January 1996	s 30(4); SI 1995/3262
Children (Scotland) Act 1995		
By virtue of s 105(8), the following provisions apply to England and Wales		
• ss 18, 26(2), 33, 44, 70(4), 74, 82, 83, 93, 104, Schs 4 (paras 8, 10, 19, 31, 37, 41(1), (2), (7)–(9), 48–52, 54, 55), 5★	no date	s 105(1)(b)
• s 105(1), (2), (6)–(10)	19 July 1995	s 105(1)(b)
• s 104	1 November 1995	s 105(1); SI 1995/2787
Church of England (Miscellaneous Provisions) Measure 1995		
• s 6	no date	s 15(2)
• remaining provisions	1 September 1995	s 15(2)
Civil Evidence Act 1995	no date	s 16(2)
Coal Industry Act 1994		
• s 24	31 January 1995	s 68(4); SI 1995/159
• Sch 11 (Pt III★)	1 March 1995	s 68(4), (5)(a); SI 1995/273
• Sch 11 (Pt III★)	30 June 1995	s 68(4), (5)(a); SI 1995/1507
• appointed day for the purposes of s 23(1)(a)–(d)	30 June 1995	s 23(1); SI 1995/1507
Commonwealth Development Corporation Act 1995	28 June 1995	
Companies Act 1989		
• Schs 19 (para 20), 24★	3 July 1995	s 215(2); SI 1995/1352
• ss 171, 176, 181	4 July 1995	s 215(2); SI 1995/1591
Consolidated Fund Act 1995	23 March 1995	
Courts and Legal Services Act 1990		
• s 82	6 March 1995	s 124(3); SI 1995/641
Criminal Appeal Act 1995		
• ss 3, 5, 7★, 8, 9, 11, 13–25, 31(1)(a), Schs 1, 2 (paras 3, 4(4), 7, 8, 10, 14, 16, 19), 3★	no date	s 32
• ss 1, 2, 4, 6, 7★, 26, 28, 30, 31(1)(b), (2), 32–34, Schs 2 (paras 1, 2, 4(1)–(3), 4(5), 5, 15, 17), 3★	1 January 1996	s 32; SI 1995/3061
Criminal Injuries Compensation Act 1995	8 November 1995	

STATUTE	COMMENCEMENT	AUTHORITY
Criminal Justice Act 1993		
• ss 27, 28	3 February 1995	s 78(3); SI 1995/43
• Sch 5 (para 1)	14 August 1995	s 78(3); SI 1995/1958
Criminal Justice and Public Order Act 1994		
• ss 17, 18, 23, 24, 31–33, 40–43, 46–51, 64(1)–(3)★, 66(6), (10)–(13), 67(3)–(5), (8), (9), 72–74, 84(1)–(4), 85, 86(1), 88, 91, 92, 136, 137, 138(1)–(5), 141, 152(1), 154, 155, 157(1)–(6), (9), 160–164, 169, 170, Schs 9 (paras 1–33, 35, 36, 37(1), (2), 39, 40, 42–45, 47–53), 10 (paras 7, 8, 11, 13, 14, 17, 18, 28, 29, 31, 37, 38, 45, 47, 52, 63(2), 68), 11★	3 February 1995	s 172(2); SI 1995/127
• ss 25–30, 34–39, 54–60, 62, 64(4)–(6), 66(1)–(5), (7)–(9), 67(1), (2), (6), (7), 156, Schs 3, 9 (para 37(3)), 10 (paras 1–3, 5, 6, 10, 15, 19–23, 32–34, 41–44, 48, 51, 54–58, 61, 62, 67, 71), 11★	10 April 1995	s 172(2); SI 1995/721
• s 19	30 May 1995	s 172(2); SI 1995/1378
• ss 75, 76, Sch 10 (para 53)	24 August 1995	s 172(2); SI 1995/1957
• Schs 5, 10 (para 65)	4 September 1995	s 172(2); SI 1995/1957
• s 89	1 November 1995	s 172(2); SI 1995/1957
Criminal Justice (Scotland) Act 1995		
By virtue of s 118(5), (6), the following provisions apply to England and Wales		
• ss 108, 110, Sch 4	no date	s 118(2)
Criminal Law (Consolidation) (Scotland) Act 1995		
By virtue of s 53(4), the following provisions apply to England and Wales		
• ss 27–29, 35(10)–(12), 53	1 April 1996	s 53(2)
Criminal Procedure (Consequential Provisions) (Scotland) Act 1995		
By virtue of s 7(4), (5), the following provisions apply to England and Wales		
• s 7, Sch 3 (para 5), Sch 4★	1 April 1996	s 7(2)
Criminal Procedure (Scotland) Act 1995		
By virtue of s 309(4), the following provisions apply to England and Wales		
• ss 44, 47, 209(3), (7), 234(4)–(11), 244, 252★, 303(4), 309	1 April 1996	s 309(2)
Crown Agents Act 1995	19 July 1995	
• appointed day for the purposes of s 1(1)	no date	s 1(1)
• dissolution date for the purposes of s 8(4)	no date	s 8(4)
Deregulation and Contracting Out Act 1994		
• Schs 5, 11 (para 6)	1 July 1995	s 82(4); SI 1995/1433
• ss 38, 42–50, 52, 53, 56, 59, 61, 63, 65, 66, 80, Schs 12, 13 (paras 1–13, 14(1)(a), (b), (e), (2)–(6), 15–18), 14 (paras 1★, 2, 4, 5(2)(a), 6–8), 17★	1 January 1996	s 82(4); SI 1995/2835

STATUTE	COMMENCEMENT	AUTHORITY
Disability Discrimination Act 1995		
• ss 1–49, 53–69, 70(4), (5), (7), Schs 1–4, 6, 7	no date	s 70(3)
• s 70(1)–(3), (6), (8), Sch 8	8 November 1995	s 70(2)
• ss 50–52, Sch 5	1 January 1996	s 70(3); SI 1995/3330
Environment Act 1995		
• ss 2, 3(1), 5, 6, 8, 10, 11, 13–18, 37(3)–(8), 41★, 53–55, 57★, 58★, 60, 80–92, 104, 108–114, 115(1)★, (2)★, (6)★, 117–119, Schs 4, 5, 7 (para 7(2)), 10 (paras 10(2), 22(1), (2), (4)(c), (6), (7), 27, 32(14), 33(6)–(8), 35★, 38(2)), 11, 12, 15 (paras 1–12, 14(2), (3), 15, 16, 18, 22–24, 26(2)), 18–20, 21 (paras 1, 2(4)), 22 (paras 1–3, 5–30, 32–36, 37(2), (3), (5)–(8), 40, 41, 43–75, 76(2), (4)–(7), (8)(b), 77–79, 80(3), 81, 82(1)★, (2)–(4), (5)★, 83–132, 133(2), 134, 136, 140–146, 148–152, 154–161, 162★, 163–181, 183–186, 187(2), 188–191, 193–212, 213(2)(a), (4), (5), 214–222, 223(1)(a), (b), (2), 224–233), 23 (paras 1–13, 14(1)–(4), (7), (8)★, 15–24), 24★	no date	s 125(2)
• ss 74, 125, Sch 22 (paras 76(8)(a), 135)	19 July 1995	s 125(3)
• ss 1, 3(2)–(8), 4, 7, 9, 12, 37(1), (2), (9), 38–40, 43–52, 56, 120(1)★, (4)–(6), 121–124, Schs 1, 2, 3, 22 (paras 4, 31, 42, 213(1), (2)(b), (3), 223(1)(c))	28 July 1995	s 125(3); SI 1995/1983
• ss 61–73, 75–77, 79, Schs 7 (paras 1–6, 7(1), (3)–(5), 8–20), 8, 9	19 September 1995	s 125(2), (3)
• ss 41★, 42, 57★, 58★, 93–95, 97–103, Schs 15 (paras 25, 26(1)), 21 (para 2(1)–(3)), 22 (paras 37(1), (4), 38, 39, 76(1), (3), 80(1), (2), 82(5)★, 133(1), 137–139, 147, 153, 162★, 182, 187(1), 192), 24★	21 September 1995	s 125(3); SI 1995/1983
• ss 96(2), (4)–(6), Schs 13, 14, 24★	1 November 1995	s 125(3); SI 1995/2765
• Sch 10 (paras 1, 2(1), (3)–(8), (9)(a), (c), (d), 3–7, 8(2), 9, 10(1), (3), 11, 12, 14, 15, 17–19, 21, 23, 28–31, 32(1)–(13), (15–(18), 33(1)–(5), 34, 35★, 36, 37, 38(1))	23 November 1995	s 125(3); SI 1995/2950
• s 115(1)★, (2)★, (3), (4), (6)★, Sch 10 (paras 2(2), (9)(b), 8(1), (3), 13, 16, 20, 22(3), (4)(a), (b), (5))	1 April 1996	s 125(3) ; SI 1995/2950
• Schs 15 (paras 13, 14(1), (4), 17, 20, 26(2)), 23 (para 14(5), (6), (8)★), 24★	1 January 1999	s 125(3); SI 1995/1983
Environmental Protection Act 1990		
• s 62	11 August 1995	s 164(3); SI 1995/2152
European Communities (Finance) Act 1995	16 January 1995	
Finance Act 1993		
• appointed day for the purposes of s 11	1 December 1995	s 11(5); SI 1995/2715

STATUTE	COMMENCEMENT	AUTHORITY
Finance Act 1994		
• appointed day for the purposes of s 105(3), (4)(b)	1 January 1996	s 105(5); SI 1995/3125
Finance Act 1995		
• ss 5, 26, Sch 2	no date	ss 5(6), 26(3)
• appointed day for the purposes of s 139, Schs 27, 29 (Pt VIII(21))	no date	s 139(3)
• ss 6, 10, 144, 154(1), (3)★	29 November 1994 (ss 6, 10: at 6 pm)	ss 6(5), 10(2), 144(2), 154(4)
• ss 2, 3, 7, 11	1 January 1995	ss 2(2), 3(4), 7(2), 11(2)
• Sch 24 (paras 8–12)	23 March 1995	Sch 24 (para 7)
• appointed day for the purposes of s 24, Sch 29 (Pt VI(3))	1 June 1995	s 24(2); SI 1995/1374
• s 8, Schs 4 (Pt II (paras 2–5)), 29 (Pt V(1))	1 July 1995	s 8(3), Schs 4 (Pt II (para 5)), 29 (Pt V(1))
• appointed day for the purposes of Sch 12 (para 4(3))	31 July 1995	s 65, Sch 12 (para 4(3)); SI 1995/1778
• appointed day for the purposes of s 20	1 December 1995	s 20(5); SI 1995/2892
• appointed day for the purposes of s 63(2)	1 January 1996	s 63(5); SI 1995/3236
• appointed day for the purposes of s 82	2 January 1996	s 82(4); SI 1995/2933
• Sch 29 (Pt VIII(7))	5 May 1996	Sch 29 (Pt VIII(7))
• remaining provisions (subject to the exception that certain provisions are expressed to take effect on various dates)	1 May 1995	see various provisions of the Act
Financial Services Act 1986		
• Sch 17★	19 June 1995	s 211(1); SI 1995/1538
Gas Act 1995		
• ss 8(2), 11(1)–(5), 12, 13, 17(1), (2), 18, Schs 5, 6★	8 November 1995	s 18(2)
• remaining provisions	no date	s 18(2)
Geneva Conventions (Amendment) Act 1995	no date	s 7(2)
Goods Vehicles (Licensing of Operators) Act 1995		
• Sch 5	no date	ss 50(2), 61
• remaining provisions	1 January 1996	s 61; SI 1995/2181
Health Authorities Act 1995		
• ss 1(1)★, (2), 2(1)★, (2), (3), 3, 4(1)★, (2), 5(1)★, (2), 6–10, Schs 1–3★	28 June 1995	s 8(1)
• ss 1(1)★, 2(1)★, 4(1)★, Schs 1–3★	1 April 1996	ss 1(2), 2(3), 4(2), 5(2), 8(1)
Home Energy Conservation Act 1995 *The Act has not yet been brought into force in Wales*		
• ss 3(1), 4(1), (2) (England)	15 January 1996	s 9(2), (3); SI 1995/3340
• remaining provisions (England)	1 April 1996	s 9(2), (3); SI 1995/3340

STATUTE	COMMENCEMENT	AUTHORITY
Income and Corporation Taxes Act 1988		
• appointed day for the purposes of s 737A (inserted by Finance Act 1994, s 122)	1 May 1995	SI 1995/1007
• appointed day for the purposes of s 51A (inserted by Finance Act 1995, s 77)	2 January 1996	SI 1995/2932
Insurance Companies (Reserves) Act 1995		
• ss 1, 3	no date	s 4(2)
• ss 2, 4	19 July 1995	
Jobseekers Act 1995		
• ss 1, 2(1)(a), (b), (c)★, (d), (2), (3), (4)(a), (b)★, (c), 3(1)(a)–(e), (f)(i), (ii), (iii)★, (2)–(4)★, 4(1)(a), (b)★, (2)★, (3), (4)★, (5)★, (6)–(11), (12)★, 5(1), (2), (3)★, 6(1), (2)–(5)★, (6), (7)★, (8)★, (9), 7(1), (2)–(6)★, (7), (8)★, 8★, 9(1)★, (2)–(7), (8)★, (9), (10)–(12)★, 10(1)★, (2)–(5), (6)(a), (b), (c)★, (d), (7)★, (8), 11(1), (2)★, (3), (4), (5)★, (6), (7)★, (8)★, (9), 12★, 13★, 14, 15(1)★, (2)(a)–(c), (d)★, (3), (4), (5)★, (6)★, (7)–(10), 16, 17(1)★, (2)–(5), 18, 19(1), (2)★, (3), (4)★, (5), (6), (7)★, (8)★, (9), (10)(b), (c)★, 20(1), (2), (3)–(8)★, 21★, 22★, 23(1)★, (2), (3)★, (4)★, (5), 24, 25, 26★, 31★, 32, 38(1)(a), (2)–(4), (6)–(8), 40★, Schs 1★, 2 (paras 2–4, 6, 7, 11–29, 30(1)–(4), 31–40, 42–76), 3★	no date	s 41(2)
• ss 39, 41(1)–(3), (6)	28 June 1995	s 41(2)
• ss 2(1)(c)★, (4)(b)★, 3(1)(f)(iii)★, (2)–(4)★, 4(1)(b)★, (2)★, (4)★, (5)★, (12)★, 5(3)★, 6(2)–(5)★, (7)★, (8)★, 7(2)–(6)★, (8)★, 8★, 9(1)★, (8)★, (10)–(12)★, (13), 10(1)★, (6)(c)★, (7)★, 11(2)★, (5)★, (7)★, (8)★, 12★, 13★, 15(1)★, (2)(d)★, (5)★, (6)★, 17(1)★, 19(2)★, (4)★, (7)★, (8)★, (10)(a), (c)★, 20(3)–(8)★, 21★, 22★, 23(1)★, (3)★, (4)★, 26–28★, 31★, 34(3)★, (7)★, 35–37, 40★, Schs 1★, 2 (para 30(5))	12 December 1995	s 41(2); SI 1995/3228
• s 29	1 January 1996	s 41(2); SI 1995/3228
• ss 28★, 30, Sch 3★	1 April 1996	s 41(2); SI 1995/3228
• ss 27★, 33, 34(1), (2), (3)★, (4)–(6), (7)★, 38(1)(b), (5), Sch 2 (para 41)	6 April 1996	s 41(2); SI 1995/3228
Judicial Pensions and Retirement Act 1993	31 March 1995	s 31(2); SI 1995/631
Landlord and Tenant (Covenants) Act 1995	1 January 1996	s 31; SI 1995/2963
Law of Property (Miscellaneous Provisions) Act 1994		
• Sch 1, para 2	15 February 1995	s 23; SI 1995/145
• remaining provisions	1 July 1995	s 23; SI 1995/1317
Law Reform (Succession) Act 1995	8 November 1995	
Licensing (Sunday Hours) Act 1995	6 August 1995	s 5; SI 1995/1930
Local Government and Housing Act 1989		
• s 71★	1 April 1995	s 195(2); SI 1995/841

STATUTE	COMMENCEMENT	AUTHORITY
Local Government (Wales) Act 1994		
• appointed day for the purposes of s 39(1)	1 February 1995	s 39(1); SI 1995/103
• ss 1(5)★, (8)★, 2, 4, 17★, Schs 15 (para 6), 16 (para 68(6), (7)★, (8)★, (9), (13)–(15), (16)★, (19)), 17 (paras 7, 8), 18★	20 March 1995	s 66(3); SI 1995/546; 851
• ss 1(5)★, (6)★, (8)★, 5, 14, 15, 18(1)–(6)★, 19, 23(2)–(6), 25–38, 42, 44, 45, 51, 53, 56–60, Schs 2 (paras 8, 9), 6 (paras 2–4, 11, 12, 21, 23, 24(1)(b)), 7 (para 1★), 10 (para 14), 12, 15 (paras 3, 20, 23, 26, 55), 16 (paras 57(1)–(5), 82(1)–(4), (5)★, 84–86, 96, 97, 106), 17 (paras 2, 3, 5, 10–14, 18–23), 18★	3 April 1995	s 66(3); SI 1995/852
• ss 1(5)★, (8)★, Schs 2 (para 13), 6 (para 24(10)(b), (17)(a), 7 (para 27(4)), 8 (para 3(2)), 15 (paras 10(1), 52, 58–61), 16 (paras 12, 26, 98), 18★	1 October 1995	s 66(3); SI 1995/2490
• Schs 16 (para 54(2)), 18★	1 January 1996	s 66(3); SI 1995/3198
• ss 1(5)★, (6)★, (8)★, 8–13, 16, 20(1)–(3), 23(1), 49, 50, 62, Schs 2 (paras 1–3, 6, 7, 10–12), 4, 5, 17 (paras 15, 17)	1 April 1996	s 66(3); SI 1995/3198
Marriage Act 1994		
• s 1(2)★, (3)★, Schedule (para 5)	24 February 1995	s 3(2); SI 1995/424
• ss 1(1), (2)★, (3)★, 2(1)★, Schedule (paras 1–4, 6–9)	1 April 1995	s 3(2); SI 1995/424
Medical (Professional Performance) Act 1995	no date	s 6
Mental Health (Patients in the Community) Act 1995	1 April 1996	s 7(2)
Merchant Shipping Act 1970		
• s 51, Sch 5	1 May 1995	s 101(4); SI 1995/965
• Sch 5★	1 August 1995	s 101(4); SI 1995/1426
Merchant Shipping Act 1995		
• ss 60, 80(2), (4), 111, 115, 116, 118, 119(2), (3), 127, Sch 12★	no date	Sch 14 (para 5)
• ss 1–59, 61–79, 80(1), (3), 81–110, 112–114, 117, 119(1), 120–126, 128–313, 314(2)–(4), 315, 316, Schs 1–11, 12★, 13, 14	1 January 1996	s 316(2)
Motor Cycle Noise Act 1987	1 August 1996	s 2(3); SI 1995/2367
National Health Service (Amendment) Act 1995		
• ss 1★, 2★	no date	s 14(3), (4)
• ss 13, 14(1), (3)–(6)	19 July 1995	s 14(3), (4)
• ss 1★, 2★, 3–6, Schedule	21 December 1995	s 14(3), (4); SI 1995/3090
Northern Ireland (Remission of Sentences) Act 1995	no date	s 2
Olympic Symbol etc (Protection) Act 1995	20 September 1995	s 19(2); SI 1995/2472

STATUTE	COMMENCEMENT	AUTHORITY
Pensions Act 1995		
• ss 1–38, 40–61, 67–89, 91–116, 117★, 118, 119, 120★, 121★, 123, 124★, 125, 135–155, 157–167, 174★, 175★, 176, 178, 180, 181, Schs 1, 2, 3 (paras 1–28, 30, 31, 38, 39(a), (c), (d), 40, 41, 43, 44(a)(ii), (b), 45, 46), 5, 6 (paras 2–16), 7 (Pts I, III, IV★)	no date	s 180
• ss 127–134, 168, 170, 171, 179, Schs 4, 7 (Pts II, IV★)	19 July 1995	s 180
• ss 90, 156, 169, 172, 174★, 175★, Sch 6 (para 1)	2 October 1995	s 180(1); SI 1995/2548
• ss 62–66★, 117★, 120★, 121★, 124★, 174★, 175★	4 December 1995	s 180(1); SI 1995/3104
• ss 39, 62–66★, 117★, 120★, 121★, 124★, 174★, 175★, Sch 3 (paras 29, 32–37, 39(b), 42, 44(a)(i), 47)	1 January 1996	s 180(1); SI 1995/3104
Police and Magistrates' Courts Act 1994		
• Sch 8 (para 19(1), (2))	3 February 1995	s 94(1), (2); SI 1995/42
• ss 1–4★, 5–7, 8★, 9, 10★, 11★, 12, 14–16★, 20, 21, 23, 24, 26★, 29, 30, 31★, 39(2), (3), 40, 45★, 72(1)–(5), (6)★, 73, 75★, 76–77, 80, 81, 83(1)★, (2)★, 84, 88(6), 91(2), (3), Schs 1★, 2★, 4 (paras 1–4, 5–14★, 15(1)★, (2), (3)★, (4)★, 16–41★, 42, 43–63★), 5 (paras 2–4, 5★, 6, 7, 8 (paras 5, 10–16, 18, 19(1), (3), 20, 21, 25–32, 33(1)–(4), (6), 34), 9, 10(2), 13, 14, 15★, 17–20★, 22, 24(a), 29, 30, 35–38), 9★	1 April 1995	s 94(1), (2); SI 1995/246, 685, 899
• s 72(6)★	1 October 1995	s 94(2); SI 1995/685
• s 72(6)★	1 January 1996	s 94(2); SI 1995/685
Prisoners (Return to Custody) Act 1995	5 September 1995	s 3(2); SI 1995/2021
Private International Law (Miscellaneous Provisions) Act 1995		
• ss 1–4, 9–15	no date	s 16(1), (3)
• ss 16–19	8 November 1995	
• ss 5, 6, 8, Schedule	8 January 1996	s 16(2)
Proceeds of Crime Act 1995		
• ss 14, 16	28 June 1995	s 16(4)
• remaining provisions	1 November 1995	s 16(3); SI 1995/2650
Proceeds of Crime (Scotland) Act 1995 *By virtue of s 50(4), (5), the following provisions apply to England and Wales*		
• ss 42, 44, 50, Sch 2	1 April 1996	s 50(2)
Road Traffic (New Drivers) Act 1995	no date	s 10(2)
Sale of Goods (Amendment) Act 1995	19 September 1995	s 3(2)
Shipping and Trading Interests (Protection) Act 1995	1 January 1996	s 9(4)
South Africa Act 1995	23 March 1995	
Statute Law (Repeals) Act 1995	8 November 1995	

STATUTE	COMMENCEMENT	AUTHORITY
Team and Group Ministries Measure 1995		
• ss 1, 3–20, Schs 1, 2	no date	s 20(2)
• s 2	28 June 1995	s 20(2)
Town and Country Planning (Costs of Inquiries etc) Act 1995	8 November 1995	

2801 Interpretation—ambiguous cases—reference to proceedings in Parliament

The plaintiffs wished to refer to speeches made by ministers in Parliament in order to support their argument relating to interpretation of the Banking Acts 1979 and 1987. The defendant claimed that the plaintiffs were not entitled to rely on the speeches under the strict criteria expounded in *Pepper v Hart* [1992] STC 898, HL (1992 Abr para 2498) and *Melluish v BMI (No 3) Ltd* [1995] STC 964, HL. *Held*, the *Pepper* and *Melluish* cases, in which the criteria were laid down, could be distinguished from the present case because they considered the purpose or object of a statute rather than the construction of a particular statutory provision and, in addition, the court in those cases was dealing with domestic legislation. The criteria did not apply so narrowly in a case where the legislation was intended to introduce the provisions of an international convention or European Directive into English law. In this case, the purpose and objects of the Banking Acts were relevant to the issues between the parties arising out of a European Directive and it was therefore important to ascertain the true purpose of the Acts. The plaintiffs would therefore be entitled to admit the ministers' speeches as evidence.

Three Rivers District Council v Governor and Co of the Bank of England (No 2) (1995) Independent, 22 December, (1996) Times, 8 January (Queen's Bench Division: Clarke J).

2802 Interpretation—infringement of trade mark—introduction of EC Council meetings as evidence

See *Wagamama Ltd v City Centre Restaurants plc*, para 2955.

2803 Retrospection—presumption against retrospection—creation of new obligation

See *Bates v Robert Barrow Ltd, Ansell v Robert Barrow Ltd,* para 1726.

2804 Statute Law (Repeals) Act 1995

The Statute Law (Repeals) Act 1995 reforms statute law by the repeal, in accordance with recommendations of the Law Commission, of enactments which (except in so far as their effect is preserved) are no longer of practical utility. The Act received the royal assent on 8 November 1995 and came into force on that date.

Section 1, Schs 1 and 2 effect the necessary repeals and consequential provisions. Sections 2 and 3 deal with extent and short title.

STOCK EXCHANGE

Halsbury's Laws of England (4th edn) Vol 45, paras 1–300

2805 Articles

Alternative Investment Market, Michael Murphy: Tax Journal, Issue 300, p 12

How Good is the Stock Exchange's AIM? Marcus Andreen (on the Alternative Investment Market): 139 SJ 684

A POSitive Framework for Offers of Unlisted Securities, Michael Howlett (on the Public Offers of Securities Regulations 1995, SI 1995/1537): 139 SJ 1018

Share of the Action, Andrew Sparrow (on the Alternative Investment Market): LS Gaz, 31 Aug 1995, p 18

2806   Securities—dealings in securities—unlicensed representative—validity of investment agreement

The Prevention of Fraud (Investments) Act 1958, s 1 (repealed) prohibited unlicensed persons from engaging in the business of dealing in securities. Dealings in securities by unlicensed persons acting on behalf of those engaged in such a business were also prohibited.

The plaintiffs entered into various investment management agreements with the defendant company, and remitted funds to it for the purchase of shares on their behalf. The defendant held a licence to deal in securities under the 1958 Act. However, the individual who had made and signed the agreements with the plaintiffs on the defendant's behalf did not, at the relevant time, hold a representative's licence under the 1958 Act. After a fall in the securities market, the plaintiffs sought to recover their losses from the defendant. The claim was dismissed at first instance. The plaintiffs appealed. *Held*, the 1958 Act was enacted to protect the investing public from unlicensed dealers in securities. The public interest under the statute was fully met by the imposition of criminal sanctions on those who, as principals or agents, dealt in securities without a licence. Such sanctions were clearly directed at the dealers themselves, and not against the deals or the contracting parties. The plaintiffs were wrong in their proposition that because the defendant's representative had been unlicensed when the contracts between the parties were made, the contracts had been rendered void by the 1958 Act. The contracts were neither expressly nor impliedly forbidden. Accordingly, the appeal would be dismissed.

Hughes v Asset Managers plc [1995] 3 All ER 669 (Court of Appeal: Nourse, Hirst and Saville LJJ).

The carrying on of investment business is now regulated by the Financial Services Act 1986, Pt I (ss 1–128C).

2807   Securities—insider dealing—information in respect of offences—international co-operation

See para 496.

2808   Securities—uncertificated securities—transfer—transfer without written instrument

See para 520.

TELECOMMUNICATIONS AND BROADCASTING

Halsbury's Laws of England (4th edn) Vol 45, paras 301–900

2809   Articles

Another Step Towards a Right of Privacy? John Gardiner (on *R v Central Independent Television plc* [1994] 3 All ER 641 (1994 Abr para 454)): 145 NLJ 225

The Banned Broadcasting Corporation, Colin Munro (on the banning of a Panorama programme by the Scottish courts): 145 NLJ 518

A Break in Transmission, David Aitman (on inconsistencies in international media law): LS Gaz, 5 January 1995, p 18

The Changing Role of the Telecoms Regulator, Caroline Easter: [1995] 5 CTLR 139

The Commission Green Paper on Mobile and Personal Communications in Europe, Jeremy Newton: [1995] EIPR 195

Convergence Between Media and Telecommunications: Towards a New Regulatory Framework, Yves Poullet, Jean-Paul Traille, François van der Mensbrugghe and Valerie Willems: [1995] 11 CLSR 174

Is There a Role for an Essential Facilities' Doctrine in Europe? Stewart White: [1995] 1 CTLR 110

Pressing for De-Regulation, Santha Rasaiah and David Newell (on media regulation): LS Gaz, 15 March 1995, p 16

Satellite Wars: Encryption, Piracy and the Law, Matthew Harris, Nick Gardner and Bill Moodie: [1995] 1 CTLR 123

Trial by Media, David Bentley (on sensational press and television coverage of trials): 139 SJ 243

2810   Broadcasting—advertisement of a political nature

The Broadcasting Act 1990, s 92(2)(a)(i) provides that the Radio Authority must do all that it can to secure that a licensed service does not include any advertisement which is inserted by or on behalf of a body whose objects are wholly or mainly of a political nature.

The applicant decided to run a radio advertising campaign to draw attention to the plight of people in certain African countries. The respondent Radio Authority refused to broadcast the advertisement because they considered that some of its objects were political and therefore contrary to the 1990 Act, s 92(2)(a)(i). The applicant applied for judicial review of the decision, arguing that having regard to the right of freedom of speech guaranteed by the European Convention on Human Rights, the respondent had misconstrued s 92(2)(a)(i). *Held*, there were a number of competing rights which had to be considered, and in relation to which a balance had to be struck. It was therefore impossible to provide a definition of a political advertisement which gave a precise indication as to what was acceptable, and a large measure of discretion had to be left to the respondent. Here, there was nothing to suggest that the respondent had misunderstood or misinterpreted s 92(2)(a)(i), nor was their decision irrational. Accordingly, the application would be dismissed.

R v Radio Authority, ex p Amnesty International British Section (1995) Independent, 1 August (Queen's Bench Division: Kennedy LJ and McCullough J).

2811   Broadcasting—Broadcasting Complaints Commission—jurisdiction to hear complaint—complaint by person with direct interest—meaning of 'direct interest'

The Broadcasting Act 1990, s 144(2) provides that a complaint must not be entertained by the Broadcasting Complaints Commission (BCC) unless made by the person affected. Section 150 provides that 'the person affected' means a participant in the programme in question who was the subject of that treatment or a person who, whether such a participant or not, had a direct interest in the subject-matter of that treatment.

A television corporation had made a television programme purporting to show racism in a village. The parish council complained that the corporation had given the impression of serious racism in the village and had then failed to interview a parish councillor who felt able to refute the allegations. The corporation sought to prohibit the BCC from hearing or determining the parish council's complaint and also sought a declaration that the parish council was not a person affected. *Held*, the BCC had a discretion to entertain the application of persons who had a direct interest in the subject matter of the treatment complained of but whose interest was not sufficiently direct to justify the making of a complaint with the applicant as the person affected. This indicated that the term 'direct interest' in s 150 was to be construed broadly. The parish council did have a direct interest and, accordingly, the corporation's application would be dismissed.

R v Broadcasting Complaints Commission, ex p Channel Four Television Corpn (1995) Times, 4 January (Queen's Bench Division: Schiemann J).

A pressure group representing one-parent families submitted a complaint to the Broadcasting Complaints Commission concerning a television documentary. It was claimed by the pressure group that certain facts had been misrepresented in the programme and that the programme had then been relied on by government policy makers to the detriment of the parents whom the group represented. The question arose whether the commission had jurisdiction to hear the complaint. Since the pressure group was not a participant in the making of the programme, it had locus standi to make a complaint only if it could properly be said to have a direct interest in the subject-matter of the complaint. *Held*, the constitution and functions of the commission were set out in the Broadcasting Act 1990, Pt V and Sch 13. The term 'direct interest' had a personal, limited and specific nature. Parliament could not have intended 'direct interest' to be so widely construed as to allow the commission to entertain complaints made by national bodies on behalf of the people they claimed to represent. In the present case the pressure group's interest was clearly an indirect interest and accordingly the commission had no jurisdiction to hear it. However, the court also stated that its decision in this case did not mean that those who collectively, as opposed to individually, were aggrieved by what they regarded as biased, unbalanced representations of contemporary issues had no right of complaint.

R v Broadcasting Complaints Commission, ex p British Broadcasting Corpn [1995] EMLR 241 (Queen's Bench Division: Brooke J). *R v Broadcasting Complaints Commission, ex p Granada Television Ltd* (1994) Times, 16 December (1994 Abr para 2672) and *R v Broadcasting Complaints Commission, ex p Channel Four Television Corpn* (1995) Times, 4 January supra not followed.

2812   Broadcasting—decision to prevent broadcast of programme—leave to appeal against decision—practical considerations—urgency and importance of case

Scotland

The BBC proposed to broadcast an extended interview with the Prime Minister only three days before local government elections. Two election candidates sought an injunction to prevent the broadcast and, at first instance, the judge had to determine whether the broadcast would be in breach of the BBC's duty to treat controversial subjects with due impartiality and whether the balance of convenience favoured the granting of an injunction to prevent broadcasting until the close of the poll. The judge found in favour of the candidates and granted an injunction to prevent the broadcast until after 9 pm on the day of the elections. The BBC appealed, raising a further argument that the candidates had not made out a prima facie case that they had a title and interest to bring the proceedings. The matter came before the court half an hour before the broadcast was due and the court found that the candidates had made out a prima facie case. The BBC applied for leave to appeal to the House of Lords. *Held*, unless the case could be regarded as one of extreme urgency and importance there was no reasonable prospect of the steps involved in an appeal being completed in time. At best, the process would be completed in order for the programme to be shown on the evening before the elections were due to take place. The BBC had failed to show the court that the issues in the programme were of such a nature that it was a matter of urgency that it be broadcast. The practical considerations far outweighed any advantage that the BBC was likely to achieve by showing the programme one day earlier than they could lawfully do under the terms of the injunction. Accordingly, leave to appeal would be refused.

Houston v British Broadcasting Corpn 1995 SLT 1305 (Inner House).

2813   Broadcasting—independent productions

The Broadcasting (Independent Productions) (Amendment) Order 1995, SI 1995/1925 (in force on 21 July 1995), amends the 1991 Order, SI 1991/1408, so as to: (1) raise the maximum shareholding that a producer may hold in a broadcaster and that one broadcaster may hold in a producer from 15 per cent to 25 per cent, and to provide that two or more broadcasters may hold up to 50 per cent of the shares in a producer without the producer thereby losing his status as an independent producer; (2) enable a producer established in the European Economic Area to hold any quantity of shares in a broadcaster outside it without losing his status of being an independent producer; and (3) exclude from the definition of 'broadcaster' the providers of teletext and similar services.

2814   Broadcasting—media ownership—government proposals

The government has completed the review of media ownership regulation which it announced in 1994 and has set out its conclusions in a policy document, *Media Ownership* (Cm 2872). It is intended to consult on its longer term proposals, but at the same time a number of immediate changes have been announced to which effect will be given by legislation. In the longer term, an independent media regulator will be established. The media markets will be defined, and their overall size established through the measurement of audience or revenue share. The value of shares in one media sector will be expressed in terms of shares in another; the necessary weightings might be based on the relative influence or market power of different media. Thresholds of ownership will be established by reference to national, sectoral and regional media markets; acquisitions beyond such thresholds will have to be referred to the independent media regulator, who will apply public interest principles and procedures laid down by statute.

The measures which will be implemented in the shorter term are the allowance of common ownership between newspaper groups and television and radio licensees within specified limits. More flexible rules will be applied to ownership of television companies. The definition of control in the Broadcasting Act 1990 will be clarified, although the existing provisions applying to related persons will continue to apply. The ownership limits for the nominated news provider for Channel 3 services (see s 32(9)) will be amended. There will be consultation regarding the encouragement of the independent production sector. The present restrictions on the radio sector will be relaxed. The existing newspaper merger provisions will be relaxed so that the circulation threshold for reference of mergers to the Monopolies and Mergers Commission will be 50,000.

2815   Broadcasting—restrictions on the holding of licences—licences to provide radio services—increase in upper limit

The Broadcasting (Restrictions on the Holding of Licences) (Amendment) Order 1995, SI 1995/1924 (in force on 21 July 1995), amends the Broadcasting Act 1990, Sch 2, Pt III, para

2(1)(e), so as to increase the upper limit on the number of licences to provide local radio services that may be held by any one person from twenty to thirty-five. The order also amends the 1991 Order, SI 1991/1176, so as to remove a number of restrictions on the holding of licences to provide certain categories of local and national radio services, and to make an amendment consequential on the amendment to the 1990 Act.

2816 Broadcasting—television—licences—fees

The Wireless Telegraphy (Television Licence Fees) (Amendment) Regulations 1995, SI 1995/655 (in force on 1 April 1995), further amend the 1991 Regulations, SI 1991/436, (1) by increasing the amount of the basic fee for television licences from £28 to £28.50 in the case of monochrome, and from £84.50 to £86.50 in the case of colour; (2) by increasing the issue fee for the standard instalment licence from £42.26 to £43.26, with instalments increased from £21.12 to £21.62; (3) by increasing the issue fee for the premium instalment licence from £22.39 to £22.89, with instalments increased from £22.37 to £22.87; (4) in respect of the budget instalment licence which may be paid for by one of thirteen specified issue fees and five equal instalments thereafter, in each case the total amount payable being £86.50.

2817 Electromagnetic compatibility—wireless telegraphy apparatus—vehicles, components and separate technical units

The Electromagnetic Compatibility (Amendment) Regulations 1995, SI 1995/3180 (in force on 1 January 1996), further amend the 1992 Regulations, SI 1992/2372, to give effect to Commission Directive (EC) 95/34, art 1.4, which adapts to technical progress and amends Council Directive (EC) 72/245, and Council Directive (EC) 89/336, art 2.2. The 1992 Regulations no longer apply in respect of 'vehicles', 'components' and 'separate technical units'.

2818 Telecommunications—registers

The Telecommunications (Registers) Order 1995, SI 1995/232 (in force on 1 March 1995), prescribes the hours during which the registers kept by the Director General of Telecommunications under the Telecommunications Act 1984 are to be open for public inspection and the fees payable for supplying certified copies of, or extracts from, the registers.

2819 Telecommunications—satellite communications services

The Satellite Communications Services Regulations 1995, SI 1995/1947 (in force on 14 August 1995), make provision, by amending specified licences, for the removal of special and exclusive rights relating to fixed satellite communication services, other than public voice telephony, between the United Kingdom and other Community member states or states which are contracting parties to the European Economic Area Agreement, and of the market for satellite earth station equipment.

2820 Telecommunications—Telecommunications Code—easement—fair and reasonable consideration

The Telecommunications Code, para 7(1)(a) (as set out in the British Telecommunications Act 1984, Sch 2), provides that where an order has been made dispensing with the need for a person's agreement, the terms and conditions in the order must include such terms with respect to the payment of consideration in respect of the giving of the agreement, or the exercise of rights to which the order relates, as it appears to the court would have been fair and reasonable if the agreement had been given willingly and subject to the other provisions of the order.

The applicant, a licensed telecommunications operator, sought permission to lay and use ducts under a private road owned by the respondent company, so that it could connect its main telecommunications centre to the business development area being established on part of the respondent's land. The respondent had previously granted the applicant the right to erect ducts and to run trunk cable under its land, and it was agreed between the parties that additional ducts were needed to enable the applicant to cater properly for the business development area. One of the terms of the proposed deed of grant was that the applicant was to pay an annual sum in consideration for the grant, with provision for an annual review. When the respondent refused to enter into the agreement voluntarily, the applicant applied under the Telecommunications Code for an order authorising it to execute the necessary works without the need for the respondent's agreement. On the issue of the amount of consideration that the applicant was to pay to the respondent, *held,* fair and reasonable consideration could not always be decided by reference to the market value of the right sought. Moreover, compulsory purchase principles, and consequently the *Pointe Gourde* principle, did not apply to the Telecommunications Code, para 7(1)(a), nor was it appropriate to have regard to the value of the benefit which would be conferred on an applicant if it was granted the right that it sought. Instead, it was necessary to determine the matter having regard to the concept of willing agreement. In particluar, the issue of fair and reasonable consideration was to be decided by reference to comparable transactions, having regard to the bargaining power of the parties.

Mercury Communications Ltd v London and India Dock Investments Ltd (1993) P & CR 135 (Mayor's and City of London County Court: Judge Hague QC).

2821 Telecommunications—terminal equipment

The Telecommunications Terminal Equipment (Amendment) Regulations 1995, SI 1995/144 (in force on 30 January 1995), correct defects in the 1992 Regulations, SI 1992/2423, and the 1994 Regulations, SI 1994/3129, by (1) making it an offence to make an EC declaration of conformity to type or an EC declaration of conformity in circumstances where the terminal equipment does not comply with the essential requirements or the conformity assessment requirements have not been complied with; (2) defining the declaration of conformity which a manufacturer or his authorised representative must make in relation to receive-only satellite earth station equipment if he elects to conform with the Community internal production control procedure under Council Directive (EC) 93/97; (3) making it clear that, in relation to satellite earth station equipment capable of terrestrial connection to the public telecommunications network but not intended to be so connected, that the conformity assessment requirements must be complied with; (4) allowing for proceedings to be brought where a person makes the declaration of conformity referred to in (3) where the equipment does not comply with the essential requirements or the conformity assessment requirements have not been complied with; (5) requiring the declaration of conformity to be made.

2822 Wireless telegraphy—apparatus for wireless telegraphy—citizens' band and amateur radio apparatus—restrictions

The Wireless Telegraphy (Citizens' Band and Amateur Apparatus) (Various Provisions) (Amendment) Order 1995, SI 1995/2588 (in force on 27 October 1995), amends the 1988 Order, SI 1988/1215, by making various changes to the restrictions which govern the importation, manufacture, sale, hire, offer or advertisement for sale or hire, custody and control of certain specified citizens' band apparatus and the import and manufacture of certain specified amateur radio apparatus.

2823 Wireless telegraphy—Isle of Man

The Wireless Telegraphy (Isle of Man) Order 1995, SI 1995/268 (in force on 8 March 1995), extends to the Isle of Man, with exceptions, adaptations and modifications, specified provisions of the Telecommunications Act 1984 and the Broadcasting Act 1990. The 1981 Order, SI 1981/1113, is varied.

2824 Wireless telegraphy—licence—charges

The Wireless Telegraphy (Licence Charges) Regulations 1995, SI 1995/1331 (in force on 1 July 1995), replace the 1991 Regulations, SI 1991/542, so as to (1) specify new and revised classes of wireless telegraphy licences for the purposes of the Wireless Telegraphy Act 1949; (2) revise the provision for fees to be paid in respect of such licences; and (3) extend the range of licences for which qualifying charities can claim a fee discount. The sector headings for the revised classes of licence are: Aeronautical; Broadcasting and Ancillary Services; Fixed Services; Hobby Radio; Maritime; Private Mobile Radio; Public Mobile Radio; Satellite Services; and Other Licences (Temporary Use and Testing and Development). SI 1995/244 is revoked.

THEATRES AND OTHER PLACES OF ENTERTAINMENT

Halsbury's Laws of England (4th edn) Vol 45, paras 901–1100

2825 Sex establishments—control

The Local Government (Miscellaneous Provisions) Act 1982, Sch 3, para 3A provides that no premises which have a music and dancing licence and which are for the time being used for a purpose for which a licence is required are to be regarded as a sex encounter establishment. Paragraph 3A also provides that a sex encounter establishment includes premises at which entertainments which are not unlawful are provided by one or more persons who are without clothes, or who expose their breasts or genital, urinary or excretory organs during the entertainment.

The plaintiff was the tenant of premises in the basement of which it operated a peep show, whereby a customer watched a sexually explicit display by one or more naked women to an accompaniment of loud pop music through the window of a booth. The plaintiff held a music and dancing licence in respect of the premises. An officer of the defendant local authority entered the premises with a warrant and seized items of property which it intended to ask the court to forfeit. The plaintiff argued that the issue and execution of the warrant were unlawful and that the officer was trespassing, on the ground that no offence had been committed because, as the premises had a music and dancing licence, under the 1982 Act, Sch 3, para 3A they did not require a sex establishment licence. On the plaintiff's appeal against the dismissal of its application for summary judgment for damages for the alleged trespass, *held*, the activities of the women in question, in the context of how they were viewed, did not fall within the licence obtained by the plaintiff because they were neither music nor public entertainment of the like kind. The plaintiff's premises were therefore not being used for a purpose for which their music and dancing licence was required. They were being used as a sex encounter establishment for which no appropriate licence had been granted. Accordingly, the warrant and its execution were lawful and the appeal would be dismissed.

Willowcell Ltd v Lord Mayor and Citizens of the City of Westminster (1995) 160 JP 101 (Court of Appeal: Roch and Ward LJJ).

It has been held that where an entertainment licence for public music and dancing is in force, the conditions attached to that licence can properly regulate the sexual content of any entertainment performed at the premises.

Westminster City Council v North (1995) Independent, 27 April (Queen's Bench Division: Balcombe LJ and French J).

2826   Theatres—advance ticket sales—value added tax

See *Customs and Excise Comrs v Richmond Theatre Management Ltd*, para 3039.

2827   Video recordings—classification—exempted work—work designed to stimulate or encourage sexual activity—computer game

The defendant produced erotic computer games on disk. One such game contained short moving images of naked women which appeared upon completion of the game. A local authority brought a prosecution against the defendant on the ground that the game had been produced and supplied without classification certificates being obtained under the Video Recordings Act 1984, ss 9, 10. The defendant claimed that the game was not a moving picture under the 1984 Act, s 1(2)(b), and that, in addition, it was an exempted work under the 1984 Act, s 2 because it was a video game that did not either depict human sexual activity or stimulate or encourage human sexual activity. In addition, it was claimed that the game did not display human genital organs, which in the case of females were internal only. The defendant was acquitted. On appeal by the authority, *held*, although the game itself did not fall into the category of a video work, the sequence featuring the naked women did. Provided there was a sequence showing continuous movement, that was sufficient to be described as a moving picture. Activity short of masturbation could be described as human sexual activity and the depiction of female genitalia was not confined to the internal organs and therefore, the work in question was not exempted. It was not relevant that the sequence was not hard pornograhy or offensive when deciding whether the work was designed to stimulate or encourage human sexual activity and, accordingly, the appeal would be allowed.

Kent County Council v Multi Media Marketing (Canterbury) Ltd (1995) Times, 9 May (Queen's Bench Division: Simon Brown LJ and Curtis J).

For earlier related proceedings see (1994) Times, 7 December (1994 Abr para 823).

2828   Video recordings—classification—review of determinations

The Video Recordings (Review of Determinations) Order 1995, SI 1995/2551 (in force on 1 November 1995), enables the authority responsible for the classification of video works to review any determination made by it before 3 November 1994 as to the suitability of a video work. The authority may issue a different classification certificate from that previously issued or it may refuse to classify the work and revoke the existing certificate. A decision to withdraw a work's classification certificate takes effect after two weeks, and a decision to re-classify a work takes effect after three months. The order also requires the authority to notify certain interested persons of any decision affecting the classification of a previously classified work.

2829   Video recordings—labelling

The Video Recordings (Labelling) (Amendment) Regulations 1995, SI 1995/2550 (in force on 1 November 1995), amend the 1985 Regulations, SI 1985/911, by specifying that labels on recordings of new video works (ie those only available after 31 October 1995) will contain the unique title (as defined) assigned to them upon classification. A new explanatory statement is introduced for works which are considered to be particularly suitable for young children.

TIME

Halsbury's Laws of England (4th edn) Vol 45, paras 1101–1200

2830   Day—separate days—last moment before midnight and first moment after midnight

See *Mannai Investment Co Ltd v Eagle Star Life Assurance Co Ltd,* para 1802.

TORT

Halsbury's Laws of England (4th edn) Vol 45, paras 1201–1536

2831   Articles

Change of Position, Paul Key (on the availability of a defence of change of position to an action for restitution): 58 MLR 505

Excising Estoppel by Representation as a Defence to Restitution, Paul Key: (1995) CLJ 388

The Final Emergence of the Tort of Harassment? Tim Lawson-Cruttenden: [1995] Fam Law 625

Paying For Blame, Sarah Gibbons (on the Hillsborough tragedy and ability of on duty police officers to sue for compensation): Police Review, 10 February 1995, p 18

Striking the Balance in the Law of Restitution, Graham Virgo: [1995] LMCLQ 362

Tort, Insurance and Ideology, Jane Stapleton: 58 MLR 820

Tort or Contract? Clive Boxer (on *Henderson v Merrett Syndicate* [1994] 3 WLR 761, HL (1994 Abr para 1687)): 139 SJ 136

Tort: When Are Local Authorities Liable? Christopher Baker (on *X (Minors) v Bedfordshire County Council* (1995) Times, Independent, 30 June, HL)): 139 SJ 706

'Unjust Enrichment', Steve Hedley: (1995) 54 CLJ 578

With Malice Aforethought, John Simister (on malicious prosecution): LS Gaz, 27 September 1995, p 24

2832   Breach of statutory duty—liability of employer

See HEALTH AND SAFETY AT WORK.

2833   Breach of statutory duty—public authority—superimposition of common law duty of care

In the first two cases, the plaintiffs alleged that public authorities had negligently carried out or failed to carry out their statutory duties to protect children from child abuse. In the other cases, the plaintiffs alleged failures by local education authorities in the performance of their statutory duties to children with special educational needs. Two of the plaintiffs also alleged that the authorities were in breach of their common law duty to provide for those needs. *Held*, in each case, the court had to consider whether the statutory provisions gave rise to a private law claim in damages and then whether there was a common law duty of care owed to the plaintiff.

In the child abuse cases, all the legislation designed to protect children in need of care and protection was concerned to establish an administrative system designed to promote the social welfare of the community. Exceptionally clear statutory language would be required to show that Parliament had intended that those responsible for carrying out those functions should be liable in damages. While a direct common law duty of care would not require the court to consider policy matters which were not justiciable, it was not just and reasonable to superimpose a common law duty of care on the authorities in relation to the performance of their statutory duties to protect children. The professionals, such as psychiatrists, retained by a public authority to advise it but not to advise or treat the plaintiffs were under no separate duty of care to the plaintiffs. Their actions would fail.

In the education cases, the courts should be slow to impose a common law duty of care in the exercise of discretionary powers conferred by Parliament for social welfare purposes. However, the position of psychologists in education cases was different from that of doctors in child abuse cases. An education authority was not liable at common law for the negligent exercise of the statutory discretions under the education legislation, but it could be liable, directly and vicariously, for negligence in the operation of its psychology service and negligent advice given by its officers. The plaintiffs' claims in these cases would succeed in part.

X (Minors) v Bedfordshire County Council; M (a Minor) v Newham London Borough Council; E (a Minor) v Dorset County Council [1995] 3 All ER 353 (House of Lords: Lords Jauncey of Tullichettle, Lane, Ackner, Browne-Wilkinson and Nolan). Decision of Court of Appeal in M v Newham London Borough Council; X v Bedfordshire County Council [1994] 4 All ER 602 (1994 Abr para 363) affirmed and in E (a Minor) v Dorset County Council; Christmas v Hampshire County Council; Keating v Bromley London Borough Council [1994] 3 WLR 853 (1994 Abr para 1102) affirmed in part.

2834 Conversion—measure of damages—unlawful detention of gas cooker

See *Jackson v Wylie*, para 992.

2835 Defences—interference with goods—wheelclamping

The plaintiffs' car was wheelclamped by the defendant after it was parked on private land without authority, despite the plaintiffs having seen a notice which stated that vehicles left there without authority would be wheelclamped and a fee charged for their release. They refused to pay the release fee and removed the wheelclamps themselves later that night. They subsequently brought an action for compensation and damages for malicious falsehood and tortious interference with their car. The defendant successfully advanced two defences to the action and the plaintiffs' claim was dismissed. They appealed. *Held*, the judge had erred in his finding that the medieval defence of distress damage feasant applied. That remedy enabled a landowner to seize and withhold property found causing damage on his land until compensation had been paid. It generally applied to damage caused by straying livestock and, although it could be applied to inanimate objects, its application to the present facts was remote from anything contemplated by those who developed the remedy. The defendant could, however, rely on the defence of volenti non fit injuria. By voluntarily accepting the risk that their car might be clamped, the plaintiffs had consented both to the otherwise tortious act of clamping and to the otherwise tortious act of detaining the car until payment of a reasonable release charge. The defence was available in the present circumstances because the release fee was reasonable, easily payable and, had it been paid, the vehicle would have been released without delay. Accordingly, the appeal would be dismissed.

Arthur v Anker (1995) Times, 1 December (Court of Appeal: Sir Thomas Bingham MR, Neill and Hirst LJJ).

2836 False imprisonment—lawfully detained prisoner—prison regulations—segregation—right of action

Canada

Following a prison riot, the prison authorities decided that the plaintiff had participated in or been an instigator of it. Acting under the relevant prison regulations, the plaintiff was segregated from other prisoners for several weeks whilst an investigation into the disturbance took place. The investigation concluded that there was no evidence to support the allegation against the plaintiff, and he was therefore returned to the general prison population. On the plaintiff's claim for damages for false imprisonment, negligence and breach of his constitutional rights, *held*, the essence of the tort of false imprisonment was the imprisonment of someone who was otherwise free. As a convicted prisoner was already in prison, he could not allege false imprisonment in relation to interference with his residual liberty. It was only where prison authorities acted in bad faith, or where prison conditions were intolerable, that a prisoner might be able to rely on the tort. Although prison authorities had a duty to take reasonable care for the safety of prisoners and could therefore be liable for negligence, having regard to the facts, the prison authorities had not been in breach of that duty either at the time of the riot, nor in placing the plaintiff in segregated custody thereafter without giving him an opportunity to make representations. The plaintiff was considered to have influence over other prisoners, and during the investigation into the riot none of the prisoners would implicate him or any other prisoners. As such, although there had been no direct evidence linking the plaintiff to the riot, he was suspected of complicity in the riot because of his position of influence, and had been placed in separate custody for the security and order of the prison. The prison authorities had therefore acted reasonably in exercising their discretion under the prison regulations, and the plaintiff had been returned to the general prison population as soon as it became clear that he had not been involved in the riot. It followed that the plaintiff's constitutional right to life, liberty and security of the person had not been violated, and even if it had been, it was justifiable. Accordingly, the claims would be dismissed.

Hill v The Queen (in Right of British Colombia) (1995) 127 DLR (4th) 362 (Supreme Court). *R v Deputy Governor of Parkhurst Prison, ex p Hague; Weldon v Secretary of State for the Home Department* [1991] 3 All ER 733, HL (1991 Abr para 2386) applied.

2837 Joint tortfeasors—company and directors—release of company from liability

New Zealand
Under the terms of a debenture trust deed, a company was required to furnish regularly to the trustee reporting certificates in respect of certain matters signed by at least two of the company's directors on behalf of them all. The company was unable to repay the sums advanced. Two debenture holders brought proceedings against the trustee seeking to recover the balance of sums due to them. The trustee joined as third parties to the proceedings the directors of the company at the material time, alleging that they had prepared the certificates negligently. By a deed to which the directors were not parties, the trustee released the company from all its liabilities to the trustee. The directors sought to have the proceedings against them struck out, contending that the company's release also released them from liability to the trustee. *Held*, in preparing the certificates, the directors were acting as agents of the company within the scope of their authority. Although the directors owed a personal duty to the trustee to exercise reasonable care and skill in preparing the certificates, the company was vicariously liable for their negligence in so doing, even if it owed no direct duty of care to the trustee in relation to the preparation of the certificates. That vicarious liability had not been excluded by the terms of the trust deed so that the company and the directors were joint tortfeasors. The release of the company from liability also released the directors and, accordingly, they would be struck out as third parties to the proceedings.

New Zealand Guardian Trust Co Ltd v Brooks [1995] 1 WLR 96 (Privy Council: Lords Keith of Kinkel, Oliver of Aylmerton, Mustill, Lloyd of Berwick and Nicholls of Birkenhead). Dictum of Blackburn J in *McGowan & Co Ltd v Dyer* (1873) LR 8 QB 141 at 145, DC, applied. Dicta of Lord Lowry in *Kuwait Asia Bank EC v National Mutual Life Nominees Ltd* [1990] 3 All ER 404 at 423–425 (1990 Abr para 1895) not followed.

2838 Joint tortfeasors—defence to action—defence available to one tortfeasor only

See *Watts v Times Newspapers*, para 1882.

2839 Joint tortfeasers—recovery of contribution—authorisation of payments unjustly requested

The plaintiff company entered into an agreement with developers to share the costs of a particular project. The defendant surveyors were engaged by the plaintiff to check and authorise the plaintiff's share of development costs. Over a period of years the developers submitted a number of claims, each of which included a notional figure for interest. The defendant recommended that the sums should be paid. The plaintiff later claimed damages for negligence and breach of contract from the defendant for its failure to advise that the bills submitted by the developers included notional interest. The defendant issued proceedings against the developers, claiming compensation pursuant to the Civil Liability (Contribution) Act 1978, ss 1, 6. It appealed against the striking out of their claims. *Held*, there were three heads under which the claim could be considered: quasi-contract, breach of trust and breach of contract. Under the head of quasi-contract, it was argued that no restitutionary claim could be made in respect of a mistake of law and that the payment of sums on a mistaken construction of the agreement was a mistake of law. However, the present case involved a mistake of fact. Under the head of breach of trust, it had to be emphasised that the reference to 'responsibility' in the 1978 Act, s 2(1) would not be narrowly construed so as to restrict the wide language of s 6(1). The developers became trustees of the sums if they knew at the time of their receipt that they were not entitled to them and it was even possible that they became trustees without such knowledge. Under the head of breach of contract, the existence of an implied term as to reasonable care was proposed. In this instance there was no necessity to imply a term as the situation fell within the original agreement. Accordingly, the appeal would be allowed and the original order set aside.

Friends' Provident Life Office v Hillier Parker May & Rowden (a firm) (Estates and General plc, third parties) [1995] 4 All ER 260 (Court of Appeal: Rose, Saville and Auld LJJ).

2840   Joint tortfeasors—recovery of contribution—entitlement—whether liability in respect of same damage

The Civil Liability (Contribution) Act 1978, s 1(1) provides that any person liable in respect of any damage suffered by another person may recover contribution from any other person liable in respect of the same damage.

A building and civil engineering contractor was awarded a contract after tender by a water authority for the design and construction of a reservoir. The contractor retained a firm of consulting engineers in the preparation of the tender and for the design of the project. An engineer employed by the authority was appointed as the construction engineer who had to issue all necessary certificates. The construction of the reservoir was defective and the authority made a claim against the contractor. The claim was settled by agreement under which the contractor agreed to construct a new reservoir at its own expense. The contractor made a claim for financial losses against the firm of consulting engineers and the firm sought a contribution from the engineer employed by the authority. It fell to be determined whether the liability of the engineer to the authority was a liability in respect of the same damage as that of the firm to the contractor within the meaning of the 1978 Act. At first instance, the judge held that the firm was able to claim a contribution from the engineer since, as a matter of construction, the 1978 Act provided a remedy regardless of the causes of action which gave rise to the liability. On the engineer's appeal, *held*, the 1978 Act, s 1(1) was to be construed directly and simply. The loss suffered by the authority in not having a completed properly working reservoir at the time that it expected, the loss sustained by the contractor in having to construct a second reservoir or the damages which the firm of consulting engineers might have to pay the contractor or for which the engineer might be liable to the authority were not for 'the same damage' within the meaning of s 1(1). The judge had erred in holding that the engineer was liable and, accordingly, the appeal would be allowed.

Birse Construction Ltd v Haiste Ltd [1996] 2 All ER 1 (Court of Appeal: Nourse and Roch LJJ and Sir John May).

2841   Libel and slander

See LIBEL AND SLANDER.

2842   Malicious prosecution—false complaint—action taken by police—whether complainant responsible for prosecution

The parties were neighbours between whom acrimonious relations had existed for many years. The defendant made allegations that the plaintiff had indecently exposed himself to her. She called the police, who arrested and charged the plaintiff. No evidence was offered by the prosecution and the plaintiff was discharged. He thereupon brought an action for malicious prosecution against the defendant. The plaintiff was awarded damages at first instance, a decision that was reversed on appeal. On further appeal by the plaintiff, the issue was whether or not the defendant was properly to be regarded as having set the law in motion against the plaintiff. *Held*, the fact that a defendant in an action of malicious prosecution was not technically the prosecutor should not enable him to escape liability where he was in substance the person responsible for the prosecution having been brought. The mere fact that an individual had given information to the police which led to their bringing a prosecution did not make that individual the prosecutor. However, where an individual falsely and maliciously gave police information indicating that some person was guilty of a criminal offence and stated that he was willing to give evidence in court of the matters in question, it was properly to be inferred that he desired and intended that the person he named should be prosecuted. Where, as in the present case, the facts relating to the alleged offence could be within the knowledge only of the complainant, it became virtually impossible for the police officer to exercise any independent discretion or judgment, and if a prosecution was instituted by the police officer the proper view was that the prosecution had been procured by the complainant. Accordingly, the judge at first instance had been correct in concluding that the defendant was to be regarded as a prosecutor and the appeal would be allowed.

Martin v Watson [1995] 3 All ER 559 (House of Lords: Lords Keith of Kinkel, Slynn of Hadley, Lloyd of Berwick, Nicholls of Birkenhead and Steyn). Decision of Court of Appeal [1994] 2 All ER 606 (1994 Abr para 2709) reversed.

2843 Negligence

See NEGLIGENCE.

2844 Nuisance

See NUISANCE.

2845 Waiver of tort—deceit—mortgage obtained by fraud—retention of surplus funds by building society

The plaintiff building society gave a 100 per cent mortgage advance to the defendant based on his fraudulent misrepresentations. The defendant defaulted on interest payments and the building society obtained an order for possession. Upon sale of the defendant's house, the building society recouped all the sums that were due to it under the mortgage and placed the surplus in a suspense account, claiming that it was entitled to retain the surplus for its own use and benefit. In criminal proceedings brought against the defendant, a confiscation order was made in respect of the surplus and accrued interest and the Crown Prosecution Service (CPS) subsequently obtained a charging order over those assets. The building society claimed they were either entitled to a remedy in tort, namely damages in deceit or, alternatively, waiver of tort with restitution for the recovery of the benefit taken by the defendant. At first instance, the court dismissed the building society's claim to the surplus as against the defendant and the CPS. On appeal, *held*, the building society had no right to the surplus in tort as the law could not accord a restitutionary remedy to a secured creditor which had elected not to avoid a mortgage but to affirm it and, in doing so, had received full satisfaction. In addition, it would be wrong to treat the unjust enrichment of the defendant as having been gained at the expense of the building society, which was not the case in the circumstances in issue. Although the law did not intend to allow a person to benefit from his wrong, this did not automatically mean that in every case there would be restitution of benefit from a wrong. A constructive trust had not been created because English law had not followed other jurisdictions where constructive trusts had become a remedy for unjust enrichment. Accordingly, the building society was not entitled to the surplus, having discharged the mortgage, and the appeal would be dismissed.

Halifax Building Society v Thomas [1995] 4 All ER 673 (Glidewell, Simon Brown and Peter Gibson LJJ).

TOWN AND COUNTRY PLANNING

Halsbury's Laws of England (4th edn) Vol 46 (reissue), paras 1–768

2846 Articles

Chartered Surveyors and Land Quality Statements, Philip Wilbourn: Estates Gazette, 4 March 1995, p 311
Compensation for Adverse Decisions, Gill Castorina: Estates Gazette, 27 May 1995, p 117
Current Trends in Local Planning and Political Discretion, Alan Joyner: [1995] JP (S) 24
Golf Courses and Planning Law, H W WIlkinson: 145 NLJ 121
How the System Operates, Sir John Banham: [1995] JPL (S) 1
The Impact of Environmental Assessment on Public Inquiry Decisions, Carys Jones and Christopher Wood: [1995] JPL 890
Planning and Conservation Areas—Where do we Stand Following PPG 15, and Whatever Happened to Steinberg? D J Hughes: [1995] JPL 679
Planning and Copyright: Copyright and Planning, Alec Samuels: 159 JP Jo 212

Planning Control and Special Industrial Uses: B2 or Not 2B, Cameron Blackhall: [1995] JPL 3
Planning Decisions and Nuisance, Gill Murphy and Leslie Rutherford: 139 SJ 388
Planning, Pollution and Noise Control, Richard Stein and Sean Humber: 139 SJ 12
Planning Yesterday and Today, J F Garner: 145 NLJ 1663
The Power of the People, Susan Hamilton: [1995] JP (S) 15
Reflections on Section 54A [of the Town and Country Planning Act 1990] and 'Plan-led' Decision-making, Nicholas Herbert-Young: [1995] JPL 292
The Role and Status of Supplementary Planning Guidance, Sean White and Mark Tewdwr-Jones: [1995] JPL 471
Structure Plans—the Conduct and Conventions of Examination in Public, Richard Phelps: [1995] JPL 95
'Structures' in Planning Law, H W Wilkinson: 145 NLJ 465
Third Party Appeals: Will They Work? Do We Need Them? Stephen Crow (on third party planning appeals)): [1995] JPL 376
Town and Country Planning (Costs of Inquiries etc) Act 1995, Gregory Jones: 139 SJ 1263
Tree Preservation and Nuisance, Leslie Rutherford and Sheila Bone: [1995] JPL 102
Tree Preservation Orders, Gordon Wignall and Barry Stanton: 139 SJ 814
Who is my Neighbour?—A Response, Jane Taussik and Jane Pitson (on publicity of planning applications): [1995] JPL 12

2847 Advertisements—control of display—deemed consent for advertisement displayed on business premises—goods sold on premises

Under the Town and Country Planning (Control of Advertisements) Regulations 1992, SI 1992/666, reg 5 no advertisement may be displayed without either consent granted by the local planning authority or the Secretary of State or, in certain circumstances, by deemed consent granted under reg 6. Deemed consent is granted under reg 6 for the display of advertisements falling within Sch 3, ie any advertisement displayed on business premises wholly with reference to any or all of the following matters, namely the business carried on, the goods sold or the services provided, on those premises.

An advertisement for brands of cigars and cigarettes was displayed on the wall of restaurant premises. Cigars and cigarettes were sold in the restaurant but there was no indication on the posters that they were. The local authority charged the company responsible for the posters with displaying an advertisement without consent contrary to the 1992 Regulations. The authority contended that 'goods' in Sch 3 meant goods which were the main purpose of the business carried on within the premises rather than mere incidental items and that the company did not have deemed consent under reg 5, requiring instead an express grant of consent. A magistrates' court concluded that the regulations should be interpreted strictly and found that the company was entitled to avail itself of the provisions for deemed consent. On the authority's appeal, *held*, an advertisement displayed on business premises could advertise goods sold on the premises notwithstanding the fact that the goods were unrelated to the principal business carried on, goods sold or services provided on the premises. Such an advertisement could advertise specific product brands sold on the premises. The magistrates had been entitled to conclude that the advertisements were displayed with deemed consent and, accordingly, the appeal would be dismissed.

Berridge v Vision Posters Ltd (1995) 159 JP 218 (Queen's Bench Division: Balcombe LJ and McCullough J).

2848 Blight notice—land subject to resolution to compulsorily acquire—whether land blighted land

The Town and Country Planning Act 1990, s 150(1) provides that where the whole or part of a hereditament or agricultural unit is comprised in blighted land and a person claims that (1) he is entitled to a qualifying interest in the hereditament or unit; (2) he has made reasonable endeavours to sell that interest or the land falls within Sch 13, paras 21 or 22 and the powers of compulsory acquisition remain exercisable; and (3) in consequence of the fact that the hereditament or blighted land was or was likely to be comprised in blighted land, he has been unable to sell that interest except at a price substantially lower than that which he might have otherwise reasonably expected, he may serve on the appropriate authority notice requiring them to purchase that interest. Sch 13, para 22(a) describes a category of blighted land as land in respect of which a compulsory purchase order is in force and the appropriate authority has power to serve, but have not served, notice to treat in respect of the land.

A local council made a resolution to compulsorily acquire a building, although the compulsory purchase order was never made and they later resolved not to proceed with the purchase. The claimants occupied and held the freehold interest in the building and served a blight notice on the council under s 150(1) requiring it to purchase their interest on the grounds that the land was blighted and they were unable to sell it other than at a price substantially lower than would otherwise have been the case. The council objected to the notice. *Held*, as there was no compulsory purchase order in force and the council did not have the power to serve a notice to treat, the land did not fall within Sch 13, para 22(a). A mere resolution to compulsorily purchase was not enough, and the council's objection was therefore well founded.

Jones Son & Vernon v Sandwell Metropolitan Borough Council (1994) 68 P & CR 563 (Lands Tribunal: P H Clarke FRICS).

2849 Caravan sites—site for gipsies—breach of statutory duty to provide site—whether defence to breach of injunction

The defendant, a gipsy, purchased land situated in the green belt and moved two mobile homes and a caravan onto the site in which he and his wife, children and parents lived. The council obtained an injunction restraining the defendant and his family from using the site as a private gipsy caravan site but the defendant and his family continued to do so, in breach of the injunction. The council then obtained a committal order against the gipsies who appealed on the ground that the council was in breach of it's statutory duty to provide adequate accommodation for them under the Caravan Sites Act 1968, s 6(1). *Held*, although a council's breach of statutory duty was not a defence to a claim for an injunction by the council, it was a factor to be taken into account in considering whether to commit to prison for breach of the injunction. In this case, breach of the injunction had continued for a considerable period of time and refusal of the offer of temporary accommodation at a different site had been unreasonably refused. The committal orders against the wife, children and parents would be discharged on compassionate grounds but the one relating to the defendant would be upheld.

Waverley Borough Council v Marney (1994) 93 LGR 86 (Court of Appeal: Stuart-Smith and Russell LJJ).

2850 Caravan sites—site for gipsies—caravans on land in contravention of planning controls—enforcement measures—violation of human rights

See *Buckley v United Kingdom*, para 1583.

2851 Caravan sites—site for gipsies—local plan policy prohibiting further sites—lawfulness of policy

The applicant, a gipsy, bought land which she used as a residential caravan site. The respondent borough council had refused to grant planning permission for the retention of mobile homes on the site, on the basis that the local plan policy stated that there would be no grant of permission for further gipsy caravan sites in the area. The borough had been designated under the Caravan Sites Act 1968, s 12 (repealed) as an area which had enough caravan sites. The respondent obtained an injunction against the applicant restraining her from using the land as a caravan site, and following further breaches applied for committal proceedings against her. She then applied for leave to apply for judicial review of the respondent's decision to initiate the proceedings against her, claiming that the gipsy policy in its local plan was discriminatory and unlawful under the Race Relations Act 1976. *Held*, in the context of the local plan policy, the term 'gipsy' did not refer to Romany gipsies as an ethnic minority. It referred, in a broader sense, to any person of nomadic habit of life, whatever their race or origin. The policy marked a shift from treating gipsies as having special status, to treating them in the same way as everyone else. This did not amount to discrimination. Furthermore, the effect of the designation of the borough under the 1968 Act was to raise a presumption that such development would be inappropriate within the Green Belt. That presumption applied equally to all persons. The local plan policy was neither unlawful nor discriminatory against gipsies. Accordingly, leave to apply for judicial review would be refused.

R v Runnymede Borough Council, ex p Smith (1994) 70 P & CR 244 (Queen's Bench Division: Owen J).

2852 Costs—discretion to award costs—multiple representation—guidelines

In a case concerning planning permission for a proposed development on an out of town site, the Secretary of State and two development companies ('the first developer' and 'the second developer') were separately represented in their successful appeal against an order of the Court of Appeal. On the matter of costs, *held*, where there was multiple representation in a case, the losing party would not normally be required to pay more than one set of costs unless that was justified in all the circumstances. Although costs were in the discretion of the court, certain propositions could be made, namely that (1) the Secretary of State was entitled to the whole of his costs if he was successful in defending his original decision, and would not normally be required to share his award by apportionment with any other successful party, (2) a developer would not normally be entitled to his costs unless he could show that there was likely to be a separate issue on which he was entitled to be heard, or unless he had an interest which required separate representation. The mere fact that he was a developer would not, of itself, justify a second set of costs, (3) a second set of costs was more likely to be awarded at first instance than in the Court of Appeal or the House of Lords, by which time the issues and the extent to which there were separate interests should have become clear, and (4) an award of a third set of costs would rarely be justified, even if there were three or more separate interests. On the facts of the instant case, the Secretary of State was entitled to the whole of his costs. Even though all the issues in the case could have been put forward by counsel for the Secretary of State, the first developer was also entitled to the whole of its costs, because the case raised difficult questions of principle arising out of the change in government policy towards out of town development between the date of application and the final decision, because of the exceptional scale of the development and the importance of the outcome of the case, and because it was unusual for neighbouring local authorities to oppose a planning permission application. However, the second developer was not entitled to its costs, as the issues in its case were identical to those of the first developer.

Bolton Metropolitan District Council v Secretary of State for the Environment [1995] 1 All ER 184 (House of Lords: Lords Goff of Chieveley, Mustill, Slynn of Hadley, Lloyd of Berwick and Steyn).

For earlier related proceedings, see (1995) Times, 25 May (para 2886).

2853 Local inquiry—costs—order against planning authority—circumstances in which order may be made

A property development company applied for full planning permission to build a number of dwellings on a development site in a residential area. The local authority did not determine the application within the required period, but gave putative reasons for refusing the application, namely that the proposed development would be detrimental to the character and visual amenity of the area, and that it would result in increased traffic on the existing roads. Following a public inquiry, a planning inspector dismissed the company's appeal against the decision on the ground of inadequate landscaping. He also decided that the local authority had not properly established the reasons for refusal that it had previously put forward, and therefore awarded the company the costs that it had incurred in refuting those reasons. On the local authority's application for judicial review of the costs order, *held*, a planning inspector was obliged to give clear and intelligible reasons for a decision on costs. Although the court was reluctant to interfere with costs decisions, in the instant case, the planning inspector's reasons were so inadequate that they were prejudicial to the local authority. He had been obliged to exercise his discretion in accordance with the guidance provided by Circular 2/87, *Award of Costs Incurred in Planning and Compulsory Purchase Order Proceedings*. Paragraph 5 of the circular set out the general basis on which costs were awarded, and imposed a test of whether a local authority had acted unreasonably in refusing to grant planning permission, thereby causing the other party to incur unnecessary expense. Unreasonableness in the context of an application for costs had to be considered on the basis of *Wednesbury* principles. Paragraph 7 required a local authority to produce evidence to substantiate its reasons for refusal and gave examples of the kind of evidence that would support a refusal, but it was not inevitable that a failure to produce such evidence would lead to a finding of unreasonableness. As the planning inspector had made no findings of unreasonableness, nor a finding that the local authority had failed to produce evidence to substantiate its reasons for refusal, it was unclear whether he had had regard to the circular. Accordingly, the appeal would be allowed.

R v Secretary of State for the Environment, ex p North Norfolk District Council [1994] 2 PLR 78 (Queen's Bench Division: Auld J).

Circular 2/87 now Circular 8/93.

A local planning authority ('the applicant') refused to grant a development company ('the respondent') outline planning permission for the extension of an industrial park, and it also failed to consider the respondent's application for redevelopment of the park within the statutory time limit. The respondent appealed to the Secretary of State, who appointed an inspector to determine the matter. Following an inquiry, the parties agreed that the applicant would withdraw its opposition to the grant of outline planning permission and request the inspector to allow the appeal, subject to certain conditions as to access routes and road improvements. It was also agreed that the respondent would not ask for the costs of the inquiry. However, further disputes arose, as a result of which the respondent decided that it was not precluded from seeking its costs. The inspector determined the matter by granting outline planning permission and awarding the respondent the costs of the inquiry. The applicant applied for judicial review of the inspector's decision in relation to costs, arguing that it was perverse and unreasonable. *Held*, generally, there was an obligation on the part of both a local planning authority and a developer to reach agreement where possible. As the failure to do so in the instant case could not, as the inspector had concluded, be attributed wholly to the applicant, his decision in that respect was unreasonable and perverse. In determining the issue of costs, the inspector should have considered whether the parties had behaved reasonably towards each other. In particular, he should have had regard to the fact that the respondent had agreed at one stage that it would not pursue the costs of the inquiry. That was a material consideration which the inspector ought to have taken into consideration. Moreover, the inspector was wrong to award costs in respect of the appeal against refusal of outline planning permission as the respondent had withdrawn that appeal. Accordingly, the application would be allowed.

R v Secretary of State for the Environment, ex p London Borough of Bexley (1994) 70 P & CR 522 (Queen's Bench Division: Tucker J).

2854 Development—access land—valuation of land

The owners of a piece of land constructed an access road from it to a public highway. It was constructed across a verge owned by the local authority. The authority contended that the owners were not entitled to a right of way across the verge and the parties reached a compromise which imposed an obligation on the owners to pay to the authority, in the event of the owners' land being sold for development or the owners developing the land themselves, 30 per cent of the difference between its value taking into account its development potential and its current value. An additional obligation provided that the surveyor be guided by the approach adopted in *Stokes v Cambridge Corpn*, where the tribunal started with the value of the land if sold in plots with all services available and then made deductions of 15 per cent for the developers' profits and the costs of roads, sewers, fencing, consents and contingencies. When the owners obtained planning permission for the residential development of their land and agreed to sell it to a developer, the parties respective surveyors could not agree as to the proper application of the *Stokes* principle. *Held*, as a matter of construction, the opening valuation had to assume that development of some kind had taken place on the owners' land and had to be on the same scheme of valuation as in *Stokes*, namely on a service plot basis.

Challock Parish Council v Shirley [1995] 2 EGLR 137 (Chancery Division: Parker J). *Stokes v Cambridge Corpn* (1961) 180 Estates Gazette 839 considered.

2855 Development—appeal—determination by appointed person—prescribed classes

The Town and Country Planning (Determination of Appeals by Appointed Persons) (Prescribed Classes) (Amendment) Regulations 1995, SI 1995/2259 (in force on 2 October 1995), amend SI 1981/1804 so as to provide that the Secretary of State, and not a person appointed by him, is to determine enforcement appeals in relation to development for which an environmental statement is required under the Town and Country Planning (Environmental Assessment and Unauthorised Development) Regulations 1995, SI 1995/2258.

2856 Development—general development order—miscellaneous amendments

The Town and Country Planning General Development (Amendment) Order 1995, SI 1995/298 (in force on 9 March 1995), amends the 1988 Order, SI 1988/1813, so as to provide that permitted development is subject to the provisions of the Conservation (Natural Habitats, &c) Regulations 1994, SI 1994/2716, regs 60–63, which relate to the conservation of natural habitats and of wild fauna and flora. New Classes F and G of the 1988 Order are inserted, permitting a change of use of a building from Class A1 or Class A2 to a mixed use and as a single flat, and from such a mixed use to Class A1 or Class A2 use. It is not permitted to change the use of a building from Class A2 to Class A1 or from Class A1 to Class A2. The definition of 'protected building' in the 1988 Order is amended to exclude reference to buildings used for special industrial uses. Provision is also made for permitted development rights for the erection of certain buildings on the site of any school, college, university or hospital.

2857 Development—general development order—procedure

The Town and Country Planning (General Development Procedure) Order 1995, SI 1995/419 (in force on 3 June 1995), revokes (so far as it is not revoked by SI 1995/418) the Town and Country Planning General Development Order 1988, SI 1988/1813 (as amended), and consolidates, with amendments, the procedural provisions of the 1988 Order as amended. The order specifies the procedures connected with planning applications, appeals to the Secretary of State and related matters so far as these are not laid down in the Town and Country Planning Act 1990 and the Town and Country Planning (Applications) Regulations 1988, SI 1988/1812. The order also deals with the maintenance of registers of planning applications, applications for certificates of lawful use or development, and other related matters. The main change made by the order is the inclusion of a requirement for a local planning authority, before granting planning permission, to consult the Historic Buildings and Monuments Commission for England in relation to development likely to affect any registered Grade I or Grade II* garden or park of special historic interest.

2858 Development—general development order—procedure—Welsh forms

The Town and Country Planning (General Development Procedure) (Welsh Forms) Order 1995, SI 1995/3336 (in force on 14 February 1996), prescribes Welsh versions of the forms prescribed by the 1995 Order, SI 1995/419, which may be used in respect of land in Wales. The forms are (1) the letter sent by a local planning authority to an applicant on receipt of an application for planning permission or certificate of lawful use or development; (2) notification to be sent to an applicant when an authority refuses planning permission or grants it subject to conditions; (3) notices of an application or appeal for planning permission to be published by an applicant in a newspaper or served on an owner or tenant; (4) certificates for use with applications and appeals for planning permission relating to ownership of land and notice to be given to an agricultural tenant; (5) notices issued by an authority to publicise applications for planning permission; (6) certificate of lawful use or development.

2859 Development—general permitted development

The Town and Country Planning (General Permitted Development) Order 1995, SI 1995/418 (in force on 3 June 1995), partly revokes the Town and Country Planning General Development Order 1988, SI 1988/1813 (as amended), and consolidates, with amendments, the permitted development provisions of the 1988 Order as amended. The order revokes SI 1990/457, 2032, 1991/1536, 2268, 1992/609, 1280. The remaining provisions of the 1988 Order which deal with procedures connected with planning applications and related matters are revoked and consolidated in SI 1995/419. This order provides that planning permission may be granted for certain classes of development without any requirement for an application to be made under the Town and Country Planning Act 1990, Pt III, although in some circumstances the permission given is subject to extensive qualifications and restrictions. Sch 2 to the order, which is subject to the provisions of the order and to the Conservation (Natural Habitats, &c) Regulations 1994, SI 1994/2716, regs 60–63, sets out these classes of development in detail. The main changes made by the order are (1) the inclusion of provisions which relate to the further implementation in England and Wales of Council Directive (EC) 85/337, (2) the inclusion of provisions enabling a local planning authority to issue a direction withdrawing certain permitted development rights, within the whole or any part of a conservation area, in relation to all or any particular development, (3) the inclusion of permitted development rights for the demolition of gates, fences, walls or other means of enclosure, and (4) the inclusion of permitted development rights for closed circuit television cameras.

2860 Development—material change of use of land—operation of helicopters along and on river

Developers planned to establish a floating heliport operating along the Thames. The court's determination was sought as to whether (i) helicopters landing on a floating, unmoored vessel would amount to operational development or a change of use of land within the meaning of the Town and Country Planning Act 1990, ss 55, 57, 336; (i) the use of the heliport along the river would constitute a material change of use of land within s 55 of that Act; and (iii) the proposed operation constituted development permitted by virtue of the Town and Country Planning General Development Order 1988, SI 1988/1813, Sch 2, Pt 4, Class B. *Held*, in order to determine whether the landing and taking off of helicopters on the vessel was a use of 'land' within the meaning of the 1990 Act, s 336, it was necessary to consider that the purpose of the

Act was to prevent uncontrolled development and a broad construction would accordingly be adopted. The water of a river lay on the land and thus the use of it was a use of land. Accordingly, the proposed use of helicopters in conjunction with the vessel was a material change in the use of land, as was the operation of a heliport along the river. The proposed operation of a floating heliport constituted Class B permitted development based on the whole of a stretch of river affected rather than the individual landing and taking-off sites. Therefore, use for a total of 28 days in one year would be permitted for the whole area and not 28 days for each individual site.

Thames Heliport v London Borough of Tower Hamlets [1995] JPL 526 (Queen's Bench Division: Sir Haydn Tudor Evans). *A-G (ex rel Yorkshire Derwent Trust Ltd) v Brotherton* [1992] 1 All ER 230, HL (1991 Abr para 2589) distinguished.

2861 Development—minerals

The Town and Country Planning (Minerals) Regulations 1995, SI 1995/2863 (in force on 3 November 1995), replace the 1971 Regulations, SI 1971/756, and modify certain provisions of the Town and Country Planning Act 1990 as they apply to development consisting of the winning and working of minerals or involving the depositing of mineral waste.

2862 Development—prohibition order—order prohibiting the resumption of quarrying—Secretary of State's refusal to confirm order

A mineral planning authority wanted to prohibit the resumption of quarrying at a quarry and made an order to that effect pursuant to the Town and Country Planning Act 1990, Sch 9, para 3. The owner of the quarry and other parties objected to the order and, at a public local inquiry, the objectors gave evidence that renewed interest had been shown in the resumption of quarrying. The inspector at the inquiry gave weight to the new evidence and recommended to the Secretary of State that the order should not be confirmed. The recommendation was accepted by the Secretary of State and the authority unsuccessfully applied for judicial review of his decision. On appeal, it fell to be determined whether the Secretary of State should have reviewed the authority's decision at the date of the order or whether he was entitled to consider the position at the date of his decision. *Held*, it was not possible to deduce from Sch 9, para 3 that the function of the Secretary of State was only to review the decision of the authority as to whether or not it was properly open to the authority, on the material before it at the time, to make the prohibition order. Such a limited function would be unduly restrictive and might cause great unfairness to the owner and other objectors who would not have had the opportunity to put material before the authority which might be highly relevant. Schedule 9, para 3 would only be construed to limit the evidence entitled to be considered where there was no other tenable construction. It could not be accepted that the decision in the present case was one which no reasonable Secretary of State could have reached. In reaching his decision upon the evidence available at the date of the order and the later evidence the Secretary of State had applied the correct test and reached a conclusion which was justified. Accordingly, the appeal would be dismissed.

R v Secretary of State for Wales, ex p Mid-Glamorgan County Council [1995] JPL 1146 (Court of Appeal: Balcombe, Roch and Saville LJJ).

2863 Development—shopping centre—agreement by developer to use reasonable endeavours to obtain lettings—reverse premiums

See *P & O Property Holdings v Norwich Union Life Insurance Society*, para 1847.

2864 Development—use classes

The Town and Country Planning (Use Classes) (Amendment) Order 1995, SI 1995/297 (in force on 9 March 1995), amends the 1987 Order, SI 1987/764, by omitting classes B4 to B7. Industrial processes that were previously within those classes now fall within class B2.

2865 Development plan—determination in accordance with plan—interpretation of plan

The Town and Country Planning Act 1990, s 54A states that where, in making any determination under the Planning Acts, regard is to be had to a development plan, determination is to be made in accordance with the plan unless material considerations indicate otherwise.

The applicant built an outdoor tennis court and mower shed on a wooded strip of land adjoining his house and garden. The land lay within the Green Belt. His application for planning permission for a change of use from woodland to residential garden including a tennis court, was refused. On his appeal against an inspector's decision to uphold the respondent council's decision, *held*, the inspector had erred in law in interpreting the development plan. There was no justification for his qualification to the statutory guidance that an exception in favour of outdoor sports was intended to be restricted to public sports. However, the inspector had also concluded that the development was harmful to the surroundings, and was in conflict with the development plan for the area. That finding rendered his error in law immaterial, since he had not found any material consideration which indicated that the presumption in favour of the development plan should be rebutted. Accordingly, the appeal would be dismissed.

Houghton v Secretary of State for the Environment (1995) 70 P & CR 178 (Queen's Bench Division: Malcolm Spence QC).

2866 Enforcement notice—appeals—appeals in respect of separate parts of one site— consideration as composite application

A borough council served individual enforcement notices in respect of five separate parts of a site, a collection of former agricultural buildings. The buildings were individually occupied by the applicants who carried out commercial trading activities there. The notices required them to cease their unauthorised commercial uses. The applicants' appeals against the enforcement notices were dismissed by an inspector, and the enforcement notices were upheld. The applicants subsequently applied by notice of motion to challenge the decision. *Held*, the Town and Country Planning Act 1990, ss 174, 177 read together imposed a duty on an inspector considering separate appeals against enforcement notices to treat each individual appeal as a separate application for planning permission. Each appeal was to be treated individually and on its own merits. The inspector had erred in law in treating the five separate sites as a series of interlinked planning applications that formed part of a greater whole. Had he considered the appeals individually, the same decision might well have been reached since he would have been entitled to consider the effect of the precedent of the one on the other. Nevertheless, each case should have been considered on its own merits. Accordingly, the court would remit the decision to the Secretary of State for rehearing and redetermination.

Bruschweiller v Secretary of State for the Environment (1994) 70 P & CR 150 (Queen's Bench Division: R M K Gray QC).

2867 Enforcement notice—appeal—application for leave to appeal refused by High Court—jurisdiction of Court of Appeal to grant leave

The Town and Country Planning Act 1990, s 289(6), as amended, provides that no appeal to the Court of Appeal is to be brought except with the leave of the Court of Appeal or the High Court.

The appellants applied for leave to appeal against the decision of an inspector on enforcement notices in respect of land. The High Court refused the appellants leave to appeal to it against the inspector's decision and they then applied to the Court of Appeal for leave to appeal against that refusal, claiming that the Court of Appeal had jurisdiction to hear the application by virtue of the Supreme Court Act 1981, s 16(1), which conferred jurisdiction to hear appeals from any judgment or order. *Held*, the 1990 Act, s 289(6) provided a filter to prevent unmeritorious appeals being brought. Appeals against a refusal of leave to appeal to a court below were not within the jurisdiction of a higher court to entertain. The requirement of leave was to deter frivolous and unmeritorious appeals and that object would be frustrated if the refusal of leave itself was to become the subject of an appeal. There was nothing in the 1981 Act, s 16(1) or the 1990 Act, s 289(6) which conferred a right of appeal to the Court of Appeal and, accordingly, the applications would be dismissed.

Huggett v Secretary of State for the Environment; Wendy Fair Markets Ltd v Secretary of State for the Environment; Bello v Secretary of State for the Environment (1995) 159 LG Rev 769 (Court of Appeal: Sir Thomas Bingham MR, Kennedy and Millett LJJ).

2868 Enforcement notice—appeal—deemed planning permission—challenge by person aggrieved

A landowner was granted planning permission to build a bungalow, subject to an agricultural occupancy condition. Following his failure to comply with the condition, the local authority issued an enforcement notice. On his appeal against the notice, a planning inspector granted deemed planning permission for the retention of the bungalow without the need to comply with the agricultural occupancy condition. The applicant, who owned land which adjoined the bungalow and over which access to the bungalow was obtained, applied under the Town and

Country Planning Act 1990, s 288 for an order quashing the planning inspector's decision. *Held*, the access way to the bungalow was the subject of dispute between the parties. The applicant had made representations to the local authority when planning permission had originally been granted, had attended the local inquiry relating to the appeal against the enforcement notice, and had made written representations to the planning inspector. It was also the case that the extent and user of the access across the applicant's land might be affected by the existence or otherwise of the agricultural occupancy condition. The applicant was therefore an aggrieved person for the purposes of the 1988 Act, s 288, with standing to make the application. The planning inspector's finding that the agricultural occupancy condition had not been properly imposed was not a finding on the legal validity of the condition, but a finding that the condition was not justified on planning grounds. However, in considering whether the condition should be retained, the planning inspector should have taken account of the circumstances prevailing at the time that he granted deemed planning permission and not those in existence at the time when the condition was originally imposed. Accordingly, the application would be granted.

Bannister v Secretary of State for the Environment [1994] 2 PLR 90 (Queen's Bench Division: David Widdicombe QC). *Turner v Secretary of State for the Environment* (1973) 28 P & CR 123, applied.

2869 Enforcement notice—appeal—evidence

An enforcement notice alleged that the respondent had erected a barn on agricultural land without planning permission. It required him to remove the barn and restore the land to agricultural use. On the respondent's appeal against the notice, the inspector reduced the area of land to which the notice applied and extended the period for its removal. The respondent's further appeal to the High Court was allowed on the ground that the construction of the barn constituted permitted development and that the inspector's decision was perverse. The Secretary of State appealed. *Held*, the High Court should not have received any of the evidence given to the inspector because it had not been argued that he had not summarised properly or had disregarded material evidence. The receipt of such evidence led, in part, to a finding of fact which should not have been made. It was for the inspector to decide whether the barn was reasonably necessary for the purposes of the activities that might be conducted on the respondent's land. The test of reasonable necessity had to be related to the barn which was the subject of the alleged permission within the Town and Country Planning General Development Order 1988, SI 1988/1813. To that extent, the inspector had used the correct test. He had concentrated on what was actually planned by the respondent. He was not required to consider other possible, but unlikely, activities for which the respondent had not actually sought permission. The appeal would be allowed.

Clarke v Secretary of State for the Environment (1992) 160 LGR 50 (Court of Appeal: Fox, Glidewell and Boreham LJJ).

2870 Enforcement notice—appeal—procedure—conformity with European Convention on Human Rights

See *Bryan v United Kingdom*, para 1576.

2871 Enforcement notice—non-compliance—alleged invalidity of enforcement notice

The appellant had been charged with failure to take steps required by an enforcement notice within the compliance period contrary to the Town and Country Planning Act 1990, s 179. He had changed his plea to guilty after a ruling by the judge that the alleged invalidity of an enforcement notice not bad on its face could not be raised as a defence to the charge. On appeal, *held*, so long as the enforcement notice was not a nullity, patently defective on its face, it would remain effective until quashed. For an offence under s 179 to be proved in criminal proceedings there was no requirement to prove that the decision of the local planning authority to issue the notice was valid and within its powers. Only the High Court had the jurisdiction to quash an enforcement notice and to consider the relevant policy documents to determine whether the issuing of the enforcement notice was perverse in a *Wednesbury* sense. No criminal court had that power. The appropriate procedure would be for the defendant to raise the validity of the council's decision as the basis of an application for an adjournment, with an undertaking to apply for judicial review to quash the notice. Accordingly, the appeal would be dismissed.

R v Wicks (1995) 93 LGR 377 (Court of Appeal: Lord Taylor of Gosforth CJ, Mantell and Keene JJ). *Wednesbury Corpn v Associated Provincial Picture Houses Ltd* [1948] KB 223, considered.

2872 Enforcement notice—replacement notice—limitation period

An unauthorised change of use of land began more than ten years before the issue of enforcement notices, issued under the Town and Country Planning Act 1990, s 171B(4), which replaced notices issued a year earlier which had been found to be defective and withdrawn. Section 171B(4) permits further enforcement action to be taken in respect of a breach of planning control within four years of any previous actual or purported action in relation to that breach. It fell to be determined whether the uses in question were immune from enforcement action under a ten-year limitation period which came into force before the replacement notices were issued. *Held*, a breach of planning control had to be distinguished from the limitation period applying to enforcement action in respect of the breach of control. The breach of planning control alleged in a 'second bite' enforcement notice under s 171B(4) had to be the same as that alleged in the first defective enforcement notice. The original notices were issued under transitional provisions continuing the original limitation period; the replacement notices were issued after the expiry of those provisions and the coming into force of the new limitation period. Those notices were governed by the ten-year limitation period and could only relate to an unauthorised change of use occurring since the introduction of that limitation period.

William Boyer (Transport) Ltd v Secretary of State for the Environment (1994) 69 P & CR 630 (Queen's Bench Division: Jeremy Sullivan QC).

2873 Existing use certificate—grant of temporary planning permission—effect

The use of the applicants' land for repairing and storing motor vehicles had been begun prior to the beginning of 1964 without planning permission and had continued ever since. In 1987 temporary permission for that use for a period of two years had been granted. A further application by the applicants to continue the temporary use was refused and subsequently an enforcement notice was issued against them. The applicants applied for an existing use certificate in respect of the use of the land. This was refused and the applicants appealed. *Held*, the provisions of the Town and Country Planning Act 1990, ss 191, 192 gave to an established use of land an immunity from enforcement action. However, the sections did not go further than that and the use remained in breach of planning control. Accordingly, the established use referred to in s 191 was necessarily an unlawful one. Immediately before the applicants were granted the temporary planning permission their use of the land was an established use within s 191. If the applicants, instead of applying for planning permission, had applied for an existing use certificate, the council would have been bound to have granted it. The effect of the planning permission was to render that which had been unlawful lawful and accordingly the established use no longer continued. Section 191 ceased to apply and with it ceased the applicants' entitlement to the grant of an existing use certificate. Accordingly, the appeal would be dismissed.

Bailey v Secretary of State for the Environment [1995] 8 LS Gaz R40 (Court of Appeal: Nourse and Henry LJJ and Potts J). *Bolivian and General Tin Trust Ltd v Secretary of State for the Environment* [1972] 1 WLR 1481 affirmed.

2874 Listed building—enforcement notice—appeal against notice—administrative error

See *O'Brien v Secretary of State for the Environment*, para 2196.

2875 Local inquiry—inspector—possibility of bias—cross-examination of inspector

The applicants, a father and his son, applied for permission to change the use of a barn. The local authority refused the application and an inspector dismissed their appeal following an inquiry. The applicants claimed that at the inquiry the inspector said a planning officer giving evidence had visited his office and that, after the close of the inquiry, the inspector and a council representative looked at a document together. The applicants sought to quash the inspector's decision and to cross-examine him on the grounds that (1) there was a real possibility of bias on the inspector's part having regard to his behaviour before and after the close of the inquiry, (2) the inspector took into consideration new evidence not raised at the inquiry without affording them an opportunity to comment on it, and (3) the inspector's failure to allow them to comment on new evidence after the close of the inquiry was in breach of the rules of natural justice. The inspector denied the allegations. At first instance, the judge read the parties' affidavits and held that all the evidence had been given in good faith and that any differences were no more than differences of recollection. He refused the applicants leave to cross-examine. On appeal, *held*, the court was unable to understand on what basis the judge had been able to find as he did. If the applicants' evidence stood alone it would be insufficient to establish their grounds of complaint. However, the difficulty arose from the inspector's denial of the parties' precise movements after the close of the inquiry as set out in the applicant's affidavits. Although it was usually undesirable that a person holding a quasi-judicial office should be exposed to cross-examination, justice to the parties and the inspector required that the disputed questions of fact be tested in the normal way by cross-examination. Accordingly, the appeal would be allowed.

Jones v Secretary of State for Wales (1995) 159 LG Rev 689 (Court of Appeal: Balcombe, Roch and Saville LJJ).

2876 Local plan—objection to proposal to include land as green belt—inquiry—burden of proof

Developers objected to the deposited draft of a local plan which designated an area of their land as green belt and for cemetery use. The local authority accepted the objections and modified the proposals to designate the land for development as a business park. A number of organisations objected to the modifications and a local plan inquiry was held. The inspector's recommendations, in effect, reinstated the original proposals and the local authority's adopted local plan reflected that. The developers unsuccessfully requested a second inquiry and then applied to quash the local plan in so far as it designated their land as green belt and for cemetery use. They submitted that the inspector (1) approached the matter as if there was a burden of proof on the objectors to the green belt proposal to justify exclusion from the green belt, and (2) did not treat the case as if the extension of the green belt boundaries required exceptional circumstances. *Held*, (1) no such burden of proof existed upon those objecting to a proposed green belt. On the contrary, it was for the body promoting the alteration to apply the relevant government policy. (2) It was not absolutely necessary for the inspector to find that exceptional circumstances existed before a green belt boundary was altered. However, he had to have regard to the government's green belt policy and apply it or depart from it giving adequate reasons. The question at the inquiry was whether the land should be included in the green belt, not whether it should have been excluded. The inspector had been seriously at fault. On the correct approach, there would have been a realistic prospect that the land would not have been included in the green belt and therefore that part of the local plan would be quashed. The application would be allowed accordingly.

Swan Hill Developments Ltd v Southend-on-Sea Borough Council [1994] 3 PLR 14 (Queen's Bench Division: Malcolm Spence QC).

2877 Planning permission—application—application called in by Secretary of State—policy guidelines

Company A applied for planning permission to build a supermarket on a site outside a town. Shortly afterwards Company B also applied for permission to build a supermarket on a site in the town centre which had been designated for development in the local plan. The town could only support one new supermarket. Company B's application was called in for determination by the Secretary of State, but he refused the local authority's request to call in the other application and to hold a joint inquiry. The authority applied to quash that decision and were successful at first instance when the judge held that (1) in a case where there was no obligation to give reasons for a decision, if all the facts and circumstances pointed to a particular decision but the actual decision was different, it was open to the court to infer that there was no valid reason for the decision, and (2) under an unofficial guideline for call-in, which was further to the official guidelines on the recovery of cases for decision by the Secretary of State published in *Planning Appeals, Call-in and Major Public Inquiries* (Cm 43), where two proposals could be considered as potential alternatives, the court was entitled to expect reasons why the Secretary of State had not followed and applied the guidelines. On appeal by the Secretary of State and Company A, *held*, the Secretary of State did not have to give reasons for calling in an application, although he had in any event done so in the present case. Further, it could not be accepted that any unofficial guideline to which the judge referred existed. The judge had been wrong and, accordingly, the appeals would be allowed.

Secretary of State for the Environment v South Northamptonshire District Council (1995) 70 P & CR 124 (Court of Appeal: McCowan, Roch and Ward LJJ). *Padfield v Minister of Agriculture, Fisheries and Food* [1968] 1 All ER 694, HL, and *R v Secretary of State for the Environment, ex p Allied London Property Developments Ltd* (unreported, 11 April 1990) considered.

2878 Planning permission—application—Crown land—modification of statutory provisions

The Town and Country Planning (Crown Land Applications) Regulations 1995, SI 1995/1139 (in force on 3 June 1995), replace the 1992 Regulations, SI 1992/2683, and modify provisions of the Town and Country Planning Act 1990 and the Town and Country Planning (General Development Procedure) Order 1995, SI 1995/419, in their application to Crown land. The modifications relate to applications in respect of Crown land for planning permission and for lawful development certificates.

2879 Planning permission—assumption of obligations—certainty of operations and activities

The Town and Country Planning Act 1990, s 106(1)(b) provides that any person interested in land in the area of a local planning authority may, by agreement or otherwise, enter into an obligation requiring specified operations or activities to be carried out in, on, under or over the land.

Trustees of an estate applied for planning permission for a golf course. They stated that their purpose in doing so was to generate funds for the repair of listed buildings on the estate. They appealed to the Secretary of State against the planning authority's failure to determine their application. They subsequently entered into a unilateral undertaking to dispose of the golf course and to use the income so generated for the repair of the buildings over a twenty year period in accordance with a yearly schedule to be submitted to the council. Planning permission was granted at a public inquiry by an inspector appointed by the Secretary of State. The council applied to quash the decision on the grounds that the unilateral undertaking did not constitute a planning obligation under the 1990 Act, s 106(1)(b) and that since the undertaking was contingent on uncertain events it was unenforceable. *Held*, the yearly schedule of intended works would have the effect of defining the operations and activities as required by s 106(1)(b). Where, in the case of a unilateral undertaking, the matter is being considered by an appellate tribunal, the question to be asked is whether the agreement is likely to achieve the local planning authority's objectives, which in the present case it did. Furthermore, the undertaking was capable of being enforced under s 106. Accordingly, the application would be dismissed.

South Oxfordshire District Council v Secretary of State for the Environment (1994) 68 P & CR 551 (Queen's Bench Division: Sir Graham Eyre QC).

2880 Planning permission—change of use class—solicitor's office—place providing services to visiting members of the public

A local authority planning inspector refused to grant a solicitor planning permission to change the use of a retail shop to a solicitor's office within class A2 of the Town and Country Planning (Use Classes) Order 1987, SI 1987/764. The decision was upheld on appeal. On the solicitor's further appeal, *held*, a solicitor's office had to be providing services principally to visiting members of the public in order to fall within class A2. As citizens' advice bureaux and law centres were included in class A2, there was no reason why the office of a profit-making legal adviser should not also qualify as class A2 use. The fact that a solicitor operated an appointments system was not conclusive of the matter, as it could not be assumed that appointments had not originally been made by those who had walked in off the street. Although some solicitors' practices were definitely not within class A2 because their services were provided principally by telephone and correspondence, some solicitors did provide services principally to visiting members of the public. As such, as long as an applicant could plausibly say that his legal services would be principally for visiting members of the public, planning permission was to be granted. Accordingly, the appeal would be allowed.

Kalra v Secretary of State for the Environment (1995) Times, 13 November (Court of Appeal: Staughton, Henry and Pill LJJ). Decision of David Widdicombe QC [1994] 2 PLR 99 reversed.

2881 Planning permission—conditional permission—agricultural workers' occupancy condition—removal—planning policy guidance notes

A local planning authority granted planning permission for a dwelling house, subject to a condition that it could be occupied only by a person employed locally in agriculture or forestry, or by the dependants of such a person ('the occupancy condition'). Over 20 years later, the occupant applied for permission to remove the occupancy condition. At the time that the application was considered, a planning policy guidance note provided that when determining an application for the removal of an occupancy condition, there had to be a realistic assessment of the continuing need for it, bearing in mind the need for a dwelling for someone employed in agriculture in the area as a whole, and not just on the particular holding to which the application related. The local planning authority refused the occupant's application, but in reliance on the guidance note, an inspector allowed the occupant's appeal and also made an order for costs against the local planning authority. On the local planning authority's appeal against the substantive decision and application for judicial review of the costs decision, *held*, it was not appropriate in planning matters to apply legalistic canons of construction to planning policy statements. The guidance note was lawful and raised a relevant material consideration, and the inspector had expressly had regard to it in reaching his decision, in particular to the need to make a realistic assessment of whether or not the occupancy condition was still necessary in the area as a whole. It was also material to take account of the probability that an agricultural planning condition would not be imposed if a contemporary application for planning permission was to be made. As such, the inspector had not erred in law in deciding to allow the appeal. As regards costs, the inspector had made an order for costs against the local planning authority because he considered that it had behaved unreasonably and that the occupant had thereby incurred unnecessary expense. That decision was not unreasonable. Accordingly both the appeal and the application for judicial review would be dismissed.

Hambleton District Council v Secretary of State for the Environment (1994) 70 P & CR 549 (Queen's Bench Division: May J).

2882 Planning permission—conditional permission—application for amendment of conditions—time limit

The Town and Country Planning Act 1990, s 73(4) contains an exception where the previous planning permission was granted subject to a condition as to the time within which the development to which it related was to be begun and where that time expired without the development being begun.

Developers obtained three consecutive planning permissions in respect of a particular site, the last of which was granted subject to conditions. Those conditions included an application for approval of reserved matters within two years from the date of the permission. They submitted an application for approval of certain reserved matters just within the two year period and then applied under the 1990 Act, s 73 for amendment to the conditions of the planning permission. They later appealed to the Secretary of State against the non-determination of their application under that section. He decided that an application under s 73 could be made provided it was begun within the time limit for beginning the development. The planning authority applied for an order of certiorari quashing the decision, arguing that the planning permission had lapsed under its own conditions and that an application under s 73 could only be made if the planning permission to which the conditions attached had not expired. *Held*, there was nothing to prevent the making of applications under s 73 after the expiry of the period for the application for approval of reserved matters; s 73(4) referred to a previous planning permission and not an application for approval of reserved matters. Accordingly, the application would be dismissed.

R v Secretary of State for the Environment, ex p Corby Borough Council (1994) 68 P & CR 544 (Queen's Bench Division: Pill J).

2883 Planning permission—conditional permission—application to dispense with condition—appeal against refusal

The respondents owned a former farm and were granted planning permission for five years to use it as hackney livery stables. They were also granted permission to create a dwelling-house out of former farm outbuildings on condition that the house was occupied only by the trainer/manager of the hackney stables, or persons employed locally in agriculture or forestry. They were later granted planning permission subject to a different condition, which limited occupation to themselves or persons employed in agriculture or forestry. The respondents' application for permission to dispense with the later condition was refused by the local planning authority, but an inspector appointed by the Secretary of State allowed their appeal against the refusal. On the local planning authority's appeal, *held*, the inspector had been entitled to consider whether it had been appropriate to impose the condition and to conclude that it had not been appropriate. However, having regard to the Town and Country Planning Act 1990, ss 73 and 73A, he had failed to inquire whether the condition was justified at the time that he determined the appeal and, accordingly, the appeal would be allowed.

Sevenoaks District Council v Secretary of State for the Environment (1995) 69 P & CR 87 (Queen's Bench Division: Gerald Moriarty QC).

2884 Planning permission—environmental assessment—planning authority's opinion

The Town and Country Planning (Environmental Assessment and Permitted Development) Regulations 1995, SI 1995/417 (in force on 3 June 1995), enable a person who wishes to undertake a development to seek an opinion from a planning authority as to whether an application for proposed development would or would not be a Schedule 1 or Schedule 2 application within the meaning of the Town and Country Planning (Assessment of Environmental Effects) Regulations 1988, SI 1988/1199. Any such opinion may be referred to the Secretary of State for his direction and any application where the relevant planning authority is the prospective developer or one of joint developers may be referred to the Secretary of State for his opinion. All opinions, directions and statements of reasons given must be open to public inspection.

2885 Planning permission—environmental information

The Town and Country Planning (Environmental Assessment and Unauthorised Development) Regulations 1995, SI 1995/2258 (in force on 2 October 1995), implement Council Directive (EC) 85/337. In particular (1) where an application has been made for planning permission in respect of which an enforcement notice has been issued and in respect of which an environmental assessment would have been required for the purposes of SI 1988/1199, the 1995 Regulations preclude the Secretary of State from granting planning permission on the determination of the enforcement notice appeal without first considering an environmental statement relating to the development, (2) if a local planning authority believes that the matters to which an enforcement notice relate constitute development to which the 1988 Regulations would have applied, it must inform the recipient of the enforcement notice, the Secretary of State, and the persons who would have been consulted if an application for planning permission had been made, of its belief, and also require any appeal to the Secretary of State to be accompanied by an environmental statement, (3) where such information has been given to a person, he may seek a direction from the Secretary of State and obtain information relevant to the preparation of his environmental statement from the local planning authority and any other person, (4) where an appellant has not provided an environmental statement, the Secretary of State may require him to do so, unless he has provided such a statement in connection with a parallel appeal against the refusal of planning permission for the same development as that to which the enforcement notice relates, (5) the Secretary of State must give specified persons the opportunity to make representations in relation to environmental statements, (6) where the Secretary of State requires an appellant to provide further information and evidence, he must give specified persons the opportunity to make representations in relation to such further information, (7) the local planning authority must advertise the fact that it has received an environmental statement, and must indicate the procedure for making representations to the Secretary of State, (8) documents issued and received by local planning authorities under the regulations must be made available for public inspection, and (9) provision is made for service of documents and for appeals to the High Court where planning permission has been granted in contravention of the regulations.

2886 Planning permission—grant—decision of Secretary of State—form of decision

The plaintiff had, on appeal, successfully applied for the quashing of a decision of the Secretary of State to grant planning permission for the construction of a shopping centre and sports complex on land which was part of an urban development area, on the ground that the Secretary of State had failed to consider the urban regeneration implications. On further appeal by the Secretary of State, *held*, in reaching his decision the Secretary of State had to state his reasons in sufficient detail for a reader to ascertain what conclusions he had reached as regards the most controversial and important issues and it would be an unjustifiable burden to expect him to refer to every material consideration and argument, however insignificant. In this case, the Secretary of State had stated his conclusion on the urban regeneration implications and although his reasons were not very full and were in certain respects badly expressed, they were adequate. Although government policy had shifted between the original planning application and the Secretary of State's final decision, whether this was sufficient to justify reopening the inquiry or refusing permission was a matter for his planning judgment. His decision showed that he had taken into account this policy shift and accordingly, the appeal would be allowed.

Bolton Metropolitan District Council v Secretary of State for the Environment [1996] 1 All ER 184 (House of Lords: Lords Goff of Chieveley, Mustill, Slynn of Hadley, Lloyd of Berwick and Steyn). Decision of Court of Appeal (1994) 69 P & CR 324 reversed.

2887 Planning permission—grant—decision of Secretary of State—unsuccessful challenge by local authority—award of costs

The Secretary of State granted planning permission to a developer in respect of land within the area of a local authority. The authority unsuccessfully applied to quash the Secretary of State's decision pursuant to the Town and Country Planning Act 1990, s 288. Although costs were awarded to the developer, who was intent on upholding the Secretary of State's conclusion, the judge declined to order that the authority should pay the Secretary of State's costs. On the

Secretary of State's appeal, *held*, the judge was plainly wrong not to award any costs in favour of the Secretary of State. It was the Secretary of State's decision that was being attacked and his counsel bore the burden of presenting the arguments. The only question for the judge was whether the developer should have been awarded some part of his costs in addition to an award in favour of the Secretary of State. Where issues argued by two respondents were identical, the court should be disposed to make only one order for costs and, if it did, it would be appropriate to afford the parties the opportunity of determining for themselves what the appropriate apportionment should be between them. Provision should be made for recourse to the court so as to make an order in default of agreement. The only way in which the situation could be rectified would be by allowing the appeal and awarding costs to the Secretary of State in addition to the order already made in favour of the developer.

Wychavon District Council v Secretary of State for the Environment [1994] 69 P & CR 394 (Court of Appeal: Leggatt, Roch and Morritt LJJ).

2888 Planning permission—grant—grant specifying floor area greater than area in outline permission—whether grant limited to smaller area

A local authority sold a site, which had outline planning permission, to a developer. The outline permission provided for the creation of 1055 sq m of additional floor area. When the developer applied for planning permission he made reference to the outline permission but stated that the proposed additional floor area to be created was 1530 sq m. The authority refused to approve the development because of the 45 per cent increase in area. The Secretary of State appointed an inspector to determine whether the developer's proposal was outside the terms of the original planning permission because of the increased floor area. The inspector found that it did not fall outside the original permission. The authority sought judicial review of the inspector's decision but its application was dismissed. On appeal, the authority submitted that it lacked jurisdiction to grant permission for substantially more than had been applied for. *Held*, it did not follow that an enlargement of the application site was ipso facto invalid. The real question was whether the permission as granted was invalid having regard to the application which was limited to 1055 sq m. If the validity of a permission was to be challenged on the ground that it substantially exceeded what was applied for, such challenge had to be made promptly, otherwise the permission would be taken to be valid. In the present case, the time for challenge had long since passed and, accordingly, the appeal would be dismissed.

Slough Borough Council v Secretary of State for the Environment (1995) 159 LG Rev 969 (Court of Appeal: Stuart-Smith, Morritt and Ward LJJ).

2889 Planning permission—grant—material considerations—motorist service area

In a written representation appeal against the refusal of planning permission for a motorist service area on the applicant's land, it fell to be determined whether the relative merits of alternative sites should have been taken into consideration in considering his planning application. *Held*, that depended on the existence of (1) the presence of a clear public convenience or advantage in the application under consideration, (2) the existence of inevitable and adverse effects or disadvantages to the public in the application, (3) the existence of an alternative site for the same project which would not have those effects or would have them to the same extent, and (4) a situation in which there could only be one permission granted for such development or at least only a very limited number of permissions. The alternative sites in question had been the subject of planning applications and a number of them were the subject of appeals. They were material considerations which should have been taken into consideration.

Secretary of State for the Environment v Edwards (1994) 69 P & CR 607 (Court of Appeal: Sir Stephen Brown P, Russell and Roch LJJ). *Greater London Council v Secretary of State for the Environment* (1985) 52 P & CR 158, CA, applied.

2890 Planning permission—grant—material considerations—need for housing of a particular type

The Town and Country Planning Act 1990, s 70(2) provides that in dealing with an application for planning permission, a local planning authority must have regard to the provisions of the development plan, so far as material to the application, and to any other material considerations.

The appellant applied to the local authority for planning permission to change the use of his property from a house in multiple occupation, namely 20 bedsitting rooms, to seven self-contained flats. When the local authority failed to determine the application within the prescribed period, the appellant appealed to the Secretary of State. It was the local authority's policy that there was a need for all types of housing in the area in which the appellant's property was situated, in particular for cheap multiple occupation housing, and the proposed conversion of his house into more expensive accommodation was therefore contrary to that policy. Although the policy was not part of the local authority's official development plan, it was included in its draft unitary development plan. The Secretary of State agreed with the policy, and therefore refused to grant planning permission. On appeal, the issue was whether the policy was a material consideration within the meaning of the 1990 Act, s 70(2). *Held*, material considerations were those which served a planning purpose, and a planning purpose was one which related to the character of the use of land. Material considerations included not only matters relating to the environment or amenities, but also to the need for housing in a particular area, as such a need related to the character or the use of the land. There was no distinction between a need for housing generally and a need for a particular type of housing, and the fact that the need for housing was dictated by cost or type of tenure was irrelevant. Moreover, the local authority's policy was not an attempt to transfer its statutory obligations as regards the provision of housing to the private sector. Accordingly, the appeal would be dismissed.

Mitchell v Secretary of State for the Environment (1994) 69 P & CR 60 (Court of Appeal: Balcombe and Saville LJJ, and Sir Roger Parker).

2891 Planning permission—grant—material considerations—offer to fund highway improvements

A developer offered to provide funding for certain highway improvements if it was granted planning permission to build a new foodstore. At a public inquiry, the inspector took account of the offer and recommended approval of the developer's application. The Secretary of State, however, refused the application and granted planning permission to a rival development on a nearby site. In doing so, the Secretary of State applied his published policy that, to enforce the rule that planning consent should not be bought and sold, planning obligations which were not directly related to the proposed development should not be used to extract payments in cash or kind from developers as the price of planning permission. The court quashed the Secretary of State's decision on the ground that he had failed to take into account the material consideration of the offer of the funding, contrary to the Town and Country Planning Act 1990, s 70(2). The Secretary of State's appeal was allowed on the ground that he had not failed to treat the developer's offer of funding as material but had simply declined to attach any significant weight to it. On appeal by the developer, *held*, for the purposes of the 1990 Act, s 70(2) a 'material' consideration meant a relevant consideration. Whether a consideration was relevant was a matter for the court to decide but it was entirely for the decision maker to attribute to a relevant consideration such weight as he thought fit and unless he acted unreasonably in doing so the court would not interfere with his decision. An offered planning obligation which had nothing to do with the proposed development, apart from the fact that it was offered by the developer, was plainly not a material consideration and could only be regarded as an attempt to buy planning permission. However, if it had some connection with the proposed development which was not de minimis, then regard had to be had to it. On the other hand, the extent, if any, to which it affected the decision was a matter entirely within the discretion of the decision maker, and if the decision maker was the Secretary of State he was entitled in exercising that discretion to have regard to his established policy. On the facts, the Secretary of State had not disregarded the applicant's offer of funding as being immaterial. On the contrary, he had given it careful consideration and therefore his decision was not open to challenge. The appeal would therefore be dismissed.

Tesco Stores Ltd v Secretary of State for the Environment [1995] 2 All ER 636 (House of Lords: Lords Keith of Kinkel, Ackner, Browne-Wilkinson, Lloyd of Berwick and Hoffmann). Decision of Court of Appeal (1994) 68 P & CR 219 (1994 Abr para 2751) affirmed.

2892 Planning permission—market—creation of market right

See *Delyn Borough Council v Solitaire (Liverpool) Ltd*, para 2023.

2893 Planning permission—nuisance—authorisation of nuisance by grant of planning permission

See *Wheeler v J J Saunders Ltd*, para 2186.

2894 Planning permission—outline planning permission—approval of reserved matters—application to quash decision of Secretary of State

The Town and Country Planning Act 1990, s 54A provides that where, in making any determination under the Planning Acts, regard is to be had to the development plan, the determination must be made in accordance with the plan unless material considerations indicate otherwise.

Developers were granted outline planning permission on appeal for residential development of land. They submitted two separate detailed schemes for the local authority's approval, but the authority failed to give the developers notice of its decision in respect of the first scheme within the prescribed time limit and it refused the second scheme. The developers appealed to the Secretary of State but an inspector dismissed both appeals. They then applied for the Secretary of State's decisions to be quashed on the grounds that (1) the 1990 Act, s 54A did not apply to an application for reserved matters, and (2) the inspector had redetermined the principle of development which had been established by the outline permission. *Held*, (1) there was no doubt that the 1990 Act required that s 54A should apply to such an appeal. The Secretary of State therefore had to have regard to the provisions of the development plan and had to act in accordance with s 54A. Further, s 54A applied because the development plan was a material consideration and regard had to be paid to such a consideration. (2) Consideration of the decision letter indicated consistency between the inspector's decision and the outline permission, that he was mindful that the principle of development had been established and that he properly restricted himself to reserved matters. Accordingly, the application would be dismissed.

St George Developments Ltd v Secretary of State for the Environment [1994] 3 PLR 33 (Queen's Bench Division: Nigel Macleod QC).

2895 Planning permission—refusal—reasons for refusal

A district council challenged a decision of the Secretary of State whereby he quashed three enforcement notices and granted retrospective planning permission for the change of use of three plots of land from former agricultural use to residential use. The council contended that the inspector ('the second inspector') on whose advice the Secretary of State had acted, had failed to take into account the decision of an inspector ('the first inspector') who, only six months earlier, had refused planning permission in respect of the same land which he believed to be Green Belt land. *Held*, the second inspector had to reach his own conclusions. He had clearly had regard to the first inspector's decision. In his decision letter, the second inspector had explained why he did not agree with the first inspector as to the visual impact of the development. Where aesthetic matters were concerned, a short reason for differing from an earlier decision sufficed. The second inspector, in stating that the first inspector's decision was material, had indicated that he was well aware of the need to secure consistency in the decision-making process. The second inspector, who had received information that the land in question was not Green Belt land, was obliged to exercise his own planning judgment and was not obliged to perpetuate the error of the first inspector as to the Green Belt issue. The council's application would be dismissed.

Aylesbury Vale District Council v Secretary of State for the Environment (1993) 68 P & CR 276 (Queen's Bench Division: Jeremy Sullivan QC).

2896 Planning permission—renewal—application—material considerations—affordable housing policy

A local authority had granted the developer outline planning permission for a residential development. Before the permission expired the developer unsuccessfully applied to renew it. On appeal, an inspector concluded that, because the application was made before the permission lapsed, it should only have been refused if a material change in planning circumstances required it. The authority had adopted a planning policy for local needs housing and a housing strategy statement following the advice contained in a Planning Policy Guidance Note which indicated that a community's need for affordable housing was a material consideration. Although the affordable housing policy did not apply to the developer's site, the inspector held that the developer's proposal did not make secure provision for affordable housing appropriate to the site and refused to grant planning permission. The developer applied to quash the inspector's decision contending that the Secretary of State did not advise, even where there was such a policy, that planning permission could be refused for a proposal which was acceptable in every other respect solely on the basis that the scheme did not make provision for affordable housing where the policy was non-statutory. *Held*, there was no authority for the proposition that a material consideration, which was to be found outside the wording of the statutory policies which were relevant to the decision, or which arose only by implication, was not capable of being treated by an inspector as a matter of considerable weight. Nor was there authority for the proposition that such a consideration, derived from matters arising outside the language of the development plan, could not justify refusal on the grounds that to allow the permission would give rise to demonstrable harm. Accordingly, the application would be dismissed.

ECC Construction Ltd v Secretary of State for the Environment [1994] 69 P & CR 51 (Queen's Bench Division: Gerald Moriarty QC).

2897   Purchase notice—validity—notice served in respect of only part of land refused planning permission

The Town and Country Planning Act 1990, s 137(1)(a) (service of purchase notices) applies where on an application for planning permission to develop any land, permission is refused or is granted subject to conditions.

The claimants purchased a disused railway cutting and applied to the local authority for planning permission for residential development of a certain area of the land. When the application was refused, the claimants served a purchase notice on the local authority under the Town and Country Planning Act 1990, s 137(2)(a), requiring it to purchase their freehold interest in the land. A preliminary issue was whether the purchase notice was valid, as it related to only part of the land for which planning permission had been refused. *Held*, the use of the words 'the land' throughout s 137 was a reference to the whole of the land that had been refused planning permission. A landowner therefore could not serve a purchase notice in respect of only part of that land, as there was no express provision in s 137 to that effect, nor could words be implied into s 137 to give it such a meaning. The purchase notice procedure in s 137 was governed by the extent of the land in the refusal or conditional grant of planning permission, and accordingly, the application would be refused.

Cook v Winchester City Council (1994) P & CR 99 (Lands Tribunal: PH Clarke FRICS). *Smart & Courtney Dale Ltd v Dover Rural District Council* (1972) P & CR 408, and *Wain v Secretary of State for the Environment* (1981) 44 P & CR 289 (1981 Abr para 488) considered.

2898   Structure plan—priority given to development near city centre—application of government policy

The plaintiff applied for planning permission to build a superstore on a site located outside a city centre, but was turned down by the local planning authority. An appeal to a planning inspector failed on the ground that the county structure plan, which was based on the Government's Planning Policy Guidance document number 6 (PPG 6), stated that priority had to be given to retail schemes located in or adjacent to a city centre. Preference would therefore be given to a rival superstore which had applied to build on a site adjacent to the city centre provided the plaintiff's application was not granted. The plaintiff appealed further on the ground that the inspector had grossly misunderstood government policy as formulated in PPG 6 when considering the plaintiff's application. *Held*, in the present circumstances, the word 'priority' indicated that preference ought to be given to sites adjacent to, or in, city centres. PPG 6 was merely a background on which to formulate structure plan policy. As there was material to show that there was a real possibility of a separate development which would meet the identified need for more retail floorspace taking place on a more appropriate site, according to the structure plan policy, that was a justification for refusing permission for an out-of-centre site. Accordingly, the plaintiff's appeal would be dismissed.

Carter Commercial Developments Ltd v Secretary of State for the Environment (1994) 69 P & CR 359 (Queen's Bench Division: Latham J).

2899   Town and Country Planning (Costs of Inquiries etc) Act 1995

The Town and Country Planning (Costs of Inquiries etc) Act 1995 provides for certain local authorities to make payments to specified persons for the administration of certain local inquiries. The Act received the royal assent on 8 November 1995 and came into force on that day.

Section 1 allows the Secretary of State to recover the costs of appointing inspectors to carry out public inquiries from local planning authorities. He may also make regulations prescribing the standard daily amount and travel and subsistence allowances payable to persons, other than inspectors, who conduct examinations-in-public into structure plans. Section 2 validates, with retrospective effect, the payment by local authorities of certain costs relating to local inquiries and examinations to the Secretary of State. Sections 3 and 4 apply to Scotland. Section 5 deals with short title, interpretation, financial provision and extent.

2900   Tree preservation order—confirmation of order—substitution of different order—extent of modifications made to order

The Town and Country Planning Act 1990, s 199(1) provides that a tree preservation order will not take effect until it is confirmed by the local planning authority and the local authority may confirm any such order either without modification or subject to such modifications as they consider expedient.

A tree preservation order was made in respect of a landowner's site specifying an area of mixed broadleaved trees, including willow and alder, and conifers. When the order was confirmed it was modified so as to specify woodland comprising mixed broadleaved trees, including willow, alder, ash and sycamore, and a scots pine. The landowner applied to have the order quashed but the judge held that the modification was one which should not be regarded as so significant as to take it outside the powers of s 199(1). On appeal, it fell to be determined whether, on the facts of the case, the modification was permitted by the 1990 Act. *Held*, it would not be right to treat the provision contained in s 199(1) as one which should be narrowly and strictly construed. However, the change from an area to a woodland order had the effect of producing a different order by bringing within the scope of the order new trees. The modification produced by that change was outside the powers to modify contained in s 199(1) and therefore outside the powers of the Act. Accordingly, the appeal would be allowed.

Evans v Waverley Borough Council (1995) Times, 18 July (Court of Appeal: Neill, Roch and Hutchison LJJ).

2901   Tree preservation order—prevention of construction by tree preservation order—claim for interest and professional fees

A site was purchased with conditional planning permission for the erection of dwellings. However, the defendant authority made a tree preservation order for a tree which was on one of the building plots. The authority initially refused the plaintiff purchaser permission to prune the tree. The purchaser contended that the tree preservation order and the initial refusal of consent under it had delayed construction. It claimed compensation for interest charged in funding the purchase moneys and building costs and for professional fees incurred in eventually procuring the defendant's permission to prune the tree. *Held*, the question to be considered in such circumstances was whether any loss suffered by the claimant was such as might fairly and reasonably be considered as arising naturally. The officers of the authority would have been well aware that the refusal of their consent to the pruning of the tree with the consequential delay in building work would have been likely to give rise to losses such as those claimed. Accordingly, compensation would be ordered in respect of the professional fees and the interest charges.

Factorset Ltd v Selby District Council [1995] 40 EG 133 (Lands Tribunal: M St J Hopper FRICS). *Hadley v Baxendale* (1854) 9 Exch 341 followed.

2902   Unauthorised campers—power to order removal—factors to be considered by local authority

The applicants were travellers who had been made subject to removal orders issued by local authorities under powers given by the Criminal Justice and Public Order Act 1994, s 77. It was claimed by the applicants that the authorities had taken insufficient account of material considerations before giving removal directions and seeking removal orders and, accordingly, they sought judicial review. *Held*, when a local authority contemplated whether to give a removal direction, the considerations to which the authority had to have regard, which were not statutory, were considerations of common humanity, which could not be ignored when dealing with the fundamental human needs of shelter and a modicum of security. Provided a local authority had had regard to those considerations, a removal order made by it could not be struck down unless one or more of the removal directions was not validly given. As a local authority had an initial discretion whether or not to give a removal direction, it had necessarily to apply its mind to the people who were for the time being residing there as well as local residents and strike a responsible balance between competing and conflicting needs. The power to make removal orders operated in personam rather than in rem and therefore a removal direction under s 77 could only apply to persons who were on the land at the time when the direction was made, and so could be contravened only by such persons. It was at the initial stage of deciding whether or not to give a removal direction, and to whom to give it, that it was necessary for the local authority to consider the relationship of its proposed action to the various statutory and humanitarian considerations which would be called into play and to decide accordingly. In this case, neither local authority had failed to make material inquiries prior to making removal directions and, accordingly, the application would be granted and the removal orders quashed.

R v Wealden District Council, ex p Wales; R v Same, ex p Stratford; R v Lincolnshire County Council, ex p Atkinson (1995) Times, 22 September, Independent, 3 October (Queen's Bench Division: Sedley J).

TRADE DESCRIPTIONS

Halsbury's Laws of England (4th edn) Vol 41, Supp paras 963–1006

2903 Articles

Comparative Advertising: Should it be Allowed? Belinda Mills: [1995] EIPR 417

Consumer Protection: Trading Standards Officer, Enforcement and the Police and Criminal Evidence Act 1984, Geoff Holgate: 159 JP Jo 284

The Protection of Geographical Indications in the European Economic Community, Bertold Schwab: [1995] EIPR 242

2904 False representations—statement as to personal qualifications

The Trade Descriptions Act 1968, s 14(1)(a) provides that it is an offence for any person in the course of any trade or business to make a statement which he knows to be false, and s 14(1)(b) provides that it is an offence for any person in the course of any trade or business recklessly to make a statement which is false. The matters about which a false statement may be made include, under subparagraph (i), the provision of any services, accommodation or facilities and, under subparagraph (iii), the time at which, manner in which or persons by whom the services, accommodation or facilities are provided.

The appellant was convicted of recklessly making in the course of his trade or business a false statement as to the provision of a service, contrary to the 1968 Act, s 14(1)(b)(i), in that by using the logo of the Guild of Master Craftsmen on his notepaper he had made a statement that he was a member of the guild. The trial judge had, however, directed the jury that the appellant had committed an offence under s 14(1)(i). On appeal, the appellant submitted that as he had only made an implied statement that he was a member of the guild, he had not made a statement for the purposes of s 14(1). *Held*, a person committed an offence under the 1968 Act, s 14(1)(a)(i) if he adopted the use of a personal qualification which he did not have. However, as there was an overlap between the subparagraphs of s 14(1), there would sometimes be cases in which the facts fell within more than one of the subparagraphs. The instant case could have been brought under subparagraph (iii), but it would have sufficed if the particulars of the offence had been confined to the assertion that the appellant had recklessly made a statement which was false, namely that he was a member of the guild. Accordingly, the appeal would be dismissed.

R v Piper (1996) 160 JP 116 (Court of Appeal: Roch LJ, Scott Baker and Jowitt JJ). *R v Breeze* [1973] 1 WLR 994, CA applied.

2905 False representations—statement as to services—insurance leaflet—effect of disclaimer referring consumer to terms and conditions of policy

A consumer took out a travel insurance policy to cover her family's overseas holiday. The text of the insurer's leaflet contained a heading that stated 'Delayed departure: Individual £100, Family £200', followed by the words 'if your departure is delayed by eight hours or more . . . '. Overleaf in the main text, the leaflet referred to the insurance certificate and advised the reader to refer to it for the full terms of the policy. In the event, the consumer and her family's flight was delayed by over ten hours and she made a claim for £200 in compensation. The insurers offered only £40, the sum having been calculated in accordance with the terms and conditions stated on the rear of insurance certificate. These restricted the amount payable to a sum dependent upon the length of the delay. The insurers were charged with recklessly making false statements as to the nature of services provided in the course of a trade or business, contrary to the Trade Descriptions Act 1968, s 14(1)(b). The justices accepted a plea of no case to answer. On appeal, *held*, the justices had erred in their finding that the leaflet and the insurance certificate were to be construed as a single document. The leaflet was to be read in isolation when deciding whether the statement offended s 14. Although the leaflet referred the reader to the insurance certificate, that reference would need to be as bold as the trade description itself if it were to be an effective disclaimer. It was not so bold and compelling as the statement and was not effective to correct the ordinary consumer's impression. The leaflet offended s 14 if, an ordinary consumer reading the statement would believe that a payment of £200 would be made if his flight was delayed for more than eight hours. Taken in isolation, it was arguable that the statement was capable of being read in that sense by the consumer. Accordingly, the matter would be remitted to the justices to reconsider their decision.

Smallshaw v PKC Associates Ltd (1995) 159 JP 730 (Queen's Bench Division: Beldam LJ and Buxton J).

2906 False trade description—export of calves—veterinary surgeon signing certificate for export without inspecting whole consignment

The Trade Descriptions Act 1968, s 1(1) provides that any person who, in the course of a trade or business, applies a false trade description to any goods or supplies or offers to supply any goods to which a false trade description is applied is guilty of an offence.

The defendants were veterinary inspectors appointed by the Minister of Agriculture, Fisheries and Food to inspect calves being exported to Europe. They had carried out inspections on behalf of an export company to which they were contracted and issued export health certificates after examining the calves and establishing that each was fit to travel. It was alleged that they had only examined approximately half the calves specified on the certificate and had thus applied a false trade description to those calves not examined. *Held*, there was no need for the defendants to be a party to the exports for them to be guilty of a charge under s 1(1). The provision of the certificates was an essential, integral and direct part of the export of the consignment of calves. Without the certificates there could be no supply. Furthermore, the expression 'trade or business' in s 1(1) included professions. There was no reason for excluding professionals from the scope of the legislation. Accordingly, the case would be remitted with a direction that the defendants be convicted.

Roberts v Leonard (1995) 159 JP 711 (Queen's Bench Division: Simon Brown LJ and Curtis J).

2907 False trade description—motor car—odometer reading—defence of reasonable precaution and due diligence—inadequate disclaimer—failure to consult all previous owners

The defendant was prosecuted by a local authority for offering to supply, and subsequently supplying, a motor car with a false mileage reading, contrary to the Trade Descriptions Act 1968, s 1. He pleaded the statutory defence, set out in the 1968 Act, s 24(1), that he had relied on information supplied to him by the person who sold him the car and that he had taken all reasonable precautions and exercised all due diligence to avoid the commission of the offence. He had also displayed a disclaimer relating to the accuracy of the mileage. The justices found that the disclaimer had not been displayed sufficiently prominently but, despite that, he had satisfied the statutory defence even though he had not checked the mileage with one of the previous owners. On appeal by the local authority, *held*, the authorities suggested it was not necessary in every case for there to be an effective disclaimer in order to show that all reasonable precautions had been taken. In addition, there was no general rule that a dealer can never have taken reasonable precautions unless he has consulted a previous owner of whom he is aware. Accordingly, the appeal would be dismissed.

London Borough of Ealing v Taylor (1994) 159 JP 460 (Queen's Bench Division: Staughton LJ and Buckley J).

2908 False trade description—motor car—odometer reading—qualification to reading

The appellant was convicted of applying a false trade description to goods, contrary to the Trade Descriptions Act 1968, s 1(1)(a). In particular, it was alleged that the appellant applied a false trade description to a motor vehicle in the course of his car sales business by means of an odometer reading entered on the sales invoice. On appeal, *held*, the statement on the sales invoice that the appellant was unable to confirm the mileage on the odometer was a qualification to the odometer reading which was part of the trade description and not merely a disclaimer. On the facts, the trade description could not be regarded as false and, accordingly, the appeal would be allowed.

R v Bull (1995) Times, 4 December (Court of Appeal: Swinton Thomas LJ, Waterhouse and Harrison JJ).

2909 Offences—investigation—obstruction of authorised officer

The Trade Descriptions Act 1968, s 29(1) provides that any person who without reasonable cause fails to give a trading standards officer any assistance or information which he may reasonably require of him for the purpose of the performance of his functions under the Act is guilty of an offence. If any person, in giving any such information, makes any statement which he knows to be false, he is also guilty of an offence: s 29(2).

When the defendant was interviewed under caution by a trading standards officer he made a statement which he knew to be false and was charged with an offence under the 1968 Act, s 29(2). The defendant submitted that, because he had been under caution, s 29(2) did not apply. He claimed that the word 'require' in s 29(1) had a mandatory element and an offence under s 29(2) could only be committed where an interviewee was bound to answer a question. On his appeal against conviction of the offence, *held*, the situation referred to in s 29(2) arose in the present case because information was sought which the officer reasonably required of the defendant for the purpose of the performance of the officer's functions under the 1968 Act. The defendant did not have to answer the officer's questions because he had been cautioned. If he had declined to do so, he would not have been guilty of any offence under s 29(1) because he would have had reasonable cause for failing to give information, namely that he had been cautioned and told that he need not give it. However, if an interviewee chose to give information which was false he put himself plainly within the scope of s 29(2). Accordingly, the appeal would be dismissed.

R v Page (1995) Times, 20 December (Court of Appeal: Kennedy LJ, Judge and Clarke JJ).

TRADE, INDUSTRY AND INDUSTRIAL RELATIONS

Halsbury's Laws of England (4th edn) Vol 47 (reissue), paras 1–1522

2910 Articles

Accepting a Relevant Restriction by Accepting Something Else, Oliver Black: [1995] ECLR 354

Decentralisation, the Public Interest and the 'Pursuit of Certainty', Barry J Rodger: [1995] ECLR 395

Comparative Advertising: Should it be Allowed? Belinda Mills: [1995] EIPR 417

Debunking the Myth of the Kite Mark, Penelope Silver (on the BS5750 kite mark): 145 NLJ 19

Keeping CCT Truly Competitive, Stephen Cirell and John Bennett (on the problems of cartels and restrictive practices in the performance of public services): 139 SJ 842

Price Promise, Christine Clayson (on contradictory holiday price indications): 139 SJ 400

Product Liability, Computer Software and Insurance Issues - the St Albans and Salvage Association Cases, E Susan Singleton: 10 CLP 167

Regulation of Travel Promotions—'A Free for All'? Martin Briggs: 145 NLJ 554

The Restrictive Trade Practices Act 1976 and the 1989 Exemption Orders: Defects of Form? Adam Collinson: [1995] ECLR 252

Sales Promotions Disasters, Peter Shears: 145 NLJ 1682, 1754, 1792

Some Frequently Asked Questions About the UK 1994 Trade Marks Act, Anselm Kamperman Sanders: [1995] EIPR 67

What is the Difference Between a Term and A Restriction? Associated Dairies and the Scope of Section 9(3) RTPA, Oliver Black (on *Associated Dairies v Baines* (para 2939)): [1995] ECLR 99

2911 Competition law—EC

See EUROPEAN COMMUNITIES.

2912 Consumer protection

See CONSUMER PROTECTION.

2913 Deregulation—contracting out—registration of companies

See para 517.

2914   Deregulation and Contracting Out Act 1994—commencement

The Deregulation and Contracting Out Act 1994 (Commencement No 4 and Transitional Provisions) Order 1995, SI 1995/2835, brings the Act into force on 1 January 1996 so far as it has not already been brought into force, or is not brought into force as part of the Goods Vehicles (Licensing of Operators) Act 1995. Transitional provision is also made. For a summary of the Act, see 1994 Abr para 2760. For details of commencement, see the commencement table in the title STATUTES.

See also para 473.

2915   Export controls

See CUSTOMS AND EXCISE.

2916   Export of live animals for slaughter—trade disrupted by protesters—port authorities' exclusion of trade—authorities' discretion to exclude

See *R v Coventry Airport, ex p Phoenix Aviation; R v Dover Harbour Board, ex p Peter Gilder and Sons; R v Associated British Ports, ex p Plymouth City Council*, para 2313.

2917   Films—European Convention on Cinematographic Co-production

The European Convention on Cinematographic Co-production (Amendment) Order 1995, SI 1995/1298 (in force on 7 June 1995), further amends the 1994 Order, SI 1994/1065, by adding Slovakia to the list of countries specified in the order.

The European Convention on Cinematographic Co-production (Amendment) (No 2) Order 1995, SI 1995/1963 (in force on 16 August 1995), further amends the 1994 Order supra by adding the Federal Republic of Germany and the Kingdom of the Netherlands to the list of countries specified in the order.

The European Convention on Cinematographic Co-production (Amendment) (No 3) Order 1995, SI 1995/2730 (in force on 8 November 1995), further amends the 1994 Order supra by adding the Republic of Finland to the list of countries specified in the order.

2918   Import controls

See CUSTOMS AND EXCISE.

2919   Industrial relations—industrial action—ballot—participation of new union members

The Trade Union and Labour Relations (Consolidation) Act 1992, s 226(1) provides that an act done by a trade union to induce a person to take part in industrial action is not protected by the statutory immunity against liability for certain economic torts unless the industrial action in which he has been induced to take part has the support of a ballot.

In the course of a trade dispute between the parties, the union called on its members to take part in industrial action consisting of a series of short-term strikes. The union gave the employer notice of its intention to hold a ballot, and served a list of the names of all its members entitled to vote in the ballot. The union notified the employer that a majority of its members had voted in favour of industrial action, and also gave notice of its intention to call for industrial action, listing members whom it intended to call on to take part in the action. In serving a second notice of the dates of further strikes, the union listed members who were to take part, some of whom were new members who had joined the union since the initial ballot. The employer was granted an injunction preventing the union from inducing new members from participating in strike action. On appeal, the issue was whether or not the union had lost its immunity from suit in calling on new members to participate in industrial action even though they had not voted in the ballot. *Held*, the participation of particular individuals in collective industrial action was distinct from the industrial action itself. It was the latter which had to have the support of a ballot, and not the participation of those induced to take part in it. Moreover, Parliament must have appreciated that there would be constant changes in the membership of a large union and that significant numbers of new members might join between the date on which an employer was given notice of a ballot, the holding of the ballot, and the taking of the industrial action. As there was no statutory provision which prevented the union from including in industrial action new members who were not balloted because they were not members at the time that the ballot was held, the union had not lost its immunity from suit and, accordingly, the appeal would be allowed.

London Underground Ltd v National Union of Rail, Maritime and Transport Workers [1995] IRLR 636 (Court of Appeal: Butler-Sloss, Millett and Ward LJJ).

2920 Industrial relations—industrial action—picketing—criminal liability

See *DPP v Todd*, para 904.

2921 Industrial relations—trade unions—ballots—code of practice

The Employment Code of Practice (Industrial Action Ballots and Notice to Employers) Order 1995, SI 1995/1729 (in force on 17 November 1995), brings into force the revised Code of Practice on Industrial Action Ballots and Notice to Employers, issued under the Trade Union and Labour Relations (Consolidation) Act 1992, s 203. The revised Code takes effect from 17 November 1995, and replaces the whole of the Code of Practice on Trade Union Ballots and Industrial Action.

2922 Industrial relations—trade unions—ballots—limited members—right to vote in ballot on transfer of engagements

The Trade Union and Labour Relations (Consolidation) Act 1992, s 100B provides that entitlement to vote in a ballot on the transfer of a trade union's engagements must be accorded equally to all members of the trade union.

The appellant trade union had five types of membership, including limited membership. When limited members were excluded from the right to vote in a ballot on a resolution to transfer the union's engagements to another trade union, a union officer commenced proceedings against the union under the 1992 Act, s 103(1). The Certification Officer declared that limited members were 'members' within the meaning of the 1992 Act, s 100B and therefore should have been allowed to vote. On the union's appeal, *held*, there were significant differences in the relationship between each class of members and the union, and a detailed consideration of the membership rules led to the conclusion that only full members were entitled to vote on questions of amalgamations and transfers of the union's engagements. As limited members did not have a substantial right to participate in the principal purposes of the union, the reference to 'members' in s 100B did not include limited members. Accordingly, the appeal would be allowed.

National Union of Mineworkers (Yorkshire District) v Millward [1995] ICR 482 (Employment Appeal Tribunal: Mummery J presiding).

2923 Industrial relations—trade unions—Certification Officer—fees

The Certification Officer (Amendment of Fees) Regulations 1995, SI 1995/483 (in force on 1 April 1995), further amend SI 1975/536, so as to alter certain fees payable to the Certification Officer. The fee for an application for approval of an instrument of amalgamation or transfer of engagement is increased to £1543; the fee for an inspection of documents kept by the Certification Officer in respect of amalgamations or transfers of engagements is decreased to £43; the fee for entry of the name of an amalgamated organisation in the lists maintained by the Certification Officer where the name is already entered is increased to £51; the fee for an application by an organisation of workers to have its name entered on the list of trade unions maintained by the Certification Officer is increased to £132; the fee for an application by an organisation of employers to have its name entered on the list of employers' associations maintained by the Certification Officer is increased to £132; and the fee payable for an application by a trade union for a certificate of independence is increased to £2583.

2924 Industrial relations—trade unions—derecognition of union—effect on individual member

The Employment Protection (Consolidation) Act 1978, s 23(1)(a) provides that every employee must have the right not to have action short of dismissal taken against him as an individual by his employer for the purpose of preventing him or deterring him from being or seeking to become a member of an independent trade union, or penalising him for doing so. 'Action' is defined in s 153(1) as including omission, and references to doing an act or taking action are to be construed accordingly.

A newspaper company negotiated with its employees' union under a collective bargaining agreement as to their terms and conditions of employment. The company later terminated the agreement and invited all those who had been employed on the basis of the terms of the agreement to sign individual contracts. Although the terms of the new contracts did not differ significantly from those of the old contracts, the effect was that employees no longer had the right to union representation. The company offered all those who were willing to enter into individual contracts a back-dated increase in pay, whereas those who did not do so did not receive the increase. The circumstances in a second case were similar to those of the first case. In both cases, industrial tribunals upheld the claims of employees who had refused to enter the new contracts that their union rights under the 1978 Act, s 23(1) had been infringed, but the Employment Appeal Tribunal allowed the employers' appeals. The Court of Appeal allowed the employees' appeal, and on the employers' further appeal, the question was whether or not the extended meaning of 'action' within the 1978 Act, s 153(1) applied to s 23(1). *Held*, as the proper interpretation of s 23(1) gave rise to a real and substantial difficulty which could not be resolved by applying the usual canons of construction, the court was entitled to have regard to the legislative history of the section in order to interpret it. On that basis, it was impossible to conclude that the omission to offer the pay increase to the employees who had not accepted the new individual contracts constituted 'action' within the meaning of s 23(1). Moreover, employers were entitled to decide whether or not to enter into or continue with a collective bargaining agreement with trade unions, and on the facts of the cases whatever the employers' purpose had been in offering an inducement to the employees to sign individual contracts, it was not done with the intention of deterring them from continuing as union members. Accordingly, the appeal would be allowed.

Associated Newspapers Ltd v Wilson; Associated British Ports v Palmer [1995] 2 All ER 100 (House of Lords: Lords Keith of Kinkel, Bridge of Harwich, Browne-Wilkinson, Slynn of Hadley, and Lloyd of Berwick). Decision of Court of Appeal [1994] ICR 97 (1993 Abr para 2554) reversed. *National Coal Board v Ridgway* [1987] 3 All ER 582 overruled.

2925 Industrial relations—trade unions—elections—scrutineer's report—election of candidate—cancellation of election

The defendant trade union held an election for the position of general president. The plaintiff emerged with the highest number of votes and was duly elected. The defendant had allowed the ballot to go ahead despite knowing that during the campaign several candidates, including the plaintiff, had been in breach of the rules governing the election. Following a complaint by an unsuccessful candidate that the election had been unfair, the ballot was set aside. The plaintiff claimed that the defendant was not entitled to order a new election. *Held*, once a candidate with the highest number of votes was declared elected following a favourable report by the independent scrutineer, a trade union had no power to cancel the election unless either such a power was expressly given under the rules, or the whole election process was a nullity. The defendant did not have any express power to cancel the election and there was no evidence that the irregularities could reasonably have affected the validity of the election process. Accordingly, the plaintiff's claim would succeed. An order would be made requiring the defendant to give effect to the result of the ballot.

Douglas v Graphical Paper and Media Union [1995] IRLR 426 (Queen's Bench Division: Morison J).

2926 Industrial relations—trade unions—membership—discrimination against member—refusal of employment

The Trade Union and Labour Relations (Consolidation) Act 1992, s 137(1)(a) provides that it is unlawful to refuse a person employment because he is or is not a member of a trade union.

The appellant was employed as a social worker for 16 years by the respondent local authority, during which time he was an active union member and a shop steward. He left the respondent's employment, but later applied to work for them again. When his application was refused, he complained that he had been unlawfully refused employment because of his trade union membership. The local authority argued that it was not the fact of the appellant's trade union membership alone that had led to the refusal of employment, but his anti-managerial and confrontational attitude in carrying out his trade union activities. An industrial tribunal found that the main reason for the refusal of employment was the appellant's trade union activities, but held that there had been no breach of the 1992 Act, s 137(1)(a) because that section referred only to trade union membership and not to trade union activities. On appeal, *held*, having regard to the wording of s 137(1)(a), the industrial tribunal had adopted too narrow an interpretation of the provision. Trade union membership and activities overlapped, and if a person was refused employment because he was a trade union activist or because of his trade union activities, an industrial tribunal was entitled to find that the refusal was in breach of s 137(1)(a). The purpose of the provision was to protect people from being discriminated against on grounds relating to union membership, and on the facts of the instant case, there had been discrimination. Accordingly, the appeal would be allowed.

Harrison v Kent County Council [1995] ICR 434 (Employment Appeal Tribunal: Mummery J presiding).

2927 Monopolies and mergers—newspaper merger references—Secretary of State's discretion to consent

The Fair Trading Act (Amendment) (Newspaper Mergers) Order 1995, SI 1995/1351 (in force on 13 June 1995), amends the Fair Trading Act 1973, s 58(4), thereby increasing to 50,000 the circulation threshold below which the Secretary of State has a discretion to give his consent to a newspaper merger without referring the matter to the Monopolies and Mergers Commission.

2928 Promotion of trade—export and investment guarantees—increase in foreign currency commitments

The Export and Investment Guarantees (Limit on Foreign Currency Commitments) Order 1995, SI 1995/1988 (in force on 27 July 1995), increases the limit in the Export and Investment Guarantees Act 1991, s 6(1)(b), so as to increase the amount of the aggregate foreign currency commitments of the Secretary of State, under arrangements made pursuant to that Act in relation to exports and insurance, from 15,000 million special drawing rights to 20,000 million special drawing rights.

2929 Public procurement—supply contracts

The Public Supply Contracts Regulations 1995, SI 1995/201 (in force on 21 February 1995), implement Council Directive (EC) 93/36 (co-ordination of procedures for the award of public supply contracts). The regulations apply to specified public bodies ('contracting authorities') seeking offers in relation to certain contracts for the purchase and hire of goods and deal with the treatment to be accorded to suppliers or potential suppliers who are nationals of and established in member states of the European Community, Hungary, Poland, Iceland, Norway and, from a specified date, Liechtenstein. The regulations provide that, in seeking offers in relation to a public supply contract, a contracting authority must use one of the following procedures: (1) the open procedure, under which any person who is interested may submit a tender, (2) the restricted procedure, under which only those persons selected by the contracting authority may submit tenders, and (3) the negotiated procedure, under which the contracting authority negotiates the terms of the contract with one or more persons selected by it. Provision is made for the advertisement by a contracting authority of its intention to seek offers in relation to public supply contracts, the matters to which the contracting authority may have regard in treating suppliers as ineligible or in selecting suppliers to tender for or to negotiate the contract, and for the selection of suppliers. Where a contracting authority decides to award a public supply contract, it must do so on the basis either of the offer which quotes the lowest price or the one which is the most economically advantageous. If requested by an unsuccessful supplier, the contracting authority must provide reasons why the supplier was unsuccessful. The regulations also implement certain provisions of Council Directive (EC) 89/665 (co-ordination of laws relating to the application of review procedures to the award of public supply and public works contracts). The obligation on a contracting authority to comply with the regulations, and with any enforceable Community obligation in relation to the award of a public supply contract, is a duty owed to suppliers, a breach of which is not a criminal offence but is actionable by a supplier.

2930 Restraint of trade—remedies—interlocutory injunction

See *Newport Association Football Club Ltd v Football Association of Wales Ltd*, para 1707.

2931 Restraint of trade—restrictive covenant—severance of unlawful terms

See *Marshall v NM Financial Management Ltd*, para 40.

2932 Restrictive trade practices—electrical contracting services—London exhibition halls

See para 1889.

2933   Restrictive trade practices—price regulation—delegation of regulatory powers

See *Bundesanstalt für den Güterfernverkehr v Gebrüder Reiff GmbH & Co KG*, para 3164.

2934   Restrictive trade practices—registered agreement—reference—representative respondent

Scotland

The Restrictive Practices Court Rules 1976, SI 1976/1897, r 3(1) provides that proceedings under the Restrictive Trade Practices Act 1976 must be instituted by a notice of reference stating that the agreements to which the notice applies are referred to the court. Rule 3(3) provides that a notice of reference must sufficiently identify the agreement or agreements to which it applies. By r 5(1), where several persons have a common interest in the proceedings by reason that they are all parties to the same agreement or have entered into substantially similar agreements, the Director General of Fair Trading may nominate any of those persons to represent all or some of them ('the representative respondent').

The Director General of Fair Trading referred an agreement to the court which related to the activities of a property centre used by several firms of solicitors. The agreement was made up of a number of documents, and its rules applied not only to firms which were members of the centre but also to firms which were occasional users of the centre. When the director nominated a member of the centre as the representative respondent, it applied for an order revoking the nomination, arguing that the director (1) had not complied with the 1976 Rules, r 3(3), and (2) had not identified the common interest between members and occasional users. *Held*, (1) it was sufficient compliance with r 3(3) that the notice of reference referred to the documentation which had been filed in the register of agreements. The rule did not also require the director to state in the notice of reference the interpretation that he wished to give to the agreement. (2) The agreement showed that both the members and the users of the centre had the same rights as regards use of the centre's facilities, and were bound by the same rules. That was sufficient evidence to establish a common interest in the proceedings for the purposes of r 5(1) and, accordingly, the application would be dismissed.

Mackie & Dewar v Director General of Fair Trading 1995 SLT 1028 (Restrictive Practices Court).

2935   Restrictive trade practices—selective distribution systems—guarantees

See *Metro SB-Großmärkte GmbH & Co KG v Cartier SA*, para 3158.

2936   Restrictive trade practices—standards and arrangements—goods

The Restrictive Trade Practices (Standards and Arrangements) (Goods) Order 1995, SI 1995/3129 (in force on 29 December 1995), approves standards of dimension, design, quality or performance of goods and manufacturing processes and arrangements as to the provision of information or advice, all of which have been adopted by Electricity Association Services Limited on 31 October 1995. The effect of the order is that, for the purpose of determining whether an agreement is one to which the Restrictive Trade Practices Act 1976 applies, no account is taken of any term in the agreement by which the parties or any of them agree to comply with, or to apply, the standards and arrangements so approved.

2937   Restrictive trade practices—standards and arrangements—services

The Restrictive Trade Practices (Standards and Arrangements) (Services) Order 1995, SI 1995/3130 (in force on 29 December 1995), approves standards of performance in the provision of services, and standards of dimension, design, quality or performance in respect of goods used in providing them and an arrangement as to the provision of information or advice, all of which have been adopted by Electricity Association Services Limited on 31 October 1995. The effect of the order is that, for the purpose of determining whether an agreement is one to which the Restrictive Trade Practices Act 1976 applies, no account is taken of any term in the agreement by which the parties or any of them agree to comply with, or to apply, the standards and arrangements so approved.

2938   Restrictive trade practices—undertaking—international organisation

See *SAT Flugesellschaft mbH v European Organisation for the Safety of Air Navigation (Eurocontrol)*, para 3162.

2939   Restrictive trade practices—unregistered agreement—enforcement

The Restrictive Practices Act 1976, s 9(3) provides that in determining whether an agreement for the supply of goods or for the application of any process of manufacture to goods is an agreement to which the Act applies, no account is to be taken of any term which relates exclusively to the goods supplied or to which the process is applied in pursuance of the agreement.

A contract between the plaintiff, a large wholesale distributor of milk, and the defendant, a milkman, included a clause which provided that the defendant was to purchase milk exclusively from the plaintiff for five years and that he was not to sell milk by way of retail to the plaintiff's customers. In breach of the clause, the defendant obtained milk supplies from a third party, upon which the plaintiff obtained an interlocutory injunction to prevent further breach. The defendant argued that the clause was not enforceable because the agreement had not been registered as required by the 1976 Act, s 1, and because details of the agreement had not been given to the Director General of Fair Trading. However, having regard to the 1976 Act, s 9(3), a judge decided that the clause was to be disregarded in determining whether or not the agreement was registrable, on the basis that the word 'term' in s 9(3) was to be read as if it were 'restriction', and that the relevant clause contained two separate restrictions. On the defendant's appeal, *held*, the 1976 Act was enacted on the basis that restrictive agreements might be contrary to the public interest. There was no significant hardship involved in giving details of an agreement to the Director General so that he could determine whether or not an agreement was registrable. Moreover, there was a potential public disadvantage in allowing borderline agreements to go unchecked by the Director General. The judge's interpretation of s 9(3) was at odds with the wording of the section, as it distinguished throughout between terms and restrictions. Having regard to the restrictive clause in the instant case, the agreement should have been registered and, accordingly, the appeal would be allowed.

Associated Dairies Limited v Baines (1995) Times, 6 July (Court of Appeal: Stuart-Smith, Hirst and Schiemann LJJ). Decision of Sir John Vinelott [1995] ICR 296 reversed.

2940   Secretary of State—payment of fees—specified functions

The Department of Trade and Industry (Fees) (Amendment) Order 1995, SI 1995/1294 (in force on 11 May 1995), amends the 1988 Order, SI 1988/93, by specifying, for the purposes of the Finance (No 2) Act 1987, functions and matters which are to be taken into account in the determination of fees prescribed by the Secretary of State in respect of his functions in relation to insurance companies and the members of Lloyd's.

TRADE MARKS AND TRADE NAMES

Halsbury's Laws of England (4th edn) Vol 48 (reissue), paras 1–500

2941   Articles

Applying Traditional Property Laws to Intellectual Property Transactions, Mark Anderson: [1995] EIPR 236

Comparative Advertising: Should it be Allowed? Belinda Mills: [1995] EIPR 417

Design Copyright Licences of Right: How Will They work in Practice? Caroline Bodley: [1995] EIPR 180

Does the First Trade Marks Directive Allow International Exhaustion of Rights? Nicholas Shea: [1995] EIPR 463

European Intellectual Property Rights: A Tabular Guide, Claire Burke: [1995] EIPR 466

The Fine Line Between Trade Names, Anthony Mosawi (on the Trade Marks Act 1994): 145 NLJ 410

Harmonising Intellectual Property Laws in the European Union: Past, Present and Future, Thomas Vinje: [1995] EIPR 361

International Intellectual Property Conventions: A Tabular Guide, Claire Burke: [1995] EIPR 477

Making a Name for Yourself—And Stopping it Being Taken in Vain, Michael Golding and Patrick Wheeler (on trade marks for a broad specification of goods such as computer software): [1995] 6 CTLR 182

New States of Mind, Eugene Gott and Mark Singley (on the new intellectual property antitrust guidelines proposed by the United States): LS Gaz, 5 April 1995, p 20

Own Label Products and the 'Lookalike' Phenomenon: A Lack of Trade Dress and Unfair Competition Protection? Belinda Mills: [1995] EIPR 116

Patent Problems, Philip Sloan (on patent damages inquiries): LS Gaz, 11 May 1995, p 15

Refusals to Licence I P, E Susan Singleton: 139 SJ 532

The Principle of Exhaustion of Trade Mark Rights Pursuant to Directive 89/104 (and Regulation 40/94), Jesper Rasmussen: [1995] EIPR 174

The Right of Nationals of Non-Madrid Union Countries to Own International Registrations, George Souter: [1995] EIPR 333

The 'Threats' Section in the UK Trade Marks Act 1994: Can a Person Still Wound Without Striking? Lim Heng Gee: [1995] EIPR 138

Trade Marks: Intellectual Property Protection on the Information Super Highway, David Kelly and Kathleen Kumor: [1995] EIPR 481

The UK Trade Marks Act 1994: An Invitation to an Olfactory Occasion? Helen Burton (on registration of scents as trade marks): [1995] EIPR 378

2942 Business and company names—control over names—words requiring approval

See para 505.

2943 Hallmarks—convention hallmarks—Czech Republic

The Hallmarking (International Convention) (Amendment) Order 1995, SI 1995/2488 (in force on 23 October 1995), further amends the 1976 Order, SI 1976/730, consequent upon the ratification by the Czech Republic of the 1972 Vienna Convention on the Control and Marking of Articles of Precious Metals. The control mark of the Prague Czech Republic Assay Office is added to the list of foreign assay office marks in the 1976 Order.

2944 Offences—confiscation orders

See para 2602.

2945 Olympic Symbol etc (Protection) Act 1995

The Olympic Symbol etc (Protection) Act 1995 makes provision in relation to the use for commercial purposes of the Olympic symbol and certain words associated with the Olympic games. The Act received the royal assent on 19 July 1995 and came into force on 1 September 1995: SI 1995/2472.

The Olympics association right is created by s 1, conferring rights and remedies which are exercisable by a person appointed by the Secretary of State ('the proprietor'), by order made by statutory instrument. Section 2 provides that the Olympics association right confers exclusive rights in relation to use of the Olympic symbol, Olympic motto and certain protected words (as defined in s 18). Although the proprietor may exploit the right for gain and give his consent to certain acts, he may not dispose of the right or any interest in or over it. In addition, the Act does not permit a proprietor to do anything which would infringe a right which subsisted before the Act comes into force, or which was created by the registration of a design under the Registered Designs Act 1949 or the registration of a trade mark under the Trade Marks Act 1994.

By s 3, a person infringes the Olympics association right if, in the course of trade, he uses a representation of the Olympic symbol, Olympic motto or a protected word, or uses a representation of something so similar to the Olympic symbol or the Olympic motto, that it would be likely to create an association with it ('a controlled representation'). The section sets out the particular circumstances in which an infringement occurs, subject to ss 4 and 5, which respectively prescribe the circumstances in which the Olympics association right is not infringed, and empower the Secretary of State to specify additional circumstances in which the Olympics association right is not infringed.

Section 6 allows a proprietor to commence proceedings in respect of an infringement of his Olympics association right, claiming the same relief as is available in respect of an infringement of a property right. In relation to infringing goods, material and articles (as defined), s 7 allows the Secretary of State to make regulations corresponding to certain provisions of the 1994 Act.

Section 8 provides for offences and penalties as regards the use of a controlled representation in relation to infringing goods, material and articles, and by s 10, the provision of the 1994 Act which relates to offences committed by bodies corporate and partnerships, applies to offences under the 1995 Act. In addition, by s 11, the provision of the 1994 Act which provides for forfeiture of certain goods, material or articles in the possession of anyone in connection with the investigation or prosecution of a relevant offence, applies to the 1995 Act.

By s 13, the provisions of the 1949 Act and the 1994 Act which relate to the registration of designs, now include a provision that a design may not be registered if it consists of or contains a controlled representation, unless the registration application is made by a proprietor or a person to whom a proprietor has given his consent to use the Olympic association right. Similarly, s 14 provides that the provision of the Copyright, Designs and Patents Act 1988 which relates to design rights in original designs, now includes a provision that design right does not subsist in a design which consists of or contains a controlled representation.

A proprietor is obliged by s 15 to comply with any directions given by the Secretary of State as regards the exercise of the Olympics association right. Where a proprietor wrongly threatens another person with infringement proceedings, s 16 allows that person to bring proceedings for relief. Moreover, in civil proceedings under the Act, s 17 obliges a proprietor to show the use that was made of a controlled representation. Sections 9 and 12 make provision for offences and forfeiture in Scotland, and s 19 deals with the title and extent of the Act.

2946 Olympics association right—appointment of proprietor

The Olympics Association Right (Appointment of Proprietor) Order 1995, SI 1995/2473 (in force on 18 October 1995), appoints the British Olympic Association as the proprietor of the Olympics association right, thereby allowing it to exercise the rights provided by the Olympic Symbol etc (Protection) Act 1995 in relation to the symbol of the Olympic Committee, its motto, the words 'Olympiad', 'Olympiads', 'Olympian', 'Olympians', 'Olympic', 'Olympics', and representations similar to the symbol and motto.

2947 Olympics association right—infringement proceedings

The Olympics Association Right (Infringement Proceedings) Regulations 1995, SI 1995/3325 (in force on 12 January 1996), make provision in respect of orders which the court may make in an action for infringement of the Olympics association right conferred by the Olympic Symbol etc (Protection) Act 1995. In particular, the regulations (1) provide that the court may order the erasure of the offending representation involving use of the Olympic symbol or motto from the infringing goods, material or articles, or for the destruction of those items, (2) permit the proprietor of the Olympics association right to apply to the court for an order that the infringing goods, material or articles are to be delivered up to the proprietor or such other person as the court directs, such application being subject to specified time limits, (3) permit the proprietor of the Olympics association right to apply to the court for an order that infringing goods, material or articles which have been delivered up are to be destroyed or forfeited, and (4) confer a power to make rules of court providing for notice to be given to anyone who might have an interest in any infringing goods, material or articles.

2948 Passing off—misrepresentation—goodwill—descriptive name—matters to be taken into consideration

The plaintiff, an American company which carried on business from America, was engaged in producing software templates used to devise business plans. The defendant was an English company which republished for use in the United Kingdom computer software which had been prepared abroad. The parties entered into negotiations with a view to producing an English version of one of the plaintiff's successful products called 'BizPlan Builder'. When the parties failed to reach agreement, the defendant launched its own product designed to perform the same function as the plaintiff's 'BizPlan Builder', calling it 'BusinessPlan Builder'. On commencing proceedings against the defendant for passing off, the plaintiff sought an interim injunction to prevent the defendant from using the name 'BusinessPlan Builder'. *Held*, one of the matters which the plaintiff had to prove was that there was goodwill attached to the name 'BizPlan Builder' in the United Kingdom, as reputation alone was not enough and goodwill in the name in America was irrelevant. Goodwill could be evidenced by the extent of the plaintiff's customers in the United Kingdom, and in considering that point, it was necessary to take account of the nature of the product, in particular the fact that it was neither ephemeral nor an item of everyday household use. It was also necessary to include sales of the product in the United Kingdom which had been generated by sources outside the United Kingdom. Taking those matters into account, the plaintiff had sufficient customers such that goodwill existed in the United Kingdom, and it followed that there was a triable issue as to whether or not that goodwill should be protected. Although the name 'BizPlan Builder' had a strong descriptive element, the word 'Builder' was used in a metaphorical sense. In addition, the use of a capital 'P' in the middle of the word 'BizPlan' and 'BusinessPlan' suggested that the defendant was emulating the plaintiff's typography, rather than using it for any other reason, and the two names were identical in meaning and not merely similar. As there was therefore a possibility of confusion between the two products, there was a serious issue to be tried as to whether the defendant was guilty of misrepresentation. Having considered the balance of convenience, the plaintiff was entitled to an interim injunction preventing use of the name 'BusinessPlan Builder'. Accordingly, the application would be granted.

Jian Tools for Sales Inc v Roderick Manhattan Group Ltd [1995] FSR 924 (Chancery Division: Knox J).

2949 Passing off—misrepresentation—goodwill—misrepresentation that product licensed by regulatory authority

The plaintiffs marketed a fungicide with an active ingredient called chlorothalonil. The product was fully approved by the Ministry of Agriculture, Fisheries and Foods (MAFF), in accordance with regulations controlling the manufacture, supply and sale of pesticides. Accordingly, the plaintiffs were entitled to use a MAFF number in relation to their product. The defendant marketed chlorothalonil and sold it bearing a MAFF number that it was not entitled to use. The product was made using a different formula to that of the plaintiffs. However, the two products were of a similar grey colour and the instructions on each container stated that the product was suitable for application to peas. The plaintiffs' claim included allegations that the defendant had passed off its product as that of the plaintiffs and as a product of a trader entitled to use a MAFF number. On applications by the plaintiff for summary judgment and by the defendant to strike out the proceedings, *held*, the recommendation by the defendant that its product was suitable for application to peas did not amount to a misrepresentation that its product was that of the plaintiffs. The use of the grey colour might amount to such a misrepresentation, even though the defendant sold its product in opaque containers and there was another grey product on the market. The essence of the first limb of the plaintiffs' claim was that the defendant had damaged the reputation and goodwill attached to a MAFF approved product by misrepresenting that its product was also approved. The plaintiffs claimed to be entitled to a share in that goodwill as members of a class of traders lawfully marketing chlorothalonil with MAFF approval. There was some uncertainty as to whether the law of passing off extended to give a cause of action to a plaintiff in such circumstances. Accordingly, the applications would be dismissed.

SDS Biotech UK Ltd v Power Agrichemicals [1995] FSR 797 (Chancery Division: Aldous J).

2950 Passing off—misrepresentation—sale of replacement parts—interlocutory injunction

The plaintiff sold helmets which complied with safety regulations. The defendant sold spare lenses which were said to suit the helmets. It was unlawful to use equipment which did not comply with the regulations and, when the helmets were fitted with the lenses, they did not comply. The plaintiff applied for an interlocutory injunction against the defendant for passing off on the ground that selling lenses 'to suit' the helmets amounted to a representation that when the lenses were fitted to the helmets they would comply with the regulations. After proceedings were issued, the defendant applied for the relevant safety approval and, although it had not been granted at the time of the hearing, the necessary safety tests had been satisfactorily conducted. *Held*, (1) even if there was a misrepresentation, it was debatable whether there was a cause of action in a case where the plaintiff's standing arose out of the fact that he complied with certain regulations while the defendant did not. In the present case, the plaintiff's argument succeeded to the necessary standard on an application for an interlocutory injunction. (2) It was arguable that selling lenses to a customer who required the products to comply with certain regulations could amount to a representation, unless he was warned, that he could lawfully use them. (3) The suggestion that an accident caused by a spare lens would reflect badly on the plaintiff was speculative, particularly as the defendant had established that its product was up to the standard for safety approval and was likely to get such approval. It was unlikely that the defendant could not meet any claim for damages. However, it would be a hardship on the defendant to be excluded from selling its product when other companies were continuing to do so. On balance, it would be a greater injustice if an injunction was granted and the application would be refused accordingly.

Hodge Clemco Ltd v Airblast Ltd [1995] FSR 806 (Chancery Division: Jacob J).

2951 Passing off—trade name—passing off by similarity in name

The plaintiff association was a charity, first named the 'Diabetic Association' and then the 'British Diabetic Association'. It had about 140,000 members and an annual income of about £10m, two-thirds of which came from donations and legacies from the public. The defendant society, a new charity with similar ends and similarly named, was subsequently founded. The plaintiff commenced proceedings against the defendant for passing off, seeking to restrain it from using the name 'Diabetic Society' or 'British Diabetic Society', on the grounds that the plaintiff enjoyed exclusive reputation and goodwill in those names as well as in the names 'British Diabetic Association' and 'Diabetic Association' and, in the alternative, that the defendant's names were deceptively similar to the names in which the plaintiff admittedly had reputation and goodwill in the sense that the defendant's use of its own name would be likely to lead the public to deal with the defendant (by becoming subscribing members of, or leaving bequests to, the defendant) on the faith of the plaintiff's reputation. *Held*, the scope of a passing-off action was wide enough to include deception of the public by one fund-raising charity in a way that tended to appropriate and so damage another fund-raising charity's goodwill, namely the other charity's 'attractive force' in obtaining financial support from the public. On the balance of probabilities, the plaintiff did not enjoy reputation and goodwill in any name other than 'British Diabetic Association' and 'Diabetic Association' and, although mistakes in the plaintiff's name were made from time to time, the scale of the incorrect references to the plaintiff as the 'British Diabetic Society' or the 'Diabetic Society' did not amount to anything more than a sporadic and erroneous usage. However, the words 'association' and 'society' were very similar in derivation and meaning and not wholly dissimilar in form and, in the particular circumstances of the case, it was clear that there was insufficient differentiation between the two words. Accordingly, the defendant's continued use of the name 'British Diabetic Society' would amount to deception, even though unintended deception, calculated to damage the plaintiff's reputation and goodwill. An injunction would be granted restraining the defendant from using the names 'British Diabetic Society' or 'Diabetic Society'.

British Diabetic Association v Diabetic Society Ltd [1995] 4 All ER 812 (Chancery Division: Robert Walker J). *Office Cleaning Services Ltd v Westminster Window and General Cleaners Ltd* [1946] 1 All ER 320n, HL, considered.

### 2952	Trade marks—Community trade marks—fees

The Community Trade Marks (Fees) Regulations 1995, SI 1995/3175 (in force on 1 January 1996), enable the registrar of trade marks to charge a fee of £15 for receiving and forwarding applications for a Community trade mark to the Office for Harmonisation in the Internal Market by way of the Patent Office.

See also para 3155.

### 2953	Trade marks—counterfeit goods—EC provisions

The Trade Marks (EC Measures Relating to Counterfeit Goods) Regulations 1995, SI 1995/1444 (in force on 1 July 1995), make consequential amendments to the Trade Marks Act 1994, s 89(3), to take account of Council Regulation (EC) 3295/94, which replaces Council Regulation (EC) 3842/86 from 1 July 1995 and lays down measures to prohibit the release for free circulation, export, re-export or entry for a suspensive procedure of counterfeit and pirated goods.

### 2954	Trade marks—infringement—injunction—order to disclose information

See *Coca-Cola Co v Gilbey*, para 1700.

### 2955	Trade marks—infringement—interpretation of statute—introduction of EC Council minutes as evidence

The Trade Marks Act 1994, s 10 provides that a person infringes a registered trade mark if he uses, in the course of trade, a sign where, because the sign is identical with or similar to the trade mark and is used in relation to goods or services identical with or similar to those for which the trade mark is registered, there exists a likelihood of confusion on the part of the public, which includes the likelihood of association with the trade mark.

The defendant opened a restaurant with a name which was very similar to one owned by the plaintiff restaurant operator. The plaintiff brought an action for trade mark infringement under the 1994 Act, s 10. Both parties agreed that s 10 covered 'classical infringement' by confusion as to the source or origin of goods or services. The plaintiff claimed that it went further by also covering the situation where a customer, on seeing the defendant's mark, called to mind the plaintiff's registered mark, even if there was no possibility of the customer being under any misapprehension as to the origin of the goods. As evidence of this, the plaintiff wished to introduce a copy of the minute of the relevant EC Council meeting which had discussed the Directive on which the 1994 Act was eventually based. *Held*, it was not permissible to refer to confidential council minutes in construing European legislation and it would be wrong and dangerous to rely on rumours as to the origin and meaning of such legislation, no matter how commonly believed they were. It was not right for an English court to follow the route adopted by the courts of another member state when it was firmly of a different view simply because the other court expressed a view first. The scope of European legislation was too important to be decided on a first past the post basis. If the plaintiff's broader interpretation of s 10 were to be adopted, the 1994 Act would be creating a new type of monopoly not related to the proprietor's trade but in the trade mark itself as a quasi-copyright in the mark. There appeared to be little commercial justification for any such extension of trade mark rights and the language of the 1994 Act was consistent with the rights being restricted to classical infringement. Section 10 was therefore confined to 'classical infringement' and had been breached by the defendant. Accordingly, judgment would be given for the plaintiff.

Wagamama Ltd v City Centre Restaurants plc [1995] FSR 713 (Chancery Division: Laddie J).

2956 Trade marks—infringement—use of registered name as book title

Scotland

The Trade Marks Act 1994, s 11(2)(b) provides that a registered trade mark is not infringed by the use of indications concerning the characteristics of goods or services provided the use is in accordance with honest practices in industrial or commercial matters.

The petitioner was the owner of a trade mark which was the name of a popular music group with a world-wide following. The respondent, a publishing company, was publishing a book on the group which had the group's name in the title. The petitioner sought an injunction against the use of the registered name in the book's title. *Held*, the respondent was using the trade mark as an 'indication', namely to indicate that it was a book concerning the group. It would be a bizarre result of trade marks legislation if it could be used to prevent publishers from using the protected name in the title of a book about the company or product. If that had been Parliament's intention, that would have been made plain. The use of the name in the present case therefore fell within the 1994 Act, s 11(2)(b) and, accordingly, the application for an injunction would be refused.

Bravado Merchandising Services Ltd v Mainstream Publishing (Edinburgh) Ltd (1995) Times, 20 November (Outer House).

2957 Trade marks—priority applications—relevant countries

The Trade Marks (Claims to Priority from Relevant Countries) (Amendment) Order 1995, SI 1995/2997 (in force on 1 January 1996), amends the 1994 Order, SI 1994/2803, and specifies Antigua and Barbuda, Bahrain, Belize, Bolivia, Botswana, Brunei Darussalam, Colombia, Djibouti, Dominica, Ecuador, Guatemala, Hong Kong, India, Jamaica, Kuwait, Macau, Maldives, Mozambique, Myanmar, Namibia, Nicaragua, Pakistan, Sierra Leone and Thailand as relevant non-Convention countries in which an application for registration of a trade mark confers priority in respect of an application for the registration of the trade mark in the United Kingdom. The claim to priority must be made within six months from the date of filing the application in the relevant country.

TRANSPORT

2958 Articles

Animal Transportation, Simon Brooman and Deborah Legge: 145 NLJ 1131

Passenger Transport, Peter Hewitt (on VAT on certain types of passenger transport): Tax Journal, Issue 303, p 6

2959 Common transport policy

See EUROPEAN COMMUNITIES.

2960 Goods vehicles—drivers' hours—rest period—circumstances in which requirements do not apply

See *Re Bird*, para 2969.

2961   Goods vehicles—international road haulage permits—revocation

The Goods Vehicles (International Road Haulage Permits) (Revocation) Regulations 1995, SI 1995/1290 (in force on 12 June 1995), revoke the 1975 Regulations, SI 1975/2234, as amended, by virtue of which commercial goods vehicles registered in the United Kingdom and proceeding on specified journeys were required to carry an appropriate permit issued by the Secretary of State.

2962   Goods Vehicles (Licensing of Operators) Act 1995

The Goods Vehicles (Licensing of Operators) Act 1995 consolidates the Transport Act 1968, Pt V and related provisions concerning the licensing of operators of certain goods vehicles. The Act received the royal assent on 19 July 1995 and came into force, except s 50, Sch 5 (which come into force on a day to be appointed and require certain documents to be carried by the drivers of large goods vehicles and make other provision in connection with such vehicles), on 1 January 1996: SI 1995/2181. A table showing the destination of enactments consolidated appears opposite.

DESTINATION TABLE

This table shows in column (1) the enactments and subordinate legislation repealed or revoked by the Goods Vehicles (Licensing of Operators) Act 1995 ante, and in column (2) the provisions of that Act corresponding thereto.

In certain cases the provision in column (1), though having a corresponding provision in column (2) is not, or not wholly, repealed or revoked as it is still required, or partly required, for the purposes of other legislation. Where this is the case, the provision is marked with a †, meaning it is not repealed or revoked, or with a *, meaning it is only partially repealed or revoked.

A "dash" in the right hand column means that the repealed or revoked provision to which it corresponds in the left hand column is spent, unnecessary or for some other reason not specifically reproduced.

† Not repealed
* Repealed in part

1	2	1	2
Road Traffic Act 1960 (c 16)	**Goods Vehicles (Licensing of Operators) Act 1995** (c 23)	s 62(5).	s 8(6)
		s 63(1).	s 10(1)
		s 63(2).	Applied to Scotland
		s 63(3).	s 12(1)–(3)
		s 63(4).	ss 10(2), 12(6), (9)
		s 63(4A)	ss 12(8), 19(11)
s 233(1).	s 38(2)	s 63(5).	Rep 1994 c 40, ss 57(1), 81(1), Sch 13, Pt I, para 2(1), Sch 17
s 233(2).	s 38(1), (4)		
s 233(3).	s 38(3)		
s 235(1).	s 39(1)		
s 235(2).	Rep 1972 c 20, s 205(1), Sch 9, Pt I	s 63(6).	s 12(12)
		s 64(1).	s 13(1), (2)
s 235(3).	s 39(2)	s 64(2)–(9)	s 13(4)–(11)
s 244*.	s 51	s 64A	s 15(1)–(4)
s 253(1)†.	s 58(1)	s 64B	s 21
s 255†.	s 53	s 65.	Rep 1982 c 49, s 74, Sch 5, para 6, Sch 6
s 257(1)†.	s 58(1)		
s 263(1).	s 55	s 66(1).	s 22(1)
s 263(2).	Rep 1981 c 14, s 88(3), Sch 8	s 66(2).	s 22(6)
		s 67.	s 16
s 265(1).	Rep 1981 c 14, s 88(3), Sch 8	s 67A(1), (2)	s 24(1), (2)
		s 67A(3)–(7).	s 24(4)–(8)
s 265(2).	—	s 67A(8)	s 24(3)
s 269†.	s 54	s 68(1).	s 17(1)
		s 68(2).	—
Transport Act 1968 (c 73)	**Goods Vehicles (Licensing of Operators) Act 1995** (c 23)	s 68(3)–(6)	s 17(2)–5
		s 68A	s 25(1)–(6)
		s 69(1), (2)	s 26(1), (2)
		s 69(2A)	s 26(3)
		s 69(3).	s 26(4)
		s 69(3A)	s 26(5)
s 59(1).	s 1(1)	s 69(4).	s 26(1), (5), Sch 2, paras 5, 6
s 59(2).	s 1(2)		
s 59(3).	Rep 1985 c 67, s 139(3), Sch 8	s 69(5).	s 28(1)
		s 69(5A), (5B)	s 28(2), (3)
s 59(4).	Rep 1969 c 35, s 47(2), Sch 6	s 69(6), (7)	s 28(4), (5)
		s 69(7A)	s 26(6), (7)
s 60(1).	s 2(1)	s 69(8).	s 26(8)
s 60(2).	s 2(2)	s 69(8A)	s 28(6)
s 60(3).	s 2(4)	s 69(9).	s 29(1)
s 60(4).	Sch 1	s 69(10).	s 29(2)–(4)
s 60(4A)	s 2(3)	s 69(10A)	ss 26(9), 28(7)
s 60(5).	s 2(5)	s 69(11).	s 28(8)
s 61(1).	s 5(1)	s 69A(1)	s 7(1)
s 61(1A)	s 5(2)	s 69A(2)	s 8(3)
s 61(1B).	s 5(3)	s 69A(3)	s 8(5)
s 61(2).	s 5(4), (5)	s 69A(3A)	s 8(6)
s 61(3)–(6)	s 5(6)–(9)	s 69A(4)	s 7(2)
s 61A	s 6	s 69B(1)	ss 12(1), 14(1)
s 62(1).	s 8(1), (2)	s 69B(2)	ss 12(4), (5), 14(1)
s 62(2).	s 8(3)	s 69B(3)	s 14(1), (2)
s 62(3).	Rep 1982 c 49, s 74(2), Sch 6	s 69B(4)	s 14(1), (2)
		s 69B(5)	s 14(3)
s 62(4).	s 8(4), Sch 2, paras 1–4	s 69B(5A), (5B)	s 14(4), (5)
s 62(4A)	s 9(1), (2), (4)	s 69B(6)	s 14(6)
s 62(4B).	ss 9(3), 51	s 69B(6A)	s 14(7)

1	2
s 69B(7)	Rep 1994 c 40, ss 57(1), 81(1), Sch 13, Pt I, para 6(5), Sch 17
s 69C(1)--(3)	s 23(1)--(3)
s 69C(4)	Rep 1994 c 40, s 57(1), Sch 13, Pt I, para 7(2)
s 69C(5)	s 23(4)
s 69C(5A)	s 23(5)
s 69C(6)	s 23(6)
s 69D	s 19
s 69E(1)	ss 11(1), 18(1)
s 69E(2)	s 18(2)
s 69E(3)	ss 11(2), 18(3)
s 69E(4)	ss 11(3), 18(4)
s 69E(5)	ss 11(4), 18(5)
s 69EA	s 30
s 69EB	s 31
s 69EC	s 32
s 69ED	s 33
s 69F	Rep 1994 c 40, ss 57(1), 81(1), Sch 13, Pt I, para 8, Sch 17
s 69G(1)	ss 12(9), (10), 19(10), 31(5)
s 69G(2)	ss 12(7), 19(10), 31(5)
s 69G(3)	s 10(2)
s 69G(4)	ss 12(8), 19(11), 31(5)
s 69H	s 34
s 69I	s 44
s 69J	s 36
s 70(1)	s 37(1)--(6)
s 70(2)--(8)	s 37(1)--(7)
s 71(1)-(5)	Rep 1980 c 34, s 69, Sch 9, Pt II
s 71(6)	Sch 5, para 1(1)-(5)
s 71(7)	Rep 1980 c 34, s 69, Sch 9, Pt II
s 71(8)	Sch 5, para 1(6)
s 71(9), (10)	Rep 1980 c 34, s 69, Sch 9, Pt II
ss 72–80	Rep 1980 c 34, s 69, Sch 9, Pt II
s 81(1)	Sch 5, para 2(1)
s 81(2)	Sch 5, para 2(2)-(4)
s 81(3), (4)	Sch 5, para 2(5), (6)
s 82(1)	Sch 5, para 3(1), (5)
s 82(2)	Sch 5, para 3(2), (3), (5)
s 82(3)	Sch 5, para 3(4)
s 82(4)	s 40(1)
s 82(5)	s 40(2), Sch 5, para 3(6)
s 82(6)	s 41(1)-(4)
s 82(7)	Applied to Scotland
s 82(8)	s 42(1), Sch 5, para 3(7)
s 82(9)	s 42(2), Sch 5, para 3(8)
s 83	Sch 5, para 4
s 84	s 43
s 85	s 46(1), (2)
s 85A	s 47
s 86(1)--(4)	s 48(1)--(4)
s 86(5)	s 48(6)
s 87(1)	s 35(1)
s 87(2)	Rep 1980 c 34, s 69, Sch 9, Pt II
s 87(3), (4)	s 35(2), (3)
s 87(4)	s 35(3)
s 87(5)	s 35(4), (5)
s 88	Rep 1985 c 67, s 139(3), Sch 8
s 89	s 45
s 90	Rep 1985 c 67, s 139(3), Sch 8
s 91(1)	s 57(1), (2)

1	2
s 91(2)	s 57(4)
s 91(3)	—
s 91(4)	s 57(6)
s 91(4A)	s 57(7)
s 91(5), (6)	s 57(8), (9)
s 91(6A)	s 57(10)
s 91(7), (8)	s 57(11), (12)
s 92(1)	ss 7(3), 58(1), Sch 5, para 1(6)
s 92(2)	s 58(2)
s 92(2A)	s 58(3)
s 92(2B)	ss 24(9), 25(7)
s 92(3)	s 26(11)
s 92(4)	Applied to Scotland
s 92(4A)	ss 16(5), 48(5)
s 92(5)	s 58(1)
s 92(6)	s 58(5)
s 93	Rep 1994 c 40, s 81(1), Sch 17
s 94(1), (2)	Rep 1994 c 40, s 81(1), Sch 17
s 94(3)	Rep 1982 c 49, s 74(2), Sch 6
s 94(4)–(6)	Rep 1980 c 34, s 69, Sch 9, Pt II
s 94(7), (8)	—
s 94(9)	Rep 1994 c 40, s 81(1), Sch 17
s 94(10)	Rep 1993 c 19, s 51, Sch 10; 1994 c 40, s 81(1), Sch 17
s 157†	s 57(13)
s 158(1)★	—
s 159(1)†	ss 21(5), 58(1)
s 159(3)(a), (b)†	s 12(12)
s 166(2)†	s 50(2)
Sch 8A	
para 1(1)--(6)	Sch 4, para 1(1)--(6)
para 1(7)	Sch 4, para 1(7), (8)
para 2	Sch 4, para 2
para 3(1)--(6)	Sch 4, para 3(1)--(6)
para 3(7)	Sch 4, para 3(7), (8)
para 4	Sch 4, para 4
Sch 10	
Pt I	ss 38(2), 39(1), 53, 54, 56
Pt II	ss 38(2), 55, remainder rep 1972 c 20, s 205(1), Sch 9, Pt I; 1980 c 42, s 20(3), Sch 2; 1981 c 14, s 88, Sch 8; 1985 c 67, s 139(3), Sch 8

Vehicle and Driving Licences Act 1969 (c 27)	Goods Vehicles (Licensing of Operators) Act 1995 (c 23)
Sch 2, para 11†	s 51

European Communities Act 1972 (c 68)	Goods Vehicles (Licensing of Operators) Act 1995 (c 23)
s 2(3)(b)†	s 49(6)

1	2	1	2
Local Government Act 1972 (c 70)	Goods Vehicles (Licensing of Operators) Act 1995 (c 23)	Public Passenger Vehicles Act 1981 (c 14)	Goods Vehicles (Licensing of Operators) Act 1995 (c 23)

s 179(3)† . . . . s 12(12)

Sch 7, para 9 . . . . —

1	2	1	2
Powers of Criminal Courts Act 1973 (c 62)	Goods Vehicles (Licensing of Operators) Act 1995 (c 23)	Forgery and Counterfeiting Act 1981 (c 45)	Goods Vehicles (Licensing of Operators) Act 1995 (c 23)

s 30† . . . . s 38(3), Sch 5, para 4(2)

s 12★ . . . . s 38(4)

1	2	1	2
Road Traffic Act 1974 (c 50)	Goods Vehicles (Licensing of Operators) Act 1995 (c 23)	Transport Act 1982 (c 49)	Goods Vehicles (Licensing of Operators) Act 1995 (c 23)

s 16 . . . . —
Sch 4
  para 1 . . . . ss 9, 51
  paras 2, 3 . . . . Rep 1994 c 40, s 81(1), Sch 17
  para 4(1) . . . . Rep 1994 c 40, s 81(1), Sch 17
  para 4(2) . . . . Sch 2, paras 5, 6
  para 4(3) . . . . Rep 1994 c 40, s 81(1), Sch 17
  para 4(4) . . . . s 26(6), (7)
  para 4(5) . . . . Rep 1994 c 40, s 81(1), Sch 17
  para 4(6) . . . . s 29(1)
  para 4(7) . . . . —
  para 5 . . . . Rep 1994 c 40, s 81(1), Sch 17
Sch 5, Pt I† . . . . s 39(2)

s 52(1) . . . . s 7(3)
s 52(2), (3) . . . . —
s 76(5) . . . . —
Sch 4, Pt I . . . . ss 7(1), (2), 8(3), (5), 12(1), (4), 14(1), (2), 23(2), (6)
Sch 4, Pt II
  para 1(a), (b) . . . . —
  para 1(c) . . . . s 12(1)
  paras 2–5 . . . . Rep 1994 c 40, s 81(1), Sch 17
  para 6(a) . . . . s 57(2)
  para 6(b) . . . . Rep 1994 c 40, s 81(1), Sch 17
  para 7(a) . . . . s 58(1)
  para 7(b) . . . . s 26(11)
  para 8(a) . . . . s 12(2)
  para 8(b) . . . . s 12(12)
Sch 5, para 6 . . . . s 46(2)

1	2	1	2
International Road Haulage Permits Act 1975 (c 46)	Goods Vehicles (Licensing of Operators) Act 1995 (c 23)	Road Traffic Regulation Act 1984 (c 27)	Goods Vehicles (Licensing of Operators) Act 1995 (c 23)

s 3(1) . . . . Sch 2, para 5
s 3(2)–(5) . . . . Rep 1988 c 54, s 3, Sch 1, Pt I

Sch 13, para 6 . . . . Sch 2, paras 5, 6

1	2	1	2
Road Traffic (Drivers' Ages and Hours of Work) Act 1976 (c 3)	Goods Vehicles (Licensing of Operators) Act 1995 (c 23)	Roads (Scotland) Act 1984 (c 54)	Goods Vehicles (Licensing of Operators) Act 1995 (c 23)

s 2(2) . . . . s 13(5), Sch 2, para 1

Sch 9, para 66(10)(d)† . . . s 21(5)

1	2	1	2
Hydrocarbon Oil Duties Act 1979 (c 5)	Goods Vehicles (Licensing of Operators) Act 1995 (c 23)	Companies Consolidation (Consequential Provisions) Act 1985 (c 9)	Goods Vehicles (Licensing of Operators) Act 1995 (c 23)

Sch 6, para 2 . . . . Sch 2, para 5

Sch 2★ . . . . s 28(8)

1	2	1	2
Transport Act 1980 (c 34)	Goods Vehicles (Licensing of Operators) Act 1995 (c 23)	Insolvency Act 1985 (c 65)	Goods Vehicles (Licensing of Operators) Act 1995 (c 23)

s 66(2) . . . . —
Sch 4★ . . . . —

Sch 8, para 16 . . . . —

1	2
Transport Act 1985 (c 67)	Goods Vehicles (Licensing of Operators) Act 1995 (c 23)

s 3(4) . . . . s 1(1)
Sch 4, para 9(1)★ . . . . . . —

1	2
Road Traffic Act 1988 (c 52)	Goods Vehicles (Licensing of Operators) Act 1995 (c 23)

s 85★ . . . . —
s 86★ . . . . —

1	2
Road Traffic (Consequential Provisions) Act 1988 (c 54)	Goods Vehicles (Licensing of Operators) Act 1995 (c 23)

Sch 3
  para 2(1) . . . . s 38(3)
  para 2(2)† . . . . s 51
  para 6(1) . . . . s 51
  para 6(2)(a)–(c) . . . . . . Sch 2, para 5
  para 6(2)(d) . . . . s 26(1)
  para 6(4) . . . . —
  para 6(8)† . . . . s 58(1)

1	2
Companies Act 1989 (c 40)	Goods Vehicles (Licensing of Operators) Act 1995 (c 23)

Sch 18, para 7 . . . . —

1	2
Planning (Consequential Provisions) Act 1990 (c 11)	Goods Vehicles (Licensing of Operators) Act 1995 (c 23)

Sch 2, para 22(1) . . . . . . s 12(12)

1	2
Environmental Protection Act 1990 (c 43)	Goods Vehicles (Licensing of Operators) Act 1995 (c 23)

Sch 15, para 10(2) . . . . . Sch 2, para 5

1	2
Road Traffic Act 1991 (c 40)	Goods Vehicles (Licensing of Operators) Act 1995 (c 23)

Sch 4, para 1 . . . . s 42(1), Sch 5, para 3(7)

1	2
Trade Union and Labour Relations (Consolidation) Act 1992 (c 52)	Goods Vehicles (Licensing of Operators) Act 1995 (c 23)

Sch 2, para 2 . . . . s 12(12)

1	2
Local Government (Wales) Act 1994 (c 19)	Goods Vehicles (Licensing of Operators) Act 1995 (c 23)

Sch 7, Pt II, para 35† . . . . s 12(12)

1	2
Deregulation and Contracting Out Act 1994 (c 40)	Goods Vehicles (Licensing of Operators) Act 1995 (c 23)

s 41 . . . . —
s 42(1) . . . . s 5(1)–(3)
s 42(2) . . . . s 5(6), (7)
s 42(3) . . . . s 6
s 43 . . . . ss 12(8), 19(11)
s 44(1) . . . . ss 13(1), (2), (4)–(11), 15(1)–(4)
s 44(2) . . . . s 14(3)–(5)
s 45 . . . . s 21
s 46 . . . . ss 16, 24(1)–(8)
s 47(1) . . . . ss 17(1), (3)–(6), 25(1)–(6)
s 47(2) . . . . s 19(1)–(9)
s 48(1) . . . . ss 26(1)–(3), (8), 28(1)–(3), (5), (6)
s 48(2) . . . . s 26(1)–(3)
s 48(3) . . . . s 28(1)–(3)
s 48(4) . . . . s 28(5)
s 48(5) . . . . ss 26(8), 28(6)
s 49 . . . . ss 11, 18
s 50(1) . . . . ss 30, 31(1)–(4), 32, 33
s 50(2) . . . . —
s 51 . . . . s 44
s 52 . . . . s 36
s 53 . . . . s 37
s 54 . . . . s 47
s 55 . . . . s 48
s 56 . . . . s 45
s 57 . . . . —
Sch 12 . . . . Sch 4
Sch 13, Pt I
  para 1(1) . . . . —
  para 1(2) . . . . Sch 2, para 1
  para 2(1) . . . . s 12(1)
  para 2(2), (3) . . . . —
  para 3 . . . . s 22(1)
  para 4(1) . . . . Sch 2, para 5
  para 4(2) . . . . —
  para 4(3) . . . . s 28(5)
  para 4(4) . . . . s 26(6), (7)
  para 4(5) . . . . s 29(1)
  para 4(6) . . . . s 29(2)
  para 4(7) . . . . ss 26(9), 28(7)
  para 5(1) . . . . s 7(1)
  para 5(2) . . . . s 8(5)
  para 5(3) . . . . s 8(6)
  para 6(1) . . . . ss 12(1), (4), 14(1)
  para 6(2) . . . . s 14(1), (2)
  para 6(3) . . . . s 14(1), (2)
  para 6(4) . . . . s 14(6), (7)
  para 6(5) . . . . —
  para 7(1) . . . . s 23(1)
  para 7(2) . . . . s 23(3)
  para 7(3) . . . . s 23(4), (5)
  para 8 . . . . —
  para 9 . . . . ss 10(2), 12(7)–(10), 19(10), (11), 31(5), 34
  para 10 . . . . s 40(1)
  para 11 . . . . s 43(2)

1	2	1	2
Goods Vehicles (Operators' Licences, Qualifications and Fees) (Amendment) Regulations 1990, SI 1990/1849	Goods Vehicles (Licensing of Operators) Act 1995 (c 23)	Goods Vehicles (Operators' Licences, Qualifications and Fees) (Amendment) (No 2) Regulations 1991, SI 1991/2239	Goods Vehicles (Licensing of Operators) Act 1995 (c 23)

reg 2(3) . . . . Sch 3, para 6(4)
reg 3(a)† . . . . Sch 3, paras 1(3), 5(2)
reg 3(b)†, (c)† . . . . s 58(1)
reg 4 . . . . —
reg 6 . . . . s 4
reg 7(a) . . . . Sch 3, paras 2–5, 12
reg 7(b) . . . . Sch 3, para 6
reg 7(c) . . . . Sch 3, para 8(2)(a)
reg 7(d) . . . . Sch 3, para 10
reg 7(e) . . . . Sch 3, paras 10, 11

reg 4(1), (2) . . . .—
reg 4(3) . . . . .s 49(6)
reg 4(4) . . . .—
reg 7 . . . . .Sch 3, para 15

Goods Vehicles (Operators' Licences, Qualifications and Fees) (Amendment) (No 2) Regulations 1990, SI 1990/2640	Goods Vehicles (Licensing of Operators) Act 1995 (c 23)

Goods Vehicles (Operators' Licences, Qualifications and Fees) (Amendment) Regulations 1992, SI 1992/2319	Goods Vehicles (Licensing of Operators) Act 1995 (c 23)

reg 4 . . . .—

reg 1† . . . . Sch 3, para 14
reg 2(2)† . . . . Sch 3, para 14
reg 3† . . . . s 58(1)
reg 4 . . . . Sch 3, para 13(1)(a), (2)

Goods Vehicles (Community Authorisations) Regulations 1992 (SI 1992/3077)	Goods Vehicles (Licensing of Operators) Act 1995 (c 23)

reg 14(1) . . . . .s 2(2), (3)
reg 14(2), (3) . . . . .s 2(2), (3)

2963 Goods vehicles—operator's licence

The Goods Vehicles (Licensing of Operators) Regulations 1995, SI 1995/2869 (in force on 1 January 1996), replace the 1984 Regulations, SI 1984/176, as amended, except for operators' qualification requirements (now contained in the Goods Vehicles (Licensing of Operators) Act 1995 (see para 2962) and fees provisions (now contained in the Goods Vehicles (Licensing of Operators) (Fees) Regulations 1995 (see para 2964). Provision is made, as a result of certain changes to be made to the goods vehicle licensing system by the Deregulation and Contracting Out Act 1994, for continuous licensing and review of operating centres, and for partnerships. The Goods Vehicles (Licensing of Operators) Regulations 1995 prescribe matters relating to licence applications, objections and representations, operating centres, inquiries held by a traffic commissioner, the content, publication and availability of statements known as applications and decisions by a traffic commissioner, and the provision of reasons for his decisions. SI 1995/1488 is revoked.

2964 Goods vehicles—operator's licence—fees

The Goods Vehicles (Licensing of Operators) (Fees) Regulations 1995, SI 1995/3000 (in force on 1 January 1996), replace provisions of the 1984 Regulations, SI 1984/176, concerning fees in respect of goods vehicle operators' licences. The fee (1) for the issue of a licence is increased from £185 to £250; (2) for the issue of a publishable variation is decreased from £185 to £160; (3) for the issue of an interim licence is £160; (4) for the continuation in force of a licence is £250. The additional fee for motor vehicles specified on the licence is now £7 per vehicle (if paid five-yearly in advance) or £8.50 per motor vehicle per quarter (if paid annually in advance). The additional fee for motor vehicles specified on an interim licence is now £10 per vehicle. The regulations also enable charges to be made by the traffic commissioner if he makes certain arrangements with the licence holder for administrative purposes, provide for refunds of unused vehicle fees covering 12-month periods in certain circumstances, and enable a licence holder to transfer vehicle fees paid from a vehicle which is removed from the licence to a vehicle which is added to it. SI 1995/1488 is revoked.

2965 Goods vehicles—plating and testing

The Goods Vehicles (Plating and Testing) (Amendment) Regulations 1995, SI 1995/1456 (in force on 1 July 1995), further amend the 1988 Regulations, SI 1988/1478, by exempting from the requirement to undergo examinations for plating and annual tests vehicles that are used on roads for distances not exceeding an aggregate of 6 miles a week.

2966 Goods vehicles—restriction—breach of permit—penalty

The Road Traffic Regulation Act 1984, s 8(1) provides that any person who acts in contravention of, or fails to comply with, an order under s 6 (orders regulating traffic in Greater London) is guilty of an offence.

The plaintiff, a company which delivered newspapers, was the operator of goods vehicles. Two of its drivers had failed to minimise their use of restricted roads and had therefore been in breach of conditions attached to permits granted under the Greater London (Restriction of Goods Vehicles) Traffic Order 1985, SI 1985/343. The regulations were made under the 1984 Act, s 6. The plaintiff was convicted of offences committed contrary to s 8(1) and, on appeal, it claimed that to have avoided using restricted roads would have delayed journeys, thereby making them less commercially feasible. *Held*, there was a clear obligation under a condition attached to the permit not to leave excluded roads until as near as possible to the planned stopping place and to take the shortest practicable route from the stopping place to the nearest excluded road or to the next planned stopping place. That condition did not incorporate commercial considerations but meant practicable in the sense of the vehicle being physically capable of going on the route. Accordingly, the appeal would be dismissed.

TNT Express (UK) Ltd v Richmond-upon-Thames London Borough Council (1995) Times, 27 June (Queen's Bench Division: McCowan LJ and Waller J). *Post Office v London Borough of Richmond* (1994) 158 JP 919 (1994 Abr para 2403) considered.

2967 Licensing and testing—fees—matters to be taken into account

The Department of Transport (Fees) (Amendment) Order 1995, SI 1995/1684 (in force on 1 July 1995), further amends SI 1988/811 by introducing provisions which, in particular, (1) specify the functions and matters which are to be taken into account in determining the fees and charges fixed by the Secretary of State under the Road Traffic Act 1988, (2) make provision in respect of the charges for the supply of test certificate forms, (3) remove references to the former test for motor bicycles, (4) specify the functions and matters to be taken into account in fixing fees for entering a person's name in the register of approved disabled driving instructors, and (5) specify the functions and matters to be taken into account in determining the fees for the issue of certificates which state the design weight of a vehicle.

2968 Passenger and goods vehicles—buses—overnight parking for buses in depot— liability to non-domestic rates on depot

See *Barnet London Borough Council v London Transport Property*, para 2461.

2969 Passenger and goods vehicles—drivers' hours—rest period—circumstances in which requirements do not apply

Council Regulation (EC) 3820/85, art 6 provides that the driving period between any two daily rest periods or between a daily rest period and a weekly rest period must not exceed nine hours, and art 7 provides that after four and a half hours' driving, the driver must observe a break of at least 45 minutes. By art 12, provided that road safety is not thereby jeopardised and to enable him to reach a suitable stopping place, the driver may depart from the provisions of the regulation to the extent necessary to ensure the safety of persons, of the vehicle or of its load.

A lorry driver was convicted of infringing arts 6 and 7 of the 1985 Regulation. The driver and his employer had anticipated before he began the relevant journey that he would not be able to comply with those provisions, as his load consisted of highly valuable goods. On appeal, the driver sought to rely on the derogation provided by art 12. The case was referred to the European Court of Justice for a preliminary ruling as to whether or not he was entitled to do so, given that he knew in advance of his journey that he would breach the regulation. *Held*, art 12 could be relied on only by a driver, and not his employer. As it was for the driver to decide whether it was necessary to derogate from the regulation, chose a suitable stopping place and record the reason for the derogation in his duty roster or recording equipment, it was clear that art 12 applied only when it unexpectedly became impossible to comply with the regulation during the course of a journey. Moreover, having regard to the condition that road safety could not be jeopardised, it was impossible for a driver and his employer to know before a journey was commenced whether or not that condition would be satisfied. It was therefore when an unforeseen event occurred that a driver had to decide whether or not he would still able to ensure road safety before derogating from the regulation. Moreover, the aim of the regulation, namely the improvement of road safety, would be defeated if drivers were allowed to derogate from the regulation even before commencing their journey.

Case C-235/94: Re Bird [1996] All ER (EC) 165 (ECJ: First Chamber).

2970 Passenger and goods vehicles—drivers' hours—use of recording equipment— meaning of 'daily working period'

Tachograph records from a driver's vehicle were inspected and disclosed breaches of regulations governing drivers' hours. Council Regulation (EC) 3821/85, art 15(2) provided that where tachograph equipment was installed, drivers had to use a record sheet for each day on which they drove, starting from when they took over the vehicle until the end of the daily working period. Article 15(3) required drivers to record separately on the tachograph driving time, all other periods of work, other periods of availability, breaks in work and daily rest periods. It was alleged that the driver, an employee of a transport company, used two sheets in the tachograph in one day. The driver claimed that he was able to do so because, having completed his daily working period and having left the company's premises, he had then undertaken a new assignment. The court had to determine what was meant by 'the end of the daily working period' and since it considered that the interpretation in the regulations was not clear, the court referred the matter to the European Court of Justice for a preliminary ruling. *Held*, in a previous decision the court held that a driver's daily period of activity commenced at the time when he activated the tachograph following a weekly or daily rest period. Where that rest period was taken in separate periods, the period of activity began at the end of a rest period of at least eight hour's duration. Consequently, the end of a daily working period coincided with the beginning of a daily rest period, or where appropriate, at the beginning of a rest period extending over a minimum of eight consecutive hours.

Case C-394/92: Criminal proceedings against Michielsen [1995] IRLR 171 (ECJ: Sixth Chamber).
Case C-313/92: Criminal proceedings against Van Swieten BV [1994] ECR 2177, ECJ considered.

2971 Passenger and goods vehicles—driving tests

The Motor Vehicles (Driving Licences) (Large Goods and Passenger-Carrying Vehicles) (Amendment) Regulations 1995, SI 1995/1162 (in force on 29 May 1995), amend the 1990 Regulations, SI 1990/2612, so as to increase from 5 clear days to 10 clear days the period of notice to be given by a candidate who cancels an appointment for a driving test in order for the Secretary of State to be able to repay the test fee.

The Motor Vehicles (Driving Licences) (Large Goods and Passenger-Carrying Vehicles) (Amendment) (No 2) Regulations 1995, SI 1995/2075 (in force on 15 August 1995), further amend the 1990 Regulations, SI 1990/2612, so that vehicles which were exempt from duty under the Vehicle Excise and Registration Act 1994, Sch 2, para 21 (repealed) by virtue of the fact that they were not intended to be used on public roads for an aggregate distance exceeding 6 miles per week remain exempt from duty and vehicles exempt from duty under Sch 2, para 20A (namely, agricultural, horticultural and forestry vehicles used on public roads for distances of no more than 1.5 km at a time) are also exempt.

2972 Public service vehicles—conditions of fitness, equipment, use and certification

The Public Service Vehicles (Conditions of Fitness, Equipment, Use and Certification) (Amendment) Regulations 1995, SI 1995/305 (in force on 14 March 1995), further amend the 1981 Regulations, SI 1981/257, so as to require every public service vehicle to carry a fire extinguisher that complies with certain British Standard specifications or with one of two prescribed levels of test under such a specification.

2973 Public service vehicles—conduct of drivers, inspectors, conductors and passengers

The Public Service Vehicles (Conduct of Drivers, Inspectors, Conductors and Passengers) (Amendment) Regulations 1995, SI 1995/186 (in force on 1 March 1995), amend SI 1990/1020, so as to provide that passengers on a public service vehicle are not prohibited from speaking to the driver when the vehicle is not in motion.

2974 Public service vehicles—lost property

The Public Service Vehicles (Lost Property) (Amendment) Regulations 1995, SI 1995/185 (in force on 1 March 1995), further amend SI 1978/1684 by (1) amending the definition of 'vehicle' to exclude vehicles used under permits granted to educational and other bodies under the Transport Act 1985, s 19, (2) reducing the period during which the operator of a public service vehicle must keep a record of lost property delivered to him from 12 months to six months, (3) setting the charge for the return of property at a maximum of £2 in all cases if demanded, and (4) providing that lost property may be disposed of if it is not claimed, or a claim is not substantiated, within one month of its delivery to an operator or his representative.

2975 Public service vehicles—operators' licences

The Public Service Vehicles (Operators' Licences) Regulations 1995, SI 1995/2908 (in force on 1 January 1996), consolidate the 1986 Regulations, SI 1986/1668, as amended, and make modifications in consequence of the Deregulation and Contracting Out Act 1994, Pt I, Ch IV, (ss 58–68). New provisions are introduced in relation to the expiry of discs, the election to pay for discs annually and the forms of notices to be given. SI 1995/689 is revoked.

The Public Service Vehicles (Operators' Licences) (Fees) Regulations 1995, SI 1995/2909 (in force on 1 January 1996), replace the 1986 Regulations supra, regs 19 and 20. A new fee structure for operators' licences and discs is introduced and provision is made for refunds of fees paid to be given in specified circumstances where discs are not used.

2976 Railways

See RAILWAYS, INLAND WATERWAYS AND PIPE-LINES.

2977 Road traffic

See ROAD TRAFFIC.

2978 Taxi cabs—fares—London

The London Cab (No 2) Order 1995, SI 1995/1181 (in force on 22 April 1995), increases the fares payable for the hiring of a motor cab in the Metropolitan Police District and the City of London in respect of all journeys beginning and ending there.

2979 Taxi cabs—licensing—requirements

The London Cab Order 1995, SI 1995/837 (in force on 18 April 1995), applies to applications for a cab licence in respect of a motor cab registered on or after 1 August 1979 and propelled by a diesel engine. It requires that a certificate, indicating that the vehicle has passed a specified exhaust emissions test, is to be handed to the public carriage examiner when the cab is presented to him for examination prior to the grant of a cab licence. The order prescribes the form of the certificate, the time within which it must be signed and the persons who can sign it, as well as giving the examiner power to require a further certificate to be produced in certain circumstances.

TRUSTS

Halsbury's Laws of England (4th edn) Vol 48 (reissue), paras 501–986

2980 Articles

Attorney-General v Reid: The Company Law Implications, A J Boyle (on *Attorney-General for Hong Kong v Reid* [1994] 1 All ER 1, PC (1993 Abr para 2576)): 16 Comp Lawyer 131

Attorneys as Trustees, Richard Oerton (on sale of a co-owned property where one co-owner is represented by someone with an enduring power of attorney): LS Gaz, 22 March 1995, p 18

Can We Now Forget About Breach of Trust? Nicholas Patten (on *Target Holdings Ltd v Redferns* [1995] 3 All ER 785, HL (para 2981)): 139 SJ 894

A Constructive Judgment, Colin Passmore and Nick Sieve (on *Royal Brunei Airlines Sdn Bhs v Tan* [1995] 3 All ER 97, PC (para 2982)): 145 NLJ 1379

Constructive Trusts—a Practical Guide, Tim Lawson-Cruttenden and Adetutu Odutola: [1995] Fam Law 560

The Home: Excuses and Contributions, Patrick Milne (on the developing law of beneficial co-ownership under constructive and resulting trusts): 145 NLJ 423

A Position of Trust, John Snape and Gary Watt (on *Royal Brunei Airlines Sdn Bhd v Philip Tan Kok Ming* [1995] 3 All ER 97, PC (para 2982)): LS Gaz, 19 July 1995, p 20

A Problem in the Construction of Gifts to Unincorporated Associations, Paul Matthews: [1995] Conv 302

Secret and Semi-Secret Trusts: Justifying Distinctions Between the Two, David Wilde: [1995] Conv 366

Trust Clauses—For Lawyers or Their Clients? Ann Kenny: 139 SJ 556

A Trustee's Lot is Not a Happy One, Robin Towns (on the position of trustees and personal representatives under the system of implied covenants for title): 145 NLJ 1410

Trustees' Duty to Disclose, Patrick O'Hagan: 145 NLJ 1414

Whose Property is it Anyway, Ann Kenny: 139 SJ 926

2981 Breach of trust—damages for breach—measure of damages

It has been held, in a case involving breach of trust by a solicitor, that the principles governing the award of damages at common law are equally applicable in equity. The basic right of a beneficiary is to have the trust duly administered in accordance with the trust instrument and with the general law. In relation to a traditional trust where the fund is held in trust for a number of beneficiaries having different, usually successive, equitable interests, the right of each beneficiary is to have the whole fund vested in the trustees so as to be available to satisfy his equitable interest when and if it falls into possession. The equitable rules of compensation for breach of trust have been largely developed in relation to such traditional trusts, where the only way in which all the beneficiaries' rights could be protected was to restore to the trust fund what ought to be there. Although the fundamental principles of equity apply to trusts arising out of commercial and financial dealings, it is wrong to apply specialist rules developed in relation to traditional trusts to such commercial trusts. Where moneys are paid to a solicitor by a client as part of a conveyancing transaction, the purpose of the transaction is to achieve the client's commercial objective. The depositing of money with the solicitor is but one aspect of the arrangements between the parties, which for the most part are contractual. The circumstances under which the solicitor can part with money from client accounts are regulated by the client's instructions and are not part of the trusts on which the property is held. Until the underlying commercial transaction is completed, the solicitor can be required to restore to client account moneys wrongly paid away, but is not under an obligation to restore the trust fund once the transaction is completed. The equitable compensation for breach of trust has to be assessed as at the date of judgment and not at an earlier date. Equitable compensation for breach of trust is designed to make good a loss in fact suffered by the beneficiaries and which, using hindsight and common sense, can be seen to have been caused by the breach.

Target Holdings Ltd v Redferns (a firm) [1995] 3 All ER 785 (House of Lords: Lords Keith of Kinkel, Ackner, Jauncey of Tullichettle, Browne-Wilkinson and Lloyd of Berwick). Decision of Court of Appeal [1994] 1 WLR 1089 (1993 Abr para 2577) reversed. *Re Dawson (Dec'd)* [1966] 2 NSWR 211 and dicta of McLachlin J in *Canson Enterprises Ltd v Boughton and Co* (1991) 85 DLR (4th) 129 approved. *Jaffray v Marshall* [1994] 1 All ER 143 (1994 Abr para 2835) disapproved.

2982 Breach of trust—loss to beneficiaries—liability of third parties

Brunei

The appellant airline appointed a company to act as its agent for the sale of transportation. The company was required to account to the airline for all sums received from such sales and was a trustee of those sums for the airline. The company used the money for its own business purposes and its payments to the airline fell into arrears, whereupon the airline terminated the agreement and began proceedings against the respondent, the company's managing director and principal shareholder, in respect of the unpaid sums. The respondent successfully appealed against a decision that he was liable to the airline as a constructive trustee. On appeal by the airline, the issue was whether the breach of trust which was a prerequisite to accessory liability had to be itself a dishonest and fraudulent breach of trust by the trustee. *Held*, in the context of accessory liability, acting dishonestly meant simply not acting as an honest person would in the circumstances, and this was an objective standard. Although honesty had a strong subjective element, this did not mean that individuals were free to set their own standards of honesty in particular circumstances. Ultimately, in most cases, an honest person should have little difficulty in knowing whether a proposed transaction, or his participation in it, would offend the normally accepted standards of honest conduct. When called upon to decide whether a person was acting honestly, a court had to look at all the circumstances known to the third party at the time and also have regard to his personal attributes. Where third parties were dealing with dishonest trustees, the question was whether the third parties owed a duty of care to the beneficiaries to, in effect, check that a trustee was not misbehaving. Although there might be cases where a third party would owe such a duty, in general beneficiaries could not reasonably expect that everyone dealing with their trustees should owe them a duty to take care lest the trustees were behaving dishonestly. Dishonesty was a necessary, and also a sufficient, ingredient of accessory liability. A liability in equity to make good resulting loss attached to a person who dishonestly procured or assisted in a breach of trust or fiduciary obligation. It was not necessary that the trustee was acting dishonestly. The appeal would be allowed.

Royal Brunei Airlines Sdn Bhd v Tan [1995] 3 All ER 97 (Privy Council: Lords Goff of Chieveley, Ackner, Nicholls of Birkenhead and Steyn and Sir John May).

Following a robbery at the plaintiff company's warehouse, a large quantity of gold and other valuables were stolen. In order to recover the proceeds, the plaintiff brought civil proceedings against numerous defendants, one of whom was the wife of a person who had been convicted in criminal proceedings of laundering the stolen gold for another convicted person. The plaintiff claimed that because the gold had been stolen with the assistance of a dishonest employee, it had an equity to trace the proceeds. The plaintiff's case against the defendant was that she knew that her husband was involved in laundering the proceeds of the stolen gold, or at least believed that he was engaged in a dishonest transaction, and was therefore liable to account to the plaintiff in equity because of her dishonest assistance in the breach of trust. *Held*, although the defendant had accompanied her husband on the foreign trips that he had made to courier the proceeds of the stolen gold, she went on the trips only in her capacity as a wife, and her mere presence did not constitute relevant assistance in furtherance of a breach of trust. An accessory could not be made accountable to the beneficiary of a constructive trust regardless of whether or not he knew of the existence of the trust, and the law did not give a beneficiary a remedy against an accessory who dealt with a trustee in ignorance that he was a trustee, or who knew that he was a trustee but did not know or suspect that the transaction in which he was assisting was a breach of trust. Accordingly, the plaintiff's claim would be dismissed.

Brinks Ltd v Abu-Saleh (No 3) (1995) Times, 23 October (Chancery Division: Rimer J). *Royal Brunei Airlines v Tan* [1995] 3 All ER 97, PC considered.

2983 Constructive trust—matrimonial home—title registered in name of one spouse only

The plaintiff wife and the defendant husband had bought a property together which was conveyed into the defendant's sole name. The plaintiff had contributed 40 per cent of the purchase price and also contributed to the cost of various conversions. She left the property after the defendant formed a relationship with another woman, and sought a declaration from the court that the defendant held the property in trust for both of them in equal shares or such shares as the court might think fit. It was suggested to the court that it did not matter whether the terminology used was concerned with a constructive trust or a resulting trust. The court assessed the plaintiff's interest at 19.4 per cent and she appealed. *Held*, to assume that the terminology used to describe a trust was irrelevant would create a potent source of confusion. All that was needed for a constructive trust to exist was a common intention that the party who was not the legal owner would have a beneficial interest and that that party would act to his or her detriment in reliance on that intention. That was the case here and therefore, a constructive interest existed. Accordingly, the appeal would be allowed and the plaintiff's share would be increased to one third.

Drake v Whipp (1995) Times, 19 December (Court of Appeal: Hirst and Peter Gibson LJJ and Forbes J).

2984 Declaration of trust—matrimonial home—loans secured on trust property—lender unaware of trust

See *Midland Bank plc v Wyatt*, para 1369.

2985 Public Trustee—fees

The Public Trustee (Fees) (Amendment) Order 1995, SI 1995/1425 (in force on 1 July 1995), further amends the 1985 Order, SI 1985/373, so that where notices affecting land would have been served on a person but due to his death are served on the Public Trustee under the Law of Property (Miscellaneous Provisions) Act 1994, s 18, the Public Trustee may make a charge for entering details of such documents on the register (£20 for each deceased person) and for causing searches of the register to be made (£10 for each name or variation of a name).

2986 Public Trustee—notices affecting land—title on death—filing of notices

The Public Trustee (Notices Affecting Land) (Title on Death) Regulations 1995, SI 1995/1330 (in force on 1 July 1995), make provision for the Public Trustee to file notices affecting land that would have been served on a person but for his death and which are served on the Public Trustee in accordance with the Law of Property (Miscellaneous Provisions) Act 1994, s 18 and to keep a register of details taken from such notices. The regulations also allow the public to requisition searches of the register.

2987 Public Trustee—vesting of intestate's property—service of notice to quit

Senior District Judge Angel has issued the following *Practice Direction* ([1995] 3 All ER 192).

Following the coming into force on 1 July 1995 of the Law of Property (Miscellaneous Provisions) Act 1994, s 14, estates which would previously have vested in the President of the Family Division, will vest in the Public Trustee.

As from that date, notice to quit in such cases must be served on the Public Trustee at the Public Trust Office, PO Box 3010, London WC2B 6JS, telephone no 0171–269–7196.

Practice Direction [1985] 1 All ER 832, is cancelled with effect from 1 July 1995.

2988 Resulting trust—purchase of property—illegality—effect on claim under trust

Australia

A mother, the widow of a naval worker, provided the purchase money for a house ('the first house') which was transferred into the names of her son and daughter. The purpose of the arrangement was to enable the mother to obtain a subsidised advance under legislation which applied to widows of naval workers, and she would not have been eligible for such an advance if she already owned a house. When the mother later purchased another house ('the second house') for herself, she applied for and received the subsidised advance, having falsely declared that she did not own or have a financial interest in a house other than that for which the advance was sought. When the first house was sold, the mother claimed to be entitled to all of the proceeds, but the daughter claimed that she was entitled to half of the proceeds. The daughter's claim was upheld, and the mother unsuccessfully appealed against the decision. On further appeal, *held*, although the resulting trust in respect of the proceeds of sale of the first house was illegal because of its association with, or furtherance of, a purpose which was contrary to the legislation, the general principle that the court would not assist a plaintiff who founded his cause of action on an immoral or illegal act was not determinative of a case, nor was it appropriate to apply the principle that the loss should lie where it fell. The purpose of the legislation was to provide public money to facilitate the purchase of housing by eligible persons, provided that such persons did not own another house. That purpose was sufficiently protected by the penalties provided for by the legislation, and the denial of the resulting trust in the instant case would simply prejudice the mother without furthering that purpose. Moreover, the purchase of the first house did not involve any fraud, and the relevance of any illegal purpose was, at most, to explain why the purchase did not constitute a gift to the mother's son and daughter. The presumption of advancement arose, and the resulting trust in the mother's favour was to be enforced. Accordingly, the appeal would be allowed.

Nelson v Nelson (1995) ALR 133 (High Court of Australia). *Tinsley v Milligan* [1993] 3 All ER 65, HL (1993 Abr para 2583) considered.

2989 Trust by imposition of condition—lottery syndicate—duty of treasurer

See *Taylor v Smith*, para 223.

2990 Trust for sale—joint tenants—notice of intention to quit—requirement for consultation

The Law of Property Act 1925, s 26(3) provides that trustees for sale must, so far as practicable, consult persons beneficially interested in possession in the rents and profits of the land until sale and must, so far as is consistent with the general interest of the trust, give effect to the wishes of such persons.

The defendant and his wife were joint tenants and, consequently, trustees for sale of a council flat. The defendant's wife left the flat and applied to the plaintiff council for accommodation as a homeless person. The plaintiff informed her that she was not homeless until she terminated her joint tenancy and recommended that she serve notice of intention to quit without informing the defendant and without his consent. She served a notice on the plaintiff and, upon the defendant refusing to vacate, obtained a possession order. After his appeal against the order was dismissed, the defendant made further appeal on the ground that the 1925 Act, s 26(3) required a joint tenant to consult the other joint tenants before terminating his tenancy and that the plaintiff's encouragement for the wife to serve the notice meant that it was procuring a breach of trust from which it could not benefit. *Held*, s 26(3) required consultation by a trustee for sale before he did a positive act. A notice by a joint tenant stating that she did not wish the tenancy to continue beyond its current four-week term was not a positive act and so s 26(3) did not apply. Accordingly, the defendant's appeal would be dismissed.

Crawley Borough Council v Ure [1995] 1 All ER 724 (Court of Appeal: Glidewell, Hobhouse and Aldous LJJ). *Hammersmith and Fulham London Borough Council v Monk* [1992] 1 All ER 1 (1991 Abr para 1495) applied.

2991 Trustee—charity trustee—investments

See para 326.

2992 Trustee—conflict of duty—jurisdiction of court

The plaintiffs were trustees of a company pension scheme under which they were also beneficiaries. The scheme made provision for its own dissolution in the event of the company going into liquidation and gave the trustees a discretion to apportion any surplus funds. It fell to be determined whether the court had jurisdiction to give directions in respect of a scheme proposed by trustees who were also beneficiaries. *Held*, the general rule of equity by virtue of which a person was prevented from placing himself in a position where his fiduciary duty and personal interest conflicted was a positive rule and did not necessarily require a consideration of morality or wrongdoing. However, in view of the adaptability of the rules of equity and the examples of exceptions to and relaxation of the general rule, the court had jurisdiction to give directions in spite of the fact that the proposals for winding up the scheme had been instituted by trustees in a position of conflict. Since the proposed scheme had, on examination, commended itself to the court and had been considered by counsel and solicitors especially appointed to consider the conflicting interests of its members, none of whom opposed it, and had been considered by the trustees' own separate legal and pension advisers, the court, in exercising its discretion, would direct that the trustees be at liberty to implement the scheme.

Re Drexel Burnham Lambert UK Pension Plan [1995] 1 WLR 32 (Chancery Division: Lindsay J). Bray v Ford [1896] AC 44, HL; Re William Makin & Sons Ltd [1992] PLR 177 and British Coal Corpn v British Coal Staff Superannuation Scheme Trustees Ltd [1993] PLR 303, considered.

2993 Trustee—discretion—exercise of discretion—reasons for exercise of discretion

See Wilson v Law Debenture Trust Corpn plc, para 2262.

2994 Trustee—overseas trust—capital gains tax

See De Rothschild v Lawrenson, para 307.

2995 Trustee—powers of investment—additional powers

The Trustee Investments (Additional Powers) Order 1995, SI 1995/768 (in force on 18 April 1995), amends the Trustee Investments Act 1961 so as to add Liechtenstein to the list of relevant states in the 1961 Act, Sch 1, Pt IV, thus extending the range of securities set out in Sch 1, Pts II and III, and makes a minor amendment to the definition of a gilt unit trust scheme in Sch 1, Pt II.

2996 Trustee—remuneration—matters for which remuneration may be granted—past and future services

The trustees of a cricket club decided to sell an area of land belonging to the club because of the club's continuing financial difficulties. It took nearly 20 years to effect the sale, during which time the trustees encountered legal and practical difficulties. On their application for remuneration for past and future services to the club, and for approval of their expenses incurred in carrying out the trusts of the indenture under which the land was held, held, it was well-established that a trustee was entitled to reimbursement for his expenses, although the court had no jurisdiction to award interest on that sum. It was also settled that a trustee was not entitled to remuneration for his time and trouble unless there was an express provision to that effect in the trust instrument. Although the court could exercise its inherent power to grant remuneration, a trustee could not demand remuneration for past services as a condition of continuing in office. Here, a fixed sum would be allowed as remuneration for the trustees' past services in respect of the sale of the club's land. The court would not, however, allow any amount for future services, as the matters with which the trustees would have to deal did not require any particular expertise.

Foster v Spencer (1995) Times, 14 August (Chancery Division: Judge Paul Baker QC).

VALUE ADDED TAX

Halsbury's Laws of England (4th edn) Vol 12, paras 864–990

2997 Articles

Can the VAT Burden Be Relieved? Ian Dawes (on the VAT burden on charities): Tax Journal, Issue 319, p10

Dispelling a Myth, Miranda Cass and Nick Cronkshaw: Tax Journal, Issue 324, p 12

The End of the Road, Daron Gunson (on tax planning on the cessation of a corporate business): Tax Journal, Issue 321, p 13

French Leaseback Fears, Henry Dyson (on buying French holiday property free of VAT): 139 SJ 426

Is There a Link? Richard Pincher (on VAT treatment of reverse consideration): [1995] BTR 306

Legislative Cleansing, Peter Jenkins (on the progress being made in simplifying the transitional VAT system currently in place in the European Union): Tax Journal, Issue 311, p 15

More Going Concerns for Property People, Richard Pincher (on classifying property as a going concern for VAT purposes): Estates Gazette, 4 November 1995, p 132

One Door Closes; Another Opens, Stephen Coleclough (on *Case C-4/94: BLP Group plc v Customs and Excise Comrs* [1995] STC 424 (para 3167)): Tax Journal, Issue 336, p 6

Passenger Transport, Peter Hewitt (on VAT on certain types of passenger transport): Tax Journal, Issue 303, p 6

A Problem Only for the Poorly Advised, Mark Stapleton (on the Value Added Tax Act 1994, Sch 10, para 2(3A)): Tax Journal, Issue 319, p 14

Proving Comparables, Jim Cotter (on the effect of the Civil Evidence Bill on use of comparable evidence in valuations): Estates Gazette, 5 August 1995, p 66

Schools, Colleges and Universities, David Rudling (on VAT relating to education): Tax Journal, Issue 318, p 15

The Sixth VAT Directive and the need for Reform, S D Coleclough: [1995] BTR 378

Solicitors and VAT, Stanley Dencher: 139 SJ 528

Tax Pitfalls on Business Start-Ups, Daron Gunson: Tax Journal, Issue 316, p 16

Ultimately Funded Training, Ian Fleming (on overcoming VAT complications relating to funding of vocational training): Tax Journal, Issue 315, p 8, Issue 316, p 14, Issue 317, p 14

VAT: A New Source of Income, Glenn Havenhand (on the reclamation of VAT by charities): Tax Journal, Issue 301, p 16

VAT and Cars, Peter Hewitt: Tax Journal, Issue 292, p 15

VAT: Business and the Predominant Concern Test, Jean Warburton: [1995] BTR 534

VAT Issues for Pension Funds, Peter Hewitt: Tax Journal, Issue 314, p 22

VAT on Financial Services, Peter Hewitt: Tax Journal, Issue 308, p 14

2998 Appeal—appeal against commissioners' exercise of discretion—discretion to make assessment to default surcharge

See *Dollar Land (Feltham) Ltd v Customs and Excise Comrs*, para 3005.

2999 Appeal—appeal against requirement of security—nature of appeal

The Commissioners of Customs and Excise required the taxpayer, under the Value Added Tax Act 1983, Sch 7, para 5(2), to provide security as a condition of its making taxable supplies. On the taxpayer's appeal against that decision, a value added tax tribunal decided that the commissioners had misdirected themselves in law by failing first to seek financial information from the taxpayer in order to assist them in reaching a fair decision, but it nevertheless dismissed the appeal. On the taxpayer's further appeal, questions arose as to the nature of the tribunal's decision on an appeal under s 40(1)(n) from a discretionary decision of the commissioners. *Held*, under Sch 7, para 5(2), the commissioners had to assess whether a given state of affairs existed and, if it did, to determine what action or decision should be taken and the steps which ought to be taken to give effect to that decision. If a tribunal could only review the decision on a point of law, s 40 would have said so. Its jurisdiction was appellate, not supervisory. As it did not have the same knowledge and experience as the commissioners for the purpose of substituting its own exercise of discretion in place of that which the commissioners ought to have exercised in order to settle, or otherwise determine, what the amount of any assessment or deposit should be, once the tribunal was satisfied that the commissioners' original decision was wrong because of their failure to take into account relevant matter, it should simply have allowed the taxpayer's appeal and left the commissioners free to take a fresh decision if they thought fit on the facts as they had become at the date of the fresh decision. A hearing before the tribunal was in the nature of an appeal simpliciter; it did not give a right to a rehearing. The appeal would be allowed.

John Dee Ltd v Customs and Excise Comrs [1995] STC 265 (Queen's Bench Division: Turner J).

1983 Act, s 40(1)(n), Sch 7, para 5(2) now Value Added Tax Act 1994, s 83(l), Sch 11, para 4(2).

3000 Assessment—assessment to best of commissioners' judgment—meaning of best judgment

The taxpayer carried on the business of a take-away food shop most of the sales from which were of hot food subject to value added tax at the standard rate. It used a cash till with a memory facility which, as well as recording transactions on till rolls, kept cumulative grand totals of all amounts entered. Such totals appeared to indicate to customs officers the suppression of takings which the taxpayer subsequently admitted. Assessments were made under the Value Added Tax Act 1983, Sch 7, para 4(1)(a) in respect of underdeclared output tax based on a weekly suppression rate derived from the till grand total. That was assumed to be tax-exclusive and, with an adjustment for zero-rated sales, value added tax was added. A deduction was made from the tax-inclusive total to allow for keying errors, training and other non-transaction entries. The taxpayer appealed against the assessments, contending that they had not been made to the best of the commissioners' judgment. *Held*, the issue of 'best judgment' had to be viewed by a value added tax tribunal objectively in two stages. It had first to decide as a question of fact what information, of that which had been before the commissioners at the time of the assessment, had been relied upon for making the assessment. Then, it had to make a value judgment as to the way in which they had arrived at their assessment. The tribunal's function was supervisory and was not to be exercised at too high a threshold, but at a reasonable standard. Given that the commissioners relied only on the grand total till memory readings for their assessment, and given that the supervisory function of the tribunal was to adjudge objectively whether the method used had supplied sufficient information to the commissioners to form a 'best judgment', any other material accumulated in the course of the investigation, but specifically not relied upon to arrive at any assessment, was not in point. All the evidence adduced at the hearings before the tribunal which related to observations, suppressed purchases, and other extraneous matters was irrelevant to the tribunal's task to determine whether the best of the commissioners' judgment, objectively viewed, was reasonably arrived at by exclusive reliance on the grand total till memory readings. The appeal would be dismissed.

Georgiou v Customs and Excise Comrs [1995] STC 1101 (Queen's Bench Division: Sir Louis Blom Cooper). Dicta of Bridge J in *Mountview Court Properties Ltd v Devlin* (1970) 21 P&CR 689 at 695, 696, DC, applied.

1983 Act, Sch 7, para 4(1) now Value Added Tax Act 1994, s 73(1).

This decision has been affirmed: [1996] STC 463.

3001   Assessment—input tax—prescribed accounting period

The Value Added Tax Act 1983, Sch 7, para 4(2) provides that where, for any prescribed accounting period, there has been paid or credited to any person as being a repayment or refund of value added tax or as being due to him as a value added tax credit an amount which ought not to have been so paid or credited, or which would not have been so paid or credited had the facts been known as they later turned out to be, the Commissioners may assess that amount as being value added tax due from him for that period and notify him accordingly.

In February 1991, the taxpayer paid £2m compensation for termination of an agreement. Its value added tax accounting period ended on 31 March 1991 and a claim for input tax was paid in the value added tax accounting period ending on 30 September 1991. A deduction of input tax of £260,869 was allowed by the commissioners on 4 September 1991 on the condition that it would be repaid if it was later determined that the £2m compensation was not consideration for a taxable supply. The commissioners later determined that the £2m was not such a consideration and in June 1993 assessed the £260,869 as tax due from the taxpayer. It appealed but the tribunal did not hear the substantive hearing, instead determining that the assessment made in June 1993 was outside the two-year time limit under the 1983 Act, Sch 7, para 4(5). On appeal by the commissioners, *held*, the question was whether 'the prescribed accounting period' was the accounting period to 31 March 1991 or to 30 June 1991. Thus the key word in Sch 7, para 4(2) was 'for'. That word should be construed in the same way as s 15, as 'so much of the input tax for that period'. Thus, the input tax was for the period ending on 31 March 1991 regardless of when it became claimable or was claimed and the assessment in June 1993 was out of time. Accordingly, the appeal would be dismissed.

Customs and Excise Comrs v Croydon Hotel & Leisure Company Ltd [1995] STC 855 (Queen's Bench Division: Popplewell J).

1983 Act, Sch 7, para 4(2) now Value Added Tax Act 1994, s 73(2). 1983 Act, s 15 now 1994 Act, s 26.

3002   Assessment—notice of assessment—multi-period assessment

The taxpayer received a notice of assessment of value added tax from the Commissioners of Customs and Excise in respect of his undeclared value added tax for a period covering several accounting periods. The notice gave only the total of the assessment. However, an accompanying letter contained three schedules from which it was possible to calculate the sum of the assessment for each prescribed accounting period. It fell to be determined whether a global assessment of value added tax could be made in circumstances where it was possible to make separate assessments for each relevant accounting period, and if so whether the taxpayer had been given sufficient notification of the assessment. At first instance, it was held that adequate notice had been given and the notification was valid. The taxpayer appealed. *Held*, a global assessment of value added tax made by the commissioners could be made in respect of separate accounting periods notwithstanding that it was possible to calculate individually the tax for each of the separate accounting periods. Whether there had been sufficient notification depended on whether the schedules to the letter could be treated as part of the assessment. There was no statutory provision dealing with the form of notice. However, as the taxpayer had received a notice of assessment and the schedules to the accompanying letter showed clearly how the sums were made up, common sense would prevail and the taxpayer would be deemed to have been given proper notification of the assessment. Accordingly, the appeal would be dismissed.

House v Customs and Excise Comrs [1996] STC 154 (Court of Appeal: Stuart-Smith and Pill LJJ and Sir John Balcombe). Decision of May J [1994] STC 211 (1994 Abr para 2856) affirmed. *International Language Centres Ltd v Customs and Excise Comrs* [1983] STC 394 (1983 Abr para 3470) considered and *Customs and Excise Comrs v Le Rififi Ltd* [1995] STC 103, CA (1994 Abr para 2855) followed.

3003 Assessment—tax recovered or recoverable by assessment—interest on tax

The Value Added Tax Act 1994 (Interest on Tax) (Prescribed Rate) Order 1995, SI 1995/521 (in force on 6 March 1995), increases the prescribed rate of interest, for the purposes of the 1994 Act, s 74, on tax recovered or recoverable by assessment, from 6.25 per cent to 7 per cent.

3004 Assessment—time limit—single or divisible assessment

The taxpayer's accounts and records were subject to continuous monitoring by the Commissioners of Customs and Excise through a special value added tax control unit for large traders' accounts. Each return was checked against the supporting documents and calculations. Since 1984, the taxpayer had used a method, in calculating its output tax, which did not comply with the commissioners' guidance on such calculations. The discrepancy in its calculations was not noticed until 1992. It appealed against two assessments to recover output tax, contending that the first had not been made within six years of the period to which it related as required by the Value Added Tax Act 1983, s 22(1) (repealed), that the second was global, and that both of them were made more than one year after the commissioners had sufficient information to justify making them, contrary to Sch 7, para 4(5)(b). *Held*, under Sch 7, para 4(5)(b), an assessment had to be made within one year of the date when evidence of facts, sufficient in the opinion of the commissioners to justify making the assessment, came to their knowledge. The question as to when they had sufficient information to justify making the assessments involved a question of mixed law and fact. The principle of law to be applied to the facts was not when the error in the computation should have been discovered by the commissioners but when the evidence of the facts had come to their knowledge; Sch 7, para 4(5)(b) did not encompass constructive knowledge. The form of notifying an assessment was not prescribed so that it was permissible to consider the notice of assessment as consisting of both the notice (form VAT 655) and the schedules to it containing summaries of the recalculation of the quarterly figures. Further, form VAT 655 made provision for notifying on the same form one or more assessments. The question whether the notice of assessment and the schedules to it comprised a single assessment or separate assessments for each accounting period, was one of mixed law and fact. The legislation distinguished between the making of an assessment and the notification of it. The assessment had been made within the six-year time limit prescribed by s 22. The appeal would be dismissed.

Customs and Excise Comrs v Post Office [1995] STC 749 (Queen's Bench Division: Potts J). *Customs and Excise Comrs v Le Rififi Ltd* [1995] STC 103, CA (1994 Abr para 2855), followed. 1983 Act, Sch 7, para 4(5)(b) now Value Added Tax Act 1994, s 73(6)(b).

3005 Default surcharge—commissioners' exercise of discretion to make assessment to surcharge—right of appeal against discretionary power

Under the Value Added Tax Act 1983, s 40(1), an appeal lies to a value added tax tribunal against a decision of the commissioners of customs and excise with respect to any of the following matters: (o) any liability to a penalty or surcharge, and (p) the amount of any penalty, interest or surcharge specified in an assessment.

It has been held that the words 'with respect to any of the following matters' in s 40(1) do not provide a basis for concluding that s 40(1)(o) and (p) give rise to implied rights to appeal against the commissioners' exercise of their discretionary power to decide to make an assessment in respect of a default surcharge. The remedy against the improper exercise of that power is an appeal to the High Court by way of judicial review.

Dollar Land (Feltham) Ltd v Customs and Excise Comrs [1995] STC 414 (Queen's Bench Division: Judge J).

1983 Act, s 40(1) now Value Added Tax Act 1994, s 83.

3006 Exempt supply—buildings—sale of property used in part as private dwelling

See *Finanzamt Uelzen v Armbrecht*, para 3168.

3007 Exempt supply—education—private tuition

The taxpayer taught mathematics privately to pupils under contracts with their parents. She used a method of teaching under a licence by virtue of which she was supplied by the proprietors of the method with teaching materials, which they granted her the right to use, and a back-up service. In return, she paid the proprietors a lump sum fee per pupil and a proportion of her fee income. It fell to be determined whether the services supplied by her were exempt from value added tax being services falling within the Value Added Tax Act 1983, Sch 6, Group 6, item 3 as 'tuition given privately'. *Held*, the taxpayer was supplying teaching services, not merely providing management services for the proprietors of the teaching method used by her. Both Council Directive (EC) 77/388, art 13(A)(1)(j) and the 1983 Act, s 17, which implemented that provision, exempted private teaching from value added tax. 'Tuition given privately' in either its English or French text covered the taxpayer's teaching activities. Having regard to the licence agreement between the taxpayer and the proprietors, those activities were clearly covered by art 13(A)(1)(j) of the Directive and by the equivalent provision of the 1983 Act. Accordingly, the teaching services supplied by the taxpayer were exempt from value added tax.

Ellicott v Customs and Excise Comrs [1995] 1 CMLR 813 (Value added tax tribunal).

1983 Act, s 17, Sch 6, Group 6, item 3 now Value Added Tax Act 1994, s 31, Sch 9, Group 6, item 2.

3008 Exempt supply—health and welfare—bodies and organisations

See *Bulthuis-Griffioen v Inspecteur der Omzetbelasting*, para 3170.

3009 Exempt supply—health and welfare—supply of spectacles and services of dispensing optician

The taxpayer carried on business as opticians employing ophthalmic opticians to carry out eye tests and issue prescriptions, and dispensing opticians to take measurements of patients' eyes, give advice, prepare and check specifications for lenses and frames, fit the spectacles and make any modifications required. It fell to be determined whether the supply of spectacles by the taxpayer was a single standard-rated supply of goods to which the dispensing opticians' services were merely ancillary or whether the services of dispensing opticians were separate exempt supplies and that the consideration received for the spectacles should be apportioned accordingly. *Held*, in substance and reality, there were two separate supplies, one of spectacles, the other of the services of the dispensing optician. The legislative history of the Value Added Tax Act 1983, Sch 6, Group 7, item 1(b) suggested that Parliament intended that the services of dispensing opticians should be exempted. Moreover, such a conclusion avoided practical difficulties and took account of the roughly even balance of the two elements.

Customs and Excise Comrs v Leightons Ltd; Customs and Excise Comrs v Eye-Tech Opticians (No 1) and Eye-Tech Opticians (No 2) [1995] STC 458 (Queen's Bench Division: McCullough J). Decision of Value added tax tribunal in *Leightons Ltd v Customs and Excise Comrs* [1994] 2 CMLR 308 (1994 Abr para 2860) affirmed.

1983 Act, Sch 6, Group 7, item 1(b) now Value Added Tax Act 1994, Sch 9, Pt II, Group 7, item 1(b).

3010 Exempt supply—land—grant of interest or right over land

The Value Added Tax (Land) Order 1995, SI 1995/282 (in force on 1 March 1995), amends the Value Added Tax Act 1994, Sch 9, Group 1, by exempting from value added tax, with some exceptions, the grant of any interest in or right over land, providing a revised definition of 'grant' which extends exemption to the surrender of an interest and also to reverse surrenders, as defined, and by making a number of consequential amendments.

3011   Finance Act 1995

See para 2489.

3012   General regulations

The Value Added Tax Regulations 1995, SI 1995/2518 (in force on 20 October 1995), replace, with amendments, all the regulations relating to value added tax, including SI 1995/152, 913, 1069, 1280. The following are among the main changes of substance. (1) A value added tax invoice provided to a person in another member state must contain the quantity of goods or extent of services, the rate of value added tax and the amount payable, excluding value added tax, expressed in sterling. (2) A retailer may now issue single invoices showing supplies which are subject to different rates of value added tax. (3) Registered persons who are approved to defer payment of excise duty on goods removed from an excise warehouse may also defer payment of any value added tax which would otherwise be due when such goods are removed. Provision is made for the determination of the latest time at which the value added tax is payable, and a distinction is made between hydrocarbon oils and other goods subject to excise duty according to the different arrangements which apply to them for the payment of excise duty; and these provisions are applied to goods which are relieved from payment of excise duty. (4) Lease purchases and supplies where full payment of the amount shown on the invoice is not due for more than 12 months from the date of issue of the invoice are now excluded from the cash accounting scheme. (5) Supplies of petroleum gases and other gaseous hydrocarbons in a gaseous state are now covered by the time of supply provisions relating to water, gas, or any form of power, heat, refrigeration or ventilation. (6) Input tax must now be adjusted when a capital item is disposed of, and its disposal is not deemed to be a supply in the course or furtherance of a business because the value added tax on the deemed supply would not be more than £250. (7) In consequence of the accession of Finland to the European Union, the Aland Islands are now to be treated for the purposes of the Value Added Tax Act 1994 as excluded from the territory of the Community. (8) Provisions corresponding to those in relation to Community traders concerning false, altered or incorrect claims now apply to third country traders. (9) Revised forms for application for registration for value added tax, partnership particulars at registration, the transfer of a going concern, a value added tax return, and a final value added tax return are included in the Schedule.

The Value Added Tax (Trading Stamps) Regulations 1995, SI 1995/3043 (in force on 1 June 1996), (in force on 1 June 1996), amend the principal 1995 Regulations, SI 1995/2518, supra by revoking Pt X (regs 76–80) which made special provision for the valuation, for value added tax purposes, of goods supplied under trading stamps schemes.

The Value Added Tax (Amendment) Regulations 1995, SI 1995/3147 (in force on 1 January 1996), amend the principal 1995 Regulations supra, in particular by inserting an additional requirement so that a person providing a value added tax invoice relating to the leasing of certain motor cars is required to state on the invoice whether the motor vehicle is a qualifying vehicle under the Value Added Tax (Input) Order 1992, SI 1992/3222, art 7(2A); and extending the time limit for the exportation of goods by an overseas visitor.

3013   Input tax—deduction—goods or services used for exempt transaction

See *BLP Group plc v Customs and Excise Comrs*, para 3167.

3014   Input tax—deduction—goods used partly for business and partly for private purposes

See *Lennartz v Finanzamt München III*, para 3174.

3015   Input tax—deduction—imported goods

See *BP Supergas Anonimos Etairia Geniki Emporiki-Viomichaniki kai Antiprossopeion v Greece*, para 3171.

3016   Input tax—deduction—input tax on professional fees—acquisiton of equipment leasing companies by bank

A bank carried on an equipment leasing business in addition to its principal banking activities. In order to extend that business the bank acquired three leasing companies. The companies became the bank's dormant subsidiaries and their leasing businesses were carried on by the bank itself. For value added tax purposes, the bank made both taxable and exempt supplies. Under the terms of a special partial exemption method agreed with the Commissioners of Customs and Excise, input tax was to be attributed between taxable and non-taxable supplies to the fullest possible extent and input tax attributable to taxable outputs was recoverable in full. The bank claimed that the terms of the special method were applicable to the acquisition of the three companies and that input tax charged on professional fees incurred in connection with the acquisitions was wholly attributable to taxable supplies of leasing and accordingly ought to be recoverable in full. The commissioners determined that only a proportion of the input tax was recoverable on the ground that the professional fees had been used in the acquisition of pre-existing businesses which, until acquired, were not the bank's business, and accordingly could not be said to have been used in making taxable supplies. The bank appealed, and a tribunal found that all of the input tax in question was attributable to taxable outputs and was recoverable in full. On further appeal by the commissioners, *held*, the only purpose underlying the bank's acquisition of the shares and the transfer of the business of the three leasing companies was to enable the bank to expand its leasing business and to make taxable supplies of leasing. Accordingly, the input tax incurred on the professional fees was wholly attributable to taxable supplies of leasing and ought to be recovered in full. The commissioners' appeal would therefore be dismissed.

Customs and Excise Comrs v UBAF Bank Ltd [1995] STC 250 (Queen's Bench Division: MacPherson J).

3017 Input tax—deduction—right to deduct—exceptions

The Value Added Tax (Input Tax) (Amendment) (No 3) Order 1995, SI 1995/1666 (in force on 1 August 1995), further amends the 1992 Order, SI 1992/3222, by (1) enabling value added tax to be charged on the supply, acquisition from another member state or importation of motor cars to be recovered as input tax in a wider range of circumstances, (2) introducing a new 50 per cent input tax recovery restriction on leasing charges where there is any private use of the motor car, and (3) excluding from recovery as input tax any value added tax charged on a supply of a motor car supplied under the margin scheme applicable to motor cars which have been subject to an earlier input tax restriction.

3018 Input tax—deduction—supply for purposes of business—business entertainment

The Value Added Tax (Special Provisions) Order 1981, SI 1981/1741, art 9(1) provides that input tax on the supply to a taxable person of goods or services used by him for the purpose of business entertainment must be excluded from the credit provisions of the Value Added Tax Act 1983.

The plaintiff designed and manufactured electronic equipment which it exhibited and sold at airshows. It claimed input tax in respect of expenditure incurred on the construction of hospitality chalets used at the airshows but, although the commissioners accepted that the chalets were partly used for business purposes, they claimed that input tax incurred thereon was wholly excluded from credit under art 9(1) because the chalets had been supplied to the plaintiff for the purpose of business entertainment. The plaintiff sought an apportionment of the income tax incurred to reflect the business use of the chalets, which was granted by the court. The commissioners appealed. *Held*, in the case of an indivisible supply of goods or services used or to be used both for business entertainment and to a measurable extent for other business purposes, the taxpayer was entitled to a partial credit in respect of the input tax based on an apportionment of the tax between the entertainment and the other business uses. This had to be implied in art 9(1) because (1) that article was not plain and unambiguous but was grammatically capable of supporting several meanings, (2) credit would have been given if the supply had been for business and non-business purposes and Parliament could not have intended to treat supplies for business entertainment less favourably than those for non-business purposes, and (3) if no apportionment were made the company would be denied the basic right of deduction set out in Council Directive (EC) 77/388, art 17. Accordingly, the appeal would be dismissed.

Thorn EMI plc v Customs and Excise Comrs [1995] STC 674 (Court of Appeal: Stuart-Smith, Hobhouse and Millett LJJ). Decision of Turner J [1994] STC 469 (1994 Abr para 2872) affirmed.

1983 Act now Value Added Tax Act 1994.

3019 Input tax—motor cars

The Value Added Tax (Cars) (Amendment) Order 1995, SI 1995/1269 (in force on 1 June 1995), amends the 1992 Order, SI 1992/3122, by inserting a new definition of 'auctioneer'; and excluding from the scope of value added tax, services in connection with a supply of a motor car by an auctioneer acting in his own name to the purchaser or vendor where the consideration for those services is taken into account when calculating the profit margin on the supply of the vehicle.

The Value Added Tax (Cars) (Amendment) (No 2) Order 1995, SI 1995/1667 (in force on 1 August 1995), further amends the 1992 Order supra, by (1) providing that the letting of a motor car on hire free of charge or for a nominal consideration and the making available of a motor car for private use, whether or not for a consideration, are to be treated as neither supplies of goods nor supplies of services, (2) disapplying the normal value added tax supply rules applicable to the private use of business assets where the asset is a motor vehicle and it is used or made available in circumstances which would, but for those rules, be the subject of a self-supply, (3) amending the self-supply provisions so as to reflect the changes to the rules relating to recovery of input tax on motor cars used exclusively for business purposes, (4) applying to the self-supply provisions the definition of use exclusively for business purposes which applies for input tax recovery, and (5) enabling secondhand motor cars which have been supplied to a taxable person under the margin scheme applicable to the supply of motor cars which are subject to restriction of input tax recovery to be sold under the secondhand car margin scheme. SI 1993/2951 is revoked.

3020 Input tax—special provisions

The Value Added Tax (Input Tax) (Amendment) (No 2) Order 1995, SI 1995/1267 (in force on 1 June 1995), amends the 1992 Regulations, SI 1992/3222, by (1) omitting references to certain itemised goods which are now included in the definition of 'second-hand goods'; (2) providing definitions of 'works of art', 'antiques' and 'collectors' items'; (3) extending the circumstances in which value added tax on certain itemised goods are excluded from credit as input tax as a condition of a wider range of goods being eligible to be supplied under the margin scheme; and (4) providing that the exclusion from credit as input tax does not apply where goods are not, and are not to be, supplied under the margin scheme.

3021 Input tax—speculative and contract builders—parity of treatment

The Value Added Tax (Input Tax) (Amendment) Order 1995, SI 1995/281 (in force on 1 March 1995), further amends the 1992 Order, SI 1992/3222, by (1) ensuring that parity of treatment between speculative and contract builders is maintained in consequence of changes made by the Value Added Tax (Construction of Buildings) Order 1995, SI 1995/280, para 3053, and by the Value Added Tax (Protected Buildings) Order 1995, SI 1995/283, para 3055; (2) applying the input tax restriction to speculative builders of all buildings rather than just dwellings; and (3) replacing certain references to the Value Added Tax Act 1994 for references to the Value Added Tax Act 1983.

3022 Offences—evasion of tax—conduct involving dishonesty—director of company— apportionment of penalty

A company's liability for value added tax had been fraudulently concealed. The taxpayer, one of its three directors, who had taken an active part in running the business and to whose dishonesty the company's dishonest conduct could partly be attributed, was assessed to a penalty in a sum representing 100 per cent of the penalty to which the company was liable under the Finance Act 1985, s 13. He appealed against the assessment. *Held*, the 1985 Act, s 21(1) permitted the Commissioners of Customs and Excise to assess the amount due by way of penalty from the person liable and to notify him accordingly. Assessment of a penalty under s 21 was one function and was required by s 21(2) to relate to prescribed accounting periods. Notification under s 21 was a separate and subsequent function which called for no more than a communication of the amount assessed as due. Section 21(2) dealt with assessment alone, not with notification. In the present case, each assessment of penalty related to a prescribed accounting period. From it, an aggregate sum was derived which, by virtue of s 13(1), became the amount of the penalty and, by virtue of the Finance Act 1986, s 14, became exigible wholly or partially from the taxpayer who had been duly notified of it. The assessment of the penalty had been arrived at lawfully by reference to prescribed accounting periods and notified to the taxpayer lawfully as a single and unapportioned amount. In determining the appropriate proportion of the penalty to be recovered from a named officer of a body corporate under s 14, his relative culpability compared to other named officers was a material consideration. However, where directors had collaborated in procuring a company's dishonest conduct, each was prima facie responsible for the whole. Although the relative culpability was a material consideration in determining the appropriate proportion of the penalty to be recovered from a named officer, relative culpability was not determined by asking whether the commissioners had shown that the director in question was any more to blame than the other directors. The question was whether, on the evidence, he was shown to be any less to blame than the other directors with whom he had colluded in bringing about the company's dishonest conduct. There was no evidence to show that the taxpayer was any less to blame than his fellow directors and, accordingly, his appeal would be dismissed.

Customs and Excise Comrs v Bassimeh [1995] STC 910 (Queen's Bench Division: Sedley J).

1985 Act, ss 13, 21 now Value Added Tax Act 1994, ss 60, 76. 1986 Act, s 14 now 1994 Act, s 61.

3023 Offences—evasion of tax—offender not registered for value added tax—amount of tax evaded

The Finance Act 1985, s 13(1) provides that where a person does any act or omits to take any action for the purpose of evading tax and his conduct involves dishonesty he is liable to a penalty equal to the amount of tax evaded or sought to be evaded by his conduct. Section 13(3) provides that the reference to the amount of tax evaded in s 13(1) is to be construed in relation to tax itself as a reference to the aggregate of the amount falsely claimed by way of credit for input tax and the amount by which output tax was falsely understated.

A company was not registered for value added tax and made no returns. The commissioners imposed a penalty on the company for evasion of tax under the 1985 Act, s 13(1) and sought to recover the whole of the penalty from the defendant, the director of the company and the person allegedly responsible for the omission. On appeal, the defendant contended that as the company was unregistered it had made neither false claims nor understatements of output tax and the amount of the penalty was therefore nil. The tribunal upheld the appeal on the ground that the 1985 Act, s 13(3) provided an exhaustive definition of the words 'amount of tax evaded' in s 13(1). On appeal by the commissioners, *held*, a failure to register or to make any returns were acts of omission for the purposes of evading tax within the meaning of the 1985 Act, s 13(1). Liability to a penalty thereunder was in no way limited or defined by s 13(3) which merely provided how 'the amount of tax evaded' was to be calculated in certain particular cases of tax evasion; s 13(3) was not exhaustive of the circumstances giving rise to the imposition of a penalty in s 13(1). Accordingly, the company's failure to register was an act of omission which gave rise to a liability to a penalty. The commissioners' appeal would therefore be allowed.

Customs and Excise Comrs v Stevenson [1995] STC 667 (Queen's Bench Division: Buxton J).

1985 Act, s 13(1), (3) now Value Added Tax Act 1994, s 60(1), (3).

3024 Payment—interim payment—advance payment

See *Balocchi v Ministero delle Finanze dello Stato*, para 3166.

3025 Payment—payments on account

The Value Added Tax (Payments on Account) (Amendment) Order 1995, SI 1995/291 (in force on 2 March 1995), amends the 1993 Order, SI 1993/2001, so as to make provision for (1) the basic period, which determines a taxable person's liability for inclusion in the payments on account scheme, (2) the reference period, which determines the amount of payments on account to be made, and (3) the periods in respect of which there is a duty to make payments on account, to roll forward on an annual basis.

3026 Refund of tax

The Value Added Tax (Refund of Tax) Order 1995, SI 1995/1978 (in force on 18 August 1995), permits the Environment Agency, established under the Environment Act 1995, s 1, to claim refunds of value added tax under the Value Added Tax Act 1994, s 33, on supplies to, or acquisitions or importations by it, if those supplies, acquisitions or importations are not for the purposes of any business carried on by it.

The Value Added Tax (Refund of Tax) (No 2) Order 1995, SI 1995/2999 (in force on 15 December 1995), entitles National Park authorities, established under the Environment Act 1995, s 63, and fire authorities, constituted by a combination scheme made under the Fire Services Act 1947, s 6, to claim refunds of value added tax under the Value Added Tax Act 1994, s 33 on supplies to, or acquisitions or importations by them if those supplies, acquisitions or importations are not for the purpose of any business carried on by them.

3027 Registration—liability to be registered—increase of limits

The Value Added Tax (Increase of Registration Limits) Order 1995, SI 1995/3037 (in force in part on 29 November 1995 and in part on 1 January 1996), increases the value added tax registration limits for taxable supplies and acquisitions from £46,000 to £47,000, with effect from 29 November 1995 in the case of taxable supplies and with effect from 1 January 1996 in the case of acquisitions. The order also increases the limit for cancellation of registration in the case of taxable supplies from £44,000 to £45,000, with effect from 29 November 1995, and in the case of acquisitions from £46,000 to £47,000, with effect from 1 January 1996.

3028 Relief—imported goods

The Value Added Tax (Imported Goods) Relief (Amendment) Order 1995, SI 1995/3222 (in force on 1 January 1996), further amends the 1984 Order, SI 1984/746, by increasing to £18 the maximum value for relief from value added tax on final importations of certain goods.

3029 Relief—secondhand goods—cessation of relief

See para 2489.

3030 Supply of goods and services—continuous supply—overpayments credited to subsequent invoices—whether overpayments constituting consideration for future supply

A number of customers of a telephone company paid more than the amount stated on their invoices. Where such overpayment was unintentional and the customer did not request repayment, the company credited any excess to the customer and took it into account when calculating the next invoice. No account was taken of output tax on the overpayment until the next invoice was issued. The Commissioners of Customs and Excise made an assessment for output tax on overpayments against which the company successfully appealed at a value added tax tribunal. On the commissioners' appeal, it fell to be determined whether overpayments became subject to output tax at the time of receipt. *Held*, a payment made in respect of continuous services had to be consideration if the recipient was chargeable to tax upon receipt of the payment. Only a supply of services for a consideration was subject to value added tax and the taxable amount in respect of services was the consideration that had been obtained or was to be obtained from a customer. For a supply of services to be taxable there had to be a direct link between the service provided and the consideration received. There was no direct link between a payment in respect of continuing supplies not yet provided and those services unless a customer agreed that his payment should be credited to a future invoice in respect of those services. There could be no such link where a customer had made an unintentional overpayment and had not subsequently agreed to allocate that payment to any particular future supply. It followed that the making of an unintentional payment was not consideration and, accordingly, the appeal would be dismissed.

Customs and Excise Comrs v British Telecom plc [1995] STC 239 (Queen's Bench Division: Dyson J).

3031 Supply of goods and services—fuel for private use—consideration for fuel—increase

The Value Added Tax (Increase of Consideration for Fuel) Order 1995, SI 1995/3040 (in force in relation to a taxable person from the beginning of the first of his prescribed accounting periods beginning after 5 April 1996), increases by 5 per cent the fixed scales used as the basis for charging value added tax on road fuel provided by businesses for private motoring, set out in the Value Added Tax Act 1994, s 57(3), Table A.

3032 Supply of goods and sevices—goods—special provisions

The Value Added Tax (Special Provisions) Order 1995, SI 1995/1268 (in force on 1 June 1995), replaces the Value Added Tax (Horses and Ponies) Order 1983, SI 1983/1088), the Value Added Tax (Special Provisions) Order 1992, SI 1992/3129, and the Value Added Tax (Special Provisions) (Amendment) Order 1995, SI 1995/957). The main changes include (1) a definition of the wider range of goods made eligible for the margin scheme by virtue of specified Community Directives; (2) the extension of the range of goods the disposal of which by mortgagees, finance houses and insurers are excluded from the scope of value added tax; (3) the exclusion from the scope of value added tax, in certain circumstances, of the transfer of assets of a business, on the transfer as a going concern of the business, or of a part of the business which is capable of separate operation; (4) the treatment of certain exchanges of reconditioned articles for similar unserviceable articles as a supply of services, and not as a supply of goods; (5) the exclusion from the scope of value added tax of acquisitions from another member state of goods removed to the United Kingdom in pursuance of a supply to a taxable person made by a person in another member state where value added tax on that supply is to be accounted for and paid in that other member state on the profit margin in accordance with specified Directives; (6) the exclusion from the scope of value added tax, by treating the transaction in question as neither a supply of goods nor a supply of services, of the removal of goods to the United Kingdom in pursuance of a supply to a person, made by a person in another member state where value added tax on that supply is to be accounted for and paid in another member state by reference to the profit margin on the supply by virtue of the law of that member state corresponding to the Value Added Tax Act 1994, s 50A; (7) the exclusion from the scope of value added tax of services in connection with a supply of goods provided by an agent acting in his own name to the purchaser where the consideration for those services is taken into account in calculating the profit margin on the supply of the goods; (8) the exclusion from the scope of value added tax of services in connection with a sale of goods provided by an auctioneer acting in his own name to the purchaser or the vendor where the consideration for those services is taken into account in calculating the profit margin on the sale of the goods; (9) the permitting of taxable persons to opt to use the margin scheme in specified circumstances and for the specified range of goods; and (10) the enabling of taxable persons who have opted to use the scheme under (9) to choose a simplified system of accounting for certain goods, whereby value added tax is calculated on the profit margin between the total purchase price and total selling price in each accounting period.

The Value Added Tax (Special Provisions) Order 1995 (Amendment) Order 1995, SI 1995/1385 (in force on 1 June 1995), corrects an error in the Value Added Tax (Special Provisions) Order 1995 supra, so as to ensure that the desupply provisions do not apply to reimported goods which were previously exported from the United Kingdom or the Isle of Man free of value added tax chargeable under the Value Added Tax Act 1994 or under Isle of Man legislation by reason of zero rating provisions of either the 1994 Act or the Isle of Man legislation or regulations made under either of them.

3033   Supply of goods and services—place of supply—advertising services

See *EC Commission v France; EC Commission v Luxembourg; EC Commission v Spain*, para 3172.

3034   Supply of goods and services—reinsurance services—legal expenses incurred in determining reinsurers liability—deduction from output tax

The taxpayer company incurred legal expenses in relation to the determination of its liability to meet certain claims arising from reinsurance contracts it had entered into. The Commissioners of Customs and Excise claimed that the input tax on the legal services was only partly deductible from the output tax on the reinsurance supplies as part of general overhead expenses. The company claimed the legal services were wholly attributable to its taxable, although zero-rated, supply of reinsurance, and it was this view that was upheld by a tribunal. On appeal by the commissioners, *held*, the supply of reinsurance constituted more than just entering into the contract and maintaining the cover but included an undertaking to make payment upon the occurrence of an insurable event. Legal services obtained to determine liability for claims were causally connected with the making of the payment if and when it was made and were therefore wholly or exclusively incurred in making taxable supplies. Accordingly, the appeal would be dismissed.

    Customs and Excise Comrs v Deutsche Ruck UK Reinsurance Company Ltd [1995] STC 495 (Queen's Bench Division: Auld J).

3035   Supply of goods and services—self-supply—business services—motor vehicle hired for private purposes

The Value Added Tax (Supply of Services) (Amendment) Order 1995, SI 1995/1668 (in force on 1 August 1995), amends the 1993 Order, SI 1993/1507, by excluding from the scope of value added tax the use by a taxable person of a motor car which has been let to him on hire for private purposes or for purposes other than those of his business if the leasing charge has been subject to a 50 per cent restriction on input tax recovery.

3036 Supply of goods and services—self-supply—interest in land and buildings

The taxpayer, an independent school, charged fees for educational services (exempt services) supplied to its pupils. It developed an area of disused farmland owned by it for use as playing fields and ancillary facilities and granted a 12-year lease to a company, formed for the commercial exploitation of the playing fields, in return for a premium and an annual rent payable by the company to the taxpayer. The company granted the taxpayer a non-exclusive licence to use the playing fields and ancillary facilities on payment of an annual fee. The company retained the right to exploit the property by charging fees for its use by other organisations. The taxpayer and the company were registered for value added tax. They each waived their right to exemption from value added tax in respect of the grant of any interest in or right over land. It fell to be determined whether, when the taxpayer began to use the land for its educational purposes, it was deemed, by virtue of the Value Added Tax Act 1983, Sch 6A, paras 5, 6, to have supplied itself with its interest in the land and buildings for the purpose of its business. *Held*, for the purposes of Community value added tax legislation, it was not permissible to take a global view of a series of transactions in the chain of supply; each transaction in the chain had to be examined separately to ascertain objectively what output tax was payable and what input tax was deductible. Council Directive (EC) 70/388, arts 5(7)(a), 6(3) permitted the self-supply of goods or services to be treated as a taxable transaction in a case in which, had the goods or services been acquired from a third person, the value added tax on them would not have been wholly deductible. They were therefore capable of being applied only where the goods or services had not in fact been acquired from a third person but had been brought into existence by the taxpayer himself. If the goods or services were acquired from a third person, then the question of whether the input tax payable on that acquisition was deductible was determined in the ordinary way, namely according to whether it could be attributed to a taxable supply. The use which the taxpayer made of the playing fields was pursuant to services (ie the licence) supplied by it to a third party, namely the company and it was irrelevant that it had developed the land at an earlier stage. It followed that there could be no room for a self-supply charge within the terms of the Directive. The 1983 Act, Sch 6A, paras 5, 6 were not consistent with the Directive. As the Directive was directly applicable and binding on the Commissioners of Customs and Excise, they could not rely as against the taxpayer upon inconsistent domestic legislation.

Customs and Excise Comrs v Robert Gordon's College [1995] STC 1093 (House of Lords: Lords Keith of Kinkel, Lloyd of Berwick, Nicholls of Birkenhead, Steyn and Hoffmann). Decision of Inner House [1994] STC 698 (1994 Abr para 2886) reversed. *Case C-4/94: BLP Group plc v Customs and Excise Comrs* [1995] STC 424, ECJ (para 3167) applied.

1983 Act, Sch 6A, paras 5, 6 now Value Added Tax Act 1994, Sch 10, paras 5, 6

3037 Supply of goods and services—services—place of supply

The Value Added Tax (Place of Supply of Services) (Amendment) Order 1995, SI 1995/3038 (in force on 1 January 1996), amends the 1992 Order, SI 1992/3121, so as to (1) move, in certain circumstances, the place of supply of valuations of, or work on, goods, from the place where the services are physically performed to the customer's member state; and (2) remove the requirement that business customers belonging in another member state must have a value added tax registration number in that member state before certain services listed in the Value Added Tax Act 1994, Sch 5 are treated as supplied where the customer belongs.

3038 Supply of goods and services—supply for a consideration—discount cards

The taxpayer produced and distributed discount cards which were purchased by the public either directly or through intermediaries. The cards entitled the holder to a complimentary main course meal and a bottle of wine at certain restaurants on up to 12 occasions. It fell to be determined whether amounts received on the sale of the cards should be disregarded for the purposes of value added tax at all stages of the supply under the Value Added Tax Act 1983, Sch 4, para 6 as consideration for a right to receive goods or services for the amount stated on a token, stamp or voucher. *Held*, the cards did not grant any right to receive goods or services. All that was granted by the card was a discount which was not a right but an expectation. No right to receive goods or services was granted for a consideration. The discount cards were not vouchers of the kind contemplated by Sch 4, para 6 which, accordingly, did not apply to any stage of the supply of the cards and all such supplies were subject to value added tax.

Customs and Excise Comrs v Granton Marketing Ltd; Customs and Excise Comrs v Wentwalk Ltd [1995] STC 510 (Queen's Bench Division: Tucker J). *Customs and Excise Comrs v Showmarch Marketing Ltd* [1994] STC 19 (1994 Abr para 2892) not followed.

1983 Act, Sch 4, para 6 now Value Added Tax Act 1994, Sch 6, para 5.

3039   Supply of goods and services—time of supply—advance theatre tickets—legal ownership of ticket receipts

A theatre claimed that money it received for advance tickets was held on trust for ticket buyers and that legal ownership did not vest in the theatre until the relevant performance took place. It therefore argued that no output tax was due on the date it received such payment. A value added tax tribunal supported the theatre's argument and the commissioners appealed. *Held*, it would be inequitable to treat a customer as the beneficiary of a trust and thereby give him the right to trace and place him in a better position than any other unsecured creditor of the theatre. No proprietary interest had been given to customers over the money paid and received and, accordingly, output tax was due at the time of payment. The commissioners' appeal would be allowed.

   Customs and Excise Comrs v Richmond Theatre Management Ltd [1995] STC 257 (Queen's Bench Division: Dyson J).

3040   Supply of goods and services—time of supply—deemed supply—agency

The taxpayer council engaged a building contractor to carry out certain works. A finance company agreed to pay the contractor the sums due under the building contracts; the taxpayer agreed to repay those sums to the company. The latter appointed the taxpayer as its agent for the purposes of the contracts so that the taxpayer received the building services as the company's agent. The taxpayer claimed input tax credit for the value added tax element of sums invoiced for the accounting periods during which those sums were invoiced but did not claim reimbursement from the company or account for output tax in respect of its supplies of the building services to the company until a later date. It fell to be determined whether the taxpayer should have accounted for output tax at the same time as it claimed the input tax credit. *Held*, under the Value Added Tax Act 1983, s 32(4), the supply of building services to the taxpayer as agent for the company was treated both as a supply by the contractor to the taxpayer and a supply by the latter to the company. On its true construction, s 32(4) deemed what would have been a single supply to be two simultaneous supplies, the tax points for the two supplies being what would have been the tax points for the single supply, so that the tax point for the deemed supplies were the respective dates of the issue of the contractor's invoices. The supplies in question were the services supplied by the contractor to the taxpayer. Tax on those services became due at the time of supply. The taxpayer did not supply such services to the company but was deemed to have supplied such services. The Value Added Tax (General) Regulations 1985, SI 1985/886, reg 26, concerning supplies in the construction industry, had no application to deemed supplies but was concerned with actual supplies of services 'under a contract'. The taxpayer's supplies of services to the company were neither actual nor 'under a contract'. The statutory provisions could only be sensibly understood and enforced if the tax point for the 'deemed supplies' by the agent to its principal was fixed by reference to the time of the actual supplies made by the contractor to the agent. Accordingly, the taxpayer was liable to account for output tax on its receipt, as agent, of the building services.

   Wirral Metropolitan Borough v Customs and Excise Comrs [1995] STC 597 (Queen's Bench Division: Potts J). Decision of value added tax tribunal [1994] 1 CMLR 341 affirmed.

   1983 Act, s 32(4) now Value Added Tax Act 1994, s 47(3).

3041   Supply of goods and services—time of supply—derogation—receipt of price

See *Ufficio IVA di Trapani v Italittica SpA*, para 3173.

3042   Supply of goods and services—tour operators

The Value Added Tax (Tour Operators) (Amendment) Order 1995, SI 1995/1495 (in force on 1 January 1996), revokes provisions of the 1987 Order, SI 1987/1806, and the 1990 Order, SI 1990/751, by virtue of which relief from value added tax was provided for the portion of the margin on a supply of designated travel services that related to transport and education services enjoyed within the Community. Accordingly, only that portion of the margin that relates to supplies enjoyed outside the territory of the Community is now relieved from value added tax.

3043   Supply of goods and services—treatment of transactions

The Value Added Tax (Treatment of Transactions) Order 1995, SI 1995/958 (in force on 1 May 1995), relieves from value added tax certain transactions relating to second-hand goods and works of art while they are subject to temporary importation arrangements by treating such transactions as neither a supply of goods nor a supply of services.

The Value Added Tax (Treatment of Transactions) (Trading Stamps) Order 1995, SI 1995/3042 (in force on 1 June 1996), revokes the 1973 Order, SI 1973/325, which removed from the scope of value added tax certain supplies of trading stamps.

3044 Supply of goods and services—value of supply—modification of retail scheme

The taxpayer sold goods by mail order through agents who received a ten per cent rebate in respect of goods ordered for themselves and a ten per cent commission in respect of goods ordered for customers. With the agreement of the Commissioners of Customs and Excise, the taxpayer operated a modified version of a retail scheme to mitigate the problems in discriminating between standard-rated and zero-rated supplies of goods in its value added tax returns. In order to make a further distinction between the agents' own purchases and customer purchases when calculating output tax under the scheme, the commissioners and the taxpayer entered into an arrangement whereby the taxpayer's gross takings were reduced by an agreed percentage, arrived at after sampling exercises and adjusted at three-year intervals, to reflect the amount of receipts attributable to the agents' own purchases. A sampling exercise having revealed that there had been an error in the approach previously used so that the percentage applied had been too low and excessive value added tax paid, the taxpayer used a newly-determined percentage figure in its subsequent returns. It sought to recover tax which it claimed had been overpaid for the earlier periods. *Held*, the commissioners had a specific statutory power to adapt any retail scheme by agreement with a retailer and also had authority under their general powers of care and management to conclude a binding free-standing agreement. The question was simply whether the taxpayer and the commissioners had entered into a binding agreement. That was a question of fact to be resolved by reference to the correspondence between the parties read in context. Such correspondence read as a whole evidenced a binding agreement which came into existence when the taxpayer submitted its first return taking advantage of newly-determined percentage figures. However, the taxpayer was precluded from altering the agreed basis for calculation within a three-year period except with the agreement of the commissioners. Accordingly, its claim would be dismissed.

GUS Merchandise Corpn Ltd v Customs and Excise Comrs (No 2); Customs and Excise Comrs v GUS Merchandise Corpn Ltd (No 2) [1995] STC 279 (Court of Appeal: Steyn and Saville LJJ and Sir John May). Decision of Hutchison J [1993] STC 738 (1993 Abr para 2626) affirmed.

3045 Supply of goods and services—value of supply—retail sales

The taxpayer, a retailer of food and funeral directing services, also carried on the business of a motor dealership. It sold motor cars and spare parts both to customers who were registered for value added tax and to customers who were not so registered. During a period when all such sales were retail sales, the taxpayer used retail scheme B to account for its output tax. The Commissioners of Customs and Excise refused it permission to calculate its output tax using that scheme on the ground that Customs and Excise Notice 727, para 1 required that all supplies made to other value added tax registered traders be excluded from the retail schemes. On appeal against the commissioners' decision, the taxpayer contended that, in determining whether a supply was a retail sale it was irrelevant that the purchaser was or was not a value added tax registered business, and that the reference in Notice 727, para 1 to supplies to other value added tax registered businesses was an example of a supply which was not likely to be a retail sale and the direction to account for such supplies outside the scheme did not have statutory force. *Held*, para 1 was intended to have statutory force and effect. It did not contain mere advice or recommendations and clearly required that supplies to other value added tax registered businesses should be accounted for outside the retail schemes. Accordingly, the taxpayer was not eligible to use retail scheme B and its appeal would be dismissed.

Oxford, Swindon and Gloucester Co-operative Society v Customs and Excise Comrs [1995] STC 583 (Queen's Bench Division: Dyson J).

3046 Taxable person—receiver appointed by mortgagee under statutory powers

It fell to be determined whether a receiver appointed under the Law of Property Act 1925, s 101(1)(iii) to collect rents from the tenants of mortgaged properties, in respect of which the mortgagor company had failed to make certain repayments to the mortgagee bank in respect of the mortgage debt, was liable to account for value added tax on such rents or whether he could apply it in discharge of the debt. The mortgagor, having waived its right to exemption from value added tax on the rents, was registered for value added tax. *Held*, the Value Added Tax (General) Regulations 1985, SI 1985/886, reg 11, which provided for persons who carried on the business of a company which was a taxable person which had gone into liquidation or receivership to be treated as taxable persons, seemed to contemplate a general incapacity which would make it impossible for any business to be carried on by the taxable person. The question was whether the appointment of the receiver had resulted in the mortgagor going into receivership. 'Going into receivership' in reg 11(3) meant the general incapacity which would result from, for example, administrative receivership, liquidation or administration; it connoted a state of affairs where the management of the mortgagor's business was taken out of the hands of its directors and placed in the care of a third party. It did not mean the partial incapacity, as in the present case, resulting from the appointment of a receiver of specific properties under the 1925 Act or an equivalent power. Under s 109(8), the value added tax was a tax affecting the mortgaged property and the receiver could not, in the proper exercise of his discretion, use it in discharge of the debts due to the mortgagee. The receiver owed duties to the mortgagor as well as to the mortgagee. The mortgagor had not required the receiver to account for the value added tax but the receiver still retained a discretion which he had to exercise properly. Accordingly, although he was not a taxable person under the 1985 Regulations, reg 11, he was obliged to account for value added tax under the 1925 Act, s 109(8).

Sargent v Customs and Excise Comrs [1995] STC 398 (Court of Appeal: Nourse and Waite LJJ and Sir Tasker Watkins). Decision of Judge Paul Baker QC [1994] STC 1 (1993 Abr para 2622) affirmed in part.

3047 Tribunal—refusal to refer question to European Court of Justice—judicial review

A value added tax and duties tribunal refused to refer a case to the European Court of Justice as it considered Community law on the issue in question to be clear. An application for judicial review of that decision was dismissed on the ground that it was not amenable to judicial review and that the alternative remedy of a statutory appeal, under the Tribunals and Inquiries Act 1992, s 11, should have been pursued. Although the taxpayer's application for leave to appeal against that decision was dismissed, it was granted leave to appeal under s 11. *Held*, the approach to be adopted by the court when hearing such an appeal against a tribunal's refusal to refer a question to the European Court on the ground that the point at issue was 'acte claire' was different to the correct approach to be adopted in a judicial review of that decision. An appeal under s 11 lay only on a point of law. In order to determine whether the tribunal's decision constituted an error of law, the court had to assess whether its decision that the application of Community law was clear so that a ruling from the European Court was not required was wrong and not whether that decision was perverse. As there was an arguable point on the issue in question, it could not be said that Community law was so obvious as to leave no scope for any reasonable doubt. If the matter had not been acte claire, the tribunal would have been disposed to refer the question to the European Court. Accordingly, the appeal would be allowed and the matter would be remitted to the tribunal to decide whether to refer the question to the European Court in the light of the present conclusion that the answer was not act claire.

Conoco Ltd v Customs and Excise Comrs [1995] STC 1022 (Queen's Bench Division: Harrison J). *R v Pharmaceutical Society of Great Britain, ex p Association of Pharmaceutical Importers* [1987] 3 CMLR 951 considered. For judicial review proceedings, see [1995] STC 468.

3048 Zero rating—books etc—diaries and address books

The question arose whether the supply of diaries and address books by the taxpayer company, which traded as general printers, was zero-rated as 'books' or 'booklets' within the Value Added Tax Act 1983, Sch 5, Group 3, item 1. The Commissioners of Customs and Excise contended that the diaries and address books, the main purpose of which was to provide blank spaces to be written in, did not fall within that provision, the essential characteristic of articles falling within which was that they were reading material conveying information. *Held*, the ordinary meaning of the word 'book' (and 'booklet') was limited to an object having the minimum characteristics of a book which was to be read or looked at. A blank diary or a blank address book was not, in the ordinary sense of the word, a book. Accordingly, the diaries and address books supplied by the taxpayer were not 'books' or 'booklets' within Sch 5, Group 3, item 1 and their supply should not be zero-rated.

Customs and Excise Comrs v Colour Offset Ltd [1995] STC 85 (Queen's Bench Division: May J).

1983 Act, Sch 5, Group 3, item 1 now Value Added Tax Act 1994, Sch 8, Pt II, Group 3, item 1.

3049 Zero rating—building work—construction of building—supply of articles of a kind ordinarily installed by builders as fixtures

The taxpayers undertook joinery work to customers' specific requirements in connection with alterations to certain listed properties. The work involved the construction of roof timbers, window frames, windows, fire screens, doors, and door frames. The joinery work was done by the taxpayers off site and then delivered to the properties. For the work to three properties, the taxpayers made an initial site visit to take measurements and in every case the taxpayers would have attended on site if any problems had arisen from their work. The taxpayers appealed against an assessment to value added tax and default interest in respect of work which they had treated as zero-rated in returns. The commissioners considered that, as the articles had not been fitted on site by the taxpayers, there had been no supplies of services in the course of an approved alteration accompanying the supplies of goods and, therefore, the supplies did not qualify for zero-rating under the Value Added Tax Act 1983, Sch 5, Group 8, item 3. *Held,* the work for each of the properties involved no more than a contract for the supply of goods. In reality, the services of the taxpayers did not form a wholly discrete and separate item from the supply of goods, but were merely the normal obligations imposed by law upon any seller of goods. Such services did not fall within Sch 5, Group 8, item 3. The taxpayers had made a single supply of goods which did not qualify for zero-rating. Accordingly, the appeal would be dismissed.

Customs and Excise Comrs v Jeffs (t/a J & J Joinery) [1995] STC 759 (Queen's Bench Division: Ognall J).

1983 Act, Sch 5, Group 8, item 3 now Value Added Tax Act 1994, Sch 8, Pt II, Group 5, item 3.

3050 Zero rating—building work—conversion, reconstruction, alteration or enlargement of existing building

The taxpayer constructed an office block on the site of a former industrial building. The old building, comprising three floors and a basement, was largely demolished but the reinforced concrete frame structure, concrete floor slabs, some brick party walls and the foundations were retained and incorporated in the office block. The external walls were demolished and the lifts and stairs were removed. About one-third of the concrete frame and 15 per cent of the concrete floor slabs had to be replaced and the basement floor was new. The office block included an additional, mansard floor and was substantially different in appearance from the building it replaced. An assessment to value added tax was made on the basis that the construction works constituted the conversion, reconstruction, alteration or enlargement of the former industrial building so that they were excluded from zero rating under the Value Added Tax Act 1983, Sch 5, Group 8, note (1A). On appeal by the taxpayer, *held,* in order to determine whether the works in question constituted the conversion, reconstruction, alteration or enlargement of any existing building within Sch 5, Group 8, note (1A), it was necessary to consider the situation before any works were carried out, and the situation when they were completed. Where substantial works were carried out which started with an existing building, it was a question of fact and degree whether the end product was a new building or not and the crucial question was whether the original building still existed in the sense of its identity having survived the works. It could not be concluded that the works had resulted in a new building and, accordingly, the appeal would be dismissed.

Customs and Excise Comrs v Marchday Holdings Ltd [1995] STC 898 (Queen's Bench Division: Laws J). *Customs and Excise Comrs v London Diocesan Fund* [1993] STC 369 (1993 Abr para 2640) and *Wimpey Group Services Ltd v Customs and Excise Comrs* [1988] STC 625, CA (1988 Abr para 2627) applied.

1983 Act, Sch 5, Group 8, note (1A) now Value Added Tax Act 1994, Sch 8, Pt II, Group 5, note (9).

3051 Zero rating—building work—protected building—approved alteration

The supply, in the course of an approved alteration of a protected building, of any services other than the services of an architect, surveyor or any person acting as consultant or in a supervisory capacity is zero-rated: Value Added Tax Act 1983, Sch 5, Group 8A, item 2. 'Alteration' does not include repair or maintenance: Sch 5, Group 8A, note (6).

Listed building consent was obtained for work to the roof of a listed building owned by the taxpayer. The old roof was to be replaced by a new roof structure of a higher specification. The entire roof covering was removed. The original cast lead of the large leaded areas, which had deteriorated, was replaced with materials which improved the efficiency of the roof in shedding and collecting water, reduced stresses on the lead sheets, and provided better insulation. Changes were made to the gutters to improve drainage and reduce the risk of flooding. Old slates were removed and sorted, and broken slates were replaced with new slates different in character and appearance, which were used where their different appearance would not be conspicuous from below. The slated pitches were raised by counter-battening with a view to possible future attic conversions to provide additional accommodation in the building. It fell to be determined whether the services supplied to the taxpayer in the course of the replacement of the roof were works of repair or maintenance which did not qualify for zero-rating as services supplied in the course of approved alteration of a protected building. *Held*, the questions to be determined were whether the work in question amounted to an alteration and whether the works fell properly within Sch 5, Group 8A, item 2, as confined by note (6). It could unequivocally be concluded that the works in question were works of repair or maintenance. The raising of the pitch of the roof was to a degree equivocal but, as it was an integral part of wider works of repair or maintenance, it fell to be treated likewise. Apart from the elevated roof pitch, the remainder of the work done was work of repair or maintenance and admitted of no other proper conclusion. In so far as there were any differences in the ultimate physical features of the roof, they were either de minimis or dictated exclusively by the nature and use of modern building materials in the exercise of proper repair or maintenance. Accordingly, the services in question were standard-rated.

Customs and Excise Comrs v Windflower Housing Association [1995] STC 860 (Queen's Bench Division: Ognall J).

1983 Act, Sch 5, Group 8A, item 2, note (6) now Value Added Tax Act 1994, Sch 8, Pt II, Group 6, item 2, note (6).

The taxpayer owned a listed farmhouse. He obtained planning permission and listed building consent for the replacement of a barn with a building to house a swimming pool. The new building was connected to the farmhouse by a covered walkway with open sides and a brick wall running between the side of the house and the swimming pool building. It fell to be determined whether the building works should be zero-rated for value added tax purposes as services supplied in the course of an approved alteration of a protected building within the meaning of the Value Added Tax Act 1983, Sch 5, Group 8A, item 2 or standard rated by virtue of Sch 5, Group 8A, note (6A) on the ground that the new building was separate from the taxpayer's house so that the building works did not constitute an alteration of a protected building. *Held*, applying the dictionary definition of the word 'separate' and the opinion of the local planning officer that the new building could be considered as an extension to the taxpayer's house, it would be concluded that the new building was not separate from the house so that the building works were to be zero-rated.

Customs and Excise Comrs v Arbib [1995] STC 490 (Queen's Bench Division: Latham J). Dicta of Lord Reid in *Brutus v Cozens* [1973] AC 854 at 861, HL, considered.

1983 Act, Sch 5, Group 8A, item 2, note (6A) now Value Added Tax Act 1994, Sch 8, Group 6, item 2, note (7).

3052 Zero rating—buildings and land

The Value Added Tax (Buildings and Land) Order 1995, SI 1995/279 (in force on 1 March 1995), further amends the Value Added Tax Act 1994, Sch 10 (Buildings and Land), by (1) adding two further categories of property transaction which cannot be taxed under an election to waive exemption, namely, a pitch for a residential caravan and the facilities for mooring a residential houseboat; (2) further defining the term 'residential houseboat', and extending the term 'mooring' to include anchoring or berthing; (3) in the provision which treats more than one building as a single building for the purposes of the election to waive exemption, replacing the words 'parades, precincts and complexes divided into separate units' with 'complexes consisting of a number of units grouped around a fully enclosed concourse'; (4) omitting the provision which extends an election to waive exemption on agricultural land to all contiguous agricultural land in the same ownership; (5) permitting, with the approval of the Commissioners of Customs and Excise, the revocation of an election to waive exemption within three months of it having effect, provided it has not been put into practical effect through the charging of value added tax or the recovery of input tax, and provided that the property in question has not been sold with a business which is a going concern, or 20 or more years after it has had effect; (6) providing that, to have effect, all elections to waive exemption must be notified in writing to the commissioners within 30 days or such later time specified, and preserve existing elections to waive exemption made before 1 March 1995 which did not at the time need to be notified; (7) automatically giving prior permission to waive exemption in certain circumstance to be described in a notice issued by the commissioners; (8) omitting the provision which required the first rent payment when an election to waive exemption is made to be apportioned; (9)

gradually abolishing the developer's self-supply charge; (10) providing that any building or civil engineering work the construction of which commences after 28 February 1995 does not fall within the self-supply provisions; (11) facilitating the removal from the self-supply charge of any building or civil engineering work started before, but still being constructed on, 1 March 1995, provided that any input tax claimed on account of a self-supply charge is repaid and no such input tax is claimed thereafter; (12) creating a final deemed self-supply on 1 March 1997 for all buildings and civil engineering works still within the scope of the self-supply charge, which includes buildings and civil engineering works still under construction where construction commenced before 1 March 1995 and specified provisions have not been applied; (13) ensuring that input tax on acquisitions from other member states is included when determining whether a person is a fully taxable person; (14) ensuring that the provisions concerning the self-supply charge on new buildings apply similarly to existing buildings which have been reconstructed, enlarged or extended; (15) making provision in respect of the basis of the deemed self-supply charge on 1 March 1997 for developments still in progress; and (16) providing that where a deemed self-supply on 1 March 1997 takes place and there has been no earlier self-supply, the person liable to the charge is not required to notify his landlord, lessor or licensor of the fact for the purposes of the 1994 Act, Sch 9, Group 1, item 1(b).

3053 Zero rating—construction of buildings

The Value Added Tax (Construction of Buildings) Order 1995, SI 1995/280 (in force on 1 March 1995), amends the Value Added Tax Act 1994, Sch 8, by substituting a new Group 5 (construction of buildings etc). The order provides, in particular (1) that persons converting non-residential property to create new dwellings or buildings for other relevant residential purposes may zero-rate the grant of a major interest in the building or a part of the building; (2) that the construction of a self-contained annex used for a relevant charitable purpose may be zero-rated, even if there is secondary access to it through an existing building; (3) that supplies of services relating in part to the construction or conversion of a qualifying building and in part to other matters may be apportioned; and (4) a stricter definition of an existing building.

3054 Zero rating—medical goods and services—pharmaceutical goods supplied by doctors on behalf of the National Health Service

The Value Added Tax (Supply of Pharmaceutical Goods) Order 1995, SI 1995/652 (in force on 1 April 1995), varies the Value Added Tax Act 1994, Sch 8, Group 12, by introducing a new item which provides for the zero-rating of goods supplied by doctors who are required or authorised to provide pharmaceutical services on behalf of the National Health Service.

3055 Zero rating—protected buildings

The Value Added Tax (Protected Buildings) Order 1995, SI 1995/283 (in force on 1 March 1995), amends the Value Added Tax Act 1994, Sch 8, by substituting a new Group 6 (protected buildings), in consequence of the substitution of Sch 8, Group 5 (construction of buildings etc) by the Value Added Tax (Construction of Buildings) Order 1995, SI 1995/280, para 3053. The main changes include (1) the insertion of a new Group 6, item 3 providing for zero-rate relief for the supply of certain goods together with eligible services in the course of an approved alteration; (2) a definition of 'dwelling' in Note (2); (3) a new definition of approved alteration in relation to ecclesiastical buildings; and (4) a clarification of the distinction between alteration and repairs.

3056 Zero rating—tax free shops

The Value Added Tax (Tax Free Shops) Order 1995, SI 1995/3041 (in force on 1 January 1996), increases to £75 the value of goods, other than wines, spirits, perfume and toilet water and tobacco products, that can be supplied in a tax free shop at the zero rate to a traveller making a journey to a destination in another member state.

3057 Zero rating—transport—air navigation services

The Value Added Tax (Transport) Order 1995, SI 1995/653 (in force on 1 April 1995), amends the Value Added Tax Act 1994, Sch 8, Group 8, by providing for zero-rating of air navigation services, as defined in the Civil Aviation Act 1982, when they are supplied in respect of aircraft which are of a description zero-rated under the 1994 Act, Sch 8, Group 8, item 2 or to a person who receives them for the purpose of a business carried on by him and who belongs outside the United Kingdom.

3058 Zero rating—transport—car service to and from airport in course of air transport

The taxpayers provided a chauffeur-driven limousine service to transport their upper class passengers to and from airports at no extra charge. The Commissioners of Customs and Excise decided that such supplies were separate standard-rated supplies. The taxpayers appealed against the decision of a value added tax tribunal upholding that decision, contending that the supply of the flight and the supply of the limousine service constituted a single zero-rated supply of international transport from a place within to a place outside the United Kingdom within the meaning of the Value Added Tax Act 1983, Sch 5, Group 10, item 4(d), that the word 'place' meant not airports but the places from which the transfer to the airports started and the ultimate destination beyond the arrival airport or, alternatively, that the supply of the limousine service was an integral or incidental part of the zero-rated supply of air transport within Sch 5, Group 10, item 4(a) or (c). *Held,* although the main purpose of the contract between the taxpayers and their passengers was the transport by way of scheduled flight (to which the provision of the limousine service was subsidiary to the main purpose of the contract), it was nevertheless one indivisible contract that the parties made. The concept of 'scheduled flight' under Sch 5, Group 10, item 4(c) was narrower than 'from a place within to a place outside the United Kingdom' under Sch 5, Group 10, item 4(d), in which 'place' meant something other than the airport. Whatever final arrangements a passenger made regarding the details of the service to be provided, he paid one indivisible and irreducible price. Further, the phrase 'any scheduled flight' in Sch 5, Group 10, item 4(c) was wide enough to embrace, as integral or incidental, the provision of the limousine service. Although the limousine service was physically separate from the flight, it was not, without great difficulty, economically dissociable from the price paid for the package offered by the taxpayers to their upper class passengers. It would be unrealistic to apportion the price paid to the taxpayers according to the provision of the limousine service on the one hand and the flight on the other. The appeals would succeed.

Virgin Atlantic Airways Ltd v Customs and Excise Comrs; Canadian Airlines International Ltd v Customs and Excise Comrs [1995] STC 341 (Queen's Bench Division: Turner J).

1983 Act, Sch 5, Group 10, item 4(a), (c), (d) now Value Added Tax Act 1994, Sch 8, Pt II, Group 8, item 4(a), (c), (d).

3059 Zero rating—transport—ships and aircraft

The Value Added Tax (Ships and Aircraft) Order 1995, SI 1995/3039 (in force on 1 January 1996), amends the Value Added Tax Act 1994, Sch 8, Group 8, so as to (1) maintain zero rating for the modification and conversion of qualifying ships and aircraft; (2) extend zero rating to supplies of certain parts and equipment for qualifying ships and aircraft; (3) extend zero rating to the making of arrangements for the supply of the parts and equipment referred to in (2); (4) define 'qualifying ships' and 'qualifying aircraft' for the purposes of Group 8; (5) provide zero-rating for the letting on hire of the goods zero-rated under (2); and (6) exclude certain supplies of parts and equipment to government departments from zero-rating under (2).

VALUERS AND APPRAISERS

Halsbury's Laws of England (4th edn) Vol 49, paras 1–100

3060 Articles

Damages and BBL: A Better Way? John Murdoch (on *Banque Bruxelles Lambert SA v Eagle Star Insurance Co Ltd* (1995) Times, 21 February, Independent, 24 February, CA (para 3062)): Estates Gazette, 11 March 1995, p 115

Negligence—A Field Day for Lenders and Borrowers, Marcel Haniff and Dolf Darnton (on the implications of negligent valuations for lenders and borrowers): Estates Gazette, 6 May 1995, p 113

Negligent Valuations, Thomas Grant and Hugh Tomlinson: 139 SJ 237

Peeping at Toms, Peter Hewitt (on the tour operators' margin scheme): Tax Journal, Issue 323, p 8

The Value Judgment, Myfanwy Badge (on *Banque Bruxelles Lambert SA v Eagle Star Insurance Co Ltd* (1995) Times, 21 February, Independent, 24 February, CA (para 3062)): LS Gaz, 22 March 1995, p 16

Valuers or Indemnifiers? H W Wilkinson (on *Banque Bruxelles Lambert SA v Eagle Star Insurance Co Ltd* (1995) Times, 21 February, Independent, 24 February, CA (para 3062)): 145 NLJ 973

3061   Valuer—duty of care—valuation of land used as security—overvaluation—loss of money invested in business

A husband and wife obtained a mortgage on the basis of a valuation made by the defendant valuers. Part of the mortgage was used to discharge a previous mortgage on the couple's house and the rest was invested in the husband's business. The business subsequently failed and it was found that the valuation had been excessive. The couple brought an action in negligence against the valuers. At first instance, the statement of claim was struck out for disclosing no cause of action but, on appeal, it was re-instated. On further appeal by the valuers, *held*, if the alleged damage was the creation of the mortgage as security for the loan, that disclosed no cause of action. The loss of the money invested in the husband's business was not the kind of damage which the valuers could or ought to have foreseen and, therefore, to declare them liable for that loss would be unfair, unjust and unreasonable. Accordingly, the appeal would be allowed.

   Saddington v Colleys Professional Services (1995) Times, 22 June (Court of Appeal: Balcombe, Otton and Aldous LJJ).

3062   Valuer—duty of care—valuation of land used as security—overvaluation—loss resulting from fall in property market

It fell to be determined whether damages awarded to a lender which had advanced money to a borrower on the security of negligently overvalued property, which advance the lender would not have made at all if it had received a proper valuation, should include the loss suffered as a result of a collapse of the property market. *Held*, the valuation was not sought to protect the lender against a decline in the property market. If a rise in the property market contributed to the lender suffering no loss, that contribution would not be ignored, in assessing the lender's damages, so as to treat the lender as sustaining a financial loss which in fact he had not sustained. If a fall in the market contributed to the lender's overall loss, on a straightforward application of the restitutionary principle, the lender should be entitled to recover that element of his loss against the negligent party. Since the valuer's negligence caused the lender to enter into the transaction which he would not otherwise have done and because he could not escape from the transaction at will, that negligence was the effective cause of the loss which the lender suffered as a result. The collapse of the market could not be seen as a new intervening cause; it could not be said to have broken the link between the valuer's negligence and the damage suffered. If the valuer had valued the property competently, he would not have been liable no matter how disastrous the investment. However, once it was established that his negligence led the lender to make a loan he would not otherwise have made, the lender was entitled to be compensated for the damage suffered.

   Banque Bruxelles Lambert SA v Eagle Star Insurance Co Ltd [1995] 2 All ER 769 (Court of Appeal: Sir Thomas Bingham MR, Rose and Morritt LJJ). Decision of Phillips J [1995] 2 All ER 769 (1994 Abr para 2907), of Arden J in *Mortgage Express Ltd v Bowerman & Partners (a Firm)* [1994] 34 EG 116 (1994 Abr para 2655), and of Judge James Fox-Andrews QC in *BNP Mortgages Ltd v Goadsby & Harding Ltd* [1994] 42 EG 150 (1994 Abr para 2000), reversed. *Baxter v F W Gapp & Co Ltd* [1939] 2 KB 271, CA, and *Swingcastle Ltd v Alastair Gibson* [1991] 2 All ER 353, HL (1991 Abr para 2573) applied. *Banque Financière de la Cité SA v Westgate Insurance Co Ltd* [1990] 2 All ER 947, HL (1990 Abr para 1373) distinguished.

WAR, ARMED CONFLICT AND EMERGENCY

Halsbury's Laws of England (4th edn) Vol 49, paras 101–200

3063   Northern Ireland

See NORTHERN IRELAND.

3064   Pensions

See PENSIONS AND SUPERANNUATION.

3065   War and emergency legislation—exports—control

See *R v Blackledge; R v Grecian; R v Mason; R v Phillips*, para 952.

WATER

Halsbury's Laws of England (4th edn) Vol 49, paras 201–939
Taking the Waters, Peter Carty (on the law governing water abstraction): 139 SJ 946
Turning Off the Tap, Alan Murdie (on advising those threatened with disconnection of their domestic water supply): 139 SJ 421
Water Pollution and the Causing Offence, Neil Parpworth: 159 JP Jo 244

3066　Environment Act 1995

See para 1289.

3067　Navigation on the Thames—operation of helicopters along and on river—material change of use of land

See *Thames Heliport v London Borough of Tower Hamlets*, para 2860.

3068　Pollution—pollution of controlled waters

See ENVIRONMENT.

3069　Reservoir—defective construction of reservoir—reconstruction of reservoir—claim for contribution to financial loss

See *Birse Construction Ltd v Haiste Ltd*, para 2840.

3070　Water supply—water intended for human consumption—enforcement of duty to supply wholesome water

A declaration was made by the European Court of Justice that the United Kingdom had failed to properly implement and apply Council Directive (EC) 80/778. In particular, the United Kingdom had failed to ensure that the quality of water supplied conformed with the Directive's requirements regarding nitrates. In order to rectify the breach of the Directive, the Secretary of State decided that he would accept undertakings from two water companies that they would take appropriate steps to comply with their duties under the Water Industry Act 1991 in relation to the supply of wholesome water. He also decided that he would not make enforcement orders against the companies under the 1991 Act, s 18. On the applicants' application for judicial review of the decisions, a judge held that the United Kingdom's obligation was to rectify the breach of the Directive as soon as possible and not merely as soon as practicable, but that it might not be possible to achieve a result earlier than was practicable. On the facts, he concluded that in accepting the undertakings, the Secretary of State had not adopted too leisurely an approach to the United Kingdom's obligations. On the applicants' appeal against the dismissal of their application, *held,* the judge had correctly recognised the nature and extent of the United Kingdom's duty to remedy the breach of its obligations. However, there were practical difficulties in bringing all drinking water up to the required standard. The issue of what was practicable entered into the question of what was possible, and there was no principle of European or domestic law which required the court to ignore practicalities. Moreover, the fact that the Secretary of State had accepted the undertakings did not preclude him from serving an enforcement notice at a later stage. Accordingly, the appeal would be dismissed.

　　R v Secretary of State for the Environment, ex p Friends of the Earth Ltd [1996] 1 CMLR 117 (Court of Appeal: Balcombe, Roch and Pill LJJ). Decision of Schiemann J [1994] 2 CMLR 760 (1994 Abr para 2922) affirmed.

WEIGHTS AND MEASURES

Halsbury's Laws of England (4th edn) Vol 50, paras 1–200

3071　Measuring equipment—capacity measures and testing equipment

The Measuring Equipment (Capacity Measures and Testing Equipment) Regulations 1995, SI 1995/735 (in force on 10 April 1995), prescribe certain dry and liquid capacity measures for use in trade and replace the Weights and Measures Regulations 1963, SI 1963/1710, Pts III and IV. The regulations do not apply to capacity measures used for measuring and serving intoxicating liquor for consumption on the premises at which it is sold or for the making up or checking of specified packages. The effect of prescription is to make it unlawful to use capacity measures for trade purposes unless they have been tested, passed as fit for such use and stamped by an inspector of weights and measures. The regulations make changes of substance relating to the transfer of intoxicating liquor from a capacity measure to another container, the testing of measures, dispensing measures for pharmaceutical purposes, the permissible limits of error and line measures.

3072 Measuring equipment—liquid fuel and lubricants

The Measuring Equipment (Liquid Fuel and Lubricants) Regulations 1995, SI 1995/1014 (in force on 4 May 1995), replace the 1988 Regulations, SI 1988/128, and apply to equipment used for trade, for any purpose, to measure liquid fuel (other than liquefied petroleum gas) in a quantity of 100 litres (or until 1 October 1995, 20 gallons) or less. They make provision as to the principles of construction and marking of measuring equipment for liquid fuel, inspection, testing, passing as fit for trade use, stamping of measuring equipment (and obliteration of stamps on such equipment) and the prescribed limits of error.

3073 Measuring equipment—liquid fuel delivered from road tankers

The Measuring Equipment (Liquid Fuel Delivered from Road Tankers) (Amendment) Regulations 1995, SI 1995/3117 (in force on 29 December 1995), further amend the 1983 Regulations, SI 1983/1390, so as to (1) withdraw the requirement that, on or after 1 September 1988, every dipstick measuring system incorporated in a bottom loaded compartment be made in accordance with a pattern in respect of which a pattern approval certificate is in force, and (2) provide for the acceptance of test results for measuring equipment imported from other member states of the European Union or contracting parties to the European Economic Area Agreement.

3074 Measuring instruments—EC requirements

The Measuring Instruments (EC Requirements) (Electrical Energy Meters) Regulations 1995, SI 1995/2607 (in force on 1 November 1995), replace the 1980 Regulations, SI 1980/886. The regulations implement certain Council Directives relating to measuring instruments and methods of metrological control and Directives relating to particular categories of instruments. The effect of the Electricity Act 1989 is modified to ensure compliance with certain Directives that prohibit restrictions on the placing on the market or entry into service of EC approved measuring equipment. The powers to grant EC pattern approvals in respect of electrical energy meters and give directions as to the manner in which applications for EC initial verifications are to be made are transferred from the Secretary of State to the Director General of Electrical Supply.

3075 Measuring instruments—non-automatic weighing machines—EC requirements— fees

The Measuring Instruments (EEC Requirements) (Fees) (Amendment) Regulations 1995, SI 1995/1376 (in force on 1 July 1995), amend the 1993 Regulations, SI 1993/798. The regulations make provision for the amendment of fees payable in connection with services undertaken by the Department of Trade and Industry, including services undertaken in connection with the variation or amendment of approvals granted to, and the periodic inspection of, designated bodies.

3076 Units of measurement—implementation of EC Directive

The Units of Measurement Regulations 1995, SI 1995/1804 (in force on 1 October 1995), implement Council Directives (EC) 71/354 and 80/181 which relate to the use of units of measurement. They provide for the phasing out of the use of imperial units of measurement for economic, public health, public safety or administrative purposes. Certain exceptions are made which permit the continued use of imperial measurements until 31 December 1999.

3077 Weighing equipment—non-automatic weighing machines

The Non-automatic Weighing Machines and Non-automatic Weighing Instruments (Amendment) Regulations 1995, SI 1995/428 (in force on 27 March 1995), amend the 1988 Regulations, SI 1988/876, and the 1992 Regulations, SI 1992/1579, so as to forbid the use for trade of equipment for the weighing of gold and other precious metals, precious stones or pearls and drugs or other pharmaceutical products outside the equipment's prescribed weighing range. In addition, the 1988 Regulations are amended to permit the import of non-automatic weighing machines which have been tested in another member state or an EEA state and the 1992 Regulations are amended to enable the Secretary of State to vary his approval of a body to carry out functions under the regulations and to enable him to inspect its performance of those functions.

3078 Weighing instruments—non-automatic weighing instruments—EC requirements

The Non-automatic Weighing Instruments (EEC Requirements) Regulations 1995, SI 1995/1907 (in force on 1 September 1995), replace the 1992 Regulations, SI 1992/1579. Provisions relating to the testing, examination and surveillance of non-automatic weighing instruments, the penalties and forfeiture for non-compliance with the regulations, or for the obstruction or failure to assist authorised persons, and the prosecution of offences remain the same. Modifications to the 1992 Regulations relate to the affixing of the EC mark of conformity, the procedures for EC verification to permit a manufacturer or his authorised representative to apply the CE marking, the procedure for EC declaration of type conformity, conformity with other Directives and the simplification of provisions relating to the wrongful affixing of the CE marking.

3079 Weights and Measures Act 1985—designated countries

The Weights and Measures (Guernsey and Alderney) Order 1995, SI 1995/1011 (in force on 1 June 1995), declares that Guernsey and Alderney are to be designated countries for the purposes of the Weights and Measures Act 1985.

WILLS

Halsbury's Laws of England (4th edn) Vol 50, paras 201–655

3080 Articles

Administration of Estates, Philip Rossdale (on the Law of Property (Miscellaneous Provisions) Act 1994): 139 SJ 747

The Effect of Divorce on Wills, Roger Kerridge: [1995] Conv 12

Intestacy, Divorce and Wills, Gareth Miller: 145 NLJ 1693

Joint Wills, Ramnik Shah: 139 SJ 195

Lack of Good Will, Andrew Paton (on *White v Jones* (1994) Times, 17 February (para 2780)): LS Gaz, 1 March 1995, p 15

Law Reform (Succession) Act 1995, Lesley King: 139 SJ 1252

Post-Death Rearrangements, Matthew Hutton: 139 SJ 1092, 1121, 1148

The Quick and the Dead, David R Harris: [1995] BTR 390

Shall We Tell the President?, Catherine Saunders (on the changes brought about by the Law of Property (Miscellaneous Provisions) Act 1994, Pt II and the new procedure for service of notices affecting land): 139 SJ 580

The Lords' View of a Solicitor, Clive Boxer (on *White v Jones* [1995] 1 All ER 691, HL (para 2780)): 139 SJ 372

Probate and Administering Estates: Dealing With Delay, Philip Rossdale: 139 SJ 424

Provision for Adult Children under the Inheritance (Provision for Family and Dependants) Act 1975, Gareth Miller: [1995] Conv 22

Reform of Intestacy: The Best We Can Do? S M Cretney: (1995) 111 LQR 77

When a Grant of Representation Should be Renounced, Philip Rossdale: 139 SJ 10

Whose Property is it Anyway, Ann Kenny: 139 SJ 926

Wills and the Mentally Disabled Beneficiary, Gordon Ashton: 145 NLJ 1578

Wills Made Easy—For the Client, John Pare: 139 SJ 1007

3081 Attestation—signature or acknowledgment of signature—validity

Scotland

The deceased executed a will, leaving her only substantial asset to one of her eight children. Five of the other children claimed that the will was invalid because it was not properly attested by the second witness. They alleged that he was not present at the time that the deceased signed the will, nor had the deceased acknowledged her signature to him. On an application for a declaration that the will was invalid, *held*, it was unlikely that the second witness had signed the will in the deceased's presence, as there was evidence that the intended beneficiary had merely given the second witness a folded, unsigned document to sign, without explaining the nature of the document to him. Although the court would be slow to accept that a person would purport to witness a document which he had not seen or read, such a situation sometimes occurred. Moreover, if acknowledgment was by words, they had to be unambiguous, and if it was by acts, they had to be precise. In any event, an acknowledgement had to leave no doubt in a witness's mind that the signature which he was attesting was that of the testator. Here, there was insufficient evidence to infer that the deceased had clearly acknowledged her signature to the second witness. Accordingly, the application would be granted.

Lindsay v Milne 1995 SLT 487 (Outer House).

3082   Conditional will—condition impossible to fulfil—effect on gift

The testator bequeathed half his estate to Charity A. The remainder was left to Charity B on the condition that it looked after the testator's pets; if it did not agree to do so, the gift was to go to Charity A. Those instructions were sent to the testator's solicitor with a note containing the proviso that any pets the testator might leave behind were to be properly cared for. The testator had a dog at the time the will was made but it died before him and at the testator's death he had no other pet. Charity A claimed that Charity B could not fulfil the condition imposed by the testator and therefore could not take the gift. *Held*, (1) where words were used which imposed a condition on a donee taking a gift and at the testator's death it had become impossible to fulfil that condition by reason of the impossibility of the condition, the condition was spent and the gift could be taken absolutely. The words were not to be construed too widely and without reference to the facts of a particular case, in which the purpose of construction was always to collect the testator's intention from the words used. In the present case, the wording of the will clearly meant that Charity B should care for any pets the testator might have when he died and that if there were none the gift would pass absolutely. (2) If the construction of the will meant that the provision was ambiguous when related to the circumstances of the testator's death, the court could let in extrinsic evidence of intention. There was in existence the testator's note and the executor had no doubt that the testator intended, if he had no pets at his death, that Charity B should still benefit and that the gift should only pass if the testator died leaving pets which Charity B for some reason refused to look after. Accordingly, half the estate would go to Charity A and the other half to Charity B.

Watson v National Children's Home (1995) Times, 31 October (Chancery Division: Judge Colyer QC).

3083   Construction of will—ambiguity—extrinsic evidence

In her will, the deceased included a clause specifying that the residue of her estate was to be bequeathed to beneficiaries living at her death, who were named in two lists, in such a way that the beneficiaries in list A were to receive 3.2 times as much as the beneficiaries in list B. Some beneficiaries in both lists were charities and two beneficiaries had died. The executor of the will applied to court to determine whether: (1) list A beneficiaries should receive 3.2 times the sum taken by each of the list B beneficiaries or whether list A beneficiaries should share a fund 3.2 times the size of the fund shared by list B beneficiaries; (2) in view of the Inheritance Tax Act 1984, s 41 which precluded tax attributable to a chargeable share of residue falling on any exempt share of residue, the non-charitable beneficiaries should receive their share subject to inheritance tax or whether their shares should be grossed up; (3) the shares of beneficiaries who had died should be applied to the payment of funeral and testamentary expenses and debts. *Held*, (1) extrinsic evidence would be admitted under the Administration of Justice Act 1982, s 21 to assist in the interpretation of the will because the clause was not so clear that it could be said there was no real doubt or ambiguity. On the evidence, it appeared that while the list A and B beneficiaries took as between themselves in equal shares, the residue available for list A beneficiaries was a fund 3.2 times the size available to those in list B. (2) The plain intention was that each beneficiary, whether charitable or not, should receive the same amount and the non-charitable beneficiaries should therefore receive grossed-up shares so they all received the same. (3) To have a share in the residue a beneficiary had to be in one of the lists and living at the date the deceased died. Beneficiaries who did not qualify had to be deleted from the lists and the two funds divided equally between the beneficiaries in the lists in relevant proportions. Therefore, no share became applicable for the payment of expenses or debts. Orders would be made accordingly.

Re Benham's Will Trusts; Lockhart v Harker [1995] STC 210 (Chancery Division: R M K Gray QC).

3084 Construction of will—rectification—'clerical error'

A testator wanted to establish a trust fund out of his residuary estate to be used for 21 years for the benefit of his poor and needy relatives to relieve hardship. Thereafter, the fund was to be applied in the same way to any needy relatives, and then to charities at the trustees' discretion. His solicitor drafted a clause of the will requiring the trust fund to be used for the assistance of the 'poor and needy' of a class of persons set out in a schedule to the will. On his own initiative, the solicitor also drafted a proviso to the clause, which provided that if any member of the class died during the testator's lifetime or within 21 years of his death, then that person's issue would stand in his place and would be eligible to benefit under the clause. A gift over clause was added for the benefit of charitable institutions or for charitable purposes. The testator subsequently provided the solicitor with the schedule, which listed six named family members and the 'issue' (who were not named) of five of them. The solicitor omitted to re-evaluate the need for his own proviso and the will was duly executed. After the testator's death, the beneficiaries of the trust sought rectification of the will by deletion of the solicitor's proviso. Questions also arose as to whether the will contained valid charitable gifts and, if so, whether they were exempt transfers within the Inheritance Act 1984, s 23(1). Held, the solicitor's proviso failed to carry out the testator's intentions that all the persons described in the schedule, named individuals and issue, would be eligible to benefit from the trust throughout the 21-year period. Instead, it operated to restrict the class of persons eligible to benefit during the 21-year period to the named individuals and to exclude the issue of those individuals while their named ancestors were still alive. The solicitor's failure, through inadvertence, to delete the proviso from the draft will once he had received the schedule for inclusion could properly be regarded as a clerical error. Accordingly, rectification would be allowed and the proviso would be deleted. The critical question for the court in determining whether a gift for the relief of poverty was a valid charitable gift was whether, on its true construction, the gift was for the relief of poverty amongst poor people of a particular class or, alternatively, a gift to particular poor persons, the relief of poverty among them being the motive of the gift. The testator had selected the members of the class on the basis that the named individuals were persons who might need financial help in the future. The class would continue to expand with the birth of unknown issue after the testator's death. Therefore, he must have intended a gift for the relief of poverty amongst the class of which those after-born issue would become members. Both the gift for the assistance of the needy members of the class during the 21-year period and the gift for distribution to them after that period were valid charitable gifts and were not disqualified because of the restricted nature of the class. Accordingly, they were valid charitable gifts. These and the gift over to charitable institutions and for charitable purposes, being for exclusively charitable purposes, were exempt transfers for the purposes of the 1984 Act, s 23(1).

Re Segelman [1995] 3 All ER 676 (Chancery Division: Chadwick J). Wordingham v Royal Exchange Trust Co Ltd [1992] 3 All ER 204 (1991 Abr para 2601), Dingle v Turner [1972] 1 All ER 878, HL, and Re Scarisbrick's Will Trusts, Cockshott v Public Trustee [1951] 1 All ER 822, CA, considered.

3085 Law Reform (Succession) Act 1995

See para 1358.

3086 Mutual wills—application of doctrine—effect of re-marriage of surviving testator

A husband and wife executed wills in identical forms leaving their respective estates to their son after the death of the survivor of them. After the death of the wife, the husband remarried and made a new will leaving everything to his second wife and appointing her as executrix. After the death of the husband, the son sought a declaration that the second wife held the husband's estate on trust to give effect to the provisions of the mutual wills. He also brought a claim against his father's estate for financial provision under the Inheritance (Provision for Family and Dependents) Act 1975. Held, if a clear agreement could be found, either in the will or elsewhere, that two wills were to be mutually binding, equity would give effect to that intention by way of a floating trust which became irrevocable upon the death of the first testator and crystallised upon the death of the second. The floating trust was not destroyed by the remarriage of the surviving testator. On the facts, the evidence fell short of establishing that the wills were mutually binding in law since the mere fact that the wills were simultaneous and identical was not sufficient. Accordingly, the Wills Act 1837, s 18 applied and the husband's first will was revoked by operation of law upon his remarriage. As to the claim for financial provision under the 1975 Act, a claim by an adult son who was able to earn his own living might, in exceptional circumstances, succeed where there was the existence of a moral obligation to make such provision. As the wills of the husband and his first wife were not mutually binding, the husband was legally and morally free to deal as he wished with the property he held jointly with his wife prior to her death. However, in relation to that part of the joint estate which belonged previously to his wife, the husband owed a moral obligation to give effect to her understanding that her husband would give effect to what she believed to be their mutual intentions. Accordingly, that moral obligation gave rise to an exceptional circumstance that justified the making of an order for financial provision in favour of the son under the 1975 Act.

Re Goodchild, Goodchild v Goodchild [1995] 1 All ER 670 (Chancery Division: Carnwath J).

3087 Probate

See EXECUTORS AND ADMINISTRATORS.

EUROPEAN COMMUNITIES

Halsbury's Laws of England (4th edn) Vols 51 and 52

The material below comprises cases heard before the European Court of Justice and important legislative developments from the EC Council and Commission. The arrangement of the material conforms with Vols 51 and 52.

3088 Articles

Access to Justice and Alternatives to Courts: European Procedural Justice Compared, Erhard Blankenburg: [1995] 14 CJQ 176

Are Member States Being Lead to Slaughter, Marie Demetriou (on *Francovich v Italy* [1993] 2 CMLR 66, ECJ): 145 NLJ 1102

Buying Power and Sophisticated Buyers in Merger Control Law: The Need for a More Sophisticated Approach, Jan Nordemann: [1995] 5 ECLR 270

The Commission Green Paper on Mobile and Personal Communications in Europe, Jeremy Newton: [1995] EIPR 195

Compliance Programmes, Julian Armstrong (on *Director General of Fair Trading v Pioneer Concrete (UK) Ltd* [1995] 1 All ER 135, HL (1994 Abr para 1219)): [1995] ECLR 147

The Conceptualization of European Labour Law, Brian Bercusson: (1995) 24 ILJ 3

Consolidation or Confusion? Meryll Dean (on the EC Directive on Unfair Contract Terms (93/13/EC)): 145 NLJ 28

Decentralisation, the Public Interest and the 'Pursuit of Certainty', Barry J Rodger: [1995] 7 ECLR 395

Deregulation: How Does the New Act Affect Competition Law? Mark Furse: 139 SJ 86

Does the United Kingdom or the European Community Need an Unfair Competition Law? Aidan Robertson and Audrey Horton: [1995] EIPR 568

The Essential Facilities' Doctrine in Community Law, Mark Furse: [1995] ECLR 469

The European Administration and the Public Administration of Member States with Regard to Competition Law, C D Ehlermann: [1995] ECLR 454

The EC Commission's Draft Regulation on Motor Vehicle Distribution: Alea Lacta Est? Frank Wijckmans and Alain Vanderelst: [1995] ECLR 225

EC Law and the Dismissal of Pregnant Servicewomen, Anthony Arnull: (1995) 24 ILJ 215

EC Packaging Directive, Caroline London and Michael Llamas (on the EC Directive on Packaging and Packaging Waste): 145 NLJ 221

Equality of Treatment: A Variable Concept? Philippa Watson: (1995) 24 ILJ 33

Forum Non Conveniens and the Brussels Convention, Alan Reed and T P Kennedy: 145 NLJ 1697, 1788

Forum Non Conveniens in Europe, Wendy Kennet: (1995) 54 CLJ 552

Future Directions in European Union Social Policy Law, Erika Szyszczak (on the impact of the European Union on British labour law): (1995) 24 ILJ 19

'Good Arguable Case' and RSC Ord 12, r 8: a Time to Quarrel? Philip Moser: 139 SJ 1224

Interpretation of European Community Law, Andrew Bowen: LA, June 1995, p 10

Is There a Role for an Essential Facilities' Doctrine in Europe? Stewart White: [1995] 1 CTLR 110

Joint Venture Analysis: The Latest Chapter, Alec Burnside and Judy Mackenzie Stuart (on treatment of joint ventures under EC competition rules): [1995] ECLR 138

Jurisdiction Within the UK, Jonathan Tecks and Tom Coates (on the jurisdiction of the European Court): 145 NLJ 425

Liability of Successor Undertakings for Infringements of EC Competition Law Committed Prior to Corporate Reorganisations, Laurent Garzaniti and Giuseppe Scassellati-Sforzolini: [1995] ECLR 348

Market Integration and Social Policy in the Court of Justice, Paul Davies: (1995) 24 ILJ 49

Nuclear Testing and Europe, Sven Deimann and Gerrit Betlam: 145 NLJ 1236

One Door Closes; Another Opens, Stephen Coleclough (on *Case C-4/94: BLP Group plc v Customs and Excise Comrs* [1995] STC 424 (para 3167)): Tax Journal, Issue 336, p 6

Passport Control, Elspeth Guild (on EU nationals' rights to cross borders of member states without passport checks): LS Gaz, 15 March 1995, p 15

Prevention is Better than Cure, Julie Nazerali (proposing an EU Competition Compliance Programme): 139 SJ 718

The Protection of Geographical Indications in the European Economic Community, Bertold Schwab: [1995] EIPR 242

The Publisher in the Electronic Age: Caught in the Area of Conflict of Copyright and Competition Law, Harald Heker: [1995] EIPR 75

Sexual Orientation Discrimination and Europe, Frances Russell: 145 NLJ 338

The Starting Point, Geoffrey Bindman (on EC measures against racism): 145 NLJ 62

Time for a Wellcome Change, Richard Pincher (on European notions of what constitutes a business): Tax Journal, Issue 302, p 16, Issue 303, p 11

Trading in Europe, Tony Holland: 145 NLJ 120

US Technology Licensing Arrangements: Do New Enforcement Guidelines in the United States Mirror Developments in the European Community? Howard W Fogt Jr and Ilene Knable Gotts: [1995] ECLR 215

Unjust Enrichment, Richard Pincher: Tax Journal, Issue 293, p 14, Issue 294, p 14, Issue 295, p 14

THE COMMUNITIES

3089 Administration—education—European Year of Lifelong Learning

Decision 2493/95 of the European Parliament and of the Council establishes 1996 as the European Year of Lifelong Learning. During the year, information, awareness-raising and promotional actions will be undertaken concerning opportunities for lifelong learning. The following are some of the main themes for the European Year: the importance of a high quality general education; the promotion of vocational training leading to qualifications for all young people; the promotion of continuing education and training; motivation for individuals for lifelong learning; and the raising of awareness of parents of the importance of education and training of children and young people. The financial framework for the implementation of the programme is 8m ecus. The decision takes effect as from 26 October 1995. (OJ L256 26.10.95 p 45.)

3090 Community institutions—EU Council—documents—public access—confidentiality

Council Decision (EC) 93/731, art 4(2) provides that access to a document of the EU Council may be refused in order to protect the confidentiality of the Council's proceedings. Council Decision (EC) 93/662 (rules of procedure), art 5(1) provides that the deliberations of the Council are covered by the obligation of professional secrecy, except in so far as the Council decides otherwise.

The editor of a national newspaper wrote to the Council, seeking access to the preparatory reports of the Committee of Permanent Representatives, and the minutes and voting records of particular Councils of Ministers. Having received some of the requested documents, the editor was informed that they should not have been sent to him and that he would not be allowed access to the other documents because they all related directly to the deliberations of the Council and were therefore confidential. The editor sought an annulment of the decision, arguing that it infringed Decision 93/731, art 4(2) in that it amounted to a blanket refusal to allow access to certain types of document. *Held*, as the objective of Decision 93/731 was to allow the public to have wide access to Council documents, the Council was obliged, when exercising its discretion under art 4(2), to balance the interests of citizens in having such access against its own interest in maintaining the confidentiality of its deliberations. In the instant case, the Council had assumed that disclosure of the requested documents would be in breach of Decision 93/662, art 5(1) because the documents referred to Council deliberations and that it was therefore obliged to refuse the editor's request. However, the Council had not also carried out the necessary balancing exercise. Accordingly, the application would be granted.

Case T-194/94: Carvel v EU Council [1995] 3 CMLR 359 (CFI: Second Chamber).

3091   Community institutions—European Parliament—general budget of European Union for 1996—adoption

On 21 December 1995, the European Parliament adopted the general budget of the European Union for the financial year 1996. The total revenue available amounts to 81,888,440,991 ecus. The revenue for 1995 was 75,438,426,452 ecus, and for 1994 for the corresponding figure was 66,002,143,762.76 ecus. (OJ L22 29.1.96 p 1.)

3092   Community institutions—European Parliament—right of inquiry—procedure

On 6 March 1995 the European Parliament, the Council and the Commission issued a Decision relating to the exercise of the European Parliament's right of inquiry. Article 2 establishes that the European Parliament may, at the request of one-quarter of its members, set up a temporary committee of inquiry to investigate alleged contravention or maladministration in the implementation of Community law.

The decision lays down detailed provisions governing the right of inquiry procedure, including the following: the committee may not investigate matters at issue before a national or Community court until such time as the legal proceedings have been completed; the committee has the right to conduct proceedings in secrecy if so required; and the information obtained by the committee must be used solely for the performance of its duties, and it may not be made pubic if it contains material of a secret or confidential nature. The decision entered into force on 6 April 1995. (OJ L78 6.4.95 p 1.)

3093   Community revenue—protection of financial interests against fraud

Council Regulation 2988/95 was adopted on 18 December, by virtue of the EC Treaty, art 235 and the Euratom Treaty, art 203 for the purpose of protecting the Communities' financial interests. The Regulation lays down rules relating to homogenous checks and administrative measures concerning irregularities with regard to Community law. Article 1(2) defines 'irregularities' as 'any infringement of a provision of Community law resulting from an act or omission by an economic operator, which has, or would have, the effect of prejudicing the general budget (either by reducing or losing revenue accruing from own resources collected directly on behalf of the Communities, or by an unjustified item of expenditure'.

Intentional irregularities, or those caused by negligence, may attract the penalties laid down in art 5, which include: the payment of an administrative fine; and total or partial removal of an advantage granted by Community rules.

Article 8 provides that member states are to take the measures necessary to ensure the 'regularity and reality of transactions involving the Communities' financial interests'. These measures must be appropriate to the specific nature of each sector and proportionate to the objectives pursued. The Regulation entered into force on 26 December 1995. (OJ L312 23.12.95 p 1.)

3094   Community treaty—agreement between member states and the Russian Federation

The Communities (Definition of Treaties) (Partnership and Co-operation Agreement between the European Communities and their Member States and the Russian Federation) Order 1995, SI 1995/1618 (in force on a date to be notified in the London Gazette), declares that the Partnership and Co-operation Agreement between the European Communities and their Member States on the one hand and the Russian Federation on the other hand, is a Community treaty for the purposes of the European Communities Act 1972, s 1(2). The agreement establishes a partnership which has several objectives, including the provision of a framework for political dialogue between the parties, the promotion of trade and investment, the support of democracy and a market economy in Russia, and the creation of conditions for a future free trade area between the Community and Russia. The main effect of declaring the agreement to be a Community treaty is that it utilises the provisions of the 1972 Act, s 2, which provides for the implementation of Community treaties.

3095 Community treaty—agreement between member states and Ukraine

The European Communities (Definition of Treaties) (Partnership and Co-operation Agreement between the European Communities and their Member States, and Ukraine) Order 1995, SI 1995/1619 (in force on a date to be notified in the London Gazette), declares that the Partnership and Co-operation Agreement between the European Communities and their Member States on the one hand and the Ukraine on the other hand, is a Community treaty for the purposes of the European Communities Act 1972, s 1(2). The agreement establishes a partnership which has several objectives, including the provision of a framework for political dialogue between the parties, the promotion of trade and investment, the provision of a basis for different aspects of co-operation, and the support of democracy and a market economy in Ukraine. The main effect of declaring the agreement to be a Community treaty is that it utilises the provisions of the 1972 Act, s 2 relating to the implementation of such treaties.

3096 Community treaty—agreement establishing the World Trade Organisation

The European Communities (Definition of Treaties) (The Agreement Establishing the World Trade Organisation) Order 1995, SI 1995/265 (in force on a date to be notified in the London Gazette), declares the Agreement Establishing the World Trade Organisation, signed at Marrakesh on 15 April 1994 by the Community, the member states and many other states, to be a Community Treaty as defined in the European Communities Act 1972, s 1(2). The Agreement establishes the organisation to provide a common institutional framework for the conduct of trade relations among its members. The agreements and associated legal instruments included in Annexes 1, 2 and 3, the Multilateral Trade Agreements, are integral parts of the Agreement and bind all members. The principal effect of declaring the 1994 Agreement to be a Community Treaty as so defined is to bring into play in relation to it the provisions of the 1972 Act, s 2 which provides for the implementation of treaties so specified.

3097 Criminal law—extradition—procedure between member states

On 10 March 1995 the Council of the European Union adopted an Act drawing up the Convention on simplified extradition procedures between member states of the European Union. The Convention was drawn up on the basis of the Maastricht Treaty on European Union, art K.3. The purpose of the Convention is to improve judicial co-operation between the member states in criminal matters with regard to proceedings and the execution of sentences. The provisions of the European Convention on Extradition of 13 December 1957 remain applicable for all matters not covered by the 1995 Convention. The 1995 Convention enters into force 90 days after the date of ratification, acceptance or approval by the last member state to carry out this formality. (OJ L78 30.3.95 p 1).

3098 General provisions—duties of member states—Justice and Home Affairs— displaced persons

The EC Council adopted a Resolution on 25 September 1995 on burden-sharing with regard to the admission and residence of displaced persons on a temporary basis. The Resolution, which was issued by virtue of the Treaty on European Union, art K.1, states that member states will, where possible, give temporary refuge to people whose lives or health are under threat as a result of armed conflict or civil war, but where such a situation arises it is desirable that the conditions for admission and residence should be arranged in a concerted fashion and in a spirit of solidarity between member states. (OJ C262 7.10.95 p 1.)

THE COURT OF JUSTICE

3099 Ancillary and other proceedings—interim measures—circumstances in which national court may grant interim relief

A company commenced proceedings against a federal department, contesting banana import quotas which had been imposed in accordance with a Community regulation. The national court stayed the proceedings pending a reference to the European Court of Justice for a preliminary ruling as to the validity of the regulation, and also ordered the federal department to provisionally grant the company additional banana import licences. On the question of whether a national court had power to grant interim relief, and the conditions under which such relief could be granted, *held*, where an annulment of a Community provision was sought, the EC Treaty authorised national courts to suspend the application of the provision, or national measures adopted to implement the provision, and also authorised it to prescribe any necessary interim measures. The interim protection had to be the same whether an individual sought suspension of a national administrative rule adopted to implement a Community regulation, or the grant of interim relief to regulate the legal position or relationship between the parties for their own benefit. The conditions which had to be satisfied before such relief could be granted were that (1) the court had to have serious doubts as to the validity of the Community provision in question, and had to itself refer the provision for a preliminary ruling if that had not already been done, (2) there was urgency, in the sense that interim relief was necessary to avoid serious and irreparable damage being caused to the party seeking relief, (3) the court had to take account of the Community interest, and (4) the court had to have regard to relevant decisions as to the lawfulness of the regulation.

Case C-465/93: Atlanta Fruchthandelsgesellschaft mbH v Bundesamt für Ernährung und Forstwirtschaft [1996] All ER (EC) 31 (ECJ: Full Court).

3100 Court of First Instance—Rules of Procedure—amendment

On 6 July 1995, the Court of First Instance (CFI) amended its Rules of Procedure. A new section, Title IV (arts 130–136), has been added to the original rules in order to take account of the specific features of proceedings relating to intellectual property which the CFI is called upon to hear, in particular by virtue of Regulation 40/94 on the Community trade mark and Regulation 2100/94 on Community plant variety rights. (OJ L172 22.7.95 p 3.)

Prior to the adoption of the above amendments, the EU Council amended art 46 of the Protocol on the Statute of the Court of Justice to enable such amendment to take place; see Council Decision 95/208. (OJ L131 15.6.95 p 33.)

The CFI rules were previously amended on 15 September 1994 (OJ L249 24.9.94 p 17) and 17 February 1995. (OJ L44 28.2.95 p 64.)

3101 European Court of Justice—Rules of Procedure—amendment

The Rules of Procedure of the European Court of Justice, and the Court of First Instance have been amended as a result of the coming into force of the Treaty on European Union, and the Agreement on the European Economic Area. The amendments enter into force on the first day of the second month after their publication in the Official Journal of the European Communities; see OJ L2 8.2.95 pp 61, 64.

3102 Reference from national court—construction of earlier decision of European Court of Justice—patent—circumstances in which patent is infringed

See *Merck & Co Inc v Primecrown Ltd,* para 2220.

3103 Reference from national court—Convention jurisdiction—enforcement of judgment in another member state

Under the 1968 Convention on Jurisdiction and the Enforcement of Judgments in Civil and Commercial Matters, art 37(1), an appeal against a decision authorising enforcement of a judgment given in a contracting state must be lodged with the High Court. The judgment on appeal against enforcement may be contested only by a single further appeal to the Court of Appeal on a point of law: art 37(2). The court with which the appeal under art 37(1) is lodged may stay the proceedings if an ordinary appeal has been lodged against the judgment in the state in which judgment was given: art 38.

In proceedings in France, the plaintiff obtained a provisionally enforceable judgment against the defendant for infringement of copyright. The plaintiff then obtained an order for registration of the judgment in England. The defendant lodged an appeal against the order. The High Court stayed the order pending the outcome of an appeal in France against the judgment. That appeal was refused. The stay of the order for registration was subsequently lifted and the defendant's appeal against the registration order was dismissed. It fell to be determined whether, if the High Court, under art 37(1), refused to grant a stay or removed a stay already imposed, the Court of Appeal had the power, under art 37(2), to impose or reimpose such a stay. *Held*, arts 37, 38 were to be interpreted as meaning that a decision by which a court of a contracting state, seised of an appeal against authorisation to enforce an enforceable judgment of a court in another contracting state, refused a stay or lifted a stay previously ordered, could not be contested by an appeal limited to the examination of points of law only. Further, the court seised of such an appeal on a point of law under art 37 had no jurisdiction to impose or reimpose such a stay.

Case C-432/93: Société d'Information Service Réalisation Organisation (SISRO) v Ampersand Software BV [1996] 2 WLR 30 (ECJ: Sixth Chamber).

3104 Reference from national court—Convention jurisdiction—interpretation for purposes of corresponding national legislation

The plaintiff, an English bank, had made a number of payments to the defendant, a Scottish local authority, under interest rate swap contracts which had been held to be void. The plaintiff brought proceedings in England to recover the sums paid to the defendant. It contended that the English court had jurisdiction in the matter as the defendant was being sued either in matters relating to contract within the Civil Jurisdiction and Judgments Act 1982, Sch 4, art 5(1) or in matters relating to tort, delict or quasi-delict within Sch 4, art 5(3). The defendant claimed that the proceedings ought to be brought in Scotland where it was domiciled. The Court of Appeal sought a preliminary ruling from the European Court of Justice (ECJ) as to the interpretation of corresponding provisions of the 1968 Brussels Convention on Jurisdiction and the Enforcement of Judgments in Civil and Commercial Matters, on which the English legislation in question was modelled. Held, the 1982 Act rendered the Convention applicable in the United Kingdom and also provided for the allocation of civil jurisdiction as between the three separate jurisdictions, of England and Wales, Scotland and Northern Ireland, within the United Kingdom. For that purpose, the 1982 Act, Sch 4 contained certain provisions modelled on the Convention. The English court was seeking a ruling on the interpretation of the provisions of the Convention to enable it to decide on the application, not of the Convention, but of the national law. Where the 1982 Act applied, it required the national court only to have regard to the ECJ's case law on the interpretation of corresponding provisions of the Convention, but where the Convention applied, the national court was bound to determine the case in accordance with principles laid down by and any relevant decision of the ECJ. The role of the ECJ was not to give advice that was without binding effect. As the national court was free in the present case to decide whether the interpretation given by the ECJ was equally valid for the purposes of the application of the national law based on the Convention, the ECJ had no jurisdiction to give a preliminary ruling.

Case C-346/93: Kleinwort Benson Ltd v City of Glasgow District Council (1995) Times, 17 April (ECJ: Full Court). For proceedings in the Court of Appeal, see [1994] 4 All ER 865 (1994 Abr para 568).

3105 Reference from national court—Convention jurisdiction—special jurisdiction— tort—place where harmful event occurred

By virtue of the 1968 Brussels Convention on Jurisdiction and the Enforcement of Judgments in Civil and Commercial Matters, art 5(3), a person domiciled in a contracting state may, in another contracting state, be sued in matters relating to tort, in the courts for the place where the harmful event occurred.

The plaintiff was arrested in England and promissory notes which he had lodged with the defendant, an English bank, were sequestered. He was subsequently released. He brought proceedings in Italy against the defendant for payment of the exchange value of the notes and for compensation for the damage allegedly suffered by him as a result of his arrest, for breach of several contracts and for injury to his reputation. The defendant challenged the jurisdiction of the Italian court on the ground that the alleged damage had occurred in England. It fell to be determined whether 'place where the harmful event occurred' in art 5(3) meant only the place where physical harm was caused to persons or things, or whether it meant also the place where damage to the plaintiff's assets occurred. Held, the general principle laid down by art 2, that a person domiciled in a contracting state should be sued in that state, would be negated if the rule of special jurisdiction in art 5(3), the choice of which was a matter for the plaintiff, were extended beyond the particular circumstances which justified it. The rule in art 5(3) was based on the existence of a particularly close connecting factor between the dispute and courts other than those of the state of the defendant's domicile, which justified the attribution of jurisdiction to those courts for those reasons relating to the sound administration of justice and the efficacious conduct of proceedings. It was already established that the place of the event giving rise to the damage, as much as the place where the damage occurred, could constitute a significant connecting factor from the point of view of jurisdiction. Although it was recognised that 'place where the harmful event occurred' could cover both the place where the damage occurred and the place of the event giving rise to it, it could not be construed so extensively as to encompass any place where the adverse consequences of an event that had already caused actual damage elsewhere could be felt. Accordingly, it could not be construed as including the place where the victim claimed to have suffered financial damage consequential upon initial damage arising and suffered by him in another contracting state.

Case C-364/93: Marinari v Lloyd's Bank plc [1996] All ER (EC) 84 (ECJ: Full Court).

3106 Specific principles of Community law—equality—employment and social affairs— rights of the individual

See para 3177.

3107 Specific principles of Community law—equality—equality of treatment—women and men

See para 3180.

APPLICATION OF COMMUNITY LAW IN NATIONAL COURTS

3108 Community law in the United Kingdom—application and enforcement— interpretation—EC Council minutes

See *Wagamama Ltd v City Centre Restaurants plc*, para 2955.

3109 Direct effect of Community law—frontier and passport controls between United Kingdom and other member states

See *Flynn v Secretary of State for the Home Department*, para 262.

3110 Implementation of Community law in the United Kingdom—statutory instruments—judicial review

See *R v Customs and Excise, ex p Eurotunnel plc*, para 28.

EXTERNAL RELATIONS

3111 Common commercial policy—exports—permissible member state restrictions

The defendants were charged with having delivered plant, plant parts and chemical products to Iraq without the export licences required under German law. On a reference to the European Court of Justice, questions arose concerning the EC Treaty, art 113 on the common commercial policy and Council Regulation (EC) 2603/69 on common rules for exports. *Held*, rules restricting exports to non-member countries of goods which could be used for both military and civil purposes fell within the scope of the EC Treaty, art 113 in respect of which the Community had exclusive competence. Accordingly, the competence of member states was excluded except where the Community granted them specific authorisation. Where there was a threat to public security, a matter to be considered by the national court, a requirement that an applicant for an export licence prove that goods to be exported would be used exclusively for civil purposes, or a refusal to issue an export licence if the goods could objectively be used for military purposes, could be consistent with the principle of proportionality. National authorities were not prevented by Community law from imposing criminal penalties for breaches of the licensing procedure provided that such penalties did not exceed what appeared to be proportionate in relation to the public aim pursued.

Case C-83/94: Re Leifer (1995) Times, 2 November (ECJ: Full Court).

3112 Intra-EEA trade—free movement of goods—import authorisation—discrimination

A Finnish statutory alcohol monopoly refused to authorise a trader to import whisky from Germany and wine from Italy unless it disclosed certain information and documents, including the names of the sellers, the price and the names of the restaurants in Finland buying the whisky and wine. The trader objected to disclosing such information on the ground that it constituted business secrets. It fell to be determined whether the requirement to obtain an authorisation to import alcoholic beverages and to put them into free circulation resulted in an impediment to intra-EEA trade and constituted a quantitative restriction on imports prohibited by the EEA Agreement and whether the conferring of the exclusive right to import alcoholic beverages on a statutory state monopoly was contrary to the Agreement. *Held*, wherever there was identity between the EEA provision and the related EC provision, the EFTA Court should follow precedents of the European Court of Justice (ECJ). Whisky and wine were covered by the EEA rules on free movement of goods. The need to obtain authorisation from the state monopoly was equivalent to a state import licence. Following the ECJ decision in *Case 51–54/71: International Fruit Co NV v Produktschap voor Groentenen Fruit* [1971] ECR 1107, such an authorisation was prohibited by the EEA Agreement even if granted automatically. Although the policy underlying the Finnish alcohol monopoly was public health, the requirement of an import authorisation was disproportionate and was not exempt from the prohibition. Following also the ECJ decision in *Case 59/75: Pubblico Ministero v Manghera* [1976] ECR 91 (1976 Abr para 1124), the monopoly's exclusive right to import alcoholic drinks into Finland was contrary to provisions prohibiting discrimination regarding the conditions under which goods were procured or marketed. Accordingly, the import monopoly in respect of whisky and wine was illegal.

Case E-1/94: Ravintoloitsijain Liiton Kustannus Oy Restamark v Helsingin Piiritullikamari [1995] 1 CMLR 161 (EFTA Court).

INDUSTRIAL POLICY AND INTERNAL MARKET

3113 Industrial development—individual industries—drugs and cosmetics—medicines for human use—labelling

See *EC Commission v Germany*, para 3133.

3114 Industrial development—individual industries—shipbuilding—development aid

See *Germany v EC Commission*, para 3115.

STATE AIDS AND REGIONAL POLICY

3115 State aids—development aid—shipbuilding

Germany proposed to grant development aid to China in the form of aid credit for the financing of three container vessels that were to be built in German shipyards on the order of a Chinese state-owned shipping company which intended to operate the vessels. Although the EC Commission decided that the loan complied with criteria laid down by the Organisation for Economic Co-operation and Development (OECD), it formed the view that the Chinese company did not need development aid in order to contribute to the general development of China. Germany sought to annul the Commission's decision refusing to exempt the aid from the prohibition on aid incompatible with the Common Market in the EC Treaty, art 92. *Held*, by virtue of Council Directive (EC) 90/684, art 4(7), state aid relating to shipbuilding that was granted as development assistance to a developing country might be deemed compatible with the Common Market under art 92(3) of the Treaty if it complied with certain OECD criteria. The Commission had a discretion under art 92(3)(d) whether to grant exemption and also had a duty to confirm that the aid in question was genuine development aid, a criterion to be distinguished from the criteria laid down by the OECD. It was entitled to assess whether the aid was necessary to contribute to the advancement of the developing country which was to receive it. The Commission had properly used the appropriate test and, accordingly, the action to annul its decision would be dismissed.

Case C-400/92: Germany v EC Commission [1995] 2 CMLR 461 (ECJ: Full Court).

3116 State aids—regional aid—state-owned company—insolvency—capital investment by state

The Spanish government created a public company 69 per cent of which was owned by the Ministry of Finance and 31 per cent by a public body attached to the Ministry of Agriculture. The government increased the company's capital to cover its large and increasing deficit. The EC Commission, which had not been informed of this, decided that this constituted a state aid contrary to the EC Treaty, art 92 and ordered the company to repay the sum in question to the

Spanish government. The company, which had ceased trading, was by then in liquidation. The Spanish government sought the annulment of the Commission's decision. *Held*, the increase in capital constituted state aid and, in being used to close down one particularly loss-making division of the company, was not a satisfactory restructuring measure and was prohibited by art 92(1). The aid in question affected inter-state trade. In so far as it might be justified as regional aid under art 92(3)(a), (c), because of the company's importance for the local economy it would be necessary to restore the company to a state of commercial viability for which purpose the new capital was inadequate and, therefore, could not be exempted and was unlawful. Accordingly, the application would be dismissed.

Case C-42/93: Spain v EC Commission [1995] 2 CMLR 702 (ECJ: Full Court).

ENVIRONMENT AND CONSUMERS

3117 Consumers—active implantable medical devices

See para 612.

3118 Consumers—Consumer Committee

Commission Decision (EC) 95/260 setting up a Consumer Committee was adopted on 13 June 1995. This new committee is designed to replace the former Consumers' Consultative Council, set up by Decision 90/55, which did not adequately meet the needs of the Commission as regards effectiveness and speed of consultation.

The Consumer Committee is to be composed of 20 members. Fifteen members are to be selected to represent national and regional consumer organisations and institutes, and the remaining five are to represent European consumer organisations. The objective of the committee is to advise the Commission on all problems relating to the protection of consumer interests at Community level. The decision took effect as from 13 June 1995. (OJ L162 13.7.95 p 37.)

3119 Consumers—consumer safety—gas appliances—approximation of laws of member states

See para 616.

3120 Consumers—foodstuff additives—conditions of use

Directive (EC) 95/2 of the Council and European Parliament on food additives was adopted on 20 February 1995. The Directive concerns all additives other than colours and sweeteners, and emphasises that the prime consideration for regulation of food additives is the need to protect the consumer. Article 1(2) states that only additives which satisfy the requirements laid down by the Scientific Committee for Food may be used in foodstuffs.

Annexes I–V list the types of additives that may be used in foodstuffs and stipulate certain conditions of use. Annex VI lays down strict rules governing the use of additives in food for infants and young children. The Directive is to be implemented in the member states by 25 September 1996. (OJ L61 18.3.95 p 1.)

3121 Consumers—medicinal products—labelling requirements

See *EC Commission v Germany*, para 3133.

3122 Consumers—medicinal products—presentation—foodstuffs

Herbal teas imported from South America were sold by the importer without any indication of their therapeutic or prophylactic properties. Such information appeared on an explanatory brochure which would be sent to a purchaser by a third party on request. The brochure stated that the teas were regarded as complementing any medicines being taken. In criminal proceedings against the importer for failing to register the teas as medicinal products, it fell to be determined whether the teas were medicinal products within Council Directive (EC) 65/65, art 1(2), which gave two definitions of medicinal products, one according to their presentation and the other according to their functions. *Held*, a product that was generally regarded as a foodstuff with no therapeutic properties was a medicinal product by representation if it was intended to appear to have such properties in the opinion of an average well-informed customer. It was immaterial that such properties were only indicated in a publication sent at the request of a purchaser after purchase; it was also immaterial that the brochure was sent by a third party provided that the third party was acting on behalf of or in connection with the importer. It was for the national courts to decide whether the third party concerned had acted independently and whether the product was intended to appear as a medicinal product. The freedom of expression under the European Convention on Human Rights, art 10 applied to Community legislation, including Directive 65/65. However, it was subject to an exception for the protection of public health in accordance with art 10(2) of the Convention which protected the right of a truly independent third party to publish views or information. That exception might defeat the right to freedom of expression in so far as the third party's conduct could be attributed to the importer.

Case C-219/91: Re Ter Voort [1995] 2 CMLR 591 (ECJ: Fifth Chamber).

3123 Environment—conservation—migratory birds

In pursuance of Council Directive (EC) 79/409, art 7(4), French provincial authorities set hunting season dates for individual species of migratory birds in their respective territories. However, if one species was hunted at a time when another species was protected, the health and survival rate of the latter species would be affected. It fell to be determined whether the setting of dates in this manner contravened the Directive. *Held*, a single date applicable to all protected species simultaneously would have to be set unless it could be scientifically established that staggered dates did not have such an effect. The date so set must provide complete protection for the whole period of migration, not merely for the period of maximum movement, although such date must not be based merely on an average date of commencement of movement. So long as specifically local migration dates were followed, different dates might be fixed in different regions. Subordinate authorities, such as the provincial authorities, might legitimately be empowered to fix the dates although national legislation should lay down parameters to the exercise of such local power in order to ensure the complete protection required by the Directive.

Case C-435/92: Association pour la Protection des Animaux Sauvages v Prefet de Maine-et-Loire [1994] 3 CMLR 685 (ECJ: Full Court).

ENERGY OTHER THAN FROM COAL

3124 European Energy Charter—implementation by Treaty

Council Decision (EC) 94/988 on the provisional application of the Energy Charter Treaty by the European Communities and their member states was adopted on 15 December 1994. The Treaty has been drawn up in order to provide a secure and binding international legal framework for the principles and objectives set out in the European Energy Charter, signed on 17 December 1991. A copy of the Treaty is annexed to the decision, as is a copy of the Energy Charter Protocol on energy efficiency and related environmental aspects. The Treaty is to enter into force on the 90th day after the date of deposit of the 30th instrument of ratification. (OJ L380 31.12.94 p 1.)

UNDERTAKINGS

3125 Commercial transactions—contractual payment periods—compensation for late payment

Commission Recommendation (EC) 95/198 on payment periods in commercial transactions has been adopted. The objective of the recommendation is to encourage member states to introduce legislation to ensure adherence to contractual payment periods in commercial transactions and to improve payment periods for public procurement contracts. Article 3 refers to compensation for late payment and suggests that a creditor be suitably compensated for damages incurred through late payment by a debtor.

In relation to public procurement contracts, art 6 suggests that public authorities adhere to a period of 60 days for payment, without prejudice to any shorter times currently in effect. In addition it is suggested that regular checks be made of the payment periods of public authorities and the results be made available in an official publication. The recommendation was adopted on 12 May 1995 but, by virtue of the EC Treaty, art 189, it is not binding on member states. (OJ L127 10.6.95 p 19.)

3126 Public contracts—public supply contracts

See para 2929.

CUSTOMS UNION AND FREE MOVEMENT OF GOODS

3127 Customs duties and equivalent charges—transit charges—customs clearance

A private company operated an international road station near Paris. Customs authorities had their offices within the station where they carried out customs clearance procedures. The company rented offices and services at the station to forwarding agents who were also entitled to use the road and rail transport facilities there. In addition to rent, the agents were charged a flat-rate transit charge for each vehicle in international transit which completed the customs clearance formalities at the station. They refused to pay the charge on the ground that, as it was originally intended to offset the costs incurred by the company in building and maintaining a TIR parking area used by the customs authorities, it was no longer justified because the authorities had agreed to carry out clearance operations on the agents' premises. It fell to be determined whether the charges were lawfully imposed. *Held*, the EC Treaty, arts 9, 12 prohibited member states from passing on to traders the costs of customs inspections and administrative formalities. The transit charge applied to all vehicles clearing customs within the station and there were no special advantages gained by the agents to justify the charge. The services supplied by the customs authorities were only those that should be paid for by the state. Articles 9, 12 prohibited the passing on of that cost to traders such as the agents. Although the company, not the state, passed the charges on, they were illegally imposed.

Case C-16/94: Edouard Dubois et Fils SA v Garonor Exploitation SA [1995] 2 CMLR 771 (ECJ: Fifth Chamber).

3128 Free movement of goods—quantitative restrictions and equivalent measures—derogations—exchange of information

Decision 3052/95 of the European Parliament and of the Council was adopted on 13 December 1995 and establishes a procedure for the exchange of information on national measures derogating from the principle of the free movement of goods within the Community. Pursuant to art 100b of the Treaty, the EC Commission has drawn up an inventory of national laws which fall under art 100a and which have not been harmonised.

The inventory has revealed that most of the obstacles to trade reported by member states are dealt with either by measures taken under art 100a or through proceedings initiated under art 169 for failure to fulfil obligations under art 30. Accordingly, by virtue of Decision 3052/95, art 1, the Council and the Parliament have ruled that where a member state takes steps to prevent the free movement, or placing on the market, of a particular model or type of product lawfully produced or marketed in another member state, it must notify the Commission where the direct or indirect effect of the measure is a general ban on the goods, a refusal to allow the goods to be placed on the market, the modification of the model or type of product concerned before it can be placed or kept on the market, or withdrawal of the goods from the market. The Decision is to take effect as from 1 January 1997. (OJ L321 30.12.95 p 1.)

3129 Free movement of goods—quantitative restrictions and equivalent measures—export controls—dual-use goods

Council Regulation 3381/94 (EC) and Council Decision 94/942/CFSP were adopted on 19 December 1994 and concern the setting up of a Community regime for the control of exports of dual-use goods. For the purposes of Regulation 3381/94, 'dual-use goods' are defined as goods which can be used for both civil and military purposes. According to art 3 of the regulation, an authorisation is required for the export of the dual-use goods listed in Annex I of Decision 94/942. In deciding whether to grant an export authorisation, the competent authorities must consider the common guidelines set out in Annex III to the decision.

By virtue of art 14 of the regulation, the exporter must keep detailed records of all transactions. Such records must include, in particular, commercial documents such as invoices, transport documents, etc, which contain sufficient information to allow the identification of the description of the dual-use goods; the quantity of the dual-use goods; the name and address of the exporter and of the consignee; and, where known, the end-use and end-user of the dual-use goods. These records must be kept for at least three years from the end of the calendar year in which the export took place. Both the regulation and the decision came into force on 31 December 1994. The date of application of both acts was originally 1 March 1995 but this date was changed by virtue of Council Regulation 837/95 and Council Decision 95/127, respectively, to 1 July 1995. (OJ L367 31.12.94 p 1.)

3130 Free movement of goods—quantitative restrictions and equivalent measures—import controls—controlled drugs

In consequence of the United Nations Convention on Narcotic Drugs 1961 and the Misuse of Drugs Act 1971, s 3(2)(b), the Secretary of State gave the applicants the exclusive right to manufacture, process and market diamorphine in the United Kingdom, and prohibited the importation of the drug. The Secretary of State subsequently granted a licence to another company to import diamorphine from a member state. That decision was made on the basis that the previous policy was contrary to the EC Treaty, art 30, in that it impeded intra-Community trade. The applicants sought a declaration that the Secretary of State's decision should be set aside. In particular, it was argued that if the 1961 Convention was incompatible with the EC Treaty, arts 30 and 36, the treaty provisions did not apply because art 234 provided that rights and obligations arising from agreements concluded between member states and third countries before the treaty came into force were not affected by the treaty. The court referred several questions as to the interpretation of arts 30, 36 and 234 to the European Court of Justice. *Held*, in determining whether or not a Community measure could be deprived of its effect by an earlier international agreement, national courts had to examine whether such an agreement imposed on the member states concerned obligations which were owed to non-member states who were parties to it, and the extent to which such obligations had the effect of disapplying arts 30 and 36. Here, the national court had to decide whether the obligations owed to non-member states required the United Kingdom to allocate quotas among the companies concerned with the production and marketing of diamorphine, and whether allowing imports would make it impossible for the United Kingdom to exercise the degree of control that the convention required. Where an international agreement allowed, but did not require, member states to adopt measures which appeared to be contrary to Community law, member states had to refrain from adopting such measures. Additionally, although art 36 allowed member states to restrict or prohibit trade in certain circumstances, those derogations related only to non-economic matters. As such, measures which restricted intra-Community trade in order to safeguard a particular company's survival were not justifiable on any of the grounds of derogation set out in art 36. Moreover, although the need to ensure that member states had reliable supplies of a drug for essential medical purposes could be justified under art 36, in that they were necessary for the protection of the health and life of humans, that derogation did not apply if less restrictive means could be used to achieve that aim.

   Case C-324/93: R v Secretary of State for the Home Department, ex p Evans Medical Ltd (Generics (UK) Ltd, intervener) [1995] All ER (EC) 481 (ECJ: Full Court).

3131 Free movement of goods—quantitative restrictions and equivalent measures—import controls—copyright—infringing material

See para 681.

3132 Free movement of goods—quantitative restrictions and equivalent measures—import controls—freshwater fish

It fell to be determined whether a prohibition under German law on the unlicensed importation of any species of live freshwater crayfish for commercial purposes, either for consumption or for release into private waters, infringed Community law. A licence was only issued if the applicant complied with certain health measures intended to prevent the crayfish from being released into the environment and to ensure that the water in which they were kept was disinfected. *Held*, as the prohibition had an effect on imports from other member states or from non-member states in free circulation in the Community, it was contrary to the EC Treaty, art 30, which precluded the application to intra-Community trade of national legislation which maintained a requirement, even as a pure formality, for import licences or any other similar procedure. It was immaterial that a large number of licences had been granted even though the importers had not fully used them. Rules restricting intra-Community trade were compatible with the Treaty only in so far as they were indispensable for the purposes of providing effective protection for the health and life of animals. Accordingly, if that aim might be achieved as effectively by measures having less restrictive effects on intra-Community trade, the import prohibition could not be covered by the derogation provided for in art 36. As less restrictive measures than the prohibition, such as making consignments of imports subject to health checks and sample checks, could have been used to prevent the risk of crayfish plague and of faunal distortion in Germany, the law in question was contrary to art 30 and not justified by art 36.

   Case C-131/93: EC Commission v Germany [1995] 2 CMLR 278 (ECJ: Sixth Chamber).

3133   Free movement of goods—quantitative restrictions and equivalent measures— medicinal products—labelling

German law restricted to two a year the expiry dates that might be indicated on the packaging of medicinal products and of non-reusable sterile medical instruments. Germany failed to inform the EC Commission of a draft regulation introducing new technical regulations for the marketing of such medical instruments. The Commission claimed that, by obliging importers to alter the original packaging and reducing the market period of the imported products, Germany had failed to fulfil its Community obligations. *Held*, so restricting the expiry dates constituted a measure having equivalent effect to an import restriction contrary to the EC Treaty, art 30 because the period of marketing imported products was thereby reduced. As harmonisation in this field was incomplete, member states had to choose the means of protecting public health in their territory. The bringing forward of the expiry date was a disproportionate measure as it did not protect public health. As Germany had failed to notify the Commission of the draft regulation, it had also contravened Council Directive (EC) 83/189.

Case C-317/92: EC Commission v Germany [1995] 2 CMLR 653 (ECJ: Full Court).

3134   Free movement of goods—quantitative restrictions and equivalent measures— exemption for goods for personal consumption—goods purchased by agent

See *R v Customs and Excise Comrs, ex p EMU Tabac Sàrl (Imperial Tobacco Co intervening)*, para 944.

AGRICULTURE

See AGRICULTURE.

FREEDOM OF MOVEMENT FOR WORKERS

3135   Derogations—public security—exclusion order—review by competent authority

Council Directive (EC) 64/221, art 9(1) provides that where there is no right of appeal to a court of law, or where such appeal may be only in respect of the legal validity of the decision, or where the appeal cannot have suspensory effect, a decision refusing renewal of a residence permit from the territory is not to be taken by the administrative authority, save in the case of urgency, until an opinion has been obtained from a competent authority of the host country before which the person concerned enjoys such rights of defence and of assistance or representation as the domestic law of that country provides for. The authority must not be the same as that empowered to take the decision refusing renewal of the residence permit or ordering expulsion.

The applicant, an Irish national, was convicted in Ireland of possessing rifles for unlawful purposes. While in the United Kingdom, he was arrested under the Prevention of Terrorism (Temporary Provisions) Act 1989 Act and served with an exclusion order. Having been removed from the United Kingdom, the applicant raised objection to the exclusion order, and was interviewed by a person nominated by the Secretary of State. However, the applicant was not told of the reason for his exclusion, nor did the nominee reveal his identity. On reconsidering the case, the Secretary of State upheld the decision to make an exclusion order. The applicant then contended that his exclusion was contrary to Directive 64/221, art 9(1), as he had not been given a chance to make representations nor to meet the Secretary of State's nominee. On a reference to the European Court of Justice for a preliminary ruling as to the interpretation of art 9(1), *held*, the object of art 9(1) was to ensure minimum procedural safeguards for persons affected by a decision refusing renewal of a residence permit or ordering the expulsion of a residence permit holder, and the purpose of the competent authority was to enable an exhaustive examination of all the facts and circumstances to be carried out before the decision was finally taken. However, the Directive did not require the competent authority to be appointed by a court, or composed of members of the judiciary, nor did it require members of the authority to be appointed for a specific period. The essential requirements were that the competent authority performed its duties independently, without being subject to control by the administrative authority, and that it followed a procedure which enabled the person concerned to present his defence. Although the person had to be notified of the authority's opinion, the Directive did not require the opinion to name the members of the authority or indicate their professional status. However, it was for the national court to determine whether those requirements were satisfied.

Case C-175/94: R v Secretary of State for the Home Department, ex p Gallagher [1996] 1 CMLR 557 (ECJ: Sixth Chamber).

3136 Material scope—employment—equality of treatment—taxation

Under German law, tax on income from employment was deducted at source by the employer and paid to the tax authorities. Workers who were permanently or usually resident in Germany were given certain tax advantages, but those who were not were excluded from those advantages and subject to additional disadvantages. The applicant lived in Belgium with his wife and children and was employed in Germany, where his wages were taxed. When he was refused entitlement to a particular tax relief, he commenced proceedings against the tax authorities. The German court referred the matter to the European Court of Justice for a ruling on whether German tax laws were contrary to the right of free movement for workers guaranteed by the EC Treaty, art 48. *Held*, although direct taxation was not within the ambit of the Community's powers, the powers retained by member states in that respect had to be exercised consistently with Community law. In addition to the express provisions of Council Regulation (EC) 1612/68, art 7, Community law prohibited not only overt discrimination by reference to nationality, but also covert discrimination by the application of other kinds of criteria which differentiated between nationals and thereby had the same discriminatory result. Even if a tax law was applied irrespective of the taxpayer's nationality, the effect of a distinction based on residence was to discriminate against nationals of other member states, as they were more likely to be non-residents. However, in relation to direct taxes, the situation of residents and non-residents was not comparable, as the income received in a member state by a non-resident was usually only part of his total income, whereas the major part of a resident's income usually came from the state of residence. Article 48 did not preclude rules under which a non-resident worker was more heavily taxed than a resident worker, but that was not so if a non-resident received most of his income in the member state in which he was employed and was not entitled to the tax benefits available there. In those circumstances, he suffered indirect discrimination because his personal and family circumstances were not taken into account in either his state of residence or his state of employment. Such discrimination was not justifiable. Moreover, discrimination arose where non-residents were deprived of the right to rely on the procedural measures which would have given them the right to claim tax refunds, and that was so even if there were discretionary provisions which allowed the tax authorities to remedy some of the procedural discrimination.

Case C-279/93: Finanzamt Köln-Altstadt v Schumacker [1995] All ER (EC) 319 (ECJ: Full Court).

3137 Material scope—employment—equality of treatment—employed or self-employed person in another member state—dependant

A Belgian national had lived in Germany for more than 20 years from the age of two years. He received an orphan's allowance on account of the death of his father; he was not dependent on his mother. His application for an education allowance to continue his university studies in the United Kingdom was rejected on the ground that he was over 21 and was not dependent on his parents. It fell to be determined whether the right to equal treatment for dependants of a national of a member state who was pursuing an activity as an employed or self-employed person in the territory of another member state, set out in Council Regulation (EC) 1612/68, art 12, could be relied upon by a migrant worker's child who was 21 or over and no longer dependent on that worker. *Held*, the principle of equal treatment set out in art 12 extended to all forms of education and required that the child of a migrant worker be able to continue his studies in order to complete his education successfully. Article 12 encompassed financial assistance for students who were already at an advanced state of their education, even if they were not already 21 or older and were no longer dependants of their parents. The definition of 'child' for the purposes of art 12 was not subject to the same conditions of age or dependency as were the rights governed by arts 10(1), 11, to which art 12 made no reference.

Case C-7/94: Landesamt für Ausbildungsförderung Nordrhein-Westfalen v Gaal (Oberbundesanwalt beim Bundesverwaltungsgericht, intervening) [1995] 3 CMLR 17 (ECJ: Sixth Chamber).

3138 Material scope—travel documents—visa requirements—third countries—external borders of member states

The EC Treaty, art 100c requires the Council of the European Union to determine the third countries whose nationals must be in possession of a visa when crossing the external borders of the member states. Council Regulation (EC) 2317/95 of 25 September 1995 includes a common list of such third countries. Article 2 enables individual member states to determine the visa requirements of nationals of third countries not on the common list, of stateless persons and of recognised refugees. Any measure enacted by member states pursuant to art 2 is to be communicated to the EC Commission within ten working days of the entry into force of the Regulation (see art 2(4)), and the Commission must then publish such information. Article 4 allows member states to exempt certain nationals of third countries including holders of diplomatic passports. However, under art 4(2), this information is to be communicated to the Commission under the same conditions as those imposed by art 2(4). The Regulation is due to enter into force six months after its publication in the Official Journal (3 October 1995), with the exception of arts 2(4), 4(2), which entered into force on the day following publication. (OJ L234 3.10.95 p 1.)

3139 Personal scope—worker—nationality—indirect discrimination

An Italian national held a post as a foreign language assistant at a German University under two contracts of employment, the first for one year and the second for four years. Under German law, certain specialist teaching posts at universities might be filled using fixed term contracts provided they were justified on objective grounds. Fixed term contracts might also be imposed on foreign language assistants solely on the basis of the nature of the work involved; such contracts were subject to a maximum limit of five years. An application to have the second contract continued after its expiry date was refused. It fell to be determined whether this refusal was compatible with the EC Treaty, art 48(2) on the free movement of workers. *Held*, as the overwhelming majority of foreign language teachers were foreigners, to treat them differently in such a manner was likely to put them at a disadvantage by comparison with German nationals and, therefore, was a form of indirect discrimination contrary to art 48(2). The need to ensure up-to-date tuition did not justify such discrimination.

Case C-272/92: Spotti v Freistaat Bayern [1994] 3 CMLR 629 (ECJ: Full Court).

3140 Personal scope—worker—failure to find work in host state

The applicants were Italian and Portuguese citizens living in the United Kingdom. They were in receipt of income support while they looked for work. The Secretary of State informed them that, as they had no real chance of obtaining work, they were in the United Kingdom in a non-economic capacity and had become a burden on public funds so that they were unlawfully resident and required to leave the country. Although they were not deported, the effect of the decision was to end their entitlement to income support. On their applications for judicial review of the decisions, *held*, the applicants could not claim that they were entitled to remain in the United Kingdom on the basis of the EC Treaty, art 48, and their right to remain on the basis of art 8a was subject to the limitations and conditions expressly imposed by that article. Although the applicants had exercised their Community law rights as workers when entering the United Kingdom and had therefore not required leave to enter, they had since ceased to be economically active. In those circumstances, the Secretary of State had been entitled to write to the applicants in the terms that he had done, as their presence was no longer lawful and they had not sought leave to remain. One of the consequences of their unlawful presence was that they were not entitled to income support. Accordingly, the applications would be dismissed.

R v Secretary of State for the Home Department, ex p Vitale; R v Secretary of State for the Home Department, ex p Do Amaral (1995) Times, 18 April (Queen's Bench Division: Judge J).

RIGHT OF ESTABLISHMENT AND FREEDOM TO PROVIDE SERVICES

3141 General—prohibition of contacting potential clients in other member states—investment advice

A company established in The Netherlands specialised in commodities futures. It had clients in The Netherlands, Belgium, France and the United Kingdom. The question arose whether a Dutch rule prohibiting the company from contacting potential clients by telephone or in person, including such clients in other member states, unless they had first expressly authorised the company in writing so to contact them was contrary to the EC Treaty, art 59 on freedom to provide services. *Held*, the Dutch prohibition did not fall outside the scope of art 59 simply because it was imposed by the state in which the provider of services was established rather than that where the potential recipient was established. Article 59 covered services which the provider offered by telephone to potential recipients established in other member states and provided without moving from the member state in which he was established. Rules such as the one in question constituted a restriction on freedom to provide services within the meaning of art 59. However, that provision did not preclude national rules which, in order to protect investor confidence in national financial markets, prohibited the practice of making unsolicited telephone calls to potential clients resident in other member states to offer them services linked to investment in commodities futures.

Case C-384/93: *Alpine Investments BV v Minister van Financiën* [1995] 2 BCLC 214 (ECJ: Full Court).

3142   General—right of establishment—legal services—guidelines

The plaintiff, a member of the German bar, opened his own chambers in Italy. However, he was suspended from practice by an Italian provincial bar council on the ground that he had contravened an Italian law by practising in Italy on a permanent basis using the title 'avvocato'. In proceedings challenging the decision, the bar council made a reference to the European Court of Justice for a preliminary ruling on Council Directive (EC) 77/249 relating to the freedom of lawyers to provide services. *Held*, as the plaintiff pursued a professional activity on a stable and continuous basis in a host member state where he had an established professional base, he came within the provisions of the EC Treaty relating to the right of establishment, and not those relating to the provision of services. The concept of establishment was broad, whereas the provision of services implied that a person was pursuing his activities in a host member state on a temporary basis, that being determined by reference to the duration of the provision of the services, and also their regularity or continuity. However, the fact that the provision of services was temporary did not mean that a person could not equip himself with some form of infrastructure in the host member state, such as an office or chambers. Although membership of a particular body might be a condition of pursuing a particular profession, it did not affect the right of establishment, and where the taking up or pursuing of an activity was subject to conditions imposed by the host member state, a national of another member state who intended to pursue that activity had to comply with them. Where national rules hindered or made it less attractive for a person to establish himself in another member state, such rules (1) had to be applied in a non-discriminatory manner, (2) had to be justified by imperative requirements which were in the general interest, (3) had to be suitable for attaining the objective which they pursued, and (4) could not go beyond what was necessary to attain that objective. It was also necessary for a host member state to take account of the equivalence of qualifications obtained in another member state, comparing the knowledge and qualifications required under national rules with those of the person concerned.

Case C-55/94: *Gebhard v Consiglio dell'Ordine degli Avvocati e Procuratori di Milano* [1996] All ER (EC) 189 (ECJ: Full Court).

3143   General—scope of principle of non-discrimination—non-resident—tax relief

The taxpayer, a Belgian national resident in Belgium, derived his sole income from a physiotherapy practice in the Netherlands of which he was a partner. Under Dutch law, resident self-employed persons were entitled to have their taxable income reduced by the amount of business profits they had added to their pension reserve so that taxation on the contributions was deferred until such time as amounts were withdrawn from the pension reserve or it was liquidated. It fell to be determined whether the refusal of the taxpayer's claim to deduct his contribution to a pension reserve was contrary to the EC Treaty, art 52. *Held*, discrimination arose through the application of different rules to comparable situations or the application of the same rule to different situations. While a difference in treatment between resident and non-resident taxpayers could not in itself be categorised as discrimination, a non-resident taxpayer, whether employed or self-employed, who received all or almost all of his income in the state where he worked was objectively in the same situation concerning income tax as a resident of that state who did the same work there. Accordingly, a non-resident taxpayer who received all or almost all of his income in the state where he worked but who was not entitled to set up a pension reserve qualifying for deductions under the same tax conditions as a resident taxpayer suffered discrimination. The effect of double taxation conventions was that fiscal cohesion was not secured by a strict correlation between the deductibility of contributions and the taxation of pensions but was shifted to another level, that of the reciprocity of the rules applicable in the contracting states. Since fiscal cohesion was achieved by a bilateral convention concluded with another member state, that principle could not be invoked to justify the discrimination caused by the Dutch law in question. Accordingly, such discrimination was contrary to art 52.

Case C-80/94: Wielockx v Inspecteur der Directe Belastingen [1996] 1 WLR 84 (ECJ: Full Court).

3144 Specific sectors—banks and financial and credit institutions—credit institutions—solvency ratios

Commission Directive (EC) 95/15 amending Commission Directive (EC) 89/647 on solvency ratios for credit institutions was adopted on 31 May 1995. The 1989 Directive is amended in relation to the technical definition of 'Zone A' and in respect of the weighting of asset items constituting claims carrying the explicit guarantee of the European Communities. The member states are to introduce implementing measures by 30 September 1995. (OJ L125 8.6.95 p 23.)

3145 Specific sectors—banks and financial and credit institutions—financial undertakings—prudential supervision

On 29 June 1995, the European Parliament and EU Council adopted Directive (EC) 95/26 amending the framework Directives in the financial services sector with a view to reinforcing prudential supervision. The Directive strengthens the powers of supervisors, making them better equipped to prevent cases of fraud and other irregularities in the financial services sector. Recital 7 of the preamble states that member states' competent authorities should not grant or should withdraw authorisation where factors indicate clearly that a financial undertaking has opted for the legal system of one member state for the purpose of evading the stricter standards in force in another member state. The Directive also makes provision for greater transparency of group structures by empowering competent authorities to refuse authorisation if they feel that it is difficult to carry out effective supervision of financial undertakings because of 'close links' between different entities.

The Directives amended by Directive 95/26 are Directives 77/780 and 89/646 in the field of credit institutions, Directives 73/239 and 92/49 in the field of non-life insurance, Directives 79/267 and 92/96 in the field of life insurance, Directive 93/22 in the field of investment firms and Directive 85/611 in the field of undertakings for collective investment in transferable securities.

The Directive is to be implemented in the member states no later than 18 July 1996. (OJ L168 18.7.95 p 7.)

3146 Specific sectors—government procurement—government supply contract—procedure

A contract notice for the concession for the computerisation of the national lottery was published by the government in the Italian national press. Only undertakings the majority of whose capital was held by the Italian public sector were permitted to tender for the contract. It fell to be determined whether the restriction on the right to tender was contrary to Community law because it favoured Italian undertakings and excluded those from other member states and whether the invitation to tender complied with the procedural requirements prescribed by Council Directive (EC) 77/62, arts 9, 17–25 (criteria for qualitative selection and for award of public supply contracts). *Held*, the EC Treaty, art 55 on the exemption of state activities from the right of establishment and freedom to provide services did not apply because the introduction of the system of computerisation did not constitute the exercise of official authority as there was no transfer to the concessionaire of any of the responsibilities in respect of the various operations inherent in the lottery. The activities involved in running the computerised system were of a technical nature and did not appear to differ in principle from those considered in *EC Commission v Italy* [1991] 2 CMLR 115, ECJ (1991 Abr para 2647) where a legislative restriction similar to the present one was held to be unlawful under the EC Treaty, art 52 on freedom of establishment and art 59 on freedom to provide services. Accordingly, art 55 did not apply and there was a breach of arts 52, 59. As the contract under consideration did not involve any transfer of responsibilities to the concessionaire constituting the exercise of a public authority, and as some of the activities contracted comprised the supply of some goods to the administration, it was subject to the procedural requirements of Directive 77/62. It was irrelevant that the products supplied did not become the property of the administration or that their price was fixed in abstract terms by way of an annual payment in proportion to the revenue accrued. As the sole real contracting authority for the contract was the Italian Finance Ministry, not the administrative body conducting the lottery, the contract was not excepted from the advertising rules contained in the Directive. The invitation to tender, therefore, did not comply with the requirements of Directive 77/62.

Case C-272/91: EC Commission v Italy [1995] 2 CMLR 673 (ECJ: Full Court).

Council Directive (EC) 77/62 replaced by Council Directive (EC) 93/36.

3147 Specific sectors—professional education and training—mutual recognition of qualifications

Commission Directive (EC) 95/43 amending the list of education and training courses subject to mutual recognition within the European Community, as contained in Annexes C and D to Council Directive 92/51 on a second general system for the recognition of professional education, was adopted on 20 July 1995.

The amendments are necessary as a result of requests from the Dutch and Austrian governments for the inclusion of additional education and training courses. Amended versions of the lists contained in Annexes C and D are attached to the Directive. The member states are requested to implement the Directive no later than 31 October 1995. (OJ L184 3.8.95 p 21.)

TRANSPORT

3148 Inland transport—road transport—carriage of goods by road—driving periods—circumstances in which requirements do not apply

See *Re Bird*, para 2969.

3149 Inland transport—road transport—dangerous goods—approximation of laws

Council Directive (EC) 94/55 on the approximation of the laws of the member states with regard to the transport of dangerous goods prohibits the transport by road of certain dangerous goods. The Directive is to be read in conjunction with the European Agreement concerning the International Carriage of Dangerous Goods by Road, concluded at Geneva on 30 September 1957. For those goods whose transport is not prohibited by the Directive, certain conditions are laid down, such as packaging and labelling requirements and the proper operation of the vehicles carrying the goods in question. The Directive is to be implemented in the member states by 1 January 1997. (OJ L319 12.12.94 p 7.)

3150 Sea transport—competition—block exemption—shipping consortia

Commission Regulation (EC) 870/95 was adopted on 20 April 1995 and concerns the application of the EC Treaty, art 85(3) to certain categories of agreements, decisions and concerted practices between liner shipping companies (consortia) pursuant to Regulation 479/92. The scope of Regulation 870/95 extends to consortia only in so far as they provide international liner transport services from or to one or more Community ports.

The EC Commission may withdraw the benefit of the regulation where it finds in a particular case that an agreement, decision, or concerted practice exempted under the regulation nevertheless has certain effects which are incompatible with the competition rules of the EC Treaty; particular examples of such are laid down in the regulation which entered into force on 22 April 1995 and is valid for a period of 5 years. (OJ L89 21.4.95 p 7.)

3151 Sea transport—sea transport between member states—freedom to provide services

France charged passengers travelling between a French port and a port of another member state both when they embarked and disembarked. Passengers travelling between ports in France were charged only on embarkation. Rates for services to French ports were lower than those for services to ports of other member states. It fell to be determined whether, in favouring operators of domestic services against those providing cross-border services, this system was contrary to Council Regulation (EC) 4055/86, which applies the principle of freedom to provide services to maritime transport between member states and member states and third countries. *Held*, by virtue of art 1, all the provisions of the EC Treaty on freedom to provide services applied to maritime transport between member states. That freedom could be relied on by undertakings against the member state in which they were established where the recipient of the service was established in another member state. Council Regulation (EC) 3577/92, art 6, which excluded French cabotage from the rules concerning the freedom to provide transport services until

January 1999 was inapplicable because it was only concerned with access to the domestic market for cabotage. The French scheme of charges constituted a restriction on the freedom to provide maritime services contrary to Regulation 4055/86 to the extent that it favoured internal transport against intra-Community transport. It was irrelevant that the charges affected all operators running cross-border services including those established in France.

Case C-381/93: EC Commission v France [1995] 2 CMLR 485 (ECJ: Full Court).

COMPETITION

3152 Application of rules of competition—abuse of dominant position—exercise of intellectual property rights

There was no comprehensive weekly television guide available in Ireland or Northern Ireland, but the appellants, the three television companies in those countries, granted licences to newspapers to publish daily listings and highlights of the week, and they each published a guide covering their own programmes. When a new company tried to publish a comprehensive weekly television guide, the appellants relied on national copyright laws to obtain injunctions preventing it from doing so. The EC Commission decided that the appellants had breached the EC Treaty, art 86. Their application for an annulment of the decision was dismissed, and on appeal, *held*, although mere ownership of intellectual property rights did not create a dominant position, the appellants enjoyed a monopoly over the information used to compile television programme listings. As they were in a position to prevent effective competition on the market in weekly television magazines, they occupied a dominant position. In the absence of Community laws on the matter, the conditions and procedures for protecting intellectual property rights were matters for the national laws of member states. However, a proprietor's exercise of an exclusive right could amount to abusive conduct within the meaning of art 86. Here, the appellants' reliance on national copyright laws in order to refuse to supply basic information had prevented the appearance on the market of a comprehensive weekly guide to television programmes, even though they did not offer such a product, and for which there was a demand. Such a refusal was an abuse of a dominant position and there was no justification for it. Moreover, by their actions, the appellants had reserved to themselves the market in weekly television guides by excluding all competition on that market. Accordingly, the appeal would be dismissed.

Cases C-241/91–242/91P: Radio Telefis Eireann and Independent Television Publications Ltd (Intellectual Property Owners Inc intervening) v EC Commission (Magill TV Guide Ltd intervening) [1995] 4 CMLR 718 (ECJ: Full Court). Decision of CFI [1991] 4 CMLR 586 (1991 Abr para 2686) affirmed.

3153 Application of rules of competition—concerted behaviour—companies in same group

A parent company required its subsidiaries to restrict the distribution of its products to allocated territories, and to refer orders from customers in other member states to the subsidiary established in the same member state as the customer. The applicant, an unrelated company, claimed that the policy infringed the EC Treaty, art 85(1) in so far as its aim was to preserve national markets and to partition them from each other in order to prevent, restrict or distort competition within the common market. The EC Commission rejected the complaint on the basis that art 85 did not apply, not only because the parent company and its subsidiaries were one economic unit whereby the subsidiaries did not enjoy any real autonomy to determine their course of action in the market, but also because the distribution arrangement did not exceed what was necessary for the division of tasks within the group of companies. The applicant sought annulment of the Commission's decision. *Held*, the parent company owned 100 per cent of the capital of some of its subsidiaries, and the sales and marketing activities of all the subsidiaries were controlled by an area team appointed by the parent company. The Commission had therefore not erred in classifying the group of companies as one economic unit within which the subsidiaries had no autonomy to determine their own course of action. Where there was no consensus of intent between economically independent entities, relations within an economic unit did not amount to a concerted practice between undertakings which restricted competition, within the meaning of art 85(1). In the instant case, although the subsidiaries were separate legal entities, they could not freely determine their conduct on the market and had to carry out the instructions given by the parent company by which they were wholly controlled. In those circumstances, art 85(1) did not apply, and that was so even though the possible effect of the parent company's distribution policy was to preserve and partition national markets. Accordingly, the application would be dismissed.

Case T-102/92: Viho Europe BV v EC Commission (Parker Pen Ltd, intervening) [1995] All ER (EC) 371 (Court of First Instance).

3154 Application of rules of competition—exclusive dealing and selective distribution—motor vehicle distribution agreements—block exemption

Commission Regulation (EC) 1475/95 on the application of the EC Treaty, art 85(3) to certain categories of motor vehicle distribution and servicing agreements was adopted on 28 June 1995.

Article 1 of the regulation declares that the EC Treaty, art 85(1) is not to apply to agreements to which only two undertakings are party and in which one contracting party agrees to supply, within a defined territory of the Common Market only to the other party, or only to the other party and to a specified number of other undertakings within the distribution system, for the purpose of resale, certain new motor vehicles intended for use on public roads and having three or more road wheels, together with spare parts for them.

The regulation replaces the earlier motor vehicle distribution block exemption (Commission Regulation (EC) 123/85), and comes into force on 1 July 1995. It applies from 1 October 1995 until 30 September 2002. The provisions of Regulation 123/85 continue to apply until 30 September 1995. (OJ L145 29.6.95 p 25.)

3155 Application of rules of competition—intellectual property rights—Community trade mark—fees

Council Regulations (EC) 2868/95 and 2869/95 were adopted on 13 December 1995 in order to implement Council Regulation (EC) 40/94 on the Community trade mark. Regulation 2868/95 lays down 101 implementing rules governing such matters as the application procedure, the registration procedure, renewal, revocation and invalidity, and the appeals procedure.

Regulation 2869/95 concerns the fees payable to the Office for Harmonisation in the Internal Market pursuant to Regulations 40/94 and 2868/95. Article 2 contains a table of the relevant fees. These fees are expressed in ecus but payments in cash can be made in the currency of the member state where the office has its seat (pursuant to art 6). Both Regulations entered into force on 22 December 1995. (OJ L303 15.12.95 pp 1, 33.)

3156 Application of rules of competition—intellectual property rights—patents—block exemption

Commission Regulation (EC) 2131/95 amends Regulation 2349/85 on the application of the EC Treaty, art 85(3) to certain categories of patent licensing, extending its application until 31 December 1995.

Regulation 2349/85 was due to be replaced by the proposed Technology Transfer Regulation (see OJ C178 30.6.94 p 3), but procedural requirements concerning the completion of the text have necessitated the extension of the original block exemption until the end of the year. (OJ L214 8.9.95 p 6.)

3157 Application of rules of competition—prohibited agreements or practices—negative clearance

Commission Regulation (EC) 3385/94 replaces Commission Regulation (EC) 27 of 3 May 1962, on the implementation of Council Regulation (EC) 17 of 6 February 1962. A new Form A/B is created; it allows undertakings and associations of undertakings to apply to the EC Commission for negative clearance in relation to agreements or practices which may fall within the prohibitions of the EC Treaty, arts 85(1), 86, or within the EEA Agreement, arts 53(1), 54. The form is also used to apply for an exemption to the EC Treaty, art 85(1) by virtue of art 85(3), or from the prohibition set out in the EEA Agreement, art 53(1) by virtue of the provisions of art 53(3). The regulation entered into force on 1 March 1995. (OJ L377 31.12.94 p 28.)

3158 Application of rules of competition—selective distribution systems—guarantees

A supplier of luxury watches operated a selective distribution system approved by the EC Commission by virtue of which the supplier only granted guarantees free of charge in respect of watches sold by its authorised dealers. German law required manufacturers who used selective distribution systems to ensure that their products were not sold by unauthorised dealers. It fell to be determined whether the supplier's refusal to honour guarantees free of charge in respect of watches sold by an unauthorised dealer in Germany who had obtained the watches from non-member states was compatible with the EC Treaty, art 85. *Held*, so long as the selective distribution system itself was valid under art 85, the restricting of guarantees to watches sold by authorised dealers was also valid.

Case C-376/92: Metro SB-Großmärkte GmbH & Co KG v Cartier SA [1994] 5 CMLR 331 (ECJ: Fifth Chamber).

3159 Application of rules of competition—shipping consortia—block exemption

See para 3150.

3160 Rules of competition—abuse of dominant position—control of concentrations—notifications, time limits and hearings

Commission Regulation (EC) 3384/94 on the notifications, time limits and hearings provided for in Council Regulation (EC) 4064/89, on the control of concentrations between undertakings, has been adopted in view of the need to improve upon certain procedural aspects contained in the previous regulation, Commission Regulation (EC) 2367/90. A new Form CO is created; it specifies the information that must be provided by an undertaking when notifying the Commission of a concentration with a Community dimension. The regulation entered into force on 1 March 1995. (OJ L377 31.12.94 p 1.)

3161 Rules of competition—exemption—restrictions indispensable to attainment of objectives—net book agreement

The EC Treaty, art 85(3) provides that the rule against the restriction of competition by member states is inapplicable where an agreement contributes to improving the production or distribution of goods or to promoting technical or economic progress, while allowing consumers a fair share of the resulting benefit and only imposes, on undertakings concerned, restrictions which are indispensable to the attainment of these objectives.

The EC Commission held that the net book agreement introduced by the plaintiff, by which publishers fixed the price at which books might be sold, was in breach of competition rules and that art 85(3) did not apply as the restrictions imposed were indispensable to the objectives of the agreement. The Commission's findings were upheld by the Court of First Instance and the plaintiff appealed on the ground that the court had upheld the Commission's decision without establishing that the objectives of the agreement had actually been attained, and had not taken account of the existence of a single language area which formed a single market for books in the United Kingdom and Ireland. *Held*, art 85(3) was not to be interpreted so as to provide that agreements conferring certain benefits, like the one in issue, were subject to the condition that such benefits must occur in the territory of the member state or states in which the undertakings who were parties to the agreement were established and not in the territory of other member states. Evidence relating to the single language area had been insufficiently considered and accordingly, the appeal would be allowed and the Court of First Instance's judgment would be set aside.

Case C-360/92P: Publishers Association v EC Commission [1995] 5 CMLR 33 (ECJ: Fifth Chamber).

3162 Rules of competition—personal application—undertaking—meaning

The defendant, an international organisation having responsibility for the supervision of air traffic control services within the air space of certain states party to the 1960 Brussels Convention on co-operation for the safety of air navigation, sought to recover charges levied for such services from an air navigation company. The latter contended that the procedure followed by the organisation in fixing charges at different rates for equivalent services, of an amount varying from state to state and from year to year, constituted an abuse of a dominant position within the meaning of the EC Treaty, art 86. The organisation contended that, as an international organisation, whose relations with the Community were governed by the rules of public international law, it could not be subject to Community rules on competition. On a reference to the European Court of Justice, *held*, the organisation's activities in respect of the collection of charges could not be separated from its other activities. Such activities, taken as a whole, related to the control and supervision of air space which were typically those of a public authority and not of an economic nature. Accordingly, the organisation did not constitute an undertaking subject to the provisions of arts 86, 90.

Case C-364/92: SAT Flugesellschaft mbH v European Organisation for the Safety of Air Navigation (Eurocontrol) [1994] 5 CMLR 208 (ECJ: Full Court).

3163 Rules of competition—territorial application—external relations—United States of America

Decision of the EC Council and the EC Commission 95/145 (EC, ECSC) of 10 April 1995 concerns the conclusion of an agreement between the European Community and the United States of America regarding the application of their competition laws. The Commission felt that international co-operation in the field of competition law needed to be strengthened, in view of the increasing pronouncement of the international dimension to competition problems, and so it negotiated the agreement for that purpose.

The stated purpose of the agreement is to 'promote co-operation and co-ordination and to lessen the possibility or impact of differences between the parties in the application of their competition laws'. Under the agreement, each party has agreed to notify the other whenever its competition authorities become aware that its enforcement activities may affect important interests of the other party. Enforcement activities as to which notification would ordinarily be appropriate include those that (1) are relevant to enforcement activities of the other party, (2) involve anti-competitive activities, other than a merger or acquisition, carried out in significant part in the other party's territory, (3) involve a merger or acquisition in which one or more of the parties to the transaction, or a company controlling one or more of the parties to the transaction, is a company incorporated or organised under the laws of the other party or one of its states or member states, (4) involve conduct believed to have been required, encouraged or approved by the other party, or (5) involve remedies that would, in significant respects, require or prohibit conduct in the other party's territory.

Officials from the competition authorities of each party must meet at least twice a year to exchange information on their current enforcement activities and priorities, exchange information on economic sectors of common interest, discuss policy changes which they are considering, and discuss other matters of mutual interest relating to the application of competition laws.

The agreement is to apply with effect from 23 September 1991, the date of the signing of the agreement. The agreement is annexed to the decision. (OJ L95 27.4.95 p 5.)

3164 Scope of rules of competition—price regulation—delegation of powers

Under German law, a system had been established for the setting of mandatory long distance haulage rates by tariff boards. The members of the boards were experts in the sectors concerned in the long distance transport of goods and were chosen by the Federal Minister of Transport from among persons proposed by firms or associations acting in the sector concerned. If a client was invoiced for less than a fixed tariff, the haulier was obliged to claim the difference; and if he failed to do so, the claim would be assigned to the national authorities. It fell to be determined whether the rendering compulsory, by their approval by ministerial order, of tariffs for the carriage of goods by road which were set by boards whose members were appointed by the public authority on a proposal by carriers was contrary to Community law. *Held*, member states were prohibited from keeping in force measures which could render the competition rules ineffective. The existence of a prohibited agreement within the meaning of the EC Treaty, art 85 was not precluded by the fact that the representatives of the industry fixing prices were appointed by the government. However, as the experts so appointed acted independently of the firms or associations which sponsored them, they could not be regarded as representing them for the purpose of price regulation. The German government had not delegated to private enterprise its powers to fix tariffs because it could still be involved in the decision-making of the boards and, where prices fixed by them were not in the general interest, the government could alter them.

Case C-185/91: Bundesanstalt für den Güterfernverkehr v Gebrüder Reiff GmbH & Co KG [1995] 5 CMLR 145 (ECJ: Full Court).

TAXATION

3165 Capital duty—reduced rate—transfer of part of business

A bank transferred several of its branches to a joint subsidiary. It fell to be determined whether the transfers should be taxed at a reduced rate on the basis that the branches could not form part of the bank's business in so far as their activities were not distinct from those of the bank and were not entirely autonomous. *Held*, it was unnecessary for a branch to carry on a distinct business or have legal personality even if it was funded by the parent company and subject to its instructions. In order to benefit from the reduced rate, it was sufficient that a branch was composed of assets and persons capable of contributing to the performance of the business to which it was transferred.

Case C-50/91: Commerz-Credit-Bank AG-Europartner v Finanzamt Saarbrücken [1995] 1 CMLR 800 (ECJ: First Chamber).

3166 Value added tax—chargeable event—interim payment

The taxpayer's business consisted in the management of immovable property in Italy where he was subject to value added tax the payment of which he was required, because of the amount of his annual turnover, to make every three months. Under Italian law, taxable persons were required, before 20 December each year, to make a payment on account amounting to 65 per cent of the net amount of value added tax which had to be paid, for the entire quarter (ie 1 October–31 December), by 5 March of the following year. A summary tax return had also to be submitted by the latter date. As the net amount of tax could not be determined with certainty before the end of the quarter, the payment on account had to be calculated on the basis of the payment for the corresponding quarter of the previous year or, if a trader anticipated that the net amount would be less, on the basis of his own estimate. A surcharge of 20 per cent of the unpaid amounts was imposed for failure to pay all or part of the amount due. It fell to be determined whether these requirements were contrary to Community law. *Held*, Council Directive (EC) 77/388, art 10 on chargeable events and chargeability to tax was concerned with the time at which value added tax became payable, not when it was payable, which was dealt with by art 22(4), (5). Member states were allowed to demand interim payments based on the turnover of taxpayers in the previous year provided they also had the option of using an estimate of their actual turnover for the relevant period where it had dropped from the previous year and there were no sanctions for underestimates made in good faith. The Italian law in question might result in taxpayers being assessed in advance for a period (ie 21 December–31 December) which had not elapsed and paying value added tax on transactions which had not taken place if their turnover had dropped in comparison with the previous year, if they made a mistake in estimating their actual turnover for the present period or if a large part of their turnover was obtained in the final 11 days of December. Accordingly, those requirements of Italian law were not in accordance with Council Directive 77/388, arts 10, 22(4), (5).

Case C-10/92: Balocchi v Ministero delle Finanze dello Stato [1995] 1 CMLR 486 (ECJ: Full Court).

3167 Value added tax—deduction—professional fees incurred in connection with disposal of shares in subsidiary

The taxpayer, a holding management company, sold shares it held in a subsidiary company in order to raise funds to pay off debts which had arisen directly from its taxable transactions. It fell to be determined whether it was entitled to deduct as input tax value added tax paid on invoices for professional services supplied by merchant bankers, solicitors and accountants in connection with the sale of the shares. *Held*, the right to deduct under Council Directive (EC) 77/388, art 17(2) arose only in respect of goods and services which had a direct and immediate link with taxable transactions; the ultimate aim pursued by the taxable person was irrelevant. The services in question had been used for the purpose of an exempt transaction and it was only by way of exception that the Directive provided for the right to deduct value added tax on goods or services used for exempt transactions. Except in the cases expressly provided for, where a taxable person supplied services to another taxable person who used them for an exempt transaction, the latter person was not entitled to deduct the value added tax paid, even if the ultimate purpose of the transaction was the carrying out of a taxable transaction. Accordingly, the taxpayer was not entitled to deduct the tax in question.

Case C-4/94: BLP Group plc v Customs and Excise Comrs [1995] STC 424 (ECJ: Fifth Chamber).

3168 Value added tax—exempt supply—buildings—sale of property used in part as private dwelling

Council Directive (EC) 77/388, art 13(B) provides that member states must exempt from value added tax the supply of buildings or parts thereof. Article 13(C) provides that member states may allow taxpayers a right of option for taxation in respect of such supply, but may restrict the scope of this right of option and must fix the details of its use. Article 17(2)(a) provides that in so far as goods and services are used for the purposes of his taxable transactions, the taxable person is entitled to deduct from the tax which he is liable to pay value added tax due or paid in respect of goods or services supplied to him by another taxable person.

Transactions governed by German law on land transfer tax were exempted from turnover tax, but German turnover tax law allowed taxable persons to treat such transfers as taxable when they were made to another trader for the purposes of his business. The plaintiff, a hotelier, sold a property consisting of a guest house, restaurant and premises used as a private dwelling. In making his value added tax declaration, the plaintiff regarded only the sale of the building used for business purposes as subject to value added tax, and treated the sum received for the private dwelling as exempt. The plaintiff therefore invoiced the purchaser for value added tax only in respect of the former part of the building, but the tax office imposed value added tax on the sale of the private dwelling as well. In proceedings in which the plaintiff challenged the decision, the German court referred several questions to the European Court of Justice regarding the interpretation of Council Directive (EC) 77/388. *Held*, a taxable person performing a transaction in a private capacity was not acting as a taxable person, and such a transaction was therefore not subject to value added tax. Moreover, if a taxable person wished to retain part of a property as part of his private assets, the Directive did not preclude him from excluding it from the value added tax system. If he did so, apportionment between the part allocated to business activities and the part retained for private use had to be based on the proportions of private and business use in the year of acquisition, and the taxable person also had to show that during his ownership of the property, he intended to retain part of it as part of his private assets. In any event, the right of option provided by art 13(C) of the Directive did not enable a supply which did not fall within the scope of value added tax to be transformed into a taxable supply. As regards the right to deduction under art 17(2)(a), if a taxable person chose to exclude part of an item of property from his business assets, that part did not fall within the scope of the value added tax system and was not to be taken into account for the purposes of art 17(2)(a).

Case C-291/92: Finanzamt Uelzen v Armbrecht [1995] All ER (EC) 882 (ECJ: Full Court).

3169 Value added tax—exempt supply—education—private tuition

See *Ellicott v Customs and Excise Comrs*, para 3007.

3170 Value added tax—exempt supply—health and welfare—bodies and organisations

The taxpayer operated a day nursery in the Netherlands. Under Dutch law, she was considered to be a trader subject to value added tax. The receipts of the nursery exceeded the amount of the costs incurred. The operating surpluses were paid to the taxpayer as remuneration. In the belief that the nursery services were exempt under Dutch law, she did not account for value added tax on the value of those services on her tax return. The law in question, which corresponded to Council Directive 77/388 (EC), art 13(A)(1)(g), exempted from value added tax supplies of goods or services of a social or cultural nature. It further provided, in accordance with art 13(A)(2)(a), that the exemption was not applicable if the trader who supplied the services aimed to make a profit. It fell to be determined whether a trader such as the taxpayer who was a natural person, who had structurally set out to achieve a positive result so that his income exceeded his expenditure, but that positive result could not be higher than what might be regarded as reasonable remuneration for the work performed by the trader himself, was to be regarded as systematically aiming to make a profit within the meaning of art 13(A)(2)(a). *Held*, art 13(A)(1) was to be interpreted as meaning that a trader who was a natural person could not claim exemption under art 13(A)(1)(g), which expressly reserved the exemption to bodies governed by public law or other organisations recognised as charitable by the member state concerned. Accordingly, a trader such as the taxpayer, a natural person, was not a person covered by art 13A(1)(g) and that fact was sufficient to bar her from the exemption available under that provision. It was, therefore, no longer relevant to determine whether a trader who structurally set out to achieve a positive result so that his income exceeded his expenditure but that positive result could not be higher than what might be regarded as reasonable remuneration for the work performed by the trader was 'systematically aiming to make a profit' within the meaning of art 13(A)(2)(a).

Case C-453/93: Bulthuis-Griffioen v Inspecteur der Omzetbelasting [1995] STC 954 (ECJ: Second Chamber).

3171 Value added tax—imports—refund of tax

The taxpayer marketed petroleum and related products in Greece, where the price of petrol was fixed. Value added tax was collected on the full consumer price, which incorporated the profit margin of intermediaries in the marketing chain as well as transport and storage costs, at the beginning of the marketing process. As companies marketing petroleum, filling stations and other retailers and distributors were, therefore, not required to account for tax on their supplies of such products, they were expressly deprived of the right to deduct value added tax levied directly on input transactions. Questions arose as to the compatibility of this special method for taxing petroleum products with the provisions of Council Directive (EC) 77/388, in particular arts 2, 11 and 17. *Held*, the fundamental principle underlying the value added tax system was that value added tax applied to each transaction by way of production or distribution after deduction had been made of the value added tax which had been levied directly on transactions relating to inputs. By virtue of art 11, value added tax was to be applied at each marketing stage on the price or value of the goods at that stage. The right of deduction under art 17 was an integral part of the value added tax scheme and in principle could not be limited except in the case of an authorised derogation. Articles 2, 11 and 17 precluded national rules which made the importation of finished petroleum products subject to value added tax calculated on the basis of a basic price different to that provided for in art 11 and which, by exempting traders in the petroleum sector from the obligation to submit returns, deprived them of the right to deduct value added tax charged directly on transactions relating to inputs. Article 14(1)(i) required member states to exempt the supply of services in connection with the importation of goods where the value of such services was included in the taxable amount in accordance with art 11(B)(3)(b), namely the transport costs incurred up to the first place of destination or to another known place of destination within the territory of the member state. A general exemption from value added tax on all transport and storage of petroleum products went beyond the exemption in art 14 and deprived the trader of the right to deduct value added tax charged on services in respect of transport and storage after the transport of petroleum products to a second place of destination. The provisions of the Directive, in particular arts 13–17, precluded an exemption from value added tax on services in respect of the transport and storage of petroleum products that were unconnected with the transport of those products from a first destination to another named destination.

Case C-62/93: BP Supergas Anonimos Etairia Geniki Emporiki-Viomichaniki kai Antiprossopeion v Greece [1995] All ER (EC) 684 (ECJ: Sixth Chamber).

3172   Value added tax—supply of services—place of supply—advertising services

In legislation intended to implement Council Directive (EC) 77/388, art 9(2)(e), by virtue of which cross-border advertising services were to be paid in the home state of the customer, France excluded a series of economic transactions from the concept of 'advertising services' by making a conceptual distinction between 'advertising' and 'promotion'; Luxembourg excluded a series of economic transactions, in particular, press conferences, seminars, cocktail parties, social functions and organised leisure activities, and the letting of sites for advertisements, from that concept; and Spain maintained a value added tax system which excluded a number of services, such as promotional activities, from the concept. It fell to be determined whether they had failed to fulfil their obligations under the Directive. *Held*, 'advertising services' was a Community concept which had to be interpreted uniformly in order to avoid instances of double taxation or non-taxation which might result from conflicting interpretations. The definition of those services within the meaning of art 9(2)(e) was not restricted to placing advertisements in the media; it extended to other means of promotion. Where other means were used exclusively, all the circumstances surrounding the service in question had to be taken into account to determine whether it constituted advertising. Although a service was supplied by an advertising agency, it was not an essential condition, in order for the service to be characterised as an advertising service, that the supplier be an advertising agency. The complaint against Luxembourg was inadmissible in so far as it related to the letting of sites for advertising purposes. All the remaining activities concerned were aimed at publicising products and services in order to increase sales; that was sufficient for them to constitute advertising. A breach of the Directive could not be defended on the ground that the Community institutions had failed adequately to define 'advertising services'. Declarations would be granted to the effect that the three member states had failed to fulfil their obligations under the Directive.

Cases C-68/92: EC Commission v France; C-69/92: EC Commission v Luxembourg; C-73/92: EC Commission v Spain [1995] 2 CMLR 1 (ECJ: Full Court).

3173   Value added tax—supply of services—time of supply—derogation—receipt of price

A builder issued a pro forma invoice for the sum outstanding in respect of building works supplied to the taxpayer. The invoice made no reference to value added tax. In its balance sheet, the taxpayer included the value of the works carried out and, under the heading 'outstanding invoices', it included the debt payable to the builder in the amount shown on the invoice. The taxpayer subsequently paid the debt shown on the invoice and the builder issued an invoice in due form, showing the value added tax. A pecuniary penalty was imposed for the breach of a domestic law which provided that while the supplier of the goods or services had the primary obligation to charge value added tax to the recipient and to pay it to the value added tax office, the recipient of the supply had a secondary obligation to pay the tax to that office if an irregular invoice which did not mention the value added tax had been issued. The taxpayer did not pay the tax relying on another domestic law which provided, pursuant to the derogation in Council Directive (EC) 77/388, art 10(2), that value added tax on all supplies of services became chargeable on receipt of the price. It fell to be determined whether the domestic provisions were compatible with Community law. *Held*, the power in art 10(2) to derogate from the general rule that value added tax was chargeable on the performance of a supply of services, which entitled member states to provide that the tax should become chargeable, for certain transactions or for certain categories of taxable persons, no later than receipt of the price, was to be construed broadly. Article 10(2) allowed member states to provide that receipt of the price was to be regarded as the event upon which, for all supplies of services, tax should become chargeable. A member state which availed itself of the derogation provided for in art 10(2) was not required to lay down a specified period from the date of the chargeable event within which the invoice or document serving as invoice had to be issued even where the price had not yet been received. Apart from the general obligation on the taxpayer to keep accounts in sufficient detail to permit application of the tax and inspection by the tax authority, there was no obligation on the member states to require documents or records to be drawn up other than the invoice, or other document serving as invoice. Member states might impose such other obligations as they deemed necessary for the correct levying and collection of the tax and for the prevention of fraud.

Case C-144/94: Ufficio IVA di Trapani v Italittica SpA [1995] STC 1059 (ECJ: Fifth Chamber).

3174 Value added tax—taxable person—economic activity—input tax—deductibility

The taxpayer worked partly as an employed person and partly as a self-employed tax consultant. He submitted annual value added tax declarations in respect of his self-employed activity. When he opened his own tax consultancy office, he brought into the business a car which he had hitherto used mainly for private purposes and only to a limited extent for business purposes. He sought to deduct input tax amounting to a proportion of the value added tax paid on the acquisition of the vehicle. Questions arose as to the criteria to be used for determining whether a person had acquired goods in his capacity as a taxable person, and as to whether a person who had so acquired goods was entitled to deduct input tax even where the goods in question were used initially only to a limited extent for business purposes. *Held*, whether an individual had acquired goods for the purposes of his economic activity within the meaning of Council Directive (EC) 77/388, art 4 was a question of fact which had to be determined in the light of all the circumstances of the case, including the nature of the goods concerned and the period between the acquisition of the goods and their use for the purposes of his economic activity. A taxable person who used goods for the purposes of an economic activity had the right, on the acquisition of those goods, to deduct input tax in accordance with the rules laid down in art 17, however small the proportion of business use.

Case C-97/90: Lennartz v Finanzamt München III [1995] STC 514 (ECJ: Sixth Chamber).

SOCIAL POLICY

3175 Education and training—'Youth for Europe' programme—third phase

Decision 818/95 (EC) of the European Parliament and the Council was adopted on 14 March 1995 and concerns the third phase of the 'Youth for Europe' programme. The main objective of the programme is to contribute to the educational process of young people by developing exchange activities within the Community. The framework of the decision concerns measures for young people in the specific socio-pedagogical context of the youth field and its aims include enabling young people to become aware of the importance of democracy; encouraging independence, creativity and entrepreneurial spirit among young people; allowing young people to express their opinion on the organisation of society; and promoting an awareness of the dangers relating to racism and xenophobia.

The third phase of the programme is to run for 5 years as from 1 January 1995. The financial framework for implementation of the entire programme is 126m ecus. The decision entered into force on 20 April 1995. (OJ L87 20.4.95 p 1.)

3176 Education and training—'Socrates' programme

Decision 819/95 (EC) of the European Parliament and of the Council establishing the Community action programme 'Socrates' was adopted on 14 March 1995. The objective of the programme is to encourage co-operation between member states in the field of education. Specific aims of the programme include the development of the European dimension in education at all levels, so as to strengthen the spirit of European citizenship, drawing on the cultural heritage of each member state; the promotion of knowledge of the languages of the European Union; the increased mobility of both teachers and students; and the increased academic recognition of diplomas, periods of study and other qualifications. The financial framework for implementation of the programme for the period 1 January 1995 to 31 December 1999 is 850m ecus. (OJ L87 20.4.95 p 10.)

3177 Employment and working conditions—employment and social affairs—rights of the individual—racial discrimination

The Treaty of European Union, art F(2) requires the European Union to respect fundamental rights, as guaranteed by the European Convention for the Protection of Human Rights and Fundamental Freedoms. On 5 October 1995, the Council and the representatives of the governments of the member states adopted a resolution on the fight against racism and xenophobia in the fields of employment and social affairs. The resolution calls upon the member states to ratify the international instruments concerning the fight against all forms of racial discrimination; to develop a respect for diversity and the equality of human beings in all teaching systems, vocational training establishments, and in training programmes for public servants and business executives; to support organisations actively committed, by democratic means, to the fight against racism and xenophobia; and to ensure the promotion of effective instruments of self-regulation, such as codes of good conduct, for the media professions. (OJ C296 10.11.95 p 13.)

3178 Employment and working conditions—transfer of undertakings—continuity of employment—effect of Community provision

See *Milligan v Securicor Cleaning*, para 1248.

3179 Employment and working conditions—transfer of undertakings—liability of transferee—stable economic activity

A contract between a building works contractor and a firm of carpenters provided that part of certain construction works which the carpenters had started was to be continued by the defendant firm. In addition, the contract provided that the cost of materials already supplied and paid for by the carpenters was to be refunded by the defendant which was also to take on two of the carpenters' employees for a short period. The plaintiff, an employee of the carpenters, was transferred to the defendant, but was later given notice of dismissal. On his claim against the defendant for damages for wrongful dismissal, it fell to be determined whether Council Directive (EC) 77/187 was applicable. *Held*, the decisive criterion for determining whether there had been a transfer of an undertaking to which the Directive applied was whether the business retained its identity, in particular whether the operation of the entity was actually continued or resumed by the new employer with the same or similar economic activities. This presupposed that the transfer related to a stable economic entity whose activity was not limited to performing one specific works contract. Where an undertaking transferred one of its building works to another undertaking for the work to be completed, the transfer came within the Directive only if it included the transfer of a body of assets enabling the activities or certain activities of the transferor to be carried on in a stable way. As the carpenters merely made available to the defendant certain workers and material for carrying out the work, the Directive was not applicable.

    Case C-48/94: Ledernes Hovedorganisation (acting for Rygaard) v Dansk Arbejdsgiverforening (acting for Strø Mølle Akustik A/S) [1996] IRLR 51 (ECJ: Full Court).

3180 Equal pay and treatment—advertising—image of women and men

On 5 October 1995, the Council and the representatives of the governments of the member states adopted a resolution on the image of women and men portrayed in advertising and the media. The resolution calls upon the member states to promote a diversified and realistic picture of the skills and potential of women and men in society and to take action aimed at disseminating this image by implementing measures with a view to ensuring the absence of discrimination on grounds of sex; promoting the balanced participation of women and men in production bodies, administrative bodies and decision-making posts; and encouraging advertising agencies and the media to promote new ideas to reflect the diversity of the roles of women and men, and to highlight the negative effects which sexual stereotyping may have on the physical and mental health of the public. (OJ C296 10.11.95 p 15.)

3181 Equal pay and treatment—equal opportunities—action programme for 1996–2000

Council Decision (EC) 95/593 was adopted on 22 December 1995. This decision establishes a medium-term action programme on equal opportunities for men and women for the period 1 January 1996 to 31 December 2000. The programme is intended to promote the integration of equal opportunities for men and women in the process of preparing, implementing and monitoring all policies and activities of the European Union and the member states. The funding for the programme is 30m ecus. The stated aims of the programme include (1) the promotion of a gender balance in decision-making; and (2) the reconciliation of working and family life for men and women. Implementation of the programme is to be by the Commission, in consultation with the member states. (OJ L335 30.12.95 p 37.)

3182 Equal pay and treatment—equal opportunities—Advisory Committee—composition and terms of reference

Commission Decision 95/420 (EC) has been adopted in order to amend Decision 82/43 relating to the setting up of the Advisory Committee on Equal Opportunities for Women and Men. The Heads of State and Government meeting within the European Council on 10 and 11 December emphasised that equality of opportunities is a paramount task of the European Union, and as a result a decision was made to adapt the original composition and terms of reference of the Advisory Committee to take account of current and future developments, particularly in relation to the new medium-term action programme outlined in the Commission's Communication of 19 July 1995. The new Decision replaces arts 2, 3, 6, adds a third paragraph to art 8 and replaces arts 10, 11. The Decision is effective as of 1 January 1996. (OJ L249 17.10.95 p 43.)

3183 Equal pay and treatment—occupational pension scheme—army pension—exclusionary provision—sex discrimination

See *Howard v Ministry of Defence*, para 2664.

3184 Equal pay and treatment—occupational pension scheme—criterion for determining whether scheme is an occupational pension scheme

Dutch civil servants were covered by both a national general pension scheme and a statutory pension scheme which applied to civil servants only. To prevent overlap between the two schemes, the amount of the general pension was deducted from an employee's pension entitlement. Following an alteration to the general pension scheme rules to eliminate discrimination against married women, married women became entitled to a general pension in their own right. The civil service pension scheme was amended to eliminate similar discrimination, but for periods of employment prior to the amendment, the old system of calculating married women's pension entitlement under the scheme was maintained. The applicant, a married man who was employed in the civil service, was adversely affected by the changes to the civil service pension scheme and complained that the scheme was more favourable to married women than to married men in respect of periods of service prior to the alteration of the scheme. His claim that the scheme was incompatible with Council Directive (EC) 79/7 was upheld, but on the pension fund's appeal, the Dutch court stayed the proceedings and referred several questions as to the interpretation of the Directive to the European Court of Justice, in particular whether the civil service pension scheme fell within art 3(1) of the Directive or the EC Treaty, art 119. *Held*, the fact that a pension scheme was governed by statute was a strong indication that the benefits provided by it were social security benefits. However, even if a scheme was adopted in accordance with legislation, it was not a social security benefit if it was based on an agreement between an employer and his employees' representatives, was financed entirely by the employer, and had the effect of supplementing benefits payable under generally applicable national laws. The only decisive criterion as to whether or not a pension scheme fell within art 119 was whether the scheme provided benefits which were consideration received by an employee from his employer by reason of the employment relationship between the employee and the employer. Moreover, if the pension concerned only a particular category of employees, was directly related to a period of service, and was calculated by reference to the employee's last salary, such a pension was comparable to an occupational pension scheme funded by a private employer. Here, as the pension for civil servants was paid to them because of the employment relationship, art 119 was applicable and not the Directive. Article 119 precluded national legislation which applied different rules for calculating the pension entitlement of married men and married women. Here, the legislation was directly discriminatory, as it placed married men at a disadvantage, whereas they were entitled to be treated in the same way and have the same scheme applied to them as was applied to married women.

Case C-7/93: Bestuur Van Het Algemeen Burgerlijk Pensioenfonds v Beune [1995] IRLR 103 (ECJ: Full Court).

3185 Equal pay and treatment—part-time and full-time workers—indirect discrimination

In six separate cases, collective agreements provided that full and part-time employees were entitled to overtime supplements for time worked in addition to the normal working hours set by the agreements. However, part-time employees were entitled to overtime rates only if the hours which they worked in excess of their own contractual hours amounted to more than the normal working hours. The part-time employees claimed that the policy was indirectly discriminatory and that they were therefore entitled to overtime supplements at the same rate as that which applied to full-time employees. The relevant courts referred several questions to the European Court of Justice as to whether the provision in the collective agreements was contrary to the EC Treaty, art 119 and Council Directive (EC) 75/117. *Held*, art 119 applied not only to statutory and administrative provisions, but also to collective agreements and individual employment contracts. Here, part-time employees who worked the same number of hours as full-time employees received the same overall pay. Moreover, part-time employees received the same overall pay as full-time employees if they worked more than the normal working hours fixed by the collective agreements, because they became entitled to overtime supplements when they did so. As such, the collective agreements did not apply different treatment as between part-time employees and full-time employees and, therefore, there was no discrimination contrary to art 119 or the Directive.

Cases C-399/92, C-409/92, C-425/92, C-34/93, C-50/93, C-78/93: Stadt Lengerich v Helmig; Schmidt v Deutsche Angestellten-Krankenkasse; Lange v Bundesknappschaft Bochum; Kussfeld v Firma Detlef Bogdol GmbH; Ludewig v Kreis Segeberg [1995] IRLR 216 (ECJ: Sixth Chamber).

3186 Equal pay and treatment—pay in lieu of notice—discrimination on grounds of maternity

See *Clark v Secretary of State for Employment*, para 1230.

3187 Equal pay and treatment—piece work

Two groups of employees of a ceramics producer, the first group of whom were automatic machine operators all of whom were men and the second group of whom were blue-pattern painters all but one of whom were women, were covered by the same collective agreement. About 70 per cent of them were paid by the piece, their pay consisting of a fixed element, paid as a basic hourly wage, and a variable element, paid by reference to the number of items produced. The average hourly piece work pay of the blue-pattern painters was considerably less than that of the automatic machine operators. In this context, it fell to be determined whether the Community principle of equal pay for men and women applied to piece work pay schemes. *Held*, the EC Treaty, art 119 and Council Directive (EC) 75/117 applied to piece work pay schemes in which pay depended entirely or in large measure on the individual output of each worker. The mere finding that in such a scheme the average pay of a group of workers consisting largely of women carrying out one type of work was appreciably lower than that of a group of workers consisting largely of men carrying out another type of work to which equal value was attributed was not in itself sufficient to establish that there was discrimination with regard to pay. However, where the pay consisted of a variable element, depending on each worker's output and a fixed element, differing according to the group of workers concerned, and it was not possible to identify the factors determining the variable element, the employer might have to bear the burden of proving that differences in pay were not due to sex discrimination. Groups chosen for comparison had to be large enough to ensure that differences in pay were not due to fortuitous or short-term factors or to differences in individual workers' individual output.

Case C-400/93: Specialarbejdforbundet i Danmark v Dansk Industri [1995] All ER (EC) 577 (ECJ: Full Court).

3188 Equal pay and treatment—promotion in employment—automatic priority where women under-represented—sex discrimination

Under a German law, where men and women employees applying for promotion to the same post were equally qualified, women were to be given priority in sectors where they were under-represented. A male and female employee were short-listed for a managerial post in a town parks department. A recommendation that the male employee be appointed was rejected on the ground that, as both employees were equally qualified and women were under-represented in the department, the female employee had to be appointed. It fell to be determined whether the law in question was prohibited by Council Directive (EC) 76/207 on equal treatment for men and women as regards access to employment. *Held*, art 2(1) prohibited sex discrimination but art 2(4) provided that the Directive was to be without prejudice to measures to promote equal opportunity for men and women, in particular by removing existing inequalities which affected women's opportunities in employment, including promotion. The German law involved discrimination on the ground of sex. Although art 2(4) of the Directive permitted national measures relating to access to employment, including promotion, which gave a specific advantage to women with a view to improving their ability to compete on the labour market and to pursue a career on an equal footing with men, it had to be interpreted strictly. A national rule which guaranteed absolute and unconditional priority to women for appointment or promotion exceeded the limits of the exception in art 2(4). Accordingly, the German law in question was contrary to Community law.

Case C-450/93: Kalanke v Freie Hansestadt Bremen [1996] All ER (EC) 66 (ECJ: Full Court).

3189 Equal pay and treatment—termination of employment—pregnancy—temporary unavailability for work—sex discrimination

See *Webb v EMO Air Cargo (UK) Ltd (No 2)*, para 2649.

3190 General principles—right of privacy—processing of personal data—protection of the individual

EC Directive 95/46 of the European Parliament and of the Council was adopted on 24 October 1995 and concerns the protection of individuals with regard to the processing of personal data. The Directive applies to the processing of personal data 'wholly or partly by automatic means, and to the processing otherwise than by automatic means of personal data which form part of a filing system or are intended to form part of a filing system': art 3(1). According to art 6, personal data must be (1) processed fairly and lawfully, (2) collected for specified, explicit and legitimate purposes, and not further processed in a way incompatible with those purposes, (3) adequate, relevant and not excessive in relation to the purposes for which they were collected, (4) accurate and, where necessary, kept up-to-date, and (5) kept in a form which permits identification of data subjects for no longer than is necessary for the purposes for which the data were collected.

Article 7 specifies the criteria for making data processing legitimate. The data may only be processed if (1) the data subject has unambiguously given his consent, or (2) processing is necessary for the performance of a contract to which the data subject is a party, or (3) processing is necessary for compliance with a legal obligation to which the controller is subject, or (4) processing is necessary in order to protect the vital interests of the data subject, or (5) processing is necessary for the performance of a task carried out in the public interest, or (6) processing is necessary for the purposes of legitimate interests pursued. Article 8 limits the circumstances in which data can be processed revealing racial or ethnic origin, political opinions, religious or philosophical beliefs, trade union membership and details of health or sex life. Articles 8–12 concern the information to be given to the data subject and the right of access. The data subject may object to the processing of personal data on 'compelling legitimate grounds relating to his particular situation': art 14.

Member states are to implement the Directive no later than 24 October 1998. However, by way of derogation, member states may provide that the processing of data already held in manual filing systems can be delayed for up to 12 years from the date of adoption. (OJ L281 23.11.95 p 31.)

3191 Social security—contributions—defaulting sub-contractor—liability of main contractor

It fell to be determined whether a Dutch law which made main contractors liable for social security contributions which had not been paid by sub-contractors on behalf of their employees, was compatible with Community law. *Held*, Council Regulation (EC) 1408/71 on the application of social security schemes to employed persons, to self-employed persons and to members of their families moving within the Community, was not restricted to national laws aimed specifically at the various areas of social security set out in art 4(1) but could extend to more general co-ordinating laws such as the one in question. As there was only an indirect link between the Dutch law and the branches of social security mentioned in art 4(1), the Dutch law did not fall within the scope of Regulation 1408/71.

Case C-327/92: Rheinhold & Mahla NV v Bestuur van de Bedrijsfsvereniging voor de Mataalnijverheid [1995] 2 CMLR 786 (ECJ: Sixth Chamber).

3192 Social security—exemption from prescription charges—sex discrimination

The National Health Service (Charges for Drugs and Appliances) Regulations 1989, SI 1989/419, reg 6(1)(c) provides that no charge is payable for the supply of drugs and appliances by doctors and chemists to a man who has attained the age of 65 years, or a woman who has attained the age of 60 years. Council Directive (EC) 79/7, art 3(1)(a) provides that the Directive applies to statutory schemes which provide protection against risks including sickness. Article 7(1)(a) provides that the Directive is without prejudice to the right of member states to exclude from its scope the determination of pensionable age for the purposes of granting old age and retirement pensions and the possible consequences thereof for other benefits.

The applicant sought judicial review of the 1989 Regulations, reg 6(1)(c), contending that it constituted unlawful sex discrimination, contrary to Council Directive 79/7. A preliminary ruling was sought from the European Court of Justice as to (1) whether the 1989 Regulations, reg 6 fell within Directive 79/7, art 3(1), (2) whether art 7(1)(a) of the Directive applied, and (3) whether the direct effect of the Directive could be relied upon to support a claim for damages for periods prior to the date of the court's decision. *Held*, (1) the provision in the 1989 Regulations, reg 6(1)(c) was provided for by statute and implemented by regulations, and therefore formed part of a statutory scheme. It also afforded direct and effective protection against the risk of sickness, in that the exemption from prescription charges was conditional on the occurrence of sickness. Therefore, reg 6 fell within art 3(1)(a) of the Directive, and it was irrelevant that the 1989 Regulations were not strictly part of the social security rules. (2) One of the circumstances in which the derogation under art 7(1)(a) of the Directive could apply was where discrimination was objectively necessary to avoid disturbing the equilibrium of the social security system or to ensure coherence between the retirement pension scheme and other benefit schemes. However, a benefit granted under a non-contributory scheme in circumstances which did not relate to a person's entitlement to old age pension had no direct influence on the financial equilibrium of contributory pension schemes. Moreover, as the exemption from prescription charges arose only once a person had reached pensionable age and was no longer able to pay national insurance contributions, the removal of sex discrimination from the exemption would not affect the financial equilibrium of the pension system. As discrimination in the exemption was therefore not objectively necessary, it was not covered by the derogation. In addition, although the fact that elderly people generally incurred more prescription charges than younger people might justify exempting them from such charges above a certain age, the exemption did not have to be linked to the statutory pensionable age and thereby be granted at different ages for men and women. (3) The court's ruling was to take effect from the date on which the 1989 Regulations, reg 6(1)(c) came into force, and could not be limited in time because of its financial consequences.

Case C-137/94: R v Secretary of State for Health, ex p Richardson [1995] All ER (EC) 865 (ECJ: Sixth Chamber).

3193 Social security—family credit—eligibility—sex discrimination

The applicant, a single parent, applied for family credit for herself and her daughter. In calculating the applicant's net income, no deduction was made in respect of childcare costs, and her application was rejected on the basis that her income exceeded the prescribed level. On appeal, the applicant argued that the failure to deduct childcare costs discriminated against single parents and also indirectly discriminated against women. On a reference to the European Court of Justice, it fell to be determined whether family credit fell within the scope of Council Directive (EC) 76/207. *Held*, the aim of family credit was to ensure that families were no worse off in work than they would be if they were not working. It was, therefore, intended to keep poorly paid workers in employment and, moreover, the prospect of receiving family credit was an incentive to the unemployed to accept low paid work. In addition, one of the conditions of entitlement to family credit was that a claimant had to be engaged in remunerative work. For those reasons, family credit was concerned with access to employment, within the meaning of art 3 of the Directive. As it was linked to an employment relationship, it also constituted a working condition, within the meaning of art 5. Family credit, therefore, fell within the scope of the Directive.

Case C-116/94: Meyers v Adjudication Officer [1995] IRLR 498 (ECJ: Fourth Chamber).

3194   Social security—income support—residence condition

See *R v Secretary of State for Social Services, ex p Sarwar*, para 2743.

3195   Social security—invalidity benefit—migrant worker—member of family

The claimant, a German national, had been an official of the European Organisation for the Safety of Air Navigation and settled in Belgium. He had been a member of the organisation's own social security scheme before his retirement. His claim for state benefits for his handicapped adult daughter was refused on the ground that, as she had never worked, she had never been subject to the social security system of Belgium or any member state and that she was a German national and the payment of the benefits claimed was subject to Belgian nationality. On a reference to the European Court of Justice, certain questions arose concerning the scope of Council Regulation (EC) 1408/71. *Held*, under that regulation, the members of the family of a worker acquired rights through their status as a member of the family of the worker. Accordingly, arts 2, 3 could not be relied upon by a dependent child of a migrant worker in order to obtain a handicapped person's allowance because they were personal to the recipient and not granted by reason of being a member of a worker's family. However, Council Regulation (EC) 1612/68, art 7(2) on freedom of movement for workers within the Community could be relied upon by a national of a member state, a former civil servant of an international organisation, in order to obtain an allowance for a handicapped adult, as provided for by the law of the member state where he resided, other than his state of origin. To make the allowance conditional on the beneficiary having Belgian nationality was incompatible with art 7(2).

Case C-310/91: Schmid v Belgium [1995] 2 CMLR 803 (ECJ: Sixth Chamber).

3196   Social security—invalidity benefit—pensionable age—sex discrimination

Under the Social Security Contributions and Benefits Act 1992, s 33 (repealed), invalidity pension was payable in certain circumstances to persons under pensionable age, set at 65 for men and 60 for women, and to persons over that age who had deferred or elected not to receive their state retirement pension. Invalidity allowance was payable under s 34 (repealed), in addition to the invalidity pension, to persons who were more than five years under pensionable age on the first day of their incapacity for work.

The claimant became incapacitated for work after reaching the age of 55. She was paid invalidity pension at the full rate until she reached pensionable age when she opted to continue receiving invalidity pension. Her pension was reduced in accordance with s 33 as she did not fulfil the contribution conditions for the grant of a full state retirement pension. She was refused invalidity allowance. The Court of Appeal found that the provisions of ss 33, 34 were discriminatory. On a reference to the European Court of Justice, it fell to be determined whether those provisions were lawful under Council Directive (EC) 79/7, art 7(1)(a), which permitted member states to exclude from the scope of the principle of equal treatment for men and women in social security the determination of pensionable age for the purposes of granting old-age and retirement pensions and the possible consequences of that for other benefits. *Held*, where a member state set the pensionable age for women at 60 and that for men at 65, art 7(1)(a) also allowed it to provide that the rate of invalidity pension payable to persons becoming incapacitated for work before they reached pensionable age was to be limited to the actual rate of retirement pension from the age of 60 in the case of women and 65 in the case of men. That provision also allowed the state to reserve entitlement to invalidity allowance, paid in addition to invalidity pension, to women aged under 55 and men aged under 60 when they first became incapacitated for work. Accordingly, the English legislation in question was lawful.

Case C-92/94: Graham v Secretary of State for Social Security [1995] All ER (EC) 736 (ECJ: Sixth Chamber).

3197   Social security—invalidity benefit—sex discrimination

The claimant's invalidity benefit was withdrawn when she was granted a widow's pension on the death of her husband. It fell to be determined whether Community law prevented a national court from interpreting the 1966 International Covenant on Civil and Political Rights, art 26, which extended the principle of equal treatment to survivors' benefits, an area that was not yet covered by Council Directive (EC) 79/7, if that area was only temporarily excluded from the jurisdiction of the Community. *Held*, as the Directive did not cover survivors' benefits, they were governed by national law and international law applicable in the member states. National law prohibiting discrimination based on art 26 of the Covenant did not prevent the future extension of that principle under the Directive itself to such benefits. Accordingly, a national court was free to apply that provision. The application of Directive 79/7 could not be withheld from a withdrawal of invalidity benefit on the ground that it followed on from the grant of a survivor's benefit. Such a withdrawal was discriminatory in breach of art 4(1) of the Directive in view of the fact that, at the relevant time, widowers continued to receive invalidity benefit as there was no equivalent national provision for transferring to a widower's pension. It could only be saved by the fact that the benefit was voluntarily surrendered in favour of the pension if the claimant had been fully informed of the financial consequences. Article 4(1) had direct effect and prevailed over any conflicting national rules which then became applicable. However, this did not prevent the national court remedying any discrimination in accordance with domestic procedures where, for example, invalidity benfit exceeded a pension.

Case C-337/91: *Van Gemert-Derks v Bestuur van de Nieuwe Industriële Bedrijfsvereniging* [1995] 1 CMLR 773 (ECJ: Full Court).

3198   Social security—pension—national pension scheme—discrimination

The claimant worked in the United Kingdom for 13 years during which period he acquired entitlement to 53 quarterly periods of old-age insurance and then in France where he acquired entitlement to 120 such quarterly periods until he was made redundant at the age of 61. He was refused French unemployment benefit because, although his qualifying periods totalled 173 periods, French law excluded claimants aged over 60 years who had completed 150 qualifying periods recognised for the purposes of pension insurance. His French pension was reduced by one-fifth because his French qualifying periods were only four-fifths of the maximum. On a reference to the European Court of Justice, questions arose as to the interpretation of Council Regulation (EC) 1408/71, arts 3(1), 49 on the application of social security schemes to employed persons, self-employed persons and members of their families moving within the Community. *Held*, as the claimant was not yet 65 and did not qualify for a British partial pension, art 49 applied so that the French pension authorities had to base entitlement to pension on the periods of insurance completed by him in France. The reduced pension reached by ignoring the United Kingdom qualifying periods as compared with a higher pension if the claimant had been employed for those periods in France resulted from the autonomous separateness of the national pension schemes underlying the EC Treaty, art 51. There was no discrimination contrary to Regulation 1408/71, art 3(1), although that provision and art 49 did not prevent the French authorities from taking account of the United Kingdom periods.

Case C-146/93: *McLachlan v Caisse Nationale d'Assurance Vieillesse des Travailleurs Salariés* [1995] 2 CMLR 540 (ECJ: First Chamber).

3199   Social security—retirement pension—derived entitlements of spouse—sex discrimination

The claimant was employed in the Netherlands for 37 years and in Belgium for eight years. On reaching the age of 65, he received a Dutch pension based on his work in the Netherlands at the statutory rate of 50 per cent personal pension, supplemented by a family pension of 50 per cent in respect of his wife who had never worked and who was not yet 65. He received a Belgian pension based on his Belgian employment at the 75 per cent rate. When his wife reached 65, she received her own Dutch personal pension and the Dutch family pension of 50 per cent was cancelled. The claimant's Belgian pension was reclassified from 75 per cent to 60 per cent on the ground that his wife was now in receipt of a Dutch pension. He contended that his Belgian pension should not have been downgraded. *Held*, as Council Directive (EC) 79/7, art 7(1)(c) authorised member states to exclude from the scope of the Directive on equal treatment for men and women the granting of entitlement to old-age benefits by virtue of the derived entitlements of a spouse, the sex discrimination prohibition in art 4(1) did not apply. The difference between Belgian and Dutch pensions law arose out of differences between legal rules which themselves applied equally to domestic and migrant workers and, therefore, did not constitute a barrier to the free movement of persons under the EC Treaty, arts 48, 51. The Belgian rules had been applied within the quite different context of the Dutch pensions system. In a case with both Belgian and Dutch elements, account should be taken of the unplanned consequences of a blind literal application of the Belgian rules. The Belgian courts should interpret the Belgian rules in the light of the free movement aims of arts 48, 51, in particular so as not to discourage a migrant worker from exercising his right to freedom of movement.

Case C-165/91: Van Munster v Rijksdienst voor Pensioenen [1995] 2 CMLR 513 (ECJ: Full Court).

3200 Social security—retirement pension—increase in respect of dependent spouse—sex discrimination

The claimant was refused an increase in her retirement pension in respect of her dependent husband because she did not meet the conditions of the Social Security Act 1975, s 45A, under which a woman was only entitled to have her retirement pension increased in respect of a dependent husband if she had been in receipt of other benefits which had been increased because of a dependent husband immediately prior to the beginning of her retirement pension. No such limitations were imposed by s 45 under which a man could claim a pension increase in respect of a dependent wife. It fell to be determined whether such discriminatory provisions were contrary to Council Directive (EC) 79/7, art 4(1) on the basic principle of equal treatment for men and women. *Held*, art 7(1)(d) on the progressive implementation of the principle of equal treatment for men and women in matters of social security did not preclude a member state which provided for increases in long-term old-age benefits in respect of a dependent spouse to be granted only to men from abolishing that discrimination solely with regard to women who fulfilled certain conditions. Accordingly, Community law afforded the claimant no entitlement to the increase sought by her.

Case C-420/92: Bramhill v Chief Adjudication Officer [1995] 2 CMLR 35 (ECJ: Fifth Chamber). 1975 Act, ss 45, 45A now Social Security Contributions and Benefits Act 1992, ss 83, 84.

INDEX

The titles under which the *Abridgment* is arranged are listed on pp *9–11*. The references in the list and in this index are to paragraphs, not pages.

administrative law
declaration, interim relief, interlocutory injunction, 1707
judicial review. *See* judicial review
misconduct in public office, local authority employees, 909
natural justice—
breach of, owner not informed of order to destroy dog, 102
fair hearing—
deportation order, 250
principles of fairness, 32
Parliamentary Commissioner for Administration, investigations by, 33

Admiralty
action in rem, arrest of ship—
arrest of more than one ship, 34
Admiralty Court, practice, 35

adoption
See under children and young persons

agency
agent—
company director, scope of authority, 2837
contract of engagement, restraint of trade, 40
fraud, liability of principal, 1740
goods or services supplied through agent, deemed supplies, value added tax liability, 3040
holding funds for principal, winding up, existence of trust, 532
estate agent—
duty of care—
client's loss through fraud, 43
negligent mis-statement, 42
relations between principal and third persons, notice to agent, knowledge imputed to principal, 2110

agriculture
agricultural business, grants, 47
agricultural holdings—
garden centre, 49
non-payment of rent, service of notice, 1838
succession to tenancy—
calculation of annual income of land, 52
principal source of livelihood, 53
valuation for inheritance tax, 51
agricultural marketing—
fruit plant material, 54
grants, 65
ornamental plant material, 56
vegetable plant material, 57
wine, 58, 59
agricultural processing, grants, 65
agricultural tenancies, 60
apples, orchards, grubbing up, 61
arable crops, compensatory payments, 62

agriculture—*continued*
common agricultural policy—
agricultural methods, environmental protection—
nitrate sensitive areas, 63
salt marshes, 64
basic principles, non-discrimination between producers and consumers, 59
registration of pure-bred animals, 67
control of pests, potatoes, importation from the Netherlands, 69
eggs, marketing standards, 70
employment, wages, 48
feeding stuffs, 72
fertilisers, Commission Directive, implementation, 73
hill livestock, compensatory allowances, 74
Home-Grown Cereals Authority, levy scheme, 75
livestock—
artificial insemination, 76
beef special premium, 77
bovine embryo, 78
extensification, moorland, 79
meat, hygiene and inspection—
farmed game bird, 1428
poultry, 1428
rabbit meat, 1428
milk, quota system, partnership requirements, 55
pesticides, maximum residue levels, 80
plant breeders' rights—
fees, 81
plant variety rights office, 82
schemes, 83
plant health—
forestry, 1449
general, 84
plant protection products, 85
rural development grants, 88
seeds—
cereal seeds, 89
national lists of varieties, fees, 90
sheep, annual premium, 91
suckler cows, premiums, 92
sugar beet, research and education, 93
surplus food, regulations, 94

allotments and smallholdings
allotment, sale, allotment holder, displacement of, 95

animals
bovine animals, records, identification and movement, 98
diseases—
enzootic bovine leukosis, 100
equine viral arteritis, 101
dog, dangerous dog—
destruction of dog ordered, failure to inform owner, 102

PUBLISHERS' ANNOUNCEMENT

HALSBURY'S

Laws of England

1995 ANNUAL ABRIDGMENT

As part of the comprehensive service to *Halsbury's Laws of England* fourth edition we have pleasure in sending you herewith the *Annual Abridgment* volume covering the calendar year 1995.

This volume is complementary to both the *Current Service* and the *Cumulative Supplement* and will provide a comprehensive and permanent record of the development of English law during the year.

New subscribers to the fourth edition may not have the earlier *Abridgment* volumes which cover the years 1974 to 1994. Missing volumes may be obtained from the publishers. A discount is available if a complete set is ordered.

BUTTERWORTHS

May 1996

Printed in England